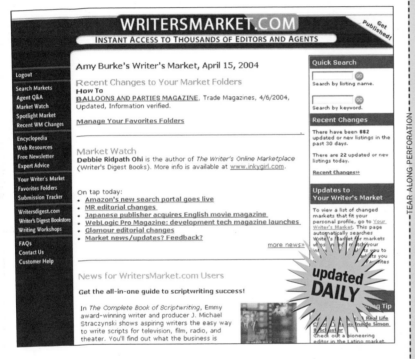

P9-CAR-782

4/6

2/7

N	market new to this edition
A	market accepts agented submissions only
⊘	market does not accept unsolicited manuscripts
🍁	Canadian market
🌐	market located outside of the U.S. and Canada
💻	online opportunity
$	market pays 0-9¢/word or $0-$150/article
$$	market pays 10-49¢/word or $151-$750/article
$$$	market pays 50-99¢/word or $751-$1,500/article
$$$$	market pays $1/word or over $1,500/article
•	comment offering additional market information from the editor of *Writer's Market*
0→	tips to break in to a specific market

ms, mss manuscript(s)

b&w black & white (photo)

SASE self-addressed, stamped envelope

SAE self-addressed envelope

IRC International Reply Coupon, for use in countries other than your own

(For words and expressions relating specifically to writing and publishing, see the Glossary in the back of this book)

—TEAR ALONG PERFORATION—

2005 WRITER'S MARKET
KEYS TO SYMBOLS

 N market new to this edition

 market accepts agented submissions only

 market does not accept unsolicited manuscripts

 Canadian market

 market located outside of the U.S. and Canada

 online opportunity

$ market pays 0-9¢/word or $0-$150/article

$ $ market pays 10-49¢/word or $151-$750/article

$ $ $ market pays 50-99¢/ word or $751-$1,500/ article

$ $ $ $ market pays $1/ word or over $1,500/article

• comment offering additional market information from the editor of *Writer's Market*

O— tips to break in to a specific market

ms, mss manuscript(s)

b&w black & white (photo)

SASE self-addressed, stamped envelope

SAE self-addressed envelope

IRC International Reply Coupon, for use in countries other than your own

(For words and expressions relating specifically to writing and publishing, see the Glossary in the back of this book)

— TEAR ALONG PERFORATION —

WRITERSMARKET.COM

Here's what you'll find at WritersMarket.com:

More than 5,600 listings — At WritersMarket.com, you'll find thousands of listings that couldn't fit in the book! It's the most comprehensive database of verified markets available.

Easy-to-use searchable database — Looking for a specific magazine or book publisher? Just type in the title or keyword for broad category results.

Listings updated daily — It doesn't look good to address your query letter to the wrong editor or agent. . .and with WritersMarket.com, that will never happen. You'll be on top of all the industry developments. . .as soon as they happen!

Personalized for you — Stay on top of your publishing contacts with Submission Tracker; Store your best-bet markets in Favorites Folders; and get updates to your publishing areas of interest, every time you log in.

Subscribe today and save $10!

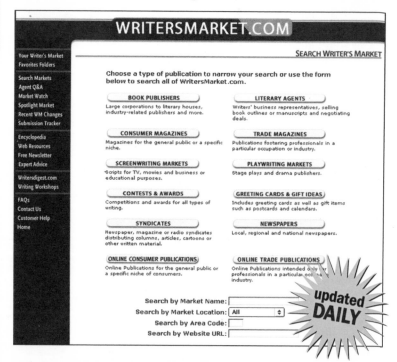

Tear out your handy bookmark
for fast reference to symbols and abbreviations used in this book

WM05

2005 Writer's Market®

Kathryn S. Brogan, Editor

Robert Lee Brewer, Assistant Editor

WRITER'S DIGEST BOOKS
CINCINNATI, OH

Complaint Procedure

If you feel you have not been treated fairly by a listing in *Writer's Market* or *Writer's Market Deluxe Edition*, we advise you to take the following steps:

- First try to contact the listing. Sometimes one phone call or a letter can quickly clear up the matter.

- Document all your correspondence with the listing. When you write to us with a complaint, provide the details of your submission, the date of your first contact with the listing and the nature of your subsequent correspondence.

- We will enter your letter into our files and attempt to contact the listing.

- The number and severity of complaints will be considered in our decision whether to delete the listing from the next edition.

Editorial Director, Writer's Digest Books: Barbara Kuroff
Managing Editor, Writer's Digest Books: Alice Pope

Writer's Market Website: www.writersmarket.com

Writer's Digest Website: www.writersdigest.com

2005 Writer's Market. Copyright © 2004 by Writer's Digest Books. Published by F&W Publications, 4700 East Galbraith Rd., Cincinnati, Ohio 45236. Printed and bound in the United States of America. All rights reserved. No part of this book may be reproduced in any form or by any electronic or mechanical means including information storage and retrieval systems without written permission from the publisher. Reviewers may quote brief passages to be printed in a magazine or newspaper.

Library of Congress Catalog Number 31-20772
International Standard Serial Number 0084-2729
International Standard Book Number 1-58297-271-0
International Standard Book Number 1-58297-272-9 (*Writer's Market Deluxe Edition*)

Attention Booksellers: This is an annual directory of F&W Publications. Return deadline for this edition is December 31, 2005.

Contents

CONSUMER MAGAZINES

TRADE JOURNALS

CONTESTS & AWARDS

RESOURCES

INDEXES

From the Editor

When I was little, my dad used to tell me bedtime stories about a girl named "Katie White." (Obviously, a modification of the fictional character Snow White.) As I grew older, too old for bedtime stories, or so I thought, he would modify these tales, and tell them to me as a means of conveying important life lessons or morals. After I graduated from college, moved away from home, and started a career, he still managed to work in an encouraging Katie White tale from time to time—just like he did today.

When my dad e-mailed me the most recent Katie White story, he did so knowing I was on deadline for this book. He encouraged me to look into my "magic mirror" to find the comfort and reassurance for which I was searching. The most important thing I learned when I looked into the mirror was: No matter how often or how much things change, you can always find one thing that remains the same. And that's definitely the case with this edition of *Writer's Market*.

I know when you went to your local bookstore to purchase this book, you probably thought, "What happened? This doesn't look like the *Writer's Market* I know." As you quickly thumbed through the pages, your curiosity, or in some cases your panic, piqued. "What are these tabs and charts? If the book looks this different, is the information still complete and accurate?" Remember what I just said: No matter how often or how much things change, there's always one thing that remains the same. *Writer's Market* is still the freelance writer's bible, and it will continue to be in the future.

Since 1921, *Writer's Market* has been bringing you the most up-to-date information that every writer needs. Whether it's contact information and submission guidelines for publishers like HarperCollins and Random House, Inc., magazines like *Good Housekeeping* and *National Geographic*, or articles and interviews with best-selling authors Julia Cameron and Dave Barry, *Writer's Market* remains the most trusted source to help you get published and get paid for what you write.

I encourage you to dive into this edition and use it to find publishers for what you write. I also challenge you to look at the new design elements, and see how they improve the way you use the information presented. The other thing I challenge you to do is look into your own magic mirror, which in many cases is the pages in this book, and think about the old saying, "The more things change, the more they stay the same."

Kathryn Struckel Brogan

Kathryn Struckel Brogan, Editor, *Writer's Market*
writersmarket@fwpubs.com

Getting Started

How to Use Writer's Market

Writer's Market is here to help you decide where and how to submit your writing to appropriate markets. Each listing contains information about the editorial focus of the market, how it prefers material to be submitted, payment information, and other helpful tips.

WHAT'S INSIDE?

Since 1921, *Writer's Market* has been giving you the important information you need to knowledgeably approach a market. We've continued to search out improvements to help you access that information more efficiently.

New! Navigational tools. We've taken the pages of *Writer's Market* and redesigned them with you, the user, in mind. Within the pages you will find a fresh, new look including more **readable market listings** and **accessible charts and graphs**. For example, one such chart can be found in the ever-popular **How Much Should I Charge?** We've taken all of the updated information in this feature and put it into an easy-to-read and navigate chart, making it easier than ever for you to find the freelance jobs you are looking for and the rates that accompany each job.

New! Tabs. We've added user-friendly tabs to each section of *Writer's Market* so you can quickly find the section you need most.

Symbols. There are a variety of symbols that appear before each listing. A key to all of the symbols appears on the back inside cover and on a removable bookmark. However, there are a few symbols we'd like to point out. In book publishers, the ⚷ quickly sums up a publisher's interests. In Consumer Magazines the ⚷ zeroes in on what areas of that market are particularly open to freelancers to help you break in to that market. Other symbols let you know whether a listing is new to the book (**N**), a book publisher accepts only agented writers (**A**), comparative pay rates for a magazine (**$**-**$$$$**), and more.

Acquisition names, royalty rates, and advances. In the Book Publishers section we identify acquisition editors with the boldface word **Acquisitions** to help you get your manuscript to the right person. Royalty rates and advances are highlighted in boldface, as well as other important information on the percentage of first-time writers and unagented writers the company publishes, the number of books published, and the number of manuscripts received each year.

Editors, pay rates, and percentage of material written by freelance writers. In the Consumer Magazines and Trade Journal sections, we identify who to send your query or article to by the boldface word **Contact**. The amount (percentage) of material accepted from freelance writers, and the pay rates for features, columns and departments, and fillers are also highlighted in boldface to help you quickly identify the information you need to know when considering whether to submit your work.

Query formats. We asked editors how they prefer to receive queries and have indicated in the listings whether they prefer queries by mail, e-mail, fax, or phone. Be sure to check an editor's individual preference before sending your query.

Articles. All of the articles, with the exception of a few standard pieces, are new to this edition. Newer, unpublished writers should be sure to read the articles in the **For Beginning Writers** section, while more experienced writers should focus on those in **The Business of Writing** section. In addition to these sections, there is also a section of **Interviews** with industry professionals and other career-oriented professionals, as well as best-selling authors.

IF *WRITER'S MARKET* IS NEW TO YOU . . .

A quick look at the **Contents** pages will familiarize you with the arrangement of *Writer's Market*. The three largest sections of the book are the market listings of Book Publishers;

Important listing information

Important

1. Listings are based on editorial questionnaires and interviews. They are not advertisements; publishers do not pay for their listings. The markets are not endorsed by *Writer's Market* editors. F+W Publications, Inc., Writer's Digest Books, and its employees go to great effort to ascertain the validity of information in this book. However, transactions between users of the information and individuals and/or companies are strictly between those parties.

2. All listings have been verified before publication of this book. If a listing has not changed from last year, then the editor said the market's needs have not changed and the previous listing continues to accurately reflect its policies.

3. *Writer's Market* reserves the right to exclude any listing.

4. When looking for a specific market, check the index. A market may not be listed for one of these reasons:

   - It doesn't solicit freelance material.

   - It doesn't pay for material.

   - It has gone out of business.

   - It has failed to verify or update its listing for this edition.

   - It hasn't answered *Writer's Market* inquiries satisfactorily. (To the best of our ability, and with our readers' help, we try to screen fraudulent listings.)

5. Individual markets that appeared in last year's edition but are not listed in this edition are included in the General Index, with a notation giving the reason for their exclusion.

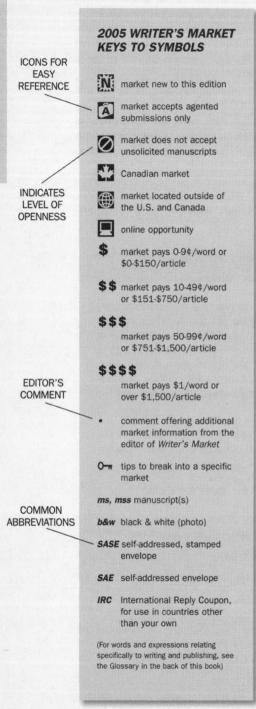

ICONS FOR
EASY
REFERENCE

INDICATES
LEVEL OF
OPENNESS

EDITOR'S
COMMENT

COMMON
ABBREVIATIONS

2005 WRITER'S MARKET KEYS TO SYMBOLS

N market new to this edition

A market accepts agented submissions only

⊘ market does not accept unsolicited manuscripts

🍁 Canadian market

🌐 market located outside of the U.S. and Canada

▣ online opportunity

$ market pays 0-9¢/word or $0-$150/article

$ $ market pays 10-49¢/word or $151-$750/article

$$$
market pays 50-99¢/word or $751-$1,500/article

$$$$
market pays $1/word or over $1,500/article

• comment offering additional market information from the editor of *Writer's Market*

O─ tips to break into a specific market

ms, mss manuscript(s)

b&w black & white (photo)

SASE self-addressed, stamped envelope

SAE self-addressed envelope

IRC International Reply Coupon, for use in countries other than your own

(For words and expressions relating specifically to writing and publishing, see the Glossary in the back of this book)

Consumer Magazines; and Trade Journals. You will also find other sections of market listings for Literary Agents and Contests & Awards.

Narrowing your search

After you've identified the market categories you're interested in, you can begin researching specific markets within each section.

Book Publishers are categorized, in the **Book Publishers Subject Index**, according to types of books they are interested in. If, for example, you plan to write a book on a religious topic, simply turn to the Book Publishers Subject Index on page 1077 and look under the Religion subhead in Nonfiction for the names and page numbers of companies that publish such books.

Consumer Magazines and Trade Journals are categorized by subject within their respective sections to make it easier for you to identify markets for your work. If you want to publish an article dealing with retirement, you could look under the Retirement category of Consumer Magazines to find an appropriate market. You would want to keep in mind, however, that magazines in other categories might also be interested in your article (for example, women's magazines publish such material as well).

Interpreting the markets

Once you've identified companies or publications that cover the subjects in which you're interested, you can begin evaluating specific listings to pinpoint the markets most receptive to your work and most beneficial to you.

In evaluating an individual listing, first check the location of the company, the types of material it is interested in seeing, submission requirements, and rights and payment policies. Depending upon your personal concerns, any of these items could be a deciding factor as you determine which markets you plan to approach. Many listings also include a reporting time, which lets you know how long it will typically take for the publisher to respond to your initial query or submission. (We suggest that you allow an additional two months for a response, just in case your submission is under further review or the publisher is backlogged.)

Check the Glossary in the back of the book for unfamiliar words. Specific symbols and abbreviations are explained in the key appearing on the back inside cover as well as on a removable bookmark. The most important abbreviation is SASE—self-addressed, stamped envelope. Always enclose a SASE when you send unsolicited queries, proposals, or manuscripts.

A careful reading of the listings will reveal that many editors are very specific about their needs. Your chances of success increase if you follow directions to the letter. Often companies do not accept unsolicited manuscripts and return them unread. If a company does not accept unsolicited manuscripts (⊘), it is indicated in the listing.

Whenever possible, obtain writer's guidelines before submitting material. You can usually obtain guidelines by sending a SASE to the address in the listing. Magazines often post their guidelines on their website as well. Most of the listings indicate how writer's guidelines are made available. You should also familiarize yourself with the company's publications. Many of the listings contain instructions on how to obtain sample copies, catalogs, or market lists. The more research you do upfront, the better your chances of acceptance, publication, and payment.

Guide to listing features

Below is an example of the market listings you'll find in each section of *Writer's Market*. Note the callouts that identify various format features of the listing.

LISTING PAYING $1/WORD OR OVER $1,500/ARTICLE

WHERE TO SEND QUERY OR ARTICLE

WHEN TO FOLLOW UP

WHO TO CONTACT

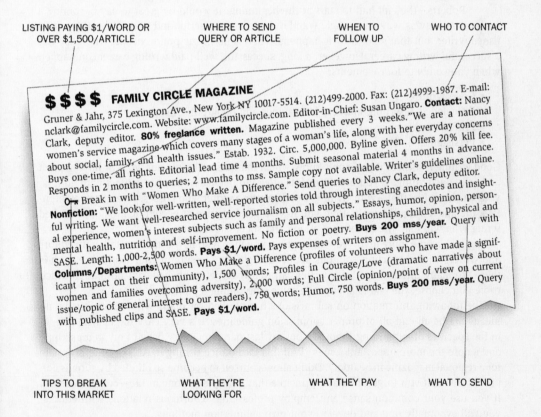

$$$$ FAMILY CIRCLE MAGAZINE
Gruner & Jahr, 375 Lexington Ave., New York NY 10017-5514. (212)499-2000. Fax: (212)4999-1987. E-mail: nclark@familycircle.com. Website: www.familycircle.com. Editor-in-Chief: Susan Ungaro. **Contact:** Nancy Clark, deputy editor. **80% freelance written.** Magazine published every 3 weeks."We are a national women's service magazine which covers many stages of a woman's life, along with her everyday concerns about social, family, and health issues." Estab. 1932. Circ. 5,000,000. Byline given. Offers 20% kill fee. Buys one-time, all rights. Editorial lead time 4 months. Submit seasonal material 4 months in advance. Responds in 2 months to queries; 2 months to mss. Sample copy not available. Writer's guidelines online.

O→ Break in with "Women Who Make A Difference." Send queries to Nancy Clark, deputy editor.

Nonfiction: "We look for well-written, well-reported stories told through interesting anecdotes and insightful writing. We want well-researched service journalism on all subjects." Essays, humor, opinion, personal experience, women's interest subjects such as family and personal relationships, children, physical and mental health, nutrition and self-improvement. No fiction or poetry. **Buys 200 mss/year.** Query with SASE. Length: 1,000-2,500 words. **Pays $1/word.** Pays expenses of writers on assignment.

Columns/Departments: Women Who Make a Difference (profiles of volunteers who have made a significant impact on their community), 1,500 words; Profiles in Courage/Love (dramatic narratives about women and families overcoming adversity), 2,000 words; Full Circle (opinion/point of view on current issue/topic of general interest to our readers), 750 words; Humor, 750 words. **Buys 200 mss/year.** Query with published clips and SASE. **Pays $1/word.**

TIPS TO BREAK INTO THIS MARKET

WHAT THEY'RE LOOKING FOR

WHAT THEY PAY

WHAT TO SEND

Before Your First Sale

Everything in life has to start somewhere and that somewhere is always at the beginning. The same is true for writers. Stephen King, J.K. Rowling, John Grisham, Nora Roberts—they all had to start at the beginning. It would be great to say becoming a writer is as easy as waving a magic wand over your manuscript and "Poof!" you're a published writer, but that's not how it happens. There's no magic potion or one true "key" to a successful writing career. However, a long, successful, well-paid writing career *can* happen when you combine four elements:

- Good writing
- Knowledge of writing markets (magazines and book publishers)
- Professionalism
- Persistence

Good writing is useless if you don't know which markets will buy your work or how to pitch and sell your writing. If you aren't professional and persistent in your contact with editors, your writing is just that—your writing. But if you are a writer who possesses, and can manipulate, the above four elements, then you have a good chance at becoming a paid, published writer who will reap the benefits of a long and successful career.

As you become more involved with writing, you may read new articles or talk with editors and writers with conflicting opinions about the right way to submit your work. The truth is there are many different routes a writer can follow to get published, but no matter which route you choose, the end is always the same—becoming a published writer.

The following information on submissions has worked for many writers, but it is by no means the be-all-end-all of proper submission guidelines. It's very easy to get wrapped up in the specifics of submitting (Should I put my last name on every page of my manuscript?) and ignore the more important issues (Will this idea on ice fishing in Alaska be appropriate for a regional magazine in Seattle?). Don't allow yourself to become so blinded by submission procedures that you forget the basic principle that guides everyone in life—common sense. If you use your common sense and employ professional, courteous relations with editors, you will eventually find and develop your own submission methods.

DEVELOP YOUR IDEAS, THEN TARGET THE MARKETS

Writers often think of an interesting story, complete the manuscript, and then begin the search for a suitable publisher or magazine. While this approach is common for fiction, poetry, and screenwriting, it reduces your chances of success in many nonfiction writing areas. Instead, try choosing categories that interest you and study those sections in *Writer's*

Market. Select several listings you consider good prospects for your type of writing. Sometimes the individual listings will even help you generate ideas.

Next, make a list of the potential markets for each idea. Make the initial contact with markets using the method stated in the market listings. If you exhaust your list of possibilities, don't give up. Instead, reevaluate the idea or try another angle. Continue developing ideas and approaching markets with the ideas. Identify and rank potential markets for an idea and continue the process.

As you submit to the various publications listed in *Writer's Market*, it's important to remember that every magazine is published with a particular audience and slant in mind. Probably the number one complaint we receive from editors is the submissions they receive are completely wrong for their magazines. The first mark of professionalism is to know your market well. That knowledge starts in *Writer's Market*, but you should also do your own detective work. Search out back issues of the magazines you wish to write for, pick up recent issues at your local newsstand, or visit magazines' websites—anything that will help you figure out what subjects specific magazines publish. This research is also helpful in learning what topics have been covered ad nauseum—the topics you should stay away from or approach in a fresh, new way. Magazine's websites are invaluable as most websites post the current issue of the magazine as well as back issues of the magazine, and most offer writer's guidelines.

Prepare for rejection and the sometimes lengthy wait. When a submission is returned, check your file folder of potential markets for that idea. Cross off the market that rejected the idea. If the editor has given you suggestions or reasons why the manuscript was not accepted, you might want to incorporate these suggestions when revising your manuscript. After revising your manuscript mail it to the next market on your list.

Take rejection with a grain of salt

Rejection is a way of life in the publishing world. It's inevitable in a business that deals with such an overwhelming number of applicants for such a limited number of positions. Anyone who has published has lived through many rejections, and writers with thin skin are at a distinct disadvantage. A rejection letter is not a personal attack. It simply indicates your submission is not appropriate for that market. Writers who let rejection dissuade them from pursuing their dream or who react to an editor's "No" with indignation or fury do themselves a disservice. Writers who let rejection stop them do not publish. Resign yourself to facing rejection now. You will live through it, and you'll eventually overcome it.

Reminder

QUERY AND COVER LETTERS

A query letter is a brief, one-page letter used as a tool to hook an editor and get him interested in your idea. When you send a query letter to a magazine, you are trying to get an editor to buy your idea or article. When you query a book publisher, you are attempting to get an editor interested enough in your idea to request your book proposal or your entire manuscript. (*Note:* Some book editors prefer to receive book proposals on first contact. Check individual listings for which method editors prefer.)

While there are no set-in-stone rules for writing query letters, there are some basic guidelines to help you write a polished, well-organized query:

- **Limit it to one page, single-spaced,** and address the editor by name (Mr. or Ms. and the surname). *Note:* Do not assume that a person is a Mr. or Ms. unless it is obvious from the name listed. For example, if you are contacting a D.J. Smith, do not assume that D.J. should be preceded by Mr. or Ms. Instead, address the letter to D.J. Smith.

- **Grab the editor's interest with a strong opening.** Some magazine queries begin with a paragraph meant to approximate the lead of the intended article.
- **Indicate how you intend to develop the article or book.** Give the editor some idea of the work's structure and content.
- **Let the editor know if you have photos** or illustrations available to accompany your magazine article.
- **Mention any expertise or training that qualifies** you to write the article or book. If you've been published before, mention it; if not, don't.
- **End with a direct request to write the article** (or, if you're pitching a book, ask for the go-ahead to send in a full proposal or the entire manuscript). Give the editor an idea of the expected length and delivery date of your manuscript.

Another question that arises is: If I don't hear from an editor in the reported response time, how do I know when I can safely send the query to another market? Many writers find it helpful to indicate in their query that if they don't receive a response from the editor (slightly after the listed reporting time), they will assume the editor is not interested. It's best to take this approach, particularly if your topic is timely.

A brief, single-spaced cover letter is helpful when sending a manuscript as it helps personalize the submission. However, if you have previously queried the editor, use the cover letter to politely and briefly remind the editor of that query—when it was sent, what it contained, etc. "Here is the piece on low-fat cooking that I queried you about on December 12. I look forward to hearing from you at your earliest convenience." Do not use the cover letter as a sales pitch.

See Also

If you are submitting to a market that accepts unsolicited manuscripts, a cover letter is useful because it personalizes your submission. You can, and should, include information about the manuscript, yourself, your publishing history, and your qualifications.

The Query Letter Clinic on page 20 offers eight different query letters, some that work and some that don't, as well as editors' comments on why the letters were either successful or failed to garner an assignment.

Query letter resources

For More Info

The following list of books provide you with more detailed information on writing query letters, cover letters, and book proposals. All titles are published by Writer's Digest Books.

- *Formatting & Submitting Your Manuscript, Edition 2*, by Cynthia Laufenberg and the Editors of Writer's Digest Books.
- *How to Write Attention-Grabbing Query & Cover Letters*, by John Wood.
- *How to Write a Book Proposal, 3rd Edition*, by Michael Larsen.
- *The Marshall Plan for Getting Your Novel Published*, by Evan Marshall.
- *The Writer's Digest Writing Clinic*, edited by Kelly Nickell.
- *Writer's Market Companion, 2nd Edition*, by Joe Feiertag and Mary Cupito.

Querying for fiction

Fiction is sometimes queried, but more often not. Many fiction editors won't decide on a submission until they have seen the complete manuscript. When submitting a fiction book idea, most editors prefer to see at least a synopsis and sample chapters (usually the first three). For fiction published in magazines, most editors want to see the complete short story manuscript. If an editor does request a query for fiction, it should include a description of the main theme and story line, including the conflict and resolution. Take a look at individual listings to see what editors prefer to receive.

NONFICTION BOOK PROPOSALS

Most nonfiction books are sold by a book proposal—a package of materials that details what your book is about, who its intended audience is, and how you intend to write the book. It includes some combination of a cover or query letter, an overview, an outline, author's information sheet, and sample chapters. Editors also want to see information about the audience for your book and about titles that compete with your proposed book.

Submitting a nonfiction book proposal

A proposal package should include the following items:

- **A cover or query letter.** This letter should be a short introduction to the material you include in the proposal.
- **An overview.** This is a brief summary of your book. For nonfiction, it should detail your book's subject and give an idea of how that subject will be developed. If you're sending a synopsis of a novel, cover the basic plot.
- **An outline.** The outline covers your book chapter by chapter and should include all major points covered in each chapter. Some outlines are done in traditional outline form, but most are written in paragraph form.
- **An author's information sheet.** This information should acquaint the editor with your writing background and convince her of your qualifications to write about the subject of your book.
- **Sample chapters.** Many editors like to see sample chapters, especially for a first book. Sample chapters show the editor how you write and develop ideas from your outline.
- **Marketing information.** Facts about how and to whom your book can be successfully marketed is now expected to accompany every book proposal. If you can provide information about the audience for your book and suggest ways the book publisher can reach those people, you will increase your chances of acceptance.
- **Competitive title analysis.** Check the *Subject Guide* to *Books in Print* for other titles on your topic. Write a one- or two-sentence synopsis of each. Point out how your book differs and improves upon existing topics.

A WORD ABOUT AGENTS

An agent represents a writer's work to buyers, negotiates contracts, follows up to see that contracts are fulfilled, and generally handles a writer's business affairs, leaving the writer free to write. Effective agents are valued for their contacts in the publishing industry, their savvy about which publishers and editors to approach with which ideas, their ability to guide an author's career, and their business sense.

While most book publishers listed in *Writer's Market* publish books by unagented writers, some of the larger houses are reluctant to consider submissions that have not reached them through a literary agent. Companies with such a policy are noted by an (🅐) icon at the beginning of the listing, as well as in the submission information within the listing.

Writer's Market includes a list of 50 literary agents who are all members of the Association of Authors' Representatives and who are also actively seeking new and established writers. For a more comprehensive resource on finding and working with an agent, see *2005 Guide to Literary Agents*.

MANUSCRIPT FORMAT

You can increase your chances of publication by following a few standard guidelines regarding the physical format of your manuscript. It should be your goal to make your manuscript readable. Use these suggestions as you would any other suggestions: Use what works for you and discard what doesn't.

In general, when submitting a manuscript, you should use white, $8\frac{1}{2} \times 11$, 20 lb. paper, and you should also choose a legible, professional looking font (i.e., Times New Roman)— no all-italic or artsy fonts. Your entire manuscript should be double-spaced with a $1\frac{1}{2}$-inch margin on all sides of the page. Once you are ready to print your manuscript, you should print either on a laser printer or an ink-jet printer.

ESTIMATING WORD COUNT

Many computers will provide you with a word count of your manuscript. Your editor will count again after editing the manuscript. Although your computer is counting characters, an editor or production editor is more concerned about the amount of space the text will occupy on a page. Several small headlines or subheads, for instance, will be counted the same by your computer as any other word of text. However, headlines and subheads usually employ a different font size than the body text, so an editor may count them differently to be sure enough space has been estimated for larger type.

For short manuscripts, it's often quickest to count each word on a representative page and multiply by the number of pages. You can get a very rough count by multiplying the number of pages in your manuscript by 250 (the average number of words on a double-spaced typewritten page).

PHOTOGRAPHS AND SLIDES

In some cases, the availability of photographs and slides can be the deciding factor as to whether an editor will accept your submission. This is especially true when querying a publication that relies heavily on photographs, illustrations, or artwork to enhance the article (i.e., craft magazines, hobby magazines, etc.). In some instances, the publication may offer additional payment for photographs or illustrations.

Check the individual listings for photograph submission guidelines and to find out which magazines review photographs. Most publications prefer that you do not send photographs with your submission. However, if photographs or illustrations are available, you should indicate as such in your query. As with manuscripts, never send the originals of your photographs or illustrations. Instead, send prints or duplicates of slides and transparencies.

SEND PHOTOCOPIES

If there is one hard-and-fast rule in publishing, it's this: *Never* send the original (or only) copy of your manuscript. Most editors cringe when they find out a writer has sent the only copy of their manuscript. You should always send photocopies of your manuscript.

Some writers choose to send a self-addressed, stamped postcard with a photocopied submission. In their cover letter they suggest if the editor is not interested in their manuscript, it may be tossed out and a reply sent on the postcard. This method is particularly helpful when sending your submissions to international markets.

Manuscript formatting checklist

1 Type your real name (even if you use a pseudonym) and contact information.

2 Double-space twice.

3 Estimated word count and the rights you are offering.

4 Type your title in capital letters, double-space and type "by," double-space again, and type your name (or pseudonym if you're using one).

5 Double-space twice, then indent first paragraph and start text of your manuscript.

6 On subsequent pages, type your name, a dash, and the page number in the upper left or right corner.

Your name   50,000 words
Your street address   World rights
City, State ZIP code
Day and evening phone numbers
E-mail address

TITLE

by

Your Name

You can increase your chances of publication by following a few standard guidelines regarding the physical format of your article or manuscript. It should be your goal to make your manuscript readable. Use these suggestions as you would any other suggestions: Use what works for you and discard what doesn't.

In general, when submitting a manuscript, you should use white, 8½ x 11, 20-lb. bond paper, and you should also choose a legible, professional-looking font (i.e., Times New Roman)—no all-italic or artsy fonts. Your entire manuscript should be double-spaced with a 1½ -inch margin

---

Your Name - 2

on all sides of the page. Once you are ready to print your article or manuscript, you should print either on a laser printer or an ink-jet printer.

Remember, though, articles should either be written after you send a one-page query letter to an editor, and the editor then asks you to write the article. If, however, you are sending an article "on spec" to an editor, you should send both a query letter and the complete article.

Fiction is a little different from nonfiction articles, in that it is only sometimes queried, but more often not. Many fiction editors won't decide on a submission until they have seen the complete manuscript. When submitting a fiction book idea, most editors prefer to see at least a synopsis and sample chapters (usually the first three). For fiction that is published

Mailing manuscripts

For More Info

- Fold manuscripts under five pages into thirds, and send in a #10 SASE.
- Mail manuscripts five pages or more unfolded in a 9×12 or 10×13 SASE.
- For return envelope, fold the envelope in half, address it to yourself, and add a stamp or, if going to Canada or another international destination, International Reply Coupons (available at most main branches of your local post office).
- Don't send by Certified mail—this is a sign of an amateur.

Useful Websites

MAILING SUBMISSIONS

No matter what size manuscript you're mailing, always include a self-addressed, stamped envelope (SASE) with sufficient return postage. The website for the U.S. Postal Service (www.usps.gov) and the website for the Canadian Post (www.canadapost.ca) both have postage calculators if you are unsure of how much postage you'll need to affix.

A book manuscript should be mailed in a sturdy, well-wrapped box. Enclose a self-addressed mailing label and paper clip your return postage to the label. However, be aware that some book publishers do not return unsolicited manuscripts, so make sure you know the practice of the publisher before sending any unsolicited material.

Types of mail service

There are many different mailing service options available to you whether you are sending a query letter or a complete manuscript. You can work with the U.S. Postal Service, United Parcel Service, Federal Express, or any number of private mailing companies. The following are the five most common types of mailing services offered by the U.S. Postal Service.

- **First Class** is an expensive way to mail a manuscript, but many writers prefer it. First-Class mail generally receives better handling and is delivered more quickly than Standard mail.
- **Priority mail** reaches its destination within two or three days.
- **Standard mail** rates are available for packages, but be sure to pack your materials carefully because they will be handled roughly. To make sure your package will be returned to you if it is undeliverable, print "Return Postage Guaranteed" under your address.
- **Certified mail** must be signed for when it reaches its destination.
- **Registered mail** is a high-security method of mailing where the contents are insured. The package is signed in and out of every office it passes through, and a receipt is returned to the sender when the package reaches its destination.

Entry-Level Opportunities

10 Gigs for Rookie Writers

by Robert W. Bly

What markets, publications, clients, and opportunities welcome rookie writers with open arms? Following are ten writing gigs you might want to consider. All ten are areas open to working with unpublished and inexperienced novice writers who have a lot of talent but few credentials.

Once you get some experience, satisfied clients, and clips under your belt with these assignments, you'll have the credentials and portfolio to move up to bigger, better-paying, and more demanding markets.

1. Local newspapers

The easiest place to get published is as a reporter for your town newspaper. Check the help-wanted classifieds of your local weekly paper. Almost every week there will be a "reporters-wanted" ad placed by that paper.

Many local newspapers have trouble finding writers because the pay is lousy, the prestige is low, the assignments dull, and the hours inconvenient. But by taking on this assignment, you can earn a few spare-time dollars—and more important, get your byline in a real newspaper.

Save every article you write. You'll soon have a file full of clips that can help you secure writing assignments at larger daily, regional, or even national newspapers. Also, take a basic journalism course at your local adult-education program or community college to learn proper newspaper style.

2. Trade publications

Big consumer magazines can be tough for rookies to break into. However, thousands of business magazines, known as "trade journals," are eager to hire rookie writers—as long as you can fill their pages with relevant, well-written material for their specialized audience. (Note: A complete list of Trade Journals begins on page 820).

What stories would a trade editor assign to a freelancer like you? A popular format is the case history, where you tell how one company solved a particular problem—including what

See Also

ROBERT W. BLY has earned a six-figure annual income as a freelance writer for more than two decades. He is the author of more than 50 books including *Secrets of a Freelance Writer* (Henry Holt & Co., 1997) and *101 Ways to Make Every Second Count* (Career Press, 1999). Bob may be reached on the Web at www.bly.com or www.selling-yourself.com.

the problem was, the solutions they considered, the method or product they chose to solve the problem, how they implemented the solution, and the results achieved.

Another is the industry round up, where you might do brief profiles of products or companies in a particular area, i.e., for a construction magazine, a discussion of the available types of building insulation. Many trade journals run articles on business skills or management topics such as how to be a better leader or reduce stress on the job.

Pay scales for trade publications are generally lower than for consumer publications, but the editors are not as demanding, requiring fewer interviews and rewrites.

Writing for trade publications is a great way to break into magazines, get a byline, hone your skills, and build a folder of published articles. The best place to start: Look at the trade journals you get at work. The reason: Your familiarity with your industry and the publication gives you a better feel for how to talk to the editor's readers.

3. Comic books

Suddenly super heroes are undergoing a renaissance, thanks to blockbuster movies like *X-Men II* and *Daredevil*. You can you get in on the action by writing for comic books. One thing comic book editors look for is a demonstrated ability to tell a story. So, if you've written and published fiction, even for literary magazines that pay in contributor's copies, say so.

What's the best way to break into writing for Superman and the Hulk? "Do it yourself," says freelance comic book writer Andrew Helfer. "By that I mean you should find an artist (lots of aspiring ones prowling the Internet), put together an original comic, and publish it yourself (pretty cheap to do: black and white, around $1,000). Before printing, however, send copies to Diamond Comics Distributors, Inc. (www.diamondcomics.com) to see if they'd be willing to distribute it.

Useful Websites

"The point is to have a professional looking comic that you can send to mainstream comic publishers. Comic editors don't want to read scripts, but they may be inclined to read a comic if it looks interesting enough. They also like to hedge their bets. If you manage to get an assignment and the subsequent script doesn't meet with approval, the editor can always say you were *supposed* to be a professional—you even had a comic published! How was he to know you were a one-hit wonder?"

4. Nonfiction books

"Write what you know" is an oft-repeated piece of advice to rookie writers. Well, everybody knows something—and that something can be the topic for your first book.

How-to books are one of the most popular types of books, and one of the easiest to write and get published. An Amazon.com search found 63,703 books with the words "how to" in the title.

What do you know better than others? Your life experience usually yields the answer. If you had cancer, you are an authority on surviving cancer. If you were a guest on *Oprah*, you know how to get on *Oprah*. Your credentials—the work or life experience that prompted you to write the book—are what will sell an editor on you as the author. Many people might want to write a book about coping with children who have attention deficit disorder (ADD), but the fact that your child has ADD adds a depth and authority other writers cannot match.

If you're passionate about your topic and want to stay involved with it beyond writing a single book—maybe make it your writing specialty—consider starting a website on that topic. Publishers call this a "platform"—a built-in readership who knows you and will buy your book—and editors look for that when they are signing new authors. Having an e-mail list of 25,000 subscribers to your monthly online newsletter on ADD is mighty attractive to a publisher thinking of hiring you to write a book for them on that topic because they can count on sales to that audience.

5. Self-publishing and print on demand

If you can't find a publisher for your nonfiction book, don't despair. You can self-publish it or take it to a print-on-demand (POD) publishing house.

The authoritative guide to self-publishing your book is *The Self-Publishing Manual* (Para Publishing, 2000), by Dan Poynter. According to Poynter, self-publishers have more control over their work, get it to market faster, and keep more of the profits from book sales.

There are several nontraditional publishers that publish books on a POD basis: The books are printed only when ordered, using POD technology that prints books one at a time (as opposed to traditional book printing which has a minimum print run of thousands of copies). These POD publishers, which include AuthorHouse (formerly 1stBooks) and Xlibris, are halfway between self-publishing and traditional publishing. They don't typically pay an advance, but the royalty payments are higher than with a mainstream publishing house. And you do get to see your book in print—a great way to accelerate your writing career.

6. E-books

Another option open to authors is to write an e-book on a topic of interest to your potential buyers and format it as a downloadable PDF file, which you offer for sale on a website.

You drive potential buyers to your site through a variety of promotional methods, including ads and articles in other people's online newsletters (e-zines), banner advertising, sending e-mails, and "affiliate deals." An affiliate deal involves arranging with another online marketer to sell your e-book to his audience in exchange for a cut of the revenue—ranging from 30 percent to 50 percent.

7. Ghostwriting

A ghostwriter is someone who writes books and materials for other people. The ghostwriter does the actual writing, but the material is published under your client's byline, and the client is credited as the author.

"All it takes to become a ghostwriter is the ability to put your ego aside while writing for a client, study his or her word patterns, have perfect communication with the client, and be an expert in people skills," writes Eva Shaw in her book *Ghostwriting: How to Get Into the Business* (Paragon House, 1991).

Celebrities often work with ghostwriters to get their books written, but those engagements usually go to experienced ghostwriters. As a novice, you're more likely to be hired by professionals, businesses, or individuals who want to write and publish a book but don't want to do the work themselves.

8. Copywriting

Writing promotional and educational materials for local and national businesses can be extremely lucrative. Business clients hire freelancers to produce a wide range of materials, from annual reports and radio commercials to websites and direct-mail letters.

Your target prospect is the marketing director at a large business, or the president or owner at a small company. Pick up the phone or send a letter offering your services as a freelance business writer. Surprisingly, some of these clients are open to working with writers who have little or no previous experience.

9. Travel writing

Almost all regional or state daily newspapers have travel sections, and this section is the easiest to break into for the beginning writer. The editors of these sections are always looking for articles on museums, amusement parks, gardens, historical houses, shopping malls, wineries, and other things to do on the weekend, as well as pieces on vacation getaways.

Tip

The best way to get started: If you're going to an exotic destination for business or pleasure, contact the paper's travel editor and propose a story with an interesting hook (i.e., diving for treasure in the Cayman Islands).

Travel writers don't make a fortune, but they get published and the travel is a nice perk—often worth as much or more as the fees they get for their articles. "In nearly two decades, I've written hundreds of stories about destinations as far-flung as Poland and Mexico," says freelance travel writer Steenie Harvey. "Editors actually pay my expenses as I travel the globe reporting on their behalf."

10. Résumé writing

Okay, résumé writing won't lead to a gig writing articles for *The New York Times*, books for Random House, or annual reports for Coca-Cola, but it's an easy way to make a relatively high hourly wage doing what you love: writing.

Learning the craft isn't difficult. You can buy handbooks of model résumés that show you how to format and organize résumés—and which method is best for your client. You can create résumés on your PC using either a word-processing program such as Microsoft Word or a desktop publishing application such as Adobe InDesign. Most résumé writing software does a lot of the formatting for you, so your job is to fill in the client's education and employment history, which you get from his old résumé and by asking questions.

Clients are not difficult to get: Run a small classified ad (with your phone number) in the Sunday business section of your local paper offering, "résumé preparation services." A small Yellow Pages ad will also get the phone ringing.

Once you become proficient, it might take you just an hour or two to prepare a résumé, and you can charge anywhere from $100 to $300 each—the low end if your client is a student, the high end if she's a high-paid executive. On an hourly basis, expect to earn $50 to $150—not a bad wage for a novice writer.

How do you turn résumé writing into a bigger opportunity? Let clients know you also do freelance business writing. So when they land a job, they can call you for reports, letters, proposals, and other corporate-writing assignments their new employer needs done.

Popular Magazines

How to Break In

by Jenna Glatzer

You get that wistful look in your eyes as you stand at the grocery checkout line. You sigh a little, fingering the glossy covers of those gloriously popular magazines. A single tear forms as you realize that, for the 35th month in a row, your byline is in none of them.

Sure, you have your little successes. Your work has appeared in smaller magazines. Maybe your articles even show up regularly in local publications, on websites, in trade magazines, or in those mid-sized consumer magazines that never quite make the cut at the supermarket.

But you can't deny you ache to finally crack those glossies and feel like you're a member of the upper echelon of freelance writers.

How do I know? I've been there. And now that I've had the exciting experience of casually flipping to my articles and pointing them out to my friendly supermarket cashiers, I want to help you do the same.

Aim big, but think small

If you don't have a bio and clips to die for, major magazine editors aren't likely to trust you with a long feature assignment right away. Instead, aim for the short articles in the front of the magazine, and stay on the lookout for appropriate ideas you can flesh out in a few hundred words or less. For truly short articles, you can skip the query and just write the whole thing if you prefer—it usually requires about the same amount of effort.

Linda Wasmer Andrews has now written 1,700 articles for a wide list of impressive magazines, but says her first big break came in 1985 when she sold several short pieces to *American Health*. "Back in those prehistoric days, you couldn't just surf the Internet for leads, so I would go to the local medical library and spend hours combing through the current issues of medical journals looking for quirky ideas that would make my queries stand out," she says. "The first one that sold was a short item about the air quality in ice-skating rinks. Other successful pitches included seatbelts for dogs and a curved-bristle toothbrush. Those short clips in a big magazine landed me long assignments from small magazines, which landed me long assignments from big magazines—my ultimate goal, of course."

Find local subjects

Savvy freelancers never discount their local newspapers, and radio and television stations. You never know when you're going to find out about one of your neighbors who has a story

Tip

JENNA GLATZER is the editor of Absolute Write (www.absolutewrite.com) and the author of *Make a Real Living as a Freelance Writer* (Nomad Press, 2004), which you can read about at www.absolutewrite.com/jenna/books.htm.

worthy of a national audience. Be especially aware of local volunteers, extraordinary human-interest stories and town projects, and interesting entrepreneurs—many magazines are on the lookout for these subjects. And don't ignore kids' accomplishments—teen magazines use plenty of stories about outstanding youth.

Sheri Bell-Rehwoldt broke into *American Profile* by paying attention to her surroundings. "I pitched the magazine a story on Delaware City, a forgotten town that was trying to entice tourists so it could regain some of its former grandeur." Bell-Rehwoldt and her husband had been gallivanting around town, and were smart enough to stop by the visitor's center for research material.

Write your own story

Your personal experiences are potential goldmines. Think about the important life lessons you've learned, the challenges you've overcome, the stories that have captivated your friends and inspired other people. A story that is uniquely yours cannot be assigned to another writer, so your bio and clips are not as important in this area as your compelling tale.

While working at a public radio station, Andrea Cooper sold a first-person story about the station's Celtic music program to *The Christian Science Monitor*. My first major credit was from *Woman's World*, where I told the story of how my fiancé helped me overcome agoraphobia.

Meet editors

If you have a chance to meet editors at conferences or networking events, do it! Sometimes you'll have an opportunity to pitch (sell a magazine idea) on the spot; other times, it's considered poor form to do business at an event, but you can listen to the editor talk and then pitch by e-mail later. Some freelancers also got their starts by landing internships or entry-level positions at magazines and using the time, in part, to make contacts.

At a writers' conference many years ago, Veda Eddy listened to a *Sports Illustrated* editor speak about her need for "quirky pieces" on sports-related subjects. Although Eddy had never read the magazine, she pitched the editor an article about the ways racehorses are named. "She said it sounded promising and asked me to follow up with a written query," says Veda. "That was the first of about six articles I wrote for *Sports Illustrated*, and it would never have happened if I hadn't had that personal contact with the editor."

Write "on spec"

Writing on speculation ("on spec") is a controversial issue among writers, but there's no denying that it can pay off. If you have no clips, or nothing you feel would impress the editor enough to assign you a particular piece, it may be worth it for you to write the article and hope it'll sell. Study the magazine's format to get an idea of the right word count and style, and then give it your best shot.

That's what Lisa Marie Beamer and Janine Adams did. Beamer won a writing contest sponsored by an online writers' group, and entrants were encouraged to submit their work to paying markets after the contest ended. She edited her entry until she thought it was marketable, and then sent it to *FamilyFun*. "I was shocked beyond belief when, two months later, a senior editor called to tell me they were interested in using my essay for their 'My Good Idea' column!" Adams queried *Good Housekeeping* about a profile of an animal-rescue activist, and they asked for the story on spec. It was published in 1997, and since then, Adams has written for many other national magazines.

Work harder than everyone else

If you're trying to break in, be willing to do extra work up front to give the editor confidence in your ability to handle the assignment. Research, nail down experts, perfect your lead, find anecdotes, and suggest sidebars and visuals where appropriate.

"I had been writing for trade publications and smaller magazines for a few years—and unsuccessfully pitching the big women's pubs—when I learned that editors like to see a lot of research in your queries," says Linda Formichelli, a freelancer who has written for *Family Circle*, *Woman's Day*, and *Redbook*.

Tip

No magic key

Many writers believe if they can just land one article in a well-known magazine, they'll be set and will never lack assignments again. The truth is most freelancers find that getting a byline in a major magazine helps, but it doesn't guarantee future sales. Jane Louise Boursaw's first major sale was to *Woman's Day*, and she says, "I felt like the queen of the world after getting that byline. That story helped me get my foot in the door and gave me the confidence to keep going, but I still had to keep chugging forward with queries."

Ditch the idea of a "magic key" market that's going to unlock the magazine industry's door, and instead, plan to knock on many doors before you make it to the V.I.P. suite.

Keep on querying

It may help if you give yourself a weekly "query quota." Boursaw suggests two or three well-crafted queries per week, whereas Bell-Rehwoldt aims for five.

Rather than shooting the same query letter to dozens of magazines at once, though, challenge yourself to make your pitch a perfect fit. Think of a magazine as a puzzle; your article must have all the right grooves, be the right size, and match the overall picture. If you can tell an editor just where your article belongs in the magazine and why her readers will be interested, your odds greatly improve.

And if you don't hear back from an editor, Adams says you should always follow up by e-mail or phone: "Don't take silence as a 'no.' "

Be audacious

There are many avenues that can lead you to your first big sale, but you have to be willing to take a risk. Beamer says she didn't have any confidence her first essay would sell. "I could have easily talked myself out of sending it, but I didn't. It sounds cliché, but you have to take what might seem like unrealistic chances if you're going to succeed. You never know which chance might pay off."

When the odds seem insurmountable, remember: Every successful freelancer once had a blank list of credits. Keep learning, keep building those clips, and don't be afraid to shoot for the top. Today might just be your day.

For Beginning Writers

Query Letter Clinic

by Kathryn S. Brogan and Cynthia Laufenberg

The query letter is the catalyst in the chemical reaction of publishing. Overall, writing a query letter is a fairly simple process that serves one purpose—selling an article.

There are two types of queries, a query for a finished manuscript, and a query for an idea that has yet to be developed into an article. Either way, a query letter is the tool that sells an idea using brief, attention-getting prose.

WHAT SHOULD I INCLUDE IN A QUERY LETTER?

A query should tell an editor how you plan to handle and develop the proposed article. Many writers even include the lead of the article as the first sentence of their query as a sales pitch to the editor. A query letter should also show that you are familiar with the publication and tell the editor why you are the most qualified person to write the article.

Beyond the information mentioned above, a query letter is also the appropriate place to state the availability of photographs or artwork. Do not send photographs with your query. You can also include a working title and a projected word count. Some writers also indicate whether a sidebar or other accompanying short would be appropriate, and the type of research they plan to conduct. It is also appropriate to include a tentative deadline and to indicate if the query is being simultaneously submitted.

WHAT SHOULD I *NOT* INCLUDE IN A QUERY LETTER?

The query letter is not the place to discuss pay rates. By mentioning what you would like to be paid, you are prematurely assuming the editor is going to buy your article. Plus, if you are really just looking to get published and get paid some amount of money, you could be doing yourself a disservice. If you offer a rate that is higher than what the editor is willing to pay, you could lose the assignment. And, if you offer a figure that's too low, you are short-changing yourself on what could possibly be a lucrative assignment.

Another thing you should avoid is requesting writer's guidelines or a sample copy of the publication. This is a red flag to the editor because it indicates you are not familiar with the magazine or its content. Don't use the query letter to list pages of qualifications. Only list those qualifications you feel would best help you land the gig. If you have too many qualifica-

KATHRYN S. BROGAN is the editor of *Writer's Market*, *Writer's Market Deluxe Edition*, and *Guide to Literary Agents*.

CYNTHIA LAUFENBERG is former managing editor of Writer's Digest Books and the author of *Formatting & Submitting Your Manuscript, Edition 2* (Writer's Digest Books). She lives in Narberth, Pennsylvania.

Things to avoid

1. **Don't try any cute attention-getting devices,** like marking the envelope "Personal." This also includes fancy stationery that lists every publication you've ever sold to, or "clever" slogans.

2. **Don't talk about fees.**

3. **Keep your opinions to yourself.**

4. **Don't tell the editors what others you've shown the idea think of it.** ("Several of my friends have read this and think it's marvelous . . ." is a certain sign of the amateur writer.) The same goes for comments from other editors.

5. **Don't name drop.** However, if you do know somebody who works for that magazine, or writes for it, or if you know an editor on another magazine who has bought your work and likes it, say so.

6. **Don't try to soft soap the editor** by telling him how great the magazine is, but definitely make it clear that you read it.

7. **Don't send any unnecessary enclosures,** such as a picture of yourself (or your prize-winning Labrador Retriever).

8. **Don't offer irrelevant information about yourself.** Simply tell the editor what there might be in your background that qualifies you to write this story.

9. **Know the magazine,** and send only those ideas that fit the format. Don't offer comments like, "I never read your magazine, but this seems to be a natural . . ." or "I know you don't usually publish articles about mountain-climbing, but . . ."

10. **Don't ask for a meeting** to discuss your idea further. If the editor feels this is necessary, he will suggest it.

11. **Don't ask for advice,** like, "If you don't think you can use this, could you suggest another magazine that could?"

12. **Don't offer to rewrite,** as this implies you know the article's not good enough as you've submitted it. Again, editors will ask for rewrites, if necessary, and they usually are.

13. **Don't make threats** like, "If I don't hear from you within four weeks I'll submit it elsewhere."

14. **Don't include a multiple-choice reply card,** letting the editor check a box to indicate whether he likes the idea.

From *Magazine Writing That Sells*, by Don McKinney (Writer's Digest Books).

For Beginning Writers

tions that you still feel would convince the editor to give you the assignment, include them as a separate page. Finally, never admit if five other editors rejected the query. This is your chance to shine, and sell the best article ever written.

HOW DO I FORMAT A QUERY LETTER?

There are no hard-and-fast rules when it comes to formatting your query letter. But there are some general, widely accepted guidelines like those listed below from *Formatting & Submitting Your Manuscript, Edition 2*, by Cynthia Laufenberg and the Editors of Writer's Digest Books (Writer's Digest Books).

- Use a standard font or typeface (avoid bold, script, or italics, except for publication titles).

For Beginning Writers

Clips and e-mail queries

When you send an e-mail query, you can provide clips five ways. Generally, there are no accepted standards for which is best, but the pros and cons of each method are described below.

1. **Include a line telling the editor that clips are available** on request. Then, mail, fax, or e-mail clips according to the editor's preference. This is a convenient solution for the writer, but not necessarily for the editor. The clips aren't available immediately, so you potentially slow the decision process by adding an additional step, and you lose any speed you've gained by e-mailing the query in the first place.

2. **Include electronic versions of the clips in the body** of the e-mail message. This can make for an awfully long e-mail, and it doesn't look as presentable as other alternatives, but it may be better than making the editor wait to download attachments or log on to a website.

3. **Include electronic versions of the articles as attachments.** The disadvantage here is the editor has to download the clips, which can take several minutes. Also, if there's a format disparity, the editor may not be able to read the attachment. The safest bet is to attach the documents as ".rtf" or ".txt" files, which should be readable with any word processing software, although you will lose formatting.

4. **Send the clips as a separate e-mail message.** This cuts the download time and eliminates software-related glitches, but it clutters the editor's e-mail queue.

5. **Set up a personal web page** and include your clips as hypertext links in or at the end of the e-mail (e.g., www.aolmembers.com/jackneff/smallbusinessclips). Setting up and maintaining the page takes a considerable amount of effort, but it may be the most convenient and reliable way for editors to access your clips electronically.

From *Formatting & Submitting Your Manuscript, Edition 2*, by Cynthia Laufenberg and the Editors of Writer's Digest Books (Writer's Digest Books).

- Your name, address, and phone number (plus e-mail and fax, if possible) should appear in the top right corner or on your letterhead.
- Use a 1-inch margin on all sides.
- Address the query to a specific editor, preferably the editor assigned to handle freelance submissions or who handles the section you're writing for. Note: The listings in *Writer's Market* provide a contact name for most submissions.
- Keep it to one page. If necessary, use a résumé or list of credits attached separately to provide additional information.
- Include a SASE or postcard for reply; state you have done so, either in the body of the letter or in a listing of enclosures.
- Use block format (no indentations).
- Single-space the body of the letter and double-space between paragraphs.
- When possible, mention that you can send the manuscript on disk or via e-mail.
- Thank the editor for considering your proposal.

WHEN SHOULD I FOLLOW UP?

Sometimes things happen, and your query never reaches the editor's hands. Problems can arise with the mail delivery, the query may have been sent to a different department, or the editor may have inadvertently thrown the query away. Whatever the reason, there are a few simple guidelines you should use when you send a follow-up letter.

You should wait to follow up on your query at least until after the reported response time in the *Writer's Market* listing for that publication. If, after two months, you have not received a response to your query, you should compose a brief follow-up letter. The letter should describe the original query sent, the date the query was sent, and a reply postcard or a SASE. Some writers find it helpful to include a photocopy of the original query to help jog the editor's memory.

Above all, though, be polite and businesslike when following up. Don't take the lack of response personal. Editors are only human—situations can arise that are beyond their control.

WHAT THE CLINIC SHOWS YOU

Unpublished writers wonder how published writers break into print. It's not a matter of luck. Published writers know how to craft a well-written, hard-hitting query. What follows are eight actual queries submitted to editors (names and addresses have been altered). Four queries are strong; four are not. Detailed comments from the editors show what the writer did and did not do to secure a sale. As you'll see, there is not a cut-and-dry "good" query format; every strong query works because of its own merit.

Good nonfiction magazine query

Cute. I'm already charmed and eager to go on reading.

Hooray! Got a couple of professionals on my hands.

The proposed topic is perfect subject matter for our magazine, which covers 20th century design, and there's a timely news peg to boot.

They lay out a clear angle for the story right upfront, and there's even a bit of controversy to keep things interesting.

This paragraph shows me the authors have already done a fair amount of research and made some initial contacts.

Reassuring to know the authors are on top of things in terms of excellent sources and photos.

The clips were impressive and clinched the assignment.

July 14, 2004

Cara Greenberg
Modernism Magazine
333 N. Main St.
Lambertville, NJ 08530

Dear Ms. Greenberg:

We just saw our first issue of *Modernism Magazine*. A friend brought it over to see if we have an authentic Saarinen table, and we do. We're full-time freelance writers who often write about art, architecture, and design.

Boston and its suburbs are well-endowed with Modernist gems. Bauhaus founder Walter Gropius' own home, which reopens to the public in May, is less than 10 miles away in Lincoln. The good news is the project has raised philosophical and curatorial issues about dealing with deteriorating modern materials. The "bad" news is The Society for the Preservation of New England Antiquities, decided not to refurbish the original furnishings.

Gropius had several Breuer prototype chairs. When the chrome began to flake during his lifetime, he sent them out to be re-chromed. Under their guidelines for conservation of artistic works, SPNEA is trying to protect the others from further flaking and rusting. Dealing with the house itself has raised curatorial issues, as Michael Lynch, VP of Properties, told us. A chemical analysis of the paint found Gropius used the very first version of latex paint as a primer. It was unstable, preventing all subsequent paint from sticking.

Gropius' daughter is coming to Boston at the end of April to help SPNEA place furnishings in the house, and will be available for interviews. SPNEA has done extensive documentation of the restoration project in 35mm slides, and they are available for a fee.

We've enclosed samples of our work from *American Craft* and *Metalsmith* magazines.

We look forward to hearing from you.

Sincerely,

Susan Scribe and Peter Penman
57 Pleasant Circle
Adroit, MA 45697
(508)865-7453
writers@email.com

Comments provided by Cara Greenberg, former editor-in-chief of *Modernism Magazine*.

Bad nonfiction magazine query

No contact information other than an e-mail address.

A bit presumptuous using my first name, but I'm not particularly offended, and it wouldn't have made any difference if the query had been a usable one.

This proposal is neither inappropriate, subject-wise, nor is it poorly written, but it suffers from utter vagueness. Since we are a special-interest magazine about 20th-century design and most of our readership is familiar with the Eames' work already, we would need a more unusual take on the subject than just a general overview of the designers' careers.

In other words, the writer has never been published before, and it's unlikely she knows the difference between a term paper and effective magazine writing.

To: Cara Greenberg
From: Ashley Adequate
aa@email.com

Dear Cara:

Charles and Ray Eames were the design titans of the Modernist movement, particularly during the 1950s. Their most famous creation, the Eames lounge chair and ottoman, is still a symbol of excellent design and taste. Especially in view of the resurgence of interest in mid-century furniture, an article on the background, design philosophy, and accomplishments of this remarkable couple would be timely and informative.

My qualifications to submit this article include a degree in interior design and a BFA in art history. I have written a short research paper on the Eameses that my professor feels is good enough for publication. I look forward to hearing of your interest in my proposed article.

Sincerely,

Ashley Adequate

Comments provided by Cara Greenberg, former editor-in-chief of *Modernism Magazine*.

For Beginning Writers

Good fiction magazine query

The author gave the name of the story being submitted.

The author named the target theme for which the story was intended, making it clear that she knows our journal.

The author indicated that a SASE for reply only was included in the submission.

Complete contact information provided.

This is a good letter by *THEMA* standards because it contains all that is necessary—the name of the story or poem being submitted, the target theme, what is enclosed, and contact information.

June 21, 2004

Virginia Howard, Editor
THEMA
Box 8747
Metairie, LA 70011-8747

Dear Ms. Howard,

My submission, "Paper Dolls," written for your premise: Stone, Paper, Scissors, is enclosed. A SASE for your reply only is also attached.

Sincerely,

Cathy Concise
21 Short Lane
Published, PA 19073
(215)555-9282
cathy@email.com

Comments provided by Virginia Howard, editor of *THEMA*.

Bad fiction magazine query

Know the name of the journal—it's *THEMA*, not *THELMA*.

Most of the information in this paragraph is superfluous. A simple, "I have an MA in literary theory" would have sufficed.

This paragraph is pure torture. Either give your credentials or don't, but don't play coy. Trying too hard to be cute in a query letter will not endear your manuscript to the editor.

Don't ever pretend you're familiar with a journal if you've never seen it. *THEMA* is theme-related, but this author obviously did not know that. Praising a journal, sight unseen, is a dangerous ploy. Had this author been "a reader, and a fan, of *THEMA*," he would have known he needed to designate the target theme for which his work was intended.

Peter Poorly
73 Minor St.
Subpar, SD 38847
(605)555-3540
poorly@email.com

July 3, 2004

Virginia Howard
Thelma
Box 8747
Metairie, LA 70011

Dear Ms. Howard,

I have recently completed a novel titled *Wrong Number*, and I am sending along an excerpt that I would be honored to see appear in *Thema*.

Since completing my MA in literary theory, I have spent the last few years writing and refining several short stories, as well as completing the first draft of a novel. Oh, and I also have a day job that enables me to pay bills.

I could talk about how I'm already at work on a second novel, and how I've written a dozen or so short stories and some half dozen poems (but no one reads poems anymore, right?). I should probably point out that I've had several stories and poems published in a variety of literary magazines. Perhaps it would behoove me to mention that I worked at a major Web company (in the halcyon days of the mid-to-late 90s) and wrote original content for a—at the time—cutting-edge website.

Having been a reader, and a fan, of *Thema*, I wanted to wait until I had the appropriate submission, and I feel the themes and energy of this particular piece might be an appropriate match for your publication. I hope you agree.

Thanks in advance for your consideration, I look forward to hearing from you.

Best regards,

Peter Poorly

Comments provided by Virginia Howard, editor of *THEMA*.

For Beginning Writers

Good nonfiction book query

This is a good summary of the book. It's short, succinct, and lets me know what to expect. The author has done her homework and can name two related books and how they are selling.

Although this is a bit exaggerated, it's good she's enthusiastic and has done some research about her audience.

Good brief bio. Although it indicates she hasn't done any published writing before, since she didn't list any publications. It shows her experience and willingness to work with the book.

Again, nice to know there's more material out there. I'd be interested to know if it includes a sample chapter.

I like how she includes her full name and contact information so I have options to reach her.

To: rachel@parallax.org
Re: Nonfiction book proposal query letter for The Bright Side

Dear Ms. Neumann:

I am a fan of Parallax Press and have visited your website. I would like to query whether the contents of *The Bright Side* would be of interest to Parallax Press.

The Bright Side is an autobiographical/motivational memoir of a Buddhist practitioner. Two books that have done well and are similar in style to *The Bright Side* are David Pelzer's *A Child Called It* and Wayne Dyer's *You'll See It When You Believe It*. Using my own experiences of an abusive childhood, depression, divorce, and a violent car crash, *The Bright Side* focuses on how simply changing my perception of those events has enriched my life.

Does the market need this book? Yes! My motivational speaking career has shown me hundreds of people in desperate need of acceptance, love, and healing, all of which must come from themselves. That is where the healing must begin. Current statistics indicate that 40 percent of the population will suffer a serious depressive episode at least once in their lifetime. Many people believe they are "not good enough." *The Bright Side* will prove that you are.

I am a 42-year-old mom of three incredible girls. I am a graduate of Northeastern College and currently hold an executive position for an international marketing firm. I am active in Toastmasters International and Dale Carnegie. I am more than prepared to promote and market the merits of *The Bright Side* in conjunction with Parallax. If you would like a more comprehensive bio, please visit my website. If *The Bright Side* has peaked your interest, please let me know, and I will gladly forward the complete proposal package.

Warm regards,

Sarah Sold
224 Ash St.
Happy, MA 78676
(781)555-7292 day
(781)555-2727 evening
www.thebrightsidebook.com

Bad nonfiction book query

For Beginning Writers

Not only has this person not done the research to find out the specific name of the editor, but he has also made the assumption the editor is a man. I almost always stop reading right here.

It's good he's had some publishing experience and has some published work, but because he doesn't list the publishers, my guess is they're self-published, which he should say straight out. Also, he doesn't say anything about why we would be interested.

This doesn't really tell me anything, as people often list and have their friends list reviews on sites like Amazon. It's better if he could quote from a publication that reviewed the book.

This comparison is so often used and so old.

Dear Sir:

Hi! My name is Rick Rejected, and I am the author of the novel, *Looking Into Your Eyes* and the book of poetry, *Flying Quietly*. These books are published by two separate, small publishers, one of which is now defunct. I am writing you with the hope that you may consider me as a client.

The novel, *Looking Into Your Eyes*, has sold 700 copies without any representation at all and has received nothing but good reviews. It is listed on Amazon with only 5-star reviews. The subject of the novel is the mental breakdown of a 14-year-old honor roll student. It is authentic in that it is a true story of my life. I have listed it as fiction because I wanted to keep anonymity. It is a book with every emotion, and it can be compared to *The Catcher in the Rye*, by J.D. Salinger.

In the past, I have been very busy and haven't found proper representation enough to get these books on the bigger market. I honestly believe they belong there.

I will send you copies of the books if you are willing to consider them for representation.

Thank you for your time and consideration.

Rick Rejected
rickr@email.com

He only includes an e-mail address. I prefer to have a phone number and mailing address so I can reach people.

We publish Buddhist and social justice books; it's clear from this short description he has not narrowed his search to publishers who are interested in his genre.

This is not enough information about why these books would do well in a bigger market.

Comments provided by Rachel Neumann, senior editor at Parallax Press.

Good fiction book query

Carol Competent
34 Sixth Ave.
Published, NY 18978
(212)555-2487
carol@email.com

June 15, 2004

Ms. Erin Cartwright-Niumata, Editiorial Director
Avalon Books
Thomas Bouregy and Co., Inc.
160 Madison Ave., 5th Floor
New York, NY 10016

Dear Ms. Cartwright-Niumata:

Please consider my finished novel, *Road Games*, for publication. I've always enjoyed romantic comedy, both reading and writing it. This particular manuscript was *this close* to being published in 1993, by Meteor, who suddenly went out of business and subsequently returned all rights to me. I turned to writing mysteries about then, as you can see from my enclosed biography. I would love, though, to see *Road Games* in print.

I know Avalon has had a policy of no explicit sex or violence. Neither of those is a problem in *Road Games*, which has no strong language either. However, I'm not sure whether the premise—the heroine is in danger from her boyfriend Rolly who works for a mobster—is acceptable to your house. That aspect of the plot is all off stage, and Rolly is more dimwit than menace. If that part of the story line is permissible, would you review the enclosed synopsis and first 30 pages of the 50,000-word novel? Again, I wasn't sure whether the scene on pages eight and nine would fit within your specification, but if it would not, I could rewrite so that Gillian and Jeff begin their walk together at the restaurant.

Thanks for considering this query. My SASE is for your response only, not for the return of any materials.

Very truly yours,

Carol Competent

She asks for us to consider her manuscript for publication along with the title and information about the former contact she had with another publishing house. ——

She has done her homework on Avalon and states it. She gives a brief summary that meets our requirements. She states the word count, which is acceptable. She is willing to rewrite and draws attention to something that may not work within our guidelines.

She has included a SASE as —— requested

Comments provided by Erin Cartwright-Niumata, editorial director of Avalon Books.

Bad fiction book query

Starts out well—she addressed the letter to me and states the title and her intentions in the first sentence.

Here she goes wrong. We do not publish this genre. Clearly she has not carefully read our guidelines.

She states the word count at 85,000, which is 15,000 words too long for us.

She closes with information about herself, which is good, but we have already decided to reject it.

July 12, 2004
Avalon Books, Thomas Bouregy & Co., Inc.
160 Madison Ave., 5th Floor
New York, NY 10016

Acquisitions: Erin Cartwright

Dear Editor Cartwright,

I am writing to inquire if I might submit for your consideration my manuscript, *Two Pioneering Women*.

The story first follows the life of a 15-year-old girl who makes the journey from Vermont to Kansas, mostly by stagecoach. Her life in Kansas portrays the social life and problems in the mid-1800s. The social life is church oriented, the economic period affected by national events and natural disasters. The second part of the story pictures the life of her daughter who marries and goes to live in Oregon. There she experiences the life of a pioneer horsewoman and deals with the birth and death of a blind and deaf child, whom her husband rejects.

I have carefully researched stagecoach travel and local histories of the settings. I have several journals and diaries on which I have loosely based the story. It is approximately 85,000 words long.

Enclosed are three sample chapters, the first chapter, one from the middle of the book, and one from the second section. A self-addressed, stamped envelope is also enclosed for return of the material if you are not interested.

I am a freelance writer. My stories are mainly set in the West, I was born and raised on an Oregon ranch. Enclosed is a list of my published credits since 1994.

Sincerely,

Nora Notgood
23 S. Chestnut St.
Slushpile, WI 86487

Comments provided by Erin Cartwright-Niumata, editorial director of Avalon Books.

What Really Happens?

Understanding the Publishing Process

by Brenda Copeland

You've done it. All that hard work has finally paid off, and you've sold your manuscript to a publishing house. You're going to be a published author. Riding high with the elation of finally having made the deal, you've phoned family and friends and your third-grade teacher to announce the heady news. You've been to the bookstore to see where your title will be shelved; you've perfected your signature for book signings; and you've prepared for your *Today Show* interview. Now what? What should you expect? What *can* you expect?

The publishing process is fraught with excitement, and more than a little anxiety. Those months between submitting your manuscript and receiving that first finished book will be filled with a lot of activity—and a lot of downtime too.

So, what really happens?

THE EDITORIAL PROCESS

Editing comes first. You may have spent many years on your manuscript, and chances are you'll be breathing a sigh of relief now that you've submitted it to your editor; but do know that, despite much industry talk of editors who don't edit, you can expect your manuscript will receive a rigorous going over. The extent of work to be done varies widely from editor to editor and project to project. Editing, like writing, is a very subjective process. Depending on the state of your manuscript and the expectations of your editor, you may simply be required to incorporate the suggestions of a line-edit (where your editor will have made changes at the sentence level), or you may have to carry out deeper structural changes involving adjustments to the construction of your manuscript. Chances are the work required will fall somewhere in the middle of this spectrum.

Editing—the time frame

How long does this part of the process take? That's a very good question. Again, the answer depends on a number of variables, not the least of which is your editor's workload and schedule of upcoming titles. Like so many professionals whose businesses are determined by production cycles and deadlines, your editor will organize her time in a sort of triage, where editorial resources will be sorted and allocated according to factors like publication

BRENDA COPELAND joined Simon & Schuster as an intern, rising quickly through the ranks to her present position as Senior Editor at Atria Books. She publishes literary and commercial fiction, narrative nonfiction, and health and lifestyle books.

date, state of the manuscript, and track record of the author. (It should come as no surprise to learn that best-selling authors don't have to wait in line.)

It's important to keep in touch with your editor after you've submitted your manuscript, but it's equally important to be flexible, and—dare I say it—patient. Your editor is constantly adapting to dozens of shifting demands, which may affect the date by which she is able to return your edited manuscript to you. Publishing is a dynamic and often high-pressure industry, and it's not always possible to predict what the day will bring. Sometimes, for example, an editor will start to work on a manuscript, only to have to put it aside for a crash project that has just been acquired. And it's always possible she'll have to delay editing the project submitted on time to attend to an author whose manuscript has come in weeks or months late. These are the same sort of people who are ushered past you at airport security when you've arrived the requisite 90 minutes prior to takeoff. It may be frustrating, but rest assured that while these people may take your place in the queue, they most certainly will not take your place at the gate. So try to be patient and understand the bigger picture. It will certainly pay off in the end.

When your editor sends her edits, make sure you ask when she expects the revisions to be returned. Even though the answer will invariably be, "as soon as possible," do know your editor will want you to return the manuscript in the best possible shape. If you need more time, ask for it. You only get one chance to publish your book, so make sure it's the best book possible.

Important

For Beginning Writers

THE PRODUCTION PROCESS

Once you and your editor are satisfied that your manuscript is the best it can be, it's time for your project to be "passed for press"—a procedure that takes place nine months prior to publication. Pass for press is the first stage in the long process of getting your book ready for production. Procedures vary from house to house, but not by much. Typically, your editor and her assistant will complete a pile of paperwork to be transmitted to the managing editor. The paperwork will include, among other things, a copyright registration form; a CIP data sheet (to register your book with the Library of Congress); directions to the copy editor; a castoff and design form to estimate the page length of your book and alert the production department to any special design considerations; and, depending on the subject and content of your book, a request for a legal read. Once all these forms have been completed, your editor will submit your manuscript (along with any accompanying artwork) to the managing editor.

The managing editor

The managing editor tracks all the material relating to your book, inside and out. From the moment your title is scheduled to the point at which books reach the warehouse, he'll have your book tracked on grids, schedules, and calendars. Part project manager, part traffic controller, the managing editor is responsible for ensuring all deadlines are met and all material is transmitted to each department in a timely manner. Not an easy assignment.

The production editor

After the managing editor has received the materials for your book and is satisfied that everything has been done according to house procedure, he will forward your manuscript to a production editor who will assign a copy editor and draw up a schedule detailing the estimated dates for each stage of production. Your editor will pass along these dates to you, along with the admonition that dates *must* be kept, or the release date of your book may be in jeopardy.

Common words and phrases

For More Info

- **Line-edit.** A line-edit involves making changes at the sentence level as opposed to deeper structural changes that involve adjustments to the construction of your entire manuscript.

- **Pass for press.** This stage usually occurs nine months prior to publication and is the first stage in getting your book ready for production. During this stage, required paperwork is filled out, schedules are set, and copyediting occurs.

- **Legal read.** A legal read is required when a book is based on real people or events.

- **Light copyedit.** A light copyedit is when a copy editor fixes typos and poor grammar, incorrect punctuation, capitalization and spelling, and points out repetition and possible ambiguities.

- **Heavy copyedit.** A heavy copyedit generally is not done by a copy editor unless the editor requests it (i.e., if the editor thinks the manuscript could benefit from this kind of edit). If a heavy copyedit is requested, the copy editor can rewrite, cut, and reparagraph the manuscript.

- **First-pass pages (sometimes called "galleys").** First-pass pages are the typeset pages of your book, and you will usually receive them four to six weeks after you receive your copyedited pages.

- **Blues.** So-called because they are printed in blue ink, blues are flat sheets that have been folded and gathered to form "signatures" (see below) which together form your book. Usually, blues are the last stage of the publishing process before your printed and bound book.

- **Signatures.** Sixteen-page segments of your manuscript that, together with blues, form your book.

The copyedited manuscript

Approximately four weeks after your project has been passed for press, your editor will send you the copyedited version of your manuscript. While your acquiring editor probably spent a lot of time on concept and structure—the big-picture stuff—your copy editor will have spent his time checking grammar, punctuation, spelling, and facts—the small-picture stuff. He will also have reviewed your manuscript for sense and consistency. Copy editors are the Felix Ungers of the publishing world. It's their job to examine details and ensure your reader isn't distracted by inconsistencies, typos, or errors of grammar or fact.

The level of thoroughness applied by your copy editor will be dictated, in part, by your editor. If your editor has requested a "light" copyedit, the copy editor will fix typos and poor grammar, incorrect punctuation, capitalization, and spelling, point out repetition, and possible ambiguities. He will also query inconsistencies, such as "that dress was blue on page 8, but on page 43 it's green—intentional?" A copy editor will not suggest rewrites, cuts, or reparagraph, unless your editor feels your manuscript could benefit from such treatment.

Authors usually have two weeks to go over the copyedited manuscript—less if your book is on a tight deadline. You will be expected to read every suggested change and respond to every query (i.e., questions). Copy editor's changes will be marked directly on the page, but queries will usually be noted on colored flags attached to the side of the page. It's hard to know who dreads those queries more: the author who has to answer them, or the assistant who has to photocopy them.

It's important to understand this is the last time you will see your project in its rough manuscript form. The next stage in the process involves first-pass pages (some houses call them galleys), which are the typeset pages of your book. If you have any changes to make to your book, make them at the copyedit stage when changes can still be incorporated without additional cost. Changes made at a later date can be expensive for both the author and the publisher. So while you address the comments made by the copy editor (and do use a colored pencil), you should also take this opportunity to make sure that the manuscript is exactly as you want it to be. If you need to add a page or subtract a page, do it now!

Reminder

Sample pages

Before you receive your copy of the first-pass pages, you'll get sample pages from your editor showing the proposed layout and design of your book. Very possibly your editor will have already selected a design by thumbing through a binder of templates. She will have chosen the format carefully, keeping in mind the subject, length, and proposed audience of the book. If you disagree with your editor's choice you will certainly have an opportunity to ask for revisions, but do know in most cases the final word on design rests with the editor and the publisher. That's why, if you have strong preferences regarding the layout of your book (font size, style, etc.), it's best to advise your editor early on in the process. It's always much easier to contribute to a decision than to have a decision reversed.

First-pass pages (or galleys)

You'll receive your set of first-pass pages anywhere from four to six weeks after returning your copyedited manuscript. For many authors, seeing those first-pass pages is a "pinch me"

For Beginning Writers

Who are these people?

For More Info

- **Editor.** The editor oversees the process of taking your book from manuscript form to book form, and his roles vary greatly depending on workload, availability, etc. How an editor ultimately works varies widely from editor to editor and project to project.

- **Managing Editor.** The managing editor is part project manager and part traffic controller, as he is the person who is responsible for making sure all deadlines are met and that all material related to your book is transmitted to the appropriate departments/people in a timely manner.

- **Production Editor.** The production editor assigns your manuscript to a copyeditor (see below) and draws up a schedule detailing the estimated dates for each stage of the production process.

- **Copy Editor.** The copy editor spends his time on the "small-picture stuff," i.e., grammar, punctuation, spelling, and facts, and he also reviews your manuscript for sense and consistency.

moment, final proof that, yes, this book is going to happen. Savor the moment. You've worked hard for it.

Reviewing first-pass pages might just be one of the most pleasant parts of the process. After all, you get to see how your words stand on the page. But don't get carried away and think you can enjoy those pages as a reader. You have an important job to do, and this is no time to let down your guard. Authors must read their pages thoroughly for sense, content, and consistency, to make sure all the changes from the copyedited manuscript have been incorporated. Your book will also be simultaneously read by a proofreader (although not by your editor). Nevertheless, it's always a good idea to mark any typos you see. Again, it's very costly to make extensive changes at this stage, so refrain from rewriting or reworking the text.

Some authors expect to see another set of pages with the changes incorporated. Sorry to say, that practice went the way of bow ties. Your production editor will monitor the changes and see that typos have been rectified and the last stage of edits have been incorporated. And she will, of course, alert you and your editor to any potential problems. But, in most cases, you will not see second-pass pages.

First the blues, then the book

The final stage of the process is know as "blues" (so-called because they are printed in blue ink). Blues are flat sheets that have been folded and gathered to form "signatures," 16-page segments that together form your book. Your production editor and editor will each review the blues for your book before giving the final okay to the printer.

And then . . . well, it's hard to believe, but in as little as two weeks after blues, your beautiful book will be born. Congratulations!

Reality Check

Things You Need to Know
Before Your Book Comes Out

by M.J. Rose

Congratulations. You've signed the contract and mailed it back to your agent. It's real. You've sold your first book. Hopefully you and your family will pop the cork on a bottle of champagne and make a toast to your success. But what will happen when you wake up the next morning and the 364 mornings after that until the day when your book hits the shelves?

What's next? What can you expect? What should you watch out for? What should you ask for? When can you complain? Who can you believe?

Unfortunately, your publisher isn't going to tell you, and while your agent will be happy to answer all your questions, she doesn't have the time to educate you about the business. And that's what it is now that the book is done—writing is an art, but publishing is a business. The more you know about how the business works, the better prepared you'll be.

Usually a book comes out 12 to 18 months after it's bought and the contract is signed. There will be periods in that year where you'll have a ton of work to do, and stretches where you never hear from your agent or your editor and there's nothing to do but start your next book. (Which you should be doing as soon as the contract is signed. Nothing is better than to be working on a new book when the first comes out—it keeps you centered and makes you more of a writer.)

So what should you expect?

You don't send me flowers

Don't expect your agent or your editor to send that big bouquet when you sign the contract. While your agent is probably thrilled for you, she's also probably sold hundreds of books in her career. She's done her job, and she will have more to do, but in terms of hugs, flowers, or excited phone calls, she's a businesswoman, not a mom. As for your editor, she's also bought hundreds of books and probably has a roster anywhere from 20 to 75 authors who she works with every year. So while your book matters to her, she's not going to send anything either—except the check.

Show me the money

You don't get the money the day you sign the contract. You don't even get it that week, or even the next. It can take from six to eight weeks until the first payment comes. Talk to your

---

M.J. ROSE (www.mjrose.com) is the author of five novels including *The Halo Effect* (MIRA, 2004), and two nonfiction books.

agent if it goes longer than that. Knowing the payment schedule will help you figure out if you can quit your day job or not. Not is more usual than unusual.

Everything is changing

The most important thing you'll do in the first months after the contract is signed is work on your book. Again. And maybe even again. And then once again. No one is quite prepared for how many times they're going to have to read and revise their books.

The first communication you'll get from your editor in e-mail or snail mail is the editorial notes. These usually arrive one to three months after the contract is signed, but that time depends on when your book is scheduled to be released. The "notes" you receive are your editor's big suggestions, changes, and requests. This is the time for the hard questions and the big decisions.

This letter can be anywhere from 1 page to 10 pages. I've even heard of 20-page letters. It isn't the line edit, there won't be comments about an actual word here or there. Rather, you'll get notes like: "Add a chapter that shows how the character reacts to the murder"; or, "I don't understand your main character's motivation in running away from home. We need to set this up better."

Tip

Usually you'll have three to six weeks to address these notes (sometimes longer depending on your book's publication date). Feel free to call your editor and discuss her edits—she wants you to. She does not expect you to smile and accept every change she is suggesting. On the other hand, however, she does expect you to take her requests seriously. Almost every author I know has issues with some of the suggestions in the notes—don't hesitate to discuss them with your editor.

Cover up or down

About nine months before your book's publication date, you'll get an overnight package that contains a cover for your book. Why so early? The publisher needs the cover for the sales conference and the catalog (which the bookseller gets about six months prior to your book's publication date). These catalogs are important. Often, they are the only way the book buyer will find out about your book.

Do you love the cover? Like the cover? Despise the cover? Don't call you editor in a fury. Call your agent. There are some things you can call the editor directly about (like editorial conversations), but complaints with the cover should go to your agent first. Let your agent argue and fight with your editor. It's better for your editor to get mad at your agent than at you.

What if your agent likes the cover but you don't? Talk it out with her. Sometimes the publisher and the agent understand the market better than you do. Even if you don't think the cover fits your book, it still may be the right cover for the book. Unless you're a book designer or a bookseller, it's probably best to go with what you publisher thinks the cover should like.

Edits again?

Yes, this is the year of edits. Once you've sent the revised manuscript back to your editor, she will read it again and mark it up. This is called a line-edit. This edited version will include cut sentences, suggestions for word replacements, questions about specific phrases, or comments on weak transitions or chapters that end too abruptly. You'll probably have two weeks to look over this edit and make changes.

Do you need to make every change? No, of course not, but you do need to take every change seriously and come up with good reasons not to make the suggested changes.

And more edits?

About a month later—which brings us to about six or seven months pre-publication, you'll get the copy edit. This edit is done by a copy editor, not your editor. It corrects the punctuation and grammar in your manuscript. You can break those rules and take issue with the copy editor's suggestions, but again, you need to have a reason. Usually you'll have two weeks to look over this version of your book. Do it carefully because you'll only have one more chance after this to see your book before it goes to print.

The last read

About three to six months before the book comes out, you'll get to see first-pass pages. Editors don't expect you to change much at this stage—a dozen words here, two sentences there. This is not the time for you to rewrite the book, but rather read the final book to make sure there are no typos.

When do the ARCs come?

Advanced reading copies (ARCs) are created about six months prior to your book's publication date and are sent out to reviewers and bookstores five months before the publication of your book. Lately, publishers have been making ARCs out of your pre-edited manuscript to save time. Talk to your agent after the contract is signed, and make sure she talks to your editor about getting the manuscript edited before the ARCs are made. Since the ARCs are what the reviewers see, you want them to be as close to the final book as possible.

Does I get ARCs? Yes, your editor or someone from the publicity department should call and ask you how many ARCs you want. This should happen about eight months before your publication date. If no one calls, you should call your agent and see if she wants to handle this, or see if she wants you to call your editor.

How many ARCs to ask for depends on how many "big mouth" people you know. If you have ten friends who have newspaper columns or run big book clubs, you want to make sure you give them all an ARC. If you are really friendly with your local bookstore owner, you want to give him a personalized copy. Ideally, you want 5 to 30 ARCs to give to people who can get buzz started for your book because word of mouth is the best advertising a book can get.

Tip

You need a marketing meeting

It's important to meet as many of the people working on your book as possible—especially your publicist and the in-house marketing staff. Call your editor seven months before your book comes out and ask if you can have a marketing meeting. Offer to fly in for it. Beg for it. It is one of the most important things you can do for your book.

The purpose of a marketing meeting is to find out what the publisher is going to do to market your book. The reality is: Few books get enough publicity or marketing—it's just the economics of the business. Publishers are publishing more books than ever and don't have the time or money to support them all.

If you can find out what your publisher is doing, you can figure out what you can do yourself to add to these marketing efforts. Some authors take their entire advance and hire outside publicists, while others take part of their advance and go on tours they set up themselves. There are literally hundreds of things you can do to add to what your publisher is going to do. (Note: For more information on what to ask at a marketing meeting see What Should I Ask? on page 40.)

See Also

The big switch

What do you do if you get shifted off to an assistant or your book is delayed? This can happen to the best of us. Know that the assistant doesn't do anything without your editor knowing about it, and that delays do not mean the house has lost interest in your book. If this happens to you, talk to your agent. Let her help you through the process.

Sweet dreams

About three weeks before the your book's publication date, you'll get a surprise package. In it will be a copy of your book. Finished. All done. This means the print run is in the warehouse, and the book's being shipped to bookstores.

There's a superstition among writers that when you receive that first copy of your book, you're supposed to sleep with it under your pillow that night for luck.

Today's the day

What will happen on the day of your book's publication? Not much. You've waited for this day for 2, 3, 4, or 40 years, and you wake up on the release date and nothing happens. The editor doesn't call. The agent doesn't call. The TV crews don't show up. Over 300 books come out every day. So while your book is everything to you, it's business as usual to the rest of the world.

Plan your own celebration. Enjoy the day. Go to the bookstores and see if the book is out. Sometimes books don't get unpacked in time and aren't on the shelf on the day of the book's scheduled release, but don't worry it will be on the shelves soon.

It can be depressing, but remember: Writing is an art, but publishing is a business—and the course of business doesn't always run smooth. What's important is that your book is done, and you're on your way to starting all over again with your second book.

What should I ask?

For More Info

It's important to find out what the marketing staff is doing to promote your book, but you need to do it without being antagonistic or sounding like a prima donna. So this is what I suggest you say:

"I know you guys are great and know how to do promotion, but I also know the realities of the business and know how many books you have in house. So, what are the things you think would help my book but that just require too much time or personal attention for you to do in-house? I really hope you'll be honest with me, I won't be upset. You guys have 100 books a quarter, I only have one a year, so what can I do to help?"

After you make your pitch to the team, you can use the following six questions to help you navigate through the meeting:

- How many advanced reading copies are you printing?

- When will the ARCs go out?

- Are you planning any kind of book tour?

- What are you hoping to do for the book?

- Are you taking out any ads? If so, where?

- Are you doing any kind of follow-up mailing to the ARC mailing?

Free Resources for Writers

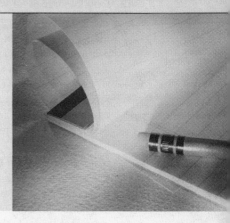

by Anthony Tedesco

One thing's for sure about us as writers: We know exactly how hard it is to be a writer. This shared struggle is what makes the writing community so quick to help its own. Case in point: I put out a hopeful call online for professional writers to share the free resources that have helped them the most in their writing careers—and I received nearly 1,000 replies.

Here I give you the best of the best. Print, online, or otherwise, these are the free resources recommended most often and most emphatically by the paid-and-published writers who use them to get paid and get published.

RESOURCES AND THEIR USES

Absolute Write (www.absolutewrite.com)

Jennifer M. Hollowell, editor of J.M.H. Creative Solutions and a writer for many publications including *The Beehive* and *Write Success Newsletter*, says she uses the resources at Absolute Write "pretty much every working day," with its newsletter and message boards being especially crucial to her goal of "sending out five query letters per day." Each newsletter is packed with tips on both the business and personal sides of being a writer, and the "Paying Markets" section of the board is packed with opportunities to put those tips into action.

Google (www.google.com)

For writers, Google has long been synonymous with "research tool I cannot live without so don't even try to take it from me." But writers like Cliff Allen, author of *One-to-One Web Marketing, 2nd Ed.* (John Wiley & Sons, 2001) and CEO of the CRM software company Coravue, Inc., also praise Google's lesser-known features like PageRank (available through the toolbar download and general search results), which, in simple terms, gauges how many popular sites already link to the listed site. Allen says that a low PageRank instantly tells him "it might be an undiscovered site worth writing about."

Useful Websites

The Grammar Hotline (800-279-9708)

Stumped by some grammar or punctuation quandary? Fear not. The Grammar Lady, aka Mary Newton Bruder, is happy to rescue your query from the rejection pile, as she's done

---

ANTHONY TEDESCO is co-author of the free e-books, *Top 250 Free Resources for Writers: Working Writers Share the Wealth of Free Resources That Have Helped Them the Most in Their Careers* and *Words of the Wise: Working Writers Share the Celebrity Writing Advice That Has Helped Them the Most in Their Careers* (both available for free downloading only at MarketsForWriters.com/wm.html).

for countless writers. Whether you're wondering about commas or compound subjects, you can expect your entire call to last about one minute, says Bruder, because most questions are repeats that don't require her to consult any source but herself. (Yes, "herself.")

As a one-woman cavalry, she understandably charges a fee for any e-mail questions she receives through GrammarLady.com (www.grammarlady.com/hotline.html), but she's generously managed to keep her Grammar Hotline service free since its 1997 inception—Monday through Friday, 9 a.m.-5 p.m. EST.

MediaBistro.com (www.mediabistro.com)

Rachel Sklar, a freelancer who has written for *The New York Times*, *Glamour*, and numerous other publications, says, "MediaBistro.com has been the single most helpful resource—online or offline—for building my writing career." Sklar's especially appreciative of the querying assistance from MediaBistro.com's articles and community forums, which has "led directly to multiple published stories." Kelly James-Enger, author of *Did You Get the Vibe* (Kensington Publishing Corp., 2003) and freelancer for over 45 national publications, further recommends MediaBistro.com's comprehensive newsfeed as a vital resource to keep apprised of "what's happening in the world of magazines and other media."

Merriam-Webster Online (www.m-w.com)

Linda Parker, author of *FabJob Guide to Become a Professional Golfer* (FabJob.com, 2003) and *The San of Africa* (Lerner Publications, 2002), relies on Merriam-Webster OnLine so often she's saved the link onto her desktop. In addition to the site's extensive dictionary functions (i.e., definition, etymology, correct alternatives to misspelled searches, etc.) and companion thesaurus, she's especially grateful for Merriam-Webster OnLine's pronunciation feature, an invaluable ally that keeps writers from mispronouncing their phone and face-to-face pitches. "Like many writers," says Parker, "my writing vocabulary is greater than my speaking vocabulary."

MomWriters (www.momwriters.com)

"This site is for every woman who says, 'I'd love to write, but I have kids,'" says Sharon Wren, a mother of two and a food columnist for *The Grapevine* and *Low Carb Energy*. "It's really inspiring to hear about others who juggle writing and take care of a family." Through its listserv, bulletin boards, and chats, the MomWriters community gives moms (and dads) the practical and personal support they need to be professional writers.

National Writers Union (www.nwu.org)

The National Writers Union (NWU) welcomes the full gamut of writers into its labor-union fold, but even nonmembers have expressed gratitude for the NWU's many free resources, including advocacy reports, writer alerts, and union documents to help freelancers. Abigail R. Esman, a published freelance writer specializing in art, political issues, and contemporary culture, was particularly grateful for the site's "extremely helpful advice on contracts."

Poynter Online (www.poynter.org)

"By far, Poynter Online has been the best all-around resource for improving my professional journalism career," says Lisa Palmer, a correspondent for *The Boston Globe* and *The Standard-Times* and a contributing writer to *American Style* magazine. "Not only do they provide story ideas daily, via 'Al's Morning Meeting,' they're a great resource for writing tips." Many writers also recommended Poynter's column "Romenesko's MediaNews" as the best news roundup of its kind.

Useful
Websites

For Beginning Writers

Preditors & Editors (www.anotherealm.com/prededitors)

"Preditors & Editors is a site every writer should know," says M.J. Rose, who has authored five novels, including *Lip Service* (Pocket Star, 1999) and her latest *The Halo Effect* (MIRA, 2004), and written for *Poets & Writers*, *Wired.com*, and many other publications. In particular, Rose urges writers to use the site for researching "which agents are reputable and which aren't." Writers also said they relied on Preditors & Editors' contests and publisher sections, and the reader feedback the site frequently posts along with each listing.

ProfNet (www.profnet.com)

"When I'm on deadline and need an expert to quote, this site is my first stop," says Absolute Write's editor-in-chief Jenna Glatzer, who's also a freelancer and author of *Make a Real Living as a Freelance Writer* (Nomad Press, 2004) and *Outwitting Writer's Block and Other Problems of the Pen* (The Lyons Press, 2003). Judy D'Mello, a freelance writer whose work has appeared in *The New York Times* and *The New York Observer*, among other publications, also praises ProfNet for its breadth of expertise ("whether you're writing about shoes or rocket science").

The Publishing Law Center (www.publaw.com/index.html)

Tish Davidson, author of books for middle school readers, including *Prejudice* (Franklin Watts, 2003) and *School Conflict* (Franklin Watts, 2003), relies on The Publishing Law Center because it has "anything you want to know about copyright and trademark usage in easy-to-understand language" and even covers "a broader area than the U.S. Copyright Office's site (www.copyright.gov)," including information on Internet and electronic issues.

Storyarts (members.core.com/CD/15/ppekin)

Storyarts' free six-week online workshop, "Writing Short Fiction" was recommended first by Radhika Meganathan, managing editor of Universal Personality (www.upandp.net) and author of *The Budding Writer's Guide to FREE Tutorials and Interactive Workshops On the Net* (Words-Worth ePress, 2004). Writers also applauded the site's free nonfiction workshop, its listserv for getting feedback on work in a monitored environment, and director Paul Pekin's generous commitment to "no advertising" on the site.

Useful
Websites

U.S. Census Bureau (www.census.gov)

I know it sounds like a punch line, but it's true: This site is from the government and it's here to help you. Farai Chideya, syndicated arts-and-politics columnist and author of *The Color of Our Future* (William Morrow, 1999), put it at the top of her list of recommended free resources. Of the site's profuse housing and population information—everything from ancestry and disabilities to utilities costs and vehicles available—Chideya says the "TIGER" demographics search (enabling geographic boundaries right down to address ranges) is especially helpful to her writing research.

Linda Formichelli, co-author of *The Renegade Writer: A Totally Unconventional Guide to Freelance Writing Success* (Marion Street Press, 2003), and who has freelanced for more than 100 magazines, including *Family Circle* and *Men's Fitness*, lauds the Census site for the paying assignments it helps her secure. "Writers can use free census data to liven up their queries and articles with facts and figures, or to add credibility to the market research sections of their book proposals."

WritersDigest.com (www.writersdigest.com)

I know this is an article for a Writer's Digest Books publication, but what's fair is fair: Writers Digest.com was emphatically recommended by droves of grateful writers like Jennifer L.

For Beginning Writers

Baum, a freelancer and regular contributor to *ePregnancy* magazine. Baum not only finds the site's daily writing prompts and highlighted markets very helpful to her career, she actually credits WritersDigest.com for making writing a career for her at all. She explains, "I earned my first paid clip by using an article I found on WritersDigest.com about the best online markets for writers."

Lynne Lepley is just as indebted to this resource. She's a campus minister/adjunct English instructor and now a published author who insists "WritersDigest.com's e-mail newsletter has had the greatest single impact on my writing career." The first time she considered working with an agent was when one of the newsletter's issues listed several agencies for writers. She contacted one ("on a whim"), signed with them, and then landed a publishing deal for her first book, *Three in One: A Book About God* (Abingdon Press, 2004).

WritersWeekly.com (www.writersweekly.com)

Many writers recommended WritersWeekly.com for its timely content, including market listings and interview request columns, but the site's ability to protect writers was most passionately cited as its qualification for "best." Cheryl Wright, print and online journalist, and author of *Think Outside the Square: Writing Publishable (Short) Stories* (Writer2Writer.com), says, "Its biggest advantage is that [publisher] Angela Hoy is an advocate for writers. If there's a warning about a market, she'll tell you about it."

Your local library and its website

Useful Websites

Libraries coast-to-coast have come a long way since ol' Mrs. Curmudgeon shushed you into total embarrassment. "Writers would be amazed at the things their local libraries are doing with the Internet," says Seattle's Jade Walker, an author, freelancer, and editor of *Siren Song Magazine* (www.sirensongmagazine.com), who relies on The Seattle Public Library for free access to "a variety of expensive databases." She also uses the library's website (www.spl. org) to search through its entire catalog and order whatever materials she needs for her writing.

New York City freelancer Lance Contrucci, whose work has appeared in *Cosmopolitan*, *The New York Times*, and many other publications, similarly vouches for The New York Public Library's website (www.nypl.org), describing it as "an invaluable tool to any writer." From home he freely accesses such databases as Newspaper Source ("159 regional papers"), Gale's full-text archives of *The New York Times* and *New York Post*, and MasterFILEPremier (1,800 periodicals), which, he says, is "handy not only for researching an article but for researching a magazine to see if they've run something similar."

Publishers' Roundtable

Five New York Publishers Speak Up

by I.J. Schecter

Writers spend a lot of time imagining the inner workings of publishing houses and the day-to-day lives of the people who run them. Who are these people, and what motivates them to do what they do? As the following roundtable interview with five senior New York publishing executives reveals, they're ordinary people who happen to share a passion for the craft of writing, the process of publishing, and the thrill of a great manuscript.

Terry Adams is the vice president and director of the Trade Paperback Division of Little, Brown.

Jonathan Galassi is the president and publisher of Farrar, Straus and Giroux.

Bob Miller is the president of Hyperion Books.

Sally Richardson is the president of the Trade and Mass Market Divisions and the publisher of the Trade Division of St. Martin's Press.

David Rosenthal is the executive vice president and publisher of Simon & Schuster.

What makes your publishing house tick?

Adams: Only a true team effort does the job, and it's our job to make sure everyone feels part of it.

Galassi: Similarly, what makes Farrar, Straus and Giroux work is a sense of shared mission—everyone working there wants to work there. We get the best out of people because they're really doing something they want to do.

Miller: When Hyperion's at its best, everyone is part of the collaboration; everyone has the same intensity and investment in the book.

Richardson: St. Martin's ticks because it's a no-star system. Everyone pulls together. We're very careful about who we hire—we want someone with taste and talent but not someone whose ego will get in the way of the whole machine.

Photo by Virginia Read

Terry Adams

Rosenthal: When so many moving parts are involved, there is indeed a sense of exhilaration when everyone, from the top of the house to the bottom, is committed. At Simon & Schuster, what also matters is a sense of range—that we can go from publishing very commer-

I.J. SCHECTER (www.ijschecter.com) writes for a number of leading magazines, newspapers, and websites, including *Golf Monthly*, *Men's Exercise*, *The Globe & Mail*, and iParenting.com. He's also the author of the recent short story collection, *The Bottom of the Mug* (Aegina Press, 1998).

cial works to more serious-minded ones, but that we strive to make sure each of them will be the best of their sort.

What proportion of the day do you spend reviewing manuscripts?

Richardson: I don't think any of us spends time during the day reading manuscripts. Certainly weekends and nights, but never in the office.

How many evenings or weekends do you work?

Galassi: This job could honestly take up every minute of every day if you let it.

Miller: During the day, I take care of e-mails, phone calls, and attend meetings. At home, between dinner and going to sleep—or very early in the morning—I read proposals and manuscripts. But those are very different kinds of work, two different switches.

Rosenthal: Often you don't end up going to bed until 1:30 or 2:00 a.m. because you want to spend quality time with your family. I have a 5-year-old daughter and 10-year-old son, and until I spend time with them I don't get to the other stuff.

Jonathan Galassi

Photo by Miriam Berkley

What is the best piece of advice you've ever received?

Adams: A colleague of mine taught me to make the three phone calls you least want to make, or do the three things you least want to do, first. Once they're out of the way, your day can only improve.

Galassi: When I was first offered a job in the movie tie-in division of Bantam, someone asked me, "Is this really what you want to do?" I said, "No." She said, "Keep looking." And that small piece of advice made all the difference to how I approached my first job.

Miller: Larry Kirshbaum, my former boss at Warner, told me, at the beginning of each day, before you have to start reacting to things, write down three things you want to get done and make a point of attending to them. I still do that.

Tip

Would you say your role is most similar to a juggler, an acrobat, a diplomat, or a clairvoyant—or a combination of all four?

Miller: You can picture the different balls in the air as the different parts of the publishing process. I think people imagine a publisher sitting over one book at any given time, when of course we're actually always dealing with a great number of books at various parts in the funnel.

Richardson: A juggler and a diplomat.

Rosenthal: I'd say a juggler.

Bob Miller

Photo by Steve Fenn

How much of a manuscript do you need to read before knowing if it's a winner?

Galassi: You can often tell in a page or two that you don't want the book. It's the ones that keep you reading—and reading—that matter.

Miller: Sometimes you've read a whole manuscript, you're talking about it the next day, criticizing it vigorously to your colleagues, and then you realize you all read the entire thing.

Richardson: You don't know until you've read it all.

Rosenthal: If an editor gives you a manuscript to read and you put it down and don't feel the urge to pick it up again, that also says something.

Interviews

What's your biggest pet peeve as it relates to writing?

Adams: Writing in the second person. Often, writing this way feels like an artificial attempt to put you inside the narrative.

Galassi: " . . . for Julia and I."

Miller: Not closing a parenthesis you've opened—someone could be left hanging for days looking for the end of the thing.

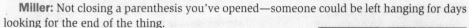

Important

Richardson: People who write "for free." Something is free or for nothing; it isn't for free.

Rosenthal: I mostly hate illogic—particularly when you're reading fiction, and you come upon a development in chapter eight or nine that simply can't be reconciled with something you read in chapter one.

What recent title are you most proud of, or what is your greatest manuscript find?

Adams: Many years ago I worked on a novel called *Geek Love* (Alfred A. Knopf, 1989) by Katherine Dunn, who had

Sally Richardson

published two novels 20 years before. We were totally in sync, and the world responded in a way that totally exceeded our expectations. It was what you live for in publishing.

Galassi: The most satisfying publishing experience for me during the past few years was with *The Corrections* (Farrar, Straus and Giroux, 2001), because Jonathan Franzen and I had been working together since 1987, and I'd always felt he was enormously gifted—endowed with everything it takes to be a major writer. His first novel got a lot of attention; his second wasn't a success. Then he wrote this truly great book, and we were able to publish it in the way it deserved. It was highly rewarding to see someone we'd been backing for a long time go all the way.

Miller: A little collection of thoughts from the late Mr. Rogers, called *The World According to Mr. Rogers: Important Things to Remember* (Hyperion, 2003). It represents the kind of book I always feel best about—those I had something to do with creating, as opposed to a manuscript submitted to many publishers that anyone, in theory, could have ended up with. I'd met Fred Rogers a few times and talked to him about the possibility of this kind of book. I felt like I was with Gandhi when I was with this man.

Richardson: I don't have a one-book answer. My main gratification comes from situations where we've already bought a book and it's in the works, but I'm able to recognize it as something much bigger than what we've planned. Something isn't just a diet book, for instance; it's a whole lifestyle book. This happens right across the list and with every type of book.

Rosenthal: There are a couple of authors whose books I'm very proud of having edited. The first is Rick Russo, particularly with *Nobody's Fool* (Knopf Publishing Group, 1994), because it's such a brilliant novel that early on had a structural question that we somehow rectified.

Also, Jon Krakauer. Before I'd ever heard of Jon, I came across his book *Into the Wild* (Random House, 1997), about a man who, for some reason, walks off into the Alaskan wilderness. I supported the book strongly, and it ended up a bestseller. Following that, and Jon's involvement with the disaster on Mt. Everest, we came up with the notion of doing *Into Thin Air* (Sagebrush Education Resources, 1998), which he didn't want to do at first but ultimately felt it might help him achieve some catharsis.

What makes a good—or bad—agent?

Galassi: The best agent-publisher relationship is a collaboration. An agent should strongly represent the author's interests while understanding we all need to be working together

Interviews

toward the same goal which is: The realization of the author's potential to the fullest possible extent.

Miller: The best agent is a translator of both the author's and publisher's needs. It comes from some awareness of what the publishing process actually consists of, as opposed to being an advocate of the author's desires.

Richardson: An honest, intelligent agent should be able to step in if he or she thinks the author or publisher is asking too much. I'll listen to a good agent's point of view.

Rosenthal: The main thing is honesty—that the agent doesn't misrepresent a situation. That he or she really thinks through what's best for the author before communicating a publisher's offer or going through with an auction.

Photo by Blaise Haywood

David Rosenthal

Can you spot a bad agent right away—during the first conversation?

Adams: It's like dating—by the second date, you know.

Galassi: You can spot a bad agent when he or she doesn't know how the publishing process works. Many agents, unfortunately, don't.

Rosenthal: You know by the second conversation. The worst thing is dealing with an agent who doesn't know what the deal is, what the contract is, what you're proposing, or when you're saying something that might actually be advantageous to the author.

Tip

Complete this sentence: _____ is the most important thing you need to make it in this business.

Adams: Luck.

Galassi: Taste. Doggedness. Persistence.

Miller: Diplomacy. Creativity. Sense of humor. Optimism.

Richardson: Energy. Commitment.

Rosenthal: Trust in yourself. Thick skin.

What's the difference between a good writer and a great writer?

Galassi: It isn't our job to decide which writers are great. Other people (i.e., readers) will decide that. I do think, though, a great book defines the time that it lives in, which we may only be able to see later.

Miller: A great title—sometimes that alone is what allows a great writer to be discovered.

Rosenthal: A million copies. Just kidding. A book that endures for 100 or 200 years. So we won't really know which of today's authors are great for some time.

What do most writers have a more difficult time with—plot or character?

Galassi: Often, so-called literary books are short on plot, and the writers of those books could benefit from exploiting plot conventions. And then, there are a lot of genre writers who don't know how to create characters.

Miller: Sometimes you read a great character, but you want to say to the author, "Just give him an obstacle—anything!" If you don't have a character we care about, who does something—as opposed to just having things happen to him—it doesn't matter what type of book it is, it isn't going to work.

Richardson: Plot.

Rosenthal: There are some very good plotters who fall flat on their face when doing characterization. Even good books are sometimes purely plot-driven, which I find less satisfying.

Interviews

Give me three pieces of advice for writers.

Adams: Go to the bookstores, and familiarize yourself with the category. But don't stop there. Get specific about research. Read acknowledgements. If I get a letter from somebody that says, "I know you were associated with this book . . ." it's very flattering and it shows me they're diligent. Few writers do that.

Galassi: When you're looking for a publisher, do your homework—look for one who publishes the kind of writing you're writing. Many authors don't bother. Second, be realistic about advice you get. Listen to the criticism that somewhere in your gut sounds right, even if it hurts. Third, believe in yourself. If you're too scared to test yourself in the market, you shouldn't be doing this. You have to be able to weather the slings and arrows of rejection.

Miller: Read other authors in your area, and try to get to know them. Join the community of writers you want to belong to. Go to readings, conferences. Also, try to get endorsements prior to submission. If a manuscript comes in with blurbs already in hand, it's amazingly effective—and this is so rarely done.

Tip

Richardson: In the 1980s we started a mass-market line, and we saw this slew of authors who would just read romances from the supermarket, and they'd say, "I can do this." They'd teach themselves how to do it. They'd just read, read, read, and work, work, work. A lot of authors on today's best-seller lists started out this way.

Rosenthal: Read. Look in the bookstores and see what attracts you. Know what's out there. The worst thing is getting a proposal on a subject you've seen two other books and four other proposals on in the past 18 months. It makes you say, "Why should I take this person seriously?" The other thing is perseverance. Know you probably won't get a quick answer. Try to be published somewhere other than by the big New York houses. Look to regional publishers, even university presses, which will position you to move up the food chain.

How do you reconcile the focus on the bottom line with the desire to publish good books?

Miller: The two aren't mutually exclusive. In fact, they often go hand in hand. If you read a book you think is of quality for its type and its audience, then that is a book, if you have spent appropriately to acquire and publish, you have a greater chance of making money on. Those two things are often set up as dichotomies. Every publishing decision is an incredible leap of faith. You have to be a romantic to be in this business, and I think we all are.

Richardson: Day to day, you're not running around thinking, "How are we going to make more money?" You're thinking, "How can I get better books in, how can I make faster decisions, how can I get better jackets?" And, inherent in all that is you're doing it to make money, but it's not the overriding thing in your mind. People tend to think publishing is driven solely by profit and therefore you're in a money-driven frenzy all the time. You're not.

Rosenthal: In the end, you're answering to yourself. You're acquiring books you like. Even if it were your own money, you'd make the same decisions.

Interviews

Julia Cameron

Developing a Creative Career

Photo by Aloma

by Jerry Jackson, Jr.

I f you ask Julia Cameron to describe herself, she'll likely tell you she's a "writing fool." Cameron has a long list of writing credits that include 15 books, several musical compositions, and countless TV, film, and theater scripts. She wrote, produced, and directed the award-winning independent feature film, *God's Will*. Cameron's also taught at The Smithsonian and Northwestern University, where she served as writer-in-residence in film. Her international bestseller, *The Artist's Way* (J.P. Tarcher/Putnam, 2002), is based on the popular creativity workshops she has taught for two decades. *The Artist's Way* has been published in a dozen languages with worldwide sales of more than 1 million copies.

In her quest to help people discover their creativity, she also wrote *The Right to Write* (J.P. Tarcher/Putnam, 1999) and *The Vein of Gold* (J.P. Tarcher/Putnam, 1996), books that help heal and rehabilitate the artist's soul in each of us. One of Cameron's keys to success has been the philosophy that writers write. "I am lucky in that I've always been stubborn and cantankerous," she says. "I never needed to be paid to write. I was always willing to go ahead and write something on spec [without contract]. When you have that kind of willingness as a writer, things tend to get bought. I don't want to make it sound like I had a career plan. I don't think careers evolve in a linear fashion—particularly writing careers."

Humble beginnings

Cameron began her professional career as a writer when she graduated from Georgetown University in 1970 with a degree in English. Shortly after that, she got a job at *The Washington Post*—where she opened mail. "When I was hired, they said, 'I hope you don't think you're a writer.' I said, 'I am a writer. I hope you don't think I'm a journalist.'" Within six months, at the age of 23, Cameron was writing features and book criticisms for *The Washington Post*. She later worked as a special correspondent for *The Chicago Tribune*.

Later on in her career, Cameron worked as a freelance writer for *Rolling Stone*, where one of her assignments was to interview director Martin Scorsese. After that interview, Scorsese asked Cameron to read a script for him—and she ended up rewriting several scenes. Shortly thereafter, in 1975, Cameron and Scorsese were married. The two collaborated on three films before they divorced a few years later.

JERRY JACKSON, JR. is a Cincinnati-based freelance writer. This interview originally appeared in the March 2003 issue of *Writer's Digest*.

Creative recovery

It was during this time that Cameron came to a major turning point in her life, which also led to her well-known philosophy about creativity. "In 1978, I got sober. I discovered I associated writing and drinking a little bit like scotch and soda: They went together," she says. "I needed to find a method of writing that was more grounded."

Cameron decided to let the "Great Creator" write through her. "I wasn't trying to be brilliant. I just listened to whatever was trying to come through me."

"I don't think careers evolve in a linear fashion—particularly writing careers."

The Artist's Way evolved from Cameron's desire to help other writers use the creative tools inside of them to improve their writing. She refers to her work as "creative recovery"—a process whereby people rediscover their creative potential. According to Cameron, creativity is not something only a select few possess. "Creativity is as natural to human beings as having blood and bone. It's part of our spiritual DNA."

Morning pages

According to Cameron realizing your potential as an artist means breaking through various creativity blocks—both physical and mental. "Writers at any level will tell you, 'I wish I had more money, more time, and more solitude.' Those issues always remain the same." Cameron says the myth that real writers don't have day jobs contributes to the problem. "The truth is, having a day job often facilitates not only doing work, but also the quality of the work that gets done. Artists thrive on structure, and we need regularity to our days."

To that end, Cameron says the most useful tool for an ongoing creative career is what she calls "morning pages"—three pages of stream-of-consciousness written in longhand. "These pages help move you into a creative flow because there is no wrong way to do morning pages." Cameron is quick to point out, too, that morning pages are not just busy work. "A writing career is like an athletic career. If you're training for a marathon, you need to run 10 slow miles for every sprint mile. Morning pages are the slow miles you need in order to run the sprint mile."

Tip

Cameron is also a big fan of writing in longhand. "There's something in longhand writing: It's almost as if your hand knows the story. I was on a panel with six top Hollywood writers several years ago, and I was surprised to learn that all six of them wrote in longhand and then transferred the writing to a computer. Using your own hand helps you find your own voice."

Your voice

Finding one's own voice is essential for anyone who wants to write, and, in most cases, it's finding that voice that is the most difficult task. While Cameron encourages writers to read her books, she hopes they go beyond simply reading the books, and, instead, apply what they have read to their own writing. "Reading a book about creativity doesn't help as much as actually doing the tasks and exercises presented in the book. If you actually put forth the effort, I think you will be satisfied with the work. My hope for writers is that my words enable other writers to put more words on the page."

Interviews

Successful Freelancers

Four Writers Share Their Secrets

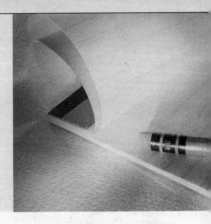

by Kelly Kyrik

I n 1995, the National Writers Union released the results of the American Writers Survey; a rather disheartening study which revealed that only 16 percent of all full-time freelancers earned more than $30,000 per year.

Suddenly, the definition of freelance "success" came attached to a dollar figure, and many writers were dismayed to realize that they had come up short. Some began to question the viability of their chosen career, many more wondered if it was time to give up their dream and slink back to the day job they'd left behind. Still, there were some hopeful writers who dared to ask: Is it really possible to be successful—i.e., make a decent living—as a freelance writer?

Now, as then, the answer is a resounding, "Yes." Although there are no current statistics on the subject, the truth is many full-time writers earn enough to comfortably support themselves and their families. Not without some struggle, perhaps, and not without many setbacks along the way, but it is clear that determined writers can and do succeed in this business.

The four writers profiled below have certainly achieved "success"—calculated as approximately $36,000 a year—as full-time freelancers. Not surprisingly, they share 3 traits: a passion for writing, the will and perseverance to succeed, and a strong belief that what they're doing is worthwhile, both for themselves as well as for others.

Interestingly enough, however, aside from those similarities, their theories on what it takes to succeed as a freelancer are as varied as the genres in which they write.

Don Vaughan, general nonfiction, www.donaldvaughan.com

"I actually owe my career to the fact that I'm terrible at math," says Don Vaughan, 46, who has been writing professionally since 1978. "In my junior year of high school, I found myself failing algebra. I didn't need the math credit, so I dropped out and took a course called, 'Mass Media,' which was essentially a class on freelance writing. I loved every minute of it, and aced it with no problem at all. From that moment on, my destiny was set."

Soon after, Vaughan began his career as a staff writer for

Don Vaughan

Photo by Leena Taimela

KELLY KYRIK (kyrik@comcast.net) has been a professional freelancer for about six years. She writes mostly for magazines and newspapers, and her published credits include the *Chicago Tribune*, *Writer's Digest*, *Cat Fancy*, and the *Weekly World News*, among others.

various newspapers and magazines before taking the freelance plunge in 1991, and he's never looked back. Now he can count more than 1,000 published credits in publications as diverse as *Veterinary Practice News*, *Today's Officer Online*, and *MAD* magazine. In addition, he's written 17 books, including the *The Everything Civil War Book* (Adams Media, 2000). His success didn't happen overnight, though.

"Freelance success comes with time and perseverance," he notes. "Anyone who thinks they can quit their job and make $30,000 their first year freelancing is fooling themselves, unless they have remarkable contacts."

Vaughan believes his success is due in large part to the fact that he has developed a reputation among magazine and book editors as a writer who can deliver good, clean copy, and, even more importantly perhaps, he can deliver it on time.

"The editors who I work with regularly know I like the challenge of a tight deadline, and that I won't let them down, so they keep coming back," he explains. "I'm also not afraid to tackle articles and books on subjects about which I know absolutely nothing. I believe it's good for a writer to work outside his or her comfort zone."

In addition, Vaughan believes very strongly that sharing the wealth benefits all writers, and he makes it a point to mentor aspiring freelancers through the class he teaches at Wake Technical Community College in Raleigh, North Carolina.

"What really makes it worthwhile is taking what I've learned over the years and sharing it with the people who take my freelance writing class," he says. "Over six weeks I teach them everything I know about the craft and the business of freelance writing, then I turn them loose. I mentor my most promising students through monthly get-togethers, and nothing pleases me more than hearing about their first magazine sale because their success is my success."

Words of Wisdom

"Network with fellow writers, editors, agents, and publishers at every opportunity. I've received a tremendous amount of work, including lucrative book deals, through referrals from other writers and editors. I also refer other writers when I feel they're appropriate for a project, or have an idea in which I think an editor would be interested." —**Don Vaughan**

Christina Wood, copywriter, www.christinawood.com

"I've been freelancing full time since May of 1996," explains Christina Wood, 43, who makes her living mainly as a copywriter although she also writes for national magazines. "Before that I worked in public broadcasting, where I used my writing skills but was not employed as a writer, and before that I worked as a marketing writer at a major daily newspaper. Whether it was writing the newsletter for a law firm I once worked for or writing grants when I was employed in the nonprofit sector, I always enjoyed using my writing abilities, regardless of my position."

Christina Wood

Over the past eight years, Wood has provided creative marketing and advertising solutions, press releases, and Web content for a variety of clients on subjects as diverse as cardiac care, computer technology, Irish theater, and custom-closet arrangements.

Wood believes it's very important for a writer to be disciplined enough to create some kind of structure when working from home, and says those who want to write for a living must accept that there is no such thing as writer's block. In addition, she is of the opinion that it takes an equal measure of both talent and skill for a freelancer to achieve his or her goals.

"I believe there are two main components to success as a professional writer," she says. "First, there is the talent with which you are born. Secondly, there is the skill that must be learned and developed. You can make an analogy with music—you can be musically gifted, but if you don't practice the piano, you'll never be any good. With writing, you develop that skill not only by using it but by reading what other people are doing."

For Wood, it's the variety and stimulation that makes writing worthwhile and keeps her coming back for more.

"One of the things I like best about what I do is that there are always new challenges," she explains. "I'm very lucky that I have long-standing relationships with several clients, but each assignment is different. There's very little opportunity to get bored. Working as a writer is like being a perpetual student, except I get paid to learn about new things—and I rarely have to deal with rush hour traffic!"

Words of Wisdom

"Writing for yourself can be extremely satisfying on a personal level, and for many people, that's enough. If you want to make a living at it, you have to understand you're writing for other people. It's important to have an awareness of who will be reading your work. Ask yourself: For whom am I writing this?" **—Christina Wood**

Jenna Glatzer, general nonfiction, www.absolutewrite.com

Photo by Mark Glatzer

Jenna Glatzer

"I got hit by a whammy of a panic disorder straight out of college and wound up agoraphobic and housebound," says Jenna Glatzer, 27, of her rather abrupt initiation into freelance writing. "I had to find a way to make a living from home, and writing seemed the best option. So I bought *Writer's Market*, learned all I could from writers' e-zines and books, and commenced making egregious mistakes—from which I eventually learned."

Glatzer has written in many genres, although she currently specializes in health topics, and she has hundreds of published credits in magazines such as *Physical*, *Woman's World*, and *Writer's Digest*. She's also the author of nine books, including the recent *Make a Real Living as a Freelance Writer* (Nomad Press, 2004), and is an optioned screenwriter, produced playwright, and author of hundreds of greeting cards and copy for plaques, T-shirts, mugs, and buttons, as well as the editor of Absolute Write, an online resource for writers.

Glatzer attributes her success to four things: perfectionism, a steel ego, flexibility, and the ability to target a market.

"I never miss a deadline, I don't take rejections personally, and I'm willing to take on nearly any topic or media," she explains. "I'll stay up all night to meet an editor's crazy deadline and not complain about rewrites. I also know how to study a magazine—a skill few beginning writers understand. I don't send queries in the hopes that my story will be appropriate for a magazine; I send queries when I'm sure the story will be appropriate, because I've studied the publication and figured out where my work belongs."

For Glatzer, success is often its own reward. "What makes it worthwhile is that I get paid to learn about things that interest me, and I get to do it in sweatpants with my cat on my lap," she says. "I still get a thrill every time a query is accepted and every time I see my work in print. I hope that never goes away."

Words of Wisdom
"Be prolific, be daring, never stop learning, and ignore any guru who spouts out advice without credentials to back it up. If someone with credits from *Redbook* and *Woman's Day* wants to teach you how to write articles for women's magazines, great! But forget the ones who aren't already successful in the fields they purport to teach." **—Jenna Glatzer**

Jeremiah Healy, fiction, www.jeremiahhealy.com

Photo by Jim Norman

Jeremiah Healy

"My first manuscript, *Blunt Darts* (Walker & Co., 1984), was rejected by 28 publishing houses before the 29th bought it," admits Jeremiah Healy, 56, now a highly successful crime fiction writer. It was a frustrating time, but his persistence in the face of such rejection handsomely paid off. "Six months after publication, *The New York Times* put the book on its holiday list as one of the seven best mysteries of the year."

In the 20 years since that fortuitous sale, the award-winning Healy has penned 17 novels, including the John Francis Cuddy private investigator series and the Mairead O'Clare legal-thriller series (written under the pseudonym Terry Devane). In addition, he's had over 60 short stories published and, in 2000, he became the first American to be elected worldwide president of the International Association of Crime Writers.

A former lawyer and professor at the New England School of Law, Healy attributes his success to dogged determination and the ability to shake off the rejections and frustrations that often deter the less-resolute writer.

"Having been a trial attorney, I knew I could lose a case without feeling unsuccessful," he says. "Accordingly, I simply never stop trying. Negative reviews, nonrenewal of a series; you just have to shake these off—like a lawyer or an athlete shakes off a defeat—and drive on."

For Healy, success came early—his first novel garnered critical praise and subsequent novels earned hefty advances in addition to warm reviews—but for him the writing itself is equally satisfying. Long a fan of private-investigator fiction written by the likes of Robert B. Parker and Marcia Muller, he truly enjoys what he writes. He does admit, however, to enjoying the notoriety, as well. "Seeing my name on a book in a store or library is a form of immortality."

Words of Wisdom
"If the process of writing is what makes you lose track of the passage of time as you do it, then writing is for you. Now all you have to do is figure out a way to get somebody to pay you for doing it." **—Jeremiah Healy**

Interviews

Dave Barry

The Award-Winning Humor Columnist Talks About Writing

Photo by *Miami Herald*

by Doug White

I f you conduct an exhaustive inventory of Dave Barry's many humor books and columns, one fact becomes clear: The man can work the word "poop" into just about any sentence. But for a guy who drops more references to bodily functions than the average fourth grader, the writing process is no laughing matter. Not that you'd necessarily discern that from the title of his book, *Boogers Are My Beat: More Lies, but Some Actual Journalism* (Crown Publishers, 2003). While he's loved by the masses and lauded by the critics, Barry, despite enjoying the pinnacle of publishing success, still struggles with his craft and isn't afraid to open up about it.

"I'm unbelievably nit-picky about every word, every syllable," says the author and syndicated columnist for *The Miami Herald* (since 1983), who won a Pulitzer Prize for commentary in 1988. "I'm very obsessive about it. I'm not like that about anything else in my life, but I am really obsessive about my words and very protective of them."

Barry says that like all former English majors, he wrestles with the subtle nuances of writing. He constantly agonizes over employing just the right word to make the rhythm of his jokes flow perfectly. He instills this same obsession in his fiction writing.

While Barry's internal word-choice debates may go on for hours, he's never short on potential topics to tackle. His philosophy on finding inspiration and subject matter is simple: Keep pen and paper close at all times. "I'm always leaving notes to myself and tearing out articles to save," says Barry. "There are certain topics I know sooner or later I've got to use—ducks attacking a hunter, for instance. Not relying on memory is a key technique for me. That's the way I work. I could never turn something in until I've dealt with every semicolon five times. I'm a constant rewriter more than an editor."

But for someone who rewrites so frequently, it seems Barry's always writing something new. He's authored more than 25 books and pens a weekly column that appears in more than 500 newspapers across the country. Despite this, Barry says there's a myth about how prolific he is. "The truth—and this is probably not going to make me popular—is not so much that I'm prolific but that a lot of writers don't write that much.

"The reason I'm considered prolific is every day I write something. The minimum I'll produce every week is a column. But more likely it's a column and part of a chapter. You keep doing that for, in my case, 20-something years and it seems like a huge output, but it's really not." Many people would argue that point, but Barry remains steadfast in his basic

DOUG WHITE is assistant editor of *HOW* magazine and a freelance writer. This interview originally appeared in the November 2003 issue of *Writer's Digest*.

contention that to be a writer, one must write. He holds little regard for whining about real or imagined constraints. He says lack of discipline—not time—is the real problem. "If you want to be a writer, find a couple of hours in the morning or evening, and do nothing but write. That's plenty of time to be a productive writer. The biggest impediment for almost everybody is the fact that it's harder than you think to just sit there and stare at the computer and pound something out. But finding the time is not the issue as much as finding the will to do it."

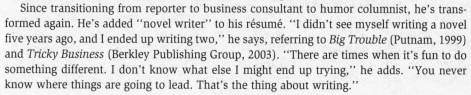

 **"I am really obsessive about my words and very protective of them."**

And what does he do on the days when he's not in the groove? You guessed it: He writes. And like most writers, he occasionally thinks his work is mind-numbing drivel. But unlike many writers, he doesn't allow that to stop him. "There are days when I do think I've wasted ten hours on nothing," he says. "I'll say, 'I'll never be any good. I'll never write another funny thing as long as I live, and I'm a fraud.' Ask my wife how many times a month I'll go to her and say, 'This is it! I'm going to become an insurance agent. I need to find a job I can do because I can't do this.'

"I think most writers go through that," says Barry. "That's why so many people don't write. They haven't had the experience of going through that enough times to realize it's part of the process. You don't necessarily give up in despair just because it didn't flow easily this day. There are going to be days like that. And even from that day you thought you wasted, there's usually something salvageable."

Barry stays fresh and avoids those dreaded deadbeat days by doing what he's done throughout his career: trying new things. He got his start writing for the *Daily Local News* of West Chester, Pennsylvania, and then the Associated Press. Later he headed to Burger Associates to teach business writing to professionals. During his teaching travels, Barry began writing observational humor pieces for fun while living in different hotel rooms.

Since transitioning from reporter to business consultant to humor columnist, he's transformed again. He's added "novel writer" to his résumé. "I didn't see myself writing a novel five years ago, and I ended up writing two," he says, referring to *Big Trouble* (Putnam, 1999) and *Tricky Business* (Berkley Publishing Group, 2003). "There are times when it's fun to do something different. I don't know what else I might end up trying," he adds. "You never know where things are going to lead. That's the thing about writing."

Tip

Interviews

Minding the Details

Writers who've been successful in getting their work published know that publishing requires two different mind-sets. The first is the actual act of writing the manuscript. The second is the business of writing—the marketing and selling of the manuscript. This shift in perspective is necessary if you want to become a successful career writer. That said, you need to keep the business side of writing in mind as you develop your writing.

Each of the following sections and accompanying sidebars discusses a writing business topic that affects anyone selling a manuscript. Our treatment of the business topics that follow is necessarily limited, so look for short blocks of information and resources throughout this section to help you further research the content.

CONTRACTS AND AGREEMENTS

If you've ever been a freelance writer, you know that contracts and agreements vary from publisher to publisher. Very rarely will you find two contracts that are exactly the same. Some magazine editors work only by verbal agreement, as do many agents; others have elaborate documents you must sign in duplicate and return to the editor before you even begin the assignment. It is essential that you consider all of the elements involved in a contract, whether verbal or written, and know what you stand to gain and lose by agreeing to the contract. Maybe you want to repurpose the article and resell it to a market that is different from the first publication to which you sold the article. If that's the case, then you need to know what rights you want to sell.

In contract negotiations, the writer is usually interested in licensing the work for a particu-

Contracts and contract negotiation

For More Info

- **The Authors Guild** (www.authorsguild.org), 31 E. 28th St., 10th Floor, New York NY 10016-7923. (212)563-5904. Fax: (212)564-5363. E-mail: staff@authorsguild.org.

- **National Writers Union** (www.nwu.org), 113 University Place, 6th Floor, New York NY 10003. (212)254-0279. Fax: (212)254-0673. E-mail: nwu@wu.org.

lar use, but limiting the publisher's ability to make other uses of the work in the future. It's in the publisher's best interest, however, to secure as many rights as possible, both now and later on. Those are the basic positions of both parties. The contract negotiation is a process of compromise on questions relating to those basic points—and the amount of compensation to be given the writer for his work. If at any time you are unsure about any part of the contract, it is best to consult a lawyer who specializes in media law and contract negotiation.

A contract is rarely a take-it-or-leave-it proposition. If an editor tells you his company will allow no changes to the contract, you will then have to decide how important the assignment is to you. However, most editors are open to negotiations, so you need to learn how to compromise on points that don't matter to you, and stand your ground on those that do matter.

RIGHTS AND THE WRITER

A creative work can be used in many different ways. As the author of the work, you hold all rights to the work in question. When you agree to have your work published, you are granting a publisher the right to use your work in any number of ways. Whether that right is to publish the manuscript for the first time in a publication or to publish it as many times and in many different ways as a publisher wishes is up to you—it all depends on the agreed-upon terms. As a general rule, the more rights you license away, the less control you have over your work and the money you're paid. You should strive to keep as many rights to your work as you can.

Writers and editors sometimes define rights in a number of different ways. Below you will find a classification of terms as they relate to rights.

- **First Serial Rights**—Rights that the writer offers a newspaper or magazine to publish the manuscript for the first time in any periodical. All other rights remain with the writer. Sometimes the qualifier "North American" is added to these rights to specify a geographical limitation to the license.

    When content is excerpted from a book scheduled to be published, and it appears in a magazine or newspaper prior to book publication, this is also called first serial rights.

- **One-Time Rights**—Nonexclusive rights (rights that can be licensed to more than one market) purchased by a periodical to publish the work once (also known as simultaneous rights). That is, there is nothing to stop the author from selling the work to other publications at the same time.

- **Second Serial (Reprint) Rights**—Nonexclusive rights given to a newspaper or magazine to publish a manuscript after it has already appeared in another newspaper or magazine.

- **All Rights**—This is exactly what it sounds like. All rights mean an author is selling every right they have to a work. If you license all rights to your work, you forfeit the right to ever use the work again. If you think you may want to use the article again, you should avoid submitting to such markets or refuse payment and withdraw your material.

- **Electronic Rights**—Rights that cover a broad range of electronic media, from online magazines and databases to CD-ROM magazine anthologies and interactive games. The contract should specify if—and which—electronic rights are included. The presumption is unspecified rights remain with the writer.

- **Subsidiary Rights**—Rights, other than book publication rights, that should be covered in a book contract. These may include various serial rights; movie, TV, audiotape, and other electronic rights; translation rights, etc. The book contract should specify who controls the rights (author or publisher) and what percentage of sales from the licensing of these rights goes to the author.

- **Dramatic, TV, and Motion Picture Rights**—Rights for use of material on the stage, in TV, or in the movies. Often a one-year option to buy such rights is offered (generally for 10 percent of the total price). The party interested in the rights then tries to sell the idea to other people—actors, directors, studios, or TV networks. Some properties are optioned numerous times, but most fail to become full productions. In those cases, the writer can sell the rights again and again.

Sometimes editors don't take the time to specify the rights they are buying. If you sense that an editor is interested in getting stories, but doesn't seem to know what his and the writer's responsibilities are, be wary. In such a case, you'll want to explain what rights you're offering (preferably one-time or first serial rights only) and that you expect additional payment for subsequent use of your work.

The Copyright Law that went into effect January 1, 1978, states writers are primarily selling one-time rights to their work unless they—and the publisher—agree otherwise in writing. Book rights are covered fully by contract between the writer and the book publisher.

SELLING SUBSIDIARY RIGHTS

The primary right in book publishing is the right to publish the book itself. All other rights (movie rights, audio rights, book club rights, etc.) are considered secondary, or subsidiary, to the right to print publication. In contract negotiations, authors and their agents traditionally try to avoid granting the publisher subsidiary rights they feel comfortable marketing themselves. Publishers, on the other hand, want to obtain as many of the subsidiary rights as they can.

Larger agencies have experience selling subsidiary rights, and many authors represented

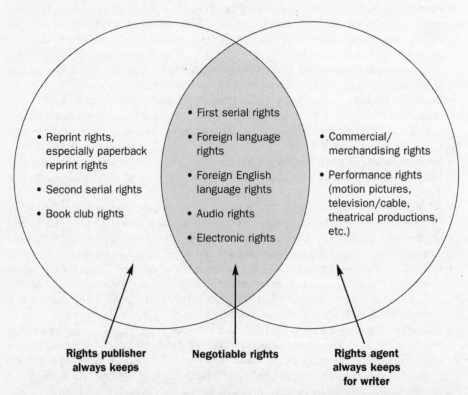

- Reprint rights, especially paperback reprint rights

- Second serial rights

- Book club rights

- First serial rights

- Foreign language rights

- Foreign English language rights

- Audio rights

- Electronic rights

- Commercial/merchandising rights

- Performance rights (motion pictures, television/cable, theatrical productions, etc.)

Rights publisher always keeps **Negotiable rights** **Rights agent always keeps for writer**

Some subsidiary rights are always granted to the publisher. Some should always be retained by the author. The remainder are negotiable, and require knowledgeable advice from a literary agent or attorney in deciding whether it is more advantageous to grant the rights to the publisher or to reserve them.

The Business of Writing

by such agents prefer to retain those rights and let their agents do the selling. On the other hand, book publishers have subsidiary rights departments whose sole job is to exploit the subsidiary rights the publisher was able to retain during the contract negotiation.

The marketing of electronic rights can be tricky. With the proliferation of electronic and multimedia formats, publishers, agents, and authors are going to great lengths to make sure contracts specify exactly which electronic rights are being conveyed (or retained). Compensation for these rights is a major source of conflict because many book publishers seek control of them, and many magazines routinely include electronic rights in the purchase of all rights, often with no additional payment.

COPYRIGHT

Copyright law exists to protect creators of original works. It is also designed to encourage the production of creative works by ensuring that artists and writers hold the rights by which they can profit from their hard work.

The moment you finish a piece of writing—or in fact, the second you begin to pen the manuscript—the law recognizes only you can decide how the work is used. Copyright protects your writing, recognizes you (its sole creator) as its owner, and grants you all the rights and benefits that accompany ownership. With very few exceptions, anything you write today will enjoy copyright protection for your lifetime, plus 70 years. Copyright protects "original works of authorship" that are fixed in a tangible form of expression. *Copyright law cannot protect titles, ideas, and facts.*

Some writers are under the mistaken impression that a registered copyright with the U.S. Copyright Office (www.copyright.gov) is necessary to protect their work, and that their work is not protected until they "receive" their copyright paperwork from the government. *This is not true.* You don't have to register your work with the U.S. Copyright Office for it to be protected. Registration for your work does, however, offer some additional protection (specifically, the possibility of recovering punitive damages in an infringement suit) as well as legal proof of the date of copyright.

Useful Websites

Most magazines are registered with the U.S. Copyright Office as single collective entities themselves; that is, the individual works that make up the magazine are *not* copyrighted individ-

Filing for copyright

To register you work with the U.S. Copyright Office, you need to complete the following steps.

For More Info

1 **Fill out an application form** (Form TX), which is available by calling (202)707-9100 or downloading from www.copyright.gov/forms.

2 **Send the application form,** a nonreturnable copy of the work in question, and a check (or money order) for $30 to:

The Library of Congress
U.S. Copyright Office
Register of Copyrights
101 Independence Ave. SE
Washington DC 20559-6000

The Business of Writing

ually in the names of the authors. You'll need to register your article yourself if you wish to have the additional protection of copyright (your name, the year of first publication, and the copyright symbol ©) appended to any published version of your work. You may use the copyright symbol regardless of whether your work has been registered with the U.S. Copyright Office.

One thing you need to pay particular attention to is work-for-hire arrangements. If you sign a work-for-hire agreement, you are agreeing that your writing will be done as a work for hire, and you will not control the copyright of the completed work—the person or organization who hired you will be the copyright owner. These agreements and transfers of exclusive rights must appear in writing to be legal. However, it's a good idea to get every publishing agreement you negotiate in writing before the sale.

FINANCES AND TAXES

You will find that as your writing business expands, so will your need to keep track of writing-related expenses and incomes. Keeping a close eye on these details will prove very helpful when it comes time to report your income to the IRS. It will also help you pay as little tax as possible and keep you aware of the state of your freelance writing as a business. This means you need to set up a detailed tracking and organizing system to log all expenses and income. Without such a system, your writing as a business will eventually fold. If you dislike handling finance-related tasks, you can always hire a professional to oversee these duties for you. However, even if you do hire a professional, you still need to keep all original records.

The following tips will help you keep track of the finance-related tasks associated with your freelance business.

Tip

- Keep accurate records.
- Separate your writing income and expenses from your personal income and expenses.
- Maintain a separate bank account and credit card for business-related expenses.
- Record every transaction (expenses and earnings) related to your writing.
- Begin keeping records when you make your first writing-related purchase.
- Establish a working, detailed system of tracking expenses and income. Include the date; the source of income (or the vendor of your purchase); a description of what was sold or bought; how the payment was rendered (cash, check, credit card); and the amount of the transaction.
- Keep all check stubs and receipts (cash purchases and credit cards).
- Set up a record-keeping system, such as a file folder system, to store all receipts.

Tax information

Important

While we cannot offer you tax advice or interpretations, we can suggest several sources for the most current information.

- Check the IRS website (www.irs.gov).

- Call your local IRS office.

- Obtain basic IRS publications by phone or by mail; most are available at libraries and some post offices.

Getting Great Interviews

Three Writers Offer Interview Tips

by Will Allison

As any reporter can tell you, nothing makes a story come to life like good quotes. But getting good quotes involves more than finding good sources; it also requires well-honed interviewing skills. In the following article, four successful writers share advice on the art of interviewing, covering everything from pacing and research to the best way of handling tough questions.

Pamela Colloff holds a bachelor's degree in English literature from Brown University and was raised in New York City. Before joining the staff of *Texas Monthly* in 1997, she wrote for *Details*, *Spin*, and *The Village Voice*, among other publications. In 2001, her article on school prayer was nominated for a National Magazine Award. The *Columbia Journalism Review* named her one of "Ten Young Writers on the Rise" in 2002.

David Martin is a staff writer at *Scene*, a New Times-owned alternative newsweekly in Cleveland. He was recently named Best Reporter in Ohio by the state Society of Professional Journalists. He is a graduate of Miami University (Ohio) and the Kiplinger Program for Public Affairs Journalism at The Ohio State University in Columbus, Ohio, the city where he was born.

Alison Owings is the author of two nonfiction books, *Hey, Waitress! The USA from the Other Side of the Tray* (University of California Press, 2002) and *Frauen: German Women Recall the Third Reich* (Rutgers University Press, 1993), a *New York Times* Notable Book. For years she was a news writer at CBS Television in New York for Walter Cronkite, Charles Kuralt, and Dan Rather, among others. Today she's planning an oral history about urban Native Americans. She also owns Oral Portraits, a service for clients who want to be interviewed for posterity.

How important is background research prior to an interview?

Colloff: Research is essential. Your answers will often be as interesting (or predictable) as your questions. The more you know, the more detailed you can be in your line of questioning.

Martin: Questions and answers will be more substantive if the interviewer is familiar with the subject. That said, a writer can waste time chasing information that an interview would show to be irrelevant. Be prepared—but don't get cute.

Owings: It depends entirely on how much time you are given, or give yourself, the prickli-

WILL ALLISON is a staff member at the Squaw Valley Community of Writers and teaches creative writing at Butler University and Indiana University-Purdue University at Indianapolis. He has served as executive editor of *Story* and editor-at-large for *Zoetrope: All-Story*.

ness of the subject, or the prickliness of the interviewee. Better to know too much than too little, but an outsider's naiveté, I've found, can be a help.

Do you prefer tape recording, taking notes, or both?

Colloff: I don't use a tape recorder very often. Magazine stories often require talking to several dozen people, at length. If you tape record all your interviews, you can easily spend weeks transcribing your tapes. I find I listen better if I'm not taping. There are exceptions, of course; if a source might be hard to reach in the future (like an inmate), or if they have a really distinctive voice or vernacular you want to capture on the page (especially if you plan on using long quotes), taping can be helpful.

Photo by Meredith Pangrace

David Martin

Martin: Always notes. I record the conversation if I know the source speaks quickly; will be quoted extensively; and/or may be litigious.

Owings: Tape recording—no contest. Quotes then can be completely accurate. You just have to introduce first time interviewees—the virgins, I call them—to your machine. I take notes, too, but mostly to record gestures, and other nonaural matters.

What's the ideal setting for an interview?

Colloff: I like to interview people in their homes, but only if we can have privacy from family members. (Otherwise, people can get self-conscious.) If the person takes a lot of pride in their work, interview them at the office. Men are often more comfortable talking while they're doing something else, like driving. Sitting down and going through a list of questions is helpful, but it's not the only way to conduct an interview. After I do a sit-down interview, I like to spend time with the main people who I'll be writing about as they go about their day. I ask questions along the way, and talk to them more casually.

Martin: I like to interview people as they're doing something else. Seeing the subject in action is instructive. Also, it forgives lulls in the conversation that in another setting might result in the interview's premature conclusion.

Owings: A quiet place.

How do you put an interview subject at ease?

Tip

Colloff: The less nervous you appear to be, the more at ease your interview subject will be. It's important to speak to them like you would a friend—don't rush headlong into questions when you first sit down to talk. Also, be familiar enough with your questions that you can have a normal flow to the conversation. (There's nothing worse than interviewers who leave lots of awkward silences while they consult their notebook for the next question.) And don't dress more formally than your interview subject. If you're interviewing someone in a rural community, for example, don't arrive in a suit; wear jeans.

Photo by Alison Owings

Alison Owings

Martin: By asking about their background. It gives sources a chance to establish their credentials and, by extension, feel good about themselves.

Owings: Variously—by expressing my gratitude, by offering, or accepting, a glass of wine, and by going through a little dance that Studs Terkel told me he also uses: needing the interviewee's pre-interview assistance (like helping me find an outlet for my tape recorder). This method reduces the interviewee's nervousness and helps make us equal.

How much time does a good interview take?

Colloff: Magazine stories are different than newspaper stories, in that you need to develop characters and a sense of place. So the more time you have with someone, the better. If someone figures largely in a story, you might visit them multiple times, and spend many hours with them. If I'm profiling someone, I basically spend time with him or her until I'm bordering on being rude, and they are starting to get tired of me being around.

Martin: How ever long it takes! Although, I find I need a cookie and a nap after more than a few hours. Listening is hard work!

Owings: Some of the women in my book *Frauen: German Women Recall the Third Reich* talked with me for perhaps ten hours or more, over days, or years. Some of the women in *Hey, Waitress!: The USA from the Other Side of the Tray* met with me for the period of a lunch break. In sum, it depends. Do you want them or their information?

How do you determine the order in which you ask your questions?

Colloff: For a sit-down interview, I like to go chronologically through the events that I'll be writing about. Often, I like to schedule a follow-up interview, since the first round of answers often provokes a whole new set of questions later in the reporting process.

Martin: I don't script precise questions in advance, much less the order. This may be the time to say that I don't mind seeming to be scatterbrained in an interview. Unless you're the host of *Fresh Air* or a *60 Minutes* correspondent, your performance is irrelevant. In fact, sometimes it is to the interviewer's advantage to play the fool. The source, in a rescue effort, may divulge more than he should. One thought on the subject of timing: Sometimes sources say the most revealing things just as the interview begins or ends, when they're stepping in and out of character.

Owings: For difficult topics, I start with nonloaded questions and move slowly into, say, genocide. I use a set of questions only as a backup.

Any tips on handling especially tough questions?

Colloff: Be straightforward. Don't preface tough questions with "I know this is a hard subject, but . . ." If you're comfortable and confident asking the question, the person you're interviewing will be more likely to answer without hesitating and getting nervous.

Martin: Don't be afraid—the source is probably prepared for the worst. In really sticky situations, it may help to tender a piece of misinformation in the hopes the source will correct it with the sought response. I'm thinking of the film version of *All the President's Men*. In one scene, a man connected to the Nixon campaign tells Bob Woodward (played by Robert Redford) he has a winter home in Florida. "Was that Miami?" Woodward asks. "Boca Raton," the man says without missing a beat.

Tip

Owings: Don't start with them.

What's the most difficult aspect of getting a good interview?

Colloff: People who are very shy can, obviously, be hard to draw out. Sometimes it helps to interview them with a friend, spouse, or co-worker, who can help get them talking.

Martin: Getting details that make stories pop. Sources typically do not speak in anecdotes; you have to elicit them. Suppose you're writing a profile, and you're interviewing an old friend of the subject's. The old friend says things like "He's kind" or "She's loyal." Well, kindness and loyalty are nice attributes, but they don't bring subjects to life. Often, the

The Business of Writing

interviewer needs to press the source for examples. Ask questions like, "Can you think of a time when . . .?" or "Do you remember an instance . . .?"

Owings: Finding a good interviewee. (And shutting up during the answers.)

Any special advice for phone interviews?

Colloff: Don't do them unless you're calling someone for basic background information. If you absolutely have to do a phone interview, and the interviewee is an important part of your story, make a point of calling him or her several times over the course of your reporting so you can establish some kind of a rapport.

Martin: Many colleagues type at their keyboard as they conduct phone interviews. I find it makes sources self-conscious. An advantage of the phone is the illusion of invisibility— i.e., the recording device or notepad is "offstage." Why spoil it? It should go without saying, but the phone is a real time-saver. Inexperienced reporters and writers often schedule face-to-face interviews with minor sources whose one or two quotes could have been obtained easily by phone.

Who was your most memorable interview and why?

Colloff: A few years ago, I interviewed a man named Tom Cherry whose father was being investigated by the FBI for having bombed a black church in Birmingham, Alabama, in 1963, killing four black girls. I had no access to the father, so I wrote the article about Tom, and his difficulty coming to terms with his father's past. We talked on and off over the course of several months. Tom talked about his feelings for his father—how much he loved his father but hated what he had done. (His father has since been convicted). I'll always remember Tom's honesty and willingness to talk about a crime the rest of his family wanted to forget.

Martin: I once conducted an interview over a dead body. I was writing a feature about young morticians, and a gracious one let me tag along as he prepared for a morning funeral service. As we stood before the open casket, he described his decision to leave the deceased's second shirt button undone so he'd spend eternity in comfort. It wasn't at all creepy. In fact, it was kind of touching.

Owings: Frau Erna Dubnack of Berlin. From 1943 to 1945, she hid a Jewish friend, Hilda Naumann, in her apartment, next door to Nazis, risking her own life and that of her young son. I don't know what affected me more: Frau Dubnack's modesty, or my awareness that the interview was taking place in the very apartment where she had hidden her friend.

Online Opportunities

Living the Freelance Life Online

by Robert Spiegel

In 1997, I needed a job. After 10 years as the publisher of *Chile Pepper* magazine, I wanted to return to my writing roots. I sold my magazine and started looking for writing jobs I could deliver from New Mexico. I was a single dad with three kids, so I wanted to work from home. I wasn't willing to move to New York, Boston, or Chicago for a job, so I turned to the Internet to see what type of work might be there for an enterprising writer.

Over the next seven years, I found work entirely over the Internet. I discovered a wealth of online writing work. Sometimes it was an actual staff position, telecommuting as a senior editor at a trade publication, while other jobs were contract or freelance work. I worked for companies in England, Amsterdam, and Indonesia. I ghostwrote books and articles, and I authored my own books, sending in final drafts as e-mail attachments. I wrote for newsletters, magazines, and online news services. All of the work had one thing in common: I could do it from home in my bathrobe while taking care of my kids.

Online job sites

One reliable tactic to find work online is to simply go to job sites to see what's posted for writers. There are general job sites like **Monster.com** (www.monster.com) and **HotJobs.com** (hotjobs.yahoo.com) that offer a wide range of jobs. You can search these sites using "writer," "editor," "journalist," or even "public relations" to find listings. Most of the jobs on these general sites are aimed at employees who walk into the company's building each day, but I've found work at these sites by simply suggesting they consider a telecommuter. These sites also post jobs specifically aimed at freelancers.

Specialized job sites are more productive for finding writing work. The two major job sites for writers are **JournalismJobs.com** (www.journalismjobs.com) and **MediaBistro.com** (www.mediabistro.com/joblistings). JournalismJobs.com focuses on jobs at newspapers, news services, and magazines, and MediaBistro.com is the industry site for magazine and book publishers. There is about a 10 percent overlap on the two sites. Although most of the listings are for staff positions, both sites also present projects specifically for freelancers.

Useful Websites

The job listings on these sites explain what the publisher wants you to include in your application. Typically, this includes a cover letter, résumé, and writing samples (also called

---

ROBERT SPIEGEL is a freelance writer who makes his living writing magazine articles, books, and newsletters. He is the editor of the newsletter *Marketing Smarter* with Google. Spiegel finds, researches, and delivers all of his writing projects online.

"clips"). The downside to job sites like these, though, is they attract a large number of job seekers, so you can get lost among the flood of résumés.

Auction sites

Useful
Websites

There are a number of auction sites that provide projects for writers. The two main sites are **Elance** (www.elance.com) and **Guru.com** (www.guru.com). Both sites charge a membership fee accompanied by a transaction fee for work obtained through the site. The monthly subscription rates range from $25 to $45, with transaction fees ranging from 2.5 percent to 5 percent. These fees are fine if you're doing plenty of business through the site, but they're hefty, perhaps prohibitive, if you're only a part-time writer.

The positive side of auction sites is there are new projects posted daily, and they're all tailored toward freelancers. I spent most of one year getting a good portion of my freelance mix from auction sites. In the long run, though, it's hard to build a strong freelancing portfolio of clients from the countless one-off projects you get through these sites.

Another difficulty of auction sites is they don't attract the best clients. The auction format puts price at the top of the list of qualifiers for writers. There are always unqualified writers who will low-bid a job, but even when the low-bidders are filtered out, qualified writers bid down their rates. When a low fee is the primary qualifier, you get clients who are seeking a deal, rather than high-quality work.

Freelancing sites

Useful
Websites

There are numerous sites on the Internet that informally post freelance projects. **NewsJobs.Net** (www.newsjobs.net/usa/default.asp) is one site, and it offers a list of about 200 freelance and job sites for writers and journalists. Some of these sites only offer new projects about once every two weeks, while others regularly offer writing opportunities. Freelance sites offer more offbeat online jobs than general job sites, like writing daily affirmations or verses for greeting cards, and I've found plenty of fun work through freelance sites. However, the work on freelance sites usually pays minimally and sometimes the work on the sites is offered by shoestring operations.

Cold calls and the Internet

One of the most successful tactics for finding work online is to make cold calls to the publishing companies you find attractive. The best way to cold call over the Internet is to send an e-mail to a specific editor asking if the publication has freelance work available. The advantage to cold calling is you may find an editor who has freelance needs before the company puts out the word, so you're not competing with dozens, even hundreds of other writers. Most of my successful long-term projects and jobs came from cold calling.

Cold calling works particularly well if you have substantial experience. If you're starting out, this may be your least productive method for finding online work. For trade and business publications, a cold call e-mail is the best approach, since most trade and business publications plan their editorial content a year in advance and, as a result, are not interested in receiving queries. I suggest getting a number of articles and projects under your belt before you send notes to editors asking if they have freelance assignments available.

Online queries

Sending a traditional query by e-mail can be a successful way to get assignments online—this is particularly true for consumer magazines. Many editors prefer e-mail queries, and they certainly answer them more quickly than they respond to paper queries. The query itself should look very much like a paper query, so you can follow the rules set out in the query section of this book. But there are a few notable differences between e-mail and paper queries.

One difference is you can't include clips in an e-mail query. Attachments from unknown senders are usually discarded, so you need to get all your information into the body of the e-mail. I suggest including clips in one of two ways. If you have clips online, you can enter a link to your articles. If not, you can paste the first three paragraphs of an article at the end of your e-mail. Explain that the full-length article is available on request. Most editors can get a feel for your skills by looking at the first three paragraphs of a published article. (For additional tips, see Clips and E-mail Queries on page 22.)

See Also

Getting the right e-mail address is often a challenge. If you can't find the editor's e-mail address in this book or on the publication's website, here's a tip that works. First look on

Job and project websites

Useful
Websites

Here is a partial list of job and project sites for writers that were selected for their longevity. Sites such as SunOasis.com and NewsJobs.Net include links to dozens of other work-related sites for freelance writers.

JOB SITES:

- **American Society of Business Publication Editors:** www.asbpe.org

- **HotJobs.com:** hotjobs.yahoo.com

- **J-Jobs:** journalism.berkeley.edu/jobs

- **JobLink for Journalists:** newslink.org/newjoblinksearch.html

- **JournalismJobs.com:** www.journalismjobs.com

- **The Journalist's Toolbox:** journaliststoolbox.com/newswriting/jobs.html

- **MediaBistron.com:** www.mediabistro.com/joblistings

- **Monster.com:** www.monster.com

- **Net-Temps:** www.net-temps.com

- **NewsJobs:** newsjobs.net/usa

AUCTION SITES:

- **Contractedwork.com:** contractedwork.com

- **Elance.com:** www.elance.com

- **Guru.com:** www.guru.com

FREELANCING SITES:

- **AllFreelanceWork:** allfreelancework.com

- **PoeWar.com:** poewar.com/jobs/index.html

- **SunOasis.com:** www.sunoasis.com

- **The Write Jobs:** www.writejobs.com

- **WritersWeekly.com:** www.writersweekly.com

The Business of Writing

the publication's website, and find the name of the editor to whom you wish to submit. For feature articles, you can query the section editor (food, health, travel). If the right section isn't clear, send your query to the managing editor and ask that it be forwarded to the appropriate editor. Once you have the editor's name, go to the advertising/sales section of the website (the people in sales and advertising usually make their e-mail addresses available online). Then, look to see how the e-mail addresses are formatted—you can usually figure out how contact names correspond to e-mail addresses.

The life of freelancing online

As you roll up your sleeves and search for work online, remember that it takes time to get the hang of it. You need to find a handful of sites that you check daily. Once or twice a week is not enough. When you comb through the sites daily, you catch opportunities that only exist for a few hours. Many publishers will put the word out and find a collection of qualified writers the very first day the ad posts.

Not all online writing jobs are satisfactory experiences. There is always the danger you will deliver satisfactory work and not get paid. Because of this, it is common for a client to make a partial payment up front. If the job is particularly large, you can negotiate multiple payments tied to portions of the overall project. If the company refuses to pay a portion (25 to 50 percent) up front, then you're best off turning down the job.

Finally, remember the quality of your work and your ability to meet deadlines will determine whether you get follow-up work. If you deliver great stories on time, you'll be able to build a small group of clients that will keep you busy. It's okay to work in your bathrobe while taking care of your kids, as long as your work is excellent and on time.

How Much Should I Charge?

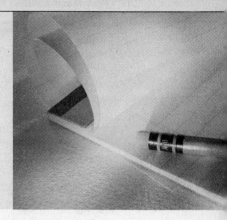

by Lynn Wasnak

Want to turn your love of words into a reliable income? The good news is thousands of professional freelance writers and editors across the United States do exactly that each year. Some freelance writers earn six figures, though incomes in the $50,000 to $75,000 range are more common. Freelance editors often achieve annual incomes of $35,000 to $50,000, while specialists in technical or medical editing report earnings of $75,000.

On the other hand, can a writer or editor go broke freelancing? Yes—successful freelancing with words is not a cakewalk; it's a business in flux. Markets churn. Editors come and go. Market research, networking, negotiating, and sound financial sense are critical.

Important

As a serious freelancer, you must develop a fair hourly rate. Unlike a staffed employee, you personally have to fund health insurance, vacations, retirement savings, self-employment tax, and office supplies—not to mention equipment, rent, and phone. Some take annual expenses and divide by 1,050 billable hours per year to determine a satisfactory hourly rate. Others simply double the hourly rate a staffer would earn. Or, for a $50,000 annual income, figure $50-$75 per hour; for a $100,000 annual income, $100 per hour is typical. Walk away from jobs that pay less.

You may not get top dollar if you're just starting out, but don't be afraid to negotiate for the best deal you can get. Your time and skills are valuable. Editors expect you to negotiate for more money, for better contract terms, or both.

Learn the nitty-gritty details of freelancing by joining professional organizations. In these groups you'll find helpful, experienced freelancers who offer tips like these:

Tip

- **Don't write without a signed contract.** If a client doesn't present a contract, write one yourself and request a signature before you begin.
- **To make more money, faster,** find an area you enjoy and in which you can specialize.
- **Market a lot.** With many queries circulating, each rejection hurts less. Rejection comes with the freelance territory; grow a thick skin.
- **Translate dollars per word into dollars per hour** by tracking your time. A $3 per word assignment may not be worth it if the research, writing, and revision take forever.
- **Put limits in your contracts**—number of revisions, total hours—with a clause that starts the hourly-rate clock ticking when limits are surpassed.
- **Invest in your profession.** Attend conferences, buy books, or take online classes.

LYNN WASNAK (www.lynnwasnak.com) is a life-long freelancer specializing in medical and business writing, and schmoozing with fellow writers.

That's the pep talk. Now let's cut to the chase. The following report cites current fees paid to professional writers for their work. This report is based on input from sales finalized in 2003 and 2004 only. The data is generated from voluntary surveys completed by freelance members of numerous professional writers' and editors' organizations and specialty groups. We thank these responding groups, listed below, and their members for generously sharing information. Also, we welcome any writers who would like to contribute their rate experience to request a survey anytime. Your figures will be included in the next edition of *Writer's Market*. Request a survey from lwasnak@fuse.net.

Organizations

For more information on determining freelance pay rates, negotiating contracts, etc., you can visit the following organizations.

- **American Literary Translators Association (ALTA):** www.utdallas.edu/research/cts/alta.htm
- **Association of Personal Historians (APH):** www.personalhistorians.org
- **American Society of Journalists and Authors (ASJA):** www.asja.org
- **American Society of Media Photographers (ASMP):** www.asmp.org
- **American Society of Picture Professionals (ASPP):** www.aspp.com
- **American Translators Association (ATA):** www.atanet.org
- **Editorial Freelancers Association (EFA):** www.the-efa.org
- **Freelance Success (FLX):** www.freelancesuccess.com
- **Independent Writers of Chicago (IWOC):** www.iwoc.org
- **International Association of Business Communicators (IABC):** www.iabc.com
- **Investigative Reporters and Editors, Inc. (IRE):** www.ire.org
- **Media Communicators Association International (MCA-I):** www.mca-i.org
- **National Writers Union (NWU):** www.nwu.org
- **Society of Professional Journalists (SPJ):** www.spj.org
- **Society for Technical Communication (STC):** www.stc.org
- **The Cartoon Bank:** www.cartoonbank.com
- **Washington Independent Writers (WIW):** www.washwriter.org
- **Women in Film (WIF):** www.wif.org
- **Writers Guild of America, East (WGAE):** www.wgae.org
- **Writers Guild of America, West (WGA):** www.wga.org

Advertising, Copywriting & Public Relations

	PER HOUR			PER PROJECT			OTHER		
	HIGH	LOW	AVG	HIGH	LOW	AVG	HIGH	LOW	AVG
Advertising copywriting	$150	$43	$83	$4,500	$215	$1,273	$2/word	$1/word	$1.50/word
Book jacket copywriting	$100	$30	$67	n/a	n/a	n/a	n/a	n/a	n/a
Campaign development or product launch	$125	$30	$76	$7,500	$1,500	$3,740	n/a	n/a	n/a
Catalog copywriting	$150	$30	$70	n/a	n/a	n/a	n/a	n/a	n/a
Copyediting for advertising	$55	$33	$40	n/a	n/a	n/a	n/a	n/a	n/a
Direct-mail copywriting	$125	$50	$78	$15,000	$500	$5,000	$2/word	$1/word	$1.50/word
Event promotions/publicity	$100	$40	$80	n/a	n/a	n/a	n/a	n/a	n/a
Fundraising campaign brochure	$100	$45	$85	$2,000	$1,000	$1,500	n/a	n/a	n/a
E-mail ad copywriting	$95	$25	$62	n/a	n/a	n/a	n/a	n/a	n/a
Political campaigns, public relations	$150	$50	$85	n/a	n/a	n/a	n/a	n/a	n/a
Press kits	$100	$45	$86	$5,000	$1,000	$2,334	n/a	n/a	n/a
Press/news release	$125	$40	$74	$500	$125	$280	n/a	n/a	n/a
Public relations for businesses	$100	$30	$73	n/a	n/a	n/a	n/a	n/a	n/a
Public relations for government	$60	$40	$50	n/a	n/a	n/a	n/a	n/a	n/a
Public relations for organizations or nonprofits	$100	$35	$60	n/a	n/a	n/a	n/a	n/a	n/a
Public relations for schools or libraries	$100	$50	$85	n/a	n/a	n/a	n/a	n/a	n/a
Speechwriting/editing (general)[1]	$167	$85	$110	$6,000	$2,700	$4,064	n/a	n/a	n/a
Speechwriting for government officials	$125	$30	$76	n/a	n/a	n/a	n/a	n/a	n/a
Speechwriting for political candidates	$150	$60	$92	n/a	n/a	n/a	n/a	n/a	n/a

[1] Per project figures based on 30-minute speech.

The Business of Writing

The Business of Writing

Audiovisuals & Electronic Communications

	PER HOUR			PER PROJECT			OTHER		
	HIGH	LOW	AVG	HIGH	LOW	AVG	HIGH	LOW	AVG
Book summaries (narrative synopsis) for film producers[1]	n/a	n/a	n/a	n/a	$800	n/a	$1,161/15 min	$1,934/30 min	$3,666/60 min
Copyediting audiovisuals	$85	$35	$53	n/a	n/a	n/a	n/a	n/a	n/a
Business film scripts[2] (training and info)	$100	$65	$84	n/a	n/a	n/a	$500/run min	$100/run min	$300/run min
Educational/training film scripts	$100	$35	$60	n/a	n/a	n/a	$500/run min	$100/run min	$300/run min
Corporate product film	$100	$30	$70	n/a	n/a	n/a	$500/run min	$100/run min	$300/run min
Movie novelization	n/a	n/a	n/a	$10,000	$5,000	$7,500	n/a	n/a	n/a
Radio editorials & essays (no production)	$70	$50	$60	n/a	n/a	n/a	n/a	n/a	n/a
Radio commercials/PSAs	$85	$30	$56	n/a	n/a	n/a	n/a	n/a	n/a
Screenwriting (original screenplay)	n/a	n/a	n/a	$97,068	$52,705	$74,887	n/a	n/a	n/a
Scripts for nontheatrical films for education, business, industry	$100	$55	$75	$5,000	$3,000	$4,083	$500/run min	$100/run min	$300/run min
TV news story/feature[3]	$100	$70	$90	n/a	n/a	n/a	n/a	n/a	n/a
TV scripts (nontheatrical)	$150	$70	$100	n/a	n/a	n/a	$1,000/day	$550/day	$800/day
TV scripts (teleplay/MOW)[4]	n/a	n/a	n/a	n/a	n/a	n/a	$500/run min	$100/run min	$300/run min
TV commercials/PSAs	$85	$60	$73	n/a	n/a	n/a	n/a	n/a	n/a

Book Publishing

	PER HOUR			PER PROJECT			OTHER		
	HIGH	LOW	AVG	HIGH	LOW	AVG	HIGH	LOW	AVG
Abstracting and abridging	$35	$30	$33	n/a	n/a	n/a	n/a	n/a	n/a
Anthology editing	n/a	n/a	n/a	$3,000	$1,200	$2,050	n/a	n/a	n/a

1 Other figures based on length of speech (min=minute).
2 Run min=run minute.
3 $1,201 Writers Guild of America minimum/story.
4 TV scripts 30 minutes or less average $6,535/story, $19,603 with teleplay; TV scripts 60 minutes or less average $11,504/story, $28,833 with teleplay.

	PER HOUR			PER PROJECT			OTHER		
	HIGH	LOW	AVG	HIGH	LOW	AVG	HIGH	LOW	AVG
Book proposal consultation	$150	$25	$69	$500	$350	$425	n/a	n/a	n/a
Book proposal writing	$100	$40	$73	$12,500	$2,500	$5,857	n/a	n/a	n/a
Book query critique	$50	$25	$38	n/a	n/a	n/a	n/a	n/a	n/a
Book query writing	n/a	n/a	n/a	$500	$120	$200	n/a	n/a	n/a
Children's book writing (advance against royalties)	n/a	n/a	n/a	n/a	n/a	n/a	$4,000	$800	$2,760
Children's book writing (work for hire)	$75	$50	$63	n/a	n/a	n/a	$5/word	$1/word	$3/word
Content editing (scholarly)	$63	$23	$43	n/a	n/a	n/a	$10/page	$4/page	$6/page
Content editing (textbook)	$63	$19	$42	n/a	n/a	n/a	$5/page	$3/page	$4/page
Content editing (trade)	$100	$15	$49	n/a	n/a	n/a	$6/page	$3.75/page	$4.75/page
Copyediting	$60	$17	$34	n/a	n/a	n/a	$7/page	$2/page	$4.20/page
Ghostwriting, as told to[1]	$100	$25	$55	$100,000	$10,000	$40,555	n/a	n/a	n/a
Ghostwriting, no credit	$113	$25	$67	$100,000	$7,500	$37,091	n/a	n/a	n/a
Indexing	$40	$30	$35	n/a	n/a	n/a	$8/page	$2.35/page	$4/page
Manuscript evaluation and critique	$150	$20	$56	$2,000	$200	$840	n/a	n/a	n/a
Nonfiction book writing (own) (advance against royalties)	n/a	n/a	n/a	n/a	n/a	n/a	$100,000	$1,000	$25,475
Nonfiction book writing (collaborative) (advance against royalties)	$100	$40	$64	n/a	n/a	n/a	$160,000	$2,000	$33,750
Novel synopsis (general)	$60	$45	$51	n/a	n/a	n/a	n/a	n/a	n/a
Proofreading	$45	$15	$25	n/a	n/a	n/a	$3/page	$1/page	$2.25/page
Research for writers or book publishers	$100	$17	$44	n/a	n/a	n/a	n/a	n/a	n/a
Rewriting	$200	$20	$62	$15,000	$3,000	$8,500	n/a	n/a	n/a
Translation (fiction)[2]	n/a	n/a	n/a	$10,000	$7,000	$8,500	12¢	6¢	9¢

1 Per project figures do not include royalty arrangements, which vary from publisher to publisher.
2 Other figures in cents are per target word.

The Business of Writing

The Business of Writing

	PER HOUR			PER PROJECT			OTHER		
	HIGH	LOW	AVG	HIGH	LOW	AVG	HIGH	LOW	AVG
Translation (nonfiction)[1]	n/a	n/a	n/a	n/a	n/a	n/a	15¢	8¢	10¢
Translation (poetry)	n/a	n/a	n/a	n/a	n/a	n/a	$15/page	$0/page	$7.50/page
Business									
Annual reports	$125	$40	$81	n/a	n/a	n/a	n/a	n/a	n/a
Associations and organizations (writing for)	$150	$40	$67	$17,600	$250	$5,130	n/a	n/a	n/a
Brochures, fliers, booklets for business	$100	$35	$72	$6,000	$330	$2,276	$375/page	$125/page	$271/page
Business editing (general)	$100	$30	$59	n/a	n/a	n/a	n/a	n/a	n/a
Business letters	$100	$45	$74	n/a	n/a	n/a	n/a	n/a	n/a
Business plan	$100	$88	$94	n/a	n/a	n/a	n/a	n/a	n/a
Business-writing seminars	$200	$65	$83	$3,500	$1,000	$2,250	n/a	n/a	n/a
Catalogs for businesses	$90	$60	$78	$10,000	$2,000	$5,000	n/a	n/a	n/a
Consultation on communications	$150	$60	$98	n/a	n/a	n/a	$1,200/day	$500/day	$850/day
Copyediting for businesses	$100	$24	$52	n/a	n/a	n/a	$4/page	$2/page	$3/page
Corporate histories	$100	$75	$92	$160,000	$30,000	$84,375	$2/word	$1/word	$1.50/word
Corporate periodicals, editing	$75	$50	$63	n/a	n/a	n/a	n/a	n/a	n/a
Corporate periodicals, writing	$100	$40	$79	n/a	n/a	n/a	$2/word	$1/word	$1.50/word
Corporate profile	$100	$75	$85	n/a	n/a	n/a	n/a	n/a	n/a
Ghostwriting for business (usually trade magazine articles for business columns)	$150	$50	$95	n/a	n/a	n/a	n/a	n/a	n/a
Government research	$75	$50	$60	n/a	n/a	n/a	n/a	n/a	n/a
Government writing	$75	$50	$55	n/a	n/a	n/a	n/a	n/a	n/a
Grant proposal writing for nonprofits	$80	$19	$57	$3,000	$1,800	$2,400	n/a	n/a	n/a

1 Other figures in cents are per target word.

	PER HOUR			PER PROJECT			OTHER		
	HIGH	LOW	AVG	HIGH	LOW	AVG	HIGH	LOW	AVG
Newsletters, desktop publishing/production[1]	$100	$35	$73	$3,800	$1,000	$2,520	n/a	n/a	n/a
Newsletters, editing	$100	$35	$59	n/a	n/a	n/a	n/a	n/a	n/a
Newsletters, writing	$125	$35	$73	n/a	n/a	n/a	$5/word	$1/word	$2/word

Computer, Scientific & Technical

	PER HOUR			PER PROJECT			OTHER		
	HIGH	LOW	AVG	HIGH	LOW	AVG	HIGH	LOW	AVG
Computer-related manual writing	$100	$30	$67	n/a	n/a	n/a	n/a	n/a	n/a
E-mail copywriting	$100	$40	$76	n/a	n/a	n/a	n/a	n/a	n/a
Medical and science editing	$100	$21	$54	n/a	n/a	n/a	$4/page	$3/page	$3.50/page
Medical and science proofreading	$100	$20	$44	n/a	n/a	n/a	n/a	n/a	n/a
Medical and science writing	$150	$30	$75	$5,000	$2,500	$3,750	$3/word	50¢/word	$1.71/word
Online editing	$75	$30	$50	n/a	n/a	n/a	$4/page	$3/page	$3.50/page
Technical editing	$75	$21	$42	n/a	n/a	n/a	n/a	n/a	n/a
Technical writing	$160	$68	$84	n/a	n/a	n/a	n/a	n/a	n/a
Web page design	$75	$35	$56	$4,000	$500	$2,000	n/a	n/a	n/a
Web page editing	$100	$30	$62	n/a	n/a	n/a	n/a	n/a	n/a
Web page writing	$120	$40	$73	n/a	n/a	n/a	$1/word $150/page	50¢/word $50/page	80¢/word $100/page
White Papers	$125	$50	$89	n/a	n/a	n/a	n/a	n/a	n/a

Editorial/Design Packages[2]

	PER HOUR			PER PROJECT			OTHER		
	HIGH	LOW	AVG	HIGH	LOW	AVG	HIGH	LOW	AVG
Desktop publishing	$150	$25	$65	n/a	n/a	n/a	n/a	n/a	n/a
Greeting card ideas	n/a	n/a	n/a	n/a	n/a	n/a	$300/card	$25/card	$125/card
Photo brochures	$75	$65	$70	n/a	n/a	n/a	n/a	n/a	n/a

1 Per project figures based on four-page newsletters.
2 For more information about photography rates, see 2005 Photographer's Market.

The Business of Writing

The Business of Writing

	PER HOUR			PER PROJECT			OTHER		
	HIGH	LOW	AVG	HIGH	LOW	AVG	HIGH	LOW	AVG
Picture editing	$100	$40	$70	n/a	n/a	n/a	n/a	n/a	n/a
Photo research	$70	$35	$48	n/a	n/a	n/a	n/a	n/a	n/a

Educational & Literary Services

	PER HOUR			PER PROJECT			OTHER		
	HIGH	LOW	AVG	HIGH	LOW	AVG	HIGH	LOW	AVG
Educational consulting and designing business/adult education courses	$200	$30	$87	$20,000	$600	$7,700	n/a	n/a	n/a
Educational grant and proposal writing	$100	$19	$51	$2,500	$600	$1,550	n/a	n/a	n/a
Manuscript evaluation for theses/dissertations	$95	$20	$50	$1,550	$250	$700	n/a	n/a	n/a
Poetry manuscript critique	$200	$75	$100	n/a	n/a	n/a	n/a	n/a	n/a
Presentations at regional writers' conferences[1]	n/a	n/a	n/a	n/a	n/a	n/a	$10,000	$50	$720
Presentations to local groups, librarians or teachers	n/a	n/a	n/a	n/a	n/a	n/a	$250/event	$35/event	$112/event
Readings by poets, fiction writers (highest fees for celebrity writers)	n/a	n/a	n/a	n/a	n/a	n/a	$3,000/event	$50/event	$200/event
Short story manuscript critique	$150	$50	$75	n/a	n/a	n/a	n/a	n/a	n/a
Teaching college course/seminar (includes adult education)	$335	$35	$70	$25,000	$500	$2,000	$550/day	$150/day	$367/day
Writers' workshops	n/a	n/a	n/a	n/a	n/a	n/a	$284/event	$60/event	$123/event
Writing for scholarly journals	n/a	n/a	n/a	n/a	n/a	n/a	$450/article	$155/article	$300/article

Magazines & Trade Journals[2]

	PER HOUR			PER PROJECT			OTHER		
	HIGH	LOW	AVG	HIGH	LOW	AVG	HIGH	LOW	AVG
Article manuscript critique	$100	$25	$55	n/a	n/a	n/a	n/a	n/a	n/a
Arts reviewing	$300	$25	$142	n/a	n/a	n/a	$1.25/word	25¢/word	75¢/word
Book reviews	n/a	n/a	n/a	$500	$25	$133	$1/word	5¢/word	44¢/word

1 Figures are per event.
2 For specific pay rate information for feature articles, columns/departments, fillers, etc., see individual market listings.

	PER HOUR			PER PROJECT			OTHER		
	HIGH	LOW	AVG	HIGH	LOW	AVG	HIGH	LOW	AVG
Consultation on magazine editorial	$200	$35	$103	n/a	n/a	n/a	n/a	n/a	n/a
Content editing	$60	$25	$43	n/a	n/a	n/a	$6,500/issue	$2,000/issue	$4,250/issue
Copyediting magazines	$95	$25	$43	n/a	n/a	n/a	n/a	n/a	n/a
Fact checking	$80	$15	$45	n/a	n/a	n/a	n/a	n/a	n/a
Ghostwriting articles (general)	$175	$40	$100	$3,500	$1,000	$2,167	$1.50/word	80¢/word	$1.08/word
City magazine, calendar of events column	n/a	n/a	n/a	n/a	n/a	n/a	$150/column	$25/column	$75/column
Consumer magazine column	n/a	n/a	n/a	n/a	n/a	n/a	$3.50/word $500/column	30¢/word $100/column	$1.35/word $317/column
Consumer magazine feature articles	n/a	n/a	n/a	$3,000	$300	$1,325	$5/word	25¢/word	$1.61/word
Magazine research	$100	$50	$67	n/a	n/a	n/a	$150/item	$100/item	$125/item
Reprint fees	n/a	n/a	n/a	$1,500	$100	$568	n/a	n/a	n/a
Proofreading	$50	$20	$41	n/a	n/a	n/a	n/a	n/a	n/a
Rewriting	$95	$25	$50	n/a	n/a	n/a	n/a	n/a	n/a
Trade journal column	$70	$35	$56	n/a	n/a	n/a	$1.50/word $550/column	60¢/word $100/column	90¢/word $340/column
Trade journal feature article	$200	$40	$122	n/a	n/a	n/a	$3.34/word	26¢/word	$1.03/word

Newspapers

	PER HOUR			PER PROJECT			OTHER		
	HIGH	LOW	AVG	HIGH	LOW	AVG	HIGH	LOW	AVG
Arts reviewing	n/a	n/a	n/a	n/a	n/a	n/a	60¢/word	10¢/word	37¢/word
Book reviews	n/a	n/a	n/a	n/a	n/a	n/a	60¢/word	25¢/word	40¢/word
Column, local	n/a	n/a	n/a	n/a	n/a	n/a	$300/column	$25/column	$150/column
Copyediting	$35	$17.50	$25	n/a	n/a	n/a	n/a	n/a	n/a
Feature	n/a	n/a	n/a	$1,000	$85	$410	75¢/word	25¢/word	57¢/word
Obituary copy	n/a	n/a	n/a	n/a	n/a	n/a	$225/story	$35/story	$112/story
Proofreading	$22	$18	$20	n/a	n/a	n/a	n/a	n/a	n/a
Stringing	n/a	n/a	n/a	n/a	n/a	n/a	$400/story	$78/story	$288/story

The Business of Writing

The Business of Writing

	PER HOUR			PER PROJECT			OTHER		
	HIGH	LOW	AVG	HIGH	LOW	AVG	HIGH	LOW	AVG
Syndicated column, self-promoted (rate depends on circulation)	n/a	n/a	n/a	n/a	n/a	n/a	$35/insertion	$4/insertion	$8/insertion

Miscellaneous

	PER HOUR			PER PROJECT			OTHER		
	HIGH	LOW	AVG	HIGH	LOW	AVG	HIGH	LOW	AVG
Comedy writing for nightclub entertainers	n/a	n/a	n/a	n/a	n/a	n/a	$50/joke	$5/joke	$38/joke
Cartoons (gag, plus illustration)	n/a	n/a	n/a	n/a	n/a	n/a	$575	$15	$100
Craft projects with instructions	n/a	n/a	n/a	$350	$50	$200	n/a	n/a	n/a
Encyclopedia articles	n/a	n/a	n/a	n/a	n/a	n/a	$200/article 50¢/word	$50/article 30¢/word	$125/article 40¢/word
Family histories	n/a	n/a	n/a	$40,000	$1,000	$5,000	$80/word	$30/word	$65/word
Manuscript typing	n/a	n/a	n/a	n/a	n/a	n/a	$2.50/page	95¢/page	$1.27/page
Published plays	n/a	n/a	n/a	n/a	n/a	n/a	$100/10-min	$300/1-act	$400/3-act
Résumés	n/a	n/a	n/a	$500	$200	$300	n/a	n/a	n/a
Writing contest judging[1]	n/a	n/a	n/a	$250	$0	$55	n/a	n/a	n/a

1 Some pay in gift certificates or books. Judging of finalists may be duty included in workshop speaker's fee.

The Game of the Name

Writing Under a Pseudonym

by Allison Block

In a famous quote from Shakespeare's *Romeo and Juliet*, Juliet asks, "What's in a name? That which we call a rose by any other name would smell as sweet." But, for our purpose, we must instead ask, "Will using a name, i.e., a pseudonym, bring an author sweet success?"

It has for many writers, including Donald Westlake, a prolific writer whose five-decade portfolio includes comic capers like *The Hot Rock* (Simon & Schuster, 1970); hard-boiled mysteries like *Firebreak* (Mysterious Press, 2001); and a brief biography of Elizabeth Taylor. Westlake is among the ranks of celebrated scribes—Mark Twain, O. Henry, Lewis Carroll, and George Orwell, to name a few—who, throughout literature, have hidden behind a *nom de plume*.

WHY ADOPT A PEN NAME?
You can sell more than one book or project at a time
"I had a contract with Random House to write one hardcover mystery novel a year," says Westlake, who once wrote five books in a year. "Whatever I did under my own name (Donald Westlake), I had to show them first." Eager to tap into the original paperback market at the same time as the mainstream hardcover market, Westlake approached his publisher and got the nod to move forward—as long as he used another name. So, in the early 1960s, Westlake wrote *The Hunter* (Pocket Books, 1962), the first in a series of novels centered on a cold-hearted detective named Parker, under the pseudonym Richard Stark. He chose "Richard" for Richard Widmark, the late noir actor famous for his portrayal of the giggling, psychopathic gangster in the 1947 melodrama *Kiss of Death*, and "Stark" as a constant reminder that his hard-boiled novels should feature lean, economical prose.

You can write in as many styles as you would like
For those who write in various genres, a pseudonym (or pseudonyms) provides a distinct label for each literary endeavor, says Westlake, whose books under the Tucker Coe pen name feature guilt-ridden ex-cop Mitchell Tobin, the emotional flipside to the remorseless Parker.

Some writers make no mystery of their multiple personalities, placing the phrase "writing as" on a book's front cover. While a double identity may hinder an author from gaining fame

ALLISON BLOCK (her real name!) is a freelance writer and book critic based in Solana Beach, California. A former editor at *San Jose: The Magazine for Silicon Valley*, her articles have appeared in regional and national publications including *Business Traveler, Luxury Living, Booklist, BookPage, Publishers Weekly*, and the *San Francisco Chronicle*.

for one name, it can also protect a reputation if the author comes out with a book that's not what the author expected. For example, Westlake cites science fiction writer Poul Anderson who wrote fantasy and hard science fiction, then comical prose. "He did this all under his own name," says Westlake. "Some of it I loved, some of it I really didn't like. If a Poul Anderson book came along, I would hesitate before I would pick it up and look at it."

You can enjoy anonymity . . . or set yourself apart

Pen names can help writers protect their privacy or the privacy of others, says Jennifer Redmond, publications coordinator at Sunbelt Publications, an independent publishing company specializing in titles on California and Baja California. "One author wanted to remain anonymous so she could write about her childhood experiences without hurting the feelings of anyone in her family," she says. "However, she also wanted to use her son's names—so she combined their first names to use as her pen name."

Scribes with a less-than-stellar track record often use a pseudonym as a way to sidestep the stigma attached to previous works, says Meg Ruley, a literary agent with the Jane Rotrosen Agency in New York. "If they take on a new name, it's like a fresh start."

In the 1960s, Westlake used the pseudonym Curt Clark to escape his past. "I wrote an article in a science fiction magazine about what was wrong with science fiction," says Westlake, who, several years later, had an idea for a novel in that genre. "I'd pretty much burned my bridges. So I thought, 'Let's see if I can find a pontoon.'"

Taking on a new name wasn't a matter of choice for *New York Times* best-selling romance writer Jennifer Crusie, whose first novel was published in the Harlequin-sister series, Silhouette. "They ask all writers to have a pseudonym as a condition of publication," says Crusie, whose books include *Crazy for You* (1999), *Fast Women* (2001), and *Bet Me* (2004), all published by St. Martin's Press. Though it was an inconvenience at the time, Crusie says there were definite perks to hiding behind her prose. "I was teaching high school at the time, and I didn't want the senior boys reading my sex scenes aloud in class," she says. "Also, my real name is Jennifer Smith, the most common name for a woman in the United States. It wasn't going to be a real grabber—you know, Jane Doe on a book." Because Crusie had to have a pseudonym, she looked to her grandmother, whose maiden name was Crusie, and she took it. These days, her last name is very much a part of her identity. "There are so many people who know me as Jennifer Crusie that it's really become my name," she says. "Somebody yells, 'Crusie,' I turn around."

You can represent a collective effort

Collaboration is key for Vancouver-based criminal attorney Jay Clarke and his daughter Rebecca, who team up to terrify readers under the moniker Michael Slade. "Rebecca literally grew up with Slade," says Clarke. Clarke began writing horror novels in 1981 (when Rebecca was three) about the psycho hunters who make up the Special X unit of the Royal Canadian Mounted Police. In her teens, Rebecca helped research the novels, and when she graduated from college with a degree in English literature and history it was a natural progression for her to write the novels too.

Clarke also writes with law partners, John Banks and Richard Covell, and his wife, Lee, who Clarke credits for the creation of the Michael Slade pseudonym. According to Clarke, "Michael" is a Biblical name that has sensitivity. "Lee never met a woman who didn't like it. And 'Slade,' he's tough as nails." Material gathered during his murder cases provides plenty of raw material for Clarke, who relies on a group of friends he calls the "Anvil Chorus" to hammer out the rough spots in his drafts.

Labels reflecting creative liaisons are also popular in nonfiction books. "One guidebook

Tip

author I worked with wanted to have some additional research done by his associates, so he came up with a pseudonym that represented their collective work," says Redmond.

You can spruce up a dull or difficult name

Another reason a writer may adopt a new name is to replace one that's hard to remember or pronounce, or the writer may settle on a surname that will position them on the bookstore shelf beside best-selling authors.

THE PERKS OF THE PSEUDONYMOUS
You have the freedom to choose any label

Writers may select any pen name they see fit, and, according to Ruley, they will find reams of advice as to what works best. "One of the popular theories is if your last name actually means something, like 'King' or 'Steel,' you'll have commercial success." One of Westlake's Random House editors had a specific formula for generating a memorable moniker: "She believed that a name worked if you used an unusual first name and a usual last name." For example, Tucker Coe, one of Westlake's pen names, was inspired by former New York Giants running back Tucker Frederickson.

You can enjoy the liberties of writing undercover

Clarke, whose books have been attracting loyal "Sladists" for decades, says that for many writers, a literary disguise can be liberating. "Masks allow people to recreate themselves. Slade is both the author and a character who writes about fellow characters—the imagined face we wear to face those who embrace his fantasy world." However, Clarke says many writers worry about whether a particular word or thought might reflect badly on their good name, but, he says, "We never worry. We can always blame Slade."

CHALLENGES POSED BY A PEN NAME
Your true identity may be doubted

Clarke, whose debut novel was *Headhunter* (William Morrow, 1985), knows all about the slippery situations a literary persona can present. "Alice Cooper liked *Headhunter* and invited me to see a concert and go backstage in Seattle," he says. "It was a long drive through a deluge of rain, and when I went to the will-call booth at the concert arena to get my ticket and pass, they asked for my ID, which read, 'Jay Clarke.' The tickets had been reserved for Michael Slade. "My alter ego could get into the concert, while I couldn't!'"

The publisher and the government want to know who you are

A novelist might protect his true identity from the public, but not from a publisher, who must inform the IRS (via Form 1099) of all payments it makes to the writer. "We require our authors to deal with us using their real names and Social Security numbers," says Redmond. "Library of Congress Cataloging-in-Publication data must be filed with both the writer's legal name and pen name, plus birth date." A writer who is determined to keep his identity hidden may handle payment through an agent, but he will still have to fess up to Uncle Sam.

Reminder

Sometimes the freedom a pen name provides for a writer, can pose challenges for a publisher. "Problems arise when someone wants a signed copy, or wants an author to appear at an event," says Redmond. "In some cases you have no author to do so or else an author who doesn't want to appear in person."

Can you keep a secret?

As tough as it might be, pseudonymous writers, like Westlake and Crusie, should keep tight-lipped about their tandem identities. "Don't blow your cover," says Westlake. "You should

The Business of Writing

always be prepared to act as if you've just been arrested for a crime you committed. Deny it! Don't ever stop denying it!'' There came a point when Westlake thought he had completed his journey as Richard Stark, but then a paperback house wanted to reissue the novels. ''I thought, 'Oh, he's never coming back.'' But, ten years later, Westlake resurrected Richard Stark.

A pseudonymous writer should never assume his identity is hermetically sealed. ''If someone wants to find you, they'll find you,'' says Westlake.

Registering a pen name

Important

Writing under a pen name involves minimal red tape, but there are two things you need to do when writing under a pen name:

1 File a Fictitious Business Statement. To open a bank or credit card account under anything other than your legal name, you must file a Fictitious Business Statement, also known as a ''Doing Business As'' (DBA) statement. To file a DBA, contact your county clerk's office. For $25, your name will be registered and published in the local paper, and you'll need to renew the DBA every five years.

2 Register with the U.S. Copyright Office. The U.S. Copyright Office offers several ways to register pseudonymous works. The first, and safest, is to record your legal name under the ''Name of Author'' portion of the registration, followed by your pseudonym (i.e., Bob Smith, writing as Benedict Surprise). You should also check ''Yes'' to the question, ''Was this author's contribution to the work pseudonymous?''

If you prefer not to have your legal identity revealed in the Copyright Office records, you can either provide only your pseudonym (and identify it as such, i.e., Benedict Surprise, pseudonym''), or leave the ''Name of Author'' space blank on the registration.

You can also use your pseudonym in the ''Copyright Claimant'' line of the registration, but the Copyright Office warns that using a fictitious name in this space could raise legal problems regarding copyright ownership. So, as with all documents, it's a good idea to consult a lawyer before you proceed.

Book Marketing 101

by Sean Murphy

I t's no secret the publishing world is changing. Many authors, particularly first-timers who've signed on with a large publishing house, feel more than a little adrift when they encounter this realm of corporate offices, busy editors and thousands of employees, advance orders and royalty statements. In other words, when they come face-to-face in an inescapable way with the fact that book publishing is not simply about art; it's a business as well. One of the biggest aspects of that business, at least as far as the author is concerned, is promotion. While a publishing house can be expected to put a certain amount of promotional effort behind all their titles, the energy, time, and money devoted vary enormously from book to book. Increasingly, the responsibility of ensuring that the most thorough possible marketing takes place falls upon the author.

"Self-promotion by authors is essential," says Peter Rubie, of the Peter Rubie Literary Agency, and author of *Telling the Story: How to Write and Sell Narrative Nonfiction* (HarperResource, 2003). "Publishing has evolved over the last decades from a more genteel literary endeavor to an overtly commercial enterprise of large conglomerates. Publishers produce more books than ever before. They essentially pick in advance which books to put a promotional push behind, and leave the others to perform however they will. The canny author is advised to beat as many bushes as possible to gain attention for themselves and their work."

There are two important reasons, says Rubie, for authors to be involved in promotion. "First, to let your core audience know the book is available. Many books have become successful simply because they appealed to a particular audience, and the author was willing and able to market the hell out of it." The second reason is author empowerment. "Self-promotion," says Rubie, "gives you a lot more control over the fate of your books and your career."

Important

Benefits of self-promotion

Simply put, authors who are willing to promote are, generally speaking, more likely to be successful. In general, their books will sell better; and for better or worse, selling better, in today's publishing climate, is the surest key to getting your next book contract. And agents and editors are more likely to put a strong effort behind writers who are willing to participate in the process.

SEAN MURPHY's novel *The Hope Valley Hubcap King* (Bantam/Dell, 2002) won the Hemingway Award for a First Novel and was featured on the American Booksellers Association Book Sense 76 list of recommended books. He has two new novels in 2004, *The Finished Man* and *The Time of New Weather*, both by Bantam/Dell.

"I've found that authors often underestimate the impact their own efforts can have on the marketing of a book," says Liz Scheier, editor at New American Library (NAL), a division of Penguin Putnam. "From signings at local bookstores to e-mail newsletters to bookmarks or magnets with the cover of his or her book on them, an enterprising author can do wonders for a book's visibility. This is especially helpful for genre authors, who have conferences and fairs and specialty bookstores to help their efforts, and for nonfiction authors, who often have contacts in their own fields that can be immensely helpful to their publishers."

All this is not to say an aspiring author has to be a marketing genius, a born extrovert, or have heart-throb charisma. What it does mean is you have to be willing to plunge in, take risks, and learn as you go. When my first two books were published in the same year, I knew nothing about marketing. Although I didn't realize it, I was signing on for a crash course in the subject. For those who find themselves in a similar position, the following will serve as a basic outline of where to start marketing your book, and a hands-on guide to take charge of your own career.

Bookstores

It is important to remember to start planning all publicity some months before your book's publication date to give bookstores sufficient time to order it, and to allow for media publishing deadlines. Also, your first few months of sales are key; so don't wait until your book is in stores to begin. One of my early decisions when I began promoting my first novel, *The Hope Valley Hubcap King* (Bantam/Dell, 2002), was that I would make contact with booksellers a priority. I soon discovered, however, it was impossible for an author to directly influence buyers for major chains like Barnes & Noble. The same does not hold true, however, for independent bookstores.

Through extensive Internet searches, I uncovered contact information for thousands of independent booksellers. This took persistence, as there is no single site that provides all this information. The best resource I found was the American Booksellers Association (ABA) directory (www.bookweb.org) of over 2,200 independent bookstores. This site, however, is organized by city, and the process of paging through to the contact details is laborious. NewPages (www.newpages.com), on the other hand, is more browsable than the ABA site, but it doesn't include zip codes or e-mail addresses, which must be looked up separately. There are many smaller organizations with more user-friendly sites, including the Northern California Independent Booksellers Association (NCIBA), at www.nciba.com.

Useful Websites

Once I created my contact list, I wrote a friendly, personal letter introducing myself as a first-time novelist, describing my book and including quotes from reviews and other writers. I sent over 1,000 of these letters out, several months before the publishing date. The result? *The Hope Valley Hubcap King* made the ABA's Book Sense 76 list of recommended titles for January/February 2003—an achievement that had a significant effect on sales, as well as a gratifying influence on my publisher, who bought my next two novels.

It is also important to consider specialty and regional booksellers who might have an interest in your work. As a Southwestern author, I prioritized bookstores in New Mexico, Arizona, and Colorado. For my second novel, *The Finished Man* (Bantam/Dell, 2004), which takes place in Southern California, I added every California retailer I could find to my list. Charles Frazier, author of the Civil War novel *Cold Mountain*, wrote to booksellers across the South, letting them know that his subject might interest their readers.

It's a good idea to visit as many stores as possible, not just in your area, but when traveling elsewhere. Ask to speak to the manager or owner, and offer to sign any of your books they have in stock.

The Business of Writing

Readings and signings

It's essential for authors to participate in readings and book signings. These are not merely for the benefit of the customers who generally turn out for such events—although small scale, one-to-one contacts are important in building an audience. But these also have a ripple effect, fostering relationships with booksellers who may recommend your books, and order subsequent titles, long after the event. Also, such events provide a "news hook" for contacting local media. I have sometimes been able to spin out a reading into a half-dozen articles, reviews, and interviews that reach hundreds more potential readers. Start by calling or visiting your local bookstore and asking the owner or manager whether they sponsor readings. Be careful to check back with these contacts when scheduling other area events to make sure you don't step on anyone's toes.

Book signings offer an alternative to readings. These usually involve a table set up with books and promotional materials, giving the author an opportunity to chat informally with bookstore customers. Although these can be a refreshing alternative for authors who find performing before an audience difficult, they have their own pitfalls, as I learned when promoting *The Hope Valley Hubcap King*. I had two signings scheduled for branches of the same bookstore, several weeks before Christmas—an ideal time to sell books. The first was a disaster; the table was in a corner, away from traffic areas, and there were no refreshments or other enticements to attract customers. I sold only a few copies, most to a friend who bought several as gifts. When I walked into the second store, my heart sank. The table was stacked with more copies of my books than I'd ever seen in one place. Given the last performance, I was sure most would still be there when I left—but I couldn't have been more wrong. This time the table was right beside the entrance. Not only that, the manager had provided cookies and a pot of coffee, so I was able to offer refreshments and strike up natural conversations with passersby. Within two hours I'd sold every copy, and set the store sales record for the week. Now I never organize a signing without checking table placement in advance—and I carry my own supply of cookies, just in case!

Other possibilities to investigate for setting up book signings and readings are writers' conferences and book fairs. Libraries can often provide information on groups, including readers' clubs and literary organizations, which sponsor readings and events. Your publisher's publicist will likely want to be involved, and should be consulted about anything you arrange.

Tip

Media

Newspapers are forever looking for news, and the lives of authors always seem to be of interest to a public that doesn't realize we spend most of our time alone in small rooms staring at computer screens! The first thing to remember in dealing with the media is that we're providing a service—giving them a story to fill their pages or airwaves. So don't be shy. The most basic means for spreading the news about your publication is a press release: a brief, one-page summary of your book, your bio, and publishing information, sent to the appropriate editor—the literary or arts pages, book review, local news supplement, or if it's a nonfiction book, the section relating to its subject (i.e., the sports page if it's a sports biography). Press releases should go out in advance of readings or other events.

For small publications, you may be able to follow up with a phone call, describing your book and explaining realistically why it is of interest to their particular audience. For larger publications this is generally not possible; the "contact" page on most publication websites provides staff e-mail addresses, which can be used to write to the appropriate editor or writer. Don't be dismayed if you don't get a response; sometimes these contacts bear fruit months later.

The same process applies to radio and TV too. I've had excellent results by phoning local radio hosts, explaining that I live in their area, and would like to discuss my book, and perhaps read an excerpt on their show. I include anything that sounds like a good story—in the case of *The Hope Valley Hubcap King*, that it took me 12 years to write, but I finally won the Hemingway Award for a First Novel, a hopeful story for any aspiring writer. Be patient—these people are busy, and everyone wants their attention. Don't be discouraged by rejection; it comes with the turf. Treat every contact as though it was of equal importance, but try not to be attached to the outcome. If you carry on, you will get results. If you continue, these will multiply.

Another option, if you have a good topic for radio talk shows, is to buy a listing in *Radio-TV InterviewReport* (www.rtir.com). This publication goes to radio producers across the country. It is said to yield excellent results, although the service is rather pricey. Planned Television Arts (PTA) (www.plannedtvarts.com) provides a similar service for television programs.

Useful Websites

It's also worth considering the PR Leads Expert Resource Network for speakers, authors, and other experts (www.prleads.com). This company will forward requests from journalists looking for spokespeople on different topics, an excellent way of generating publicity for you and your book. This service works best if your book is nonfiction and you have expertise in a specialized area such as health, parenting, business, etc. Even if such services are beyond your budget, it's well worth visiting their websites because they often offer free tips that can spark ideas for your own efforts.

Provide your publisher with a list of publications that might be interested in receiving review copies of your work. Particularly in nonfiction, your knowledge of the market can be of key importance to your publisher's efforts. One strategy that has proved successful for me in nonfiction has been publishing excerpts and spin-off articles. With the assistance of my

"Self-promotion gives you a lot more control over the fate of your books and your career."

publisher, I placed segments from my book *One Bird, One Stone* (Renaissance/St. Martin's, 2002) or related articles in *Yoga Journal*, *The Sun*, *Tricycle*, and others. Several of these publications went on to review the book, and subsequent titles, too. Remember, if you've published a book on your subject, you're an expert in the eyes of the public. You can take advantage of this expertise to publish articles that will not only promote your book, but they may earn you some pocket money as well.

Public speaking, organizations, and teaching

So you've just published a book on harness racing? You should be contacting every harness racing organization in the nation to see if they'd like to review you in their newsletter or host you for a speaking engagement. Don't like public speaking? Many a successful speaker has started out with an aversion to the field—and ended up loving it. Why not give it a try? At the very least, you'll sell some books, and you may receive payment for your efforts. Also contact universities and civic organizations, many of whom have a budget for speakers. Don't forget literary organizations and book clubs, too. Consider alumni groups and religious organizations—they may include publication announcements in their newsletters. Letters to groups that might have an interest in your work can have a significant impact. When promoting *One Bird, One Stone*, I sent a mailing to meditation centers and spiritual organizations across the country. When I'd worked my way through these organizations, I sent e-mails to Unitarian Churches, which have historically exhibited an interest in Eastern philosophies.

Networking

Every contact helps build connections, which contribute not only to your success, but that of others around you. F. Scott Fitzgerald knew Ernest Hemingway, who knew Gertrude Stein, who knew Ezra Pound, who knew T.S. Eliot—and they all knew James Joyce. If you don't belong to a writers' organization, consider joining one. Such organizations can pay off enormously in terms of networking, spreading the word about your writing, and most importantly, fellowship—the support and friendship of other writers working toward similar goals.

If you teach a writing workshop, or are involved in any promotional event, have a sign-up sheet for those who want to hear about future events or publications. Once you have enough contacts on your mailing list, you can periodically send out a newsletter. Be sensitive, though; swamping people with unwanted communications may have the opposite effect to that intended.

Cyber-marketing

The importance of setting up and maintaining an attractive, user-friendly website cannot be overstated. Your website has the potential to reach countless readers. The Authors Guild (www.authorsguild.org) has a low-cost, easy-to-maintain member website service that doesn't require extensive computer knowledge; many organizations offer similar services. Make sure your website address is printed on your book jacket. If you set up your site so visitors can post messages about your work, you can add their contact information to your mailing list. Also, if anyone mentions that they enjoyed your book, ask if they'd take a minute to post a review at one of the online bookstores like Amazon.com.

Useful
Websites

Your regular e-mail correspondence also provides an opportunity to spread the word about your book. I include a short, unobtrusive "blurb" about my latest book in the signature/return address portion at the bottom of my e-mail template. This blurb can include a link to online bookstores and can be easily customized and updated. Many correspondents have realized I'm a novelist through this means and have gone on to inquire about and purchase my books.

Creative alternatives

The possibilities of promotion are only limited by the imagination—promotional postcards, pens, buttons, refrigerator magnets, and skywriting are just a few options to consider. Contact libraries via the Internet and convince them to buy your books. Get your titles into the school system. Remember: Don't be too pushy. You'll win some and you'll lose some. The ones who are successful are the ones who keep going. Apply as much creativity to the process of promotion as you did to the process of creation.

Publishers and Their Imprints

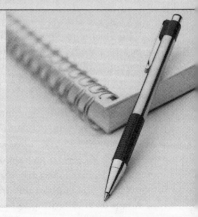

The publishing world is constantly changing and evolving. With all of the buying, selling, reorganizing, consolidating, and dissolving, it's hard to keep publishers and their imprints straight. To help you make sense of these changes, we offer this breakdown of major publishers (and their divisions)—who owns whom and which imprints are under each company umbrella. Keep in mind that this information is constantly changing. We have provided the websites of each of the publishers so you can continue to keep an eye on this ever-evolving business.

HARPERCOLLINS

www.harpercollins.com

HarperCollins Australia/New Zealand
Angus & Robertson
Flamingo
Fourth Estate
HarperCollins
HarperReligious
HarperSports
Voyager

HarperCollins Canada
HarperFlamingoCanada
PerennialCanada

HarperCollins Children's Books Group
Amistad
Julie Andrews Collection
Avon
Joanna Cotler books
Eos
Laura Geringer Books
Greenwillow Books
HarperAudio
HarperCollins Children's Books
HarperFestival
HarperTempest
HarperTrophy
Rayo
Katherine Tegen Books

HarperCollins General Books Group
Access
Amistad
Avon
Caedmon
Ecco
Eos
Fourth Estate
HarperAudio
HarperBusiness
HarperCollins
HarperEntertainment
HarperLargePrint
HarperResource
HarperSanFrancisco
HarperTorch
Harper Design International

William Morrow
William Morrow Cookbooks
Perennial
PerfectBound
Quill
Rayo
ReganBooks

HarperCollins Publishers
Beech Tree Books
Greenwillow Books
HarperCollins
Hearst Books
Lothrup, Lee & Shepard Books
Morrow Junior Books
Mulberry Books
Quill Trade Paperbacks

HarperCollins UK
Bartholomew Maps
Collins
Collins Crime
Collins Education
HarperCollins Children's Books
Thorsons/Element
Voyager Books

Zondervan
Inspirio
Vida
Zonderkidz
Zondervan

HOLTZBRINCK PUBLISHERS

www.holtzbrinck.com

Audio Renaissance
Bedford/St. Martin's
Tom Doherty Associates LLC
Aerie Books
Forge Books
Orb Books
Starscape
Tor
Tor Teen

Farrar, Straus & Giroux
Faber & Faber (division)
Farrar, Straus & Giroux Books for Young
    Readers
Hill & Wang (division)
MIRASOL Libros Juvenile
North Point Press
Sunburst Books

Henry Holt and Co. LLC
Books for Young Readers
John Macrae Books
Metropolitan Books
Owl Books
Red Feather Books
Times Books

Nature America, Inc.
Picador
St. Martin's Press LLC
Thomas Dunne Books
Griffin
Minotaur
Palgrave MacMillan (division)
Priddy Books
St. Martin's Press Paperback & Reference
    Group
St. Martin's Press Trade Division
Truman Talley Books

PENGUIN GROUP (USA), INC.

www.penguingroup.com

Penguin Adult Division
Ace Books
Alpha Books
Avery
Berkley Books

Dutton
Gotham Books
HPBooks
Jove
New American Library

Penguin
   Penguin
   Penguin Classics
   Penguin Compass
   Penguin 20th Century Classics
Perigree
Plume
Portfolio
G.P. Putnam's Sons
Riverhead
Jeremy P. Tarcher
Viking

Penguin Audiobooks
Arkangel Shakespeare
Penguin*HighBridge Audio

Penguin Children's Division
Dial Books for Young Readers
Dutton Children's Books

Dutton Interactive
Firebird
Phyllis Fogelman Books
Grosset & Dunlap
   Planet Dexter
   Platt & Munk
Philomel
Playskool
Price Stern Sloan
PSS
Puffin Books
G.P. Putnam's Sons
   PaperStar
Viking Children's Books
Frederick Warne

RANDOM HOUSE, INC.

www.randomhouse.com

Ballantine Publishing Group
Ballantine Books
Ballantine Reader's Circle
Del Rey
Del Rey/Lucas Books
Fawcett
Ivy
One World
Wellspring

Bantam Dell Publishing Group
Bantam Hardcover
Bantam Mass Market
Bantam Trade Paperback
Crimeline
Delacorte Press
Dell
Delta
The Dial Press
Domain
DTP
Fanfare
Island
Spectra

Crown Publishing Group
Shaye Arehart Books
Bell Tower
Clarkson Potter
Crown Forum
Crown Publishers, Inc.
Harmony Books
Prima
Three Rivers Press

Doubleday Broadway Publishing Group
Anchor Books
Broadway Books
Currency
Doubleday
Doubleday Image
Doubleday Religious Publishing
   Three Leaves Press
Main Street Books
Nan A. Talese

Knopf Publishing Group

Everyman's Library
Alfred A. Knopf
Knopf Travel Guides
National Audobon Guides
Pantheon Books
Schocken Books
Vintage Anchor Publishing
   Anchor Books
   Vintage Books

Random House Audio Publishing Group

Listening Library
Random House Audible
Random House Audio
Random House Audio Assets
Random House Audio Dimensions
Random House Audio Roads
Random House Audio Voices
Random House Price-less

Random House Children's Books

BooksReportsNow.com
GoldenBooks.com
Junie B. Jones
Kids@Random
Knopf/Delacorte/Dell Young
Readers Group
   Bantam
   Crown
   David Fickling Books
   Delacorte Press
   Dell Dragonfly
   Dell Laurel-Leaf
   Dell Yearling Books
   Doubleday
   Alfred A. Knopf
   Wendy Lamb Books
Random House Young Readers Group
   Akiko
   Arthur
   Barbie
   Beginner Books
   The Berenstain Bears
   Bob the Builder
   Disney
   Dragon Tales
   First Time Books
   Golden Books

   Landmark Books
   Little Golden Books
   Lucas Books
   Mercer Mayer
   Nickelodeon
   Nick, Jr.
   pat the bunny
   Picturebacks
   Precious Moments
   Richard Scarry
   Sesame Street Books
   Step Into Reading
   Stepping Stones
   Star Wars
   Thomas the Tank Engine and Friends
Seussville
Teachers@Random
Teens@Random

Random House Direct, Inc.

Bon Apetit
Gourmet Books
Pillsbury

Random House Information Group

Fodor's Travel Publications
Living Language
Prima Games
The Princeton Review
Random House Español
Random House Puzzles & Games
Random House Reference

Random House International

Arete
McClelland & Stewart Ltd.
Plaza & Janes
Random House Australia
Random House of Canada Ltd.
Random House of Mondadori
Random House South America
Random House United Kingdom
Transworld UK
Verlagsgruppe Random House

The Business of Writing

Random House Large Print
Random House Publishing Group
Ballantine Books
Del Rey
Modern Library
One World
Presidio Press
Random House
Random House Trade Paperbacks
Villard

Random House Reference Publishing
Boston Globe Puzzle Books
Chicago Tribune Crosswords
House of Collectibles

Los Angeles Times Crosswords
McKay Chess Library
Random House Websters
Washington Post Crosswords

Random House Value Publishing
Children's Classics
Crescent
Gramercy
Testament
Wings

Waterbrook Press
Fisherman Bible Study Guides
Shaw Books
Waterbrook Press

SIMON & SCHUSTER

www.simonsays.com

Simon & Schuster Adult Publishing
Atria Books
    Washington Square Press
The Free Press
    Simon & Schuster Source
    Wall Street Journal Books
Kaplan
Pocket Books
    Downtown Press
    MTV Books
    Paraview Pocket
    Pocket Star
    Star Trek
    VH-1 Books
    World Wrestling Entertainment
Scribner
    Lisa Drew Books
    Scribner Classics
    Scribner Paperback Fiction
Simon & Schuster
    Simon & Schuster Classic Editions
Simon & Schuster Trade Paperbacks
    Fireside
    Libros en Español
    Touchstone

Simon & Schuster Australia
Audio
Fireside
Kangaroo Press
Martin Books
Pocket Books
Scribner
Simon & Schuster
Touchstone

Simon & Schuster Children's Publishing
Aladdin Paperbacks
Atheneum Books for Young Readers
    Richard Jackson Books
    Anne Schwartz Books
Libros Para Niños
Little Simon
Margaret K. McElderry Books
Simon & Schuster Books for Young Readers
    Paula Wiseman Books
Simon Pulse
Simon Spotlight
Simon Spotlight Entertainment

The Business of Writing

Simon & Schuster New Media

Simon & Schuster Audio
- Encore
- Nightingale-Conant
- Pimsleur Language Programs
- Simon & Schuster Audioworks
- Simon & Schuster Sound Ideas

Simon & Schuster Online
Simon & Schuster UK

Fireside

The Free Press

Martin Books

Pocket Books

Scribner

Simon & Schuster

Simon & Schuster Audio

Touchstone

Town House

TIME WARNER BOOK GROUP

www.twbookmark.com

Warner Books

Aspect

Bulfinch Press

Little, Brown, and Co. Adult Trade Division
- Back Bay Books

Little, Brown, and Co. Children's Publishing
- Megan Tingley Books

Mysterious Press

Time Warner Audio Books

Walk Worthy

Warner Faith

Warner Forever

Warner Vision

Literary Agents

The 50 literary agencies listed in this section are either actively seeking new clients ◯ or seeking both new and established writers ◑ , and they all generate 98 to 100 percent of their income from commission on sales.

All 50 agencies are members of the Association of Authors' Representatives (AAR), which means they do not charge for reading, critiquing, or editing. Some agents in this section may charge clients for office expenses such as photocopying, foreign postage, long-distance phone calls, or express mail services. Make sure you have a clear understanding of what these expenses are before signing any agency agreement.

FOR MORE ON THE SUBJECT . . .

The *2005 Guide to Literary Agents* (Writer's Digest Books) offers more than 600 listings for both literary and script agents, as well as information on production companies, independent publicists, and writers' conferences. It also offers a wealth of information on the author/agent relationship and other related topics.

SUBHEADS

Each listing is broken down into subheads to make locating specific information easier. In the first section, you'll find contact information for each agency. Further information is provided which indicates an agency's size, its willingness to work with a new or previously unpublished writer, and its general areas of interest.

Member Agents: Agencies comprised of more than one agent list member agents and their individual specialties to help you determine the most appropriate person for your query letter.

Represents: Here agencies specify what nonfiction and fiction subjects they consider.

⟿ Look for the key icon to quickly learn an agent's areas of specialization or specific strengths.

How to Contact: In this section agents specify the type of material they want to receive, how they want to receive material, and how long you should wait for their response.

Recent Sales: To give a sense of the types of material they represent, agents provide specific titles they've sold as well as a sampling of clients' names.

Terms: Provided here are details of an agent's commission, whether a contract is offered, and what additional office expenses you might have to pay if the agent agrees to represent you. Standard commissions range from 10 to 15 percent for domestic sales, and 15 to 20 percent for foreign or dramatic sales.

Writers' Conferences: Here agents list the conferences they attend.

Tips: Agents offer advice and additional instructions for writers looking for representation.

N ⬚ CAROLE ABEL LITERARY AGENT

160 W. 87th St., New York NY 10024. Fax: (212)724-1384. E-mail: caroleabel@aol.com. Member of AAR. 50% of clients are new/unpublished writers. Currently handles: nonfiction books.

Represents Nonfiction books.

How to Contact Query with SASE by mail only. No e-mail or fax queries.

Recent Sales *Instant Self Hypnosis*, by Forbes Blair (Sourcebooks); *Word Play*, by L. Myers/L. Goodman (McGraw Hill).

⬚ LINDA ALLEN LITERARY AGENCY

1949 Green St., Suite 5, San Francisco CA 94123-4829. (415)921-6437. **Contact:** Linda Allen. Estab. 1982. Member of AAR. Represents 35-40 clients.

Represents Novels (adult). **Considers these fiction areas:** Literary; mainstream/contemporary.

How to Contact Query with SASE. Considers simultaneous queries. Responds in 3 weeks to queries. Returns materials only with SASE. Obtains most new clients through recommendations from others.

Recent Sales This agency prefers not to share information on specific sales.

Terms Agent receives 15% commission on domestic sales. Charges for photocopying.

⬚ ALTAIR LITERARY AGENCY, LLC

P.O. Box 11656, Washington DC 20008. (202)237-8282. Website: www.altairliteraryagency.com. Estab. 1996. Member of AAR. Represents 60 clients. 50% of clients are new/unpublished writers. Currently handles: 80% nonfiction books; 5% novels; 15% children's novelty/activity only.

Member Agents Andrea Pedolsky, partner; Nicholas Smith, partner.

Represents Nonfiction books. **Considers these nonfiction areas:** History; money/finance (published journalists only); popular culture; science/technology (history of); sports; illustrated; current events/contemporary issues, museum, organization, and corporate-brand books. **Considers these fiction areas:** Historical (pre-20th century mysteries only).

O→ This agency specializes in nonfiction with an emphasis on authors who have credentials and professional recognition for their topic, and a high level of public exposure. Actively seeking solid, well-informed authors who have a public platform for the subject specialty.

How to Contact Query with SASE or see website for more specific query information. Considers simultaneous queries. Responds in 2-4 weeks to queries; 1 month to mss. Obtains most new clients through recommendations from others, solicitations, author queries.

Recent Sales *Stillpoint Dhammapada*, by Geri Larkin (Harper SF); *Cutting Edge Runner*, by Matt Fitzgerald (Rodale); *Rules for a Pretty Woman*, by Suzette Francis (Avon); *Genealogy 101*, by Barbara Renick, NGS Series (Rutledge Hill Press); *Solar System*, by Christine Corning Malloy with the American Museum of Natural History (Chronicle Children's Books); *The Introvert Advantage*, by Marti Laney (Workman).

Terms Agent receives 15% commission on domestic sales; 20% commission on foreign sales. Offers written contract, binding for 1 year; 2-month notice must be given to terminate contract. Charges clients for postage, copying, messengers, and FedEx and UPS.

⬚ MIRIAM ALTSHULER LITERARY AGENCY

53 Old Post Rd. N., Red Hook NY 12571. (845)758-9408. Fax: (845)758-3118. **Contact:** Miriam Altshuler. Estab. 1994. Member of AAR. Represents 40 clients. Currently handles: 45% nonfiction books; 45% novels; 5% story collections; 5% juvenile books.

• Ms. Altshuler has been an agent since 1982.

Represents Nonfiction books, novels, short story collections, juvenile books. **Considers these nonfiction areas:** Biography/autobiography; ethnic/cultural interests; history; language/literature/criticism; memoirs; multicultural; music/dance; nature/environment; popular culture; psychology; sociology; theater/film; women's issues/studies. **Considers these fiction areas:** Literary; mainstream/contemporary; multicultural; thriller.

O→ Does not want self-help. mystery, how-to, romance, horror, spiritual, or screenplays.

How to Contact Query with SASE. Prefers to read materials exclusively. No e-mail or fax queries. Considers simultaneous queries. Responds in 2 weeks to queries; 3 weeks to mss. Returns materials only with SASE. Obtains most new clients through recommendations from others.

Terms Agent receives 15% commission on domestic sales; 20% commission on foreign sales. No written contract. Charges clients for overseas mailing, photocopies, overnight mail when requested by author.

Writers' Conferences Bread Loaf Writers' Conference (Middlebury VT, August); Washington Independent Writers Conference (Washington DC, June).

☑ BETSY AMSTER LITERARY ENTERPRISES

P.O. Box 27788, Los Angeles CA 90027-0788. **Contact:** Betsy Amster. Estab. 1992. Member of AAR. Represents over 65 clients. 35% of clients are new/unpublished writers. Currently handles: 65% nonfiction books; 35% novels.

- Prior to opening her agency, Ms. Amster was an editor at Pantheon and Vintage for 10 years, and served as editorial director for the Globe Pequot Press for 2 years. "This experience gives me a wider perspective on the business and the ability to give focused editorial feedback to my clients."

Represents Nonfiction books, novels. **Considers these nonfiction areas:** Biography/autobiography; child guidance/parenting; ethnic/cultural interests; gardening; health/medicine; history; money/finance; psychology; sociology; women's issues/studies; career. **Considers these fiction areas:** Ethnic; literary; mystery/suspense (quirky); thriller (quirky); women's (high quality).

- ☐ Actively seeking "strong narrative nonfiction, particularly by journalists; outstanding literary fiction (the next Michael Chabon or Jhumpa Lahiri); witty, intelligent, commercial women's fiction (the next Elinor Lipman or Jennifer Weiner); and high-profile, self-help and psychology, preferably research based." Does not want to receive poetry, children's books, romances, westerns, science fiction.

How to Contact For fiction, send query, first 3 pages, and SASE. For nonfiction, send query or proposal with SASE. No e-mail or fax queries. Considers simultaneous queries. Responds in 1 month to queries; 2 months to mss. Obtains most new clients through recommendations from others, solicitations, conferences.

Recent Sales *Rejuvenile: How a New Species of Reluctant Adults is Redefining Maturity*, by Christopher Noxon (Crown); *My Therapist's Dog*, by Diana Wells (Algonquin); *The Reluctant Tuscan*, by Phil Doran (Gotham); *Pen on Fire*, by Barbara DeMarco-Barrett (Harcourt). Other clients include Dwight Allen, Dr. Elaine N. Aron, Dr. Helen Brenner, Robin Chotzinoff, Frank Clifford, Rob Cohen & David Wollock, Jan DeBlieu, Margaret Lobenstine, Paul Mandelbaum, Wendy Mogel, Sharon Montrose, Joy Nicholson, Katie Singer, Louise Steinman.

Terms Agent receives 15% commission on domestic sales; 20% commission on foreign sales. Offers written contract, binding for 1-2 years; 3-month notice must be given to terminate contract. Charges for photocopying, postage, long distance phone calls, messengers, and galleys and books used in submissions to foreign and film agents and to magazines for first serial rights.

Writers' Conferences Squaw Valley; San Diego Writers Conference; UCLA Extension Writer's Program; The Loft Literary Center (Minneapolis).

☒ ☑ ARCADIA

31 Lake Place North, Danbury CT 06810. E-mail: arcadialit@att.net. **Contact:** Victoria Gould Pryor. Member of AAR.

Represents Nonfiction books (readable, serious), novels. **Considers these nonfiction areas:** Biography/autobiography; business/economics; current affairs; history; memoirs; psychology; science/technology; self-help/personal improvement; true crime/investigative; women's issues/studies; medicine; investigative journalism; culture; classical music; life transforming. **Considers these fiction areas:** "I'm drawn to character-driven, well-plotted, imaginative, and unusual fiction, both literary and commercial."

- ☐ "I'm a very hands-on agent, necessary in this competitive marketplace. I work with authors on revisions until whatever we present to publishers is as perfect as it can be. I represent talented, dedicated, intelligent, and ambitious writers who are looking for a long-term relationship based on professional success and mutual respect."

How to Contact Query with SASE. E-mail queries accepted without attachments.

Recent Sales This agency prefers not to share information on specific sales.

☑ BALKIN AGENCY, INC.

P.O. Box 222, Amherst MA 01004. (413)548-9835. Fax: (413)548-9836. **Contact:** Rick Balkin, president. Estab. 1972. Member of AAR. Represents 50 clients. 10% of clients are new/unpublished writers. Currently handles: 85% nonfiction books; 5% scholarly books; 5% textbooks; 5% reference books.

- Prior to opening his agency, Mr. Balkin served as executive editor with Bobbs-Merrill Company.

Represents Nonfiction books, scholarly books, textbooks. **Considers these nonfiction areas:** Animals; anthropology/archaeology; biography/autobiography; current affairs; health/medicine; history; how-to; language/literature/criticism; music/dance; nature/environment; popular culture; science/technology; sociology; translation; travel; true crime/investigative.

- ☐ This agency specializes in adult nonfiction. Does not want to receive fiction, poetry, screenplays, computer books.

How to Contact Query with SASE, proposal package, outline. No e-mail or fax queries. Responds in 1 week to queries; 2 weeks to mss. Returns materials only with SASE. Obtains most new clients through recommendations from others.

Recent Sales Sold 30 titles in the last year. *The Liar's Tale*, (W.W. Norton Co.); *Adolescent Depression*, (Henry Holt); *Eliz. Van Lew: A Union Spy in the Heart of the Confederacy*, (biography, Oxford U.P.).

Terms Agent receives 15% commission on domestic sales; 20% commission on foreign sales. Offers written contract, binding for 1 year. Charges clients for photocopying and express or foreign mail.

Tips "I do not take on books described as bestsellers or potential bestsellers. Any nonfiction work that is either unique, paradigmatic, a contribution, truly witty, or a labor of love is grist for my mill."

ⓓ LORETTA BARRETT BOOKS, INC.

101 Fifth Ave., New York NY 10003. (212)242-3420. Fax: (212)807-9579. E-mail: mail@lorettabarrettbooks.com. **Contact:** Loretta A. Barrett or Nick Mullendore. Estab. 1990. Member of AAR. Represents 90 clients. Currently handles: 60% nonfiction books; 40% novels.

• Prior to opening her agency, Ms. Barrett was vice president and executive editor at Doubleday for 25 years.

Represents Nonfiction books, novels. **Considers these nonfiction areas:** Americana; animals; anthropology/ archaeology; biography/autobiography; business/economics; child guidance/parenting; computers/electronic; cooking/foods/nutrition; crafts/hobbies; creative nonfiction; current affairs; education; ethnic/cultural interests; gay/lesbian issues; government/politics/law; health/medicine; history; how-to; language/literature/criticism; memoirs; money/finance; multicultural; music/dance; nature/environment; New Age/metaphysics; philosophy; popular culture; psychology; religious/inspirational; science/technology; self-help/personal improvement; sociology; spirituality; sports; women's issues/studies. **Considers these fiction areas:** Action/ adventure; confession; contemporary issues; detective/police/crime; ethnic; family saga; feminist; gay/lesbian; glitz; historical; literary; mainstream/contemporary; mystery/suspense; psychic/supernatural; thriller.

○┓ This agency specializes in general interest books. No children's or juvenile.

How to Contact Query with SASE. No e-mail or fax queries. Considers simultaneous queries. Responds in 6 weeks to queries. Returns materials only with SASE.

Recent Sales *A Lady First*, by Letitia Baldrige (Viking); *The Singularity is Near*, by Ray Kurzweil (Viking); *Flesh Tones*, by MJ Rose (Ballantine Books); *The Lake of Dead Languages*, by Carol Goodman (Ballantine Books); *The Bad Witness*, by Laura Van Wormer (Mira Books).

Terms Agent receives 15% commission on domestic sales; 20% commission on foreign sales. Offers written contract. Charges clients for shipping and photocopying.

Writers' Conferences San Diego State University Writer's Conference; Maui Writer's Conference.

ⓓ MEREDITH BERNSTEIN LITERARY AGENCY

2112 Broadway, Suite 503A, New York NY 10023. (212)799-1007. Fax: (212)799-1145. Estab. 1981. Member of AAR. Represents 85 clients. 20% of clients are new/unpublished writers. Currently handles: 50% nonfiction books; 50% fiction.

• Prior to opening her agency, Ms. Bernstein served in another agency for 5 years.

Member Agents Meredith Bernstein, Elizabeth Cavanaugh.

Represents Nonfiction books, fiction of all kinds. **Considers these nonfiction areas:** Any area of nonfiction in which the author has an established. **Considers these fiction areas:** Literary; mystery/suspense; romance; thriller; women's.

○┓ This agency does not specialize, "very eclectic."

How to Contact Query with SASE. No e-mail or fax queries. Considers simultaneous queries. Obtains most new clients through recommendations from others, conferences, also develops and packages own ideas.

Recent Sales Nancy Pickard, 3-book (women's fiction) deal with Ballantine; *Secret of O Milagre*, by Catherine Mulvaney (Pocket Books); Elizabeth Pantley, untitled book on sleep solutions for kids 2-6 (McGraw Hill).

Terms Agent receives 15% commission on domestic sales; 20% commission on foreign sales. Charges clients $75 disbursement fee/year.

Writers' Conferences SouthWest Writers Conference (Albuquereque, August); Rocky Moutnain Writers' Conference (Denver, September); Golden Triangle (Beaumont TX, October); Pacific Northwest Writers Conference; Austin League Writers Conference; Willamette Writers Conference (Portland, OR); Lafayette Writers Conference (Lafayette, LA); Surrey Writers Conference (Surrey, BC.); San Diego State University Writers Conference (San Diego, CA).

ⓓ BRANDT & HOCHMAN LITERARY AGENTS, INC.

1501 Broadway, New York NY 10036. (212)840-5760. Fax: (212)840-5776. **Contact:** Carl Brandt; Gail Hochman; Marianne Merola; Charles Schlessiger; Bill Contardi. Estab. 1913. Member of AAR. Represents 200 clients.

Represents Nonfiction books, novels, short story collections, juvenile books, journalism. **Considers these nonfiction areas:** Biography/autobiography; current affairs; ethnic/cultural interests; government/politics/law;

Literary Agents

history; women's issues/studies. **Considers these fiction areas:** Contemporary issues; ethnic; historical; literary; mainstream/contemporary; mystery/suspense; romance; thriller; young adult.

How to Contact Query with SASE. No e-mail or fax queries. Considers simultaneous queries. Responds in 1 month to queries. Returns materials only with SASE. Obtains most new clients through recommendations from others.

Recent Sales Sold 50 titles in the last year. This agency prefers not to share information on specific sales. Other clients include Scott Turow, Carlos Fuentes, Ursula Hegi, Michael Cunningham, Mary Pope Osborne, Julia Glass.

Terms Agent receives 15% commission on domestic sales; 20% commission on foreign sales. Charges clients for "manuscript duplication or other special expenses agreed to in advance."

Tips "Write a letter which will give the agent a sense of you as a professional writer, your long-term interests as well as a short description of the work at hand."

CURTIS BROWN, LTD.

10 Astor Place, New York NY 10003-6935. (212)473-5400. Also: 1750 Montgomery St., San Fancisco CA 94111. (415)954-8566. **Contact:** Perry Knowlton, chairman; Timothy Knowlton, CEO; Peter L. Ginsberg, president. Member of AAR; signatory of WGA.

Member Agents Laura Blake Peterson; Ellen Geiger; Emilie Jacobson, vice president; Maureen Walters, vice president; Virginia Knowlton (literary, adult, children's); Timothy Knowlton (film, screenplays, plays; Ed Wintle (film, screenplays, plays); Mitchell Waters; Elizabeth Harding; Kristen Manges; Dave Barber (translation rights).

Represents Nonfiction books, novels, short story collections, novellas, juvenile books, poetry books, movie scripts, feature film, TV scripts, TV movie of the week, stage plays. **Considers these nonfiction areas:** Agriculture/horticulture; Americana; animals; anthropology/archaeology; art/architecture/design; biography/autobiography; business/economics; child guidance/parenting; computers/electronic; cooking/foods/nutrition; crafts/hobbies; creative nonfiction; current affairs; education; ethnic/cultural interests; gardening; gay/lesbian issues; government/politics/law; health/medicine; history; how-to; humor/satire; interior design/decorating; juvenile nonfiction; language/literature/criticism; memoirs; military/war; money/finance; multicultural; music/dance; nature/environment; New Age/metaphysics; philosophy; photography; popular culture; psychology; recreation; regional; religious/inspirational; science/technology; self-help/personal improvement; sex; sociology; software; spirituality; sports; theater/film; translation; travel; true crime/investigative; women's issues/studies; young adult. **Considers these fiction areas:** Action/adventure; comic books/cartoon; confession; contemporary issues; detective/police/crime; erotica; ethnic; experimental; family saga; fantasy; feminist; gay/lesbian; glitz; gothic; hi-lo; historical; horror; humor/satire; juvenile; literary; mainstream/contemporary; military/war; multicultural; multimedia; mystery/suspense; New Age; occult; picture books; plays; poetry; poetry in translation; psychic/supernatural; regional; religious/inspirational; romance; science fiction; short story collections; spiritual; sports; thriller; translation; westerns/frontier; young adult; women's. **Considers these script subject areas:** Action/adventure; comedy; detective/police/crime; ethnic; feminist; gay/lesbian; historical; horror; mainstream; mystery/suspense; psychic/supernatural; romantic comedy; romantic drama; thriller; western/frontier.

How to Contact Query with SASE. Prefers to read materials exclusively. *No unsolicited mss.* No e-mail or fax queries. Responds in 3 weeks to queries; 5 weeks to mss. Obtains most new clients through recommendations from others, solicitations, conferences.

Recent Sales This agency prefers not to share information on specific sales.

Terms Offers written contract. Charges for photocopying, some postage.

SHEREE BYKOFSKY ASSOCIATES, INC.

16 W. 36th St., 13th Floor, New York NY 10018. Website: www.shereebee.com. **Contact:** Sheree Bykofsky. Estab. 1984, incorporated 1991. Member of AAR, ASJA, WNBA. Currently handles: 80% nonfiction books; 20% novels.

● Prior to opening her agency, Ms. Bykofsky served as executive editor of The Stonesong Press and managing editor of Chiron Press. She is also the author or co-author of more than 17 books, including *The Complete Idiot's Guide to Getting Published*. Ms. Bykofsky teaches publishing at NYU and The 92nd St. Y.

Member Agents Janet Rosen, associate; Megan Buckley, associate.

Represents Nonfiction books, novels. **Considers these nonfiction areas:** Americana; animals; art/architecture/design; biography/autobiography; business/economics; child guidance/parenting; cooking/foods/nutrition; crafts/hobbies; creative nonfiction; current affairs; education; ethnic/cultural interests; gardening; gay/lesbian issues; government/politics/law; health/medicine; history; how-to; humor/satire; interior design/decorating; language/literature/criticism; memoirs; military/war; money/finance (personal finance); multicultural; music/dance; nature/environment; New Age/metaphysics; philosophy; photography; popular culture; psychology; recreation; regional; religious/inspirational; science/technology; self-help/personal improvement; sex; sociology; spirituality; sports; theater/film; translation; travel; true crime/investigative; women's issues/studies; anthropolgy. **Considers these fiction areas:** Literary; mainstream/contemporary; mystery/suspense.

> O— This agency specializes in popular reference nonfiction, commercial fiction with a literary quality, and mysteries. "I have wide-ranging interests, but it really depends on quality of writing, originality, and how a particular project appeals to me (or not). I take on fiction when I completely love it—it doesn't matter what area or genre." Does not want to receive poetry, material for children, screenplays, westerns, horror, science fiction, or fantasy.

How to Contact Query with SASE. No unsolicited mss or phone calls. Considers simultaneous queries. Responds in 1 week to queries with SASE. Responds in 1 month to requested mss. Returns materials only with SASE. Obtains most new clients through recommendations from others.

Recent Sales Sold 100 titles in the last year. *10 Sure Signs a Movie Character Is Doomed and Other Surprising Movie Lists*, by Richard Roeper (Hyperion); *What Is Love?*, by Taro Gold (Andrews & McMeel); *How to Make Someone Love You in 90 Minutes or Less—And Make it Last Forever*, by Nick Boothman.

Terms Agent receives 15% commission on domestic sales; 20% commission on foreign sales. Offers written contract, binding for 1 year. Charges for postage, photocopying and fax.

Writers' Conferences ASJA (New York City); Asilomar (Pacific Grove CA); St. Petersburg; Whidbey Island; Jacksonville; Albuquerque; Austin; Columbus; Southwestern Writers; Willamette (Portland); Dorothy Canfield Fisher (San Diego); Writers Union (Maui); Pacific NW; IWWG; and many others.

Tips "Read the agent listing carefully, and comply with guidelines."

◨ MARIA CARVAINIS AGENCY, INC.

1350 Avenue of the Americas, Suite 2905, New York NY 10019. (212)245-6365. Fax: (212)245-7196. E-mail: mca@mariacarvainisagency.com. **Contact:** Maria Carvainis, president. Estab. 1977. Member of AAR, Authors Guild, Women's Media Group, ABA, MWA, RWA; signatory of WGA. Represents 60 clients. 10% of clients are new/unpublished writers. Currently handles: 34% nonfiction books; 65% novels; 1% poetry.

> • Prior to opening her agency, Ms. Carvainis spent more than 10 years in the publishing industry as a senior editor with Macmillan Publishing, Basic Books, Avon Books, and Crown Publishers. Ms. Carvainis has served as a member of the AAR Board of Directors and AAR Treasurer, as well as serving as chair of the AAR Contracts Committee. She presently serves on the AAR Royalty Committee.

Member Agents Moira Sullivan (literary assistant); David Harvey (literary assistant); Anna Del Vecchio (contracts manager).

Represents Nonfiction books, novels. **Considers these nonfiction areas:** Biography/autobiography; business/economics; history; memoirs; science/technology (pop science); women's issues/studies. **Considers these fiction areas:** Historical; literary; mainstream/contemporary; mystery/suspense; thriller; middle grade and young adult, women's fiction.

> O— Does not want to receive science fiction or children's picture books.

How to Contact Query with SASE. Responds in 1 week to queries; 3 months to mss. Obtains most new clients through recommendations from others, conferences, 60% from conferences/referrals; 40% from query letters.

Recent Sales *Slightly Dangerous*, by Mary Balogh (Delacorte); *White Hot*, by Sandra Brown (Simon & Schuster); *Winterset*, by Candace Camp (MIRA); *Collara Killer*, by Lee Charles Kelley (Morrow/Avon); *Love and Madness*, by Martin Levy (William Morrow); *Island of Bones*, by P.J. Parrish (Kensington); *Women of America*, by Charlie Smith (W.W. Norton); *Some Danger Involved*, by Will Thomas (Touchstone Fireside). Other clients include Sue Erikson Bloland, Pam Conrad, S.V. Date, Michael G. Downs, Phillip DePoy, Carlos Dews, Tyler Dilts, Keith Dunlap, Cindy Gerard, Ellen Newmark, Kristine Rolofson, Janet Mansfield Soares, Christine Sneed, Ernest Suarez.

Terms Agent receives 15% commission on domestic sales; 20% commission on foreign sales. Offers written contract, binding for 2 years on a book-by-book basis. Charges clients for foreign postage, bulk copying.

Writers' Conferences BEA; Frankfurt Book Fair; London Book Fair.

◨ CASTIGLIA LITERARY AGENCY

1155 Camino Del Mar, Suite 510, Del Mar CA 92014. (858)755-8761. Fax: (858)755-7063. **Contact:** Julie Castiglia. Estab. 1993. Member of AAR, PEN. Represents 50 clients. Currently handles: 55% nonfiction books; 45% novels.

Member Agents Winifred Golden, Julie Castiglia.

Represents Nonfiction books, novels. **Considers these nonfiction areas:** Animals; anthropology/archaeology; biography/autobiography; business/economics; child guidance/parenting; cooking/foods/nutrition; current affairs; ethnic/cultural interests; health/medicine; history; language/literature/criticism; money/finance; nature/environment; New Age/metaphysics; psychology; religious/inspirational; science/technology; self-help/personal improvement; sociology; women's issues/studies. **Considers these fiction areas:** Contemporary issues; ethnic; literary; mainstream/contemporary; mystery/suspense; women's (especially).

O-- Does not want to receive horror, screenplays, or academic nonfiction.

How to Contact Query with SASE. No fax queries. Responds in 2 months to mss. Returns materials only with SASE. Obtains most new clients through recommendations from others, solicitations, conferences.

Recent Sales Sold 22 titles in the last year. 3 untitle novels by Susan Squires (St. Martin's); *Maya Running*, by Anjali Banerjee (Random House).

Terms Agent receives 15% commission on domestic sales; 25% commission on foreign sales. Offers written contract; 6-week notice must be given to terminate contract. Charges clients for Fed Ex or Messenger.

Writers' Conferences Southwestern Writers Conference (Albuquerque NM, August); National Writers Conference; Willamette Writers Conference (OR); San Diego State University (CA); Writers at Work (Utah); Austin Conference (TX).

Tips "Be professional with submissions. Attend workshops and conferences before you approach an agent."

RUTH COHEN, INC., LITERARY AGENCY

P.O. Box 2244, La Jolla CA 92038-2244. (858)456-5805. **Contact:** Ruth Cohen. Estab. 1982. Member of AAR, Authors Guild, Sisters in Crime, RWA, SCBWI. Represents 39 clients. 15% of clients are new/unpublished writers. Currently handles: 60% novels; 40% juvenile books.

• Prior to becoming an agent, Ms. Cohen served as directing editor at Scott Foresman & Co.(now Pearson).

Represents Novels (adult), juvenile books. **Considers these fiction areas:** Ethnic; historical; juvenile; literary; mainstream/contemporary; mystery/suspense; young adult.

O-- This agency specializes in "quality writing in contemporary fiction, women's fiction, mysteries, thrillers and juvenile fiction." Does not want to receive poetry, westerns, film scripts, or how-to books.

How to Contact Submit outline, 1 sample chapter(s). Responds in 3 weeks to queries. Returns materials only with SASE. Obtains most new clients through recommendations from others, solicitations.

Recent Sales This agency prefers not to share information on specific sales.

Terms Agent receives 15% commission on domestic sales; 25% commission on foreign sales. Offers written contract, binding for 1 year. Charges for foreign postage, phone calls, photocopying submissions, and overnight delivery of mss when appropriate.

Tips "As the publishing world merges and changes, there seem to be fewer opportunities for new writers to succeed in the work that they love. We urge you to develop the patience, persistence, and preseverance that have made this agency so successful. Prepare a well-written and well-crafted manuscript, and our combined best efforts can help advance both our careers."

CORNERSTONE LITERARY, INC.

4500 Wilshire Blvd., 3rd floor, Los Angeles CA 90010. (323)930-6039. Fax: (323)930-0407. Website: www.corner stoneliterary.com. **Contact:** Helen Breitwieser. Estab. 1998. Member of AAR; Author's Guild; MWA; RWA. Represents 40 clients. 30% of clients are new/unpublished writers.

• Prior to founding her own boutique agency, Ms. Breitwieser was a literary agent at The William Morris Agency.

Represents Novels. **Considers these fiction areas:** Detective/police/crime; erotica; ethnic; family saga; glitz; historical; literary; mainstream/contemporary; multicultural; mystery/suspense; romance; thriller.

O-- Actively seeking first fiction, literary. Does not want to receive science fiction, westerns, children's books, poetry, screenplays, fantasy, gay/lesbian, horror, self-help, psychology, business.

How to Contact Query with SASE. Responds in 6-8 weeks to queries; 2 months to mss. Returns materials only with SASE. Obtains most new clients through recommendations from others.

Recent Sales Sold 38 titles in the last year. *The Earth Moved*, by Carmen Reid (Pocket); *The Delta Sisters*, by Kayla Perrin (St. Martin's Press); *The Sweetest Taboo*, by Carole Matthews (HarperCollins). Other clients include Stan Diehl, Elaine Coffman, Danielle Girard, R.J. Kaiser, Rachel Lee.

Terms Agent receives 15% commission on domestic sales; 20% commission on foreign sales. Offers written contract, binding for 1 year; 2-month notice must be given to terminate contract.

Tips "Don't query about more than 1 manuscript. Do not e-mail queries/submissions."

JAMES R. CYPHER, THE CYPHER AGENCY

816 Wolcott Ave., Beacon NY 12508-4261. Phone/fax: (845)831-5677. E-mail: jimcypher@prodigy.net. Website: pages.prodigy.net/jimcypher/. **Contact:** James R. Cypher. Estab. 1993. Member of AAR, Authors Guild. Represents 40 clients. 40% of clients are new/unpublished writers. Currently handles: 100% nonfiction books.

• Prior to opening his agency, Mr. Cypher worked as a corporate public relations manager for a Fortune 500 multi-national computer company for 28 years.

Represents Nonfiction books. **Considers these nonfiction areas:** Biography/autobiography; current affairs; ethnic/cultural interests; gay/lesbian issues; government/politics/law; health/medicine; history; how-to; language/literature/criticism; memoirs (travel); money/finance; music/dance; nature/environment; popular culture; psychology; science/technology; self-help/personal improvement; sociology; sports; theater/film; travel (memoirs); true crime/investigative; women's issues/studies.

    O⌐ Actively seeking a wide variety of topical nonfiction. Does not want to receive humor, pets, gardening, cooking books, crafts, spiritual, religious, or New Age topics.

How to Contact Query with SASE, proposal package, outline, 2 sample chapter(s). Accepts e-mail and fax queries. Considers simultaneous queries. Responds in 2 weeks to queries; 6 weeks to mss. Obtains most new clients through recommendations from others, conferences, networking on online computer service.

Recent Sales Sold 5 titles in the last year. *The Night the Defeos Died: Reinvestigating the Amityville Murders*, by Ric Osuna (Katco Literary & Media); *Revolution in Zanzibar: An American's Cold War Tale*, by Donald Petterson (Westview Press); *Once Upon a Word: True Tales of Word Origins*, by Rob Kyff (Tapestry Press).

Terms Agent receives 15% commission on domestic sales; 20% commission on foreign sales. Offers written contract; 1-month notice must be given to terminate contract. 100% of business is derived from commissions on ms sales. Charges clients for postage, photocopying, overseas phone calls and faxes.

◙ DARHANSOFF, VERRILL, FELDMAN LITERARY AGENTS

236 W. 26th St., Suite 802, New York NY 10001. (917)305-1300. Fax: (917)305-1400. Estab. 1975. Member of AAR. Represents 120 clients. 10% of clients are new/unpublished writers. Currently handles: 25% nonfiction books; 60% novels; 15% story collections.

Member Agents Liz Darhansoff, Charles Verrill, Leigh Feldman.

Represents Novels, short story collections. **Considers these nonfiction areas:** Narrative nonfiction.

    O⌐ Specializes in literary fiction.

How to Contact Obtains most new clients through recommendations from others.

◙ LIZA DAWSON ASSOCIATES

240 W. 35th St., Suite 500, New York NY 10001. (212)465-9071. **Contact:** Liza Dawson, Caitlin Blasdell. Member of AAR, MWA, Women's Media Group. Represents 50 clients. 15% of clients are new/unpublished writers. Currently handles: 60% nonfiction books; 40% novels.

    • Prior to becoming an agent, Ms. Dawson was an editor for 20 years, spending 11 years at William Morrow as vice president and 2 at Putnam as executive editor. Ms. Blasdell was a senior editor at HarperCollins and Avon.

Member Agents Liza Dawson, Caitlin Blasdell.

Represents Nonfiction books, novels, scholarly books. **Considers these nonfiction areas:** Biography/autobiography; business/economics; child guidance/parenting; health/medicine; history; memoirs; psychology; sociology; women's issues/studies. **Considers these fiction areas:** Ethnic; family saga; historical; literary; mystery/suspense; regional; science fiction (Blasdell only); thriller.

    O⌐ This agency specializes in readable literary fiction, thrillers, mainstream historicals, and women's fiction, academics, historians, business, journalists, and psychology. Does not want to receive westerns, sports, computers, juvenile.

How to Contact Query with SASE. Responds in 3 weeks to queries; 6 weeks to mss. Obtains most new clients through recommendations from others, conferences.

Recent Sales Sold 40 titles in the last year. *IDA B.*, by Karen E. Quinones Miller (Simon and Schuster); *Mayada: Daughter of Iraq* by Jean Sasson (Dutton); *The Nanny Murders*, by Merry Jones (St. Martin's); *WORDCRAFT: How to Write Like a Professional*, by Jack Hart (Pantheon); *...And a Time to Die: How Hospitals Shape the End of Life Experience*, by Dr. Sharon Kaufman (Scribner).

Terms Agent receives 15% commission on domestic sales; 20% commission on foreign sales. Offers written contract. Charges clients for photocopying and overseas postage.

◙ DUNHAM LITERARY, INC.

156 Fifth Ave., Suite 625, New York NY 10010-7002. (212)929-0994. Website: www.dunhamlit.com. **Contact:** Jennie Dunham. Estab. 2000. Member of AAR. Represents 50 clients. 15% of clients are new/unpublished writers. Currently handles: 25% nonfiction books; 25% novels; 50% juvenile books.

    • Prior to opening her agency, Ms. Dunham worked as a literary agent for Russell & Volkening. The Rhoda Weyr Agency is now a division of Dunham Literary, Inc.

Represents Nonfiction books, novels, short story collections, juvenile books. **Considers these nonfiction areas:** Anthropology/archaeology; biography/autobiography; ethnic/cultural interests; government/politics/law; health/medicine; history; language/literature/criticism; nature/environment; popular culture; psychology; science/technology; women's issues/studies. **Considers these fiction areas:** Ethnic; juvenile; literary; mainstream/contemporary; picture books; young adult.

How to Contact Query with SASE. No e-mail or fax queries. Responds in 1 week to queries; 2 months to mss. Obtains most new clients through recommendations from others, solicitations.

Recent Sales *Alice in Wonderland*, by Robert Sabuda; *Dahlia*, by Barbara McClintock; *Living Dead Girl*, by Tod Goldberg; *In My Mother's House*, by Margaret McMulla; *Black Hawk Down*, by Mark Bowden; *Look Back All the Green Valley*, by Fred Chappell; *Even Now*, by Susan S. Kelly.

Terms Agent receives 15% commission on domestic sales; 20% commission on foreign sales. Writers reimbursed for office fees after the sale of ms.

DYSTEL & GODERICH LITERARY MANAGEMENT

1 Union Square W., Suite 904, New York NY 10003. (212)627-9100. Fax: (212)627-9313. E-mail: miriam@dystel. com. Website: www.dystel.com. **Contact:** Miriam Goderich. Estab. 1994. Member of AAR. Represents 300 clients. 50% of clients are new/unpublished writers. Currently handles: 65% nonfiction books; 25% novels; 10% cookbooks.

● Dystel & Goderich Literary Management recently acquired the client list of Bedford Book Works.

Member Agents Stacey Glick; Jane Dystel; Miriam Goderich; Michael Bourret; Jessica Papin; Jim McCarthy.

Represents Nonfiction books, novels, cookbooks. **Considers these nonfiction areas:** Animals; anthropology/archaeology; biography/autobiography; business/economics; child guidance/parenting; cooking/foods/nutrition; current affairs; education; ethnic/cultural interests; gay/lesbian issues; government/politics/law; health/medicine; history; humor/satire; military/war; money/finance; New Age/metaphysics; popular culture; psychology; religious/inspirational; science/technology; true crime/investigative; women's issues/studies. **Considers these fiction areas:** Action/adventure; contemporary issues; detective/police/crime; ethnic; family saga; gay/lesbian; literary; mainstream/contemporary; mystery/suspense; thriller (especially).

○━ This agency specializes in commercial and literary fiction and nonfiction, plus cookbooks.

How to Contact Query with SASE. Considers simultaneous queries. Responds in 1 month to queries; 6 weeks to mss. Obtains most new clients through recommendations from others, solicitations, conferences.

Recent Sales *The Gift of Jazzy*, by Cindy Adams; *Whiskey Sour*, by J.A. Konrath; *Bittersweet*, by Alice Medrich; *Douglass' Women*, by Jewell Parker Rhodes; *Taste: Pure and Simple*, by Michel Nischan; *The Mapmaker's Wife*, by Robert Whitaker; *Kushiel's Avatar*, by Jacqueline Carey; *The Last Goodbye*, by Reed Arvin; *Boy Gets Grill*, by Bobby Flay.

Terms Agent receives 15% commission on domestic sales; 19% commission on foreign sales. Offers written contract, binding for book-to-book basis. Charges for photocopying. Galley charges and book charges from the publisher are passed on to the author.

Writers' Conferences West Coast Writers Conference (Whidbey Island WA, Columbus Day weekend); University of Iowa Writer's Conference; Pacific Northwest Writer's Conference; Pike's Peak Writer's Conference; Santa Barbara Writer's Conference; Harriette Austin's Writer's Conference; Sandhills Writers Conference; ASU Writers Conference.

Tips "Work on sending professional, well-written queries that are concise and addressed to the specific agent the author is contacting. No dear Sirs/Madam."

ELAINE P. ENGLISH

Graybill & English, LLC, 1875 Connecticut Ave. NW, Suite 712, Washington DC 20009. (202)588-9798, ext. 143. Fax: (202)457-0662. E-mail: elaineengl@aol.com. Website: www.graybillandenglish.com. **Contact:** Elaine English. Member of AAR. Represents 18 clients. 50% of clients are new/unpublished writers. Currently handles: 100% novels.

● Ms. English is also an attorney specializing in media and publishing law.

Member Agents Elaine English (women's fiction, including romance and mysteries).

Represents Novels. **Considers these fiction areas:** Historical; mainstream/contemporary; multicultural; mystery/suspense; romance (including single titles); thriller; women's.

○━ "While not as an agent, per se, I have been working in publishing for over 15 years. Also, I'm affiliated with other agents who represent a broad spectrum of projects." Actively seeking women's fiction, including single-title romances. Does not want to receive anything other than above.

How to Contact Submit synopsis first, 3 chapters, SASE. Responds in 6 weeks to queries; 6 months to mss. Returns materials only with SASE. Obtains most new clients through solicitations.

Terms Agent receives 15% commission on domestic sales; 20% commission on foreign sales. Offers written contract; 30-day notice must be given to terminate contract. Charges only for expenses directly related to sales of manuscript (long distance, postage, copying).

Writers' Conferences Washington Romance Writers (Harpers Ferry VA, April); RWA Nationals (Dallas TX, July; SEAK Medical Fiction Writing for Physcians (Cape Cod, September); Emerald City (Seattle WA, October).

FELICIA ETH LITERARY REPRESENTATION

555 Bryant St., Suite 350, Palo Alto CA 94301-1700. (650)375-1276. Fax: (650)401-8892. E-mail: feliciaeth@aol.c om. **Contact:** Felicia Eth. Estab. 1988. Member of AAR. Represents 25-35 clients. Works with established and new writers. Currently handles: 85% nonfiction books; 15% adult novels.

Represents Nonfiction books, novels. **Considers these nonfiction areas:** Animals; anthropology/archaeology; biography/autobiography; business/economics; child guidance/parenting; current affairs; ethnic/cultural interests; gay/lesbian issues; government/politics/law; health/medicine; history; nature/environment; popular culture; psychology; science/technology; sociology; true crime/investigative; women's issues/studies. **Considers these fiction areas:** Ethnic; feminist; gay/lesbian; literary; mainstream/contemporary; thriller.

    O→ This agency specializes in "provocative, intelligent, thoughtful nonfiction on a wide array of subjects which are commercial, and high-quality fiction—preferably mainstream and contemporary."

How to Contact Query with SASE, outline. Considers simultaneous queries. Responds in 3 weeks to queries; 4-6 weeks to mss.

Recent Sales Sold 7-10 titles in the last year. *Jane Austen in Boca*, by Paula Marantz Cohen (St. Martin's Press); *Beyond Pink and Blue*, by Dr. Leonard Sax (Doubleday/Random House); *Lavendar Road to Success*, by Kirk Snyder (Ten Speed Press).

Terms Agent receives 15% commission on domestic sales; 20% commission on foreign sales; 20% commission on dramatic rights sales. Charges clients for photocopying, express mail service—extraordinary expenses.

Writers' Conferences Independent Writers of LA (Los Angeles); Conference of National Coalition of Independent Scholars (Berkley CA); Writers Guild.

Tips "For nonfiction, established expertise is certainly a plus, as is magazine publication—though not a prerequisite. I am highly dedicated to those projects I represent, but highly selective in what I choose."

N ◙ DIANA FINCH LITERARY AGENCY

116 W. 23rd St., Suite 500, New York NY 10011. (646)375-2081. Fax: (212)851-8405. E-mail: diana.finch@verizon.net. **Contact:** Diana Finch. Estab. 2003. Member of AAR. Represents 35 clients. 20% of clients are new/unpublished writers. Currently handles: 60% nonfiction books; 25% novels; 5% story collections; 5% juvenile books; 5% multimedia.

    • Prior to becoming an agent, Ms. Finch was an assistant editor at St. Martin's Press.

Represents Nonfiction books, novels, scholarly books. **Considers these nonfiction areas:** Biography/autobiography; business/economics; child guidance/parenting; computers/electronic; current affairs; ethnic/cultural interests; government/politics/law; health/medicine; history; how-to; humor/satire; memoirs; military/war; money/finance; music/dance; nature/environment; photography; popular culture; psychology; science/technology; self-help/personal improvement; sports; theater/film; translation; true crime/investigative; women's issues/studies; juvenile. **Considers these fiction areas:** Action/adventure; detective/police/crime; ethnic; historical; literary; mainstream/contemporary; thriller; young adult.

    O→ Actively seeking narrative nonfiction, popular science, and health topics. Does not want romance, mysteries, or children's picture books.

How to Contact Query with SASE. Considers simultaneous queries. Returns materials only with SASE. Obtains most new clients through recommendations from others.

Recent Sales Untitled nonfiction, by Greg Palast (Penguin US and UK); *Journey of the Magi*, by Tudor Parfitt (Farrar, Straus, & Giroux); *Sixth Grade*, by Susie Morgenstern (Viking Children's); *We Were There: African-American Vets*, by Yvonne Latty and Ron Tarver (HarperCollins). Other clients include Keith Devlin, Daniel Duane, Thomas Goltz, Hugh Pope, Sebastian Matthews, Joan Lambert, Dr. Robert Marion.

Terms Agent receives 15% commission on domestic sales; 20% commission on foreign sales. Offers written contract. "I charge for photocopying, overseas postage, galleys, and books purchased, and try to recap these costs from earnings received for a client, rather than charging outright."

Tips "Do as much research as you can on agents before you query. Have someone critique your query letter before you send it. It should be only 1 page and describe your book clearly—and why you are writing it—but also demonstrate creativity and a sense of your writing style."

◙ GELFMAN, SCHNEIDER, LITERARY AGENTS, INC.

250 W. 57th St., New York NY 10107. (212)245-1993. Fax: (212)245-8678. **Contact:** Jane Gelfman, Deborah Schneider. Estab. 1981. Member of AAR. Represents 300+ clients. 10% of clients are new/unpublished writers.

Represents Nonfiction books, novels, "We represent adult, general, hardcover fiction and nonfiction, literary and commercial, and some mysteries." **Considers these fiction areas:** Literary; mainstream/contemporary; mystery/suspense.

    O→ Does not want to receive romances, science fiction, westerns, or children's books.

How to Contact Query with SASE. No e-mail queries accepted. Responds in 1 month to queries; 2 months to mss. Obtains most new clients through recommendations from others.

Terms Agent receives 15% commission on domestic sales; 20% commission on foreign sales. Offers written contract. Charges clients for photocopying, messengers and couriers.

SANFORD J. GREENBURGER ASSOCIATES, INC.

55 Fifth Ave., New York NY 10003. (212)206-5600. Fax: (212)463-8718. Website: www.greenburger.com. **Contact:** Heide Lange. Estab. 1945. Member of AAR. Represents 500 clients.

Member Agents Heide Lange, Faith Hamlin, Theresa Park, Elyse Cheney, Dan Mandel, Julie Barer, Matthew Bialer.

Represents Nonfiction books, novels. **Considers these nonfiction areas:** Agriculture/horticulture; Americana; animals; anthropology/archaeology; art/architecture/design; biography/autobiography; business/economics; child guidance/parenting; computers/electronic; cooking/foods/nutrition; crafts/hobbies; current affairs; education; ethnic/cultural interests; gardening; gay/lesbian issues; government/politics/law; health/medicine; history; how-to; humor/satire; interior design/decorating; juvenile nonfiction; language/literature/criticism; memoirs; military/war; money/finance; multicultural; music/dance; nature/environment; New Age/metaphysics; philosophy; photography; popular culture; psychology; recreation; regional; religious/inspirational; science/technology; self-help/personal improvement; sex; sociology; software; sports; theater/film; translation; travel; true crime/investigative; women's issues/studies; young adult. **Considers these fiction areas:** Action/adventure; contemporary issues; detective/police/crime; ethnic; family saga; feminist; gay/lesbian; glitz; historical; humor/satire; literary; mainstream/contemporary; mystery/suspense; psychic/supernatural; regional; sports; thriller.

○─ Does not want to receive romances or westerns.

How to Contact Query with SASE. Considers simultaneous queries. Responds in 3 weeks to queries; 2 months to mss.

Recent Sales Sold 200 titles in the last year. This agency prefers not to share information on specific sales. Other clients include Andrew Ross, Margaret Cuthbert, Nicholas Sparks, Mary Kurcinka, Linda Nichols, Edy Clarke, Brad Thor, Dan Brown, Sallie Bissell.

Terms Agent receives 15% commission on domestic sales; 20% commission on foreign sales. Charges for photocopying, books for foreign and subsidiary rights submissions.

HOPKINS LITERARY ASSOCIATES

2117 Buffalo Rd., Suite 327, Rochester NY 14624-1507. (585)352-6268. **Contact:** Pam Hopkins. Estab. 1996. Member of AAR, RWA. Represents 30 clients. 5% of clients are new/unpublished writers. Currently handles: 100% novels.

Represents Novels. **Considers these fiction areas:** Historical; mainstream/contemporary; romance; women's.

○─ This agency specializes in women's fiction, particularly historical, contemporary, and category romance as well as mainstream work.

How to Contact Submit outline, 3 sample chapter(s). No e-mail or fax queries. Considers simultaneous queries. Responds in 2 weeks to queries; 1 month to mss. Returns materials only with SASE. Obtains most new clients through recommendations from others, solicitations, conferences.

Recent Sales Sold 50 titles in the last year. *The First Mistake*, by Merline Lovelace (Mira); *The Romantic*, by Madeline Hunter (Bantam); *The Damsel in this Dress*, by Marianne Stillings (Avon).

Terms Agent receives 15% commission on domestic sales; 20% commission on foreign sales. No written contract.

Writers' Conferences Romance Writers of America.

LINDA KONNER LITERARY AGENCY

10 W. 15th St., Suite 1918, New York NY 10011-6829. (212)691-3419. E-mail: ldkonner@cs.com. **Contact:** Linda Konner. Estab. 1996. Member of AAR, ASJA; signatory of WGA. Represents 65 clients. 5-10% of clients are new/unpublished writers. Currently handles: 100% nonfiction books.

Represents Nonfiction books (adult only). **Considers these nonfiction areas:** Gay/lesbian issues; health/medicine (diet/nutrition/fitness); how-to; money/finance (personal finance); popular culture; psychology; self-help/personal improvement; women's issues/studies; business, parenting, relationships.

○─ This agency specializes in health, self-help, and how-to books.

How to Contact Query with SASE, outline, sufficient return postage. Prefers to read materials exclusively for 2 weeks. Considers simultaneous queries. Obtains most new clients through recommendations from others, occasional solicitation among established authors/journalists.

Recent Sales Sold 26 titles in the last year. *The Ultimate Body*, by Liz Neporent (Ballantine); *Strength for Their Journey: The Five Disciplines Every African-American Parent Must Teach Her Child*, by Robert Johnson, MD, and Paulette Stanford, MD, (Doubleday).

Terms Agent receives 15% commission on domestic sales; 25% commission on foreign sales. Offers written contract. Charges $85 one-time fee for domestic expenses; additional expenses may be incurred for foreign sales.

Writers' Conferences American Society of Journalists and Authors (New York City, Spring).

☑ NANCY LOVE LITERARY AGENCY

250 E. 65th St., New York NY 10021-6614. (212)980-3499. Fax: (212)308-6405. E-mail: nloveag@aol.com. **Contact:** Nancy Love. Estab. 1984. Member of AAR. Represents 60-80 clients. 25% of clients are new/unpublished writers. Currently handles: 90% nonfiction books; 10% novels.

Member Agents Nancy Love; Miriam Tager (mysteries, thrillers).

Represents Nonfiction books, novels (mysteries and thrillers only). **Considers these nonfiction areas:** Biography/autobiography; child guidance/parenting; cooking/foods/nutrition; current affairs; ethnic/cultural interests; government/politics/law; health/medicine; history; how-to; nature/environment; New Age/metaphysics; popular culture; psychology; religious/inspirational; science/technology; self-help/personal improvement; sociology; spirituality; travel (armchair only, no how-to travel); true crime/investigative; women's issues/studies. **Considers these fiction areas:** Mystery/suspense; thriller.

　　O━ This agency specializes in adult nonfiction and mysteries. Actively seeking health and medicine (including alternative medicine), parenting, spiritual, and inspirational. Does not want to receive novels other than mysteries and thrillers.

How to Contact For nonfiction, send a proposal, chapter summary, and sample chapter. For fiction, query first. Fiction is only read on an exclusive basis. No e-mail or fax queries. Considers simultaneous queries. Responds in 3 weeks to queries; 6 weeks to mss. Returns materials only with SASE. Obtains most new clients through recommendations from others, solicitations.

Recent Sales Sold 20 titles in the last year. Books 3 and 4 in Blanco County Mystery Series, by Ben Rehder (St. Martin's Press); *Back Pain*, by Emile Hiesinger, M.D., and Marian Bettaucourt (Pocket Books); *The Tools People Use to Quit Addictions*, by Stanton Peele, Ph.D. (Crown); *All the Shah's Men: The Hidden Story of the CIA's Coup in Iran*, by Steven Kinzer (John Wiley).

Terms Agent receives 15% commission on domestic sales; 20% commission on foreign sales. Offers written contract. Charges clients for photocopying "if it runs over $20."

Tips "Nonfiction author and/or collaborator must be an authority in subject area and have a platform. Send a SASE if you want a response."

☑ DONALD MAASS LITERARY AGENCY

160 W. 95th St., Suite 1B, New York NY 10025. (212)866-8200. Website: www.maassagency.com. **Contact:** Donald Maass, Jennifer Jackson, or Rachel Vater. Estab. 1980. Member of AAR, SFWA, MWA, RWA. Represents over 100 clients. 5% of clients are new/unpublished writers. Currently handles: 100% novels.

　　● Prior to opening his agency, Mr. Maass served as an editor at Dell Publishing (New York) and as a reader at Gollancz (London). He is the current president of AAR.

Member Agents Donald Maass (mainstream, literary, mystery/suspense, science fiction); Jennifer Jackson (commercial fiction, especially romance, science fiction, fantasy, mystery/suspense); Rachel Vater (chick lit, mystery, thriller, fantasy, commercial, literary).

Represents Novels. **Considers these fiction areas:** Detective/police/crime; fantasy; historical; horror; literary; mainstream/contemporary; mystery/suspense; psychic/supernatural; romance (historical, paranormal, time travel); science fiction; thriller; women's.

　　O━ This agency specializes in commercial fiction, especially science fiction, fantasy, mystery, romance, suspense. Actively seeking "to expand the literary portion of our list and expand in romance and women's fiction." Does not want to receive nonfiction, children's, or poetry.

How to Contact Query with SASE. Returns material only with SASE. Considers simultaneous queries. Responds in 2 weeks to queries; 3 months to mss.

Recent Sales Sold over 100 titles in the last year. *Shoulder the Sky*, by Anne Perry (Ballantine); *The Longest Night*, by Gregg Keizer (G.P. Putnam's Sons).

Terms Agent receives 15% commission on domestic sales; 20% commission on foreign sales.

Writers' Conferences *Donald Maass:* World Science Fiction Convention; Frankfurt Book Fair; Pacific Northwest Writers Conference; Bouchercon and others; *Jennifer Jackson:* World Science Fiction and Fantasy Convention; RWA National, and others.

Tips "We are fiction specialists, also noted for our innovative approach to career planning. Few new clients are accepted, but interested authors should query with SASE. Subagents in all principle foreign countries and Hollywood. No nonfiction or juvenile works considered."

☑ CAROL MANN AGENCY

55 Fifth Ave., New York NY 10003. (212)206-5635. Fax: (212)675-4809. E-mail: emily@carolmannagency.com. **Contact:** Emily Nurkin. Estab. 1977. Member of AAR. Represents 200 clients. 25% of clients are new/unpublished writers. Currently handles: 70% nonfiction books; 30% novels.

Member Agents Carol Mann (literary fiction, nonfiction); Emily Nurkin (fiction and nonfiction).

Represents Nonfiction books, novels. **Considers these nonfiction areas:** Anthropology/archaeology; art/architecture/design; biography/autobiography; business/economics; child guidance/parenting; current affairs; ethnic/cultural interests; government/politics/law; health/medicine; history; money/finance; psychology; self-help/personal improvement; sociology; women's issues/studies. **Considers these fiction areas:** Literary; commercial.

    O→ This agency specializes in current affairs; self-help; popular culture; psychology; parenting; history. Does not want to receive "genre fiction (romance, mystery, etc.)."

How to Contact Query with outline/proposal and SASE. Responds in 3 weeks to queries.

Recent Sales Other clients include novelists Paul Auster and Marita Golden; journalists Tim Egan, Hannah Storm, Willow Bay, Pulitzer Prize-winner Fox Butterfield; best-selling essayist Shelby Steele; sociologist Dr. William Julius Wilson; economist Thomas Sowell; best-selling diet doctors Mary Dan and Michael Eades; ACLU president Nadine Strossen; pundit Mona Charen; memoirist Lauren Winner; photography project editors Rick Smolan and David Cohen (*America 24/7*); and Kevin Liles, president of Def Jam Records.

Terms Agent receives 15% commission on domestic sales; 20% commission on foreign sales. Offers written contract.

CLAUDIA MENZA LITERARY AGENCY

1170 Broadway, Suite 807, New York NY 10001. (212)889-6850. **Contact:** Claudia Menza. Estab. 1983. Member of AAR. Represents 111 clients. 50% of clients are new/unpublished writers.

    • Prior to becoming an agent, Ms. Menza was an editor/managing editor at a publishing company.

Represents Nonfiction books, novels. **Considers these nonfiction areas:** Current affairs; education; ethnic/cultural interests (especially African-American); health/medicine; history; multicultural; music/dance; photography; psychology; theater/film.

    O→ This agency specializes in African-American fiction and nonfiction, and editorial assistance.

How to Contact Submit outline, 25 pages. Prefers to read materials exclusively. Responds in 2 weeks to queries; 2-4 months to mss. Returns materials only with SASE. Obtains most new clients through recommendations from others.

Recent Sales This agency prefers not to share information on specific sales.

Terms Agent receives 15% commission on domestic sales; 20% (if co-agent is used) commission on foreign sales; 20% commission on dramatic rights sales. Offers written contract.

WILLIAM MORRIS AGENCY, INC.

1325 Avenue of the Americas, New York NY 10019. (212)586-5100. Fax: (212)903-1418. Website: www.wma.com. California office: 151 El Camino Dr., Beverly Hills CA 90212. Member of AAR.

Member Agents Owen Laster, Jennifer Rudolph Walsh, Suzanne Gluck, Joni Evans, Tracy Fisher, Mel Berger, Jay Mandel, Manie Barron.

Represents Nonfiction books, novels.

How to Contact Query with SASE. Considers simultaneous queries.

Recent Sales This agency prefers not to share information on specific sales.

Terms Agent receives 15% commission on domestic sales; 20% commission on foreign sales.

L. PERKINS ASSOCIATES

16 W. 36 St., New York NY 10018. (212)279-6418. Fax: (718)543-5354. E-mail: lperkinsagency@yahoo.com. **Contact:** Lori Perkins. Estab. 1990. Member of AAR. Represents 50 clients. 10% of clients are new/unpublished writers.

    • Ms. Perkins has been an agent for 18 years. Her agency has an affiliate agency, Southern Literary Group. She is also the author of *The Insider's Guide to Getting an Agent* (Writer's Digest Books).

Represents Nonfiction books, novels. **Considers these nonfiction areas:** Popular culture. **Considers these fiction areas:** Fantasy; horror; literary (dark); science fiction.

    O→ All of Ms. Perkins' clients write both fiction and nonfiction. "This combination keeps my clients publishing for years. I am also a published author so I know what it takes to write a book." Actively seeking a Latino *Gone With the Wind* and *Waiting to Exhale,* and urban ethnic horror. Does not want to receive "anything outside of the above categories, i.e., westerns, romance."

How to Contact Query with SASE. Considers simultaneous queries. Responds in 6 weeks to queries; 3 months to mss. Returns materials only with SASE. Obtains most new clients through recommendations from others, solicitations, conferences.

Recent Sales Sold 100 titles in the last year. *The Illustrated Ray Bradbury*, by Jerry Weist (Avon); *The Poet in Exile*, by Ray Manzarek (Avalon); *Behind Sad Eyes: The Life of George Harrison*, (St. Martin's Press).

Terms Agent receives 15% commission on domestic sales; 20% commission on foreign sales. No written contract. Charges clients for photocopying.

Writers' Conferences San Diego Writer's Conference; NECON; BEA; World Fantasy.

Tips "Research your field and contact professional writers' organizations to see who is looking for what. Finish your novel before querying agents. Read my book, *An Insider's Guide to Getting an Agent* to get a sense of how agents operate."

PINDER LANE & GARON-BROOKE ASSOCIATES, LTD.

159 W. 53rd St., Suite 14C, New York NY 10019-6005. (212)489-0880. E-mail: pinderl@interport.net. **Contact:** Robert Thixton. Member of AAR; signatory of WGA. Represents 30 clients. 20% of clients are new/unpublished writers. Currently handles: 25% nonfiction books; 75% novels.

Member Agents Dick Duane, Robert Thixton.

Represents Nonfiction books, novels. **Considers these fiction areas:** Contemporary issues; detective/police/crime; family saga; fantasy; gay/lesbian; literary; mainstream/contemporary; mystery/suspense; romance; science fiction.

 Oₙ This agency specializes in mainstream fiction and nonfiction. Does not want to receive screenplays, TV series teleplays, or dramatic plays.

How to Contact Query with SASE. *No unsolicited mss.* Responds in 3 weeks to queries; 2 months to mss. Obtains most new clients through referrals, queries.

Recent Sales Sold 20 titles in the last year. *Diana & Jackie—Maidens, Mothers & Myths*, by Jay Mulvaney (St. Martin's Press); *The Sixth Fleet* (series), by David Meadows (Berkley); *Dark Fires*, by Rosemary Rogers (Mira Books).

Terms Agent receives 15% commission on domestic sales; 30% commission on foreign sales. Offers written contract, binding for 3-5 years.

Tips "With our literary and media experience, our agency is uniquely positioned for the current and future direction publishing is taking. Send query letter first giving the essence of the manuscript, and a personal or career bio with SASE."

HELEN REES LITERARY AGENCY

376 North St., Boston MA 02113-2013. (617)227-9014. Fax: (617)227-8762. E-mail: reesliterary@aol.com. **Contact:** Joan Mazmanian, Ann Collette, Helen Rees, or Lorin Rees. Estab. 1983. Member of AAR, PEN. Represents 80 clients. 50% of clients are new/unpublished writers. Currently handles: 60% nonfiction books; 40% novels.

Member Agents Ann Collette (literary fiction, women's studies, health, biography, history); Helen Rees (business, money/finance/economics, government/politics/law, contemporary issues, literary fiction); Lorin Rees (business, memoir).

Represents Nonfiction books, novels. **Considers these nonfiction areas:** Biography/autobiography; business/economics; current affairs; government/politics/law; health/medicine; history; money/finance; women's issues/studies. **Considers these fiction areas:** Contemporary issues; historical; literary; mainstream/contemporary; mystery/suspense; thriller.

How to Contact Query with SASE, outline, 2 sample chapter(s). No e-mail or fax queries. Responds in 2-3 weeks to queries. Obtains most new clients through recommendations from others, solicitations, conferences.

Recent Sales Sold 30 titles in the last year. *Why Smart Executives Fail*, by Sydney Finkelstein (Portfolio); *What (Really) Works*, by William Joyce, Nitin Nohria, Bruce Roberson (Harper Business); *It's Your Ship: Management Techniques for the Best Damn Ship in the Navy*, by Capt. D. Michael Abrashoff (Warner); *The Watson Dynasty: The Fiery Reign and Troubled Legacy of IBM's Founding Father and Son*, by Richard St. Tedlow (Harper Business); *Video & DVD Guide 2004* (annual), by Mick Martin and Marsha Porter (Ballantine); *The Case for Israel*, by Alan Dershowitz (John Wiley & Sons); *A Call to Service: My Vision for a Better America*, by John Kerry (Viking); *GUTS!: Companies that Blow the Doors Off Business-As-Usual*, by Kevin and Jackie Freiberg (Currency).

Terms Agent receives 15% commission on domestic sales; 20% commission on foreign sales.

REGAL LITERARY AGENCY

52 Warfield St., Montclair NJ 07043. (973)509-5767. Fax: (973)509-0259. E-mail: bess@regal-literary.com. Website: www.regal-literary.com. **Contact:** Bess Reed. Estab. 2002. Member of AAR. Represents 60 clients. 20% of clients are new/unpublished writers. Currently handles: 48% nonfiction books; 46% novels; 2% story collections; 2% novellas; 2% poetry.

 ● Prior to becoming agents, Gordon Kato was a psychologist, Jospeh Regal was a musician, and Dan Kois was an actor/comedian.

Member Agents Gordon Kato (literary fiction, commercial fiction, pop culture); Joseph Regal (literary fiction, science, history, memoir); Dan Kois (literary fiction, history, sports, pop culture, memoir).

Represents Nonfiction books, novels, short story collections, novellas. **Considers these nonfiction areas:** Anthropology/archaeology; art/architecture/design; biography/autobiography; business/economics; cooking/foods/nutrition; current affairs; ethnic/cultural interests; gay/lesbian issues; government/politics/law; history;

humor/satire; language/literature/criticism; memoirs; military/war; music/dance; nature/environment; photography; popular culture; psychology; religious/inspirational (includes inspirational); science/technology (includes technology); sports; translation; true crime/investigative; women's issues/studies. **Considers these fiction areas:** Comic books/cartoon; detective/police/crime; ethnic; historical; literary; mystery/suspense; thriller; contemporary.

> O➤ "We have discovered more than a dozen successful literary novelists in the last 5 years. We are small, but are extraordinarily responsive to our writers. We are more like managers than agents, with an eye toward every aspect of our writers' careers, including publicity and other media." Actively seeking literary fiction and narrative nonfiction. Does not want romance, science fiction, horror, screenplays, or children's books.

How to Contact Query with SASE, submit 5-15 sample pages. No e-mail or fax queries. Considers simultaneous queries. Responds in 2-3 weeks to queries; 4-12 to mss. Returns materials only with SASE. Obtains most new clients through recommendations from others, unsolicited submissions.

Recent Sales Sold 23 titles in the last year. Other clients include James Reston, Jr., Tim Winton, Pascale La Draoulec, Tony Earley, Dennie Hughes, Mark Lee, Jake Page, Cheryl Bernard, Daniel Wallace, Paul Wilkes, John Marks, Keith Scribner, Jack Passarella, Alex Abella.

Terms Agent receives 15% commission on domestic sales; 20% commission on foreign sales. No written contract. Charges clients for typical, major office expenses, such as photocopying and foreign postage.

✓ JODIE RHODES LITERARY AGENCY

8840 Villa La Jolla Dr., Suite 315, La Jolla CA 92037-1957. (858)625-0544. Fax: (858)625-0544. **Contact:** Jodie Rhodes, president. Estab. 1998. Member of AAR. Represents 50 clients. 60% of clients are new/unpublished writers. Currently handles: 60% nonfiction books; 35% novels; 5% middle to young adult books.

> • Prior to opening her agency, Ms. Rhodes was a university-level, creative writing teacher, workshop director, published novelist, and Vice President Media Director at the N.W. Ayer Advertising Agency.

Member Agents Jodie Rhodes, president; Clark McCutcheon (fiction); Bob McCarter (nonfiction).

Represents Nonfiction books, novels, juvenile books. **Considers these nonfiction areas:** Biography/autobiography; child guidance/parenting; ethnic/cultural interests; government/politics/law; health/medicine; history; memoirs; military/war; science/technology; women's issues/studies. **Considers these fiction areas:** Contemporary issues; ethnic; family saga; historical; juvenile; literary; mainstream/contemporary; mystery/suspense; thriller; young adult; women's.

> O➤ Actively seeking "writers passionate about their books with a talent for richly textured narrative, an eye for details, and a nose for research." Nonfiction writers must have recognized credentials and expert knowledge of their subject matter. Does not want to receive erotica, horror, fantasy, romance, science fiction, children's books, religious, or inspirational books.

How to Contact Query with brief synopsis, first 30-50 pages, and SASE. No e-mail or fax queries. Considers simultaneous queries. Responds in 10 days to queries. Returns materials only with SASE. Obtains most new clients through recommendations from others, agent sourcebooks.

Recent Sales Sold 26 titles in the last year. *The Myrtles*, by Frances Kermeen (Warner); *Inside the Crips*, by Ann Pearlman (St. Martin's); *Home is East*, by Mary Ly (Bantam); *For Matrimonial Purposes*, by Kavita Daswani (Putnam); *Taming of the Chew*, by Denise Lamothe (Penguin); *Living in a Black & White World*, by Ann Pearlman (John Wiley & Sons).

Terms Agent receives 15% commission on domestic sales; 20% commission on foreign sales. Offers written contract; 1-month notice must be given to terminate contract. Charges clients for fax, photocopying, phone calls, and postage. "Charges are itemized and approved by writers upfront."

Tips "Think your book out before you write it. Do your research, know your subject matter intimately, write vivid specifics, not bland generalities. Care deeply about your book. Don't imitate other writers. Find your own voice. We never take on a book we don't believe in, and we go the extra mile for our writers. We welcome talented, new writers."

🅽 ✓ BARBARA RIFKIND LITERARY AGENCY

132 Perry St., 6th Floor, New York NY 10014. (212)229-0453. Fax: (212)229-0454. E-mail: barbara@barbararifki nd.net. **Contact:** Barbara Rifkind. Estab. 2002. Member of AAR. Represents 20 clients. 50% of clients are new/ unpublished writers. Currently handles: 80% nonfiction books; 10% scholarly books; 10% textbooks.

> • Prior to becoming an agent, Ms. Rifkind was an acquisitions editor, editorial manager, and a general manager in educational publishing (Addison Wesley).

Represents Nonfiction books, scholarly books, textbooks. **Considers these nonfiction areas:** Anthropology/archaeology; art/architecture/design; biography/autobiography; business/economics; child guidance/parenting; current affairs; ethnic/cultural interests; government/politics/law; health/medicine; history; language/

literature/criticism; money/finance; popular culture; psychology; science/technology; sociology; women's is-sues/studies.

○┅ "We represent writers of smart nonfiction—academics, journalists, scientists, thinkers, people who've done something real and have something to say—writing for general trade audiences and occassionally for trade scholarly or textbook markets. We like to work in the areas of history; science writing; business and economics; applications of social sciences to important issues; public affairs and current events; narrative nonfiction; women's issues and parenting from a discipline." Actively seeking smart nonfic-tion from credentialed thinkers or published writers in selected areas of interest. Does not want commer-cial or category fiction, juvenile, and other nonselected areas.

How to Contact Query with SASE, submit proposal package, outline. Accepts e-mail queries. No fax queries. Responds in 2 weeks to queries. Obtains most new clients through recommendations from others.

Recent Sales Sold 6 titles in the last year. Other clients include Zvi Bodie, Juan Enriquez, Nancy Folbre, Walter Friedman, James Hoopes, Herminia Ibarra, Milind Lele, Barry Nalebuff, Raghu Rajan, Steven Wall, Luigi Zingales, Ian Ayres, Greg Stone, Bill Hammack.

Terms Agent receives 15% commission on domestic sales; 10% commission on foreign sales. Offers written contract, binding for 6 months; immediate upon written notice notice must be given to terminate contract.

◪ B.J. ROBBINS LITERARY AGENCY

5130 Bellaire Ave., North Hollywood CA 91607-2908. (818)760-6602. Fax: (818)760-6616. E-mail: robbinsliterar y@aol.com. **Contact:** (Ms.) B.J. Robbins. Estab. 1992. Member of AAR. Represents 40 clients. 50% of clients are new/unpublished writers. Currently handles: 50% nonfiction books; 50% novels.

Member Agents Regina Su Mangum.

Represents Nonfiction books, novels. **Considers these nonfiction areas:** Biography/autobiography; child guid-ance/parenting; current affairs; ethnic/cultural interests; health/medicine; how-to; humor/satire; memoirs; music/dance; popular culture; psychology; self-help/personal improvement; sociology; sports; theater/film; true crime/investigative; women's issues/studies. **Considers these fiction areas:** Contemporary issues; detec-tive/police/crime; ethnic; literary; mainstream/contemporary; mystery/suspense; sports; thriller.

How to Contact Submit 3 sample chapter(s), outline/proposal, SASE. E-mail queries OK; no attachments. No fax queries. Considers simultaneous queries. Responds in 2 weeks to queries; 6 weeks to mss. Returns materials only with SASE. Obtains most new clients through conferences, referrals.

Recent Sales Sold 15 titles in the last year. *The Sex Lives of Cannibals*, by J. Maarten Troost (Broadway); *Quickening*, by Laura Catherine Brown (Random House/Ballantine); *Snow Mountain Passage*, by James D. Houston (Knopf); *The Last Summer*, by John Hough, Jr. (Simon & Schuster); *Last Stand on the Little Bighorn*, by James M. Donovan (Little, Brown).

Terms Agent receives 15% commission on domestic sales; 20% commission on foreign sales. Offers written contract; 3-month notice must be given to terminate contract. 100% of business is derived from commissions on ms sales. Charges clients for postage and photocopying only. Writers charged for fees only after the sale of ms.

Writers' Conferences Squaw Valley Fiction Writers Workshop (Squaw Valley CA, August); SDSU Writers Con-ference (San Diego CA, January).

◪ RITA ROSENKRANZ LITERARY AGENCY

440 West End Ave., Suite 15D, New York NY 10024-5358. (212)873-6333. **Contact:** Rita Rosenkranz. Estab. 1990. Member of AAR. Represents 30 clients. 20% of clients are new/unpublished writers. Currently handles: 98% nonfiction books; 2% novels.

● Prior to opening her agency, Rita Rosenkranz worked as an editor in major New York publishing houses.

Represents Nonfiction books. **Considers these nonfiction areas:** Animals; anthropology/archaeology; art/ architecture/design; biography/autobiography; business/economics; child guidance/parenting; computers/ electronic; cooking/foods/nutrition; crafts/hobbies; current affairs; ethnic/cultural interests; gay/lesbian issues; government/politics/law; health/medicine; history; how-to; humor/satire; interior design/decorating; lan-guage/literature/criticism; military/war; money/finance; music/dance; nature/environment; New Age/meta-physics; photography; popular culture; psychology; religious/inspirational; science/technology; self-help/per-sonal improvement; sports; theater/film; women's issues/studies.

○┅ "This agency focuses on adult nonfiction. Stresses strong editorial development and refinement before submitting to publishers, and brainstorms ideas with authors." Actively seeking authors "who are well paired with their subject, either for professional or personal reasons."

How to Contact Submit proposal package, outline, SASE. No e-mail or fax queries. Considers simultaneous queries. Responds in 2 weeks to queries. Obtains most new clients through solicitations, conferences, word of mouth.

Recent Sales Sold 35 titles in the last year. *Forbidden Fruit: True Love Stories from the Underground Railroad*, by Betty DeRamus (Atria Books); *Should I Medicate My Child?*, by Lisa Charis (Perigee); *Customer Branded Service*, by Janelle Barlow and Paul Stewart (Berrett-Koehler).

Terms Agent receives 15% commission on domestic sales; 20% commission on foreign sales. Offers written contract, binding for 3 years; 3-month written notice must be given to terminate contract. 100% of business is derived from commissions on ms sales. Charges clients for photocopying. Makes referrals to editing service.

Tips ''Identify the current competition for your project to make sure the project is valid. A strong cover letter is very important.''

◙ THE SAGALYN AGENCY

7201 Bethesda Ave., Suite 675, Bethesda MD 20814. (301)718-6440. Fax: (310)718-6444. E-mail: agency@Sagaly n.com. Website: Sagalyn.com. **Contact:** Rebeca Sagalyn. Estab. 1980. Member of AAR. Currently handles: 85% nonfiction books; 5% novels; 10% scholarly books.

Member Agents Raphael Sagalyn, Rebeca Sagalyn.

Represents Nonfiction books (history, science, business).

   ○━ Does not want to receive stage plays, screenplays, poetry, science fiction, romance, children's books, or young adult books.

How to Contact Please send e-mail queries only, no attachments. Include 1 of these words in subject line: Query, submission, inquiry. Response time depends on number of current queries, generally within 3 weeks.

Recent Sales See website for sales information.

Tips ''We receive between 1,000-1,200 queries a year, which in turn lead to 2 or 3 new clients.''

Ⓝ ◙ WENDY SCHMALZ AGENCY

Box 831, Hudson NY 12534. (518)672-7697. Fax: (518)672-7662. E-mail: wschmalz@earthlink.net. **Contact:** Wendy Schmalz. Estab. 2002. Member of AAR. Represents 30 clients. 10% of clients are new/unpublished writers. Currently handles: 25% nonfiction books; 25% novels; 50% juvenile books.

Represents Nonfiction books, novels, YA novels. **Considers these nonfiction areas:** Biography/autobiography; current affairs; gay/lesbian issues; popular culture; juvenile nonfiction. **Considers these fiction areas:** Gay/ lesbian; juvenile; literary; young adult; contemporary issues.

   ○━ No picture book texts.

How to Contact Query with SASE. Accepts e-mail queries. No fax queries. Responds in 2 weeks to queries; 6 weeks to mss. Returns materials only with SASE. Obtains most new clients through recommendations from others.

Terms Agent receives 15% commission on domestic sales; 20% commission on foreign sales. No written contract. Charges authors actual expenses incurred by agent for photocopying and Fed Ex charges incurred for Fed Ex mss.

◙ WENDY SHERMAN ASSOCIATES, INC.

450 Seventh Ave., Suite 3004, New York NY 10123. (212)279-9027. Fax: (212)279-8863. E-mail: wendy@wsher man.com. **Contact:** Wendy Sherman. Estab. 1999. Member of AAR. Represents 30 clients. 30% of clients are new/unpublished writers. Currently handles: 50% nonfiction books; 50% novels.

   ● Prior to opening the agency, Ms. Sherman worked for The Aaron Priest agency and was vice president, executive director of Henry Holt, associate publisher, subsidary rights director, sales and marketing director.

Member Agents Tracy Brown, Wendy Sherman.

Represents Nonfiction books, novels. **Considers these nonfiction areas:** Psychology; narrative nonfiction, practical. **Considers these fiction areas:** Literary; women's (suspense).

   ○━ ''We specialize in developing new writers as well as working with more established writers. My experi-ence as a publisher has proven to be a great asset to my clients.''

How to Contact Query with SASE, or send outline/proposal, 1 sample chapter. No e-mail queries. Considers simultaneous queries. Responds in 1 month to queries. Returns materials only with SASE. Obtains most new clients through recommendations from others.

Recent Sales Sold 16 titles in the last year. Other clients include Greg Baer, M.D., Liam Callanan, Lise Friedman, Rabbi Mark Borowitz, Alan Eisenstock, D.W. Buffa, William Lashner, Nani Power, Sarah Stonich, American Dance Foundation, Howard Bahr, Lundy Bancroft, Tom Schweich, Suzanne Chazin, Al Hudler, Mary Sharratt, Libby Street.

Terms Agent receives 15% commission on domestic sales; 20% commission on foreign sales. Offers written contract. Charges for photocopying of ms, messengers, express mail services, etc. (reasonable, standard ex-penses).

☑ IRENE SKOLNICK LITERARY AGENCY

22 W. 23rd St., 5th Floor, New York NY 10010. (212)727-3648. Fax: (212)727-1024. E-mail: sirene35@aol.com. **Contact:** Irene Skolnick. Estab. 1993. Member of AAR. Represents 45 clients. 75% of clients are new/unpublished writers.

Member Agents Irene Skolnick.

Represents Nonfiction books (adult), novels (adult). **Considers these nonfiction areas:** Biography/autobiography; current affairs; cultural history. **Considers these fiction areas:** Contemporary issues; literary; mainstream/contemporary.

How to Contact Query with SASE, outline, sample chapter(s). Accepts e-mail queries. No fax queries. Considers simultaneous queries. Responds in 1 month to queries. Returns materials only with SASE.

Recent Sales *Two Lives*, by Vikram Seth; *Don't Get Too Comfortable*, by David Rakoff (Doubleday); *The Pieces from Berlin*, by Michael Pye (Knopf).

Terms Agent receives 15% commission on domestic sales; 20% commission on foreign sales. Sometimes offers criticism service. Charges for international postage, photocopying over 40 pages.

☑ STEELE-PERKINS LITERARY AGENCY

26 Island Lane, Canandaigua NY 14424. (585)396-9290. Fax: (585)396-3579. E-mail: pattiesp@aol.com. **Contact:** Pattie Steele-Perkins. Member of AAR, RWA. Currently handles: 100% Romance and mainstream women's fiction.

Represents Novels. **Considers these fiction areas:** Mainstream/contemporary; multicultural; romance; women's.

o— Actively seeking romance, women's fiction, and multicultural works.

How to Contact Submit outline, 3 sample chapter(s), SASE. Considers simultaneous queries. Responds in 6 weeks to queries. Returns materials only with SASE. Obtains most new clients through recommendations from others, queries/solicitations.

Recent Sales This agency prefers not to share information on specific sales.

Terms Agent receives 15% commission on domestic sales. Offers written contract, binding for 1 year; 1-month notice must be given to terminate contract.

Writers' Conferences National Conference of Romance Writers of America; Book Expo America Writers' Conferences.

Tips "Be patient. E-mail rather than call. Make sure what you are sending is the best it can be."

☑ WALES LITERARY AGENCY, INC.

P.O. Box 9428, Seattle WA 98109-0428. (206)284-7114. E-mail: waleslit@waleslit.com. Website: www.waleslit.com. **Contact:** Elizabeth Wales, Meg Lemke. Estab. 1988. Member of AAR, Book Publishers' Northwest, Pacific Northwest Booksellers Association, PEN. Represents 65 clients. 10% of clients are new/unpublished writers. Currently handles: 60% nonfiction books; 40% fiction.

● Prior to becoming an agent, Ms. Wales worked at Oxford University Press and Viking Penguin.

Member Agents Elizabeth Wales, Adrienne Reed.

o— This agency specializes in narrative nonfiction, and quality, mainstream and literary fiction. Does not handle screenplays, children's literature, genre fiction, most category nonfiction.

How to Contact Query with cover letter, writing sample (approx. 30 pages), and SASE. No phone or fax queries. Prefers regular mail queries, but accepts 1-page e-mail queries with no attachments. Considers simultaneous queries. Responds in 3 weeks to queries; 6 weeks to mss. Returns materials only with SASE.

Recent Sales *Michelangelo's Mountains*, by Eric Scigliano (Simon & Schuster); *In Praise of Small Things*, by Lynda Lynn Haupt (Little, Brown & Co.); *Against Gravity*, by Farnoosh Moshini (Penguin).

Terms Agent receives 15% commission on domestic sales; 20% commission on foreign sales.

Writers' Conferences Pacific NW Writers Conference (Seattle); Writers at Work (Salt Lake City); Writing Rendezvous (Anchorage); Willamette Writers (Portland).

Tips "Especially interested in work that espouses a progressive cultural or political view, projects a new voice, or simply shares an important, compelling story. Encourages writers living in the Pacific Northwest, West Coast, Alaska, and Pacific Rim countries, and writers from historically underrepresented groups, such as gay and lesbian writers and writers of color, to submit work (but does not discourage writers outside these areas). Most importantly, whether in fiction or nonfiction, the agency is looking for talented storytellers."

☑ LYNN WHITTAKER, LITERARY AGENT

Graybill & English, LLC, 1875 Connecticut Ave. NW, Suite 712, Washington DC 20009. (202)588-9798, ext. 127. Fax: (202)457-0662. E-mail: lynnwhittaker@aol.com. Website: www.graybillandenglish.com. Estab. 1998. Member of AAR. Represents 24 clients. 10% of clients are new/unpublished writers. Currently handles: 80% nonfiction books; 20% novels.

● Prior to becoming an agent, Ms. Whittaker was an editor, owner of a small press, and taught at the college level.

Represents Nonfiction books, novels. **Considers these nonfiction areas:** Animals; biography/autobiography; current affairs; ethnic/cultural interests; health/medicine; history; memoirs; money/finance; multicultural; nature/environment; popular culture; science/technology; sports; women's issues/studies. **Considers these fiction areas:** Detective/police/crime; ethnic; historical; literary; multicultural; mystery/suspense; sports.

O→ "As a former editor, I especially enjoy working closely with writers to polish their proposals and manuscripts." Actively seeking literary fiction, sports, history, mystery/suspense. Does not want to receive romance/women's commercial fiction, children's/young adult, religious, fantasy/horror.

How to Contact Query with SASE, submit proposal package, outline, 2 sample chapter(s). Responds in 2 weeks to queries; 1 month to mss. Returns materials only with SASE. Obtains most new clients through recommendations from others.

Recent Sales *O' Artful Death* (mystery), by Sarah Stewart Taylor (St. Martin's); *The Cincinnati Arch*, by John Tallmadge (University of Georgia Press); *Leadership the Katherine Graham Way*, by Robin Gerber (Portfolio/Penguin Putnam). Other clients include Michael Wilbon, Mariah Burton Nelson, Leonard Shapiro, Phyllis George, Dorothy Sucher, James McGregor Burns, Susan McCullough.

Terms Agent receives 15% commission on domestic sales; 20% commission on foreign sales. Offers written contract; 1-month notice must be given to terminate contract. Direct expenses for photocopying of proposals and mss, UPS/FedEx.

Writers' Conferences Creative Nonfiction Conference, (Goucher College MD, August); Washington Independent Writers, (Washington DC, May); Hariette Austin Writers Conference, (Athens GA, July); Boucheron (various cities).

◢ WRITERS HOUSE

21 W. 26th St., New York NY 10010. (212)685-2400. Fax: (212)685-1781. Estab. 1974. Member of AAR. Represents 440 clients. 50% of clients are new/unpublished writers. Currently handles: 25% nonfiction books; 40% novels; 35% juvenile books.

Member Agents Albert Zuckerman (major novels, thrillers, women's fiction, important nonfiction); Amy Berkower (major juvenile authors, women's fiction, art and decorating, psychology); Merrilee Heifetz (quality children's fiction, science fiction and fantasy, popular culture, literary fiction); Susan Cohen (juvenile and YA fiction and nonfiction, Judaism, women's issues); Susan Ginsburg (serious and popular fiction, true crime, narrative nonfiction, personality books, cookbooks); Michele Rubin (serious nonfiction); Robin Rue (commercial fiction and nonfiction, YA fiction); Jennifer Lyons (literary, commercial fiction, international fiction, nonfiction, and illustrated); Jodi Reamer (juvenile and YA fiction and nonfiction, adult commercial fiction, popular culture); Simon Lipskar (literary and commercial fiction, narrative nonfiction); Nicole Pitesa (juvenile and YA fiction, literary fiction); Steven Malk (juvenile and YA fiction and nonfiction).

Represents Nonfiction books, novels, juvenile books. **Considers these nonfiction areas:** Animals; art/architecture/design; biography/autobiography; business/economics; child guidance/parenting; cooking/foods/nutrition; health/medicine; history; interior design/decorating; juvenile nonfiction; military/war; money/finance; music/dance; nature/environment; psychology; science/technology; self-help/personal improvement; theater/film; true crime/investigative; women's issues/studies. **Considers these fiction areas:** Action/adventure; comic books/cartoon; confession; contemporary issues; detective/police/crime; erotica; ethnic; experimental; family saga; fantasy; feminist; gay/lesbian; glitz; gothic; hi-lo; historical; horror; humor/satire; juvenile; literary; mainstream/contemporary; military/war; multicultural; multimedia; mystery/suspense; New Age; occult; picture books; plays; poetry; poetry in translation; psychic/supernatural; regional; religious/inspirational; romance; science fiction; short story collections; spiritual; sports; thriller; translation; westerns/frontier; young adult; women's.

O→ This agency specializes in all types of popular fiction and nonfiction. Does not want to receive scholarly, professional, poetry, plays, or screenplays.

How to Contact Query with SASE. No e-mail or fax queries. Responds in 1 month to queries. Obtains most new clients through recommendations from others.

Recent Sales Sold 200-300 titles in the last year. *Moneyball*, by Michael Lewis (Norton); *Art of Deception*, by Ridley Pearson (Hyperion); *Report from Ground Zero*, by Dennis Smith (Viking); *The Villa*, by Nora Roberts (Penguin/Putnam); *Captain Underpants*, by Dan Pilkey (Scholastic); *Junie B. Jones*, by Barbara Park (Random House). Other clients include Francine Pascal, Ken Follett, Stephen Hawking, Linda Howard, F. Paul Wilson, Neil Gaiman, Laurel Hamilton, V.C. Andrews, Lisa Jackson.

Terms Agent receives 15% commission on domestic sales; 20% commission on foreign sales. Offers written contract, binding for 1 year. Agency charges fees for copying mss and proposals, and overseas airmail of books.

Tips "Do not send manuscripts. Write a compelling letter. If you do, we'll ask to see your work."

◙ SUSAN ZECKENDORF ASSOC., INC.

171 W. 57th St., New York NY 10019. (212)245-2928. **Contact:** Susan Zeckendorf. Estab. 1979. Member of AAR. Represents 15 clients. 25% of clients are new/unpublished writers. Currently handles: 50% nonfiction books; 50% novels.

• Prior to opening her agency, Ms. Zeckendorf was a counseling psychologist.

Represents Nonfiction books, novels. **Considers these nonfiction areas:** Biography/autobiography; child guidance/parenting; health/medicine; history; music/dance; psychology; science/technology; sociology; women's issues/studies. **Considers these fiction areas:** Detective/police/crime; ethnic; historical; literary; mainstream/contemporary; mystery/suspense; thriller.

O→ Actively seeking mysteries, literary fiction, mainstream fiction, thrillers, social history, parenting, classical music, biography. Does not want to receive science fiction, romance. "No children's books."

How to Contact Query with SASE. No e-mail or fax queries. Considers simultaneous queries. Responds in 10 days to queries; 3 weeks to mss. Returns materials only with SASE.

Recent Sales *How to Write a Damn Good Mystery*, by James N. Frey (St. Martin's); *Moment of Madness*, by Una-Mary Parker (Headline); *The Handscrabble Chronicles* (Berkley); *Something to Live For (The Susan McCorkle Story)* (Northeastern University Press).

Terms Agent receives 15% commission on domestic sales; 20% commission on foreign sales. Charges for photocopying, messenger services.

Writers' Conferences Central Valley Writers Conference; The Tucson Publishers Association Conference; Writer's Connection; Frontiers in Writing Conference (Amarillo TX); Golden Triangle Writers Conference (Beaumont TX); Oklahoma Festival of Books (Claremont OK); SMU Writers Conference (NYC).

Tips "We are a small agency giving lots of individual attention. We respond quickly to submissions."

Book Publishers

The markets in this year's Book Publishers section offer opportunities in nearly every area of publishing. Large, commercial houses are here as are their smaller counterparts.

The **Book Publishers Subject Index** is the best place to start your search. You'll find it in the back of the book, before the General Index. Subject areas for both fiction and nonfiction are broken out for all of the book publisher listings, including Canadian and international publishers and small presses.

When you have compiled a list of publishers interested in books in your subject area, read the detailed listings. Pare down your list by cross-referencing two or three subject areas and eliminating the listings only marginally suited to your book. When you have a good list, send for those publishers' catalogs and manuscript guidelines, or check publishers' websites, which often contain catalog listings, manuscript preparation guidelines, current contact names, and other information helpful to prospective authors. You want to use this information to make sure your book idea is in line with a publisher's list but is not a duplicate of something already published.

You should also visit bookstores and libraries to see if the publisher's books are well represented. When you find a couple of books the house has published that are similar to yours, write or call the company to find out who edited those books. This extra bit of research could be the key to getting your proposal to precisely the right editor.

Publishers prefer different methods of submission on first contact. Most like to see a one-page query with SASE, especially for nonfiction. Others will accept a brief proposal package that might include an outline and/or a sample chapter. Some publishers will accept submissions from agents only. Each listing in the Book Publishers section includes specific submission methods, when provided by the publisher. Make sure you read each listing carefully to find out exactly what the publisher wants to receive.

When you write your one-page query, give an overview of your book, mention the intended audience, the competition for your book (check local bookstore shelves), and what sets your book apart from the competition. You should also include any previous publishing experience or special training relevant to the subject of your book.

Personalize your query by addressing them individually and mentioning what you know about a company from its catalog or books you've seen. Never send a form letter as a query. Envelopes addressed to "Editor" or "Editorial Department" end up in the dreaded slush pile. Under the heading **Acquisitions**, we list the names of editors who acquire new books for each company, along with the editors' specific areas of expertise. Try your best to send your query to the appropriate editor. Editors move around all the time, so it's in your best interest to look online or call the publishing house to make sure the editor you are addressing your query to is still employed by that publisher.

Author-subsidy publishers' not included

Writer's Market is a reference tool to help you sell your writing, and we encourage you to work with publishers that pay a royalty. Subsidy publishing involves paying money to a publishing house to publish a book. The source of the money could be a government, foundation, or university grant, or it could be the author of the book. If one of the publishers listed here offers you an author-subsidy arrangement (sometimes called "cooperative publishing," "co-publishing," or "joint venture"), asks you to pay for part or all of the cost of any aspect of publishing (editing services, manuscript critiques, printing, advertising, etc.), or to guarantee the purchase of any number of the books yourself, we would like you to let us know about that company immediately.

INFORMATION AT-A-GLANCE

There are a number of icons at the beginning of each listing to quickly convey certain information. In the Book Publisher sections, these icons identify new listings (⊞), Canadian markets (⊠), publishers located outside of the U.S. and Canada (⊕), publishers that accept agented submissions only (⊠), and publishers who do not accept unsolicited manuscripts (⊘). Different sections of *Writer's Market* include other symbols; check the back inside cover for an explanation of all the symbols used throughout the book.

How much money? What are my odds?

We've also highlighted important information in boldface, the "quick facts" you won't find in any other market guide but should know before you submit your work. These items include: how many manuscripts a publisher buys per year; how many manuscripts from first-time authors; how many manuscripts from unagented writers; the royalty rate a publisher pays; and how large an advance is offered. Standard royalty rates for paperbacks generally range from $7\frac{1}{2}$ to $12\frac{1}{2}$ percent, for hardcovers from 10 to 15 percent. Royalty rates for children's books are often lower, generally ranging from 5 to 10 percent; 10 percent for picture books (split between the author and the illustrator).

Publishers, their imprints, and how they are related

In this era of big publishing—and big mergers—the world of publishing has grown even more intertwined. A "family tree" on page 90 lists the imprints and divisions of the largest conglomerate publishers.

Keep in mind that most of the major publishers listed in this family tree do not accept unagented submissions or unsolicited manuscripts. You will find many of these publishers and their imprints listed within the Book Publishers section, and many contain only basic contact information. If you are interested in pursuing any of these publishers, we advise you to see each publisher's website for more information.

For a list of publishers according to their subjects of interest, see the Nonfiction and Fiction sections of the Book Publishers Subject Index. Information on book publishers listed in the previous edition of *Writer's Market*, but not included in this edition, can be found in the General Index.

[N] ABDO PUBLISHING CO.

4940 Viking Dr., Edina MN 55435. (952)831-1317. Fax: (952)831-1632. E-mail: info@abdopub.com. Website: www.abdopub.com. **Acquisitions:** Paul Abdo, editor-in-chief. Publishes hardcover originals. **Publishes 200 titles/year; imprint publishes 50 titles/year. Receives 300 queries and 100 mss/year. 5% of books from first-time authors; 100% from unagented writers. Makes outright purchase of $700-1,500.**
Imprints ABDO & Daughters, Buddy Books, Checkerboard Library, SandCastle.

    O⌐ ABDO publishes nonfiction children's books (pre-kindergarten to 6th grade) for school and public libraries—mainly history, sports, and biography.

Nonfiction Biography, children's/juvenile, how-to. Subjects include animals, history, sports. Query with SASE.
Recent Title(s) *Lewis and Clark*, by John Hamilton (children's nonfiction); *Tiger Woods*, by Paul Joseph (children's biography).

ABI PROFESSIONAL PUBLICATIONS

P.O. Box 149, St. Petersburg FL 33731. (727)556-0950. Fax: (727)556-2560. E-mail: abipropub@vandamere.com. Website: www.abipropub.com. **Acquisitions:** Art Brown, publisher/editor-in-chief (prosthetics, rehabilitation, dental/medical research). Publishes hardcover and trade paperback originals. **Publishes 10 titles/year. Receives 20-30 queries and 5-10 mss/year. 25% of books from first-time authors; 100% from unagented writers. Pays royalty on revenues generated. Offers small advance.** Publishes book 1 + years after acceptance of ms. Accepts simultaneous submissions. Responds in 6 months to queries.

    ● No registered, certified, return-receipt submissions accepted.

Nonfiction Reference, technical, textbook. Subjects include health/medicine. Submit proposal package including outline, representative sample chapter(s), author bio, or submit complete ms. Reviews artwork/photos as part of ms package. Send photocopies.
Recent Title(s) *Cleft Palate Dentistry*, by Robert McKinstry (dental text); *Managing Stroke*, by Paul R. Rao and John E. Toerge (rehabilitation).
Tips Audience is allied health professionals, dentists, researchers, patients undergoing physical rehabilitation. "We will not review electronic submissions."

ABINGDON PRESS

Imprint of The United Methodist Publishing House, 201 Eighth Ave. S., Nashville TN 37203. (615)749-6000. Fax: (615)749-6512. Website: www.abingdonpress.com. President/Publisher: Neil M. Alexander. Senior Vice President/Publishing: Harriett Jane Olson. **Acquisitions:** Robert Ratcliff, senior editor (professional clergy and academic); Peg Augustine, editor (children's); Ron Kidd, senior editor (general interest). Estab. 1789. Publishes hardcover and paperback originals; church supplies. **Publishes 120 titles/year. Receives 3,000 queries and 250 mss/year. Small% of books from first-time authors; 85% from unagented writers. Pays 7½% royalty on retail price.** Publishes book 2 years after acceptance of ms. Does not accept simultaneous submissions. Responds in 2 months to queries. Book catalog free; ms guidelines online.
Imprints Dimensions for Living, Cokesbury, Abingdon Press.

    O⌐ Abingdon Press, America's oldest theological publisher, provides an ecumenical publishing program dedicated to serving the Christian community—clergy, scholars, church leaders, musicians, and general readers—with quality resources in the areas of Bible study, the practice of ministry, theology, devotion, spirituality, inspiration, prayer, music and worship, reference, Christian education, and church supplies.

Nonfiction Children's/juvenile, gift book, reference, textbook, religious-lay, and professional, scholarly. Subjects include education, music/dance, religion. Query with outline and samples only.
Recent Title(s) *The Delany Sisters Reach High*, by Hearth (children's); *What Do Other Faiths Believe?*, by Stroble; *What About the Soul? Neuroscience and Christian Anthropology*, by Green.

HARRY N. ABRAMS, INC.

La Martiniere Groupe, 100 Fifth Ave., New York NY 10011. (212)206-7715. Fax: (212)645-8437. E-mail: submissions@abramsbooks.com. Website: www.abramsbooks.com. President: Steven Parr. **Acquisitions:** Eric Himmel, editor-in-chief. Estab. 1949. Publishes hardcover and "a few" paperback originals. **Publishes 150 titles/year. Pays royalty. Offers variable advance.** Publishes book 2 years after acceptance of ms. Does not accept simultaneous submissions. Responds in 6-8 weeks to queries. Book catalog for $5.

    O⌐ "We publish *only* high-quality illustrated art books, i.e., art, art history, museum exhibition catalogs, written by specialists and scholars in the field."

Nonfiction Illustrated book. Subjects include art/architecture, nature/environment, recreation (outdoor). Requires illustrated material for art and art history, museums. Submit outline, sample chapter(s), illustrations. Reviews artwork/photos as part of ms package.
Tips "We are one of the few publishers who publish almost exclusively illustrated books. We consider ourselves

the leading publishers of art books and high-quality artwork in the U.S. Once the author has signed a contract to write a book for our firm the author must finish the manuscript to agreed-upon high standards within the schedule agreed upon in the contract."

ABSEY & CO.
23011 Northcrest Dr., Spring TX 77389. (281)257-2340. Fax: (281)251-4676. E-mail: abseyandco@aol.com. Website: www.absey.com. **Acquisitions:** Edward Wilson, editor-in-chief. Publishes hardcover, trade paperback, and mass market paperback originals. **Publishes 6-10 titles/year. 50% of books from first-time authors; 50% from unagented writers. Royalty and advance vary.** Publishes book 1 year after acceptance of ms. Does not accept simultaneous submissions. Responds in 3 months to queries; 9 months to mss. Ms guidelines online.

O→ "Our goal is to publish original, creative works of literary merit." Currently emphasizing educational, young adult literature. De-emphasizing self-help.

Nonfiction Subjects include education, language/literature (language arts), general nonfiction. "We will not open anything without a return address. All submissions sent without return or insufficient postage are discarded." Query with SASE.

Fiction Juvenile, mainstream/contemporary, short story collections. "Since we are a small, new press, we are looking for book-length manuscripts with a firm intended audience." Query with SASE.

Poetry Publishes the Writers and Young Writers Series. Interested in thematic poetry collections of literary merit. Query.

Recent Title(s) *Dragonfly*, by Alice McLerran (fiction); *Where I'm From*, by George Ella Lyon (poetry).

Tips "We work closely and attentively with authors and their work." Does not accept e-mail submissions.

ACADEMY CHICAGO PUBLISHERS
363 W. Erie St., Suite 7E., Chicago IL 60610-3125. (312)751-7300. Fax: (312)751-7306. E-mail: info@academychicago.com. Website: www.academychicago.com. **Acquisitions:** Anita Miller, editorial director/senior editor. Estab. 1975. Publishes hardcover originals and trade paperback reprints. **Publishes 10 titles/year. Receives 2,000 submissions/year. Pays 7-10% royalty on wholesale price. Offers modest advance.** Publishes book 18 months after acceptance of ms. Responds in 3 months to queries. Book catalog and ms guidelines online.

O→ "We publish quality fiction and nonfiction. Our audience is literate and discriminating. No novelized biography, history, or science fiction."

Nonfiction Biography. Subjects include history, travel. No religion or self-help. Submit proposal package including outline, 3 sample chapter(s), author bio.

Fiction Historical, mainstream/contemporary, military/war, mystery. "We look for quality work, but we do not publish experimental, avant garde novels." Submit proposal package including 3 sample chapter(s), synopsis.

Recent Title(s) *Letters in the Attic*, by Bonnie Shimko; *Tinder Box: The Iroquois Theatre Disaster 1903*, by Anthony Hatch.

Tips "At the moment, we are looking for good nonfiction; we certainly want excellent original fiction, but we are swamped. No fax queries, no disks. No electronic submissions. We are always interested in reprinting good out-of-print books."

ACE SCIENCE FICTION AND FANTASY
Imprint of The Berkley Publishing Group, Penguin Group (USA), Inc., 375 Hudson St., New York NY 10014. (212)366-2000. Website: www.penguin.com. **Acquisitions:** Anne Sowards, editor; John Morgan, editor. Estab. 1953. Publishes hardcover, paperback, and trade paperback originals and reprints. **Publishes 75 titles/year. Pays royalty. Offers advance.** Publishes book 1-2 years after acceptance of ms. Does not accept simultaneous submissions. Responds in 2 months to queries; 6 months to mss. Ms guidelines for #10 SASE.

O→ Ace publishes science fiction and fantasy exclusively.

Fiction Fantasy, science fiction. No other genre accepted. No short stories. Query first with SASE.

Recent Title(s) *In the King's Service*, by Katherine Kurtz; *All Tomorrow's Parties*, by William Gibson.

ACEN PRESS
DNA Press, P.O. Box 572, Eagleville PA 19408. Fax: (501)694-5495. E-mail: dnapress@yahoo.com. Website: www.dnapress.net. **Acquisitions:** Xela Schenk, operations manager (New Age). Estab. 1998. Publishes trade paperback originals. **Publishes 10 titles/year; imprint publishes 5 titles/year. Receives 500 queries and 400 mss/year. 90% of books from first-time authors; 100% from unagented writers. Pays 10-15% royalty.** Publishes book 4 months after acceptance of ms. Accepts simultaneous submissions. Responds in 6 weeks to mss. Book catalog and ms guidelines free.

O→ Book publisher for young adults, children, and adults.

Nonfiction Children's/juvenile (explaining science), how-to. Subjects include education, science. "We publish books for children which teach scientific concepts as part of the general context; or how-to for adults which carry scientific knowledge and contribute to learning." Submit complete ms. Reviews artwork/photos as part of ms package. Send photocopies.

Fiction Juvenile, science fiction, young adult. "All books should be oriented to explaining science even if they do not fall 100% under the category of science fiction." Submit complete ms.

Recent Title(s) *College Knowledge*; *DNA Array Image Analysis*.

Tips "Quick response, great relationships, high commission/royalty."

ACTA PUBLICATIONS

4848 N. Clark St., Chicago IL 60640-4711. Fax: (773)271-7399. E-mail: actapublications@aol.com. Website: www.actapublications.com. **Acquisitions:** Gregory F. Augustine Pierce. Estab. 1958. Publishes trade paperback originals. **Publishes 12 titles/year. Receives 100 queries and 25 mss/year. 50% of books from first-time authors; 90% from unagented writers. Pays 10-12% royalty on wholesale price.** Publishes book 1 year after acceptance of ms. Does not accept simultaneous submissions. Responds in 1 month to proposals. Book catalog and ms guidelines for #10 SASE.

○→ ACTA publishes nonacademic, practical books aimed at the mainline religious market.

Nonfiction Self-help. Subjects include religion, spirituality. Submit outline, 1 sample chapter(s). Reviews artwork/photos as part of ms package. Send photocopies.

Recent Title(s) *Invitation to Catholicism*, by Alice Camille (religious education); *Protect Us from All Anxiety: Meditations for the Depressed*, by William Burke (self-help).

Tips "Don't send a submission unless you have read our catalog or 1 of our books."

N AD LIB BOOKS, LLC

217 E. Foxwood Dr., Raymore MO 64083. Phone/Fax: (816)331-6160. E-mail: info@adlibbooks.com. Website: www.adlibbooks.com. **Acquisitions:** Julie Henry, publication director (general fiction, all genres). Estab. 2004. Publishes trade paperback originals. **Publishes 12 titles/year. 95% of books from first-time authors; 100% from unagented writers. Pays 7% royalty on wholesale price.** Publishes book 4 months after acceptance of ms. Accepts simultaneous submissions. Responds in 1 month to queries; 3 months to mss. Ms guidelines for #10 SASE or online.

Fiction Adventure, experimental, fantasy, historical, horror, humor, juvenile, literary, mainstream/contemporary, military/war, mystery, romance, science fiction, spiritual, sports, suspense. Query with SASE.

Recent Title(s) *The Spring Habit*, by David Hanson (humor); *A Matter of Time*, by Julie Mears Henry (romance).

ADAMS MEDIA CORP.

57 Littlefield St., Avon MA 02322. (508)427-7100. Fax: (800)872-5628. E-mail: submissions@adamsmedia.com. Website: www.adamsmedia.com. **Acquisitions:** Gary M. Krebs, publishing director; Jill Alexander, editor; Tracy Quinn McLennan, associate editor; Danielle Chiotti, project editor; Kate Epstein, assistant editor; Courtney Nolan, editorial assistant; Bethany Brown, associate editor; Eric Hall, project editor. Estab. 1980. Publishes hardcover originals, trade paperback originals and reprints. **Publishes 160 titles/year. Receives 5,000 queries and 1,500 mss/year. 40% of books from first-time authors; 40% from unagented writers. Pays standard royalty or makes outright purchase. Offers variable advance.** Publishes book 1 year after acceptance of ms. Accepts simultaneous submissions. Responds in 3 months to queries. Ms guidelines online.

○→ Adams Media publishes commercial nonfiction, including self-help, inspiration, women's issues, pop psychology, relationships, business, parenting, New Age, gift books, cookbooks, how-to, reference. Does not return unsolicited materials. Does not accept electronic submissions. Submit outline.

Recent Title(s) *Why Men Love Bitches*, by Sherry Argov; *Small Miracles for the Jewish Heart*, by Yitta Halberstam and Judith Leventhal; *God Is My CEO*, by Larry Julian.

N ADAMS-BLAKE PUBLISHING

8041 Sierra St., Fair Oaks CA 95628. (916)962-9296. Website: www.adams-blake.com. Vice President: Paul Raymond. **Acquisitions:** Monica Blane, senior editor. Estab. 1992. Publishes trade paperback originals and reprints. **Publishes 10-15 titles/year. Receives 150 queries and 90 mss/year. 90% of books from first-time authors; 90% from unagented writers. Pays 10% royalty on wholesale price.** Publishes book 6 months after acceptance of ms. Accepts simultaneous submissions. Responds in 3 months to mss. Ms guidelines online.

○→ Adams-Blake Publishing is looking for business, technology, and finance titles as well as data that can be bound/packaged and sold to specific industry groups at high margins. "We publish technical and training material we can sell to the corporate market. We are especially looking for 'high ticket' items that sell to the corporate market for prices between $100-300." Currently emphasizing technical, computers, technology. De-emphasizing business, management.

Nonfiction How-to, technical. Subjects include business/economics, computers/electronic, health/medicine, money/finance, software. Query with sample chapters or complete ms. Reviews artwork/photos as part of ms package. Send photocopies.

Recent Title(s) *Success From Home,* by Alan Canton.

Tips "We will take a chance on material the big houses reject. Since we sell the majority of our material directly, we can publish material for a very select market. This year we seek niche market material that we can Docutech and sell direct to the corporate sector. Author should include a marketing plan. Sell us on the project!"

ADDICUS BOOKS, INC.

P.O. Box 45327, Omaha NE 68145. (402)330-7493. Website: www.addicusbooks.com. **Acquisitions:** Acquisitions Editor. Estab. 1994. **Publishes 5-10 nonfiction titles/year. 70% of books from first-time authors; 60% from unagented writers. Pays royalty on retail price. Offers advance.** Publishes book 9 months after acceptance of ms. Accepts simultaneous submissions. Responds in 1 month to proposals. Ms guidelines online.

   O→ Addicus Books, Inc. seeks mss with strong national or regional appeal.

Nonfiction How-to, self-help. Subjects include Americana, business/economics, health/medicine, psychology, regional, true crime, true crime. "We are expanding our line of consumer health titles." Query with SASE. Do not send entire ms unless requested. When querying electronically, send only 1-page e-mail, giving an overview of your book and its market. Please do not send attachments unless invited to do so. Additional submission guidelines online.

Recent Title(s) *A Simple Guide to Thyroid Disorders*, by Paul Ruggieri, M.D; *Understanding Lumpectomy—A Guide to Breast Cancer Treatment*, by Rosalind Benedet, R.N. and Mark Rounsaville, M.D.

Tips "We are looking for quick-reference books on health topics. Do some market research to make sure the market is not already flooded with similar books. We're also looking for good true-crime manuscripts, with an interesting story, with twists and turns, behind the crime."

ADIRONDACK MOUNTAIN CLUB, INC.

814 Goggins Rd., Lake George NY 12845-4117. (518)668-4447. Fax: (518)668-3746. E-mail: pubs@adk.org. Website: www.adk.org. **Acquisitions:** John Kettlewell, editor (all titles); Neal Burdick, editor (*Adirondac* magazine, published bimonthly). Publishes hardcover and trade paperback originals and reprints. **Publishes 34 titles/year. Receives 36 queries and 12 mss/year. 95% of books from first-time authors; 95% from unagented writers. Pays 6-10% royalty on retail price. Offers $250-1,000 advance.** Publishes book 1-3 years after acceptance of ms. Does not accept simultaneous submissions. Responds in 3 months to queries; 4 months to proposals; 4 months to mss. Book catalog free and online; ms guidelines free.

   O→ "Our main focus is recreational guides to the Adirondack and Catskill Parks; however, our titles continue to include natural, cultural, and literary histories of these regions. Our main interest is in protecting the resource through environmental education. This is the focus of our magazine, *Adirondac*, as well."

Nonfiction Reference. Subjects include nature/environment, recreation, regional, sports, travel, trail maps. Query with SASE, or submit proposal package including outline, 1-2 sample chapter(s), with proposed illustrations and visuals. Reviews artwork/photos as part of ms package. Send photocopies.

Recent Title(s) *Canoe and Kayak Guide: East-Central New York State; Catskill Day Hikes for All Seasons.*

Tips "Our audience consists of outdoors people interested in muscle-powered recreation, natural history, and 'armchair traveling' in the Adirondacks and Catskills. Bear in mind the educational mandate implicit in our organization's mission. Note range of current ADK titles."

AERONAUTICAL PUBLISHERS

1 Oakglade Circle, Hummelstown PA 17036-9525. (717)566-0468. Fax: (717)566-6423. E-mail: aeronauticalpubs @aol.com. Website: www.aeronauticalpublishers.com. **Acquisitions:** Mike Markowski, publisher; Marjie Markowski, editor-in-chief. Estab. 1981. Publishes trade paperback originals. **Pays variable royalty.** Responds in 2 months to queries. Ms guidelines online.

Imprints American Aeronautical Archives, Aviation Publishers.

   O→ "Our mission is to help people learn more about aviation and model aviation through the written word."

Nonfiction How-to, technical, general. Subjects include history (aviation), hobbies, recreation, radio control, free flight, indoor models, micro radio control, homebuilt aircraft, ultralights, and hang gliders. Prefers submission by e-mail.

Recent Title(s) *Flying Models*, by Don Ross.

Tips "Our focus is on books of short to medium length that will serve the emerging needs of the hobby. We also want to help youth get started, while enhancing everyone's enjoyment of the hobby. We are looking for authors that are passionate about the hobby, and will champion the messages of their books."

AKTRIN FURNITURE INFORMATION CENTER

164 S. Main St., P.O. Box 898, High Point NC 27261. (336)841-8535. Fax: (336)841-5435. E-mail: aktrin@aktrin.c om. Website: www.furniture-info.com. **Acquisitions:** Donna Fincher, director of operations. Estab. 1985. Pub-

lishes trade paperback originals. **Publishes 8 titles/year. Receives 5 queries/year. 20% of books from first-time authors; 20% from unagented writers. Makes outright purchase of $1,500 minimum. Offers $300-600 advance.** Publishes book 2 months after acceptance of ms. Accepts simultaneous submissions. Responds in 1 month to queries. Book catalog free.

Imprints AKTRIN Furniture Information Center-Canada (151 Randall St., Oakville ON L6J 1P5 Canada. (905)845-3474. Contact: Stefan Wille).

> **O→** AKTRIN is a full-service organization dedicated to the furniture industry. "Our focus is on determining trends, challenges, and opportunities, while also identifying problems and weak spots." Currently emphasizing the wood industry.

Nonfiction Reference. Subjects include business/economics. "We are writing only about the furniture industry. Have an understanding of business/economics." Query.

Recent Title(s) *The American Demand for Household Furniture and Trends*, by Thomas McCormick (in-depth analysis of American household furniture market).

Tips Audience is executives of furniture companies (manufacturers and retailers), and suppliers and consultants to the furniture industry.

ALASKA NORTHWEST BOOKS

Graphic Arts Center Publishing, P.O. Box 10306, Portland OR 97296-0306. (503)226-2402. Fax: (503)223-1410. Website: www.gacpc.com. **Acquisitions:** Tricia Brown. Estab. 1959. Publishes hardcover and trade paperback originals and reprints. **Publishes 12 titles/year. Receives hundreds of submissions/year. 10% of books from first-time authors; 90% from unagented writers. Pays 10-14% royalty on net revenues. Buys mss outright (rarely). Offers advance.** Publishes book an average of 2 years after acceptance of ms. Accepts simultaneous submissions. Responds in 6 months to queries. Book catalog for 9 × 12 SAE with 6 first-class stamps; ms guidelines online.

Nonfiction Children's/juvenile, cookbook. Subjects include nature/environment, recreation, sports, travel, Native American culture, adventure, the arts. "All written for a general readership, not for experts in the subject." Submit outline, sample chapter(s).

Recent Title(s) *The Winterlake Lodge Cookbook: Culinary Adventures in the Wilderness*; *Portrait of the Alaska Railroad*; *Big-Enough Anna: The Little Sled Dog Who Braved the Arctic* (children's book).

Tips "Book proposals that are professionally written and polished with a clear understanding of the market, receive our most careful consideration. We are looking for originality. We publish a wide range of books for a wide audience. Some of our books are clearly for travelers, others for those interested in outdoor recreation or various regional subjects. If I were a writer trying to market a book today, I would research the competition (existing books) for what I have in mind, and clearly (and concisely) express why my idea is different and better. I would describe the book buyers (and readers)—where they are, how many of them are there, how they can be reached (organizations, publications), why they would want or need my book."

ALBA HOUSE

2187 Victory Blvd., Staten Island NY 10314-6603. (718)761-0047. Fax: (718)761-0057. E-mail: albabooks@aol.com. Website: www.albahouse.org. **Acquisitions:** Edmund C. Lane, S.S.P., editor. Estab. 1961. Publishes hardcover, trade paperback, and mass market paperback originals. **Publishes 24 titles/year. Receives 300 queries and 150 mss/year. 20% of books from first-time authors; 100% from unagented writers. Pays 7-10% royalty.** Publishes book 9 months after acceptance of ms. Does not accept simultaneous submissions. Responds in 1 month to queries; 1 month to proposals; 2 months to mss. Book catalog and ms guidelines free.

> **O→** Alba House is the North American publishing division of the Society of St. Paul, an International Roman Catholic Missionary Religious Congregation dedicated to spreading the Gospel message.

Nonfiction Manuscripts which contribute, from a Roman Catholic perspective, to the personal, intellectual, and spiritual growth of individuals in the following areas: Scripture, theology and the Church, saints (their lives and teachings), spirituality and prayer, religious life, marriage and family life, liturgy and homily preparation, pastoral concerns, religious education, bereavement, moral and ethical concerns. Reference, textbook. Subjects include education, philosophy, psychology, religion, spirituality. Reviews artwork/photos as part of ms package. Send photocopies.

Recent Title(s) *Fulton J. Sheen*, by Kathleen Riley, Ph.D.

N ALEF DESIGN GROUP

4423 Fruitland Ave., Los Angeles CA 90058. (800)238-6724. Fax: (323)585-0327. Website: www.alefdesign.com. **Acquisitions:** Jane Golub. Estab. 1990. Publishes hardcover and trade paperback originals. **Publishes 25 titles/year; imprint publishes 10 titles/year. Receives 30 queries and 30 mss/year. 80% of books from first-time authors; 100% from unagented writers. Pays 10% royalty. Offers advance.** Publishes book 3 years after acceptance of ms. Does not accept simultaneous submissions. Responds in 6 months to mss. Ms guidelines for 9×12 SAE with 10 first-class stamps.

◯━ The Alef Design Group publishes books of Judaic interest only.

Nonfiction Children's/juvenile, textbook. Subjects include language/literature (Hebrew), religion (Jewish). Query with SASE. Reviews artwork/photos as part of ms package. Send photocopies.

Fiction Juvenile, religious, young adult. "We publish books of Judaic interest only." Query with SASE.

Recent Title(s) *Talmud with Training Wheels* (nonfiction); *Let's Talk About God,* by Dorothy K. Kripke (juvenile nonfiction).

ALEXANDER BOOKS

Imprint of Creativity, Inc., 65 Macedonia Rd., Alexander NC 28701. (828)252-9515. Fax: (828)255-8719. E-mail: sales@abooks.com. Website: www.abooks.com. **Acquisitions:** Pat Roberts, acquisitions editor. Publishes hardcover originals, and trade paperback originals and reprints. **Publishes 15-20 titles/year. Receives 200 queries and 100 mss/year. 10% of books from first-time authors; 75% from unagented writers. Pays royalty on net receipts. Offers rare advance.** Publishes book 18 months after acceptance of ms. Book catalog and ms guidelines online.

Imprints Farthest Star (classic science fiction, very few new titles); Mountain Church (mainline Protestant material).

◯━ Alexander Books publishes mostly nonfiction national titles, both new and reprints.

Nonfiction Biography, how-to, reference, self-help. Subjects include computers/electronic, government/politics, history, regional, religion, travel, collectibles. "We are interested in large, niche markets." Query, or submit 3 sample chapters and proposal package, including marketing plans with SASE. Reviews artwork/photos as part of ms package. Send photocopies.

Fiction Mainstream/contemporary, mystery, regional (Western North Carolina), science fiction, western. "We prefer local or well-known authors or local interest settings." Query with SASE, or submit 3 sample chapter(s), synopsis.

Recent Title(s) *Sanders Price Guide to Autographs, 5th Ed.*, by Sanders and Roberts; *Birthright*, by Mike Resnick.

Tips "Send well-proofed manuscripts in final form. We will not read first rough drafts. Know your market."

ALGONQUIN BOOKS OF CHAPEL HILL

Workman Publishing, P.O. Box 2225, Chapel Hill NC 27515-2225. (919)967-0108. Website: www.algonquin.com. **Acquisitions:** Editorial Department. Publishes hardcover originals. **Publishes 24 titles/year.** query by mail before submitting work. No phone, e-mail or fax queries or submissions. Visit our website for full submission policy to queries. Ms guidelines online.

◯━ Algonquin Books publishes quality literary fiction and literary nonfiction.

ALGORA PUBLISHING

222 Riverside Dr., 16th Floor, New York NY 10025-6809. (212)678-0232. Fax: (212)666-3682. E-mail: editors@algora.com. Website: www.algora.com. **Acquisitions:** Martin DeMers, editor (sociology/philosophy/economics); Claudiu A. Secara, publisher (philosophy/international affairs). Publishes hardcover and trade paperback originals and reprints. **Publishes 25 titles/year. Receives 1,500 queries and 800 mss/year. 20% of books from first-time authors; 85% from unagented writers. Pays 7½-12% royalty on net receipts. Offers $0-1,000 advance.** Publishes book 10 months after acceptance of ms. Accepts simultaneous submissions. Responds in 1 month to queries; 1 month to proposals; 2 months to mss. Book catalog and ms guidelines online; ms guidelines online.

◯━ Algora Publishing is an academic-type press, focusing on works by American, European or Asian authors for the educated general reader.

Nonfiction General nonfiction for the educated reader. Subjects include anthropology/archeology, business/economics, creative nonfiction, education, government/politics, history, language/literature, military/war, money/finance, music/dance, nature/environment, philosophy, psychology, religion, science, sociology, translation, women's issues/studies. Query by e-mail (preferred) or submit proposal package including outline, 3 sample chapters or complete ms.

Recent Title(s) *Soul Snatchers—The Mechanics of Cults*, by Jean-Marie Abgrall (sociology); *Russian Intelligence Services*, by Vladimir Plougin (history).

Tips "We welcome first-time writers; we help them outline their project, crafting an author's raw manuscript into a literary work."

ALL ABOUT KIDS PUBLISHING

117 Bernal Rd. #70, PMB 405, San Jose CA 95119. (408)846-6060. Fax: (408)846-1835. E-mail: lguevara@aakp.com. Website: www.aakp.com. **Acquisitions:** Linda Guevara, editor. Publishes hardcover originals. **Publishes 10-12 titles/year. Receives 250 queries and 7,500 mss/year. 80% of books from first-time authors; 75% from unagented writers. Pays 3-5% royalty. Offers $1,000 advance.** Publishes book 2 years after acceptance

of ms. Accepts simultaneous submissions. Responds in 3 months to mss. Book catalog for $3.50 or on website; ms guidelines online.

Nonfiction Children's/juvenile, cookbook. Subjects include animals, art/architecture, cooking/foods/nutrition, education, ethnic. Submit complete ms. No queries, please. Reviews artwork/photos as part of ms package. Send photocopies.

Fiction Adventure, ethnic, fantasy, humor, juvenile, picture books, young adult. Submit complete ms. No queries please.

ALLWORTH PRESS

10 E. 23rd St., Suite 510, New York NY 10010-4402. Fax: (212)777-8261. E-mail: pub@allworth.com. Website: www.allworth.com. Publisher: Tad Crawford. **Acquisitions:** Nicole Potter, senior editor. Estab. 1989. Publishes hardcover and trade paperback originals. **Publishes 36-40 titles/year. Offers advance.** Does not accept simultaneous submissions. Responds in 1 month to queries; 1 month to proposals. Book catalog and ms guidelines free; ms guidelines online.

O→ Allworth Press publishes business and self-help information for artists, designers, photographers, authors and film and performing artists, as well as books about business, money and the law for the general public. The press also publishes the best of classic and contemporary writing in art and graphic design. Currently emphasizing photography, film, video, music and theater.

Nonfiction How-to, reference. Subjects include art/architecture, business/economics, film/cinema/stage, music/dance, photography, film, television, graphic design, performing arts, writing, as well as business and legal guides for the public. Query.

Recent Title(s) *Citizen Brand*, by Marc Gobé; *Talking Photography*, by Frank Van Riper; *Hollywood Dealmaking*, by Dina Appleton and Daniel Yankelevits.

Tips "We are trying to give ordinary people advice to better themselves in practical ways—as well as helping creative people in the fine and commercial arts."

ALPINE PUBLICATIONS

225 S. Madison Ave., Loveland CO 80537. (970)667-9317. Fax: (970)667-9157. E-mail: alpinepubl@aol.com. Website: alpinepub.com. **Acquisitions:** Ms. B.J. McKinney, publisher. Estab. 1975. Publishes hardcover and trade paperback originals and reprints. **Publishes 6-10 titles/year. 40% of books from first-time authors; 95% from unagented writers. Pays 8-15% royalty on wholesale price. Offers advance.** Publishes book 18 months after acceptance of ms. Accepts simultaneous submissions. Responds in 1-3 months to queries; 1 month to proposals; 1 month to mss. Book catalog free; ms guidelines online.

Imprints Blue Ribbon Books.

Nonfiction How-to, illustrated book, reference. Subjects include animals. "Alpine specializes in books that promote the enjoyment of and responsibility for companion animals with emphasis on dogs and horses." Reviews artwork/photos as part of ms package. Send photocopies.

Recent Title(s) *New Secrets of Successful Show Dog Handling*, by Peter Green and Mario Migliorini (dog); *Training for Trail Horse Classes*, by Laurie Truskauskas (horse); *The Japanese Chin*, by Elisabeth Legl (dogs).

Tips "Our audience is pet owners, breeders, and exhibitors, veterinarians, animal trainers, animal care specialists, and judges. Look up some of our titles before you submit. See what is unique about our books. Write your proposal to suit our guidelines."

AMACOM BOOKS

American Management Association, 1601 Broadway, New York NY 10019-7406. (212)903-8417. Fax: (212)903-8083. Website: www.amanet.org. President and Publisher: Hank Kennedy. **Acquisitions:** Adrienne Hickey, editorial director (management, human resources development, leadership, organizational effectiveness, strategic planning); Ellen Kadin, senior acquisitions editor (marketing, sales, customer service, careers); Jacquie Flynn, executive editor (personal development training, emerging science and technology, self-help, finance); Christina McLaughlin, acquisitions editor (real estate, project management, supply chain management). Estab. 1923. Publishes hardcover and trade paperback originals, professional books in various formats. **Publishes 60-70 titles/year. Receives 800 submissions/year. 50% of books from first-time authors; 70% from unagented writers. Pays 10-15% royalty on net receipts. Offers advance.** Publishes book 6-9 months after acceptance of ms. Responds in 2 months to queries. Book catalog free; ms guidelines online.

O→ Amacom is the publishing arm of the American Management Association, the world's largest training organization for managers and executives. Amacom publishes books on business issues, strategies, and tasks to enhance organizational and individual effectiveness, as well as self-help books for more personal and professional growth, and books on science, current events, history. Currently emphasizing leadership/management skills, real estate, self-help. De-emphasizing small-business management, job-finding, information technology.

Nonfiction Publishes business books of all types, including management, business strategy, organizational effectiveness, sales, marketing, training, technology applications, finance, career, professional skills for retail, direct mail, college, and corporate markets. Publishes books on public policy, science, current events, history, self-help. Query, or submit outline/synopsis, sample chapters, résumé.

Recent Title(s) *The Wright Way*, by Mark Eppler; *eBay the Smart Way, 3rd Ed.*, by Joseph T. Sinclair; *Conquering Consumerspace*, by Michael R. Solomon.

⋈ AMBASSADOR BOOKS, INC.

91 Prescott St., Worcester MA 01605. (508)756-2893. Fax: (508)757-7055. Website: www.ambassadorbooks.c om. **Acquisitions:** Kathryn Conlan, acquisitions editor. Publishes hardcover and trade paperback originals. **Publishes 9 titles/year. Receives 2,000 queries and 100 mss/year. 50% of books from first-time authors; 90% from unagented writers. Pays 8-10% royalty on retail price.** Publishes book 1 year after acceptance of ms. Accepts simultaneous submissions. Responds in 3-4 months to queries. Book catalog free or online at website.

　　⛉ "We are a Christian publishing company looking for books of intellectual and/or spiritual excellence."

Nonfiction Books with a spiritual theme. Biography, children's/juvenile, illustrated book, self-help. Subjects include creative nonfiction, regional, religion, spirituality, sports, Catholic and Christian books. Query with SASE, or submit complete ms. Reviews artwork/photos as part of ms package. Send photocopies.

Fiction Books with a spiritual/religious theme. Juvenile, literary, picture books, religious, spiritual, sports, young adult, women's. Query with SASE, or submit complete ms.

Recent Title(s) *A Farewell to Glory: The Rise and Fall of an Epic Football Rivalry—Boston College vs. Holy Cross*, by Wally Carew; *Stitches*, by Kevin Morrison; *The Man Who Met the King*, by Gerard Goggins.

⋈ AMBER BOOKS PUBLISHING

Imprint of Amber Communications Group, Inc., 1334 E. Chandler Blvd., Suite 5-D67, Phoenix AZ 85048. (480)460-1660. Fax: (480)283-0991. E-mail: amberbk@aol.com. Website: www.amberbooks.com. **Acquisitions:** Tony Rose, publisher (self-help/Career Guides, African-American celebrity bios, novels, etc.); Yvonne Rose, senior editor (African-American fashion, style, etc.). Estab. 1998. Publishes trade paperback and mass market paperback originals. **Publishes 5-10 titles/year. Receives 100-150 queries and 50 mss/year. 80% of books from first-time authors; 100% from unagented writers. Pays 10-15% royalty on wholesale price.** Publishes book 1 year after acceptance of ms. Accepts simultaneous submissions. Responds in 1-2 months to queries. Book catalog free or online.

　　⛉ "Amber Books is the nation's largest African-American publisher of self-help and Career Guide books. In July 2000, the company expanded to include Busta Books, the celebrity bio imprint. In September 2001, Colossus Books emerged as the hot, new imprint, which features world-renowned personalities and history-making topics. Amber/Wiley Books was founded in 2002 as the result of a co-publishing/ imprint deal between John Wiley & Sons, Inc., and Amber Books. January 2003 marked the beginning of Ambrosia Books, the imprint for nonfiction and fiction, novels and docudramas."

Nonfiction Biography (celebrity), children's/juvenile, how-to, self-help, Career Guides. Subjects include fashion/beauty, multicultural, personal finance, relationship advice. Submit proposal or outline with author biography. Please do not e-mail or mail mss unless requested by publisher. Reviews artwork/photos as part of ms package. Send photocopies.

Fiction Historic docudramas. Wants African-American topics and interest. Submit proposal or outline with author biography. Please do not e-mail or mail mss unless requested by publisher. Reviews artwork/photos as part if ms package. Send photocopies.

Recent Title(s) *Fighting for Your Life: The African-American Criminal Justice Survival Guide*, by John V. Elmore, Esq.; *The Afrocentric Bride: A Style Guide*, by Therez Fleetwood; *The African-American Woman's Guide to Great Sex, Happiness and Marital Bliss*, by Jel D. Lewis-Jones.

Tips "The goal of Amber Books is to expand our catalog comprised of self-help books, and celebrity bio books; and expand our fiction department in print and on software, which pertain to, about, and for the African-American population."

AMERICA WEST PUBLISHERS

P.O. Box 2208, Carson City NV 89702-2208. (775)885-0700. Fax: (877)726-2632. E-mail: global@nohoax.com. Website: www.nohoax.com. **Acquisitions:** George Green, president. Estab. 1985. Publishes hardcover and trade paperback originals and reprints. **Publishes 20 titles/year. Receives 150 submissions/year. 90% of books from first-time authors; 90% from unagented writers. Pays 10% royalty on wholesale price. Offers $300 average advance.** Publishes book 6 months after acceptance of ms. Accepts simultaneous submissions. Responds in 1 month to queries. Book catalog and ms guidelines free.

Imprints Bridger House Publishers, Inc.

O→ America West seeks the "other side of the picture," political cover-ups, and new health alternatives.
Nonfiction Subjects include business/economics, government/politics, health/medicine (holistic self-help), New Age, UFO-metaphysical. Submit outline, sample chapter(s). Reviews artwork/photos as part of ms package.

Recent Title(s) *Psychokinesiology*, by Dr. Alec Halub.

Tips "We currently have materials in all bookstores that have areas of UFOs; also political and economic nonfiction."

N AMERICAN ATHEIST PRESS

P.O. Box 5733, Parsippany NJ 07054-6733. (908)276-7300. Fax: (908)276-7402. E-mail: editor@atheists.org. Website: www.atheists.org. **Acquisitions:** Frank Zindler, editor. Estab. 1963. Publishes trade paperback originals and reprints. Publishes quarterly journal, *American Atheist*, for which articles of interest to atheists are needed. **Publishes 12 titles/year. Receives 200 submissions/year. 40-50% of books from first-time authors; 100% from unagented writers. Pays 5-10% royalty on retail price.** Publishes book within 2 years after acceptance of ms. Accepts simultaneous submissions. Responds in 4 months to queries. Book catalog for 6½×9½ SAE; ms guidelines for 9×12 SAE.

Imprints Gustav Broukal Press.

O→ "We are interested in books that will help atheists gain a deeper understanding of atheism, improve their ability to critique religious propaganda, and assist them in fighting to maintain the 'wall of separation between state and church.'" Currently emphasizing the politics of religion, science and religion. De-emphasizing Biblical criticism (but still doing some).

Nonfiction Biography, reference, general. Subjects include general nonfiction, government/politics, history (of religion and atheism, of the effects of religion historically), philosophy (from an atheist perspective, particularly criticism of religion), religion, atheism (particularly the lifestyle of atheism; the history of atheism; applications of atheism. "We would like to see more submissions dealing with the histories of specific religious sects, such as the L.D.S., the Worldwide Church of God, etc." Submit outline, sample chapter(s). Reviews artwork/photos as part of ms package.

Fiction Humor (satire of religion or of current religious leaders), anything of particular interest to atheists. "We rarely publish any fiction. But we have occasionally released a humorous book. No mainstream. For our press to consider fiction, it would have to tie in with the general focus of our press, which is the promotion of atheism and free thought." Submit outline, sample chapter(s).

Recent Title(s) *Living in the Light: Freeing Your Child from the Dark Ages*, by Anne Stone (rearing atheist children); *The Jesus the Jews Never Knew (Against the Historicity of Jesus)*, by Frank R. Zindler.

Tips "We will need more how-to types of material—how to argue with creationists, how to fight for state/church separation, etc. We have an urgent need for literature for young atheists."

AMERICAN BAR ASSOCIATION PUBLISHING

(formerly American Bar Association Book Publishing), 750 N. Lake Shore Dr., Chicago IL 60611. (312)988-5000. Fax: (312)988-6030. Website: www.abanet.org/abapubs/home.html. **Acquisitions:** Adrienne Cook, Esq., director of new product development. Estab. 1878. Publishes hardcover and trade paperback originals. **Publishes 100 titles/year. Receives 50 queries/year. 20% of books from first-time authors; 95% from unagented writers. Pays 5-15% royalty on net receipts.** Publishes book 6 months after acceptance of ms. Accepts simultaneous submissions. Responds in 1 month to queries; 1 month to proposals; 3 months to mss. Book catalog and ms guidelines on website; ms guidelines online.

O→ "We are interested in books that will help lawyers practice law more effectively whether it's help in handling clients, structuring a real estate deal or taking an antitrust case to court."

Nonfiction All areas of legal practice. How-to (in the legal market), reference, technical. Subjects include business/economics, computers/electronic, money/finance, software, legal practice. "Our market is not, generally, the public. Books need to be targeted to lawyers who are seeking solutions to their practice problems. We rarely publish scholarly treatises." Query with SASE.

Recent Title(s) *The Attorney-Client Privilege and the Work-Product Doctrine*; *A Practical Guide to Real Estate Transactions*; *The Spine at Trial*.

Tips "ABA books are written for busy, practicing lawyers. The most successful books have a practical, reader-friendly voice. If you can build in features like checklists, exhibits, sample contracts, flow charts, and tables of cases, please do so." The Association also publishes over 50 major national periodicals in a variety of legal areas. Contact Kathleen Welton, director of book publishing, at the above address for guidelines.

N AMERICAN CHEMICAL SOCIETY

Publications/Books Division, 1155 16th St. NW, Washington DC 20036. (202)452-2120. Fax: (202)452-8913. E-mail: b_hauserman@acs.org. Website: pubs.acs.org/books/. **Acquisitions:** Bob Hauserman, acquisitions editor. Estab. 1876. Publishes hardcover originals. **Publishes 35 titles/year. Pays royalty.** Accepts simultaneous submissions. Responds in 2 months to proposals. Book catalog free; ms guidelines online.

O→ American Chemical Society publishes symposium-based books for chemistry.

Nonfiction Technical, semi-technical. Subjects include science. "Emphasis is on meeting-based books."

Recent Title(s) *Infrared Analysis of Peptides and Proteins*, edited by Singh.

AMERICAN CORRECTIONAL ASSOCIATION

4380 Forbes Blvd., Lanham MD 20706. (301)918-1800. Fax: (301)918-1886. E-mail: aliceh@aca.org. Website: www.corrections.com/aca. **Acquisitions:** Alice Heiserman, manager of publications. Estab. 1870. Publishes hardcover and trade paperback originals. **Publishes 18 titles/year. Receives 40 submissions/year. 90% of books from first-time authors; 100% from unagented writers. Pays 10% royalty on net receipts.** Publishes book 1 year after acceptance of ms. Responds in 4 months to queries. Book catalog free; ms guidelines online.

O→ American Correctional Association provides practical information on jails, prisons, boot camps, probation, parole, community corrections, juvenile facilities and rehabilitation programs, substance abuse programs, and other areas of corrections.

Nonfiction "We are looking for practical, how-to texts or training materials written for the corrections profession." How-to, reference, technical, textbook, correspondence courses. Subjects include corrections and criminal justice. No autobiographies or true-life accounts by current or former inmates or correctional officers, theses, or dissertations. No fiction or poetry. Query with SASE. Reviews artwork/photos as part of ms package.

Recent Title(s) *Working with Women Offenders in Correctional Institutions*, by Dr. Joann Brown Morton; *The Full Spectrum: Essays on Staff Diversity in Corrections*, edited by Carla Smalls; *Recess is Over: Managing Youthful Offenders in Adult Correctional Systems*, by Barry Glick, Ph.D., William Sturgeon.

Tips Authors are professionals in the field and corrections. "Our audience is made up of corrections professionals and criminal justice students. No books by inmates or former inmates." This publisher advises out-of-town freelance editors, indexers, and proofreaders to refrain from requesting work from them.

AMERICAN COUNSELING ASSOCIATION

5999 Stevenson Ave., Alexandria VA 22304-3300. (703)823-9800. **Acquisitions:** Carolyn C. Baker, director of publications. Estab. 1952. Publishes paperback originals. **Publishes 10-15 titles/year. Receives 75 submissions/year. 5% of books from first-time authors; 90% from unagented writers. Pays 10-15% royalty on net receipts.** Publishes book 7 months after acceptance of ms. Accepts simultaneous submissions. Responds in 2 months to queries; 2 months to proposals; 4 months to mss. Ms guidelines free.

O→ The American Counseling Association is dedicated to promoting public confidence and trust in the counseling profession. "We publish scholarly texts for graduate level students and mental health professionals. We do not publish books for the general public."

Nonfiction Reference, scholarly, textbook (for professional counselors). Subjects include education, gay/lesbian, health/medicine, multicultural, psychology, religion, sociology, spirituality, women's issues/studies. ACA does not publish self-help books or autobiographies. Query with SASE, or submit proposal package including outline, 2 sample chapter(s), vitae.

Recent Title(s) *Assessment in Counseling, 3rd Ed.*, by Albert Hood and Richard Johnson; *Documentation in Counseling Records, 2nd Ed.*, by Robert Mitchell.

Tips "Target your market. Your books will not be appropriate for everyone across all disciplines."

AMERICAN FEDERATION OF ASTROLOGERS

6535 S. Rural Rd., Tempe AZ 85283. (480)838-1751. Fax: (480)838-8293. E-mail: afa@msn.com. Website: www.astrologers.com. **Acquisitions:** Kris Brandt Riske, publications manager. Estab. 1938. Publishes trade paperback originals and reprints. **Publishes 10-15 titles/year. Receives 10 queries and 20 mss/year. 50% of books from first-time authors; 100% from unagented writers. Pays 10% royalty. Offers advance.** Publishes book 10 months after acceptance of ms. Accepts simultaneous submissions. Responds in 6 months to mss. Book catalog for $2; ms guidelines free.

O→ American Federation of Astrologers publishes astrology books, calendars, charts, and related aids.

Nonfiction Subjects include astrology. Submit complete ms.

Recent Title(s) *The Vertex*, by Donna Henson.

AMERICAN PRESS

28 State St., Suite 1100, Boston MA 02109. (617)247-0022. **Acquisitions:** Jana Kirk, editor. Estab. 1911. Publishes college textbooks. **Publishes 25 titles/year. Receives 350 queries and 100 mss/year. 50% of books from first-time authors; 90% from unagented writers. Pays 5-15% royalty on wholesale price.** Publishes book 9 months after acceptance of ms. Does not accept simultaneous submissions. Responds in 3 months to queries.

Book Publishers

Nonfiction Technical, textbook. Subjects include agriculture/horticulture, anthropology/archeology, art/architecture, business/economics, education, government/politics, health/medicine, history, music/dance, psychology, science, sociology, sports. "We prefer that our authors actually teach courses for which the manuscripts are designed." Query, or submit outline with tentative table of contents. No complete mss.

Recent Title(s) *Athletic Administration*, by Wm. F. Stier, Jr.; *Business Law 2e*, by Frank Shaw; *Programming in C++*, by A. Ebrahimi.

AMERICAN QUILTER'S SOCIETY

Schroeder Publishing, P.O. Box 3290, Paducah KY 42002-3290. (270)898-7903. Fax: (270)898-1173. E-mail: editor@aqsquilt.com. Website: www.aqsquilt.com. **Acquisitions:** Barbara Smith, executive book editor (primarily how-to and patterns, but other quilting books sometimes published). Estab. 1984. Publishes hardcover and trade paperback originals. **Publishes 20 titles/year. Receives 300 queries/year. 60% of books from first-time authors; 100% from unagented writers. Pays 5% royalty on retail price.** Publishes book 11 months after acceptance of ms. Accepts simultaneous submissions. Responds in same day to queries; 2 months to proposals. Book catalog and ms guidelines free; ms guidelines online.

    O-π American Quilter's Society publishes how-to and pattern books for quilters (beginners through intermediate skill level).

Nonfiction Coffee table book, how-to, reference, technical (about quilting). Subjects include creative nonfiction, hobbies (about quilting). Query with SASE, or submit proposal package including outline, 2 sample chapter(s), photos and patterns (if available). Reviews artwork/photos as part of ms package. Send photocopies; slides and drawings are also acceptable for a proposal.

Recent Title(s) *Guide to Machine Quilting*, by Diane Gaudynski; *Quiltscapes*, by Rebecca Barker; *Birds and Flowers Album*, by Bea Oglesby.

AMERICAN SOCIETY FOR TRAINING AND DEVELOPMENT

1640 King St., Alexandria VA 22313. (800)628-2783. Fax: (703)683-9591. E-mail: mmorrow@astd.org. Website: www.astd.org. **Acquisitions:** Mark Morrow, manager ASTD Press (acquisitions and development). Estab. 1944. Publishes trade paperback originals. **Publishes 10-12 titles/year. Receives 50 queries and 25-50 mss/year. 25% of books from first-time authors; 99% from unagented writers. Pays 10% royalty on net receipts. Offers $500-1,000 advance.** Publishes book up to 1 year after acceptance of ms. Accepts simultaneous submissions. Responds in 1 month to queries; 1 month to proposals; 1 month to mss. Book catalog and ms guidelines free.

Nonfiction Trade books for training and performance improvement professionals. Subjects include training and development. Submit proposal package including outline, 1 sample chapter(s). Reviews artwork/photos as part of ms package.

Recent Title(s) *Leading E-Learning*, by William Horton; *Training on the Job*, by Diane Walter; *Return on Investment, Vol. 3*, by Jack Phillips.

Tips Audience includes training professionals including frontline trainers, training managers and executives; performance professionals, including performance consultants; organizational development and human resource development professionals. "Send a good proposal targeted to our audience providing how-to advice that readers can apply now!"

AMERICAN WATER WORKS ASSOCIATION

6666 W. Quincy Ave., Denver CO 80235. (303)794-7711. Fax: (303)794-7310. E-mail: cmurcray@awwa.org. Website: www.awwa.org. **Acquisitions:** Colin Murcray, senior acquisitions editor. Estab. 1881. Publishes hardcover and trade paperback originals. **Publishes 100 titles/year. Receives 200 queries and 35 mss/year. 30% of books from first-time authors; 100% from unagented writers. Pays 15% royalty on wholesale or retail price.** Publishes book 1 year after acceptance of ms. Does not accept simultaneous submissions. Responds in 4 months to queries. Book catalog and ms guidelines free.

    O-π AWWA strives to advance and promote the safety and knowledge of drinking water and related issues to all audiences—from kindergarten through post-doctorate.

Nonfiction Subjects include nature/environment, science, software, drinking water-related topics. Query with SASE, or submit outline, 3 sample chapter(s), author bio. Reviews artwork/photos as part of ms package. Send photocopies.

Recent Title(s) *The Evolving Water Utility*, by Gary Westerhoff, et. al.

AMERICANA PUBLISHING, INC.

303 San Mateo N.E., Suite 104 A, Albuquerque NM 87108. (505)265-6121. Fax: (505)255-6189. E-mail: editor@americanabooks.com. Website: www.americanabooks.com. **Acquisitions:** Managing Editor. Publishes audiobooks, most previously published in print, and a few trade paperbacks. **Publishes 150 + titles/year. Receives**

500+ queries and 300+ mss/year. 5% of books from first-time authors; 50% from unagented writers. Pays 10% royalty. Publishes book 1-2 years after acceptance of ms. Accepts simultaneous submissions. Responds in 6 months to queries; 6 months to proposals; 6 months to mss. Book catalog online; ms guidelines by e-mail.

Fiction Adventure, fantasy (space fantasy), historical, military/war, mystery (amateur, sleuth, cozy, police procedural, private eye/hardboiled), science fiction, western. Does not accept short stories. Prefer 30,000-60,000 words. Prefer series. Does not want nonfiction, children's, poetry, sexually explicit (soft or hard porn), autobiographies, juvenile, gratuitous violence. Query with SASE, or submit 2 sample chapter(s). E-mail queries accepted as well.

Tips "Publish samples online."

AMG PUBLISHERS

6815 Shallowford Rd., Chattanooga TN 37421-1755. (423)894-6060. Fax: (423)894-9511. E-mail: danp@amginte rnational.org. Website: www.amgpublishers.com. **Acquisitions:** Dr. Warren Baker, senior editor; Richard Steele, Jr., associate editor; Dan Penwell, manager of product development and acquisitions. Publishes hardcover and trade paperback originals and reprints, and mass market paperback and electronic originals. **Publishes 35 titles/year; imprint publishes 15 titles/year. Receives 1,000 queries and 500 mss/year. 20% of books from first-time authors; 50% from unagented writers. Pays 10-16% royalty on wholesale price.** Publishes book 9-12 months after acceptance of ms. Accepts simultaneous submissions. Responds in 1 week to queries; 4 months to proposals; 4 months to mss. Book catalog and ms guidelines online.

Imprints Living Ink.

Nonfiction Reference, textbook, workbook, Bibles, commentaries. Looking for books that facilitate interaction with Bible, encourage and facilitate spiritual growth. Subjects include Christian living, women's, men's, and family issues, single and divorce issues, devotionals, inspirationals, prayer, contemporary issues, Biblical reference, applied theology and apologetics, Christian ministry and Bible study in the Following God Series format. Note our Following God Series (www.followinggod.com) covers a variety of Bible study topics. This Bible study is designed in an interactive format. Prefer queries by e-mail.

Recent Title(s) *Hungry for More God*, by Dr. Rob Currie; *Dear God Send Me a Soul Mate*, by Rose Sweet; *A Guide Book for New Believers*, by Bette Nordberg.

Tips "The AMG readership consists largely of adults involved in personal Bible study. We rarely accept books outside of our current genres, so be sure what you're submitting will fit in with our current works."

AMHERST MEDIA, INC.

175 Rano St., Suite 200, Buffalo NY 14207. (716)874-4450. Fax: (716)874-4508. E-mail: amherstmed@aol.com. Website: www.AmherstMedia.com. **Acquisitions:** Craig Alesse, publisher. Estab. 1974. Publishes trade paperback originals and reprints. **Publishes 30 titles/year. Receives 100 submissions/year. 60% of books from first-time authors; 90% from unagented writers. Pays 6-8% royalty on retail price. Offers advance.** Publishes book 1 year after acceptance of ms. Accepts simultaneous submissions. Responds in 2 months to queries. Book catalog and ms guidelines free.

O╍ Amherst Media publishes how-to photography books.

Nonfiction How-to. Subjects include photography. "Looking for well-written and illustrated photo books." Query with outline, 2 sample chapters, and SASE. Reviews artwork/photos as part of ms package.

Recent Title(s) *Portrait Photographer's Handbook*, by Bill Hurter.

Tips "Our audience is made up of beginning to advanced photographers. If I were a writer trying to market a book today, I would fill the need of a specific audience and self-edit in a tight manner."

THE AMWELL PRESS

P.O. Box 5385, Clinton NJ 08809-0385. (908)638-9033. Fax: (908)638-4728. President: James Rikhoff. Corporate Secretary: Genevieve Symonds. **Acquisitions:** Monica Sullivan, vice president. Estab. 1976. Publishes hardcover originals. **Publishes 4 titles/year.** Publishes book 18 months after acceptance of ms. Responds in 2 months to queries.

O╍ The Amwell Press publishes hunting and fishing nonfiction, but not how-to books on these subjects.

Nonfiction Subjects include hunting and fishing stories/literature (not how-to). Mostly limited editions. No fiction. Query with SASE.

Recent Title(s) *Handy to Home*, by Tom Hennessey; *Beyond Hill Country*, by Rikhoff and Sullivan; *Timber and Tide*, by Bob Elman.

ANCHORAGE PRESS PLAYS, INC.

P.O. Box 2901, Louisville KY 40201. (502)583-2288. Fax: (502)583-2281. E-mail: applays@bellsouth.net. Website: www.applays.com. **Acquisitions:** Marilee Miller, publisher. Estab. 1935. Publishes hardcover and trade paperback originals. **Publishes up to 10 titles/year. Receives 45-90 submissions/year. 50% of books from** first-time authors; 80% from unagented writers. **Pays 10-15% royalty. Playwrights also receive 50-75% royalties.** Publishes book 1-2 years after acceptance of ms. Accepts simultaneous submissions. Responds in 6 months to mss. Book catalog and ms guidelines online.

○┅ "We are an international agency for plays for young people. First in the field since 1935."

Nonfiction Textbook, plays. Subjects include education, theater, child drama, plays. "We are looking for texts for teachers of drama/theater." Query. Reviews artwork/photos as part of ms package.

Recent Title(s) *Curtain Time is Magic Time*, by Michael H. Hibbard; *The Rose of Treason*, by James DeVita; *The Pied Piper of Hamelin*, by Tim Wright.

WILLIAM ANDREW, INC.

(formerly William Andrew/Noyes Publishing), 13 Eaton Ave., Norwich NY 13815. (607)337-5000. Fax: (607)337-5090. E-mail: editorial@williamandrew.com. Website: www.williamandrew.com. **Acquisitions:** Millicent Treloar, senior editor. Estab. 1989. Publishes hardcover originals. **Publishes 15 titles/year. 100% from unagented writers.** Publishes book 1 year after acceptance of ms. Accepts simultaneous submissions. Book catalog online.

○┅ William Andrew, Inc., publishes post-baccalaureate book and database references for practicing scientists and engineers. Currently emphasizing advanced materials for food science, materials science and process technologies, plastics and polymers.

Nonfiction Reference, scholarly, technical. Subject areas include nanotechnology, industrial processing, formulations, applied chemistry (coatings, adhesives, solvents, industrial cleaning products, food ingredients, personal care products), water treatment, safety, semiconductors. Submit outline with book propsal, SASE. Reviews artwork/photos as part of ms package. Send photocopies.

Recent Title(s) *Nanostructured Materials*, by Koch; *Handbook of Molded Part Shrinkage and Warpage*, by Fischer; *Fluoroplastics, Volumes 1 and 2*, by Ebnesajjad.

Ⓐ ANDREWS McMEEL UNIVERSAL

4520 Main St., Kansas City MO 64111-7701. (816)932-6700. **Acquisitions:** Christine Schillig, vice president/editorial director. Estab. 1973. Publishes hardcover and paperback originals. **Publishes 200 titles/year. Pays royalty on retail price, or net receipts. Offers advance.**

○┅ Andrews McMeel publishes general trade books, humor books, miniature gift books, calendars, and stationery products.

Nonfiction How-to, humor, inspirational. Subjects include contemporary culture, general trade, relationships. Also produces gift books. *Agented submissions only.*

Recent Title(s) *The Complete Far Side*, by Gary Larsen.

ANKER PUBLISHING CO., INC.

P.O. Box 249, Bolton MA 01740-0249. (978)779-6190. E-mail: info@ankerpub.com. Website: www.ankerpub.com. **Acquisitions:** James D. Anker, president and publisher. Publishes hardcover and paperback professional books. **Publishes 6 titles/year. Pays royalty. Offers advance.** Publishes book 4 months after acceptance of ms. Accepts simultaneous submissions.

○┅ Publishes professional development books for higher education faculty and administrators.

Nonfiction Professional development. Subjects include education. Query with SASE, or submit proposal package including outline, 3 sample chapter(s).

Ⓝ APA BOOKS

American Psychological Association, 750 First St., NE, Washington DC 20002-4242. E-mail: books@apa.org. Website: www.apa.org. Publishes hardcover and trade paperback originals. **Publishes 75 titles/year.** Book catalog and ms guidelines online.

Imprints Magination Press.

Nonfiction Reference, scholarly, textbook, professional. Subjects include education, gay/lesbian, multicultural, psychology, science, social sciences, sociology, women's issues/studies. Submit proposal package including outline, 1-3 sample chapter(s), curriculum vitae of all authors/editors.

Tips "Our press features scholarly books on empirically supported topics for professionals and students in all areas of psychology."

APPALACHIAN MOUNTAIN CLUB BOOKS

5 Joy St., Boston MA 02108. Fax: (617)523-0722. Website: www.outdoors.org. **Acquisitions:** Beth Krusi, publisher/editor. Estab. 1897. Publishes hardcover and trade paperback originals. **Publishes 10-15 titles/year. Receives 100 queries and 30 mss/year. 30% of books from first-time authors; 90% from unagented writers.**

Pays 7-9% royalty on retail price. Offers modest advance. Publishes book 12-18 months after acceptance of ms. Accepts simultaneous submissions. Responds in 3 months to proposals. Ms guidelines online.

○┱ Appalachian Mountain Club publishes hiking guides, paddling guides, nature, conservation, and mountain-subject guides for America's Northeast. "We connect recreation to conservation and education."

Nonfiction Subjects include nature/environment, recreation, regional (Northeast outdoor recreation), literary nonfiction, guidebooks. "Writers should avoid submitting proposals on Appalachia (rural southern mountains)." Query. Accepts electronic submissions. Reviews artwork/photos as part of ms package. Send photocopies or transparencies.

Recent Title(s) *Women on High*; *Northeastern Wilds*; *Outdoor Leadership, White Mountain Guide, 27th Ed.*

Tips "Our audience is outdoor recreationists, conservation-minded hikers and canoeists, family outdoor lovers, armchair enthusiasts. Visit our website for proposal submission guidelines and more information."

A-R EDITIONS, INC.

8551 Research Way, Suite 180, Middleton WI 53562. (608)836-9000. Fax: (608)831-8200. Website: www.areditions.com. **Acquisitions:** Paul L. Ranzini, managing editor (Recent Researches music editions); James L. Zychowicz, managing editor (Computer Music and Digital Audio Series). Estab. 1962. **Publishes 30 titles/year. Receives 40 queries and 30 mss/year. 75% of books from first-time authors; 100% from unagented writers. Pays royalty or honoraria.** Does not accept simultaneous submissions. Responds in 1 month to queries; 3 months to proposals; 6 months to mss. Book catalog and ms guidelines online.

○┱ A-R Editions publishes modern critical editions of music based on current musicological research. Each edition is devoted to works by a single composer or to a single genre of composition. The contents are chosen for their potential interest to scholars and performers, then prepared for publication according to the standards that govern the making of all reliable, historical editions.

Nonfiction Subjects include computers/electronic, music/dance, software, historical music editions. Computer Music and Digital Audio Series titles deal with issues tied to digital and electronic media, and include both textbooks and handbooks in this area. Query with SASE, or submit outline.

Recent Title(s) *Audio Recording Handbook*, by Alan P. Kefauver; *Charles Ives: 129 Songs*, edited by H. Wiley Hitchcock; *Hyperimprovisation*, by Roger Dean.

ARABESQUE

BET Books, 850 Third Ave., 16th Floor, New York NY 10022. (212)407-1500. Website: www.bet.com/books. **Acquisitions:** Karen Thomas, editorial director; Chandra Taylor, consulting editor. Publishes mass market paperback originals. **Publishes 60 titles/year. 30-50% of books from first-time authors; 50% from unagented writers. Pays royalty on retail price, varies by author. Offers varying advance.** Publishes book 18 months after acceptance of ms. Accepts simultaneous submissions. Responds in 3 months to mss. Book catalog for #10 SASE; ms guidelines online.

○┱ Arabesque publishes contemporary romances about African-American couples.

Fiction Multicultural (romance), romance. "Arabesque books must be 85,000-100,000 words in length, and are contemporary genre romances only." Submit proposal package including 3 sample chapter(s), synopsis.

Recent Title(s) *His 1-800 Wife*, by Shirley Hailstock.

Tips "Please do not phone to see if your manuscript was received or returned, or to find out what we thought of it. A self-addressed, stamped postcard can be enclosed with your submission if you want confirmation of its arrival. Specify whether you would like your manuscript returned or recycled if it is not right for us."

ⒶARCADE PUBLISHING

141 Fifth Ave., New York NY 10010. (212)475-2633. Website: www.arcadepub.com. **Acquisitions:** Richard Seaver, president/editor-in-chief; Jeannette Seaver, publisher/executive editor; Cal Barksdale, senior editor; Greg Comer, editor; Darcy Falkerhager, associate editor; Casey Ebro, assistant editor. Estab. 1988. Publishes hardcover originals, trade paperback reprints. **Publishes 45 titles/year. 5% of books from first-time authors. Pays royalty on retail price. 10 author's copies. Offers advance.** Publishes book within 18 months after acceptance of ms. Responds in 1 month to queries. Book catalog and ms guidelines for #10 SASE.

○┱ Arcade prides itself on publishing top-notch literary nonfiction and fiction, with a significant proportion of foreign writers.

Nonfiction Biography, general nonfiction. Subjects include general nonfiction, government/politics, history, nature/environment, travel, popular science. *Agented submissions only*. Reviews artwork/photos as part of ms package. Send photocopies.

Fiction Ethnic, historical, humor, literary, mainstream/contemporary, mystery, short story collections, suspense. No romance, science fiction. *Agented submissions only*.

Recent Title(s) *Black Dahlia Avenger*, by Steve Hodel; *Zelda Fitzgerald*, by Sally Cline; *Nehru*, by Shashi Tharoor.

Ⓝ ARCADIA PUBLISHING

Imprint of Tempus Publishing Group, 420 Wando Park Blvd., Mt. Pleasant SC 29464. (843)853-2070. Fax: (843)853-0044. E-mail: sales@arcadiapublishing.com. Website: www.arcadiapublishing.com. **Acquisitions:** Keith Ulrich, publisher (Midwest and West); Amy Sutton, publisher (North); Christine Riley, publisher (South); Mark Berry, publisher (narrative local history); Jane Elliot, director of publishing. Estab. 1993. Publishes mass market paperback originals. **Publishes 500 titles/year; imprint publishes 350 titles/year. 80% of books from first-time authors; 95% from unagented writers.** Accepts simultaneous submissions. Responds in 1 month to queries. Book catalog and ms guidelines online.

    ○┐ Arcadia publishes photographic regional histories. "We have more than 1,000 in print in our Images of America Series. We have expanded our program to include Midwest and West Coast locations." Currently emphasizing local history, oral history, Civil War history, college histories, African-American history.

Nonfiction Coffee table book, gift book. Subjects include history, military/war, regional, sports, pictorial history, local history, African-American history, postcard history, sports history, college history, oral history, Civil War history, local, national, and regional publications. Query with SASE. Reviews artwork/photos as part of ms package. Send photocopies.

Recent Title(s) *Charleston: Alone Among the Cities*, by The South Carolina Historical Society.

Tips "Writers should know that we only publish history titles. The majority of our books are on a city or region, and are pictorial in nature. We are beginning new series, including oral histories, sports histories, black histories, and college histories."

ARDEN PRESS, INC.

P.O. Box 418, Denver CO 80201-0418. (303)697-6766. Fax: (303)697-3443. **Acquisitions:** Susan Conley, publisher. Estab. 1980. Publishes hardcover and trade paperback originals and reprints. **Publishes 4-6 titles/year. Receives 600 submissions/year. 20% of books from first-time authors; 80% from unagented writers. Pays 8-15% royalty on wholesale price. Offers $2,000 average advance.** Publishes book 6 months after acceptance of ms. Accepts simultaneous submissions. Responds in 2 months to queries. Ms guidelines free.

    ○┐ Arden Press publishes nonfiction on women's history and women's issues. "We sell to general and women's bookstores as well as public and academic libraries. Many of our titles are adopted as texts for use in college courses."

Nonfiction Subjects include women's issues/studies. No personal memoirs or autobiographies. Query with outline/synopsis and sample chapters.

Recent Title(s) *Whatever Happened to the Year of the Woman?*, by Amy Handlin.

Tips "Writers have the best chance selling us nonfiction on women's subjects. If I were a writer trying to market a book today, I would learn as much as I could about publishers' profiles *then* contact those who publish similar works."

ARKANSAS RESEARCH, INC.

P.O. Box 303, Conway AR 72033. (501)470-1120. Fax: (501)470-1120. E-mail: desmond@ipa.net. **Acquisitions:** Desmond Walls Allen, owner. Estab. 1985. Publishes hardcover originals and trade paperback originals and reprints. **Publishes 20 titles/year. 90% of books from first-time authors; 100% from unagented writers. Pays 5-10% royalty on retail price.** Publishes book 6 months after acceptance of ms. Does not accept simultaneous submissions. Responds in 1 month to queries. Book catalog for $1; ms guidelines free.

Imprints Research Associates.

    ○┐ "Our company opens a world of information to researchers interested in the history of Arkansas."

Nonfiction All Arkansas-related subjects. How-to (genealogy), reference, self-help. Subjects include Americana, ethnic, history, hobbies (genealogy), military/war, regional. "We don't print autobiographies or genealogies about 1 family." Query with SASE. Reviews artwork/photos as part of ms package. Send photocopies.

Recent Title(s) *Life & Times from The Clay County Courier Newspaper Published at Corning, Arkansas, 1893-1900.*

ARTE PUBLICO PRESS

University of Houston, 452 Cullen Performance Hall, Houston TX 77204-2004. Fax: (713)743-3080. Website: www.artepublicopress.com. **Acquisitions:** Nicolas Kanellos, editor. Estab. 1979. Publishes hardcover originals, trade paperback originals and reprints. **Publishes 36 titles/year. Receives 1,000 queries and 2,000 mss/year. 50% of books from first-time authors; 80% from unagented writers. Pays 10% royalty on wholesale price. Provides 20 author's copies; 40% discount on subsequent copies. Offers $1,000-3,000 advance.** Publishes book 2 years after acceptance of ms. Accepts simultaneous submissions. Responds in 1 month to queries; 1 month to proposals; 4 months to mss. Book catalog free; ms guidelines online.

Imprints Piñata Books.

○┅ "We are a showcase for Hispanic literary creativity, arts and culture. Our endeavor is to provide a national forum for U.S.-Hispanic literature."
Nonfiction Children's/juvenile, reference. Subjects include ethnic, language/literature, regional, translation, women's issues/studies. Hispanic civil rights issues for new series: The Hispanic Civil Rights Series. Query with SASE, or submit outline, 2 sample chapter(s).
Fiction Ethnic, literary, mainstream/contemporary, written by U.S.-Hispanic authors. Query with SASE, or submit outline/proposal, 2 sample chapter(s), synopsis, or submit complete ms.
Poetry Submit 10 sample poems.
Recent Title(s) *Shadows and Supposes*, by Gloria Vando (poetry); *Home Killings*, by Marcos McPeek Villatoro (mystery); *Message to Aztlár*, by Rodolfo "Corky" Gonzales (Hispanic Civil Rights Series book).

ASA, AVIATION SUPPLIES & ACADEMICS
7005 132nd Pl. SE, Newcastle WA 98059. (425)235-1500. Fax: (425)235-0128. Website: www.asa2fly.com. Director of Operations: Mike Lorden. Editor: Jennifer Trerise. **Acquisitions:** Fred Boyns, controller; Jacqueline Spanitz, curriculum director and technical advisor (pilot and aviation educator). **Publishes 25-40 titles/year. 100% from unagented writers.** Publishes book 9 months or more after acceptance of ms. Does not accept simultaneous submissions. Book catalog free.
○┅ ASA is an industry leader in the development and sales of aviation supplies, publications, and software for pilots, flight instructors, flight engineers and aviation technicians. All ASA products are developed by a team of researchers, authors and editors.
Nonfiction All subjects must be related to aviation education and training. How-to, technical. Subjects include education. "We are primarily an aviation publisher. Educational books in this area are our specialty; other aviation books will be considered." Query with outline. Send photocopies.
Recent Title(s) *The Savvy Flight Instructor: Secrets of the Successful CFI*, by Greg Brown.
Tips "Two of our specialty series include ASA's *Focus Series*, and ASA *Aviator's Library*. Books in our *Focus Series* concentrate on single-subject areas of aviation knowledge, curriculum and practice. The *Aviator's Library* is comprised of titles of known and/or classic aviation authors or established instructor/authors in the industry, and other aviation specialty titles."

ASCE PRESS
(formerly American Society of Civil Engineers Press), 1801 Alexander Bell Dr., Reston VA 20191-4400. (703)295-6275. Fax: (703)295-6278. E-mail: ascepress@asce.org. Website: www.pubs.asce.org. **Acquisitions:** Bernadette Capelle, acquisitions editor. Estab. 1988. **Publishes 15-20 titles/year. 50% of books from first-time authors; 100% from unagented writers. Pays 10% royalty.** Accepts simultaneous submissions. Request ASCE Press book proposal submission guidelines; ms guidelines online.
○┅ ASCE Press publishes technical volumes that are useful to both practicing civil engineers and graduate level civil engineering students. "We publish books by individual authors and editors to advance the civil engineering profession." Currently emphasizing management, construction engineering, geotechnical, hydrology, structural engineering, and bridge engineering. De-emphasizing highly specialized areas with narrow scope.
Nonfiction "We are looking for topics that are useful and instructive to the engineering practitioner." Subjects include civil engineering. Query with outline, sample chapters and cv.
Recent Title(s) *Ten Commandments of Better Contracting*, by Francis T. Hartman; *Managing and Leading: 52 Lessons Learned for Engineers*, by Stuart Walesh, Ph.D.; *Guide to the Use of the Wind Load Provisions of ASCE 7-02*, by Kishor Mehta and James Delahay.
Tips "ASCE Press is a book publishing imprint of ASCE and produces authored and edited applications-oriented books for practicing civil engineers and graduate level civil engineering students. All proposals and manuscripts undergo a vigorous review process."

ASIAN HUMANITIES PRESS
Jain Publishing Co., P.O. Box 3523, Fremont CA 94539. (510)659-8272. Fax: (510)659-0501. E-mail: mail@jainpub.com. Website: www.jainpub.com. **Acquisitions:** M.K. Jain, editor-in-chief. Estab. 1989. Publishes hardcover and trade paperback originals and reprints. **Publishes 6 titles/year. Receives 200 submissions/year. 100% from unagented writers. Pays 5-15% royalty on net receipts.** Publishes book 1-2 years after acceptance of ms. Does not return proposal material. Responds in 3 months to mss. Book catalog and ms guidelines online.
○┅ Asian Humanities Press publishes in the areas of humanities and social sciences pertaining to Asia, commonly categorized as "Asian Studies." Currently emphasizing undergraduate-level textbooks.
Nonfiction Reference, textbook, general trade books. Subjects include language/literature, philosophy, psychology, religion, spirituality, Asian classics, social sciences, art/culture. Submit proposal package including vita, list of prior publications. Reviews artwork/photos as part of ms package. Send photocopies.
Recent Title(s) *Adhidharmasamuccaya*, by Walpola Rahula.

ASM INTERNATIONAL

9639 Kinsman Rd., Materials Park OH 44073-0002. (440)338-5151, ext. 5706. Fax: (440)338-4634. E-mail: sdhenry@asminternational.org. Website: www.asminternational.org. **Acquisitions:** Scott D. Henry, assistant director of reference publications (metallurgy/materials). Publishes hardcover originals. **Publishes 15-20 titles/year. Receives 50 queries and 10 mss/year. 50% of books from first-time authors; 100% from unagented writers. Pays royalty on wholesale price or makes outright purchase.** Does not accept simultaneous submissions. Responds in 1 month to queries; 4 months to proposals; 2 months to mss. Book catalog free or online at website; ms guidelines free.

　O→ "We focus on practical information related to materials selection and processing."

Nonfiction Reference, technical, textbook. Subjects include engineering reference. Submit proposal package including outline, 1 sample chapter(s), author credentials. Reviews artwork/photos as part of ms package. Send photocopies.

Recent Title(s) *Introduction to Aluminum Alloys and Tempers*, by J.G. Kaufman; *Titanium: A Technical Guide, 2nd Ed.*, by M.J. Donachie, Jr.

Tips "Our audience consists of technically trained people seeking practical information on metals and materials to help them solve problems on the job."

ASSOCIATION FOR SUPERVISION AND CURRICULUM DEVELOPMENT

1703 N. Beauregard St., Alexandria VA 22311. (703)575-5693. Fax: (703)575-5400. E-mail: swillis@ascd.org. Website: www.ascd.org. **Acquisitions:** Scott Willis, acquisitions director. Estab. 1943. Publishes trade paperback originals. **Publishes 24-30 titles/year. Receives 100 queries and 100 mss/year. 50% of books from first-time authors; 95% from unagented writers. Pays negotiable royalty on actual monies received.** Publishes book 1 year after acceptance of ms. Accepts simultaneous submissions. Responds in 3 months to proposals. Book catalog and ms guidelines free or online.

　O→ ASCD publishes high-quality professional books for educators.

Nonfiction Subjects include education (for professional educators). Submit outline, 2 sample chapter(s). Reviews artwork/photos as part of ms package. Send photocopies.

Recent Title(s) *Leadership for the Learning: How to Help Students Succeed*, by Carl Glickman; *The Multiple Intelligences of Reading and Writing*, by Thomas Armstrong; *Educating Oppositional and Defiant Children*, by Philip S. Hall, Nancy D. Hall.

ASTRAGAL PRESS

P.O. Box 239, Mendham NJ 07945. (973)543-3045. Fax: (973)543-3044. E-mail: info@astragalpress.com. Website: www.astragalpress.com. Estab. 1983. Publishes hardcover and trade paperback originals and reprints. **Publishes 4-6 titles/year. Receives 50 queries/year. Pays 10% royalty on net receipts.** Publishes book 1 year after acceptance of ms. Does not accept simultaneous submissions. Responds in 1 month to queries. Book catalog and ms guidelines free.

　O→ "Our primary audience includes those interested in collecting and working with old tools (hand tools especially) and working in traditional early trades. We also publish books on railroads."

Nonfiction Books on early tools, trades & technology, and railroads. Query. Send photocopies.

Recent Title(s) *A Field Guide to the Makers of American Wooden Planes*, by Thomas L. Elliott; *A Price Guide to Antique Tools, 3rd Ed.*, by Herbert P. Kean.

Tips "We sell to niche markets. We are happy to work with knowledgeable amateur authors in developing titles."

ATHENOS PUBLISHING

P.O. Box 782054, Wichita KS 67278-2054. E-mail: athenos_info@lycos.com. Website: www.athenospublishing.com. **Acquisitions:** Quinn Aubrey, editor. Estab. 2000. Publishes hardcover and trade paperback originals. **Publishes 5-10 titles/year. 99% of books from first-time authors; 100% from unagented writers. Pays 5-10% royalty on retail price. Offers $500-1,000 advance.** Publishes book 1 year after acceptance of ms. Accepts simultaneous submissions. Responds in 1 month to queries; 2 months to proposals. Book catalog for #10 SASE; ms guidelines online.

Nonfiction Biography, children's/juvenile, self-help. Subjects include alternative lifestyles, anthropology/archeology, community, contemporary culture, creative nonfiction, ethnic, gay/lesbian, general nonfiction, government/politics, history, humanities, multicultural, religion, sex, social sciences, women's issues/studies, world affairs. The current publishing program emphasizes multicultural interests, anthropology, current events, gay/lesbian/gender issues, religious interests and societal concerns, and women's studies/interests. Query with SASE. **All unsolicited mss returned unopened.** Reviews artwork/photos as part of ms package. Send photocopies or If color, send color photocopies.

Recent Title(s) *Natural Blues*, by Jheri Shayler; *The World I Know*, by Melanie Price; *Southern Ritual*, by Nella Banks.

Tips "Query with a short overview of the book's main theme(s), also include some background on the author or contributors. If we like the sound of a proposal, we will contact you to request sample sections or a completed manuscript."

N ATRIAD PRESS, LLC

13820 Methuen Green, Dallas TX 75240. (972)671-0002. E-mail: editor@atriadpress.com. Website: www.atriad-press.com; www.hauntedencounters.com. President: Ginnie Bivona. **Acquisitions:** Mitchel Whitington, senior editor. Estab. 2003. Publishes trade paperback originals. **Publishes 8 titles/year. Receives 200 queries and 1,000 mss/year. 50% of books from first-time authors; 90% from unagented writers. Pays royalty on wholesale price.** Publishes book 1 year after acceptance of ms. Accepts simultaneous submissions. Responds in 1 month to queries; 1 month to proposals; 3 months to mss. Book catalog and ms guidelines online.

Nonfiction Ghost stories, haunted experiences. Does not want UFO or angels. Submit proposal package including outline, 3 sample chapter(s).

Recent Title(s) *Haunted Encounters: Real-Life Stories of Supernatural Experiences* (anthology).

Tips "The market for ghost stories is huge! It seems to be very broad—and ranges from young to old. Currently, our books are for adults, but we would consider the teen market. Please check your manuscript carefully for errors in spelling and structure."

AUGSBURG BOOKS

Imprint of Augsburg Fortress Publishers, P.O. Box 1209, Minneapolis MN 55440-1209. (612)330-3300. Website: www.augsburgbooks.com. Publisher: Scott Tunseth. **Acquisitions:** Lois Wallentine. Publishes trade and mass market paperback originals and reprints, hardcover picture books. **Publishes 40 titles/year. 2-3% of books from first-time authors. Pays royalty.** Publishes book 18 months after acceptance of ms. Responds in 3 months to queries. Book catalog for 9×12 SAE with 3 first-class stamps; ms guidelines online.

  O— Augsburg Books is the popular religious book imprint of Augsburg Fortress Publishers, the publishing house of the Evangelical Lutheran Church in America. Augsburg Books are meant to nurture faith in daily life, enhancing the lives of Christians in their homes, churches, and schools.

Nonfiction Children's/juvenile, self-help. Subjects include religion, spirituality (adult), grief/healing/wholeness, parenting, interactive books for children and families, seasonal and picture books. Submit outline, 1-2 sample chapters (if requested).

Recent Title(s) *God Created*, by Mark Francisco Bozutti-Jones; *Martin Luther*, by James A. Nestingen; *Executive Values*, by Kurt Senske.

AVALON BOOKS

Thomas Bouregy & Co., Inc., 160 Madison Ave., 5th Floor, New York NY 10016. (212)598-0222. Fax: (212)979-1862. E-mail: avalon@avalonbooks.com. Website: www.avalonbooks.com. **Acquisitions:** Erin Cartwright-Niumata, editorial director. Estab. 1950. Publishes hardcover originals. **Publishes 60 titles/year. Receives 2,000 queries and 1,200 mss/year. 65% of books from first-time authors; 80% from unagented writers. Pays 5-15% royalty. Offers $1,000+ advance.** Publishes book 10-12 months after acceptance of ms. Responds in 1 month to queries. Book catalog and ms guidelines online.

  O— "We publish wholesome fiction. We're the 'Family Channel' of publishing. We try to make what we publish suitable for anybody in the family." Currently seeking contemporary romances, historicl romances, mysteries, series, westerns, good writing, developed characters, interesting story lines. De-emphasizing romantic suspense.

Fiction Historical (romance), mystery, romance, western. "We publish wholesome contemporary romances, mysteries, historical romances and westerns. Our books are read by adults as well as teenagers, and the characters are all adults. All mysteries are contemporary. We publish contemporary romances (four every two months), historical romances (two every two months), mysteries (two every two months) and westerns (two every two months). Submit first 3 sample chapters, a 2-3 page synopsis and SASE. The manuscripts should be between 40,000 to 70,000 words. Manuscripts that are too long will not be considered. Time period and setting are the author's preference. The historical romances will maintain the high level of reading expected by our readers. The books shall be wholesome fiction, without graphic sex, violence or strong language." Query with SASE.

Recent Title(s) *Mr. Perfect*, by Shelagh McEachern (romance); *Willow*, by Carolyn Brown (historical romance); *A Hanging in Hidetown*, By Kent Conwell.

Tips "We are looking for love stories, heroines who have interesting professions, and we are actively seeking new authors. We do accept unagented manuscripts, and we do publish first novels. Right now we are concentrating on finding talented new mystery and historical romance writers with solid story-telling skills. Read our guidelines carefully before submitting."

N AVALON TRAVEL PUBLISHING

Avalon Publishing Group, 1400 65th St., Suite 250, Emeryville CA 94608. (510)595-3664. Fax: (510)595-4228. E-mail: info@travelmatters.com. Submissions E-mail: acquisitions@avalonpub.com. Website: www.travelmatt ers.com. Publisher/Acquisitions: Bill Newlin. **Acquisitions:** Rebecca Browning, acquisitions editor. Estab. 1973. Publishes trade paperback originals. **Publishes 100 titles/year. Receives 100-200 submissions/year. 50% of books from first-time authors; 95% from unagented writers. Pays royalty on net receipts. Offers up to $10,000 advance.** Publishes book an average of 9 months after acceptance of ms. Accepts simultaneous submissions. Responds in 4 months to queries; 4 months to proposals.

Imprints *Series:* Adapter Kit; City Smart; Dog Lover's Companion; Moon Handbooks; Rick Steves; Road Trip USA.

O➤ "Avalon Travel Publishing publishes comprehensive, articulate travel information to North and South America, Asia and the Pacific. We have an interest in outdoor recreation including camping/hiking/biking."

Nonfiction Subjects include regional, travel.

Tips "Avalon Travel Publishing produces books that are designed by and for independent travelers seeking the most rewarding travel experience possible. Please visit our acquisitions website at www.travelmatters.com/acquisitions before submitting materials."

N AVANT-GUIDE

Empire Press Media, Empire State Building, Suite 7814-78th Floor, 350 5th Ave., New York NY 10118. E-mail: editor@avantguide.com. Website: www.avantguide.com. **Acquisitions:** Dan Levine, editor-in-chief (travel). Estab. 1997. Publishes trade paperback and electronic originals. **Publishes 20 titles/year. Receives 200 queries and 10 mss/year. 20% of books from first-time authors; 100% from unagented writers. Makes outright purchase of $10,000-30,000.** Publishes book 10 months after acceptance of ms. Accepts simultaneous submissions. Responds in 1 month to queries; 1 month to proposals; 1 month to mss. Book catalog free; ms guidelines online.

Nonfiction Subjects include travel (guide books). "Avant-Guide books live at the intersection of travel and style. They co-opt the best aspects of the guidebook genre—namely, being thorough and trustworthy. Then they add dynamic prose, innovative design and a brutally honest cosmopolitan perspective. Each new title in this boutique travel guidebook series is comprehensive in scope and includes authoritative reports on essential sights, as well as hip new restaurants, nightclubs, hotels, and shops—all while making a fashion statement all its own. In a soundbite, Avant-Guide is the first and only travel guidebook series for globally aware travelistas." Query by e-mail.

Tips "Avant-Guide readers are style-conscious, well-dressed, well-traveled city dwelling 25-49 year old men and women. They are sophisticated, brand-savvy, well-heeled, 21st century consumers searching for understated, cutting edge experiences. While they like to travel stylishly, our readers are busy people who don't have time to wade through exhaustive lists. When they travel they want to know only about the best hotels, restaurants, shops and nightlife. Our core audience resides in affluent city areas and gentrified multi-ethnic areas. They are predominantly single or unmarried-couples, highly qualified executives and creative professionals."

AVANYU PUBLISHING, INC.

P.O. Box 27134, Albuquerque NM 87125. (505)341-1280. Fax: (505)341-1281. Website: www.avanyu-publishin g.com. **Acquisitions:** J. Brent Ricks, president. Estab. 1984. Publishes hardcover and trade paperback originals and reprints. **Publishes 4 titles/year. Receives 40 submissions/year. 30% of books from first-time authors; 90% from unagented writers. Pays 8% maximum royalty on wholesale price. Offers advance.** Publishes book 1 year after acceptance of ms. Does not accept simultaneous submissions. Responds in 2 months to queries. Book catalog for #10 SASE.

O➤ Avanyu publishes highly-illustrated, history-oriented books on American Indians and adventures in the Southwest.

Nonfiction Biography, children's/juvenile, coffee table book, illustrated book, reference, scholarly. Subjects include Americana (Southwest), anthropology/archeology, art/architecture, ethnic, history, multicultural, photography, regional, sociology, spirituality. Query with SASE. Reviews artwork/photos as part of ms package.

Recent Title(s) *Kachinas Spirit Beings of the Hopi*; *Mesa Verde Ancient Architecture*; *Hopi Snake Ceremonies*.

Tips "Our audience consists of libraries, art collectors, and history students. We publish subjects dealing with modern and historic American Indian matters of all kinds."

AVERY

Imprint of Penguin Group (USA), Inc., 375 Hudson St., New York NY 10014. (212)366-2000. Website: www.peng uin.com. Megan Newman, publisher. Estab. 1976. Publishes hardcover and trade paperback originals. **Publishes 25 titles/year. 50% of books from first-time authors; 25% from unagented writers. Pays royalty.**

Offers advance. Publishes book 1 year after acceptance of ms. Accepts simultaneous submissions. Responds in 1 month to queries; 1 month to proposals; 6 weeks to mss. Book catalog and ms guidelines free.

○┐ Avery specializes in health, nutrition, alternative medicine, and fitness.

Nonfiction "We generally do not publish personal accounts of health topics unless they outline a specific plan that covers all areas of the topic." Submit proposal package including outline, author bio, cover letter, table of contents, preface, SASE.

Recent Title(s) *Natural Highs*, by Hyla Cass, M.D. and Patrick Holford; *Dare to Lose*, by Shari Lieberman, Ph.D.; *Prescription for Nutritional Healing*, by Phyllis A. Balch, CNC.

Tips "Our mission is to enable people to improve their health through clear and up-to-date information."

AVISSON PRESS, INC.

3007 Taliaferro Rd., Greensboro NC 27408. Fax: (336)288-6989. **Acquisitions:** M.L. Hester, editor. Estab. 1994. Publishes hardcover originals and trade paperback originals and reprints. **Publishes 8-10 titles/year. Receives 600 queries and 400 mss/year. 5% of books from first-time authors; 90% from unagented writers. Pays 8-10% royalty on wholesale price. Offers occasional small advance.** Publishes book 15 months after acceptance of ms. Accepts simultaneous submissions. Responds in 1 week to queries; 1 week to proposals; 2 months to mss. Book catalog for #10 SASE.

○┐ Currently emphasizing young-adult biography only. No fiction or poetry.

Nonfiction Biography. Subjects include ethnic, sports, women's issues/studies. Query with SASE, or submit outline, 1-3 sample chapter(s).

Recent Title(s) *Go, Girl!: Young Women Superstars of Pop Music*, by Jacqueline Robb; *The Experimenters: Eleven Great Chemists*, by Margery Everden.

Tips Audience is primarily public and school libraries.

ⓝ ⊘ AVOCET PRESS, INC.

19 Paul Court, Pearl River NY 10965. E-mail: books@avocetpress.com. Website: www.avocetpress.com. Estab. 1997. Publishes hardcover and trade paperback originals. **Publishes 6 titles/year. Receives 1,200 queries and 120 mss/year. 40% of books from first-time authors; 80% from unagented writers. Pays royalty on wholesale price.** Publishes book 18 months after acceptance of ms. Does not accept simultaneous submissions. Responds in 3 months to queries; 6 months to mss. Book catalog and ms guidelines online.

Imprints Memento Mori (mysteries).

● Currently not accepting any mss. Check online for updates.

Fiction Feminist, literary, mainstream/contemporary, multicultural, mystery, poetry. "Read our books! Plot and characters are very important." Query with SASE.

Poetry "Read our books! Must have already published in literary journals." Submit 4 sample poems.

Tips "Avocet Press, Inc., is a small, independent publisher of a wide variety of quality literature. Our offerings range from important contemporary poetry to mysteries to beautifully written historical fiction. We are particularly interested in work that is different, exciting, and awakens us to angles of the world that we haven't noticed before."

BACKCOUNTRY GUIDES

Imprint of The Countryman Press, P. O. Box 748, Woodstock VT 05091-0748. (802)457-4826. Fax: (802)457-1678. E-mail: countrymanpress@wwnorton.com. Website: www.countrymanpress.com. **Acquisitions:** Kermit Hummel, editorial director. Publishes trade paperback originals. **Publishes 15 titles/year. Receives 1,000 queries and a few mss/year. 25% of books from first-time authors; 75% from unagented writers. Pays 6-8% royalty on retail price. Offers $1,500-2,500 advance.** Publishes book 18 months after acceptance of ms. Accepts simultaneous submissions. Responds in 2 months to proposals. Book catalog free; ms guidelines online.

○┐ Backcountry Guides publishes guidebooks that encourage physical fitness and appreciation for and understanding of the natural world, self-sufficiency, and adventure. "We publish several series of regional destination guidebooks to outdoor recreation. They include: 50 Hikes Series; Backroad Bicycling Series; Trout Streams Series; Bicycling America's National Parks Series; and a paddling (canoeing and kayaking) series."

Nonfiction Subjects include nature/environment, recreation (bicycling, hiking, canoeing, kayaking, fly fishing, walking, guidebooks, and series), sports. Query with SASE, or submit proposal package including outline, market analysis, 50 sample pages.

Recent Title(s) *Bicycling America's National Parks: California*, by David Story; *Kayaking the Maine Coast*, by Dorcas Miller.

Tips "Look at our existing series of guidebooks to see how your proposal fits in."

BAEN PUBLISHING ENTERPRISES

P.O. Box 1403, Riverdale NY 10471-0671. (718)548-3100. E-mail: slush@baen.com. Website: www.baen.com. **Acquisitions:** Jim Baen, editor-in-chief; Toni Weisskopf, executive editor. Estab. 1983. Publishes hardcover, trade paperback and mass market paperback originals and reprints. **Publishes 120 titles/year. Receives 5,000 submissions/year. 5% of books from first-time authors; 50% from unagented writers. Pays royalty on retail price. Offers advance.** Does not accept simultaneous submissions. Responds in 8 months to queries; 8 months to proposals; 1 year to mss. Book catalog free; ms guidelines online.

- Electronic submissions are strongly preferred.
- "We publish books at the heart of science fiction and fantasy."

Fiction Fantasy, science fiction. Interested in science fiction novels (based on real science) and fantasy novels "that at least strive for originality." Submit outline, 3 consecutive sample chapter(s), synopsis, or submit complete ms.

Recent Title(s) *War of Honor*, by David Weber.

Tips "See our books before submitting. Send for our writers' guidelines. We recommend *Writing to the Point*, by Algis Budrys."

N BAKER ACADEMIC

Imprint of Baker Book House Co., P.O. Box 6287, Grand Rapids MI 49516-6287. (616)676-9185. Fax: (616)676-2315. Website: www.bakeracademic.com. Director of Publications: Jim Kinney. Estab. 1939. Publishes hardcover and trade paperback originals. **Publishes 40 titles/year. 10% of books from first-time authors; 85% from unagented writers. Offers advance.** Publishes book 1 year after acceptance of ms. Book catalog for $9\frac{1}{2} \times 12\frac{1}{2}$ SAE with 3 First-Class stamps; ms guidelines for #10 SASE.

- "Baker Academic publishes religious academic and professional books for students and church leaders. Most of our authors and readers are Christians with academic interests, and our books are purchased from all standard retailers." Does accept unsolicited proposals from credentialed academics.

Nonfiction Illustrated book, multimedia, reference, scholarly, textbook, dictionary, encyclopedia, reprint, professional book, CD-ROM. Subjects include anthropology/archeology, education, psychology, religion, women's issues/studies, Biblical studies, Christian doctrine, books for pastors and church leaders, contemporary issues.

Recent Title(s) *360-Degree Preaching*, by Michael J. Quicke (professional); *New Testament History*, by Ben Witherington III; *Deconstructing Evangelism*, by D.G. Hart.

BAKER BOOK HOUSE CO.

P.O. Box 6287, Grand Rapids MI 49516-6287. (616)676-9185. Fax: (616)676-2315. Website: www.bakerbooks.com. **Imprints** Baker Academic, Baker Books, Bethany House, Brazos Press, Chosen, Fleming H. Revell.

BAKER BOOKS

Imprint of Baker Book House Co., P.O. Box 6287, Grand Rapids MI 49516-6287. (616)676-9185. Fax: (616)676-2315. Website: www.bakerbooks.com. Director of Publications: Don Stephenson. Estab. 1939. Publishes hardcover and trade paperback originals, and trade paperback reprints. **Publishes 75 titles/year. 10% of books from first-time authors; 85% from unagented writers. Pays on net receipts. Offers advance.** Publishes book within 1 year after acceptance of ms. Does not accept unsolicited proposals. Book catalog for $9\frac{1}{2} \times 12\frac{1}{2}$ SAE with 3 first-class stamps; ms guidelines for #10 SASE.

- "Baker Books publishes popular religious nonfiction reference books and professional books for church leaders. Most of our authors and readers are evangelical Christians, and our books are purchased from Christian bookstores, mail-order retailers, and school bookstores." Does not accept unsolicited proposals.

Nonfiction Biography, multimedia, reference, self-help, textbook, CD-ROM. Subjects include child guidance/parenting, psychology, religion, women's issues/studies, Christian doctrine, books for pastors and church leaders, seniors' concerns, singleness, contemporary issues.

Recent Title(s) *Love, Sex and Lasting Relationships*, by Chip Ingram (marriage and family issues); *The Healing Power of Prayer*, by Chester Tolson and Harold Koenig (religion).

BALCONY PRESS

512 E. Wilson, Suite 213, Glendale CA 91206. (818)956-5313. E-mail: ann@balconypress.com. **Acquisitions:** Ann Gray, publisher. Publishes hardcover and trade paperback originals. **Publishes 6-8 titles/year. Pays 10% royalty on wholesale price.** Accepts simultaneous submissions. Responds in 1 month to queries; 1 month to proposals; 3 months to mss. Book catalog free.

- "We also now publish *LA Architect* magazine focusing on contemporary architecture and design in Southern California. Editor: Jesse Brink."

Nonfiction Subjects include art/architecture, ethnic, gardening, history (relative to design, art, and architecture), regional. "We are interested in the human side of design as opposed to technical or how-to. We like to think our books will be interesting to the general public who might not otherwise select an architecture or design book." Query by e-mail or letter. Submit outline and 2 sample chapters with introduction, if applicable.

Recent Title(s) *Iron: Erecting the Walt Disney Concert Hall*, by Gil Garcetti.

Tips Audience consists of architects, designers, and the general public who enjoy those fields. "Our books typically cover California subjects, but that is not a restriction. It's always nice when an author has strong ideas about how the book can be effectively marketed. We are not afraid of small niches if a good sales plan can be devised."

BALE BOOKS

Bale Publications, 5121 St. Charles Ave., Suite #13, New Orleans LA 70115. **Acquisitions:** Don Bale, Jr, editor-in-chief. Estab. 1963. Publishes hardcover and paperback originals and reprints. **Publishes 10 titles/year. Receives 25 submissions/year. 50% of books from first-time authors; 90% from unagented writers. Offers standard 10-12½% royalty contract on wholesale or retail price; sometimes makes outright purchases of $500.** Publishes 3 years after acceptance of ms. Does not accept simultaneous submissions. Responds in 3 months to queries. Book catalog for #10 SAE with 2 first-class stamps.

○━ "Our mission is to educate numismatists about coins, coin collecting, and investing opportunities."

Nonfiction Numismatics. Subjects include hobbies, money/finance. "Our specialties are coin and stock market investment books; especially coin investment books and coin price guides." Submit outline, 3 sample chapter(s).

Recent Title(s) *How to Find Valuable Old & Scarce Coins*, by Jules Penn.

Tips "Most of our books are sold through publicity and ads in the coin newspapers. We are open to any new ideas in the area of numismatics. Write for a teenage through adult level. Lead the reader by the hand like a teacher, building chapter by chapter. Our books sometimes have a light, humorous treatment, but not necessarily. We look for good English, construction and content, and sales potential."

BALL PUBLISHING

335 N. River St., Batavia IL 60510. (630)208-9080. Fax: (630)208-9350. E-mail: info@ballpublishing.com. Website: www.ballpublishing.com. **Acquisitions:** Rick Blanchette, managing editor (floriculture, horticulture, gardening). Publishes hardcover and trade paperback originals. **Publishes 4-6 titles/year. Receives 25 queries and 10 mss/year. 20% of books from first-time authors; 95% from unagented writers. Pays 10-15% royalty on wholesale price. Offers up to $3,000 advance.** Publishes book 12-18 months after acceptance of ms. Accepts simultaneous submissions. Responds in 2 months to queries. Book catalog for 8½×11 SAE with 3 first-class stamps.

○━ "We publish for the book trade and the horticulture trade. Books on both home gardening/landscaping and commercial production are considered."

Nonfiction How-to, reference, technical, textbook. Subjects include agriculture/horticulture, gardening, floriculture. Query with SASE, or submit proposal package including outline, 2 sample chapter(s). Reviews artwork/photos as part of ms package. Send photocopies.

Recent Title(s) *Contain Yourself*, by Kerstin Ouellet; *The Ball Redbook, 17th Ed.*

Tips "We are expanding our book line to home gardeners, while still publishing for green industry professionals. Gardening books should be well thought out and unique in the market. Actively looking for photo books on specific genera and families of flowers and trees."

Ⓐ BALLANTINE PUBLISHING GROUP

Imprint of Random House, Inc., 1745 Broadway, New York NY 10019. (212)782-9000. Website: www.randomho use.com/bb. Publisher: Gina Centrello. Senior VP/Editor-in-Chief: Nancy Miller. VP/Editorial Director: Linda Marrow. **Acquisitions:** Joe Blades, vice president/executive editor (*fiction*: suspense, mystery, *nonfiction*: pop culture, film history and criticism, travel); Tracy Brown, senior editor (*fiction*: literary, quality commerical, paperback reprint *nonfiction*: history, travel, issue-oriented, nature, narrative, biography, paperback reprint); Allison Dickens, assistant editor (*fiction*: literary, women's fiction, commercial, *nonfiction*: biography, narrative, history (art, culinary, travel); Charlotte Herscher, associate editor (*fiction*: historical and contemporary romance); Linda Marrow, vice president/editorial director (*fiction*: suspense, women's, crime); Nancy Miller, senior vice president/editor-in-chief (*nonfiction*: serious commercial, narrative, memoirs, issue-oriented health, parenting); Maureen O'Neal, vice president/editorial director (*nonfiction*: health, childcare, parenting, narrative, diet, *fiction*: women's, quality commercial, Southern fictiom, Ballantine Reader's Circle, trade paperback); Patricia Peters, assistant editor (*nonfiction*: biography, history, travel, narrative, *fiction*: commercial, literary, mysteries); Dan Smetanka, senior editor (*nonfiction*: adventure, narrative, science, religion, *fiction*: literary, quality commercial paperback reprint, story collections); Shauna Summers, senior editor (*fiction*: historical and contemporary romance, general women's fiction, thrillers, suspense); Zach Schisgal, senior editor (*nonfiction*: pop culture, health/fitness, self-help, military history, celebrity/media tie-in). Estab. 1952. Publishes hardcover, trade paperback, mass market paperback originals. **Pays 8-15% royalty. Offers variable advance.** Ms guidelines online.

Imprints Ballantine Books, Ballantine Reader's Circle, Del Rey, Del Rey/Lucas Books, Fawcett, Ivy, One World, Wellspring.

O→ Ballantine Books publishes a wide variety of nonfiction and fiction.

Nonfiction Biography, gift book, how-to, humor, self-help. Subjects include animals, child guidance/parenting, community, cooking/foods/nutrition, creative nonfiction, education, gay/lesbian, general nonfiction, health/medicine, history, language/literature, memoirs, military/war, recreation, religion, sex, spirituality, travel, true crime, women's issues/studies. *Agented submissions only.* Reviews artwork/photos as part of ms package. Send photocopies.

Fiction Confession, ethnic, fantasy, feminist, gay/lesbian, historical, humor, literary, mainstream/contemporary (women's), military/war, multicultural, mystery, romance, short story collections, spiritual, suspense, general fiction. *Agented submissions only.*

BANCROFT PRESS

P.O. Box 65360, Baltimore MD 21209-9945. (410)358-0658. Fax: (410)764-1967. E-mail: bruceb@bancroftpress. com. Website: www.bancroftpress.com. **Acquisitions:** Bruce Bortz, publisher (health, investments, politics, history, humor); Fiction Editor (literary novels, mystery/thrillers, young adult). Publishes hardcover and trade paperback originals. Also packages books for other publishers (no fee to authors). **Publishes 6 titles/year. Pays 6-8% royalty. Pays various royalties on retail price. Offers $750 advance.** Publishes book up to 3 years after acceptance of ms. Accepts simultaneous submissions. Responds in 6-12 months to queries; 6-12 months to proposals; 6-12 months to mss. Ms guidelines online.

O→ Bancroft Press is a general trade publisher. "We are currently moving into soley publishing young adult fiction and adult fiction for young adults (single titles and series). Please, nothing that would be too graphic for anyone under 17 years old."

Nonfiction "Our No. 1 priority is publishing books appropriate for young adults, ages 10-18. All quality books on any subject that fit that category will be considered." Biography, how-to, humor, self-help. Subjects include business/economics, government/politics, health/medicine, money/finance, regional, sports, women's issues/studies, popular culture, essays. "We advise writers to visit the website." Submit proposal package including outline, 2 sample chapter(s), competition/market survey.

Fiction "Our No. 1 priority is publishing books appropriate for young adults, ages 10-18. All quality books on any subject that fit that category will be considered." Ethnic (general), feminist, gay/lesbian, historical, humor, literary, mainstream/contemporary, military/war, mystery (amateur sleuth, cozy, police procedural, private eye/hardboiled), regional, science fiction (hard science/technological, soft/sociological), young adult (historical, problem novels, series), thrillers. Query with SASE, or submit outline, 2 sample chapter(s), synopsis, by mail or e-mail, or submit complete ms.

Recent Title(s) *Paul & Juliana*, by Richard Hawley; *A Farewell to Legs*, by Jeffrey Cohen; *Chain Thinking*, by Elliott Light.

🄽 🄰 ∅ BANTAM BOOKS FOR YOUNG READERS

Imprint of Random House Children's Books/Random House, Inc., 1745 Broadway, New York NY 10019. (212)782-9000. Website: www.randomhouse.com/kids.

● Not seeking mss at this time.

O→ Movie tie-ins, and media driven projects.

🄰 ∅ BANTAM DELL PUBLISHING GROUP

Imprint of Random House, Inc., 1745 Broadway, New York NY 10019. (212)782-9000. Website: www.bantamdel l.com. **Acquisitions:** Toni Burbank (nonfiction: self-help, health/medicine, nature, spirituality, philosophy); Jackie Cantor (fiction: general commercial, literary, women's fiction, memoir); Tracy Devine (fiction and nonfiction: narrative nonfiction, history, adventure, military, science, women's fiction, general upscale commercial fiction, suspense); Wendy McCurdy (fiction: romance, women's fiction); Beth Rashbaum (nonfiction: health, psychology, self-help, women's issues, Judaica, history, memoir); John Flicker (fiction and nonfiction: crime fiction, thrillers/suspense, current events, history, biography/memoir, politics); Anne Groell (fiction: fantasy, science fiction); Ann Harris (fiction and nonfiction: general commercial, literary, science, medicine, politics); Susan Kamil (The Dial Press: literary fiction and nonfiction); Bill Massey (fiction and nonfiction: thrillers, suspense, historical, military, nature/outdoors, adventure, popular science); Kate Miciak (fiction: mystery, suspense, historical fiction); Philip Rappaport (nonfiction: self-help, health, lifestyle, popular culture, general nonfiction); Juliet Ulman (fiction: fantasy, science fiction). Estab. 1945. Publishes hardcover, trade paperback and mass market paperback originals; mass market paperback reprints. **Publishes 350 titles/year. Offers advance.** Publishes book 1 year after acceptance of ms. Accepts simultaneous submissions.

Imprints Bantam Hardcover, Bantam Mass Market, Bantam Trade Paperback, Crimetime, Delacorte Press, Dell, Delta, The Dial Press, Domain, DTP, Fanfare, Island, Spectra.

    O↗ Bantam Dell is a division of Random House, Inc., publishing both fiction and nonfiction. *No unsolicited mss. Agented submissions only.* No e-mail submissions.

Nonfiction Biography, how-to, humor, self-help. Subjects include Americana, child guidance/parenting, cooking/foods/nutrition, government/politics, health/medicine, history, humor, military/war, New Age, philosophy, psychology, religion, science, sociology, spirituality, sports, true crime, women's issues/studies, fitness, mysticism/astrology.

Fiction Adventure, fantasy, historical, horror, literary, military/war, mystery, science fiction, suspense, women's fiction, general commercial fiction.

Recent Title(s) *The Cottage*, by Danielle Steel (Delacorte, fiction); *A Painted House*, by John Grisham (Dell, fiction); *Body of Lies*, by Iris Johansen (Bantam, fiction).

Ⓐ ⊘ BANTAM DOUBLEDAY DELL BOOKS FOR YOUNG READERS

Random House Children's Publishing, Random House, Inc., 1745 Broadway, New York NY 10019. (212)782-9000. Fax: (212)782-8234. Website: www.randomhouse.com/kids. Vice President/Publisher: Beverly Horowitz. **Acquisitions:** Michelle Poploff, editorial director. Publishes hardcover, trade paperback and mass market paperback series originals, trade paperback reprints. **Publishes 300 titles/year. Receives thousands queries/year. 10% of books from first-time authors; small% from unagented writers. Pays royalty. Offers varied advance.** Publishes book 2 years after acceptance of ms. Does not accept simultaneous submissions. Responds in 2 months to queries. Book catalog for 9×12 SASE.

Imprints Delacorte Press Books for Young Readers, Doubleday Books for Young Readers, Dell Laurel Leaf (YA), Dell Yearling (middle grade).

    O↗ "Bantam Doubleday Dell Books for Young Readers publishes award-winning books by distinguished authors and the most promising new writers." The best way to break in to this market is through its 2 contests, the Marguerite de Angeli Contest and the Delacorte Press Contest for a First Young Adult Novel.

Nonfiction Children's/juvenile. "Bantam Doubleday Dell Books for Young Readers publishes a very limited number of nonfiction titles." *No unsolicited mss.*

Fiction Adventure, fantasy, historical, humor, juvenile, mainstream/contemporary, mystery, picture books, suspense, chapter books, middle-grade. *No unsolicited mss.* Accepts unsolicited queries only.

Recent Title(s) *Sisterhood of the Traveling Pants*, by Ann Brashares; *Cuba 15,* by Nancy Osa.

BARBOUR PUBLISHING, INC.

P.O. Box 719, Uhrichsville OH 44683. (740)922-6045. Fax: (740)922-5948. Website: www.barbourpublishing.com. **Acquisitions:** Paul Muckley, editorial director (nonfiction); Rebecca Germany, senior editor (women's fiction); Shannon Hill, editor-at-large (mystery, thriller, suspense fiction). Estab. 1981. Publishes hardcover, trade paperback and mass market paperback originals and reprints. **Publishes 200 titles/year. Receives 500 queries and 1000 mss/year. 40% of books from first-time authors; 95% from unagented writers. Pays 0-12% royalty on net price or makes outright purchase of $500-5,000. Offers $500-5,000 advance.** Publishes book 2 years after acceptance of ms. Accepts simultaneous submissions. Responds in 1 month to queries. Book catalog online or for 9×12 SAE with 2 first-class stamps; ms guidelines for #10 SASE or online.

Imprints Heartsong Presents (contact Rebecca Germany, managing editor).

    O↗ Barbour Books publishes mostly devotional material that is nondenominational and evangelical in nature; Heartsong Presents publishes Christian romance. "We're a Christian evangelical publisher."

Nonfiction Biography, gift book, humor, reference, devotional, Bible trivia. Subjects include child guidance/parenting, cooking/foods/nutrition, money/finance, religion (evangelical Christian), women's issues/studies. "We look for book ideas with mass appeal—nothing in narrowly-defined niches. If you can appeal to a wide audience with an important message, creatively presented, we'd be interested to see your proposal." Submit outline, 3 sample chapter(s), SASE. Reviews artwork/photos as part of ms package. Send photocopies.

Fiction Mystery, romance (historical and contemporary), suspense, women's issues, futuristic, thriller. "Heartsong romance is 'sweet'—no sex, no bad language. Other genres may be 'grittier'—real-life stories. All must have Christian faith as an underlying basis. Commom writer's mistakes are a sketchy proposal, an unbelieveable story, and a story that doesn't fit our guidelines for inspirational romances." Submit 3 sample chapter(s), synopsis, SASE.

Recent Title(s) *Faith that Breathes*, by Michael Ross (devotional); *A Treasure Deep*, by Alton Gansky (fiction); *You're Late Again Lord*, by Karon Phillips Goodman (women's issues).

Tips "Audience is evangelical/Christian conservative, nondenominational, young and old. We're looking for great concepts, not necessarily a big name author or agent. We want to publish books that will sell millions, not just 'flash in the pan' releases. Send us your ideas!"

BAREFOOT BOOKS

2067 Massachusettes Ave., Cambridge MA 02140. (617)576-0660. Fax: (617)576-0049. Website: www.barefootb ooks.com. Publishes hardcover and trade paperback originals. **Publishes 30 titles/year. Receives 2,000 queries and 3,000 mss/year. 35% of books from first-time authors; 60% from unagented writers. Pays 2½-5% royalty on retail price, or makes outright purchase of $5.99-19.99. Offers advance.** Publishes book 2 years after acceptance of ms. Accepts simultaneous submissions. Responds in 2 months to queries; 2 months to proposals; 3 months to mss. Book catalog for 9×12 SAE stamped with $1.80 postage; ms guidelines online.

    ○→ We are a small, independent publishing company that publishes high-quality picture books for children of all ages and specializes in the work of artists and writers from many cultures. We focus on themes that support independence of spirit, encourage openness to others, and foster a life-long love of learning. Does not accept unsolicited mss, but does accept query letters and first pages of mss.

Fiction Juvenile. Barefoot Books only publishes children's picture books and anthologies of folktales. "We do not publish novels. We are no longer accepting unsolicited manuscripts. We do accept query letters, and we encourage authors to send the first page of their manuscript with the query letter." Query with SASE, or submit first page of ms. Anthology collection with SASE and one sample story.

Recent Title(s) *We All Went on Safari: A Counting Journey through Tanzania,* by Laurie Krebs (early learning picture book); *The Fairie's Gift,* by Tanya Robyn Batt (picture book); *The Lady of Ten Thousand Names: Goddess Stories from Many Cultures,* by Borleigh Mutein (illustrated anthology).

Tips "Our audience is made up of children and parents, teachers and students, of many different ages and cultures. Since we are a small publisher, and we definitely publish for a 'niche' market, it is helpful to look at our books and our website before submitting, to see if your book would fit into the type of book we publish."

BARNEGAT LIGHT PRESS

Pine Barrens Press, P.O. Box 607, 3959 Rt. 563, Chatsworth NJ 08019-0607. (609)894-4415. Fax: (609)894-2350. **Acquisitions:** R. Marilyn Schmidt, publisher. Publishes trade paperback originals. **Publishes 4 titles/year. Receives 50 queries and 30 mss/year. 0% of books from first-time authors; 100% from unagented writers. Makes outright purchase.** Publishes book 6 months after acceptance of ms. Responds in 1 month to queries. Book catalog free or online at website.

Imprints Pine Barrens Press.

    ○→ "We are a regional publisher emphasizing the mid-Atlantic region. Areas concerned are gardening, cooking, and travel."

Nonfiction Cookbook, how-to, illustrated book. Subjects include agriculture/horticulture, cooking/foods/nutrition, gardening, regional, travel. Query with SASE. Reviews artwork/photos as part of ms package. Send photocopies.

Recent Title(s) *Churches and Graveyards of the Pine Gardens,* R. Marilyn Schmidt.

BARRICADE BOOKS, INC.

185 Bridge Plaza N., Suite 308A, Fort Lee NJ 07024-5900. (201)944-7600. Fax: (201)944-6363. **Acquisitions:** Carole Stuart, publisher. Estab. 1991. Publishes hardcover and trade paperback originals, trade paperback reprints. **Publishes 30 titles/year. Receives 200 queries and 100 mss/year. 80% of books from first-time authors; 50% from unagented writers. Pays 10-12% royalty on retail price for hardcover. Offers advance.** Publishes book 18 months after acceptance of ms. Responds in 1 month to queries. Book catalog for $3.

    ○→ Barricade Books publishes nonfiction, "mostly of the controversial type, and books we can promote with authors who can talk about their topics on radio and television and to the press."

Nonfiction Biography, how-to, reference, self-help. Subjects include business/economics, ethnic, gay/lesbian, government/politics, health/medicine, history, nature/environment, psychology, sociology, women's issues/studies. Query with SASE, or submit outline, 1-2 sample chapter(s). Material will not be returned or responded to without SASE. Reviews artwork/photos as part of ms package. Send photocopies.

Recent Title(s) *Conversations with a Pedophile,* by Dramy Zabin; *Sex and the Single Girl,* by Helen Gurley Brown (reprint).

Tips "Do your homework. Visit bookshops to find publishers who are doing the kinds of books you want to write. Always submit to a person—not just 'Editor.' Always enclose a SASE or you may not get a response."

BARRON'S EDUCATIONAL SERIES, INC.

250 Wireless Blvd., Hauppauge NY 11788. (800)645-3476. Fax: (631)434-3723. Website: barronseduc.com. **Acquisitions:** Wayne Barr, acquisitions editor. Estab. 1941. Publishes hardcover, paperback and mass market originals and software. **Publishes 400 titles/year. Receives 2,000 queries and 1,000 submissions/year. 40% of books from first-time authors; 75% from unagented writers. Pays 12-14% royalty on net receipts. Offers $3-4,000 advance.** Publishes book 18 months after acceptance of ms. Accepts simultaneous submissions. Responds in 3 months to queries; 8 months to mss. Book catalog free; ms guidelines online.

Book Publishers

○⊸ Barron's tends to publish series of books, both for adults and children. "We are always on the lookout for creative nonfiction ideas for children and adults."

Nonfiction Children's/juvenile, cookbook, textbook, student test prep guides. Subjects include art/architecture, business/economics, child guidance/parenting, cooking/foods/nutrition, education, health/medicine, hobbies, language/literature, New Age, sports, translation, travel, adult education, foreign language, review books, guidance, pets, literary guides. Query with SASE, or submit outline, 2-3 sample chapter(s). Reviews artwork/photos as part of ms package.

Fiction Juvenile. Submit sample chapter(s), synopsis.

Recent Title(s) *A Book of Magical Herbs*, by Margaret Picton; *Family Gardener*, by Lucy Peel.

Tips "Audience is mostly educated self-learners and hobbyists. The writer has the best chance of selling us a book that will fit into one of our series. Children's books have less chance for acceptance because of the glut of submissions. SASE must be included for the return of all materials. Please be patient for replies."

[N] BARTON BOOK PRESS

P.O. Box 3201, Erie PA 16508. Phone/fax: (814)453-6363. E-mail: bartonbooks@hotmail.com. **Acquisitions:** Michelle Parent, acquisitions editor (mass market fiction, mystery/suspense, horror, thriller, action/adventure); J.P. Parent, editor (fantasy, science fiction, gay/lesbian, occult, juvenile). Estab. 1999. Publishes hardcover and mass market paperback originals and reprints. **Publishes 8 titles/year; imprint publishes 4 titles/year. Receives 50-100 queries and 60+ mss/year. 80% of books from first-time authors; 75% from unagented writers. Pays negotiable, competitive royalty. Advance varies.** Publishes book 9-24 months after acceptance of ms. Accepts simultaneous submissions. Responds in 1 month to queries; 6 months to mss. Ms guidelines for #10 SASE.

Imprints Barton Books, Fantasia (contact Kyle Drey, managing editor, or Ken Leclair, assistant).

Fiction Adventure, fantasy, gay/lesbian, horror, humor, juvenile, literary, mainstream/contemporary, mystery, occult, picture books, science fiction, suspense, thriller. "We want full-length, quality fiction, and edited novels displaying strong characterization, plot, theme, and believable settings." No nonfiction, romance, erotica, western, poetry, or sports. Query with SASE and 2 sample chapters.

Recent Title(s) *Shrouded Insanity*, by Jamian Snow (mystery/thriller).

Tips "Our audience is interested in the highest quality fiction with solid characterization and ingenious story lines. Interesting series welcome. An agent is not always necessary if your writing is strong."

BASIC BOOKS

Perseus Books, 387 Park Ave. S., 12th Floor, New York NY 10016. (212)340-8100. Website: www.basicbooks.com. **Acquisitions:** Elizabeth Maguire, VP, associate publisher, editorial director; Jo Ann Miller, executive editor; Bill Frucht, executive editor. Publishes hardcover originals and reprints, trade paperback originals and reprints. **Publishes 100 titles/year. Receives 500 queries and 300 mss/year. 5% of books from first-time authors; 10% from unagented writers. Pays 10-15% royalty on retail price. Offers less than $10,000 advance.** Publishes book 1 year after acceptance of ms. Accepts simultaneous submissions. Responds in 3 months to queries; 3 months to proposals; 6 months to mss. Book catalog and ms guidelines free.

Nonfiction Biography, serious adult trade. Subjects include Americana, anthropology/archeology, business/economics, child guidance/parenting, computers/electronic, creative nonfiction, education, ethnic, gay/lesbian, government/politics, health/medicine, history, language/literature, memoirs, military/war, money/finance, multicultural, music/dance, nature/environment, philosophy, psychology, regional, religion, science, sex, sociology, spirituality, translation, women's issues/studies. "Because of the current post 9/11 situation, we are not currently accepting any unsolicited submissions. This is subject to change without notice." Specific submission guidelines online.

Recent Title(s) *The Mystery of Capital*, by Hernando de Soto (economics); *The Hidden Hitler*, by Lothar Machton (history/biography); *The Truth Will Set You Free*, by Alice Miller (psychology).

BASIC HEALTH PUBLICATIONS, INC.

8200 Boulevard E., 25F, North Bergen NJ 07047. (201)868-8336. Fax: (201)868-2842. E-mail: ngoldfind@basiche althpub.com. Website: www.letsliveonline.com. **Acquisitions:** Norman Goldfind, publisher (health, alternative medicine, nutrition, fitness). Estab. 2001. Publishes trade paperback and mass market paperback originals and reprints. **Publishes 30 titles/year; imprint publishes 30 titles/year. Receives 100 queries and 75 mss/year. 10% of books from first-time authors; 10% from unagented writers. Pays 10-20% royalty on wholesale price. Offers $2,500-25,000 advance.** Publishes book 1 year after acceptance of ms. Accepts simultaneous submissions. Responds in 1 month to queries; 1 month to proposals; 2 months to mss. Book catalog online; ms guidelines for #10 SASE.

Nonfiction Booklets, trade paperback, mass market paperback. Subjects include health/medicine. "We are very highly focused on health, alternative medicine, nutrition, and fitness. Must be well researched and documented with appropriate references. Writing should be aimed at lay audience but also be able to cross over to professional market." Submit proposal package including outline, 2-3 sample chapter(s), introduction.

Recent Title(s) *Stopping the Clock: Longevity for the New Millennium*, by Ronald Klatz, M.D., D.O. & Robert Goldman, M.D., D.O., Ph.D.; *Dr. Earl Mindell's Natural Remedies for 101 Ailments*, by Earl Mindell, R.Ph., Ph.D.

Tips "Our audience is over 30, well educated, middle to upper income. We prefer writers with professional credentials (M.D.s, Ph.D.s, N.D.s, etc.), or writers with backgrounds in health and medicine."

BATTELLE PRESS

Battelle Memorial Institute, 505 King Ave., Columbus OH 43201. (614)424-6393. Fax: (614)424-3819. E-mail: press@battelle.org. Website: www.battelle.org. **Acquisitions:** Joe Sheldrick. Estab. 1980. Publishes hardcover and paperback originals and markets primarily by direct mail. **Publishes 15 titles/year. Pays 10% royalty on wholesale price.** Publishes book 6 months after acceptance of ms. Accepts simultaneous submissions. Responds in 1 month to queries. Book catalog free; ms guidelines online.

> O→ Battelle Press strives to be a primary source of books and software on science and technology management.

Nonfiction Subjects include science. "We are looking for management, leadership, project management and communication books specifically targeted to engineers and scientists." Query with SASE. Returns submissions with SASE only by writer's request. Reviews artwork/photos as part of ms package. Send photocopies.

Recent Title(s) *Managing the Industry/University Cooperative Research Center*; *Project Manager's Survival Guide.*

Tips Audience consists of engineers, researchers, scientists and corporate researchers and developers.

BAY/SOMA PUBLISHING, INC.

444 DeHaro St., Suite 130, San Francisco CA 94107. (415)252-4350 and (415)252-4360. Fax: (415)252-4352. E-mail: info@baybooks.com. Website: www.baybooks.com. President/Publisher: James Connolly (james.connolly@baybooks.com). **Acquisitions:** Floyd Yearout, editorial director (floyd.yearout@baybooks.com). Publishes hardcover originals, trade paperback originals and reprints. **Publishes 20 titles/year. Receives 300 queries/year. 10% of books from first-time authors. Royalties vary substantially. Offers $0-25,000 advance.** Publishes book 18 months after acceptance of ms. Accepts simultaneous submissions. Responds in 1 year to queries. Book catalog for 9×12 SAE with 3 first-class stamps or see website.

Nonfiction Coffee table book, cookbook, gift book, how-to, humor, illustrated book. Subjects include cooking/foods/nutrition, gardening, health/medicine, nature/environment, interior design. Query with SASE.

Recent Title(s) *Savor the Southwest*, by Barbara Fenzl (cooking); *Low-Carb Meals in Minutes*, by Linda Gassenheimer; *Designs for a Healthy Home*, by Dan Phillips.

BAYCREST BOOKS

P.O. Box 2009, Monroe MI 48161. E-mail: ceo@baycrestbooks.com. Submissions E-mail: submissions@baycrestbooks.com. Website: www.baycrestbooks.com. **Acquisitions:** Nadine Meeker, CEO/publisher; Kate Orlando, senior editor. Estab. 2002. Publishes trade paperback originals. **Publishes 6 titles/year; imprint publishes 1 title/year. 100% of books from first-time authors. Pays 7-10% royalty on retail price.** Publishes book 12-18 months after acceptance of ms. Accepts simultaneous submissions. Responds in 2 months to queries; 2 months to proposals; 4 months to mss. Book catalog and ms guidelines online.

Imprints Finger Print (mystery); One in Ten (gay/lesbian fiction); Storm Front (action); Orange Moon (young adult); Sunset Rapids (mainstream/romance); StarPoint (science fiction).

Fiction Adventure, erotica, fantasy, feminist, gay/lesbian, historical, horror, literary, mainstream/contemporary, mystery, romance, science fiction, suspense, western, young adult. "Writers seeking to publish with us should visit our website to see which divisions we carry, and what we are looking for in each division. In short, we are looking for fiction that captivates readers and 're-writes' the genre, taking it to a new level. We seek character-driven pieces with characters you love or love to hate. Think pulp fiction with a literary edge. We want stories from fresh, new authors (or published authors) who can think 'outside the box' and marketplace. We don't want a re-manufactured version of the hottest trends. We look for books that set the trends and engage the readers. Give us something that hasn't 'been done' before." Submit proposal package including synopsis.

Recent Title(s) *One Belief Away*, by C.N. Winters (historical lesbian fiction); *Inferno*, by Trish Shields (contemporary lesbian fiction).

Tips "We want our books to appeal to the 'common man,' yet have characters and plots which grab the literature reader as well. If your query doesn't capture our attention, we feel your books will bore us as well. We're not interested in what your neighbor or best friend thinks about your book. We'll be the judge. Prior publishing experience is welcome but not an automatic ticket to publish with us. Be sure to carefully proof everything you send, and be sure to follow our guidelines to the letter.''

BAYLOR UNIVERSITY PRESS

P.O. Box 97363, Waco TX 76798. (254)710-3164. Fax: (254)710-3440. Website: www.baylorpress.com. **Acquisitions:** Carey C. Newman, editor. Publishes hardcover and trade paperback originals. **Publishes 5 titles/year. Pays 10% royalty on wholesale price.** Publishes book 6 months after acceptance of ms. Does not accept simultaneous submissions. Responds in 2 months to proposals. Ms guidelines online.

Imprints Markham Press Fund.

- ○ "We publish contemporary and historical scholarly works on religion, ethics, church-state studies, and oral history, particularly as these relate to Texas and the Southwest." Currently emphasizing religious studies, history. De-emphasizing art, archaeology.

Nonfiction Subjects include anthropology/archeology, history, regional, religion, women's issues/studies. Submit outline, 1-3 sample chapter(s).

Recent Title(s) *Houses of the Interpreter: Reading Scripture, Reading Culture*, by David Lyle Jeffrey; *Horton Foote: Genesis of an American Playwright*, edited by Marion Castleberry; *Acts: A Handbook on the Greek Text*, by Mikeal C. Parsons and Martin M. Culy.

Tips "We publish contemporary and historical scholarly works on religion, ethics, church-state studies, and oral history, particularly as these relate to Texas and the Southwest." Currently emphasizing religious studies, history. De-emphasizing art, archaeology.

BAYWOOD PUBLISHING CO., INC.

26 Austin Ave., P.O. Box 337, Amityville NY 11701. (631)691-1270. Fax: (631)691-1770. E-mail: baywood@baywood.com. Website: www.baywood.com. **Acquisitions:** Stuart Cohen, managing editor. Estab. 1964. **Publishes 25 titles/year. Pays 7-15% royalty on retail price. Offers advance.** Publishes book within 1 year after acceptance of ms. Does not accept simultaneous submissions. Book catalog and ms guidelines free; ms guidelines online.

- ○ Baywood Publishing publishes original and innovative books in the humanities and social sciences, including areas such as health sciences, gerontology, death and bereavement, psychology, technical communications and archaeology.

Nonfiction Scholarly, technical, scholarly. Subjects include anthropology/archeology, computers/electronic, education, health/medicine, nature/environment, psychology, sociology, women's issues/studies, gerontology, imagery, labor relations, death/dying, drugs. Submit proposal package.

Recent Title(s) *Common Threads: Nine Widows' Journeys Through Love, Loss and Healing*, by Diane S. Kaimann; *Invitation to the Life Course: Toward New Understandings of Later Life*, edited by Richard A. Settersten, Jr.; *Exploding Steamboats, Senate Debates and Technical Reports: The Convergence of Technology, Politics and Rhetoric in the Steamboat Bill of 1838*, by R. John Brockmann.

BEACON HILL PRESS OF KANSAS CITY

Nazarene Publishing House, P.O. Box 419527, Kansas City MO 64141. (816)931-1900. Fax: (816)753-4071. **Acquisitions:** Judi Perry, consumer editor. Publishes hardcover and paperback originals. **Publishes 30 titles/year. Pays royalty.** Publishes book 1 year after acceptance of ms. Responds in 3 months to queries.

- ○ "Beacon Hill Press is a Christ-centered publisher that provides authentically Christian resources faithful to God's word and relevant to life."

Nonfiction Doctrinally must conform to the evangelical, Wesleyan tradition. Accent on holy living; encouragement in daily Christian life. Subjects include applied Christianity, spiritual formation, leadership resources, contemporary issues, and Christian care. No fiction, autobiography, poetry, short stories, or children's picture books. Query with SASE, or submit proposal package. Average ms length: 30,000-60,000.

Recent Title(s) *My Faith Still Holds*, by Joyce Williams.

BEACON PRESS

25 Beacon St., Boston MA 02108-2892. (617)742-2110. Fax: (617)723-3097. E-mail: cvyce@beacon.org. Website: www.beacon.org. Director: Helene Atwan. **Acquisitions:** Gayatri Patnaik, senior editor (African-American, Asian-American, Latino, Native American, Jewish, and gay and lesbian studies, anthropology); Joanne Wyckoff, executive editor (child and family issues, environmental concerns); Amy Caldwell, associate editor (poetry, gender studies, gay/lesbian studies, and Cuban studies); Christopher Vyce, assistant editor. Estab. 1854. Publishes hardcover originals and paperback reprints. **Publishes 60 titles/year. Receives 4,000 submissions/year. 10% of books from first-time authors. Pays royalty. Offers advance.** Accepts simultaneous submissions. Responds in 3 months to queries.

Imprints Bluestreak Series (innovative literary writing by women of color).

O→ Beacon Press publishes general interest books that promote the following values: the inherent worth and dignity of every person; justice, equity, and compassion in human relations; acceptance of one another; a free and responsible search for truth and meaning; the goal of world community with peace, liberty, and justice for all; respect for the interdependent web of all existence. Currently emphasizing innovative nonfiction writing by people of all colors. De-emphasizing poetry, children's stories, art books, self-help.

Nonfiction Scholarly. Subjects include anthropology/archeology, child guidance/parenting, education, ethnic, gay/lesbian, nature/environment, philosophy, religion, women's issues/studies, world affairs. General nonfiction including works of original scholarship, religion, women's studies, philosophy, current affairs, anthropology, environmental concerns, African-American, Asian-American, Native American, Latino, and Jewish studies, gay and lesbian studies, education, legal studies, child and family issues, Irish studies. *Strongly prefers agented submissions.* Query with SASE, or submit outline, sample chapter(s), résumé, CV. *Strongly prefers referred submissions, on exclusive.*

Recent Title(s) *Radical Equation*, by Robert Moses and Charles Cobb; *All Souls*, by Michael Patrick McDonald; *Speak to Me*, by Marcie Hershman.

Tips "We probably accept only 1 or 2 manuscripts from an unpublished pool of 4,000 submissions/year. No fiction, children's book, or poetry submissions invited. An academic affiliation is helpful."

BEARMANOR MEDIA

P.O. Box 750, Boalsburg PA 16827. E-mail: info@ritzbros.com. Website: www.bearmanormedia.com. Estab. 2001. Publishes trade paperback originals and reprints. **Publishes 6 titles/year. 50% of books from first-time authors; 100% from unagented writers. Pays 20% royalty on retail price.** Publishes book 8 months after acceptance of ms. Accepts simultaneous submissions. Responds in 1 month to queries; 1 month to proposals; 2 months to mss. Book catalog for #10 SASE; ms guidelines by e-mail.

Nonfiction Autobiography, biography. Subjects include general nonfiction, old-time radio, voice actors, old movies. Query with SASE, or submit proposal package including outline, list of credits on the subject.

Recent Title(s) *The Great Gildersleeve*, by Charles Stumpf (radio biography); *Hollywood's Golden Age*, by Edward Dmytryk (Hollywood biography); *Information, Please*, by Martin Grams, Jr.

Tips "My readers love the past. Radio, old movies, old television. My own tastes include voice actors and scripts, especially of radio and television no longer available. I prefer books on subjects that haven't previously been covered as full books. Doesn't matter to me if you're a first-time author or have a track record. Just know your subject!"

BEARPAW PUBLISHING

9120 Thorton Rd., #343, Stockton CA 95209. (800)books04. E-mail: stories@bearpawpublishing.com. Website: www.bearpawpublishing.com. **Acquisitions:** Jiana Behr, owner (gay fiction). Estab. 2002. Publishes trade paperback originals. **Publishes 5 titles/year. Receives 30 queries and 20 mss/year. 50% of books from first-time authors; 100% from unagented writers. Pays 10% royalty on wholesale price.** Publishes book 10 months after acceptance of ms. Does not accept simultaneous submissions. Responds in 1 month to queries; 2 months to mss. Book catalog and ms guidelines online.

Fiction Adventure, confession, erotica, ethnic, fantasy, gay/lesbian, gothic, historical, horror, humor, mainstream/contemporary, military/war, multicultural, mystery, occult, romance, science fiction, short story collections, spiritual, sports, suspense, western. All submissions should include gay characters as the main characters. Sex in the book is requested but not required. Submit complete ms.

Recent Title(s) *Cost of Love*, by Alexis Rogers (contemporary).

Tips "Audience is gay men. I prefer submissions via e-mail in text format. I will accept attachments and large loads."

BEAVER POND PUBLISHING

P.O. Box 224, Greenville PA 16125. (724)588-3492. Fax: (724)588-2486. E-mail: oj@zoominternet.net. Website: www.beaverpondpublishing.com. **Acquisitions:** Rich Faler, publications director. Estab. 1990. Publishes trade paperback originals and reprints. **Publishes 4 titles/year. Receives 30 queries and 20 mss/year. 50% of books from first-time authors; 100% from unagented writers. On most contracts, pays 8-10% royalty on net sales, or makes outright purchase.** Publishes book 1 year after acceptance of ms. Accepts simultaneous submissions. Responds in 1 month to queries. Book catalog free; ms guidelines online.

O→ Beaver Pond publishes primarily outdoor-oriented books and magazines.

Nonfiction How-to. Subjects include nature/environment, photography (outdoor), sports, hunting, fishing. "We are actively seeking shorter length manuscripts suitable for 20-40 page booklets, in addition to longer length books. Don't offer too general a title with no 'meat.'" Query with SASE, or submit outline, 2 sample chapter(s). Reviews artwork/photos as part of ms package.

Recent Title(s) *Allegheny Angler: Fifty Years a Fly Fisher*, by John Buch; *Crow Shooting Secrets #2*, by Dick Mermon.

Tips "Audience is active outdoor people that want to excel at their craft. Write the book that you would have wanted when you first began a specific outdoor activity. The manuscript needs to completely cover a narrow topic in depth."

BEEMAN JORGENSEN, INC.

7510 Allisonville Rd., Indianapolis IN 46250. (317)841-7677. Fax: (317)849-2001. **Acquisitions:** Brett Johnson, president (automotive/auto racing). Publishes hardcover and trade paperback originals and hardcover reprints. **Publishes 4 titles/year. Receives 10 queries/year. 50% of books from first-time authors; 100% from unagented writers. Pays 15-30% royalty on wholesale price. Offers up to $1,000 advance.** Publishes book 8 months after acceptance of ms. Responds in 1 month to queries; 2 months to proposals. Book catalog free.

Nonfiction Publishes books on automobiles and auto racing. Coffee table book, illustrated book, reference. Subjects include sports (auto racing). Query with SASE, or submit proposal package including outline, 1 sample chapter(s).

Recent Title(s) *Drag Racing Basics*, by Cindy Crawford (illustrated book); *Road America*, by Tom Schultz (illustrated book); *Porshe 356, Guide to D-I-Y Restoration*, by Jim Kellogg (illustrated book).

Tips Audience is automotive enthusiasts, specific marque owners/enthusiasts, auto racing fans, and participants.

BEHRMAN HOUSE, INC.

11 Edison Place, Springfield NJ 07081. (973)379-7200. Fax: (973)379-7280. Website: www.behrmanhouse.com. **Acquisitions:** David Behrman. Estab. 1921. **Publishes 20 titles/year. Receives 200 submissions/year. 20% of books from first-time authors; 95% from unagented writers. Pays 2-10% on wholesale price or retail price or makes outright purchase of $500-10,000. Offers $1,000 average advance.** Publishes book 18 months after acceptance of ms. Accepts simultaneous submissions. Responds in 2 months to queries. Book catalog free; ms guidelines online.

O─╖ "Behrman House publishes quality books of Jewish content—history, Bible, philosophy, holidays, ethics, Israel, Hebrew—for children and adults."

Nonfiction Children's/juvenile (ages 1-18), reference, textbook. Subjects include ethnic, philosophy, religion. "We want Jewish textbooks for the el-hi market." Query with SASE.

Recent Title(s) *Great Israel Scavenger Hunt*, by Scott Blumenthal (Israel); *Rediscovering the Jewish Holidays*, by Nina Beth Cardin and Gila Gevirtz (Jewish Holidays).

FREDERIC C. BEIL, PUBLISHER, INC.

609 Whitaker St., Savannah GA 31401. (912)233-2446. Fax: (912)233-6456. E-mail: beilbook@beil.com. Website: www.beil.com. **Acquisitions:** Mary Ann Bowman, editor. Estab. 1982. Publishes hardcover originals and reprints. **Publishes 13 titles/year. Receives 3,500 queries and 13 mss/year. 80% of books from first-time authors; 100% from unagented writers. Pays 7½% royalty on retail price.** Publishes book 20 months after acceptance of ms. Accepts simultaneous submissions. Responds in 2 weeks to queries. Book catalog free.

Imprints The Sandstone Press, Hypermedia, Inc.

O─╖ Frederic C. Beil publishes in the fields of history, literature, biography, books about books, and the book arts.

Nonfiction Biography, children's/juvenile, illustrated book, reference, general trade. Subjects include art/architecture, general nonfiction, history, language/literature, book arts. Query with SASE. Reviews artwork/photos as part of ms package. Send photocopies.

Fiction Historical, literary, regional, short story collections, biography. Query with SASE.

Recent Title(s) *Joseph Jefferson: Dean of the American Theatre*, by Arthur Bloom; *Goya, Are You With Me Now?*, by H.E. Francis.

Tips "Our objectives are (1) to offer to the reading public carefully selected texts of lasting value; (2) to adhere to high standards in the choice of materials and in bookmaking craftsmanship; (3) to produce books that exemplify good taste in format and design; and (4) to maintain the lowest cost consistent with quality."

BENTLEY PUBLISHERS

Automotive Publishers, 1734 Massachusetts Ave., Cambridge MA 02138-1804. (617)547-4170. Website: www.bentleypublishers.com. **Acquisitions:** Janet Barnes, director of publishing. Estab. 1950. Publishes hardcover and trade paperback originals and reprints. **Publishes 15-20 titles/year. 20% of books from first-time authors; 95% from unagented writers. Pays 10-15% royalty on net price or makes outright purchase. Offers negotiable advance.** Publishes book 1 year after acceptance of ms. Does not accept simultaneous submissions. Responds in 6 weeks to queries. Book catalog and ms guidelines for 9×12 SAE with 4 first-class stamps. Proposal guidelines online.

O→ Bentley Publishers publishes books for automotive enthusiasts.

Nonfiction Automotive subjects only. How-to, technical, theory of operation. Subjects include sports (motor sports). Query with SASE, or submit outline, sample chapter(s). Reviews artwork/photos as part of ms package.

Recent Title(s) *Corvette from the Inside*, by Dave McLellan (reference); *Zora Arkus-Duntov: The Legend Behind the Corvette*, by Jerry Burton (biography); *Mercedes-Benz E-class (W124) Owner's Bible™: 1986-1995* (how-to).

Tips "Our audience is composed of serious, intelligent automobile, sports car, and racing enthusiasts, automotive technicians and high-performance tuners."

ℕ ⊘ THE BERKLEY PUBLISHING GROUP

Penguin Putnam, Inc., 375 Hudson St., New York NY 10014. (212)366-2000. Website: www.penguinputnam.com. **Acquisitions:** Denise Silvestro, senior editor (general nonfiction, business); Tom Colgan, senior editor (history, business, inspiration, biography, suspense/thriller, mystery, adventure); Gail Fortune, senior editor (women's fiction, romance, mystery); Martha Bushko, associate editor (mystery, literary fiction, narrative nonfiction, history, suspense/thriller); Kimberly Waltemyer, editor (adult western, romance, mystery); Christine Zika, senior editor (women's fiction, romance, mystery, health, diet, parenting, self-help, New Age, relationships); Allison McCabe, senior editor (women's fiction, literary fiction, narrative nonfiction, suspense/thriller, romance). Estab. 1955. Publishes paperback and mass market originals and reprints. **Publishes approximately 800 titles/year. Small% of books from first-time authors; 1% from unagented writers. Pays 4-15% royalty on retail price. Offers advance.** Publishes book 2 years after acceptance of ms. Does not accept simultaneous submissions. Responds in 6 weeks to queries.

Imprints Ace Science Fiction, Berkley, Boulevard, Jove, Prime Crime.

• Currently not accepting unsolicited submissions.

O→ The Berkley Publishing Group publishes a variety of general nonfiction and fiction including the traditional categories of romance, mystery and science fiction.

Nonfiction Biography, how-to, reference, self-help. Subjects include business/economics, child guidance/parenting, creative nonfiction, gay/lesbian, general nonfiction, health/medicine, history, New Age, psychology, true crime, women's issues/studies, job-seeking communication, positive thinking, general commercial publishing. No memoirs or personal stories. *Prefers agented submissions.*

Fiction Adventure, historical, literary, mystery, romance, spiritual, suspense, western, young adult. No occult fiction. *Prefers agented submissions.*

Recent Title(s) *Tom Clancy's Rainbow Six*, by Tom Clancy (novel); *Meditations from Conversations with God*, by Neale Donald Walsch (inspiration).

ℕ BET BOOKS

1235 W St. NE, Washington DC 20018. Website: www.bet.com/books. **Acquisitions:** Linda Gill, VP/publisher. Estab. 1998. **Publishes 40 titles/year.**

Tips "Please do not phone to see if your manuscript was received or returned, or to find out what we thought of it. A self-addressed, stamped postcard can be enclosed with your submission if you want confirmation of its arrival. Specify whether you would like your manuscript returned or recycled if it is not right for us."

⊘ BETHANY HOUSE PUBLISHERS

11400 Hampshire Ave. S., Minneapolis MN 55438. (952)829-2500. Fax: (952)996-1304. Website: www.bethanyhouse.com. Estab. 1956. Publishes hardcover and trade paperback originals, mass market paperback reprints. **Publishes 90-100 titles/year. 2% of books from first-time authors; 50% from unagented writers. Pays negotiable royalty on net price. Offers negotiable advance.** Publishes book 1 year after acceptance of ms. Accepts simultaneous submissions. Responds in 3 months to queries. Book catalog for 9×12 SAE with 5 first-class stamps; ms guidelines online.

O→ Bethany House Publishers specializes in books that communicate Biblical truth and assist people in both spiritual and practical areas of life. "While we do not accept unsolicited queries or proposals via telephone or e-mail, we will consider 1-page queries sent by fax and directed to Adult Nonfiction, Adult Fiction, or Young Adult/Children. Queries of interest to us should receive a reply in 4-6 weeks."

Nonfiction Gift book, how-to, reference, self-help, spiritual growth. Subjects include child guidance/parenting, Biblical disciplines, personal and corporate renewal, emerging generations, devotional, marriage and family, applied theology, inspirational. **All unsolicited mss returned unopened.**

Fiction Historical, juvenile, young adult, contemporary.

Recent Title(s) *Mischief from the Back Row*, by Todd and Jedd Hafer (humor); *The Still of the Night*, by Kristen Heitzmann (fiction); *Finding Favor with the King*, by Tommy Tenney (nonfiction).

Tips "Bethany House Publishers' publishing program relates Biblical truth to all areas of life—whether in the framework of a well-told story, of a challenging book for spiritual growth, or of a Bible reference work. We are seeking high quality fiction and nonfiction that will inspire and challenge our audience.''

BEYOND WORDS PUBLISHING, INC.

20827 NW Cornell Rd., Suite 500, Hillsboro OR 97124. (503)531-8700. Fax: (503)531-8773. E-mail: info@beyond word.com. Website: www.beyondword.com. **Acquisitions:** Cynthia Black, editor-in-chief (adult books); Jennifer Angell, acquisitions editor (children's books). Estab. 1983. Publishes hardcover and trade paperback originals and paperback reprints. **Publishes 20-25 titles/year. Receives 4,000 queries and 2,000 mss/year. 65% of books from first-time authors; 50% from unagented writers. Pays 10-15% royalty on publishers proceeds. Offers advance.** Publishes book 12-18 months after acceptance of ms. Accepts simultaneous submissions. Responds in 6 months to queries; 4 months to proposals; 6 months to mss. Book catalog and ms guidelines for #10 SASE or online; ms guidelines online.

• No electronic submissions or queries.

Nonfiction Children's/juvenile, coffee table book, gift book, how-to, self-help. Subjects include animals, child guidance/parenting, health/medicine, photography (selectively), psychology, spirituality, women's issues/studies. Query with SASE, or submit proposal package including outline, 3 sample chapter(s). Reviews artwork/photos as part of ms package. Send photocopies.

Fiction Ethnic (picture book), religious (children's). Does not accept adult fiction. Only wants children's/young adult fiction. Query with SASE, or submit, or submit complete ms.

Tips *"Beyond Words* markets to cultural, creative people, mostly women ages 30-60. Study our list before you submit and check out our website to make sure your book is a good fit for our list.''

BICK PUBLISHING HOUSE

307 Neck Rd., Madison CT 06443. (203)245-0073. Fax: (203)245-5990. E-mail: bickpubhse@aol.com. Website: www.bickpubhouse.com. **Acquisitions:** Dale Carlson, president (psychology); Hannah Carlson (special needs, disabilities); Irene Ruth (wildlife). Estab. 1994. Publishes trade paperback originals. **Publishes 4 titles/year. Receives 100 queries and 100 mss/year. 55% of books from first-time authors; 55% from unagented writers. Pays 10% royalty on net receipts. Offers $500-1,000 advance.** Publishes book 1 year after acceptance of ms. Responds in 1 month to queries; 2 months to proposals; 3 months to mss. Book catalog free; ms guidelines for #10 SASE.

○➞ Bick Publishing House publishes step-by-step, easy-to-read professional information for the general adult public about physical, psychological, and emotional disabilities or special needs. Currently emphasizing science, psychology for teens.

Nonfiction Subjects include health/medicine (disability/special needs), psychology, young adult or teen science, psychology, wildlife rehabilitation. Query with SASE, or submit proposal package including outline, 3 sample chapter(s), résumé.

Recent Title(s) *The Courage to Lead Support Groups: Mental Illnesses and Addictions,* by Hannah Carlson; *In and Out of Your Mind Teen Science,* by Dale Carlson; *Who Said What, Philosophy Quotes for Teens: What Are You Doing with Your Life?,* by J. Krishnamurti.

BKMK PRESS

University of Missouri-Kansas City, 5101 Rockhill Rd., Kansas City MO 64110-2499. (816)235-2558. Fax: (816)235-2611. E-mail: bkmk@umkc.edu. Website: www.umkc.edu/bkmk. **Acquisitions:** Ben Furnish, managing editor. Estab. 1971. Publishes trade paperback originals. **Publishes 5-6 titles/year. Receives 450-500 queries and 250 mss/year. 20% of books from first-time authors; 100% from unagented writers. Pays 10% royalty on wholesale price.** Publishes book 1 year after acceptance of ms. Accepts simultaneous submissions. Responds in 8 months to queries; 8 months to mss. Ms guidelines online.

○➞ BkMk Press publishes fine literature. Reading period January-June.

Nonfiction Subjects include creative nonfiction. Query with SASE.

Fiction Literary, short story collections. Query with SASE.

Poetry Submit 10 sample poems.

Recent Title(s) *The Alibi Cafe,* by Mary Troy; *Beyond the Reach,* by Deborah Cummins (poetry).

Tips ''We skew toward readers of literature, particularly contemporary writing. Because of our limited number of titles published per year, we discourage apprentice writers or 'scattershot' submissions.''

Ⓝ BLACK DOME PRESS CORP.

1011 Route 296, Hensonville NY 12439. (518)734-6357. Website: www.blackdomepress.com. **Acquisitions:** Deborah Allen, publisher (New York state history). Estab. 1990. Publishes hardcover and trade paperback originals and reprints. **Publishes 6 titles/year. Receives 150 queries and 25 mss/year. 20% of books from first-time authors; 80% from unagented writers. Pays 10% royalty on wholesale price.** Publishes book 2 years after acceptance of ms. Accepts simultaneous submissions. Responds in 3 months to queries; 3 months to proposals; 3 months to mss. Book catalog online.

Nonfiction Subjects include history, nature/environment, regional (New York state). New York state regional material only. Submit proposal package including outline, 1 sample chapter(s), author bio.

Recent Title(s) *Catskill Trails*, by Edward G. Henry (hiking guide); *Kingston, New York: The Architectural Guide*, by William B. Rhoads (architectural history).

Tips "Our audience is comprised of New York state residents, tourists, and visitors."

BLACK HERON PRESS

P.O. Box 95676, Seattle WA 98145. Website: www.blackheronpress.com. **Acquisitions:** Jerry Gold, publisher. Estab. 1984. Publishes hardcover and trade paperback originals. **Publishes 4 titles/year. Pays 8-9% royalty on retail price.** Accepts simultaneous submissions. Responds in 3 months to queries; 6 months to proposals; 6 months to mss.

○➤ "Black Heron Press publishes literary fiction—lately we've tended toward surrealism/science fiction (not fantasy) and social fiction; writers should look at some of our titles. We're especially interested in books on the social or historical significances of independent publishing. We've already done 2 titles."

Fiction High quality, innovative fiction. Humor, literary, mainstream/contemporary, science fiction (surrealism), Vietnam war novel - literary. "We don't want to see fiction written for the mass market. If it sells to the mass market, fine, but we don't see ourselves as a commercial press." Query with SASE.

Recent Title(s) *Obscure in the Shade of the Giants*, by Jerome Gold; *The Bathhouse*, by Farnoosh Moshiri.

Tips "Readers should look at some of our books before submitting—they are easily available. Most submissions we see are done competently but have been sent to the wrong place. We do not publish self-help books or romances."

Ⓝ BLACKBIRCH PRESS, INC.

Gale, 10911 Technology Place, San Diego CA 92127. Website: www.galegroup.com/blackbirch/. **Acquisitions:** Publisher-Blackbirch Press. Estab. 1992. Publishes hardcover and trade paperback originals. **Publishes 70-90 titles/year. Receives 400 queries and 75 mss/year. 100% from unagented writers. Pays 4-8% royalty on net price or makes outright purchase. Offers $1,000-5,000 advance.** Publishes book 1 year after acceptance of ms. Accepts simultaneous submissions. Replies only if interested to queries. Manuscript guidelines free.

○➤ Blackbirch Press publishes juvenile and young adult nonfiction and fiction titles.

Nonfiction Biography, children's/juvenile, illustrated book, reference. Subjects include animals, anthropology/archeology, art/architecture, education, health/medicine, history, nature/environment, science, sports, travel, women's issues/studies. Publishes in series—6-8 books at a time. "No proposals for adult readers, please." *No unsolicited mss or proposals. No phone calls.* Query with SASE. Cover letters and résumés are useful for identifying new authors. Reviews artwork/photos as part of ms package. Send photocopies.

Recent Title(s) *A Whale on Her Own: The True Story of Wilma the Whale*, by Brian Skerry; *Flies*, by Elaine Pascoe.

Tips "We cannot return submissions or send guidelines/replies without an enclosed SASE."

BLOOMBERG PRESS

Imprint of Bloomberg L.P., 100 Business Park Dr., P.O. Box 888, Princeton NJ 08542-0888. Website: www.bloomberg.com/books. **Acquisitions:** Kathleen Peterson, senior acquisitions editor. Estab. 1995. Publishes hardcover and trade paperback originals. **Publishes 18-22 titles/year. Receives 200 queries and 20 mss/year. 45% from unagented writers. Pays negotiable, competitive royalty. Offers negotiable advance.** Publishes book 9 months after acceptance of ms. Accepts simultaneous submissions. Responds in 1 month to queries. Book catalog for 10×13 SAE with 5 first-class stamps.

Imprints Bloomberg Personal Bookshelf, Bloomberg Professional Library.

○➤ Bloomberg Press publishes professional books for practitioners in the financial markets, and finance and investing books for informed investors, entrepreneurs, and consumers. "We publish commercially successful, very high-quality books that stand out clearly from the competition by their brevity, ease of use, sophistication, and abundance of practical tips and strategies; books readers need, will use, and appreciate."

Nonfiction How-to, reference, technical. Subjects include business/economics, money/finance, current affairs, personal finance and investing for consumers, professional books on finance, investment and financial services, and books for financial advisors. "We are looking for authorities and for experienced service journalists. We are looking for original solutions to widespread problems, and books offering fresh investment opportunities. Do not send us unfocused books containing general information already covered by books in the marketplace." Submit outline, sample chapter(s), SAE with sufficient postage, or submit complete ms.

Tips "*Bloomberg Professional Library*: Audience is upscale, financial professionals—traders, dealers, brokers, planners and advisors, financial managers, money managers, company executives, sophisticated investors. *Bloomberg Personal Bookshelf:* Audience is upscale consumers and individual investors. Authors are experienced business and financial journalists and/or financial professionals nationally prominent in their specialty for some time who have proven an ability to write a successful book. Research Bloomberg and look at our books in a library or bookstore, and peruse our website."

☑ BLUE MOON BOOKS, INC.

Imprint of Avalon Publishing Group, 245 W. 17th St., 11th Floor, New York NY 10011. (212)981-9919. Fax: (646)375-2571. E-mail: tmpress@aol.com. Website: www.avalonpub.com. **Acquisitions:** Gayle Watkins, editor. Estab. 1987. Publishes trade paperback and mass market paperback originals. **Publishes 50-60 titles/year. Receives 1,000 queries and 500 mss/year. Pays 6% royalty on retail price for mass market books, and 7¹/₂% royalty on trade paperback books. Offers $500 and up advance.** Publishes book 1 year after acceptance of ms. Responds in 2 months to queries. Book catalog free.

    ○┯ "Blue Moon Books is strictly an erotic press; largely fetish-oriented material, B&D, S&M, etc."

Fiction Erotica. *No unsolicited mss.*

Recent Title(s) *Sex Practice*, by Ray Gordon; *66 Chapters About 33 Women*, by Michael Hemmingson.

BLUE/GRAY BOOKS

Imprint of Creativity, Inc., 65 Macedonia Rd., Alexander NC 28701. (828)252-9515. Fax: (828)255-8719. Website: abooks.com. **Acquisitions:** Pat Roberts, acquisitions editor. Publishes trade paperback originals and reprints. **Publishes 4 titles/year. Pays negotiable royalty on wholesale price. Offers advance.** Publishes book 18 months after acceptance of ms.

    ○┯ Blue/Gray Books specializes in Civil War history.

Nonfiction Biography. Subjects include military/war (Civil War). Query with SASE, or submit proposal package including 3 sample chapter(s), original book if wanting reprint. Reviews artwork/photos as part of ms package. Send photocopies.

Recent Title(s) *Deo Vindice: Heroes in Gray Forever*, by Lee Jacobs.

BLUEWOOD BOOKS

Imprint of The Siyeh Group, Inc., P.O. Box 689, San Mateo CA 94401. (650)548-0754. Fax: (650)548-0654. E-mail: bluewoodb@aol.com. **Acquisitions:** Richard Michaels, director. Publishes trade paperback originals. **Publishes 8 titles/year. 20% of books from first-time authors; 100% from unagented writers. Makes work-for-hire assignments—fee depends upon book and writer's expertise. Offers ¹/₃ fee advance.** Does not accept simultaneous submissions.

    ○┯ "We are looking for qualified writers for nonfiction series—history and biography oriented."

Nonfiction Biography, illustrated book. Subjects include Americana, anthropology/archeology, art/architecture, business/economics, government/politics, health/medicine, history, military/war, multicultural, science, sports, women's issues/studies. Query with SASE.

Recent Title(s) *True Stories of Baseball's Hall of Famers*, by Russell Roberts (baseball history/biography); *100 Native Americans Who Shaped American History*, by Bonnie Juetner (American history/biography).

Tips "Our audience consists of adults and young adults. Our books are written on a newspaper level—clear, concise, well organized, and easy to understand. We encourage potential writers to send us a résumé, providing background qualifications and references."

BNA BOOKS

Imprint of The Bureau of National Affairs, Inc., 1231 25th St. NW, Washington DC 20037-1165. (202)452-4343. Fax: (202)452-4997. E-mail: books@bna.com. Website: www.bnabooks.com. **Acquisitions:** Jim Fattibene, acquisitions manager. Estab. 1929. Publishes hardcover and softcover originals. **Publishes 35 titles/year. Receives 50 submissions/year. 20% of books from first-time authors; 95% from unagented writers. Pays 10-15% royalty on net receipts. Offers $500 average advance.** Publishes book 1 year after acceptance of ms. Accepts simultaneous submissions. Responds in 3 months to queries. Book catalog and ms guidelines online.

    ○┯ BNA Books publishes professional reference books written by lawyers, for lawyers. Currently emphasizing employment, intellectual property, and health law.

Nonfiction Reference, scholarly. Subjects include labor and employment law, health law, legal practice, labor relations law, intellectual property law. No fiction, biographies, bibliographies, cookbooks, religion books, humor, or trade books. Submit detailed table of contents or outline.

Recent Title(s) *Fair Labor Standards Act; Intellectual Property Law in Cyberspace; Health Care Fraud and Abuse.*

Tips "Our audience is made up of practicing lawyers and law librarians. We look for authoritative and comprehensive treatises that can be supplemented or revised every year or 2 on legal subjects of interest to those audiences."

BOA EDITIONS, LTD.

260 East Ave., Rochester NY 14604. (585)546-3410. Fax: (585)546-3913. E-mail: boaedit@frontiernet.net. Website: www.boaeditions.org. **Acquisitions:** Thom Ward, editor. Estab. 1976. Publishes hardcover and trade paperback originals. **Publishes 11-13 titles/year. Receives 1,000 queries and 700 mss/year. 15% of books from first-time authors; 90% from unagented writers. Negotiates royalties. Offers variable advance.** Publishes book 18 months after acceptance of ms. Accepts simultaneous submissions. Responds in 1 week to queries; 5 months to mss. Ms guidelines online.

○〒 BOA Editions publishes distinguished collections of poetry and poetry in translation. "Our goal is to publish the finest American contemporary poetry and poetry in translation."

Poetry Query by mail after January 1, 2004. Boa offers a first book poetry prize of $1,500 and book publication for the winner. For guidelines, see the home page of our website.

Recent Title(s) *Owner of the House*, by Louis Simpson; *Book of My Nights*, by Li-Young Lee.

Tips "Readers who, like Whitman, expect of the poet to 'indicate more than the beauty and dignity which always attach to dumb real objects. They expect him to indicate the path between reality and their souls,' are the audience of BOA's books."

N THE BOLD STRUMMER, LTD.

P.O. Box 2037, Westport CT 06880-2037. (203)227-8588. Fax: (203)227-8775. E-mail: theboldstrummer@msn.com. Website: www.boldstrummerltd.com. **Acquisitions:** Nicholas Clarke. Estab. 1973. Publishes hardcover and trade paperback originals and reprints. **Publishes 6-8 titles/year. Receives 5 queries and 2 mss/year. 50% of books from first-time authors; 100% from unagented writers. Pays 10% royalty on retail price.** Publishes book 1 year after acceptance of ms. Book catalog and ms guidelines free.

○〒 "The Bold Strummer, Ltd., or our associate publisher Pro/Am Music resources, publishes most good quality work that is offered in our field(s). BSL publishes guitar and related instrument books (guitar, violin, drums). We are now the sole distributor of Pro/Am's publications."

Nonfiction Subjects include music/dance (guitar and piano-related books). Query with SASE. Reviews artwork/photos as part of ms package. Send photocopies.

Tips "Bold Strummer has also become a leading source of books about Flamenco Gypsies. Pro/AM specializes in piano books, composer biography, etc. Very narrow niche publishers."

N BOOKHOME PUBLISHING

P.O. Box 5900, Navarre FL 32566. (850)936-4184. Fax: (850)939-4953. E-mail: info@bookhome.com. Website: www.bookhome.com. **Acquisitions:** Shirley Siluk Gregory, publisher. Estab. 1996. Publishes hardcover and trade paperback originals. **Publishes 5 titles/year. Receives 100 queries and 100 mss/year. 50% of books from first-time authors; 50% from unagented writers. Pays 7-12% royalty on wholesale price. Offers $0-1,000 advance.** Publishes book 1 year after acceptance of ms. Accepts simultaneous submissions. Responds in 2 months to proposals. Book catalog for #10 SAE with 2 first-class stamps; ms guidelines online.

○〒 "Our goal is to help people live better lives by crafting lifestyles and businesses that are ideal for them."

Nonfiction How-to, self-help. Subjects include business/economics, creative nonfiction, Lifestyles, career. Query with SASE, or submit proposal package including 2 sample chapter(s). Marketing plan.

Recent Title(s) *Get Published Get Paid*, by Janet Groene.

Tips "Ask for our guidelines (include SASE) or review our guidelines at our website. Do your homework, then make your proposal irresistible!Make sure a publicity plan is part of your proposal. We work hard to tell the world about our wonderful books, and we expect our authors to do the same."

BOOKWORLD, INC./BLUE STAR PRODUCTIONS

9666 E. Riggs Rd., #194, Sun Lakes AZ 85248. (480)895-7995. Fax: (480)895-6991. E-mail: bookworldinc@earthlink.net. Website: bluestarproductions.net. **Acquisitions:** Barbara DeBolt, editor. Publishes trade paperback originals. **Publishes 10-12 titles/year. Receives thousands of submissions/year. 75% of books from first-time authors; 90% from unagented writers. Pays royalty.** Does not accept simultaneous submissions. Responds in 8 months to queries; 16 or more months to mss. Book catalog online.

○〒 "We focus on UFOs, the paranormal, metaphysical, angels, psychic phenomena, visionary fiction, spiritual—both fiction and nonfiction."

Nonfiction "To save time and reduce the amount of paper submissions, we are encouraging e-mail queries and submissions (no downloads or attachments), or disk submissions formatted for Windows 95, using WordPerfect or Microsoft Word. Our response will be via e-mail so no SASE will be needed in these instances, unless the disk needs to be returned. For those without computer access, a SASE is a must, and we prefer seeing the actual manuscript, a query letter. No phone queries."

Tips "Authors selected for publication must be prepared to promote their books via public appearances and/or work with a publicist."

BOYDS MILLS PRESS

Highlights for Children, 815 Church St., Honesdale PA 18431-1895. (570)253-1164. Website: www.boydsmillspress.com. Publisher: Kent L. Brown. **Acquisitions:** Larry Rosler, editorial director. Estab. 1990. Publishes hardcover originals and trade paperback reprints. **Publishes 50 titles/year. Receives 10,000 queries and 7,500 mss/year. 40% of books from first-time authors; 60% from unagented writers. Pays royalty on retail price. Offers variable advance.** Accepts simultaneous submissions. Responds in 1 month to mss. Book catalog online.
Imprints Wordsong (poetry).

- Boyds Mill Press, the book-publishing arm of *Highlights for Children*, publishes a wide range of children's books of literary merit, from preschool to young adult. Currently emphasizing picture books and novels (but no fantasy, romance, or horror). Time between acceptance and publication depends on acceptance of ms.

Nonfiction Children's/juvenile. Subjects include agriculture/horticulture, animals, ethnic, history, nature/environment, sports, travel. "Nonfiction should be accurate, tailored to young audience. Prefer simple, narrative style, but in compelling, evocative language. Too many authors overwrite for the young audience and get bogged down in minutiae. Boyds Mills Press is not interested in manuscripts depicting violence, explicit sexuality, racism of any kind, or which promote hatred. We also are not the right market for self-help books." Query with SASE, or submit proposal package including outline. Reviews artwork/photos as part of ms package.

Fiction Adventure, ethnic, historical, humor, juvenile, mystery, picture books, young adult (adventure, animal, contemporary, ethnic, historical, humor, mystery, sports). "We look for imaginative stories or concepts with simple, lively language that employs a variety of literary devices, including rhythm, repitition, and when composed properly, rhyme. The stories may entertain or challenge, but the content must be age appropriate for children. For middle and young adult fiction we look for stories told in strong, considered prose driven by well-imagined characters." No fantasy, romance, horror. Query with SASE. Submit outline/synopsis and 3 sample chapters for novel or complete ms.

Poetry "Poetry should be appropriate for young audiences, clever, fun language, with easily understood meaning. Too much poetry is either too simple and static in meaning, or too obscure." Collections should have a unifying theme.

Recent Title(s) *Rat*, by Jan Cheripko (novel); *The Alligator in the Closet*, by David Harrison (poetry).

Tips "Our audience is pre-school to young adult. Concentrate first on your writing. Polish it. Then—and only then—select a market. We need primarily picture books with fresh ideas and characters—avoid worn themes of 'coming-of-age,' 'new sibling,' and self-help ideas. We are always interested in multicultural settings. Please—no anthropomorphic characters."

BRANCH AND VINE PUBLISHERS, LLC

P.O. Box 1297, Radford VA 24143-1297. (540)639-3096. Fax: (540)639-3096. E-mail: branchandvine@aol.com. Website: www.branchandvinepublishers.com. **Acquisitions:** Steven Macon and James Armentrout, editors (science fiction, fantasy, alternate history). Estab. 1995. Publishes hardcover and trade paperback originals, as well as electronic originals and reprints. **Publishes 10 titles/year. Receives 50-100 queries and 70+ mss/year. 50% of books from first-time authors; 75% from unagented writers. Pays 10% royalty on retail price.** Publishes book 6-12 months after acceptance of ms. Does not accept simultaneous submissions. Responds in 4-6 months to queries; 4-6 months to proposals; 4-6 months to mss. Book catalog and ms guidelines online.

Nonfiction Booklets, children's/juvenile, how-to, humor, reference, scholarly, self-help, textbook. Subjects include Americana, art/architecture, child guidance/parenting, computers/electronic, cooking/foods/nutrition, creative nonfiction, education, gardening, general nonfiction, government/politics, health/medicine, history, hobbies, military/war, nature/environment, psychology, religion, science, spirituality, sports, travel, world affairs. Submit proposal package including outline, 3 sample chapter(s). Reviews artwork/photos as part of ms package. Send photocopies.

Fiction Adventure, fantasy, historical, horror, humor, juvenile, literary, mainstream/contemporary, military/war, mystery, poetry, religious, science fiction, short story collections, spiritual, suspense, western, alternate history, plays, and dramatic subjects. "Follow guidelines on our website." Submit 3 sample chapter(s), synopsis.

Tips "Audience is anyone that appreciates good fiction and likes to be surprised by plot twists and living characters. Know your market. Here's a secret: Editors are concerned about only 1 thing, 'Will this manuscript make money?' Other than that, know how to tell a story. Don't be afraid of revisions, and read, read, read! Also check website for updates; submissions are not open all year."

⊘ BRANDEN PUBLISHING CO., INC.

P.O. Box 812094, Wellesley MA 02482. (781)235-3634. Fax: (781)790-1056. Website: www.branden.com. **Acquisitions:** Adolph Caso, editor. Estab. 1965. Publishes hardcover and trade paperback originals, reprints, and software. **Publishes 15 titles/year. Receives 1,000 submissions/year. 80% of books from first-time authors;**

90% from unagented writers. Pays 5-10% royalty on net receipts. 10 author's copies. Offers $1,000 maximum advance. Publishes book 10 months after acceptance of ms. Responds in 1 month to queries.

Imprints International Pocket Library and Popular Technology, Four Seas and Brashear.

○━ Branden publishes books by or about women, children, military, Italian-American, or African-American themes.

Nonfiction Biography, children's/juvenile, illustrated book, reference, technical, textbook. Subjects include Americana, art/architecture, computers/electronic, contemporary culture, education, ethnic, general nonfiction, government/politics, health/medicine, history, military/war, music/dance, photography, sociology, software, classics. Especially looking for "about 10 manuscripts on national and international subjects, including biographies of well-known individuals. Currently specializing in Americana, Italian-American, African-American." No religion or philosophy. *No unsolicited mss.* Paragraph query only with author's vita and SASE. No telephone, e-mail, or fax inquiries. Reviews artwork/photos as part of ms package.

Fiction Ethnic (histories, integration), historical, literary, military/war, religious (historical-reconstructive), short story collections. Looking for "contemporary, fast pace, modern society." No science, mystery, experimental, horor, or pornography. *No unsolicited mss.* Query with SASE. Paragraph query only with author's vita and SASE. No telephone, e-mail, or fax inquiries.

Recent Title(s) *Quilt of America*, by Carole Gariepy; *The Wisdom of Angels*, by Martha Cummings; *Kaso English to Italian Dictionary*, by Adolph Caso.

BRASSEY'S, INC.

22841 Quicksilver Dr., Dulles VA 20166. (703)661-1548. Fax: (703)661-1547. E-mail: djacobs@booksintl.com. Website: www.brasseysinc.com. **Acquisitions:** Don McKeon, vice president/publisher; Don Jacobs, associate acquisitions editor (general inquiries). Estab. 1984. Publishes hardcover and trade paperback originals and reprints. **Publishes 100 titles/year. Receives 900 queries/year. 20% of books from first-time authors; 70% from unagented writers. Pays 8-12% royalty on wholesale price. Offers $30,000 maximum advance.** Publishes book 1 year after acceptance of ms. Accepts simultaneous submissions. Responds in 2 months to queries. Book catalog free; ms guidelines for 9×12 SAE with 4 first-class stamps.

Imprints Brassey's Sports.

○━ Brassey's specializes in national and international affairs, history (military), biography, intelligence, foreign policy, defense, transportation, reference, and sports. "We are seeking to build our history and international affairs college textbook lists."

Nonfiction Biography, coffee table book, reference, textbook. Subjects include government/politics, history, military/war, sports, world affairs, national and international affairs, intelligence studies. When submitting nonfiction, be sure to include sufficient biographical information (e.g., track records of previous publications), and "make clear in the proposal how your work might differ from other such works already published and with which yours might compete." Query with SASE, or submit proposal package including outline, 2 sample chapter(s), author bio, analysis of book's competition. Reviews artwork/photos as part of ms package. Send photocopies.

Recent Title(s) *Imperial Hubris: Why the West is Losing the War on Terror; Cold War Submarines: U.S. and Soviet Design and Construction*, by Norman Polmar and K.J. Moore; *Getting in the Game: Inside Baseball's Winter Meetings*, by Josh Lewin.

Tips "Our audience consists of military personnel, government policymakers, professors, undergraduate and graduate students, and general readers with an interest in our subjects."

BREAKAWAY BOOKS

P.O. Box 24, Halcottsville NY 12438. (212)898-0408. E-mail: information@breakawaybooks.com. Website: www.breakawaybooks.com. **Acquisitions:** Garth Battista, publisher. Estab. 1994. Publishes hardcover and trade paperback originals. **Publishes 8-10 titles/year. Receives 400 queries and 100 mss/year. 35% of books from first-time authors; 75% from unagented writers. Pays 6-15% royalty on retail price. Offers $2,000-3,000 advance.** Publishes book 9 months after acceptance of ms. Accepts simultaneous submissions. Responds in 1 month to queries; 1 month to proposals; 2 months to mss. Book catalog and ms guidelines free; ms guidelines online.

○━ "Breakaway Books is a sports literature specialty publisher—only fiction and narrative nonfiction. No how-tos."

Nonfiction Subjects include sports (narrative only, not how-to). Query with SASE or by e-mail.

Fiction Short story collections (sports stories). Query with SASE, or submit complete ms.

Recent Title(s) *The Runner and the Path*, by Dean Ottati; *Becoming an Ironman*, by Kara Douglass Thom; *Running Through the Wall*, by Neal Jamison.

Tips Audience is intelligent, passionately committed to athletes. "We're starting a new children's book line—

only children's books dealing with running, cycling, swimming, triathlon, plus boating (canoes, kayaks and sailboats)."

[N] BRENNER MICROCOMPUTING, INC.

Imprint of Brenner Information Group, P.O. Box 721000, San Diego CA 92172. (858)538-0093. Fax: (858)538-0380. E-mail: brenner@brennerbooks.com. Website: www.brennerbooks.com. **Acquisitions:** Jenny Hanson, acquisitions manager (pricing & ranges). Estab. 1982. Publishes trade paperback and electronic originals. **Publishes 15 titles/year. Receives 10 queries and 1 mss/year. 5% of books from first-time authors; 95% from unagented writers. Pays 5-15% royalty on wholesale price, or retail price, or net receipts. Offers $0-1,000 advance.** Publishes book 1 year after acceptance of ms. Accepts simultaneous submissions. Responds in 1 month to queries; 1 month to proposals; 1 month to mss. Book catalog free; ms guidelines for #10 SASE.

Nonfiction How-to, reference, self-help, technical. Subjects include business/economics, computers/electronic, marketing & pricing for small businesses.

BREVET PRESS, INC.

P.O. Box 1404, Sioux Falls SD 57101. **Acquisitions:** Donald P. Mackintosh, publisher (business); Peter E. Reid, managing editor (technical); A. Melton, editor (Americana); B. Mackintosh, editor (history). Estab. 1972. Publishes hardcover and paperback originals and reprints. **Publishes 15 titles/year. Receives 40 submissions/year. 50% of books from first-time authors; 100% from unagented writers. Pays 5% royalty. Offers $1,000 average advance.** Publishes book 1 year after acceptance of ms. Accepts simultaneous submissions. Responds in 2 months to queries. Book catalog free.

    0–¬ Brevet Books seeks nonfiction with "market potential and literary excellence."

Nonfiction Technical. Subjects include Americana, business/economics, history. Query with SASE. Reviews artwork/photos as part of ms package. Send photocopies.

Tips "Keep sexism out of the manuscripts."

BRIDGE WORKS PUBLISHING CO.

Box 1798, 221 Bridge Lane, Bridgehampton NY 11932. (631)537-3418. Fax: (631)537-5092. E-mail: bap@hamptons.com. **Acquisitions:** Barbara Phillips, editor/publisher. Estab. 1992. Publishes hardcover originals and reprints. **Publishes 6-9 titles/year. Receives 1,000 queries and 1,000 mss/year. 50% of books from first-time authors; 40% from unagented writers. Offers $1,000 advance.** Publishes book 1 year after acceptance of ms. Responds in 1 month to queries; 1 month to proposals; 2 months to mss. Book catalog and ms guidelines for #10 SASE.

    0–¬ "Bridge Works is a small press dedicated to mainstream quality fiction. Also mysteries and short story collections."

Nonfiction Query with SASE, or submit proposal package including outline.

Fiction Literary (novels), mystery, short story collections. "Query with SASE before submitting manuscript. First-time authors should have manuscripts vetted by freelance editors before submitting. We do not accept or read multiple submissions."

Recent Title(s) *The Beginning of Calamities*, by Tom House; *What Else But Home*, by Sharon Rolens.

Tips "Query letters should be 1 page, giving general subject or plot of the book and stating who the writer feels is the audience for the work. In the case of novels, a portion of the work could be enclosed. We do not publish how-to's, self-help, romances, or cookbooks."

[N] BRIGHTON PUBLICATIONS, INC.

P.O. Box 120706, St. Paul MN 55112-0706. (800)536-2665. Fax: (651)636-2220. E-mail: sharon@partybooks.com. Website: www.partybooks.com. **Acquisitions:** Sharon E. Dlugosch, editor. Estab. 1977. Publishes trade paperback originals. **Publishes 4 titles/year. Receives 100 queries and 100 mss/year. 50% of books from first-time authors; 100% from unagented writers. Pays 10% royalty on wholesale price.** Accepts simultaneous submissions. Responds in 3 months to queries. Book catalog and ms guidelines for #10 SASE.

    0–¬ Brighton Publications publishes books on celebration or seasonal how-to parties and anything that will help to give a better party such as activities, games, favors, and themes. Currently emphasizing games for meetings, annual parties, picnics, etc., celebration themes, and party/special event planning.

Nonfiction How-to. Subjects include games, tabletop, party themes. "We're interested in topics telling how to live any part of life well." Query with SASE, or submit outline, 2 sample chapter(s).

Recent Title(s) *Installation Ceremonies for Every Group: 26 Memorable Ways to Install New Officers*, by Pat Hines; *Meeting Room Games: Getting Things Done in Committees*, by Nan Booth.

BRISTOL FASHION PUBLICATIONS, INC.

P.O. Box 4676, Harrisburg PA 17111-4676. (800)478-7147. E-mail: jpk@bfpbooks.com. Website: www.bfpbooks.com. **Acquisitions:** John Kaufman, publisher. Publishes trade paperback originals. **Publishes 15-25 titles/**

year. Receives 250 queries and 100 mss/year. **50% of books from first-time authors; 100% from unagented writers. Pays 7-11% royalty on retail price.** Responds in 1 month to queries. Ms guidelines online.

> ⚓ Bristol Fashion Publications, Inc. (BFP, Inc.) publishes books on boats and boating. Publishes book 3 months after final ms is received from the author.

Nonfiction General interest relating to boats and boating. How-to, reference. Subjects include history. "We are interested in any title which relates to these fields. Query with a list of ideas. Include phone number. This is a fast-changing market. Our title plans rarely extend past 6 months, although we know the type and quantity of books we will publish over the next 2 years. We prefer good knowledge with simple-to-understand writing style containing a well-rounded vocabulary." Query with SASE, or the guidelines on the website. Reviews artwork/photos as part of ms package. Send photocopies or JPEG files on CD.

Recent Title(s) *Madison—Hydroplane Heritage; Electric Propulsion for Boats; VHF Marine Radio Handbook.*

Tips "All of our staff and editors are boaters. As such, we publish what we would want to read relating to boats. Our audience is generally boat owners or expected owners who are interested in learning about boats, boat repair and boating. Keep it easy and simple to follow. Use nautical terms where appropriate. Do not use complicated technical jargon, terms or formulas without a detailed explanation of same. Use experienced craftsmen as a resource for knowledge. Please read our guidelines before submitting your manuscript."

BRISTOL PUBLISHING ENTERPRISES

2714 McCone Ave., Hayward CA 94545. Fax: (510)783-5492. Website: bristolcookbooks.com. **Acquisitions:** Aidan Wylde. Estab. 1988. Publishes trade paperback originals. **Publishes 10-20 titles/year. Receives 100-200 queries/year. 25% of books from first-time authors; 100% from unagented writers. Pays 6% royalty on net proceeds or makes outright purchase. Offers small advance.** Publishes book 1 year after acceptance of ms. Accepts simultaneous submissions. Responds in 4 months to queries. Book catalog online.

Imprints Nitty Gritty cookbooks, The Best 50 Recipe Series, Pet Care Series.

Nonfiction Cookbook, craft books, pet care books. Subjects include cooking/foods/nutrition. Send a proposal, or query with possible outline, brief note about author's background, sample of writing, or chapter from ms.

Recent Title(s) *Cooking on the Indoor Grill,* by Catherine Fulde; *Vegetarian Slow Cooker,* by Joanna White; *Best 50 Bar Drinks,* by Dona Z. Mellach.

Tips Readers of cookbooks are novice cooks. "Our books educate without intimidating. We require our authors to have some form of background in the food industry."

BROADMAN & HOLMAN PUBLISHERS

(formerly Broadman & Holman), LifeWay Christian Resources, 127 Ninth Ave. N., Nashville TN 37234. (615)251-2392. Fax: (615)251-3752. Website: www.broadmanholman.com. Publisher: David Shepherd. **Acquisitions:** Leonard G. Goss, editorial director. Estab. 1934. Publishes hardcover and paperback originals. **Publishes 90-100 titles/year. Pays negotiable royalty.** Accepts simultaneous submissions. Responds in 3 months to queries; 2 months to mss. Book catalog free; ms guidelines for #10 SASE.

> ⚓ Broadman & Holman Publishers publishes books that provide Biblical solutions that spiritually transform individuals and cultures. Currently emphasizing inspirational/gift books, general Christian living and books on Christianity and society.

Nonfiction Children's/juvenile, gift book, illustrated book, reference, textbook, devotional journals. Subjects include religion, spirituality. Christian living, devotionals, prayer, women, youth, spiritual growth, Christian history, parenting, home school, Biblical studies, science and faith, current events, marriage and family concerns, church life, pastoral helps, preaching, evangelism. "We are open to freelance submissions in all areas. Materials in these areas must be suited for an evangelical Christian readership." No poetry, biography, or sermons. Query with SASE.

Fiction Adventure, mystery, religious (general religious, inspirational, religious fantasy, religious mystery/suspense, religious thriller, religious romance), western. "We publish fiction in all the main genres. We want not only a very good story, but also one that sets forth Christian values. Nothing that lacks a positive Christian emphasis (but do not preach, however); nothing that fails to sustain reader interest." Query with SASE.

Recent Title(s) *A Greater Freedom,* by Oliver North; *The Beloved Disciple,* by Beth Moore; *Against All Odds,* by Chuck Norris.

Ⓐ BROADWAY BOOKS

Imprint of Doubleday Broadway Publishing Group, Random House, Inc., 1745 Broadway, New York NY 10019. (212)782-9000. Fax: (212)782-9411. Website: www.broadwaybooks.com. **Acquisitions:** Gerald Howard, editor-at-large; Kristine Puopolo, senior editor (general nonfiction, health, self-help); Patricia Medved, senior editor (parenting, self-help); Becky Cole, associate editor (nonfiction, popular culture); Charles Conrad, vice president and executive editor (general nonfiction); Jennifer Josephy, vice president and executive editor (cookbooks); Ann Campbell, senior editor (psychology/self-help, parenting, health). Estab. 1995.

O→ Broadway publishes general interest nonfiction and fiction for adults.

Nonfiction Biography, cookbook, illustrated book, reference, General interest adult books. Subjects include business/economics, child guidance/parenting, contemporary culture, cooking/foods/nutrition, gay/lesbian, general nonfiction, government/politics, health/medicine, history, memoirs, money/finance, multicultural, New Age, psychology, sex, spirituality, sports, travel (narrative), women's issues/studies, current affairs, motivational/inspirational, popular culture, consumer reference. *Agented submissions only.*

Fiction Publishes a limited list of commercial fiction, mainly chick-lit women's fiction. *Agented submissions only.*

Recent Title(s) *A Short History of Nearly Everything*, by Bill Bryson; *The Automatic Millionaire*, by David Bach; *Babyville*, by Jane Green.

BUCKNELL UNIVERSITY PRESS

Lewisburg PA 17837. (570)577-3674. Fax: (570)577-3797. E-mail: clingham@bucknell.edu. Website: www.departments.bucknell.edu/univ_press. **Acquisitions:** Greg Clingham, director. Estab. 1969. Publishes hardcover originals. **Publishes 35-40 titles/year. Receives 400 submissions/year. 20% of books from first-time authors; 99% from unagented writers. Pays royalty.** Publishes book 12-18 months after acceptance of ms. Does not accept simultaneous submissions. Responds in 1 month to queries. Book catalog free; ms guidelines online.

O→ "In all fields, our criteria are scholarly excellence, critical originality, and interdisciplinary and theoretical expertise and sensitivity."

Nonfiction Scholarly. Subjects include art/architecture, history, language/literature, philosophy, religion, sociology, English and American literary criticism, literary theory and cultural studies, historiography, art history, modern languages, classics, anthropology, ethnology, cultural and political geography, Hispanic and Latin American studies. Series: Bucknell Studies in Eighteenth-Century Literature and Culture, Bucknell Studies in Latin American Literature and Theory, Eighteenth-Century Scotland. Query with SASE.

Recent Title(s) *Being in Common: Nation, Subject, and Community in Latin American Literature and Culture*, by Silva Rosman; *Freedom, Slavery, and Absolutism: Corneille, Pascal, Racine*, by Zia Elmarsafy; *Staging Modern Playwrights: From Director's Concept to Performance*, by Sidney Homan.

BUILDERBOOKS™

National Association of Home Builders, 1201 15th St. NW, Washington DC 20005-2800. (800)368-5242. Fax: (202)266-8559. E-mail: publishing@nahb.com. Website: www.builderbooks.com. Managing Director: Bruce T. Holmes. **Acquisitions:** Doris M. Tennyson, senior acquisitions editor (business and construction management for remodelers; computerization, marketing and selling for builders, remodelers, developers, suppliers, manufacturers, and their sales and marketing directors; customer relations; legal issues; seniors housing); Theresa Minch, executive editor (business and construction management for builders, developers, and others; construction how-to; computerization, multifamily, safety). Publishes "educational books and electronic products for builders, remodelers, developers, sales and marketing professionals, and consumers in the residential construction industry. Writers must be experts." **Publishes 20 titles/year. 33% of books from first-time authors; 99% from unagented writers. Pays royalty.** Publishes book 6-9 months after acceptance of ms. Does not accept simultaneous submissions. Responds in 1-2 months to queries. Book catalog free or on website; ms guidelines by e-mail.

Nonfiction "We prefer a detailed outline on a strong residential construction industry topic. Our readers like step-by-step, educational books and electronic products, no history or philosophy of the industry." How-to, reference, technical. Subjects include home building, remodeling, business and construction management, sales and marketing, customer service, computerization, multifamily, safety, financial management. Query first. E-mail queries accepted. Include electronic and hard copy artwork/photos as part of ms package. Send photocopies.

Recent Title(s) *Build a Successful Sales Program*, by Perry Goldman; *Estimator Pro™, 5.0 (An Estimating Spreadsheet Template)*, by Jay Christofferson; *Jobsite Phrasebook*, by Kent Shepard.

Tips "Ask for a sample outline." Audience is primarily home builders, remodelers, developers, sales and marketing professionals, and consumers in the residential construction industry.

BULFINCH PRESS

Imprint of Time Warner Book Group, Time Life Bldg., 1271 Avenue of the Americas, New York NY 10020. (212)522-8700. Website: www.bulfinchpress.com. VP/Publisher: Jill Cohen. **Acquisitions:** Jared Silverman, assistant to the publisher. Publishes hardcover and trade paperback originals. **Publishes 70-80 titles/year. Receives 600 queries/year. Pays variable royalty on wholesale price. Offers variable advance.** Publishes book 18 months after acceptance of ms. Accepts simultaneous submissions. Responds in 2 months to proposals.

O→ Bulfinch Press publishes large format art books. "We are the home of Ansel Adams and Irving Penn."

Nonfiction Coffee table book, cookbook, gift book, illustrated book. Subjects include art/architecture, cooking/

foods/nutrition, gardening, photography, interior design, lifestyle. Query with SASE, or submit sample artwork, outline. Reviews artwork/photos as part of ms package. Send color photocopies, slides, or laser prints.

Recent Title(s) *Remembering Jack: Intimate and Unseen Photographs of the Kennedys*, photographs by Jacques Lowe, text by Hugh Sidey, and forward by Robert F. Kennedy, Jr.; *100 Years of Harley Davidson*, by Willie G. Davidson; *Preston Bailey's Design for Entertaining*, by Preston Bailey.

Ꙩ BULL PUBLISHING CO.

P.O. Box 1377, Boulder CO 80306. (800)676-2855. Fax: (303)545-6354. E-mail: jim.bullpublishing@comcast.net. Website: www.bullpub.com. **Acquisitions:** James Bull, publisher (self-care, nutrition, women's health, weight control); Lansing Hays, publisher (self-help, psychology). Estab. 1974. Publishes hardcover and trade paperback originals. **Publishes 6-8 titles/year. Pays 10-16% royalty on wholesale price (net to publisher).** Publishes book 6 months after acceptance of ms. Book catalog free.

　　○ℼ Bull Publishing publishes health and nutrition books for the public with an emphasis on self-care, nutrition, women's health, weight control and psychology.

Nonfiction How-to, self-help. Subjects include cooking/foods/nutrition, education, health/medicine, women's issues/studies. Subjects include self-care, nutrition, fitness, child health and nutrition, health education, mental health. "We look for books that fit our area of strength: responsible books on health that fill a substantial public need, and that we can market primarily through professionals." Submit outline, sample chapter(s). Reviews artwork/photos as part of ms package.

Recent Title(s) *Child of Mine, 3rd Ed.*, by Ellyn Satter.

THE BUREAU FOR AT-RISK YOUTH

P.O. Box 760, Plainview NY 11803-0760. (516)349-5520. Fax: (516)349-5521. E-mail: info@at-risk.com. Website: www.at-risk.com. **Acquisitions:** Sally Germain, editor-in-chief. Estab. 1988. **Publishes 25-50 titles/year. Receives hundreds submissions/year. 100% from unagented writers. Pays 10% maximum royalty on selling price. Offers variable advance.** Publishes book 1 year after acceptance of ms. Accepts simultaneous submissions. Responds in 8 months to queries. Book catalog free if appropriate after communication with author.

　　○ℼ Publishes materials on youth guidance topics, such as drugs and violence prevention, character education and life skills for young people in grades K-12, and the educators, parents, mental health and juvenile justice professionals who work with them. "We prefer a workbook/activity book, curriculum, or book/booklet series format."

Nonfiction Educational materials for parents, educators and other professionals who work with youth. Booklets. Subjects include child guidance/parenting, education. "The materials we publish are curriculum, book series, workbook/activity books or how-to-oriented pieces tailored to our audience. They are generally not single book titles and our series are rarely book length." Query with SASE.

Recent Title(s) *Helping Kids Heal*, by Rebecca Carman.

Tips "Publications are sold through direct mail catalogs and Internet. Writers whose expertise is a fit with our customers' interests should send query or proposals since we tailor everything very specifically to meet our audience's needs."

BURFORD BOOKS

32 Morris Ave., Springfield NJ 07081. (973)258-0960. Fax: (973)258-0113. **Acquisitions:** Peter Burford, publisher. Estab. 1997. Publishes hardcover originals, trade paperback originals and reprints. **Publishes 25 titles/ year. Receives 300 queries and 200 mss/year. 30% of books from first-time authors; 60% from unagented writers. Pays royalty on wholesale price.** Publishes book 18 months after acceptance of ms. Accepts simultaneous submissions. Responds in 1 month to queries; 1 month to proposals; 2 months to mss. Book catalog and ms guidelines free.

　　○ℼ Burford Books publishes books on all aspects of the outdoors, from backpacking to sports, practical and literary.

Nonfiction How-to, illustrated book. Subjects include animals, cooking/foods/nutrition, hobbies, military/war, nature/environment, recreation, sports, travel. Query with SASE, or submit outline. Reviews artwork/photos as part of ms package. Send photocopies.

Recent Title(s) *Gettysburg: You Are There*, by Robert Clasby; *The GPS Handbook*, by Bob Egbert and Joe King.

BUTTE PUBLICATIONS, INC.

P.O. Box 1328, Hillsboro OR 97123-1328. (503)648-9791. Fax: (503)693-9526. Website: www.buttepublications. com. **Acquisitions:** M. Brink, president. Estab. 1992. **Publishes 6-8 titles/year. Receives 30 queries and 20 mss/year. 50% of books from first-time authors; 100% from unagented writers. Pays 8-12% royalty on net receipts.** Publishes book 1 year after acceptance of ms. Accepts simultaneous submissions. Responds in (usually) 1 month to queries; 4 months to proposals; 6 months to mss. Book catalog and ms guidelines for #10 SASE or online; ms guidelines online.

⚭ Butte Publications, Inc., publishes classroom books related to deafness and language.

Nonfiction Children's/juvenile, textbook. Subjects include education (all related to field of deafness and education). Submit proposal package, including author bio, synopsis, market survey, and complete ms, if completed. Reviews artwork/photos as part of ms package. Send photocopies.

Recent Title(s) *Myths*, by Paris and Tracy; *Lessons In Syntax*, by McCarr; *El Jardin Silencioso*, by Ogden.

Tips "Audience is students, teachers, parents, and professionals in the arena dealing with deafness and hearing loss. We are not seeking autobiographies or novels."

C&T PUBLISHING

1651 Challenge Dr., Concord CA 94520. (925)677-0377. Fax: (925)677-0374. E-mail: ctinfo@ctpub.com. Website: www.ctpub.com. **Acquisitions:** Jan Grigsby, editor. Estab. 1983. Publishes hardcover and trade paperback originals. **Publishes 32 titles/year. Receives 300 submissions/year. 20% of books from first-time authors; 100% from unagented writers. Pays 5-10% royalty on net receipts.** Accepts simultaneous submissions. Responds in 3 months to queries. Book catalog free; proposal guidelines online.

⚭ "C&T publishes well-written, beautifully designed books on quilting, dollmaking, fiber arts, and ribbonwork."

Nonfiction How-to (quilting), illustrated book. Subjects include art/architecture, hobbies, quilting books, primarily how-to, occasional quilt picture books, quilt-related crafts, wearable art, needlework, fiber and surface embellishments, other books relating to fabric crafting. Extensive proposal guidelines are available on the company's website.

Recent Title(s) *Laurel Burch Quilts*, by Laurel Burch; *Machine Embroidery and More*, by Kristen Dibbs.

Tips "In our industry, we find that how-to books have the longest selling life. Quiltmakers, sewing enthusiasts, needle artists, and fiber artists are our audience. We like to see new concepts or techniques. Include some great samples, and you'll get our attention quickly. Dynamic design is hard to resist, and if that's your forte, show us what you've done."

CADENCE JAZZ BOOKS

Cadence Building, Redwood NY 13679. (315)287-2852. Fax: (315)287-2860. E-mail: cjb@cadencebuilding.com. Website: www.cadencebuilding.com. **Acquisitions:** Bob Rusch, Larry Raye. Estab. 1992. Publishes trade paperback and mass market paperback originals. **Publishes 5 titles/year. 90% of books from first-time authors; 100% from unagented writers. Pays royalty or makes outright purchase. Offers advance.** Publishes book 6-12 months after acceptance of ms. Responds in 1 month to queries.

⚭ Cadence publishes jazz histories and discographies.

Nonfiction Biography, reference. Subjects include music/dance, jazz music biographies, discographies and reference works. Submit outline, sample chapter(s), SASE. Reviews artwork/photos as part of ms package. Send photocopies.

Recent Title(s) *The Earthly Recordings of Sun Ra*, by Robert L. Campbell (discography).

CAMBRIDGE EDUCATIONAL

2572 Brunswick Ave., Lawrenceville NJ 08648-4128. (800)468-4227. Fax: (800)FAX-ON-US. Website: www.cambridgeeducational.com. President: Betsy Sherer. Subsidiaries include: Cambridge Parenting and Cambridge Job Search. **Acquisitions:** Julian Chiabella, manager of acquisitions. Estab. 1981. Publishes supplemental educational products. **Publishes 30-40 titles/year. Receives 200 submissions/year. 20% of books from first-time authors; 90% from unagented writers. Makes outright purchase of $1,500-4,000. Occasional royalty arrangement.** Publishes book 8 months after acceptance of ms. Accepts simultaneous submissions.

⚭ "We are known in the education industry for guidance-related and career search programs." Currently emphasizing social studies and science.

Nonfiction Subjects include child guidance/parenting, cooking/foods/nutrition, education, health/medicine, money/finance, science, social sciences, career guidance, social studies. "We are looking for scriptwriters in the same subject areas and age group. We only publish books written for young adults and primarily sold to libraries, schools, etc. We do not seek books targeted to adults or written at high readability levels." Query or submit outline/synopsis and sample chapters. Does not respond unless interested. Reviews artwork/photos as part of ms package.

Recent Title(s) *6 Steps to Getting a Job for People with Disabilities*, by Wayne Forster.

Tips "We encourage the submission of high-quality books on timely topics written for young adult audiences at moderate to low readibility levels. Call and request a copy of all our current catalogs, talk to the management about what is timely in the areas you wish to write on, thoroughly research the topic, and write a manuscript that will be read by young adults without being overly technical. Low to moderate readibility yet entertaining, informative and accurate.''

CAMINO BOOKS, INC.

P.O. Box 59026, Philadelphia PA 19102. (215)413-1917. Fax: (215)413-3255. Website: www.caminobooks.com. **Acquisitions:** E. Jutkowitz, publisher. Estab. 1987. Publishes hardcover and trade paperback originals. **Publishes 8 titles/year. Receives 500 submissions/year. 20% of books from first-time authors. Pays 6-12% royalty on net receipts. Offers $1,000 average advance.** Publishes book 1 year after acceptance of ms. Responds in 2 weeks to queries. Ms guidelines online.

O¬ Camino Books, Inc., publishes nonfiction of regional interest to the Mid-Atlantic states.

Nonfiction Biography, children's/juvenile, cookbook, how-to. Subjects include agriculture/horticulture, Americana, art/architecture, child guidance/parenting, cooking/foods/nutrition, ethnic, gardening, government/politics, history, regional, travel. Query with SASE, or submit outline, sample chapter(s).

Tips ''The books must be of interest to readers in the Middle Atlantic states, or they should have a clearly defined niche, such as cookbooks.''

⊘ CANDLEWICK PRESS

2067 Massachusetts Ave., Cambridge MA 02140. (617)661-3330. Fax: (617)661-0565. Website: www.candlewick.com. President/Publisher: Karen Lotz. **Acquisitions:** Deb Wayshak (fiction); Jamie Michalak, editor; Joan Powers, editor-at-large (picture books); Liz Bicknell, editorial director/associate publisher (poetry, picture books, fiction); Mary Lee Donovan, executive editor (picture books, nonfiction/fiction); Kara LaReau, senior editor; Sarah Ketchersid, editor (board, toddler). Estab. 1991. Publishes hardcover originals, trade paperback originals and reprints. **Publishes 200 titles/year. Receives 10,000-12,000 submissions/year. 5% of books from first-time authors; 40% from unagented writers.**

O¬ Candlewick Press publishes high-quality, illustrated children's books for ages infant through young adult. ''We are a truly child-centered publisher.''

Nonfiction Children's/juvenile. ''Good writing is essential; specific topics are less important than strong, clear writing.''

Fiction Juvenile, picture books, young adult.

Recent Title(s) *Fairieality*, by Ellwand, Downton, and Bird; *Feed*, by M.T. Anderson (National Book Award finalist); *Judy Moody*, by Megan McDonald.

Tips ''We no longer accept unsolicited mss. See our website for further information about us.''

⦿ CANON PRESS

P.O. Box 9025, Moscow ID 83843. (208)892-8074. Fax: (208)892-8143. E-mail: canonads@moscow.com. Website: www.canonpress.org. **Acquisitions:** Jeffrey C. Evans, marketing manager. Estab. 1988. Publishes hardcover and trade paperback originals. **Publishes 10 titles/year. Receives 250 queries and 250 mss/year. 10% of books from first-time authors; 100% from unagented writers. Pays 10-15% royalty on wholesale price, or retail price.** Publishes book 18 months after acceptance of ms. Accepts simultaneous submissions. Responds in 1 month to queries; 1 month to proposals; 1 month to mss. Book catalog and ms guidelines online.

Nonfiction Subjects include creative nonfiction, education, humanities, language/literature, religion. ''As we are generally dissatisfied with contemporary, evangelical Christian nonfiction, we recommend visiting our website and perusing our recent titles before submitting.'' Submit proposal package including outline, 3 sample chapter(s).

Fiction Adventure, historical, humor, juvenile, literary, poetry, poetry in translation, religious, short story collections. Submit proposal package including 3 sample chapter(s), synopsis.

Poetry ''As we are generally dissatisfied with contemporary, evangelical Christian poetry (or lack thereof), we recommend perusing our website and new titles before submitting.'' Submit 15 sample poems.

Recent Title(s) *Against Christianity*, by Peter Leithart (theology); *A Serrated Edge*, by Douglas Wilson (satire); *The Lord's Service*, by Jeffrey J. Meyers (worship).

Tips ''We seek to encourage Christians with God-honoring, Biblical books. Writers should possess a Trinitarian understanding of the good, true, and beautiful, and their submissions should reflect their understanding.''

CAPITAL BOOKS

22841 Quicksilver Dr., Dulles VA 20166. (703)661-1571. Fax: (703)661-1547. E-mail: jennifer@booksintl.com. Website: www.capital-books.com. **Acquisitions:** Kathleen Hughes, publisher (reference, how-to, gardening, women's studies); Noemi Taylor, senior acquisitions editor (regional travel, pets, lifestyle, cookbooks). Estab. 1998. Publishes hardcover and trade paperback originals, and trade paperback reprints. **Publishes 40 titles/ year. Receives 200 queries and 300 mss/year. 10% of books from first-time authors; 50% from unagented writers. Pays 1-10% royalty on net receipts. Offers $1,000-5,000 advance.** Publishes book 9 months after acceptance of ms. Accepts simultaneous submissions. Responds in 1 month to queries; 2 months to proposals; 3 months to mss. Book catalog free; ms guidelines online.

Nonfiction Cookbook, how-to, reference, self-help. Subjects include animals, business/economics, child guidance/parenting, contemporary culture, cooking/foods/nutrition, gardening, general nonfiction, health/medicine, money/finance, multicultural, nature/environment, psychology, regional, social sciences, travel, women's issues/studies. "We are looking for lifestyle and business books by experts with their own marketing and sales outlets." No religious titles, fiction, or children's books. Submit proposal package including outline, 3 sample chapter(s), query letter. Reviews artwork/photos as part of ms package. Send photocopies.

Recent Title(s) *The Color Answer Book*, by Leatrice Eiseman; *Nosithimia: The Greek-American Family Cookbook*, by Georgia Sarianides; *Learning Sickness*, by James Lang.

Tips "Our audience is comprised of enthusiastic readers who look to books for answers and information. Do not send fiction or religious titles. Please tell us how you, the author, can help market and sell the book."

⊘ CAPSTONE PRESS

P.O. Box 669, Mankato MN 56002. (507)388-6650. Fax: (507)625-4662. Website: www.capstone-press.com. **Acquisitions:** Eric Kudalis, product planning manager (nonfiction for students grades K-12). Publishes hardcover originals. **Publishes 400 titles/year. Receives 100 queries/year. 5% of books from first-time authors. Makes outright purchase; payment varies by imprint. Offers advance.** Responds in 3 months to queries. Book catalog and ms guidelines online.

Imprints Capstone Books, Blue Earth Books, Bridgestone Books, Pebble Books, LifeMatters.

   ⊶ Capstone Press publishes nonfiction children's books for schools and libraries.

Nonfiction Children's/juvenile. Subjects include Americana, animals, child guidance/parenting, cooking/foods/nutrition, health/medicine, history, military/war, multicultural, nature/environment, recreation, science, sports. "We do not accept proposals or manuscripts. Authors interested in writing for Capstone Press can request an author's brochure." Query via website.

Recent Title(s) *Downhill In-Line Skating*, by Nick Cook; *The Nez Perce Tribe*, by Allison Lassieur.

Tips Audience is made up of elementary, middle school, and high school students who are just learning how to read, who are experiencing reading difficulties, or who are learning English. Capstone Press does not publish unsolicited mss submitted by authors, and it rarely entertains proposals. Instead, Capstone hires freelance authors to write on nonfiction topics selected by the company. Authors may request a brochure via website.

CARDOZA PUBLISHING

857 Broadway, 3rd Floor, New York NY 10003. E-mail: submissions@cardozapub.com. Website: www.cardoza pub.com. **Acquisitions:** Michelle Knoetgen, acquisitions editor (gaming, gambling, card and casino games, and board games). Estab. 1981. Publishes trade paperback originals and reprints. **Publishes 35-40 titles/year. Receives 20-30 queries and 20-30 mss/year. 50% of books from first-time authors; 90% from unagented writers. Pays 5-6% royalty on retail price. Offers $1,000-10,000 advance.** Publishes book 7 months after acceptance of ms. Accepts simultaneous submissions. Responds in 1-2 months to queries; 1-2 months to proposals; 2-3 months to mss. Book catalog online; ms guidelines by e-mail.

Nonfiction How-to. Subjects include hobbies, gaming, gambling, backgammon chess, card games. "Cardoza Publishing publishes exclusively gaming and gambling titles. In the past, we have specialized in poker and chess titles. While we always need more of those, we are currently seeking more books on various noncasino card games, such as bridge, hearts, spades, gin rummy, or canasta." Query with SASE, or submit complete ms. Reviews artwork/photos as part of ms package. Send photocopies.

Recent Title(s) *Poker Wisdom of a Champion*, by Doyle Brunson (poker); *Learning from Bobby Fischer's Greatest Games*, by Eric Schiller (chess); *Ken Warren Teaches Texas Hold 'Em*, by Ken Warren (poker).

Tips Audience is professional and recreational gamblers, chess players, card players. "We prefer not to deal with agents whenever possible. We publish only titles in a very specific niche market; please do not send us material that will not be relevant to our business."

THE CAREER PRESS, INC.

Box 687, 3 Tice Rd., Franklin Lakes NJ 07417. (201)848-0310; (800)227-3371. Fax: (201)848-0310. Website: www.careerpress.com; www.newpagebooks.com. **Acquisitions:** Michael Lewis, senior acquisitions editor. Estab. 1985. Publishes hardcover and paperback originals. **Publishes 70 titles/year. Receives 300 queries and 1,000 mss/year. 10% of books from first-time authors; 10% from unagented writers. Offers advance.** Publishes book up to 6 months after acceptance of ms. Does not accept simultaneous submissions. Ms guidelines online.

Imprints New Page Books.

   ⊶ Career Press publishes books for adult readers seeking practical information to improve themselves in careers, college, finance, parenting, retirement, spirituality and other related topics, as well as manage-

ment philosophy titles for a small business and management audience. New Page Books publishes in the areas of New Age, health, parenting, and weddings/entertaining. Currently de-emphasizing Judaica.
Nonfiction How-to, reference, self-help. Subjects include business/economics, money/finance, recreation, nutrition. "Look through our catalog; become familiar with our publications. We like to select authors who are specialists on their topic." Query with SASE, or submit outline, 1-2 sample chapter(s).
Recent Title(s) *Hollywood Urban Legends*, by Richard Roeper; *100 Ways to Motivate Yourself,* by Steve Chandler.

CAROLRHODA BOOKS, INC.
Imprint of Lerner Publishing Group, 241 First Ave. N., Minneapolis MN 55401. (612)332-3344. *No phone calls.* Fax: (612)332-7615. Website: www.lernerbooks.com. **Acquisitions:** Zelda Wagner, fiction submissions editor. Estab. 1969. Publishes hardcover originals. **Publishes 50-60 titles/year. Receives 2,000 submissions/year. 10% of books from first-time authors; 90% from unagented writers. Pays royalty on wholesale price, or makes outright purchase. Negotiates payments of advance against royalty. Offers varied advance.** Accepts simultaneous submissions. Responds in 8 months to queries. Book catalog for 9×12 SAE with $3.50 postage; ms guidelines online.
- Accepts submissions from November 1-30 only. Submissions received at other times of the year will be returned to sender.
- O→ Carolrhoda Books is a children's publisher focused on producing high-quality, socially conscious nonfiction and fiction books with unique and well-developed ideas and angles for young readers that help them learn about and explore the world around them.

Nonfiction Carolrhoda Books seeks creative children's nonfiction. Biography. Subjects include ethnic, nature/environment, science. "We are always interested in adding to our biography series. Books on the natural and hard sciences are also of interest." Query with SASE. Reviews artwork/photos as part of ms package. Send photocopies.
Fiction Historical, juvenile, multicultural, picture books, young reader, middle grade and young adult fiction. "We continue to add fiction for middle grades and 8-10 picture books per year. Not looking for folktales or anthropomorphic animal stories." Carolrhoda does not publish alphabet books, puzzle books, song books, textbooks, workbooks, religious subject matter, or plays. Query with SASE, or submit complete ms.
Recent Title(s) *The War*, by Anais Vaugelade; *Little Wolf's Haunted Hall for Small Horrors,* by Ian Whybrow.

Ⓐ CARROLL & GRAF PUBLISHERS, INC.
Avalon Publishing Group, 161 William St., 16th Floor, New York NY 10038. (646)375-2570. Fax: (646)375-2571. Website: www.avalonpub.com; www.carrolandgraf.com. **Acquisitions:** Herman Graf, publisher; Phillip Turner, executive editor; Tina Pohlman, senior editor. Estab. 1982. Publishes hardcover and trade paperback originals. **Publishes 120 titles/year. 10% of books from first-time authors. Pays 10-15% royalty on retail price for hardcover, 6-7½% for paperback. Offers advance commensurate with the work.** Publishes book 9-18 months after acceptance of ms. Responds in a timely fashion to queries. Book catalog free.
- O→ Carroll and Graf Publishers offers quality fiction and nonfiction for a general readership.

Nonfiction Publish general trade books; interested in developing long term relations with authors. Biography, reference, self-help. Subjects include business/economics, contemporary culture, health/medicine, history, memoirs, military/war, psychology, sports, true crime, adventure/exploration. *Agented submissions only.*
Fiction Literary, mainstream/contemporary, mystery, science fiction, suspense, thriller. No romance. *Agented submissions only.* Query with SASE.
Recent Title(s) *Ziff: A Life?*, by Alan Lelchuk; *Hell Hath No Fury: Women's Letters from the End of the Affair*, edited by Anna Holmes; *Robert Maxwell: Israel's Superspy,* by Gordon Thomas and Martin Dillon.

CARSON-DELLOSA PUBLISHING CO., INC.
P.O. Box 35665, Greensboro NC 27425-5665. (336)632-0084. Fax: (336)856-9414. Website: www.carson-dellosa. com. **Acquisitions:** Pamela Hill, product acquistions. **Publishes 70-80 titles/year. Receives 100-150 submissions/year. 25% of books from first-time authors; 95% from unagented writers. Makes outright purchase.** Accepts simultaneous submissions. Responds in 2 months to proposals. Book catalog online; ms guidelines free.
Nonfiction We publish supplementary educational materials, such as teacher resource books, workbooks, and activity books. Subjects include education (including Christian education). No textbooks or trade children's books, please. Submit proposal package including sample chapters or pages, SASE. Reviews artwork/photos as part of ms package. Send photocopies.
Tips "Our audience consists of pre-K through grade 8 educators, parents, and students. Ask for our submission guidelines and a catalog before you send us your materials. We do not publish fiction or nonfiction storybooks."

CARSTENS PUBLICATIONS, INC.

Hobby Book Division, P.O. Box 700, Newton NJ 07860-0700. (973)383-3355. Fax: (973)383-4064. E-mail: hal@c
arstens-publications.com. Website: www.carstens-publications.com. **Acquisitions:** Harold H. Carstens, publisher. Estab. 1933. Publishes paperback originals. **Publishes 8 titles/year. 100% from unagented writers.
Pays 10% royalty on retail price. Offers advance.** Publishes book 1 year after acceptance of ms. Responds in
2 months to queries. Book catalog for #10 SASE.

O–π Carstens specializes in books about railroads, model railroads, and airplanes for hobbyists.

Nonfiction Subjects include model railroading, toy trains, model aviation, railroads, and model hobbies. "Authors must know their field intimately because our readers are active modelers. Writers cannot write about
somebody else's hobby with authority. If they do, we can't use them. Our railroad books presently are primarily
photographic essays on specific railroads." Query with SASE. Reviews artwork/photos as part of ms package.

Recent Title(s) *Modeling the Wild West*, edited by Harold H. Carstens; *Seaboard Coastline*, by Bob Warren.

Tips "We need lots of good photos. Material must be in model, hobby, railroad, and transportation field only."

▣ CARTWHEEL BOOKS

Imprint of Scholastic Trade Division, 557 Broadway, New York NY 10012. (212)343-6100. Website: www.schola
stic.com. Vice President/Editorial Director: Ken Geist. **Acquisitions:** Grace Maccarone, executive editor. Estab.
1991. Publishes novelty books, easy readers, board books, hardcover and trade paperback originals. **Publishes
85-100 titles/year. Receives 1,200 mss/year. Pays royalty on retail price. or flat fee. Offers advance.** Publishes book 2 years after acceptance of ms. Accepts simultaneous submissions. Responds in 1-4 months to
queries; 6 months to mss. 9×12 SASE; ms guidelines free.

O–π Cartwheel Books publishes innovative books for children, up to age 8. "We are looking for 'novelties'
that are books first, play objects second. Even without its gimmick, a Cartwheel Book should stand
alone as a valid piece of children's literature."

Nonfiction Children's/juvenile. Subjects include animals, history, music/dance, nature/environment, recreation, science, sports. "Cartwheel Books publishes for the very young, therefore nonfiction should be written
in a manner that is accessible to preschoolers through 2nd grade. Often writers choose topics that are too
narrow or 'special' and do not appeal to the mass market. Also, the text and vocabulary are frequently too
difficult for our young audience." Accepts mss from agents, previously published authors only. Reviews art-
work/photos as part of ms package. Please do not send original artwork.

Fiction Humor, juvenile, mystery, picture books. "Again, the subject should have mass market appeal for very
young children. Humor can be helpful, but not necessary. Mistakes writers make are a reading level that is too
difficult, a topic of no interest or too narrow, or manuscripts that are too long." Accepts mss from agents,
previously published authors only.

Tips Audience is young children, ages 0-8. "Know what types of books the publisher does. Some manuscripts
that don't work for one house may be perfect for another. Check out bookstores or catalogs to see where your
writing would 'fit' best."

CATHOLIC UNIVERSITY OF AMERICA PRESS

620 Michigan Ave. NE, Washington DC 20064. (202)319-5052. Fax: (202)319-4985. E-mail: cua-press@cua.edu.
Website: cuapress.cua.edu. **Acquisitions:** Dr. Gregory F. Lanave, acquisitions editor (philosophy, theology);
Dr. David J. McGonagle, director (all other fields). Estab. 1939. **Publishes 20-25 titles/year. Receives 100
submissions/year. 50% of books from first-time authors; 100% from unagented writers. Pays variable
royalty on net receipts.** Publishes book 2 years after acceptance of ms. Responds in 6 months to queries. Book
catalog for #10 SASE; ms guidelines online.

O–π The Catholic University of America Press publishes in the fields of history (ecclesiastical and secular),
literature and languages, philosophy, political theory, social studies, and theology. "We have interdisciplinary emphasis on patristics, medieval studies, and Irish studies. Our principal interest is in works of
original scholarship intended for scholars and other professionals, and for academic libraries, but we
will also consider manuscripts whose chief contribution is to offer a synthesis of knowledge of the
subject which may be of interest to a wider audience or suitable for use as supplementary reading
material in courses."

Nonfiction Scholarly. Subjects include government/politics, history, language/literature, philosophy, religion,
Church-state relations. No unrevised doctoral dissertations. Length: 80,000-200,000 words. Query with outline,
sample chapter, cv, and list of previous publications.

Recent Title(s) *Mediapolitik: How the Mass Media Have Transformed World Politics*, by Lee Edwards.

Tips "Scholarly monographs and works suitable for adoption as supplementary reading material in courses
have the best chance."

CATO INSTITUTE

1000 Massachusetts Ave. NW, Washington DC 20001. (202)842-0200. Website: www.cato.org. **Acquisitions:** Gene Healy, senior editor. Estab. 1977. Publishes hardcover originals, trade paperback originals and reprints. **Publishes 12 titles/year. Receives 50 submissions/year. 25% of books from first-time authors; 90% from unagented writers. Makes outright purchase of $1,000-10,000. Offers advance.** Publishes book 9 months after acceptance of ms. Accepts simultaneous submissions. Responds in 3 months to queries. Book catalog online.

> Cato Institute publishes books on public policy issues from a free-market or libertarian perspective.

Nonfiction Scholarly. Subjects include business/economics, education, government/politics, health/medicine, money/finance, sociology, public policy, foreign policy, monetary policy. Query with SASE.

Recent Title(s) *Toward Liberty*, edited by David Boaz; *Voucher Wars*, by Clint Bolick.

CAXTON PRESS

312 Main St., Caldwell ID 83605-3299. (208)459-7421. Fax: (208)459-7450. Website: caxtonpress.com. Publisher: Scott Gipson. **Acquisitions:** Wayne Cornell, editor (Western Americana, regional nonfiction). Estab. 1907. Publishes hardcover and trade paperback originals. **Publishes 6-10 titles/year. Receives 250/year submissions/year. 50% of books from first-time authors; 60% from unagented writers. Pays royalty. Offers advance.** Publishes book 18 months after acceptance of ms. Accepts simultaneous submissions. Responds in 3 months to queries. Book catalog for 9×12 SAE; ms guidelines online.

> "Western Americana nonfiction remains our focus. We define Western Americana as almost any topic that deals with the people or culture of the west, past and present." Currently emphasizing regional issues—primarily Pacific Northwest. De-emphasizing "coffee table" or photograph-intensive books.

Nonfiction Biography, children's/juvenile, cookbook, scholarly. Subjects include Americana, history, regional. "We need good Western Americana, especially the Northwest, emphasis on serious, narrative nonfiction." Query. Reviews artwork/photos as part of ms package.

Recent Title(s) *Forlorn Hope: The Nez Perce Victory at White Bird Canyon*, by John D. McDermott; *Do Them No Harm: Lewis and Clark Among the Nez Perce*, by Zoa Swayne; *Shoshoni Pony*, by Carol Lynn MacGregor.

Tips "Books to us never can or will be primarily articles of merchandise to be produced as cheaply as possible and to be sold like slabs of bacon or packages of cereal over the counter. If there is anything that is really worthwhile in this mad jumble we call the 21st century, it should be books."

CELESTIAL ARTS

Ten Speed Press, P.O. Box 7123-S, Berkeley CA 94707. (510)559-1600. Fax: (510)524-1629. Website: www.tenspeed.com. **Acquisitions:** Jo Ann Deck, publisher; Veronica Randall, managing editor. Estab. 1966. Publishes trade paperback originals and reprints. **Publishes 40 titles/year. Receives 500 queries and 200 mss/year. 30% of books from first-time authors; 10% from unagented writers. Pays 15% royalty on wholesale price. Offers modest advance.** Accepts simultaneous submissions. Responds in 2 months to queries. Book catalog and ms guidelines online.

> Celestial Arts publishes nonfiction for a forward-thinking, open-minded audience interested in psychology, self-help, spirituality, health and parenting.

Nonfiction Cookbook, how-to, reference, self-help. Subjects include child guidance/parenting, cooking/foods/nutrition, education, health/medicine, New Age, psychology, women's issues/studies. "We specialize in parenting, alternative health, how-to and spirituality. And please, no poetry!" Submit proposal package including outline, 1-2 sample chapter(s), author bio, SASE. Reviews artwork/photos as part of ms package. Send photocopies.

Recent Title(s) *How to Be Happy, Dammit: A Cynic's Guide to Enlightenment*, by Karen Salmansohn.

Tips Audience is fairly well-informed, interested in psychology and sociology-related topics, open-minded, innovative, forward-thinking. "The most completely thought-out (developed) proposals earn the most consideration."

Ⓝ CENTER FOR THANATOLOGY RESEARCH & EDUCATION, INC.

391 Atlantic Ave., Brooklyn NY 11217. (718)858-3026. E-mail: rhalporn@pipeline.com. Website: www.thanatology.org. **Acquisitions:** Roberta Halporn, director (gravestone studies, death & dying). Estab. 1980. **Publishes 7 titles/year. Receives 10 queries and 3 mss/year. 15% of books from first-time authors; 100% from unagented writers. Pays 10% royalty on wholesale price.** Publishes book 9 months after acceptance of ms. Does not accept simultaneous submissions. Responds in 1 month to queries; 1 month to proposals. Book catalog and ms guidelines free.

Nonfiction Children's/juvenile, scholarly, self-help. Subjects include education, health/medicine, humanities, psychology, religion, social sciences, sociology, women's issues/studies, anthropology. "All proposals we feel are applicable are sent to a board of professional readers for comment." Query with SASE. Reviews artwork/photos as part of ms package. Send photocopies.

Poetry "We are open to appropriate submissions." Query.

Recent Title(s) *Mourning the Living: Coping with the Problems of Substance Abuse*, by F. Selder, Ph.D. (academic/scientific); *Getting the Most Out of Cemetery Visits*, by R. Halporn, M.A. (for educators); *Counting to Zero: Poems on Miscarriage*, by Marion Cohen (poetry on women's grief).

Tips "We serve 2 different audiences: One is physicians/social workers/nurses dealing with dying patients and bereaved families. The second relates to all aspects of cemetery lore: recording, preservation, description, art of."

CENTERSTREAM PUBLICATIONS

P.O. Box 17878, Anaheim Hills CA 92807. (714)779-9390. Fax: (714)779-9390. E-mail: centerstrm@aol.com. Website: www.centerstream-usa.com. **Acquisitions:** Ron Middlebrook, Cindy Middlebrook, owners. Estab. 1980. Publishes hardcover and mass market paperback originals, trade paperback and mass market paperback reprints. **Publishes 12 titles/year. Receives 15 queries and 15 mss/year. 80% of books from first-time authors; 100% from unagented writers. Pays 10-15% royalty on wholesale price. Offers $300-3,000 advance.** Publishes book 8 months after acceptance of ms. Accepts simultaneous submissions. Responds in 3 months to queries. Book catalog and ms guidelines for #10 SASE.

O⟶ Centerstream publishes music history and instructional books.

Nonfiction How-to. Subjects include history, music/dance. Query with SASE.

Recent Title(s) *History of Dobro Guitars*.

CHALICE PRESS

P.O. Box 179, St. Louis MO 63166. (314)231-8500. Fax: (314)231-8524. E-mail: chalice@cbp21.com. Website: www.chalicepress.com. **Acquisitions:** Dr. Jane E. McAvoy, editorial director. Publishes hardcover and trade paperback originals. **Publishes 40 titles/year. Receives 500 queries and 400 mss/year. 15% of books from first-time authors; 100% from unagented writers. Pays 14% royalty on net receipts.** Publishes book 1 year after acceptance of ms. Accepts simultaneous submissions. Responds in 1 month to queries; 2 months to proposals; 3 months to mss. Book catalog and ms guidelines online.

Nonfiction Textbook. Subjects include religion, Christian spirituality. Submit proposal package including outline, 1-2 sample chapter(s).

Recent Title(s) *Embracing a Beautiful God*, by Patricia Farmer; *The Process Perspective*, by John B. Cobb, Jr.; *Strike Terror No More*, edited by Jon Berquist.

Tips "We publish for both professional and lay Christian readers."

Ⓝ CHAPULTEPEC PRESS

4222 Chambers, Cincinnati OH 45223. (513)681-1976. E-mail: chapultepecpress@hotmail.com. Website: www.tokyoroserecords.com. **Acquisitions:** David Garza. Estab. 2001. Publishes trade paperback originals. **Publishes 5 titles/year. Receives 50 queries and 10 mss/year. 75% of books from first-time authors; 100% from unagented writers. Pays 10-50% royalty on wholesale price.** Publishes book 6 months after acceptance of ms. Accepts simultaneous submissions. Responds in 2 months to queries; 2 months to proposals; 2 months to mss. Book catalog online; ms guidelines by e-mail.

Nonfiction Autobiography, biography, booklets, general nonfiction, humor, illustrated book, multimedia. Subjects include alternative lifestyles, art/architecture, contemporary culture, creative nonfiction, ethnic, government/politics, history, humanities, language/literature, literary criticism, memoirs, multicultural, music/dance, nature/environment, philosophy, photography, recreation, regional, translation, world affairs. Submit proposal package including outline, 2-3 sample chapter(s), artwork samples. Reviews artwork/photos as part of ms package. Send photocopies.

Fiction Comic books, erotica, ethnic, experimental, humor, literary, multicultural, multimedia, occult, picture books, plays, poetry, poetry in translation, regional, short story collections, translation. Submit proposal package including 2-3 sample chapter(s), synopsis, artwork samples.

Poetry Submit 5-15 sample poems.

Recent Title(s) *The Compact Duchamp*, by Guy R. Beining; *A Beautiful Woman*, by Roesing Ape.

Tips Chapultepec Press specializes in shorter-length publications (100 pages or less).

CHARISMA HOUSE

Strang Communications, 600 Rinehart Rd., Lake Mary FL 32746. (407)333-0600. Fax: (407)333-7100. E-mail: charismahouse@strang.com. Website: www.charismahouse.com. **Acquisitions:** Atalie Anderson, acquisitions assistant. Publishes hardcover and trade paperback originals. **Publishes 40-50 titles/year. Receives 600 mss/year. 2% of books from first-time authors; 95% from unagented writers. Pays 4-18% royalty on retail**

price. Offers $1,500-5,000 advance. Publishes book 9 months after acceptance of ms. Accepts simultaneous submissions. Allow 1 year for review to proposals. Ms guidelines online.

Imprints Creation House Press (customized publications of Christian fiction and nonfiction); Siloam (emphasizing healthy living in mind, body and spirit).

○━ "Charisma House publishes books for the Pentecostal/Charismatic Christian market to inspire and equip people to live a Christian life and to walk in the divine purpose for which they were created. We are interested in fiction but have not yet begun a fiction line."

Nonfiction Biography, cookbook, gift book, self-help. Subjects include child guidance/parenting, cooking/foods/nutrition, health/medicine, religion (Christian), sex, spirituality (charismatic), women's issues/studies, spirit-filled interest. Request ms guidelines to receive Project Appraisal Form Questionnaire.

Recent Title(s) *Gatekeeper*, by Terry Craig (fiction); *Matters of the Heart*, by Juanita Bynum, Ph.D. (nonfiction).

Tips "For all book submission requests, we send a Project Appraisal Questionnaire Form to all who want to submit a manuscript. They must complete and return the form. This allows a thorough review without weeding through excess information."

THE CHARLES PRESS, PUBLISHERS

117 S. 17th St., Suite 310, Philadelphia PA 19103. (215)496-9616. Fax: (215)496-9637. E-mail: mailbox@charlesp resspub.com. Website: www.charlespresspub.com. **Acquisitions:** Lauren Meltzer, publisher. Estab. 1982. Publishes hardcover and trade paperback originals. **Publishes 10-16 titles/year. Receives 1,500 queries and 500 mss/year. Pays 7½-12% royalty. Advances commensurate with first year sales potential.** Publishes book 4-12 months after acceptance of ms. Accepts simultaneous submissions. Responds in 1 month to queries; 2 months to proposals; 3 months to mss. Book catalog and ms guidelines online.

○━ Currently emphasizing true crime, criminology, psychology (including suicide, anger and violence).

Nonfiction Subjects include child guidance/parenting, health/medicine (allied), psychology, counseling, criminology, true crime. No fiction or poetry. Query or submit proposal package that includes a description of the book, a few representative sample chapters, intended audience, author's qualifications/background and SASE. No e-mailed submissions. Reviews artwork/photos as part of ms package. Send photocopies or transparencies.

Recent Title(s) *The Golden Age of Medical Science and the Dark Age of Healthcare Delivery*, by Sylvan Weinberg, M.D.

CHARLES RIVER MEDIA

10 Downer Ave., Hingham MA 02043-1132. (781)740-0400. Fax: (781)740-8816. E-mail: info@charlesriver.com. Website: www.charlesriver.com. **Acquisitions:** David Pallai, president (networking, Internet related); Jennifer Niles, publisher (computer graphics, animation, game programming). Publishes hardcover and trade paperback originals. **Publishes 50 titles/year. Receives 1,000 queries and 250 mss/year. 20% of books from first-time authors; 90% from unagented writers. Pays 5-20% royalty on wholesale price. Offers $3,000-20,000 advance.** Publishes book 4 months after acceptance of ms. Accepts simultaneous submissions. Responds in 1 month to queries. Book catalog for #10 SASE; ms guidelines online.

○━ "Our publishing program concentrates on 4 major areas: Internet, networking, game development, and graphics. The majority of our titles are considered intermediate, not high-level research monographs, and not for lowest-level general users."

Nonfiction Multimedia (Win/Mac format), reference, technical. Subjects include computers/electronic. Query with SASE, or submit proposal package including outline, 2 sample chapter(s), résumé. Reviews artwork/photos as part of ms package. Send photocopies or GIF, TIFF, or PDF files.

Recent Title(s) *Game Programming Gems 3*, edited by Dante Treglia; *Security + Exam Guide*, by C. Crayton.

Tips "We are very receptive to detailed proposals by first-time or nonagented authors. Consult our website for proposal outlines. Manuscripts must be completed within 6 months of contract signing."

CHARLESBRIDGE PUBLISHING, SCHOOL DIVISION

85 Main St., Watertown MA 02472. (800)225-3214. Fax: (800)926-5775. E-mail: schooleditorial@charlesbridge.c om. Website: www.charlesbridge.com/school. **Acquisitions:** Elena Dworkin Wright, vice president school division. Estab. 1980. Publishes educational curricula and hardcover and paperback nonfiction and fiction children's picture books. **Publishes 20 titles/year. Receives 1,000 submissions/year. 10-20% of books from first-time authors; 80% from unagented writers. Royalty and advance vary.** Publishes book 2 years after acceptance of ms. Ms guidelines online.

○━ "We're looking for compelling story lines, humor and strong educational content."

Nonfiction Children's/juvenile, textbook. Subjects include education, multicultural, nature/environment, science, math, astronomy, physical science, problem solving. Submit complete ms.

Fiction Multicultural, nature, science, social studies, bedtime, etc. Non-rhyming stories. Submit complete ms.

Recent Title(s) *A Place for Zero*, by Angeline Spraivagna Lo Presti; *Sir Cumference and the Sword in the Cone*, by Cindy Neuschwander.

CHARLESBRIDGE PUBLISHING, TRADE DIVISION

85 Main St., Watertown MA 02472. (617)926-0329. Fax: (617)926-5720. E-mail: tradeeditorial@charlesbridge.com. Website: www.charlesbridge.com. **Acquisitions:** Submission Editor. Estab. 1980. Publishes hardcover and trade paperback nonfiction children's picture picture books (80%) and fiction picture books for the trade and library markets. **Publishes 30 titles/year. Receives 2,500 submissions/year. 10-20% of books from first-time authors; 80% from unagented writers. Pays royalty. Offers advance.** Publishes book 2-4 years after acceptance of ms. Ms guidelines online.

Imprints Charlesbridge.

O── "We're always interested in innovative approaches to a difficult genre, the nonfiction picture book. No novels or books for older children." Currently emphasizing nature, science, multiculturalism.

Nonfiction Children's/juvenile. Subjects include animals, creative nonfiction, history, multicultural, nature/environment, science, social science. Strong interest in nature, environment, social studies, and other topics for trade and library markets. *Exclusive submissions only.*

Fiction "Strong stories with enduring themes." *Exclusive submissions only.*

Recent Title(s) *The Beetle Alphabet Book*, by Jerry Pallotta; *Mung-Mung*, by Linda Sue Park; *Florida*, by Sandra Friend.

CHATHAM PRESS

Box A, Greenwich CT 06870. **Acquisitions:** Jane Andrassi. Estab. 1971. Publishes hardcover and paperback originals, reprints, and anthologies. **Publishes 10 titles/year. Receives 50 submissions/year. 25% of books from first-time authors; 75% from unagented writers.** Publishes book 6 months after acceptance of ms. Responds in 2 months to queries. Book catalog and ms guidelines for 6×9 SAE with 6 first-class stamps.

O── Chatham Press publishes "books that relate to the U.S. coastline from Maine to the Carolinas and which bring a new insight, visual or verbal, to the nonfiction topic."

Nonfiction Illustrated book. Subjects include history, nature/environment, regional (Northeast seaboard), translation (from French and German), natural history. Query with SASE. Reviews artwork/photos as part of ms package.

Recent Title(s) *Exploring Old Martha's Vineyard.*

Tips "Illustrated New England-relevant titles have the best chance of being sold to our firm. We have a slightly greater (15%) skew toward cooking and travel titles."

CHELSEA GREEN PUBLISHING CO.

P.O. Box 428, 85 N. Main St., White River Junction VT 05001-0428. (802)295-6300. Fax: (802)295-6444. Website: www.chelseagreen.com. **Acquisitions:** Ben Watson, senior editor. Estab. 1984. Publishes hardcover and trade paperback originals and reprints. **Publishes 8-12 titles/year. Receives 300-400 queries and 200-300 mss/year. 30% of books from first-time authors; 80% from unagented writers. Pays royalty on publisher's net. Offers $2,500-10,000 advance.** Publishes book 18 months after acceptance of ms. Responds in 1 week to queries; 1 month to proposals; 1 month to mss. Book catalog free or online; ms guidelines online.

O── Chelsea Green publishes and distributes books relating to issues of sustainability with a special concentration on books about nature, the environment, independent living and enterprise, organic gardening, renewable energy, and alternative or natural building techniques. The books reflect positive options in a world of environmental turmoil. Emphasizing food/agriculture/gardening, innovative shelter and natural building, renewable energy, sustainable business, and enterprise. De-emphasizing nature/natural history.

Nonfiction Cookbook, how-to, reference, technical. Subjects include agriculture/horticulture, art/architecture, cooking/foods/nutrition, gardening, health/medicine, money/finance, nature/environment, forestry, current affairs/politics. Query with SASE, or submit proposal package including outline, 1-2 sample chapter(s). Reviews artwork/photos as part of ms package.

Recent Title(s) *The Slow Food Guide to New York City*, by Slow Food USA; *The Straw Bale House*, by Steen, Steen, Bainbridge; *Gaia's Garden*, by Toby Hemenway.

Tips "Our readers are passionately enthusiastic about ecological solutions for contemporary challenges in construction, energy harvesting, agriculture, and forestry. Our books are also carefully and handsomely produced to give pleasure to bibliophiles of a practical bent. It would be very helpful for prospective authors to have a look at several of our current books, as well as our catalog and website. For certain types of book, we are the perfect publisher, but we are exceedingly focused on particular areas."

CHELSEA HOUSE PUBLISHERS

Haights Cross Communications, 1974 Sproul Rd., Suite 400, Broomall PA 19008-0914. (800)848-BOOK. Fax: (800)780-7300. E-mail: editorial@chelseahouse.com. Website: www.chelseahouse.com. **Acquisitions:** Editorial Assistant. Publishes hardcover originals and reprints. **Publishes 350 titles/year. Receives 1,000 queries and 500 mss/year. 25% of books from first-time authors; 98% from unagented writers. Makes outright purchase of $1,500-3,500.** Publishes book 16 months after acceptance of ms. Accepts simultaneous submissions. Responds in 1 month to queries; 3 months to proposals; 3 months to mss. Book catalog online; ms guidelines for #10 SASE.

⚬→ "We publish a nonfiction education series primarly for the library market/schools."

Nonfiction Biography (must be common format, fitting under a series umbreall a), children's/juvenile. Subjects include Americana, animals, anthropology/archeology, ethnic, gay/lesbian, government/politics, health/medicine, history, hobbies, language/literature, military/war, multicultural, music/dance, nature/environment, recreation, regional, religion, science, sociology, sports, travel, women's issues/studies. "We are interested in expanding our topics to include more on the physical, life and environmental sciences." Query with SASE, or submit proposal package including outline, 2-3 sample chapter(s), résumé. Reviews artwork/photos as part of ms package. Send photocopies.

Recent Title(s) *Ireland* (Modern World Nation Series—geography); *Moliere* (Bloom's Major Dramatists Series—literary criticism); *Right to Privacy* (Point/Counterpoint Series).

Tips "Know our product. Do not waste your time or ours by sending something that does not fit our market. Be professional. Send clean, clear submissions that show you read the preferred submission format. Always include SASE."

CHEMICAL PUBLISHING CO., INC.

527 Third Ave., #427, New York NY 10016-4168. (212)779-0090. Fax: (212)889-1537. E-mail: chempub@aol.com. Website: www.chemicalpublishing.com. **Acquisitions:** Ms. S. Soto-Galicia, publisher. Estab. 1934. Publishes hardcover originals. **Publishes 8 titles/year. Receives 20 queries/year. 50% of books from first-time authors; 100% from unagented writers. Pays 10% royalty on retail price or makes negotiable outright purchase. Offers negotiable advance.** Publishes book 8 months after acceptance of ms. Does not accept simultaneous submissions. Responds in 3 weeks to queries; 5 weeks to proposals; 2 months to mss. Book catalog free; ms guidelines online.

⚬→ Chemical Publishing Co., Inc., publishes professional chemistry-technical titles aimed at people employed in the chemical industry, libraries and graduate courses.

Nonfiction How-to, reference, applied chemical technology (cosmetics, cement, textiles). Subjects include agriculture/horticulture, cooking/foods/nutrition, health/medicine, nature/environment, science, analytical methods, chemical technology, cosmetics, dictionaries, engineering, environmental science, food technology, formularies, industrial technology, medical, metallurgy, textiles. Submit outline, few pages of 3 sample chapter(s), SASE. Reviews artwork/photos as part of ms package.

Recent Title(s) *Cooling Water Treatment, Principles and Practice*; *Harry's Cosmeticology, 8th Ed.*; *Library Handbook for Organic Chemists.*

Tips Audience is professionals in various fields of chemistry, corporate and public libraries, college libraries. "We request a fax letter with an introduction of the author and the kind of book written. Afterwards, we will reply. If the title is of interest, then we will request samples of the manuscript."

CHICAGO REVIEW PRESS

814 N. Franklin, Chicago IL 60610-3109. (312)337-0747. Fax: (312)337-5110. E-mail: csherry@chicagoreviewpress.com. Submissions E-mail: ytaylor@chicagoreviewpress.com. Website: www.chicagoreviewpress.com. **Acquisitions:** Cynthia Sherry, executive editor (general nonfiction, children's); Yuval Taylor, senior editor (African-American and performing arts); Jerome Pohlen, senior editor (educational resources). Estab. 1973. Publishes hardcover and trade paperback originals, and trade paperback reprints. **Publishes 40-50 titles/year. Receives 400 queries and 800 mss/year. 50% of books from first-time authors; 50% from unagented writers. Pays 7-12½% royalty. Offers $3,000-10,000 average advance.** Publishes book 18 months after acceptance of ms. Accepts simultaneous submissions. Responds in 3 months to queries. Book catalog for $3.50; ms guidelines for #10 SASE or online at website.

Imprints Lawrence Hill Books; A Capella Books (contact Yuval Taylor); Zephyr Press (contact Jerome Pohlen).

⚬→ Chicago Review Press publishes intelligent nonfiction on timely subjects for educated readers with special interests.

Nonfiction Children's/juvenile (activity books only), how-to. Subjects include art/architecture, child guidance/parenting, creative nonfiction, education, gardening (regional), health/medicine, history, hobbies, memoirs, multicultural, nature/environment, recreation, regional, music. Query with outline, TOC, and 1-2 sample chapters. Reviews artwork/photos as part of ms package.

Recent Title(s) *Snake Hips*, by Anne Thomas Soffee.

Tips "Along with a table of contents and 1-2 sample chapters, also send a cover letter and a list of credentials with your proposal. Also, provide the following information in your cover letter: audience, market, and competition—who is the book written for and what sets it apart from what's already out there."

CHILD WELFARE LEAGUE OF AMERICA

440 First St. NW, 3rd Floor, Washington DC 20001. (202)638-2952. Fax: (202)638-4004. E-mail: books@cwla.org. Website: www.cwla.org. **Acquisitions:** Acquisitions Editor. Publishes hardcover and trade paperback originals. **Publishes 4-5 trade titles/year; 10-20 professional titles/year. Receives 750 submissions/year. 95% from unagented writers. Pays 0-10% royalty on net domestic sales.** Publishes book 2 years after acceptance of ms. Responds in 6-9 months to queries. Book catalog and ms guidelines online.

Imprints CWLA Press (child welfare professional publications); Child & Family Press (children's books and parenting books for the general public).

> **O—** CWLA is a privately supported, nonprofit, membership-based organization committed to preserving, protecting, and promoting the well-being of all children and their families.

Nonfiction Children's/juvenile. Subjects include child guidance/parenting, sociology. Submit complete ms.

Recent Title(s) *The Coffee Can Kid* (children's); *Respectful Parenting* (parenting).

Tips "We are looking for positive, kid-friendly books for ages 3-9. We are looking for books that have a positive message—a feel-good book."

CHILDSWORK/CHILDSPLAY, LLC

Imprint of The Guidance Channel, 135 Dupont St., P.O. Box 760, Plainview NY 11803-0760. (516)349-5520. Website: www.childswork.com. **Acquisitions:** Karen Schader, editor (psychological books and games for use with children). Publishes trade paperback originals and reprints. **Publishes 10-12 titles/year. Receives 250 queries and 50 mss/year. 5% of books from first-time authors; 100% from unagented writers. Makes outright purchase of $500-3,000.** Publishes book 9 months after acceptance of ms. Accepts simultaneous submissions. Responds in 1 month to queries; 1 month to proposals; 3 months to mss. Book catalog and ms guidelines for 9×12 SAE with 4 first-class stamps.

> **O—** Our target market includes therapists, counselors, and teachers working with children who are experiencing behavioral, emotional, and social difficulties.

Nonfiction Psychological storybooks and workbooks, psychological games. Subjects include child guidance/parenting, education, health/medicine, psychology. All books and games are psychologically based and well researched. Query with SASE.

Fiction Children's storybooks must deal with some aspect of psychological development or difficulty (e.g., ADHD, anger management, social skills, OCD, etc.). "Be in our files (résumé, writing samples), and we will contact you when we develop new projects." Submit complete ms.

Recent Title(s) *Sometimes I Worry Too Much*; *Anger Control Games*.

Tips "Our market is comprised of mental health and education professionals who are primarily therapists, guidance counselors, and teachers. A majority of our projects are assignments rather than submissions. Impress us with your writing ability and your background in psychology and education. If submitting rather seeking work on assignment, demonstrate that your work is marketable and profitable."

CHINA BOOKS

Imprint of Long River Press, 2929 24th St., San Francisco CA 94110-4126. (415)282-2994. Fax: (415)282-0994. Website: www.chinabooks.com. **Acquisitions:** Greg Jones, editor (language study, health, history). Estab. 1960. Publishes hardcover and trade paperback originals. **Publishes 5 titles/year. Receives 300 submissions/year. 10% of books from first-time authors; 95% from unagented writers. Pays 6-8% royalty on net receipts. Offers negotiable advance.** Publishes book 1 year after acceptance of ms. Accepts simultaneous submissions. Responds in 3 months to queries. Book catalog free; ms guidelines online.

> **O—** China Books is the main importer and distributor of books and magazines from China, providing an ever-changing variety of useful tools for travelers, scholars, and others interested in China and Chinese culture. "We are looking for original book ideas, especially in the areas of language study, children's books, history, and culture, all relating to China." Currently emphasizing language study. De-emphasizing art, fiction, poetry.

Nonfiction "Important: All books must be on topics related to China or Chinese-Americans. Books on China's history, politics, environment, women, art/architecture; language textbooks, acupuncture, and folklore." Biography, children's/juvenile, coffee table book, how-to, self-help, textbook. Subjects include agriculture/horticulture, art/architecture, business/economics, cooking/foods/nutrition, education, ethnic, gardening, government/politics, health/medicine, history, language/literature, music/dance, nature/environment, religion, sociology, translation, travel, women's issues/studies. Reviews artwork/photos as part of ms package.

Recent Title(s) *Scotty's Goal*, by Zhao Yu; *Complementary Education and Culture*, by Joe Fong.

Tips ''We are looking for original ideas, especially in language study, children's education, adoption of Chinese babies, or health issues relating to traditional Chinese medicine.''

CHITRA PUBLICATIONS

2 Public Ave., Montrose PA 18801. (570)278-1984. Fax: (570)278-2223. E-mail: chitraed@epix.net. Website: www.quilttownusa.com. **Acquisitions:** Acquisitions Editors. Publishes trade paperback originals. **Publishes 6 titles/year. Receives 70-80 queries and 10-20 mss/year. Pays royalty.** Publishes book 6-12 months after acceptance of ms. Does not accept simultaneous submissions. Responds in 2 weeks to queries; 3 weeks to proposals; 1 month to mss. Book catalog and ms guidelines for #10 SASE; ms guidelines online.

○┅ ''We publish quality quilting magazines and pattern books that recognize, promote, and inspire self expression.''

Nonfiction How-to. Subjects include quilting. Query with SASE. Reviews artwork/photos as part of ms package. Send photocopies or transparencies.

Ⓝ CHIVALRY BOOKSHELF

4226 Cambridge Way, Union City CA 94587. (510)471-2944. Fax: (978)418-4774. E-mail: chronique_editor@yahoo.com. Submissions E-mail: csr@chivalrybookshelf.com. Website: www.chivalrybookshelf.com. **Acquisitions:** Brian R. Price, publisher (history, art, philosophy, political science, military, martial arts, fencing); Gregory Mele, martial arts editor (martial arts, fencing, history). Estab. 1996. Publishes hardcover and trade paperback originals and reprints. **Publishes 12 titles/year. Receives 75 queries and 25 mss/year. 50% of books from first-time authors; 90% from unagented writers. Pays 5-12% royalty.** Publishes book 6 months after acceptance of ms. Does not accept simultaneous submissions. Responds in 1 month to queries; 1 month to proposals; 2 months to mss. Book catalog free; ms guidelines online.

Nonfiction Biography, booklets, children's/juvenile, coffee table book, gift book, how-to, humor, illustrated book, scholarly, technical. Subjects include art/architecture, creative nonfiction, education, general nonfiction, government/politics, history, military/war, recreation, sports (martial arts/fencing especially), translation. ''Chivalry Bookshelf began focusing on new works and important reprints relating to arms and armour, medieval knighthood, and related topics. Since then, we have become the largest publisher of books relating to 'Western' or 'historical' martial arts, including translations, interpretations, and fascimile reproductions done in partnership with major museums such as the J. Paul Getty Museum and the British Royal Armouries. During 2004, we are expanding our history and military line dramatically and will be seeking manuscripts, especially translations and biographies, relating to classical, medieval, Renaissance, or pre-21st century history. During 2005 we plan to launch a new imprint dealing with modern politics and military issues. Manuscripts that deal with military memoirs, arms and armour, martial arts, and medieval history will receive particular consideration.'' Query with SASE, or submit proposal package including outline, 1 sample chapter(s), sample illustrations, or submit complete ms. Reviews artwork/photos as part of ms package.

Recent Title(s) *The Medieval Art of Swordsmanship*, translated and interpreted by Dr. Jeffrey L. Forgeng, co-published with the British Royal Armouries (art history); *Jousts & Tournaments*, by Dr. Stephen Muhlberger (scholarly/popular translation); *Arte of Defence*, by William E. Wilson (historical fencing).

Tips ''The bulk of our books are intended for serious amateur scholars and students of history and martial arts. The authors we select tend to have a strong voice, are well read in their chosen field, and submit relatively clean manuscripts.''

CHOSEN BOOKS PUBLISHING CO., LTD.

3985 Bradwater St., Fairfax VA 22031-3702. (703)764-8250. Fax: (703)764-3995. E-mail: jecampbell@aol.com. Website: www.bakerbooks.com. **Acquisitions:** Jane Campbell, editorial director. Estab. 1971. Publishes hardcover and trade paperback originals. **Publishes 20-25 titles/year. Receives 500 submissions/year. 15% of books from first-time authors; 99% from unagented writers. Offers small advance.** Publishes book 12-18 months after acceptance of ms. Accepts simultaneous submissions. Responds in 3 months to queries. Ms guidelines for #10 SASE.

○┅ ''We publish well-crafted books that recognize the gifts and ministry of the Holy Spirit, and help the reader live a more empowered and effective life for Jesus Christ.''

Nonfiction Subjects include religion (Christianity). ''We publish books reflecting the current acts of the Holy Spirit in the world, books with a charismatic Christian orientation.'' No New Age, poetry, fiction, autobiographies, biographies, compilations, Bible studies, booklets, academic, or children's books. Submit synopsis, chapter outline, résumé, 2 chapters and SASE. No computer disks or e-mail attachments; brief query only by e-mail.

Recent Title(s) *Healing the Nations: A Call to Global Intercession*, by John Sandford.

Tips ''We look for solid, practical advice for the growing and maturing Christian from authors with professional or personal experience platforms. No conversion accounts or chronicling of life events, please. State the topic or theme of your book clearly in your cover letter.''

CHRISTIAN ED. PUBLISHERS

P.O. Box 26639, San Diego CA 92196. (858)578-4700. Fax: (858)578-2431. Website: www.christianedwarehouse. com. **Acquisitions:** Janet Ackelson, assistant editor. **Publishes 80 titles/year. Makes outright purchase of 3¢/ word.** Responds in 3 months on assigned material. Book catalog for 9×12 SAE with 4 first-class stamps; ms guidelines for #10 SASE.

O→ Christian Ed. Publishers is an independent, nondenominational, evangelical company founded nearly 50 years ago to produce Christ-centered curriculum materials based on the Word of God for thousands of churches of different denominations throughout the world. ''Our mission is to introduce children, teens, and adults to a personal faith in Jesus Christ, and to help them grow in their faith and service to the Lord. We publish materials that teach moral and spiritual values while training individuals for a lifetime of Christian service.'' Currently emphasizing Bible curriculum for preschool through preteen ages.

Nonfiction Children's/juvenile. Subjects include education (Christian), religion. ''All subjects are on assignment.'' Query with SASE.

Fiction ''All writing is done on assignment.'' Query with SASE.

Recent Title(s) *All-Stars for Jesus: Bible Curriculum for Preteens.*

Tips ''Read our guidelines carefully before sending us a manuscript. All writing is done on assignment only and must be age appropriate (preschool-6th grade).''

CHRONICLE BOOKS

85 Second St., 6th Floor, San Francisco CA 94105. (415)537-4200. Fax: (415)537-4460. E-mail: frontdesk@chroni clebooks.com. Website: www.chroniclebooks.com. **Acquisitions:** Jay Schaefer (fiction); Bill LeBlond (cookbooks); Leslie Jonath (lifestyle); Alan Rapp (art and design); Sarah Malarky (licensing and popular culture); Mikyla Bruder (crafts and lifestyle); Steve Mockus (popular culture); Debra Lande (gift books); Victoria Rock (children's). Estab. 1966. Publishes hardcover and trade paperback originals. **Publishes 175 titles/year.** Publishes book 18 months after acceptance of ms. Accepts simultaneous submissions. Responds in 3 months to queries. Book catalog for 11x14 SAE with 5 first-class stamps; ms guidelines online.

Imprints Chronicle Books for Children, GiftWorks (ancillary products, such as stationery, gift books).

O→ ''Inspired by the enduring magic and importance of books, our objective is to create and distribute exceptional publishing that is instantly recognizable for its spirit, creativity and value. This objective informs our business relationships and endeavors, be they with customers, authors, suppliers or colleagues.''

Nonfiction Coffee table book, cookbook, gift book. Subjects include art/architecture, cooking/foods/nutrition, gardening, nature/environment, photography, recreation, regional, design, pop culture, interior design. Query or submit outline/synopsis with artwork and sample chapters.

Fiction Submit complete ms.

Recent Title(s) *The Beatles Anthology*, by The Beatles; *Worst-Case Scenario Survival Handbook*, by David Borgenicht and Joshua Piven.

CHRONICLE BOOKS FOR CHILDREN

85 Second St., 6th Floor, San Francisco CA 94105. (415)537-4200. Fax: (415)537-4460. E-mail: frontdesk@chroni clebooks.com. Website: www.chroniclekids.com. **Acquisitions:** Victoria Rock, associate publisher; Beth Weber, managing editor; Jennifer Vetter, editor; Susan Pearson, editor-at-large; Samantha McFerrin, assistant editor. Publishes hardcover and trade paperback originals. **Publishes 40-50 titles/year. Receives 20,000 submissions/ year. 5% of books from first-time authors; 25% from unagented writers. Pays 8% royalty. Offers variable advance.** Publishes book 18 months after acceptance of ms. Accepts simultaneous submissions. Responds in 2-18 weeks to queries; 6 months to mss. Book catalog for 9×12 SAE with 3 first-class stamps; ms guidelines online.

O→ Chronicle Books for Children publishes an eclectic mixture of traditional and innovative children's books. ''Our aim is to publish books that inspire young readers to learn and grow creatively while helping them discover the joy of reading. We're looking for quirky, bold artwork and subject matter.'' Currently emphasizing picture books. De-emphasizing young adult.

Nonfiction Biography, children's/juvenile (for ages 8-12), illustrated book, picture books (for ages up to 8 years). Subjects include animals, art/architecture, multicultural, nature/environment, science. Query with synopsis and SASE. Reviews artwork/photos as part of ms package.

Fiction Mainstream/contemporary, multicultural, young adult, picture books; middle grade fiction; young adult projects. ''We do not accept proposals by fax, via e-mail, or on disk. When submitting artwork, either as a part of a project or as samples for review, do not send original art. Please be sure to include an SASE large enough to hold your materials. Projects submitted without an appropriate SASE will be recycled." Query with SASE. Send complete ms with SASE for picture books.

Recent Title(s) *Ghost Wings*; *Dream Carver*; *Star in the Darkness*.

Tips "We are interested in projects that have a unique bent to them—be it in subject matter, writing style, or illustrative technique. As a small list, we are looking for books that will lend our list a distinctive flavor. Primarily we are interested in fiction and nonfiction picture books for children ages up to eight years, and nonfiction books for children ages up to twelve years. We publish board, pop-up, and other novelty formats as well as picture books. We are also interested in early chapter books, middle grade fiction, and young adult projects."

CHURCH GROWTH INSTITUTE

P.O. Box 7, Elkton MD 21922-0007. (434)525-0022. Fax: (434)525-0608. E-mail: cgimail@churchgrowth.org. Website: www.churchgrowth.org. **Acquisitions:** Cindy Spear, administrator/resource development director. Estab. 1978. Publishes trade paperback originals, 3-ring-bound manuals, mixed media resource packets. **Publishes 4 titles/year. Pays 6% royalty on retail price.** Publishes book 1 year after acceptance of ms. Accepts simultaneous submissions. Responds in 3 months to queries. Book catalog for 9×12 SAE with 4 first-class stamps; ms guidelines given after query and outline is received.

> O→ "Our mission is to provide practical resources to help pastors, churches, and individuals reach their potential for Christ; to promote spiritual and numerical growth in churches, thereby leading Christians to maturity and lost people to Christ; and to equip pastors so they can equip their church members to do the work of the ministry."

Nonfiction "Material should originate from a conservative Christian view and cover topics that will help churches grow, through leadership training, self-evaluation, and new or unique ministries, or enhancing existing ministries. Self-discovery inventories regarding spiritual growth, relationship improvement, etc., are hot items." How-to. Subjects include education, religion (church-growth related), ministry, how-to manuals, spiritual growth, relationship-building, evangelism. "Accepted manuscripts will be adapted to our resource packet, manual, or inventory format. All material must be practical and easy for the average Christian to understand." Query, or submit outline and brief explanation of what the packet will accomplish in the local church and whether it is leadership or lay oriented. Queries accepted by mail or e-mail. No phone queries. Reviews artwork/photos as part of ms package. Send photos or images on CD (in TIFF, EPS, or PDF format).

Recent Title(s) *Ministry Descriptions*; *Ask Me to Pray for You*; *Evaluating Your Friendship Skills*.

Tips "We are not publishing many textbooks. Concentrate on how-to manuals and ministry evaluation and diagnostic tools and spiritual or relationship-oriented 'inventories' for individual Christians."

CIRCLET PRESS, INC.

1770 Massachusetts Ave., #278, Cambridge MA 02140. E-mail: circlet-info@circlet.com. Submissions E-mail: editorial@circlet.com. Website: www.circlet.com. **Acquisitions:** Cecilia Tan, publisher/editor. Estab. 1992. Publishes hardcover and trade paperback originals. **Publishes 4-6 titles/year. Receives 50-100 queries and 500 mss/year. 90% from unagented writers. Pays 4-12% royalty on retail price, or makes outright purchase. Also pays in books, if author prefers.** Publishes book 18 months after acceptance of ms. Accepts simultaneous submissions. Responds in 1 months to queries; 6-18 months to mss. Book catalog for 10 SAE with 2 first-class stamps; ms guidelines online.

Imprints The Ultra Violet Library (gay and lesbian science fiction and fantasy "these books will not be as erotic as our others"); Circumflex (erotic and sexual nonfiction titles, how-to and essays).

> O→ "Circlet Press publishes science fiction/fantasy short stories which are too erotic for the mainstream and to promote literature with a positive view of sex and sexuality, which celebrates pleasure and diversity. We also publish other books celebrating sexuality and imagination with our imprints: The Ultra Violet Library and Circumflex."

Fiction Ethnic, science fiction, short stories only. "Fiction must combine both the erotic and the fantastic. The erotic content needs to be an integral part of a science fiction story, and vice versa. Writers should not assume that any sex is the same as erotica. No horror! No exploitative sex, murder or rape. No degradation." No novels. Query with SASE. Submit full short stories up to 10,000 words between April 15 and August 31. Manuscripts received outside this reading period are discarded. Queries only via e-mail.

Recent Title(s) *Nymph*, by Francesca Lia Block; *The Darker Passions: Dracula*, by Amarantha Knight.

Tips "Our audience is adults who enjoy science fiction and fantasy, especially the works of Anne Rice, Storm Constantine, Samuel Delany, who enjoy vivid storytelling and erotic content. Seize your most vivid fantasy, your deepest dream and set it free onto paper. That is at the heart of all good speculative fiction. Then if it has an erotic theme as well as a science fiction one, send it to me. No horror, rape, death or mutilation! I want to see stories that *celebrate* sex and sexuality in a positive manner. Please write for our guidelines as each year we have a specific list of topics we seek. Short stories only, *no* novels.''

CLARION BOOKS

Houghton Mifflin Co., 215 Park Ave. S., New York NY 10003. Website: www.houghtonmifflinbooks.com. **Acquisitions:** Dinah Stevenson, editorial director; Jennifer B. Greene, editor (contemporary fiction, picture books for all ages, nonfiction); Jennifer Wingertzahn, editor (fiction, picture books); Lynne Polvino, associate editor (fiction, nonfiction, picture books). Estab. 1965. Publishes hardcover originals for children. **Publishes 50 titles/year. Pays 5-10% royalty on retail price. Offers minimum of $4,000 advance.** Publishes book 2 years after acceptance of ms. Responds in 2 months to queries Prefers no multiple submissions to mss. Ms guidelines for #10 SASE or online.

O—¬ Clarion Books publishes picture books, nonfiction, and fiction for infants through grade 12. Avoid telling your stories in verse unless you are a professional poet.

Nonfiction Biography, children's/juvenile, photo essay. Subjects include Americana, history, language/literature, nature/environment, photography, holiday. No unsolicited mss. Query with SASE, or submit proposal package including sample chapter(s), SASE. Reviews artwork/photos as part of ms package. Send photocopies.

Fiction Adventure, historical, humor, mystery, suspense, strong character studies. Clarion is highly selective in the areas of historical fiction, fantasy, and science fiction. A novel must be superlatively written in order to find a place on the list. Mss that arrive without an SASE of adequate size will *not* be responded to or returned. Accepts fiction translations. No unsolicited mss. Submit complete ms. No queries, please. Send to only *one* Clarion editor.

Recent Title(s) *Opera Cat*, by Tess Weaver; *The Same Stuff as Stars*, by Katherine Paterson.

Tips Looks for ''freshness, enthusiasm—in short, life.''

ℕ Ⓐ CLARKSON POTTER

The Crown Publishing Group, Random House, Inc., 1745 Broadway, 13th Floor, New York NY 10019. (212)782-9000. Website: www.clarksonpotter.com. Lauren Shakely, editorial director. Estab. 1959. Publishes hardcover and trade paperback originals. Accepts agented submissions only. **Publishes 55 titles/year. 15% of books from first-time authors. Offers advance.** Does not accept simultaneous submissions. Responds in 3 months to queries; 3 months to proposals.

O—¬ Clarkson Potter specializes in publishing cooking books, decorating and other around-the-house how-to subjects.

Nonfiction Biography, how-to, humor, self-help, crafts, cooking and foods; decorating; design gardening. Subjects include art/architecture, child guidance/parenting, cooking/foods/nutrition, humor, language/literature, memoirs, nature/environment, photography, psychology, translation. *Agented submissions only.* Query or submit outline and sample chapter with tearsheets from magazines and artwork copies (e.g.—color photocopies or duplicate transparencies).

CLEAR LIGHT PUBLISHERS

823 Don Diego, Santa Fe NM 87505-4224. (505)989-9590. E-mail: publish@clearlightbooks.com. **Acquisitions:** Harmon Houghton, publisher. Estab. 1981. Publishes hardcover and trade paperback originals. **Publishes 20-24 titles/year. Receives 100 queries/year. 10% of books from first-time authors; 50% from unagented writers. Pays 10% royalty on wholesale price. Offers advance, a percent of gross potential.** Publishes book 1 year after acceptance of ms. Accepts simultaneous submissions. Responds in 3 months to queries. Book catalog free.

O—¬ Clear Light publishes books that ''accurately depict the positive side of human experience and inspire the spirit.''

Nonfiction Biography, coffee table book, cookbook. Subjects include Americana, anthropology/archeology, art/architecture, cooking/foods/nutrition, ethnic, history, nature/environment, philosophy, photography, regional (Southwest). Query with SASE. Reviews artwork/photos as part of ms package. Send photocopies.

Recent Title(s) *American Indian History*, by Robert Venables; *Celebrations Cookbook*, by Myra Baucom; *American Indian Love Stories*, by Herman Grey.

CLEIS PRESS

P.O. Box 14684, San Francisco CA 94114-0684. (415)575-4700. Fax: (415)575-4705. Website: www.cleispress.c om. **Acquisitions:** Frederique Delacoste. Estab. 1980. Publishes trade paperback originals and reprints. **Publishes 20 titles/year. 10% of books from first-time authors; 90% from unagented writers. Pays variable royalty on retail price.** Publishes book 2 years after acceptance of ms. Responds in 1 month to queries. Book catalog for #10 SAE with 2 first-class stamps.

0→ Cleis Press specializes in feminist and gay/lesbian fiction and nonfiction.

Nonfiction Subjects include gay/lesbian, women's issues/studies, sexual politics, erotica, human rights, African-American studies. "We are interested in books on topics of sexuality, human rights and women's and gay and lesbian literature. Please consult our website first to be certain that your book fits our list." Query or submit outline and sample chapters.

Fiction Feminist, gay/lesbian, literary. "We are looking for high quality fiction by women and men." No romances. Submit complete ms. *Writer's Market* recommends sending a query with SASE first.

Recent Title(s) *Black Like Us* (fiction); *Whole Lesbian Sex Book* (nonfiction); *No Place Like Home: Echoes from Kosovo* (nonfiction).

Tips "Be familiar with publishers' catalogs; be absolutely aware of your audience; research potential markets; present fresh new ways of looking at your topic; avoid 'PR' language and include publishing history in query letter."

CLEVELAND STATE UNIVERSITY POETRY CENTER

R.T. 1841, Cleveland State University, 2121 Euclid Ave., Cleveland OH 44115-2214. (216)687-3986. Fax: (216)687-6943. E-mail: poetrycenter@csuohio.edu. Website: www.csuohio.edu/poetrycenter. **Acquisitions:** Rita Grabowski, coordinator. Estab. 1962. Publishes trade paperback originals. **Publishes 4 titles/year. Receives 500 queries and up to 1,000 mss/year. 60% of books from first-time authors; 100% from unagented writers. CSU Poetry Series pays one-time, lump-sum royalty of $300, plus 50 copies; Cleveland Poets Series (Ohio poets only) pays 100 copies. $1,000 prize for best full-length ms each year in 2 categories.** Accepts simultaneous submissions. Responds in 1 month to queries; 8 months to mss. Manuscript guidelines for SASE. Manuscripts are not returned.

Poetry Send SASE for guidelines or check website. Submit only November-January. Charges $20 reading fee. Reviews artwork/photos only if applicable (e.g., concrete poetry). No light verse, inspirational, or greeting card verse. ("This does not mean that we do not consider poetry with humor or philosophical/religious import.")

Recent Title(s) *The Job of Being Everybody*, by Douglas Goetsch; *Guide to Native Beasts*, by Mary Quade.

Tips "Our books are for serious readers of poetry, i.e., poets, critics, academics, students, people who read *Poetry*, *FIELD*, *American Poetry Review*, etc. Trends include movement away from 'confessional' poetry; greater attention to form and craftsmanship. Project an interesting, coherent personality; link poems so as to make coherent unity, not just a miscellaneous collection. Especially need poems with mystery, i.e., poems that suggest much, but do not tell all."

ℕ CLOVER PARK PRESS

P.O. Box 5067, Santa Monica CA 90409-5067. (310)452-7657. E-mail: cloverparkpr@earthlink.net. Website: home.earthlink.net/~cloverparkpr. **Acquisitions:** Martha Grant, acquisitions editor. Estab. 1991. Publishes hardcover and trade paperback originals. **Publishes 6-10 titles/year. Receives 60 queries and 20 mss/year. 80% from unagented writers. Pays royalty, or makes outright purchase. Offers modest advance.** Publishes book less than 1 year after acceptance of ms. Accepts simultaneous submissions. Responds in 2 months to queries; 2 months to proposals; 4 months to mss. Book catalog online; ms guidelines for #10 SASE.

Nonfiction Biography, general nonfiction. Subjects include creative nonfiction, memoirs, multicultural, nature/environment, regional, science, travel, women's issues/studies, world affairs. "We are accepting queries in the above subjects in order to expand our list." Query with SASE, or submit proposal package including outline, author bio, 30-50 pages (including the first chapter), SASE.

Recent Title(s) *Harmattan: A Journey Across the Sahara*, by Geraldine Kennedy (travel memoir); *From the Center of the Earth: Stories Out of the Peace Corps*, edited by G. Kennedy (multicultural anthology).

Tips "Our audience is women, high school, and college students, readers with curiosity about the world. Initial contact by e-mail or query letter. We welcome good writing. Have patience, we will respond."

COACHES CHOICE

P.O. Box 1828, Monterey CA 93942. (888)229-5745. Fax: (831)372-6075. E-mail: info@healthylearning.com. Website: www.coacheschoice.com. **Acquisitions:** Sue Peterson, general manager (sports). Publishes trade paperback originals and reprints. **Publishes 75 titles/year. Receives 100 queries and 60 mss/year. 50% of books from first-time authors; 95% from unagented writers. Pays 10-15% royalty.** Publishes book 1 year after acceptance of ms. Accepts simultaneous submissions. Responds in 2 months to queries. Book catalog free; ms guidelines online.

0→ "We publish books for anyone who coaches a sport or has an interest in coaching a sport—all levels of competition."

Nonfiction How-to, reference. Subjects include sports, sports specific training, general physical conditioning. Submit proposal package including outline, 2 sample chapter(s), résumé. Reviews artwork/photos as part of ms package. Send photocopies or diagrams.

Recent Title(s) *Coaching the Multiple West Coast Offense*, by Ron Jenkins.

COASTAL CAROLINA PRESS

2231 Wrightsville Ave., Wilmington NC 28403. Website: www.coastalcarolinapress.org. **Acquisitions:** Nicole Smith, editor. Estab. 1999. Hardcover, trade paperback and mass market paperback originals and trade paperback reprints. **Publishes 4 titles/year. 70% of books from first-time authors; 100% from unagented writers. Pays royalty.** Publishes book 1 year after acceptance of ms. Book catalog and ms guidelines online.

 ○➡ "We are a non-profit corporation dedicated to publishing materials about the history, culture and activities of coastal North & South Carolina. We do not publish poetry or religious titles."

Nonfiction Coffee table book, cookbook, how-to, humor. Subjects include agriculture/horticulture, art/architecture, cooking/foods/nutrition, creative nonfiction, education, ethnic, gardening, history, language/literature, memoirs, military/war, multicultural, music/dance, nature/environment, photography, recreation, regional, sociology, travel, women's issues/studies. Publishes books with regional niche. Query with SASE.

Fiction Adventure, ethnic, historical, humor, juvenile, literary, mainstream/contemporary, military/war, multicultural, mystery, regional, short story collections, suspense, young adult. Mss must be written by authors living on the coast of the Carolinas and/or feature a coastal theme or setting. Query with SASE.

Recent Title(s) *Searching for Virginia Dave: A Fool's Errand*, by Marjorie Hudson (historical non-fiction/memoir); *Island Murders*, by Wanda Campbell (fiction).

COFFEE HOUSE PRESS

27 N. Fourth St., Suite 400, Minneapolis MN 55401. Fax: (612)338-4004. Publisher: Allan Kornblum. **Acquisitions:** Chris Fischbach, senior editor. Estab. 1984. Publishes hardcover and trade paperback originals. **Publishes 14 titles/year. Receives 5,000 queries and 3,000 mss/year. 75% from unagented writers. Pays 8% royalty on retail price. Provides 15 author's copies.** Publishes book 18 months after acceptance of ms. Responds in 1 month to queries; up to 6 months to mss. Book catalog and ms guidelines for #10 SASE with 2 first-class stamps; ms guidelines for #10 SAE with 55¢ first-class stamps.

Fiction Ethnic, experimental, literary, mainstream/contemporary, short story collections, novels. No genre. Query with SASE. Query first with samples and SASE.

Poetry Full-length collections.

Recent Title(s) *Miniatures*, by Norah Labiner (fiction); *Avalanche*, by Quincy Troupe (poetry).

Tips "Look for our books at stores and libraries to get a feel for what we like to publish. No phone calls, e-mails, or faxes."

COLLECTORS PRESS, INC.

P.O. Box 230986, Portland OR 97281-0986. (503)684-3030. Fax: (503)684-3777. Website: www.collectorspress.com. **Acquisitions:** Richard Perry, publisher. Estab. 1992. Publishes hardcover and trade paperback originals. **Publishes 20 titles/year. Receives 500 queries and 200 mss/year. 75% of books from first-time authors; 75% from unagented writers. Pays royalty.** Publishes book 1 year after acceptance of ms. Responds in 1 month to queries. Book catalog and ms guidelines free.

 ○➡ Collectors Press, Inc., publishes award-winning popular-culture coffee table and gift books on 20th century, and modern collections and interests.

Nonfiction Illustrated book, reference. Subjects include art/architecture, photography, nostalgic pop culture, science-fiction art, fantasy art, graphic design, comic art, magazine art, historical art, poster art, genre-specific art. Submit proposal package, including market research, outline, 2 sample chapters, and SASE. Reviews artwork/photos as part of ms package. Send transparencies or very clear photos.

Recent Title(s) *Silver Age of Comic Book Art*; *Candy: The Sweet History*.

Tips "Your professional package must be typed. No computer disks accepted."

🄽 COLLEGE CENTRAL PRESS

141 W. 28th St., 9th Floor, New York NY 10001. (212)714-1731. E-mail: info@collegecentralpress.com. Submissions E-mail: submissions@collegecentralpress.com. **Acquisitions:** Jeff Gardner, Debbie Kuo. Estab. 2003. Publishes trade paperback, mass market, and electronic originals and reprints. **Publishes 25 titles/year. Pays 30-70% royalty on retail price.**

Nonfiction Audiocassettes, booklets, how-to, reference, self-help, general nonfiction. Subjects include art/architecture, business/economics, computers/electronic, cooking/foods/nutrition, education, gay/lesbian, health/medicine, hobbies, money/finance, music/dance, nature/environment, recreation, sex, software, sports, travel, women's issues/studies, world affairs, jobs, communications, counseling/career guidance, entertainment/games, house & home, real estate, young adult. Submit proposal package including outline, 2 sample chapter(s), or submit complete ms. Reviews artwork/photos as part of ms package. Send photocopies.

Tips "Our audience includes graduating seniors at colleges, universities, and technical schools, as well as entry-level job seekers and employers."

COLLEGE PRESS PUBLISHING CO.

P.O. Box 1132, Joplin MO 64802. (417)623-6280. Website: www.collegepress.com. **Acquisitions:** Acquisitions Editor. Estab. 1959. Publishes hardcover and trade paperback originals and reprints. **Publishes 15-20 titles/ year. Receives 400 queries and 300 mss/year. 25% of books from first-time authors; 90% from unagented writers. Pays 5-15% royalty on wholesale price.** Publishes book 6 months after acceptance of ms. Accepts simultaneous submissions. Responds in 3 months to proposals. Book catalog for 9×12 SAE with 5 first-class stamps; ms guidelines online.

Imprints HeartSpring Publishing (nonacademic Christian, inspirational, devotional and Christian fiction).

O₋ "College Press is an evangelical Christian publishing house primarily associated with the Christian churches/Church of Christ."

Nonfiction "We seek textbooks used in Christian colleges and universities—leaning toward an Arminian and an amillennial mindset." Textbook (Christian textbooks and small group studies). Subjects include religion, Christian apologetics, historical biographies of Christians. Query with SASE, or submit proposal package including 3 sample chapter(s), author bio, synopsis.

Recent Title(s) *Encounters with Christ*, by Mark E. Moore.

Tips "Our core market is Christian Churches/Churches of Christ and conservative evangelical Christians. Have your material critically reviewed prior to sending it. Make sure that it is non-Calvinistic and that it leans more amillennial (if it is apocalyptic writing)."

COMMON COURAGE PRESS

One Red Barn Rd. Box 702, Monroe ME 04951. Fax: (207)525-3068. Website: www.commoncouragepress.com. **Acquisitions:** Ms. Flic Shooter, publisher (leftist political literature). Estab. 1991. Publishes hardcover and trade paperback originals and trade paperback reprints. **Publishes 12 titles/year. Receives 50 queries and 200 mss/ year. 50% of books from first-time authors; 100% from unagented writers. Pays 10% royalty on wholesale price.** Publishes book 9 months after acceptance of ms. Accepts simultaneous submissions. Responds in 1 month to queries. Book catalog and ms guidelines online.

• Query by mail or fax or use e-mail form on website.

O₋ "Nonfiction leftist, activist, political, history, feminist, media issues are our niche."

Nonfiction Reference, textbook. Subjects include anthropology/archeology, creative nonfiction, ethnic, gay/ lesbian, government/politics, health/medicine, history, military/war, multicultural, nature/environment, science. Query with SASE or submit proposal package, including outline or submit completed ms. Reviews artwork/photos as part of ms package.

Recent Title(s) *New Military Humanism*, by Noam Chomsky (leftist political); *Rogue State*, by William Blum (leftist political).

Tips Audience consists of left-wing activists, college audiences.

CONCORDIA PUBLISHING HOUSE

3558 S. Jefferson Ave., St. Louis MO 63118-3968. (314)268-1187. Fax: (314)268-1329. Website: www.cph.org. **Acquisitions:** Peggy Kuethe, production editor (children's product, adult devotional, teaching resources); Mark Sell, senior editor (adult nonfiction on Christian spirituality and culture, academic works of interest in Lutheran markets). Estab. 1869. Publishes hardcover and trade paperback originals. **Publishes 50 titles/year.** Ms guidelines online.

O₋ Concordia publishes Protestant, inspirational, theological, family, and juvenile material. All mss must conform to the doctrinal tenets of The Lutheran Church—Missouri Synod. No longer publishes fiction.

Nonfiction Children's/juvenile, adult. Subjects include child guidance/parenting (in Christian context), religion, inspirational.

Recent Title(s) *Faithfully Parenting Tweens: A Proactive Approach*, by John Bucka (parenting); *A Tree for Christmas*, by Dandi Daley Mackall (children's picture).

Tips "Call for information about what we are currently accepting."

CONTEMPORARY BOOKS

Imprint of McGraw-Hill Co., 130 E. Randolph St., Suite 900, Chicago IL 60601. (312)233-6500. Fax: (312)233-7570. Website: www.books.mcgraw-hill.com. Also, 2 Penn Plaza, 11th Floor, New York NY 10121. (212)904-2000. Vice President: Philip Ruppel. **Acquisitions:** Chicago: Monica Stoll, associate editor (general trade); Christopher Brown, executive editor (world languages and test prep); Garret Lemoi, associate editor (world languages). New York: Judith McCarthy, senior editor (health and self-help); Michele Pezzuti, associate editor (self-help); Mark Weinstein, editor (sports). Estab. 1947. Publishes hardcover originals and trade paperback originals and reprints. **Publishes 300 titles/year. Receives 5,000 submissions/year. 10% of books from first-time authors; 25% from unagented writers. Pays 6-15% royalty on retail price. Offers advance.** Publishes book 1 year after acceptance of ms. Accepts simultaneous submissions. Responds in 2 months to queries. Ms guidelines for #10 SASE.

Imprints Contemporary Books, VGM Career Books, McGraw-Hill.

O→ "We are a midsize, niche-oriented, backlist-oriented publisher. We publish exclusively nonfiction in general interest trade categories."

Nonfiction How-to, reference (popular and general), self-help. Subjects include child guidance/parenting, cooking/foods/nutrition, health/medicine, psychology, sports, careers, foreign languages. Query with SASE, or submit outline, sample chapter(s). Reviews artwork/photos as part of ms package.

Recent Title(s) *Raising Resilient Children*, by Robert Brooks and Sam Goldstein; *The Last-Minute Party Girl*, by Erika Lenkert.

N CONTINUUM INTERNATIONAL PUBLISHING GROUP, LTD.

15 E. 26th St., Suite 1703, New York NY 10010. (212)953-5858 and (800)561-7704. Fax: (212)953-5944. E-mail: info@continuum-books.com. Website: www.continuumbooks.com/index. **Acquisitions:** Robin Baird-Smith, publishing director (religious books); Anthony Haynes, publishing director (philosophy, education, linguistics, literature, reference). Publishes hardcover originals and paperback textbooks. **Publishes 350-400 titles/year. Receives 1,000 queries and 400 mss/year. 10% of books from first-time authors; 99% from unagented writers. Pays 0-15% royalty. Offers advance.** Publishes book 9 months after acceptance of ms. Does not accept simultaneous submissions. Responds in 1 month to proposals. Book catalog and ms guidelines free.

Imprints Continuum, Pinter, Thoemmes Continuum, Geoffrey Chapman, Mowbray, Mansell, Anthlone Press, T & T Clark, Burns & Oates, Sheffield Academic Press.

O→ Continuum publishes textbooks, monographs, and reference works in the humanities, arts, and social sciences for students, teachers, and professionals worldwide.

Nonfiction Reference, technical, textbook. Subjects include anthropology/archeology, business/economics, education, film/cinema/stage (performance), government/politics, history, language/literature, music/dance (popular), philosophy, religion, sociology, travel (tourism), therapy culture studies, linguistics. Submit outline.

Recent Title(s) *New History of Jazz*, by Alyn Shipton; *The Continuum Companion to Twentieth Century Theatre*, edited by Colin Chambers.

COOPER SQUARE PRESS

Rowman and Littlefield Publishing Group, 200 Park Ave. S., Suite 1109, New York NY 10003. (212)529-3888. Fax: (212)529-4223. Website: www.coopersquarepress.com. **Acquisitions:** Ross Plotkin, acquisitions editor. Estab. 1984. Publishes hardcover originals, trade paperback originals and reprints. **Publishes 40 titles/year. Receives 1,200 submissions/year. 15% of books from first-time authors; 65% from unagented writers. Pays 10-15% royalty on net receipts.** Publishes book 1 year after acceptance of ms. Responds in 2 months to queries. Book catalog and ms guidelines for 9×12 SAE with 4 first-class stamps.

Nonfiction Biography, reference (trade). Subjects include contemporary culture, history, contemporary affairs, music, film, theater, art, nature writing, exploration, women's studies, African-American studies, literary studies. No unsolicited mss. Query with SASE, or submit outline, sample chapter(s).

O COPPER CANYON PRESS

P.O. Box 271, Port Townsend WA 98368. (360)385-4925. Fax: (360)385-4985. E-mail: poetry@coppercanyonpress.org. Website: www.coppercanyonpress.org. **Acquisitions:** Sam Hamill, editor. Estab. 1972. Publishes trade paperback originals and occasional cloth-bound editions. **Publishes 18 titles/year. Receives 2,000 queries and 1,500 mss/year. 10% of books from first-time authors; 95% from unagented writers. Pays royalty.** Publishes book 2 years after acceptance of ms. Responds in 4 months to queries. Book catalog free; ms guidelines online.

O→ Copper Canyon Press is dedicated to publishing poetry in a wide range of styles and from a full range of the world's many cultures.

Poetry "First, second, and third book manuscripts are considered only for our Hayden Carruth Award, presented annually." Send SASE for entry form in September of each year. *No unsolicited mss.*

Recent Title(s) *Steal Away*, by C.D. Wright; *Nightworks*, by Marvin Bell; *The Complete Poems of Kenneth Rexroth*.

CORNELL MARITIME PRESS, INC.

P.O. Box 456, Centreville MD 21617-0456. (410)758-1075. Fax: (410)758-6849. E-mail: cornell@crosslink.net. **Acquisitions:** Charlotte Kurst, managing editor. Estab. 1938. Publishes hardcover originals and quality paperbacks. **Publishes 7-9 titles/year. Receives 150 submissions/year. 80% of books from first-time authors; 99% from unagented writers.** Publishes book 1 year after acceptance of ms. Responds in 2 months to queries. Book catalog for 10×13 SAE with 5 first-class stamps.

Imprints Tidewater (regional history, folklore, and wildlife of the Chesapeake Bay and the Delmarva Peninsula).
O→ Cornell Maritime Press publishes books for the merchant marine and a few recreational boating books for professional mariners and yachtsmen.
Nonfiction How-to (on maritime subjects), technical, manuals. Subjects include marine subjects (highly technical). Query first, with writing samples and outlines of book ideas.
Recent Title(s) *Chesapeake Bay Buyboats*, by Larry S. Chowning; *Majesty from Assateague*, by Harvey Hagman, illustrated by David Aiken; *American Merchant Seaman's Manual*, 7th Ed., by William B. Hayler.

CORNELL UNIVERSITY PRESS

Sage House, 512 E. State St., Ithaca NY 14850. (607)277-2338. Fax: (607)277-2374. Website: www.cornellpress.cornell.edu. Estab. 1869. Publishes hardcover and paperback originals. **Publishes 150 titles/year. Pays royalty. Offers $0-5,000 advance.** Publishes book 1 year after acceptance of ms. Accepts simultaneous submissions. Book catalog and ms guidelines online.
Imprints Comstock (contact Peter J. Prescott, science editor), ILR Press (contact Frances Benson).
O→ Cornell Press is an academic publisher of nonfiction with particular strengths in anthropology, Asian studies, biological sciences, classics, history, labor and business, literary criticism, politics and international relations, psychology, women's studies, Slavic studies, philosophy. Currently emphasizing sound scholarship that appeals beyond the academic community.
Nonfiction Biography, reference, scholarly, textbook. Subjects include agriculture/horticulture, anthropology/archeology, art/architecture, business/economics, education, ethnic, gay/lesbian, government/politics, history, language/literature, military/war, music/dance, philosophy, psychology, regional, religion, science, sociology, translation, women's issues/studies. Submit résumé, cover letter, and prospectus.
Recent Title(s) *Ermengard of Narbonne and the World of the Troubadours*, by Fredric L. Cheyette; *Russia's Unfinished Revolution*, by Michael McFaul; *The Birds of Ecuador*, by Robert S. Ridgely and Paul J. Greenfield.

CORWIN PRESS, INC.

2455 Teller Rd., Thousand Oaks CA 91320. (805)499-9734. Fax: (805)499-2692. E-mail: robb.clouse@corwinpress.com. **Acquisitions:** Robb Clouse, editorial director; Elizabeth Brenkus, acquisitions editor (administration, leadership); Kylee Liegl, acquisitions editor (curriculum and content areas, classroom management, special and gifted education); Rachel Livsey, acquisitions editor (professional development, assessment, diversity and bilingualism, adult learning); Faye Zucker, executive editor (teaching methods, learning styles). Estab. 1990. Publishes hardcover and paperback originals. **Publishes 90 titles/year.** Publishes book 7 months after acceptance of ms. Responds in 1 month to queries. Ms guidelines for #10 SASE.
O→ Corwin Press, Inc., publishes leading-edge, user-friendly publications for education professionals.
Nonfiction Professional-level publications for administrators, teachers, school specialists, policymakers, researchers and others involved with K-12 education. Subjects include education. Seeking fresh insights, conclusions, and recommendations for action. Prefers theory or research-based books that provide real-world examples and practical, hands-on strategies to help busy educators be successful. No textbooks that simply summarize existing knowledge or mass-market books. Query with SASE.
Recent Title(s) *Differentiated Instructional Strategies*, by Gayle H. Gregory and Carolyn Chapman; *Evaluating Professional Development*, by Thomas R. Guskey; *Refaming the Path to School Leadership*, by Lee G. Bolman and Terrence E. Deal.

COUNCIL OAK BOOKS/WILDCAT CANYON PRESS

2105 E. 15th St., Suite B, Tulsa OK 74104. (918)743-BOOK. Fax: (918)583-4995. E-mail: pmillichap@bigplanet.com. **Acquisitions:** Paulette Millichap, publisher (stories about women and relationships, Native American history and spirituality, memoir, small, inspirational gift books, Americana). Estab. 1984. Publishes hardcover originals, trade paperback originals, and reprints. **Publishes 10-12 titles/year. Receives 1,000 queries/year. 35% of books from first-time authors; 75% from unagented writers. Pays 10-15% royalty on net receipts.** Publishes book 9-12 months after acceptance of ms. Accepts simultaneous submissions. Responds in 1 month to queries; 1 month to proposals. Book catalog and ms guidelines for #10 SASE.
Nonfiction Autobiography, gift book, illustrated book. Subjects include Americana, memoirs, Native American studies. Query with SASE. Reviews artwork/photos as part of ms package. Send photocopies.
Recent Title(s) *Native New Yorkers*, by Evan Pritchard.

COUNCIL ON SOCIAL WORK EDUCATION

1725 Duke St., Suite 500, Alexandria VA 22314-3457. (703)683-8080. Fax: (703)683-8099. E-mail: publications@cswe.org. Website: www.cswe.org. **Acquisitions:** Michael J. Monti, director of publications. Estab. 1952. Publishes trade paperback originals. **Publishes 4 titles/year. Receives 12 queries and 8 mss/year. 25% of books from first-time authors; 100% from unagented writers. Pays sliding royalty scale, starting at 10%.** Publishes book 1 year after acceptance of ms. Responds in 2 months to queries; 3 months to proposals; 3 months to mss. Book catalog and ms guidelines free via website or with SASE.

> O— Council on Social Work Education produces books and resources for social work educators, students and practitioners.

Nonfiction Subjects include education, sociology, social work. Books for social work and other educators. Query with proposal package, including cv, outline, 2 sample chapters and SASE. Reviews artwork/photos as part of ms package. Send photocopies.

Recent Title(s) *Group Work Education in the Field*, by Julianne Wayne and Carol S. Cohen; *Ethics Education in Social Work*, by Frederic G. Reamer.

Tips Audience is "Social work educators and students and others in the helping professions. Check areas of publication interest on website."

THE COUNTRYMAN PRESS

P.O. Box 748, Woodstock VT 05091-0748. (802)457-4826. Fax: (802)457-1678. E-mail: countrymanpress@wwn orton.com. Website: www.countrymanpress.com. Editorial Director: Kermit Hummel. Estab. 1973. Publishes hardcover originals, trade paperback originals and reprints. **Publishes 35 titles/year. Receives 1,000 queries/ year. 30% of books from first-time authors; 70% from unagented writers. Pays 5-15% royalty on retail price. Offers $1,000-5,000 advance.** Publishes book 18 months after acceptance of ms. Accepts simultaneous submissions. Responds in 2 months to proposals. Book catalog free; ms guidelines online.

Imprints Backcountry Guides, Berkshire House.

> O— Countryman Press publishes books that encourage physical fitness and appreciation for and understanding of the natural world, self-sufficiency, and adventure.

Nonfiction "We publish several series of regional recreation guidebooks—hiking, bicycling, walking, fly-fishing, canoeing, kayaking—and are looking to expand them. We're also looking for books of national interest on travel, gardening, rural living, nature, and fly-fishing." How-to, guidebooks; general nonfiction. Subjects include cooking/foods/nutrition, gardening, general nonfiction, history (New England), nature/environment, recreation, regional (New England), travel, country living. Submit proposal package including outline, 3 sample chapter(s), author bio, market information, SASE. Reviews artwork/photos as part of ms package. Send photocopies.

Recent Title(s) *The King Arthur Flour Baker's Companion: The All-Purpose Baking Cookbook*; *The Green Mountain Spinnery Knitting Book*; *Dog Friendly New York*.

Ⓝ COUNTRYSPORT PRESS

Down East Enterprises, P.O. Box 679, Camden ME 04843. (207)594-9544. Fax: (207)594-0147. E-mail: msteere@ countrysportpress.com. Website: www.countrysportpress.com. **Acquisitions:** Michael Steere, managing editor. Estab. 1988. Publishes hardcover originals and reprints. **Publishes 4 titles/year. 20% of books from first-time authors; 90% from unagented writers. Pays royalty on wholesale or retail price. Offers variable advance.** Publishes book 1 year after acceptance of ms. Accepts simultaneous submissions. Responds in 1 month to queries; 3 months to proposals; 3 months to mss. Book catalog free via website or with SASE.

> • E-mail queries only. Submissions of mss or proposals via e-mail will not be considered.
>
> O— "Our audience is upscale sportsmen with interests in wingshooting, fly fishing, fine guns and other outdoor activities."

Nonfiction Coffee table book, how-to, illustrated book. Subjects include sports, wingshooting, fly fishing, fine guns, other outdoor-related subjects. "We are looking for high-quality writing that is often reflective, anecdotal, and that offers a complete picture of an outdoor experience." Query with SASE, or submit outline, 3 sample chapter(s).

Recent Title(s) *The Best Guns (revision)*, by Michael McIntosh.

COVENANT COMMUNICATIONS, INC.

Box 416, American Fork UT 84003-0416. (801)756-1041. Website: www.covenant-lds.com. **Publishes 50 + titles/year. 35% of books from first-time authors; 100% from unagented writers. Pays 6½-15% royalty on retail price.** Publishes book 6-12 months after acceptance of ms. Responds in 4 months to mss. Ms guidelines online.

> O— Currently emphasizing inspirational, devotional, historical, biography. Our fiction is also expanding, and we are looking for new approaches to LDS literature and storytelling.

Nonfiction Biography, children's/juvenile, coffee table book, gift book, humor, illustrated book, multimedia (CD-ROM), reference, scholarly. Subjects include child guidance/parenting, creative nonfiction, history, memoirs, religion (LDS or Mormon), spirituality. Submit complete ms with synopsis and 1-page cover letter.

Fiction "We publish exclusively to the 'Mormon' (The Church of Jesus Christ of Latter-Day Saints) market. All work must appeal to that audience." Adventure, historical, humor, juvenile, literary, mainstream/contemporary, mystery, picture books, regional, religious, romance, spiritual, suspense, young adult. Submit complete ms with synopsis and 1-page cover letter.

Recent Title(s) *Between Husband and Wife*, by Brinley and Lamb (marriage/self-help); *Land of Promise*, by S. Michael Wilcox; *Saints at War II, Korea and Vietnam*, by Robert Freeman and Dennis Wright.

Tips ''Our audience is exclusively LDS (Latter-Day Saints, 'Mormon').''

ℕ CQ PRESS

1255 22nd St. NW, Suite 400, Washington DC 20037. (202)729-1800. Fax: (202)729-1806. E-mail: ckiino@cqpress.com. Website: www.cqpress.com. **Acquisitions:** Doug Goldenberg-Hart, Shana Wagger (library/reference); Brenda Carter, Clarisse Kiino (college/political science), John Lewis Needham (online). Estab. 1945. Publishes hardcover and online paperback titles. **Publishes 50-70 titles/year. 95% from unagented writers. Pays college or reference royalties or fees. Offers occasional advance.** Publishes book an average of 1 year after acceptance of ms. Accepts simultaneous submissions. Responds in 3 months to queries. Book catalog free.

Imprints CQ Press, College/Political Science, Library/Reference, Directory.

   O—π CQ Press seeks ''to educate the public by publishing authoritative works on American and international government and politics.''

Nonfiction ''We are interested in American government, public administration, comparative government, and international relations.'' Reference, textbook (all levels of college political science texts), information directories (on federal and state governments, national elections, international/state politics and governmental issues). Subjects include government/politics, history. Submit proposal package including outline.

Tips ''Our books present important information on American government and politics, and related issues, with careful attention to accuracy, thoroughness, and readability.''

CRAFTSMAN BOOK CO.

6058 Corte Del Cedro, Carlsbad CA 92009-9974. (760)438-7828 or (800)829-8123. Fax: (760)438-0398. E-mail: jacobs@costbook.com. Website: www.craftsman-book.com. **Acquisitions:** Laurence D. Jacobs, editorial manager. Estab. 1957. Publishes paperback originals. **Publishes 12 titles/year. Receives 50 submissions/year. 85% of books from first-time authors; 98% from unagented writers. Pays 7½-12½% royalty on wholesale price or retail price.** Publishes book 2 years after acceptance of ms. Accepts simultaneous submissions. Responds in 2 months to queries. Book catalog and ms guidelines free.

   O—π Publishes how-to manuals for professional builders. Currently emphasizing construction software.

Nonfiction All titles are related to construction for professional builders. How-to, technical. Subjects include building, construction. Query with SASE. Reviews artwork/photos as part of ms package.

Recent Title(s) *Steel-Frame House Construction*, by Tim Waite.

Tips ''The book should be loaded with step-by-step instructions, illustrations, charts, reference data, forms, samples, cost estimates, rules of thumb, and examples that solve actual problems in the builder's office and in the field. The book must cover the subject completely, become the owner's primary reference on the subject, have a high utility-to-cost ratio, and help the owner make a better living in his chosen field.''

CRANE HILL PUBLISHERS

Southern Lights Custom Publishing, 3608 Clairmont Ave., Birmingham AL 35222. (205)714-3007. Fax: (205)714-3008. E-mail: cranemail@cranehill.com. Website: www.cranehill.com. Estab. 1992. Publishes hardcover and trade paperback originals. **Publishes 8-12 titles/year. Receives 200-300 queries and 100 mss/year. 65% of books from first-time authors; 95% from unagented writers. Pays royalty.** Publishes book 2 years after acceptance of ms. Accepts simultaneous submissions. Responds in 2-3 months to queries; 6 months to proposals. Book catalog free; ms guidelines by e-mail.

   O—π ''Crane Hill Publishers is dedicated to the publication of America's indigenous cultural traditions. Our mission is to build a tradition of quality books that reflect the history, perceptions, experience, and customs of people in regional locales around the United States.''

Nonfiction Biography, coffee table book, cookbook, gift book, reference, self-help. Subjects include Americana, art/architecture, cooking/foods/nutrition, creative nonfiction, gardening, general nonfiction, history, travel. Query with SASE. Reviews artwork/photos as part of ms package. Send photocopies.

Fiction Literary, mainstream/contemporary. Query with SASE.

CREATIVE HOMEOWNER

24 Park Way, Upper Saddle River NJ 07458. (201)934-7100. Fax: (201)934-7541. E-mail: jennifer.doolittle@creativehomeowner.com. Website: www.creativehomeowner.com. **Acquisitions:** Tim Bakke, editorial director; Fran Donegan, senior editor (home improvement/repair); Kathie Robitz, senior editor (home decorating/design). Estab. 1978. Publishes trade paperback originals. **Publishes 12-16 titles/year. Receives dozens of queries mss/year. 50% of books from first-time authors; 98% from unagented writers. Pays royalty, or makes

outright purchase of $8,000-35,000. Publishes book 16 months after acceptance of ms. Responds in 6 months to queries. Book catalog free.

○ᵣ Creative Homeowner is the one source for the largest selection of quality home-related how-to books, idea books, booklets, and project plans.

Nonfiction How-to, illustrated book. Subjects include gardening, crafts/hobbies, home remodeling/building, home repairs, home decorating/design, ideas, inspiration. Query, or submit proposal package, including competitive books (short analysis), outline, and SASE. Reviews artwork/photos as part of ms package.

Recent Title(s) *Pools & Spas,* by Fran Donegan and David Short; *Design Ideas for Decks*; *Bathrooms: Plan, Remodel, Build.*

CRICKET BOOKS

Imprint of Carus Publishing, 30 Grove St., Suite C, Peterborough NH 03458. (603)924-7209. Fax: (603)924-7380. Website: www.cricketbooks.net. **Acquisitions:** Submissions Editor. Estab. 1999. Publishes hardcover originals. **Publishes 10 titles/year. Receives 1,500 queries and 5,000 mss/year. Pays 10% royalty on net receipts. Open to first-time and unagented authors. Pays up to 10% royalty on retail price. Offers $1,500 and up advance.** Publishes book 18 months after acceptance of ms. Accepts simultaneous submissions. Responds in 4 months to queries; 4 months to proposals; 6 months to mss. Ms guidelines online.

• Currently not accepting queries or ms. Check website for submissions details and updates.

○ᵣ Cricket Books publishes picture books, chapter books, and middle-grade novels.

Nonfiction Children's/juvenile. Send proposal, including sample chapters, table of contents, and description of competition.

Fiction Juvenile (adventure, easy-to-read, fantasy/science fiction, historical, horror, mystery/suspense, problem novels, sports, western), early chapter books and middle-grade fiction. Submit complete ms.

Recent Title(s) *Breakout,* by Paul Fleischman; *Dare to be Scared*, by Robert San Souci; *Freedom Roads*, by Joyce Hansen and Gary McGowan.

Tips "Take a look at the recent titles to see what sort of materials we're interested in, especially for nonfiction. Please note that we aren't doing the sort of strictly educational nonfiction that other publishers specialize in."

CROSSQUARTER PUBLISHING GROUP

P.O. Box 8756, Santa Fe NM 87504. (505)438-9846. E-mail: info@crossquarter.com. Website: www.crossquarter. com. **Acquisitions:** Anthony Ravenscroft. Publishes case and trade paperback originals and reprints. **Publishes 5-10 titles/year. Receives 250 queries/year. 90% of books from first-time authors. Pays 8-10% royalty on wholesale or retail price.** Publishes book 1 year after acceptance of ms. Accepts simultaneous submissions. Responds in 3 months to queries. Book catalog for $1.75; ms guidelines online.

• Query letters are required. No unsolicited mss.

○ᵣ "We emphasize personal sovereignty, self responsibility and growth with pagan or pagan-friendly emphasis for young adults and adults."

Nonfiction Biography, how-to, self-help. Subjects include health/medicine, nature/environment, New Age, philosophy, psychology, religion (pagan only), spirituality, autobiography. Query with SASE. Reviews artwork/photos as part of ms package. Send photocopies.

Fiction Science fiction, visionary fiction. Query with SASE.

Recent Title(s) *Dead as I'll Ever Be: Psychic Adventures that Changed My Life*, by Pamela Evans; *Beyond One's Own*, by Gabriel Constans; *The Shamrock and The Feather*, by Dori Dalton.

Tips "Audience is earth-conscious people looking to grow into balance of body, mind, heart and spirit."

CROWN BUSINESS

Random House, Inc., 1745 Broadway, New York NY 10019. (212)572-2275. Fax: (212)572-6192. E-mail: jmahaney@randomhouse.com. Website: www.crownbusiness.com. **Acquisitions:** John Mahaney, executive editor. Estab. 1995. Publishes hardcover and trade paperback originals. **Publishes 20-25 titles/year. 50% of books from first-time authors; 15% from unagented writers. Pays standard hardcover and trade paperback royalties. Offers negotiable advance.** Publishes book 9 months after acceptance of ms. Accepts simultaneous submissions. Responds in 1 month to proposals. Book catalog online.

Nonfiction Subjects include business/economics, money/finance, management, technology. Query with proposal package including outline, 1-2 sample chapters, market analysis and SASE.

Recent Title(s) *Execution: The Discipline of Getting Things Done*, by Larry Bossidy and Ram Charan.

Ⓝ Ⓐ ⊘ CROWN PUBLISHING GROUP

Imprint of Random House, Inc., 1745 Broadway, New York NY 10019. (212)782-9000. Website: www.randomhouse.com/crown. Estab. 1933.

Imprints Bell Tower, Clarkson Potter, Crown Business, Crown Forum, Crown Publishers, Inc., Harmony Books, Prima, Shaye Arehart Books, Three Rivers Press.
- See website for more details.

⃞Ⓝ Ⓞ CRYSTAL DREAMS PUBLISHING

P.O. Box 698, Dover TN 37058. Website: www.crystaldreamspub.com. Estab. 2001. Publishes trade paperback originals and reprints. **Publishes 20 titles/year. Receives 500 queries and 300 mss/year. 90% of books from first-time authors; 90% from unagented writers. Pays 40% royalty on net receipts.** Publishes book 6 months after acceptance of ms. Accepts simultaneous submissions. Responds in 1 month to queries; 2 months to proposals; 2 months to mss. Book catalog and ms guidelines online.
- "Crystal Dreams is currently closed to new submissions so we may concentrate our energy on our current submissions."

Nonfiction Children's/juvenile, humor. Subjects include alternative lifestyles, animals, creative nonfiction, gay/lesbian, general nonfiction, history, hobbies, memoirs, military/war, New Age, regional, religion, science, spirituality, world affairs. Submit proposal package including outline, 3 sample chapter(s), preliminary marketing plan.

Fiction Adventure, experimental, fantasy, feminist, gay/lesbian, gothic, historical, horror, humor, juvenile, literary, mainstream/contemporary, military/war, mystery, occult, plays, poetry, regional, religious, romance, science fiction, short story collections, spiritual, sports, suspense, western, young adult. Submit proposal package including 3 sample chapter(s), synopsis, preliminary marketing plan.

Poetry "We are looking for poets who can get out and sell themselves to the public. All forms of poetry are accepted." Submit complete ms.

Recent Title(s) *Hunting Breeds of Laika*, by Vladimir Beregovoy (pets); *Final Chapter*, by T.W. Miller (sci-fi/thriller); *Sounds of Sylence*, by Sylence Campbell (poetry).

Tips "Our audience varies a lot. We have readers who range from school children to retired persons. Wow us! Show us that you are an author who is willing to work and be known."

CSLI PUBLICATIONS

Ventura Hall, Stanford University, Stanford CA 94305-4115. (650)723-1839. Fax: (650)725-2166. E-mail: pubs@csli.stanford.edu. Website: cslipublications.stanford.edu. **Acquisitions:** Dikran Karagueuzian, director (linguistics, philosophy, logic, computer science). Publishes hardcover and scholarly paperback originals. **Publishes 40 titles/year. Receives 200 queries and 50 mss/year. Pays 3-10% royalty; honorarium.** Publishes book 1 year after acceptance of ms. Does not accept simultaneous submissions. Responds in 1 month to queries; 4 months to proposals; 6 months to mss. Book catalog free; ms guidelines online.
- No unsolicited mss.
- ⃗ "CSLI Publications, part of the Center for the Study of Language and Information, specializes in books in the areas of formal linguistics, logic, philosophy, computer science and human-computer interaction." Currently emphasizing human-computer interaction, computers and media, voice technology, pragmatic linguistics.

Nonfiction Reference, technical, textbook, scholarly. Subjects include anthropology/archeology, computers/electronic, language/literature (linguistics), science, logic, cognitive science. Query with SASE or by email.

Recent Title(s) *Computer Prediction*, by Stefan Muller; *On the Formal Way to Chinese Languages*, edited by Sao-Wing Zang and Chen-Sheng Luthan Liu; *Collaborative Language Engineering*, edited by Stephan Oepen, et. al.

CUMBERLAND HOUSE PUBLISHING

431 Harding Industrial Dr., Nashville TN 37211. (615)832-1171. Fax: (615)832-0633. E-mail: info@cumberlandhouse.com. Website: www.cumberlandhouse.com. **Acquisitions:** Tilly Katz, acquisitions editor. Estab. 1996. Publishes hardcover, trade paperback and mass market originals and reprints. **Publishes 60 titles/year; imprint publishes 5 titles/year. Receives 3,000 queries and 500 mss/year. 30% of books from first-time authors; 80% from unagented writers. Pays 10-15% royalty on net receipts. Offers $500-5,000 advance.** Publishes book an average of 12 months after acceptance of ms. Accepts simultaneous submissions. Responds in 6 months to queries; 6 months to proposals; 1 year to mss. Book catalog for 8×10 SAE with 4 first-class stamps; ms guidelines online.

Imprints Cumberland House Hearthside, Highland Books.
- Accepts mss by US mail only. No electronic or telephone queries will be accepted.
- ⃗ Cumberland House publishes "market specific books. We evaluate in terms of how sure we are that we can publish the book successfully and then the quality or uniqueness of a project." Currently emphasizing nonfiction. Deemphasizing fiction and mystery.

Nonfiction Cookbook, gift book, how-to, humor, reference. Subjects include Americana, cooking/foods/nutrition, government/politics, history, military/war, recreation, regional, sports, travel, popular culture, civil war. Query or submit outline. Reviews artwork/photos as part of ms package. Send photocopies only; not original copies.

Fiction Historical, mystery. Writers should know "the odds are really stacked against them." Query with SASE.

Recent Title(s) *Why a Daughter Needs a Dad*, by Greg Lang.

Tips Audience is "adventuresome people who like a fresh approach to things. Writers should tell what their idea is, why it's unique and why somebody would want to buy it—but don't pester us."

Ⓐ CURRENCY

1745 Broadway, New York NY 10019. (212)782-9000. E-mail: rscholl@randomhouse.com. Website: www.rand omhouse.com/doubleday/currency. **Acquisitions:** Roger Scholl, editorial director. Estab. 1989. **Pays 7¹/₂-15% royalty on retail price. Offers advance.** Publishes book 1 year after acceptance of ms.

○➼ Currency publishes "business books for people who want to make a difference, not just a living."

Nonfiction Subjects include marketing, investment. *Agented submissions only.*

Recent Title(s) *Managing Up*; *Don't Mess with My Money*.

CYCLE PUBLISHING

1282 Seventh Ave., San Francisco CA 94122-2526. (415)665-8214. Fax: (415)753-8572. **Acquisitions:** Rob van der Plas, publisher/editor. Estab. 1997. Publishes hardcover and trade paperback originals. **Publishes 6 titles/ year. Receives 15 submissions/year. 10% of books from first-time authors; 100% from unagented writers. Pays 12% royalty on net receipts.** Publishes book an average of 1 year after acceptance of ms. Accepts simultaneous submissions. Responds in 3 months to queries. Book catalog and ms guidelines for #10 SASE.

Nonfiction How-to, technical. Subjects include recreation, sports, travel, manufactured homes. Submit complete ms. Reviews artwork/photos as part of ms package.

Recent Title(s) *Mountain Bike Maintenance*; *Buying a Manufactured Home*.

Tips "Writers have a good chance selling us books with better and more illustrations and a systematic treatment of the subject. First check what is on the market and ask yourself whether you are writing something that is not yet available and wanted."

DA CAPO PRESS

Perseus Books Group, 11 Cambridge Center, Cambridge MA 02142. Website: www.dacapopress.com. Estab. 1975. Publishes hardcover originals and trade paperback originals and reprints. **Publishes 115 titles/year; imprint publishes 115 titles/year. Receives 500 queries and 300 mss/year. 25% of books from first-time authors; 1% from unagented writers. Pays 7-15% royalty. Offers $1,000-225,000 advance.** Publishes book 1 year after acceptance of ms. Accepts simultaneous submissions. Responds in 2-3 months to queries; 2-3 months to proposals; 2-3 months to mss. Book catalog and ms guidelines online.

Nonfiction Autobiography, biography, coffee table book, gift book. Subjects include art/architecture, contemporary culture, creative nonfiction, general nonfiction, government/politics, history, language/literature, memoirs, military/war, social sciences, sports, translation, travel, world affairs. Does not accept electronic submissions or take phone calls regarding submissions. Query with SASE, or submit proposal package including outline, 3 sample chapter(s), c.v. Reviews artwork/photos as part of ms package. Send photocopies.

Recent Title(s) *Arthur Miller*, by Martin Gottfried; *Da Capo Best Music Writing 2003*, edited by Matt Groening; *The Bedford Boys*, by Alex Kershaw.

DAN RIVER PRESS

Conservatory of American Letters, P.O. Box 298, Thomaston ME 04861-0298. (207)354-0998. E-mail: cal@ameri canletters.org. Website: www.americanletters.org. **Acquisitions:** Richard S. Danbury, fiction editor. Estab. 1977. Publishes hardcover and paperback originals. **Publishes 8-10 titles/year. Pays 10-15% royalty, 10 author's copies. Offers occassional advance.** Publishes book 3-4 months after acceptance of ms. Accepts simultaneous submissions. Responds in 2-3 days to queries. Book catalog for 6×9 SAE with 60¢ postage affixed; ms guidelines online.

○➼ "Small press publisher of fiction and biographies owned by a nonprofit foundation."

Fiction Accepts anything but porn, sedition, evangelical, and children's literature. Submit publishing history, synopsis, author bio. Cover letter or query should include estimated word count, brief bio, and brief publishing history. Query should also deal with marketing ideas. Be specific ("'All Women' is not a marketing idea we can work with") and social security number, #10 SASE. "We do not read electronic submissions or queries."

Poetry Publishes poetry and fiction anthology (submission guidelines to *Dan River Anthology* on the Web or send #10 SASE).

Recent Title(s) *Dan River Anthology 2004*, by R.S. Danbury III, editor (poetry and short stories); *Ash: Adam Pachter, a Story Told By a Dead Man*; *In the Rivers' Flow*, by Jim Ainsworth (fiction).

Tips "Spend some time developing a following. Forget the advice that says, 'Your first job is to find a publisher!' That's nonsense. Your first job as a writer is to develop an audience. Do that and a publisher will find you."

DANA PRESS

900 15th St. NW, Washington DC 20005. (202)408-8800. Fax: (202)408-5599. Website: www.dana.org/books/press. **Acquisitions:** Jane Nevins, editor-in-chief; Dan Gordon, editor. Publishes hardcover and trade paperback originals. **Publishes 4 titles/year. Receives 10 queries and 3 mss/year. 50% of books from first-time authors; 90% from unagented writers. Pays 7-10% royalty on list price. Offers $10,000-35,000 advance.** Publishes book 1 year after acceptance of ms. Accepts simultaneous submissions. Responds in 2 weeks to queries; 1 month to proposals; 2 months to mss. Book catalog and ms guidelines online.

Nonfiction Biography, coffee table book, self-help, brain-related health books. Subjects include health/medicine, memoirs, psychology, science. "We focus almost exclusively on the brain." Reviews artwork/photos as part of ms package. Send photocopies.

Recent Title(s) *Striking Back at Stroke: A Doctor Patient Journal,* by Cleo Hutton and Louis R. Caplan, M.D.; *The Bard on the Brain: Understanding the Mind Through the Art of Shakespeare and the Science of Imaging,* by Paul Matthews, M.D., and Jeffrey McQuain, Ph.D.; *Back from the Brink: How Crises Spur Doctors to New Discoveries About the Brain,* by Edward J. Sylvester.

Tips "Coherent, thought-out proposals are key. What is the scope of the book? Who is the reader? It's important to have an angle."

DANTE UNIVERSITY OF AMERICA PRESS, INC.

P.O. Box 812158, Wellesley MA 02482. Fax: (781)790-1056. E-mail: danteu@danteuniversity.org. Website: www.danteuniversity.org/dpress.html. **Acquisitions:** Adolph Caso, president. Estab. 1975. Publishes hardcover and trade paperback originals and reprints. **Publishes 5 titles/year. Receives 50 submissions/year. 50% of books from first-time authors; 50% from unagented writers. Pays royalty. Offers negotiable advance.** Publishes book 10 months after acceptance of ms. Responds in 2 months to queries.

○ᴦ "The Dante University Press exists to bring quality, educational books pertaining to our Italian heritage as well as the historical and political studies of America. Profits from the sale of these publications benefit the Foundation, bringing Dante University closer to a reality."

Nonfiction Biography, reference, scholarly, reprints. Subjects include history (Italian-American), humanities, translation (from Italian and Latin), general scholarly nonfiction, Renaissance thought and letter, Italian language and linguistics, Italian-American culture, bilingual education. Query with SASE. Reviews artwork/photos as part of ms package.

Fiction Translations from Italian and Latin. Query with SASE.

Poetry "There is a chance that we would use Renaissance poetry translations."

Recent Title(s) *The Prince,* by Machiavelli (social sciences); *The Kaso Dictionary—English-Italian* (reference).

MAY DAVENPORT, PUBLISHERS

26313 Purissima Rd., Los Altos Hills CA 94022. (650)947-1275. Fax: (650)947-1373. E-mail: mdbooks@earthlink.net. Website: www.maydavenportpublishers.com. **Acquisitions:** May Davenport, editor/publisher. Estab. 1976. Publishes hardcover and paperback originals. **Publishes 4 titles/year. Receives 1,500 submissions/year. 95% of books from first-time authors; 100% from unagented writers. Pays 15% royalty on retail price. Offers no advance.** Publishes book 1 year after acceptance of ms. Responds in 1 month to queries. Book catalog and ms guidelines for #10 SASE.

Imprints md Books (nonfiction and fiction).

○ᴦ May Davenport publishes "literature for teenagers (before they graduate from high schools) as supplementary literary material in English courses nationwide." Looking particularly for authors able to write for the "teen Internet" generation who don't like to read in-depth. Currently emphasizing more upper-level subjects for teens.

Nonfiction Subjects include Americana, language/literature, humorous memoirs for chldren/young adults. "For children ages 6-8: stories to read with pictures to color in 500 words. For preteens and young adults: Exhibit your writing skills and entertain them with your literary tools." Query with SASE.

Fiction Humor, literary. "We want to focus on novels junior and senior high school teachers can share with their reluctant readers in their classrooms." Query with SASE.

Recent Title(s) *Senioritis,* by Tate Thompson; *Significant Footsteps,* by Ashleigh E. Grange (fiction); *The Lesson Plan,* by Irvin Gay (fiction).

Tips "If you have to write only about the ills of today's society of incest, murders, homelessness, divorce, 1-parent families, just write your fictional novel humorously. If you can't write that way, create youthful characters so teachers, as well as 15-18-year-old high school readers, will laugh at your descriptive passages and contemporary dialogue. Avoid 1-sentence paragraphs. The audience we want to reach is past Nancy Drew and Hardy Boy readers.''

JONATHAN DAVID PUBLISHERS, INC.

68-22 Eliot Ave., Middle Village NY 11379-1194. (718)456-8611. Fax: (718)894-2818. E-mail: info@jdbooks.c om. Website: www.jdbooks.com. **Acquisitions:** Alfred J. Kolatch, editor-in-chief. Estab. 1948. Publishes hardcover and trade paperback originals and reprints. **Publishes 20-25 titles/year. 50% of books from first-time authors; 90% from unagented writers. Pays royalty, or makes outright purchase.** Publishes book 18 months after acceptance of ms. Responds in 1 month to queries; 1 month to proposals; 2 months to mss. Book catalog and ms guidelines online.

0₋ₙ Jonathan David publishes ''popular Judaica.'' Currently emphasizing projects geared toward children.
Nonfiction Biography, children's/juvenile, coffee table book, cookbook, gift book, how-to, humor, illustrated book, reference, self-help. Subjects include cooking/foods/nutrition, creative nonfiction, ethnic, humor, multicultural, religion, sex, sports. Query with SASE, or submit proposal package including outline, 3 sample chapter(s), résumé. Reviews artwork/photos as part of ms package. Send photocopies.
Recent Title(s) *Drawing a Crowd*, by Bill Gallo (sports cartoons/memoir).

DAVIS PUBLICATIONS, INC.

50 Portland St., Worcester MA 01608. (508)754-7201. Fax: (508)753-3834. **Acquisitions:** David Coen, managing editor. Estab. 1901. **Publishes 5-10 titles/year. Royalty varies by project, 5-10%. Offers advance.** Publishes book 1 year after acceptance of ms. Does not accept simultaneous submissions. Book catalog for 9×12 SAE with $2 U.S. postage; ms guidelines for #10 SASE.

0₋ₙ Davis publishes art, design, and craft books for the elementary through high school art education markets. ''Our mission is to produce materials that help art teachers do their job better.''
Nonfiction Illustrated book. Subjects include art/architecture, education, history. Submit outline, sample chapter(s). Reviews artwork/photos as part of ms package.
Recent Title(s) *From Ordinary to Extraordinary, Art and Design Problem-Solving*, by Ken Vieth; *Creative Coloring*, by Art Sherwyn; *You Can Weave!*, by Kathleen Monaghan.
Tips ''Keep in mind the intended audience. Our readers are visually oriented. Photos should be good quality transparencies. Well-selected illustrations should explain, amplify, and enhance the text. We average 2-4 photos/page. We like to see technique photos as well as illustrations of finished artwork, by a variety of artists, including students. Recent books have been on using technology in art teaching, printmaking, art education profession, history through art timeline. We do not publish fiction or poetry in any form!''

DAW BOOKS, INC.

Imprint of Penguin Putnam, Inc., 375 Hudson St., 3rd Floor, New York NY 10014-3658. (212)366-2096. Fax: (212)366-2090. E-mail: daw@us.penguingroup.com. Website: www.dawbooks.com. Publishers: Elizabeth Wollheim and Sheila Gilbert. **Acquisitions:** Peter Stampfel, submissions editor. Estab. 1971. Publishes hardcover and paperback originals and reprints. **Publishes 60-80 titles/year. Pays in royalties with an advance negotiable on a book-by-book basis.** Responds in 6 weeks to queries. Book catalog free; ms guidelines online.

● Simultaneous submissions ''returned unread at once, unless prior arrangements are made by agent.''
0₋ₙ DAW Books publishes science fiction and fantasy.
Fiction Fantasy, science fiction. ''We are interested in science fiction and fantasy novels. We need science fiction more than fantasy right now, but we're still looking for both. We like character-driven books with appealing characters. We accept both agented and unagented manuscripts. Long books are absolutely not a problem. We are not seeking collections of short stories or ideas for anthologies. We do not want any nonfiction manuscripts.'' Query with SASE. Simultaneous submissions ''returned unread at once unless prior arrangements are made by agent.''
Recent Title(s) *Alta*, by Mercedes Lacky (fantasy); *The War of the Flowers*, by Tad Williams (fantasy).

DAWN PUBLICATIONS

12402 Britney Springs Rd., Nevada City CA 95959. (530)274-7775. Fax: (530)274-7778. Website: www.dawnpub .com. **Acquisitions:** Glenn Hovemann, editor. Estab. 1979. Publishes hardcover and trade paperback originals. **Publishes 6 titles/year. Receives 550 queries and 2,500 mss/year. 15% of books from first-time authors; 90% from unagented writers. Pays royalty on net receipts. Offers advance.** Publishes book 1 to 2 years after acceptance of ms. Accepts simultaneous submissions. Responds in 2 months to queries. Book catalog and ms guidelines online.

0₋ₙ Dawn Publications is dedicated to inspiring in children a sense of appreciation for all life on earth. Dawn looks for nature awareness and appreciation titles that promote a relationship with the natural world and specific habitats, usually through inspiring treatment and nonfiction.

Nonfiction Children's/juvenile. Subjects include animals, nature/environment. Query with SASE.
Recent Title(s) *Salmon Stream*, by Carol Reed-Jones; *In One Tidepool*, by Anthony Fredericks; *The Okomi Series*, with Jane Goodall.
Tips Publishes mostly nonfiction with lightness and inspiration.

DBS PRODUCTIONS

P.O. Box 1894, Charlottesville VA 22903. (800)745-1581. Fax: (434)293-5502. E-mail: robert@dbs-sar.com. Website: www.dbs-sar.com. **Acquisitions:** Bob Adams, publisher. Estab. 1989. Publishes hardcover and trade paperback originals. **Publishes 6 titles/year. Receives 5 queries/year. 5% of books from first-time authors; 100% from unagented writers. Pays 5-20% royalty on retail price.** Publishes book 1 year after acceptance of ms. Does not accept simultaneous submissions. Responds in 2 months to queries. Book catalog on request or on website; ms guidelines for #10 SASE.

○━ dbS Productions produces search and rescue and outdoor first-aid related materials and courses. It offers a selection of publications, videotapes, management kits and tools, and instructional modules.

Nonfiction Technical, textbook. Subjects include health/medicine. Submit proposal package including outline, 2 sample chapter(s). Reviews artwork/photos as part of ms package. Send photocopies.
Recent Title(s) *Field Operations Guide for Search and Rescue, 2nd Ed.*, by R. Koester.

DEAD END STREET, LLC

813 Third St., Hoquiam WA 98550. (415)378-7401. E-mail: submissions@deadendstreet.com. Website: deadend street.com. Director of Publications: Ivan Black. **Acquisitions:** John Rutledge, director of submissions. Estab. 1997. Publishes all genres and seeks "cutting edge authors who represent the world's dead end streets." **Pays 10-40% royalties, and 10 author's copies.** Publishes book 6 months after acceptance of ms. Accepts simultaneous submissions. Responds in 1 month to submissions to queries. Book catalog and ms guidelines online.

Poetry Accepts poetry written by children. Sample books available on website. "We require electonic submissions via e-mail in MS Word or Word Perfect." Cover letter required.

IVAN R. DEE, PUBLISHER

Imprint of The Rowman & Littlefield Publishing Group, 1332 N. Halsted St., Chicago IL 60622-2694. (312)787-6262. Fax: (312)787-6269. E-mail: elephant@ivanrdee.com. Submissions E-mail: editorial@ivanrdee.com. Website: www.ivanrdee.com. **Acquisitions:** Ivan R. Dee, president; Hilary Meyer, managing editor. Estab. 1988. Publishes hardcover originals and trade paperback originals and reprints. **Publishes 60 titles/year. 10% of books from first-time authors; 80% from unagented writers. Pays royalty. Offers advance.** Publishes book 8 months after acceptance of ms. Accepts simultaneous submissions. Responds in 1 month to queries; 1 month to proposals; 1 month to mss. Book catalog free.

Imprints Elephant Paperbacks, New Amsterdam Books, J.S. Sanders Books.

○━ Ivan R. Dee publishes serious nonfiction for general-informed readers.

Nonfiction Biography. Subjects include art/architecture, film/cinema/stage, government/politics, history, language/literature, world affairs, contemporary culture, film/cinema/stage, baseball. "We publish history, biography, literature and letters, theater and drama, politics and current affairs, and literary baseball." Submit outline, sample chapter(s). "We do not accept electronic submissions." Reviews artwork/photos as part of ms package.
Recent Title(s) *Oppenheimer*, by Jeremy Bernstein; *Open World*, by Philippe Legrain; *Ivan R. Dee Guide to Plays and Playwrights*, by Trevor Griffiths.
Tips "We publish for an intelligent lay audience and college course adoptions."

Ⓐ DEL REY BOOKS

Imprint of Random House Publishing Group, 1745 Broadway, 18th Floor, New York NY 10019. (212)782-9000. E-mail: delrey@randomhouse.com. Website: www.randomhouse.com/delrey. **Acquisitions:** Betsy Mitchell, VP & editor-in-chief (science fiction, fantasy); Shelly Shapiro, editorial director (science fiction, fantasy); Steve Saffel, editorial director/media projects (fantasy, alternate history, media tie-ins); Chris Schluep, editor (science fiction, fantasy). Estab. 1977. Publishes hardcover, trade paperback, and mass market originals and mass market paperback reprints. **Publishes 120 titles/year. Receives 1,900 submissions/year. 10% of books from first-time authors. Pays royalty on retail price. Offers competitive advance.** Publishes book 1 year after acceptance of ms. Does not accept simultaneous submissions.

○━ Del Rey publishes top level fantasy, alternate history, and science fiction.

Fiction Fantasy (should have the practice of magic as an essential element of the plot), science fiction (well-plotted novels with good characterizations, exotic locales and detailed alien creatures), alternate history. *Agented submissions only.*

Recent Title(s) *Altered Carbon*, by Richard K. Morgan; *Tanequil*, by Terry Brooks; *Iron Council*, by China Miéville.

Tips "Del Rey is a reader's house. Pay particular attention to plotting, strong characters, and dramatic, satisfactory conclusions. It must be/feel believable. That's what the readers like. In terms of mass market, we basically created the field of fantasy bestsellers. Not that it didn't exist before, but we put the mass into mass market."

N A Ø DELACORTE BOOKS FOR YOUNG READERS

Imprint of Random House Children's Books/Random House, Inc., 1745 Broadway, New York NY 10019. (212)782-9000. Website: www.randomhouse.com/kids.
- Although not currently seeking unsolicited mss, mss are being sought for 2 contests: Delacorte Dell Yearling Contest for a First Middle-Grade Novel and Delacorte Press Contest for a First Young Adult Novel. Submission guidelines can be found online.

N A Ø DELL DRAGONFLY BOOKS FOR YOUNG READERS

Imprint of Random House Children's Books/Random House, Inc., 1745 Broadway, New York NY 10019. (212)782-9000. Website: www.randomhouse.com/kids.
- Quality reprint paperback imprint for paperback books. Does not accept mss.

N A Ø DELL LAUREL LEAF BOOKS FOR YOUNG READERS

Imprint of Random House Children's Books/Random House, Inc., 1745 Broadway, New York NY 10019. (212)782-9000. Website: www.randomhouse.com/teens.
- Quality reprint paperback imprint for young adult paperback books. Does not accept mss.

N A Ø DELL YEARLING BOOKS FOR YOUNG READERS

Imprint of Random House Children's Books/Random House, Inc., 1745 Broadway, New York NY 10019. (212)782-9000. Website: www.randomhouse.com/kids.
- Quality reprint paperback imprint for middle grade paperback books. Does not accept unsolicited mss.

Ø THE DENALI PRESS

P.O. Box 021535, Juneau AK 99802-1535. (907)586-6014. Fax: (907)463-6780. E-mail: denalipress@alaska.com. Website: www.denalipress.com. **Acquisitions:** Alan Schorr, editorial director; Sally Silvas-Ottumwa, editorial associate. Estab. 1986. Publishes trade paperback originals. **Publishes 5 titles/year. Receives 120 submissions/year. 50% of books from first-time authors; 80% from unagented writers. Pays 10% royalty on wholesale price, or makes outright purchase. Offers advance.** Publishes book 1 year after acceptance of ms. Accepts simultaneous submissions. Responds in 1 month to queries.
- ⊙→ The Denali Press looks for reference works suitable for the educational, professional, and library market. "Though we publish books on a variety of topics, our focus is most broadly centered on multiculturalism, public policy, Alaskana, and general reference works."

Nonfiction Reference. Subjects include Americana, anthropology/archeology, ethnic, government/politics, history, multicultural, recreation, regional. "We need reference books—ethnic, refugee, and minority concerns." Query with SASE, or submit outline, sample chapter(s). **All unsolicited mss returned unopened.**

Recent Title(s) *Winning Political Campaigns: A Comprehensive Guide to Electoral Success*, by William S. Bike.

DEVORSS & CO.

DeVorss Publications, P.O. Box 1389, Camarillo CA 93011-1389. E-mail: editorial@devorss.com. Website: www. devorss.com. Publishes hardcover and trade paperback originals and reprints. **Receives 700 queries and 300 mss/year. 95% of books from first-time authors; 100% from unagented writers. 10% maximum royalty on retail price.** Publishes book 6 months after acceptance of ms. Accepts simultaneous submissions. Responds in 1 month to mss. Book catalog for #10 SASE; ms guidelines for #10 SASE.

Nonfiction Children's/juvenile, gift book, self-help, Body, Mind, and Spirit. Subjects include creative nonfiction, philosophy, psychology, spirituality, Body, Mind, and Spirit. Query with SASE. Reviews artwork/photos as part of ms package. Send photocopies.

Recent Title(s) *Little Green Apples*, by O.C. Smith and James Shaw.

Tips "Our audience is people using their mind to improve health, finances, relationships, life changes, etc. Ask for guidelines first. Don't submit outlines, proposals, or manuscripts. Don't call. Please send submissions and inquiries by mail only."

A DIAL BOOKS FOR YOUNG READERS

Imprint of Penguin Group USA, 345 Hudson St., 14th Floor, New York NY 10014. (212)366-2000. Website: www.penguinputnam.com. President/Publisher: Nancy Paulsen. Associate Publisher/Editorial Director: Lauri

Hornik. **Acquisitions:** Submissions Editor. Estab. 1961. Publishes hardcover originals. **Publishes 50 titles/ year. Receives 5,000 queries/year. 20% of books from first-time authors. Pays royalty. Offers varies advance.** Does not accept simultaneous submissions. Responds in 4 months to queries. Book catalog for 9 x12 SAE with 4 first-class stamps.

○━ Dial Books for Young Readers publishes quality picture books for ages 18 months-8 years; lively, believable novels for middle readers and young adults; and occasional nonfiction for middle readers and young adults.

Nonfiction Children's/juvenile, illustrated book. Accepts unsolicited queries.

Fiction Adventure, fantasy, juvenile, picture books, young adult. Especially looking for "lively and well-written novels for middle grade and young adult children involving a convincing plot and believable characters. The subject matter or theme should not already be overworked in previously published books. The approach must not be demeaning to any minority group, nor should the roles of female characters (or others) be stereotyped, though we don't think books should be didactic, or in any way message-y. No topics inappropriate for the juvenile, young adult, and middle grade audiences. No plays." Query with SASE. Accepts unsolicited queries and up to 10 pages for longer works and unsolicited mss for picture books.

Recent Title(s) *A Cool Moonlight*, by Angela Johnson; *A Year Down Yonder*, by Richard Peck; *A Penguin Pup for Pinkerton*, by Steven Kellogg.

Tips "Our readers are anywhere from preschool age to teenage. Picture books must have strong plots, lots of action, unusual premises, or universal themes treated with freshness and originality. Humor works well in these books. A very well-thought-out and intelligently presented book has the best chance of being taken on. Genre isn't as much of a factor as presentation."

[N] DIAMOND EYES PUBLISHING

2309 Mountain Spruce St., Ocoee FL 34761. (407)654-6652. E-mail: info@depublishing.com. Submissions E-mail: wordsarelife@yahoo.com. Website: www.depublishing.com. **Acquisitions:** Jessica Adriel, senior editor (fiction). Estab. 1999. Publishes trade paperback originals. **Publishes 5 titles/year; imprint publishes 2 titles/ year. Receives 300 queries and 50 mss/year. 80% of books from first-time authors; 100% from unagented writers. Pays 7-10% royalty on retail price.** Publishes book 1 year after acceptance of ms. Accepts simultaneous submissions. Responds in 2 months to queries; 4 months to mss. Book catalog and ms guidelines online.

Imprints Lauren's Box; Trident Books.

Nonfiction Self-help. Subjects include general nonfiction, money/finance, religion, true crime, motivational books, workbooks, church dramas, plays. "Diamond Eyes is looking for 'How-to Manuals' that can be marketed to churches. We are especially interested in leadership ideas for teens, and ideas for how to grow/develop a drama department. We are looking for shorts plays to comprise for churches or youth organizations. Biblical finance or controversial biblical topics welcome. Authors should note that we have a charismatic viewpoint on most issues." Query via e-mail.

Fiction Mainstream/contemporary, plays, young adult. "Trident Books is seeking fresh ideas for mainstream fiction, or any story that teaches a moral or lesson. Books are marketed toward a secular audience but teach a moral or ethical virtue. We are also interested in books that possess supernatural perspectives or characters. Lauren's Box is a women's fiction imprint of Diamond Eyes and is looking for authors who write about everyday characters who embrace grief, trauma divorce, or any other issue except medical that women face today. We are looking for romance novels as well. Submit your ideas on all subjects if you are looking for a publisher who is interested in the purpose of your book and not just publishing another title." Query via e-mail.

Poetry "We only publish the winners of our contest. The winners will be published in a gift book along with inspirational photos. The fee to enter the contest is $7/poem. There is no deadline. Our goal is to enhance the meaning and purpose of poetry by sharing the beauty of the writer through their own expression. We welcome poems on various topics. Entrants can view the topics on our website."

Recent Title(s) *Writing His Way*, by Jessica Adriel (Christian manual writing); *Everybody Fails*, by Lauren Ali (young adult); *Bloodland*, by John Roberts (general).

Tips "We are a Christian publisher looking for fiction that has a message and provides the reader with more than just entertainment. Read a few articles on query letters, and know how the industry works. Understand that writing talent is secondary to how an author conducts him/herself. Your query is your first impression. Do not rush, be more than prepared when you send out your query."

DISCOVERY ENTERPRISES, LTD.

31 Laurelwood Dr., Carlisle MA 01741. (978)287-5401. Fax: (978)287-5402. E-mail: ushistorydocs@aol.com. **Acquisitions:** JoAnne W. Deitch, president (plays for Readers Theatre, on American history). Publishes trade paperback originals. **Publishes 10 titles/year. Receives 50 queries and 20 mss/year. 5% of books from first-time authors; 90% from unagented writers. Pays 20-20% royalty.** Publishes book 3 months after acceptance

of ms. Accepts simultaneous submissions. Responds in 1 month to queries. Book catalog for 6×9 SAE with 3 first-class stamps.

Fiction "We're interested in 40-minute plays (reading time) for students in grades 4-10 on topics in U.S. history." Historical, plays. Query with SASE, or submit complete ms.

Recent Title(s) *Life on the Road to Freedom: Sojourner Truth*, by Sharon Fennessey; *Salem Witch Hunt*, by Hilary Weisman; *Lewis and Clark: Across a Vast Land*, by Harold Torrance.

Tips "Call or send query letter on topic prior to sending ms for plays. We currently need a play on early colonists in Jamestown or Plymouth; a play on post-Civil War South; a play on the Revolutionary War, focusing on George Washington."

ⓃDISKUS PUBLISHING

P.O. Box 43, Albany IN 47320. E-mail: editor@diskuspublishing.com. Submissions E-mail: diskussubs@aol.com. Website: www.diskuspublishing.com. Editor-in-Chief: Marilyn Nesbitt. **Acquisitions:** Joyce McLaughlin, inspirational and children's editor; Holly Janey, submissions editor. Estab. 1996. Publishes e-books. **Publishes 50 titles/year. Pays 40% royalty.** Publishes book 6-8 months after acceptance of ms. Accepts simultaneous submissions. Book catalog for #10 SASE; ms guidelines for #10 SASE or online.

Fiction Adventure, ethnic (general), fantasy (space fantasy), historical, horror, humor, juvenile, literary, mainstream/contemporary, military/war, multicultural (general), mystery, religious, romance, science fiction, short story collections, suspense, western, young adult. Submit publishing history, author bio, Estimated Word Count and Genre, or submit complete ms.

Recent Title(s) *The Best Laid Plans*, by Leta Nolan Childers (romance); *Brazen*, by Lori Foster (adventure/romance); *A Change of Destiny*, by Marilyn Mansfield (science fiction/futuristic).

ⓃDNA PRESS

P.O. Box 572, Eagleville PA 19408. (610)489-8404. Fax: (208)692-2855. E-mail: dnapress@yahoo.com. **Acquisitions:** Alexander Kuklin, Ph.D., managing editor (popular science and children scientific books); Xela Schenk, operations manager (New Age). Estab. 1998. Publishes trade paperback originals. **Publishes 10 titles/year; imprint publishes 5 titles/year. Receives 75 queries and 20 mss/year. 90% of books from first-time authors; 100% from unagented writers. Pays 10-20% royalty.** Publishes book 6 months after acceptance of ms. Accepts simultaneous submissions. Responds in 6 weeks to mss. Book catalog and ms guidelines free.

• Book publisher for young adults, children, and adults.

Nonfiction Children's/juvenile (explaining science), how-to. Subjects include education, New Age, science. "We publish books for children or how-to for adults which carry scientific knowledge and contribute to learning." Submit complete ms. Reviews artwork/photos as part of ms package. Send photocopies.

Fiction Juvenile, science fiction, young adult. "All books should be oriented to explaining science even if they do not fall 100% under the category of science fiction." Submit complete ms.

Recent Title(s) *How to DNA Test Our Family Relationships*, by Terrence Carmichael and Alexander Kuklin; *DNA Array Image Analysis*, by Kamberova and Shah; *Microarrays Methods and Applications*, by Hardiman.

Tips "We publish under the series 'Nuts & Bolts.' We offer quick response, great relationships, high commission/royalty."

DO-IT-YOURSELF LEGAL PUBLISHERS

60 Park Place, Suite 103, Newark NJ 07102. (973)639-0400. Fax: (973)639-1801. **Acquisitions:** Dan Benjamin, associate editor; Anne Torrey, editorial director. Estab. 1978. Publishes trade paperback originals. **Publishes 6 titles/year; imprint publishes 2 titles/year. Receives 25 queries/year. Pays 15-20% royalty on wholesale price.** Publishes book 6 months after acceptance of ms. Accepts simultaneous submissions. Responds in 1 month to queries; 1 month to proposals; 3 months to mss.

Imprints Selfhelper Law Press of America.

○┐ "The fundamental premise underlying our works is that the simplest problems can be effectively handled by anyone with average common sense and a competent guidebook."

Nonfiction Subject matter should deal with self-help law topics that instruct the lay person on how to undertake legal tasks without the use of attorney or other high cost experts. How-to, self-help. Subjects include law. Query with SASE.

Recent Title(s) *The National Mortgage Qualification Kit*, by Benji O. Anosike, Ph.D.

ⓃDOLLAR$MART BOOKS

4320-C Ridgecrest, #150, Rio Rancho NM 87124. (505)681-2880. **Acquisitions:** Cheryl Gorder, publisher (financial education and business); Robin, editor (spirituality and New Age). Estab. 1985. Publishes trade paperback and electronic originals. **Publishes 12 titles/year. Receives 100 queries and 75 mss/year. 90% of books from first-time authors; 90% from unagented writers. Pays 10-15% royalty on retail price, or makes outright**

purchase of $500-3,000. Publishes book 3 months after acceptance of ms. Accepts simultaneous submissions. Responds in 1 month to queries; 1 month to mss. Book catalog free; ms guidelines for #10 SASE.

Nonfiction How-to, reference, self-help. Subjects include business/economics, education, money/finance, New Age, spirituality, real estate. Submit complete ms. Reviews artwork/photos as part of ms package. Send photocopies.

Fiction "The only fiction we publish is 'spiritual warrior' type." Submit complete ms.

Recent Title(s) *Dollar$mart Resource Guide for Kids*; *Dollar$mart Kid's Education at Home*.

Tips "We would prefer to see complete manuscripts, and we will return manuscripts if they are accompanied by an envelope with sufficient postage."

DORAL PUBLISHING, INC.

2501 W. Behrend Dr., #43, Phoenix AZ 85027. (623)875-2057. Fax: (623)875-2059. E-mail: doralpub@mindspring.com. Website: www.doralpub.com. **Acquisitions:** Alvin Grossman, publisher; Joe Liddy, marketing manager (purebred dogs). Estab. 1986. Publishes hardcover and trade paperback originals. **Publishes 10 titles/year. Receives 30 queries and 15 mss/year. 85% from unagented writers. Pays 10% royalty on wholesale price.** Publishes book 6 months after acceptance of ms. Does not accept simultaneous submissions. Responds in 2 months to queries. Book catalog free; ms guidelines for #10 SASE.

    O⊸ Doral Publishing publishes only books about dogs and dog-related topics, mostly geared for pure-bred dog owners and showing. Currently emphasizing breed books.

Nonfiction Children's/juvenile, how-to, reference. Subjects include animals, health/medicine. "We are looking for new ideas. No flowery prose. Manuscripts should be literate, intelligent, but easy to read." Subjects must be dog-related. Query with SASE, or submit outline, 2 sample chapter(s). Reviews artwork/photos as part of ms package. Send photocopies.

Fiction Juvenile. Subjects must center around dogs. Either the main character should be a dog or a dog should play an integral role. Query with SASE.

Recent Title(s) *The Bernese Mountain Dog*; *How Wiliy Got His Wings*.

Tips "We are currently expanding and are looking for new topics and fresh ideas while staying true to our niche. While we will steadfastly maintain that market—we are always looking for excellent breed books—we also want to explore more 'mainstream' topics."

DORCHESTER PUBLISHING CO., INC.

200 Madison Ave., Suite 2000, New York NY 10016. (212)725-8811. Fax: (212)532-1054. Website: www.dorchesterpub.com. **Offers advance.** Does not accept simultaneous submissions. Ms guidelines online.

Imprints Love Spell (romance), Leisure Books (romance, westerns, horror), Smooch (young adult).

    • No submissions via e-mail or fax.

Ⓝ Ⓐ ⊘ DORLING KINDERSLEY

Pearson Plc, 375 Hudson St., New York NY 10014. (212)213-4800. Website: www.dk.com. **Pays royalty or flat fee.**

    O⊸ Publishes picture books for middle-grade and older readers. Also, illustrated reference books for adults and children.

Fiction *Agented submissions only.*

Ⓝ Ⓐ ⊘ DOUBLEDAY BOOKS FOR YOUNG READERS

Imprint of Random House Children's Books/Random House, Inc., 1745 Broadway, New York NY 10019. (212)782-9000. Website: www.randomhouse.com/kids.

    • Trade picture book list, from preschool to age 8. Not accepting any unsolicited book mss at this time.

Ⓐ DOUBLEDAY BROADWAY PUBLISHING GROUP

Imprint of Random House, Inc., 1745 Broadway, New York NY 10019. (212)782-9000. Fax: (212)782-9700. Website: www.randomhouse.com/doubleday/. Vice President/Editor-in-Chief: William Thomas. Estab. 1897. Publishes hardcover originals. **Publishes 70 titles/year. Receives thousands of queries and thousands of mss/year. 30% of books from first-time authors. Pays royalty on retail price. Offers advance.** Publishes book 1 year after acceptance of ms. Does not accept simultaneous submissions.

Imprints Anchor Books, Broadway Books, Currency, Doubleday, Doubleday Image, Doubleday Religious Publishing, Main Street Books, Nan A. Talese.

    • Does not accept any unagented submissions. No exceptions.

    O⊸ Doubleday publishes high-quality fiction and nonfiction.

Nonfiction Biography. Subjects include Americana, anthropology/archeology, business/economics, computers/electronic, education, ethnic, government/politics, health/medicine, history, language/literature, money/fi-

nance, nature/environment, philosophy, religion, science, sociology, software, sports, translation, women's issues/studies. *Agented submissions only.*
Fiction Adventure, confession, ethnic, experimental, feminist, gay/lesbian, historical, humor, literary, mainstream/contemporary, religious, short story collections. *Agented submissions only.*
Recent Title(s) *The DaVinci Code*, by Dan Brown.

[A] DOUBLEDAY RELIGIOUS PUBLISHING

Imprint of Doubleday Broadway Publishing Group, Division of Random House, Inc., 1745 Broadway, New York NY 10019. (212)782-9000. Website: www.randomhouse.com. **Acquisitions:** Michelle Rapkin, vice president, religious division; Trace Murphy, editor-in-chief; Andrew Corbin, editor. Estab. 1897. Publishes hardcover and trade paperback originals and reprints. **Publishes 45-50 titles/year; imprint publishes 12 titles/year. Receives 1,000 queries and 500 mss/year. 3% from unagented writers. Pays 7½-15% royalty. Offers advance.** Publishes book 1 year after acceptance of ms. Accepts simultaneous submissions. Responds in 3 months to proposals. Book catalog for SAE with 3 first-class stamps.
Imprints Image Books, Anchor Bible Commentary, Anchor Bible Reference, Galilee, New Jerusalem Bible, Three Leaves Press.
Nonfiction Historical, philosophical, religious. *Agented submissions only.*
Fiction Religious. *Agented submissions only.*
Recent Title(s) *God Has a Dream*, by Desmond Tutu; *Introduction to the Gospel of John*, by Raymond Brown; *Tibetan Book of Yoga*, by Geshe Michael Roach.

DOUBLEDAY/IMAGE

Doubleday Broadway Publishing Group, Random House, Inc., 1745 Broadway, New York NY 10019. (212)782-9000. Fax: (212)302-7985. Website: www.randomhouse.com. **Acquisitions:** Trace Murphy, executive editor. Estab. 1956. Publishes hardcover, trade and mass market paperback originals and reprints. **Publishes 12 titles/year. Receives 500 queries and 300 mss/year. 10% of books from first-time authors. Pays royalty on retail price. Offers varied advance.** Publishes book 18 months after acceptance of ms. Accepts simultaneous submissions. Responds in 3 months to proposals.
  O─ Image Books has grown from a classic Catholic list to include a variety of current and future classics, maintaining a high standard of quality as the finest in religious paperbacks. Also publishes Doubleday paperbacks/hardcovers for general religion, spirituality, including works based in Buddhism, Islam, Judaism.
Nonfiction Biography, gift book, how-to, illustrated book, reference, self-help. Subjects include philosophy, psychology, religion, women's issues/studies. Query with SASE. Reviews artwork/photos as part of ms package. Send photocopies.
Recent Title(s) *Papal Sin*, by Garry Wills; *Soul Survivor*, by Philip Yancey; *The Lamb's Supper*, by Scott Hahn.

DOVER PUBLICATIONS, INC.

31 E. 2nd St., Mineola NY 11501. (516)294-7000. Fax: (516)873-1401. Website: www.doverpublications.com. **Acquisitions:** Paul Negri, editor-in-chief; John Grafton (math/science reprints). Estab. 1941. Publishes trade paperback originals and reprints. **Publishes 660 titles/year. Makes outright purchase.** Accepts simultaneous submissions. Book catalog online.
Nonfiction Biography, children's/juvenile, cookbook, how-to, humor, illustrated book, textbook. Subjects include agriculture/horticulture, Americana, animals, anthropology/archeology, art/architecture, cooking/foods/nutrition, health/medicine, history, hobbies, language/literature, music/dance, nature/environment, philosophy, photography, religion, science, sports, translation, travel. Publishes mostly reprints. Accepts original paper doll collections, game books, coloring books (juvenile). Query with SASE. Reviews artwork/photos as part of ms package.
Recent Title(s) *The Waning of the Middle Ages*, by John Huizenga.

[N] DOWN EAST BOOKS

Imprint of Down East Enterprise, Inc., P.O. Box 679, Camden ME 04843-0679. Fax: (207)594-7215. **Acquisitions:** Chris Cornell, editor (Countrysport); Michael Steere, associate editor (general). Estab. 1967. Publishes hardcover and trade paperback originals, trade paperback reprints. **Publishes 24-30 titles/year. Receives 1,000 submissions/year. 50% of books from first-time authors; 90% from unagented writers. Pays 10-15% royalty on net receipts. Offers $500 average advance.** Publishes book 1 year after acceptance of ms. Accepts simultaneous submissions. Responds in 3 months to queries. Send SASE for ms guidlines. Send 9 × 12 SASE for guidelines, plus recent catalog.
Imprints Countrysport Press (fly fishing and wing-shooting market; Chris Cornell, editor, e-mail: ccornell@downeast.com).

⚬ Down East Books publishes books that capture and illuminate the unique beauty and character of New England's history, culture, and wild places.

Nonfiction Children's/juvenile. Subjects include Americana, history, nature/environment, recreation, regional, sports. Books about the New England region, Maine in particular. "All of our regional books must have a Maine or New England emphasis." Query with SASE. Reviews artwork/photos as part of ms package.

Fiction Juvenile, mainstream/contemporary, regional. "We publish 2-4 juvenile titles/year (fiction and nonfiction), and 0-1 adult fiction titles/year." Query with SASE.

Recent Title(s) *The Maine Poets*, by Wesley McNair; *Visiting Aunt Sylvia's*, by Heather Austin; *Maine Sail*, by Margaret McCrea.

Ⓝ DOWN THE SHORE PUBLISHING

Box 3100, Harvey Cedars NJ 08008. (609)978-1233. Website: www.down-the-shore.com. **Acquisitions:** Leslee Ganss, associate editor. Publishes hardcover and trade paperback originals and reprints. **Publishes 5-8 titles/ year. Receives 200 queries and 20 mss/year. 80% of books from first-time authors; 100% from unagented writers. Pays royalty on wholesale price or retail price, or makes outright purchase. Offers occasional advance.** Publishes book 1-2 years after acceptance of ms. Accepts simultaneous submissions. Responds in 3 months to queries. Book catalog for 8×10 SAE with 2 first-class stamps or on website; ms guidelines online.

⚬ "Bear in mind that our market is regional—New Jersey, the Jersey Shore, the mid-Atlantic, and seashore and coastal subjects."

Nonfiction Children's/juvenile, coffee table book, gift book, illustrated book. Subjects include Americana, art/ architecture, history, nature/environment, regional. Query with SASE, or submit proposal package including outline, 1 sample chapter(s). Reviews artwork/photos as part of ms package. Send photocopies.

Fiction Regional. Query with SASE, or submit proposal package including 1 sample chapter(s), synopsis.

Poetry "We do not publish poetry, unless it is to be included as part of an anthology."

Recent Title(s) *Shore Chronicles: Diaries and Travelers' Tales from the Jersey Shore 1764-1955*, by Margaret Thomas Buchholz, editor (nonfiction); *Shore Stories: An Anthology of the Jersey Shore*, edited by Rich Youmans (fiction).

Tips "Carefully consider whether your proposal is a good fit for our established market."

Ⓝ DOWN THERE PRESS

Subsidiary of Open Enterprises Cooperative, Inc., 938 Howard St., #101, San Francisco CA 94103-4100. Website: www.goodvibes.com/dtp/dtp.html. Estab. 1975. Publishes paperback originals. **Publishes 1-2 titles/year. Pays royalty.** Publishes book 18 months after acceptance of ms. Accepts simultaneous submissions. Responds in 9 months to mss. Book catalog for #10 SASE; ms guidelines for #10 SASE.

Fiction Erotica, feminist, sex education/sex-positive nonfiction. Prefers book proposals rather than entire ms.

Ⓐ ⊘ LISA DREW BOOKS

Imprint of Scribner, Simon & Schuster Adult Publishing Group, 1230 Avenue of the Americas, New York NY 10020. (212)698-7000. Website: www.simonsays.com. **Acquisitions:** Lisa Drew, publisher. Publishes hardcover originals. **Publishes 10-14 titles/year. Receives 600 queries/year. 10% of books from first-time authors. Pays royalty on retail price. Offers variable advance.** Publishes book 1 year after acceptance of ms. Accepts simultaneous submissions. Responds in 1 month to queries. Book catalog free.

⚬ "We publish reading books; nonfiction that tells a story, not 'Fourteen Ways to Improve Your Marriage.'"

Nonfiction Subjects include government/politics, history, women's issues/studies. No unsolicited material. *Agented submissions only.*

Ⓐ THOMAS DUNNE BOOKS

Imprint of St. Martin's Press, 175 Fifth Ave., New York NY 10010. (212)674-5151. Website: www.stmartins.com. **Acquisitions:** Tom Dunne, publisher; Peter J. Wolverton, associate publisher; Ruth Cavin, associate publisher (mysteries). Publishes hardcover originals, trade paperback originals, and reprints. **Publishes 210 titles/year. Receives 1,000 queries/year. 20% of books from first-time authors. Pays royalty. Pays 10-15% royalty on retail price for hardcover, 7½% for paperback. Offers varying advance.** Publishes book 1 year after acceptance of ms. Accepts simultaneous submissions. Responds in 2 months to queries. Book catalog and ms guidelines free.

⚬ Thomas Dunne publishes a wide range of fiction and nonfiction. Accepts submissions from agents only.

Nonfiction Biography. Subjects include government/politics, history, sports, political commentary. "Author's attention to detail is important. We get a lot of manuscripts that are poorly proofread and just can't be considered." Agents submit query, or an outline and 100 sample pages. Reviews artwork/photos as part of ms package. Send photocopies.

Fiction Mainstream/contemporary, mystery, suspense, thrillers, women's. Agents submit query, or submit synopsis and 100 sample pages.

Recent Title(s) *Grant Comes East*, by Newt Gingrich; *Big Lies*, by Joe Canason.

DUQUESNE UNIVERSITY PRESS

600 Forbes Ave., Pittsburgh PA 15282. (412)396-6610. Fax: (412)396-5984. Website: www.dupress.duq.edu. **Acquisitions:** Susan Wadsworth-Booth, director. Estab. 1927. Publishes hardcover and trade paperback originals. **Publishes 8-12 titles/year. Receives 500 queries and 75 mss/year. 30% of books from first-time authors; 95% from unagented writers. Pays royalty on net price. Offers (some) advance.** Publishes book 1 year after acceptance of ms. Responds in 1 month to proposals; 3 months to mss. Book catalog and ms guidelines for #10 SASE; ms guidelines online.

- ◦┯ Duquesne publishes scholarly monographs in the fields of literary studies (medieval & Renaissance), continental philosophy, ethics, religious studies, existential psychology, and creative nonfiction for a general readership.

Nonfiction Scholarly (academic). Subjects include creative nonfiction, language/literature, philosophy (continental), psychology (existential), religion. "We look for quality of scholarship." For scholarly books, query or submit outline, 1 sample chapter, and SASE. For creative nonfiction, submit 1 copy of ms.

Recent Title(s) *Walking My Dog, Jane*, by Ned Rozell; *The Last Settlers*, by Jennifer Brice and Charles Mason; *Shanghai Quartet*, by Min-Zhan Lu.

DURBAN HOUSE PUBLISHING CO.

7502 Greenville Ave., Suite 500, Dallas TX 75231. (214)890-4050. Fax: (214)890-9295. E-mail: info@durbanhous e.com. Website: www.durbanhouse.com. **Acquisitions:** Robert Middlemiss, acquisitions editor (all areas consistent with house interest). Estab. 2000. Publishes hardcover and trade paperback originals. **Publishes 8-12 titles/year. 50% of books from first-time authors; 60% from unagented writers. Pays 8-15% royalty on wholesale price. Offers up to $2,000 advance.** Publishes book 1 year-18 months after acceptance of ms. Accepts simultaneous submissions. Book catalog and ms guidelines online.

Nonfiction Autobiography, biography, how-to, self-help. Subjects include alternative lifestyles, ethnic, gay/ lesbian, general nonfiction, health/medicine, New Age, psychology, sex, spirituality. "We are actively looking for titles consistent with house interests. Writers should have established platform and appropriate credentials before querying. Query only. No phone queries." Query with SASE, or submit proposal package including outline, 3 sample chapter(s), author bio.

Fiction Adventure, historical, horror, literary, mainstream/contemporary, mystery, suspense. "We are concentrating on mystery/thriller/suspense titles. Query only. No phone queries." Query with SASE, or submit 3 sample chapter(s), synopsis, author bio, and platform details.

Recent Title(s) *Spores, Plagues and History: The Story of Anthrax*, by Chris Holmes; *Behind the Mountain*, by Nick Williams; *Designed to Kill*, by Chester Campbell.

Tips "Readers look for quality in writing, story, and plot."

Ⓐ ⊘ DUTTON ADULT TRADE

Imprint of Penguin Group (USA), Inc., 375 Hudson St., New York NY 10014. (212)366-2000. Website: www.peng uinputnam.com. Editor-in-Chief, Editorial Director: Brian Tart. Estab. 1852. Publishers hardcover originals. **Publishes 40 titles/year. Pays royalty. Offers negotiable advance.** Publishes book 12-18 months after acceptance of ms. Accepts simultaneous submissions. Responds in 6 months to queries. Book catalog for #10 SASE.

- ◦┯ Dutton publishes hardcover, original, mainstream, and contemporary fiction and nonfiction in the areas of memoir, self-help, politics, psychology, and science for a general readership.

Nonfiction Humor, reference, self-help, Memoir. Subjects include general nonfiction. *Agented submissions only. No unsolicited mss.*

Fiction Adventure, historical, literary, mainstream/contemporary, mystery, short story collections, suspense. *Agented submissions only. No unsolicited mss.*

Recent Title(s) *Lies and the Lying Liars Who Tell Them*, by Al Franken; *The Privilege of You*, by Dave Pelzer; *Quitting America*, by Randall Robinson.

Tips "Write the complete manuscript and submit it to an agent or agents. They will know exactly which editor will be interested in a project."

DUTTON CHILDREN'S BOOKS

Imprint of Penguin Group (USA), Inc., 345 Hudson St., New York NY 10014. (212)414-3700. Fax: (212)414-3397. Website: www.penguin.com. **Acquisitions:** Stephanie Owens Lurie, president and publisher (picture books and fiction); Maureen Sullivan, executive editor (books for all ages with distinctive narrative style); Lucia Monfried, senior editor (picture books, easy-to-read books, fiction). Estab. 1852. Publishes hardcover originals as well as novelty formats. **Publishes 100 titles/year. 15% of books from first-time authors. Pays royalty on retail price. Offers advance.**

O→ Dutton Children's Books publishes high-quality fiction and nonfiction for readers ranging from preschoolers to young adults on a variety of subjects. Currently emphasizing picture books and middle-grade and young adult novels that offer a fresh perspective. De-emphasizing photographic nonfiction and picture books that teach a lesson.

Nonfiction Children's/juvenile, for preschoolers to young adults. Subjects include animals, history (US), nature/environment, science. Query with SASE.

Fiction Dutton Children's Books has a diverse, general interest list that includes picture books; easy-to-read books; and fiction for all ages, from "first chapter" books to young adult readers. Query with SASE and letter only.

Recent Title(s) *Creation*, by Gerald McDermott (picture book); *Leonardo, Beautiful Dreamer*, by Robert Byrd (nonfiction); *The Boy Who Spoke Dog*, by Clay Morgan (novel).

Ⓝ E-DIGITAL BOOKS, LLC

1155 S. Havana St. #11-364, Aurora CO 80012. Submissions E-mail: submissions@edigitalbooks.com. Website: www.edigitalbooks.com; www.edigitalcatholic.com. **Acquisitions:** T.R. Allen, manager and editor-in-chief (photography, art, travel, history, literary and short story collections, poetry, how-to, utility products, and Christian religious). Estab. 1999. **Publishes 10-15 titles/year. Receives 5 queries and 5 mss/year. 50% of books from first-time authors; 100% from unagented writers. Pays 30-60% royalty on retail price.** Publishes book 6 months after acceptance of ms. Accepts simultaneous submissions. Responds in 6 months to queries. Book catalog and ms guidlines by e-mail.

Nonfiction Children's/juvenile, illustrated book. Subjects include animals, art/architecture, creative nonfiction, ethnic, general nonfiction, history, language/literature, photography, religion, spirituality, travel. Query via e-mail with "Nonfiction Query" in the subject line. Reviews artwork/photos as part of ms package. Send JPEG initially.

Fiction Adventure, ethnic, fantasy, historical, humor, juvenile, literary, mainstream/contemporary, military/war, multicultural, multimedia, mystery, picture books, poetry, religious (Christian), romance (no), short story collections, spiritual, suspense, western, young adult. "General guidelines: family audience with respect to language and subject matter." Query via e-mail with "Fiction Query" in subject line.

Poetry "We are interested in Christian religious or secular poetry that embraces uplifting, positive, and inspirational themes." Query.

Recent Title(s) *Everywhere You Turn*, by Cathy Lynn (travel photography); *E-Digital E-Stickers*, by E-Digital Books staff (utility).

Tips "Audience is family, Christian, travel oriented, interested in the efficacy and convenience of our published utility e-books. Overall, we are specifically interested in subject matter that involves bringing a positive light into the world. We will consider material that is of a darker and more complicated matter if it provides informed and intelligent solutions to whatever area of difficulty that is examined or problem that is presented."

EAKIN PRESS/SUNBELT MEDIA, INC.

P.O. Box 90159, Austin TX 78709-0159. (512)288-1771. Fax: (512)288-1813. Website: www.eakinpress.com. **Acquisitions:** Angela Buckley, associate editor. Estab. 1978. Publishes hardcover and paperback originals and reprints. **Publishes 60 titles/year. Receives 1,500 submissions/year. 50% of books from first-time authors; 90% from unagented writers. Pays royalty. Pays 10-12-15% royalty on net sales.** Publishes book 18 months after acceptance of ms. Accepts simultaneous submissions. Responds in 3 months to queries. Book catalog for $1.25; ms guidelines online.

Imprints Eakin Press, Nortex Press, Sunbelt Eakin.

• No electronic submissions.

O→ Eakin specializes in Texana and Western Americana for adults and juveniles. Currently emphasizing women's studies.

Nonfiction Biography, cookbook (regional). Subjects include Americana (Western), business/economics, cooking/foods/nutrition, ethnic, history, military/war, regional, sports, African American studies, Civil War, Texas history. Juvenile nonfiction: includes biographies of historic personalities, prefer with Texas or regional interest, or nature studies; and easy-read illustrated books for grades 1-3. Query with SASE.

Fiction Historical, juvenile. Juvenile fiction for grades K-12, preferably relating to Texas and the Southwest or contemporary. Nonfiction adult with Texas or Southwest theme. No adult fiction. Query or submit outline/synopsis and sample chapters.

Recent Title(s) *The Golden Bay*, by John J. Nance; *Red Zone*, by Red McCombs.

⬛ EASTERN WASHINGTON UNIVERSITY PRESS

705 W. 1st Ave., Spokane WA 99201. (509)623-4284. Fax: (509)623-4283. E-mail: ewupress@ewu.edu. Website: ewupress.ewu.edu. **Acquisitions:** Scott Poole, assitant director (poetry); Joelean Copeland, managing editor (nonfiction). Estab. 1994. Publishes hardcover and trade paperback originals and reprints. **Publishes 7 titles/ year. Receives 100 queries/year. 50% of books from first-time authors. Pays 10% royalty.** Publishes book 2-4 years after acceptance of ms. Accepts simultaneous submissions. Responds in 1 month to queries; 3 months to proposals; 6-9 months to mss. Book catalog and ms guidelines free.

Nonfiction Subjects include anthropology/archeology, creative nonfiction, government/politics, history, language/literature, philosophy, regional, translation. "Looking to go from 2-4 titles a year within the next two years." Query with SASE.

Fiction Short story collections. Query with SASE.

Poetry "Looking to increase from 3-6 titles a year." Submit complete ms.

ECLIPSE PRESS

The Blood-Horse, Inc., 1736 Alexandria Dr., Lexington KY 40504. Website: www.eclipsepress.com. **Acquisitions:** Jacqueline Duke, editor (equine). Estab. 1916. Publishes hardcover and trade paperback originals. **Publishes 12-15 titles/year. Receives 100 queries and 50 mss/year. 50% of books from first-time authors; 40% from unagented writers. Pays 10-15% royalty on net receipts, or makes outright purchase. Offers $3,000-12,000 advance.** Publishes book 18 months after acceptance of ms. Accepts simultaneous submissions. Responds in 2-3 months to queries; 2-3 months to proposals; 2-3 months to mss. Book catalog free.

Nonfiction Subjects include sports (equine, equestrian). "We only accept nonfiction works on equine and equestrian topics." Query with SASE, or submit outline, sample chapter(s). Reviews artwork/photos as part of ms package.

Tips "Our audience is sports, horse, and racing enthusiasts."

EDEN PUBLISHING

P.O. Box 20176, Keizer OR 97307-0176. Phone/fax: (503)390-9013. Website: www.edenpublishing.com. **Acquisitions:** Barbara Griffin, managing editor. Publishes trade paperback originals. **Receives 1,200 queries and 10 mss/year. 40% of books from first-time authors; 100% from unagented writers. Pays royalty on retail price.** Publishes book 4-6 months after acceptance of ms. Responds in 2 weeks to queries.

➤ Eden publishes books with strong Christian theme. Also, recently added literary poetry to the list they market to educators and libraries.

Nonfiction Self-help. Subjects include education, religion, spirituality (Christian only, nondenominational). Query with SASE. **All unsolicited mss returned unopened.**

Recent Title(s) *At the Foot of the Cross: Easter Dramatic Readings*, by Barbara Dan (drama); *Poetry Grand Slam Finale*, by Alan MacDougall (poetry); *Night (Die Nacht)*, by Richard Exner (bilingual text).

Tips "Our primary target market is mainstream Christians, pastors and Christian colleges. Our secondary target market is academic libraries."

⬛ EDUCATOR'S INTERNATIONAL PRESS, INC.

18 Colleen Rd., Troy NY 12180. (518)271-9886. Fax: (518)266-9422. E-mail: sarah@edint.com. Website: www.e dint.com. **Acquisitions:** Sarah J. Biondello, publisher/acquisitions editor. Estab. 1996. Publishes hardcover and trade paperback originals and reprints. **Publishes 10-12 titles/year. Receives 50 queries and 50 mss/year. 50% of books from first-time authors; 98% from unagented writers. Pays 3-15% royalty on wholesale price.** Publishes book 1 year after acceptance of ms. Accepts simultaneous submissions. Responds in 2 months to queries; 2 months to proposals; 3 months to mss. Book catalog and ms guidelines free.

➤ Educator's International publishes books in all aspects of education, broadly conceived, from pre-kindergarten to postgraduate. "We specialize in texts, professional books, videos and other materials for students, faculty, practitioners and researchers. We also publish a full list of books in the areas of women's studies, and social and behavioral sciences."

Nonfiction Textbook, supplemental texts; conference proceedings. Subjects include education, gay/lesbian, language/literature, philosophy, psychology, software, women's issues/studies. Submit table of contents, outline, 2-3 chapters, résumé with SASE. Reviews artwork/photos as part of ms package.

Recent Title(s) *Our Sons Were Labeled Behavior Disordered*, by Joy-Ruth Mickelson.

Tips Audience is professors, students, researchers, individuals, libraries.

EDUCATORS PUBLISHING SERVICE

P.O. Box 9031, Cambridge MA 02139-9031. (617)547-6706. Fax: (617)547-3805. Website: www.epsbooks.com. **Acquisitions:** Charles H. Heinle, vice president, Publishing Group. Estab. 1952. **Publishes 26 titles/year. Receives 400 queries and 400 mss/year. 50% of books from first-time authors; 100% from unagented** writers. **Pays 5-12% royalty on retail price.** Publishes book 8 months (minimum) after acceptance of ms. Accepts simultaneous submissions. Responds in 1 month to queries; 3 months to proposals; 3 months to mss. Book catalog and ms guidelines free; ms guidelines online.

    O→ EPS accepts queries from educators writing for a school market, authoring materials (primarily K-8) in the reading and language areas. "We are interested in materials following pedagogical restraints (such as decodable tests and leveled readers) that we can incorporate into ongoing or future projects."

Nonfiction Workbooks (language arts) and some professional books. Subjects include education (reading comprehension, phonics vocabulary development and writing), supplementary texts and workbooks (reading and language arts). Query with SASE.

Recent Title(s) *Words Are Wonderful, Book 3*, by Dorothy Grant Hennings; *Ten Essential Vocabulary Strategies*, by Lee Mountain; *Write About Me*, by Elsie Wilmerding.

Tips Teacher, students (K-adult) audiences.

EDUPRESS, INC.

208 Avenida Fabricante #200, San Clemente CA 92672. (949)366-9499. Fax: (949)366-9441. E-mail: info@edupressinc.com. Website: www.edupressinc.com. **Acquisitions:** Kathy Rogers, product coordinator. Estab. 1979. Publishes trade paperback originals. **Publishes 40 titles/year. Receives 20 queries and 100 mss/year. 25% of books from first-time authors.** Publishes book 1 year after acceptance of ms. Responds in 2 months to queries; 5 months to mss. Book catalog and ms guidelines free.

    O→ Edupress, Inc., publishes supplemental resources for classroom curriculum. Currently emphasizing more science, math, language arts emphasis than in the past.

Nonfiction Subjects include education (resources for pre-school through middle school). Submit proposal package, including ms copy, outline, 1 sample chapter, and SASE. Reviews artwork/photos as part of ms package. Send photocopies.

Recent Title(s) Phonics-Based Writing Series; *Classroom Plays for Social Studies*.

Tips Audience is classroom teachers and homeschool parents.

EERDMANS BOOKS FOR YOUNG READERS

William B. Eerdmans Publishing Co., 255 Jefferson Ave. SE, Grand Rapids MI 49503. (616)459-4591. Fax: (616)459-6540. Website: www.eerdmans.com. **Acquisitions:** Judy Zylstra, editor. Publishes picture books and middle reader and young adult fiction and nonfiction. **Publishes 12-15 titles/year. Receives 3,000 submissions/year. Pays 5-7½% royalty on retail price.** Publishes book Publishes middle reader and YA books in 1 year; publishes picture books in 2-3 years after acceptance of ms. Accepts simultaneous submissions. Responds in 6 weeks to queries. Book catalog for #10 SASE; ms guidelines online.

    • No queries or submissions via e-mail or fax.

    O→ "We publish books for children and young adults that deal with spiritual themes—but never in a preachy or heavy-handed way. Some of our books are clearly religious, while others (especially our novels) look at spiritual issues in very subtle ways. We look for books that are honest, wise and hopeful." Currently emphasizing general picture books (also picture book biographies), novels (middle reader and YA). De-emphasizing retellings of Bible stories.

Nonfiction Children's/juvenile, picture books, middle reader, young adult nonfiction. "Do not send illustrations unless you are a professional illustrator." Submit complete mss for picture books and novels or biographies under 200 pages with SASE. For longer books, send query letter and 3 or 4 sample chapters with SASE. Reviews artwork/photos as part of ms package. Send color photocopies rather than original art.

Fiction Juvenile, picture books, young adult, middle reader. "Do not send illustrations unless you are a professional illustrator." Submit complete mss for picture books and novels or biographies under 200 pages with SASE. For longer books, send query letter and 3 or 4 sample chapters with SASE.

Recent Title(s) *A Bird or Two: A Story about Henri Matisse*, written and illustrated by Bijou Le Tord; *When Daddy Prays*, written by Nikki Grimes, illustrated by Tim Ladwig; *Secrets in the House of Delgado*, by Gloria Miklowitz.

WILLIAM B. EERDMANS PUBLISHING CO.

255 Jefferson Ave. SE, Grand Rapids MI 49503. (616)459-4591. Fax: (616)459-6540. E-mail: sales@eerdmans.com. Website: www.eerdmans.com. **Acquisitions:** Jon Pott, editor-in-chief; Judy Zylstra, editor-in-chief (children's books). Estab. 1911. Publishes hardcover and paperback originals and reprints. **Publishes 120-130 titles/year. Receives 3,000-4,000 submissions/year. 10% of books from first-time authors; 95% from unagented writers. Pays royalty. Offers occasional advance.** Publishes book usually within 1 year after acceptance of ms. Accepts simultaneous submissions. Responds in 6 weeks to queries. Book catalog and ms guidelines free.

Imprints Eerdmans Books for Young Readers (Judy Zylstra, editor).

O—π "The majority of our adult publications are religious and most of these are academic or semi-academic in character (as opposed to inspirational or celebrity books), though we also publish general trade books on the Christian life. Our nonreligious titles, most of them in regional history or on social issues, aim, similarly, at an educated audience."

Nonfiction Children's/juvenile, reference, textbook, monographs. Subjects include history (religious), language/literature, philosophy (of religion), psychology, regional (history), religion, sociology, translation, Biblical studies, theology, ethics. "We prefer that writers take the time to notice if we have published anything at all in the same category as their manuscript before sending it to us." Query with outline, 2-3 sample chapters, and SASE for return of ms. Reviews artwork/photos as part of ms package.

Fiction Religious (children's, general, fantasy). Query with SASE.

Recent Title(s) *The Dwelling of the Light: Praying with Icons of Christ*, by Rowan Williams; *Inge: A Girl's Journey Through Nazi Europe*, by Inge Joseph Bleier and David E. Gumpert; *Familiar Stranger: An Introduction to Jesus of Nazareth*, by Michael J. McClymond.

N ELDER BOOKS

P.O. Box 490, Forest Knolls CA 94933. (415)488-9002. E-mail: info@elderbooks.com. Website: www.elderbooks. com. **Acquisitions:** Carmel Sheridan, director. Estab. 1987. Publishes trade paperback originals. **Publishes 6-10 titles/year. Receives 200 queries and 50 mss/year. 50% of books from first-time authors; 50% from unagented writers. Pays 7% royalty on retail price; No advance.** Publishes book 9 months after acceptance of ms. Responds in 3 months to queries. Book catalog free.

O—π Elder Books is dedicated to publishing practical, hands-on guidebooks for family and professional caregivers of persons with Alzheimer's.

Nonfiction Gift book, how-to, self-help. Subjects include child guidance/parenting, education, health/medicine, money/finance, psychology, women's issues/studies, Senior issues, Alzheimer's disease. Submit outline, 2 sample chapters. Reviews artwork/photos as part of ms package. Send photocopies.

Recent Title(s) *Coping With Caring: Daily Reflections for Alzheimer's Caregivers*, by Lyn Roche.

Tips "Our books are written in a style that is user-friendly and nontechnical, presenting key information on caregiver concerns including: how to keep the person engaged through meaningful activities, prevent caregiver burnout, cope with wandering and organize a search in the event the person disappears, deal with difficult behaviors."

ELECTRIC WORKS PUBLISHING

605 Ave. C.E., Bismarck ND 58501. (701)255-0356. E-mail: editors@electricpublishing.com. Website: www.elec tricpublishing.com. **Acquisitions:** James R. Bohe, editor-in-chief. Publishes digital books. **Publishes 15 titles/year. Receives 80 queries and 250 mss/year. 90% of books from first-time authors; 95% from unagented writers. Pays royalty on wholesale price.** Publishes book 3 months after acceptance of ms. Accepts simultaneous submissions. Responds in 5 months to queries. Book catalog and ms guidelines online.

O—π Digital publisher offering a wide range of subjects.

Nonfiction Biography, children's/juvenile, cookbook, how-to, humor, self-help, technical. Subjects include child guidance/parenting, computers/electronic, cooking/foods/nutrition, creative nonfiction, education, history, hobbies, military/war, money/finance, multicultural, nature/environment, recreation, regional, religion, science, sociology, spirituality, women's issues/studies. *Electronic submissions only.* Submit entire ms in digital format. Reviews artwork/photos as part of ms package.

Fiction Adventure, ethnic, experimental, fantasy, gothic, historical, horror, humor, juvenile, literary, mainstream/contemporary, military/war, multicultural, multimedia, mystery, occult, regional, religious, romance, science fiction, short story collections (of 40,000 words or more), spiritual, sports, suspense, western, young adult. *Electronic submissions only.* Submit ms in digital format.

Recent Title(s) *We Never Cried at Babylon*, by Ashi Ke Nashi; *Ravenna's Heart*, by Cassandra Stout; *The Hitler Quarter*, by Maynard Soull.

ELEPHANT BOOKS

65 Macedonia Rd., Alexander NC 28701. (828)252-9515. Fax: (828)255-8719. E-mail: sales@abooks.com. Website: abooks.com. **Acquisitions:** Pat Roberts, acquisitions editor. Publishes trade paperback originals and reprints. **Publishes 8 titles/year. Receives 100 queries and 50 mss/year. 90% of books from first-time authors; 80% from unagented writers. Pays 12-15% royalty on wholesale price. Seldom offers advance.** Publishes book 18 months after acceptance of ms. Book catalog and ms guidelines online.

Imprints Blue/Gray Books (contact Ralph Roberts, Civil War history).

Nonfiction Cookbook. Subjects include cooking/foods/nutrition, history, military/war (Civil War). Query, or submit outline with 3 sample chapters and proposal package, including potential marketing plans with SASE. Reviews artwork/photos as part of ms package. Send photocopies.

Recent Title(s) *Rebel Boast*, by Manly Wade Wellman.

ⓝ ELLORA'S CAVE PUBLISHING, INC.

P.O. Box 787, Hudson OH 44236. (330)689-1118. Fax: (330)689-1119. E-mail: service@ellorascave.com. Submissions E-mail: submissions@ellorascave.com. Website: www.ellorascave.com. **Acquisitions:** Sheri Ross Carucci, editor-in-chief (erotic romance); Raelene Gorlinsky, managing editor. Estab. 2000. Publishes trade paperback and electronic originals and reprints. **Publishes 208 titles/year. Receives 300 queries and 300 mss/year. 75% of books from first-time authors; 95% from unagented writers. Pays 8-40% royalty on net receipts.** Publishes book 9 months after acceptance of ms. Accepts simultaneous submissions. Responds in 2 months to queries; 2 months to proposals; 2 months to mss. Book catalog and ms guidelines online.

Fiction Erotica, fantasy, gay/lesbian, gothic, historical, horror, mainstream/contemporary, multicultural, mystery, romance, science fiction, suspense, western. All must be under genre romance. All must have erotic content or author be willing to add sex during editing. Submit proposal package including 3 sample chapter(s), synopsis. Send via e-mail in .doc or .rtf format.

Recent Title(s) *The Empress' New Clothes*, by Jaid Black; *Fighting Fear*, by Christine Warren.

Tips "Our audience is romance readers who want to read more sex, more detailed sex. They come to us, because we offer not erotica, but Romantica™. Sex with romance, plot, emotion. Remember Ellora's Cave is a Romantica™ site. We publish romance books with an erotic nature. More sex is the motto, but there has to be a storyline—a logical plot and a happy ending."

EMPEROR'S NEW CLOTHES PRESS

E-mail: info@encpress.com. Submissions E-mail: publisher@encpress.com. Website: www.encpress.com. **Acquisitions:** Olga Gardner Galvin, publisher/editor-in-chief. Estab. 2003. Publishes trade paperback originals. **Publishes 4-6 titles/year. 90% of books from first-time authors; 100% from unagented writers. Pays 50% royalty on retail price.** Publishes book 18 months after acceptance of ms. Does not accept simultaneous submissions. Responds in 2-3 weeks to queries; 3-4 months to mss. Book catalog and ms guidelines online.

Fiction Adventure, humor, literary, mainstream/contemporary, science fiction, suspense, political satire, utopias/dystopias, social satire, picaresque novel. Query through e-mail.

Recent Title(s) *Don't Call It "Virtual,"* by Beth Elliott (political satire/utopia/lesbian); *Season of Ash*, by Justin Bryant (South Africa/politics/contemporary); *Moon Beaver*, by Andrew Hook (adventure/humor/social satire).

Tips Audience is well-informed, socially liberal, fiscally conservative, decidedly not politically correct readers. "Don't be afraid to offend. We're not publishing for the 'broadest possible audience.' We're publishing for the politically incorrect audience with a good sense of humor. If it's not at all funny, we don't want to read it."

EMPIRE PUBLISHING SERVICE

P.O. Box 1344, Studio City CA 91614-0344. **Acquisitions:** Joseph Witt. Estab. 1960. Publishes hardcover reprints and trade paperback originals and reprints. **Publishes 40 titles/year; imprint publishes 15 titles/year. Receives 500 queries and 85 mss/year. 50% of books from first-time authors; 95% from unagented writers. Pays 6-10% royalty on retail price. Offers variable advance.** Publishes book up to 2 years after acceptance of ms. Does not accept simultaneous submissions. Responds in 1 month to queries; 2 months to proposals; up to 1 year to mss. Book catalog for #10 SASE; ms guidelines for $1 or #10 SASE.

Imprints Gaslight Publications, Gaslight Books, Empire Publications, Empire Books, Empire Music.

○━ "Submit only Sherlock Holmes, performing arts and health."

Nonfiction How-to, humor, reference, technical, textbook. Subjects include health/medicine, humor, music/dance, Sherlock Holmes. Query with SASE. Reviews artwork/photos as part of ms package. Send photocopies.

Fiction Historical (pre-18th century), mystery (Sherlock Holmes). Query with SASE.

Recent Title(s) *On the Scent with Sherlock Holmes*, by Jacy Tracy; *Elementary My Dear Watson*, by William Alan Landes; *The Magic of Food*, by James Cohen.

ENCOUNTER BOOKS

665 Third St., Suite 330, San Francisco CA 94107-1951. (415)538-1460. Fax: (415)538-1461. Website: www.encounterbooks.com. **Acquisitions:** Peter Collier, publisher. Hardcover originals and trade paperback reprints. **Publishes 12-20 titles/year. Receives 500 queries and 200 mss/year. 10% of books from first-time authors; 40% from unagented writers. Pays 7-10% royalty on retail price. Offers $2,000-25,000 advance.** Publishes book 18 months after acceptance of ms. Accepts simultaneous submissions. Responds in 3 months to queries; 4 months to proposals; 4 months to mss. Book catalog free or online; ms guidelines online.

○━ Encounter Books publishes serious nonfiction—books that can alter our society, challenge our morality, stimulate our imaginations. Currently emphasizing history, culture, social criticism, and politics.

Nonfiction Biography, reference. Subjects include child guidance/parenting, education, ethnic, government/politics, health/medicine, history, language/literature, memoirs, military/war, multicultural, philosophy, psychology, religion, science, sociology, women's issues/studies, gender studies. Submit proposal package, including outline and 1 sample chapter.

Recent Title(s) *Anti-Americanism*, by Jean-Francis Revel; *Mexifornia: A State of Becoming*, by Victor Davis Hanson; *BioEvolution: How Biotechnology is Changing Our World*, by Michael Fumento.

ENSLOW PUBLISHERS, INC.

40 Industrial Rd., Box 398, Berkeley Heights NJ 07922. (973)771-9400. Website: www.enslow.com. **Acquisitions:** Brian D. Enslow, editor. Estab. 1977. Publishes hardcover originals. 10% require freelance illustration. **Publishes 250 titles/year. Pays royalty on net price with advance or flat fee. Offers advance.** Publishes book 1 year after acceptance of ms. Responds in 1 month to queries. Ms guidelines for #10 SASE.

�○➧ Enslow publishes hardcover nonfiction series books for young adults and school-age children.

Nonfiction Biography, children's/juvenile, reference. Subjects include health/medicine, history, recreation (Sports), science, sociology. Interested in new ideas for series of books for young people. No fiction, fictionalized history, or dialogue.

Recent Title(s) *TV News: Can It Be Trusted?*, by Ray Spangenburg and Kit Moser; *Resisters and Rescuers—Standing Up Against the Holocaust*, by Linda Jacobs Attman.

Tips "We love to receive résumés from experienced writers with good research skills who can think like young people."

ENTREPRENEUR PRESS

2445 McCabe Way, Irvine CA 92614. (949)261-2325. Fax: (949)261-7729. Website: www.smallbizbooks.com. **Acquisitions:** Jere Calmes, editorial director; Leanne Harvey, marketing director. Publishes quality hardcover and trade paperbacks. **Publishes 50 titles/year. Receives 1,200 queries and 600 mss/year. 40% of books from first-time authors; 60% from unagented writers. Pays 2-15% royalty, or makes $2,000-10,000 outright purchase.** Accepts simultaneous submissions. Book catalog and ms guidelines free.

Nonfiction Subjects include business/economics, start-up, marketing, finance, personal finance, accounting, motivation, leadership, and management. Query with SASE, or submit proposal package including outline, 2 sample chapter(s), author bio, preface or executive summary, competition. Reviews artwork/photos as part of ms package. Send transparencies.

Recent Title(s) *Start Your Business, 3rd Ed.*, by Lesonsky; *Many Miles to Go*, by Brian Tracy.

Tips Audience is "people who are thinking about starting or growing their own business, and people who want to become successful and effective in business and management. Also general business skills, including finance, marketing, presentation, leadership, etc."

Ⓐ ⊘ EOS

Imprint of HarperCollins General Books Group, 10 E. 53rd St., New York NY 10022. (212)207-7000. Submissions E-mail: eossubs@harpercollins.com. Website: www.eosbooks.com. Estab. 1998. Publishes hardcover originals, trade and mass market paperback originals, and reprints. **Publishes 40-46 titles/year. 10% of books from first-time authors. Pays royalty on retail price. Offers variable advance.** Publishes book 18-24 months after acceptance of ms. Responds in 6 months to queries. Ms guidelines for #10 SASE.

�○➧ Eos publishes "quality science fiction/fantasy with broad appeal."

Fiction Fantasy, science fiction. No horror or juvenile. *Agented submissions only.* **All unsolicited mss returned unopened.** *No unsolicited submissions.*

Recent Title(s) *The Magician's Guild*, by Trudi Canavan; *City of Pearl*, by Karen Traviss; *King of Foxes*, by Raymond E. Feist.

Tips "The official HarperCollins submissions policy has changed, and we can no longer accept unsolicited submissions. To submit your science fiction or fantasy novel to Eos, please query first. We strongly urge you to query via e-mail. Your query should be brief—no more than a 2-page description of your book. Do not send chapters or full synopsis at this time. You will receive a response—either a decline or a request for more material—in approximately 1-2 months."

EPICENTER PRESS, INC.

P.O. Box 82368, Kenmore WA 98028. (425)485-6822. Fax: (425)481-8253. E-mail: info@epicenterpress.com. Website: www.epicenterpress.com. **Acquisitions:** Kent Sturgis, publisher. Estab. 1987. Publishes hardcover and trade paperback originals. **Publishes 10 titles/year. Receives 200 queries and 100 mss/year. 75% of books from first-time authors; 90% from unagented writers.** Publishes book 1-2 years after acceptance of ms. Responds in 2 months to queries. Book catalog and ms guidelines on website.

�○➧ "We are a regional press founded in Alaska whose interests include but are not limited to the arts, history, environment, and diverse cultures and lifestyles of the North Pacific and high latitudes.

Nonfiction "Our focus is Alaska and the Pacific Northwest. We do not encourage nonfiction titles from outside this region." Biography, coffee table book, gift book, humor. Subjects include animals, art/architecture, ethnic, history, nature/environment, photography, recreation, regional, women's issues/studies. Submit outline and 3 sample chapters. Reviews artwork/photos as part of ms package. Send photocopies.

Recent Title(s) *Raising Ourselves*, by Velma Wallis.

ETC PUBLICATIONS

700 E. Vereda Sur, Palm Springs CA 92262-4816. (760)325-5352. Fax: (760)325-8841. **Acquisitions:** Dr. Richard W. Hostrop, publisher (education and social sciences); Lee Ona S. Hostrop, editorial director (history and works suitable below the college level). Estab. 1972. Publishes hardcover and paperback originals. **Publishes 6-12 titles/year. Receives 100 submissions/year. 75% of books from first-time authors; 90% from unagented writers. Offers 5-15% royalty, based on wholesale and retail price.** Publishes book 9 months after acceptance of ms.

O— ETC publishes works that "further learning as opposed to entertainment."

Nonfiction Textbook, educational management, gifted education, futuristics. Subjects include education, translation (in above areas). Submit complete ms with SASE. Reviews artwork/photos as part of ms package.

Recent Title(s) *The Internet for Educators and Homeschoolers*, by Steve Jones, Ph.D.

Tips "Special consideration is given to those authors who are capable and willing to submit their completed work in camera-ready, typeset form. We are particularly interested in works suitable for both the Christian school market and homeschoolers; e.g., state history texts below the high school level with a Christian-oriented slant."

EVAN-MOOR EDUCATIONAL PUBLISHERS

18 Lower Ragsdale Dr., Monterey CA 93940-5746. (831)649-5901. Fax: (831)649-6256. E-mail: editorial@evan-moor.com. Website: www.evan-moor.com. **Acquisitions:** Acquisitions Editor. Estab. 1979. Publishes teaching materials. **Publishes 50-60 titles/year. Receives 50 queries and 100 mss/year. 1% of books from first-time authors; 100% from unagented writers. Makes outright purchase.** Publishes book 1 year after acceptance of ms. Accepts simultaneous submissions. Responds in 3 months to queries. Book catalog and ms guidelines free or on website.

O— "Our books are teaching ideas, lesson plans, and blackline reproducibles for grades PreK-6 in all curriculum areas except music and bilingual." Currently emphasizing writing/language arts, practice materials for home use. De-emphasizing thematic materials. "We do not publish children's literary fiction or literary nonfiction."

Nonfiction Subjects include education, teaching materials, grade pre-K-6. No children's fiction or nonfiction literature. Submit proposal package, including outline and 3 sample chapters.

Recent Title(s) *Daily Paragraph Editing* (5-book series, grades 2-6); *Look, Listen, & Speak* (10-book series for grades K-3 combining print materials and interactive CD-ROM to teach basic vocabulary to English-language learners).

Tips "Writers should know how classroom/educational materials differ from trade publications. They should request catalogs and submission guidelines before sending queries or manuscripts. Visiting our website will give writers a clear picture of the type of materials we publish."

[N] [A] M. EVANS AND CO., INC.

216 E. 49th St., New York NY 10017-1502. (212)688-2810. Fax: (212)486-4544. E-mail: editorial@mevans.com. Website: www.mevans.com. **Acquisitions:** Editor. Estab. 1960. Publishes hardcover and trade paperback originals. **Publishes 30-40 titles/year. 5% from unagented writers. Pays negotiable royalty. Offers advance.** Publishes book 8 months after acceptance of ms. Responds in 2 months to queries. Book catalog for 9×12 SAE with 3 first-class stamps; ms guidelines online.

O— Evans has a strong line of health and self-help books but is interested in publishing quality titles on a wide variety of subject matters. "We publish a general trade list of adult nonfiction, cookbooks and semi-reference works. The emphasis is on selectivity, publishing commercial works with quality." Currently emphasizing health, relationships, nutrition.

Nonfiction Cookbook, self-help. Subjects include cooking/foods/nutrition, general nonfiction, health/medicine, relationships. "Our most successful nonfiction titles have been related to health and the behavioral sciences. No limitation on subject." No memoirs. Query with SASE. *No unsolicited mss.*

Fiction "Our very small general fiction list represents an attempt to combine quality with commercial potential. We publish no more than one novel per season." "Small, general trade publisher specializing in nonfiction titles on health, nutrition, diet, cookbooks, parenting, popular psychology." Query with SASE. *No unsolicited mss.*

Recent Title(s) *Dr. Atkins' Diet Revolution* (health); *This Is How Love Works*, by Steven Carter.

Tips "A writer should clearly indicate what his book is all about, frequently the task the writer performs least well. His credentials, although important, mean less than his ability to convince this company that he understands his subject and that he has the ability to communicate a message worth hearing. Writers should review our book catalog before making submissions."

EXCALIBUR PUBLICATIONS

P.O. Box 89667, Tucson AZ 85752-9667. (520)575-9057. E-mail: excalibureditor@earthlink.net. **Acquisitions:** Alan M. Petrillo, editor. Publishes trade paperback originals. **Publishes 4-6 titles/year. Pays royalty or makes outright purchase.** Responds in 1 month to queries; 1 month to mss.

○┐ Excalibur publishes historical and military works from all time periods.

Nonfiction Subjects include history (military), military/war (strategy and tactics, as well as the history of battles, firearms, arms, and armour), historical personalities. "We are seeking well-researched and documented works. Unpublished writers are welcome." Query with outline, first 3 chapters, SASE. Include notes on photos, illustrations, and maps.

Recent Title(s) *Famous Faces of World War II*, by Robert Van Osdol; *Present Sabers: A History of the U.S. Horse Cavalry*, by Allan Heninger.

Tips "Know your subject matter, and present it in a clear and precise manner. Please give us a brief description of your background or experience as it relates to your submission, as well as any marketing insight you might have on your subject."

EXCELSIOR CEE PUBLISHING

P.O. Box 5861, Norman OK 73070. (405)329-3909. Fax: (405)329-6886. **Acquisitions:** J.C. Marshall. Estab. 1989. Publishes hardcover and trade paperback originals. **Publishes 15 titles/year. Receives 400 queries/ year. Pays royalty, or makes outright purchase (both negotiable); will consider co-op publishing some titles.** Publishes book 1 year after acceptance of ms. Accepts simultaneous submissions. Responds in 1 month to queries. Book catalog for #10 SASE.

○┐ "All of our books speak to the reader through words of feeling—whether they are how-to, educational, humor, or memoir, the reader comes away with feeling, truth, and inspiration." Currently emphasizing how-to, family history, memoirs, inspiration. De-emphasizing childrens.

Nonfiction Biography, gift book, how-to, humor, self-help, inspiration. Subjects include Americana, education, history, language/literature, memoirs, women's issues/studies, general nonfiction, writing. Query with SASE.

Recent Title(s) *Goodbye Kite*, by Lois Redpath; *About Face . . . Forward March*, by Robert Seikel; *Oklahoma Jim*, by James Shears.

Tips "We have a general audience, bookstore browsers interested in nonfiction reading. We publish titles that have a mass appeal and can be enjoyed by a large reading public."

EXECUTIVE EXCELLENCE PUBLISHING

1366 E. 1120 S., Provo UT 84606. (800)304-9782. Fax: (801)377-5960. E-mail: editorial@eep.com. Website: www.eep.com. **Acquisitions:** Ken Shelton, editor in chief. Estab. 1984. Publishes hardcover and trade paperback originals and trade paperback reprints. **Publishes 10 titles/year. Receives 300 queries and 150 mss/ year. 35% of books from first-time authors; 95% from unagented writers. Pays 15% on cash received and 50% of subsidiary right proceeds.** Publishes book 6-9 months after acceptance of ms. Accepts simultaneous submissions. Responds in 1 month to queries; 1 month to proposals; 1 month to mss. Book catalog free or on website.

○┐ Executive Excellence publishes business and self-help titles. "We help you—the busy person, executive or entrepreneur—to find a wiser, better way to live your life and lead your organization." Currently emphasizing business innovations for general management and leadership (from the personal perspective). De-emphasizing technical or scholarly textbooks on operational processes and financial management or workbooks.

Nonfiction Self-help. Subjects include business/economics, leadership/management, entrepreneurship, career, motivational. Submit proposal package, including outline, 1-2 sample chapters and author bio, company information.

Recent Title(s) *Spirit of Leadership*, by Robert J. Spitzer; *Traits of Champions*, by Andrew Wood and Brian Tracy.

Tips "Executive Excellence Publishing is an established publishing house with a strong niche in the marketplace. Our magazines, *Executive Excellence*, *Sales and Marketing Excellence* and *Personal Excellence*, are distributed monthly in countries across the world. Our authors are on the cutting edge in their fields of leadership, self-help and business and organizational development. We are always looking for strong new talent with something to say, and a burning desire to say it."

FACTS ON FILE, INC.

132 W. 31st St., 17th Floor, New York NY 10001. (212)967-8800. Fax: (212)967-9196. E-mail: llikoff@factsonfile. com. Website: www.factsonfile.com. **Acquisitions:** Laurie Likoff, editorial director (science, fashion, natural

history); Frank Darmstadt (science & technology, nature, reference); Nicole Bowen, senior editor (American history, women's studies, young adult reference); James Chambers, trade editor (health, pop culture, true crime, sports); Jeff Soloway, acquisitions editor (language/literature). Estab. 1941. Publishes hardcover originals and reprints. **Publishes 135 titles/year. 25% from unagented writers. Pays 10% royalty on retail price. Offers $5,000-10,000 advance.** Accepts simultaneous submissions. Responds in 2 months to queries. Book catalog free; ms guidelines online.

Imprints Checkmark Books.

   O⊶ Facts on File produces high-quality reference materials on a broad range of subjects for the school library market and the general nonfiction trade.

Nonfiction "We publish serious, informational books for a targeted audience. All our books must have strong library interest, but we also distribute books effectively to the trade. Our library books fit the junior and senior high school curriculum." Reference. Subjects include contemporary culture, education, health/medicine, history, language/literature, multicultural, recreation, religion, sports, careers, entertainment, natural history, popular culture. No computer books, technical books, cookbooks, biographies (except YA), pop psychology, humor, fiction or poetry. Query or submit outline and sample chapter with SASE. No submissions returned without SASE.

Tips "Our audience is school and public libraries for our more reference-oriented books and libraries, schools and bookstores for our less reference-oriented informational titles."

FAIRLEIGH DICKINSON UNIVERSITY PRESS

285 Madison Ave., Madison NJ 07940. (973)443-8564. Fax: (973)443-8364. E-mail: fdupress@fdu.edu. **Acquisitions:** Harry Keyishian, director. Estab. 1967. Publishes hardcover originals. **Publishes 45 titles/year. Receives 300 submissions/year. 33% of books from first-time authors; 95% from unagented writers.** Publishes book 1 year after acceptance of ms. Responds in 2 weeks to queries.

   ● "Contract is arranged through Associated University Presses of Cranbury, New Jersey. We are a selection committee only." Nonauthor subsidy publishes 2% of books.

   O⊶ Fairleigh Dickinson publishes scholarly books for the academic market.

Nonfiction Biography, reference, scholarly, scholarly books. Subjects include art/architecture, business/economics, ethnic, film/cinema/stage, gay/lesbian, government/politics, history, music/dance, philosophy, psychology, sociology, women's issues/studies, Civil War, film, Jewish studies, literary criticism, scholarly editions. Looking for scholarly books in all fields; no nonscholarly books. Query with outline and sample chapters. Reviews artwork/photos as part of ms package.

Recent Title(s) *The Carlyle Encyclopedia*, edited by Mark Cummings; *Sleuthing Ethnicity: The Detective in Multiethnic Crime Fiction*, edited by D. Fischer-Hornung and Monika Mueller; *Whig's Progress: Tom Wharton Between Revolutions*, by J. Kent Clark.

Tips "Research must be up to date. Poor reviews result when bibliographies and notes don't reflect current research. We follow *Chicago Manual of Style* (14th edition) style in scholarly citations. We welcome collections of unpublished conference papers or essay collections, if they relate to a strong central theme and have scholarly merit."

FAIRVIEW PRESS

2450 Riverside Ave., Minneapolis MN 55454. (800)544-8207. Fax: (612)672-4980. E-mail: press@fairview.org. Website: www.fairviewpress.org. **Acquisitions:** Lane Stiles, director; Stephanie Billecke, senior editor. Estab. 1988. Publishes hardcover and trade paperback originals and reprints. **Publishes 8-12 titles/year. Receives 3,000 queries and 1,500 mss/year. 40% of books from first-time authors; 65% from unagented writers. Advance and royalties negotiable.** Publishes book 1 year after acceptance of ms. Accepts simultaneous submissions. Responds in 6 months to proposals. Book catalog free; ms guidelines online.

   O⊶ Fairview Press currently publishes books and related materials emphasizing aging, end-of-life issues, caregiving, grief, and bereavement.

Nonfiction Reference, self-help. Subjects include health/medicine, women's issues/studies, aging, grief and bereavement, patient education, nutrition. "Manuscripts that are essentially 1 person's story are rarely salable." Submit proposal package including outline, 2 sample chapter(s), author bio, marketing ideas, SASE. Reviews artwork/photos as part of ms package. Send photocopies.

Tips Audience is general reader, especially families. "Tell us what void your book fills in the market; give us an angle. Tell us who will buy your book. We have moved away from recovery books and have focused on health and medical issues."

FAITH KIDZ BOOKS

Cook Communications Ministries, 4050 Lee Vance View, Colorado Springs CO 80918. Fax: (719)536-3265. Website: www.cookministries.com. **Acquisitions:** Heather Gemmen, acquisitions editor. Publishes hardcover

Book Publishers

and paperback originals. **Publishes 40-50 titles/year. Receives 1,000-1,500 mss/year. Pays 1 flat fee. Rarely offers advance.** Publishes book 18 months after acceptance of ms. Accepts simultaneous submissions. Responds in 6 months to queries.

O— Faith Kids Books publishes inspirational works for children, ages 0-12, with a strong underlying Christian theme or clearly stated Biblical value, designed to foster spiritual growth in children and positive interaction between parent and child. Currently emphasizing Bible storybooks, Christian living books, life issue books, early readers, and picture books.

Nonfiction Biography, children's/juvenile. Subjects include religion (Bible stories, devotionals), picture books on nonfiction subjects. Submit proposal package including cover letter, SASE.

Fiction Historical, juvenile, picture books, religious, toddler books. "Picture books, devotionals, Bible storybooks, for an age range of 1-12. We're particularly interested in materials for beginning readers." No teen fiction. Query with SASE. Previously published or agented authors preferred.

Recent Title(s) *Tale of Three Trees*, by Angela Hunt (fiction); *Learn-to-Read Bible*, by Heather Gemmen.

FANTAGRAPHICS BOOKS

7563 Lake City Way NE, Seattle WA 98115. Website: www.fantagraphics.com. Co-owners: Gary Groth, Kim Thompson. **Acquisitions:** Submissions Editor. Estab. 1976. Publishes original trade paperbacks. Responds in 3 months to queries; 3 months to proposals; 3 months to mss. Book catalog and ms guidelines online.

Fiction Comic books. "Fantagraphics is an independent company with a modus operandi different from larger, factory-like corporate comics publishers. If your talents are limited to a specific area of expertise (i.e. inking, writing, etc.), then you will need to develop your own team before submitting a project to us. We want to see an idea that is fully fleshed-out in your mind, at least, if not on paper. Submit a minimum of 5 fully-inked pages of art, a synopsis, and a brief note stating approximately how many issues you have in mind."

Recent Title(s) *Zippy Annual*, by Bill Griffith; *Don't Call Me Stupid*, by Steve Weissman; *Hey, Wait . . .*, by Jason.

Tips "Take note of the originality and diversity of the themes and approaches to drawing in such Fantagraphics titles as *Love & Rockets* (stories of life in Latin America and Chicano L.A.), *Palestine* (journalistic autobiography in the Middle East), *Eightball* (surrealism mixed with kitsch culture in stories alternately humorous and painfully personal), and *Naughty Bits* (feminist humor and short stories which both attack and commiserate). Try to develop your own, equally individual voice; originality, aesthetic maturity, and graphic storytelling skill are the signs by which Fantagraphics judges whether or not your submission is ripe for publication."

Ⓐ FARRAR, STRAUS & GIROUX

Holtzbrinck Publishers, 19 Union Square West, New York NY 10003. (212)741-6900. E-mail: fsg.editorial@fsgbooks.com. Website: www.fsgbooks.com. Estab. 1946. Publishes hardcover and trade paperback books. **Publishes 180 titles/year. Receives 1,500-2,000 queries and mss/year.** Responds in 2 months to queries; 2 months to proposals. Ms guidelines free.

Imprints Faber & Faber (division), Farrar, Straus & Giroux Books for Young Readers, Hill & Wang (division), MIRASOL Libros Juvenile, North Point Press, Sunburst Books.

Nonfiction Subjects include literary.

Fiction Literary.

FARRAR, STRAUS & GIROUX BOOKS FOR YOUNG READERS

Farrar Straus Giroux, Inc., 19 Union Square W., New York NY 10003. (212)741-6900. Fax: (212)633-2427. **Acquisitions:** Margaret Ferguson, editorial director. Estab. 1946. Publishes hardcover originals and trade paperback reprints. **Publishes 75 titles/year. Receives 6,000 queries and mss/year. 5% of books from first-time authors; 50% from unagented writers. Pays royalty. Pays 2-6% royalty on retail price for paperbacks, 3-10% for hardcovers. Offers $3,000-25,000 advance.** Publishes book 18 months after acceptance of ms. Accepts simultaneous submissions. Responds in 2 months to queries; 4 months to mss. Book catalog for 9×12 SAE with $1.95 postage; ms guidelines for #10 SAE.

Imprints Frances Foster Books, Melanie Kroupa Books.

O— "We publish original and well-written material for all ages."

Fiction Juvenile, picture books, young adult, nonfiction. "Do not query picture books; just send manuscript. Do not fax queries or manuscripts." Query with SASE.

Recent Title(s) *Jack Adrift*, by Jack Gautos (ages 12 up); *The Canning Season*, by Polly Horvath (Newberry Honor Book, 10-14); *Tree of Life*, by Peter Sis (ages 4-8).

Tips Audience is full age range, preschool to young adult. Specializes in literary fiction.

N A FAWCETT

The Ballantine Publishing Group, A Division of Random House, Inc., 1745 Broadway, New York NY 10019. E-mail: bfi@randomhouse.com. Website: www.randomhouse.com. Estab. 1955. Publishes paperback originals and reprints.

O⊶ Major publisher of mystery mass market and trade paperbacks.

Fiction Mystery. *Agented submissions only.* **All unsolicited mss returned unopened.**

FC2

Publications Unit, Campus Box 4241, Illinois State University, Normal IL 61790-4241. (850)644-2260. E-mail: fc2@english.fsu.edu. Website: fc2.org. **Acquisitions:** R.M. Berry, publisher (fiction). Estab. 1974. Publishes hardcover and paperback originals. **Publishes 6 titles/year. 95% from unagented writers. Pays 10% royalty.** Publishes book 1-3 years after acceptance of ms. Accepts simultaneous submissions. Responds in 3 weeks to queries; 2-6 months to mss. Ms guidelines online.

O⊶ Publisher of innovative fiction.

Fiction Experimental, feminist, gay/lesbian, innovative; modernist/postmodern; avant-garde; anarchist; minority; cyberpunk. Query with SASE, or submit outline, publishing history, synopsis, author bio.

Recent Title(s) *Book of Lazarus*, by Richard Grossman; *Is It Sexual Harassment Yet?*, by Cris Mazza; *Liberty's Excess*, by Lidia Yuknavitch.

Tips "Be familiar with our list."

FREDERICK FELL PUBLISHERS, INC.

2131 Hollywood Blvd., Suite 305, Hollywood FL 33020. (954)925-5242. Fax: (954)925-5244. E-mail: info@fellpub.com. Website: www.fellpub.com. **Acquisitions:** Barnara Newman, senior editor. Publishes hardcover and trade paperback originals. **Publishes 40 titles/year. Receives 4,000 queries and 1,000 mss/year. 95% of books from first-time authors; 95% from unagented writers. Pays negotiable royalty on retail price. Offers up to $10,000 advance.** Publishes book 1 year after acceptance of ms. Accepts simultaneous submissions. Responds in 1 month to queries; 3 months to proposals. Ms guidelines for #10 SASE.

O⊶ "Fell has just launched 25 titles in the *Know-It-All* series. We will be publishing over 125 titles in all genres. Prove to us that your title is the best in this new exciting format."

Nonfiction "We are reviewing in all categories. Advise us of the top three competitive titles for your work and the reasons why the public would benefit by having your book published." How-to, reference, self-help. Subjects include business/economics, child guidance/parenting, education, ethnic, film/cinema/stage, health/medicine, hobbies, money/finance, spirituality. Submit proposal package, including outline, 3 sample chapters, author bio, publicity ideas, market analysis. Reviews artwork/photos as part of ms package. Send photocopies.

Recent Title(s) *Venus & Serena: My Seven Years as Hitting Coach for the Williams Sisters.*

Tips "We are most interested in well-written, timely nonfiction with strong sales potential. We will not consider topics that appeal to a small, select audience. Learn markets and be prepared to help with sales and promotion. Show us how your book is unique or better than the competition."

N FERGUSON PUBLISHING CO.

Imprint of Facts on File, 132 W. 31st St., 17th Floor, New York NY 10001. (800)322-8755. E-mail: editorial@factsonfile.com. Website: www.fergpubco.com. **Acquisitions:** Editorial Director. Estab. 1940. Publishes hardcover and trade paperback originals. **Publishes 50 titles/year. Pays by project.** Responds in 6 months to queries. Ms guidelines online.

O⊶ "We are primarily a career education publisher that publishes for schools and libraries. We need writers who have expertise in a particular career or career field (for possible full-length books on a specific career or field)."

Nonfiction "We publish work specifically for the elementary/junior high/high school/college library reference market. Works are generally encyclopedic in nature. Our current focus is career encyclopedias. We consider manuscripts that cross over into the trade market." Reference. Subjects include careers. "No mass market, poetry, scholarly, or juvenile books, please." Query or submit an outline and 1 sample chapter.

Recent Title(s) *Ferguson Career Biographies: Colin Powell, Bill Gates, etc.* (20 total books in series); *Careers in Focus: Geriatric Care, Design, etc.*

Tips "We like writers who know the market—former or current librarians or teachers or guidance counselors."

N FILBERT PUBLISHING

140 3rd St., Box 326, Kandiyohi MN 56251. E-mail: filbertpublishing@filbertpublishing.com. Submissions E-mail: filbertpublishing@filbertpublishing.com. Website: www.filbertpublishing.com. **Acquisitions:** Maurice Erickson, director of acquistions. Estab. 1995. Publishes trade paperback originals and reprints, and electronic originals. **Publishes 6 titles/year. Receives 120 queries and 60 mss/year. 70% of books from first-time**

authors; **100% from unagented writers. Pays 10-15% royalty on retail price.** Publishes book 4-6 months after acceptance of ms. Accepts simultaneous submissions. Responds in 2 months to queries; 2 months to proposals; 3 months to mss. Book catalog for 6×9 SAE with 4 first-class stamps; ms guidelines online.

Nonfiction Booklets, how-to, reference. Subjects include business/economics, creative nonfiction, general nonfiction, hobbies, regional. "Writers who keep their eye on *Writing Etc.* (our free e-mag for writers) will get a feel for the style we're looking for." Query with SASE, or submit proposal package including outline, 2 sample chapter(s), strong query. Reviews artwork/photos as part of ms package. Send photocopies.

Fiction Adventure, historical, mainstream/contemporary, mystery, regional, romance, suspense. "If your manuscript follows a formula of any kind, please submit it elsewhere. We enjoy unpredictable plots and strong characters supported by great writing." Query with SASE, or submit proposal package including 2 sample chapter(s), synopsis, strong query.

Recent Title(s) *Writing Wide (September 03)*, by Billie A. Williams; *Heart Songs*, by Beth Ann Erickson.

Tips "The people who purchase our books tend to be very educated, discriminating readers. Many are writers who are interested in finding information that will make their jobs easier and more profitable." "I'd suggest that authors subscribe to our e-magazine, *Writing Etc.* It's free and will give them a feel for what we're looking for. We also use *Writing Etc.* as a way to promote our author's books as well as keep in touch with our readership. When you know *Writing Etc.*, you know a lot about Filbert Publishing."

FILTER PRESS, LLC

P.O. Box 95, Palmer Lake CO 80133-0095. (719)481-2420. Fax: (719)481-2420. E-mail: filter.press@prodigy.net. Website: www.filterpressbooks.com. **Acquisitions:** Doris Baker, president. Estab. 1956. Publishes trade paperback originals and reprints. **Publishes 4-6 titles/year. Pays 10-12% royalty on wholesale price.** Publishes book 1 year after acceptance of ms.

   O➤ Filter Press specializes in nonfiction of the West.

Nonfiction Subjects include Americana, anthropology/archeology, ethnic, history, memoirs, regional, crafts and crafts people of the Southwest. Query with outline and SASE. Reviews artwork/photos as part of ms package.

Recent Title(s) *Kokopelli Drumin' Belly*, by Gail E. Haley (children's picture book); *Meadow Lark*, by Mary Peace Finley (YA fiction).

FIRE ENGINEERING BOOKS & VIDEOS

Imprint of PennWell Corp., 1421 S. Sheridan Rd., Tulsa OK 74112-6600. (918)831-9420. Fax: (918)832-9319. E-mail: jaredw@pennwell.com. Website: www.pennwellbooks.com. **Acquisitions:** Jared Wicklund, supervising editor. Publishes hardcover and softcover originals. **Publishes 10 titles/year. Receives 24 queries/year. 75% of books from first-time authors; 100% from unagented writers. Pays variable royalty on net sales.** Publishes book 1 year after acceptance of ms. Does not accept simultaneous submissions. Responds in 3 months to proposals. Book catalog free.

   O➤ Fire Engineering publishes textbooks relevant to firefighting and training. Currently emphasizing strategy and tactics, reserve training, preparedness for terrorist threats, natural disasters, first response to fires and emergencies.

Nonfiction Reference, technical, textbook. Subjects include firefighter training, public safety. Submit outline, 2 sample chapter(s), résumé, author bio, table of contents, SASE.

Recent Title(s) *The Fire Chief's Handbook, 6th Ed.*, edited by Robert C. Barr and John Eversole; *Firefighter Rescue & Survival*, by Richard Kolomay and Robert Hoff.

Tips "No human-interest stories, technical training only."

⒩ FLORICANTO PRESS

Inter American Corp., 650 Castro St., Suite 120-331, Mountain View CA 94041. (415)552-1879. Fax: (415)793-2662. E-mail: editor@floricantopress.com. Website: www.floricantopress.com. Publishes hardcover and trade paperback originals and reprints. **Publishes 6 titles/year. Receives 200 queries/year. 60% of books from first-time authors; 5% from unagented writers. Pays 5% royalty on wholesale price. Offers $500-1,500 advance.** Rejected mss destroyed. Responds in 3 months to queries; 7 months to mss. Book catalog for #10 SASE; ms guidelines online.

   O➤ Floricanto Press is "dedicated to promoting Latino thought and culture." Currently emphasizing biographies, women's studies, history. De-emphasizing poetry.

Nonfiction Biography, cookbook, reference. Subjects include anthropology/archeology, cooking/foods/nutrition, ethnic (Hispanic), health/medicine, history, language/literature, psychology, women's issues/studies. "We are looking primarily for nonfiction popular (but serious) titles that appeal to the general public on Hispanic subjects." Submit outline and sample chapter(s).

Fiction Adventure, erotica, ethnic (Hispanic), literary, occult, romance, short story collections. "On fiction we prefer contemporary works and themes." Submit synopsis and 1 sample chapter.

Recent Title(s) *Far from My Mother's Home*, by Barbara Jujica (short stories); *Love & Riot in Los Angeles*, nonfiction.

Tips Audience is general public interested in Hispanic culture. "Submit material as described, on DOS disk, graphic art for cover. We need authors that are willing to promote their work heavily."

FLORIDA ACADEMIC PRESS

P.O. Box 540, Gainesville FL 32602. (352)332-5104. Fax: (352)331-6003. E-mail: fapress@worldnet.att.net. **Acquisitions:** Max Vargas, CEO and managing editor; Sam Decalo, acquisitions editor (scholarly, self-help); Florence Dusek, assistant editor (fiction). Publishes hardcover and trade paperback originals. **Publishes 6 titles/year. Receives 300+ queries and 100+ mss/year. 50% of books from first-time authors; 100% from unagented writers. Pays 5-8% royalty on retail price, depending if paperback or hardcover.** Publishes book 3-5 months after acceptance of ms. Responds in 2-6 months to mss.

> O—¬ "We are primarily an academic/scholarly publisher. We do publish self-help books if assessed as original. Our interest in serious fiction is secondary, and our criteria is strict. No poetry, science fiction, religious, autobiography, polemical, children's books, or collections of stories."

Nonfiction Reference, scholarly, self-help. Subjects include government/politics, history, third world. Submit complete ms. Reviews artwork/photos as part of ms package. Send photocopies.

Fiction Literary criticism. Submit complete ms.

Recent Title(s) *Complete Publishers Resource Manual*, by Linda Able (reference); *Civil-Military Relations in Africa*, by Samuel Decalo (history); *Orpheus in Brooklyn*, by Bertrand Mathieu (literary criticism).

Tips Considers complete mss only. "Manuscripts we decide to publish must be re-submitted in camera-ready form."

ℕ FOCAL PRESS

Imprint of Elsevier (USA), Inc., 200 Wheeler Rd., Burlington MA 01803. Fax: (781)221-1615. Website: www.focalpress.com. **Acquisitions:** Jenny Ridout, publisher; for further editorial contacts, visit the contacts page on the company's website. Estab. US, 1981; UK, 1938. Publishes hardcover and paperback originals and reprints. **Publishes 80-120 UK-US titles/year; entire firm publishes over 1,000 titles/year. Receives 500-700 submissions/year. 25% of books from first-time authors; 90% from unagented writers. Pays 10-12% royalty on net receipts. Offers modest advance.** Publishes book 9-12 months after acceptance of ms. Accepts simultaneous submissions. Responds in 2 months to queries. Book catalog for #10 SASE; ms guidelines online.

> O—¬ Focal Press books provide professional excellence for students, advanced amateurs, and working professionals involved in all areas of media technology. Topics of interest include film/video, audio, broadcasting, and cinematography, through to journalism, radio, television, video, and writing. Currently emphasizing graphics, animation, and multimedia.

Nonfiction How-to, reference, scholarly, technical, textbook, media arts. Subjects include film/cinema/stage, photography, film, cinematography, broadcasting, theater and performing arts, audio, sound and media technology. "We do not publish collections of photographs or books composed primarily of photographs." Query preferred, or submit outline and sample chapters. Reviews artwork/photos as part of ms package.

Recent Title(s) *Adobe Photoshop 7.0 for Photographers*, by Martin Evening (nonfiction).

FOCUS PUBLISHING, INC.

P.O. Box 665, Bemidji MN 56619. (218)759-9817. Fax: (218)751-7210. Website: www.focuspublishing.com. **Acquisitions:** Jan Haley, president. Estab. 1993. Publishes hardcover and trade paperback originals and reprints. **Publishes 4-6 titles/year. Receives 300 queries and 200 mss/year. 90% of books from first-time authors; 100% from unagented writers. Pays 7-10% royalty on retail price.** Publishes book 1 year after acceptance of ms. Responds in less than 6 months to queries. Book catalog free.

> O—¬ "Focus Publishing is a small press primarily devoted to adult Christian books with a Bible study emphasis."

Nonfiction Subjects include religion, Christian living, Bible studies for men and women. Submit proposal package, including marketing ideas with SASE. Reviews artwork/photos as part of ms package. Send photocopies.

Recent Title(s) *The Lord's Table: A Biblical Approach to Weight Loss*, by Mike Cleveland; *Living in His Forgiveness*, by Sandy Day.

ℕ FODOR'S TRAVEL PUBLICATIONS, INC.

Imprint of Random House, Inc., 1745 Broadway, New York NY 10019. Website: www.fodors.com. **Acquisitions:** Karen Cure, editorial director. Estab. 1936. Publishes trade paperback originals. **Publishes 300 titles/year. Receives 100 queries and 4 mss/year. Most titles are collective works, with contributions as works for hire. Most contributions are updates of previously published volumes; however,.** Publishes book 1 year after acceptance of ms. Accepts simultaneous submissions. Responds in 2 months to queries. Book catalog free.

O→ Fodor's publishes travel books on many regions and countries.

Nonfiction How-to (travel), illustrated book (travel), travel guide. Subjects include travel. "We are interested in unique approaches to favorite destinations. Writers seldom review our catalog or our list and often query about books on topics that we're already covering. Beyond that, it's important to review competition and to say what the proposed book will add. Do not send originals without first querying as to our interest in the project. We're not interested in travel literature or in proposals for general travel guidebooks." Query, or submit outline, sample chapter(s) and proposal package, including competition review and review of market with SASE.

Recent Title(s) *Peru*; *Holland*; *Traveling Solo*.

Tips "In preparing your query or proposal, remember that it's the only argument Fodor's will hear about why your book will be a good one, and why you think it will sell; and it's also best evidence of your ability to create the book you propose. Craft your proposal well and carefully so that it puts your best foot forward."

Ⓝ FOGHORN OUTDOORS

Avalon Travel Publishing, Avalon Publishing Group, 1400 65th St., Suite 250, Emeryville CA 94608. (510)595-3664. Fax: (510)595-4228. E-mail: acquisitions@avalonpub.com. Website: www.travelmatters.com; www.foghorn.com. **Acquisitions:** Acquisitions Assistant. Estab. 1985. Publishes trade paperback originals and reprints. **Publishes 30 titles/year. Receives 500 queries and 200 mss/year. 10% of books from first-time authors; 98% from unagented writers. Pays 12% royalty on wholesale price; occasional work-for-hire.** Publishes book 18 months after acceptance of ms. Accepts simultaneous submissions. Responds in 1 month to queries; 2 months to proposals; 2 months to mss. Book catalog free; ms guidelines online.

O→ Foghorn publishes outdoor recreation guidebooks. Editorial mission is "to produce current, informative and complete travel information for specific types of travelers."

Nonfiction Outdoor recreation guidebooks. Subjects include nature/environment, recreation (camping, biking, fishing), sports, outdoors, leisure. Query first with SASE, Attn: acquisitions assistant.

Recent Title(s) *Foghorn Outdoors: California Camping*, by Tom Stienstra.

Tips "We are expanding our list nationally in the formats we already publish (camping, hiking, fishing, dogs) as well as developing new formats to test California."

FORDHAM UNIVERSITY PRESS

University Box L, Bronx NY 10458. Fax: (718)817-4785. Website: www.fordhampress.com. **Acquisitions:** Helen Tartar, editorial director. Publishes hardcover and trade paperback originals and reprints. **Publishes 30 titles/year. Receives 450 queries and 100 mss/year. 25% of books from first-time authors; 100% from unagented writers. Pays 4-7% royalty on retail price.** Publishes book 6-24 months after acceptance of ms. Responds in 2 months to proposals; 2 months to mss. Book catalog and ms guidelines free.

O→ "We are a publisher in humanities, accepting scholarly monographs, collections, occasional reprints and general interest titles for consideration."

Nonfiction Biography, textbook, scholarly. Subjects include Americana, anthropology/archeology, art/architecture, government/politics, history, language/literature, military/war (World War II), philosophy, regional (New York), religion, sociology, translation. No fiction. Submit outline, 2-5 sample chapter(s).

Recent Title(s) *Palisades: 100,000 Acres in 100 years*, by Robert Binnewies.

Tips "We have an academic and general audience."

FOREIGN POLICY ASSOCIATION

470 Park Ave. S., New York NY 10016. (212)481-8100. Fax: (212)481-9275. Website: www.fpa.org. **Acquisitions:** Karen Rohan, editor-in-chief. Publishes 2 periodicals and an occasional hardcover and trade paperback original. **Publishes 5-6 titles/year. Receives 12 queries and 6 mss/year. 99% from unagented writers. Makes outright purchase of $2,500-4,000.** Publishes book 9 months after acceptance of ms. Accepts simultaneous submissions. Responds in 2 months to queries. Book catalog free.

Imprints Headline Series (quarterly), Great Decisions (annual).

O→ "The Foreign Policy Association, a nonpartisan, not-for-profit educational organization founded in 1918, is a catalyst for developing awareness, understanding of and informed opinion on U.S. foreign policy and global issues. Through its balanced, nonpartisan publications, FPA seeks to encourage individuals in schools, communities and the workplace to participate in the foreign policy process."

Nonfiction Reference, textbook. Subjects include government/politics, history, foreign policy, social studies. Query, submit outline.

Recent Title(s) *NATO and Transatlantic Relations in the Twenty-First Century*, by Stanley R. Sloan.

Tips Audience is students and people with an interest, but not necessarily any expertise, in foreign policy and international relations.

FORTRESS PRESS

Box 1209, Minneapolis MN 55440-1209. (612)330-3300. Website: www.fortresspress.com. **Acquisitions:** J. Michael West, editor-in-chief; Dr. K.C. Hanson, editor. Publishes hardcover and trade paperback originals. **Publishes 60 titles/year. Receives 1,000 queries/year. 5-10% of books from first-time authors. Pays royalty on retail price.** Publishes book within 1 year after acceptance of ms. Accepts simultaneous submissions. Responds in 3 months to proposals. Book catalog free (call 1-800-328-4648); ms guidelines online.

○➡ Fortress Press publishes academic books in Biblical studies, theology, Christian ethics, church history, and professional books in pastoral care and counseling.

Nonfiction Subjects include religion, women's issues/studies, church history, African-American studies. Query with annotated toc, brief cv, sample chapter (introduction) and SASE. Please study guidelines before submitting.

Recent Title(s) *The Writings of The New Testament*, by Luke Timothy Johnson; *The Wrath of Jonah: The Crisis of Religious Nationalism in the Israli-Palestinian Conflict*, by Rosemary Radford Ruether and Herman J. Ruether.

FORUM PUBLISHING CO.

383 E. Main St., Centerport NY 11721. (631)754-5000. Fax: (631)754-0630. Website: www.forum123.com. **Acquisitions:** Martin Stevens. Estab. 1981. Publishes trade paperback originals. **Publishes 12 titles/year. Receives 200 queries and 25 mss/year. 75% of books from first-time authors; 75% from unagented writers. Makes outright purchase of $250-750.** Publishes book 4 months after acceptance of ms. Accepts simultaneous submissions. Responds in 1 month to mss. Book catalog free.

○➡ "Forum publishes only business titles."

Nonfiction Subjects include business/economics, money/finance. Submit outline. Reviews artwork/photos as part of ms package. Send photocopies.

Recent Title(s) *Selling Information By Mail*, by Glen Gilcrest.

FORWARD MOVEMENT PUBLICATIONS

412 Sycamore St., Cincinnati OH 45202. (513)721-6659. Fax: (513)721-0729. E-mail: esgleason@forwarddaybyday.com. Website: www.forwardmovement.org. **Acquisitions:** The Rev. Dr. Edward S. Gleason, editor and director. Estab. 1934. Publishes trade and mass market paperback originals, trade paperback reprints and tracts. **Publishes 6 titles/year. Receives 1,000 queries and 300 mss/year. 30% of books from first-time authors; 100% from unagented writers. Pays one-time honorarium.** Responds in 1 month to queries; 1 month to proposals; 2 months to mss. Book catalog and ms guidelines free.

○➡ "Forward Movement was established 'to help reinvigorate the life of the church.' Many titles focus on the life of prayer, where our relationship with God is centered, death, marriage, baptism, recovery, joy, the Episcopal Church and more." Currently emphasizing prayer/spirituality.

Nonfiction "We publish a variety of types of books, but they all relate to the lives of Christians. We are an agency of the Episcopal Church." Biography, children's/juvenile, reference, self-help (about religion and prayer). Subjects include religion. Query with SASE or submit complete ms.

Fiction Episcopal for middle school (ages 8-12) readers. Juvenile. Query with SASE.

Recent Title(s) *God Is Not in the Thesaurus*, by Bo Don Cox (nonfiction).

Tips Audience is primarily Episcopalians and other Christians.

Ⓝ WALTER FOSTER PUBLISHING, INC.

23062 La Cadena Dr., Laguna Hills CA 92653. (800)426-0099. Fax: (949)380-7575. E-mail: info@walterfoster.com. Website: www.walterfoster.com. **Acquisitions:** Sydney Sprague, associate publisher. Publishes trade paperback originals. **Publishes 30-40 titles/year. Receives 20-30 queries/year. 50% of books from first-time authors; 100% from unagented writers. Makes outright purchase.** Publishes book 1 year after acceptance of ms. Accepts simultaneous submissions. Responds in 2 months to queries; 6 months to proposals; 6 months to mss. Book catalog free.

○➡ Walter Foster publishes instructional how-to/craft instruction as well as licensed products.

Nonfiction How-to. Subjects include arts and crafts. Submit proposal package, including query letter, color photos/examples of artwork. Reviews artwork/photos as part of ms package. color photocopies or color photos. Samples cannot be returned.

Recent Title(s) *Glass Painting; Ceramic Painting; Paper Crafts* (art instruction).

FOUR WALLS EIGHT WINDOWS

39 W. 14th St., Room 503, New York NY 10011. (212)206-8965. Fax: (212)206-8799. Website: www.4w8w.com. Publisher: John Oakes. **Acquisitions:** Acquistions Editor. Estab. 1987. Publishes hardcover originals, trade paperback originals and reprints. **Publishes 35 titles/year. Receives 3,000 submissions/year. 15% of books from first-time authors; 50% from unagented writers. Pays royalty on retail or net price, depending on contract. Offers variable advance.** Publishes book 1-2 years after acceptance of ms. Accepts simultaneous

submissions. Responds in 2 months to queries. Book catalog for 6 X 9 SAE with 3 first-class stamps.
Imprints No Exit, Axoplasm.

○┓ Emphasizing fine literature and quality nonfiction, Four Walls Eight Windows has a reputation for carefully edited and distinctive books.

Nonfiction Subjects include history, nature/environment, science. No New Age. Query with outline and SASE. All mss without SASE discarded.

Fiction Feminist, gay/lesbian, nonfiction. "No romance, popular." Query with SASE. "Query letter accompanied by sample chapter, outline and SASE is best. Useful to know if writer has published elsewhere, and if so, where."

Recent Title(s) *The Mystery of the Aleph*, by Amir D. Aczel (science); *Valentine*, by Lucius Shepard (fiction); *Sizzling Chops, Dazzling Spins: Ping-Pong and the Art of Staying Alive*, by Jerome Charyn (history/memoir).

FOX CHAPEL PUBLISHING

1970 Broad St., East Petersburg PA 17520. (717)560-4703. Fax: (717)560-4702. E-mail: editors@carvingworld.com. Website: www.foxchapelpublishing.com. **Acquisitions:** Alan Giagnocavo, publisher; Peg Couch, acquisitions editor; Ayleen Stellhorn, editor. Publishes hardcover and trade paperback originals and trade paperback reprints. **Publishes 25-40 titles/year. 50% of books from first-time authors; 100% from unagented writers. Pays royalty or makes outright purchase. Offers variable advance.** Publishes book 6-18 months after acceptance of ms. Accepts simultaneous submissions. Responds in 2 months to queries.

○┓ Fox Chapel publishes woodworking and woodcarving titles for professionals and hobbyists.

Nonfiction Subjects include woodworking, wood carving, scroll saw and woodturning. Write for query submission guidelines. Reviews artwork/photos as part of ms package. Send photocopies.

Recent Title(s) *Fireplace Mantel Ideas*; *Woodcarving the Nativity*; *Pen Turner's Workbook*.

Tips "We're looking for knowledgeable artists, woodworkers first, writers second to write for us. Our market is for avid woodworking hobbyists and professionals."

FPMI/STAR MOUNTAIN, INC.

4901 University Square, Suite 3, Huntsville AL 35816. (256)539-1850. Fax: (256)539-0911. E-mail: jsoutherland @fpmi.com. Website: www.fpmi.com. **Acquisitions:** John Southerland, publications director. Estab. 1985. Publishes trade paperback originals. **Publishes 4-6 titles/year. Receives 4-5 submissions/year. 60% of books from first-time authors; 100% from unagented writers. Pays 15% on retail price.** Publishes book an average of 1 year after acceptance of ms. Accepts simultaneous submissions. Responds in 3 weeks to queries; 2 months to mss. Book catalog free or online.

○┓ "Our primary audience is federal managers and supervisors—particularly first and second level."

Nonfiction Technical. Subjects include government/politics, labor relations, personnel issues. "We will be publishing books for government and business on topics such as sexual harassment, human resources, and how to deal with leave abuse by employees. Our books are practical, how-to books for a supervisor or manager. Scholarly theoretical works do not interest our audience." Submit outline/synopsis and sample chapters or send complete ms.

Recent Title(s) *Building the Optimum Organization for Federal Agencies*, by C. Robert Nelson, DPA; *Workplace Harassment: A Handbook for Supervisors, Managers and EEO and Human Resources Professions*, by Marilyn L. (Teplitz) Mattingly.

Tips "We are interested in books that are practical, easy-to-read, and less than 150 pages. If I were a writer trying to market a book today, I would emphasize practical topics with plenty of examples in succinct, concrete language."

FREE PRESS

Simon & Schuster, 1230 Avenue of the Americas, New York NY 10020. (212)698-7000. Fax: (212)632-4989. Website: www.simonsays.com. Publisher: Martha Levin. **Acquisitions:** Bruce Nichols, vice president/senior editor (history/serious nonfiction); Leslie Meredith, vice president/senior editor (psychology/sprituality/self-help); Fred Hills (business/serious nonfiction); Bill Rosen, vice president/executive editor (serious nonfiction/illustrated/reference); Amy Scheibe, senior editor (literary fiction); Elizabeth Stein, senior editor (history, current events, biography, memoir); Dominick Anfuso, vice president/editorial director (self-help/literary fiction). Estab. 1947. **Publishes 120 titles/year. Receives 3,000 submissions/year. 15% of books from first-time authors; 50% from unagented writers. Pays variable royalty. Offers advance.** Publishes book 1 year after acceptance of ms. Responds in 2 months to queries.

○┓ The Free Press publishes a wide variety of fiction and nonfiction.

Nonfiction Does not accept unagented submissions. Query with 1-3 sample chapters, outline before submitting mss.

Recent Title(s) *Self Matters*, by Phil McGraw; *American Jihad*, by Steven Emerson.

FREE SPIRIT PUBLISHING, INC.

217 Fifth Ave. N., Suite 200, Minneapolis MN 55401-1260. (612)338-2068. Fax: (612)337-5050. E-mail: help4kids @freespirit.com. Website: www.freespirit.com. Publisher: Judy Galbraith. **Acquisitions:** Acquisitions Editor. Estab. 1983. Publishes trade paperback originals and reprints. **Publishes 20 titles/year. 25% of books from first-time authors; 50% from unagented writers. Offers advance.** Book catalog and ms guidelines free; ms guidelines online.

Imprints Self-Help for Kids, Learning to Get Along Series, Self-Help for Teens.

○┐ "We believe passionately in empowering kids to learn to think for themselves and make their own good choices."

Nonfiction Children's/juvenile (young adult), self-help (parenting). Subjects include child guidance/parenting, education (pre-K-12, study and social skills, special needs, differentiation but not textbooks or basic skills books like reading, counting, etc.), health/medicine (mental/emotional health for/about children), psychology (for/about children), sociology (for/about children). "Many of our authors are educators, mental health professionals, and youth workers involved in helping kids and teens." No fiction or picture storybooks, poetry, single biographies or autobiographies, books with mythical or animal characters, or books with religious or New Age content. Query with cover letter stating qualifications, intent, and intended audience and how your book stands out from the field, along with outline, 2 sample chapters, résumé, SASE. Do not send original copies of work.

Recent Title(s) *See Jane Win for Girls*; *Life Lists for Teens*; *How to Take the Grrrr Out of Anger*.

Tips "Our books are issue-oriented, jargon-free, and solution-focused. Our audience is children, teens, teachers, parents and youth counselors. We are especially concerned with kids' social and emotional well-being and look for books with ready-to-use strategies for coping with today's issues at home or in school—written in everyday language. We are not looking for academic or religious materials, or books that analyze problem's with the nation's school systems. Instead, we want books that offer practical, positive advice so kids can help themselves and parents and teachers can help kids succeed."

FRONT STREET

862 Haywood Rd., Asheville NC 28806. (828)236-3097. Fax: (828)236-3098. E-mail: contactus@frontstreetbooks. com. Website: www.frontstreetbooks.com. **Acquisitions:** Joy Neaves, editor. Estab. 1994. Publishes hardcover originals. **Publishes 10-15 titles/year; imprint publishes 6-12 titles/year. Receives 2,000 queries and 5,000 mss/year. 50% of books from first-time authors; 80% from unagented writers. Pays royalty on retail price. Offers advance.** Publishes book 1 year after acceptance of ms. Accepts simultaneous submissions. Responds in 1 month to queries; 2 months to proposals; 3 months to mss. Book catalog and ms guidelines online.

Imprints Front Street/Lemniscant Books.

○┐ "We are an independent publisher of books for children and young adults."

Nonfiction Children's/juvenile, humor, illustrated book.

Fiction Adventure, historical, humor, juvenile, literary, picture books, young adult (adventure, fantasy/science fiction, historical, mystery/suspense, problem novels, sports). Query with SASE. Submit complete ms, if under 100 pages, with SASE. Keeps illustration samples on file. Reviews artwork/photos with ms. Send photocopies.

Poetry Submit 25 sample poems.

Recent Title(s) *Honeysuckle House*, by Andrea Cheng (YA novel); *Hunger Moon*, by Sarah Lamstein; *Black Brothers*, by Lisa Tetzner and Hans Binder (YA graphic novel).

FUTURE HORIZONS

721 W. Abram St., Arlington TX 76013. (817)277-0727. Fax: (817)277-2270. E-mail: victoria@futurehorizons-autism.com. Website: www.futurehorizons-autism.com. **Acquisitions:** Victoria Ulmer. Publishes hardcover originals, trade paperback originals and reprints. **Publishes 10 titles/year. Receives 250 queries and 125 mss/year. 75% of books from first-time authors; 95% from unagented writers. Pays 10% royalty, or makes outright purchase.** Publishes book 2 months after acceptance of ms. Accepts simultaneous submissions. Responds in 1 month to queries; 2 months to proposals. Book catalog free; ms guidelines online.

Nonfiction Children's/juvenile (pertaining to autism), cookbook (for autistic individuals), humor (about autism), self-help (detailing with autism/Asperger's syndrome). Subjects include education (about autism/Asperger's syndrome), autism. Submit proposal package including outline. Reviews artwork/photos as part of ms package. Send photocopies.

Recent Title(s) *Diagnosing Jefferson*, by Norm Ledgin (nonfiction); *Tobin Learns to Make Friends*, by Diane Murrell (childrens fiction).

Tips Audience is parents, teachers, professionals dealing with individuals with autism or Asperger's syndrome. "Books that sell well, have practical and useful information on how to help individuals and/or care givers of individuals with autism. Personal stories, even success stories, are usually not helpful to others in a practical way."

GATF PRESS

Graphic Arts Technical Foundation, 200 Deer Run Rd., Sewickley PA 15143-2600. (412)741-6860. Fax: (412)741-2311. E-mail: poresick@gatf.org. Submissions E-mail: awoodall@gatf.org. Website: www.gain.net. **Acquisitions:** Peter Oresick, director of publications; Tom Destree, editor in chief; Amy Woodall, managing editor (graphic arts, communication, book publishing, printing). Estab. 1924. Publishes trade paperback originals and hardcover reference texts. **Publishes 20 titles/year. Receives 25 submissions/year. 50% of books from first-time authors; 100% from unagented writers. Pays 5-15% royalty on wholesale price.** Publishes book 18 months after acceptance of ms. Responds in 1 month to queries. Book catalog for 9×12 SAE with 2 first-class stamps; ms guidelines for #10 SASE.

> O—¬ "GATF's mission is to serve the graphic communications community as the major resource for technical information and services through research and education." Currrently emphasizing career guides for graphic communications and turnkey training curriculums."

Nonfiction How-to, reference, technical, textbook. Subjects include printing/graphic communications, electronic publishing. "We primarily want textbook/reference books about printing and related technologies. However, we are expanding our reach into electronic communications." Query with SASE, or submit outline, sample chapters, and SASE. Reviews artwork/photos as part of ms package.

Recent Title(s) *Color and Its Reproduction, 3rd Ed.*, by Gary G. Field; *To Be a Profitable Printer*, by Michael Moffit.

Tips "We are publishing titles that are updated more frequently, such as *On-Demand Publishing*. Our scope now includes reference titles geared toward general audiences interested in computers, imaging, and Internet, as well as print publishing."

GEM GUIDES BOOK CO.

315 Cloverleaf Dr., Suite F, Baldwin Park CA 91706-6510. (626)855-1611. Fax: (626)855-1610. E-mail: gembooks @aol.com. Website: www.gemguidesbooks.com. **Acquisitions:** Kathy Mayerski, editor. Estab. 1965. **Publishes 6-8 titles/year. Receives 20 submissions/year. 60% of books from first-time authors; 100% from unagented writers. Pays 6-10% royalty on retail price.** Publishes book 1 year after acceptance of ms. Accepts simultaneous submissions. Responds in 5 months to queries.

Imprints Gembooks.

> O—¬ "Gem Guides prefers nonfiction books for the hobbyist in rocks and minerals; lapidary and jewelry-making; travel and recreation guide books for the West and Southwest; and other regional local interest." Currently emphasizing how-to, field guides, West/Southwest regional interest. De-emphasizing stories, history, poetry.

Nonfiction Subjects include history (Western), hobbies (lapidary and jewelry-making), nature/environment, recreation, regional (Western US), science (earth), travel. Query with outline/synopsis and sample chapters with SASE. Reviews artwork/photos as part of ms package.

Recent Title(s) *Fee Mining and Rockhounding Adventures in the West*, by James Martin Monaco and Jeannette Hathaway Monaco; *The GPS Guide to Western Gem Trails*, by David Kelty; *Baby's Day Out in Southern California: Fun Plaes to Go with Babies and Toddlers*, by JoBea Holt.

Tips "We have a general audience of people interested in recreational activities. Publishers plan and have specific book lines in which they specialize. Learn about the publisher and submit materials compatible with that publisher's product line."

[N] GENESIS PRESS, INC.

1213 Hwy. 45 N., Columbus MS 39705. (662)329-9927. Fax: (662)329-9399. E-mail: books@genesis-press.com. Website: www.genesis-press.com. **Acquisitions:** Sharon Morgan. Publishes hardcover and trade paperback originals and reprints. **Publishes 30 titles/year. Receives 100 queries and 100-150 mss/year. 50% of books from first-time authors; 90% from unagented writers. Pays 6-12% royalty on invoice price. Offers $750-5,000 advance.** Publishes book 1 year after acceptance of ms. Responds in 2 months to queries; 4 months to mss. Ms guidelines online.

> O—¬ Genesis is interested in high quality, mainstream or literary fiction, especially by African-American authors. "We specialize in the African-American niche." Currently emphasizing African-American romance, erotica, ethnic or multicultural women's fiction, and literary. De-emphasizing nonfiction.

Nonfiction Biography, humor. Subjects include history. Query with SASE, or submit outline, 3 sample chapter(s).

Fiction Erotica, ethnic, literary, multicultural, romance, women's. Query with SASE, or submit 3 sample chapter(s), synopsis.

Recent Title(s) *Hitler, the War and the Pope*, by Ronald J. Rychlak; *Cherish the Flame*, by Beverly Clark; *No Apologies*, by Seressia Glass.

Book Publishers

Tips "Be professional. Always include a cover letter and SASE. Follow the submission guidelines posted on our website or send SASE for a copy."

GGC, INC./PUBLISHING

5107 13th St. NW, Washington DC 20011. (202)541-9700. Fax: (202)541-9750. E-mail: info@ggcinc.com. Website: www.gogardner.com. **Acquisitions:** Garth Gardner, publisher (computer graphics, animation cartoons); Bonney Ford, editor (GGC, art, animation). Publishes trade paperback reprints. **Publishes 10 titles/year; imprint publishes 2 titles/year. Receives 50 queries and 25 mss/year. 80% of books from first-time authors; 70% from unagented writers. Pays 10-15% royalty on wholesale price or makes outright purchase.** Publishes book 3 months after acceptance of ms. Accepts simultaneous submissions. Responds in 1 month to queries. Book catalog and ms guidelines online.

O— GGC publishes books on the subjects of computer graphics, animation, new media, multimedia, art, cartoons, drawing.

Nonfiction How-to, multimedia, reference, self-help, technical, textbook. Subjects include art/architecture, education, history, computer graphics. Submit proposal package including 2 sample chapter(s), résumé, cover letter. Reviews artwork/photos as part of ms package. Send photocopies.

Recent Title(s) *Career Diary of an Animation Studio Owner*, by Joseph L. Daniels; *Career Diary of an Animation Producer*, by Sue Riedl.

GLENBRIDGE PUBLISHING, LTD.

19923 E. Long Ave., Centennial CO 80016. (720)870-8381. Fax: (720)870-5598. E-mail: glenbr@eazy.net. **Acquisitions:** James A. Keene, editor. Estab. 1986. Publishes hardcover originals and reprints, trade paperback originals. **Publishes 6-8 titles/year. Pays 10% royalty.** Publishes book 1 year after acceptance of ms. Accepts simultaneous submissions. Responds in 2 months to queries. Book catalog online; ms guidelines for #10 SASE.

O— "Glenbridge has an eclectic approach to publishing. We look for titles that have long-term capabilities."

Nonfiction Subjects include Americana, business/economics, cooking/foods/nutrition, health/medicine, history, philosophy, psychology, sociology, music. Query with outline/synopsis, sample chapters, and SASE.

Recent Title(s) *Susan Smith—Victim or Murderer*, by George Rekers, Ph.D; *Three Minute Therapy: Change Your Thinking/Change Your Life*, by Dr. Michael Edelstein with David R. Steele.

THE GLOBE PEQUOT PRESS, INC.

P.O. Box 480, Guilford CT 06437. (203)458-4500. Fax: (203)458-4604. Website: www.globepequot.com. President/Publisher: Linda Kennedy. **Acquisitions:** Shelley Wolf, submissions editor. Estab. 1947. Publishes paperback originals, hardcover originals and reprints. **Publishes 600 titles/year. Receives 3,000 submissions/year. 30% of books from first-time authors; 70% from unagented writers. Average print order for a first book is 4,000-7,500. Makes an outright purchase, or pays 10% royalty on net price. Offers advance.** Publishes book 1 year after acceptance of ms. Accepts simultaneous submissions. Responds in 3 months to queries. Ms guidelines online.

O— Globe Pequot is the largest publisher of regional travel books and outdoor recreation in the United States and offers the broadest selection of travel titles of any vendor in this market.

Nonfiction Humor (regional), regional travel guidebooks, outdoor recreation guides, natural history field guides. Subjects include cooking/foods/nutrition (regional), history (popular, regional), nature/environment, recreation, regional travel. No doctoral theses, fiction, genealogies, travel memoirs, poetry, or textbooks. Submit brief synopsis of work, table of contents or outline, sample chapter, résumé/vita, definition of target audience, and an analysis of competing titles. Reviews artwork/photos as part of ms package. Do not send originals.

Recent Title(s) *Arizona Curiosities*; *Hiking Arkansas*; *Exploring the Great Texas Coastal Birding Trail*.

🅰 DAVID R. GODINE, PUBLISHER, INC.

9 Hamilton Place, Boston MA 02108. (617)451-9600. Fax: (617)350-0250. E-mail: info@godine.com. Website: www.godine.com. Estab. 1970. Publishes hardcover and trade paperback originals and reprints. **Publishes 35 titles/year. Pays royalty on retail price.** Publishes book 3 years after acceptance of ms. Book catalog for 5×8 SAE with 3 first-class stamps.

O— "Our particular strengths are books about the history and design of the written word, literary essays, and the best of world fiction in translation. We also have an unusually strong list of children's books, all of them printed in their entirety with no cuts, deletions, or side-stepping to keep the political watchdogs happy."

Nonfiction Biography, children's/juvenile, coffee table book, cookbook, illustrated book. Subjects include Americana, art/architecture, gardening, nature/environment, photography, literary criticism, book arts, typography. *No unsolicited mss.* Query with SASE.

Fiction Historical, literary. *No unsolicited mss.* Query with SASE.

Recent Title(s) *The Penelopeia*, by Jane Rawlings; *A Year with Emerson*, selected and edited by Richard Grossman; *Henrietta & the Golden Eggs*, by Hanna Johansen, pictures by Kaethi Bhend.

Tips "Please visit our website for more information about our books and detailed submission policy. No phone calls, please."

🅽 GOVERNMENT INSTITUTES/ABS.

4 Research Place, Suite 200, Rockville MD 20850-3226. (301)921-2300. Fax: (301)921-0373. Website: www.govinst.com. **Acquisitions:** Ken Lawrence, senior consulting editor (occupational safety and health, quality, ISO 9000 risk and reliability); Charlene Ikonomou (environmental compliance and sciences, marine industry), editor. Estab. 1973. Publishes hardcover and softcover originals and CD-ROM/disk products. **Publishes 45 titles/year. Receives 100 submissions/year. 50% of books from first-time authors; 100% from unagented writers. Pays royalty or makes outright purchase.** Publishes book 5 months after acceptance of ms. Responds in 2 months to queries. Book catalog free.

○┓ "Our mission is to be the leading global company providing practical, accurate, timely and authoritative information desired by people concerned with environment, health and safety, telecommunications, and other regulatory and technical topics." Currently emphasizing practical information for the business community. De-emphasizing books on issues and theories.

Nonfiction Reference, technical. Subjects include environmental law, occupational safety and health, real estate with an envionmental slant, management systems, quality, ISO 9000, risk and reliability. Needs professional-level titiles in those areas. Also looking for international environmental topics. Submit outline, at least one sample chapter(s).

Recent Title(s) *Environmental Guide to the Internet*, by Murphy/Briggs-Erickson.

Tips "We also conduct courses. Authors are frequently invited to serve as instructors."

THE GRADUATE GROUP

P.O. Box 370351, West Hartford CT 06137-0351. (860)233-2330. Fax: (860)233-2330. E-mail: graduategroup@hotmail.com. Website: www.graduategroup.com. **Acquisitions:** Mara Whitman, partner; Amy Gibson, partner; Robert Whitman, vice president. Estab. 1964. Publishes trade paperback originals. **Publishes 50 titles/year. Receives 100 queries and 70 mss/year. 60% of books from first-time authors; 85% from unagented writers. Pays 20% royalty on retail price.** Publishes book 3 months after acceptance of ms. Accepts simultaneous submissions. Responds in 1 month to queries. Book catalog free; ms guidelines online.

○┓ "The Graduate Group helps college and graduate students better prepare themselves for rewarding careers and helps people advance in the workplace." Currently emphasizing test preparation, career advancement, and materials for prisoners, law enforcement, books on unique careers.

Nonfiction Reference. Subjects include business/economics, education, government/politics, health/medicine, money/finance, law enforcement. Submit complete ms and SASE with sufficient postage.

Recent Title(s) *Real Life 101: Winning Secrets You Won't Find in Class*, by Debra Yergen; *Getting In: Applicant's Guide to Graduate School Admissions*, by David Burrell.

Tips Audience is career planning offices; colleges, graduate schools, and public libraries. "We are open to all submissions, especially those involving career planning, internships, and other nonfiction titles. Looking for books on law enforcement, books for prisoners, and reference books on subjects/fields students would be interested in. We want books on helping students and others to interview, pass tests, gain opportunity, understand the world of work, network, build experience, prepare for advancement, prepare to enter business, improve personality, and build relationships."

GRAND CANYON ASSOCIATION

P.O. Box 399, 1 Tonto St., Grand Canyon AZ 86023. (928)638-2481. Fax: (928)638-2484. E-mail: tberger@grandcanyon.org. Website: www.grandcanyon.org. **Acquisitions:** Todd R. Berger, managing editor (Grand Canyon-related geology, natural history, outdoor activities, human history, photography, ecology, etc., posters and other nonbook products). Estab. 1932. Publishes hardcover originals and reprints, and trade paperback originals and reprints. **Publishes 6 titles/year. Receives 100 queries and 100 submissions/year. 70% of books from first-time authors; 99% from unagented writers. Pays royalty on wholesale price, or makes outright purchase.** Publishes book 1 month-1 year after acceptance of ms. Accepts simultaneous submissions. Responds in 2 months to queries; 2 months to proposals; 2 months to mss. Book catalog online; ms guidelines by e-mail.

Nonfiction Autobiography, biography, booklets, children's/juvenile, coffee table book, gift book, how-to, illustrated book, scholarly. Subjects include animals, anthropology/archeology, art/architecture, creative nonfiction, general nonfiction, history, nature/environment, photography, recreation, regional, science, sports, travel, geology. Grand Canyon Association (GCA) is a nonprofit organization established in 1932 to support education, research, and other programs for the benefit of Grand Canyon National Park and its visitors. GCA operates bookstores throughout the park, publishes books and other materials related to the Grand Canyon region,

Book Publishers

supports wildlife surveys and other research, funds acquisitions for the park's research library, and produces a wide variety of free publications and exhibits for park visitors. Since 1932 GCA has provided Grand Canyon National Park with over $15 million in aid. All publications and other products are related to Grand Canyon National Park and the surrounding region. Query with SASE, or submit proposal package including outline, 3-4 sample chapter(s), list of publication credits, and samples of previous work, or submit complete ms. Reviews artwork/photos as part of ms package. Send transparencies or color or b&w prints are OK, as are digital scans of images.

Recent Title(s) *Phantom Ranch*, by Scott Thybony (illustrated history); *Grand Canyon: The Vault of Heaven*, by Susan Lamb (photograhic scenic book); *An Introduction to Grand Canyon Geology*, by L. Greer Price (illustrated geology).

Tips "All books, articles, and other products must be about the Grand Canyon. We also publish some things, to a much lesser extent, on the surrounding region, particularly geology-related titles with a connection to the Grand Canyon."

GRAYWOLF PRESS

2402 University Ave., Suite 203, St. Paul MN 55114. Website: www.graywolfpress.org. Editor/Publisher: Fiona McCrae. Executive Editor: Anne Czarniecki. Poetry Editor: Jeffrey Shotts. **Acquisitions:** Katie Dublinski, editor (nonfiction, fiction). Estab. 1974. Publishes trade cloth and paperback originals. **Publishes 20 titles/year. Receives 2,500 queries/year. 20% of books from first-time authors; 50% from unagented writers. Pays royalty on retail price. Offers $1,000-15,000 advance.** Publishes book 18 months after acceptance of ms. Responds in 3 months to queries. Book catalog free; ms guidelines online.

> Graywolf Press is an independent, nonprofit publisher dedicated to the creation and promotion of thoughtful and imaginative contemporary literature essential to a vital and diverse culture.

Nonfiction Subjects include contemporary culture, language/literature, culture. Query with SASE, or submit 30-page sample.

Fiction Literary, short story collections. "Familiarize yourself with our list first." No genre books (romance, western, science fiction, suspense). Query with SASE and 30-page sample. "Please do not fax or e-mail queries or submissions."

Poetry "We are interested in linguistically challenging work." Query with SASE and 10-poem sample.

Recent Title(s) *What Narcissism Means to Me*, by Tony Hoagland; *One Vacant Chair*, by Joe Coomer; *The Black Interior*, by Elizabeth Alexander.

GREAT POTENTIAL PRESS

P.O. Box 5057, Scottsdale AZ 85261. (602)954-4200. Fax: (602)954-0185. E-mail: info@giftedbooks.com. Website: www.giftedbooks.com. **Acquisitions:** Janet Gore, editor (gifted curriculum in schools); James Webb, president (parenting and social and emotional needs). Estab. 1986. Publishes trade paperback originals. **Publishes 4-5 titles/year. Receives 10 queries and 10-15 mss/year. 25% of books from first-time authors; 100% from unagented writers. Pays 10% royalty on retail price.** Publishes book 6-12 months after acceptance of ms. Accepts simultaneous submissions. Responds in 2 months to queries; 3 months to proposals; 4 months to mss. Book catalog free or on website; ms guidelines online.

> Great Potential Press publishes books on the social/emotional/interpersonal/creative needs of gifted and talented children and adults for parents and teachers of gifted and talented youngsters. Currently emphasizing books regarding gifted and talented children, their parents and teachers. De-emphasizing research-based books.

Nonfiction Biography, children's/juvenile, humor, reference, self-help, textbook, assessment scales, advocacy, parenting tips. Subjects include child guidance/parenting, education, multicultural, psychology, translation, travel, women's issues/studies, gifted/talented children and adults. No research-based books, dissertations. Submit proposal package, including preface or introduction, TOC, outline, 3 sample chapters and an explanation of how work differs from similar published books.

Recent Title(s) *Helping Gifted Children Soar*, by Carol Strip, Ph.D; *Raisin' Brains: Surviving My Smart Family*, by Karen Isaacson; *Some of My Best Friends Are Books, 2nd Ed.*, by Judith Halste.

Tips "Manuscripts should be clear, cogent, and well-written and should pertain to gifted, talented, and creative persons and/or issues."

GREAT QUOTATIONS PUBLISHING

8102 Lemont Rd., #300, Woodridge IL 60517. (630)390-3580. **Acquisitions:** Tami Suits, acquisitions editor (humor, relationships, Christian); Jan Stob, acquisitions editor (children's). Estab. 1991. **Publishes 30 titles/ year. Receives 1,500 queries and 1,200 mss/year. 50% of books from first-time authors; 80% from unagented writers. Pays 3-8% royalty on net receipts.** Publishes book 6 months after acceptance of ms. Accepts simultaneous submissions. Responds in 6 months with SASE to queries. Book catalog for $2; ms guidelines for #10 SASE.

    O⇥ Great Quotations seeks original material for the following general categories: humor, inspiration, motivation, success, romance, tributes to mom/dad/grandma/grandpa, etc. Currently emphasizing humor, relationships. De-emphasizing poetry, self-help. "We publish new books twice a year, in July and in January."

Nonfiction Humor, illustrated book, self-help. Subjects include business/economics, child guidance/parenting, nature/environment, religion, sports, women's issues/studies. "We look for subjects with identifiable markets, appealing to the general public. We publish humorous books or others requiring multicolor illustration on the inside. We don't publish highly controversial subject matter." Submit outline, 2 sample chapter(s). Reviews artwork/photos as part of ms package. Send photocopies or transparencies.

Recent Title(s) *Stress or Sanity*; *If My Teacher Sleeps at School*.

Tips "Our books are physically small and generally a very quick read. They are available at gift shops and book shops throughout the country. We are aware that most of our books are bought on impulse and given as gifts. We need strong, clever, descriptive titles; beautiful cover art; and brief, positive, upbeat text. Be prepared to submit final manuscript on computer disk, according to our specifications. (It is not necessary to try to format the typesetting of your manuscript to look like a finished book.)"

GREENE BARK PRESS

P.O. Box 1108, Bridgeport CT 06601. (203)372-4861. Fax: (203)371-5856. Website: www.greenebarkpress.com. **Acquisitions:** Thomas J. Greene, publisher; Michele Hofbauer, associate publisher. Estab. 1991. Publishes hardcover originals. **Publishes 5 titles/year. Receives 100 queries and 6,000 mss/year. 60% of books from first-time authors; 100% from unagented writers. Pays 10-15% royalty on wholesale price.** Publishes book 1 year after acceptance of ms. Accepts simultaneous submissions. Responds in 1 month to queries; 6 months to mss. Book catalog for $2; ms guidelines for SASE.

    O⇥ Greene Bark Press only publishes books for children and young adults, mainly picture and read-to books. "All of our titles appeal to the imagination and encourage children to read and explore the world through books. We only publish children's fiction—all subjects—but in reading picture book format appealing to ages 3-9 or all ages."

Fiction Juvenile. Submit complete ms. No queries or ms by e-mail.

Recent Title(s) *The Magical Trunk*, by Gigi Tegge; *Hey! There's a Goblin Under My Throne!*, by Rhett Ransom Pennell.

Tips Audience is "children who read to themselves and others. Mothers, fathers, grandparents, godparents who read to their respective children, grandchildren. Include SASE, be prepared to wait, do not inquire by telephone."

Ø GREENHAVEN PRESS, INC.

10911 Technology Place, San Diego CA 92127. Website: www.greenhaven.com. **Acquisitions:** Chandra Howard, aquisitions editor. Estab. 1970. Publishes approximately 135 anthologies/year; all anthologies are works for hire. **Makes outright purchase of $1,000-3,000.** Book catalog for 9×12 SAE with 3 first-class stamps or online.

    O⇥ Greenhaven Press publishes hard and softcover educational supplementary materials and (nontrade) nonfiction anthologies on contemporary issues, literary criticism, and history for high school and college readers. These anthologies serve as supplementary educational material for high school and college libraries and classrooms. Currently emphasizing historical topics and social-issue anthologies.

Nonfiction Subjects include history, social issues. "We produce tightly formatted anthologies on contemporary issues and history for high school and college-level readers. We are looking for freelance book editors to research and compile these anthologies; we are not interested in submissions of single-author manuscripts. Each series has specific requirements. Potential book editors should familiarize themselves with our catalog and anthologies." Send query letter and résumé. *No unsolicited ms.*

Recent Title(s) *Opposing Viewpoints: Abortion*; *Examining Pop Culture: Violence in Film and TV*; *At Issue in History: The Cuban Missle Crisis*.

GREENLINE PUBLICATIONS

P.O. Box 590780, San Francisco CA 94159-0780. (415)386-8646, ext. 35. Fax: (415)386-8049. E-mail: funrises2@ aol.com. Website: www.greenlinepub.com. **Acquisitions:** Alan Davis, executive editor (travel publications); Samia Afra, associate publisher. Estab. 1998. Publishes trade paperback originals. **Publishes 6 titles/year; imprint publishes 4 (Fun); 2 (Historic) titles/year. Makes outright purchase of $15,000-20,000. Offers $5,000 advance.** Does not accept simultaneous submissions. Responds in 2 months to queries; 2 months to proposals; 2 months to mss. Book catalog free.

Imprints Fun Seeker's Guides, Greenline Historical Travel Guides.

Nonfiction Subjects include history, travel. Submit proposal package including outline. Reviews artwork/photos as part of ms package.

Recent Title(s) *The 25 Best World War II Sites: Pacific Theater*, by Chuck Thompson (travel); *The Fun Seeker's Las Vegas*, by Norine Dwoykin (travel); *The Fun Seeker's Los Angeles*, by Jordan Rane (travel).

Tips Audience is adult travelers.

◎ GREENWILLOW BOOKS

HarperCollins Publishers, 1350 Avenue of the Americas, New York NY 10019. (212)261-6500. Website: www.harperchildrens.com. Senior Editor: Rebecca Davis. Estab. 1974. Publishes hardcover originals and reprints. **Publishes 50-60 titles/year. 1% of books from first-time authors; 30% from unagented writers. Pays 10% royalty. on wholesale price for first-time authors. Offers variable advance.** Publishes book 2 years after acceptance of ms.

    ○ᴦ Greenwillow Books publishes quality picture books and fiction for young readers of all ages, and nonfiction primarily for children under seven years of age.

Fiction Juvenile. Fantasy, humor, literary, mystery, picture books.

Recent Title(s) *Whale Talk*, by Chris Crutcher.

Tips "Currently not accepting unsolicited mail, mss or queries. Please call (212)261-6627 for an update."

GREENWOOD PRESS

Greenwood Publishing Group, 88 Post Rd. W., Box 5007, Westport CT 06881. (203)226-3571. Fax: (203)222-1502. E-mail: editorial@greenwood.com. Website: www.greenwood.com. **Acquisitions:** Gary Kuris, editorial director; Emily Birch, managing editor. Publishes hardcover originals. **Publishes 200 titles/year. Receives 1,000 queries/year. 25% of books from first-time authors. Pays variable royalty on net price. Offers rare advance.** Publishes book 1 year after acceptance of ms. Accepts simultaneous submissions. Responds in 6 months to queries. Book catalog and ms guidelines online; ms guidelines online.

    ○ᴦ Greenwood Press publishes reference materials for high school, public and academic libraries in the humanities and the social and hard sciences.

Nonfiction Reference, scholarly. Subjects include humanities, social sciences, humanities and the social and hard sciences. Query with proposal package, including scope, organization, length of project, whether complete ms is available or when it will be, cv or résumé and SASE. *No unsolicited mss.*

Recent Title(s) *All Things Shakespeare*, by Kirstin Olsen.

GREENWOOD PUBLISHING GROUP

Reed-Elsevier (USA) Inc., 88 Post Rd. W, Box 5007, Westport CT 06881. (203)226-3571. Fax: (203)222-1502. Website: www.greenwood.com. **Acquisitions:** Reference—George Butler (literature, drama, gbutler@greenwood.com); Debbie Carvalko (psychology); Eric Levy (art and architecture, music and dance, popular culture, elevy@greenwood.com). Secondary School Reference—Heather Staines (history and military studies, hstaines@greenwood.com). **Publishes 700 titles/year. Pays variable royalty on net price. Offers advance rarely. Offers rare advance.** Publishes book 1 year after acceptance of ms. Accepts simultaneous submissions. Book catalog and ms guidelines online.

Imprints Praeger, Greenwood Press.

    ○ᴦ The Greenwood Publishing Group consists of two distinguished imprints with one unifying purpose: to provide the best possible reference and general interest resources in the humanities and the social and hard sciences.

Nonfiction Reference, scholarly. Subjects include business/economics, child guidance/parenting, education, government/politics, history, humanities, language/literature, music/dance, psychology, religion, social sciences, sociology, sports, women's issues/studies. Query with proposal package, including scope, organization, length of project, whether a complete ms is available or when it will be, cv or résumé and SASE. *No unsolicited mss.*

Tips "No interest in fiction, drama, poetry—looking for reference materials and materials for educated general readers. Most of our authors are college professors who have distinguished credentialsa and who have published research widely in their fields." Greenwood Publishing maintains an excellent website, providing complete catalog, ms guidelines and editorial contacts.

Ⓐ ◎ GROSSET & DUNLAP PUBLISHERS

Penguin Putnam Inc., 345 Hudson St., New York NY 10014. President/Publisher: Debra Dorfman. Estab. 1898. Publishes hardcover (few) and paperback originals. **Publishes 175 titles/year. Pays royalty. Offers advance.** Publishes book 18 months after acceptance of ms. Does not accept simultaneous submissions. Responds in 2 months to queries.

● Not currently accepting submissions.

O— Grosset & Dunlap publishes children's books that show children that reading is fun, with books that speak to their interests, and that are affordable so that children can build a home library of their own. Focus on licensed properties, series and readers.

Nonfiction Children's/juvenile. Subjects include nature/environment, science. *Agented submissions only.*

Fiction Juvenile. *Agented submissions only.*

Recent Title(s) *Katie Kazoo* (series); *Dish* (series); *Strawberry Shortcake* (license).

Tips "Nonfiction that is particularly topical or of wide interest in the mass market; new concepts for novelty format for preschoolers; and very well-written easy readers on topics that appeal to primary graders have the best chance of selling to our firm."

GROUP PUBLISHING, INC.

1515 Cascade Ave., Loveland CO 80538. (970)669-3836. Fax: (970)679-4370. E-mail: kloesche@grouppublishing. com. Website: www.grouppublishing.com. **Acquisitions:** Kerri Loesche, editorial assistant. Estab. 1974. Publishes trade paperback originals. **Publishes 40 titles/year. Receives 500 queries and 500 mss/year. 40% of books from first-time authors; 95% from unagented writers. Pays up to 10% royalty on wholesale price or makes outright purchase or work for hire. Offers up to $1,000 advance.** Publishes book 18 months after acceptance of ms. Accepts simultaneous submissions. Responds in 1 month to queries; 6 months to proposals; 6 months to mss. Book catalog for 9×12 SAE with 2 first-class stamps; ms guidelines online.

O— "Our mission is to equip churches to help children, youth, and adults grow in their relationship with Jesus."

Nonfiction Children's/juvenile, how-to, multimedia, textbook. Subjects include education, religion. "We're an interdenominational publisher of resource materials for people who work with adults, youth or children in a Christian church setting. We also publish materials for use directly by youth or children (such as devotional books, workbooks or Bibles stories). Everything we do is based on concepts of active and interactive learning as described in *Why Nobody Learns Much of Anything at Church: And How to Fix It*, by Thom and Joani Schultz. We need new, practical, hands-on, innovative, out-of-the-box ideas—things that no one's doing . . . yet." Query with SASE, or submit proposal package including outline, 3 sample chapter(s), cover letter, introduction to book, and sample activities if appropriate.

Recent Title(s) *An Unstoppable Force*, by Erwin McManus; *The 1 Thing*, by Thom and Joani Schultz (effective teaching and learning).

Tips "Our audience consists of pastors, Christian education directors and Sunday school teachers."

Ⓝ Ⓐ Ⓩ GROVE/ATLANTIC, INC.

841 Broadway, 4th Floor, New York NY 10003. (212)614-7850. Fax: (212)614-7886. Estab. 1952. Publishes hardcover and trade paperback originals, and reprints. **Publishes 60-70 titles/year. Receives thousands of queries/year. 10-15% of books from first-time authors. Pays 7½-15% royalty on retail price. Offers considerably varies advance.** Publishes book 1 year after acceptance of ms. Accepts simultaneous submissions. Book catalog free.

Imprints Grove Press (estab. 1952), Atlantic Monthly Press (estab. 1917).

O— Grove/Atlantic publishes serious nonfiction and literary fiction.

Nonfiction Biography. Subjects include government/politics, history, travel. Query with SASE. *No unsolicited mss.*

Fiction Experimental, literary. *Agented submissions only.* Query with SASE. *No unsolicited mss.*

Poetry "We try to publish at least one volume of poetry every list." *No unsolicited mss.* Query.

Recent Title(s) *Triangle: The Fire That Changed America*, by David von Drehle; *Black Hawk Dawn: A Story of Modern War*, by Mark Bowden.

ALDINE DE GRUYTER

Walter de Gruyter, Inc., 200 Saw Mill River Rd., Hawthorne NY 10532. (914)747-0110, ext. 19. Fax: (914)747-1326. E-mail: rkoffler@degruyterny.com. Website: www.degruyter.com. **Acquisitions:** Dr. Richard Koffler, executive editor. Publishes hardcover and academic paperback originals. **Publishes 15-25 titles/year. Receives several hundred queries and 100 mss/year. 15% of books from first-time authors; 99% from unagented writers. Pays 7½-10% royalty on net receipts.** Publishes book 9 months after acceptance of ms. Accepts simultaneous submissions. Responds in 2 months to proposals. Book catalog free; ms guidelines only after contract.

O— Aldine de Gruyter is an academic nonfiction publisher.

Nonfiction Scholarly, textbook (rare), course-related monographs; edited volumes. Subjects include anthropology/archeology, humanities, psychology (evolutionary), sociology, social psychology (not clinical), human services. "Aldine's authors are academics with Ph.D.'s and strong publication records. No poetry or fiction."

Submit proposal package including 1-2 sample chapter(s), cv, market, competing texts, reviews of early work.
Recent Title(s) *Images of Terror*, by Philip Jenkins.
Tips Audience is professors and upper level and graduate students. "Never send unsolicited manuscripts; always query before sending anything."

GRYPHON HOUSE, INC.

P.O. Box 207, Beltsville MD 20704. (301)595-9500. Fax: (301)595-0051. Website: www.gryphonhouse.com. **Acquisitions:** Kathy Charner, editor-in-chief. Estab. 1971. Publishes trade paperback originals. **Publishes 12-15 titles/year. Pays royalty on wholesale price.** Does not accept simultaneous submissions. Responds in 3-6 months to queries. Ms guidelines online.

   O— Gryphon House publishes books that teachers and parents of young children (birth-age 8) consider essential to their daily lives.

Nonfiction Children's/juvenile, how-to. Subjects include child guidance/parenting, education (early childhood). Currently emphasizing reading; de-emphasizing after-school activities. Submit outline, 2-3 sample chapter(s), SASE.
Recent Title(s) *The Busy Family's Guide to Volunteering*, by Jenny Friedman; *Science Is Simple*, by Peggy Ashbrook; *Zen Parenting*, by Judith Costello and Jurgen Haver.

GRYPHON PUBLICATIONS

P.O. Box 209, Brooklyn NY 11228. **Acquisitions:** Gary Lovisi, owner/publisher. Publishes trade paperback originals and reprints. **Publishes 10 titles/year. Receives 500 queries and 1,000 mss/year. 20% of books from first-time authors; 90% from unagented writers. Makes outright purchase by contract, price varies. Offers no advance.** Publishes book 1-2 years after acceptance of ms. Responds in 1 month to queries to queries. Book catalog and ms guidelines for #10 SASE.
Imprints Paperback Parade Magazine, Hardboiled Magazine, Gryphon Books, Gryphon Doubles.

   O— "I publish very genre-oriented work (science fiction, crime, pulps) and nonfiction on these topics, authors and artists. It's best to query with an idea first."

Nonfiction Reference, scholarly, bibliography. Subjects include hobbies, language/literature, book collecting. "We need well-written, well-researched articles, but query first on topic and length. Writers should not submit material that is not fully developed/researched." Query with SASE. Reviews artwork/photos as part of ms package. Send photocopies; slides, transparencies may be necessary later.
Fiction Crime, hard-boiled fiction. "We want cutting-edge fiction, under 3,000 words with impact." For short stories, query or submit complete ms. For novels, send 1-page query letter with SASE.
Recent Title(s) *Barsom: Edgar Rice Burroughs & the Martian Myth*, by Richard A. Lysoff; *Sherlock Holmes & the Terror Out of Time*, by Ralph Vaughan; *A Trunk Full of Murder*, by Julius Fast.
Tips "We are very particular about novels and book-length work. A first-timer has a better chance with a short story or article. On anything over 4,000 words do not send manuscript, send only query letter with SASE."

HACHAI PUBLISHING

156 Chester Ave., Brooklyn NY 11218. (718)633-0100. Website: www.hachai.com. **Acquisitions:** Devorah Leah Rosenfeld, editor. Estab. 1988. Publishes hardcover originals. **Publishes 4 titles/year. Makes outright purchase of $600 and up.** Accepts simultaneous submissions. Responds in 2 months to mss. Book catalog free; ms guidelines online.

   O— "Hachai is dedicated to producing high quality Jewish children's literature, ages 2-10. Story should promote universal values such as sharing, kindness, etc."

Nonfiction Children's/juvenile. Subjects include ethnic, religion. Submit complete ms, SASE. Reviews artwork/ photos as part of ms package. Send photocopies.
Recent Title(s) *When the World was Quiet*, by Phyllis Nutkis; *Bedtime*, by Nechama Dina Adelman; *Once Upon a Time*, by Draizy Zelcer.
Tips "We are looking for books that convey the traditional Jewish experience in modern times or long ago; traditional Jewish observance such as Sabbath and holidays and mitzvos such as mezuzah, blessings etc; positive character traits (middos) such as honesty, charity, respect, sharing, etc. We are also interested in historical fiction for young readers (7-10) written with a traditional Jewish perspective and highlighting the relevance of Torah in making important choices. Please, no animal stories, romance, violence, preachy sermonizing."

HALF HALT PRESS, INC.

P.O. Box 67, Boonsboro MD 21713. (301)733-7119. Fax: (301)733-7408. E-mail: hhpress@aol.com. Website: www.halfhaltpress.com. **Acquisitions:** Elizabeth Carnes, publisher. Estab. 1986. Publishes 90% hardcover and trade paperback originals and 10% reprints. **Publishes 15 titles/year. Receives 150 submissions/year. 25%**

of books from first-time authors; 50% from unagented writers. **Pays 10-12½% royalty on retail price.** Publishes book 1 year after acceptance of ms. Does not accept simultaneous submissions. Responds in 1 month to queries. Book catalog for 6×9 SAE 2 first-class stamps.

O─┑ "We publish high-quality nonfiction on equestrian topics, books that help riders and trainers do something better."

Nonfiction How-to. Subjects include animals (horses), sports. "We need serious instructional works by authorities in the field on horse-related topics, broadly defined." Query with SASE. Reviews artwork/photos as part of ms package.

Recent Title(s) *Dressage in Harmony*, by Walter Zettl.

Tips "Writers have the best chance selling us well-written, unique works that teach serious horse people how to do something better. If I were a writer trying to market a book today, I would offer a straightforward presentation, letting the work speak for itself, without hype or hard sell. Allow the publisher to contact the writer, without frequent calling to check status. They haven't forgotten the writer but may have many different proposals at hand; frequent calls to 'touch base,' multiplied by the number of submissions, become an annoyance. As the publisher/author relationship becomes close and is based on working well together, early impressions may be important, even to the point of being a consideration in acceptance for publication."

ALEXANDER HAMILTON INSTITUTE

70 Hilltop Rd., Ramsey NJ 07446-1119. (201)825-3377. Fax: (201)825-8696. Website: www.ahipubs.com. **Acquisitions:** Brian L.P. Zevnik, editor-in-chief; Gloria Ju, editor. Estab. 1909. Publishes 3-ring binder and paperback originals. **Publishes 5-10 titles/year. Receives 50 queries and 10 mss/year. 25% of books from first-time authors; 95% from unagented writers. Pays 5-8% royalty on retail price, or makes outright purchase of $3,500-7,000. Offers $3,500-7,000 advance.** Publishes book 10 months after acceptance of ms. Accepts simultaneous submissions. Responds in 1 month to queries; 2 months to mss.

O─┑ Alexander Hamilton Institute publishes management books for upper-level managers and executives. Currently emphasizing legal issues for HR/personnel.

Nonfiction The main audience is US personnel executives and high-level management. Subjects include legal personnel matters. "These books combine court case research and practical application of defensible programs."

Recent Title(s) *Employer's Guide to Record-Keeping Requirements*.

Tips "We sell exclusively by direct mail or through electronic means to managers and executives. A writer must know his/her field and be able to communicate legal and practical systems and programs."

HAMPTON ROADS PUBLISHING CO., INC.

1125 Stoney Ridge Rd., Charlottesville VA 22902. (434)296-2772. Fax: (434)296-5096. E-mail: hrpc@hrpub.com. Website: www.hrpub.com. **Acquisitions:** Frank DeMarco, chief editor (metaphysical/visionary fiction); Robert S. Friedman, president (metaphysical, spiritual, inspirational, self-help); Richard Leviton, senior editor (alternative medicine). Estab. 1989. Publishes hardcover and trade paperback originals. Publishes and distributes hardcover and paperback originals on subjects including metaphysics, health, complementary medicine, visionary fiction, and other related topics. **Publishes 35-40 titles/year. Receives 1,000 queries and 1,500 mss/year. 50% of books from first-time authors; 70% from unagented writers. Pays royalty. Offers $1,000-50,000 advance.** Publishes book 1 year after acceptance of ms. Accepts simultaneous submissions. Responds in 2-4 months to queries; 2-4 months to proposals; 6-12 months to mss. Ms guidelines online.

O─┑ "Our reason for being is to impact, uplift, and contribute to positive change in the world. We publish books that will enrich and empower the evolving consciousness of mankind."

Nonfiction How-to, illustrated book, self-help. Subjects include New Age, spirituality. Query with SASE, or submit synopsis, SASE. Reviews artwork/photos as part of ms package. Send photocopies.

Fiction Literary, spiritual, Visionary fiction, past-life fiction based on actual memories. "Fiction should have 1 or more of the following themes: spiritual, inspirational, metaphysical, i.e., past-life recall, out-of-body experiences, near-death experience, paranormal." Query with SASE, or submit outline, 2 sample chapter(s), synopsis, or submit complete ms.

Recent Title(s) *The Beethoven Factor*, by Paul Pearsall; *The Natural Way to Heal*, by Walter Last; *Phoenix Lights*, by Lynn D. Kitei, M.D.

HANCOCK HOUSE PUBLISHERS

1431 Harrison Ave., Blaine WA 98230-5005. (604)538-1114. Fax: (604)538-2262. E-mail: david@hancockwildlif e.org. Website: www.hancockwildlife.org. David Hancock, publisher. **Acquisitions:** Yvonne Lund, promotional manager. Estab. 1971. Publishes hardcover and trade paperback originals and reprints. **Publishes 12-20 titles/ year. Receives 300 submissions/year. 50% of books from first-time authors; 90% from unagented writers. Pays 10% royalty.** Publishes book up to 1 year after acceptance of ms. Accepts simultaneous submissions. Book catalog free; ms guidelines online.

Book Publishers

○━ Hancock House Publishers is the largest North American publisher of wildlife and Native Indian titles. "We also cover Pacific Northwest, fishing, history, Canadiana, biographies. We are seeking agriculture, natural history, animal husbandry, conservation, and popular science titles with a regional (Pacific Northwest), national, or international focus." Currently emphasizing nonfiction wildlife, cryptozoology, guide books, native history, biography, fishing.

Nonfiction "Centered around Pacific Northwest, local history, nature guide books, international ornithology, and Native Americans." Biography, how-to, reference, technical, Pacific Northwest history and biography. Subjects include agriculture/horticulture, animals, ethnic, history, nature/environment, regional. Submit proposal package including outline, 3 sample chapter(s), selling points, SASE. Reviews artwork/photos as part of ms package. Send photocopies.

Recent Title(s) *Arabian Falconry*, by Roger Upton; *Estrildid Finches*, by Matthew Vriends.

HANSER GARDNER PUBLICATIONS

6915 Valley Ave., Cincinnati OH 45244. (513)527-8894. Fax: (513)527-8801. Website: www.hansergardner.com. **Acquisitions:** Woody Chapman (metalworking—wchapman@gardnerweb.com); Christine Strohm (plastics—cstrohm@gardnerweb.com). Estab. 1993. Publishes hardcover and paperback originals, and digital educational and training programs. **Publishes 10-15 titles/year. Receives 100 queries and 10-20 mss/year. 50% of books from first-time authors; 100% from unagented writers. Pays 10-15% royalty on net receipts.** Publishes book 10 months after acceptance of ms. Accepts simultaneous submissions. Responds in 2 weeks to queries; 1 month to proposals; 1 month to mss. Book catalog free; ms guidelines online.

○━ Hanser Gardner publishes books and electronic media for the manufacturing (both metalworking and plastics) industries. Publications range from basic training materials to advanced reference books.

Nonfiction "We publish how-to texts, reference, and technical books, and computer-based learning materials for the manufacturing industries. Titles include award-winning management books, encyclopedic references, and leading references." Submit outline, sample chapter(s), résumé, preface, and comparison to competing or similar titles.

Recent Title(s) *Modern Machine Shop's Handbook for the Metalworking Industries*, by W. Chapman; *Polymer Extrusion, 4th Ed.*, by Chris Rauwendaal.

Tips "E-mail submissions speed up response time."

HARBOR HOUSE

629 Stevens Crossing, Augusta GA 30907. (706)738-0354. Fax: (706)738-0354. Website: harborhousebooks.com. Estab. 1997. Publishes hardcover originals and paperback originals. **Pays 10% royalty. Offers $5,000 advance.** Publishes book 6-18 months after acceptance of ms. Accepts simultaneous submissions. Responds in 4 weeks to queries; 2 months to mss. Book catalog and ms guidelines online.

Fiction Historical (biography), horror (psychological, supernatural), mainstream/contemporary, military/war, romance (historical), young adult (horror, mystery/suspense), civil war. Submit outline, 3 sample chapter(s). Query.

HARBOR PRESS

5713 Wollochet Dr. NW, Gig Harbor WA 98335. Fax: (253)851-5191. E-mail: info@harborpress.com. Website: www.harborpress.com. President/Publisher: Harry R. Lynn. **Acquisitions:** Deborah Young, senior editor. Submissions address: Harbor Press, 5 Glen Dr., Plainview NY 11803. Estab. 1985. Publishes hardcover and trade paperback originals and reprints. **Publishes 4-6 titles/year. Negotiates competitive royalties on wholesale price, or makes outright purchase.** Does not accept simultaneous submissions.

○━ Harbor Press publishes books that will help readers achieve better health and more successful lives. Currently emphasizing diet and weight loss, parenting, psychology/human relationships, successful living books. Credentialed authors only.

Nonfiction How-to, self-help. Subjects include child guidance/parenting, cooking/foods/nutrition (diet and weight loss only), health/medicine, psychology. Query with SASE, or submit proposal package including outline, 3 sample chapter(s), synopsis. Reviews artwork/photos as part of ms package. Send photocopies.

Recent Title(s) *The Prostate Diet Cookbook*, by Buffy Sanders; *Yes! Your Teen Is Crazy: Loving Your Kid Without Losing Your Mind*, by Michael Bradley.

⊘ HARCOURT, INC., CHILDREN'S BOOK DIVISION

525 B St., Suite 1900, San Diego CA 92101. (619)281-6616. Fax: (619)699-6777. Website: www.harcourtbooks. com/htm/childrens_index.asp. Estab. 1919. Publishes hardcover originals and trade paperback reprints.

Imprints Harcourt Children's Books, Gulliver Books, Red Wagon Books, Harcourt Young Classics, Green Light Readers, Voyager Books/Libros Viajeros, Harcourt Paperbacks, Odyssey Classics, Magic Carpet Books.

○┐ Harcourt, Inc., owns some of the world's most prestigious publishing imprints—imprints which distinguish quality products for the juvenile, educational, scientific, technical, medical, professional and trade markets worldwide.

Nonfiction *No unsolicited mss or queries.* No phone calls.

Fiction Young adult. *No unsolicited mss or queries.* No phone calls.

Recent Title(s) *A Northern Light*, by Jennifer Donnelly; *How I Became a Pirate*, by Melinda Long, illustrated by David Shannon.

Ⓐ ⊘ HARCOURT, INC., TRADE DIVISION

525 B St., Suite 1900, San Diego CA 92101. (619)699-6560. Fax: (619)699-5555. Website: www.harcourtbooks.com. **Acquisitions:** David Hough, managing editor; Drenka Willen, senior editor (poetry, fiction in translation, history); Andrea Schulz (nonfiction, American fiction, history, science); Ann Patty (American fiction). Publishes hardcover and trade paperback originals and trade paperback reprints. **Publishes 120 titles/year. 5% of books from first-time authors; 5% from unagented writers. Pays 6-15% royalty on retail price. Offers $2,000 minimum advance.** Accepts simultaneous submissions. Book catalog for 9×12 SAE; ms guidelines online.

Imprints Harvest Books (contact Andre Bernard).

○┐ Harcourt, Inc., owns some of the world's most prestigious publishing imprints—imprints which distinguish quality products for the juvenile, educational, scientific, technical, medical, professional, and trade markets worldwide. Currently emphasizing science and math.

Nonfiction Biography, children's/juvenile, coffee table book, gift book, illustrated book, multimedia, reference, technical. Subjects include anthropology/archeology, art/architecture, child guidance/parenting, creative non-fiction, education, ethnic, gay/lesbian, general nonfiction, government/politics, health/medicine, history, language/literature, memoirs, military/war, multicultural, philosophy, psychology, religion, science, sociology, spirituality, sports, translation, travel, women's issues/studies. Published all categories except business/finance (university texts), cookbooks, self-help, sex. *No unsolicited mss. Agented submissions only.*

Fiction Historical, mystery, picture books. *Agented submissions only.*

Recent Title(s) *Life of Pi*, by Yann Martel (fiction); *Baudolino*, by Umberto Eco (fiction); *Odd Girl Out*, by Rachel Simmons (nonfiction).

Ⓝ Ⓐ HARPERBUSINESS

Imprint of HarperCollins General Books Group, 10 E. 53rd St., New York NY 10022. (212)207-7000. Website: www.harpercollins.com. **Acquisitions:** Leah Spiro, senior editor; Herb Schaffner, senior editor. Estab. 1991. Publishes hardcover, trade paperback originals, hardcover and trade paperback reprints. **Publishes 30-40 titles/year. Receives 500 queries and and mss/year. 1% of books from first-time authors; 0% from unagented writers. Pays royalty on retail price. Offers advance.** Accepts simultaneous submissions.

○┐ HarperBusiness publishes "the inside story on ideas that will shape business practices with cutting-edge information and visionary concepts."

Nonfiction Biography (economics). Subjects include business/economics, Marketing subjects. "We don't publish how-to, textbooks or things for academic market; no reference (tax or mortgage guides), our reference department does that. Proposals need to be top notch. We tend not to publish people who have no business standing. Must have business credentials." *Agented submissions only.*

Ⓝ Ⓐ ⊘ HARPERCOLLINS

10 E. 53rd St., New York NY 10022. (212)207-7000. Website: www.harpercollins.com. Executive Editor: Mark Bryant. Publishes hardcover and paperback originals and paperback reprints. **Publishes 120-150 (trade) titles/year. Pays royalty. Offers negotiable advance.** Responds in 6 weeks to queries.

Imprints HarperCollins Australia/New Zealand: Angus & Robertson, Flamingo, Fourth Estate, HarperBusiness, HarperCollins, HarperReligious, HarperSports, Voyager; **HarperCollins Canada:** HarperFlamingoCanada, PerennialCanada; **HarperCollins Children's Books Group:** Amistad, Julie Andrews Collection, Avon, Joanna Cotler Books, Eos, Laura Geringer Books, Greenwillow Books, HarperAudio, HarperCollins Children's Books, HarperFestival, HarperTempest, HarperTrophy, Rayo, Katherine Tegen Books; **HarperCollins General Books Group:** Access, Amistad, Avon, Caedmon, Ecco, Eos, Fourth Estate, HarperAudio, HarperBusiness, HarperCollins, HarperEntertainment, HarperLargePrint, HarperResource, HarperSanFrancisco, HarperTorch, Harper Design International, Perennial, PerfectBound, Quill, Rayo, ReganBooks, William Morrow, William Morrow Cookbooks; **HarperCollins Publishers:** Beech Tree Books, Greenwillow Books, HarperCollins, Hearst Books, Lothrup, Lee & Shepard Books, Morrow Junior Books, Mulberry Books, Quill Trade Paperbacks; **HarperCollins UK:** Bartholomew Maps, Collins, Collins Crime, Collins Education, HarperCollins Children's Books, Thorsons/Element, Voyager Books; **Zondervan:** Inspirio, Vida, Zonderkidz, Zondervan.

○┐ "HarperCollins, one of the largest English language publishers in the world, is a broad-based publisher with strengths in academic, business and professional, children's, educational, general interest, and religious and spiritual books, as well as multimedia titles."

Nonfiction *Agented submissions only.*

Fiction Adventure, fantasy, gothic, historical, literary, mystery, science fiction, suspense, western. "We look for a strong story line and exceptional literary talent." *Agented submissions only.* **All unsolicited mss returned unopened.**

Recent Title(s) *The Tennis Partner*, by Abraham Verghese; *The Professor and the Madman*, by Simon Winchester; *I Know This Much Is True*, by Wally Lamb.

Tips "We do not accept any unsolicited material."

HARPERCOLLINS CHILDREN'S BOOKS GROUP

Imprint of HarperCollins Children's Books Group, 1350 Avenue of the Americas, New York NY 10019. (212)265-6500. Website: www.harperchildrens.com. Publishes hardcover and paperback originals. **Publishes 525-550 titles/year.**

Imprints Amistad, Julie Andrews Collection, Avon, Joanna Cotler Books, Eos, Laura Geringer Books, Greenwillow Books, HarperAudio, HarperCollins Children's Books, HarperFestival, HarperTempest, HarperTrophy, Rayo, Katherine Tegen Books.

  ○➤ No unsolicited mss and/or unagented mss or queries. "The volume of these submissions is so large that we cannot give them the attention they deserve. Such submissions will not be reviewed or returned."

Nonfiction Picture books, middle grade, young adult, board books, novelty books, TV/Movie tie-ins. *No unsolicited mss or queries. Agented submissions only.*

Fiction Picture books, young adult, chapter books, middle grade, early readers. *Agented submissions only. No unsolicited mss or queries.*

HARPERCOLLINS GENERAL BOOKS GROUP

Division of HarperCollins Publishers, 10 E. 53 St., New York NY 10022. (212)207-7000. Fax: (212)207-7633. Website: www.harpercollins.com.

Imprints Access, Amistad, Avon, Caedmon, Ecco, Eos, Fourth Estate, HarperAudio, HarperBusiness, HarperCollins, HarperEntertainment, HarperLargePrint, HarperResource, HarperSanFranciso, HarperTorch, Harper Design International, Perennial, PerfectBound, Quill, Rayo, ReganBooks, William Morrow, William Morrow Cookbooks.

  • See website for further details.

HARPERCOLLINS PUBLISHERS

Imprint of HarperCollins, 10 E. 53 St., New York NY 10022. (212)207-7000. Fax: (212)207-7145. Website: www.harpercollins.com.

Imprints Beech Tree Books, Greenwillow Books, HarperCollins, Hearst Books, Lothrup, Lee & Shepard Books, Morrow Junior Books, Mulberry Books, Quill Trade Paperbacks.

  • See website for more details.

HARPERSANFRANCISCO

Imprint of HarperCollins General Books Group, 353 Sacramento St., Suite 500, San Francisco CA 94111-3653. (415)477-4400. Fax: (415)477-4444. E-mail: hcsanfrancisco@harpercollins.com. **Acquisitions:** Stephen Hanselman, senior vice president/publisher (Christian spirituality, history, biography); Michael Maudlin, editorial director (Christian spirituality, religious history and biography, Biblical studies, Christian theology); John Loudon, executive editor (religious studies, Biblical studies, psychology/personal growth, Eastern religions, Catholic, spirituality, inspiration); Eric Brandt, senior editor (religious studies, world religions, academic/reference, psychology, philosophy, sociology); Gideon Weil, editor (general nonfiction, spiritual fiction, self-help, psychology, Eastern religions, gift, inspiration, Judaica); Renee Sedliar, associate editor (general nonfiction, spiritual/religious fiction, inspiration, self-help). Estab. 1977. Publishes hardcover originals, trade paperback originals and reprints. **Publishes 75 titles/year. Receives about 10,000 submissions/year. 5% of books from first-time authors. Pays royalty. Offers advance.** Publishes book within 18 months after acceptance of ms.

  ○➤ HarperSanFrancisco "strives to be the preeminent publisher of the most important books across the full spectrum of religion and spiritual literature, adding to the wealth of the world's wisdom by respecting all traditions."

Nonfiction Biography, how-to, reference, self-help. Subjects include psychology (inspiration), religion, spirituality. *No unsolicited mss.*

Recent Title(s) *The Good Book*, by Peter J. Gomes; *The Call*, by Oriah Mountain Dreamer; *When Religion Becomes Evil*, by Charles Kimball.

Book Publishers

N A Ø HARPERTORCH

Imprint of HarperCollins General Books Group, 10 E. 53rd St., New York NY 10022. (212)207-7000. Fax: (212)207-7901. Publisher: Michael Morrison. **Acquisitions:** Sarah Durand. Publishes paperback originals and reprints. **Pays royalty. Offers advance.**

Fiction Fantasy, mainstream/contemporary, mystery, romance (contemporary, historical, romantic suspense), science fiction, suspense. Query with SASE through agent.

HARTMAN PUBLISHING, INC.

8529-A Indian School NE, Albuquerque NM 87112. (505)291-1274. Fax: (505)291-1284. E-mail: susan@hartman online.com. Website: www.hartmanonline.com. **Acquisitions:** Susan Alvare, managing editor (healthcare education). Publishes trade paperback originals. **Publishes 5-10 titles/year. Receives 50 queries and 25 mss/ year. 50% of books from first-time authors; 100% from unagented writers. Pays 6-12% royalty on wholesale or retail price, or makes outright purchase of $200-600.** Publishes book 4-12 months after acceptance of ms. Accepts simultaneous submissions. Responds in 2 months to proposals; 3 months to mss. Book catalog free; ms guidelines online.

Imprints Care Spring (Mark Hartman, publisher).

    ○┓ We publish educational and inspirational books for employees of nursing homes, home health agencies, hospitals, and providers of eldercare.

Nonfiction Textbook. Subjects include health/medicine. "Writers should request our books-wanted list, as well as view samples of our published material." Submit proposals via e-mail.

HARVARD BUSINESS SCHOOL PRESS

Imprint of Harvard Business School Publishing Corp., 60 Harvard Way, Boston MA 02163. (617)783-7400. Fax: (617)783-7489. E-mail: bookpublisher@hbsp.harvard.edu. Website: www.hbsp.harvard.edu. Director: David Goehring. **Acquisitions:** Hollis Heimbouch, editorial director; Kirsten Sandberg, executive editor; Melinda Adams Merino, executive editor; Jeff Kehoe, senior editor; Jacque Murphy, senior editor. Estab. 1984. Publishes hardcover originals. **Publishes 40-50 titles/year. Pays escalating royalty on retail price. Advances vary widely depending on author and market for the book.** Accepts simultaneous submissions. Responds in 1 month to proposals; 1 month to mss. Book catalog and ms guidelines online.

    ○┓ The Harvard Business School Press publishes books for an audience of senior and general managers and business scholars. HBS Press is the source of the most influential ideas and conversations that shape business worldwide.

Nonfiction Trade and professional. Subjects include business, general management, strategy, leadership, marketing, technology management and innovation, human resources. Submit proposal package including outline, sample chapter(s).

Recent Title(s) *The Innovator's Solution*, by Clayton Christense and Michael Raynor; *Why Not?*, by Barry Nalebuff and Ian Ayres; *Changing Minds*, by Howard Gardner.

Tips "Take care to look into the type of business books we publish. They are generally not policy-oriented, dissertations, or edited collections."

THE HARVARD COMMON PRESS

535 Albany St., Boston MA 02118-2500. (617)423-5803. Fax: (617)695-9794. Website: www.harvardcommonpre ss.com. Publisher/President: Bruce P. Shaw. **Acquisitions:** Pamela Hoenig, executive editor. Estab. 1976. Publishes hardcover and trade paperback originals and reprints. **Publishes 16 titles/year. Receives 1,000 submissions/year. 20% of books from first-time authors; 40% from unagented writers. Pays royalty. Offers average $4,000 advance.** Publishes book 1 year after acceptance of ms. Accepts simultaneous submissions. Responds in 2 months to queries. Book catalog for 9×12 SAE with 3 first-class stamps; ms guidelines for #10 SASE or online.

Imprints Gambit Books.

    ○┓ "We want strong, practical books that help people gain control over a particular area of their lives." Currently emphasizing cooking, child care/parenting, health. De-emphasizing general instructional books, travel.

Nonfiction Subjects include child guidance/parenting, cooking/foods/nutrition, health/medicine. "A large percentage of our list is made up of books about cooking, child care, and parenting; in these areas we are looking for authors who are knowledgeable, if not experts, and who can offer a different approach to the subject. We are open to good nonfiction proposals that show evidence of strong organization and writing, and clearly demonstrate a need in the marketplace. First-time authors are welcome." Submit outline, 1-3 sample chapter(s). Reviews artwork/photos as part of ms package.

Recent Title(s) *Icebox Pies*, by Lauren Chattman; *Real Stew*, by Clifford A. Wright.

Tips "We are demanding about the quality of proposals; in addition to strong writing skills and thorough knowledge of the subject matter, we require a detailed analysis of the competition."

Ⓐ ∅ HARVEST HOUSE PUBLISHERS

990 Owen Loop N., Eugene OR 97402. (541)343-0123. Fax: (541)302-0731. Website: www.harvesthousepublish ers.com. Estab. 1974. Publishes hardcover originals and reprints, trade paperback originals and reprints, and mass market paperback originals and reprints. **Publishes 160 titles/year. Receives 1,500 queries and 1,000 mss/year. 1% of books from first-time authors; 5% from unagented writers. Pays royalty.** Book catalog free.

- Harvest House is no longer accepting unsolicited manuscripts.

Nonfiction Reference, self-help. Subjects include anthropology/archeology, business/economics, child guidance/parenting, health/medicine, money/finance, religion, women's issues/studies, Bible studies. *No unsolicited mss. Agented submissions only.*

Fiction *No unsolicited mss, proposals, or artwork. Agented submissions only.*

Recent Title(s) *Power of a Praying Husband*, by Stormie Omartial (Christian living); *Life Management for Busy Women*, by Elizabeth George (Christian living); *After Anne*, by Roxanne Henke (relationship).

Tips "For first time/nonpublished authors we suggest building their literary résumé by submitting to magazines, or perhaps accruing book contributions. First: Build slowly."

HASTINGS HOUSE/DAYTRIPS PUBLISHERS

(formerly Hastings House), LINI LLC, 2601 Wells Ave., Suite 161, Fern Park FL 32730-2000. (407)339-3600. Fax: (407)339-5900. E-mail: hastings_daytrips@earthlink.net. Website: www.hastingshousebooks.com. Publisher: Peter Leers. **Acquisitions:** Earl Steinbicker, senior travel editor (edits Daytrips Series). Publishes trade paperback originals and reprints. **Publishes 20 titles/year. Receives 600 queries and 900 mss/year. 10% of books from first-time authors; 40% from unagented writers. Pays 8-10% royalty on net receipts.** Publishes book 6-10 months after acceptance of ms. Responds in 2 months to queries.

- "We are primarily focused on expanding our Daytrips Travel Series (facts/guide) nationally and internationally." Currently de-emphasizing all other subjects.

Nonfiction Subjects include travel. Submit outline. Query.

Recent Title(s) *Daytrips Eastern Australia*, by James Postell; *Daytrips Quebec*, by Karen Desrosiers; *Daytrips Scotland & Wales*, by Judith Frances Duddle.

HAWK PUBLISHING GROUP

7107 S. Yale Ave., #345, Tulsa OK 74136. (918)492-3677. Fax: (918)492-2120. Website: www.hawkpub.com. Estab. 1999. Publishes hardcover and trade paperback originals. **Publishes 6-8 titles/year. 25% of books from first-time authors; 50% from unagented writers. Pays royalty.** Publishes book 1-2 years after acceptance of ms. Accepts simultaneous submissions. Ms guidelines online.

- "Please visit our website and read the submission guidelines before sending anything to us. The best way to learn what might interest us is to visit the website, read the information there, look at the books, and perhaps even read a few of them."

Nonfiction Looking for subjects of broad appeal and interest. Queries by e-mail are welcome.

Fiction Looking for good books of all kinds. Not interested in juvenile, poetry, or short story collections. Does not want childrens or young adult books. Submissions will not be returned, so send only copies. No SASE. No submissions by e-mail or by "certified mail or any other service that requires a signature." Replies "only if interested. If you have not heard from us within 3 months after the receipt of your submission, you may safely assume that we were not able to find a place for it in our list."

Recent Title(s) *The Darkest Night*, by Jodie Larsen; *Mama Used to Say*, by Hannibal B. Johnson; *When the Levee Breaks*, by Patrick Chalfant.

THE HAWORTH PRESS, INC.

10 Alice St., Binghamton NY 13904. (607)722-5857. Fax: (607)771-0012. Website: www.haworthpress.com. **Acquisitions:** Bill Palmer, vice president, publications. Estab. 1973. Publishes hardcover and trade paperback originals. **Publishes 100 titles/year. Receives 500 queries and 250 mss/year. 60% of books from first-time authors; 98% from unagented writers. Pays 7¹/₂-15% royalty on wholesale price.** Publishes book 1 year after acceptance of ms. Responds in 2 months to proposals. Ms guidelines online.

Imprints Best Business Books; Food Products Press; Harrington Park Press; Alice Street Editions; Southern Tier Editions; International Business Press; Pharmaceutical Products Press; The Haworth Clinical Practice Press; The Haworth Hispanic/Latino Press; The Haworth Herbal Press; The Haworth Hospitality Press; The Haworth Information Press; The Haworth Integrative Healing Press; The Haworth Maltreatment & Trauma Press; The

Haworth Medical Press; The Haworth Pastoral Press; The Haworth Social Work Practice Press; The Haworth Reference Press; The Haworth Political Press; The Haworth Judaic Press.

O→ The Haworth Press is primarily a scholarly press.

Nonfiction Reference, scholarly, textbook. Subjects include agriculture/horticulture, business/economics, child guidance/parenting, cooking/foods/nutrition, gay/lesbian, health/medicine, money/finance, psychology, sociology, women's issues/studies. Submit proposal package including outline, 1-3 sample chapter(s), author bio. Reviews artwork/photos as part of ms package. Send photocopies.

Recent Title(s) *The Body Bears the Burden: Trauma, Dissociation, and Disease*; *The Mental Health Diagnostic Desk Reference: Visual Guides and More for Learning to Use the Diagnostic and Statistical Manual (DSM-IV-TR)*, *2nd Ed.*; *Handbook of Psychotropic Herbs: A Scientific Analysis of Herbal Remedies for Psychiatric Conditions*.

HAY HOUSE, INC.

P.O. Box 5100, Carlsbad CA 92018-5100. (760)431-7695. Fax: (760)431-6948. E-mail: slittrell@hayhouse.com. Website: www.hayhouse.com. Editorial Director: Jill Kramer. **Acquisitions:** Shannon Littrell, acquisitions editor. Estab. 1985. Publishes hardcover and trade paperback originals. **Publishes 50 titles/year. Receives 1,200 submissions/year. 5% of books from first-time authors. Pays standard royalty.** Publishes book 12-15 months after acceptance of ms. Accepts simultaneous submissions. Responds in 2 months to mss. No e-mail submissions; ms guidelines online.

Imprints Astro Room, Hay House Lifestyles, Smiley Books.

● Hay House will not accept submissions of any kind until January 2004, and then, only from agents.

O→ "We publish books, audios, and videos that help heal the planet."

Nonfiction Biography, self-help. Subjects include cooking/foods/nutrition, education, health/medicine, money/finance, nature/environment, New Age, philosophy, psychology, sociology, women's issues/studies. "Hay House is interested in a variety of subjects as long as they have a positive self-help slant to them. No poetry, children's books, or negative concepts that are not conducive to helping/healing ourselves or our planet." *Agented submissions only.*

Recent Title(s) *10 Secrets for Success and Inner Peace*, by Wayne Dyer.

Tips "Our audience is concerned with our planet, the healing properties of love, and general self-help principles. If I were a writer trying to market a book today, I would research the market thoroughly to make sure there weren't already too many books on the subject I was interested in writing about. Then I would make sure I had a unique slant on my idea. SASE a must! Simultaneous submissions from agents must include SASEs. No e-mail submissions."

HAZELDEN PUBLISHING AND EDUCATIONAL SERVICES

P.O. Box 176, Center City MN 55012. (651)257-4010. Website: www.hazelden.org. Rebecca Post, editorial director. Estab. 1954. Publishes trade paperback originals and educational materials (videos, workbooks, pamphlets, etc.) for treatment centers, schools, hospitals, and correctional institutions. **Publishes 100 titles/year. Receives 2,500 queries and 2,000 mss/year. 30% of books from first-time authors; 50% from unagented writers. Pays 8% royalty on retail price. Offers variable advance.** Publishes book 1 year after acceptance of ms. Accepts simultaneous submissions. Responds in 6 months to queries. Book catalog and ms guidelines online.

O→ Hazelden is a trade, educational and professional publisher specializing is psychology, self-help, and spiritual books that help enhance the quality of people's lives. Products include gift books, curriculum, workbooks, audio and video, computer-based products, and wellness products. "We specialize in books on addiction/recovery, spirituality/personal growth, and prevention topics related to chemical and mental health."

Nonfiction How-to, multimedia, self-help. Subjects include child guidance/parenting, memoirs, psychology, sex (sexual addiction), spirituality, addiction/recovery, eating disorders, codependency/family issues. Query with SASE.

Recent Title(s) *52 Weeks of Conscious Contact*, by Melody Beattie; *Raising Depression-Free Children*, by Kathleen Panula Hockey.

Tips Audience includes "consumers and professionals interested in the range of topics related to chemical and emotional health, including spirituality, self-help, and addiction recovery."

HEALTH COMMUNICATIONS, INC.

3201 SW 15th St., Deerfield Beach FL 33442. (954)360-0909. Fax: (954)360-0034. Website: www.hcibooks.com. **Acquisitions:** Bret Witter, editorial director; Allison Janse, executive editor; Susan Heim, religion editor; Elisabeth Rinaldi, editor. Estab. 1976. Publishes hardcover and trade paperback nonfiction only. **Publishes 50 titles/ year.** Responds in 3 months to queries; 3 months to proposals. Ms guidelines online.

○┓ "We are the Life Issues Publisher. Health Communications, Inc., strives to help people grow and improve their lives, from physical and emotional health to finances and interpersonal relationships."
Nonfiction Self-help. Subjects include child guidance/parenting, health/medicine, psychology, women's issues/studies.
Recent Title(s) *How to Be Like Women of Influence*, by Pat Williams; *A Teen's Guide to Christian Living*, by Bettie Youngs; *How Not to Be My Patient*, by Edward T. Creagan, M.D.

HEALTH PRESS

P.O. Box 37470, Albuquerque NM 87176. (505)888-1394. Fax: (505)888-1521. E-mail: goodbooks@healthpress.com. Website: www.healthpress.com. **Acquisitions:** K. Frazer, editor. Estab. 1988. Publishes hardcover and trade paperback originals. **Publishes 8 titles/year. 90% of books from first-time authors; 90% from unagented writers. Pays standard royalty on wholesale price.** Publishes book 1 year after acceptance of ms. Accepts simultaneous submissions. Responds in 3 months to proposals. Book catalog free; ms guidelines online.
○┓ Health Press publishes books by healthcare professionals on cutting-edge patient education topics.
Nonfiction How-to, reference, self-help, textbook. Subjects include education, health/medicine. Submit proposal package including outline, 3 complete sample chapter(s), résumé. Reviews artwork/photos as part of ms package. Send photocopies.
Recent Title(s) *Keeping a Secret: A Story about Juvenile Rheumatoid Arthritis*; *Peanut Butter Jam: A Story about Peanut Allergy*; *Health and Nutrition Secrets*.

HEALTH PROFESSIONS PRESS

P.O. Box 10624, Baltimore MD 21285-0624. (410)337-9585. Fax: (410)337-8539. E-mail: acquis@healthpropress.com. Website: www.healthpropress.com. **Acquisitions:** Mary Magnus, director of publications (aging, long-term care, health administration). Publishes hardcover and trade paperback originals. **Publishes 6-8 titles/year. Receives 70 queries and 12 mss/year. 50% of books from first-time authors; 100% from unagented writers. Pays 8-18% royalty on wholesale price.** Publishes book 10 months after acceptance of ms. Accepts simultaneous submissions. Responds in 1 month to queries; 3 months to proposals; 4 months to mss. Book catalog free or online; ms guidelines online.
○┓ "We are a specialty publisher. Our primary audiences are professionals, students, and educated consumers interested in topics related to aging and eldercare."
Nonfiction How-to, reference, self-help, textbook. Subjects include health/medicine, psychology. Query with SASE, or submit proposal package including outline, 1-2 sample chapter(s), résumé, cover letter.
Recent Title(s) *Transitions in Dying and Bereavement: A Psychological Guide to Hospice and Palliative Care*, by Victoria Hospice Society, et al; *The Past in the Present: Using Reminiscence in Health and Social Care*, by Gibson; *Navigating the Alzheimer's Journey: A Compass for Caregiving*.

WILLIAM S. HEIN & CO., INC.

1285 Main St., Buffalo NY 14209-1987. (716)882-2600. Fax: (716)883-8100. E-mail: mail@wshein.com. Website: www.wshein.com. **Acquisitions:** Sheila Jarrett, publications manager. Estab. 1961. **Publishes 50 titles/year. Receives 80 queries and 40 mss/year. 20% of books from first-time authors; 100% from unagented writers. Pays 10-20% royalty on net price.** Publishes book 9 months after acceptance of ms. Accepts simultaneous submissions. Responds in 2 months to queries. Book catalog online; ms guidelines for #10 SASE.
○┓ William S. Hein & Co. publishes reference books for law librarians, legal researchers, and those interested in legal writing. Currently emphasizing legal research, legal writing, and legal education.
Nonfiction Law, reference, scholarly. Subjects include education, government/politics, women's issues/studies, world affairs, legislative histories.
Recent Title(s) *1000 Days to the Bar*, by Dennis J. Tonsing; *Librarian's Copyright Companion*, by James S. Heller.

Ⓝ HEINEMANN

Reed Elsevier (USA) Inc., 361 Hanover St., Portsmouth NH 03801-3912. (603)431-7894. Fax: (603)431-7840. E-mail: proposals@heinemann.com. Website: www.heinemann.com. **Acquisitions:** Leigh Peake, editorial director (education); Lisa Barnett, senior editor (performing arts); William Varner, acquisitions editor (literacy); Lisa Luedeke, acquisitions editor (Boynton/Cook). Estab. 1977. Publishes hardcover and trade paperback originals. **Publishes 80-100 titles/year. 50% of books from first-time authors; 75% from unagented writers. Pays royalty on wholesale price. Offers variable advance.** Does not accept simultaneous submissions. Responds in 6-8 weeks to proposals. Book catalog free; ms guidelines online.
Imprints Boynton/Cook Publishers.
○┓ Heinemann specializes in theater and education titles. "Our goal is to offer a wide selecton of books that satisfy the needs and interests of educators from kindergarten to college." Currently emphasizing literacy education, social studies, mathematics, science, K-12 education through technology.

Nonfiction How-to, reference. Subjects include child guidance/parenting, education, film/cinema/stage, gay/lesbian, language/literature, women's issues/studies. "Our goal is to provide books that represent leading ideas within our niche markets. We publish very strictly within our categories. We do not publish classroom textbooks." Query with SASE, or submit proposal package including outline, 1-2 sample chapter(s), table of contents.

Recent Title(s) *Word Matters*, by Irene Fountas and Gay-sa Pirrell.

Tips "Keep your queries (and manuscripts!) short, study the market, be realistic and prepared to promote your book."

HELLGATE PRESS

Division of PSI Research, P.O. Box 3727, Central Point OR 97502-0032. (541)245-6502. Fax: (541)245-6505. Website: www.hellgatepress.com. **Acquisitions:** Emmett Ramey, president. Estab. 1996. **Publishes 20-25 titles/year. Pays royalty.** Publishes book 6 months after acceptance of ms. Responds in 2 months to queries. Book catalog for catalog envelope with SASE; ms guidelines online.

○┐ Hellgate Press specializes in military history, other military topics, and travel.

Nonfiction Subjects include history, memoirs, military/war, travel. Query with SASE, or submit outline, sample chapter(s). Reviews artwork/photos as part of ms package. Send photocopies.

Recent Title(s) *Code to Keep*, by Ernest Brace; *Where We Were in Vietnam*, by Michael P. Kelley; *Piloto: Migrant Worker to Jet Pilot*, by Lt. Col. Henry Cervantes, USAF (Ret).

Ⓝ Ø HELM PUBLISHING

3923 Seward Ave., Rockford IL 61108. (815)398-4660. E-mail: sales@publishersdrive.com. Submissions E-mail: dianne@publishersdrive.com. Website: www.publishersdrive.com. **Acquisitions:** Dianne Helm, CEO (fiction); Richard Oury, senior editor (nonfiction). Estab. 1997. Publishes trade paperback and mass market originals and reprints. **Publishes 10 titles/year. Receives 800 queries and 80 mss/year. 75% of books from first-time authors; 100% from unagented writers. Pays 40% royalty on wholesale price.** Publishes book 6 months after acceptance of ms. Accepts simultaneous submissions. Responds in 1 month to queries; 2 months to proposals; 4 months to mss. Book catalog and ms guidelines online.

Nonfiction Autobiography, biography, booklets, children's/juvenile, coffee table book, cookbook, humor. Subjects include agriculture/horticulture, Americana, contemporary culture, cooking/foods/nutrition, creative nonfiction, education, gardening, gay/lesbian, general nonfiction, government/politics, history, humanities, memoirs, military/war, nature/environment, New Age, philosophy, psychology, regional, science, spirituality, sports, travel, women's issues/studies. Accepts phone calls, query first about subject area. Query with SASE, or submit proposal package including outline, 3 sample chapter(s), author bio, writer experience, market plans, background experience on subject area. **All unsolicited mss returned unopened.** Reviews artwork/photos as part of ms package. Send photocopies or e-mail JPEGs, no originals.

Fiction Adventure, comic books, fantasy, gay/lesbian, gothic, hi-lo, historical, horror, humor, juvenile, literary, mainstream/contemporary, military/war, mystery, plays, poetry, regional, science fiction, short story collections, spiritual, suspense, young adult. Accepts phone calls. Query first about subject area. Query with SASE, or submit proposal package including 3 sample chapter(s), synopsis, author bio, background writer experience, including association and group affiliations, and marketing plans. **All unsolicited mss returned unopened.**

Poetry List previous poems published and publications. Query, or submit 5-10 sample poems.

Recent Title(s) *Stick Your Head Under the Water*, by Bruce Muench (nonfiction science); *Incident at Pittston Crossing*, by C. Burton Nelson (fiction Civil War); *Geography of My Bones*, by Olivia Diamond (poetry).

Tips "Readers of all ages and types of books make up audience. Follow the guidelines for submission, be patient, and write well."

HENDRICK-LONG PUBLISHING CO., INC.

10635 Toweroaks D., Houston TX 77070. (832)912-7323. Fax: (832)912-7353. E-mail: hendrick-long@worldnet.att.net. Website: hendricklongpublishing.com. **Acquisitions:** Vilma Long. Estab. 1969. Publishes hardcover and trade paperback originals and hardcover reprints. **Publishes 4 titles/year. Receives 500 submissions/year. 90% from unagented writers. Pays royalty. Pays royalty on selling price. Offers advance.** Publishes book 18 months after acceptance of ms. Does not accept simultaneous submissions. Responds in 1 month to queries, 2 months if more than 1 query is sent. Book catalog for 8½×11 or 9×12 SASE with 4 first-class stamps; ms guidelines online.

○┐ Hendrick-Long publishes historical fiction and nonfiction primarily about Texas and the Southwest for children and young adults.

Nonfiction Biography, children's/juvenile. Subjects include history, regional. Query, or submit outline and 2 sample chapters. Reviews artwork/photos as part of ms package. Send photocopies.

Fiction Juvenile, young adult. Query with SASE, or submit outline, 2 sample chapter(s), synopsis.
Recent Title(s) *Little Bit of Texas Part 1 and 2*; *The Official THEA Study Guide.*

Ⓝ HENDRICKSON PUBLISHERS, INC.

140 Summit St., P.O. Box 3473, Peabody MA 01961-3473. Fax: (978)531-8146. E-mail: dharrell@hendrickson.com. **Acquisitions:** Shirley Decker-Lucke, editorial director. Estab. 1983. Publishes trade reprints and scholarly material in the areas of New Testament; Hebrew Bible; religion and culture; patristics; Judaism; and practical, historical, and Biblical theology. **Publishes 35 titles/year. Receives 300 submissions/year. 10% of books from first-time authors; 90% from unagented writers.** Publishes book an average of 1 year after acceptance of ms. Does not accept simultaneous submissions. Responds in 2 months to queries. Book catalog and ms guidelines for #10 SASE.

○┐ Hendrickson is an academic publisher of books that "give insight into Bible understanding (academically) and encourage spiritual growth (popular trade)." Currently emphasizing Biblical helps and reference, ministerial helps, Biblical studies and de-emphasizing fiction and biography.

Nonfiction Reference. Subjects include religion. "We will consider any quality manuscript specifically related to Biblical studies and related fields." Submit outline, sample chapter(s), and CV.
Recent Title(s) *Encyclopedia of Contemporary Christian Music*, by Mark Allan Powell.

Ⓝ JOSEPH HENRY PRESS

National Academy Press, 500 5th St., NW, Lockbox 285, Washington DC 20001. (202)334-3336. Fax: (202)334-2793. E-mail: jrobbins@nas.edu. Website: www.jhpress.org. **Acquisitions:** Jeffrey Robbins, senior editor. Publishes hardcover and trade paperback originals. **Publishes 15-20 titles/year. Receives 200 queries and 60 mss/year. 40% of books from first-time authors; 80% from unagented writers. Pays 10% royalty on net receipts. Offers occasional, varying advance.** Publishes book 18 months after acceptance of ms. Accepts simultaneous submissions. Responds in 1 month to queries.

● Submit to: Jeffrey Robbins, senior editor, The Joseph Henry Press, 36 Dartmouth St. #810, Malden MA 02148. (781)324-4786. Fax: (781)397-8255.

○┐ "The Joseph Henry Press seeks manuscripts in general science and technology that will appeal to young scientists and established professionals or to interested lay readers within the overall categories of science, technology and health. We'll be looking at everything from astrophysics to the environment to nutrition."

Nonfiction Technical. Subjects include health/medicine, nature/environment, psychology, science, technology, nutrition. Submit proposal package including author bio, table of contents, prospectus, SASE.
Recent Title(s) *Einstein's Unfinished Symphony: Listening to the Sounds of Space-Time*, by Marcia Bartusiak; *Buzzwords: A Scientist Muses on Sex, Bugs and Rock 'n' Roll*, by May R. Berenbaum.

HENSLEY PUBLISHING

6116 E. 32nd St., Tulsa OK 74135-5494. (918)664-8520. E-mail: editorial@hensleypublishing.com. Website: www.hensleypublishing.com. **Acquisitions:** Acquisitions Department. Publishes trade paperback originals. **Publishes 5-10 titles/year. Receives 800 submissions/year. 50% of books from first-time authors; 50% from unagented writers.** Publishes book 18 months after acceptance of ms. Responds in 2 months to queries. Ms guidelines online.

○┐ Hensley Publishing publishes Bible studies and curriculum that offer the reader a wide range of topics. Currently emphasizing 192-page workbook studies.

Nonfiction Subjects include child guidance/parenting, money/finance, religion, women's issues/studies, marriage/family. "We do not want to see anything non-Christian." No New Age, poetry, plays, sermon collections. Query with synopsis and sample chapters.
Recent Title(s) *Seven Keys to Hearing God's Voice*, by Craig Von Buseck; *Five Steps to Financial Freedom*, by James Wise; *The Fear Factor*, by Dr. Wayne Mack and Joshua Mack.
Tips "Submit something that crosses denominational lines directed toward the large Christian market, not small specialized groups. We serve an interdenominational market—all Christian persuasions. Our goal is to get readers back into studying their Bible instead of studying about the Bible."

HERITAGE BOOKS, INC.

1540-C Pointer Ridge Place, Bowie MD 20716-1859. (301)390-7708. Fax: (301)390-7153. Submissions E-mail: submissions@heritagebooks.com. **Acquisitions:** Editorial Director. Estab. 1978. Publishes hardcover and paperback originals and reprints. **Publishes 200 titles/year. Receives 300 submissions/year. 25% of books from first-time authors; 100% from unagented writers. Pays 10% royalty on list price.** Accepts simultaneous submissions. Responds in 3 months to queries. Book catalog and ms guidelines free.

○┳ "Our goal is to celebrate life by exploring all aspects of American life: settlement, development, wars, and other significant events, including family histories, memoirs, etc." Currently emphasizing early American life, early wars and conflicts, ethnic studies.

Nonfiction Biography, how-to (genealogical, historical), reference, scholarly. Subjects include Americana, ethnic (origins and research guides), history, memoirs, military/war, regional (history). Query with SASE. Submit outline via e-mail. Reviews artwork/photos as part of ms package.

Fiction Historical (relating to early American life, 1600-1900). Query with SASE. Submit outline via e-mail.

Tips "The quality of the book is of prime importance; next is its relevance to our fields of interest."

HEYDAY BOOKS

Box 9145, Berkeley CA 94709-9145. Fax: (510)549-1889. E-mail: heyday@heydaybooks.com. Website: www.heydaybooks.com. **Acquisitions:** Jeannine Gendar, editorial director. Estab. 1974. Publishes hardcover originals, trade paperback originals and reprints. **Publishes 12-15 titles/year. Receives 200 submissions/year. 50% of books from first-time authors; 90% from unagented writers. Pays 8% royalty on net price.** Publishes book 10 months after acceptance of ms. Does not accept simultaneous submissions. Responds in 2 months to queries; 2 months to mss. Book catalog for 7×9 SAE with 3 first-class stamps.

○┳ Heyday Books publishes nonfiction books and literary anthologies with a strong California focus. "We publish books about Native Americans, natural history, history, literature, and recreation, with a strong California focus."

Nonfiction Books about California only. Subjects include Americana, ethnic, history, nature/environment, recreation, regional, travel. Query with outline and synopsis. Reviews artwork/photos as part of ms package.

Recent Title(s) *Dark God of Eros: A William Everson Reader*, edited by Albert Gelpi; *The High Sierra of California*, by Gary Snyder and Tom Killion; *Under the Fifth Sun: Latino Literature from California*, edited by Rick Heidre.

HIDDENSPRING

997 Macarthur Blvd., Mahwah NJ 07430. (201)825-7300. Fax: (201)825-8345. Website: www.hiddenspringbooks.com. **Acquisitions:** Paul McMahon, managing editor (nonfiction/spirituality). Publishes hardcover and trade paperback originals and reprints. **Publishes 10-12 titles/year. 5% of books from first-time authors; 10% from unagented writers. Royalty varies. Offers variable advance.** Accepts simultaneous submissions. Responds in 1 month to queries.

○┳ "Books should always have a spiritual angle—nonfiction with a spiritual twist."

Nonfiction Biography, self-help. Subjects include Americana, anthropology/archeology, art/architecture, creative nonfiction, ethnic, gardening, history, multicultural, music/dance, psychology, religion, travel. Submit proposal package including outline, 1 sample chapter(s), SASE.

Recent Title(s) *The Spiritual Traveler: Boston and New England*, by Jana Riess; *Christian Mystics*, by Ursula King; *Tolkien and C.S. Lewis*, by Colin Durie.

HIGH PLAINS PRESS

P.O. Box 123, 539 Cassa Rd., Glendo WY 82213. (307)735-4370. Fax: (307)735-4590. E-mail: editor@highplainspress.com. Website: www.highplainspress.com. **Acquisitions:** Nancy Curtis, publisher. Estab. 1986. Publishes hardcover and trade paperback originals. **Publishes 4 titles/year. Receives 300 queries and 200 mss/year. 80% of books from first-time authors; 95% from unagented writers. Pays 10% royalty on wholesale price. Offers $200-800 advance.** Publishes book 2 years after acceptance of ms. Accepts simultaneous submissions. Responds in 1 month to queries; 3 months to proposals; 3 months to mss. Book catalog for 9×12 SASE; ms guidelines online.

○┳ "What we sell best is history of the Old West, particularly things relating to Wyoming. We also publish 1 book of poetry a year in our Poetry of the American West series."

Nonfiction "We focus on books of the American West, mainly history. We like books on the history and culture of Wyoming and the West." Biography. Subjects include Americana, art/architecture, history, nature/environment, regional. Submit outline, 3 sample chapter(s). Reviews artwork/photos as part of ms package. Send photocopies.

Poetry "We only seek poetry closely tied to the Rockies. Do not submit single poems." Query, or submit complete ms.

Recent Title(s) *Tom Horn: Blood on the Moon*, by Chip Carlson; *Coyotes & Canaries: Characters that Made the West Wild and Wonderful*, by Larry K. Brown; *Sheepwagon: Home on the Range*, by Nancy Weidel.

HIGH TIDE PRESS

3650 W. 183rd St., Homewood IL 60430-2603. (708)206-2054. Fax: (708)206-2044. E-mail: managing.editor@hightidepress.com. Website: www.hightidepress.com. **Acquisitions:** Monica Regan, managing editor. Publishes hardcover and trade paperback originals. **Publishes 8 titles/year. Receives 200 queries and 100 mss/year.**

50% of books from first-time authors; 80% from unagented writers. Offers $500-1,000 advance. Publishes book 1 year after acceptance of ms. Accepts simultaneous submissions. Responds in 1-6 months to queries; 1-6 months to proposals; 1-6 months to mss. Book catalog free or on website.

Nonfiction Subjects include psychology, nonprofit management, mental illness, and developmental disabilities. Reviews artwork/photos as part of ms package.

Recent Title(s) *Lessons in Grief & Death: Supporting People with Developmental Disabilities in the Healing Process*, by Linda Van Dyke; *Cold Cash for Warm Hearts: 101 Best Moneymaking Ideas for Nonprofit Organizations*, by Richard Steckel, et al.

Tips "Our audience consists of professionals in these fields: mental health/psychology, disabilities, business, marketing, nonprofit leadership, and management. You should send us a 1-page query with SASE, giving a brief overview of the book, its market, and your background. If we are interested, we will request a book proposal. The book proposal outlines the nature of your work, who your market is, and information about your background. Please do not send a complete manuscript unless we request one."

HILL AND WANG

Farrar Straus & Giroux, Inc., 19 Union Square W., New York NY 10003. (212)741-6900. Fax: (212)633-9385. Website: www.fsgbooks.com. **Acquisitions:** Elisabeth Sifton, publisher; Thomas LeBien, editor. Estab. 1956. Publishes hardcover and trade paperbacks. **Publishes 12 titles/year. Receives 1,500 queries/year. 50% of books from first-time authors; 50% from unagented writers. Pays 10% royalty on retail price to 5,000 copies sold, 12½% to 10,000 copies, 15% thereafter on hardcover; 7½% on retail price for paperback.** Publishes book 1 year after acceptance of ms. Accepts simultaneous submissions. Book catalog free.

○━ Hill and Wang publishes serious nonfiction books, primarily in history and the social sciences.

Nonfiction Subjects include government/politics, history (American), women's issues/studies. Submit outline, sample chapter(s). SASE and a letter explaining rationale for book.

Fiction Not considering new fiction, drama or poetry.

Recent Title(s) *Pox Americana: The Great Smallpox Epidemic of 1775-82*, by Elizabeth A. Fenn; *1831: Year of Eclipse*, by Louis P. Masur.

HILL STREET PRESS

191 E. Broad St., Suite 209, Athens GA 30601-2848. (706)613-7200. Fax: (706)613-7204. E-mail: editorial@hillstreetpress.com. Website: www.hillstreetpress.com. **Acquisitions:** Judy Long, editor-in-chief. Estab. 1998. Publishes hardcover originals, trade paperback originals and reprints. **Publishes 20 titles/year. Receives 300 queries/year. 5% of books from first-time authors; 2% from unagented writers. Pays 9-12½% royalty on wholesale price.** Publishes book 1 year after acceptance of ms. Accepts simultaneous submissions. Responds in 1 month to queries; 3 months to proposals; 6 months to mss. Book catalog and ms guidelines online.

○━ "HSP is a Southern regional press. While we are not a scholarly or academic press, our nonfiction titles must meet the standards of research for an exacting general audience."

Nonfiction Biography, coffee table book, cookbook, gift book, humor, illustrated book. Subjects include Americana, cooking/foods/nutrition, creative nonfiction, gardening, gay/lesbian, history, memoirs, nature/environment, recreation, regional (Southern), sports, travel. Submit proposal package including outline, 3 sample chapter(s), résumé.

Fiction Must have a strong connection with the American South. Gay/lesbian, historical, humor, literary, mainstream/contemporary, military/war, regional (southern US), religious, sports, African-American. "Reasonable length projects (50,000-85,000 words) stand a far better chance of review. Do not submit proposals for works in excess of 125,000 words in length." No short stories. "No cornball moonlight-and-magnolia stuff." Query with SASE, or submit proposal package including 3 sample chapter(s), résumé, synopsis, press clips. "Let us know at the point of submission if you are represented by an agent."

Recent Title(s) *Strange Birds in the Tree of Heaven*, by Karen Salyer McElmurray (literary fiction); *The Worst Day of My Life, So Far*, by M.A. Harper (literary fiction); *How I Learned to Snap* (memoir).

Tips "Audience is discerning with an interest in the fiction, history, current issues, and food of the American South"

HIPPOCRENE BOOKS, INC.

171 Madison Ave., New York NY 10016. (212)685-4371. Fax: (212)779-9338. E-mail: hippocrene.books@verizon.net. Website: www.hippocrenebooks.com. President/Publisher: George Blagowidow. **Acquisitions:** Anne E. McBride, editor-in-chief (food and wine, nonfiction reference); Nicholas Williams, editor (foreign language, dictionaries, language guides); Anne Kemper, editor (history). Estab. 1971. Publishes hardcover and trade paperback originals. **Publishes 60-80 titles/year. Receives 400 submissions/year. 10% of books from first-time authors; 95% from unagented writers. Pays 6-10% royalty on retail price. Offers $2,000 advance.**

Publishes book 16 months after acceptance of ms. Accepts simultaneous submissions. Responds in 2 months to queries. Book catalog for 9 x12 SAE with 5 first-class stamps; ms guidelines for #10 SASE.

    ○→ "We focus on ethnic-interest and language-related titles, particularly on lesser published and often overlooked ones." Currently emphasizing concise foreign language dictionaries. De-emphasizing military history.

Nonfiction Biography, cookbook, reference. Subjects include cooking/foods/nutrition, ethnic, history, language/literature, military/war, multicultural, travel. Submit proposal package including outline, 2 sample chapter(s), table of contents.

Recent Title(s) *Yoruba Practical Dictionary*; *A History of the Islamic World*; *Secrets of Colombian Cooking*.

Tips "Our recent successes in publishing general books considered midlist by larger publishers is making us more of a general trade publisher. We continue to do well with reference books like dictionaries, atlases, and language studies. We ask for proposal, sample chapter, and table of contents. We then ask for material if we are interested."

HOBBY HOUSE PRESS

1 Corporate Dr., Grantsville MD 21536. (301)895-3792. Fax: (301)895-5029. Website: www.hobbyhouse.com. Publishes hardcover and trade paperback originals. **Publishes 20 titles/year. Receives 50 queries and 25 mss/ year. 85% of books from first-time authors; 95% from unagented writers. Pays 10% royalty on net receipts.** Publishes book 6 months after acceptance of ms. Accepts simultaneous submissions. Responds in 2 weeks to queries; 1 month to proposals. Book catalog and ms guidelines free.

Nonfiction Gift book, how-to, reference, price guides. Subjects include gardening, hobbies (collecting/antiques). Query with SASE, or submit outline, 1 sample chapter(s), photos. Reviews artwork/photos as part of ms package. Send prints.

Recent Title(s) *A Century of Crayola Collectibles*; *Comic Book Survival and Price Guide*; *Teddy Bear Artist Pattern Book*.

N: HOHM PRESS

P.O. Box 31, Prescott AZ 86302. (800)381-2700. Fax: (928)717-1779. Website: www.hohmpress.com. **Acquisitions:** Regina Sara Ryan, managing editor. Estab. 1975. Publishes hardcover and trade paperback originals. **Publishes 6-8 titles/year. 50% of books from first-time authors. Pays 10% royalty on net sales.** Publishes book 18 months after acceptance of ms. Accepts simultaneous submissions. Responds in 3 months to queries.

    ○→ Hohm Press publishes a range of titles in the areas of transpersonal psychology and spirituality, herbistry, alternative health methods, and nutrition. Currently emphasizing health alternatives. Not interested in personal health survival stories.

Nonfiction Subjects include health/medicine (natural/alternative health), philosophy, religion (Hindu, Buddhist, Sufi, or translations of classic texts in major religious traditions), yoga. "We look for writers who have an established record in their field of expertise. The best buy of recent years came from 2 women who fully substantiated how they could market their book. We believed they could do it. We were right." Query with SASE. No e-mail inquiries, please.

Poetry "We are not accepting poetry at this time except for translations of recognized religious/spiritual classics."

HOLIDAY HOUSE, INC.

425 Madison Ave., New York NY 10017. (212)688-0085. Fax: (212)421-6134. Editor-in-Chief: Regina Griffin. Estab. 1935. Publishes hardcover originals and paperback reprints. **Publishes 60 titles/year. Receives 8,000 submissions/year. 2-5% of books from first-time authors; 50% from unagented writers. Pays royalty on list price, range varies. Offers Flexible, depending on whether the book is illustrated. advance.** Publishes book 1-2 years after acceptance of ms. Does not accept simultaneous submissions. Ms guidelines for #10 SASE.

    ○→ Holiday House publishes children's and young adult books for the school and library markets. "We have a commitment to publishing first-time authors and illustrators. We specialize in quality hardcovers from picture books to young adult, both fiction and nonfiction, primarily for the school and library market." Currently emphasizing literary middle-grade novels.

Nonfiction Subjects include Americana, history, science, Judaica. Query with SASE. Reviews artwork/photos as part of ms package. Send photocopies—no originals—to Claire Counihan, art director.

Fiction Adventure, historical, humor, literary, mainstream/contemporary, Judaica and holiday, animal stories for young readers. Children's books only. Query with SASE. "No phone calls, please."

Recent Title(s) *In Defense of Liberty: The Story of America's Bill of Rights*, by Russell Freedman; *Blues Journey*, by Walter Dean Myers, illustrated by Christopher Myers.

Tips "We need novels with strong stories and writing. We do not publish board books or novelties."

Ⓝ HOLLOWAY HOUSE PUBLISHING CO.

8060 Melrose Ave., Los Angeles CA 90046. (323)653-8060. Fax: (323)655-9452. Estab. 1960. Publishes paperback originals. Publishes book 6-12 months after acceptance of ms. Does not accept simultaneous submissions.
Fiction Comic books, erotica, ethnic, multicultural, African-American, nonfiction. Query with SASE.

HOLMES & MEIER PUBLISHERS, INC.

East Building, 160 Broadway, New York NY 10038. (212)374-0100. Fax: (212)374-1313. E-mail: info@holmesan dmeier.com. Website: www.holmesandmeier.com. Publisher: Miriam H. Holmes. **Acquisitions:** Maggie Kennedy, managing editor. Estab. 1969. Publishes hardcover and paperback originals. **Publishes 20 titles/year. Pays royalty.** Publishes book an average of 18 months after acceptance of ms. Does not accept simultaneous submissions. Responds in 6 months to queries. Book catalog free.
Imprints Africana Publishing Co.

　　○➛ "We are noted as an academic publishing house and are pleased with our reputation for excellence in the field. However, we are also expanding our list to include books of more general interest."
Nonfiction Biography, reference. Subjects include art/architecture, business/economics, ethnic, government/ politics, history, regional, translation, women's issues/studies. Query first with outline, sample chapters, cv and idea of intended market/audience.

HENRY HOLT & CO. BOOKS FOR YOUNG READERS

Imprint of Henry Holt & Co., LLC, 115 W. 18th St., New York NY 10011. (212)886-9200. Website: www.henryhol t.com. Associate Publisher and Editorial Director: Laura Godwin. Executive Editor: Christy Ottaviano. Editor-at-Large: Nina Ignatowicz. Editor: Reka Simonsen. Associate Editor: Adriane Fry. Editor: Kate Farrell. **Acquisitions:** Submissions Editor. Estab. 1866 (Holt). Publishes hardcover originals of picture books, chapter books, middle grade and young adult novels. **Publishes 70-80 titles/year. 10% of books from first-time authors; 50% from unagented writers. Pays royalty on retail price. Offers $3,000 and up advance.** Publishes book 18-36 months after acceptance of ms. Does not accept simultaneous submissions. Responds in 3-4 months to queries. Book catalog for $8\frac{1}{2} \times 11$ SAE with $1.75 postage; ms guidelines online.

　　○➛ "Henry Holt Books for Young Readers publishes highly original and cutting-edge fiction and nonfiction for all ages, from the very young to the young adult."
Nonfiction Children's/juvenile, illustrated book. Submit complete ms.
Holtzbrinck Publishers, **Fiction** Adventure, fantasy, historical, mainstream/contemporary, multicultural, picture books, young adult. Juvenile: adventure, animal, contemporary, fantasy, history, multicultural. Picture books: animal, concept, history, mulitcultural, sports. Young adult: contemporary, fantasy, history, multicultural, nature/environment, problem novels, sports. Submit complete ms.
Recent Title(s) *Hondo and Fabian*, by Peter McCarty; *Keeper of the Night*, by Kimberly Willis Holt.

Ⓞ HENRY HOLT & CO. LLC

Holtzbrinck Publishers, 115 W. 18th St., New York NY 10011. (212)886-9200. Fax: (212)633-0748. Website: www.henryholt.com. President and Publisher: John Sterling. **Acquisitions:** Jennifer Barth, editor-in-chief (adult literary fiction, narrative nonfiction); Sara Bershtel, associate publisher of Metropolitan Books (literary fiction, politics, history); Vanessa Mobley, editor, adult trade; Paul Gozob, editorial director, Times Books (science, culture, history, health); Lisa Considine, senior editor, adult trade (lifestyle, health, self-help, parenting); Laura Godwin, associate publisher, Books for Young Readers (picture books, young adult novels). Estab. 1866. Does not accept simultaneous submissions.
Imprints Books for Young Readers, John Macrae Books, Metropolitan Books, Owl Books, Red Feather Books, Times Books.

　　● Does not accept unsolicited queries or mss.
　　○➛ Holt is a general-interest publisher of quality fiction and nonfiction. Currently emphasizing narrative nonfiction. De-emphasizing cooking, gardening.
Recent Title(s) *An Army at Dawn*, by Rick Atkinson; *Blue Latitudes*, by Tony Horwitz; *Nickel and Dimed*, by Barbara Ehrenreich.

Ⓝ HOLY CROSS ORTHODOX PRESS

Hellenic College, 50 Goddard Ave., Brookline MA 02445. (617)850-1321. Fax: (617)850-1457. E-mail: press@hch c.edu. **Acquisitions:** Herald Gjura. Estab. 1974. Publishes trade paperback originals. **Publishes 8 titles/year; imprint publishes 2 titles/year. Receives 10-15 queries and 10-15 mss/year. 85% of books from first-time authors; 100% from unagented writers. Pays 8-12% royalty on retail price.** Publishes book 18 months after acceptance of ms. Accepts simultaneous submissions. Responds in 6 months to mss. Book catalog free.
Imprints Holy Cross Orthodox Press, Hellenic College Press.

O→ Holy Cross publishes titles that are rooted in the tradition of the Eastern Orthodox Church.

Nonfiction Academic. Subjects include ethnic, religion (Greek Orthodox). "Holy Cross Orthodox Press publishes scholarly and popular literature in the areas of Orthodox Christian theology and Greek letters. Submissions are often far too technical usually with a very limited audiences." Submit outline, or submit complete ms. Reviews artwork/photos as part of ms package. Send photocopies.

Recent Title(s) *Christianity: Lineaments of a Sacred Tradition*, by Philip Sherrard.

HOMA & SEKEY BOOKS

P.O. Box 103, Dumont NJ 07628. (201)384-6692. Fax: (201)384-6055. E-mail: info@homabooks.com. Submissions E-mail: submission@homabooks.com. Website: www.homabooks.com. **Acquisitions:** Shawn Ye, editor (fiction and nonfiction). Estab. 1997. Publishes hardcover originals and trade paperback originals and reprints. **Publishes 10 titles/year. Receives 300-500 queries and 100-200 mss/year. 50% of books from first-time authors; 90% from unagented writers. Pays 5-10% royalty on retail price.** Publishes book 1 year after acceptance of ms. Accepts simultaneous submissions. Responds in 2 months to queries; 3 months to proposals; 4 months to mss. Book catalog and ms guidelines online.

Nonfiction Autobiography, biography, coffee table book, illustrated book, reference, scholarly, textbook. Subjects include alternative lifestyles, art/architecture, business/economics, contemporary culture, creative nonfiction, ethnic, general nonfiction, health/medicine, history, language/literature, memoirs, multicultural, New Age, photography, social sciences, translation, travel, world affairs. "We publish books on Asian topics. Books should have something to do with Asia." Submit proposal package including outline, 2 sample chapter(s), or submit complete ms. Reviews artwork/photos as part of ms package. Send photocopies.

Fiction Adventure, ethnic, feminist, historical, literary, multicultural, mystery, plays, poetry, poetry in translation, romance, short story collections, young adult. "We publish books on Asian topics. Books should be Asia-related." Submit proposal package including 2 sample chapter(s), synopsis, or submit complete ms.

Poetry "We publish books on Asian topics. Poetry should have things to do with Asia." Submit complete ms.

Recent Title(s) *The Haier Way: The Making of a Chinese Business Leader and a Global Brand*, by Dr. Jeannie Yi; *Father and Son*, by Han Sung-won (novel); *Selected Short Stories*, by Korean women writers (Korean translation).

Tips General readership with a leaning on Asian cultures. "Authors should be willing to participate in publicity and promotion activities."

N A HONOR BOOKS

Cook Communications Ministries, 4050 Lee Vance View, Colorado Springs CO 80918. E-mail: info@honorbooks.com. Website: www.honorbooks.com. Publishes hardcover and trade paperback originals. **Publishes 60 titles/year. Pays royalty on wholesale price, makes outright purchase or assigns work for hire. Offers negotiable advance.** Publishes book 2 years after acceptance of ms.

- Proposals can be submitted using form on website.

O→ "We are a Christian publishing house with a mission to inspire and encourage people to draw near to God and to enjoy His love and grace. We are no longer accepting unsolicited mss from writers." Currently emphasizing humor, personal and spiritual growth, children's books, devotions, personal stories.

Nonfiction Subjects include religion, motivation, devotionals. Subjects are geared toward the "felt needs" of people. No autobiographies or teaching books.

Recent Title(s) *My Personal Promise Bibles*; *Quiet Moments with God*.

Tips "Our books are for busy, achievement-oriented people who are looking for a balance between reaching their goals and knowing that God loves them unconditionally. Our books encourage spiritual growth, joyful living and intimacy with God. Write about what you are for and not what you are against. We look for scripts that are biblically based and which inspire readers."

HOUGHTON MIFFLIN BOOKS FOR CHILDREN

Imprint of Houghton Mifflin Trade & Reference Division, 222 Berkeley St., Boston MA 02116. (617)351-5959. Fax: (617)351-1111. E-mail: children's_books@hmco.com. Website: www.houghtonmifflinbooks.com. **Acquisitions:** Hannah Rodgers, editorial associate; Ann Rider, Margaret Raymo, Eden Edwards, senior editors; Kate O'Sullivan, editor. Publishes hardcover originals and trade paperback originals and reprints. **Publishes 100 titles/year. Receives 5,000 queries and 14,000 mss/year. 10% of books from first-time authors; 60% from unagented writers. Pays 5-10% royalty on retail price. Offers variable advance.** Publishes book 18-24 months after acceptance of ms. Accepts simultaneous submissions. Responds in 4 months to queries. Book catalog for 9×12 SASE with 3 first-class stamps; ms guidelines online.

Imprints Sandpiper Paperback Books, Graphia (Eden Edwards, senior editor).

- Does not respond to mss unless interested.

O→ "Houghton Mifflin gives shape to ideas that educate, inform, and above all, delight."

Nonfiction Biography, children's/juvenile, humor, illustrated book. Subjects include animals, anthropology/

archeology, art/architecture, ethnic, history, language/literature, music/dance, nature/environment, science, sports. Interested in innovative books and subjects about which the author is passionate. Query with SASE, or submit sample chapter(s), synopsis. **Note:** Mss not returned without appropriate-sized SASE. Reviews artwork/photos as part of ms package. Send photocopies.

Fiction Adventure, ethnic, historical, humor, juvenile (early readers), literary, mystery, picture books, suspense, young adult, board books. Submit complete ms with appropriate-sized SASE.

Recent Title(s) *Henry Climbs a Mountain*, by D.B. Johnson; *Mosque*, by David Macaulay; *Ollie the Stomper*, by Olivier Dunrea.

Tips "Faxed or e-mailed manuscripts and proposals are not considered. Complete submission guidelines available on website."

Ⓐ HOUGHTON MIFFLIN CO.

222 Berkeley St., Boston MA 02116. Website: www.hmco.com. Executive Vice President: Theresa D. Kelly. Editor-in-Chief/Publisher, Adult Books: Janet Silver. **Acquisitions:** Submissions Editor. Estab. 1832. Publishes hardcover originals and trade paperback originals and reprints. **Publishes 250 titles/year; imprint publishes 25 titles/year. Receives 1,000 queries and 2,000 mss/year. 10% of books from first-time authors. Hardcover: pays 10-15% royalty on retail price, sliding scale or flat rate based on sales; paperback: 7½% flat rate, but negotiable. Offers variable advance.** Publishes book 3 years after acceptance of ms. Accepts simultaneous submissions. Book catalog online.

Imprints American Heritage Dictionaries; Clarion Books; Great Source; Houghton Mifflin; Houghton Mifflin Books for Children; Houghton Mifflin Paperbacks; Mariner Books; McDougal Littell; Peterson Field Guides; Riverside Publishing Company; Sunburst Technology; Taylor's Gardening Guides.

> ⦿ "Houghton Mifflin gives shape to ideas that educate, inform and delight. In a new era of publishing, our legacy of quality thrives as we combine imagination with technology, bringing you new ways to know."

Nonfiction Audiocassettes, autobiography, biography, children's/juvenile, cookbook, gift book, how-to, illustrated book, reference, self-help. Subjects include agriculture/horticulture, animals, anthropology/archeology, cooking/foods/nutrition, ethnic, gardening, gay/lesbian, general nonfiction, health/medicine, history, memoirs, military/war, social sciences. "We are not a mass market publisher. Our main focus is serious nonfiction. We do practical self-help but not pop psychology self-help." *Agented submissions only.*

Fiction Literary. "We are not a mass market publisher. Study the current list." *Agented submissions only.*

Recent Title(s) *Fast Food Nation*, by Eric Schlosser (nonfiction); *Why I Am Catholic*, by Garry Wills (nonfiction); *The Best American Short Stories*.

Tips "Our audience is high end literary."

HOUSE OF COLLECTIBLES

Imprint of Random House, Inc., 1745 Broadway, 15th Floor, New York NY 10019. Website: www.houseofcollectibles.com. **Acquisitions:** Dorothy Harris, director. Publishes trade and mass market paperback originals. **Publishes 30-35 titles/year. Receives 200 queries/year. 7% of books from first-time authors; 75% from unagented writers. Royalty on retail price varies. Offers varied advance.** Does not accept simultaneous submissions. Book catalog free.

Imprints Official Price Guide series.

> ⦿ "One of the premier publishing companies devoted to books on a wide range of antiques and collectibles, House of Collectibles publishes books for the seasoned expert and the beginning collector alike."

Nonfiction How-to (related to collecting antiques and coins), reference. Subjects include art/architecture (fine art), sports, comic books, American patriotic memorabilia, clocks, character toys, coins, stamps, costume jewelry, knives, books, military, glassware, records, arts and crafts, Native American collectibles, pottery, fleamarkets. Accepts unsolicited proposals.

Recent Title(s) *The Official Price Guide to Records*, by Jerry Osborne; *The One-Minute Coin Expert*, by John Travers; *Instant Expert: Collection Watches*, by Cooksey Schugart.

Tips "We have been publishing price guides and other books on antiques and collectibles for over 35 years and plan to meet the needs of collectors, dealers, and appraisers well into the 21st century."

HOWELL PRESS, INC.

1713-2D Allied Lane, Charlottesville VA 22903. (434)977-4006. Fax: (434)971-7204. E-mail: rhowell@howellpress.com. Website: www.howellpress.com. **Acquisitions:** Ross A. Howell, president; Dara Parker, editor. Estab. 1985. **Publishes 8-10 titles/year. Receives 500 submissions/year. 10% of books from first-time authors; 80% from unagented writers. Pays 5-10% royalty. Offers advance.** Publishes book 18 months after acceptance of ms. Book catalog for 9×12 SAE with 4 first-class stamps; ms guidelines online.

o— "While our aviation, history, and transportation titles are produced for the enthusiast market, writing must be accessible to the general adult reader." Currently emphasizing regional (Mid-Atlantic and Southeast), travel, ghost stories, wine and wine making, gift books, quilts and quilt history.

Nonfiction Illustrated book. Subjects include history, regional, aviation, transportation, gourmet, quilts. "Generally open to most ideas, as long as writing is accessible to average adult reader. Our line is targeted, so it would be advisable to look over our catalog before querying to better understand what Howell Press does." Query with SASE, or submit outline, sample chapter(s). Does not return mss without SASE. Reviews artwork/photos as part of ms package.

Recent Title(s) *Old Virginia: The Pursuit of a Pastoral Ideal*, by William Rasmussen and Robert Tilton; *Cooking in the Nude: For Barbecue Buffs*, by Debbie and Stephen Cornwell.

Tips "Focus of our program has been illustrated books, but we will also consider nonfiction manuscripts that would not be illustrated."

HOWELLS HOUSE

P.O. Box 9546, Washington DC 20016-9546. (202)333-2182. **Acquisitions:** W.D. Howells, publisher. Estab. 1988. Publishes hardcover and trade paperback originals and reprints. **Publishes 4 titles/year; imprint publishes 2-3 titles/year. Receives 2,000 queries and 300 mss/year. 50% of books from first-time authors; 60% from unagented writers. Pays 15% net royalty or makes outright purchase. May offer advance.** Publishes book 8 months after acceptance of ms. Does not accept simultaneous submissions. Responds in 2 months to proposals.

Imprints The Compass Press, Whalesback Books.

o— "Our interests are institutions and institutional change."

Nonfiction Biography, illustrated book, textbook. Subjects include Americana, anthropology/archeology, art/architecture, business/economics, education, government/politics, history, photography, science, sociology, translation, women's issues/studies. Query.

Fiction Historical, literary, mainstream/contemporary. Query.

N HQN BOOKS

Imprint of Harlequin, 233 Broadway, 10th Floor, New York NY 10279. **Acquisitions:** Tracy Farrell, executive editor. Publishes hardcover, trade paperback, and mass market paperback originals. **Pays royalty. Offers advance.**

Fiction Romance (contemporary and historical). Accepts unagented material. Does not accept e-mail queries.

HUDSON HILLS PRESS, INC.

74-2 Union St., Box 205, Manchester VT 05254. (802)362-6450. Fax: (802)362-6459. E-mail: sbutterfield@hudsonhills.com. Website: www.hudsonhills.com. **Acquisitions:** Sarah Butterfield, assistant to publisher. Estab. 1978. Publishes hardcover and paperback originals. **Publishes 15+ titles/year. Receives 50-100 submissions/year. 15% of books from first-time authors; 90% from unagented writers. Pays 4-6% royalty on retail price. Offers $3,500 average advance.** Publishes book 1 year after acceptance of ms. Accepts simultaneous submissions. Responds in 2 months to queries. Book catalog for 6×9 SAE with 2 first-class stamps.

o— Hudson Hills Press publishes books about art and photography, including monographs.

Nonfiction Subjects include art/architecture, photography. Query first, then submit outline and sample chapters. Reviews artwork/photos as part of ms package.

Recent Title(s) *Natural Seduction*, by Michele Oka Doner.

HUMAN KINETICS PUBLISHERS, INC.

P.O. Box 5076, Champaign IL 61825-5076. (800)747-4457. Fax: (217)351-1549. E-mail: webmaster@hkusa.com. Website: www.humankinetics.com. CEO: Brian Holding. President: Rainer Martens. **Acquisitions:** Ted Miller, vice president and director (trade); Martin Barnard, trade senior acquisitions editor (fitness, running, golf, tennis); Ed McNeely, trade acquisitions editor (strength training, cycling, martial arts, minor spa); Scott Wikgren, HPERD director (health, physical education, recreation, dance); Bonnie Pettifor, acquisitions editor, HPERD; Gayle Kassing, acquisitions editor, HPERD; Mike Bahrke, STM acquisitions editor (scientific, technical, medical); Loarn Robertson, STM acquisitions editor (biomechanics, anatomy, athletic training, cardiac rehab, test/measurement); Judy Wright, HPERD acquisitions editor (dance, motor, learning/behavior/performance/development, gymnastics, adapted physical education, older adults); Amy Clocksin, acquisitions editor. Estab. 1974. Publishes hardcover and paperback text and reference books, trade paperback originals, software and audiovisual. **Publishes 120 titles/year. Receives 300 submissions/year. 30% of books from first-time authors; 90% from unagented writers. Pays 10-15% royalty on net income.** Publishes book up to 18 months after acceptance of ms. Accepts simultaneous submissions. Responds in 2 months to queries. Book catalog free; ms guidelines online.

Book Publishers

Imprints HK.

O→ Human Kinetics publishes books which provide expert knowledge in sport and fitness training and techniques, physical education, sports sciences and sports medicine for coaches, athletes and fitness enthusiasts and professionals in the physical action field.

Nonfiction How-to, multimedia, reference, self-help, technical, textbook. Subjects include education, health/medicine, psychology, recreation, sports (sciences). Submit outline, sample chapter(s). Reviews artwork/photos as part of ms package.

Recent Title(s) *Fitness and Health*, by Brian J. Sharkey; *Artistry on Ice*, by Nancy Kerrigan.

HUNTER HOUSE

P.O. Box 2914, Alameda CA 94501. (510)865-5282. Fax: (510)865-4295. E-mail: acquisitions@hunterhouse.com. Website: www.hunterhouse.com. **Acquisitions:** Jeanne Brondino, acquisitions editor; Kiran S. Rana, publisher. Estab. 1978. Publishes hardcover and trade paperback originals and reprints. **Publishes 24 titles/year. Receives 200-300 queries and 100 mss/year. 50% of books from first-time authors; 80% from unagented writers. Pays 12% royalty on net receipts, defined as selling price. Offers $500-3,000 advance.** Publishes book 1-2 years after acceptance of ms. Accepts simultaneous submissions. Responds in 2 months to queries; 3 months to proposals; 6 months to mss. Book catalog for 8 æ × 11 SAE with 3 first-class stamps; ms guidelines online.

O→ Hunter House publishes health books (especially women's health), self-help health, sexuality and couple relationships, violence prevention and intervention. De-emphasizing reference, self-help psychology.

Nonfiction Subjects include alternative lifestyles, health/medicine, self-help, women's health, fitness, relationships, sexuality, personal growth, and violence prevention. "Health books (especially women's health) should focus on emerging health issues or current issues that are inadequately covered and be written for the general population. Family books: Our current focus is sexuality and couple relationships, and alternative lifestyles to high stress. Community topics include violence prevention/violence intervention. We also publish specialized curricula for counselors and educators in the areas of violence prevention and trauma in children." Query with proposal package, including synopsis, TOC, and chapter outline, sample chapter, target audience information, competition, and what distinguishes the book. Reviews artwork/photos as part of ms package. Send photocopies, proposals generally not returned, requested mss returned with SASE. Reviews artwork/photos as part of ms package.

Recent Title(s) *The Complete Guide to Joseph H. Pilates' Techniques of Physical Conditioning*, by Allan Menezes; *Pocket Book of Foreplay*, Richard Craze; *Living Beyond Multiple Sclerosis—A Women's Guide*, by Judith Lynn Nichols.

Tips Audience is concerned people who are looking to educate themselves and their community about real-life issues that affect them. "Please send as much information as possible about who your audience is, how your book addresses their needs, and how you reach that audience in your ongoing work."

HUNTER PUBLISHING, INC.

130 Campus Dr., Edison NJ 08818. Fax: (772)546-8040. E-mail: hunterp@bellsouth.net. Website: www.hunterpublishing.com. President: Michael Hunter. **Acquisitions:** Kim Andre, editor; Lissa Dailey. Estab. 1985. **Publishes 100 titles/year. Receives 300 submissions/year. 10% of books from first-time authors; 75% from unagented writers. Pays royalty. Offers negotiable advance.** Publishes book 5 months after acceptance of ms. Accepts simultaneous submissions. Responds in 3 weeks to queries; 1 month to mss. Book catalog for #10 SAE with 4 first-class stamps.

Imprints Adventure Guides, Romantic Weekends Guides, Alive Guides.

O→ Hunter Publishing publishes practical guides for travelers going to the Caribbean, U.S., Europe, South America, and the far reaches of the globe.

Nonfiction Reference. Subjects include regional, travel (travel guides). "We need travel guides to areas covered by few competitors: Caribbean Islands, South and Central America, Europe, Australia, New Zealand from an active 'adventure' perspective." No personal travel stories or books not directed to travelers. Query, or submit outline/synopsis and sample chapters. Reviews artwork/photos as part of ms package.

Recent Title(s) *Adventure Guide to Canada's Atlantic Provinces*, by Barbara Radcliffe-Rogers.

Tips "Guides should be destination-specific, rather than theme-based alone. Thus, 'Travel with Kids' is too broad; 'Italy with Kids' is OK. Make sure the guide doesn't duplicate what other guide publishers do."

IBEX PUBLISHERS

P.O. Box 30087, Bethesda MD 20824. (301)718-8188. Fax: (301)907-8707. E-mail: info@ibexpub.com. Website: www.ibexpub.com. Publishes hardcover and trade paperback originals and reprints. **Publishes 10-12 titles/year. Payment varies.** Accepts simultaneous submissions. Book catalog free.

Imprints Iranbooks Press.

O— IBEX publishes books about Iran and the Middle East.

Nonfiction Biography, cookbook, reference, textbook. Subjects include cooking/foods/nutrition, language/literature. Query with SASE, or submit propsal package, including outline and 2 sample chapters.

Poetry Translations of Persian poets will be considered.

THE ICON EDITIONS

Imprint of Westview Press, Perseus Books Group, 5500 Central Ave., Boulder CO 80301-2877. (720)562-3281. Fax: (720)406-7337. Website: www.westviewpress.com. **Acquisitions:** Sarah Warner. Estab. 1973. Publishes hardcover and trade paperback originals. **Publishes 5 titles/year. Receives hundreds of queries/year. 10% of books from first-time authors; 50% from unagented writers. Royalty and advance vary.** Publishes book 6-9 months after acceptance of ms. Accepts simultaneous submissions. Book catalog free.

O— The Icon Editions focus on books in art history, art criticism, and architecture for the textbook and trade markets.

Nonfiction Textbook, general readership titles. Subjects include art/architecture, art history, art criticism. Query with SASE. Reviews artwork/photos as part of ms package.

Recent Title(s) *Italian Renaissance Art*, by Laurie Schneider Adams; *Matisse and Picasso*, by Jack Flam.

ICONOGRAFIX, INC.

1830A Hanley Rd., P.O. Box 446, Hudson WI 54016. (715)381-9755. Fax: (715)381-9756. E-mail: iconogfx@spac estar.net. **Acquisitions:** Dylan Frautschi, acquisitions manager (transportation). Estab. 1992. Publishes trade paperback originals. **Publishes 24 titles/year. Receives 100 queries and 20 mss/year. 50% of books from first-time authors; 100% from unagented writers. Pays 8-12$\frac{1}{2}$% royalty on wholesale price or makes outright purchase of $1,000-3,000. Offers $1,000-3,500 advance.** Publishes book 1 year after acceptance of ms. Accepts simultaneous submissions. Responds in 1 month to queries; 3 months to proposals; 3 months to mss. Book catalog and ms guidelines free.

O— Iconografix publishes special, historical-interest photographic books for transportation equipment enthusiasts. Currently emphasizing emergency vehicles, buses, trucks, railroads, automobiles, auto racing, construction equipment.

Nonfiction Interested in photo archives. Coffee table book, illustrated book (photographic), photo albums. Subjects include Americana (photos from archives of historic places, objects, people), history, hobbies, military/ war, transportation (older photos of specific vehicles). Query with SASE, or submit proposal package, including outline. Reviews artwork/photos as part of ms package. Send photocopies.

Recent Title(s) *Greyhound Buses 1914-2000 Photo Archive*, by William A. Luke; *Indianapolis Racing Cars of Frank Kurtis, 1941-1963 Photo Archive*, by Gordon Eliot White; *The American Ambulance 1900-2002: An Illustrated History*, by Walter M.P. McCall.

ICS PUBLICATIONS

Institute of Carmelite Studies, 2131 Lincoln Rd. NE, Washington DC 20002. (202)832-8489. Fax: (202)832-8967. Website: www.icspublications.org. **Acquisitions:** John Sullivan, O.C.D. Publishes hardcover and trade paperback originals and reprints. **Publishes 6 titles/year. Receives 10-20 queries and 10 mss/year. 10% of books from first-time authors; 90-100% from unagented writers. Pays 2-6% royalty on retail price or makes outright purchase. Offers $500 advance.** Publishes book 2 years after acceptance of ms. Responds in 4 months to proposals. Book catalog for 7×10 SAE with 2 first-class stamps; ms guidelines for #10 SASE.

O— "Our audience consists of those interested in the Carmelite tradition and in developing their life of prayer and spirituality."

Nonfiction "We are looking for significant works on Carmelite history, spirituality, and main figures (Saints Teresa, John of the Cross, Therese of Lisieux, etc.)." Religious (should relate to Carmelite spirituality and prayer). "Too often we receive proposals for works that merely repeat what has already been done, are too technical for a general audience, or have little to do with the Carmelite tradition and spirit." Query or submit outline and 1 sample chapter.

Recent Title(s) *The Science of the Cross*, by St. Edith Stein.

IDYLL ARBOR, INC.

P.O. Box 720, Ravensdale WA 98051. (425)432-3231. Fax: (425)432-3726. E-mail: editors@idyllarbor.com. Website: www.idyllarbor.com. **Acquisitions:** Tom Blaschko. Publishes hardcover and trade paperback originals, and trade paperback reprints. **Publishes 6 titles/year. 50% of books from first-time authors; 100% from unagented writers. Pays 8-15% royalty on wholesale price or retail price.** Publishes book 1 year after acceptance of ms. Accepts simultaneous submissions. Responds in 1 month to queries; 2 months to proposals; 4 months to mss. Book catalog and ms guidelines free.

Imprints Issues Press, Pine Winds Press.

○━ Idyll Arbor publishes practical information on the current state and art of healthcare practice. Currently emphasizing therapies (recreational, aquatic, occupational, music, horticultural), activity directors in long-term care facilities, and social service professionals.

Nonfiction Reference, technical, textbook. Subjects include health/medicine (for therapists, social service providers and activity directors), psychology, recreation (as therapy), horticulture (used in long-term care activities or health care therapy). "Idyll Arbor is currently developing a line of books under the imprint Issues Press, which treats emotional issues in a clear-headed manner. The latest books are *Female Sex Offenders: What Therapists, Law Enforcement and Child Protective Services Need to Know* and *Situational Mediation: Sensible Conflict Resolution*. Another series of *Personal Health* books explains a condition or a closely related set of medical or psychological conditions. The target audience is the person or the family of the person with the condition. We want to publish a book that explains a condition at the level of detail expected of the average primary care physician so that our readers can address the situation intelligently with specialists. We look for manuscripts from authors with recent clinical experience. Good grounding in theory is required, but practical experience is more important." Query preferred with outline and 1 sample chapter. Reviews artwork/photos as part of ms package. Send photocopies.

Recent Title(s) *The Enduring Human Spirit: Thought-Provoking Stories on Caring for Our Elders*, by Charles Tindell; *Aquatic Therapy: Techniques and Interventions*, by Luis G. Varg.

Tips "The books must be useful for the health practitioner who meets face to face with patients or the books must be useful for teaching undergraduate and graduate level classes. We are especially looking for therapists with a solid clinical background to write on their area of expertise."

ILR PRESS

Cornell University Press, Sage House, 512 E. State St., Ithaca NY 14850. (607)277-2338. Fax: (607)277-2374. **Acquisitions:** Frances Benson, editorial director (fgb2@cornell.edu), or Sheryl Englund, acquisitions editor (sae7@cornell.edu). Estab. 1945. Publishes hardcover and trade paperback originals and reprints. **Publishes 10-12 titles/year. Pays royalty.** Does not accept simultaneous submissions. Responds in 2 months to queries. Book catalog free.

○━ "We are interested in manuscripts with innovative perspectives on current workplace issues that concern both academics and the general public."

Nonfiction Subjects include business/economics, government/politics, history, sociology. All titles relate to industrial relations and/or workplace issues including relevant work in the fields of history, sociology, political science, economics, human resources, and organizational behavior. Developing a new series on the work of health care. Query with SASE, or submit outline, sample chapter(s), cv.

Recent Title(s) *Code Green: Money-driven Hospitals and the Dismantling of Nursing*, by Dana Beth Weinberg; *The Working Class Majority: America's Best Kept Secret*, by Michael Zweig; *State of Working America*, by Lawrence Mishel, et. al.

Tips "Manuscripts must be well documented to pass our editorial evaluation, which includes review by academics in related fields."

IMAGES SI, INC.

Imprint of Images Publishing, 109 Woods of Arden Rd., Staten Island NY 10312. (718)966-3694. Fax: (718)966-3695. Website: www.imagesco.com. **Acquisitions:** Ronald Chironna. Estab. 1990. Publishes hardcover originals, trade paperback originals and audio. **Publishes 5 titles/year. 10% of books from first-time authors; 75% from unagented writers. Pays 10-20% royalty on wholesale price. Offers $1,000-5,000 advance.** Publishes book 6 months after acceptance of ms. Accepts simultaneous submissions. Responds in 2 months to queries; 2 months to proposals; 2 months to mss. Book catalog online.

○━ "We are currently looking for science fiction and fantasy stories and books more than anything else."

Nonfiction Audiocassettes, booklets, how-to, technical, CDs. Subjects include computers/electronic, photography, science, software. Query with SASE.

Fiction Fantasy, science fiction, audiocassetes, CDs, and printed books. "We are looking for short stories as well as full-length novels." Query with SASE.

Recent Title(s) *The Exiles of Damaria/Book One/Riddles and Dreams*, by Ardath Mayhar (fanatsy print book); *Nova-Audio, Issues 1-3*, by Hoyt, Franklin, Schoen, Wild, Silverberg, and Catelli (science fiction audio); *Kirlian Photography*, by John Iovine (photo/how-to).

IMPACT PUBLISHERS, INC.

P.O. Box 6016, Atascadero CA 93423-6016. (805)466-5917. Fax: (805)466-5919. E-mail: info@impactpublishers. com. Website: www.impactpublishers.com. **Acquisitions:** Freeman Porter, acquisitions editor. Estab. 1970. Publishes trade paperback originals. **Publishes 6-10 titles/year. Receives 250 queries and 250 mss/year. 20%**

of books from first-time authors; **60% from unagented writers. Pays 10% royalty on net receipts. Offers advance.** Publishes book 12-18 months after acceptance of ms. Accepts simultaneous submissions. Responds in 5 months to proposals. Book catalog free; ms guidelines online.

Imprints American Source Books, Little Imp Books, Rebuilding Books, Practical Therapist series.

O→ "Our purpose is to make the best human services expertise available to the widest possible audience: children, teens, parents, couples, individuals seeking self-help and personal growth, and human service professionals." Currently emphasizing books on divorce recovery for The Rebuilding Books Series. De-emphasizing children's books.

Nonfiction "All our books are written by qualified human service professionals and are in the fields of mental health, personal growth, relationships, aging, families, children, and professional psychology." Children's/juvenile, self-help. Subjects include child guidance/parenting, health/medicine, psychology (professional), caregiving/eldercare. "We do not publish general fiction for children. We do not publish poetry." Submit proposal package, including short résumé or vita, book description, audience description, outline, 1-3 sample chapters, and SASE.

Recent Title(s) *Time for a Better Marriage: Training in Marriage Enrichment*, by Jon Carlson, Ph.D. and Don Dinkmeyer, Sr., Ph.D.

Tips "Don't call to see if we have received your submission. Include a self-addressed, stamped postcard if you want to know if your manuscript arrived safely. We prefer a nonacademic, readable style. We publish only popular psychology and self-help materials written in 'everyday language' by professionals with advanced degrees and significant experience in the human services."

INAUDIO

(formerly Commuters Library), P.O. Box 3168, Falls Church VA 22043. (703)790-8250. Fax: (703)790-8234. E-mail: jlangenfeld@inaudio.biz. Website: www.inaudio.biz. **Acquisitions:** Joe Langenfeld, editor. Estab. 1991. Publishes audiobooks. **Publishes 80 titles/year. Pays 5-10% royalty. Offers $200-1,000 advance.** Publishes book 1 year after acceptance of ms. Accepts simultaneous submissions. Ms guidelines online.

O→ "Small publisher of audiobooks (many classics) with plans to publish new works of fiction and nonfiction, primarily novellas."

Nonfiction Audiocassettes, children's/juvenile, humor. Subjects include government/politics, current affairs, environment. Query with SASE, or submit outline, 1 sample chapter(s), Synopsis; Estimated Word Count. Does not accept unsolicited mss. Responds only with SASE.

Fiction Adventure, fantasy, historical, horror, humor, literary, mainstream/contemporary, military/war, mystery, suspense, western, young adult. Does not accept unsolicited mss. Responds only with SASE. Query with SASE, or submit outline, 1 sample chapter(s), synopsis.

Tips "Audiobooks are growing in popularity. Authors should consider going directly to audio for special works. Give us good writing 10,000 to 20,000 words in length."

INCENTIVE PUBLICATIONS, INC.

3835 Cleghorn Ave., Nashville TN 37215-2532. (615)385-2934. Fax: (615)385-2967. E-mail: comments@incentiv epublications.com. Website: www.incentivepublications.com. **Acquisitions:** Patience Camplair, editor. Estab. 1970. Publishes paperback originals. **Publishes 25-30 titles/year. Receives 350 submissions/year. 25% of books from first-time authors; 100% from unagented writers. Pays royalty, or makes outright purchase.** Publishes book an average of 1 year after acceptance of ms. Responds in 1 month to queries. Ms guidelines online.

O→ Incentive publishes developmentally appropriate teacher/parent resource materials and educational workbooks for children in grades K-12. Currently emphasizing primary material. Also interested in character education, English as a second language programs, early learning, current technology, related materials.

Nonfiction Subjects include education. Teacher resource books in pre-K through 12th grade. Query with synopsis and detailed outline.

Recent Title(s) *The Ready to Learn Book Series*, by Imogene Forte (Grades pre K-K); *Drumming to the Beat of a Different Marcher*, by Debbie Silver; *As Reading Programs Come and Go, This Is What You Need to Know*, by Judith Cochran.

INDIANA HISTORICAL SOCIETY PRESS

450 W. Ohio St., Indianapolis IN 46202-3269. (317)233-6073. Fax: (317)233-0857. **Acquisitions:** Judith Q. McMullen, assistant editor. Estab. 1830. Publishes hardcover originals. **Publishes 7 titles/year. Pays 6% royalty. net revenue received.** Responds in 1 month to queries.

Nonfiction Biography. Subjects include agriculture/horticulture, art/architecture, business/economics, ethnic, government/politics, history, military/war, sports, children's books. All topics must relate to Indiana. "We seek book-length manuscripts that are solidly researched and engagingly written on topics related to Indiana: biography, history, literature, music, politics, transportation, sports, agriculture, architecture, and children's books." Query with SASE.

Recent Title(s) *Carole Lombard: The Hoosier Tornado*, by Wes D. Gehring; *Casper and Catherine Move to America: An Immigrant Family's Adventure, 1849-1850*, by Brian Hasler.

INFO NET PUBLISHING

21142 Canada Rd., Unit 1-C, Lake Forest CA 92630. (949)458-9292. Fax: (949)462-9595. E-mail: herb@infonetpublishing.com. Website: www.infonetpublishing.com. **Acquisitions:** Herb Wetenkamp, president. Estab. 1987. Publishes hardcover and trade paperback originals. **Publishes 6 titles/year. Receives 50 queries and 20 mss/year. 80% of books from first-time authors; 85% from unagented writers. Pays 7-10% royalty on wholesale price, or makes outright purchase of $1,000-5,000. Offers $1,000-2,000 advance in some cases.** Publishes book 10 months after acceptance of ms. Accepts simultaneous submissions. Responds in 2 months to queries. Book catalog for 10×12 SAE with 2 first-class stamps; ms guidelines for #10 SASE.

   O— Info Net publishes for easily identified niche markets; specific markets with some sort of special interest, hobby, avocation, profession, sport, or lifestyle. New emphasis on collectibles and a series of books on retailing with CD-Roms.

Nonfiction Biography, children's/juvenile, gift book, how-to, reference, self-help, technical. Subjects include Americana (and collectibles), business/economics (retailing), history, hobbies, military/war, nature/environment (and environment), recreation, regional, sports, travel, women's issues/studies, aviation/aircraft archaeology. "We are looking for specific niche market books, not general titles, other than self-help. Do not repeat same formula as other books. In other words, offer something new." Submit outline, 3 sample chapters, proposal package, including demographics, marketing plans/data with SASE. Reviews artwork/photos as part of ms package. Send photocopies.

Recent Title(s) *Aircraft Wrecks in the Mountains and Deserts of California, 3rd Ed.*

Tips "Please check to be sure similar titles are not already published covering the exact same subject matter. Research the book you are proposing."

INFORMATION TODAY, INC.

143 Old Marlton Pike, Medford NJ 08055. (609)654-6266. Fax: (609)654-4309. E-mail: jbryans@infotoday.com. Website: www.infotoday.com. **Acquisitions:** John B. Bryans, editor-in-chief. Publishes hardcover and trade paperback originals. **Publishes 15-20 titles/year. Receives 100 queries and 30 mss/year. 30% of books from first-time authors; 90% from unagented writers. Pays 10-15% royalty on wholesale price. Offers $500-2,500 advance.** Publishes book 9 months after acceptance of ms. Accepts simultaneous submissions. Responds in 1 month to queries; 2 months to proposals; 3 months to mss. Book catalog free or on website; ms guidelines free or via e-mail as attachment.

Imprints ITI (academic, scholarly, library science); CyberAge Books (high-end consumer and business technology books—emphasis on Internet/WWW topics including online research).

   O— "We look for highly-focused coverage of cutting-edge technology topics, written by established experts and targeted to a tech-savvy readership. Virtually all our titles focus on how information is accessed, used, shared, and transformed into knowledge that can benefit people, business, and society." Currently emphasizing Internet/online technologies, including their social significance; biography, how-to, technical, reference. De-emphasizing fiction.

Nonfiction Biography, how-to, multimedia, reference, self-help, technical, scholarly. Subjects include business/economics, computers/electronic, education, science, Internet and cyberculture, library and information science. Query with SASE. Reviews artwork/photos as part of ms package. Send photocopies.

Recent Title(s) *Web Deception: Misinformation on the Internet*, edited by Anne P. Mintz; *Naked in Cyberspace: How to Find Personal Information Online, 2nd Ed.*, by Carole A. Lane.

Tips "Our readers include scholars, academics, indexers, librarians, information professionals (ITI imprint), as well as high-end consumer and business users of Internet/WWW/online technologies, and people interested in the marriage of technology with issues of social significance (i.e., cyberculture)."

INNER OCEAN PUBLISHING, INC.

P.O. Box 1239, Makawao HI 96768. (808)573-8000. Fax: (808)573-0700. E-mail: info@innerocean.com. Website: www.innerocean.com. **Acquisitions:** Karen Bouris, associate publisher. Estab. 1999. Publishes hardcover originals and trade paperback originals and reprints. **Publishes 20+ titles/year. Pays 10-15% roaylty on net sales. Offers modest advance.** Accepts simultaneous submissions. Responds in 2-3 months to queries. Book catalog free; ms guidelines online.

Nonfiction General trade. Subjects include spirituality, women's issues/studies, personal growth, sexuality, environmental, and political call to action. Query with SASE. Do not send complete ms.

Recent Title(s) *Spiritual Gardening*; *MoveOn's 50 Ways to Love Your Country*; *Sexy Mamas: Keeping Your Sex Life Alive While Raising Kids*.

Tips Audience is a wide range of readers interested in improving their lives through self-awareness, personal empowerment, and community involvement.

INNER TRADITIONS

Bear & Co., P.O. Box 388, Rochester VT 05767. (802)767-3174. Fax: (802)767-3726. E-mail: submissions@gotoit. com. Website: www.innertraditions.com. Managing Editor: Jennie Levitan. **Acquisitions:** Jon Graham, editor. Estab. 1975. Publishes hardcover and trade paperback originals and reprints. **Publishes 60 titles/year. Receives 3,000 submissions/year. 10% of books from first-time authors; 20% from unagented writers. Pays 8-10% royalty on net receipts. Offers $1,000 average advance.** Publishes book 1 year after acceptance of ms. Responds in 3 months to queries; 6 months to mss. Book catalog and ms guidelines free; ms guidelines online.

Imprints Destiny Audio Editions, Destiny Books, Destiny Recordings, Healing Arts Press, Inner Traditions, Inner Traditions En Espanol, Inner Traditions India, Park Street Press, Bear & Company, Bear Cub, Bindu Books.

> **O—** Inner Traditions publishes works representing the spiritual, cultural and mythic traditions of the world and works on alternative medicine and holistic health that combine contemporary thought with the knowledge of the world's great healing traditions. Currently emphasizing sacred sexuality, indigenous spirituality, ancient history.

Nonfiction "We are interested in the relationship of the spiritual and transformative aspects of world cultures." Children's/juvenile, self-help. Subjects include animals, art/architecture, child guidance/parenting, contemporary culture, ethnic, fashion/beauty, health/medicine (alternative medicine), history (ancient history and mythology), music/dance, nature/environment (and environment), New Age, philosophy (esoteric), psychology, religion (world religions), sex, spirituality, women's issues/studies, indigenous cultures, ethnobotany business. No fiction. Query or submit outline and sample chapters with SASE. Does not return mss without SASE. Reviews artwork/photos as part of ms package.

Recent Title(s) *Pilates on the Ball*, by Colleen Craig; *The Biology of Transcendence*, by Joseph Chilton Pearce; *The Templars and the Assassins*, by James Wasserman.

Tips "We are not interested in autobiographical stories of self-transformation. We do accept electronic submissions (via e-mail). We are not currently looking at fiction."

INSTITUTE OF POLICE TECHNOLOGY AND MANAGEMENT

University of North Florida, 12000 Alumni Dr., Jacksonville FL 32224-2678. (904)620-4786. Fax: (904)620-2453. E-mail: rhodge@unf.edu. Website: www.iptm.org. **Acquisitions:** Richard C. Hodge, editor. Estab. 1980. Usually publishes trade paperback originals. **Publishes 8 titles/year. Receives 30 queries and 12 mss/year. 50% of books from first-time authors; 100% from unagented writers. Pays 25% royalty on actual sale price, or makes outright purchase of $300-2,000.** Publishes book 6 months after acceptance of ms. Does not accept simultaneous submissions. Responds in 3 weeks to queries.

> **O—** "Our publications are principally for law enforcement. Will consider works in nearly every area of law enforcement."

Nonfiction Illustrated book, reference, technical, textbook. Subjects include traffic crash investigation and reconstruction, management and supervision, criminal investigations, security. "Our authors are mostly active or retired law enforcement officers with excellent, up-to-date knowledge of their particular areas. However, some authors are highly regarded professionals in other specialized fields that in some way intersect with law enforcement." Reviews artwork/photos as part of ms package.

Tips "Manuscripts should not be submitted before the author has contacted IPTM's editor by e-mail or telephone. It is best to make this contact before completing a lengthy work such as a manual."

INTERCULTURAL PRESS, INC.

P.O. Box 700, Yarmouth ME 04096. (866)372-2665 or (207)846-5168. Fax: (207)846-5181. E-mail: books@interc|ulturalpress.com. Website: www.interculturalpress.com. **Acquisitions:** Judy Carl-Hendrick, managing editor. Estab. 1980. Publishes hardcover and paperback originals. **Publishes 8-12 titles/year. Receives 50-80 submissions/year. 50% of books from first-time authors; 95% from unagented writers. Pays royalty. Offers small advance occasionally.** Publishes book within 18 months after acceptance of ms. Accepts simultaneous submissions. Responds in 1 month to queries. Book catalog free; ms guidelines online.

> **O—** Intercultural Press publishes materials related to intercultural relations, including the practical concerns of living and working in foreign countries, the impact of cultural differences on personal and professional relationships, and the challenges of interacting with people from unfamiliar cultures, whether at home or abroad. Currently emphasizing international business.

Nonfiction "We want books with an international or domestic intercultural or multicultural focus, including those on business operations (how to be effective in intercultural business activities), education (textbooks for teaching intercultural subjects, for instance), and training (for Americans abroad or foreign nationals coming to the United States).'' Reference, textbooks, theory. Subjects include world affairs, business, education, diversity and multicultural, relocation and cultural adaptation, culture learning, training materials, country-specific guides. ''Our books are published for educators in the intercultural field, business people engaged in international business, managers concerned with cultural diversity in the workplace, and anyone who works in an occupation where cross-cultural communication and adaptation are important skills. No manuscripts that don't have an intercultural focus.'' Accepts nonfiction translations. Submit proposals, outline, résumé, cv, and potential market information.

Recent Title(s) *The Cultural Imperative: Global Trends in the 21st Century*, by Richard D. Lewis; *Exploring Culture: Excercises, Stories and Synthetic Cultures*, by Gert Jan Hofstede, Paul B. Pedersen and Geert Hofstede.

INTERLINK PUBLISHING GROUP, INC.

46 Crosby St., Northampton MA 01060. (413)582-7054. Fax: (413)582-7057. E-mail: info@interlinkbooks.com. Website: www.interlinkbooks.com. **Acquisitions:** Michel Moushabeck, publisher. Estab. 1987. Publishes hardcover and trade paperback originals. **Publishes 50 titles/year. Receives 600 submissions/year. 30% of books from first-time authors; 50% from unagented writers. Pays 6-8% royalty on retail price. Offers small advance.** Publishes book 18 months after acceptance of ms. Accepts simultaneous submissions. Responds in 3 months to queries. Book catalog free; ms guidelines online.

Imprints Crocodile Books, USA; Interlink Books; Olive Branch Press.

    ○┯ Interlink publishes a general trade list of adult fiction and nonfiction with an emphasis on books that have a wide appeal while also meeting high intellectual and literary standards.

Nonfiction Subjects include world travel, world history and politics, ethnic cooking, world music. Submit outline and sample chapters.

Fiction Ethnic, international. ''Adult—We are looking for translated works relating to the Middle East, Africa or Latin America.'' No science fiction, romance, plays, erotica, fantasy, horror. Query with SASE, or submit outline, sample chapter(s).

Recent Title(s) *House of the Winds*, by Mia Yun.

Tips ''Any submissions that fit well in our publishing program will receive careful attention. A visit to our website, your local bookstore, or library to look at some of our books before you send in your submission is recommended.''

ⓝ INTERNATIONAL CITY/COUNTY MANAGEMENT ASSOCIATION

777 N. Capitol St., NE, Suite 500, Washington DC 20002. (202)962-4262. Fax: (202)962-3500. Website: www.icma.org. **Acquisitions:** Christine Ulrich, editorial director. Estab. 1914. Publishes hardcover and paperback originals. **Publishes 10-15 titles/year. Receives 50 queries and 20 mss/year. 20% of books from first-time authors; 100% from unagented writers. Makes negotiable outright purchase. Offers occasional advance.** Publishes book 18 months after acceptance of ms. Responds in 2 months to queries. Book catalog and ms guidelines online.

    ○┯ ''Our mission is to create excellence in local government by developing and fostering professional local government management worldwide.''

Nonfiction Reference, textbook, training manuals. Subjects include government/politics. Query with outline and 1 sample chapter. Reviews artwork/photos as part of ms package. Send photocopies.

Recent Title(s) *Homeland Security: Best Practices for Local Government*; *Economic Development: Strategies for State and Local Practice*.

Tips ''Our mission is to enhance the quality of local government and to support and assist professional local administrators in the United States and other countries.''

INTERNATIONAL FOUNDATION OF EMPLOYEE BENEFIT PLANS

P.O. Box 69, Brookfield WI 53008-0069. (262)786-6700. Fax: (262)786-8780. E-mail: books@ifebp.org. Website: www.ifebp.org. **Acquisitions:** Dee Birschel, senior director of publications. Estab. 1954. Publishes trade paperback originals. **Publishes 10 titles/year. Receives 20 submissions/year. 15% of books from first-time authors; 80% from unagented writers. Pays 5-15% royalty on wholesale and retail price.** Publishes book 1 year after acceptance of ms. Responds in 3 months to queries. Book catalog free; ms guidelines for #10 SASE.

    ○┯ IFEBP publishes general and technical monographs on all aspects of employee benefits—pension plans, health insurance, etc.

Nonfiction Subjects limited to health care, pensions, retirement planning and employee benefits and compensation. Reference, technical, textbook. Subjects include consumer information. Query with outline.

Recent Title(s) *Integrated Disability Management: An Employers Guide*, by Janet R. Douglas.

Tips ''Be aware of interests of employers and the marketplace in benefits topics, for example, how AIDS affects employers, healthcare cost containment.''

INTERNATIONAL MARINE

The McGraw-Hill Companies, P.O. Box 220, Camden ME 04843-0220. (207)236-4838. Fax: (207)236-6314. Website: www.internationalmarine.com. Editorial Director: Jonathan Eaton (boating, marine nonfiction). **Acquisitions:** Tris Coburn. Estab. 1969. Publishes hardcover and paperback originals. **Publishes 50 titles/year. Receives 500-700 mss/year. 30% of books from first-time authors; 60% from unagented writers. Pays standard royalties based on net price. Offers advance.** Publishes book 1 year after acceptance of ms. Responds in 2 months to queries. Ms guidelines online.

Imprints Ragged Mountain Press (sports and outdoor books that take you off the beaten path).

○━ International Marine publishes "the best books about boats."

Nonfiction Publishes "a wide range of subjects include: sea stories, seamanship, boat maintenance, etc." Subjects include marine and outdoor nonfiction. All books are illustrated. "Material in all stages welcome." Query first with outline and 2-3 sample chapters. Reviews artwork/photos as part of ms package.

Recent Title(s) *How to Read a Nautical Chart*, by Nigel Caulder; *By the Grace of the Sea: A Woman's Solo Odyssey Around the World*, by Pat Henry; *Coaching Girls' Lacrosse: A Baffled Parent's Guide*, by Janine Tucker.

Tips "Writers should be aware of the need for clarity, accuracy and interest. Many progress too far in the actual writing."

INTERNATIONAL MEDICAL PUBLISHING

1313 Dolley Madison Blvd., Suite 302, McLean VA 22101. (703)356-2037. Fax: (703)734-8987. E-mail: contact@ medicalpublishing.com. Website: www.medicalpublishing.com. **Acquisitions:** Thomas Masterson, MD, editor. Estab. 1991. Publishes mass market paperback originals. **Publishes 30 titles/year. Receives 100 queries and 20 mss/year. 5% of books from first-time authors; 100% from unagented writers. Pays royalty on gross receipts.** Publishes book 8 months after acceptance of ms. Responds in 2 months to queries.

○━ IMP publishes books to make life easier for doctors in training. "We're branching out to also make life easier for people with chronic medical problems."

Nonfiction Reference, textbook. Subjects include health/medicine. "We distribute only through medical and scientific bookstores. Think about practical material for doctors-in-training. We are interested in handbooks. Online projects are of interest." Query with outline.

Recent Title(s) *Healthy People 2010*, by the US Department of Health and Human Services; *Day-by-Day Diabetes*, by Resa Levetan.

Ⓝ INTERNATIONAL PRESS

P.O. Box 43503, Somerville MA 02143. Fax: (617)623-3101. E-mail: orders@intlpress.com. Submissions E-mail: hugh@intlpress.com. Website: www.intlpress.com. **Acquisitions:** Hugh Rutledge, managing editor (research math and physics). Estab. 1992. Publishes hardcover originals and reprints. **Publishes 12 titles/year. Receives 200 queries and 500 mss/year. 10% of books from first-time authors; 100% from unagented writers. Pays 3-10% royalty.** Publishes book 6 months after acceptance of ms. Does not accept simultaneous submissions. Responds in 5 months to queries; 5 months to proposals; 1 year to mss. Book catalog free; ms guidelines online.

Nonfiction Reference, scholarly. Subjects include science. "All our books will be in research mathematics. Authors need to provide ready to print latex files." Submit complete ms. Reviews artwork/photos as part of ms package. EPS files.

Recent Title(s) *Selected Works on Ricci Flow*; *Current Developments in Mathematics*; *Surveys in Differential Geometry*.

Tips "Audience is Ph.D. mathematicians and students."

INTERNATIONAL PUBLISHERS CO., INC.

239 W. 23 St., New York NY 10011. (212)366-9816. Fax: (212)366-9820. E-mail: service@intpubnyc.com. Website: www.intpubnyc.com. **Acquisitions:** Betty Smith, president. Estab. 1924. Publishes hardcover originals, trade paperback originals and reprints. **Publishes 5-6 titles/year. Receives 50-100 mss/year. 10% of books from first-time authors. Pays 5-7½% royalty on paperbacks; 10% royalty on cloth.** Publishes book 6 months after acceptance of ms. Accepts simultaneous submissions. Responds in 1 month to queries; 6 months to mss. Book catalog and ms guidelines for SAE with 60¢ postage.

○━ International Publishers Co., Inc., emphasizes books based on Marxist science.

Nonfiction Subjects include art/architecture, government/politics, history, philosophy, economics, social sciences, Marxist-Leninist classics. "Books on labor, black studies, and women's studies based on Marxist science have high priority." Query, or submit outline, sample chapters, and SASE. Reviews artwork/photos as part of ms package.

Recent Title(s) *Choice: A Doctor's Experience with the Abortion Dilemma*, by Don Sloan, M.D.; *People vs. Profits: Selections from the Writings of Victor Perlo*.

Tips No fiction or poetry.

INTERNATIONAL SOCIETY FOR TECHNOLOGY IN EDUCATION (ISTE)

480 Charnelton St., Eugene OR 97401. (541)434-8928. E-mail: sharter@iste.org. Website: www.iste.org. **Acquisitions:** Scott Harter, acquisitions editor. Publishes trade paperback originals. **Publishes 20 titles/year. Receives 150 queries and 50 mss/year. 75% of books from first-time authors; 95% from unagented writers. Pays 12% royalty on retail price.** Publishes book 5 months after acceptance of ms. Accepts simultaneous submissions. Responds in 1 month to queries; 1 month to proposals; 1 month to mss. Book catalog and ms guidelines free.

   O➥ Currently emphasizing curriculum integration and standards-based program development books. De-emphasizing how-to books.

Nonfiction Reference, technical, curriculum. Subjects include educational technology, educational software, educational administration. Submit proposal package including outline, sample chapter(s), TOC, vita. Reviews artwork/photos as part of ms package. Send photocopies.

Recent Title(s) *Palm Handheld Computers—A Complete Resource for Classroom Teachers*, by Michael Curtis, et al.

Tips "Our audience is teachers, technology coordinators, administrators."

INTERNATIONAL WEALTH SUCCESS

P.O. Box 186, Merrick NY 11570-0186. (516)766-5850. Fax: (516)766-5919. **Acquisitions:** Tyler G. Hicks, editor. Estab. 1967. **Publishes 10 titles/year. Receives 100 submissions/year. 100% of books from first-time authors; 100% from unagented writers. Pays 10% royalty on wholesale or retail price. Offers usual advance of $1,000, but this varies depending on author's reputation and nature of book. Buys all rights.** Publishes book 4 months after acceptance of ms. Responds in 1 month to queries. Book catalog and ms guidelines for 9×12 SAE with 3 first-class stamps.

   O➥ "Our mission is to publish books, newsletters, and self-study courses aimed at helping beginners and experienced business people start, and succeed in, their own small business in the fields of real estate, import-export, mail order, licensing, venture capital, financial brokerage, etc. The large number of layoffs and downsizings have made our publications of greater importance to people seeking financial independence in their own business, free of layoff threats and snarling bosses."

Nonfiction How-to, self-help. Subjects include business/economics, financing, business success, venture capital, etc. "Techniques, methods, sources for building wealth. Highly personal, how-to-do-it with plenty of case histories. Books are aimed at wealth builders and are highly sympathetic to their problems. These publications present a wide range of business opportunities while providing practical, hands-on, step-by-step instructions aimed at helping readers achieve their personal goals in as short a time as possible while adhering to ethical and professional business standards." Length: 60,000-70,000 words. Query. Reviews artwork/photos as part of ms package.

Recent Title(s) *How to Buy and Flip Real Estate for a Profit*, by Rod L. Griffin.

Tips "With the mass layoffs in large and medium-size companies there is an increasing interest in owning your own business. So we focus on more how-to, hands-on material on owning—and becoming successful in—one's own business of any kind. Our market is the BWB—Beginning Wealth Builder. This person has so little money that financial planning is something they never think of. Instead, they want to know what kind of a business they can get into to make some money without a large investment. Write for this market and you have millions of potential readers. Remember—there are a lot more people without money than with money."

Ø INTERVARSITY PRESS

P.O. Box 1400, Downers Grove IL 60515. (630)734-4000. Fax: (630)734-4200. E-mail: mail@ivpress.com. Website: www.ivpress.com. **Acquisitions:** David Zimmerman, associate editor; Andy Le Peau, editorial director; Jim Hoover, associate editorial director (academic, reference); Cindy Bunch, editor (Bible study, Christian living); Gary Deddo, associate editor (academic); Dan Reid, editor (reference, academic); Al Hsu, associate editor (general). Estab. 1947. Publishes hardcover originals, trade paperback and mass market paperback originals. **Publishes 80-90 titles/year. Receives 1,500 queries and 1,000 mss/year. 15% of books from first-time authors; 85% from unagented writers. Pays negotiable flat fee or royalty on retail price. Offers negotiable advance.** Publishes book 1 year after acceptance of ms. Accepts simultaneous submissions. Responds in 3 months to proposals. Book catalog for 9×12 SAE and 5 first-class stamps; ms guidelines online.

Imprints Academic (contact Gary Deddo); Bible Study (contact Cindy Bunch); General (contact Al Hsu); Reference (contact Dan Reid).

   O➥ InterVarsity Press publishes a full line of books from an evangelical Christian perspective targeted to an open-minded audience. "We serve those in the university, the church, and the world, by publishing books from an evangelical Christian perspective."

Nonfiction Subjects include religion. Query with SASE. *No unsolicited mss.*

Recent Title(s) *A Fragile Stone*, by Michael Card; *The Design Revolution*, by William Dembski.

INTERWEAVE PRESS

201 E. 4th St., Loveland CO 80537. (970)669-7672. Fax: (970)667-8317. Website: www.interweave.com. **Acquisitions:** Betsy Armstrong, book editorial director. Estab. 1975. Publishes hardcover and trade paperback originals. **Publishes 16-20 titles/year. Receives 50 submissions/year. 60% of books from first-time authors; 98% from unagented writers. Pays 10% royalty on net receipts.** Publishes book 1-3 years after acceptance of ms. Accepts simultaneous submissions. Responds in 2 months to queries. Book catalog and ms guidelines free.

> Oᴿ Interweave Press publishes instructive and inspirational titles relating to the fiber arts and beadwork topics.

Nonfiction Subjects limited to fiber arts—basketry, spinning, knitting, dyeing and weaving—and beadwork topics. How-to, technical. Submit outline, sample chapter(s). Reviews artwork/photos as part of ms package.

Recent Title(s) *Beading in the Native American Tradition*, by David Dean.

Tips "We are looking for very clear, informally written, technically correct manuscripts, generally of a how-to nature, in our specific fiber and beadwork fields only. Our audience includes a variety of creative self-starters who appreciate inspiration and clear instruction. They are often well educated and skillful in many areas."

THE INVISIBLE COLLEGE PRESS

P.O. Box 209, Woodbridge VA 22194-0209. (703)590-4005. E-mail: submissions@invispress.com. Website: www.invispress.com. **Acquisitions:** Dr. Phillip Reynolds, editor (nonfiction); Paul Mossinger, submissions editor (fiction). Publishes trade paperback originals and reprints. **Publishes 12 titles/year. Receives 120 queries and 30 mss/year. 75% of books from first-time authors; 75% from unagented writers. Pays 10-25% royalty on wholesale price. Offers $100 advance.** Publishes book 4 months after acceptance of ms. Accepts simultaneous submissions. Responds in 1 month to queries; 1 month to proposals; 3 months to mss. Book catalog and ms guidelines online.

Nonfiction Reference. Subjects include creative nonfiction, government/politics, religion, spirituality, conspiracy. "We only publish nonfiction related to conspiracies, UFOs, government cover-ups, and the paranormal." Query with SASE, or submit proposal package including outline, 1 sample chapter(s).

Fiction Experimental, fantasy, gothic, horror, literary, mainstream/contemporary, occult, religious, science fiction, spiritual, suspense, conspiracy. "We only publish fiction related to conspiracies, UFOs, government cover-ups, and the paranormal." Query with SASE, or submit proposal package including 1 sample chapter(s), synopsis.

Recent Title(s) *UFO Politics at the White House*, by Larry Bryant (nonfiction); *City of Pillars*, by Dominic Peloso (fiction); *The Third Day*, by Mark Graham (fiction).

Tips "Our audience tends to be fans of conspiracies and UFO mythology. They go to UFO conventions, they research who shot JFK, they believe that they are being followed by Men in Black, they wear aluminum-foil hats to stop the CIA from beaming them thought-control rays. We are only interested in work dealing with established conspiracy/UFO mythology. Rosicrucians, Illuminatti, Men in Black, Area 51, Atlantis, etc. If your book doesn't sound like an episode of the *X-Files*, we probably won't consider it."

IRON GATE PUBLISHING

P.O. Box 999, Niwot CO 80544-0999. (303)530-2551. Fax: (303)530-5273. E-mail: editor@irongate.com. Website: www.irongate.com; www.reunionsolutions.com. **Acquisitions:** Dina C. Carson, publisher (how-to, genealogy). Publishes hardcover and trade paperback originals. **Publishes 6-10 titles/year; imprint publishes 2-6 titles/year. Receives 100 queries and 20 mss/year. 30% of books from first-time authors; 10% from unagented writers. Pays royalty on a case-by-case basis.** Publishes book 1 year after acceptance of ms. Accepts simultaneous submissions. Responds in 2 months to proposals. Book catalog free or on website; ms guidelines online.

Imprints Reunion Solutions Press, KinderMed Press.

> Oᴿ "Our readers are people who are looking for solid, how-to advice on planning reunions or self-publishing a genealogy."

Nonfiction Subjects include child guidance/parenting, health/medicine, hobbies. Query with SASE, or submit proposal package, including outline, 2 sample chapters, and marketing summary. Reviews artwork/photos as part of ms package. Send photocopies.

Recent Title(s) *The Genealogy and Local History Researcher's Self-Publishing Guide*; *Reunion Solutions: Everything You Need to Know to Plan a Family, Class, Military, Association or Corporate Reunion*.

Tips "Please look at the other books we publish and tell us in your query letter why your book would fit into our line of books."

ITALICA PRESS

595 Main St., Suite 605, New York NY 10044-0047. (212)935-4230. Fax: (212)838-7812. E-mail: inquiries@italica press.com. Website: www.italicapress.com. **Acquisitions:** Ronald G. Musto and Eileen Gardiner, publishers.

Estab. 1985. Publishes trade paperback originals. **Publishes 6 titles/year. Receives 600 queries and 60 mss/ year. 5% of books from first-time authors; 100% from unagented writers. Pays 7-15% royalty on wholesale price. author's copies.** Publishes book 1 year after acceptance of ms. Accepts simultaneous submissions. Responds in 1 month to queries; 2 months to mss. Book catalog and ms guidelines online.

   O→ Italica Press publishes English translations of modern Italian fiction and medieval and Renaissance nonfiction.

Nonfiction Subjects include translation. "We publish English translations of medieval and Renaissance source materials and English translations of modern Italian fiction." Query with SASE. Reviews artwork/photos as part of ms package. Send photocopies.

Fiction Translations of 20th century Italian fiction. Query with SASE.

Poetry Poetry titles are generally dual language.

Tips "We are interested in considering a wide variety of medieval and Renaissance topics (not historical fiction), and for modern works we are only interested in translations from Italian fiction by well-known Italian authors."

🆕 LEE JACOBS PRODUCTIONS

Box 362, Pomeroy OH 45769. (740)992-5208. Fax: (740)992-0616. Website: LeeJacobsProductions.com. **Acquisitions:** Lee Jacobs, president. Publishes hardcover and trade paperback originals and reprints. **Publishes 5 titles/year. Receives 5 queries and 5 mss/year. 10% of books from first-time authors; 90% from unagented writers. Pays 5% royalty or makes outright purchase of $100-5,000.** Publishes book 6 months after acceptance of ms. Responds in 1 month to queries; 1 month to proposals; 6 months to mss. Book catalog for $5 or on website.

   O→ Lee Jacobs Productions publishes books about magic, comedy and entertainment.

Nonfiction Biography, coffee table book, how-to, humor, illustrated book, reference, technical, textbook. Subjects include history, hobbies, humor, memoirs, money/finance, photography, psychology, recreation. Query with SASE. Reviews artwork/photos as part of ms package.

Tips Audience is magicians, comedians, pro entertainers, mentalists.

JAIN PUBLISHING CO.

P.O. Box 3523, Fremont CA 94539. (510)659-8272. Fax: (510)659-0501. E-mail: mail@jainpub.com. Website: www.jainpub.com. **Acquisitions:** M.K. Jain, editor-in-chief. Estab. 1989. Publishes hardcover and paperback originals and reprints. **Publishes 6 titles/year. Receives 300 queries/year. 100% from unagented writers. Pays 5-15% royalty on net sales.** Publishes book 1-2 years after acceptance of ms. Responds in 3 months to mss. Book catalog and ms guidelines online; ms guidelines online.

Imprints Asian Humanities Press.

   O→ Jain Publishing Co. publishes college textbooks as well as professional and scholarly references.

Nonfiction Reference, textbook. Subjects include humanities, social sciences, communication, English & literature, religious studies, business, scientific/technical. Submit proposal package including publishing history. Reviews artwork/photos as part of ms package. Send photocopies.

Recent Title(s) *A Student Guide to College Composition*, by William Murdiek.

ALICE JAMES BOOKS

238 Main St., Farmington ME 04938. (207)778-7071. Fax: (207)778-7071. E-mail: ajb@umf.maine.edu. Website: www.alicejamesbooks.org. **Acquisitions:** April Ossmann, director (poetry). Publishes trade paperback originals. **Publishes 4 titles/year. Receives 1,000 mss/year. 75% of books from first-time authors; 99% from unagented writers. Pays through competition awards.** Publishes book 1 year after acceptance of ms. Accepts simultaneous submissions. Responds in 1 month to queries; 4 months to mss. Book catalog for free or on website; ms guidelines for #10 SASE or on website.

   O→ Alice James Books is a nonprofit poetry press.

Poetry Query.

Recent Title(s) *The Art of the Lathe*, by B.H. Fairchild; *The River at Wolf*, by Jean Valentine; *Pity the Bathtub Its Forced Embrace of the Human Form*, by Matthea Harvey.

Tips "Send SASE for contest guidelines or check website. Do not send work without consulting current guidelines."

JAYJO BOOKS, LLC

Imprint of The Guidance Channel, P.O. Box 760, 135 Dupont St., Plainview NY 11803-0769. (516)349-5520. Fax: (516)349-5521. **Acquisitions:** Sally Germain, editor-in-chief (for elementary school age youth). Publishes trade paperback originals. **Publishes 8-12 titles/year. Receives 100 queries/year. 25% of books from first-time authors; 100% from unagented writers. Makes outright purchase of $500-1,000.** Publishes book 9 months after acceptance of ms. Accepts simultaneous submissions. Responds in 2 months to queries; 2 months to proposals; 2 months to mss. Book catalog and writer's guidelines for #10 SASE.

Imprints Each book published is for a specific series. Series include: Special Family and Friends, Health Habits for Kids, Substance Free Kids, Special Kids in School. Series publish 1-5 titles/year.

Nonfiction Children's/juvenile, illustrated book. Subjects include health/medicine (issues for children). "JayJo Books is a publisher of nonfiction books to help teachers, parents, and children cope with chronic illnesses, special needs, and health education in classroom, family, and social settings. Each JayJo series has a particular style and format it must follow. Writers should send query letter with areas of expertise or interest and suggested focus of book." No animal character books or illustrated books. Query with SASE.

Tips "Send a query letter—since we only publish books adapted to our special formats—we contact appropriate potential authors and work with them to customize manuscript."

JEWISH LIGHTS PUBLISHING

LongHill Partners, Inc., P.O. Box 237, Sunset Farm Offices, Rt. 4, Woodstock VT 05091. (802)457-4000. Fax: (802)457-4004. Website: www.jewishlights.com. Editor: Stuart Matlins. **Acquisitions:** Acquisitions Editor. Estab. 1990. Publishes hardcover and trade paperback originals, trade paperback reprints. **Publishes 30 titles/ year. Receives 1,000 submissions/year. 30% of books from first-time authors; 99% from unagented writers. Pays royalty on net sales, 10% on first printing, then increases.** Publishes book 1 year after acceptance of ms. Accepts simultaneous submissions. Responds in 3 months to queries. Book catalog and ms guidelines free.

- O—¬ "People of all faiths and backgrounds yearn for books that attract, engage, educate and spiritually inspire. Our principal goal is to stimulate thought and help all people learn about who the Jewish people are, where they come from, and what the future can be made to hold."

Nonfiction Children's/juvenile, illustrated book, reference, self-help. Subjects include business/economics (with spiritual slant, finding spiritual meaning in one's work), health/medicine (healing/recovery, wellness, aging, life cycle), history, nature/environment, philosophy, religion (theology), spirituality (and inspiration), women's issues/studies. "We do *not* publish haggadot, biography, poetry, or cookbooks." Submit proposal package, including cover letter, table of contents, 2 sample chapters and SASE (postage must cover weight of ms). Reviews artwork/photos as part of ms package. Send photocopies.

Recent Title(s) *The Rituals and Practices of a Jewish Life: A Handbook for Personal Spiritual Renewal*, by Kerry M. Oliteky and Daniel Judson; *The Jewish Prophet: Visionary Words from Moses and Miriam to Henrietta Szold and A.J. Heschel*, by Michael J. Shire; *Noah's Wife: The Story of Naamah*, by Sandy Eisenberg Sasso.

Tips "We publish books for all faiths and backgrounds that also reflect the Jewish wisdom tradition."

JIST PUBLISHING, INC.

8902 Otis Ave., Indianapolis IN 46216-1033. (317)613-4200. Fax: (317)613-4304. E-mail: info@jist.com. Website: www.jist.com. **Acquisitions:** Susan Pines, associate publisher (career reference and career assessment mss); Lori Cates Hand, acquisitions and development editor (trade mss); Randy Haubner, acquisitions editor (workbook mss and all KIDSRIGHTS/JIST Life mss). Estab. 1981. Publishes practical, self-directed tools and training materials that are used in employment and training education, and business settings. Whether reference books, trade books, assessment tools, workbooks, or videos, JIST products foster self-directed job-search attitudes and behaviors. Trade and institutional hardcover and paperback originals and reprints. **Publishes 50 titles/year. Receives 150 submissions/year. 25% of books from first-time authors. Pays 5-10% royalty on wholesale price or makes outright purchase (negotiable).** Publishes book 1-2 years after acceptance of ms. Accepts simultaneous submissions. Responds in 5-6 months to queries. Book catalog and ms guidelines online.

Imprints JIST Works (job search, career development, and occupational information titles); Park Avenue (education, business, self-help, and life skills titles); Your Domain Publishing (public domain and government agency data and information titles); JIST Life (adults); KIDSRIGHTS (children).

- O—¬ "Our purpose is to provide quality job search, career development, occupational, character education, and life skills information, products, and services that help people manage and improve their lives and careers—and the lives of others."

Nonfiction Specializes in job search, career development, occupational information, character education, and domestic abuse topics. "We want text/workbook formats that would be useful in a school or other institutional setting. We also publish trade titles for all reading levels. Will consider books for professional staff and educators, appropriate software and videos." Query with SASE. Reviews artwork/photos as part of ms package.

Recent Title(s) *The Very Quick Job Search, Third Ed.*, by Michael Farr; *Young Person's Occupational Outlook Handbook, Fourth Ed.*, by the editors of JIST; *Gallery of Best Résumés, Third Ed.*, by David Noble.

Tips "Our primary audience is institutions and staff who work with people of all reading and academic skill levels, making career and life decisions, and people who are looking for jobs."

ⓃÎ THE JOHNS HOPKINS UNIVERSITY PRESS

2715 N. Charles St., Baltimore MD 21218. (410)516-6900. Fax: (410)516-6968. E-mail: tcl@mail.press.jhu.edu. Website: www.press.jhu.edu. **Acquisitions:** Trevor Lipscombe, editor-in-chief (science; tcl@mail.press.jhu.edu); Jacqueline C. Wehmueller, executive editor (consumer health, history of medicine, education; jwehmueller @mail.press.jhu.edu); Henry Y.K. Tom, executive editor (social sciences; htom@mail.press.jhu.edu); Wendy Harris, senior acquisitions editor (clinical medicine, public health, health policy; wharris@mail.press.jhu.edu); Robert J. Brugger, senior acquisitions editor (American history, history of science and technology, regional books; rbrugger@mail.press.jhu.edu); Vincent J. Burke, acquisitions editor (biology; vjb@mail.press.jhu.edu); Michael B. Lonegro, acquisitions editor (humanities, classics, and ancient studies; mlonegro@mail.press.jhu.edu). Estab. 1878. Publishes hardcover originals and reprints, and trade paperback reprints. **Publishes 125 titles/ year. Pays royalty.** Publishes book 1 year after acceptance of ms.

Nonfiction Biography, reference, scholarly, textbook. Subjects include general nonfiction, government/politics, health/medicine, history, humanities, regional, religion, science, social sciences. Submit proposal package including outline, 1 sample chapter(s), curriculum vita. Reviews artwork/photos as part of ms package. Send photocopies.

Recent Title(s) *In Albert's Shadow*, by Milan Popovic (collection of letters); *An Alliance at Risk*, by Laurent Cohen-Tanugi, translated by George A. Holoch, Jr. (international relations); *Living with Rheumatoid Arthritis*, by Tammi L. Shlotzhauer, M.D., and James L. McGuire, M.D. (health).

JOHNSON BOOKS

Johnson Publishing Co., 1880 S. 57th Court, Boulder CO 80301. (303)443-9766. Fax: (303)998-7594. E-mail: books@jpcolorado.com. **Acquisitions:** Stephen Topping, editorial director. Estab. 1979. Publishes hardcover and paperback originals and reprints. **Publishes 10-12 titles/year. Receives 500 submissions/year. 30% of books from first-time authors; 90% from unagented writers. Royalties vary.** Publishes book 1 year after acceptance of ms. Responds in 3 months to queries. Book catalog for 9×12 SAE with 5 first-class stamps.

Imprints Spring Creek Press.

0–ʀ Johnson Books specializes in books on the American West, primarily outdoor, ''useful'' titles that will have strong national appeal.

Nonfiction Subjects include anthropology/archeology, history, nature/environment (environmental subjects), recreation (outdoor), regional, science, travel (regional), general nonfiction, books on the West, natural history, paleontology, geology. ''We are primarily interested in books for the informed popular market, though we will consider vividly written scholarly works.'' Looks for ''good writing, thorough research, professional presentation, and appropriate style. Marketing suggestions from writers are helpful.'' Submit outline/synopsis and 3 sample chapters.

Recent Title(s) *Life Lessons from a Ranch Horse*, by Mark Roshid (horses); *Libby, Montana*, by Andrea Peacock (environment); *Denver's Glitch Gardens*, by Betty Hull (local history).

JOSSEY-BASS/PFEIFFER

John Wiley & Sons, Inc., 989 Market St., San Francisco CA 94103. (415)433-1740. Fax: (415)433-0499. Website: www.josseybass.com; www.pfeiffer.com. **Acquisitions:** Paul Foster, publisher (health, education, nonprofit, psychology, religion); Cedric Crocker, publisher (business & management, Pfeiffer). **Publishes 250 titles/year. Pays variable royalties. Offers occasional advance.** Publishes book 1 year after acceptance of ms. Accepts simultaneous submissions. Responds in 2 months to queries. Ms guidelines online.

Nonfiction Subjects include business/economics, education, health/medicine, money/finance, psychology, religion. Jossey-Bass publishes first-time and unagented authors. Publishes books on topics of interest to a wide range of readers: business & management, conflict resolution, mediation and negotiation, K-12 education, higher and adult education, healthcare management, psychology/behavioral healthcare, nonprofit & public management, religion, human resources & training. Also publishes 25 periodicals.

Recent Title(s) *Leading in a Culture of Change*, by Michael Fullan; *Fighting for Your Marriage*, by Howard J. Markman and Susan L. Blumberg; *Building Moral Intelligence*, by Michele Borba.

JOURNEYFORTH

Imprint of BJU Press, 1700 Wade Hampton Blvd., Greenville SC 29614-0001. (864)242-5100, ext. 4350. E-mail: jb@bjup.com. Website: www.bjup.com. **Acquisitions:** Nancy Lohr, manuscript editor (juvenile fiction). Estab. 1974. Publishes paperback original and reprints. **Publishes 10 titles/year. Pays royalty.** Publishes book 12-18 months after acceptance of ms. Accepts simultaneous submissions. Responds in 1 month to queries; 3 months to mss. Book catalog free; ms guidelines online.

0–ʀ ''Small independent publisher of excellent, trustworthy novels, information books, audio tapes and ancillary materials for readers pre-school through high school. We desire to develop in our children a love for and understanding of the written word, ultimately helping them love and understand God's word."

Fiction Adventure (children's/juvenile, young adult), historical (children's/juvenile, young adult), juvenile (animal, easy-to-read, series), mystery (children's/juvenile, young adult), sports (children's/juvenile, young adult), suspense (young adult), western (young adult), young adult (series). "Our fiction is all based on a moral and Christian worldview." Query with SASE, or submit outline, 5 sample chapter(s), or submit complete ms.

Recent Title(s) *Case of the Sassy Parrot*, by Milly Howard (fiction, ages 7-9); *Daniel Colton Kid Knapped*, by Elaine Schulte (historical nonfiction, ages 9-12); *Children of the Storm: The Autobiography of Natasha Vins* (young adult).

Tips "Study the publisher's guidelines. Make sure your work is suitable or you waste time for you and the publisher."

JUDAICA PRESS

123 Ditmas Ave., Brooklyn NY 11218. (718)972-6200. Fax: (718)972-6204. E-mail: info@judaicapress.com. Website: www.judaicapress.com. **Acquisitions:** Nachum Shapiro, managing editor. Estab. 1963. Publishes hardcover and trade paperback originals and reprints. **Publishes 12 titles/year.** Responds in 3 months to queries. Book catalog in print and online.

O→ "We cater to the Orthodox Jewish market."

Nonfiction "Looking for Orthodox Judaica in all genres." Children's/juvenile, cookbook, textbook, outreach books. Subjects include religion (Bible commentary), prayer, holidays, life cycle. Submit ms with SASE.

Fiction Novels.

Recent Title(s) *Scattered Pieces*, by Allison Cohen; *The Practical Guide to Kashrus*, by Rabbi Shaul Wagschal; *How Mitzvah Giraffe Got His Long, Long Neck*, by David Sokoloff.

JUSTICE HOUSE PUBLISHING, INC.

P.O. Box 4233, Spanaway WA 98387. (253)262-0205. Fax: (253)475-2158. E-mail: submissions@justicehouse.com. Website: www.justicehouse.com. Publishes trade paperback originals. **Publishes 20-30 titles/year. Receives 5-10 queries and 1-5 mss/year. 100% of books from first-time authors; 100% from unagented writers. Pays 10-15% royalty on wholesale price.** Publishes book 2 years after acceptance of ms. Does not accept simultaneous submissions. Responds in 2-3 months to queries; 2-3 months to proposals; 3-6 months to mss. Book catalog free; ms guidelines online.

● All submissions must be made via e-mail.

Fiction Fantasy, feminist, gay/lesbian, mystery, romance, science fiction, short story collections. "We specialize in lesbian fiction." Submit complete ms.

Recent Title(s) *Tropical Storm*, by Melissa Good (lesbian fiction); *The Deal*, by Maggie Ryan (lesbian fiction); *Kona Dreams*, by Shari J. Berman.

Tips Audience is comprised of 18 and older eductated lesbian females.

KAEDEN BOOKS

P.O. Box 16190, Rocky River OH 44116-0190. (440)617-1400. Fax: (440)617-1403. E-mail: jhoyer@kaeden.com. Website: www.kaeden.com. **Acquisitions:** Craig Urmston, fiction editor (children's grades preK-3). Estab. 1990. Publishes paperback originals. **Publishes 8-16 titles/year. Pays flat fee or royalty by individual arrangement with author depending on book.** Publishes book 6-24 months after acceptance of ms. Ms guidelines online.

O→ "Children's book publisher for education K-3 market: reading stories, fiction/nonfiction, chapter books, science, math, and social studies materials, also poetry."

Nonfiction Grades K-3 only. Needs all subjects, especially biography, science, nature, and history. Query with outline, publishing history, author bio, and synopsis. Send a disposable copy of ms. Responds only, "if interested."

Fiction Grades K-3 only. Adventure, ethnic, fantasy, historical, humor, mystery, science fiction (soft/sociological), short story collections, sports, suspense (amateur sleuth). Query with outline, publishing history, synopsis, and author bio. Send a disposable copy of ms. Responds only "if interested."

Tips "Our line is expanding with particular interest in nonfiction for grades K-3 only. Material must be suitable for use in the public school classroom, be multicultural, and be high interest with appropriate word usage and a positive tone for the respective grade."

KALMBACH PUBLISHING CO.

21027 Crossroads Circle, P.O. Box 1612, Waukesha WI 53187-1612. (262)796-8776. Fax: (262)798-6468. E-mail: books@kalmbach.com. Website: corporate.kalmbach.com. **Acquisitions:** Candice St. Jacques, editor-in-chief; Kent Johnson, senior acquisitions editor. Estab. 1934. Publishes hardcover and paperback originals, paperback reprints. **Publishes 15-20 titles/year. Receives 100 submissions/year. 75% of books from first-time authors;**

99% from unagented writers. Pays 7% royalty on net receipts. Offers $2,500 advance. Publishes book 18 months after acceptance of ms. Responds in 2 months to queries.

Nonfiction Kalmbach publishes reference materials and how-to publications for hobbyists. Concentration in the railfan, model railroading, plastic modeling, and toy train collecting/operating hobbies. "Our book publishing effort is mostly in railroading and similar hobby how-to-do-it titles. However, we are now looking to acquire how-to titles on beading and fashionable jewelry making." Query with 2-3 page detailed outline, sample chapter with photos, drawings, and how-to text. Reviews artwork/photos as part of ms package.

Recent Title(s) *The Art of Lionel Trains*, by Roger Carp; *Faces of Railroading*, by Carl Swanson; *Basic Painting and Weathering for Model Railroaders*, by Jeff Wilson.

Tips "Our hobby books are about half text and half illustrations. Any hobby author who wants to publish with us must be able to furnish good photographs and rough drawings before we'll consider his or her book."

KAR-BEN PUBLISHING

Submissions address: 6800 Tildenwood Lane, Rockville MD 20852. (301)984-8826. Fax: (301)881-9195. E-mail: karben@aol.com. Website: www.karben.com. **Acquisitions:** Madeline Wikler and Judye Groner, editors (juvenile Judaica). Estab. 1976. Publishes hardcover and trade paperback originals. **Publishes 10-15 titles/year. Receives 50-100 queries and 300-400 mss/year. 5% of books from first-time authors; 100% from unagented writers. Pays 5-8% royalty on net receipts. Offers $500-2,500 advance.** Accepts simultaneous submissions. Responds in 1 month to queries. Book catalog free or on website; ms guidelines online.

○ Kar-Ben Publishing publishes high-quality materials on Jewish themes for young children and families.

Nonfiction "Jewish themes only!" Children's/juvenile (Judaica only). Subjects include religion. Submit complete ms.

Fiction "Jewish themes and young kids only!" Juvenile, religious.

Recent Title(s) *Ilan Ramon*; *Matzah Meals*; *Keeping the Promise*.

Tips "Do a literature search to make sure similar title doesn't already exist."

KAYA PRODUCTION

116 Pinehurst Ave. #E51, New York NY 10033. (212)740-3519. E-mail: kaya@kaya.com. Website: www.kaya.com. **Acquisitions:** Sunyoung Lee, editor. For submissions: 2121 James M. Wood Blvd. #423, Los Angeles CA 90006. Publishes hardcover originals and trade paperback originals and reprints. Accepts simultaneous submissions. Responds in 6 months to mss. Book catalog free; ms guidelines online.

● "We do not accept electronic submissions."

○ "Kaya is an independent literary press dedicated to the publication of innovative literature from the Asian diaspora."

Nonfiction Subjects include multicultural. "Kaya publishes Asian, Asian American and Asian diasporic materials. We are looking for innovative writers with a commitment to quality literature." Submit proposal package including outline, sample chapter(s), previous publications, SASE. Reviews artwork/photos as part of ms package. Send photocopies.

Fiction "Kaya publishes Asian, Asian-American and Asian diasporic materials. We are looking for innovative writers with a commitment to quality literature." Submit 2-4 sample chapter(s), synopsis, SASE.

Poetry Submit complete ms.

Recent Title(s) *Where We Once Belonged*, by Sia Figiel (novel); *The Anchored Angel: Selected Writings*, by Jose Garcia Villa, edited by Gileen Tabios.

Tips Audience is people interested in a high standard of literature and who are interested in breaking down easy approaches to multicultural literature.

KENSINGTON PUBLISHING CORP.

850 Third Ave., 16th Floor, New York NY 10022. (212)407-1500. Fax: (212)935-0699. Website: www.kensingtonbooks.com. **Acquisitions:** Michaela Hamilton, editor-in-chief (thrillers, mysteries, mainstream fiction, true crime, current events); Kate Duffy, editorial director, romance and women's fiction (historical romance, Regency romance, Brava erotic romance, women's contemporary fiction); John Scognamiglio, editorial director, fiction (historical romance, Regency romance, women's contemporary fiction, gay and lesbian fiction and nonfiction, mysteries, suspense, mainstream fiction); Karen Thomas, editorial director, Dafina Books/Arabesque romances (African-American fiction and nonfiction); Bruce Bender, managing director, Citadel Press (popular nonfiction, film, television, wicca, gambling, current events); Ann LaFarge, executive editor, Zebra Books and Citadel Press (women's fiction, thrillers, westerns, commercial nonfiction); Bob Shuman, senior editor, Citadel Press (politics, military, wicca, business, Judaica, sports); Elaine Sparber, senior editor (health, alternative health, pets, New Age, self-help); Margaret Wolf, senior editor, Citadel Press (psychology, women's issues, women's health, entertainment, current events, cookbooks); Jeremie Ruby-Strauss, senior editor (nonfiction, pop culture, pop reference, true crime); Richard Ember, editor, Citadel Press (biography, film, sports, New Age, spirituality);

Miles Lott, assistant editor (mainstream fiction, thrillers, horror, women's fiction, general nonfiction, popular culture, entertainment); Hilary Sares, consulting editor (historical romance, Regency romance, women's fiction); Lisa Filippattos, consulting editor (contemporary and historical romance, Regency romances, Brava erotic romance, women's fiction, thrillers); Lee Heiman, consulting editor (alternative health). Estab. 1975. Publishes hardcover and trade paperback originals, mass market paperback originals and reprints. **Publishes over 500 titles/year. Receives 5,000 queries and 2,000 mss/year. 10% of books from first-time authors. Pays 8-15% royalty on retail price, or makes outright purchase. Offers $2,000 and up advance.** Publishes book 9-12 months after acceptance of ms. Accepts simultaneous submissions. Responds in 1 month to queries; 1 month to proposals; 4 months to mss. Book catalog online.

Imprints Kensington Books; Brava Books; Citadel Press; Dafina Books; Pinnacle Books; Zebra Books.

● Kensington recently purchased the assets of Carol Publishing Group.

O→ Kensington focuses on profitable niches and uses aggressive marketing techniques to support its books.

Nonfiction Biography, cookbook, gift book, how-to, humor, illustrated book, reference, self-help. Subjects include Americana, animals, business/economics, child guidance/parenting, contemporary culture, cooking/foods/nutrition, gay/lesbian, health/medicine (alternative), history, hobbies, memoirs, military/war, money/finance, multicultural, nature/environment, philosophy, psychology, recreation, regional, sex, sports, travel, true crime, women's issues/studies, pop culture, true crime, current events. *Agented submissions only. No unsolicited mss.* Reviews artwork/photos as part of ms package. Send photocopies.

Fiction Ethnic, gay/lesbian, historical, horror, mainstream/contemporary, multicultural, mystery, occult, romance (contemporary, historical, regency,), suspense, western (epic), thrillers; women's. No science fiction/fantasy, experimental fiction, business texts or children's titles. *Agented submissions only. No unsolicited mss.*

Recent Title(s) *Green Calder Grass*, by Janet Dailey (fiction); *Unfinished Business*, by Harlan Ullman (nonfiction).

Tips Agented submissions only, except for submissions to Arabesque, Ballad, Bouquet, Encanto and Precious Gems. For those imprints, query with SASE or submit proposal package including 3 sample chapter(s), synopsis.

KENT STATE UNIVERSITY PRESS

P.O. Box 5190, Kent OH 44242-0001. (330)672-7913. Fax: (330)672-3104. Website: www.kentstateuniversitypress.com. **Acquisitions:** Joanna H. Craig, editor-in-chief. Estab. 1965. Publishes hardcover and paperback originals and some reprints. **Publishes 30-35 titles/year. Nonauthor subsidy publishes 20% of books. Standard minimum book contract on net sales.** Responds in 3 months to queries. Book catalog free.

O→ Kent State publishes primarily scholarly works and titles of regional interest. Currently emphasizing US history, literary criticism.

Nonfiction Biography, scholarly. Subjects include anthropology/archeology, art/architecture, general nonfiction, history, language/literature, regional, true crime, literary criticism, material culture, textile/fashion studies, US foreign relations. Especially interested in scholarly works in history and literary studies of high quality, any titles of regional interest for Ohio, scholarly biographies, the arts, and general nonfiction. Send a letter of inquiry before submitting mss. Decisions based on in-house readings and 2 by outside scholars in the field of study. Enclose return postage.

N A Ø ALFRED A. KNOPF AND CROWN BOOKS FOR YOUNG READERS

Imprint of Random House, 1745 Broadway, New York NY 10019. (212)782-9000. Website: www.randomhouse.com/kids.

● Distinguished juvenile fiction and nonfiction for ages 0-18. Send query with SASE. Address envelope to Acquisitions Editor, Knopf & Crown Books for Young Readers, Random House, 1745 Broadway, 9-3, New York NY 10019.

KNOPF PUBLISHING GROUP

Imprint of Random House, Inc., 1745 Broadway, 21st Floor, New York NY 10019. Website: www.aaknopf.com. **Acquisitions:** Senior Editor. Estab. 1915. Publishes hardcover and paperback originals. **Publishes 200 titles/year. 15% of books from first-time authors; 30% from unagented writers. Pays 10-15% royalty. Royalty and advance vary. Offers advance.** Publishes book 1 year after acceptance of ms. Accepts simultaneous submissions. Responds in 3-5 months to queries. Book catalog for $7\frac{1}{2} \times 10\frac{1}{2}$ SAE with 5 first-class stamps; ms guidelines online.

Imprints Alfred A. Knopf, Everyman's Library, Knopf Travel Guides, National Audobon Guides, Pantheon Books, Shocken Books, Vintage Anchor Publishing (Vintage Books, Anchor Books).

O→ Knopf is a general publisher of quality nonfiction and fiction.

Nonfiction Scholarly, book-length nonfiction, including books of scholarly merit. Subjects include general nonfiction, general scholarly nonfiction. "A good nonfiction writer should be able to follow the latest scholarship in any field of human knowledge, and fill in the abstractions of scholarship for the benefit of the general reader

Book Publishers

by means of good, concrete, sensory reporting.'' **Preferred length: 50,000-150,000 words**. Query with SASE. Reviews artwork/photos as part of ms package.

Fiction Publishes book-length fiction of literary merit by known or unknown writers. Length: 40,000-150,000 words. Query with SASE, or submit sample chapter(s).

Recent Title(s) *Amateur Marriage*, by Anne Tyler; *Stalin*, by Simon Montefiore; *The Spiral Staircase*, by Karen Armstrong.

KOENISHA PUBLICATIONS

3196 53rd St., Hamilton MI 49419-9626. (269)751-4100. Fax: (269)751-4100. E-mail: koenisha@macatawa.org. Website: www.koenisha.com. **Acquisitions:** Sharolett Koenig, publisher; Flavia Crowner, proof editor; Earl Leon, acquisition editor. Publishes trade paperback originals. **Publishes 10-12 titles/year. Receives 50 queries and 50 mss/year. 95% of books from first-time authors; 100% from unagented writers. Pays 15-25% royalty on net receipts.** Publishes book 1 year after acceptance of ms. Accepts simultaneous submissions. Responds in 2 months to queries; 3 months to proposals; 3 months to mss. Book catalog and ms guidelines free or on website; ms guidelines online.

Nonfiction Autobiography, children's/juvenile, cookbook, how-to. Subjects include gardening, hobbies, memoirs, nature/environment. Query with SASE, or submit complete ms. Reviews artwork/photos as part of ms package. Send photocopies.

Fiction Humor, mainstream/contemporary, mystery, romance, suspense, young adult. ''We do not accept manuscripts that contain unnecessary foul language, explicit sex or gratuitous violence.'' Query with SASE, or submit proposal package including 3 sample chapter(s), synopsis.

Poetry Submit 3 sample poems.

Recent Title(s) *Lost and Found Love*, by Anne Skalitza (young adult romance); *Crucial Judgment*, by Al Blanchard (mystery); *A Writer's Concordance: Every Thing the Bible Says About Writing*, by Sharolett Koenig (inspirational).

Tips ''We're not interested in books written to suit a particular line or house or because it's trendy. Instead write a book from your heart—the inspiration or idea that kept you going through the writing process.''

H.J. KRAMER, INC.

Imprint of New World Library, P.O. Box 1082, Tiburon CA 94920. (415)435-5367. Fax: (415)435-5364. E-mail: hjkramer@jps.net. **Acquisitions:** Jan Phillips, managing editor. Estab. 1984. Publishes hardcover and trade paperback originals. **Publishes 5 titles/year. Receives 1,000 queries and 500 mss/year. 20% of books from first-time authors. Advance varies.** Publishes book 18 months after acceptance of ms. Book catalog free.

Imprints Starseed Press Children's Illustrated Books.

Nonfiction Subjects include health/medicine (holistic), spirituality, metaphysical.

Fiction Juvenile, picture books with themes of self-esteem, nonviolence, and spirituality. Prospective authors please note: Kramer's list is selective and is normally fully slated several seasons in advance.

Recent Title(s) *Truth in Dating*, by Dr. Susan Campbell (nonfiction); *Smudge Bunny*, by Dr. Bernie Sigel (fiction).

Tips ''Our books are for people who are interested in personal growth and consciousness-raising. We are not interested in personal stories unless they have universal appeal. We do not accept e-mail submissions of mss although queries will be answered.''

KRAUSE PUBLICATIONS

Imprint of F+W Publications, Inc., 700 E. State, Iola WI 54990. (715)445-2214. Fax: (715)445-4087. E-mail: info@krause.com. Website: www.krause.com. **Acquisitions:** Acquisitions Editor. Publishes hardcover and trade paperback originals. **Publishes 170 titles/year. Receives 400 queries and 40 mss/year. 10% of books from first-time authors; 90% from unagented writers. Pays 9-12% royalty on net or makes outright purchase of $2,000-10,000. Offers $1,500-4,000 advance.** Publishes book 1 year after acceptance of ms. Does not accept simultaneous submissions. Responds in 2 months to proposals; 2 months to mss. Book catalog for free or on website; ms guidelines free.

    ○┓ ''We are the world's largest hobby and collectibles publisher.''

Nonfiction How-to, illustrated book, reference, technical, price guides. Subjects include hobbies (antiques, collectibles, toys), sports (outdoors, hunting, fishing), coins, stamps, firearms, knives, records, sewing, quilting, ceramics. Submit proposal package, including outline, 1-3 sample chapters, and letter explaining your project's unique contributions. Reviews artwork/photos as part of ms package. Send sample photos.

Recent Title(s) *Antique Trunks—An Identification and Price Guide*, by Pat Morse and Linda Edelstein (reference/price guide); *Sewing with Nancy's Favorite Hints*, by Nancy Zieman (how-to); *Standard Catalog of® Ferrari 1947-2003*, by Mike Covello (how-to/reference).

Tips Audience consists of serious hobbyists. "Your work should provide a unique contribution to the special interest."

KREGEL PUBLICATIONS

Kregel, Inc., P.O. Box 2607, Grand Rapids MI 49501. (616)451-4775. Fax: (616)451-9330. Website: www.kregelp ublications.com. **Acquisitions:** Dennis R. Hillman, publisher. Estab. 1949. Publishes hardcover and trade paperback originals and reprints. **Publishes 90 titles/year. Receives 1,000 queries and 300 mss/year. 10% of books from first-time authors; 90% from unagented writers. Pays 8-16% royalty on wholesale price. Offers $200-2,000 advance.** Publishes book 14 months after acceptance of ms. Accepts simultaneous submissions. Responds in 3 months to queries. Book catalog for 9X12 SASE; ms guidelines online.

Imprints Editorial Portavoz (Spanish-language works), Kregel Academic & Professional, Kregel Kidzone.

> **O¬** "Our mission as an evangelical Christian publisher is to provide—with integrity and excellence—trusted, Biblically-based resources that challenge and encourage individuals in their Christian lives. Works in theology and Biblical studies should reflect the historic, orthodox Protestant tradition."

Nonfiction "We serve evangelical Christian readers and those in career Christian service."

Fiction Religious (children's, general, inspirational, mystery/suspense, relationships), young adult. Fiction should be geared toward the evangelical Christian market. Wants "books with fast-paced, contemporary storylines presenting a strong Christian message in an engaging, entertaining style."

Recent Title(s) *Unveiling Islam*, by Ergun Caner and Emir Caner (contemporary issues); *Praying the Attributes of God*, by Rosemary Jensen (devotional); *Romance Rustlers and Thunderbird Thieves*, by Sharon Dunn (mystery).

Tips "Our audience consists of conservative, evangelical Christians, including pastors and ministry students. Think through very clearly the intended audience for the work."

KRIEGER PUBLISHING CO.

P.O. Box 9542, Melbourne FL 32902-9542. (321)724-9542. Fax: (321)951-3671. E-mail: info@krieger-publishing. com. Website: www.krieger-publishing.com. **Acquisitions:** Sharan B. Merriam and Ronald M. Cervero, series editor (adult education); Donald M. Waltz, series editor (space sciences); David E. Kyvig, series director (local history); Hans Trefousse, series editor (history); James B. Gardner, series editor (public history). Estab. 1969. Publishes hardcover and paperback originals and reprints. **Publishes 30 titles/year. Receives 100 submissions/year. 30% of books from first-time authors; 100% from unagented writers. Pays royalty on net price.** Publishes book 18 months after acceptance of ms. Responds in 3 months to queries. Book catalog free.

Imprints Anvil Series, Orbit Series, Public History, Professional Practices in Adult Education and Lifelong Learning Series.

> **O¬** "We are a short-run niche publisher providing accurate and well-documented scientific and technical titles for text and reference use, college level and higher."

Nonfiction Reference, technical, textbook, scholarly. Subjects include agriculture/horticulture, animals, education (adult), history, nature/environment, science (space), herpetology, chemistry, physics, engineering, veterinary medicine, natural history, math. Query with SASE. Reviews artwork/photos as part of ms package.

Recent Title(s) *Amphibian Medicine & Captive Husbandry*, edited by Kevin R. Wright and Brent R. Whitaker; *A History of Christian Education: Protestant, Catholic, and Orthodox Perspectives*, by John L. Elias.

LAKE CLAREMONT PRESS

4650 N. Rockwell St., Chicago IL 60625. (773)583-7800. Fax: (773)583-7877. E-mail: sharon@lakeclaremont.c om. Website: www.lakeclaremont.com. **Acquisitions:** Sharon Woodhouse, publisher. Publishes trade paperback originals. **Publishes 5-7 titles/year. Receives 300 queries and 50 mss/year. 50% of books from first-time authors; 100% from unagented writers. Pays 10-15% royalty on wholesale price. Offers $250-2,000 advance.** Publishes book 8 months after acceptance of ms. Accepts simultaneous submissions. Responds in 1 month to queries; 2 months to proposals; 2-6 months to mss. Book catalog online.

> **O¬** "We specialize in books on the Chicago area and its history, and may consider regional titles for the Midwest. We also like nonfiction books on ghosts and cemeteries."

Nonfiction Subjects include Americana, ethnic, history, nature/environment (regional), regional, travel, women's issues/studies, film/cinema/stage (regional), urban studies. Query with SASE, or submit proposal package, including outline and 2 sample chapters, or submit complete ms (e-mail queries and proposals preferred).

Recent Title(s) *The Chicago River: A Natural and Unnatural History*, by Libby Hill; *Chicago's Midway Airport: The First Seventy-Five Years*, by Christopher Lynch.

Tips "Please include a market analysis in proposals (who would buy this book and where) and an analysis of similar books available for different regions. Please know what else is out there."

WENDY LAMB BOOKS

Imprint of Random House Children's Books/Random House, Inc., 1745 Broadway, New York NY 10019. (212)782-9000. Website: www.randomhouse.com/kids. **Acquisitions:** Wendy Lamb, editorial director/acquisitions editor; Alison Root, editorial. Estab. 2001. Publishes hardcover originals. **Publishes 12 titles/year. Receives 300-400 submissions/year. 15% of books from first-time authors; 10% from unagented writers. Pays royalty.** Accepts simultaneous submissions. Responds in 1 month to queries. Ms guidelines for #10 SASE.

- Literary fiction and nonfiction for readers 8-15. Query via e-mail or hard copy. Include SASE for response.

Nonfiction Children's/juvenile.

Fiction Juvenile (ages 2-18).

Poetry Submit 4 sample poems.

Recent Title(s) *Bud, Not Buddy*, by Christopher Paul Curtis; *The Beet Fields*, by Gary Paulsen; *Nory Ryan's Song*, by Patricia Reilly Cliff.

Tips "A query letter should briefly describe the book you want to write, the intended age group, and your publishing credentials, if any. If you like, you may send no more than 5 pages of the manuscript of shorter works (picture books) and a maximum of 10 pages of longer works (novels). Please do not send more than the specified amount. Also, do not send cassette tapes, videos, or other materials along with your query or excerpt. Manuscript pages will not be returned. Do not send original art."

LANGENSCHEIDT PUBLISHING GROUP

46-35 54th Rd., Maspeth NY 11378. (800)432-6277. Fax: (718)784-0640. E-mail: spohja@langenscheidt.com. **Acquisitions:** Sue Pohja, director of acquisitions. Estab. 1983. Publishes hardcover and trade paperback originals. **Publishes 200 titles/year. Receives 100 queries and 50 mss/year. 90% from unagented writers. Pays royalty, or makes outright purchase.** Publishes book 6 months after acceptance of ms. Accepts simultaneous submissions. Responds in 2 months to proposals. Book catalog free.

Imprints ADC Map, American Map, Hagstrom Map, Insight Guides, Hammond World Atlas Corp., Langenscheidt Trade, Berlitz Publishing.

- Langenscheidt Publishing Group publishes maps, travel guides, language reference, and dictionary titles, world atlases, educational materials, and language learning audio products.

Nonfiction Reference. Subjects include education, travel, foreign language. "Any title that fills a gap in our line is welcome for review." Submit outline and 2 sample chapters (complete ms preferred). For return of unsolicited queries, include a SASE.

Recent Title(s) *Berlitz Intermediate Spanish*; *Insight Guide Colorado*; *Hammond World Atlas*.

Tips "Any item related to our map, foreign language dictionary, audio, atlas, and travel lines could have potential for us. Of particular interest are titles that have a sizeable potential customer base and have little in the way of good competition."

LARK

Sterling Publishing, 67 Broadway, Asheville NC 28801. (828)253-0467. Fax: (828)253-7952. Website: www.lark books.com. Director of Publishing: Carol Taylor. **Acquisitions:** Nicole Tuggle, submissions coordinator. Estab. 1976. Publishes hardcover and trade paperback originals and reprints. **Publishes 50 titles/year. Receives 300 queries and 100 mss/year. 80% of books from first-time authors; 90% from unagented writers. Offers up to $4,000 advance.** Publishes book 1 year after acceptance of ms. Accepts simultaneous submissions. Responds in 3 months to queries. Ms guidelines online.

- Lark Books publishes high quality, highly illustrated books, primarily in the crafts/leisure markets celebrating the creative spirit. We work closely with bookclubs. Our books are either how-to, 'gallery' or combination books."

Nonfiction Children's/juvenile, coffee table book, how-to, illustrated book. Subjects include gardening, hobbies, nature/environment, crafts. Query first. If asked, submit outline and 1 sample chapter, sample projects, table of contents, visuals. Reviews artwork/photos as part of ms package. Send transparencies.

Recent Title(s) *Gorgeous Leather Crafts*.

Tips "We publish both first-time and seasoned authors. In either case, we need to know that you have substantial expertise on the topic of the proposed book—that we can trust you to know what you're talking about. If you're great at your craft but not so great as a writer, you might want to work with us as a coauthor or as a creative consultant."

LARSON PUBLICATIONS/PBPF

4936 Rt. 414, Burdett NY 14818-9729. (607)546-9342. Fax: (607)546-9344. E-mail: larson@lightlink.com. Website: www.larsonpublications.org. **Acquisitions:** Paul Cash, director. Estab. 1982. Publishes hardcover and trade paperback originals. **Publishes 4-5 titles/year. Receives 1,000 submissions/year. 5% of books from first-time authors. Pays variable royalty. Seldom offers advance.** Publishes book 1-2 years after acceptance of ms. Accepts simultaneous submissions. Responds in 4-6 months to queries. Visit website for book catalog.

Nonfiction Subjects include philosophy, psychology, religion, spirituality. Query with SASE and outline.

Recent Title(s) *Astonoesis*, by Anthony Damiani.

Tips "We look for original studies of comparative spiritual philosophy or personal fruits of independent (trans-sectarian viewpoint) spiritual research/practice."

LAWYERS & JUDGES PUBLISHING CO.

P.O. Box 30040, Tucson AZ 85751-0040. (520)323-1500. Fax: (520)323-0055. E-mail: sales@lawyersandjudges.c om. Website: www.lawyersandjudges.com. Editorial Assistant: Jill Ciotti. **Acquisitions:** Steve Weintraub, president. Estab. 1963. Publishes professional hardcover and trade paperback originals. **Publishes 15 titles/year. Receives 200 queries and 30 mss/year. 15% of books from first-time authors; 100% from unagented writers. Pays 7-10% royalty on net receipts.** Publishes book 5 months after acceptance of ms. Accepts simultaneous submissions. Responds in 2 months to queries. Book catalog free; ms guidelines online.

　　O→ Lawyers & Judges is a highly specific publishing company, reaching the legal, accident reconstruction, insurance, and medical fields.

Nonfiction Reference. Subjects include law, insurance, forensics, accident reconstruction. "Unless a writer is an expert in the forensics/legal/insurance areas, we are not interested." Submit proposal package including outline, sample chapter(s).

Recent Title(s) *Human Factors in Traffic Safety.*

LEE & LOW BOOKS

95 Madison Ave., New York NY 10016. (212)779-4400. Fax: (212)532-6035. Website: www.leeandlow.com. **Acquisitions:** Louise May, executive editor. Estab. 1991. Publishes hardcover originals—picture books, middle-grade works only. **Publishes 12-16 titles/year. Pays royalty. Offers advance.** Accepts simultaneous submissions. Responds in 2-4 months to queries; 2-4 months to mss. Book catalog for SASE with $1.75 postage; ms guidelines online.

　　O→ "Our goals are to meet a growing need for books that address children of color, and to present literature that all children can identify with. We only consider multicultural children's books." Currently emphasizing material for 5-12 year olds. Sponsors a yearly New Voices Award for first-time picture book authors of color. Contest rules online at website or for SASE.

Nonfiction Children's/juvenile, illustrated book. Subjects include ethnic, multicultural.

Fiction Ethnic, juvenile, multicultural, illustrated. "We do not consider folktales, fairy tales, or animal stories." Send complete ms with cover letter or through an agent.

Recent Title(s) *The Pot that Juan Built*, by Nancy Andrews-Goebel; *Summer Sun Risin'*, by W. Nikola-Lisa.

Tips "Of special interest are stories set in contemporary America. We are interested in fiction as well as nonfiction."

LEGACY PRESS

Imprint of Rainbow Publishers, P.O. Box 261129, San Diego CA 92196. (858)668-3260. **Acquisitions:** Christy Scannell, editor. Estab. 1997. **Publishes 20 titles/year. Receives 250 queries and 100 mss/year. 50% of books from first-time authors. Pays royalty based on wholesale price. Offers negotiable advance.** Publishes book 1-3 years after acceptance of ms. Accepts simultaneous submissions. Book catalog for 9×12 SAE with 2 first-class stamps; ms guidelines for #10 SASE.

　　O→ "Legacy Press strives to publish Bible-based materials that inspire Christian spiritual growth and development in children." Currently emphasizing nonfiction for kids, particularly pre-teens and more specifically girls, although we are publishing boys and girls 2-12. No picture books, fiction without additional activities, poetry or plays.

Nonfiction Subjects include creative nonfiction, education, hobbies, religion. Query with SASE, or submit outline, 3-5 sample chapter(s), market analysis.

Recent Title(s) *The Official Christian Babysitting Guide*, by Rebecca P. Totilo; *The Ponytail Girls*, by Bonnie Compton Hanson (5-book series).

Tips "We are looking for Christian versions of general market nonfiction for kids, as well as original ideas."

LEGEND BOOKS

69 Lansing St., Auburn NY 13021. (315)258-8012. **Acquisitions:** Joseph P. Berry, editor. Publishes paperback monographs, scholarly books, and college textbooks. **Publishes 15 titles/year. Receives 100 queries and 60 mss/year. 50% of books from first-time authors; 100% from unagented writers. Pays 20% royalty on net sales.** Publishes book 9 months after acceptance of ms. Accepts simultaneous submissions. Responds in 2 months to queries; 2 months to proposals; 2 months to mss.

　　O→ Legend Books publishes a variety of books used in the college classroom, including workbooks. However, it does not publish any books on mathematics or hard sciences.

Nonfiction Biography, scholarly, textbook, community/public affairs, speech/mass communication. Subjects include business/economics, child guidance/parenting, community, education, government/politics, health/

medicine, history, humanities, philosophy, psychology, recreation, social sciences, sociology, sports, journalism, public relations, television. Query with SASE, or submit complete ms (include SASE if ms is to be returned). Reviews artwork/photos as part of ms package. Send photocopies.

Recent Title(s) *The Conversion of the King of Bissau*, by Timothy Coates, Ph.D. (world history); *Values, Society & Evolution*, by H. James Birx, Ph.D. (anthropology and sociology).

Tips "We seek college professors who actually teach courses for which their books are designed."

LEHIGH UNIVERSITY PRESS

Linderman Library, 30 Library Dr., Lehigh University, Bethlehem PA 18015-3067. (610)758-3933. Fax: (610)758-6331. E-mail: inlup@lehigh.edu. Website: fpl.cc.lehigh.edu/inlup. **Acquisitions:** Philip A. Metzger, director. Estab. 1985. Publishes hardcover originals. **Publishes 10 titles/year. Receives 90-100 queries and 50-60 mss/year. 70% of books from first-time authors; 100% from unagented writers. Pays royalty.** Publishes book 18 months after acceptance of ms. Accepts simultaneous submissions. Responds in 3 months to queries. Book catalog and ms guidelines free.

○┓ "Currently emphasizing works on 18th-century studies, history of technology, East-Asian studies, and literary criticism. Accepts all subjects of academic merit."

Nonfiction Lehigh University Press is a conduit for nonfiction works of scholarly interest to the academic community. Biography, reference, scholarly. Subjects include Americana, art/architecture, history, language/literature, science. Submit proposal package including 1 sample chapter(s).

Recent Title(s) *The Terror of Our Days: Four American Poets Respond to the Holocaust*, by Harriet L. Parmet; *One Woman Determined to Make a Difference: The Life of Madeleine Zabruskie Doty*, by Alice Duffy Rinehart.

LEISURE BOOKS

Imprint of Dorchester Publishing Co., 200 Madison Ave., Suite 2000, New York NY 10016. (212)725-8811. Fax: (212)532-1054. Website: www.dorchesterpub.com. **Acquisitions:** Micaela Bombard and Jessica McDonnell, editorial assistants; Kate Seaver, editor; Alicia Condon, editorial director; Don D'Auria, executive editor (westerns, thrillers, horror); Christopher Keeslar, senior editor. Estab. 1970. Publishes mass market paperback originals and reprints. Publishes romances, westerns, horrors, young adult, chick lit, and thrillers only. **Publishes 240 titles/year. Receives thousands of submissions/year. 20% of books from first-time authors; 20% from unagented writers. Pays royalty on retail price. Offers negotiable advance.** Publishes book 18 months after acceptance of ms. Does not accept simultaneous submissions. Responds in 6 months to queries. Book catalog for free by calling (800)481-9191; ms guidelines online.

Imprints Love Spell (romance); Leisure (romance, western, thriller, horror).

○┓ Leisure Books/Love Spell is seeking historical, contemporary, time travel, and paranormal romances.

Fiction Historical (romance), horror, romance, western, chick lit. "All historical romance should be set pre-1900. Horrors and westerns are growing as well. No sweet romance, science fiction, erotica, mainstream, or action/adventure. New YA line, contemporary, and paranormal, 45,000 words." Query with SASE, or submit outline, first 3 sample chapter(s), synopsis. "All manuscripts must be typed, double-spaced on one side, and left unbound."

Recent Title(s) *Dark Destiny*, by Christine Feehan (romance); *To Wake the Dead*, by Richard Laymon (horror).

ARTHUR A. LEVINE BOOKS

Imprint of Scholastic Trade Division, 557 Broadway, New York NY 10012. (212)343-4436. Website: www.scholastic.com. **Acquisitions:** Arthur Levine, editorial director. **Publishes 10-14 titles/year. Pays variable royalty on retail price. Offers variable advance.** Book catalog for 9×12 SASE.

Fiction Juvenile, picture books, young adult, middle grade novels. Query with SASE. "We are willing to work with first-time authors, with or without an agent."

Recent Title(s) *Frida*, by Jonah Winter; *Millicent Min, Girl Genius*, by Lisa Yee; *The Story of a Seagull and the Cat Who Taught Her How to Fly*, by Luis Sepulveda.

LIBRARIES UNLIMITED, INC.

88 Post Rd. W., Westport CT 06881. (800)225-5800. Fax: (203)222-1502. E-mail: mdillon@lu.com. Website: www.lu.com. **Acquisitions:** Martin Dillon, director of acquisitions; Barbara Ittner, acquisitions editor (public library titles); Sharon Coatney (school library titles). Estab. 1964. Publishes hardcover originals. **Publishes 100 titles/year. Receives 400 queries and 100 mss/year. 50% of books from first-time authors; 100% from unagented writers.** Publishes book 9 months after acceptance of ms. Accepts simultaneous submissions. Responds in 1 month to queries; 2 months to proposals; 2 months to mss. Book catalog and ms guidelines online.

○┓ Libraries Unlimited publishes resources for libraries, librarians, and educators. "We are currently emphasizing readers' advisory guides, academic reference works, readers' theatre, storytelling, biographical dictionary."

Nonfiction Biography (collections), reference, textbook. Subjects include agriculture/horticulture, anthropology/archeology, art/architecture, business/economics, education, ethnic, health/medicine, history, language/literature, music/dance, philosophy, psychology, religion, science, sociology, women's issues/studies, technology. "We are interested in library applications and tools for all subject areas." Submit proposal package including outline, 1 sample chapter(s), résumé. Reviews artwork/photos as part of ms package. Send photocopies.

Recent Title(s) *Information Literacy: Essential Skills for the Information Age*, by Michael B. Eisenberg, Carrie A. Lowe, and Kathleen L. Spitzer; *Picture This! Using Picture Books for Character Education in the Classroom*, by Claire Gatrell Stephens.

Tips "We welcome any ideas that combine professional expertise, writing ability, and innovative thinking. Audience is librarians (school, public, academic, and special) and teachers (K-12)."

LIGUORI PUBLICATIONS

One Liguori Dr., Liguori MO 63057. (636)464-2500. Fax: (636)464-8449. Website: www.liguori.org. Publisher: Harry Grile. **Acquisitions:** Hans Christoffersen, editorial director. Estab. 1947. Publishes paperback originals and reprints under the Ligouri and Libros Ligouri imprints. **Publishes 30 titles/year. Pays royalty, or makes outright purchase. Offers varied advance.** Publishes book 2 years after acceptance of ms. Does not accept simultaneous submissions. Responds in 2 months to queries; 2 months to proposals; 3 months to mss. Ms guidelines online.

Imprints Libros Liguori, Liguori Books, Liguori/Triumph, Liguori Lifespan.

○━ Liguori Publications, faithful to the charism of St. Alphonsus, is an apostolate within the mission of the Denver Province. Its mission, a collaborative effort of Redemptorists and laity, is to spread the gospel of Jesus Christ primarily through the print and electronic media. It shares in the Redemptorist priority of giving special attention to the poor and the most abandoned. Currently emphasizing practical spirituality, prayers and devotions, "how-to" spirituality.

Nonfiction Manuscripts with Catholic sensibility. Self-help. Subjects include computers/electronic, religion, spirituality. Mostly adult audience; limited children/juvenile. Query with SASE, or submit outline, 1 sample chapter(s).

Ⓝ LILLENAS PUBLISHING CO.

Imprint of Lillenas Drama Resources, 2923 Troost Ave., Kansas City MO 64109. (816)931-1900. Fax: (816)412-8390. E-mail: drama@lillenas.com. Website: www.lillenasdrama.com. **Acquisitions:** Kim Messer, product manager (Christian drama). Publishes mass market paperback and electronic originals. **Publishes 50 + titles/year; imprint publishes 12 + titles/year. Pays royalty on wholesale price, or makes outright purchase.**

Nonfiction Plays, collections of scripts. Subjects include religion, life issues. Query with SASE, or submit complete ms.

LIMELIGHT EDITIONS

Proscenium Publishers, Inc., 118 E. 30th St., New York NY 10016. Fax: (212)532-5526. E-mail: limelighteditions @earthlink.net. Website: www.limelighteditions.com. **Acquisitions:** Melvyn B. Zerman, president; Jenna Young, associate publisher. Estab. 1983. Publishes hardcover and trade paperback originals, trade paperback reprints. **Publishes 14 titles/year. Receives 150 queries and 40 mss/year. 15% of books from first-time authors; 20% from unagented writers. Pays 7½-10% royalty on retail price. Offers $500-2,000 advance.** Publishes book 10 months after acceptance of ms. Does not accept simultaneous submissions. Responds in 1 month to queries; 1 month to proposals; 3 months to mss. Book catalog and ms guidelines free.

○━ Limelight Editions publishes books on film, theater, music, and dance history. "Our books make a strong contribution to their fields and deserve to remain in print for many years."

Nonfiction "All books are on the performing arts *exclusively*." Biography, how-to (instructional), humor, illustrated book. Subjects include film/cinema/stage, history, multicultural, music/dance. Query with SASE, or submit proposal package including outline, 2-3 sample chapter(s). Reviews artwork/photos as part of ms package. Send photocopies.

Recent Title(s) *Transformational Acting*, by Sande Shurin; *The Spy Who Thrilled Us*, by Mike Di Leo; *The Nashville Chronicles*, by Jan Stuart.

LIMITLESS DARE 2 DREAM PUBLISHING

Limitless Corp., Dare 2 Dream Publishing, 100 Pin Oak Ct., Lexington SC 29073. (803)359-2881. Fax: (803)356-8231. E-mail: limitlessd2d@aol.com. Website: www.limitlessd2d.net. **Acquisitions:** Samantha E. Ruskin, CEO; Anne M. Clarkson, CIO (purchasing and marketing). Estab. 2002. Publishes trade paperback originals and reprints. **Publishes 35-50 titles/year; imprint publishes at least 35-50 titles/year. Receives 1,000 + queries and 800-1,200 mss/year. Pays 12-20% royalty on purchase price.** Publishes book 3-12 months after acceptance of ms. Does not accept simultaneous submissions. Responds in 1 month to queries; 3-5 months to mss. Book catalog for #10 SASE; ms guidelines for #10 SASE.

Imprints Dare 2 Dream.

O→ "We do not do books that demean women in any way or books where the women are helpless females waiting to be rescued. We do not do anything of a religious nature at all, so please do not send it. Other than that writers will find us quite open minded and willing to read and consider their manuscripts. The criteria at D2D is good stories, good writing, and hold the reader's interest."

Nonfiction Audiocassettes, reference. Subjects include alternative lifestyles, animals, creative nonfiction, general nonfiction, history, hobbies, humanities, memoirs, military/war, philosophy, photography, psychology, regional, spirituality, women's issues/studies. Query with SASE, or submit complete ms. Reviews artwork/photos as part of ms package. Send photocopies or e-mail attachments or burned onto a CD.

Fiction Adventure, erotica, fantasy, feminist, gay/lesbian, historical, horror, humor, mainstream/contemporary, military/war, multimedia, mystery, occult, poetry, regional, romance, science fiction, short story collections, spiritual, suspense, western. Query with SASE, or submit complete ms.

Poetry "Poetry can be a tough market, but we do publish volumes of poetry. All we can say is try us. If it is very good poetry, you have a good chance with us." Query, or submit any number of sample poems, or submit complete ms.

Recent Title(s) *Home to Ohio*, by Deborah E. Warr (mainstream); *Return of the Warrior*, by Katherine E. Standell (lesbian fiction); *Journeys*, by Anne Azel (lesbian fiction).

Tips "Our audience is primarily women in all walks of life and from all educational levels. This company was created by 2 women who know the struggle to get into print, so our best advice is to just go ahead and do it—send the manuscript to us and give it a try. We promise to treat it with honor and respect."

LIONHEARTED PUBLISHING, INC.

P.O. Box 618, Zephyr Cove NV 89448-0618. (775)588-1388. E-mail: admin@lionhearted.com. Website: www.lionhearted.com. **Acquisitions:** Historical or Contemporary Acquistions Editor. Estab. 1994. Publishes trade and mass market paperback originals and e-books. **Publishes 6-24 titles/year. 90% from unagented writers. Royalties of 10% maximum on paperbacks; 30% on electronic books. Offers $100 advance.** Publishes book 18-24 months after acceptance of ms. Does not accept simultaneous submissions. Responds in 1 month to queries; 3 months to mss. Book catalog and ms guidelines online.

O→ "Multiple award-winning, independent publisher of single title, mass market paperback and e-book, romance novels."

Fiction Romance (contemporary, futuristic/time travel, historical, regency period, romantic suspense; over 65,000 words only), romantic comedies. Query with SASE, or submit outline, 3 sample chapter(s), publishing history, synopsis, estimated word count, cover letter, and 1-paragraph story summary in cover letter. Do not send ms by regular mail unless invited by editor. Send sample chapters in body of e-mail or label each attachment with the title.

Recent Title(s) *The Only One*, by Karen Woods (contemporary romance); *The Magic Token*, by Susan Christina (Regency romance); *Suddenly Love*, by Catherine Sellers (contemporary).

Tips "If you are not an avid reader of romance, don't attempt to write romance. Please read a few of our single-title releases (they are a bit different) before submitting your romance novel."

▲ LISTEN & LIVE AUDIO, INC.

P.O. Box 817, Roseland NJ 07068. (973)781-1444. Fax: (973)781-0333. E-mail: alisa@listenandlive.com. Website: www.listenandlive.com. **Acquisitions:** Alisa Weberman, publisher (mss/books for audiobook consideration). **Publishes 20 titles/year. Receives 200 mss/year. Offers advance.** Publishes book 3-6 months after acceptance of ms. Accepts simultaneous submissions. Responds in 1 month to mss. Book catalog online.

Imprints Defiance Audio, Appleseed Audio.

O→ Listen & Live publishes fiction and nonfiction books on audio cassette/CD.

Nonfiction Multimedia (audio format), self-help, true life. Subjects include business/economics, relationships. *Agented submissions only.*

Fiction Mystery, young adult, contemporary, women's fiction, children's. *Agented submissions only.*

Recent Title(s) *The Darwin Awards I & II*; *Jump the Shark*; *No One Left Behind.*

Tips Agents/publishers only may submit mss/books.

▲ ⊘ LITTLE SIMON

Imprint of Simon & Schuster Children's Publishing Division, Simon & Schuster, 1230 Avenue of the Americas, New York NY 10020. (212)698-1295. Fax: (212)698-2794. Website: www.simonsayskids.com. Executive Vice President/Publisher: Robin Corey. **Acquisitions:** Cindy Alvarez, vice president/editorial director; Erin Molta, senior editor. Publishes novelty and branded books only. **Publishes 50 titles/year. 5% of books from first-time authors. Offers advance and royalties.** Publishes book 2 years after acceptance of ms.

- Currently not accepting unsolicited mss.
- ⚬⊸ "Our goal is to provide fresh material in an innovative format for preschool to age 8. Our books are often, if not exclusively, format driven."

Nonfiction "We publish very few nonfiction titles." Children's/juvenile. No picture books. Query with SASE.

Fiction "Novelty books include many things that do not fit in the traditional hardcover or paperback format, such as pop-up, board book, scratch and sniff, glow in the dark, lift the flap, etc." Children's/juvenile. No picture books. Large part of the list is holiday-themed.

Recent Title(s) *Alice in Wonderland*, by Robert Sabuda; *Chanukah Bugs*, by David Carter; *It's the Great Pumpkin, Charlie Brown*, by Charles M. Schultz.

Ⓐ LITTLE, BROWN AND CO. ADULT TRADE BOOKS

Division of Time Warner Book Group, 1271 Avenue of the Americas, New York NY 10020. (212)522-8700. Fax: (212)522-2067. Website: www.twbookmark.com. Estab. 1837. Publishes hardcover originals and paperback originals and reprints.

Ⓐ LITTLE, BROWN AND CO. CHILDREN'S PUBLISHING

Subsidiary of Time Warner Book Group, Time Life Bldg., 1271 Avenue of the Americas, 11th Floor, New York NY 10020. (212)522-8700. Website: www.twbookmark.com. Editor-in-Chief/V-P, Associate Publisher: Megan Tingley. Marketing Director VP/Associate Publisher: Bill Boedeker. Senior Editor: Cindy Eagan. Editor: Jennifer Hunt. Estab. 1837. Publishes hardcover originals, trade paperback reprints. **Publishes 70-100 titles/year. Pays royalty on retail price. Offers negotiable advance.** Publishes book 2 years after acceptance of ms. Accepts simultaneous submissions. Responds in 1 month to queries; 2 months to proposals; 2 months to mss.

Imprints Megan Tingley Books (Megan Tingley, editorial director).

- ⚬⊸ Little, Brown and Co. Children's Publishing publishes all formats including board books, picture books, middle grade fiction, and nonfiction YA titles. "We are looking for strong writing and presentation, but no predetermined topics."

Nonfiction Children's/juvenile. Subjects include animals, art/architecture, ethnic, gay/lesbian, history, hobbies, nature/environment, recreation, science, sports. Writers should avoid "looking for the 'issue' they think publishers want to see, choosing instead topics they know best and are most enthusiastic about/inspired by." *Agented submissions only.*

Fiction Adventure, ethnic, fantasy, feminist, gay/lesbian, historical, humor, juvenile, mystery, picture books, science fiction, suspense, young adult. "We are looking for strong fiction for children of all ages in any area, including multicultural. We always prefer full manuscripts for fiction." *Agented submissions only.*

Recent Title(s) *Gossip Girl*, by Cecily von Ziegesar; *Little Brown Bear Won't Take a Nap*, by Jane Dyer; *The Feel Good Book*, by Todd Parr.

Tips "Our audience is children of all ages, from preschool through young adult. We are looking for quality material that will work in hardcover—send us your best."

Ⓝ Ⓐ LITTLE, BROWN AND CO., INC.

Subsidiary of Time Warner Book Group, 1271 Avenue of the Americas, New York NY 10017. Website: www.twbookgroup.com. Publisher/Editor-in-Chief: Michael Pietsch. **Acquisitions:** Editorial Department, Trade Division. Estab. 1837. Publishes adult and juvenile hardcover and paperback originals, and reprints. **Pays royalty. Offers varying advance.** Does not accept simultaneous submissions. Ms guidelines online.

Imprints Little, Brown and Co; Back Bay Books.

- ⚬⊸ "The general editorial philosophy for all divisions continues to be broad and flexible, with high quality and the promise of commercial success as always the first considerations."

Nonfiction Autobiography, biography, cookbook. Subjects include contemporary culture, cooking/foods/nutrition, history, memoirs, nature/environment, science, sports. No unsolicited mss or proposals.

Fiction Experimental, literary, mainstream/contemporary, mystery, short story collections, suspense, thrillers/espionage, translations. *Agented submissions only.*

Recent Title(s) *The Lovely Bones*, by Alice Sebold; *Fear Itself*, by Walter Mosley.

LIVINGSTON PRESS

University of West Alabama, Station 22, Livingston AL 35470. E-mail: jwt@uwa.edu. Website: www.livingstonpress.uwa.edu. **Acquisitions:** Joe Taylor, director. Estab. 1984. Publishes hardcover and trade paperback originals. **Publishes 9 titles/year. 50% of books from first-time authors; 99% from unagented writers. Pays a choice of 12% of initial run or a combination of contributor's copies and 10% royalty of net.** Publishes book 18 months after acceptance of ms. Accepts simultaneous submissions. Responds in 1 month to queries; 1 year to mss. Book catalog for SASE; ms guidelines online.

Imprints Swallow's Tale Press.

- Reads mss from December 1-January 15 only.
- O→ Livingston Press publishes topics such as Southern literature and quirky fiction. Currently emphasizing short stories. De-emphasizing poetry.

Fiction Experimental, literary, short story collections, off-beat or Southern. "We are interested in form and, of course, style." Query with SASE. Accepts unsoliced mss only during December.

Poetry "We publish very little poetry, mostly books we have asked to see." Query.

Recent Title(s) *Partita In Venice*, by Curt Leviant; *Flight From Valhalla*, by Michael Bugeja (poetry); *B. Horror and Other Stories*, by Wendell Mayo.

Tips "Our readers are interested in literature, often quirky literature that emphasizes form and style. Please visit our website for current needs."

LLEWELLYN PUBLICATIONS

Imprint of Llewellyn Worldwide, Ltd., P.O. Box 64383, St. Paul MN 55164-0383. (651)291-1970. Fax: (651)291-1908. E-mail: lwlpc@llewellyn.com. Website: www.llewellyn.com. **Acquisitions:** Nancy J. Mostad, acquisitions manager (New Age, metaphysical, occult, astrology, tarot, wicca, pagan, magick, alternative health, self-help, how-to books). Estab. 1901. Publishes trade and mass market paperback originals. **Publishes 100 titles/year. Receives 2,000 submissions/year. 30% of books from first-time authors; 90% from unagented writers. Pays 10% royalty on wholesale price, or retail price.** Accepts simultaneous submissions. Responds in 3 months to queries. Book catalog for 9×12 SAE with 4 first-class stamps; ms guidelines online.

- O→ Llewellyn publishes New Age fiction and nonfiction exploring "new worlds of mind and spirit." Currently emphasizing astrology, wicca, alternative health and healing, tarot. De-emphasizing fiction, channeling.

Nonfiction How-to, self-help. Subjects include cooking/foods/nutrition, health/medicine, nature/environment, New Age, psychology, women's issues/studies. Submit outline, sample chapter(s). Reviews artwork/photos as part of ms package.

Fiction "Authentic and educational, yet entertaining." Occult, spiritual (metaphysical).

Recent Title(s) *Authentic Spirituality*, by Richard N. Potter; *The Sophisticated Gourmet*, by Noel Tyl.

LOFT PRESS, INC.

P.O. Box 150, Fort Valley VA 22652. (540)933-6210. Website: www.loftpress.com. **Acquisitions:** Ann A. Hunter, editor-in-chief. Publishes hardcover and trade paperback originals and reprints. **Publishes 12-20 titles/year; imprint publishes 6-8 titles/year. Receives 200 queries and 150 mss/year. 50% of books from first-time authors; 100% from unagented writers. Pays royalty on net receipts.** Publishes book 6 months after acceptance of ms. Ms guidelines online.

Imprints Punch Press, Eschat Press, Far Muse Press (for all contact Stephen R. Hunter, publisher).

Nonfiction Biography, coffee table book, how-to, technical, textbook. Subjects include Americana, art/architecture, business/economics, computers/electronic, government/politics, history, language/literature, memoirs, philosophy, regional, religion, science. Submit proposal package including outline, 1 sample chapter(s). Reviews artwork/photos as part of ms package. Send photocopies.

Fiction Literary, plays, poetry, poetry in translation, regional, short story collections. Submit proposal package including 1 sample chapter(s), synopsis.

Poetry Submit 5 sample poems.

Recent Title(s) *Who Is God*, by Mohan Rao; *Light Ruck*, by Tom Lacombe.

LONE EAGLE PUBLISHING CO.

1024 N. Orange Dr., Hollywood CA 90038. (323)308-3411; (800)815-0503. E-mail: jblack@ifilm.com. Website: www.hdconline.com. **Acquisitions:** Jeff Black, editor. Estab. 1982. Publishes perfectbound and trade paperback originals. **Publishes 15 titles/year. Receives 100 submissions/year. 50% from unagented writers. Pays 10% royalty. Offers $2,500-5,000 average advance.** Publishes book 1 year after acceptance of ms. Accepts simultaneous submissions. Responds quarterly to queries. Book catalog free.

- O→ Lone Eagle Publishing Company publishes reference directories that contain comprehensive and accurate credits, personal data, and contact information for every major entertainment industry craft. Lone Eagle also publishes many how-to books for the film production business, including books on screenwriting, directing, budgeting and producing, acting, editing, etc. Lone Eagle is broadening its base to include general entertainment titles.

Nonfiction Biography, how-to, reference, technical. Subjects include film/cinema/stage, entertainment. "We are looking for books in film and television, related topics or biographies." Submit outline, sample chapter(s). Reviews artwork/photos as part of ms package.

Recent Title(s) *Elements of Style for Screenwriters*, by Paul Argentina; *1001: A Video Odyssey*, by Steve Tathan.

Tips "A well-written, well-thought-out book on some technical aspect of the motion picture (or video) industry has the best chance. Pick a subject that has not been done to death, make sure you know what you're talking about, get someone well-known in that area to endorse the book and prepare to spend a lot of time publicizing the book. Completed manuscripts have the best chance for acceptance."

LOOMPANICS UNLIMITED

P.O. Box 1197, Port Townsend WA 98368-0997. Fax: (360)385-7785. E-mail: editorial@loompanics.com. Website: www.loompanics.com. **Acquisitions:** Michael Hoy, editor. Estab. 1975. Publishes trade paperback originals. **Publishes 12 titles/year. Receives 500 submissions/year. 40% of books from first-time authors; 100% from unagented writers. Pays 10-12% royalty on wholesale and/or retail sales, or makes outright purchase of $100-1,200. Offers $500 average advance.** Publishes book 6 months after acceptance of ms. Accepts simultaneous submissions. Responds in 3 months to queries. Book catalog for $5, postage paid; ms guidelines online.

 "Our motto 'No more secrets-no more excuses-no more limits' says it all, whatever the subject. Our books are somewhat 'edgy.' From computer hacking to gardening to tax avoision, we are the name in beat-the-system books." Always emphasizing unusual takes on subjects that are controversial and how-to books. "We do not want anything that's already been done or New Age."

Nonfiction "In general, we like works on edgy topics or obscure-but-useful technology written with confidence in a matter-of-fact way. We are looking for how-to books in the fields of espionage, investigation, the underground economy, police methods, how to beat the system, crime and criminal techniques." How-to, reference, self-help, technical. Subjects include agriculture/horticulture, Americana, anthropology/archeology, computers/electronic, government/politics, health/medicine, money/finance, psychology, science, film/cinema/stage. "We are also looking for articles on similar subjects for our catalog and its supplements." Query with SASE, or submit outline, sample chapter(s). Reviews artwork/photos as part of ms package.

Recent Title(s) *Rancho Costa Nada: The Dirt Cheap Desert Homestead*, by Phil Garlington; *Speak Up, Speak Out and Be Heard: How to Protest and Make It Count*, by Jeremy Holcomb; *Uberhacker II! More Ways to Break into a Computer*, by Carolyn Meinel.

Tips "Our audience is primarily young males looking for hard-to-find information on alternatives to 'The System.' Your chances for success are greatly improved if you can show us how your proposal fits in with our catalog."

LOST HORSE PRESS

105 Lost Horse Lane, Sandpoint ID 83864. (208)255-4410. Fax: (208)255-1560. E-mail: losthorsepress@mindspring.com. Website: www.losthorsepress.org. **Acquisitions:** Christine Holbert, editor (novels, novellas). Estab. 1998. Publishes hardcover and paperback originals. **Publishes 4 titles/year.** Publishes book 1-2 years after acceptance of ms. Responds in 3 months to queries; 6-9 months to mss. Book catalog free; ms guidelines for #10 SASE.

Fiction Literary, poetry, regional (Pacific Northwest), short story collections. Accepts queries by e-mail. Accepts submissions on disk. Query with SASE, or submit publishing history, author bio, SASE, or submit complete ms. Submit cover letter.

Recent Title(s) *Woman on the Cross*, by Pierre Delattre (novel); *Iron Fever*, by Stephan Torre (poetry); *Hiding from Salesmen*, by Scott Poole (poetry).

LOUISIANA STATE UNIVERSITY PRESS

P.O. Box 25053, Baton Rouge LA 70894-5053. (225)578-6618. Fax: (225)578-6461. Website: www.lsu.edu/lsupress. **Acquisitions:** Sylvia Frank Rodrigue, editor-in-chief. Estab. 1935. Publishes hardcover and paperback originals, and reprints. **Publishes 70-80 titles/year. Receives 800 submissions/year. 33% of books from first-time authors; 95% from unagented writers. Pays royalty.** Publishes book 1 year after acceptance of ms. Does not accept simultaneous submissions. Responds in 1 month to queries. Book catalog and ms guidelines free.

Nonfiction Biography. Subjects include art/architecture, ethnic, government/politics, history, language/literature, music/dance, photography, regional, women's issues/studies. Query with SASE, or submit outline, sample chapter(s).

Recent Title(s) *The Ha-Ha*, by David Kirby (poetry); *Days of Glory: The Army of the Cumberland, 1861-1865*, by Larry J. Daniel (history); *The Great Southern Babylon: Sex, Race, and Respectability in New Orleans, 1865-1920*, by Alecia P. Long (history).

Tips "Our audience includes scholars, intelligent laymen, general audience."

LOVE SPELL

Imprint of Dorchester Publishing Co., Inc., 200 Madison Ave., Suite 2000, New York NY 10016. (212)725-8811. Fax: (212)532-1054. Website: www.dorchesterpub.com. **Acquisitions:** Micaela Bombard and Jessica McDonnell, editorial assistants; Kate Seaver, editor; Christopher Keeslar, senior editor. Publishes mass market paperback originals. **Publishes 48 titles/year. Receives 1,500-2,000 queries and 150-500 mss/year. 30% of books from first-time authors; 25-30% from unagented writers. Pays 4% royalty on retail price. Offers $2,000 average advance.** Publishes book 1 year after acceptance of ms. Does not accept simultaneous submissions. Responds in 6 months to mss. Book catalog for free or by calling (800)481-9191; ms guidelines online.

O→ Love Spell publishes the quirky sub-genres of romance: time-travel, paranormal, futuristic. "Despite the exotic settings, we are still interested in character-driven plots."

Fiction Romance (futuristic, time travel, paranormal, historical), whimsical contemporaries. "Books industry-wide are getting shorter; we're interested in 90,000 words." Query with SASE, or submit 3 sample chapter(s), synopsis. No material will be returned without SASE. Query first. No queries by fax. "All manuscripts must be typed, double-spaced on one side, and left unbound."

Recent Title(s) *A Girl's Guide to Vampires*, by Katie MacAlister.

LOYOLA PRESS

3441 N. Ashland Ave., Chicago IL 60657-1397. (773)281-1818. Fax: (773)281-0152. E-mail: editorial@loyolapress.com. Website: www.loyolapress.org. **Acquisitions:** Joseph Durepos, acquisitions editor. Publishes hardcover and trade paperback. **Publishes 30-40 titles/year. Receives 500 queries/year. Pays standard royalties. Offers reasonable advance.** Accepts simultaneous submissions. Book catalog and ms guidelines online.

Imprints Jesuit Way (focus on Jesuit life and history as well as on Ignatian spirituality and ministry).

Nonfiction Subjects include religion, spirituality, inspirational, prayer, Catholic life, grief and loss, marriage and family. *Jesuit Way* books focus on Jesuit life and history as well as on Ignatian spirituality and ministry. Query with SASE.

Recent Title(s) *Heroic Leadership*, by Chris Lowney; *The New Faithful*, by Colleen Carroll; *The Holy War*, by Paula Huston.

Tips "We're looking for authors who have a fresh approach to religion and spirituality, especially for readers looking for a way to respond to God in their daily lives."

⊘ LUCENT BOOKS

10911 Technology Place, San Diego CA 92127. **Acquisitions:** Chandra Howard, acquisitions editor. Estab. 1988. **Publishes 200 titles/year. 10% of books from first-time authors; 90% from unagented writers. Makes outright purchase of $2,500-3,000.**

O→ Lucent Books is a nontrade publisher of nonfiction for the middle school audience providing students with resource material for academic studies and for independent learning.

Nonfiction Children's/juvenile. Subjects include history, world affairs, cultural and social issues. Tightly formatted books for middle grade readers. Each series has specific requirements. Potential writers should familiarize themselves with the material. All are works for hire, by assignment only. *No unsolicited mss.* Query with cover letter, résumé, list of publications.

Recent Title(s) *J.K. Rowling*, by Bradley Steffens; *Life in the Trenches*, by Stephen Currie; *Women of the American Revolution*, by Louise Chipley Slavicek.

Tips "We expect writers to do thorough research using books, magazines, and newspapers. Biased writing, whether liberal or conservative, has no place in our books. We prefer to work with writers who have experience writing nonfiction for middle grade students. We are looking for experienced writers, especially those who have written nonfiction books at young adult level."

THE LYONS PRESS

Imprint of The Globe Pequot Press, Inc., Box 480, 246 Goose Lane, Guilford CT 06437. (203)458-4500. Fax: (203)458-4668. Website: www.lyonspress.com. VP-GPP/Publisher: Tony Lyons. **Acquisitions:** Lilly Golden, editor-at-large (fiction, memoirs, narrative nonfiction); Jay Cassell, editorial director (fishing, hunting, survival, military, history); Jay McCullough, editor (narrative nonfiction, travelogues, adventure, military, espionage, international current events, history); Tom McCarthy, senior editor (sports & fitness, history, outdoor adventure, memoirs); Ann Treistman, editor (narrative nonfiction, travelogues, adventure, sports, animals, cooking); Holly Rubino, production editor (narrative nonfiction, home); Lisa Purcell, editor-at-large (history, adventure, narrative nonfiction, cooking); George Donahue, senior editor (military history, martial arts, narrative nonfiction, sports, travel, current affairs); Enrica Gadler, editor-at-large; Alicia Solis. Estab. 1984 (Lyons & Burford), 1997 (The Lyons Press). Publishes hardcover and trade paperback originals and reprints. **Publishes 300 titles/year. 50% of books from first-time authors; 30% from unagented writers. Pays 5-10% royalty on wholesale price. Offers $2,000-7,000 advance.** Publishes book 1 year after acceptance of ms. Accepts simultaneous submissions. Responds in 1 month to queries; 1 month to proposals; 2 months to mss. Book catalog and ms guidelines online.

- The Lyons Press has teamed up to develop books with L.L. Bean, *Field & Stream*, Orvis, Outward Bound, Buckmasters, and *Golf Magazine*.
- O⊸ The Lyons Press publishes practical and literary books, chiefly centered on outdoor subjects—natural history, all sports, gardening, horses, fishing. Currently emphasizing adventure, sports. De-emphasizing hobbies, travel.

Nonfiction Biography, cookbook, how-to, reference. Subjects include agriculture/horticulture, Americana, animals, anthropology/archeology, cooking/foods/nutrition, gardening, health/medicine, history, hobbies, military/war, nature/environment (environment), recreation, science, sports, travel. "Visit our website and note the featured categories." Query with SASE, or submit proposal package including outline, 3 sample chapter(s), and marketing description. Reviews artwork/photos as part of ms package. Send photocopies or nonoriginal prints.

Fiction Historical, military/war, short story collections (fishing, hunting, outdoor, nature), sports. Query with SASE, or submit proposal package including outline, 3-5 sample chapter(s).

Recent Title(s) *Embedded*, by William Katovsky (current events); *Spotted in France*, by Gregory Edmond (travel); *Facing Ali*, by Stephen Brunt (sports).

THE MAGNI GROUP, INC.

7106 Wellington Point Rd., McKinney TX 75070. (972)540-2050. Fax: (972)540-1057. E-mail: info@magnico.com. Website: www.magnico.com. **Acquisitions:** Evan Reynolds, president. Publishes hardcover originals and trade paperback reprints. **Publishes 5-10 titles/year. Receives 20 queries and 10-20 mss/year. 50% of books from first-time authors; 80% from unagented writers. Pays royalty on wholesale price, or makes outright purchase. Offers advance.** Publishes book 6 months after acceptance of ms. Does not accept simultaneous submissions. Responds in 2 months to queries. Book catalog and ms guidelines online.

Imprints Magni Publishing.

Nonfiction Cookbook, how-to, self-help. Subjects include child guidance/parenting, cooking/foods/nutrition, health/medicine, money/finance, sex. Submit complete ms. Reviews artwork/photos as part of ms package. Send photocopies.

Recent Title(s) *Eat Like the Stars Cookbook*; *Holiday Planner*; *Eat Yourself Thin Like I Did* (cookbook).

MAISONNEUVE PRESS

P.O. Box 2980, Washington DC 20013-2980. (301)277-7505. Fax: (301)277-2467. E-mail: editors@maisonneuve press.com. Website: www.maisonneuvepress.com. **Acquisitions:** Robert Merrill, editor (politics, literature, philosophy); Dennis Crow, editor (architecture, urban studies, sociology). Publishes hardcover and trade paperback originals. **Publishes 6 titles/year. 5% of books from first-time authors; 100% from unagented writers. Pays 5% royalty on cover price or $2,000 maximum outright purchase.** Publishes book 1 year after acceptance of ms. Accepts simultaneous submissions. Responds in 1 month to queries; 1 month to proposals; 1 month to mss. Book catalog free; Send letter for guidelines, individual response.

- O⊸ "Maisonneuve provides solid, first-hand information for serious adult readers: academics and political activists."

Nonfiction Biography. Subjects include education, ethnic, gay/lesbian, government/politics, history, language/literature, military/war, philosophy, psychology, sociology, translation, women's issues/studies, literary criticism, social theory, economics, essay collections. "We make decisions on completed manuscripts only. Will correspond on work in progress. Some books submitted are too narrowly focused; not marketable enough. We are eager to read manuscripts on the current crisis and war. The commercial media—TV and newspapers—are not doing a very good job of cutting through the government propaganda." Query with SASE, or submit complete ms. Reviews artwork/photos as part of ms package. Send photocopies.

Recent Title(s) *Morse Peckham, Man's Rage for Chaos: Biology, Behavior and the Arts.*

Ⓝ MANDALA PUBLISHING

17 Paul Dr., San Rafael CA 94903. (415)526-1380. Fax: (415)532-3281. E-mail: info@mandala.org. **Acquisitions:** Lisa Fitzpatrick, associate publisher (Hindu philosophy, music, and art). Estab. 1989. Publishes hardcover, trade paperback, and electronic originals. **Publishes 12 titles/year. Receives 200 queries and 100 mss/year. 40% of books from first-time authors; 100% from unagented writers. Pays 3-15% royalty on retail price.** Publishes book 8 months after acceptance of ms. Accepts simultaneous submissions. Responds in 6 months to queries; 6 months to proposals; 6 months to mss. Book catalog online.

Nonfiction Biography, children's/juvenile, coffee table book, scholarly, self-help. Subjects include alternative lifestyles, cooking/foods/nutrition, education, health/medicine, philosophy, photography, religion, spirituality. "We specialize in preserving and promoting the Vedic tradition by producing high quality, fully illustrated coffee table books, gift items, stationery, posters, etc., for modern general audiences." Query with SASE. Reviews artwork/photos as part of ms package. Send photocopies or thumbnails.

Fiction Juvenile, religious, spiritual. Query with SASE.

Recent Title(s) *Prince of Dharma*, by Ranchor Prinie (illustrated biography); *The Gita Deck*, by Mandala Publishing (inspirational card deck).

☑ MARLOR PRESS, INC.

4304 Brigadoon Dr., St. Paul MN 55126. (651)484-4600. E-mail: marlin.marlor@minn.net. **Acquisitions:** Marlin Bree, publisher. Estab. 1981. Publishes trade paperback originals. **Publishes 6 titles/year. Receives 100 queries and 25 mss/year. Pays 8-10% royalty on wholesale price.** Publishes book 1 year after acceptance of ms. Does not accept simultaneous submissions. Responds in 3-6 weeks to queries. Ms guidelines for #10 SASE.

    ○━ Currently emphasizing general interest nonfiction children's books and nonfiction boating books. De-emphasizing travel.

Nonfiction Children's/juvenile, how-to. Subjects include travel, boating. "Primarily how-to stuff." *No unsolicited mss.* No anecdotal reminiscences or biographical materials. No fiction or poetry. Query first; submit outline with sample chapters only when requested. Do not send full ms. Reviews artwork/photos as part of ms package.

Recent Title(s) *Going Abroad: The Bathroom Survival Guide*, by Eva Newman; *Wake of the Green Storm: A Survivor's Tale*, by Marlin Bree.

N ☑ MARLOWE & CO.

Imprint of Avalon Publishing Group, 245 W. 17th St., 11th Floor, New York NY 10011. (646)375-2570. Fax: (212)375-2571. Website: www.avalonpub.com. Publisher: Matthew Lore. Estab. 1994.

    ○━ Marlowe & Co., an imprint of Avalon Publishing Group, publishes widely in the areas of health and fitness, food and cooking, psychology and personal growth, religion and spirituality, current affairs, pregnancy and parenting, and folklore and mythology. About 50 books a year are published by the imprint, roughly 30% of which are commissioned by the publisher."

Nonfiction Subjects include health and fitness, food and cooking, psychology and personal growth, religion and spirituality, current affairs, pregnancy and parenting, and folklore and mythology. *No unsolicited mss.*

Recent Title(s) *The Glucose Revolution*, by Jennie Brand-Miller; *Going the Other Way*, by Billy Bean; *Party of One*, by Anneli Rufus.

N MAUPIN HOUSE PUBLISHING, INC.

P.O. Box 90148, Gainesville FL 32607. (800)524-0634. Fax: (352)373-5546. E-mail: info@maupinhouse.com. Website: www.maupinhouse.com. **Acquisitions:** Julia Graddy, publisher. Publishes trade paperback originals and reprints. **Publishes 7 titles/year. Pays 10% royalty on retail price.** Responds in 2 months to queries.

    ○━ Maupin House publishes professional resource books for language arts teachers K-12.

Nonfiction How-to. Subjects include education, language/literature, writing workshop, reading instruction. "We are looking for practical, in-classroom resource materials, especially in the field of language arts and writing workshops. Classroom teachers are our top choice as authors." Query with SASE.

Recent Title(s) *Primary Literacy Centers*; *Beyond Book Reports*.

N MBI PUBLISHING CO.

Galtier Plaza, Suite 200, 380 Jackson St., St. Paul MN 55101. (651)287-5100. Fax: (651)287-5101. Website: www.motorbooks.com. Sr. VP, Global Publishing: Tim Parker; VP, Publishing: Zack Miller. **Acquisitions:** Lee Klancher, senior editor; Darwin Holmstrom (motorcycles); Peter Bodensteiner (racing, how-to); Dennis Pernu (Americana, trains & boats); Steve Gansen (military, aviation, tractors). Estab. 1973. Publishes hardcover and paperback originals. **Publishes 200 titles/year. Receives 300 queries and 50 mss/year. 95% from unagented writers. Pays royalty on net receipts. Offers $5,000 average advance.** Publishes book 1 year after acceptance of ms. Accepts simultaneous submissions. Responds in 3 months to queries. Book catalog free; ms guidelines for #10 SASE.

Imprints Motorbooks International, Crestline.

    ○━ MBI is a transportation-related publisher: cars, motorcycles, racing, trucks, tractors, boats, bicycles—also Americana, aviation and military history.

Nonfiction Transportation-related subjects. Coffee table book, gift book, how-to, illustrated book, narrative nonfiction. Subjects include Americana, history, hobbies, military/war, photography, translation (nonfiction). "State qualifications for doing book." Query with SASE. Reviews artwork/photos as part of ms package. Send photocopies.

Recent Title(s) *Jesse James: The Man and His Machines*, by Mike Seate; *How to Customize Damn Near Anything*, edited by Lee Klancher; *Corvette: 50 Years*, by Phil Berg.

N MC PRESS

125 N. Woodland Trail, Double Oak TX 75077. Fax: (682)831-0701. E-mail: mlee@mcpressonline.com. Website: www.mcpressonline.com. **Acquisitions:** Merrikay Lee, president (computer). Estab. 2001. Publishes trade paperback originals. **Publishes 40 titles/year; imprint publishes 20 titles/year. Receives 100 queries and 50 mss/year. 5% of books from first-time authors; 5% from unagented writers. Pays 10-16% royalty on wholesale price.** Publishes book 9 months after acceptance of ms. Accepts simultaneous submissions. Responds in 1 month to queries; 1 month to proposals; 1 month to mss. Book catalog and ms guidelines free.
Imprints MC Press, IBM Press.
Nonfiction Technical. Subjects include computers/electronic. ''We specialize in computer titles targeted at the IBM marketplace.'' Submit proposal package including outline, 2 sample chapter(s), abstract. Reviews artwork/photos as part of ms package. Send photocopies.
Recent Title(s) *Understanding the IBM Web Facing Tool*, by Claus Weiss and Emily Bruner (computer); *Eclipse Step-by-Step*, by Jae Pluta (computer).

McBOOKS PRESS

1D Booth Building, 520 N. Meadow St., Ithaca NY 14850. (607)272-2114. Fax: (607)273-6068. E-mail: mcbooks @mcbooks.com. Website: www.mcbooks.com. Publisher: Alexander G. Skutt. **Acquisitions:** Jackie Swift, editorial director. Estab. 1979. Publishes trade paperback and hardcover originals and reprints. **Publishes 20 titles/year. Pays 5-10% royalty on retail price. Offers $1,000-5,000 advance.** Accepts simultaneous submissions. Responds in 1 month to queries; 2 months to proposals. Ms guidelines online.
- ''We are booked nearly solid for the next few years. We can only consider the highest quality projects in our narrow interest areas.''
- O—¬ Currently emphasizing nautical and military historical fiction.
Nonfiction Subjects include regional (New York state), vegetarianism, and veganism. ''Authors' ability to promote a plus.'' *No unsolicited mss.* Query with SASE.
Fiction Historical (nautical), nautical and military historical. Query with SASE.
Recent Title(s) *Man of War*, by Alexander Kent; *Battlecruiser*, by Douglas Reeman; *On a Making Tide*, by David Donachie.

McDONALD & WOODWARD PUBLISHING CO.

431-B E. Broadway, Granville OH 43023-1310. (740)321-1140. Fax: (740)321-1141. Website: www.mwpubco.com. **Acquisitions:** Jerry N. McDonald, managing partner/publisher. Estab. 1986. Publishes hardcover and trade paperback originals. **Publishes 8 titles/year. Receives 100 queries and 20 mss/year. 50% of books from first-time authors; 100% from unagented writers. Pays 10% royalty on net receipts.** Publishes book 1 year after acceptance of ms. Accepts simultaneous submissions. Responds in 2 weeks to queries. Book catalog free.
- O—¬ ''McDonald & Woodward publishes books in natural and cultural history.'' Currently emphasizing travel, natural and cultural history. De-emphasizing self-help.
Nonfiction Biography, coffee table book, illustrated book. Subjects include Americana, anthropology/archeology, ethnic, history, nature/environment, science, travel. Query with SASE, or submit outline, sample chapter(s). Reviews artwork/photos as part of ms package. Send photocopies.
Recent Title(s) *The Carousel Keepers: An Oral History of American Carousels*, by Carrie Papa; *A Guide to Common Freshwater Invertebrates of North America*, by J. Reese Voshell; *Juan Ponce de Leon and the Spanish Discovery of Puerto Rico and Florida*, by Robert H. Fuson.
Tips ''We are especially interested in additional titles in our Guides to the American Landscape Series. Should consult titles in print for guidance. We want well-organized, clearly written, substantive material.''

MARGARET K. McELDERRY BOOKS

Imprint of Simon & Schuster Children's Publishing Division, Simon & Schuster, 1230 Sixth Ave., New York NY 10020. (212)698-2761. Fax: (212)698-2796. Website: www.simonsayskids.com. Vice President/Publisher: Brenda Bowen. **Acquisitions:** Emma D. Dryden, vice president/editorial director (books for preschoolers to 18-year-olds); Karen Wojtyla, senior editor; Sarah Nielsen, assistant editor. Estab. 1971. Publishes quality material for preschoolers to 18-year-olds. Publishes hardcover originals. **Publishes 30 titles/year. Receives 4,000 queries/year. 15% of books from first-time authors; 50% from unagented writers. Average print order is 5,000-10,000 for a first middle grade or young adult book; 7,500-20,000 for a first picture book. Pays royalty on hardcover retail price: 10% fiction; picture book, 5% author and 5% illustrator. Offers $5,000-8,000 advance for new authors.** Publishes book up to 3 years after acceptance of ms. Ms guidelines for #10 SASE.
- O—¬ ''We are more interested in superior writing and illustration than in a particular 'type' of book.'' Currently emphasizing young picture books and funny middle grade fiction.
Nonfiction Biography, children's/juvenile. Subjects include history, adventure. ''Read. The field is competitive. See what's been done and what's out there before submitting. Looks for originality of ideas, clarity and felicity

Book Publishers

of expression, well-organized plot and strong characterization (fiction) or clear exposition (nonfiction); quality. Accept query letters with SASE only." *No unsolicited mss.*

Fiction Adventure, fantasy, historical, mainstream/contemporary, mystery, picture books, young adult (or middle grade), All categories (fiction and nonfiction) for juvenile and young adult. "We will consider any category. Results depend on the quality of the imagination, the artwork, and the writing." *No unsolicited mss.* Send query letter with SASE only for picture books; query letter with first 3 chapters, SASE for middle grade and young adult novels.

Poetry *No unsolicited mss.* Query, or submit 3 sample poems.

Recent Title(s) *Bear Wants More*, by Karma Wilson and Jane Chapman (picture book); *Shout, Sister, Shout!*, by Roxane Orgill (nonfiction); *Aleutian Sparrow*, by Karen Hesse (middle grade fiction).

Tips "Read! The children's book field is competitive. See what's been done and what's out there before submitting. We look for high quality: an originality of ideas, clarity and felicity of expression, a well-organized plot, and strong character-driven stories."

McGRAW-HILL TRADE

Imprint of The McGraw-Hill Companies, 2 Penn Plaza, 11th Floor, New York NY 10121. (212)904-2000. Fax: (212)904-6096. Website: www.books.mcgraw-hill.com/business/contact.html. Publisher: Philip Ruppel. **Publishes 550 titles/year. Receives 1,200 queries and 1,200 mss/year. Offers advance.** Publishes book 1 year after acceptance of ms. Accepts simultaneous submissions. Responds in 3 months to queries. Ms guidelines online.

- • Publisher not responsible for returning mss or proposals.
- ○→ "McGraw Hill Trade is a major nonfiction reference publisher in four distinct areas: business reference, self-help/health, sports/fitness, and education reference."

Nonfiction How-to, reference, self-help, technical. Subjects include business/economics, child guidance/parenting, education (study guides), health/medicine, money/finance, sports (fitness), management, consumer reference, English and foreign language reference. "Current, up-to-date, original ideas are needed. Good self-promotion is key." Submit proposal package including outline, TOC, concept of book.

Recent Title(s) *No Cry Sleep Solution*; *Leadership Secrets of Colin Powell*; *Fat Flush Plan.*

MEADOWBROOK PRESS

5451 Smetana Dr., Minnetonka MN 55343. (952)930-1100. Fax: (952)930-1940. Website: www.meadowbrookpress.com. **Acquisitions:** Submissions Editor. Estab. 1975. Publishes trade paperback originals and reprints. **Publishes 12 titles/year. Receives 1,500 queries/year. 10% of books from first-time authors. Pays 10% royalty. Offers small advance.** Publishes book 1 year after acceptance of ms. Accepts simultaneous submissions. Responds in 4 months to queries. Book catalog for #10 SASE; ms guidelines online.

- ○→ Meadowbrook is a family-oriented press which specializes in parenting and pregnancy books, party planning books.

Nonfiction How-to, reference. Subjects include child guidance/parenting, cooking/foods/nutrition, pregnancy, childbirth, party planning, children's activities, relationships. "We prefer a query first; then we will request an outline and/or sample material." Send for guidelines. No children's fiction, poetry, academic, or biography. Query with SASE, or submit outline, sample chapter(s).

Recent Title(s) *365 Toddler Tips*, by Penny Warner (parenting); *Themed Baby Showers*, by Becky Long (party planning).

Tips "Always send for guidelines before submitting material. We do not accept unsolicited picture book submissions."

N MEDALLION PRESS, INC.

225 Seabreeze, Palm Beach FL 33480. Website: www.medallionpress.com. **Acquisitions:** Peggy McMillan, acquisitions (all fiction—no erotica). Estab. 2003. Publishes trade paperback and mass market paperback originals. **Publishes 30 titles/year. 80% of books from first-time authors; 80% from unagented writers. Pays 6-8% royalty. Offers advance.** Publishes book 1 year after acceptance of ms. Accepts simultaneous submissions. Responds in 3 months to queries; 6 months to mss. Book catalog and ms guidelines online.

Imprints Gold (mass market paperback fiction); Silver (trade paperback fiction); Bronze (young adult fiction).

Fiction Adventure, fantasy, historical, horror, military/war, multicultural, mystery, romance, science fiction, suspense, western, young adult. Currently seeking adventure/thriller, suspense, mystery, horror, and science fiction. Query with SASE, or submit proposal package including 3 sample chapter(s), synopsis.

Recent Title(s) *The Last Dance*, by Nan Ryan (historical romance mass market); *To Tame a Viking*, by Leslie Burbank (fantasy romance trade paperback).

Tips "Audience is general mainstream adults and young adults."

MERIWETHER PUBLISHING, LTD.

885 Elkton Dr., Colorado Springs CO 80907-3557. (719)594-4422. Fax: (719)594-9916. E-mail: merpeds@aol.com. Website: www.meriwetherpublishing.com; www.contemporarydrama.com. **Acquisitions:** Arthur Zapel, Theodore Zapel, Rhonda Wray, editors. Estab. 1969. Publishes paperback originals and reprints. **Receives 1,200 submissions/year. 50% of books from first-time authors; 90% from unagented writers. Pays 10% royalty on retail price, or makes outright purchase.** Publishes book 6-12 months after acceptance of ms. Accepts simultaneous submissions. Responds in 3 weeks to queries; 2 months to mss. Book catalog and ms guidelines for $2 postage.

- Meriwether publishes theater books, games and videos; speech resources; plays, skits, and musicals; and resources for gifted students. "We specialize in books on the theatre arts and religious plays for Christmas, Easter, and youth activities. We also publish musicals for high school performers and churches." Currently emphasizing how-to books for theatrical arts and church youth activities.

Nonfiction "We publish unusual textbooks or trade books related to the communication of performing arts and how-to books on staging, costuming, lighting, etc." How-to, reference, textbook. Subjects include performing arts, theater/drama. "We prefer mainstream religion theatre titles." Query, or submit outline/synopsis and sample chapters.

Fiction Plays and musical comedies for middle grades through college only. Mainstream/contemporary, plays (and musicals), religious (children's plays and religious Christmas and Easter plays), suspense, all in playscript format, comedy. Query with SASE.

Recent Title(s) *Sketch-O-Frenia*, by Dessler/Phillus; *Introduction to Theatre Arts*, by Suzi Zimmerman.

Tips "Our educational books are sold to teachers and students at college, high school, and middle school levels. Our religious books are sold to youth activity directors, pastors, and choir directors. Our trade books are directed at the public with a tie to the performing arts. Another group of buyers is the professional theater, radio, and TV category. We focus more on books of plays and short scenes and textbooks on directing, staging, make-up, lighting, etc."

MERRIAM PRESS

218 Beech St., Bennington VT 05201-2611. (802)447-0313. Fax: (802)217-1051. E-mail: ray@merriam-press.com. Website: www.merriam-press.com. Publishes hardcover and softcover originals and reprints. **Publishes 12 + titles/year. Receives 300 submissions/year. 70-90% of books from first-time authors; 95% from unagented writers. Pays 10% royalty on actual selling price.** Publishes book 1 year or less after acceptance of ms. Does not accept simultaneous submissions. Responds quickly to queries; e-mail preferred to queries. Book catalog for $1 or visit website to view all available titles and access writer's guidelines and info.

- Merriam Press publishes only World War II military history.

Nonfiction Biography, illustrated book, reference, technical. Subjects include military/war (World War II). Query with SASE or by e-mail first. Reviews artwork/photos as part of ms package. Send photocopies or on floppy disk/CD.

Recent Title(s) *The Cow Spoke French: The Story of Sgt. William True, An American Paratrooper in World War II*, By William True, Company F, 2nd Battalion, 506th Parachute Infantry Regiment, 101st Airborne Division, ETO, and Deryck Tufts True; *Dogface Soldiers: The Story of B Company, 15th Regiment, 3rd Infantry Division, From Fedala to Salzburg: Audie Murphy and His Brothers in Arms*, by Daniel R. Champagne; *Not All Were Heroes: A Private in the Corps of Engineers in the Pacific During World War II*, by Herbert L. Martin.

Tips "Our books are geared for WWII historians, collectors, model kit builders, wargamers, veterans, general enthusiasts. We do not publish any fiction or poetry, only WWII military history."

MEYERBOOKS, PUBLISHER

P.O. Box 427, Glenwood IL 60425-0427. (708)757-4950. **Acquisitions:** David Meyer, publisher. Estab. 1976. Publishes hardcover and trade paperback originals and reprints. **Publishes 5 titles/year. Pays 10-15% royalty on wholesale or retail price.** Responds in 3 months to queries.

Imprints David Meyer Magic Books, Waltham Street Press.

- "We are currently publishing books on stage magic history. We only consider subjects which have never been presented in book form before. We are not currently considering books on health, herbs, cookery, or general Americana."

Nonfiction Reference. Subjects include history of stage magic. Query with SASE.

Recent Title(s) *Inclined Toward Magic: Encounters with Books, Collectors and Conjurors' Lives*, by David Meyer; *Houdini and the Indescribable Phenomenon*, by Robert Lund.

MICHIGAN STATE UNIVERSITY PRESS

1405 S. Harrison Rd., Manly Miles Bldg., Suite 25, East Lansing MI 48823-5202. (517)355-9543. Fax: (517)432-2611. E-mail: msupress@msu.edu. Website: www.msupress.msu.edu. **Acquisitions:** Martha Bates, acquisi-

Book Publishers

tions editor. Estab. 1947. Publishes hardcover and softcover originals. **Publishes 35 titles/year. Receives 2,400 submissions/year. 75% of books from first-time authors; 100% from unagented writers. Pays variable royalty.** Publishes book 18 months after acceptance of ms. Does not accept simultaneous submissions. Book catalog and manuscript guidelines for 9 × 12 SASE; ms guidelines online.

Imprints Colleagues, University of Calgary Press, Penumbra, National Museum of Science and Industry (UK), Lynx House, African Books Collective, University of Alberta Press.

⊶ Michigan State University publishes scholarly books that further scholarship in their particular field. In addition, they publish nonfiction that addresses, in a more contemporary way, social concerns, such as diversity, civil rights, and the environment.

Nonfiction Scholarly. Subjects include Americana (American studies), business/economics, creative nonfiction, ethnic (Afro-American studies), government/politics, history (contemporary civil rights), language/literature, regional (Great Lakes regional, Canadian studies), women's issues/studies. Reviews artwork/photos as part of ms package.

Recent Title(s) *A Sinner of Memory*, essays by Melita Schaum (memoir); *On the Brink: The Great Lakes in the 21st Century*, by Dave Dempsey (environmental); *Death in Reverse: A Love Story*, by Ruth L. Schwartz (memoir).

MID-LIST PRESS

4324 12th Ave S., Minneapolis MN 55407-3218. (612)822-3733. Fax: (612)823-8387. Website: www.midlist.org. Publisher: Lane Stiles. Estab. 1989. Publishes hardcover and trade paperback originals. **Publishes 4 titles/year. Pays 40-50% royalty on net receipts. Offers $1,000 advance.** Publishes book 12-18 months after acceptance of ms. Accepts simultaneous submissions. Responds in 3 weeks to queries; 3 months to mss. Ms guidelines online.

⊶ Mid-List Press publishes books of high literary merit and fresh artistic vision by new and emerging writers.

Fiction General fiction. No children's, juvenile, romance, young adult. Send query letter first. Previously published authors only. See guidelines.

Recent Title(s) *The Trouble with You Is*, by Susan Jackson Rodgers (short fiction); *Not So the Chairs*, by Donald Finkel (poetry); *Odd Men In*, by Michael Milburn (creative nonfiction).

Tips Mid-List Press is an independent press. In addition to publishing the annual winners of the Mid-List Press First Series Awards, Mid-List Press publishes fiction, poetry, and creative nonfiction by established writers.

Ⓞ MIGHTYBOOK

10924 Grant Rd., #225, Houston TX 77070. (281)955-9855. Fax: (281)890-4818. E-mail: reaves@mightybook.com. Website: www.mightybook.com. **Acquisitions:** Richard Eaves, acquisitions editor. Estab. 1991. Publishes electronic books. **Publishes 30-50 titles/year. Pays royalties of 20% gross.** Publishes book 6-9 months after acceptance of ms.

Fiction Very short children's picture books (100-200 words). *No unsolicited mss.*

Recent Title(s) *When I Find Courage*, by Robin McKay Pimental; *A Bug Time Story*, by Naomi Tola.

MILKWEED EDITIONS

1011 Washington Ave. S., Suite 300, Minneapolis MN 55415. (612)332-3192. Fax: (612)215-2550. Website: www.milkweed.org and www.worldashome.org. **Acquisitions:** Emerson Blake, editor-in-chief; Elisabeth Fitz, first reader (fiction, nonfiction, children's fiction, poetry). Estab. 1980. Publishes hardcover originals and paperback originals and reprints. **Publishes 15 titles/year. Receives 3,000 submissions/year. 30% of books from first-time authors; 70% from unagented writers. Pays 7% royalty on retail price. Offers varied advance.** Publishes book 1-2 years after acceptance of ms. Accepts simultaneous submissions. Responds in 2 months to queries; 6 months to mss. Book catalog for $1.50 postage; ms guidelines online.

Imprints Milkweeds for Young Readers.

● Reads poetry in January and June only.

⊶ Milkweed Editions publishes literary fiction for adults and middle grade readers, nonfiction, and poetry. "Our vision is focused on giving voice to writers whose work is of the highest literary quality and whose ideas engender personal reflection and cultural action."

Nonfiction Literary. Subjects include nature/environment, human community. Submit complete ms with SASE.

Fiction Literary. Novels for adults and for readers 8-13. High literary quality. For adult readers: literary fiction, nonfiction, poetry, essays. For children (ages 8-13): literary novels. Translations welcome for both audiences. No romance, mysteries, science fiction. Send for guidelines first, then submit complete ms.

Recent Title(s) *Ordinary Wolves*, by Seth Kanter (fiction); *Cross-Pollinations*, by Gary Paul Nabhan (nonfiction); *Playing the Black Piano*, by Bill Holm (poetry).

Tips "We are looking for excellent writing with the intent of making a humane impact on society. Send for guidelines. Acquaint yourself with our books in terms of style and quality before submitting. Many factors influence our selection process, so don't get discouraged. Nonfiction is focused on literary writing about the natural world, including living well in urban environments."

MINNESOTA HISTORICAL SOCIETY PRESS

Minnesota Historical Society, 345 Kellogg Blvd. W., St. Paul MN 55102-1906. (651)296-2264. Fax: (651)297-1345. Website: www.mnhs.org/mhspress. **Acquisitions:** Gregory M. Britton, director; Ann Regan, managing editor. Estab. 1849. Publishes hardcover and trade paperback originals, trade paperback reprints. **Publishes 20 titles/year; imprint publishes 1-4 titles/year. Receives 100 queries and 25 mss/year. 50% of books from first-time authors; 85% from unagented writers. Royalties are negotiated. Offers advance.** Publishes book 14 months after acceptance of ms. Accepts simultaneous submissions. Responds in 1 month to queries. Book catalog free.

Imprints Borealis Books.

☞ Minnesota Historical Society Press publishes both scholarly and general interest books that contribute to the understanding of the Midwest.

Nonfiction Regional works only. Biography, coffee table book, cookbook, illustrated book, reference, scholarly. Subjects include anthropology/archeology, art/architecture, cooking/foods/nutrition, ethnic, history, memoirs, photography, regional, women's issues/studies. Query with SASE, or submit proposal package including outline, 1 sample chapter(s). Reviews artwork/photos as part of ms package. Send photocopies.

Recent Title(s) *The Language of Blood: A Memoir*, by Jane Jeong Trenka; *Red River Rising: The Anatomy of a Flood and the Survival of an American City*, by Ashley Shelby.

Tips A regional connection is required.

☑ MITCHELL LANE PUBLISHERS, INC.

P.O. Box 196, Hockessin DE 19711. (302)234-9426. Fax: (302)234-4742. **Acquisitions:** Barbara Mitchell, publisher. Estab. 1993. Publishes hardcover and library bound originals. **Publishes 55 titles/year. Receives 100 queries and 5 mss/year. 0% of books from first-time authors; 90% from unagented writers. Makes outright purchase on work-for-hire basis.** Publishes book 1 year after acceptance of ms. Does not accept simultaneous submissions. Responds only if interested to queries. Book catalog free.

☞ "Mitchell Lane publishes multicultural biographies for children and young adults."

Nonfiction Biography, children's/juvenile. Subjects include ethnic, multicultural. Query with SASE. **All unsolicited mss returned unopened.**

Recent Title(s) *The Life and Times of Johann Sebastian Bach* (Masters of Music); *Alfred Nobel and the Story Behind the Nobel Prize* (Great Achievement Awards); *Eminem* (Blue Banner Biographies).

Tips "We hire writers on a 'work-for-hire' basis to complete book projects we assign. Send résumé and writing samples that do not need to be returned."

MODERN LANGUAGE ASSOCIATION OF AMERICA

26 Broadway, 3rd Floor, New York NY 10004-1789. (646)576-5000. Fax: (646)458-0030. Director of MLA Book Publications: David G. Nicholls. **Acquisitions:** Joseph Gibaldi, director of book acquisitions and development; Sonia Kane, acquisitions editor. Estab. 1883. Publishes hardcover and paperback originals. **Publishes 15 titles/year. Receives 125 submissions/year. 100% from unagented writers. Pays 4-8% royalty on net receipts.** Publishes book 1 year after acceptance of ms. Does not accept simultaneous submissions. Responds in 2 months to mss. Book catalog free.

☞ The MLA publishes on current issues in literary and linguistic research and teaching of language and literature at postsecondary level.

Nonfiction Reference, scholarly, professional. Subjects include education, language/literature, translation (with companion volume in foreign language, for classroom use). No critical monographs. Query with SASE, or submit outline.

Recent Title(s) *Disability Studies: Enabling the Humanities*, edited by Sharon L. Snyder, Brenda Jo Brueggeman, and Rosemarie Garland-Thomson; *Twilight: A Drama in Five Acts*, by Elsa Bernstein.

MOMENTUM BOOKS, LLC

117 W. Third St., Royal Oak MI 48067. (800)758-1870. Fax: (248)691-4531. E-mail: momentumbooks@glis.net. Website: www.momentumbooks.com. **Acquisitions:** Franklin Foxx, editor. Estab. 1987. **Publishes 6 titles/year. Receives 100 queries and 30 mss/year. 95% of books from first-time authors; 100% from unagented writers. Pays 10-15% royalty.** Does not accept simultaneous submissions. Ms guidelines online.

☞ Momentum Books publishes regional books and general interest nonfiction.

Nonfiction Biography, cookbook, guides. Subjects include cooking/foods/nutrition, history, memoirs, sports, travel, automotive, current events. Submit proposal package including outline, 3 sample chapter(s), marketing outline.

Recent Title(s) *Rockin' Down the Dial*, by David Carson (regional history); *Offbeat Cruises & Excursions*, by Len Barnes (travel); *Will of Iron: Principles for Healthy Living*, by Peter Nielsen (health/fitness).

MORNINGSIDE HOUSE, INC.

Morningside Bookshop, 260 Oak St., Dayton OH 45410. (937)461-6736. Fax: (937)461-4260. E-mail: msbooks@e rinet.com. Website: www.morningsidebooks.com. **Acquisitions:** Robert J. Younger, publisher. Publishes hardcover and trade paperback originals. **Publishes 10 titles/year; imprint publishes 5 titles/year. Receives 30 queries and 10 mss/year. 20% of books from first-time authors; 80% from unagented writers. Pays 10% royalty on retail price. Offers $1,000-2,000 advance.** Publishes book 15 months after acceptance of ms. Accepts simultaneous submissions. Book catalog for $5 or on website.

Imprints Morningside Press, Press of Morningside Bookshop.

☞ Morningside publishes books for readers interested in the history of the American Civil War.

Nonfiction Subjects include history, military/war. Query with SASE, or submit complete ms. Reviews artwork/photos as part of ms package. Send photocopies.

Recent Title(s) *The Mississippi Brigade of Brig. Gen. Joseph R. Davis*, by T.P. Williams; *The 16th Michigan Infantry*, by Kim Crawford.

Tips "We are only interested in previously unpublished material."

Ⓐ MORROW/AVON BOOKS

HarperCollins, 10 E. 53rd St., New York NY 10022. E-mail: avonromance@harpercollins.com. Website: www.av onbooks.com. **Acquisitions:** Editorial Submissions. Estab. 1941. Publishes hardcover trade and mass market paperback originals and reprints. **Publishes 400 titles/year. Royalty negotiable. Offers advance.** Publishes book 2 years after acceptance of ms. Accepts simultaneous submissions. Responds in 3 months to queries. Ms guidelines for #10 SASE.

Imprints Avon, Eos, HarperEntertainment, HarperTorch.

● Agented submissions only for all genres except romance. Look on website for romance guidelines.

Nonfiction Biography, how-to, self-help. Subjects include business/economics, government/politics, health/ medicine, history, military/war, psychology (popular), sports. No textbooks. Query with SASE.

Fiction Fantasy, mystery, romance (contemporary, historical), science fiction, suspense. Query with SASE.

Recent Title(s) *The Reluctant Suitor*, by Kathleen Woodiwiss.

Ⓝ MOTORCYCLING

a Watermark of Bristol Fashion Publications, Inc., P.O. Box 4676, Harrisburg PA 17111-4676. (800)478-7147. E-mail: jpk@bfpbooks.com. Website: www.bfpbooks.com. **Acquisitions:** John Kaufman, publisher. Publishes trade paperback originals and limited hardback. **Publishes 15-25 titles/year. Receives 100 queries and 50 mss/year. 50% of books from first-time authors; 99% from unagented writers. Pays 7-11% royalty on retail price.** Publishes book 3 months after acceptance of ms. Responds in 1 month to queries. Ms guidelines online.

● Motorcycling (BFP, Inc.) publishes books on motorcycling and motorcycling history.

Nonfiction General interest relating to touring, guide books, how-to subjects, and motorcycling history. "We are interested in any title related to these fields. Query with a list of ideas. Include phone number. Our title plans rarely extend past 6 months, although we know the type and quantity of books we will publish over the next 2 years. We prefer good knowledge with simple-to-understand writing style containing a well-rounded vocabulary." Query with SASE. Reviews artwork/photos as part of ms package. Send photocopies or JPEG files on CD.

Tips "All of our staff and editors are riders. As such, we publish what we would want to read relating to the subject. Our audience in general are active riders at the beginner and intermediate level of repair knowledge and riding skills, and history buffs wanting to learn more about the history of motorcycles in this country. Many are people new to motorcycles, attempting to learn all they can before starting out on that first long ride or even buying their first bike. Keep it easy and simple to follow. Use motorcycle jargon sparingly. Do not use complicated technical jargon, terms, or formulas without a detailed explanation of the same. Use experienced riders and mechanics as a resource for knowledge."

MOUNT OLIVE COLLEGE PRESS

Mount Olive College, 634 Henderson St., Mount Olive NC 28365. (919)658-2502. **Acquisitions:** Dr. Pepper Worthington, director (nonfiction, fiction, poetry, children's stories). Estab. 1990. Publishes trade paperback originals. **Publishes 5 titles/year. Receives 2,500 queries/year. 75% of books from first-time authors.** Does not accept simultaneous submissions.

Nonfiction Biography, children's/juvenile, scholarly, self-help. Subjects include creative nonfiction, general nonfiction, history, humanities, language/literature, memoirs, philosophy, psychology, religion, sociology, travel, women's issues/studies. Submit 3 sample chapter(s). Reviews artwork/photos as part of ms package. Send photocopies.

Fiction Literary, poetry, religious, short story collections, spiritual. Submit 3 sample chapter(s).

Poetry Submit 10 sample poems.

MOUNTAIN PRESS PUBLISHING CO.

P.O. Box 2399, Missoula MT 59806-2399. (406)728-1900 or (800)234-5308. Fax: (406)728-1635. E-mail: info@mt npress.com. Website: www.mountain-press.com. **Acquisitions:** Gwen McKenna, editor (history); Jennifer Carey, editor (Roadside Geology, Field Guides, and Tumbleweed Series, natural history, science). Estab. 1948. Publishes hardcover and trade paperback originals. **Publishes 15 titles/year. Receives 250 submissions/year. 50% of books from first-time authors; 90% from unagented writers. Pays 7-12% royalty on wholesale price.** Publishes book 2 years after acceptance of ms. Responds in 3 months to queries. Book catalog online.

- Expanding children's/juvenile nonfiction titles.
- "We are expanding our Roadside Geology, Geology Underfoot, and Roadside History series (done on a state-by-state basis). We are interested in well-written regional field guides—plants and flowers—and readable history and natural history."

Nonfiction How-to. Subjects include animals, history (Western), nature/environment, regional, science (Earth science). "No personal histories or journals." Query with SASE, or submit outline, sample chapter(s). Reviews artwork/photos as part of ms package.

Recent Title(s) *Plants of the Lewis and Clark Expedition*, by H. Wayne Phillips; *Loons: Diving Birds of the North*, by Donna Love; *Encyclopedia of Indian Wars*, by Gregory F. Michno.

Tips "Find out what kind of books a publisher is interested in and tailor your writing to them; research markets and target your audience. Research other books on the same subjects. Make yours different. Don't present your manuscript to a publisher—sell it. Give the information needed to make a decision on a title. Please learn what we publish before sending your proposal. We are a 'niche' publisher."

Ⓐ Ⓔ MULTNOMAH PUBLISHERS, INC.

P.O. Box 1720, Sisters OR 97759. (541)549-1144. Fax: (541)549-8048. Website: www.multnomahbooks.com. **Acquisitions:** Rod Morris, senior editor (general fiction). Estab. 1987. Publishes hardcover and trade paperback originals. **Publishes 75 titles/year. 2% of books from first-time authors; 50% from unagented writers. Pays royalty on wholesale price. Provides 100 author's copies. Offers advance.** Publishes book 1-2 years after acceptance of ms. Accepts simultaneous submissions. Ms guidelines online.

Imprints Multnomah Books, Multnomah Gifts, Multnomah Fiction.

- Multnomah is currently not accepting unsolicited queries, proposals, or mss. Queries will be accepted through agents and at writers' conferences at which a Multnomah representative is present.
- Multnomah publishes books on Christian living, family enrichment, devotional and gift books, and fiction.

Nonfiction Subjects include child guidance/parenting, religion, Christian living. *Agented submissions only.*

Fiction Adventure, historical, humor, literary, mystery, religious, romance, suspense, western. *Agented submissions only.*

Recent Title(s) *The Prayer of Jabez*, by Bruce Wilkinson (nonfiction); *The Rescuer*, by Dee Henderson (fiction); *Night Light for Parents*, by James Dobson (nonfiction).

MUSTANG PUBLISHING CO.

P.O. Box 770426, Memphis TN 38177-0426. Website: www.mustangpublishing.com. **Acquisitions:** Rollin Riggs, editor. Estab. 1983. Publishes hardcover and trade paperback originals. **Publishes 10 titles/year. Receives 1,000 submissions/year. 50% of books from first-time authors; 90% from unagented writers. Pays 6-8% royalty on retail price. Offers advance.** Publishes book 1 year after acceptance of ms. Accepts simultaneous submissions. Responds in 1 month to queries. Book catalog for $2 and #10 SASE. No phone calls, please.

- Mustang publishes general interest nonfiction for an adult audience.

Nonfiction How-to, humor, self-help. Subjects include Americana, general nonfiction, hobbies, humor, recreation, sports, travel. "Our needs are very general—humor, travel, how-to, etc.—for the 18-to 60-year-old market." Query with SASE, or submit outline, sample chapter(s). Reviews artwork/photos as part of ms package. Send photocopies.

Recent Title(s) *Medical School Admissions: The Insider's Guide*, by Zebala (career); *The Complete Book of Golf Games*, by Johnston (sports).

Tips "We are not interested in first-person travel accounts or memoirs."

Ⓐ THE MYSTERIOUS PRESS

Imprint of Warner Books, 1271 Avenue of the Americas, New York NY 10020. (212)522-7200. Fax: (212)522-7990. Website: www.mysteriouspress.com. **Acquisitions:** Kristin Weber, editor. Estab. 1976. Publishes hard-

Book Publishers

cover, trade paperback and mass market editions. **Publishes 20 titles/year. Pays standard, but negotiable, royalty on retail price. Offers negotiable advance.** Publishes book an average of 1 year after acceptance of ms. Ms guidelines online.

- Agented submissions only.
- The Mysterious Press publishes well-written crime/mystery/suspense fiction.

Fiction Mystery, suspense, Crime/detective novels. No short stories. *Agented submissions only.*

Recent Title(s) *Open and Shut*, by David Rosenfelt; *Last Lessons of Summer*, by Margaret Maron.

N MYSTIC RIDGE BOOKS

Subsidiary of Mystic Ridge Productions, Inc., P.O. Box 66930, Albuquerque NM 87193-6930. (505)899-2121. **Acquisitions:** Richard Brown, president (books of quality, unique to their subject, of a marketable nature). Estab. 1999. Publishes hardcover, trade paperback, and mass market paperback originals, and trade paperback and mass market paperback reprints. **Publishes 6 + titles/year. Receives 500 + queries and 200 + mss/year. 50% of books from first-time authors; 90% from unagented writers. Pays 10% royalty on wholesale price.** Publishes book 9 months after acceptance of ms. Accepts simultaneous submissions. Responds in 1 month to queries; 1-2 months to proposals; 1-3 months to mss. Book catalog and ms guidelines online.

Nonfiction Audiocassettes, autobiography, biography, children's/juvenile, cookbook, how-to, humor, self-help, general nonfiction. Subjects include Americana, animals, anthropology/archeology, business/economics, child guidance/parenting, contemporary culture, cooking/foods/nutrition, creative nonfiction, government/politics, health/medicine, history, hobbies, language/literature, memoirs, money/finance, philosophy, psychology, recreation, science, sex, social sciences, spirituality, translation, women's issues/studies. "The writer should have a unique angle on a subject (it would be a plus if they are an expert in their field). The topic should not be too narrow a market; in other words, the target readership should be fairly large. The writer must also be a good self-promoter, willing to be proactive in getting publicity." Query with SASE. Reviews artwork/photos as part of ms package. Send photocopies.

Fiction Erotica, fantasy, historical, humor, juvenile, literary, mainstream/contemporary, mystery, romance, suspense, young adult. "Works must be original, with something new to offer, of a topic that caters to many. No knock-offs, please, or imitations of other works. The writer must also be a good self-promoter, willing to be proactive in getting publicity." Query with SASE.

Recent Title(s) *Baring It All*, edited by Layla Shilkret (nonfiction—women's erotica); *Cutting Edge Blackjack*, by Richard Harvey (nonfiction—games/gaming); *Dudley's Christmas Gift*, by Reginald D'Oji (children's fiction).

Tips "An agent is not necessary. Quality is key. It is helpful if the author has a dynamic, charismatic personality, who is intent on developing a high, public profile."

MYSTIC SEAPORT

(formerly Mystic Seaport Museum), 75 Greenmanville Ave., Mystic CT 06355-0990. (860)572-0711. Fax: (860)572-5348. **Acquisitions:** Andy German, publications director. Estab. 1970. Publishes hardcover and trade paperback originals and reprints. **Publishes 8-10 titles/year. Pays royalty on wholesale price. Offers advance.** Does not accept simultaneous submissions. Responds in 3 months to proposals.

Imprints American Maritime Library.

- "We strive to publish significant new work in the areas of American maritime, yachting and small-craft history and biography." Mystic Seaport Museum has enlarged its focus from New England to North America.

Nonfiction Biography, how-to, reference, studies of economic, social, artistic, or musical elements of American maritime (not naval) history; books on traditional boat and ship types and construction (how to). Subjects include Americana, art/architecture, history. "We need serious, well-documented biographies, studies of economic, social, artistic, or musical elements of American maritime history; books on traditional boat and ship types and construction (how-to). We are now interested in all North American maritime history—not, as in the past, principally New England. We like to see anything and everything, from queries to finished work." Query with SASE, or submit outline, 3 sample chapter(s).

Recent Title(s) *America and the Sea: A Maritime History*, Benjamin W. Labaree, et. al.

THE NAUTICAL & AVIATION PUBLISHING CO.

2055 Middleburg Lane, Mt. Pleasant SC 29464. (843)856-0561. Fax: (843)856-3164. **Acquisitions:** Melissa A. Pluta, acquisitions editor. Estab. 1979. Publishes hardcover originals and reprints. **Publishes 10-12 titles/ year. Receives 500 submissions/year. Pays 10-12% royalty on net receipts. Offers rare advance.** Accepts simultaneous submissions. Responds in 3 weeks to queries. Book catalog free.

- The Nautical & Aviation Publishing Co. publishes naval and military history, fiction, and reference.

Nonfiction Reference. Subjects include military/war (American), naval history. Query with SASE, or submit 3 sample chapter(s), synopsis. Reviews artwork/photos as part of ms package.

Fiction Historical, military/war (Revolutionary War, War of 1812, Civil War, WW I and II, Persian Gulf, and Marine Corps history). Looks for "novels with a strong military history orientation." Submit complete ms with cover letter and brief synopsis.

Recent Title(s) *The Civil War in the Carolinas*, by Dan L. Morrill; *Christopher and the Quasi War with France*, by William P. Mack; *A Guide to Airborne Weapons*, by David Crosby.

Tips "We are primarily a nonfiction publisher, but we will review historical fiction of military interest with strong literary merit."

NAVAL INSTITUTE PRESS

US Naval Institute, 291 Wood Ave., Annapolis MD 21402-5034. (410)268-6110. Fax: (410)295-1084. E-mail: esecunda@usni.org. Website: www.usni.org. Press Director: Mark Gatlin. **Acquisitions:** Paul Wilderson, executive editor; Tom Cutler, senior acquisitions editor; Eric Mills, acquisitions editor. Estab. 1873. **Publishes 80-90 titles/year. Receives 700-800 submissions/year. 50% of books from first-time authors; 90% from unagented writers.** Ms guidelines online.

> ○┱ The Naval Institute Press publishes trade and scholarly nonfiction and some fiction. "We are interested in national and international security, naval, military, military jointness, intelligence, and special warfare, both current and historical."

Nonfiction Submit proposal package including outline/table of contents, sample chapter(s), author bio, page count, number of illustrations, ms completion date, intended market, or submit complete ms. Send SASE with sufficient postage for return of ms.

NEAL-SCHUMAN PUBLISHERS, INC.

100 William St., Suite 2004, New York NY 10038-4512. (212)925-8650. Fax: (212)219-8916. E-mail: miguel@neal-schuman.com. Website: www.neal-schuman.com. **Acquisitions:** Miguel A. Figueroa, director of publishing. Estab. 1976. Publishes trade paperback originals. **Publishes 30 titles/year. Receives 500 submissions/year. 75% of books from first-time authors; 90% from unagented writers. Pays 10% royalty on net receipts. Offers infrequent advance.** Publishes book 4 months after acceptance of ms. Does not accept simultaneous submissions. Responds in 1 month to proposals. Book catalog and ms guidelines free.

> ○┱ "Neal-Schuman publishes books about libraries, information science, and the use of information technology, especially in education and libraries." Especially soliciting proposals for undergraduate information studies, knowledge management textbooks.

Nonfiction Reference, technical, textbook, professional. Subjects include computers/electronic, education, software, Internet guides, library and information science. "We are looking for many books about the Internet." Submit proposal package including outline, sample chapter(s), résumé, preface.

Recent Title(s) *Fundamentals of Information Studies*, by June Lester and Wallace C. Koehler, Jr; *Developing and Maintaining Practical Archives, 2nd Ed.*, by Gregory S. Hunter; *The Medical Library Association Encyclopedic Guide to Searching and Finding Health Information on the Web*, by P.F. Anderson and Nancy J. Allee.

NETIMPRESS PUBLISHING, INC.

3186 Michael's Ct., Green Cove Springs FL 32043. (513)464-2082. E-mail: rtrent@netimpress.com. Submissions E-mail: acquisitions@netimpress.com. Website: www.netimpress.com. **Acquisitions:** Rod Trent, owner (technology); Brian Knight, owner (technology). Estab. 2002. Publishes trade paperback and electronic originals. **Publishes 50 titles/year; imprint publishes 25 titles/year. Receives 150 queries and 50 mss/year. 50% of books from first-time authors; 80% from unagented writers. Pays 50% royalty on retail price.** Publishes book 4 months after acceptance of ms. Accepts simultaneous submissions. Responds in 1 month to queries; 1 month to proposals; 1 month to mss. Book catalog online; ms guidelines by e-mail.

Imprints Start To Finish Guide, Just the FAQs.

Nonfiction Booklets, how-to, reference, self-help, technical. Subjects include computers/electronic, software. "Our goal is to publish e-books that are 50-150 pages in length. These books should be a no-frills technical guide or how-to for a specific subject in the technology industry." Query with SASE, or submit proposal package including outline, 1 sample chapter(s). Reviews artwork/photos as part of ms package. Electronic images.

Recent Title(s) *Start To Finish Guide To SMS Delivery*, by Dana Daugherty (technology); *Start To Finish Guide To SQL Server Performance*, by Brian Kelley (technology); *Just the FAQs for SMS*, by Cliff Hobbs (technology).

Tips "Our audience is a group of people heavily involved in technology and technology support for companies for which they are employed. These include consultants and IT. Writers must understand the proposed topic very well. They must also be able to communicate technical expertise into easy-to-understand text."

THE NEW ENGLAND PRESS, INC.

P.O. Box 575, Shelburne VT 05482. (802)863-2520. Fax: (802)863-1510. E-mail: info@nepress.com. Website: www.nepress.com. **Acquisitions:** Christopher A. Bray, managing editor. Estab. 1978. Publishes hardcover and trade paperback originals. **Publishes 6-8 titles/year. Receives 600 queries and 300 mss/year. 10% of books from first-time authors; 90% from unagented writers. Pays royalty on wholesale price.** Publishes book 15 months after acceptance of ms. Accepts simultaneous submissions. Responds in 6-9 months to queries. Book catalog free; ms guidelines online.

○► The New England Press publishes high-quality trade books of regional northern New England interest. Currently emphasizing young adult biography and oral histories.

Nonfiction Biography, illustrated book, young adult. Subjects include history, nature/environment, regional, world affairs, Vermontiana. "Nonfiction submissions must be based in Vermont and have northern New England topics. No memoirs or family histories. Identify potential markets and ways to reach them in cover letter." Query with SASE, or submit outline, 3 sample chapter(s). Reviews artwork/photos as part of ms package. Send copies only; no original art.

Fiction Historical (Vermont, New Hampshire, Maine). "We look for very specific subject matters based on Vermont history and heritage, including historical novels for young adults set in northern New England. We do not publish contemporary adult fiction of any kind." Query with SASE, or submit 2 sample chapter(s), synopsis.

Recent Title(s) *Men Against Granite*; *Rumrunners and Revenuers: Prohibition in Vermont* (history); *Vermont Quiz Book.*

Tips "Our readers are interested in all aspects of Vermont and northern New England, including history and humor, young adult historical fiction, and biography. No agent is needed, but our market is extremely specific and our volume is low, so send a query or outline and writing samples first. Sending the whole manuscript is discouraged. We will not accept projects that are still under development or give advances."

NEW HARBINGER PUBLICATIONS

5674 Shattuck Ave., Oakland CA 94609. (510)652-0215. Fax: (510)652-5472. E-mail: proposals@newharbinger.com. Website: www.newharbinger.com. **Acquisitions:** Catharine Sutker, acquisitions manager; Melissa Kirk, senior acquisitions editor. Estab. 1973. **Publishes 50 titles/year. Receives 1,000 queries and 300 mss/year. 60% of books from first-time authors; 75% from unagented writers. Pays 10% royalty on net receipts.** Publishes book 1 year after acceptance of ms. Accepts simultaneous submissions. Responds in 1 month to queries; 1 month to proposals; 2 months to mss. Book catalog free; ms guidelines online.

○► "We look for step-by-step self-help titles on psychology, health, and balanced living that teach the average reader how to master essential skills. Our books are also read by mental health professionals who want simple, clear explanations of important psychological techniques and health issues."

Nonfiction Self-help (psychology/health). Subjects include health/medicine, psychology, women's issues/studies, balanced living, anger management, anxiety, coping. "Authors need to be qualified psychotherapists or health practitioners to publish with us." Submit proposal package including outline, 2 sample chapter(s), competing titles, and a compelling, supported reason why the book is unique.

Recent Title(s) *The Anxiety & Phobia Workbook, 3rd ed.*, by Edmund J. Bourne; *Rosacea: A Self-Help Guide*, by Arlen Brownstein; *Brave New You*, by Mary and John Valentis.

Tips Audience includes psychotherapists and lay readers wanting step-by-step strategies to solve specific problems. "Our definition of a self-help psychology or health book is one that teaches essential life skills. The primary goal is to train the reader so that, after reading the book, he or she can deal more effectively with health and/or psychological challenges."

NEW HOPE PUBLISHERS

Woman's Missionary Union, P.O. Box 12065, Birmingham AL 35202-2065. (205)991-8100. Fax: (205)991-4015. E-mail: new_hope@wmu.org. Website: www.newhopepubl.com. **Acquisitions:** Acquisitions Editor. **Publishes 27-32 titles/year. Receives several hundred queries/year. 25% of books from first-time authors; small% from unagented writers. Pays royalty on net receipts.** Publishes book 2 years after acceptance of ms. Responds in 2 months to mss. Book catalog for 9×12 SAE with 3 first-class stamps; ms guidelines online.

Imprints New Hope.

○► "Our goal is to create unique books that help women and families to grow in Christ and share His hope."

Nonfiction "We publish books dealing with all facets of Christian life for women and families, including health, discipleship, missions, ministry, Bible studies, spiritual development, parenting, and marriage. We currently do not accept adult fiction or children's picture books. We are particularly interested in niche categories and books on lifestyle development and change." Children's/juvenile (religion). Subjects include child guidance/parenting (from Christian perspective), education (Christian church), health/medicine (Christian), multicultural, religion (spiritual development, Bible study, life situations from Christian perspective, ministry), women's issues/studies (Christian), church leadership, evangelism. Prefers a query and prospectus but will evaluate a complete ms.

Recent Title(s) *Called and Accountable*, by Henry Blackaby; *Refuge: A Pathway Out of Domestic Violence & Abuse*, by Det. Sgt. Donald Stewart; *Growing Godly Women*, by Donna Margaret Greene.

NEW HORIZON PRESS

P.O. Box 669, Far Hills NJ 07931. (908)604-6311. Fax: (908)604-6330. E-mail: nhp@newhorizonpressbooks.com. Website: www.newhorizonpressbooks.com. **Acquisitions:** Dr. Joan S. Dunphy, publisher (nonfiction, social issues, true crime). Estab. 1983. Publishes hardcover and trade paperback originals. **Publishes 12 titles/ year. 90% of books from first-time authors; 50% from unagented writers. Pays standard royalty on net receipts. Offers advance.** Publishes book 2 years after acceptance of ms. Accepts simultaneous submissions. Book catalog free; ms guidelines online.

Imprints Small Horizons.

○➤ New Horizon publishes adult nonfiction featuring true stories of uncommon heroes, true crime, social issues, and self help.

Nonfiction Biography, children's/juvenile, how-to, self-help. Subjects include child guidance/parenting, creative nonfiction, government/politics, health/medicine, nature/environment, psychology, women's issues/ studies, true crime. Submit proposal package including outline, 3 sample chapter(s), résumé, author bio, photo, marketing information.

Recent Title(s) *Dead Center*, by Frank J. Daniels; *Mending Wounded Minds*, by Beth Friday Henry; *Race Against Evil*, by David Race Bannon.

Tips "We are a small publisher, thus it is important that the author/publisher have a good working relationship. The author must be willing to promote his book."

Ⓝ NEW SPIRIT

Imprint of BET Books, 850 Third Ave., 16th Floor, New York NY 10022. Website: www.bet.com/books. **Acquisitions:** Glenda Howard, senior editor. Responds in 4 months to proposals.

Nonfiction "Our nonfiction books objective is to encourage and motivate readers by offering messages advocating personal growth, empowerment, and strong personal relationships." Submit proposal package including outline, 3 sample chapter(s).

Fiction "We are looking to acquire fiction novels that are well crafted, and will feature strong characters who overcome challenges and obstacles through the power of prayer and faith. The New Spirit fiction titles will appeal to a broad audience because they will address contemporary issues such as love, betrayal, tragedy, and triumph over adversity, while keeping a spiritual message throughout." Submit proposal package including 3 sample chapter(s), synopsis.

Tips "Please do not phone to see if your manuscript was received or returned, or to find out what we thought of it. A self-addressed, stamped postcard can be enclosed with your submission if you want confirmation of its arrival. Specify whether you would like your manuscript returned or recycled if it is not right for us."

NEW VOICES PUBLISHING

Imprint of KidsTerrain, Inc., P.O. Box 560, Wilmington MA 01887. (978)658-2131. Fax: (978)988-8833. E-mail: rschiano@kidsterrain.com. Website: www.kidsterrain.com. **Acquisitions:** Rita Schiano, executive editor (children's books). Estab. 2000. Publishes hardcover and trade paperback originals. **Publishes 5 titles/year. Receives 30 queries and 20 mss/year. 95% of books from first-time authors; 95% from unagented writers. Pays 10-15% royalty on wholesale price.** Publishes book 1 year after acceptance of ms. Does not accept simultaneous submissions. Responds in 1 month to queries; 3 months to proposals; 3 months to mss. Book catalog and ms guidelines online.

○➤ The audience for this company is children ages 4-9.

Nonfiction Children's/juvenile, illustrated book. Subjects include child guidance/parenting. Query with SASE. Reviews artwork/photos as part of ms package. Send photocopies.

Fiction Juvenile. Query with SASE.

Recent Title(s) *The Magic in Me*, by Maggie Moran (children's fiction); *Aunt Rosa's House*, by Maggie Moran (children's fiction); *Last Night I Left Earth for Awhile*, by Natalie Brown-Douglas (children's fiction).

Tips "Know, specifically, what your story/book is about."

NEW WORLD LIBRARY

14 Pamaron Way, Novato CA 94949. (415)884-2100. Fax: (415)884-2199. E-mail: escort@nwlib.com. Website: www.newworldlibrary.com. Publisher: Marc Allen. Senior Editor: Jason Gardner. **Acquisitions:** Georgia Hughes, editorial director. Estab. 1979. Publishes hardcover and trade paperback originals and reprints. **Publishes 40 titles/year. 20% of books from first-time authors; 50% from unagented writers. Pays 12-20% royalty on wholesale price for hardcover. Offers $0-30,000 advance.** Publishes book 12-18 months after

acceptance of ms. Accepts simultaneous submissions. Responds in 3 months to queries. Book catalog free; ms guidelines online.

Imprints Nataraj, H.J. Kramer.

> O─ "NWL is dedicated to publishing books and audio projects that inspire and challenge us to improve the quality of our lives and our world."

Nonfiction Gift book, self-help. Subjects include alternative lifestyles (health), business/economics (prosperity), ethnic (African/American, Native American), health/medicine (natural), money/finance, nature/environment, psychology, religion, spirituality, women's issues/studies, personal growth, parenting. Query with SASE, or submit outline, 2-3 sample chapter(s), author bio, SASE. Reviews artwork/photos as part of ms package. Send photocopies.

Recent Title(s) *The Seven Whispers*, by Christina Baldwin; *The Power of Now*, by Eckhart Tolle; *Goal Sisters*, by Ann Leach and Michelle Pillen.

NEW YORK UNIVERSITY PRESS

838 Broadway, New York NY 10003. (212)998-2575. Fax: (212)995-3833. Website: www.nyupress.org. **Acquisitions:** Eric Zinner (cultural studies, literature, media, history); Jennifer Hammer (Jewish studies, psychology, religion, women's studies); Ilene Kalish (social sciences); Deborah Gershenowitz (law, American history). Estab. 1916. Hardcover and trade paperback originals. **Publishes 100 titles/year. Receives 800-1,000 queries/year. 30% of books from first-time authors; 90% from unagented writers. Pays royalty on net receipts.** Publishes book 9-11 months after acceptance of ms. Accepts simultaneous submissions. Responds in 1-4 months (peer reviewed) to proposals. Ms guidelines online.

> O─ New York University Press embraces ideological diversity. "We often publish books on the same issue from different poles to generate dialogue, engender and resist pat categorizations."

Nonfiction Subjects include anthropology/archeology, business/economics, ethnic, gay/lesbian, government/politics, history, language/literature, military/war, psychology, regional, religion, sociology, sports, women's issues/studies. Query with SASE, or submit proposal package including outline, 1 sample chapter(s). Reviews artwork/photos as part of ms package. Send photocopies.

NO STARCH PRESS, INC.

555 De Haro St., Suite 250, San Francisco CA 94107. (415)863-9900. Fax: (415)863-9950. E-mail: info@nostarch.com. Website: www.nostarch.com. **Acquisitions:** William Pollock, publisher. Estab. 1994. Publishes trade paperback originals. **Publishes 20-25 titles/year. Receives 100 queries and 5 mss/year. 80% of books from first-time authors; 90% from unagented writers. Pays 10-15% royalty on wholesale price. Offers advance.** Publishes book 4 months after acceptance of ms. Accepts simultaneous submissions. Book catalog free.

Imprints Linux Journal Press.

> O─ No Starch Press, Inc., is an independent publishing company committed to producing easy-to-read and information-packed computer books. Currently emphasizing open source, Web development, computer security issues, programming tools, and robotics. "More stuff, less fluff."

Nonfiction How-to, reference, technical. Subjects include computers/electronic, hobbies, software (Open Source). Submit outline, 1 sample chapter(s), author bio, market rationale. Reviews artwork/photos as part of ms package. Send photocopies.

Recent Title(s) *Hacking: The Art of Exploitation*, by Jon Erickson; *Art of Assembly Language*, by Randall Hyde; *Hacking the XBox*, by Andrew "bunnie" Huang.

Tips "No fluff—content, content, content or just plain fun. Understand how your book fits into the market. Tell us why someone, anyone, will buy your book. Be enthusiastic."

NODIN PRESS

530 N. Third St., Suite 120, Minneapolis MN 55401. (612)333-6300. Fax: (612)333-6303. E-mail: nstill4402@aol.com. **Acquisitions:** Norton Stillman, publisher. Publishes hardcover and trade paperback originals. **Publishes 5 titles/year. Receives 20 queries and 20 mss/year. 75% of books from first-time authors; 100% from unagented writers. Pays 7½% royalty.** Publishes book 6 months after acceptance of ms. Accepts simultaneous submissions. Responds in 6 months to queries. Book catalog and ms guidelines free.

> O─ Nodin Press publishes Minnesota regional titles: nonfiction, memoir, sports, poetry.

Nonfiction Biography, regional guide book. Subjects include history (ethnic), regional, sports, travel. Query with SASE.

Poetry Regional (Minnesota poets). Submit 10 sample poems.

Recent Title(s) *Cloud Unfold*, by Brenda Veland; *Mountain Upside Down*, by John Toren; *Batter Up: Century of Minnesota Baseball*, by Ross Bernstein.

NOMAD PRESS

2456 Christian St., White River Junction VT 05001. (802)649-1995. Fax: (802)649-2667. E-mail: info@nomadpress.net. Website: www.nomadpress.net. **Publisher:** Alex Kahan. **Acquisitions:** Lauri Berkenkamp. Publishes trade paperback originals. **Publishes 8 + titles/year. 10% of books from first-time authors; 90% from unagented writers. Pays royalty on retail price, or makes outright purchase. Offers negotiable advance.** Publishes book 1 year after acceptance of ms. Does not accept simultaneous submissions. Responds in 1-2 months to mss. Book catalog and ms guidelines online.

Nonfiction Parenting, how-to, teaching/education, sailing/marine titles. Subjects include child guidance/parenting, sports, teacher training/education, writing/journalism. Actively seeking well-written nonfiction. No disorder-specific parenting mss, cookbooks, poetry, or technical manuals. Submit complete ms. Reviews artwork/photos as part of ms package. Send photocopies.

Recent Title(s) *Maximum Sail Power: The Complete Guide to Sails, Sail Technology and Performance*, by Brian Hancock (sports); *The Land of War Elephants: Travels Beyond the Pale in Afghanistan, Pakistan, and India*, by Mathew Wilson (travel); *"Because I Said So!" Family Squabbles and How to Handle Them, a Go Parents! Guide*, by Lauri Berkenkamp and Steven Atkins, Psy.D. (teaching).

Ø NONETHELESS PRESS

20332 W. 98th St., Lenexa KS 66220. (913)254-7266. Fax: (913)393-3245. E-mail: info@nonethelesspress.com. Website: www.nonethelesspress.com. **Acquisitions:** Marie-Christine Ebershoff. Estab. 2002. Publishes hardcover, trade paperback and electronic originals and reprints. **Publishes 10-16 titles/year. Receives 400 queries and 100 mss/year. 50% of books from first-time authors; 60% from unagented writers. Pays 20% royalty on wholesale price.** Publishes book 8 months after acceptance of ms. Accepts simultaneous submissions. Responds in 3 months to queries; 3 months to proposals; 3 months to mss. Book catalog and ms guidelines online.

Nonfiction Biography, general nonfiction, reference, scholarly, textbook, general nonfiction. Subjects include art/architecture, contemporary culture, creative nonfiction, history, humanities, language/literature, multicultural, philosophy, religion, world affairs, women's studies. Nonetheless Press is a new publisher that is following the best traditions of the small press movement, with an ambitious initial list. At a time when most independent publishers are crowding their titles into ever smaller niches, Nonetheless defies that convention and chooses mss for the best of all possible reasons—because they are good. Query with SASE. **All unsolicited mss returned unopened.** Reviews artwork/photos as part of ms package. Send photocopies.

Fiction Historical, literary, short story collections, spiritual. Query with SASE. **All unsolicited mss returned unopened.**

Recent Title(s) *Strange Birds from Zoroaster's Nest*, by Laina Farhat-Holzman (religion/world affairs); *The Ecumenical Cruise*, by Walter Benesch (philosophy/short story collection); *Secrets of Successful Query Letters*, by Pam Brodowsky (reference/writing).

Tips "Provide a detailed, specific proposal. Don't waste your time or ours with half-formed ideas vaguely expressed."

NORTH CAROLINA OFFICE OF ARCHIVES AND HISTORY

Historical Publications Section, 4622 Mail Service Center, Raleigh NC 27699-4622. (919)733-7442. Fax: (919)733-1439. E-mail: donna.kelly@ncmail.net. Website: www.ah.dcr.state.nc.us/sections/hp. **Acquisitions:** Donna E. Kelly, administrator (North Carolina and southern history). Publishes hardcover and trade paperback originals. **Publishes 4 titles/year. Receives 20 queries and 25 mss/year. 5% of books from first-time authors; 100% from unagented writers. Makes one-time payment upon delivery of completed ms.** Publishes book 2 years after acceptance of ms. Accepts simultaneous submissions. Responds in 1 week to queries; 1 week to proposals; 2 months to mss. Ms guidelines for $3.

> **O→** "We publish *only* titles that relate to North Carolina. The North Carolina Office of Archives and History also publishes the *North Carolina Historical Review*, a scholarly journal of history."

Nonfiction Hardcover and trade paperback books relating to North Carolina. Subjects include history (related to North Carolina), military/war (related to North Carolina), regional (North Carolina and Southern history). Query with SASE. Reviews artwork/photos as part of ms package. Send photocopies.

Recent Title(s) *The North Carolina State Fair: The First 150 Years*, by Melton A. McLaurin; *Paving Tobacco Road: A Century of Progress*, by the North Carolina Department of Transportation, by Walter R. Turner; *A History of African Americans in North Carolina*, by Crow, Escott and Hatley.

Tips Audience is public school and college teachers and students, librarians, historians, genealogists, North Carolina citizens, tourists.

NORTH POINT PRESS

Imprint of Farrar Straus & Giroux, Inc., 19 Union Square W., New York NY 10003. (212)741-6900. Fax: (212)633-9385. **Acquisitions:** Rebecca Saletan, editorial director; Stacia Decker, editorial assistant. Estab. 1980. Publishes hardcover and paperback originals. **Publishes 25 titles/year. Receives 100 queries and 100 mss/year. 20% of books from first-time authors. Pays standard royalty. Offers varied advance.** Publishes book 18 months after acceptance of ms. Accepts simultaneous submissions. Responds in 2 months to queries; 3 months to proposals; 3 months to mss. Ms guidelines for #10 SASE.

Oᴙ "We are a broad-based literary trade publisher—high quality writing only."

Nonfiction Subjects include history, memoirs, nature/environment, religion (no New Age), sports, travel, music, cooking/food. "Be familiar with our list. No genres." Query with SASE, or submit outline, 1-2 sample chapter(s).

Recent Title(s) *The Birds of Heaven*, by Peter Matthiessen; *Cradle to Cradle*, by William McDonough and Michael Braungart; *American Ground*, by William Langewiesche.

NORTHEASTERN UNIVERSITY PRESS

360 Huntington Ave., 416CP, Boston MA 02115. (617)373-5480. Fax: (617)373-5483. Website: www.nupress.ne u.edu. **Acquisitions:** Robert Gormley, editor-in-chief (history, political science, law, and society); Sarah Rowley, editor (women's studies, American studies, music, criminal justice). Estab. 1977. Publishes hardcover originals and trade paperback originals and reprints. **Publishes 40 titles/year. Receives 500 queries and 100 mss/year. 50% of books from first-time authors; 90% from unagented writers. Pays 5-15% royalty on wholesale price. Offers $500-20,000 advance.** Publishes book 1 year after acceptance of ms. Accepts simultaneous submissions. Book catalog free; ms guidelines online.

Oᴙ Northeastern University Press publishes scholarly and general interest titles in the areas of American history, political science, criminal justice, women's studies, music, and reprints of African-American literature. Currently emphasizing American studies. De-emphasizing literary studies.

Nonfiction Biography, scholarly, adult trade, scholarly monographs. Subjects include Americana, history, regional, women's issues/studies, music, criminal justice. Query with SASE, or submit proposal package including outline, 1-2 sample chapter(s). Reviews artwork/photos as part of ms package. Send photocopies.

Recent Title(s) *A Rose for Mary: The Hunt for the Real Boston Strangler*, by Casey Sherman; *The Politics of Terror: The U.S. Response to 9/11*, edited by William Crotty; *Dynasty's End: Bill Russell and the 1968-69 World Champion Boston Celtics*, by Thomas J. Whalen.

NORTHERN ILLINOIS UNIVERSITY PRESS

310 N. Fifth St., DeKalb IL 60115-2854. (815)753-1826. Fax: (815)753-1845. Director/Editor-in-Chief: Mary L. Lincoln. **Acquisitions:** Melody Herr, acquisitions editor (history, politics). Estab. 1965. **Publishes 20-22 titles/ year. Pays 10-15% royalty on wholesale price. Offers advance.** Does not accept simultaneous submissions. Book catalog free.

Oᴙ NIU Press publishes scholarly work and books of general interest to the informed public. "We publish mainly history, politics, anthropology, and other social sciences. We are interested also in studies on the Chicago area and Midwest, and in literature in translation." Currently emphasizing history, the social sciences, and cultural studies.

Nonfiction "Publishes mainly history, political science, social sciences, philosophy, literary and cultural studies, and regional studies." Subjects include anthropology/archeology, government/politics, history, language/literature, philosophy, regional, social sciences, translation, cultural studies. No collections of previously published essays, no unsolicited poetry. Query with SASE, or submit outline, 1-3 sample chapter(s).

Recent Title(s) *Possessed: Women, Witches and Demons in Imperial Russia.*

☑ NORTHLAND PUBLISHING, INC.

(formerly Northland Publishing, LLC), P.O. Box 1389, Flagstaff AZ 86002-1389. (928)774-5251. Fax: (928)774-0592. Website: www.northlandpub.com. **Acquisitions:** Tammy Gales, managing editor; Theresa Howell, children's editor (picture books, especially with Southwest appeal). Estab. 1958. Publishes hardcover and trade paperback originals. **Publishes 8-10 titles/year; imprint publishes 8-10 titles/year. Receives 2,000 submissions/year. 20% of books from first-time authors; 20% from unagented writers. Pays royalty. Offers advance.** Publishes book 1-2 years after acceptance of ms. Accepts simultaneous submissions. Responds in 3 months to queries. Call for book catalog; ms guidelines online.

Imprints Rising Moon (books for children).

● Rising Moon has temporarily suspended consideration of unsolicited manuscripts. No e-mail submissions accepted.

Oᴙ "Northland Publishing acquires nonfiction books intended for general trade audiences on the American West and Southwest, including Native American arts, crafts, and culture; Mexican culture; regional cookery; Western lifestyle; and interior design and architecture. Northland is also accepting samples from entertaining travel writers and photographers from around the U.S. Samples will be considered on a work-for-hire basis for Northland's new visual tour series. Northland is not accepting poetry or fiction at this time."

Nonfiction Query with SASE, or submit outline, 2-3 sample chapter(s). No fax or e-mail submissions. Reviews artwork/photos as part of ms package. Picture books. Submit complete ms.
Recent Title(s) *Outdoor Style*, by Suzanne Pickett Martinson; *Simply 7*, by Kelley Cleary Coffeen; *Sedona: Treasure of the Southwest*, by Kathleen Bryant.
Tips "Our audience is composed of general-interest readers."

NORTHWORD PRESS
Imprint of Creative Publishing International, Inc., 18705 Lake Dr. E., Chanhassen MN 55317. (952)936-4700. Fax: (952)988-0201. Website: www.northwordpress.com. **Acquisitions:** Bryan Trandem (adult books); Aimee Jackson (children's books). Estab. 1984. Publishes hardcover and trade paperback originals. **Publishes 15-20 titles/year. Receives 600 submissions/year. 25% of books from first-time authors; 50% from unagented writers. Pays 10-12% royalty on wholesale price. Offers $2,000-10,000 advance.** Publishes book 1-2 years after acceptance of ms. Accepts simultaneous submissions. Responds in 3 months to queries. Ms guidelines for #10 SASE.
  O— NorthWord Press exclusively publishes nature and wildlife titles for adults and children.
Nonfiction Children's/juvenile, coffee table book, illustrated book, introductions to wildlife and natural history. Subjects include animals, nature/environment. Query with SASE, or submit outline, sample chapter(s).
Recent Title(s) *Trout, Trout, Trout!*, by April Pulley Sayre, illustrated by Trip Park; *Everything Bug*, by Cherie Winner (nonfiction, ages 8-11); *Starting Life: Duck*, by Claire Llewellyn, illustrated by Simon Mendez (nonfiction ages 5-8).
Tips "Visit our website before submitting to see if your submission is a good fit for our list."

NOVA PRESS
11659 Mayfield Ave., Suite 1, Los Angeles CA 90049. (310)207-4078. Fax: (310)571-0908. E-mail: novapress@aol.com. Website: www.novapress.net. **Acquisitions:** Jeff Kolby, president. Estab. 1993. Publishes trade paperback originals. **Publishes 4 titles/year. Pays 10-22½% royalty on net receipts. Offers advance.** Publishes book 6 months after acceptance of ms. Does not accept simultaneous submissions. Book catalog free.
  O— Nova Press publishes only test prep books for college entrance exams (SAT, GRE, GMAT, LSAT, etc.), and closely related reference books, such as college guides and vocabulary books.
Nonfiction How-to, self-help, technical, test prep books for college entrance exams. Subjects include education, software.
Recent Title(s) *The MCAT Chemistry Book*, by Ajikumar Aryangat.

NURSESBOOKS.ORG
(formerly American Nurses Publishing), American Nurses Association, 600 Maryland Ave. SW, #100 West, Washington DC 20024-2571. (202)651-7212. Fax: (202)651-7003. **Acquisitions:** Rosanne O'Connor, publisher; Eric Wurzbacher, editor/project manager. Publishes professional paperback originals and reprints. **Publishes 15 titles/year. Receives 300 queries and 8-10 mss/year. 75% of books from first-time authors; 100% from unagented writers. Pays 12% royalty on net receipts. Offers negotiable advance.** Publishes book 4 months after acceptance of ms. Does not accept simultaneous submissions. Responds in 3 months to proposals; 3 months to mss. Book catalog online; ms guidelines free.
  O— Nursebooks.org publishes books designed to help professional nurses in their work and careers. Through the publishing program, Nursebooks.org provides nurses in all practice settings with publications that address cutting-edge issues and form a basis for debate and exploration of this century's most critical health care trends.
Nonfiction Reference, technical, textbook, handbooks; resource guides. Subjects include health/medicine. Subjects include advanced practice, computers, continuing education, ethics, human rights, health care policy, managed care, nursing administration, psychiatric and mental health, quality, research, workplace issues, key clinical topics. Submit outline, 1 sample chapter, cv. Reviews artwork/photos as part of ms package. Send photocopies.
Recent Title(s) *Nursing and the Law*; *End-of-Life Care*; *Critical Practice Management Strategies*.

OAK KNOLL PRESS
310 Delaware St., New Castle DE 19720. (302)328-7232. Fax: (302)328-7274. E-mail: oakknoll@oakknoll.com. Website: www.oakknoll.com. **Acquisitions:** John Von Hoelle, director of publishing. Estab. 1976. Publishes hardcover and trade paperback originals and reprints. **Publishes 40 titles/year. Receives 250 queries and 100 mss/year. 50% of books from first-time authors; 100% from unagented writers.** Publishes book 12 months after acceptance of ms. Accepts simultaneous submissions. Ms guidelines online.
  O— Oak Knoll specializes in books about books and manuals on the book arts—preserving the art and lore of the printed word.

Nonfiction How-to. Subjects include book arts, printing, papermaking, bookbinding, book collecting, etc. Reviews artwork/photos as part of ms package. Send photocopies.

Recent Title(s) *Historical Scripts*, by Stan Knight; *The Great Libraries*, by Stan Staikos.

THE OAKLEA PRESS

6912-B Three Chopt Rd., Richmond VA 23226. (804)281-5872. Fax: (804)281-5686. E-mail: info@oakleapress.com. Website: www.oakleapress.com. **Acquisitions:** John Gotschalk, editor; S.H. Martin, publisher. Publishes hardcover and trade paperback originals. **Receives 300 queries and 50 mss/year. 50% of books from first-time authors; 90% from unagented writers. Pays 10-20% royalty on wholesale price.** Publishes book 6 months after acceptance of ms. Accepts simultaneous submissions. Responds in 1 month to queries; 1 month to proposals; 3 months to mss. Book catalog online.

Nonfiction How-to, self-help. Subjects include business management, lean enterprise. "We like how-to books and currently are actively looking for those that can help businesses and organizations increase the productivity of workers and staff." Submit proposal package including outline, 1 sample chapter(s).

Recent Title(s) *Buried Alive! Digging Out of a Management Dumpster*, by Anna Versteeg et al; *Secrets of Success: Key Insights for Life's Journey from the Great Western Myths*, by Gerald W. Morton, Ph.D.

OHIO STATE UNIVERSITY PRESS

1070 Carmack Rd., Columbus OH 43210-1002. (614)292-6930. Fax: (614)292-2065. E-mail: ohiostatepress@osu.edu. Website: www.ohiostatepress.org. **Acquisitions:** Malcolm Litchfield, director; Heather Miller, acquisitions editor. Estab. 1957. **Publishes 30 titles/year. Pays royalty. Offers advance.** Responds in 3 months to queries. Ms guidelines online.

○━ Ohio State University Press publishes scholarly nonfiction, and offers short fiction and short poetry prizes. Currently emphasizing history, literary studies, political science, women's health, classics, Victoria studies.

Nonfiction Scholarly. Subjects include business/economics, education, general nonfiction, government/politics, history (American), language/literature, multicultural, regional, sociology, women's issues/studies, criminology, literary criticism, women's health. Query with SASE.

Recent Title(s) *Saving Lives*, by Albert Goldbarth (poetry); *Ohio: History of People*, by Andrew Cayton (nonfiction).

OHIO UNIVERSITY PRESS

Scott Quadrangle, Athens OH 45701. (740)593-1155. Fax: (740)593-4536. Website: www.ohio.edu/oupress/. **Acquisitions:** Gillian Berchowitz, senior editor (American history and popular culture, legal history, African studies, Appalachian studies); David Sanders, director (literature, literary criticism, midwest and frontier studies, Ohioana). Estab. 1964. Publishes hardcover and trade paperback originals and reprints. **Publishes 45-50 titles/year. Receives 500 queries and 50 mss/year. 20% of books from first-time authors; 95% from unagented writers. Pays 7-10% royalty on net receipts.** Publishes book 1 year after acceptance of ms. Responds in 1 month to queries; 1 month to proposals; 2 months to mss. Book catalog free; ms guidelines online.

Imprints Ohio University Research in International Studies (Gillian Berchowitz); Swallow Press (David Sanders, director).

○━ Ohio University Press publishes and disseminates the fruits of research and creative endeavor, specifically in the areas of literary studies, regional works, philosophy, contemporary history, African studies, and frontier Americana. Its charge to produce books of value in service to the academic community and for the enrichment of the broader culture is in keeping with the university's mission of teaching, research and service to its constituents.

Nonfiction Reference, scholarly. Subjects include Americana, anthropology/archeology, art/architecture, ethnic, gardening, government/politics, history, language/literature, military/war, nature/environment, philosophy, regional, sociology, travel, women's issues/studies, African studies. "We prefer queries or detailed proposals, rather than manuscripts, pertaining to scholarly projects that might have a general interest. Proposals should explain the thesis and details of the subject matter, not just sell a title." Query with SASE. Reviews artwork/photos as part of ms package. Send photocopies.

Recent Title(s) *Acquamarine Blue Five: Personal Stories of College Students with Autism*, edited by Dawn Prince-Hughes; *John Reed and the Writing of a Revolution*, by Daniel W. Lehman; *The Inclusive Corporation: The Disability Handbook for Business Professionals*, edited by Griff Hogan.

Tips "Rather than trying to hook the editor on your work, let the material be compelling enough and well-presented enough to do it for you."

THE OLIVER PRESS, INC.

5707 W. 36th St., Minneapolis MN 55416-2510. (952)926-8981. Fax: (952)926-8965. E-mail: queries@oliverpress.com. Website: www.oliverpress.com. **Acquisitions:** Denise Sterling, editor. Estab. 1991. Publishes hardcover originals. **Publishes 10 titles/year. Receives 100 queries and 20 mss/year. 10% of books from first-time authors; 100% from unagented writers.** Publishes book up to 2 years after acceptance of ms. Accepts simultaneous submissions. Responds in 6 months to queries. Book catalog for 9×12 SAE with 4 first-class stamps; ms guidelines online.

O— "We publish collective biographies for ages 10 and up. Although we cover a wide array of subjects, all are published in this format. We are looking for titles for our Innovators series (history of technology) and Business Builders series."

Nonfiction Collective biographies only. Children's/juvenile. Subjects include business/economics, ethnic, government/politics, health/medicine, history (history of technology), military/war, nature/environment, science. Query with SASE.

Recent Title(s) *Business Builders in Fast Food*, by Nathan Aaseng; *Women with Wings*, by Jacqueline McLean.

Tips "Audience is primarily junior and senior high school students writing reports."

ONSTAGE PUBLISHING

214 E. Moulton St. NE, Decatur AL 35601. (256)308-2300. Website: www.onstagebooks.com. **Acquisitions:** Dianne Hamilton, senior editor. Estab. 1999. Publishes hardcover and mass market paperback originals. **Publishes 5 titles/year. Receives 300 queries and 500 mss/year. 80% of books from first-time authors; 95% from unagented writers. Pays royalty on wholesale price. Offers variable advance.** Publishes book 1-2 years after acceptance of ms. Accepts simultaneous submissions. Responds in 1-2 months to queries; 1-2 months to proposals; 2-4 months to mss. Book catalog for 9×12 SASE with 3 first-class stamps or online at website; ms guidelines for #10 SASE or online at website.

Nonfiction Biography, children's/juvenile, coffee table book. Subjects include education, history, music/dance, photography, sports. "We want nonfiction that reads like a story and is well referenced." Submit proposal package including outline, first 3 chapters, or submit complete ms, if less than 50 pages. Reviews artwork/photos as part of ms package. Send photocopies.

Fiction Adventure, fantasy, historical, humor, juvenile, literary, mainstream/contemporary, mystery, picture books, regional, romance, science fiction, short story collections, sports, suspense, young adult. "We pride ourselves in scouting out new talent and publishing works by new writers. We publish mainly children's titles." Submit proposal package including outline, first 3 chapters, synopsis. Submit complete ms, if less than 50 pages. Submit art work to Senior Editor, copies only.

Recent Title(s) *Fat Tuesday*, by Susan Vaught (contemporary YA novel); *The Legacy of Bletchley Park*, by Annie Laura Smith (WWII historical, middle grade mystery); *Secret of Crybaby Hollow*, by Darren Butler (middle grade mystery book, ages 8-12, the third book in the Abbie Girl Spy Adventures).

Tips "Our audience is pre-K to young adult. Study our catalog, and get a sense of the kind of books we publish, so that you know whether your project is likely to be right for us."

OPEN ROAD PUBLISHING

P.O. Box 284, Cold Spring Harbor NY 11724. (631)692-7172. Fax: (631)692-7193. E-mail: Jopenroad@aol.com. Website: openroadpub.com. Publisher: Jonathan Stein. Publishes trade paperback originals. **Publishes 22-27 titles/year. Receives 200 queries and 75 mss/year. 30% of books from first-time authors; 98% from unagented writers. Pays 5-6% royalty on retail price. Offers $1,000-5,000 advance.** Publishes book 3 months after acceptance of ms. Accepts simultaneous submissions. Responds in 1 month to queries; 2 months to proposals. Book catalog and ms guidelines free.

O— Open Road publishes travel guides and has expanded into other areas with its new imprint, Cold Spring Press, particularly sports/fitness, topical, biographies, history, fantasy.

Nonfiction How-to. Subjects include travel. Query with SASE.

Recent Title(s) *Tahiti & French Polynesia Guide*, by Jon Prince; *Arizona Guide*, by Larry Ludmer; *Caribbean with Kids*, by Paris Permenter & John Bigley.

ORANGE FRAZER PRESS, INC.

P.O. Box 214, Wilmington OH 45177. (937)382-3196. Fax: (937)383-3159. Website: www.orangefrazer.com. **Acquisitions:** Marcy Hawley, editor. Publishes hardcover and trade paperback originals and reprints. **Publishes 25 titles/year. Receives 50 queries and 40 mss/year. 50% of books from first-time authors; 99% from unagented writers. Pays 10-12% royalty on wholesale price. Offers advance.** Publishes book 18 months after acceptance of ms. Accepts simultaneous submissions. Responds in 2 months to queries; 1 month to proposals; 1 month to mss. Book catalog free.

O— Orange Frazer Press accepts Ohio-related nonfiction only; corporate histories; town celebrations; anniversary books.

Nonfiction Accepts Ohio nonfiction only. Biography, coffee table book, cookbook, gift book, humor, illustrated book, reference, textbook. Subjects include art/architecture, cooking/foods/nutrition, education, history, memoirs, nature/environment, photography, recreation, regional (Ohio), sports, travel, women's issues/studies. Submit proposal package including outline, 1 sample chapter(s), SASE. Reviews artwork/photos as part of ms package. Send photocopies or transparencies.

Recent Title(s) *Party Animals, Washington, D.C.*; *Building Ohio, A Traveler's Guide to Rural Ohio*; *The Ohio Almanac, 3rd ed.*

Tips "We do many high-end company and corporate histories."

N ⊘ ORCHARD BOOKS

Imprint of Scholastic Trade Division, 557 Broadway, New York NY 10012. (212)343-6100. Website: www.scholastic.com. Estab. 1987. Publishes hardcover and trade paperback originals. **Publishes 60-70 titles/year. Receives 3,000 queries/year. 25% of books from first-time authors; 50% from unagented writers. Pays 6-10% royalty on retail price. Offers varied advance.** Publishes book 1 year after acceptance of ms. Responds in 3 months to queries.

> ○➦ Orchard specializes in children's picture books. Currently emphasizing picture books and middle grade novels (ages 8-12). De-emphasizing young adult.

Nonfiction Children's/juvenile, illustrated book. Subjects include animals, history, nature/environment. *"No unsolicited mss. Queries only. Be as specific and enlightening as possible about your book."* Query with SASE. Reviews artwork/photos as part of ms package. Send photocopies.

Fiction Picture books, young adult, middle reader; novelty. *No unsolicited mss.* Query with SASE.

Recent Title(s) *Stuart's Cape*, by Sara Pennypacker, illustrated by Martin Matje; *Talkin' About Bessie*, by Nikki Grimes, illustrated by E.B. Lewis.

Tips "Go to a bookstore and read several Orchard Books to get an idea of what we publish. Write what you feel and query us if you think it's 'right.' It's worth finding the right publishing match."

N ORCHISES PRESS

P.O. Box 20602, Alexandria VA 22320-1602. (703)683-1243. Fax: (703)993-1161. E-mail: lathbury@gmu.edu. Website: mason.gmu.edu/~rlathbur. **Acquisitions:** Roger Lathbury, editor-in-chief. Estab. 1983. Publishes hardcover and trade paperback originals and reprints. **Publishes 4-5 titles/year. Receives 600 queries and 200 mss/year. 1% of books from first-time authors; 95% from unagented writers. Pays 36% of receipts after Orchises has recouped its costs.** Publishes book 1 year after acceptance of ms. Accepts simultaneous submissions. Responds in 3 months to queries. Book catalog for #10 SASE; ms guidelines online.

> ○➦ Orchises Press is a general literary publisher specializing in poetry with selected reprints and textbooks. No new fiction or children's books.

Nonfiction Biography, how-to, humor, reference, technical, textbook. Subjects include literary. No real restrictions on subject matter. Query with SASE. Reviews artwork/photos as part of ms package. Send photocopies.

Poetry Poetry must have been published in respected literary journals. Publishes free verse, but has strong formalist preferences. Query, or submit 5 sample poems.

Recent Title(s) *Library*, by Stephen Akey (nonfiction); *I Think I Am Going to Call My Wife Paraguay*, by David Kirby (poetry).

Tips "Show some evidence of appealing to a wider audience than simply people you know. Publication in a nationally prominent venue is not required, but it helps."

OREGON STATE UNIVERSITY PRESS

101 Waldo Hall, Corvallis OR 97331-6407. (541)737-3873. Fax: (541)737-3170. Website: oregonstate.edu/dept/press. **Acquisitions:** Mary Elizabeth Braun, acquiring editor. Estab. 1962. Publishes hardcover and paperback originals. **Publishes 15-20 titles/year. Receives 400 submissions/year. 75% of books from first-time authors; 100% from unagented writers. Pays royalty on net receipts.** Publishes book 1 year after acceptance of ms. Does not accept simultaneous submissions. Responds in 3 months to queries. Book catalog for 6×9 SAE with 2 first-class stamps; ms guidelines online.

> ○➦ Oregon State University Press publishes several scholarly and specialized books, and books of particular importance to the Pacific Northwest. "OSU Press plays an essential role by publishing books that may not have a large audience, but are important to scholars, students, and librarians in the region."

Nonfiction Publishes scholarly books in history, biography, geography, literature, natural resource management, with strong emphasis on Pacific or Northwestern topics. Reference, scholarly. Subjects include regional, science. Submit outline, sample chapter(s).

Recent Title(s) *Gathering Moss: A Natural & Cultural History of Mosses*, by Robin Wall Kimmerer; *Oregon's Promise: An Interpretive History*, by David Peterson del Mar; *Living with Earthquakes in the Pacific Northwest*, by Robert S. Yeats.

Ⓐ THE OVERLOOK PRESS
Distributed by Penguin Putnam, 141 Wooster St., New York NY 10012. (212)673-2210. Fax: (212)673-2296. Publisher: Peter Mayer. **Acquisitions:** (Ms.) Tracy Carns, associate publisher. Estab. 1971. Publishes hardcover and trade paperback originals and hardcover reprints. **Publishes 40 titles/year. Receives 300 submissions/year. Pays 3-15% royalty on wholesale price, or retail price. Offers advance.** Does not accept simultaneous submissions. Responds in 5 months to queries. Book catalog free.
Imprints Elephant's Eye, Tusk Books.
➔ Overlook Press publishes fiction, children's books, and nonfiction.
Nonfiction Biography. Subjects include art/architecture, film/cinema/stage, history, regional (New York State), current events, design, health/fitness, how-to, lifestyle, martial arts. No pornography. *Agented submissions only.*
Fiction Literary, some commercial, foreign literature in translation. *Agented submissions only.*

THE OVERMOUNTAIN PRESS
P.O. Box 1261, Johnson City TN 37605. (423)926-2691. Fax: (423)929-2464. E-mail: submissions@overmtn.com. Website: www.overmountainpress.com. **Acquisitions:** Jason Weems, editor. Estab. 1970. Publishes hardcover and trade paperback originals and reprints. **Publishes 15-20 titles/year. Receives 500 queries and 100 mss/year. 50% of books from first-time authors; 100% from unagented writers. Pays 7¹/₂-15% royalty on wholesale price.** Publishes book 1 year after acceptance of ms. Accepts simultaneous submissions. Responds in 6 months to proposals; 6 months to mss. Book catalog free; ms guidelines online.
Imprints Silver Dagger Mysteries.
➔ The Overmountain Press publishes primarily Appalachian history. Audience is people interested in history of Tennessee, Virginia, North Carolina, Kentucky, and all aspects of this region—Revolutionary War, Civil War, county histories, historical biographies, etc. Currently reviewing only regional. De-emphasizing general interest children's fiction, poetry.
Nonfiction Regional works only. Biography, children's/juvenile, coffee table book, cookbook. Subjects include Americana, cooking/foods/nutrition, ethnic, history, military/war, nature/environment, photography, regional, women's issues/studies, Native American. Submit proposal package including outline, 3 sample chapter(s), marketing suggestions. Reviews artwork/photos as part of ms package. Send photocopies.
Fiction Picture books.
Recent Title(s) *Apple Doll*, by Kathleen Phillips Poulsen (children's picture books); *Southwest Virginia Crossroads*, by Joe Tennis.
Tips "Please submit a proposal. Please, no phone calls."

RICHARD C. OWEN PUBLISHERS, INC.
P.O. Box 585, Katonah NY 10536. (914)232-3903. Website: www.rcowen.com. **Acquisitions:** Janice Boland, director, children's books; Amy Finney, project editor (professional development, teacher-oriented books). Estab. 1982. Publishes hardcover and paperback originals. **Publishes 23 titles/year. Receives 50 queries and 1,000 mss/year. 99% of books from first-time authors; 100% from unagented writers. Pays 5% royalty on wholesale price. Books for Young Learners Anthologies: flat fee for all rights.** Publishes book 2-5 years after acceptance of ms. Accepts simultaneous submissions. Responds in 1 month to queries; 1 month to proposals; 5 months to mss. Ms guidelines online.
➔ "In addition to publishing good literature, stories for 8-9-year-old children, we are also seeking manuscripts for 8-9-year-old children. Subjects include humor, careers, mysteries, science fiction, folktales, women, fashion trends, sports, music, myths, journalism, history, inventions, planets, architecture, plays, adventure, technology, vehicles."
Nonfiction Children's/juvenile. Subjects include animals, art/architecture, fashion/beauty, gardening, history, music/dance, nature/environment, recreation, science, sports, women's issues/studies, contemporary culture. "Our books are for kindergarten, first- and second-grade children to read on their own. The stories are very brief—under 1,000 words—yet well structured and crafted with memorable characters, language, and plots." Send for ms guidelines, then submit complete ms with SASE via mail only or visit website.
Fiction Picture books. "Brief, strong story line, believable characters, natural language, exciting—child-appealing stories with a twist. No lists books, alphabet, or counting books." Seeking short, snappy stories and articles for 7-8-year-old children (2nd grade). Subjects include humor, careers, mysteries, science fiction, folktales, women, fashion trends, sports, music, mysteries, myths, journalism, history, inventions, planets, architecture, plays, adventure, technology, vehicles. Send for ms guidelines, then submit full ms with SASE via mail only. No e-mail submissions, please.
Poetry "Poems that excite children are fun, humorous, fresh, and interesting. If rhyming, must be without force or contrivance. Poems should tell a story or evoke a mood or atmostphere and have rhythmic language." No jingles. Submit complete ms.

Recent Title(s) *Powwow*, by Rhonda Cox (nonfiction); *Concrete*, by Ellen Javernich (fiction); *Bunny Magic*, by Suzanne Hardin (humor).

Tips "We don't respond to queries or e-mails. Please do *not* fax or e-mail us. Because our books are so brief it is better to send entire manuscript. We publish story books with inherent educational value for young readers—books they can read with enjoyment and success. We believe students become enthusiastic, independent, life-long learners when supported and guided by skillful teachers using good books. The professional development work we do and the books we publish support these beliefs."

OXFORD UNIVERSITY PRESS

198 Madison Ave., New York NY 10016. (212)726-6000. Website: www.oup.com/us. **Acquisitions:** Joan Bossert, vice president/editorial director; Laura Brown, president. Publishes hardcover and trade paperback originals and reprints. **Publishes 1,500 titles/year. 40% of books from first-time authors; 80% from unagented writers. Pays 0-15% royalty on wholesale price, or retail price. Offers $0-40,000 advance.** Publishes book 10 months after acceptance of ms. Accepts simultaneous submissions. Responds in at least 3 months to proposals. Book catalog free; ms guidelines online.

   ⊶ "We publish books that make a significant contribution to the literature and research in a number of disciplines, which reflect the departments at the University of Oxford."

Nonfiction Oxford is an academic, scholarly press. Biography, children's/juvenile, reference, technical, textbook. Subjects include anthropology/archeology, art/architecture, business/economics, computers/electronic, gay/lesbian, government/politics, health/medicine, history, language/literature, military/war, money/finance, music/dance, nature/environment, philosophy, psychology (and psychiatry), religion, science, sociology, women's issues/studies, law. Submit outline, sample chapter(s), cv. Reviews artwork/photos as part of ms package.

ℕ P & R PUBLISHING CO.

P.O. Box 817, Phillipsburg NJ 08865. Fax: (908)454-0859. Website: www.prpbooks.com. **Acquisitions:** Allan Fisher, director of publications (nonfiction—adults); Melissa Craig, acquisitions editor (children's). Estab. 1930. Publishes hardcover originals and trade paperback originals and reprints. **Publishes 40 titles/year. Receives 300 queries and 100 mss/year. 5% of books from first-time authors; 95% from unagented writers. Pays 10-14% royalty on wholesale price.** Accepts simultaneous submissions. Responds in 1 month to queries; 2 months to proposals; 4 months to mss. Book catalog free; ms guidelines online.

Nonfiction Biography, booklets, children's/juvenile, gift book, scholarly. Subjects include history, religion, spirituality, translation. Query with SASE.

Recent Title(s) *The Prophet and His Message*, by Michael J. Williams (Biblical studies); *Fine China Is for Single Women Too*, by Lydia Brownback (women); *King's Arrow*, by Douglas Bond (children's historical fiction).

Tips "Our audience is evangelical Christians, other Christians, and seekers. All of our publications are consistent with Biblical teaching, as summarized in the Westminster Standards."

PACIFIC BOOKS, PUBLISHERS

P.O. Box 558, Palo Alto CA 94302-0558. Phone/Fax: (650)856-6400. **Acquisitions:** Henry Ponleithner, editor. Estab. 1945. **Publishes 6-12 titles/year. Pays 7½-15% royalty.** Does not accept simultaneous submissions. Responds in 1 month to queries. Book catalog for 9×12 SAE; ms guidelines for 9×12 SAE.

   ⊶ Pacific Books publishes general interest and scholarly nonfiction including professional and technical books, and college textbooks.

Nonfiction General interest, professional, technical, and scholarly nonfiction trade books. Reference, scholarly, technical, textbook. Subjects include Americana (western), general nonfiction, regional, translation, Hawaiiana. Looks for "well-written, documented material of interest to a significant audience." Also considers text and reference books for high school and college. Query with SASE, or submit outline. Reviews artwork/photos as part of ms package.

Recent Title(s) *How to Choose a Nursery School: A Parents' Guide to Preschool Education*, by Ada Anbar.

PACIFIC PRESS PUBLISHING ASSOCIATION

Trade Book Division, P.O. Box 5353, Nampa ID 83653-5353. (208)465-2500. Fax: (208)465-2531. E-mail: booksubmissions@pacificpress.com. Website: www.pacificpress.com. **Acquisitions:** Tim Lale, acquisitions editor (children's stories, biography, Christian living, spiritual growth); David Jarnes, book editor (theology, doctrine, inspiration). Estab. 1874. Publishes hardcover and trade paperback originals and reprints. **Publishes 35 titles/year. Receives 600 submissions/year. 35% of books from first-time authors; 100% from unagented writers. Pays 8-16% royalty on wholesale price.** Publishes book up to 2 years after acceptance of ms. Does not accept simultaneous submissions. Responds in 3 months to queries. Ms guidelines online.

   ⊶ "We publish books that fit Seventh-day Adventist beliefs only. All titles are Christian and religious. For guidance, see www.adventist.org/beliefs/index.html. Our books fit into the categories of this retail site: www.adventistbookcenter.com."

Book Publishers

Nonfiction Biography, booklets, children's/juvenile, cookbook (vegetarian), how-to, humor. Subjects include child guidance/parenting, cooking/foods/nutrition (vegetarian only), health/medicine, history, nature/environment, philosophy, religion, spirituality, women's issues/studies, family living, Christian lifestyle, Bible study, Christian doctrine, eschatology. Query with SASE or e-mail, or submit 3 sample chapters, cover letter with overview of book. Electronic submissions accepted. Reviews artwork/photos as part of ms package.

Fiction Religious. "Pacific Press rarely publishes fiction, but we're interested in developing a line of Seventh-day Adventist fiction in the future. Only proposals accepted; no full manuscripts."

Recent Title(s) *Graffiti in the Holy of Holies*, by Clifford Goldstein (doctrine); *Parenting by the Spirit*, by Sally Hohnberger (practical Christianity); *I Miss Grandpa*, by Karen Holford (children's).

Tips "Our primary audience is members of the Seventh-day Adventist denomination. Almost all are written by Seventh-day Adventists. Books that do well for us relate the Biblical message to practical human concerns and focus more on the experiential rather than theoretical aspects of Christianity. We are assigning more titles, using less unsolicited material—although we still publish manuscripts from freelance submissions and proposals."

PALADIN PRESS

P.O. Box 1307, Boulder CO 80306-1307. (303)443-7250. Fax: (303)442-8741. E-mail: editorial@paladin-press.com. Website: www.paladin-press.com. **President/Publisher:** Peder C. Lund. **Acquisitions:** Jon Ford, editorial director. Estab. 1970. Publishes hardcover originals and paperback originals and reprints. **Publishes 50 titles/year. 50% of books from first-time authors; 100% from unagented writers. Pays 10-15% royalty on net receipts. Offers advance.** Publishes book 1 year after acceptance of ms. Accepts simultaneous submissions. Responds in 2 months to proposals. Book catalog free.

Imprints Sycamore Island Books, Flying Machines Press, Outer Limits Press.

- ⊶ Paladin Press publishes the "action library" of nonfiction in military science, police science, weapons, combat, personal freedom, self-defense, survival.

Nonfiction "Paladin Press primarily publishes original manuscripts on military science, weaponry, self-defense, personal privacy, financial freedom, espionage, police science, action careers, guerrilla warfare, and fieldcraft." How-to, reference. Subjects include government/politics, military/war. "If applicable, send sample photographs and line drawings with complete outline and sample chapters." Query with SASE.

Recent Title(s) *The Advanced Tactical Marksman*, by Dave Lauck.

Tips "We need lucid, instructive material aimed at our market and accompanied by sharp, relevant illustrations and photos. As we are primarily a publisher of 'how-to' books, a manuscript that has step-by-step instructions, written in a clear and concise manner (but not strictly outline form) is desirable. No fiction, first-person accounts, children's, religious, or joke books. We are also interested in serious, professional videos and video ideas (contact Michael Janich)."

Ⓝ PALARI PUBLISHING

P.O. Box 9288, Richmond VA 23227-0288. (804)883-6112. Fax: (804)883-5234. E-mail: palaripub@aol.com. Website: www.palari.net. **Acquisitions:** David Smitherman, publisher (nonfiction, cultural, gay/lesbian, mystery, historical). Estab. 1998. Publishes hardcover and trade paperback originals. **Imprint publishes 4 titles/year. Receives 400 queries and 200 mss/year. 80% of books from first-time authors; 100% from unagented writers. Pays royalty.** Publishes book 1 year after acceptance of ms. Does not accept simultaneous submissions. Responds in 1 month to queries; 1 month to proposals; 2-3 months to mss. Book catalog free; ms guidelines online.

Nonfiction Subjects include alternative lifestyles, Americana, anthropology/archeology, contemporary culture, creative nonfiction, ethnic, gay/lesbian, general nonfiction, history, multicultural, photography, social sciences. "Have a well-presented, well-researched proposal to submit." Query with SASE. Reviews artwork/photos as part of ms package. Send photocopies.

Fiction Adventure, ethnic, gay/lesbian, historical, literary, mainstream/contemporary, multicultural, mystery, suspense. "Tell why your idea is unique or interesting. Make sure we are interested in your genre before submitting." Query with SASE.

Recent Title(s) *We're Still Here: Contemporary Virginia Indians Tell Their Stories*, by Sandra Waugaman (cultural/history); *Red, White & Blue in the USA*, by Esther Chao (photography, coffee table book, patriotism); *In and Out in Hollywood*, by Ben Patrick Johnson (comedy, industry entertainment, gay).

Tips "When submitting, tell about yourself and your experiences, and why you are qualified to write about your subject."

Ⓝ PANTHEON BOOKS

Imprint of Knopf Publishing Group, Division of Random House, Inc., 1745 Broadway 21-2, New York NY 10019. (212)782-9000. Fax: (212)572-6030. Website: www.pantheonbooks.com. **Editorial Director:** Dan Frank. **Senior Editors:** Shelley Wanger, Deborah Garrison. **Executive Editor:** Erroll McDonald. **Acquisitions:** Adult Editorial

Department. Estab. 1942. Publishes hardcover and trade paperback originals and trade paperback reprints. **Pays royalty. Offers advance.** Does not accept simultaneous submissions.

O━ Pantheon Books publishes both Western and non-Western authors of literary fiction and important nonfiction.

Nonfiction Autobiography, biography, literary; international. Subjects include general nonfiction, government/politics, history, memoirs, science, travel.

Fiction Quality fiction and nonfiction. Query with cover letter and sample material.

Recent Title(s) *Jimmy Corrigan*, by Chris Ware; *Nigger*, by Randall Kennedy; *Three Junes*, by Julie Glass.

PARACLETE PRESS

P.O. Box 1568, Orleans MA 02653. (508)255-4685. Fax: (508)255-5705. **Acquisitions:** Editorial Review Committee. Estab. 1981. Publishes hardcover and trade paperback originals. **Publishes 20 titles/year. Receives 250 mss/year.** Publishes book up to 2 years after acceptance of ms. Accepts simultaneous submissions. Responds in 2 months to queries; 2 months to mss. Book catalog for $8^1/_2 \times 11$ SASE; ms guidelines for #10 SASE.

O━ Publisher of Christian classics, devotionals, new editions of classics, books on prayer, Christian living, compact discs, and videos.

Nonfiction Subjects include religion. No poetry or children's books. Query with SASE, or submit 2-3 sample chapter(s), table of contents, chapter summaries.

Recent Title(s) *The Illumined Heart*, by Frederica Mathewes-Green; *Seeking His Mind*, by M. Basil Pennington, O.C.S.O; *Radical Hospitality*, by Lonni Collins Pratt and Daniel Homan, O.S.B.

PARADISE CAY PUBLICATIONS

P.O. Box 29, Arcata CA 95518-0029. (707)822-7038. Fax: (707)822-9163. E-mail: paracay@humboldt1.com. Website: www.paracay.com. **Acquisitions:** Matt Morehouse, publisher (nautical). Publishes hardcover and trade paperback originals and reprints. **Publishes 5 titles/year; imprint publishes 2 titles/year. Receives 30-40 queries and 20-30 mss/year. 10% of books from first-time authors; 100% from unagented writers. Pays 10-15% royalty on wholesale price, or makes outright purchase of $1,000-10,000. Offers $0-2,000 advance.** Publishes book 4 months after acceptance of ms. Responds in 1 month to queries; 1 month to proposals; 2 months to mss. Book catalog and ms guidelines free on request or online.

Imprints Pardey Books.

Nonfiction Cookbook, how-to, illustrated book, reference, technical, textbook. Subjects include cooking/foods/nutrition, recreation, sports, travel. Query with SASE, or submit proposal package including 2-3 sample chapter(s), call first. Reviews artwork/photos as part of ms package. Send photocopies.

Fiction Adventure (nautical, sailing). All fiction must have a nautical theme. Query with SASE, or submit proposal package including 2-3 sample chapter(s), synopsis.

Recent Title(s) *American Practical Navigator*, by Nathaniel Bowditch; *Voyage Toward Vengeance* (fiction); *How to Rename Your Boat*.

Tips Audience is recreational sailors and powerboaters. Call Matt Morehouse (publisher) before submitting anything.

PARAGON HOUSE PUBLISHERS

2285 University Ave. W., Suite 200, St. Paul MN 55114-1635. (651)644-3087. Fax: (651)644-0997. E-mail: paragon@paragonhouse.com. Website: www.paragonhouse.com. **Acquisitions:** Rosemary Yokoi, acquisitions editor. Estab. 1962. Publishes hardcover and trade paperback originals and trade paperback reprints. **Publishes 12-15 titles/year; imprint publishes 2-5 titles/year. Receives 1,500 queries and 150 mss/year. 7% of books from first-time authors; 90% from unagented writers. Offers $500-1,500 advance.** Publishes book 1 year after acceptance of ms. Accepts simultaneous submissions. Ms guidelines online.

Imprints PWPA Books (Dr. Gordon L. Anderson); Athena Books; New Era Books; ICUS Books

O━ "We publish general-interest titles and textbooks that provide the readers greater understanding of society and the world." Currently emphasizing religion, philosophy.

Nonfiction Biography, reference, textbook. Subjects include child guidance/parenting, government/politics, memoirs, multicultural, nature/environment, philosophy, religion, sex, sociology, women's issues/studies, world affairs. Submit proposal package including outline, 2 sample chapter(s), market breakdown, SASE.

Recent Title(s) *Righteous Gentiles of the Holocaust*, by David Gushee; *The Sacred Mirror*, by John J. Prendergast; *Kaballah Simply Stated*, by Robert Waxman.

PARALLAX PRESS

United Buddhist Church, Inc., P.O. Box 7355, Berkeley CA 94707. (510)525-0101, ext. 113. Fax: (510)525-7129. E-mail: rachel@parallax.org. Website: www.parallax.org. **Acquisitions:** Rachel Neumann, senior editor (Buddhism, engaged Buddhism, social responsibility, spirituality). Estab. 1985. Publishes hardcover and trade paperback originals. **Publishes 8 titles/year. Receives 200-6,000 queries and 200 mss/year. 2% of books from first-time authors; 10% from unagented writers. Pays 20-30% royalty on wholesale price, or makes outright purchase of $500-2,000.** Publishes book 6-9 months after acceptance of ms. Does not accept simultaneous submissions. Responds in 1 month to queries; 3 months to proposals; 3 months to mss. Book catalog for 1 SAE with 3 first-class stamps; ms guidelines for #10 SASE.

Nonfiction Children's/juvenile, coffee table book, self-help. Subjects include multicultural, religion, spirituality. Query with SASE, or submit proposal package including outline, 2 sample chapter(s). Reviews artwork/photos as part of ms package. Send photocopies.

Recent Title(s) *Mindfulness in the Marketplace*, by Allan Hunt Badiner (collection of essays); *Be Free Where You Are*, by Thich Nhat Hanh (nonfiction); *Thomas Merton and Thich Nhat Hanh*, by Robert H. King (nonfiction).

PARKWAY PUBLISHERS, INC.

Box 3678, Boone NC 28607. (828)265-3993. Fax: (828)265-3993. E-mail: parkwaypub@hotmail.com. Website: www.parkwaypublishers.com. **Acquisitions:** Rao Aluri, president. Publishes hardcover and trade paperback originals. **Publishes 10-12 titles/year. Receives 15-20 queries and 20 mss/year. 75% of books from first-time authors; 100% from unagented writers.** Publishes book 8 months after acceptance of ms. Does not accept simultaneous submissions.

  ⚬━ Parkway publishes books on the local history and culture of western North Carolina. "We are located on Blue Ridge Parkway and our primary industry is tourism. We are interested in books which present the history and culture of western North Carolina to the tourist market." Will consider fiction if it highlights the region.

Nonfiction Technical. Subjects include history, psychology, regional. Query with SASE, or submit complete ms.

Recent Title(s) *Letter from James*, by Ruth Layng (historical fiction).

Ⓝ PASSEGGIATA PRESS

420 West 14th St., Pueblo CO 81003-3404. (719)544-1038. Fax: (719)544-7911. E-mail: passeggiata@compuserve.com. **Acquisitions:** Donald E. Herdeck, publisher/editor-in-chief; Harold Ames, Jr., general editor. Estab. 1973. Publishes hardcover and paperback originals. **Publishes 10-20 titles/year. Receives 200 submissions/year. 15% of books from first-time authors; 99% from unagented writers. Pays 5-10% royalty. Foundation or institution receives 20-30 copies of book and at times royalty on first printing. Pays royalties once yearly (against advance) as a percentage of net paid receipts. Offers $300 average advance.** Accepts simultaneous submissions. Responds in 1 week to queries; 1 month to mss.

  ⚬━ "We search for books that will make clear the complexity and value of non-Western literature and culture. Mostly we do fiction in translation." Currently emphasizing criticism of non-Western writing (Caribbean, Latin American, etc.). De-emphasizing poetry.

Nonfiction Specializes in African, Caribbean, Middle Eastern (Arabic and Persian), and Asian-Pacific literature, criticism and translation, Third World literature and history, fiction, poetry, criticism, history and translations of creative work. Scholarly. Subjects include ethnic, history, language/literature, multicultural, regional, translation. Query with SASE, or submit outline, TOC. Reviews artwork/photos as part of ms package. State availability of photos/illustrations.

Fiction "We publish original fiction only by writers from Africa, the Caribbean, the Middle East, Asia, and the Pacific. Query with SASE, or submit outline, table of contents. State "origins (non-Western), education and previous publications. "Send inquiry letter first and ms only if so requested by us. We are not a subsidy publisher, but do a few specialized titles a year with grants. In those cases we accept institutional subventions."

Poetry Submit 5-10 sample poems.

Recent Title(s) *History of Syriac Literature and Sciences*; *Ghost Songs: A Palestinian Love Story*.

Tips "We are always interested in genuine contributions to understanding non-Western culture. We need a polished translation, or original prose or poetry by non-Western authors only. Critical and cross-cultural studies are accepted from any scholar from anywhere."

Ⓒ PAULINE BOOKS AND MEDIA

Daughters of St. Paul, 50 St. Paul's Ave., Jamaica Plain MA 02130-3491. (617)522-8911. Fax: (617)524-9805. Website: www.pauline.org. **Acquisitions:** Sr. Madonna Ratliff, FSP, acquisitions editor (adult); Sr. Patricia Jablonski, acquisitions editor (children). Estab. 1948. Publishes trade paperback originals and reprints. **Publishes 50-60 titles/year. Receives 1,500 submissions/year. Pays 8-12% royalty on net receipts. Offers advance.** Publishes book 1-2 years after acceptance of ms. Does not accept simultaneous submissions. Responds in 6-8 weeks to queries. Book catalog for 9×12 SAE with 4 first-class stamps; ms guidelines online.

  ⚬━ "As a Catholic publishing house, PBM publishes in the areas of spirituality (prayer/holiness of life/ Biblical); religious faith formation (adults/children); family life (parenting, activities, etc.); teacher resources (reproducibles, activities, games, crafts, etc.); biographies of saints; mariology; prayer books;

and books for young people and children. Submissions are evaluated on adherence to Gospel values, harmony with the Catholic tradition, relevance of topic, and quality of writing. Does not publish fiction for adults, autobiographical works, or poetry.''

Nonfiction No strictly nonreligious works considered. *No unsolicited mss.* Query with SASE.

Fiction Children only. No strictly nonreligious works considered. *No unsolicited mss.* Query only with SASE.

Recent Title(s) *St. John of the Cross: Man and Mystic*, by Richard P. Hardy; *Theology of the Body Explained: A Commentary on John Paul II's ''Gospel of the Body,''* by Christopher West; *Surviving Depression: A Catholic Approach*, by Kathryn J. Hermes, FSP.

[N] PAULIST PRESS

997 MacArthur Blvd., Mahwah NJ 07430. (201)825-7300. Fax: (201)825-8345. E-mail: info@paulistpress.com. Website: www.paulistpress.com. **Acquisitions:** Lawrence Boadt, C.S.P., editorial director for general submissions; Christopher Bellitto, academic editor; Susan O'Keefe, children's editor; Donald Brophy, senior editor (liturgy and catechetics). Estab. 1865. Publishes hardcover and paperback originals and paperback reprints. **Publishes 90-100 titles/year. Receives 500 submissions/year. 5-8% of books from first-time authors; 95% from unagented writers. Usually pays royalty on net, but occasionally on retail price. Offers advance.** Publishes book 10 months after acceptance of ms. Does not accept simultaneous submissions. Responds in 2 months to queries. Ms guidelines online.

> ○┐ ''The editorial mission of the Paulist Press is to publish books in the area of religious thought, especially, but not exclusively, Catholic religious thought. The major topics would be religious children's books, college theological textbooks, spirituality of prayer and religious classical works.'' Current areas of special interest are books that appeal to the religious and spiritual searching of unchurched people, children's books on Catholic subjects, and theology textbooks for college courses in religion. Less desired at this time are books in philosophy and biography, poetry, and fiction.

Nonfiction Self-help, textbook (religious). Subjects include philosophy, religion. ''We would like to see theology (Catholic and ecumenical Christian), popular spirituality, liturgy, and religious education texts.'' Submit outline, 2 sample chapter(s). Reviews artwork/photos as part of ms package.

Recent Title(s) *101 Questions & Answers on Vatican II*, by Maureen Sullivan; *Show Us Your Mercy and Love*, by Justin Rigali; *Francis of Assisi*, by Adrian House.

PEACHTREE CHILDREN'S BOOKS

Peachtree Publishers, Ltd., 1700 Chattahoochee Ave., Atlanta GA 30318-2112. (404)876-8761. Fax: (404)875-2578. E-mail: hello@peachtree-online.com. Website: www.peachtree-online.com. **Acquisitions:** Helen Harriss, submissions editor. Publishes hardcover and trade paperback originals. **Publishes 30 titles/year. 25% of books from first-time authors; 25% from unagented writers. Pays royalty on retail price; Advance varies.** Publishes book 1 year or more after acceptance of ms. Accepts simultaneous submissions. Responds in 6 months to queries; 6 months to mss. Book catalog for 6 first-class stamps; ms guidelines online.

Imprints Freestone, Peachtree Jr.

> ○┐ ''We publish a broad range of subjects and perspectives, with emphasis on innovative plots and strong writing.''

Nonfiction Children's/juvenile. Subjects include animals, child guidance/parenting, creative nonfiction, education, ethnic, gardening, health/medicine, history, language/literature, multicultural, music/dance, nature/environment, recreation, regional, science, social sciences, sports, travel. No e-mail or fax queries of mss. Submit complete ms with SASE.

Fiction Juvenile, picture books, young adult. Looking for very well-written middle grade and young adult novels. No collections of poetry or short stories; no romance or science fiction. Submit complete ms with SASE.

Recent Title(s) *About Amphibians*, Cathryn Sill (children's picture book); *Yellow Star*, by Carmen Agra Deedy; *My Life and Death by Alexandra Canarsie*, by Susan Heyboer O'Keefe.

PELICAN PUBLISHING CO.

P.O. Box 3110, Gretna LA 70054. (504)368-1175. Website: www.pelicanpub.com. **Acquisitions:** Nina Kooij, editor-in-chief. Estab. 1926. Publishes hardcover, trade paperback and mass market paperback originals and reprints. **Publishes 90 titles/year. Receives 5,000 submissions/year. 15% of books from first-time authors; 80% from unagented writers. Pays royalty on actual receipts. Advance considered.** Publishes book 9-18 months after acceptance of ms. Does not accept simultaneous submissions. Responds in 1 month to queries; 3 months to mss. Book catalog for SASE; Writer's guidelines for SASE or on website.

> ○┐ ''We believe ideas have consequences. One of the consequences is that they lead to a best-selling book. We publish books to improve and uplift the reader.'' Currently emphasizing business titles.

Nonfiction Biography, children's/juvenile, coffee table book (limited), cookbook, gift book, illustrated book, self-help. Subjects include Americana (especially Southern regional, Ozarks, Texas, Florida, and Southwest), art/architecture, contemporary culture, ethnic, government/politics, history (popular), multicultural, regional, religion (for popular audience mostly, but will consider others), sports, travel (regional and international), motivational (with business slant), inspirational (author must be someone with potential for large audience), Scottish, Irish, editorial cartoon. "We look for authors who can promote successfully. We require that a query be made first. This greatly expedites the review process and can save the writer additional postage expenses." No multiple queries or submissions. Query with SASE. Reviews artwork/photos as part of ms package.

Fiction Historical, juvenile (regional or historical focus). "We publish maybe 1 novel a year, usually by an author we already have. Almost all proposals are returned. We are most interested in historical Southern novels." No young adult, romance, science fiction, fantasy, gothic, mystery, erotica, confession, horror, sex, or violence. Also no "psychological" novels. Query with SASE, or submit outline, 2 sample chapter(s), synopsis, SASE. "Not responsible if writer's only copy is sent."

Recent Title(s) *Douglas Southall Freeman*, by David E. Johnson (biography).

Tips "We do extremely well with cookbooks, travel, popular histories, and some business. We will continue to build in these areas. The writer must have a clear sense of the market and knowledge of the competition. A query letter should describe the project briefly, give the author's writing and professional credentials, and promotional ideas."

N ⊘ PENDRAGON PUBLISHING, INC.

P.O. Box 31665, Chicago IL 60631. (847)720-0600. Fax: (847)720-0601. E-mail: info@pendragonpublishinginc.com. Website: www.pendragonpublishinginc.com. **Acquisitions:** Kate Palandech, managing director (all areas). Estab. 2002. Publishes hardcover, trade paperback, and mass market originals. **Publishes 10 titles/year. 75% of books from first-time authors; 75% from unagented writers. Pays 10-15% royalty on retail price. Offers $500-1,000 advance.** Publishes book 1 year after acceptance of ms. Accepts simultaneous submissions. Responds in 6 months to queries; 6 months to proposals; 6 months to mss. Book catalog and ms guidelines online.

Nonfiction Gift book, self-help. Subjects include creative nonfiction, general nonfiction, health/medicine, New Age, psychology, spirituality. "Review our titles in our online catalog. We are looking for writers who can inspire their readers by bringing a fresh perspective or new knowledge to their subject matter. We are happy to consider first-time authors." Submit proposal package including outline, 2 sample chapter(s). **All unsolicited mss returned unopened.** Reviews artwork/photos as part of ms package. Send photocopies.

Recent Title(s) *The Joy Formula for Health & Beauty*, by Dr. Laura Humphrey (self-help/psychology/personal growth); *Pathways of the Soul*, by Nancy Miller Ogren (mind/body/spirit book/card/CD set).

Tips "Our readers are seeking personal growth either through self-help, mind/body/spirit (New Age), or any subject matter that will inspire them to lead more satisfying lives. Our motto is: 'To inspire the soul to soar.' We are a small publishing house that works very closely with our authors in the entire process from manuscript drafts to marketing and sales. We allow our authors great input, but certain final decisions (i.e., final titles and cover art) will always rest with Pendragon. Authors must be flexible and open to the creative process that is publishing."

⊘ PENGUIN GROUP (USA), Inc.

375 Hudson St., New York NY 10014. (212)366-2000. Website: www.penguin.com. General interest publisher of both fiction and nonfiction. Ms guidelines online.

Imprints Penguin Adult Division: Ace Books, Alpha Books, Avery, Berkley Books, Dutton, Gotham Books, HPBooks, Jove, New American Library, Penguin (Penguin, Penguin Classics, Penguin Compass, Penguin 20th Century Classics), Perigee, Plume, Portfolio, G.P. Putnam's Sons, Riverhead, Jeremy P. Tarcher, Viking; **Penguin Audiobooks:** Arkangel Shakespeare, Penguin*HighBridge Audio; **Penguin Children's Division:** Dial Books for Young Readers, Dutton Children's Books, Dutton Interactive, Firebird, Phyllis Fogelman Books, Grosset & Dunlap (Planet Dexter, Platt & Munk), Philomel, Playskool, Price Stern Sloan,PSS, Puffin Books, G.P. Putnam's Sons (PaperStar), Viking Children's Books, Frederick Warne.

N A ⊘ PENGUIN YOUNG READERS GROUP

Division of Penguin Group (USA), Inc., a member of Pearson, 345 Hudson St., New York NY 10014. (212)366-2000. Website: penguinputnam.com. Estab. 1838. Publishes hardcover and paperback originals.

Imprints Dial Books for Young Readers, Dutton Children's Books, Dutton Interactive, Grosset & Dunlap, Paperstar, Philomel, Planet Dexter, Platt & Munk, Playskool, PSS, Puffin Books, G P Putnam's Sons, Viking Children's Books, Frederick Warren.

N PENMARIN BOOKS, INC.

1044 Magnolia Way, Roseville CA 95661. (916)771-5869. Fax: (916)771-5879. E-mail: penmarin@jps.net. Website: www.penmarin.com. **Acquisitions:** Hal Lockwood, editor-in-chief (all categories). Estab. 1987. Publishes hardcover and trade paperback originals. **Publishes 4 titles/year. Receives 200 queries and 100 mss/year.**

40% of books from first-time authors; 60% from unagented writers. Pays 7-15% royalty on retail price. **Offers $3,000-10,000 advance.** Publishes book 1 year after acceptance of ms. Accepts simultaneous submissions. Responds in 2 days to queries; 1 month to proposals. Book catalog and ms guidelines online.

Nonfiction Autobiography, biography, illustrated book, self-help. Subjects include child guidance/parenting, contemporary culture, general nonfiction, health/medicine, history, memoirs, psychology, world affairs. Submit proposal package including outline, 1-3 sample chapter(s), and all material listed in proposal/submission guidelines on website. Query by e-mail first. Reviews artwork/photos as part of ms package. Send photocopies.

Recent Title(s) *Hit Me with Your Best Shot*, by Kallen (self-help/success); *Farewell America: The Plot to Kill JFK*, by Hepburn (investigative journalism); *Carl Rogers: The Quiet Revolutionary*, by Rogers/Russell (oral history/biography).

PENNSYLVANIA HISTORICAL AND MUSEUM COMMISSION

Commonwealth of Pennsylvania, Keystone Bldg., 400 North St., Harrisburg PA 17120-0053. (717)787-8099. Fax: (717)787-8312. Website: www.phmc.state.pa.us. **Acquisitions:** Diane B. Reed, chief, publications and sales division. Estab. 1913. Publishes hardcover and paperback originals and reprints. **Publishes 6-8 titles/ year. Receives 25 submissions/year. Pays 5-10% royalty on retail price or makes outright purchase.** Publishes book 18-24 months after acceptance of ms. Accepts simultaneous submissions. Responds in 4 months to queries. Prepare ms according to the *Chicago Manual of Style*.

• "We are a public history agency and have a tradition of publishing scholarly and reference works, as well as more popularly styled books that reach an even broader audience interested in some aspect of Pennsylvania's history and heritage."

Nonfiction All books must be related to Pennsylvania, its history or culture. "The Commission considers manuscripts on Pennsylvania, specifically on archaeology, history, art (decorative and fine), politics, and biography." Illustrated book, reference, technical. Subjects include anthropology/archeology, art/architecture, government/ politics, history, travel (historic). Guidelines and proposal forms available. No fiction. Query with SASE, or submit outline, sample chapter(s).

Recent Title(s) *Classification Guide for Arrowheads and Spearpoints of Eastern Pennsylvania and the Central Middle Atlantic*, by Jay Custer.

Tips "Our audience is diverse—students, specialists, and generalists—all of them interested in 1 or more aspects of Pennsylvania's history and culture. Manuscripts must be well researched and documented (footnotes not necessarily required depending on the nature of the manuscript) and interestingly written. Manuscripts must be factually accurate, but in being so, writers must not sacrifice style."

PERIGEE BOOKS

Imprint of Penguin Group (USA), Inc., 375 Hudson St., New York NY 10014. (212)366-2000. Publisher: John Duff. **Acquisitions:** Sheila Curry Oakes, executive editor (child care, health); Michelle Howry, editor (personal growth, personal finance, women's issues). Publishes hardcover and trade paperback originals and reprints. **Publishes 55-60 titles/year. Receives hundreds queries and 300 + submissions/year. 30% of books from first-time authors; 10% from unagented writers. Pays 6-7½% royalty. Offers $5,000-150,000 advance.** Publishes book within 18 months after acceptance of ms. Accepts simultaneous submissions. Responds in 2 months to queries. Book catalog free; ms guidelines given on contract.

• Publishes in all areas of self-help and how-to. Currently emphasizing popular psychology, women's issues in health, fitness, and careers and lifestyles.

Nonfiction How-to, reference (popular), self-help, prescriptive books. Subjects include animals, child guidance/ parenting, cooking/foods/nutrition, health/medicine, hobbies, money/finance (personal finance), psychology, sex, sports, women's issues/studies, fashion/beauty. Prefers agented mss, but accepts unsolicited queries. Query with SASE, or submit outline.

THE PERMANENT PRESS/SECOND CHANCE PRESS

4170 Noyac Rd., Sag Harbor NY 11963. (631)725-1101. Fax: (631)725-8215. Website: www.thepermanentpress. com. **Acquisitions:** Judith Shepard, editor. Estab. 1978. Publishes hardcover originals. **Publishes 12 titles/ year. Receives 7,000 submissions/year. 60% of books from first-time authors; 60% from unagented writers. Pays 10-15% royalty on wholesale price. Offers $1,000 advance for Permanent Press books; royalty only on Second Chance Press titles.** Publishes book 18 months after acceptance of ms. Accepts simultaneous submissions. Responds in 3 weeks to queries; 6 months to mss. Book catalog for 8×10 SAE with 7 first-class stamps; ms guidelines for #10 SASE.

• Permanent Press publishes literary fiction. Second Chance Press devotes itself exclusively to re-publishing fine books that are out of print and deserve continued recognition. "We endeavor to publish quality writing—primarily fiction—without regard to authors' reputations or track records." Currently emphasizing literary fiction. No poetry, short story collections.

Nonfiction Autobiography, biography. Subjects include history, memoirs. No scientific and technical material, academic studies. Query with SASE.

Fiction Literary, mainstream/contemporary, mystery. Especially looking for high-line literary fiction, "artful, original and arresting." Accepts any fiction category as long as it is a "well-written, original full-length novel." Query with SASE and first 20 pages. No queries by fax.

Recent Title(s) *A Good Divorce*, by John Keegan; *Angels In the Morning*, by Sasha Troyan; *Hail to the Chiefs*, by Barbara Holland.

Tips "Audience is the silent minority—people with good taste. We are interested in the writing more than anything and dislike long outlines. The SASE is vital to keep track of things, as we are receiving ever more submissions. No fax queries will be answered. We aren't looking for genre fiction but a compelling, well-written story." Permanent Press does not employ readers and the number of submissions it receives has grown. If the writer sends a query or manuscript that the press is not interested in, a reply may take 6 weeks. If there is interest, it may take 3-6 months.

PETER PAUPER PRESS, INC.

202 Mamaroneck Ave., White Plains NY 10601-5376. E-mail: nbeilenson@peterpauper.com. **Acquisitions:** Nick Beilenson, editorial director. Estab. 1928. Publishes hardcover originals. **Publishes 40-50 titles/year. Receives 100 queries and 150 mss/year. 5% from unagented writers. Makes outright purchase only. Offers advance.** Publishes book 1 year after acceptance of ms. Does not accept simultaneous submissions. Responds in 1 month to queries. Manuscript guidelines for #10 SASE or may request via e-mail for a faxed copy (include fax number in e-mail request).

> PPP publishes small and medium format, illustrated gift books for occasions and in celebration of specific relationships such as mom, sister, friend, teacher, grandmother, granddaughter. PPP has expanded into the following areas: books for teens and tweens, books on popular topics of nonfiction for adults and licensed books by best-selling authors.

Nonfiction Gift book. Subjects include specific relationships or special occasions (graduation, Mother's Day, Christmas, etc.). "We do publish interactive journals and workbooks but not narrative manuscripts or fiction. We publish brief, original quotes, aphorisms, and wise sayings. Please do not send us other people's quotes." Query with SASE.

Recent Title(s) *The Essential Writer's Notebook*, by Natalie Goldberg; *The Feng Shui Journal*, by Teresa Polanco; *My Life as a Baby*.

Tips "Our readers are primarily female, age 10 and over, who are likely to buy a 'gift' book or gift book set in a stationery, gift, book, or boutique store or national book chain. Writers should become familiar with our previously published work. We publish only small- and medium-format, illustrated, hardcover gift books and sets of between 1,000-4,000 words. We have no interest in work aimed at men."

PFLAUM PUBLISHING GROUP

N90 W16890 Roosevelt Dr., Menomonee Falls WI 53051-7933. (262)502-4222. Fax: (262)502-4224. E-mail: kcannizzo@pflaum.com. **Acquisitions:** Karen A. Cannizzo, editorial director. **Publishes 20 titles/year. Payment may be outright purchase, royalty, or down payment plus royalty.** Book catalog and ms guidelines free.

> "Pflaum Publishing Group, a division of Peter Li, Inc., serves the specialized market of religious education, primarily Roman Catholic. We provide high quality, theologically sound, practical, and affordable resources that assist religious educators of and ministers to children from preschool through senior high school."

Nonfiction Religious education programs and catechetical resources. Query with SASE.

Recent Title(s) *Totally Lent! A Teen's Journey to Easter 2004*; *Changing Lives*; *Transformational Ministry and Today's Teens*.

PHAIDON PRESS

180 Varick St., Suite 1420, New York NY 10014. (212)652-5400. Fax: (212)652-5410. Website: www.phaidon.com. **Acquisitions:** Editorial Submissions. Publishes hardcover and trade paperback originals and reprints. **Publishes 100 titles/year. Receives 500 mss/year. 40% of books from first-time authors; 90% from unagented writers. Pays royalty on wholesale price, if appropriate. Offers advance, if appropriate.** Publishes book 1 year after acceptance of ms. Accepts simultaneous submissions. Responds in 3 months to proposals. Book catalog free; ms guidelines online.

Imprints Phaidon.

Nonfiction Subjects include art/architecture, photography, design. Submit proposal package and outline, or submit complete ms. Reviews artwork/photos as part of ms package. Send photocopies.

PHI DELTA KAPPA EDUCATIONAL FOUNDATION

P.O. Box 789, Bloomington IN 47402. (812)339-1156. Fax: (812)339-0018. E-mail: special.pubs@pdkintl.org. Website: www.pdkintl.org. **Acquisitions:** Donovan R. Walling, director of publications and research. Estab. 1906. Publishes hardcover and trade paperback originals. **Publishes 24-30 titles/year. Receives 100 queries and 50-60 mss/year. 50% of books from first-time authors; 100% from unagented writers. Pays honorarium of $500-5,000.** Publishes book 9 months after acceptance of ms. Does not accept simultaneous submissions. Responds in 3 months to proposals. Book catalog and ms guidelines free.

> O— "We publish books for educators—K-12 and higher education. Our professional books are often used in college courses but are never specifically designed as textbooks."

Nonfiction How-to, reference, scholarly, essay collections. Subjects include child guidance/parenting, education, legal issues. Query with SASE, or submit outline, 1 sample chapter(s). Reviews artwork/photos as part of ms package.

Recent Title(s) *The ABC's of Behavior Change*, by Frank J. Sparzo; *American Overseas Schools*, edited by Robert J. Simpson and Charles R. Duke.

⊘ PHILOMEL BOOKS

Imprint of Penguin Group (USA), Inc., 345 Hudson St., New York NY 10014. (212)414-3610. **Acquisitions:** Patricia Lee Gauch, editor-at-large; Michael Green, editorial director. Estab. 1980. Publishes hardcover originals. **Publishes 20-25 titles/year. Receives 2,600 submissions/year. 15% of books from first-time authors; 30% from unagented writers. Pays royalty. author's copies. Offers negotiable advance.** Publishes book 1-2 years after acceptance of ms. Accepts simultaneous submissions. Responds in 3 months to queries; 4 months to mss. Book catalog for 9×12 SAE with 4 first-class stamps; ms guidelines for #10 SASE.

> O— "We look for beautifully written, engaging manuscripts for children and young adults."

Fiction Adventure, ethnic, fantasy, historical, juvenile (5-9 years), literary, picture books, regional, short story collections, western (young adult), young adult (10-18 years). Children's picture books (ages 3-8); middle-grade fiction and illustrated chapter books (ages 7-10); young adult novels (ages 10-15). Looking for "story-driven novels with a strong cultural voice but which speak universally." No series or activity books. No "generic, mass-market oriented fiction." Query with SASE, or submit outline, 3 sample chapter(s), synopsis. *No unsolicited mss,*.

Recent Title(s) *Eagle Strike*, by Anthony Horowitz; *Triss*, by Brian Jacques; *Gisfor Goat*, by Patricia Palacco.

Tips "We prefer a very brief synopsis that states the basic premise of the story. This will help us determine whether or not the manuscript is suited to our list. If applicable, we'd be interested in knowing the author's writing experience or background knowledge. We try to be less influenced by the swings of the market than in the power, value, essence of the manuscript itself."

PHILOSOPHY DOCUMENTATION CENTER

P.O. Box 7147, Charlottesville VA 22906-7147. (434)220-3300. Fax: (434)220-3301. E-mail: order@pdcnet.org. Website: www.pdcnet.org. **Acquisitions:** Dr. George Leaman, director. Estab. 1966. **Publishes 4 titles/year. Receives 4-6 queries and 4-6 mss/year. 50% of books from first-time authors. Pays 2½-10% royalty. Offers advance.** Publishes book 1 year after acceptance of ms. Does not accept simultaneous submissions. Responds in 2 months to queries. Book catalog free.

> O— The Philosophy Documentation Center works in cooperation with publishers, database producers, software developers, journal editors, authors, librarians, and philosophers to create an electronic clearinghouse for philosophical publishing.

Nonfiction Reference, textbook, guidebooks; directories in the field of philosophy. Subjects include philosophy, software. "We want to increase our range of philosophical titles and are especially interested in electronic publishing." Query with SASE, or submit outline.

Recent Title(s) *Proceedings of the World Congress of Philosophy*; *2002-2003 Directory of American Philosophers*.

🅐 ⊘ PICADOR USA

Subsidiary of Holtzbrinck Publishers Holdings LLC, 175 Fifth Ave., New York NY 10010. Website: www.picadorusa.com. Estab. 1994. Publishes hardcover and trade paperback originals and reprints.

> ● *No unsolicited mss or queries. Agented submissions only.*
> O— Picador publishes high-quality literary fiction and nonfiction.

PICCADILLY BOOKS, LTD.

P.O. Box 25203, Colorado Springs CO 80936-5203. (719)550-9887. Website: www.piccadillybooks.com. **Acquisitions:** Submissions Department. Estab. 1985. Publishes hardcover originals and trade paperback originals and reprints. **Publishes 5-8 titles/year. Receives 120 submissions/year. 70% of books from first-time authors; 95% from unagented writers. Pays 6-10% royalty on retail price.** Publishes book 1 year after acceptance of ms. Accepts simultaneous submissions. Responds only if interested, unless accompanied by a SASE to queries.

○┐ Picadilly publishes nonfiction, diet, nutrition, and health-related books with a focus on alternative and natural medicine.

Nonfiction How-to, reference, self-help. Subjects include cooking/foods/nutrition, health/medicine, performing arts, writing, small business. "Do your research. Let us know why there is a need for your book, how it differs from other books on the market, and how you will promote the book." No phone calls. Submit outline and sample chapters.

Recent Title(s) *Heart Frauds*, by Charles T. McGee, M.D.

Tips "We publish nonfiction, general interest, self-help books currently emphasizing alternative health."

PICTON PRESS

Picton Corp., P.O. Box 250, Rockport ME 04856-0250. (207)236-6565. Fax: (207)236-6713. E-mail: sales@picton press.com. Website: www.pictonpress.com. Publishes hardcover and mass market paperback originals and reprints. **Publishes 30 titles/year. Receives 30 queries and 15 mss/year. 50% of books from first-time authors; 100% from unagented writers. Pays 0-10% royalty on wholesale price, or makes outright purchase. Offers advance.** Publishes book 6 months after acceptance of ms. Does not accept simultaneous submissions. Responds in 2 months to queries; 2 months to proposals; 3 months to mss. Book catalog free.

Imprints Cricketfield Press, New England History Press, Penobscot Press, Picton Press.

○┐ "Picton Press is one of America's oldest, largest, and most respected publishers of genealogical and historical books specializing in research tools for the 17th, 18th, and 19th centuries."

Nonfiction Reference, textbook. Subjects include Americana, history, hobbies, genealogy, vital records. Query with SASE, or submit outline.

Recent Title(s) *Nemesis At Potsdam*, by Alfred de Zayas.

THE PILGRIM PRESS

700 Prospect Ave. E., Cleveland OH 44115-1100. (216)736-3755. Fax: (216)736-2207. E-mail: stavetet@ucc.org. Website: www.thepilgrimpress.com. **Acquisitions:** Timothy G. Staveteig, publisher. Publishes hardcover and trade paperback originals. **Publishes 55 titles/year. 60% of books from first-time authors; 80% from unagented writers. Pays standard royalties. Offers advance.** Publishes book an average of 18 months after acceptance of ms. Does not accept simultaneous submissions. Responds in 3 months to queries. Book catalog and ms guidelines online.

Nonfiction Scholarly. Subjects include business/economics, gay/lesbian, government/politics, nature/environment, religion, ethics, social issues with a strong commitment to justice—addressing such topics as public policy, sexuality and gender, human rights and minority liberation—primarily in a Christian context, but not exclusively.

Tips "We are concentrating more on academic and trade submissions. Writers should send books about contemporary social issues. Our audience is liberal, open-minded, socially aware, feminist, church members and clergy, teachers, and seminary professors."

PIÑATA BOOKS

Imprint of Arte Publico Press, University of Houston, Houston TX 77204-2004. (713)743-2841. Fax: (713)743-3080. Website: www.artepublicopress.com. **Acquisitions:** Nicolas Kanellos, director. Estab. 1994. Publishes hardcover and trade paperback originals. **Publishes 10-15 titles/year. 60% of books from first-time authors. Pays 10% royalty on wholesale price. Offers $1,000-3,000 advance.** Publishes book 2 years after acceptance of ms. Accepts simultaneous submissions. Responds in 1 month to queries; 6 months to mss. Book catalog and ms guidelines available via website or with #10 SASE.

○┐ Piñata Books is dedicated to the publication of children's and young adult literature focusing on US Hispanic culture by US Hispanic authors.

Nonfiction "Piñata Books specializes in publication of children's and young adult literature that authentically portrays themes, characters and customs unique to U.S. Hispanic culture." Children's/juvenile. Subjects include ethnic. Query with SASE, or submit outline, 2 sample chapter(s), synopsis.

Fiction Adventure, juvenile, picture books, young adult. Query with SASE, or submit 2 sample chapter(s), synopsis, SASE.

Poetry Appropriate to Hispanic theme. Submit 10 sample poems.

Recent Title(s) *Walking Stars*, by Victor Villasenor; *The Bakery Lady*, by Pat Mora.

Tips "Include cover letter with submission explaining why your manuscript is unique and important, why we should publish it, who will buy it, etc."

PINEAPPLE PRESS, INC.

P.O. Box 3889, Sarasota FL 34230. (941)359-0886. Fax: (941)351-9988. Website: www.pineapplepress.com. **Acquisitions:** June Cussen, editor. Estab. 1982. Publishes hardcover and trade paperback originals. **Publishes**

25 titles/year. Receives 1,500 submissions/year. 20% of books from first-time authors; 80% from un-agented writers. Pays 6½-15% royalty on net receipts. Offers rare advance. Publishes book 18 months after acceptance of ms. Accepts simultaneous submissions. Responds in 3 months to queries. Book catalog for 9 × 12 SAE with $1.25 postage.

○─ "We are seeking quality nonfiction on diverse topics for the library and book trade markets."

Nonfiction Biography, how-to, reference. Subjects include animals, gardening, history, nature/environment, regional (Florida). "We will consider most nonfiction topics. Most, though not all, of our fiction and nonfiction deals with Florida." No pop psychology or autobiographies. Query, or submit outline/brief synopsis, sample chapters, and SASE.

Fiction Historical, literary, mainstream/contemporary, regional (Florida). No romance or science fiction. Query with SASE, or submit outline, sample chapter(s), synopsis. Submit outline/brief synopsis and sample chapters.

Recent Title(s) *Ornamental Tropical Shrubs*, by Amanda Jarrett.

Tips "Learn everything you can about book publishing and publicity, and agree to actively participate in promoting your book. A query on a novel without a brief sample seems useless."

⊘ PIPPIN PRESS

229 E. 85th St., P.O. Box 1347, Gracie Station, New York NY 10028. (212)288-4920. Fax: (732)225-1562. **Acquisitions:** Barbara Francis, publisher and editor-in-chief; Joyce Segal, senior editor. Estab. 1987. Publishes hardcover originals. **Publishes 4-6 titles/year. Receives 1,500 queries/year. 80% from unagented writers. Pays royalty. Offers advance.** Publishes book 2 years after acceptance of ms. Does not accept simultaneous submissions. Responds in 3 weeks to queries. Book catalog for 6 × 9 SASE; ms guidelines for #10 SASE.

○─ Pippin publishes general nonfiction and fiction for children ages 4-12.

Nonfiction Biography, children's/juvenile, humor, autobiography. Subjects include animals, history (American), memoirs, science, literature, general nonfiction for children ages 4-12. *No unsolicited mss.* Query with SASE only. Reviews artwork/photos as part of ms package. Send photocopies.

Fiction Historical, humor, mystery, picture books. "We're especially looking for small chapter books for 7- to 11-year olds, especially by people of many cultures." Also interested in humorous fiction for ages 7-11. "At this time, we are especially interested in historical novels, 'autobiographical' novels, historical, and literary biographies, and humor." Query with SASE only.

Recent Title(s) *A Visit from the Leopard: Memories of a Ugandan Childhood*, by Catherine Mudiko-Piwang and Edward Frascino; *Abigail's Drum*, by John A. Minahan, illustrated by Robert Quackenbush (historical fiction).

Tips "Read as many of the best children's books published in the last 5 years as you can. We are looking for multi-ethnic fiction and nonfiction for ages 7-10, as well as general fiction for this age group. I would pay particular attention to children's books favorably reviewed in *School Library Journal*, *The Booklist*, *The New York Times Book Review*, and *Publishers Weekly*."

PLANNERS PRESS

Imprint of the American Planning Association, 122 S. Michigan Ave., Chicago IL 60603. Fax: (312)431-9985. E-mail: slewis@planning.org. Website: www.planning.org. **Acquisitions:** Sylvia Lewis, director of publications. Estab. 1978. Publishes hardcover and trade paperback originals. **Publishes 4-6 titles/year. Receives 20 queries and 6-8 mss/year. 50% of books from first-time authors; 100% from unagented writers. Pays 7½-12% royalty on retail price. Offers advance.** Publishes book 1 year after acceptance of ms. Does not accept simultaneous submissions. Responds in 1 month to queries; 2 months to proposals; 2 months to mss. Book catalog and ms guidelines free.

○─ "Our books have a narrow audience of city planners and often focus on the tools of city planning."

Nonfiction Technical (public policy and city planning). Subjects include government/politics. Submit 2 sample chapters and table of contents. Reviews artwork/photos as part of ms package. Send photocopies.

Recent Title(s) *Redesigning Cities—Principles, Practice, Implementation*; *Making Places Special—Stories of Real Places Made Better by Planning*; *Above and Beyond—Visualizing Change in Small Towns and Rural Areas.*

PLAYERS PRESS, INC.

P.O. Box 1132, Studio City CA 91614-0132. (818)789-4980. **Acquisitions:** Robert W. Gordon, vice president, editorial. Estab. 1965. Publishes hardcover originals and trade paperback originals and reprints. **Publishes 35-70 titles/year. Receives 200-1,000 submissions/year. 15% of books from first-time authors; 80% from unagented writers. Pays royalty on wholesale price. Offers advance.** Publishes book 3 months-2 years after acceptance of ms. Does not accept simultaneous submissions. Book catalog for 9 × 12 SAE with 5 first-class stamps; ms guidelines for #10 SASE.

○─ Players Press publishes support books for the entertainment industries: theater, film, television, dance and technical. Currently emphasizing plays for all ages, theatre crafts, monologues and short scenes for ages 5-9, 11-15, and musicals.

Nonfiction Children's/juvenile, theatrical drama/entertainment industry. Subjects include film/cinema/stage, performing arts, costume, theater crafts, film crafts, dance. Needs quality plays and musicals, adult or juvenile. Query with SASE. Reviews music as part of ms package.

Fiction Plays: Subject matter includes adventure, confession, ethnic, experimental, fantasy, historical, horror, humor, mainstream, mystery, religious romance, science fiction, suspense, western. Submit complete ms for theatrical plays only. Plays must be previously produced. "No novels or story books are accepted."

Recent Title(s) *Women's Wear of the 1930's*, by Hopper/Countryman; *Rhyme Tyme*, by William-Alan Landes; *Borrowed Plumage*, by David Crawford.

Tips "Plays, entertainment industry texts, theater, film and TV books have the only chances of selling to our firm."

⊘ PLAYHOUSE PUBLISHING

1566 Akron-Peninsula Rd., Akron OH 44313. (330)926-1313. Fax: (330)926-1315. E-mail: webmaster@playhous epublishing.com. Website: www.playhousepublishing.com. **Acquisitions:** Children's Acquisitions Editor. Publishes hardcover originals and novelty board books. **Publishes 10-15 titles/year; imprint publishes 3-5 titles/ year. Work-for-hire. Makes outright purchase.** Publishes book 18-24 months after acceptance of ms. Accepts simultaneous submissions. Responds in 2 months to proposals. Book catalog and ms guidelines online.

Imprints Picture Me Books (board books with photos); Nibble Me Books (board books with edibles).

- Playhouse Publishing will no longer accept unsolicited mss sent for review in the mail. Any items sent in the mail will be destroyed. The company encourages writers to submit query letters/book proposals electronically to webmaster@playhousepublishing.com. All copy must be contained in the body of an e-mail. Attachments will not be opened.

- O→ "We publish novelty board books and juvenile fiction appropriate for children from birth to first grade. All Picture Me Books titles incorporate the 'picture me' photo concept. All Nibble Me Books titles incorporate an edible that completes the illustrations."

Fiction Juvenile.

Recent Title(s) *My Grandma & Me*, by Merry North; *Pretend & Play Princess*, by Cathy Hapka; *My Little Red Lunchbox*, by Carol Pugliano-Martin.

PLEASANT COMPANY PUBLICATIONS

8400 Fairway Place, Middleton WI 53562. Fax: (608)828-4768. Website: www.americangirl.com. **Acquisitions:** Submissions Editor. Estab. 1986. Publishes hardcover and trade paperback originals. **Publishes 50-60 titles/ year. Receives 500 queries and 800 mss/year. 90% from unagented writers. Offers varying advance.** Publishes book 3-12 months after acceptance of ms. Accepts simultaneous submissions. Responds in 3 months to queries; 4 months to mss. Book catalog for #10 SASE; ms guidelines for for SASE or on the website.

Imprints The American Girls Collection, American Girl Library, AG Fiction, History Mysteries, Girls of Many Lands.

- O→ Pleasant Company publishes fiction and nonfiction for girls 7-12.

Nonfiction Children's/juvenile (for girls 7-12), how-to. Subjects include Americana, history, contemporary lifestyle, activities. Query with SASE.

Fiction Contemporary. "Contemporary fiction submissions should capture the spirit of contemporary American girls and also illuminate the ways in which their lives are personally touched by issues and concerns affecting America today. We are seeking strong, well-written contemporary, told from the perspective of a middle-school-age girl. No romance, picture books, poetry." Stories must feature an American girl, aged 10-13; reading level 4th-6th grade. Query with SASE, or submit complete ms (preferred).

Recent Title(s) *Smoke Screen*, by Amy Goldman Koss; *Nowhere, Now Here*, by Ann Howard Creel.

PLEXUS PUBLISHING, INC.

143 Old Marlton Pike, Medford NJ 08055-8750. (609)654-6500. Fax: (609)654-4309. E-mail: jbryans@infotoday. com. **Acquisitions:** John B. Bryans, editor-in-chief. Estab. 1977. Publishes hardcover and paperback originals. **Publishes 4-5 titles/year. Receives 30-60 submissions/year. 70% of books from first-time authors; 90% from unagented writers. Pays 10-15% royalty on net receipts. Offers $500-1,000 advance.** Accepts simultaneous submissions. Responds in 3 months to proposals. Book catalog and ms guidelines for 10×13 SAE with 4 first-class stamps.

- O→ Plexus publishes mainly regional-interest (southern New Jersey) fiction and nonfiction including mysteries, field guides, history. Also health/medicine, biology, botany, ecology, botony, astronomy.

Nonfiction How-to, illustrated book, reference, textbook, natural, historical references, and scholarly. Subjects include agriculture/horticulture, education, gardening, health/medicine, history (southern New Jersey), nature/environment, recreation, regional (southern New Jersey), science, botany, medicine, biology, ecology, astronomy. "We will consider any book on a nature/biology subject, particularly those of a reference (permanent) nature that would be of lasting value to high school and college audiences, and/or the general reading public (ages 14 and up). Authors should have authentic qualifications in their subject area, but qualifications may be by experience as well as academic training.'' Also interested in mss of about 20-40 pages in length for feature articles in *Biology Digest* (guidelines available for SASE). No gardening, philosophy, or psychology; generally not interested in travel but will consider travel that gives sound ecological information. Query with SASE. Reviews artwork/photos as part of ms package. Send photocopies.

Fiction Mysteries and literary novels with a strong regional (southern New Jersey) angle. Query with SASE.

Recent Title(s) *Boardwalk Empire: The Birth, High Times, and Corruption of Atlantic City*, by Nelson Johnson; *Wildflowers of the Pine Barrens of New Jersey*, by Howard P. Boyd.

N A PLUME

Division of Penguin Group (USA), Inc., 375 Hudson St., New York NY 10014. (212)366-2000. Website: www.penguinputnam.com. Estab. 1948. Publishes paperback originals and reprints. **Pays in royalties and author's copies. Offers advance.** Publishes book 12-18 months after acceptance of ms. Accepts simultaneous submissions. Responds in 3 months to queries. Book catalog for SASE.

Nonfiction Serious and historical nonfiction, including pop culture, current events, politics. *Agented submissions only.* Query with SASE.

Fiction ''All kinds of commercial and litearary fiction, including mainstream, historical, New Age, western, erotica, gay. Full-length novels and collections.'' *Agented submissions only.* Query with SASE. ''State type of book and past publishing projects.''

POLYCHROME PUBLISHING CORP.

4509 N. Francisco, Chicago IL 60625. (773)478-4455. Fax: (773)478-0786. E-mail: polypub@earthlink.net. Website: www.polychromebooks.com. Estab. 1990. Publishes hardcover originals and reprints. **Publishes 4 titles/year. Receives 3,000 queries and 7,500-8,000 mss/year. 50% of books from first-time authors; 100% from unagented writers. Pays royalty. Offers advance.** Publishes book 2 years after acceptance of ms. Accepts simultaneous submissions. Responds in 8 months to mss. Book catalog for #10 SASE; ms guidelines for #10 SASE or on the website.

Nonfiction Children's/juvenile. Subjects include ethnic. Subjects emphasize ethnic, particularly multicultural/Asian-American. Submit outline, 3 sample chapter(s). Reviews artwork/photos as part of ms package. Send photocopies.

Fiction Ethnic, juvenile, multicultural (particularly Asian-American), picture books, young adult. ''We do not publish fables, folktales, fairy tales, or anthropomorphic animal stories.'' Submit synopsis and 3 sample chapters, for picture books submit whole ms.

Recent Title(s) *Striking It Rich: Treasures from Gold Mountain*; *Char Siu Bao Boy*.

POPULAR WOODWORKING BOOKS

F+W Publications, 4700 Galbraith Rd., Cincinnati OH 45236. (513)531-2690. **Acquisitions:** Jim Stack, acquisitions editor. Publishes trade paperback originals and reprints. **Publishes 10-12 titles/year. Receives 30 queries and 10 mss/year. 50% of books from first-time authors; 95% from unagented writers. Pays 10-20% royalty on net receipts. Offers $5,000 advance.** Publishes book 1 year after acceptance of ms. Accepts simultaneous submissions. Responds in 1 month to queries. Book catalog for 9×12 SAE with 6 first-class stamps; ms guidelines for 9×12 SAE with 6 first-class stamps.

   0→ Popular Woodworking publishes how-to woodworking books that use photos with captions to show and tell the reader how to build projects. Technical illustrations and materials lists supply all the rest of the information needed. Currently emphasizing woodworking jigs and fixtures, furniture and cabinet projects, smaller finely crafted boxes, all styles of furniture. De-emphasizing woodturning, woodcarving, scroll saw projects.

Nonfiction ''We publish heavily illustrated how-to woodworking books that show, rather than tell, our readers how to accomplish their woodworking goals.'' How-to, illustrated book. Subjects include hobbies, woodworking/wood crafts. Query with SASE, or submit proposal package including outline, transparencies. Reviews artwork/photos as part of ms package.

Recent Title(s) *Jigs & Fixtures Bible*, by R.J. DeCristoforo; *Build Your Own Home Office Furniture*, by Danny Proulx; *Jim Tolpin's Table Saw Magic, 2nd Ed.*, by Jim Toplin.

Tips ''Our books are for beginning to advanced woodworking enthusiasts.''

POSSIBILITY PRESS

One Oakglade Circle, Hummelstown PA 17036-9525. (717)566-0468. Fax: (717)566-6423. E-mail: possibilitypress@aol.com. Website: www.possibilitypress.com. **Acquisitions:** Mike Markowski, publisher; Marjie Markowski, editor-in-chief. Estab. 1981. Publishes trade paperback originals. **Publishes 5-10 titles/year. Receives 1,000** submissions/year. 90% of books from first-time authors; 95% from unagented writers. Royalties vary. Responds in 2 months to queries. Ms guidelines online.

Imprints Aeronautical Publishers, Possibility Press.

O→ "Our mission is to help the people of the world grow and become the best they can be, through the written and spoken word."

Nonfiction How-to, self-help, inspirational. Subjects include business/economics, psychology (pop psychology), success/motivation, inspiration, entrepreneurship, sales marketing, network, MLM and home-based business topics, and human interest success stories. Prefers submissions to be mailed. Include SASE.

Fiction Parables that teach lessons about life and success.

Recent Title(s) *The Power of Having Desire*, by Bruce Garrabrandt; *Leading Leaders to Leadership*, by John Fuhrman; *The Power of Meeting New People*, by Debra Fine.

Tips "Our focus is on creating and publishing short- to medium-length bestsellers written by authors who speak and consult. We're looking for kind and compassionate authors who are passionate about making a difference in the world, and on a mission to do so."

PRB PRODUCTIONS

963 Peralta Ave., Albany CA 94706-2144. (510)526-0722. Fax: (510)527-4763. E-mail: prbprdns@aol.com. Website: www.prbpro.com; www.prbmusic.com. **Acquisitions:** Peter R. Ballinger, publisher (early and contemporary music for instruments and voices). **Publishes 10-15 titles/year. Pays 10% royalty on retail price.** Accepts simultaneous submissions. Responds in 1 month to queries; 3 months to mss. Book catalog free on request or on website.

Nonfiction Textbook, sheet music. Subjects include music/dance. Query with SASE, or submit complete ms.

Recent Title(s) *Two String Quartets*, by Nathaniel Stookey (contemporary); *Complete 6-Part Viol Consorts of Charles Coleman*; *G.P. Telemann, Jesu, meine Freude, Cantata for SATB Soloists/Chorus, Chamber Orchestra*, edited by Ann Kersting-Meulman.

Tips Audience is music schools, universities, libraries, professional music educators, and amateur/professional musicians.

Ⓝ PREP PUBLISHING

Prep, Inc., 1110½ Hay St., Fayetteville NC 28305. E-mail: preppub@aol.com. Website: www.prep-pub.com. **Acquisitions:** Anne McKinney, editor (nonfiction, careers). Estab. 1995. Publishes hardcover and trade paperback originals. **Publishes 10-12 titles/year; imprint publishes 2 each titles/year. Receives 1,000 queries and 40 mss/year. 90% of books from first-time authors; 70% from unagented writers. Pays 6-10% royalty on retail price.** Publishes book 3 months after acceptance of ms. Accepts simultaneous submissions. Response time varies to queries; 1 month to mss. Book catalog and ms guidelines online.

Imprints Judeo-Christian Ethics, Real-Résumés, Government Jobs, Business Success.

Nonfiction Biography, how-to, self-help. Subjects include business/economics, computers/electronic, creative nonfiction, education, health/medicine, money/finance, religion, spirituality. Query with SASE.

Fiction Literary, mainstream/contemporary, military/war, mystery, spiritual. Query with SASE.

PRICE STERN SLOAN, INC.

Penguin Group (USA), 345 Hudson, New York NY 10014. (212)414-3590. Fax: (212)414-3396. **Acquisitions:** Debra Dorfman, publisher. Estab. 1963. **Publishes 80 titles/year. Makes outright purchase. Offers advance.** Does not accept simultaneous submissions. Responds in 3 months to queries. Book catalog for 9×12 SAE with 5 first-class stamps; ms guidelines for #10 SASE. Address to Book Catalog or Manuscript Guidelines.

Imprints Mad Libs, Mad Libs Jr., Mr. Men & Little Miss, Serendipity, Wee Sing.

O→ Price Stern Sloan publishes quirky mass market novelty series for children as well as licensed tie-in books.

Nonfiction Children's/juvenile, humor. "Most of our titles are unique in concept as well as execution." Do not send *original* artwork or ms. *No unsolicited mss.*

Fiction "Quirky, funny picture books, novelty books and quirky full color series."

Recent Title(s) *Elf*; *Fear Factor Mad Libs*; *Super Silly Mad Libs Jr.*

Tips "Price Stern Sloan has a unique, humorous, off-the-wall feel."

Ⓝ PRINCETON ARCHITECTURAL PRESS

37 E. 7th St., New York NY 10003. (212)995-9620. Fax: (212)995-9454. E-mail: editorial@papress.com. Submissions E-mail: clare@papress.com. Website: www.papress.com. **Acquisitions:** Clare Jacobson, editorial director; Mark Lamstrer, senior editor. Publishes hardcover and trade paperback originals. **Publishes 50 titles/year. Receives 300 queries and 150 mss/year. 65% of books from first-time authors; 95% from unagented writers. Pays royalty on wholesale price.** Publishes book 1 year after acceptance of ms. Accepts simultaneous submis-

sions. Responds in 2 months to queries; 2 months to proposals; 2 months to mss. Book catalog and ms guidelines online.

Nonfiction Coffee table book, gift book, how-to, illustrated book, multimedia, reference, scholarly, technical, textbook. Subjects include art/architecture, general nonfiction. Submit proposal package including outline, 1 sample chapter(s), table of contents, sample of art, and survey of competitive titles. Reviews artwork/photos as part of ms package. not originals.

Recent Title(s) *45 RPM: A Visual History of the Seven-Inch Record*, edited by Spencer Drate (pictorial collection of record covers); *Inside Design Now: The National Design Triennial*, edited by Donald Albrecht, et. al. (museum catalog of new design work); *Rural Studio*, by Andrea Oppenheimer Dean and Timothy Hursley (monograph on design/build studio).

Tips "Princeton Architecture Press publishes fine books on architecture, design, photography, landscape, and visual culture. Our books are acclaimed for their strong and unique editorial vision, unrivaled design sensibility, and high production values at affordable prices."

PRINCETON BOOK CO.

614 Route 130, Hightstown NJ 08520. (609)426-0602. Fax: (609)426-1344. E-mail: pbc@dancehorizons.com. Website: www.dancehorizons.com. **Acquisitions:** Charles Woodford, president (dance and adult nonfiction). Publishes hardcover and trade paperback originals and reprints. **Publishes 5-6 titles/year. Receives 50 queries and 100 mss/year. 80% of books from first-time authors; 100% from unagented writers. Pays negotiable royalty on retail price. Offers negotiable advance.** Publishes book 9-12 months after acceptance of ms. Accepts simultaneous submissions. Responds in 1 week to queries; 1 week to proposals. Book catalog free on request or on website; ms guidelines online.

Imprints Dance Horizons, Elysian Editions.

Nonfiction "We publish all sorts of dance-related books including ones on fitness and health." Biography, children's/juvenile, gift book, how-to, illustrated book, reference. Subjects include music/dance. Submit proposal package including outline, 3 sample chapter(s). Reviews artwork/photos as part of ms package. Send photocopies.

Recent Title(s) *Playful Family Yoga*, by Teressa Asencia; *Relax Your Neck, Liberate Your Shoulders*, by Eric Franklin; *Good-bye to Bad Backs*, by Judith Scott.

PROFESSIONAL PUBLICATIONS, INC.

1250 Fifth Ave., Belmont CA 94002-3863. (650)593-9119. Fax: (650)592-4519. E-mail: acquisitions@ppi2pass.com. Website: www.ppi2pass.com. **Acquisitions:** George Seki, acquisitions editor. Estab. 1975. Publishes hardcover, electronic and paperback originals, video and audio cassettes, CD-ROMs. **Publishes 10 titles/year. Receives 10-20 submissions/year.** Publishes book 18 months after acceptance of ms. Accepts simultaneous submissions. Responds in 1 month to queries. Book catalog and ms guidelines free.

O— PPI publishes for professionals preparing to take examinations for national licensing and certification. Professional Publications wants only professionals practicing in the field to submit material. Currently emphasizing engineering exam review.

Nonfiction Multimedia, reference, technical, textbook. Subjects include science, architecture, landscape architecture, engineering mathematics, engineering, land surveying, interior design, and other professional licensure and development subjects. Especially needs "review and reference books for all professional licensing examinations." Please submit ms and proposal outlining market potential, etc. Proposal template available upon request. Reviews artwork/photos as part of ms package.

Recent Title(s) *Six-Minute Solutions for the Civil PE Exam*, various authors.

Tips "We specialize in books for working professionals: engineers, architects, land surveyors, interior designers, etc. The more technically complex the manuscript, the happier we are. We love equations, tables of data, complex illustrations, mathematics, etc. Facts, figures, and estimates about the market—and marketing ideas from the author—will help sell us on the work."

PROMETHEUS BOOKS

59 John Glenn Dr., Amherst NY 14228-2197. (716)691-0133 ext. 207. Fax: (716)564-2711. E-mail: editorial@prometheusmail.com. Website: www.prometheusbooks.com. **Acquisitions:** Steven L. Mitchell, editor-in-chief (Prometheus/Humanity Books, philosophy, social science, social issues in journalism, political science, history, consumer health, psychology, general nonfiction); Dr. Ann O'Hear, acquisitions editor (Humanity Books, scholarly and professional works in philosophy, social science); Linda Greenspan Regan, executive editor (Prometheus, popular science, popular health, popular psychology, criminology); Jeremy Sauer, editorial assistant (permissions). Estab. 1969. Publishes hardcover originals, trade paperback originals and reprints. **Publishes 85-100 titles/year. Receives 2,500 submissions/year. 25% of books from first-time authors; 50% from unagented writers. Pays 10-15% royalty on wholesale price. Offers $0-3,000 advance.** Publishes book 18 months after

acceptance of ms. Accepts simultaneous submissions. Responds in 1 month to queries; 2 months to proposals; 4 months to mss. Book catalog free or online; ms guidelines for #10 SASE.

Imprints Humanity Books (scholarly and professional monographs in philosophy, social science, sociology, archaeology, black stuides, womens studies, Marxist studies, etc.).

O—¬ "Prometheus Books is a leading independent publisher in philosophy, popular science, and critical thinking. We publish authoritative and thoughtful books by distinguished authors in many categories. We are a niche, or specialized, publisher that features critiques of the paranormal and pseudoscience, critiques of religious extremism and right wing fundamentalism and creationism; Biblical and Koranic criticism: human sexuality, etc. Currently emphasizing popular science, health, psychology, social science."

Nonfiction Biography, children's/juvenile, reference, self-help, general, historical, popular. Subjects include education, government/politics, health/medicine, history, language/literature, New Age (critiquing of), philosophy, psychology, religion (not religious, but critiquing), contemporary issues, current events, Islamic studies, law, popular science, critiques of the paranormal and UFO sightings, sexuality. "Ask for a catalog, go to the library or our website, look at our books and others like them to get an idea of what our focus is." Submit proposal package including outline, synopsis, and a well-developed query letter with SASE. Reviews artwork/photos as part of ms package. Send photocopies.

Recent Title(s) *Cracking Cases*, by Henry Lee; *Mortal Evidence*, by Cyril Wecht.

Tips "Audience is highly literate with multiple degrees; an audience that is intellectually mature and knows what it wants. They are aware, and we try to provide them with new information on topics of interest to them in mainstream and related areas."

PRUETT PUBLISHING

7464 Arapahoe Rd., Suite A-9, Boulder CO 80303. (303)449-4919. Fax: (303)443-9019. E-mail: pruettbks@aol.com. **Acquisitions:** Jim Pruett, publisher. Estab. 1959. Publishes hardcover and trade paperback originals and reprints. **Publishes 10-15 titles/year. 60% of books from first-time authors; 95% from unagented writers. Pays 10-12% royalty on net receipts. Offers advance.** Publishes book 18 months after acceptance of ms. Accepts simultaneous submissions. Responds in 2 months to queries. Book catalog and ms guidelines free.

O—¬ "Pruett Publishing strives to convey to our customers and readers a respect of the American West, in particular the spirit, traditions, and attitude of the region. We publish books in the following subject areas: outdoor recreation, regional history, environment and nature, travel and culture. We especially need books on outdoor recreation."

Nonfiction "We are looking for nonfiction manuscripts and guides that focus on the Rocky Mountain West." Guidebooks. Subjects include Americana (Western), anthropology/archeology (Native American), cooking/foods/nutrition (Native American, Mexican, Spanish), ethnic, history (Western), nature/environment, recreation (outdoor), regional, sports (cycling, hiking, fly fishing), travel. Submit proposal package. Reviews artwork/photos as part of ms package.

Recent Title(s) *Flyfishing the Texas Coast: Back Country Flats to Bluewater*, by Chuck Scales and Phil Shook, photography by David J. Sams; *Trout Country: Reflections on Rivers, Flyfishing & Related Addictions*, by Bob Saile; *Rocky Mountain Christmas*, by John H. Monnett.

Tips "There has been a movement away from large publisher's mass market books toward small publisher's regional-interest books, and in turn distributors and retail outlets are more interested in small publishers. Authors don't need to have a big name to have a good publisher. Look for similar books that you feel are well produced—consider design, editing, overall quality, and contact those publishers. Get to know several publishers, and find the one that feels right—trust your instincts."

N̄ ⌀ PUFFIN BOOKS

Imprint of Penguin Putnam, Inc., 375 Hudson St., New York NY 10014. (212)366-2000. Website: www.penguinputnam.com. President/Publisher: Tracy Tang. **Acquisitions:** Sharyn November, senior editor; Kristin Gilson, executive editor. Publishes trade paperback originals and reprints. **Publishes 175-200 titles/year. Receives 300 queries and 300 mss/year. 1% of books from first-time authors; 5% from unagented writers. Royalty varies. Offers varies advance.** Publishes book 1 year after acceptance of ms. Does not accept simultaneous submissions. Responds in 3 months to mss. Book catalog for 9×12 SAE with 7 first-class stamps.

O—¬ Puffin Books publishes high-end trade paperbacks and paperback reprints for preschool children, beginning and middle readers, and young adults.

Nonfiction Biography, children's/juvenile, illustrated book, Young children's concept books (counting, shapes, colors). Subjects include education (for teaching concepts and colors, not academic), history, women's issues/studies. Query with SASE. *No unsolicited mss.*

Fiction Picture books, young adult, middle grade, easy-to-read grades 1-3. "We publish mostly paperback reprints. We do very few original titles. We do not publish original picture books." *No unsolicited mss.*

Tips "Our audience ranges from little children 'first books' to young adult (ages 14-16). An original idea has the best luck." .

N PULPIT PUBLISHING

1370 University Ave., #507, Berkeley CA 94702. E-mail: editor@pulplit.com. Submissions E-mail: submissions@pulplit.com. Website: www.pulplit.com. **Acquisitions:** John O'Brien, editor-in-chief (fiction, nonfiction, and criticism); Ben Henry, poetry editor. Estab. 2002. Publishes hardcover, trade paperback, and electronic originals. **Publishes 4 titles/year. 100% of books from first-time authors; 100% from unagented writers. Pays 5-10% royalty on wholesale price.** Publishes book 3 months after acceptance of ms. Accepts simultaneous submissions. Responds in 1 month to queries; 1 month to proposals; 3 months to mss. Book catalog and ms guidelines online.

Nonfiction Booklets, humor, scholarly. Subjects include humanities. Submit complete ms. Reviews artwork/photos as part of ms package.

Fiction Adventure, comic books, erotica, experimental, fantasy, gothic, hi-lo, historical, humor, juvenile, literary, mainstream/contemporary, plays, poetry, science fiction, short story collections, western, young adult. Want edgy, smart, hip, and sassy. Submit complete ms.

Poetry "To give you some idea, we enjoy Simic, Russell Edson, Nash, Kerouac, and Ferlinghetti to name but a few. We look for humor, topic, but always resonance and never for meter. Flow is more important than anything." Submit complete ms.

Recent Title(s) *Frustrated Young Men*, by John O'Brien (short story collection).

Tips "Audience is computer-literate, college students. We're tiny. We sell primarily through the website. We're risky but full of heart."

A Ø G.P. PUTNAM'S SONS HARDCOVER

Imprint of Penguin Group (USA), Inc., 375 Hudson, New York NY 10014. (212)366-2000. Fax: (212)366-2664. Website: www.penguinputnam.com. Publisher: Neil Nyren. Publishes hardcover originals. **Pays variable royalties on retail price. Offers varies advance.** Accepts simultaneous submissions. Responds in 6 months to queries. Request book catalog through mail order department.

Nonfiction Biography, cookbook, self-help. Subjects include animals, business/economics, child guidance/parenting, contemporary culture, cooking/foods/nutrition, health/medicine, military/war, nature/environment, religion, science, sports, travel, women's issues/studies, celebrity-related topics. *Agented submissions only. No unsolicited mss.*

Fiction Adventure, literary, mainstream/contemporary, mystery, suspense, women's. Prefers agented submissions. *Agented submissions only. No unsolicited mss.*

Recent Title(s) *Blow Fly*, by Patricia Cornwell (fiction); *The Teeth of the Tiger*, by Tom Clancy (fiction).

QUEST BOOKS

Imprint of Theosophical Publishing House, 306 W. Geneva Rd., Wheaton IL 60187. (630)665-0130. Fax: (630)665-8791. E-mail: questpermissions@theosmail.net. Website: www.questbooks.net. **Acquisitions:** Brenda Rosen. Publishes hardcover originals and trade paperback originals and reprints. **Publishes 10-12 titles/year. Receives 500 submissions/year. 75% of books from first-time authors; 90% from unagented writers. Pays royalty. Offers varying advance.** Publishes book 20 months after acceptance of ms. Accepts simultaneous submissions. Responds in 2 months to queries. Book catalog free; ms guidelines online.

> **O—π** "Quest Books is the imprint of the Theosophical Publishing House, the publishing arm of the Theosophical Society of America. Since 1965, Quest books has sold millions of books by leading cultural thinkers on such increasingly popular subjects as transpersonal psychology, comparative religion, deep ecology, spiritual growth, the development of creativity, and alternative health practices."

Nonfiction Subjects include anthropology/archeology, art/architecture, health/medicine, music/dance, nature/environment, philosophy (holistic), psychology (transpersonal), religion (Eastern and Western), science, spirituality (Native American, etc.), travel, women's issues/studies, biography, self-help, theosophy, comparative religion, men's and women's spirituality, holistic implications in science, health and healing, yoga, meditation, astrology. "Our speciality is high-quality spiritual nonfiction with a self-help aspect. Great writing is a must. We seldom publish 'personal spiritual awakening' stories. No submissions accepted that do not fit the needs outlined above." Accepts nonfiction translations. No fiction, poetry, children's books, or any literature based on channeling or personal psychic impressions. Query with SASE, or submit proposal package including sample chapter(s), author bio, TOC. Reviews artwork/photos as part of ms package. Send photocopies.

Recent Title(s) *The Templars and the Grail*; *The Genesis Meditations*; *The Zen of Listening*.

Tips "Our audience includes cultural creatives, seekers in all religions, students of religion, general public, professors, and health professionals. Read a few recent Quest titles. Know our books and our company goals.

Explain how your book or proposal relates to other Quest titles. Quest gives preference to writers with established reputations/successful publications."

QUILL DRIVER BOOKS/WORD DANCER PRESS

1831 Industrial Way #101, Sanger CA 93657. (559)876-2170. Fax: (559)876-2180. Website: www.quilldriverboo ks.com. **Acquisitions:** Stephen Blake Mettee, publisher. Publishes hardcover and trade paperback originals and reprints. **Publishes 10-12 (Quill Driver Books: 6-8/year, Word Dancer Press: 4/year) titles/year. 50% of books from first-time authors; 95% from unagented writers. Pays 4-10% royalty on retail price. Offers $500-5,000 advance.** Publishes book 9 months after acceptance of ms. Accepts simultaneous submissions. Responds in 1 month to queries; 1 month to proposals; 3 months to mss. Book catalog and ms guidelines for #10 SASE.

○┐ "We publish a modest number of books per year, each of which, we hope, makes a worthwhile contribution to the human community, and we have a little fun along the way. We are strongly emphasizing our 2 new book series: The Best Half of Life series—on subjects which will serve to enhance the lifestyles, life skills, and pleasures of living for those over 50. The Fast Track Course series—short how-to or explanatory books on any subject."

Nonfiction Biography, how-to, reference, general. Subjects include general nonfiction, regional (California), writing, aging. Query with SASE, or submit proposal package. Reviews artwork/photos as part of ms package. Send photocopies.

Recent Title(s) *Pitching Hollywood: How to Sell Your TV and Movie Ideas*, by Jonathan Koch and Robert Kosberg with Tanya Meurer Norman; *If You Want It Done Right, You Don't Have to Do It Yourself*, by Donna M. Genett, Ph.D; *The Fast Track Course on How to Write a Nonfiction Book Proposal*, by Stephen Blake Mettee.

QUITE SPECIFIC MEDIA GROUP, LTD.

7 Old Fulton St., Brooklyn Heights NY 11201. (212)725-5377. Fax: (212)725-8506. E-mail: info@quitespecificme dia.com. Website: www.quitespecificmedia.com. **Acquisitions:** Ralph Pine, editor-in-chief. Editorial Office: 7373 Pyramid Place, Hollywood CA 90046. Estab. 1967. Publishes hardcover originals, trade paperback originals and reprints. **Publishes 12 titles/year. Receives 300 queries and 100 mss/year. 75% of books from first-time authors; 85% from unagented writers. Pays royalty on wholesale price. Offers varies advance.** Publishes book 18 months after acceptance of ms. Accepts simultaneous submissions. Responds to queries. Book catalog online; ms guidelines free.

Imprints Costume & Fashion Press, Drama Publishers, By Design Press, Entertainment Pro, Jade Rabbit.

○┐ Quite Specific Media Group is an umbrella company of 5 imprints specializing in costume and fashion, theater and design.

Nonfiction For and about performing arts theory and practice: acting, directing; voice, speech, movement; makeup, masks, wits; costumes, sets, lighting, sound; design and execution; technical theater, stagecraft, equipment; stage management; producing; arts management, all varieties; business and legal aspects; film, radio, television, cable, video; theory, criticism, reference; theater and performance history; costume and fashion. How-to, multimedia, reference, textbook, guides; manuals; directories. Subjects include fashion/beauty, film/ cinema/stage, history, translation. Accepts nonfiction and technical works in translations also. Query with SASE, or submit 1-3 sample chapter(s). No complete ms. Reviews artwork/photos as part of ms package.

⊞ RAILROADING

a Watermark of Bristol Fashion Publications, Inc., P.O. Box 4676, Harrisburg PA 17111-4676. (800)478-7147. E-mail: jpk@bfpbooks.com. Website: www.bfpbooks.com. **Acquisitions:** John Kaufman, publisher. Publishes trade paperback originals and limited hardback. **Publishes 15-25 titles/year. Receives 100 queries and 50 mss/year. 50% of books from first-time authors; 99% from unagented writers. Pays 7-11% royalty on retail price.** Publishes book 3 months after acceptance of ms. Responds in 1 month to queries. Ms guidelines online.

● Railroading (BFP, Inc.) publishes books on model railroading and railroad history.

Nonfiction How-to, reference. Subjects include general nonfiction (relating to model railroading and railroad history). "We are interested in any title related to these fields. Query with a list of ideas. Include phone number. This is a fast-changing market. Our title plans rarely extend past 6 months, although we know the type and quantity of books we will publish over the next 2 years. We prefer good knowledge with simple-to-understand writing style containing a well-rounded vocabulary." Query with SASE. Reviews artwork/photos as part of ms package. Send photocopies or JPEG files on CD.

Recent Title(s) *Track Plans for Beginners in N-Scale; Track Plans for Beginners in HO-Scale; Track Plans for Beginners in O-Scale.*

Tips "All of our staff and editors are model railroaders. As such, we publish what we would want to read relating to the subject. Our audience in general are active model railroaders at the beginner and intermediate level, and history buffs wanting to learn more about the history of railroads in this country. Many are people new to the hobby, attempting to learn all they can before starting their first layout. Keep it easy and simple to follow. Use railroad terms and jargon sparingly. Do not use complicated technical jargon, terms, or formulas without detailed explanation of the same. Use experienced craftsmen as a resource for knowledge. Please read our guidelines before submitting your manuscript.''

N A Ø RANDOM HOUSE CHILDREN'S BOOKS

Imprint of Random House, Inc., 1745 Broadway, New York NY 10019. (212)782-9000. Website: www.randomho use.com/kids. Estab. 1925.

Imprints BooksReportsNow.com, GoldenBooks.com, Junie B. Jones, Kids@Random; **Knopf/Delacorte/ Dell Young Readers Group:** Bantam, Crown, David Fickling Books, Delacorte Press, Dell Dragonfly, Dell Laurel-Leaf, Dell Yearling, Doubleday, Alfred A. Knopf, Wendy Lamb Books; **Random House Young Readers Group:** Akiko, Arthur, Barbie, Beginner Books, The Berenstain Bears, Bob the Builder, Disney, Dragon Tales, First Time Books, Golden Books, Landmark Books, Little Golden Books, Lucas Books, Mercer Mayer, Nickelodeon, Nick, Jr., pat the bunny, Picturebacks, Precious Moments, Richard Scarry, Sesame Street Books, Step Into Reading, Stepping Stones, Star Wars, Thomas the Tank Engine and Friends; Seusville, Teachers@Random, Teens@Random.

- See website for more details.

N A Ø RANDOM HOUSE, INC.

Division of Bertelsmann Book Group, 1745 Broadway, New York NY 10019. (212)782-9000. Website: www.rand omhouse.com. Estab. 1925. **Pays royalty. Offers advance.**

Imprints Ballantine Publishing Group: Ballantine Books, Ballantine Reader¥s Circle, Del Rey, Del Rey/Lucas Books, Fawcett, Ivy, One World, Wellspring; **Bantam Dell Publishing Group:** Bantam Hardcover, Bantam Mass Market, Bantam Trade Paperback, Crimeline, Delacorte Press, Dell, Delta, The Dial Press, Domain, DTP, Fanfare, Island, Spectra; **Crown Publishing Group:** Bell Tower, Clarkson Potter, Crown Business, Crown Forum, Crown Publishers, Inc., Harmony Books, Prima, Shaye Arehart Books, Three Rivers Press; **Doubleday Broadway Publishing Group:** Anchor Books, Broadway Books, Currency, Doubleday, Doubleday Image, Doubleday Religious Publishing, Main Street Books, Nan A. Talese; **Knopf Publishing Group:** Alfred A. Knopf, Everyman¥s Library, Knopf Travel Guides, National Audobon Guides, Pantheon Books, Schocken Books, Vintage Anchor Publishing (Vintage Books, Anchor Books); **Random House Audio Publishing Group:** Listening Library, Random House Audible, Random House Audio, Random House Audio Assets, Random House Audio Dimensions, Random House Audio Roads, Random House Audio Voices, Random House Price-less; **Random House Children¥s Books:** BooksReportsNow.com, GoldenBooks.com, Junie B. Jones, Kids@Random, Knopf/ Delacorte/Dell Young Readers Group (Alfred A. Knopf, Bantam, Crown, David Fickling Books, Delacorte Press, Dell Dragonfly, Dell Laurel-Leaf, Dell Yearling Books, Doubleday, Wendy Lamb Books), Random House Young Readers Group (Akiko, Arthur, Barbie, Beginner Books, The Berenstain Bears, Bob the Builder, Disney, Dragon Tales, First Time Books, Golden Books, Landmark Books, Little Golden Books, Lucas Books, Mercer Mayer, Nickelodeon, Nick, Jr., pat the bunny, Picturebacks, Precious Moments, Richard Scarry, Sesame Street Books, Step Into Reading, Stepping Stones, Star Wars, Thomas the Tank Engine and Friends), Sesussville, Teachers@-Random, Teens@Random; **Random House Direct, Inc.:** Bon Appetit, Gourmet Books, Pillsbury; **Random House Information Group:** Fodor¥s Travel Publications, Living Language, Prima Games, The Princeton Review, Random House Espanol, Random House Puzzles & Games, Random House Reference; **Random House International:** Arete, McClelland & Stewart Ltd., Plaza & Janes, Random House Australia, Random House of Canada Ltd., Random House Mondadori, Random House South America, Random House United Kingdom, Transworld UK, Verlagsgruppe Random House; **Random House Large Print; Random House Publishing Group:** Ballantine Books, Del Rey, Modern Library, One World, Presidio Press, Random House, Random House Trade Paperbacks, Villard; **Random House Reference Publishing:** Boston Globe Puzzle Books, Chicago Tribune Crosswords, House of Collectibles, Los Angeles Time Crosswords, McKay Chess Library, Random House Websters, Washington Post Crosswords; **Random House Value Publishing:** Children¥s Classics, Crescent, Gramercy, Testament, Wings; **Waterbrook Press:** Fisherman Bible Study Guides, Shaw Books, Waterbrook Press.

- See website for complete list of imprints. Agented submissions only. *No unsolicited mss.*
- "Random House has long been committed to publishing the best literature by writers both in the United States and abroad.''

N A Ø RANDOM HOUSE PUBLISHING GROUP

Division of Random House, Inc., 1745 Broadway, New York NY 10019. (212)782-9000. Website: www.randomh ouse.com. Estab. 1925. Publishes hardcover and paperback trade books. **Publishes 120 titles/year. Receives 3,000 submissions/year.**

Imprints Ballantine Books, Del Rey, Modern Library, One World, Presidio Press, Random House, Random House Trade Paperbacks, Villard.

• See website for details.

○➤ "Random House is the world's largest English-language general trade book publisher. It includes an array of prestigious imprints that publish some of the foremost writers of our time—in hardcover, trade paperback, mass market paperback, electronic, multimedia and other formats."

Nonfiction *Agented submissions only.*

Fiction *Agented submissions only.*

Ⓐ Ⓓ RANDOM HOUSE YOUNG READERS GROUP

Imprint of Random House Children's Books, a Division of Random House, Inc., 1745 Broadway, New York NY 10019. (212)782-9000. Fax: (212)782-9698. Website: www.randomhouse.com/kids. Accepts simultaneous submissions. Responds in 4 months to queries.

Imprints Akiko, Arthur, Barbie, Beginner Books, The Berenstain Bears, Bob the Builder, Disney, Dragon Tales, First Time Books, Golden Books, Landmark Books, Little Golden Books, Lucas Books, Mercer Mayer, Nickelodeon, Nick, Jr., pat the bunny, Picturebacks, Precious Moments, Richard Scarry, Sesame Street Books, Step Into Reading, Stepping Stones, Star Wars, Thomas the Tank Engine and Friends.

Fiction "Random House publishes a select list of first chapter books and novels, with an emphasis on fantasy and historical fiction." Chapter books, middle-grade, young adult. *Agented submissions only.* No queries by fax.

Ⓐ Ⓓ RANDOM HOUSE/GOLDEN BOOKS FOR YOUNG READERS GROUP

Imprint of Random House Children's Books/Random House, Inc., 1745 Broadway, New York NY 10019. (212)782-9000. Website: www.randomhouse.com/kids. Vice President/Publisher: Kate Klimo. Vice President/Publisher (Random House): Mallory Loehr. Associate Publisher (Golden Books): Amy Jarashow. Estab. 1935. Publishes hardcover, trade paperback, and mass market paperback originals and reprints. **Publishes 375 titles/year. Receives 1,000 queries/year. Pays 1-6% royalty, or makes outright purchase. Offers variable advance.** Accepts simultaneous submissions. Book catalog free.

Imprints Beginner Books, Disney, First Time Books, Landmark Books, Picturebacks, Sesame Workshop, Step into Reading, Stepping Stones, Little Golden Books.

• Color & activity; board & novelty; fiction and nonfiction for beginning readers; hardcover and paperback fiction for kids ages 7-YA.

○➤ "Our aim is to create books that nurture the hearts and minds of children, providing and promoting quality books and a rich variety of media that entertain and educate readers from birth to 16 years."

Nonfiction Children's/juvenile. Subjects include animals, history, nature/environment, science, sports, popular culture. *No unsolicited mss. Agented submissions only.*

Fiction Horror, juvenile, mystery, picture books, young adult. "Familiarize yourself with our list. We look for original, unique stories. Do something that hasn't been done." *Agented submissions only. No unsolicited mss.*

Recent Title(s) *The Best Place to Read*, by Debbie Bertram & Susan Bloom; *Top-Secret, Personal Beeswax: A Journal by Junie B. (and Me)*, by Barbara Park; *The Pup Speaks Up*, by Anna Jane Hays.

Ⓝ RAVEN TREE PRESS, LLC

200 S. Washington St., Suite 306, Green Bay WI 54301. (920)438-1605. Fax: (920)438-1607. E-mail: amy@ravent reepress.com. Website: www.raventreepress.com. **Acquisitions:** Amy Crane Johnson, editor (children's picture books). Estab. 2000. Publishes hardcover and trade paperback originals. **Publishes 10 titles/year. Receives 1,500 mss/year. 75% of books from first-time authors; 100% from unagented writers. Pays royalty. Offers variable advance.** Publishes book 2 years after acceptance of ms. Accepts simultaneous submissions. Responds in 4 months to mss. Book catalog and ms guidelines online.

Nonfiction Children's/juvenile. Stories will be translated upon acceptance. Submit complete ms. Reviews artwork/photos as part of ms package. Send photocopies.

Fiction Juvenile, picture books. Looking for lower reading levels (K-3)—math, science, social studies. Bilingual—no wordplay, no rhyming, 500 words or less. Submit complete ms.

Recent Title(s) *On the Banks of the Amazon*, by Nancy Kelly Allen; *Oh, Crumps!*, by Lee Bock (bilingual children's picture book).

Tips "Follow submission guidelines on website."

RED HEN PRESS

P.O. Box 3537, Granada Hills CA 91394. (818)831-0649. Fax: (818)831-6659. E-mail: editor@redhen.org. Website: www.redhen.org. **Acquisitions:** Mark E. Cull, publisher/editor (fiction); Katherine Gale, poetry editor (poetry, literary fiction). Estab. 1993. Publishes trade paperback originals. **Publishes 10 titles/year. Receives 2,000 queries and 500 mss/year. 10% of books from first-time authors; 90% from unagented writers.**

Publishes book 1 year after acceptance of ms. Accepts simultaneous submissions. Responds in 1 month to queries; 2 months to proposals; 3 months to mss. Book catalog free; ms guidelines online.

O— Red Hen Press is a nonprofit organization specializing in literary fiction and nonfiction. Currently de-emphasizing poetry.

Nonfiction Biography, children's/juvenile. Subjects include ethnic, gay/lesbian, language/literature, memoirs, women's issues/studies, political/social interest. Query with SASE. Reviews artwork/photos as part of ms package. Send photocopies.

Fiction "We prefer high-quality literary fiction." Ethnic, experimental, feminist, gay/lesbian, historical, literary, mainstream/contemporary, poetry, poetry in translation, short story collections. "We prefer high-quality literary fiction." Query with SASE.

Poetry Query, or submit 5 sample poems.

Recent Title(s) *The Misread City: New Literary Los Angeles*, edited by Dana Gioia and Scott Timberg; *Rebel*, by Tom Hayden.

Tips "Audience reads poetry, literary fiction, intelligent nonfiction. If you have an agent, we may be too small since we don't pay advances. Write well. Send queries first. Be willing to help promote your own book."

RED WHEEL/WEISER AND CONARI PRESS

(formerly Red Wheel/Weiser), 368 Congress St., Boston MA 02210. (617)542-1324. Fax: (617)482-9676. Website: www.redwheelweiser.com. **Acquisitions:** Pat Bryce, acquisitions editor. Estab. 1956. Publishes hardcover and trade paperback originals and reprints. **Publishes 60-75 titles/year; imprint publishes 20-25 titles/year. Receives 2,000 queries and 2,000 mss/year. 20% of books from first-time authors; 50% from unagented writers. Pays royalty.** Publishes book 1 year after acceptance of ms. Accepts simultaneous submissions. Responds in 3 months to queries; 3-6 months to proposals; 3-6 months to mss. Book catalog free; ms guidelines online.

Imprints Red Wheel, Conari Press, Weiser.

Nonfiction Gift book, self-help, inspirational, esoteric subjects including magic, Wicca, astrology, tarot. Subjects include New Age, spirituality, women's issues/studies, parenting. Query with SASE, or submit proposal package including outline, 2 sample chapter(s), TOC. Reviews artwork/photos as part of ms package. Send photocopies.

Recent Title(s) *Snap Out of It*, by Ilene Segalove; *The Odd Girls' Book of Spells*, by Cal Garrison; *How to Live in the World and Still Be Happy*, by Hugh Prather.

REFERENCE PRESS INTERNATIONAL

P.O. Box 4126, Greenwich CT 06831. (203)622-6860. Fax: (707)929-0282. **Acquisitions:** Cheryl Lacoff, senior editor. Publishes hardcover and trade paperback originals. **Publishes 6 titles/year. Receives 50 queries and 20 mss/year. 75% of books from first-time authors; 90% from unagented writers. Pays royalty, or makes outright purchase. Offers determined by project advance.** Publishes book 6 months after acceptance of ms. Accepts simultaneous submissions. Responds in 3 months to queries.

O— Reference Press specializes in gift books, instructional, reference, and how-to titles.

Nonfiction Gift book, how-to, illustrated book, multimedia (audio, video, CD-ROM), reference, technical, instructional. Subjects include anything related to the fine arts or crafts field. "Follow the guidelines as stated concerning subjects and types of books we're looking for." Query with SASE, or submit outline, 1-3 sample chapter(s). Reviews artwork/photos as part of ms package. Send photocopies.

Recent Title(s) *Who's Who in the Peace Corps* (alumni directory).

REFERENCE SERVICE PRESS

5000 Windplay Dr., Suite 4, El Dorado Hills CA 95762. (916)939-9620. Fax: (916)939-9626. E-mail: findaid@aol.com. Website: www.rspfunding.com. **Acquisitions:** Stuart Hauser, acquisitions editor. Estab. 1977. Publishes hardcover originals. **Publishes 10-20 titles/year. 100% from unagented writers. Pays 10% royalty. Offers advance.** Publishes book 6 months after acceptance of ms. Accepts simultaneous submissions. Responds in 2 months to queries. Book catalog for #10 SASE.

O— Reference Service Press focuses on the development and publication of financial aid resources in any format (print, electronic, e-book, etc.). We are interested in financial aid publications aimed at specific groups (e.g., minorities, women, veterans, the disabled, undergraduates majoring in specific subject areas, specific types of financial aid, etc.).

Nonfiction Specializes in financial aid opportunities for students in or having these characteristics: women, minorities, veterans, the disabled, etc. Subjects include agriculture/horticulture, art/architecture, business/economics, education, ethnic, health/medicine, history, religion, science, sociology, women's issues/studies, disabled. Submit outline, sample chapter(s).

Recent Title(s) *Financial Aids for Women, 2003-2005*.

Tips "Our audience consists of librarians, counselors, researchers, students, re-entry women, scholars, and other fundseekers."

REPUBLIC OF TEXAS PRESS

Imprint of Taylor Trade Publishing, 3164 Harbinger Lane, Dallas TX 75287. Phone/Fax: (972)307-1186. E-mail: dundeeh@aol.com. **Acquisitions:** Janet Harris, acquisitions editor. Publishes trade and paperback originals. **Publishes 10-15 titles/year. 95% from unagented writers. Pays industry-standard royalty on net receipts. Offers small advance.** Publishes book 9 months-1 year after acceptance of ms. Accepts simultaneous submissions. Responds in 1 month to queries.

O—¬ Republic of Texas Press specializes in Texas history and general Texana nonfiction.

Nonfiction Subjects include ethnic, general nonfiction, history, nature/environment, regional, sports, travel, women's issues/studies, Old West, Texas military, ghost accounts. Submit TOC, 2 sample chapters, target audience, author bio, and SASE.

Recent Title(s) *Texas Bandits: From Real to Reel*, by Mona Sizer; *Texas Women in World War II*, by Cindy Wiegand; *Alamo Traces: New Evidence and New Conclusions*, by Thomas Ricks Lindley.

Tips "We are interested in anything relating to Texas. From the wacky to the most informative, any nonfiction concept will be considered. Our market is adult."

RESURRECTION PRESS

Imprint of Catholic Book Publishing Co., 77 W. End Rd., Totowa NJ 07512-1405. Fax: (973)890-2410. **Acquisitions:** Emilie Cerar, editor. Publishes trade paperback originals and reprints. **Publishes 8-10 titles/year. Receives 100 queries and 100 mss/year. 25% of books from first-time authors; 100% from unagented writers. Pays 5-10% royalty. Offers $250-2,000 advance.** Publishes book 1 year after acceptance of ms. Accepts simultaneous submissions. Responds in 1 month to queries; 1 month to proposals; 2 months to mss. Book catalog and ms guidelines free.

O—¬ Resurrection Press publishes religious, devotional, and inspirational titles.

Nonfiction Self-help. Subjects include religion. Query with SASE, or submit outline, 2 sample chapter(s). Reviews artwork/photos as part of ms package. Send photocopies.

Recent Title(s) *Mourning Sickness*, by Keith Smith; *Sabbath Moments*, by Adolfo Quezada.

Ⓐ Ⓞ FLEMING H. REVELL PUBLISHING

Imprint of Baker Book House, P.O. Box 6287, Grand Rapids MI 49516. Fax: (616)676-2315. Website: www.baker books.com. **Acquisitions:** Lonnie Hull DuPont, director of acquisitions; Bill Petersen, senior acquisitions editor; Jane Campbell, editorial director (Chosen Books). Estab. 1870. Publishes hardcover, trade paperback and mass market paperback originals. **Publishes 75 titles/year. Pays 14-18% royalty on wholesale price. Offers advance.** Publishes book 1 year after acceptance of ms.

● No longer accepts unsolicited mss.

O—¬ Revell publishes to the heart (rather than to the head). For 125 years, Revell has been publishing evangelical books for the personal enrichment and spiritual growth of general Christian readers.

Nonfiction How-to, self-help. Subjects include child guidance/parenting, religion, Christian living.

Fiction Religious.

Recent Title(s) *Making Children Mind Without Losing Yours*, by Dr. Kevin Leman (nonfiction); *Woman of Grace*, by Kathleen Morgan (fiction).

MORGAN REYNOLDS PUBLISHING

620 S. Elm St., Suite 223, Greensboro NC 27406. (336)275-1311. Fax: (336)275-1152. E-mail: editorial@morganr eynolds.com. Website: www.morganreynolds.com. Founder/Publisher: John Riley. **Acquisitions:** Angie De-Cola, editor. Estab. 1994. Publishes hardcover originals. **Publishes 25 titles/year. Receives 250-300 queries and 100-150 mss/year. 50% of books from first-time authors; 100% from unagented writers. Pays advance and 10% royalty.** Publishes book 12-18 months after acceptance of ms. Accepts simultaneous submissions. Responds in 3 months to queries. Book catalog and ms guidelines online.

O—¬ Morgan Reynolds publishes nonfiction books for young-adult readers. "We prefer lively, well-written biographies of interesting, contemporary and historical figures for our biography series. Books for our Great Events Series should be insightful and exciting looks at critical periods. We are interested in more well-known subjects rather than the esoteric." Currently emphasizing great scientists, composers, philosophers, world writers. De-emphasizing sports figures.

Nonfiction "We do not always publish the obvious subjects. Don't shy away from less-popular subjects. We also publish nonfiction related to great events." Biography. Subjects include Americana (young-adult oriented), business/economics, government/politics, history, language/literature, military/war, money/finance, women's issues/studies. No children's books, picture books, or fiction. Query with SASE.

Recent Title(s) *Marcus Garvey: Black Nationalist*, by Peggy Caravantes; *Isak Dinesen: Gothic Storyteller*, by Roger Leslie; *Galileo Galilei and the Science of Motion*, by William J. Boerst.

Tips "Request our writer's guidelines, and visit our website. We will be happy to send a catalog if provided with 80 cents postage."

RFF PRESS

Resources for the Future, 1616 P St., NW, Washington DC 20036. (202)328-5086. Fax: (202)328-5137. E-mail: rffpress@rff.org. Website: www.rffpress.org. **Acquisitions:** Don Reisman, publisher. Publishes hardcover, trade paperback and electronic originals. **Publishes 20 titles/year. Pays royalty on wholesale price.** Publishes book 6 months after acceptance of ms. Accepts simultaneous submissions. Responds in 1 month to queries; 1 month to proposals; 2 months to mss. Book catalog online; ms guidelines free.

Nonfiction "We focus on social science approaches to environmental and natural resource issues." Reference, technical, textbook, trade. Subjects include agriculture/horticulture, business/economics, government/politics, history, nature/environment, science. "We do not publish works that are purely opinion driven. Inquire via e-mail or letter; no phone calls." Submit proposal package including outline. Reviews artwork/photos as part of ms package. Send photocopies.

Recent Title(s) *Northern Landscapes: The Struggle for Wilderness Alaska*, by Daniel Nelson; *Private Rights and Public Resources: Equity and Property Allocation in Market-Based Environmental Policy*, by Leigh Raymond; *True Warnings and False Alarms: Evaluating Fears About the Health Risks of Technology, 1948-1971*, by Allan C. Mazur.

Tips Audience is scholars, policy makes, activists, businesses, the general public.

N: RIO NUEVO PUBLISHERS

Imprint of Treasure Chest Books, P.O. Box 5250, Tucson AZ 85703. Fax: (520)624-5888. E-mail: info@rionuevo.com. Submissions E-mail: cooper@rionuevo.com. Website: www.rionuevo.com. **Acquisitions:** Lisa Cooper, editor-in-chief (adult nonfiction titles about the Southwest). Estab. 1975. Publishes hardcover and trade paperback originals and reprints. **Publishes 12-20 titles/year. Receives 20 queries and 10 mss/year. 30% of books from first-time authors; 100% from unagented writers. Pays 4-10% royalty on net receipts, or makes outright purchase. Offers $1,000-4,000 advance.** Publishes book 1 year after acceptance of ms. Accepts simultaneous submissions. Responds in 6 months to queries; 6 months to proposals; 6 months to mss. Book catalog online; ms guidelines by e-mail.

Nonfiction Cookbook, gift book, illustrated book. Subjects include animals, cooking/foods/nutrition, gardening, general nonfiction, history, nature/environment, regional, religion, spirituality, travel. "We cover the Southwest but prefer titles that are not too narrow in their focus. We want our books to be of broad enough interest that people from other places will also want to read them." Query with SASE, or submit proposal package including outline, 2 sample chapter(s). Reviews artwork/photos as part of ms package. Send photocopies.

Recent Title(s) *Listening with Your Heart: Lessons from Native America*; *Folk Saints of the Borderlands: Victims, Bandits, and Healers*; *Our Sonoran Desert*.

Tips "We have a general audience of intelligent people interested in the Southwest—nature, history, culture. Many of our books are sold in gift shops throughout the region; we are also distributed nationally by W.W. Norton."

RISING MOON

Imprint of Northland Publishing, Inc., P.O. Box 1389, Flagstaff AZ 86002-1389. (928)774-5251. Fax: (928)774-0592. E-mail: editorial@northlandpub.com. Website: www.northlandpub.com. **Acquisitions:** Theresa Howell, kids editor. Estab. 1988. Publishes hardcover and trade paperback originals. **Publishes 8-10 titles/year. Receives 1,000 submissions/year. 20% of books from first-time authors; 20% from unagented writers. Pays royalty. Sometimes pays flat fee. Offers advance.** Publishes book 1-2 years after acceptance of ms. Accepts simultaneous submissions. Responds in 3 months to queries. Call for book catalog; ms guidelines online.

O➨ Rising Moon's objective is to provide children with entertaining and informative books that follow the heart and tickle the funny bone. Rising Moon is no longer publishing middle-grade children's fiction.

Fiction Picture books (with Southwest or Latino themes). "We are looking for exceptional bilingual stories (Spanish/English), fractured fairy tales, and original stories with a Southwest flavor." Submit complete ms with SASE of adequate size and postage. No e-mail submissions.

Recent Title(s) *The Seed and the Giant Saguaro*, by Jennifer Ward, illsutrated by Mike Rangner.

Tips "Our audience is composed of regional Southwest-interest readers."

RIVER CITY PUBLISHING

River City Publishing, LLC, 1719 Mulberry St., Montgomery AL 36106. (334)265-6753. Fax: (334)265-8880. E-mail: agordon@rivercitypublishing.com. Website: www.rivercitypublishing.com. **Acquisitions:** Ashley Gordon, editor. Estab. 1989. Publishes hardcover and trade paperback originals and reprints. **Publishes 12 titles/ year. Receives 1,250 queries and 200 mss/year. 20% of books from first-time authors; 75% from unagented writers. Pays 10% royalty on net revenue. Offers $500-5,000 advance.** Publishes book 1 year after acceptance of ms. Accepts simultaneous submissions. Responds in 3 months to queries; 4 months to proposals; 1 year to mss. Ms guidelines free.

Imprints Starrhill Press, Elliott & Clark, River City Kids.

Nonfiction Biography, coffee table book, illustrated book. Subjects include art/architecture, creative nonfiction, ethnic, government/politics, history, language/literature, memoirs, multicultural, music/dance, photography, regional, sports, travel. Submit proposal package including outline, 2 sample chapter(s), author's bio/résumé. Reviews artwork/photos as part of ms package. Send photocopies.

Fiction Ethnic, historical, literary, multicultural, poetry, regional (southern), short story collections. Submit proposal package including 3 sample chapter(s), résumé, synopsis, author bio.

Poetry Query.

Recent Title(s) *Speaks the Nightbird*, by Robert McCammon (historical fiction); *My Mother's Witness*, by Carolyn Haines (creative nonfiction); *Love to the Spirits*, by Stephen March (short story).

🅰 ROC BOOKS

Imprint of New American Library, A Division of Penguin Putnam, Inc., 375 Hudson St., New York NY 10014. (212)366-2000. Website: www.penguinputnam.com. **Acquisitions:** Jennifer Heddle, editor. Publishes mass market, trade, and hardcover originals. **Publishes 48 titles/year. Receives 500 queries/year. Pays royalty. Offers negotiable advance.** Accepts simultaneous submissions. Responds in 2-3 months to queries.

　　☞ "We're looking for books that are a good read, that people will want to pick up time and time again."

Fiction Fantasy, horror, science fiction. "Roc tries to strike a balance between fantasy and science fiction. We strongly discourage unsolicited submissions." Query with SASE, or submit 1-2 sample chapter(s), synopsis.

Recent Title(s) *The House of Gaian*, by Anne Bishop; *Dies the Fire*, by S.M. Stirling.

Ⓝ JAMES A. ROCK & CO., PUBLISHERS

9170 Traville Gateway Dr., #305, Rockville MD 20850. Fax: (301)294-1683. Website: www.rockpublishing.com. **Acquisitions:** James A. or Lynne A. Rock, editors. Estab. 1977. Publishes hardcover, trade paperback, and electronic originals and reprints. **Publishes 10-15 titles/year; imprint publishes 3-7 titles/year. 10% of books from first-time authors; 25% from unagented writers. Pays 5-15% royalty. Offers $0-2,000 advance.** Publishes book 9 months after acceptance of ms. Does not accept simultaneous submissions. Responds in 1 month to queries; 1 month to proposals; 1 month to mss. Book catalog and ms guidelines online.

Imprints Sense of Wonder Press, Yellow Back Mysteries, Castle Keep Press.

Nonfiction Audiocassettes, autobiography, biography, booklets, children's/juvenile, coffee table book, cookbook, gift book, how-to, humor, illustrated book, multimedia, reference, scholarly, self-help, technical, textbook, bibliography. Subjects include Americana, animals, anthropology/archeology, art/architecture, business/ economics, child guidance/parenting, community, computers/electronic, contemporary culture, cooking/ foods/nutrition, creative nonfiction, education, gardening, general nonfiction, government/politics, health/ medicine, history, hobbies, humanities, language/literature, memoirs, military/war, money/finance, multicultural, music/dance, nature/environment, New Age, philosophy, science, software, travel, women's issues/ studies, world affairs. "Grammar, language, punctuation, and spelling count heavily. We edit all manuscripts for style and content, and we do not want to read sloppy, unschooled, or badly written manuscripts. If you are composing in English, we expect you to be in control of your instrument. We are rather conservative when it comes to punctuation." Query with SASE. Reviews artwork/photos as part of ms package. Send photocopies.

Fiction Adventure, comic books, experimental, fantasy, gothic, horror, humor, juvenile, literary, mainstream/ contemporary, multicultural, multimedia, mystery, picture books, plays, poetry, poetry in translation, regional, religious, romance, science fiction, short story collections, suspense, young adult, ghost. Query with SASE.

Poetry "Good poetry sometimes develops its own conventions. Feel free to do so if you feel up to it." Submit 5 sample poems.

Recent Title(s) *Rex Stout: A Majesty's Life*, by John McAleer (biography); *Sci-Fi Womanthology*, edited by Forrest J. Ackerman and Pam Keesey (short story anthology).

Tips "Exhibit a love of language, of Western Culture, and of writing. A 'gift of laughter and sense that the world is mad' won't hurt."

ROSE PUBLISHING

4455 Torrance Blvd., #259, Torrance CA 90503. (310)370-8962. Fax: (310)370-7492. E-mail: rosepubl@aol.com. Website: www.rose-publishing.com. **Acquisitions:** Carol R. Witte, editor. **Publishes 5-10 titles/year. 5% of books from first-time authors; 100% from unagented writers. Makes outright purchase.** Publishes book 18 months after acceptance of ms. Accepts simultaneous submissions. Responds in 3 months to proposals; 2 months to mss. Book catalog free.

O— "We publish Bible reference materials in chart, pamphlet, and Powerpoint form, easy-to-understand and appealing to children, teens or adults on Bible study, prayer, basic beliefs, Scripture memory, salvation, sharing the gospel, worship, abstinence, creation, apologetics, marriage, family, grief, and comfort."

Nonfiction Reference, pamphlets, group study books. Subjects include religion, science, sex, spirituality, Bible studies, Christian history, counseling aids, cults/occult, curriculum, Christian discipleship, evangelism/witnessing, Christian living, marriage, prayer, creation, singles issues. No fiction or poetry. Submit proposal package including outline, photocopies of chart contents or poster artwork. Reviews artwork/photos as part of ms package. Send photocopies.

Recent Title(s) *Charts and Pamphlets of Fruit of the Spirit*; *Bible Overview*; *The Twelve Disciples*.

Tips Audience includes both church (Bible study leaders, Sunday school teachers [all ages], pastors, youth leaders), and home (parents, home schoolers, children, youth, high school, and college). Open to topics that supplement Sunday School curriculum or Bible study, junior high creation materials, Bible study, reasons to believe, books of the Bible.

ROUTLEDGE

(formerly Routledge, Inc.), part of Taylor and Francis plc, 29 W. 35th St., New York NY 10001-2299. (212)216-7800. Fax: (212)563-2269. Website: routledge-ny.com. **Acquisitions:** Mary MacInnes, vice president/publisher. Estab. 1836. **Publishes 200 titles/year. 10% of books from first-time authors; 95% from unagented writers. Pays royalty. Offers advance.** Publishes book 1 year after acceptance of ms. Accepts simultaneous submissions. Responds in 3 months to queries. Ms guidelines online.

Imprints Theatre Arts Books, Routledge Falmer, Brunner-Routledge.

O— The Routledge list includes humanities, social sciences, reference, monographs, reference works, hardback and paperback upper-level texts, scholarly research, student supplementary books.

Nonfiction Reference, textbook. Subjects include education, ethnic, gay/lesbian, government/politics, history, music/dance, psychology, literary criticism, social sciences, geography, cultural studies, urban studies and planning. Query with proposal package, including TOC, intro, sample chapter, readership, suggested academic reviewers, overall prospectus, cv, and SASE.

ROXBURY PUBLISHING CO.

P.O. Box 491044, Los Angeles CA 90049. (310)473-3312. **Acquisitions:** Claude Teweles, publisher. Estab. 1981. Publishes hardcover and paperback originals and reprints. **Publishes 15-20 titles/year. Pays royalty.** Accepts simultaneous submissions. Responds in 2 months to queries.

O— Roxbury publishes college textbooks in the humanities and social sciences only.

Nonfiction Textbook (college-level textbooks and supplements only). Subjects include humanities, social sciences, sociology, political science, family studies, criminology, criminal justice. Query with SASE, or submit outline, sample chapter(s), synopsis, or submit complete ms.

ROYAL FIREWORKS PUBLISHING

1 First Ave., P.O. Box 399, Unionville NY 10988. (845)726-4444. Fax: (845)726-3824. E-mail: mail@rfwp.com. Website: www.rfwp.com. **Acquisitions:** William Neumann, editor (young adult); Dr. T.M. Kemnitz, editor (education). Estab. 1977. Publishes library binding and trade paperback originals, reprints and textbooks. **Publishes 75-140 titles/year. Receives 1,000 queries and 400 mss/year. 30-50% of books from first-time authors; 98% from unagented writers. Pays 5-10% royalty on wholesale price.** Publishes book 9 months after acceptance of ms. Does not accept simultaneous submissions. Responds in 1 month to mss. Book catalog for $3.85; ms guidelines for #10 SASE.

Nonfiction Textbook. Subjects include child guidance/parenting, education. "We do books for gifted children, their parents and teachers." Submit complete ms. Reviews artwork/photos as part of ms package. Send photocopies.

Fiction Young adult. "We do novels for children from 8-16. We do a lot of historical fiction, science fiction, adventure, mystery, sports, etc. We are concerned about the values." No drugs, sex, swearing. Submit complete ms.

Recent Title(s) *Grammar Voyage*, by Michael Thompson; *Double Vision*, by Jerry Chris; *A Few Screws Loose*, by Maryann Easley.

Tips Audience is comprised of gifted children, their parents and teachers, and children (8-18) who read.

RUTGERS UNIVERSITY PRESS

100 Joyce Kilmer Ave., Piscataway NJ 08854-8099. (732)445-7762. Fax: (732)445-7039. Website: rutgerspress.rutgers.edu. **Acquisitions:** Leslie Mitchner, editor-in-chief/associate director (humanities); Kristi Long, senior

editor (social sciences); Audra Wolfe, editor (science, health & medicine); Melanie Halkias, editor (history, American studies, Asian-American studies). Estab. 1936. Publishes hardcover and trade paperback originals, and reprints. **Publishes 90 titles/year. Receives 1,500 queries and 300 mss/year. 30% of books from first-time authors; 70% from unagented writers. Pays 7½-15% royalty. Offers $1,000-10,000 advance.** Publishes book 1 year after acceptance of ms. Responds in 1 month to proposals. Book catalog online or with SASE; ms guidelines online.

  O→ "Our Press aims to reach audiences beyond the academic community with accessible scholarly and regional books."

Nonfiction Reference. Subjects include art/architecture (art history), ethnic, film/cinema/stage, gay/lesbian, government/politics, health/medicine, history, multicultural, nature/environment, regional, religion, sociology, women's issues/studies, African-American studies, Asian-American studies, history of science and technology, literature, literary criticism, human evolution, ecology, media studies. Books for use in undergraduate courses. Submit outline, 2-3 sample chapter(s). Reviews artwork/photos as part of ms package. Send photocopies.

Recent Title(s) *The Great Communication Gap: Why Americans Feel So Alone*, by Laura Pappano.

Tips Both academic and general audiences. "Many of our books have potential for undergraduate course use. We are more trade-oriented than most university presses. We are looking for intelligent, well-written, and accessible books. Avoid overly narrow topics."

RUTLEDGE HILL PRESS

Imprint of Thomas Nelson, P.O. Box 141000, Nashville TN 37214-1000. (615)902-2333. Fax: (615)902-2340. Website: www.rutledgehillpress.com. **Acquisitions:** Lawrence Stone, publisher. Estab. 1982. Publishes hardcover and trade paperback originals and reprints. **Publishes 40-50 titles/year. Receives 1,000 submissions/year. 40% of books from first-time authors; 80% from unagented writers. Pays royalty. Offers advance.** Publishes book 10 months after acceptance of ms. Responds in 2 months to queries. Book catalog for 9×12 SASE; ms guidelines for #10 SASE.

  O→ "We are a publisher of market-specific books, focusing on particular genres or regions."

Nonfiction "We have recently made a strategic decision to focus our publishing in 4 areas: cookbooks, how-to books, health and nutrition, and gift and inspirational (not religious) books. The book should have a unique marketing hook. Books built on new ideas and targeted to a specific U.S. region are welcome. Please, no fiction, children's, academic, poetry or religious works, and we won't even look at *Life's Little Instruction Book* spinoffs or copycats." Submit cover letter that includes brief marketing strategy and author bio, outline, and sample chapters. Reviews artwork/photos as part of ms package.

Recent Title(s) *A Gentleman Entertains*, by John Bridges and Bryan Curtis; *101 Secrets a Good Dad Knows*, by Walter Browder and Sue Ellen Browder; *I Hope You Dance*, by Tia Sillers and Mark Sanders.

Ⓝ SABLE PUBLISHING

P.O. Box 4496, Palm Springs CA 92263. (760)408-1881. E-mail: sablepublishing@aol.com. Website: www.sable publishing.com. Ed Baron, CEO. **Acquisitions:** Glory Harley, submissions editor. Estab. 2000. Publishes hardcover and trade paperback originals and reprints. **Publishes 24 titles/year. Receives 300 + queries and 100 + submissions/year. 40% of books from first-time authors; 90% from unagented writers. Pays 7-12% royalty on retail price.** Publishes book 18 months after acceptance of ms. Accepts simultaneous submissions. Responds in 3 months to queries; 3 months to proposals; 3 months to mss. Book catalog online; ms guidelines by e-mail.

Nonfiction Autobiography, biography, how-to, humor, illustrated book, self-help. Subjects include alternative lifestyles, contemporary culture, cooking/foods/nutrition, creative nonfiction, ethnic, hobbies, humanities, language/literature, memoirs, money/finance, multicultural, New Age, philosophy, photography, psychology, regional, religion, sex, social sciences, sociology, spirituality, women's issues/studies. Query with SASE, or submit proposal package including outline, 3 sample chapter(s), author bio. Reviews artwork/photos as part of ms package. Send photocopies.

Fiction Adventure, confession, erotica, ethnic, experimental, fantasy, feminist, gothic, horror, humor, literary, mainstream/contemporary, multicultural, multimedia, mystery, occult, poetry, regional, religious, romance, science fiction, short story collections, spiritual, suspense, western. "We look for originality, and we are interested in screenplays for motion pictures, scripts for half-hour TV shows, and scripts for TV series." Query with SASE, or submit proposal package including 3 sample chapter(s), synopsis, author bio.

Poetry "We love epic poems, rhyming poetry that isn't forced, and expressions of complete ideas expressed in a poetic form. We especially love illustrated poetry." Query, or submit 10 sample poems, or submit complete ms.

Recent Title(s) *The Jewish Maven Cookbook*, by Shoshana Barer (cooking, advice, humor, wisdom); *Creativity, Making Your Mark*, by Hyacinthe Baron (how-to, self-help-art, self-improvement); *Pure Gold, An Economic Goldmine*, by Jack Bentley (economics, business, finance, self-help).

SAE INTERNATIONAL

Society of Automotive Engineers, 400 Commonwealth Dr., Warrendale PA 15096. (724)776-4841. E-mail: writea book@sae.org. Website: www.sae.org. **Acquisitions:** Jeff Worsinger, product developer; Martha Swiss, product developer; Kris Hattman, product developer; Erin Moore, product developer; Matt Miller, product manager; Theresa Wertz, product developer. Estab. 1905. Publishes hardcover and trade paperback originals, Web and CD-ROM based electronic product. **Publishes 30-40 titles/year. Receives 250 queries and 75 mss/year. 30-40% of books from first-time authors; 100% from unagented writers. Pays royalty. Offers possible advance.** Publishes book 9-10 months after acceptance of ms. Accepts simultaneous submissions. Responds in 2 months to queries. Book catalog free; ms guidelines online.

> O—¬ "Automotive means anything self-propelled. We are a professional society serving this area, which includes aircraft, spacecraft, marine, rail, automobiles, trucks, and off-highway vehicles." Currently emphasizing engineering.

Nonfiction Biography, multimedia (CD-ROM, Web-based), reference, technical, textbook. Query with SASE. Reviews artwork/photos as part of ms package. Send photocopies.

Recent Title(s) *Formula 1 Technology*; *Ford: The Dust and the Glory*.

Tips "Audience is automotive engineers, technicians, car buffs, aerospace engineers, technicians, and historians."

SAFARI PRESS, INC.

15621 Chemical Lane, Bldg. B, Huntington Beach CA 92649-1506. (714)894-9080. Fax: (714)894-4949. E-mail: info@safaripress.com. Website: www.safaripress.com. **Acquisitions:** Jacqueline Neufeld, editor. Estab. 1985. Publishes hardcover originals and reprints, and trade paperback reprints. **Publishes 25-30 titles/year. 50% of books from first-time authors; 99% from unagented writers. Pays 8-15% royalty on wholesale price.** Does not accept simultaneous submissions. Book catalog for $1; ms guidelines online.

> • The editor notes that she receives many mss outside the areas of big-game hunting, wingshooting, and sporting firearms, and these are always rejected.
>
> O—¬ Safari Press publishes books only on big-game hunting, sporting, firearms, and wingshooting; this includes African, North American, European, Asian, and South American hunting and wingshooting. Does not want books on 'outdoors' topics (hiking, camping, canoeing, etc.).

Nonfiction Biography (of hunters), how-to (hunting and wingshooting stories), hunting adventure stories. Subjects include hunting, firearms, wingshooting, "We discourage autobiographies, unless the life of the hunter or firearms maker has been exceptional. We routinely reject manuscripts along the lines of 'Me and my buddies went hunting for . . . and a good time was had by all!' No outdoors topics (hiking, camping, canoeing, fishing, etc.). Query with SASE, or submit outline.

Recent Title(s) *Royal Quest: The Hunting Saga of H.I.H. Prince Abdorreza of Iran*; *The Best of Holland & Holland: England's Premier Gunmaker*; *African Hunter II*.

SALEM PRESS, INC.

Magill's Choice, 131 N. El Molino, Suite 350, Pasadena CA 91101. (626)584-0106. Fax: (626)584-1525. Website: www.salempress.com. **Acquisitions:** Dawn P. Dawson. **Publishes 20-22 titles/year. Receives 15 queries/year. Work-for-hire pays 5-15¢/word.** Responds in 1 month to queries; 1 month to proposals. Book catalog online.

Nonfiction Reference. Subjects include business/economics, ethnic, government/politics, health/medicine, history, language/literature, military/war, music/dance, nature/environment, philosophy, psychology, science, sociology, women's issues/studies. "We accept vitas for writers interested in supplying articles/entries for encyclopedia-type entries in library reference books. Will also accept multi-volume book ideas from people interested in being a general editor." Query with SASE.

Ⓝ SALINA BOOKSHELF

1254 W. University Ave., Suite 130, Flagstaff AZ 86001. (928)527-0070. Fax: (928)526-0386. E-mail: jessier@sali nabookshelf.com. Website: www.salinabookshelf.com. **Acquisitions:** Jessie Ruffenach, editor. Publishes trade paperback originals and reprints. **Publishes 4-5 titles/year. 50% of books from first-time authors; 100% from unagented writers. Pays varying royalty. Offers advance.** Publishes book 1 year after acceptance of ms. Accepts simultaneous submissions. Responds in 3 months to queries.

Nonfiction Children's/juvenile, textbook (Navajo language). Subjects include education, ethnic, science. "We publish childrens' bilingual readers. Nonfiction should be appropriate to science and social studies curriculum grades 3-8." Query with SASE. Reviews artwork/photos as part of ms package. Send photocopies.

Fiction Juvenile. "Submissions should be in English or Navajo. All our books relate to the Navajo language and culture." Query with SASE.

Poetry "We accept poetry in English/Southwest language for children." Submit 3 sample poems.
Recent Title(s) *Dine Bizaad: Speak, Read, Write Navajo*, by Irvy W. Goossen.

SANTA MONICA PRESS LLC

P.O. Box 1076, Santa Monica CA 90406. Website: www.santamonicapress.com. **Acquisitions:** Acquistions Editor. Estab. 1991. Publishes trade paperback originals. **Publishes 15 titles/year. Receives 500+ submissions/year. 25% of books from first-time authors; 75% from unagented writers. Pays 4-10% royalty on wholesale price. Offers $500-2,500 advance.** Publishes book 6-18 months after acceptance of ms. Accepts simultaneous submissions. Responds in 1-2 months to proposals. Book catalog for 9×12 SASE with 83¢ postage; ms guidelines online.

○┓ "At Santa Monica Press, we're not afraid to cast a wide editorial net. Our vision extends from lively and modern how-to books to offbeat looks at popular culture, from film history to literature."

Nonfiction Biography, gift book, how-to, humor, illustrated book, reference. Subjects include Americana, creative nonfiction, film/cinema/stage, health/medicine, language/literature, memoirs, music/dance, spirituality, sports, travel, contemporary culture, film/cinema/stage, general nonfiction. **All unsolicited mss returned unopened.** Submit proposal package, including outline, 2-3 sample chapters, biography, marketing and publicity plans, analysis of competitive titles, SASE with appropriate postage. Reviews artwork/photos as part of ms package. Send photocopies.

Recent Title(s) *Marilyn Monroe Dyed Here: More Locations of America's Pop Culture Landmarks*, by Chris Epting; *Movie Star Homes: The Fames to the Forgotten*, by Judy Artunian and Mike Oldham; *The Dog Ate My Résumé: Survival Tips for Life After College*, by Zack Arnstein and Larry Arnstein.

Tips "Visit our website before submitting to get a clear idea of the types of books we publish. Carefully analyze your book's competition and tell us what makes your book different—and what makes it better. Also let us know what promotional and marketing opportunities you, as the author, bring to the project."

SARABANDE BOOKS, INC.

2234 Dundee Rd., Suite 200, Louisville KY 40205. (502)458-4028. Fax: (502)458-4065. E-mail: info@sarabandebooks.org. Website: www.sarabandebooks.org. **Acquisitions:** Sarah Gorham, editor-in-chief. Estab. 1994. Publishes hardcover and trade paperback originals. **Publishes 10 titles/year. Receives 500 queries and 3,000 mss/year. 35% of books from first-time authors; 75% from unagented writers. Pays royalty. 10% on actual income received. Also pays in author's copies. Offers $500-1,000 advance.** Publishes book 18 months after acceptance of ms. Accepts simultaneous submissions. Responds in 3 months to queries; 6 months to mss. Book catalog free; ms and contest guidelines for #10 SASE or on website.

○┓ "Sarabande Books was founded to publish poetry and short fiction, as well as the occasional literary essay collection. We look for works of lasting literary value. We are actively seeking creative nonfiction."

Fiction Literary, short story collections, novellas, short novels, 300 pages maximum, 150 pages minimum. Queries in September only. Query with 1 sample story or chapter. Include 1-page bio and listing of publishing credits.

Poetry "Poetry of superior artistic quality. Otherwise no restraints or specifications." Submissions in September only. Query, or submit 10 sample poems.

Recent Title(s) *Where the Long Grass Bends*, by Neela Vaswani (fiction); *Subject Matter*, by Baron Wormser (poetry).

Tips Sarabande publishes for a general literary audience. "Know your market. Read—and buy—books of literature." Sponsors contests.

SAS PUBLISHING

SAS Campus Dr., Cary NC 27513-2414. (919)531-0585. Fax: (919)677-4444. E-mail: sasbbu@sas.com. Website: support.sas.com/bbu. **Acquisitions:** Julie M. Platt, editor-in-chief. Estab. 1976. Publishes hardcover and trade paperback originals. **Publishes 40 titles/year. Receives 30 submissions/year. 50% of books from first-time authors; 100% from unagented writers. Payment negotable. Offers negotable advance.** Does not accept simultaneous submissions. Responds in 2 weeks to queries. Book catalog and ms guidelines via website or with SASE; ms guidelines online.

○┓ SAS publishes books for SAS and JMP software users, "both new and experienced."

Nonfiction Technical, textbook. Subjects include software, statistics. "SAS Publishing develops and writes books inhouse. Through Books by Users Press, we also publish books by SAS users on a variety of topics relating to SAS software. Books by Users Press titles enhance users' abilities to use SAS effectively. We're interested in publishing manuscripts that describe or illustrate using any of SAS products, including JMP software. Books must be aimed at SAS or JMP users, either new or experienced. Tutorials are particularly attractive, as are descriptions of user-written applications for solving real-life business, industry or academic problems. Books on programming techniques using SAS are also desirable. Manuscripts must reflect current or upcoming software releases, and the author's writing should indicate an understanding of SAS and the technical aspects covered in the manuscript." Query with SASE, or submit outline, sample chapter(s). Reviews artwork/photos as part of ms package.

Recent Title(s) *The Little SAS Book: A Primer, Third Edition*, by Lora D. Delwiche and Susan J. Slaughter.

Tips "If I were a writer trying to market a book today, I would concentrate on developing a manuscript that teaches or illustrates a specific concept or application that SAS users will find beneficial in their own environments or can adapt to their own needs."

SASQUATCH BOOKS

119 S. Main, Suite 400, Seattle WA 98104. (206)467-4300. Fax: (206)467-4301. E-mail: custserve@sasquatchbooks.com. Website: www.sasquatchbooks.com. President: Chad Haight. **Acquisitions:** Gary Luke, editorial director; Terence Maikels, acquisitions editor; Heidi Lenze, acquisitions editor. Estab. 1986. Publishes regional hardcover and trade paperback originals. **Publishes 30 titles/year. 20% of books from first-time authors; 75% from unagented writers. Pays royalty on cover price. Offers wide range advance.** Publishes book 6 months after acceptance of ms. Does not accept simultaneous submissions. Responds in 3 months to queries. Book catalog for 9×12 SAE with 2 first-class stamps; ms guidelines online.

   O➝ Sasquatch Books publishes books for a West Coast regional audience—Alaska to California. Currently emphasizing outdoor recreation, cookbooks, and history.

Nonfiction "We are seeking quality nonfiction works about the Pacific Northwest and West Coast regions (including Alaska to California). The literature of place includes how-to and where-to as well as history and narrative nonfiction." Reference. Subjects include animals, art/architecture, business/economics, cooking/foods/nutrition, gardening, history, nature/environment, recreation, regional, sports, travel, women's issues/studies, outdoors. Query first, then submit outline and sample chapters with SASE.

Recent Title(s) *Out of Left Field*, by Art Thiel; *Book Lust*, by Nancy Pearl; *The Traveling Curmudgeon*, by Jon Winokur.

Tips "We sell books through a range of channels in addition to the book trade. Our primary audience consists of active, literate residents of the West Coast."

Ⓐ SCHOCKEN BOOKS

Imprint of Random House, Inc., a Division of Bertlesmann AG, 1745 Broadway, New York NY 10019. (212)572-2838. Fax: (212)572-6030. Website: www.schocken.com. **Acquisitions:** Altie Karper, editorial director. Estab. 1945. Publishes hardcover and trade paperback originals and reprints. **Publishes 9-12 titles/year. Small% of books from first-time authors; small% from unagented writers. Offers varied advance.** Accepts simultaneous submissions.

   O➝ "Schocken publishes quality Judaica in all areas—fiction, history, biography, current affairs, spirituality and religious practices, popular culture, and cultural studies."

Recent Title(s) *One People Two Worlds*, by Ammiel Hirsch and Yosef Reinman; *The Rebbe's Army*, by Sue Fishkoff; *Reading the Women of the Bible*, by Tikva Frymer-Kensky.

Ⓐ SCHOLASTIC LIBRARY PUBLISHING

A division of Scholastic, Inc., 90 Sherman Turnpike, Danbury CT 06816. (203)797-3500. Fax: (203)797-3197. Website: www.scholasticlibrary.com. Estab. 1895. Publishes hardcover and trade paperback originals. Does not accept simultaneous submissions.

Imprints Children's Press, Grolier, Franklin Watts.

   • This publisher accepts agented submissions only.

   O➝ "Scholastic Library is a leading publisher of reference, educational, and children's books. We provide parents, teachers, and librarians with the tools they need to enlighten children to the pleasure of learning and prepare them for the road ahead."

Ⓐ SCHOLASTIC PRESS

Imprint of Scholastic, Inc., 557 Broadway, New York NY 10012. (212)343-6100. Fax: (212)343-4713. Website: www.scholastic.com. **Acquisitions:** Elizabeth Szabla, editorial director. Publishes hardcover originals. **Publishes 50 titles/year. Receives 2,500 queries/year. 5% of books from first-time authors. Pays royalty on retail price. Offers variable advance.** Publishes book 18-24 months after acceptance of ms. Does not accept simultaneous submissions. Responds in 2 months to queries; 6-8 months to mss.

   O➝ Scholastic Press publishes "fresh, literary picture book fiction and nonfiction; fresh, literary nonseries or nongenre-oriented middle grade and young adult fiction." Currently emphasizing "subtly handled treatments of key relationships in children's lives; unusual approaches to commonly dry subjects, such as biography, math, history, or science." De-emphasizing fairy tales (or retellings), board books, genre, or series fiction (mystery, fantasy, etc.).

Nonfiction Children's/juvenile, general interest. *Agented submissions and previously published authors only.*

Fiction Juvenile, picture books, novels. Wants "fresh, exciting picture books and novels—inspiring, new talent." *Agented submissions and previously published authors only.*

Recent Title(s) *Old Turtle and the Broken Truth*, by Douglas Wood, illustrated by Jon J. Muth; *The Red Blanket*, by Eliza Thomas, illustrated by Joe Cepeda; *A Corner of the Universe*, by Ann M. Martin.

ⓝ SCHOLASTIC PROFESSIONAL PUBLISHING

Imprint of Scholastic, Inc., 524 Broadway, New York NY 10012. Website: www.scholastic.com. Vice President/Editor-in-Chief: Terry Cooper. **Acquisitions:** Deborah Schecter, editorial director (pre-K-grade 4 teacher resource books and materials); Virginia Dooley, editorial director (grade 4-8 teacher resource books); Margery Rosnick, acquisitions editor (theory and practice). Estab. 1989. **Publishes 140 + titles/year. Offers advance.** Does not accept simultaneous submissions. Responds in 3 months to queries. Book catalog for 9×12 SASE.

    ○┱ "We publish teacher resources to help teachers in their professional growth and to help enrich the curriculum." Currently emphasizing reading and writing, math, standards, testing.

Nonfiction Subjects include education. Elementary and middle-school level theories, strategies, lessons—all subject areas, including math, science, social studies, easy art projects, phonics, writing, management techniques, teaching strategies based on personal/professional experience in the clssroom and technology ideas. Production is limited to printed matter: resource and activity books, professional development materials, reference titles. Length: 6,000-12,000 words. Offers standard contract. Query with table of contents, outline, and sample chapter.

Recent Title(s) *Irresistable ABCs*; *Nonfiction in Focus*; *Classroom Management in Photographs*.

Tips "Writer should have background working in the classroom with elementary or middle school children, teaching pre-service students, and/or solid background in developing supplementary educational materials for these markets."

SCHREIBER PUBLISHING, INC.

51 Monroe St., Suite 101, Rockville MD 20850. (301)424-7737 ext. 28. Fax: (301)424-2336. E-mail: spbooks@aol.com. Website: www.schreiberpublishing.com. President: Morry Schreiber. **Acquisitions:** Linguistics Editor; Judaica Editor. Publishes hardcover and trade paperback originals and reprints. **Publishes 8 titles/year. Receives 40 queries and 12 mss/year. 80% of books from first-time authors; 95% from unagented writers. Pays negotiable royalty on retail price.** Publishes book 6 months after acceptance of ms. Accepts simultaneous submissions. Responds in 1 month to queries; 1 month to proposals; 1 month to mss. Book catalog free or on website; ms guidelines free.

    ○┱ Schreiber publishes reference books and dictionaries for better language and translation work, as well as Judaica books emphasizing Jewish culture and religion. Currently emphasizing multicultural dictionaries and parochial books.

Nonfiction Biography, children's/juvenile, coffee table book, gift book, humor, multimedia (CD-ROM), reference, textbook. Subjects include history, language/literature, memoirs, money/finance, multicultural, religion, science, translation. Query with SASE, or submit proposal package including outline, 1 sample chapter, and TOC. Reviews artwork/photos as part of ms package. Send photocopies.

Recent Title(s) *Questioning the Bible*, by Morry Soffer; *Spanish Business Dictionary*.

SCHROEDER PUBLISHING CO., INC.

P.O. Box 3009, Paducah KY 42002-3009. (270)898-6211. Fax: (270)898-8890. E-mail: editor@collectorbooks.com. Website: www.collectorbooks.com. Estab. 1973. Publishes hardcover and trade paperback orginals. **Publishes 95 titles/year; imprint publishes 65 (Collector Books); 30 (American Quilter's Society) titles/year. Receives 150 queries and 100 mss/year. 60% of books from first-time authors; 100% from unagented writers. Pays 5% royalty on retail price.** Publishes book 6 months after acceptance of ms. Accepts simultaneous submissions. Responds in 1 month to queries; 1 month to proposals; 1 month to mss. Book catalog and ms guidelines online.

Imprints Collector Books, American Quilter's Society.

Nonfiction Coffee table book, gift book, how-to, illustrated book, reference, self-help, textbook. Subjects include general nonfiction, hobbies, antiques and collectibles. Submit proposal package including outline, 2 sample chapter(s). Reviews artwork/photos as part of ms package. Send transparencies or prints.

Recent Title(s) *Schroeder's Antiques Price Guide*, by Sharon Huxford (reference); *Vintage Golf Club Collectibles*, by Ronald John (reference); *Collector's Encyclopedia of Depression Glass*, by Gene Florence (reference).

Tips Audience consists of collectors, garage sale and flea market shoppers, antique dealers, E-bay shoppers, and quilters.

☑ SCIENCE & HUMANITIES PRESS

P.O. Box 7151, Chesterfield MO 63006-7151. (636)394-4950. E-mail: pub@sciencehumanitiespress.com. Website: www.sciencehumanitiespress.com. **Acquisitions:** Dr. Bud Banis, publisher. Publishes trade paperback originals and reprints, and electronic originals and reprints. **Publishes 20-30 titles/year. Receives 1,000 queries and 50 mss/year. 25% of books from first-time authors; 100% from unagented writers. Pays 8% royalty on retail price.** Publishes book 6-12 after acceptance of ms. Accepts simultaneous submissions. Responds in 2 months to queries; 2 months to proposals; 3 months to mss. Book catalog and ms guidelines online.

Imprints Science & Humanities Press, BeachHouse Books, MacroPrintBooks (large print editions), Heuristic Books, Early Editions Books.

Nonfiction Biography, gift book, how-to, humor, reference, self-help, technical, textbook, medical, disabilities adaptation. Subjects include Americana, business/economics, child guidance/parenting, computers/electronic, creative nonfiction, education, government/politics, health/medicine, history, hobbies, language/literature, memoirs, military/war, money/finance, philosophy, psychology, recreation, regional, science, sex, sociology, software, spirituality, sports, travel, women's issues/studies, math/statistics, management science. "Submissions are best as brief descriptions by e-mail, including some description of the author's background/credentials, and thoughts on approach to nontraditional or specialized markets. Why is the book important and who would buy it? Prefer description by e-mail. Need not be a large format proposal."

Fiction *Does not accept unsolicited mss.* Adventure, historical, humor, literary, mainstream/contemporary, military/war, mystery, plays, poetry, regional, romance, short story collections, spiritual, sports, suspense, western, young adult. "We prefer books with a theme that gives a market focus. Brief description by e-mail."

Recent Title(s) *To Norma Jeane with Love, Jimmie,* by Jim Dougherty/LC Van Savage (biography); *Growing Up on Route 66,* by Michael Lund (coming of age); *Avoiding Attendants from Hell: A Practical Guide to Finding, Hiring, and Keeping Personal Care Attendants,* by June Price.

Tips Sales are primarily through the Internet, special orders, reviews in specialized media, direct sales to libraries, special organizations and use as textbooks. "Our expertise is electronic publishing for continuous short-run, in-house production rather than mass distribution to retail outlets. This allows us to commit to books that might not be financially successful in conventional book store environments and to keep books in print and available for extended periods of time. Books should be of types that would sell steadily over a long period of time, rather than those that require rapid rollout and bookstore shelf exposure for a short time. We consider the nurture of new talent part of our mission but enjoy experienced authors as well. We are proud that many of our books are second, third, and fourth books from authors who were once our first-time authors. A good book is not a one-time accident."

☑ SCRIBNER

Imprint of Simon & Schuster Adult Publishing Group, 1230 Avenue of the Americas, New York NY 10020. (212)698-7000. Website: www.simonsays.com. **Acquisitions:** Nan Graham (literary fiction, nonfiction); Sarah McGrath (fiction, nonfiction); Susanne Kirk (fiction); Lisa Drew (nonfiction); Alexis Gargagliano (fiction, nonfiction); Brant Rumble (fiction, nonfiction); Colin Harrison (fiction, nonfiction). Publishes hardcover originals. **Publishes 70-75 titles/year. Receives thousands queries/year. 20% of books from first-time authors; 0% from unagented writers. Pays 7½-15% royalty. Offers variable advance.** Publishes book 9 months after acceptance of ms. Accepts simultaneous submissions. Responds in 3 months to queries.

Imprints Lisa Drew Books, Scribner Classics (reprints only), Scribner Poetry (by invitation only).

Nonfiction Biography. Subjects include education, ethnic, gay/lesbian, health/medicine, history, language/literature, nature/environment, philosophy, psychology, religion, science, criticism. *Agented submissions only.*

Fiction Literary, mystery, suspense. *Agented submissions only.*

Recent Title(s) *That Old Ace in the Hole,* by Annie Proulx; *Cosmopolis,* by Don DeLillo; *Random Family,* by Adrian Nicole LeBlanc.

SEAWORTHY PUBLICATIONS, INC.

207 S. Park St., Port Washington WI 53074. (262)268-9250. Fax: (262)268-9208. E-mail: publisher@seaworthy.c om. Website: www.seaworthy.com. **Acquisitions:** Joseph F. Janson, publisher. Publishes trade paperback originals, hardcover originals, and reprints. **Publishes 8 titles/year. Receives 150 queries and 40 mss/year. 60% of books from first-time authors; 100% from unagented writers. Pays 15% royalty on wholesale price. Offers $1,000 advance.** Publishes book 6 months after acceptance of ms. Does not accept simultaneous submissions. Responds in 1 month to queries. Book catalog on website or for #10 SASE; ms guidelines online.

⚬ Seaworthy Publications is a nautical book publisher that primarily publishes books of interest to recreational boaters and bluewater cruisers, including cruising guides, how-to books about boating. Currently emphasizing how-to.

Nonfiction Illustrated book, reference, technical. Subjects include hobbies (sailing, boating), regional (boating guide books). Regional guide books, first-person adventure, reference, technical—all dealing with boating.

Query with SASE, or submit 3 sample chapter(s), table of contents. Prefers electronic query via e-mail. Reviews artwork/photos as part of ms package. Send photocopies or color prints.

Recent Title(s) *Get Rid of Boat Odors*, by Peggy Hall.

Tips "Our audience consists of sailors, boaters, and those interested in the sea, sailing, or long-distance cruising."

SEEDLING PUBLICATIONS, INC.

20 W. Kanawha Ave., Columbus OH 43214-1432. Phone/Fax: (614)888-4140. E-mail: lsalem@jinl.com. Website: www.seedlingpub.com. **Acquisitions:** Josie Stewart, vice president. Estab. 1992. Publishes in an 8-, 12-, or 16-page format for beginning readers. **Publishes 10-20 titles/year. Receives 450 mss/year. 50% of books from first-time authors; 100% from unagented writers. Makes outright purchase.** Publishes book 1 year after acceptance of ms. Accepts simultaneous submissions. Responds in 6 months to queries. Ms guidelines for #10 SASE.

> O→ "We are an education niche publisher, producing books for beginning readers. Stories must include language that is natural to young children and story lines that are interesting to 5-7-year-olds and written at their beginning reading level."

Nonfiction Children's/juvenile. Science, math, or social studies concepts are considered. Does not accept mss or queries via fax. Reviews artwork/photos as part of ms package. Send photocopies.

Fiction Juvenile. Submit complete ms.

Recent Title(s) *How the Cheetah Got His Spots*, by Josie Stewar and Lynn Salem; *Beetle Jobs*, by Ryan Durney.

Tips "Follow our guidelines. Do not submit full-length picture books or chapter books. We are an education niche publisher. Our books are for children, ages 5-7, who are just beginning to read independently. We do not accept stories that rhyme or poetry at this time. Try your manuscript with young readers. Listen for text that doesn't flow when the child reads the story. Rewrite until the text sounds natural to beginning readers. Visit our website to be sure your manuscript fits our market." Does not accept manuscripts via fax. Does not accept queries at all.

Ⓝ SEPIA

Imprint of BET Books, 850 Third Ave., 16th Floor, New York NY 10022. Website: www.bet.com/books. **Acquisitions:** Glenda Howard, senior editor. Responds in 4 months to proposals.

Fiction Historical, mainstream/contemporary. "Manuscripts submitted in consideration for Sepia should be 90,000-100,000 words in length. We will review both contemporary and historical novels that display strong characters with intriguing plots." Submit proposal package including 3 sample chapter(s), synopsis.

Tips "Please do not phone to see if your manuscript was received or returned, or to find out what we thought of it. A self-addressed, stamped postcard can be enclosed with your submission if you want confirmation of its arrival. Specify whether you would like your manuscript returned or recycled if it is not right for us."

SHAMBHALA PUBLICATIONS, INC.

300 Massachusetts Ave., Boston MA 02115. (617)424-0030. Fax: (617)236-1563. E-mail: editors@shambhala.com. Website: www.shambhala.com. **Acquisitions:** Eden Steinberg, editor; Emily Bower, editor; David O'Neal, managing editor; Peter Turner, president; Beth Frankl, editor. Estab. 1969. Publishes hardcover and trade paperback originals and reprints. **Publishes 90-100 titles/year. Receives 2,000 queries and 500-700 mss/ year. 30% of books from first-time authors; 80% from unagented writers. Pays 8% royalty on retail price.** Publishes book 1 year after acceptance of ms. Accepts simultaneous submissions. Responds in 1 month to queries; 2 months to proposals; 2 months to mss. Book catalog and ms guidelines free.

Nonfiction Autobiography, biography, reference, self-help. Subjects include alternative lifestyles, anthropology/ archeology, art/architecture, creative nonfiction, general nonfiction, health/medicine, humanities, language/ literature, memoirs, philosophy, religion, spirituality, women's issues/studies. Query with SASE, or submit proposal package including outline, 2 sample chapter(s), résumé, synopsis, TOC, or submit complete ms. Reviews artwork/photos as part of ms package.

Ⓝ SHEED & WARD BOOK PUBLISHING

Imprint of Rowman & Littlefield Publishing Group, 4501 Forbes Blvd., Suite 200, Lanham MD 20706. (301)459-3366. Fax: (301)429-5748. Website: www.sheedandward.com. **Acquisitions:** Editor. Publishes hardcover and paperback originals. **Publishes 25-30 titles/year. Receives 600-1,000 queries and 600-1,000 mss/year. 25% of books from first-time authors; 90% from unagented writers. Pays 6-12% royalty on retail price. Offers $500-2,000 advance.** Publishes book 8 months after acceptance of ms. Does not accept simultaneous submissions. Responds in 1 month to queries; 2 months to proposals; 2 months to mss. Book catalog free or on website; ms guidelines online.

Ο⊓ "We are looking for books that help our readers, most of whom are college educated, gain access to the riches of the Catholic/Christian tradition. We publish in the areas of history, biography, spirituality, prayer, ethics, ministry, justice, liturgy."

Nonfiction Biography. Subjects include religion, spirituality, family life, theology, ethics. Submit proposal package including outline, 2 sample chapter(s), strong cover letter indicating why the project is unique and compelling. Reviews artwork/photos as part of ms package. Send photocopies.

Recent Title(s) *Seeing with Our Souls: Monastic Wisdom for Every Day*, by Joan Chittister, O.S.B; *Professions of Faith: Living and Working as a Catholic*, edited by James Martin, S.J., and Jeremy Langford.

Tips "We prefer that writers get our author guidelines either from our website or via mail before submitting proposals."

SHEEP MEADOW PRESS

P.O. Box 1345, Riverdale NY 10471. (718)548-5547. Fax: (718)884-0406. E-mail: poetry@sheepmeadowpress.com. **Acquisitions:** Stanley Moss, publisher. Publishes hardcover and trade paperback originals and reprints. **Publishes 10-12 titles/year. Pays 7-10% royalty on retail price.** Book catalog free.

Poetry Submit complete ms.

SIERRA CLUB BOOKS

85 Second St., San Francisco CA 94105. (415)977-5500. Fax: (415)977-5792. E-mail: danny.moses@sierraclub.org. Website: www.sierraclub.org/books. **Acquisitions:** Danny Moses, editor-in-chief. Estab. 1962. Publishes hardcover and paperback originals and reprints. **Publishes approximately 15 titles/year. Receives 1,000 submissions/year. 50% from unagented writers. Pays royalty. Offers $5,000-15,000 average advance.** Publishes book 1 year after acceptance of ms. Accepts simultaneous submissions. Responds in 1 month to queries; 2 months to proposals; 3 months to mss. Book catalog and ms guidelines online.

Imprints Sierra Club Books for Children.

• Currently not accepting unsolicited mss or proposals for children's books.

Ο⊓ The Sierra Club was founded to help people to explore, enjoy, and preserve the nation's forests, waters, wildlife, and wilderness. The books program publishes quality trade books about the outdoors and the protection of the natural world.

Nonfiction Subjects include general nonfiction, nature/environment. A broad range of environmental subjects: outdoor adventure, women in the outdoors; literature, including travel and works on the spiritual aspects of the natural world; natural history and current environmental issues. Does not want "proposals for large, color-photographic books without substantial text; how-to books on building things outdoors; books on motorized travel; or any but the most professional studies of animals." No fiction or poetry. Query with SASE. Reviews artwork/photos as part of ms package. Send photocopies.

Recent Title(s) *Downhill Slide: Why the Corporate Ski Industry is Bad for Skiing, Ski Towns, and the Environment*, by Hal Clifford; *Breaking Gridlock: Moving Towards Transportation That Works*, by Jim Motavalli; *My Story as Told by Water*, by David James Duncan.

SILHOUETTE BOOKS

233 Broadway, New York NY 10279. (212)553-4200. Fax: (212)227-8969. Website: www.eharlequin.com. Editorial Director, Silhouette Books: Tara Gavin. **Acquisitions:** Mavis Allen, associate senior editor (Silhouette Romance); Gail Chasan, senior editor (Silhouette Special Editions); Melissa Jeglinski, senior editor (Silhouette Desire); Leslie Wainger, executive editor (Silhouette Intimate Moments). Estab. 1979. Publishes mass market paperback originals. **Publishes over 350 titles/year. Receives approximately 4,000 submissions/year. Pays royalty. Offers advance.** Publishes book 1-3 years after acceptance of ms. Does not accept simultaneous submissions. Ms guidelines online.

Imprints Silhouette Romance (contemporary adult romances, 53,000-58,000 words); Silhouette Desire (contemporary adult romances, 55,000-60,000 words); Silhouette Intimate Moments (contemporary adult romances, 80,000 words); Harlequin Historicals (adult historical romances, 95,000-105,000 words); Silhouette Special Edition (contemporary adult romances, 75,000-80,000 words).

Ο⊓ Silhouette publishes contemporary adult romances.

Fiction Romance (contemporary and historical romance for adults). "We are interested in seeing submissions for all our lines. No manuscripts other than the types outlined. Manuscript should follow our general format, yet have an individuality and life of its own that will make them stand out in the readers' minds." *No unsolicited mss.* Send query letter, 2 page synopsis, and SASE to head of imprint.

Recent Title(s) *A Question of Intent*, by Merline Lovelace; *A Little Bit Pregnant*, by Susan Mallery.

Tips "The romance market is constantly changing, so when you read for research, read the latest books and those that have been recommended to you by people knowledgeable in the genre. We are actively seeking new authors for all our lines, contemporary and historical."

SILMAN-JAMES PRESS

3624 Shannon Rd., Los Angeles CA 90027. (323)661-9922. E-mail: silmanjamespress@earthlink.net. Website: www.silmanjamespress.com. **Acquisitions:** Gwen Feldman, Jim Fox, publishers. Publishes trade paperback originals and reprints. **Publishes 6-10 titles/year. Receives 75 queries and 50 mss/year. 30% of books from first-time authors; 80% from unagented writers. Pays variable royalty on retail price.** Responds in 2 months to queries; 2 months to proposals; 3 months to mss. Book catalog free.

Imprints Siles Press (publishes chess books and other nonfiction subjects).

Nonfiction Pertaining to film, theatre, music, peforming arts. Biography, how-to, reference, technical, textbook. Submit proposal package including outline, 1+ sample chapter(s), or submit complete ms. Reviews artwork/ photos as part of ms package. Send photocopies.

Recent Title(s) *Pal Benko: My Life, Games, and Compositions*; *Book on Acting: Improvisation Technique for the Professional Actor in Film, Theatre, and Television*, by Stephen Book.

Tips ''Our audience ranges from people with a general interest in film (fans, etc.) to students of film and performing arts to industry professionals. We will accept 'query' phone calls.''

SILVER MOON PRESS

160 Fifth Ave., New York NY 10010. (212)242-6499. Fax: (212)242-6799. **Acquisitions:** Hope Killcoyne, managing editor. Publishes hardcover originals. **Publishes 5-8 titles/year. Receives 600 queries and 400 mss/year. 60% of books from first-time authors; 70% from unagented writers. Pays 7-10% royalty. Offers 500-1,000 advance.** Publishes book 18 months after acceptance of ms. Accepts simultaneous submissions. Responds in 6-12 months to queries; 6-12 months to proposals; 6-12 months to mss. Book catalog for 9×12 SASE; ms guidelines for #10 SASE.

  O— Publishes educational material for grades 3-8.

Nonfiction Biography, test-prep material. Subjects include education, history, language/literature, multicultural. Query with SASE, or submit proposal package including outline, 1-3 sample chapter(s).

Fiction Historical, multicultural, biographical. Query with SASE, or submit proposal package including 1-3 sample chapter(s), synopsis.

Recent Title(s) *Ambush in the Wilderness*, by Kris Hemphill (historical fiction); *Race to Kitty Hawk*, by Edwin Raffa and Annelle Rigsby (historical fiction); *In the Hands of the Enemy*, by Robert Sheely (historical fiction).

[N] [A] [∅] SIMON & SCHUSTER

1230 Avenue of the Americas, New York NY 10020. (212)698-7000. Website: www.simonsays.com. **Pays royalty. Offers advance.** Ms guidelines online.

Imprints Simon & Schuster Adult Publishing Group: Atria Books (Washington Square Press), The Free Press (Simon & Schuster Source, Wall Street Journal Books), Kaplan, Pocket Books (Downtown Press, MTV Books, Paraview Pocket, Pocket Star, Star Trek, VH-1 Books, World Wrestling Entertainment), Scribner (Lisa Drew Books, Scribner Classics, Scribner Paperback Fiction), Simon & Schuster (Simon & Schuster Classic Editions), Simon & Schuster Trade Paperbacks Fireside, Libros en Espanol, Touchstone; **Simon & Schuster Australia:** Audio, Fireside, Kangaroo Press, Martin Books, Pocket Books, Scribner, Simon & Schuster, Touchstone; **Simon & Schuster Children's Publishing:** Aladdin Paperbacks; Atheneum Books for Young Readers (Richard Jackson Books, Anne Schwartz Books), Libros Para Ninos, Little Simon, Margaret K. McElderry Books, Simon & Schuster Books for Young Readers (Paula Weisman Books), Simon Pulse, Simon Spotlight Entertainment; **Simon & Schuster New Media:** Simon & Schuster Audio (Encore, Nightingale-Conant, Pimsleur Language Programs, Simon & Schuster Audioworks, Simon & Schuster Sound Ideas); **Simon & Schuster Online**; **Simon & Schuster Online**; **Simon & Schuster UK:** Fireside, The Free Press, Martin Books, Pocket Books, Scribner, Simon & Schuster, Simon & Schuster Audio, Touchstone, Town House.

  • See website for more details.

[N] [∅] SIMON & SCHUSTER BOOKS FOR YOUNG READERS

Imprint of Simon & Schuster Children's Publishing, 1230 Avenue of the Americas, New York NY 10020. (212)698-7000. Fax: (212)698-2796. Website: www.simonsayskids.com. **Acquisitions:** Elizabeth Law, vice president/associate publisher; Kevin Lewis, executive editor; Paula Wiseman, editorial director. Publishes hardcover originals. **Publishes 75 titles/year. Pays variable royalty on retail price.** Publishes book 4 years after acceptance of ms. Accepts simultaneous submissions. Responds in 2 months to queries; 2 months to mss. Ms guidelines for #10 SASE.

  • *No unsolicited mss.* Queries are accepted via mail.

  O— ''We publish high-quality fiction and nonfiction for a variety of age groups and a variety of markets. Above all, we strive to publish books that will offer kids a fresh perspective on their world.''

Nonfiction Children's/juvenile. Subjects include history, nature/environment, biography. **All unsolicited mss returned unopened.** Query with SASE only.

Book Publishers

Fiction Fantasy, historical, humor, juvenile, mystery, picture books, science fiction, young adult (adventure, historical, mystery, contemporary fiction). **All unsolicited mss returned unopened.** Query with SASE only.
Recent Title(s) *Duck for President*, by Doreen Cronin; *The Spider and the Fly*, by Mary Howitt, illustrated by Tony Di Terlizzi; *Pop Princess*, by Rachel Cohn.

SKINNER HOUSE BOOKS

The Unitarian Universalist Association, 25 Beacon St., Boston MA 02108. (617)742-2100 ext. 601. Fax: (617)742-7025. Website: www.uua.org/skinner. **Acquisitions:** Mary Benard, project editor. Estab. 1975. Publishes trade paperback originals and reprints. **Publishes 8-10 titles/year. 50% of books from first-time authors; 100% from unagented writers. Pays 5-10% royalty on net receipts.** Publishes book 1 year after acceptance of ms. Does not accept simultaneous submissions. Responds in 3 months to queries. Book catalog for 6×9 SAE with 3 first-class stamps; ms guidelines online.

> 0→ "We publish titles in Unitarian Universalist faith, liberal religion, history, biography, worship, and issues of social justice. We also publish inspirational titles of poetic prose and meditations. Writers should know that Unitarian Universalism is a liberal religious denomination committed to progressive ideals." Currently emphasizing social justice concerns.

Nonfiction Biography, self-help. Subjects include gay/lesbian, memoirs, religion, women's issues/studies, inspirational, church leadership. Query with SASE. Reviews artwork/photos as part of ms package. Send photocopies.
Recent Title(s) *Never Far from Home: Stories from the Radio Pulpit*, by Carl Scovel; *The Other Side of Salvation: Spiritualism and the 19th-Century Religious Experience*, by John B. Buescher; *Waking Up the Karma Fairy: Life Lessons and Holy Adventures*, by Meg Barnhouse.
Tips "From outside our denomination, we are interested in manuscripts that will be of help or interest to liberal churches, Sunday School classes, parents, ministers, and volunteers. Inspirational/spiritual and children's titles must reflect liberal Unitarian Universalist values. Fiction for youth is being considered."

GIBBS SMITH, PUBLISHER

P.O. Box 667, Layton UT 84041. (801)544-9800. Fax: (801)546-8853. E-mail: info@gibbs-smith.com. Website: www.gibbs-smith.com. **Acquisitions:** Suzanne Taylor, editorial director, humor. Estab. 1969. Publishes hardcover and trade paperback originals. **Publishes 50 titles/year. Receives 1,500-2,000 submissions/year. 8-10% of books from first-time authors; 50% from unagented writers. Pays 8-14% royalty on gross receipts. Offers $2,000-3,000 advance.** Publishes book 1-2 years after acceptance of ms. Accepts simultaneous submissions. Responds in 1 month to queries; 10 weeks to proposals; 10 weeks to mss. Book catalog for 9×12 SAE and $2.13 in postage; ms guidelines online.

> 0→ "We publish books that enrich and inspire humankind." Currently emphasizing interior decorating and design, home reference. De-emphasizing novels and short stories.

Nonfiction Humor, illustrated book, textbook, children's. Subjects include art/architecture, nature/environment, regional, interior design. Query with SASE, or submit outline, several completed sample chapter(s), author's cv. Reviews artwork/photos as part of ms package. Send sample illustrations, if applicable.
Fiction Only short works oriented to gift market. No novels or short stories. Submit synopsis with sample illustration, if applicable. Send query letter or short gift book ms directly to the editorial director.
Recent Title(s) *Unmistakably French*, by Betty Lou Phillips (nonfiction); *101 Things to Do with a Cake Mix*, by Stephanie Ashcraft (cookbook).

SOHO PRESS, INC.

853 Broadway, New York NY 10003. (212)260-1900. Fax: (212)260-1902. Website: www.sohopress.com. **Acquisitions:** Juris Jurjevics, publisher/editor-in-chief; Laura Hruska, associate publisher. Estab. 1986. Publishes hardcover and trade paperback originals. **Publishes 40 titles/year. Receives 7,000 submissions/year. 75% of books from first-time authors; 40% from unagented writers. Pays 10-15% royalty on retail price. Offers advance.** Publishes book within 1 year after acceptance of ms. Accepts simultaneous submissions. Responds in 2 months to queries; 2 months to mss. Book catalog for 6×9 SAE with 2 first-class stamps; ms guidelines online.

> 0→ Soho Press publishes literate fiction and nonfiction. Currently emphasizing mystery, literary fiction, thrillers. De-emphasizing cooking, how-to.

Nonfiction Autobiography, biography, autobiography; literary. Subjects include contemporary culture, history, memoirs, military/war, translation, travel. No self-help, how-to, or cookbooks. Submit outline, sample chapter(s).
Fiction Adventure, ethnic, feminist, historical, literary, mainstream/contemporary, mystery (police procedural), suspense. Query with SASE, or submit complete ms.
Recent Title(s) *Since the Layoffs*, by Iain Levison; *Maisie Dobbs*, by Jacqueline Winspear.

Tips "Soho Press publishes discerning authors for discriminating readers, finding the strongest possible writers and publishing them." Soho Press also publishes series: Hera (historical fiction reprints with accurate and strong female lead characters) and Soho Crime (mysteries set overseas, noir, procedurals).

SOURCEBOOKS, INC.

P.O. Box 4410, Naperville IL 60567. (630)961-3900. Fax: (630)961-2168. Website: www.sourcebooks.com. Publisher: Dominique Raccah. **Acquisitions:** Todd Stocke, editorial director (nonfiction trade); Deborah Werksman (Sourcebooks Hysteria, Sourcebooks Casablanca). Estab. 1987. Publishes hardcover and trade paperback originals. **Publishes 120 titles/year. 30% of books from first-time authors; 25% from unagented writers. Pays royalty on wholesale price. Offers advance.** Publishes book 1 year after acceptance of ms. Accepts simultaneous submissions. Responds in 3 months to queries. Book catalog and ms guidelines online.

Imprints Sourcebooks Casablanca (love/relationships); Sourcebooks Hysteria (women's humor/gift book); Sourcebooks Landmark; Sourcebooks MediaFusion (multimedia); Sphinx Publishing (self-help legal).

O→ Sourcebooks publishes many forms of nonfiction titles, generally in the how-to and reference areas, including books on parenting, self-help/psychology, business, and health. Focus is on practical, useful information and skills. It also continues to publish in the reference, New Age, history, current affairs, and travel categories. Currently emphasizing gift, women's interest, history, reference.

Nonfiction "We seek unique books on traditional subjects and authors who are smart and aggressive." Biography, gift book, how-to, illustrated book, multimedia, reference, self-help, technical, textbook. Subjects include art/architecture, business/economics, child guidance/parenting, history, military/war, money/finance, psychology, science, sports, women's issues/studies, contemporary culture. Books for small business owners, entrepreneurs, and students. "A key to submitting books to us is to explain how your book helps the reader, why it is different from the books already out there (please do your homework), and the author's credentials for writing this book. Books likely to succeed with us are self-help, parenting and childcare, psychology, women's issues, how-to, history, reference, biography, humor, gift books, or books with strong artwork." Query with SASE. 2-3 sample chapters (not the first). No complete mss. Reviews artwork/photos as part of ms package.

Recent Title(s) *Jefferson's Great Gamble*, by Charles Cerami; *40,001 Baby Names*, by Diane Stafford.

Tips "Our market is a decidedly trade-oriented bookstore audience. We also have very strong penetration into the gift-store market. Books which cross over between these 2 very different markets do extremely well with us. Our list is a solid mix of unique and general audience titles and series-oriented projects. In other words, we are looking for products that break new ground either in their own areas or within the framework of our series of imprints. We love to develop books in new areas or develop strong titles in areas that are already well developed."

SOUTH END PRESS

7 Brookline St., Cambridge MA 02139. (617)547-4002. Fax: (617)547-1333. E-mail: southend@southendpress.org. Website: www.southendpress.org. Estab. 1977. Publishes library and trade paperback originals and reprints. **Publishes 10 titles/year. Receives 400 queries and 100 mss/year. 30% of books from first-time authors; 95% from unagented writers. Pays 11% royalty on wholesale price. Offers occasionally $500-2,500 advance.** Publishes book 9 months after acceptance of ms. Accepts simultaneous submissions. Responds in up to 3 months to queries; up to 3 months to proposals. Book catalog free; ms guidelines online.

O→ South End Press publishes nonfiction political books with a left/feminist/antiracist perspective.

Nonfiction Subjects include ethnic, gay/lesbian, government/politics, health/medicine, history, nature/environment (environment), philosophy, science, sociology, women's issues/studies, economics, world affairs. Query with SASE, or submit 2 sample chapter(s), intro or conclusion, and annotated TOC. Reviews artwork/photos as part of ms package. Send photocopies.

Recent Title(s) *War Talk*, by Arundhati Roy; *Culture and Resistance*, by Edward Said.

SOUTHERN ILLINOIS UNIVERSITY PRESS

P.O. Box 3697, Carbondale IL 62902-3697. (618)453-2281. Fax: (618)453-1221. Website: www.siu.edu/~siupress. **Acquisitions:** Karl Kageff, editor-in-chief (film/theater, history, sports, poetry, regional and US history, rhetoric); Kristine Priddy, editor (civil rights, women's studies, true crime). Estab. 1956. Publishes hardcover and trade paperback originals and reprints. **Publishes 40-50 titles/year. Receives 700 queries and 300 mss/year. 40% of books from first-time authors; 99% from unagented writers. Pays 5-10% royalty on wholesale price. Rarely offers advance.** Publishes book 1-1æ years after acceptance of ms. Does not accept simultaneous submissions. Responds in 4 months to queries. Book catalog and ms guidelines free.

Imprints Shawnee Books, Shawnee Classics (regional reprint), Writing Baseball, Crab Orchard Award Series in Poetry, Theater in the Americas, Rhetorics and Feminisms, Studies in Writing and Rhetoric.

O→ "Scholarly press specializes in film and theater studies, civil rights, rhetoric and composition studies, American history, Civil War, regional and nonfiction trade, women's studies, baseball, poetry. No fiction." Currently emphasizing film and theater, American history, civil rights.

Recent Title(s) *Our Culture of Pandering,* by Paul Simon (nonfiction trade); *Film and Television After 9/11,* by Wheeler Winston Dixon (film); *Finding Susan,* by Molly Hurley Moran (true crime).

SOUTHERN METHODIST UNIVERSITY PRESS

P.O. Box 750415, Dallas TX 75275-0415. (214)768-1433. Fax: (214)768-1428. Website: www.tamu.edu/upress. **Acquisitions:** Kathryn Lang, senior editor. Estab. 1937. Publishes hardcover and trade paperback originals and reprints. **Publishes 10-12 titles/year. Receives 500 queries and 500 mss/year. 75% of books from first-time authors; 95% from unagented writers. Pays up to 10% royalty on wholesale price, 10 author's copies. Offers $500 advance.** Publishes book 1 year after acceptance of ms. Does not accept simultaneous submissions. Responds in 1 week to queries; 1 month to proposals; up to 1 year to mss. Book catalog free; ms guidelines online.

> **O→** Southern Methodist University publishes for the general, educated audience in the fields of literary fiction, sports, ethics, and human values, film and theater, regional studies. Currently emphasizing literary fiction. De-emphasizing scholarly, narrowly focused academic studies.

Nonfiction Subjects include creative nonfiction, medical, ethics/human values, film/theater, regional history. Query with SASE, or submit outline, 3 sample chapter(s), author bio, table of contents. Reviews artwork/photos as part of ms package. Send photocopies.

Fiction Literary, short story collections, novels. "We are willing to look at 'serious' or 'literary' fiction." No "mass market, science fiction, formula, thriller, romance." Query with SASE.

Recent Title(s) *How the Water Feels: Stories,* by Paul Eggers; *Requiem for a Summer Cottage: A Novel,* by Barbara Lockhart.

SPECTRA BOOKS

Subsidiary of Random House, Inc., 1745 Broadway, New York NY 10019. (212)782-8632. Fax: (212)782-9174. Website: www.bantamdell.com. Estab. 1985. Publishes hardcover originals, paperback originals, and trade paperbacks. **Pays royalty. Offers negotiable advance.** Accepts simultaneous submissions. Responds in 6 months to mss. Ms guidelines for #10 SASE.

Fiction Fantasy, literary, science fiction. Needs include novels that attempt to broaden the traditional range of science fiction and fantasy. Strong emphasis on characterization. Especially well-written, traditional science fiction and fantasy will be considered. No fiction that doesn't have at least some element of speculation or the fantastic. Query with 3 sample chapters and a short (no more that 3 double-spaced paragraphs) synopsis.

THE SPEECH BIN, INC.

1965 25th Ave., Vero Beach FL 32960-3062. (561)770-0007. **Acquisitions:** Jan J. Binney, senior editor. Estab. 1984. Publishes trade paperback originals. **Publishes 10-20 titles/year. Receives 500 mss/year. 50% of books from first-time authors; 90% from unagented writers. Pays negotiable royalty on wholesale price. Offers advance.** Publishes book 1 year after acceptance of ms. Does not accept simultaneous submissions. Responds in 3 months to queries. Book catalog for 9×12 SASE.

> **O→** Publishes professional materials for specialists in rehabilitation, particularly speech-language pathologists and audiologists, special educators, occupational and physical therapists, and parents and caregivers of children and adults with developmental and post-trauma disabilities."

Nonfiction Booklets, children's/juvenile (preschool-teen), how-to, illustrated book, reference, textbook, games for children and adults. Subjects include education, health/medicine, communication disorders, education for handicapped persons. Query with SASE, or submit outline, sample chapter(s). Reviews artwork/photos as part of ms package. Send photocopies.

Fiction "Booklets or books for children and adults about handicapped persons, especially with communication disorders. This is a potentially new market for The Speech Bin." Query with SASE, or submit outline, sample chapter(s), synopsis.

Recent Title(s) *I Can Say S; I Can Say R.*

Tips "Books and materials must be clearly presented, well written, and competently illustrated. We have added books and materials for use by other allied health professionals. We are also looking for more materials for use in treating adults and very young children with communication disorders. Please do not fax or e-mail manuscripts to us." The Speech Bin is increasing their number of books published per year and is especially interested in reviewing treatment materials for adults and adolescents.

☑ SPENCE PUBLISHING CO.

111 Cole St., Dallas TX 75207. (214)939-1700. Fax: (214)939-1800. E-mail: muncy@spencepublishing.com. Website: www.spencepublishing.com. **Acquisitions:** Mitchell Muncy, editor-in-chief. Estab. 1995. Publishes hardcover and trade paperback originals.

> • No longer accepting unsolicited proposals.

SQUARE ONE PUBLISHERS, INC.

115 Herricks Rd., Garden City Park NY 11040. (516)535-2010. Fax: (516)535-2014. Website: www.squareonepublishers.com. Publisher: Rudy Shur. **Acquisitions:** Acquisitions Editor. Publishes trade paperback originals.

Publishes 20 titles/year. Receives 500 queries and 100 mss/year. 95% of books from first-time authors; 95% from unagented writers. Pays 10-15% royalty on wholesale price. Offers variable advance. Publishes book 10 months after acceptance of ms. Accepts simultaneous submissions. Responds in 1 month to queries; 1 month to proposals; 1 month to mss. Book catalog and ms guidelines free or on website; ms guidelines online.

Nonfiction Cookbook, how-to, reference, self-help. Subjects include business/economics, child guidance/parenting, health/medicine, hobbies, money/finance, nature/environment, psychology, religion, spirituality, sports, travel, writers' guides, cooking/foods, gaming/gambling. Query with SASE, or submit proposal package including outline, author bio, introduction, synopsis, SASE. Reviews artwork/photos as part of ms package. Send photocopies.

Recent Title(s) *Talking With Your Hands, Listening with Your Eyes*, by Gabriel Grayson (reference/sign language); *Retiring Right, 3rd edition*, by Lawrence Kaplan (personal finance); *How to Publish Your Articles*, by Shirley Kawa-Jump (reference/writing).

Tips "We focus on making our books accessible, accurate, and interesting. They are written for people who are looking for the best place to start, and who don't appreciate the terms 'dummy,' 'idiot,' or 'fool,' on the cover of their books. We look for smartly written, informative books that have a strong point of view, and that are authored by people who know their subjects well."

N ST PAULS/ALBA HOUSE

Society of St Paul, 2187 Victory Blvd., Staten Island NY 10314-6603. (718)761-0047. Fax: (718)761-0057. E-mail: edmund_lane@juno.com. Website: www.alba-house.com. **Acquisitions:** Victor L. Viberti, SSP, acquisitions editor. Estab. 1957. Publishes trade paperback and mass market paperback originals and reprints. **Publishes 22 titles/year. Receives 250 queries and 150 mss/year. 10% of books from first-time authors; 100% from unagented writers. Pays 5-10% royalty.** Publishes book 10 months after acceptance of ms. Does not accept simultaneous submissions. Responds in 1 month to queries; 1 month to proposals; 2 months to mss. Book catalog and ms guidelines free.

Nonfiction Reference, scholarly, textbook, religious biographies. Subjects include philosophy, religion, spirituality. "Alba House is the North American publishing division of St. Paul, an International Roman Catholic Missionary Religious Congregation dedicated to spreading the Gospel message via the media of communications." Does not want fiction, children's books, poetry, personal testimonies, or autobiographies. Submit complete ms. Reviews artwork/photos as part of ms package. Send photocopies.

Recent Title(s) *Ethics: The Drama of the Moral Life*, by Piotr Jaroszynski and Matthew Anderson (textbook); *Have You Heard the Good News?*, by Edward T. Dowling, S.J. (homiletics).

Tips "Our audience is educated Roman Catholic readers interested in matters related to the Church, spirituality, Biblical and theological topics, moral concerns, lives of the saints, etc."

ST. ANTHONY MESSENGER PRESS

28 W. Liberty St., Cincinnati OH 45202-6498. (513)241-5615. Fax: (513)241-0399. E-mail: books@americancath olic.org. Website: www.americancatholic.org. Publisher: The Rev. Jeremy Harrington, O.F.M. **Acquisitions:** Lisa Biedenbach, editorial director. Estab. 1970. Publishes trade paperback originals. **Publishes 15-25 titles/year; imprint publishes 10-12 titles/year. Receives 200 queries and 50 mss/year. 5% of books from first-time authors; 99% from unagented writers. Pays 10-12% royalty on net receipts. Offers $1,000 average advance.** Publishes book 18 months after acceptance of ms. Responds in 1 month to queries; 2 months to proposals; 2 months to mss. Book catalog for 9×12 SAE with 4 first-class stamps; ms guidelines online.

Imprints Servant Books—publishes 10-12 titles/year.

O— "St. Anthony Messenger Press/Franciscan Communications seeks to communicate the word that is Jesus Christ in the styles of Saints Francis and Anthony. Through print and electronic media marketed in North America and worldwide, we endeavor to evangelize, inspire, and inform those who search for God and seek a richer Catholic, Christian, human life. Our efforts help support the life, ministry, and charities of the Franciscan Friars of St. John the Baptist Province, who sponsor our work." Currently emphasizing prayer/spirituality.

Nonfiction Family-based religious education programs. Subjects include education, history, religion, sex, Catholic identity and teaching, prayer and spirituality resources, Scripture study. Query with SASE, or submit outline, Attn: Lisa Biedenbach. Reviews artwork/photos as part of ms package.

Recent Title(s) *Would You Like to Be a Catholic?*, by Eugene Kennedy; *Landscape of Prayer*, by Murray Bodo; *Twelve Apostolic Women*, by Joanne Turpin.

Tips "Our readers are ordinary 'folks in the pews' and those who minister to and educate these folks. Writers need to know the audience and the kind of books we publish. Manuscripts should reflect best and current Catholic theology and doctrine." St. Anthony Messenger Press especially seeks books which will sell in bulk quantities to parishes, teachers, pastoral ministers, etc. They expect to sell at least 5,000 to 7,000 copies of a book.

🅽 🄰 ⊘ ST. MARTIN'S PRESS, LLC

Holtzbrinck Publishers, 175 Fifth Ave., New York NY 10010. (212)674-5151. Fax: (212)420-9314. Website: www.stmartins.com. Estab. 1952. Publishes hardcover, trade paperback and mass market originals. **Publishes 1,500 titles/year. Pays royalty. Offers advance.** Ms guidelines online.

Imprints Thomas Dunne Books, Griffin, Minotaur, Palgrave MacMillan (division), Priddy Books, St. Martin's Press Paperback & Reference Group, St. Martin's Press Trade Division, Truman Talley Books.

O— General interest publisher of both fiction and nonfiction.

Nonfiction Biography, cookbook, reference, scholarly, self-help, textbook. Subjects include business/economics, cooking/foods/nutrition, sports, general nonfiction, contemporary culture, true crime. *Agented submissions only. No unsolicited mss.*

Fiction Fantasy, historical, horror, literary, mainstream/contemporary, mystery, science fiction, suspense, western (contemporary), general fiction; thriller. *Agented submissions only. No unsolicited mss.*

ST. MARY'S PRESS

702 Terrace Heights, Winona MN 55987-1318. (800)533-8095. Fax: (800)344-9225. E-mail: submissions@smp.org. Website: www.smp.org. Ms guidelines online or by e-mail.

Nonfiction Subjects include religion (prayers), spirituality. Titles for Catholic youth and their parents, teachers, and youth ministers. Query with SASE, or submit proposal package including outline, 1 sample chapter(s), SASE. Brief author biography.

Recent Title(s) *Catholic Faith Handbook for Youth*; *The Total Faith Initiative*; *Living Justice and Proclaiming Peace*.

Tips "Request product catalog and/or do research online of Saint Mary Press book lists before submitting proposal."

STACKPOLE BOOKS

5067 Ritter Rd., Mechanicsburg PA 17055. Fax: (717)796-0412. E-mail: jschnell@stackpolebooks.com. Website: www.stackpolebooks.com. **Acquisitions:** Judith Schnell, editorial director (fly fishing, sports); Chris Evans, editor (history); Mark Allison, editor (nature); Ed Skender, editor (military guides); Kyle Weaver, editor (Pennsylvania). Estab. 1935. Publishes hardcover and paperback originals and reprints. **Publishes 90 titles/year. Offers industry standard advance.** Publishes book 1 year after acceptance of ms. Does not accept simultaneous submissions. Responds in 1 month to queries.

O— "Stackpole maintains a growing and vital publishing program by featuring authors who are experts in their fields, from outdoor activities to Civil War history."

Nonfiction Subjects include history (especially Civil War), military/war, nature/environment, recreation, sports, wildlife, outdoor skills, fly fishing, paddling, climbing. Query with SASE. Does not return unsolicited mss. Reviews artwork/photos as part of ms package.

Recent Title(s) *Trout from Small Streams*; *Lee's Real Plan*; *Mammal Tracks & Signs*.

Tips "Stackpole seeks well-written, authoritative manuscripts for specialized and general trade markets. Proposals should include chapter outline, sample chapter, illustrations, and author's credentials."

STANDARD PUBLICATIONS, INC.

P.O. Box 2226, Champaign IL 61825-2226. (217)898-7825. E-mail: spi@standardpublications.com. **Acquisitions:** Borislav Dzodo. Estab. 2001. publishes trade paperback originals and reprints. **Publishes 4 titles/year. Receives 20 queries and 8 mss/year. 50% of books from first-time authors; 100% from unagented writers. Pays 5-10% royalty on wholesale price, or makes outright purchase of $200-10,000.** Publishes book 8 months after acceptance of ms. Accepts simultaneous submissions. Responds in 1 month to queries; 2 months to proposals; 2 months to mss.

O— Publishes books for women at home, and for males interested in how-to information or technical content that is hard to find.

Nonfiction Biography, booklets, how-to, illustrated book, reference, technical, textbook. Subjects include business/economics, child guidance/parenting, ethnic, gardening, general nonfiction, hobbies, money/finance, recreation, sex, translation. "We have three primary focuses for the next two years. In order of priority: 1. Content of a technical nature that is difficult to find. Usually associated with trades that often restrict their knowledge or the popular public perception of legal restrictions. Examples are locksmithing, gun maintenance, magic, legal, survival. 2. How-to books in areas such as home theater, telescopes, specialized trades, etc. 3. Expanding our line of books on astrology, the occult, palm reading, horoscope, etc." Query with SASE, or submit proposal package including outline, 3 sample chapter(s), or submit complete ms. Reviews artwork/photos as part of ms package. Send photocopies.

Recent Title(s) *Visual Guide to Lock Picking*, by Mark McCloud (how-to); *Nostradamus, His Works and Prophecies*, by Theodore Garencieres.

Tips "Use Amazon.com sales rankings as a free and easy form of market research to determine the suitability of your topic matter."

STEEPLE HILL

Imprint of Harlequin Enterprises, 233 Broadway, New York NY 10279. Website: www.steeplehill.com. **Acquisitions:** Joan Marlow Golan, senior editor; Krista Stroever, editor; Anna Cory-Watson, editorial assistant; Diane Dietz, assistant editor. Estab. 1997. Publishes mass market and trade paperback originals. **Pays royalty. Offers advance.** Does not accept simultaneous submissions. Ms guidelines online.

Imprints Love Inspired.

> • "This series of contemporary, inspirational love stories portrays Christian characters facing the many challenges of life, faith, and love in today's world."

Fiction Romance (Christian, 70,000 words), inspirational romance. Query with SASE, or submit 3 sample chapter(s), synopsis.

Recent Title(s) *Hideaway*, by Hannah Alexander; *Promise of Grace*, by Bonnie K. Winn.

Tips "Drama, humor, and even a touch of mystery all have a place in Steeple Hill. Subplots are welcome and should further the story's main focus or intertwine in a meaningful way. Secondary characters (children, family, friends, neighbors, fellow church members, etc.) may all contribute to a substantial and satisfying story. These wholesome tales include strong family values and high moral standards. While there is no premarital sex between characters, in the case of romance, a vivid, exciting tone presented with a mature perspective is essential. Although the element of faith must clearly be present, it should be well integrated into the characterizations and plot. The conflict between the main characters should be an emotional one, arising naturally from the well-developed personalities you've created. Suitable stories should also impart an important lesson about the powers of trust and faith."

STENHOUSE PUBLISHERS

477 Congress St., Suite 4B, Portland ME 04101-3451. (207)253-1600. Fax: (207)253-5121. E-mail: wvarner@stenhouse.com. Website: www.stenhouse.com. **Acquisitions:** William Varner, senior editor. Estab. 1993. Publishes paperback originals. **Publishes 15 titles/year. Receives 300 queries/year. 30% of books from first-time authors; 99% from unagented writers. Pays royalty on wholesale price. Offers very modest advance.** Accepts simultaneous submissions. Responds in 1 month to queries; 3 months to mss. Book catalog free or online; ms guidelines online.

> • Stenhouse publishes exclusively professional books for teachers, K-12.

Nonfiction Subjects include education (specializing in literacy). "All our books are a combination of theory and practice." No children's books or student texts. Query with SASE, or submit outline. Reviews artwork/photos as part of ms package. Send photocopies.

Recent Title(s) *Reconsidering Read-Aloud*, by Mary Lee Hahn; *Writing for Real*, by Ross M. Burkhardt; *Knowing How*, by Mary C. McMackin and Barbara Seigel.

N STERLING PUBLISHING

387 Park Ave. S., New York NY 10016. (212)532-7160. Fax: (212)213-2495. Website: www.sterlingpub.com. **Acquisitions:** Acquisitions Editor. Estab. 1949. Publishes hardcover and paperback originals and reprints. **Publishes 350 titles/year. Pays royalty. Offers advance.** Does not accept simultaneous submissions. Responds in 4 months to queries. Ms guidelines online.

Imprints Sterling/Chapelle, Lark, Sterling/Tamos, Sterling/Prolific Impressions.

> • Sterling publishes highly illustrated, accessible, hands-on, practical books for adults and children.

Nonfiction Publishes nonfiction only. Children's/juvenile, how-to, humor, reference, adult. Subjects include alternative lifestyles, animals, art/architecture, ethnic, gardening, health/medicine, hobbies, New Age, recreation, science, sports, fiber arts, games and puzzles, children's humor, children's science, nature and activities, pets, wine, home decorating, dolls and puppets, ghosts, UFOs, woodworking, crafts, medieval, Celtic subjects, alternative health and healing, new consciousness. Query with SASE, or submit outline, 2 sample chapter(s), SASE. Reviews artwork/photos as part of ms package.

STILLWATER PUBLISHING CO.

P.O. Box 606, Stillwater MN 55082. E-mail: esbensen@pressenter.com. Website: www.stillwater-publishing.com. **Acquisitions:** Jane Esbensen Moore. Estab. 2001. Publishes harcover originals, trade paperback originals and reprints, mass market paperback originals and reprints. **Publishes 6 titles/year. Receives 250 queries and 200 mss/year. 90% of books from first-time authors; 100% from unagented writers. Pays 8-15% royalty on net receipts. Offers $500 advance.** Publishes book 9 months after acceptance of ms. Accepts simultaneous submissions. Responds in 1 month to queries; 1 month to proposals; 3 months to mss. Book catalog and ms guidelines online.

Nonfiction Autobiography, biography, children's/juvenile, coffee table book, how-to, humor, illustrated book, reference, scholarly, technical. Subjects include Americana, anthropology/archeology, art/architecture, creative nonfiction, ethnic, general nonfiction, history, hobbies, humanities, language/literature, memoirs, military/war, translation. Submit complete ms. Reviews artwork/photos as part of ms package. Send photocopies.

Fiction Adventure, comic books, historical, horror, humor, juvenile, literary, mainstream/contemporary, military/war, mystery, short story collections, suspense, western, young adult. Submit complete ms.

Recent Title(s) *Irma: Memoirs of a Vampire Gone Dry*, by Laine Jacob (fiction); *Pick Up Stick City*, by Steve Semken (fiction); *Motor Oil for the Car Guy's Soul*, by Kevin Clemens (essay).

Tips "We are willing to consider anything that's well written, except heaven/hell stories and demons."

N STIPES PUBLISHING LLC

P.O. Box 526, Champaign IL 61824-9933. (217)356-8391. Fax: (217)356-5753. E-mail: stipes@soltec.net. Website: www.stipes.com. **Acquisitions:** Benjamin H. Watts, (engineering, science, business); Robert Watts (agriculture, music, and physical education). Estab. 1925. Publishes hardcover and paperback originals. **Publishes 15-30 titles/year. Receives 150 submissions/year. 50% of books from first-time authors; 95% from unagented writers. Pays 15% maximum royalty on retail price.** Publishes book 4 months after acceptance of ms. Does not accept simultaneous submissions. Responds in 2 months to queries. Ms guidelines online.

○➤ Stipes Publishing is "oriented towards the education market and educational books with some emphasis in the trade market."

Nonfiction Technical (some areas), textbook (on business/economics, music, chemistry, CADD, agriculture/horticulture, environmental education, recreation, physical education). Subjects include agriculture/horticulture, business/economics, music/dance, nature/environment, recreation, science. "All of our books in the trade area are books that also have a college text market. No books unrelated to educational fields taught at the college level." Submit outline, 1 sample chapter(s).

Recent Title(s) *The AutoCAD 2004 Workbook*, by Philip Age and Ronald Sutliff.

N STOEGER PUBLISHING CO.

17603 Indian Head Hwy., Suite 200, Accokeek MD 20607. (301)283-6300. Fax: (301)283-6986. Website: www.stoegerindustries.com. **Acquisitions:** Jay Langston, publisher. Estab. 1925. Publishes hardback and trade paperback originals. **Publishes 12-15 titles/year. Royalty varies, depending on ms. Offers advance.** Accepts simultaneous submissions. Responds in 2 months to queries. Book catalog online.

○➤ Stoeger publishes books on hunting, shooting sports, fishing, cooking, nature, and wildlife.

Nonfiction Specializes in reference and how-to books that pertain to hunting, fishing, and appeal to gun enthusiasts. How-to, reference. Subjects include cooking/foods/nutrition, sports. Submit outline, sample chapter(s).

Recent Title(s) *Shooter's Bible 2003; Gun Trader's Guide, 26th ed.; Hunting Whitetails East & West*.

N STONE BRIDGE PRESS

P.O. Box 8208, Berkeley CA 94707. (510)524-8732. Fax: (510)524-8711. E-mail: sbpedit@stonebridge.com. Website: www.stonebridge.com. **Acquisitions:** Peter Goodman, publisher. Estab. 1989. Publishes hardcover and trade paperback originals. **Publishes 6 titles/year. Receives 100 queries and 75 mss/year. 15-20% of books from first-time authors; 90% from unagented writers. Pays royalty on wholesale price. Offers variable advance.** Publishes book 2 years after acceptance of ms. Accepts simultaneous submissions. Responds in 4 months to queries; 6 months to proposals; 8 months to mss. Book catalog for 2 first-class stamps and SASE; ms guidelines online.

Imprints The Rock Spring Collection of Japanese Literature.

○➤ Stone Bridge Press strives "to publish and distribute high-quality informational tools about Japan." Currently emphasizing art/design, spirituality. De-emphasizing business, current affairs, fiction.

Nonfiction How-to, reference, popular culture. Subjects include art/architecture, business/economics, ethnic, language/literature, philosophy, travel, popular culture. "We publish Japan- (and some Asia-) related books only." Query with SASE. Reviews artwork/photos as part of ms package. Send photocopies.

Fiction Experimental, fantasy, gay/lesbian, Japan-themed. "Primarily looking at material relating to Japan. Translations only." Query with SASE. 1-page cover letter.

Recent Title(s) *Naikan: Gratitude, Grace, and the Japanese Art of Self-Reflection*; *The Anime Encyclopedia*; *Glyphix for Visual Journaling*.

Tips Audience is "intelligent, worldly readers with an interest in Japan based on personal need or experience. No children's books or commercial fiction. Realize that interest in Japan is a moving target. Please don't submit yesterday's trends or rely on a view of Japan that is outmoded. Stay current!"

STONEYDALE PRESS

523 Main St., Stevensville MT 59870. (406)777-2729. Fax: (406)777-2521. E-mail: daleburk@montana.com. **Acquisitions:** Dale A. Burk, publisher. Estab. 1976. Publishes hardcover and trade paperback originals. **Pub-**

lishes 4-6 titles/year. **Receives 40-50 queries and 6-8 mss/year. 90% from unagented writers. Pays 12-15% royalty. Offers advance.** Publishes book 18 months after acceptance of ms. Does not accept simultaneous submissions. Responds in 2 months to queries. Book catalog available.

○┐ "We seek to publish the best available source books on big game hunting, historical reminiscence, and outdoor recreation in the Northern Rocky Mountain region."

Nonfiction How-to (hunting books). Subjects include regional, sports, historical reminiscences. Query with SASE.

Recent Title(s) *We Called This Creek Traveller's Rest*, by The Discovery Writers; *Mule Tracks: The Last of the Story*, by Howard Copenhaver; *Hunting Chukar*, by Rochard O'Toole.

STOREY PUBLISHING, LLC

210 MASS MoCA Way, North Adams MA 01247. (413)346-2100. Fax: (413)346-2196. Website: www.storey.com. **Acquisitions:** Deborah Balmuth, editorial director (building, cooking, mind/body/spirit); Deborah Burns (horses, nature, juvenile); Gwen Steege (gardening, crafts). Estab. 1983. Publishes hardcover and trade paperback originals and reprints. **Publishes 40 titles/year. Receives 600 queries and 150 mss/year. 25% of books from first-time authors; 80% from unagented writers. Pays royalty, or makes outright purchase. Offers advance.** Publishes book within 2 years after acceptance of ms. Accepts simultaneous submissions. Responds in 1 month to queries; 3 months to proposals; 3 months to mss. Book catalog free; ms guidelines online.

○┐ "We publish practical information that encourages personal independence in harmony with the environment."

Nonfiction Subjects include animals, cooking/foods/nutrition, gardening, nature/environment, home, mind/body/spirit, birds, beer and wine, crafts, building. Reviews artwork/photos as part of ms package.

Recent Title(s) *The Flower Gardener's Bible*, by Lewis and Nancy Hill; *Organizing Plain & Simple*, by Donna Smallin; *The New England Clam Shack Cookbook*, by Brooke Dojny.

STORY LINE PRESS

Three Oaks Farm, P.O. Box 1240, Ashland OR 97520-0055. (541)512-8792. Fax: (541)512-8793. E-mail: mail@storylinepress.com. Website: www.storylinepress.com. **Acquisitions:** Robert McDowell, publisher/editor. Estab. 1985. Publishes hardcover and trade paperback originals. **Publishes 12-16 titles/year. Receives 500 queries and 1,000 mss/year. 10% of books from first-time authors. Pays 10-15% royalty on net retail price or makes outright purchase of $250-1,500. Offers $0-3,000 advance.** Publishes book 1-2 years after acceptance of ms. Accepts simultaneous submissions. Responds in 1 month to queries; 3 months to mss. Book catalog free; ms guidelines for #10 SASE.

○┐ "Story Line Press exists to publish the best stories of our time in poetry, fiction, and nonfiction. Seventy-five percent of our list includes a wide range of poetry and books about poetry. Our books are intended for the general and academic reader. We are working to expand the audience for serious literature."

Nonfiction Literary. Subjects include language/literature, authors. Query with SASE.

Fiction Literary. No popular genres. Query with SASE.

Poetry Query with SASE.

Recent Title(s) *New Expansive Poetry*, by R.S. Gwynn, editor (nonfiction); *Quit Monks Or Die!*, by Maxine Kumin (fiction); *Questions for Ecclesiastes*, by Mark Jarman (poetry).

Tips "We strongly recommend that first-time poetry authors submit their book-length manuscripts in the Nicholas Roerich Poetry Contest, and first-time fiction authors send to the Three Oaks Fiction Contest."

STRIDER NOLAN PUBLISHING, INC.

68 S. Main St., Doylestown PA 18901. (215)887-3821. Fax: (215)340-3926. E-mail: msk@stridernolan.com. Submissions E-mail: submissions@stridernolan.com. Website: www.stridernolan.com. VP Marketing & Development: Jill S. Katz. President: Michael S. Katz. Publishes hardcover, trade paperback, and electronic originals. **Publishes 5-10 titles/year. Receives 50-100 queries and 25-75 mss/year. 50% of books from first-time authors; 50% from unagented writers. Pays royalty on retail price.** Accepts simultaneous submissions. Responds in 2 months to queries; 2 months to proposals; 2 months to mss. Book catalog and ms guidelines online.

Nonfiction Children's/juvenile, coffee table book, cookbook, how-to, illustrated book, reference, scholarly, self-help. Subjects include Americana, animals, art/architecture, child guidance/parenting, cooking/foods/nutrition, creative nonfiction, general nonfiction, health/medicine, history, hobbies, nature/environment, New Age, philosophy, recreation, sports, women's issues/studies, martial arts. Query with SASE. Reviews artwork/photos as part of ms package. Send photocopies.

Fiction Adventure, experimental, fantasy, gothic, historical, horror, humor, juvenile, mainstream/contemporary, military/war, mystery, occult, picture books, science fiction, short story collections, spiritual, sports, suspense, western, young adult, martial arts. Query with SASE.

Recent Title(s) *Martial Arts Student Logbook*, by Jonathan Maberry (martial arts); *The Hit-Man's Music Trivia Quizbook*, by Klotz, McCann, Hembrecht, Shames, Miller & Frederickson (music); *The Vampire Slayers Field Guide to the Undead*, by Shane MacDougall (horror/occult/folklore).

Tips "We are constantly expanding our product line to include books for adults, young adults, and children. Book lines will include The Ultimate Martial Arts Library, Children's Books, Young Adult Novels, Cookbooks, Picture Books, etc. We are a new company and we are looking for fresh, new, exciting ideas. Writers with something new to say, or a new way to say something wonderful, should consider sending their books to us first. We are very interested in working with new authors."

N STYLEWRITER, INC.

4395 N. Windsor Dr., Provo UT 84604-6301. (866)997-8953. Fax: (801)802-7888. E-mail: customerservice@swinc.org. Submissions E-mail: query@swinc.org. Website: www.swinc.org. Estab. 2001. Publishes hardcover, trade paperback, and electronic originals and reprints. **Publishes 30 titles/year; imprint publishes 5 titles/year. 99% of books from first-time authors; 99% from unagented writers. Pays 45-65% royalty on wholesale price. Offers $500-10,000 advance.** Publishes book 1 year after acceptance of ms. Accepts simultaneous submissions. Responds in 3-4 months to queries; 4-6 months to proposals; 4-6 months to mss. Book catalog and ms guidelines online.

Imprints The Early Years, Imagine, Saga, Illumination, Silhouette, Exposé Press.

Nonfiction Biography, children's/juvenile, how-to, self-help. Subjects include child guidance/parenting, cooking/foods/nutrition, creative nonfiction, education, general nonfiction, health/medicine, history, hobbies, humanities, memoirs, money/finance, New Age, philosophy, psychology, religion, science, social sciences, sociology, spirituality, translation, women's issues/studies, world affairs. Query with SASE, or submit proposal package including outline, 3 sample chapter(s). Preference of receipt by e-mail attachment in Microsoft Word. Reviews artwork/photos as part of ms package. Send JPEG or PDF via e-mail attachment to above e-mail.

Fiction Adventure, ethnic, experimental, fantasy, feminist, gothic, historical, horror, humor, juvenile, literary, mainstream/contemporary, military/war, multicultural, mystery, poetry, religious, romance, science fiction, short story collections, spiritual, suspense, western, young adult, children. Especially interested in romance, children, and horror. Submit proposal package including 3 sample chapter(s), synopsis.

Poetry Submit 5 sample poems.

Tips "Trust your vision but do the market research before querying."

SUCCESS PUBLISHING

3419 Dunham Rd., Warsaw NY 14569-9735. **Acquisitions:** Allan H. Smith, president (home-based business); Ginger Smith (business); Dana Herbison (home/craft); Robin Garretson (fiction). Estab. 1982. Publishes mass market paperback originals. **Publishes 6 titles/year. Receives 175 submissions and 10 mss/year. 90% of books from first-time authors; 100% from unagented writers. Pays 7-12% royalty. Offers $500-1,000 advance.** Publishes book 10 months after acceptance of ms. Accepts simultaneous submissions. Responds in 2 months to queries. Book catalog and ms guidelines for #10 SAE with 2 first-class stamps.

○┰ Success publishes guides that focus on the needs of the home entrepreneur to succeed as a viable business. Currently emphasizing starting a new business. De-emphasizing self-help/motivation books. Success Publishing notes that it is looking for ghostwriters.

Nonfiction Children's/juvenile, how-to, self-help. Subjects include business/economics, child guidance/parenting, hobbies, money/finance, craft/home-based business. "We are looking for books on how-to subjects such as home business and sewing." Query with SASE.

Recent Title(s) *How to Find a Date/Mate*, by Dana Herbison.

Tips "Our audience is made up of housewives, hobbyists, and owners of home-based businesses."

SUN BOOKS/SUN PUBLISHING

P.O. Box 5588, Santa Fe NM 87502-5588. (505)471-5177. E-mail: info@sunbooks.com. Website: www.sunbooks.com. **Acquisitions:** Skip Whitson, director. Publishes trade paperback originals and reprints. **Publishes 10-15 titles/year. Receives hundreds of submissions/year. 5% of books from first-time authors; 90% from unagented writers. Pays 5% royalty on retail price, or makes outright purchase.** Publishes book 16 months after acceptance of ms. Responds in 2 months to queries; 2 months to proposals; 6 months to mss. Book catalog online.

Nonfiction Biography, cookbook, how-to, humor, illustrated book, reference, self-help, technical. Subjects include Americana, anthropology/archeology, business/economics, cooking/foods/nutrition, creative nonfiction, education, government/politics, health/medicine, history, language/literature, memoirs, money/finance, multicultural, nature/environment, philosophy, psychology, regional, religion, sociology, travel, women's issues/studies, metaphysics, motivational, inspirational, Oriental studes. Query with SASE, preferably via e-mail. Reviews artwork/photos as part of ms package. Send photocopies.

Recent Title(s) *Eight Pillars of Prosperity*, by James Allen; *Ambition and Success*, by Orson Swett Marden; *Cheerfulness as a Life Power*, by Orson Swett Marden.

SUNBELT PUBLICATIONS

1250 Fayette St., El Cajon CA 92020. (619)258-4911. Fax: (619)258-4916. E-mail: mail@sunbeltpub.com. Website: www.sunbeltbooks.com. **Acquisitions:** Jennifer Redmond, publications coordinator; Lowell Lindsay, publisher. Publishes hardcover and trade paperback originals and reprints. **Publishes 6-10 titles/year. Receives 30 queries and 20 mss/year. 80% of books from first-time authors; 100% from unagented writers. Pays 10-14% royalty.** Accepts simultaneous submissions. Responds in 1 month to queries; 1 month to proposals; 3 months to mss. Book catalog free or online; ms guidelines online.

○➔ "We are interested in the cultural and natural history of the 'The Californias' in the U.S. and Mexico."

Nonfiction "We publish multi-language pictorials, natural science and outdoor guidebooks, regional references, and stories that celebrate the land and its people." Coffee table book, how-to, reference, guidebooks. Subjects include anthropology/archeology, history (regional), nature/environment (natural history), recreation, regional, travel. Query with SASE, or submit proposal package including outline, 1-2 sample chapter(s). Reviews artwork/photos as part of ms package. Send photocopies.

Recent Title(s) *Baja Legends*, by Greg Niemann (history/travel); *More Adventures with Kids in San Diego*, by Judy Botello and Kt Paxton (regional guidebook).

Tips "Our audience is interested in natural science or the cultural history of California and Baja California, Mexico. They want specific information that is accurate and up-to-date. Our books are written for an adult audience that is primarily interested in adventure and the outdoors. Our guidebooks lead to both personal and armchair adventure and travel. Authors must be willing to actively promote their book through book signings, the media, and lectures/slide shows for intended audiences."

SWEDENBORG FOUNDATION PUBLISHERS

320 North Church St., West Chester PA 19380. (610)430-3222. Fax: (610)430-7982. E-mail: editor@swedenborg.com. Website: www.swedenborg.com. **Acquisitions:** Mary Lou Bertucci, senior editor. Estab. 1849. Publishes trade paperback originals and reprints. **Publishes 5 titles/year.** Does not accept simultaneous submissions. Responds in 1 month to queries; 3 months to proposals; 3 months to mss. Book catalog free; ms guidelines online.

Imprints Chrysalis Books, Swedenborg Foundation Press.

○➔ "The Swedenborg Foundation publishes books by and about Emanuel Swedenborg (1688-1772), his ideas, how his ideas have influenced others, and related topics. A Chrysalis book is a spiritually focused book presented with a nonsectarian perspective that appeals to open-minded, well-educated seekers of all traditions. Appropriate topics include—but are not limited to—science, mysticism, spiritual growth and development, wisdom traditions, healing and spirituality, as well as subjects that explore Swedenborgian concepts, such as: near-death experience, angels, Biblical interpretation, mysteries of good and evil, etc. Although Chrysalis Books explore topics of general spirituality, a work must actively engage the thought of Emanuel Swedenborg and show an understanding of his philosophy in order to be accepted for publication."

Nonfiction Self-help, spiritual growth and development. Subjects include philosophy, psychology, religion, science. Query with SASE, or submit proposal package including outline, sample chapter(s), synopsis. "I personally prefer e-mail." Reviews artwork/photos as part of ms package. Send photocopies.

Recent Title(s) *Healing as a Sacred Path: A Story of Personal, Medical, and Spiritual Transformation*, by L. Robert Keck; *Emanuel Swedenborg: Visionary Savant in the Age of Reason*, by Ernst Benz; *Kant on Swedenborg*, edited and translated by Gregory Johnson.

Ⓝ SYBEX, INC.

1151 Marina Village Pkwy., Alameda CA 94501. (510)523-8233. Fax: (510)523-2373. E-mail: proposals@sybex.com. Website: www.sybex.com. Publisher: Rodnay Zaks. Estab. 1976. Publishes paperback originals. **Publishes 150 titles/year. Pays standard royalties. Offers competitive advance.** Publishes book 3 months after acceptance of ms. Accepts simultaneous submissions. Responds in 1 month to queries. Book catalog and ms guidelines online.

○➔ Sybex publishes computer and software titles.

Nonfiction "Manuscripts most publishable in the field of PC applications software, hardware, programming languages, operating systems, computer games, Internet/Web certification, and networking." Technical. Subjects include computers/electronic, software. Looks for "clear writing, logical presentation of material, and good selection of material such that the most important aspects of the subject matter are thoroughly covered; well-focused subject matter; clear understanding of target audience; and well thought-out organization that helps the reader understand the material." Submit outline, 2-3 sample chapter(s), résumé. Reviews artwork/photos as part of ms package. Send disk/CD.

Recent Title(s) *Photoshop Elements Solutions*, by Mikkel Haland; *Mastering Windows 2000 Server*, by Mark Minasi; *CCNA: Cisco Certified Network Associate Study Guide*, by Todd Lammle.

Tips Queries/mss may be routed to other editors in the publishing group. Also seeking freelance writers for revising existing works and as contributors in multi-author projects, and freelance editors for editing works in progress.

SYRACUSE UNIVERSITY PRESS

621 Skytop Road, Suite 110, Syracuse NY 13244-5290. (315)443-5534. Fax: (315)443-5545. Website: syracuseuniversitypress.syr.edu. **Acquisitions:** Peter B. Webber, director. Estab. 1943. **Publishes 50 titles/year. Receives 600-700 submissions/year. 25% of books from first-time authors; 75% from unagented writers. Pays royalty on net receipts. Offers advance.** Publishes book an average of 15 months after acceptance of ms. Does not accept simultaneous submissions. Book catalog for 9×12 SAE with 3 first-class stamps; ms guidelines online.

   O→ Currently emphasizing television, Jewish studies, Middle East topics. De-emphasizing peace studies.

Nonfiction Subjects include regional. "Special opportunity in our nonfiction program for freelance writers of books on New York state, sports history, Jewish studies, the Middle East, religious studies, television, and popular culture. Provide precise descriptions of subjects, along with background description of project. The author must make a case for the importance of his or her subject." Query with SASE, or submit outline, 2 sample chapter(s). Reviews artwork/photos as part of ms package.

Recent Title(s) *Islam Without Illusions: Its Past, Its Present, and Its Challenge for the Future*, by Ed Hotaling (Middle East studies); *Shohola Falls: A Novel*, by Michael Pearson; *Joyce and Reality: The Empirical Strikes Back*, by John Gordon (Irish studies).

Tips "We're seeking well-written and well-researched books that will make a significant contribution to the subject areas listed above and will be well-received in the marketplace."

NAN A. TALESE

Imprint of Doubleday, 1745 Broadway, New York NY 10019. (212)782-8918. Fax: (212)782-8448. Website: www.nantalese.com. **Acquisitions:** Nan A. Talese, publisher and editorial director; Coates Bateman, editor; Lorna Owen, associate editor. Publishes hardcover originals. **Publishes 15 titles/year. Receives 400 queries and 400 mss/year. Pays variable royalty on retail price. Offers varying advance.** Publishes book 1 year after acceptance of ms. Accepts simultaneous submissions. Responds in 1 week to queries; 2 weeks to proposals; 2 weeks to mss. Agented submissions only.

   O→ Nan A. Talese publishes nonfiction with a powerful guiding narrative and relevance to larger cultural interests, and literary fiction of the highest quality.

Nonfiction Biography. Subjects include contemporary culture, history, philosophy, sociology. *Agented submissions only.*

Fiction Literary. Well-written narratives with a compelling story line, good characterization and use of language. "We like stories with an edge." *Agented submissions only.*

Recent Title(s) *Swallows of Kabul*, by Yasmina Khadra; *Albion: The Origins of the English Imagination*, by Peter Ackroyd; *Oryx and Crake*, by Margaret Atwood.

Tips "Audience is highly literate people interested in story, information and insight. We want well-written material. See our website."

JEREMY P. TARCHER, INC.

Imprint of Penguin Group (USA), Inc., 375 Hudson St., New York NY 10014. (212)366-2000. Website: www.penguinputnam.com. Publisher: Joel Fotinos. **Acquisitions:** Mitch Horowitz, senior editor; Terri Hennessy, senior editor; Sara Carder, editor. Estab. 1972. Publishes hardcover and trade paperback originals and reprints. **Publishes 40-50 titles/year. Receives 750 queries and 750 mss/year. 10% of books from first-time authors; 5% from unagented writers. Pays royalty. Offers advance.** Accepts simultaneous submissions. Book catalog free.

   O→ Tarcher's vision is to publish ideas and works about human consciousness that are large enough to include all aspects of human experience.

Nonfiction How-to, self-help. Subjects include business/economics, child guidance/parenting, gay/lesbian, health/medicine, nature/environment, philosophy, psychology, religion, women's issues/studies. Query with SASE.

Recent Title(s) *The Hard Question*, by Susan Piver; *The Hydrogen Economy*, by Jeremy Rifkin.

Tips "Our audience seeks personal growth through books. Understand the imprint's focus and categories. We stick with the tried and true."

TCU PRESS

P.O. Box 298300, TCU, Fort Worth TX 76129. (817)257-7822. Fax: (817)257-5075. **Acquisitions:** Judy Alter, director; James Ward Lee, acquisitions editor; Susan Petty, editor. Estab. 1966. Publishes hardcover originals, some reprints. **Publishes 6-10 titles/year. Receives 100 submissions/year. 10% of books from first-time authors; 75% from unagented writers. Pays 10% royalty on net receipts.** Publishes book 16 months after acceptance of ms. Does not accept simultaneous submissions. Responds in 3 months to queries.

O— TCU publishes "scholarly works and regional titles of significance focusing on the history and literature of the American West."

Nonfiction Biography, children's/juvenile, coffee table book, scholarly. Subjects include Americana, art/architecture, contemporary culture, ethnic, history, language/literature, multicultural, regional, women's issues/studies, American studies, criticism. Query with SASE. Reviews artwork/photos as part of ms package.

Fiction Historical, young adult, contemporary. No mysteries or science fiction.

Recent Title(s) *Paul Baker and the Integration of Abilities*, edited by Robert Flynn and Eugene McKinney; *Texas Autobiographies*, by Bert Almon; *Texas Literary Outlaws*, by Steven L. Davis.

Tips "Regional and/or Texana nonfiction has best chance of breaking into our firm. Our list focuses on the history of literature of the American West, although recently we have branched out into literary criticism, women's studies, and Mexican-American studies."

TEACHING & LEARNING CO.

1204 Buchanan St., P.O. Box 10, Carthage IL 62321-0010. (217)357-2591. Fax: (217)357-6789. E-mail: customerservice@teachinglearning.com. Website: www.teachinglearning.com. **Acquisitions:** Jill Day, vice president of production. Estab. 1994. **Publishes 60 titles/year. Receives 25 queries and 200 mss/year. 25% of books from first-time authors; 98% from unagented writers. Pays royalty.** Accepts simultaneous submissions. Responds in 3 months to queries; 9 months to proposals; 9 months to mss. Book catalog and ms guidelines free.

O— Teaching & Learning Co. publishes teacher resources (supplementary activity/idea books) for grades pre K-8. Currently emphasizing "more math for all grade levels, more primary science material."

Nonfiction Children's/juvenile. Subjects include art/architecture, education, language/literature, science, teacher resources in language arts, reading, math, science, social studies, arts and crafts, responsibility education. No picture books or storybooks. Submit table of contents, introduction, 3 sample chapters with SASE. Reviews artwork/photos as part of ms package. Send photocopies.

Recent Title(s) *Group Project Student Role Sheets*, by Christine Boardman Moen (nonfiction); *Poetry Writing Handbook*, by Greta Barclay Lipson, Ed.D. (poetry); *Four Square Writing Methods (3 books)*, by Evan and Judith Gould.

Tips "Our books are for teachers and parents of pre K-8th grade children."

TEN SPEED PRESS

P.O. Box 7123, Berkeley CA 94707. (510)559-1600. Fax: (510)524-1052. E-mail: info@tenspeed.com. Website: www.tenspeed.com. **Acquisitions:** Phil Wood, president; Kirsty Melville, Ten Speed Press publisher; Lorena Jones, Ten Speed Press editorial director; Jo Ann Deck, Celestial Arts/Crossing Press publisher. Estab. 1971. Publishes trade paperback originals and reprints. **Publishes 120 titles/year; imprint publishes 70 titles/year. 40% of books from first-time authors; 40% from unagented writers. Pays 15-20% royalty on net receipts. Offers $2,500 average advance.** Publishes book 1 year after acceptance of ms. Accepts simultaneous submissions. Responds in 3 months to queries. Book catalog for 9×12 SAE with 6 first-class stamps; ms guidelines online.

Imprints Celestial Arts, Crossing Press, Tricycle Press.

O— Ten Speed Press publishes authoritative books for an audience interested in innovative ideas. Currently emphasizing cookbooks, career, business, alternative education, and offbeat general nonfiction gift books.

Nonfiction Subjects include business/economics, child guidance/parenting, cooking/foods/nutrition, gardening, health/medicine, money/finance, nature/environment, New Age (mind/body/spirit), recreation, science. "No fiction." Query with SASE, or submit proposal package including sample chapter(s).

Recent Title(s) *How to Be Happy, Dammit*, by Karen Salmansohn; *The Bread Baker's Apprentice*, by Peter Reinhart.

Tips "We like books from people who really know their subject, rather than people who think they've spotted a trend to capitalize on. We like books that will sell for a long time, rather than nine-day wonders. Our audience consists of a well-educated, slightly weird group of people who like food, the outdoors, and take a light, but serious, approach to business and careers. Study the backlist of each publisher you're submitting to and tailor your proposal to what you perceive as their needs. Nothing gets a publisher's attention like someone who knows what he or she is talking about, and nothing falls flat like someone who obviously has no idea who he or she is submitting to."

THIRD WORLD PRESS

P.O. Box 19730, Chicago IL 60619. (773)651-0700. Fax: (773)651-7286. E-mail: twpress3@aol.com. Publisher: Haki R. Madhubuti. **Acquisitions:** Bennett Johnson. Estab. 1967. Publishes hardcover and trade paperback originals and reprints. **Publishes 20 titles/year. Receives 200-300 queries and 200 mss/year. 20% of books from first-time authors; 80% from unagented writers. Pays royalty on retail price. Individual arrangement with author depending on the book, etc.** Publishes book 18 months after acceptance of ms. Accepts simultaneous submissions. Responds in 6 months to queries; 5 months to mss. Book catalog free; ms guidelines for #10 SASE.

- Third World Press is open to submissions in July only.

Nonfiction Children's/juvenile, illustrated book, reference, self-help, textbook, African-centered; African-American materials. Subjects include anthropology/archeology, education, ethnic, government/politics, health/medicine, history, language/literature, philosophy, psychology, regional, religion, sociology, women's issues/studies, Black studies, literary criticism. Query with SASE, or submit outline, 5 sample chapter(s). Reviews artwork/photos as part of ms package. Send photocopies.

Fiction Ethnic, feminist, historical, juvenile (animal, easy-to-read, fantasy, historical, contemporary), literary, mainstream/contemporary, picture books, plays, short story collections, young adult (easy-to-read/teen, folktales, historical), African-centered, African-American materials, preschool/picture book. "We primarily publish nonfiction, but will consider fiction by and about Blacks." Query with SASE, or submit outline, 5 sample chapter(s), synopsis.

Poetry African-centered and African-American materials. Submit complete ms.

Recent Title(s) *In Montgomery and Other Poems*, by Gwendolyn Brooks; *Tough Notes: A Healing Call for Creating Exceptional Black Men*, by Haki R. Madhubuti; *The Paradox of Loyalty*, edited by Julianne Malveaux and Reginna A. Green.

TIDEWATER PUBLISHERS

Cornell Maritime Press, Inc., P.O. Box 456, Centreville MD 21617-0456. (410)758-1075. Fax: (410)758-6849. **Acquisitions:** Charlotte Kurst, managing editor. Estab. 1938. Publishes hardcover and paperback originals. **Publishes 7-9 titles/year. Receives 150 submissions/year. 41% of books from first-time authors; 99% from unagented writers. Pays 7½-15% royalty on retail price.** Publishes book 1 year after acceptance of ms. Does not accept simultaneous submissions. Responds in 2 months to queries. Book catalog for 10×13 SAE with 5 first-class stamps.

O→ Tidewater Publishers issues adult nonfiction works related to the Chesapeake Bay area, Delmarva, or Maryland in general. "The only fiction we handle is juvenile, and it must have a regional focus."

Nonfiction Regional subjects only. Children's/juvenile, cookbook, illustrated book, reference. Subjects include art/architecture, history, regional, natural history, folklore, Chesapeake watercraft. Query with SASE, or submit outline, sample chapter(s). Reviews artwork/photos as part of ms package.

Fiction Regional juvenile fiction only. Query with SASE, or submit outline, sample chapter(s), synopsis.

Recent Title(s) *Perry's Baltimore Adventure*, by Peter Dans, illustrated by Kim Harrell; *Maryland Lost and Found . . . Again*, by Eugene Meyer.

Tips "Our audience is made up of readers interested in works that are specific to the Chesapeake Bay and Delmarva Peninsula area. We do not publish personal narratives, adult fiction, or poetry."

TILBURY HOUSE, PUBLISHERS

imprint of Harpswell Press, Inc., 2 Mechanic St., Gardiner ME 04345. (207)582-1899. Fax: (207)582-8227. E-mail: tilbury@tilburyhouse.com. Website: www.tilburyhouse.com. Publisher: Jennifer Bunting (New England, maritime, children's). **Acquisitions:** Audrey Maynard, children's book editor. Estab. 1990. Publishes hardcover originals, trade paperback originals. **Publishes 10 titles/year. Pays royalty.** Book catalog free; ms guidelines online.

Nonfiction Regional adult biography/history/maritime/nature, and children's picture books. Submit complete ms. Reviews artwork/photos as part of ms package. Send photocopies.

Recent Title(s) *On Wilderness: Voices from Maine* (adult nonfiction); *Life Between the Tides: Marine Plants and Animals of the Northeast* (adult nonfiction); *Life Under Ice*, by Mary Cerullo (children's nonfiction).

TIMBERWOLF PRESS, INC.

202 N. Allen Dr., Suite A, Allen TX 75013. (972)359-0911. Fax: (972)359-0525. E-mail: submissions@timberwolfpress.com. Website: www.timberwolfpress.com. **Acquisitions:** Carol Woods, senior editor. Publishes trade paperback originals, hardcovers, and audiobooks. **Publishes 24-30 titles/year. Receives 1,400+ queries and**

Book Publishers

600+ mss/year. **40% of books from first-time authors; 90% from unagented writers. Pays royalty on wholesale price. Two-tiered advance structure, depending on author's potential. Offers industry standard advance or better, or lower advance with immediate royalties.** Publishes book 1 year after acceptance of ms. Accepts simultaneous submissions. Responds in 3 months to queries; 6 months to mss. Book catalog and ms guidelines online.

Fiction Fantasy, military/war, mystery, science fiction, suspense, western, children's. "In addition to the p-book, we present each title in next generation fully-cast, dramatized, unabridged audio theater, available in the usual formats; and downloadable in all formats from our website. So our stories must maintain tension and pace. Think exciting. Think breathless. Think terrific story, terrific characters, terrific writing." Query via e-mail only.

Recent Title(s) *Galactic Convoy*, from the Helmsman Series, by Bill Baldwin (military science fiction); *Velda*, by Ron Miller (mystery).

Tips "We accept e-queries and e-submissions only. And polish that query. Grammar, punctuation, and spelling are as important in e-queries and e-submissions as they are in p-queries."

Ⓐ MEGAN TINGLEY BOOKS

Imprint of Little, Brown & Co., 1271 Avenue of the Americas, New York NY 10020. (212)522-8700. Fax: (212)522-7997. Website: www.lb-kids.com. **Acquisitions:** Megan Tingley, editor-in-chief; Sara Morling, assistant editor. Publishes hardcover and trade paperback originals and reprints. **Publishes 80-100 titles/year; imprint publishes 10-20 titles/year. Receives 500-1,000 queries and 500-1,000 mss/year. 2% of books from first-time authors; 5% from unagented writers. Pays 0-15% royalty on retail price, or makes outright purchase.** Publishes book 2 years after acceptance of ms. Accepts simultaneous submissions. Responds in 1 month to queries; 6-8 weeks to proposals; 6-8 weeks to mss.

> ○━ Megan Tingley Books is an imprint of the children's book department of Little, Brown and Company. Currently looking for all formats with special interest in humor, music, multicultural, supernatural, narrative nonfiction, poetry, and unusual art styles. No fairy tales.

Nonfiction Children's/juvenile. Subjects include animals, art/architecture, cooking/foods/nutrition, creative nonfiction, ethnic, gay/lesbian, history, hobbies, language/literature, memoirs, multicultural, music/dance, nature/environment, photography, science, sports, all juvenile interests. *Agented submissions and queries only.* Ideally, books should be about a subject that hasn't been dealt with for children before. Reviews artwork/photos as part of ms package. Send photocopies. No original pieces.

Fiction Juvenile, picture books, young adult. *Agented submissions only.* Strong, contemporary female characters preferred. No genre novels (romance, mystery, science fiction, etc.).

Recent Title(s) *Otto Goes to the Beach*, by Todd Parr; *O'Baby!*, by Leo Landry; *Keeping You a Secret*, by Julie Ann Peters.

Tips "Do your research. Know our submission policy. Do not fax or call."

THE TOBY PRESS, LTD.

P.O. Box 8531, New Milford CT 06776-8531. Fax: (203)830-8512. Website: www.tobypress.com. **Acquisitions:** Editorial Director (fiction, biography). Publishes hardcover originals and paperbacks. **Publishes 20-25 titles/year. Receives 300 queries/year. 50% of books from first-time authors; 10% from unagented writers. Offers advance.** Publishes book up to 2 year after acceptance of ms. Accepts simultaneous submissions.

> ○━ The Toby Press publishes literary fiction.

Nonfiction Biography.

Fiction Literary.

Recent Title(s) *Foiglman*, by Aharon Megged; *With*, by Donald Harington.

TRAFALGAR SQUARE PUBLISHING

P.O. Box 257, N. Pomfret VT 05053-0257. (802)457-1911. Fax: (802)457-1913. E-mail: tsquare@sover.net. Website: www.horseandriderbooks.com. Publisher: Caroline Robbins. **Acquisitions:** Martha Cook, managing editor. Estab. 1985. Publishes hardcover and trade paperback originals and reprints. **Publishes 10 titles/year. Pays royalty. Offers advance.** Responds in 2 months to queries.

> ○━ "We publish high quality instructional books for horsemen and horsewomen, always with the horse's welfare in mind."

Nonfiction "We publish books for intermediate to advanced riders and horsemen." Subjects include animals (horses). "No stories, children's books, or horse biographies." Query with SASE, or submit proposal package including 1-2 sample chapter(s), outline or table of contents, letter of writer's qualifications, and audience for book's subject.

Recent Title(s) *Horse Housing*, by Richard Klimesh and Cherry Hill; *Yoga for Equestrians*, by Linda Benedik; *It's Not Just About the Ribbons*, by Jane Savoie.

TRAILS MEDIA GROUP, INC.

P.O. Box 317, Black Earth WI 53515. (608)767-8000. Fax: (608)767-5444. E-mail: books@wistrails.com. Website: www.trailsbooks.com. Director: Michael Martin. **Acquisitions:** Stan Stoga, acquisitions editor. Publishes hardcover originals, trade paperback originals, and reprints. **Publishes 12 titles/year. Pays royalty. Offers advance.** Does not accept simultaneous submissions. Responds in 2 months to proposals.
Imprints Trails Books, Prairie Oak Press.

> **O─** Trails Media Group publishes exclusively Midwest regional nonfiction. Currently emphasizing travel, sports, recreation, home and garden.

Nonfiction ''Any work considered must have a strong tie to Wisconsin and/or the Midwest region.'' Subjects include art/architecture, gardening, general nonfiction, history, regional, sports, travel, folklore, general trade subjects. No poetry or fiction. Query with SASE, or submit outline, 1 sample chapter(s).
Tips ''When we say we publish regional works only, we mean Wisconsin, Minnesota, Michigan, Illinois, Iowa, Indiana. Please do not submit books of national interest. We cannot consider them.''

N: TRANS NATION

2715 Buford Hwy. NE, Atlanta GA 30324. Fax: (404)634-3739. E-mail: info@transnation.us. Website: www.transnation.us. **Acquisitions:** Ronald Ashley, editor (general submissions); and Juan Maldonado, editor (Spanish submissions). Estab. 2001. Publishes hardcover, trade paperback, mass market paperback originals, and electronic originals and reprints. **Publishes 10-15 titles/year. Receives 45 queries and 20 mss/year. 80% of books from first-time authors; 100% from unagented writers. Pays 15-20% royalty on wholesale price.** Publishes book 9 months after acceptance of ms. Accepts simultaneous submissions. Responds in 1 month to queries; 3 months to proposals; 3 months to mss. Book catalog online; ms guidelines by e-mail.
Nonfiction Audiocassettes, booklets, children's/juvenile, multimedia, reference, bilingual safety training materials (especially English-Spanish and Spanish-English). Subjects include contemporary culture, education, language/literature, multicultural, translation, training materials. ''We specialize in Spanish/English publications, translation, and education materials.'' Submit complete ms with cover letter and outline. Reviews artwork/photos as part of ms package. Send photocopies.
Fiction Erotica, ethnic, multicultural, will consider quality work in other categories. Does not want poetry or science fiction. ''We will begin publishing fiction in 2004, and are interested in manuscripts geared toward a multicultural audience.'' Submit proposal package including 1 sample chapter(s), synopsis.
Recent Title(s) *1,000 Spanish Commands: Public Safety*, by Irene Walsh (translation); *Ingles Rapido 1,000: Construccion*, by Irene Welsh (translation).
Tips ''Audience is multicultural, English and Spanish speakers. Please be sure to include appropriate contact information. If we are interested, we will contact you normally within 30 days of receipt of manuscript.''

TRANSNATIONAL PUBLISHERS, INC.

410 Saw Mill River Rd., Ardsley NY 10502. (914)693-5100. Fax: (914)693-4430. E-mail: info@transnationalpubs.com. Website: www.transnationalpubs.com. Publisher: Heike Fenton. Estab. 1980. **Publishes 45-50 titles/year. Receives 40-50 queries and 30 mss/year. 60% of books from first-time authors; 95% from unagented writers. Pays royalty.** Publishes book 6-9 months after acceptance of ms. Accepts simultaneous submissions. Responds in 1 month to queries. Book catalog and ms guidelines free.

> **O─** ''We provide specialized international law publications for the teaching of law and law-related subjects in law school classroom, clinic, and continuing legal education settings.'' Currently emphasizing any area of international law that is considered a current issue/event.

Nonfiction Reference, technical, textbook. Subjects include business/economics, government/politics, women's issues/studies, international law. Query with SASE, or submit proposal package including sample chapter(s), TOC, and introduction.
Recent Title(s) *Introduction to International Criminal Law*, by M. Cherif Basslouni; *Trade, Inequality & Justice*, by Frank J. Garcia; *International Criminal Evidence*, by the Honorable Richard May and Marieke Wlerda.

TRAVELERS' TALES

330 Townsend St., Suite 208, San Francisco CA 94107. (415)227-8600. Fax: (415)227-8600. E-mail: ttales@travelerstales.com. Submissions E-mail: submit@travelerstales.com. Website: www.travelerstales.com. **Acquisitions:** James O'Reilly and Larry Habegger, series editors. Publishes inspirational travel books, mostly anthologies and travel advice books. **Publishes 8-10 titles/year. Pays $100 honorarium for anthology pieces.** Accepts simultaneous submissions. Ms guidelines online.
Imprints Travelers' Tales Guides, Footsteps, Travelers' Tales Classics.
Nonfiction Subjects include all aspects of travel.
Recent Title(s) *The Best Travelers' Tales 2004*; *Hyenas Laughed at Me and Now I Know Why*; *Travelers' Tales China*.

Tips ''We publish personal nonfiction stories and anecdotes—funny, illuminating, adventurous, frightening, or grim. Stories should reflect that unique alchemy that occurs when you enter unfamiliar territory and begin to see the world differently as a result. Stories that have already been published, including book excerpts, are welcome as long as the authors retain the copyright or can obtain permission from the copyright holder to reprint the material. We do not publish fiction.''

TREBLE HEART BOOKS

1284 Overlook Dr., Sierra Vista AZ 85635. (520)458-5602. Fax: (520)458-5618. Submissions E-mail: submissions @trebleheartbooks.com. Website: www.trebleheartbooks.com. **Acquisitions:** Lee Emory, owner/publisher (fiction, nonfiction, romance, mystery, suspense, paranormal, metaphysical, historical, Westerns, thrillers—no children's books). Estab. 2001. Publishes trade paperback originals and reprints (limited), and electronic originals. **Publishes approximately 48 titles/year. Receives 500 queries and 1,000 mss/year. 50% of books from first-time authors; 90% from unagented writers. Pays 15-35% royalty on wholesale price, or retail price.** Publishes book 8-12 months after acceptance of ms. Does not accept simultaneous submissions. Responds in 3 weeks to queries; 2 months to proposals; 3-4 months to mss. Ms guidelines online.

Imprints MountainView (inspirational fiction and nonfiction, most faiths); Sundowners (Westerns).

Nonfiction How-to, humor, self-help. Subjects include creative nonfiction, general nonfiction, health/medicine, New Age, psychology, religion, spirituality, women's issues/studies. ''Writing skills must be top notch to make it here. We have 12 editors to serve. Study the guidelines and write in the lively, active voice with a fresh slant.'' Submit complete ms. Query by e-mail. Reviews artwork/photos as part of ms package. Send TIFF or PDF files on CD or via e-mail.

Fiction Adventure, fantasy, historical, horror, humor, mainstream/contemporary, mystery, occult, religious, romance, science fiction, short story collections, spiritual, suspense, western. ''Follow our guidelines. Authors are encouraged to write outside of the box here, but traditional stories and plots are also accepted if handled with a fresh twist or approach.'' Submit complete ms. Query by e-mail. Hardcopy submissions are not accepted. Please submit via e-mail only.

Recent Title(s) *Apostasy Revealed*, by Nicholoas A. Stivers (religious nonfiction); *Managing Fear*, by Stanley Popovich (nonfiction); *Death Rides a Pale Horse*, by Dusty Rhodes (western).

Tips ''We love book lovers who want to be entertained or are interested in religion, spirituality (metaphysical) fiction, and nonfiction. Ages from 13-100. We accept unagented submissions, but do not accept hard copy manuscripts. All submissions must come to us via e-mail or attachment. We now require a 90-day exclusive to have time to move the manuscript through our reading staff before you submit elsewhere. Study and follow our guidelines and style sheets.''

TRICYCLE PRESS

P.O. Box 7123, Berkeley CA 94707. (510)559-1600. Website: www.tenspeed.com. **Acquisitions:** Nicole Geiger, publisher; Abigail Samoun, project editor. Estab. 1993. Publishes hardcover and trade paperback originals. **Publishes 18-20 titles/year. 20% of books from first-time authors; 60% from unagented writers. Pays 15-20% royalty on net receipts. Offers $0-9,000 advance.** Publishes book 1-2 years after acceptance of ms. Accepts simultaneous submissions. Responds in 4-6 months to mss. Book catalog for 9×12 SASE with 3 first-class stamps or visit the website; ms guidelines online.

    O—¬ ''Tricycle Press looks for something outside the mainstream; books that encourage children to look at the world from a possibly alternative angle. We have been trying to expand into the educational market and middle grade fiction.''

Nonfiction Biography, children's/juvenile, gift book, how-to, humor, illustrated book, self-help, picture books. Subjects include animals, art/architecture, creative nonfiction, film/cinema/stage, gardening, health/medicine, multicultural, music/dance, nature/environment, photography, science, travel, health, geography, math. Submit 2-3 chapters, or 20 pages and TOC. Reviews artwork/photos as part of ms package. Send photocopies.

Fiction Preteen. ''One-off middle grade novels—quality fiction, 'tween fiction.'' Board books and picture books: Submit complete ms. Middle grade books and other longer projects: Send complete outline and 2-3 sample chapters (ages 9-14).

Recent Title(s) *Yesterday I Had the Blues*, by Jeron Frame, illustrated by Gregory Christie; *The Young Adventurer's Guide to Everest: From Avalanche to Zopkio*, by Jonathan Chester; *Don't Laugh at Me*, by Steve Seskin and Allen Shamblin, illustrated by Glin Dibley.

THE TRINITY FOUNDATION

PO Box 68, Unicoi TN 37692. (423)743-0199. Fax: (423)743-2005. E-mail: jrob1517@aol.com. Website: www.tri nityfoundation.org. **Acquisitions:** John Robbins. Publishes hardcover and paperback originals and reprints. **Publishes 5 titles/year. Makes outright purchase of $1-1,500.** Publishes book 9 months after acceptance of ms. Responds in 1 month to queries; 1 month to proposals; 3 months to mss. Book catalog online.

Nonfiction "Only books that confirm to the philosophy and theology of the Westminster Confession of Faith." Textbook. Subjects include business/economics, education, government/politics, history, philosophy, religion, science. Query with SASE. "Very few unsolicited manuscripts meet our requirements. Read at least 1 of our books before sending a query."

TRUMAN STATE UNIVERSITY PRESS

100 E. Normal St., Kirksville MO 63501-4221. (660)785-7336. Fax: (660)785-4480. E-mail: tsup@truman.edu. Website: tsup.truman.edu. **Acquisitions:** Nancy Rediger, director/editor-in-chief (regional, poetry); Raymond Mentzer (early modern history). **Publishes 10 titles/year. Pays 7% royalty on net receipts.** Ms guidelines online.
Nonfiction Early modern, regional, poetry.
Recent Title(s) *When the Railroad Leaves Town*; *Kindled Terraces: American Poets in Greece*; *Husbands, Wives, and Concubines*.

TURTLE BOOKS

866 United Nations Plaza, Suite #525, New York NY 10017. (212)644-2020. Fax: (212)223-4387. Website: www.t urtlebooks.com. **Acquisitions:** John Whitman, publisher (children's picture books). Publishes hardcover and trade paperback originals. **Publishes 6-8 titles/year. Receives 1,000 mss/year. 25% of books from first-time authors; 50% from unagented writers. Pays royalty on retail price. Offers advance.** Publishes book 12 months after acceptance of ms. Accepts simultaneous submissions.
    O─┐ Turtle Books publishes children's picture books.
Nonfiction Children's/juvenile, illustrated book. Subjects include animals, education, history, language/literature, multicultural, nature/environment, regional, any subject suitable for a children's picture book. Submit complete ms. Reviews artwork/photos as part of ms package. Send photocopies, no original art.
Fiction Adventure, ethnic, fantasy, historical, multicultural, regional, sports, western. Subjects suitable for children's picture books. "We are looking for good stories which can be illustrated as children's picture books." Submit complete ms.
Poetry Must be suitable for an illustrated children's book format. Submit complete ms.
Recent Title(s) *Keeper of the Swamp*, by Ann Garrett; *The Crab Man*, by Patricia Van West; *Alphabet Fiesta*, by Anne Miranda (children's picture books).
Tips "Our preference is for stories rather than concept books. We will consider only children's picture book manuscripts."

TURTLE PRESS

S.K. Productions, P.O. Box 290206, Wethersfield CT 06129-0206. (860)721-1198. Fax: (860)529-7775. E-mail: editorial@turtlepress.com. Website: www.turtlepress.com. **Acquisitions:** Cynthia Kim, editor. Publishes hardcover originals, trade paperback originals and reprints. **Publishes 4-8 titles/year. Pays 8-10% royalty. Offers $500-1,500 advance.** Accepts simultaneous submissions. Responds in 1 month to queries. Ms guidelines online.
    O─┐ Turtle Press publishes sports and martial arts nonfiction for a specialty niche audience. Currently emphasizing martial arts, eastern philosophy. De-emphasizing self-help.
Nonfiction How-to, self-help. Subjects include philosophy, sports, martial arts. "We prefer tightly targeted topics on which there is little or no information available in the market, particularly for our sports and martial arts titles." Query with SASE.
Recent Title(s) *Warrior Speed*, by Ted Weimann; *The Art of Harmony*, by Sang H. Kim; *Fighting Science*, by Martina Sprague.

TUTTLE PUBLISHING

153 Milk St., 4th Floor, Boston MA 02109. Publishing Director: Ed Walters. **Acquisitions:** Editorial Acquisitions. Estab. 1832. Publishes hardcover and trade paperback originals and reprints. **Publishes 125 titles/year. Receives 1,000 queries/year. 20% of books from first-time authors; 40% from unagented writers. Pays 5-10% royalty on net or retail price, depending on format and kind of book. Offers advance.** Publishes book 18 months after acceptance of ms. Accepts simultaneous submissions. Responds in 4 months to proposals.
    O─┐ "Tuttle is America's leading publisher of books on Japan and Asia."
Nonfiction Self-help. Subjects include ethnic, health/medicine, philosophy (Eastern), religion (Eastern), Taoist. Query with SASE, or submit outline. Cannot guarantee return of ms.
Recent Title(s) *Zen Master Raven*, by Robert Aitken; *Bruce Lee: The Celebrated Life of the Golden Dragon*, by John Little; *Haiku: Poetry Ancient and Modern*, by Jackie Hardy.

◙ TYNDALE HOUSE PUBLISHERS, INC.

351 Executive Dr., Carol Stream IL 60188. (630)668-8300. Website: www.tyndale.com. **Acquisitions:** Ms Review Committee. Estab. 1962. Publishes hardcover and trade paperback originals and mass paperback reprints.

Publishes 225-250 titles/year. 5% of books from first-time authors. Pays negotiable royalty. Offers negotiable advance. Publishes book 9 months after acceptance of ms. Accepts simultaneous submissions. Responds in 3 months to queries; 6 months to mss. Ms guidelines for 9×12 SAE and $2.40 for postage or visit website.

⟳ Tyndale House publishes "practical, user-friendly Christian books for the home and family."

Nonfiction Children's/juvenile, self-help (Christian growth). Subjects include child guidance/parenting, religion, devotional/inspirational, theology/Bible doctrine, contemporary/critical issues. Prefers agented submissions. Query with SASE, or submit outline. *No unsolicited mss.*

Fiction Romance, Christian (children's, general, inspirational, mystery/suspense, thriller, romance). Prefers agented submissions. Should read romance (historical, contemporary), suspense, historical, and contemporary. Christian truths must be woven into the story organically. No short story collections. Youth books: character building stories with Christian perspective. Especially interested in ages 10-14. "We primarily publish Christian historical romances, with occasional contemporary, suspense, or standalones." No short story collections. Query with SASE, or submit outline, 3 sample chapter(s), synopsis. *No unsolicited mss.*

Recent Title(s) *The Absolutes*, by James Robison; *Apocalypse Dawn*, by Mel Odom; *Into the Nevernight*, by Anne DeGraaf.

TZIPORA PUBLICATIONS, INC.

175 E. 96 St., #10-O, New York NY 10128. (212)427-5399. Fax: (413)638-9158. E-mail: tziporapub@msn.com. **Acquisitions:** Dina Grossman, publisher (success stories of immigrants in the US). Estab. 2002. Publishes hardcover, trade paperback, mass market paperback, and electronic originals. **Publishes 7 titles/year. Receives 30 queries and 2 mss/year. 90% of books from first-time authors; 100% from unagented writers. Pays 10-15% royalty. Offers $1,000 advance.** Publishes book 6 months after acceptance of ms. Accepts simultaneous submissions. Responds in 1 month to queries; 1 month to proposals; 2 months to mss. Book catalog and ms guidelines for #10 SASE.

Nonfiction Subjects include community, contemporary culture, creative nonfiction, general nonfiction, government/politics, humanities, memoirs, multicultural, philosophy, psychology, religion, social sciences, translation, women's issues/studies, world affairs, fundamentalism. "We will be concentrating on books about successes and universal opportunities immigrants find in America. Please see *Kane & Abel* by J. Archer as an example." Query with SASE, or submit proposal package including outline, 1-3 sample chapter(s), author bio. Reviews artwork/photos as part of ms package. Send photocopies or color copies, e-mail attachments.

Fiction Fiction-based or real stories. "We will be concentrating on books about successes and universal opportunities immigrants find in America. Please see *Kane & Abel* by J. Archer as an example." Query with SASE, or submit proposal package including 1-3 sample chapter(s), synopsis, author bio.

Recent Title(s) *How We Returned To Egypt*, by Dina Grossman.

Tips "Our audience is anyone who needs inspiration in order to move ahead in life. The hero of the stories will be introduced to the public in numerous ways."

UCLA AMERICAN INDIAN STUDIES CENTER

3220 Campbell Hall, Box 951548, UCLA, Los Angeles CA 90095-1548. (310)825-7315. Fax: (310)206-7060. E-mail: editor@aisc.ucla.edu. Website: www.books.aisc.ucla.edu. **Acquisitions:** Hanay Geiogamah, interim director. Estab. 1979. Publishes hardcover and trade paperback originals. **Publishes 4 titles/year. Receives 10 queries and 8 mss/year. 60% of books from first-time authors; 100% from unagented writers. Pays 8% royalty on retail price.** Publishes book 1 year after acceptance of ms. Accepts simultaneous submissions. Book catalog and ms guidelines free and on website.

⟳ "We publish nonfiction, fiction, and poetry by and about Native Americans. We publish the *American Indian Culture and Research Journal*, which accepts poetry submissions."

Nonfiction Reference, scholarly. Subjects include Americana, anthropology/archeology, ethnic, government/politics, health/medicine, history, language/literature, multicultural, religion, sociology, contemporary culture. Submit proposal package including outline, 2 sample chapter(s). Reviews artwork/photos as part of ms package. Send photocopies.

Fiction Ethnic, literary, plays, poetry, religious, short story collections, American Indian. Submit proposal package including synopsis, or submit complete ms with a cover letter.

Poetry Query, or submit complete ms.

Recent Title(s) *Cedar Smoke on Abalone Mountain*; *Keepers of the Morning Star*; *An Anthology of Native Women's Theater*.

UNION SQUARE PUBLISHING

Cardoza Publishing, 857 Broadway, 3rd Floor, New York NY 10003. E-mail: submissions@cardozapub.com. **Acquisitions:** Michelle Knoetgen (biographies, word books, cultural studies, sports, general nonfiction). Estab. 2002. Publishes hardcover originals, trade paperback originals and reprints, mass market paperback originals.

Book Publishers

Publishes 5-10 titles/year. Receives 10 queries and 5 mss/year. 80% of books from first-time authors; 95% from unagented writers. Pays 5-6% royalty on retail price. Offers $1,000-10,000 advance. Publishes book 7 months after acceptance of ms. Accepts simultaneous submissions. Responds in 1-2 months to queries; 1-2 months to proposals; 2-3 months to mss. Ms guidelines by e-mail.

Nonfiction Autobiography, biography, cookbook, how-to, self-help. Subjects include anthropology/archeology, community, contemporary culture, cooking/foods/nutrition, education, ethnic, general nonfiction, government/politics, history, hobbies, humanities, language/literature, memoirs, multicultural, music/dance, nature/environment, philosophy, recreation, religion, social sciences, sociology, spirituality, sports, translation. "Union Square Publishing is a new imprint of a long-established company, and we have yet to determine the exact role it will fill in the publishing world. We began by publishing books on writing, words, and language." Query with SASE, or submit complete ms. Reviews artwork/photos as part of ms package. Send photocopies.

Recent Title(s) *The Complete Guide to Successful Publishing*, by Avery Cardoza (how-to); *Word Master*, by J.G. Barton (language).

Tips "Audience is word lovers, aspiring publishers, bibliophiles. Potentially the general market, depending on what other titles we publish in the future."

UNITY HOUSE

Unity School of Christianity, 1901 NW Blue Pkwy., Unity Village MO 64065-0001. (816)524-3550, ext. 3190. Fax: (816)251-3552. Website: www.unityworldhq.org. **Acquisitions:** Michael Maday, editor. Estab. 1903. Publishes hardcover and trade paperback originals and reprints. **Publishes 16 titles/year. Receives 500 submissions/year. 30% of books from first-time authors; 95% from unagented writers. Pays 10-15% royalty on net receipts. Offers advance.** Publishes book 13 months after acceptance of ms. Does not accept simultaneous submissions. Responds in 2 weeks to queries; 2 weeks to proposals; 1 month to mss. Ms guidelines online.

  O— "Unity House publishes metaphysical Christian books based on Unity principles, as well as inspirational books on metaphysics and practical spirituality. All manuscripts must reflect a spiritual foundation and express the Unity philosophy, practical Christianity, universal principles, and/or metaphysics."

Nonfiction "Writers should be familiar with principles of metaphysical Christianity but not feel bound by them. We are interested in works in the related fields of holistic health, spiritual psychology, and the philosophy of other world religions." Reference (spiritual/metaphysical), self-help, inspirational. Subjects include health/medicine (holistic), philosophy (perennial/New Thought), psychology (transpersonal), religion (spiritual/metaphysical Bible interpretation/modern Biblical studies). Query with book proposal, including cover letter summarizing unique features, suggested sales and marketing strategies, TOC or project outline, and 1-3 sample chapters with SASE. Reviews artwork/photos as part of ms package. Send photocopies.

Fiction Juvenile, picture books, spiritual, young adult, visionary fiction, inspirational, metaphysical. Query with SASE.

Recent Title(s) *Looking In For Number One*, by Alan Cohen; *That's Just How My Spirit Travels*, by Rosemary Fillmore Rhea.

THE UNIVERSITY OF AKRON PRESS

374B Bierce Library, Akron OH 44325-1703. (330)972-5342. Fax: (330)972-8364. E-mail: uapress@uakron.edu. Website: www.uakron.edu/uapress. **Acquisitions:** Michael Carley, director. Estab. 1988. Publishes hardcover and trade paperback originals. **Publishes 8-12 titles/year. Receives 400-500 queries and 100 mss/year. 40% of books from first-time authors; 100% from unagented writers. Pays 5-10% royalty. Offers (possible) advance.** Publishes book 10-12 months after acceptance of ms. Responds in 2 months to queries; 2 months to proposals; 3 months to mss. Book catalog free; ms guidelines online.

  O— "The University of Akron Press strives to be the University's ambassador for scholarship and creative writing at the national and international levels." Currently emphasizing technology and the environment, Ohio history and culture, poetry, history of law, political science, and international, political, and economic history. De-emphasizing fiction.

Nonfiction Scholarly. Subjects include history, regional, science, environment, technology, law, political science. "We publish mostly in our 4 nonfiction series: Technology and the Environment; Ohio History and Culture; Law, Politics and Society, and International, Political, and Economic History." Query with SASE. Reviews artwork/photos as part of ms package. Send photocopies.

Poetry Follow the guidelines and submit manuscripts only for the contest: www.uakron.edu/uapress/poetry.html.

Recent Title(s) *Downstairs, Upstairs*, by John A. Flower; *Thick Description and Fine Texture*, edited by David B. Baker.

Tips "We have mostly an audience of general educated readers, with a more specialized audience of public historians, sociologists and political scientists for the scholarly series."

UNIVERSITY OF ALABAMA PRESS

Box 870380, Tuscaloosa AL 35487-0380. (205)348-5180. Fax: (205)348-9201. Website: www.uapress.ua.edu.
Acquisitions: Daniel J.J. Ross, director (American history, Southern history and culture, American military history, American religious history, Latin American history, Jewish studies); Daniel Waterman, acquisitions editor for humanities (American literature and criticism, rhetoric and communication, literary journalism, African-American studies, women's studies, public administration, theater, natural history and environmental studies, regional studies, including regional trade titles); Judith Knight, senior acquisitions editor (American archaeology, Caribbean archaeology, historical archaeology, ethnohistory, anthropology). Estab. 1945. Publishes nonfiction hardcover and paperbound originals, and fiction paperback reprints. **Publishes 55-60 titles/year. Receives 400 submissions/year. 70% of books from first-time authors; 95% from unagented writers. Offers advance.** Responds in 2 weeks to queries. Book catalog free.
Nonfiction Biography, scholarly. Subjects include anthropology/archeology, community, government/politics, history, language/literature, religion, translation. Considers upon merit almost any subject of scholarly interest, but specializes in communications, military history, public administration, literary criticism and biography, history, Jewish studies, and American archeology. Accepts nonfiction translations. Query with SASE. Reviews artwork/photos as part of ms package.
Fiction Reprints of works by contemporary, Southern writers. Query with SASE.
Tips Please direct inquiry to appropriate acquisitions editor. University of Alabama Press responds to an author within 2 weeks upon receiving the ms. If they think it is unsuitable for Alabama's program, they tell the author at once. If the ms warrants it, they begin the peer-review process, which may take 2-4 months to complete. During that process, they keep the author fully informed.

UNIVERSITY OF ARIZONA PRESS

355 S. Euclid Ave., Suite 103, Tucson AZ 85719-6654. (520)621-1441. Fax: (520)621-8899. E-mail: uapress@uapress.arizona.edu. Website: www.uapress.arizona.edu. **Acquisitions:** Christine Szuter, director; Patti Hartmann, senior editor; Allyson Carter, acquiring editor. Estab. 1959. Publishes hardcover and paperback originals and reprints. **Publishes 50 titles/year. Receives 300-400 submissions/year. 30% of books from first-time authors; 95% from unagented writers. Royalty terms vary; usual starting point for scholarly monography is after sale of first 1,000 copies. Offers advance.** Publishes book 1 year after acceptance of ms. Does not accept simultaneous submissions. Responds in 3 months to queries. Book catalog available via website or upon request; ms guidelines online.
O─┬ "University of Arizona is a publisher of scholarly books and books of the Southwest."
Nonfiction Subjects include Americana, anthropology/archeology, ethnic, nature/environment, regional, environmental studies, western, and environmental history. Scholarly books about anthropology, Arizona, American West, archeology, Native American studies, Latino studies, environmental science, global change, Latin America, Native Americans, natural history, space sciences, and women's studies. Query with SASE, or submit sample chapter(s), résumé. Reviews artwork/photos as part of ms package.
Recent Title(s) *Tequila: A Natural and Cultural History*, by Ana Valenzuela-Zapata and Gary Paul Nabhan (nature/food and spirits); *Loteria*, by Teresa Villegas and Ilan Stavans (art, Latino studies).
Tips "Perhaps the most common mistake a writer might make is to offer a book manuscript or proposal to a house whose list he or she has not studied carefully. Editors rejoice in receiving material that is clearly targeted to the house's list, 'I have approached your firm because my books complement your past publications in—' presented in a straightforward, businesslike manner."

THE UNIVERSITY OF ARKANSAS PRESS

201 Ozark Ave., Fayetteville AR 72701-1201. (479)575-3246. Fax: (479)575-6044. E-mail: uaprinfo@cavern.uark.edu. Website: www.uapress.com. **Acquisitions:** Lawrence J. Malley, director and editor-in-chief. Estab. 1980. Publishes hardcover and trade paperback originals and reprints. **Publishes 30 titles/year. Receives 1,000 submissions/year. 30% of books from first-time authors; 95% from unagented writers. Pays royalty on net receipts.** Publishes book 1 year after acceptance of ms. Responds in 3 months to proposals. Book catalog and ms guidelines on website or on request.
O─┬ The University of Arkansas Press publishes series on Ozark studies, the Civil War in the West, poetry and poetics, and sport and society.
Nonfiction Subjects include government/politics, history (Southern), humanities, nature/environment, regional, Arkansas, African-American studies, Middle Eastern studies, poetry/poetics. Accepted mss must be submitted on disk. Query with SASE, or submit outline, sample chapter(s), résumé.
Recent Title(s) *Promises Kept*; *Trembling Air*; *Dangerous Liaisons*.

UNIVERSITY OF CALIFORNIA PRESS

2120 Berkeley Way, Berkeley CA 94720. (510)642-4247. Website: www.ucpress.edu. Director: Lynne E. Withey. **Acquisitions:** Reed Malcolm, editor (religion and Asian studies); Doris Kretschmer, executive editor (natural history); Deborah Kirshman, editor (art); Sheila Levine, editorial director; Monica McCormick, editor (history); Naomi Schneider, executive editor (sociology, gender studies); Blake Edgar, editor (biology, archaeology, enology, viticulture); Stephanie Fay, editor (art); Stan Holwitz, editor (anthropology, public health); Laura Cerruti, editor (literature, classics); Mary Francis, editor (music, film); Charles R. Crumly, executive editor (biology). Estab. 1893. Publishes hardcover and paperback originals and reprints. **Publishes 180 titles/year. Offers advance.** Response time varies, depending on the subject. Enclose return postage to queries. Ms guidelines online.

O─ University of California Press publishes mostly nonfiction written by scholars.

Nonfiction Scholarly. Subjects include history, nature/environment, translation, art, literature, natural sciences, some high-level popularizations. No length preference. Query with SASE.

Fiction Publishes fiction only in translation.

Recent Title(s) *The Commercialization of Intimate Life*, by Arlie Hochschild; *Pathologies of Power*, by Paul Farmer; *Late Beethoven*, by Maynard Solomon.

UNIVERSITY OF GEORGIA PRESS

330 Research Dr., Athens GA 30602-4901. (706)369-6130. Fax: (706)369-6131. E-mail: books@ugapress.uga.edu. Website: www.ugapress.org. Estab. 1938. Publishes hardcover originals, trade paperback originals, and reprints. **Publishes 85 titles/year. Offers rare, varying advance.** Publishes book 1 year after acceptance of ms. Does not accept simultaneous submissions. Responds in 2 months to queries. Book catalog and ms guidelines for #10 SASE; ms guidelines online.

Nonfiction Biography. Subjects include government/politics, history (American), nature/environment, regional, environmental studies, literary nonfiction. Query with SASE, or submit 1 sample chapter(s), author bio. Reviews artwork/photos as part of ms package. Send if essential to book.

Fiction Short story collections published in Flannery O'Connor Award Competition. Query #10 SASE for guidelines and submission periods. Charges $20 submission fee. "No phone calls accepted."

Poetry Published only through contemporary poetry series competition. Query first for guidelines and submission periods. Charges $20 submission fee. #10 SASE for guidelines.

Recent Title(s) *Deep in Our Hearts: Nine White Women in the Freedom Movement*, by Connie Curry et al; *As Eve Said to the Serpent: On Landscape, Gender and Art*, by Rebecca Solnit; *Big Bend*, by Bill Roorbach.

UNIVERSITY OF IDAHO PRESS

P.O. Box 444416, Moscow ID 83844-4416. (208)885-3300. Fax: (208)885-3301. E-mail: uipress@uidaho.edu. Website: www.uidaho.edu/uipress. **Acquisitions:** Ivar Nelson, director. Estab. 1972. Publishes hardcover and trade paperback originals and reprints. **Publishes 8-10 titles/year. Receives 150-250 queries and 25-50 mss/year. 100% from unagented writers. Pays 10% royalty on net receipts. Offers occasional advance.** Publishes book 1 year after acceptance of ms. Accepts simultaneous submissions. Responds in 6 months to queries. Book catalog free; ms guidelines online.

O─ Major subjects published by the Press include the history of Idaho, the northern Rocky Mountains and the region; the natural history of the same area; Native American culture and history; mining history; Hemingway studies; Idaho human rights series; ecological literary criticism, resource, and policy studies; and literature of the region and the West.

Nonfiction Biography, reference, technical, textbook. Subjects include Americana, anthropology/archeology, ethnic, history, language/literature, nature/environment, recreation, regional, women's issues/studies, folklore. "Writers should contact us to discuss projects in advance. Be aware of the constraints of scholarly publishing, and avoid submitting queries and manuscripts in areas in which the press doesn't publish." Query with SASE, or submit proposal package including sample chapter(s), contents, and vita. Reviews artwork/photos as part of ms package. Send photocopies.

Recent Title(s) *Bold Spirit*, by Linda L. Hunt; *Common Courage*, by Andrea Vogt.

UNIVERSITY OF IOWA PRESS

100 Kuhl House, Iowa City IA 52242-1000. (319)335-2000. Fax: (319)335-2055. Website: www.uiowapress.org. **Acquisitions:** Holly Carver, director; Prasenjit Gupta, acquisitions editor. Estab. 1969. Publishes hardcover and paperback originals. **Publishes 35 titles/year. Receives 300-400 submissions/year. 30% of books from first-time authors; 95% from unagented writers. Pays 7-10% royalty on net receipts.** Publishes book 1 year after acceptance of ms. Responds in 6 months to queries. Book catalog free; ms guidelines online.

O─ "We publish authoritative, original nonfiction that we market mostly by direct mail to groups with special interests in our titles, and by advertising in trade and scholarly publications."

Nonfiction Subjects include anthropology/archeology, creative nonfiction, history (regional), language/literature, nature/environment, American literary studies. Looks for evidence of original research, reliable sources, clarity of organization, complete development of theme with documentation, supportive footnotes and/or bibliography, and a substantive contribution to knowledge in the field treated. Use *Chicago Manual of Style*. Query with SASE, or submit outline. Reviews artwork/photos as part of ms package.

Fiction Currently publishes the Iowa Short Fiction Award selections. Competition guidelines available on website. See Competition and Awards section for further information.

Poetry Currently publishes winners of the Iowa Poetry Prize Competition, Kuhl House Poets, poetry anthologies. Competition guidelines available on website.

Recent Title(s) *Fauna and Flora, Earth and Sky: Brushes with Nature's Wisdom*, by Trudy Dittmar.

Tips "Developing a series in creative nonfiction."

UNIVERSITY OF MISSOURI PRESS

2910 LeMone Blvd., Columbia MO 65201. (573)882-7641. Fax: (573)884-4498. Website: www.system.missouri. edu/upress. **Acquisitions:** (Mr.) Clair Willcox, acquisitions editor; Beverly Jarrett, editor-in-chief (American history, political philosophy, intellectual history, women's studies, African-American studies). Estab. 1958. Publishes hardcover and paperback originals and paperback reprints. **Publishes 65 titles/year. Receives 500 submissions/year. 40-50% of books from first-time authors; 90% from unagented writers. Pays up to 10% royalty on net receipts.** Publishes book within 1 year after acceptance of ms. Responds immediately to queries; 3 months to mss. Book catalog free; ms guidelines online.

> O⌐ University of Missouri Press publishes primarily scholarly nonfiction in the humanities and social sciences. Currently emphasizing American history, political philosophy, literary criticism, African-American studies, women's studies.

Nonfiction Scholarly. Subjects include history (American), regional (studies of Missouri and the Midwest), social sciences, women's issues/studies, political philosophy, African-American studies. Consult *Chicago Manual of Style*. No mathematics or hard sciences. Query with SASE, or submit outline, sample chapter(s).

Recent Title(s) *Don't Let the Fire Go Out!*, by Jean Carnahan; *Wilderness Journey: The Life of William Clark*, by William E. Foley.

UNIVERSITY OF NEBRASKA PRESS

233 N. 8th St., Lincoln NE 68588-0225. (402)472-3581. Fax: (402)472-0308. E-mail: pressmail@unl.edu. Website: nebraskapress.unl.edu. **Acquisitions:** Gary Dunham, editor-in-chief (Native American studies); Ladette Randolph, acquisitions editor (creative nonfiction). Publishes hardcover and trade paperback originals and trade paperback reprints. **Publishes 140 titles/year. Receives 1,000 queries and 100 mss/year. 60% of books from first-time authors; 95% from unagented writers. Pays 5-10% royalty on wholesale price. Offers 500-1,000 advance.** Publishes book 1 year after acceptance of ms. Responds in 1 month to queries; 1 month to proposals; 2 months to mss. Book catalog free; ms guidelines online.

Imprints Bison Books.

Nonfiction Biography, cookbook, reference, textbook. Subjects include agriculture/horticulture, animals, anthropology/archeology, creative nonfiction, history, memoirs, military/war, multicultural, nature/environment, religion, sports, translation, women's issues/studies, Native American studies, American Lives series, experimental fiction by American-Indian writers. Query with SASE.

Recent Title(s) *Local Wonders*, by Ted Kooser; *In the Shadow of Memory*, by Floyd Skloot; *Sarah Winnemucca*, by Sally Zanjani (Native American memoir).

UNIVERSITY OF NEVADA PRESS

MS 166, Reno NV 89557. (775)784-6573. Fax: (775)784-6200. E-mail: johare@unr.edu. Website: www.nvbooks. nevada.edu. **Acquisitions:** Joanne O'Hare, director and editor-in-chief (environmental arts and humanities series, western literature series, gambling series, Shepperson series in Nevada history); Sara Velez Mallea, editor (Basque studies). Estab. 1961. Publishes hardcover and paperback originals and reprints. **Publishes 25 titles/year.** Does not accept simultaneous submissions. Ms guidelines online.

> O⌐ "We are the first university press to sustain a sound series on Basque studies—New World and Old World."

Nonfiction Biography. Subjects include anthropology/archeology, community, ethnic (studies), history (regional and natural), language/literature, nature/environment (history), regional (history and geography), current affairs, gambling and gaming, Basque studies. No juvenile books. Submit proposal. No online submissions. Reviews artwork/photos as part of ms package. Send photocopies.

Fiction "We publish in Basque Studies, Gambling Studies, Western literature, and Western history." Query with SASE, or submit outline, 2-4 sample chapter(s), synopsis.

THE UNIVERSITY OF NORTH CAROLINA PRESS

P.O. Box 2288, Chapel Hill NC 27515-2288. (919)966-3561. Fax: (919)966-3829. E-mail: uncpress@unc.edu. Website: www.uncpress.unc.edu. **Acquisitions:** David Perry, editor-in-chief (regional trade, Civil War); Charles

Grench, senior editor (American history, European history, law and legal studies, business and economic history, classics, political or social science); Elaine Maisner, editor (Latin American studies, religious studies, anthropology, regional trade, folklore); Sian Hunter, editor (literary studies, gender studies, American studies, African American studies, social medicine, Appalachian studies, media studies); Mark Simpson-Vos, associate editor (electronic publishing and special projects, American-Indian studies). Publishes hardcover originals, trade paperback originals and reprints. **Publishes 90 titles/year. Receives 500 queries and 200 mss/year. 50% of books from first-time authors; 90% from unagented writers. Pays variable royalty on wholesale price. Offers variable advance.** Publishes book 1 year after acceptance of ms. Responds in 3-4 weeks to queries; 3-4 weeks to proposals; 2 weeks to mss. Book catalog free or on website; ms guidelines online.

    O→ "UNC Press publishes nonfiction books for academic and general audiences. We have a special interest in trade and scholarly titles about our region. We do not, however, publish original fiction, drama, or poetry, memoirs of living persons, or festshriften."

Nonfiction Biography, cookbook, multimedia (CD-ROM). Subjects include Americana, anthropology/archeology, art/architecture, cooking/foods/nutrition, gardening, government/politics, health/medicine, history, language/literature, military/war, multicultural, music/dance, nature/environment, philosophy, photography, regional, religion, translation, women's issues/studies, African-American studies, American studies, cultural studies, Latin-American studies, American-Indian studies, media studies, gender studies, social medicine, Appalachian studies. Submit proposal package including outline, cv, cover letter, abstract, and TOC. Reviews artwork/photos as part of ms package. Send photocopies.

UNIVERSITY OF NORTH TEXAS PRESS

P.O. Box 311336, Denton TX 76203-1336. Fax: (940)565-4590. E-mail: rchrisman@unt.edu or kdevinney@unt.edu. Website: www.unt.edu/untpress. Director: Ronald Chrisman. **Acquisitions:** Karen DeVinney, managing editor. Estab. 1987. Publishes hardcover and trade paperback originals and reprints. **Publishes 14-16 titles/ year. Receives 500 queries/year. 95% from unagented writers. Pays 7-10% royalty on net receipts.** Publishes book 1-2 years after acceptance of ms. Does not accept simultaneous submissions. Responds in 1 month to queries. Book catalog for 8½×11 SASE; ms guidelines online.

    O→ We are dedicated to producing the highest quality scholarly, academic, and general interest books. We are committed to serving all peoples by publishing stories of their cultures and experiences that have been overlooked. Currently emphasizing military history, Texas history and Texas literature, Mexican-American studies.

Nonfiction Subjects include agriculture/horticulture, Americana, ethnic, government/politics, history, language/literature, military/war, nature/environment, regional, women's issues/studies. Query with SASE. Reviews artwork/photos as part of ms package. Send photocopies.

Fiction "The only fiction we publish is the winner of the Katherine Anne Porter Prize in Short Fiction, an annual, national competition with a $1,000 prize, and publication of the winning manuscript each Fall."

Poetry "The only poetry we publish is the winner of the Vassar Miller Prize in Poetry, an annual, national competition with a $1,000 prize and publication of the winning manuscript each Spring." Query.

Recent Title(s) *Interpreters with Lewis and Clark*; *The Royal Air Force in Texas*.

Tips "We publish series called War and the Southwest; Texas Folklore Society Publications; the Western Life Series; Literary Biographies of Texas Writers; practical guide series; Al-Filo: Mexican-American studies; North Texas crime and criminal justice; Katherine Anne Porter Prize in Short Fiction."

UNIVERSITY OF OKLAHOMA PRESS

1005 Asp Ave., Norman OK 73019-6051. E-mail: cerankin@ou.edu. Website: www.oupress.com. **Acquisitions:** Charles E. Rankin, editor-in-chief. Estab. 1928. Publishes hardcover and paperback originals and reprints. **Publishes 90 titles/year. Pays standard royalty.** Does not accept simultaneous submissions. Responds promptly to queries. Book catalog for 9×12 SAE with 6 first-class stamps.

Imprints Plains Reprints.

    O→ University of Oklahoma Press publishes books for both scholarly and nonspecialist readers.

Nonfiction Subjects include political science (Congressional, area and security studies), history (regional, military, natural), language/literature (American Indian, US West), American Indian studies, classical studies. Query with SASE, or submit outline, 1-2 sample chapter(s), résumé. Use *Chicago Manual of Style* for ms guidelines. Reviews artwork/photos as part of ms package.

Recent Title(s) *The Buffalo Soldiers: A Narrative of the Black Cavalry in the West, Revised Ed.*, by William H. Leckie with Shirley A. Leckie (history); *Ojibwa Warrior*, by Dennis Banks and Richard Erdoes (American Indian studies); *Oklahoma Breeding Bird Atlas*, by Dan L. Reinking (natural history).

⊘ UNIVERSITY OF PENNSYLVANIA PRESS

4200 Pine St., Philadelphia PA 19104-4011. (215)898-6261. Fax: (215)898-0404. Website: www.upenn.edu/ pennpress. Director: Eric Halpern. **Acquisitions:** Jerome Singerman, humanities editor; Peter Agree, social sciences editor; Jo Joslyn, art and architecture editor; Robert Lockhart, history editor. Estab. 1890. Publishes hardcover and paperback originals, and reprints. **Publishes 75 titles/year. Receives 1,000 submissions/year. 20-30% of books from first-time authors; 95% from unagented writers. Royalty determined on book-by-book basis. Offers advance.** Publishes book 10 months after delivery of ms. Does not accept simultaneous submissions. Responds in 3 months to queries. Book catalog and ms guidelines online.

Nonfiction "Serious books that serve the scholar and the professional, student and general reader." Scholarly. Subjects include Americana, art/architecture, history (American, art), sociology, anthropology, literary criticism, cultural studies, ancient studies, medieval studies, urban studies, human rights. Follow the *Chicago Manual of Style. No unsolicited mss.* Query with SASE, or submit outline, résumé. Reviews artwork/photos as part of ms package. Send photocopies.

UNIVERSITY OF SCRANTON PRESS

University of Scranton, Linden and Monroe, Scranton PA 18510. (570)941-4228. Fax: (570)941-6256. E-mail: scrantonpress@scranton.edu. Website: www.scrantonpress.com. **Acquisitions:** Richard W. Rousseau, director. Estab. 1981. Publishes paperback originals. **Publishes 8 titles/year. Receives 200 queries and 45 mss/year. 60% of books from first-time authors; 100% from unagented writers. Pays 10% royalty.** Publishes book within 1 year after acceptance of ms. Does not accept simultaneous submissions. Book catalog and ms guidelines free.

Imprints Ridge Row Press.

O→ The University of Scranton Press, a member of the Association of Jesuit University Presses, publishes primarily scholarly monographs in theology, philosophy, and the culture and history of Northeast Pennsylvania.

Nonfiction Looking for clear editorial focus: theology/religious studies; philosophy/philosophy of religion; scholarly treatments; the culture of Northeast Pennsylvania. Scholarly monographs. Subjects include art/architecture, language/literature, philosophy, regional, religion, sociology. Query with SASE, or submit outline, 2 sample chapter(s).

Poetry Only poetry related to Northeast Pennsylvania.

Recent Title(s) *Not My Kid 2*, by Mary Muscari, Ph.D; *Jesuit Generals*, by Thomas E. Zeyen, S.J; *Fire and Ice*, by Mary McCullough.

UNIVERSITY OF SOUTH CAROLINA PRESS

1600 Hampton St., 5th Floor, Columbia SC 29208. (803)777-5243. Fax: (803)777-0160. Website: www.sc.edu/uscpress. **Acquisitions:** Curtis Clark, director (trade books); Barry Blose, acquisitions editor (literature, religious studies, rhetoric, communication, social work); Alexander Moore, acquisitions editor (history, regional studies). Estab. 1944. Publishes hardcover originals, trade paperback originals and reprints. **Publishes 50-55 titles/year. Receives 1,000 queries and 250 mss/year. 30% of books from first-time authors; 95% from unagented writers.** Publishes book 1 year after acceptance of ms. Accepts simultaneous submissions. Responds in 3 months to mss. Book catalog free; ms guidelines online.

O→ "We focus on scholarly monographs and regional trade books of lasting merit."

Nonfiction Biography, illustrated book, monograph. Subjects include art/architecture, history (American, Civil War, culinary, maritime, women's), language/literature, regional, religion, rhetoric, communication. "Do not submit entire unsolicited manuscripts or projects with limited scholarly value." Query with SASE, or submit proposal package and outline, and 1 sample chapter and résumé with SASE. Reviews artwork/photos as part of ms package. Send photocopies.

Recent Title(s) *The Temper of the West: A Memoir*, by William Jovanovich; *Out of Passau: Leaving a City Hitler Called Home*, by Anna Elisabeth Rosmus; *Gardens and Historic Plants of the Antebellum South*, by James R. Cothran.

UNIVERSITY OF TEXAS PRESS

P.O. Box 7819, Austin TX 78713-7819. (512)471-7233. Fax: (512)232-7178. E-mail: utpress@uts.cc.utexas.edu. Website: www.utexas.edu/utpress/. **Acquisitions:** Theresa May, assistant director/editor-in-chief (social sciences, Latin American studies); James Burr, sponsoring editor (humanities, classics); William Bishel, sponsoring editor (natural sciences, Texas history). Estab. 1952. **Publishes 90 titles/year. Receives 1,000 submissions/year. 50% of books from first-time authors; 99% from unagented writers. Pays royalty on net receipts. Offers occasional advance.** Publishes book 18-24 months after acceptance of ms. Does not accept simultaneous submissions. Responds in 3 months to queries. Book catalog free; ms guidelines online.

O→ "In addition to publishing the results of advanced research for scholars worldwide, UT Press has a special obligation to the people of its state to publish authoritative books on Texas. We do not publish fiction or poetry, except for some Latin American and Middle Eastern literature in translation."

Nonfiction Biography, scholarly. Subjects include anthropology/archeology, art/architecture, ethnic, film/cinema/stage, history, language/literature, nature/environment, regional, science, translation, women's issues/ studies, natural history, American, Latin American, Native American, Latino, and Middle Eastern studies; classics and the ancient world, film, contemporary regional architecture, geography, ornithology, biology. Also uses specialty titles related to Texas and the Southwest, national trade titles and regional trade titles. Query with SASE, or submit outline, 2 sample chapter(s). Reviews artwork/photos as part of ms package.

Fiction No poetry. Query with SASE, or submit outline, 2 sample chapter(s).

Recent Title(s) *The Hacienda in Mexico*, by Nierman and Vallejo; *Playas of the Great Plains*, by Smith; *Women's Lives in Colonial Quito*, by Gauderman.

Tips "It's difficult to make a manuscript over 400 double-spaced pages into a feasible book. Authors should take special care to edit out extraneous material. We look for sharply focused, in-depth treatments of important topics."

UNIVERSITY PRESS OF COLORADO

5589 Arapahoe, Suite 206C, Boulder CO 80303. (720)406-8849. Fax: (720)406-3443. Director: Darrin Pratt. **Acquisitions:** Sandy Crooms, editor. Estab. 1965. Publishes hardcover and paperback originals. **Publishes 30-40 titles/year. Receives 1,000 submissions/year. 50% of books from first-time authors; 95% from unagented writers. Pays 5-15% royalty on net receipts. Offers advance.** Publishes book within 2 years after acceptance of ms. Accepts simultaneous submissions. Responds in 6 months to queries. Book catalog free.

- O— "We are a university press that publishes scholarly nonfiction in the disciplines of the American West, Native-American studies, archeology, environmental studies, and regional-interest titles." Currently de-emphasizing fiction, poetry, biography.

Nonfiction Scholarly. Subjects include nature/environment, regional. Length: 250-500 pages. Query with SASE. Reviews artwork/photos as part of ms package.

Recent Title(s) *Reversing the Lens: Ethnicity Race, Gender, and Sexuality Through Film*, by Jun Xing and Lane Ryo Hirabayashi; *International Environmental Cooperation: Politics and Diplomacy in Pacific Asia*, by Paul G. Harris.

Tips "We have series on mining history and on Mesoamerican worlds."

UNIVERSITY PRESS OF KANSAS

2501 W. 15th St., Lawrence KS 66049-3905. (785)864-4154. Fax: (785)864-4586. E-mail: upress@ku.edu. Website: www.kansaspress.ku.edu. **Acquisitions:** Michael J. Briggs, editor-in-chief (military history, political science, law); Nancy Scott Jackson, acquisitions editor (western history, American studies, environmental studies, women's studies); Fred M. Woodward, director, (political science, presidency, regional). Estab. 1946. Publishes hardcover originals, trade paperback originals and reprints. **Publishes 55 titles/year. Receives 600 queries/ year. 20% of books from first-time authors; 98% from unagented writers. Pays 5-15% royalty on net receipts. Offers selective advance.** Publishes book 10 months after acceptance of ms. Does not accept simultaneous submissions. Responds in 1 month to proposals. Book catalog and ms guidelines free.

- O— The University Press of Kansas publishes scholarly books that advance knowledge and regional books that contribute to the understanding of Kansas, the Great Plains, and the Midwest.

Nonfiction Biography, scholarly. Subjects include Americana, anthropology/archeology, government/politics, history, military/war, nature/environment, philosophy, regional, sociology, women's issues/studies. "We are looking for books on topics of wide interest based on solid scholarship and written for both specialists and informed general readers. Do not send unsolicited, complete manuscripts." Submit outline, sample chapter(s), cover letter, cv, prospectus. Reviews artwork/photos as part of ms package. Send photocopies.

Recent Title(s) *The Zapruder Film: Reframing JFK's Assassination*, by David R. Wrone; *Brown V. Board of Education: Caste, Culture, and the Constitution*, by Robert J. Cottrol and Raymond T. Diamond.

UNIVERSITY PRESS OF MISSISSIPPI

3825 Ridgewood Rd., Jackson MS 39211-6492. (601)432-6205. Fax: (601)432-6217. E-mail: press@ihl.state.ms. us. **Acquisitions:** Craig Gill, editor-in-chief (regional studies, art, folklore, fiction, memoirs); Seetha Srinivasan, director (African-American studies, popular culture, literature). Estab. 1970. Publishes hardcover and paperback originals and reprints. **Publishes 60 titles/year. Receives 750 submissions/year. 20% of books from first-time authors; 90% from unagented writers. Competitive royalties and terms. Offers advance.** Publishes book 1 year after acceptance of ms. Does not accept simultaneous submissions. Responds in 3 months to queries. Book catalog for 9×12 SAE with 3 first-class stamps.

Imprints Muscadine Books (regional trade), Banner Books (literary reprints).

- O— "University Press of Mississippi publishes scholarly and trade titles, as well as special series, including: American Made Music; Conversations with Public Intellectuals; Conversations with Filmmakers; Faulkner and Yoknapatawpha; Literary Conversations; Studies in Popular Culture; Hollywood Legends; Understanding Health and Sickness; Writers and Their Work."

Nonfiction Biography, scholarly. Subjects include Americana, art/architecture, ethnic (minority studies), government/politics, health/medicine, history, language/literature, music/dance, photography, regional (Southern), folklife, literary criticism, popular culture with scholarly emphasis, literary studies. "We prefer a proposal that describes the significance of the work and a chapter outline." Submit outline, sample chapter(s), cv.
Fiction Commissioned trade editions by prominent writers.
Recent Title(s) *Fortune's Favorite Child: The Uneasy Life of Walter Anderson*, by Christopher Maurer; *Malinche's Children*, by Daniel Houston-Davila.

UNIVERSITY PRESS OF NEW ENGLAND

1 Court St., Suite 250, Lebanon NH 03766. (603)448-1533. Fax: (603)448-7006. E-mail: university.press@dartmouth.edu. Website: www.upne.com. Director: Richard Abel. **Acquisitions:** Phyllis Deutsch, senior editor; Ellen Wicklum, editor; John Landrigan, editor. Estab. 1970. Publishes hardcover originals. **Publishes 80 titles/year. Pays standard royalty. Offers occasional advance.** Responds in 2 months to queries. Book catalog and ms guidelines for 9×12 SASE and 5 first-class stamps; ms guidelines online.
Imprints Hardscrabble Books (publishing fiction of New England).
Nonfiction Biography. Subjects include Americana (New England material culture), art/architecture, music/dance, nature/environment, regional (New England), American studies, Jewish studies. Submit outline, 1-2 sample chapter(s). No electronic submissions.
Fiction Literary. Only New England novels, literary fiction, and reprints. Query with SASE, or submit sample chapter(s).
Recent Title(s) *Erasure*, by Percival Everett (fiction); *The Dickinsons of Amherst*, by Jerome Liebling (photography, biography); *The Ice Chronicles: The Quest to Understand Global Climate Change*, by Paul Mayewski and Frank White (nonfiction, science).

THE URBAN LAND INSTITUTE

1025 Thomas Jefferson St. NW, Washington DC 20007-5201. (202)624-7000. Fax: (202)624-7140. Website: www.uli.org. **Acquisitions:** Rachelle Levitt, executive vice president/publisher. Estab. 1936. Publishes hardcover and trade paperback originals. **Publishes 15-20 titles/year. Receives 20 submissions/year. 2% of books from first-time authors; 100% from unagented writers. Pays 10% royalty on gross sales. Offers $1,500-2,000 advance.** Publishes book 6 months after acceptance of ms. Does not accept simultaneous submissions. Book catalog and ms guidelines via website or 9×12 SAE.
    O— The Urban Land Institute publishes technical books on real estate development and land planning.
Nonfiction Technical. Subjects include money/finance, design and development. "The majority of manuscripts are created in-house by research staff. We acquire 2 or 3 outside authors to fill schedule and subject areas where our list has gaps. We are not interested in real estate sales, brokerages, appraisal, making money in real estate, opinion, personal point of view, or manuscripts negative toward growth and development." Query with SASE. Reviews artwork/photos as part of ms package.
Recent Title(s) *Place Making: Developing Town Centers, Main Streets, and Urban Villages; Transforming Suburban Business Districts*.

UTAH STATE UNIVERSITY PRESS

7800 Old Main Hill, Logan UT 84322-7800. (435)797-1362. Fax: (435)797-0313. Website: www.usu.edu/usupress. **Acquisitions:** Michael Spooner, director (composition, poetry); John Alley, editor (history, folklore, fiction). Estab. 1972. Publishes hardcover and trade paperback originals and reprints. **Publishes 18 titles/year. Receives 250 submissions/year. 8% of books from first-time authors. Pays royalty on net receipts.** Publishes book 18 months after acceptance of ms. Does not accept simultaneous submissions. Responds in 1 month to queries. Book catalog free; ms guidelines online.
    O— Utah State University Press publishes scholarly works in the academic areas noted below. Currently interested in book-length scholarly mss dealing with folklore studies, composition studies, Native American studies, and history.
Nonfiction Biography, reference, scholarly, textbook. Subjects include history (of the West), regional, folklore, the West, Native-American studies, studies in composition and rhetoric. Query with SASE. Reviews artwork/photos as part of ms package. Send photocopies.
Recent Title(s) *The Anguish of Snails*, by Barre Toelken; *Uranium Frenzy*, by Raye Ringholz; *The Owl Question*, by Faith Shearin.
Tips Utah State University Press also sponsors the annual May Swenson Poetry Award.

VANDAMERE PRESS

P.O. Box 149, St. Petersburg FL 33731. **Acquisitions:** Jerry Frank, senior acquistions editor. Estab. 1984. Publishes hardcover and trade paperback originals and reprints. **Publishes 8-15 titles/year. Receives 750 queries** and 2,000 mss/year. 25% of books from first-time authors; 90% from unagented writers. **Pays royalty. on revenues generated. Offers advance.** Publishes book 1-3 years after acceptance of ms. Accepts simultaneous submissions. Responds in 6 months to queries.

  O→ Vandamere publishes high-quality work with solid, well-documented research and minimum author/political bias.

Nonfiction Biography, illustrated book, reference. Subjects include Americana, education, health/medicine, history, military/war, photography, regional (Washington D.C./Mid-Atlantic), women's issues/studies, disability/healthcare issues. No New Age. Submit outline, 2-3 sample chapter(s). Send photocopies.

Fiction Adventure, humor, mystery, suspense. Submit 5-10 sample chapter(s), synopsis.

Recent Title(s) *Ask What You Can Do for Your Country*, by Dan Fleming (nonfiction); *Cry Me a River*, by Patricia Hagan (fiction).

Tips "Authors who can provide endorsements from significant published writers, celebrities, etc., will always be given serious consideration. Clean, easy-to-read, dark copy is essential. Patience in waiting for replies is essential. All unsolicited work is looked at, but at certain times of the year our review schedule will stop. No response without SASE. No electronic submissions or queries."

VANDERBILT UNIVERSITY PRESS

VU Station B 351813, Nashville TN 37235. (615)322-3585. Fax: (615)343-8823. E-mail: vupress@vanderbilt.edu. Website: www.vanderbilt.edu/vupress. **Acquisitions:** Michael Ames, director. Publishes hardcover originals and trade paperback originals and reprints. **Publishes 20-25 titles/year. Receives 500 queries/year. 25% of books from first-time authors; 90% from unagented writers. Pays 8% royalty on net receipts. Offers rare advance.** Publishes book 10 months after acceptance of ms. Accepts simultaneous submissions. Responds in 2 weeks to proposals. Book catalog free; ms guidelines online.

  • Also distributes for and co-publishes with Country Music Foundation.

  O→ "Vanderbilt University Press publishes books on healthcare, social sciences, education, and regional studies, for both academic and general audiences that are intellectually significant, socially relevant, and of practical importance."

Nonfiction Biography, scholarly, textbook. Subjects include Americana, anthropology/archeology, education, ethnic, government/politics, health/medicine, history, language/literature, multicultural, music/dance, nature/environment, philosophy, women's issues/studies. Submit prospectus, sample chapter, cv. Reviews artwork/photos as part of ms package. Send photocopies.

Recent Title(s) *A Good-Natured Riot: The Birth of the Grand Ole Opry*, by Charles K. Wolfe; *Invisible Work: Borges and Translation*, by Efrain Kristal; *Smoke in Their Eyes: Lessons Learned in Movement Leadership from the Tobacco Wars*, by Michael Pertschuk.

Tips "Our audience consists of scholars and educated, general readers."

Ⓐ VIKING

Imprint of Penguin Group (USA), Inc., 375 Hudson St., New York NY 10014. (212)366-2000. Publisher: Clare Ferraro. Publishes hardcover and originals. **Pays 10-15% royalty on retail price. Offers negotiable advance.** Publishes book 12-18 months after acceptance of ms. Accepts simultaneous submissions. Responds in 6 months to queries.

  O→ Viking publishes a mix of academic and popular fiction and nonfiction.

Nonfiction Biography. Subjects include business/economics, child guidance/parenting, cooking/foods/nutrition, health/medicine, history, language/literature, music/dance, philosophy, women's issues/studies. *Agented submissions only.*

Fiction Literary, mainstream/contemporary, mystery, suspense. *Agented submissions only.*

Recent Title(s) *Ten Minutes from Normal*, by Karen Hughes; *American Dynasty*, by Kevin Philips; *Forest Lover*, by Susan Vreeland.

VIKING CHILDREN'S BOOKS

Imprint of Penguin Group (USA), Inc., 345 Hudson St., New York NY 10014-3657. (212)414-3600. Fax: (212)414-3399. Website: www.penguin.com. **Acquisitions:** Catherine Frank, editor; Tracy Gates, executive editor; Melanie Cecka, senior editor; Jill Davis, senior editor; Anne Gunton, assistant editor. Publishes hardcover originals. **Publishes 70 titles/year. Pays 2-10% royalty on retail price or flat fee. Offers negotiable advance.** Publishes book 1-2 years after acceptance of ms. Responds in 6 months to queries; 6 months to mss. Does not accept unsolicited submissions.

  O→ Viking Children's Books publishes high-quality trade books for children including fiction, nonfiction, picture books and novelty books for pre-schoolers through young adults.

Nonfiction Children's/juvenile. Query with SASE, or submit outline, 3 sample chapters, SASE.

Fiction Juvenile, picture books, young adult. For picture books, submit complete ms and SASE. For novels, submit outline with 3 sample chapters and SASE.

Recent Title(s) *Strange Mr. Satie*, by M.T. Anderson; *Restless*, by Rich Wallace.

N A VILLARD BOOKS

Imprint of Random House Publishing Group, 1745 Broadway, New York NY 10019. (212)572-2600. Website: www.atrandom.com. Publisher: Gina Cantrello. Estab. 1983. Publishes hardcover and trade paperback originals. **Publishes 40-50 titles/year. 5% from unagented writers. Pays negotiable royalty. Offers negotiable advance.** Accepts simultaneous submissions.

O→ "Villard Books is the publisher of savvy and sometimes quirky, best-selling hardcovers and trade paperbacks."

Nonfiction Subjects include general nonfiction, commercial nonfiction. *Agented submissions only.*

Fiction Commercial fiction. *Agented submissions only.*

Recent Title(s) *The New Work of Dogs*, by Jon Katz; *Unusually Stupid Americans*, by Ross and Kathryn Petras.

A VINTAGE BOOKS & ANCHOR BOOKS

Division of Random House, Inc., 1745 Broadway Ave., New York NY 10019. Website: www.vintagebooks.com; www.anchorbooks.com. Publishes trade paperback originals and reprints. **Pays 4-8% royalty on retail price. Offers $2,500 and up advance.** Publishes book 1 year after acceptance of ms. Accepts simultaneous submissions. Responds in 6 months to queries.

Fiction Literary, mainstream/contemporary, short story collections. *Agented submissions only.*

VINTAGE IMAGES

P.O. Box 4435, Spring MD 20868. (301)879-6522. Fax: (301)879-6524. E-mail: vimages@erols.com. Website: www.vintageimages.com. **Acquisitions:** Brian Smolens, president. Publishes trade paperback originals. **Publishes 8 titles/year. Pays 4-8% royalty on wholesale price.** Publishes book 5 months after acceptance of ms. Does not accept simultaneous submissions. Ms guidelines online.

O→ "We publish photographic poster books and need writers who are exceptionally creative. This is truly a creative writing exercise."

Nonfiction Gift book, humor, illustrated book, poster books. Subjects include Americana, photography.

Recent Title(s) *Fishing Tales: A Vintage Images Poster Book*.

Tips "We are interested in creative writers who can weave a humorous/dramatic theme around 36 vintage photos (early 1900s). Note: This project will not proceed until 2005, so interested writers should submit only e-mail or mail addresses at this time."

VITAL HEALTH PUBLISHING

P.O. Box 152, Ridgefield CT 06877. (203)894-1882. Fax: (203)894-1866. E-mail: info@vitalhealthbooks.com. Website: www.vitalhealthbooks.com. **Acquisitions:** David Richard, publishing director (health, nutrition, ecology, creativity). Estab. 1997. Publishes trade paperback originals and reprints. **Publishes 10 titles/year; imprint publishes 5-6 titles/year. Receives 150 queries and 25 mss/year. 25% of books from first-time authors; 90% from unagented writers. Pays 15-20% royalty on wholesale price for top authors; pays in copies 30-40% of the time. Offers $1,000-5,000 advance.** Publishes book 6-8 months after acceptance of ms. Does not accept simultaneous submissions. Responds in 2 months to queries; 1-3 months to proposals; 2-4 months to mss. Book catalog online.

Imprints Vital Health Publishing, Enhancement Books.

O→ Nonfiction books for a health-conscious, well-educated, creative audience.

Nonfiction Audiocassettes, children's/juvenile, cookbook, self-help. Subjects include health/medicine, music/dance, New Age, philosophy, spirituality. "All titles must be related to health. Because we have a holistic philosophy, this includes nutrition, ecology, creativity, and spirituality. Submit proposal package including outline, 1 sample chapter(s), cover letter describing the project. Reviews artwork/photos as part of ms package. Send photocopies or color prints.

Recent Title(s) *Trace Your Genes to Health*, by Chris Reading, M.D. (nonfiction); *Our Children's Health*, by Bonnie Minsky, L.C.N. and Lisa Holk, N.D. (nonfiction); *On Wings of Spirit: The American Physician's Poetry Association Anthology*, by John Graham-Pole (poetry).

Tips "View our website to compare our titles to your manuscript."

WALKER AND CO.

Walker Publishing Co., 435 Hudson St., New York NY 10014. Fax: (212)727-0984. Website: www.walkeryoungreaders.com. Publisher: George Gibson. Adult Nonfiction Editor: Jacqueline Johnson. Juvenile Publisher: Emily Easton. Juvenile Editor: Timothy Travaglini. **Acquisitions:** Submissions to Adult Nonfiction Editor limited to agents, published authors, and writers wtih professional credentials in their field of expertise. Children's books to "Submissions Editor-Juvenile." Estab. 1959. Publishes hardcover trade originals. **Publishes 25 titles/year. Receives 3,500 submissions/year. Pays 6% on paperback, 10% on hardcover. Offers competitive advance.** Publishes book 1 year after acceptance of ms. Does not accept simultaneous submissions. Responds in 3 months to queries. Book catalog for 9×12 SAE with 3 first-class stamps.

Imprints Walker & Co. Books for Young Readers.

O–π Walker publishes general nonfiction on a variety of subjects as well as children's books.

Nonfiction Adult. Subjects include health/medicine, history (science and technology), nature/environment, science (popular), sports (baseball). Query with SASE. No phone calls.

Fiction Juvenile (fiction, nonfiction), picture books (juvenile). Query with SASE.

Recent Title(s) *Salt*, by Mark Kurlansky (history); *IQ Goes to School* (juvenile); *Lusitania*, by Diana Preston (history).

WALTSAN PUBLISHING, LLC

5000 Barnett St., Fort Worth TX 76103-2006. (817)492-0188. E-mail: sandra@waltsan.com. Website: www.waltsan.com. **Publishes 40-60 titles/year. Receives 1,500 queries and 1,000 mss/year. 95% of books from first-time authors; 95% from unagented writers. Pays 20% royalty on wholesale price.** Publishes book 1-2 years after acceptance of ms. Accepts simultaneous submissions. Responds in 2 months to queries; 2 months to proposals; 4-6 months to mss. Book catalog and ms guidelines online.

Nonfiction Subjects include general nonfiction. "We look at any nonfiction subject." Query with SASE or via website, or submit proposal package, including outline and 3 sample chapters, or submit complete ms. Reviews artwork/photos as part of ms package. Send photocopies.

Fiction "We look at all fiction." Full-length or collections equal to full-length only. 50,000 word minimum. Query with SASE, or submit proposal package including 3 sample chapter(s), synopsis, or submit complete ms.

Recent Title(s) *Shadows and Stones*, by Bernita Stark (dark fiction of shape changers and vampires); *Kite Paper, Papel de Barrilete*, by Sue Littleton (love poem with Spanish and English texts); *Jules Verne Classics*, edited by Walter Wellborn.

Tips Audience is computer literate, generally higher income and intelligent. "When possible, authors record their manuscript to include audio on the CD. Check our website for guidelines and sample contract." Initial queries and proposals may be submitted on paper. Manuscripts accepted for publication must be submitted electronically—no exceptions. Only publishes on CDs and other removable media.

Ⓐ WARNER ASPECT

Imprint of Warner Books, 1271 Avenue of the Americas, New York NY 10020. (212)522-7200. Website: twbookmark.com. Editor: Jaime Levine. Publishes hardcover, trade paperback, mass market paperback originals and mass market paperback reprints. **Publishes 30 titles/year. Receives 500 queries and 350 mss/year. 5-10% of books from first-time authors; 1% from unagented writers. Pays royalty on retail price. Offers $5,000-up advance.** Publishes book 14 months after acceptance of ms. Responds in 3 months to mss.

O–π "We're looking for 'epic' stories in both fantasy and science fiction. Also seeking writers of color to add to what we've already published by Octavia E. Butler, Nalo Hopkinson, Walter Mosley, etc."

Fiction Fantasy, science fiction. "Mistake writers often make is "hoping against hope that being unagented won't make a difference. We simply don't have the staff to look at unagented projects." *Agented submissions only.*

Recent Title(s) *Hidden Empire*, by Kevin J. Anderson; *The Elder Gods*, by David & Leigh Eddings.

Ⓐ Ⓞ WARNER BOOKS

Imprint of Time Warner Book Group, Time & Life Building, 1271 Avenue of the Americas, New York NY 10020. (212)522-7200. Fax: (212)522-7993. Website: www.twbookmark.com. President/Time Warner Book Group: Maureen Egen. **Acquisitions:** (Ms.) Jamie Raab, senior vice president/publisher (general nonfiction and fiction); Les Pockell, associate publisher (general nonfiction); Rick Horgan, vice president/executive editor (general nonfiction and fiction, thrillers); Amy Einhorn, editorial director, trade paperback (popular culture, business, fitness, self-help); Beth de Guzman, editorial director, mass market (fiction, romance, nonfiction); Rick Wolff, vice president/executive editor (business, humor, sports); Kristen Weber, editor-in-chief, Mysterious Press (mysteries, suspense); Caryn Karmatz Rudy, senior editor (fiction, general nonfiction, popular culture); Diana Baroni, executive editor (health, fitness, general nonfiction and fiction); John Aherne, editor (popular culture, men's health, New Age, movie tie-ins, general fiction); Rolf Zettersten, vice president/Warner Faith (books for the CBA market); (Ms.) Jaime Levine, editor/Aspect (science fiction); Karen Koszto Inyik, senior editor (women's fiction). Estab. 1960. Publishes hardcover, trade paperback and mass market paperback originals and reprints and e-books. **Publishes 250 titles/year. Pays variable royalty. Offers variable advance.** Publishes book 2 years after acceptance of ms. Accepts no unsolicited mss to queries.

Imprints Aspect; Bulfinch Press; Little, Brown, & Co. Adult Trade Division (Back Bay Books); Little, Brown, & Co. Children's Publishing (Megan Tingley Books); Mysterious Press; Walk Worthy Press; Warner Business; Warner Faith; Warner Forever; Warner Vision.

   O— Warner publishes general interest fiction and nonfiction.

Nonfiction Biography, humor, reference, self-help. Subjects include business/economics, contemporary culture, cooking/foods/nutrition, health/medicine, history, psychology, spirituality, sports, current affairs, human potential. *No unsolicited mss.*

Fiction Fantasy, horror, mainstream/contemporary, mystery, romance, science fiction, suspense, thrillers. *Agented submissions only. No unsolicited mss.*

Recent Title(s) *Up Country*, by Nelson DeMille; *Nights in Rodanthe*, by Nicholas Sparks; *Rich Dad Poor Dad*, by Robert T. Kiyosaki with Sharon L. Lechter.

WASHINGTON STATE UNIVERSITY PRESS

P.O. Box 645910, Pullman WA 99164-5910. (800)354-7360. Fax: (509)335-8568. E-mail: wsupress@wsu.edu. Website: www.wsupress.wsu.edu. **Acquisitions:** Glen Lindeman, editor. Estab. 1928. Publishes hardcover originals, trade paperback originals and reprints. **Publishes 8-10 titles/year. Receives 200-250 submissions/year. 40% of books from first-time authors. Most books from unagented writers. Pays 5% royalty graduated according to sales.** Publishes book 18 months after acceptance of ms. Responds in 2 months to queries. Ms guidelines online.

   O— WSU Press publishes books on the history, pre-history, culture, and politics of the West, particularly the Pacific Northwest.

Nonfiction Biography. Subjects include cooking/foods/nutrition (history), government/politics, history, nature/environment, regional, essays. "We seek manuscripts that focus on the Pacific Northwest as a region. No poetry, novels, literary criticism, how-to books. We welcome innovative and thought-provoking titles in a wide diversity of genres, from essays and memoirs to history, archaeology, and political science." Submit outline, sample chapter(s). Reviews artwork/photos as part of ms package.

Recent Title(s) *Copyright Law on Campus*; *Captured Honor: POW Survival in the Philippines*; *Eccentric Seattle: Pillars and Pariahs Who Made the City Not Such a Boring Place After All.*

Tips "We have developed our marketing in the direction of regional and local history and have attempted to use this as the base upon which to expand our publishing program. In regional history, the secret is to write a good narrative—a good story—that is substantiated factually. It should be told in an imaginative, clever way. Have visuals (photos, maps, etc.) available to help the reader envision what has happened. Tell the regional history story in a way that ties it to larger, national, and even international events. Weave it into the large pattern of history."

▣ WATERBROOK PRESS

Subsidiary of Random House, 2375 Telstar Dr., Suite 160, Colorado Springs CO 80920. (719)590-4999. Fax: (719)590-8977. Website: www.waterbrookpress.com. **Acquisitions:** Don Pape (nonfiction); Dudley Delffs, editor (fiction). Estab. 1996. Publishes hardcover and trade paperback originals. **Publishes 70 titles/year; imprint publishes 18 titles/year. Receives 2,000 queries/year. 15-25% of books from first-time authors; 25% from unagented writers. Pays royalty.** Publishes book 11 months after acceptance of ms. Accepts simultaneous submissions. Responds in 2-3 months to queries; 2-3 months to proposals; 2-3 months to mss. Book catalog online.

Imprints Fisherman Bible Study Guides, Shaw Books (Elisa Stanford, editor), Waterbrook Press.

Nonfiction Children's/juvenile, self-help. Subjects include child guidance/parenting, general nonfiction, health/medicine, money/finance, religion, spirituality. "We publish books on unique topics with a Christian perspective." *Agented submissions only.*

Fiction Adventure, historical, literary, mainstream/contemporary, mystery, religious (inspirational, religious mystery/suspense, religious thriller, religious romance), romance (contemporary, historical), science fiction, spiritual, suspense. *Agented submissions only.*

Recent Title(s) *Every Woman's Battle*, by Shannon Ethridge; *Hold Tight the Thread*, by Jane Kirkpatrick; *How Children Raise Parents*, by Dan Allender.

WATSON-GUPTILL PUBLICATIONS

Imprint of Billboard Publications, Inc., 770 Broadway, New York NY 10003. (646)654-5000. Fax: (646)654-5486. Website: www.watsonguptill.com. **Acquisitions:** Candace Raney, executive editor (fine art, art technique, pop culture, graphic design); Bob Nirkind, executive editor (Billboard-music, popular culture); Joy Acquilino, senior editor (crafts); Victoria Craven, senior editor (Amphoto-photography, lifestyle, architecture); Julie Mazur (children's books). Publishes hardcover and trade paperback originals and reprints. **Receives 150 queries and 50 mss/year. 50% of books from first-time authors; 75% from unagented writers. Pays royalty on wholesale

price. Publishes book 9 months after acceptance of ms. Responds in 2 months to queries; 3 months to proposals. Book catalog free; ms guidelines online.

Imprints Watson-Guptill, Amphoto, Whitney Library of Design, Billboard Books, Back Stage Books.

O⊸ Watson-Guptill is an arts book publisher.

Nonfiction How-to (instructionals). Subjects include art/architecture, music/dance, photography, lifestyle, pop culture, theater. "Writers should be aware of the kinds of books (arts, crafts, graphic designs, instructional) Watson-Guptill publishes before submitting. Although we are growing and will consider new ideas and approaches, we will not consider a book if it is clearly outside of our publishing program." Query with SASE, or submit proposal package including outline, 1-2 sample chapter(s). Reviews artwork/photos as part of ms package. Send photocopies or transparencies.

Recent Title(s) *Choosing Colors*, by Kevin McCloud; *The Golden Age of American Impressionism*, by William Gerdts; *Days of Hope and Dreams: An Intimate Portrait of Bruce Springsteen*, by Frank Stefanko.

Tips "We are an art book publisher."

WELCOME ENTERPRISES, INC.

6 W. 18th St., New York NY 10011. (212)989-3200. Fax: (212)989-3205. E-mail: info@welcomebooks.biz. Website: www.welcomebooks.biz. **Acquisitions:** Lena Tabori, publisher/editor; Natasha Tabori Fried, editor; Katrina Fried, editor; Alice Wong, editor. Estab. 1980. **Publishes 10 titles/year. Pays 7½% royalty on net receipts.**

Nonfiction Illustrated book. Subjects include art/architecture, language/literature, photography. Query with SASE.

Recent Title(s) *The Little Big Book of New York*; *Mom's Almanac.*

WESTCLIFFE PUBLISHERS

P.O. Box 1261, Englewood CO 80150. (303)935-0900. Fax: (303)935-0903. E-mail: editor@westcliffepublishers.com. Website: www.westcliffepublishers.com. Linda Doyle, associate publisher. **Acquisitions:** Jenna Samelson, managing editor. Estab. 1981. Publishes hardcover originals, trade paperback originals, and reprints. **Publishes 18 titles/year. Receives 100 queries and 60 mss/year. 50% of books from first-time authors; 100% from unagented writers. Pays royalty on retail price. Offers advance.** Publishes book 18 months after acceptance of ms. Accepts simultaneous submissions. Responds in 1 month to queries. Book catalog free; ms guidelines online.

O⊸ "Westcliffe Publishers produces the highest quality in regional photography and essays for our outdoor guidebooks, coffee table-style books, and calendars. As an eco-publisher our mission is to foster environmental awareness by showing the beauty of the natural world." Strong concentration on color guide books, outdoor sports, history.

Nonfiction Coffee table book, gift book, illustrated book, reference. Subjects include Americana, animals, gardening, history, nature/environment, photography, regional, sports (outdoor), travel. "Writers need to do their market research to justify a need in the marketplace." Submit proposal package including outline. Westcliffe will contact you for photos, writing samples.

Recent Title(s) *Colorado: 1870-2000*, by John Fielder; *Haunted Texas Vacations*, by Lisa Farwell.

Tips Audience are nature and outdoors enthusiasts and photographers. "Just call us!"

WESTERN PSYCHOLOGICAL SERVICES

Manson Western Corp., 12031 Wilshire Blvd., Los Angeles CA 90025. (310)478-2061. Fax: (310)478-2061. E-mail: smanson@wpspublish.com. Website: www.wpspublish.com; www.creativetherapystore.com. **Acquisitions:** Susan Madden, director of marketing. Estab. 1948. Publishes trade paperback originals. **Publishes 6 titles/year. Receives 60 queries and 30 mss/year. 75% of books from first-time authors; 80% from unagented writers. Pays 5-10% royalty on wholesale price.** Publishes book 1 year after acceptance of ms. Accepts simultaneous submissions. Responds in 2 months to queries. Book catalog free; ms guidelines online.

O⊸ Western Psychological Services publishes practical books used by therapists, counselors, social workers, and others in the helping professionals working with children and adults.

Nonfiction Testing, addictions, special education, autism, speech-language-hearing, marriage and family therapy, neuropsychology, school psychology, occupational therapy, sensory integration. Subjects include child guidance/parenting, education, psychology, muliticultural issues. Submit complete ms. Reviews artwork/photos as part of ms package. Send photocopies.

Fiction Children's books dealing with feelings, anger, social skills, autism, family problems, etc. Submit complete ms.

Recent Title(s) *Christopher's Anger*, by Denise Zuckerman, M.A.

▩ WESTMINSTER JOHN KNOX PRESS

Division of Presbyterian Publishing Corp., 100 Witherspoon St., Louisville KY 40202-1396. (502)569-5613. Fax: (502)569-5113. Website: www.wjkbooks.com. **Acquisitions:** Lori Dowell. Publishes hardcover and trade paperback originals and reprints. **Publishes 100 titles/year. Receives 2,500 queries and 750 mss/year. 10% of books from first-time authors. Pays royalty on retail price. Offers advance.** Publishes book up to 18 months after acceptance of ms. Accepts simultaneous submissions. Book catalog for #10 SASE; ms guidelines online.

> O→ "All WJK books have a religious/spiritual angle, but are written for various markets—scholarly, professional, and the general reader." Westminster John Knox is affiliated with the Presbyterian Church USA.

Nonfiction Biography, gift book, how-to, humor, illustrated book, multimedia, reference, self-help, textbook. Subjects include anthropology/archeology, child guidance/parenting, education, ethnic, gay/lesbian, history, multicultural, philosophy, psychology, religion, sociology, spirituality, women's issues/studies. Submit proposal package according to WJK book proposal guidelines.

WESTWINDS PRESS

Imprint of Graphic Arts Center Publishing, P.O. Box 10306, Portland OR 97296-0306. (503)226-2402. Fax: (503)223-1410. Website: www.gacpc.com. **Acquisitions:** Tricia Brown, acquisitions editor. Estab. 1999. Publishes hardcover and trade paperback originals and reprints. **Publishes 5-7 titles/year. Receives hundreds of submissions/year. 10% of books from first-time authors; 90% from unagented writers. Pays 10-14% royalty on net receipts, or makes outright purchase. Offers advance.** Publishes book an average of 2 years after acceptance of ms. Accepts simultaneous submissions. Responds in 6 months to queries. Book catalog for 9×12 SAE with 6 first-class stamps; ms guidelines online.

Nonfiction Children's/juvenile, cookbook. Subjects include history, memoirs, regional (Western regional states—nature, travel, cookbooks, Native American culture, adventure, outdoor recreation, sports, the arts, and children's books), guidebooks.

Recent Title(s) *Stone Fruit* (Northwest Homegrown cookbook series); *The Exploding Whale* (memoir); *Portland Confidential* (true crime).

Tips "Book proposals that are professionally written and polished with a clear understanding of the market receive our most careful consideration. We are looking for originality. We publish a wide range of books for a wide audience. Some of our books are clearly for travelers, others for those interested in outdoor recreation or various regional subjects. If I were a writer trying to market a book today, I would research the competition (existing books) for what I have in mind, and clearly (and concisely) express why my idea is different and better. I would describe the book buyers (and readers)—where they are, how many of them are there, how they can be reached (organizations, publications), why they would want or need my book."

WHITSTON PUBLISHING CO., INC.

1717 Central Ave., Suite 201, Albany NY 12205. (518)452-1900. Fax: (518)452-1777. E-mail: whitston@capital.net. Website: www.whitston.com. **Acquisitions:** Michael Laddin, publisher. Estab. 1969. Publishes hardcover and trade paperback originals. **Publishes 15-25 titles/year. Receives 200 submissions/year. 20% of books from first-time authors; 100% from unagented writers. Pays royalties after sale of 500 copies.** Publishes book 1 year after acceptance of ms. Does not accept simultaneous submissions. Responds in 6 months to queries.

> O→ Whitston focuses on literature, politics, history, business, and the sciences.

Nonfiction "We publish nonfiction books in the humanities. We also publish reference bibliographies and indexes." Subjects include art/architecture, business/economics, government/politics, health/medicine, history, language/literature, social sciences. Query with SASE. Reviews artwork/photos as part of ms package.

Recent Title(s) *Mark Twain Among the Scholars*; *Autobiographies by Americans of Color*; *Into the Dragon's Teeth: Warriors' Tales of the Battle of the Bulge.*

WILDER PUBLISHING CENTER

919 Lafond Ave., St. Paul MN 55104. (651)659-6013. Fax: (651)642-2061. E-mail: vlh@wilder.org. Website: www.wilder.org. **Acquisitions:** Vincent Hyman, director. Publishes professional trade paperback originals. **Publishes 6 titles/year. Receives 30 queries and 15 mss/year. 75% of books from first-time authors; 100% from unagented writers. Pays 10% royalty on net receipts. Books are sold through direct mail; average discount is 20%. Offers $1,000-3,000 advance.** Publishes book 18 months after acceptance of ms. Accepts simultaneous submissions. Responds in 1 month to queries; 1 month to proposals; 3 months to mss. Book catalog and ms guidelines free or online; ms guidelines online.

> O→ Wilder Publishing Center emphasizes community development and nonprofit organization management.

Nonfiction Subjects include nonprofit management, funder's guides, board guides, organizational development, community building. "We are seeking manuscripts that report 'best practice' methods using handbook or workbook formats for nonprofit and community development managers." Submit 3 sample chapter(s). Phone query OK before submitting proposal with detailed chapter outline, SASE, statement of the goals of the book, statement of unique selling points, identification of audience.

Recent Title(s) *The Lobbying and Advocacy Handbook for Nonprofit Organizations*; *The Wilder Nonprofit Guide to Crafting Effective Mission and Vision Statements*; *The Five Life Stages of Nonprofit Organizations*.

Tips "Writers must be practitioners with a passion for their work in nonprofit management or community building and experience presenting their techniques at conferences. We seek practical, not academic books. Our books identify professional challenges faced by our audiences and offer practical, step-by-step solutions."

WILDERNESS PRESS

1200 Fifth St., Berkley CA 94710. (510)558-1666. Fax: (510)558-1696. E-mail: editor@wildernesspress.com. Website: www.wildernesspress.com. **Acquisitions:** Managing Editor. Estab. 1967. Publishes paperback originals. **Publishes 12 titles/year.** Publishes book 8-12 months after acceptance of ms. Responds in 2 months to queries. Book catalog and ms guidelines online.

    ○➤ "Wilderness Press has a 35-year tradition of publishing the highest quality, most accurate hiking and other outdoor activity guidebooks."

Nonfiction How-to (outdoors). Subjects include nature/environment, recreation, trail guides for hikers and backpackers. "We publish books about the outdoors. Most are trail guides for hikers and backpackers, but we also publish climbing, kayaking, and other outdoor activity guides, how-to books about the outdoors. The manuscript must be accurate. The author must research an area in person. If writing a trail guide, you must walk all the trails in the area your book is about. Outlook must be strongly conservationist. Style must be appropriate for a highly literate audience." Download proposal guidelines from website.

Recent Title(s) *Backpacking Idaho*; *Sequoia National Park*; *Washington's Highest Mountains*.

WILLOW CREEK PRESS

P.O. Box 147, 9931 Highway 70 W., Minocqua WI 54548. (715)358-7010. Fax: (715)358-2807. E-mail: andread@willowcreekpress.com. Website: www.willowcreekpress.com. **Acquisitions:** Andrea Donner, managing editor. Estab. 1986. Publishes hardcover and trade paperback originals and reprints. **Publishes 25 titles/year. Receives 400 queries and 150 mss/year. 15% of books from first-time authors; 50% from unagented writers. Pays 6-15% royalty on wholesale price. Offers $2,000-5,000 advance.** Publishes book within 18 months after acceptance of ms. Accepts simultaneous submissions. Responds in 2 months to queries. Ms guidelines online.

    ○➤ "We specialize in nature, outdoor, and sporting topics, including gardening, wildlife, and animal books. Pets, cookbooks, and a few humor books and essays round out our titles." Currently emphasizing pets (mainly dogs and cats), wildlife, outdoor sports (hunting, fishing). De-emphasizing essays, fiction.

Nonfiction Coffee table book, cookbook, how-to, humor, illustrated book, reference. Subjects include animals, cooking/foods/nutrition, gardening, humor, nature/environment, recreation, sports, travel, wildlife, pets. Submit outline, 1 sample chapter(s), SASE. Reviews artwork/photos as part of ms package.

Recent Title(s) *101 Uses for a Dog*; *Castwork: Reflections of Fly-Fishing Guides & the American West*; *Lab Rules: Virtues of Canine Character*.

WILSHIRE BOOK CO.

12015 Sherman Rd., North Hollywood CA 91605-3781. (818)765-8579. Fax: (818)765-2922. E-mail: mpowers@mpowers.com. Website: www.mpowers.com. Publisher: Melvin Powers. **Acquisitions:** Rights Department. Estab. 1947. Publishes trade paperback originals and reprints. **Publishes 25 titles/year. Receives 1,800 submissions/year. 80% of books from first-time authors; 75% from unagented writers. Pays standard royalty. Offers advance.** Publishes book 6 months after acceptance of ms. Accepts simultaneous submissions. Responds in 2 months to queries. Ms guidelines online.

Nonfiction How-to, self-help, motivational/inspiration, recovery. Subjects include psychology, personal success, entrepreneurship, humor, Internet marketing, mail order, horsmanship, trick training for horses. Minimum 50,000 words. Query with SASE, or submit outline, 3 sample chapter(s), author bio, analysis of book's competition, or submit complete ms. No e-mail submissions. Reviews artwork/photos as part of ms package. Send photocopies.

Fiction Adult allegories that teach principles of psychological growth or offer guidance in living. Minimum 30,000 words. No standard fiction or short stories. Query with SASE, or submit 3 sample chapter(s), synopsis, or submit complete ms.

Recent Title(s) *The Dragon Slayer with a Heavy Heart*, by Marcia Powers; *The Secret of Overcoming Verbal Abuse*, by Albert Ellis, Ph.D., and Marcia Grad Powers; *The Princess Who Believed in Fairy Tales*, by Marcia Grad.

Tips "We are vitally interested in all new material we receive. Just as you hopefully submit your manuscript for publication, we are hopeful as we read each one submitted, searching for those we believe could be successful in the marketplace. Writing and publishing must be a team effort. We need you to write what we can sell. We suggest you read the successful books similar to the one you want to write. Analyze them to discover what elements make them winners. Duplicate those elements in your own style, using a creative new approach and fresh material, and you will have written a book we can catapult onto the bestseller list. You are welcome to telephone or e-mail us for immediate feedback on any book concept you may have. To learn more about us and what we publish, visit our website.''

WINDRIVER PUBLISHING, INC.

P.O. Box 911540, St. George UT 84791-1540. (435)634-8037. Fax: (435)688-0138. E-mail: info@windriverpublishing.com. Website: www.windriverpublishing.com. **Acquisitions:** E. Keith Howick, Jr., president; Gail Howick, vice president/editor-in-chief. Estab. 2003. Publishes hardcover originals and reprints, trade paperback originals, mass market originals. **Publishes 24 titles/year. Receives 1,000 queries and 300 mss/year. 95% of books from first-time authors; 90% from unagented writers. Pays 5-10% royalty on retail price.** Publishes book 1 year after acceptance of ms. Accepts simultaneous submissions. Responds in 1 month to queries; 4 months to proposals; 4 months to mss. Book catalog and ms guidelines online.

Nonfiction Autobiography, biography, children's/juvenile, cookbook, humor, self-help. Subjects include cooking/foods/nutrition, gardening, general nonfiction, government/politics, history, hobbies, New Age, religion, science, spirituality. Follow online instructions for submitting proposal, including synopsis and 3 sample chapters. Ms submissions by invitation only. Reviews artwork/photos as part of ms package.

Fiction Adventure, fantasy, historical, humor, juvenile, literary, military/war, mystery, religious, science fiction, spiritual, suspense, young adult. Follow online instructions for submitting proposal, including synopsis and 3 sample chapters. Ms submissions by invitation only.

Recent Title(s) *Don't Put Lipstick on the Cat!*; *The American St. Nick*; *Waldo Chicken Wakes the Dead*.

Tips "We do not accept manuscripts containing graphic or gratuitous profanity, sex, or violence. See online instructions for details."

WINDSOR BOOKS

Imprint of Windsor Marketing Corp., P.O. Box 280, Brightwaters NY 11718-0280. (631)321-7830. Website: www.windsorpublishing.com. **Acquisitions:** Jeff Schmidt, managing editor. Estab. 1968. Publishes hardcover and trade paperback originals, reprints, and very specific software. **Publishes 6 titles/year. Receives approximately 40 submissions/year. 60% of books from first-time authors; 90% from unagented writers. Pays 10% royalty on retail price; 5% on wholesale price (50% of total cost). Offers variable advance.** Publishes book an average of 6 months after acceptance of ms. Accepts simultaneous submissions. Responds in 2 weeks to queries.

O─┐ "Our books are for serious investors."

Nonfiction Interested in books on strategies, methods for investing in the stock market, options market and commodities markets. How-to, technical. Subjects include business/economics (investing in stocks and commodities), money/finance, software. Query with SASE, or submit outline, sample chapter(s). Reviews artwork/photos as part of ms package.

Tips "We sell through direct mail to our mailing list and other financial lists. Writers must keep their work original; this market tends to have a great deal of information overlap among publications."

WINDSWEPT HOUSE PUBLISHERS

P.O. Box 159, Mount Desert ME 04660-0159. (207)244-5027. Fax: (207)244-3369. E-mail: windswt@acadia.net. Website: www.booknotes.com/windswept. **Acquisitions:** Mavis Weinberger, owner. Publishes hardcover and trade paperback originals. **Publishes 4 titles/year. Pays up to 10% royalty.** Book catalog online; ms guidelines for #10 SASE.

Nonfiction Biography, children's/juvenile, illustrated book. Subjects include animals, history, memoirs, nature/environment, regional. **All unsolicited mss returned unopened.** Reviews artwork/photos as part of ms package. Send photocopies.

Recent Title(s) *In the Company of Trees*, by Shamms Mortier.

WINDWARD PUBLISHING, INC.

Imprint of the Finney Co., 3943 Meadowbrook Road, Minneapolis MN 55426. (952)938-9330. Fax: (952)938-7353. E-mail: feedback@finney-hobar.com. Website: www.finney-hobar.com. **Acquisitions:** Alan E. Krysan, president. Estab. 1973. Publishes trade paperback originals. **Publishes 6-10 titles/year. Receives 80 queries and 20 mss/year. 35% of books from first-time authors; 100% from unagented writers. Pays 10% royalty on wholesale price. Offers advance.** Publishes book 6-12 months after acceptance of ms. Accepts simultaneous submissions. Responds in 8-10 weeks to queries.

○⇥ Windward publishes illustrated natural history and recreation books.

Nonfiction Illustrated book, handbooks, field guides. Subjects include agriculture/horticulture, animals, gardening, nature/environment, recreation, science, sports, natural history. Query with SASE. Reviews artwork/photos as part of ms package.

Recent Title(s) *Sea Turtles Hatching*, by Katherine Orr; *Posionous & Hazardous Marine Life*, by Sandra Romashko; *My Little Book Series*, by Hope Irvin Marston.

WIZARDS OF THE COAST

P.O. Box 707, Renton WA 98057-0707. (425)226-6500. Website: www.wizards.com. **Acquisitions:** Peter Archer, director. Publishes hardcover and trade paperback originals and trade paperback reprints. Wizard of the Coast publishes games as well, including Dungeons & Dragons role-playing game. **Publishes 50-60 titles/year. Receives 600 queries and 300 mss/year. 25% of books from first-time authors; 35% from unagented writers. Pays 4-8% royalty on retail price. Offers $4,000-6,000 average advance.** Publishes book 1 year after acceptance of ms. Accepts simultaneous submissions. Responds in 4 months to queries. Ms guidelines for #10 SASE.

Imprints Dragonlance Books, Forgotten Realms Books, Magic: The Gathering Books, Eberron, Knights of the Silver Dragon (YA) Books.

○⇥ Wizards of the Coast publishes only science fiction and fantasy shared-world titles. Currently emphasizing solid fantasy writers. De-emphasizing gothic fiction.

Nonfiction ''All of our nonfiction books are generated in-house.''

Fiction Fantasy, short story collections. ''We currently publish only work-for-hire novels set in our trademarked worlds. No violent or gory fantasy or science fiction.'' Request guidelines, then query with outline/synopsis and a 10-page writing sample.

Recent Title(s) *The Lone Drow*, by R.A. Salvatore.

Tips ''Our audience is largely comprised of highly imaginative 12-30 year-old males.''

WOODBINE HOUSE

6510 Bells Mill Rd., Bethesda MD 20817. (301)897-3570. Fax: (301)897-5838. E-mail: ngpaul@woodbinehouse.com. Website: www.woodbinehouse.com. **Acquisitions:** Nancy Gray Paul, acquisitions editor. Estab. 1985. Publishes hardcover and trade paperback originals. **Publishes 8 titles/year. 90% from unagented writers. Pays 10-12% royalty.** Publishes book 18 months after acceptance of ms. Accepts simultaneous submissions. Responds in 8 months to queries. Book catalog for 6×9 SAE with 3 first-class stamps; ms guidelines online.

○⇥ Woodbine House publishes books for or about individuals with disabilities to help those individuals and their families live fulfilling and satisfying lives in their homes, schools, and communities.

Nonfiction Publishes books for and about children with disabilities. Reference. Subjects include health/medicine. No personal accounts or general parenting guides. Submit outline, 3 sample chapter(s). Reviews artwork/photos as part of ms package.

Fiction Picture books (children's). Submit complete ms. with SASE.

Recent Title(s) *Activity Schedules for Children with Autism: Teaching Independent Behavior*, by Lynn McClannahan and Patricia Krantz; *Children with Fragile X Syndrome: A Parents' Guide*, by Jayne Dixon Weber, Ed.

Tips ''Do not send us a proposal on the basis of this description. Examine our catalog or website and a couple of our books to make sure you are on the right track. Put some thought into how your book could be marketed (aside from in bookstores). Keep cover letters concise and to the point; if it's a subject that interests us, we'll ask to see more.''

WORKMAN PUBLISHING CO.

708 Broadway, New York NY 10003. (212)254-5900. Fax: (212)254-8098. Website: www.workman.com. Editor-in-chief: Susan Bolotin. **Acquisitions:** Suzanne Rafer, executive editor (cookbook, child care, parenting, teen interest); Ruth Sullivan, Jennifer Griffin, Margot Herrera, Richard Rosen, senior editors. David Allender, senior editor, juvenile. Estab. 1967. Publishes hardcover and trade paperback originals. **Publishes 40 titles/year. Receives thousands of queries/year. Open to first-time authors. Pays variable royalty on retail price. Offers variable advance.** Publishes book approximately 1 year after acceptance of ms. Accepts simultaneous submissions. Responds in 5 months to queries. Ms guidelines online.

Imprints Algonquin, Artisan, Greenwich Workshop Press, Storey.

○⇥ ''We are a trade paperback house specializing in a wide range of popular nonfiction. We publish no adult fiction and very little children's fiction. We also publish a full range of full-color wall and Page-A-Day calendars.''

Nonfiction Cookbook, gift book, how-to, humor. Subjects include business/economics, child guidance/parenting, cooking/foods/nutrition, gardening, health/medicine, sports, travel. Query with SASE first for guidelines. Reviews artwork/photos as part of ms package.

Recent Title(s) *The Dinner Doctor*, by Anne Byrn; *The What to Expect Baby-Sitter's Handbook*, by Heidi Murkoff.
Tips "No phone calls, please. We do not accept submissions via fax or e-mail."

WRITER'S DIGEST BOOKS

F + W Publications, 4700 E. Galbraith Rd., Cincinnati OH 45236. (513)531-2690, ext. 1408. Website: www.writer sdigest.com. Estab. 1920. Publishes primarily hardcover originals. **Publishes 15-20 titles/year. Receives 300 queries and 50 mss/year. 20% from unagented writers. Pays 10-20% royalty on net receipts. Offers average $5,000 and up advance.** Publishes book 18 months after acceptance of ms. Accepts simultaneous submissions. Responds in 2 months to queries. Book catalog for 9×12 SAE with 6 first-class stamps.

    O➔ Writer's Digest Books is the premiere source for books about writing, publishing instructional and reference books for writers. Typical mss are 80,000 words.

Nonfiction How-to, reference, instructional books for writers. "Our instruction books stress results and how specifically to achieve them. Should be well-researched, yet lively and readable. We do not want to see books telling readers how to crack specific nonfiction markets: *Writing for the Computer Market* or *Writing for Trade Publications*, for instance. We are most in need of fiction-technique books written by published authors. Be prepared to explain how the proposed book differs from existing books on the subject." No fiction or poetry. Query with SASE, or submit outline, sample chapter(s), SASE.
Recent Title(s) *Pocket Muse*, by Monica Wood; *Writing the Breakout Novel*, by Donald Maass.
Tips "Most queries we receive are either too broad (how to write fiction) or too niche (how to write erotic horror), and don't reflect a knowledge of our large backlist of 150 titles. We rarely publish books on niche topics such as songwriting, scriptwriting, or poetry, unless the author has outstanding credentials or an outstanding manuscript. We are actively seeking: briefer books (20,000-40,000 words) that distill vast amounts of writing advice into skimmable rules and principles; lighter or humorous reads about the writing life, superbly written; interactive and visual writing instruction books, similar to *Pocket Muse*, by Monica Wood; and general reference works that appeal to an audience beyond writers, such as specialized word finders, eccentric dictionaries, or pocket guides."

YAHBOOKS PUBLISHING

30799 Pinetree Rd., #356, Cleveland OH 44124. (216)233-5961. Fax: (440)247-1581. E-mail: eric@yahbooks.c om. Website: www.yahbooks.com. Estab. 2001. publishes trade paperback originals. **Publishes 5 titles/year. Pays 10-30% royalty on wholesale price, or makes outright purchase of $0-50,000.** Publishes book 0-6 months after acceptance of ms. Accepts simultaneous submissions. Responds in 1 month to queries; 1 month to proposals; 1-2 months to mss.
Nonfiction Children's/juvenile, gift book, how-to. Subjects include computers/electronic. Submit outline, sample chapter(s), or submit complete ms. Reviews artwork/photos as part of ms package. Send photocopies.
Recent Title(s) *You Are Here College Internet Guide*, by Eric Leebow (Internet/college); *You Are Here High School Internet Guide*, by Eric Leebow (Internet/teen/high school); *You Are Here Kids & Family Internet Guide*, by Eric Leebow (Internet/family).
Tips "We publish a book series of Internet guides. Variety of audiences."

YMAA PUBLICATION CENTER

4354 Washington St., Roslindale MA 02131. (617)323-7215. Fax: (617)323-7417. E-mail: ymaa@aol.com. **Acquisitions:** David Ripianzi, director. Estab. 1982. Publishes trade paperback originals and reprints. **Publishes 6 titles/year. Receives 50 queries and 20 mss/year. 25% of books from first-time authors; 100% from unagented writers. Pays 10% royalty on net receipts.** Publishes book 18 months after acceptance of ms. Accepts simultaneous submissions. Responds in 3 months to proposals. Book catalog online; ms guidelines free.

    O➔ "YMAA publishes books on Chinese Chi Kung (Qigong), Taijiquan, (Tai Chi) and Asian martial arts. We are expanding our focus to include books on healing, wellness, meditation and subjects related to Asian culture and Asian medicine." De-emphasizing fitness books.

Nonfiction "We are most interested in Asian martial arts, Chinese medicine, and Chinese Qigong. We publish Eastern thought, health, meditation, massage, and East/West synthesis." How-to, multimedia, self-help. Subjects include ethnic, health/medicine (Chinese), history, philosophy, spirituality, sports, Asian martial arts, Chinese Qigong. "We no longer publish or solicit books for children. We also produce instructional videos to accompany our books on traditional Chinese martial arts, meditation, massage, and Chi Kung." Submit proposal package including outline, 1 sample chapter(s), author bio, SASE. Reviews artwork/photos as part of ms package. Send photocopies and 1-2 originals to determine quality of photo/line art.
Recent Title(s) *Qigong Meditation-Embryonic Breathing*, by Dr. Yang Jwing-Ming; *The Martial Way and Its Virtues*, by F.J. Chu.
Tips "If you are submitting health-related material, please refer to an Asian tradition. Learn about author publicity options as your participation is mandatory."

ZONDERVAN

Division of HarperCollins Publishers, 5300 Patterson Ave. SE, Grand Rapids MI 49530-0002. (616)698-6900. Fax: (616)698-3454. E-mail: zpub@zondervan.com. Website: www.zondervan.com. Executive VP: Scott Bolinder. **Acquisitions:** Manuscript Review Editor. Estab. 1931. Publishes hardcover and trade paperback originals and reprints. **Publishes 120 titles/year. Receives 3,000 submissions/year. 10% of books from first-time authors; 60% from unagented writers. Pays 14% royalty on net amount received on sales of cloth and softcover trade editions; 12% royalty on net amount received on sales of mass market paperbacks. Offers variable advance.** Responds in 2 months to queries; 3 months to proposals; 4 months to mss. Ms guidelines online.
Imprints Inspirio, Vida, Zonderkidz, Zondervan.

- ○⌐ "Our mission is to be the leading Christian communications company meeting the needs of people with resources that glorify Jesus Christ and promote Biblical principles."

Nonfiction All religious perspective (evangelical). Autobiography, biography, children's/juvenile, reference, self-help, textbook. Subjects include history, humanities, memoirs, religion, Christian living, devotional, Bible study resources, preaching, counseling, college and seminary textbooks, discipleship, worship, and church renewal for pastors, professionals and lay leaders in ministry, theological, and Biblical reference books. Submit outline, 1 sample chapter(s).

Fiction Some adult fiction (mainstream, Biblical). Refer to nonfiction. "Inklings-style" fiction of high literary quality. Christian relevance in all cases. Will not consider collections of short stories. Query with SASE, or submit outline, 1 sample chapter(s), synopsis.

Recent Title(s) *Purpose Driven Life*, by Rick Warren (Christian living); *Cape Refuge*, by Terri Blackstock (fiction).

Canadian & International Book Publishers

C anadian and international book publishers share the same mission as their U.S. counterparts—publishing timely books on subjects of concern and interest to a targetable audience. Most of the publishers listed in this section, however, differ from U.S. publishers in that their needs tend toward subjects that are specific to their country or intended for a Canadian or international audience. Some are interested in submissions from writers outside of the U.S. only. There are many regional publishers that concentrate on region-specific subjects.

U.S. writers hoping to do business with Canadian or international publishers should follow specific paths of research to find out as much about their intended markets as possible. The listings will inform you about what kinds of books the Canadian and international companies publish and tell you whether they are open to receiving submissions from writers outside the U.S. To further target your markets and see very specific examples of the books these houses are publishing, send for catalogs from publishers, or check their websites.

Once you have determined which publishers will accept your work, it is important to understand the differences that exist between U.S. mail and international mail. U.S. postage stamps are useless on mailings originating outside of the U.S. When enclosing a SASE for return of your query or manuscript from a publisher outside the U.S. (including Canada), you must include International Reply Coupons (IRCs) or postage stamps from that country.

Canadian publishers are indicated by the ◼ icon, and markets located outside of the U.S. and Canada are indicated by the ◼ icon.

For a list of publishers according to their subjects of interest, see the Nonfiction and Fiction sections of the Book Publishers' Subject Index. Information on book publishers listed in the previous edition of *Writer's Market*, but not included in this edition, can be found in the General Index.

A&C BLACK PUBLISHERS, LTD.

Bloomsbury plc, 37 Soho Square, London W1D 3QZ England. (020)7758-0200. Fax: (020)7758-0222. **Acquisitions:** Sarah Fecher, editor (children's nonfiction); Jon Appleton, editor (children's fiction); Janet Murphy, editor (nautical); Charlotte Jenkins (sport); Linda Lambert, editor (arts and crafts); Katie Taylor, editor (theater, writing, reference); Nigel Redman, editor (ornithology). Publishes hardcover and trade paperback originals, trade paperback reprints. **Publishes 170 titles/year; imprint publishes 10-20 titles/year. Receives 3,000 queries and 650 mss/year. 5% of books from first-time authors; 70% from unagented writers. Pays royalty on retail price or net receipts; makes outright purchase very occasionally on short children's books. Offers £1,500-6,000 advance.** Publishes book 9 months after acceptance of ms. Accepts simultaneous submissions. Responds in 1 month to queries; 2 months to proposals; 2 months to mss. Book catalog free.

Imprints Adlard Coles Nautical (Janet Murphy, editor); Christopher Helm/Pica Press (Nigel Redman, editor); Herbert Press (Linda Lambert, editor).

Nonfiction Children's/juvenile, how-to, illustrated book, reference. Subjects include art/architecture, creative nonfiction, education, multicultural, music/dance, nature/environment, recreation, sports, travel, nutrition. Query with SASE, or submit proposal package including outline, 2 sample chapter(s), or submit complete ms. Reviews artwork/photos as part of ms package. Send transparencies.

Fiction Juvenile. Submit 2 sample chapter(s), synopsis, or submit complete ms.

Recent Title(s) *The Body Lean and Lifted*, by Marja Putkisto; *Women Potters*, by Moira Vincentelli; *Whitaker's Almanack* (Pocket Reference).

THE ALTHOUSE PRESS

University of Western Ontario, Faculty of Education, 1137 Western Rd., London ON N6G 1G7 Canada. (519)661-2096. Fax: (519)661-3833. E-mail: press@uwo.ca. Website: www.edu.uwo.ca/althousepress. Director: Dr. Greg Dickinson. **Acquisitions:** Katherine Butson, editorial assistant. Publishes trade paperback originals and reprints. **Publishes 1-5 titles/year. Receives 30 queries and 19 mss/year. 50% of books from first-time authors; 100% from unagented writers. Pays 10% royalty. Offers $300 advance.** Publishes book 6-12 months after acceptance of ms. Accepts simultaneous submissions. Responds in 1 month to queries; 4 months to mss. Book catalog free; ms guidelines online.

○→ "The Althouse Press publishes both scholarly research monographs in education and professional books and materials for educators in elementary schools, secondary schools, and faculties of education." De-emphasizing curricular or instructional materials intended for use by elementary or secondary school students.

Nonfiction Subjects include education (scholarly). "Do not send incomplete manuscripts that are only marginally appropriate to our market and limited mandate." Reviews artwork/photos as part of ms package. Send photocopies.

Recent Title(s) *The Best Teacher I Ever Had*, by Alex Michalos; *Questioning Leadership*, by Bob McMillan; *Writing in the Dark*, by Max Van Manen.

Tips Audience is practicing teachers and graduate education students.

AMBER LANE PRESS, LTD.

Church St., Charlbury 0X7 3PR United Kingdom. 01608 810024. Fax: 01608 810024. E-mail: info@amberlanepress.co.uk. Website: www.amberlanepress.co.uk. **Acquisitions:** Judith Scott, managing editor (drama/theater/music). Publishes hardcover and trade paperback originals, trade paperback reprints. **Publishes 5 titles/year. Receives 10 queries and 6 mss/year. 20% of books from first-time authors; 10% from unagented writers. Pays 7½-12% royalty. Offers £250-1,000 (sterling pounds) advance.** Publishes book 18 months after acceptance of ms. Accepts simultaneous submissions. Responds in 1 month to queries. Book catalog free.

○→ Amber Lane Press aims "to help promote British theater and modern drama in general."

Nonfiction Biography, how-to, reference. Subjects include music/dance. Submit proposal package including outline, 2 sample chapter(s).

Fiction Plays. "All plays need to be staged professionally by a major theater/theater company." Submit complete ms.

Recent Title(s) *Theatre in a Cool Climate*, Vera Gottlieb and Colin Chambers, eds; *Oroonoko*, Aphra Behn, adapted by Biyi Bandele (play); *Strindberg and Love*, by Eivor Martinus (biography).

Tips "Explain why the book would be different from anything else already published on the subject."

ANNICK PRESS, LTD.

15 Patricia Ave., Toronto ON M2M 1H9 Canada. (416)221-4802. Fax: (416)221-8400. E-mail: annick@annickpress.com. Website: www.annickpress.com. **Acquisitions:** Rick Wilks, director; Colleen MacMillan, associate publisher. Publishes picture books, juvenile and YA fiction and nonfiction, specializes in trade books. **Publishes**

25 titles/year. Receives 5,000 queries and 3,000 mss/year. 20% of books from first-time authors; 80-85% from unagented writers. Publishes book 2 years after acceptance of ms. Does not accept simultaneous submissions. Book catalog and ms guidelines online.

- **O—** Annick Press maintains "a commitment to high quality books that entertain and challenge. Our publications share fantasy and stimulate imagination, while encouraging children to trust their judgment and abilities." *Does not accept unsolicited mss.*

Recent Title(s) *The Mole Sisters and the Fairy Ring*, by Roslyn Schwartz; *The Dirt Eaters*, by Dennis Foon; *Archers, Alchemists, and 98 other Medieval Jobs You Might Have Loved or Loathed*, by Priscilla Galloway.

ANVIL PRESS

3008 MPO, Vancouver BC V6B 3X5 Canada. (604)876-8710. Fax: (604)879-2667. E-mail: anvil@anvilpress.com. Website: www.anvilpress.com. **Acquisitions:** Brian Kaufman. Estab. 1988. Publishes trade paperback originals. **Publishes 8-10 titles/year. Receives 300 queries/year. 80% of books from first-time authors; 70% from unagented writers. Pays 15% royalty on net receipts. Offers $500 advance.** Publishes book 8 months after acceptance of ms. Accepts simultaneous submissions. Responds in 2 months to queries; 6 months to mss. Book catalog for 9×12 SAE with 2 first-class stamps; ms guidelines online.

- Canadian authors only.
- **O—** "Anvil Press publishes contemporary adult fiction, poetry, and drama, giving voice to up-and-coming Canadian writers, exploring all literary genres, discovering, nurturing, and promoting new Canadian literary talent." Currently emphasizing urban/suburban themed fiction and poetry; de-emphasizing historical novels.

Fiction Experimental, literary, short story collections. Contemporary, modern literature—no formulaic or genre. Query with SASE.

Poetry "Get our catalog, look at our poetry. We do very little poetry—maybe 1-2 titles per year." Query, or submit 12 sample poems.

Recent Title(s) *Tight Like That*, by Jim Christy (fiction); *Rattlesnake Plantain*, by Heidi Greco (poetry).

Tips Audience is young, informed, educated, aware, with an opinion, culturally active (films, books, the performing arts). "No U.S. authors. Research the appropriate publisher for your work."

BEACH HOLME PUBLISHERS, LTD.

1010-409 Granville St., Vancouver BC V6C 1T2 Canada. (604)733-4868. Fax: (604)733-4860. E-mail: bhp@beach holme.bc.ca. Website: www.beachholme.bc.ca. **Acquisitions:** Michael Carroll, publisher (adult and young adult fiction, poetry, creative nonfiction); Jen Hamilton, production manager; Sarah Warren, publicity and marketing coordinator. Estab. 1971. Publishes trade paperback originals. **Publishes 10-14 titles/year. Receives 1,000 submissions/year. 40% of books from first-time authors; 75% from unagented writers. Pays 10% royalty on retail price. Offers $500 average advance.** Publishes book 1 year after acceptance of ms. Does not accept simultaneous submissions. Responds in 4-6 months to queries. Ms guidelines online.

Imprints Porcepic Books (literary); Sandcastle Books (children's/YA); Prospect Books (nonfiction).

- **O—** Beach Holme seeks "to publish excellent, emerging Canadian fiction, nonfiction, and poetry and to contribute to Canadian materials for children with quality young adult historical novels."

Nonfiction Subjects include creative nonfiction. Query with SASE, or submit outline, 2 sample chapter(s).

Fiction Experimental, literary, poetry, young adult (Canada historical/regional), Adult literary fiction from authors published in Canadian literary magazines. Interested in excellent quality, imaginative writing from writers published in Canadian literary magazines. Query with SASE, or submit outline, 2 sample chapter(s).

Recent Title(s) *Kameleon Man*, by Kim Barry Brunhuber; *Last Days in Africville*, by Dorothy Perkyns.

Tips "Make sure the manuscript is well written. We see so many that only the unique and excellent can't be put down. Prior publication is a must. This doesn't necessarily mean book-length manuscripts, but a writer should try to publish his or her short fiction or poetry."

BETWEEN THE LINES

720 Bathurst St., Suite #404, Toronto ON M5S 2R4 Canada. (416)535-9914. Fax: (416)535-1484. E-mail: btlbooks @web.ca. Website: www.btlbooks.com. **Acquisitions:** Paul Eprile, editorial coordinator. Publishes trade paperback originals. **Publishes 8 titles/year. Receives 350 queries and 50 mss/year. 80% of books from first-time authors; 95% from unagented writers. Pays 8% royalty.** Publishes book 1 year after acceptance of ms. Accepts simultaneous submissions. Responds in 2 months to queries; 2 months to proposals; 4 months to mss. Book catalog and ms guidelines for 8½×11 SAE and IRCs; ms guidelines online.

- **O—** "We are a small independent house concentrating on politics and public policy issues, social issues, gender issues, international development, education, and the environment. We publish mainly Canadian authors."

Nonfiction Subjects include education, gay/lesbian, government/politics, health/medicine, history, memoirs, social sciences, sociology, women's issues/studies. Submit proposal package including outline, 2-3 sample chapter(s). Reviews artwork/photos as part of ms package.

Recent Title(s) *Booze: A Distilled History*; *User Error: Resisting Computer Culture*.

⚡ THE BOOKS COLLECTIVE

214-21, 10405 Jasper Ave., Edmonton AB T5J 3S2 Canada. (780)448-0590. Fax: (780)448-0640. Website: www.bookscollective.com. Estab. 1992. Publishes hardcover and trade paperback originals. **Publishes 6-10 titles/ year; imprint publishes 2-5 titles/year. 30-60% of books from first-time authors; 90% from unagented writers. Pays 6-12% royalty on retail price. Offers $250-500 (Canadian) advance.** Publishes book 1 year after acceptance of ms. Does not accept simultaneous submissions. Responds in 1 month to queries; 1 month to proposals; 6 months to mss. Book catalog for 9×12 SAE with 4 first-class Canadian stamps or on website; ms guidelines online.

Imprints Tesseract Books, River Books, Slipstream Books.

○→ "All nonfiction projects are developed from query letters or are developed in-house. Always query first." Canadian authors only (expats or living abroad, landed immigrants OK). All non-Canadian submissions returned unread."

Nonfiction Biography, multimedia. Subjects include creative nonfiction, language/literature, memoirs, multicultural. Query with SASE, or submit proposal package including outline, 1-3 sample chapter(s), résumé. Reviews artwork/photos as part of ms package. Send photocopies.

Fiction Experimental, fantasy, feminist, gay/lesbian, horror, literary, mainstream/contemporary, multicultural, multimedia, plays, poetry, regional, science fiction, short story collections. Tesseract Books publishes an annual anthology of Canadian speculative short fiction and poetry. Query with SASE, or submit proposal package including 1-3 sample chapter(s), résumé, synopsis, or submit complete ms.

Poetry Query, or submit 5-10 sample poems, or submit complete ms.

Recent Title(s) *Tinka's New Dress*, by Ronnie Burkett (contemporary drama); *Gypsy Messenger*, by Marijan Megla (poetry); *The Healer* (speculative fiction).

Tips "Our books are geared for literate, intelligent readers of literary mainstream, cutting edge, and speculative writing. If you do not know our titles, query first or write for guidelines. Look up our titles and study suitability of your manuscript. We are a writers' co-op—expect long timelines. Unless your manuscript is of surpassing excellence, it will not survive omission of an SASE."

⊘ ⚡ BOREALIS PRESS, LTD.

110 Bloomingdale St., Ottawa ON K2C 4A4 Canada. (613)798-9299. Fax: (613)798-9747. E-mail: borealis@istar. ca. Website: www.borealispress.com. Frank Tierney, president. **Acquisitions:** Glenn Clever, senior editor. Estab. 1972. Publishes hardcover and paperback originals and reprints. **Publishes 20 titles/year. Receives 400-500 submissions/year. 80% of books from first-time authors; 95% from unagented writers. Pays 10% royalty on net receipts. 3 free author's copies.** Publishes book 18 months after acceptance of ms. Does not accept simultaneous submissions. Responds in 2 months to queries; 4 months to mss. Book catalog and ms guidelines online.

Imprints Tecumseh Press.

○→ "Our mission is to publish work which will be of lasting interest in the Canadian book market." Currently emphasizing Canadian fiction, nonfiction, drama, poetry. De-emphasizing children's books.

Nonfiction Biography, children's/juvenile, reference. Subjects include government/politics, history, language/ literature, regional. "Only material Canadian in content." Looks for "style in tone and language, reader interest, and maturity of outlook." Query with SASE, or submit outline, 2 sample chapter(s). *No unsolicited mss.* Reviews artwork/photos as part of ms package.

Fiction Adventure, ethnic, historical, juvenile, literary, mainstream/contemporary, romance, short story collections, young adult. "Only material Canadian in content and dealing with significant aspects of the human situation." Query with SASE, or submit 1-2 sample chapter(s), synopsis. *No unsolicited mss.*

Recent Title(s) *Canada's Governors General At Play*, by James Noonan; *James McGill of Montreal*, by John Cooper; *Musk Oxen of Gango*, by Mary Burpee.

⚡ THE BOSTON MILLS PRESS

132 Main St., Erin ON N0B 1T0 Canada. (519)833-2407. Fax: (519)833-2195. E-mail: books@bostonmillspress.com. Website: www.bostonmillspress.com. President: John Denison. **Acquisitions:** Noel Hudson, managing editor. Estab. 1974. Publishes hardcover and trade paperback originals. **Publishes 20 titles/year. Receives 100 submissions/year. 40% of books from first-time authors; 95% from unagented writers. Pays 8% royalty on retail price. Offers advance.** Publishes book 6 months-2 years after acceptance of ms. Accepts simultaneous submissions. Responds in 2 months to queries. Book catalog free.

○→ Boston Mills Press publishes specific market titles of Canadian and American interest including history, transportation, and regional guidebooks. "We like very focused books aimed at the North American market."

Nonfiction Coffee table book, gift book, illustrated book. Subjects include Americana, art/architecture, cooking/foods/nutrition, creative nonfiction, gardening, history, military/war, nature/environment, photography, recreation, regional, sports, travel, Canadiana. "We're interested in anything to do with Canadian or American history—especially transportation." No autobiographies. Query with SASE. Reviews artwork/photos as part of ms package. Send photocopies.

N ⊕ BRADT TRAVEL GUIDES, LTD.

19 High St., Chalfont St. Peter Buckes SL9 9QE United Kingdom. 01753 893444. Fax: 01753 892333. E-mail: info@bradt-travelguides.com. Website: www.bradt-travelguides.com. **Acquisitions:** Tricia Hayne, editorial director; Adrian Phillips, senior editor. Estab. 1974. Publishes mass market paperback originals. **Publishes 25 titles/year. Receives 150 queries and 60 mss/year. 30% of books from first-time authors; 95% from unagented writers. Pays 11½-12½% royalty on wholesale price. Offers advance.** Publishes book 6 months after acceptance of ms. Does not accept simultaneous submissions. Responds in 1 month to queries; 1 month to proposals; 1 month to mss. Book catalog online; ms guidelines by e-mail.

Nonfiction Subjects include general nonfiction, travel, and a new series of mini guides to more unusual European cities. "We specialize in unusual destinations—generally not mass market holiday regions. Wildlife, history, culture and responsible travel important." Query with SASE, or submit outline, details of competition and author's suitability for the title.

Recent Title(s) *Ukraine: The Bradt Travel Guide*, by Andrew Evans; *Macedonia: The Bradt Travel Guide*, by Thammy Evans; *Lille: The Bradt Mini Guide*, by Laurence Phillips.

Tips "Thinking, responsible travelers who are interested in destinations off the beaten tourist track. Be enthusiastic about the country you want to cover—we often commission energetic first-time authors in preference to seasoned hacks. Include an e-mail address for replies if possible."

⊡ BROKEN JAW PRESS

Box 596, Station A, Fredericton NB E3B 5A6 Canada. (506)454-5127. Fax: (506)454-5127. E-mail: jblades@nbnet.nb.ca. Website: www.brokenjaw.com. Publisher: Joe Blades. **Acquisitions:** Rob McLennan, editor (Cauldron Book Series only). Publishes Canadian-authored trade paperback originals and reprints. **Publishes 8-12 titles/year. 50% of books from first-time authors; 100% from unagented writers. Pays 10% royalty on retail price. Offers $0-100 advance.** Publishes book 18 months after acceptance of ms. Does not accept simultaneous submissions. Responds in 1 year to mss. Book catalog for 9×12 SAE with 2 first-class Canadian stamps in Canada; ms guidelines online.

Imprints Book Rat, SpareTime Editions, Dead Sea Physh Products, Maritimes Arts Projects Productions.

○→ "We are a small, mostly literary Canadian publishing house."

Nonfiction Illustrated book, self-help. Subjects include creative nonfiction, gay/lesbian, history, language/literature, regional, women's issues/studies, contemporary culture. Reviews artwork/photos as part of ms package.

Fiction Literary.

Recent Title(s) *Sunset*, by Pablo Urbanyi, translated by Hugh Hazelton (fiction); *All the Perfect Disguises*, by Lorri Neilsen Glenn (poetry).

Tips "No queries, please. Unsolicited manuscripts only in the context of the Poets' Corner Award. Please see the award guidelines on our website."

⊕ BROWN SKIN BOOKS

Pentimento, Ltd., P.O. Box 46504, London N1 3NT United Kingdom. E-mail: info@brownskinbooks.co.uk. Website: www.brownskinbooks.co.uk. **Acquisitions:** Vastiana Belfon, managing director (erotic fiction by women of color). Estab. 2002. Publishes trade paperback originals. **Publishes 7 titles/year. 75% of books from first-time authors; 80% from unagented writers. Pays 5-50% royalty, or makes outright purchase.** Publishes book 6 months after acceptance of ms. Accepts simultaneous submissions. Responds in 1 month to queries; 1 month to proposals; 2 months to mss. Book catalog and ms guidelines online.

Fiction Erotica. "We are looking for erotic short stories or novels written by women of color." Submit proposal package including 2 sample chapter(s), synopsis.

Recent Title(s) *Personal Business*, by Isabel Baptiste; *Body and Soul*, by Jade Williams.

Tips "Audience is women of color aged between 18 and 50, living in the U.S., Canada, Europe, Africa, and the Caribbean. Please make sure that there is a strong story with believable characters. This is just as important as the sex in our erotic fiction."

⬛ THE BRUCEDALE PRESS

P.O. Box 2259, Port Elgin ON N0H 2C0 Canada. (519)832-6025. Website: www.bmts.com/~brucedale. **Acquisitions:** Anne Duke Judd, editor-in-chief. Publishes hardcover and trade paperback originals. **Publishes 3 titles/ year. Receives 50 queries and 30 mss/year. 75% of books from first-time authors; 100% from unagented writers. Pays royalty.** Publishes book 1 year after acceptance of ms. Accepts simultaneous submissions. Book catalog for #10 SASE (Canadian postage or IRC) or online; ms guidelines online.

    ○➤ The Brucedale Press publishes books and other materials of regional interest and merit as well as literary, historical, and/or pictorial works. Accepts works by Canadian authors only. Submissions accepted November-December, unless invited at other times. Early submissions returned unread.

Nonfiction Biography, children's/juvenile, humor, illustrated book, reference. Subjects include history, language/literature, memoirs, military/war, nature/environment, photography. "Invitations to submit are sent to writers and writers' groups on The Brucedale Press mailing list when projects are in progress. Send a #10 SASE to have your name added to the list. Unless responding to an invitation to submit, query first, with outline and sample chapter for book-length submissions. Submit full manuscript of work intended for children. A brief résumé of your writing efforts and successes is always of interest and may bring future invitations, even if the present submission is not accepted for publication." Reviews artwork/photos as part of ms package.

Fiction Fantasy, feminist, historical, humor, juvenile, literary, mainstream/contemporary, mystery, plays, poetry, romance, short story collections, young adult.

Recent Title(s) *Barns of the Queen's Bush,* by Jon Radojkovic; *Thirty Years on Call: A Country Doctor's Family Life,* by Doris Pennington; *The Quilted Grapevine,* by Nancy-Lou Patterson.

Tips "Our focus is very regional. In reading submissions, I look for quality writing with a strong connection to the Queen's Bush area of Ontario. Suggest all authors visit our website, get a catalog, and read our books before submitting."

⬛ CANADIAN LIBRARY ASSOCIATION

328 Frank St., Ottawa ON K2P 0X8 Canada. (613)232-9625, ext. 322. Fax: (613)563-9895. E-mail: publishing@cla .ca. Website: www.cla.ca. Publishes trade paperback originals. **Publishes 4 titles/year. Receives 10 queries and 5 mss/year. 50% of books from first-time authors; 100% from unagented writers. Pays 10% royalty on wholesale price.** Publishes book 6 months after acceptance of ms. Does not accept simultaneous submissions. Responds in 1 month to queries; 3 months to proposals; 3 months to mss. Book catalog and ms guidelines free.

    ○➤ "CLA publishes practical/professional/academic materials with a Canadian focus or direct Canadian application as a service to CLA members and to contribute to the professional development of library staff."

Nonfiction Reference, textbook. Subjects include history, language/literature, library science. Query with SASE, or submit outline. Reviews artwork/photos as part of ms package. Send photocopies.

Recent Title(s) *The B2B Canadian Research Sourcebook: Your Essential Guide*; *Demystifying Copyright: A Researcher's Guide to Copyright in Canadian Libraries and Archives.*

Tips Audience is library and information scientists.

⬛ CANADIAN PLAINS RESEARCH CENTER

University of Regina, Regina SK S4S 0A2 Canada. (306)585-4795. Fax: (306)585-4699. E-mail: brian.mlazgar@ur egina.ca. Website: www.cprc.uregina.ca. **Acquisitions:** Brian Mlazgar, coordinator. Estab. 1973. Publishes scholarly paperback originals and some casebound originals. **Publishes 8-10 titles/year. Receives 15-20 submissions/year. 35% of books from first-time authors.** Publishes book 2 years after acceptance of ms. Does not accept simultaneous submissions. Responds in 6 months to queries. Book catalog and ms guidelines free.

    ○➤ Canadian Plains Research Center publishes scholarly research on the Canadian plains.

Nonfiction Biography, illustrated book, technical, textbook. Subjects include business/economics, government/ politics, history, nature/environment, regional, sociology. "The Canadian Plains Research Center publishes the results of research on topics relating to the Canadian Plains region, although manuscripts relating to the Great Plains region will be considered. Material *must* be scholarly. Do not submit health, self-help, hobbies, music, sports, psychology, recreation, or cookbooks unless they have a scholarly approach." Query with SASE, or submit complete ms. Reviews artwork/photos as part of ms package.

Recent Title(s) *Discover Saskatchewan,* by Nilson (guide to historic sites and markers).

Tips "Pay attention to manuscript preparation and accurate footnoting, according to *Chicago Manual of Style.*"

⬛ CHA PRESS

17 York St., Ottawa ON K1N 9J6 Canada. (613)241-8005, ext. 264. Fax: (613)241-5055. E-mail: chapress@cha. ca. Website: www.cha.ca. **Acquisitions:** Eleanor Sawyer, director of publishing. **Publishes 4-5 titles/year. Receives 5 queries and 3 mss/year. 40% of books from first-time authors; 90% from unagented writers.**

Pays 10-17% royalty on retail price, or makes outright purchase of $250-1,000. Offers $500-1,500 advance. Responds in 3 months to queries. Book catalog and ms guidelines free.

O-π CHA Press strives to be Canada's health administration textbook publisher. "We serve readers in our broad continuum of care in regional health authorities, hospitals, and health care facilities and agencies, which are governed by trustees." Currently emphasizing history of regionalization; accountability of boards/executives; executives and leadership. De-emphasizing hospital-based issues of any type.

Nonfiction How-to, textbook, guides. Subjects include health/medicine, history. Query with SASE, or submit outline.

Recent Title(s) *Governance for Health System Trustees*, by Jannice E. Moore; *Strengthening the Quality of Cancer Services in Ontario*, edited by Terrence Sullivan, William Evans, Helen Angus, and Alan Hudson.

Tips Audience is healthcare facility managers (senior/middle); policy analysts/researchers; nurse practitioners and other healthcare professionals; trustees. "CHA Press is looking to expand its frontlist in 2003 to include governance, risk management, security and safety, health system reform, and quality assessment. Don't underestimate amount of time it will take to write or mistake generic 'how-to health for mass media' as appropriate for CHA's specialty press."

CHEMTEC PUBLISHING

38 Earswick Dr., Toronto-Scarborough, ON M1E 1C6 Canada. (416)265-2603. Fax: (416)265-1399. E-mail: info@chemtec.org. Website: www.chemtec.org. **Acquisitions:** Anna Wypych, president. Publishes hardcover originals. **Publishes 5 titles/year. Receives 10 queries and 7 mss/year. 20% of books from first-time authors. Pays 5-15% royalty on retail price.** Publishes book 6 months after acceptance of ms. Accepts simultaneous submissions. Responds in 2 months to queries; 4 months to mss. Book catalog and ms guidelines free.

O-π Chemtec publishes books on polymer chemistry, physics, and technology. "Special emphasis is given to process additives and books which treat subject in comprehensive manner."

Nonfiction Technical, textbook. Subjects include science, environment, chemistry, polymers. Submit outline, sample chapter(s).

Recent Title(s) *Handbook of Fillers*, by George Wypych; *Handbook of Solvents*, by multiple authors.

Tips Audience is industrial research and universities.

CICERONE PRESS

2 Police Square, Milnthorpe, Cumbria LA7 7PY United Kingdom. 015395 62069. Fax: 015395 63417. E-mail: info@cicerone.co.uk. Website: www.cicerone.co.uk. **Acquisitions:** Jonathan Williams, acquisitions editor. Publishes hardcover and trade paperback originals and reprints. **Publishes 24 titles/year. Receives 50-100 queries and 50 mss/year. 35% of books from first-time authors; 100% from unagented writers.** Publishes book 1 year after acceptance of ms. Does not accept simultaneous submissions. Responds in 2 months to mss. Book catalog online.

O-π Cicerone specializes in guides to the great outdoors—hiking, climbing, cycling, mountaineering, etc. No fiction or poetry.

Nonfiction Reference. Subjects include sports, travel. Query with SASE, or submit outline, 2 sample chapter(s).

Recent Title(s) *Walking in the Alps*, by Kev Reynolds (topography nonfiction).

CIPD PUBLISHING

CIPD House, Camp Rd., Wimbledon SW19 4UX United Kingdom. Website: www.cipdpublishing.co.uk. **Acquisitions:** Ruth Lake, commissioning editor (student textbook); Mula Bhaumik, commissioning editor (practicioner products in regulatory areas); Stephen Partridge, commissioning editor (practicioner products). Publishes trade paperback originals and reprints. **Publishes 31 titles/year. Pays 2-10% royalty on wholesale price.** Publishes book 3 months after acceptance of ms. Ms guidelines online.

Nonfiction Textbook, subscription products. Subjects include business/economics, general nonfiction (HR). Submit proposal package including outline, 1 sample chapter(s).

Recent Title(s) *Employment Law for People Managers*.

Tips "Audience is HR practicioners and students, and training professionals."

COACH HOUSE BOOKS

401 Huron St. on bpNichol Lane, Toronto ON M5S 2G5 Canada. (416)979-2217. Fax: (416)977-1158. E-mail: mail@chbooks.com. Website: www.chbooks.com. **Acquisitions:** Alana Wilcox, editor. Publishes trade paperback originals. **Publishes 16 titles/year. 80% of books from first-time authors; 100% from unagented writers. Pays 10% royalty on retail price.** Publishes book 1 year after acceptance of ms. Does not accept simultaneous submissions. Responds in 6 months to queries. Ms guidelines online.

Nonfiction Artists' books. Query with SASE. **All unsolicited mss returned unopened.**

Fiction Experimental, literary, plays. "Consult website for submissions policy." **All unsolicited mss returned unopened.**

Poetry Consult website for guidelines. Query.

Recent Title(s) *Eunoia*, by Christian Bök (poetry); *Lenny Bruce Is Dead*, by Jonathan Goldstein (fiction); *All My Friends are Superheroes*, by Andrew Kaufman (fiction).

COMPENDIUM PUBLISHING, LTD.

43 Frith St., 1st Floor, London W1V 5TE United Kingdom. (0207)287-4570. Fax: (0207)494-0583. E-mail: compendiumpub@aol.com. Website: www.compendiumpublishing.com. **Acquisitions:** Alan Greene, publisher. Publishes hardcover originals and reprints, trade paperback originals and reprints. **Publishes 50 titles/year. Receives 1,000 mss/year. 70% of books from first-time authors; 80% from unagented writers. Pays 5-12½% royalty on net receipts, or makes outright purchase of $3,000-10,000.** Publishes book 18 months after acceptance of ms. Accepts simultaneous submissions. Responds in 1 month to queries; 3 months to proposals; 3 months to mss.

Nonfiction Coffee table book, cookbook, gift book, illustrated book, reference, self-help, technical. Subjects include anthropology/archeology, art/architecture, cooking/foods/nutrition, gardening, gay/lesbian, history, hobbies, military/war, nature/environment, photography, recreation, sex, sports, travel, women's issues/studies, transport. Submit outline, sample chapter(s), or submit complete ms.

Recent Title(s) *History of Science*, by Dr. Peter Whitfield; *The Art of Painting Miniatures*, by Alex Castro; *Ballparks*, by Jim Sutton.

COTEAU BOOKS

Thunder Creek Publishing Co-operative Ltd., 401-2206 Dewdney Ave., Suite 401, Regina SK S4R 1H3 Canada. (306)777-0170. Fax: (306)522-5152. E-mail: coteau@coteaubooks.com. Website: www.coteaubooks.com. **Acquisitions:** Geoffrey Ursell, publisher. Estab. 1975. Publishes trade paperback originals and reprints. **Publishes 20 titles/year. Receives 200 queries and 200 mss/year. 50% of books from first-time authors; 100% from unagented writers. Pays 10% royalty on retail price.** Publishes book 1 year after acceptance of ms. Does not accept simultaneous submissions. Responds in 2 months to queries; 6 months to mss. Book catalog free; ms guidelines online.

○━ "Our mission is to publish the finest in Canadian fiction, nonfiction, poetry, drama, and children's literature, with an emphasis on Saskatchewan and prairie writers." De-emphasizing science fiction, picture books.

Nonfiction Coffee table book, reference. Subjects include creative nonfiction, ethnic, history, language/literature, memoirs, regional, sports, travel. Canadian authors only. Submit 3-4 sample chapter(s), author bio, SASE.

Fiction Ethnic, fantasy, feminist, gay/lesbian, historical, humor, juvenile, literary, mainstream/contemporary, multicultural, multimedia, mystery, plays, poetry, regional, short story collections, spiritual, sports, young adult, novels, short fiction, middle years. *Canadian authors only*. No science fiction. No children's picture books. Submit 3-4 sample chapter(s), author bio, SASE.

Poetry Submit 20-25 sample poems, or submit complete ms.

Recent Title(s) *In the Same Boat*, juvenile fiction series for ages 8 and up (promotes familiarity with other cultures); *Penelope's Way*, by Blanche Howard (novel); *Out of Her Backpack*, by Laura Cutler (short stories).

Tips "Look at past publications to get an idea of our editorial program. We do not publish romance, horror, or picture books but are interested in juvenile and teen fiction from Canadian authors. Submissions may be made by e-mail (maximum 20 pages) with attachments."

CRESCENT MOON PUBLISHING

P.O. Box 393, Maidstone Kent ME14 5XU United Kingdom. E-mail: jrobinson@crescentmoon.org.uk. Website: www.crescentmoon.org.uk. **Acquisitions:** Jeremy Robinson, director (arts, media, cinema, literature); Cassidy Hushes (visual arts). Estab. 1988. Publishes hardcover and trade paperback originals. **Publishes 25 titles/year. Receives 300 queries and 400 mss/year. 1% of books from first-time authors; 1% from unagented writers. Pays royalty. Offers negotiable advance.** Publishes book 18 months after acceptance of ms. Accepts simultaneous submissions. Responds in 2 months to queries; 4 months to proposals; 4 months to mss. Book catalog and ms guidelines free.

Imprints Joe's Press, *Pagan America Magazine*, *Passion Magazine*.

○━ "Our mission is to publish the best in contemporary work, in poetry, fiction, and critical studies, and selections from the great writers." Currently emphasizing nonfiction (media, film, music, painting). De-emphasizing children's books.

Nonfiction Biography, children's/juvenile, illustrated book, reference, scholarly (academic), textbook. Subjects include Americana, art/architecture, gardening, language/literature, music/dance, philosophy, religion, travel, women's issues/studies. Query with SASE, or submit outline, 2 sample chapter(s). Reviews artwork/photos as part of ms package. Send photocopies.

Fiction Erotica, experimental, feminist, gay/lesbian, literary, short story collections. "We do not publish much fiction at present but will consider high quality new work." Query with SASE, or submit outline, 2 sample chapter(s), synopsis.

Poetry "We prefer a small selection of the poet's very best work at first. We prefer free or nonrhyming poetry. Do not send too much material." Query, or submit 6 sample poems.

Recent Title(s) *Nuclear War in the UK* (nonfiction); *Andy Goldworthy in Close-UP* (nonfiction).

Tips "Our audience is interested in new contemporary writing."

CRESSRELLES PUBLISHING CO., LTD.

10 Station Rd., Industrial Estate, Colwall, Malvern Worcestershire WR13 6RN United Kingdom. Phone/fax: 01684 540154. E-mail: simonsmith@cressrelles4drama.fsbusiness.co.uk. Publishes hardcover and trade paperback originals. **Publishes 10-20 titles/year. Pays royalty on retail price.** Book catalog free.

Imprints Kenyon-Deane, J. Garnet Miller, New Playwright's Network, Actinic Press.

Nonfiction Subjects include drama (plays), theater. Submit complete ms.

DAY BOOKS

Orchard Piece, Crawborough, Charlbury Oxfordshire OX7 3TX United Kingdom. E-mail: diaries@day-books.com. Submissions E-mail: ef@day-books.com. Website: www.day-books.com. **Acquisitions:** James Sanderson, managing editor (diaries and biographies). Estab. 1997. Publishes hardcover originals and trade paperback reprints. **Publishes 4 titles/year. Receives 30 queries and 30 mss/year. 10% of books from first-time authors; 80% from unagented writers. Pays 10% royalty on wholesale price. Offers $1,000-2,500 advance.** Publishes book 1 year after acceptance of ms. Accepts simultaneous submissions. Responds in 1 month to queries; 1 month to proposals; 1 month to mss. Book catalog online; ms guidelines free.

Nonfiction Autobiography, biography, scholarly. Subjects include general nonfiction, history, memoirs, regional. Query with SASE, submit proposal package, or submit complete ms. Reviews artwork/photos as part of ms package. Send photocopies.

Recent Title(s) *Inside Stalin's Russia: The Diaries of Reader Bullard, 1930-1934*, by Julian and Margaret Bullard (history/biography); *Lifting the Latch: A Life on the Land*, by Sheila Stewart (social history/biography).

DUNDURN PRESS, LTD.

8 Market St., Suite 200, Toronto ON M5E 1M6 Canada. (416)214-5544. Website: www.dundurn.com. **Acquisitions:** Acquisitions Editor. Estab. 1972. Publishes hardcover and trade paperback originals and reprints. **Receives 600 submissions/year. 50% of books from first-time authors; 85% from unagented writers. Pays 10% royalty on net receipts.** Publishes book an average of 1 year after acceptance of ms. Accepts simultaneous submissions. Responds in 1-2 months to queries. Ms guidelines online.

O— Dundurn publishes books by Canadian authors.

Nonfiction Subjects include art/architecture, history (Canadian and military), music/dance (drama), regional, art history, theater, serious and popular nonfiction.

Fiction Literary, mystery, young adult. "No romance, science fiction, or experimental." Query with SASE, and submit sample chapter(s), synopsis, author bio.

Recent Title(s) *The Glenwood Treasure*, by Kim Moritsugu (novel); *Dixie & the Dominion* (military history); *60 Years Behind the Wheel* (popular nonfiction).

ECCENOVA EDITIONS

P.O. Box 50001, 15-1594 Fairfield Rd., Victoria BC V8S 5L8 Canada. Fax: (250)595-8401. E-mail: acquisitions@eccenova.com. Website: www.eccenova.com. Estab. 2003. Publishes hardcover and trade paperback originals. **Publishes 6 titles/year. Receives 40-50 queries and 15 mss/year. 90% of books from first-time authors; 90% from unagented writers. Pays 15% royalty on wholesale price.** Publishes book 9 months after acceptance of ms. Does not accept simultaneous submissions. Responds in 1 week to e-mail queries; 1 month to proposals; 3 months to mss. Book catalog and ms guidelines online.

Nonfiction Scholarly. Subjects include anthropology/archeology, art/architecture, creative nonfiction, education (university), history, humanities, language/literature, New Age, philosophy, religion, science, social sciences, sociology, spirituality, women's issues/studies, magic/occult, theater. "We like to see solid argument construction and good research. Scholarly works should be 'toned down' for a more lay audience but must be credible and well supported, no matter how outlandish the premise! We have a preference for maverick thinkers who dare to challenge the status quo, but in order to have credibility, the author should make the most of his/her credentials and training/experience in the field. We have strong interests in religion, philosophy, and science, but are open to all humanities subjects. We can accept only greyscale/b&w images (if any) for the text-block.'' Query via e-mail or with SASE. Reviews artwork/photos as part of ms package. Send photocopies.

Recent Title(s) *Goddess in the Grass: Serpentine Mythology and the Great Goddess*, by Linda Foubister; *Black Magick Woman: The Sinister Side of the Song of Solomon*, by Janet Tyson; *The Sea's Enthrall: Memoirs of an Oceanographer*, by Dr. Timothy Parsons.

Tips ''Our audience is well educated and open minded. They appreciate a challenge to their ideas and like a good 'story' behind the research. Many are mature university students looking for support material for humanities/science courses or instructors looking for unique 'readers.' Because this company is founded on the idea of creating a unique library of human knowledge, emulating the Library at Alexandria, we are more interested in quality than quantity. We look for works that open new avenues of investigation or shed new light on old ones. We value original thought, so try not to create a book that rests solely on other people's work. Query first, explaining why you wrote the book, what your credentials are, and how you think it meets the criterion of originality.''

☑ ECRITS DES FORGES

C.P. 335, 1497 Laviolette, Trois-Rivieres QC G9A 5G4 Canada. (819)379-9813. Fax: (819)376-0774. E-mail: ecrits.desforges@tr.cgocable.ca. **Acquisitions:** Gaston Bellemare, president. Publishes hardcover originals. **Publishes 40 titles/year. Receives 30 queries and 1,000 mss/year. 10% of books from first-time authors; 90% from unagented writers. Pays 10-30% royalty. Offers 50% advance.** Publishes book 9 months after acceptance of ms. Accepts simultaneous submissions. Responds in 9 months to queries. Book catalog free.

　　○┐ Ecrits des Forges publishes only poetry written in French.

Poetry Submit 20 sample poems.

Recent Title(s) *Ode au St-Laurent*, by Gatien Lapointe (poetry).

☑ ECW PRESS

2120 Queen St. E., Suite 200, Toronto ON M4E 1E2 Canada. (416)694-3348. Fax: (416)698-9906. E-mail: info@ecwpress.com. Website: www.ecwpress.com. **Acquisitions:** Jack David, president (nonfiction); Michael Holmes, literary editor (fiction, poetry); Jennifer Hale, associate editor (pop culture, entertainment). Estab. 1979. Publishes hardcover and trade paperback originals. **Publishes 45 titles/year; imprint publishes 6 titles/year. Receives 500 queries and 300 mss/year. 30% of books from first-time authors. Pays 8-12% royalty on net receipts. Offers $300-5,000 advance.** Publishes book 18 months after acceptance of ms. Accepts simultaneous submissions. Book catalog free; ms guidelines online.

　　○┐ ECW publishes nonfiction about people or subjects that have a substantial fan base. Currently emphasizing books about music, Wicca, gambling, TV and movie stars.

Nonfiction Biography (popular), humor. Subjects include business/economics, creative nonfiction, gay/lesbian, general nonfiction, government/politics, health/medicine, history, memoirs, money/finance, regional, sex, sports, women's issues/studies, contemporary culture, Wicca, gambling, TV and movie stars. Submit proposal package including outline, 4-5 sample chapter(s), IRC, SASE. Reviews artwork/photos as part of ms package. Send photocopies.

Fiction ''We publish literary fiction and poetry from Canadian authors exclusively. Literary, mystery, poetry, short story collections, suspense. Visit company website to view submission guidelines.

Poetry ''We publish Canadian poetry exclusively.'' Query, or submit 4-5 sample poems.

Recent Title(s) *Too Close to the Falls*, by Catherine Gildiner; *Ghost Rider*, by Neil Peart; *Ashland*, by Gil Anderson (poetry).

Tips ''Visit our website and read a selection of our books.''

ℕ ☑ ÉDITIONS LA LIBERTE, INC.

3020 Chemin Ste-Foy, Ste-Foy QC G1X 3V6 Canada. (418)658-3763. Fax: (418)658-3763. **Acquisitions:** Hugues Doré, director of operations. Publishes trade paperback originals. **Publishes 4-5 titles/year. Receives 125 queries and 100 mss/year. 75% of books from first-time authors; 90% from unagented writers. Pays 10% royalty on retail price.** Publishes book 4 months after acceptance of ms. Accepts simultaneous submissions. Book catalog free.

　　○┐ Accepts only mss written in French. Specializes in history. De-emphasizing fiction and poetry.

Nonfiction Biography, children's/juvenile. Subjects include Americana, animals, anthropology/archeology, child guidance/parenting, cooking/foods/nutrition, education, government/politics, history, hobbies, language/literature, music/dance, nature/environment, psychology, science, sociology. Submit proposal package including complete ms.

Fiction Historical, juvenile, literary, mainstream/contemporary, short story collections, young adult. Query with SASE.

Recent Title(s) *Au coeur de la Litterature D'enfance et de Jeunesse*, by Charlotte Guerette (nonfiction); *Le Cahier des dix (collectif)* (history).

⊘ ⊞ FERNHURST BOOKS

Duke's Path, High St., Arundel, West Sussex United Kingdom. 01903-882277. Fax: 01903-882715. E-mail: sales@ fernhurstbooks.co.uk. Website: www.fernhurstbooks.co.uk. **Acquisitions:** Tim Davison, publisher. Publishes mass market paperback originals. **Publishes 12 titles/year. Receives 2-4 queries/year. 50% of books from first-time authors; 90% from unagented writers. Pays 10% royalty. Offers advance.** Publishes book up to 1 year after acceptance of ms. Does not accept simultaneous submissions. Book catalog free.

    ⊶ Fernhurst publishes books on watersports, producing practical, highly-illustrated handbooks on sailing and watersports. Currently emphasizing sailing and maintenance.

Nonfiction Gift book, how-to, humor. Subjects include sports. Submit proposal package including outline. *No unsolicited mss.* Reviews artwork/photos as part of ms package.

N A ⊘ ⊞ DAVID FICKLING BOOKS

31 Beaumont St., Oxford OX1 2NP England. (0)1865 339000. Website: www.davidficklingbooks.co.uk.

    ● High-quality fiction and picture books for 0-18. Submit synopsis, first few chapters, and SASE. Address to: Editor, David Fickling Books, (address as above).

⊞ FINDHORN PRESS

305A The Park, Findhorn, Forres Scotland IV36 3TE United Kingdom. 01309-690582. Fax: 01309-690036. E-mail: info@findhornpress.com. Website: www.findhornpress.com. **Acquisitions:** Thierry Bogliolo, publisher. Publishes trade paperback originals. **Publishes 12 titles/year. Receives 1,000 queries/year. 50% of books from first-time authors. Pays 10-15% royalty on wholesale price.** Publishes book 1 year after acceptance of ms. Book catalog and ms guidelines online.

Nonfiction Self-help. Subjects include health/medicine, nature/environment, spirituality. Submit proposal package including outline, 1 sample chapter, marketing plan.

⊞ FLYLEAF PRESS

(formerly Fly Leaf Press), 4 Spencer Villas, Glenageary, County Dublin Ireland. (353)1-2845906. Fax: (353)1-2806231. E-mail: flyleaf@indigo.ie. Website: www.flyleaf.ie. **Acquisitions:** James Ryan, managing editor (family history). Publishes hardcover originals. **Publishes 3 titles/year. Receives 15 queries and 10 mss/year. 60% of books from first-time authors; 100% from unagented writers. Pays 7-10% royalty on wholesale price.** Publishes book 6 months after acceptance of ms. Does not accept simultaneous submissions. Responds in 1 month to mss. Book catalog available free by request or online at website.

Nonfiction Subjects include history, hobbies, family history. Submit proposal package including outline, 1 sample chapter(s).

Recent Title(s) *Sources for Irish Family History*, by James G. Ryan; *Longford & Its People*, by David Leahy.

Tips Audience is family history hobbyists, history students, local historians.

⊘ ⊡ GUERNICA EDITIONS

Box 117, Station P, Toronto ON M5S 2S6 Canada. (416)658-9888. Fax: (416)657-8885. E-mail: guernicaeditions @cs.com. Website: www.guernicaeditions.com. **Acquisitions:** Antonio D'Alfonso, editor/publisher (poetry, nonfiction, novels); Ken Scambray, editor (US reprints). Estab. 1978. Publishes trade paperback originals, reprints, and software. **Publishes 25 titles/year. Receives 1,000 submissions and 750 mss/year. 20% of books from first-time authors; 99% from unagented writers. Pays 8-10% royalty on retail price. Or makes outright purchase of $200-5,000. Offers $200-2,000 advance.** Publishes book 15 months after acceptance of ms. Does not accept simultaneous submissions. Responds in 1 month to queries; 6 months to proposals; 1 year to mss. Book catalog online.

    ⊶ Guernica Editions is an independent press dedicated to the bridging of cultures. "We do original and translations of fine works. We are seeking essays on authors and translations with less emphasis on poetry."

Nonfiction Biography. Subjects include art/architecture, creative nonfiction, ethnic, film/cinema/stage, gay/ lesbian, government/politics, history, language/literature, memoirs, multicultural, music/dance, philosophy, psychology, regional, religion, sex, translation, women's issues/studies. Query with SASE. **All unsolicited mss returned unopened.** Reviews artwork/photos as part of ms package. Send photocopies.

Fiction Erotica, feminist, gay/lesbian, literary, multicultural, plays, poetry, poetry in translation. "We wish to open up into the fiction world and focus less on poetry. We specialize in European, especially Italian, translations." Query with SASE. **All unsolicited mss returned unopened.**

Poetry Feminist, gay/lesbian, literary, multicultural, poetry in translation. "We wish to have writers in translation. Any writer who has translated Italian poetry is welcomed. Full books only. Not single poems by different authors, unless modern, and used as an anthology. First books will have no place in the next couple of years." Query.

Recent Title(s) *Reel Canadians*, by Angela Baldassarre; *Italian Women in Black Dresses*, by Maria Mazziotti Gillan; *Song for My Father*, by Miriam Packer.

HAMBLEDON AND LONDON

102 Gloucester Ave., London NW1 8HX United Kingdom. 0044 207 586 0817. Fax: 0044 207 586 9970. E-mail: office@hambledon.co.uk. Submissions E-mail: ajm@hambledon.co.uk. Website: www.hambledon.co.uk. **Acquisitions:** Tony Morris, commissioning director (all history); Martin Sheppard, director (commissioning, editorial marketing). Publishes hardcover and trade paperback originals. **Publishes 20-30 titles/year; imprint publishes 20-30 titles/year. Receives 750 queries and 150 mss/year. 10% of books from first-time authors; 90% from unagented writers. Pays 0-10% royalty on retail price.** Publishes book 6 months after acceptance of ms. Accepts simultaneous submissions. Responds in 1 week to queries; 2 weeks to proposals; 1 month to mss. Book catalog online; ms guidelines free.

○─ "We publish high quality history at an affordable price for the general reader as well as the specialist."

Nonfiction Biography (historical). Subjects include history, language/literature. Submit outline. Reviews artwork/photos as part of ms package. Send photocopies.

Recent Title(s) *Churchill: A Study in Greatness*, by Geoffrey Best; *Pilgrimage in Medieval England*, by Diana Webb.

HARLEQUIN ENTERPRISES, LTD.

225 Duncan Mill Rd., Don Mills ON M3B 3K9 Canada. (416)445-5860. **Acquisitions:** Tara Gavin, editorial director New York (Silhouette, Harlequin, Steeple Hill, Luna); Diane Moggy, editorial director Toronto (MIRA, Red Dress Ink, HQN Books); Randall Toye, editorial director Toronto (Gold Eagle, Worldwide Library); Karin Stoecker, editorial director UK. U.S. Address: 233 Broadway, Suite 1001, New York NY 10279. (212)553-4200. UK: Eton House, 18-24 Paradise Lane, Richmond, Surrey, TW9 1SR, United Kingdom. Estab. 1949. Publishes mass market paperback, trade paperback, and hardcover originals and reprints. **Publishes 1,500 titles/year. Pays royalty. Offers advance.** Publishes book 1-2 years after acceptance of ms. Responds in 6 weeks to queries; 3 months to mss. Ms guidelines online.

Imprints Harlequin Books, Silhouette, MIRA, Gold Eagle, Luna, HQN Books, World Wide Library, Mills & Boon, Steeple Hill, Red Dress Ink.

• Websites: www.eharlequin.com; www.mirabooks.com; www.reddressink.com; www.steeplehill.com; www.luna-books.com.

Fiction Considers all types of serious romance and strong, mainstream, women's fiction. For series, query with SASE. For MIRA, *agented submissions only.*

Tips "The quickest route to success is to check www.eharlequin.com, other websites listed above, or write or call for submission guidlines. We acquire first novelists. Before submitting, read as many current titles in the imprint or line of your choice as you can. It's very important to know the genre, what readers are looking for, and the series or imprint most appropriate for your submission."

HARLEQUIN MILLS & BOON, LTD.

Harlequin Enterprises, Ltd., Eton House, 18-24 Paradise Rd., Richmond Surrey TW9 1SR United Kingdom. (44)0208-288-2800. Website: www.millsandboon.co.uk. **Acquisitions:** Bryona Green, associate senior editor (Harlequin Romance); Tessa Shapcott, senior editor (Harlequin Presents); Samantha Bell, senior editor (RDI); Linda Fildew, editor (Mills & Boon Historicals); and Sheila Hodgson, editor (Mills & Boon Medicals). Estab. 1908-1909. Publishes mass market paperback originals. **Pays advance against royalty.** Publishes book 2 years after acceptance of ms. Does not accept simultaneous submissions. Responds in 3 months to mss. Ms guidelines online.

Imprints Harlequin, Silhouette, Mills & Boon, MIRA, RDI.

○─ "World's largest publisher of brand name category romance and women's fiction; books are available for translation into more than 20 languages and distributed in more than 100 international markets."

Fiction Romance (contemporary, historical, regency period, medical). Query with SASE, or submit 3 sample chapter(s), synopsis.

Recent Title(s) *The Salvatore Marriage*, by Michelle Reid; *The Last Year of Being Single*, by Sarah Tucker; *Consultant in Crisis*, by Alison Roberts.

Tips "Study a wide selection of our current paperbacks to gain an understanding of our requirements, then write from the heart."

ⓝ ⊘ ⌖ HARPERCOLLINS CANADA, LTD.

2 Bloor St. E., 20th Floor, Toronto ON M4W 1A8 Canada. (416)975-9334. Fax: (416)975-5223. Website: www.harpercollins.ca.

 ● Harpercollins is not accepting unsolicited material at this time.

⊕ HELTER SKELTER PUBLISHING

4 Denmark St., London WC2H 8LL United Kingdom. (44)171 836 1151. Fax: (44)171 240 9880. E-mail: helter@skelter.demon.co.uk. **Acquisitions:** Sean Body, editor (music, film). Publishes hardcover and trade paperback originals and trade paperback reprints. **Publishes 10 titles/year. Receives 50 queries and 30 mss/year. 50% of books from first-time authors; 60% from unagented writers. Pays 8-12½% royalty on retail price. Offers $1,000-6,000 advance.** Publishes book 6 months after acceptance of ms. Accepts simultaneous submissions. Responds in 1 month to queries. Book catalog free.

Imprints Firefly.

 ⊶ "Our mission is to publish high quality books about music and cinema subjects of enduring appeal."

Nonfiction Biography. Subjects include music/dance. Submit outline, 2 sample chapter(s). Reviews artwork/photos as part of ms package. Send photocopies.

Recent Title(s) *Waiting for the Man*, Harry Shapiro.

Tips "The subject artist should have a career spanning at least five years."

⌖ HERITAGE HOUSE PUBLISHING CO., LTD.

301-3555 Outrigger Rd., Nanoose Bay BC V9P 9K1 Canada. (250)468-5328. Fax: (250)468-5318. E-mail: publisher@heritagehouse.ca. Website: www.heritagehouse.ca. **Acquisitions:** Rodger Touchie, publisher/president. Publishes trade paperback originals. **Publishes 10-12 titles/year. Receives 200 queries and 60 mss/year. 50% of books from first-time authors; 100% from unagented writers. Pays 9% royalty. Offers advance.** Publishes book 1 year after acceptance of ms. Does not accept simultaneous submissions. Responds in 2 months to queries. Book catalog for #10 SASE; ms guidelines online.

 ⊶ Heritage House is primarily a regional publisher of Western Canadiana and the Pacific Northwest. "We aim to publish and distribute good books that entertain and educate our readership regarding both historic and contemporary Western Canada and Pacific Northwest."

Nonfiction Biography, how-to, illustrated book. Subjects include animals, anthropology/archeology, cooking/foods/nutrition, history, nature/environment, recreation, regional, sports. "Writers should include a sample of their writing, an overview sample of photos or illustrations to support the text, and a brief letter describing who they are writing for." Query with SASE, or submit outline, 2-3 sample chapter(s). Reviews artwork/photos as part of ms package. Send photocopies.

Fiction Children's books. Very limited. Only author/illustrator collaboration.

Recent Title(s) *Daggers Unsheathed: The Political Assassination of Glen Clark*, by Judi Tyabji Wilson (political history); *Fortress of the Grizzlies: The Khutzeymateen Grizzly Bear Sanctuary*, by Dan Wakeman and Wendy Shymanski; *Born to Die: A Copy Killer's Final Message*, by Ian Macdonald and Betty O'Keefe.

Tips "Our books appeal to residents and visitors to the northwest quadrant of the continent. Present your material only after you have done your best."

⊕ HIPPOPOTAMUS PRESS

22 Whitewell Rd., Frome, Somerset BA11 4EL United Kingdom. 0173-466653. Fax: 01373-466653. **Acquisitions:** R. John, editor; M. Pargitter (poetry); Anna Martin (translation). Publishes hardcover and trade paperback originals. **Publishes 6-12 titles/year. 90% of books from first-time authors; 90% from unagented writers. Pays 7½-10% royalty on retail price. Offers advance.** Publishes book 10 months after acceptance of ms. Accepts simultaneous submissions. Responds in 1 month to queries. Book catalog free.

Imprints Hippopotamus Press, *Outposts* Poetry Quarterly, distributor for University of Salzburg Press.

 ⊶ Hippopotamus Press publishes first, full collections of verse by those well represented in the mainstream poetry magazines of the English-speaking world.

Nonfiction Subjects include language/literature, translation. Query with SASE, or submit complete ms.

Poetry "Read one of our authors! Poets often make the mistake of submitting poetry not knowing the type of verse we publish." Query, or submit complete ms.

Recent Title(s) *Mystic Bridge*, Edward Lowbury.

Tips "We publish books for a literate audience. We have a strong link to the Modernist tradition. Read what we publish."

⊕ HOW TO BOOKS, LTD.

3 Newtec Place, Magdalen Rd., Oxford OX4 1RE Great Britain. (00144)1865 793806. Fax: (00144)1865 248780. E-mail: info@howtobooks.co.uk. Website: www.howtobooks.co.uk. **Acquisitions:** Nikki Read, commissioning

editor (self-help, business, careers, home & family, living & working abroad). Publishes trade paperback originals and reprints. **Publishes 100 titles/year. Receives 200 queries and 100 mss/year. 80% of books from first-time authors; 90% from unagented writers.** Accepts simultaneous submissions. Responds in 1 month to queries; 1 month to proposals; 2 months to mss. Book catalog free or on website; ms guidelines free.

Nonfiction How-to, reference, self-help. Subjects include child guidance/parenting, creative nonfiction, money/finance, small business. "Submit a proposal you feel strongly about and can write knowledgably. Have a look at our catalog/website to see what we publish. We ask authors to send a synopsis for initial consideration." Submit proposal package including outline, 1 sample chapter.

Recent Title(s) *Our Greatest Writers*, by John Carrington; *Build Your Own Home*, by Tony Booth; *Meet Your Ancestors*, by Diane Marelli.

Tips "Our books are aimed at people who want to improve their lives, their careers, their general skills. Our authors have to have a passion and extensive knowledge about their subject area."

INSTITUTE OF PSYCHOLOGICAL RESEARCH, INC.

34 Fleury St. W., Montréal QC H3L 1S9 Canada. (514)382-3000. Fax: (514)382-3007. **Acquisitions:** Robert Chevrier, advisor; Dr. Nicholas Chevrier, vice president, scientific affairs. Estab. 1958. Publishes hardcover and trade paperback originals and reprints. **Publishes 12 titles/year. Receives 15 submissions/year. 10% of books from first-time authors; 100% from unagented writers. Pays 10-12% royalty.** Publishes book 6 months after acceptance of ms. Responds in 2 months to queries.

> ⚬━ Institute of Psychological Research publishes psychological tests and science textbooks for a varied professional audience.

Nonfiction Textbook. Subjects include philosophy, psychology, science, translation. "We are looking for psychological tests in French or English." Query with SASE, or submit complete ms.

Recent Title(s) *Épreuve individuelle d'habileté mentale*, by Jean-Marc Chevrier (intelligence test).

Tips "Psychologists, guidance counselors, professionals, schools, school boards, hospitals, teachers, government agencies and industries comprise our audience."

ISER BOOKS

Faculty of Arts Publications, Memorial University of Newfoundland, FM 2006, St. John's NF A1S 5S7 Canada. (709)737-8343. Fax: (709)737-7560. Website: www.mun.ca/iser/. **Acquisitions:** Al Potter, manager. Publishes trade paperback originals. **Publishes 3-4 titles/year. Receives 10-20 queries and 10 mss/year. 45% of books from first-time authors; 85% from unagented writers. Pays 6-10% royalty on wholesale price.** Publishes book 6 months after acceptance of ms. Does not accept simultaneous submissions. Responds in 1 month to queries; 2 months to proposals; 4 months to mss. Book catalog and ms guidelines free.

> ⚬━ Iser Books publishes research within such disciplines and in such parts of the world as are deemed of relevance to Newfoundland and Labrador.

Nonfiction Biography, reference. Subjects include anthropology/archeology, ethnic, government/politics, history, multicultural, recreation, regional, sociology, translation, women's issues/studies. Query with SASE, or submit proposal package including outline, 2-3 sample chapter(s).

Recent Title(s) *A Way of Life That Does Not Exist: Canada and the Extinguishment of the Innu*, by Colin Samson; *Narratives at Work: Women, Men, Unionization and the Fashioning of Identities*, by Linda K. Cullum.

KYLE CATHIE, LTD.

Kyle Cathie, 122 Arlington Rd., London NW1 7HP UK. (44)207-692-7215. Fax: (44)207-692-7260. E-mail: general.enquiries@kyle-cathie.com. Website: www.kyle-cathie.com. **Acquisitions:** Muna Reyal, senior editor (cookery/general); Caroline Taggart, senior editor (gardening/general); Sarah Epton, senior editor (health/general). Publishes hardcover and trade paperback originals. **Publishes 25 titles/year. Receives 300 queries/year. 15% of books from first-time authors; 10% from unagented writers. Pays 5-12½% royalty on retail price. Offers** ⅔ **of earnings on first print run as advance.** Publishes book 6 months after acceptance of ms. Accepts simultaneous submissions. Responds in 2 months to queries; 1 month to proposals; 2 weeks to mss. Book catalog free.

Nonfiction Cookbook, gift book, illustrated book, reference, self-help. Subjects include cooking/foods/nutrition, gardening, health/medicine. Reviews artwork/photos as part of ms package.

Recent Title(s) *Healthy Eating for Diabetes*, by Anthony Worrall-Thompson (cookery); *Gardeners' Question Time Plant Chooser*, by Matthew Biggs, John Cushnie, Bob Flowerdew, and Bunny Guinness (gardening); *The Exercise Bible*, by Joanna Hall (health and fitness).

Tips "We look for books which will have a long life, which contribute something new to the marketplace, and which have an angle—so we can get publicity."

◼ LES ÉDITIONS DU VERMILLON

305 St. Patrick St., Ottawa ON K1N 5K4 Canada. (613)241-4032. Fax: (613)241-3109. E-mail: leseditionsduvermil lon@rogers.com. **Acquisitions:** Jacques Flamand, editorial director. Publishes trade paperback originals. **Publishes 15-20 titles/year. Pays 10% royalty.** Publishes book 18 months after acceptance of ms. Responds in 6 months to mss. Book catalog free.

Fiction Juvenile, literary, religious, short story collections, young adult. Query with SASE.

Recent Title(s) *Ce pays qui est le mien*, by Didier Leclair (novel); *Une twiga â Ottawa*, by Mireille Messier (children, 8-10 years); *Ombres et lueurs*, by Gabrielle Poulin (poetry).

◼ LOBSTER PRESS

1620 Sherbrooke St. W, Suites C & D, Montreal QC H3H 1C9 Canada. (514)904-1100. Fax: (514)904-1101. Website: www.lobsterpress.com. **Acquisitions:** Gabriella Mancini, editorial manager. Publishes hardcover, trade paperback, and mass market paperback originals. **Publishes 25 titles/year. Receives 200 queries and 1,500 mss/year. 90% of books from first-time authors; 75% from unagented writers. Pays 5-10% royalty on retail price. Offers $1,000-6,000 (Canadian) advance.** Publishes book 2 years after acceptance of ms. Does not accept simultaneous submissions. Responds in 3 months to queries; 10 months to proposals; 1 year to mss.

● Lobster Press is presently not accepting submissions.

Nonfiction Children's/juvenile, illustrated book, self-help. Subjects include child guidance/parenting, creative nonfiction, history, sex, travel. Query with SASE (IRC or Canadian postage only), or submit complete ms. Reviews artwork/photos as part of ms package. Send photocopies.

Fiction Adventure (for children), historical (for children), juvenile, picture books, young adult. Submit complete ms.

Recent Title(s) *Sink or Swim*, by Valerie Coulman, illustrated by Ragé (picture book).

◼ LONE PINE PUBLISHING

10145 81st Ave., Edmonton AB T6E 1W9 Canada. (403)433-9333. Fax: (403)433-9646. Website: www.lonepinep ublishing.com. **Acquisitions:** Nancy Foulds, editorial director. Estab. 1980. Publishes trade paperback originals and reprints. **Publishes 30-40 titles/year. Receives 800 submissions/year. 75% of books from first-time authors; 95% from unagented writers. Pays royalty.** Does not accept simultaneous submissions. Responds in 3 months to queries. Book catalog free.

Imprints Lone Pine, Home World, Pine Candle, Pine Cone.

○➡ Lone Pine publishes natural history and outdoor recreation—including gardening—titles and some popular history and ghost story collections by region. "'The World Outside Your Door' is our motto—helping people appreciate nature and their own special place." Currently emphasizing ghost stories by region, popular history.

Nonfiction Subjects include animals, gardening, nature/environment, recreation, regional. The list is set for the next year and a half, but we are interested in seeing new material. Query with SASE, or submit outline, sample chapter(s). Reviews artwork/photos as part of ms package.

Recent Title(s) *Month-to-Month Gardening Guide for Ohio*, by Alison Beck and Debra Knapke; *Campfire Ghost Stories*, by Jo-Anne Christensen; *Bugs of Ontario*, by John Acorn and Ian Sheldon.

Tips "Writers have their best chance with recreational or nature guidebooks. Most of our books are strongly regional in nature."

◼ LTDBOOKS

200 N. Service Rd. West, Unit 1, Suite 301, Oakville ON L6M 2Y1 Canada. (905)847-6060. Fax: (905)847-6060. E-mail: editor@ltdbooks.com. Website: www.ltdbooks.com. **Acquisitions:** Dee Lloyd, editor; Terry Shiels, editor. Estab. 1999. Publishes electronic originals on disk or by download as well as selected trade paperback titles. **Publishes 15 titles/year. Pays 30% royalty on electronic titles and flat rate on trade paperbacks.** Publishes book more than 1 year after acceptance of ms. Accepts simultaneous submissions. Responds in 1-2 months to queries. Ms guidelines online.

● Only accepts electronic submissions. Paper submissions are automatically rejected.

○➡ "LTDBooks, an energetic presence in the rapidly expanding e-book market, is a multi-genre, royalty-paying fiction publisher specializing in high quality stories with strong characters and great ideas."

Fiction Adventure, fantasy (space fantasy, sword and sorcery), historical (general), horror (dark fantasy, futuristic, psychological, supernatural), literary, mainstream/contemporary, mystery (amateur sleuth, cozy, police procedural, private eye/hardboiled), romance (contemporary, futuristic/time travel, gothic, historical, regency period, romantic suspense), science fiction (hard science/technological, soft/sociological), suspense (amateur sleuth, cozy, police procedural, private eye/hardboiled), western, young adult (adventure, fantasy/science fiction, historical, horror, mystery/suspense, problem novels, romance, series, sports, thriller/espionage, western). Follow guidelines on website. Queries via e-mail only. All submissions must be in electronic format; paper submissions automatically rejected.

Recent Title(s) *Shadow Dweller Series*, by J.C. Wilder; *The Accidental Goddess*, by Linnea Sinclair writing as Megan Sybil Baker.

Tips "We publish only fiction. All of our books are electronic (as download or on disk) with ongoing additions to our new trade paperback program. All submitting authors must have a working e-mail address for correspondence."

⊠ MANOR HOUSE PUBLISHING, INC.

452 Cottingham Crescent, Ancaster ON L9G 3V6 Canada. (905)648-2193. Fax: (905)648-8369. E-mail: mdavie@t hestar.ca. Website: www.manor-house.biz. **Acquisitions:** Mike Davie, president (novels, poetry, and nonfiction). Estab. 1998. Publishes hardcover, trade paperback, and mass market paperback originals, and mass market paperback reprints. **Publishes 5-6 titles/year. Receives 30 queries and 20 mss/year. 90% of books from first-time authors; 90% from unagented writers. Pays 10-15% royalty on retail price.** Publishes book 12-14 months after acceptance of ms. Accepts simultaneous submissions. Responds in 1 month to queries; 1 month to proposals; 1 month to mss. Book catalog online; ms guidelines by e-mail.

Nonfiction Biography, coffee table book, how-to, humor, illustrated book, self-help. Subjects include alternative lifestyles, anthropology/archeology, business/economics, community, general nonfiction, history, sex, social sciences, sociology, spirituality. "We are a Canadian publisher, so manuscripts should be Canadian in content and aimed as much as possible at a wide, general audience." Query with SASE, or submit proposal package including outline, 3 sample chapter(s), author bio, or submit complete ms. Reviews artwork/photos as part of ms package. Send photocopies.

Fiction Adventure, experimental, gothic, historical, horror, humor, juvenile, literary, mainstream/contemporary, mystery, occult, poetry, regional, romance, short story collections, young adult. "Stories should have Canadian settings and characters should be Canadian, but content should have universal appeal to wide audience." Query with SASE, or submit proposal package including 3 sample chapter(s), synopsis, author bio, or submit complete ms.

Poetry "Poetry should engage, provoke, involve the reader. (I don't like yawning when I read.)" Query, or submit 12-20 sample poems, or submit complete ms.

Recent Title(s) *Political Losers*, by Michael B. Davie (politics/science); *Broken Dreams*, by Amanda Hyde (young adult novel); *Mystical Poetry*, by Deborah Morrison (poetry).

Tips "Our audience includes everyone—the general public/mass audience. Self-edit your work first, make sure it is well written with strong Canadian content."

Ⓝ ∅ ⊠ McCLELLAND & STEWART, LTD.

Imprint of The Canadian Publishers, 481 University Ave., Suite 900, Toronto ON M5G 2E9 Canada. (416)598-1114. Fax: (416)598-7764. E-mail: editorial@mcclelland.com. Website: www.mcclelland.com. Publishes hardcover, trade paperback, and mass market paperback originals and reprints. **Publishes 80 titles/year. Receives 1,500 queries/year. 10% of books from first-time authors; 30% from unagented writers. Pays 10-15% royalty on retail price (hardcover rates). Offers advance.** Publishes book 1 year after acceptance of ms. Responds in 3 months to proposals.

Imprints McClelland & Stewart, New Canadian Library, Douglas Gibson Books, Emblem Editions (Ellen Seligman, editor).

Nonfiction "We publish books by Canadian authors or on Canadian subjects." Biography, coffee table book, how-to, humor, illustrated book, reference, self-help. Subjects include agriculture/horticulture, animals, art/architecture, business/economics, child guidance/parenting, cooking/foods/nutrition, education, gardening, gay/lesbian, government/politics, health/medicine, history, hobbies, language/literature, military/war, money/finance, music/dance, nature/environment, philosophy, photography, psychology, recreation, religion, science, sociology, sports, translation, travel, women's issues/studies, Canadiana. Submit outline. **All unsolicited mss returned unopened.**

Fiction Experimental, historical, humor, literary (novels), mystery (some), short story collections. "We publish quality fiction by prize-winning authors, as well as the work of new and developing authors." **All unsolicited mss returned unopened.** Query.

Poetry "Only Canadian poets should apply. We publish only 4 titles each year." Query. *No unsolicited mss.*

Recent Title(s) *Oryx and Crake*, by Margaret Atwood; *The Island Walkers*, by John Bemrose; *The Last Crossing*, by Guy Vanderhaeghe.

🌐 MERCAT PRESS

10 Coates Crescent, Edinburgh EH3 7AL Scotland. E-mail: enquiries@mercatpress.com. Website: www.mercatp ress.com. **Acquisitions:** Sean Costello, managing editor; Tom Johnstone, managing editor. Publishes hardcover

and trade paperback originals and reprints. **Publishes 30 titles/year. Receives 200 queries and 100 mss/year. 10% of books from first-time authors; 70% from unagented writers. Pays 7½-10% royalty on retail price.** Publishes book 6 months after acceptance of ms. Accepts simultaneous submissions. Responds in 1 month to queries. Book catalog free or on website.

Nonfiction Biography, children's/juvenile, cookbook, reference, textbook, fiction. Subjects include agriculture/horticulture, art/architecture, cooking/foods/nutrition, gardening, government/politics, history, language/literature, memoirs, music/dance, nature/environment, photography, regional, sociology. Scottish interest only. Query with IRCs, or submit proposal package, including outline and 2 sample chapters.

Recent Title(s) *A Sense of Belonging to Scotland*, by Andy Hall; *Jessie's Journey*, by Jess Smith; *The One*, by Paul Reed.

Tips "Consult our website for an idea of the type of books we publish."

Ⓐ ☒ MIRA BOOKS

Imprint of Harlequin, 225 Duncan Mill Rd., Don Mills ON M3B 3K9 Canada. Website: www.mirabooks.com. **Acquisitions:** Amy Moore-Benson, senior editor. Publishes hardcover, trade paperback, and mass market originals. **Pays royalty. Offers advance.**

Fiction Relationship novels; contemporary and historical romance; political, psychological, and legal thrillers; family sagas. *Agented submissions only.* No e-mail queries.

🌐 MONARCH BOOKS

Imprint of Angus Hudson, Ltd., Concorde House, Grenville Place, London NW7 3SA United Kingdom. (44)020 8959 3668. Fax: (44)020 8959 3678. E-mail: tonyc@angushudson.com. **Acquisitions:** Tony Collins, editorial director (whole list). Estab. 1988. Publishes hardcover, trade paperback, and mass market paperback originals and reprints. **Publishes 35 titles/year. Receives 2,000 queries and 1,500 mss/year. 25% of books from first-time authors; 90% from unagented writers. Pays 10-15% royalty on wholesale price. Offers negotiable advance.** Publishes book 8 months after acceptance of ms. Accepts simultaneous submissions. Responds in 1 month to queries; 2 months to proposals; 1 month to mss. Book catalog and ms guidelines free.

Imprints Monarch.

    ○⊸ "We publish primarily for the evangelical Christian market, providing tools and resources for Christian leaders." Monarch Books publishes and distributes in the US and Canada through an arrangement with Kregel Books (Grand Rapids MI).

Nonfiction Biography, humor, reference, self-help. Subjects include child guidance/parenting, philosophy, psychology, religion, science, sex, sociology, Christian fiction. All subjects must have a Christian treatment. Query with SASE, or submit proposal package including outline, 2 sample chapter(s).

Recent Title(s) *The Heavenly Man*, by Brother Yun (biography).

Tips "Think about who you are writing for. What will a reader get as benefit from reading your book?"

☒ MOOSE ENTERPRISE BOOK & THEATRE PLAY PUBLISHING

684 Walls Side Rd., Sault Ste. Marie ON P6A 5K6 Canada. (705)779-3331. Fax: (705)779-3331. **Acquisitions:** Richard Mousseau, owner/editor (fiction, history, general); Edmond Alcid, editor (story poetry, juvenile/children, general). Publishes trade and mass market paperback originals. **Publishes 7-10 titles/year. Receives 120-180 queries and 10 mss/year. 60% of books from first-time authors; 100% from unagented writers. Pays 20-40% royalty on retail price.** Publishes book 6 months after acceptance of ms. Responds in 1 month to queries; 2 months to proposals; 2 months to mss. Book catalog and ms guidelines for #10 SASE.

Nonfiction Biography, children's/juvenile. Subjects include history, memoirs, military/war. Query with SASE, or submit proposal package including outline, 2 sample chapter(s), author bio. Reviews artwork/photos as part of ms package. Send photocopies.

Fiction Adventure, historical, horror, humor, military/war, mystery, plays, regional, science fiction, short story collections, western, young adult, story poetry. Query with SASE, or submit proposal package including 2 sample chapter(s), synopsis, author bio.

Poetry Western and story poetry. Send author's bio and summary of project, typed, double-spaced, 1-sided. Query, or submit 5 sample poems.

Recent Title(s) *A Long Exciting Trip to Peace*, by Angus Harnden (military/history); *Executor of Mercy*, by Edmond Alcid (adventure/novel); *An American Trapped in a Communist Paradise* (historical autobiography).

Tips "Send only material that is of moral quality. Send bio of author."

☒ NATURAL HERITAGE/NATURAL HISTORY, INC.

P.O. Box 95, Station O, Toronto ON M4A 2M8 Canada. (416)694-7907. Fax: (416)690-0819. E-mail: info@natural heritagebooks.com. Website: www.naturalheritagebooks.com. **Acquisitions:** Barry Penhale, publisher. Publishes trade paperback originals. **Publishes 10-12 titles/year. 50% of books from first-time authors; 85%**

from unagented writers. **Pays 8-10% royalty on retail price.** Publishes book 2-3 years after acceptance of ms. Accepts simultaneous submissions. Responds in 4 months to queries; 6 months to proposals; 6 months to mss. Book catalog free; ms guidelines online.

Imprints Natural Heritage Books.

○➤ Currently emphasizing heritage, history, nature.

Nonfiction Subjects include ethnic, history, nature/environment, recreation, regional. Submit outline.

Fiction Children's (age 8-12), biography/memoir. Query with SASE.

Recent Title(s) *Canoeing a Continent: On the Trail of Alexander Mackenzie*, by Max Finkelstein (nonfiction); *Algonquin Wildlife: Lessons in Survival*, by Norm Quinn (nonfiction); *The Underground Railroad: Next Stop, Toronto!*, by Adrienne Shadd, Afua Cooper, and Karolyn Smardz Frost (young adult nonfiction).

Tips "We are a Canadian publisher in the natural heritage and history fields. We publish only Canadian authors or books with significant Canadian content."

NEW SOCIETY PUBLISHERS

P.O. Box 189, Gabriola BC V0R 1X0 Canada. (250)247-9737. Fax: (250)247-7471. E-mail: info@newsociety.com. Website: www.newsociety.com. **Acquisitions:** Chris Plant, editor. Publishes trade paperback originals and reprints and electronic originals. **Publishes 20 titles/year. Receives 300 queries and 200 mss/year. 50% of books from first-time authors; 80% from unagented writers. Pays 10-12% royalty on wholesale price. Offers $0-5,000 advance.** Publishes book 9 months after acceptance of ms. Accepts simultaneous submissions. Responds in 1 month to queries; 2 months to proposals. Book catalog free or online; ms guidelines online.

Nonfiction Biography, how-to, illustrated book, self-help. Subjects include business/economics, child guidance/parenting, creative nonfiction, education, government/politics, memoirs, nature/environment, philosophy, regional. Query with SASE, or submit proposal package including outline, 2 sample chapter(s). Reviews artwork/photos as part of ms package. Send photocopies.

Recent Title(s) *The Party's Over: Oil, War & the Fate of Industrial Societies*, by Richard Heinberg (current affairs).

Tips Audience is activists, academics, progressive business people, managers. "Don't get an agent!"

NEWEST PUBLISHERS LTD.

201, 8540-109 St., Edmonton AB T6G 1E6 Canada. (780)432-9427. Fax: (780)433-3179. E-mail: info@newestpress.com. Website: www.newestpress.com. **Acquisitions:** Ruth Linka, general manager. Estab. 1977. Publishes trade paperback originals. **Publishes 13-16 titles/year. Receives 500 submissions/year. 40% of books from first-time authors; 85% from unagented writers. Pays 10% royalty.** Publishes book 2-3 years after acceptance of ms. Accepts simultaneous submissions. Responds in 6-8 months to queries. Book catalog for 9 × 12 SASE; ms guidelines online.

○➤ NeWest publishes Western Canadian fiction, nonfiction, poetry, and drama.

Nonfiction Literary/essays (Western Canadian authors, Western Canadian and Northern themes). Subjects include ethnic, government/politics, history (Western Canada), nature/environment (northern), Canadiana. Query.

Fiction Literary. "Our press is interested in Western Canadian writing." Submit complete ms.

Recent Title(s) *Big Rig 2*, by Don McTavish (nonfiction); *Better than Life*, by Margaret Gunning (fiction); *Playing Dead*, by Rudy Wiebe (nonfiction).

NOVALIS

Bayard Presse Canada, 49 Front St. E, Toronto ON M5E 1B3 Canada. (416)363-3303. Fax: (416)363-9409. E-mail: cservice@novalis.ca. Website: www.novalis.ca. **Acquisitions:** Kevin Burns, commissioning editor; Michael O'Hearn, publisher; Anne Louise Mahoney, managing editor. Editorial offices: Novalis, St. Paul University, 223 Main St., Ottawa ON, K1S 1C4, Canada. Phone: (613)782-3039. Fax: (613)751-4020. E-mail: kburns@ustpaul.ca. Publishes hardcover and trade paperback originals and trade paperback reprints. **Publishes 40 titles/year. 20% of books from first-time authors; 50% from unagented writers. Pays 10-15% royalty on wholesale price. Offers $300-2,000 advance.** Publishes book 9 months after acceptance of ms. Responds in 2 months to queries; 1 month to proposals; 2 months to mss. Book catalog for free or online; ms guidelines free.

○➤ "Novalis publishes books about faith, religion, and spirituality in their broadest sense. Based in the Catholic tradition, our interest is strongly ecumenical. Regardless of their denominational perspective, our books speak to the heart, mind, and spirit of people seeking to deepen their faith and understanding."

Nonfiction Biography, children's/juvenile, gift book, humor, illustrated book, reference, self-help. Subjects include child guidance/parenting, education (Christian or Catholic), memoirs, multicultural, nature/environment, philosophy, religion, spirituality. Query with SASE.

Recent Title(s) *The Human Right to Peace*, by Douglas Roche; *Becoming Fully Human: Living the Bible with*

God, Each Other, and the Environment, by Walter Vogels; *Saint Nicholas, Bishop of Myra: The Life and Times of the Original Father Christmas*, by David L. Cunn.

PACIFIC EDUCATIONAL PRESS

Faculty of Education, University of British Columbia, Vancouver BC V6T 1Z4 Canada. Fax: (604)822-6603. E-mail: pep@interchange.ubc.ca. **Acquisitions:** Catherine Edwards, director. Publishes trade paperback originals and cloth reference books. **Publishes 2-4 titles/year. Receives 60 submissions/year. 15% of books from first-time authors; 100% from unagented writers.** Accepts simultaneous submissions. Responds in 6 months to mss. Book catalog and ms guidelines for 9×12 SAE with IRCs.

- Pacific Educational Press publishes books on the subject of education for an adult audience of teachers, scholars, librarians, and parents. Currently emphasizing literature, education, social studies education, international issues, mathematics, science.

Recent Title(s) *Teaching to Wonder: Responding to Poetry in the Secondary Classroom*, by Carl Leggo; *The Canadian Anthology of Social Studies*, by Roland Case and Penney Clark; *Teaching Shakespeare on Screen*, by Neil Bechervaise.

PEDLAR PRESS

P.O. Box 26, Station P, Toronto ON M5S 2S6 Canada. (416)534-2011. Fax: (416)535-9677. E-mail: feralgrl@interl og.com. **Acquisitions:** Beth Follett, editor (fiction, poetry). Publishes hardcover and trade paperback originals. **Publishes 4-6 titles/year. Receives 50-60 mss/year. 50% of books from first-time authors; 100% from unagented writers. Pays 10% royalty on retail price. Offers $200-400 advance.** Publishes book 1 year after acceptance of ms. Accepts simultaneous submissions. Responds in 1 month to queries; 6 months to mss. Book catalog and ms guidelines for #10 SASE.

- Niche is outsider voices, experimental style, and form. Please note: Pedlar will not consider USA authors until 2005. Currently emphasizing experimental fiction.

Nonfiction Illustrated book. Subjects include creative nonfiction, gay/lesbian, language/literature, sex, women's issues/studies. Submit proposal package including outline, 5 sample chapter(s). Reviews artwork/photos as part of ms package. Send photocopies.

Fiction Erotica, experimental, feminist, gay/lesbian, humor, literary, picture books, poetry, short story collections. Query with SASE, or submit proposal package including 5 sample chapter(s), synopsis.

Recent Title(s) *Mouthing the Words*, by Camilla Gibb (fiction); *Cheez 100*, by Fiona Smyth (art book).

Tips "We select manuscripts according to our taste. Be familiar with some if not most of our recent titles."

PIPERS' ASH, LTD.

Pipers' Ash, Church Rd., Christian Malford, Chippenham, Wiltshire SN15 4BW United Kingdom. +44(01249)720-563. Fax: 0870 0568917. E-mail: pipersash@supamasu.com. Website: www.supamasu.com. **Acquisitions:** Manuscript Evaluation Desk. Estab. 1976. Publishes hardcover and paperback editions. **Publishes 12 titles/year. Receives 1,000 queries and 400 mss/year. 90% of books from first-time authors; 99% from unagented writers. Pays 10% royalty on wholesale price, and 5 author's copies.** Publishes book 6 months after acceptance of ms. Does not accept simultaneous submissions. Responds in 1 month to queries; 1 month to proposals; 3 months to mss. Book catalog for A5 SASE and on website; ms guidelines online.

Imprints Salisbury, Canterbury, Lincoln, Gloucester, Durham, Ely.

Nonfiction Autobiography, biography, how-to, self-help, children's/juvenile/teenagers. Subjects include creative nonfiction, ethnic, history, humanities, language/literature, military/war, philosophy, recreation, religion, translation. "Visit website." Query with SASE.

Fiction Adventure, confession, feminist, historical, juvenile, literary, mainstream/contemporary, military/war, plays, poetry, poetry in translation, regional, religious, romance (contemporary, romantic suspense), science fiction (hard science/technological, soft/sociological), short story collections, sports, suspense. "We publish 30,000-word novels and short story collections. Visit our website." Query with SASE, or submit sample chapter(s), 25-word synopsis (that sorts out the writers from the wafflers).

Poetry Submit 60 sample poems.

Recent Title(s) *Cross to Bear*, by Chris Spiller; *Science Quicktion*, by Steve Fitzsimmons; *Henry's Navy Blue Hair*, by Gwyneth Hughes.

Tips "Visit website."

PLAYWRIGHTS CANADA PRESS

215 Spadina Ave., Suite 230, Toronto ON M5T 2C7 Canada. (416)703-0013. Fax: (416)408-3402. Website: www.playwrightscanada.com. **Acquisitions:** Betony Main, editorial coordinator. Estab. 1972. Publishes paperback originals and reprints of plays. **Receives 40 submissions/year. 50% of books from first-time authors;**

50% from unagented writers. Pays 10% royalty on retail price. Publishes book 6 months-1 year after acceptance of ms. Responds in 2-3 months to queries. Ms guidelines online.

> O➞ Playwrights Canada Press publishes only drama by Canadian citizens or landed immigrants, which has received professional production.

Recent Title(s) *A Voice of Her Own*, edited by Sherrill Grace and Angela Rabeiro; *Home Is My Road*, by Florence Gibson; *Einstein's Gift*, by Vern Thiessen.

🌐 DAVID PORTEOUS EDITIONS

P.O. Box 5, Chudleigh, Newton Abbot, Devon TQ13 0YZ United Kingdom. E-mail: editorial@davidporteous.com. Website: www.davidporteous.com. **Acquisitions:** David Porteous, publisher (arts, crafts, hobbies). Estab. 1992. Publishes hardcover originals and trade paperback originals and reprints. **Publishes 3-5 titles/year. 90% of books from first-time authors; 99% from unagented writers.** Does not accept simultaneous submissions. Responds in 1 month to queries; 2 months to proposals; 2 months to mss. Book catalog online.

Nonfiction How-to, illustrated book. Subjects include hobbies, arts, crafts. "We publish practical, illustrated books showing step-by-step instructions." Query with SASE. Reviews artwork/photos as part of ms package. Send photocopies or digital images.

Recent Title(s) *Create Greeting Cards with Glass Painting Techniques*, by Joan Dale (craft); *Paul Riley's Watercolour Workshop*, by Paul Riley (art instruction); *Painting with Stitches*, by Sue Dove (craft).

Tips "We publish for an International market. So the content must be suitable for the U.S.A., U.K., South Africa, Australia, and New Zealand."

🔲 PRODUCTIVE PUBLICATIONS

P.O. Box 7200 Station A, Toronto ON M5W 1X8 Canada. (416)483-0634. Fax: (416)322-7434. **Acquisitions:** Iain Williamson, owner. Estab. 1985. Publishes trade paperback originals. **Publishes 24 titles/year. Receives 160 queries and 40 mss/year. 80% of books from first-time authors; 100% from unagented writers. Pays 10-15% royalty on wholesale price.** Publishes book 6 months after acceptance of ms. Accepts simultaneous submissions. Responds in 1 month to queries; 1 month to proposals; 3 months to mss. Book catalog free.

> O➞ "Productive Publications publishes books to help readers succeed and to help them meet the challenges of the new information age and global marketplace." Interested in books on business, computer software, the Internet for business purposes, investment, stock market and mutual funds, etc. Currently emphasizing computers, software, small business, business management, entrepreneurship. De-emphasizing jobs, how to get employment.

Nonfiction How-to, reference, self-help, technical. Subjects include business/economics (small business and management), computers/electronic, money/finance, software (business). "We are interested in small business/entrepreneurship/self-help (business)—100-300 pages." Submit outline. Reviews artwork/photos as part of ms package. Send photocopies.

Recent Title(s) *How to Deliver Excellent Customer Service: A Step-by-Step Guide for Every Business*, by Julie Olley; *Market Your Professional Service*, by Jerome Shure.

Tips "We are looking for books written by knowledgable, experienced experts who can express their ideas clearly and simply."

🔲 PURICH PUBLISHING

Box 23032, Market Mall Post Office, Saskatoon SK S7J 5H3 Canada. (306)373-5311. Fax: (306)373-5315. E-mail: purich@sasktel.net. Website: www.purichpublishing.com. **Acquisitions:** Donald Purich, publisher (law, Aboriginal issues); Karen Bolstad, publisher (law, history, education). Publishes trade paperback originals. **Publishes 3-5 titles/year. 20% of books from first-time authors. Pays 8-12% royalty on retail price.** Publishes book within 4 months of completion of editorial work, after acceptance of ms. Accepts simultaneous submissions. Responds in 1 month to queries; 3 months to mss. Book catalog free.

> O➞ Purich publishes books on law, Aboriginal/Native American issues, and Western Canadian history and education for the academic and professional trade reference market.

Nonfiction Reference, technical, textbook. Subjects include education, government/politics, history, Aboriginal issues. "We are a specialized publisher and only consider work in our subject areas." Query with SASE.

Recent Title(s) *Tough on Kids: Rethinking Approaches to Youth Justice*, by Ross Green and Kearney Healy; *Reclaiming Aboriginal Justice, Identity, and Community*, by Craig Proulx; *Who are Canada's Aboriginal Peoples?*, edited by Paul Chartrand.

🔲 ROCKY MOUNTAIN BOOKS

#3 Spruce Centre SW, Calgary AB T3C 3B3 Canada. (403)249-9490. Fax: (403)249-2968. E-mail: tonyd@rmbooks.com. Website: www.rmbooks.com. **Acquisitions:** Tony Daffern, publisher. Publishes trade paperback originals. **Publishes 5 titles/year. Receives 30 queries/year. 75% of books from first-time authors; 100% from** unagented writers. **Pays 12% royalty on net receipts. Rarely offers advance.** Publishes book 1 year after acceptance of ms. Does not accept simultaneous submissions. Responds in 1 month to queries. Book catalog and ms guidelines free.

○━ Rocky Mountain Books publishes on outdoor recreation, mountains, and mountaineering in Western Canada.

Nonfiction Biography, how-to. Subjects include nature/environment, recreation, regional, travel. "Our main area of publishing is outdoor recreation guides to Western and Northern Canada." Query with SASE.

Recent Title(s) *Caves of the Canadian Rockies and Columbia Mountains*, by John Rollins; *Exploring Prince George*, by Mike Nash.

RONSDALE PRESS

3350 W. 21st Ave., Vancouver BC V6S 1G7 Canada. (604)738-4688. Fax: (604)731-4548. Website: www.ronsdale press.com. **Acquisitions:** Ronald B. Hatch, director (fiction, poetry, social commentary); Veronica Hatch, managing director (children's literature). Estab. 1988. Publishes trade paperback originals. **Publishes 10 titles/ year. Receives 300 queries and 800 mss/year. 60% of books from first-time authors; 95% from unagented writers. Pays 10% royalty on retail price.** Publishes book 6 months after acceptance of ms. Accepts simultaneous submissions. Responds in 2 weeks to queries; 1 month to proposals; 3 months to mss. Book catalog for #10 SASE; ms guidelines online.

○━ Canadian authors only. Ronsdale publishes fiction, poetry, regional history, biography and autobiography, books of ideas about Canada, as well as young adult historical fiction.

Nonfiction Biography, children's/juvenile. Subjects include history (Canadian), language/literature, nature/ environment, regional.

Fiction Literary, short story collections, novels. *Canadian authors only.* Query with at least the first 80 pages. Short story collections must have some previous magazine publication.

Poetry "Poets should have published some poems in magazines/journals and should be well-read in contemporary masters." Submit complete ms.

Recent Title(s) *Adrift in Time*, by John Wilson (YA historical fiction); *When Eagles Call*, by Susan Dobbie (novel).

Tips "Ronsdale Press is a literary publishing house, based in Vancouver, and dedicated to publishing books from across Canada, books that give Canadians new insights into themselves and their country. We aim to publish the best Canadian writers."

SAXON HOUSE CANADA

P.O. Box 6947, Station A, Toronto ON M5W 1X6 Canada. (416)488-7171. Fax: (416)488-2989. **Acquisitions:** Dietrich Hummell, editor-in-chief; W.H. Wallace, general manager (history, philosophy); Carla Saxon, CEO (printed music). Publishes hardcover originals and trade paperback reprints. **Publishes 4 titles/year. Receives approximately 60 queries and 20 mss/year. 20% of books from first-time authors; 80% from unagented writers. Pays royalty on wholesale price, or makes outright purchase.** Publishes book 15 months after acceptance of ms. Accepts simultaneous submissions. Responds in 4 months to mss.

Nonfiction Illustrated book. Subjects include history, philosophy, religion, music (printed music). Submit proposal package including 3 sample chapter(s), résumé. Reviews artwork/photos as part of ms package. Send photocopies.

Fiction Historical, literary. Submit proposal package including 3 sample chapter(s), résumé.

Recent Title(s) *The Journey to Canada*, by David Mills (history); *Voices From the Lake*, by E.M. Watts (illustrated ancient American Indian legend); *The Wine of Babylon*, by David Mills (epic poem).

Tips "We want books with literary integrity, historical accuracy, and fresh narrative skills."

SCHOLASTIC CANADA, LTD.

175 Hillmount Rd., Markham ON L6C 1Z7 Canada. (905)887-7323. Fax: (905)887-3643. Website: www.scholasti c.ca. Publishes hardcover and trade paperback originals. **Publishes 40 titles/year; imprint publishes 4 titles/ year. 3% of books from first-time authors; 50% from unagented writers. Pays 5-10% royalty on retail price. Offers $1,000-5,000 (Canadian) advance.** Publishes book 1 year after acceptance of ms. Does not accept simultaneous submissions. Responds in 3 months to queries; 6 months to proposals. Book catalog for 8½×11 SAE with 2 first-class stamps (IRC or Canadian stamps only).

Imprints North Winds Press, Les Editions Scholastic.

○━ Scholastic publishes books by Canadians and/or about Canada. Currently emphasizing Canadian interest, middle-grade fiction.

Nonfiction Biography, children's/juvenile. Subjects include history, hobbies, nature/environment, recreation, science, sports. *Agented submissions only. No unsolicited mss.*

Fiction Juvenile (middle grade), young adult. *No unsolicited mss. Agented submissions only.* Canadian authors only.

Recent Title(s) *Lighthouse*, by Robert Munsch; *Dear Canada: Brothers Far from Home*, by Jean Little; *Subway Mouse*, by Barbara Reid.

STELLER PRESS, LTD.

13-4335 W. 10th Ave., Vancouver BC V6R 2H6 Canada. (604)222-2955. Fax: (604)222-2965. E-mail: info@steller press.com. **Acquisitions:** Steve Paton (outdoors/gardening). Publishes trade paperback originals. **Publishes 4 titles/year. 75% of books from first-time authors; 100% from unagented writers. Pays royalty on retail price. Offers $500-2,000 advance.** Accepts simultaneous submissions. Responds in 6 months to queries.

⊶ "All titles are specific to the Pacific Northwest." Currently emphasizing gardening, history, outdoors. De-emphasizing fiction, poetry.

Nonfiction Subjects include gardening, history, nature/environment, regional, travel.

Recent Title(s) *Roses For the Pacific Northwest*, by Christine Allen; *Herbs For the Pacific Northwest*, by Moira Carlson.

SUMAIYAH DISTRIBUTORS PVT, LTD.

422⁸/₁ Ansari Rd., Daryaganj, 2nd Floor, New Delhi Delhi 110002 India. (011)23244148. Fax: (011)23244133. E-mail: sumaiyah@vsnl.net. **Acquisitions:** Mohd. Aslam Khan, managing director (medical and allied health sciences); Mrs. Feroza Khanam, acquisitions editor (marketing sales, customer service and development). Estab. 2000. **Publishes 10 titles/year. Receives 8 queries and 5 mss/year. 90% of books from first-time authors. Pays 10-12% royalty. Offers $400-800 advance.** Publishes book 3 months after acceptance of ms. Accepts simultaneous submissions. Responds in 1 month to mss. Book catalog and ms guidelines free.

Nonfiction Illustrated book, technical, textbook, medical and allied health sciences management, quick reference manual, and self-guide book. Subjects include health/medicine. Submit complete ms. Reviews artwork/photos as part of ms package.

Recent Title(s) *Understanding Human Histology*, by Dr. Abrar Khan (textbook for undergraduate medical and allied health).

Tips "We place strong emphasis on materials that teach quick grasp of the subject for the busy student, practitioners, and researchers. And the writers should clearly indicate what book is about and audience."

THOMPSON EDUCATIONAL PUBLISHING, INC.

6 Ripley Ave., Suite 200, Toronto ON M6S 3N9 Canada. (416)766-2763. Fax: (416)766-0398. E-mail: publisher@t hompsonbooks.com. Website: www.thompsonbooks.com. **Acquisitions:** Keith Thompson, president. **Publishes 10 titles/year. Receives 15 queries and 10 mss/year. 80% of books from first-time authors; 100% from unagented writers. Pays 10% royalty on net receipts.** Publishes book 1 year after acceptance of ms. Does not accept simultaneous submissions. Responds in 1 month to queries. Book catalog free; ms guidelines online.

⊶ Thompson Educational specializes in high-quality educational texts in the social sciences and humanities.

Nonfiction Textbook. Subjects include business/economics, education, ethnic, government/politics, multicultural, sociology, sports, women's issues/studies. Submit outline, 1 sample chapter(s), résumé.

Recent Title(s) *Juvenile Justice Systems*, edited by N. Bala, J. Hornick, H.N. Snyder, and J.J. Paetsch.

TITAN BOOKS, LTD.

144 Southwark St., London SE1 OUP England. (0207)620 0200. Fax: (0207)620 0032. E-mail: editorial@titanma il.com. Website: www.titanbooks.com. **Acquisitions:** D. Barraclough, editorial manager. Publishes trade and mass market paperback originals and reprints. **Publishes about 100 titles/year. Receives 500 queries and 200 mss/year. 1% of books from first-time authors; 50% from unagented writers. Pays 6-8% royalty on retail price. Offers variable advance.** Accepts simultaneous submissions. Responds in 1 month to queries; 3 months to proposals; 6 months to mss. Ms guidelines for #10 SASE.

⊶ Titan Books publishes film and TV titles.

Nonfiction Biography, how-to, illustrated books. Subjects include film/cinema/stage, film and TV. Submit outline, sample chapter(s), SASE.

Recent Title(s) *Don't Panic: Douglas Adams & the Hitchhiker's Guide to the Galaxy*; *Tales from Development Hell*; *The Texas Chain Saw Massacre Companion*.

TOUCHWOOD EDITIONS

#6-356 Simcoe St., Victoria BC V8V 1L1 Canada. (250)360-0829. Fax: (250)385-0829. **Acquisitions:** Vivian Sinclair, managing editor. Publishes trade paperback originals and reprints. **Publishes 8-10 titles/year. 50%**

of books from first-time authors; 100% from unagented writers. **Pays 12% royalty on wholesale price.** Publishes book 6 months after acceptance of ms. Accepts simultaneous submissions. Responds in 1 month to queries. Book catalog free.

Nonfiction Biography. Subjects include anthropology/archeology, art/architecture, creative nonfiction, government/politics, history, nature/environment, recreation, regional. Query with SASE, or submit outline, 2-3 sample chapter(s), synopsis. Reviews artwork/photos as part of ms package. Send photocopies.

Recent Title(s) *A Man Called Moses*, by Bill Gallaher; *Painter, Paddler: The Art and Adventures of Stewart Marshall*, by Andrew Scott; *An Edible Journey*, by Elizabeth Levinson.

Tips "Our area of interest is Western Canada. We would like more creative nonfiction and historical fiction."

◪ TRADEWIND BOOKS

1809 Maritime Mews, Granville Island, Vancouver BC V6H 3W7 Canada. (604)662-4405. Fax: (604)730-0153. E-mail: tradewindbooks@eudoramail.com. Website: www.tradewindbooks.com. **Acquisitions:** Michael Katz, publisher (picturebooks, young adult); Carol Frank, art director (picturebooks); Tiffany Stone (acquisitions editor). Publishes hardcover and trade paperback originals. **Publishes 5 titles/year. Receives 1,000 submissions/year. 10% of books from first-time authors; 50% from unagented writers. Pays 7% royalty on retail price. Offers variable advance.** Publishes book 3 years after acceptance of ms. Accepts simultaneous submissions. Responds in 2 months to mss. Book catalog and ms guidelines online.

○➡ Tradewind Books publishes juvenile picture books and young adult novels. Requires that submissions include evidence that author has read at least 3 titles published by Tradewind Books.

Fiction Juvenile. Query with SASE, or submit proposal package including 2 sample chapter(s), synopsis.

Recent Title(s) *The Bone Collector's Son*; *The Sorcerer's Letterbox*; *For Sure For Sure*.

◪ TURNSTONE PRESS

607-100 Arthur St., Winnipeg MB R3B 1H3 Canada. (204)947-1555. Fax: (204)942-1555. E-mail: info@turnstone press.com. Website: www.turnstonepress.com. **Acquisitions:** Todd Besant, managing editor; Sharon Caseburg, acquisitions editor. Estab. 1976. Publishes trade paperback originals, mass market for literary mystery imprint. **Publishes 10-12 titles/year. Receives 1,000 mss/year. 25% of books from first-time authors; 75% from unagented writers. Pays 10% royalty on retail price, and 10 author's copies. Offers advance.** Publishes book 18 months-2 years after acceptance of ms. Does not accept simultaneous submissions. Responds in 4 months to queries. Book catalog for #10 SASE; ms guidelines online.

Imprints Ravenstone (literary mystery fiction).

○➡ Turnstone Press is a literary press that publishes Canadian writers with an emphasis on writers from, and writing on, the Canadian West. Currently emphasizing novels, nonfiction travel, adventure travel, poetry. Does not consider formula or mainstream work.

Nonfiction Subjects include travel, adventure travel, cultural/social issues, Canadian literary criticism. Query with SASE, literary curriculum vitae, and 50-page sample.

Fiction Literary, regional (Western Canada), short story collections, contemporary, novels. *Canadian authors only*. Query with SASE, literary curriculum vitae, and 50-page sample.

Poetry Submit complete ms.

Recent Title(s) *The Monitor*, by Janice MacDonald (mystery); *Kilter: 55 Fictions*, by John Gould (fiction); *Fortune*, by Tanis MacDonald (poetry).

Tips "Writers are encouraged to view our list and check if submissions are appropriate. Although we publish new authors, we prefer first-time authors to have publishing credits in literary magazines. Would like to see more adventure travel as well as eclectic novels. Would like to see 'nonformula' writing for the Ravenstone imprint, especially literary thrillers, urban mystery, and noir."

⊘ ◪ THE UNIVERSITY OF ALBERTA PRESS

Ring House 2, Edmonton AB T6G 2E1 Canada. (780)492-3662. Fax: (780)492-0719. E-mail: uap@ualberta.ca. Website: www.uap.ualberta.ca. Estab. 1969. Publishes orginals and reprints. **Publishes 18-25 titles/year. Receives 400 submissions/year. Royalties are negotiated.** Publishes book within 2 years (usually) after acceptance of ms. Does not accept simultaneous submissions. Responds in 3 months to queries. Ms guidelines online.

○➡ "Award-winning publisher The University of Alberta Press has published excellent scholarly works and fine books for general audiences. Our program is particularly strong in the areas of biography, history, literature, natural history, and books of regional interest. Within each of those broad subject areas, we have published in a variety of specific fields. We are pursuing academic manuscripts in our areas of strength and expertise, as listed above, and inviting submissions in several new areas including travel/ adventure writing, business, health, and social policy. We do not accept unsolicited novels or poetry. Please see our website for details."

Tips Query with SASE.

UNIVERSITY OF CALGARY PRESS

2500 University Dr. NW, Calgary AB T2N 1N4 Canada. (403)220-7578. Fax: (403)282-0085. Website: www.uofc press.com. **Acquisitions:** Walter Hildebrandt, director. Publishes hardcover and trade paperback originals and reprints. **Publishes 30-40 titles/year.** Publishes book 20 months after acceptance of ms. Does not accept simultaneous submissions. Responds in 1 month to queries; 2 months to proposals; 2 months to mss. Book catalog free; ms guidelines online.

○━ "University of Calgary Press is committed to the advancement of scholarship through the publication of first-rate monographs, and academic and scientific journals."

Nonfiction Scholarly. Subjects include art/architecture, philosophy, travel, women's issues/studies, world affairs. Canadian studies, post-modern studies, native studies, history, international relations, artic studies, Africa, Latin American and Caribbean studies, and heritage of the Canadian and American heartland. "The UC Press has recently launched a new Open Spaces series presenting some of the region's finest literary works that resonate with prarie themes, voices, and experiences." Submit outline, 2 sample chapter(s), SASE. Reviews artwork/photos as part of ms package. Send photocopies.

Recent Title(s) *The Citizen's Voice: Twentieth-Century Politics and Literature*, by Michael Keren; *To Be a Cowboy: Oliver Christensen's Story*, by Barbara Holliday, as told to her by Oliver Christensen; *Muskox Land: Ellesmere Island in the Age of Contact*, by Lyle Dick.

UNIVERSITY OF OTTAWA PRESS

542 King Edward, Ottawa ON K1N 6N5 Canada. (613)562-5246. Fax: (613)562-5247. E-mail: press@uottawa.ca. Website: www.uopress.uottawa.ca. **Acquisitions:** Ruth Bradley St-Cyr, editor-in-chief. Estab. 1936. **Publishes 22 titles/year. Receives 250 submissions/year. 20% of books from first-time authors; 95% from unagented writers. Pays 5-10% royalty on net receipts.** Publishes book 6-12 months after acceptance of ms. Does not accept simultaneous submissions. Responds in 1 month to queries; 6 months to mss. Book catalog and ms guidelines free.

○━ The University of Ottawa Press publishes books for the scholarly and serious nonfiction audiences. They were "the first *officially* bilingual university publishing house in Canada. Our goal is to help the publication of cutting-edge research—books written to be useful to active researchers but accessible to an interested public." Currently emphasizing French in North America, language rights, social sciences, translation, Canadian studies. De-emphasizing medieval studies, criminology.

Nonfiction Reference, textbook. Subjects include education, government/politics, history, language/literature, nature/environment, philosophy, regional, religion, sociology, translation, women's issues/studies. Submit outline, sample chapter(s).

Recent Title(s) *Philosophical Theory and the Universal Declaration of Human Rights*, edited by William Sweet; *Not Written in Stone: Jews, Constitutions, and Constitutionalism in Canada*, edited by Daniel J. Elazar, Michael Brown, and Ira Robinson.

Tips "No unrevised theses! Envision audience of academic specialists and readers of serious nonfiction."

VÉHICULE PRESS

Box 125, Place du Parc Station, Montreal QC H2X 4A3 Canada. (514)844-6073. Fax: (514)844-7543. Website: www.vehiculepress.com. **Acquisitions:** Simon Dardick, president/publisher. Estab. 1973. Publishes trade paperback originals by Canadian authors only. **Publishes 15 titles/year. Receives 250 submissions/year. 20% of books from first-time authors; 95% from unagented writers. Pays 10-15% royalty on retail price. Offers $200-500 advance.** Publishes book 1 year after acceptance of ms. Responds in 4 months to queries. Book catalog for 9×12 SAE with IRCs.

Imprints Signal Editions (poetry); Dossier Quebec (history, memoirs).

● Canadian authors only.

○━ "Montreal's Véhicule Press has published the best of Canadian and Quebec literature—fiction, poetry, essays, translations, and social history."

Nonfiction Autobiography, biography. Subjects include government/politics, history, language/literature, memoirs, regional, sociology. Especially looking for Canadian social history. Query with SASE. Reviews artwork/photos as part of ms package.

Fiction Feminist, literary, regional, short story collections. No romance or formula writing. Query with SASE.

Poetry Contact Carmine Starnino.

Recent Title(s) *Between the Wars: The Canadian Jewish Community in Transition*, by Israel Medres, translated by Vivian Felsen (nonfiction); *Merrybegot*, by Mary Dalton (poetry); *A House by the Sea*, by Sikeena Karmali (fiction).

Tips "We are interested only in Canadian authors."

▓ WALL & EMERSON, INC.

6 O'Connor Dr., Toronto ON M4K 2K1 Canada. (416)467-8685. Fax: (416)352-5368. E-mail: wall@wallbooks.com. Website: www.wallbooks.com. **Acquisitions:** Byron E. Wall, president (history of science, mathematics). Estab. 1987. Publishes hardcover originals and reprints. **Publishes 3 titles/year. Receives 10 queries and 8 mss/year. 50% of books from first-time authors; 100% from unagented writers. Pays 5-12% royalty on wholesale price.** Publishes book 1 year after acceptance of ms. Accepts simultaneous submissions. Responds in 1 month to queries; 1 month to proposals; 3 months to mss. Book catalog and ms guidelines free or online.

  O- "We are most interested in textbooks for college courses that meet well-defined needs and are targeted to their audiences." Currently emphasizing adult education, engineering. De-emphasizing social work.

Nonfiction Reference, textbook. Subjects include education, health/medicine, philosophy, science. "We are looking for any undergraduate text that meets the needs of a well-defined course in colleges in the U.S. and Canada." Submit proposal package including outline, 2 sample chapter(s).

Recent Title(s) *Princinples of Engineering Economic Analysis*; *Voices Past and Present*.

Tips "Our audience consists of college undergraduate students and college libraries. Our ideal writer is a college professor writing a text for a course he or she teaches regularly. If I were a writer trying to market a book today, I would identify the audience for the book and write directly to the audience throughout the book. I would then approach a publisher that publishes books specifically for that audience."

▓ WEIGL EDUCATIONAL PUBLISHERS, LTD.

6325 10th St. SE, Calgary AB T2H 2Z9 Canada. (403)233-7747. Fax: (403)233-7769. E-mail: info@weigl.com. Website: www.weigl.com. **Acquisitions:** Linda Weigl, president. Publishes hardcover originals and reprints, school library softcover. **Publishes 104 titles/year. 100% from unagented writers. Makes outright purchase.** Responds ASAP to queries. Book catalog free.

  O- Textbook publisher catering to juvenile and young adult audience (K-12).

Nonfiction Children's/juvenile, textbook, library series. Subjects include animals, education, government/politics, history, nature/environment, science. Query with SASE.

Recent Title(s) *American Symbols*; *Caring for Your Pet*; *Celebrating Cultures*.

▓ WHITECAP BOOKS, LTD.

351 Lynn Ave., North Vancouver BC V7J 2C4 Canada. (604)980-9852. Fax: (604)980-8197. E-mail: whitecap@whitecap.ca. Website: www.whitecap.ca. **Acquisitions:** Christine Rowlands. Publishes hardcover and trade paperback originals. **Publishes 20 titles/year. Receives 500 queries and 1,000 mss/year. 20% of books from first-time authors; 90% from unagented writers. Pays royalty. Offers negotiated advance.** Publishes book 18 months after acceptance of ms. Accepts simultaneous submissions. Responds in 3 months to proposals.

  O- Whitecap Books publishes a wide range of nonfiction with a Canadian and international focus. Currently emphasizing children's nonfiction, natural history. De-emphasizing children's illustrated fiction.

Nonfiction Children's/juvenile, coffee table book, cookbook. Subjects include animals, cooking/foods/nutrition, gardening, history, nature/environment, recreation, regional, travel. "We require an annotated outline. Writers should take the time to research our list and read the submission guidelines on our website. This is especially important for children's writers." Submit outline, 1 sample chapter(s), SASE. Reviews artwork/photos as part of ms package. Send photocopies.

Recent Title(s) *Vancouver's Glory Years*, by Heather Conn and Henry Ewert (nonfiction); *Accidental Alphabet*, by Dianne Bonder (children's illustrated fiction); *Mustang Mountain Series*, by Sharon Siamon (children's/YA fiction).

Tips "We want well-written, well-researched material that presents a fresh approach to a particular topic."

⊕ WOODHEAD PUBLISHING, LTD.

Abington Hall, Abington, Cambridge CB1 6AH United Kingdom. (pl44)1223-891358. Fax: (pl44)1223-893694. E-mail: wp@woodhead-publishing.com. Website: www.woodhead-publishing.com. **Acquisitions:** Francis Dodds (food science, technology, and nutrition); Gwen Jones (materials engineering, textile technology, welding and joining). Publishes hardcover originals. **Publishes 40 titles/year. 75% of books from first-time authors; 99% from unagented writers. Pays 10% royalty on wholesale price.** Publishes book 6 months after acceptance of ms. Does not accept simultaneous submissions. Book catalog for free or on website; ms guidelines online.

Imprints Woodhead Publishing.

Nonfiction Technical. Subjects include food science, materials engineering, textile technology, welding and joining. Submit proposal package including outline. Reviews artwork/photos as part of ms package. Send photocopies.

Recent Title(s) *Yoghurt: Science and Technology*; *Food Preservation Techniques*; *Fatigue in Composites*.

⊠ ⊡ WORLDWIDE LIBRARY

Division of Harlequin Books, 225 Duncan Mill Rd., Don Mills ON M2B 3K9 Canada. (416)445-5860. Estab. 1979. Publishes paperback originals and reprints. "Mystery program is reprint, hardcover to paperback; no originals, please." **Advance and sometimes royalties; copyright buyout.** Publishes book 1-2 years after acceptance of ms. Accepts simultaneous submissions. Responds in 10 weeks to queries.

Fiction "Action-adventure series and future fiction."

⊕ ZED BOOKS

7 Cynthia St., London N1 9JF United Kingdom. 44-71-837-4014. Fax: 44-71-833-3960. E-mail: zedbooks@zedbooks.demon.co.uk. Website: www.zedbooks.co.uk. **Acquisitions:** Robert Molten (international affairs, politics, development, environment, Third World, gender studies, cultural studies, social sciences). Publishes hardcover and trade paperback originals. **Publishes 40-45 titles/year. Receives 300 queries and 150 mss/year. 25% of books from first-time authors; 95-100% from unagented writers. Pays 7½-10% royalty on retail price, or net receipts. Offers $1,000 advance.** Publishes book 9 months after acceptance of ms. Accepts simultaneous submissions. Responds in 1 week to queries; 1 month to proposals; 3 months to mss. Book catalog free; ms guidelines online.

Nonfiction Textbook. Subjects include agriculture/horticulture, anthropology/archeology, business/economics, education, government/politics, health/medicine, history, money/finance, multicultural, nature/environment, sociology, women's issues/studies. Submit proposal package including outline, 2 sample chapter(s), or submit complete ms.

Small Presses

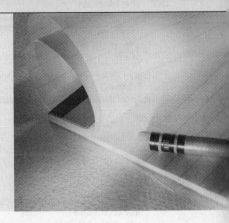

S mall press is a relative term. Compared to the dozen or so conglomerates, the rest of the book publishing world may seem to be comprised of small presses. A number of the publishers listed in the Book Publishers section consider themselves small presses and cultivate the image. For our classification, small presses are those that publish, on average, no more than six books per year.

The publishing opportunities are slightly more limited with the companies listed here than with those in the Book Publishers section. Not only are they publishing fewer books, but small presses are usually not able to market their books as effectively as larger publishers, and their print runs and royalty arrangements are usually smaller.

However, realistic small press publishers don't try to compete with Penguin Group (USA), Inc., or Random House. Most small press publishers get into book publishing for the love of it, not solely for the profit. Of course, every publisher, small or large, wants successful books, but small press publishers often measure success in different ways.

Many writers actually prefer to work with small presses. Since small publishing houses are usually based on the publisher's commitment to the subject matter, and since they work with far fewer authors than the conglomerates, small press authors and their books usually receive more personal attention than the larger publishers can afford to give them. Promotional dollars at the big houses tend to be siphoned toward a few books each season that they have decided are likely to succeed, leaving hundreds of "midlist" books underpromoted. Since small presses only commit to a very small number of books every year, they are vitally interested in the promotion and distribution of each book.

Just because they publish fewer titles than large publishing houses does not mean small press editors have the time to look at complete manuscripts. In fact, the editors with smaller staffs often have even less time for submissions. The procedure for contacting a small press with your book idea is exactly the same as it is for a larger publisher. Send a one-page query with SASE first. If the press is interested in your proposal, be ready to send an outline or synopsis, and/or a sample chapter or two.

For more information on small presses, see *Novel & Short Story Writer's Market* and *Poet's Market* (Writer's Digest Books).

For a list of publishers according to their subjects of interest, see the Nonfiction and Fiction sections of the Book Publishers Subject Index. Information on book publishers listed in the previous edition of *Writer's Market*, but not included in this edition, can be found in the General Index.

A.T. PUBLISHING

23 Lily Lake Rd., Highland NY 12528. (845)691-2021. **Acquisitions:** Anthony Prizzia, publisher (education); John Prizzia, publisher. Estab. 2001. Publishes trade paperback originals. **Publishes 1-3 titles/year. Receives 1-3 queries and 1-3 mss/year. 100% of books from first-time authors; 100% from unagented writers. Pays 15-25% royalty on retail price, or makes outright purchase of $500-2,500. Offers $500-1,000 advance.** Accepts simultaneous submissions. Responds in 1 month to queries; 2 months to proposals; 4 months to mss.
Nonfiction How-to. Subjects include cooking/foods/nutrition, education, recreation, science, sports. Query with SASE, or submit complete ms. Reviews artwork/photos as part of ms package. Send photocopies.
Recent Title(s) *It's Not Just Sauce*, by Tony Prizzia; *The Waiter and Waitress's Guide to a Bigger Income*, by Anthony Thomas (how-to).
Tips Audience is people interested in a variety of topics, general. "Submit typed manuscript for consideration, including a SASE for return of manuscript."

ACME PRESS

P.O. Box 1702, Westminster MD 21158-1702. (410)848-7577. **Acquisitions:** (Ms.) E.G. Johnston, managing editor. Estab. 1991. Publishes hardcover and trade paperback originals. **Publishes 1-2 titles/year. Pays 25 author's copies and 50% of profits. Offers small advance.** Publishes book 1 year after acceptance of ms. Accepts simultaneous submissions. Responds in 2 weeks to queries; 2 months to mss. Book catalog and ms guidelines for #10 SASE.
Fiction Humor. "We accept submissions on any subject as long as the material is humorous; prefer full-length novels. No cartoons or art (text only). No pornography, poetry, short stories, or children's material." Submit first 3-5 chapters, synopsis, and SASE.
Recent Title(s) *SuperFan*, by Lyn A. Sherwood (funny football novel).
Tips "We are always looking for the great comic novel."

ADAMS-HALL PUBLISHING

P.O. Box 491002, Los Angeles CA 90049. (800)888-4452 or (310)476-9388. E-mail: adamshallpublish@aol.com. Website: www.adams-hall.com. **Acquisitions:** Sue Ann Bacon, editorial director. Publishes hardcover and trade paperback originals and reprints. **Publishes 3-4 titles/year. Pays 10% royalty on net receipts. Offers negotiable advance.** Does not accept simultaneous submissions. Responds in 1 month to queries.
Nonfiction Subjects include money/finance, business. Small successful house that aggressively promotes select titles. Only interested in business or personal finance titles with broad appeal. Submit query, title, synopsis, your qualifications, a list of 3 competitive books and how it's widely different from other books. Do not send ms or sample chapters.
Recent Title(s) *Fail Proof Your Business*.

AMERICAN CATHOLIC PRESS

16565 S. State St., South Holland IL 60473. (312)331-5845. Fax: (708)331-5484. E-mail: acp@acpress.org. Website: www.acpress.org. **Acquisitions:** Rev. Michael Gilligan, Ph.D., editorial director. Estab. 1967. Publishes hardcover originals and hardcover and paperback reprints. **Publishes 4 titles/year. Makes outright purchase of $25-100.** Does not accept simultaneous submissions. Ms guidelines online.
Nonfiction Subjects include education, music/dance, religion, spirituality. "We publish books on the Roman Catholic liturgy—for the most part, books on religious music and educational books and pamphlets. We also publish religious songs for church use, including Psalms, as well as choral and instrumental arrangements. We are interested in new music, meant for use in church services. Books, or even pamphlets, on the Roman Catholic Mass are especially welcome. We have no interest in secular topics and are not interested in religious poetry of any kind."
Tips "Most of our sales are by direct mail, although we do work through retail outlets."

⊘ AMIGADGET PUBLISHING CO.

P.O. Box 1696, Lexington SC 29071. (803)779-3196. E-mail: amigadget@fotoartista.com. Website: www.fotoartista.com/amigadget. **Acquisitions:** Jay Gross, editor-in-chief. Publishes hardcover and trade paperback originals. **Publishes 2 titles/year.** Responds in 2 months to queries.
Nonfiction "Niche markets are our specialty. No books on Windows." **All unsolicited mss returned unopened.** Query via e-mail only.
Recent Title(s) *The Coffee Experience*, by J. Gross (travel).

ANACUS PRESS

Imprint of Finney Co., 3943 Meadowbrook Rd., Minneapolis MN 55426. (952)938-9330. Fax: (952)938-7353. E-mail: feedback@finney-hobar.com. Website: www.anacus.com. **Acquisitions:** Alan Krysan, president (bicycling guides, travel). Publishes trade paperback originals. **Publishes variable number of titles/year. Pays 10% royalty on wholesale price. Offers $500 advance.** Book catalog online.

Nonfiction Subjects include recreation, regional, travel (travel guides, travelogue). Query with SASE.

Recent Title(s) *Bed, Breakfast & Bike Mississippi Valley*, by Dale Lally (travel guide); *The Adventure of Two Lifetimes*, by Peggy & Brian Goetz (travelogue); *Bed, Breakfast & Bike Midwest*, by Robert & Theresa Russell (travel guide).

Tips Audience is cyclists and armchair adventurers.

ANHINGA PRESS

P.O. Box 10595, Tallahassee FL 32302. (850)422-1408. Fax: (850)442-6323. E-mail: info@anhinga.org. Website: www.anhinga.org. **Acquisitions:** Rick Campbell or Joann Gardner, editors. Publishes hardcover and trade paperback originals. **Publishes 3-4 titles/year. Pays 10% royalty on retail price. Offers Anhinga Prize of $2,000.** Accepts simultaneous submissions. Responds in 3 months to queries; 3 months to proposals; 3 months to mss. Book catalog for #10 SASE or online; ms guidelines online.

Poetry "We like good poetry." Query, or submit 6 sample poems.

Recent Title(s) *Summer*, by Robert Dana; *The Secret History of Water*, by Silvia Curbelo; *Mint Snowball*, by Naomi Shihab Nye.

Tips "We publish poetry only."

ANVIL PUBLISHERS, INC.

3852 Allsborough Dr., Tucker GA 30084. (770)938-0289. Fax: (770)493-7232. E-mail: anvilpub@aol.com. **Acquisitions:** Lee Xavier, editor-in-chief. Publishes hardcover and paperback originals, CD-ROMs. **Publishes 3-5 titles/year. Pays royalty.** Responds in 3 months to mss.

Nonfiction Biography. Subjects include health/medicine, history (American), military/war. Query with SASE, or submit outline.

Recent Title(s) *New Hope: Avoiding Lung Cancer*; *How To Work with Angry People and Outraged Publics*; *How To Manage Organizational Communication During Crisis*.

ARCHIMEDES PRESS, INC.

(formerly The Consumer Press), 6 Berkley Rd., Glenville NY 12302. (518)265-3269. Fax: (518)384-1313. E-mail: archimedespress@earthlink.net. Website: www.archimedespress.com. President: Kim Gorham. **Acquisitions:** Richard DiMaggio, chief editor. Estab. 2002. Publishes broad-based hardcover, trade paperback, and mass market paperback originals. **Publishes 3-6 titles/year. Pays 10% royalty.** Publishes book 6 months after acceptance of ms. Does not accept simultaneous submissions. Responds in 2 months to queries.

Nonfiction Children's/juvenile, how-to, illustrated book, multimedia, self-help. Subjects include alternative lifestyles, business/economics, child guidance/parenting, community, cooking/foods/nutrition, creative nonfiction, education, general nonfiction, government/politics, history, humanities, language/literature, money/finance, photography, sex, social sciences, travel. "E-mail submissions acceptable. Please snail mail complete manuscripts. If a consumer wants it, so do we. Emphasis originally on legal and financial issues, but looking strongly to expand to other broad-based issues. Love children's books also." Query with SASE, or submit sample chapter(s), SASE, or submit complete ms. Reviews artwork/photos as part of ms package. Send photocopies.

Recent Title(s) *Candy from Around the World*, by Stacy Cacciatore; *A Girl's Guide to Writing Her Autobiography*, by Robynn Clairday; *The Reel Deal: The Best in International Films*, by Mark Sells.

Tips "Our audience is the consumer, plain and simple. That means everyone. We are a small press and try hard to avoid the limitations of the industry. Agents are not necessary and neither are prior publications. We may be able to take you to the next level. We understand there is a lot of talent out there which is restricted by conventional wisdom in this industry. We want fresh, creative ideas and will accept unsolicited manuscripts. These, however, will not be returned without a SASE. E-mails are OK. No phone calls, please."

ARJUNA LIBRARY PRESS

Imprint of *Journal of Regional Criticism*, 1025 Garner St., D, Space 18, Colorado Springs CO 80905-1774. **Acquisitions:** Count Joseph A. Uphoff, Jr. Publishes trade paperback originals. **Publishes 3-6 titles/year. Receives 10 queries and 50 mss/year. 10% of books from first-time authors; 90% from unagented writers.** Publishes book 6 months after acceptance of ms. Accepts simultaneous submissions. Book catalog for $2; ms guidelines for #10 SASE.

o→ *The Journal of Regional Criticism* has now expressed the mission of studying distinguishments within the context of general surrealism as special surrealism to generate complex movement. This ideology presents such compounds as cultural surrealism, ethnic surrealism, or surrealist abstraction.

Nonfiction Reference, technical, experimental. Subjects include anthropology/archeology, art/architecture, creative nonfiction, philosophy, photography, science, surrealism. "The most appropriate work to send is short;

20 pages is a good size. The work should be adapted to maximize the potential of Xerox reproduction including diagrams, equations, and typography. Preferred subjects are literary, aesthetic, and relevant science.'' Currently emphasizing universal and historical surrealism; de-emphasizing traditional and eclectic delimitation of surrealism. Submit complete ms. Reviews artwork/photos as part of ms package. Send photocopies or transparencies or artcards.

Fiction Adventure, experimental, fantasy, historical, horror, literary, occult, poetry, poetry in translation, science fiction, surrealism. ''The focus being surrealism, the composition should embody principles of the theory in a spirit of experimental inquiry.'' Submit complete ms.

Poetry ''Poetry is published as single-page photocopy. It is most appropriate to send 3 or 4 poems with a résumé. A sample will be returned in any SASE. The poetry will be filed.''

Recent Title(s) *The Creative Personality*, by Professor S. Giora Shoham; *Thoughtful Fragments*, by Ryan Jackson.

ART DIRECTION BOOK CO., INC.

456 Glenbrook Rd., Glenbrook CT 06096-1800. (203)353-1441. Fax: (203)353-1371. **Acquisitions:** Don Barron, editorial director. Estab. 1959. Publishes hardcover and paperback originals. **Publishes 2 titles/year. Pays 10% royalty on retail price. Offers average $1,000 advance.** Publishes book 1 year after acceptance of ms. Does not accept simultaneous submissions. Responds in 3 months to queries. Book catalog for 6×9 SAE.
Imprints Infosource Publications.

    O→ Art Direction Book Co. is interested in books for the professional advertising art field—books for art directors, designers, etc; also entry level books for commercial and advertising art students in such fields as typography, photography, paste-up, illustration, clip-art, design, layout, and graphic arts.

Nonfiction Textbook, commercial art, ad art how-to. Subjects include art/architecture. Query with outline and 1 sample chapter. Reviews artwork/photos as part of ms package.

Recent Title(s) *The Write Book*.

ASLAN PUBLISHING

2490 Black Rock Turnpike, #342WM, Fairfield CT 06825. (203)372-0300. Fax: (203)374-4766. E-mail: barbara@aslanpublishing.com. Website: www.aslanpublishing.com. **Acquisitions:** Barbara H. Levine, creative director. **Publishes 2-4 titles/year. Pays 8-10% royalty on wholesale price.** Publishes book 18-24 months after acceptance of ms. Accepts simultaneous submissions. Responds in 2 months to queries.

    O→ ''Aslan Publishing offers readers a window to the soul via well-crafted and practical self-help books, inspirational books, and modern-day parables. Our mission is to publish books that uplift one's mind, body, and spirit. Please do not send proposals without first sending a query letter of up to 3 pages. Include SASE, e-mail address, phone number, word count.''

Nonfiction Topics vary. ''Please check our website for the types of books we publish. We are open to unusual ideas. We want authors who will do their own promotion with some guidance from us.''

Recent Title(s) *The Penis Dialogues: Handle with Care*, by Gabriel Constans, Ph.D; *Win in the Arena of Life: Living a Life You Love is Worth Fighting For*, by Ricky Anderson; *Candida—The Silent Epidemic*, by Gail Burton.

AVID READER PRESS

VWI Corp., 6705 W. Hwy 290, Suite 502-295, Austin TX 78735. (512)288-5349. Fax: (512)288-0317. E-mail: query@avidreaderpress.com. Website: www.avidreaderpress.com. **Acquisitions:** Elena Lipkowski, publisher. Publishes trade paperback originals and reprints. **Publishes 3 titles/year. 50% of books from first-time authors; 90% from unagented writers. Negotiates contracts individually.** Publishes book 1 year after acceptance of ms. Accepts simultaneous submissions. Responds in 1 month to queries; 1 month to proposals; 2 months to mss. Book catalog and ms guidelines on website.

Nonfiction Biography, coffee table book, how-to, multimedia (video), self-help. Subjects include animals, health/medicine, natural health, alternative medicine. ''We want to help people, and their pets, improve or maintain their health. We are seeking well-written, well-organized, original, or unique books on Natural Health or Alternative Medicine. Books should inform consumers about health options of which they may be unaware. However, the subject matter should be supported by research. No personal accounts unless they directly relate to a general audience. We will also consider reprinting older or under-marketed titles in these areas.'' Submit proposal package including outline, 2 sample chapter(s), SASE. Reviews artwork/photos as part of ms package. Send photocopies.

Recent Title(s) *Just Fine: Unmasking Concealed Chronic Illness and Pain*, by Carol Sveilich; *Feel Better Now . . . Meditation*, by Gary Halperin.

Tips When submitting a query, ''include a listing of current competitive books, author qualifications, and information on how your book is unique, and potential readers of your book. We look for authors who want to actively participate in the marketing of their books.''

Small Presses

◪ BANTER PRESS

520 Hudson St., Suite 139, New York NY 10014. (718)965-1613. E-mail: info@banterpress.com. Website: www. banterpress.com. **Acquisitions:** David McClintock, president (small business, software development, patient/ doctor communication). Estab. 2002. Publishes trade paperback and electronic originals and reprints. **Publishes 1-3 titles/year. Receives 50 queries and 10 mss/year. 80% of books from first-time authors; 100% from unagented writers. Pays 15-20% royalty on wholesale price.** Publishes book 1 year after acceptance of ms. Accepts simultaneous submissions. Responds in 2 weeks to queries; 2 months to proposals; 3 months to mss. Book catalog and ms guidelines online.

Imprints Banter Business, Banter Health, Banter Living.

Nonfiction Audiocassettes, biography, how-to, multimedia, self-help, technical. Subjects include business/economics, computers/electronic, creative nonfiction (business-oriented only), general nonfiction, health/medicine (written for patients), software, writing, editing, publishing. "We seek authors who are active speakers within their industry, especially those who do seminars or consulting. We're small but very experienced and selective. Currently, we're eager to see small business customer service, patient/doctor communication, and business fiction (like *The Goal* or *Fish!*). Submit proposal package including outline, maximum sample chapter(s), author bio, analysis of competing books, author's plan for promoting the book. Reviews artwork/photos as part of ms package. Send photocopies or never send originals.

Fiction Business fiction. "We only want business fiction that brings management issues to life." Submit maximum sample chapter(s), author bio, ideas for promotion.

Tips "Our readers are curious, technologically savvy professionals who need inspiring, up-to-date business and health information. Please don't mail us manuscripts! E-mail them as Word documents, PDFs, or as plain text files (.txt). Best yet, paste text into a giant e-mail. We want your words—electronically."

BARNWOOD PRESS

P.O. Box 146, Selma IN 47383. (765)288-0145. Fax: (765)285-3765. E-mail: tkoontz@bsu.edu. Website: www.barnwoodpress.org. **Acquisitions:** Tom Koontz, editor. Estab. 1975. Publishes original trade paperbacks. **Publishes 2 titles/year. Payment varies.** Responds in 1 month to queries.

Poetry Query first with a few sample poems and cover letter with brief bio and publication credits.

BEAR STAR PRESS

185 Hollow Oak Dr., Cohasset CA 95973. (530)891-0360. Website: www.bearstarpress.com. **Acquisitions:** Beth Spencer, publisher/editor. Estab. 1996. Publishes trade paperback originals. **Publishes 1-2 titles/year. Pays $1,000, and 25 copies based off annual Dorothy Brunsman contest.** Publishes book 9 months after acceptance of ms. Accepts simultaneous submissions. Responds in 2 weeks to queries. Ms guidelines online.

○┐ "Bear Star is committed to publishing the best poetry it can attract. Each year it sponsors a contest open to poets from Western and Pacific states. From time to time we add to our list other poets from our target area whose work we admire."

Poetry Wants well-crafted poems. No restrictions as to form, subject matter, style, or purpose. "Poets should enter our annual book competition. Other books are occasionally solicited by publisher, sometimes from among contestants who didn't win." Query, or submit complete ms.

Recent Title(s) *The Bandsaw Riots*, by Arlitia Jones; *Closet Drama*, by Kandie St. Germain; *The Book of Common Betrayals*, by Lynne Knight.

Tips "Send your best work, consider its arrangement. A 'wow' poem early keeps me reading."

BENDALL BOOKS

145 Tyee Dr., PMB 361, Point Roberts WA 98281. (250)743-2946. Fax: (250)743-2910. E-mail: admin@bendallbooks.com. Website: www.islandnet.com/bendallbooks. **Acquisitions:** R. Bendall, publisher. Publishes trade paperback originals. **Publishes 1 title/year. Receives 135 queries and 10 mss/year. 50% of books from first-time authors; 100% from unagented writers. Pays 5-15% royalty on wholesale price.** Publishes book 1 year after acceptance of ms. Accepts simultaneous submissions. Book catalog free; ms guidelines online.

Nonfiction Reference, textbook. Subjects include education. Query with SASE.

Recent Title(s) *Daily Meaning*, edited by Allan Neilsen; *Fiction Workshop Companion*, by Jon Volkmer.

BLISS PUBLISHING CO.

P.O. Box 920, Marlborough MA 01752. (508)480-0060. Website: www.blisspublishing.com. **Acquisitions:** Stephen H. Clouter, publisher. Publishes hardcover and trade paperback originals. **Publishes 2-4 titles/year. Pays 10-15% royalty on wholesale price.** Does not accept simultaneous submissions. Responds in 2 months to queries.

Nonfiction Biography, illustrated book, reference, textbook. Subjects include government/politics, history, music/dance, nature/environment, recreation, regional. Submit proposal package including outline, 3 sample chapter(s), résumé. SASE.

Recent Title(s) *Ninnuock, The Algonkian People of New England*, Steven F. Johnson.

BLUE POPPY PRESS

Imprint of Blue Poppy Enterprises, Inc., 5441 Western Ave., #2, Boulder CO 80301-2733. (303)447-8372. Fax: (303)245-8362. E-mail: info@bluepoppy.com. Website: www.bluepoppy.com. **Acquisitions:** Bob Flaws, editor-in-chief. Estab. 1981. Publishes hardcover and trade paperback originals. **Publishes 3-4 titles/year. Receives 50-100 queries and 20 mss/year. 30-40% of books from first-time authors; 100% from unagented writers. Pays 8-12% royalty.** Publishes book 1 year after acceptance of ms. Does not accept simultaneous submissions. Responds in 1 month to queries. Book catalog free; ms guidelines online.

> O→ Blue Poppy Press is dedicated to expanding and improving the English language literature on acupuncture and Asian medicine for both professional practitioners and lay readers.

Nonfiction Self-help, technical, textbook (related to acupuncture and Oriental medicine). Subjects include ethnic, health/medicine. "We only publish books on acupuncture and Oriental medicine by authors who can read Chinese and have a minimum of 5 years clinical experience. We also require all our authors to use Wiseman's *Glossary of Chinese Medical Terminology* as their standard for technical terms." Query with SASE, or submit outline, 1 sample chapter(s).

Recent Title(s) *Chinese Medical Psychiatry*, by Bob Flaws & James Lake, MD.

Tips Audience is "practicing acupuncturists, interested in alternatives in healthcare, preventive medicine, Chinese philosophy, and medicine."

BLUE-COLLAR BOOKS

P.O. Box 40117, Washington DC 20016. (202)489-5544. E-mail: info@bluecollarbooks.com. Submissions E-mail: submit@bluecollarbooks.com. Website: www.bluecollarbooks.com. **Acquisitions:** Sonny Shivers, acquisitions editor; Benny Pekkanen, editor (literary fiction). Publishes hardcover and trade paperback originals. **Publishes 2 titles/year. Receives 1,000 queries and 500 mss/year. 75% of books from first-time authors; 80% from unagented writers. Pays 30-50% royalty on wholesale price.** Publishes book 12-18 months after acceptance of ms. Accepts simultaneous submissions. Responds in 3 months to queries; 3-5 months to proposals; 5 months to mss. Book catalog free; ms guidelines online.

Fiction Ethnic, experimental, literary, short story collections. Submit proposal package including 20-40 pages.

Recent Title(s) *Twenty-Six* (short story collection); *Best Wishes* (experimental novel).

Ⓐ BOOK PEDDLERS

15245 Minnetonka Blvd., Minnetonka MN 55345. (952)912-0036. Fax: (952)912-0105. E-mail: vlansky@bookpeddlers.com. Website: www.bookpeddlers.com. **Acquisitions:** Vicki Lansky, publisher/editor. Publishes hardcover and trade paperback originals. **Publishes 3 titles/year. Receives 50 queries and 10 mss/year. 0% of books from first-time authors; 0% from unagented writers. Pays 10% royalty on wholesale price. Offers $500 advance.** Publishes book 1 year after acceptance of ms. Accepts simultaneous submissions. Responds in 1 week to queries; 1 week to proposals. Book catalog for #10 SASE; ms guidelines online.

Nonfiction Children's/juvenile, gift book, how-to, self-help. "We accept no fiction and practically nothing that is sent to us. A writer must be very on target for our consideration." Query with SASE.

Recent Title(s) *Coming Clean*, by Schar War (dirty little secrets from a professional housecleaner); *Dress to Impress*, by Joyce N. Shellhart; *Trouble-Free Travel with Children*, by Vicki Lansky.

Tips "See submission guidelines on website."

BOOKHAVEN PRESS, LLC

P.O. Box 1243, Moon Township PA 15108. (412)494-6926. Orders: (800)782-7424. Fax: (412)494-5479. Website: www.members.aol.com/bookhaven. Editorial Manager: Victor Richards. **Acquisitions:** Dennis Damp, publisher. Publishes trade paperback originals. **Publishes 2 titles/year. Pays 7-12% royalty on wholesale price.** Does not accept simultaneous submissions. Sends form letter for rejection, destroys originals. Responds in 3 months to queries; 1 month to proposals; 2 months to mss. Book catalog free; ms guidelines online.

Nonfiction How-to, reference. Subjects include business/economics, education, money/finance. Bookhaven Press seeks to develop complimentary titles for its existing career book line. Emphasizing health care and government employment. "We look for well-developed manuscripts from computer literate writers. All manuscripts must be available in IBM computer format (Word Perfect or Microsoft Word preferred)." Submit outline, 2 sample chapter(s).

Recent Title(s) *The Book of U.S. Government Jobs, 8th Ed.*; *Post Office Jobs, 3rd ed.*, by Dennis V. Damp.

BREWERS PUBLICATIONS

Imprint of Association of Brewers, 736 Pearl St., Boulder CO 80302. (303)447-0816. Fax: (303)447-2825. E-mail: ray@aob.org. Website: beertown.org. **Acquisitions:** Ray Daniels, publisher. Estab. 1986. Publishes hardcover and trade paperback originals. **Publishes 2 titles/year. 50% of books from first-time authors; 50% from unagented writers. Pays royalty on net receipts. Offers negotiated advance.** Publishes book 18 months after acceptance of ms. Accepts simultaneous submissions. Responds in 3 months to queries. Ms guidelines online.

O→ Brewers Publications is the largest publisher of books on beer-related subjects.

Nonfiction "We only publish books of interest to brewers and most authors have many years experience and in-depth knowledge of their subject. We are not interested in fiction, drinking games or beer/bar reviews. Those determined to fit our needs will subscribe to and read *Zymurgy* and *The New Brewer*." Query first with brief proposal and SASE.

Recent Title(s) *Standards of Brewing*, by Dr. Charles Bamforth; *The Compleat Meadmaker*, by Ken Schramm.

BRIGHT MOUNTAIN BOOKS, INC.

206 Riva Ridge Dr., Fairview NC 28730. (828)628-1768. Fax: (828)628-1755. E-mail: booksbmb@charter.net. **Acquisitions:** Cynthia F. Bright, editor. Publishes hardcover originals and trade paperback originals and reprints. **Publishes 6 titles/year. Pays 5-10% royalty on retail price.** Responds in 1 month to queries; 3 months to mss.

Imprints Historical Images.

Nonfiction Biography. Subjects include history, regional. "Our current emphasis is on regional titles set in the Southern Appalachians and Carolinas, which can include nonfiction by local writers." Query with SASE.

Recent Title(s) *Herk: Hero of the Skies*, by Joseph Dabney.

BROOKS BOOKS

3720 N. Woodridge Dr., Decatur IL 62526. (217)877-2966. E-mail: brooksbooks@q-com.com. Website: www.family-net.net/ ~ brooksbooks. **Acquisitions:** Randy Brooks, editor (haiku poetry, tanka poetry). Publishes hardcover and trade paperback originals. **Publishes 3-5 titles/year. Receives 100 queries and 25 mss/year. 10% of books from first-time authors; 100% from unagented writers. Pays 10-15% royalty on retail price or makes outright purchase of $100-500.** Publishes book 16 months after acceptance of ms. Responds in 1 month to queries; 3 months to proposals; 6 months to mss. Book catalog for #10 SASE or online at website; ms guidelines for #10 SASE.

Imprints High/Coo Press, Brooks Books.

O→ Brooks Books, formerly High/Coo Press, publishes English-language haiku books, chapbooks, magazines, and bibliographies.

Poetry Submit 10 sample poems.

Recent Title(s) *Almost Unseen: Selected Haiku of George Swede*, by George Swede; *To Hear the Rain: Selected Haiku*, by Peggy Lyles.

Tips "Our readers enjoy contemporary haiku based on the literary tradition of Japanese aesthetics (not 5-7-5 Internet jokes)."

CAGE CONSULTING, INC.

P.O. Box 69034, Tucson AZ 85737. (520)579-4318 or (888)899-CAGE. Fax: (520)744-1792. E-mail: cheryl@cagec onsulting.com. Website: www.cageconsulting.com. **Acquisitions:** Cheryl A. Cage, president. Estab. 1996. Publishes trade and mass market paperback originals. **Publishes 2-4 titles/year. 50% of books from first-time authors; 100% from unagented writers. Pays 8% minimum royalty (begins with first book sold), 15% maximum royalty (after initial investment recouped) on wholesale price.** Publishes book 6-12 months after acceptance of ms. Accepts simultaneous submissions. Responds in 1 month to proposals; 1 month to mss. Book catalog and ms guidelines online.

Nonfiction Reference (aviation and business). Subjects include Self-Employment, Career Advancement, Job Search. "Author must be viewed as an expert in the area they are discussing. First-time authors welcomed." Submit proposal package including outline, 2 sample chapter(s), résumé.

Fiction Mystery, suspense, aviation. Interested in fiction that provides the reader an "insider's" view of aviation (from any professional point of view: pilot, flight attendant, air traffic controller, aircraft accident investigator, upper level airline management, upper level airport management). Want the reader to learn a little something about the industry while being entertained. Submit proposal package including 3 sample chapter(s), résumé, synopsis.

Tips "The following describes our audience. Fiction: Any mystery or suspense fan, or an individual who is interested in the inner workings of the world of aviation. Aviation Nonfiction: Professional pilots for the Pilot Tech and Career Guides. Business Nonfiction: Career seekers, small business owners looking to enchance their bottom line. Don't allow 'flowery' writing to get in the way of telling a good story or presenting useful information. Give us a great idea presented in a focused, concise manner. No phone calls or unsolicited e-mails!''

CAROLINA WREN PRESS

120 Morris St., Durham NC 27701. (919)560-2738. E-mail: carolina@carolinawrenpress.org. Website: www.carolinawrenpress.org. Estab. 1976. ''We publish poetry, fiction, nonfiction, biography, autobiography, literary nonfiction work by, and/or about people of color, women, gay/lesbian issues, health and mental health topics in children's literature.'' Publishes book 1 year after acceptance of ms. Responds in 3 months to queries; 6 months to mss. Ms guidelines online.

• Reads unsolicited mss all year, but prefers writers to wait and enter their contests—poetry contest in Fall 2004 and 2006, fiction contest in Winter 2004-2005.

Fiction Ethnic, experimental (poetry), feminist, gay/lesbian, literary, short story collections. ''We are especially interested in children's literature on the subjects of health, illness, mental illness, healing, etc.'' Query by mail only with SASE and short (10 pp) sample.

Tips ''Manuscripts are read year-round, but reply time is long unless submitting for a contest.''

CAROUSEL PRESS

P.O. Box 6038, Berkeley CA 94706-0038. (510)527-5849. Website: www.carousel-press.com. **Acquisitions:** Carole T. Meyers, editor/publisher. Estab. 1976. Publishes trade paperback originals and reprints. **Publishes 1-2 titles/year. Pays 10-15% royalty on wholesale price. Offers $1,000 advance.** Responds in 1 month to queries.

Nonfiction Subjects include travel, travel-related. Query with SASE.

Recent Title(s) *Dream Sleeps: Castle & Palace Hotels of Europe*, by Pamela L. Barrus.

CASSANDRA PRESS

P.O. Box 228, Boulder CO 80306. (800)527-6104 or (303)444-2590. Fax: (303)444-2994. E-mail: starvibe@indra.com. Website: www.cassandrapress.com. **Acquisitions:** Fred Rubenfeld, president. Estab. 1985. Publishes trade paperback originals. **Publishes 3 titles/year. Receives 200 submissions/year. 50% of books from first-time authors; 50% from unagented writers. Pays 6-8% royalty on retail price. Offers rarely advance.** Publishes book 1 year after acceptance of ms. Accepts simultaneous submissions. Responds in 3 weeks to queries; 3 months to mss. Book catalog and ms guidelines free.

Nonfiction How-to, self-help. Subjects include cooking/foods/nutrition, government/politics, health/medicine, New Age, philosophy, psychology, religion, spirituality. ''We like to do around 3 titles a year in the general New Age, metaphysical and holistic health fields.'' No children's books or novels. Submit outline, sample chapter(s).

Recent Title(s) *Treason the New World Order*, Gurudas (political).

CAVE BOOKS

277 Clamer Rd., Trenton NJ 08628-3204. (609)530-9743. E-mail: pddb@juno.com. Website: www.cavebooks.com. **Acquisitions:** Paul Steward, editor. Estab. 1980. Publishes hardcover and trade paperback originals and reprints. **Publishes 2 titles/year. Receives 20 queries and 10 mss/year. 75% of books from first-time authors; 100% from unagented writers. Pays 10% royalty on retail price.** Publishes book 18 months after acceptance of ms. Accepts simultaneous submissions. Responds in 2 weeks to queries; 3 months to mss.

O— Cave Books publishes books only on caves, karst, and speleology.

Nonfiction Biography, technical (science), adventure. Subjects include Americana, animals, anthropology/archeology, history, nature/environment, photography, recreation, regional, science, sports (cave exploration), travel. Submit complete ms. Reviews artwork/photos as part of ms package. Send photocopies.

Fiction ''Must be realistic and centrally concerned with cave exploration. The cave and action in the cave must be central, authentic, and realistic.'' Adventure, historical, literary, caves, karst, speleology. No gothic, science fiction, fantasy, romance, mystery, or poetry. No novels that are not entirely about caves. Query with SASE, or submit complete ms.

Recent Title(s) *Hidden Beneath the Mountains: The Caves of Sequoia and Kings Canyon National Parks.*

Tips ''Our readers are interested only in caves, karst, and speleology. Please do not send manuscripts on other subjects.''

CLARITY PRESS, INC.

3277 Roswell Rd. NE, #469, Atlanta GA 30305. (877)613-1495. Fax: (404)231-3899 and (877)613-7868. E-mail: claritypress@usa.net. Website: www.claritypress.com. **Acquisitions:** Diana G. Collier, editorial director (contemporary social justice issues). Estab. 1984. Publishes hardcover and trade paperback originals. **Publishes 4 titles/year.** Accepts simultaneous submissions. Submit by e-mail, no SASE. Responds in 1 month to queries.

Nonfiction Publishes books on contemporary issues in US, Middle East and Africa. Subjects include ethnic, world affairs, human rights/socio-economic and minority issues. No fiction. Query with synopsis, table of contents, résumé, publishing history.

Recent Title(s) *State Terrorism and the United States*, by Frederick H. Gareau; *Destroying World Order*, by Francis A. Boyle.

Tips "Check our titles on website."

N CLEAR VIEW PRESS

P.O. Box 11574, Marina del Rey CA 90295. E-mail: publisher@clearviewpress.com. Website: www.clearviewpress.com. Estab. 2003. Publishes hardcover, trade paperback, and electronic originals. **Publishes 3 titles/year; imprint publishes 3 titles/year. 80% of books from first-time authors; 80% from unagented writers. Pays 10% royalty on wholesale price.** Publishes book 4-12 months after acceptance of ms. Responds in 3 months to queries; 3 months to proposals; 3 months to mss. Book catalog online; ms guidelines for #10 SASE.

Nonfiction Audiocassettes, how-to, self-help, technical. Subjects include computers/electronic, education, hobbies, memoirs, New Age, spirituality, literary criticism. Query with SASE, or submit proposal package including outline, 1 sample chapter(s).

Fiction Adventure, comic books, literary, mainstream/contemporary, spiritual. Query with SASE, or submit complete ms.

Recent Title(s) *Advanced Nanotechnology*, by Steiner (technology/science); *The River Beneath the River*, by Susan Tabin (fiction).

THE COLLEGE BOARD

College Entrance Examination Board, 45 Columbus Ave., New York NY 10023-6992. (212)713-8000. Website: www.collegeboard.com. **Acquisitions:** Thomas Vanderberg, director of publications. Publishes trade paperback originals. **Publishes 2 titles/year. Receives 30 submissions/year. 25% of books from first-time authors; 50% from unagented writers. Pays royalty on retail price. Offers advance.** Publishes book 9 months after acceptance of ms. Responds in 2 months to queries. Book catalog free.

o-π The College Board publishes guidance information for college-bound students.

Nonfiction "We want books to help students make a successful transition from high school to college." Reference. Subjects include education, college guidance. Query with SASE, or submit outline, sample chapter(s), SASE.

Recent Title(s) *The College Application Essay*, by Sarah McGinty; *Campus Visits & College Interviews*, by Zola Dincin Schneider.

CONSUMER PRESS

13326 SW 28 St., Suite 102, Ft. Lauderdale FL 33330. (954)370-9153. Fax: (954)472-1008. **Acquisitions:** Joseph Pappas, editorial director. Estab. 1989. Publishes trade paperback originals. **Publishes 2-5 titles/year. Pays royalty on wholesale price or on retail price, as per agreement.** Does not accept simultaneous submissions. Book catalog free.

Imprints Women's Publications.

Nonfiction How-to, self-help. Subjects include child guidance/parenting, health/medicine, money/finance, women's issues/studies, homeowner guides, building/remodeling, food/nutrition. Query with SASE.

Recent Title(s) *The Ritalin Free Child*, by Diana Hunter; *Before You Hire a Contractor, 2nd ed.*, by Steve Gonzalez, C.R.C.

COTTONWOOD PRESS, INC.

109-B Cameron Dr., Fort Collins CO 80525. (800)864-4297. Fax: (970)204-0761. E-mail: cottonwood@cottonwoodpress.com. Website: www.cottonwoodpress.com. **Acquisitions:** Cheryl Thurston, editor. Estab. 1986. Publishes trade paperback originals. **Publishes 2-8 titles/year. Receives 50 queries and 40 mss/year. 50% of books from first-time authors; 100% from unagented writers. Pays 10-12% royalty on net receipts.** Publishes book 1 year after acceptance of ms. Accepts simultaneous submissions. Responds in 1 month to queries; 1 month to proposals; 3 months to mss. Book catalog for 10×12 SAE with 2 first-class stamps; ms guidelines online.

o-π Cottonwood Press publishes creative and practical materials for English and language arts teachers, grades 5-12. "We believe English should be everyone's favorite subject."

Nonfiction Textbook. Subjects include education, language/literature. "We are always looking for truly original, creative materials for teachers." Query with SASE, or submit outline, 1-3 sample chapter(s).

Recent Title(s) *Plugged in to English*; *Live! From the Classroom! It's Mythology*.

Tips "We publish only supplemental textbooks for English/language arts teachers, grades 5-12, with an emphasis upon middle school and junior high materials. Don't assume we publish educational materials for all subject areas. We do not. Never submit anything to us before looking at our catalog. We have a very narrow focus and a distinctive style. Writers who don't understand that are wasting their time. On the plus side, we are eager to work with new authors who show a sense of humor and a familiarity with young adolescents.''

COUNTRY MUSIC FOUNDATION PRESS

222 Fifth Ave. S., Nashville TN 37203. (615)416-2001. Fax: (615)255-2245. Website: www.countrymusichalloffa me.com. **Acquisitions:** Jay Orr, senior museum editor; Kira Florita, director, special projects; Michael Gray, associate editor. Publishes hardcover originals and trade paperback originals and reprints. **Publishes 2-4 titles/ year. Receives 12 queries/year. Pays 10% royalty on wholesale price. Offers $1,000-5,000 advance.** Publishes book 1 year after acceptance of ms. Accepts simultaneous submissions. Responds in 2 months to queries; 3 months to proposals; 4 months to mss. Book catalog online; ms guidelines free.

- Also co-publish and hire writers (work-for-hire) for anthologies or for mass-market trade publications where CMF is authored.

- Oπ ''We publish historical, biographical and reference books about country music, many in a joint imprint with Vanderbilt University Press. We require strict factual accuracy and strive to engage an educated general audience.'' Currently emphasizes ''histories, biographies, and memoirs with a strong narrative and accessible to an educated general audience.'' De-emphasizing ''heavily academic studies.''

Nonfiction All must emphasize country music. Biography, illustrated book, reference, scholarly. Subjects include Americana, history, memoirs, music/dance, photography, regional. Query with SASE or submit proposal package, including outline, 1 sample chapter and introduction. Reviews artwork/photos as part of ms package. Send photocopies.

Recent Title(s) *Singing in the Saddle: The History of the Singing Cowboy*, by Doug Green (history); *Vinyl Hayride: Country Music Album Covers* (authored for Chronicle Books).

Tips ''Our audience is a balance between educated country music fans and scholars. Submit queries or proposals only if you are very knowledgeable about your subject. Our books are in-depth studies written by experts or by music insiders. We aren't especially receptive to inexperienced beginners.''

N DAGBOOKS

11 Penshire Circle, Penfield NY 14526. Website: www.dagbooks.com. **Acquisitions:** Dave Grass, editor. Estab. 2000. **Publishes 3-4 titles/year. 100% from unagented writers. Pays 45% on retail from website; 45% minus discounts elsewhere.** Publishes book 2 months after acceptance of ms. Accepts simultaneous submissions. Responds in 1 week to queries; 1 week to proposals; 2 weeks to mss. Book catalog online; ms guidelines by e-mail.

Nonfiction Booklets, how-to, humor, ebooks. Subjects include animals, art/architecture, business/economics (small business), general nonfiction, hobbies, pets, home-based business. ''We are especially interested in books that help readers start businesses, especially home-based, inexpensive, and/or unique ventures.'' Query with SASE, or submit proposal package including outline, 2 sample chapter(s), or submit complete ms. Or send query by e-mail. Reviews artwork/photos as part of ms package. Send photocopies or prints, digital files.

Fiction Adventure, experimental, humor, juvenile, picture books, poetry, science fiction, short story collections, young adult, cartoons. ''We are especially interested in humor, cartoons, and short story collections in regard to fiction at this time.'' Query with SASE, or submit proposal package including 2 sample chapter(s), synopsis, or 5-10 cartoons, or submit complete ms. Or send query by e-mail.

Poetry ''We are most interested in modern, avant-garde, unique, and experimental poetry that makes people think.'' Submit complete ms.

Recent Title(s) *Start Your Own Professional Pet-Sitting Service*, by Dave Grass; *Amazing Computer Art*, by Mark Terreri; *Off the Mark Cartoons, Pets and Other Animals*, by Mark Parisi.

Tips ''We started out dealing with pet-related topics, but will now consider most topics that have a potential to draw interest. Especially looking for material that is not widely available elsewhere. Our audience wants to learn and improve themselves. We publish ebooks, so try to make your material fill a void and/or contain features/benefits to readers that paper books do not.''

JOHN DANIEL AND CO.

Daniel & Daniel, Publishers, Inc., P.O. Box 2790, McKinleyville CA 95519. (707)839-3495. Fax: (707)839-3242. E-mail: jd@danielpublishing.com. Website: www.danielpublishing.com. **Acquisitions:** John Daniel, publisher. Estab. 1980. Publishes hardcover originals and trade paperback originals. Publishes poetry, fiction and nonfiction. **Publishes 4 or fewer titles/year. Pays 10% royalty on wholesale price. Offers $0-500 advance.** Publishes book 1 year after acceptance of ms. Accepts simultaneous submissions. Responds in 1 month to queries; 1 month to proposals; 2 months to mss. Book catalog and ms guidelines online.

Nonfiction Biography, essay. Subjects include creative nonfiction, memoirs. ''We seldom publish books over

70,000 words. Other than that, we're looking for books that are important and well-written." Query with SASE, or submit proposal package including outline, 50 pages.

Fiction Literary, poetry, short story collections. Publishes poetry, fiction and nonfiction; specializes in belles lettres, literary memoir. Query with SASE, or submit proposal package including synopsis, 50 pages.

Poetry "We publish very little poetry, I'm sorry to say." Query, or submit complete ms.

Recent Title(s) *Stealing Home*, by Irving Weinman (novel); *Go Where the Landshed Takes You*, by Jane Glazer (poetry).

Tips "Literate, intelligent general readers. We are very small and very cautious, and we publish fewer books each year, so any submission to us is a long shot. But we welcome your submissions. By mail only, please. We don't want submissions by phone, fax, disk, or e-mail."

DAWBERT PRESS, INC.

(formerly Dawbert Press), Submissions Department, P.O. Box 67, Duxbury MA 02331. (781)934-7202. E-mail: info@dawbert.com. Website: www.dawbert.com. **Acquisitions:** Allison Elliott, editor. Publishes mass market paperback originals. **Publishes 3 titles/year. Pays 5-10% royalty on retail price.** Publishes book months after acceptance of ms. Accepts simultaneous submissions. Ms guidelines online.

Nonfiction Reference. Subjects include travel, recreation. "We publish only travel and recreation books." Submit outline. Reviews artwork/photos as part of ms package. Send photocopies.

Recent Title(s) *On the Road Again with Man's Best Friend*, by Habgood (travel with pets); *Pets on the Go, The Definitive Pet Vacation and Accommodation Guide*; *Families on the Go!, The Inside Scoop on the Best Family Friendly Accommodations and Vacations in North America*.

DISKOTECH, INC.

7930 State Line, Suite 210, Prairie Village KS 66208. (913)432-8606. Fax: (913)432-8606*51. **Acquisitions:** Jane Locke, submissions editor. Estab. 1989. Publishes multimedia nonfiction and fiction for PC's and the Internet. **Publishes 2 titles/year. Pays 10-15% royalty on wholesale price.** Does not accept simultaneous submissions. Responds in 2 months to queries.

Nonfiction Authors must supply the multimedia, such as video, music, and animation in html format. Considers most nonfiction subjects. Query with SASE.

Fiction Authors must supply the multimedia, such as video, music, and animation and the work in html format. Considers all fiction genres. Query with SASE.

Recent Title(s) *The Martensville Nightmare CVN®*, Karen Smith (1st multimedia true crime story on CD-Rom); *Negative Space CVN®*, Holly Franking (computerized video novel on CD-ROM); *Celebrity lnk CVN®* (Hypermedia Internet Tabloid).

DUFOUR EDITIONS

P.O. Box 7, Chester Springs PA 19425. (610)458-5005 or (800)869-5677. Fax: (610)458-7103. E-mail: info@dufou reditions.com. Website: www.dufoureditions.com. **Acquisitions:** Christopher May, publisher. Estab. 1948. Publishes hardcover originals, trade paperback originals and reprints. **Publishes 3-4 titles/year. Receives 200 queries and 15 mss/year. 20-30% of books from first-time authors; 80% from unagented writers. Pays 6-10% royalty on net receipts. Offers $100-500 advance.** Publishes book 18 months after acceptance of ms. Accepts simultaneous submissions. Responds in 3 months to queries; 3 months to proposals; 6 months to mss. Book catalog free.

> O→ "We publish literary fiction by good writers which is well received and achieves modest sales." De-emphsazing poetry and nonfiction.

Nonfiction Biography. Subjects include history, translation. Query with SASE. Reviews artwork/photos as part of ms package. Send photocopies.

Fiction Literary, short story collections. "We like books that are slightly off-beat, different and well-written." Query with SASE.

Poetry Query.

Recent Title(s) *Behold Faith and Other Stories*, by Tom Noyes; *Yielding Ice About to Melt*, by Richard Penna; *Night Sounds and Other Stories*, by Karen Gettert Shoemaker.

Tips "Audience is sophisticated, literate readers especially interested in foreign literature and translations, and a strong Irish-Celtic focus, as well as work from U.S. writers. Check to see if the publisher is really a good match for your subject matter."

EAGLE'S VIEW PUBLISHING

6756 North Fork Rd., Liberty UT 84310. (801)745-0905. Fax: (801)745-0903. E-mail: eglcrafts@aol.com. Website: www.eaglesviewpub.com. **Acquisitions:** Denise Knight, editor-in-chief. Estab. 1982. Publishes trade paperback originals. **Publishes 2-4 titles/year. Receives 40 queries and 20 mss/year. 90% of books from first-**

time authors; **100% from unagented writers. Pays 8-10% royalty on net selling price.** Publishes book 1 year or more after acceptance of ms. Accepts simultaneous submissions. Responds in 1 year to proposals. Book catalog and ms guidelines for $4.

> **O-π** Eagle's View primarily publishes how-to craft books with a subject related to historical or contemporary Native American/Mountain Man/frontier crafts/bead crafts. Currently emphasizing bead-related craft books. De-emphasizing history except for historical Indian crafts.

Nonfiction How-to, Indian, mountain man, and American frontier (history and craft). Subjects include anthropology/archeology (Native American crafts), ethnic (Native American), history (American frontier historical patterns and books), hobbies (crafts, especially beadwork). "We are expanding from our Indian craft base to more general but related crafts. We prefer to do photography in-house." Submit outline, 1-2 sample chapter(s). Reviews artwork/photos as part of ms package. Send photocopies or sample illustrations.

Recent Title(s) *Treasury of Beaded Jewelry*, by Mary Ellen Harte; *Beads and Beadwork of the American Indian*, by William C. Orchard; *Hemp Masters: Getting Knotty*, by Max Lunger.

Tips "We will not be publishing any new beaded earrings books for the forseeable future. We are interested in other craft projects using seed beads, especially books that feature a variety of items, not just different designs for 1 item."

EARTH-LOVE PUBLISHING HOUSE LTD.

3440 Youngfield St., Suite 353, Wheat Ridge CO 80033. (303)233-9660. Fax: (303)233-9354. **Acquisitions:** Laodeciae Augustine, director. Publishes trade paperback originals. **Publishes 1-2 titles/year. Pays 6-10% royalty on wholesale price.** Does not accept simultaneous submissions. Responds in 1 month to queries; 1 month to proposals; 3 months to mss.

Nonfiction Reference. Subjects include minerals. Query with SASE.

Recent Title(s) *Love Is in the Earth—Kaleidoscope Pictorial Supplement Z*, by Melody (mineral reference); *Loves Is in the Earth—Crystal Tarot for the Millennium*, by Melody; *Love Is in the Earth—Reality Checque*, by Melody.

EASTLAND PRESS

P.O. Box 99749, Seattle WA 98139. (206)217-0204. Fax: (206)217-0205. E-mail: info@eastlandpress.com. Website: www.eastlandpress.com. **Acquisitions:** John O'Connor, managing editor. Estab. 1981. Publishes hardcover and trade paperback originals. **Publishes 3-4 titles/year. Receives 25 queries/year. 30% of books from first-time authors; 90% from unagented writers. Pays 12-15% royalty on receipts.** Publishes book 2 years after acceptance of ms. Accepts simultaneous submissions. Responds in 1 month to queries. Book catalog free.

> **O-π** Eastland Press is interested in textbooks for practitioners of alternative medical therapies primarily Chinese and physical therapies, and related bodywork.

Nonfiction Reference, textbook, alternative medicine (Chinese and physical therapies, and related bodywork). Subjects include health/medicine. "We prefer that a manuscript be completed or close to completion before we will consider publication. Proposals are rarely considered, unless submitted by a published author or teaching institution." Submit outline and 2-3 sample chapters. Reviews artwork/photos as part of ms package. Send photocopies.

Recent Title(s) *Cranial Sutures*, by Marc Pick; *Acupuncture in the Treatment of Children*, by Julian Scott.

THE EIGHTH MOUNTAIN PRESS

624 SE 29th Ave., Portland OR 97214. E-mail: eighthmt@pacifier.com. **Acquisitions:** Ruth Gundle, editor. Estab. 1985. Publishes original trade paperbacks. **Publishes 1 title/year. Pays 7% royalty.** Responds in 6 weeks to queries.

> **O-π** Eighth Mountain is a small press publisher of literary works by women.

Fiction Poetry.

Poetry "Our books are handsomely designed and printed on acid-free paper in both quality trade paperbacks and library editions." Initial press run for poetry is 2,500. Does not want fax submissions. E-mail submissions fine, no attachments. "We expect a query letter along with a few poems. A résumé of published work, if any, should be included. Work should be typed, double-spaced, and with your name on each page."

EIH PUBLISHING

AHU Press, P.O. Box 249, Goshen VA 24439. (540)997-0325. E-mail: hyptrainer@aol.com. Website: www.holisti ctree.com. **Acquisitions:** Dr. Allen Chips, acquisitions/publishing director (holistic texts and how-to/self-help). Estab. 1999. Publishes hardcover originals and reprints, trade paperback originals and reprints, electronic originals and reprints, and mass market paperback reprints. **Publishes 3-7 titles/year. Receives 35 queries and 20 submissions/year. 50% of books from first-time authors; 95% from unagented writers. Pays 10% royalty.** Publishes book 9-12 months after acceptance of ms. Accepts simultaneous submissions. Responds in 1 month to queries; 2 months to proposals; 3 months to mss. Book catalog and ms guidelines online.

Nonfiction Audiocassettes, how-to, self-help, textbook. Subjects include education, health/medicine, psychology, spirituality. "We are looking for textbooks, and self-help, how-to books with a holistic health or transpersonal therapy orientation." First, query to hyptrainer@aol.com. Then, submit TOC with 2 sample chapters. Reviews artwork/photos as part of ms package. Send photocopies.

Recent Title(s) *Script Magic: A Hypnotherapist's Desk Reference*, by Dr. Allen Chips, Henry Bolduc, Dr. Masud Ansari, and others; *Life Patterns: Soul Lessons & Forgiveness*, by Henry Bolduc; *Inspirational Poetry*, by Dee Chips.

Tips Audience is people desiring to learn about mind-body-spirit oriented therapies/practices that lead to healing and/or enlightenment. "The best authors are engaged in regular travel and seminars/workshops, demonstrating dedication, self-motivation, and a people orientation."

ELYSIAN EDITIONS

Imprint of Princeton Book Co., Publishers, 614 Route 130, Hightstown NJ 08520. (609)426-0602. Fax: (609)426-1344. E-mail: elysian@aosi.com. Website: www.dancehorizons.com/elysian.html. **Acquisitions:** Charles Woodford (fitness, yoga, travel, memoir, true adventure). Publishes hardcover and trade paperback originals and reprints. **Publishes 1-3 titles/year. Receives 100 queries and 30 mss/year. 25% of books from first-time authors; 50% from unagented writers. Pays royalty on retail price. Offers negotiable advance.** Publishes book 9-12 months after acceptance of ms. Accepts simultaneous submissions. Responds in 3 weeks to queries; 3 weeks to proposals; 1 month to mss. Book catalog free or on website; ms guidelines free.

Nonfiction Biography. Subjects include memoirs, travel, true adventure, fitness, yoga. Submit proposal package including outline, 3 sample chapter(s). Reviews artwork/photos as part of ms package. Send photocopies.

Recent Title(s) *Manhattan Meoics: The Gripping Story of the Men and Women of Emergency Medical Services Who Make the Streets of the City Their Career.*

EMIS, INC.

P.O. Box 820062, Dallas TX 75382-0062. Website: www.emispub.com. **Acquisitions:** Lynda Blake, president. Publishes trade paperback originals. **Publishes 2 titles/year. Pays 12% royalty on retail price.** Responds in 3 months to queries. Book catalog and ms guidelines free.

    ○→ Medical text designed for physicians; fit in the lab coat pocket as a quick reference. Currently emphasizing women's health.

Nonfiction Reference. Subjects include health/medicine, psychology, women's health/medicine. Submit 3 sample chapters with SASE.

Recent Title(s) *Managing Contraceptive Pill Patients.*

Tips Audience is medical professionals and medical product manufacturers and distributors.

ENDLESS KNOT PRODUCTIONS

P.O. Box 230312, Boston MA 02123. (617)445-4651. Fax: (617)547-1333. E-mail: alexander@endless-knot.com. Website: www.endless-knot.com. **Acquisitions:** Alexander Dwinell. Publishes trade paperback originals and reprints. **Publishes 1-2 titles/year. Pays royalty. Offers advance.** Does not accept simultaneous submissions. Responds in 2 months to queries.

Fiction New publisher of fiction. "We are looking to publish cutting-edge fiction with a subversive kick."

Tips "We are particularly interested in well-written stories which contain strong characters and plotting with a radical political subtext. The politics should be anti-authoritarian and anti-capitalist without being polemical."

⊘ EQUILIBRIUM PRESS, INC.

10736 Jefferson Blvd., #680, Culver City CA 90230. (310)204-3290. Fax: (310)204-3550. E-mail: info@equipress.com. Website: www.equipress.com. Publishes trade paperback originals. **Publishes 1-2 titles/year. Pays 10-15% royalty on net receipts. Offers variable advance.** Responds in 2 months to queries. Ms guidelines online.

    ○→ "We're looking for books that inform and inspire—all nonfiction related to women's health and wellness for an upscale, educated audience in a wide age range. No fiction, poetry, erotica."

Nonfiction "Personal memoirs unlikely to be acquired unless they offer something more than 'my story.'" Query with SASE or submit proposal package, including chapter-by-chapter outline, 1-3 sample chapters (including the introduction) and a letter answering the following questions in detail: How is the book unique? (i.e., What are the competing books?; Who is the audience?; How will you reach that audience?; Who might endorse it?; What will you do to promote the book?) *No unsolicited mss.*

Recent Title(s) *A Special Delivery: Mother-Daughter Letters from Afar*, by Mitchell & Mitchell (family/pregnancy); *The Stepmom's Guide to Simplifying Your Life*, by Goodman (family/self-help).

Tips "Do your homework—know what other books are similar and be able to say why yours is better and/or different. Know the audience and how you will reach them. Most importantly, what are *you* prepared to do to promote the book?"

ERIE CANAL PRODUCTIONS

4 Farmdale St., Clinton NY 13323. E-mail: eriecanal@juno.com. Website: www.eriecanalproductions.com. **Acquisitions:** Scott Fiesthumel, president. Estab. 2001. Publishes trade paperback originals. **Publishes 1-2 titles/year. 50% of books from first-time authors; 100% from unagented writers. Pays negotiable royalty on net profits.** Responds in 1 month to queries. Book catalog free.

Nonfiction Biography. Subjects include Americana, general nonfiction, history, sports. Query with SASE. **All unsolicited mss returned unopened.**

Recent Title(s) *The Legend of Wild Bill Setley*, by Tony Kissel, S. Fiesthumer (biography); *Tripleheader: Tales, Memories, and Notes from the Shadow of Cooperstown*, by Gene Carney, Bob Palazzo (sports essays).

Tips "We publish nonfiction books that look at historical places, events, and people along the traditional route of the Erie Canal through New York State."

THE FAMILY ALBUM

4887 Newport Rd., Kinzers PA 17535. (717)442-0220. E-mail: rarebooks@pobox.com. **Acquisitions:** Ron Lieberman. Estab. 1969. Publishes hardcover originals and reprints. **Publishes 1 title/year. Pays royalty on wholesale price.** Does not accept simultaneous submissions.

Nonfiction Subjects include art/architecture (folk art), history, regional. "Significant works in the field of (nonfiction) bibliography. Worthy submissions in the field of Pennsylvania history, folk art, and lore. We are also seeking materials relating to books, literacy, and national development. Special emphasis on Third World countries, and the role of printing in international development." No religious material or personal memoirs. Submit outline, sample chapter(s).

FAMILYLIFE PUBLISHING

FamilyLife, a division of Campus Crusade for Christ, P.O. Box 7111, Little Rock AR 72223. (800)358-6329. Website: www.familylife.com. **Acquisitions:** Mark Whitlock, acquisitions editor. Publishes hardcover and trade paperback originals. **Publishes 3-12 titles/year. Receives 250 queries and 50 mss/year. 1% of books from first-time authors; 90% from unagented writers. Pays 2-18% royalty on wholesale price, or makes outright purchase.** Publishes book 2 years after acceptance of ms. Accepts simultaneous submissions. Responds in 3 months to queries; 6 months to proposals; 6 months to mss. Book catalog online at website or for 8×10 SASE with 4 first-class stamps; ms guidelines online.

⚬— "FamilyLife is dedicated to effectively developing godly families. We publish connecting resources—books, videos, audio resources, and interactive multi-piece packs—that help husbands and wives communicate better, and parents and children build stronger relationships."

Nonfiction Audiocassettes, booklets, children's/juvenile, gift book, Interactive multi-piece activity packs. Subjects include child guidance/parenting, education, general nonfiction, religion, sex, spirituality, women's issues/studies, Marriage Communication, Marriage Preparation, Resources for Children. "FamilyLife Publishing exists to create resources to connect your family. We publish very few books. Become familiar with what we offer. Our resources are unique in the marketplace. Discover what makes us unique, match your work to our style, and then submit." Query with SASE, or submit proposal package including outline, 2 sample chapter(s). Reviews artwork/photos as part of ms package. Computer disk with 96 dpi JPGS.

Recent Title(s) *Wizards, Hobbits, and Harry Potter* (fantasy literature overview and discussion guide); *Simply Romantic Nights*, by Dennis and Barbara Rainey, et al (marriage/sexual intimacy/communication).

Tips "Before you submit to us, be sure to read our writer's guidelines and The Family Manifesto. You can find both on our website. If you don't know who we are or what we do, please send your information elsewhere. Most of what we publish is generated from inside our organization. The opportunity to be published by FamilyLife is very slim. We understand the challenges of getting your ideas in front of acquistions editors. However, our output is very small. You will probably receive a rejection letter from us."

FINNEY CO., INC.

3943 Meadowbrook Rd., Minneapolis MN 55426. (952)938-9330. Fax: (952)938-7353. E-mail: feedback@finney-hobar.com. Website: www.finney-hobar.com. **Acquisitions:** Alan E. Krysan, president. Publishes trade paperback originals. **Publishes 2 titles/year. Pays 10% royalty on wholesale price. Offers advance.** Publishes book 1 year after acceptance of ms. Responds in 8-10 weeks to queries.

Nonfiction Reference, textbook. Subjects include business/economics, education, career exploration/development. Finney publishes career development educational materials. Query with SASE. Reviews artwork/photos as part of ms package.

Recent Title(s) *Planning My Career*, by Capozziello; *Occupational Guidance for Agriculture*, by Henkel, et. al.

▣ FLAME OF THE FOREST PUBLISHING

95085 North Bank Rogue Rd., Gold Beach OR 97444-9543. (541)247-2924. Fax: (541)247-0373. E-mail: info@flameoftheforest.com. **Acquisitions:** John Morris, editor (title acquisition/development). Estab. 2003. Publishes hardcover and trade paperback originals. **Publishes 2-4 titles/year; imprint publishes 1-2 titles/year. Receives less than 500 queries and less than 500 mss/year. 50% of books from first-time authors; 100% from unagented writers. Pays 5-15% royalty on retail price, or makes outright purchase of $500-5,000. Offers $500-5,000 advance.** Does not accept simultaneous submissions. Responds in 3 months to queries; 3 months to proposals; 3 months to mss. Ms guidelines by e-mail.

Imprints Angsana.

Nonfiction Children's/juvenile, coffee table book, cookbook, gift book, illustrated book. Subjects include cooking/foods/nutrition, ethnic, general nonfiction, multicultural, nature/environment, regional, travel, world affairs. "Our title line centers on Pacific Rim regional/cultural themes." Query with SASE, or submit complete ms. Reviews artwork/photos as part of ms package. Send photocopies.

Fiction Ethnic, multicultural, picture books. "We are seeking to develop children's and regional/cultural titles with a Pacific Rim theme." Query with SASE.

Recent Title(s) *Beyond Fusion: A New Look at Ethnic Influences on Contemporary Cooking*, by Rainer Zinngrebe (high quality/coffetable style cookbook); *Terror in Bali*, by Alan Atkinson (regional/current events); *Around Asia*, by Yeoh Siew Hoon (travel).

Tips "We develop only Pacific Rim cultural/regional themes that show clear market relevance. We are small and very selective."

FOLK ART REFERENCE

61 Beekman Place, Madison CT 06443. (203)245-2246. E-mail: pfalk@cshore.com. Website: www.folkart.com. **Acquisitions:** Peter Hastings Falk, president. Estab. 1985. Publishes hardcover and trade paperback originals, dictionaries and exhibition records exclusive to fine art. Does not accept simultaneous submissions.

Recent Title(s) *Who Was Who in American Art: 1564-1975*, by Peter Falk.

Tips Currently emphasizing American art history, conservation, exhibition records.

FOOTPRINT PRESS

P.O. Box 645, Fishers NY 14453-0645. (585)421-9383. Fax: (585)421-9383. E-mail: info@footprintpress.com. Website: www.footprintpress.com. **Acquisitions:** Sue Freeman, publisher (New York state recreation). Publishes trade paperback originals. **Publishes 1 title/year. Pays 10% royalty on wholesale price.** Accepts simultaneous submissions. Responds in 1 month to queries; 1 month to proposals; 2 months to mss. Book catalog and ms guidelines for #10 SASE or online.

O→ Footprint Press publishes books pertaining to outdoor recreation in New York state.

Nonfiction How-to. Subjects include recreation, regional, sports. Query with SASE.

Recent Title(s) *Peak Experiences: Hiking the Highest Summits in New York State, County by County*, by Gary Fallesen; *Birding in Central and Western New York*, by Norman E. Wolfe; *200 Waterfalls in Central and Western New York*, by Rich and Sue Freeman.

FRIENDS UNITED PRESS

101 Quaker Hill, Richmond IN 47374. (765)962-7573. Fax: (765)966-1293. Website: www.fum.org. **Acquisitions:** Barbara Bennett Mays, editor/manager. Estab. 1968. **Publishes 3 titles/year. Receives 100 queries and 80 mss/year. 50% of books from first-time authors; 99% from unagented writers. Pays 7½% royalty on wholesale price.** Publishes book 1 year after acceptance of ms. Accepts simultaneous submissions. Responds in 3 months to queries. Book catalog and ms guidelines free.

O→ "Friends United Press publishes books that reflect Quaker religious practices and testimonies, and energize and equip Friends and others through the power of the Holy Spirit to gather people into fellowships where Jesus Christ is loved, known, and obeyed 'as Teacher and Lord.' "

Nonfiction Biography (Quaker), humor, textbook. Subjects include history, religion, theology. "Authors should be Quaker and should be familiar with Quaker history, spirituality, and doctrine." Submit proposal package. Reviews artwork/photos as part of ms package. Send photocopies.

Recent Title(s) *A Very Good Marriage*, by Tom Mullen (nonfiction); *Notes from Ramallah, 1939*, by Nancy Parker McDowell; *Imagination and Spirit: A Contemporary Quaker Reader*, edited by J. Brent Bill.

Tips "Spirituality manuscripts must be in agreement with Quaker spirituality."

FRONT ROW EXPERIENCE

540 Discovery Bay Blvd., Discovery Bay CA 94514-9454. (925)634-5710. Fax: (925)634-5710. E-mail: service@frontrowexperience.com. Website: www.frontrowexperience.com. **Acquisitions:** Frank Alexander, editor. Estab. 1974. Publishes trade paperback originals and reprints. **Publishes 1-2 titles/year. Pays 10% royalty on net receipts.** Accepts simultaneous submissions. Responds in 1 month to queries.

Imprints Kokono.

○┱ Front Row publishes books on movement education and coordination activities for pre-K to 6th grade.
Nonfiction Subjects include movement education, perceptual-motor development, sensory motor development, hand-eye coordination activities. Query.
Recent Title(s) *Perceptual-Motor Lesson Plans, Level 2.*
Tips "Be on target—find out what we want, and only submit queries."

FYOS ENTERTAINMENT, LLC

P.O. Box 2021, Philadelphia PA 19103. (215)972-8067. Fax: (215)972-8076. E-mail: info@fyos.com. Website: www.fyos.com. **Acquisitions:** Tonya Marie Evans, editor-in-chief (poetry, African-American fiction); Susan Borden Evans, general manager (African-American fiction). Publishes hardcover originals and trade paperback originals. **Publishes 2-3 titles/year. Receives 100-160 queries and 20-40 mss/year. Pays 10-15% royalty on retail price. or a 60 (publisher)/40 (author) split of net receipts. Will also consider outright purchase opportunities.** Publishes book 1 year after acceptance of ms. Accepts simultaneous submissions. Responds in 1-3 months to queries; 3-6 months to mss. Book catalog for #10 SASE; ms guidelines online.
Imprints LE Series Books (legal guides for writers).
Nonfiction Law and self-publishing topics. Subjects include self-publishing. Query with SASE.
Fiction Multicultural, poetry, short story collections. "We concentrate acquisition efforts on poetry and fiction of interest primarily to the African-American reader. We are looking for thought-provoking, well-written work that offers a 'quick and entertaining' read." Query with SASE.
Poetry "We shy away from 'rhyming form poetry' and words that are more appropriate for performance than reading." Submit 10 sample poems.
Recent Title(s) *Literary Law Guide*, by Susan Borden Evans and Tonya Evans (nonfiction/law); *Seasons of Her*, by T. Evans; *SHINE!*, by T. Evans.
Tips African-American women, age 18-55. "Neatness counts! Present yourself and your work in a highly professional manner."

GAMBLING TIMES, INC.

3883 W. Century Blvd., Inglewood CA 90303. (310)674-3365. Fax: (310)674-3205. E-mail: srs@gamblingtimes.com. Website: www.gamblingtimes.com. **Acquisitions:** Stanley R. Sludikoff, publisher. Publishes hardcover and trade paperback originals. **Publishes 2-4 titles/year. Pays 4-11% royalty on retail price.** Does not accept simultaneous submissions. Responds in 4 months to queries; 5 months to proposals; 6 months to mss.
Nonfiction How-to, reference (on gambling). No longer accepts mss from first-time writers. Query with SASE, or submit proposal package, or submit complete ms.
Recent Title(s) *Book of Tells*, by Caro (poker).
Tips "All of our books serve to educate the public about some aspect of gambling."

⊘ GAY SUNSHINE PRESS and LEYLAND PUBLICATIONS

P.O. Box 410690, San Francisco CA 94141-0690. Fax: (415)626-1802. Website: www.gaysunshine.com. **Acquisitions:** Winston Leyland, editor. Estab. 1970. Publishes hardcover originals, trade paperback originals and reprints. **Publishes 3-4 titles/year. Pays royalty, or makes outright purchase.** Responds in 6 weeks to queries; 2 months to mss. Book catalog for $1.
○┱ Gay history, sex, politics, and culture are the focus of the quality books published by Gay Sunshine Press. Leyland Publications publishes books on popular aspects of gay sexuality and culture.
Nonfiction "We're interested in innovative literary nonfiction which deals with gay lifestyles." How-to. Subjects include gay/lesbian. No long personal accounts, academic or overly formal titles. Query with SASE. **All unsolicited mss returned unopened.**
Fiction Interested in innovative well-written novels on gay themes; also short story collections. Erotica, experimental, historical, literary, mystery, science fiction, All gay male material only. "We have a high literary standard for fiction. We desire fiction on gay themes of high literary quality and prefer writers who have already had work published in literary magazines. We also pubilsh erotica—short stories and novels." Query with SASE. **All unsolicited mss returned unopened.**
Recent Title(s) *Out of the Closet Into Our Hearts: Celebration of Our Gay/Lesbian Family Members.*

⊘ GINGERBREAD HOUSE

602 Montauk Hwy., Westhampton Beach NY 11978. Website: www.gingerbreadbooks.com. Publishes hardcover and trade paperback originals and reprints. **Publishes 3-6 titles/year. Pays royalty on retail price. Offers competitive advance.** Publishes book 1 year after acceptance of ms. Book catalog online.
Nonfiction Children's/juvenile, gift book. Subjects include religion, writing tips. **All unsolicited mss returned unopened.**
Fiction Humor, juvenile, picture books, poetry, religious, young adult. **All unsolicited mss returned unopened.**

Small Presses

Recent Title(s) *In English, of Course*, by Josephine Nobisso (picture book).

Tips "We publish high-quality books for children of all ages. Our titles must possess both universal and niche appeal. Should our 'no unsolicited manuscripts' policy change, we will put out calls for submissions through all of the usual venues."

GOLDEN WEST BOOKS

P.O. Box 80250, San Marino CA 91118. (626)458-8148. Fax: (626)458-8148. E-mail: trainbook@earthlink.net. Website: www.goldenwestbooks.com. **Acquisitions:** Donald Duke, publisher. Publishes hardcover originals. **Publishes 3-4 titles/year. Receives 8-10 queries and 5 mss/year. 75% of books from first-time authors; 100% from unagented writers. Pays 8-10% royalty on wholesale price. Offers no advance.** Publishes book 3 months after acceptance of ms. Does not accept simultaneous submissions. Responds in 3 months to queries. Book catalog and ms guidelines free.

  O➥ Golden West Books specializes in railroad history.

Nonfiction Illustrated book (railroad history). Subjects include Americana, history. Query with SASE. Reviews artwork/photos as part of ms package.

Recent Title(s) *The Ulster & Delaware Railroad Through the Catskills*, by Gerald M. Best; *The Streamline Era*, by Robert C. Reed; *Electric Railways Around San Francisco Bay*, by Donald Duke.

GOOD BOOK PUBLISHING CO.

P.O. Box 837, Kihei HI 96753-0837. (808)874-4876. Fax: (808)874-4876. E-mail: dickb@dickb.com. Website: www.dickb.com/index.shtml. **Acquisitions:** Richard G. Burns, publisher. Publishes trade paperback originals. **Publishes 1 title/year. Receives 5 queries and 5 mss/year. 100% of books from first-time authors; 100% from unagented writers. Pays 10% royalty.** Publishes book 3 months after acceptance of ms. Accepts simultaneous submissions. Responds in 1 month to queries; 1 month to mss. Book catalog free.

Nonfiction Biography, self-help. Subjects include health/medicine, history, psychology, religion. Spiritual roots of Alcoholics Anonymous. Query with SASE.

Recent Title(s) *By the Power of God: A Guide to Early A.A. Groups and Forming Similar Groups Today*, by Dick Bo.

GRANITE PUBLISHING, LLC

P.O. Box 1429, Columbus NC 28722. (828)894-8444. Fax: (828)894-8454. E-mail: granitepub@5thworld.com. Website: www.5thworld.com. President: Pam Meyer. **Acquisitions:** Brian Crissey. Publishes trade paperback originals and reprints. **Publishes 3 titles/year. Receives 50 queries and 150 mss/year. 70% of books from first-time authors; 90% from unagented writers. Pays 7½-10% royalty.** Publishes book 16 months after acceptance of ms. Accepts simultaneous submissions. Responds in 6 months to mss.

Imprints Wild Flower Press, Swan-Raven & Co., Agents of Change.

  O➥ "Granite Publishing strives to preserve the Earth by publishing books that develop new wisdom about our emerging planetary citizenship, bringing information from the outerworlds to our world." Currently emphasizing indigenous ideas, planetary healing.

Nonfiction Multimedia. Subjects include New Age, planetary paradigm shift. Submit proposal. Reviews artwork/photos as part of ms package. Send photocopies.

Recent Title(s) *The Divine Nature of Plants*, by Laura Aversano; *Connecting the Dots*, by Paola Harris.

Ⓝ GREYCORE PRESS

2646 New Prospect Rd., Pine Bush NY 12566. (845)744-5081. Fax: (845)744-8081. Website: www.greycore.com. Estab. 1999. Publishes hardcover originals. **Publishes 3 titles/year. Offers $1,000 advance.** Publishes book 18 months after acceptance of ms. Accepts simultaneous submissions.

Fiction Literary, mainstream/contemporary. Query with SASE.

Ⓝ J.A. GRUBB PUBLISHING

28 W. 650 Highlake Rd., West Chicago IL 60185. Fax: (312)803-1669. E-mail: jagrubbpub@aol.com. **Acquisitions:** Jonathan Grubb, head publisher (medical research, sleep, gambling, self-improvement, diet, real estate). Estab. 2004. Publishes trade paperback and mass market paperback originals and reprints. **Publishes 2 titles/year; imprint publishes 2 titles/year. Receives 24 queries and 4 mss/year. 50% of books from first-time authors; 50% from unagented writers. Pays 5-7% royalty on retail price.** Publishes book 1 year after acceptance of ms. Accepts simultaneous submissions. Responds in 1 month to queries; 2 months to proposals; 2 months to mss.

Nonfiction Audiocassettes, autobiography, biography, booklets, general nonfiction, how-to, scholarly, self-help, technical. Subjects include art/architecture (architecture from a functional, business perspective), business/economics, cooking/foods/nutrition (diet books), health/medicine, money/finance, music/dance, New Age, philosophy, psychology, regional (related to Chicago), science, social sciences, sports (martial arts only), gambling. Submit proposal package including outline, 2-4 sample chapter(s), or submit complete ms.

Ⓝ HATALA GEROPRODUCTS

P.O. Box 42, Greentop MO 63546. E-mail: editor@geroproducts.com. Website: www.geroproducts.com. **Acquisitions:** Mark Hatala, Ph.D., president (psychology, romance, relationships). Estab. 2002. Publishes hardcover and trade paperback originals. **Publishes 1-2 titles/year. Receives 40 queries and 20 mss/year. 30% of books from first-time authors; 100% from unagented writers. Pays 5-7½% royalty on retail price. Offers $250-500 advance.** Publishes book 18 months after acceptance of ms. Accepts simultaneous submissions. Responds in 1 month to queries; 2 months to proposals; 2 months to mss. Ms guidelines online.

Nonfiction How-to, humor, self-help, senior relationships, and romance. Subjects include health/medicine, psychology, sex, travel, senior, advice. "Books should be of interest to older (60+) adults. Romance, relationships, advice, travel, how-to books are most appropriate. All books are larger print; so manuscripts should be around 50,000 words." Query with SASE, or submit proposal package including outline, 3 sample chapter(s), SASE.

Fiction Erotica, romance. Query with SASE, or submit proposal package including 3 sample chapter(s), synopsis, SASE.

Recent Title(s) *Seniors in Love*, by Robert Wolley (senior relationships); *ABC's of Aging*, by Dr. Ruth Jacobs (self-help); *Romance is in the Air*, by Ginger Binkley (romance).

Tips "Audience is men and women (but particularly women) over age 60. Books need to be pertinent to the lives of older Americans."

HEMINGWAY WESTERN STUDIES SERIES

Imprint of Boise State University, 1910 University Dr., Boise ID 83725. (208)426-1999. Fax: (208)426-4373. E-mail: ttrusky@boisestate.edu. Website: www.boisestate.edu/hemingway. **Acquisitions:** Tom Trusky, editor. Publishes multiple edition artists' books which deal with Rocky Mountain political, social, and environmental issues. **Offers advance.** Does not accept simultaneous submissions. Ms guidelines free.

Ⓝ HICKORY TALES PUBLISHING, LLC

841 Newberry St., Bowling Green KY 42103. (270)791-3242. E-mail: jadonel@aol.com. Editor: Andrew Donelson (history, historical fiction, adventure fiction) . **Acquisitions:** Jack Donelson, co-editor (religious, children's). Estab. 2000. Publishes trade paperback originals. **Publishes 1-5 titles/year. Receives 20-100 queries and 100 mss/year. 70% of books from first-time authors; 90% from unagented writers. Pays 10-15% royalty on net receipts.** Publishes book 3-6 months after acceptance of ms. Accepts simultaneous submissions. Ms guidelines for #10 SASE.

Nonfiction Autobiography, biography, children's/juvenile. Subjects include history, religion, science, etc. Photographs, drawings, and maps are a plus. Submit complete ms. Reviews artwork/photos as part of ms package. Send photocopies or transparencies.

Fiction Adventure, historical, juvenile, military/war, picture books, religious, young adult. "Let the first paragraph of each chapter entice the reader and tie the whole with a theme, a lesson, or a good come-away feeling. We want readers to hunger for your next word." Submit complete ms.

Poetry 1-2 pages max/poem. Artwork helps. Submit complete ms.

Recent Title(s) *Chalmette*, by Charles Patton (historical novel); *Andrew Jackson Donelson*, by William Beeler Satterfield (biography).

Tips "Have faith in yourself. Tell me the story in the language you would tell your best friend. Draw word pictures from your own experience. We will respond to queries and submissions, but please be patient due to backlog."

LAWRENCE HILL BOOKS

Chicago Review Press, 814 N. Franklin St., 2nd Floor, Chicago IL 60610. (312)337-0747. Fax: (312)337-5985. **Acquisitions:** Yuval Taylor, editor (black interest). Publishes hardcover originals and trade paperback originals and reprints. **Publishes 3-10 titles/year. Receives 20 queries and 10 mss/year. 40% of books from first-time authors; 50% from unagented writers. Pays 7½-12½% royalty on retail price. Offers $1,500-7,500 advance.** Publishes book 1 year after acceptance of ms. Accepts simultaneous submissions. Responds in 1 month to queries; 1 month to proposals; 1 month to mss. Book catalog free.

Nonfiction Biography, reference, general nonfiction. Subjects include ethnic, government/politics, history, multicultural. All books should appeal directly to an African American readership. Submit proposal package including outline, 2 sample chapter(s).

Recent Title(s) *When Race Becomes Real*, edited by Bernestine Singley.

HORSE CREEK PUBLICATIONS, INC.

4500 Highland Hills Dr., Norman OK 73026. (405)364-9647. Fax: (405)573-6735. E-mail: sue.schrems@horsecreekpublications.com. Website: www.horsecreekpublications.com. **Acquisitions:** Suzanne H. Schrems, publisher (nonfiction/historical fiction, history, America West, women, Oklahoma); Edward L. Schrems, publisher (conservative politics). **Publishes 3 titles/year. 70% of books from first-time authors. Pays 10% royalty on retail price.** Publishes book 9-12 months after acceptance of ms. Does not accept simultaneous submissions. Responds in 3 months to queries; 3 months to proposals; 3 months to mss. Ms guidelines free.

Nonfiction Biography, history. Subjects include Americana, government/politics, history, regional, women's issues/studies, America West, Oklahoma. "It has to be a 'good read,' not academic." Submit proposal package including 2 sample chapter(s), illustrations or photographs. Reviews artwork/photos as part of ms package. Send photocopies.

Fiction Historical. "We only accept historical fiction related to Western history." Submit 3 sample chapter(s), synopsis.

Recent Title(s) *Uncommon Women, Unmarked Trails* (nonfiction); *Oklahoma Women in Politics in the Early Twentieth Century* (nonfiction); *Donner Party Cookbook* (nonfiction).

Tips "Our audience is the adult/young reader. We are looking for solid nonfiction history that is readable, a 'good read.' We also accept manuscripts relating to the conservative politics, current and historical, and manuscripts pertaining to the history of the American West suitable for young readers."

ILLUMINATION ARTS

P.O. Box 1865, Bellevue WA 98009. (425)644-7185. Fax: (425)644-9274. E-mail: liteinfo@illumin.com. Website: www.illumin.com. **Acquisitions:** Ruth Thompson, editorial director, (ms submissions); Terri Cohlene, creative director (artwork submissions). Publishes hardcover originals. **Pays royalty on wholesale price. Offers advance for artists.** Book catalog and ms guidelines online.

○⇥ Illumination Arts publishes inspirational/spiritual (not religious), children's picture books.

Nonfiction Children's/juvenile. "Our books are all high quality and exquisitely illustrated. Stories need to be exciting and inspirational for children." Submit complete ms with SASE. Reviews artwork/photos as part of ms package. Send photocopies.

Fiction Picture books (children's), prefer under 1,000 words; 1,500 words max. No electronic submissions.

Recent Title(s) *The Errant Knight*; *The Tree*.

Tips "A smart writer researches publishing companies thoroughly before submitting and then follows submission guidelines closely."

IMPASSIO PRESS

P.O. Box 31905, Seattle WA 98103. (206)632-7675. Fax: (775)254-4073. E-mail: books@impassio.com. Website: www.impassio.com. **Acquisitions:** Olivia Dresher, publisher/editor (fragmentary writing). Publishes hardcover and trade paperback originals. **Publishes 1-3 titles/year. Receives 100 queries and 75 mss/year. 30% of books from first-time authors; 90% from unagented writers. Pays 5% royalty on retail price.** Publishes book 12-18 months after acceptance of ms. Accepts simultaneous submissions. Responds in 1 month to queries; 1 month to proposals; 2 months to mss. Book catalog for 6×9 SASE with 2 first-class stamps or online at website; ms guidelines online.

Nonfiction Biography, All forms of fragmentary writing. Subjects include language/literature, memoirs, nature/environment, philosophy, spirituality, translation, travel, women's issues/studies, diaries, journals, letters, poetic prose. "The nonfiction we publish must be in fragmentary form: journals, diaries, notebooks; letters; aphorisms; poetic prose fragments; vignettes. The writing should be personal and of literary quality." Query with SASE. Reviews artwork/photos as part of ms package. Send photocopies.

Fiction Experimental, literary. "We will only consider fiction in the form of a diary/journal/notebook or in the form of letters." Query with SASE.

Poetry "We do not accept poetry, per se; only poetic prose in fragmentary form."

Recent Title(s) *One Journal's Life*, by Audrey Borenstein (a meditation about journal keeping); *This Is How I Speak*, by Sandi Sonnenfeld (diary); *Water & Earth*, by Guy Gauthier (journal).

Tips "Our audience is college-educated adults, 18 and over. We're interested in writing that demonstrates a literary sensibility and fresh use of language. We're not interested in self-help literature."

Ⓝ INTERCONTINENTAL PUBLISHING

P.O. Box 7242, Fairfax Station VA 22039. E-mail: icpub@worldnet.att.net. Website: home.att.net/~icpub/. **Acquisitions:** H.G. Smittenaar, publisher. Publishes hardcover and trade paperback originals. **Publishes 3-4 titles/year. Pays 5% minimum royalty.** Accepts simultaneous submissions. Responds ASAP to proposals.

○⇥ Intercontinental publishes mystery and suspense novels.

Fiction Mystery, suspense. Submit proposal package, including 1-3 sample chapters, estimated word count and SASE.

Recent Title(s) *I'm Okay, You're Dead*, by Spizer (mystery); *Dekok and the Begging Death*, by Baantjer (police procedural); *Tales from Old California*, by Gerald Schiller.

Tips "Be original, write proper English, be entertaining."

JELMAR PUBLISHING CO., INC.

P.O. Box 488, Plainview NY 11803. (516)822-6861. **Acquisitions:** Joel J. Shulman, president. Publishes hardcover and trade paperback originals. **Publishes 2-5 titles/year. Pays 25% royalty.** Does not accept simultaneous submissions. Responds in 1 week to queries.

Nonfiction How-to, technical. Subjects include package printing and printing fields. "The writer must be a specialist and recognized expert in the field." Query with SASE.

Recent Title(s) *Graphic Design for Corrugated Packaging*, Donald G. McCaughey, Jr. (graphic design).

JIREH PUBLISHING CO.

P.O. Box 4263, San Leandro CA 94579-0263. E-mail: jaholman@jirehpublishing.com. Website: www.jirehpublishing.com. **Acquisitions:** Janice Holman, editor (fiction/nonfiction). Estab. 1995. Publishes hardcover, trade paperback, and electronic originals. **Publishes 2-5 titles/year. Receives 100-200 queries and 50-75 mss/year. 95% of books from first-time authors; 98% from unagented writers. Pays 10-12% royalty on wholesale price.** Publishes book 9-12 months after acceptance of ms. Accepts simultaneous submissions. Responds in 1-2 months to queries; 2 months to proposals; 3 months to mss. Book catalog and ms guidelines online.

Nonfiction Ebooks. Subjects include religion (contemporary Christian). "We want the material to involve Christian values." Query with SASE, or submit proposal package including outline, 3 sample chapter(s), SASE.

Fiction Mystery, religious (Christian ebooks, general religious, mystery/suspense, thriller, romance), suspense. "We are looking for Christian values in the books that we publish." Query with SASE.

Recent Title(s) *Accessible Bathroom Design: Tearing Down the Barriers*, by Jessie C. Jacobs (how-to reference); *In the Midst of Deceipt*, by Deborah Piccurrelli (mystery).

Tips "Our audience is adults who are eager to read books that are interesting, exciting, and promote Christian values."

N JOHNSTON ASSOCIATES, INTERNATIONAL (JASI)

P.O. Box 313, Medina WA 98039. (425)454-7333. Fax: (425)462-1355. E-mail: jasibooks@aol.com. **Acquisitions:** Priscilla Johnston, publisher. Publishes trade paperback originals. **Publishes 2-4 titles/year. Pays 12-15½% royalty on wholesale price. Offers $500-1,000 advance.** Accepts simultaneous submissions. Responds in 2-3 months to queries. Book catalog and ms guidelines for #10 SASE.

Nonfiction Regional travel guides. Query with SASE, or submit proposal package including outline, sample chapter(s). Does not accept e-mail or CD/DVD submissions.

Recent Title(s) *Discover the Southwest with Kids*, by Mary Vadsudeva; *Las Vegas on the Dime*, by Michael Toole.

KAMEHAMEHA SCHOOLS PRESS

Kamehameha Schools, 1887 Makuakane St., Honolulu HI 96817-1887. (808)842-8719. Fax: (808)842-8895. E-mail: kspress@ksbe.edu. Website: kspress.ksbe.edu. **Acquisitions:** Acquisitions Editor. Publishes hardcover and trade paperback originals and reprints. **Publishes 3-5 titles/year. 10-25% of books from first-time authors; 100% from unagented writers. Makes outright purchase.** Publishes book up to 2 years after acceptance of ms. Responds in 3 months to queries. Book catalog online or request print copy.

Imprints Kamehameha Schools Press, Kamehameha Schools, Kamehameha Schools Bishop Estate.

○━ "Only writers with substantial and documented expertise in Hawaiian history, Hawaiian culture, Hawaiian language, and/or Hawaiian studies should consider submitting to Kamehameha Schools Press. We prefer to work with writers available to physically meet at our Honolulu offices."

Nonfiction Biography, children's/juvenile, reference, textbook. Subjects include education (Hawaiian), history (Hawaiian), regional (Hawaii), translation (Hawaiian). Query with SASE. Reviews artwork/photos as part of ms package. Send photocopies.

DENIS KITCHEN PUBLISHING CO., LLC

P.O. Box 9514, North Amherst MA 01059-9514. (413)259-1627. Fax: (413)259-1812. E-mail: publishing@deniskitchen.com. Website: www.deniskitchen.com. **Acquisitions:** Denis Kitchen, publisher (graphic novels, classic comic strips, postcard books, boxed trading cards, graphics, pop culture, alternative culture). Publishes hardcover and trade paperback originals and reprints. **Publishes 4 titles/year. 15% of books from first-time authors; 50% from unagented writers. Pays 6-10% royalty on retail price. Occasionally makes deals based on percentage of wholesale if idea and/or bulk of work is done in-house. Offers $1-5,000 advance.** Publishes book 9-12 months after acceptance of ms. Does not accept simultaneous submissions. Responds in 4-6 weeks to queries; 4-6 weeks to proposals; 4-6 weeks to mss.

- This publisher strongly discourages e-mail submissions.

Nonfiction Coffee table book, illustrated book, graphic novels. Subjects include art, comic art, pop culture, alternative culture, graphic novels. Query with SASE, or submit proposal package including outline, illustrative matter, or submit complete ms. Reviews artwork/photos as part of ms package. Send photocopies or transparencies.

Fiction Adventure, erotica, historical, horror, humor, literary, mystery, occult, science fiction (only if in graphic novel form). "We do not want pure fiction. We seek cartoonists or writer/illustrator teams who can tell compelling stories with a combination of words and pictures." No pure fiction (meaning text only). Query with SASE, or submit sample illustrations/comic pages, or submit complete ms.

Recent Title(s) *The Unsyndicated Kurtzman*, by Harvey Kurtzman; *The Grasshopper and the Ant*, by Harvey Kurtzman; *Jazz Greats*, by R. Crumb.

Tips "Our audience is readers who embrace the graphic novel revolution, who appreciate historical comic strips and books, and those who follow popular and alternative culture. Readers who supported Kitchen Sink Press for 3 decades will find that Denis Kitchen Publishing continues the tradition and precedents established by KSP. We like to discover new talent. The artist who has a day job but a great idea is encouraged to contact us. The pop culture historian who has a new take on an important figure is likewise encouraged. We have few preconceived notions about manuscripts or ideas though we are decidedly selective. Historically, we have published many first-time authors and artists, some of whom developed into award-winning creators with substantial followings. Artists or illustrators who do not have confidence in their writing should send us self-promotional postcards (our favorite way of spotting new talent)."

LAHONTAN IMAGES

P.O. Box 1592, Susanville CA 96130-1592. (530)257-6747. Fax: (530)251-4801. **Acquisitions:** Tim I. Purdy, owner. Estab. 1986. Publishes hardcover and trade paperback originals. **Publishes 2 titles/year. Pays 10-15% royalty on wholesale price, or retail price.** Does not accept simultaneous submissions. Responds in 2 months to queries.

Nonfiction Subjects include regional. Publishes nonfiction books pertaining to northeastern California and western Nevada. Query with SASE.

Recent Title(s) *Maggie Greeno*, George McDow Jr. (biography).

LANGMARC PUBLISHING

P.O. Box 90488, Austin TX 78709-0488. (512)394-0989. Fax: (512)394-0829. E-mail: langmarc@booksails.com. Website: www.langmarc.com. **Acquisitions:** Lois Qualben, president (inspirational). Publishes trade paperback originals. **Publishes 3-5 titles/year; imprint publishes 1 title/year. Receives 150 queries and 80 mss/year. 60% of books from first-time authors; 100% from unagented writers. Pays 10-13% royalty on wholesale price.** Publishes book 18 months after acceptance of ms. Accepts simultaneous submissions. Responds in 3 months to queries. Book catalog free; ms guidelines online.

Imprints North Sea Press, Harbor Lights Series

Nonfiction Self-help, inspirational. Subjects include child guidance/parenting, education, health/medicine. Query with SASE. Reviews artwork/photos as part of ms package. Send photocopies.

Recent Title(s) *Honor Thy Father and Mother: Understanding the Spiritual Needs of Abuse Victims*, by Diane Stelling; *James Butler Bonham: Messenger of Defeat*, by William Bonham; *Strongheart*, by Dr. Terri Wood Jenkins.

N LIBRARY OF VIRGINIA

800 E. Broad St., Richmond VA 23219-8000. (804)692-3500. Fax: (804)692-3594. Website: www.lva.lib.va.us. **Acquisitions:** Gregg D. Kimball, assistant director (Virginia history and culture). Publishes hardcover originals and reprints. **Publishes 3-4 titles/year. Pays royalty on retail price, or makes outright purchase.** Does not accept simultaneous submissions. Responds in 1 month to queries; 1 month to proposals; 3 months to mss. Book catalog online.

Nonfiction The Library of Virginia publishes works that draw from the Library's collections. Biography, coffee table book, illustrated book. Subjects include history, regional. Submit proposal package including outline, 1 sample chapter(s).

Recent Title(s) *Regarding Ellen Glasgow*, by Taylor & Longest, eds. (literary essays); *Virginia in Maps*, by Stephenson & McKee, eds. (coffee table book).

LIGHTHOUSE POINT PRESS

100 First Ave., Suite 525, Pittsburgh PA 15222-1517. (412)323-9320. Fax: (412)323-9334. E-mail: info@yearick-millea.com. **Acquisitions:** Ralph W. Yearick, publisher (business/career/general nonfiction). Publishes hard-

cover and trade paperback originals and trade paperback reprints. **Publishes 1-2 titles/year. Pays 5-10% royalty on retail price.** Does not accept simultaneous submissions. Responds in 6 months to queries.

O— Lighthouse Point Press specializes in business/career nonfiction titles.

Nonfiction Reference. Subjects include business/economics. ''We are open to all types of submissions related to general nonfiction, but most interested in business/career manuscripts.'' Submit proposal package including outline, 1-2 sample chapter(s), or submit complete ms.

Recent Title(s) *A Passion for Winning: Fifty Years of Promoting Legendary People and Products*, by Aaron D. Cushman (business/public relations).

Tips ''When submitting a manuscript or proposal, please tell us what you see as the target market/audience for the book. Also, be very specific about what you are willing to do to promote the book.''

⊘ LINTEL

24 Blake Lane, Middletown NY 10940. (845)342-5224. **Acquisitions:** Joan Dornhoefer, editorial assistant. Estab. 1978. Publishes hardcover originals and reprints and trade paperback originals. **Pays royalty. Authors get 100 copies originally, plus royalties after expenses cleared. Offers advance.** Publishes book 6-8 months after acceptance of ms. Accepts simultaneous submissions. Responds in 2 months to queries; 3 months to mss.

● No unsolicited mss.

Nonfiction ''So far all our nonfiction titles have been textbooks.'' Query with SASE.

Fiction Experimental, feminist, gay/lesbian, regional (short fiction). Query with SASE. Accepts photocopied submissions.

Poetry Submit 5 sample poems.

Recent Title(s) *Writing a Television Play, Second Edition*, Michelle Cousin (textbook); *June*, Mary Sanders Smith (fiction); *Love's Mainland*, by Walter James Miller.

MAGNUS PRESS

P.O. Box 2666, Carlsbad CA 92018. (760)806-3743. Fax: (760)806-3689. E-mail: magnuspres@aol.com. Website: www.magnuspress.com. **Acquisitions:** Warren Angel, editorial director. Estab. 1997. Publishes trade paperback originals and reprints. **Publishes 1-3 titles/year; imprint publishes 1-3 titles/year. Receives 200 queries and 220 mss/year. 44% of books from first-time authors; 89% from unagented writers. Pays 6-15% royalty on retail price.** Publishes book 1 year after acceptance of ms. Accepts simultaneous submissions. Responds in 1 month to queries; 1 month to proposals; 1 month to mss. Book catalog for #10 SASE; ms guidelines for #10 SASE.

Imprints Canticle Books

Nonfiction Christian books, popularly written Bible studies, inspirational, devotional. Subjects include religion (from a Christian perspective.). ''Writers must be well-grounded in Biblical knowledge and must be able to communicate effectively with the lay person.'' Submit proposal package including outline, 3 sample chapter(s), author bio.

Recent Title(s) *Sports Stories and the Bible*, by Stan Nix (inspirational).

Tips Magnus Press's audience is mainly Christian lay persons, but also includes anyone interested in spirituality and/or Biblical studies and the church. ''Study our listings and catalog; learn to write effectively for an average reader; read any one of our published books.''

MARINE TECHNIQUES PUBLISHING, INC.

126 Western Ave., Suite 266, Augusta ME 04330-7252. (207)622-7984. Fax: (207)621-0821. E-mail: marinetechniques@midmaine.com. **Acquisitions:** James L. Pelletier, president/CEO (commercial marine or maritime international); Christopher S. Pelletier, vice president operations (national and international maritime related properties). **Publishes 3-5 titles/year. Receives 5-20 queries and 1-4 mss/year. 15% of books from first-time authors. Pays 25-43% royalty on wholesale or retail price.** Publishes book 6-12 months after acceptance of ms. Accepts simultaneous submissions. Responds in 2 months to queries; 4 months to proposals; 6 months to mss. Book catalog free.

O— Publishes only books related to the commercial marine industry.

Nonfiction Reference, self-help, technical, maritime company directories. Subjects include the commerical maritime industry only. Submit proposal package, including ms, with all photos (photocopies OK).

Fiction Must be commercial maritime/marine related. Submit complete ms.

Poetry Must be related to maritime/marine subject matter. Submit complete ms.

Tips Audience consists of commercial marine/maritime firms, persons employed in all aspects of the marine/maritime commercial and recreational fields, persons interested in seeking employment in the commercial marine industry; firms seeking to sell their products and services to vessel owners, operators, and managers in the commercial marine industry worldwide, etc.

MCGAVICK FIELD PUBLISHING

118 N. Cherry, Olathe KS 66061. (913)782-1702. Fax: (913)782-1765. E-mail: fhernan@prodigy.net. Website: www.abcnanny.com. **Publishes 4 titles/year.** Does not accept simultaneous submissions. Fax or e-mail for ms guidelines.

  o→ McGavick Field publishes handbooks dealing with life situations, parent care, child care. "We are looking for books that can be published in the format of *The ABCs of Hiring a Nanny*, accompanied by a companion disk and website."

Nonfiction Biography, how-to, humor, reference, self-help. Subjects include business/economics, child guidance/parenting, computers/electronic, government/politics, humor, women's issues/studies.

Recent Title(s) *The ABCs of Credit*; *Too Much Information, not enough time to read the small print.*

Tips "We are looking for manuscripts that deal with lifestyle issues and the various government agencies that are set up to protect us as consumers."

MENUS AND MUSIC

1462 66th St., Emeryville CA 94608. (510)658-9100. Fax: (510)658-1605. E-mail: info@menusandmusic.com. Website: www.menusandmusic.com. **Acquisitions:** Sharon O'Connor, president (music, food, travel). Publishes trade paperback originals and reprints. **Publishes 2 titles/year. Receives 5 queries/year. Pays 7-10% royalty.** Accepts simultaneous submissions. Responds in 1 month to queries; 1 month to proposals; 3 months to mss. Book catalog and ms guidelines free.

Nonfiction Coffee table book, cookbook, gift book. Subjects include Americana, art/architecture, cooking/foods/nutrition, gardening, hobbies, music/dance, photography, recreation, travel. Submit proposal package including outline, 1 sample chapter(s). Reviews artwork/photos as part of ms package. Send photocopies.

Fiction Humor (women), multimedia, poetry, poetry in translation. "We are especially interested in proposals that will appeal to women, gift buyers, or books that can be paired with music." Submit proposal package including 1 sample chapter(s), synopsis.

Poetry Submit 3 sample poems.

Recent Title(s) *Bistro*, by Sharon O'Connor.

Tips "Our books are primarily bought by women who are interested in cooking, music, and travel. We have excellent distribution in the gift industry and good distribution in the book trade. We are interested in high quality work—we have completed books with New York's Metropolitan Opera and the San Francisco Ballet. Our books are beautiful and sell well for years."

MIDDLE ATLANTIC PRESS

10 Twosome Dr., Box 600, Moorestown NJ 08057. (856)235-4444, ext. 249. Fax: (856)727-6914. E-mail: tdoherty @koen.com. Website: www.koen.com/midat/index.html. **Acquisitions:** Terence Doherty, associate publisher/acquisitions editor; Robert Koen, publisher. Publishes trade paperback originals and reprints, mass market paperback originals. **Publishes 2-3 titles/year. Pays 6-10% royalty on wholesale price. Offers $500-5,000 advance.** Responds in 3 weeks to queries. Book catalog for 9×6 SAE with 2 first-class stamps or online.

  o→ Middle Atlantic Press is a regional publisher of nonfiction focusing on New York, New Jersey, Pennsylvania, Delaware, and Maryland. Currently emphasizing books of information (i.e., guides, travel). De-emphasizing juvenile titles.

Nonfiction Biography, cookbook, reference. Subjects include Americana, cooking/foods/nutrition, history, memoirs, recreation, regional, sports, travel. "M.A.P. is a regional publisher specializing in nonfiction on varied subject matter. Most everything we publish, however, to a large degree, deals with some aspect of the states of the mid-Atlantic region (New York, New Jersey, Pennsylvania, Delaware, and Maryland)." Query with general description and SASE.

Recent Title(s) *The Great Philadelphia Fan Book*; *Animal Patients: 50 Years in the Life of an Animal Doctor*, by Ed Scanlon V.M.D; *George Washington's New Jersey.*

MILKWEEDS FOR YOUNG READERS

Milkweed Editions, 1011 Washington Ave. S., Suite 300, Minneapolis MN 55415. (612)332-3192. Fax: (612)215-2550. Website: www.milkweed.org. **Acquisitions:** Elisabeth Fitz, children's reader. Estab. 1984. Publishes hardcover and trade paperback originals. **Publishes 1-2 titles/year. 25% of books from first-time authors; 70% from unagented writers. Pays 7% royalty on retail price. Offers variable advance.** Publishes book 1 year after acceptance of ms. Accepts simultaneous submissions. Responds in 2 months to queries. Book catalog for $1.50; ms guidelines for #10 SASE or on the website.

  o→ "We are looking first of all for high quality literary writing. We publish books with the intention of making a humane impact on society."

Fiction Adventure, fantasy, historical, humor, mainstream/contemporary, animal, environmental. Query with SASE.

Recent Title(s) *The Trouble with Jeremy Chance*, by George Harrar; *Hard Times for Jake Smith*, by Aileen Kilgore Henderson.

MISSOURI HISTORICAL SOCIETY PRESS

The Missouri Historical Society, P.O. Box 11940, St. Louis MO 63112-0040. (314)746-4558 or (314)746-4556. Fax: (314)746-4548. E-mail: vwmonks@mohistory.org; lmm@mohistory.org. Website: www.mohistory.org. **Acquisitions:** Victoria Monks, publications manager and Lauren Mitchell, book editor (nonfiction with regional themes). Publishes hardcover originals and reprints and trade paperback originals and reprints. **Publishes 2-4 titles/year. Receives 30 queries and 20 mss/year. 10% of books from first-time authors; 80% from un-agented writers. Pays 5-10% royalty.** Responds in 1 month to queries; 1 month to proposals; 2 months to mss.

Nonfiction Biography, coffee table book, reference. Subjects include art/architecture, history, language/literature, multicultural, regional, sports, women's issues/studies, popular culture, photography, children's nonfiction. Query with SASE and request author-proposal form.

Recent Title(s) *Lewis and Clark: Across the Divide*, by Carolyn Gilman (regional history); *The Enemy Among Us: POWs in Missouri During World War II*, by David Fiedler (regional history); *A Song of Faith and Hope*, by Frankie Muse Freeman (memoir/African-American history).

Tips "We're looking for new perspectives, even if the topics are familiar. You'll get our attention with nontraditional voices and views."

MOUNT IDA PRESS

152 Washington Ave., Albany NY 12210. (518)426-5935. Fax: (518)426-4116. **Acquisitions:** Diana S. Waite, publisher. Publishes trade paperback original illustrated books. Does not accept simultaneous submissions.

    O→ Mount Ida Press specializes in high-quality publications on regional history, architecture, and building technology.

Recent Title(s) *Yin Yo Tang: Preserving Chinese Vernacular; Architecture.*

NATUREGRAPH PUBLISHERS, INC.

P.O. Box 1047, Happy Camp CA 96039. (530)493-5353. Fax: (530)493-5240. E-mail: nature@sisqtel.net. Website: www.naturegraph.com. Keven Brown, editor. **Acquisitions:** Barbara Brown, editor-in-chief. Estab. 1946. Publishes trade paperback originals. **Publishes 3 titles/year. Pays 8-10% royalty on wholesale price.** Accepts simultaneous submissions. Responds in 1 month to queries; 2 months to mss. Book catalog free.

    O→ "Naturegraph publishes books to help people learn about the natural world and Native American culture. Not so technically written to scare away beginners." Emphasizing natural history and Native American history (but not political).

Nonfiction Primarily publishes nonfiction for the layman in natural history (biology, geology, ecology, astronomy); American Indian (historical and contemporary); outdoor living (backpacking, wild edibles, etc.). How-to. Subjects include ethnic, nature/environment, science (natural history: biology, geology, ecology, astronomy), crafts. "Our primary niches are nature and Native American subjects with adult level, nontechnical language, and scientific accuracy. First, send for our free catalog. Study what kind of books we have already published." Query with SASE, or submit outline, 2 sample chapter(s).

Recent Title(s) *Scenic Byways of Northern California; The Winds Erase Your Footprints.*

Tips "Please—always send a stamped reply envelope. Publishers get hundreds of manuscripts yearly; not just yours."

NEW ENGLAND CARTOGRAPHICS, INC.

P.O. Box 9369, North Amherst MA 01059. (413)549-4124. Fax: (413)549-3621. E-mail: geolopes@crocker.com. Website: www.necartographics.com. **Acquisitions:** Valerie Vaughan, editor; Christopher Ryan, president. Publishes trade paperback originals and reprints. **Publishes 3 titles/year. Pays 5-10% royalty on retail price.** Does not accept simultaneous submissions. Responds in 2 months to queries.

Nonfiction Subjects include nature/environment, recreation, regional, sports. "We are interested in specific 'where to' in the area of outdoor recreation guidebooks of the northeast U.S." Topics of interest are hiking/backpacking, skiing, canoeing, rail-trails, etc. Query with SASE, or submit sample chapter(s). Reviews artwork/photos as part of ms package. Send photocopies.

Recent Title(s) *Hiking Green Mountain National Forest*, by Bruce Scofield.

NEWSAGE PRESS

P.O. Box 607, Troutdale OR 97060-0607. (503)695-2211. Fax: (503)695-5406. E-mail: info@newsagepress.com. Website: www.newsagepress.com. **Acquisitions:** Maureen R. Michelson, publisher; Sherry Wachter, marketing and communications. Estab. 1985. Publishes trade paperback originals. Ms guidelines online.

O⟶ "We focus on nonfiction books, no 'how to' books. No cynical, despairing books." Currently emphasizing books that explore the animal/human bond, and death and grieving, and are written intelligently. Photo-essay books in large format are no longer published by Newsage Press.

Nonfiction Subjects include animals, multicultural, nature/environment, women's issues/studies, death/dying.

Recent Title(s) *Compassion in Dying: Stories of Dignity and Choice*, by Barbara Coombs Lee; *Pets At Risk: From Allergies to Cancer, Remedies for an Unsuspected Epidemic*, by Alfred Plechner, DVM; *Life Touches Life: A Mother's Story of Stillbirth and Healing*, by Lorraine Ash.

NEXT DECADE, INC.

39 Old Farmstead Rd., Chester NJ 07930. (908)879-6625. Fax: (908)879-2920. E-mail: barbara@nextdecade.com. Website: www.nextdecade.com. **Acquisitions:** Barbara Kimmel, president (reference); Carol Rose, editor. Publishes trade paperback originals. **Publishes 2-4 titles/year. Pays 8-15% royalty on wholesale price.** Responds in 1 month to queries. Book catalog and ms guidelines online.

Nonfiction Reference. Subjects include health/medicine (women's), money/finance, multicultural, senior/retirement issues.

Recent Title(s) *Retire in Style*, by Warren Bland, Ph.D; *The Hysterectomy Hoax*, by Stanley West, M.D.

Tips "We publish books that simplify complex subjects. We are a small, award-winning press that successfully publishes a handful of books each year."

Ⓝ NICOLAS-HAYS

P.O. Box 1126, Berwick ME 03910. (207)698-1041. Fax: (207)698-1042. E-mail: info@nicolashays.com. Website: www.nicolashays.com. **Acquisitions:** Y. Paglia, acquisitions editor. Publishes hardcover originals and trade paperback originals and reprints. **Publishes 2-4 titles/year. Pays 15% royalty on wholesale price. Offers $200-500 advance.** Does not accept simultaneous submissions. Responds in 2 months to queries.

Nonfiction Self-help. Subjects include philosophy (Eastern), psychology (Jungian), religion (alternative), spirituality, women's issues/studies. Query with SASE, or submit outline, 3 sample chapter(s).

Recent Title(s) *Retire Your Family Karma*, by Ashok Bedi and Boris Matthews; *In Praise of the Goddess: The Devimahatmya and Its Meaning*, by Devadatta Kali; *The Divine Waba*, by J.M. Spiegelman.

Tips "We publish only books that are the lifework of authors—our editorial plans change based on what the author writes."

OBERLIN COLLEGE PRESS

10 N. Professor St., Oberlin College, Oberlin OH 44074. (440)775-8408. Fax: (440)775-8124. E-mail: oc.press@oberlin.edu. Website: www.oberlin.edu/ocpress. Managing Editor: Linda Slocum. **Acquisitions:** David Young, Pamela Alexander, Martha Collins, and David Walker, editors. Publishes hardcover and trade paperback originals. **Publishes 2-3 titles/year. Pays 7¹/₂-10% royalty.** Does not accept simultaneous submissions. Responds promptly to queries; 1 month to proposals; 2 months to mss.

Imprints *FIELD: Contemporary Poetry & Poetics*, a biannual magazine, FIELD Translation Series, FIELD Poetry Series, FIELD Editions.

Poetry *FIELD Magazine*—submit up to 5 poems with SASE for response; FIELD Translation Series—query with SASE and sample poems; FIELD Poetry Series—*no unsolicited mss*, enter mss in FIELD Poetry Prize held annually in May. Send SASE for guidelines after February 1.

Recent Title(s) *Random Symmetries*, by Tom Andrews; *The Lightning Field*, by Carol Moldaw; *Amnesia*, by Jonah Winter.

OCEAN VIEW BOOKS

P.O. Box 9249, Denver CO 80209. **Acquisitions:** Lee Ballentine, editor. Publishes hardcover originals and trade paperback originals. **Publishes 2 titles/year. 100% from unagented writers. Pays royalty. Offers advance.** Does not accept simultaneous submissions. Responds to queries in 2 months, if interested to queries.

Fiction Literary, science fiction. "Ocean View Books is an award-winning publisher of new speculative and slipstream fiction, poetry, criticism, surrealism."

Recent Title(s) *Missing Pieces*, by Kathryn Rantala.

OMEGA PUBLICATIONS

256 Darrow Rd., New Lebanon NY 12125-2615. (518)794-8181. Fax: (518)794-8187. E-mail: sufibooks@omegapub.com. Website: www.omegapub.com. **Acquisitions:** Jennifer Whitman. Estab. 1977. Publishes hardcover and trade paperback originals and reprints. **Publishes 2-3 titles/year. Pays 12-15% royalty on wholesale price. Offers $500-1,000 advance.** Does not accept simultaneous submissions. Responds in 3 months to mss.

Nonfiction Subjects include philosophy, religion, spirituality. "We are interested in any material related to Sufism, and only that." Query with SASE, or submit 2 sample chapter(s).

Recent Title(s) *Pearl in Wine*, by Zia Inayat Khan; *The Drunken Universe*, by P.L. Wilson.

OZARK MOUNTAIN PUBLISHING, INC.

P.O. Box 754, Huntsville AR 72740. (479)738-2348. Fax: (479)738-2348. Website: www.ozarkmt.com. **Acquisitions:** Nancy Garrison. Publishes hardcover and trade paperback originals and mass market paperback reprints. **Publishes 3-4 titles/year. Pays 10% royalty on retail price. Offers $500 advance.** Accepts simultaneous submissions. Responds in 6 months to queries. Book catalog free or online; ms guidelines online.

Nonfiction Subjects include New Age, spirituality (New Age/metaphysical). "No phone calls please." Query with SASE, or submit proposal package including outline, 2 sample chapter(s).

Recent Title(s) *Holiday in Heaven*, by Aron Abrahamsen; *Is Jehovah an E.T.?*, by Dorothy Leon; *The Ultimate Dictionary of Dream Language*, by Briceida Ryan.

PACESETTER PUBLICATIONS

P.O. Box 101330, Denver CO 80250-1330. (303)722-7200. Fax: (303)733-2626. E-mail: jsabah@aol.com. Website: www.joesabah.com. **Acquisitions:** Joe Sabah, editor (how-to). Publishes trade paperback originals and reprints. **Publishes 3 titles/year. Pays 10-15% royalty. Offers $500-2,000 advance.** Does not accept simultaneous submissions. Responds in 1 month to queries.

Nonfiction How-to, self-help. Subjects include money/finance. Query with SASE, or submit proposal package including outline, 2 sample chapter(s).

Recent Title(s) *How to Get the Job You Really Want and Get Employers to Call You.*

◎ PACIFIC VIEW PRESS

P.O. Box 2657, Berkeley CA 94702. (510)849-4213. **Acquisitions:** Pam Zumwalt, acquisitions editor. Estab. 1992. Publishes hardcover and trade paperback originals. **Publishes 3 titles/year. Pays 5-10% royalty on wholesale price. Offers $500-2,000 advance.** Responds in 2 months to queries. Book catalog free; ms guidelines for #10 SASE.

Nonfiction Pacific View Press publishes books for persons professionally/personally aware of the growing importance of the Pacific Rim and/or the modern culture of these countries, especially China. Children's/juvenile (Asia/multicultural only), reference, textbook (Chinese medicine only). Subjects include business/economics (Asia and Pacific Rim only), health/medicine (Chinese medicine), history (Asia), multicultural, regional (Pacific Rim), travel (related to Pacific Rim), contemporary Pacific Rim affairs. "We are only interested in Pacific Rim related-issues. Do not send proposals outside of our area of interest." Query with SASE. *No unsolicited mss.*

Recent Title(s) *The Great Taiwan Bubble: The Rise and Fall of an Emerging Stock Market*, by Steven R. Champion; *A Thousand Peaks: Poems from China*, by Siyu Liu and Orel Protopopescu; *Exploring Chinatown: A Children's Guide to Chinese Culture*, by Carol Stepanchuk.

Tips "We are currently only interested in Asia-related nonfiction for children 8-13."

PARADISE RESEARCH PUBLICATIONS, INC.

P.O. Box 837, Kihei HI 96753-0837. (808)874-4876. Fax: (808)874-4876. E-mail: dickb@dickb.com. Website: www.dickb.com/index.shtml. Publishes trade paperback originals. **Publishes 3 titles/year. Receives 5 queries and 1 mss/year. 20% of books from first-time authors; 100% from unagented writers. Pays 10% royalty.** Publishes book 3 months after acceptance of ms. Accepts simultaneous submissions. Responds in 1 month to queries. Book catalog online.

Nonfiction Self-help. Subjects include health/medicine, psychology, religion, spirituality. Paradise Research Publications is interested only in books on Alcoholics Anonymous and its spiritual roots. Query with SASE.

ℕ THE PARANOID PUBLICATIONS GROUP

208 Pine Lake Ave., Suite 200, La Porte IN 46350-3032. Website: www.paranoidpublications.com. **Acquisitions:** Keith W. Kimmel, owner. Estab. 2002. Publishes trade paperback and mass market paperback originals. **Publishes 2 titles/year. Receives 10 queries and 10 mss/year. 100% of books from first-time authors; 100% from unagented writers. Pays 3-20% royalty on retail price, or makes outright purchase of $20-5,000. Offers up to $500 advance.** Publishes book 6-12 months after acceptance of ms. Accepts simultaneous submissions. Responds in 2-3 months to queries; 2-3 months to proposals; 2-3 months to mss. Book catalog and ms guidelines online.

Nonfiction How-to, illustrated book, reference, technical, textbook. Subjects include agriculture/horticulture, alternative lifestyles, business/economics, computers/electronic, government/politics, health/medicine, hobbies, military/war, money/finance, nature/environment, psychology, science, world affairs, automotive, law. "Off-beat titles encouraged to submit. We are looking for titles under the 'alternative' viewpoint, works that teach our readers how to live freely, do business off the books, etc. We enjoy off-beat, nonmainstream titles targeted at specific, smaller audiences." Submit proposal package including 3 sample chapter(s), SASE. Submit complete ms with SASE preferred. Reviews artwork/photos as part of ms package. Send photocopies.

Tips "We welcome new authors. We suffer from a lack of submissions, and while most publishing houses are overburdened with submissions, we aren't getting enough. All submissions are carefully reviewed. We don't 'peek and toss.'"

PERSPECTIVES PRESS, INC.

The Infertility and Adoption Publisher, P.O. Box 90318, Indianapolis IN 46290-0318. (317)872-3055. E-mail: info@perspectivespress.com. Website: www.perspectivespress.com. **Acquisitions:** Pat Johnston, publisher. Estab. 1982. Publishes hardcover and trade paperback originals. **Publishes 1-4 titles/year. Receives 200 queries/year. 95% of books from first-time authors; 95% from unagented writers. Pays 5-15% royalty on net receipts.** Publishes book 1 year after acceptance of ms. Does not accept simultaneous submissions. Responds in 1 month to queries. Book catalog for #10 SAE and 2 first-class stamps or on website; ms guidelines online.

- "Our purpose is to promote understanding of infertility issues and alternatives, adoption and closely-related child welfare issues, and to educate and sensitize those personally experiencing these life situations, professionals who work with such clients, and the public at large."

Nonfiction Children's/juvenile, how-to, self-help. Subjects include child guidance/parenting, health/medicine, psychology, sociology. Must be related to infertility, adoption, alternative routes to family building. "No adult fiction!" Query with SASE.

Recent Title(s) *PCOS: The Hidden Epidemic*, by Samuel Thatcher MD; *Inside Transracial Adoption*, by Gail Steinberg and Beth Hall; *Attaching in Adoption*, by Deborah Gray.

Tips "For adults, we are seeking infertility and adoption decision-making materials, books dealing with adoptive or foster parenting issues, books to use with children, books to share with others to help explain infertility, adoption, foster care, third party reproductive assistance, special programming or training manuals, etc. For children, we will consider adoption or foster care-related fiction manuscripts that are appropriate for preschoolers and early elementary school children. We do not consider YA. Nonfiction manuscripts are considered for all ages. No autobiography, memoir or adult fiction. While we would consider a manuscript from a writer who was not personally or professionally involved in these issues, we would be more inclined to accept a manuscript submitted by an infertile person, an adoptee, a birthparent, an adoptive parent or a professional working with any of these."

PICKWICK PUBLICATION

215 Incline Way, San Jose CA 95139. (408)224-6777. E-mail: dyh1@aol.com. Website: www.pickwickpublications.com. **Acquisitions:** Dikran Y. Hadidian, general editor (theology, Biblical studies, church history). Publishes trade paperback originals and reprints. **Publishes 3-4 titles/year. Pays 10% royalty.** Publishes book 1 year after acceptance of ms. Accepts simultaneous submissions. Responds in 2 months to queries; 4 months to proposals; 6 months to mss. Book catalog and ms guidelines online.

Nonfiction Textbook. Subjects include philosophy, religion. Query with SASE, or submit outline, 2 sample chapter(s), or submit complete ms.

PLANNING/COMMUNICATIONS

7215 Oak Ave., River Forest IL 60305. (708)366-5200. E-mail: dl@planningcommunications.com. Website: jobfindersonline.com; dreamitdoit.net. **Acquisitions:** Daniel Lauber, president. Estab. 1979. Publishes hardcover, trade, and mass market paperback originals, trade paperback reprints. **Publishes 3-6 titles/year. Receives 30 queries and 20 mss/year. 50% of books from first-time authors; 100% from unagented writers. Pays 10-16% royalty on net receipts.** Publishes book 1 year after acceptance of ms. Accepts simultaneous submissions. Responds in 3 months to queries. Book catalog for $2 or free on website; ms guidelines online.

- Planning/Communications publishes books on careers, improving your life, dream fulfillment, ending discrimination, sociology, urban planning, and politics.

Nonfiction Self-help. Subjects include business/economics (careers), education, government/politics, money/finance, sociology, ending discrimination, careers, résumés, cover letters, interviewing. Submit outline, 3 sample chapter(s), SASE. Reviews artwork/photos as part of ms package. Send photocopies.

Recent Title(s) *Dream It Do It: Inspiring Stories of Dreams Come True*, by Sharon Cook and Graciela Sholander; *Flight Attendant Job Finder & Career Guide*, by Tim Kirkwood; *International Job Finder*, by Daniel Lauber and Kraig Rice.

Tips "Our editorial mission is to publish books that can make a difference in people's lives—books of substance, not glitz."

ℕ POGO PRESS, INC.

4 Cardinal Lane, St. Paul MN 55127-6406. (651)483-4692. E-mail: pogopres@minn.net. Website: www.pogopress.com. **Acquisitions:** Leo J. Harris, vice president. Publishes trade paperback originals. **Publishes 3 titles/year.**

Pays royalty on wholesale price. Publishes book 6 months after acceptance of ms. Does not accept simultaneous submissions. Responds in 2 months to queries. Book catalog free.

Nonfiction Illustrated book. Subjects include art/architecture, history, travel. "We limit our publishing to Breweriana, history, art, popular culture and travel odysseys. Our books are heavily illustrated." No e-mail submissions. Query with SASE. Reviews artwork/photos as part of ms package. Send photocopies.

Recent Title(s) *The History of Beer and Brewing in Chicago—1833 to 1978,* by Bob Skilnik.

✱ PONCHA PRESS

P.O. Box 280, Morrison CO 80465. Fax: (303)697-2384. E-mail: info@ponchapress.com. Website: www.ponchapress.com. **Acquisitions:** Barbara Osgood-Hartness, editor-in-chief. Publishes hardcover and trade paperback originals. **Publishes 1 title/year. Receives 400 queries/year. 100% of books from first-time authors; 100% from unagented writers. Pays royalty.** Publishes book 1 year after acceptance of ms. Accepts simultaneous submissions. Responds in 1 month to queries; 3 months to mss. Book catalog and ms guidelines on website; ms guidelines online.

Nonfiction Topics relating to contemporary social, political, and cultural issues in the United States. **All unsolicited mss returned unopened.** Query with SASE. See submission guidelines on website first. Reviews artwork/photos as part of ms package. Send photocopies.

Fiction Literary, mainstream/contemporary. Writers should consult website for submission guidelines and complete fully. Query with SASE.

Recent Title(s) *The Execution of a Serial Killer: One Man's Experience Witnessing the Death Penalty,* by Joseph D. Diaz, Ph.D.; *An English Experience: Exploring the Backroads and Byways of Gloucestire, Wiltshire and Hampshire,* by Marge D. Hansen.

Tips "Only finished and polished manuscripts on contemporary social, political, and cultural issues in the U.S. No first drafts or proposals for unwritten work."

✱ THE POST-APOLLO PRESS

35 Marie St., Sausalito CA 94965. (415)332-1458. Fax: (415)332-8045. E-mail: postapollo@earthlink.net. Website: www.postapollopress.com. **Acquisitions:** Simone Fattal, publisher,. Estab. 1982. Publishes trade paperback originals and reprints. **Publishes 4 titles/year. Pays 5-7% royalty on wholesale price.** Publishes book 1½ years after acceptance of ms. Responds in 3 months to queries. Book catalog and ms guidelines for #10 SASE.

● Not accepting new mss.

Nonfiction Essay; letters. Subjects include art/architecture, language/literature, translation, women's issues/studies. Query.

Fiction Experimental, literary (plays), spiritual. "Many of our books are first translations into English." No juvenile, horror, sports, or romance. Submit 1 sample chapter(s), SASE. "The Post-Apollo Press is not accepting manuscripts or queries currently due to a full publishing schedule."

Poetry Experimental/translations.

Recent Title(s) *Happily,* by Lyn Hejinian; *Some Life,* by Joanne Kyger; *Where the Rocks Started,* by Marc Atherton.

Tips "We are interested in writers with a fresh and original vision. We often publish foreign literature that is already well known in its original country, but new to the American reader."

PRAKKEN PUBLICATIONS, INC.

P.O. Box 8623, Ann Arbor MI 48107-8623. (734)975-2800. Fax: (734)975-2787. Publisher: George Kennedy. **Acquisitions:** Susanne Peckham, book editor. Estab. 1934. Publishes educational hardcover and paperback originals, as well as educational magazines. **Publishes 3 titles/year. Pays 10% royalty on net receipts. Offers advance.** Accepts simultaneous submissions. Responds in 2 months to queries. Book catalog for #10 SASE.

○━ "We publish books for educators in career/vocational and technology education, as well as books for the machine trades and machinists' education. Currently emphasizing machine trades.

Nonfiction Biography (of inventors, technologists, scientists), reference. Subjects include education. "We are currently interested in manuscripts with broad appeal in any of the specific subject areas of machine trades, technology education, career-technical education, and reference for the general education field." Submit outline, sample chapter(s).

Recent Title(s) *Moving Civilization: The Growth of Transportation,* by Dennis Karwatka; *Building Civilization: The Growth of Production,* by Dennis Karwatka; *Connecting Civilization: The Growth of Communication,* by Dennis Karwatka.

Tips "We have a continuing interest in magazine and book manuscripts which reflect emerging issues and trends in education, especially career-technical, industrial, and technology education."

PRECEPT PRESS

Bonus Books, 875 N. Michigan Ave., Suite 1416, Chicago IL 60611. (312)467-0580. Fax: (312)467-9271. E-mail: bb@bonus-books.com. Website: www.bonus-books.com. **Acquisitions:** Kelley Thornton, acquisitions editor. Estab. 1970. Publishes hardcover and trade paperback originals. **Publishes 3-5 titles/year. Receives 300 queries and 100 mss/year. 25% of books from first-time authors; 90% from unagented writers. Pays royalty. Offers advance.** Publishes book 1 year after acceptance of ms. Accepts simultaneous submissions. Responds in 3 months to proposals. Ms guidelines online.

O─┐ Precept Press features a wide variety of books for the medical community.

Nonfiction Reference, technical, textbook. Subjects include health/medicine (clinical medical, oncology texts), science. Query with SASE.

Recent Title(s) *Nutritional Care for High-Risk Newborns*, ed. by Groh-Wargo, Thompson & Cox.

THE PRESS AT THE MARYLAND HISTORICAL SOCIETY

201 W. Monument St., Baltimore MD 21201. (410)685-3750. Fax: (410)385-2105. E-mail: rcottom@mdhs.org. Website: www.mdhs.org. **Acquisitions:** Robert I. Cottom, publisher (Maryland-Chesapeake history); Patricia Dockman Anderson, managing editor (Maryland-Chesapeake history). Publishes hardcover and trade paperback originals, and trade paperback reprints. **Publishes 2-4 titles/year. Receives 15-20 queries and 8-10 mss/year. 50% of books from first-time authors; 100% from unagented writers. Pays 6-10% royalty on retail price.** Publishes book 1-2 years after acceptance of ms. Accepts simultaneous submissions. Responds in 2 months to queries; 2 months to proposals; 6 months to mss. Book catalog online.

O─┐ The Press at the Maryland Historical Society specializes in Maryland state and Chesapeake regional subjects.

Nonfiction Biography, children's/juvenile, illustrated book, scholarly textbook. Subjects include anthropology/ archeology, art/architecture, history. Query with SASE, or submit proposal package including outline, 1-2 sample chapter(s).

Recent Title(s) *The Chesapeake: An Environmental Biography*, by John R. Wennersten; *The Patapsco Valley: Cradle of the Industrial Revolution in Maryland*, by Henry K. Sharp.

Tips "Our audience consists of intelligent readers of Maryland/Chesapeake regional history and biography."

PUCKERBRUSH PRESS

76 Main St., Orono ME 04473-1430. (207)581-3832. **Acquisitions:** Constance Hunting, publisher/editor. Estab. 1971. Publishes trade paperback originals and reprints of literary fiction and poetry. **Publishes 3-4 titles/year. Pays 10-15% royalty on wholesale price.** Does not accept simultaneous submissions. Responds in 1 month to queries; 2 months to proposals; 3 months to mss. Book catalog for large SASE and 34¢; ms guidelines for SASE.

Nonfiction Subjects include language/literature, translation, belles lettres. Query with SASE.

Fiction Literary, short story collections. Submit complete ms, and include cover letter.

Poetry Highest literary quality. Submit complete ms.

Recent Title(s) *Settling*, by Patricia Ranzoni (poetry).

Tips "No religious subjects, crime per se, tired prose. For sophisticated readers who retain love of literature. Maine writers continue to be featured."

ℕ QUICK PUBLISHING, LLC

1610 Long Leaf Circle, St. Louis MO 63146. (314)432-3435. Fax: (314)993-0930. E-mail: quickpublishing@sbcglobal.net. **Acquisitions:** Angie Quick. Publishes trade paperback and hardback originals. **Publishes 2-5 titles/ year. Pays 8-10% royalty on net receipts.** Responds in 1 month to queries; 1 month to proposals; 3 months to mss. Ms guidelines online.

Nonfiction Scientific, outdoor guides, regional books, and self-help, including child guidance/parenting, education, senior/aging. Query with SASE, or submit outline.

Recent Title(s) *The Wisdom to Choose*, by Dixon Arnett and Wende Dawson Chan.

RED EYE PRESS, INC.

P.O. Box 65751, Los Angeles CA 90065. **Acquisitions:** James Goodwin, president. Publishes trade paperback originals. **Publishes 2 titles/year. Pays 8-12% royalty on retail price. Offers $1-2,000 advance.** Does not accept simultaneous submissions. Responds in 1 month to queries; 3 months to mss.

Nonfiction How-to, reference. Subjects include gardening. Query with SASE, or submit outline, 2 sample chapter(s).

Recent Title(s) *Great Labor Quotations—Sourcebook and Reader*, Peter Bollen.

Tips "We publish how-to and reference works that are the standard for their genre, authoritative, and able to remain in print for many years."

Small Presses

RED MILL PRESS

135 W. 20th St., 5th Floor Rear, New York NY 10011. (212)367-7575, ext. 102. Fax: (212)367-8532. E-mail: info@redmillpress.com. **Acquisitions:** Kate Simon, editor (nutrition/fitness/weight loss issues). Estab. 1999. **Publishes 2-10 titles/year. Receives 10 queries and 25 mss/year. 30% of books from first-time authors; 30% from unagented writers. Pays royalty on wholesale price. Advance.** Publishes book 1 year after acceptance of ms. Does not accept simultaneous submissions. Responds in 3-4 months to queries; 3-4 months to proposals; 3-4 months to mss.

Nonfiction Health related to weight loss, fitness, and nutrition. Subjects include cooking/foods/nutrition, Fitness, Weight Loss. "Sound, realistic advice. Writer needs to have a platform to sell books, not just an idea." Submit complete ms. Reviews artwork/photos as part of ms package. Material will not be returned.

Recent Title(s) *Breaking the Pattern*, by Charles Stuart Platkin (behavioral change/weight loss).

Tips "Our audience is women, primarily age 25-55."

RED SAGE PUBLISHING, INC.

P.O. Box 4844, Seminole FL 33775. (727)391-3847. Website: www.redsagepub.com. **Acquisitions:** Alexandria Kendall, publisher; Judith Pich, executive editor. Estab. 1995. **Publishes 4 titles/year. 50% of books from first-time authors.** Does not accept simultaneous submissions. Ms guidelines online.

   O─ Publishes books of ultra-sensual fiction, written for the adventurous woman.

Recent Title(s) *Secrets, Volume 10* (an anthology of 4 novellas); *Forever Kissed* (sexy paranormal featuring vampires).

Tips "We define romantic erotica. Sensuous, bold, spicy, untamed, hot, and sometimes politically incorrect, *Secrets* stories concentrate on the sophisticated, highly intense adult relationship. We look for character-driven stories that concentrate on the love and sexual relationship between a hero and the heroine. Red Sage is expanding into single-title books in 2004. Author voice, excellent writing, and strong emotions are all important ingredients to the fiction we publish."

RISING STAR PRESS

P.O. Box 66378, Scotts Valley CA 95067. (831)461-0604. Fax: (831)461-0445. E-mail: editor@risingstarpress.com. Website: www.risingstarpress.com. **Acquisitions:** Acquisitions Editor. Publishes hardcover originals and reprints, trade paperback originals and reprints. **Publishes 3-6 titles/year. Pays 10-15% royalty on wholesale price. Offers $1,000-8,000 advance.** Publishes book 9 months after acceptance of ms. Accepts simultaneous submissions. Responds in 2 months to proposals. Ms guidelines online.

Nonfiction Biography, reference, self-help. Subjects include education, health/medicine, language/literature, philosophy, regional, religion, sociology. "Rising Star Press publishes books that cause people to think and be inspired to act in some positive and proactive way to improve their own life as well as the lives of those around them. Authors are treated as partners in the production and marketing process. Books are selected based on the combination of fit with the company mission, consistency between the author's words and life, and marketability." Currently emphasizing social and religious issues. De-emphasizing metaphysical, personal finance. "Authors need to be able to answer these questions: Who will benefit from reading this? Why? Mistakes writers often make are not identifying their target market early and shaping the work to address it." Query with SASE, or submit outline, 2 sample chapter(s). Must include e-mail address with query/proposal.

Fiction "Must illuminate topics, as listed for nonfiction submissions, for the reader who is more drawn to fiction writing."

Recent Title(s) *Dancing with Diagnosis—Steps for Taking the Lead When Facing Cancer*, by Michelle Waters; *The Dishonest Church*, by Jack Good; *The Doghouse Angel—From the Darkness of Abuse to the Light of Healing*, by Kimberly Steward.

Ⓝ ROBBIE DEAN PRESS

2910 E. Eisenhower Pkwy., Ann Arbor MI 48108. (734)973-9511. Fax: (734)973-9475. E-mail: robbiedeanpress@aol.com. Submissions E-mail: fairyha@aol.com. Website: www.robbiedeanpress.com. Owner/Publisher: Fairy Cuttayer-Scott, Ph.D. (literature, deafness, education). **Acquisitions:** Robert M. Scott, Jr., chair of review board (general). Estab. 1991. **Publishes 3 titles/year. Receives 20-25 queries and 10-15 mss/year. 90% of books from first-time authors; 100% from unagented writers. Pays 10-20% royalty on retail price.** Publishes book 8 months after acceptance of ms. Accepts simultaneous submissions. Responds in 1 month to mss. Book catalog online; ms guidelines by e-mail.

Nonfiction Autobiography, biography, booklets, children's/juvenile, coffee table book, gift book, how-to, illustrated book, reference, scholarly, self-help, textbook. Subjects include child guidance/parenting, computers/electronic, education, ethnic, general nonfiction, health/medicine, humanities, language/literature, multicultural, photography, psychology, religion, science, spirituality. "The work must be one that the author plans to use in his or another's college class(es)." Query with SASE, or submit complete ms. Reviews artwork/photos as part of ms package. Send photocopies.

Fiction Ethnic, historical, humor, juvenile, literary, multicultural, picture books, poetry, religious, science fiction. "If the fictional work is not focused to be a college text, then do not send it to Robbie Dean Press." Query with SASE, or submit complete ms.

Poetry "Again, if the work is not for a college course use, do not submit." Query, or submit complete ms.

Recent Title(s) *Process & Voice in the Writing Workshop, 3rd Ed.*, by Gregory Shafer, Ph.D. (text); *Your Remarkable Anatomy*, by Don Lowell Fisher, Ph.D. (text/reference); *Poems of the Spirit*, by Shirley Barnett (poetry).

Tips "Our audience is students, from elementary to college. Quite honestly, Robbie Dean Press is most comfortable not working with an agent."

🅽 ROCK SPRING PRESS

6015 Morrow St. E., Suite 106, Jacksonville FL 32217. E-mail: editor@rockspringpress.com. Website: www.rockspringpress.com. Publisher: Alice Platt. Estab. 2002. Publishes hardcover originals. **Publishes 1-5 titles/year. Pays 12-15% royalty on wholesale price. Offers up to $500 advance.** Publishes book 8-18 months after acceptance of ms. Accepts simultaneous submissions. Responds in 3 months to queries; 3 months to proposals; 3 months to mss. Ms guidelines online.

Nonfiction General nonfiction. Subjects include Americana, animals, nature/environment, travel. "We are looking for descriptive travel writing that informs the reader about the experience of being in, or traveling to, a place. We are also interested in books that make nature and the environment accessible to the average reader." No travel guides. Submit proposal package including outline, 3 sample chapter(s), unique marketing suggestions for your book, or submit complete ms. Reviews artwork/photos as part of ms package. e-mail low resolution scans.

Tips "Our audience is reasonably well-educated (bachelor's degree) adults interested in travel and their natural environment. Proofread. What you send should be as good as you envision the final product. Please make sure submissions are typed and double-spaced."

SAFER SOCIETY PRESS

P.O. Box 340, Brandon VT 05733. (802)247-3132. Fax: (802)247-4233. Website: www.safersociety.org. **Acquisitions:** Publications Specialist. Estab. 1985. Publishes trade paperback originals. **Publishes 3-4 titles/year. Receives 15-20 queries and 15-20 mss/year. 90% of books from first-time authors; 100% from unagented writers. Pays 5% royalty on retail price.** Publishes book 1 year after acceptance of ms. Accepts simultaneous submissions. Book catalog free; ms guidelines online.

⚬⚮ "Our mission is the prevention and treatment of sexual abuse."

Nonfiction Self-help (sex abuse prevention and treatment). Subjects include psychology (sexual abuse). "We are a small, nonprofit, niche press. We want well-researched books dealing with any aspect of sexual abuse: treatment, prevention, understanding; works on subject in Spanish." Query with SASE, submit proposal package, or complete ms. Reviews artwork/photos as part of ms package. Send photocopies.

Recent Title(s) *Phallometric Testing with Sexual Offenders: Theory, Research, and Practice*, by William L. Marshall and Yolanda M. Fernandez; *Del Camino*, by Timothy J. Kahn, translated by Child Adolescent Services, Inc.; *Current Practices and Trends in Sexual Abuser Management: The Safer Society 2002 Nationwide Survey*, by Robert J. McGrath, Georgia F. Cumming, and Brenda L. Burchard.

Tips Audience is persons working in mental health/persons needing self-help books. Pays small fees or low royalties.

SALVO PRESS

61428 Elder Ridge St., P.O. Box 9095, Bend OR 97702. (541)330-9709. E-mail: info@salvopress.com. Website: www.salvopress.com. **Acquisitions:** Scott Schmidt, publisher. Estab. 1998. Publishes paperback originals and e-books in most formats. **Publishes 3 titles/year. Receives 500 queries/year. 50% of books from first-time authors; 80% from unagented writers. Pays 10-15% royalty.** Publishes book 9 months after acceptance of ms. Does not accept simultaneous submissions. Responds in 1 month to queries; 2 months to mss. Book catalog and ms guidelines online.

Fiction Adventure, literary, mystery (amateur sleuth, police procedural, private/hard boiled), science fiction (hard science/technological), suspense, espionage, thriller. "Our needs change. Check our website." Query with SASE.

Recent Title(s) *Superior Position*, by Evan McNamara; *House of the Rising Sun*, by Chuck Hustmyre; *Poised to Kill*, by Brian Lutterman.

THE SIDRAN INSTITUTE PRESS

(formerly The Sidran Press), 200 E. Joppa Rd., Suite 207, Baltimore MD 21286-3107. (410)825-8888. Fax: (410)337-0747. E-mail: sidran@sidran.org. Website: www.sidran.org. **Acquisitions:** Esther Giller, director. Estab. 1986. Publishes hardcover originals and trade paperback originals and reprints. **Publishes 2-3 titles/year. Pays 8-10% royalty on wholesale price.** Does not accept simultaneous submissions. Responds in 1 month to queries; 3 months to proposals; 6 months to mss. Book catalog and ms guidelines free.

Nonfiction Reference, self-help, textbook, professional. Subjects include psychology, psychiatry, expressive therapies. Specializes in trauma/abuse/domestic violence and mental health issues. "Sidran Institute Press is the publishing division of Sidran Institute, which is a nonprofit organization devoted to advocacy, education, training, and research in support of people with traumatic stress conditions and dissociative disorders." Exclusively publishes books about traumatic stress and dissociative conditions, nonfiction, practical tools for recovery, education and training materials for professionals, self-help workbooks. Currently emphasizing practical recovery tools, professional training, application of research. De-emphasizing biography, autobiography, or first-person recovery narratives. Query with proposal package including outline, 2-3 sample chapters, introduction, competing titles, market information.

Recent Title(s) *Male Victims of Same-Sex Abuse: Addressing Their Sexual Response*, by John Preble, Nick Groth; *The Essence of Being Real: Relational Peer Support for Men and Women Who Have Experienced Trauma*, by Jennifer L. Wilkerson; *The Twenty-Four Carat Buddha and Other Fables*, by Maxine Harris.

SLAPERING HOL PRESS

Imprint of The Hudson Valley Writers' Center, 300 Riverside Dr., Sleepy Hollow NY 10591. (914)332-5953. Fax: (914)332-4825. E-mail: info@writerscenter.org. Website: www.writerscenter.org. **Acquisitions:** Stephanie Strickland and Margo Stever, co-editors (poetry). Publishes chapbooks. **Publishes 1-2 titles/year. Receives 70 queries and 300 mss/year. 100% of books from first-time authors; 100% from unagented writers.** Publishes book 6 months after acceptance of ms. Accepts simultaneous submissions. Book catalog and competition guidelines for #10 SASE.

Poetry Unpublished poets are invited to submit a collection of poems (16-20 pages) for the annual chapbook competition. The winning poet receives a $1,000 cash award, publication, 10 copies, and a reading at The Hudson Valley Writers' Center.

Recent Title(s) *The Landscape of Mind*, by Jianquing Zheng; *The Scottish Cafe*, by Susan H. Case; *Days When Nothing Happens*, by David Tucker.

Tips Poets should obtain the contest guidelines before submitting.

SOCRATIC PRESS

P.O. Box 66683, St. Pete Beach FL 33736-6683. (727)367-6177. Publishes hardcover, trade paperback and electronic originals and electronic reprints. **Publishes 2-3 titles/year. Pays 15-50% royalty on retail price.**

Nonfiction How-to, humor, illustrated book, self-help. Subjects include animals, business/economics, creative nonfiction, government/politics, health/medicine, language/literature, money/finance, nature/environment, philosophy, psychology, science, sex, social sciences, spirituality. "Our principal interest is in books that are politically incorrect and are too controversial for other publishers." Query with SASE, or submit proposal package including outline.

Recent Title(s) *Handbook of the Coming American Revolution*, by Bryant.

Tips Audience is "skeptical, free-thinking, libertarian, inquisitive, unihibited, curious, iconoclastic."

SPECTACLE LANE PRESS, INC.

P.O. Box 1237, Mt. Pleasant SC 29465-1237. (843)971-9165 or (888)669-8114 (toll free). Fax: (843)971-9165. E-mail: jaskar44@aol.com. **Acquisitions:** James A. Skardon, editor. Publishes nonfiction text and/or cartoons, hardcover and trade paperback originals. **Publishes 2-3 titles/year. Pays advance against 6-10% royalty on wholesale price.** Responds in 2 weeks to queries; 1 month to mss.

    O— Emphasizes humor, but also interested in sports, lifestyle, and celebrity oriented books. All books should be related to subjects of strong current interest and promotable on radio and TV.

Nonfiction "Query first. We will request an outline, table of contents, and 3 chapters, if we are interested."

Recent Title(s) *Call Me Coach*, by George H. Baldwin (sports biography); *Money, Inc.*, by Joseph Farris (business cartoons); *Incidents and Accidents for Frazzled Women*, by Kim Burke (humor).

ST. BEDE'S PUBLICATIONS

St. Scholastica Priory, P.O. Box 545, Petersham MA 01366-0545. (978)724-3213. Fax: (978)724-3216. President: Sister Mary Clare Vincent. **Acquisitions:** Acquisitions Editor. Estab. 1977. Publishes hardcover originals, trade paperback originals and reprints. **Publishes 3-4 titles/year. Receives 100 submissions/year. 30-40% of books from first-time authors; 98% from unagented writers. Pays 5-10% royalty on wholesale price, or retail price.** Publishes book 2 years after acceptance of ms. Accepts simultaneous submissions. Responds in 2 months to queries. Book catalog and ms guidelines for 9×12 SAE with 2 first-class stamps.

⊶ St. Bede's Publications is owned and operated by the Roman Catholic nuns of St. Scholastica Priory. The publications are seen as an apostolic outreach. Their mission is to make available to everyone quality books on spiritual subjects such as prayer, scripture, theology, and the lives of holy people.

Nonfiction Textbook (theology). Subjects include history, philosophy, religion, sex, spirituality, translation, prayer, hagiography, theology, church history, related lives of saints. No submissions unrelated to religion, theology, spirituality, etc., and no poetry, fiction, or children's books. Does not return submissions without adequate postage. Query, or submit outline and sample chapters with SASE.

Recent Title(s) *Reading the Gospels with Gregory the Great*, translated by Santha Bhattacharji; *Why Catholic?*, by Father John Pasquini.

Tips "There seems to be a growing interest in monasticism among lay people, and we will be publishing more books in this area. For our theology/philosophy titles our audience is scholars, colleges and universities, seminaries, etc. For our other titles (i.e. prayer, spirituality, lives of saints, etc.) the audience is above-average readers interested in furthering their knowledge in these areas."

STEMMER HOUSE PUBLISHERS

4 White Brook Rd., Gilsum NH 03448. (800)345-6665. Fax: (603)357-2073. E-mail: stemmerhouse@pathwaybook.com. **Acquisitions:** Craig Thom, editor-in-chief (design, natural history, nonfiction, children's books). Estab. 1975. Publishes hardcover and trade paperback originals. **Publishes 2-4 titles/year; imprint publishes 2 titles/year. Receives 2,000 queries and 1,500 mss/year. 50% of books from first-time authors; 90% from unagented writers. Pays 5-10% royalty on wholesale price. Offers $300 advance.** Publishes book 1-2 years after acceptance of ms. Accepts simultaneous submissions. Responds in 1 month to queries. Book catalog for 9×12 SAE with 3 first-class stamps; ms guidelines for #10 SASE.

Imprints The International Design Library, The NatureEncyclopedia Series.

⊶ Stemmer House publishes nonfiction illustrated books for children/juveniles in the arts and humanities, children's books and CDs. Currently emphasizing natural history.

Nonfiction Biography, children's/juvenile, illustrated book. Subjects include animals, multicultural, nature/environment, arts. Query with SASE.

Ⓝ STILL WATERS POETRY PRESS

459 Willow Ave., Galloway Township NJ 08201. **Acquisitions:** Shirley A. Lake, editor. Estab. 1984. Publishes trade paperback originals and chapbooks. **Publishes 2 titles/year. Pays in copies for first press run; 10% royalty for additional press runs.** Does not accept simultaneous submissions. Responds in 1 month to queries; 1 month to proposals; 3 months to mss. Book catalog and ms guidelines for #10 SASE or online.

Poetry "Dedicated to significant poetry for, by or about women, we want contemporary themes and styles set on American soil. We don't want gay, patriarchal religion, lesbian, simple rhyme or erotic themes." "We publish chapbooks only, 20-30 pages, one author at a time. Do not expect publication of a single poem." Query with SASE then submit complete ms.

Recent Title(s) *Suzy and Her Husbands*, by Edward Mast; *Moving Expenses*, by Lori Shpunt.

Tips "Don't send manuscripts via certified mail. It wastes your money and my time."

STRATA PUBLISHING, INC.

P.O. Box 1303, State College PA 16804. (814)234-8545. Website: www.stratapub.com. **Acquisitions:** Kathleen Domenig, publisher (speech communication, journalism, mass communication, political science). Publishes college textbooks. **Publishes 1-3 titles/year. Pays royalty on wholesale price.** Publishes book about 1 year after acceptance of ms. Responds in 1 month to queries; 3 months to proposals; 3 months to mss. Book catalog and ms guidelines online.

Nonfiction Textbook. Subjects include government/politics, speech, journalism, mass communication. Query with SASE, or submit proposal package including outline, 2 sample chapter(s).

Recent Title(s) *Argumentation: Understanding and Shaping Arguments, updated ed.*, by James A. Herrick; *The Why, Who, and How of the Editorial Page, 4th ed.*, by Kenneth Rystrom; *Political Communication: Rhetoric, Government, and Citizens, 2nd ed.*, by Dan F. Hahn.

Tips "Please visit our website for a description of our publishing needs and manuscript submission guidelines."

THE SUGAR HILL PRESS

216 Stoddard Rd., Hancock NH 03449-5102. **Acquisitions:** L. Bickford, publisher. Estab. 1990. Publishes trade paperback originals. **Publishes 1 title/year. Pays 20% royalty on publisher's revenues.** Responds in 1 month to proposals.

⊶ "Our books focus on helping school personnel—secretaries, guidance counselors, administrators—make the most of their school's investment in school administration software."

Nonfiction "We publish technical manuals for users of school administrative software only. (These are supplemental materials, not the manuals which come in the box.) A successful writer will combine technical expertise with crystal-clear prose.'' Query with SASE.

Recent Title(s) *Perfect Attendance*, by Frances M. Kulak; *A Win School Primer*, by L. Bickford.

SYSTEMS CO., INC.

P.O. Box 339, Carlsborg WA 98324. (360)683-6860. **Acquisitions:** Richard H. Peetz, Ph.D., president. Estab. 1981. Publishes hardcover and trade paperback originals. **Publishes 3-5 titles/year. 50% of books from first-time authors; 100% from unagented writers. Pays 20% royalty on wholesale price after costs.** Publishes book 6 months after acceptance of ms. Accepts simultaneous submissions. Responds in 2 months to queries. Book catalog free; ms guidelines for $1.

O→ ''We publish succinct and well-organized technical and how-to-do-it books with minimum filler.'' De-emphasizing business/economics, health/medicine.

Nonfiction How-to, self-help, technical, textbook. Subjects include nature/environment, science, automotive, engineering. Submit outline, 2 sample chapter(s), SASE. Reviews artwork/photos as part of ms package. Send photocopies.

Recent Title(s) *Radiation Effects on Electronics*, by F.L. Bouquet.

Tips ''Our audience consists of people in technical occupations, people interested in doing things themselves. In submitting nonfiction, writers often make the mistake of picking a common topic with lots of published books in print.''

N TAMARACK BOOKS, INC.

P.O. Box 190313, Boise ID 83719. (800)962-6657. Fax: (208)922-5880. President/Owner: Kathy Gaudry. Publishes trade paperback originals and reprints. **Publishes 3-5 titles/year. Pays 5-15% royalty. Offers advance.** Does not accept simultaneous submissions. Responds in 4 months to queries; 6 months to mss.

O→ ''We publish nonfiction history of the American West and are avidly seeking women's books. Time period preference is for pre-1900s.'' Currently emphasizing ''pioneer women who have made a difference, whether they have name recognition or not.''

Nonfiction Illustrated book. Subjects include history, regional. ''We are looking for manuscripts for a popular audience, but based on solid research. We specialize in mountain man, women's issues, and outlaw history prior to 1940 in the West, but will look at any good manuscript on Western history prior to 1940.'' Query with SASE, or submit outline.

Recent Title(s) *Competitive Struggle, America's Western Fur Trading Posts, 1764-1865*, R.G. Robertson.

Tips ''We look for authors who want to actively participate in the marketing of their books.''

N TECHNICAL ANALYSIS OF STOCKS & COMMODITIES

Technical Analysis, Inc., 4757 California Ave. SW, Seattle WA 98116-4499. (206)938-0570. E-mail: editor@traders.com. Website: www.traders.com. **Acquisitions:** Jayanthi Gopalakrishnan, editor. Estab. 1982. Publishes trade paperback originals and reprints. **Makes outright purchase.** Responds in 6 months to queries.

Nonfiction Publishes business and economics books and software about using charts and computers to trade stocks, options, mutual funds or commodity futures. ''Know the industry and the markets using technical analysis.'' Query with SASE.

Recent Title(s) *Charting the Stock Market*, by Hutson, Weis, Schroeder (technical analysis).

Tips ''Only traders and technical analysts really understand the industry. First consideration for publication will be given to material, regardless of topic, that presents the subject in terms that are easily understandable by the novice trader. One of our prime considerations is to instruct, and we must do so in a manner that the lay person can comprehend. This by no means bars material of a complex nature, but the author must first establish the groundwork.''

TEXAS WESTERN PRESS

The University of Texas at El Paso, 500 W. University Ave., El Paso TX 79968-0633. (915)747-5688. Fax: (915)747-7515. E-mail: twp@utep.edu. Website: www.utep.edu/twp. **Acquisitions:** Dr. Jon Amastae, director. Estab. 1952. Publishes hardcover and paperback originals. **Publishes 2-3 titles/year. Pays standard 10% royalty. Offers advance.** Does not accept simultaneous submissions. Responds in 2 months to queries. Book catalog and ms guidelines free; ms guidelines online.

Imprints Southwestern Studies.

O→ Texas Western Press publishes books on the history and cultures of the American Southwest, including the US-Mexico borderlands, West Texas, New Mexico, and northern Mexico. Currently emphasizing developing border issues, economic issues of the border. De-emphasizing coffee table books.

Nonfiction Scholarly, technical. Subjects include education, health/medicine, history, language/literature, nature/environment, regional, science, social sciences. Historic and cultural accounts of the Southwest (West

Texas, New Mexico, northern Mexico). Also art, photographic books, Native American and limited regional ficiton reprints. Occasional technical titles. "Our *Southwestern Studies* use manuscripts of up to 30,000 words. Our hardback books range from 30,000 words up. The writer should use good exposition in his work. Most of our work requires documentation. We favor a scholarly, but not overly pedantic, style. We specialize in superior book design." Query with SASE, or submit outline. Follow *Chicago Manual of Style*.

Recent Title(s) *The Carvajal Family*, by Alfonso del Toro; *James Wiley Magoffin*, by W.H. Timmons.

Tips Texas Western Press is interested in books relating to the history of Hispanics in the US, will experiment with photo-documentary books, and is interested in seeing more contemporary books on border issues. "We try to treat our authors professionally, produce handsome, long-lived books and aim for quality, rather than quantity of titles carrying our imprint."

TIA CHUCHA PRESS

c/o Tia Chucha's Cate Cultural, 12737 Glenoaks Blvd., #22, Sylmar CA 91342. **Acquisitions:** Luis Rodriguez, director. Publishes trade paperback originals. **Publishes 2-4 titles/year. Receives 25-30 queries and 150 mss/ year. Pays 10% royalty on wholesale price.** Publishes book 1 year after acceptance of ms. Does not accept simultaneous submissions. Responds in 9 months to mss. Ms guidelines free.

Poetry "No restrictions as to style or content. We do cross-cultural and performance-oriented poetry. It has to work on the page, however." Submit complete ms.

Recent Title(s) *Rise*, by A. Van Jordan; *Bumtown*, by Tony Fitzpatrick; *Singing the Bones Together*, by Angela Shannon.

Tips Audience is "those interested in strong, multicultural, urban poetry—the best of bar-cafe poetry. Send letter of inquiry with 2-3 samples of your best work."

TNI BOOKS

2442 NW Market #357, Seattle WA 98107. (206)352-8695. Fax: (206)374-2625. E-mail: tnibooks@tnibooks.com. Website: www.tnibooks.com. **Acquisitions:** Adam Voith, owner. Publishes trade paperback originals and mass market paperback originals. **Publishes 2-3 titles/year. Pays royalty. Offers variable advance.** Accepts simultaneous submissions. Responds in 6 months to queries; 6 months to proposals; 6 months to mss. Book catalog and ms guidelines for #10 SASE or online; ms guidelines online.

Nonfiction Coffee table book, gift book, humor, illustrated book, multimedia. Subjects include Americana, creative nonfiction, language/literature, travel. Write or visit website for current guidelines and learn about current needs. Submit complete ms. Reviews artwork/photos as part of ms package. prints or e-mail electronic images.

Fiction Experimental, humor, literary, mainstream/contemporary, picture books, short story collections. Write or visit website for current guidelines and learn about current needs. Submit complete ms.

Recent Title(s) *Lost Joy*, by Camden Joy (fiction); *Stand Up Ernie Baxter: You're Dead*, by Adam Voith (fiction).

Tips "Visit our website and look at and/or read some of our books before submitting work."

TODD PUBLICATIONS

P.O. Box 635, Nyack NY 10960. (845)358-6213. E-mail: toddpub@aol.com. Website: www.toddpublications.c om. **Acquisitions:** Barry Klein, president. Estab. 1973. Publishes hardcover and trade paperback originals. **Publishes 2 titles/year. 1% of books from first-time authors. Pays 10% royalty on wholesale price. Offers advance.** Publishes book 3 months after acceptance of ms. Accepts simultaneous submissions. Responds in 1 month to proposals. Book catalog available via website or with SASE; ms guidelines for #10 SASE.

○━ Todd Publications publishes and distributes reference books and directories of all types.

Nonfiction How-to, reference, self-help, directories. Subjects include business/economics, ethnic, health/medicine, money/finance, travel. Submit 2 sample chapter(s).

Recent Title(s) *Mail Order Business Directory*; *Guide to American & International Directories*; *Reference Encyclopedia of the American Indian*.

TRANSPERSONAL PUBLISHING

AHU Press, P.O. Box 249, Goshen VA 24439. (540)997-0325. E-mail: hyptrainer@aol.com. Website: www.trans personalpublishing.com. **Acquisitions:** Dr. Allen Chips, acquistions/publishing director (holistic health books/ texts, metaphysical/spiritual, how-to/self-help). Estab. 1999. Publishes hardcover, trade paperback, and electronic originals and reprints; and mass market paperback reprints. **Publishes 3-7 titles/year. Receives 35 queries and 20 submissions/year. 50% of books from first-time authors; 95% from unagented writers. Pays 10% royalty.** Publishes book 9-12 months after acceptance of ms. Accepts simultaneous submissions. Responds in 1 month to queries; 2 months to proposals; 3 months to mss. Book catalog and ms guidelines online.

Nonfiction How-to, self-help, textbook. Subjects include psychology, holistic health/medicine, metaphysics/

spirituality. "We are looking for textbooks and self-help, how-to books with a holistic health or transpersonal orientation." Query by e-mail, then submit TOC with 2 sample chapters. Reviews artwork/photos as part of ms package. Send photocopies.

Recent Title(s) *Script Magic (revised edition): A Hypnotherapist's Desk Reference*, by Dr. Allen Chips, Henry Bolduc, and Dr. Masud Ansari; *Life Patterns: Soul Lessons & Forgiveness*, by Henry Bolduc; *Alive & Well: Edgar Cayce's Healthcare Wisdom*, by Bette Margolis.

Tips Audience is people desiring to learn about body-mind-soul-oriented practices or self-help concepts that lead to healing and/or enlightenment. "The best authors are engaged in regular travel and seminars/workshops demonstrating dedication, self-motivation, and a people orientation. We specialize in buying rights or sharing rights with self-published authors, or authors seeking a publisher for their backlisted or out-of-print titles that are within our genre."

UNIVERSITY PUBLISHING CO.

P.O. Box 7038, Berkeley CA 94707. E-mail: unipub@earthlink.net. Website: home.earthlink.net/~unipub/index.html. **Acquisitions:** Elizabeth Kay (screenwriting, media, fiction); Robert Allred (survivor's guide, how-to, fiction). 326 15th St., Oakland CA 94612. (510)262-9333. Publishes trade paperback and mass market paperback originals. **Publishes 1-4 titles/year. Receives 80 queries and 30 mss/year. 50% of books from first-time authors; 33% from unagented writers. Pays 7.5-12.5% royalty. Offers $500 + advance.** Publishes book 18 months after acceptance of ms. Accepts simultaneous submissions. Responds in 1 month to queries; 1 month to proposals; 1 month to mss. Ms guidelines for #10 SASE.

Nonfiction How-to, self-help, textbook. Subjects include business/economics, cooking/foods/nutrition, education, government/politics, history, hobbies, military/war, nature/environment, science, spirituality. "Open to almost any good writing." Submit proposal package including outline, first 50 pages, cover letter, SASE.

Fiction Erotica, ethnic, fantasy, historical, horror, humor, literary, mainstream/contemporary, military/war, mystery, occult, religious, romance, science fiction, suspense, western. Submit proposal package including outline, synopsis, first 50 pages, cover letter, SASE.

Recent Title(s) *Infantry Weapons of the Vietnam War*, by Sun Lee (military history).

UNSEENPRESS.COM, INC.

P.O. Box 687, Westfield IN 46074. (317)840-6456. E-mail: editor@unseenpress.com. Website: www.unseenpress.com. **Acquisitions:** Nicole Kobrowski, editor (true paranormal, anything related to ghost hunting); Michael Kobrowski, editor (paranormal general). Estab. 2001. Publishes hardcover, trade paperback, mass market paperback, and electronic originals. **Publishes 2-5 titles/year. 10% of books from first-time authors; 100% from unagented writers. Outright purchase negotiated (see guidelines).** Publishes book 6-12 months after acceptance of ms. Responds in 1 month to queries; 2 months to proposals; 2 months to mss. Book catalog online; ms guidelines by e-mail.

Nonfiction Audiocassettes, multimedia, reference. Subjects include general nonfiction, Paranormal. "We are looking for true stories with a history and some sort of theory behind them that can be somewhat substantiated or at least accepted because of some sort of evidence. We are looking for well-written articles for our website/newsletter and magazine (2003) about ghost hunting. Anything with an international slant is very desirable." Query with SASE, or submit outline/proposal, 3 sample chapter(s). Reviews artwork/photos as part of ms package. Digital images, if requested. For queries, please state availability.

Recent Title(s) *Ghosts of Hamilton County, Indiana*, by Nicole Kobrowski (true experiences); *The Definitive Ghost Hunters Guide to Investigations*, by Nicole Kobrowski (reference).

Tips "True stories which make the readers feel as though they are there with the author. Our readers prefer a good dose of history and ghost experiences versus blood and guts." "Review our website and guidelines first. Tailor your submission accordingly. Do not send anything similar to a campfire story. Legends must have some history behind them and a connection to present experiences."

VANDERWYK & BURNHAM

P.O. Box 2789, Acton MA 01720. (978)263-7595. Fax: (978)263-0696. Website: www.vandb.com. **Acquisitions:** Meredith Rutter, publisher. Publishes hardcover and trade paperback originals. **Publishes 1-3 titles/year. Pays royalty on retail price. Offers $500-2,000 advance.** Accepts simultaneous submissions. Responds in 3 months to queries. Ms guidelines online.

Nonfiction Subjects include psychology, narrative nonfiction, contemporary issues, aging. "We publish books that make a difference in people's lives, including motivational books about admirable people and programs, and self-help books for people 50 and over." Query with SASE, or submit proposal package including résumé, publishing history, synopsis.

Recent Title(s) *Are Your Parents Driving You Crazy? How to Resolve the Most Common Dilemmas with Aging Parents*; *Sisters and Brothers All These Years: Taking Another Look at the Longest Relationship in Your Life*.

VISIONS COMMUNICATIONS

200 E. 10th St., #714, New York NY 10003. (212)529-4029. Fax: (212)529-4029. E-mail: bayeun@aol.com. **Acquisitions:** Beth Bay. Estab. 1994. Visions specializes in trade and reference books. Publishes hardcover originals and paperback originals and reprints. **Publishes 5 titles/year. Pays 5-20% royalty on retail price.** Publishes book 6 months after acceptance of ms. Responds in 1 month to queries; 3 months to mss. Ms guidelines free.

Nonfiction Children's/juvenile, how-to, reference, self-help, technical, textbook. Subjects include art/architecture, business/economics, health/medicine, psychology, religion, science, women's issues/studies, scholarly, engineering. Submit proposal package including outline, 3 sample chapter(s).

Recent Title(s) *Illuminating Engineering*, by Joseph Murdoch; *Restructuring Electricity Markets*, by Charles Cichetti.

VITESSE PRESS

PMB 367, 45 State St., Montpelier VT 05601-2100. (802)229-4243. Fax: (802)229-6939. E-mail: dick@vitessepress.com. Website: www.vitessepress.com. **Acquisitions:** Richard H. Mansfield, editor. Estab. 1985. Publishes trade paperback originals. **Publishes 2 titles/year. Pays 10% royalty on net receipts.** Does not accept simultaneous submissions. Responds in 1 month to queries.

Nonfiction How-to, technical, recreation. Subjects include health/medicine, regional (mountain biking guides), sports. Especially interested in cycling-related books.

Recent Title(s) *Bicycle Touring Made Easy*, by Lise Krieger.

WAYFINDER PRESS

P.O. Box 217, Ridgway CO 81432-0217. (970)626-5452. **Acquisitions:** Marcus E. Wilson, owner. Estab. 1980. Publishes trade paperback originals. **Publishes 2 titles/year. Pays 8-10% royalty on retail price.** Does not accept simultaneous submissions. Responds in 1 month to queries.

Nonfiction Illustrated book, reference. Subjects include Americana, government/politics, history, nature/environment, photography, recreation, regional, travel. "We are looking for books on western Colorado: history, nature, recreation, photo, and travel. No books on subjects outside our geographical area of specialization." Query with SASE, or submit outline, sample chapter(s). Reviews artwork/photos as part of ms package.

Recent Title(s) *Ouray—Chief of the Utes*, P. David Smith.

Tips "Writers have the best chance selling us tourist-oriented books. Our audience is the local population and tourists."

WESTERN NEW YORK WARES INC.

P.O. Box 733, Ellicott Station, Buffalo NY 14205. (716)832-6088. E-mail: info@wnybooks.com. Website: www.buffalobooks.com. **Acquisitions:** Brian S. Meyer, publisher (regional history); Tom Connolly, marketing manager (sports, regional travel). Publishes trade paperback originals. **Publishes 3 titles/year. Pays 50% royalty on net receipts.** Publishes book 1 year after acceptance of ms. Accepts simultaneous submissions. Responds in 6 weeks to queries. Book catalog for free or on website; ms guidelines online.

Nonfiction Only regional nonfiction topics that focus on Western New York (Buffalo, Niagra Falls, Chautauqua, Allegany). Subjects include art/architecture, history, photography, travel. No fiction. Query with SASE.

Recent Title(s) *Game Night in Buffalo: A Town, Its Teams, Its Sporting Memories*, by Sal Maiorana; *Goat Island: Niagra's Scenic Retreat*, by Paul Gromosiak.

WHITFORD PRESS

Imprint of Schiffer Publishing, Ltd., 4880 Lower Valley Rd., Atglen PA 19310. (610)593-1777. **Acquisitions:** Ellen Taylor, managing editor. Estab. 1985. Publishes trade paperback originals. **Publishes 1-3 titles/year. Pays royalty on wholesale price.** Does not accept simultaneous submissions. Responds in 2 months to queries. Book catalog free.

Nonfiction How-to, reference, self-help. Subjects include New Age. "We are looking for well-written, well-organized, original books on all metaphysical subjects (except channeling and past lives). Books that empower the reader or show him/her ways to develop personal skills are preferred. New approaches, techniques, or concepts are best. No personal accounts unless they directly relate to a general audience. No moralistic, fatalistic, sexist, or strictly philosophical books." Query with SASE, or submit outline.

Tips "Our audience is knowledgeable in metaphysical fields, well read and progressive in thinking. Please check bookstores to see if your subject has already been covered thoroughly. Expertise in the field is not enough; your book must be clean, well written and well organized. A specific and unique marketing angle is a plus. No Sun-sign material; we prefer more advanced work. Please don't send entire manuscript unless we request it, and be sure to include a SASE. Let us know if the book is available on computer diskette and what type of hardware/software. Manuscripts should be between 60,000 and 110,000 words."

WOLF DEN BOOKS

5783 S.W. 40th St., #221, Miami FL 33155. E-mail: info@wolfdenbooks.com. Website: www.wolfdenbooks.com. **Acquisitions:** Gail Shivel (literary criticism); S.L. Harrison (journalism, history, political science). Estab. 2000. Publishes hardcover, trade paperback and electronic originals and reprints. **Publishes 3 titles/year. Receives 6 queries and 3 mss/year. 100% from unagented writers. Pays 5-7.5% royalty on retail price.** Publishes book 1 year after acceptance of ms. Accepts simultaneous submissions. Book catalog online; ms guidelines by e-mail.
• Do not send postage; mss are not returned.
Nonfiction Reference, scholarly, textbook. Subjects include general nonfiction, history, language/literature, political science, literary biography. "Thoughtful, idea-rich, factual, common sense prose is sought in the areas of literary criticism, political science, history and journalism." Submit complete ms. Reviews artwork/photos as part of ms package. Send photocopies.
Recent Title(s) *a.k.a. H. L. Mencken: Pseudonymous Writings*, by H.L. Mencken; *Cavalcade of Journalists, 1900-2000*, by S.L. Harrison (reference); *Criticism: The Major Texts*, edited by W.J. Bate (literary criticism text).

N WOODFIELD PRESS

2820 Los Tomases Dr. NW, Albuquerque NM 87107-1240. (505)342-1724. E-mail: hfried@hfried.com. Website: woodfieldpress.com. **Acquisitions:** Howard J. Fried, partner. Publishes hardcover, trade paperback and mass market paperback originals. **Publishes 2 titles/year. Pays 15% royalty on wholesale price.** Publishes book 4 months after acceptance of ms. Responds in 1 month to queries; 1 month to proposals; 1 month to mss. Book catalog for #10 SASE or online.
Nonfiction Biography, children's/juvenile. Subjects include aviation, biography. Query with SASE, or submit proposal package including outline, or submit complete ms.
Recent Title(s) *More Eye of Experience*, by Fried; *Still More Eye of Experience*, by Fried; *Biography of Fay Gillis Wells*.

N WORD WARRIORS PRESS

920 Blackoaks Lane, Anoka MN 55303. E-mail: gail@wordwarriorspress.com. Website: www.wordwarriorspress.com. **Acquisitions:** Gail Cerridwen, managing editor (memoir, essays, journals). Estab. 2003. Publishes trade paperback originals. **Publishes 2-4 titles/year. 100% of books from first-time authors; 100% from unagented writers. Pays 6-12% royalty on retail price.** Publishes book 6 months after acceptance of ms. Accepts simultaneous submissions. Responds in 1 month to queries; 1 month to proposals; 2 months to mss. Ms guidelines online.
Nonfiction Subjects include creative nonfiction, ethnic, gay/lesbian, memoirs, multicultural, women's issues/studies. "We publish only authors in their 20s or late teens, especially those people and stories not well represented in mainstream publishing. We're looking for edgy, uncensored material with a strong voice. Currently we are seeking manuscripts in Spanish and English (alternating pages), or Spanglish, as well as memoirs from prisoners and the homeless." Submit 2 sample chapter(s). Reviews artwork/photos as part of ms package. Send photocopies.
Recent Title(s) *Yesterday's Warrior: A Memoir*, by Heather Harrison.

WORLD LEISURE

P.O. Box 160, Hampstead NH 03841. (617)569-1966. Fax: (603)947-0838. E-mail: admin@worldleisure.com. Website: www.worldleisure.com. **Acquisitions:** Charles Leocha, president. Estab. 1977. Publishes trade paperback originals. **Publishes 3-5 titles/year. Pays royalty, or makes outright purchase.** Accepts simultaneous submissions. Responds in 2 months to queries. Book catalog and ms guidelines online.
➤ World Leisure specializes in travel books, activity guidebooks, and self-help titles.
Nonfiction Self-help. Subjects include recreation, sports (skiing/snowboarding), travel. "We will be publishing annual updates to *Ski Snowboard Europe* and *Ski Snowboard America & Canada*. Writers planning any winter resort stories should contact us for possible add-on assignments at areas not covered by our staff." Submit outline, intro sample chapter(s), annotated table of contents, SASE.
Recent Title(s) *Ski Snowboard America and Canada*, by Charles Leocha; *Ski Snowboard Europe*, by Charles Leocha.

Consumer Magazines

Selling your writing to consumer magazines is as much an exercise of your marketing skills as it is of your writing abilities. Editors of consumer magazines are looking not only for good writing, but for good writing which communicates pertinent information to a specific audience—their readers.

Approaching the consumer magazine market

Marketing skills will help you successfully discern a magazine's editorial slant, and write queries and articles that prove your knowledge of the magazine's readership. You can gather clues about a magazine's readership—and establish your credibility with the magazine's editor—in a number of ways:

- **Read** the magazine's listing in *Writer's Market*.
- **Study** a magazine's writer's guidelines.
- **Check** a magazine's website.
- **Read** several current issues of the target magazine.
- **Talk** to an editor by phone.

Writers who can correctly and consistently discern a publication's audience and deliver stories that speak to that target readership will win out every time over writers who simply write what they write and send it where they will.

What editors want

In nonfiction, editors continue to look for short feature articles covering specialized topics. Editors want crisp writing and expertise. If you are not an expert in the area about which you are writing, make yourself one through research. Always query before sending your manuscript. Don't e-mail or fax a query unless an editor specifically mentions openness to this in the listing.

Fiction editors prefer to receive complete manuscripts. Writers must keep in mind that marketing fiction is competitive, and editors receive far more material than they can publish. For this reason, they often do not respond to submissions unless they are interested in using the story. More comprehensive information on fiction markets can be found in *Novel & Short Story Writer's Market* (Writer's Digest Books).

Payment

Most magazines listed here have indicated pay rates; some give very specific payment-per-word rates, while others state a range. **(Note: All of the magazines listed in the Consumer**

Magazines section are paying markets. However, some of the magazines are not identified by payment icons (**$–$ $ $ $**) because the magazines preferred not to disclose
specific payment information.) Any agreement you come to with a magazine, whether
verbal or written, should specify the payment you are to receive and when you are to receive
it. Some magazines pay writers only after the piece in question has been published (on
publication). Others pay as soon as they have accepted a piece and are sure they are going
to use it (on acceptance). In *Writer's Market*, those magazines that pay on acceptance have
been highlighted with the phrase **pays on acceptance** set in bold type.

So what is a good pay rate? There are no standards; the principle of supply and demand
operates at full throttle in the business of writing and publishing. As long as there are more
writers than opportunities for publication, wages for freelancers will never skyrocket. Rates
vary widely from one market to the next. Smaller circulation magazines and some departments of the larger magazines will pay a lower rate.

Editors know that the listings in *Writer's Market* are read and used by writers with a wide
range of experience, from those as-yet unpublished writers just starting out, to those with a
successful, profitable freelance career. As a result, many magazines publicly report pay rates
in the lower end of their actual pay ranges. Experienced writers will be able to successfully
negotiate higher pay rates for their material. Newer writers should be encouraged that as
their reputation grows (along with their clip file), they will be able to command higher rates.
The article "How Much Should I Charge?" on page 71, gives you an idea of pay ranges for
different freelance jobs, including those directly associated with magazines.

INFORMATION AT-A-GLANCE

In the Consumer Magazine section, icons identify comparative payment rates (**$–
$ $ $ $**); new listings (**N**); and magazines that do not accept unsolicited manuscripts
(**⊘**). Different sections of *Writer's Market* include other symbols; check the inside back
cover for an explanation of all the symbols used throughout the book.

Important information is highlighted in boldface—the "quick facts" you won't find in any
other market book, but should know before you submit your work. The word **Contact** identifies the appropriate person to query at each magazine. We also highlight what percentage of
the magazine is freelance written; how many manuscripts a magazine buys per year of nonfiction, fiction, poetry, and fillers; and respective pay rates in each category.

**Information on publications listed in the previous edition of *Writer's Market*, but not
included in this edition, can be found in the General Index.**

ANIMAL

⊠ $ $ AKC GAZETTE

American Kennel Club, 260 Madison Ave., New York NY 10016. Fax: (212)696-8239. E-mail: gazette@akc.org. Website: www.akc.org/pubs/gazette_toc.cfm. **Contact:** Erika Mansourian. **85% freelance written.** Monthly magazine. "Geared to interests of fanciers of purebred dogs as opposed to commercial interests or pet owners. We require solid expertise from our contributors—we are *not* a pet magazine." Estab. 1889. Circ. 60,000. Pays on publication. Publishes ms an average of 6 months after acceptance. Byline given. Offers 10% kill fee. Buys first North American serial, electronic, international rights. Submit seasonal material 6 months in advance. Accepts queries by mail. Responds in 2 months to queries. Sample copy not available. Writer's guidelines for #10 SASE.

Nonfiction General interest, how-to, humor, interview/profile, photo feature, travel, dog art, training and canine performance sports. No poetry, tributes to individual dogs or fiction. **Buys 30-40 mss/year.** Length: 1,000-3,000 words. **Pays $300-500.** Pays expenses of writers on assignment.

Photos Photo contest guidelines for #10 SASE. State availability with submission. Reviews color transparencies, prints. Buys one-time rights. Pays $50-200/photo. Captions, identification of subjects, model releases required.

Fiction Annual short fiction contest only. Guidelines for #10 SASE.

Tips "Contributors should be involved in the dog fancy or expert in area they write about (veterinary, showing, field trialing, obedience training, dogs in legislation, dog art or history or literature). All submissions are welcome but author must be a credible expert or be able to interview and quote the experts. Veterinary articles must be written by or with veterinarians. Humorous features or personal experiences relative to purebred dogs that have broader applications. For features generally, know the subject thoroughly and be conversant with jargon peculiar to the sport of dogs."

$ $ APPALOOSA JOURNAL

Appaloosa Horse Club, 2720 West Pullman Rd., Moscow ID 83843-0903. (208)882-5578. Fax: (208)882-8150. E-mail: journal@appaloosa.com. Website: www.appaloosajournal.com. **Contact:** Robin Hendrickson, editor. **40% freelance written.** Monthly magazine covering Appaloosa horses. Estab. 1946. Circ. 25,000. Pays on publication. Publishes ms an average of 3 months after acceptance. Byline given. Buys first North American serial, electronic rights. Responds in 1 month to queries; 2 months to mss. Sample copy for free. Writer's guidelines online.

• *Appaloosa Journal* no longer accepts material for columns.

Nonfiction Historical/nostalgic, interview/profile, photo feature. **Buys 15-20 mss/year.** Query with or without published clips or send complete ms. Length: 800-2,000 words. **Pays $150-400.**

Photos Send photos with submission. Payment varies. Captions, identification of subjects required.

   ◼ The online magazine carries original content not found in the print edition. Contact: Michelle Anderson, online editor.

Tips "Articles by writers with horse knowledge, news sense, and photography skills are in great demand. If it's a strong article about an Appaloosa, the writer has a pretty good chance of publication. A good understanding of the breed and the industry, breeders, and owners is helpful. Make sure there's some substance and a unique twist."

⊠ $ $ AQUARIUM FISH MAGAZINE

Fishkeeping—the Art and the Science, Bowtie, Inc., P.O. Box 6050, Mission Viejo CA 92690. Fax: (949)855-3045. E-mail: aquariumfish@fancypubs.com. Website: www.aquariumfish.com. Editor: Russ Case. Managing Editor: Patricia Knight. **Contact:** Dave Cravotta, associate editor. **90% freelance written.** Monthly magazine covering keeping fish and other aquatic pets. "Our focus is on beginning and intermediate fish keeping. Most of our articles concentrate on general fish and aquarium care, but we will also consider other types of articles that may be helpful to those in the fishkeeping hobby. Freshwater and salt-water tanks, and ponds are covered." Estab. 1988. Pays on publication. Publishes ms an average of 6+ months after acceptance. Byline given. Buys first North American serial, electronic rights. Accepts queries by mail, e-mail, fax. Responds in 1 month to queries; 6 months to mss. Writer's guidelines for #10 SASE.

Nonfiction General interest (species profiles, natural history with home care info), interview/profile (of well-known people in fish keeping), new product (press releases only for Product Showcase section), photo feature, caring for fish in aquariums. Special issues: "We do have two annuals; freelancers should query." No fiction, anthropomorphism, articles on sport fishing, or animals that cannot be kept as pets (e.g., whales, dolphins, manatees, etc.). **Buys 60 mss/year.** Query with or without published clips or send complete ms. Length: 1,500-3,000 words. **Pays 10¢/word.**

Photos State availability with submission. Reviews 35mm transparencies, 4×5 prints. Buys first North American serial rights. Offers $15-200/photo. Identification of subjects required.

Fillers Facts, gags to be illustrated by cartoonist, newsbreaks. **Buys variable number/year.** Length: 50-200 words.

Tips "Take a look at our guidelines before submitting. Writers are not required to provide photos for submitted articles, but we do encourage it, if possible. It helps if writers are involved in fish keeping themselves. Our writers tend to be experienced fish keepers, detailed researchers, and some scientists."

$ $ CAT FANCY

Cat Care for the Responsible Owner, Fancy Publications, Inc., P.O. Box 6050, Mission Viejo CA 92690. (949)855-8822. E-mail: query@fancypubs.com. Website: www.catfancy.com. **Contact:** Susan Logan, editor. **90% freelance written.** Monthly magazine covering all aspects of responsible cat ownership. Estab. 1965. Pays on publication. Buys first North American serial rights. Editorial lead time 6 months. Responds in 3 months to queries. Writer's guidelines online.

• *Cat Fancy* does not accept unsolicited mss.

Nonfiction Engaging presentation of expert, up-to-date information. Must be cat oriented. No unsolicited mss. Writing should not be gender specific. How-to, humor, photo feature, travel, behavior, health, lifestyle, cat culture, entertainment. **Buys 70 mss/year.** Query with published clips. Length: 1,000-2,000 words. **Pays $50-450.**

Photos Seeking photos of happy, healthy, well-groomed cats and kittens in studio or indoor settings. Buys one-time rights. Negotiates payment individually. Captions, identification of subjects, model releases required.

Columns/Departments Most of our columns are written by regular contributors who are recognized experts in their fields.

Tips "No fiction or poetry. Please read recent issues to become acquainted with our style and content. Show us in your query how you can contribute something new and unique. No phone queries."

$ $ CATS USA

Guide to Buying and Caring for Purebred Kittens, Fancy Publications, Inc., P.O. Box 6050, Mission Viejo CA 92690. (949)855-8822. **Contact:** Editor. **90% freelance written.** Annual publication for purebred kitten buyers. Estab. 1993. Pays on publication. Buys first North American serial rights. Editorial lead time 6 months. Responds in 3 months to queries. Sample copy not available. Writer's guidelines for #10 SASE.

Nonfiction Healthcare, training, breed information. **Buys 20 mss/year.** Query with published clips. Length: 1,000-2,000 words. **Pays $50-450.**

Photos Looking for happy, healthy, well-groomed purebred cats and kittens in studio or indoor settings. Guidelines for #10 SASE. Buys one-time rights. Negotiates payment individually. Captions, identification of subjects, model releases required.

Tips "No fiction or poetry. Please read a recent issue to become acquainted with our style and content. Show us in your query how you can contribute something new and unique. No phone queries."

$ $ THE CHRONICLE OF THE HORSE

P.O. Box 46, Middleburg VA 20118-0046. (540)687-6341. Fax: (540)687-3937. E-mail: staff@chronofhorse.com. Website: www.chronofhorse.com. Editor: John Strassburger. Managing Editor: Trisha Booker. **Contact:** Beth Rasin, assistant editor. **80% freelance written.** Weekly magazine covering horses. "We cover English riding sports, including horse showing, grand prix jumping competitions, steeplechase racing, foxhunting, dressage, endurance riding, handicapped riding and combined training. We are the official publication for the national governing bodies of many of the above sports. We feature news, how-to articles on equitation and horse care and interviews with leaders in the various fields." Estab. 1937. Circ. 22,000. Pays for features on acceptance; news and other items on publication. Publishes ms an average of 4 months after acceptance. Byline given. Buys first North American serial rights, makes work-for-hire assignments. Submit seasonal material 3 months in advance. Accepts queries by mail, e-mail. Responds in 5-6 weeks to queries. Sample copy for $2 and 9×12 SAE. Writer's guidelines online.

O─ Break in by "clearing a small news assignment in your area ahead of time."

Nonfiction General interest, historical/nostalgic (history of breeds, use of horses in other countries and times, art, etc.), how-to (trailer, train, design a course, save money, etc.), humor (centered on living with horses or horse people), interview/profile (of nationally known horsemen or the very unusual), technical (horse care, articles on feeding, injuries, care of foals, shoeing, etc.). Special issues: Steeplechase Racing (January); American Horse in Sport and Grand Prix Jumping (February); Horse Show (March); Intercollegiate (April); Kentucky 4-Star Preview (April); Junior and Pony (April); Dressage (June); Horse Care (July); Combined Training (August); Hunt Roster (September); Amateur (November); Stallion (December). No Q&A interviews, clinic reports, Western riding articles, personal experience or wild horses. **Buys 300 mss/year.** Query with or without published clips or send complete ms. Length: 6-7 pages. **Pays $150-250.**

Photos State availability with submission. Reviews prints or color slides; accepts color for b&w reproduction. Buys one-time rights. Pays $25-30. Identification of subjects required.

Columns/Departments Dressage, Combined Training, Horse Show, Horse Care, Racing over Fences, Young Entry (about young riders, geared for youth), Horses and Humanities, Hunting, Vaulting, Handicapped Riding, Trail Riding, 1,000-1,225 words; News of major competitions ("clear assignment with us first"), 1,500 words. Query with or without published clips or send complete ms. **Pays $25-200**.

▣ The online magazine carries original content not found in the print edition and includes writer's guidelines. Contact: Melinda Goslin, online editor.

Tips "Get our guidelines. Our readers are sophisticated, competitive horsemen. Articles need to go beyond common knowledge. Freelancers often attempt too broad or too basic a subject. We welcome well-written news stories on major events, but clear the assignment with us."

Ⓝ $ COONHOUND BLOODLINES

The Complete Magazine for the Houndsman and Coon Hunter, United Kennel Club, Inc., 100 E. Kilgore Rd., Kalamazoo MI 49002-5584. (269)343-9020. Fax: (269)343-7037. E-mail: vrand@ukcdogs.com. Website: www.ukcdogs.com. **Contact:** Vicki Rand, editor. **40% freelance written.** Monthly magazine covering all aspects of the 6 Coonhound dog breeds. "Writers must retain the 'slang' particular to dog people and to our readers—many of whom are from the South." Estab. 1925. Circ. 16,000. Pays on publication. Publishes ms an average of 6 months after acceptance. Byline given. Buys first North American serial rights, makes work-for-hire assignments. Editorial lead time 6 months. Submit seasonal material 6 months in advance. Accepts queries by mail, e-mail, fax, phone. Accepts simultaneous submissions. Responds in 6 weeks to queries. Sample copy for $4.50. Writer's guidelines not available.

Nonfiction General interest, historical/nostalgic, humor, interview/profile, new product, personal experience, photo feature, breed-specific. Special issues: Six of our 12 issues are each devoted to a specific breed of Coonhound. Treeing Walker (February); English (March); Black & Tan (April); Bluetick (May); Redbone (June); Plott Hound (July), 1,000-3,000 words and photos. **Buys 12-36 mss/year.** Query. Length: 1,000-5,000 words. **Pays $100.** Sometimes pays expenses of writers on assignment.

Photos State availability with submission. Reviews contact sheets. Buys one-time rights. Negotiates payment individually. Captions, identification of subjects required.

Columns/Departments Buys 6-12 mss/year. Pays $100.

Fiction Must be about the Coonhound breeds or hunting with hounds. Adventure, historical, humorous, mystery. **Buys 3-6 mss/year.** Query. Length: 1,000-3,000 words. **Pays $100.**

Tips "Hunting with hounds is a two-century old American tradition and an important part of the American heritage, especially east of the Mississippi. It covers a lifestyle as well as a wonderful segment of the American population, many of whom still live by honest, friendly values."

$ $ DOG FANCY

Fancy Publications, Inc., P.O. Box 6050, Mission Viejo CA 92690-6050. Fax: (949)855-3045. E-mail: dogfancy@fancypubs.com. Website: www.dogfancy.com. **Contact:** Maureen Kochan, editor. **95% freelance written.** Monthly magazine for men and women of all ages interested in all phases of dog ownership. Estab. 1970. Circ. 250,000. Pays on publication. Publishes ms an average of 6 months after acceptance. Byline given. Offers negotiable kill fee. Buys first North American serial, nonexclusive electronic and other rights. Submit seasonal material 6 months in advance. Accepts queries by mail. Responds in 2 months to queries. Sample copy for $5.50. Writer's guidelines online.

Nonfiction Book excerpts, general interest, how-to, humor, inspirational, interview/profile, personal experience, photo feature, travel. "No stories written from a dog's point of view." **Buys 100 mss/year.** Query. Length: 850-1,500 words. **Pays $200-500.**

Photos State availability with submission. Reviews contact sheets, transparencies, prints. Buys electronic rights. Offers no additional payment for photos accepted with ms.

Columns/Departments Health and Medicine, 600-700 words; Training and Behavior, 800 words. **Buys 24 mss/year.** Query by mail only. **Pays $300-400.**

Tips "We're looking for the unique experience that enhances the dog/owner relationship—with the dog as the focus of the story, not the owner. Medical articles are assigned to veterinarians. Note that we write for a lay audience (nontechnical), but we do assume a certain level of intelligence. Read the magazine before making a pitch. Make sure your query is clear, concise, and relevant."

DOG WORLD

3 Burroughs, Irvine CA 92618. Website: www.dogworldmag.com. **Contact:** Maureen Kochan, editor. **95% freelance written.** Monthly magazine covering dogs. "We write for the serious dog enthusiast and participant, including breeders, veterinarians, exhibitors, groomers, agility competitors, etc., as well as a general audience

interested in in-depth information about dogs." Estab. 1915. Circ. 58,000. Pays on publication. Byline given. Buys exclusive worldwide print rights for six months and nonexclusive electronic rights. Editorial lead time 6 months. Submit seasonal material 6 months in advance. Accepts queries by mail. Responds in 3 months to queries. Writer's guidelines for #10 SASE.

Nonfiction General interest (on dogs including health care, veterinary medicine, grooming, legislation, responsible ownership, obedience training, kennel operations, dog sports, breed spotlights and histories), new product. No fluffy poems or pieces about dogs. **Buys approximately 50 mss/year.** Query by mail only with SASE. Query should include a list of points the story will cover and a list of experts the writer plans to interview. Length: 2,000-2,500 words. **Pays negotiable rate.** Sometimes pays expenses of writers on assignment.

Photos State availability with submission. Buys one-time rights. Offers no additional payment for photos accepted with ms; negotiates payment individually for professional photos. Current rate for cover photo is $500; inside color photo $50-175; b&w $25-50, depending on size used. Payment on publication.

Tips "Get a copy of the magazine and our writer's guidelines. Stories should cover a very narrowly focused topic in great depth. Be able to translate technical and medical articles into language the average reader can understand. Be ready to quote experts through live interviews."

$ $ EQUESTRIAN MAGAZINE

The Official Magazine of Equestrian Sport Since 1937, United States Equestrian Federation (USEF), 4047 Iron Works Parkway, Lexington KY 40511. (859)225-6923. Fax: (859)231-6662. E-mail: bsosby@usef.org. Website: www.usef.org. **Contact:** Brian Sosby, managing editor. **10-30% freelance written.** Magazine published 10 times/year covering the equestrian sport. Estab. 1937. Circ. 77,000. Pays on publication. Byline given. Offers 50% kill fee. Buys first North American serial, first rights. Editorial lead time 1-5 months. Accepts queries by mail, e-mail, fax, phone. Sample copy and writer's guidelines free.

Nonfiction Interview/profile, technical, all equestrian-related. **Buys 20-30 mss/year.** Query with published clips. Length: 500-3,500 words. **Pays $200-500.**

Photos State availability with submission. Reviews contact sheets. Buys one-time rights. Offers $50-200/photo. Captions, identification of subjects, model releases required.

Columns/Departments Horses of the Past (famous equines); Horse People (famous horsemen/women), both 500-1,000 words. **Buys 20-30 mss/year.** Query with published clips. **Pays $100.**

Tips "Write via e-mail in first instance with samples, résumé, then mail original clips."

$ EQUINE JOURNAL

103 Roxbury St., Keene NH 03431-8801. (603)357-4271. Fax: (603)357-7851. E-mail: editorial@equinejournal.com. Website: www.equinejournal.com. **Contact:** Kathleen Labonville, managing editor. **90% freelance written.** Monthly tabloid covering horses—all breeds, all disciplines. "To educate, entertain, and enable amateurs and professionals alike to stay on top of new developments in the field. Covers horse-related activities from all corners of New England, New York, New Jersey, Pennsylvania, and the Midwest." Estab. 1988. Circ. 26,000. Pays on publication. Byline given. Buys first North American serial, electronic rights. Editorial lead time 3 months. Submit seasonal material 4 months in advance. Accepts queries by mail, e-mail, fax, phone. Responds in 2 months to queries. Writer's guidelines online.

Nonfiction General interest, how-to, interview/profile. **Buys 100 mss/year.** Query with published clips or send complete ms. Length: 1,500-3,000 words.

Photos Send photos with submission. Reviews prints. Pays $10.

Columns/Departments Horse Health (health-related topics), 1,200-1,500 words. **Buys 12 mss/year.** Query.

Fillers Short humor. Length: 500-1,000 words. **Pays $40-75.**

EQUUS

Primedia Enthusiast Group, 656 Quince Orchard Rd., Suite 600, Gaithersburg MD 20878-1409. (301)977-3900. Fax: (301)990-9015. E-mail: equuslts@aol.com. Website: www.equisearch.com. Editor: Laurie Prinz. Monthly magazine covering equine behavior. Provides the latest information from the world's top veternarians, equine researchers, riders and trainers. Circ. 149,482. Sample copy not available.

$ $ FIELD TRIAL MAGAZINE

Androscoggin Publishing, Inc., P.O. Box 298, Milan NH 03588-0098. (617)449-6767. Fax: (603)449-2462. E-mail: birddog@ncia.net. Website: www.fielddog.com/ftm. **Contact:** Craig Doherty, editor. **75% freelance written.** Quarterly magazine covering field trials for pointing dogs. "Our readers are knowledgeable sports men and women who want interesting and informative articles about their sport." Estab. 1997. Circ. 6,000. Pays on publication. Publishes ms an average of 6 months after acceptance. Byline given. Buys first North American serial rights. Editorial lead time 3 months. Submit seasonal material 6 months in advance. Accepts queries by mail, e-mail, fax. Accepts simultaneous submissions. Responds in 2 weeks to queries; 2 months to mss. Sample copy free or online. Writer's guidelines online.

Nonfiction Book excerpts, essays, general interest, historical/nostalgic, how-to, interview/profile, opinion, personal experience. No hunting articles. **Buys 12-16 mss/year.** Query. Length: 1,000-3,000 words. **Pays $100-300.**

Photos Send photos with submission. Buys one-time rights. Offers no additional payment for photos accepted with ms. Captions, identification of subjects required.

Fiction Fiction that deals with bird dogs and field trials. **Buys 4 mss/year.** Send complete ms. Length: 1,000-2,500 words. **Pays $100-250.**

Tips "Make sure you have correct and accurate information—we'll work with a writer who has good solid info even if the writing needs work."

$ $ THE GAITED HORSE

The One Magazine for All Gaited Horses, P.O. Box 3070, Deer Park WA 99006-3070. Phone/Fax: (509)276-4930. E-mail: tgheditor@thegaitedhorse.com. Website: www.thegaitedhorse.com. **Contact:** Rhonda Hart Poe, editor. Quarterly magazine. "Subject matter must relate in some way to gaited horses." Estab. 1998. Circ. 15,000. Pays on publication. Publishes ms an average of 2 months after acceptance. Byline given. Buys first North American serial rights, makes work-for-hire assignments. Editorial lead time 4 months. Submit seasonal material 4 months in advance. Accepts queries by mail, e-mail. Accepts simultaneous submissions. Responds in 6 weeks to queries; 1 month to mss. Sample copy for $3. Writer's guidelines online.

Nonfiction Wants anything related to gaited horses, lifestyles, art, etc. Book excerpts, essays, exposé, general interest (gaited horses), historical/nostalgic, how-to, humor, interview/profile, new product, personal experience, photo feature, travel. **Buys 25 mss/year.** Query or send complete ms. Length: 1,000-2,500 words. **Pays $50-300.**

Photos State availability of or send photos with submission. Reviews prints (3×5 or larger). Buys one-time rights. Negotiates payment individually. Captions, identification of subjects, model releases required.

Columns/Departments Legal Paces (equine owners rights & responsibilities); Horse Cents (financial advice for horse owners); Health Check (vet advice); Smoother Trails (trail riding), all 500-1,000 words. **Buys 24 mss/year.** Query. **Pays $100.**

Fillers Anecdotes, short humor, NewsBits. **Buys 20/year.** Length: 5-300 words. **Pays $10-50.**

Tips "We are actively seeking to develop writers from within the various gaited breeds and equine disciplines. If you have a unique perspective on these horses, we would love to hear from you. Submit a query that targets any aspect of gaited horses and you'll have my attention."

$ THE GREYHOUND REVIEW

P.O. Box 543, Abilene KS 67410-0543. (785)263-4660. Fax: (785)263-4689. E-mail: nga@ngagreyhounds.com. Website: www.ngagreyhounds.com. Editor: Gary Guccione. **Contact:** Tim Horan, managing editor. **20% freelance written.** Monthly magazine covering greyhound breeding, training and racing. Estab. 1911. Circ. 4,000. **Pays on acceptance.** Byline given. Buys first rights. Submit seasonal material 2 months in advance. Responds in 2 weeks to queries; 1 month to mss. Sample copy for $3. Writer's guidelines free.

Nonfiction "Articles must be targeted at the greyhound industry: from hard news, special events at racetracks to the latest medical discoveries." How-to, interview/profile, personal experience. Do not submit gambling systems. **Buys 24 mss/year.** Query. Length: 1,000-10,000 words. **Pays $85-150.**

Reprints Send photocopy. Pays 100% of amount paid for original article.

Photos State availability with submission. Reviews 35mm transparencies, 8×10 prints. Buys one-time rights. Pays $10-50 photo. Identification of subjects required.

$ ⬚ HORSE & COUNTRY CANADA

Equine Publications, Inc., 422 Kitley Line 3, Toledo ON K0E 1Y0, Canada. (613)275-1684. Fax: (613)275-1807. **Contact:** Editor. **40% freelance written.** Bimonthly magazine covering equestrian issues. "A celebration of equestrian sport and the country way of life." Estab. 1994. Circ. 14,000. Pays on publication. Publishes ms an average of 3 months after acceptance. Byline sometimes given. Buys one-time rights. Accepts queries by mail.

Nonfiction Book excerpts, historical/nostalgic, how-to, inspirational, new product, travel. Query with published clips. Length: 1,200-1,700 words. **Pays $25-150.** Sometimes pays expenses of writers on assignment.

Photos Send photos with submission. Reviews prints. Buys one-time rights. Pays $15-125/photo or negotiates payment individually. Captions required.

Columns/Departments Back to Basics (care for horses); Ask the Experts (how-to with horses); Nutrition (for horses), all 800 words. Query with published clips. **Pays $25-150.**

$ $ $ HORSE & RIDER

The Magazine of Western Riding, Primedia, 4101 International Parkway, Carrollton TX 75007. (972)309-5700. Fax: (972)309-5670. E-mail: horse&rider@primediamags.com. Website: www.horseandrider.com. **Contact:** Darrell Dodds, editor/associate publisher. **10% freelance written.** Monthly magazine covering Western horse industry, competition, recreation. "*Horse & Rider*'s mission is to educate, inform, and entertain both competitive and recreational riders with tightly focused training articles, practical stable management techniques, hands-on healthcare tips, safe trail-riding practices, well-researched consumer advice, and a behind-the-scenes, you-are-there approach to major equine events." Estab. 1961. Circ. 164,000. **Pays on acceptance.** Publishes ms an average of 1 year after acceptance. Byline given. Offers $75 kill fee. Buys first North American serial rights. Editorial lead time 2 months. Submit seasonal material 6 months in advance. Accepts queries by mail. Responds in 3 months to queries; 3 months to mss. Sample copy and writer's guidelines online.

- Does *not accept* e-mail submissions.

Nonfiction Book excerpts, general interest, how-to (horse training, horsemanship), humor, interview/profile, new product, personal experience, photo feature, travel, horse health care, trail riding. **Buys 5-10 mss/year.** Send complete ms. Length: 1,000-3,000 words. **Pays $150-1,000.**

Photos State availability of or send photos with submission. Buys rights on assignment or stock. Negotiates payment individually. Captions, identification of subjects, model releases required.

The online magazine carries original content not found in the print edition. Contact: Darrell Dodds.

Tips Writers should have "patience, ability to accept critical editing, and extensive knowledge of the Western horse industry and our publication."

$ $ HORSE ILLUSTRATED

The Magazine for Responsible Horse Owners, Fancy Publications, Inc., P.O. Box 6050, Mission Viejo CA 92690-6050. (949)855-8822. Fax: (949)855-3045. E-mail: horseillustrated@fancypubs.com. Website: www.horseillustrated.com. Managing Editor: Elizabeth Moyer. **Contact:** Moira Harris, editor. **90% freelance written.** Prefers to work with published/established writers but will work with new/unpublished writers. Monthly magazine covering all aspects of horse ownership. "Our readers are adults, mostly women, between the ages of 18 and 40; stories should be geared to that age group and reflect responsible horse care." Estab. 1976. Circ. 216,930. Pays on publication. Publishes ms an average of 8 months after acceptance. Byline given. Buys one-time rights, requires first North American rights among equine publications. Submit seasonal material 6 months in advance. Accepts queries by mail. Responds in 3 months to queries. Writer's guidelines for #10 SASE.

Nonfiction "We are looking for authoritative, in-depth features on trends and issues in the horse industry. Such articles must be queried first with a detailed outline of the article and clips. We rarely have a need for fiction." General interest, historical/nostalgic, how-to (horse care, training, veterinary care), inspirational, photo feature. No "little girl" horse stories, "cowboy and Indian" stories or anything not *directly* relating to horses. **Buys 20 mss/year.** Query or send complete ms. Length: 1,000-2,000 words. **Pays $100-400.**

Photos Send photos with submission. Reviews 35mm and medium format transparencies, 4×6 prints.

Tips "Freelancers can break in at this publication with feature articles on Western and English training methods; veterinary and general care how-to articles; and horse sports articles. We rarely use personal experience articles. Submit photos with training and how-to articles whenever possible. We have a very good record of developing new freelancers into regular contributors/columnists. We are always looking for fresh talent, but certainly enjoy working with established writers who 'know the ropes' as well. We are accepting less unsolicited freelance work—much is now assigned and contracted."

$ $ THE HORSE

Your Guide to Equine Health Care, P.O. Box 4680, Lexington KY 40544-4680. (859)276-6771. Fax: (859)276-4450. E-mail: kherbert@thehorse.com. Website: www.thehorse.com. Managing Editor: Christy West. **Contact:** Kimberly S. Herbert, editor. **85% freelance written.** Monthly magazine covering equine health and care. *The Horse* is an educational/news magazine geared toward the hands-on horse owner. Estab. 1983. Circ. 60,000. **Pays on acceptance.** Publishes ms an average of 6 months after acceptance. Byline given. Buys first world and electronic rights Accepts queries by mail, e-mail. Responds in 3 months to queries. Sample copy for $2.95 or online. Writer's guidelines online.

Break in with short horse health news items.

Nonfiction How-to, technical, topical interviews. "No first-person experiences not from professionals; this is a technical magazine to inform horse owners." **Buys 90 mss/year.** Query with published clips. Length: 250-4,000 words. **Pays $50-750 for assigned articles.**

Photos Send photos with submission. Reviews transparencies. $35-350. Captions, identification of subjects required.

Columns/Departments News Front (news on horse health), 100-500 words; Equinomics (economics of horse ownership); Step by Step (feet and leg care); Nutrition; Reproduction; Back to Basics, all 1,500-2,200 words. **Buys 50 mss/year.** Query with published clips. **Pays $50-400.**

⊞ The online magazine carries original content not found in the print edition, mostly news items.

Tips "We publish reliable horse health care and management information from top industry professionals and researchers around the world. Manuscript must be submitted electronically or on disk."

$⊠ HORSEPOWER

Magazine for Young Horse Lovers, Horse Publications Group, P.O. Box 670, Aurora ON L4G 4J9, Canada. Fax: (905)841-1530. E-mail: info@horse-canada.com. Website: www.horse-canada.com. **Contact:** Susan Stafford, editor. **50% freelance written.** Bimonthly magazine covering horse care and training for teens and preteens (ages 8-16). "Safety when dealing with horses is our first priority. Also, explaining techniques, etc., in terms kids can understand without over-simplifying." Estab. 1988. Circ. 10,000. Pays on publication. Publishes ms an average of 6 months after acceptance. Byline given. Buys one-time rights. Editorial lead time 2 months. Submit seasonal material 4 months in advance. Accepts queries by mail, e-mail, fax. Accepts simultaneous submissions. Responds in 3 weeks to queries; 6 months to mss. Sample copy for $2.95. Writer's guidelines for #10 SASE.

Nonfiction How-to (horse care, grooming, training, etc.), humor, interview/profile (famouse riders). **Buys 6 mss/year.** Query or send complete ms. Length: 500-1,200 words. **Pays $50-75.** Pays in contributor copies upon request.

Reprints Accepts previously published submissions.

Photos Send photos with submission. Reviews 4×6 prints, GIF/JPEG files. Buys one-time rights. Offers $10-15/photo. Captions required.

Columns/Departments How To ... (step-by-step), 1,000 words. **Buys 3 mss/year.** Query or send complete ms. **Pays $50-75.**

Fiction Adventure, humorous, slice-of-life vignettes. Nothing too young for the readership or stories about "How I Won the Big Race," etc. **Buys 2 mss/year.** Length: 500-1,200 words. **Pays $50-75.**

Tips "Writers must have a firm grasp on all aspects of horse ownership, training, health care, etc. Most of our readers are quite intelligent and do not want to be talked down to. Articles must not be too simplistic."

Ⓝ $⊠ HORSES ALL

North Hill Publications, 278-19 St. NE, Calgary AB T2E 8P7, Canada. (403)248-9993. Fax: (403)248-8838. E-mail: horsesall@northhill.net. **Contact:** Jean Llewellyn, editor. **40% freelance written.** Eager to work with new/unpublished writers. Monthly tabloid covering horse owners and the horse industry. Estab. 1977. Circ. 25,000. Pays on publication. Publishes ms an average of 3 months after acceptance. Byline given. Buys first North American serial rights. Submit seasonal material 3 months in advance. Accepts queries by mail, e-mail, fax. Accepts previously published material. Accepts simultaneous submissions.

Nonfiction "We would prefer more general stories, no specific local events or shows." Book excerpts, essays, general interest, historical/nostalgic, how-to (training, horse care and maintenance), inspirational, interview/profile, personal experience, photo feature. **Buys 3 mss/year.** Query. Length: 800-1,400 words. **Pays $50-75 (Canadian).**

Photos Send photos with submission. Reviews 3x4 or larger prints. Buys one-time rights. Captions, identification of subjects, model releases required.

Tips "Our writers must be knowledgeable about horses and the horse industry, and be able to write features in a readable, conversational manner. While we do include coverage of major events in our publication, we generally require that these events take place in Canada. Any exceptions to this general rule are evaluated on a case-by-case basis."

$I LOVE CATS

I Love Cats Publishing, 16 Meadow Hill Lane, Armonk NY 10504. (908)222-0990. Fax: (908)222-8228. E-mail: yankee@izzy.net. Website: www.iluvcats.com. **Contact:** Lisa Allmendinger, editor. **100% freelance written.** Bimonthly magazine. "*I Love Cats* is a general interest cat magazine for the entire family. It caters to cat lovers of all ages. The stories in the magazine include fiction, nonfiction, how-to, humorous, and columns for the cat lover." Estab. 1989. Circ. 50,000. Pays on publication. Publishes ms an average of 2 years after acceptance. Byline given. Must sign copyright consent form. Buys all rights. Editorial lead time 6 months. Submit seasonal material 9 months in advance. Accepts queries by mail, e-mail. Responds in 3 months to queries. Sample copy for $5. Writer's guidelines online.

Nonfiction Essays, general interest, how-to, humor, inspirational, interview/profile, new product, opinion, personal experience, photo feature. No poetry. **Buys 100 mss/year.** Send complete ms. Length: 500-1,000 words. **Pays $50-100, contributor copies or other premiums if requested.** Sometimes pays expenses of writers on assignment.

Photos Please send copies; art will no longer be returned. Send photos with submission. Buys all rights. Offers no additional payment for photos accepted with ms. Identification of subjects required.

Fiction Adventure, fantasy, historical, humorous, mainstream, mystery, novel excerpts, slice-of-life vignettes, suspense. "This is a family magazine. No graphic violence, pornography or other inappropriate material. *I Love Cats* is strictly 'G-rated.'" **Buys 100 mss/year.** Send complete ms. Length: 500-1,000 words. **Pays $25-100.**

Fillers Anecdotes, facts, short humor. **Buys 25/year. Pays $25.**

Tips "Please keep stories short and concise. Send complete manuscript with photos, if possible. I buy lots of first-time authors. Nonfiction pieces with color photos are always in short supply. With the exception of the standing columns, the rest of the magazine is open to freelancers. Be witty, humorous, or offer a different approach to writing."

$ $ KITTENS USA

Adopting and Caring for Your Kitten, Fancy Publications, Inc., P.O. Box 6050, Mission Viejo CA 92690. (949)855-8822. **Contact:** Editor. **90% freelance written.** Annual publication for kitten buyers. Estab. 1997. Pays on publication. Buys first North American serial rights. Editorial lead time 6 months. Responds in 3 months to queries. Sample copy not available. Writer's guidelines for #10 SASE.

Nonfiction Healthcare, training, adoption. **Buys 20 mss/year.** Query with published clips. Length: 1,000-2,000 words. **Pays $50-450.**

Photos Looking for happy, healthy, well-groomed kittens in studio or indoor settings. Guidelines for #10 SASE. Buys one-time rights. Negotiates payment individually. Captions, identification of subjects, model releases required.

Tips "No fiction or poetry. Please read recent issues to become acquainted with our style and content. Show us in your query how you can contribute something new and unique. No phone queries."

$ MINIATURE DONKEY TALK

Miniature Donkey Talk, Inc., 1338 Hughes Shop Rd., Westminster MD 21158-2911. (410)875-0118. Fax: (410)857-9145. E-mail: minidonk@qis.net. Website: www.qis.net/~minidonk/mdt.htm. Bonnie Gross, editor. **65% freelance written.** Bimonthly magazine covering miniature donkeys or donkeys, with articles on healthcare, promotion, and management of donkeys for owners, breeders, or donkey lovers. Estab. 1987. Circ. 4,925. **Pays on acceptance.** Publishes ms an average of 4 months after acceptance. Byline given. Buys first, second serial (reprint) rights. Editorial lead time 2 months. Submit seasonal material 3 months in advance. Accepts queries by mail, e-mail, fax. Accepts previously published material. Responds in 2 weeks to queries; 1 month to mss. Sample copy for $5. Writer's guidelines free.

Nonfiction Book excerpts, humor, interview/profile, personal experience. **Buys 6 mss/year.** Query with published clips. Length: 700-7,000 words. **Pays $25-150.**

Photos State availability with submission. Reviews 3×5 prints. Buys one-time rights. Offers no additional payment for photos accepted with ms. Identification of subjects required.

Columns/Departments Humor, 2,000 words; Healthcare, 2,000-5,000 words; Management, 2,000 words. **Buys 50 mss/year.** Query. **Pays $25-100.**

Fiction Humorous. **Buys 6 mss/year.** Query. Length: 3,000-7,000 words. **Pays $25-100.**

Fillers Anecdotes, facts, gags to be illustrated by cartoonist, short humor. **Buys 12/year.** Length: 200-2,000 words. **Pays $15-35.**

Tips "Simply send your manuscript. If on topic and appropriate, good possibility it will be published. We accept the following types of material: breeder profiles—either of yourself or another breeder. The full address and/ or telephone number of the breeder will not appear in the article as this would constitute advertising; coverage of nonshow events such as fairs, donkey gatherings, holiday events, etc. We do not pay for coverage of an event that you were involved in organizing; detailed or specific instructional or training material. We're always interested in people's training methods; relevant, informative equine health pieces. We much prefer they deal specifically with donkeys; however, we will consider articles specifically geared toward horses. If at all possible, substitute the word 'horse' for donkey. We reserve the right to edit, change, delete, or add to health articles as we deem appropriate. Please be very careful in the accuracy of advice or treatment and review the material with a veterinarian; farm management articles; and fictional stories on donkeys."

$ $ MUSHING

Stellar Communications, Inc., P.O. Box 149, Ester AK 99725-0149. (907)479-0454. Fax: (907)479-3137. E-mail: editor@mushing.com. Website: www.mushing.com. Publisher: Todd Hoener. **Contact:** Deirdre Alida Helfferich, managing editor. Bimonthly magazine covering all aspects of the growing sports of dogsledding, skijoring, carting, dog packing, and weight pulling. "*Mushing* promotes responsible dog care through feature articles and updates on working animal health care, safety, nutrition, and training." Estab. 1987. Circ. 6,000. Pays within 3 months of publication. Publishes ms an average of 4 months after acceptance. Byline given. Buys first, second serial (reprint) rights. Submit seasonal material 4 months in advance. Accepts queries by mail, e-mail, fax, phone. Responds in 8 months to queries. Sample copy for $5 ($6 US to Canada). Writer's guidelines online.

Nonfiction "We consider articles on canine health and nutrition, sled dog behavior and training, musher profiles and interviews, equipment how-to's, trail tips, expedition and race accounts, innovations, sled dog history, current issues, personal experiences, and humor." Historical/nostalgic, how-to. Special issues: Iditarod and Long-Distance Racing (January/February); Expeditions/Peak of Race Season (March/April); Health and Nutrition (May/June); Musher and Dog Profiles, Summer Activities (July/August); Equipment, Fall Training (September/October); Races and Places (November/December). Query with or without published clips. Considers complete ms with SASE. Length: 1,000-2,500 words. **Pays $50-250.** Sometimes pays expenses of writers on assignment.

Photos "We look for good b&w and quality color for covers and specials." Send photos with submission. Reviews contact sheets, negatives, transparencies, prints. Buys one time and second reprint rights. Pays $20-165/photo. Captions, identification of subjects, model releases required.

Columns/Departments Length: 500-1,000 words. Query with or without published clips or send complete ms.

Fillers Anecdotes, facts, newsbreaks, short humor, cartoons, puzzles. Length: 100-250 words. **Pays $20-35.**

Tips "Read our magazine. Know something about dog-driven, dog-powered sports."

$ $PAINT HORSE JOURNAL

American Paint Horse Association, P.O. Box 961023, Fort Worth TX 76161-0023. (817)834-2742. Fax: (817)222-8466. E-mail: jnice@apha.com. Website: www.apha.com. **Contact:** Jennifer Nice, editor. **10% freelance written.** Works with a small number of new/unpublished writers/year. Monthly magazine for people who raise, breed and show Paint Horses. Estab. 1966. Circ. 30,000. **Pays on acceptance.** Byline given. Offers negotiable kill fee. Buys first North American serial rights. Submit seasonal material 3 months in advance. Accepts queries by mail, e-mail, fax. Sample copy for $4.50. Writer's guidelines online.

Nonfiction General interest (personality pieces on well-known owners of Paints), historical/nostalgic (Paint Horses in the past—particular horses and the breed in general), how-to (train and show horses), photo feature (Paint Horses). **Buys 4-5 mss/year.** Query. Length: 1,000-2,000 words. **Pays $100-650.**

Photos Photos must illustrate article and must include registered Paint Horses. Send photos with submission. Reviews 35mm or larger transparencies, 3×5 or larger color glossy prints, digital images on CD or DVD. Offers no additional payment for photos accepted with accompanying ms. Captions required.

Tips "Well-written first person articles are welcomed. Submit items that show a definite understanding of the horse business. Be sure you understand precisely what a Paint Horse is as defined by the American Paint Horse Association. Use proper equine terminology. Photos with copy are almost always essential."

$ROCKY MOUNTAIN RIDER MAGAZINE

Regional All-Breed Horse Monthly, P.O. Box 1011, Hamilton MT 59840. (406)363-4085. Fax: (406)363-1056. Website: www.rockymountainrider.com. **Contact:** Natalie Riehl, editor. **90% freelance written.** Monthly magazine for horse owners and enthusiasts. Estab. 1993. Circ. 14,500. Pays on publication. Publishes ms an average of 6 months after acceptance. Byline given. Buys one-time rights. Submit seasonal material 6 months in advance. Accepts simultaneous submissions. Responds in 1 month to queries; 2 months to mss. Sample copy for free. Writer's guidelines for #10 SASE.

Nonfiction Book excerpts, essays, general interest, historical/nostalgic, humor, interview/profile, new product, personal experience, photo feature, cowboy poetry, equine medical. **Buys 100 mss/year.** Send complete ms. Length: 500-2,000 words. **Pays $15-90.**

Photos Send photos with submission. Reviews 3×5 and digital prints. Buys one-time rights. Pays $5/photo. Captions, identification of subjects required.

Poetry Light verse, traditional. **Buys 25 poems/year.** Submit maximum 10 poems. Length: 6-36 lines. **Pays $10.**

Fillers Anecdotes, facts, gags to be illustrated by cartoonist, short humor. Length: 200-750 words. **Pays $15.**

Tips "*RMR* is looking for positive, human interest stories that appeal to an audience of horsepeople. We accept profiles of unusual people or animals, history, humor, anecdotes, cowboy poetry, coverage of regional events, and new products. We aren't looking for many 'how-to' or training articles, and are not currently looking at any fiction."

ART & ARCHITECTURE

$ $THE AMERICAN ART JOURNAL

Kennedy Galleries, Inc., 730 Fifth Ave., New York NY 10019. (212)541-9600. Fax: (212)977-3833. **Contact:** Jayne A. Kuchna, editor-in-chief. Prefers to work with published/established writers; works with a small number of new/unpublished writers each year. Annual magazine covering American art history of the 17th, 18th, 19th and 20th centuries, including painting, sculpture, architecture, photography, cultural history, etc., for people with a serious interest in American art, and who are already knowledgeable about the subject. Readers are scholars, curators, collectors, students of American art, or persons with a strong interest in Americana. Circ. 2,000. **Pays on acceptance.** Publishes ms an average of 6 months after acceptance. Byline given. all rights, but will reassign rights to writers. Responds in 2 months to queries. Sample copy for $18.

Nonfiction "All articles are about some phase or aspect of American art history. No how-to articles written in a casual or 'folksy' style. Writing style must be formal and serious." Historical. **Buys 10-15 mss/year.** Length: 2,500-10,000 words. **Pays $400-600.**

Photos Reviews b&w only. Purchased with accompanying ms. Captions required.

Tips "Articles must be scholarly, thoroughly documented, well-researched, well-written and illustrated. Whenever possible, all manuscripts must be accompanied by b&w photographs which have been integrated into the text by the use of numbers."

$ $ AMERICAN ARTIST

VNU Business Media, 770 Broadway, New York NY 10003-9595. (646)654-5206. Fax: (646)654-5514. E-mail: mail@myamericanartist.com. Website: www.myamericanartist.com. **Contact:** M. Stephen Doherty, editor-in-chief. Monthly magazine covering art. Written to provide information on outstanding representational artists living in the US. Estab. 1937. Circ. 116,526. Editorial lead time 18 weeks. Accepts queries by mail. Responds in 6-8 weeks to queries. Sample copy for $3.95. Writer's guidelines by e-mail.

Nonfiction Essays, exposé, interview/profile, personal experience, technical. Query with published clips and résumé. Length: 1,500-2,000 words. **Pays $500.**

N $ $ AMERICAN INDIAN ART MAGAZINE

American Indian Art, Inc., 7314 E. Osborn Dr., Scottsdale AZ 85251. (480)994-5445. Fax: (480)945-9533. Website: www.aiamagazine.com. Editor: Tobi Taylor. **Contact:** Roanne P. Goldfein, editorial director. **97% freelance written.** Works with many new/unpublished writers/year. Quarterly magazine covering Native American art, historic and contemporary, including new research on any aspect of Native American art north of the US-Mexico border. Estab. 1975. Circ. 30,000. Pays on publication. Publishes ms an average of 3 months after acceptance. Byline given. Buys first, one-time rights. Responds in 6 weeks to queries; 3 months to mss. Sample copy not available. Writer's guidelines for #10 SASE or online.

Nonfiction New research on any aspect of Native American art. No previously published work or personal interviews with artists. **Buys 12-18 mss/year.** Query. Length: 6,000-7,000 words. **Pays $75-300.**

Photos An article usually requires between 8 and 15 photographs. Buys one-time rights. Fee schedules and reimbursable expenses are decided upon by the magazine and the author.

Tips "The magazine is devoted to all aspects of Native American art. Some of our readers are knowledgeable about the field and some know very little. We seek articles that offer something to both groups. Articles reflecting original research are preferred to those summarizing previously published information."

$ $ $ AMERICANSTYLE MAGAZINE

The Rosen Group, 3000 Chestnut Ave., Suite 304, Baltimore MD 21211. (410)889-3093. Fax: (410)243-7089. E-mail: hoped@rosengrp.com. Website: www.americanstyle.com. **Contact:** Hope Daniels, editor-in-chief. **80% freelance written.** Bimonthly magazine covering arts, crafts, travel, and interior design. "*AmericanStyle* is a full-color lifestyle publication for people who love art. Our mandate is to nurture collectors with information that will increase their passion for contemporary art and craft and the artists who create it. *AmericanStyle*'s primary audience is contemporary craft collectors and enthusiasts. Readers are college-educated, age 35+, high-income earners with the financial means to collect art and craft, and to travel to national art and craft events in pursuit of their passions." Estab. 1994. Circ. 60,000. Pays on publication. Publishes ms an average of 9 months after acceptance. Buys first North American serial rights. Editorial lead time 9 months. Submit seasonal material at least 1 year in advance. Accepts queries by mail, e-mail, fax. Sample copy for $3. Writer's guidelines online. Editorial calendar online.

  ● *AmericanStyle* is especially interested in freelance ideas about arts travel, profiles of contemporary craft collectors, and established studio artists.

Nonfiction Specialized arts/crafts interests. Length: 300-1,500 words. **Pays $500-800.** Sometimes pays expenses of writers on assignment.

Photos Send photos with submission. Reviews oversized transparencies, 35mm slides, high res e-images. Negotiates payment individually. Captions required.

Columns/Departments Portfolio (profiles of emerging and established artists); Arts Walk; Origins; One on One, all 600-900 words. Query with published clips. **Pays $400-600.**

Tips "This is not a hobby-crafter magazine. Country crafts or home crafting is not our market. We focus on contemporary American craft art, such as ceramics, wood, fiber, glass, metal."

$ $ $ART & ANTIQUES

TransWorld Publishing, Inc., 2100 Powers Ferry Rd., Suite 300, Atlanta GA 30339. (770)955-5656. Fax: (770)952-0669. Editor: Barbara S. Tapp. **Contact:** Patti Verbanas, managing editor. **90% freelance written.** Magazine published 11 times/year covering fine art and antique collectibles and the people who collect them and/or create them. "*Art & Antiques* is the authoritative source for elegant, sophisticated coverage of the treasures collectors love, the places to discover them, and the unique ways collectors use them to enrich their environments." Circ. 125,800. **Pays on acceptance.** Byline given. Offers 25% kill fee or $250. Buys all rights. Editorial lead time 8 months. Submit seasonal material 8 months in advance. Accepts queries by mail. Responds in 6 weeks to queries; 2 months to mss. Sample copy and writer's guidelines free.

Nonfiction "We publish 1 'interior design with art and antiques' focus feature a month." Essays. Special issues: Designing with art & antiques (April); Asian art & antiques (February); Contemporary art (September). **Buys 200 mss/year.** Query with or without published clips. Length: 150-1,200 words. **Pays $150-1,200 for assigned articles.** Pays $50 toward expenses of writers on assignment.

Photos Scouting shots. Send photos with submission. Reviews contact sheets, transparencies, prints. Captions, identification of subjects required.

Columns/Departments Art & Antiques Update (trend coverage and timely news of issues and personalities), 100-350 words; Review (thoughts and criticisms on a variety of worldwide art exhibitions throughout the year), 600-800 words; Value Judgements (experts highlight popular to undiscovered areas of collecting), 600-800 words; Emerging Artists (an artist on the cusp of discovery), 600-800 words; Discoveries (collections in lesser-known museums and homes open to the public), 800-900 words; Studio Session (peek into the studio of an artist who is currently hot or is a revered veteran allowing the reader to watch the artist in action), 800-900 words; Then & Now (the best reproductions being created today and the craftspeople behind the work), 800-900 words; World View (major art and antiques news worldwide; visuals preferred but not necessary), 600-800 words; Travelling Collector (hottest art and antiques destinations, dictated by those on editorial calendar; visuals preferred but not necessary), 800-900 words; Essay (first-person piece tackling a topic in a nonacademic way; visuals preferred but not necessary); A&A Insider (a how-to column on collecting topics). **Buys 200 mss/year.** Query by mail only with or without published clips. **Pays $150-900.**

Fillers Facts, newsbreaks. **Buys 22/year.** Length: 150-300 words. **Pays $150-300.**

▣ The online magazine carries original content not found in the print edition, though there is no payment at this time.

Tips "Send scouting shots with your queries. We are a visual magazine and no idea will be considered without visuals. We are good about responding to writers in a timely fashion—excessive phone calls are not appreciated, but do check in if you haven't heard from us in 2 months. We like colorful, lively and creative writing."

$ $ART CALENDAR MAGAZINE

The Business Magazine for Visual Artists, P.O. Box 2675, Salisbury MD 21802. Fax: (410)749-9626. E-mail: info@artcalendar.com. Website: www.artcalendar.com. **Contact:** Carolyn Proeber, publisher. **100% freelance written.** Monthly magazine. Estab. 1986. Circ. 23,000. Pays on publication. Accepts previously published material. Sample copy for $5 prepaid. Writer's guidelines online.

● "We welcome nuts-and-bolts, practical articles of interest to serious visual artists, emerging or professional. Examples: marketing how-to's, first-person stories on how an artist has built his career or an aspect of it, interviews with artists (business/career-building emphasis), and pieces on business practices and other topics of use to artists. The tone of our magazine is practical, can-do, and uplifting. Writers may use as many or as few words as necessary to tell the whole story."

Nonfiction Essays (the psychology of creativity), how-to, interview/profile (successful artists with a focus on what made them successful — not necessarily rich and famous artists, but the guy-next-door who paints all day and makes a decent living doing it.), personal experience (artists making a difference (art teachers working with disabled students, bringing a community together, etc.), technical (new equipment, new media, computer software, Internet sites that are way cool that no one has heard of yet), Cartoons, art law, including pending legislation that affects artists (copyright law, Internet regulations, etc.). "We like nuts-and-bolts information about making a living as an artist. We do not run reviews or art historical pieces, nor do we like writing characterized by "critic-speak," philosophical hyperbole, psychological arrogance, politics, or New Age religion. Also, we do not condone a get-rich-quick attitude." Send complete ms. **Pays $200.** We can make other arrangements in lieu of pay, i.e. a subscription or copies of the magazine in which your article appears.

Reprints Send photocopy or typed ms and information about when and where the material previously appeared. Pays $50.

Photos Reviews b&w glossy or color prints. Pays $25.

Columns/Departments "If an artist or freelancer sends us good articles regularly, and based on results we feel that s/he is able to produce a column at least three times per year, we will invite him to be a Contributing Writer. If a gifted artist-writer can commit to producing an article on a monthly basis, we will offer him a regular column and the title Contributing Editor." Send complete ms.

Ⓝ $ $ ART PAPERS

Atlanta Art Papers, Inc., P.O. Box 5748, Atlanta GA 31107-0748. (404)588-1837. Fax: (404)588-1836. E-mail: editor@artpaper.org. Website: www.artpapers.org. **Contact:** Charles Reeve, editor-in-chief. **95% freelance written.** Bimonthly magazine covering contemporary art and artists. "*Art Papers*, about regional and national contemporary art and artists, features a variety of perspectives on current art concerns. Each issue presents topical articles, interviews, reviews from across the US, and an extensive and informative artists' classified listings section. Our writers and the artists they cover represent the scope and diversity of the country's art scene." Estab. 1977. Circ. 12,000. Pays on publication. Publishes ms an average of 3 months after acceptance. Byline given. Not copyrighted. Buys all rights. Editorial lead time 2 months. Submit seasonal material 2 months in advance. Sample copy not available.

Nonfiction Feature articles and reviews. **Buys 240 mss/year. Pays $60-325; unsolicited articles are on spec.**

Photos Send photos with submission. Reviews color slides, b&w prints. Offers no additional payment for photos accepted with ms. Identification of subjects required.

Columns/Departments Current art concerns and news. **Buys 8-10 mss/year.** Query. **Pays $100-175.**

Ⓝ $ ART TIMES

Commentary and Reasons for the Fine and Performing Arts, P.O. Box 730, Mount Marion NY 12456-0730. (914)246-6944. Fax: (914)246-6944. E-mail: info@arttimesjournal.com. Website: www.arttimesjournal.com. **Contact:** Raymond J. Steiner, editor. **10% freelance written.** Monthly tabloid covering the arts (visual, theater, dance, music, literary, etc.). "*Art Times* covers the art fields and is distributed in locations most frequented by those enjoying the arts. Our copies are distributed throughout upstate New York counties as well as in most of the galleries of Soho, 57th Street and Madison Avenue in the metropolitan area; locations include theaters, galleries, museums, cultural centers and the like. Our readers are mostly over 40, affluent, art-conscious and sophisticated. Subscribers are located across U.S. and abroad (Italy, France, Germany, Greece, Russia, etc.)." Estab. 1984. Circ. 27,000. Pays on publication. Publishes ms an average of 4 years after acceptance. Byline given. Buys first North American serial, first rights. Submit seasonal material 8 months in advance. Accepts simultaneous submissions. Responds in 3 months to queries; 6 months to mss. Sample copy for 9 × 12 SAE and 6 first-class stamps. Writer's guidelines for #10 SASE or on website.

Fiction Raymond J. Steiner, fiction editor. "We're looking for short fiction that aspires to be literary. No excessive violence, sexist, off-beat, erotic, sports, or juvenile fiction." Adventure, ethnic, fantasy, historical, humorous, mainstream, science fiction, contemporary. "We seek quality literary pieces. Nothing violent, sexist, erotic, juvenile, racist, romantic, political, etc." **Buys 8-10 mss/year.** Send complete ms. Length: 1,500 words maximum. **Pays $25 maximum (honorarium) and 1 year's free subscription.**

Poetry "We prefer well-crafted 'literary' poems. No excessively sentimental poetry." Raymond J. Steiner, poetry editor. Avant-garde, free verse, haiku, light verse, traditional, poet's niche. **Buys 30-35 poems/year.** Submit maximum 6 poems. Length: 20 lines maximum. **Offers contributor copies and 1 year's free subscription.**

Tips "Be advised that we are presently on an approximate 4-year lead for short stories, 2-year lead for poetry. We are now receiving 300-400 poems and 40-50 short stories per month. We only publish 2-3 poems and 1 story each issue. Be familiar with *Art Times* and its special audience. *Art Times* has literary leanings with articles written by a staff of scholars knowledgeable in their respective fields. Although an 'arts' publication, we observe no restrictions (other than noted) in accepting fiction/poetry other than a concern for quality writing—subjects can cover anything and not specifically arts."

$ 📭 ARTICHOKE

Writings About the Visual Arts, Artichoke Publishing, 208-901 Jervis St., Vancouver BC V6E 2B6, Canada. Fax: (604)683-1941. E-mail: editor@artichoke.ca. Website: www.artichoke.ca. **Contact:** Paula Gustafson, editor. **90% freelance written.** Triannual magazine. "*Artichoke* is Western Canada's visual arts magazine. Writers must be familiar with Canadian art and artists." Estab. 1989. Circ. 1,500. **Pays on acceptance.** Publishes ms an average of 6 months after acceptance. Byline given. Offers 50% kill fee. Buys one-time rights. Editorial lead time 6 months. Accepts queries by mail, e-mail, fax. Accepts simultaneous submissions. Responds in 1 week to queries; 2 weeks to mss. Sample copy for free. Writer's guidelines online.

Nonfiction Essays, interview/profile, opinion, critical reviews about Canadian visual art. "*Artichoke* does not publish fiction, poetry, or academic jargon." **Buys 100 mss/year.** Query with or without published clips or send complete ms. Length: 1,000-2,500 words. **Pays $125.**

Photos State availability of or send photos with submission. Reviews transparencies, prints. Buys one-time rights. Offers no additional payment for photos accepted with ms. Captions, identification of subjects required.

ARTNEWS
ABC, 48 W. 38th St., New York NY 10018. (212)398-1690. Fax: (212)819-0394. E-mail: info@artnewsonline.com. Website: www.artnewsonline.com. Monthly magazine. *"Artnews* reports on art, personalities, issues, trends and events that shape the international art world. Investigative features focus on art ranging from old masters to contemporary, including painting, sculpture, prints and photography. Regular columns offer exhibition and book reviews, travel destinations, investment and appreciation advice, design insights and updates on major art world figures." Estab. 1902. Circ. 82,911. Accepts queries by mail, e-mail, fax, phone. Sample copy not available.

☑ AZURE DESIGN, ARCHITECTURE AND ART
460 Richmond St. W., Suite 601, Toronto ON M5V 1Y1, Canada. (416)203-9674. Fax: (416)203-9842. E-mail: azure@azureonline.com. Website: www.azureonline.com. **Contact:** Nelda Rodger, editor. **50% freelance written.** Magazine covering design and architecture. Estab. 1985. Circ. 20,000. Pays on publication. Publishes ms an average of 1 month after acceptance. Offers variable kill fee. Buys first rights. Editorial lead time up to 45 days. Responds in 6 weeks to queries. Sample copy not available.
Nonfiction Buys 25-30 mss/year. Length: 350-2,000 words. **Payment varies.**
Columns/Departments Trailer (essay/photo on something from the built environment); and Forms & Functions (coming exhibitions, happenings in world of design), both 300-350 words. **Buys 30 mss/year.** Query. **Payment varies.**
Tips "Try to understand what the magazine is about. Writers must be well versed in the field of architecture and design. It's very unusual to get something from someone I haven't worked quite closely with and gotten a sense of who the writer is. The best way to introduce yourself is by sending clips or writing samples and describing what your background is in the field."

$ BOMB MAGAZINE
New Arts Publications, 594 Broadway, Suite 905, New York NY 10012-3289. (212)4313943. Fax: (212)4315880. E-mail: info@bombsite.com. Website: www.bombsite.com. Editor: Betsy Sussler. Managing Editor: Nell McClister. Quarterly magazine providing interviews between artists, writers, musicians, directors and actors. Written, edited and produced by industry professionals and funded by those interested in the arts. Publishes "work which is unconventional and contains an edge, whether it be in style or subject matter." Estab. 1981. Circ. 36,000. Pays on publication. Publishes ms an average of 3-6 months after acceptance. Buys first, one-time rights. Editorial lead time 3-4 months. Accepts queries by mail. Responds in 3-5 months to mss. Sample copy for $7, plus $1.42 postage and handling. Writer's guidelines by e-mail.
Fiction Send completed ms with SASE. Experimental, novel excerpts, contemporary. No genre: romance, science fiction, horror, western. Length: 10-12 pages average. **Pays $100, and contributor's copies.**
Poetry Send completed ms with SASE. Submit no more than 25 pages. Length: No more than 25 pages in length.
Tips Mss should be typed, double-spaced, proofread adn should be final drafts.

Ⓝ $ $ ☑ C
international contemporary art, C The Visual Arts Foundation, P.O. Box 5, Station B, Toronto ON M5T 2T2, Canada. (416)539-9495. Fax: (416)539-9903. E-mail: general@cmagazine.com. Website: www.cmagazine.com. **Contact:** Petra Chevrier, associate editor. **80% freelance written.** Quarterly magazine covering international contemporary art. *"C* provides a vital and vibrant forum for the presentation of contemporary art and the discussion of issues surrounding art in our culture, including feature articles, reviews and reports, as well as original artists' projects." Estab. 1983. Circ. 7,000. Pays on publication. Publishes ms an average of 4 months after acceptance. Byline given. Offers kill fee. Editorial lead time 3 months. Accepts queries by mail, e-mail, fax. Accepts simultaneous submissions. Responds in 6 weeks to queries; 4 months to mss. Sample copy for $10 (US). Writer's guidelines for #10 SASE.
Nonfiction Essays, general interest, opinion, personal experience. **Buys 50 mss/year.** Length: 1,000-3,000 words. **Pays $150-500 (Canadian), $105-350 (US).**
Photos State availability of or send photos with submission. Reviews 35mm transparencies or 8×10 prints. Buys one-time rights; shared copyright on reprints. Offers no additional payment for photos accepted with ms. Captions required.
Columns/Departments Reviews (review of art exhibitions), 500 words. **Buys 30 mss/year.** Query. **Pays $125 (Canadian).**

L.A. ARCHITECT

The Magazine of Design in Southern California, Balcony Press, 512 E. Wilson, Suite 213, Glendale CA 91206. (818)956-5313. Fax: (818)956-5904. E-mail: jesse@balconypress.com. Website: www.laarch.com. **Contact:** Jesse Brink, editor. **80% freelance written.** Bimonthly magazine covering architecture, interiors, landscape, and other design disciplines. *"L.A. Architect* is interested in architecture, interiors, product, graphics, and landscape design as well as news about the arts. We encourage designers to keep us informed on projects, techniques, and products that are innovative, new, or nationally newsworthy. We are especially interested in new and renovated projects that illustrate a high degree of design integrity and unique answers to typical problems in the urban cultural and physical environment." Estab. 1999. Circ. 20,000. Pays on publication. Publishes ms an average of 3 months after acceptance. Byline given. Makes work-for-hire assignments. Editorial lead time 4 months. Submit seasonal material 4 months in advance. Accepts queries by mail, e-mail, fax. Responds in 1 month to queries; 1 month to mss. Sample copy for $3. Writer's guidelines online.

Nonfiction Book excerpts, essays, historical/nostalgic, interview/profile, new product. "No technical, foo-foo interiors, or non-Southern California subjects." **Buys 20 mss/year.** Length: 500-2,000 words. **Payment negotiable.**

Photos State availability with submission. Buys one-time rights. Offers no additional payment for photos accepted with ms. Captions, identification of subjects, model releases required.

Tips "Our magazine focuses on contemporary and cutting-edge work either happening in Southern California or designed by a Southern California designer. We like to find little-known talent which has not been widely published. We are not like *Architectural Digest* in flavor so avoid highly decorative subjects. Each project, product, or event should be accompanied by a story proposal or brief description and select images. Do not send original art without our written request; we make every effort to return materials we are unable to use, but this is sometimes difficult and we must make advance arrangements for original art."

$ $THE MAGAZINE ANTIQUES

Brant Publications, 575 Broadway, New York NY 10012. (212)941-2800. Fax: (212)941-2819. **Contact:** Allison Ledes, editor. **75% freelance written.** Monthly magazine. "Articles should present new information in a scholarly format (with footnotes) on the fine and decorative arts, architecture, historic preservation, and landscape architecture." Estab. 1922. Circ. 61,556. Pays on publication. Publishes ms an average of 6 months after acceptance. Byline given. Buys all rights. Editorial lead time 6 months. Submit seasonal material 6 months in advance. Responds in 3 weeks to queries; 6 months to mss. Sample copy for $10.50 for back issue; $5 for current issue.

Nonfiction Historical/nostalgic, scholarly. **Buys 50 mss/year.** Length: 2,850-3,500 words. **Pays $250-500.** Sometimes pays expenses of writers on assignment.

Photos State availability with submission. Reviews contact sheets, negatives, transparencies, prints. Buys one-time rights. Captions, identification of subjects required.

$ $ $ $METROPOLIS

The Magazine of Architecture and Design, Bellerophon Publications, 61 W. 23rd St., 4th Floor, New York NY 10010. (212)627-9977. Fax: (212)627-9988. E-mail: edit@metropolismag.com. Website: www.metropolismag.com. Executive Editor: Martin Pedersen. **Contact:** Julien Devereux, managing editor. **80% freelance written.** Monthly magazine (combined issues February/March and August/September) for consumers interested in architecture and design. Estab. 1981. Circ. 45,000. Pays 60-90 days after acceptance. Publishes ms an average of 3 months after acceptance. Byline given. Makes work-for-hire assignments. Submit seasonal material 3 months in advance. Accepts queries by mail, e-mail, fax. Responds in 8 months to queries. Sample copy for $7. Writer's guidelines online.

Nonfiction Martin Pedersen, executive editor. Essays (design, architecture, urban planning issues and ideas), interview/profile (of multi-disciplinary designers/architects). No profiles on individual architectural practices, information from public relations firms, or fine arts. **Buys 30 mss/year.** Length: 1,500-4,000 words. **Pays $1,500-4,000.**

Photos Reviews contact sheets, 35mm or 4 × 5 transparencies, 8 × 10 b&w prints. Buys one-time rights. Payment offered for certain photos. Captions required.

Columns/Departments The Metropolis Observed (architecture, design, and city planning news features), 100-1,200 words, **pays $100-1,200;** Perspective (opinion or personal observation of architecture and design), 1,200 words, **pays $1,200;** Enterprise (the business/development of architecture and design), 1,500 words, **pays $1,500;** In Review (architecture and book review essays), 1,500 words, **pays $1,500.** Direct queries to Julien Devereux, managing editor. **Buys 40 mss/year.** Query with published clips.

The online magazine carries original content not found in the print edition. Contact: Julie Taraska (jtaraska@metropolismag.com).

Tips *"Metropolis* strives to tell the story of design to a lay person with an interest in the built environment, while keeping the professional designer engaged. The magazine examines the various design disciplines (architecture, interior design, product design, graphic design, planning, and preservation) and their social/cultural context. We're looking for the new, the obscure, or the wonderful. Also, be patient and don't expect an immediate answer after submission of query.''

$ $ ▢ MIX

Independent Art and Culture Magazine, Parallelogramme Artist-Run Culture and Publishing, Inc., 401 Richmond St., Suite 446, Toronto ON M5V 3A8, Canada. (416)506-1012. Fax: (416)506-0141. E-mail: info@mixmagazine.c om. Website: www.mixmagazine.com. **95% freelance written.** Quarterly magazine covering Artist-Run gallery activities. ''Mix represents and investigates contemporary artistic practices and issues, especially in the progres- sive Canadian artist-run scene.'' Estab. 1975. Circ. 3,500. Pays on publication. Publishes ms an average of 6 months after acceptance. Byline given. Offers 40% kill fee. Buys first North American serial rights. Editorial lead time 6 months. Submit seasonal material 4 months in advance. Accepts queries by mail, e-mail, fax. Responds in 2 months to queries; 3 months to mss. Sample copy for $6.95, 8½ × 10¼ SAE and 6 first-class stamps. Writer's guidelines online.

Nonfiction Essays, interview/profile. **Buys 12-20 mss/year.** Query with published clips. Length: 750-3,500 words. **Pays $100-450.**

Reprints Send photocopy of article and information about when and where the article previously appeared.

Photos State availability with submission. Buys one-time rights. Captions, identification of subjects required.

Columns/Departments Features, 1,000-3,000 words; Art Reviews, 500 words. Query with published clips. **Pays $100-450.**

▣ The online magazine carries original content not found in the print edition and includes writer's guide- lines.

Tips ''Read the magazine and other contemporary art magazines. Understand the idea 'artist-run.' We're not interested in 'artsy-phartsy' editorial but rather pieces that are critical, dynamic and would be of interest to nonartists too.''

$ $ MODERNISM MAGAZINE

333 N. Main St., Lambertville NJ 08530. (609)397-4104. Fax: (609)397-9377. E-mail: andrea@modernismmagazi ne.com. Website: www.modernismmagazine.com. Publisher: David Rago. **Contact:** Andrea Truppin, editor-in- chief. **70% freelance written.** Quarterly magazine covering 20th century art and design. ''We are interested in objects and the people who created them. Our coverage begins in the 1920s with Art Deco and related move- ments, and ends with 1980s Post-Modernism, leaving contemporary design to other magazines. Our emphasis is on the decorative arts—furniture, pottery, glass, textiles, metalwork, and so on—but we're moving toward more coverage of painting and sculpture.'' Estab. 1998. Circ. 20,000. Pays on publication. Publishes ms an average of 4 months after acceptance. Byline given. Offers 25% kill fee. Buys all rights. Editorial lead time 6 months. Submit seasonal material 6 months in advance. Accepts queries by mail, e-mail, fax. Accepts previously published material. Accepts simultaneous submissions. Responds in 1 month to queries. Sample copy for $6.95. Writer's guidelines free.

Nonfiction Book excerpts, essays, historical/nostalgic, interview/profile, new product, photo feature. ''No first- person.'' **Buys 20 mss/year.** Query with published clips. Length: 2,000-2,500 words. **Pays $400 for assigned articles.**

Reprints Accepts previously published submissions.

Photos State availability of or send photos with submission. Reviews contact sheets, transparencies, prints. Buys one-time rights. Negotiates payment individually. Captions, identification of subjects required.

Tips ''Articles should be well-researched, carefully reported, and directed at a popular audience with a special interest in the Modernist movement. Please don't assume readers have prior familiarity with your subject; be sure to tell us the who, what, why, when, and how of whatever you're discussing.''

$ $ SOUTHWEST ART

5444 Westheimer Rd., Suite 1440, Houston TX 77056. (713)296-7900. Fax: (713)850-1314. E-mail: southwestart @southwestart.com. Website: www.southwestart.com. **Contact:** Editors. **60% freelance written.** Monthly magazine ''directed to art collectors interested in artists, market trends, and art history of the American West.'' Estab. 1971. Circ. 60,000. **Pays on acceptance.** Publishes ms an average of 1 year after acceptance. Byline given. Offers $125 kill fee. Not copyrighted. Submit seasonal material 8 months in advance. Accepts queries by mail, fax. Responds in 6 months to mss.

Nonfiction Book excerpts, interview/profile. No fiction or poetry. **Buys 70 mss/year.** Query with published clips. Length: 1,400-1,600 words.

Photos ''Photographs, color print-outs, and videotapes will not be considered.'' Reviews 35mm, 2¼×2¼, 4×5 transparencies. Negotiates rights. Captions, identification of subjects required.

Tips "Research the Southwest art market, send slides or transparencies with queries, send writing samples demonstrating knowledge of the art world."

$ $WATERCOLOR

VNU Business Media, 770 Broadway, New York NY 10003. (646)654-5600. Fax: (646)654-5514. E-mail: mail@a mericanartist.com. Website: www.myamericanartist.com. **Contact:** M. Stephen Doherty, editor-in-chief. Quarterly magazine. Devoted to watermedia artists. Circ. 80,000. Editorial lead time 4 months. Sample copy not available.

Nonfiction Essays, exposé, interview/profile, personal experience, technical. Query. Length: 1,500-2,000 words. **Pays $500.**

$ $WILDLIFE ART

The Art Journal of the Natural World, Pothole Publications, Inc., 1428 E. Cliff Rd., Burnsville MN 55337. Fax: (952)736-1030. E-mail: publisher@winternet.com. Website: www.wildlifeartmag.com. Publisher: Robert Koenke. **Contact:** Mary Nelson, editor. **60% freelance written.** Bimonthly magazine. "*Wildlife Art* is the world's foremost magazine of the natural world, featuring wildlife, landscape, and western art. Features living artists as well as wildlife art masters, illustrators and conservation organizations. Special emphasis on landscape and plein-air paintings. Audience is collectors, galleries, museums, show promoters worldwide." Estab. 1982. Circ. 30,000. Pays on publication. Publishes ms an average of 6 months after acceptance. Byline given. Offers negotiable kill fee. Buys second serial (reprint) rights. Accepts queries by mail, e-mail. Responds in 6 months to queries. Sample copy for 9×12 SAE and 10 first-class stamps. Writer's guidelines online.

Nonfiction General interest, historical/nostalgic, interview/profile. **Buys 40 mss/year.** Query with published clips, include artwork samples. Length: 800-1,500 words. **Pays $150-500.**

Tips "Best way to break in is to offer concrete story ideas; new talent; a new unique twist of artistic excellence."

ASSOCIATIONS

$ $ $ $AAUW OUTLOOK

American Association of University Women, 1111 16th St. NW, Washington DC 20036. (202)785-7737. Fax: (202)872-1425. E-mail: editor@aauw.org. Website: www.aauw.org. **Contact:** Jodi Lipson, editor. **10% freelance written.** Magazine published 2-4 times/year covering women, equity, and education. Circ. 150,000. **Pays on acceptance.** Publishes ms an average of 1 month after acceptance. Byline given. Buys first North American serial rights. Editorial lead time 3 months. Accepts queries by e-mail, phone.

Nonfiction Interview/profile, photo feature, book reviews and features. **Buys 3 mss/year.** Query with published clips. Length: 1,500-2,000 words. **Pays $1,200-1,600 for assigned articles.**

Photos State availability with submission. Buys one-time rights. Offers $25-50 per photo.

Columns/Departments Book Review (women, education, equity), 500 words. **Buys 2-3 mss/year.** Query. **Pays $200-500.**

Tips "Contact us first. We plan our editorial calendar, identify topics, then hire a writer to write that specific article. Tell us where you got our name and send clips."

$ $ $ $AMERICAN EDUCATOR

American Federation of Teachers, 555 New Jersey Ave., Washington DC 20001. (202)879-4420. Fax: (202)879-4534. E-mail: amered@aft.org. Website: www.aft.org/american_educator/index.html. **Contact:** Ruth Wattenberg, editor. **50% freelance written.** Quarterly magazine covering education, condition of children, and labor issues. "*American Educator*, the quarterly magazine of the American Federation of Teachers, reaches over 800,000 public school teachers, higher education faculty, and education researchers and policymakers. The magazine concentrates on significant ideas and practices in education, civics, and the condition of children in America and around the world." Estab. 1977. Circ. 850,000. Pays on publication. Publishes ms an average of 2-6 months after acceptance. Byline given. Offers 50% kill fee. Buys one-time, electronic rights. Editorial lead time 1 year. Submit seasonal material 6 months in advance. Accepts queries by mail, e-mail, fax. Accepts previously published material. Accepts simultaneous submissions. Responds in 2 months to queries; 6 months to mss. Sample copy online. Writer's guidelines online.

Nonfiction Book excerpts, essays, historical/nostalgic, interview/profile, discussions of educational research. No pieces that are not supportive of the public schools. **Buys 8 mss/year.** Query with published clips. Length: 1,000-7,000 words. **Pays $750-3,000 for assigned articles; $300-1,000 for unsolicited articles.** Pays expenses of writers on assignment.

Photos State availability with submission. Reviews contact sheets, negatives, transparencies, 8×10 prints, GIF/

JPEG files. Buys one-time rights. Negotiates payment individually. Captions, identification of subjects, model releases required.

$ $⬚ CANADIAN ESCAPES

August Communications, 225-530 Century St., Winnipeg MB R3H 0Y3, Canada. (888)573-1136. Fax: (866)957-0217. E-mail: t.rehberg@august.ca. Managing Editor: Adam Peeler. **Contact:** Trina Rehberg, editor. **60% freelance written.** Quarterly magazine covering Canadian travel. *"Canadian Escapes* is a quarterly association magazine written for the Tourism Industry Association of Canada. It promotes Canadian travel." Estab. 2002. Circ. 1,700. Pays 1 month after publication. Publishes ms an average of 1-2 months after acceptance. Byline given. Buys all rights. Editorial lead time 4 months. Submit seasonal material 6 months in advance. Accepts queries by mail, e-mail, fax. Sample copy for free.

Nonfiction "The magazine is targeted at international buyers of Canadian tourism." General interest, historical/nostalgic, travel. **Buys 30 mss/year.** Query with published clips. Length: 1,000-2,500 words. **Pays 15-30¢/word.**

Photos State availability with submission. Reviews GIF/JPEG files. Buys all rights. Negotiates payment individually. Captions required.

Tips "Review the Tourism Industry Association of Canada's website, www.tiac-aitc.ca."

$ $DAC NEWS

Official Publication of the Detroit Athletic Club, Detroit Athletic Club, 241 Madison Ave., Detroit MI 48226. (313)442-1034. Fax: (313)442-1047. E-mail: kenv@thedac.com. **Contact:** Kenneth Voyles, editor/publisher. **20% freelance written.** Magazine published 10 times/year. *"DAC News* is the magazine for Detroit Athletic Club members. It covers club news and events, plus general interest features." Estab. 1916. Circ. 4,700. Pays on publication. Publishes ms an average of 3 months after acceptance. Byline given. Buys one-time rights, makes work-for-hire assignments. Editorial lead time 3 months. Submit seasonal material 3 months in advance. Accepts queries by mail, phone. Accepts previously published material. Responds in 1 month to queries. Sample copy for free.

Nonfiction General interest, historical/nostalgic, photo feature. "No politics or social issues—this is an entertainment magazine. We do not acccept unsolicited manuscripts or queries for travel articles." **Buys 2-3 mss/year.** Length: 1,000-2,000 words. **Pays $100-500.** Sometimes pays expenses of writers on assignment.

Photos Illustrations only. State availability with submission. Reviews transparencies, 4×6 prints. Buys one-time rights. Negotiates payment individually. Captions, identification of subjects, model releases required.

Tips "Review our editorial calendar. It tends to repeat from year to year, so a freelancer with a fresh approach to one of these topics will get our attention quickly. It helps if articles have some connection with the DAC, but this is not absolutely necessary. We also welcome articles on Detroit history, Michigan history, or automotive history."

$ $DCM

Data Center Management: Bringing Insight and Ideas to the Data Center Community, AFCOM, 742 E. Chapman Ave., Orange CA 92866. Fax: (714)997-9743. E-mail: cdrysdale@afcom.com. Website: www.afcom.com. Executive Editor: Len Eckhaus. **Contact:** Chelsey Drysdale, managing editor. **50% freelance written.** Bimonthly magazine covering data center management. *"DCM* is the slick, 4-color, bimonthly publication for members of AFCOM, the leading association for data center management." Estab. 1988. Circ. 4,000 worldwide. Pays on acceptance for assigned articles and on publication for unsolicited articles. Publishes ms an average of 3 months after acceptance. Byline given. Offers 0-10% kill fee. Buys all rights. Editorial lead time 6-12 months. Submit seasonal material 6 months in advance. Responds in 1-3 weeks to queries; 1-3 months to mss. Writer's guidelines online.

● Prefers queries by e-mail.

Nonfiction How-to, technical, management as it relates to and includes examples of data centers and data center managers. Special issues: "The January/February issue is the annual 'Emerging Technologies' issue. Articles for this issue are visionary and product neutral." No product reviews, interviews/profiles, reprints of any kind, or general tech or management articles. **Buys 15+ mss/year.** Query with published clips. Length: 2,000 word maximum. **Pays 30¢/word and up, based on writer's expertise.**

Photos "We rarely consider freelance photos." State availability with submission. Reviews GIF/JPEG files. Buys one-time rights. Offers no additional payment for photos accepted with ms. Identification of subjects, model releases required.

Tips "See 'Top 10 Reasons for Rejection' online."

$ $THE ELKS MAGAZINE

425 W. Diversey P, Chicago IL 60614-6196. (773)755-4740. E-mail: elksmag@elks.org. Website: www.elks.org/elksmag. Editor: Fred D. Oakes. **Contact:** Anna L. Idol, managing editor. **25% freelance written.** Magazine

published 10 times/year with basic mission of being the "voice of the Elks." All material concerning the news of the Elks is written in-house. Estab. 1922. Circ. 1,120,000. **Pays on acceptance.** Buys first North American serial rights. Responds in 1 week to queries Responds in 1 month with a yes/no on ms purchase to mss. Sample copy for 9 × 12 SAE with 4 first-class stamps or online. Writer's guidelines online.

● Accepts queries by mail, but purchase decision is based on final mss only.

Nonfiction "We're really interested in seeing manuscripts on business, technology, history, or just intriguing topics, ranging from sports to science." No fiction, politics, religion, controversial issues, travel, first-person, fillers, or verse. **Buys 20-30 mss/year.** Send complete ms. Length: 1,500-2,500 words. **Pays 20¢/word.**

Photos If possible, please advise where photographs may be found. Photographs taken and submitted by the writer are paid for separately at $25 each. Vertical scenics-send transparencies, slides. $475 for one-time cover rights.

Tips "Please try us first. We'll get back to you soon."

$ $ 🖂 FRANCHISE CANADA MAGAZINE

August Communications, 225-530 Century St., Winnipeg MB R3H 0Y4, Canada. Fax: (866)957-0217. E-mail: j.johnson@august.ca. Website: www.august.ca. Managing Editor: Adam Peeler. **Contact:** Jackie Johnson, editor. **70% freelance written.** Bimonthly magazine covering the franchising industry in Canada. "*Franchise Canada Magazine* is the Canadian Franchise Association publication for all franchise industry stakeholders, including current and future franchisees and franchisors." Estab. 1999. Circ. 6,500. Pays 30 days after publication. Publishes ms an average of 2 months after acceptance. Byline given. Buys all rights. Accepts queries by e-mail, fax.

Nonfiction How-to (investigate a franchise system—research methods), interview/profile (CFA franchise members/businesses), technical (aspects of franchising). **Buys 12 mss/year.** Query with published clips. Length: 1,000-1,800 words. **Pays 15-30¢/word.**

Photos State availability with submission. Reviews GIF/JPEG files. Buys all rights. Negotiates payment individually. Captions required.

Columns/Departments Franchisor Profiles (profiles of CFA members), 1,500-1,800 words. **Buys 10 mss/year.** Query with published clips. **Pays 15-30¢/word.**

Tips "Research the Canadian Franchise Association website, www.cfa.ca."

$ $ THE KEEPER'S LOG

U.S. Lighthouse Society, 244 Kearny St., San Francisco CA 94108. (415)362-7255. **Contact:** Wayne Wheeler, editor. **10% freelance written.** Quarterly magazine covering lighthouses, lightships, and human interest relating to them. "Our audience is national (some foreign members). The magazine carries historical and contemporary information (articles) relating to technical, human interest, history, etc." Estab. 1984. Circ. 11,000. Pays on publication. Publishes ms an average of 6 months after acceptance. Byline given. Buys first rights. Editorial lead time 6 months. Accepts queries by mail. Responds in 1 week to queries. Sample copy for $5. Writer's guidelines for #10 SASE.

Nonfiction Historical/nostalgic, personal experience, photo feature, technical. Ghost stories need not apply. Buys 1 mss/year. Query. Length: 2,500-5,000 words. **Pays $200-400.**

Photos State availability with submission. Reviews 5 × 7 prints. Offers no additional payment for photos accepted with ms. Identification of subjects required.

$ $ KIWANIS

3636 Woodview Trace, Indianapolis IN 46268-3196. (317)875-8755. Fax: (317)879-0204. E-mail: jbrockley@kiwanis.org. Website: www.kiwanis.org. **Contact:** Jack Brockley, managing editor. **10% freelance written.** Magazine published 6 times/year for business and professional persons and their families. Estab. 1917. Circ. 240,000. **Pays on acceptance.** Publishes ms an average of 6 months after acceptance. Byline given. Offers 40% kill fee. Buys first rights. Accepts queries by mail, e-mail, fax. Responds in 1 month to queries. Sample copy and writer's guidelines for 9 × 12 SAE with 5 first class stamps. Writer's guidelines online.

● No unsolicited mss.

Nonfiction Articles about social and civic betterment, small-business concerns, children, science, education, religion, family, health, recreation, etc. Emphasis on objectivity, intelligent analysis, and thorough research of contemporary issues. Positive tone preferred. Concise, lively writing, absence of clichés, and impartial presentation of controversy required. Articles must include information and quotations from international sources. "We have a continuing need for articles that concern helping youth, particularly prenatal through age 5: day care, developmentally appropriate education, early intervention for at-risk children, parent education, safety and health. No fiction, personal essays, profiles, travel pieces, fillers, or verse of any kind. A light or humorous approach is welcomed where the subject is appropriate and all other requirements are observed." **Buys 20 mss/year.** Length: 500-1,200 words. **Pays $300-600.** Sometimes pays expenses of writers on assignment.

Photos "We accept photos submitted with manuscripts. Our rate for a manuscript with good photos is higher than for one without." Buys one-time rights. Identification of subjects, model releases required.

Tips "We will work with any writer who presents a strong feature article idea applicable to our magazine's audience and who will prove he or she knows the craft of writing. First, obtain writer's guidelines and a sample copy. Study for general style and content. When querying, present detailed outline of proposed manuscript's focus and editorial intent. Indicate expert sources to be used, as well as possible Kiwanis sources for quotations and anecdotes. Present a well-researched, smoothly written manuscript that contains a 'human quality' with the use of anecdotes, practical examples, quotations, etc."

N $ $ LEGACY MAGAZINE

The Magazine of the National Association for Interpretation, National Association for Interpretation, P.O. Box 2246, Fort Collins CO 80522. (970)484-8283. Fax: (970)484-8179. E-mail: design@interpnet.com. Website: www .interpnet.com/interpnet/miscpages/publication.htm. **Contact:** Paul Caputo, art and publications director. **80% freelance written.** Bimonthly magazine covering heritage interpretation (national parks, museums, nature centers, aquaria, etc.). "The National Association for Interpretation's premier publication, *Legacy Magazine* offers a thought-provoking look at the field of heritage interpretation through articles about individuals who interpret natural and cultural history, biographies of important figures in or related to the field, discussions of interpretive sites, and trends in interpretation. The magazine, published 6 times a year, appeals to those interested in learning about natural or cultural heritage and interpretive sites around the world." Estab. 1989. Circ. 5,000. Pays on publication. Publishes ms an average of 4 months after acceptance. Byline given. Offers 80% kill fee. Buys first North American serial rights. Editorial lead time 6 months. Submit seasonal material 4 months in advance. Accepts queries by mail, e-mail, fax, phone. Accepts simultaneous submissions. Responds in 1 month to queries; 4 months to mss. Sample copy online. Writer's guidelines by e-mail.

Nonfiction Essays, historical/nostalgic, opinion, personal experience, photo feature, travel, heritage interpretation. **Buys 12-20 mss/year.** Query. Length: 500-2,500 words. **Pays $75-350.** Sometimes pays expenses of writers on assignment.

Photos State availability with submission. Reviews contact sheets, 4×6 prints, GIF/JPEG files. Buys one-time rights. Offers $75-100/photo. Captions required.

Columns/Departments Visitor's View (review of personal experience at a heritage interpretation site), 500 words. **Buys 6 mss/year.** Query. **Pays $75-150.**

Tips "Please review the article descriptions in our writer's guidelines before submitting a query."

$ $ THE LION

300 W. 22nd St., Oak Brook IL 60523-8815. (630)571-5466. Fax: (630)571-8890. E-mail: rkleinfe@lionsclubs.org. Website: www.lionsclubs.org. **Contact:** Robert Kleinfelder, senior editor. **35% freelance written.** Works with a small number of new/unpublished writers each year. Monthly magazine covering service club organization for Lions Club members and their families. Estab. 1918. Circ. 490,000. **Pays on acceptance.** Publishes ms an average of 5 months after acceptance. Byline given. Buys all rights. Accepts queries by mail, e-mail, fax, phone. Responds in 1 month to queries. Sample copy and writer's guidelines free.

Nonfiction Welcomes humor, if sophisticated but clean; no sensationalism. Prefers anecdotes in articles. Photo feature (must be of a Lions Club service project), informational (issues of interest to civic-minded individuals). No travel, biography, or personal experiences. **Buys 40 mss/year.** Length: 500-1,500 words. **Pays $100-750.** Sometimes pays expenses of writers on assignment.

Photos Purchased with accompanying ms. "Photos should be at least 5×7 glossies; color prints or slides are preferred. Be sure photos are clear and as candid as possible." Total purchase price for ms includes payment for photos accepted with ms. Captions required.

Tips "Send detailed description of proposed article. Query first and request writer's guidelines and sample copy. Incomplete details on how the Lions involved actually carried out a project and poor quality photos are the most frequent mistakes made by writers in completing an article assignment for us. No gags, fillers, quizzes, or poems are accepted. We are geared increasingly to an international audience. Writers who travel internationally could query for possible assignments, although only locally related expenses could be paid."

$ $ $ THE MEETING PROFESSIONAL

Meeting Professionals International, 4455 LBJ Freeway, Suite 1200, Dallas TX 75244-5903. Fax: (972)702-3096. E-mail: publications@mpiweb.org. Website: www.mpiweb.org/news. Associate Publisher: Bruce MacMillan. Editor-in-Chief: John Delavan. **Contact:** Michael Pinchera, publications coordinator. **60% freelance written.** Monthly magazine covering the global meeting idustry. "*The Meeting Professional* delivers strategic editorial content on meeting industry trends, opportunities and items of importance in the hope of fostering professional development and career enhancement. The magazine is mailed monthly to 19,000 MPI members and 11,500 qualified nonmember subscribers and meeting industry planners. It is also distributed at major industry shows, such as IT&ME and EIBTM, at MPI conferences, and upon individual request.'' Circ. 32,000. **Pays on acceptance.** Publishes ms an average of 2-3 months after acceptance. Byline given. Offers a negotiable kill fee. Buys all rights. Editorial lead time 2 months. Submit seasonal material 3 months in advance. Accepts queries by mail, e-mail, fax. Sample copy for free. Writer's guidelines by e-mail.

Nonfiction General interest, how-to, interview/profile, travel, industry-related. No duplications from other industry publications. **Buys 60 mss/year.** Query with published clips. Length: 1,000-2,500 words. **Pays 50-75¢/word for assigned articles.**

Tips ''Understand and have experience within the industry. Writers who are familiar with our magazine and our competitors are better able to get our attention, send better queries, and get assignments.''

$ $ PERSPECTIVES IN HEALTH

Pan American Health Organization, 525 23rd St. NW, Washington DC 20037-2895. (202)974-3122. Fax: (202)974-3143. E-mail: eberwind@paho.org. Website: www.paho.org. **Contact:** Donna Eberwine, editor. **80% freelance written.** Magazine published 3 times/year covering international public health with a focus on the Americas. ''*Perspectives in Health*, the popular magazine of the Pan American Health Organization (PAHO), was created in 1996 to serve as a forum on current issues in the area of international public health and human development. PAHO works with the international community, government institutions, nongovernmental organizations, universities, community groups, and others to strengthen national and local public health systems and to improve the health and well-being of the peoples of the Americas.'' Estab. 1996. Circ. 10,000. **Pays on acceptance.** Publishes ms an average of 6 months after acceptance. Byline given. Buys first North American serials rights and electronic rights to post articles on the PAHO website. Editorial lead time 2 months. Accepts queries by mail, e-mail, fax, phone. Responds in 2 months to queries. Sample copy and writer's guidelines free.

• Each issue of *Perspectives in Health* is published in English and Spanish.

Nonfiction Subject matter: Culturally insightful and scientifically sound articles related to international public health and human development issues and programs affecting North America, Latin America, and the Caribbean. The story angle should have wide relevancy—i.e., capturing national and particularly international concerns, even if the setting is local—and should be high in human interest content: ''international public health with a human face.'' General topics may include (but are not limited to) AIDS and other sexually transmitted diseases, maternal and child health, the environment, food and nutrition, cardiovascular diseases, cancer, mental health, oral health, violence, veterinary health, disaster preparedness, health education and promotion, substance abuse, water and sanitation, and issues related to the health and well-being of women, adolescents, workers, the elderly, and minority groups in the countries of the Americas. Historical pieces on the region's public health ''trail blazers'' and innovators are also welcome. General interest, historical/nostalgic, interview/profile, opinion, personal experience, photo feature. No highly technical, highly bureaucratic articles. **Buys 12 mss/year.** Query with or without published clips or send complete ms. Length: 1,500-3,000 words. **Pays $250.** Sometimes pays expenses of writers on assignment.

Photos State availability with submission. Reviews contact sheets, negatives, transparencies, prints. Buys one-time rights. Negotiates payment individually. Captions, identification of subjects, model releases required.

Columns/Departments Last Word, 750 words. **Buys 2 mss/year.** Query with or without published clips or send complete ms. **Pays $100.**

Tips ''*Perspectives* puts the human face on international public health issues and programs. All facts must be documented. Quote people involved with the programs described. Get on-site information—not simply an Internet-research story.''

$ $ RECREATION NEWS

Official Publication of the ESM Association of the Capital Region, 7339 D Hanover Pkwy., Greenbelt MD 20770. (301)474-4600. Fax: (301)474-6283. E-mail: editor@recreationnews.com. Website: www.recreationnews.com. **Contact:** Francis X. Orphe, editor. **85% freelance written.** Monthly guide to leisure-time activities for federal and private industry workers covering outdoor recreation, travel, fitness and indoor pasttimes. Estab. 1979. Circ. 110,000. Pays on publication. Publishes ms an average of 8 months after acceptance. Byline given. Buys first, second serial (reprint) rights. Submit seasonal material 10 months in advance. Accepts queries by mail, e-mail, fax, phone. Accepts previously published material. Accepts simultaneous submissions. Responds in 2 months to queries. Sample copy and writer's guidelines for 9×12 SAE with $1.05 in postage.

Nonfiction Articles Editor. Historical/nostalgic (Washington-related), personal experience (with recreation, life in Washington), travel (mid-Atlantic travel only), sports; hobbies. Special issues: skiing (December). **Buys 45 mss/year.** Query with published clips. Length: 800-2,000 words. **Pays $50-300.**

Reprints Send tearsheet or typed ms with rights for sale noted and information about when and where the material previously appeared. Pays $50.

Photos Photo Editor. Call for details.

Tips ''Our writers generally have a few years of professional writing experience and their work runs to the lively and conversational. We like more manuscripts in a wide range of recreational topics, including the off-beat. The areas of our publication most open to freelancers are general articles on travel and sports, both participational and spectator, also historic in the DC area. In general, stories on sites visited need to include info on nearby places of interest and places to stop for lunch, to shop, etc.''

$ $ $ SCOUTING

Boy Scouts of America, 1325 W. Walnut Hill Lane, P.O. Box 152079, Irving TX 75015-2079. (972)580-2367. Fax: (972)580-2367. E-mail: 103064.3363@compuserve.com. Website: www.scoutingmagazine.org. Executive Editor: Scott Daniels. **Contact:** Jon C. Halter, editor. **80% freelance written.** Magazine published 6 times/year covering Scouting activities for adult leaders of the Boy Scouts, Cub Scouts, and Venturing. Estab. 1913. Circ. 1,000,000. Pays on acceptance for major features and some shorter features. Publishes ms an average of 18 months after acceptance. Byline given. Buys first North American serial rights. Editorial lead time 1 year. Submit seasonal material 1 year in advance. Accepts queries by mail, fax. Accepts previously published material. Accepts simultaneous submissions. Responds in 1 month to queries; 2 months to mss. Sample copy for $2.50 and 9×12 SAE with 4 first-class stamps or online. Writer's guidelines online.

> O→ Break in with ''a profile of an outstanding Scout leader who has useful advice for new volunteer leaders (especially good if the situation involves urban Scouting or Scouts with disabilities or other extraordinary roles).''

Nonfiction Program activities, leadership techniques and styles, profiles, inspirational, occasional general interest for adults (humor, historical, nature, social issues, trends). Inspirational, interview/profile. **Buys 20-30 mss/year.** Query with published clips and SASE. Length: 600-1,200 words. **Pays $750-1,000 for major articles, $300-500 for shorter features.** Pays expenses of writers on assignment.

Reprints Send photocopy of article and information about when and where the article previously appeared. ''First-person accounts of meaningful Scouting experiences (previously published in local newspapers, etc.) are a popular subject.''

Photos State availability with submission. Reviews transparencies, prints. Buys one-time rights. Identification of subjects required.

Columns/Departments Way It Was (Scouting history), 600-750 words; Family Talk (family—raising kids, etc.), 600-750 words. **Buys 8-12 mss/year.** Query. **Pays $300-500.**

Fillers ''Limited to personal accounts of humorous or inspirational Scouting experiences.'' Anecdotes, short humor. **Buys 15-25/year.** Length: 50-150 words. **Pays $25 on publication.**

> ■ The online version carries original content not found in the print edition and includes writer's guidelines. Contact: Scott Daniels.

Tips ''*Scouting* magazine articles are mainly about successful program activities conducted by or for Cub Scout packs, Boy Scout troops, and Venturing crews. We also include features on winning leadership techniques and styles, profiles of outstanding individual leaders, and inspirational accounts (usually first person) or *Scouting*'s impact on an individual, either as a youth or while serving as a volunteer adult leader. Because most volunteer Scout leaders are also parents of children of Scout age, *Scouting* is also considered a family magazine. We publish material we feel will help parents in strengthening their families (because they often deal with communicating and interacting with young people, many of these features are useful to a reader in both roles as parent and Scout leader).''

$ $ SOUTH AMERICAN EXPLORER

South American Explorers, 126 Indian Creek Rd., Ithaca NY 14850. (607)277-0488. Fax: (607)277-6122. E-mail: don@saexplorers.org. Website: www.saexplorers.org. **Contact:** Don Montague, editor-in-chief. **80% freelance written.** Quarterly travel/scientific/educational journal covering exploration, conservation, anthropology, ethnography, field sports, natural history, history, archeology, linguistics, and just about anything relating to South America. ''The *South American Explorer* goes primarily (but not exclusively) to members of the South American Explorers. Readers are interested in all the above subjects as well as endangered peoples, wildlife protection, volunteer opportunities, etc.'' Estab. 1977. Circ. 10,000. Pays on publication. Publishes ms an average of 2-3 months after acceptance. Byline given. Buys first rights. Editorial lead time 3 months. Accepts queries by mail, e-mail, fax, phone. Accepts previously published material. Accepts simultaneous submissions. Responds in 1 month to queries.

Nonfiction All content must relate to South America in some way. Book excerpts, essays, exposé, general interest, historical/nostalgic, how-to, humor, inspirational, interview/profile, new product, opinion, personal experience, photo feature, religious, technical, travel. No ''My South American Vacation,'' ''The Extraterrestrial Origins of Machu Picchu,'' ''Encounters with the Amazon Yeti,'' ''My Journal of Traveling Through South America.'' **Buys 20 mss/year.** Query with or without published clips or send complete ms. Length: 1,000-4,500 words. **Pays $50-400 for assigned articles; $50-300 for unsolicited articles.**

Photos Send photos with submission. Reviews contact sheets, negatives, transparencies, prints, GIF/JPEG files. Buys one-time rights. Negotiates payment individually. Captions required.

Columns/Departments Ask the Doctor; South American Explorers; Book Reviews; Movie Reviews; News Shorts; Tips and Notes; Cyber Page. **Buys 6 mss/year.** Send complete ms. **Pays $50-250.**

Fillers Length: 500-1,500 words.

$ TRAIL & TIMBERLINE

The Colorado Mountain Club, 710 10th St., Suite 200, Golden CO 80401. (303)279-3080, ext. 105. Fax: (303)279-9690. E-mail: beckwt@cmc.org. Website: www.cmc.org. **Contact:** Tom Beckwith, editor. **80% freelance written.** Bimonthly official publication of the Colorado Mountain Club. "Articles in *Trail & Timberline* conform to the mission statement of the Colorado Mountain Club to unite the energy, interest, and knowledge of lovers of the Colorado mountains, to collect and disseminate information, to stimulate public interest, and to encourage preservation of the mountains of Colorado and the Rocky Mountain region." Estab. 1918. Circ. 10,500. Pays on publication. Publishes ms an average of 2 months after acceptance. Byline given. Buys all rights. Editorial lead time 6 months. Submit seasonal material 6 months in advance. Accepts queries by mail, e-mail. Accepts previously published material. Responds in 1 week to queries; 1 month to mss. Sample copy for $5. Writer's guidelines online.

Nonfiction Essays, humor, personal experience, photo feature, travel. **Buys 10-15 mss/year.** Query. Length: 500-2,000 words. **Pays $50.**

Photos Send photos with submission. Reviews contact sheets, 35mm transparencies, 3×5 or larger prints, GIF/JPEG files. Buys one-time rights. Offers no additional payment for photos accepted with ms. Captions, identification of subjects, model releases required.

Columns/Departments Wild Colorado (conservation/public lands issues), 1,000 words; Education (mountain education/natural history), 500-1,000 words. **Buys 6-12 mss/year.** Query. **Pays $50.**

Poetry Jared Smith, associate editor, poetry. Avant-garde, free verse, traditional. **Buys 6-12 poems/year.**

Tips "Writers should be familiar with the purposes and ethos of the Colorado Mountain Club before querying. Writer's guidelines are available and should be consulted—particularly for poetry submissions. All submissions must conform to the mission statement of the Colorado Mountain Club."

Ⓝ $ $ $ UPDATE

New York Academy of Sciences Magazine, New York Academy of Sciences, 2 E. 63rd St., New York NY 10021. E-mail: dvanatta@nyas.org. Website: www.nyas.org. **Contact:** Dan Van Atta, editor. **40% freelance written.** Magazine published 7 times/year covering science, health issues. Scientific newsletter for members of the New York Academy of Sciences. Estab. 2001. Circ. 25,000. Pays on publication. Publishes ms an average of 1 month after acceptance. Byline sometimes given. Not copyrighted. Buys first, electronic rights, makes work-for-hire assignments. Editorial lead time 2 months. Submit seasonal material 2 months in advance. Accepts queries by mail, e-mail. Sample copy online.

Nonfiction All articles "must be science or medical related in every case." Book excerpts, essays, general interest, historical/nostalgic, interview/profile, technical. No science fiction, any pieces exceeding 1,000 words, or subjects that aren't current. **Buys 6-7 mss/year.** Query. Length: 300-1,000 words. **Pays $200-1,200.** Sometimes pays expenses of writers on assignment.

Photos State availability with submission. Reviews GIF/JPEG files. Buys one-time rights. Negotiates payment individually. Captions, identification of subjects, model releases required.

Tips "Submit detailed summary or outline of the proposed article's content. Subject matter must be current and topical, as well as scientific, technical, or medical in nature. We prefer interviews with noted scientific and medical researchers whose work is cutting edge and credible. Articles should be relatively brief and contain some 'news' element, i.e., important recent development or unusual, attention-getting element. All sources must be identified and credible."

$ $ VFW MAGAZINE

Veterans of Foreign Wars of the United States, 406 W. 34th St., Kansas City MO 64111. (816)756-3390. Fax: (816)968-1169. E-mail: jcarter@vfw.org. Website: www.vfw.org. **Contact:** Rich Kolb, editor-in-chief. **40% freelance written.** Monthly magazine on veterans' affairs, military history, patriotism, defense, and current events. "*VFW Magazine* goes to its members worldwide, all having served honorably in the armed forces overseas from World War II through the war on terrorism." Circ. 1,800,000. **Pays on acceptance.** Byline given. Offers 50% kill fee. Buys first rights. Submit seasonal material 6 months in advance. Accepts queries by mail, e-mail, fax. Responds in 2 months to queries. Sample copy for 9×12 SAE with 5 first-class stamps.

⊶ Break in with "fresh and innovative angles on veterans' rights; stories on little-known exploits in U.S. military history. Will be particularly in the market for Korean War battle accounts during 2001-2003. Upbeat articles about severely disabled veterans who have overcome their disabilities; feel-good patriotism pieces; current events as they relate to defense policy; health and retirement pieces are always welcome.''

Nonfiction Veterans' and defense affairs, recognition of veterans and military service, current foreign policy, American armed forces abroad and international events affecting US national security are in demand. **Buys 25-30 mss/year.** Query with 1-page outline, résumé, and published clips. Length: 1,000 words. **Pays up to $500 maximum unless otherwise negotiated.**

Photos Send photos with submission. Reviews contact sheets, negatives, color ($2^1/_4 \times 2^1/_4$) preferred transparencies, 5×7 or 8×10 b&w prints. Buys first North American rights. Captions, identification of subjects required.

Tips ''Absolute accuracy and quotes from relevant individuals are a must. Bibliographies useful if subject required extensive research and/or is open to dispute. Counsult *The Associated Press Stylebook* for correct grammar and punctuation. Please enclose a 3-sentence biography describing your military service and your military experience in the field in which you are writing. No phone queries.''

$ $ VINTAGE SNOWMOBILE MAGAZINE

Vintage Snowmobile Club of America, P.O. Box 508, Luverne MN 56156. (507)283-1860. Fax: (507)449-0004. E-mail: info@vsca.com. Website: www.vsca.com. **Contact:** Terry Hoffman, editor. **75% freelance written.** Quarterly magazine covering vintage snowmobiles and collectors. *Vintage Snowmobile Magazine* deals with vintage snowmobiles and is sent to members of the Vintage Snowmobile Club of America. Estab. 1987. Circ. 2,400. **Pays on acceptance.** Publishes ms an average of 3 months after acceptance. Byline sometimes given. Buys first North American serial rights. Editorial lead time 2 months. Submit seasonal material 3 months in advance. Accepts queries by mail, e-mail, fax, phone. Responds in 1 month to queries; 2 months to mss.

Nonfiction General interest, historical/nostalgic, humor, photo feature, coverage of shows. Query with published clips. Length: 200-2,000 words. **Pays 10-12¢/word for assigned articles; 3-5¢/word for unsolicited articles.** Sometimes pays expenses of writers on assignment.

Photos Send photos with submission. Reviews 3×5 prints, GIF/JPEG files. Buys all rights. Negotiates payment individually.

Columns/Departments Featured Sleds Stories, 500 words. Query with published clips. **Pays 10-12¢/word.**

Fillers Gags to be illustrated by cartoonist. **Buys 3/year.**

ASTROLOGY, METAPHYSICAL & NEW AGE

$ $ $ $ BODY & SOUL

Whole Living, New Age Publishing, Inc., 42 Pleasant St., Watertown MA 02472. (617)926-0200. Website: www.bodyandsoulmag.com. Editor-in-Chief: Seth Bauer. Managing Editor: Tania Hannan. **Contact:** Editorial Department. **75% freelance written.** Works with a small number of new/unpublished writers each year. Magazine published 8 times/year emphasizing ''personal fulfillment and social change. The audience we reach is primarily female, college-educated, 25-55 years of age, concerned about social values, humanitarianism and balance in personal life.'' Estab. 1974. Circ. 230,000. Publishes ms an average of 4 months after acceptance. Byline given. Offers 25% kill fee. Buys first North American serial, electronic rights. Editorial lead time 6 months. Submit seasonal material 6 months in advance. Accepts queries by mail. Accepts simultaneous submissions. Responds in 2 months to queries; 2 months to mss. Sample copy for $5 and 9×12 SAE. Writer's guidelines online.

> ⚠ No phone calls. The process of decision making takes time and involves more than one editor. An answer cannot be given over the phone.

Nonfiction Book excerpts, essays, how-to, inspirational, interview/profile, new product, personal experience, travel, spiritual. **Buys 50 mss/year.** Query with published clips. Length: 100-2,500 words. **Pays 75¢-$1/word.** Pays expenses of writers on assignment.

Reprints Send tearsheet or photocopy.

Columns/Departments Care (health/beauty/fitness); Choose (home/natural selections); Nourish (food/nutrition); Evolve (mind/spirit/first person), 600-1,300 words. **Buys 50 mss/year.** Query with published clips. **Pays 75¢-$1/word.**

Tips ''Read the magazine and get a sense of type of writing run in column. In particular we are interested in seeing inspirational, first-person pieces that highlight an engaging idea, experience or issue. We are also looking for new cutting-edge thinking. No e-mail or phone queries, please. Begin with a query, résumé and published clips — we will contact you for the manuscript. Query first with clips. A query is one to two paragraphs—if you need more space than that to *present* the idea, then you don't have a clear grip on it.''

$ $FATE MAGAZINE

P.O. Box 460, Lakeville MN 55044. (952)431-2050. E-mail: fate@fatemag.com. Website: www.fatemag.com. **Contact:** Editor. **70% freelance written.** Estab. 1948. Circ. 20,000. Pays on publication. Byline given. Buys all rights. Responds in 3 months to queries.

Nonfiction Personal psychic and mystical experiences, 350-500 words. **Pays $25.** Articles on parapsychology, Fortean phenomena, cryptozoology, spiritual healing, flying saucers, new frontiers of science, and mystical aspects of ancient civilizations, 500-3,000 words. Must include complete authenticating details. Prefers interesting accounts of single events rather than roundups. "We very frequently accept manuscripts from new writers; the majority are individual's first-person accounts of their own psychic/mystical/spiritual experiences. We do need to have all details, where, when, why, who and what, included for complete documentation. We ask for a notarized statement attesting to truth of the article." Query. **Pays 10¢/word.**

Photos Buys slides, prints, or digital photos/illustrations with ms. Pays $10.

Fillers Fillers are especially welcomed and must be be fully authenticated also, and on similar topics. Length: 50-300 words.

Tips "We would like more stories about *current* paranormal or unusual events."

$MAGICAL BLEND MAGAZINE

A Primer for the 21st Century, 133½ Broadway, Chico CA 95928. (530)893-9037. Fax: (530)893-9076. E-mail: editor@magicalblend.com. Website: www.magicalblend.com. **Contact:** Michael Peter Langevin, editor. **50% freelance written.** Bimonthly magazine covering social and mystical transformation. "*Magical Blend* endorses no one pathway to spiritual growth, but attempts to explore many alternative possibilities to help transform the planet." Estab. 1980. Circ. 100,000. Pays on publication. Publishes ms an average of 2 months after acceptance. Byline given. Responds in 2-6 months to mss. Sample copy for free. Writer's guidelines for #10 SASE.

   0–ℸ Break in by "writing a great article that gives our readers something they can use in their daily lives or obtain 'name' interviews."

Nonfiction "Articles must reflect our standards; see our magazine." Book excerpts, essays, general interest, inspirational, interview/profile, religious, travel. No poetry or fiction. **Buys 24 mss/year.** Send complete ms. Length: 1,000-2,000 words. **Pays $35-100.**

Photos State availability with submission. Reviews transparencies. Buys all rights. Negotiates payment individually. Identification of subjects, model releases required.

Fillers Newsbreaks. **Buys 12-20/year.** Length: 300-450 words. **Pays variable rate.**

$NEW YORK SPIRIT MAGAZINE

107 Sterling Place, Brooklyn NY 11217. (800)634-0989. Fax: (718)230-3459. E-mail: office@nyspirit.com. Website: www.nyspirit.com. Bimonthly tabloid covering spirituality and personal growth and transformation. "We are a magazine that caters to the holistic health community in New York City." Circ. 50,000. **Pays on acceptance.** Publishes ms an average of 3 months after acceptance. Byline given. Buys first rights. Editorial lead time 1 month. Accepts previously published material. Accepts simultaneous submissions. Responds in 1 month to queries. Sample copy for 8×10 SAE and 10 first-class stamps. Writer's guidelines online.

Nonfiction Essays, how-to, humor, inspirational, interview/profile, photo feature. **Buys 30 mss/year.** Query with or without published clips. Length: 1,000-3,500 words. **Pays $150 maximum.**

Photos State availability with submission. Model releases required.

Columns/Departments Fitness (new ideas in staying fit), 1,500 words. **Pays $150.**

Fiction Humorous, mainstream, inspirational. **Buys 5 mss/year.** Query with published clips. Length: 1,000-3,500 words. **Pays $150.**

Tips "Be vivid and descriptive. We are *very* interested in hearing from new writers."

$PANGAIA

Earthwise Spirituality, Blessed Bee, Inc., P.O. Box 641, Point Arena CA 95468. Fax: (707)882-2793. E-mail: info@pangaia.com. Website: www.pangaia.com. Editor: Anne Newkirk Niven. Managing Editor: Elizabeth Barrette. **50% freelance written.** Quarterly magazine of Earth spirituality covering Earth-based religions. "We publish articles pertinent to an Earth-loving readership. Mysticism, science, humor, tools all are described." Estab. 1994. Circ. 8,500. Pays on publication. Publishes ms an average of 6 months after acceptance. Byline given. Offers $10 kill fee. Buys first North American serial, electronic rights. Editorial lead time 6 months. Submit seasonal material 6 months in advance. Accepts queries by mail, e-mail. Responds in 2-8 weeks to queries. Sample copy for $5. Writer's guidelines online.

Nonfiction Book excerpts, essays, how-to, humor, inspirational, interview/profile, photo feature, religious, Reviews. Special issues: "Land Before Time" (Winter 2003-2004); "Arts & Culture" (Spring 2004); "Animal Magic" (Summer 2004); "Science and Magic" (Autumn 2004). No material on unrelated topics. **Buys 30 mss/year.** Query. Length: 500-5,000 words. **Pays 1-3¢/word.** Sometimes pays with contributor copies or other premiums rather than a cash payment if negotiated/requested by writer. Sometimes pays expenses of writers on assignment.

Photos State availability with submission. Reviews 5×7 prints, GIF/JPEG files. Buys one-time rights. Negotiates payment individually. Model releases required.

Fiction Ethnic, fantasy, religious, science fiction, Pagan/Gaian. No grim or abstract stories. **Buys 5 mss/year.** Send complete ms. Length: 500-5,000 words. **Pays 1-3¢/word.**

Poetry Will consider most forms. Free verse, traditional. "Avoid clichés like the burning times. Do not send forms with rhyme/meter unless those features are executed perfectly." **Buys 12 poems/year.** Submit maximum 5 poems. Length: 3-100 lines. **Pays $10.**

Tips "Share a spiritual insight that can enlighten others. Back up your facts with citations where relevant, and make those facts sound like the neatest thing since self-lighting charcoal. Explain how to solve a problem; offer a new way to make the world a better place. We would also like to see serious scholarship on nature religion topics, material of interest to intermediate or advanced practicioners, which is both accurate and engaging."

$SHAMAN'S DRUM

A Journal of Experiential Shamanism, Cross-Cultural Shamanism Network, P.O. Box 270, Williams OR 97544. (541)846-1313. Fax: (541)846-1204. **Contact:** Timothy White, editor. **75% freelance written.** Quarterly educational magazine of cross-cultural shamanism. "*Shaman's Drum* seeks contributions directed toward a general but well-informed audience. Our intent is to expand, challenge, and refine our readers' and our understanding of shamanism in practice. Topics include indigenous medicineway practices, contemporary shamanic healing practices, ecstatic spiritual practices, and contemporary shamanic psychotherapies. Our overall focus is cross-cultural, but our editorial approach is culture-specific—we prefer that authors focus on specific ethnic traditions or personal practices about which they have significant firsthand experience. We are looking for examples of not only how shamanism has transformed individual lives but also practical ways it can help ensure survival of life on the planet. We want material that captures the heart and feeling of shamanism and that can inspire people to direct action and participation, and to explore shamanism in greater depth." Estab. 1985. Circ. 14,000. Publishes ms an average of 6 months after acceptance. Byline given. Buys first North American serial, first rights. Editorial lead time 1 year. Accepts previously published material. Responds in 3 months to queries. Sample copy for $7. Writer's guidelines for #10 SASE.

Nonfiction Book excerpts, essays, interview/profile (please query), opinion, personal experience, photo feature. No fiction, poetry, or fillers. **Buys 16 mss/year.** Send complete ms. Length: 5,000-8,000 words. **Pays 5-8¢/ word, "depending on how much we have to edit."**

Reprints Send ms with rights for sale noted and information about when and where the material previously appeared. Pays 50% of amount paid for an original article.

Photos Send photos with submission. Reviews contact sheets, transparencies, All size prints. Buys one-time rights. Offers $40-50/photo. Identification of subjects required.

Columns/Departments Judy Wells, Earth Circles. Timothy White, Reviews. Earth Circles (news format, concerned with issues, events, organizations related to shamanism, indigenous peoples, and caretaking Earth. Relevant clippings also sought. Reviews (in-depth reviews of books about shamanism or closely related subjects such as indigenous lifestyles, ethnobotany, transpersonal healing, and ecstatic spirituality), 500-1,500 words. **Buys 8 mss/year.** Query. **Pays 5¢/word.**

Tips "All articles must have a clear relationship to shamanism, but may be on topics which have not traditionally been defined as shamanic. We prefer original material that is based on, or illustrated with, first-hand knowledge and personal experience. Articles should be well documented with descriptive examples and pertinent background information. Photographs and illustrations of high quality are always welcome and can help sell articles."

AUTOMOTIVE & MOTORCYCLE

$$AMERICAN IRON MAGAZINE

TAM Communications, Inc., 1010 Summer St., Stamford CT 06905. (203)425-8777. Fax: (203)425-8775. **Contact:** Chris Maida, editor. **40% freelance written.** Family-oriented magazine publishing 13 issues/year covering Harley-Davidson and other US brands with a definite emphasis on Harleys. Circ. 159,000. Pays on publication. Publishes ms an average of 6 months after acceptance. Byline given. Not copyrighted. Responds in 6 months to queries. Sample copy for $10.

● Looking for people who are writers and motorcyclists who know the verbage. Call before submitting (stories/photos).

Nonfiction "Clean and nonoffensive. Stories include bike features, touring stories, how-to tech stories with step-by-step photos, historical pieces, events, opinion, and various topics of interest to the people who ride

Harley-Davidsons." No fiction. **Buys 60 mss/year.** Length: 1,200 words. **Pays $400 on publication for touring articles with slides to first-time writers.**

Photos Send SASE for return of photos. Reviews color slides for tour stories.

Tips "We're not looking for stories about the top 10 biker bars or do-it-yourself tattoos. We're looking for articles about motorcycling, the people, and the machines. If you understand the Harley mystique and can write well, you have a good chance of being published."

$ AMERICAN MOTORCYCLIST

American Motorcyclist Association, 13515 Yarmouth Dr., Pickerington OH 43147. (614)856-1900. Fax: (614)856-1920. E-mail: bwood@ama-cycle.org. Website: www.ama-cycle.org. **Contact:** Bill Wood, managing editor. **10% freelance written.** Monthly magazine for "enthusiastic motorcyclists, investing considerable time and money in the sport. We emphasize the motorcyclist, not the vehicle." Estab. 1947. Circ. 260,000. Pays on publication. Byline given. Buys first North American serial rights. Editorial lead time 3 months. Submit seasonal material 4 months in advance. Accepts queries by mail, e-mail. Responds in 5 weeks to queries; 6 weeks to mss. Sample copy for $1.25. Writer's guidelines free.

Nonfiction Interview/profile (with interesting personalities in the world of motorcycling), personal experience, travel. **Buys 8 mss/year.** Query with or without published clips or send complete ms. Length: 1,000-2,500 words. **Pays minimum $8/published column inch.**

Photos Send photos with submission. Reviews transparencies, prints. Buys one-time rights. Pays $50/photo minimum. Captions, identification of subjects required.

Tips "Our major category of freelance stories concerns motorcycling trips to interesting North American destinations. Prefers stories of a timeless nature."

N $ $ AUTO RESTORER

Fancy Publications, Inc., P.O. Box 6050, Mission Viejo CA 92690-6050. (949)855-8822, ext. 3412. Fax: (949)855-3045. E-mail: tkade@fancypubs.com. Website: www.autorestorermagazine.com. **Contact:** Ted Kade, editor. **85% freelance written.** Monthly magazine covering auto restoration. "Our readers own old cars and they work on them. We help our readers by providing as much practical, how-to information as we can about restoration and old cars." Estab. 1989. Pays on publication. Publishes ms an average of 3 months after acceptance. Buys first North American serial, one-time rights. Submit seasonal material 4 months in advance. Accepts queries by mail, e-mail, fax. Responds in 2 months to queries. Sample copy for $7. Writer's guidelines free.

Nonfiction How-to (auto restoration), new product, photo feature, technical, product evaluation. **Buys 60 mss/ year.** Query with or without published clips. Length: 200-2,500 words. **Pays $150/published page, including photos and illustrations.**

Photos Technical drawings that illustrate articles in black ink are welcome. Send photos with submission. Reviews contact sheets, transparencies, 5×7 prints. Offers no additional payment for photos accepted with ms.

Tips "Query first. Interview the owner of a restored car. Present advice to others on how to do a similar restoration. Seek advice from experts. Go light on history and nonspecific details. Make it something that the magazine regularly uses. Do automotive how-tos."

N Ø AUTO WORLD MAGAZINE

American Media, Inc., 1000 American Media Way, Boca Raton FL 33464-1000. (561)998-7293. Fax: (561)998-7265. Website: www.amiautoworld.com. Circ. 400,000.

- Does not buy freelance material or use freelance writers.

N $ $ AUTOMOBILE QUARTERLY

The Connoisseur's Magazine of Motoring Today, Yesterday, and Tomorrow, Automobile Heritage Publishing & Communications LLC, 137 E. Market St., New Albany IN 47150. (812)948-2886. Fax: (812)948-2816. Website: www.autoquarterly.com. Publisher: Gerald Durnell. **Contact:** Mr. Tracy L. Powell, managing editor. **85% freelance written.** Quarterly magazine covering "automotive history, with excellent photography." Estab. 1962. Circ. 8,000. **Pays on acceptance.** Publishes ms an average of 1 year after acceptance. Byline given. Buys first international serial rights. Editorial lead time 9 months. Responds in 1 month to queries; 2 months to mss. Sample copy for $19.95.

Nonfiction Historical/nostalgic, photo feature, technical, biographies. **Buys 25 mss/year.** Query. Length: 2,500-5,000 words. **Pays approximately 35¢/word or more.** Sometimes pays expenses of writers on assignment.

Photos State availability with submission. Reviews 4×5; 35mm; 120 transparencies; historical prints. Buys perpetual rights of published photography per work-for-hire freelance agreement.

Tips "Please query, with clips, via snail mail. No phone calls, please. Study *Automobile Quarterly*'s unique treatment of automotive history first."

$ $ $ $ AUTOWEEK

Crain Communications, Inc., 1155 Gratiot Ave., Detroit MI 48207. (313)446-6000. Fax: (313)446-1027. E-mail: bgritzinger@crain.com. Website: www.autoweek.com. Editor: Dutch Mandell. Managing Editor: Roger Hart. **Contact:** Bob Gritzinger, news editor. **10% freelance written,** mostly by regular contributors. Weekly magazine. "*AutoWeek* is the country's only weekly magazine for the auto enthusiast." Estab. 1958. Circ. 350,000. Pays on publication. Publishes ms an average of 1 month after acceptance. Byline given. Buys first North American serial rights. Accepts queries by mail, e-mail, fax, phone.

Nonfiction Historical/nostalgic, interview/profile, new product. **Buys 100 mss/year.** Query. Length: 100-1,500 words. **Pays $1/word.**

$ $ BACKROADS

Motorcycles, Travel & Adventure, Backroads, Inc., P.O. Box 317, Branchville NJ 07826. (973)948-4176. Fax: (973)948-0823. E-mail: editor@backroadsusa.com. Website: www.backroadsusa.com. Managing Editor: Shira Kamil. **Contact:** Brian Rathjen, editor/publisher. **80% freelance written.** Monthly tabloid covering motorcycle touring. "*Backroads* is a motorcycle tour magazine geared toward getting motorcyclists on the road and traveling. We provide interesting destinations, unique roadside attractions and eateries, plus Rip & Ride Route Sheets. We cater to all brands. If you really ride, you need *Backroads*." Estab. 1995. Circ. 40,000. Pays on publication. Publishes ms an average of 3 months after acceptance. Byline given. Buys one-time rights. Editorial lead time 1 month. Submit seasonal material 3 months in advance. Accepts queries by mail, e-mail, fax. Accepts previously published material. Responds in 3 weeks to queries. Sample copy for $2. Writer's guidelines free.

Nonfiction Shira Kamil, editor/publisher. Essays (motorcycle/touring), how-to, humor, new product, opinion, personal experience, technical, travel. "No long diatribes on 'How I got into motorcycles.'" **Buys 2-4 mss/year.** Query. Length: 500-2,500 words. **Pays 10¢/word minimum for assigned articles; 5¢/word minimum for unsolicited articles.** Pays writers contributor copies or other premiums for short pieces.

Photos Send photos with submission. Reviews contact sheets. Offers no additional payment for photos accepted with ms.

Columns/Departments We're Outta Here (weekend destinations), 500-750 words; Great All-American Diner Run (good eateries with great location), 300-800 words; Thoughts from the Road (personal opinion/insights), 250-500 words; Mysterious America (unique and obscure sights), 300-800 words; Big City Getaway (day trips), 500-750 words. **Buys 20-24 mss/year.** Query. **Pays 2¢/word-$50/article.**

Fiction Adventure, humorous. **Buys 2-4 mss/year.** Query. Length: 500-1,500 words. **Pays 2-4¢/word.**

Fillers Facts, newsbreaks. Length: 100-250 words.

Tips "We prefer destination-oriented articles in a light, layman's format, with photos (negatives or transparencies preferred). Stay away from any name-dropping and first-person references."

$ $ $ ⊠ CANADIAN BIKER MAGAZINE

735 Market St., Victoria BC V8T 2E2, Canada. (250)384-0333. Fax: (250)384-1832. E-mail: edit@canadianbiker.c om. Website: canadianbiker.com. **Contact:** John Campbell, editor. **65% freelance written.** Magazine covering motorcycling. "A family-oriented motorcycle magazine whose purpose is to unite Canadian motorcyclists from coast to coast through the dissemination of information in a non-biased, open forum. The magazine reports on new product, events, touring, racing, vintage and custom motorcycling as well as new industry information." Estab. 1980. Circ. 20,000. Publishes ms an average of 1 year after acceptance. Byline given. Buys first rights. Editorial lead time 3 months. Accepts queries by mail, e-mail, fax, phone. Responds in 6 weeks to queries; 6 months to mss. Sample copy for $5 or online. Writer's guidelines free.

Nonfiction All nonfiction must include photos and/or illustrations. General interest, historical/nostalgic, how-to, interview/profile (Canadian personalities preferred), new product, technical, travel. **Buys 12 mss/year.** Query with or without published clips or send complete ms. Length: 500-1,500 words. **Pays $100-200 for assigned articles; $80-150 for unsolicited articles.**

Photos State availability of or send photos with submission. Reviews 4×4 transparencies, 3×5 prints. Buys one-time rights. Negotiates payment individually. Captions, identification of subjects, model releases required.

Tips "We're looking for more racing features, rider profiles, custom sport bikes, quality touring stories, 'extreme' riding articles. Contact editor first before writing anything. Have original ideas, an ability to write from an authoritative point of view, and an ability to supply quality photos to accompany text. Writers should be involved in the motorcycle industry and be intimately familiar with some aspect of the industry which would be of interest to readers. Observations of the industry should be current, timely and informative."

$ $ $ $ CAR AND DRIVER

Hachette Filipacchi Magazines, Inc., 2002 Hogback Rd., Ann Arbor MI 48105-9795. (734)971-3600. Fax: (734)971-9188. E-mail: spence1cd@aol.com. Website: www.caranddriver.com. **Contact:** Steve Spence, managing editor. Monthly magazine for auto enthusiasts; college-educated, professional, median 24-35 years of age.

Estab. 1956. Circ. 1,300,000. **Pays on acceptance.** Byline given. Offers 25% kill fee. Buys first North American serial rights. Accepts queries by mail, e-mail, fax. Responds in 2 months to queries.

Nonfiction Seek stories about people and trends, including racing. Two recent freelance purchases include news-feature on cities across America banning "cruising" and feature on how car companies create "new car smells." All road tests are staff-written. "Unsolicited manuscripts are not accepted. Query letters must be addressed to the Managing Editor. Rates are generous, but few manuscripts are purchased from outside." **Buys 1 mss/year. Pays max $3,000/feature; $750-1,500/short piece.** Pays expenses of writers on assignment.

Photos Color slides and b&w photos sometimes purchased with accompanying ms.

The online magazine carries original content not found in the print edition. Contact: Ron Kiino, online editor.

Tips "It is best to start off with an interesting query and to stay away from nuts-and-bolts ideas because that will be handled in-house or by an acknowledged expert. Our goal is to be absolutely without flaw in our presentation of automotive facts, but we strive to be every bit as entertaining as we are informative. We do not print this sort of story: 'My Dad's Wacky, Lovable Beetle.' "

$ $ CITY CYCLE MOTORCYCLE NEWS

First Hudson Publishing Co., P.O. Box 808, Nyack NY 10960. (845)353-MOTO. Fax: (845)353-5240. E-mail: info@motorcyclenews.cc. Website: www.motorcyclenews.cc. **Contact:** Mark Kalan, publisher/editor. **50% freelance written.** Monthly magazine featuring "positive coverage of motorcycling in America—riding, travel, racing and tech." Estab. 1989. Circ. 60,000. Pays on publication. Publishes ms an average of 2 months after acceptance. Byline given. Buys one-time rights. Editorial lead time 3 months. Submit seasonal material 3 months in advance. Accepts previously published material. Accepts simultaneous submissions. Responds in 1 month to queries. Sample copy for $4. Writer's guidelines for #10 SASE.

Nonfiction Essays, general interest, historical/nostalgic, how-to, humor, inspirational, interview/profile, new product, personal experience, photo feature, technical, travel. Special issues: Daytona Beach Blocktober Fest; Summer touring stories—travel. **Buys 12 mss/year.** Query with published clips. Length: 1,000-2,000 words. **Pays $50-250 for assigned articles; $25-125 for unsolicited articles.** Pays expenses of writers on assignment.

Reprints Send tearsheet or photocopy. No payment.

Photos State availability with submission. Reviews contact sheets, transparencies. Buys one-time rights. Negotiates payment individually. Captions, identification of subjects, model releases required.

Columns/Departments Query with published clips.

Fiction All fiction must be motorcycle related. Adventure, fantasy, historical, romance, slice-of-life vignettes. Query with published clips. Length: 1,500-2,500 words. **Pays $50-250.**

Poetry Must be motorcycle related. Avant-garde, free verse, haiku, light verse, traditional. **Buys 6 poems/year.** Submit maximum 12 poems. Length: Length open. **Pays $10-50.**

Fillers Anecdotes, cartoons. **Buys 12/year.** Length: 100-200 words. **Pays $10-50.**

Tips "Ride a motorcycle and be able to construct a readable sentence!"

CRUISING RIDER MAGAZINE

Running in Style, P.O. Box 1943, Sedona AZ 86336. (928)282-9293. E-mail: joshua@verdenet.com. **Contact:** Joshua Placa, editor. **10% freelance written.** Pays on publication. Buys all rights.

$ $ FRICTION ZONE

Motorcycle Travel and Information, P.O. Box 530, Idyllwild CA 92549-0530. (909)659-9500. Fax: (909)659-8182. E-mail: editor@friction-zone.com. Website: www.friction-zone.com. **Contact:** Amy Holland, editor/publisher. **60% freelance written.** Monthly magazine covering motorcycles. Estab. 1999. Circ. 23,000. Pays on publication. Publishes ms an average of 1 month after acceptance. Byline given. Buys first North American serial rights. Editorial lead time 6 weeks. Submit seasonal material 2 months in advance. Sample copy for $4.50 or on website.

Nonfiction General interest, historical/nostalgic, how-to, humor, inspirational, interview/profile, new product, opinion, photo feature, technical, travel, medical (relating to motorcyclists), book reviews (relating to motorcyclists). Does not accept first-person writing. **Buys 1 mss/year.** Query. Length: 1,000-3,000 words. **Pays 20¢/word.** Sometimes pays expenses of writers on assignment.

Photos Send photos with submission. Reviews negatives, slides. Buys one-time rights. Offers $15/published photo. Captions, identification of subjects, model releases required.

Columns/Departments Health Zone (health issues relating to motorcyclists); Motorcycle Engines 101 (basic motorcycle mechanics); Road Trip (California destination review including hotel, road, restaurant), all 2,000 words. **Buys 60 mss/year.** Query. **Pays 20¢/word.**

Fiction Amy Holland. "Want stories concerning motorcycling or motorcyclists. No 'first-person' fiction." Query. Length: 1,000-2,000 words. **Pays 20¢/word.**

Fillers Anecdotes, facts, gags to be illustrated by cartoonist, newsbreaks, short humor. Length: 2,000-3,000 words. **Pays 20¢/word.**

Tips "Query via e-mail with sample writing. Visit our website for more detailed guidelines."

Ⓝ $ $ IN THE WIND

Paisano Publications, LLC, P.O. Box 3000, Agoura Hills CA 91376-3000. (818)889-8740. Fax: (818)889-1252. E-mail: kpeterson@easyriders.net. Website: www.easyriders.com. Editor: Kim Peterson. **50% freelance written.** Quarterly magazine. "Geared toward the custom (primarily Harley-Davidson) motorcycle rider and enthusiast, *In the Wind* is driven by candid pictorial-action photos of bikes being ridden, and events, with a monthly travel piece—Travelin' Trails." Estab. 1978. Circ. 90,000. Pays on publication. Publishes ms an average of 9 months after acceptance. Byline given. Buys all rights. Editorial lead time 6 months. Accepts queries by mail, e-mail. Responds in 2 weeks to queries; 2 months to mss. Sample copy not available.

Nonfiction Photo feature, event coverage. No long-winded tech articles. **Buys 6 mss/year.** Length: 1,000-2,000 words. **Pays $250-600.** Sometimes pays expenses of writers on assignment.

Photos Send SASE for return. Send photos with submission. Reviews transparencies, digital images, b&w, color prints. Buys all rights. Identification of subjects, model releases, on obviously posed and partially nude photos, required.

Tips "Know the subject. Looking for submissions from people who ride their own bikes."

LATINOS ON WHEELS

On Wheels, Inc., 585 E. Larned St., Suite 100, Detroit MI 48226-4369. (313)963-2209. Fax: (313)963-7778. E-mail: editor@onwheelsinc.com. Website: www.onwheelsinc.com/lowmagazine. Editor: Lyndon Conrad Bell. Quarterly magazine. Supplement to leading Latino newspapers in the U.S. Provides Latino car buyers and car enthusiasts with the most relevant automotive trends. Circ. 500,000. Sample copy not available.

LOWRIDER MAGAZINE

Primedia Enthusiast Group, 2100 E. Howell Ave., Suite 209, Anaheim CA 92806. E-mail: ralph.fuentes@primedia.com. Website: www.lowridermagazine.com. Editor: Ralph Fuentes. Monthly magazine. Covers the national and international lowriding scene with high impact, full-color vehicle and event features. Circ. 212,500. Editorial lead time 3 months. Sample copy not available.

MOMENTUM

Hachette Filipacchi Media U.S., Inc., 1633 Broadway, 40th Floor, New York NY 10019. (212)767-6000. Fax: (212)767-4757. Managing Editor: Nancy Alfaro. Magazine published 3 times/year. Published excluxively for the Mercedes-Benz owner who appreciates quality, elegance, adventure and style. Circ. 750,000. Sample copy not available.

MOTOR AGE

Advanstar Communications, Inc., 150 Strafford Ave., Suite 210, Wayne PA 19087-3114. (610)687-2587. Fax: (610)687-1419. E-mail: motorage@advanstar.com. Website: www.motorage.com. Editor: Bill Cannon. Monthly magazine. Edited as a technical journal for automotive service dealers and technicians in the U.S. Circ. 143,147. Sample copy not available.

$ $ $ MOTOR TREND

Primedia, 6420 Wilshire Blvd., Los Angeles CA 90048. (323)782-2220. E-mail: motortrend@primedia.com. Website: www.motortrend.com. **Contact:** Matt Stone, executive editor. **5-10% freelance written.** Only works with published/established writers. Monthly magazine for automotive enthusiasts and general interest consumers. Circ. 1,250,000. Publishes ms an average of 3 months after acceptance. Buys all rights. Accepts queries by mail. Responds in 1 month to queries. Sample copy not available.

Nonfiction "Automotive and related subjects that have national appeal. Emphasis on domestic and imported cars, road tests, driving impressions, auto classics, auto, travel, racing, and high-performance features for the enthusiast. Packed with facts. Freelancers should confine queries to photo-illustrated exotic drives and other feature material; road tests and related activity are handled inhouse. Fact-filled query suggested for all freelancers."

Photos Buys photos of prototype cars and assorted automotive matter. Pays $25-500 for transparencies.

Columns/Departments Car care (query Matt Stone, senior editor).

OUTLAW BIKER

Outlaw Biker Enterprises, Inc., 5 Marine View Plaza, Suite 207, Hoboken NJ 07030. (201)653-2700. Fax: (201)653-7892. E-mail: editor@outlawbiker.com. Website: www.outlawbiker.com. **50% freelance written.**

Magazine published 6 times/year covering bikers and their lifestyle. "All writers must be insiders of biker lifestyle. Features include coverage of biker events, profiles, and humor." Estab. 1983. Circ. 150,000. Pays on publication. Publishes ms an average of 3 months after acceptance. Byline given. Buys first rights. Editorial lead time 3 months. Submit seasonal material 5 months in advance. Accepts queries by mail, e-mail, fax. Accepts previously published material. Accepts simultaneous submissions. Responds in 2 weeks to queries; 2 months to mss. Sample copy for $5.98. Writer's guidelines for #10 SASE.

Nonfiction Historical/nostalgic, humor, new product, personal experience, photo feature, travel. Special issues: Daytona Special, Sturgis Special (annual bike runs). "No first time experiences—our readers already know." **Buys 10-12 mss/year.** Send complete ms. Length: 100-1,000 words.

Photos Send photos with submission. Reviews transparencies, prints. Buys one-time rights. Offers $0-10/photo. Captions, identification of subjects, model releases required.

Columns/Departments Buys 10-12 mss/year. Send complete ms.

Fiction Adventure, erotica, fantasy, historical, humorous, romance, science fiction, slice-of-life vignettes, suspense. No racism. **Buys 10-12 mss/year.** Send complete ms. Length: 500-2,500 words.

Poetry Avant-garde, free verse, haiku, light verse, traditional. **Buys 10-12 poems/year.** Submit maximum 12 poems. Length: 2-1,000 lines.

Fillers Anecdotes, facts, gags to be illustrated by cartoonist, newsbreaks, short humor. **Buys 10-12/year.** Length: 500-2,000 words.

The online version of *Outlaw Biker* carries original content not found in the print edition.

Tips "Writers must be insiders of the biker lifestyle. Manuscripts with accompanying photographs as art are given higher priority."

POPULAR HOT RODDING

Primedia Enthusiast Group, 2400 E. Katella Ave., Suite 1100, Anaheim CA 92806. (714)939-2400. E-mail: john.h unkins@primedia.com. Website: www.popularhotrodding.com. Editor: John Hunkins. Monthly magazine. Written for the automotive enthusiast by highlighting features that emphasize performance, bolt-on accessories, replacement parts, safety and the sport of drag racing. Circ. 182,000. Sample copy not available.

• Query first.

$ $ RIDER MAGAZINE

Ehlert Publishing Group, 2575 Vista Del Mar Dr., Ventura CA 93001. E-mail: editor@ridermagazine.com. Website: www.ridermagazine.com. **Contact:** Mark Tuttle, editor. **60% freelance written.** Monthly magazine covering motorcycling. "*Rider* serves the all-brand motorcycle lifestyle/enthusiast with a slant toward travel and touring." Estab. 1974. Circ. 107,000. Pays on publication. Publishes ms an average of 6-12 months after acceptance. Byline given. Offers 25% kill fee. Buys first North American serial, electronic rights. Editorial lead time 4 months. Submit seasonal material 6 months in advance. Accepts queries by mail. Responds in 2 months to queries. Sample copy for $2.95. Writer's guidelines for #10 SASE.

"The articles we do buy often share the following characteristics: 1. The writer queried us in advance by regular mail (not by telephone or e-mail) to see if we needed or wanted the story. 2. The story was well written and of proper length. 3. The story had sharp, uncluttered photos taken with the proper film—*Rider* does not buy stories without photos."

Nonfiction General interest, historical/nostalgic, how-to (re: motorcycling), humor, interview/profile, personal experience, travel. Does not want to see "fiction or articles on 'How I Began Motorcycling.'" **Buys 40-50 mss/year.** Query. Length: 750-2,000 words. **Pays $150-750.**

Photos Send photos with submission. Reviews contact sheets, transparencies, 5×7 (b&w only) prints. Buys one-time and electronic rights. Offers no additional payment for photos accepted with ms. Captions required.

Columns/Departments Favorite Rides (short trip), 850-1,100 words. **Buys 12 mss/year.** Query. **Pays $150-750.**

Tips "We rarely accept manuscripts without photos (slides or b&w prints). Query first. Follow guidelines available on request. We are most open to feature stories (must include excellent photography) and material for 'Rides, Rallies and Clubs.' Include information on routes, local attractions, restaurants, and scenery in favorite ride submissions."

$ $ ROAD BIKE

TAM Communications, 1010 Summer St., Stamford CT 06905. (203)425-8777. Fax: (203)425-8775. E-mail: jessicap@roadbikemag.com. **Contact:** Jessica Prokup, editor. **50% freelance written.** Monthly magazine covering motorcycling—tour, travel, project and custom bikes, products, and tech. Estab. 1993. Circ. 50,000. Pays on publication. Publishes ms an average of 6 months after acceptance. Byline given. Editorial lead time 4 months. Submit seasonal material 6 months in advance. Accepts queries by mail, fax. Writer's guidelines free.

Nonfiction How-to (motorcycle, travel, camping), interview/profile (motorcycle related), new product, photo feature (motorcycle events or gathering places with minimum of 1,000 words text), travel. No fiction. **Buys 100 mss/year.** Query with or without published clips or send complete ms. Length: 1,000-3,500 words. **Pays $15-400.**

Photos Send photos with submission (slides preferred, prints and high-res digital images accepted). Buys one-time rights. Offers no additional payment for photos accepted with ms. Captions required.

Columns/Departments Reviews (products, media, all motorcycle related), 300-750 words, plus 1 or more photos. Query with published clips or send complete ms. **Pays $15-400.**

Fillers Facts.

$ $ ROAD KING

Parthenon Publishing, 28 White Bridge Rd., Suite 209, Nashville TN 37205. Fax: (615)627-2197. Website: www.roadking.com. **Contact:** Lisa Waddle, editor. **25% freelance written.** Bimonthly magazine covering the trucking industry. **Pays on acceptance.** Publishes ms an average of 3 months after acceptance. Byline given. Offers 30% kill fee. Buys first North American serial, all electronic rights. Editorial lead time 3-4 months. Submit seasonal material 4 months in advance. Accepts queries by mail, fax. Accepts previously published material. Accepts simultaneous submissions. Responds in 3-4 weeks to queries. Sample copy for #10 SASE. Writer's guidelines free.

Nonfiction Book excerpts, general interest, how-to, humor, new product, health. **Buys 12 mss/year.** Query with published clips. Length: 100-1,000 words. **Pays $50-700.** Pays expenses of writers on assignment.

Photos Michael Nott, art director. Send photos with submission. Negotiates payment individually.

SPORT COMPACT CAR

Primedia Enthusiast Group, 774 S. Placentia Ave., Placentia CA 92870. (714)939-2584. E-mail: scott.oldham@primedia.com. Website: www.sportcompactcarweb.com. Editor: Scott Oldham. Monthly magazine. Targeted to owners and potential buyers of new compacts who seek inside information regarding performance, personalization and cosmetic enhancement of the vehicles. Circ. 117,000. Editorial lead time 4 months. Sample copy not available.

SPORT TRUCK

Primedia Enthusiast Group, 774 S. Placentia Ave., Placentia CA 92870. E-mail: sporttruck@primedia.com. Website: www.sporttruck.com. Editor: Kevin Wilson. Monthly magazine. Covers the entire range of light duty trucks and sport utility vehicles with an emphasis on performance and personalization. Circ. 200,357. Sample copy not available.

SUPER CHEVY

Primedia Enthusiast Group, 2400 Katella Ave., 11th Floor, Anaheim CA 92806-5945. (714)939-2540. Fax: (714)572-1864. E-mail: terry.cole@primedia.com. Website: www.superchevy-web.com. Editor: Terry Cole. Monthly magazine. Reports on various forms of motorsports where Cheverolet cars and engines are in competition. Circ. 198,995. Sample copy not available.

N TRAINS

Kalmbach Publishing Co., P.O. Box 1612, Waukesha WI 53187-1612. (262)796-8776. Fax: (262)796-1142. E-mail: editor@trainsmag.com. Website: www.trainsmag.com. Editor: Mark Hemphill. Monthly magazine. Appeals to consumers interested in learning about the function and history of the train industry. Circ. 130,385. Editorial lead time 2 months. Sample copy not available.

N $ $ $ VELOCITY MAGAZINE

Journal of the Honda Acura Club, Honda Acura Club International, 4324 Promenade Way, Suite 109, Marina del Rey CA 90292. (310)822-6163. Fax: (310)822-5030. E-mail: staff@hondaclub.com. Website: www.hondaclub.com. Managing Editor: Suzanne Peauralto. **Contact:** Peter Frey, editor. **50% freelance written.** Quarterly magazine covering Honda and Acura autos and products for automotive general interest and enthusiasts. Estab. 1999. Circ. 50,000. Pays on publication. Publishes ms an average of 2 months after acceptance. Byline given. Offers 50% kill fee. Buys all rights. Editorial lead time 2 months. Submit seasonal material 2 months in advance. Accepts queries by mail, fax. Accepts previously published material. Sample copy for $3. Writer's guidelines free.

Nonfiction General interest, historical/nostalgic, new product, photo feature, automotive. **Buys 50 mss/year.** Query with published clips. Length: 400-1,000 words. **Pays 50¢/word.** Sometimes pays expenses of writers on assignment.

Reprints Accepts previously published submissions.

Photos Send photos with submission. Buys all rights. Negotiates payment individually. Captions, identification of subjects required.

N $ $ $ $VIPER MAGAZINE

The Magazine for Dodge Viper Enthusiasts, J.R. Thompson Co., 26970 Haggerty Rd., Farmington Hills MI 48331-3407. (248)553-4566. Fax: (248)553-2138. E-mail: jrt@jrthompson.com. Website: www.vipermagazine.com. Editor-in-Chief: Mark Giannotta. **Contact:** John Thompson, editorial director. **20% freelance written.** Quarterly magazine covering all Vipers—all the time. Also the official magazine of the Viper Club of America. "Speak to *VM* readers from a basis of Viper knowledge and enthusiasm. We take an honest, journalistic approach to all stories, but we're demonstrably and understandably proud of the Dodge Viper sports car, its manufacturer and employees." Estab. 1995. Circ. 15,000. **Pays on acceptance.** Publishes ms an average of 4 months after acceptance. Byline given. Buys first, second serial (reprint) rights. Editorial lead time 5 months. Submit seasonal material 6 months in advance. Accepts queries by mail, e-mail, fax, phone. Accepts previously published material. Responds in 1 week to queries. Writer's guidelines for #10 SASE or by e-mail.

Nonfiction Query. Length: 400-1,500 words. **Pays $1/word.** Sometimes pays expenses of writers on assignment. and information about when and where the material previously appeared. payment varies.

Photos State availability of or send photos with submission. Buys all rights. Negotiates payment individually. Captions, identification of subjects, model releases required.

Columns/Departments SnakeBites (coverage of Viper Club of America events such as local chapter activities, fundraising, track days, etc.), under 200 words; Competition (competitive Viper events such as road-racing, drag-racing, etc.), under 200 words. **Pays $1/word.**

Fillers Anecdotes, facts, gags to be illustrated by cartoonist, newsbreaks, short humor. Length: 25-100 words. **Pays $1/word.**

Tips "Being a Viper owner is a good start, since you have been exposed to our 'culture' and probably receive the magazine. This is an even more specialized magazine than traditional auto-buff books, so knowing Vipers is essential."

AVIATION

$ $ $ $AIR & SPACE MAGAZINE

Smithsonian Institution, P.O. Box 37012, Victor Bldg. 7100, MRC 951, Washington DC 20013-7012. (202)275-1230. Fax: (202)275-1886. E-mail: editors@airspacemag.com. Website: www.airspacemag.com. Editor: George Larson. **Contact:** Linda Shiner, executive editor (features); Pat Trenner, senior editor (departments). **80% freelance written.** Bimonthly magazine covering aviation and aerospace for a nontechnical audience. "The emphasis is on the human rather than the technological, on the ideas behind the events. Features are slanted to a technically curious, but not necessarily technically knowledgeable audience. We are looking for unique angles to aviation/aerospace stories, history, events, personalities, current and future technologies, that emphasize the human-interest aspect." Estab. 1985. Circ. 225,000. **Pays on acceptance.** Byline given. Offers kill fee. Buys first North American serial rights. Accepts queries by mail, e-mail, fax. Responds in 3 months to queries. Sample copy for $5. Writer's guidelines online.

⊶ "We're looking for 'reader service' articles—a collection of helpful hints and interviews with experts that would help our readers enjoy their interest in aviation. An example: An article telling readers how they could learn more about the space shuttle, where to visit, how to invite an astronaut to speak to their schools, what books are most informative, etc. A good place to break in is our 'Soundings' department."

Nonfiction The editors are actively seeking stories covering space and general or business aviation. Book excerpts, essays, general interest (on aviation/aerospace), historical/nostalgic, humor, photo feature, technical. **Buys 50 mss/year.** Query with published clips. Length: 1,500-3,000 words. **Pays $1,500-3,000.** Pays expenses of writers on assignment.

Photos Refuses unsolicited material. State availability with submission. Reviews 35 mm transparencies, digital files.

Columns/Departments Above and Beyond (first person), 1,500-2,000 words; Flights and Fancy (whimsy), approximately 800 words. Soundings (brief items, timely but not breaking news), 500-700 words. **Buys 25 mss/year.** Query with published clips. **Pays $150-300.**

▣ The online version carries original content not found in the print edition. Contact: Linda Shiner, Pat Trenner.

Tips "We continue to be interested in stories about space exploration. Also, writing should be clear, accurate, and engaging. It should be free of technical and insider jargon, and generous with explanation and background. The first step every aspiring contributor should take is to study recent issues of the magazine."

$ $AIR LINE PILOT

The Magazine of Professional Flight Deck Crews, Air Line Pilots Association, 535 Herndon Pkwy., P.O. Box 1169, Herndon VA 20172. (703)481-4460. Fax: (703)689-4370. E-mail: magazine@alpa.org. Website: www.alpa.org.

Contact: Gary DiNunno, editor. **10% freelance written.** Prefers to work with published/established writers; works with a small number of new/unpublished writers each year. Magazine published 10 times/year for airline pilots covering commercial aviation industry information—economics, avionics, equipment, systems, safety—that affects a pilot's life in a professional sense. Also includes information about management/labor relations trends, contract negotiations, etc. Estab. 1931. Circ. 95,000. **Pays on acceptance.** Publishes ms an average of 6 months after acceptance. Offers 50% kill fee. all rights except book rights Submit seasonal material 6 months in advance. Responds in 2 months to queries. Sample copy for $2. Writer's guidelines online.

Nonfiction Humor, inspirational, photo feature, technical. **Buys 20 mss/year.** Query with or without published clips or send complete ms and SASE. Length: 700-3,000 words. **Pays $100-600 for assigned articles; $50-600 for unsolicited articles.**

Reprints Send photocopy of article or typed ms with rights for sale noted and information about when and where the material previously appeared. Payment varies.

Photos "Our greatest need is for strikingly original cover photographs featuring ALPA flight deck crew members and their airlines in their operating environment. See list of airlines with ALPA Pilots online." Send photos with submission. Reviews contact sheets, 35mm transparencies, 8×10 prints, digital acceptable, but must be very high resolution (300 dpi at 8x11). Will review low res thumbnail images. Buys all rights for cover photos, one-time rights for inside color. Offers $10-35/b&w photo, $30-50 for color used inside and $450 for color used as cover. For cover photography, shoot vertical rather than horizontal. Identification of subjects required.

Tips "For our feature section, we seek aviation industry information that affects the life of a professional pilot's career standpoint. We also seek material that affects a pilot's life from a job security and work environment standpoint. Any airline pilot featured in an article must be an Air Line Pilot Association member in good standing. Our readers are very experienced and require a high level of technical accuracy in both written material and photographs."

$BALLOON LIFE

Balloon Life Magazine, Inc., 2336 47th Ave. SW, Seattle WA 98116-2331. (206)935-3649. Fax: (206)935-3326. E-mail: tom@balloonlife.com. Website: www.balloonlife.com. **Contact:** Tom Hamilton, editor-in-chief. **75% freelance written.** Monthly magazine covering sport of hot air ballooning. Publishes material "about the sport of hot air ballooning. Readers participate as pilots, crew, official observers at events and spectators." Estab. 1986. Circ. 4,000. Pays on publication. Publishes ms an average of 3-4 months after acceptance. Byline given. Offers 50-100% kill fee. Buys first North American serial, one-time rights. Buys nonexclusive, all rights. Submit seasonal material 4 months in advance. Accepts queries by e-mail, fax. Accepts previously published material. Accepts simultaneous submissions. Responds in 3 weeks to queries; 1 month to mss. Sample copy for 9×12 SAE with $2 postage. Writer's guidelines for #10 SASE.

Nonfiction Book excerpts, general interest, how-to (flying hot air balloons, equipment techniques), interview/profile, new product, technical, events/rallies, safety seminars, balloon clubs/organizations, letters to the editor. **Buys 150 mss/year.** Query with or without published clips or send complete ms. Length: 1,000-1,500 words. **Pays $50-75 for assigned articles; $25-50 for unsolicited articles.** Pays expenses of writers on assignment.

Reprints Send tearsheet, photocopy or typed ms with rights for sale noted and information about when and where the material previously appeared. Pays 100% of amount paid for an original article or story.

Photos Send photos with submission. Reviews transparencies, prints. Buys nonexclusive, all rights. Offers $15/inside photos, $50/cover. Identification of subjects required.

Columns/Departments Hangar Flying (real-life flying experience that others can learn from), 800-1,500 words; Crew Quarters (devoted to some aspect of crewing), 900 words; Preflight (a news and information column), 100-500 words; **pays $50.** Logbook (recent balloon events—events that have taken place in last 3-4 months), 300-500 words; **pays $20. Buys 60 mss/year.** Send complete ms. **Pays $20-50.**

Fiction Tom Hamilton, editor. Humorous, related to hot air ballooning. **Buys 3-5 mss/year.** Send complete ms. Length: 800-1,900 words. **Pays $25-75 and contributor's copies.**

Tips "This magazine slants toward the technical side of ballooning. We are interested in articles that help to educate and provide safety information. Also stories with manufacturers, important individuals, and/or of historic events and technological advances important to ballooning. The magazine attempts to present articles that show 'how-to' (fly, business opportunities, weather, equipment). Both our Feature Stories section and Logbook section are where most manuscripts are purchased."

FLYING MAGAZINE

Hachette Filipacchi Media U.S., Inc., 500 W. Putnam Ave., Greenwich CT 06830. (203)622-2706. Fax: (203)622-2725. E-mail: flyedit@hfmus.com. Website: www.flyingmag.com. Editor: J. Mac McClellan. Managing Editor: Elizabeth Murray. Monthly magazine covering aviation. Edited for active pilots through coverage of new product development and application in the general aviation market. Estab. 1927. Circ. 303,000. Editorial lead time 3 months. Accepts queries by mail, e-mail, fax. Sample copy for $3.99.

• *Flying* is almost entirely staff written, use of freelance material is limited.

Nonfiction "We are looking for the most unusual and best-written material that suits *Flying*. Most subjects in aviation have already been done so fresher ideas and approaches to stories are particularly valued. We buy 'I Learned About Flying From That' articles, as well as an occasional feature with and without photographs supplied." Send complete ms.

$ $ GENERAL AVIATION NEWS

Flyer Media, Inc., P.O. Box 39099, Lakewood WA 98439-0099. (888)333-5937. Fax: (253)471-9911. E-mail: janice@generalaviationnews.com. Website: www.generalaviationnews.com. **Contact:** Janice Wood, editor. **30% freelance written.** Prefers to work with published/established writers. Biweekly tabloid covering general, regional, national, and international aviation stories of interest to pilots, aircraft owners, and aviation enthusiasts. Estab. 1949. Circ. 35,000. Pays 1 month after publication. Publishes ms an average of 3 months after acceptance. Byline given. Buys first North American serial, second serial (reprint) rights. Submit seasonal material 6 months in advance. Accepts queries by mail, e-mail, fax, phone. Responds in 2 months to queries. Sample copy for $3.50. Writer's guidelines online.

• Always query first. Unsolicited mss will not be considered.

O➔ Break in by having "an aviation background, including a pilot's license, being up to date on current events, and being able to write. A 1,000-word story with good photos is the best way to see your name in print.

Nonfiction "News is covered by our staff. What we're looking for from freelancers is personality features, including stories of people who use their aircraft in an unusual way, builder and pilot reports, and historical features." **Buys 100 mss/year.** Query with published clips. Length: 500-2,000 words. **Pays $75-500.** Sometimes pays expenses of writers on assignment.

Photos Shoot clear, up-close photos, preferably color prints or slides. Send photos with submission. Payment negotiable. Captions, identification of subjects required.

Tips "The longer the story, the less likely it is to be accepted. If you are covering controversy, send us both sides of the story. Most of our features and news stories are assigned in response to a query."

$ $ PLANE AND PILOT

Werner Publishing Corp., 12121 Wilshire Blvd., Suite 1200, Los Angeles CA 90025. (310)820-1500. Fax: (310)826-5008. E-mail: editors@planeandpilotmag.com. Website: www.planeandpilotmag.com. Editor: Lyn Freeman. **Contact:** Katherine Diaz, managing editor. **80% freelance written.** Monthly magazine covering general aviation. "We think a spirited, conversational writing style is most entertaining for our readers. We are read by private and corporate pilots, instructors, students, mechanics and technicians—everyone involved or interested in general aviation." Estab. 1964. Circ. 150,000. Pays on publication. Publishes ms an average of 4 months after acceptance. Byline given. Offers kill fee. Buys all rights. Submit seasonal material 4 months in advance. Accepts previously published material. Responds in 4 months to queries. Sample copy for $5.50. Writer's guidelines online.

Nonfiction How-to, new product, personal experience, technical, travel, pilot efficiency, pilot reports on aircraft. **Buys 75 mss/year.** Query. Length: 1,200 words. **Pays $200-500.** Pays expenses of writers on assignment.

Reprints Send tearsheet, photocopy or typed ms with rights for sale noted and information about when and where the material previously appeared. Pays 50% of amount paid for original article.

Photos Submit suggested heads, decks and captions for all photos with each story. Submit b&w photos, 8×10 prints with glossy finish. Submit color photos in the form of 2¼×2¼ or 4×5 or 35mm transparencies in plastic sleeves. Buys all rights. Offers $50-300/photo.

Columns/Departments Readback (any newsworthy items on aircraft and/or people in aviation), 1,200 words; Jobs & Schools (a feature or an interesting school or program in aviation), 900-1,000 words. **Buys 30 mss/ year.** Send complete ms. **Pays $200-500.**

Tips "Pilot proficiency articles are our bread and butter. Manuscripts should be kept under 1,800 words, 1,200 words is ideal."

$ $ PRIVATE PILOT

Y-Visionary, Inc., 265 S. Anita Dr., #120, Orange CA 92868. (714)939-9991, ext. 234. Fax: (714)939-9909. E-mail: bfedorko@earthlink.net. Website: www.privatepilotmag.com. **Contact:** Bill Fedorko, editoral director. **40% freelance written.** Monthly magazine covering general aviation. "*Private Pilot* is edited for owners and pilots of single and multi-engine aircraft." Estab. 1965. Circ. 85,000. Pays on publication. Publishes ms an average of 4 months after acceptance. Byline given. Offers 15% or $75 kill fee. Buys first North American serial rights. Editorial lead time 3 months. Submit seasonal material 6 months in advance. Accepts queries by mail, fax. Responds in 2 months to queries. Writer's guidelines for #10 SASE.

Nonfiction General interest, historical/nostalgic, how-to, humor, inspirational, interview/profile, new product, opinion, personal experience, technical, travel, aircraft types. **Buys 12-15 mss/year.** Query. Length: 800-3,000 words. **Pays $250-650.** Sometimes pays expenses of writers on assignment.

Photos State availability with submission. Reviews 35mm transparencies. Buys one-time rights. Negotiates payment individually. Captions, identification of subjects, model releases required.

Tips "Send good queries. Readers are pilots who want to read about aircraft, places to go, and ways to save money."

Ⓝ SKY

Pace Communications, Inc., 1301 Carolina St., Greensboro NC 27401. (336)378-6065. Fax: (336)383-5699. E-mail: editorial@delta-sky.com. Website: www.delta-sky.com. Managing Editor: Mickey McLean. Monthly magazine. Circ. 500,000. Editorial lead time 6 months. Sample copy for $7.50.

Tips "With all correspondence, please include your address and a daytime telephone number."

BUSINESS & FINANCE

NATIONAL

$ $ THE BUSINESS JOURNAL

Serving San Jose and Silicon Valley, American City Business Journals, Inc., 96 N. Third St., Suite 100, San Jose CA 95112. (408)294-1837. Fax: (408)295-5028. E-mail: sanjose@bizjournals.com. Website: www.amcity.com/sanjose. Editor: Norman Bell. **Contact:** Robert Celaschi, managing editor. **2-5% freelance written.** Weekly tabloid covering a wide cross-section of industries. "Our stories are written for business people. Our audience is primarily upper-level management." Estab. 1983. Circ. 13,200. Pays on publication. Byline given. Offers $75 kill fee. Buys all rights. Editorial lead time 1 month. Accepts queries by e-mail. Responds in 2 weeks to queries. Sample copy for free. Writer's guidelines free.

Nonfiction News/feature articles specifically assigned. **Buys 300 mss/year.** Query. Length: 700-2,500 words. **Pays $175-400.**

Photos State availability with submission. Reviews 5×7 prints. Offers $25/photo used.

Tips "Just call or e-mail (preferable) and say you are interested. We give almost everyone a chance."

$ $ $ $ BUSINESS 2.0 MAGAZINE

Time, Inc., One California St., 29th Floor, San Francisco CA 94134. Fax: (415)656-8660. E-mail: freelancers@business2.com. Website: www.business2.com. **Contact:** Josh Quittner, editor. Monthly magazine covering business in the Internet economy. Estab. 1998. Circ. 350,000. Pays on publication. Publishes ms an average of 3 months after acceptance. Byline given. Offers 20% kill fee. Buys all rights. Editorial lead time 2 months. Submit seasonal material 4 months in advance. Accepts queries by e-mail. Accepts simultaneous submissions. Sample copy for free. Writer's guidelines online.

O→ Break in with fresh ideas on web-enabled business transformation—from the way companies are conceived and financed to how they develop markets and retain customers.

Nonfiction Essays, exposé, new product, opinion, travel, new business ideas for the Internet. **Buys 40-50 mss/year.** Query with published clips. Length: 150-3,000 words. **Pays $1/word.** Pays expenses of writers on assignment.

Ⓝ ⊘ BUSINESSWEEK

McGraw-Hill, Inc., 1221 Avenue of the Americas, 43rd Floor, New York NY 10020-1001. (212)512-2511. Fax: (212)512-4938. Website: www.businessweek.com. Publisher: William Kupper. Weekly magazine. Circ. 991,000. Pays on other.

● *BusinessWeek* does not accept freelance submissions.

$ $ DOLLARS AND SENSE: THE MAGAZINE OF ECONOMIC JUSTICE

Economic Affairs Bureau, 740 Cambridge St., Cambridge MA 02141-1401. (617)876-2434. Fax: (617)876-0008. E-mail: dollars@dollarsandsense.org. Website: www.dollarsandsense.org. **Contact:** Amy Gluckman or Adria Scharf, co-editors. **10% freelance written.** Bimonthly magazine covering economic, environmental, and social justice. "We explain the workings of the U.S. and international economics, and provide left perspectives on current economic affairs. Our audience is a mix of activists, organizers, academics, unionists, and other socially concerned people." Estab. 1974. Circ. 8,000. Pays on publication. Publishes ms an average of 4 months after acceptance. Byline given. Editorial lead time 3 months. Submit seasonal material 2 months in advance. Accepts queries by mail, e-mail, fax, phone. Sample copy for $5 or on website. Writer's guidelines online.

Nonfiction Exposé, political economics. **Buys 6 mss/year.** Query with published clips. Length: 700-2,500 words. **Pays $0-200.** Sometimes pays expenses of writers on assignment.

Photos State availability with submission. Buys one-time rights. Negotiates payment individually. Captions, identification of subjects required.

Tips "Be familiar with our magazine and the types of communities interested in reading us. *Dollars and Sense* is a progressive economics magazine that explains in a popular way both the workings of the economy and struggles to change it. Articles may be on the environment, the World Bank, community organizing, urban conflict, inflation, unemployment, union reform, welfare, changes in government regulation—a broad range of topics that have an economic theme. Find samples of our latest issue on our homepage."

N $ $ ENTREPRENEUR MAGAZINE

Entrepreneur Media, 2445 McCabe Way, Suite 400, Irvine CA 92614. (949)261-2325. Fax: (949)261-0234. E-mail: pbennett@entrepreneur.com. Website: www.entrepreneur.com. **Contact:** Peggy Reeves Bennett, articles editor. **60% freelance written.** *Entrepreneur* readers already run their own businesses. They have been in business for several years and are seeking innovative methods and strategies to improve their business operations. They are also interested in new business ideas and opportunities, as well as current issues that affect their companies. Circ. 540,000. **Pays on acceptance.** Publishes ms an average of 5 months after acceptance. Byline given. first international rights. Submit seasonal material 6 months in advance. Accepts queries by mail, e-mail, fax. Responds in 3 months to queries. Sample copy for $7.20 from Order Department or on website. Writer's guidelines for #10 SASE or by e-mail.

Nonfiction A few columns are now open to freelancers: "Smarts," "Money Buzz," "Marketing Buzz," and "Management Buzz." How-to (information on running a business, dealing with the psychological aspects of running a business, profiles of unique entrpreuers), current news/trends (and their effect on small business). **Buys 10-20 mss/year.** Query with published clips. Length: 2000 words. **Payment varies.**

Photos "Ask for photos or transparencies when interviewing entrepreneurs; send them with the article." Buys one-time rights.

Tips "Read several issues of the magazine! Study the feature articles versus the columns. Probably 75 percent of our freelance rejections are for article ideas covered in one of our regular columns. Go beyond the typical, flat 'business magazine query'—how to write a press release, how to negotiate with vendors, etc.—and instead investigate a current trend and develop a story on how that trend affects small business. In your query, mention companies you'd like to use to illustrate examples and sources who will provide expertise on the topic."

FORBES

Forbes, Inc., 60 5th Ave., New York NY 10011. (212)660-2200. Fax: (212)620-1873. E-mail: readers@forbes.com. Website: www.forbes.com. Editor-in-Chief: Steve Forbes. Editor: William Baldwin. Biweekly magazine. Edited for top business management professionals and for those aspiring to positions of corporate leadership. Circ. 1,000,000. Editorial lead time 2 months. Sample copy not available.

N Ø FORTUNE

Time, Inc., 1271 Avenue of The Americas, New York NY 10020. (212)522-1212. Fax: (212)522-0810. E-mail: fortunemail_letters@fortunemail.com. Website: www.fortune.com. Editor: Peter Petre. Biweekly magazine. Edited primarily for high-demographic business people. Specializes in big stories about companies, business personalities, technology, managing, Wall Street, media, marketing, personal finance, politics and policy. Circ. 1,066,000. Editorial lead time 6 weeks. Sample copy not available.

• Does not accept freelance submissions.

$ $ $ $ HISPANIC BUSINESS

Hispanic Business, Inc., 425 Pine Ave., Santa Barbara CA 93117. Fax: (805)964-5539. E-mail: robert.macias@hbinc.com. Website: www.hispanicbusiness.com. Editor: Jesus Chavarria. **Contact:** Robert Macias, deputy managing editor. **50-60% freelance written.** Monthly magazine covering Hispanic business. "For more than 2 decades, *Hispanic Business* magazine has documented the growing affluence and power of the Hispanic community. Our magazine reaches the most educated, affluent Hispanic business and community leaders. Stories should have relevance for the Hispanic business community." Estab. 1979. Circ. 220,000 (rate base); 990,000 (readership base). Pays on publication. Publishes ms an average of 1 month after acceptance. Byline given. Offers 50% kill fee. Buys all rights. Editorial lead time 1-3 months. Submit seasonal material 2 months in advance. Accepts queries by mail, e-mail. Accepts simultaneous submissions. Responds in 3 weeks to queries; 1 month to mss. Sample copy for free.

Nonfiction Interview/profile, travel. **Buys 120 mss/year.** Query with published clips. Length: 650-2,000 words. **Pays $50-1,500.** Sometimes pays expenses of writers on assignment.

Photos State availability with submission. Reviews GIF/JPEG files. Buys all rights. Negotiates payment individually. Captions required.
Columns/Departments Tech Pulse (technology); Money Matters (financial), both 650 words. **Buys 40 mss/year.** Query with published clips. **Pays $50-450.**
Tips "E-mail or snail mail queries with published clips are the most effective."

$ $ $ $ INDUSTRYWEEK

Leadership in Manufacturing, Penton Media, Inc., Penton Media Bldg., 1300 E. 9th St., Cleveland OH 44114. (216)696-7000. Fax: (216)696-7670. E-mail: tvinas@industryweek.com. Website: www.industryweek.com. Editor-in-Chief: Patricia Panchak. **Contact:** Tonya Vinas, managing editor. **30% freelance written.** Magazine published 12 times/year. "*IndustryWeek* provides information that helps manufacturers drive continuous improvement throughout the enterprise. Every issue of *IndustryWeek* is edited for the management teams of today's most competitive manufacturing companies, as well as decision-makers in the service industries that support manufacturing growth and productivity." Estab. 1970. Circ. 200,000. **Pays on acceptance.** Publishes ms an average of 2 months after acceptance. Byline given. Buys all rights. Accepts queries by e-mail. Responds in 1 month to queries. Sample copy and writer's guidelines online.
Nonfiction Book excerpts, exposé, interview/profile. "No first-person articles." **Buys 25 mss/year.** Query with published clips. Length: 1,800-3,000 words. **Pays average of $1/word for all articles; reserves right to negotiate.** Sometimes pays expenses of writers on assignment.
Photos Reviews contact sheets, negatives, transparencies, prints. Buys one-time rights. Negotiates payment individually. Captions, identification of subjects required.
Tips "Pitch wonderful ideas targeted precisely at our audience. Read, re-read, and understand the writer's guidelines and stories published. *IndustryWeek* readers are primarily senior executives—people with the title of vice president, executive vice president, senior vice president, chief executive officer, chief financial officer, chief information officer, chairman, managing director, and president. *IW*'s executive readers oversee global corporations. While *IW*'s primary target audience is a senior executive in a U.S. firm, your story should provide information that any executive anywhere in the world can use. *IW*'s audience is primarily in companies in manufacturing and manufacturing-related industries."

$ $ $ LATIN TRADE

Your Business Source for Latin America, 95 Merrick Way, Suite 600, Coral Gables FL 33134. (305)358-8373. Fax: (305)358-9166. Website: www.latintrade.com. **Contact:** Greg Brown, editor. **55% freelance written.** Monthly magazine covering Latin American business. "*Latin Trade* covers cross-border business in Latin America for top executives doing business with the region." Estab. 1993. Circ. 82,000. Pays on publication. Publishes ms an average of 3 months after acceptance. Byline given. Offers 25% kill fee. Buys all rights, makes work-for-hire assignments. Editorial lead time 3 months. Submit seasonal material 6 months in advance. Accepts queries by mail, e-mail. Responds in 2 weeks to queries. Writer's guidelines free.
Nonfiction Exposé, interview/profile, travel, business news. No one-source stories or unsolicited stories. **Buys 50 mss/year.** Query with published clips. Length: 800-2,000 words. **Pays $200-1,000.** Sometimes pays expenses of writers on assignment.
Photos Digital submissions preferred. State availability with submission. Buys one-time rights. Negotiates payment individually. Identification of subjects required.

☑ MONEY

Time, Inc., 1271 Avenue of the Americas, 32nd Floor, New York NY 10020. (212)522-1212. Fax: (212)522-0189. E-mail: money_letters@moneymail.com. Website: money.cnn.com. Editor: Norman Pearlstine. Managing Editor: Robert Safian. Monthly magazine covering finance. "*Money* magazine offers sophisticated coverage in all aspects of personal finance for individuals, business executives, and personal investors." Estab. 1972. Circ. 1,945,265. Editorial lead time 2 months. Sample copy for $3.95.
• "*Money* magazine does not accept unsolicited manuscripts and almost never uses freelance writers."

$ $ $ MYBUSINESS MAGAZINE

Hammock Publishing, 3322 W. End Ave., Suite 700, Nashville TN 37203. Fax: (615)690-3401. E-mail: sscully@hammock.com. Website: www.mybusinessmag.com. **Contact:** Shannon Scully, managing editor. **75% freelance written.** Bimonthly magazine for small businesses. "We are a guide to small business success, however that is defined in the new small business economy. We explore the methods and minds behind the trends and celebrate the men and women leading the creation of the new small business economy." Estab. 1999. Circ. 600,000. **Pays on acceptance.** Publishes ms an average of 4 months after acceptance. Byline given. Offers 30% kill fee. Buys first North American serial, electronic rights. Editorial lead time 4 months. Submit seasonal material 5 months in advance. Accepts queries by mail, fax. Accepts simultaneous submissions. Responds in 3 weeks to queries. Sample copy free. Writer's guidelines online.

Nonfiction Book excerpts, how-to (small business topics), new product. **Buys 8 mss/year.** Query with published clips. Length: 200-1,800 words. **Pays $75-1,000.** Pays expenses of writers on assignment.

Tips *MyBusiness* is sent bimonthly to the 600,000 members of the National Federation of Independent Business. "We're here to help small business owners by giving them a range of how-to pieces that evaluate, analyze, and lead to solutions."

$ $ THE NETWORK JOURNAL

Black Professional and Small Business News, The Network Journal Communication, 29 John St., Suite 1402, New York, NY 10038. (212)962-3791. Fax: (212)962-3537. E-mail: editors@tnj.com. Website: www.tnj.com. Editor: Rosalind McLymont. **Contact:** Aziz Adetimirn, publisher. **25% freelance written.** Monthly magazine covering business and career articles. *The Network Journal* caters to Black professionals and small-business owners, providing quality coverage on business, financial, technology and career news germane to the Black community. Estab. 1993. Circ. 15,000. Pays on publication. Byline given. Buys all rights. Editorial lead time 2 months. Submit seasonal material 3 months in advance. Accepts queries by mail, e-mail, fax, phone. Accepts previously published material. Accepts simultaneous submissions. Sample copy for $1 or online. Writer's guidelines for SASE or online.

Nonfiction How-to, interview/profile. Send complete ms. Length: 1,200-1,500 words. **Pays $150-200.** Sometimes pays expenses of writers on assignment.

Photos Send photos with submission. Buys one-time rights. Offers $25/photo. Identification of subjects required.

Columns/Departments Book reviews, 700-800 words; career management and small business development, 800 words. **Pays $100.**

The online magazine carries original content not found in the print version and includes writer's guidelines.

Tips "We are looking for vigorous writing and reporting for our cover stories and feature articles. Pieces should have gripping leads, quotes that actually say something and that come from several sources. Unless it is a column, please do not submit a 1-source story. Always remember that your article must contain a nutgraph—that's usually the third paragraph telling the reader what the story is about and why you are telling it now. Editorializing should be kept to a minimum. If you're writing a column, make sure your opinions are well-supported."

PERDIDO

Leadership with a Conscience, High Tide Press, 3650 W. 183rd St., Homewood IL 60430-2603. (708)206-2054. Fax: (708)206-2044. E-mail: editor1@hightidepress.com. Website: www.perdidomagazine.com. **Contact:** Mary Rundell-Holmes, editor. **60% freelance written.** Quarterly magazine covering leadership and management as they relate to mission-oriented organizations. "We are concerned with what's happening in organizations that are mission-oriented—as opposed to merely profit-oriented. *Perdido* is focused on helping conscientious leaders put innovative ideas into practice. We seek pragmatic articles on management techniques as well as esoteric essays on social issues. The readership of *Perdido* is comprised mainly of CEOs, executive directors, vice presidents, and program directors of nonprofit and for-profit organizations. We try to make the content of *Perdido* accessible to all decision-makers, whether in the nonprofit or for-profit world, government, or academia. *Perdido* actively pursues diverse opinions and authors from many different fields." Estab. 1994. Circ. 6,000. Pays on publication. Publishes ms an average of 3 months after acceptance. Byline given. Buys first North American serial, second serial (reprint) rights. Editorial lead time 4 months. Submit seasonal material 6 months in advance. Accepts queries by mail, e-mail, fax, phone. Accepts previously published material. Accepts simultaneous submissions. Responds in 2 months to queries. Sample copy for 6×9 SASE with 2 first-class stamps or online. Writer's guidelines for #10 SASE or by e-mail.

Nonfiction Book excerpts, humor, inspirational, interview/profile, informative articles. **Buys 6-10 mss/year.** Query with published clips. Length: 1,000-5,000 words.

Photos State availability with submission. Reviews 5×7 prints. Buys one-time rights. Negotiates payment individually. Captions, identification of subjects, model releases required.

Columns/Departments Book Review (new books on management/leadership), 800 words.

Tips "Potential writers for *Perdido* should rely on the magazine's motto—Leadership with a Conscience—as a starting point. We're looking for thoughtful reflections on management that help people succeed. While instructive articles are good, we avoid step-by-step recipes. Data and real life examples are very important."

PROFESSIONAL BUILDER

Reed Business Information, 2000 Clearwater Dr., Oak Brook IL 60523. (630)288-8190. Fax: (630)288-8145. E-mail: hmccune@reedbusiness.com. Website: www.housingzone.com/pb. **Contact:** Heather McCune, editor.

Magazine published 17 times/year covering the business of building. Designed as a resource to help builders run succesful and profitable businesses. Circ. 127,277. Editorial lead time 1 month. Accepts queries by mail, e-mail. Sample copy not available.
Nonfiction Query.

$ $ $ $⊡ PROFIT

Your Guide to Business Success, 1 Mt. Pleasant Rd., 11th Floor, Toronto ON M4Y 2Y5, Canada. (416)764-1402. Fax: (416)764-1404. E-mail: profit@profit.rogers.com. Website: www.profitguide.com. Publisher: Kerry Mitchell. **Contact:** Ian Portsmouth, editor. **80% freelance written.** Magazine published 6 times/year covering small and medium businesses. ''We specialize in specific, useful information that helps our readers manage their businesses better. We want Canadian stories only.'' Estab. 1982. Circ. 110,000. **Pays on acceptance.** Publishes ms an average of 2 months after acceptance. Byline given. Offers variable kill fee. Buys first North American serial, electronic rights. Submit seasonal material 6 months in advance. Accepts queries by mail, e-mail, fax, phone. Responds in 1 month to queries; 6 weeks to mss. Sample copy for 9×12 SAE with 84¢ postage. Writer's guidelines free.
Nonfiction How-to (business management tips), strategies and Canadian business profiles. **Buys 50 mss/year.** Query with published clips. Length: 800-2,000 words. **Pays $500-2,000.** Pays expenses of writers on assignment.
Columns/Departments Finance (info on raising capital in Canada), 700 words; Marketing (marketing strategies for independent business), 700 words. **Buys 80 mss/year.** Query with published clips. **Pays $150-600.**

▣ The online magazine carries original content not found in the print edition. Contact: Ian Portsmouth, editor.

Tips ''We're wide open to freelancers with good ideas and some knowledge of business. Read the magazine and understand it before submitting your ideas—which should have a Canadian focus.''

$ $TECHNICAL ANALYSIS OF STOCKS & COMMODITIES

The Traders' Magazine, Technical Analysis, Inc., 4757 California Ave. SW, Seattle WA 98116-4499. (206)938-0570. Fax: (206)938-1307. E-mail: editor@traders.com. Website: www.traders.com. Publisher: Jack K. Hutson. **Contact:** Jayanthi Gopalakrishnan, editor. **85% freelance written.** Magazine covers methods of investing and trading stocks, bonds and commodities (futures), options, mutual funds, and precious metals using technical analysis. Estab. 1982. Circ. 65,000. Pays on publication. Publishes ms an average of 6 months after acceptance. Byline given. Buys all rights. Accepts previously published material. Responds in 2 months to queries. Sample copy for $5. Writer's guidelines online.

• Eager to work with new/unpublished writers.

Nonfiction How-to (trade), humor (cartoons), technical (trading and software aids to trading), reviews, utilities, real world trading (actual case studies of trades and their results). ''No newsletter-type, buy-sell recommendations. The article subject must relate to technical analysis, charting or a numerical technique used to trade securities or futures. Almost universally requires graphics with every article.'' **Buys 150 mss/year.** Query with published clips or send complete ms. Length: 1,000-4,000 words. **Pays $100-500.**
Reprints Send tearsheet with rights for sale noted and information about when and where the material previously appeared.
Photos Christine M. Morrison, art director. State availability with submission. Buys one time and reprint rights. Pays $60-350 for b&w or color negatives with prints or positive slides. Captions, identification of subjects, model releases required.
Columns/Departments Length: 800-1,600 words. **Buys 100 mss/year.** Query. **Pays $50-300.**
Fillers Karen Wasserman, fillers editor. Must relate to trading stocks, bonds, options, mutual funds, commodities, or precious metals. Cartoons on investment humor. **Buys 20/year.** Length: 500 words. **Pays $20-50.**
Tips ''Describe how to use technical analysis, charting, or computer work in day-to-day trading of stocks, bonds, commodities, options, mutual funds, or precious metals. A blow-by-blow account of how a trade was made, including the trader's thought processes, is the very best-received story by our subscribers. One of our primary considerations is to instruct in a manner that the layperson can comprehend. We are not hypercritical of writing style.''

REGIONAL

$ $ALASKA BUSINESS MONTHLY

Alaska Business Publishing, 501 W. Northern Lights Blvd., Suite 100, Anchorage AK 99503-2577. (907)276-4373. Fax: (907)279-2900. E-mail: editor@akbizmag.com. Website: www.akbizmag.com. **Contact:** Debbie Cutler, editor. **80% freelance written.** Magazine covering Alaska-oriented business and industry. ''Our audience is Alaska businessmen and women who rely on us for timely features and up-to-date information about doing business in Alaska.'' Estab. 1985. Circ. 10,000. Pays on publication. Publishes ms an average of 4 months after

acceptance. Byline given. Offers $50 kill fee. Buys all rights. Editorial lead time 5 months. Submit seasonal material 5 months in advance. Accepts queries by mail, e-mail, fax. Accepts previously published material. Responds in 1 month to queries. Sample copy for 9 × 12 SAE and 4 first-class stamps. Writer's guidelines free.
Nonfiction General interest, how-to, interview/profile, new product (Alaska), opinion. No fiction, poetry, or anything not pertinent to Alaska. **Buys approximately 130 mss/year.** Send complete ms. Length: 500-2,000 words. **Pays $150-300.** Sometimes pays expenses of writers on assignment.
Photos State availability with submission.
Columns/Departments Required Reading (business book reviews); Right Moves; Alaska this Month; Monthly Calendars (all Alaska related), all 500-1,200 words. **Buys 12 mss/year.** Send complete ms. **Pays $50-75.**
Tips "Send a well-written manuscript on a subject of importance to Alaska businesses. We seek informative, entertaining articles on everything from entrepreneurs to heavy industry. We cover all Alaska industry to include mining, tourism, timber, transportation, oil and gas, fisheries, finance, insurance, real estate, communications, medical services, technology, and construction. We also cover Native and environmental issues, and occasionally feature Seattle and other communities in the Pacific Northwest."

$ $⊡ ATLANTIC BUSINESS MAGAZINE
Communications Ten, Ltd., 197 Water St., St. John's NL A1C 6E7, Canada. (709)726-9300. Fax: (709)726-3013. E-mail: dchafe@atlanticbusinessmagazine.com. Website: www.atlanticbusinessmagazine.com. Managing Editor: Edwina Hutton. **Contact:** Dawn Chafe, editor. **80% freelance written.** Bimonthly magazine covering business in Atlantic Canada. "We discuss positive business developments, emphasizing that the 4 Atlantic provinces are a great place to do business." Estab. 1989. Circ. 30,000. Pays on publication. Publishes ms an average of 2 months after acceptance. Byline given. Buys one-time rights. Editorial lead time 2 months. Accepts queries by mail, e-mail, fax. Sample copy and writer's guidelines free.
Nonfiction Exposé, general interest, interview/profile, new product. "We don't want religious, technical, or scholarly material. We are not an academic magazine." **Buys 36 mss/year.** Query with published clips. Length: 1,200-2,500 words. **Pays $300-750.** Sometimes pays expenses of writers on assignment.
Photos Send photos with submission. Reviews contact sheets, transparencies, prints. Buys one-time rights. Negotiates payment individually. Captions, identification of subjects required.
Columns/Departments Query with published clips.
Tips "Writers should submit their areas of interest as well as samples of their work and, if possible, suggested story ideas."

Ⓝ $ $ $⊡ BCBUSINESS
Canada Wide Magazines & Communications, Ltd., 4180 Lougheed Hwy., 4th Floor, Burnaby BC V5C 6A7, Canada. (604)299-7311. Fax: (604)299-9188. E-mail: bcb@canadawide.com. Managing Editor: Noel Hulsman. **Contact:** Bonnie Irving, editor. **80% freelance written.** Monthly magazine covering significant issues and trends shaping the province's business environment. "Stories are lively, topical and extensively researched." Circ. 30,000. Pays 2 weeks prior to being published. Publishes ms an average of 2 months after acceptance. Byline given. Offers kill fee. Buys first rights. Editorial lead time 4 months. Submit seasonal material 4 months in advance. Accepts queries by e-mail. Accepts simultaneous submissions. Responds in 6 weeks to queries. Writer's guidelines free.
Nonfiction Query with published clips. Length: 1,500-2,000 words. **Pays 40-65¢/word, depending on length and complexity of story.** Sometimes pays expenses of writers on assignment.
Photos State availability with submission.

$ $⊡ BUSINESS LONDON
Bowes Publishers, 1147 Gainsburough Rd., London ON N5Y 4X3, Canada. (519)472-7601. Fax: (519)473-7859. **Contact:** Gord Delamont, editor. **70% freelance written.** Monthly magazine covering London business. "Our audience is primarily small and medium businesses and entrepreneurs. Focus is on success stories and how to better operate your business." Estab. 1987. Circ. 14,000. Pays on publication. Publishes ms an average of 3 months after acceptance. Byline given. Offers 50% kill fee. Buys first rights. Editorial lead time 3 months. Responds in 3 months to mss. Sample copy for #10 SASE. Writer's guidelines free.
Nonfiction How-to (business topics), humor, interview/profile, new product (local only), personal experience (must have a London connection). **Buys 30 mss/year.** Query with published clips. Length: 250-1,500 words. **Pays $125-500.**
Photos Send photos with submission. Reviews contact sheets, transparencies. Buys one-time rights. Negotiates payment individually. Identification of subjects required.
Tips "Phone with a great idea. The most valuable thing a writer owns is ideas. We'll take a chance on an unknown if the idea is good enough."

$ $ BUSINESS NEW HAVEN

Second Wind Media, Ltd., 1221 Chapel St., New Haven CT 06511. Fax: (203)781-3482. E-mail: news@businessnewhaven.com. Website: www.businessnewhaven.com. **Contact:** Michael C. Bingham, editor. **33% freelance written.** Biweekly regional business publication covering the Connecticut business community. *"Business New Haven* is a business-to-business vehicle targeted to business owners and managers." Estab. 1993. Circ. 14,000. Pays on publication. Byline given. Buys one-time, all rights. Editorial lead time 1 month. Accepts queries by mail, e-mail, fax. Sample copy online. Writer's guidelines by e-mail. Editorial calendar online.

Nonfiction How-to, interview/profile, new product, technical. **Buys 40 mss/year.** Query with published clips. Length: 500-2,500 words. **Pays $25-200.** Sometimes pays expenses of writers on assignment.

Photos State availability with submission. Buys all rights. Negotiates payment individually. Identification of subjects required.

Tips "We publish only stories specific to Connecticut business."

BUSINESS NH MAGAZINE

670 N. Commercial St., Suite 110, Manchester NH 03101-1831. (603)626-6354. Fax: (603)626-6359. E-mail: edit@businessnhmagazine.com. **Contact:** Stephanie McLaughlin, editor. **25% freelance written.** Monthly magazine covering business, politics and people of New Hampshire. "Our audience consists of the owners and top managers of New Hampshire businesses." Estab. 1983. Circ. 15,000. Pays on publication. Publishes ms an average of 2 months after acceptance. Byline given. Accepts queries by e-mail, fax.

Nonfiction How-to, interview/profile. "No unsolicited manuscripts; interested in New Hampshire writers only." **Buys 24 mss/year.** Query with published clips and résumé. Length: 750-2,500 words. **Payment varies.**

Photos Both b&w and color photos used. Buys one-time rights. Payment varies.

Tips "I *always* want clips and résumé with queries. Freelance stories are almost always assigned. Stories *must* be local to New Hampshire."

CANADIAN MONEYSAVER

Canadian MoneySaver, Inc., Box 370, Bath ON K0H 1G0, Canada. (613)352-7448. Fax: (613)352-7700. E-mail: moneyinfo@canadianmoneysaver.ca. Website: www.canadianmoneysaver.ca. **Contact:** Dale Ennis, editor. **10% freelance written.** Monthly magazine covering personal finance. *"Canadian MoneySaver* contains practical money articles on tax, investment, retirement, and financial planning for everyday use." Estab. 1981. Circ. 76,300. Pays on publication. Publishes ms an average of 1 month after acceptance. Byline given. Buys first rights. Editorial lead time 1 month. Accepts queries by mail, e-mail, fax, phone. Responds in 2 weeks to queries; 1 month to mss. Sample copy online. Writer's guidelines free.

Nonfiction How-to (personal finance), personal experience. Query with published clips. Length: 800-2,000 words. **Pays negotiable rates for assigned articles.**

$ CRAIN'S DETROIT BUSINESS

Crain Communications, Inc., 1155 Gratiot, Detroit MI 48207-2997. (313)446-0419. Fax: (313)446-1687. E-mail: sselby@crain.com. Website: www.crainsdetroit.com. Editor: Mary Kramer. Executive Editor: Cindy Goodaker. **Contact:** Shawn Selby, special sections editor. **15% freelance written.** Weekly tabloid covering business in the Detroit metropolitan area—specifically Wayne, Oakland, Macomb, Washtenaw, and Livingston counties. Estab. 1985. Circ. 150,000. Pays on publication. Publishes ms an average of 1 month after acceptance. Byline given. Buys all rights. Accepts queries by mail, e-mail. Sample copy for $1.50. Writer's guidelines online.

• *Crain's Detroit Business* uses only area writers and local topics.

Nonfiction New product, technical, business. **Buys 50 mss/year.** Query with published clips. Length: 30-40 words/column inch. **Pays $10-15/column inch.** Pays expenses of writers on assignment.

Photos State availability with submission.

Tips "Contact special sections editor in writing with background and, if possible, specific story ideas relating to our type of coverage and coverage area. We only use *local* writers."

FINANCIAL TIMES

Financial Times, Ltd., One Southwark Bridge, London England SE1 9HL, United Kingdom. (44207)873-3000. Website: www.ft.com. Editor: Andrew Gowers. Daily magazine. Provides information on world business, politics, finance and economics, as well managagement topics, technology and communications. Circ. 229,423. Editorial lead time 8 days. Sample copy not available.

$ IN BUSINESS WINDSOR

Cornerstone Publications, Inc., 1775 Sprucewood Ave., Unit 1, LaSalle ON N9J 1X7, Canada. (519)250-2880. Fax: (519)250-2881. E-mail: editor@inbusinesswindsor.com. Website: www.inbusinesswindsor.com. **Contact:** Gary Baxter, general manager/publisher; Kelly O'Sullivan, editor. **70% freelance written.** Monthly magazine

covering business. "We focus on issues/ideas which are of interest to businesses in and around Windsor and Essex County (Ontario). Most stories deal with business and finance; occasionally we will cover health and sports issues that affect our readers." Estab. 1988. Circ. 10,000. **Pays on acceptance.** Byline given. Buys first rights. Editorial lead time 3 months. Submit seasonal material 3 months in advance. Accepts queries by mail, e-mail, fax. Responds in 2 weeks to queries; 1 month to mss. Sample copy for $3.50.
Nonfiction General interest, how-to, interview/profile. **Buys 25 mss/year.** Query with published clips. Length: 800-1,500 words. **Pays $70-150.** Sometimes pays expenses of writers on assignment.

$ $INGRAM'S

Show-Me Publishing, Inc., 306 E. 12th St., Suite 1014, Kansas City MO 64106. (816)842-9994. Fax: (816)474-1111. E-mail: editorial@ingramsonline.com. **Contact:** Editor. **50% freelance written.** Monthly magazine covering Kansas City business/executive lifestyle for "upscale, affluent business executives and professionals. Looking for sophisticated writing with style and humor when appropriate." Estab. 1974. Circ. 96,000. Pays 1 month after publication. Publishes ms an average of 2 months after acceptance. Byline given. Buys first, electronic rights. Editorial lead time 2 months. Submit seasonal material 3 months in advance. Accepts queries by mail, fax. Responds in 6 weeks to queries. Sample copy for $3.
● Only accepts local writers and guest columnist are not paid articles.
Nonfiction "All articles must have a Kansas City angle. We don't accept unsolicited manuscripts except for opinion column." General interest, how-to (business and personal finance related), interview/profile (Kansas City execs, politicians, celebrities), opinion, technical. **Buys 30 mss/year.** Query with published clips. Length: 500-3,000 words. **Pays $175-350.** Sometimes pays expenses of writers on assignment.
Columns/Departments Say So (opinion), 1,500 words. **Buys 12 mss/year. Pays $100 max.**
📷 All articles published are also published on the website, and writers must agree to those terms.
Tips "Writers must understand the publication and the audience—knowing what appeals to a business executive, entrepreneur, or professional in Kansas City. Do not call."

N $ $THE LANE REPORT

Lane Communications Group, 201 E. Main St., 14th Floor, Lexington KY 40507. (859)244-3500. Fax: (859)244-3555. E-mail: editorial@lanereport.com. Website: www.kybiz.com. Editor: Tim Hunt. **Contact:** Karen Baird, associate editor. **50% freelance written.** Monthly magazine covering statewide business. Estab. 1986. Circ. 15,000. Pays on publication. Byline given. Buys one-time rights. Editorial lead time 6 weeks. Submit seasonal material 3 months in advance. Accepts queries by mail, e-mail, fax. Accepts previously published material. Accepts simultaneous submissions. Responds in 1 month to queries. Sample copy and writer's guidelines free.
Nonfiction Essays, interview/profile, new product, photo feature. No fiction. **Buys 30-40 mss/year.** Query with published clips. Length: 500-2,000 words. **Pays $100-375.** Sometimes pays expenses of writers on assignment.
Photos State availability with submission. Reviews contact sheets, negatives, transparencies, prints. Buys one-time rights. Negotiates payment individually. Identification of subjects required.
Columns/Departments Technology and Business in Kentucky; Advertising; Exploring Kentucky; Perspective; Spotlight on the Arts, all less than 1,000 words.
📷 The online magazine carries original content not included in the print edition. Contact: Karen Baird, online editor.
Tips "As Kentucky's only statewide business and economics publication, we look for stories that incorporate perspectives from the Commonwealth's various regions and prominent industries—tying it into the national picture when appropriate. We also look for insightful profiles and interviews of Kentucky's entrepreneurs and business leaders."

N $ $ $ $☑ OREGON BUSINESS

MEDIAmerica, Inc., 610 SW Broadway, Suite 200, Portland OR 97205. (503)223-0304. Fax: (503)221-6544. E-mail: queries@oregonbusiness.com. Website: www.oregonbusiness.com. **Contact:** Gillian Floren, editor. **20-30% freelance written.** Monthly magazine covering business in Oregon. "Our subscribers inlcude owners of small and medium-sized businesses, government agencies, professional staffs of banks, insurance companies, ad agencies, attorneys and other service providers. We accept *only* stories about Oregon businesses, issues and trends." Estab. 1981. Circ. 50,000. Pays on publication. Byline given. Buys first North American serial, electronic rights. Editorial lead time 2 months. Accepts queries by mail, e-mail. Sample copy for $4. Writer's guidelines online.
Nonfiction Features should focus on "major trends shaping the state; noteworthy businesses, practices, and leaders; stories with sweeping implications across industry sectors." Query with résumé and 2-3 published clips. Length: 1,200-3,000 words.
Columns/Departments First Person (opinion piece on an issue related to business), 750 words; Around the State (recent news and trends, and how they might shape the future), 100-600 words; Business Tools (practical,

how-to suggestions for business managers and owners), 400-600 words; In Character (profile of interesting or "quirky" member of the business community), 850 words. Query with résumé and 2-3 published clips.

Tips "An *Oregon Business* story must meet at least two of the following criteria: **Size and location**. The topic must be relevant to Northwest businesses. Companies (including franchises) must be based in Oregon or Southwest Washington with at least five employees and annual sales above $250,000. **Service**: Our sections (1,200 words) are reserved largely for service pieces focusing on finance, marketing, management or other general business topics. These stories are meant to be instructional, emphasizing problem-solving by example. **Trends**: These are sometimes covered in a section piece, or perhaps a feature story. We aim to be the state's leading business publication so we want to be the first to spot trends that affect Oregon companies. **Exclusivity or strategy**: of an event, whether it's a corporate merger, a dramatic turnaround, a marketing triumph or a PR disaster."

$ ROCHESTER BUSINESS JOURNAL

Rochester Business Journal, Inc., 55 St. Paul St., Rochester NY 14604. (585)546-8303. Fax: (585)546-3398. E-mail: rackley@rbj.net. Website: www.rbjdaily.com. Editor: Paul Ericson. Managing Editor: Mike Dickinson. **Contact:** Reid Ackley, associate editor. **10% freelance written.** Weekly tabloid covering local business. "The *Rochester Business Journal* is geared toward corporate executives and owners of small businesses, bringing them leading-edge business coverage and analysis first in the market." Estab. 1984. Circ. 10,000. Pays on publication. Publishes ms an average of 1 month after acceptance. Byline given. Buys first, second serial (reprint), electronic rights. Editorial lead time 6 weeks. Accepts queries by mail, e-mail, fax. Responds in 1 week to queries. Sample copy for free or by e-mail. Writer's guidelines online.

Nonfiction How-to (business topics), news features, trend stories with local examples. Do not query about any topics that do not include several local examples—local companies, organizations, universities, etc. **Buys 110 mss/year.** Query with published clips. Length: 1,000-2,000 words. **Pays $150.**

Tips "The *Rochester Business Journal* prefers queries from local published writers who can demonstrate the ability to write for a sophisticated audience of business readers. Story ideas should be about business trends illustrated with numerous examples of local companies participating in the change or movement."

$ $ VERMONT BUSINESS MAGAZINE

2 Church St., Burlington VT 05401-4445. (802)863-8038. Fax: (802)863-8069. E-mail: mcq@vermontbiz.com. Website: www.vermontbiz.com. **Contact:** Timothy McQuiston, editor. **80% freelance written.** Monthly tabloid covering business in Vermont. Circ. 8,000. Pays on publication. Publishes ms an average of 1 month after acceptance. Byline given. Buys one-time rights. Responds in 2 months to queries. Sample copy for 11×14 SAE and 7 first-class stamps.

Nonfiction Business trends and issues. **Buys 200 mss/year.** Query with published clips. Length: 800-1,800 words. **Pays $100-200.**

Reprints Send tearsheet and information about when and where the material previously appeared.

Photos Send photos with submission. Reviews contact sheets. Offers $10-35/photo. Identification of subjects required.

Tips "Read daily papers and look for business angles for a follow-up article. We look for issue and trend articles rather than company or businessman profiles. Note: Magazine accepts Vermont-specific material only. The articles must be about Vermont."

CAREER, COLLEGE & ALUMNI

$ $ AMERICAN CAREERS

Career Communications, Inc., 6701 W. 64th St., Overland Park KS 66202. (800)669-7795. Fax: (913)362-7788. Website: www.carcom.com. **Contact:** Mary Pitchford, editor. **50% freelance written.** High school and technical school student publication covering careers, career statistics, skills needed to get jobs. "*American Careers* provides career, salary, and education information to middle school and high school students. Self-tests help them relate their interests and abilities to future careers. Articles on résumés, interviews, etc., help them develop employability skills." Estab. 1989. Circ. 500,000. Pays 1 month after acceptance. Byline given. Buys all rights, makes work-for-hire assignments. Accepts queries by mail. Accepts simultaneous submissions. Sample copy for $3. Writer's guidelines for #10 SASE.

   ○━ Break in by "sending us query letters with samples and résumés. We want to 'meet' the writer before making an assignment."

Nonfiction Career and education features related to career paths, including arts and communication, business, law, government, finance, construction, technology, health services, human services, manufacturing, engineering, and natural resources and agriculture. "No preachy advice to teens or articles that talk down to students."

Buys 20 mss/year. Query by mail only with published clips. Length: 300-1,000 words. **Pays $100-450.** Pays expenses of writers on assignment.

Photos State availability with submission. Buys all rights. Negotiates payment individually. Captions, identification of subjects, model releases required.

Tips "Letters of introduction or query letters with samples and résumés are ways we get to know writers. Samples should include how-to articles and career-related articles. Articles written for teenagers also would make good samples. Short feature articles on careers, career-related how-to articles, and self-assessment tools (10-20 point quizzes with scoring information) are primarily what we publish."

$ $ THE BLACK COLLEGIAN

The Career & Self Development Magazine for African-American Students, IMDiversity, Inc., 909 Poydras St., 34th Floor, New Orleans LA 70112. (504)523-0154. Fax: (504)523-0271. E-mail: michelle@black-collegian.com. Website: www.black-collegian.com. **Contact:** Press Edwards, vice president/editor. **25% freelance written.** Semiannual magazine for African-American college students and recent graduates with an interest in career and job information, African-American cultural awareness, personalities, history, trends, and current events. Estab. 1970. Circ. 122,000. Pays 1 month after publication. Byline given. Buys one-time rights. Submit seasonal material 2 months in advance. Accepts queries by mail, e-mail, fax. Responds in 6 months to queries. Sample copy for $5 (includes postage) and 9×12 SAE. Writer's guidelines for #10 SASE.

Nonfiction Material on careers, sports, black history, news analysis. Articles on problems and opportunities confronting African-American college students and recent graduates. Book excerpts, exposé, general interest, historical/nostalgic, how-to (develop employability), inspirational, interview/profile, opinion, personal experience. Query. Length: 900-1,900 words. **Pays $100-500 for assigned articles.**

Photos State availability of or send photos with submission. Reviews 8×10 prints. Captions, identification of subjects, model releases required.

The online magazine carries original content in addition to what's included in the print edition. Contact: Press Edwards.

Tips Articles are published under primarily 5 broad categories: job hunting information, overviews of career opportunities and industry reports, self-development information, analyses and investigations of conditions and problems that affect African-Americans, and celebrations of African-American success.

$ $ $ $ BROWN ALUMNI MAGAZINE

Brown University, Box 1854, Providence RI 02912-1854. (401)863-2873. Fax: (401)863-9599. E-mail: alumni_magazine@brown.edu. Website: www.brownalumnimagazine.com. Editor: Norman Boucher. **Contact:** Elizabeth Smith, office manager. Bimonthly magazine covering the world of Brown University and its alumni. "We are an editorially independent, general interest magazine covering the on-campus world of Brown University and the off-campus world of its alumni." Estab. 1900. Circ. 80,000. **Pays on acceptance.** Publishes ms an average of 3 months after acceptance. Byline given. Offers 25-30% kill fee. Buys North American serial and Web rights. Editorial lead time 3 months. Submit seasonal material 4 months in advance. Accepts queries by mail, e-mail, fax. Responds in 1 month to queries; 2 months to mss. Sample copy for free. Writer's guidelines not available.

Nonfiction Book excerpts, essays, exposé, general interest, historical/nostalgic, humor, interview/profile, opinion, personal experience, photo feature, travel, profiles. No articles unconnected to Brown or its alumni. **Buys 50 mss/year.** Query with published clips. Length: 150-4,000 words. **Pays $200-2,000 for assigned articles; $100-1,500 for unsolicited articles.** Pays expenses of writers on assignment.

Photos State availability with submission. Reviews contact sheets, transparencies, prints. Buys one-time rights. Negotiates payment individually. Captions, identification of subjects required.

Columns/Departments Under the Elms (news items about campus), 100-400 words; Arts & Culture (reviews of Brown-authored works), 200-500 words; Alumni P.O.V. (essays by Brown alumni), 750 words; Sports (reports on Brown sports teams and athletes), 200-500 words. **Buys 10-20 mss/year.** Query with published clips. **Pays $100-500.**

Tips "Be imaginative and be specific. A Brown connection is required for all stories in the magazine, but a Brown connection alone does not guarantee our interest. Ask yourself: Why should readers care about your proposed story? Also, we look for depth and objective reporting, not boosterism."

$ $ CIRCLE K MAGAZINE

3636 Woodview Trace, Indianapolis IN 46268-3196. (317)875-8755. Fax: (317)879-0204. E-mail: ckimagazine@kiwanis.org. Website: www.circlek.org. **Contact:** Shanna Mooney, executive editor. **60% freelance written.** Magazine published 5 times/year. "Our readership consists almost entirely of above-average college students interested in voluntary community service and leadership development. They are politically and socially aware and have a wide range of interests." Circ. 15,000. **Pays on acceptance.** Byline given. Buys first North American serial rights. Accepts queries by mail, e-mail, fax. Responds in 2 months to queries. Sample copy for large SAE with 3 first-class stamps or on website. Writer's guidelines online.

O➥ Break in by offering "fresh ideas for stories dealing with college students who are not only concerned with themselves. Our readers are concerned with making their communities better."

Nonfiction Articles published in *Circle K* are of 2 types—serious and light nonfiction. "We are interested in general interest articles on topics concerning college students and their lifestyles, as well as articles dealing with careers, community concerns, and leadership development." "No first-person confessions, family histories, or travel pieces." Query. Length: 1,500-2,000 words. **Pays $150-400.**

Photos Purchased with accompanying ms; total price includes both photos and ms. Captions required.

Tips "Query should indicate author's familiarity with the field and sources. Subject treatment must be objective and in-depth, and articles should include illustrative examples and quotes from persons involved in the subject or qualified to speak on it. We are open to working with new writers who present a good article idea and demonstrate that they've done their homework concerning the article subject itself, as well as concerning our magazine's style. We're interested in college-oriented trends, for example: entrepreneur schooling, high-tech classrooms, music, leisure, and health issues."

Ⓝ $ $ EQUAL OPPORTUNITY

The Nation's Only Multi-Ethnic Recruitment Magazine for African-American, Hispanic, Native-American & Asian-American College Grads, Equal Opportunity Publications, Inc., 445 Broad Hollow Rd., Suite 425, Melville NY 11747. (631)421-9421. Fax: (631)421-0359. E-mail: jschneider@eop.com. Website: www.eop.com. **Contact:** James Schneider, editor. **70% freelance written.** Prefers to work with published/established writers. Triannual magazine covering career guidance for minorities. "Our audience is 90% college juniors and seniors; 10% working graduates. An understanding of educational and career problems of minorities is essential." Estab. 1967. Circ. 11,000. Pays on publication. Publishes ms an average of 6 months after acceptance. Byline given. Buys first rights. Editorial lead time 6 months. Submit seasonal material 6 months in advance. Accepts queries by mail, e-mail, fax, phone. Accepts previously published material. Responds in 2 weeks to queries; 1 month to mss. Sample copy and writer's guidelines for 9×12 SAE with 5 first-class stamps.

• Distributed through college guidance and placement offices.

Nonfiction General interest (specific minority concerns), how-to (job hunting skills, personal finance, better living, coping with discrimination), interview/profile (minority role models), opinion (problems of minorities), personal experience (professional and student study experiences), technical (on career fields offering opportunities for minorities), coverage of minority interests. **Buys 10 mss/year.** Query with or without published clips or send complete ms. Length: 1,000-2,000 words. **Pays 10¢/word.** Sometimes pays expenses of writers on assignment.

Reprints Send information about when and where the material previously appeared. Pays 10¢/word.

Photos Reviews 35mm color slides and b&w. Buys all rights. Pays $15/photo use. Captions, identification of subjects required.

Tips "Articles must be geared toward questions and answers faced by minority and women students. We would like to see role-model profiles of professions."

$ FLORIDA LEADER

(for college students), P.O. Box 14081, Gainesville FL 32604-2081. (352)373-6907. Fax: (352)373-8120. E-mail: stephanie@studentleader.com. Website: www.floridaleader.com. Publisher: W.H. Oxendine, Jr. **Contact:** Stephanie Reck, editor. **10% freelance written.** Triannual magazine. College magazine, feature-oriented, especially activities, events, interests and issues pertaining to college students. Estab. 1983. Circ. 50,000. Pays on publication. Publishes ms an average of 2 months after acceptance. Byline given. Submit seasonal material 6 months in advance. Accepts queries by mail, e-mail, fax. Responds in 2 months to queries. Sample copy for $3.50, 9×12 SAE with 5 first-class stamps. Writer's guidelines online.

Nonfiction Practical tips for going to college, student life and leadership development. How-to, humor, interview/profile, Feature (All multi-sourced and Florida college related). "No lengthy individual profiles or articles without primary and secondary sources of attribution." Length: 900 words. **Pays $35-75.** Sometimes pays expenses of writers on assignment.

Photos State availability with submission. Reviews negatives, transparencies. Captions, identification of subjects, model releases required.

Columns/Departments College Life, The Lead Role, In Every Issue (quizzes, tips), Florida Forum (features Florida high school students), 250-1,000 words. **Buys 2 mss/year.** Query.

Tips "Read other high school and college publications for current issues, interests. Send manuscripts or outlines for review. All sections open to freelance work. Always looking for lighter, humorous articles as well as features on Florida colleges and universities, careers, jobs. Multi-sourced (5-10) articles are best."

$ $ $ $ HARVARD MAGAZINE

Harvard Magazine, Inc., 7 Ware St., Cambridge MA 02138. (617)495-5746. Fax: (617)495-0324. Website: www.harvardmagazine.com. **Contact:** John S. Rosenberg, editor. **35-50% freelance written.** Bimonthly magazine for Harvard University faculty, alumni, and students. Estab. 1898. Circ. 225,000. Pays on publication. Publishes ms an average of 4 months after acceptance. Byline given. Buys one-time print and website rights. Editorial lead time 1 year. Accepts queries by mail, fax. Responds in 1 month to queries; 1 month to mss. Sample copy online. Writer's guidelines not available.

Nonfiction Book excerpts, essays, interview/profile, journalism on Harvard-related intellectual subjects. **Buys 20-30 mss/year.** Query with published clips. Length: 800-10,000 words. **Pays $250-2,000.** Pays expenses of writers on assignment.

$ $ $ $ NOTRE DAME MAGAZINE

University of Notre Dame, 538 Grace Hall, Notre Dame IN 46556-5612. (574)631-5335. Fax: (574)631-6767. E-mail: ndmag@nd.edu. Website: www.nd.edu/~ndmag. Managing Editor: Carol Schaal. **Contact:** Kerry Temple, editor. **75% freelance written.** Quarterly magazine covering news of Notre Dame and education and issues affecting contemporary society. "We are a university magazine with a scope as broad as that found at a university, but we place our discussion in a moral, ethical, spiritual context reflecting our Catholic heritage." Estab. 1972. Circ. 142,000. **Pays on acceptance.** Publishes ms an average of 1 year after acceptance. Byline given. Buys first, electronic rights. Accepts queries by mail, e-mail, fax. Responds in 2 months to queries. Sample copy online. Writer's guidelines online.

Nonfiction Opinion, personal experience, religious. **Buys 35 mss/year.** Query with published clips. Length: 600-3,000 words. **Pays $250-3,000.** Sometimes pays expenses of writers on assignment.

Photos State availability with submission. Reviews transparencies, 8×10 prints, b&w contact sheets. Buys one-time and electronic rights. Identification of subjects, model releases required.

Columns/Departments Perspectives (essays, often written in first person, deal with a wide array of issues—some topical, some personal, some serious, some light). Query with or without published clips or send complete ms.

   The online version carries original content not found in the print edition and includes writer's guidelines. Contact: Carol Schaal.

Tips "The editors are always looking for new writers and fresh ideas. However, the caliber of the magazine and frequency of its publication dictate that the writing meet very high standards. The editors value articles strong in storytelling quality, journalistic technique, and substance. They do not encourage promotional or nostalgia pieces, stories on sports, or essays which are sentimentally religious."

$ $ OREGON QUARTERLY

The Magazine of the University of Oregon, 5228 University of Oregon, 130 Chapman Hall, Eugene OR 97403-5228. (541)346-5048. Fax: (541)346-5571. E-mail: gmaynard@uoregon.edu. Website: www.uoregon.edu/~oq. Associate Editor: Ross West. **Contact:** Guy Maynard, editor. **50% freelance written.** Quarterly magazine covering people and ideas at the University of Oregon and the Northwest. Estab. 1919. Circ. 100,000. **Pays on acceptance.** Publishes ms an average of 3 months after acceptance. Byline given. Buys first North American serial rights. Accepts queries by mail, e-mail. Accepts previously published material. Responds in 2 months to queries. Sample copy for 9×12 SAE with 4 first-class stamps or on website. Writer's guidelines online.

   Break in to the magazine with a profile (400 or 800 words) of a University of Oregon alumnus. Best to query first.

Nonfiction Northwest issues and culture from the perspective of UO alumni and faculty. **Buys 30 mss/year.** Query with published clips. Length: 250-2,500 words. **Pays $100-750.** Sometimes pays expenses of writers on assignment.

Reprints Send photocopy and information about when and where the material previously appeared. Pays 50% of amount paid for an original article.

Photos State availability with submission. Reviews 8×10 prints. Buys one-time rights. Offers $10-25/photo. Identification of subjects required.

Fiction Publishes novel excerpts.

Tips "Query with strong, colorful lead; clips."

THE PENN STATER

Penn State Alumni Association, Hintz Family Alumni Center, University Park PA 16802. (814)865-2709. Fax: (814)863-5690. E-mail: pennstater@psu.edu. Website: www.alumni.psu.edu. **Contact:** Tina Hay, editor. **75% freelance written.** Bimonthly magazine covering Penn State and Penn Staters. Estab. 1910. Circ. 123,000. **Pays on acceptance.** Publishes ms an average of 4 months after acceptance. Byline given. Offers 50% kill fee. Buys first North American serial, second serial (reprint) rights. Editorial lead time 3 months. Submit seasonal material

8 months in advance. Accepts queries by mail, e-mail, fax. Accepts previously published material. Accepts simultaneous submissions. Responds in 3 months to queries. Sample copy and writer's guidelines free.

Nonfiction Stories must have Penn State connection. Book excerpts (by Penn Staters), general interest, historical/nostalgic, interview/profile, personal experience, photo feature, book reviews, science/research. No unsolicited mss. **Buys 20 mss/year.** Query with published clips. Length: 200-3,000 words. **Pays competitive rates.** Pays expenses of writers on assignment.

Reprints Send photocopy and information about when and where the material previously appeared. Payment varies.

Photos Send photos with submission. Reviews transparencies, prints. Buys one-time rights. Negotiates payment individually. Captions required.

Tips "We are especially interested in attracting writers who are savvy in creative nonfiction/literary journalism. Most stories must have a Penn State tie-in. No phone calls."

$ $THE PURDUE ALUMNUS

Purdue Alumni Association, Dick and Sandy Dauch Alumni Center, 403 W. Wood St., West Lafayette IN 47907-2007. (765)494-5182. Fax: (765)494-9179. E-mail: slmartin@purdue.edu. Website: www.purdue.edu/PAA. **Contact:** Sharon Martin, editor. **50% freelance written.** Prefers to work with published/established writers; works with small number of new/unpublished writers each year. Bimonthly magazine covering subjects of interest to Purdue University alumni. Estab. 1912. Circ. 65,000. Pays on publication. Publishes ms an average of 2 months after acceptance. Byline given. Buys first rights, makes work-for-hire assignments. Submit seasonal material 6 months in advance. Accepts queries by mail. Accepts previously published material. Accepts simultaneous submissions. Responds in 6 weeks to queries. Sample copy for 9×12 SAE with 2 first-class stamps. Writer's guidelines online.

Nonfiction Focus is on alumni, campus news, issues, and opinions of interest to 65,000 members of the Alumni Association. Feature style, primarily university-oriented. Issues relevant to education. General interest, historical/nostalgic, humor, interview/profile, personal experience. **Buys 12-20 mss/year.** Length: 1,500-2,500 words. **Pays $250-500 for assigned articles.** Pays expenses of writers on assignment.

Photos State availability with submission. Reviews 5×7 prints, b&w contact sheets.

Tips "We have more than 350,000 living, breathing Purdue alumni. If you can find a good story about one of them, we're interested. We use local freelancers to do campus pieces."

$ $ $ $RUTGERS MAGAZINE

Rutgers University, Davidson Hall, 96 Davidson Rd., New Brunswick NJ 08854. (732)445-3710. Fax: (732)932-6950. E-mail: rutgersmagazine@ur.rutgers.edu. **Contact:** Renee Olson, editor. **30% freelance written.** Published 3 times/year, university magazine of "general interest, but articles must have a Rutgers University or alumni tie-in." Circ. 70,000. **Pays on acceptance.** Publishes ms an average of 4 months after acceptance. Byline given. Offers kill fee. Buys first North American serial rights. Submit seasonal material 8 months in advance. Accepts queries by mail, e-mail, fax. Responds in 1 month to queries. Sample copy for $3 and 9×12 SAE with 5 first-class stamps.

Nonfiction Essays, general interest, historical/nostalgic, interview/profile, photo feature, science/research; art/humanities. No articles without a Rutgers connection. **Buys 10-15 mss/year.** Query with published clips. Length: 1,200-3,500 words. **Pays $1,200-2,200.** Pays expenses of writers on assignment.

Photos State availability with submission. Buys one-time rights. Payment varies. Identification of subjects required.

Columns/Departments Sports; Alumni Profiles (related to Rutgers), all 1,200-1,800 words. **Buys 4-6 mss/year.** Query with published clips. **Pays competitively.**

Tips "Send an intriguing query backed by solid clips. We'll evaluate clips and topic for most appropriate use."

SCHOLASTIC ADMINISTR@TOR MAGAZINE

Scholastic, Inc., 557 Broadway, New York NY 10012. (212)343-6100. Fax: (212)343-4799. E-mail: lrenwick@scholastic.com. Website: www.scholastic.com/administrator. Senior Managing Editor: Lucile Renwick. Magazine published 8 times/year. Focuses on helping today's school administrators and education technology leaders in their efforts to improve the management of schools. Circ. 100,000. Editorial lead time 1 month. Sample copy for free.

$SUCCEED

The Magazine for Continuing Education, classesUSA.com, 1200 South Ave., Suite 202, Staten Island NY 10314. (718)761-4800. Fax: (718)761-3300. E-mail: editorial@collegebound.net. **Contact:** Gina LaGuardia, editor-in-chief. **85% freelance written.** Quarterly magazine. "*SUCCEED*'s readers are interested in continuing education, whether it be for changing careers or enhancing their current career." Estab. 1994. Circ. 155,000. Pays on publication. Publishes ms an average of 4 months after acceptance. Byline given. Buys first, second serial (reprint) rights. Editorial lead time 4 months. Submit seasonal material 4 months in advance. Accepts queries by mail, e-mail. Accepts previously published material. Accepts simultaneous submissions. Responds in 5 weeks to queries. Sample copy for $1.87. Writer's guidelines for 9×12 SASE.

○ᴿ Break in with "an up-to-date, expert-driven article of interest to our audience with personal, real-life anecdotes as support—not basis—for exploration."

Nonfiction Essays, exposé, general interest, how-to (change careers), interview/profile (interesting careers), new product, opinion, personal experience. **Buys 25 mss/year.** Query with published clips. Length: 1,000-1,500 words. **Pays $75-150.** Sometimes pays expenses of writers on assignment.

Reprints Send photocopy.

Photos Send photos with submission. Reviews negatives, prints. Buys one-time rights. Offers no additional payment for photos accepted with ms. Captions, identification of subjects required.

Columns/Departments Tech Zone (new media/technology), 300-700 words; To Be... (personality/career profile), 600-800 words; Financial Fitness (finance, money management), 100-300 words; Memo Pad (short, newsworthy items that relate to today's changing job market and continuing education); Solo Success (how readers can "do it on their own," with recommended resources, books, and software). **Buys 10 mss/year.** Query with published clips. **Pays $50-75.**

Fillers Facts, newsbreaks. **Buys 5/year.** Length: 50-200 words.

Tips "Stay current and address issues of importance to our readers—lifelong learners and those in career transition. They're ambitious, hands-on, and open to advice, new areas of opportunity, etc."

TRANSFORMATIONS

A Journal of People and Change, Worcester Polytechnic Institute, 100 Institute Rd., Worcester MA 01609-2280. Fax: (508)831-5820. E-mail: transformations@wpi.edu. Website: www.wpi.edu/+Transformations. **Contact:** Michael Dorsey, interim editor. **50% freelance written.** Quarterly alumni magazine covering science and engineering/education/business personalities and related technologies and issues for 25,000 alumni, primarily engineers, scientists, managers, media. Estab. 1897. Circ. 30,000. Pays on publication. Publishes ms an average of 6 months after acceptance. Byline given. Buys one-time rights. Accepts queries by mail, e-mail. Accepts previously published material. Accepts simultaneous submissions. Responds in 1 month to queries. Sample copy online.

Nonfiction Interview/profile (alumni in engineering, science, etc.), photo feature, features on people and programs at WPI. Query with published clips. Length: 300-3,000 words. **Pays negotiable rate.** Sometimes pays expenses of writers on assignment.

Photos State availability with submission. Reviews contact sheets. Pays negotiable rate. Captions required.

▣ The online magazine carries original content not found in the print edition.

Tips "Submit outline of story, story idea or published work. Features are most open to freelancers with excellent narrative skills, and an ability to understand and convey complex technologies in an engaging way. Keep in mind that this is an alumni magazine, so most articles focus on the college and its graduates."

Ⓝ $ $U.S. BLACK ENGINEER/HISPANIC ENGINEER

And Information Technology, Career Communications Group, Inc., 729 E. Pratt St., Suite 504, Baltimore MD 21202-3101. (410)244-7101. Fax: (410)752-1837. E-mail: editors@ccgmag.com. Website: www.blackengineer.com. **Contact:** Eric Addison, managing editor. **80% freelance written.** Quarterly magazine. "Both of our magazines are designed to bring technology issues home to people of color. We look at careers in technology and what affects career possibilities, including education. But we also look at how technology affects Black Americans and Latinos." Estab. 1976. Circ. 40,000. Pays on publication. Publishes ms an average of 1 month after acceptance. Byline given. Offers 50% kill fee. Makes work-for-hire assignments. Editorial lead time 2 months. Accepts queries by mail, e-mail, fax, phone. Responds in 2 months to queries. Sample copy for #10 SASE. Writer's guidelines for #10 SASE.

Nonfiction How-to (plan a career, get a first job, get a good job), interview/profile, new product, technical (new technologies and people of color involved with them), Capitol Hill/federal reportage on technology and EEO issues. No opinion pieces, first-person articles, routine profiles with no news peg or grounding in science/technology issues. Length: 650-1,800 words. **Pays $250-600 for assigned articles.** Sometimes pays expenses of writers on assignment.

Photos State availability with submission. Buys all rights. Negotiates payment individually. Captions, identification of subjects, model releases required.

Columns/Departments Dot-Comets (rising new economy entrepreneurs); Color of Technology (Did you know that...?), 800 words; Pros on the Move (Black/Hispanic career moves), 500 words; My Greatest Challenge (up from the roots), 650 words; E-Commerce (websites of interest), 650 words; TechDollars (technology and finance), 650 words; Community News (related to science and technology), 650 words; Technology for Kids, 650 words; Technology Overseas, 650 words. **Buys 30 mss/year. Pays $250-300.**

Tips "Call or come see me. Also contact us about covering our conferences, Black Engineer of the Year Awards and Women of Color Technology Awards."

CHILD CARE & PARENTAL GUIDANCE

$ $ ALL ABOUT KIDS MAGAZINE

Midwest Parenting Publications, 1901 Broad Ripple Ave., Indianapolis IN 46220. E-mail: jasonjones@aak.com. Website: www.aak.com. **Contact:** Tom Wynne, editor. **100% freelance written.** Monthly magazine covering a myriad of parenting topics and pieces of information relative to families and children in greater Cincinnati. Estab. 1985. Circ. 60,000. Pays on publication. Publishes ms an average of 6 months after acceptance. Byline given. Buys first, electronic rights. Editorial lead time 3 months. Submit seasonal material 6 months in advance. Accepts queries by mail. Writer's guidelines online.

Nonfiction Exposé, general interest, historical/nostalgic, how-to (family projects, crafts), humor, inspirational, interview/profile, opinion, photo feature, travel. Special issues: Maternity (January); Special Needs Children (May). No product or book reviews. **Buys 50 mss/year.** Send complete ms. Length: 750-3,000 words. **Pays $50-250 for assigned articles; $50-100 for unsolicited articles.**

Photos State availability with submission.

Fillers Anecdotes, facts, gags to be illustrated by cartoonist, short humor. **Buys 20/year.** Length: 350-800 words. **Pays $50-100.**

Tips "Submit full-text articles with query letter. Keep in mind the location of the magazine and try to include relevant sidebars, sources, etc."

Ⓝ $ $ $ AMERICAN BABY MAGAZINE

For Expectant and New Parents, Meredith Corp., 125 Park Ave., 16th Floor, New York NY 10017. (212)557-6600. Fax: (212)445-1345. Website: www.americanbaby.com. **Contact:** Sarah Jones, assistant editor. **70% freelance written.** Monthly magazine covering health, medical and childcare concerns for expectant and new parents, particularly those having their first child or those whose child is between the ages of birth and 2 years old. Mothers are the primary readers, but fathers' issues are equally important. Estab. 1938. Circ. 2,000,000. **Pays on acceptance.** Publishes ms an average of 6 months after acceptance. Byline given. Offers 25% kill fee. Buys first North American serial rights. Editorial lead time 5 months. Submit seasonal material 6 months in advance. Accepts queries by mail. Accepts previously published material. Accepts simultaneous submissions. Responds in 3 months to queries; 3 months to mss. Sample copy for 9 × 12 SAE with 6 first-class stamps. Writer's guidelines for #10 SASE.

● Prefers to work with published/established writers; works with a small number of new/unpublished writers each year.

Nonfiction Full-length articles should offer helpful expert information on some aspect of pregnancy or child care; should cover a common problem of child-raising, along with solutions; or should give expert advice on a psychological or practical subject. Articles about products, such as toys and nursery furniture, are not accepted, as these are covered by staff members. Book excerpts, essays, general interest, how-to (some aspect of pregnancy or child care), humor, new product, personal experience, Fitness; Beauty; Health. "No 'hearts and flowers' or fantasy pieces." **Buys 60 mss/year.** Query with or without published clips or send complete ms. Length: 1,000-2,000 words. **Pays $750-1,200 for assigned articles; $600-800 for unsolicited articles.** Pays expenses of writers on assignment.

Reprints Send photocopy and information about when and where the material previously appeared. Pays 50%.

Photos State availability with submission. Reviews transparencies, Prints. Buys one-time rights. Identification of subjects, model releases required.

Columns/Departments Personal Experience, 700-1,000 words, Short Items, Crib Notes (news and feature items) and Medical Update, 50-250 words. **Pays $200-1,000.**

Tips "Get to know our style by thoroughly reading a recent issue of the magazine. Don't send something we recently published. Our readers want to feel connected to other parents, both to share experiences and to learn from one another. They want reassurance that the problems they are facing are solvable and not uncommon. They want to keep up with the latest issues affecting their new family, particularly health and medical news, but they don't have a lot of spare time to read. We forgo the theoretical approach to offer quick-to-read, hands-on information that can be put to use immediately. A simple, straightforward, clear approach is mandatory."

$ ATLANTA PARENT/ATLANTA BABY

2346 Perimeter Park Dr., Suite 101, Atlanta GA 30341. (770)454-7599. Fax: (770)454-7699. E-mail: atlantaparent @atlantaparent.com. Website: www.atlantaparent.com. Publisher: Liz White. **Contact:** Amy Dusek, managing editor. **50% freelance written.** Pays on publication. Publishes ms an average of 3 months after acceptance.

Byline given. Buys one-time rights. Submit seasonal material 6 months in advance. Accepts queries by mail, e-mail. Accepts previously published material. Responds in 4 months to queries. Sample copy for $3.

Nonfiction General interest, how-to, humor, interview/profile, travel. Special issues: Private School (January); Camp (February); Birthday Parties (March and September); Maternity and Mothering (May and October); Childcare (July); Back-to-School (August); Teens (September); Holidays (November/December). No religious or philosophical discussions. **Buys 60 mss/year.** Query with or without published clips or send complete ms. Length: 800-1,500 words. **Pays $5-50.** Sometimes pays expenses of writers on assignment.

Reprints Send tearsheet or photocopy with rights for sale noted and information about when and where the material previously appeared. **Pays $30-50.**

Photos State availability of or send photos with submission. Reviews 3×5 photos. Buys one-time rights. Offers $10/photo.

Tips "Articles should be geared to problems or situations of families and parents. Should include down-to-earth tips and be clearly written. No philosophical discussions. We're also looking for well-written humor."

N $ $ $ $ BABY TALK

Time, Inc., 530 Fifth Ave., 4th Floor, New York NY 10036. (212)522-8989. Fax: (212)522-8699. E-mail: letters@babytalk.com. Website: www.babytalk.com. Managing Editor: Sally Tusa. **Contact:** Editor. **Mostly freelance written.** magazine published 10 times/year. *"Baby Talk* is written primarily for women who are considering pregnancy or who are expecting a child, and parents of children from birth through 18 months, with the emphasis on pregnancy through first six months of life." Estab. 1935. Circ. 2,000,000. Byline given. Accepts queries by mail. Responds in 2 months to queries.

Nonfiction Features cover pregnancy, the basics of baby care, infant/toddler health, growth and development, juvenile equipment and toys, work and day care, marriage and sex, "approached from a how-to, service perspective. The message—Here's what you need to know and why—is delivered with smart, crisp style. The tone is confident and reassuring (and, when appropriate, humorous and playful), with the backing of experts. In essence, *Baby Talk* is a training manual of parents facing the day-to-day dilemmas of new parenthood." No phone calls. Query with SASE. Length: 1,000-2,000 words. **Pays $500-2,000 depending on length, degree of difficulty and the writer's experience.**

Columns/Departments 100-1,250 words. Several departments are written by regular contributors. Query with SASE. **Pays $100-1,000.**

Tips "Please familiarize yourself with the magazine before submitting a query. Take the time to focus your story idea; scattershot queries are a waste of everyone's time. Does not accept poetry."

$ BIG APPLE PARENT/QUEENS PARENT/WESTCHESTER PARENT

Family Communications, Inc., 9 E. 38th St., 4th Floor, New York NY 10016. (212)889-6400. Fax: (212)689-4958. E-mail: hellonwheels@parentsknow.com. Website: www.parentsknow.com. **Contact:** Helen Freedman, executive editor. **90% freelance written.** Monthly tabloid covering New York City family life. *"BAP* readers live in high-rise Manhattan apartments; it is an educated, upscale audience. Often both parents are working full time in professional occupations. Child-care help tends to be one on one, in the home. Kids attend private schools for the most part. While not quite a suburban approach, some of our *QP* readers do have backyards (though most live in high-rise apartments). It is a more middle-class audience in Queens. More kids are in day care centers; majority of kids are in public schools. Our Westchester county edition is for suburban parents." Estab. 1985. Circ. 80,000, *Big Apple*; 70,000, *Queens Parent*; 70,000, *Westchester Parent*. Pays 2 months after publication. Byline given. Offers 50% kill fee. Buys first New York area rights. Submit seasonal material 3 months in advance. Accepts queries by mail, e-mail, fax. Accepts simultaneous submissions. Responds immediately to queries. Sample copy and writer's guidelines free.

> **O—** Break in with "Commentary (op ed); newsy angles—but everything should be targeted to parents. We love journalistic pieces (as opposed to essays, which is what we mostly get)."

Nonfiction Book excerpts, exposé, general interest, how-to, inspirational, interview/profile, opinion, personal experience, family health, education. "We're always looking for news and coverage of controversial issues." **Buys 150 mss/year.** Query with or without published clips or send complete ms. Length: 600-1,000 words. **Pays $35-50.** Sometimes pays expenses of writers on assignment.

Reprints Send tearsheet or typed ms with rights for sale noted and information about when and where the material previously appeared. Pays same as article rate.

Columns/Departments Dads; Education; Family Finance. **Buys 50-60 mss/year.** Send complete ms.

Tips "We have a very local focus; our aim is to present articles our readers cannot find in national publications. To that end, news stories and human interest pieces must focus on New York and New Yorkers. We are always looking for news and newsy pieces; we keep on top of current events, frequently giving issues that may relate to parenting a local focus so that the idea will work for us as well. We are not currently looking for essays, humor, general child raising, or travel."

$ BOISE FAMILY MAGAZINE

Magazine for Treasure Valley Parents, 13191 W. Scotfield St., Boise ID 83713-0899. (208)938-2119. Fax: (208)938-2117. E-mail: boisefamily@cs.com. Website: www.boisefamily.com. **Contact:** Liz Buckingham, editor. **90% freelance written.** Monthly magazine covering parenting, education, child development. "Geared to parents with children 12 years and younger. Focus on education, interest, activities for children. Positive parenting and healthy families." Estab. 1993. Circ. 19,000. Pays on publication. Publishes ms an average of 3 months after acceptance. Byline given. Offers 50% kill fee. Buys first North American serial rights. Editorial lead time 3 months. Submit seasonal material 3 months in advance. Accepts queries by mail, e-mail. Accepts simultaneous submissions. Responds in 2 months to queries. Sample copy for $1.50. Writer's guidelines online.

Nonfiction Essays, how-to, interview/profile, new product. Special issues: Health and Wellness (January); Birthday Party Fun (February); Education; Home & Garden (March); Summer Camps (April); Kids' Sports Guide (May); Summer, Family Travel; Arts Fairs & Festivals (June/July); Back-to-School; the Arts (August/September); Fall Fun; Children's Health (October); Winter Family Travel; Holiday Ideas (November); Holiday Crafts and Traditions (December). No political or religious affiliation-oriented articles. **Buys 10 mss/year.** Query with published clips. Length: 900-1,300 words. **Pays $50-100.** Sometimes pays expenses of writers on assignment.

Reprints Accepts previously published submissions.

Photos State availability with submission. Reviews 3×5 prints. Buys one-time rights. Negotiates payment individually. Captions required.

Columns/Departments Crafts, travel, finance, parenting. Length: 700-900 words. Query with published clips. **Pays $50-100.**

$ CATHOLIC PARENT

Our Sunday Visitor, 200 Noll Plaza, Huntington IN 46750-4310. (260)356-8400. Fax: (260)356-8472. E-mail: cparent@osv.com. Website: www.osv.com. **95% freelance written.** Bimonthly magazine. "We look for practical, realistic parenting articles written for a primarily Roman Catholic audience. The key is practical, not pious." Estab. 1993. Circ. 36,000. **Pays on acceptance.** Publishes ms an average of 6 months after acceptance. Byline given. Offers variable kill fee. Buys first North American serial rights. Editorial lead time 6 months. Submit seasonal material 6 months in advance. Accepts simultaneous submissions. Responds in 2 months to queries. Sample copy for $3.

- *Catholic Parent* is extremely receptive to first-person accounts of personal experiences dealing with parenting issues that are moving, emotionally engaging and uplifting for the reader. Bear in mind the magazine's mission to provide practical information for parents.

Nonfiction Essays, how-to, humor, inspirational, personal experience, religious. **Buys 50 mss/year.** Send complete ms. Length: 800 words. **Payment varies.** Sometimes pays expenses of writers on assignment.

Photos State availability with submission.

Columns/Departments This Works (parenting tips), 200 words. **Buys 50 mss/year.** Send complete ms. **Pays $15-25.**

Tips No poetry or fiction.

Ⓝ $ CHESAPEAKE FAMILY

Jefferson Communications, 1202 West St., Suite 100, Annapolis MD 21401. (410)263-1641. Fax: (410)280-0255. E-mail: mail@chesapeakefamily.com. Website: www.chesapeakefamily.com. **Contact:** Suzette Guiffré, editor. **80% freelance written.** Monthly magazine covering parenting. "*Chesapeake Family* is a free, regional parenting publication serving readers in the Anne Arundel, Calvert, Prince George's, and Queen Anne's counties of Maryland. Our goal is to identify tips, resources, and products that will make our readers' lives easier. We answer the questions they don't have time to ask, doing the research for them so they have the information they need to make better decisions for their families' health, education, and well-being." Estab. 1990. Circ. 40,000. Publishes ms an average of 2 months after acceptance. Byline given. Buys first, one-time, second serial (reprint), electronic rights, makes work-for-hire assignments. Editorial lead time 3-6 months. Submit seasonal material 4 months in advance. Accepts queries by mail, e-mail, fax. Accepts previously published material. Accepts simultaneous submissions. Sample copy for SASE with 3 First-Class stamps. Writer's guidelines online.

Nonfiction How-to (parenting topics: sign your kids up for sports, find out if your child needs braces, etc.), interview/profile (local personalities), travel (family-fun destinations). No general, personal essays (however, personal anecdotes leading into a story with general applicability is fine). **Buys 25 mss/year.** Send complete ms. Length: 800-1,200 words. **Pays $75-125; $35-50 for unsolicited articles.**

Photos State availability with submission. Reviews prints, GIF/JPEG files. Offers no additional payment for photos accepted with ms, unless original, assigned photo is selected for the cover. Model releases required.

Columns/Departments Buys 25 mss/year. **Pays $35-50.**

Tips "A writer's best chance is to know the issues specific to our local readers. Know how to research the issues well, answer the questions our readers need to know, and give them information they can act on—and present it in a friendly, conversational tone.''

$ $ CHICAGO PARENT

Wednesday Journal, Inc., 141 S. Oak Park Ave., Oak Park IL 60302-2972. (708)386-5555. Fax: (708)524-8360. E-mail: sschultz@chicagoparent.com. Website: www.chicagoparent.com. **Contact:** Susy Schultz, editor. **60% freelance written.** Monthly tabloid. *"Chicago Parent* has a distinctly local approach. We offer information, inspiration, perspective and empathy to Chicago-area parents. Our lively editorial mix has a 'we're all in this together' spirit, and articles are thoroughly researched and well written." Estab. 1988. Circ. 125,000 in three zones covering the 6-county Chicago metropolitan area. Pays on publication. Publishes ms an average of 2 months after acceptance. Byline given. Offers 10-50% kill fee. Buys first, electronic rights. Editorial lead time 4 months. Submit seasonal material 4 months in advance. Accepts queries by mail. Responds in 6 weeks to queries. Sample copy for $3.95 and 11×17 SAE with $1.65 postage. Writer's guidelines for #10 SASE.

> ○➔ Break in by "writing 'short stuff' items (front-of-the-book short items on local people, places and things of interest to families)." Local writers only.

Nonfiction Essays, exposé, how-to (parent-related), humor, interview/profile, travel, local interest; investigative features. Special issues: include Chicago Baby and Healthy Child. "No pot-boiler parenting pieces, simultaneous submissions, previously published pieces or non-local writers (from outside the 6-county Chicago metropolitan area)." **Buys 40-50 mss/year.** Query with published clips. Length: 200-2,500 words. **Pays $25-300 for assigned articles; $25-100 for unsolicited articles.** Pays expenses of writers on assignment.

Photos State availability with submission. Reviews contact sheets, negatives, prints. Buys one-time rights. Offers $0-40/photo; negotiates payment individually. Captions, identification of subjects required.

Columns/Departments Healthy Child (kids' health issues), 850 words; Getaway (travel pieces), up to 1,200 words; other columns not open to freelancers. **Buys 30 mss/year.** Query with published clips or send complete ms. **Pays $100.**

Tips "We don't like pot-boiler parenting topics and don't accept many personal essays unless they are truly compelling."

$ $ $ $ CHILD

Gruner + Jahr, 375 Lexington Ave., New York NY 10017-5514. (212)499-2000. Fax: (212)499-2038. Website: www.child.com. Editor-in-Chief: Miriam Arond. Managing Editor: Polly Chevalier. **Contact:** Submissions. **95% freelance written.** Monthly magazine covering parenting. Estab. 1986. Circ. 1,020,000. **Pays on acceptance.** Byline given. Offers 25% kill fee. Buys all rights. Editorial lead time 8 months. Submit seasonal material 6 months in advance. Accepts queries by mail. Responds in 2 months to queries. Sample copy for $3.95. Writer's guidelines for #10 SASE.

Nonfiction Book excerpts, essays, interview/profile, personal experience, travel, health, timely trend stories on topics that affect today's parents. No poetry or fiction. **Buys 50 feature, 20-30 short mss/year.** Query with published clips. Length: 650-2,500 words. **Pays $1/word and up for assigned articles.** Sometimes pays expenses of writers on assignment.

Photos State availability with submission. Reviews transparencies. Buys one-time rights. Negotiates payment individually.

Columns/Departments What I Wish Every Parent Knew (personal essay); How They Do It (highlighting the experience of real parents in unique situations, explaining how they keep their lives in balance). **Buys 10 mss/ year.** Query with published clips. **Pays $1/word and up.**

> ▣ The online magazine carries original content not found in the print edition. Contact: Kathleen Tripp, online editor.

Tips "Stories should include opinions from experts as well as anecdotes from parents to illustrate the points being made. Lifestyle is key. Send a well-written query that meets our editorial needs. *Child* receives too many inappropriate submissions. Please consider your work carefully before submitting."

Ⓝ $ CONNECTICUT'S COUNTY KIDS

Journal Register Co., 877 Post Rd. E., Westport CT 06880-5224. (203)226-8877, ext. 125. Fax: (203)221-7540. E-mail: countykids@ctcentral.com. Website: www.countykids.com. **Contact:** Linda Greco, editor. **80-90% freelance written.** Monthly tabloid covering parenting. "We publish positive articles (nonfiction) that help parents of today raise children." Estab. 1987. Circ. 35,000. Pays on publication. Publishes ms an average of 2 months after acceptance. Byline given. Buys first North American serial, first, one-time, second serial (reprint) rights. Editorial lead time 6 weeks. Submit seasonal material 2-3 months in advance. Accepts queries by e-mail. Accepts previously published material. Sample copy not available. Writer's guidelines by e-mail.

Nonfiction Essays, general interest, humor, inspirational, new product, opinion, personal experience. Special issues: Birthday; Maternity and Birthing Services. No fiction. **Buys 24-35 mss/year.** Send complete ms. Length: 600-1,500 words. **Pays $40-100 for assigned articles; $25-40 for unsolicited articles.**

Columns/Departments Mom's View (humorous experiences), 800-1,000 words; Pediatric Health (medical situations), 800 words; Active Family (events shared as a family), 800 words. **Buys 15-20 mss/year.** Send complete ms. **Pays $25-40.**

Tips "We like to use Connecticut writers when we can, but we do use writers from all over the U.S. We like all kinds of writing styles."

$ $⬚ EXPECTING

Family Communications, 65 The East Hall, Toronto ON M8Z 5W3, Canada. (416)537-2604. Fax: (416)538-1794. **Contact:** Tracy Cooper, editor. **100% freelance written.** Semiannual digest-sized magazine. Writers must be Canadian health professionals. Articles address all topics relevant to expectant parents. Estab. 1995. Circ. 100,000. **Pays on acceptance.** Publishes ms an average of 6 months after acceptance. Byline given. Buys all rights. Editorial lead time 6 months. Accepts queries by mail, fax. Responds in 2 months to queries.

Nonfiction Medical. **Buys 6 mss/year.** Query with published clips. Length: 1,000-2,000 words. **Pays $300 (more for some articles).** Sometimes pays expenses of writers on assignment.

Photos State availability with submission. Buys all rights. Negotiates payment individually. Identification of subjects required.

$ $ FAMILY DIGEST

The Black Mom's Best Friend!, Family Digest Association, 696 San Ramon Valley Blvd., #349, Danville CA 94526. Fax: (925)838-4948. E-mail: editor@familydigest.com. **Contact:** John Starch, associate editor. **90% freelance written.** Quarterly magazine. "Our mission: Help black moms/female heads-of-household get more out of their roles as wife, mother, homemaker. Editorial coverage includes parenting, health, love and marriage, travel, family finances, and beauty and style. All designed to appeal to black moms." Estab. 1997. Circ. 400,000. Pays on publication. Publishes ms an average of 6 months after acceptance. Buys first North American serial, all rights. Editorial lead time 2 months. Submit seasonal material 3 months in advance. Accepts queries by e-mail. Accepts previously published material. Accepts simultaneous submissions. Responds in 1 month to queries. Writer's guidelines by e-mail.

Nonfiction "We are not political. We do not want articles that blame others. We do want articles that improve the lives of our readers." Book excerpts, general interest (dealing with relationships), historical/nostalgic, how-to, humor, inspirational, interview/profile, personal experience. Query with published clips. Length: up to 3,000 words. **Pays $100-500.** Sometimes pays expenses of writers on assignment.

Photos Reviews negatives, transparencies, prints. Offers no additional payment for photos accepted with ms. Captions, identification of subjects, model releases required.

Columns/Departments Food; Travel; Family; Parenting; Love and Marriage; Health; Family Finances; Beauty and Style. **Buys 100 mss/year.** Query with published clips. **Pays $100-500.**

Fiction Erotica, ethnic, historical, humorous, novel excerpts, romance. Query with published clips.

Fillers Anecdotes, facts, gags to be illustrated by cartoonist, short humor. **Buys 100 mss/year.** Length: 50-250 words.

$ THE FAMILY DIGEST

P.O. Box 40137, Fort Wayne IN 46804. **Contact:** Corine B. Erlandson, manuscript editor. **95% freelance written.** Bimonthly magazine. "*The Family Digest* is dedicated to the joy and fulfillment of the Catholic family and its relationship to the Catholic parish." Estab. 1945. Circ. 150,000. Pays within 1-2 months of acceptance. Byline given. Buys first North American serial rights. Submit seasonal material 7 months in advance. Accepts queries by mail. Accepts previously published material. Responds in 1-2 months to queries. Sample copy and writer's guidelines for 6×9 SAE with 2 first-class stamps.

Nonfiction Family life, parish life, prayer life, Catholic traditions. How-to, inspirational, religious. **Buys 60 unsolicited mss/year.** Send complete ms. Length: 750-1,200 words. **Pays $40-60 for accepted articles.**

Reprints Send ms with rights for sale noted and information about when and where the material previously appeared.

Fillers Anecdotes, tasteful humor based on personal experience. **Buys 18/year.** Length: 25-100 words. **Pays $25.**

Tips "Prospective freelance contributors should be familiar with the publication and the types of articles we accept and publish. We are especially looking for upbeat articles which affirm the simple ways in which the Catholic faith is expressed in daily life. Articles on family and parish life, including seasonal articles, how-to pieces, inspirational, prayer, spiritual life, and Church traditions, will be gladly reviewed for possible acceptance and publication."

Consumer Magazines

$ $ $ $ FAMILYFUN

Disney Magazine Publishing, Inc., 244 Main St., Northampton MA 01060-3107. (413)585-0444. Fax: (413)586-5724. Website: www.familyfun.com. **Contact:** Jean Graham, editorial assistant. Magazine covering activities for families with kids ages 3-12. *"Family Fun* is about all the great things families can do together. Our writers are either parents or authorities in a covered field." Estab. 1991. Circ. 1,850,000. **Pays on acceptance.** Byline sometimes given. Offers 25% kill fee. Buys simultaneous rights, makes work-for-hire assignments. Editorial lead time 6 months. Submit seasonal material 6 months in advance. Accepts simultaneous submissions. Responds in 3 months to queries. Sample copy for $3. Writer's guidelines online.

Nonfiction Book excerpts, essays, general interest, how-to (crafts, cooking, educational activities), humor, interview/profile, personal experience, photo feature, travel. **Buys dozens of mss/year.** Query with published clips. Length: 850-3,000 words. **Pays $1.25/word.** Pays expenses of writers on assignment.

Photos State availability with submission. Reviews contact sheets, negatives, transparencies. Buys all rights. Offers $75-500/photo. Identification of subjects, model releases required.

Columns/Departments Family Almanac, Nicole Blasenak, assistant editor (simple, quick, practical, inexpensive ideas and projects—outings, crafts, games, nature activities, learning projects, and cooking with children), 200-400 words; query or send ms; **pays $100-$200/article or $150 for ideas.** Family Traveler, Adrienne Stolarz, (brief, newsy items about family travel, what's new, what's great, and especially, what's a good deal), 100-125 words; send ms; **pays $100, also pays $50 for ideas.** Family Ties, Kathy Whittemore, senior editor (first-person column that spotlights some aspect of family life that is humorous, inspirational, or interesting); 1,300 words; send ms; **pays $1,625.** My Great Idea, Mary Giles, senior editor (explains fun and inventive ideas that have worked for writer's own family); 800-1,000 words; query or send ms; **pays $1,250 on acceptance;** also publishes best letters from writers and readers following column, send to My Great Ideas Editor, 100-150 words, **pays $75 on publication. Buys 60-80 letters/year; 10-12 mss/year.**

Tips "Many of our writers break into *FF* by writing for Family Almanac or Family Traveler (front-of-the-book departments)."

N $ GRAND RAPIDS FAMILY

Gemini Publications, 549 Ottawa Ave., NW, Grand Rapids MI 49503. (616)459-4545. Fax: (616)459-4800. E-mail: cvalde@geminipub.com. Website: www.geminipub.com. **Contact:** Carole Valade, editor. Monthly magazine covering local parenting issues. *"Grand Rapids Family* seeks to inform, instruct, amuse and entertain its readers and their families." Circ. 30,000. Pays on publication. Byline given. Offers $25 kill fee. Buys first North American serial, simultaneous, all rights, makes work-for-hire assignments. Editorial lead time 3 months. Submit seasonal material 4 months in advance. Accepts simultaneous submissions. Responds in 2 months to queries; 6 months to mss. Writer's guidelines for #10 SASE.

Nonfiction "The publication recognizes that parenting is a process that begins before conception/adoption and continues for a lifetime. The issues are diverse and ever changing. *Grand Rapids Family* seeks to identify these issues and give them a local perspective, using local sources and resources." Query. **Pays $25-50.**

Photos State availability with submission. Reviews contact sheets. Buys one-time or all rights. Offers $25/photo. Captions, identification of subjects, model releases required.

Columns/Departments All local: law, finance, humor, opinion, mental health. **Pays $25.**

HEALTHY BEGINNINGS, HEALTHY GROWING, HEALTHY CHOICES

Bridge Communications, Inc., 1450 Pilgrim Rd., Birmingham MI 48009-1006. (248)646-1020. E-mail: bridgecomm@aol.com. Website: www.bridge-comm.com. Editor: Alice R. McCarthy, Ph.D. Semiannual (March and October publication dates) 4-page, 4-color newsletters written for parents of children in grades preK-3, 4-5, and 6-8. Mental and physical health topics, plus strong support for school health programs including student health education. No advertising except books related to children's health. Circ. 100,000 yearly. Editorial lead time 4 months. Sample copies available.

$ HOME EDUCATION MAGAZINE

P.O. Box 1083, Tonasket WA 98855. (509)486-1351. E-mail: hem-editor@home-ed-magazine.com. Website: www.home-ed-magazine.com. **Contact:** Helen E. Hegener, managing editor. **80% freelance written.** Bimonthly magazine covering home-based education. We feature articles which address the concerns of parents who want to take a direct involvement in the education of their children—concerns such as socialization, how to find curriculums and materials, testing and evaluation, how to tell when your child is ready to begin reading, what to do when homeschooling is difficult, teaching advanced subjects, etc. Estab. 1983. Circ. 32,000. **Pays on acceptance.** Publishes ms an average of 4 months after acceptance. Byline given. Buys first North American serial, first, one-time, electronic rights. Submit seasonal material 6 months in advance. Accepts queries by mail, e-mail. Responds in 2 months to queries. Sample copy for $6.50. Writer's guidelines for #10 SASE or via e-mail.

○➤ Break in by "reading our magazine, understanding how we communicate with our readers, having an understanding of homeschooling, and being able to communicate that understanding clearly."

Nonfiction Essays, how-to (related to home schooling), humor, interview/profile, personal experience, photo feature, technical. **Buys 40-50 mss/year.** Query with or without published clips or send complete ms. Length: 750-2,500 words. **Pays $50-100.** Sometimes pays expenses of writers on assignment.

Photos Send photos with submission. Reviews enlargements, 35mm prints, b&w, CD-ROMs. Buys one-time rights. Pays $100/cover; $12/inside b&w photos. Identification of subjects required.

Tips "We would like to see how-to articles (that don't preach, just present options); articles on testing, accountability, working with the public schools, socialization, learning disabilities, resources, support groups, legislation, and humor. We need answers to the questions that homeschoolers ask. Please, no teachers telling parents how to teach. Personal experience with homeschooling is the preferred approach."

$ HOMESCHOOLING TODAY

P.O. Box 468, Barker TX 77413. Fax: (832)201-7620. E-mail: publisher@homeschooltoday.com. Website: www. homeschooltoday.com. **Contact:** Stacy McDonald, editor. **75% freelance written.** Bimonthly magazine covering homeschooling. "We are a practical magazine for homeschoolers with a broadly Christian perspective." Estab. 1992. Circ. 25,000. Pays on publication. Publishes ms an average of 1 year after acceptance. Byline given. Offers 25% kill fee. Buys first rights. Editorial lead time 6 months. Submit seasonal material 1 year in advance. Accepts queries by mail, e-mail, fax. Accepts simultaneous submissions. Responds in 1 month to queries; 2 months to mss. Sample copy and writer's guidelines free.

Nonfiction Book excerpts, how-to, inspirational, interview/profile, new product. No fiction or poetry. **Buys 30 mss/year.** Query. Length: 500-2,500 words. **Pays 8¢/word.**

Photos State availability with submission. Buys one-time rights. Offers no additional payment for photos accepted with ms. Captions, identification of subjects required.

INSTRUCTOR MAGAZINE

For Teachers of Grades K-8, Scholastic, Inc., 524 Broadway, New York NY 10012. (212)343-6100. Fax: (212)965-7497. E-mail: instructor@scholastic.com. Website: www.scholastic.com/instructor. Editor: Terry Cooper. Managing Editor: Jennifer Prescott. 8 times/ year Geared toward teachers, curriculum coordinators, principals and supervisors of kindergarten through 8th grade classes. Circ. 200,391. Editorial lead time 2 months. Submit seasonal material 6 months in advance. Accepts queries by mail. Responds in 3 months to queries; 3 months to mss. Sample copy available by calling (866)436-2455. Writer's guidelines online.

Nonfiction Features Department. (Classroom management and practice; education trends and issues; professional development; lesson plans). Query with or without published clips or send complete ms. Length: 800-1,200 words.

Columns/Departments Departments Editor. Activities and Tips (activities and tips for teachers), 250 words; Lesson Units (lesson- planning units on a specific curriculum area or theme) 400-800 words; Cyber Hunt Activities (tech-based activities in the classroom)250 words; End of the Day (personal essays about a teacher's experience with kids) 400-500 words. Query with or without published clips or send complete ms.

Tips "As you write, think: How can I make this article most useful for teachers? Write in your natural voice. We shy away from wordy, academic prose. Let us know what grade/subject you teach and name and location of your school."

$ $ METRO PARENT MAGAZINE

Metro Parent Publishing Group, 24567 Northwestern Hwy., Suite 150, Southfield MI 48075. (248)352-0990. Fax: (248)352-5066. E-mail: sdemaggio@metroparent.com. Website: www.metroparent.com. **Contact:** Susan DeMaggio, editor. **75% freelance written.** Monthly magazine covering parenting, women's health, education. "We are a local magazine on parenting topics and issues of interest to Detroit-area parents. Related issues: *Ann Arbor Parent; African/American Parent; Metro Baby Magazine.*" Circ. 85,000. Pays on publication. Publishes ms an average of 3 months after acceptance. Byline given. Buys first rights. Editorial lead time 3 months. Submit seasonal material 3 months in advance. Accepts queries by mail, e-mail. Accepts previously published material. Accepts simultaneous submissions. Responds in 2 weeks to queries; 3 months to mss. Sample copy for $2.50.

Nonfiction Essays, humor, inspirational, personal experience. **Buys 100 mss/year.** Send complete ms. Length: 1,500-2,500 words. **Pays $50-300 for assigned articles.**

Photos State availability with submission. Buys one-time rights. Offers $100-200/photo or negotiates payment individually. Captions required.

Columns/Departments Women's Health (latest issues of 20-40 year olds), 750-900 words; Solo Parenting (advice for single parents); Family Finance (making sense of money and legal issues); Tweens 'N Teens (handling teen "issues"), 750-800 words. **Buys 50 mss/year.** Send complete ms. **Pays $75-150.**

N $ METROFAMILY MAGAZINE

Inprint Publishing, 1015 Waterford Pkwy., Suite G, Box H-1, Edmond OK 73034. (405)340-1404. E-mail: editor@ metrofamilymagazine.com. Website: www.metrofamilymagazine.com. Publisher: Sarah Taylor. **Contact:** Denise Springer, editor. **60% freelance written.** Monthly tabloid covering parenting. *"MetroFamily Magazine* provides local parenting and family fun information for our Central Oklahoma readers. Send us information parents can use and relate to. Keep it light and bring on the humor."* Circ. 20,000. Pays on publication. Publishes ms an average of 1-2 months after acceptance. Byline given. Offers 100% kill fee. Buys first North American serial, second serial (reprint), simultaneous, electronic rights. Editorial lead time 2-3 months. Submit seasonal material 3 months in advance. Accepts queries by mail, e-mail. Accepts previously published material. Accepts simultaneous submissions. Responds in 3 weeks to queries; 1 month to mss. Sample copy for 10 × 13 SAE and 3 first-class stamps. Writer's guidelines for #10 SASE.

Nonfiction How-to (parenting issues, education), humor, inspirational, travel. No poetry, fiction, or anything that doesn't support good, solid family values. Send complete ms. Length: 300-600 words. **Pays $25-50, plus 1 contributor copy.**

Photos State availability with submission. Reviews GIF/JPEG files. Buys one-time rights. Negotiates payment individually. Captions, identification of subjects, model releases required.

Columns/Departments Sandwich Generation (parents with older parents), 600 words. **Buys 12 mss/year.** Send complete ms. **Pays $25-35.**

Fillers Facts, short humor. **Buys 12/year.** Length: 300-600 words. **Pays $25-35.**

$ METROKIDS MAGAZINE

The Resource for Delaware Valley Families, Kidstuff Publications, Inc., 1080 N. Delaware Ave., #702, Philadelphia PA 19125-4330. (215)291-5560. Fax: (215)291-5563. E-mail: editor@metrokids.com. Website: www.metro kids.com. **Contact:** Nancy Lisagor, Ph.D., editor-in-chief. **25% freelance written.** Monthly tabloid providing information for parents and kids in Philadelphia, South Jersey, and surrounding counties. Estab. 1990. Circ. 125,000. Pays on publication. Byline given. Buys one-time rights. Submit seasonal material 4 months in advance. Accepts queries by e-mail. Accepts previously published material. Writer's guidelines by e-mail.

• Responds only if interested.

Nonfiction General interest, how-to, new product, travel, parenting, health. Special issues: Educator's Edition (March & September; field trips, school enrichment, teacher, professional development); Camps (December-June); Special Kids (August; children with special needs); Vacations and Theme Parks (May, June); What's Happening (January; guide to events and activities); Kids 'N Care (July; guide to childcare). **Buys 40 mss/year.** Query with published clips. Length: 800-1,500 words. **Pays $1-50.** Sometimes pays expenses of writers on assignment.

Reprints Send photocopy and information about when and where the material previously appeared. Pays $20-40.

Photos State availability with submission. Buys one-time rights. Captions required.

Columns/Departments Techno Family (CD-ROM and website reviews); Body Wise (health); Style File (fashion and trends); Woman First (motherhood); Practical Parenting (financial parenting advice); all 800-1,000 words. **Buys 25 mss/year.** Query. **Pays $1-50.**

Tips "We prefer e-mail queries or submissions. Because they're so numerous, we don't reply unless interested. We are interested in feature articles (on specified topics) or material for our regular departments (with a regional/seasonal base). Articles should cite expert sources and the most up-to-date theories and facts. We are looking for a journalistic-style of writing. Editorial calendar available on request. We are also interested in finding local writers for assignments."

$ $ $ $ PARENTING MAGAZINE

Time, Inc., 530 Fifth Ave., 4th Floor, New York NY 10036. (212)522-8989. Fax: (212)522-8699. E-mail: letters@p arenting.com. Website: www.parenting.com. Editor-in-Chief: Janet Chan. Executive Editor: Lisa Bain. **Contact:** Articles Editor. Magazine published 10 times/year "for mothers of children from birth to 12, and covering both the emotional and practical aspects of parenting." Estab. 1987. Circ. 2,100,000. **Pays on acceptance.** Byline given. Offers 25% kill fee. Buys a variety of rights, including electronic rights. Sample copy for $2.95 and 9 × 12 SAE with 5 first-class stamps. Writer's guidelines for #10 SASE.

Nonfiction Book excerpts, personal experience, child development/behavior/health; investigative reports. **Buys 20-30 mss/year.** Query with or without published clips. Length: 1,000-2,500 words. **Pays $1,000-3,000.** Pays expenses of writers on assignment.

Columns/Departments Query to the specific departmental editor. Ages and Stages (child development and behavior), 100-400 words; Children's Health, 100-350 words. **Buys 50-60 mss/year.** Query. **Pays $50-400.**

Tips "The best guide for writers is the magazine itself. Please familiarize yourself with it before submitting a query."

N PARENTS

Gruner + Jahr, 375 Lexington Ave., 10th Floor, New York NY 10017. (212)499-2000. Fax: (212)499-2083. Website: www.parents.com. Monthly magazine. Estab. 1,700,000. Responds in 6 weeks to queries. Writer's guidelines online.

Nonfiction "Before you query us, please take a close look at our magazine at the library or newsstand. This will give you a good idea of the different kinds of stories we publish, as well as their tempo and tone. In addition, please take the time to look at the masthead to make sure you are directing your query to the correct department." Query.

Tips "We're a national publication, so we're mainly interested in stories that will appeal to a wide variety of parents. We're always looking for compelling human-interest stories, so you may want to check your local newspaper for ideas. Keep in mind that we can't pursue stories that have appeared in competing national publications."

$ PEDIATRICS FOR PARENTS

Pediatrics for Parents, Inc., P.O. Box 63716, Philadelphia PA 19147-3321. Fax: (419)858-7221. E-mail: rich.sagall @pobox.com. **Contact:** Richard J. Sagall, editor. **10% freelance written.** Monthly newsletter covering children's health. "*Pediatrics For Parents* emphasizes an informed, common-sense approach to childhood health care. We stress preventative action, accident prevention, when to call the doctor and when and how to handle a situation at home. We are also looking for articles that describe general, medical and pediatric problems, advances, new treatments, etc. All articles must be medically accurate and useful to parents with children—prenatal to adolescence." Estab. 1981. Circ. 500. Pays on publication. Publishes ms an average of 4 months after acceptance. Byline given. Buys first North American serial, electronic rights. Accepts queries by mail, e-mail, fax. Accepts previously published material. Accepts simultaneous submissions. Responds in 1 month to queries. Sample copy online. Writer's guidelines online.

Nonfiction Medical. No first person or experience. **Buys 10 mss/year.** Query with or without published clips or send complete ms. Length: 500-1,000 words. **Pays $10-50.**

Reprints Accepts previously published submissions.

$ SAN DIEGO FAMILY MAGAZINE

San Diego County's Leading Resource for Parents & Educators Who Care! P.O. Box 23960, San Diego CA 92193-3960. (619)685-6970. Fax: (619)685-6978. Website: www.sandiegofamily.com. **Contact:** Claire Yezbak Fadden, editor. **75% freelance written.** Monthly magazine for parenting and family issues. "*SDFM* strives to provide informative, educational articles emphasizing positive parenting for our typical readership of educated mothers, ages 25-45, with an upper-level income. Most articles are factual and practical, a few are humor and personal experience. Editorial emphasis is uplifting and positive." Estab. 1982. Circ. 120,000. Pays on publication. Byline given. Buys first, one-time, second serial (reprint) rights. Editorial lead time 2 months. Submit seasonal material 3 months in advance. Accepts previously published material. Responds in 2 months to queries; 3 months to mss. Sample copy for $4.50 with 9×12 SAE. Writer's guidelines online.

● No e-mail or fax queries.

Nonfiction How-to, interview/profile (influential or noted persons or experts included in parenting or the welfare of children), parenting, new baby help, enhancing education, family activities, articles of specific interest to San Diego. "No rambling, personal experience pieces." **Buys 75 mss/year.** Send complete ms. Length: 800-1,200 words. **Pays $1.25/column inch.**

Reprints Send ms with rights for sale noted and information about when and where the material previously appeared.

Photos State availability with submission. Reviews contact sheets, 3½×5 or 5×7 prints. Buys one-time rights. Negotiates payment individually. Identification of subjects required.

Columns/Departments Kids' Books (topical book reviews—women's interest, grandparenting, fitness, health, cooking, home and garden), 800 words. **Buys 12 mss/year.** Query. **Pays $1.25/column inch.**

Fillers Facts, newsbreaks (specific to family market). **Buys 10/year.** Length: 50-200 words. **Pays $1.25/column inch minimum.**

$ $ SOUTH FLORIDA PARENTING

5555 Nob Hill Rd., Sunrise FL 33351. (954)747-3050. Fax: (954)747-3055. E-mail: vmccash@sfparenting.com. Website: www.sfparenting.com. **Contact:** Vicki McCash Brennan, managing editor. **90% freelance written.** Monthly magazine covering parenting, family. "*South Florida Parenting* provides news, information, and a calendar of events for readers in Southeast Florida. The focus is on positive parenting and things to do or information about raising children in South Florida." Estab. 1990. Circ. 110,000. Pays on publication. Byline given. Buys one-time, second serial (reprint) rights, makes work-for-hire assignments. Editorial lead time 4 months. Submit seasonal material 5 months in advance. Accepts queries by mail, e-mail, fax. Accepts previously published material. Accepts simultaneous submissions. Responds in 2 months to queries; 6 months to mss. Sample copy for 9×12 SAE with $2.95 postage. Writer's guidelines for #10 SASE.

- Preference given to writers based in South Florida.
- O→ Best bet to break in: "Be a local South Florida resident (particular need for writers from the Miami-Dade area) and address contemporary parenting topics and concerns."

Nonfiction How-to (parenting issues), interview/profile, family and children's issues. Special issues: Education/Women's Health (January); Birthday Party (February); Summer Camp (March); Maternity (April); Florida/Vacation Guide (May); Kid Crown Awards (July); Back to School (August); Education (September); Holiday (December). **Buys 60+ mss/year.** Query with published clips or send complete ms. Length: 500-2,000 words. **Pays $40-300.**

Reprints Send photocopy or e-mail on spec. **Pays $25-50.**

Photos State availability with submission. Reviews negatives, transparencies, prints. Buys one-time rights. Sometimes offers additional payment for photos accepted with ms.

Columns/Departments Baby Basics (for parents of infants); Preteen Power (for parents of preteens); Family Money (family finances), all 500-750 words.

Tips "We want information targeted to the South Florida market. Multicultural and well-sourced is preferred. A unique approach to a universal parenting concern will be considered for publication. Profiles or interviews of courageous parents. Opinion pieces on child rearing should be supported by experts and research should be listed. First-person stories should be fresh and insightful. All writing should be clear and concise. Submissions can be typewritten, double-spaced, but the preferred format is on diskette or by e-mail attachment."

⚟ TODAY'S PARENT

Today's Parent Group, One Mt. Pleasant Rd., 8th Floor, Toronto ON M4Y 2Y5, Canada. (416)764-2883. Fax: (416)764-2801. Website: www.todaysparent.com. **Contact:** Denny Manchee, managing editor. Monthly magazine. Edited for parents with children up to the age of twelve. Circ. 175,000. Editorial lead time 5 months. Sample copy not available.

$ $ $ $⚟ TODAY'S PARENT PREGNANCY & BIRTH

One Mt. Pleasant Rd., 8th Floor, Toronto ON M4Y 2Y5, Canada. (416)764-2883. Fax: (416)764-2801. Website: www.todaysparent.com. **Contact:** Editor. **100% freelance written.** Magazine published 3 times/year. "*P&B* helps, supports and encourages expectant and new parents with news and features related to pregnancy, birth, human sexuality and parenting." Estab. 1973. Circ. 200,000. **Pays on acceptance.** Publishes ms an average of 8 months after acceptance. Buys first North American serial rights. Editorial lead time 6 months. Responds in 6 weeks to queries. Sample copy and writer's guidelines for #10 SASE.

Nonfiction Features about pregnancy, labor and delivery, post-partum issues. **Buys 12 mss/year.** Query with published clips. Length: 1,000-2,500 words. **Pays $700-1,500.** Sometimes pays expenses of writers on assignment.

Photos State availability with submission. Rights negotiated individually. Pay negotiated individually.

Tips "Our writers are professional freelance writers with specific knowledge in the childbirth field. *P&B* is written for a Canadian audience using Canadian research and sources."

Ⓝ $ $ TOLEDO AREA PARENT NEWS

Adams Street Publishing, 1120 Adams St., Toledo OH 43624-1509. (419)244-9859. Fax: (419)244-9871. E-mail: editor@toldeoparent.com. Website: www.toledoparent.com. **Contact:** Eric Lawrence, editor. Monthly tabloid for Northwest Ohio/Southeast Michigan parents. Estab. 1992. Circ. 42,000. Pays on publication. Publishes ms an average of 1 month after acceptance. Byline given. Editorial lead time 3 months. Accepts queries by mail, e-mail, fax. Responds in 1 month to queries. Sample copy for $1.50.

- O→ Break in with "local interest articles—Ohio/Michigan regional topics and examples preferred."

Nonfiction "We use only local writers by assignment. We accept queries and opinion pieces only. Send cover letter to be considered for assignments." General interest, interview/profile, opinion. **Buys 10 mss/year.** Length: 1,000-2,500 words. **Pays $75-125.**

Photos State availability with submission. Buys all rights. Negotiates payment individually. Identification of subjects required.

Tips "We love humorous stories that deal with common parenting issues or features on cutting-edge issues."

$ $ TWINS

The Magazine for Parents of Multiples, The Business Word, Inc., 11211 E. Arapahoe Rd., Suite 100, Centennial CO 80112-3851. (303)290-8500 or (888)55TWINS. Fax: (303)290-9025. E-mail: twins.editor@businessword.com. Website: www.twinsmagazine.com. Editor-in-Chief: Susan J. Alt. **Contact:** Sharon Withers, managing editor. **80% freelance written.** Bimonthly magazine covering parenting multiples. "*TWINS* is an international publication that provides informational and educational articles regarding the parenting of twins, triplets, and more. All articles must be multiple specific and have an upbeat, hopeful, and/or positive ending." Estab. 1984. Circ. 55,000. Pays on publication. Byline given. Buys first North American serial rights. Editorial lead time 6 months. Submit seasonal material 8 months in advance. Accepts queries by mail, e-mail, fax. Response time varies to queries. Sample copy for $5 or on website. Writer's guidelines online.

Nonfiction Interested in seeing twin-specific discipline articles. Personal experience (first-person parenting experience), professional experience as it relates to multiples. Nothing on cloning, pregnancy reduction or fertility issues. **Buys 12 mss/year.** Query with or without published clips or send complete ms. Length: 1,300 words. **Pays $25-250 for assigned articles; $25-100 for unsolicited articles.**

Photos State availability with submission. Offers no additional payment for photos accepted with ms. Identification of subjects required.

Columns/Departments Special Miracles (miraculous stories about multiples with a happy ending), 800-850 words. **Buys 12-20 mss/year.** Query with or without published clips or send complete ms. **Pays $40-75.**

Tips "All department articles must have a happy ending, as well as teach a lesson helpful to parents of multiples."

$WESTERN NEW YORK FAMILY

Western New York Family, Inc., 3147 Delaware Ave., Suite B, Buffalo NY 14217. (716)836-3486. Fax: (716)836-3680. E-mail: wnyfamily@aol.com. Website: www.wnyfamilymagazine.com. **Contact:** Michele Miller, editor/publisher. **90% freelance written.** Monthly magazine covering parenting in Western New York State. "Readership is largely composed of families with children ages newborn to 14 years. Although most subscriptions are in the name of the mother, 91% of fathers also read the publication. Strong emphasis is placed on how and where to find family-oriented events, as well as goods and services for children, in the Buffalo/Niagara Falls area." Estab. 1984. Circ. 22,500. Pays on publication. Publishes ms an average of 3 months after acceptance. Byline given. Buys one-time, second serial (reprint), simultaneous rights. Editorial lead time 2 months. Submit seasonal material 3 months in advance. Accepts previously published material. Accepts simultaneous submissions. Responds only if interested to queries. Sample copy for $2.50 and 9×12 SAE with $1.06 postage. Writer's guidelines online.

　　O─┐ Break in with either a "cutting edge" topic that is new and different in its relevance to current parenting challenges and trends or a "timeless" topic which is "evergreen" and can be kept on file to fill last minute holes.

Nonfiction How-to (craft projects for kids, holiday, costume, etc.), humor (as related to parenting), personal experience (parenting related), travel (family destinations). Special issues: Birthday Celebrations (January); Cabin Fever (February); Seeking Spring/Eldercare Guide (March); Having a Baby/Home Buying, Building & Beautifying; (April); Mother's Day (May); Father's Day (June); Summer Fun (July and August); Back to School (September); Halloween Happenings (October); Family Issues (November); and Holiday Happenings/Exploring Education (December). **Buys 100 mss/year.** Send complete ms by mail or e-mail. Unsolicited e-mail attachments are not accepted; paste text of article into body of e-mail. Length: 750-3,000 words. **Pays $50-150 for assigned articles; $25-50 for unsolicited articles.** Sometimes pays expenses of writers on assignment.

Reprints Accepts previously published submissions.

Photos State availability with submission. Reviews 3×5 prints, JPEG files via e-mail. Buys one-time rights. Offers no additional payment for photos accepted with ms. Captions, identification of subjects, model releases required.

Tips "We are interested in well-researched, nonfiction articles on surviving the newborn, preschool, school age, and adolescent years. Our readers want practical information on places to go and things to do in the Buffalo area and nearby Canada. They enjoy humorous articles about the trials and tribulations of parenthood as well as 'how-to' articles (i.e., choosing a musical instrument for your child, keeping your sanity while shopping with preschoolers, ideas for holidays and birthdays, etc.). Articles on making a working parent's life easier are of great interest as are articles written by fathers. We also need more material on preteen and young teen (13-15) issues. More material on multicultural families and their related experiences, traditions, etc., would be of interest in 2003. We prefer a warm, conversational style of writing."

$ $⊠ WHAT'S UP KIDS? FAMILY MAGAZINE

496 Metler Rd., Ridgeville ON L0S 1M0, Canada. E-mail: susan@whatsupkids.com. Website: www.whatsupkids .com. **Contact:** Susan Pennell-Sebekos, managing editor. **95% freelance written.** Bimonthly magazine covering topics of interest to young families. "Editorial is aimed at parents of kids brith-age 10 (approximately). Kids Fun Section offers a section just for kids. We're committed to providing top-notch content." Estab. 1997. Circ. 200,000. **Pays on acceptance.** Publishes ms an average of 4 months after acceptance. Byline given. Buys all rights. Editorial lead time 6 months. Submit seasonal material 6 months in advance. Accepts queries by mail,

e-mail. Accepts previously published material. Responds in 2-4 weeks to queries. Sample copy for free. Writer's guidelines online at website or by e-mail.

Nonfiction General interest, humor, inspirational, interview/profile, new product, personal experience, travel. No religious (one sided) or op-ed. **Buys 50 mss/year.** Query with published clips. Length: 1,000-3,500 words. **Pays $100-350 for assigned articles.** Sometimes pays expenses of writers on assignment.

Photos State availability with submission. Reviews GIF/JPEG files. Buys all rights. Offers $50/photo. Captions, identification of subjects, model releases required.

Columns/Departments What's Up in Health (general family health), 800-1,000 words; What's Up in Finance (family finance advice), 800-1,000 words; What's Up in Crafts (craft ideas), 800-1,000 words; Parent to Parent (personal experience), 1,000-1,500 words. **Buys variable number of mss/year.** Query with published clips. **Pays $150.**

Tips "Currently, we only accept submissions from Canadian writers. Writers should send résumé, clips, and query. Be patient! I will respond as quickly as possible. We're growing and as we grow, payment will grow too!"

WORKING MOTHER MAGAZINE

260 Madison Ave., 3rd Floor, New York NY 10016. (212)351-6400. Fax: (212)351-6487. E-mail: editors@working mother.com. Website: www.workingmother.com. **Contact:** Articles Department. **90% freelance written.** Prefers to work with published/established writers; works with a small number of new/unpublished writers each year. Monthly magazine for women who balance a career with the concerns of parenting. Circ. 925,000. Publishes ms an average of 4 months after acceptance. Byline given. Offers kill fee. Buys all rights. Submit seasonal material 6 months in advance. Accepts queries by mail. Sample copy for $5; available by calling (800)925-0788. Writer's guidelines online.

Nonfiction Service, humor, child development, material pertinent to the working mother's predicament. Humor, service; child development; material perinent to the working mother's predicament. **Buys 9-10 mss/year.** Query. Length: 700-1,500 words. Pays expenses of writers on assignment.

Tips "We are looking for pieces that help the reader. In other words, we don't simply report on a trend without discussing how it specifically affects our readers' lives and how they can handle the effects. Where can they look for help if necessary?"

COMIC BOOKS

$THE COMICS JOURNAL

Fantagraphics Books, 7563 Lake City Way NE, Seattle WA 98115. (206)524-1967. Fax: (206)524-2104. E-mail: milo@tcj.com. Website: www.tcj.com. **Contact:** Milo George, managing editor. Monthly magazine covering the comics medium from an arts-first perspective. *The Comics Journal* is one of the nation's most respected single-arts magazines, providing its readers with an eclectic mix of industry news, professional interviews, and reviews of current work. Due to its reputation as the American magazine with an interest in comics as an art form, the *Journal* has subscribers worldwide, and in this country serves as an important window into the world of comics for several general arts and news magazines. Byline given. Buys exclusive rights to articles that run in print or online versions for 6 months after initial publication. Rights then revert back to the writer. Accepts queries by mail, e-mail. Writer's guidelines online.

Nonfiction "We're not the magazine for the discussion of comic 'universes,' character re-boots, and Spider-Man's new costume—beyond, perhaps, the business or cultural implications of such events." Essays, general interest, how-to, humor, interview/profile, opinion. Send complete ms. Length: 2,000-3,000 words. **Pays 4¢/word, and 1 contributor's copy.**

Columns/Departments On Theory, Art and Craft (2,000-3,000 words); Firing Line (600-1,000 words); Bullets (100 words); Comics Library (up to 5,000 words). Send complete ms. **Pays 4¢/word, and 1 contributor's copy.**

Contact: Dirk Deppey, webmaster (dirk@fantagraphics.com).

Tips "Like most magazines, the best writers guideline is to look at the material within the magazine and give something that approximates that material in terms of approach and sophistication. Anything else is a waste of time."

CONSUMER SERVICE & BUSINESS OPPORTUNITY

CONSUMER REPORTS

Consumers Union of U.S., Inc., 101 Truman Ave., Yonkers NY 10703-1057. (914)378-2000. Fax: (914)378-2904. Website: www.consumerreports.org. Managing Editor: Kimberly Kleman. **Contact:** Margot Slade, editor. **5%**

freelance written. Monthly magazine. "*Consumer Reports* is the leading product-testing and consumer-service magazine in the U.S. We buy very little freelance material, mostly from proven writers we have used before for finance and health stories." Estab. 1936. Circ. 14,000,000. **Pays on acceptance.** Publishes ms an average of 2 months after acceptance. Offers negotiable kill fee. Buys all rights. Editorial lead time 4 months. Submit seasonal material 6 months in advance. Accepts queries by mail.

Nonfiction Technical, personal finance, personal health. **Buys 12 mss/year.** Query. Length: 1,000 words. **Pays variable rate.**

$ $ HOME BUSINESS MAGAZINE

United Marketing & Research Co., Inc., 9582 Hamilton Ave., PMB 368, Huntington Beach CA 92646. Fax: (714)962-7722. E-mail: admin@homebusinessmag.com. Website: www.homebusinessmag.com. **Contact:** Stacy Henderson, online editor. **75% freelance written.** "*Home Business Magazine* covers every angle of the home-based business market including: cutting edge editorial by well-known authorities on sales and marketing, business operations, the home office, franchising, business opportunities, network marketing, mail order and other subjects to help readers choose, manage and prosper in a home-based business; display advertising, classified ads and a directory of home-based businesses; technology, the Internet, computers and the future of home-based business; home-office editorial including management advice, office set-up, and product descriptions; business opportunities, franchising and work-from-home success stories." Estab. 1993. Circ. 80,000. Pays on publication. Publishes ms an average of 6 months after acceptance. Byline given. Makes work-for-hire assignments. Editorial lead time 4 months. Submit seasonal material 6 months in advance. Accepts queries by mail, e-mail, fax. Accepts previously published material. Accepts simultaneous submissions. Sample copy for 9×12 SAE and 8 first-class stamps. Writer's guidelines for #10 SASE.

Nonfiction Book excerpts, general interest, how-to (home business), inspirational, interview/profile, new product, personal experience, photo feature, technical, mail order; franchise; business management; internet; finance network marketing. No non-home business related topics. **Buys 40 mss/year.** Send complete ms. Length: 200-1,000 words. **Pays 20¢/word for assigned articles; $0-65 for unsolicited articles.**

Photos Send photos with submission. Buys one-time rights. Offers no additional payment for photos accepted with ms. Identification of subjects required.

Columns/Departments Marketing & Sales; Money Corner; Home Office; Management; Technology; Working Smarter; Franchising; Network Marketing, all 650 words. Send complete ms.

■ The online magazine carries original content not found in the print edition. Contact: Herb Wetenkamp, online editor.

Tips "Send complete information by mail as per our writer's guidelines and e-mail if possible. We encourage writers to submit Feature Articles (2-3 pages) and Departmental Articles (1 page). Please submit polished, well-written, organized material. It helps to provide subheadings within the article. Boxes, lists and bullets are encouraged because they make your article easier to read, use and reference by the reader. A primary problem in the past is that articles do not stick to the subject of the title. Please pay attention to the focus of your article and to your title. Please don't call to get the status of your submission. We will call if we're interested in publishing the submission."

KIPLINGER'S PERSONAL FINANCE

1729 H St. NW, Washington DC 20006. (202)887-6400. Fax: (202)331-1206. Website: www.kiplinger.com. Editor: Fred W. Frailey. **Contact:** Dayl Sanders, office manager. **10% freelance written.** Prefers to work with published/established writers. Monthly magazine for general, adult audience intersted in personal finance and consumer information. "*Kiplinger's* is a highly trustworthy source of information on saving and investing, taxes, credit, home ownership, paying for college, retirement planning, automobile buying, and many other personal finance topics." Estab. 1947. Circ. 1,300,000. **Pays on acceptance.** Publishes ms an average of 2 months after acceptance. Buys all rights. Responds in 1 month to queries.

Nonfiction "Most material is staff-written, but we accept some freelance. Thorough documentation is required for fact-checking." Query with published clips. Pays expenses of writers on assignment.

Tips "We are looking for a heavy emphasis on personal finance topics. Currently all work is provided by in-house writers."

$ $ ⊡ LIVING SAFETY

A Canada Safety Council Publication for Safety in the Home, Traffic and Recreational Environments, 1020 Thomas Spratt Place, Ottawa ON K1G 5L5, Canada. (613)739-1535. Fax: (613)739-1566. E-mail: jsmith@safety-council.org. Website: www.safety-council.org. **Contact:** Jack Smith, editor-in-chief. **65% freelance written.** Quarterly magazine covering off-the-job safety. "Off-the-job health and safety magazine covering topics in the home, traffic, and recreational environments. Audience is the Canadian employee and his/her family." Estab. 1983. Circ. 100,000. **Pays on acceptance.** Publishes ms an average of 2 months after acceptance. Byline given.

Buys all rights. Editorial lead time 4 months. Submit seasonal material 6 months in advance. Accepts queries by mail. Accepts previously published material. Accepts simultaneous submissions. Responds in 1 month to queries. Sample copy and writer's guidelines free.

Nonfiction General interest, how-to (safety tips, health tips), personal experience. **Buys 24 mss/year.** Query with published clips. Length: 1,000-2,500 words. **Pays $500 maximum.** Sometimes pays expenses of writers on assignment.

Reprints Send tearsheet.

Photos State availability with submission. Reviews contact sheets, negatives, transparencies, prints. Offers no additional payment for photos accepted with ms. Identification of subjects required.

CONTEMPORARY CULTURE

$ $ $ $ A&U

America's AIDS Magazine, Art & Understanding, Inc., 25 Monroe St., Suite 205, Albany NY 12210-2729. (888)245-4333. Fax: (888)790-1790. E-mail: editor@aumag.org. Website: www.aumag.org. **Contact:** David Waggoner, editor-in-chief. **50% freelance written.** Monthly magazine covering cultural, political, and medical responses to AIDS/HIV. Estab. 1991. Circ. 205,000. Pays 2 months after publication. Publishes ms an average of 3 months after acceptance. Byline given. Offers 20% kill fee. Buys first North American serial rights. Editorial lead time 6 months. Accepts queries by mail, fax, phone. Accepts simultaneous submissions. Responds in 1 month to queries; 2 months to mss. Sample copy for $5. Writer's guidelines online.

Nonfiction Book excerpts, essays, general interest, how-to, humor, interview/profile, new product, opinion, personal experience, photo feature, travel, reviews (film, theater, art exhibits, video, music, other media), medical news. **Buys 120 mss/year.** Query with published clips. Length: 800-4,800 words. **Pays $250-2,500 for assigned articles.** Sometimes pays expenses of writers on assignment.

Photos State availability with submission. Reviews contact sheets, up to 4×5 transparencies, 4×5 to 8×10 prints. Buys one-time rights. Offers $50-500/photo. Captions, identification of subjects, model releases required.

Columns/Departments The Culture of AIDS (reviews of books, music, film), 800 words; Viewpoint (personal opinion), 900-1,500 words. **Buys 100 mss/year.** Send complete ms. **Pays $100-250.**

Fiction Unpublished work only; accepts prose, poetry, and drama. Send complete ms. Length: less than 3,500 words. **Pays $50-200.**

Poetry Any length/style (shorter works preferred). **Pays $50.**

▣ The online magazine carries original content not found in the print edition. Contact: David Waggoner.

Tips "We're looking for more articles on youth and HIV/AIDS; more international coverage; more small-town America coverage."

$ $ $ ▧ ADBUSTERS

Journal of the Mental Environment, The Media Foundation, 1243 W. 7th Ave., Vancouver BC V6H 1B7, Canada. (604)736-9401. Fax: (604)737-6021. Website: www.adbusters.org. Managing Editor: Tim Querengesser. **Contact:** Kalle Lasn, editor. **50% freelance written.** Bimonthly magazine. "We are an activist journal of the mental environment." Estab. 1989. Circ. 90,000. Pays 1 month after publication. Byline given. Buys first rights. Accepts queries by mail, e-mail, fax. Accepts simultaneous submissions. Writer's guidelines online.

Nonfiction Essays, exposé, interview/profile, opinion. **Buys variable mss/year.** Query. Length: 250-3,000 words. **Pays $100/page for unsolicited articles; 50¢/word for solicited articles.**

Fiction Inquire about themes.

Poetry Inquire about themes.

$ $ THE AMERICAN SCHOLAR

Phi Beta Kappa, 1606 New Hampshire Ave. NW, Washington DC 20009. (202)265-3808. Fax: (202)265-0083. E-mail: scholar@pbk.org. Editor: Anne Fadiman. **Contact:** Jean Stipicevic, managing editor. **100% freelance written.** Quarterly journal. "Our intent is to have articles written by scholars and experts but written in nontechnical language for an intelligent audience. Material covers a wide range in the arts, sciences, current affairs, history, and literature." Estab. 1932. Circ. 25,000. Pays on publication. Publishes ms an average of 1 year after acceptance. Byline given. Offers 50% kill fee. Buys first rights. Editorial lead time 6 months. Submit seasonal material 6 months in advance. Accepts queries by mail, e-mail, fax. Responds in 2 weeks to queries; 2 months to mss. Sample copy for $9. Writer's guidelines for #10 SASE.

Nonfiction Essays, historical/nostalgic, humor. **Buys 40 mss/year.** Query. Length: 3,000-5,000 words. **Pays $500 maximum.**

Poetry "We have no special requirements of length, form, or content for original poetry." Rob Farnsworth, poetry editor. **Buys 25 poems/year.** Submit maximum 3-4 poems. **Pays $50.**

BACK STAGE

VNU Business Media, 770 Broadway, New York NY 10003. (646)654-5500. Fax: (646)654-5743. E-mail: backstage@backstage.com. Website: www.backstage.com. **Editor:** Sherry Eaker. **Managing Editor:** David Sheward. Weekly magazine covering performing arts. *"Back Stage* was created for actors, singers, dancers, and associated performing arts professionals." Circ. 33,000. Accepts queries by mail. Sample copy for $3.25.

$BOSTON REVIEW

E53-407, M.I.T., Cambridge MA 02139. (617)258-0805. Fax: (617)252-1549. E-mail: review@mit.edu. Website: www.bostonreview.net. **Editors:** Deb Chasman and Josh Cohen. **Contact:** Joshua J. Friedman, managing editor. **90% freelance written.** Bimonthly magazine of cultural and political analysis, reviews, fiction, and poetry. "The editors are committed to a society and culture that foster human diversity and a democracy in which we seek common grounds of principle amidst our many differences. In the hope of advancing these ideals, the *Review* acts as a forum that seeks to enrich the language of public debate." Estab. 1975. Circ. 20,000. Publishes ms an average of 4 months after acceptance. Byline given. Buys first North American serial, first rights. Accepts simultaneous submissions. Responds in 4 months to queries. Sample copy for $5 or online. Writer's guidelines online.

Nonfiction Critical essays and reviews. "We do not accept unsolicited book reviews. If you would like to be considered for review assignments, please send your résumé along with several published clips." **Buys 50 mss/year.** Query with published clips.

Fiction Junot Diaz, fiction editor. "I'm looking for stories that are emotionally and intellectually substantive and also interesting on the level of language. Things that are shocking, dark, lewd, comic, or even insane are fine so long as the fiction is *controlled* and purposeful in a masterly way. Subtlety, delicacy, and lyricism are attractive too." Ethnic, experimental, contemporary, prose poem. "No romance, erotica, genre fiction." **Buys 5 mss/year.** Send complete ms. Length: 1,200-5,000 words. **Pays $50-100, and 5 contributor's copies.**

Poetry Mary Jo Bang and Timothy Donnelly, poetry editors.

N $ $BRUTARIAN

The Magazine of Brutiful Art, 9405 Ulysses Ct., Burke VA 22015. E-mail: brutarian@msn.com. Website: www.brutarian.com. **Contact:** Dominick J. Salemi, publisher/editor. **100% freelance written.** Quarterly magazine covering trash, carnival culture, the ridiculous and the sublime. "A healthy knowledge of the great works of antiquity and an equally healthy contempt for most of what passes today as culture." Estab. 1991. Circ. 5,000. Pays on publication. Publishes ms an average of 3 months after acceptance. Byline given. Buys first, electronic rights. Editorial lead time 2 months. Submit seasonal material 3 months in advance. Accepts queries by mail. Accepts simultaneous submissions. Responds in 1 week to queries; 2 months to mss. Sample copy for $6. Writer's guidelines online.

O⊷ Break in with an interview with an interesting musical group, film actor/actress or director, or unusual writer.

Nonfiction Book excerpts, essays, exposé, general interest, historical/nostalgic, humor, interview/profile, opinion, photo feature, travel, reviews of books, film, and music. **Buys 30 mss/year.** Send complete ms. Length: No length limits. **Pays up to 10¢/word.** Sometimes pays expenses of writers on assignment.

Reprints Send ms with rights for sale noted and information about when and where the material previously appeared. Pays 50% of amount paid for an original article.

Photos State availability with submission. Reviews contact sheets. Buys one-time rights. Offers no additional payment for photos accepted with ms. Captions, identification of subjects, model releases required.

Columns/Departments Celluloid Void (critiques of cult and obscure films), 500-1,000 words; Brut Library (critiques of books), 500-1,000 words. **Buys 20-30 mss/year.** Send complete ms. **Pays $50 average for book reviews; 5-10¢/word for feature articles.**

Fiction Adventure, confessions, erotica, experimental, fantasy, horror, humorous, mystery, novel excerpts, suspense. **Buys 8-10 mss/year.** Send complete ms. Length: No length limit. **Pays up to 10¢/word.**

Poetry Avant-garde, free verse, traditional. **Buys 10-15 poems/year.** Submit maximum 3 poems. Length: 25-1,000 lines. **Pays $20-200.**

Tips "Send résumé with completed manuscript. Avoid dry tone and excessive scholasticism. Do not cover topics or issues which have been done to death unless you have a fresh approach or new insights on the subject. Pays $25/illustration; $100 for cover art."

$ CANADIAN DIMENSION

Dimension Publications, Inc., 91 Albert St., Room 2-B, Winnipeg MB R3B 1G5, Canada. (204)957-1519. E-mail: info@canadiandimension.mb.ca. Website: www.canadiandimension.mb.ca. **Contact:** Kevin Matthews. **80% freelance written.** Bimonthly magazine covering socialist perspective. "We bring a socialist perspective to bear on events across Canada and around the world. Our contributors provide in-depth coverage on popular movements, peace, labour, women, aboriginal justice, environment, third world and eastern Europe." Estab. 1963. Circ. 2,000. Pays on publication. Publishes ms an average of 6 months after acceptance. Accepts previously published material. Accepts simultaneous submissions. Responds in 6 weeks to queries. Sample copy for $2. Writer's guidelines online.

Nonfiction Interview/profile, opinion, reviews; political commentary and analysis; journalistic style. **Buys 8 mss/year.** Length: 500-2,000 words. **Pays $25-100.**

Reprints Send ms with rights for sale noted and information about when and where the material previously appeared.

$ $ $COMMENTARY

American Jewish Committee, 165 E. 56th St., New York NY 10022. (212)891-1400. Fax: (212)891-6700. E-mail: editorial@commentarymagazine.com. Website: www.commentarymagazine.com. Editor: Neal Kozodoy. Managing Editor: Gary Rosen. **Contact:** Benjamin Balint, assistant editor. Monthly magazine. Pays on publication. Publishes ms an average of 2 months after acceptance. Byline given. Buys all rights. Accepts queries by mail, e-mail. Writer's guidelines not available.

Nonfiction Essays, opinion. **Buys 4 mss/year.** Query. Length: 2,000-8,000 words. **Pays $400-1,200.**

Tips "Unsolicited manuscripts must be accompanied by a self-addressed, stamped envelope."

$ $ COMMON GROUND

Common Ground Publishing, 201-3091 W. Broadway, Vancouver BC V6K 2G9, Canada. (604)733-2215. Fax: (604)733-4415. E-mail: editor@commonground.ca. Website: www.commonground.ca. Senior Editor: Joseph Roberts. **90% freelance written.** Monthly tabloid covering health, environment, spirit, creativity, and wellness. "We serve the cultural creative community." Estab. 1982. Circ. 65,900. Pays on publication. Publishes ms an average of 1 month after acceptance. Byline given. Buys one-time, second serial (reprint) rights. Editorial lead time 2 months. Submit seasonal material 3 months in advance. Accepts queries by e-mail. Accepts simultaneous submissions. Responds in 6 weeks to queries; 3 months to mss. Sample copy for $5. Writer's guidelines online.

Nonfiction Topics include health, personal growth, creativity, spirituality, ecology, or short inspiring stories on environment themes. Book excerpts, how-to, inspirational, interview/profile, opinion, personal experience, travel, call to action. **Buys 12 mss/year.** Send complete ms. Length: 500-2,500 words. **Pays 10¢/word (Canadian).**

Reprints Accepts previously published submissions.

Photos State availability with submission. Buys one-time rights. Captions, photo credits required.

$ $ $FIRST THINGS

Institute on Religion & Public Life, 156 Fifth Ave., Suite 400, New York NY 10010. (212)627-1985. Fax: (212)627-2184. E-mail: ft@firstthings.com. Website: www.firstthings.com. Editor-in-Chief: Richard John Neuhaus. Managing Editor: Matthew Boudway. **Contact:** Damon Linker, editor. **70% freelance written.** "Intellectual journal published 10 times/year containing social and ethical commentary in broad sense, religious and ethical perspectives on society, culture, law, medicine, church and state, morality and mores." Estab. 1990. Circ. 32,000. Pays on publication. Publishes ms an average of 4 months after acceptance. Byline given. Buys all rights. Editorial lead time 2 months. Submit seasonal material 5 months in advance. Responds in 3 weeks to mss. Sample copy and writer's guidelines for #10 SASE.

Nonfiction Essays, opinion. **Buys 60 mss/year.** Send complete ms. Length: 1,500-6,000 words. **Pays $400-1,000.** Sometimes pays expenses of writers on assignment.

Poetry Joseph Bettum, poetry editor. Traditional. **Buys 25-30 poems/year.** Length: 4-40 lines. **Pays $50.**

Tips "We prefer complete manuscripts (hard copy, double-spaced) to queries, but will reply if unsure."

$ $ $ FW MAGAZINE

FW Omni Media Corp., 460 Richmond St. W., Toronto ON M5V 1Y1, Canada. (416)591-6537. Fax: (416)591-2390. E-mail: editors@myfw.com. Website: www.myfw.com. **80% freelance written.** Bimonthly magazine. "We are a lifestyle magazine that is geared to both males and females. Our readership is between 18-34 years old. We focus on the hottest new trends for our readers. We profile people in their 20s doing exciting ventures." Estab. 1993. Circ. 500,000. Pays on publication. Byline given. Offers 50% kill fee. Buys first, electronic rights. Editorial lead time 2 months. Submit seasonal material 3 months in advance. Accepts queries by fax, phone. Accepts simultaneous submissions. Responds to queries in 1 month if interested to queries; 2 months to mss. Sample copy for free. Writer's guidelines online.

Nonfiction Exposé, general interest, how-to, interview/profile, new product, personal experience, photo feature, travel. **Buys 83 mss/year.** Query with published clips. Length: 500-3,000 words. **Pays $300-1,000.** Sometimes pays expenses of writers on assignment.

Photos State availability with submission. Reviews contact sheets, negatives. Buys one-time rights. Negotiates payment individually. Captions, identification of subjects, model releases required.

Columns/Departments Body (the newest trends in fitness); Travel (the new "hotspots" on a budget); Work (interesting jobs for people in their 20s); Fashion (profile new designers and trends); all 1,000 words. **Buys 50 mss/year.** Query. **Pays $300-1,000.**

$ GENERATION X NATIONAL JOURNAL

Speaking for Our Generation, 411 W. Front, Wayland IA 52654. (319)256-4221. E-mail: genxjournal12004@yaho o.com. Editor: Les Stoops. **Contact:** Kathy Stoops, managing editor. **95% freelance written.** Bimonthly creative journal covering the generation who came of age in the late '80s and early '90s. Estab. 2003. Pays on publication. Publishes ms an average of 3 months after acceptance. Buys one-time rights. Editorial lead time 4 months. Submit seasonal material 6 months in advance. Accepts queries by mail, e-mail. Accepts simultaneous submissions. Responds in 2 months to queries; 3 months to mss. Sample copy for $3. Writer's guidelines for #10 SASE.

Nonfiction Book excerpts, essays, general interest, historical/nostalgic, how-to, humor, inspirational, interview/profile, opinion, personal experience, religious (but practical), travel. No sexually explicit material; religious pieces are fine, but cannot be preachy. Send complete ms. Length: 500-2,500 words. **Pays $5-10.**

Columns/Departments Politicrat Corner (any political views), 500-2,000 words; Ethnic View (views life from a minority's perspective), 500-2,000 words; Gen-X Poetry (realistic, humorous poetry), 5-15 lines; Success Stories (a Gen-xer who is successful, how they did it, etc.), 500-2,000 words. **Pays $5-10.**

Fiction Adventure, confessions, ethnic, experimental, fantasy, historical, humorous, mainstream, religious, romance, slice-of-life vignettes, political pieces, success stories. No erotica or horror. Length: 500-2,500 words. **Pays $5-10.**

Poetry "Share your heritage. Discuss the challenges of gaining understanding of one another's differences." Avant-garde, free verse, haiku, light verse, traditional. Submit maximum 5 poems. Length: 5-25 lines.

Fillers Anecdotes, short humor. Length: 10-100 words. **Pays $5-10.**

Tips "Be thought provoking in your ideas. Gen-X can spot half-baked thinking and are ruthlessly realistic. We are seeking classy material. Seeking to escape the gutter, meaning: No reality TV crass, date arranging stuff. Let's stay away from trash talk and curse words. Good writers don't need shock and awe. We are looking for optimism. Keep in touch with Kathy and learn more about monthly contests coming in the near future."

$ $ ☑ HEADS MAGAZINE

Worldwide Heads, P.O. Box 1319, Hudson QC J0P 1H0, Canada. (450)458-1934. Fax: (450)458-2977. E-mail: stuff@headsmagazine.com. Website: www.headsmagazine.com. **Contact:** Editor. **100% freelance written.** Magazine published every 6 weeks covering the marijuana lifestyle. "*Heads Magazine* is a counter-culture publication concerning the lifestyle surrounding marijuana use and propogation." Estab. 2000. Circ. 75,000. Pays 3 months after publication. Publishes ms an average of 3 months after acceptance. Byline given. Buys all rights. Editorial lead time 3 months. Submit seasonal material 4 months in advance. Accepts queries by mail, e-mail, fax. Accepts simultaneous submissions. Sample copy for $5 (US) or online at website. Writer's guidelines for $5 (US) or by e-mail.

● The editor will contact the writer only if query/ms is usable.

Nonfiction Book excerpts, exposé, general interest, how-to (grow info), humor, interview/profile, new product, opinion, personal experience, photo feature, travel. **Buys 150 mss/year.** Query with published clips or send complete ms. Length: 600-1,500 words. **Pays $50-200.**

Photos Send photos with submission. Reviews contact sheets, prints, GIF/JPEG files. Buys all rights. Negotiates payment individually. Captions, model releases required.

Columns/Departments Marijuana Notes & News (news items about marijuana), 80-150 words; Heads Destination (travel stories), 1,000-2,000 words; Heads Musician (feature story about a musician—pot oriented), 1,000-2,000 words; Ahead of Their Times (groundbreaking member of the counter-culture), 600-1,000 words. **Buys 64 mss/year.** Send complete ms. **Pays $50-200.**

Fillers Facts, newsbreaks. Length: 50-150 words. **Pays $5-15.**

N $ $ $ $ KARMA MAGAZINE

Karma Magazine, Inc., 185 Berry St., Suite 5411, San Francisco CA 94107. E-mail: editorial@karma-magazine.c om. Website: www.karma-magazine.com. Editor: Eric Eslao. **Contact:** Ali Fard, managing editor. Quarterly magazine covering nightlife culture. "*Karma* provides outstanding nightlife and cultural perspectives to 21- to 34-year-old urban professionals across the nation. We cover bars, clubs, restaurants, style, celebrity, music, film, and art culture." Estab. 2003. Circ. 100,000. Pays on publication. Publishes ms an average of 3 months after acceptance. Byline given. Offers 25% kill fee. Buys first North American serial, first, one-time, electronic, all rights. Editorial lead time 3 months. Submit seasonal material 3 months in advance. Accepts queries by e-mail. Accepts simultaneous submissions. Responds in 1 month to queries. Sample copy online. Writer's guidelines by e-mail.

Nonfiction Essays, general interest, how-to, interview/profile, new product, opinion, photo feature, technical, travel. No self-congratulatory or self-obsessed personal experiences about the nightclub scene; no story ideas without original angles. **Buys 30 mss/year.** Query with published clips. Length: 500-3,000 words. **Pays 10-50¢/word.** Sometimes pays expenses of writers on assignment.

Photos Chad Smavatkul, photo editor. State availability with submission. Reviews contact sheets, prints, GIF/JPEG files. Buys one-time rights or all rights. Negotiates payment individually. Captions, identification of subjects required.

Columns/Departments Ali Fard, managing editor, or Starla Estrada, editorial coordinator. Secondary Feature (profile of international hotspot with active nightlife), 2,500 words; Zen (cultural criticism, general-interest features), 1,000 words; Utility (nightlife community/celebrity interviews, profiles), 1,000 words; Access/Reincarnations/File (reviews and nightlife profiles of clubs, bars, restaurants), 300-800 words. Query with published clips. **Pays 50¢-$1/word.**

Fillers Anecdotes, facts, newsbreaks, short humor. **Buys 100/year.** Length: 100-300 words.

Tips "Stories must have a pulse for nightlife and present original and thought-provoking subjects. Writers interested in covering or reviewing clubs and restaurants must have great understanding of their subjects and provide an original angle on their function in the scene."

$ 🖳 THE LIST

The List, Ltd., 14 High St., Edinburgh EH1 1TE, Scotland. (0131) 550 3050. Fax: (0131) 557 8500. E-mail: editor@list.co.uk. Website: www.list.co.uk. Publisher/General Editor: Robin Hodge. **Contact:** Nick Barley, editor. **25% freelance written.** Biweekly magazine covering Glasgow and Edinburgh arts, events, listings, and lifestyle. "*The List* is pitched at educated 18-35 year olds." Estab. 1985. Circ. 15,000. Pays on publication. Publishes ms an average of 2 weeks after acceptance. Byline given. Offers 100% kill fee. Buys first, second serial (reprint) rights. Editorial lead time 1 month. Submit seasonal material 1 month in advance. Accepts queries by mail, e-mail. Accepts simultaneous submissions. Sample copy not available.

Nonfiction Interview/profile, opinion, travel. Query with published clips. Length: Word Length: 300 words. **Pays £60-80.** Sometimes pays expenses of writers on assignment.

Columns/Departments Reviews, 50-650 words, **pays £16-35/word**; Book Reviews, 150 words, **pays £14/word**; Comic Reviews, 100 words, **pays £10/word**; TV/Video Reviews, 100 words, **pays £10/word**; Record Reviews, 100 words, **pays £10/word**. Query with published clips.

$ $ $ $ MOTHER JONES

Foundation for National Progress, 731 Market St., Suite 600, San Francisco CA 94103. (415)665-6637. Fax: (415)665-6696. E-mail: query@motherjones.com. Website: www.motherjones.com. **Contact:** Clara Jeffery, deputy editor; Alastair Paulin, managing editor; Roger Cohn, editor-in-chief; Monika Bauerlein, senior editor; Tim Dickinson, articles editor. **80% freelance written.** Bimonthly magazine covering politics, investigative reporting, social issues, and pop culture. "*Mother Jones* is a 'progressive' magazine—but the core of its editorial well is reporting (i.e., fact-based). No slant required. MotherJones.com is an online sister publication." Estab. 1976. Circ. 175,000. Pays on publication. Publishes ms an average of 4 months after acceptance. Byline given. Offers 33% kill fee. Buys first North American serial, first, one-time, electronic rights. Editorial lead time 4 months. Submit seasonal material 6 months in advance. Responds in 2 months to queries. Sample copy for $6 and 9×12 SAE. Writer's guidelines online.

Nonfiction Exposé, interview/profile, photo feature, current issues; policy; investigative reporting. **Buys 70-100 mss/year.** Query with published clips. Length: 2,000-5,000 words. **Pays $1/word.** Sometimes pays expenses of writers on assignment.

Columns/Departments Outfront (short, newsy and/or outrageous and/or humorous items), 200-800 words; Profiles of "Hellraisers," 500 words. **Pays $1/word.**

Tips "We're looking for hard-hitting, investigative reports exposing government cover-ups, corporate malfeasance, scientific myopia, institutional fraud or hypocrisy; thoughtful, provocative articles which challenge the conventional wisdom (on the right or the left) concerning issues of national importance; and timely, people-oriented stories on issues such as the environment, labor, the media, health care, consumer protection, and cultural trends. Send a great, short query and establish your credibility as a reporter. Explain what you plan to cover and how you will proceed with the reporting. The query should convey your approach, tone and style, and should answer the following: What are your specific qualifications to write on this topic? What 'ins' do you have with your sources? Can you provide full documentation so that your story can be fact-checked?"

$ NEW HAVEN ADVOCATE

News & Arts Weekly, New Mass Media, Inc., 900 Chapel St., Suite 1100, New Haven CT 06510. (203)789-0010. Fax: (203)787-1418. E-mail: pbass@newhavenadvocate.com. Website: www.newhavenadvocate.com. **Contact:**

Paul Bass, managing editor. **10% freelance written.** Weekly tabloid. "Alternative, investigative, cultural reporting with a strong voice. We like to shake things up." Estab. 1975. Circ. 55,000. Pays on publication. Byline given. Buys one-time rights. Buys on speculation Editorial lead time 1 month. Submit seasonal material 2 months in advance. Accepts simultaneous submissions. Responds in 1 month to queries. Sample copy not available.

Nonfiction Book excerpts, essays, exposé, general interest, humor, interview/profile. **Buys 15-20 mss/year.** Query with published clips. Length: 750-2,000 words. **Pays $50-150.** Sometimes pays expenses of writers on assignment.

Photos State availability with submission. Buys one-time rights. Captions, identification of subjects, model releases required.

Tips "Strong local focus; strong literary voice, controversial, easy-reading, contemporary, etc."

$ $ SHEPHERD EXPRESS

Alternative Publications, Inc., 413 N. Second St., Suite 150, Milwaukee WI 53203. (414)276-2222. Fax: (414)276-3312. E-mail: editor@shepherd-express.com. Website: www.shepherd-express.com. **50% freelance written.** Weekly tabloid covering "news and arts with a progressive news edge and a hip entertainment perspective." Estab. 1982. Circ. 58,000. Pays on publication. Publishes ms an average of 2 weeks after acceptance. Submit seasonal material 1 month in advance. Accepts simultaneous submissions. Sample copy for $3.

Nonfiction Book excerpts, essays, exposé, opinion. **Buys 200 mss/year.** Query with published clips or send complete ms. Length: 900-2,500 words. **Pays $35-300 for assigned articles; $10-200 for unsolicited articles.** Sometimes pays expenses of writers on assignment.

Photos State availability with submission. Reviews prints. Buys one-time rights. Negotiates payment individually. Captions, identification of subjects, model releases required.

Columns/Departments Opinions (social trends, politics, from progressive slant), 800-1,200 words; Books Reviewed (new books only: Social trends, environment, politics), 600-1,200 words. **Buys 10 mss/year.** Send complete ms.

Tips "Include solid analysis with point of view in tight but lively writing. Nothing cute. Do not tell us that something is important, tell us why."

UTNE READER

1624 Harmon Place, Suite 330, Minneapolis MN 55403. (612)338-5040. Fax: (612)338-6043. E-mail: editor@utne.com. Website: www.utne.com. Accepts queries by mail, e-mail, fax. Writer's guidelines online.

• The *Utne Reader* has been a finalist three times for the National Magazine Award for general excellence.

Reprints Send tearsheet or photocopy with rights for sale noted and information about when and where the material previously appeared.

Tips "State the theme(s) clearly, let the narrative flow, and build the story around strong characters and a vivid sense of place. Give us rounded episodes, logically arranged."

$ YES!

A Journal of Positive Futures, Positive Futures Network, P.O. Box 10818, Bainbridge Island WA 98110. (206)842-0216. Fax: (206)842-5208. E-mail: editors@futurenet.org. Website: www.futurenet.org. Executive Editor: Sarah Ruth van Gelder. Quarterly magazine covering sustainability and community. "Interested in stories on building a positive future: sustainability, overcoming divisiveness, ethical business practices, etc." Estab. 1996. Circ. 23,000. Pays on publication. Byline given. Editorial lead time 4 months. Accepts queries by mail. Accepts previously published material. Accepts simultaneous submissions. Responds in 1 month to queries; 3 months to mss. Sample copy and writer's guidelines online.

Nonfiction "Please check website for a detailed call for submission before each issue." Book excerpts, essays, humor, interview/profile, personal experience, photo feature, technical, environmental. Query with published clips. Length: 200-3,500 words. **Pays up to $100/page for original, researched material.** Pays writers with 1-year subscription and 2 contributor copies.

Reprints Send photocopy or typed ms with rights for sale noted and information about when and where the material previously appeared. Pays 100% of amount paid for an original article.

Photos State availability with submission. Reviews contact sheets, negatives, transparencies, prints. Buys one-time rights. Offers $20-75/photo. Identification of subjects required.

Tips "Read and become familiar with the publication's purpose, tone and quality. We are about facilitating the creation of a better world. We are looking for writers who want to participate in that process. *Yes!* is less interested in bemoaning the state of our problems than in highlighting promising solutions. We are highly unlikely to accept submissions that simply state the author's opinion on what needs to be fixed and why. Our readers know *why* we need to move towards sustainability; they are interested in *how* to do so."

DETECTIVE & CRIME

$P I MAGAZINE

Journal of Professional Investigators, P I Magazine, Inc., 4400 Route 9 S., Suite 1000, P.O. Box 7198, Freehold NJ 07728-7198. (732)308-3800. Fax: (732)308-3314. E-mail: editor@pimagazine.com. Website: www.pimagazine.com. Publisher/Editor-in-Chief: Jimmie Mesis. **Contact:** Don Johnson, editor. **90% freelance written.** Magazine published 6 times/year. "Audience includes U.S., Canada, and professional investigators in 20-plus countries, law enforcement, attorneys, process servers, paralegals, and other legal professionals." Estab. 1988. Pays on publication. Accepts queries by mail, e-mail. Sample copy for free. Writer's guidelines online.

• No payment for unsolicited materials.

Nonfiction "Manuscripts must include educational material for professional investigators. Profiles are accepted if they offer information on how other professionals can use the knowledge or expertise utilized by the person profiled. Accounts of real cases are used only as part of an educational piece. Investigators with special expertise should query for educational articles to exceed 1,000 words." **Buys up to 75 mss/year.** Query. Length: 1,000-2,000 words. **Pays $50-150 for articles up to 1,000 words; $10-50 for articles of 500 words or less.**

Photos State availability with submission. May offer additional payment for photos accepted with ms. Identification of subjects, model releases required.

Tips "*P I Magazine* has a new publisher and editor-in-chief, a new editor, and a new focus! Please review the current issue online to understand the magazine before submitting a query. Avoid clichés and television inspired concepts of PIs. Great way to get the editor's attention: There are numerous special sections that need shorts of 500 words or less. $10-50."

DISABILITIES

$ $⊠ ABILITIES

Canada's Lifestyle Magazine for People with Disabilities, Canadian Abilities Foundation, 650-340 College St., Toronto ON M5T 3A9, Canada. (416)923-1885. Fax: (416)923-9829. E-mail: able@abilities.ca. Website: www.abilities.ca. Editor: Raymond Cohen. **Contact:** Lisa Bendall, managing editor. **50% freelance written.** Quarterly magazine covering disability issues. "*Abilities* provides information, inspiration, and opportunity to its readers with articles and resources covering health, travel, sports, products, technology, profiles, employment, recreation, and more." Estab. 1987. Circ. 45,000. Pays on publication. Publishes ms an average of 3 months after acceptance. Byline given. Offers 50% kill fee. Buys first rights. Editorial lead time 3 months. Submit seasonal material 4 months in advance. Accepts queries by mail, e-mail, fax. Responds in 3 months to queries. Sample copy for free. Writer's guidelines for #10 SASE, online, or by e-mail.

Nonfiction Book excerpts, general interest, how-to, humor, inspirational, interview/profile, new product, opinion, personal experience, photo feature, travel. Does not want "articles that 'preach to the converted'—contain info that people with disabilities likely already know, such as what it's like to have a disability." **Buys 30-40 mss/year.** Query or send complete ms. Length: 500-2,500 words. **Pays $50-400 (Canadian) for assigned articles; $50-300 (Canadian) for unsolicited articles.**

Reprints Sometimes accepts previously published submissions (if stated as such).

Photos State availability with submission.

Columns/Departments The Lighter Side (humor), 600 words; Profile, 1,200 words.

Tips "Do not contact by phone—send something in writing. Send a great idea that we haven't done before, and make a case for why you'd be able to do a good job with it. Be sure to include a relevant writing sample."

$ $ $ $ARTHRITIS TODAY

Arthritis Foundation, 1330 W. Peachtree St., Atlanta GA 30309. (404)872-7100. Fax: (404)872-9559. E-mail: atmail@arthritis.org. Website: www.arthritis.org. Editor: Marcy O'Koon Moss. Managing Editor: Lissa Poirot. Medical Editor: Donna Siegfried. Lifestyle Editor: Amy Brayfield. **50% freelance written.** Bimonthly magazine covering living with arthritis; latest in research/treatment. "*Arthritis Today* is a consumer health magazine and is written for the more than 70 million Americans who have arthritis and for the millions of others whose lives are touched by an arthritis-related disease. The editorial content is designed to help the person with arthritis live a more productive, independent, and pain-free life. The articles are upbeat and provide practical advice, information and inspiration." Estab. 1987. Circ. 650,000. **Pays on acceptance.** Byline given. Offers kill fee. Buys first North American serial, second serial (reprint), electronic rights. Editorial lead time 6 months. Submit seasonal material 6 months in advance. Accepts queries by mail, e-mail, fax. Accepts simultaneous submissions. Responds in 2 months to queries. Sample copy for 9×11 SAE with 4 first-class stamps. Writer's guidelines online.

Nonfiction General interest, how-to (tips on any aspect of living with arthritis), inspirational, new product (arthritis related), opinion, personal experience, photo feature, technical, travel (tips, news), service, nutrition, general health, lifestyle. **Buys 12 unsolicited mss/year.** Query with published clips. Length: 150-2,500 words. **Pays $100-2,500.** Pays expenses of writers on assignment.

Photos Send photos with submission. Reviews prints. Buys one-time rights. Negotiates payment individually. Identification of subjects required.

Columns/Departments Nutrition, 100-600 words; Fitness, 100-600 words; Balance (emotional coping), 100-600 words; MedWatch, 100-800 words; Solutions, 100-600 words; Life Makeover, 400-600 words.

Fillers Facts, gags to be illustrated by cartoonist, short humor. **Buys 2/year.** Length: 40-100 words. **Pays $80-150.**

Tips "Our readers are already well informed. We need ideas and writers that give in-depth, fresh, interesting information that truly adds to their understanding of their condition and their quality of life. Quality writers are more important than good ideas. The staff generates many of our ideas but needs experienced, talented writers who are good reporters to execute them. Please provide published clips. In addition to articles specifically about living with arthritis, we look for articles to appeal to an older audience on subjects such as hobbies, general health, lifestyle, etc."

$ $ ASTHMA MAGAZINE

Taking Control of Asthma and Allergies, Mosby, Inc., P.O. Box 473, Hingham MA 02043. (781)740-0221. E-mail: asthmamagazine@verizon.net. Website: www.mosby.com/asthma. Publisher: Jeff Ryals. **Contact:** Rachel Butler, editor-in-chief. **50% freelance written.** Bimonthly magazine. "*Asthma Magazine* offers unbiased education for people with asthma. We are an independent publication (not sponsored by any drug company) and we provide indepth education to help the asthmatic manage his/her disease and live an active and healthy life." Estab. 1995. Circ. 65,000. Pays on publication. Publishes ms an average of 1 month after acceptance. Byline given. Offers 25% kill fee. Buys all rights. Editorial lead time 6 months. Submit seasonal material 3 months in advance. Accepts queries by mail, e-mail, fax, phone. Sample copy for free. Writer's guidelines for free.

Nonfiction Buys 4 features/issue. How-to, inspirational, interview/profile, new product (usually a news blurb, not a full article), personal experience, technical, travel. **Buys 12-15 mss/year.** Query with published clips. Length: 1,000-1,200 words. **Pays $200-500.**

Photos State availability with submission. Reviews Prints. Buys all rights. Offers no additional payment for photos accepted with ms.

Columns/Departments Hear My Story (personal experience of a person with asthma or article about someone who has accomplished something significant despite their asthma, or someone in the asthma/medical field). Query with published clips. **Pays $250.**

Tips "We look for writers who have had experience writing for the medical community for either clinicians or patients. Writing must be clear, concise and easy to understand (7th-9th grade reading level), as well as thoroughly researched and medically accurate."

$ $ CAREERS & THE DISABLED

Equal Opportunity Publications, 445 Broad Hollow Rd., Suite 425, Melville NY 11747. (631)421-9421. Fax: (631)421-0359. E-mail: jschneider@eop.com. Website: www.eop.com. **Contact:** James Schneider, editor. **60% freelance written.** Quarterly magazine offering "role-model profiles and career guidance articles geared toward disabled college students and professionals, and promotes personal and professional growth." Estab. 1967. Circ. 10,000. Pays on publication. Publishes ms an average of 6 months after acceptance. Byline given. Buys first North American serial rights. Editorial lead time 6 months. Submit seasonal material 6 months in advance. Accepts queries by mail, e-mail, fax, phone. Accepts previously published material. Accepts simultaneous submissions. Responds in 3 weeks to queries. Sample copy for 9×12 SAE with 5 first-class stamps.

Nonfiction Essays, general interest, how-to, interview/profile, new product, opinion, personal experience. **Buys 30 mss/year.** Query. Length: 1,000-2,500 words. **Pays 10¢/word.** Sometimes pays expenses of writers on assignment.

Reprints Accepts previously published submissions and information about when and where the material previously appeared.

Photos Reviews transparencies, prints. Buys one-time rights. Offers $15-50/photo. Captions, identification of subjects, model releases required.

Tips "Be as targeted as possible. Role-model profiles and specific career guidance strategies that offer advice to disabled college students are most needed."

$ $ DIABETES HEALTH

(formerly *Diabetes Interview*), 6 School St., Suite 160, Fairfax CA 94930. (415)258-2828. Fax: (415)387-3604. Website: www.diabetesinterview.com. **Contact:** Daniel Trecroci, managing editor. **40% freelance written.** Monthly tabloid covering diabetes care. "*Diabetes Interview* covers the latest in diabetes care, medications, and patient advocacy. Personal accounts are welcome as well as medical-oriented articles by MDs, RNs, and CDEs (certified diabetes educators)." Estab. 1991. Circ. 40,000. Pays on publication. Publishes ms an average of 2 months after acceptance. Byline given. Buys all rights. Editorial lead time 2 months. Submit seasonal material 2 months in advance. Accepts queries by mail, e-mail, fax, phone. Sample copy online. Writer's guidelines free.

Nonfiction Essays, how-to, humor, inspirational, interview/profile, new product, opinion, personal experience. **Buys 25 mss/year.** Query. **Pays 20¢/word.**

Reprints Accepts previously published submissions.

Photos State availability of or send photos with submission. Negotiates payment individually.

Tips "Be actively involved in the diabetes community or have diabetes. However, writers need not have diabetes to write an article, but it must be diabetes-related."

$ $ DIABETES SELF-MANAGEMENT

R.A. Rapaport Publishing, Inc., 150 W. 22nd St., Suite 800, New York NY 10011-2421. (212)989-0200. Fax: (212)989-4786. E-mail: editor@diabetes-self-mgmt.com. Website: www.diabetesselfmanagement.com. **Contact:** Ingrid Strauch, managing editor. **20% freelance written.** Bimonthly magazine. "We publish how-to health care articles for motivated, intelligent readers who have diabetes and who are actively involved in their own health care management. All articles must have immediate application to their daily living." Estab. 1983. Circ. 480,000. Pays on publication. Byline given. Offers 20% kill fee. Buys all rights. Submit seasonal material 6 months in advance. Accepts queries by mail, e-mail, fax. Responds in 6 weeks to queries. Sample copy for $4 and 9×12 SAE with 6 first-class stamps or online. Writer's guidelines for #10 SASE.

• "We are extremely generous regarding permission to republish."

O— Break in by having extensive knowledge of diabetes.

Nonfiction How-to (exercise, nutrition, diabetes self-care, product surveys), technical (reviews of products available, foods sold by brand name, pharmacology), travel (considerations and prep for people with diabetes). No personal experiences, personality profiles, exposés, or research breakthroughs. **Buys 10-12 mss/year.** Query with published clips. Length: 2,000-2,500 words. **Pays $400-700 for assigned articles; $200-700 for unsolicited articles.**

Tips "The rule of thumb for any article we publish is that it must be clear, concise, useful, and instructive, and it must have immediate application to the lives of our readers. If your query is accepted, expect heavy editorial supervision."

$ DIALOGUE

Blindskills, Inc., P.O. Box 5181, Salem OR 97304-0181. (800)860-4224; (503)581-4224. Fax: (503)581-0178. E-mail: blindskl@teleport.com. Website: www.blindskills.com. **Contact:** Carol M. McCarl, editor. **60% freelance written.** Quarterly journal covering the visually impaired. Estab. 1961. Circ. 1,100. Pays on publication. Publishes ms an average of 8 months after acceptance. Byline given. Buys first rights. Editorial lead time 3 months. Accepts queries by mail, e-mail, fax. One free sample on request. Available in Braille, 4-track audio cassette, large print, and disk (for compatible IBM computer). Writer's guidelines online.

O— Break in by "using accurate punctuation, grammar, and structure, and writing about pertinent subject matter."

Nonfiction Mostly features material written by visually impaired writers. Essays, general interest, historical/nostalgic, how-to (life skills methods used by visually impaired people), humor, interview/profile, personal experience, sports, recreation, hobbies. No controversial, explicit sex, religious, or political topics. **Buys 80 mss/year.** Send complete ms. Length: 500-1,200 words. **Pays $10-35 for assigned articles; $10-25 for unsolicited articles.**

Columns/Departments All material should be relative to blind and visually impaired readers. Careers, 1,000 words; Hear's How (dealing with sight loss), 1,000 words. **Buys 80 mss/year.** Send complete ms. **Pays $10-25.**

Fiction Publishes material by visually impaired writers. Adventure, humorous, slice-of-life vignettes, first-person experiences. No controversial, explicit sex, religious, or political topics. **Buys 6-8 mss/year.** Send complete ms. Length: 800-1,200 words. **Pays $15-25.**

$ KALEIDOSCOPE

Exploring the Experience of Disability Through Literature and the Fine Arts, Kaleidoscope Press, 701 S. Main St., Akron OH 44311-1019. (330)762-9755. Fax: (330)762-0912. E-mail: mshiplett@udsakron.org. Website: www.udsakron.org. **Contact:** Gail Willmott, editor-in-chief. **75% freelance written.** Eager to work with new/unpublished writers. Semiannual magazine. Subscribers include individuals, agencies, and organizations that assist people with disabilities and many university and public libraries. Appreciates work by established writers as well. Especially interested in work by writers with a disability, but features writers both with and without disabilities. "Writers without a disability must limit themselves to our focus, while those with a disability may explore any topic (although we prefer original perspectives about experiences with disability)." Estab. 1979.

Circ. 1,000. Pays on publication. Byline given. Buys first, reprints permitted with credit given to original publication rights. Rights return to author upon publication. Accepts queries by mail, fax. Accepts previously published material. Accepts simultaneous submissions. Responds in 3 weeks to queries; 6 months to mss. Sample copy for $6 prepaid. Writer's guidelines online.

O┐ Submit photocopies with SASE for return of work. Please type submissions (double spaced). Include SASE with sufficient postage for return of work. All submissions should be accompanied by an autobiographical sketch. May include art or photos that enhance works, prefer b&w with high contrast.

Nonfiction Articles related to disability. Book excerpts, essays, humor, interview/profile, personal experience, book reviews, articles related to disability. Special issues: Mental Illness (January 2005, deadline August 2004); Parents and Children (July 2005, deadline March 2005). **Buys 8-15 mss/year.** Length: 5,000 words maximum. **Pays $25-125, plus 2 copies.**

Reprints Send ms with rights for sale noted and information about when and where the material previously appeared.

Photos Send photos with submission.

Fiction Fiction Editor. Short stories, novel excerpts. Traditional and experimental styles. Works should explore experiences with disability. Use people-first language. "We look for well-developed plots, engaging characters and realistic dialogue. We lean toward fiction that emphasizes character and emotions rather than action-oriented narratives." "No fiction that is stereotypical, patronizing, sentimental, erotic, or maudlin. No romance, religious or dogmatic fiction; no children's literature." Length: 5,000 words maximum. **Pays $10-125, and 2 contributor's copies; additional copies $6.**

Poetry "Do not get caught up in rhyme scheme. High quality with strong imagery and evocative language." Reviews any style. **Buys 12-20 poems/year.** Submit maximum 5 poems.

Tips "Articles and personal experiences should be creative rather than journalistic and with some depth. Writers should use more than just the simple facts and chronology of an experience with disability. Inquire about future themes of upcoming issues. Sample copy very helpful. Works should not use stereotyping, patronizing, or offending language about disability. We seek fresh imagery and thought-provoking language."

ENTERTAINMENT

$ CINEASTE

America's Leading Magazine on the Art and Politics of the Cinema, Cineaste Publishers, Inc., 304 Hudson St., 6th Floor, New York NY 10013-1015. (212)366-5720. Fax: (212)366-5724. E-mail: cineaste@cineaste.com. **Contact:** Gary Crowdus, editor-in-chief. **30% freelance written.** Quarterly magazine covering motion pictures with an emphasis on social and political perspective on cinema. Estab. 1967. Circ. 11,000. Pays on publication. Publishes ms an average of 4 months after acceptance. Byline given. Offers 50% kill fee. Buys first North American serial rights. Editorial lead time 3 months. Submit seasonal material 4 months in advance. Accepts queries by mail, e-mail, fax. Responds in 1 month to queries. Sample copy for $5. Writer's guidelines for #10 SASE.

O┐ Break in by "being familiar with our unique editorial orientation—we are not just another film magazine."

Nonfiction Book excerpts, essays, exposé, historical/nostalgic, humor, interview/profile, opinion. **Buys 20-30 mss/year.** Query with published clips. Length: 2,000-5,000 words. **Pays $30-100.**

Photos State availability with submission. Reviews transparencies, 8 × 10 prints. Buys one-time rights. Offers no additional payment for photos accepted with ms. Identification of subjects required.

Columns/Departments Homevideo (topics of general interest or a related group of films); A Second Look (new interpretation of a film classic or a reevaluation of an unjustly neglected release of more recent vintage); Lost and Found (film that may or may not be released or otherwise seen in the U.S. but which is important enough to be brought to the attention of our readers), all 1,000-1,500 words. Query with published clips. **Pays $50 minimum.**

Tips "We dislike academic jargon, obtuse Marxist terminology, film buff trivia, trendy 'buzz' phrases, and show biz references. We do not want our writers to speak of how they have 'read' or 'decoded' a film, but to view, analyze, and interpret. The author's processes and quirks should be secondary to the interests of the reader. Warning the reader of problems with specific films is more important to us than artificially 'puffing' a film because its producers or politics are agreeable. One article format we encourage is an omnibus review of several current films, preferably those not reviewed in a previous issue. Such an article would focus on films that perhaps share a certain political perspective, subject matter, or generic concerns (e.g., films on suburban life, or urban violence, or revisionist Westerns). Like individual film reviews, these articles should incorporate a very brief synopsis of plots for those who haven't seen the films. The main focus, however, should be on the social issues manifested in each film, and how it may reflect something about the current political/social/ esthetic climate."

$⬚ DANCE INTERNATIONAL

Scotiabanti Dance Centre, 677 Davie St., Vancouver BC V6B 2G6, Canada. (604)681-1525. Fax: (604)681-7732. E-mail: danceint@direct.ca. Website: www.danceinternational.org. **Contact:** Maureen Riches, editor. **100% freelance written.** Quarterly magazine covering dance arts. "Articles and reviews on current activities in world dance, with occasional historical essays; reviews of dance films, video, and books." Estab. 1973. Circ. 4,500. Pays on publication. Publishes ms an average of 3 months after acceptance. Byline given. Offers 50% kill fee. Buys one-time rights. Editorial lead time 3 months. Submit seasonal material 6 weeks in advance. Accepts queries by mail, e-mail, fax, phone. Responds in 2 weeks to queries; 1 month to mss. Sample copy for $7. Writer's guidelines for #10 SASE.

Nonfiction Book excerpts, essays, historical/nostalgic, interview/profile, personal experience, photo feature. **Buys 100 mss/year.** Query. Length: 1,200-2,200 words. **Pays $40-150.**

Photos Send photos with submission. Reviews prints. Offers no additional payment for photos accepted with ms. Identification of subjects required.

Columns/Departments Dance Bookshelf (recent books reviewed), 700-800 words; Regional Reports (events in each region), 1,200 words. **Buys 100 mss/year.** Query. **Pays $80.**

Tips "Send résumé and samples of recent writings."

$ DANCE SPIRIT

Lifestyle Ventures, LLC, 250 W. 57th St., Suite 420, New York NY 10107. (212)265-8890. Fax: (212)265-8908. E-mail: editor@dancespirit.com. Website: www.dancespirit.com. **Contact:** Sara Jarrett, features editor. **50% freelance written.** Monthly magazine covering all dance disciplines. "*Dance Spirit* is a special interest teen magazine for girls and guys who study and perform either through a studio or a school dance performance group." Estab. 1997. Circ. 130,000. Pays on publication. Publishes ms an average of 4 months after acceptance. Byline given. Offers 25% kill fee. Buys all rights. Editorial lead time 3 months. Submit seasonal material 8 months in advance. Accepts queries by mail, e-mail, fax. Responds in 3 months to queries; 4 months to mss. Sample copy for $4.95.

Nonfiction Personal experience, photo feature, dance-related articles only. **Buys 100 mss/year.** Query with published clips. Length: 600-1,200 words. **Pays $100.** Sometimes pays expenses of writers on assignment.

Photos Reviews transparencies. Buys all rights. Negotiates payment individually. Captions, identification of subjects, model releases required.

Columns/Departments Ballet; Jazz; Tap; Swing; Hip Hop; Lyrical; Pom; Body; Beauty; City Focus; Choreography; Stars; Nutrition.

⬚ The online magazine carries original content not found in the print edition. Contact: Sara Jarrett.

Tips "Reading the magazine can't be stressed enough. We look for writers with a dance background and experienced dancers/choreographers to contribute; succinct writing style, hip outlook."

$ $ DIRECTED BY

The Cinema Quarterly, Visionary Media, P.O. Box 1722, Glendora CA 91740-1722. Fax: (626)963-0235. E-mail: visionarycinema@yahoo.com. Website: www.directed-by.com. **Contact:** Carsten Dau, editor. **25% freelance written.** Quarterly magazine covering the craft of directing a motion picture. "Our articles are for readers particularly knowledgeable about the art and history of movies from the director's point of view. Our purpose is to communicate our enthusiasm and interest in the craft of cinema." Estab. 1998. Circ. 42,000. Pays on publication. Publishes ms an average of 3 months after acceptance. Byline given. Offers 50% kill fee. Buys all rights. Editorial lead time 3 months. Submit seasonal material 3 months in advance. Accepts queries by mail, e-mail. Accepts simultaneous submissions. Responds in 6 weeks to queries. Sample copy for $5. Writer's guidelines free or by e-mail.

Nonfiction Essays, historical/nostalgic, interview/profile, photo feature, on-set reports. No gossip, celebrity-oriented material, or movie reviews. **Buys 12 mss/year.** Query. Length: 500-7,500 words. **Pays $50-750.** Sometimes pays expenses of writers on assignment.

Photos State availability with submission. Reviews contact sheets. Buys all rights. Offers no additional payment for photos accepted with ms. Captions, identification of subjects required.

Columns/Departments Trends (overview/analysis of specific moviemaking movements/genres/subjects), 1,500-2,000 words; Focus (innovative take on the vision of a contemporary director), 1,500-2,000 words; Appreciation (overview of deceased/foreign director), 1,000-1,500 words; Final Cut (spotlight interview with contemporary director), 3,000 words; Perspectives (interviews/articles about film craftspeople who work with a featured director), 1,500-2,000 words. **Buys 12 mss/year.** Query. **Pays $50-750.**

Tips "We have been inundated with 'shelf-life' article queries and cannot publish even a fraction of them. As such, we have restricted our interest in freelancers to writers who have direct access to a notable director of a current film which has not been significantly covered in previous issues of magazines; said director must be willing to grant an exclusive peronal interview to *DIRECTED BY*."

⊡ ⊘ DISNEY MAGAZINE

Disney Publishing Worldwide, 244 Main St., Northampton MA 01060-3886. (413)585-0444. Fax: (413)587-9335. E-mail: letters.familyfun@disney.com. Website: www.disneymagazine.com. Quarterly magazine. Circ. 480,000.

- Does not buy freelance material or use freelance writers.

$ $ EAST END LIGHTS

The Quarterly Magazine for Elton John Fans, P.O. Box 621, Joplin MO 64802-0621. Phone/Fax: (417)776-4120. E-mail: eel@accessthemusic.com. **Contact:** Mark Norris, publisher. **90% freelance written.** Quarterly magazine covering Elton John. "In one way or another, a story must relate to Elton John, his activities or associates (past and present). We appeal to discriminating Elton fans. No gushing fanzine material. No current concert reviews." Estab. 1990. Circ. 1,700. Pays 3 weeks after publication. Publishes ms an average of 3 months after acceptance. Byline given. Offers 100% kill fee. Buys first, second serial (reprint) rights. Submit seasonal material 6 months in advance. Accepts queries by mail, e-mail, fax. Accepts previously published material. Responds in 2 months to queries. Sample copy for $5.

Nonfiction Book excerpts, essays, exposé, general interest, historical/nostalgic, humor, interview/profile. **Buys 20 mss/year.** Query with or without published clips or send complete ms. Length: 400-1,000 words. **Pays $20-250 for assigned articles; $20-150 for unsolicited articles.** Pays in contributor copies only when author requests it.

Reprints Send tearsheet or photocopy with rights for sale noted and information about when and where the material previously appeared. Pays 50%.

Photos State availability with submission. Reviews negatives, 5×7 prints, high-resolution digital files. Buys one-time and all rights. Offers $20-200/photo.

Columns/Departments Clippings (nonwire references to Elton John in other publications), maximum 200 words. **Buys 12 mss/year.** Send complete ms. **Pays $20-50.**

Tips "Approach us with a well-thought-out story idea. We prefer interviews with Elton-related personalities—past or present; try to land an interview we haven't done. We are particularly interested in music/memorabilia collecting of Elton material."

⊡ ELECTRONIC GAMING MONTHLY

Ziff-Davis Media, Inc., 701 2nd St., 8th Floor, San Francisco CA 94105. (415)547-8000. Fax: (415)547-8777. E-mail: egm@ziffdavis.com. Website: www.egmmag.com. Editor: Dan Hsu. Monthly magazine. Focuses on electronic games for console video game units. Circ. 600,000. Sample copy not available.

⊡ ⊘ ENTERTAINMENT WEEKLY

Time, Inc., 1675 Broadway, 30th Floor, New York NY 10019. (212)522-5600. Fax: (212)522-0074. Website: www.ew.com. Editor: Norman Pearlstine. Weekly magazine. Written for readers who want the latest reviews, previews and updates of the entertainment world. Circ. 1,600,000. Editorial lead time 4 weeks. Sample copy not available.

- Does not buy freelance material or use freelance writers.

$ $ FANGORIA

Horror in Entertainment, Starlog Communications, Inc., 475 Park Ave. S., 7th Floor, New York NY 10016. (212)689-2830. Fax: (212)889-7933. Website: www.fangoria.com. **Contact:** Anthony Timpone, editor. **95% freelance written.** Works with a small number of new/unpublished writers each year. Magazine published 10 times/year covering horror films, TV projects, comics, videos, and literature, and those who create them. "We provide an assignment sheet (deadlines, info) to writers, thus authorizing queried stories that we're buying." Estab. 1979. Pays on publication. Publishes ms an average of 3 months after acceptance. Byline given. Buys all rights. Submit seasonal material 4 months in advance. Accepts queries by mail. Responds in 6 weeks to queries. Sample copy for $8 and 10×13 SAE with 4 first-class stamps. Writer's guidelines for #10 SASE.

    ○⌐ Break in by "reading the magazine regularly and exhibiting a professional view of the genre."

Nonfiction Book excerpts, interview/profile of movie directors, makeup FX artists, screenwriters, producers, actors, noted horror/thriller novelists and others—with genre credits; special FX and special makeup FX how-it-was-dones (on filmmaking only). Occasional "think" pieces, opinion pieces, reviews, or sub-theme overviews by industry professionals. Avoids most articles on science-fiction films—see listing for sister magazine *Starlog* in *Writer's Market* science fiction consumer magazine section. **Buys 120 mss/year.** Query with published clips. Length: 1,000-3,500 words. **Pays $100-250.** Sometimes pays expenses of writers on assignment.

Photos State availability with submission. Reviews transparencies, prints (b&w, color) electronically. Captions, identification of subjects required.

Columns/Departments Monster Invasion (exclusive, early information about new film productions; also mini-interviews with filmmakers and novelists). Query with published clips. **Pays $45-75.**

◼ The online magazine carries original content not found in the print edition.

Tips "Other than recommending that you study one or several copies of *Fangoria*, we can only describe it as a horror film magazine consisting primarily of interviews with technicians and filmmakers in the field. Be sure to stress the interview subjects' words—not your own opinions as much. We're very interested in small, independent filmmakers working outside of Hollywood. These people are usually more accessible to writers, and more cooperative. *Fangoria* is also sort of a *de facto* bible for youngsters interested in movie makeup careers and for young filmmakers. We are devoted only to *reel* horrors—the fakery of films, the imagery of the horror fiction of a Stephen King or a Clive Barker—*we do not* want nor would we *ever* publish articles on real-life horrors, murders, etc. A writer must *like* and *enjoy* horror films and horror fiction to work for us. If the photos in *Fangoria* disgust you, if the sight of (*stage*) blood repels you, if you feel 'superior' to horror (and its fans), you aren't a writer for us and we certainly aren't the market for you. We love giving new writers their *first* chance to break into print in a national magazine. We are currently looking for Arizona- and Las Vegas-based correspondents."

$ FILMFAX

The Magazine of Unusual Film, Television, and Retro Pop Culture, Filmfax, Inc., P.O. Box 1900, Evanston IL 60204. (847)866-7155. E-mail: filmfax@speedsite.com. Website: www.filmfax.com. **Contact:** James J.J. Wilson, managing editor/story editor. **100% freelance written.** Quarterly magazine covering films and television for the silent era through the 1970s, focusing mainly on horror, science fiction, westerns, and comedy. *Filmfax* also has recently absorbed all the features of *Outre Magazine*, which focused on the quirky side of American pop pop culture of the post-war era through the 1960s. "Most of our features are interviews with actors, directors, writers, artists, musicians, and the other people involved in making classic genre films and pop culture of that era, although we do publish articles on films and people if the material is comprehensive and beyond common knowledge. We also publish reviews of current releases in video/DVD, books, and CDs related to our general subject." Estab. 1986. Circ. 30,000. Pays on publication. Publishes ms an average of 6-12 months after acceptance. Byline given. Buys first North American serial rights. Editorial lead time 6-12 months. Accepts queries by mail, e-mail. Accepts previously published material. Responds in 1-2 weeks to queries; 1 month to mss. Sample copy for free. Writer's guidelines online.

Nonfiction Prefers first-hand interviews, but will consider queries on other topics. No general criticism or pieces which do not contain information not commonly known to genre film fans. **Buys 60 mss/year.** Query. Length: 300-15,000 words. **Pays 3¢/word.**

Photos State availability with submission. Buys one-time rights. Offers no additional payment for photos accepted with ms. Identification of subjects required.

Columns/Departments Accepts reviews of books, CDs, and videos/DVDs. **Buys 50 mss/year.** Query. **Pays 3¢/word.**

Fiction "We publish fiction very seldom, less than 1 story/year. Inquire in advance."

Tips "Send us an e-mail or letter describing what ideas you have that may fit our format. As a specialty publication, reading the magazine is the best way to get a feel for what we like to publish."

$ 5678 MAGAZINE

Champion Media, P.O. Box 8886, Gaithersburg MD 20898. (301)871-7160. Fax: (301)519-1019. E-mail: durand5678@aol.com. Website: www.5678magazine.com. **Contact:** Barry Durand, publisher. **50% freelance written.** Bimonthly magazine covering dance: Couples, line, country, swing. "All articles with a dance or dance music slant. Interviews, reviews, features—today's social dance." Estab. 1999. Circ. 10,000. Pays on publication. Publishes ms an average of 2 months after acceptance. Byline given. Buys first rights. Editorial lead time 2 months. Accepts queries by e-mail. Sample copy for free. Writer's guidelines by e-mail.

Nonfiction Historical/nostalgic, how-to, humor, interview/profile, photo feature. **Buys 60 mss/year.** Query. Length: 600-2,000 words. **Pays $35-100.** Sometimes pays expenses of writers on assignment.

Photos Send photos with submission. Buys one-time rights. Negotiates payment individually. Captions, identification of subjects required.

Fiction Humorous, slice-of-life vignettes. **Buys 10 mss/year.** Query. Length: 600-1,500 words. **Pays $35-100.**

ℕ INTERVIEW

Brant Publications, Inc., 575 Broadway, 5th Floor, New York NY 10012. (212)941-2900. Fax: (212)941-2934. E-mail: brantinter@aol.com. Website: www.interviewmagazine.com. Editor: Ingrid Sischy. Monthly magazine. Explores the inside world of music, film, fashion, art, TV, photography, sports, contemporary life and politics through celebrity interviews. Circ. 200,000. Editorial lead time 2 months. Sample copy not available.

$ $ MOVIEMAKER MAGAZINE

MovieMaker Publishing Co., 349 Broadway, Third Floor, New York NY 10013. (212)625-3377. Fax: (212)625-3373. E-mail: jwood@moviemaker.com. Website: www.moviemaker.com. Editor: Timothy Rhys. **Contact:** Jennifer Wood, managing editor. **95% freelance written.** Quarterly magazine covering film, independent cinema, and Hollywood. *"MovieMaker*'s editorial is a progressive mix of in-depth interviews and criticism, combined with practical techniques and advice on financing, distribution, and production strategies. Behind-the-scenes discussions with Hollywood's top moviemakers, as well as independents from around the globe, are routinely found in *MovieMaker*'s pages." Estab. 1993. Circ. 50,000. Pays within 1 month upon publication. Publishes ms an average of 2 months after acceptance. Byline given. Offers variable kill fee. Buys all rights. Editorial lead time 3 months. Submit seasonal material 4 months in advance. Accepts queries by mail, e-mail, fax. Accepts simultaneous submissions. Responds in 2 months to queries; 2 months to mss. Sample copy online. Writer's guidelines by e-mail.

• E-mail queries preferred.

Nonfiction Exposé, general interest, historical/nostalgic, how-to, interview/profile, new product, technical. **Buys 10 mss/year.** Query with published clips. Length: 800-3,000 words. **Pays $75-500 for assigned articles.**

Photos State availability with submission. Rights purchased negotiable. Payment varies for photos accepted with ms. Identification of subjects required.

Columns/Departments Documentary; Home Cinema (home video/DVD reviews); How They Did It (first-person filmmaking experiences); Festival Beat (film festival reviews); World Cinema (current state of cinema from a particular country). Query with published clips. **Pays $75-300.**

Tips "The best way to begin working with *MovieMaker* is to send a list of 'pitches' along with your résumé and clips. As we receive a number of résumés each week, we want to get an early sense of not just your style of writing, but the kinds of subjects that interest you most as they relate to film. E-mail is the preferred method of correspondence, and please allow 2-4 weeks before following up on a query or résumé. Queries should be submitted in writing, rather than phone calls."

N Ø PREMIERE MAGAZINE

Hachette Filipacchi Magazines, 1633 Broadway, 41st Floor, New York NY 10019. (212)767-5400. Fax: (212)767-5450. Website: www.premiere.com. Magazine published 10 times/year.

• Does not buy freelance material or use freelance writers.

$ $ RUE MORGUE

Horror in Culture & Entertainment, Marrs Media, Inc., 700 Queen St. E., Toronto ON M4M 1G9, Canada. E-mail: info@rue-morgue.com. Website: www.rue-morgue.com. Editor: Rod Gudino. Associate Editor: Mary Beth Hollyer. **Contact:** Jen Vuckovic, managing editor. **50% freelance written.** Bimonthly magazine covering horror entertainment. "A knowledge of horror entertainment (films, books, games, toys, etc.)." Estab. 1997. Pays on publication. Publishes ms an average of 4 months after acceptance. Byline given. Buys all rights. Editorial lead time 2 months. Submit seasonal material 4 months in advance. Accepts queries by e-mail. Responds in 6 weeks to queries; 2 months to mss. Sample copy not available. Writer's guidelines by e-mail.

Nonfiction Essays, exposé, historical/nostalgic, interview/profile, new product, travel. No fiction. Reviews done by staff writers. **Buys 10 mss/year.** Query with published clips or send complete ms. Length: 500-2,000 words. **Pays $75-300.**

Columns/Departments Classic Cut (historical essays on classic horror films, books, games, comic books, music), 500-700 words. **Buys 1-2 mss/year.** Query with published clips. **Pays $60.**

Tips "The editors are most responsive to special interest articles and analytical essays on cultural/historical topics relating to the horror genre—published examples: Leon Theremin, Soren Kierkegaard, Horror in Fine Art, Murderbilia."

N Ø SOAP OPERA DIGEST

Primedia Broad Reach Magazines, 216 Madison Ave., 10th Floor, New York NY 10016. Website: www.soapdigest.com. Weekly magazine. Edited for the day time and prime time soap opera viewer. Circ. 1,040,142.

• Does not buy freelance material or use freelance writers.

$ $ $ $ SOUND & VISION

Hachette Filipacchi Magazines, Inc., 1633 Broadway, New York NY 10019. (212)767-6000. Fax: (212)767-5615. E-mail: soundandvision@hfmus.com. Website: www.soundandvisionmag.com. Editor-in-Chief: Bob Ankosko. Entertainment Editor: Ken Richardson. **Contact:** Michael Gaughn, features editor. **50% freelance written.** Published 10 times/year. Provides readers with authoritive information on the entertainment technologies and products that will impact their lives. Estab. 1958. Circ. 450,000. **Pays on acceptance.** Publishes ms an average of 4 months after acceptance. Byline given. Buys first North American serial, electronic rights. Accepts queries by mail, e-mail, fax. Sample copy for 9×12 SAE and 11 first-class stamps.

Nonfiction Home theater, audio, video and multimedia equipment plus movie and music reviews, how-to-buy and how-to-use A/V gear, interview/profile. **Buys 25 mss/year.** Query with published clips. Length: 1,500-3,000 words. **Pays $1,000-1,500.**

Tips "Send proposals or outlines, rather than complete articles, along with published clips to establish writing ability. Publisher assumes no responsibility for return or safety of unsolicited art, photos or manuscripts."

$ $⬛ TAKE ONE

Film & Television in Canada, Canadian Independent Film & Television Publishing Association, 252-128 Danforth Ave., Toronto ON M4K 1N1, Canada. (416)944-1096. Fax: (416)465-4356. E-mail: takeone@interlog.com. Website: www.takeonemagazine.ca. **Contact:** Wyndham Wise, editor-in-chief. **100% freelance written.** Quarterly magazine covering Canadian film and television. "*Take One* is a special interest magazine that focuses exclusively on Canadian cinema, filmmakers, and Canadian television." Estab. 1992. Circ. 5,000/issue. Pays on publication. Publishes ms an average of 2 months after acceptance. Byline given. Offers 50% kill fee. Buys one-time, electronic rights. Editorial lead time 3 months. Submit seasonal material 3 months in advance. Accepts queries by mail, e-mail, fax, phone. Sample copy online.

Nonfiction Essays, historical/nostalgic, interview/profile, opinion. Query. Length: 2,000-4,000 words. **Pays 12¢/word.** Sometimes pays expenses of writers on assignment.

Ⓝ ⊘ VARIETY

Reed Business Information, 5700 Wilshire Blvd., Suite 120, Los Angeles CA 90036. (323)965-4476. Fax: (323)857-0494. E-mail: news@reedbusiness.com. Website: www.variety.com. Weekly magazine. Circ. 34,000.
• Does not buy freelance material or use freelance writers.

$ $ $ $ XXL MAGAZINE

Harris Publications, 1115 Broadway, 8th Floor, New York NY 10010. (212)462-9500. E-mail: zenat@harris-pub.com. **Contact:** Zena Tsarfin, managing editor. **50% freelance written.** Monthly magazine "XXL is hip-hop on a higher level, an upscale urban lifestyle magazine." Estab. 1997. Circ. 350,000. Pays on publication. Byline given. Offers 25% kill fee. Buys all rights. Editorial lead time 2 months. Submit seasonal material 3 months in advance. Accepts queries by mail, e-mail. Sample copy not available.

Nonfiction Interview/profile, music; entertainment; luxury materialism. Query with published clips. Length: 200-5,000 words. **Pays $1/word.** Pays expenses of writers on assignment.

Photos State availability with submission. Reviews contact sheets, transparencies, prints. Buys 3 month "no-see" rights. Captions, model releases required.

Tips Please send clips, query and cover letter by mail or e-mail.

ETHNIC & MINORITY

$ AIM MAGAZINE

Aim Publishing Co., P.O. Box 1174, Maywood IL 60153. (708)344-4414. Fax: (206)543-2746. E-mail: mapilado@aol.com. Website: aimmagazine.org. **Contact:** Dr. Myron Apilado, editor. **75% freelance written.** Works with a small number of new/unpublished writers each year. Quarterly magazine on social betterment that promotes racial harmony and peace for high school, college and general audience. Publishes material "to purge racism from the human bloodstream through the written word - that is the purpose of *Aim Magazine*." Estab. 1975. Circ. 10,000. Pays on publication. Publishes ms an average of 3 months after acceptance. Byline given. Offers 60% kill fee. Buys first, one-time rights. Submit seasonal material 6 months in advance. Accepts queries by mail, e-mail. Accepts simultaneous submissions. Responds in 2 months to queries; 1 month to mss. Sample copy and writer's guidelines for $4 and 9×12 SAE with $1.70 postage or online.

Nonfiction Exposé (education), general interest (social significance), historical/nostalgic (Black or Indian), how-to (create a more equitable society), interview/profile (one who is making social contributions to community), book reviews; reviews of plays. No religious material. **Buys 16 mss/year.** Send complete ms. Length: 500-800 words. **Pays $25-35.**

Photos Reviews b&w prints. Captions, identification of subjects required.

Fiction Ruth Apilado, associate editor. "Fiction that teaches the brotherhood of man." Ethnic, historical, mainstream, suspense. Open. No "religious" mss. **Buys 20 mss/year.** Send complete ms. Length: 1,000-1,500 words. **Pays $25-35.**

Poetry Avant-garde, free verse, light verse. No "preachy" poetry. **Buys 20 poems/year.** Submit maximum 5 poems. Length: 15-30 lines. **Pays $3-5.**

Fillers Anecdotes, newsbreaks, short humor. **Buys 30/year.** Length: 50-100 words. **Pays $5.**

Tips ''Interview anyone of any age who unselfishly is making an unusual contribution to the lives of less fortunate individuals. Include photo and background of person. We look at the nations of the world as part of one family. Short stories and historical pieces about Blacks and Indians are the areas most open to freelancers. Subject matter of submission is of paramount concern for us rather than writing style. Articles and stories showing the similarity in the lives of people with different racial backgrounds are desired.''

$ $ AMBASSADOR MAGAZINE

National Italian American Foundation, 1860-19 St. NW, Washington DC 20009. (202)387-0600. Fax: (202)387-0800. E-mail: kevin@niaf.org. Website: www.niaf.org. **Contact:** Kevin Heitz. **40% freelance written.** Magazine for Italian-Americans covering Italian-American history and culture. ''We publish nonfiction articles on little-known events in Italian-American history and articles on Italian-American culture, traditions, and personalities living and dead.'' Estab. 1989. Circ. 25,000. Pays on approval of final draft. Byline given. Offers $100 kill fee. Buys second serial (reprint) rights. Editorial lead time 3 months. Accepts queries by mail, e-mail, fax. Accepts previously published material. Accepts simultaneous submissions. Responds in 1 month to queries. Sample copy and writer's guidelines free.

Nonfiction Historical/nostalgic, interview/profile, personal experience, photo feature. **Buys 12 mss/year.** Send complete ms. Length: 1,500-2,000 words. **Pays $250.**

Photos Send photos with submission. Reviews contact sheets, prints. Buys one-time rights. Offers no additional payment for photos accepted with ms. Captions, identification of subjects required.

Tips ''Good photos, clear prose, and a good storytelling ability are all prerequisites.''

$ $ $ B'NAI B'RITH MAGAZINE

(formerly *The B'nai B'rith IJM*), B'nai B'rith International, 2020 K St. NW, Washington DC 20006. (202)857-2708. Fax: (202)857-2781. E-mail: ijm@bnaibrith.org. Website: bbinet.org. **Contact:** Elana Harris, managing editor. **90% freelance written.** Quarterly magazine ''specializing in social, political, historical, religious, cultural, 'lifestyle,' and service articles relating chiefly to the Jewish communities of North America and Israel. Write for the American Jewish audience, i.e., write about topics from a Jewish perspective, highlighting creativity and innovation in Jewish life.'' Estab. 1886. Circ. 110,000. Pays on publication. Publishes ms an average of 6 months after acceptance. Byline given. Offers 25% kill fee. Buys first rights. Editorial lead time 3 months. Submit seasonal material 5 months in advance. Accepts queries by mail, e-mail, fax. Accepts simultaneous submissions. Responds in 1 month to queries; 6 weeks to mss. Sample copy for $2. Writer's guidelines for #10 SASE or by e-mail.

Nonfiction General interest pieces of relevance to the Jewish community of US and abroad. Interview/profile, photo feature, religious, travel. ''No Holocaust memoirs, first-person essays/memoirs, fiction, or poetry.'' **Buys 14-20 mss/year.** Query with published clips. Length: 1,000-2,500 words. **Pays $300-800 for assigned articles; $300-700 for unsolicited articles.** Sometimes pays expenses of writers on assignment.

Photos ''Rarely assigned.'' Buys one-time rights.

Columns/Departments Up Front (book, CD reviews, small/short items with Jewish interest), 150-200 words. **Buys 3 mss/year.** Query. **Pays $50.**

Tips ''Know what's going on in the Jewish world. Look at other Jewish publications also. Writers should submit clips with their queries. Read our guidelines carefully and present a good idea expressed well. Proofread your query letter.''

$ ⊡ CELTIC HERITAGE

Clansman Publishing, Ltd., P.O. Box 8805, Station A, Halifax NS B3K 5M4, Canada. (902)835-6244. Fax: (902)835-0080. E-mail: celtic@hfx.eastlink.ca. Website: www.celticheritage.ns.ca. **Contact:** Alexa Thompson, managing editor. **95% freelance written.** Bimonthly magazine covering culture of North Americans of Celtic descent. ''The magazine chronicles the stories of Celtish people who have settled in North America, with a focus on the stories of those who are not mentioned in history books. We also feature Gaelic language articles, history of Celtic people, traditions, music, and folklore. We profile Celtic musicians and include reviews of Celtic books, music, and videos.'' Estab. 1987. Circ. 8,000 (per issue). Pays on publication. Publishes ms an average of 2 months after acceptance. Byline given. Buys all rights. Editorial lead time 2 months. Submit seasonal material 3 months in advance. Accepts queries by mail, e-mail, fax, phone. Accepts previously published material. Responds in 1 week to queries; 1 month to mss. Sample copy for free. Writer's guidelines online.

Nonfiction Essays, general interest, historical/nostalgic, interview/profile, opinion, personal experience, travel, Gaelic language, Celtic music reviews, profiles of Celtic musicians, Celtic history, traditions, and folklore. No fiction, poetry, historical stories already well publicized. **Buys 100 mss/year.** Query or send complete ms.

Length: 800-2,500 words. **Pays $50-75 (Canadian). All writers receive a complimentary subscription.** "We have, on rare occasion, run an advertisement for a writer in lieu of payment."

Photos State availability with submission. Reviews 35mm transparencies, 5×7 prints, GIF/JPEG files (200 dpi). Buys one-time rights. Negotiates payment individually. Captions, identification of subjects, model releases required.

Columns/Departments "We do not have specific columns/departments. Suggest writers send query first if interested in developing a column." Length: 800-2,500 words. Query. **Pays $50-75 (Canadian).**

Fillers Anecdotes, facts. **Buys 2-3/year.** Length: 300-500 words. **Pays $30-50 (canadian).**

Tips "The easiest way to get my attention is to submit a query by e-mail. We are so short staffed that we do not have much time to start a correspondence by regular post."

CONGRESS MONTHLY

American Jewish Congress, 15 E. 84th St., New York NY 10028. (212)879-4500. **Contact:** Rochelle Mancini, managing editor. **90% freelance written.** Bimonthly magazine. "*Congress Monthly*'s readership is popular, but well-informed; the magazine covers political, social, economic, and cultural issues of concern to the Jewish community in general and to the American Jewish Congress in particular." Estab. 1933. Circ. 35,000. Pays on publication. Publishes ms an average of 3 months after acceptance. Byline given. Buys one-time rights. Submit seasonal material 2 months in advance. Responds in 2 months to queries.

Nonfiction General interest ("current topical issues geared toward our audience"). Travel, book, film, and theater reviews. No technical material. Query. Length: 1,000-2,500 words. **Pays amount determined by article length and author experience.**

Photos State availability with submission. Reviews b&w prints.

$ FILIPINAS

A Magazine for All Filipinos, Filipinas Publishing, Inc., 1486 Huntington Ave., Suite 300, South San Francisco CA 94080. (650)872-8650. Fax: (650)872-8651. E-mail: editorial@filipinasmag.com. Website: www.filipinasmag.com. **Contact:** Mona Lisa Yuchengco, editor/publisher. Monthly magazine focused on Filipino-American affairs. "*Filipinas* answers the lack of mainstream media coverage of Filipinos in America. It targets both Filipino immigrants and American-born Filipinos, gives in-depth coverage of political, social, cultural events in the Philippines and in the Filipino-American community. Features role models, history, travel, food and leisure, issues, and controversies." Estab. 1992. Circ. 40,000. Pays on publication. Publishes ms an average of 5 months after acceptance. Byline given. Offers $10 kill fee. Buys first, all rights. Editorial lead time 2 months. Submit seasonal material 4 months in advance. Accepts queries by mail, e-mail, fax. Responds in 3 weeks to queries; 5 months to mss. Writer's guidelines for 9½×4 SASE or on website.

> O→ Break in with "a good idea outlined well in the query letter. Also, tenacity is key. If one idea is shot down, come up with another."

Nonfiction Interested in seeing "more issue-oriented pieces, unusual topics regarding Filipino-Americans and stories from the Midwest and other parts of the country other than the coasts." Exposé, general interest, historical/nostalgic, inspirational, interview/profile, opinion, personal experience, travel. No academic papers. **Buys 80-100 mss/year.** Query with published clips. Length: 800-1,500 words. **Pays $50-75.**

Photos State availability with submission. Reviews 2¼×2¼ and 4×5 transparencies. Buys one-time rights. Offers $15-35/photo. Captions, identification of subjects required.

Columns/Departments Cultural Currents (Filipino traditions, beliefs), 1,500 words. Query with published clips. Pays $50-75.

$ $ GERMAN LIFE

Zeitgeist Publishing, Inc., 1068 National Hwy., LaVale MD 21502. (301)729-6190. Fax: (301)729-1720. E-mail: mslider@germanlife.com. Website: www.germanlife.com. **Contact:** Mark Slider, editor. **50% freelance written.** Bimonthly magazine covering German-speaking Europe. "*German Life* is for all interested in the diversity of German-speaking culture, past and present, and in the various ways that the United States (and North America in general) has been shaped by its German immigrants. The magazine is dedicated to solid reporting on cultural, historical, social, and political events." Estab. 1994. Circ. 40,000. Pays on publication. Byline given. Buys first North American serial rights. Editorial lead time 4 months. Submit seasonal material 6 months in advance. Accepts queries by mail, e-mail. Responds in 2 months to queries; 3 months to mss. Sample copy for $4.95 and SAE with 4 first-class stamps. Writer's guidelines online.

Nonfiction General interest, historical/nostalgic, interview/profile, photo feature, travel. Special issues: Oktoberfest-related (October); Seasonal Relative to Germany, Switzerland, or Austria (December); Travel to German-speaking Europe (April). **Buys 50 mss/year.** Query with published clips. Length: 800-1,500 words. **Pays $200-500 for assigned articles; $200-350 for unsolicited articles.**

Photos State availability with submission. Reviews color transparencies, 5×7 color or b&w prints. Buys one-time rights. Offers no additional payment for photos accepted with ms. Identification of subjects required.

Columns/Departments German-Americana (regards specific German-American communities, organizations, and/or events past or present), 1,200 words; Profile (portrays prominent Germans, Americans, or German-Americans), 1,000 words; At Home (cuisine, etc. relating to German-speaking Europe), 800 words; Library (reviews of books, videos, CDs, etc.), 300 words. **Buys 30 mss/year.** Query with published clips. **Pays $50-150.**

Fillers Facts, newsbreaks. Length: 100-300 words. **Pays $50-150.**

Tips "The best queries include several informative proposals. Writers should avoid overemphasizing autobiographical experiences/stories."

$HERITAGE FLORIDA JEWISH NEWS

207 O'Brien Rd., Suite 101, Fern Park FL 32730. (407)834-8787. E-mail: heritagefl@aol.com. Website: www.heritagefl.com. **20% freelance written.** Weekly tabloid on Jewish subjects of local, national and international scope, except for special issues. "Covers news of local, national and international scope of interest to Jewish readers and not likely to be found in other publications." Estab. 1976. Circ. 3,500. Pays on publication. Byline given. Buys first North American serial, first, one-time, second serial (reprint), simultaneous rights. Submit seasonal material 3 months in advance. Accepts queries by mail, e-mail. Accepts previously published material. Responds in 1 month to queries. Sample copy for $1 and 9 × 12 SASE.

Nonfiction "Especially needs articles for these annual issues: Rosh Hashanah, Financial, Chanukah, Celebration (wedding and bar mitzvah), Passover, Health and Fitness, Education, Travel and Savvy Seniors. No ficion, poems, first-person experiences." General interest, interview/profile, opinion, photo feature, religious, travel. **Buys 50 mss/year.** Send complete ms. Length: 500-1,000 words. **Pays 50¢/column inch.**

Reprints Send ms with rights for sale noted.

Photos State availability with submission. Reviews 8 X 10 prints. Buys one-time rights. Offers $5/photo. Captions, identification of subjects required.

$HORIZONS

The Jewish Family Journal, Targum Press, 22700 W. Eleven Mile Rd., Southfield MI 48034. Fax: (888)298-9992. E-mail: horizons@netvision.net.il. Website: www.targum.com. Managing Editor: Moshe Dombey. **Contact:** Miriam Zakon, chief editor. **100% freelance written.** Quarterly magazine covering the Orthodox Jewish family. "We include fiction and nonfiction, memoirs, essays, historical, and informational articles, all of interest to the Orthodox Jew." Estab. 1994. Circ. 5,000. Pays 4-6 weeks after publication. Publishes ms an average of 6 months after acceptance. Byline given. Buys one-time rights. Editorial lead time 6 months. Submit seasonal material 8 months in advance. Accepts queries by mail, e-mail, fax. Accepts simultaneous submissions. Responds in 1 week to queries; 2 months to mss. Writer's guidelines available.

Nonfiction Essays, historical/nostalgic, humor, inspirational, interview/profile, opinion, personal experience, photo feature, travel. **Buys 150 mss/year.** Send complete ms. Length: 350-3,000 words. **Pays $5-150.**

Photos State availability with submission. Buys one-time rights. Offers no additional payment for photos accepted with ms.

Fiction Historical, humorous, mainstream, slice-of-life vignettes. Nothing not suitable to Orthodox Jewish values. **Buys 10-15 mss/year.** Send complete ms. Length: 300-3,000 words. **Pays $20-100.**

Poetry Free verse, haiku, light verse, traditional. **Buys 30-35 poems/year.** Submit maximum 4 poems. Length: 3-28 lines. **Pays $5-10.**

Fillers Anecdotes, short humor. **Buys 20/year.** Length: 50-120 words. **Pays $5.**

Tips "*Horizons* publishes for the Orthodox Jewish market and therefore only accepts articles that are of interest to this market. We do not accept submissions dealing with political issues or Jewish legal issues. The tone is light and friendly and we therefore do not accept submissions that are of a scholarly nature. Our writers must be very familiar with our market. Anything that is not suitable for our readership doesn't stand a chance, no matter how high its literary merit."

$INTERNATIONAL EXAMINER

622 S. Washington, Seattle WA 98104. (206)624-3925. Fax: (206)624-3046. E-mail: editor@iexaminer.org. Website: www.iexaminer.org. **Contact:** Nhien Nguyen, managing editor. **75% freelance written.** Biweekly journal of Asian-American news, politics, and arts. "We write about Asian-American issues and things of interest to Asian-Americans. We do not want stuff about Asian things (stories on your trip to China, Japanese Tea Ceremony, etc. will be rejected). Yes, we are in English." Estab. 1974. Circ. 12,000. Pays on publication. Publishes ms an average of 1 month after acceptance. Buys one-time rights. Editorial lead time 1 month. Submit seasonal material 2 months in advance. Accepts simultaneous submissions. Writer's guidelines for #10 SASE.

Nonfiction Essays, exposé, general interest, historical/nostalgic, humor, interview/profile, opinion, personal experience, photo feature. **Buys 100 mss/year.** Query by mail, fax, or e-mail with published clips. Length: 750-

5,000 words depending on subject. **Pays $25-100.** Sometimes pays expenses of writers on assignment.

Reprints Accepts previously published submissions (as long as not published in same area). Send typed ms with rights for sale noted and information about when and where the material previously appeared. Payment negotiable.

Photos State availability with submission. Reviews contact sheets. Buys one-time rights. Negotiates payment individually. Captions, identification of subjects required.

Fiction Asian-American authored fiction by or about Asian-Americans. Novel excerpts. **Buys 1-2 mss/year.** Query.

Tips "Write decent, suitable material on a subject of interest to Asian-American community. All submissions are reviewed; all good ones are contacted. It helps to call and run idea by editor before or after sending submissions."

$ $ ITALIAN AMERICA

Official Publication of the Order Sons of Italy in America, Order Sons of Italy in America, 219 E St. NE, Washington DC 20002. (202)547-2900. Fax: (202)546-8168. E-mail: nationaloffice@osia.org. Website: www.osia.org. **Contact:** Dr. Dona De Sanctis, editor/deputy executive director. **20% freelance written.** Quarterly magazine. "*Italian America* provides timely information about OSIA, while reporting on individuals, institutions, issues, and events of current or historical significance in the Italian-American community." Estab. 1996. Circ. 65,000. Pays on publication. Publishes ms an average of 3 months after acceptance. Byline given. Offers 50% kill fee. Buys worldwide nonexclusive rights. Editorial lead time 3 months. Accepts queries by mail, e-mail, fax. Accepts simultaneous submissions. Sample copy for free. Writer's guidelines online.

Nonfiction Historical (little known historical facts that must relate to Italian Americans), interview/profile, opinion, current events. **Buys 10 mss/year.** Query with published clips. Length: 1,000-1,200 words. **Pays $50-250.**

Tips "We pay particular attention to the quality of graphics that accompany the stories. We are interested in little known facts about historical/cultural Italian America."

$ $ JEWISH ACTION

Union of Orthodox Jewish Congregations of America, 11 Broadway, New York NY 10004. (212)613-8146. Fax: (212)613-0646. E-mail: ja@ou.org. Website: www.ou.org. Editor: Nechama Carmel. **Contact:** Diane Chabbott, assistant editor. **80% freelance written.** Quarterly magazine covering a vibrant approach to Jewish issues, Orthodox lifestyle, and values. Circ. 40,000. Pays 2 months after publication. Byline given. Not copyrighted. Submit seasonal material 4 months in advance. Responds in 3 months to queries. Sample copy online. Writer's guidelines for #10 SASE or by e-mail.

● Prefers queries by e-mail. Mail and fax OK.

O→ Break in with a query for "Just Between Us" column.

Nonfiction Current Jewish issues, history, biography, art, inspirational, humor, music, book reviews. "We are not looking for Holocaust accounts. We welcome essays about responses to personal or societal challenges." **Buys 30-40 mss/year.** Query with published clips. Length: 1,000-3,000 words. **Pays $100-400 for assigned articles; $75-150 for unsolicited articles.**

Photos Send photos with submission. Identification of subjects required.

Columns/Departments Just Between Us (personal opinion on current Jewish life and issues), 1,000 words. Buys 4 mss/year.

Fiction Must have relevance to Orthodox reader. Length: 1,000-2,000 words.

Poetry Buys limited number of poems/year. **Pays $25-75.**

Tips "Remember that your reader is well educated and has a strong commitment to Orthodox Judaism. Articles on the holidays, Israel, and other common topics should offer a fresh insight. Because the magazine is a quarterly, we do not generally publish articles which concern specific timely events."

$ KHABAR

The Community Magazine, Khabar, Inc., 3790 Holcomb Bridge Rd., Suite 101, Norcross GA 30092. (770)451-3067. Fax: (770)234-6115. E-mail: editor@khabar.com. Website: www.khabar.com. **Contact:** Parthiv N. Parekh, editor. **50% freelance written.** Monthly magazine covering the Asian and Indian community in Georgia. "Content relating to Indian-American and/or immigrant experience." Estab. 1992. Circ. 14,000. Pays on publication. Publishes ms an average of 2 months after acceptance. Offers 35% kill fee. Buys one-time, second serial (reprint), simultaneous, electronic rights. Editorial lead time 2 months. Submit seasonal material 2 months in advance. Accepts queries by mail, e-mail. Accepts previously published material. Accepts simultaneous submissions. Sample copy for free. Writer's guidelines free or by e-mail.

Nonfiction Essays, interview/profile, opinion, personal experience, travel. **Buys 5 mss/year.** Query with or without published clips or send complete ms. Length: 750-4,000 words. **Pays $50-125 for assigned articles; $25-100 for unsolicited articles.**

Reprints Accepts previously published submissions.

Photos State availability of or send photos with submission. Negotiates payment individually. Captions, identification of subjects required.

Columns/Departments Book Review, 1,200 words; Music Review, 800 words; Spotlight (profiles), 1,200-3,000 words. All columns must feature Indian or Asian Americans. **Buys 5 mss/year.** Query with or without published clips or send complete ms. **Pays $25-100.**

Fiction Ethnic. **Buys 5 mss/year.** Query with or without published clips or send complete ms. **Pays $25-100.**

Tips "Ask for our 'content guidelines' document by e-mail or otherwise by writing to us."

$ $ $ $ LATINA MAGAZINE

Latina Media Ventures, 1500 Broadway, 7th Floor, New York NY 10036. (212)642-0200. E-mail: editor@latina.com. Website: www.latina.com. **40-50% freelance written.** Monthly magazine covering Latina lifestyle. "*Latina Magazine* is the leading bilingual lifestyle publication for Hispanic women in the United States today. Covering the best of Latino fashion, beauty, culture, and food, the magazine also features celebrity profiles and interviews." Estab. 1996. Circ. 250,000. Pays on publication. Publishes ms an average of 2-3 months after acceptance. Byline given. Offers 25% kill fee. Buys first, second serial (reprint), electronic rights. Editorial lead time 3 months. Submit seasonal material 4-5 months in advance. Accepts queries by e-mail. Responds in 1 month to queries; 1-2 months to mss. Sample copy online.

● Editors are in charge of their individual sections and pitches should be made directly to them. Do not make pitches directly to the editor-in-chief or the editorial director as they will only be routed to the relevant section editor. E-mail addresses for specific editors are listed next to the contact names in each section.

Nonfiction Essays, how-to, humor, inspirational, interview/profile, new product, personal experience. Special issues: The 10 Latinas Who Changed the World (December). "We do not feature an extensive amount of celebrity content or entertainment content, and freelancers should be sensitive to this. The magazine does not contain book or album reviews, and we do not write stories covering an artist's new project. We do not attend press junkets and do not cover press conferences. Please note that we are a lifestyle magazine, not an entertainment magazine." **Buys 15-20 mss/year.** Query with published clips. Length: 300-2,200 words. **Pays $1/word.** Pays expenses of writers on assignment.

Photos State availability with submission. Reviews contact sheets, transparencies, GIF/JPEG files. Buys one-time rights. Negotiates payment individually. Identification of subjects required.

Tips "*Latina*'s features cover a wide gamut of topics, including fashion, beauty, wellness, and personal essays. The magazine runs a wide variety of features on news and service topics (from the issues affecting Latina adolescents to stories dealin with anger). If you are going to make a pitch, please keep the following things in mind.All pitches should include statistics or some background reporting that demonstrates why a developing trend is important. Also, provide examples of women who can provide a personal perspective. Profiles and essays need to have a strong personal journey angle. We will not cover someone just because they are Hispanic. When pitching stories about a particular person, please let us know the following: timeliness (Is this someone who is somehow tied to breaking news events? Has their story been heard?); the 'wow' factor (Why is this person remarkable? What elements make this story a standout? What sets your subject apart from other women?); target our audience (please note that the magazine targets acculturated, English-dominant Latina women between the ages of 18-39)."

N $ $ $ MOMENT

The Magazine of Jewish Culture, Politics and Religion, 4710 41st St. NW, Washington DC 20016. (202)364-3300. Fax: (202)364-2636. E-mail: editor@momentmag.com. Website: www.momentmag.com. Publisher/Editor: Hershel Shanks. **90% freelance written.** Bimonthly magazine. "*Moment* is an independent Jewish bimonthly general interest magazine that specializes in cultural, political, historical, religious, and 'lifestyle' articles relating chiefly to the North American Jewish community and Israel." Estab. 1975. Circ. 65,000. Pays on publication. Publishes ms an average of 6 months after acceptance. Byline given. Buys first North American serial rights. Editorial lead time 3 months. Submit seasonal material 6 months in advance. Accepts queries by mail, e-mail, fax. Accepts simultaneous submissions. Responds in 1 month to queries; 3 months to mss. Sample copy for $4.50 and SAE. Writer's guidelines online.

Nonfiction "We look for meaty, colorful, thought-provoking features and essays on Jewish trends and Israel. We occasionally publish book excerpts, memoirs, and profiles." **Buys 25-30 mss/year.** Query with published clips. Length: 2,500-4,000 words. **Pays $200-1,200 for assigned articles; $40-500 for unsolicited articles.**

Photos State availability with submission. Buys one-time rights. Negotiates payment individually. Identification of subjects required.

Columns/Departments 5762—snappy pieces of not more than 250 words about quirky events in Jewish communities, news and ideas to improve Jewish living; Olam (The Jewish World)—first-person pieces, humor, and colorful reportage of 600-1,500 words; Book reviews (fiction and nonfiction) are accepted but generally assigned, 400-800 words. **Buys 30 mss/year.** Query with published clips. **Pays $50-250.**

Tips "Stories for *Moment* are usually assigned, but unsolicited manuscripts are often selected for publication. Successful features offer readers an in-depth journalistic treatment of an issue, phenomenon, institution, or individual. The more the writer can follow the principle of 'show, don't tell,' the better. The majority of the submissions we receive are about The Holocaust and Israel. A writer has a better chance of having an idea accepted if it is not on these subjects."

$ $ NA'AMAT WOMAN

Magazine of NA'AMAT USA, the Women's Labor Zionist Organization of America, NA'AMAT USA, 350 Fifth Ave., Suite 4700, New York NY 10118. (212)563-5222. Fax: (212)563-5710. **Contact:** Judith A. Sokoloff, editor. **80% freelance written.** Magazine published 4 times/year covering Jewish themes and issues, Israel, women's issues, and social and political issues. "Magazine covering a wide variety of subjects of interest to the Jewish community—including political and social issues, arts, profiles; many articles about Israel; and women's issues. Fiction must have a Jewish theme. Readers are the American Jewish community." Estab. 1926. Circ. 20,000. Pays on publication. Byline given. Buys first North American serial, first, one-time, second serial (reprint) rights, makes work-for-hire assignments. Accepts queries by mail, fax. Responds in 3 months to queries; 3 months to mss. Sample copy for 9×11½ SAE and $1.20 postage. Writer's guidelines for #10 SASE.

Nonfiction "All articles must be of particular interest to the Jewish community." Exposé, general interest (Jewish), historical/nostalgic, interview/profile, opinion, personal experience, photo feature, travel, art, music, social, and political issues, Israel. **Buys 20 mss/year.** Query with or without published clips or send complete ms. **Pays 10-15¢/word.**

Photos State availability with submission. Buys one-time rights. Pays $25-55 for 4×5 or 5×7 prints. Captions, identification of subjects required.

Columns/Departments Film and book reviews with Jewish themes. **Buys 20 mss/year.** Query with published clips or send complete ms. **Pays 10¢/word.**

Fiction "Intelligent fiction with Jewish slant. No maudlin nostalgia or trite humor." Ethnic, historical, humorous, novel excerpts, women-oriented. **Buys 3 mss/year.** Query with published clips or send complete ms. Length: 2,000-3,000 words. **Pays 10¢/word and 2 contributor's copies.**

$ $ NATIVE PEOPLES

(formerly *Native Peoples Magazine*), 5333 N. 7th St., Suite 224, Phoenix AZ 85012. (602)265-4855. Fax: (602)265-3113. E-mail: dgibson@nativepeoples.com. Website: www.nativepeoples.com. **Contact:** Daniel Gibson, editor. Bimonthly magazine covering Native Americans. "High-quality reproduction with full color throughout. The primary purpose of this magazine is to offer a sensitive portrayal of the arts and lifeways of Native peoples of the Americas." Estab. 1987. Circ. 50,000. Pays on publication. Byline given. Buys one-time rights. Accepts queries by mail, e-mail, fax. Responds in 2 months to queries. Writer's guidelines online.

Nonfiction Pathways (travel section) and Viewpoint (opinion) most open to freelancers. Looking for articles on educational, economic and political development; occasional historic pieces; Native events. Interview/profile (of interesting and leading Natives from all walks of life, with an emphasis on arts), personal experience. **Buys 35 mss/year.** Query with published clips. Length: 1,000-2,500 words. **Pays 25¢/word.**

Photos State availability with submission. Reviews transparencies, prefers 35mm slides. Also accepts high res electronic photo images, inquire for details. Buys one-time rights. Offers $45-150/page rates, $250/cover photos. Identification of subjects required.

Tips "We are focused upon authenticity and a positive portrayal of present-day Native American life and cultural practices. Our stories portray role models of Native people, young and old, with a sense of pride in their heritage and culture. Therefore, it is important that the Native American point of view be incorporated in each story."

$ $ RUSSIAN LIFE

RIS Publications, P.O. Box 567, Montpelier VT 05601. (802)223-4955. E-mail: info@rispubs.com. Website: www.rispubs.com. Editor: Lina Rozovskya. **Contact:** Paul Richardson, publisher. **75% freelance written.** Bimonthly magazine covering Russian culture, history, travel and business. "Our readers are informed Russophiles with an avid interest in all things Russian. But we do not publish personal travel journals or the like." Estab. 1956. Circ. 15,000. Pays on publication. Publishes ms an average of 2 months after acceptance. Byline given. Offers $25 kill fee. Buys first rights. Editorial lead time 2 months. Submit seasonal material 3 months in advance. Accepts queries by mail. Accepts previously published material. Responds in 1 month to queries. Sample copy for 9×12 SAE and 6 first-class stamps. Writer's guidelines online.

○┐ Break in with a "good travel essay piece covering remote regions of Russia."

Nonfiction General interest, photo feature, travel. No personal stories, i.e., "How I came to love Russia." **Buys 15-20 mss/year.** Query. Length: 1,000-6,000 words. **Pays $100-300.**

Reprints Accepts previously published submissions

Photos Send photos with submission. Reviews contact sheets. Buys one-time rights. Negotiates payment individually. Captions required.

■ The online magazine carries original content not found in the print editions.

Tips "A straightforward query letter with writing sample or manuscript (not returnable) enclosed."

$ $ SCANDINAVIAN REVIEW

The American-Scandinavian Foundation, 58 Park Ave., New York NY 10016. (212)879-9779. E-mail: editor@am scan.org. Website: www.amscan.org. **75% freelance written.** Triannual magazine for contemporary Scandinavia. Audience: Members, embassies, consulates, libraries. Slant: Popular coverage of contemporary affairs in Scandinavia. Estab. 1913. Circ. 4,000. Pays on publication. Publishes ms an average of 2 months after acceptance. Byline given. Buys first North American serial, second serial (reprint) rights. Editorial lead time 3 months. Submit seasonal material 3 months in advance. Accepts previously published material. Responds in 6 weeks to queries. Sample copy online. Writer's guidelines free.

Nonfiction General interest, interview/profile, photo feature, travel (must have Scandinavia as topic focus). Special issues: Scandinavian travel. No pornography. **Buys 30 mss/year.** Query with published clips. Length: 1,500-2,000 words. **Pays $300 maximum.**

Photos Reviews 3×5 transparencies, prints. Buys one-time rights. Pays $25-50/photo; negotiates payment individually. Captions required.

ℕ $ TODAY'S LATINO MAGAZINE

217 N. Broad St., Middletown DE 19709. (302)981-5131. Fax: (302)376-1129. E-mail: mdelgado@todayslatino.c om. Website: www.todayslatino.com. Managing Editor: Hector Correa. **Contact:** Milton Delgado, editor. **80% freelance written.** Quarterly magazine covering issues and stories affecting latinos. "We seek to inform, educate and entertain the upwardly mobile Latino and English speaking people interested in our rich culture and language." Estab. 2003. Circ. 5,000. Pays on publication. Publishes ms an average of 2 months after acceptance. Byline given. Buys one-time rights. Editorial lead time 1 month. Submit seasonal material 1 month in advance. Accepts queries by mail, e-mail, fax, phone. Accepts previously published material. Accepts simultaneous submissions. Sample copy for free. Writer's guidelines free.

Nonfiction Length: 500-1,500 words. **Pays $75-125.** Sometimes pays expenses of writers on assignment.

Photos Send photos with submission. Reviews GIF/JPEG files. Buys one-time rights. Pays $25-100. Captions, identification of subjects, model releases required.

Columns/Departments Politics; Celebrities; Travel, all 1,000 words. **Buys 10 mss/year.** Query with or without published clips. **Pays $75-125.**

Fiction Ethnic. Does not want vulgar, street urban. **Buys 1 mss/year.** Send complete ms.

Poetry Avant-garde, free verse, traditional. Does not want vulgar writing. **Buys 4 poems/year.** Submit maximum 4 poems. Length: 5-20 lines.

Fillers Anecdotes, facts, newsbreaks, short humor. **Buys 4/year.** Length: 500-750 words. **Pays $75-100.**

Tips "I really appreciate a professional writer who can write in English and Spanish, and whose style would be attractive for the professional Latino."

UPSCALE MAGAZINE

Bronner Brothers, 600 Bronner Brothers Way, Atlanta GA 30310. (404)758-7467. Fax: (404)755-9892. Website: www.upscalemagazine.com. **Contact:** Joyce E. Davis, senior editor. Monthly magazine covering topics for "upscale African-American/black interests. *Upscale* offers to take the reader to the 'next level' of life's experience. Written for the black reader and consumer, *Upscale* provides information in the realms of business, news, lifestyle, fashion and beauty, and arts and entertainment." Estab. 1989. Circ. 250,000. Pays on publication. Publishes ms an average of 4 months after acceptance. Byline given. Offers 25% kill fee. Buys first North American serial rights. Editorial lead time 3-4 months. Accepts queries by mail. Accepts simultaneous submissions. Responds in 1 month to queries; 2 months to mss. Sample copy online. Writer's guidelines online.

Photos State availability with submission. Negotiates payment individually. Captions, identification of subjects, model releases required.

Columns/Departments Constance Clemons, office manager. News & Business (factual, current); Lifestyle (travel, home, wellness, etc.); Beauty & Fashion (tips, trends, upscale fashion, hair); and Arts & Entertainment (artwork, black celebrities, entertainment). **Buys 6-10 mss/year.** Query with published clips. **Payment different for each department.**

Tips "Make queries informative and exciting. Include entertaining clips. Be familiar with issues affecting black readers. Be able to write about them with ease and intelligence."

N $⊠ WINDSPEAKER

Aboriginal Multi-Media Society of Alberta, 13245-146 St., Edmonton AB T5L 4S8, Canada. (800)661-5469. Fax: (780)455-7639. E-mail: edwind@ammsa.com. Website: www.ammsa.com. **Contact:** Debora Steel, editor-in-chief. **25% freelance written.** Monthly tabloid covering native issues. "Focus on events and issues that affect and interest native peoples, national or local." Estab. 1983. Circ. 27,000. Pays on publication. Publishes ms an average of 1 month after acceptance. Byline given. Offers kill fee. Buys first rights. Editorial lead time 1 month. Submit seasonal material 2 months in advance. Accepts queries by mail, e-mail, phone. Accepts simultaneous submissions. Sample copy for free. Writer's guidelines online.

Nonfiction Interview/profile, opinion, photo feature, travel, Reviews: books, music, movies. Special issues: Powwow (June); Travel supplement (May). **Buys 200 mss/year.** Query with published clips and SASE or by phone. Length: 500-800 words. **Pays $3-3.60/published inch.** Sometimes pays expenses of writers on assignment.

Photos Send photos with submission. Buys one-time rights. Offers $25-100/photo. Will pay for film and processing. Identification of subjects required.

Tips "Knowledge of Aboriginal culture and political issues is a great asset."

FOOD & DRINK

$ $ $ $ BON APPETIT

America's Food and Entertaining Magazine, Conde Nast Publications, Inc., 6300 Wilshire Blvd., 10th Floor, Los Angeles CA 90048. (323)965-3600. Fax: (323)937-1206. Website: www.bonappetit.com. Editor-in-Chief: Barbara Fairchild. Senior Editor: Hugh Garvey. **Contact:** Victoria von Biel, executive editor. **50% freelance written.** Monthly magazine covering fine food, restaurants, and home entertaining. "*Bon Appetit* readers are upscale food enthusiasts and sophisticated travelers. They eat out often and entertain 4-6 times a month." Estab. 1975. Circ. 1,300,000. **Pays on acceptance.** Byline given. Buys all rights. Submit seasonal material 1 year in advance. Accepts queries by mail. Responds in 6 weeks to queries. Writer's guidelines for #10 SASE.

Nonfiction Travel (food-related), food feature, personal essays. "No cartoons, quizzes, poetry, historic food features, or obscure food subjects." **Buys 50 mss/year.** Query with published clips. No phone calls or e-mails. Length: 150-2,000 words. **Pays $100-2,000.** Pays expenses of writers on assignment.

Photos Never send photos.

Tips "We are not generally interested in receiving specific queries, but we do look for new good writers. They must have a good knowledge of *Bon Appetit* and the related topics of food and entertaining (as shown in accompanying clips). A light, lively style is a plus. Nothing long and pedantic, please."

N ⊘ COOK'S ILLUSTRATED

Boston Common Press, 17 Station St., Brookline MA 02445-7995. (617)232-1000. Fax: (617)232-1572. E-mail: cooks@bcpress.com. Website: cooksillustrated.com. Bimonthly magazine. Circ. 500,000.

• Does not buy freelance material or use freelance writers.

N ⊘ COOKING LIGHT

Southern Progress Corp., P.O. Box 1748, Birmingham AL 35201-1748. (205)445-6000. Fax: (205)445-6600. E-mail: cookinglight@spc.com. Website: www.cookinglight.com. Monthly magazine. Circ. 1,500,000.

• Does not buy freelance material or use freelance writers.

N ⊘ FOOD & WINE

American Express Publishing Corp., 1120 Avenue of the Americas, 9th Floor, New York NY 10036. (212)382-5600. Fax: (212)764-2177. E-mail: food&wine@axepub.com. Website: www.foodandwine.com. Monthly magazine. Designed for the reader who enjoys the finer things in life, editorial focuses on upscale dining, covering resturants, entertaining at home and travel destinations. Circ. 964,000. Editorial lead time 6 months. Sample copy not available.

• Does not buy freelance material or use freelance writers.

N $ $ HOME COOKING

House of White Birches, 306 E. Parr Rd., Berne IN 46711. (260)589-4000 ext. 396. Fax: (260)589-8093. E-mail: editor@homecookingmagazine.com. Website: www.homecookingmagazine.com. Project Supervisor: Barb Sprunger. **Contact:** Shelly Vaughan James, editor. **35% freelance written.** Bimonthly magazine. Circ. 58,000. Pays within 45 days after acceptance. Publishes ms an average of 4 months after acceptance. Byline given. Buys all rights. Editorial lead time 6 months. Submit seasonal material 6 months in advance. Accepts queries by mail, e-mail. Accepts simultaneous submissions. Responds in 1 month to queries. Sample copy for 6×9 SAE and 5 first-class stamps.

Nonfiction How-to, humor, personal experience, recipes, all in food/cooking area. No health/fitness or travel articles. **Buys 36 mss/year.** Query or send complete manuscript. Length: 250-750 words plus 6-8 recipes. **Pays $25-250 for assigned articles; $25-200 for unsolicited articles.**

Columns/Departments Pinch of Sage (hints for the home cook), 200-500 words; Kitchen Know-How, 250-1,000 words. **Buys 12 mss/year.** Query or send complete manuscript. **Pays $25-200.**

Tips "You must request our writer's guidelines and editorial calendar for issue themes. We will gladly e-mail or mail them to you. Please follow our guidelines and schedule for all submissions."

$ $ PRIMO RISTORANTE

Foley Publishing, P.O. Box 73, Liberty Corner NJ 07938. (908)766-6006. Fax: (908)766-6607. E-mail: info@primo ristorante.com. Website: www.primoristorante.com. **Contact:** Raymond Foley, publisher or Jaclyn Foley, editor. **75% freelance written.** Bimonthly magazine covering "Italian anything!" *"Primo Ristorante—The magazine for the Italian Connoisseur.* For Italian restaurants and those who love Italian food, travel, wine and all things Italian!" Estab. 1994. Circ. 40,000. Pays on publication. Publishes ms an average of 3 months after acceptance. Byline sometimes given. Buys first North American serial, one-time rights. Editorial lead time 3 months. Submit seasonal material 3 months in advance. Accepts previously published material. Responds in 1 month to queries; 2 months to mss. Sample copy and writer's guidelines for 9×12 SAE and 4 first-class stamps.

Nonfiction Book excerpts, general interest, historical/nostalgic, how-to (prepare Italian foods), humor, new product, opinion, personal experience, travel. **Buys 25 mss/year.** Send complete ms. Length: 100-1,000 words. **Pays $100-350 for assigned articles; $75-300 for unsolicited articles.** Sometimes pays expenses of writers on assignment.

Reprints Send tearsheet or photocopy and information about when and where the material previously appeared. Pays 25% of amount paid for an original article.

Photos Send photos with submission. Reviews 3×5 prints. Buys one-time rights. Negotiates payment individually. Captions, model releases required.

Columns/Departments Send complete ms. **Pays $50-200.**

Fillers Anecdotes, facts, short humor. **Buys 10/year. Pays $10-50.**

$ $ WINE PRESS NORTHWEST

Tri-City Herald, 107 N. Cascade St., Kennewick WA 99336. (509)582-1564. Fax: (509)582-7221. E-mail: editor@ winepressnw.com. Website: www.winepressnw.com. Associate Editor: Eric Degerman. **Contact:** Andy Perdue, editor. **50% freelance written.** Quarterly magazine covering Pacific Northwest wine (Washington, Oregon, British Columbia, Idaho). "We focus narrowly on Pacific Northwest wine. If we write about travel, it's where to go to drink NW wine. If we write about food, it's what goes with NW wine. No beer, no spirits." Estab. 1998. Circ. 12,000. Pays on publication. Publishes ms an average of 3 months after acceptance. Byline given. Offers 20% kill fee. Buys first North American serial, electronic rights. Editorial lead time 3 months. Submit seasonal material 3 months in advance. Accepts queries by mail, e-mail, fax. Accepts simultaneous submissions. Responds in 1 month to queries. Sample copy free or online. Writer's guidelines free.

Nonfiction General interest, historical/nostalgic, interview/profile, new product, photo feature, travel. No "beer, spirits, non-NW (California wine, etc.)" **Buys 30 mss/year.** Query with published clips. Length: 1,500-2,500 words. **Pays $300.** Sometimes pays expenses of writers on assignment.

Photos State availability with submission. Reviews contact sheets. Buys one-time rights. Negotiates payment individually. Identification of subjects required.

The online magazine carries original content not found in the print edition. Contact: Andy Perdue, online editor.

Tips "Writers must be familiar with *Wine Press Northwest* and should have a passion for the region, its wines, and cuisine."

$ $ $ WINE SPECTATOR

M. Shanken Communications, Inc., 387 Park Ave. S., 8th Floor, New York NY 10016. (212)481-8610. Fax: (212)684-5424. E-mail: winespec@mshanken.com. Website: www.winespectator.com. **Contact:** Thomas Matthews, executive editor. **20% freelance written.** Prefers to work with published/established writers. Biweekly news magazine. Estab. 1976. Circ. 350,000. Pays within 30 days of publication. Publishes ms an average of 2 months after acceptance. Byline given. Buys all rights, makes work-for-hire assignments. Submit seasonal material 4 months in advance. Accepts queries by mail, fax. Responds in 3 months to queries. Sample copy for $5. Writer's guidelines for #10 SASE.

Nonfiction General interest (news about wine or wine events), interview/profile (of wine, vintners, wineries), opinion, photo feature, travel, dining and other lifestyle pieces. No "winery promotional pieces or articles by writers who lack sufficient knowledge to write below just surface data." Query. Length: 100-2,000 words. **Pays $100-1,000.**

Photos Send photos with submission. Buys all rights. Pays $75 minimum for color transparencies. Captions, identification of subjects, model releases required.

■ The online magazine carries original content not found in the print edition. Contact: Dana Nigro, news editor.

Tips "A solid knowledge of wine is a must. Query letters essential, detailing the story idea. New, refreshing ideas which have not been covered before stand a good chance of acceptance. *Wine Spectator* is a consumer-oriented news magazine, but we are interested in some trade stories; brevity is essential."

GAMES & PUZZLES

$THE BRIDGE BULLETIN

American Contract Bridge League, 2990 Airways Blvd., Memphis TN 38116-3847. (901)332-5586, ext. 1291. Fax: (901)398-7754. E-mail: editor@acbl.org. Website: www.acbl.org. Managing Editor: Paul Linxwiler. **Contact:** Brent Manley, editor. **20% freelance written.** Monthly magazine covering duplicate (tournament) bridge. Estab. 1938. Circ. 155,000. Pays on publication. Publishes ms an average of 3 months after acceptance. Byline given. Buys first, second serial (reprint) rights. Editorial lead time 2 months. Accepts queries by mail, e-mail. Accepts previously published material. Accepts simultaneous submissions.

○━ Break in with a "humorous piece about bridge."

Nonfiction Book excerpts, essays, how-to (play better bridge), humor, interview/profile, new product, personal experience, photo feature, technical, travel. **Buys 6 mss/year.** Query. Length: 500-2,000 words. **Pays $100/ page.**

Photos Color required. State availability with submission. Buys all rights. Negotiates payment individually. Identification of subjects required.

Tips "Articles must relate to contract bridge in some way. Cartoons on bridge welcome."

$ $CHESS LIFE

United States Chess Federation, 3054 US Route 9W, New Windsor NY 12553-7698. (845)562-8350, ext. 152. Fax: (845)236-4852. E-mail: editor@uschess.org. Website: www.uschess.org. **Contact:** Kalev Pehme, editor. **15% freelance written.** Works with a small number of new/unpublished writers/year. Monthly magazine. "*Chess Life* is the official publication of the United States Chess Federation, covering news of most major chess events, both here and abroad, with special emphasis on the triumphs and exploits of American players." Estab. 1939. Circ. 70,000. Publishes ms an average of 8 months after acceptance. Byline given. Buys first rights. Submit seasonal material 8 months in advance. Accepts queries by mail, e-mail, fax, phone. Accepts simultaneous submissions. Responds in 3 months to mss. Sample copy and writer's guidelines for 9×11 SAE with 5 first-class stamps.

Nonfiction All must have some relation to chess. General interest, historical/nostalgic, humor, interview/profile (of a famous chess player or organizer), photo feature (chess centered), technical. No "stories about personal experiences with chess." **Buys 30-40 mss/year.** Query with samples if new to publication. Length: 3,000 words maximum. **Pays $100/page (800-1,000 words).** Sometimes pays expenses of writers on assignment.

Reprints Send tearsheet, photocopy or typed ms with rights for sale noted and information about when and where the material previously appeared.

Photos Reviews b&w contact sheets and prints, and color prints and slides. Buys all or negotiable rights. Pays $25-35 inside; $100-300 for covers. Captions, identification of subjects, model releases required.

Columns/Departments Chess Review (brief articles on unknown chess personalities) and "Chess in Everyday Life."

Fillers Submit with samples and clips. Buys first or negotiable rights to cartoons and puzzles. **Pays $25 upon acceptance.**

Tips "Articles must be written from an informed point of view—not from view of the curious amateur. Most of our writers are specialized in that they have sound credentials as chess players. Freelancers in major population areas (except New York and Los Angeles, which we already have covered) who are interested in short personality profiles and perhaps news reporting have the best opportunities. We're looking for more personality pieces on chess players around the country; not just the stars, but local masters, talented youths, and dedicated volunteers. Freelancers interested in such pieces might let us know of their interest and their range. Could be we know of an interesting story in their territory that needs covering. Examples of published articles include a locally produced chess television program, a meeting of chess set collectors from around the world, chess in our prisons, and chess in the works of several famous writers."

N $ $ $GAMES MAGAZINE

Games Publications, a division of Kappa Publishing Group, Inc., 7002 W. Butler Pike, Ambler PA 19002. (215)643-6385. Fax: (215)628-3571. E-mail: games@kappapublishing.com. **Contact:** R. Wayne Schmittberger, editor-in-chief. **50% freelance written.** Magazine published 10 times/year covering puzzles and games. *"Games is a magazine of puzzles, contests, and features pertaining to games and ingenuity. It is aimed primarily at adults and has an emphasis on pop culture."* Estab. 1977. Circ. 100,000. Pays on publication. Publishes ms an average of 4 months after acceptance. Byline given. Offers 25% kill fee. Buys first North American serial, first, one-time, second serial (reprint), all rights, makes work-for-hire assignments. Editorial lead time 3 months. Submit seasonal material 6 months in advance. Accepts queries by mail, e-mail. Accepts previously published material. Accepts simultaneous submissions. Responds in 6 weeks to queries; 3 months to mss. Sample copy for $5. Writer's guidelines for #10 SASE.

Nonfiction Photo feature, puzzles; games. **Buys 100 puzzles/year and 3 mss/year.** Query. Length: 1,500-2,500 words. **Pays $500-1,200.** Sometimes pays expenses of writers on assignment.

Photos State availability with submission. Reviews contact sheets, negatives, transparencies, prints. Buys one-time rights. Negotiates payment individually. Captions, identification of subjects, model releases required.

Columns/Departments Gamebits (game/puzzle news), 250 words; Games & Books (product reviews), 350 words; Wild Cards (short text puzzles), 100 words. **Buys 50 mss/year.** Query. **Pays $25-250.**

Fiction Adventure, mystery. **Buys 1-2 mss/year.** Query. Length: 1,500-2,500 words. **Pays $500-1,200.**

Tips "Look for real-life people, places, or things that might in some way be the basis for a puzzle."

N GIANT CROSSWORDS

Scrambl-Gram, Inc., Puzzle Buffs International, 41 Park Dr., Port Clinton OH 43452. (419)734-2600. **Contact:** S. Bowers, managing editor. **50% freelance written.** Eager to work with new/unpublished writers. Quarterly magazine with crossword puzzles and word games. Estab. 1970. **Pays on acceptance.** Publishes ms an average of 1 month after acceptance. Buys all rights. Responds in 1 month to queries.

Nonfiction Crosswords only. **Pays according to size of puzzle and/or clues.**

Tips "We are expanding our syndication of original crosswords and our publishing schedule to include new titles and extra issues of current puzzle books. Submit one sample of work with inquiry."

GAY & LESBIAN INTEREST

N $ $THE ADVOCATE

Liberation Publications, Inc., 6922 Hollywood Blvd., Suite 1000, Los Angeles CA Z90028-6148. (323)871-1225. Fax: (323)467-6805. E-mail: newsroom@advocate.com. Website: www.advocate.com. **Contact:** Bruce Steele, editor-in-chief. Biweekly magazine covering national news events with a gay and lesbian perspective on the issues. Estab. 1967. Circ. 100,000. Pays on publication. Byline given. Buys first North American serial rights. Responds in 1 month to queries. Sample copy for $3.95. Writer's guidelines for #10 SASE.

Nonfiction "Here are elements we look for in all articles: *Angling*: An angle is the one editorial tool we have to attract a reader's attention. An *Advocate* editor won't make an assignment unless he or she has worked out a very specific angle with you. Once you've worked out the angle with an editor, don't deviate from it without letting the editor know. Some of the elements we look for in angles are: a news hook; an open question or controversy; a 'why' or 'how' element or novel twist; national appeal; and tight focus. *Content*: Lesbian and gay news stories in all areas of life: arts, sciences, financial, medical, cyberspace, etc. *Tone*: Tone is the element that makes an emotional connection. Some characteristics we look for: toughness; edginess; fairness and even-handedness; multiple perspectives." Exposé, interview/profile, News reporting and investigating. Special issues: gays on campus, coming out interviews with celebrities, HIV and health. Query. Length: 1,200 words. **Pays $550.**

Columns/Departments Arts & Media (news and profiles of well-known gay or lesbians in entertainment) is most open to freelancers; 750 words. Query. **Pays $100-500.**

Fiction

Tips *"The Advocate* is a unique newsmagazine. While we report on gay and lesbian issues and are published by one of the country's oldest and most established gay-owned companies, we also play by the rules of main-stream-not gay-community-journalism."

$ECHO MAGAZINE

ACE Publishing, Inc., P.O. Box 16630, Phoenix AZ 85011-6630. (602)266-0550. Fax: (602)266-0773. E-mail: editor@echomag.com. Website: www.echomag.com. **Contact:** Buddy Early, managing editor. **30-40% freelance written.** Biweekly magazine covering gay and lesbian issues. *"Echo Magazine* is a newsmagazine for gay, lesbian, bisexual, and transgendered persons in the Phoenix metro area and throughout the state of Arizona.

Editorial content needs to be pro-gay, that is, supportive of GLBT equality in all areas of American life." Estab. 1989. Circ. 15,000-18,000. Pays on publication. Publishes ms an average of less than 1 month after acceptance. Byline given. Buys all rights. Editorial lead time 1-2 months. Submit seasonal material 1-2 months in advance. Accepts queries by e-mail. Responds in 2 weeks to queries; 1 month to mss. Sample copy online. Writer's guidelines by e-mail.

Nonfiction Book excerpts, essays, historical/nostalgic, humor, interview/profile, opinion, personal experience, photo feature, travel. Special issues: Pride Festival (April); Arts issue (August); Holiday Gift/Decor (December). No "articles on topics unrelated to our GLBT readers, or anything that is not pro-gay." **Buys 10-20 mss/year.** Query. Length: 500-2,000 words. **Pays $30-40.**

Photos State availability with submission. Reviews contact sheets, GIF/JPEG files. Buys all rights. Negotiates payment individually. Captions, identification of subjects, model releases required.

Columns/Departments Guest Commentary (opinion on GLBT issues), 500-1,000 words; Arts/Entertainment (profiles of GLBT or relevant celebrities, or arts issues), 800-1,500 words. **Buys 5-10 mss/year.** Query. **Pays $30-40.**

Tips "Know Phoenix (or other areas of Arizona) and its GLBT community. Please don't send nongay-related or nonpro-gay material. Research your topics thoroughly and write professionally. Our print content and online contenty are very similar."

$ $ GIRLFRIENDS MAGAZINE

Lesbian Culture, Politics, and Entertainment, 3415 Cèsar Châvez, Suite 101, San Francisco CA 94110. (415)648-9464. Fax: (415)648-4705. E-mail: editorial@girlfriendsmag.com. Website: www.girlfriendsmag.com. **Contact:** Mignon Freeman, managing editor. Monthly lesbian magazine. "*Girlfriends* provides its readers with intelligent, entertaining and visually pleasing coverage of culture, politics, and entertainment—all from an informed and critical lesbian perspective." Estab. 1994. Circ. 75,000. Pays on publication. Publishes ms an average of 6 months after acceptance. Byline given. Offers 50% kill fee. Buys first, use for advertising/promoting *girlfriends* rights. Editorial lead time 3 months. Submit seasonal material 6 months in advance. Accepts queries by mail, e-mail. Accepts simultaneous submissions. Responds in 3 weeks to queries; 2 months to mss. Sample copy for $4.95 plus $1.50 s/h or online. Writer's guidelines online.

• *Girlfriends* is not accepting fiction, poetry or fillers.

○┓ Break in by sending a letter detailing interests and story ideas, plus résumé and published samples.

Nonfiction Book excerpts, essays, exposé, historical/nostalgic, humor, interview/profile, new product, opinion, personal experience, photo feature, religious, technical, travel, investigative features. Special issues: Sex, music, bridal, sports and Hollywood issues, breast cancer issue. Special features: Best lesbian restaurants in the US; best places to live. **Buys 20-25 mss/year.** Query with published clips. Length: 1,000-3,500 words. **Pays 10-25¢/word.**

Reprints Send photocopy or typed ms with rights for sale noted and information about when and where the material previously appeared. Negotiable payment.

Photos Send photos with submission. Reviews contact sheets, 4×5 or 2¼ × 2¼ transparencies, prints. Buys one-time rights. Offers $30-250/photo. Captions, identification of subjects, model releases required.

Columns/Departments Book reviews, 900 words; Music reviews, 600 words; Travel, 600 words; Opinion pieces, 1,000 words; Humor, 600 words. Query with published clips. **Pays 15¢/word.**

Tips "Be unafraid of controversy—articles should focus on problems and debates raised in lesbian culture, politics, and sexuality. Avoid being 'politically correct.' We don't just want to know what's happening in the lesbian world, we want to know how what's happening in the world affects lesbians."

$ $ THE GUIDE

To Gay Travel, Entertainment, Politics, and Sex, Fidelity Publishing, P.O. Box 990593, Boston MA 02199-0593. (617)266-8557. Fax: (617)266-1125. E-mail: letters@guidemag.com. Website: www.guidemag.com. **25% freelance written.** Monthly magazine on the gay and lesbian community. Estab. 1981. Circ. 30,000. **Pays on acceptance.** Publishes ms an average of 2 months after acceptance. Offers negotiable kill fee. Buys first rights. Submit seasonal material 2 months in advance. Accepts queries by mail, e-mail. Accepts previously published material. Accepts simultaneous submissions. Responds in 3 months to queries. Sample copy for 9×12 SAE and 8 first-class stamps. Writer's guidelines for #10 SASE.

Nonfiction Book excerpts (if yet unpublished), essays, exposé, general interest, historical/nostalgic, humor, interview/profile, opinion, personal experience, photo feature, religious. **Buys 24 mss/year.** Query with or without published clips or send complete ms. Length: 500-5,000 words. **Pays $85-240.**

Reprints Occasionally buys previously published submissions. Pays 100% of amount paid for an original article.

Photos Send photos with submission. Reviews contact sheets. Buys one-time rights. Pays $15/image used. Captions, identification of subjects, model releases required.

Tips "Brevity, humor, and militancy appreciated. Writing on sex, political analysis, and humor are particularly appreciated. We purchase very few freelance travel pieces; those that we do buy are usually on less commercial destinations.''

$HX MAGAZINE

Two Queens, Inc., 230 W. 17th St., 8th Floor, New York NY 10011. (212)352-3535. Fax: (212)352-3596. E-mail: editor@hx.com. Website: www.hx.com. **Contact:** Trent Straube, editor. **25% freelance written.** Weekly magazine covering gay New York City nightlife and entertainment. Estab. 1991. Circ. 39,000. Pays on publication. Publishes ms an average of 1 month after acceptance. Byline given. Buys first North American serial, second serial (reprint), electronic rights. Editorial lead time 2 months. Submit seasonal material 2 months in advance. We must be exclusive East Coast publisher to accept. Only responds if interested to queries. Sample copy not available.

Nonfiction General interest, arts and entertainment; celebrity profiles; reviews. **Buys 50 mss/year.** Query with published clips. Length: 500-2,000 words. **Pays $50-150; $25-100 for unsolicited articles.**

Reprints Send tearsheet or photocopy with rights for sale noted and information about when and where the material previously appeared. Pays 50% of amount paid for an original article.

Photos State availability with submission. Reviews contact sheets, negatives, 8×10 prints. Buys one-time, reprint and electronic reprint rights. Captions, identification of subjects, model releases required.

Columns/Departments Buys 200 mss/year. Query with published clips. **Pays $25-125.**

$ $IN THE FAMILY

The Magazine for Queer People and Their Loved Ones, Family Magazine, Inc., 7850 N. Silverbell Rd., Suite 114-188, Tucson AZ 85743. (520)579-8043. E-mail: lmarkowitz@aol.com. Website: www.inthefamily.com. **Contact:** Laura Markowitz, editor. **20% freelance written.** Quarterly magazine covering lesbian, gay, transgender, and bisexual family relationships. ''Using the lens of psychotherapy, our magazine looks at the complexities of L/G/B/T family relationships as well as professional issues for L/G/B/T therapists.'' Estab. 1995. Circ. 3,000. Pays on publication. Publishes ms an average of 3 months after acceptance. Byline given. Offers 25% kill fee. Buys first rights. Editorial lead time 6 months. Submit seasonal material 4 months in advance. Responds in 1 month to queries; 3 months to mss. Sample copy for $6.50. Writer's guidelines online.

Nonfiction Essays, exposé, humor, opinion, personal experience, photo feature. ''No autobiography or erotica.'' **Buys 4 mss/year.** Length: 2,500-4,000 words. **Pays $100-300 for assigned articles; $35-150 for unsolicited articles.** Sometimes pays expenses of writers on assignment.

Photos State availability with submission. Reviews contact sheets. Buys one-time rights. Negotiates payment individually. Captions, identification of subjects, model releases required.

Columns/Departments Ellen Elgart, senior editor. Family Album (aspects of queer family life), 1,500 words; A Look at Research (relevant social science findings), 1,500 words; The Last Word (gentle humor), 800 words. **Buys 4 mss/year.** Send complete ms. **Pays $35-150.**

Fiction Helena Lipstadt, fiction editor. Ethnic, slice-of-life vignettes, family life theme for G/L/B/Ts. No erotica, science fiction, horror, romance, serialized novels, or westerns. **Buys 4 mss/year.** Send complete ms. Length: 1,000-2,500 words. **Pays $35-100.**

Poetry Helena Lipstadt, fiction editor. Avant-garde, free verse, haiku, light verse, traditional. **Buys 4 poems/year.** Submit maximum 6 poems. Length: 10-35 lines. **Pays $35.**

Tips ''*In the Family* takes an in-depth look at the complexities of lesbian, gay, transgender, and bisexual family relationships, including couples and intimacy, money, sex, extended family, parenting, and more. Readers include therapists of all sexual orientations as well as family members of lesbian, gay, and bisexuals, and also queer people who are interested in what therapists have to say about such themes as how to recover from a gay bashing; how to navigate single life; how to have a good divorce; how to understand bisexuality; how to come out to children; how to understand fringe sexual practices; how to reconcile homosexuality and religion. Therapists read it to learn the latest research about working with queer families, to learn from the regular case studies and clinical advice columns. Family members appreciate the multiple viewpoints in the magazine. We look for writers who know something about these issues and who have an engaging, intelligent, narrative style. We are allergic to therapy jargon and political rhetoric.''

$ $INSTINCT MAGAZINE

Instinct Publishing, 15335 Morrison St., Suite 325, Sherman Oaks CA 91403. (818)205-9033. Fax: (818)205-9093. E-mail: editor@instinctmag.com. Website: www.instinctmag.com. Editor: Parker Ray. **Contact:** Alexander Cho, associate editor. **60% freelance written.** Monthly magazine covering gay men's life and style issues. ''*Instinct* is a blend of *Cosmo* and *Maxim* for gay men. We're smart, sexy, irreverent, and more than a bit un-PC, a unique style that has made us the No. 1 gay men's magazine in the U.S.'' Estab. 1997. Circ. 60,000 + . Pays on publication. Byline given. Offers 20% kill fee. Buys all rights. Editorial lead time 2 months. Accepts queries by mail, e-mail, phone. Accepts simultaneous submissions. Sample copy online. Writer's guidelines online.

Nonfiction "Be inventive and specific—an article on 'dating' isn't saying much and will need a twist, for example." Exposé, general interest, humor, interview/profile, travel. Does not want first-person accounts or articles. Query with or without published clips. Length: 800-2,400 words. **Pays $150-300.** Sometimes pays expenses of writers on assignment.

Photos Buys all rights. Negotiates payment individually. Captions, identification of subjects, model releases required.

Columns/Departments Health (gay, off-kilter), 800 words; Fitness (irreverent), 500 words; Movies, Books (edgy, sardonic), 800 words; Music, Video Games (indie, underground), 800 words. **Pays $150-250.**

Tips "While *Instinct* publishes a wide variety of features and columns having to do with gay men's issues, we maintain our signature irreverent, edgy, un-PC tone throughout. When pitching stories (e-mail is preferred), be as specific as possible, and try to think beyond the normal scope of 'gay relationship' features. An article on 'Dating Tips,' for example, will not be considered, while an article on 'Tips on Dating Two Guys At Once' is more our slant. We rarely accept finished articles. We keep a special eye out for pitches on investigational/ exposé-type stories geared toward our audience."

$ $ $ METROSOURCE

MetroSource Publishing, Inc., 180 Varick St., 5th Floor, New York NY 10014. (212)691-5127. Fax: (212)741-2978. Website: www.metrosource.com. **70% freelance written.** Magazine published 5 times/year. "*MetroSource* is an upscale, glossy, 4-color lifestyle magazine targeted to an urban, professional gay and lesbian readership." Estab. 1990. Circ. 85,000. Pays on publication. Publishes ms an average of 2 months after acceptance. Byline given. Editorial lead time 3 months. Submit seasonal material 4 months in advance. Accepts queries by mail, e-mail, fax, phone. Accepts simultaneous submissions. Sample copy for $5.

Nonfiction Exposé, interview/profile, opinion, photo feature, travel. **Buys 20 mss/year.** Query with published clips. Length: 1,000-2,500 words. **Pays $100-900.**

Photos State availability with submission. Negotiates payment individually. Captions, model releases required.

Columns/Departments Book, film, television, and stage reviews; health columns; and personal diary and opinion pieces. Word lengths vary. Query with published clips. **Pays $200.**

OUT

245 W. 17th St., Suite 1200, New York NY 10011. (212)242-8100. Fax: (212)242-8338. E-mail: letters@out.com. Website: www.out.com. **Contact:** Department Editor. **80% freelance written.** Monthly national magazine covering gay and lesbian general-interest topics. "Our subjects range from current affairs to culture, from fitness to finance." Estab. 1992. Circ. 120,000. Pays on publication. Publishes ms an average of 3 months after acceptance. Byline given. Offers 25% kill fee. Buys first North American serial rights. second serial (reprint) rights for anthologies (additional fee paid) and 30-day reprint rights (additional fee paid if applicable) Editorial lead time 3 months. Submit seasonal material 5 months in advance. Accepts queries by mail. Accepts simultaneous submissions. Responds in 6 weeks to queries; 2 months to mss. Sample copy for $6. Writer's guidelines for #10 SASE.

Nonfiction Book excerpts, essays, exposé, general interest, historical/nostalgic, humor, interview/profile, new product, opinion, personal experience, photo feature, travel, fashion/lifestyle. **Buys 200 mss/year.** Query with published clips and SASE. Length: 50-1,500 words. **Pays variable rate.** Sometimes pays expenses of writers on assignment.

Photos State availability with submission. Reviews contact sheets, transparencies, prints. Buys one-time rights. Negotiates payment individually. Captions, identification of subjects, model releases required.

Tips "*Out*'s contributors include editors and writers from the country's top consumer titles: Skilled reporters, columnists, and writers with distinctive voices and specific expertise in the fields they cover. But while published clips and relevant experience are a must, the magazine also seeks out fresh, young voices. The best guide to the kind of stories we publish is to review our recent issues—is there a place for the story you have in mind? Be aware of our long lead time. No phone queries, please."

OUTSMART

Up & Out Communications, 3406 Audubon Place, Houston TX 77006. (713)520-7237. Fax: (713)522-3275. Website: www.outsmartmagazine.com. **70% freelance written.** Monthly magazine concerned with gay, lesbian, bisexual, and transgender issues. "*OutSmart* offers vibrant and thoughtful coverage of the stories that appeal most to an educated gay audience." Estab. 1994. Circ. 60,000. Pays on publication. Byline given. Buys one-time, simultaneous rights. Permission to publish on website. Editorial lead time 3 months. Submit seasonal material 4 months in advance. Accepts queries by mail, e-mail, fax. Accepts previously published material. Accepts simultaneous submissions. Responds in 6 weeks to queries; 2 months to mss. Sample copy and writer's guidelines online.

Nonfiction Historical/nostalgic, interview/profile, opinion, personal experience, photo feature, travel, health/

wellness; local/national news. **Buys 24 mss/year.** Send complete ms. Length: 450-2,000 words. **Negotiates payment individually.**

Reprints Send photocopy.

Photos State availability with submission. Reviews 4×6 prints. Buys one-time rights. Negotiates payment individually. Identification of subjects required.

■ The online magazine carries original content not found in the print edition and includes writer's guidelines.

Tips *"OutSmart* is a mainstream publication that covers culture, politics, personalities, entertainment, and health/wellness as well as local and national news and events. It is our goal to address the diversity of the lesbian, gay, bisexual, and transgender community, fostering understanding among all Houston's citizens."

$WISCONSIN IN STEP

In Step, Inc., 1661 N. Water St., Suite 411, Milwaukee WI 53202. (414)278-7840. Fax: (414)278-5868. E-mail: instepnews@aol.com. Website: www.instepnews.com. **30% freelance written.** Biweekly consumer tabloid for gay and lesbian readers. Estab. 1984. Circ. 15,000. Buys first North American serial, second serial (reprint) rights. Submit seasonal material 2 months in advance. Accepts queries by mail, e-mail. Accepts simultaneous submissions. Responds in 3 weeks to queries; 1 month to mss. Sample copy for $3. Writer's guidelines for #10 SASE.

Nonfiction Book excerpts, exposé, historical/nostalgic, interview/profile, new product, opinion, religious, travel. Query. Length: 500-2,000 words. **Pays $15-100.**

Photos State availability with submission. Reviews 5×7 prints. Buys one-time rights. Negotiates payment individually. Captions, identification of subjects, model releases required.

■ The online magazine carries original content not found in the print edition.

Tips "E-mail flawless copy samples to get my attention. Be patient."

GENERAL INTEREST

Ⓝ $ $ THE AMERICAN LEGION MAGAZINE

P.O. Box 1055, Indianapolis IN 46206-1055. (317)630-1200. Fax: (317)630-1280. E-mail: magazine@legion.org. Website: www.legion.org. Editorial Administrator: Patricia Marschand. **Contact:** John Raughter, editor. **70% freelance written.** Prefers to work with published/established writers, but works with a small number of new/unpublished writers each year. Monthly magazine. "Working through 15,000 community-level posts, the honorably discharged wartime veterans of The American Legion dedicate themselves to God, country and traditional American values. They believe in a strong defense; adequate and compassionate care for veterans and their families; community service; and the wholesome development of our nation's youth. We publish articles that reflect these values. We inform our readers and their families of significant trends and issues affecting our nation, the world and the way we live. Our major features focus on the American flag, national security, foreign affairs, business trends, social issues, health, education, ethics and the arts. We also publish selected general feature articles, articles of special interest to veterans, and question-and-answer interviews with prominent national and world figures." Estab. 1919. Circ. 2,800,000. **Pays on acceptance.** Publishes ms an average of 6 months after acceptance. Byline given. Buys first North American serial rights. Accepts queries by mail, e-mail, fax. Responds in 2 months to queries. Sample copy for $3.50 and 9×12 SAE with 6 first-class stamps. Writer's guidelines for #10 SASE.

Nonfiction Well-reported articles or expert commentaries cover issues/trends in world/national affairs, contemporary problems, general interest, sharply-focused feature subjects. Monthly Q&A with national figures/experts. General interest, interview/profile. No regional topics or promotion of partisan political agendas. No personal experiences or war stories. **Buys 50-60 mss/year.** Query with SASE should explain the subject or issue, article's angle and organization, writer's qualifications and experts to be interviewed. Length: 300-2,000 words. **Pays 40¢/word and up.**

Photos On assignment.

Tips "Queries by new writers should include clips/background/expertise; no longer than 1½ pages. Submit suitable material showing you have read several issues. *The American Legion Magazine* considers itself 'the magazine for a strong America.' Reflect this theme (which includes economy, educational system, moral fiber, social issues, infrastructure, technology and national defense/security). We are a general interest, national magazine, not a strictly military magazine. We are widely read by members of the Washington establishment and other policy makers."

AMERICAN PROFILE

Publishing Group of America, 341 Cool Springs Blvd., Suite 400, Franklin TN 37067. (615)468-6000. Fax: (615)468-6100. E-mail: editorial@americanprofile.com. Website: www.americanprofile.com. **95% freelance**

written. Weekly magazine with national and regional editorial celebrating the people, places, and experiences of hometowns across America. The 4-color magazine is distributed through small to medium-size community newspapers. Estab. 2000. Circ. 4,600,000. **Pays on acceptance.** Byline given. Buys first, electronic, 6-month exclusive rights rights. Editorial lead time 3 months. Submit seasonal material 6 months in advance. Accepts queries by mail. Responds in 1 month to queries; 1 month to mss. Writer's guidelines online.

- In addition to a query, first-time writers should include 2-3 published clips.

Nonfiction General interest, how-to, interview/profile. No fiction, nostalgia, poetry, essays. **Buys 250 mss/ year.** Query with published clips. Length: 450-1,200 words. Pays expenses of writers on assignment.

Photos State availability with submission. Reviews transparencies. Buys one-time rights, nonexclusive after 6 months. Negotiates payment individually. Captions, identification of subjects, model releases required.

Columns/Departments Health; Family; Finances; Home; Gardening.

Tips "We appreciate hard-copy submissions and 1-paragraph queries for short manuscripts (fewer than 500 words) on food, gardening, nature, profiles, health, and home projects for small-town audiences. Must be out of the ordinary. Please visit the website to see our writing style."

$ $ $ $ THE ATLANTIC MONTHLY

77 N. Washington St., Boston MA 02114. (617)854-7749. Fax: (617)854-7877. Website: www.theatlantic.com. Managing Editor: Cullen Murphy. **Contact:** C. Michael Curtis, senior editor. Monthly magazine of arts and public affairs. General magazine for an educated readership with broad cultural interests. Estab. 1857. Circ. 500,000. **Pays on acceptance.** Byline given. Buys first North American serial rights. Accepts queries by mail. Responds in 2 months to mss. Writer's guidelines online.

Nonfiction Reportage preferred. Book excerpts, essays, general interest, humor, personal experience, religious, travel. Query with or without published clips or send complete ms. All unsolicited mss must be accompanied by SASE. Length: 1,000-6,000 words. **Payment varies.** Sometimes pays expenses of writers on assignment.

Fiction "Seeks fiction that is clear, tightly written with strong sense of 'story' and well-defined characters." Literary and contemporary fiction. **Buys 10-12 mss/year.** Send complete ms. Length: 2,000-6,000 words. **Pays $3,000.**

Poetry Peter Davison, poetry editor. **Buys 40-60 poems/year.**

- The online magazine carries original content not found in the print edition. Contact: Kate Bacon, online editor.

Tips Writers should be aware that this is not a market for beginner's work (nonfiction and fiction), nor is it truly for intermediate work. Study this magazine before sending only your best, most professional work. When making first contact, "cover letters are sometimes helpful, particularly if they cite prior publications or involvement in writing programs. Common mistakes: melodrama, inconclusiveness, lack of development, unpersuasive characters and/or dialogue."

$ ⊘ BIBLIOPHILOS

A Journal of History, Literature, and the Liberal Arts, The Bibliophile Publishing Co., Inc., 200 Security Building, Fairmont WV 26554. (304)366-8107. **Contact:** Dr. Gerald J. Bobango, editor. **65-70% freelance written.** Quarterly literary magazine concentrating on 19th century American and European history and literature. "We see ourself as a forum for new and unpublished writers, historians, philosophers, literary critics and reviewers, and those who love animals. Audience is academic-oriented, college graduate, who believes in traditional Aristotelian-Thomistic thought and education, and has a fair streak of the Luddite in him/her. Our ideal reader owns no television, has never sent nor received e-mail, and avoids shopping malls at any cost. He loves books." Estab. 1981. Circ. 400. Pays on publication. Publishes ms an average of 1 year after acceptance. Byline given. Buys first North American serial rights. Editorial lead time 6 months. Submit seasonal material 6 months in advance. Accepts queries by mail. Responds in 2 weeks to queries; 1 month to mss. Sample copy for $5.25., Writer's guidelines for 9½ × 4 SAE with 2 first-class Stamps.

- Closed to submissions in 2004. Wait until next year. Query first only, unaccompanied by any manuscript.
- ⚬⚯ Break in with "either prose or poetry which is illustrative of man triumphing over and doing without technology, pure Ludditism, if need be. Send material critical of the socialist welfare state, constantly expanding federal government (or government at all levels), or exposing the inequities of affirmative action, political correctness, and the mass media packaging of political candidates. We want to see a pre-1960 worldview."

Nonfiction Book excerpts, essays, general interest, historical/nostalgic, humor, interview/profile, opinion, personal experience, photo feature, travel, book review-essay, literary criticism. Special issues: Upcoming theme issues include an annual all book-review issue, containing 10-15 reviews and review-essays, or poetry about books and reading. Does not want to see "anything that Oprah would recommend, or that Erma Bombeck or Ann Landers would think humorous or interesting. No 'I found Jesus and it changed my life' material." **Buys**

25-30 mss/year. Query by mail only first, not with any manuscript included. Length: 1,500-3,000 words. **Pays $5-35.**

Photos State availability with submission. Reviews b&w 4×6 prints. Buys one-time rights. Negotiates payment individually. Identification of subjects required.

Columns/Departments Features (fiction and nonfiction, short stories), 1,500-3,000 words; Poetry (batches of 5, preferably thematically related), 3-150 lines; Reviews (book reviews or review essays on new books or individual authors, current and past), 1,000-1,500 words; Opinion (man triumphing over technology and technocrats, the facade of modern education, computer fetishism), 1,000-1,500 words. **Buys 20 mss/year.** Query by mail only. **Pays $25-40.**

Fiction Gerald J. Bobango, editor. Adventure, ethnic, historical, horror, humorous, mainstream, mystery, novel excerpts, romance, slice-of-life vignettes, suspense, western, utopian, Orwellian. "No 'I found Jesus and it turned my life around'; no 'I remember Mama, who was a saint and I miss her terribly'; no gay or lesbian topics; no drug culture material; nothing harping on political correctness; nothing to do with healthy living, HMOs, medical programs, or the welfare state, unless it is against statism in these areas." **Buys 25-30 mss/ year.** Length: 1,500-3,000 words. **Pays $25-40.**

Poetry "Formal and rhymed verse gets read first." Free verse, light verse, traditional, political satire, doggerel.

ℕ BLACK DIASPORA MAGAZINE

Black Diaspora Communications, Ltd., P.O. Box 828, New York NY 10163. (212)268-8348. Fax: (212)268-8370. E-mail: blakdias@earthlink.net. Publisher: René John-Sandy. **Contact:** Benesia Babb and Jerry King, managing editors. Bimonthly magazine covering "general topics in all facets of their lives." *Black Diaspora Magazine* is a "general interest publication for African-Americans, Caribbeans, Africans, Hispanics." Estab. 1979. Circ. 210,000. Publishes ms an average of 3 months after acceptance. Byline given. Buys first North American serial, one-time rights. Accepts queries by mail. Accepts previously published material. Responds in 3 weeks to queries. Sample copy for $5. Writer's guidelines for #10 SASE.

Nonfiction Essays, general interest.

Poetry Wants "long and short poems—creatively done. Sonnets are good. They should all follow editorial guidelines. Be imaginative." Reviews books of poetry in 200-300 words, single book format. Open to unsolicited reviews. No 5-page poems. Submit maximum 2 poems.

Tips "Please do not call editors. They're very busy and don't have time for all calls. Be patient. Make friends with editorial assistants and assistant editors."

ℕ $CAPPER'S

Ogden Publications, Inc., 1503 SW 42nd St., Topeka KS 66609-1265. (785)274-4300. Website: www.cappers.c om. **25% freelance written.** Works with a small number of new/unpublished writers each year. Biweekly tabloid emphasizing home and family for readers who live mainly in the rural Midwest. "*Capper's* is upbeat, focusing on the homey feelings people like to share, as well as hopes and dreams." Estab. 1879. Circ. 240,000. Pays for poetry and fiction on acceptance; articles on publication. Publishes ms an average of 2-12 months after acceptance. Byline given. Buys first North American serial rights. Submit seasonal material 4 months in advance. Accepts queries by mail. Responds in 2-3 months to queries; 6 months to mss. Sample copy online. Writer's guidelines online.

Nonfiction General interest, historical/nostalgic (local museums, etc.), inspirational, travel, nostalgic, human interest, family-oriented. **Buys 75 mss/year.** Send complete ms. Length: 900 words maximum. **Pays $2.50/ printed inch. Pays additional $5 if used on website.**

Reprints Accepts occasionally from noncompeting venues. Send typed ms with rights for sale noted and information about when and where the material previously appeared.

Photos Send photos with submission. Buys one-time rights. Pays $5-15 for b&w glossy prints; $20-40 for color prints (inside); $40 for cover. Captions required.

Columns/Departments Heart of the Home (letters sharing humorous, heartwarming, poignant & nostalgic experiences of life, recipes, hints), 400 words maximum. Send complete ms. **Pays approximately $2 per printed inch. Payment for recipes is $5. Hints used earn $2 gift certificate.**

Fiction "We buy very few fiction pieces—longer than short stories, shorter than novels." Adventure, historical, humorous, mainstream, mystery, romance, serialized novels, western. No explicit sex, violence, profanity, or alcohol use. **Buys 4-5 mss/year.** Length: 7,500-50,000 words. **Pays $100-400.**

Poetry "The poems that appear in *Capper's* are not too difficult to read. They're easy to grasp. We're looking for everyday events and down-to-earth themes." Free verse, light verse, traditional, nature, inspiration. **Buys 150 poems/year.** Submit maximum 5-6 poems. Length: 4-16 lines. **Pays $10-15.**

Tips "Study a few issues of our publication. Most rejections are for material that is too long, unsuitable or out of character for our magazine (too sexy, too much profanity, wrong kind of topic, etc.). On occasion, we must cut material to fit column space. No electronic submissions."

$ $ CIA—CITIZEN IN AMERICA

CIA—Citizen in America, Inc., 30 Ford St., Glen Cove, Long Island NY 11542. (516)671-4047. E-mail: ciamc@we
btv.net. Website: www.citizeninamerica.com. **Contact:** John J. Maddox, magazine coordinator. **100% free-lance written.** Magazine published 9 times/year covering first amendment responsibilities. *"CIA—Citizen in
America* trys to strengthen democracy here and abroad by allowing the freedom of expression in all forms
possible through the press. *CIA* does not shy away from controversy." Estab. 2002. Pays on publication. Publishes ms an average of 3 months after acceptance. Byline sometimes given. Buys one-time rights. Accepts
queries by mail, e-mail. Accepts previously published material. Accepts simultaneous submissions. Responds
in 2 weeks to queries; 1-2 months to mss. Sample copy for $6.95. Writer's guidelines for #10 SASE, e-mail or
on website.

Nonfiction Essays, exposé, general interest, historical/nostalgic, humor, inspirational, opinion, personal experience, religious, travel. Does not want "any manuscript that deliberately exploits or promotes racial, religious,
or gender bigotry." **Buys 150 + mss/year.** Send complete ms. Length: 2,500 words maximum. **Pays $40-100,
plus 1 contributor copy.**

Photos State availability with submission. Offers no additional payment for photos accepted with ms.

Columns/Departments There are numerous columns where paid articles are accepted. See writer's guidelines
for details. Send complete ms.

Fiction Adventure, erotica, ethnic, experimental, historical, humorous, mainstream, religious, romance, science
fiction, slice-of-life vignettes, western, war stories. No screen or plays. No works that deliberately promote
racism, prejudice, or gender oriented violence. Send complete ms. Length: 250-2,500 words.

Poetry Avant-garde, free verse, light verse, traditional. Submit maximum 5 poems. Length: 25 lines maximum.

Fillers Anecdotes, facts, short humor.

Tips "Writers should consciously shy away from getting an 'ego' or 'celebrity' boost in this publication. Therefore, writers should have a fervent desire to publish work for others to read. Rule of thumb is: If the writer
feels good writing it, *CIA* will feel the same reading and, hopefully, publishing it. The purchase of sample copy
is strongly recommended before submission."

N DEPARTURES

American Express Publishing Corp., 1120 Avenue of the Americas, 9th Floor, New York NY 10036. (212)382-5600. Fax: (212)827-6497. Website: www.departures.com. Editor: Richard David Story. Associate Editor: Stellene Volandes. Bimonthly magazine. Contains features articles on travel, art and culture, men's and women's
style and interior design with an eye on global adventures and purchases. Circ. 680,000. Editorial lead time 4
months. Sample copy not available.

$ $ $ $ DIVERSION

1790 Broadway, New York NY 10019. (212)969-7500. Fax: (212)969-7563. E-mail: shartford@hearst.com. Website: www.diversion.com. **Contact:** Shari Hartford. Monthly magazine covering travel and lifestyle, edited for
physicians. *"Diversion* offers an eclectic mix of interests beyond medicine. Regular features include stories on
domestic and foreign travel destinations, food and wine, sports cars, gardening, photography, books, electronic
gear, and the arts. Although *Diversion* doesn't cover health subjects, it does feature profiles of doctors who
excel at nonmedical pursuits or who engage in medical volunteer work." Estab. 1973. Circ. 176,000. Pays 3
months after acceptance. Byline given. Offers 25% kill fee. Editorial lead time 4 months. Responds in 1 month
to queries. Sample copy for $4.50. Guidelines available.

　　o→ Break in by "querying with a brief proposal describing the focus of the story. It should be on a topic
　　in which you have demonstrated expertise."

Nonfiction "We get so many travel and food queries that we're hard pressed to even read them all. Far better
to query us on culture, the arts, sports, technology, etc." **Buys 50 mss/year.** Query with proposal, published
clips, and author's credentials. Length: 1,800-2,000 words. **Pays 50¢-$1/word.**

Columns/Departments Travel, food & wine, photography, gardening, cars, technology. Length: 1,200 words.

EBONY

Johnson Publishing Co., Inc., 820 S. Michigan Ave., Chicago IL 60605. (312)322-9200. Fax: (312)322-9375.
Website: www.ebony.com. Monthly magazine covering topics ranging from education and history to entertainment, art, government, health, travel, sports and social events. African-American oriented consumer interest
magazine. Circ. 1,728,986. Editorial lead time 3 months. Sample copy not available.

$ EDUCATION IN FOCUS

Books for All Times, Inc., P.O. Box 202, Warrenton VA 20188. (540)428-3175. E-mail: staff@bfat.com. Website:
www.bfat.com. **Contact:** Joe David, editor. **80% freelance written.** Semiannual newsletter for public interested
in education issues at all levels. "We are always looking for intelligent articles that provide educationally sound

ideas that enhance the understanding of what is happening or what should be happening in our schools today. We are not looking for material that might be published by the Department of Education. Instead we want material from liberated and mature thinkers and writers, tamed by reason and humanitarianism." Estab. 1989. Circ. 1,000. **Pays on acceptance.** Publishes ms an average of 2 months after acceptance. Byline given. Buys first, one-time, second serial (reprint), book, newsletter and internet rights rights. Editorial lead time 2 months. Accepts queries by mail, e-mail. Accepts simultaneous submissions. Responds in 1 month to queries. Sample copy for #10 SASE.

Nonfiction "We prefer documented, intelligent articles that deeply inform. The best way to be quickly rejected is to send articles that defend the public school system as it is today, or was!" Book excerpts, exposé, general interest. **Buys 4-6 mss/year.** Query with published clips or send complete ms. Length: 3,000 words. Some longer articles can be broken into 2 articles—1 for each issue. **Pays $25-75.**

Tips "Maintain an honest voice and a clear focus on the subject."

N̄ $ $ $FRIENDLY EXCHANGE

C-E Publishers: Publishers, Friendly Exchange Business Office, P.O. Box 2120, Warren MI 48090-2120. (586)753-8325. Fax: (586)558-5802. E-mail: friendlyexchange@aol.com. Website: www.friendlyexchange.com. **Contact:** Dan Grantham, editor. **80% freelance written.** Quarterly magazine for policyholders of Farmers Insurance Group of Companies exploring travel, health, home, auto, financial, lifestyle and leisure topics of interest to active families. "These are traditional families (median adult age 39) who live primarily in the area bounded by Ohio on the east and the Pacific Ocean on the west, along with Tennessee, Alabama, and Virginia." Estab. 1981. Circ. 5,400,000. **Pays on acceptance.** Publishes ms an average of 5 months after acceptance. Offers 25% kill fee. Buys all rights. Submit seasonal material 1 year in advance. Accepts simultaneous submissions. Responds in 2 months to queries. Sample copy for 9×12 SAE and 5 first-class stamps. Writer's guidelines for #10 SASE.

Nonfiction "We provide readers with 'news they can use' through articles that help them make smart choices about lifestyle issues. We focus on home, auto, health, personal finance, travel and other lifestyle/consumer issues of interest to today's families. Readers should get a sense of the issues involved, and information that could help them make those decisions. Style is warm and colorful, making liberal use of anecdotes and quotes." **Buys 32 mss/year.** Query. Length: 200-1,200 words. **Pays $500-1,000, including expenses.**

Columns/Departments Consumer issues, health, finances and leisure are topics of regular columns.

Tips "We concentrate on providing readers information relating to current trends. We prefer tightly targeted stories that provide new information to help readers make decisions about their lives. We don't take queries or mss on first-person essays or humorous articles. We prefer e-mail queries."

$ $GRIT

American Life and Traditions, Ogden Publications, 1503 SW 42nd St., Topeka KS 66609-1265. (785)274-4300. Fax: (785)274-4305. E-mail: grit@grit.com. Website: www.grit.com. **Contact:** Ann Crahan, editor-in-chief. **90% freelance written.** Open to new writers. Monthly "*Grit* is good news. As a wholesome, family-oriented magazine published for more than a century and distributed nationally, *Grit* features articles about family lifestyles, traditions, values, and pastimes. *Grit* accents the best of American life and traditions—past and present. Our readers are ordinary people doing extraordinary things, with courage, heart, determination, and imagination. Many of them live in small towns and rural areas across the country; others live in cities but share many of the values typical of small-town America." Estab. 1882. Circ. 90,000. Pays on publication. Byline given. Buys first North American serial rights. Submit seasonal material 6 months in advance. Accepts queries by mail. Sample copy and writer's guidelines for $4 and 11X14 SASE with 4 first-class stamps. Sample articles on website.

○– Break in through Departments such as Best Friends, Looking Back, Poetry.

Nonfiction The best way to sell work is by reading each issue cover to cover. Humor, interview/profile, features (timely, newsworthy, touching but with a *Grit* angle), readers' true stories, outdoor hobbies, collectibles, gardening, crafts, hobbies, leisure pastimes. Query by mail only. Prefers full ms with photos. Length: Main features run 1,200-1,500 words. Department features average 800-1,000 words. **Pays 15¢/word for features; plays flat rate for departments.**

Photos Professional quality photos (b&w prints or color slides/prints) increase acceptability of articles. Send photos with submission. Pays up to $25 each in features according to quality, placement, and color/b&w. Payment for department photos included in flat rate.

Fiction Short stories, 1,500-3,500 words; may also purchase accompanying art if of high quality and appropriate. Need serials (romance, westerns, mysteries), 3,500-10,000 words. Send ms with SASE to Fiction Dept. Adventure, condensed novels, mainstream, mystery, religious, romance, western, nostalgia. "No sex, violence, drugs, obscene words, abuse, alcohol, or negative diatribes."

Tips "Articles should be directed to a national audience, mostly 40 years and older. Sources identified fully. Our readers are warm and loving. They want to read about others with heart. Tell us stories about someone unusual, an unsung hero, an artist of the backroads, an interesting trip with an emotional twist, a memory with a message, an ordinary person accomplishing extraordinary things. Tell us stories that will make us cry with joy.'' Send complete ms with photos for consideration.

$ $ $ $ HARPER'S MAGAZINE

666 Broadway, 11th Floor, New York NY 10012. (212)420-5720. Fax: (212)228-5889. Website: www.harpers.o rg. Editor: Lewis H. Lapham. **Contact:** Ann Gollin, editor's assistant. **90% freelance written.** Monthly magazine for well-educated, socially concerned, widely read men and women who value ideas and good writing. *"Harper's Magazine* encourages national discussion on current and significant issues in a format that offers arresting facts and intelligent opinions. By means of its several shorter journalistic forms—Harper's Index, Readings, Forum, and Annotation—as well as with its acclaimed essays, fiction, and reporting, *Harper's* continues the tradition begun with its first issue in 1850: to inform readers across the whole spectrum of political, literary, cultural, and scientific affairs.'' Estab. 1850. Circ. 230,000. **Pays on acceptance.** Publishes ms an average of 3 months after acceptance. Offers negotiable kill fee. Vary with author and material. Accepts previously published material. Responds in 6 weeks to queries. Sample copy for $5.95.

Nonfiction "For writers working with agents or who will query first only, our requirements are: public affairs, literary, international and local reporting, and humor.'' Publishes 1 major report/issue. Length: 4,000-6,000 words. Publishes 1 major essay/issue. Length: 4,000-6,000 words. "These should be construed as topical essays on all manner of subjects (politics, the arts, crime, business, etc.) to which the author can bring the force of passionate and informed statement.'' Humor. No interviews; no profiles. No unsolicited poems will be accepted. **Buys 2 mss/year.** Complete ms and query must include SASE. Length: 4,000-6,000 words.

Reprints Accepted for Readings section. Send typed ms with rights for sale noted and information about when and where the article previously appeared.

Photos Occasionally purchased with ms; others by assignment. Stacey Clarkson, art director. State availability with submission. Pays $50-500.

Fiction Lewis H. Lapham, editor. Publishes 1 short story/month. Will consider unsolicited fiction. Humorous. Query. Length: 3,000-5,000 words. **Generally pays 50¢-$1/word.**

Tips "Some readers expect their magazines to clothe them with opinions in the way that Bloomingdale's dresses them for the opera. The readers of *Harper's Magazine* belong to a different crowd. They strike me as the kind of people who would rather think in their own voices and come to their own conclusions.''

N $ $ $ $ NATIONAL GEOGRAPHIC MAGAZINE

1145 17th St. NW, Washington DC 20036. (202)857-7000. Fax: (202)492-5767. Website: www.nationalgeograph ic.com. Editor-in-Chief: William Allen. **Contact:** Oliver Payne, senior editor. **60% freelance written.** Prefers to work with published/established writers. Monthly magazine for members of the National Geographic Society. "Timely articles written in a compelling, 'eyewitness' style. Arresting photographs that speak to us of the beauty, mystery, and harsh realities of life on earth. Maps of unprecedented detail and accuracy. These are the hallmarks of *National Geographic* magazine. Since 1888, the *Geographic* has been educating readers about the world.'' Estab. 1888. Circ. 7,800,000.

> Before querying, study recent issues and check a *Geographic Index* at a library since the magazine seldom returns to regions or subjects covered within the past 10 years.

Nonfiction Senior Editor: Oliver Payne. *National Geographic* publishes general interest, illustrated articles on science, natural history, exploration, cultures and geographical regions. Of the freelance writers assigned, a few are experts in their fields; the remainder are established professionals. Fewer than 1% of unsolicited queries result in assignments. Query (500 words with clips of published articles by mail to Senior Assitant Editor Oliver Payne. Do not send mss. Length: 2,000-8,000 words. Pays expenses of writers on assignment.

Photos Query in care of the Photographic Division.

> The online magazine carries original content not included in the print edition. Contact: Valerie May, online editor.

Tips "State the theme(s) clearly, let the narrative flow, and build the story around strong characters and a vivid sense of place. Give us rounded episodes, logically arranged.''

NEW YORK TIMES UPFRONT

Scholastic, Inc., 557 Broadway, New York NY 10012-3999. (212)343-6100. Fax: (212)343-4808. Website: www.u pfrontmagazine.com. Editor: Elliott Rebhun. Biweekly magazine. Collaboration between The New York Times and Scholastic, Inc. designed as a news magazine specifically for teenagers. Circ. 200,000. Editorial lead time 1-2 months. Sample copy not available.

THE NEW YORKER

The New Yorker, Inc., 4 Times Square, New York NY 10036. (212) 286-5900. Website: www.newyorker.com. Weekly magazine. A quality magazine of interesting, well-written stories, articles, essays and poems for a literate audience. Estab. 1925. Circ. 750,000. **Pays on acceptance.** Accepts queries by e-mail. Responds in 3 months to mss. Writer's guidelines online.

- • *The New Yorker* receives approximately 4,000 submissions per month.
- **O–** For e-mail submissions: fiction@newyorker.com (fiction); talkofthetown@newyorker.com (Talk of the Town); shouts@newyorker.com (Shouts & Murmurs); poetry@newyorker.com (poetry); newsbreaks-@newyorker.com (newsbreaks).

Fiction Publishes 1 ms/issue. Send complete ms. **Payment varies.**

Poetry Send poetry to ''Poetry Department.''

Tips ''Be lively, original, not overly literary. Write what you want to write, not what you think the editor would like.''

⩍ $ $ $ NEWSWEEK

251 W. 57th St., 17th Floor, New York NY 10019. (212)445-4000. Fax: (212)445-5146. E-mail: myturn@newswee k.com. Website: www.newsweek.com. **Contact:** Pamela Hamer, assistant editor. ''*Newsweek* is edited to report the week's developments on the newsfront of the world and the nation through news, commentary and analysis.'' Accepts unsolicited mss for *My Turn*, a column of personal opinion. The 850-900 word essays for the column must be original, not published elsewhere and contain verifiable facts. **Payment is $1,000** on publication. Circ. 3,180,000. non-exclusive world-wide rights. Responds in 2 months only on submissions with SASE to mss.

$ $ $ THE OLD FARMER'S ALMANAC

Yankee Publishing, Inc., Main St., Dublin NH 03444. (603)563-8111. Fax: (603)563-8252. Website: www.almana c.com. **Contact:** Janice Stillman, editor. **95% freelance written.** Annual magazine covering weather, gardening, history, oddities, lore. ''*The Old Farmer's Almanac* is the oldest continuously published periodical in North America. Since 1792, it has provided useful information for people in all walks of life: tide tables for those who live near the ocean; sunrise tables and planting charts for those who live on the farm or simply enjoy gardening; recipes for those who like to cook; and forecasts for those who don't like the question of weather left up in the air. The words of the *Almanac*'s founder, Robert B. Thomas, guide us still. 'Our main endeavor is to be useful, but with a pleasant degree of humour.''' Estab. 1792. Circ. 3,750,000. **Pays on acceptance.** Publishes ms an average of 9 months after acceptance. Byline given. Offers 25% kill fee. Buys first North American serial, electronic, all rights. Editorial lead time 6 months. Submit seasonal material 1 year in advance. Accepts queries by mail. Responds in 3 weeks to queries; 2 months to mss. Sample copy for $5 at bookstores or online. Writer's guidelines online.

Nonfiction General interest, historical/nostalgic, how-to (garden, cook, save money), humor, weather, natural remedies, obscure facts, history, popular culture. No personal weather recollections/accounts, personal/family histories. Query with published clips. Length: 800-2,500 words. **Pays 65¢/word.** Sometimes pays expenses of writers on assignment.

Fillers Anecdotes, short humor. **Buys 1-2/year.** Length: 100-200 words. **Pays 50¢/word.**

▪ The online magazine carries original content not found in the print edition.

Tips ''Read it. Think differently. Read writer's guidelines online.''

OPEN SPACES

Open Spaces Publications, Inc., PMB 134, 6327-C SW Capitol Hwy., Portland OR 97239-1937. (503)227-5764. Fax: (503)227-3401. E-mail: info@open-spaces.com. Website: www.open-spaces.com. President: Penny Harrison. Managing Editor: James Bradley. **Contact:** Elizabeth Arthur, editor. **95% freelance written.** Quarterly general interest magazine. ''*Open Spaces* is a forum for informed writing and intelligent thought. Articles are written by experts in various fields. Audience is varied (CEOs and rock climbers, politicos and university presidents, etc.) but is highly educated and loves to read good writing.'' Estab. 1997. Pays on publication. Publishes ms an average of 6 months after acceptance. Byline given. Offers 20% kill fee. Rights purchased vary with author and material. Editorial lead time 9 months. Accepts queries by mail, fax. Accepts simultaneous submissions. Sample copy for $10. Writer's guidelines online.

Nonfiction Essays, general interest, historical/nostalgic, how-to (if clever), humor, interview/profile, personal experience, travel. **Buys 35 mss/year.** Query with published clips. Length: 1,500-2,500 words; major articles: 2,500-6,000 words. **Pays variable amount.**

Photos State availability with submission. Buys one-time rights. Captions, identification of subjects required.

Columns/Departments David Williams, departments editor. Books (substantial topics such as the Booker Prize, The Newbery, etc.); Travel (must reveal insight); Sports (past subjects include rowing, swing dancing, and ultimate); Unintended Consequences, 1,500-2,500 words. **Buys 20-25 mss/year.** Query with published clips or send complete ms. **Payment varies.**

Fiction Ellen Teicher, fiction editor. ''Quality is far more important than type. Read the magazine.'' ''Excellence is the issue - not subject matter." **Buys 8 mss/year.** Length: 2,000-6,000 words. **Payment varies.**

Poetry "Again, quality is far more important than type." Susan Juve-Hu Bucharest, poetry editor. Submit maximum 3 poems with SASE.

Fillers Anecdotes, short humor, cartoons; interesting or amusing Northwest facts; expressions, etc.

Tips "*Open Spaces* reviews all manuscripts submitted in hopes of finding writing of the highest quality. We present a Northwest perspective as well as a national and international one. Best advice is read the magazine."

$ $ $ $ PARADE

The Sunday Magazine, Parade Publications, Inc., 711 Third Ave., New York NY 10017. (212)450-7000. Fax: (212)450-7284. Website: www.parade.com. Editor: Lee Kravitz. Managing Editor: Dakila Divina. **Contact:** Articles Editor. **95% freelance written.** Weekly magazine for a general interest audience. Estab. 1941. Circ. 81,000,000. **Pays on acceptance.** Publishes ms an average of 5 months after acceptance. Kill fee varies in amount. Buys worldwide exclusive rights for 7 days, plus nonexclusive electronic and other rights in perpetuity. Editorial lead time 1 month. Accepts queries by mail, fax. Accepts simultaneous submissions. Sample copy online. Writer's guidelines online.

• Does not accept e-mail queries.

Nonfiction Publishes general interest (on health, trends, social issues or anything of interest to a broad general audience), interview/profile (of news figures, celebrities and people of national significance), and "provocative topical pieces of news value." Spot news events are not accepted, as *Parade* has a 2-month lead time. No fiction, fashion, travel, poetry, cartoons, nostalgia, regular columns, personal essays, quizzes, or fillers. Unsolicited queries concerning celebrities, politicians, sports figures, or technical are rarely assigned. **Buys 150 mss/ year.** Query with published clips. Length: 1,000-1,200 words. **Pays $2,500 minimum.** Pays expenses of writers on assignment.

Tips "If the writer has a specific expertise in the proposed topic, it increases a writer's chances for breaking in. Send a well-researched, well-written 1-page proposal and enclose a SASE. Do not submit completed manuscripts."

⊘ PEOPLE

Time, Inc., 1271 Avenue of the Americas, New York NY 10020. (212)522-1212. Fax: (212)522-1359. E-mail: editor@people.com. Website: www.people.com. Editor-in-Chief: Noman Pearlstine. Managing Editor: Martha Nelson. Weekly magazine. Designed as a forum for personality journalism through the use of short articles on contemporary news events and people. Circ. 3,617,127. Editorial lead time 3 months. Sample copy not available.

• Does not buy freelance materials or use freelance writers.

Ⓝ PORTLAND MAGAZINE

Maine's City Magazine, 722 Congress St., Portland ME 041012. (207)775-4339. Fax: (207)775-2334. Website: www.portlandmagazine.com. **Contact:** Colin Sargent, editor. Monthly "City lifestyle magazine—fiction, style, business, real estate, controversy, fashion, cuisine, interviews and art relating to the Maine area." Estab. 1985. Circ. 100,000. Pays on publication. Buys first North American serial rights.

Fiction Colin Sargent, editor. Send complete ms. Length: "Fiction below 700 words, please." 3 double-spaced typed pages.

Ⓝ $ $ READER'S DIGEST

The Reader's Digest Association, Inc., Box 100, Pleasantville NY 10572-0100. Website: rd.com. Monthly magazine.

Columns/Departments Life in These United States; All in a Day's Work; and Humor in Uniform, **pays $300.** Laughter, the Best Medicine; and Quotable Quotes, **pays $100.** Address your submission to the appropriate humor category. Please note your name, address, and phone number with all submissions. Previously published material must include the name, date, and page number of the source. Original items should be less than 100 words, and become our property upon publication and payment. All contributions may be edited and cannot be acknowledged or returned.

Tips "Original articles are usually assigned to regular contributors to the magazine. We do not accept or return unpublished manuscripts. We do, however, accept one-page queries that clearly detail the article idea—with special emphasis on the arc of the story, your interview access to the main characters, your access to special documents, etc. We look for dramatic narratives, articles about everyday heroes, crime dramas, adventure stories. Do include a separate page of your writing credits. We are not interested in poetry, fiction, or opinion pieces. Please submit article proposals on the rd.com website."

$ $ $ $ ⊡ READER'S DIGEST (CANADA)

1125 Stanley St., Montreal QC H3B 5H5, Canada. (514)940-0751. E-mail: editor@readersdigest.ca. Website: www.readersdigest.ca. Editor-in-Chief: Murray Lewis. **Contact:** Ron Starr, senior editor. **10-25% freelance**

written. Monthly magazine of general interest articles and subjects. Estab. 1948. Circ. 1,300,000. **Pays on acceptance for original works.** Pays on publication for "pickups." Byline given. Offers $500 (Canadian) kill fee. one-time rights (for reprints), all rights (for original articles). Submit seasonal material 5 months in advance. Accepts queries by mail, e-mail. Accepts previously published material. Responds in 5 weeks to queries. Writer's guidelines for #10 SASE with Canadian postage or #10 SAE with 1 IRC.

Nonfiction "We're looking for true stories that depend on emotion and reveal the power of our relationships to help us overcome adversity; also for true first-person accounts of an event that changed a life for the better or led to new insight. No fiction, poetry or articles too specialized, technical or esoteric—read *Reader's Digest* to see what kind of articles we want." General interest, how-to (general interest), inspirational, personal experience. Query with published clips. Length: 3,000-5,000 words. **Pays minimum of $2,700.** Pays expenses of writers on assignment.

Reprints Send previously published material to Peter Des Lauriers, senior editor. Payment is negotiable.

Photos State availability with submission.

🖥 The online magazine carries original content not found in the print edition. Contact: Peter Des Lauriers.

Tips "*Reader's Digest* usually finds its freelance writers through other well-known publications in which they have previously been published. There are guidelines available and writers should read *Reader's Digest* to see what kind of stories we look for and how they are written. We do not accept unsolicited manuscripts."

$ REUNIONS MAGAZINE

P.O. Box 11727, Milwaukee WI 53211-0727. (414)263-4567. Fax: (414)263-6331. E-mail: reunions@execpc.com. Website: www.reunionsmag.com. **Contact:** Edith Wagner, editor. **75% freelance written.** Bimonthly magazine covering reunions—all aspects and types. "*Reunions Magazine* is primarily for people actively planning family, class, military, and other reunions. We want easy, practical ideas about organizing, planning, researching/searching, attending, or promoting reunions." Estab. 1990. Circ. 18,000. Pays on publication. Publishes ms an average of 1 year after acceptance. Byline given. Buys one-time rights. Editorial lead time 6 months. Submit seasonal material 1 year in advance. Accepts queries by mail, e-mail, fax. Accepts previously published material. Responds in about 1 year to queries. Sample copy and writer's guidelines for #10 SASE or online.

Nonfiction "We can't get enough about reunion activities, particularly family reunions with multigenerational activities. We would also like more reunion food-related material." Needs reviewers for books, videos, software (include your requirements). Special features: Ethnic/African-American family reunions; food, kids stuff, theme parks, small venues (bed & breakfasts, dormitories, condos); golf, travel and gaming features; themes, cruises, ranch reunions and reunions in various US locations. Historical/nostalgic, how-to, humor, interview/profile, new product, personal experience, photo feature, travel. **Buys 50 mss/year.** Query with published clips. Length: 500-2,500 (prefers work on the short side). **Pays $25-50.** Often rewards with generous copies.

Reprints Send tearsheet, photocopy or typed ms with rights for sale noted and information about when and where the material previously appeared. Usually pays $10.

Photos Always looking for vertical cover photos screaming: "Reunion!" Prefer print pictures; e-mail pictures (TIFF or JPG). State availability with submission. Reviews contact sheets, negatives, 35mm transparencies, prints. Offers no additional payment for photos accepted with ms. Captions, identification of subjects, model releases required.

Fillers Must be reunion-related. Anecdotes, facts, short humor. **Buys 20-40/year.** Length: 50-250 words. **Pays $5.**

🖥 The online magazine carries original content and includes writer's guidelines and articles. Contact: Edith Wagner, online editor.

Tips "All copy must be reunion-related with strong, real reunion examples and experiences. Write a lively account of an interesting or unusual reunion, either upcoming or soon after while it's hot. Tell readers why the reunion is special, what went into planning it, and how attendees reacted. Our "Masterplan" section, about family reunion planning, is a great place for a freelancer to start by telling her/his own reunion. Send us how-tos or tips about any of the many aspects of reunion organizing. Open your minds to different types of reunions—they're all around!"

$ $ $ $ ROBB REPORT

The Magazine for the Luxury Lifestyle, Curtco Media Labs, 1 Acton Place, Acton MA 01720. (978)264-7500. Fax: (978)264-7505. E-mail: miken@robbreport.com. Website: www.robbreport.com. **Contact:** Mike Nolan, editor. **60% freelance written.** Monthly magazine. "We are a lifestyle magazine geared toward active, affluent readers. Addresses upscale autos, luxury travel, boating, technology, lifestyles, watches, fashion, sports, investments, collectibles." Estab. 1976. Circ. 111,000. Pays on publication. Byline given. Offers 25% kill fee. Buys first North American serial, all rights. Submit seasonal material 5 months in advance. Accepts queries by mail, fax. Responds in 2 months to queries; 1 month to mss. Sample copy for $10.95, plus shipping and handling. Writer's guidelines for #10 SASE.

Nonfiction General interest (autos, lifestyle, etc), interview/profile (prominent personalities/entrepreneurs), new product (autos, boats, consumer electronics), travel (international and domestic). Special issues: Home issue (October); Recreation (March). **Buys 60 mss/year.** Query with published clips. Length: 500-3,500 words. **Pays $150-2,000.** Sometimes pays expenses of writers on assignment.

Photos State availability with submission. Buys one-time rights. Payment depends on article.

⬛ The online magazine carries original content not found in the print edition. Contact: Mike Nolan.

Tips "Show zest in your writing, immaculate research, and strong thematic structure, and you can handle most any assignment. We want to put the reader there, whether the article is about test driving a car, fishing for marlin, touring a luxury home, or profiling a celebrity. The best articles will be those that tell compelling stories. Anecdotes should be used liberally, especially for leads, and the fun should show in your writing."

$ $ THE SATURDAY EVENING POST

The Saturday Evening Post Society, P.O. Box 567, Indianapolis IN 46206. (317)634-1100. Fax: (317)637-0126. E-mail: letters@satevepost.org. Website: www.satevepost.org. Travel Editor: Holly Miller. **30% freelance written.** Bimonthly general interest, family-oriented magazine focusing on physical fitness, preventive medicine. "Ask almost any American if he or she has heard of *The Saturday Evening Post*, and you will find that many have fond recollections of the magazine from their childhood days. Many readers recall sitting with their families on Saturdays awaiting delivery of their *Post* subscription in the mail. *The Saturday Evening Post* has forged a tradition of 'forefront journalism.' *The Saturday Evening Post* continues to stand at the journalistic forefront with its coverage of health, nutrition, and preventive medicine." Estab. 1728. Circ. 350,000. Pays on publication. Publishes ms an average of 3 months after acceptance. Byline given. Buys second serial (reprint), all rights. Submit seasonal material 4 months in advance. Accepts queries by mail, fax. Accepts simultaneous submissions. Responds in 1 month to queries; 6 weeks to mss. Writer's guidelines online.

Nonfiction Book excerpts, how-to (gardening, home improvement), humor, interview/profile, travel, medical; health; fitness. "No political articles or articles containing sexual innuendo or hypersophistication." **Buys 25 mss/year.** Query with or without published clips or send complete ms. Length: 750-2,500 words. **Pays $150 minumum, negotiable maximum.** Sometimes pays expenses of writers on assignment.

Photos State availability with submission. Reviews negatives, transparencies. Buys one-time or all rights. Offers $50 minimum, negotiable maximum per photo. Identification of subjects, model releases required.

Columns/Departments Travel (destinations); Post Scripts (well-known humorists); Post People (activities of celebrities). Length 750-1,500. **Buys 16 mss/year.** Query with published clips or send complete ms. **Pays $150 minimum, negotiable maximum.**

Poetry Light verse.

Fillers Post Scripts Editor: Steve Pettinga. Anecdotes, short humor. **Buys 200/year.** Length: 300 words. **Pays $15.**

Tips "Areas most open to freelancers are Health, Fitness, Research Breakthroughs, Nutrition, Post Scripts and Travel. For travel we like text-photo packages, pragmatic tips, side bars and safe rather than exotic destinations. Query by mail, not phone. Send clips."

$ $ $ $ SMITHSONIAN MAGAZINE

MRC 951, P.O. Box 37012, Washington DC 20013-7012. (202)275-2000. E-mail: articles@simag.si.edu. Website: www.smithsonianmag.si.edu. Editor-in-chief: Carey Winfrey. **Contact:** Marlane A. Liddell, articles editor. **90% freelance written.** Monthly magazine for associate members of the Smithsonian Institution; 85% with college education. "*Smithsonian Magazine's* mission is to inspire fascination with all the world has to offer by featuring unexpected and entertaining editorial that explores different lifestyles, cultures and peoples, the arts, the wonders of nature and technology and much more. The highly educated, innovative readers of *Smithsonian* share a unique desire to celebrate life, seeking out the timely as well as timeless, the artistic as well as the academic and the thought-provoking as well as the humorous." Circ. 2,300,000. **Pays on acceptance.** Publishes ms an average of 6 months after acceptance. Offers 33% kill fee. Buys first North American serial rights. Editorial lead time 2 months. Submit seasonal material 3 months in advance. Accepts queries by e-mail. Responds in 2 months to queries. Sample copy for $5, c/o Judy Smith. Writer's guidelines online.

⊙╍ "We consider focused subjects that fall within the general range of Smithsonian Institution interests, such as: cultural history, physical science, art and natural history. We are always looking for offbeat subjects and profiles. We do not consider fiction, poetry, political and news events, or previously published articles. We publish only twelve issues a year, so it is difficult to place an article in *Smithsonian*, but please be assured that all proposals are considered."

Nonfiction "Our mandate from the Smithsonian Institution says we are to be interested in the same things which now interest or should interest the Institution: Cultural and fine arts, history, natural sciences, hard sciences, etc." **Buys 120-130 feature (up to 5,000 words) and 12 short (500-650 words) mss/year.** Query with published clips. **Pays various rates per feature, $1,500 per short piece.** Pays expenses of writers on assignment.

Photos Purchased with or without ms and on assignment. "Illustrations are not the responsibility of authors, but if you do have photographs or illustration materials, please include a selection of them with your submission. In general, 35mm color transparencies or black-and-white prints are perfectly acceptable. Photographs published in the magazine are usually obtained through assignment, stock agencies, or specialized sources. No photo library is maintained and photographs should be submitted only to accompany a specific article proposal." Send photos with submission. Pays $400/full color page. Captions required.

Columns/Departments Last Page humor, 550-700 words. **Buys 12-15 department articles/year.** Length: 1,000-2,000 words. Send complete ms. **Pays $1,000-1,500.**

Tips "We prefer a written proposal of one or two pages as a preliminary query. The proposal should convince us that we should cover the subject, offer descriptive information on how you, the writer, would treat the subject and offer us an opportunity to judge your writing ability. Background information and writing credentials and samples are helpful. All unsolicited proposals are sent to us on speculation and you should receive a reply within eight weeks. Please include a self-addressed stamped envelope. We also accept proposals via electronic mail at articles@simag.si.edu. If we decide to commission an article, the writer receives full payment on acceptance of the manuscript. If the article is found unsuitable, one-third of the payment serves as a kill fee."

$ $ $ THE SUN

The Sun Publishing Co., 107 N. Roberson St., Chapel Hill NC 27516. (919)942-5282. Fax: (919)932-3101. Website: www.thesunmagazine.org. **Contact:** Sy Safransky, editor. **90% freelance written.** Monthly magazine. "We are open to all kinds of writing, though we favor work of a personal nature." Estab. 1974. Circ. 60,000. Pays on publication. Publishes ms an average of 6-12 months after acceptance. Byline given. Buys first, one-time rights. Accepts previously published material. Sample copy for $5. Writer's guidelines online.
- Responds in 3-6 months.

Nonfiction Book excerpts, essays, general interest, interview/profile, opinion, personal experience, spiritual. **Buys 50 mss/year.** Send complete ms. Length: 7,000 words maximum. **Pays $300-1,250.** Complimentary subscription is given in addition to payment (applies to payment for *all* works, not just nonfiction).

Reprints Send photocopy and information about when and where the material previously appeared. Pays 50% of amount paid for original article or story.

Photos Send photos with submission. Reviews b&w prints. Buys one-time rights. Offers $50-200/photo. Model releases required.

Fiction "We avoid stereotypical genre pieces like science fiction, romance, western, and horror. Read an issue before submitting." Literary. **Buys 20 mss/year.** Send complete ms. Length: 7,000 words maximum. **Pays $300-750.**

Poetry Free verse, prose poems, short and long poems. **Buys 24 poems/year.** Submit maximum 6 poems. **Pays $50-250.**

N ⊘ TIME

Time Inc. Magazine, Time & Life Bldg., 1271 Avenue of the Americas, New York NY 10020. (212)522-1212. Fax: (212)522-0323. E-mail: letters@time.com. Website: www.time.com. **Contact:** Jim Kelly, managing editor. Weekly magazine. "*Time* covers the full range of information that is important to people today—breaking news, national and world affairs, business news, societal and lifestyle issues, culture and entertainment news and reviews." Estab. 1923. Circ. 4,150,000. Sample copy not available.
- *Time* does not accept unsolicited material for publication. The magazine is entirely staff written and produced.

$ $ $ $ TOWN & COUNTRY

The Hearst Corp., 1700 Broadway, New York NY 10019. (212)903-5000. Fax: (212)262-7107. Website: www.townandcountrymag.com. Editor-in-Chief: Pamela Fiori. **40% freelance written.** Monthly lifestyle magazine. "*Town & Country* is a lifestyle magazine for the affluent market. Features focus on fashion, beauty, travel, interior design, and the arts, as well as individuals' accomplishments and contributions to society." Estab. 1846. Circ. 488,000. **Pays on acceptance.** Byline given. Offers 25% kill fee. Buys first North American serial, electronic rights. Accepts queries by mail. Responds in 2 months to queries.

Nonfiction "We're looking for engaging service articles for a high income, well-educated audience, in numerous categories: travel, personalities, interior design, fashion, beauty, jewelry, health, city news, the arts, philanthropy." General interest, interview/profile, travel. Rarely publishes work not commissioned by the magazine. Does not publish poetry, short stories, or fiction. **Buys 25 mss/year.** Query by mail only with relevant clips before submitting. Length: Column items, 100-300 words; feature stories, 800-2,000 words. **Pays $2/word.**

Tips "We have served the affluent market for over 150 years, and our writers need to be expert in the needs and interests of that market. Most of our freelance writers start by doing short pieces for our front-of-book columns, then progress from there.''

N ⊘ VERANDA

The Hearst Corp., 455 E. Paces Ferry Road NE, Suite 216, Atlanta GA 30305-3319. (404)261-3603. Fax: (404)364-9772. E-mail: mmevans@hearst.com. Website: www.veranda.com. Bimonthly magazine. Written as a southern lifestyle and interior design publication. Circ. 380,890. Editorial lead time 5 months. Sample copy not available.

• Does not buy freelance materials or use freelance writers.

$ THE WORLD & I

The Magazine for Lifelong Learners, News World Communications, Inc., 3600 New York Ave. NE, Washington DC 20002. (202)635-4000. Fax: (202)269-9353. E-mail: editor@worldandimag.com. Website: www.worldandi.com. Editor: Morton A. Kaplan. Associate Executive Editor: Eric P. Olsen. **Contact:** Gary Rowe, editorial office manager. **90% freelance written.** Monthly magazine. ''A broad interest magazine for the thinking, educated person.'' Estab. 1986. Circ. 30,000. Pays on publication. Publishes ms an average of 6 months after acceptance. Byline given. Offers 20% kill fee. Submit seasonal material 5 months in advance. Accepts queries by mail. Accepts previously published material. Responds in 6 weeks to queries; 10 weeks to mss. Sample copy for $5 and 9×12 SASE. Writer's guidelines online.

Nonfiction ''Description of Sections: Current Issues: Politics, economics and strategic trends covered in a variety of approaches, including special report, analysis, commentary and photo essay. The Arts: International coverage of music, dance, theater, film, television, craft, design, architecture, photography, poetry, painting and sculpture—through reviews, features, essays, opinion pieces and a 6-page Gallery of full-color reproductions. Life: Surveys all aspects of life in 22 rotating subsections which include: Travel and Adventure (first person reflections, preference given to authors who provide photographic images), Profile (people or organizations that are 'making a difference'), Food and Garden (must be accompanied by photos), Education, Humor, Hobby, Family, Consumer, Trends, and Health. Send SASE for complete list of subsections. Natural Science: Covers the latest in science and technology, relating it to the social and historical context, under these headings: At the Edge, Impacts, Nature Walk, Science and Spirit, Science and Values, Scientists: Past and Present, Crucibles of Science and Science Essay. Book World: Excerpts from important, timely books (followed by commentaries) and 10-12 scholarly reviews of significant new books each month, including untranslated works from abroad. Covers current affairs, intellectual issues, contemporary fiction, history, moral/religious issues and the social sciences. Currents in Modern Thought: Examines scholarly research and theoretical debate across the wide range of disciplines in the humanities and social sciences. Featured themes are explored by several contributors. Investigates theoretical issues raised by certain current events, and offers contemporary reflection on issues drawn from the whole history of human thought. Culture: Surveys the world's people in these subsections: Peoples (their unique characteristics and cultural symbols), Crossroads (changes brought by the meeting of cultures), Patterns (photo essay depicting the daily life of a distinct culture), Folk Wisdom (folklore and practical wisdom and their present forms), and Heritage (multicultural backgrounds of the American people and how they are bound to the world). Photo Essay: Patterns, a 6- or 8-page photo essay, appears monthly in the Culture section. Emphasis is placed on comprehensive photographic coverage of a people or group, their private or public lifestyle, in a given situation or context. Accompanying word count: 300-500 words. Photos must be from existing stock, no travel subsidy. Life & Ideals, a 6- or 8-page photo essay, occasionally appears in the Life section. First priority is given to those focused on individuals or organizations that are 'making a difference.' Accompanying word count: 700-1,000 words.'' No *National Enquirer*-type articles. **Buys 1,200 mss/year.** Query with published clips. Length: 1,000-5,000 words. **Pays per article basis for assigned articles.** Seldom pays expenses of writers on assignment.

Reprints Send ms with rights for sale noted and information about when and where the material previously appeared.

Photos State availability with submission. Reviews contact sheets, transparencies, prints. Buys one-time rights. Payment negotiable. Identification of subjects, model releases required.

Fiction Novel excerpts.

Poetry Arts Editor. Avant-garde, free verse, haiku, light verse, traditional. **Buys 4-6 poems/year.** Submit maximum 5 poems. **Pays $30-75.**

Tips ''We accept articles from journalists, but also place special emphasis on scholarly contributions. It is our hope that the magazine will enable the best of contemporary thought, presented in accessible language, to reach a wider audience than would normally be possible through the academic journals appropriate to any given discipline.''

HEALTH & FITNESS

$ $ AMERICAN FITNESS

15250 Ventura Blvd., Suite 200, Sherman Oaks CA 91403. (818)905-0040. Fax: (818)990-5468. Website: www.af aa.com. Publisher: Roscoe Fawcett. **Contact:** Dr. Meg Jordan, editor. **75% freelance written.** Bimonthly magazine covering exercise and fitness, health, and nutrition. "We need timely, in-depth, informative articles on health, fitness, aerobic exercise, sports nutrition, age-specific fitness, and outdoor activity." Absolutely no first-person accounts. Need well-reserched articles for professional readers. Circ. 42,000. Pays 6 weeks after publication. Publishes ms an average of 6 months after acceptance. Byline given. Submit seasonal material 4 months in advance. Accepts queries by mail, fax. Accepts previously published material. Accepts simultaneous submissions. Responds in 6 weeks to queries. Sample copy for $3 and SAE with 6 first-class stamps.

Nonfiction Needs include health and fitness, including women's issues (pregnancy, family, pre- and postnatal, menopause, and eating disorders); new research findings on exercise techniques and equipment; aerobic exercise; sports nutrition; sports medicine; innovations and trends in aerobic sports; tips on teaching exercise and humorous accounts of fitness motivation; physiology; youth and senior fitness. Historical/nostalgic (history of various athletic events), inspirational, interview/profile (fitness figures), new product (plus equipment review), personal experience (successful fitness story), photo feature (on exercise, fitness, new sport), travel (activity adventures). No articles on unsound nutritional practices, popular trends, or unsafe exercise gimmicks. **Buys 18-25 mss/year.** Query with published clips or send complete ms. Length: 800-1,200 words. **Pays $200 for features, $80 for news.** Sometimes pays expenses of writers on assignment.

Photos Sports, action, fitness, aquatic aerobics competitions, and exercise class. "We are especially interested in photos of high-adrenalin sports like rock climbing and mountain biking." Reviews transparencies, prints. Usually buys all rights; other rights purchased depend on use of photo. Pays $35 for transparencies. Captions, identification of subjects, model releases required.

Columns/Departments Research (latest exercise and fitness findings); Alternative paths (nonmainstream approaches to health, wellness, and fitness); Strength (latest breakthroughs in weight training); Clubscene (profiles and highlights of fitness club industry); Adventure (treks, trails, and global challenges); Food (low-fat/nonfat, high-flavor dishes); Homescene (home-workout alternatives); Clip 'n' Post (concise exercise research to post in health clubs, offices or on refrigerators). Length: 800-1,000 words. Query with published clips or send complete ms. **Pays $100-200.**

Tips "Make sure to quote scientific literature or good research studies and several experts with good credentials to validate exercise trend, technique, or issue. Cover a unique aerobics or fitness angle, provide accurate and interesting findings, and write in a lively, intelligent manner. Please, no first-person accouts of 'how I lost weight or discovered running.' *AF* is a good place for first-time authors or regularly published authors who want to sell spin-offs or reprints."

$ $ $ $ AMERICAN HEALTH & FITNESS

CANUSA Publishing, 5775 McLaughlin Rd., Mississauga ON L5R 3P7, Canada. Fax: (905)507-2372. E-mail: editorial@ahfmag.com. Website: www.ahfmag.com. Publisher: Robert Kennedy. **Contact:** Kerrie-Lee Brown, editor-in-chief. Bimonthly magazine. "*American Health & Fitness* is designed to help male fitness enthusiasts (18-39) stay fit, strong, virile, and healthy through sensible diet and exercise." Estab. 2000. Circ. 310,000. **Pays on acceptance.** Publishes ms an average of 6 months after acceptance. Byline given. Buys all rights. Editorial lead time 4 months. Submit seasonal material 6 months in advance. Accepts queries by mail, e-mail, fax. Responds in 4 months to queries; 4 months to mss. Sample copy for $5.

Nonfiction How-to, humor, inspirational, interview/profile, new product, personal experience, photo feature, bodybuilding and weight training, health & fitness tips, diet, medical advice, workouts, nutrition. **Buys 80-100 mss/year.** Send complete ms. Length: 1,500 words maximum. **Pays for assigned and unsolicited articles.**

Photos Send photos with submission. Reviews 35mm transparencies, 8×10 prints. Buys all rights. Offers $35 and up/photo. Captions, identification of subjects required.

Columns/Departments Personal Training; Strength & Conditioning; Fitness; Longevity; Natural Health; Sex. **Buys 40 mss/year.** Send complete ms.

Fillers Anecdotes, facts, gags to be illustrated by cartoonist, newsbreaks (fitness, nutrition, health), short humor. **Buys 50-100/year.** Length: 100-200 words. **Pays 35¢ and up/word.**

$ $ ASCENT MAGAZINE

Yoga for an Inspired Life, Timeless Books, 837 Rue Gilford, Montreal QC H2J 1P1, Canada. (514)499-3999. Fax: (514)499-3904. E-mail: info@ascentmagazine.com. Website: www.ascentmagazine.com. Editor: Clea McDougall. **Contact:** Juniper Glass, managing editor. **75% freelance written.** Quarterly magazine covering engaged spirituality, with a focus on yoga philosophy and practice. "*Ascent* publishes unique and personal perspectives on yoga and spirituality. Our goal is to explore what it means to be truly human, to think deeply, and live a meaningful life in today's world." Estab. 1999. Circ. 6,000. Pays on publication. Publishes ms an average of 3 months after acceptance. Byline given. Offers 20% kill fee. Buys first North American serial, with exclusive rights for 6 months after publication. Editorial lead time 4 months. Submit seasonal material 6 months in advance. Accepts queries by e-mail. Responds in 1 month to queries; 1 month to mss. Sample copy for $5. Writer's guidelines online.

Nonfiction Essays, interview/profile, personal experience, photo feature, religious. Special issues: Travel (Summer 2004); Health & Fitness (Fall 2004); Liberation (Winter 2004). No academic articles or promotional articles for specific yoga school or retreats. **Buys 30 mss/year.** Query with published clips. Length: 800-3,500 words. **Pays 20¢/word (Canadian).** Sometimes pays expenses of writers on assignment.

Photos Joe Ollmann, designer. Reviews GIF/JPEG files. Buys one-time rights. Negotiates payment individually.

Columns/Departments Reviews (books and CDs), 500 words. **Buys 10 mss/year.** Query with published clips. **Pays $50-150 (Canadian).**

Tips "*Ascent* publishes mainly personal, reflective nonfiction. Make sure to tell us how you will bring a personal, intimate tone to your article. Send a detailed query with writing samples. Give us a good idea of your potential as a writer."

N ⊘ BALLY TOTAL FITNESS MAGAZINE

RB Publishing, Inc., 2901 International Lane, Suite 200, Madison WI 53704-3177. (608)241-8777. Fax: (608)241-8666. E-mail: editor@ballyfitness.com. Quarterly magazine. Circ. 500,000.

 • Does not buy freelance material or use freelance writers.

N $ $ BETTER HEALTH

Better Health Magazine, 1450 Chapel St., New Haven CT 06511-4440. (203)789-3972. Fax: (203)789-4053. **Contact:** Cynthia Wolfe Boynton, editor/publishing director. **90% freelance written.** Prefers to work with published/established writers; will consider new/unpublished writers. Query first, do not send article. Bimonthly magazine devoted to health, wellness and medical issues. Estab. 1979. Circ. 500,000. **Pays on acceptance.** Byline given. Offers 20% kill fee. Buys first rights. Sample copy for $2.50. Writer's guidelines for #10 SASE.

Nonfiction Wellness/prevention issues are of primary interest. New medical techniques or nonmainstream practices are not considered. No fillers, poems, quizzes, seasonal, heavy humor, inspirational or personal experience. Length: 1,500-3,000 words. **Pays $300-700.**

$ $ $ BETTER NUTRITION

Active Interest Media, 301 Concourse Blvd., Suite 350, Glen Allen VA 23059. (804)346-0990. Fax: (804)346-1223. E-mail: editorial@betternutrition.com. Website: www.betternutrition.com. **Contact:** Jerry Shaver, managing editor. **57% freelance written.** Monthly magazine covering nutritional news and approaches to optimal health. "The new *Better Nutrition* helps people (men, women, families, old and young) integrate nutritious food, the latest and most effective dietary supplements, and exercise/personal care into healthy lifestyles." Estab. 1938. Circ. 460,000. Pays on publication. Publishes ms an average of 2 months after acceptance. Byline given. Buys varies according to article rights. Editorial lead time 3 months. Accepts queries by mail, e-mail. Sample copy for free.

Nonfiction Each issue has multiple features, clinical research crystallized into accessible articles on nutrition, health, alternative medicine, disease prevention. **Buys 120-180 mss/year.** Query. Length: 400-1,200 words. **Pays $400-1,000.**

Photos State availability with submission. Reviews 4×5 transparencies, 3×5 prints. Buys one time rights or non-exclusive reprint rights. Negotiates payment individually. Captions, identification of subjects, model releases required.

Tips "Be on top of what's newsbreaking in nutrition and supplementation. Interview experts. Fact-check, fact-check, fact-check. Send in a résumé (including Social Security/IRS number), a couple of clips and a list of article possibilities."

$ $ CLIMBING

Primedia Enthusiast Group, 0326 Highway 133, Suite 190, Carbondale CO 81623. (970)963-9449. Fax: (970)963-9442. E-mail: climbing@climbing.com. Website: www.climbing.com. Editor: Jeff Achey. Magazine published 9 times/year covering climbing and mountaineering. Provides features on rock climbing and mountaineering worldwide. Estab. 1970. Circ. 51,000. Pays on publication. Editorial lead time 6 weeks. Accepts queries by e-mail. Sample copy for $ 4.99. Writer's guidelines online.

Nonfiction SASE returns. Interview/profile (Interesting climbers), personal experience (Climbing adventures), Surveys of different areas. Query. Length: 2,000-5,000 words. **Pays 35¢/word.**

Photos State availability with submission. Reviews negatives, 35mm transparencies, prints. Pays $75 minimum / $700 maximum.

Columns/Departments Roadworthy (destination mini-features), 500-1,500 words; High and Wild (well-known and obscure mountain destinations), 1,000-2,000 words; Training, 1,000-1,500 words; Medicine, 1,000-1,500 words; Equipment, (reviews technical climbing gear) 1,000-2,000 words; Just Out, (review of one piece of equipment), 500-600 words; Tech Tip, (how-to description of techniques), 250-500 words; Players (profiles of climbers), 750 words; Reviews (reviews books, guidebooks, films, CD-Roms and videos), 200-300 words; Perspective (personal opinion or experience), 200-300 words. Query. **Payment varies.**

Ⓝ Ⓞ FIT PREGNANCY

American Media, Inc., 21100 Erwin St., Woodland Hills CA 91367-3712. (818)884-6800. Fax: (818)992-6895. Website: www.fitpregnancy.com. Bimonthly magazine. Circ. 505,000.
• Does not buy freelance material or use freelance writers.

Ⓝ $ $ FIT.STYLE

A Bally Total Fitness Magazine, RB Publishing, Inc., 2901 International Lane, Madison WI 53704. Fax: (608)241-8666. E-mail: erin.e@rbpub.com. Website: www.rbpub.com. Editor: Jon Harris. **Contact:** Erin M. Eagan, managing editor. **75% freelance written.** Quarterly magazine. "A national newsstand publication that is also distributed in all Bally Total Fitness clubs. The magazine is geared towards women in their 20's and 30's, and read by over 5 million Americans. Each issue educates readers on achieving balance in their lives and provides them with the tools they need to live a fit, healthy, and active lifestyle." Estab. 1999. Circ. 300,000. Pays on publication. Publishes ms an average of 2 months after acceptance. Byline given. Offers 20% kill fee. Not copyrighted. Buys all rights. Editorial lead time 4 months. Submit seasonal material 4 months in advance. Accepts queries by mail, e-mail, fax. Accepts simultaneous submissions. Responds in 2 months to mss. Sample copy for #10 SASE. Writer's guidelines by e-mail.

Nonfiction General interest, interview/profile, photo feature, travel. **Buys 5-6 mss/year.** Query with published clips. Length: 500-1,200 words. **Pays 50¢/word.**

Photos State availability with submission. Reviews GIF/JPEG files. Buys one-time rights. Negotiates payment individually. Captions, identification of subjects, model releases required.

Columns/Departments EverythingFITNESS (celeb bits on fitness routines, information, etc.); EverythingNUTRITION (celeb bits on nutrition habits, diets, etc.). **Buys 8 mss/year.** Query with published clips. **Pays 50¢/word.**

Ⓝ $ $ $ $ FITNESS MAGAZINE

15 E. 26th St., 5th Floor, New York NY 10010-1536. (646)758-0430. Fax: (646)758-0550. **Contact:** Trish Calvo, senior editor (features). Monthly magazine for women in their twenties and thirties who are interested in fitness and living a healthy life. "Do not call." **Pays on acceptance.** Byline given. Offers 20% kill fee. Buys first North American serial rights. Responds in 2 months to queries. Writer's guidelines for #10 SASE.

Nonfiction "We need timely, well-written nonfiction articles on exercise and fitness, beauty, health, diet/nutrition, and psychology. We always include boxes and sidebars in our stories." **Buys 60-80 mss/year.** Query. Length: 1,500-2,500 words. **Pays $1,500-2,500.** Pays expenses of writers on assignment.

Reprints Send photocopy. Negotiates fee.

Columns/Departments Length:600-1,200 words. **Buys 30 mss/year.** Query. **Pays $800-1,500.**

Tips "Our pieces must get inside the mind of the reader and address her needs, hopes, fears and desires. *Fitness* acknowledges that getting and staying fit is difficult in an era when we are all time-pressured."

$ $ HEALING LIFESTYLES & SPAS

P.O. Box 90110, Santa Barbara CA 93190. (202)441-9557. Fax: (805)684-4397. E-mail: editorial@healinglifestyles.com. Website: www.healinglifestyles.com. Editor: Melissa Scott. **90% freelance written.** "*Healing Lifestyles & Spas* is a bimonthly magazine committed to healing, health, and living a well-rounded, more natural life. In each issue we cover retreats, spas, organic living, natural food, herbs, beauty, yoga, alternative medicine, bodywork, spirituality, and features on living a healthy lifestyle." Estab. 1996. Circ. 45,000. Pays on publication. Publishes ms an average of 2-10 months after acceptance. Editorial lead time 6 months. Submit seasonal material 6-9 months in advance. Accepts queries by mail, e-mail. Responds in 6 weeks to queries.

Nonfiction "We will consider all in-depth features relating to spas, retreats, lifestyle issues, mind/body well being, yoga, enlightening profiles, and women's health issues." Travel (domestic and international). No fiction or poetry. Query. Length: 1,000-2,000 words. **Pays $150-500, depending on length, research, experience, and availability and quality of images.**

Photos "If you will be providing your own photography, you must use slide film or provide a Mac formatted CD with image resolution of at least 300 dpi." Send photos with submission. Captions required.

Columns/Departments All Things New & Natural (short pieces outlining new health trends, alternative medicine updates, and other interesting tidbits of information), 50-200 words; Guinea Pig (first-hand information on new modalities, fitness classes, etc.), 100-200 words; Media Reviews, 100 words; Urban Retreats (focuses on a single city and explores its natural side), 1,200-1,600 words; Health (features on relevant topics ranging from nutrition to health news and updates), 900-1,200 words; Good For You (organic natural food articles and recipes), 1,000-1,200 words; Day Spa (unique day spas around the country), 400-500 words; Spa a la carte (explores a new treatment or modality on the spa menu), 600-1,000 words; Insight (focuses on profiles or theme-related articles), 1,000-2,000 words. Query.

$ $ $ $HEALTH

Time, Inc., Southern Progress Corp., 2100 Lakeshore Dr., Birmingham AL 35209. (205)445-6000. Fax: (205)445-5123. E-mail: health@timeinc.com. Website: www.health.com. Vice President/Editor: Doug Crichton. Magazine published 10 times/year covering health, fitness, and nutrition. "Our readers are predominantly college-educated women in their 30s, 40s, and 50s. Edited to focus not on illness, but on wellness events, ideas, and people." Estab. 1987. Circ. 1,360,000. **Pays on acceptance.** Byline given. Offers 33% kill fee. Buys first publication and online rights rights. Accepts queries by mail, fax. Accepts simultaneous submissions. Responds in 2 months to queries to mss. Sample copy for $5 to Back Issues. Writer's guidelines for #10 SASE.
Nonfiction No unsolicited mss. **Buys 25 mss/year.** Query with published clips and SASE. Length: 1,200 words. **Pays $1-1.50/word.** Pays expenses of writers on assignment.
Columns/Departments Food, Mind, Healthy Looks, Fitness, Relationships.
Tips "We look for well-articulated ideas with a narrow focus and broad appeal. A query that starts with an unusual local event and hooks it legitimately to some national trend or concern is bound to get our attention. Use quotes, examples and statistics to show why the topic is important and why the approach is workable. We need to see clear evidence of credible research findings pointing to meaningful options for our readers. Stories should offer practical advice and give clear explanations."

$ $HEPATITIS

Management and Treatment—A Practical Guide for Patients, Families, and Friends, Quality Publishing, Inc., 523 N. Sam Houston Tollway E., Suite 300, Houston TX 77060. (281)272-2744. Fax: (281)847-5440. E-mail: editor@hepatitismag.com. Website: www.hepatitismag.com. **Contact:** Managing Editor. **70-80% freelance written.** Quarterly magazine covering Hepatitis health news. Estab. 1999. Circ. 25,000. Pays on publication. Publishes ms an average of 2 months after acceptance. Byline given. Buys first North American serial, electronic rights. Editorial lead time 6 months. Submit seasonal material 4 months in advance. Accepts queries by mail, e-mail. Accepts simultaneous submissions. Responds in 6 weeks to queries. Sample copy and writer's guidelines free.
Nonfiction Inspirational, interview/profile, new product, personal experience. "We do not want any one-source or no-source articles." **Buys 42-48 mss/year.** Query with or without published clips. Length: 1,500-2,500 words. Sometimes pays expenses of writers on assignment.
Photos Send photos with submission. Reviews transparencies, prints, GIF/JPEG files. Rights negotiated, usually purchases one-time rights. Offers no additional payment for photos accepted with ms. Identification of subjects required.
Columns/Departments General news or advice on Hepatitis written by a doctor or healthcare professional, 1,500-2,000 words. **Buys 12-18 mss/year.** Query. **Pays $375-500.**
Tips "Be specific in your query. Show me that you know the topic you want to write about. And show me that you can write a solid, well-rounded story."

⊞ HERE'S HEALTH

Emap, Greater London House, Hampstead Rd., London NW1 7EJ, England. (020) 7347 1893. Fax: (020) 7347 1897. Editor: Sarah Wilson. **Contact:** Lisa Howells, deputy editor. **80% freelance written.** Monthly magazine covering complementary and alternative health. "*Here's Health* focuses on holistic health and well being." Estab. 1950. Circ. 25,000. **Pays on acceptance.** Publishes ms an average of 3 months after acceptance. Byline given. Buys all rights. Editorial lead time 3-4 months. Submit seasonal material 3-4 months in advance. Accepts queries by mail, fax. Accepts simultaneous submissions. Sample copy for 1 SAE and 2 first-class stamps.
Photos Angela Ryan, art editor. State availability with submission. Reviews contact sheets, transparencies, prints. Buys all rights. Negotiates payment individiually. Captions, identification of subjects, model releases required.

$ $ $ $MAMM MAGAZINE

Courage, Respect & Survival, MAMM, LLC, 54 W. 22nd St., 4th Floor, New York NY 10010. (646)365-1355. Fax: (646)365-1369. E-mail: editorial@mamm.com. Website: www.mamm.com. Managing Editor: Liz Galst.

80% freelance written. Magazine published 10 times/year covering cancer prevention, treatment, and survival for women. "*MAMM* gives its readers the essential tools and emotional support they need before, during and after diagnosis of breast, ovarian and other female reproductive cancers. We offer a mix of survivor profiles, conventional and alternative treatment information, investigative features, essays, and cutting-edge news." Estab. 1997. Circ. 100,000. Pays within 45 days of publication. Publishes ms an average of 3 months after acceptance. Byline given. Offers 50% kill fee. Buys exclusive rights up to 3 months after publishing, first rights after that. Editorial lead time 4 months. Submit seasonal material 4 months in advance. Accepts simultaneous submissions. Sample copy and writer's guidelines free.

Nonfiction Book excerpts, essays, exposé, historical/nostalgic, how-to, humor, inspirational, interview/profile, opinion, personal experience, photo feature. **Buys 90 mss/year.** Query with published clips. Length: 200-3,000 words. **Pays $50-1,500.** Sometimes pays expenses of writers on assignment.

Photos Send photos with submission. Reviews contact sheets, negatives. Buys first rights. Negotiates payment individually. Identification of subjects required.

Columns/Departments Cancer Girl (humor/experience); Opinion (cultural/political); International Dispatch (experience), all 600 words. **Buys 30 mss/year.** Query with published clips. **Pays $250-300. Buys 6 mss/year.** Query with published clips.

$ $ $ $ MEN'S HEALTH

Rodale, 33 E. Minor St., Emmaus PA 18098. (610)967-5171. Fax: (610)967-7725. E-mail: bill.stieg@rodale.com. Website: www.menshealth.com. Editor-in-Chief: David Zinczenko. Executive Editor: Peter Moore. **Contact:** Bill Stieg, senior editor. **50% freelance written.** Magazine published 10 times/year covering men's health and fitness. "*Men's Health* is a lifestyle magazine showing men the practical and positive actions that make their lives better, with articles covering fitness, nutrition, relationships, travel, careers, grooming, and health issues." Estab. 1986. Circ. 1,600,000. **Pays on acceptance.** Offers 25% kill fee. Buys all rights. Accepts queries by mail, fax. Responds in 3 weeks to queries. Writer's guidelines for #10 SASE.

O— Freelancers have the best chance with the front-of-the-book piece, Malegrams.

Nonfiction "Authoritative information on all aspects of men's physical and emotional health. We rely on writers to seek out the right experts and to either tell a story from a first-person vantage or get good anecdotes." **Buys 30 features/year; 360 short mss/year.** Query with published clips. Length: 1,200-4,000 words for features, 100-300 words for short pieces. **Pays $1,000-5,000 for features; $100-500 for short pieces.**

Columns/Departments Length: 750-1,500 words. **Buys 80 mss/year. Pays $750-2,000.**

The online magazine carries original content not included in the print edition. Contact: Fred Zahradnick, online associate.

Tips "We have a wide definition of health. We believe that being successful in every area of your life is being healthy. The magazine focuses on all aspects of health, from stress issues to nutrition to exercise to sex. It is 50% staff written, 50% from freelancers. The best way to break in is not by covering a particular subject, but by covering it within the magazine's style. There is a very particular tone and voice to the magazine. A writer has to be a good humor writer as well as a good service writer. Prefers mail queries. No phone calls, please."

$ NATURAL BEAUTY & HEALTH MAGAZINE

A Primer for Holistic Health and Natural Living, P.O. Box 600, Chico CA 95927. (530)893-9076. E-mail: editor@ magicalblend.com. Website: www.nbhonline.com. **50% freelance written.** Bimonthly magazine covering alternative healing practices, bodywork, self-help, and spiritual perspectives on wellness. "*Natural Beauty & Health Magazine* exists to aid individuals in achieving better lives, both physically and spiritually. We hold that health is as much a state of the mind as a condition of the body." Estab. 2001. Circ. 100,000. Pays on publication. Publishes an average of 2 months after acceptance. Byline given. Responds in 2-6 months to mss. Sample copy for free. Writer's guidelines for #10 SASE.

O— Break in by "writing an engaging article about some unique perspective on healthy or balanced living or some form of healing trasnformation with practical advice for readers on how to achieve it or interview a recognizable celebrity with a natural lifestyle."

Nonfiction "Articles must reflect our standards; see our magazine." Book excerpts, essays, general interest, inspirational, interview/profile, travel, spiritual. No poetry or fiction. **Buys 24 mss/year.** Send complete ms. Length: 500-2,000 words. **Pays $35-100.**

Photos State availability with submission. Reviews transparencies. Buys all rights. Negotiates payment individually. Identification of subjects, model releases required.

Fillers Alternative health news. **Buys 12-20/year.** Length: 200-500 words. **Pays variable rate.**

N $ $ $ OXYGEN!

Serious Fitness for Serious Women, Canusa Products/St. Ives, Inc., 5775 McLaughlin Rd., Mississauga ON L5R 3P7, Canada. (905)507-3545. Fax: (905)507-2372. E-mail: editorial@oxygenmag.com. Website: www.oxygenm

ag.com. **Contact:** Kerri Lee Brown, editor-in-chief. **70% freelance written.** Monthly magazine covering women's health and fitness. *"Oxygen encourages various exercise, good nutrition to shape and condition the body."* Estab. 1997. Circ. 340,000. **Pays on acceptance.** Publishes ms an average of 4 months after acceptance. Byline given. Offers 25% kill fee. Buys all rights. Editorial lead time 3 months. Submit seasonal material 6 months in advance. Accepts queries by mail, fax. Responds in 5 weeks to queries; 2 months to mss. Sample copy for $5.

○➤ Break in with *"a really strong query proving that it is well researched."*

Nonfiction Exposé, how-to (training and nutrition), humor, inspirational, interview/profile, new product, personal experience, photo feature. No *"poorly researched articles that do not genuinely help the readers towards physical fitness, health and physique."* **Buys 100 mss/year.** Send complete ms. Length: 1,400-1,800 words. **Pays $250-1,000.** Sometimes pays expenses of writers on assignment.

Reprints Send tearsheet, photocopy or typed ms with rights for sale noted and information about when and where the material previously appeared. Pay varies.

Photos State availability of or send photos with submission. Reviews contact sheets, 35mm transparencies, prints. Buys all rights. Offers $35-500. Identification of subjects required.

Columns/Departments Nutrition (low-fat recipes), 1,700 words; Weight Training (routines and techniques), 1,800 words; Aerobics (how-tos), 1,700 words. **Buys 50 mss/year.** Send complete ms. **Pays $150-500.**

▣ The online magazine carries original content not found in the print edition.

Tips *"Every editor of every magazine is looking, waiting, hoping and praying for the magic article. The beauty of the writing has to spring from the page; the edge imparted has to excite the reader because of its unbelievable information."*

Ⓝ $ $ $ $ POZ

POZ Publishing, LLC, One Little W. 12th St., 6th Floor, New York NY 10014. (212)242-2163. Fax: (212)675-8505. E-mail: poz-editor@poz.com. Website: www.poz.com. Managing Editor: Angelo Ragaza. **Contact:** Walter Armstrong, editor. **100% freelance written.** Monthly national magazine for people impacted by HIV and AIDS. *"POZ is a trusted source of conventional and alternative treatment information, investigative features, survivor profiles, essays and cutting-edge news for people living with AIDS and their caregivers. POZ is a lifestyle magazine with both health and cultural content."* Estab. 1994. Circ. 91,000. Pays 45 days after acceptance. Publishes ms an average of 3 months after acceptance. Byline given. Offers 20% kill fee. Buys first rights. Editorial lead time 4 months. Submit seasonal material 4 months in advance. Accepts simultaneous submissions. Sample copy and writer's guidelines free.

Nonfiction Book excerpts, essays, exposé, historical/nostalgic, how-to, humor, inspirational, interview/profile, opinion, personal experience, photo feature. **Buys 180 mss/year.** Query with published clips. *"We take unsolicited mss on speculation only."* Length: 200-3,000 words. **Pays $50-1,000.** Sometimes pays expenses of writers on assignment.

Photos Send photos with submission. Reviews contact sheets, negatives. Buys first rights. Negotiates payment individually. Identification of subjects required.

Columns/Departments Life (personal experience); Back Page (humor); Data Dish (opinion/experience/information), all 600 words. **Buys 120 mss/year.** Query with published clips. **Pays $200-3,000.**

Fiction Buys 10 mss/year. Send complete ms. Length: 700-2,000 words. **Payment negotiable.**

Poetry Avant-garde, free verse, haiku, light verse, traditional. **Buys 12 poems/year.** Submit maximum 3 poems. Length: 10-40 lines. **Payment negotiable.**

Fillers Anecdotes, facts, gags to be illustrated by cartoonist, newsbreaks, short humor. **Buys 90/year.** Length: 50-150 words. **Pays $50-75.**

Ⓩ PREVENTION

Rodale, Inc., 33 E. Minor St., Emmaus PA 18098-0099. E-mail: prevention@rodale.com. Website: www.prevention.com. Monthly magazine covering health and fitness. Written to motivate, inspire and enable male and female readers ages 35 and over to take charge of their health, to become healthier and happier, and to improve the lives of family and friends. Estab. 1950. Circ. 3,150,000.

• *Prevention* does not accept, nor do they acknowledge, unsolicited submissions.

Ⓝ Ⓩ PREVENTION'S GUIDE TO WEIGHT LOSS

Rodale, Inc., 33 E. Minor St., Emmaus PA 18098-0001. (610)967-5171. Fax: (610)967-7726. E-mail: preventionspecials@rodale.com. Website: www.prevention.com. Executive Editor: Cindi Caciolo. Biannual magazine. Edited to help readers make the positive lifestyle changes necessary to shed weight permanently and in the most healthful manner possible. Circ. 425,000. Sample copy not available.

• Does not buy freelance materials or use freelance writers.

Ⓝ Ⓩ PREVENTION'S GUIDE: FIT AND FIRM AT 35 PLUS

Rodale, Inc., 33 E. Minor St., Emmaus PA 18098-7726. (610)967-5171. Fax: (610)967-7654. E-mail: preventionspecials@rodale.com. Website: www.prevention.com. Executive Editor: Cindi Caciolo. Semiannual magazine.

Targeted to the 35+ women who want to look and feel their best. Circ. 650,000. Sample copy not available.

- Does not buy freelance materials or use freelance writers.

ℕ ⊘ PREVENTION'S GUIDE: WALKING FIT

Rodale, Inc., 33 E. Minor St., Emmaus PA 18098-0001. (610)967-5171. Fax: (610)967-7654. E-mail: preventionsp ecials@rodale.com. Website: www.prevention.com. Executive Editor: Cindi Caciolo. Biannual magazine. Serves as a guide for those looking to experience the many benefits of fitness walking. Circ. 650,000. Sample copy not available.

- Does not buy freelance materials or use freelance writers.

$ $ $ $ SHAPE MAGAZINE

Weider Publications, Inc., 21100 Erwin St., Woodland Hills CA 91367. (818)595-0593. Fax: (818)704-7620. Website: www.shapemag.com. Editor-in-Chief: Anne Russell. **Contact:** Lynn Perkin, EIC assistant. **70% freelance written.** Prefers to work with published/established writers. Monthly magazine covering women's health and fitness. "*Shape* reaches women who are committed to healthful, active lifestyles. Our readers are participating in a variety of fitness-related activities, in the gym, at home and outdoors, and they are also proactive about their health and are nutrition conscious." Estab. 1981. Circ. 1,600,000. **Pays on acceptance.** Offers 33% kill fee. Buys second serial (reprint), all rights. Submit seasonal material 8 months in advance. Responds in 2 months to queries. Sample copy for 9×12 SAE and 4 first-class stamps.

Nonfiction "We use some health and fitness articles written by professionals in their specific fields." Book excerpts, exposé (health, fitness, nutrition related), how-to (get fit), health/fitness, recipes. "No articles that haven't been queried first." **Buys 27 features/year and 36-54 short mss/year.** Query by mail only with published clips. Length: 2,500 words for features, 1,000 words for shorter pieces. **Pays $1.50/word, on average.**

Tips "Review a recent issue of the magazine. Not responsible for unsolicited material. We reserve the right to edit any article."

$ $ VIBRANT LIFE

A Magazine for Healthful Living, Review and Herald Publishing Association, 55 W. Oak Ridge Dr., Hagerstown MD 21740-7390. (301)393-4019. Fax: (301)393-4055. E-mail: vibrantlife@rhpa.org. Website: www.vibrantlife.c om. **Contact:** Charles Mills, editor. **80% freelance written.** Enjoys working with published/established writers; works with a small number of new/unpublished writers each year. Bimonthly magazine covering health articles (especially from a prevention angle and with a Christian slant). "The average length of time between acceptance of a freelance-written manuscript and publication of the material depends upon the topics: some immediately used; others up to 2 years." Estab. 1885. Circ. 50,000. **Pays on acceptance.** Byline given. Offers 50% kill fee. Buys first serial, first world serial, or sometimes second serial (reprint) rights. Submit seasonal material 9 months in advance. Accepts queries by mail, e-mail, fax. Accepts previously published material. Responds in 1 month to queries. Sample copy for $1. Writer's guidelines online.

Nonfiction "We seek practical articles promoting better health and a more fulfilled life. We especially like features on breakthroughs in medicine, and most aspects of health. We need articles on how to integrate a person's spiritual life with their health. We'd like more in the areas of exercise, nutrition, water, avoiding addictions of all types, and rest—all done from a wellness perspective." Interview/profile (with personalities on health). **Buys 50-60 feature articles/year and 6-12 short mss/year.** Send complete ms. Length: 500-1,500 words for features, 25-250 words for short pieces. **Pays $75-300 for features, $50-75 for short pieces.**

Reprints Send tearsheet and information about when and where the material previously appeared. Pays 50% of amount paid for an original article.

Photos Not interested in b&w photos. Send photos with submission. Reviews 35mm transparencies.

Columns/Departments Buys 12-18 department articles/year. Length: 500-650 words. **Pays $75-175.**

Tips "*Vibrant Life* is published for baby boomers, particularly young professionals, age 40-55. Articles must be written in an interesting, easy-to-read style. Information must be reliable; no faddism. We are more conservative than other magazines in our field. Request a sample copy, and study the magazine and writer's guidelines."

$ $ $ $ VIM & VIGOR

America's Family Health Magazine, 1010 E. Missouri Ave., Phoenix AZ 85014-2601. (602)395-5850. Fax: (602)395-5853. E-mail: betht@mcmurry.com. **Contact:** Beth Tomkiw, editorial director. **75% freelance written.** Quarterly magazine covering health and healthcare. Estab. 1985. Circ. 650,000. **Pays on acceptance.** Publishes ms an average of 3 months after acceptance. Byline given. Buys all rights. Sample copy for 9×12 SAE with 8 first-class stamps. Writer's guidelines for #10 SASE.

Nonfiction "Absolutely no complete manuscripts will be accepted/returned. All articles are assigned. Send published samples for assignment consideration. Any queries regarding story ideas will be placed on the following year's conference agenda and will be addressed on a topic-by-topic basis." Health, disease, medical breakthroughs, exercise/fitness trends, wellness, healthcare. **Buys 12 mss/year.** Send published clips by mail or e-mail. Length: 500-1,500 words. **Pays 90¢-$1.20/word.** Pays expenses of writers on assignment.

Tips "Writers must have consumer healthcare experience."

WEIGHT WATCHERS MAGAZINE

W/W Publishing Group, 747 3rd Ave., 24th Floor, New York NY 10017. (212)207-8800. Fax: (212)588-1733. E-mail: wwmeditor@wwpublishinggroup.com. Website: www.weightwatchers.com. Editor-in-Chief: Nancy Gagliardi. Executive Editor: Geri Anne Fennessey. Associate Editor: Lisa Harris. **70% freelance written.** Bimonthly magazine mostly for women interested in weight loss, including healthy lifestyle/behavior information/advice, news on health, nutrition, fitness, beauty, fashion, psychology and food/recipes. Estab. 1968. Circ. 1,200,000. **Pays on acceptance.** Offers 25% kill fee. Buys first North American serial rights. Editorial lead time 3-12 months. Accepts queries by mail.

Nonfiction Covers diet, nutrition, motivation/psychology, food, spas, and products for both the kitchen and an active lifestyle. Articles have an authoritative, yet friendly tone. How-to and service information crucial for all stories. Query with published clips. Length: 700-1,500 words.

Columns/Departments Accepts editorial in health, fitness, diet, inspiration, nutrition.

Tips "Well-developed, tightly written queries always a plus, as are trend pieces. We're always on the lookout for a fresh angle on an old topic. Sources must be reputable; we prefer subjects to be medical professionals with university affiliations who are published in their field of expertise. Lead times require stories to be seasonal, long-range, and forward-looking. We're looking for fresh, innovative stories that yield worthwhile information for women interested in losing weight—the latest exercise alternatives, a suggestion of how they can reduce stress, nutritional information that may not be common knowledge, reassurance about their lifestyle or health concerns, etc. Familiarity with the Weight Watchers philosophy/program is a plus."

$ $ YOGA FOR EVERYBODY

EGW Publishing Co., 1041 Shary Circle, Concord CA 94518. Fax: (925)671-5573. E-mail: editor@yoga4everybody.com. Website: www.yoga4everybody.com. **Contact:** Kelly Townsend, editor. **100% freelance written.** Quarterly magazine covering yoga, health, stress reduction, and alternative health remedies. "*Yoga for EveryBody* is dedicated to the encouragement and practice of yoga for all types of people. We are more interested in the pursuit of yoga at the beginner and intermediate level and less so in the professional level." Estab. 2003. Circ. 20,000. Pays half on acceptance, half on publication; kill fee is first payment. Publishes ms an average of 3-12 months after acceptance. Byline given. Offers 50% kill fee. Buys all rights. Editorial lead time 3 months. Submit seasonal material 3-6 months in advance. Accepts queries by mail, e-mail, fax. Accepts simultaneous submissions. Sample copy not available. Writer's guidelines online.

Nonfiction Essays, how-to (descriptions of postures and asanas), interview/profile, new product, personal experience, photo feature, technical (yoga postures), travel (retreats), book reviews. No music reviews or unsolicited poetry and cartoons. **Buys 12-16 mss/year.** Query with or without published clips. Length: 1,000-2,000 words. **Pays $100-300 for assigned articles.** Pays in contributor copies in exchange for advertisement.

Photos State availability with submission. Buys all rights. Pays up to $150 for 5-10 photos. Model releases required.

Columns/Departments Working Wellness (where yoga and stress reduction is incorporated into the workplace and business world); Studio Review (favorite yoga studios); Millennial Wisdom (leaders in the field); Yoga Solutions (where yoga has advanced physical or emotional healing); Yoga Fun (retreats, conferences, and workshops); On the Mat (new and notable yoga products); Cross Culture (yoga around the world). **Buys up to 60 mss/year.** Query with or without published clips. **Pays $100.**

$ $ $ $ YOGA JOURNAL

2054 University Ave., Suite 600, Berkeley CA 94704. (510)841-9200. Fax: (510)644-3101. E-mail: editorial@yogajournal.com. Website: www.yogajournal.com. **Contact:** Kathryn Arnold, editorial director. **75% freelance written.** Bimonthly magazine covering the practice and philosophy of yoga. Estab. 1975. Circ. 130,000. Pays within 90 days of acceptance. Publishes ms an average of 10 months after acceptance. Byline given. Offers kill fee on assigned articles. Buys first North American serial rights. Submit seasonal material 4 months in advance. Accepts queries by mail. Accepts previously published material. Responds in 3 months to queries. Sample copy for $4.99. Writer's guidelines online.

Nonfiction "Yoga is a main concern, but we also highlight other conscious living/New Age personalities and endeavors (nothing too 'woo-woo'). In particular we welcome articles on the following themes: 1. Leaders, spokepersons, and visionaries in the yoga community; 2. The practice of hatha yoga; 3. Applications of yoga to everyday life; 4. Hatha yoga anatomy and kinesiology, and therapeutic yoga; 5. Nutrition and diet, cooking, and natural skin and body care." Book excerpts, how-to (yoga, exercise, etc.), inspirational, interview/profile, opinion, photo feature, travel (yoga-related). Does not want unsolicited poetry or cartoons. "Please avoid New

Age jargon and in-house buzz words as much as possible.'' **Buys 50-60 mss/year.** Query with SASE. Length: 2,500-6,000 words. **Pays $800-2,000.**

Reprints Send tearsheet or photocopy with rights for sale noted and information about when and where the material previously appeared.

Columns/Departments Health (self-care; well-being); Body-Mind (hatha Yoga; other body-mind modalities; meditation; yoga philosophy; Western mysticism); Community (service; profiles; organizations; events), Length: 1,500-2,000 words. **Pays $400-800.** Living (books; video; arts; music), 800 words. **Pays $200-250.** World of Yoga, Spectrum (brief yoga and healthy living news/events/fillers), 150-600 words. **Pays $50-150.** ''We encourage a well-written query letter outlining your subject and describing its appeal.''

Tips ''Please read our writer's guidelines before submission. Do not e-mail or fax unsolicited manuscripts.''

YOUR HEALTH & FITNESS

General Learning Communications, 900 Skokie Blvd., Northbrook IL 60062-1574. (847)205-3000. Fax: (847)564-8197. Website: www.glcomm.com. **Contact:** Debb Bastian, editorial director (adult healthcare). **90% freelance written.** Works with published/established writers with substantial experience in health/healthcare writing. Quarterly assignments made. Assigns educational pieces on health, fitness, and safety that successfully translate specific, timely, and relevant health information for a consumer audience. Estab. 1969. Circ. 1,000,000. Pays after acceptance and medical review, approximately 6 months. Buys all rights.

> ○━ ''Appropriate queries will be reviewed. If you're interested in writing for the magazine, send a cover letter, résumé/curriculum vitae, and writing samples. Topics are determined approximately one year in advance on a rolling schedule. No unsolicited manuscripts.''

Nonfiction All article topics are assigned. Consumer health. **Buys approximately 65 mss/year.** Send a résumé and cover letter accompanied by several published writing samples on health and/or health-related topics. Length: 300-1,000 words. **Payment varies, commensurate with experience and complexity of assignment.**

Tips ''Submissions should be made via mail. Writers must have consumer health writing experience and provide published clips. No phone queries.''

HISTORY

$ $ AMERICA'S CIVIL WAR

Primedia History Group, 741 Miller Dr., SE, Suite D-2, Leesburg VA 20175-8920. (703)771-9400. E-mail: americas civilwar@thehistorynet.com. Website: www.thehistorynet.com. Managing Editor: Carl von Wodtke. **Contact:** Dana Shoaf, editor. **95% freelance written.** Bimonthly magazine covering ''popular history and straight historical narrative for both the general reader and the Civil War buff covering strategy, tactics, personalities, arms and equipment.'' Estab. 1988. Circ. 78,000. Pays on publication. Publishes ms an average of 2 years after acceptance. Byline given. Buys all rights. Accepts queries by mail, e-mail, fax. Responds in 3 months to queries; 6 months to mss. Sample copy for $5. Writer's guidelines for #10 SASE or online.

Nonfiction Historical/nostalgic, book notices; preservation news. No fiction or poetry. **Buys 24 mss/year.** Query. Length: 3,500-4,000 words and should include a 500-word sidebar. **Pays $300 and up.**

Photos Send photos with submission or cite sources. ''We'll order.'' Captions, identification of subjects required.

Columns/Departments Personality (profiles of Civil War personalities); Men & Material (about weapons used); Commands (about units); Eyewitness to War (historical letters and diary excerpts). Length: 2,000 words. **Buys 24 mss/year.** Query. **Pays $150 and up.**

> ▣ The online magazine carries original content not found in the print edition and includes writer's guidelines. Contact: Roger Vance.

Tips ''All stories must be true. We do not publish fiction or poetry. Write an entertaining, well-researched, informative and unusual story that grabs the reader's attention and holds it. Include suggested readings in a standard format at the end of your piece. Manuscript must be typed, double-spaced on one side of standard white 8½×11, 16 to 30 pound paper—no onion skin paper or dot matrix printouts. All submissions are on speculation. Prefer subjects to be on disk (IBM- or Macintosh-compatible floppy disk) as well as a hard copy. Choose stories with strong art possibilities.''

AMERICAN HERITAGE

28 W. 23rd St., New York NY 10010. (212)367-3100. E-mail: mail@americanheritage.com. Website: www.ameri canheritage.com. **Contact:** Richard Snow, editor. **70% freelance written.** Magazine published 6 times/year. ''*American Heritage* writes from a historical point of view on politics, business, art, current and international affairs, and our changing lifestyles. The articles are written with the intent to enrich the reader's appreciation of the sometimes nostalgic, sometimes funny, always stirring panorama of the American experience.'' Circ. 350,000. **Pays on acceptance.** Publishes ms an average of 6-12 months after acceptance. Byline given. Buys

first North American serial, all rights. Submit seasonal material 1 year in advance. Responds in 2 months to queries. Writer's guidelines for #10 SASE.

• Before submitting material, "check our index to see whether we have already treated the subject."

Nonfiction Wants "historical articles by scholars or journalists intended for intelligent lay readers rather than for professional historians." Emphasis is on authenticity, accuracy, and verve. "Interesting documents, photographs, and drawings are always welcome. Style should stress readability and accuracy." Historical/nostalgic. **Buys 30 unsolicited mss/year.** Query. Length: 1,500-6,000 words. **Payment varies.** Sometimes pays expenses of writers on assignment.

Tips "We have over the years published quite a few 'firsts' from young writers whose historical knowledge, research methods, and writing skills met our standards. The scope and ambition of a new writer tell us a lot about his or her future usefulness to us. A major article gives us a better idea of the writer's value. Everything depends on the quality of the material. We don't really care whether the author is 20 and unknown, or 80 and famous, or vice versa. No phone calls, please."

$ $ AMERICAN HISTORY

741 Miller Dr., Suite D2 SE, Leesburg VA 20175. (703)771-9400. Website: www.thehistorynet.com. **Contact:** Douglas Brinkley, editor. **60% freelance written.** Bimonthly magazine of cultural, social, military, and political history published for a general audience. Estab. 1966. Circ. 95,000. **Pays on acceptance.** Byline given. Buys first rights. Responds in 10 weeks to queries. Sample copy and guidelines for $5 (includes 3rd class postage) or $4 and 9×12 SAE with 4 first-class stamps. Writer's guidelines for #10 SASE or online.

Nonfiction Features events in the lives of noteworthy historical figures and accounts of important events in American history. Also includes pictorial features on artists, photographers, and graphic subjects. "Material is presented on a popular rather than a scholarly level." **Buys 20 mss/year.** Query by mail only with published clips and SASE. Length: 2,000-4,000 words depending on type of article. **Pays $500-600.**

Photos Welcomes suggestions for illustrations.

The online magazine occasionally carries some original content not included in the print edition. Contact: Christine Techky, managing editor.

Tips "Key prerequisites for publication are thorough research and accurate presentation, precise English usage, and sound organization, a lively style, and a high level of human interest. Unsolicited manuscripts not considered. Inappropriate materials include: fiction, book reviews, travelogues, personal/family narratives not of national significance, articles about collectibles/antiques, living artists, local/individual historic buildings/landmarks, and articles of a current editorial nature. Currently seeking articles on significant Civil War subjects. No phone, fax, or e-mail queries, please."

$ THE ARTILLERYMAN

Historical Publications, Inc., 234 Monarch Hill Rd., Tunbridge VT 05077. (802)889-3500. Fax: (802)889-5627. E-mail: mail@civilwarnews.com. **Contact:** Kathryn Jorgensen, editor. **60% freelance written.** Quarterly magazine covering antique artillery, fortifications, and crew-served weapons 1750-1900 for competition shooters, collectors, and living history reenactors using artillery. "Emphasis on Revolutionary War and Civil War but includes everyone interested in pre-1900 artillery and fortifications, preservation, construction of replicas, etc." Estab. 1979. Circ. 2,000. Pays on publication. Publishes ms an average of 6 months after acceptance. Byline given. Not copyrighted. Buys one-time rights. Accepts queries by mail, e-mail, fax. Accepts previously published material. Accepts simultaneous submissions. Responds in 3 weeks to queries. Sample copy and writer's guidelines for 9×12 SAE with 4 first-class stamps.

○→ Break in with a historical or travel piece featuring artillery—the types and history of guns and their use.

Nonfiction Interested in "artillery *only*, for sophisticated readers. Not interested in other weapons, battles in general." Historical/nostalgic, how-to (reproduce ordnance equipment/sights/implements/tools/accessories, etc.), interview/profile, new product, opinion (must be accompanied by detailed background of writer and include references), personal experience, photo feature, technical (must have footnotes), travel (where to find interesting antique cannon). **Buys 24-30 mss/year.** Send complete ms. Length: 300 words minimum. **Pays $20-60.** Sometimes pays expenses of writers on assignment.

Reprints Send tearsheet or photocopy and information about when and where the material previously appeared. Pays 100% of amount paid for an original article.

Photos Send photos with submission. Pays $5 for 5×7 and larger b&w prints. Captions, identification of subjects required.

Tips "We regularly use freelance contributions for Places-to-Visit, Cannon Safety, The Workshop, and Unit Profiles departments. Also need pieces on unusual cannon or cannon with a known and unique history. To judge whether writing style and/or expertise will suit our needs, writers should ask themselves if they could knowledgeably talk *artillery* with an expert. Subject matter is of more concern than writer's background."

$ $ AVIATION HISTORY

Primedia History Group, 741 Miller Dr., SE, Suite D-2, Leesburg VA 20175-8920. (703)771-9400. Fax: (703)779-8345. E-mail: AviationHistory@thehistorynet.com. Website: www.thehistorynet.com. Managing Editor: Carl von Wodtke. **Contact:** Arthur Sanfelici, editor. **95% freelance written.** Bimonthly magazine covering military and civilian aviation from first flight to the jet age. It aims to make aeronautical history not only factually accurate and complete, but also enjoyable to a varied subscriber and newsstand audience. Estab. 1990. Circ. 60,000. Pays on publication. Publishes ms an average of 2 years after acceptance. Byline given. Buys all rights. Editorial lead time 6 months. Submit seasonal material 1 year in advance. Accepts queries by mail, e-mail, fax. Accepts simultaneous submissions. Responds in 3 months to queries; 6 months to mss. Sample copy for $5. Writer's guidelines for #10 SASE or online.

Nonfiction Historical/nostalgic, interview/profile, personal experience. **Buys 24 mss/year.** Query. Length: Feature articles should be 3,500-4,000 words, each with a 500-word sidebar, author's biography, and book suggestions for further reading. **Pays $300.**

Photos State availability of art and photos with submissions, cite sources. "We'll order." Reviews contact sheets, negatives, transparencies. Buys one-time rights. Identification of subjects required.

Columns/Departments People and Planes; Enduring Heritage; Aerial Oddities; Art of Flight, all 2,000 words. **Pays $150.** Book reviews, 300-750 words, **pays minimum $40.**

▣ The online magazine carries original content not found in the print edition and includes writer's guidelines. Contact: Roger Vance.

Tips "Choose stories with strong art possibilities. Include a hard copy as well as an IBM- or Macintosh-compatible floppy disk. Write an entertaining, informative, and unusual story that grabs the reader's attention and holds it. All stories must be true. We do not publish fiction or poetry."

BRITISH HERITAGE

Primedia Enthusiast Group, 6405 Flank Dr., Harrisburg PA 17112. (717)657-9555. Fax: (717)657-9552. Website: www.thehistorynet.com. Managing Editor: Bruce Heydt. Bimonthly magazine covering British heritage. Presents comprehensive information and background of British culture for admirers and those interested in learning about life (past and present) in England, Scotland, and Wales. Circ. 77,485. **Pays on acceptance.** Buys all rights. Editorial lead time 6 months. Accepts queries by mail, e-mail. Sample copy not available. Writer's guidelines by e-mail.

Nonfiction Historical/nostalgic (British History), interview/profile, travel. **Buys 30 mss/year.** Send complete ms.

Columns/Departments In History's Court (two writers take up opposing sides in a historical debate), 1,500 words; Great Britons (biographical sketches of interesting British personalities), 2,000 words; Rendezvous with Destiny (highlight a specific historical personality focusing on a historic turning point) 1,500 words; It Happened Here (describe a historic home, castle, cathedral, etc.) 2,000 words; Wayfaring (travel oriented features) 2,000 words; Historymakers (interviews with eyewitnesses to historic events) 2,000 words. . British Heritage does not accept unsolicited manuscripts in "In History's Court" The following departments are generally written by the editorial staff or by a regularly commissioned contributing editor; The Game's Afoot, Hindsight, Timeline, The Private Side, Keepsakes, and Reviews.

$ $ CIVIL WAR TIMES

6405 Flank Dr., Harrisburg PA 17112. (717)657-9555. Fax: (717)657-9552. E-mail: civilwartimes.magazine@primedia.com. Website: www.thehistorynet.com. Editor: Jim Kushlan. **Contact:** Carl Zebrowski, managing editor (book and product reviews contact). **90% freelance written.** Works with a small number of new/unpublished writers each year. Magazine published 6 times/year. "*Civil War Times* is the full-spectrum magazine of the Civil War. Specifically, we look for nonpartisan coverage of battles, prominent military and civilian figures, the home front, politics, military technology, common soldier life, prisoners and escapes, period art and photography, the naval war, blockade-running, specific regiments, and much more." Estab. 1962. Circ. 108,000. **Pays on acceptance.** Publishes ms an average of 18 months after acceptance. Buys unlimited usage rights. Submit seasonal material 1 year in advance. Responds in 3-6 months to queries. Sample copy for $6. Writer's guidelines for #10 SASE.

Nonfiction Interview/profile, photo feature, Civil War historical material. "Don't send us a comprehensive article on a well-known major battle. Instead, focus on some part or aspect of such a battle, or some group of soldiers in the battle. Similar advice applies to major historical figures like Lincoln and Lee. Positively no fiction or poetry." **Buys 20 freelance mss/year.** Query with clips and SASE. **Pays $75-750.**

Photos Jeff King, art director.

Tips "We're very open to new submissions. Send query after examining writer's guidelines and several recent issues. Include photocopies of photos that could feasibly accompany the article. Confederate soldiers' diaries and letters are especially welcome."

$ $ GATEWAY HERITAGE

Missouri Historical Society, P.O. Box 11940, St. Louis MO 63112-0040. (314)746-4558. Fax: (314)746-4548. E-mail: vwmonks@mohistory.org. Website: www.mohistory.org. **Contact:** Victoria W. Monks, editor. **75% freelance written.** Quarterly magazine covering Missouri history and culture. *"Gateway Heritage* is a popular cultural history magazine that is primarily a member benefit of the Missouri Historical Society. Thus, we have a general audience with an interest in the history and culture of Missouri, and St. Louis in particular." Estab. 1980. Circ. 9,000. Pays on publication. Publishes ms an average of 6 months after acceptance. Byline given. Offers $100 kill fee. Buys first North American serial rights. Editorial lead time 6 months. Submit seasonal material 1 year in advance. Accepts queries by mail, e-mail, fax. Responds in 2 weeks to queries; 2 months to mss. Sample copy for 9×12 SAE and 7 first-class stamps. Writer's guidelines for #10 SASE.

Nonfiction Book excerpts, interview/profile, photo feature, historical, scholarly essays, Missouri biographies, viewpoints on events, first-hand historical accounts, regional architectural history, literary history. No genealogies. **Buys 12-15 mss/year.** Query with published clips. Length: 3,500-5,000 words. **Pays $300-400 (average).**

Photos State availability with submission.

Columns/Departments Origins (essays on the beginnings of organizations, movements, and immigrant communities in St. Louis and Missouri), 1,500-2,500 words; Missouri Biographies (biographical sketches of famous and interesting Missourians), 1,500-2,500 words; Gateway Conversations (interviews); Letters Home (excerpts from letters, diaries, and journals), 1,500-2,500 words. **Buys 6-8 mss/year.** Query with published clips. **Pays $250-300.**

Tips "Submitting articles for our departments is a good way to break in to *Gateway Heritage.*"

$ GOOD OLD DAYS

America's Premier Nostalgia Magazine, House of White Birches, 306 E. Parr Rd., Berne IN 46711. E-mail: editor@goodolddaysonline.com. Website: www.goodolddaysonline.com. **Contact:** Ken Tate, editor. **75% freelance written.** Monthly magazine of first person nostalgia, 1935-1960. "We look for strong narratives showing life as it was in the first half of the 20th century. Our readership is comprised of nostalgia buffs, history enthusiasts, and the people who actually lived and grew up in this era." Pays on contract. Publishes ms an average of 8 months after acceptance. Byline given. Prefers all rights, but will negotiate for First North American serial and one-time rights. Submit seasonal material 10 months in advance. Responds in 2 months to queries. Sample copy for $2. Writer's guidelines online.

● Queries accepted, but are not necessary.

Nonfiction Regular features: Good Old Days on Wheels (transportation auto, plane, horse-drawn, tram, bicycle, trolley, etc.); Good Old Days In the Kitchen (favorite foods, appliances, ways of cooking, recipes); Home Remedies (herbs and poultices, hometown doctors, harrowing kitchen table operations). Historical/nostalgic, humor, personal experience, photo feature, favorite food/recipes, year-round seasonal material, biography, memorable events, fads, fashion, sports, music, literature, entertainment. No fiction accepted. **Buys 350 mss/ year.** Query or send complete ms. Length: 500-1,500 words. **Pays $20-100, depending on quality and photos.**

Photos "Send original or professionally copied photographs. Do not submit laser-copied prints." Send photos with submission. Identification of subjects required.

Tips "Most of our writers are not professionals. We prefer the author's individual voice, warmth, humor, and honesty over technical ability."

$ LIGHTHOUSE DIGEST

Lighthouse Digest, P.O. Box 1690, Wells ME 04090. (207)646-0515. Fax: (207)646-0516. E-mail: timh@lhdigest.com. Website: www.lighthousedigest.com. **Contact:** Tim Harrison, editor. **15% freelance written.** Monthly magazine covering historical, fiction and news events about lighthouses and similar maritime stories. Estab. 1989. Circ. 24,000. Pays on publication. Publishes ms an average of 4 months after acceptance. Byline given. Buys one-time, electronic rights. Editorial lead time 3 months. Submit seasonal material 3 months in advance. Accepts queries by e-mail. Accepts simultaneous submissions. Responds in 6 weeks to queries. Sample copy for free. Writer's guidelines not available.

Nonfiction Exposé, general interest, historical/nostalgic, humor, inspirational, personal experience, photo feature, religious, technical, travel. No historical data taken from books. **Buys 30 mss/year.** Send complete ms. Length: 2,500 words maximum. **Pays $75.**

Photos Send photos with submission. Reviews prints. Buys all rights. Offers no additional payment for photos accepted with ms. Captions, identification of subjects required.

Fiction Adventure, historical, humorous, mystery, religious, romance, suspense. **Buys 2 mss/year.** Send complete ms. Length: 2,500 words maximum. **Pays $75-150.**

Tips "Read our publication and visit the website."

Ⓝ $ $ $ $ MHQ

The Quarterly Journal of Military History, Primedia History Group, 741 Miller Dr. SE, Suite D-2, Leesburg VA 20175-8920. (703)771-9400. Fax: (703)779-8345. E-mail: mhq@thehistory.net.com. Website: www.thehistoryn et.com. Editor: Rod Paschall. Managing Editor: Carl von Wodtke. **Contact:** Richard Latture, associate editor. **100% freelance written.** Quarterly journal covering military history. *"MHQ* offers readers in-depth articles on the history of warfare from ancient times into the 20th century. Authoritative features and departments cover military strategies, philosophies, campaigns, battles, personalities, weaponry, espionage and perspectives, all written in a lively and readable style. Articles are accompanied by classic works of art, photographs and maps. Readers include serious students of military tactics, strategy, leaders and campaigns, as well as general world history enthusiasts. Many readers are currently in the military or retired officers." Estab. 1988. Circ. 40,000. Pays on publication. Byline given. Buys all rights. Editorial lead time 1 year. Submit seasonal material 1 year in advance. Accepts queries by mail, e-mail, fax. Accepts simultaneous submissions. Responds in 3 months to queries; 6 months to mss. Sample copy for $23 (hardcover), $13 (softcover); some articles on website. Writer's guidelines for #10 SASE or online.

Nonfiction Historical/nostalgic, personal experience, photo feature. No fiction or stories pertaining to collectibles or reenactments. **Buys 50 mss/year.** Query preferred; also accepts complete ms. Length: 1,500-6,000 words. **Pays $500-2,000 for assigned articles; $400-2,000 for unsolicited articles.**

Photos Send photos/art with submission. Reviews transparencies, prints. Buys all rights. Negotiates payment individually. Identification of subjects required.

Columns/Departments Artists on War (description of artwork of a military nature); Experience of War (first-person accounts of military incidents); Strategic View (discussion of military theory, strategy); Arms & Men (description of military hardware or unit), all up to 2,500 words. **Buys 20 mss/year.** Send complete ms. **Pays $400-800.**

🔲 The online magazine carries original content not included in the print edition and includes writer's guidelines. Contact: Roger Vance.

Tips "All stories must be true—we publish no fiction. Although we are always looking for variety, some subjects—World War II, the American Civil War, and military biography, for instance—are the focus of so many proposals that we are forced to judge them by relatively rigid criteria. We are always glad to consider articles on these subjects. However, less common ones—medieval, Asian, or South American military history, for example—are more likely to attract our attention. The likelihood that articles can be effectively illustrated often determines the ultimate fate of manuscripts. Many otherwise excellent articles have been rejected due to a lack of suitable art or photographs. Regular departments—columns on strategy, tactics, and weaponry—average 1,500 words. While the information we publish is scholarly and substantive, we prefer writing that is light, anecdotal, and above all, engaging, rather than didactic."

$ $ MILITARY HISTORY

Primedia History Group, 741 Miller Dr., SE, Suite D-2, Leesburg VA 20175-8920. (703)771-9400. Fax: (703)779-8345. E-mail: militaryhistory@thehistorynet.com. Website: www.thehistorynet.com. Managing Editor: Carl von Wodtke. **Contact:** Jon Guttman, editor. **95% freelance written.** "We'll work with anyone, established or not, who can provide the goods and convince us of its accuracy." Bimonthly magazine covering all military history of the world. "We strive to give the general reader accurate, highly readable, often narrative popular history, richly accompanied by period art." Circ. 112,000. 30 days after publication. Publishes ms an average of 2 years after acceptance. Byline given. Buys all rights. Submit seasonal material 1 year in advance. Accepts queries by mail, e-mail, fax. Responds in 3 months to queries; 6 months to mss. Sample copy for $5. Writer's guidelines for #10 SASE or online.

Nonfiction "The best way to break into our magazine is to write an entertaining, informative and unusual story that grabs the readers attention and holds it." Historical/nostalgic, interview/profile (military figures of commanding interest), personal experience (only occasionally). **Buys 30 mss/year.** Query with published clips. "Submit a short, self-explanatory query summarizing the story proposed, its highlights, and/or significance. State also your own expertise, access to sources or proposed means of developing the pertinent information." Length: 4,000 words with a 500-word sidebar. **Pays $400.**

Columns/Departments Intrigue; Weaponry; Perspectives; Personality; Reviews (books, video, CD-ROMs, software—all relating to military history). Length: 2,000 words. **Buys 24 mss/year.** Query with published clips. **Pays $200.**

🔲 The online magazine contains content not found in the print edition and includes writer's guidelines. Contact: Roger Vance.

Tips "We would like journalistically 'pure' submissions that adhere to basics, such as full name at first reference, same with rank, and definition of prior or related events, issues cited as context or obscure military 'hardware.' Read the magazine, discover our style, and avoid subjects already covered. Pick stories with strong art possibilities (real art and photos), send photocopies, tell us where to order the art. Avoid historical overview; focus upon an event with appropriate and accurate context. Provide bibliography. Tell the story in popular but elegant style. Include a hard copy as well as an IBM- or Macintosh-compatible floppy disk.''

Ⓝ $ NOSTALGIA MAGAZINE

Enriching Today with the Stories of Yesterday, King's Publishing Group, Inc., 1703 N. Normandie St., Spokane WA 99205. (800)723-2086 or (509)323-2086. Fax: (509)323-2096. E-mail: editor@nostalgiamagazine.net. Website: www.nostalgiamagazine.us. **Contact:** Mark Carter, editor. **90% freelance written.** Monthly magazine covering stories and photos of personal, historical, nostalgic experiences: ''I remember when...'' *Nostalgia Magazine* is a journal that gathers photos, personal remembrance stories, diaries, and researched stories of well-known—and more often little-known—people, places, and events, and puts them into one monthly volume. ''We glean the best of the past to share now to enrich life now.'' Estab. 1999. Circ. 5,000. Pays on publication. Publishes ms an average of 3 months after acceptance. Byline given. Buys simultaneous, reprints in our regional editions rights. Editorial lead time 3 months. Submit seasonal material 4 months in advance. Accepts queries by mail, e-mail. Accepts previously published material. Accepts simultaneous submissions. Responds in 2 months to queries; 3 months to mss. Sample copy for $5. Writer's guidelines online.

Nonfiction Book excerpts, essays, exposé, general interest, historical/nostalgic, how-to, humor, inspirational, interview/profile, new product, personal experience, photo feature, religious, technical, travel. Does not want genealogies, current events/news, divisive politics (in historical setting sometimes OK), or glorification of immorality. **Buys 120 mss/year.** Send complete ms. Length: 400-2,000 words. **Pays $10-100.**

Photos Send photos with submission. Reviews negatives, transparencies, prints, GIF/JPEG files. Buys use in all publications only. Mss with exceptional photos will receive primary consideration and payment. Captions, identification of subjects required.

Poetry Free verse, light verse, traditional, historical. Does not want avant-garde, contemporary/modern experiences, sappy junk. **Buys 6 poems/year.** Submit maximum 1 poems.

Fillers Anecdotes, facts, gags to be illustrated by cartoonist, short humor. **Buys 50/year.** Length: 50-200 words. **Pays $10.**

Tips ''Start with an interesting photograph from the past you know, or your own past. Good photos are the key to people reading an interesting story in our magazine. Write the who, what, when, where, why, and how. We need one interesting photo for every 400 words text. If you have a great story and no photos, we can often guide the writer in how to find a photo.''

$ $ PERSIMMON HILL

National Cowboy & Western Heritage Museum, 1700 NE 63rd St., Oklahoma City OK 73111. (405)478-6404. Fax: (405)478-4714. E-mail: editor@nationalcowboymuseum.org. Website: www.nationalcowboymuseum.org. **Contact:** M.J. Van Deventer, editor. **70% freelance written.** Prefers to work with published/established writers; works with a small number of new/unpublished writers each year. Quarterly magazine for an audience interested in Western art, Western history, ranching, and rodeo, including historians, artists, ranchers, art galleries, schools, and libraries. Estab. 1970. Circ. 15,000. Pays on publication. Publishes ms an average of 2 years after acceptance. Byline given. Buys first rights. Responds in 3 months to queries. Sample copy for $10.50, including postage. Writer's guidelines for #10 SASE or on website.

● The editor of *Persimmon Hill* reports: ''We need more material on rodeo, both contemporary and historical. And we need more profiles on contemporary working ranches in the West.''

Nonfiction Historical and contemporary articles on famous Western figures connected with pioneering the American West, Western art, rodeo, cowboys, etc. (or biographies of such people), stories of Western flora and animal life and environmental subjects. ''We want thoroughly researched and historically authentic material written in a popular style. May have a humorous approach to subject.'' ''No broad, sweeping, superficial pieces; i.e., the California Gold Rush or rehashed pieces on Billy the Kid, etc.'' **Buys 35-50 mss/year.** Query by mail only with clips. Length: 1,500 words. **Pays $150-250.**

Photos Purchased with ms or on assignment. Reviews color transparencies, glossy b&w prints. Pays according to quality and importance for b&w and color photos. Captions required.

Tips ''Send us a story that captures the spirit of adventure and individualism that typifies the Old West or reveals a facet of the Western lifestyle in contemporary society. Excellent illustrations for articles are essential! We lean towards scholarly, historical, well-researched articles. We're less focused on Western celebrities than some of the other contemporary Western magazines.''

PRESERVATION MAGAZINE

National Trust for Historic Preservation, 1785 Massachusetts Ave. NW, Washington DC 20036. (202)588-6388. Fax: (202)588-6266. E-mail: preservation@nthp.org. Website: www.preservationonline.org. **Contact:** James Conaway, editor-in-chief. **75% freelance written.** Prefers to work with published/established writers. Bimonthly magazine covering preservation of historic buildings in the US. ''We cover subjects related in some way to place. Most entries are features, department, or opinion pieces." Circ. 250,000. Pays on publication. Publishes ms an average of 1 month after acceptance. Byline given. Offers variable kill fee. Buys one-time rights. Accepts queries by mail, e-mail, fax. Responds in 2 months to queries. Writer's guidelines online.

Nonfiction Book excerpts, essays, historical/nostalgic, humor, interview/profile, new product, opinion, photo feature, travel, features. **Buys 30 mss/year.** Query with published clips. Length: 500-3,500 words. Sometimes pays expenses of writers on assignment, but not long-distance travel.

    ■ The online magazine carries original content not found in the print edition. Contact: Margaret Foster.

Tips "Do not send or propose histories of buildings, descriptive accounts of cities or towns or long-winded treatises. Best bet for breaking in is via Preservation Online, Preservation News (news features, 500-1,000 words), Bricks & Mortar (brief profile or article, 250-500 words)."

$ $ $TIMELINE

Ohio Historical Society, 1982 Velma Ave., Columbus OH 43211-2497. (614)297-2360. Fax: (614)297-2367. E-mail: timeline@ohiohistory.org. **Contact:** Christopher S. Duckworth, editor. **90% freelance written.** Works with a small number of new/unpublished writers each year. Bimonthly magazine covering history, prehistory, and the natural sciences, directed toward readers in the Midwest. Estab. 1984. Circ. 19,000. **Pays on acceptance.** Publishes ms an average of 1 year after acceptance. Byline given. Offers $75 minimum kill fee. Buys first North American serial, all rights. Submit seasonal material 6 months in advance. Accepts queries by mail, e-mail, fax. Responds in 3 weeks to queries; 6 weeks to mss. Sample copy for $6 and 9×12 SAE. Writer's guidelines for #10 SASE.

Nonfiction Topics include the traditional fields of political, economic, military, and social history; biography; the history of science and technology; archaeology and anthropology; architecture; the fine and decorative arts; and the natural sciences including botany, geology, zoology, ecology, and paleontology. Book excerpts, essays, historical/nostalgic, interview/profile (of individuals), photo feature. **Buys 22 mss/year.** Query. Length: 1,500-6,000 words. Also vignettes of 500-1,000 words. **Pays $100-900.**

Photos Submissions should include ideas for illustration. Send photos with submission. Reviews contact sheets, transparencies, 8×10 prints. Buys one-time rights. Captions, identification of subjects, model releases required.

Tips "We want crisply written, authoritative narratives for the intelligent lay reader. An Ohio slant may strengthen a submission, but it is not indispensable. Contributors must know enough about their subject to explain it clearly and in an interesting fashion. We use high-quality illustration with all features. If appropriate illustration is unavailable, we can't use the feature. The writer who sends illustration ideas with a manuscript has an advantage, but an often-published illustration won't attract us."

$ $TRACES OF INDIANA AND MIDWESTERN HISTORY

Indiana Historical Society, 450 W. Ohio St., Indianapolis IN 46202-3269. (317)232-1877. Fax: (317)233-0857. E-mail: rboomhower@indianahistory.org. Website: www.indianahistory.org/traces.htm. **Contact:** Ray E. Boomhower, managing editor. **80% freelance written.** Quarterly magazine on Indiana history. "Conceived as a vehicle to bring to the public good narrative and analytical history about Indiana in its broader contexts of region and nation, *Traces* explores the lives of artists, writers, performers, soldiers, politicians, entrepreneurs, homemakers, reformers, and naturalists. It has traced the impact of Hoosiers on the nation and the world. In this vein, the editors seek nonfiction articles that are solidly researched, attractively written, and amenable to illustration, and they encourage scholars, journalists, and freelance writers to contribute to the magazine." Estab. 1989. Circ. 10,000. **Pays on acceptance.** Publishes ms an average of 6 months after acceptance. Byline given. Buys one-time rights. Submit seasonal material 1 year in advance. Responds in 3 months to mss. Sample copy and writer's guidelines for $5.25 (make checks payable to Indiana Historical Society) and 9×12 SAE with 7 first-class stamps or on website. Writer's guidelines for #10 SASE.

Nonfiction Book excerpts, historical essays, historical photographic features on topics of biography, literature, folklore, music, visual arts, politics, economics, industry, transportation, and sports. **Buys 20 mss/year.** Send complete ms. Length: 2,000-4,000 words. **Pays $100-500.**

Photos Send photos with submission. Reviews contact sheets, transparencies, photocopies, prints. Buys one-time rights. Pays "reasonable photographic expenses." Captions, identification of subjects, permissions required.

Tips "Freelancers should be aware of prerequisites for writing history for a broad audience. Should have some awareness of this magazine and other magazines of this type published by Midwestern historical societies. Preference is given to subjects with an Indiana connection and authors who are familiar with *Traces*. Quality of potential illustration is also important."

$ $ $TRUE WEST

True West Publishing, Inc., P.O. Box 8008, Cave Creek AZ 85327. (888)687-1881. Fax: (480)575-1903. E-mail: editor@truewestmagazine.com. Website: www.truewestmagazine.com. Executive Editor: Bob Boze Bell. **Con-**

tact: R.G. Robertson, editor. **70% freelance written.** Works with a small number of new/unpublished writers each year. Magazine published 10 times/year. covering Western American history from prehistory 1800 to 1930. "We want reliable research on significant historical topics written in lively prose for an informed general audience. More recent topics may be used if they have a historical angle or retain the Old West flavor of trail dust and saddle leather." Estab. 1953. Pays on publication. Byline given. Buys first North American serial rights. Editorial lead time 3 months. Accepts queries by mail, e-mail. Sample copy for $3 and 9×12 SASE. Writer's guidelines online. Editorial calendar online.

- • No unsolicited mss.
- O⚬ "We are looking for historically accurate stories on the Old West that make you wonder 'What happens next?'"

Nonfiction No fiction, poetry, or unsupported, undocumented tales. **Buys 30 mss/year.** Query. Length: 1,000-3,000 words. **Pays $50-800.**

Photos State availability with submission. Reviews contact sheets, negatives, 4×5 transparencies, 4×5 prints. Buys one-time rights. Offers $10-75/photo. Captions, identification of subjects, model releases required.

Columns/Departments Book Reviews, 50-60 words (no unsolicited reviews). **Pays $25.**

Fillers Anecdotes, facts, gags to be illustrated by cartoonist, newsbreaks, short humor. **Buys 30/year.** Length: 50-600 words.

Tips "Read our magazines and follow our guidelines. A freelancer is most likely to break in with us by submitting thoroughly researched, lively prose on relatively obscure topics or by being assigned to write for 1 of our departments. First-person accounts rarely fill our needs. Historical accuracy and strict adherence to the facts are essential. We much prefer material based on primary sources (archives, court records, documents, contemporary newspapers and first-person accounts) to those that rely mainly on secondary sources (published books, magazines, and journals)."

$ $ VIETNAM

Primedia History Group, 741 Miller Dr., SE, #D-2, Leesburg VA 20175-8920. (703)771-9400. Fax: (703)779-8345. E-mail: vietnam@thehistorynet.com. Website: www.thehistorynet.com. Managing Editor: Carl von Wodtke. **Contact:** David T. Zabecki, editor. **90% freelance written.** Bimonthly magazine providing in-depth and authoritative accounts of the many complexities that made the war in Vietnam unique, including the people, battles, strategies, perspectives, analysis, and weaponry. Estab. 1988. Circ. 46,000. Pays on publication. Publishes ms an average of 1-2 years after acceptance. Byline given. Buys all rights. Accepts queries by mail, e-mail, fax. Responds in 3 months to queries; 6 months to mss. Sample copy for $5. Writer's guidelines for #10 SASE.

Nonfiction Historical/nostalgic (military), interview/profile, personal experience. "Absolutely no fiction or poetry; we want straight history, as much personal narrative as possible, but not the gung-ho, shoot-'em-up variety, either." **Buys 24 mss/year.** Query. Length: 4,000 words maximum; sidebars 500 words. **Pays $300 for features.**

Photos Send photos with submission or state availability and cite sources. Identification of subjects required.

Columns/Departments Arsenal (about weapons used, all sides); Personality (profiles of the players, all sides); Fighting Forces (various units or types of units: air, sea, rescue); Perspectives. Length: 2,000 words. Query. **Pays $150.**

▪ The online magazine contains content not found in the print edition and includes writer's guidelines. Contact: Claudia Gary Annis.

Tips "Choose stories with strong art possibilities. Send hard copy plus an IBM- or Macintosh-compatible floppy disk. All stories must be true. We do not publish fiction or poetry. All stories should be carefully researched, third-person articles or firsthand accounts that give the reader a sense of experiencing historical events."

$ $ WILD WEST

Primedia History Group, 741 Miller Dr., SE, Suite D-2, Leesburg VA 20175-8920. (703)771-9400. Fax: (703)779-8345. E-mail: wildwest@thehistorynet.com. Website: www.thehistorynet.com. Managing Editor: Carl von Wodtke. **Contact:** Gregory Lalire, editor. **95% freelance written.** Bimonthly magazine covering the history of the American frontier, from its eastern beginnings to its western terminus. "*Wild West* covers the popular (narrative) history of the American West—events, trends, personalities, anything of general interest." Estab. 1988. Circ. 83,500. Pays on publication. Publishes ms an average of 2 years after acceptance. Byline given. Not copyrighted. Buys all rights. Editorial lead time 10 months. Submit seasonal material 1 year in advance. Accepts queries by mail, e-mail. Accepts simultaneous submissions. Responds in 3 months to queries; 6 months to mss. Sample copy for $6. Writer's guidelines for #10 SASE or online.

Nonfiction Historical/nostalgic (Old West). No excerpts, travel, etc. Articles can be "adapted from" book. No fiction or poetry—nothing current. **Buys 36 mss/year.** Query. Length: 3,500 words with a 500-word sidebar. **Pays $300.**

Photos State availability with submission. Reviews negatives, transparencies. Buys one-time rights. Offers no additional payment for photos accepted with ms. Captions, identification of subjects required.

Columns/Departments Gunfighters & Lawmen, 2,000 words; Westerners, 2,000 words; Warriors & Chiefs, 2,000 words; Western Lore, 2,000 words; Guns of the West, 1,500 words; Artists West, 1,500 words; Books Reviews, 250 words. **Buys 36 mss/year.** Query. **Pays $150 for departments; book reviews paid by the word, minimum $40.**

▣ The online magazine carries original content not found in the print edition. Contact: Roger Vance, online editor.

Tips "Always query the editor with your story idea. Successful queries include a description of sources of information and suggestions for color and b&w photography or artwork. The best way to break into our magazine is to write an entertaining, informative and unusual story that grabs the reader's attention and holds it. We favor carefully researched, third-person articles that give the reader a sense of experiencing historical events. Include a hard copy as well as an IBM- or Macintosh-compatible floppy disk."

$ $WORLD WAR II

Primedia History Group, 741 Miller Dr., SE, Suite D-2, Leesburg VA 20175-8920. (703)771-9400. Fax: (703)779-8345. E-mail: worldwarii@thehistorynet.com. Website: www.thehistorynet.com. Managing Editor: Carl von Wodtke. **Contact:** Christopher Anderson, editor. **95% freelance written.** Prefers to work with published/established writers. Bimonthly magazine covering "military operations in World War II—events, personalities, strategy, national policy, etc." Estab. 1986. Circ. 146,000. Pays on publication. Publishes ms an average of 2 years after acceptance. Byline given. Buys all rights. Accepts queries by mail, e-mail, fax. Responds in 3 months to queries; 6 months to mss. Sample copy for $5. Writer's guidelines for #10 SASE or online.

Nonfiction World War II military history. Submit anniversary-related material 1 year in advance. No fiction. **Buys 24 mss/year.** Query. Length: Length: 4,000 words with a 500-word sidebar. **Pays $300 and up.**

Photos For photos and other art, send photocopies and cite sources. "We'll order." State availability with submission. Captions, identification of subjects required.

Columns/Departments Undercover (espionage, resistance, sabotage, intelligence gathering, behind the lines, etc.); Personality (WWII personalities of interest); Armament (weapons, their use and development); Commands (unit histories); One Man's War (personal profiles), all 2,000 words. Book reviews, 300-750 words. **Buys 30 (plus book reviews) mss/year.** Query. **Pays $150 and up.**

▣ The online magazine contains content not found in the print edition and includes writer's guidelines. Contact: Roger Vance.

Tips "List your sources and suggest further readings in standard format at the end of your piece—as a bibliography for our files in case of factual challenge or dispute. All submissions are on speculation. Include a hard copy as well as an IBM- or Macintosh-compatible floppy disk. All stories must be true. We do not publish fiction or poetry. Stories should be carefully researched."

HOBBY & CRAFT

⒩ $ANTIQUE JOURNAL

Krause Publications, 500 Fesler St., Suite 201, El Cajon CA 92020. (619)593-2931. Fax: (619)447-7187. E-mail: antiquejournal@krause.com. Website: www.collect.com. **Contact:** Jennifer Edwards, editor. **90% freelance written.** Monthly magazine covering antiques and collectibles. *Antique Journal* serves antique dealers and collectors in Northern California, Washington, Oregon and Nevada. Estab. 1992. Circ. 25,000. Pays on publication. Publishes ms an average of 1 month after acceptance. Byline given. Buys first North American serial rights. Editorial lead time 1 month. Submit seasonal material 2 months in advance. Accepts queries by mail, e-mail, fax, phone. Accepts previously published material. Accepts simultaneous submissions. Responds in 2 weeks to queries. Sample copy for $2.50. Writer's guidelines free.

Nonfiction General interest, historical/nostalgic, how-to (start a collection display and sell antiques), interview/profile. Does not want religious articles, opinion pieces, exposés. Query. Length: 500-700 words. **Pays $25-60.**

Photos Send photos with submission. Reviews 5×7 transparencies, 5×7 prints, GIF/JPEG files. Buys all rights. Offers no additional payment for photos accepted with ms. Identification of subjects required.

Columns/Departments Cover Stories (on specific antique merchandise or trends), 1,000 words; Show Producer Profile (profiles antiques show promoters), 500-700 words; California Profile, Washington Profile, Nevada Profile, Oregon Profile (profiles antiques shops/malls in specific states), 500 words; Vintage Fashions (on vintage clothing, hats, shoes, etc.), 500-700 words. **Buys 108 mss/year.** Query. **Pays $25-60.**

Tips "Talk directly to the editor or publisher either by phone or e-mail."

$ $ANTIQUE REVIEW

Krause Publications, P.O. Box 1050, Dubuque IA 52004-1050. (800)482-4150. E-mail: kunkell@krause.com. Website: www.collect.com. **Contact:** Linda Kunkel, editor. **60% freelance written.** Eager to work with new/

unpublished writers. Monthly tabloid for an antique-oriented readership, "generally well-educated, interested in Early American furniture and decorative arts, as well as folk art." Estab. 1975. Circ. 6,000. Pays on publication. Publishes ms an average of 3 months after acceptance. Byline given. Buys first North American serial, second serial (reprint) rights. Accepts queries by mail, e-mail, phone. Accepts previously published material. Responds in 3 months to queries. Inquire for sample copy.

Nonfiction "The articles we desire concern history and production of furniture, pottery, china, and other quality Americana. In some cases, contemporary folk art items are acceptable. We are also interested in reporting on antiques shows and auctions with statements on conditions and prices." Query should show "author's familiarity with antiques, an interest in the historical development of artifacts relating to early America, and an awareness of antiques market." **Buys 30-45 mss/year.** Query with published clips. Length: 600-1,500 words. **Pays $100-200.** Sometimes pays expenses of writers on assignment.

Reprints Send tearsheet, photocopy or typed ms with rights for sale noted and information about when and where the material previously appeared.

Photos Articles with photographs receive preference. Accepts and prefers digital photos (200 dpi, JPEG format). Send photos with submission. Reviews 3×5 or larger glossy b&w or color prints. Payment included in ms price. Captions required.

Tips "Give us a call and let us know of specific interests. We are most concerned with the background in antiques than in writing abilities. The writing can be edited, but the knowledge imparted is of primary interest. A frequent mistake is being too general, not becoming deeply involved in the topic and its research. We are interested in primary research into America's historic material culture."

N $ $ ANTIQUE TRADER

Krause Publications, 700 E. State St., Iola WI 54990-0001. (715)445-2214. Fax: (715)445-4087. E-mail: antiquetrader@krause.com. Website: www.collect.com. Features Editor: Lisa Jacobsen. **Contact:** Sharon Korbeck, editor. **80-90% freelance written.** Weekly tabloid covering antiques. "We publish quote-heavy stories of timely interest in the antiques field. We cover antiques shows, auctions, and news events." Estab. 1957. Circ. 30,000. Pays on publication. Publishes ms an average of 1-3 months after acceptance. Byline given. Offers 50% kill fee. Buys exclusive rights. Editorial lead time 2 months. Accepts queries by mail, e-mail, fax. Responds in 1 week to queries; 2 months to mss. Sample copy for cover price, plus postage. Writer's guidelines online.

Nonfiction Book excerpts, general interest, interview/profile, personal experience, show and auction coverage. Does not want the same, dry textbook, historical stories on antiques that appear elsewhere. "I want personality and timeliness." **Buys 1,000+ mss/year.** Query with or without published clips or send complete ms. Length: 750-1,200 words. **Pays $50-200, plus contributor copy.** Sometimes pays expenses of writers on assignment. Reviews transparencies, prints, GIF/JPEG files. Buys one-time rights. Offers no additional payment for photos accepted with ms. Identification of subjects required.

Columns/Departments Holy Grail (best items in an antiques genre), 750-1,000 words; Collector Profile (interviews with interesting collectors), 750-1,000 words. **Buys 30-60 mss/year.** Query with or without published clips or send complete ms.

$ ANTIQUE & COLLECTABLES NEWSMAGAZINE

Krause Publications, 500 Fesler St., Suite 201, El Cajon CA 92022. (619)593-2933. Fax: (619)447-7187. E-mail: ac@krause.com. Website: www.collect.com. **Contact:** Manny Cruz, managing editor. **90% freelance written.** Monthly magazine covering antiques and collectibles. *Antique & Collectables Newsmagazine* serves dealers, collectors and the general public in Southern California, Arizona and Southern Nevada on the antiques and collectibles industry. Estab. 1979. Circ. 27,500. Pays on publication. Publishes ms an average of 1 month after acceptance. Byline given. Buys first North American serial rights. Editorial lead time 1 month. Submit seasonal material 2 months in advance. Accepts queries by mail, e-mail, fax, phone. Accepts previously published material. Accepts simultaneous submissions. Responds in 2 weeks to queries. Sample copy for $2.50. Writer's guidelines free.

Nonfiction General interest, historical/nostalgic, how-to (start a collection, display and sell antiques), interview/profile, photo feature. Does not want religious articles, opinion pieces, and exposés. Query. Length: 500-700 words. **Pays $25-70.**

Photos Send photos with submission. Reviews 5×7 transparencies, 5×7 prints, GIF/JPEG files. Buys all rights. Offers no additional payment for photos accepted with ms.

Columns/Departments Focus on San Diego (antique shops, malls and dealers), 500-600 words; Focus on Old Towne Orange (antique shops, malls and dealers), 500-600 words; Focus on Arizona (antique shops, malls and dealers), 500-600 words; Collector's Spotlight (collectors of antiques), 700-900 words; On with the Show (profiles on show producers), 700-900 words; Cover Stories (on specific antique merchandise or trends), 1,000 words. **Buys 96 mss/year.** Query. **Pays $25-70.**

Tips "Talk directly to the editor or publisher either by phone or e-mail."

$ $ANTIQUES & COLLECTING MAGAZINE

1006 S. Michigan Ave., Chicago IL 60605. (312)939-4767. Fax: (312)939-0053. E-mail: acmeditor@interaccess.com. **Contact:** Therese Nolan, editor. **80% freelance written.** Monthly magazine covering antiques and collectibles. Estab. 1931. Circ. 20,000. Pays on publication. Publishes ms an average of 6 months after acceptance. Byline given. Buys first rights. Editorial lead time 3 months. Submit seasonal material 6 months in advance. Accepts queries by mail, e-mail, fax, phone. Responds in 6 weeks to queries; 2 months to mss. Sample copy for free. Writer's guidelines for free or by e-mail.

Nonfiction Book excerpts, general interest, historical/nostalgic, how-to, interview/profile, opinion, personal experience, photo feature, features about antiques and collectibles made before 1970. **Buys 40-50 mss/year.** Query. Length: 1,000-1,600 words. **Pays $150-250, plus 4 copies.**

Photos Send photos with submission. Reviews transparencies, prints. Buys one-time rights. Offers no additional payment for photos accepted with ms. Captions, identification of subjects required.

Fillers Anecdotes, facts.

N ARTS & CRAFTS

Krause Publications, Inc., 700 E. State St., Iola WI 54990-0001. (715)445-4612. Fax: (715)445-4087. E-mail: arts&crafts@krause.com. Website: www.artsandcraftsmag.com. Editor: Althea Reetz. Magazine published 7 times/year featuring unique arts and crafts for home decor, gifts and fashion. Written for craft enthusiasts throughout the U.S. and Canada. Circ. 100,000. Editorial lead time 14 weeks. Sample copy not available.

$ $BEAD & BUTTON

Kalmbach Publishing, 21027 Crossroads Circle, Waukesha WI 53186. (262)796-8776. E-mail: akorach@beadandbutton.com. Website: www.beadandbutton.com. Editor: Mindy Brooks. **Contact:** Lora Groszkiewicz, editorial assistant. **50% freelance written.** *"Bead & Button* is a bimonthly magazine devoted to techniques, projects, designs and materials relating to beads, buttons, and accessories. Our readership includes both professional and amateur bead and button makers, hobbyists, and enthusiasts who find satisfaction in making beautiful things." Estab. 1994. Circ. 80,000. **Pays on acceptance.** Publishes ms an average of 4 months after acceptance. Byline given. Offers $75 kill fee. Buys all rights. Accepts queries by mail, e-mail, fax. Writer's guidelines online.

Nonfiction Historical/nostalgic (on beaded jewelry history), how-to (make beaded jewelry and accessories), humor (or inspirational —1 endpiece for each issue), interview/profile. **Buys 24-30 mss/year.** Send complete ms. Length: 750-3,000 words. **Pays $75-300.**

Photos Send photos with submission. Offers no additional payment for photos accepted with ms. Identification of subjects required.

Columns/Departments Chic & Easy (fashionable jewelry how-to); Beginner (easy-to-make jewelry how-to); Simply Earrings (fashionable earring how-to); Fun Fashion (trendy jewelry how-to), all 1,000 words. **Buys 12 mss/year.** Send complete ms. **Pays $75-150.**

Tips *"Bead & Button* magazine primarily publishes how-to articles by the artists who have designed the piece. We publish two profiles and one historical piece per issue. These would be the only applicable articles for non-artisan writers. Also our humorous and inspirational endpiece might apply."

N $ $BIG REEL

Movie, Video & Hollywood Collectibles, Krause Publications, P.O. Box 1050, Dubuque IA 52004. (800)482-4143. Fax: (800)531-0880. E-mail: fliessc@krause.com. Website: www.bigreel.com. **Contact:** Claire R. Fliess, editor. **95% freelance written.** Monthly tabloid covering movie, video and Hollywood collectibles. "The audience is 50+ years old, deals with film (most advertisers) and old movies, serials." Circ. 5,870. Pays on publication. Publishes ms an average of 9 months after acceptance. Byline given. Offers $25 kill fee. Buys all rights. Editorial lead time 2 months. Submit seasonal material 2 months in advance. Accepts queries by mail, e-mail, fax, phone. Accepts simultaneous submissions. Responds in 1 month to mss. Sample copy for free. Writer's guidelines free.

Nonfiction Essays, historical/nostalgic, interview/profile, personal experience, photo feature. Special issues: Western (April); Horror (October); Poster (June). Does not want opinion pieces. **Buys 120 mss/year.** Query. Length: 1,500-3,000 words. **Pays $100-300.**

Photos Send photos with submission. Reviews 8×10 prints, JPEG files. Buys all rights. Offers no additional payment for photos accepted with ms. Captions, identification of subjects, model releases required.

Tips "Ask if we would be interested in the topic, or send manuscript."

$ $BLADE MAGAZINE

The World's #1 Knife Publication, Krause Publications, 700 E. State St., Iola WI 54990-0001. (715)445-2214. Fax: (715)445-4087. E-mail: blademagazine@krause.com. Website: www.blademag.com. Editor: Steve Shackleford. **Contact:** Joe Kertzman, managing editor. **5% freelance written.** Monthly magazine covering working, using, collectible, popular knives. "*Blade* prefers indepth articles focusing on groups of knives, whether military, collectible, high-tech, pocket knives or hunting knives and how they perform." Estab. 1973. Circ. 39,000. Pays on publication. Publishes ms an average of 9 months after acceptance. Byline given. Buys all rights. Editorial lead time 9 months. Submit seasonal material 9 months in advance. Accepts queries by mail, e-mail, fax. Responds in 3 months to queries; 6 months to mss. Sample copy for $4.99., Writer's guidelines for 8×11 SAE with 3 first-class Stamps.

Nonfiction General interest, historical/nostalgic, how-to, interview/profile, new product, photo feature, technical. Query with or without published clips or send complete ms. Length: 700-1,400 words. **Pays $200-350.**

Photos Send photos with submission. Reviews transparencies, prints. Buys all rights. Offers no additional payment for photos accepted with ms. Captions, identification of subjects required.

Fillers Anecdotes, facts, newsbreaks. **Buys 1-2/year.** Length: 50-200 words. **Pays $25-50.**

Tips "We are always willing to read submissions from anyone who has read a few copies and studied the market. The ideal article for us is a piece bringing out the romance, legend, and love of man's oldest tool—the knife. We like articles that place knives in peoples' hands—in life saving situations, adventure modes, etc. (Nothing gory or with the knife as the villain.) People and knives are good copy. We are getting more and better written articles from writers who are reading the publication beforehand. That makes for a harder sell for the quickie writer not willing to do his homework. Go to knife shows and talk to the makers and collectors. Visit knifemakers' shops and knife factories. Read anything and everything you can find on knives and knifemaking."

$BREW YOUR OWN

The How-to Homebrew Beer Magazine, Battenkill Communications, 5053 Main St., Suite A, Manchester Center VT 05255. (802)362-3981. Fax: (802)362-2377. E-mail: edit@byo.com. Website: www.byo.com. **Contact:** Chris Colby, editor. **85% freelance written.** Monthly magazine covering home brewing. "Our mission is to provide practical information in an entertaining format. We try to capture the spirit and challenge of brewing while helping our readers brew the best beer they can." Estab. 1995. Circ. 40,000. **Pays on acceptance.** Publishes ms an average of 4 months after acceptance. Byline given. Offers 25% kill fee. Buys all rights. Editorial lead time 3 months. Submit seasonal material 3 months in advance. Accepts queries by mail, e-mail, fax. Responds in 2 months to queries. Writer's guidelines online.

    O→ Break in by "sending a detailed query in 1 of 2 key areas: how to brew a specific, interesting style of beer (with step-by-step recipes) or how to build your own specific piece of brewing equipment."

Nonfiction Informational pieces on equipment, ingredients, and brewing methods. Historical/nostalgic, how-to (home brewing), humor (related to home brewing), interview/profile (of professional brewers who can offer useful tips to home hobbyists), personal experience, trends. **Buys 75 mss/year.** Query with published clips or description of brewing expertise. Length: 800-3,000 words. **Pays $50-150, depending on length, complexity of article and experience of writer.** Sometimes pays expenses of writers on assignment.

Photos State availability with submission. Reviews contact sheets, transparencies, 5×7 prints, slides, and electronic images. Buys all rights. Negotiates payment individually. Captions required.

Columns/Departments News (humorous, unusual news about homebrewing), 50-250 words; Last Call (humorous stories about homebrewing), 700 words. **Buys 12 mss/year.** Query with or without published clips. **Pays $50.**

Tips "*Brew Your Own* is for anyone who is interested in brewing beer, from beginners to advanced all-grain brewers. We seek articles that are straightforward and factual, not full of esoteric theories or complex calculations. Our readers tend to be intelligent, upscale, and literate."

$ $CERAMICS MONTHLY

735 Ceramic Place, Westerville OH 43081. (614)895-4213. Fax: (614)891-8960. E-mail: editorial@ceramicsmonthly.org. Website: www.ceramicsmonthly.org. **Contact:** Renée Fairchild, assistant editor. **70% freelance written.** Monthly magazine (except July and August) covering the ceramic art and craft field. "Each issue includes articles on potters and ceramics artists from throughout the world, exhibitions, and production processes, as well as critical commentary, book and video reviews, clay and glaze recipes, kiln designs and firing techniques, advice from experts in the field, and ads for available materials and equipment. While principally covering contemporary work, the magazine also looks back at influential artists and events from the past." Estab. 1953. Circ. 39,000. Pays on publication. Byline given. Editorial lead time 3 months. Submit seasonal material 6 months in advance. Accepts queries by mail, e-mail, fax, phone. Responds in 2 months to mss. Writer's guidelines online.

Nonfiction Essays, how-to, interview/profile, opinion, personal experience, technical. **Buys 100 mss/year.** Send complete ms. Length: 500-3,000 words. **Pays 10¢/word.**

Photos Send photos with submission. Reviews original slides or 2¼ or 4×5 transparencies. Offers $25 for photos. Captions required.

Columns/Departments Upfront (workshop/exhibition review), 500-1,000 words. **Buys 20 mss/year.** Send complete ms.

$ $CLASSIC TOY TRAINS

Kalmbach Publishing Co., 21027 Crossroads Circle, Waukesha WI 53187. (262)796-8776. Fax: (262)796-1142. E-mail: editor@classictoytrains.com. Website: www.classictoytrains.com. **Contact:** Neil Besougloff, editor. **80% freelance written.** Magazine published 9 times/year covering collectible toy trains (O, S, Standard, G scale, etc.) like Lionel, American Flyer, Marx, Dorfan, etc. "For the collector and operator of toy trains, *CTT* offers full-color photos of layouts and collections of toy trains, restoration tips, operating information, new product reviews and information, and insights into the history of toy trains." Estab. 1987. Circ. 65,000. **Pays on acceptance.** Publishes ms an average of 1 year after acceptance. Byline given. Buys all rights. Editorial lead time 3 months. Submit seasonal material 6 months in advance. Accepts queries by mail, e-mail. Responds in 3 weeks to queries; 1 month to mss. Sample copy for $5.50, plus s&h. Writer's guidelines online.

Nonfiction General interest, historical/nostalgic, how-to (restore toy trains; design a layout; build accessories; fix broken toy trains), interview/profile, personal experience, photo feature, technical. **Buys 90 mss/year.** Query. Length: 500-5,000 words. **Pays $75-500.** Sometimes pays expenses of writers on assignment.

Photos Send photos with submission. Reviews 4×5 transparencies, 5×7 prints or 35mm slides preferred. Buys all rights. Offers no additional payment for photos accepted with ms or $15-75/photo. Captions required.

Fillers Uses cartoons. **Buys 6/year. Pays $30.**

Tips "It's important to have a thorough understanding of the toy train hobby; most of our freelancers are hobbyists themselves. One-half to two-thirds of *CTT*'s editorial space is devoted to photographs; superior photography is critical."

$ 🖂 COLLECTIBLES CANADA

Canada's Guide to Contemporary Collectible Art, Trajan Publishing, 103 Lakeshore Rd., Suite 202, St. Catharines ON L2N 2T6, Canada. (905)646-7744, ext. 229. Fax: (905)646-0995. E-mail: susanpennell@look.ca. Website: www.collectiblescanada.ca. Editor: Susan Pennell. Executive Editor: Mary Lynn McCauley. **90% freelance written.** Quarterly magazine covering contemporary collectible art and gifts. "We provide news and profiles of limited edition collectible art from a positive perspective. We are an informational tool for collectors who want to read about the products they love." Circ. 12,000. Pays 1 month after publication. Publishes ms an average of 3 months after acceptance. Byline given. Buys first North American serial rights. Editorial lead time 3 months. Submit seasonal material 3 months in advance. Accepts queries by mail, e-mail, fax. Responds in 1 month to queries. Sample copy for $3.95 (Canadian) and $2.50 IRC. Writer's guidelines for #10 SASE.

Nonfiction Historical/nostalgic (collectibles), interview/profile, new product, technical, collectible art such as figurines, dolls, bears, prints, etc. No articles on antique-related subjects ("we cover contemporary collectibles"). No articles about stamp, coin, or sports collecting. **Buys 16 mss/year.** Query with published clips. Length: 500-1,200 words. **Pays $75-120 (Canadian).** Sometimes pays expenses of writers on assignment.

Photos State availability with submission. Reviews negatives, transparencies, prints. Buys one-time rights. Negotiates payment individually. Identification of subjects required.

Columns/Departments Book reviews (positive slant, primarily informational). Length: 500-800 words.

Tips "Read the magazine first. Writers who can offer an article with a unique angle based on collectibles. Examples of past article ideas: 'The History of Fabergé,' 'Crossing the Lines: How Collectibles Go From Art Print To Figurine, To Plate To Doll.' Send an e-mail with your idea and I'll evaluate it promptly."

Ⓝ $ $COLLECTOR MAGAZINE & PRICE GUIDE

Krause Publications, P.O. Box 1050, Dubuque IA 52004. (800)482-4143. Fax: (800)531-0880. E-mail: fliessc@krause.com. Website: www.collect.com. **Contact:** Claire R. Fliess, editor. **20% freelance written.** Monthly magazine covering collectibles—all kinds. "Our readers like all collectibles. Antiques, furniture, glass, and ceramics are most often written about." Estab. 1994. Circ. 23,173. Byline given. Offers $25 kill fee. Buys all rights. Editorial lead time 3 months. Submit seasonal material 3 months in advance. Accepts queries by mail, e-mail, fax, phone. Accepts simultaneous submissions. Responds in 1 month to mss. Sample copy for free. Writer's guidelines free.

Nonfiction Essays, historical/nostalgic, interview/profile, show reports, price guide information. Does not want opinion pieces. **Buys 40 mss/year.** Query. Length: 1,000-2,000 words. **Pays $100-300.**

Photos Send photos with submission. Reviews 8 X 10 prints, JPEG files. Buys all rights. Offers no additional payment for photos accepted with ms. Captions, identification of subjects, model releases required.

Columns/Departments Toys Remembered (one toy type—history and prices), 500 words and picture. **Buys 20 mss/year.** Query. **Pays $100-150.**

Tips "This magazine stresses prices of collectible items. We are open to all subjects."

$COLLECTORS NEWS

P.O. Box 306, Grundy Center IA 50638. (319)824-6981. Fax: (319)824-3414. E-mail: collectors@collectors-news.com. Website: collectors-news.com. **Contact:** Linda Kruger, managing editor. **20% freelance written.** Works with a small number of new/unpublished writers each year. Monthly magazine-size publication on offset, glossy cover, covering antiques, collectibles, and nostalgic memorabilia. Estab. 1959. Circ. 9,000. Pays on publication. Publishes ms an average of 1 year after acceptance. Byline given. Buys first rights, makes work-for-hire assignments. Submit seasonal material 3 months in advance. Accepts queries by mail, e-mail, fax, phone. Responds in 2 weeks to queries; 6 weeks to mss. Sample copy for $4 and 9×12 SAE. Writer's guidelines free.

   ○→ Break in with articles on collecting online; history and values of collectibles and antiques; collectors with unique and/or extensive collections; using collectibles in the home decor; and any 20th century and timely subjects.

Nonfiction General interest (any subject re: collectibles, antique to modern), historical/nostalgic (relating to collections or collectors), how-to (display your collection, care for, restore, appraise, locate, add to, etc.), interview/profile (covering individual collectors and their hobbies, unique or extensive; celebrity collectors, and limited edition artists), technical (in-depth analysis of a particular antique, collectible, or collecting field), travel ("hot" antiquing places in the US). Special issues: 12-month listing of antique and collectible shows, flea markets, and conventions (January includes events January-December; June includes events June-May); Care & Display of Collectibles (September); holidays (October-December). **Buys 36 mss/year.** Query with sample of writing. Length: 800-1,000 words. **Pays $1.10/column inch.**

Photos "Articles must be accompanied by photographs for illustration." A selection of 2-8 images is suggested. "Articles are eligible for full-color front page consideration when accompanied by quality color prints, high resolution electronic images and/or color transparencies. Only 1 article is highlighted on the cover/month. Any article providing a color photo selected for front page use receives an additional $25." Reviews color or b&w images. Buys first rights. Payment for photos included in payment for ms. Captions required.

Tips "Present a professionally written article with quality illustrations—well-researched and documented information."

COUNTRY ALMANAC

Harris Publications, Inc., 1115 Broadway, New York NY 10010. (212)807-7100. Fax: (212)463-9958. E-mail: countryletters@yahoo.com. Website: www.countryalmanacmag.com. Editor: Jodi Zucker. Quarterly magazine. Written as a home service magazine containing articles ranging from country crafts, home-spun decorating and making heirlooms, to the best in affordable mail-order collectibles. Circ. 302,111. Editorial lead time 2 months. Sample copy not available.

N COUNTRY MARKETPLACE

707 Kautz Rd., Saint Charles IL 60174-5330. (630)377-8000. Fax: (630)377-8194. Website: www.sampler.com. Editor: Amy Wiegman. Bimonthly magazine. Edited for active crafters who are interested in current crafting trends, ideas and products. Circ. 300,000. Editorial lead time 3 months. Sample copy not available.

$CQ AMATEUR RADIO

The Radio Amateur's Journal, CQ Communications, Inc., 25 Newbridge Rd., Hicksville NY 11801. (516)681-2922. Fax: (516)681-2926. E-mail: cq@cq-amateur-radio.com. Website: www.cq-amateur-radio.com. Managing Editor: Gail Schieber. **Contact:** Richard Moseson, editor. **40% freelance written.** Monthly magazine covering amateur (ham) radio. "CQ is published for active ham radio operators and is read by radio amateurs in over 100 countries. All articles must deal with amateur radio. Our focus is on operating and on practical projects. A thorough knowledge of amateur radio is required." Estab. 1945. Circ. 60,000. Pays on publication. Publishes ms an average of 6 months after acceptance. Byline given. Buys first North American serial rights. Editorial lead time 4 months. Submit seasonal material 4 months in advance. Accepts queries by mail, e-mail, fax. Responds in 3 weeks to queries; 3 months to mss. Sample copy for free. Writer's guidelines online.

Nonfiction Historical/nostalgic, how-to, interview/profile, personal experience, technical, all related to amateur radio. **Buys 50-60 mss/year.** Query. Length: 2,000-4,000 words. **Pays $40/published page.**

Photos State availability with submission. Reviews contact sheets, 4×6 prints, TIFF or JPEG files with 300 dpi resolution. Buys one-time rights. Offers no additional payment for photos accepted with ms. Captions, identification of subjects, model releases required.

Tips "You must know and understand ham radio and ham radio operators. Most of our writers (95%) are licensed hams. Because our readers span a wide area of interests within amateur radio, don't assume they are already familiar with your topic. Explain. At the same time, don't write down to the readers. They are intelligent, well-educated people who will understand what you're saying when written and explained in plain English."

$ $ ⊡ THE CRAFT FACTOR

Saskatchewan Craft Council, 813 Broadway Ave., Saskatoon SK S7N 1B5, Canada. (306)653-3616. E-mail: scc.editor@shaw.ca. **Contact:** Gale Alaie, editor. **100% freelance written.** Semiannual magazine covering craft and related subjects. Estab. 1975. Circ. 1,500. Pays on publication. Byline sometimes given. Offers $50 kill fee. Buys first rights. Editorial lead time 2 months. Accepts queries by mail, e-mail, phone. Sample copy for free. Writer's guidelines free.

Nonfiction Historical/nostalgic, interview/profile, technical. Length: 500-1,500 words. **Pays $75-250.** Sometimes pays expenses of writers on assignment.

Photos Reviews transparencies, slides.

$ $ CROCHET WORLD

House of White Birches, P.O. Box 776, Henniker NH 03242. Fax: (219)589-8093. E-mail: editor@crochet-world.com. Website: www.whitebirches.com. **Contact:** Susan Hankins, editor. **100% freelance written.** Bimonthly magazine covering crochet patterns. "*Crochet World* is a pattern magazine devoted to the art of crochet. We also feature a Q&A column, letters (swap shop) column, and occasionally nonpattern manuscripts, but it must be devoted to crochet." Estab. 1978. Circ. 75,000. Pays on publication. Byline given. Buys all rights. Editorial lead time 4 months. Submit seasonal material 6 months in advance. Responds in 1 month to queries. Sample copy for $2. Writer's guidelines free.

Nonfiction How-to (crochet). **Buys 0-2 mss/year.** Send complete ms. Length: 500-1,500 words. **Pays $50.**

Columns/Departments Touch of Style (crocheted clothing); It's a Snap! (quick 1-night simple patterns); Pattern of the Month, each issue. **Buys dozens of mss/year.** Send complete pattern. **Pays $40-300.**

Poetry Strictly crochet-related. **Buys 0-5 poems/year.** Submit maximum 2 poems. Length: 6-10 lines. **Pays $10-20.**

Fillers Anecdotes, facts, short humor. **Buys 0-10/year.** Length: 25-200 words. **Pays $5-30.**

Tips "Be aware that this is a pattern-generated magazine for crochet designs. I prefer the actual item sent along with complete directions/graphs etc., over queries. In some cases a photo submission or good sketch will do. Crocheted designs must be well-made and original and directions must be complete. Write for designer's guidelines which detail how to submit designs. Noncrochet items, such as fillers, poetry *must* be crochet-related, not knit, not sewing, etc."

$ $ DECORATIVE ARTIST'S WORKBOOK

F + W Publications, Inc., 4700 E. Galbraith Rd., Cincinnati OH 45236. (513)531-2690, ext. 1461. E-mail: dawedit@fwpubs.com. Website: www.decorativeartist.com. **Contact:** Anne Hevener, editor. **75% freelance written.** Bimonthly magazine covering decorative painting step-by-step projects. Offers "straightforward, personal instruction in the techniques of decorative painting." Estab. 1987. Circ. 85,000. **Pays on acceptance.** Byline given. Offers 25% kill fee. Buys first North American serial rights. Submit seasonal material 8 months in advance. Accepts queries by mail, e-mail. Responds in 3 weeks to queries. Sample copy for $8 and 9×12 SAE with 5 first-class stamps. Writer's guidelines online.

Nonfiction How-to (related to decorative painting projects), new product, technique. **Buys 30 mss/year.** Query with slides or photos. Length: 1,200-1,800 words. **Pays 15-25¢/word.**

■ The online magazine carries original content not found in the print edition. Contact: Anne Hevener, online editor.

Tips "Create a design, surface, or technique that is fresh and new to decorative painting. I'm looking for experts in the field who, through their own experience, can accurately describe the techniques involved. How-to articles are most open to freelancers skilled in decorative painting. Be sure to query with photo/slides, and show that you understand the extensive graphic requirements for these pieces and can provide painted progressives—painted illustrations that show painting in progress."

$ $ DOLLHOUSE MINIATURES

Kalmbach Publishing Co., 21027 Crossroads Circle, Waukesha WI 53187-1612. (262)796-8776. Fax: (262)796-1383. E-mail: mbuellesbach@dhminiatures.com. Website: www.dhminiatures.com. Editor: Melanie Buellesbach. **50% freelance written.** Monthly magazine covering dollhouse scale miniatures. "*Dollhouse Miniatures* is America's best-selling miniatures magazine and the definitive resource for artisans, collectors, and hobbyists. It promotes and supports the large national and international community of miniaturists through club columns, short reports, and by featuring reader projects and ideas." Estab. 1971. Circ. 25,000. **Pays on acceptance.** Byline given. Buys all rights. Editorial lead time 6 months. Submit seasonal material 6 months in advance. Accepts queries by mail, e-mail. Responds in 1 month to queries; 2 months to mss. Sample copy for $4.95. Writer's guidelines online.

Nonfiction How-to (miniature projects of various scales in variety of media), interview/profile (artisans, collectors), photo feature (dollhouses, collections, museums). No articles on miniature shops or essays. **Buys 50-60**

mss/year. Query with or without published clips or send complete ms. Length: 500-1,500 words. **Pays $50-350 for assigned articles; $0-200 for unsolicited articles.**

Photos Send photos with submission. Reviews 35mm slides and larger, 3×5 prints. Buys all rights. Photos are paid for with ms. Seldom buys individual photos. Captions, identification of subjects required.

Tips "Familiarity with the miniatures hobby is very helpful. Accuracy to scale is extremely important to our readers. A complete package (manuscripts/photos) has a better chance of publication."

N $ $ DOLLS

Jones Publishing, Inc., E 17 Passaic Ave., Hasbrouck Heights NJ 07684. (715)445-5000. Fax: (715)445-4053. E-mail: nrdollsmagazine@earthlink.net. Website: www.jonespublishing.com. Assistant Editor: Trina Laube. **Contact:** Nayda Rondon, editor. **75% freelance written.** Magazine published 10 times/year covering dolls, doll artists and related topics of interest to doll collectors and enthusiasts. "*Dolls* enhances the joy of collecting by introducing readers to the best new dolls from around the world, along with the artists and designers who create them. It keeps readers up-to-date on shows, sales and special events in the doll world. With beautiful color photography, *Dolls* offers an array of easy-to-read, informative articles that help our collectors select the best buys." Estab. 1982. Circ. 100,000. Pays on publication. Byline given. Buys first North American serial rights. Accepts queries by mail, e-mail. Responds in 1 month to queries.

Nonfiction Historical/nostalgic, how-to, interview/profile, new product, photo feature. **Buys 55 mss/year.** Query with published clips or send complete ms. Length: 750-1,200 words. **Pays $75-300.**

Photos Send photos with submission. Reviews transparencies. Buys one-time rights. Offers no additional payment for photos accepted with ms. Captions, identification of subjects, model releases required.

Tips "Know the subject matter and artists. Having quality artwork and access to doll artists for interviews are big pluses. We need original ideas of interest to doll lovers."

$ $ $ FAMILY TREE MAGAZINE

F+W Publications, 4700 E. Galbraith Rd., Cincinnati OH 45236. (513)531-2690. Fax: (513)891-7153. E-mail: ftmedit@fwpubs.com. Website: www.familytreemagazine.com. **Contact:** Allison Stacy, editor. **75% freelance written.** Bimonthly magazine covering family history, heritage, and genealogy research. "*Family Tree Magazine* is a general-interest consumer magazine that helps readers discover, preserve, and celebrate their family's history. We cover genealogy, ethnic heritage, genealogy websites and software, scrapbooking, photography and photo preservation, and other ways that families connect with their past." Estab. 1999. Circ. 85,000. **Pays on acceptance.** Publishes ms an average of 6 months after acceptance. Byline given. Offers 25% kill fee. Buys first, electronic rights. Editorial lead time 8 months. Submit seasonal material 8 months in advance. Accepts queries by mail, e-mail. Responds in 1 month to queries. Sample copy for $7 from website. Writer's guidelines online.

- Break in by suggesting a "useful, timely idea for our Toolkit section on a resource that our readers would love to discover."

Nonfiction "Articles are geared to beginners but never talk down to the audience. We emphasize sidebars, tips, and other reader-friendly 'packaging,' and each article aims to give the reader the resources necessary to take the next step in his or her quest for the past." Book excerpts, historical/nostalgic, how-to (genealogy), new product (photography, computer), technical (genealogy software, photography equipment). **Buys 60 mss/year.** Query with published clips. Length: 250-3,500 words. **Pays $25-800.**

Photos State availability with submission. Reviews color transparencies. Buys one-time rights. Negotiates payment individually. Captions required.

Tips "Always query with a specific story idea. Look at sample issues before querying to get a feel for appropriate topics and angles. We see too many broad, general stories on genealogy or records, and personal accounts of 'How I found great-aunt Sally' without how-to value."

$ $ FIBERARTS

The Magazine of Textiles, Interweave Press, 201 E. Fourth St., Loveland CO 80537. (970)613-9679. Fax: (970)669-6110. E-mail: assteditor@fiberartsmagazine.com. Website: www.fiberartsmagazine.com. **Contact:** Sunita Patterson, editor. **90% freelance written.** Magazine published 5 times/year covering textiles as art and craft (contemporary trends in fiber sculpture, weaving, quilting, surface design, stitchery, papermaking, basketry, felting, wearable art, knitting, fashion, crochet, mixed textile techniques, ethnic dying, eccentric tidbits, etc.) for textile artists, craftspeople, collectors, teachers, museum and gallery staffs, and enthusiasts. Estab. 1975. Circ. 22,500. Pays on publication. Publishes ms an average of 4 months after acceptance. Byline given. Buys first rights. Accepts queries by mail. Sample copy for $6. Writer's guidelines online.

Nonfiction "Please be very specific about your proposal. Also, an important consideration in accepting an article is the kind of photos that you can provide as illustration. We like to see photos in advance." Essays, interview/profile (artist), opinion, personal experience, photo feature, technical, education, trends, exhibition reviews, textile news, book reviews, ethnic. Query with brief synopsis, SASE, and visuals. No phone queries. Length: 250-2,000 words. **Pays $70-550.**

Photos Color slides, large-format transparencies, or 300 dpi 5″ high TIFF images must accompany every query. The more photos to choose from, the better. Please include caption information. The names and addresses of those mentioned in the article or to whom the visuals are to be returned are necessary.

Columns/Departments Commentary (thoughtful opinion on a topic of interest to our readers), 400 words; Notable Events; Worldwide Connections; The Creative Process; Fiber Hot Spots; Collections; Practical Matters, 450 words and 2-4 photos; Profile (focuses on one artist), 450 words and 1 photo; Reviews (exhibits and shows; summarize quality, significance, focus and atmosphere, then evaluate selected pieces for aesthetic quality, content and technique—because we have an international readership, brief biographical notes or quotes might be pertinent for locally or regionally known artists), 500 words and 3-5 photos. (Do not cite works for which visuals are unavailable; you are not eligible to review a show in which you have participated as an artist, organizer, curator or juror.) **Pays $100-150.**

Tips "Our writers are very familiar with the textile field, and this is what we look for in a new writer. Familiarity with textile techniques, history or events determines clarity of an article more than a particular style of writing. The writer should also be familiar with *Fiberarts* magazine. The professional is essential to the editorial depth of *Fiberarts* and must find timely information in the pages of the magazine, but our editorial philosophy is that the magazine must provide the non-professional textile enthusiast with the inspiration, support, useful information and direction to keep him or her excited, interested and committed. Although we address serious issues relating to the fiber arts as well as light, we're looking for an accessible rather than overly scholarly tone."

$ 🖼 FIBRE FOCUS

Magazine of the Ontario Handweavers and Spinners, 10 Teanaustaye Dr., Hillsdale ON L0L 1V0, Canada. E-mail: jettevdm@sympatico.ca. Website: www.ohs.on.ca. **Contact:** Jette Vandermeiden, editor. **90% freelance written.** Quarterly magazine covering handweaving, spinning, basketry, beading, and other fibre arts. "Our readers are weavers and spinners who also do dyeing, knitting, basketry, feltmaking, papermaking, sheep raising, and craft supply. All articles deal with some aspect of these crafts." Estab. 1957. Circ. 1,000. Pays within 30 days after publication. Byline given. Buys one-time rights. Editorial lead time 6 months. Submit seasonal material 6 months in advance. Accepts previously published material. Responds in 1 month to queries. Sample copy for $5 Canadian. Writer's guidelines online.

Nonfiction How-to, interview/profile, new product, opinion, personal experience, technical, travel, book reviews. **Buys 40-60 mss/year.** Length: Varies. **Pays $30 Canadian/published page.**

Photos Send photos with submission. Reviews 4×6 color prints. Buys one-time rights. Offers additional payment for photos accepted with ms. Captions, identification of subjects required.

Fiction Humorous, slice-of-life vignettes. **Pays $30 Canadian/published page.**

Tips "Visit the OHS website for current information."

$ $ FINE TOOL JOURNAL

Antique & Collectible Tools, Inc., 27 Fickett Rd., Pownal ME 04069. (207)688-4962. Fax: (207)688-4831. E-mail: ceb@finetoolj.com. Website: www.finetoolj.com. **Contact:** Clarence Blanchard, president. **90% freelance written.** Quarterly magazine specializing in older or antique hand tools from all traditional trades. Readers are primarily interested in woodworking tools, but some subscribers have interests in such areas as leatherworking, wrenches, kitchen, and machinist tools. Readers range from beginners just getting into the hobby to advanced collectors and organizations. Estab. 1970. Circ. 2,500. Pays on publication. Publishes ms an average of 6 months after acceptance. Byline given. Offers $50 kill fee. Buys first, second serial (reprint) rights. Editorial lead time 9 months. Submit seasonal material 6 months in advance. Accepts queries by mail. Accepts previously published material. Responds in 2 months to queries; 3 months to mss. Sample copy for $5. Writer's guidelines for #10 SASE.

Nonfiction "We're looking for articles about tools from all trades. Interests include collecting, preservation, history, values and price trends, traditional methods and uses, interviews with collectors/users/makers, etc. Most articles published will deal with vintage, pre-1950, hand tools. Also seeking articles on how to use specific tools or how a specific trade was carried out. However, how-to articles must be detailed and not just of general interest. We do on occasion run articles on modern toolmakers who produce traditional hand tools." General interest, historical/nostalgic, how-to (make, use, fix and tune tools), interview/profile, personal experience, photo feature, technical. **Buys 24 mss/year.** Send complete ms. Length: 400-2,000 words. **Pays $50-200.** Pays expenses of writers on assignment.

Photos Send photos with submission. Reviews 4×5 prints. Buys all rights. Negotiates payment individually. Identification of subjects, model releases required.

Columns/Departments Stanley Tools (new finds and odd types), 300-400 words; Tips of the Trade (how to use tools), 100-200 words. **Buys 12 mss/year.** Send complete ms. **Pays $30-60.**

Tips "The easiest way to get published in the *Journal* is to have personal experience or know someone who can supply the detailed information. We are seeking articles that go deeper than general interest and that knowledge requires experience and/or research. Short of personal experience, find a subject that fits our needs and that interests you. Spend some time learning the ins and outs of the subject and with hard work and a little luck you will earn the right to write about it."

N $ $ FINE WOODWORKING

The Taunton Press, P.O. Box 5506, Newtown CT 06470-5506. (800)926-8776. Fax: (203)270-6753. E-mail: fw@taunton.com. Website: www.taunton.com. Publisher: Tim Schreiner. **Contact:** Anatole Burkin, executive editor. Bimonthly magazine on woodworking in the small shop. "All writers are also skilled woodworkers. It's more important that a contributor be a woodworker than a writer. Our editors (also woodworkers) will provide assistance." Estab. 1975. Circ. 270,000. **Pays on acceptance.** Byline given. Offers variable kill fee. Buys first rights. Rights to republish in anthologies and use in promo pieces Submit seasonal material 6 months in advance. Accepts simultaneous submissions. Responds in 2 months to queries. Writer's guidelines free and online.

> ○→ "We're looking for good articles on almost all aspects of woodworking from the basics of tool use, stock preparation and joinery to specialized techniques and finishing. We're especially keen on articles about shop-built tools, jigs and fixtures or any stage of design, construction, finishing and installation of cabinetry and furniture. Whether the subject involves fundamental methods or advanced techniques, we look for high-quality workmanship, thoughtful designs, safe and proper procedures."

Nonfiction How-to (woodworking). "No specs—our editors would rather see more than less." **Buys 120 mss/year.** Query with proposal letter. **Pays $150/magazine page for assigned articles.** Sometimes pays expenses of writers on assignment.

Photos Send photos with submission. Reviews contact sheets, negatives, transparencies, Prints. Buys one-time rights. Captions, identification of subjects, model releases required.

Columns/Departments Notes & Comment (topics of interest to woodworkers); Question & Answer (woodworking Q&A); Methods of Work (shop tips); Tools & Materials (short reviews of new tools). **Buys 400 mss/year. Pays $10-150/published page.**

> The online magazine carries original content not found in the print edition. Contact: Mark Schofield, online editor.

Tips "Look for authors guidelines and follow them. Stories about woodworking reported by non-woodworkers are *not* used. Our magazine is essentially reader-written by woodworkers."

$ FINESCALE MODELER

Kalmbach Publishing Co., 21027 Crossroads Circle, P.O. Box 1612, Waukesha WI 53187. (414)796-8776. Fax: (414)796-1383. E-mail: mthompson@finescale.com. Website: www.finescale.com. **Contact:** Dick McNally, managing editor. **80% freelance written.** Eager to work with new/unpublished writers. Magazine published 10 times/year "devoted to how-to-do-it modeling information for scale model builders who build non-operating aircraft, tanks, boats, automobiles, figures, dioramas, and science fiction and fantasy models." Circ. 60,000. **Pays on acceptance.** Publishes ms an average of 14 months after acceptance. Byline given. Buys all rights. Responds in 6 weeks to queries; 3 months to mss. Sample copy for 9×12 SAE and 3 first-class stamps.

● *Finescale Modeler* is especially looking for how-to articles for car modelers.

Nonfiction How-to (build scale models), technical (research information for building models). Query or send complete ms. Length: 750-3,000 words. **Pays $55 published page minimum.**

Photos Send photos with submission. Reviews transparencies, color prints. Buys one-time rights. Pays $7.50 minimum for transparencies and $5 minimum for color prints. Captions, identification of subjects required.

Columns/Departments *FSM* Showcase (photos plus description of model); *FSM* Tips and Techniques (model building hints and tips). **Buys 25-50 mss/year.** Send complete ms. **Pays $25-50.**

Tips "A freelancer can best break in first through hints and tips, then through feature articles. Most people who write for *FSM* are modelers first, writers second. This is a specialty magazine for a special, quite expert audience. Essentially, 99% of our writers will come from that audience."

N $ $ GENEALOGICAL COMPUTING

MyFamily.com, Inc., 360 W. 4800 N., Provo UT 84604. (801)705-7000. Fax: (801)705-7001. E-mail: liz@ancestordetective.com. Website: www.ancestry.com. **Contact:** Liz Kerstens, managing editor. **85% freelance written.** Quarterly magazine covering genealogy and computers. Estab. 1980. Circ. 16,000. Pays on publication. Publishes ms an average of 4 months after acceptance. Byline given. Buys all rights. Editorial lead time 4 months. Submit seasonal material 4 months in advance.

Nonfiction How-to, interview/profile, new product, technical. **Buys 40 mss/year.** Query. Length: 1,500-2,500 words. **Pays $75-500.**

Reprints Accepts previously published submissions. Pays 75% of amount paid for an original article.

$ $THE HOME SHOP MACHINIST

2779 Aero Park Dr., Traverse City MI 49686. (616)946-3712. Fax: (616)946-3289. E-mail: nknopf@villagepress.com. Website: www.villagepress.com. **Contact:** Neil Knopf, editor. **95% freelance written.** Bimonthly magazine covering machining and metalworking for the hobbyist. Circ. 34,000. Pays on publication. Publishes ms an average of 2 years after acceptance. Byline given. Buys first North American serial rights. Responds in 2 months to queries. Sample copy for free. Writer's guidelines for 9×12 SASE.

Nonfiction How-to (projects designed to upgrade present shop equipment or hobby model projects that require machining), technical (should pertain to metalworking, machining, drafting, layout, welding or foundry work for the hobbyist). No fiction or "people" features. **Buys 40 mss/year.** Query with or without published clips or send complete ms. Length: open—"whatever it takes to do a thorough job." **Pays $40/published page, plus $9/published photo.**

Photos Send photos with submission. Pays $9-40 for 5×7 b&w prints; $70/page for camera-ready art; $40 for b&w cover photo. Captions, identification of subjects required.

Columns/Departments Book Reviews; New Product Reviews; Micro-Machining; Foundry. Length: 600-1,500 words. "Become familiar with our magazine before submitting." **Buys 25-30 mss/year.** Query. **Pays $40-70.**

Fillers Machining tips/shortcuts. **Buys 12-15/year.** Length: 100-300 words. **Pays $30-48.**

Tips "The writer should be experienced in the area of metalworking and machining; should be extremely thorough in explanations of methods, processes—always with an eye to safety; and should provide good quality b&w photos and/or clear dimensioned drawings to aid in description. Visuals are of increasing importance to our readers. Carefully planned photos, drawings and charts will carry a submission to our magazine much farther along the path to publication."

$ $KITPLANES

For Designers, Builders, and Pilots of Experimental Aircraft, A Primedia Publication. (973)227-7660. Fax: (973)227-7630. E-mail: editorial@kitplanes.com. Website: www.kitplanes.com. **Contact:** Brian Clark, editor. **80% freelance written.** Eager to work with new/unpublished writers. Monthly magazine covering self-construction of private aircraft for pilots and builders. Estab. 1984. Circ. 72,000. Pays on publication. Publishes ms an average of 3 months after acceptance. Byline given. Buys complete rights, except book rights. Submit seasonal material 6 months in advance. Accepts queries by mail, e-mail. Responds in 2 weeks to queries; 6 weeks to mss. Sample copy for $6. Writer's guidelines online.

Nonfiction "We are looking for articles on specific construction techniques, the use of tools, both hand and power, in aircraft building, the relative merits of various materials, conversions of engines from automobiles for aviation use, installation of instruments and electronics." General interest, how-to, interview/profile, new product, personal experience, photo feature, technical. No general-interest aviation articles, or "My First Solo" type of articles. **Buys 80 mss/year.** Query. Length: 500-3,000 words. **Pays $70-600 including story photos for assigned articles.**

Photos State availability of or send photos with submission. Buys one-time rights. Pays $300 for cover photos. Captions, identification of subjects required.

Tips "*Kitplanes* contains very specific information—a writer must be extremely knowledgeable in the field. Major features are entrusted only to known writers. I cannot emphasize enough that articles must be directed at the individual aircraft builder. We need more 'how-to' photo features in all areas of homebuilt aircraft."

KNITTING DIGEST

House of White Birches, 306 E. Parr Rd., Berne IN 46711. (260)589-4000. Fax: (260)589-8093. E-mail: editor@knittingdigest.com. Website: www.whitebirches.com. **Contact:** Jeanne Stauffer, editor. **100% freelance written.** Bimonthly magazine covering knitting designs and patterns. "We print only occasional articles, but are always open to knitting designs and proposals." Estab. 1993. Circ. 50,000. Pays within 6 months. Publishes ms an average of 11 months after acceptance. Byline given. Offers 100% kill fee. Buys all rights. Accepts queries by mail, e-mail. Responds in 2 months to queries; 6 months to mss. Sample copy not available. Writer's guidelines for #10 SASE.

Nonfiction How-to (knitting skills), technical (knitting field). **Buys 4-6 mss/year.** Send complete ms. Length: 500 words maximum. **Pays variable amount. Also pays in contributor copies.**

Tips "Clear concise writing. Humor is appreciated in this field, as much as technical tips. The magazine is a digest, so space is limited. All submissions must be typed and double-spaced."

$ $ KNIVES ILLUSTRATED

The Premier Cutlery Magazine, 265 S. Anita Dr., Suite 120, Orange CA 92868-3310. (423)894-8319. Fax: (423)892-7254. E-mail: editorial@knivesillustrated.com. Website: www.knivesillustrated.com. **40-50% freelance written.** Bimonthly magazine covering high-quality factory and custom knives. "We publish articles on different types of factory and custom knives, how-to make knives, technical articles, shop tours, articles on knife makers and artists. Must have knowledge about knives and the people who use and make them. We feature the full range of custom and high tech production knives, from miniatures to swords, leaving nothing untouched. We're also known for our outstanding how-to articles and technical features on equipment, materials and knife making supplies. We do not feature knife maker profiles as such, although we do spotlight some makers by featuring a variety of their knives and insight into their background and philosophy." Estab. 1987. Circ. 35,000. Pays on publication. Byline given. Editorial lead time 3 months. Accepts queries by mail, e-mail, fax. Responds in 2 weeks to queries. Sample copy available. Writer's guidelines for #10 SASE.

Nonfiction General interest, historical/nostalgic, how-to, interview/profile, new product, photo feature, technical. **Buys 35-40 mss/year.** Query. Length: 400-2,000 words. **Pays $100-500.**

Photos Send photos with submission. Reviews 35mm, $2^{1}/_{4} \times 2^{1}/_{4}$, 4×5 transparencies, 5×7 prints, electronic images in TIFF, GIP or JPEG Mac format. Negotiates payment individually. Captions, identification of subjects, model releases required.

Tips "Most of our contributors are involved with knives, either as collectors, makers, engravers, etc. To write about this subject requires knowledge. A 'good' writer can do OK if they study some recent issues. If you are interested in submitting work to *Knives Illustrated* magazine, it is suggested you analyze at least two or three different editions to get a feel for the magazine. It is also recommended that you call or mail in your query to determine if we are interested in the topic you have in mind. While verbal or written approval may be given, all articles are still received on a speculation basis. We cannot approve any article until we have it in hand, whereupon we will make a final decision as to its suitability for our use. Bear in mind we do not suggest you go to the trouble to write an article if there is doubt we can use it promptly."

LAPIDARY JOURNAL

60 Chestnut Ave., Suite 201, Devon PA 19333-1312. (610)964-6300. Fax: (610)293-0977. E-mail: lj.editorial@primedia.com. Website: www.lapidaryjournal.com. **70% freelance written.** Monthly magazine covering gem, bead and jewelry arts. "Our audience is hobbyists who usually have some knowledge of and proficiency in the subject before they start reading. Our style is conversational and informative. There are how-to projects and profiles of artists and materials." Estab. 1947. Circ. 53,000. **Pays on acceptance.** Publishes ms an average of 4 months after acceptance. Byline given. one-time and worldwide rights. Editorial lead time 3 months. Accepts queries by mail, e-mail. Sample copy online.

Nonfiction Looks for conversational and lively narratives with quotes and anecdotes; Q&A's; interviews. How-to (jewelry/craft), interview/profile, new product, personal experience, technical, travel. Special issues: Bead Annual, Gemstone Annual, Jewelry Design issue. **Buys 100 mss/year.** Query. Length: 1,500-2,500 words preferred; 1,000-3,500 words acceptable; longer works occasionally published serially. Pays some expenses of writers on assignment.

Reprints Send photocopy.

Tips "Some knowledge of jewelry, gemstones and/or minerals is a definite asset. *Jewelry Journal* is a section within *Lapidary Journal* that offers illustrated, step-by-step instruction in gem cutting, jewelry making, and beading. Please request a copy of the *Jewelry Journal* guidelines for greater detail."

$ $ THE LEATHER CRAFTERS & SADDLERS JOURNAL

331 Annette Court, Rhinelander WI 54501-2902. (715)362-5393. Fax: (715)362-5391. E-mail: journal@newnorth .net. Managing Editor: Dorothea Reis. **Contact:** William R. Reis, publisher. **100% freelance written.** Bimonthly magazine. "A leather-working publication with how-to, step-by-step instructional articles using full-size patterns for leathercraft, leather art, custom saddle, boot and harness making, etc. A complete resource for leather, tools, machinery, and allied materials, plus leather industry news." Estab. 1990. Circ. 9,000. Pays on publication. Publishes ms an average of 2 months after acceptance. Byline given. Buys first North American serial, second serial (reprint) rights. Submit seasonal material 6 months in advance. Accepts queries by mail, e-mail, fax, phone. Accepts previously published material. Accepts simultaneous submissions. Responds in 1 month to mss. Sample copy for $5. Writer's guidelines for #10 SASE.

    Break in with a how-to, step-by-step leather item article from beginner through masters and saddlemaking.

Nonfiction "I want only articles that include hands-on, step-by-step, how-to information." How-to (crafts and arts, and any other projects using leather). **Buys 75 mss/year.** Send complete ms. Length: 500-2,500 words. **Pays $20-250 for assigned articles; $20-150 for unsolicited articles.**

Reprints Send tearsheet or photocopy. Pays 50% of amount paid for an original article.

Photos Send good contrast color print photos and full-size patterns and/or full-size photo-carve patterns with submission. Lack of these reduces payment amount. Captions required.

Columns/Departments Beginners; Intermediate; Artists; Western Design; Saddlemakers; International Design; and Letters (the open exchange of information between all peoples). Length: 500-2,500 words on all. **Buys 75 mss/year.** Send complete ms. **Pays 5¢/word.**

Fillers Anecdotes, facts, gags to be illustrated by cartoonist, newsbreaks. Length: 25-200 words. **Pays $5-20.**

Tips "We want to work with people who understand and know leathercraft and are interested in passing on their knowledge to others. We would prefer to interview people who have achieved a high level in leathercraft skill."

$LOST TREASURE, INC.

P.O. Box 451589, Grove OK 74345. (918)786-2182. Fax: (918)786-2192. E-mail: managingeditor@losttreasure.com. Website: www.losttreasure.com. **Contact:** Janet Warford-Perry, managing editor. **75% freelance written.** Monthly and annual magazines covering lost treasure. Estab. 1966. Circ. 55,000. Pays on publication. Byline given. Buys all rights. Accepts queries by mail, e-mail, fax. Responds in 1 month to queries; 2 months to mss. Sample copy for #10 SASE. Writer's guidelines for 10×13 SAE with $1.47 postage or online.

Nonfiction *Lost Treasure*, a monthly, is composed of lost treasure stories, legends, how-to articles, treasure hunting club news, who's who in treasure hunting, tips. Length: 500-1,200 words. *Treasure Cache*, an annual, contains stories about documented treasure caches with a sidebar from the author telling the reader how to search for the cache highlighted in the story. **Buys 225 mss/year.** Query on *Treasure Cache* only. Length: 1,000-2,000 words. **Pays 4¢/word.**

Photos Black & white or color prints, hand-drawn or copied maps, art with source credit with mss will help sell your story. We are always looking for cover photos with or without accompanying ms. Pays $100/published cover photo. Must be 35mm color slides or negatives, vertical. Pays $5/published photo. Captions required.

Tips "We are only interested in treasures that can be found with metal detectors. Queries welcome but not required. If you write about famous treasures and lost mines, be sure we haven't used your selected topic recently and story must have a new slant or new information. Source documentation required. How-tos should cover some aspect of treasure hunting and how-to steps should be clearly defined. If you have a *Treasure Cache* story we will, if necessary, help the author with the sidebar telling how to search for the cache in the story. *Lost Treasure* articles should coordinate with theme issues when possible."

N MICHAEL'S CREATE!

Krause Publications, 700 E. State St., Iola WI 54990-0001. (715)445-2214. Fax: (715)445-4087. Website: www.krause.com. Editor: Jane Beard. **Contact:** Sandra Sparks, associate editor. Bimonthly magazine. Pays on publication. Publishes ms an average of 6 months after acceptance. Byline given. Buys all rights. Editorial lead time 6 months. Submit seasonal material 6 months in advance. Accepts queries by mail, e-mail. Sample copy not available. Writer's guidelines free.

Nonfiction How-to. **Buys 20-24 mss/year.** Query. **Pays variable amount.**

$MINIATURE QUILTS

Chitra Publications, 2 Public Ave., Montrose PA 18801. (570)278-1984. Fax: (570)278-2223. E-mail: chitraed@epix.net. Website: www.quilttownusa.com. **Contact:** Phyllis Montange, production coordinator. **40% freelance written.** Bimonthly magazine on miniature quilts. "We seek articles of an instructional nature (all techniques), profiles of talented quiltmakers, and informational articles on all aspects of miniature quilts. Miniature is defined as quilts made up of blocks smaller than 5 inches." Estab. 1990. Circ. 70,000. Pays on publication. Publishes ms an average of 6 months after acceptance. Byline given. Buys second serial (reprint) rights. Submit seasonal material 8 months in advance. Accepts queries by mail, fax. Responds in 2 months to queries. Writer's guidelines online.

O── "Best bet—a quilter writing about a new or unusual quilting technique."

Nonfiction How-to, interview/profile (quilters who make small quilts), photo feature (about noteworthy miniature quilts or exhibits). Query. Length: 1,500 words maximum. **Pays $75/published page of text.**

Photos Send photos with submission. Reviews 35mm slides and larger transparencies. Offers $20/photo. Captions, identification of subjects, model releases required.

$MODEL RAILROADER

P.O. Box 1612, Waukesha WI 53187. Fax: (262)796-1142. E-mail: mrmag@mrmag.com. Website: www.trains.com. **Contact:** Russ Larson, publisher or Terry Thompson, editor. Monthly magazine for hobbyists interested in scale model railroading. "We publish articles on all aspects of model-railroading and on prototype (real) railroading as a subject for modeling." Byline given. Buys exclusive rights. Accepts queries by mail, e-mail, fax. Responds in 2 months to queries.

○→ "Study publication before submitting material." First-hand knowledge of subject almost always necessary for acceptable slant.

Nonfiction Wants construction articles on specific model railroad projects (structures, cars, locomotives, scenery, benchwork, etc.). Also photo stories showing model railroads. Query. **Pays base rate of $90/page.**

Photos Buys photos with detailed descriptive captions only. Pays $15 and up, depending on size and use. Full color cover earns $200.

Tips "Before you prepare and submit any article, you should write us a short letter of inquiry describing what you want to do. We can then tell you if it fits our needs and save you from working on something we don't want."

$ MONITORING TIMES

Grove Enterprises, Inc., 7540 Hwy. 64 W., Brasstown NC 28902-0098. (828)837-9200. Fax: (828)837-2216. E-mail: editor@monitoringtimes.com. Website: www.monitoringtimes.com. Publisher: Robert Grove. **Contact:** Rachel Baughn, editor. **15% freelance written.** Monthly magazine for radio hobbyists. Estab. 1982. Circ. 20,000. Pays on publication. Publishes ms an average of 4 months after acceptance. Byline given. Buys first North American serial, second serial (reprint) rights. Submit seasonal material 4 months in advance. Accepts queries by mail, e-mail. Accepts previously published material. Responds in 1 month to queries. Sample copy for 9 × 12 SAE and 9 first-class stamps. Writer's guidelines online.

○→ Break in with a shortwave station profile or topic, or scanning topics of broad interest.

Nonfiction General interest, how-to, humor, interview/profile, personal experience, photo feature, technical. **Buys 50 mss/year.** Query. Length: 1,500-3,000 words. **Pays average of $50/published page.**

Reprints Send photocopy and information about when and where the material previously appeared. Pays 25% of amount paid for an original article.

Photos Send photos with submission. Buys one-time rights. Captions required.

Columns/Departments "Query managing editor."

Tips "Need articles on radio communications systems and shortwave broadcasters. We are accepting more technical projects."

$ NUMISMATIST MAGAZINE

American Numismatic Association, 818 N. Cascade Ave., Colorado Springs CO 80903-3279. (719)632-2646. Fax: (719)634-4085. E-mail: magazine@money.org. **Contact:** Barbara Gregory, editor. Monthly magazine covering numismatics (study of coins, tokens, medals, and paper money). Estab. 1888. Circ. 30,000. Pays on publication. Publishes ms an average of 1 year after acceptance. Byline given. Buys perpetual, but nonexclusive rights. Editorial lead time 2 months. Sample copy for free.

Nonfiction "Submitted material should present new information and/or constitute a contribution to numismatic education for the experienced collector and beginner alike." Book excerpts, essays, historical/nostalgic, opinion, technical. **Buys 60 mss/year.** Query or send complete ms. Length: 2,500 words maximum. **Pays 7¢/word.** Sometimes pays expenses of writers on assignment.

Photos Send photos with submission. Negotiates payment individually. Captions, identification of subjects required.

Columns/Departments Send complete ms. **Pays $25-100.**

N $ $ OP

The Magazine of Book Culture & Collecting, Stewart & Brown Publishing, LLC, P.O. Box 106, Eureka CA 95502. E-mail: writers@opmagazine.com. Website: www.opmagazine.com. Editor: Dee Stewart. **Contact:** P. Scott Brown, managing editor. **90% freelance written.** Bimonthly magazine covering used and antiquarian bookselling and book collecting. "We cover all aspects of selling and collecting out-of-print books. We emphasize good writing, interesting people, and unexpected view points." Estab. 2002. Circ. 2,000. Pays on publication. Publishes ms an average of 4 months after acceptance. Byline given. Offers negotiable kill fee. Buys first North American serial, second serial (reprint), electronic rights, makes work-for-hire assignments. Editorial lead time 4 months. Submit seasonal material 4 months in advance. Accepts queries by mail, e-mail. Accepts previously published material. Accepts simultaneous submissions. Responds in 1 month to queries; 2 months to mss. Sample copy for $5. Writer's guidelines online.

Nonfiction Book excerpts, essays, exposé, general interest, historical/nostalgic, how-to, humor, interview/profile, opinion, personal experience, photo feature, travel. Does not want tales of the "gold in my attic" vein; stories emphasizing books as an investment. **Buys 40 mss/year.** Query with published clips. Length: 1,000-5,000 words. **Pays $100-300.** Sometimes pays expenses of writers on assignment.

Photos State availability with submission. Reviews GIF/JPEG files. Buys one-time, plus nonexclusive electronic rights. Negotiates payment individually. Captions, identification of subjects required.

Columns/Departments Shop Talk (news about collectors, booksellers, and bookselling), 350 words; On the

Shelf (reviews of books about books, writers, publishers, collecting), 800 words; Endpaper (outstanding personal essay on books or collecting), 850 words; Book Scout (profiles of book places), 2,000 words. **Buys 20 mss/year.** Send complete ms. **Pays $25-200.**

Tips "Tell compelling stories about people and the passion for book collecting. We aim to make academic writing on books accessible to a broad audience and to enliven the writing of aficionados with solid editing and story development."

PACK-O-FUN

Projects For Kids & Families, Clapper Communications, 2400 Devon Ave., Des Plaines IL 60018-4618. (847)635-5800. Fax: (847)635-6311. Website: www.craftideas.com. Editor: Billie Ciancio. **Contact:** Irene Mueller, managing editor. **85% freelance written.** Bimonthly magazine covering crafts and activities for kids and those working with kids. Estab. 1951. Circ. 102,000. Pays 45 days after signed contract. Byline given. Buys all rights. Editorial lead time 6 months. Submit seasonal material 6 months in advance. Accepts queries by mail, fax. Accepts previously published material. Accepts simultaneous submissions. Responds in 2 months to queries. Sample copy for $3.50 or online.

Nonfiction "We request quick and easy, inexpensive crafts and activities. Projects must be original, and complete instructions are required upon acceptance." **Payment negotiable.**

Reprints Send tearsheet and information about when and where the material previously appeared.

Photos Photos of project may be submitted in place of project at query stage.

Tips "*Pack-O-Fun* is looking for original how-to projects for kids and those working with kids. Write simple instructions for crafts to be done by children ages 5-13 years. We're looking for recyclable ideas for throwaways. We accept fiction if accompanied by a craft or in skit form (appropriate for classrooms, scouts or Bible school groups). It would be helpful to check out our magazine before submitting."

N $ $ PAPERCRAFTS MAGAZINE

14901 S. Heritagecrest Way, Bluffdale UT 84065. (801)984-2070. Fax: (801)984-2080. E-mail: editor@craftsmag.com. Website: www.craftsmag.com. Magazine published 10 times/year designed to help readers make creative and rewarding handmade crafts. The main focus is fresh, craft-related projects our reader can make and display in her home or give as gifts. Estab. 1978. Circ. 300,000. **Pays on acceptance.** Byline given. Buys all rights. Editorial lead time 6 months. Accepts queries by mail, e-mail. Responds in 1 month to queries. Writer's guidelines for #10 SASE.

Nonfiction How-to. **Buys 300 mss/year.** Query with photo or sketch of how-to project. Do not send the actual project until request. **Pays $100-500 for assigned articles.**

Tips "We are looking for projects that are fresh, innovative, and in sync with today's trends. We accept projects made with a variety of techniques and media. Projects can fall in several categories, ranging from home decor to gifts, garden accessories to jewelry, and other seasonal craft projects. Submitted projects must be original, never-before-published, copyright-free work that use readily available materials."

$ PIECEWORK MAGAZINE

Interweave Press, Inc., 201 E. 4th St., Loveland CO 80537-5655. (970)669-7672. Fax: (970)667-8317. E-mail: piecework@interweave.com. Website: www.interweave.com. **90% freelance written.** Bimonthly magazine covering needlework history. "*PieceWork* celebrates the rich tradition of needlework and the history of the people behind it. Stories and projects on embroidery, cross-stitch, knitting, crocheting, and quilting, along with other textile arts, are featured in each issue." Estab. 1993. Circ. 60,000. Pays on publication. Byline given. Offers 30% kill fee. Buys first North American serial rights. Editorial lead time 6 months. Submit seasonal material 6 months in advance. Accepts queries by mail, e-mail, fax, phone. Responds in 6 months to queries. Sample copy and writer's guidelines free.

Nonfiction Book excerpts, historical/nostalgic, how-to, interview/profile, new product. No contemporary needlework articles. **Buys 25-30 mss/year.** Send complete ms. Length: 1,000-5,000 words. **Pays $100/printed page.**

Photos State availability of or send photos with submission. Reviews transparencies, prints. Buys one-time rights. Captions, identification of subjects, model releases required.

Tips "Submit a well-researched article on a historical aspect of needlework complete with information on visuals and suggestion for accompanying project."

$ POPULAR COMMUNICATIONS

CQ Communications, Inc., 25 Newbridge Rd., Hicksville NY 11801. (516)681-2922. Fax: (516)681-2926. E-mail: popularcom@aol.com. Website: www.popular-communications.com. **Contact:** Harold Ort, editor. **25% freelance written.** Monthly magazine covering the radio communications hobby. Estab. 1982. Circ. 40,000. Pays on publication. Publishes ms an average of 6 months after acceptance. Byline given. Buys first North

American serial rights. Editorial lead time 3 months. Submit seasonal material 6 months in advance. Accepts queries by mail, e-mail. Responds in 1 month to queries; 2 months to mss. Sample copy for free. Writer's guidelines for #10 SASE.

Nonfiction General interest, how-to (antenna construction), humor, new product, photo feature, technical. **Buys 6-10 mss/year.** Query. Length: 1,800-3,000 words. **Pays $35/printed page.**

Photos State availability with submission. Negotiates payment individually. Captions, identification of subjects, model releases required.

Tips "Either be a radio enthusiast or know one who can help you before sending us an article."

N $ $ $ $ POPULAR MECHANICS

Hearst Corp., 810 Seventh Ave., 6th Floor, New York NY 10019. (212)649-2000. Fax: (212)586-5562. E-mail: popularmechanics@hearst.com. Website: www.popularmechanics.com. **Contact:** Joe Oldham, editor-in-chief; Sarah Deem, managing editor. **up to 50% freelance written.** Monthly magazine on automotive, home improvement, science, boating, outdoors, electronics. "We are a men's service magazine that tries to address the diverse interests of today's male, providing him with information to improve the way he lives. We cover stories from do-it-yourself projects to technological advances in aerospace, military, automotive and so on." Estab. 1902. Circ. 1,200,000. **Pays on acceptance.** Publishes ms an average of 6 months after acceptance. Byline given. Offers 25% kill fee. Buys all rights. Submit seasonal material 6 months in advance. Responds in 3 weeks to queries; 1 month to mss. Writer's guidelines for SASE or online.

Nonfiction General interest, how-to (shop projects, car fix-its), new product, technical. Special issues: Boating Guide (February); Home Improvement Guide (April); Consumer Electronics Guide (May); New Cars Guide (October); Woodworking Guide (November). No historical, editorial, or critique pieces. **Buys 2 mss/year.** Query with or without published clips or send complete ms. Length: 500-1,500 words. **Pays $500-1,500 for assigned articles; $300-1,000 for unsolicited articles.** Sometimes pays expenses of writers on assignment.

Photos Usually assigns a photographer. "If you have photos, send with submission." Reviews prints, slides. Buys all rights. Offers no additional payment for photos accepted with ms. Captions, identification of subjects, model releases required.

Columns/Departments New Cars (latest and hottest cars out of Detroit and Europe), Car Care (Maintenance basics, How It Works, Fix-Its and New products: send to Don Chaikin. Electronics, Audio, Home Video, Computers, Photography: send to Tobey Grumet. Boating (new equipment, how-tos, fishing tips), Outdoors (gear, vehicles, outdoor adventures): send to Cliff Gromer. Home & Shop Journal: send to Steve Willson. Science (latest developments), Tech Update (breakthroughs) and Aviation (sport aviation, homebuilt aircraft, new commercial aircraft, civil aeronautics): send to Jim Wilson. All columns are about 800 words.

The online magazine contains material not found in the print edition. Contact: Ken Juran, online editor.

$ $ POPULAR WOODWORKING

F+W Publications, 4700 E. Galbraith Rd., Cincinnati OH 45236. (513)531-2690, ext 1308. E-mail: popwood@fw pubs.com. Website: www.popularwoodworking.com. Editor/Publisher: Steve Shanesy. Executive Editor: Christopher Schwarz. **Contact:** Kara Gebhart, associate editor. **45% freelance written.** Magazine published 7 times/year. "*Popular Woodworking* invites woodworkers of all levels into a community of professionals who share their hard-won shop experience through in-depth projects and technique articles, which help the readers hone their existing skills and develop new ones. Related stories increase the readers' understanding and enjoyment of their craft. Any project submitted must be aesthetically pleasing, of sound construction and offer a challenge to readers. On the average, we use four freelance features per issue. Our primary needs are 'how-to' articles on woodworking. Our secondary need is for articles that will inspire discussion concerning woodworking. Tone of articles should be conversational and informal, as if the writer is speaking directly to the reader. Our readers are the woodworking hobbyist and small woodshop owner. Writers should have an extensive knowledge of woodworking, or be able to communicate information gained from woodworkers." Estab. 1981. Circ. 200,000. **Pays on acceptance.** Publishes ms an average of 10 months after acceptance. Byline given. Buys first world rights rights. Submit seasonal material 6 months in advance. Accepts queries by mail, e-mail, fax, phone. Accepts previously published material. Responds in 2 months to queries. Sample copy for $4.50 and 9×12 SAE with 6 first-class stamps or online. Writer's guidelines online.

O— "The project must be well-designed, well-constructed, well-built and well-finished. Technique pieces must have practical application."

Nonfiction How-to (on woodworking projects, with plans), humor (woodworking anecdotes), technical (woodworking techniques). Special issues: Workshop issue, tool buying guide. No tool reviews. **Buys 40 mss/year.** Query with or without published clips or send complete ms. **Pay starts at $150/published page.**

Reprints Send photocopy with rights for sale noted and information about when and where the material previously appeared. Pays 25% of amount paid for an original article.

Photos Photographic quality affects acceptance. Need sharp close-up color photos of step-by-step construction process. Send photos with submission. Reviews color only, slides and transparencies, 3×5 glossies acceptable. Captions, identification of subjects required.

Columns/Departments Tricks of the Trade (helpful techniques), Out of the Woodwork (thoughts on woodworking as a profession or hobby, can be humorous or serious), 500-1,500 words. **Buys 20 mss/year.** Query.

☐ The online version of this publication contains material not found in the print edition. Contact: Michael A. Rabkin.

Tips "Write an 'Out of the Woodwork' column for us and then follow up with photos of your projects. Submissions should include materials list, complete diagrams (blueprints not necessary), and discussion of the step-by-step process. We have become more selective on accepting only practical, attractive projects with quality construction. We are also looking for more original topics for our other articles."

Ⓝ $ $POSTCARD COLLECTOR

Krause Publications, P.O. Box 1050, Dubuque IA 52004. (800)482-4143. Fax: (800)531-0880. E-mail: fliessc@krause.com. Website: www.postcardcollector.com. **Contact:** Claire R. Fliess, editor. **98% freelance written.** Monthly magazine covering postcard collecting. "The publication prints columns and articles about postcard collections. Sometimes they are historical—some are modern. Dealers and collectors subscribe." Estab. 1983. Circ. 6,165. Pays on publication. Publishes ms an average of 9 months after acceptance. Byline given. Offers $25 kill fee. Buys all rights. Editorial lead time 3 months. Submit seasonal material 3 months in advance. Accepts queries by mail, e-mail, fax, phone. Accepts simultaneous submissions. Responds in 1 month to mss. Sample copy for free. Writer's guidelines free.

Nonfiction Essays, historical/nostalgic, interview/profile, personal experience, photo feature. Does not want poorly researched articles. **Buys 120 mss/year.** Query. Length: 800-1,500 words. **Pays $75-200.**

Photos Send photos with submission. Reviews 4 X 6 prints, JPEG files. Buys negotiable rights. Offers no additional payment for photos accepted with ms. Captions, identification of subjects required.

Columns/Departments Book Reviews (review of content including images), 500-800 words. **Buys 120 mss/year.** Query. **Pays $75-200.**

Tips "Need good images of postcards, well-researched article—unusual topic."

$THE PYSANKA

Starwind Press, P.O. Box 98, Ripley OH 45167. (937)392-4549. E-mail: susannah@techgallery.com. **Contact:** Susannah West, editor. **90% freelance written.** Quarterly newsletter covering wax-resist egg decoration. "*The Pysanka* examines the art of wax-resist egg decoration (pysanky). Its audience is artists and hobbyists who create this style egg." Estab. 2000. Circ. 100. **Pays on acceptance.** Publishes ms an average of 3 months after acceptance. Byline given. Offers 100% kill fee. Buys first North American serial rights. Editorial lead time 3 months. Submit seasonal material 3 months in advance. Accepts queries by mail, e-mail. Accepts previously published material. Responds in 2 months to queries; 2 months to mss. Sample copy for $3.50. Writer's guidelines for #10 SASE.

Nonfiction Historical/nostalgic, how-to, interview/profile, new product, opinion, personal experience, photo feature, travel. **Buys 16-20 mss/year.** Query or send complete ms. Length: 500-900 words. **Pays $10.**

Reprints Accepts previously published submissions.

Photos State availability with submission. Negotiates payment individually. Identification of subjects required.

Columns/Departments Around and About (reviews of interesting places to visit related to the craft), 300-500 words; Passing the Torch (workshop experiences), 200-500 words; On the Pysanky Bookshelf (book reviews), 100-200 words; Issues and Answers (issues of interest), 500-900 words. **Buys 8-12 mss/year.** Query. **Pays $5-10.**

Fiction Ethnic. **Buys 4 mss/year.** Send complete ms. Length: 2,000-5,000 words. **Pays 1¢/word.**

Tips "The writer should be familiar with the wax-resist style of egg decoration, ideally an artist or hobbyist who makes this style of egg."

QUILTER'S NEWSLETTER MAGAZINE

Primedia Enthusiast Group, 741 Corporate Circle, Suite A, Golden CO 80401. (303)278-1010. Fax: (303)277-0307. E-mail: questions@qnm.com. Website: www.quiltersnewsletter.com. Editor: Mary Leman Austin. Magazine published 10 times/year covering quilt making. Written for quilt enthusiasts. Estab. 1969. Circ. 185,000. Pays on publication. Publishes ms an average of 1 year after acceptance. Accepts queries by mail. Responds in 6-8 weeks to mss. Sample copy online. Writer's guidelines online.

Nonfiction SASE Returns. Historical/nostalgic, how-to (design techniques, presentation of a single technique or concept with step-by-step approach), interview/profile, new product, reviews- quilt books and videos. Send complete ms.

Photos Color only, no b&w. Reviews 2×2, 4×5 or larger transparencies, 35mm slides. Negotiates payment individually. Captions required.

Tips "Our decision will be based on the freshness of the material, the interest of the material to our readers, whether we have recently published similar material or already have something similar in our inventory, how well it fits into the balance of the material we have on hand, how much rewriting or editing we think it will require, and the quality of the slides, photos or illustrations you include."

N $ QUILTER'S WORLD

House of White Birches, 306 E. Parr Rd., Berne IN 46711. (260)589-8741. Fax: (260)589-8093. E-mail: editor@quilters-world.com. Website: www.quilters-world.com. **Contact:** Sandra L. Hatch, editor. **100% freelance written.** Works with a small number of new/unpublished writers each year. Bimonthly magazine covering quilting. *"Quilter's World* is a general quilting publication. We accept articles about special quilters, techniques, coverage of unusual quilts at quilt shows, special interest quilts, human interest articles and patterns. We include 12-17 patterns in every issue. Reader is 30-70 years old, midwestern." Circ. 130,000. Pays 45 days after acceptance. Byline given. Buys first, one-time, all rights. Submit seasonal material 10 months in advance. Accepts queries by mail, e-mail. Responds in 3 months to queries. Writer's guidelines for #10 SASE.

Nonfiction How-to, interview/profile (quilters), new product (quilt products), photo feature, technical. **Buys 18-24 mss/year.** Query or send complete ms. Length: Open. **Pays $50-100.**

Reprints Send photocopy and information about when and where the material previously appeared.

Tips "Read several recent issues for style and content."

$ $ THE QUILTER

All American Crafts, Inc., 243 Newton-Sparta Rd., Newton NJ 07860. (973)383-8080. Fax: (973)383-8133. E-mail: editors@thequiltermag.com. Website: www.thequiltermag.com. **Contact:** Laurette Koserowski, editor. **45% freelance written.** Bimonthly magazine on quilting. Estab. 1988. Pays on publication. Publishes ms an average of 6 months after acceptance. Byline given. Submit seasonal material 6 months in advance. Accepts queries by mail, phone. Responds in 2 months to queries. Sample copy for 9×12 SAE and 4 first-class stamps. Writer's guidelines online.

Nonfiction Quilts and quilt patterns with instructions, quilt-related projects, interview/profile, photo feature—all quilt related. Query with published clips. Length: 350-1,000 words. **Pays 10-12¢/word.**

Photos Send photos with submission. Reviews transparencies, prints. Buys one-time or all rights. Offers $10-15/photo. Captions, identification of subjects required.

Columns/Departments Feature Teacher (qualified quilt teachers with teaching involved—with slides); Profile (award-winning and interesting quilters). Length: 1,000 words maximum. **Pays 10¢/word, $15/photo.**

$ QUILTWORKS TODAY

Chitra Publications, 2 Public Ave., Montrose PA 18801. (570)278-1984. Fax: (570)278-2223. E-mail: chitraed@epix.net. Website: www.quilttownusa.com. **Contact:** Connie Ellsworth, production manager. **40% freelance written.** Bimonthly magazine covering quilting, traditional and contemporary. "We seek articles with 1 or 2 magazine pages of text, and quilts that illustrate the content. (Each page of text is approximately 750 words, 6,500 characters, or 3 double-spaced typewritten pages.) Please submit double-spaced manuscripts with wide margins. Submit your article in both hard copy and on a MacIntosh formatted disk, or if using a PC, save as MS-DOS text." Estab. 2002. Circ. 70,000. Pays on publication. Publishes ms an average of 6 months after acceptance. Byline given. Buys second serial (reprint) rights. Submit seasonal material 8 months in advance. Accepts queries by mail, e-mail, fax. Responds in 1 month to queries; 2 months to mss. Writer's guidelines online.

Nonfiction How-to (for various quilting techniques), interview/profile, new product, personal experience, photo feature, instructional, quilting education. **Buys 12-18 mss/year.** Query or send complete ms. **Pays $75/full page of published text.**

Reprints Send photocopy and information about when and where the material previously appeared.

Photos Send photos with submission. Reviews 35mm slides and larger transparenices (color). Offers $20/photo. Captions, identification of subjects required.

Tips "Our publication appeals to new and experienced traditional quilters."

$ RENAISSANCE MAGAZINE

division of Queue, Inc., 1450 Barnum Ave., Suite 207, Bridgeport CT 06610. (800)232-2224. Fax: (800)775-2729. E-mail: editor@renaissancemagazine.com. Website: www.renaissancemagazine.com. **Contact:** Kim Guarnaccia, managing editor. **90% freelance written.** Bimonthly magazine covering the history of the Middle Ages and the Renaissance. "Our readers include historians, reenactors, roleplayers, medievalists, and Renaissance Faire enthusiasts." Estab. 1996. Circ. 33,000. Pays on publication. Publishes ms an average of 1 year after acceptance. Byline given. Buys first North American serial rights. Editorial lead time 6 months. Submit seasonal material 4 months in advance. Accepts queries by mail, e-mail, fax, phone. Accepts previously published material. Responds in 3 weeks to queries; 2 months to mss. Sample copy for $9. Writer's guidelines online.

● The editor reports an interest in seeing costuming "how-to" articles; and Renaissance Festival "insider" articles.

○━ Break in by submitting short (500-1,000 word) articles as fillers or querying on upcoming theme issues.

Nonfiction Essays, exposé, historical/nostalgic, how-to, interview/profile, new product, opinion, photo feature, religious, travel. **Buys 25 mss/year.** Query or send ms. Length: 1,000-5,000 words. **Pays 8¢/word.**

Photos State availability with submission. Reviews contact sheets, negatives, transparencies, prints. Buys all rights. Pays $7.50/photo. Captions, identification of subjects, model releases required.

Columns/Departments Book reviews, 500 words. Include original or good copy of book cover. "For interested reviewers, books can be supplied for review; query first." **Pays 8¢/word.**

Tips "Send in all articles in the standard manuscript format with photos/slides or illustrations for suggested use. Writers *must* be open to critique, and all historical articles should also include a recommended reading list. A SASE must be included to receive a response to any submission."

$ $ROCK & GEM

The Earth's Treasures, Minerals and Jewelry, Miller Magazines, Inc., 4880 Market St., Ventura CA 93003-7783. (805)644-3824, ext. 29. Fax: (805)644-3875. E-mail: editor@rockngem.com. Website: www.rockngem.com. **Contact:** Lynn Varon, managing editor. **99% freelance written.** Monthly magazine covering rockhounding field trips, how-to lapidary projects, minerals, fossils, gold prospecting, mining, etc. "This is not a scientific journal. Its articles appeal to amateurs, beginners, and experts, but its tone is conversational and casual, not stuffy. It's for hobbyists." Estab. 1971. Circ. 55,000. Pays on publication. Byline given. Buys first North American serial rights. Editorial lead time 4 months. Submit seasonal material 6 months in advance. Accepts queries by mail. Writer's guidelines online.

Nonfiction General interest, how-to, personal experience, photo feature, travel. Does not want to see "The 25th Anniversary of the Pet Rock," or anything so scientific that it could be a thesis. **Buys 156-200 mss/year.** Send complete ms. Length: 2,000-4,000 words. **Pays $100-250.**

Photos Accepts prints, slides or digital art on disk or CD only (provide thumbnails). Send photos with submission. Offers no additional payment for photos accepted with ms. Captions required.

Tips "We're looking for more how-to articles and field trips with maps. Read writers guidelines very carefully and follow all instructions in them. Then be patient. Your manuscript may be published within a month or even a year from date of submission."

$ $RUG HOOKING MAGAZINE

Stackpole Magazines, 1300 Market St., Suite 202, Lemoyne PA 17043-1420. (717)234-5091. Fax: (717)234-1359. E-mail: rughook@paonline.com. Website: www.rughookingonline.com. Editor: Virginia P. Stimmel. **Contact:** Lisa McMullen, assistant editor. **75% freelance written.** Magazine published 5 times/year covering the craft of rug hooking. "This is the only magazine in the world devoted exclusively to rug hooking. Our readers are both novices and experts. They seek how-to pieces, features on fellow artisans and stories on beautiful rugs, new and old." Estab. 1989. Circ. 11,000. **Pays on acceptance.** Publishes ms an average of 1 year after acceptance. Byline given. Buys all rights. Editorial lead time 6 months. Submit seasonal material 6 months in advance. Accepts queries by mail, e-mail, fax. Responds in 2 months to queries. Sample copy for $5.

Nonfiction Also buys 2, 100-page books/year. How-to (hook a rug or a specific aspect of hooking), personal experience. **Buys 30 mss/year.** Query with published clips. Length: 825-2,475 words. **Pays $72-283.50.** Sometimes pays expenses of writers on assignment.

Reprints Send photocopy and information about when and where the material previously appeared.

Photos Send photos with submission. Reviews 2×2 transparencies, 3×5 prints. Buys all rights. Negotiates payment individually. Identification of subjects required.

$SCALE AUTO

(formerly *Scale Auto Enthusiast*), Kalmbach Publishing Co., 21027 Crossroads Circle, P.O. Box 1612, Waukesha WI 53187-1612. (262)796-8776. Fax: (262)796-1383. E-mail: jhaught@kalmbach.com. Website: www.scaleauto mag.com. **Contact:** Jim Haught, editor. **70% freelance written.** Bimonthly magazine covering model car building. "We are looking for model builders, collectors, and enthusiasts who feel their models and/or modeling techniques and experiences would be of interest and benefit to our readership." Estab. 1979. Circ. 35,000. Pays on publication. Publishes ms an average of 1 year after acceptance. Byline given. Buys all rights. Editorial lead time 4 months. Submit seasonal material 4 months in advance. Accepts queries by mail, e-mail, fax, phone. Responds in 3 months to queries; 3 months to mss. Sample copy and writer's guidelines free or on website.

Nonfiction Book excerpts, historical/nostalgic, how-to (build models, do different techniques), interview/profile, personal experience, photo feature, technical. Query or send complete ms. Length: 750-3,000 words. **Pays $60/published page.**

Photos When writing how-to articles be sure to take photos *during* the project. Send photos with submission. Reviews negatives, 35mm color transparencies, color glossy. Buys all rights. Negotiates payment individually. Captions, identification of subjects, model releases required.

Columns/Departments Buys 50 mss/year. Query. **Pays $60/page.**

Tips "First and foremost, our readers like how-to material: how-to paint, how-to scratchbuild, how-to chop a roof, etc. Basically, our readers want to know how to make their own models better. Therefore, any help or advice you can offer is what modelers want to read. Also, the more photos you send, taken from a variety of views, the better choice we have in putting together an outstanding article layout. Send us more photos than you would ever possibly imagine we could use. This permits us to pick and choose the best of the bunch."

$ $ SEW NEWS

The Fashion Magazine for People Who Sew, Primedia Enthusiast Group, 741 Corporate Circle, Suite A, Golden CO 80401. (303)278-1010. Fax: (303)277-0370. E-mail: sewnews@sewnews.com. Website: www.sewnews.c om. **Contact:** Linda Turner Griepentrog, editor. **90% freelance written.** Works with a small number of new/unpublished writers each year. Monthly magazine covering fashion and home-dec sewing. "Our magazine is for the beginning home sewer to the professional dressmaker. It expresses the fun, creativity, and excitement of sewing." Estab. 1980. Circ. 175,000. **Pays on acceptance.** Publishes ms an average of 6 months after acceptance. Byline given. Buys all rights. Submit seasonal material 6 months in advance. Accepts queries by mail, e-mail, fax. Responds in 2 months to mss. Sample copy for $5.99. Writer's guidelines for #10 SAE with 2 first-class stamps or online.

  • All stories submitted to *Sew News* must be on disk or by e-mail.

Nonfiction How-to (sewing techniques), interview/profile (interesting personalities in home-sewing field). **Buys 200-240 mss/year.** Query with published clips if available. Length: 500-2,000 words. **Pays $25-500 for assigned articles.**

Photos Prefers color photos or slides, or e-mail submission. Send photos with submission. Buys all rights. Payment included in ms price. Identification of subjects required.

  ▣ The online magazine carries some original content not found in the print edition and includes writer's guidelines. *Sew News* has a free online newsletter.

Tips "Query first with writing sample and outline of proposed story. Areas most open to freelancers are how-to and sewing techniques; give explicit, step-by-step instructions, plus rough art. We're using more home decorating and soft craft content."

$ SHUTTLE SPINDLE & DYEPOT

Handweavers Guild of America, Inc., 1255 Buford Hwy., Suite 211, Suwanee GA 30024. (678)730-0010. Fax: (678)730-0836. E-mail: hga@weavespindye.org. Website: www.weavespindye.org. Assistant Editor: Trish Fowler. Advertising Manager: Dorothy Holt. **Contact:** Sandra Bowles, editor-in-chief. **60% freelance written.** Quarterly magazine. "Quarterly membership publication of the Handweavers Guild of America, Inc., *Shuttle Spindle & Dyepot* magazine seeks to encourage excellence in contemporary fiber arts and to support the preservation of techniques and traditions in fiber arts. It also provides inspiration for fiber artists of all levels and develops public awareness and appreciation of the fiber arts. *Shuttle Spindle & Dyepot* appeals to a highly educated, creative and very knowledgeable audience of fiber artists and craftsmen—weavers, spinners, dyers and basket makers." Estab. 1969. Circ. 30,000. Pays on publication. Publishes ms an average of 6 months after acceptance. Byline given. Buys first North American serial, second serial (reprint), electronic rights. Editorial lead time 8 months. Submit seasonal material 8 months in advance. Accepts queries by mail, e-mail, fax, phone. Sample copy for $7.50 plus shipping. Writer's guidelines online.

  ⌖ Articles featuring up-and-coming artists, new techniques, cutting-edge ideas and designs, fascinating children's activities, and comprehensive fiber collections are a few examples of "best bet" topics.

Nonfiction Inspirational, interview/profile, new product, personal experience, photo feature, technical, travel. "No self-promotional and no articles from those without knowledge of area/art/artists." **Buys 40 mss/year.** Query with published clips. Length: 1,000-2,000 words. **Pays $75-150.**

Photos State availability with submission. Offers no additional payment for photos accepted with ms. Captions, identification of subjects, model releases required.

Columns/Departments Books and Videos, News and Information, Calendar and Conference, Travel and Workshop, Guildview (all fiber/art related).

Tips "Become knowledgeable about the fiber arts and artists. The writer should provide an article of importance to the weaving, spinning, dyeing and basket making community. Query by telephone (once familiar with publication) by appointment helps editor and writer.

$SPORTS COLLECTORS DIGEST

Voice for the Hobby, Krause Publications, 700 E. State St., Iola WI 54990. (715)445-2214. Fax: (715)445-4087. E-mail: scd@krause.com. Website: www.sportscollectorsdigest.com; www.krause.com. **Contact:** T.S. O'Connell, editor. **10% freelance written.** Weekly tabloid covering sports collectibles. ''Sports collectibles columns only.'' Estab. 1973. Circ. 30,000. Pays on publication. Publishes an average of 2 months after acceptance. Byline given. Makes work-for-hire assignments. Editorial lead time 2 months. Submit seasonal material 1 month in advance. Accepts queries by e-mail. Sample copy for free. Writer's guidelines not available.

Nonfiction General interest (new card issues, research older sets), historical/nostalgic (old stadiums, old collectibles, etc.), how-to (buy cards, sell cards and other collectibles, display collectibles, ways to get autographs, jerseys and other memorabilia), interview/profile (well-known collectors, ball players—but must focus on collectibles), new product (new card sets), personal experience (what I collect and why-type stories). No sports stories. ''We are not competing with *The Sporting News*, *Sports Illustrated* or your daily paper. Sports collectibles only.'' **Buys 50-75 mss/year.** Query. Length: 300-3,000 words. **Pays $100-150.**

Reprints Send tearsheet. Pays 100% of amount paid for an original article.

Photos Unusual collectibles. Send photos with submission. Buys all rights. Pays $25-150 for b&w prints. Identification of subjects required.

Columns/Departments Length: 500-1,500 words. ''We have all the columnists we need but welcome ideas for new columns.'' **Buys 100-150 mss/year.** Query. **Pays $90-150.**

Tips ''Sports collectibles submissions only, e-mailed or mailed to T.S. O'Connell.''

$ $TATTOO REVUE

Art & Ink Enterprises, Inc., 5 Marine View Plaza, Suite 207, Hoboken NJ 07030. (201)653-2700. Fax: (201)653-7892. E-mail: inked@skinartmag.com. Website: www.skinart.com. Editor: Jean Chris Miller. **Contact:** Managing Editor. **25% freelance written.** Interview and profile magazine published 10 times/year covering tattoo artists, their art and lifestyle. ''All writers must have knowledge of tattoos. Features include interviews with tattoo artists and collectors. Estab. 1990. Circ. 100,000. Pays on publication. Publishes ms an average of 3 months after acceptance. Byline given. Buys one-time rights. Editorial lead time 3 months. Submit seasonal material 5 months in advance. Accepts queries by mail, e-mail, fax. Responds in 2 weeks to queries. Sample copy for $5.98. Writer's guidelines for #10 SASE.

Nonfiction Book excerpts, historical/nostalgic, humor, interview/profile, photo feature. Special issues: Publishes special convention issues—dates and locations provided upon request. ''No first-time experiences—our readers already know.'' **Buys 10-30 mss/year.** Query with published clips or send complete ms. Length: 500-2,500 words. **Pays $25-200.**

Photos Send photos with submission. Reviews transparencies, prints. Buys one-time rights. Offers $0-10/photo. Captions, identification of subjects, model releases required.

Columns/Departments Buys 10-30 mss/year. Query with or without published clips or send complete ms. **Pays $25-50.**

Fillers Anecdotes, facts, gags to be illustrated by cartoonist, newsbreaks, short humor. **Buys 10-20/year.** Length: 50-2,000 words.

🖥 The online magazine carries original content not found in the print edition. Contact: Chris Miller.

Tips ''All writers must have knowledge of tattoos! Either giving or receiving.''

ⓝ $ $TEDDY BEAR REVIEW

Jones Publishing, Inc., N7450 Aanstad Rd., P.O. Box 5000, Iola WI 54945. (715)445-5000. E-mail: editor@teddyb earreview.com. Website: www.teddybearreview.com. **65% freelance written.** Works with a small number of new/unpublished writers each year. Bimonthly magazine on teddy bears for collectors, enthusiasts and bear-makers. Estab. 1985. Payment upon publication on the last day of the month the issue is mailed. Byline given. Contact editor for copy of freelance contributor agreement. Submit seasonal material 6 months in advance. Sample copy and writer's guidelines for $2 and 9×12 SAE.

Nonfiction Historical/nostalgic, how-to, interview/profile. No articles from the bear's point of view. **Buys 30-40 mss/year.** Query with published clips. Length: 900-1,500 words. **Pays $100-350.**

Photos Send photos with submission. Reviews transparencies, prints. Buys one-time rights. Offers no additional payment for photos accepted with ms. Captions required.

Tips ''We are interested in good, professional writers around the country with a strong knowledge of teddy bears. Historical profile of bear companies, profiles of contemporary artists, and knowledgeable reports on museum collections are of interest.''

$ $THREADS

Taunton Press, 63 S. Main St., P.O. Box 5506, Newtown CT 06470. (203)426-8171. Fax: (203)426-3434. E-mail: th@taunton.com. Website: www.threadsmagazine.com. Bimonthly magazine covering sewing, garment construction, home decor and embellishments (quilting and embroidery). "We're seeking proposals from hands-on authors who first and foremost have a skill. Being an experienced writer is of secondary consideration." Estab. 1985. Circ. 165,000. Byline given. Offers $150 kill fee. Buys one-time, second serial (reprint) rights. Editorial lead time 4 months. Responds in 1-2 months to queries. Writer's guidelines for free or online.

Nonfiction "We prefer first-person experience." **Pays $150/page.**

Columns/Departments Product reviews; Book reviews; Tips; Closures (stories of a humorous nature). Query. **Pays $150/page.**

Tips "Send us a proposal (outline) with photos of your own work (garments, samplers, etc.).''

$ $TOY FARMER

Toy Farmer Publications, 7496 106 Ave. SE, LaMoure ND 58458-9404. (701)883-5206. Fax: (701)883-5209. E-mail: zekesez@aol.com. Website: www.toyfarmer.com. President/Publisher: Cathy Scheibe. **Contact:** Cheryl Hegvik, editorial assistant. **80% freelance written.** Monthly magazine covering farm toys. Estab. 1978. Circ. 27,000. Pays on publication. Byline given. Buys first North American serial rights. Editorial lead time 3 months. Submit seasonal material 3 months in advance. Accepts queries by mail, e-mail, fax, phone. Accepts previously published material. Responds in 1 month to queries; 2 months to mss. Sample copy for $4. Writer's guidelines available upon request.

• Youth involvement is strongly encouraged.

Nonfiction General interest, historical/nostalgic, humor, interview/profile, new product, personal experience, technical, book introductions. **Buys 100 mss/year.** Query with published clips. Length: 800-1,500 words. **Pays 10¢/word.** Sometimes pays expenses of writers on assignment.

Photos Must be 35mm originals. State availability with submission. Reviews transparencies. Buys one-time rights. Offers no additional payment for photos accepted with ms.

Columns/Departments "We have regular monthly columns; so freelance work should not duplicate column subjects.''

$ $TOY SHOP

Krause Publications, 700 E. State St., Iola WI 54990-0001. (715)445-4612. Fax: (715)445-4087. E-mail: toyshop@krause.com. Website: www.toyshopmag.com.; www.collect.com. **Contact:** Tom Bartsch, editor. **20% freelance written.** Biweekly tabloid covering toys. "Our publication features writing that's easy to understand and lively." Estab. 1988. Circ. 20,000. Pays on publication. Publishes ms an average of 4 months after acceptance. Byline given. Offers $50 kill fee. Editorial lead time 2 months. Submit seasonal material 2 months in advance. Accepts queries by mail, e-mail, phone. Accepts previously published material. Accepts simultaneous submissions. Responds in 1 week to queries; 1 month to mss. Sample copy for free. Writer's guidelines free.

Nonfiction General interest, historical/nostalgic, humor, interview/profile, personal experience. **Buys 60 mss/year.** Query. Length: 600-800 words. **Pays $125-175.** Sometimes pays expenses of writers on assignment.

Reprints Send photocopy and information about when and where the material previously appeared.

Photos Send photos with submission. Reviews 5×7 prints, GIF/JPEG files. Offers no additional payment for photos accepted with ms. Captions, identification of subjects required.

Columns/Departments Buys 20 mss/year. Query. **Pays $125-175.**

Tips "Submit well worded queries. Know our magazine and style before submitting.''

$ $TOY TRUCKER & CONTRACTOR

Toy Farmer Publications, 7496 106th Ave. SE, LaMoure ND 58458-9404. (701)883-5206. Fax: (701)883-5209. E-mail: zekesez@aol.com. Website: www.toytrucker.com. President/Publisher: Cathy Scheibe. **Contact:** Cheryl Hegvik, editorial assistant. **80% freelance written.** Monthly magazine covering collectible toys. "We are a magazine on hobby and collectible toy trucks and construction pieces." Estab. 1990. Circ. 6,500. Pays on publication. Byline given. Buys first North American serial rights. Editorial lead time 3 months. Submit seasonal material 3 months in advance. Accepts queries by mail, e-mail, fax, phone. Accepts previously published material. Responds in 1 month to queries; 2 months to mss. Sample copy for $4. Writer's guidelines available on request.

Nonfiction Historical/nostalgic, interview/profile, new product, personal experience, technical. **Buys 35 mss/year.** Query. Length: 800-2,400 words. **Pays 10¢/word.** Sometimes pays expenses of writers on assignment.

Photos Must be 35mm originals. Send photos with submission. Offers no additional payment for photos accepted with ms. Captions, identification of subjects, model releases required.

Tips "Send sample work that would apply to our magazine. Also, we need more articles on collectors or builders. We have regular columns, so a feature should not repeat what our columns do.''

Ⓝ TUFF STUFF

Krause Publications, 700 E. State St., Iola WI 54990-0001. (715)445-2214. Fax: (715)445-4087. E-mail: tuffstuff@krause.com. Website: www.tuffstuff.com. Editor: Rocky Landsverk. **Contact:** Tom Huttman, managing editor.

Monthly magazine covering sports collectibles. "Collectibles expertise is necessary." Estab. 1984. Circ. 190,000. Pays on publication. Publishes ms an average of 2 months after acceptance. Byline given. Offers negotiable kill fee. Makes work-for-hire assignments. Editorial lead time 3 months. Submit seasonal material 3 months in advance. Accepts queries by e-mail. Sample copy for free. Writer's guidelines not available.

Photos State availability with submission. Reviews GIF/JPEG files. Buys one-time rights. Negotiates payment individually.

Tips "No general interest sports submissions. Collectibles writers only."

Ⓝ VOGUE KNITTING

Soho Publishing Co., Inc., 233 Spring St., 8th Floor, New York NY 10013. (212)937-2555. Fax: (646)336-3960. E-mail: webmaster@vogueknitting.com. Website: www.vogueknitting.com. Editor-in-Chief: Trisha Malcolm. Executive Editor: Carla Scott. Quarterly magazine created for participants in and enthusiasts of high fashion knitting. Circ. 175,000.

$WESTERN & EASTERN TREASURES

People's Publishing Co., Inc., P.O. Box 219, San Anselmo CA 94979. E-mail: treasurenet@prodigy.net. Website: www.treasurenet.com. **Contact:** Rosemary Anderson, managing editor. **100% freelance written.** Monthly magazine covering hobby/sport of metal detecting/treasure hunting. "*Western & Eastern Treasures* provides concise, yet comprehensive coverage of every aspect of the sport/hobby of metal detecting and treasure hunting with a strong emphasis on current, accurate information; innovative, field-proven advice and instruction; and entertaining, effective presentation." Estab. 1966. Circ. 50,000. Pays on publication. Publishes ms an average of 3 months after acceptance. Byline given. Buys all rights. Editorial lead time 4 months. Submit seasonal material 3-4 months in advance. Responds in 3 months to mss. Sample copy for 9×12 SAE and 5 first-class stamps. Writer's guidelines for #10 SASE.

Nonfiction How-to (tips and finds for metal detectorists), interview/profile (only people in metal detecting), personal experience (positive metal detector experiences), technical (only metal detecting hobby-related), helping in local community with metal detecting skills (i.e., helping local police locate evidence at crime scenes—all volunteer basis). Special issues: Silver & Gold Annual (editorial deadline February each year)—looking for articles 1,500 words maximum, plus photos on the subject of locating silver and/or gold using a metal detector. No fiction, poetry, or puzzles. **Buys 150+ mss/year.** Send complete ms. Length: 600-1,500 words. **Pays 2¢/ word for assigned articles.** Sometimes pays in contributor copies as trade for advertising space.

Photos Steve Anderson, vice president. Send photos with submission. Reviews 35mm transparencies, prints, digital scans (minimum 300 dpi). Buys all rights. Offers $5 minimum/photo. Captions, identification of subjects required.

$ $WOODSHOP NEWS

Soundings Publications, Inc., 10 Bokum Rd., Essex CT 06426-1185. (860)767-8227. Fax: (860)767-0645. E-mail: editorial@woodshopnews.com. Website: www.woodshopnews.com. **Contact:** A.J. Hamler, editor. **20% freelance written.** Monthly tabloid "covering woodworking for professionals. Solid business news and features about woodworking companies. Feature stories about interesting professional woodworkers. Some how-to articles." Estab. 1986. Circ. 85,000. Pays on publication. Publishes ms an average of 3 months after acceptance. Byline given. Offers 25% kill fee. Buys first North American serial rights. Submit seasonal material 4 months in advance. Accepts queries by mail, e-mail, fax. Responds in 1 month to queries. Sample copy online. Writer's guidelines free.

● *Woodshop News* needs writers in major cities in all regions except the Northeast. Also looking for more editorial opinion pieces.

Nonfiction How-to (query first), interview/profile, new product, opinion, personal experience, photo feature. Key word is "newsworthy." No general interest profiles of "folksy" woodworkers. **Buys 15-25 mss/year.** Query with published clips or send complete ms. Length: 100-1,200 words. **Pays $50-500 for assigned articles; $40-250 for unsolicited articles.** Pays expenses of writers on assignment.

Photos Send photos with submission. Reviews contact sheets, prints. Buys one-time rights. Offers $20-35/color photo; $250/color cover, usually with story. Captions, identification of subjects required.

Columns/Departments Pro Shop (business advice, marketing, employee relations, taxes, etc., for the professional written by an established professional in the field); Finishing (how-to and techniques, materials, spray-booths, staining; written by experienced finishers), both 1,200-1,500 words. **Buys 18 mss/year.** Query. **Pays $200-300.**

Fillers Small filler items, briefs, or news tips that are followed up by staff reporters. **Pays $10.**

Tips "The best way to start is a profile of a professional woodworker in your area. Find a unique angle about the person or business and stress this as the theme of your article. Avoid a broad, general-interest theme that would be more appropriate to a daily newspaper. Our readers are professional woodworkers who want more depth and more specifics than would a general readership. If you are profiling a business, we need standard business information such as gross annual earnings/sales, customer base, product line and prices, marketing strategy, etc. Color 35mm or high-res digital photos are a must. We need more freelance writers from the Mid-Atlantic, Midwest, and West Coast.''

$ $ WOODWORK

A Magazine For All Woodworkers, Ross Periodicals, 42 Digital Dr., #5, Novato CA 94949. (415)382-0580. Fax: (415)382-0587. E-mail: woodwork@rossperiodicals.com. Publisher: Tom Toldrian. **Contact:** John Lavine, editor. **90% freelance written.** Bimonthly magazine covering woodworking. ''We are aiming at a broad audience of woodworkers, from the enthusiast to professional. Articles run the range from intermediate to complex. We cover such subjects as carving, turning, furniture, tools old and new, design, techniques, projects, and more. We also feature profiles of woodworkers, with the emphasis being always on communicating woodworking methods, practices, theories, and techniques. Suggestions for articles are always welcome.'' Estab. 1986. Circ. 50,000. Pays on publication. Byline given. Buys first North American serial, second serial (reprint) rights. Accepts queries by mail, e-mail, fax. Sample copy for $5 and 9×12 SAE with 6 first-class stamps. Writer's guidelines for #10 SASE.

Nonfiction How-to (simple or complex, making attractive furniture), interview/profile (of established woodworkers that make attractive furniture), photo feature (of interest to woodworkers), technical (tools, techniques). ''Do not send a how-to unless you are a woodworker.'' Query. Length: 1,500-2,000 words. **Pays $150/ published page.**

Photos Send photos with submission. Reviews 35mm slides. Buys one-time rights. Pays higher page rate for photos accepted with ms. Captions, identification of subjects required.

Columns/Departments Tips and Techniques column, **pays $35-75.** Interview/profiles of established woodworkers (bring out woodworker's philosophy about the craft, opinions about what is happening currently). Good photos of attractive furniture a must. Section on how-to desirable. Query with published clips.

Tips ''Our main requirement is that each article must directly concern woodworking. If you are not a woodworker, the interview/profile is your best, really only chance. Good writing is essential as are good photos. The interview must be entertaining, but informative and pertinent to woodworkers' interests. Include sidebar written by the profile subject.''

HOME & GARDEN

$ THE ALMANAC FOR FARMERS & CITY FOLK

Greentree Publishing, Inc., 840 S. Rancho Dr., Suite 4-319, Las Vegas NV 89106. (702)387-6777. Website: www.thealmanac.com. **Contact:** Lucas McFadden, editor. **30-40% freelance written.** Annual almanac of ''down-home, folksy material pertaining to farming, gardening, homemaking, animals, etc.'' Deadline: March 31. Estab. 1983. Circ. 400,000. Pays on publication. Publishes ms an average of 6 months after acceptance. Byline given. Buys first North American serial rights. Sample copy for $4.99. Writer's guidelines not available.

○— Break in with short, humorous solutions to everyday problems; gardening; or how-to pieces.

Nonfiction Essays, general interest, historical/nostalgic, how-to (any home or garden project), humor. No fiction or controversial topics. ''Please, no first-person pieces!'' **Buys 30 mss/year.** No queries please. Editorial decisions made from ms only. Send complete ms by mail. Length: 350-1,400 words. **Pays $45/page.**

Poetry Buys 1-6 poems/year. **Pays $45 for full pages, otherwise proportionate share thereof.**

Fillers Uses 60/year. Anecdotes, facts, short humor, gardening hints. Length: 125 words maximum. **Pays $10-45.**

Tips ''Typed submissions essential as we scan manuscript. Short, succinct material is preferred. Material should appeal to a wide range of people and should be on the 'folksy' side, preferably with a thread of humor woven in. *No first-person pieces.*''

$ $ THE AMERICAN GARDENER

A Publication of the American Horticultural Society, 7931 E. Boulevard Dr., Alexandria VA 22308-1300. (703)768-5700. Fax: (703)768-7533. E-mail: editor@ahs.org. Website: www.ahs.org. Managing Editor: Mary Yee. **Contact:** David J. Ellis, editor. **70% freelance written.** Bimonthly magazine covering gardening and horticulture. ''*The American Gardener* is the official publication of the American Horticultural Society (AHS), a national, nonprofit, membership organization for gardeners, founded in 1922. The AHS mission is 'to open the eyes of all Americans to the vital connection between people and plants, and to inspire all Americans to become responsible caretakers of the earth, to celebrate America's diversity through the arts and sciences of horticulture, and to lead this effort by sharing the Society's unique national resources with all Americans.'' All articles in *The American Gardener* are also published on members-only website. Estab. 1922. Circ. 33,000. Pays on publication. Publishes ms an average of 6 months after acceptance. Byline given. Offers 25% kill fee. Buys first North American serial rights. Editorial lead time 4 months. Submit seasonal material at least 1 year in advance. Accepts queries by mail. Responds in 3 months to queries. Sample copy for $5. Writer's guidelines by e-mail.

Nonfiction "Feature-length articles include in-depth profiles of individual plant groups; profiles of prominent American horticulturists and gardeners (living and dead); profiles of unusual public or private gardens; descriptions of historical developments in American gardening; descriptions of innovative landscape design projects (especially relating to use of regionally native plants or naturalistic gardening); and descriptions of important plant breeding and research programs tailored to a lay audience. We run a few how-to articles; these should address relatively complex or unusual topics that most other gardening magazines won't tackle—photography needs to be provided." **Buys 30 mss/year.** Query with published clips. Length: 1,500-2,500 words. **Pays $300-500, depending on complexity and author's experience.**

Reprints Rarely purchases second rights. Send photocopy of article with information about when and where the material previously appeared. Payment varies.

Photos Must be accompanied by postage-paid return mailer. State availability with submission. Reviews transparencies. Buys one-time rights, plus limited rights to run article on members-only website. Offers $60-300/photo. Identification of subjects required.

Columns/Departments Conservationist's Notebook (addresses issues in plant conservation that are relevant or of interest to gardeners); Natural Connections (explains a natural phenomenon—plant and pollinator relationships, plant and fungus relationships, parasites—that may be observed in nature or in the garden), 750-1,200 words. **Buys 10 mss/year.** Query with published clips. **Pays $100-250.**

Tips "The majority of our readers are advanced, passionate amateur gardeners; about 20 percent are horticultural professionals. Most prefer not to use synthetic chemical pesticides. Our articles are intended to bring this knowledgeable group new information, ranging from the latest scientific findings that affect plants to in-depth profiles of specific plant groups, and the history of gardening and gardens in America."

$ $ AUSTIN HOME & LIVING

Publications & Communications, Inc., 11675 Jollyville Rd., Suite 150, Austin TX 78759. (512)381-0576. Fax: (512)331-3950. E-mail: bronas@pcinews.com. Website: www.austinhomeandliving.com. Editor: Taylor Bowles. **Contact:** Brona Stockton, associate publisher. **75% freelance written.** Bimonthly magazine. "*Austin Home & Living* showcases the homes found in Austin and provides tips on food, gardening, and decorating." Estab. 1994. Circ. 20,000. Pays on publication. Publishes ms an average of 4 months after acceptance. Byline given. Offers 100% kill fee. Buys all rights. Editorial lead time 4 months. Submit seasonal material 6 months in advance. Accepts queries by mail, e-mail, fax. Responds in 1 month to queries; 2 months to mss. Sample copy for free. Writer's guidelines online.

Nonfiction How-to, interview/profile, new product, travel. **Buys 18 mss/year.** Query with published clips. Length: 500-2,000 words. **Pays $200 for assigned articles.** Pays expenses of writers on assignment.

Photos State availability of or send photos with submission. Reviews negatives, transparencies, prints. Buys all rights. Offers no additional payment for photos accepted with ms. Captions required.

$ BACKHOME

Your Hands-On Guide to Sustainable Living, Wordsworth Communications, Inc., P.O. Box 70, Hendersonville NC 28793. (828)696-3838. Fax: (828)696-0700. E-mail: backhome@ioa.com. Website: www.backhomemagazine.com. **Contact:** Lorna K. Loveless, editor. **80% freelance written.** Bimonthly magazine. *BackHome* encourages readers to take more control over their lives by doing more for themselves: productive organic gardening; building and repairing their homes; utilizing alternative energy systems; raising crops and livestock; building furniture; toys and games and other projects; creative cooking. *BackHome* promotes respect for family activities, community programs, and the environment. Estab. 1990. Circ. 26,000. Pays on publication. Publishes ms an average of 1 year after acceptance. Byline given. Offers $25 kill fee at publisher's discretion. Buys first North American serial rights. Editorial lead time 3 months. Submit seasonal material 6 months in advance. Accepts queries by mail, e-mail, fax, phone. Accepts previously published material. Responds in 6 weeks to queries; 2 months to mss. Sample copy $5 or online. Writer's guidelines online.

- The editor reports an interest in seeing "more alternative energy experiences, *good* small houses, workshop projects (for handy persons, not experts), and community action others can copy."

- Break in by writing about personal experience (especially in overcoming challenges) in fields in which *BackHome* focuses.

Nonfiction How-to (gardening, construction, energy, homebusiness), interview/profile, personal experience, technical, self-sufficiency. No essays or old-timey reminiscences. **Buys 80 mss/year.** Query. Length: 750-5,000 words. **Pays $35 (approximately)/printed page.**

Reprints Send photocopy and information about when and where the material previously appeared. Pays $35/printed page.

Photos Send photos with submission. Reviews color prints, 35mm slides, JPEG photo attachments of 300 dpi. Buys one-time rights. Offers additional payment for photos published. Identification of subjects required.

Tips "Very specific in relating personal experiences in the areas of gardening, energy, and homebuilding how-to. Third-person approaches to others' experiences are also acceptable but somewhat less desirable. Clear color photo prints, especially those in which people are prominent, help immensely when deciding upon what is accepted."

N BEDROOMS & BATHS

Harris Publications, Inc., 1115 Broadway, 8th Floor, New York NY 10010-3455. (212)807-7100. Fax: (212)627-4678. E-mail: nyjacksier@aol.com. Editor: Barbara Jacksier. Quarterly magazine. The source of decorating ideas for creating beautiful bedrooms and baths. Circ. 300,000. Editorial lead time 6 months. Sample copy not available.

N $ $ $ $ BETTER HOMES AND GARDENS

1716 Locust St., Des Moines IA 50309-3023. (515)284-3044. Fax: (515)284-3763. Website: www.bhg.com. Editor-in-Chief: Karol DeWulf Nickell; Editor (Building): Laura O' Neil; Editor (Food & Nutrition): Nancy Hopkins; Editor (Garden/Outdoor Living): Elvin McDonald; Editor (Health): Christian Millman; Editor (Education & Parenting): Stephen George; Editor (Automotive): Lamont Olson; Editor (Home Design): Oma Ford; Editor (Features and Family Matters): Stephen George. **10-15% freelance written.** Magazine "providing home service information for people who have a serious interest in their homes." "We read all freelance articles, but much prefer to see a letter of query rather than a finished manuscript." Estab. 1922. Circ. 7,605,000. **Pays on acceptance.** Buys all rights. Sample copy not available. Writer's guidelines not available.

Nonfiction Travel, Education, gardening, health, cars, home, entertainment. "We do not deal with political subjects or with areas not connected with the home, community, and family." No poetry or fiction. **Pay rates vary.**

Tips Most stories published by this magazine go through a lengthy process of development involving both editor and writer. Some editors will consider *only* query letters, not unsolicited manuscripts. Direct queries to the department that best suits your story line.

$ $ BIRDS & BLOOMS

Reiman Publications, 5400 S. 60th St., Greendale WI 53129. (414)423-0100. E-mail: editors@birdsandblooms.com. Website: www.birdsandblooms.com. **15% freelance written.** Bimonthly magazine focusing on the "beauty in your own backyard. *Birds & Blooms* is a sharing magazine that lets backyard enthusiasts chat with each other by exchanging personal experiences. This makes *Birds & Blooms* more like a conversation than a magazine, as readers share tips and tricks on producing beautiful blooms and attracting feathered friends to their backyards." Estab. 1995. Circ. 1,900,000. Pays on publication. Publishes ms an average of 7 months after acceptance. Byline given. Buys all rights. Editorial lead time 2 months. Submit seasonal material 4 months in advance. Accepts queries by mail, e-mail. Accepts simultaneous submissions. Responds in 2 months to queries; 2 months to mss. Sample copy for $2, 9×12 SAE and $1.95 postage. Writer's guidelines for #10 SASE.

Nonfiction Essays, how-to, humor, inspirational, personal experience, photo feature, natural crafting and plan items for building backyard accents. No bird rescue or captive bird pieces. **Buys 12-20 mss/year.** Send complete ms. Length: 250-1,000 words. **Pays $100-400.**

Photos Trudi Bellin, photo coordinator. Send photos with submission. Reviews transparencies, prints. Buys one-time rights. Identification of subjects required.

Columns/Departments Backyard Banter (odds, ends and unique things); Bird Tales (backyard bird stories); Local Lookouts (community backyard happenings), all 200 words. **Buys 12-20 mss/year.** Send complete ms. **Pays $50-75.**

Fillers Anecdotes, facts, gags to be illustrated by cartoonist. **Buys 25/year.** Length: 10-250 words. **Pays $10-75.**

Tips "Focus on conversational writing—like you're chatting with a neighbor over your fence. Manuscripts full of tips and ideas that people can use in backyards across the country have the best chance of being used. Photos that illustrate these points also increase chances of being used."

$ $ CALIFORNIA HOMES

The Magazine of Architecture, the Arts and Distinctive Design, McFadden-Bray Publishing Corp., P.O. Box 8655, Newport Beach CA 92658. (949)640-1484. Fax: (949)640-1665. E-mail: edit@calhomesmagazine.com. **Contact:** Susan McFadden, editor. **80% freelance written.** Bimonthly magazine covering California interiors, architecture, some food, travel, history, current events in the field. Estab. 1997. Circ. 80,000. Pays on publication. Publishes ms an average of 3 months after acceptance. Byline given. Offers 50% kill fee. Buys first North American serial rights. Editorial lead time 3 months. Submit seasonal material 6 months in advance. Accepts queries by mail, e-mail, fax. Responds in 1 month to queries; 2 months to mss. Sample copy for $7.50. Writer's guidelines for #10 SASE.

Nonfiction Query. Length: 500-1,000 words. **Pays $250-750.** Sometimes pays expenses of writers on assignment.
Photos State availability with submission. Buys one-time rights. Negotiates payment individually. Captions required.

$ $ $ $⌨ CANADIAN GARDENING MAGAZINE

Avid Media, Inc., 340 Ferrier St., Suite 210, Markham ON L3R 2Z5, Canada. (905)475-8440. Fax: (905)475-9246. E-mail: satterthwaite@canadiangardening.com. Website: www.canadiangardening.com. Managing Editor: Christina Selby. **Contact:** Aldona Satterthwaite, editor. Mostly freelance written. Magazine published 8 times/year covering Canadian gardening. *"Canadian Gardening* is a national magazine aimed at the avid home gardener. Our readers are city gardeners with tiny lots, country gardeners with rolling acreage, indoor gardeners, rooftop gardeners, and enthusiastic beginners and experienced veterans. Estab. 1990. Circ. 152,000. **Pays on acceptance.** Byline given. Offers 25-50% kill fee. Buys electronic rights. Editorial lead time 3 months. Submit seasonal material 3 months in advance. Accepts queries by mail, e-mail, fax. Accepts simultaneous submissions. Responds in 3 months to queries. Writer's guidelines online.

Nonfiction How-to (planting and gardening projects), humor, personal experience, technical, plant and garden profiles, practical advice. **Buys 100 mss/year.** Query. Length: 200-2,000 words. **Pays $50-1,500 (Canadian).** Sometimes pays expenses of writers on assignment.
Photos Send photos with submission. Reviews color transparencies. Negotiates payment individually.

$ $ $ $⌨ CANADIAN HOME WORKSHOP

The Do-It-Yourself Magazine, Avid Media, Inc., 340 Ferrier St., Suite 210, Markham ON L3R 2Z5, Canada. (905)475-8440. Fax: (905)475-9246. E-mail: letters@canadianhomeworkshop.com. Website: www.canadianhomeworkshop.com. **Contact:** Douglas Thomson, editor. **90% freelance written**, half of these are assigned. Magazine published 9 times/year covering the "do-it-yourself" market including woodworking projects, renovation, restoration, and maintenance. Circ. 120,000. Pays 1 month after receipt. Byline given. Offers 50% kill fee. Rights are negotiated with author. Submit seasonal material 6 months in advance. Responds in 6 weeks to queries. Sample copy for 9×12 SAE. Writer's guidelines for #10 SASE.

Nonfiction How-to (home maintenance, renovation, woodworking projects, and features). **Buys 40-60 mss/ year.** Query with published clips. Length: 1,500-2,500 words. **Pays $800-2,000.** Pays expenses of writers on assignment.
Photos Send photos with submission. Payment for photos, transparencies negotiated with the author. Captions, identification of subjects, model releases required.
Tips "Freelancers must be aware of our magazine format. Products used in how-to articles must be readily available across Canada. Deadlines for articles are four months in advance of cover date. How-tos should be detailed enough for the amateur but appealing to the experienced. Articles must have Canadian content: sources, locations, etc."

$ $⌨ CANADIAN HOMES & COTTAGES

The In-Home Show, Ltd., 2650 Meadowvale Blvd., Unit 4, Mississauga ON L5N 6M5, Canada. (905)567-1440. Fax: (905)567-1442. E-mail: jnaisby@homesandcottages.com. Website: www.homesandcottages.com. Assistant Editor: Steven Chester. **Contact:** Janice Naisby, editor-in-chief. **75% freelance written.** Magazine published 6 times/year covering building and renovating; "technically comprehensive articles." Estab. 1987. Circ. 79,000. Pays on publication. Publishes ms an average of 2 months after acceptance. Byline given. Offers 10% kill fee. Buys first North American serial rights. Editorial lead time 3 months. Submit seasonal material 3 months in advance. Accepts queries by mail. Sample copy for SAE. Writer's guidelines for #10 SASE.

Nonfiction Looking for how-to projects and simple home improvement ideas. Humor (building and renovation related), new product, technical. **Buys 32 mss/year.** Query. Length: 1,000-2,000 words. **Pays $300-750.** Sometimes pays expenses of writers on assignment.
Photos Send photos with submission. Reviews transparencies, prints. Buys one-time rights. Negotiates payment individually. Captions, identification of subjects required.
Tips "Read our magazine before sending in a query. Remember that you are writing to a Canadian audience."

⌨ CANADIAN LIVING

Transcontinental Media, Inc., 25 Sheppard Ave. W., Suite 100, Toronto ON M2N 6S7, Canada. (416)733-7600. E-mail: letters@canadianliving.com. Website: www.canadianliving.com. **Contact:** Submissions Editor. Monthly magazine covering Canadian lifestyles. Written as a family lifestyle magazine with emphasis on practical information for women at home and in business. Circ. 542,815. Editorial lead time 3 months. Accepts queries by mail, e-mail. Sample copy not available. Writer's guidelines by e-mail.

Nonfiction General interest, how-to, interview/profile. Travel articles or features dealing with career or workplace issues. Query. Length: 750-2,500 words.

$ $ COLORADO HOMES & LIFESTYLES

Wiesner Publishing, LLC, 7009 S. Potomac St., Centennial CO 80112-4029. (303)397-7600. Fax: (303)397-7619. E-mail: submissions@coloradohomesmag.com. Website: www.coloradohomesmag.com. **75% freelance written.** Upscale shelter magazine published 9 times/year containing beautiful homes, landscapes, architecture, calendar, antiques, etc. All of Colorado is included. Geared toward home-related and lifestyle areas, personality profiles, etc. Estab. 1981. Circ. 36,000. **Pays on acceptance.** Publishes ms an average of 3 months after acceptance. Byline given. Offers 15% kill fee. Buys first North American serial rights. Editorial lead time 3 months. Submit seasonal material 1 year in advance. Accepts queries by mail, e-mail. Accepts simultaneous submissions. Responds in 2 months to queries. Sample copy for #10 SASE.

Nonfiction Fine homes and furnishings, regional interior design trends, shopping information, interesting personalities and lifestyles—all with a Colorado slant. No personal essays, religious, humor, technical. **Buys 50-75 mss/year.** Query with published clips. Length: 900-1,500 words. **Pays $200-400.** Sometimes pays expenses of writers on assignment.

Photos Send photos with submission. Reviews transparencies, b&w glossy prints, CDs, digital images, slides. Identification of subjects, title and caption suggestions appreciated. photographic credits required.

Tips "Send query, lead paragraph, clips. Send ideas for story or stories. Include some photos, if applicable. The more interesting and unique the subject the better. A frequent mistake made by writers is failure to provide material with a style and slant appropriate for the magazine, due to poor understanding of the focus of the magazine."

$ $ CONCRETE HOMES

Publications and Communications, Inc. (PCI), 11675 Jollyville Rd., Suite 150, Austin TX 78759. Fax: (512)331-3950. E-mail: homes@pcinews.com. Website: concretehomesmagazine.com. Editor: Larry Storer. **Contact:** Brona Stockton, associate publisher . **85% freelance written.** Bimonthly magazine covering homes built with concrete. "*Concrete Homes* is a publication designed to be informative to consumers, builders, contractors, architects, etc., who are interested in concrete homes. The magazine profiles concrete home projects (they musy be complete) and offers how-to and industry news articles." Estab. 1999. Circ. 25,000. Pays on publication. Publishes ms an average of 2 months after acceptance. Byline given. Offers 100% kill fee. Buys all rights. Editorial lead time 2 months. Submit seasonal material 3-4 months in advance. Accepts queries by mail, e-mail. Accepts simultaneous submissions. Responds in 1 month to queries; 1 month to mss. Sample copy online. Writer's guidelines online.

Nonfiction How-to, interview/profile, new product, technical. **Buys 30-40 mss/year.** Query or query with published clips. Length: 800-2,000 words. **Pays $200-250.** Sometimes pays expenses of writers on assignment.

Photos State availability with submission. Reviews 8 × 10 transparencies, prints, GIF/JPEG files. Buys all rights. Offers no additional payment for photos accepted with ms. Captions required.

Tips "Demonstrate awareness of concrete homes and some knowledge of the construction/building industry."

$ $ $ $ 🖳 COTTAGE LIFE

Quarto Communications, 54 St. Patrick St., Toronto ON M5T 1V1, Canada. (416)599-2000. Fax: (416)599-4070. E-mail: editorial@cottagelife.com. Website: www.cottagelife.com. Managing Editor: Penny Caldwell. **Contact:** Michelle Kelly, associate editor. **80% freelance written.** Bimonthly magazine. "*Cottage Life* is written and designed for the people who own and spend time at waterfront cottages throughout Canada and bordering U.S. states, with a strong focus on Ontario. The magazine has a strong service slant, combining useful 'how-to' journalism with coverage of the people, trends, and issues in cottage country. Regular columns are devoted to boating, fishing, watersports, projects, real estate, cooking, design and decor, nature, personal cottage experience, and environmental, political, and financial issues of concern to cottagers." Estab. 1988. Circ. 70,000. **Pays on acceptance.** Publishes ms an average of 2 months after acceptance. Byline given. Offers 50-100% kill fee. Buys first North American serial rights. Sample copy not available. Writer's guidelines free.

Nonfiction Book excerpts, exposé, historical/nostalgic, how-to, humor, interview/profile, personal experience, photo feature, technical. **Buys 90 mss/year.** Query with published clips and SAE with Canadian postage or IRCs. Length: 1,500-3,500 words. **Pays $100-3,000.** Pays expenses of writers on assignment.

Columns/Departments On the Waterfront (front department featuring short news, humor, human interest, and service items). Length: 300 words maximum. **Pays $50-300.** Cooking, Real Estate, Fishing, Nature, Watersports, Decor, Personal Experience and Issues. Length: 150-1,200 words. Query with published clips and SAE with Canadian postage or IRCs. **Pays $100-1,200.**

Tips "If you have not previously written for the magazine, the 'On the Waterfront' section is an excellent place to break in."

COUNTRY DECORATING IDEAS

Harris Publications, Inc., 1115 Broadway, New York NY 10010. (212)807-7100. Fax: (212)627-4678. E-mail: countryletters@yahoo.com. Website: www.countrydecoratingideas.com. Quarterly magazine. Offers features on do-it-yourself ideas and affordable advice on country decorating for the home. Circ. 360,183. Editorial lead time 2 months. Sample copy not available.

🅝 $ $ $ $ COUNTRY HOME

Meredith Corp., 1716 Locust St., Des Moines IA 50309-3023. (515)284-3000. Fax: (515)284-2552. E-mail: country h@meredith.com. Website: www.countryhome.com. Editor-in-Chief: Carol Sama Sheehan. **Contact:** Assignments Editor. Magazine published 10 times/year for people interested in the country way of life. "*Country Home* magazine is a lifestyle publication created for readers who share passions for American history, style, craftsmanship, tradition, and cuisine. These people, with a desire to find a simpler, more meaningful lifestyle, live their lives and design their living spaces in ways that reflect those passions." Estab. 1979. Circ. 1,250,000. Pays on completion of assignment. Publishes ms an average of 5 months after acceptance. Byline given. Submit seasonal material 6 months in advance. Accepts queries by mail. Responds in 6 weeks to queries. Sample copy for $4.95. Writer's guidelines not available.

　　○ᴨ "We are not responsible for unsolicited manuscripts, and we do not encourage telephone queries."
Nonfiction Architecture and Design, Families at Home, Travel, Food and Entertaining, Art and Antiques, Gardens and Outdoor Living, Personal Reflections. Query by mail only with writing samples and SASE. Length: 750-1,500 words. **Pays $500-1,500.**
Columns/Departments Length: 500-750 words. Include SASE. Query with published clips. **Pays $300-500.**
　　■ The online magazine carries original content not found in the print edition. Contact: Susan Weaver, online editor.

🅝 COUNTRY KITCHENS

Harris Publications, Inc., 1115 Broadway, 8th Floor, New York NY 10010. (212)807-7100. Fax: (212)627-4678. Editor: Barbara Jacksier. Semiannual magazine. Provides innovative ideas for designing your kitchen in the ever popular country style. Circ. 325,000. Sample copy not available.

COUNTRY LIVING

The Hearst Corp., 224 W. 57th St., 7th Floor, New York NY 10019. (212)649-3500. E-mail: countryliving@hearst. com. **Contact:** Charlotte Barnard, deputy editor. Monthly magazine covering home design and interior decorating with an emphasis on country style. "A lifestyle magazine for readers who appreciate the warmth and traditions associated with American home and family life. Each monthly issue embraces American country decorating and includes features on furniture, antiques, gardening, home building, real estate, cooking, entertaining and travel." Estab. 1978. Circ. 1,600,000. Sample copy not available. Writer's guidelines not available.
Nonfiction Most open to freelancers: Antiques articles from authorities. **Buys 20-30 mss/year.** Send complete ms and SASE. **Payment varies.**
Columns/Departments Query first.
Tips "Know the magazine, know the market and know how to write a good story that will interest *our* readers."

COUNTRY SAMPLER

Country Sampler, Inc., 707 Kautz Rd., St. Charles IL 60174. (630)377-8000. Fax: (630)377-8194. Website: www.s ampler.com. Bimonthly magazine. "*Country Sampler* is a country decorating, antiques, and collectibles magazine and a country product catalog." Estab. 1984. Circ. 426,771. Accepts queries by mail, fax. Sample copy not available.
Nonfiction "Furniture, accessories, and decorative accents created by artisans throughout the country are displayed and offered for purchase directly from the maker. Fully decorated room settings show the readers how to use the items in their homes to achieve the warmth and charm of the country look."
Tips "Send photos and story idea for a country-style house tour. Story should be regarding decorating tips and techniques."

🅝 $ $ EARLY AMERICAN LIFE

Firelands Media Group LLC, P.O. Box 221230, Shaker Heights OH 44122-0996. E-mail: queries@firelandsmedia. com. Website: www.ealonline.com. **Contact:** Jeanmarie Andrews, managing editor. **60% freelance written.** Bimonthly magazine for "people who are interested in capturing the warmth and beauty of the 1600-1840 period and using it in their homes and lives today. They are interested in antiques, traditional crafts, architecture, restoration, and collecting.'' Estab. 1970. Circ. 90,000. **Pays on acceptance.** Publishes ms an average of 1 year after acceptance. Byline given. Buys worldwide rights. Accepts queries by mail, e-mail. Responds in 3 months to queries. Sample copy and writer's guidelines for 9×12 SAE with 4 first-class stamps.

O→ Break in ''by offering highly descriptive, entertaining, yet informational articles on social culture, decorative arts, antiques, or well-restored and appropriately furnished homes that reflect middle-class American life prior to 1850.''

Nonfiction ''Social history (the story of the people, not epic heroes and battles), travel to historic sites, antiques and reproductions, restoration, architecture, and decorating. We try to entertain as we inform. We're always on the lookout for good pieces on any of our subjects. Would like to see more on how real people did something great to their homes.'' **Buys 40 mss/year.** Query with or without published clips or send complete ms. Length: 750-3,000 words. **Pays $100-600, additionally for photos.**

Tips ''Our readers are eager for ideas on how to bring early America into their lives. Conceive a new approach to satisfy their related interests in arts, crafts, travel to historic sites, and especially in houses decorated in the Early American style. Write to entertain and inform at the same time. We are visually oriented to having photos available or helping us with sources for illustrations.''

$ $ $ FINE GARDENING

Taunton Press, 63 S. Main St., P.O. Box 5506, Newtown CT 06470-5506. (203)426-8171. Fax: (203)426-3434. E-mail: fg@taunton.com. Website: www.finegardening.com. **Contact:** Todd Meier, executive editor. Bimonthly magazine. ''High-value magazine on landscape and ornamental gardening. Articles written by avid gardeners— first person, hands-on gardening experiences.'' Estab. 1988. Circ. 200,000. **Pays on acceptance.** Publishes ms an average of 6 months after acceptance. Byline given. Buys all rights. Editorial lead time 1 year. Submit seasonal material 1 year in advance. Accepts queries by mail, e-mail, fax. Sample copy not available. Writer's guidelines free.

Nonfiction How-to, personal experience, photo feature, Book review. **Buys 60 mss/year.** Query. Length: 1,000-3,000 words. **Pays $300-1,200.**

Photos Send photos with submission. Reviews digital. Serial rights.

Columns/Departments Book, video and software reviews (on gardening); Last Word (essays/serious, humorous, fact or fiction). Length: 250-500 words. **Buys 30 mss/year.** Query. **Pays $50- 200.**

Tips ''It's most important to have solid first-hand experience as a gardener. Tell us what you've done with your own landscape and plants.''

$ $ FINE HOMEBUILDING

The Taunton Press, 63 S. Main St., P.O. Box 5506, Newtown CT 06470-5506. (203)426-8171. Fax: (203)426-3434. E-mail: fh@taunton.com. Website: www.taunton.com. Bimonthly magazine for builders, architects, contractors, owner/builders and others who are seriously involved in building new houses or reviving old ones. Estab. 1981. Circ. 300,000. Pays half on acceptance, half on publication. Publishes ms an average of 1 year after acceptance. Byline given. Offers on acceptance payment as kill fee. Buys first rights. Reprint rights Responds in 1 month to queries. Sample copy not available. Writer's guidelines for SASE and on website.

Nonfiction ''We're interested in almost all aspects of home building, from laying out foundations to capping cupolas.'' Query with outline, description, photographs, sketches and SASE. **Pays $150/published page.**

Photos ''Take lots of work-in-progress photos. Color print film, ASA 400, from either Kodak or Fuji works best. If you prefer to use slide film, use ASA 100. Keep track of the negatives; we will need them for publication. If you're not sure what to use or how to go about it, feel free to call for advice.''

Columns/Departments Tools & Materials, Reviews, Questions & Answers, Tips & Techniques, Cross Section, What's the Difference?, Finishing Touches, Great Moments, Breaktime, Drawing Board (design column). Query with outline, description, photographs, sketches and SASE. **Payment varies.**

Tips ''Our chief contributors are home builders, architects and other professionals. We're more interested in your point of view and technical expertise than your prose style. Adopt an easy, conversational style and define any obscure terms for non-specialists. We try to visit all our contributors and rarely publish building projects we haven't seen, or authors we haven't met.''

Ⓝ $ $ $ $ GARDEN SHED

Meredith Corp., 1716 Locust St., Des Moines IA 50309-3038. (515)284-3000. Fax: (515)284-3697. Editor-in-Chief: Doug Jimerson. Editor: Susan Appleget Hurst. Magazine published twice/year. Created for gardening and landscape enthusiasts. Circ. 475,000. Editorial lead time 6 months. Sample copy not available.

$ $ $ GARDENING HOW-TO

North American Media Group, 12301 Whitewater Dr., Minnetonka MN 55343. (952)988-7474. Fax: (952)936-9333. E-mail: mpestel@namginc.com. Website: www.gardeningclub.com. **Contact:** Mary Pestel, associate editor. **40% freelance written.** Bimonthly magazine covering gardening/horticulture. *"Gardening How-To* is the bimonthly publication of the National Home Gardening Club, headquartered in Minnetonka, Minnesota. As the primary benefit of membership in the Club, the magazine's aim is to provide timely, interesting, and inspiring editorial that will appeal to our audience of intermediate- to advanced-level home gardeners." Estab. 1996. Circ. 600,000. **Pays on acceptance.** Publishes ms an average of 4 months after acceptance. Byline given. Offers 25% kill fee. Buys one-time rights. Editorial lead time 6 months. Submit seasonal material 6 months in advance. Accepts queries by mail, e-mail, fax. Sample copy for $3. Writer's guidelines for free or by e-mail.

Nonfiction Buys 36 mss/year. Query with published clips. Length: 1,000-2,000 words. **Pays $200-1,000.** Sometimes pays expenses of writers on assignment.

Photos State availability with submission. Buys one-time rights. Negotiates payment individually.

THE HERB COMPANION

Ogden Publications, Inc., 1503 SW 42nd St., Topeka KS 66609. (785)274-4300. Fax: (785)274-4305. E-mail: editor@herbcompanion.com. Website: www.herbcompanion.com. **Contact:** Dawna Edwards, editor. **80% freelance written.** Bimonthly magazine about herbs: culture, history, culinary, crafts and some medicinal use for both experienced and novice herb enthusiasts. Pays on publication. Byline given. Buys all rights. Editorial lead time 4 months. Accepts queries by mail, e-mail, fax. Responds in 2 months to queries. Sample copy for $6. Writer's guidelines online.

Nonfiction Practical horticultural, original recipes, historical, herbal crafts, helpful hints, and book reviews. How-to, interview/profile. Submit by mail only detailed query or ms. Length: 4 pages or 1,000 words. **Pays according to length, story type, and experience.**

Photos Returns photos and artwork. Send photos with submission. Reviews transparencies.

Tips "New approaches to familiar topics are especially welcome. If you aren't already familiar with the content, style and tone of the magazine. Technical accuracy is essential. Please use scientific as well as popular names for plants and cover the subject in depth while avoiding overly academic presentation. Information should be made accessible to the reader, and we find this is best accomplished by writing from direct personal experience where possible and always in an informal style."

$ $ THE HERB QUARTERLY

EGW Publishing Co., 1041 Shary Circle, Concord CA 94518. (925)671-9852. E-mail: jenniferbarrett@earthlink.n et. Website: www.herbquarterly.com. **Contact:** Jennifer Barrett, editor. **95% freelance written.** Quarterly magazine covering herbs and their uses. "Now in its 25th year, *The Herb Quarterly* brings readers the joy of herbs and the herb garden each season, with recipes, remedies, and growing advice." Estab. 1978. Circ. 45,000. Pays on publication. Publishes ms an average of 3 months after acceptance. Byline given. Offers 25% kill fee. Buys first North American serial rights. Editorial lead time 6 months. Submit seasonal material 6-12 months in advance. Accepts queries by mail, e-mail. Responds in 1 month to queries; 2 months to mss. Sample copy for free. Writer's guidelines free.

Nonfiction Book excerpts, historical/nostalgic, how-to (cooking, crafts, gardening), interview/profile (herbalist), new product, opinion, personal experience, photo feature, technical (gardening), travel (gardeners around the world). **Buys 21 + mss/year.** Query with or without published clips or send complete ms. Length: 250-2,500 words. **Pays $50-350.** Provides contributor copies in addition to payment. Sometimes pays expenses of writers on assignment.

Tips "Please read the magazine before submitting. We prefer specific information (whether natural health approaches or gardening advice) rather than general."

$ ☒ HOME DIGEST

Your Guide to Home and Life Improvement, Home Digest International, Inc., 268 Lakeshore Rd. E., Unit 604, Oakville ON L6J 7S4, Canada. (905)844-3361. Fax: (905)849-4618. E-mail: homedigesteditor@sympatico.ca. Website: www.home-digest.com. **Contact:** William Roebuck, editor. **25% freelance written.** Quarterly magazine covering home and life management for families in the greater Toronto region. *"Home Digest* has a strong service slant, combining useful how-to journalism with coverage of the trends and issues of home ownership and family life. In essence, our focus is on the concerns of families living in their own homes." Estab. 1995. Circ. 700,000. Pays on publication. Publishes ms an average of 3 months after acceptance. Byline given. Buys first North American serial rights and the rights to archive articles on the magazine's website. Editorial lead time 3 months. Submit seasonal material 5 months in advance. Accepts queries by mail, e-mail. Accepts previously published material. Accepts simultaneous submissions. Responds in 1 month to queries. Sample copy for 9×6 SAE and 2 Canadian first-class stamps. Writer's guidelines online.

Nonfiction General interest, how-to (household hints, basic home renovation, decorating), humor (living in Toronto). No opinion, fashion, or beauty. **Buys 8 mss/year.** Query. Length: 350-700 words. **Pays $35-100 (Canadian).**

Photos Send photos with submission. Reviews prints. Buys one-time rights. Pays $10-20/photo. Captions, identification of subjects, model releases required.

Columns/Departments Household Hints (tested tips that work); Home Renovation Tips; all 300-350 words. **Buys 4-6 mss/year.** Query. **Pays $40-50 (Canadian).**

Tips "Base your ideas on practical experiences. We're looking for 'uncommon' advice that works."

$ $ $ $ HORTICULTURE

Gardening at Its Best, F+W Publications, 98 N. Washington St., Boston MA 02114. (617)742-5600. Fax: (617)367-6364. E-mail: tfischer@hortmag.com. Website: www.hortmag.com. **Contact:** Thomas Fischer, executive editor. Bimonthly magazine. "*Horticulture*, the country's oldest gardening magazine, is designed for active amateur gardeners. Our goal is to offer a blend of text, photographs and illustrations that will both instruct and inspire readers." Circ. 240,000. Byline given. Offers kill fee. Buys first North American serial, one-time rights. Submit seasonal material 10 months in advance. Accepts queries by mail, e-mail, fax. Responds in 3 months to queries. Sample copy not available. Writer's guidelines for SASE or by e-mail.

Nonfiction "We look for an encouraging personal experience, anecdote and opinion. At the same time, a thorough article should to some degree place its subject in the broader context of horticulture." **Buys 15 mss/ year.** Query with published clips, subject background material and SASE. Length: 1,000-2,000 words. **Pays $600-1,500.** Pays expenses of writers on assignment if previously arranged with editor.

Columns/Departments Length: 100-1,500 words. Query with published clips, subject background material and SASE. Include disk where possible. **Pays $50-750.**

Tips "We believe every article must offer ideas or illustrate principles that our readers might apply on their own gardens. No matter what the subject, we want our readers to become better, more creative gardeners."

HOUSE & GARDEN

Condé Nast Publications, Inc., 4 Times Square, New York NY 10036. (212)286-4580. Fax: (212)286-8533. E-mail: letters@houseandgarden.com. Website: www.houseandgarden.com. Editor: Dominique Browning. Written as the definitive voice of the best design and style for the home and garden, *House & Garden* provides access to top home design projects from the best architects, decorators, and landscape designers from around the world. Circ. 753,186. Editorial lead time 4 months. Sample copy not available.

[N] $ $ $ $ HOUSE BEAUTIFUL

The Hearst Corp., 1700 Broadway, 29th Floor, New York NY 10019. (212)903-5000. Fax: (212)765-8292. Website: www.housebeautiful.com. Editor: Marc Mayfield. Monthly magazine. Targeted toward affluent, educated readers ages 30-40. Covers home design and decoration, gardening and entertaining, interior design, architecture and travel. Circ. 865,352. Editorial lead time 3 months. Sample copy not available.

$ $ $ LAKESTYLE

Celebrating Life on the Water, Bayside Publications, Inc., P.O. Box 170, Excelsior MN 55331. (952)470-1380. Fax: (952)470-1389. E-mail: editor@lakestyle.com. Website: www.lakestyle.com. **Contact:** Nancy Henke, editor. **50% freelance written.** Quarterly magazine. "*Lakestyle* is committed to celebrating the lifestyle chosen by lake home and cabin owners." Estab. 2000. Circ. 40,000. Pays on publication. Publishes ms an average of 3 months after acceptance. Byline given. Offers 10% kill fee. Buys all rights. Editorial lead time 2 months. Submit seasonal material 3 months in advance. Accepts queries by mail, e-mail, fax, phone. Accepts previously published material. Responds in 3 weeks to queries; 1 month to mss. Sample copy for $5. Writer's guidelines online.

Nonfiction Essays, historical/nostalgic, how-to, humor, inspirational, interview/profile, new product, photo feature. No direct promotion of product. **Buys 15 mss/year.** Query with or without published clips or send complete ms. Length: 500-2,500 words. **Pays 25-50¢/word for assigned articles; 10-25¢/word for unsolicited articles.** Sometimes pays expenses of writers on assignment.

Photos State availability of or send photos with submission. Rights purchased vary. Offers no additional payment for photos accepted with ms. Captions, identification of subjects, model releases required.

Columns/Departments Lakestyle Entertaining (entertaining ideas); Lakestyle Gardening (gardening ideas); On the Water (boating/playing on the lake); Hidden Treasures (little known events); At the Cabin (cabin owner's information); all approximately 1,000 words. **Buys 10 mss/year.** Query with or without published clips or send complete ms. **Pays 10-25¢/word.**

Tips "*Lakestyle* is interested in enhancing the lifestyle chosen by our readers, a thorough knowledge of cabin/ lake home issues helps writers fulfill this goal."

$ $ LOG HOME LIVING

Home Buyer Publications, Inc., 4125-T Lafayette Center Dr., Suite 100, Chantilly VA 20151. (703)222-9411. Fax: (703)222-3209. Website: www.loghomeliving.com. **90% freelance written.** Monthly magazine for enthusiasts who are dreaming of, planning for, or actively building a log home. Estab. 1989. Circ. 132,000. **Pays on acceptance.** Publishes ms an average of 6 months after acceptance. Byline given. Offers $100 kill fee. Buys first, second serial (reprint) rights. Editorial lead time 6 months. Submit seasonal material 6 months in advance. Accepts queries by mail. Accepts previously published material. Responds in 6 weeks to queries. Sample copy for $4. Writer's guidelines for #10 SASE.

Nonfiction Book excerpts, how-to (build or maintain log home), interview/profile (log-home owners), personal experience, photo feature (log homes), technical (design/decor topics), travel. "We do not want historical/nostalgic material." **Buys 6 mss/year.** Query. Length: 1,000-2,000 words. **Pays $250-500.** Pays expenses of writers on assignment.

Reprints Send tearsheet or photocopy and information about when and where the material previously appeared. Pays $100-200 for reprint rights.

Photos State availability with submission. Reviews contact sheets, 4×5 transparencies, 4×6 prints. Buys one-time rights. Negotiates payment individually.

Tips *"Log Home Living* is devoted almost exclusively to modern manufactured and handcrafted kit log homes. Our interest in historical or nostalgic stories of very old log cabins, reconstructed log homes, or one-of-a-kind owner-built homes is secondary and should be queried first."

MIDWEST HOME AND GARDEN

U.S. Trust Bldg., 730 S. Second Ave., Minneapolis MN 55402. Fax: (612)371-5801. E-mail: awoods@minnesotamonthly.com. Website: www.minnesotamonthly.com. **Contact:** Amy Woods, editor. **50% freelance written.** *"Midwest Home and Garden* is an upscale shelter magazine showcasing innovative architecture, interesting interior design, and beautiful gardens of the Midwest." Estab. 1997. Circ. 80,000. **Pays on acceptance.** Byline given. Accepts queries by mail, e-mail, fax. Writer's guidelines online.

Nonfiction Profiles of regional designers, architects, craftspeople related to home and garden. Photo-driven articles on home decor and design, and gardens. Book excerpts, essays, how-to (garden and design), interview/profile (brief), new product, photo feature. Query with résumé, published clips, and SASE. Length: 300-1,000 words. **Payment negotiable.**

Columns/Departments Back Home (essay on home/garden topics), 800 words; Design Directions (people and trends in home and garden), 300 words.

Tips "We are always looking for great new interior design, architecture, and gardens—in Minnesota and in the Midwest."

$ $ MOUNTAIN LIVING

Wiesner Publishing, 7009 S. Potomac St., Englewood CO 80112. (303)397-7600. Fax: (303)397-7619. E-mail: irawlings@mountainliving.com. Website: www.mountainliving.com. **Contact:** Irene Rawlings, editor-in-chief. **50% freelance written.** Bimonthly magazine covering "shelter and lifestyle issues for people who live in, visit, or hope to live in the mountains." Estab. 1994. Circ. 35,000. **Pays on acceptance.** Publishes ms an average of 4 months after acceptance. Byline given. Offers 15% kill fee. Buys all rights. Editorial lead time 6 months. Submit seasonal material 6 months in advance. Accepts queries by mail, e-mail, phone. Responds in 6 weeks to queries; 2 months to mss. Sample copy for $5 or on website.

Nonfiction Photo feature, travel, home features. **Buys 30 mss/year.** Query with published clips. Length: 1,200-2,000 words. **Pays $250-500.** Sometimes pays expenses of writers on assignment.

Photos Provide photos (slides, transparencies, or on disk, saved as TIFF and at least 300 dpi). State availability with submission. Buys one-time rights. Negotiates payment individually.

Columns/Departments Art; Insider's Guide; Entertaining. Length: 300-1,500 words. **Buys 35 mss/year.** Query with published clips. **Pays $50-500.**

Tips "A deep understanding of and respect for the mountain environment is essential. Think out of the box. We love to be surprised. Write a brilliant, short query, and always send clips."

$ $ PEOPLE, PLACES & PLANTS

512 Memorial Hwy., N. Yarmouth ME 04097. (207)827-4783. Fax: (207)829-6814. E-mail: paul@ppplants.com. Website: newenglandgardening.com. Paul Tukey, editor-in-chief. **50% freelance written.** Gardening magazine published 6 times/year focused on New England. "We now publish 2 editions: One focuses on New England and New York state, the other focuses on the Mid-Atlantic states (metro New York to Virginia)." Circ. 52,000. **Pays on acceptance.** Publishes ms an average of 3 months after acceptance. Buys first rights. Responds in 1 month to queries. Sample copy by e-mail. Writer's guidelines by e-mail.

Nonfiction Know the subject at hand; anecdotes help get readers interested in stories. Query. **Pays $50-500.**

Photos Reviews slides. $50-500.

Consumer Magazines

$ $ ROMANTIC HOMES

Y-Visionary Publishing, 265 Anita Dr., Suite 120, Orange CA 92868. (714)939-9991. Fax: (714)939-9909. Website: www.romantichomesmag.com. Editor-in-Chief: Gretchen Keene. **Contact:** Abella Carroll, executive managing editor. **70% freelance written.** Monthly magazine covering home decor. *"Romantic Homes* is the magazine for women who want to create a warm, intimate, and casually elegant home—a haven that is both a gathering place for family and friends and a private refuge from the pressures of the outside world. The *Romantic Homes* reader is personally involved in the decor of her home. Features offer unique ideas and how-to advice on decorating, home furnishings, and gardening. Departments focus on floor and wall coverings, paint, textiles, refinishing, architectural elements, artwork, travel, and entertaining. Every article responds to the reader's need to create a beautiful, attainable environment, providing her with the style ideas and resources to achieve her own romantic home." Estab. 1994. Circ. 200,000. Pays 30-60 days upon receipt of invoice. Publishes ms an average of 4 months after acceptance. Byline given. Buys all rights. Editorial lead time 5 months. Submit seasonal material 6 months in advance. Accepts queries by mail, fax. Accepts simultaneous submissions. Responds in 2 weeks to queries; 2 months to mss. Writer's guidelines for #10 SASE.

Nonfiction "Not just for dreaming, *Romantic Homes* combines unique ideas and inspirations with practical how-to advice on decorating, home furnishings, remodeling, and gardening for readers who are actively involved in improving their homes. Every article responds to the reader's need to know how to do it and where to find it." Essays, how-to, new product, personal experience, travel. **Buys 150 mss/year.** Query with published clips. Length: 1,000-1,200 words. **Pays $500.**

Photos State availability of or send photos with submission. Reviews transparencies. Buys all rights. Captions, identification of subjects, model releases required.

Columns/Departments Departments cover antiques, collectibles, artwork, shopping, travel, refinishing, architectural elements, flower arranging, entertaining, and decorating. Length: 400-600 words. **Pays $250.**

Tips "Submit great ideas with photos."

$ $ SAN DIEGO HOME/GARDEN LIFESTYLES

McKinnon Enterprises, Box 719001, San Diego CA 92171-9001. (858)571-1818. Fax: (858)571-6379. E-mail: carlson@sdhg.net; ditler@sdhg.net. **Contact:** Wayne Carlson, editor; Eva Ditler, managing editor. **50% freelance written.** Monthly magazine covering homes, gardens, food, intriguing people, real estate, art, culture, and local travel for residents of San Diego city and county. Estab. 1979. Circ. 50,000. Pays on publication. Publishes ms an average of 3 months after acceptance. Byline given. Buys first North American serial rights. Submit seasonal material 3 months in advance. Accepts queries by mail, e-mail, fax, phone. Responds in 3 months to queries. Sample copy for $4.

Nonfiction Residential architecture and interior design (San Diego-area homes only), remodeling (must be well-designed—little do-it-yourself), residential landscape design, furniture, other features oriented toward upscale readers interested in living the cultured good life in San Diego. Articles must have a local angle. Query with published clips. Length: 700-2,000 words. **Pays $50-350 for assigned articles.**

Tips "No out-of-town, out-of-state subject material. Most freelance work is accepted from local writers. Gear stories to the unique quality of San Diego. We try to offer only information unique to San Diego—people, places, shops, resources, etc."

$ $ SEATTLE HOMES AND LIFESTYLES

Wiesner Publishing, LLC, 1221 E. Pike St., Suite 305, Seattle WA 98122-3930. (206)322-6699. Fax: (206)322-2799. E-mail: falbert@seattlehomesmag.com. Website: www.seattlehomesmag.com. **Contact:** Fred Albert, editor-in-chief. **60% freelance written.** Magazine published 8 times/year covering home design and lifestyles. *"Seattle Homes and Lifestyles* showcases the finest homes and gardens in the Northwest, and the personalities and lifestyles that make this region special. We try to help our readers take full advantage of the resources the region has to offer with in-depth coverage of events, entertaining, shopping, food, and wine. And we write about it with a warm, personal approach that underscores our local perspective." Estab. 1996. Circ. 30,000. **Pays on acceptance.** Publishes ms an average of 2 months after acceptance. Byline given. Offers 25% kill fee. Buys first, electronic rights. Editorial lead time 3 months. Submit seasonal material 4 months in advance. Accepts previously published material. Accepts simultaneous submissions. Responds in 4 months to queries.

Nonfiction General interest, how-to (decorating, cooking), interview/profile, photo feature. "No essays, journal entries, sports coverage." **Buys 95 mss/year.** Query with published clips via mail. Length: 300-1,500 words. **Pays $125-375.**

Photos State availability with submission. Reviews contact sheets, transparencies, prints. Buys one-time rights. Negotiates payment individually. Captions, identification of subjects, model releases required.

Tips "We're always looking for experienced journalists with clips that demonstrate a knack for writing engaging, informative features. We're also looking for writers knowledgeable about architecture and decorating who can communicate a home's flavor and spirit through the written word. Since all stories are assigned by the editor, please do not submit manuscripts. Send a résumé and 3 published samples of your work. Story pitches are not encouraged. Please mail all submissions—do not e-mail or fax. Please don't call—we'll call you if we have an assignment. Writers from the Seattle area only."

SOUTHERN ACCENTS

Southern Progress Corp., 2100 Lakeshore Dr., Birmingham AL 35209. (205)445-6000. Fax: (205)445-6990. Website: www.southernaccents.com. **Contact:** Frances MacDougall, executive editor. "*Southern Accents* celebrates the finest of the South." Estab. 1977. Circ. 370,000. Accepts queries by mail. Responds in 2 months to queries.
Nonfiction "Each issue features the finest homes and gardens along with a balance of features that reflect the affluent lifestyles of its readers, including architecture, antiques, entertaining, collecting, and travel." Query by mail with SASE, bio, clips, and photos.

■ The online magazine carries original content not found in the print edition. Contact: Christina Bennett, assistant online editor.

Tips "Query us only with specific ideas targeted to our current columns."

MARTHA STEWART LIVING

Time Publishing, Inc., 11 W. 42nd St., 25th Floor, New York NY 10036. Fax: (212)827-8289. E-mail: mstewart@marthastewart.com. Website: www.marthastewart.com. **Contact:** Editorial. Monthly magazine offering readers a unique combination of inspiration and how-to information focusing on our 8 core areas: Home, Cooking & Entertaining, Gardening, Crafts, Holidays, Keeping, Weddings, and Baby.

$ $ $ STYLE AT HOME

Transcontinental Media, Inc., 25 Sheppard Ave. W., Suite 100, Toronto ON M2N 6S7, Canada. (416)733-7600. Fax: (416)218-3632. E-mail: letters@styleathome.com. Managing Editor: Laurie Grassi. **Contact:** Gail Johnston Habs, editor-in-chief. **85% freelance written.** Magazine published 10 times/year. "The number one magazine choice of Canadian women aged 25 to 54 who have a serious interest in decorating. Provides an authoritative, stylish collection of inspiring and accessible Canadian interiors, decor projects; reports on style design trends." Estab. 1997. Circ. 230,000. **Pays on acceptance.** Byline given. Offers 50% kill fee. Buys first, electronic rights. Editorial lead time 4 months. Submit seasonal material 6 months in advance. Accepts queries by e-mail. Responds in 1 month to queries; 2 weeks to mss. Writer's guidelines by e-mail.

О–г Break in by "familiarizing yourself with the type of interiors we show. Be very up to date with the design and home decor market in Canada. Provide a lead to a fabulous home or garden."

Nonfiction Interview/profile, new product. "No how-to; these are planned in-house." **Buys 80 mss/year.** Query with published clips; include scouting shots with interior story queries. Length: 300-700 words. **Pays $300-1,000.** Sometimes pays expenses of writers on assignment.
Columns/Departments Humor (fun home decor/renovating experiences), 500 words. Query with published clips. **Pays $250-500.**

$ $ TEXAS GARDENER

The Magazine for Texas Gardeners, by Texas Gardeners, Suntex Communications, Inc., P.O. Box 9005, Waco TX 76714-9005. (254)848-9393. Fax: (254)848-9779. E-mail: suntex@calpha.com. **Contact:** Chris Corby, editor. **80% freelance written.** Works with a small number of new/unpublished writers each year. Bimonthly magazine covering vegetable and fruit production, ornamentals, and home landscape information for home gardeners in Texas. Estab. 1981. Circ. 30,000. Pays on publication. Publishes ms an average of 4 months after acceptance. Byline given. Buys first North American serial, all rights. Submit seasonal material 6 months in advance. Accepts queries by mail, e-mail, fax. Responds in 2 months to queries. Sample copy for $2.95 and SAE with 5 first-class stamps. Writer's guidelines for #10 SASE.
Nonfiction "We use articles that relate to Texas gardeners. We also like personality profiles on hobby gardeners and professional horticulturists who are doing somehting unique." How-to, humor, interview/profile, photo feature. **Buys 50-60 mss/year.** Query with published clips. Length: 800-2,400 words. **Pays $50-200.**
Photos "We prefer superb color and b&w photos; 90% of photos used are color." Send photos with submission. Reviews contact sheets, 2¼×2¼ or 35mm color transparencies, 8×10 b&w prints. Pays negotiable rates. Identification of subjects, model releases required.
Columns/Departments Between Neighbors. **Pays $25.**
Tips "First, be a Texan. Then come up with a good idea of interest to home gardeners in this state. Be specific. Stick to feature topics like 'How Alley Gardening Became a Texas Tradition.' Leave topics like 'How to Control Fire Blight' to the experts. High quality photos could make the difference. We would like to add several writers to our group of regular contributors and would make assignments on a regular basis. Fillers are easy to come up with in-house. We want good writers who can produce accurate and interesting copy. Frequent mistakes

made by writers in completing an article assignment for us are that articles are not slanted toward Texas gardening, show inaccurate or too little gardening information, or lack good writing style.''

$ $TIMBER FRAME HOMES

Home Buyer Publications, 4125 Lafayette Center Dr., Suite 100, Chantilly VA 20151. Fax: (703)222-3209. E-mail: editor@timberframehomes.com. Website: www.timberframehomes.com. **50% freelance written.** Quarterly magazine for people who own or are planning to build contemporary timber frame homes. It is devoted exclusively to timber frame homes that have a freestanding frame and wooden joinery. Our interest in historical, reconstructed timber frames and one-of-a-kind owner-built homes is secondary and should be queried first. Estab. 1991. Circ. 92,500. **Pays on acceptance.** Publishes ms an average of 3 months after acceptance. Byline given. Offers $100 kill fee. Buys first rights. Accepts queries by mail, e-mail. Sample copy for $4. Writer's guidelines for #10 SASE.

Nonfiction Book excerpts, general interest, how-to, interview/profile, new product, photo feature, technical. No historical articles. **Buys 15 mss/year.** Query with published clips. Length: 1,200-1,400 words. **Pays $300-500.** Sometimes pays expenses of writers on assignment.

Photos State availability with submission. Reviews contact sheets, transparencies, prints. Buys one-time rights. Negotiates payment individually.

Columns/Departments Constructive Advice (timber frame construction); Interior Elements (decorating); Drawing Board (design), all 1,200-1,400 words. **Buys 6 mss/year.** Query with published clips. **Pays $300-500.**

ℕ TRADITIONAL HOME

Meredith Corp., 1716 Locust St., Des Moines 50309-3038. (515)284-3000. Fax: (515)284-2083. E-mail: traditional home@mdp.com. Website: www.traditionalhome.com. Executive Editor: Marsha Leisch. Garden Editor: Ethne Clark. Magazine published 8 times/year. Features articles on building and decorating homes in the traditional style. Circ. 925,000. Editorial lead time 6 months. Sample copy not available.

$ $UNIQUE HOMES

Network Communications, 327 Wall St., Princeton NJ 08540. (609)688-1110. Fax: (609)688-0201. E-mail: lkim@uniquehomes.com. Website: www.uniquehomes.com. Editor: Kathleen Carlin-Russell. **Contact:** Lauren Baier Kim, managing editor. **30% freelance written.** Bimonthly magazine covering luxury real estate for consumers and the high-end real estate industry. "Our focus is the luxury real estate market, i.e., the business of buying and selling luxury homes, as well as regional market trends.'' Pays on publication. Publishes ms an average of 3 months after acceptance. Byline given. Buys all rights. Editorial lead time 4 months. Submit seasonal material 4 months in advance. Accepts queries by mail, e-mail, fax. Responds in 1 month to queries; 4 months to mss. Sample copy online. Writer's guidelines not available.

Nonfiction Looking for high-end luxury real estate profiles on cities and geographical regions. Luxury real estate, interior design, landscaping, home features. Special issues: Golf Course Living; Resort Living; Ski Real Estate; Farms, Ranches and Country Estates; Waterfront Homes; International Homes. **Buys 36 mss/year.** Query with published clips and résumé. Length: 500-1,500 words. **Pays $150-500.**

Photos State availability with submission. Reviews transparencies, prints. Buys one-time rights. Offers no additional payment for photos accepted with ms. Captions required.

Tips "For profiles on specific geographical areas, seeking writers with an in-depth personal knowledge of the luxury real estate trends in those locations.''

ℕ $ $VICTORIAN HOMES

Y-Visionary Publishing, LP, 265 S. Anita Dr., Suite 120, Orange CA 92868-3310. (714)939-9991. Fax: (714)939-9909. E-mail: editorial@victorianhomes.com. Website: www.victorianhomesmag.com. **90% freelance written.** Bimonthly magazine covering Victorian home restoration and decoration. "*Victorian Homes* is read by Victorian home owners, restorers, house museum management and others interested in the Victorian revival. Feature articles cover home architecture, interior design, furnishings and the home's history. Photography is *very* important to the feature.'' Estab. 1981. Circ. 100,000. **Pays on acceptance.** Publishes ms an average of 1 year after acceptance. Byline given. Offers $50 kill fee. Buys first North American serial, one-time rights. Editorial lead time 4 months. Submit seasonal material 1 year in advance. Accepts queries by mail, e-mail, fax. Accepts simultaneous submissions. Responds in 6 weeks to queries; 2 months to mss. Sample copy and writer's guidelines for SAE.

O─ Break in with "access to good photography and reasonable knowledge of the Victorian era.''

Nonfiction "Article must deal with structures—no historical articles on Victorian people or lifestyles.'' How-to (create period style curtains, wall treatments, bathrooms, kitchens, etc.), photo feature. **Buys 30-35 mss/year.** Query. Length: 800-1,800 words. **Pays $300-500.** Sometimes pays expenses of writers on assignment.

Photos State availability with submission. Reviews 2¼×2¼ transparencies. Buys one-time rights. Negotiates payment individually. Captions required.

ℕ $ $WATER GARDENING

The Magazine for Pondkeepers, The Water Gardeners, Inc., P.O. Box 607, St. John IN 46373. (219)374-9419. Fax: (219)374-9052. E-mail: wgmag@watergardening.com. Website: www.watergardening.com. **Contact:** Sue Speichert, editor. **50% freelance written.** Bimonthly magazine. *Water Gardening* is for hobby water gardeners. "We prefer articles from a first-person perspective." Estab. 1996. Circ. 25,000. Pays on publication. Publishes ms an average of 6 months after acceptance. Byline given. Offers 50% kill fee. Buys first North American serial rights. Editorial lead time 6 months. Submit seasonal material 6-12 months in advance. Accepts queries by mail, e-mail, fax. Responds in 1 month to queries; 3 months to mss. Sample copy for $3. Writer's guidelines for #10 SASE.

Nonfiction How-to (construct, maintain, improve ponds, water features), interview/profile, new product, personal experience, photo feature. **Buys 18-20 mss/year.** Query. Length: 600-1,500 words.

Photos State availability with submission. Reviews contact sheets, 3×5 transparencies, 3×5 prints. Buys one-time rights. Negotiates payment individuallly. Captions, identification of subjects, model releases required.

HUMOR

$COMEDY WRITERS ASSOCIATION NEWSLETTER

(also called *Jokewriters Guild Newsletter*), P.O. Box 605, Times Plaza Station, 542 Atlantic Ave., Brooklyn NY 11217-0605. (718)855-3351. E-mail: makinsonrobert@hotmail.com. Website: www.angelfire.com/bizz/rbmaki nson/index.html. **Contact:** Robert Makinson, editor. **10% freelance written.** Semiannual newsletter on comedy writing for association members. Estab. 1989. **Pays on acceptance.** Publishes ms an average of 3 months after acceptance. Byline given. Buys all rights. Accepts queries by mail, e-mail. Responds in 2 weeks to queries; 1 month to mss. Sample copy for $5. Writer's guidelines for #10 SASE.

Nonfiction "You may submit articles and byline will be given if used, but at present payment is only made for jokes. Emphasis should be on marketing, not general humor articles." How-to (articles about marketing, directories, Internet, new trends). Query. Length: 250-500 words.

Tips "The easiest way to be mentioned in the publication is to submit short jokes. (Payment is $2-4/joke). Jokes for professional speakers preferred. Include SASE when submitting jokes."

$FUNNY TIMES

A Monthly Humor Review, Funny Times, Inc., P.O. Box 18530, Cleveland Heights OH 44118. (216)371-8600. Fax: (216)371-8696. E-mail: ft@funnytimes.com. Website: www.funnytimes.com. **Contact:** Raymond Lesser, Susan Wolpert, editors. **10% freelance written.** Monthly tabloid for humor. "*Funny Times* is a monthly review of America's funniest cartoonists and writers. We are the *Reader's Digest* of modern American humor with a progressive/peace-oriented/environmental/politically activist slant." Estab. 1985. Circ. 63,000. Pays on publication. Publishes ms an average of 3 months after acceptance. Byline given. Buys one-time, second serial (reprint) rights. Editorial lead time 2 months. Accepts previously published material. Accepts simultaneous submissions. Responds in 3 months to mss. Sample copy for $3 or 9×12 SAE with 4 first-class stamps (83¢ postage). Writer's guidelines online.

Nonfiction "We only publish humor or interviews with funny people (comedians, comic actors, cartoonists, etc.). Everything we publish is very funny. If your piece isn't extremely funny then don't bother to send it. Don't send us anything that's not outrageously funny. Don't send anything that other people haven't already read and told you they laughed so hard they peed their pants." Essays (funny), humor, interview/profile, opinion (humorous), personal experience (absolutely funny). **Buys 36 mss/year.** Send complete ms. Length: 500-700 words. **Pays $50 minimum.**

Reprints Accepts previously published submissions.

Columns/Departments Query with published clips.

Fiction Ray Lesser and Susan Wolpert, editors. Humorous. "Anything funny." **Buys 6 mss/year.** Query with published clips. Length: 500-700 words. **Pays $50-150.**

Fillers Short humor. Buys 6/year. Pays $20.

Tips "Send us a small packet (1-3 items) of only your very funniest stuff. If this makes us laugh we'll be glad to ask for more. We particularly welcome previously published material that has been well-received elsewhere."

ℕ $ $MAD MAGAZINE

1700 Broadway, New York NY 10019. (212)506-4850. Website: www.madmag.com. **Contact:** Editorial Dept. **100% freelance written.** Monthly magazine "always on the lookout for new ways to spoof and to poke fun at hot trends." Estab. 1952. **Pays on acceptance.** Publishes ms an average of 6 months after acceptance. Byline given. Buys all rights. Submit seasonal material 6 months in advance. Responds in 10 weeks to queries. Sample copy online. Writer's guidelines online.

Nonfiction "Submit a premise with three of four examples of how you intend to carry it through, describing the action and visual content. Rough sketches desired but not necessary. One-page gags: two- to eight-panel cartoon continuities as minimum very funny, maximum hilarious!" Satire; parody. "We're *not* interested in formats we're already doing or have done to death like 'what they say and what they really mean.' *Don't* send previously published submissions, riddles, advice columns, TV or movie satires, book manuscripts, top ten lists, articles about Alfred E. Neuman, poetry, essays, short stories or other text pieces." **Buys 400 mss/year. Pays minimum of $400/*MAD* page.**

Tips "Have fun! Remember to think visually! Surprise us! Freelancers can best break in with satirical nontopical material. Include SASE with each submission. Originality is prized. We like outrageous, silly and/or satirical humor."

INFLIGHT

$ $ $ $ ATTACHÉ MAGAZINE

Pace Communications, 1301 Carolina St., Greensboro NC 27401. (336)378-6065. Fax: (336)378-8278. E-mail: attacheedit@attachemag.com. Website: www.attachemag.com. **Contact:** Submissions Editor. **60% freelance written.** Monthly magazine for travelers on U.S. Airways. "We focus on 'the best of the world' and use a humorous view." Estab. 1997. Circ. 441,000. **Pays on acceptance.** Publishes ms an average of 4 months after acceptance. Byline given. Offers kill fee. Buys first global serial rights. Editorial lead time 3 months. Accepts queries by mail, e-mail. Responds in 6 weeks to queries; 1 month to mss. Sample copy for $7.50 or online. Writer's guidelines online.

Nonfiction Features are highly visual, focusing on some unusual or unique angle of travel, food, business, or other topic approved by an *Attaché* editor. Book excerpts, essays, general interest, personal experience, travel, food; lifestyle; sports. **Buys 50-75 mss/year.** Query with published clips. Length: 350-2,500 words. **Pays $350-2,500.** Sometimes pays expenses of writers on assignment.

Photos State availability with submission. Reviews contact sheets, negatives, transparencies. Buys one-time rights. Negotiates payment individually. Identification of subjects, model releases required.

Columns/Departments Passions includes several topics such as "Vices," "Food," "Golf," "Sporting," "Shelf Life," and "Things That Go;" Paragons features short lists of the best in a particular field or category, as well as 400-word pieces describing the best of something—for example, the best home tool, the best ice cream in Paris, and the best reading library. Each piece should lend itself to highly visual art. Informed Sources are departments of expertise and first-person accounts; they include "How It Works," "Home Front," "Improvement," and "Genius at Work." **Buys 50-75 mss/year.** Query. **Pays $500-2,000.**

Tips "We look for cleverly written, entertaining articles with a unique angle, particularly pieces that focus on 'the best of' something. Study the magazine for content, style and tone. Queries for story ideas should be to the point and presented clearly. Any correspondence should include SASE."

$ $ $ HEMISPHERES

Pace Communications for United Airlines, 1301 Carolina St., Greensboro NC 27401. (336)383-5800. E-mail: hemiedit@aol.com. Website: www.hemispheresmagazine.com. **Contact:** Mr. Randy Johnson, editor; Mr. Selby Bateman, senior editor. **95% freelance written.** Monthly magazine for the educated, sophisticated business and recreational frequent traveler on an airline that spans the globe. "*Hemispheres* is an inflight magazine that interprets 'inflight' to be a mode of delivery rather than an editorial genre. As such, Hemispheres' task is to engage, intrigue and entertain its primary readers—an international, culturally diverse group of affluent, educated professionals and executives who frequently travel for business and pleasure on United Airlines. The magazine offers a global perspective and a focus on topics that cross borders as often as the people reading the magazine. That places our emphasis on ideas, concepts, and culture rather than products. We present that perspective in a fresh, artful and sophisticated graphic enviroment." Estab. 1992. Circ. 500,000. **Pays on acceptance.** Publishes ms an average of 4-6 months after acceptance. Byline given. Offers 20% kill fee. Buys first worldwide rights. Editorial lead time 8 months. Submit seasonal material 8 months in advance. Accepts queries by mail. Responds in 2 months to queries; 4 months to mss. Sample copy for $7.50. Writer's guidelines for #10 SASE.

Nonfiction "Keeping 'global' in mind, we look for topics that reflect a modern appreciation of the world's cultures and environment. No 'What I did (or am going to do) on a trip to....'" General interest, humor, personal experience. Query with published clips. Length: 500-3,000 words. **Pays 50¢/word and up.**

Photos Reviews photos "only when we request them." State availability with submission. Buys one-time rights.

Negotiates payment individually. Captions, identification of subjects, model releases required.

Columns/Departments Making a Difference (Q&A format interview with world leaders, movers, and shakers. A 500-600 word introduction anchors the interview. "We want to profile an international mix of men and women representing a variety of topics or issues, but all must truly be making a difference. No puffy celebrity profiles."); 15 Fascinating Facts (a snappy selection of 1- or 2-sentence obscure, intriguing, or travel-service-oriented items that the reader never knew about a city, state, country, or destination.); Executive Secrets (things that top executives know); Case Study (Business strategies of international companies or organizations. No lionizations of CEOs. Strategies should be the emphasis. "We want international candidates."); Weekend Breakway (Takes us just outside a major city after a week of business for several activities for a physically active, action-packed weekend. This isn't a sedentary "getaway" at a "property."); Roving Gourmet (Insider's guide to interesting eating in major city, resort area, or region. The slant can be anything from ethnic to expensive; not just "best." The 4 featured eateries span a spectrum from "hole in the wall," to "expense account lunch," and on to "big deal dining."); Collecting (occasional 800-word story on collections and collecting that can emphasize travel); Eye on Sports (global look at anything of interest in sports); Vintage Traveler (options for mature, experienced travelers); Savvy Shopper (Insider's tour of best places in the world to shop. Savvy Shopper steps beyond all those stories that just mention the great shopping at a particular destination. A shop-by-shop, gallery-by-gallery tour of the best places in the world.); Science and Technology (Substantive, insightful stories on how technology is changing our lives and the business world. Not just another column on audio components or software. No gift guides!); Aviation Journal (For those fascinated with aviation. Topics range widely.); Terminal Bliss (a great airports guide series); Grape And Grain (wine and spirits with emphasis on education, not one-upmanship); Show Business (films, music, and entertainment); Musings (humor or just curious musings); Quick Quiz (tests to amuse and educate); Travel Trends (brief, practical, invaluable, global, trend-oriented); Book Beat (Tackles topics like the Wodehouse Society, the birth of a book, the competition between local bookshops and national chains. Please, no review proposals.); What the World's Reading (residents explore how current bestsellers tell us what their country is thinking). Length: 1,400 words. Query with published clips. **Pays 50¢/word and up.**

Fiction Lisa Fann, fiction editor and Selby Bateman, senior editor. Adventure, ethnic, historical, humorous, mainstream, mystery, explorations of those issues common to all people but within the context of a particular culture. **Buys 14 mss/year.** Send complete ms. Length: 1,000-4,000 words. **Pays 50¢/word and up.**

Tips "We increasingly require writers of 'destination' pieces or departments to 'live whereof they write.' Increasingly want to hear from US, UK, or other English-speaking/writing journalists (business & travel) who reside outside the US in Europe, South America, Central America, and the Pacific Rim—all areas that United flies. We're not looking for writers who aim at the inflight market. *Hemispheres* broke the fluffy mold of that tired domestic genre. Our monthly readers are a global mix on the cutting edge of the global economy and culture. They don't need to have the world filtered by US writers. We want a Hong Kong restaurant writer to speak for that city's eateries, so we need English-speaking writers around the globe. That's the 'insider' story our readers respect. We use resident writers for departments such as Roving Gourmet, Savvy Shopper, On Location, 3 Perfect Days, and Weekend Breakaway, but authoritative writers can roam in features. Sure we cover the US, but with a global view: No 'in this country' phraseology. 'Too American' is a frequent complaint for queries. We use UK English spellings in articles that speak from that tradition and we specify costs in local currency first before US dollars. Basically, all of above serves the realization that today, 'global' begins with respect for 'local.' That approach permits a wealth of ways to present culture, travel, and business for a wide readership. We anchor that with a reader-service mission that grounds everything in 'how to do it.'"

$ MIDWEST AIRLINES MAGAZINE

Paradigm Communications Group, 2701 First Ave., Suite 250, Seattle WA 98121. **Contact:** Eric Lucas, managing editor. **90% freelance written.** Bimonthly magazine for Midwest Airlines. "Positive depiction of the changing economy and culture of the U.S., plus travel and leisure features." Estab. 1993. Circ. 35,000. Pays on publication. Byline given. Buys first North American serial rights. Editorial lead time 9 months. Accepts queries by mail. Responds in 6 weeks to queries. Sample copy for 9×12 SASE. Writer's guidelines free.

• *Midwest Airlines Magazine* continues to look for *sophisticated* travel and golf writing.

Nonfiction Travel, business, sports and leisure. Special issues: "Need good ideas for golf articles in spring." No humor, how-to, or fiction. **Buys 20-25 mss/year.** Query by mail only with published clips and résumé. Length: 250-3,000 words. **Pays $100 minimum.** Sometimes pays expenses of writers on assignment.

Columns/Departments Preview (arts and events), 200-400 words; Portfolio (business), 200-500 words. **Buys 12-15 mss/year.** Query with published clips. **Pays $100-150.**

Tips "Article ideas *must* encompass areas within the airline's route system. We buy quality writing from reliable writers. Editorial philosophy emphasizes innovation and positive outlook. Do not send manuscripts unless you have no clips."

$ $ $ $ SOUTHWEST AIRLINES SPIRIT

4255 Amon Carter Blvd., Fort Worth TX 76155. (817)967-1804. Fax: (817)967-1571. E-mail: john@spiritmag.com. Website: www.spiritmag.com. **Contact:** John Clark, editor. Monthly magazine for passengers on Southwest Airlines. Estab. 1992. Circ. 380,000. **Pays on acceptance.** Byline given. Buys first North American serial, electronic rights. Responds in 1 month to queries.

Nonfiction "Seeking lively, accessible, entertaining, relevant, and trendy travel, business, lifestyle, sports, celebrity, food, tech-product stories on newsworthy/noteworthy topics in destinations served by Southwest Airlines; well-researched and reported; multiple source only. Experienced magazine professionals only." **Buys about 40 mss/year.** Query by mail only with published clips. Length: Length: 1,500 words (features). **Pays $1/word.** Pays expenses of writers on assignment.

Columns/Departments Length: 800-900 words. **Buys about 21 mss/year.** Query by mail only with published clips.

Fillers Buys 12/year. Length: 250 words. **Pays variable amount.**

Tips "*Southwest Airlines Spirit* magazine reaches more than 2.8 million readers every month aboard Southwest Airlines. Our median reader is a college-educated, 32-40-year-old traveler with a household income around $90,000. Writers must have proven magazine capabilities, a sense of fun, excellent reporting skills, a smart, hip style, and the ability to provide take-away value to the reader in sidebars, charts, and/or lists."

$ $ SPIRIT OF ALOHA

The Inflight Magazine of Aloha Airlines and Island Air, Honolulu Publishing Co., Ltd., 707 Richards St., Suite 525, Honolulu HI 96813. (808)524-7400. Fax: (808)531-2306. E-mail: tchapman@honpub.com. Website: www.spiritofaloha.com. **Contact:** Tom Chapman, editor. **80% freelance written.** Bimonthly magazine covering Hawaii, and other Aloha Airlines destinations. Estab. 1978. Circ. 100,000. **Pays on acceptance.** Publishes ms an average of 2 months after acceptance. Byline given. Buys first rights. Editorial lead time 2 months. Submit seasonal material 4 months in advance. Accepts queries by mail, e-mail. Responds in 1 month to queries. Writer's guidelines by e-mail.

Nonfiction Should be related to Hawaii and other mainland and Pacific destinations of airline. **Buys 40 mss/year.** Query with published clips. Length: 1,500-2,000 words. **Pays $500 and up.**

Photos State availability with submission. Reviews transparencies. Buys one-time rights. Negotiates payment individually. Captions, identification of subjects, model releases required.

$ $ $ WASHINGTON FLYER MAGAZINE

1707 L St., NW, Suite 800, Washington DC 20036. (202)331-9393. Fax: (202)331-2043. E-mail: jessica@themagazinegroup.com. Website: www.fly2dc.com. **Contact:** Jessica Bizik, editor-in-chief. **60% freelance written.** Bimonthly magazine for business and pleasure travelers at Washington National and Washington Dulles International airports INSI. "Primarily affluent, well-educated audience that flies frequently in and out of Washington, DC." Estab. 1989. Circ. 182,000. **Pays on acceptance.** Byline given. Offers 25% kill fee. Buys first North American serial rights. Submit seasonal material 4 months in advance. Accepts queries by mail, e-mail, fax. Responds in 10 weeks to queries. Sample copy and writer's guidelines for 9×12 SAE with $2 postage. Writer's guidelines online. Editorial calendar online.

O— "First understand the magazine—from the nuances of its content to its tone. Best departments to get your foot in the door are 'Washington Insider' and 'Mini Escapes.' The former deals with new business, the arts, sports, etc. in Washington. The latter: getaways that are within four hours of Washington by car. Regarding travel, we're less apt to run stories on sedentary pursuits (e.g., inns, B&Bs, spas). Our readers want to get out and discover an area, whether it's DC or Barcelona. Action-oriented activities work best. Also, the best way to pitch is via e-mail. Our mail is sorted by interns, and sometimes I never get queries. E-mail is so immediate, and I can give a more personal response."

Nonfiction One international destination feature per issue, determined 6 months in advance. One feature per issue on aspect of life in Washington. General interest, interview/profile, travel, business. No personal experiences, poetry, opinion or inspirational. **Buys 20-30 mss/year.** Query with published clips. Length: 800-1,200 words. **Pays $500-900.**

Photos State availability with submission. Reviews negatives, almost always color transparencies. Buys one-time rights. Considers additional payment for top-quality photos accepted with ms. Identification of subjects required.

Columns/Departments Washington Insider, Travel, Hospitality, Airports and Airlines, Restaurants, Shopping, all 800-1,200 words. Query. **Pays $500-900.**

Tips "Know the Washington market and issues relating to frequent business/pleasure travelers as we move toward a global economy. With a bimonthly publication schedule it's important that stories remain viable as possible during the magazine's two-month 'shelf life.' No telephone calls, please and understand that most assignments are made several months in advance. Queries are best sent via e-mail."

JUVENILE

N $ADVENTURES

6401 The Paseo Blvd., Kansas City MO 64131-1213. (816)333-7000. Fax: (816)333-4439. E-mail: acallison@naza rene.org. **Contact:** Andrea Callison. **75% freelance written.** Published by Adventures for children ages 6-8. Correlates to the weekly Sunday school lesson. Pays on publication. Publishes ms an average of 1 year after acceptance. Buys all rights. Accepts queries by mail, fax. Responds in 2 months to queries. Sample copy for #10 SASE. Writer's guidelines for #10 SASE.

Columns/Departments Fiction and Nonfiction Stories, 250 words, **Pays $25**; Rebus Stories, 125-150 words, **Pays $25**; Interesting Facts/Trivia, 100-125 words, **Pays $15**; Recipes & Crafts, **Pays $15**; Activities, **Pays $15**. Send complete ms.

Fiction Accepts life application stories that show early elementary children dealing with the issues related to the Bible story, Bible Truth, or lesson goals. Children may interact with friends, family, or other individuals in the stories. Make characters and events realistic. Avoid placing characters in a perfect world or depicting spiritually precocious children. Length: 250 words. **Pays $25.**

Poetry Short, fun, easy-to-understand, age-appropriate poetry that correlates with the Bible story, Bible Truth, or lesson goals is welcome. "We prefer rhythmic, pattern poems, but will accept free verse if reads smoothly out loud." Length: 4-8 lines. **25¢/line, min. $2.**

$ $AMERICAN GIRL

8400 Fairway Place, Middleton WI 53562. (608)836-4848. E-mail: im_agmag_editor@pleasantco.com. Website: www.americangirl.com. Executive Editor: Kristi Thom. Managing Editor: Barbara Stretchberry. **Contact:** Maga zine Department Assistant. **5% freelance written.** Bimonthly 4-color magazine covering hobbies, crafts, pro files, and history of interest to girls ages 8-12. "Four-color bimonthly magazine for girls age 8-12. We want thoughtfully developed children's literature with good characters and plots." Estab. 1992. Circ. 700,000. **Pays on acceptance.** Byline given for larger features, not departments. Offers 50% kill fee. Buys first North American serial, all rights. Editorial lead time 6 months. Submit seasonal material 6 months in advance. Accepts queries by mail. Accepts previously published material. Accepts simultaneous submissions. Responds in 3 months to queries. Sample copy for $3.95 (check made out to *American Girl*) and 9×12 SAE with $1.98 postage. Writer's guidelines online.

   ○⇁ Best opportunity for freelancers is the Girls Express section. "We're looking for short profiles of girls who are into sports, the arts, interesting hobbies, cultural activities, and other areas. A key: The girl must be the 'star' and the story must be from her point of view. Be sure to include the age of the girls you're pitching to us. If you have any photo leads, please send those, too. We also welcome how-to stories—how to send away for free things, hot ideas for a cool day, how to write the President and get a response. In addition, we're looking for easy crafts that can be explained in a few simple steps. Stories in Girls Express have to be told in no more than 175 words. We prefer to receive ideas in query form rather than finished manuscripts."

Nonfiction Pays $300 minimum for feature articles. Pays expenses of writers on assignment.

Photos "We prefer to shoot." State availability with submission. Buys all rights.

Columns/Departments Girls Express (short profiles of girls with unusual and interesting hobbies that other girls want to read about), 175 words; Giggle Gang (puzzles, games, etc.—especially looking for seasonal). Query.

Fiction Magazine Department Assistant. Adventure, condensed novels, ethnic, historical, humorous, slice-of life vignettes. No romance, science fiction, fantasy. **Buys 6 mss/year.** Query with published clips. Length: 2,300 words maximum. **Pays $500 minimum.**

$ $ARCHAEOLOGY'S DIG MAGAZINE

Cobblestone Publishing, 30 Grove St., Suite C, Peterborough NH 03458-1454. (603)924-7209. Fax: (603)924-7380. E-mail: cfbakeriii@meganet.net. Website: www.digonsite.com. **Contact:** Rosalie Baker, editor. **75% free lance written.** Magazine published 9 times/year covering archaeology for kids ages 9-14. Estab. 1999. Circ. 20,000. Pays on publication. Publishes ms an average of 4 months after acceptance. Byline given. Buys all rights. Editorial lead time 6 months. Submit seasonal material 3 months in advance. Accepts queries by mail. Responds in several months to queries; 1 month to mss. Sample copy for $4.95 with 8x11 SASE or $9 without SASE. Writer's guidelines online.

   ● Does *not* accept unsolicited material.

Nonfiction Personal experience, photo feature, travel, archaeological excavation reports. No fiction. Occasional paleontology stories accepted. **Buys 30-40 mss/year.** Query with published clips. Length: 100-1,000 words. **Pays 20-25¢/word.**

Photos State availability with submission. Buys one-time rights. Negotiates payment individually. Identification of subjects required.

Tips "Please remember that this is a children's magazine for kids ages 9-14 so the tone is as kid-friendly as possible given the scholarship involved in researching and describing a site or a find."

$ BABYBUG

Carus Publishing Co., P.O. Box 300, Peru IL 61354. (815)224-5803, ext. 656. Editor-in-Chief: Marianne Carus. **Contact:** Paula Morrow, executive editor. **50% freelance written.** Board-book magazine published monthly except for combined May/June and July/August issues. *"Babybug* is 'the listening and looking magazine for infants and toddlers,' intended to be read aloud by a loving adult to foster a love of books and reading in young children ages 6 months-2 years." Estab. 1994. Circ. 45,000. Pays on publication. Publishes ms an average of 18 months after acceptance. Byline given. Buys variable rights. Editorial lead time 10 months. Submit seasonal material 1 year in advance. Accepts simultaneous submissions. Sample copy for $5. Writer's guidelines online.

Nonfiction General interest. **Buys 10-20 mss/year.** Send complete ms. Length: up to 4 short sentences. **Pays $25.**

Fiction Anything for infants and toddlers. Adventure, humorous. **Buys 10-20 mss/year.** Send complete ms. Length: 2-8 short sentences. **Pays $25 and up.**

Poetry Buys 30 poems/year. Submit maximum 5 poems. Length: 2-8 lines. **Pays $25.**

Tips "Imagine having to read your story or poem—out loud—50 times or more! That's what parents will have to do. Babies and toddlers demand, 'Read it again'—your material must hold up under repetition."

$ $ $ $ BOYS' LIFE

Boy Scouts of America, P.O. Box 152079, Irving TX 75015-2079. (972)580-2366. Fax: (972)580-2079. Website: www.boyslife.org. **Contact:** Michael Goldman, senior editor. **75% freelance written.** Prefers to work with published/established writers; works with small number of new/unpublished writers each year. Monthly magazine covering activities of interest to all boys ages 6-18. Most readers are Boy Scouts or Cub Scouts. *"Boys' Life* covers Boy Scout activities and general interest subjects for ages 8 to 18, Boy Scouts, Cub Scouts and others of that age group." Estab. 1911. Circ. 1,300,000. **Pays on acceptance.** Publishes ms an average of 1 year after acceptance. Buys one-time rights. Accepts queries by mail, fax. Responds in 2 months to queries. Sample copy for $3.60 and 9×12 SAE. Writer's guidelines for #10 SASE or online.

Nonfiction Subject matter is broad, everything from professional sports to American history to how to pack a canoe. Look at a current list of the BSA's more than 100 merit badge pamphlets for an idea of the wide range of subjects possible. Uses strong photo features with about 500 words of text. Separate payment or assignment for photos. How-to, photo feature, hobby and craft ideas. **Buys 60 mss/year.** Query with SASE. No phone queries. Length: Major articles run 500-1,500 words; preferred length is about 1,000 words, including sidebars and boxes. **Pays $400-1,500.** Pays expenses of writers on assignment.

Columns/Departments Darrin Scheid, associate editor. "Science, nature, earth, health, sports, space and aviation, cars, computers, entertainment, pets, history, music are some of the columns for which we use 300-750 words of text. This is a good place to show us what you can do." **Buys 75-80 mss/year.** Query. **Pays $250-300.**

Fiction Rich Haddaway, associate editor. Include SASE. Adventure, humorous, mystery, science fiction, western, sports. **Buys 12-15 mss/year.** Send complete ms. Length: 1,000-1,500 words. **Pays $750 minimum.**

Fillers Freelance comics pages and scripts.

Tips "We strongly recommend reading at least 12 issues of the magazine before you submit queries. We are a good market for any writer willing to do the necessary homework."

$ BREAD FOR GOD'S CHILDREN

Bread Ministries, Inc., P.O. Box 1017, Arcadia FL 34265. (863)494-6214. Fax: (863)993-0154. E-mail: bread@sun line.net. Editor: Judith M. Gibbs. **Contact:** Donna Wade, editorial secretary. **10% freelance written.** Published 6-8 times/year. "An interdenominational Christian teaching publication published 6-8 times/year written to aid children and youth in leading a Christian life." Estab. 1972. Circ. 10,000. Pays on publication. Publishes ms an average of 6 months after acceptance. Byline given. Buys first rights. Accepts queries by mail. Accepts simultaneous submissions. Responds in 6 months to mss. Three sample copies for 9×12 SAE and 5 first-class stamps. Writer's guidelines for #10 SASE.

    Break in with a good story about a 6-10 year old gaining insight into a spiritual principle—without an adult preaching the message to him.

Reprints Send tearsheet and information about when and where the material previously appeared.

Columns/Departments Let's Chat (children's Christian values), 500-700 words; Teen Page (youth Christian values), 600-800 words; Idea Page (games, crafts, Bible drills). **Buys 5-8 mss/year.** Send complete ms. **Pays $30.**

Fiction "We are looking for writers who have a solid knowledge of Biblical principles and are concerned for the youth of today living by those principles. Our stories must be well written, with the story itself getting the message across—no preaching, moralizing, or tag endings." No fantasy, science fiction, or nonChristian themes. **Buys 15-20 mss/year.** Send complete ms. Length: 600-800 words (young children), 900-1,500 words (older children). **Pays $40-50.**

Tips "We're looking for more submissions on healing miracles and reconciliation/restoration. Follow usual guidelines for careful writing, editing, and proofreading. We get many manuscripts with misspellings, poor grammar, careless typing. Know your subject—writer should know the Lord to write about the Christian life. Study the publication and our guidelines."

$CADET QUEST MAGAZINE

(formerly *Crusader Magazine*), P.O. Box 7259, Grand Rapids MI 49510-7259. (616)241-5616. Fax: (616)241-5558. E-mail: submissions@calvinistcadets.org. Website: www.calvinistcadets.org. **Contact:** G. Richard Broene, editor. **40% freelance written.** Works with a small number of new/unpublished writers each year. Magazine published 7 times/year. "*Cadet Quest Magazine* shows boys 9-14 how God is at work in their lives and in the world around them." Estab. 1958. Circ. 10,000. **Pays on acceptance.** Publishes ms an average of 4-11 months after acceptance. Byline given. Buys first North American serial, one-time, second serial (reprint), simultaneous rights. Rights purchased vary with author and material. Accepts previously published material. Accepts simultaneous submissions. Responds in 2 months to submissions. Sample copy for 9×12 SASE. Writer's guidelines for #10 SASE.

● Accepts submissions by mail, or by e-mail (must include ms in text of e-mail). Will not open attachments.

Nonfiction Articles about young boys' interests: sports (articles about athletes and developing Christian character through sports; photos appreciated), outdoor activities (camping skills, nature study, survival exercises; practical 'how to do it' approach works best. 'God in nature' themes appreciated), science, crafts, and problems. Emphasis is on a Christian perspective, but no simplistic moralisms. How-to, humor, inspirational, interview/profile, personal experience, informational. Special issues: Write for new themes list in February. **Buys 20-25 mss/year.** Send complete ms. Length: 500-1,500 words. **Pays 2-5¢/word.**

Reprints Send ms with rights for sale noted. Payment varies.

Photos Pays $4-25 for photos purchased with ms.

Columns/Departments Project Page (uses simple projects boys 9-14 can do on their own made with easily accessible materials; must provide clear, accurate instructions).

Fiction "Considerable fiction is used. Fast-moving stories that appeal to a boy's sense of adventure or sense of humor are welcome." Adventure, religious, spiritual, sports, comics. "Avoid preachiness. Avoid simplistic answers to complicated problems. Avoid long dialogue and little action." No fantasy, science fiction, fashion, horror or erotica. Send complete ms. Length: 900-1,500 words. **Pays 4-6¢/word, and 1 contributor's copy.**

Fillers Short humor, any type of puzzles.

Tips "Best time to submit stories/articles is early in calendar year (February-April). Also remember readers are boys ages 9-14. Stories must reflect or add to the theme of the issue."

$ $CALLIOPE

Exploring World History, Cobblestone Publishing Co., 30 Grove St., Suite C, Peterborough NH 03458-1454. (603)924-7209. Fax: (603)924-7380. Website: www.cobblestonepub.com. Editors: Rosalie and Charles Baker. **Contact:** Rosalie F. Baker, editor. **More than 50% freelance written.** Magazine published 9 times/year covering world history (East and West) through 1800 AD for 8 to 14 year olds. Articles must relate to the issue's theme. "*Calliope* covers world history (east/west) and lively, original approaches to the subject are the primary concerns of the editors in choosing material. For 8-14 year olds." Estab. 1990. Circ. 11,000. Pays on publication. Byline given. Buys all rights. Responds in several months (if interested, responds 5 months before publication date) to mss. Sample copy for $4.50 and 7½×10½ SASE with 4 first-class stamps or online. Writer's guidelines for #10 SAE and 1 first-class stamp or on website.

○ Break in with a "well-written query on a topic that relates directly to an upcoming issue's theme, a writing sample that is well-researched and concise and a bibliography that includes new research."

Nonfiction Articles must relate to the theme. Essays, general interest, historical/nostalgic, how-to (activities), humor, interview/profile, personal experience, photo feature, technical, travel, recipes. No religious, pornographic, biased, or sophisticated submissions. **Buys 30-40 mss/year.** Query by mail only with published clips. Length: 700-800 words for feature articles; 300-600 words for supplemental nonfiction. **Pays 20-25¢/printed word.**

Photos State availability with submission. Reviews contact sheets, color slides and b&w prints. Buys one-time rights. Pays $15-100 (color cover negotiated).

Columns/Departments Activities (crafts, recipes, projects), up to 700 words. Query by mail only with published clips. **Pays on individual basis.**

Fiction Rosalie Baker, editor. All fiction must be theme-related. **Buys 10 mss/year.** Query with or without published clips. Length: 1,000 words maximum. **Pays 20-25¢/word.**

Fillers Puzzles and games (no word finds); crossword and other word puzzles using the vocabulary of the issue's theme; mazes and picture puzzles that relate to the theme. **Pays on individual basis.**

Tips "A query must consist of all of the following to be considered (please use nonerasable paper): a brief cover letter stating the subject and word length of the proposed article; a detailed 1-page outline explaining the information to be presented in the article; an extensive bibliography of materials the author intends to use in preparing the article; a self-addressed stamped envelope. (Authors are urged to use primary resources and up-to-date scholarly resources in their bibliography.) Writers new to *Calliope* should send a writing sample with the query. In all correspondence, please include your complete address as well as a telephone number where you can be reached."

N $ CHARACTERS

Kids Short Story & Poetry Outlet, Davis Publications, P.O. Box 708, Newport NH 03773-0708. (603)863-5896. Fax: (603)863-8198. E-mail: hotdog@nhvt.net. **Contact:** Cindy Davis, editor. **100% freelance written.** Quarterly magazine for kids. "We accept submissions by all, but give preference to ones written by kids." Estab. 2003. Pays on publication. Publishes ms an average of 8 months after acceptance. Byline given. Not copyrighted. Buys one-time, second serial (reprint) rights. Editorial lead time 4 months. Submit seasonal material 6 months in advance. Accepts queries by mail, e-mail. Accepts previously published material. Accepts simultaneous submissions. Responds in 2 weeks to queries; 1 month to mss. Sample copy for $5. Writer's guidelines by e-mail.

Fiction All genres accepted. **Buys 40 mss/year.** Send complete ms. Length: 1,500 words maximum. **$5, plus contributor copy.**

Poetry Light verse, traditional. **Buys 8 poems/year.** Submit maximum 2 poems. Length: up to 18 lines.

$ $ CHILDREN'S MAGIC WINDOW MAGAZINE

ProMark Publishing, P.O. Box 390, Perham MN 56573. Website: www.childrensmagicwindow.com. Editor: Joan Foster. Managing Editor: George Rowel. **Contact:** Mike Hoffman, production director. **70% freelance written.** Bimonthly magazine covering children's stories. "*Children's Magic Window* is a bimonthly, full-color magazine for all 6-12 year olds. Features 96 colorful pages of educational and entertaining stories, games, puzzles, magic, jokes, riddles, mazes, and fun facts. Challenging, yet lots of fun. Features sports and celebrity profiles, articles on health, history, nutrition, animals, and more." Estab. 1999. Circ. 10,000. Pays on publication. Publishes ms an average of 5 months after acceptance. Byline given. Offers 25% kill fee. Buys all rights. Editorial lead time 5 months. Submit seasonal material 8 months in advance. Accepts queries by mail. Responds in 6 weeks to queries; 5 months to mss. Writer's guidelines for #10 SASE.

Nonfiction General interest, historical/nostalgic, humor, photo feature. "We avoid all topics involving sex, drugs, alcohol, or violence." **Buys 20 mss/year.** Query with published clips or send complete ms. Length: 400-1,000 words. **Pays $0-400.** Pays in contributor copies upon author request.

Photos Send photos with submission. Reviews contact sheets, up to 8×10 prints. Buys all rights. Negotiates payment individually. Model releases required.

Columns/Departments Fun Facts (short explanation of any topic), up to 70 words; Science Fun (2-page spread involving interesting science projects); Make It Yourself (2-page spread of a craft or skill); Magic (2-page spread of a unique trick and how to perfom it). **Buys 1 or 2 for each department for each issue.** Send complete ms. **Pays up to $80.**

Fiction Joan Foster, editor. "Fiction should be written for the 9-12 age group. Must challenge the reader and yet be easily understood. Look for pieces that are exciting and fresh." Experimental, fantasy, historical, humorous, mystery, suspense. "We avoid all topics involving sex, drugs, alcohol, or violence." **Buys 28 mss/year.** Send complete ms. Length: Length: Up to 1,000. **Pays up to $400.**

Poetry Joan Foster, editor. Light verse. **Buys 20 poems/year.** Submit maximum 2 poems. Length: Up to 10 lines maximum.

Fillers Anecdotes, facts, gags to be illustrated by cartoonist, short humor. **Buys 50/year.** Length: Up to 80 words maximum. **Pays up to $20.**

Tips "We are mostly concerned about finding entertaining, yet educational; fun, yet challenging material. We are looking for pieces that are entertaining for kids and at the same time can be interesting for adults. We want the contents of our magazine to make reading fun for the young reader."

N $ $ CHILDREN'S PLAYMATE MAGAZINE

Children's Better Health Institute, P.O. Box 567, Indianapolis IN 46206-0567. Website: www.childrensplaymate mag.org. **40% freelance written.** Eager to work with new/unpublished writers. Magazine published 8 times/year for children ages 6-8. "We are looking for articles, poems, and activities with a health, fitness, or nutrition oriented theme. We try to present our material in a positive light, and we try to incorporate humor and a light approach wherever possible without minimizing the seriousness of what we are saying." Estab. 1929. Circ. 114,907. Pays on publication. Byline given. Buys all rights. Submit seasonal material 8 months in advance. Responds in 3 months to queries. Sample copy for $1.75. Writer's guidelines for SASE or on website.

● May hold mss for up to 1 year before acceptance/publication.

○ Include word count. Material will not be returned unless accompanied by a SASE.

Nonfiction "We are especially interested in material concerning sports and fitness, including profiles of famous amateur and professional athleters; 'average' atheletes (especially children) who have overcome obstacles to excel in their arears; and new or unusual sports, particularly those in whcich childrent can participate. Nonfiction articles dealing with health subjects should be fresh and creative. Avoid encyclopedic or 'preachy' approach. We try to present our health material in a positive manner, incorporate humor and a light approach wherever possible without minimizing the seriousness of the message." Interview/profile (famous amateurs and professional athletes), photo feature, Recipes (ingredients should be healthfu). **Buys 25 mss/year.** Send complete ms. Length: 300-700 words. **Pays up to 17¢/word.**

Photos State availability with submission. Buys one-time rights. $15 minimum. Captions, model releases required.

Fiction Terry Harshman, editor. Not buying much fiction right now except for rebus stories of 100-300 words and occasional poems. Vocabulary suitable for ages 6-8. Include word count. No adult or adolescent fiction. Send complete ms. Length: 300-700 words. **Pays minimum of 17¢/word and 10 contributor's copies.**

Fillers Recipes, puzzles, dot-to-dots, color-ins, hidden pictures, mazes. Prefers camara-ready activities. Activity guidelines for #10 SASE. **Buys 25/year. Pays variable amount.**

Tips "We would especially like to see more holiday stories, articles and activities. Please send seasonal material at least eight months in advance."

$CLUB CONNECTION

A Missionettes Magazine for Girls, The General Council of the Assemblies of God, 1445 N. Boonville Ave., Springfield MO 65802. (417)862-2781. Fax: (417)862-0503. E-mail: clubconnection@ag.org. Website: missionettes.ag.org/clubconnection. Editor: Debby Seler. Managing Editor: Lori VanVeen. **Contact:** Kelly Kirksey, assistant editor. **25% freelance written.** Quarterly magazine covering Christian discipleship. "*Club Connection* is a Christian-based magazine for girls ages 6-12." Estab. 1997. Circ. 12,000. Pays on publication. Publishes ms an average of 6-12 months after acceptance. Buys first, one-time rights. Editorial lead time 6 months. Submit seasonal material 9-12 months in advance. Accepts queries by mail, e-mail, fax. Responds in 1 month to queries; 1-2 months to mss. Sample copy for free. Writer's guidelines online.

Nonfiction Historical/nostalgic, how-to (fun activities for girls), humor, inspirational, interview/profile, personal experience, religious. Special issues: A Look At Nature: trees, flowers, insects, butterflies, etc. (Spring 2003); A View of the World: geography, mountains, oceans and seas, summer vacation (Summer 2003); The Bigger Picture: science, the universe, astronauts, back to school (Fall 2003); The Perfect Plan: God's unique design in all creation, Jesus, salvation, Christmas (Winter 2003). No songs or poetry. **Buys 8 mss/year.** Send complete ms. Length: 250-800 words. **Pays $35-50 for assigned articles; $25-40 for unsolicited articles.**

Photos Send photos with submission. Reviews 3½×5 prints. Buys one-time rights. Offers $10/photo. Captions, identification of subjects required.

Fiction Adventure, confessions, ethnic, historical, humorous, mainstream, mystery, religious. No songs or poetry. **Buys 8 mss/year.** Send complete ms. Length: 250-800 words. **Pays $25-50.**

Tips "Our goal is to offer a Christ-centered, fun magazine for girls. We look for word count, age appropriateness, and relevancy to today's girls when selecting articles. Writing to theme's is also helpful. They can be found on our website."

$CLUBHOUSE JR.

Focus on the Family, 8605 Explorer Dr., Colorado Springs CO 80920. Editor: Annette Bourland. **Contact:** Suzanne Hadley, associate editor. Monthly magazine for 4-8 year olds. Estab. 1988. Circ. 96,000. Publishes ms an average of 1 year after acceptance. Byline given. Buys first rights. Accepts queries by mail. Accepts simultaneous submissions. Responds in 2 months to queries. Sample copy for $1.25 and 8×10 SASE. Writer's guidelines for #10 SASE.

Poetry "Poetry should have a strong message that supports traditional values. No cute but pointless work." Submit maximum 5 poems. **Pays $50-100.**

$ $CLUBHOUSE MAGAZINE

Focus on the Family, 8605 Explorer Dr., Colorado Springs CO 80920. (719)531-3400. Website: www.clubhousemagazine.org. Editor: Jesse Florea. **Contact:** Suzanne Hadley, associate editor. **25% freelance written.** Monthly magazine. "*Clubhouse* readers are 8-12 year old boys and girls who desire to know more about God and the

Bible. Their parents (who typically pay for the membership) want wholesome, educational material with Scriptural or moral insight. The kids want excitement, adventure, action, humor, or mystery. Your job as a writer is to please both the parent and child with each article." Estab. 1987. Circ. 114,000. **Pays on acceptance.** Publishes ms an average of 6-12 months after acceptance. Byline given. Buys first North American serial, first, one-time, electronic rights. Editorial lead time 5 months. Submit seasonal material 7 months in advance. Responds in 2 months to mss. Sample copy for $1.50 with 9×12 SASE. Writer's guidelines for #10 SASE.

Nonfiction Jesse Florea, editor. Essays, how-to, humor, inspirational, interview/profile, personal experience, photo feature, religious. "Avoid Bible stories without a unique format or overt visual appeal. Avoid informational-only, science, or educational articles. Avoid biographies told encyclopedia or textbook style." **Buys 3 mss/year.** Send complete ms. Length: 800-1,200 words. **Pays $25-450 for assigned articles; 10-25¢/word for unsolicited articles.**

Fiction Jesse Florea, editor. Adventure, humorous, mystery, religious, suspense, holiday. Avoid contemporary, middle-class family settings (existing authors meet this need), poems (rarely printed), stories dealing with boy-girl relationships. "No science fiction." **Buys 10 mss/year.** Send complete ms. Length: 400-1,500 words. **Pays $200 and up for first time contributor and 5 contributor's copies; additional copies available.**

Fillers Facts, newsbreaks. **Buys 2/year.** Length: 40-100 words.

$ $ COBBLESTONE

Discover American History, Cobblestone Publishing, 30 Grove St., Suite C, Peterborough NH 03458. Fax: (603)924-7380. E-mail: mchorlian@yahoo.com. Website: www.cobblestonepub.com. **Contact:** Meg Chorlian, editor. Monthly magazine (September-May) covering American history for children ages 8-14. Prefers to work with published/established writers "Each issue presents a particular theme, making it exciting as well as informative. Half of all subscriptions are for schools." All material must relate to monthly theme. Estab. 1979. Circ. 30,000. Pays on publication. Publishes ms an average of 4 months after acceptance. Byline given. Offers 50% kill fee. Buys all rights. Editorial lead time 8 months. Accepts queries by mail, fax. Responds in 4 months to queries. Sample copy for $4.95 and 7½×10½ SAE with 4 first-class stamps. Writer's guidelines for #10 SASE and 1 first-class stamp or on website.

Nonfiction "Request a copy of the writer's guidelines to find out specific issue themes in upcoming months." Historical/nostalgic, interview/profile, personal experience, plays, biography, recipes, activities. No material that editorializes rather than reports. **Buys 80 mss/year.** Query by mail with published clips, outline, and bibliography. Length: Feature articles 600-800 words; supplemental nonfiction 300-500 words. **Pays 20-25¢/ printed word.**

Photos Photos must relate to theme. State availability with submission. Reviews contact sheets, transparencies, prints. Buys one-time rights. Offers $15-50 for nonprofessional quality, up to $100 for professional quality. Captions, identification of subjects required.

Columns/Departments Puzzles and Games (no word finds); crosswords and other word puzzles using the vocabulary of the issue's theme.

Fiction Adventure, ethnic, historical, biographical fiction relating to theme. Has to be very strong and accurate. **Buys 5 mss/year.** Query with published clips. Length: 500-800 words. **Pays 20-25¢/word.**

Poetry Must relate to theme. Free verse, light verse, traditional. **Buys 3 poems/year.** Length: Up to 50 lines.

Tips "Review theme lists and past issues of magazine to see what we look for."

$ $ CRICKET

Carus Publishing Co., P.O. Box 300, Peru IL 61354-0300. (815)224-5803. **Contact:** Marianne Carus, editor-in-chief. Monthly magazine for children ages 9-14. Magazine for children, ages 9-14. Estab. 1973. Circ. 73,000. Pays on publication. Publishes ms an average of 6-24 months after acceptance. Byline given. Rights vary. Submit seasonal material 1 year in advance. Accepts previously published material. Responds in 3 months to mss. Sample copy for $5 and 9×12 SAE. Writer's guidelines for SASE and on website.

• *Cricket* is looking for more fiction and nonfiction for the older end of its 9-14 age range. It also seeks humorous stories and mysteries (*not* detective spoofs), fantasy and original fairy tales, stand-alone excerpts from unpublished novels, and well-written/researched science articles.

Nonfiction A bibliography is required for all nonfiction articles. Travel, adventure, biography, foreign culture, geography, history, natural science, science, social science, sports, technology. Send complete ms. Length: 200-1,500 words. **Pays 25¢/word maximum.**

Reprints Send ms with rights for sale noted and information about when and where the material previously appeared. Pays 50% of amount paid for an original article.

Fiction Adventure, ethnic, fantasy, historical, humorous, mystery, novel excerpts, science fiction, suspense, western, folk and fairy tales. No didactic, sex, religious, or horror stories. **Buys 75-100 mss/year.** Send complete ms. Length: 200-2,000 words. **Pays 25¢/word maximum, and 6 contributor's copies; $2.50 charge for extras.**

Poetry Buys 20-30 poems/year. Length: 25 lines maximum. **Pays $3/line maximum.**

$DISCOVERIES

Word Action Publishing Co., 6401 The Paseo, Kansas City MO 64131. (816)333-7000, ext. 2728. Fax: (816)333-4439. E-mail: jjsmith@nazarene.org. Editor: Virginia Folsom. **Contact:** Julie Smith, editorial assistant. **80% freelance written.** Weekly Sunday school take-home paper. "Our audience is third and fourth graders. We require that the stories relate to the Sunday school lesson for that week." Circ. 18,000. **Pays on acceptance.** Publishes ms an average of 1-2 year after acceptance. Byline given. Buys multi-use rights. Accepts queries by mail, e-mail, fax. Accepts previously published material. Accepts simultaneous submissions. Responds in 6 weeks to queries. Sample copy for SASE. Writer's guidelines for SASE.

    ○→ "Query before sending submissions. Make sure content is Biblically correct and relevant where necessary."

Fiction Submit contemporary, true-to-life portrayals of 8-10 year olds, written for a third- to fourth-grade reading level. Religious themes. Must relate to our theme list. No fantasy, science fiction, abnormally mature or precocious children, personification of animals. Nothing preachy. No unrealistic dialogue. **Buys 50 mss/year.** Send complete ms. **Pays $25.**

Fillers Spot cartoons, puzzles (related to the theme), trivia (any miscellaneous area of interest to 8-10 year olds). Length: 50-100 words. **Pays $10 for trivia, puzzles, and cartoons.**

Tips "Follow our theme list, read the Bible verses that relate to the theme."

$ $DISCOVERY TRAILS

Gospel Publishing House, 1445 N. Boonville Ave., Springfield MO 65802-1894. (417)831-8000. Fax: (417)862-6059. E-mail: rl-discoverytrails@gph.org. Website: www.radiantlife.org. **Contact:** Sinda S. Zinn, editor. **50% freelance written.** Weekly 4-page Sunday school take-home paper. *Discovery Trails* is written for boys and girls 10-12 (slanted toward older group). Fiction, adventure stories showing children applying Christian principles in everyday living are used in the paper. Estab. 1954. Circ. 20,000. **Pays on acceptance.** Publishes ms an average of 18 months after acceptance. Byline given. Buys one-time, second serial (reprint), simultaneous rights. Editorial lead time 18 months. Submit seasonal material 18 months in advance. Accepts simultaneous submissions. Sample copy for #10 SASE. Writer's guidelines online.

Nonfiction Wants articles with reader appeal, emphasizing some phase of Christian living or historical, scientific, or natural material which includes a spiritual lesson. Submissions should include a bibliography of facts. **Buys 15-20 mss/year.** Send complete ms. Length: 400 words maximum. **Pays 7-10¢/word.**

Reprints Send ms with rights for sale noted and information about when and where the material previously appeared. Pays 7¢/word.

Fiction Wants fiction that presents realistic characters working out their problems according to Bible principles, presenting Christianity in action without being preachy. Serial stories acceptable. Adventure, historical, humorous, mystery, religious, spiritual, sports. No Bible fiction, "Halloween," "Easter Bunny", "Santa Claus" or science fiction stories. **Buys 80-90 mss/year.** Send complete ms. Length: 500-800 words. **Pays 7-10¢/word and 3 contributor's copies.**

Fillers Bits & Bytes of quirky facts, puzzles, interactive activities, quizzes, word games, and fun activities that address social skills on a focused topic with accurate research, vivid writing, and spiritual emphasis. Crafts, how-to articles, recipes should be age appropriate, safe and cheap, express newness/originality and accuracy, a clear focus, and an opening that makes kids want to read and do it. **Buys 8-10/year.** Length: 300 words maximum.

Tips "Follow the guidelines, remember the story should be interesting—carried by dialogue and action rather than narration—and appropriate for a Sunday school take-home paper. Don't send groups of stories in 1 submission."

Ⓝ $ $FACES

People, Places and Cultures, Cobblestone Publishing, 30 Grove St., Suite C, Peterborough NH 03458. (603)924-7209. Fax: (603)924-7380. E-mail: facesmag@yahoo.com. Website: www.cobblestonepub.com. **Contact:** Elizabeth Crooker, editor. **90-100% freelance written.** Monthly magazine published during school year. "*Faces* covers world culture for ages 9-14. It stands apart from other children's magazines by offering a solid look at one subject and stressing strong editorial content, color photographs throughout and original illustrations. *Faces* offers an equal balance of feature articles and activities, as well as folktales and legends." Estab. 1984. Circ. 15,000. Pays on publication. Publishes ms an average of 4 months after acceptance. Byline given. Offers 50% kill fee. Buys all rights. Editorial lead time 1 year. Accepts queries by mail, e-mail. Accepts simultaneous submissions. Sample copy for $4.95 and 7½ × 10½ (or larger) SAE with $2 postage or online. Writer's guidelines for SASE or on website.

    ○→ All material must relate to the theme of a specific upcoming issue in order to be considered. Writers new to *Faces* should send a writing sample with the query.

Nonfiction Historical/nostalgic, humor, interview/profile, personal experience, photo feature, travel, recipes, activities, puzzles, mazes. All must relate to theme. **Buys 45-50 mss/year.** Query with published clips. Length: 800 words for feature articles; 300-600 for supplemental nonfiction; up to 700 words for activities. **Pays 20-25¢/word.**

Photos State availability of photos with submission or send copies of related images for photo researcher. Reviews contact sheets, transparencies, prints. Buys one-time rights. Captions, identification of subjects, model releases required.

Fiction Ethnic, historical, retold legends or folktales. Depends on theme. Query with published clips. Length: Up to 800 words. **Pays 20-25¢/word.**

Poetry Avant-garde, free verse, haiku, light verse, traditional. Length: 100 words maximum.

Tips "Freelancers should send for a sample copy of magazine and a list of upcoming themes and writer's guidelines. The magazine is based on a monthly theme (upcoming themes include Kalahari Life, Poland, Prairie Provinces of Canada, Palestinians). We appreciate professional queries that follow our detailed writer's guidelines."

$ $ THE FRIEND

50 E. North Temple, Salt Lake City UT 84150-3226. Fax: (801)240-2270. **Contact:** Vivian Paulsen, managing editor. **50% freelance written.** Eager to work with new/unpublished writers as well as established writers. Monthly Publication of The Church of Jesus Christ of Latter-Day Saints for children ages 3-11. Circ. 275,000. **Pays on acceptance.** Buys all rights. Submit seasonal material 1 year in advance. Responds in 2 months to mss. Sample copy and writer's guidelines for $1.50 and 9×12 SAE with 4 first-class stamps.

Nonfiction "*The Friend* is particularly interested in stories based on true experiences." Special issues: Christmas, Easter. Submit complete ms with SASE. No queries, please. Length: 1,000 words maximum. **Pays $100 (200-300 words); $250 (400 words and up) minimum.**

Poetry Serious, humorous, holiday. Any form with child appeal. **Pays $50 minimum.**

Tips "Do you remember how it feels to be a child? Can you write stories that appeal to children ages 3-11 in today's world? We're interested in stories with an international flavor and those that focus on present-day problems. Send material of high literary quality slanted to our editorial requirements. Let the child solve the problem—not some helpful, all-wise adult. No overt moralizing. Nonfiction should be creatively presented—not an array of facts strung together. Beware of being cutesy."

$ $ GIRLS' LIFE

Monarch Publishing, 4517 Harford Rd., Baltimore MD 21214. E-mail: karen@girlslife.com. Website: www.girlsli fe.com. **Contact:** Karen Bokram, editor. Bimonthly magazine covering girls ages 9-15. Estab. 1994. Circ. 2,000,000. Pays on publication. Publishes ms an average of 3 months after acceptance. Byline given. Buys all rights. Editorial lead time 4 months. Submit seasonal material 5 months in advance. Accepts queries by mail. Responds in 1 month to queries. Sample copy for $5 or online. Writer's guidelines online.

Nonfiction Book excerpts, essays, general interest, how-to, humor, inspirational, interview/profile, new product, travel, beauty, relationship, sports. Special issues: Back to School (August/September); Fall, Halloween (October/November); Holidays, Winter (December/January); Valentine's Day, Crushes (February/March); Spring, Mother's Day (April/May); and Summer, Father's Day (June/July). **Buys 40 mss/year.** Query by mail with published clips. Submit complete mss on spec only. Length: 700-2,000 words. **Pays $350/regular column; $500/feature.**

Photos State availability with submission. Reviews contact sheets, negatives, transparencies. Negotiates payment individually. Captions, identification of subjects, model releases required.

Columns/Departments Buys 20 mss/year. Query with published clips. **Pays $150-450.**

Tips Send queries with published writing samples and detailed résumé. "Have new ideas, a voice that speaks to our audience—not *down* to our audience—and supply artwork source."

$ GUIDE

True Stories Pointing to Jesus, Review and Herald Publishing Association, 55 W. Oak Ridge Dr., Hagerstown MD 21740. (301)393-4037. Fax: (301)393-4055. E-mail: guide@rhpa.org. Website: www.guidemagazine.org. **Contact:** Randy Fishell, editor, or Rachel Whitaker, assistant editor. **90% freelance written.** Weekly magazine featuring all-true stories showing God's involvement in 10- to 14-year-olds' lives. Estab. 1953. Circ. 33,000. **Pays on acceptance.** Publishes ms an average of 8 months after acceptance. Byline given. Buys first North American serial, second serial (reprint) rights. Editorial lead time 8 months. Submit seasonal material 8 months in advance. Accepts queries by mail, e-mail, fax. Responds in 1 month to queries. Sample copy for SAE and 2 first-class stamps. Writer's guidelines online.

    ○ᴦ Break in with "a true story that shows in a clear way that God is involved in a 10- to 14-year-old's life."

Nonfiction Religious. "No fiction. Nonfiction should set forth a clearly evident spiritual application." **Buys 300 mss/year.** Send complete ms. Length: 750-1,500 words. **Pays $25-125.**

Reprints Send photocopy. Pays 50% of usual rates.

Fillers Games, puzzles, religious. **Buys 75/year. Pays $25-40.**

Tips "The majority of 'misses' are due to the lack of a clearly evident (not 'preachy') spiritual application."

$ HIGH ADVENTURE

General Council of the Assemblies of God/Royal Rangers, 1445 N. Boonville Ave., Springfield MO 65802-1894. (417)862-2781, ext. 4177. Fax: (417)831-8230. E-mail: royalrangers@ag.org. Website: www.royalrangers.ag.org. **Contact:** Rev. Jerry Parks, editor. **60-70% freelance written.** Quarterly magazine. "*High Adventure* is a quarterly Royal Rangers magazine for boys. This 16-page, 4-color periodical is designed to provide boys with worthwhile leisure reading to challenge them to higher ideals and greater spiritual dedication; and to perpetuate the spirit of Royal Rangers ministry through stories, crafts, ideas, and illustrations." Estab. 1971. Circ. 87,000. Pays on publication. Publishes ms an average of 6-12 months after acceptance. Buys one-time, electronic rights. Buys first or all rights. Editorial lead time 3 months. Submit seasonal material 3 months in advance. Accepts queries by mail, e-mail, fax. Accepts previously published material. Accepts simultaneous submissions. Responds in 4-6 weeks to queries; 3-6 months to mss. Sample copy and writer's guidelines for 9×12 SAE and 2 first-class stamps. Writer's guidelines for SASE, by e-mail or fax. Editorial calendar for #10 SASE.

Nonfiction General interest, historical/nostalgic, humor, inspirational, personal experience, religious. No objectionable language, innuendo, immoral, or non-Christian materials. **Buys 10-12 mss/year.** Send complete ms. Length: 200-1,000 words. **Pays 6¢/word for assigned articles.**

Fiction Rev. Jerry Parks, editor. Adventure, historical, humorous, religious, camping. No objectionable language, innuendo, immoral, or non-Christian materials. **Buys 30 mss/year.** Send complete ms. Length: 200-1,000 words. **Pays 6¢/word, plus 3 contributor's copies.**

Fillers Anecdotes, facts, short humor. **Buys 25-30/year.** Length: 25-100 words. **Pays 6¢/word.**

Tips "Consider the (middle/upper elementary) average age of readership when making a submission."

$ HIGHLIGHTS FOR CHILDREN

803 Church St., Honesdale PA 18431-1824. (570)253-1080. Fax: (570)251-7847. Website: www.highlights.com. Editor: Christine French Clark. **Contact:** Manuscript Submissions. **80% freelance written.** Monthly magazine for children ages 2-12. "This book of wholesome fun is dedicated to helping children grow in basic skills and knowledge, in creativeness, in ability to think and reason, in sensitivity to others, in high ideals, and worthy ways of living—for children are the world's most important people. We publish stories for beginning and advanced readers. Up to 500 words for beginners (ages 3-7), up to 800 words for advanced (ages 8-12)." Estab. 1946. Circ. 2,500,000. **Pays on acceptance.** Buys all rights. Accepts queries by mail. Responds in 2 months to queries. Sample copy for free. Writer's guidelines for SASE or on website.

Nonfiction "We need articles on science, technology, and nature written by persons with strong backgrounds in those fields. Contributions always welcomed from new writers, especially engineers, scientists, historians, teachers, etc., who can make useful, interesting facts accessible to children. Also writers who have lived abroad and can interpret the ways of life, especially of children, in other countries in ways that will foster world brotherhood. Sports material, arts features, biographies, and articles of general interest to children. Direct, original approach, simple style, interesting content, not rewritten from encyclopedias. State background and qualifications for writing factual articles submitted. Include references or sources of information. Articles geared toward our younger readers (3-7) especially welcome, up to 400 words. Also buys original party plans for children ages 4-12, clearly described in 300-600 words, including drawings or samples of items to be illustrated. Also, novel but tested ideas in crafts, with clear directions. Include samples. Projects must require only free or inexpensive, easy-to-obtain materials. Especially desirable if easy enough for early primary grades. Also, fingerplays with lots of action, easy for very young children to grasp and to dramatize. Avoid wordiness. We need creative-thinking puzzles that can be illustrated, optical illusions, brain teasers, games of physical agility, and other 'fun' activities." Query. Length: 800 words maximum. **Pays $50 for party plans; $25 for craft ideas; $25 for fingerplays.**

Photos Reviews color 35mm slides, photos, or electronic files.

Fiction Unusual, meaningful stories appealing to both girls and boys, ages 2-12. "Vivid, full of action. Engaging plot, strong characterization, lively language." Prefers stories in which a child protagonist solves a dilemma through his or her own resources. Seeks stories that the child ages 8-12 will eagerly read, and the child ages 2-7 will like to hear when read aloud (400-800 words). "Stories require interesting plots and a number of illustration possiblities. Also need rebuses (picture stories 125 words or under), stories with urban settings, stories for beginning readers (100-400 words), sports and humorous stories and mysteries. We also would like to see more material of 1-page length (300-400 words), both fiction and factual. War, crime, and violence are taboo."

Adventure, fantasy, historical, humorous, animal, contemporary, folktales, multi-cultural, problem-solving, sports. "No war, crime or violence." Send complete ms. **Pays $100 minimum.**

■ The online magazine carries original content not found in the print edition.

Tips "We are pleased that many authors of children's literature report that their first published work was in the pages of *Highlights*. It is not our policy to consider fiction on the strength of the reputation of the author. We judge each submission on its own merits. With factual material, however, we do prefer that writers be authorities in their field or people with first-hand experience. In this manner we can avoid the encyclopedic article that merely restates information readily available elsewhere. We don't make assignments. Query with simple letter to establish whether the nonfiction subject is likely to be of interest. A beginning writer should first become familiar with the type of material that *Highlights* publishes. Include special qualifications, if any, of author. Write for the child, not the editor. Write in a voice that children understand and relate to. Speak to today's kids, avoiding didactic, overt messages. Even though our general principles haven't changed over the years, we are contemporary in our approach to issues. Avoid worn themes.''

$ $⊘ HUMPTY DUMPTY'S MAGAZINE

Children's Better Health Institute, P.O. Box 567, Indianapolis IN 46206-0567. (317)636-8881. Fax: (317)684-8094. E-mail: cbhiseif@tcon.net. Website: www.humptydumptymag.org. **Contact:** Nancy S. Axelrad, editor. **25% freelance written.** Magazine published 8 times/year covering health, nutrition, hygiene, fitness, and safety for children ages 4-6. "Our publication is designed to entertain and to educate young readers in healthy lifestyle habits. Fiction, poetry, pencil activities should have an element of good nutrition or fitness." Estab. 1948. Circ. 350,000. Pays on publication. Publishes ms an average of 8 months after acceptance. Byline given. Buys all rights. Editorial lead time 8 months. Submit seasonal material 10 months in advance. Accepts simultaneous submissions. Sample copy for $1.75. Writer's guidelines for SASE or on website.

● All work is on speculation only; queries are not accepted nor are stories assigned.

Nonfiction "Material must have a health theme—nutrition, safety, exercise, hygiene. We're looking for articles that encourage readers to develop better health habits without preaching. Very simple factual articles that creatively teach readers about their bodies. We use several puzzles and activities in each issue—dot-to-dot, hidden pictures, and other activities that promote following instructions, developing finger dexterity, and working with numbers and letters.'' Include word count. **Buys 3-4 mss/year.** Send complete ms. Length: 300 words maximum. **Pays 22¢/word.**

Photos Send photos with submission. Buys all rights. Offers no additonal payment for photos accepted with ms.

Columns/Departments Mix & Fix (no-cook recipes), 100 words. All ingredients must be nutritious—low fat, no sugar, etc.—and tasty. **Buys 8 mss/year.** Send complete ms. **Payment varies.**

Fiction Phyllis Lybarger, editor. "We use some stories in rhyme and a few easy-to-read stories for the beginning reader. All stories should work well as read-alouds. Currently we need health/sports/fitness stories. We try to present our health material in a positive light, incorporating humor and a light approach wherever possible. Avoid stereotyping. Characters in contemporary stories should be realistic and reflect good, wholesome values.'' Include word count. Juvenile health-related material. "No inanimate talking objects, animal stories and science fiction.'' **Buys 4-6 mss/year.** Send complete ms. Length: 350 words maximum. **Pays 22¢/word for stories, plus 10 contributor's copies.**

Tips "We would like to see more holiday stories, articles and activities. Please send seasonal material at least eight months in advance.''

$ $ JACK AND JILL

Children's Better Health Institute, P.O. Box 567, Indianapolis IN 46206-0567. (317)636-8881. Fax: (317)684-8094. E-mail: cbhiseif@tcon.net. Website: www.jackandjillmag.org. **Contact:** Daniel Lee, editor. **50% freelance written.** Bimonthly Magazine published 8 times/year for children ages 7-10. "Material will not be returned unless accompanied by SASE with sufficient postage.'' No queries. May hold material being seriously considered for up to 1 year. Estab. 1938. Circ. 200,000. Pays on publication. Publishes ms an average of 8 months after acceptance. Byline given. Buys all rights. Submit seasonal material 8 months in advance. Responds in 10 weeks to mss. Sample copy for $1.75. Writer's guidelines online.

○➔ Break in with nonfiction about ordinary kids with a news hook—something that ties in with current events, matters the kids are seeing on television and in mainstream news—i.e., space exploration, scientific advances, sports, etc.

Nonfiction "Because we want to encourage youngsters to read for pleasure and for information, we are interested in material that will challenge a young child's intelligence *and* be enjoyable reading. Our emphasis is on good health, and we are in particular need of articles, stories, and activities with health, safety, exercise, and nutrition themes. We try to present our health material in a positive light—incorporating humor and a light approach wherever possible without minimizing the seriousness of what we are saying. Straight factual articles are OK if they are short and interestingly written. We would rather see, however, more creative alternatives to the straight factual article. Items with a news hook will get extra attention. We'd like to see articles about interesting kids involved in out-of-the-ordinary activities. We're also interested in articles about people with unusual hobbies for our Hobby Shop department." **Buys 10-15 mss/year.** Send complete ms. Length: 500-800 words. **Pays 17¢/word minimum.**

Photos When appropriate, photos should accompany ms. Reviews sharp, contrasting b&w glossy prints. Sometimes uses color slides, transparencies, or good color prints. Buys one-time rights. Pays $15/photo.

Fiction May include, but is not limited to, realistic stories, fantasy, adventure—set in past, present, or future. "All stories need a well-developed plot, action, and incident. Humor is highly desirable. Stories that deal with a health theme need not have health as the primary subject." Adventure, historical, humorous, mystery, science fiction, sports. Wants health-related stories with a subtle lesson. **Buys 20-25 mss/year.** Send complete ms. Length: 500-800 words. **Pays 15¢/word minimum.**

Fillers Puzzles (including various kinds of word and crossword puzzles), poems, games, science projects, and creative craft projects. "We get a lot of these. To be selected, an item needs a little extra spark and originality. Instructions for activities should be clearly and simply written and accompanied by models or diagram sketches. We also have a need for recipes. Ingredients should be healthful; avoid sugar, salt, chocolate, red meat, and fats as much as possible. In all material, avoid references to eating sugary foods, such as candy, cakes, cookies, and soft drinks."

Tips "We are constantly looking for new writers who can tell good stories with interesting slants—stories that are not full of out-dated and time-worn expressions. We like to see stories about kids who are smart and capable, but not sarcastic or smug. Problem-solving skills, personal responsibility, and integrity are good topics for us. Obtain *current* issues of the magazine and *study* them to determine our present needs and editorial style."

N $ $ $ JUNIOR SCHOLASTIC

Scholastic, Inc., 557 Broadway, 4th Floor, New York NY 10012-3902. (212)343-6100. Fax: (212)343-6945. E-mail: junior@scholastic.com. Website: www.juniorscholastic.com. Editor: Suzanne McCabe. Magazine published 18 times/year. Edited for students aged 11-14. Circ. 535,000. Editorial lead time 6 weeks. Sample copy not available.

$ $ LADYBUG

The Magazine for Young Children, Carus Publishing Co., P.O. Box 300, Peru IL 61354-0300. (815)224-5803 ext. 656. Editor-in-Chief: Marianne Carus. **Contact:** Paula Morrow, executive editor. Monthly magazine for children ages 2-6. "We look for quality writing—quality literature, no matter the subject. For young children, ages 2-6." Estab. 1990. Circ. 134,000. Pays on publication. Byline given. For recurring features, pays flat fee and copyright becomes property of Cricket Magazine Group. Buys second serial (reprint), all rights. Rights purchased vary. Submit seasonal material 1 year in advance. Accepts previously published material. Responds in 3 months to mss. Sample copy for $5 and 9×12 SAE. Guidelines only for #10 SASE or online.

• *Ladybug* needs imaginative activities based on concepts and interesting, appropriate nonfiction. See sample issues. Also needs articles and parent-child activities for its online parent's companion.

Nonfiction Can You Do This?, 1-2 pages; The World Around You, 2-4 pages; activities based on concepts (size, color, sequence, comparison, etc.), 1-2 pages. "Most *Ladybug* nonfiction is in the form of illustration. We'd like more simple science, how-things-work, and behind the scenes on a preschool level." **Buys 35 mss/year.** Send complete ms; no queries. Length: 250-300 words. **Pays 25¢/word.**

Fiction Marianne Carus, editor-in-chief; Paula Morrow, editor. "Looking for age-appropriate read-aloud stories for preschoolers." **Buys 30 mss/year.** Send complete ms. Length: 800 words maximum. **Pays 25¢/word (less for reprints).**

Poetry Light verse, traditional, humorous. **Buys 40 poems/year.** Submit maximum 5 poems. Length: 20 lines maximum. **Pays $3/line, with $25 minimum.**

Fillers "We welcome interactive activities: rebuses, up to 100 words; *original* fingerplays and action rhymes (up to 8 lines)." Anecdotes, facts, short humor. **Buys 10/year.** Length: 100 words maximum. **Pays 25¢/word.**

Tips "Reread manuscript *before* sending in. Keep within specified word limits. Study back issues before submitting to learn about the types of material we're looking for. Writing style is paramount. We look for rich, evocative language and a sense of joy or wonder. Remember that you're writing for preschoolers—be age-appropriate but not condescending. A story must hold enjoyment for both parent and child through repeated read-aloud sessions. Remember that people come in all colors, sizes, physical conditions, and have special needs. Be inclusive!"

$ MY FRIEND

The Catholic Magazine for Kids, Pauline Books & Media/Daughters of St. Paul, 50 Saint Pauls Ave., Jamaica Plain, Boston MA 02130-3491. (617)522-8911. Fax: (617)541-9805. E-mail: myfriend@pauline.org. Website:

www.myfriendmagazine.org. Editor-in-Chief: Sister Donna William Giaimo. **Contact:** Sister Maria Grace Dateno, editor. **25% freelance written.** Magazine published 10 times/year for children ages 7-12. *"My Friend* is a 32-page monthly Catholic magazine for boys and girls. Its goal is to communicate religious truths and positive values in an enjoyable and attractive way." Theme list available. Send a SASE to the above address, or see website (click on "For Contributors"). Estab. 1979. Circ. 8,000. **Pays on acceptance.** Publishes ms an average of 6 months after acceptance. Buys worldwide publication rights. Responds in 2 months to mss. Sample copy for $2 and 9×12 SASE ($1.29). Writer's guidelines and theme list for #10 SASE.

Fiction "We are looking for stories that immediately grab the imagination of the reader. Good dialogue, realistic character development, current lingo are necessary. A child protagonist must resolve a dilemma through his or her own resources. Not all the stories of each issue have to be directly related to the theme. We continue to need stories that are simply fun and humorous. We also appreciate an underlying awareness of current events and current global tensions. Ever since September 11, kids are very sensitive to such realities." Religious, sports. Send complete ms. Length: 600-1,200 words. **Pays $75-150.**

Tips "For fiction, we prefer the submission of manuscripts to query letters. If you are not sure whether a story would be appropriate for *My Friend*, please request our complete guidelines, theme list, and a sample issue (see above). For nonfiction articles, you may query by e-mail, but most are written by staff and contributing authors."

$ NATURE FRIEND

Carlisle Press, 2673 TR 421, Sugarcreek OH 44681. (330)852-1900. Fax: (330)852-3285. **Contact:** Marvin Wengerd, editor. **80% freelance written.** Monthly magazine covering nature. *"Nature Friend* includes stories, puzzles, science experiments, nature experiments—all submissions need to honor God as creator." Estab. 1983. Circ. 13,000. Pays on publication. Byline given. Buys first, one-time rights. Editorial lead time 4 months. Submit seasonal material 3 months in advance. Accepts simultaneous submissions. Responds in 6 months to mss. Sample copy and writer's guidelines for $4 postage paid.

    O⇥ Break in with a "conversational story about a nature subject that imparts knowledge and instills Christian values."

Nonfiction How-to (nature, science experiments), photo feature, articles about interesting/unusual animals. No poetry, evolution, animals depicted in captivity. **Buys 50 mss/year.** Send complete ms. Length: 250-900 words. **Pays 5¢/word.**

Photos Send photos with submission. Reviews prints. Buys one-time rights. Offers $35-50/photo. Captions, identification of subjects required.

Columns/Departments Learning By Doing, 500-900 words. "I need more hands-on, how-to articles." **Buys 20 mss/year.** Send complete ms.

Fillers Facts, puzzles, short essays on something current in nature. **Buys 35/year.** Length: 150-250 words. **Pays 5¢/word.**

Tips "We want to bring joy and knowledge to children by opening the world of God's creation to them. We endeavor to create a sense of awe about nature's creator and a respect for His creation. I'd like to see more submissions on hands-on things to do with a nature theme (not collecting rocks or leaves—real stuff). Also looking for good stories that are accompanied by good photography."

$ $ NEW MOON

The Magazine for Girls & Their Dreams, New Moon Publishing, Inc., 34 E. Superior St., #200, Duluth MN 55802. (218)728-5507. Fax: (218)728-0314. E-mail: girl@newmoon.org. Website: www.newmoon.org. **Contact:** Editorial Department. **25% freelance written.** Bimonthly magazine covering girls ages 8-14, edited by girls aged 8-14. "In general, all material should be pro-girl and feature girls and women as the primary focus. *New Moon* is for every girl who wants her voice heard and her dreams taken seriously. *New Moon* celebrates girls, explores the passage from girl to woman, and builds healthy resistance to gender inequities. The *New Moon* girl is true to herself and *New Moon* helps her as she pursues her unique path in life, moving confidently into the world." Estab. 1992. Circ. 30,000. Pays on publication. Publishes ms an average of 6 months after acceptance. Byline given. Buys all rights. Editorial lead time 6 months. Submit seasonal material 8 months in advance. Accepts queries by mail, e-mail, fax. Accepts simultaneous submissions. Responds in 2 months to mss. Sample copy for $6.75 or online. Writer's guidelines for SASE or online.

    O⇥ Adult writers can break in with "Herstory articles about less well-known women from all over the world, especially if it relates to one of our themes. Same with Women's Work articles. Girls can break in with essays and articles (nonfiction) that relate to a theme."

Nonfiction Essays, general interest, humor, inspirational, interview/profile, opinion, personal experience (written by girls), photo feature, religious, travel, multicultural/girls from other countries. No fashion, beauty, or dating. **Buys 20 mss/year.** Query with or without published clips or send complete ms. Length: 600 words. **Pays 6-12¢/word.**

Photos State availability with submission. Buys one-time rights. Negotiates payment individually. Captions, identification of subjects required.

Columns/Departments Women's Work (profile of a woman and her job(s) relating the the theme), 600 words; Herstory (historical woman relating to theme), 600 words. **Buys 10 mss/year.** Query. **Pays 6-12¢/word.**

Fiction Prefers girl-written material. All girl-centered. Adventure, fantasy, historical, humorous, slice-of-life vignettes. **Buys 6 mss/year.** Send complete ms. Length: 900-1,200 words. **Pays 6-12¢/word.**

Poetry No poetry by adults.

Tips "We'd like to see more girl-written feature articles that relate to a theme. These can be about anything the girl has done personally, or she can write about something she's studied. Please read *New Moon* before submitting to get a sense of our style. Writers and artists who comprehend our goals have the best chance of publication. We love creative articles—both nonfiction and fiction—that are not condescending to our readers. Keep articles to suggested word lengths; avoid stereotypes. Refer to our guidelines and upcoming themes."

$ON THE LINE

Mennonite Publishing House, 616 Walnut Ave., Scottdale PA 15683-1999. (724)887-8500. Fax: (724)887-3111. E-mail: ofl@mph.org. Website: www.mph.org. **Contact:** Mary Clemens Meyer, editor. **90% freelance written.** Works with a small number of new/unpublished writers each year. Monthly Christian magazine for children ages 9-14. "*On the Line* helps upper elementary and junior high children understand and appreciate God, the created world, themselves, and others." Estab. 1908. Circ. 5,500. **Pays on acceptance.** Publishes ms an average of 1 year after acceptance. Byline given. Buys one-time rights. Submit seasonal material 6 months in advance. Accepts queries by e-mail. Accepts previously published material. Accepts simultaneous submissions. Responds in 1 month to mss. Sample copy for 9×12 SAE and 2 first-class stamps. Writer's guidelines for 9X12 SAE and 2 first-class stamps.

Nonfiction How-to (things to make with easy-to-get materials including food recipes), informational (300-500 word articles on wonders of nature, people who have made outstanding contributions). **Buys 95 mss/year.** Send complete ms. **Pays $15-35.**

Reprints Send ms with rights for sale noted and information about when and where the material previously appeared. Pays 75% of amount paid for an original article.

Photos Pays $50-75. Buying color photos of kids, ages 10-14, for cover use. Digital photos or electronic image files only.

Fiction Mary Clemens Meyer. Adventure, humorous, religious, everyday problems. No fantasy or fictionalized Bible stories. Wants more mystery and humorous. **Buys 50 mss/year.** Send complete ms. Length: 1,000-1,800 words. **Pays 3-5¢/word.**

Poetry Light verse, religious. Length: 3-12 lines. **Pays $10-25.**

Fillers Appropriate puzzles, cartoons, and quizzes.

Tips "Study the publication first. We need short, well-written how-to and craft articles; also more puzzles. Don't send query; we prefer to see the complete manuscript."

$ $POCKETS

The Upper Room, 1908 Grand Ave., P.O. Box 340004, Nashville TN 37203-0004. (615)340-7333. Fax: (615)340-7267. E-mail: pockets@upperroom.org. Website: www.pockets.org.; www.upperroom.org/pockets. **Contact:** Lynn Gilliam, editor. **60% freelance written.** Monthly (except February) magazine covering children's and families' spiritual formation. "We are a Christian, inter-denominational publication for children 6-11 years of age. Each issue reflects a specific theme." Estab. 1981. Circ. 94,000. **Pays on acceptance.** Publishes ms an average of 1 year to 18 months after acceptance. Byline given. Buys first North American serial rights. Submit seasonal material 1 year in advance. Accepts previously published material. Responds in 6 weeks to mss. Sample copy for 9×12 SAE and 4 first-class stamps. Writer's guidelines, themes, and due dates available online.

• *Pockets* publishes fiction and poetry, as well as short-short stories (no more than 600 words) for children 5-7. They publish 1 of these stories/issue. Eager to work with new/unpublished writers.

Nonfiction Each issue reflects a specific theme; themes available online or send #10 SASE. Interview/profile, personal experience, religious (retold scripture stories). No violence or romance. **Buys 5 mss/year.** Length: 400-1,000 words. **Pays 14¢/word.**

Reprints Accepts one-time previously published submissions. Send typed ms with rights for sale noted and information about when and where the material previously appeared.

Photos No photos unless they accompany an article. Send photos with submission. Reviews contact sheets, transparencies, prints. Buys one-time rights. Pays $25/photo.

Columns/Departments Poetry and Prayer (related to themes), maximum 24 lines; Pocketsful of Love (family communications activities), 300 words; Peacemakers at Work (profiles of children working for peace, justice, and ecological concerns), 300-800 words. **Pays 14¢/word.** Activities/Games (related to themes). **Pays $25 and**

up. Kids Cook (simple recipes children can make alone or with minimal help from an adult). **Pays $25. Buys 20 mss/year.**

Fiction Lynn W. Gilliam, associate editor. "Submissions do not need to be overtly religious. They should reflect daily living, lifestyle, and problem-solving based on living as faithful disciples. They should help children experience the Christian life that is not always a neatly wrapped moral package but is open to the continuing revelation of God's will for their lives." Adventure, ethnic, historical, religious, slice-of-life vignettes. No fantasy, science fiction, talking animals. **Buys 44 mss/year.** Send complete ms. Length: 600-1,400 words. **Pays 14¢/word, plus 2-5 contributor's copies.**

Poetry Buys 22 poems/year. Length: 4-24 lines. **Pays $2/line, $25 minimum.**

■ The online magazine carries original content not found in the print edition and includes writer's guidelines, themes, and fiction-writing contest guidelines. Contact: Lynn Gilliam, associate editor.

Tips "Theme stories, role models, and retold scripture stories are most open to freelancers. Poetry is also open. It is very helpful if writers read our writer's guidelines and themes on our website. We have an annual fiction writing contest. Contest guidelines available with #10 SASE or on our website."

SCIENCE WORLD

Scholastic, Inc., 557 Broadway, New York NY 10012-3902. (212)343-6100. Fax: (212)343-6945. E-mail: scienceworld@scholastic.com. Website: www.scholastic.com. Editor: Patty Jones. Biweekly magazine. Science publication for students grades 7-10. Circ. 404,597. Editorial lead time 3 weeks. Sample copy not available.

[N] $ SHINE BRIGHTLY

GEMS Girls' Clubs, P.O. Box 7259, Grand Rapids MI 49510. (616)241-5616. Fax: (616)241-5558. E-mail: sara@gemsgc.org. Website: www.gospelcom.net/gems. Editor: Jan Boone. **Contact:** Sara Lynne Hilton, managing editor. **80% freelance written.** Works with new and published/established writers. Monthly magazine "to show girls ages 9-14 how God is at work in their lives and in the world around them. Our purpose is to lead girls into a living relationship with Jesus Christ and to help them see how God is at work in their lives and the world around them. Puzzles, crafts, stories, and articles for girls ages 9-14." Estab. 1971. Circ. 13,000. Pays on publication. Publishes ms an average of 1 year after acceptance. Byline given. Buys first North American serial, second serial (reprint), simultaneous rights. Submit seasonal material 1 year in advance. Accepts previously published material. Accepts simultaneous submissions. Responds in 2 months to queries. Sample copy for 9×12 SAE with 3 first class stamps and $1. Writer's guidelines online.

Nonfiction "We do not want easy solutions or quick character changes from good to bad. No pietistic characters. No 'new girl at school starting over after parents' divorce' stories. Constant mention of God is not necessary if the moral tone of the story is positive. We do not want stories that always have a happy ending." Needs include: biographies and autobiographies of "heroes of the faith," informational (write for issue themes), multicultural materials. Humor (need much more), inspirational, interview/profile, personal experience (avoid the testimony approach), photo feature (query first), religious, travel. **Buys 35 unsolicited mss/year.** Send complete ms. Length: 200-800 words. **Pays 3¢/word, plus 2 copies.**

Reprints Send ms with rights for sale noted and information about when and where the material previously appeared.

Photos Purchased with or without ms. Appreciate multicultural subjects. Reviews 5×7 or 8×10 clear color glossy prints. Pays $25-50 on publication.

Columns/Departments How-to (crafts); puzzles and jokes; quizzes. Length: 200-400 words. Send complete ms. **Pay varies.**

Fiction Adventure, ethnic, historical, humorous, mystery, religious, romance, slice-of-life vignettes, suspense. **Buys 20 mss/year.** Send complete ms. Length: 400-1,000 words. **Pays $20-50.**

Poetry Free verse, haiku, light verse, traditional.

Tips "Prefers not to see anything on the adult level, secular material, or violence. Writers frequently oversimplify the articles and often write with a Pollyanna attitude. An author should be able to see his/her writing style as exciting and appealing to girls ages 9-14. The style can be fun, but also teach a truth. Subjects should be current and important to *SHINE brightly* readers. Use our theme update as a guide. We would like to receive material with a multicultural slant."

$ $ SPIDER

The Magazine for Children, Cricket Magazine Group, P.O. Box 300, Peru IL 61354. (815)224-5803. Fax: (815)224-6615. Website: www.cricketmag.com. Editor: Heather Delabre. **Contact:** Submissions Editor. **85% freelance written.** Monthly magazine covering literary, general interest. "*Spider* introduces 6- to 9-year-old children to the highest quality stories, poems, illustrations, articles, and activities. It was created to foster in beginning readers a love of reading and discovery that will last a lifetime. We're looking for writers who respect children's intelligence." Estab. 1994. Circ. 79,000. Pays on publication. Publishes ms an average of 2-3 years after accep-

.tance. Byline given. Rights vary. Editorial lead time 9 months. Accepts previously published material. Accepts simultaneous submissions. Responds in 3 months to mss. Sample copy for $5. Writer's guidelines for #10 SASE or on website.

Nonfiction A bibliography is required with all nonfiction submissions. Nature, animals, science & technology, environment, foreign culture, history. Send complete ms. Length: 300-800 words. **Pays 25¢/word.**

Reprints Send photocopy with rights for sale noted and information about when and where the material previously appeared.

Photos Send photos with submission. Reviews contact sheets, 35mm to 4×4 transparencies, 8×10 prints. Buys one-time rights. Offers $35-50/photo. Captions, identification of subjects, model releases required.

Fiction Marianne Carus, editor-in-chief; Heather Delabre, editor. Adventure, ethnic, fantasy, historical, humorous, mystery, science fiction, suspense, realistic fiction, folk tales, fairy tales. No romance, horror, religious. Send complete ms. Length: 300-1,000 words. **Pays 25¢/word and 2 contributor's copies; additional copies $2.**

Poetry Free verse, traditional, nonsense, humorous, serious. No forced rhymes, didactic. Submit maximum 5 poems. Length: 20 lines maximum. **Pays $3/line maximum.**

Fillers Puzzles, crafts, recipes, mazes, games, brainteasers, engaging math and word activities. **Payment depends on type of filler.**

Tips "We'd like to see more of the following: engaging nonfiction, fillers, and 'takeout page' activities; folktales, fairy tales, science fiction, and humorous stories. Most importantly, do not write down to children."

Ⓝ $ $ $ SPORTS ILLUSTRATED FOR KIDS

Time-Warner, Sports Illustrated Building, 135 W. 50th St., 4th Floor, New York NY 10020. (212)522-3112. Fax: (212)522-0120. Website: www.sikids.com. Publisher: Peter Krieger. **Contact:** Editorial Administrator. **20% freelance written.** Monthly magazine on sports for children 8 years old and up. Content is divided 20/80 between sports as played by kids, and sports as played by professionals. Estab. 1989. **Pays on acceptance.** Publishes ms an average of 3 months after acceptance. Byline given. Offers 25% kill fee. Buys all rights. Accepts queries by mail, fax. For sample copy call (800)992-0196. Writer's guidelines for #10 SASE.

Nonfiction General interest, how-to, humor, inspirational, interview/profile, photo feature, Games, puzzles. **Buys 15 mss/year.** Query with published clips. Length: 100-1,500 words. **Pays $75-1,000 for assigned articles; $75-800 for unsolicited articles.** Pays expenses of writers on assignment.

Photos State availability with submission. Buys one-time rights.

> ▣ The online magazine carries original content not found in the print edition. Contact: Peter Kay, Director of New Media.

$ STONE SOUP

The Magazine by Young Writers and Artists, Children's Art Foundation, P.O. Box 83, Santa Cruz CA 95063-0083. (831)426-5557. Fax: (831)426-1161. E-mail: editor@stonesoup.com. Website: www.stonesoup.com. **Contact:** Ms. Gerry Mandel, editor. **100% freelance written.** Bimonthly magazine of writing and art by children, including fiction, poetry, book reviews, and art by children through age 13. Audience is children, teachers, parents, writers, artists. "We have a preference for writing and art based on real-life experiences; no formula stories or poems." Estab. 1973. Circ. 20,000. Pays on publication. Publishes ms an average of 4 months after acceptance. Buys all rights. Submit seasonal material 6 months in advance. Sample copy for $5 or online. Writer's guidelines online.

> ● Don't send queries, just submissions. No e-mail submissions. "Please do not enclose a SASE. We only respond to work we want to publish. If you do not hear from us within 6 weeks, it means we could not use your work."

Nonfiction Historical/nostalgic, personal experience, book reviews. **Buys 12 mss/year. Pays $40.**

Fiction Adventure, ethnic, experimental, fantasy, historical, humorous, mystery, science fiction, slice-of-life vignettes, suspense. "We do not like assignments or formula stories of any kind." **Buys 60 mss/year.** Send complete ms. Length: 150-2,500 words. **Pays $40 for stories. Authors also receive 2 copies, a certificate, and discounts on additional copies and on subscriptions.**

Poetry Avant-garde, free verse. **Buys 12 poems/year. Pays $40/poem.**

> ▣ The online magazine carries original content not found in the print edition and includes writer's guidelines. Contact: Ms. Gerry Mandel, online editor.

Tips "All writing we publish is by young people ages 13 and under. We do not publish any writing by adults. We can't emphasize enough how important it is to read a couple of issues of the magazine. We have a strong preference for writing on subjects that mean a lot to the author. If you feel strongly about something that happened to you or something you observed, use that feeling as the basis for your story or poem. Stories should have good descriptions, realistic dialogue, and a point to make. In a poem, each word must be chosen carefully. Your poem should present a view of your subject, and a way of using words that are special and all your own."

$ $ TURTLE MAGAZINE FOR PRESCHOOL KIDS

Children's Better Health Institute, P.O. Box 567, Indianapolis IN 46206-0567. Website: www.turtlemag.org. Bimonthly magazine. General interest, interactive magazine with the purpose of helping preschoolers develop healthy minds and bodies. Magazine of picture stories and articles for preschool children 2-5 years old. Estab. 1978. Circ. 300,000. Pays on publication. Byline given. Buys all rights. Submit seasonal material 8 months in advance. Responds in 3 months to queries. Sample copy for $1.75. Writer's guidelines for #10 SASE.

• May hold mss for up to 1 year before acceptance/publication.

Nonfiction "We use very simple science experiments. These should be pretested. We also publish simple, healthful recipes." Length: 100-300 words. **Pays up to 22¢/word.**

Fiction "Not buying much fiction right now except for rebus stories. All material should have a health or fitness slant. We no longer buy stories about 'generic' turtles because we now have PokeyToes, our own trade-marked turtle character. All should 'move along' and lend themselves well to illustration. Writing should be energetic, enthusiastic, and creative—like preschoolers themselves. No queries, please." No queries. Send complete ms. Length: 150-300 words. **Pays up to 22¢/word, plus 10 contributor's copies.** "We use short verse on our inside front cover and back cover."

Tips "We are looking for more short rebus stories, easy science experiments, and simple, nonfiction health articles. We are trying to include more material for our youngest readers. Material must be entertaining and written from a healthy lifestyle perspective."

LITERARY & "LITTLE"

N $ THE ABSINTHE LITERARY REVIEW

P.O. Box 328, Spring Green WI 53588. Website: www.absinthe-literary-review.com. **Contact:** Charles Allen Wyman, editor. "*ALR* publishes short stories, novel excerpts, poems and literary essays. Our target audience is the literate individual who enjoys creative language use, character-driven fiction and the clashing of worlds— real and surreal, poetic and prosaic, sacred and transgressive." Accepts queries by mail, e-mail. Sample copy not available.

Fiction "Transgressive works dealing with sex, death, disease, madness, and the like; the clash of archaic with modern-day; archetype, symbolism; surrealism, philosophy, physics; existential and post-modern flavoring; experimental or flagrantly textured (but not sloppy or casual) fiction; intense crafting of language from the writer's writer. See website for information on the Absinthe Editors' Prize. Anathemas: mainstream storytellers, 'Oprah' fiction, high school or beginner fiction, poetry or fiction that contains no capital letters or punctuation, 'hot' trends, genre prose or poetry, first, second or third drafts, pieces that exceed our stated word count (5,000 max.) by thousands of words, writers who do not read and follow our onsite guidelines." **Pays $2-10.**

Poetry Pays $1-10.

$ AFRICAN AMERICAN REVIEW

Saint Louis University, Shannon Hall 119, 220 N. Grand Blvd., St. Louis MO 63103-2007. (314)977-3703. Fax: (314)977-3649. E-mail: keenanam@slu.edu. Website: aar.slu.edu. Editor: Joe Weixlmann. **Contact:** Aileen Keenan, managing editor. **65% freelance written.** Quarterly magazine covering African-American literature and culture. "Essays on African-American literature, theater, film, art and culture generally; interviews; poetry and fiction by African-American authors; book reviews." Estab. 1967. Circ. 2,067. Pays on publication. Publishes ms an average of 1-2 years after acceptance. Byline given. Buys first North American serial rights. Editorial lead time 1 year. Responds in 1 month to queries; 6 months to mss. Sample copy for $12. Writer's guidelines online.

Nonfiction Essays, interview/profile. **Buys 30 mss/year.** Query. Length: 3,500-6,000 words. **Pays $50-150.** Pays in contributors copies upon request.

Photos State availability with submission. Pays $100 for covers. Captions required.

Fiction Joe Weixlmann, editor. Ethnic, experimental, mainstream. "No children's/juvenile/young adult/teen." **Buys 5 mss/year.** Length: 2,500-5,000 words. **Pays $25-100, 3 contributor's copies and 10 offprints.**

$ AGNI

Dept. NM, Creative Writing Program, Boston University, 236 Bay State Rd., Boston MA 02215. (617)353-7135. Fax: (617)353-7134. E-mail: agni@bu.edu. Website: agni.bu.edu. **Contact:** Sven Birkerts, editor. Biannual magazine. "Eclectic literary magazine publishing first-rate poems, essays, translations, and stories." Estab. 1972. Circ. 4,000. Pays on publication. Publishes ms an average of 6 months after acceptance. Byline given. Buys first North American serial rights. Rights to reprint in *AGNI* anthology (with author's consent). Editorial lead time 1 year. Accepts queries by mail. Accepts simultaneous submissions. Responds in 2 weeks to queries; 4 months to mss. Sample copy for $10 or online. Writer's guidelines for #10 SASE or email agni@bu.edu.

• Reading period September 1-May 31 only.

Fiction Stories, prose poems. "No science fiction or romance." **Buys 6-12 mss/year. Pays $10/page up to $150, 2 contributor's copies, 1-year subscription, and 4 gift copies.**

Poetry Buys more than 140 poems/year. Submit maximum 5 poems. with SASE **Pays $20-150.**

▣ The online magazine carries original content not found in the print edition. Contact: Sven Birkerts, editor.

Tips "We're looking for extraordinary translations from little-translated languages. It is important to look at a copy of *AGNI* before submitting, to see if your work might be compatible. Please write for guidelines or a sample."

$ $ALASKA QUARTERLY REVIEW

ESB 208, University of Alaska-Anchorage, 3211 Providence Dr., Anchorage AK 99508. (907)786-6916. E-mail: ayaqr@uaa.alaska.edu. Website: www.uaa.alaska.edu/aqr. **Contact:** Ronald Spatz, executive editor. **95% freelance written.** Semiannual magazine publishing fiction, poetry, literary nonfiction, and short plays in traditional and experimental styles. *AQR* "publishes fiction, poetry, literary nonfiction and short plays in traditional and experimental styles." Estab. 1982. Circ. 3,500. Honorariums on publication when funding permits. Publishes ms an average of 6 months after acceptance. Byline given. Buys first North American serial rights. Upon request, rights will be transferred back to author after publication. Accepts queries by mail. Responds in 1 month to queries; 6 months to mss. Sample copy for $6. Writer's guidelines online.

• *Alaska Quarterly* reports they are always looking for freelance material and new writers.

Nonfiction Literary nonfiction: essays and memoirs. **Buys 0-5 mss/year.** Query. Length: 1,000-20,000 words. **Pays $50-200 subject to funding.** Pays in contributor's copies and subscription when funding is limited.

Fiction Ronald Spatz, fiction editor. Experimental and traditional literary forms. No romance, children's, or inspirational/religious. Publishes novel excerpts. **Buys 20-26 mss/year.** Also publishes drama: experimental and traditional one-act plays. **Buys 0-2 mss/year.** Experimental, contemporary, prose poem. "If the works in *Alaska Quarterly Review* have certain characteristics, they are these: freshness, honesty, and a compelling subject. What makes a piece stand out from the multitude of other submissions? The voice of the piece must be strong—idiosyncratic enough to create a unique persona. We look for the demonstration of craft, making the situation palpable and putting it in a form where it becomes emotionally and intellectually complex. One could look through our pages over time and see that many of the pieces published in the *Alaska Quarterly Review* concern everyday life. We're not asking our writers to go outside themselves and their experiences to the absolute exotic to catch our interest. We look for the experiential and revelatory qualities of the work. We will, without hesitation, champion a piece that may be less polished or stylistically sophisticated, if it engages me, surprises me, and resonates for me. The joy in reading such a work is in discovering something true. Moreover, in keeping with our mission to publish new writers, we are looking for voices our readers do not know, voices that may not always be reflected in the dominant culture and that, in all instances, have something important to convey." Length: not exceeding 100 pages. **Pays $50-200 subject to funding; pays in contributor's copies and subscriptions when funding is limited.**

Poetry Avant-garde, free verse, traditional. No light verse. **Buys 10-30 poems/year.** Submit maximum 10 poems. **Pays $10-50 subject to availability of funds; pays in contributor's copies and subscriptions when funding is limited.**

▣ The online magazine carries original content not found in the print edition and includes writer's guidelines.

Tips "All sections are open to freelancers. We rely almost exclusively on unsolicited manuscripts. *AQR* is a nonprofit literary magazine and does not always have funds to pay authors."

N $AMBITIONS MAGAZINE

The City of Light Magazine, P.O. Box 13486, St. Petersburg FL 33733. E-mail: ambitionscoffee@hotmail.com. **Contact:** Ben Scarlato, publisher. **100% freelance written.** Monthly magazine covering "great fiction." "*Ambitions* is a 20-page literary magazine photocopied at the local copy shop. Right now, *Ambitions* is growing trying to reach everyone throughout America. This magazine is opening all doorways of free expression to bring out the artist within." Estab. 2003. Circ. 100. Pays on publication. Publishes ms an average of 3 months after acceptance. Byline sometimes given. Buys one-time rights. Accepts queries by mail, e-mail. Accepts simultaneous submissions. Responds in 3 weeks to mss. Writer's guidelines by e-mail.

Nonfiction Essays, humor, personal experience. Query. Length: Length: 200 words. **Pays 1¢/word.** Pays in contributor copies for fiction because of length.

Columns/Departments Mr. Advice and Mrs. Crow (a fun, organized advice column about anything); Science Table (astronomy and NASA experiments); The Culture Searchlight (writer's point of view of life and what can be improved); all 200 words. **Buys 10 mss/year.** Query. **Pays 1-2¢/word.**

Fiction Adventure, condensed novels, experimental, fantasy, historical, mystery, novel excerpts, science fiction, serialized novels, suspense. No pornography or anything offensive, no blood-shed stories, and nothing mainstream. **Buys 12 mss/year.** Length: 1,000-2,000 words. **Pays 3 contributor copies.**

Poetry Avant-garde, free verse, light verse. Nothing racist or mainstream. **Buys 12 poems/year.** Submit maximum 3 poems. Length: 5-30 lines.

Fillers Gags to be illustrated by cartoonist. **Buys 20/year.** Length: 10-30 words. **Pays 1¢/word.**

Tips "Be interesting and break away from the mainstream storm. Be yourself, this is a creative magazine. Nothing childish will be accepted. Be daring and serious with your art. Paint your words with a kindness and a willingness to be rebellious to the rest of the world. Have surprises and forget the mainstream artist world. This magazine is growing in a new roadway of expression."

$ THE AMERICAN DISSIDENT

ContraOstrich Press, 1837 Main St., Concord MA 01742. E-mail: enmarge@aol.com. Website: www.geocities. com/enmarge. **Contact:** G. Tod Slone, editor. **100% freelance written.** Semiannual magazine "offering hardcore criticism of all American icons and institutions in English, French, or Spanish. Writers must be free of dogma, clear in mind, critical in outlook, and courageous in behavior." Estab. 1998. Circ. 200. Pays on publication. Publishes ms an average of 9 months after acceptance. Byline given. Buys first North American serial, one-time rights. Editorial lead time 6 months. Accepts queries by mail. Responds in 3 weeks to queries; 2 months to mss. Sample copy for $8. Writer's guidelines online.

Nonfiction Essays, interview/profile, opinion, personal experience. **Buys 2-4 mss/year.** Query. Length: 250-750 words. **Pays $5 for assigned articles.** Pays in contributor's copies for poetry submissions and book reviews.

Photos State availability with submission. Reviews prints. Buys one-time rights. Negotiates payment individually. Identification of subjects required.

Poetry Free verse. Poetry with a message, not poetry for the sake of poetry. Submit maximum 3-5 poems.

Tips "*The American Dissident* is subversive and samizdat in nature, providing a forum for the questioning, challenging, and angering (if need be) of entrenched professors, poets, writers, editors, actors, workshop leaders, MFA program directors, town mothers & fathers, and whoever else has sold out to the machine. It fights, satirizes, and exposés, wielding logic and reason against celebrity, diversion, groupthink, herd mentality, and conformity."

$ ANCIENT PATHS

Christian Literary Magazine, P.O. Box 7505, Fairfax Station VA 22039. E-mail: ssburris@msn.com. Website: www.literatureclassics.com/ancientpaths/magazine/table.html. **Contact:** Skylar Hamilton Burris, editor. **99% freelance written.** Annual magazine with subtle Christian and general religious themes. "*Ancient Paths* publishes quality fiction and creative nonfiction for a literate Christian audience. Religious themes are usually subtle, and the magazine has non-Christian readers as well as some content by non-Christian authors. However, writers should be comfortable appearing in a Christian magazine." Estab. 1998. Circ. 175-200. Pays on publication. Publishes ms an average of 2 months after acceptance. Byline given. Not copyrighted. Buys one-time rights. Submit seasonal material 3 months in advance. Accepts queries by mail, e-mail. Accepts previously published material. Accepts simultaneous submissions. Responds in 1 week to queries; 4-5 weeks to mss. Sample copy for $3.50; make checks payable to Skylar Burris *not* to *Ancient Paths*. Writer's guidelines online. Editorial calendar online.

Nonfiction Book excerpts, historical/nostalgic, religious, Book reviews of poetry chapbooks. No devotions, sermons, or lessons. **Buys 1-10 mss/year.** Send complete ms. Length: 250-2,500 words. **Pays $2, 1 copy, and discount on additional copies.**

Fiction Fantasy, historical, humorous, mainstream, mystery, novel excerpts, religious, science fiction, slice-of-life vignettes, western. No retelling of Bible stories. Literary fiction favored over genre fiction. **Buys 4-10 mss/ year.** Send complete ms. Length: 250-2,500 words. **Pays $2, 1 copy, and discount on additional copies.**

Poetry Free verse, traditional. No avant-garde, prose poetry, or poor meter. **Buys 25-60 poems/year.** Submit maximum 5 poems. Length: 4-60 lines. **Pays $1/poem, 1 copy, and discount on additional copies.**

Tips "Make the reader think as well as feel. Do not simply state a moral message; no preaching, nothing didactic. You should have something meaningful to say, but be subtle. Show, don't tell."

Ⓝ $ ANTIETAM REVIEW

Washington County Arts Council, 41 S. Potomac, Hagerstown MD 21740-5512. (301)791-3132. Fax: (240)420-1754. E-mail: antietamreview@washingtoncountyarts.com. Website: www.washingtoncountyarts.com. **Contact:** Mary Jo Vincent, managing editor. **90% freelance written.** Annual magazine covering fiction (short stories), poetry and b&w photography. Estab. 1982. Circ. 1,000. Pays on publication. Publishes ms an average of 2-3 months after acceptance. Byline given. Buys first North American serial rights. Accepts queries by mail, e-mail, phone. Responds in 4 months to queries. Sample copy for $6.30 (back issue); $8.40 (current issue). Writer's guidelines for #10 SASE.

Fiction Winnie Wagaman, managing editor. Condensed novels, ethnic, experimental, novel excerpts, short stories of a literary quality. No religious, romance, erotica, confession, or horror. **Buys 9 mss/year.** Query with published clips or send complete ms. Length: No more than 5,000 words. **Pays $50-100 and 2 contributor's copies.**

Poetry Avant-garde, free verse, traditional. Does not want to see haiku, religious and most rhyme. **Buys 20-25 poems/year.** Submit maximum 3 poems. Length: 30 lines maximum. **Pays $25.**

Tips "We seek high-quality, well-crafted work with significant character development and shift. We look for work that is interesting, involves the reader, and teaches us a new way to view the world. A manuscript stands out because of its energy and flow. Most of our submissions reflect the times (news/current events) more than industry trends. Works should have a compelling voice, originality, magic."

$⊡ THE ANTIGONISH REVIEW

St. Francis Xavier University, P.O. Box 5000, Antigonish NS B2G 2W5, Canada. (902)867-3962. Fax: (902)867-5563. E-mail: tar@stfx.ca. Website: www.antigonishreview.com. Managing Editor: Josephine Mensch. **Contact:** B. Allan Quigley or Jeanette Lynes, co-editors. **100% freelance written.** Quarterly magazine. Literary magazine for educated and creative readers. Estab. 1970. Circ. 850. Pays on publication. Publishes ms an average of 8 months after acceptance. Byline given. Offers variable kill fee. Rights retained by author. Editorial lead time 4 months. Submit seasonal material 4 months in advance. Accepts queries by mail, fax. Responds in 1 month to queries; 6 months to mss. Sample copy for $7 or online. Writer's guidelines for #10 SASE or online.

Nonfiction Essays, interview/profile, book reviews/articles. No academic pieces. **Buys 15-20 mss/year.** Query. Length: 1,500-5,000 words. **Pays $50-150.**

Fiction Literary. Contemporary, prose poem. No erotica. **Buys 35-40 mss/year.** Send complete ms. Length: 500-5,000 words. **Pays $50 for stories.**

Poetry Buys 100-125 poems/year. Submit maximum 5 poems. **Pays in copies.**

Tips "Send for guidelines and/or sample copy. Send ms with cover letter and SASE with submission."

$ ANTIOCH REVIEW

P.O. Box 148, Yellow Springs OH 45387-0148. Website: www.antioch.edu/review. **Contact:** Robert S. Fogarty, editor. Quarterly magazine for general, literary, and academic audience. "Literary and cultural review of contemporary issues, and literature for general readership." Estab. 1941. Circ. 5,100. Pays on publication. Publishes ms an average of 10 months after acceptance. Byline given. Buys first, one-time rights. Rights revert to author upon publication. Accepts queries by mail. Responds in 2 months to mss. Sample copy for $6. Writer's guidelines online.

● Responds in 3 months.

Nonfiction "Contemporary articles in the humanities and social sciences, politics, economics, literature, and all areas of broad intellectual concern. Somewhat scholarly, but never pedantic in style, eschewing all professional jargon. Lively, distinctive prose insisted upon. We *do not* read simultaneous submissions." Length: 2,000-8,000 words. **Pays $10/printed page.**

Fiction Fiction editor. "Quality fiction only, distinctive in style with fresh insights into the human condition." Experimental, contemporary. No science fiction, fantasy, or confessions. Length: generally under 8,000. **Pays $10/printed page.**

Poetry "No light or inspirational verse."

$⊡ ARC

Canada's National Poetry Magazine, Arc Poetry Society, Box 7219, Ottawa ON K1L 8E4, Canada. E-mail: arc.poetry@cyberus.ca. Website: www.cyberus.ca/~arc.poetry. **Contact:** Anita Lahey, managing editor. Semiannual magazine featuring poetry, poetry-related articles, and criticism. "Our focus is poetry, and Canadian poetry in general, although we do publish writers from elsewhere. We are looking for the best poetry from new and established writers. We often have special issues. Send a SASE for upcoming special issues and contests." Estab. 1978. Circ. 1,500. Pays on publication. Publishes ms an average of 6 months after acceptance. Byline given. Buys one-time rights. Responds in 4 months to queries. Writer's guidelines for #10 SASE.

Nonfiction Essays, interview/profile, book reviews. Query first. Length: 500-4,000 words. **Pays $30/printed page (Canadian), and 2 copies.**

Photos Query first. Buys one-time rights. Pays $300 for 10 photos.

Poetry Avant-garde, free verse. **Buys 60 poems/year.** Submit maximum 6 poems. **Pays $30/printed page (Canadian).**

Tips "Please include brief biographical note with submission."

$ ARTFUL DODGE

Dept. of English, College of Wooster, Wooster OH 44691. (330)263-2577. Website: www.wooster.edu/artfuldodge. **Contact:** Philip Brady, poetry editor. Annual magazine that "takes a strong interest in poets who are

Consumer Magazines

continually testing what they can get away with successfully in regard to subject, perspective, language, etc., but who also show mastery of the current American poetic techniques—its varied textures and its achievement in the illumination of the particular. There is no theme in this magazine, except literary power. We also have an ongoing interest in translations from Central/Eastern Europe and elsewhere.'' Estab. 1979. Circ. 1,000. Buys first North American serial rights. Accepts queries by mail. Accepts simultaneous submissions. Responds in 1 year to mss. Sample copy for $7. Writer's guidelines for #10 SASE.

Fiction Experimental, prose poem. ''We judge by literary quality, not by genre. We are especially interested in fine English translations of significant prose writers. Translations should be submitted with original texts.'' **Pays 2 contributor's copies and honorarium of $5/page, ''thanks to funding from the Ohio Arts Council.''**

Poetry ''We are interested in poems that utilize stylistic persuasions both old and new to good effect. We are not afraid of poems which try to deal with large social, political, historical, and even philosophical questions—especially if the poem emerges from one's own life experience and is not the result of armchair pontificating. We don't want cute, rococo surrealism, someone's warmed-up, left-over notion of an avant-garde that existed 10-100 years ago, or any last bastions of rhymed verse in the civilized world.'' **Buys 20 poems/year.** Submit maximum 6 poems.

Tips ''Poets may send books for review consideration; however, there is no guarantee we can review them.''

$ARTS & LETTERS

Journal of Contemporary Culture, Georgia College & State University, Campus Box 89, Milledgeville GA 31061. E-mail: al@gcsu.edu. Website: al.gcsu.edu. **Contact:** Martin Lammon, editor. Semiannual magazine covering poetry, fiction, creative nonfiction, and commentary on contemporary culture. ''The journal features the mentors interview series and the world poetry translation series. Also, it is the only journal nationwide to feature authors and artists that represent such an eclectic range of creative work.'' Estab. 1999. Circ. 1,500. Pays on publication. Publishes ms an average of 6-12 months after acceptance. Rights revert to author after publication. Responds in 2 months to mss. Sample copy for $5, plus $1 for postage. Writer's guidelines online.

Nonfiction Karen Salyer McElmurray, creative nonfiction editor. Looking for creative nonfiction.

Fiction Allen Gee, fiction editor. No genre fiction. **Buys 6 mss/year.** Length: 3,000-7,500 words. **Pays $50 minimum or $10/published page.**

Poetry Alice Friman, poetry editor.

Tips ''An obvious, but not gimmicky, attention to fresh usage of language. A solid grasp of the craft of story writing. Fully realized work.''

BELLINGHAM REVIEW

Mail Stop 9053, Western Washington University, Bellingham WA 98225. (360)650-4863. E-mail: bhreview@cc. wwu.edu. Website: www.wwu.edu/~bhreview. Editor: Brenda Miller. **Contact:** Poetry, Fiction, or Creative Nonfiction Editor. **100% freelance written.** Semiannual nonprofit magazine. *Bellingham Review* seeks literature of palpable quality; stories, essays, and poems that nudge the limits of form or execute traditional forms exquisitely. Estab. 1977. Circ. 1,600. Pays on publication when funding allows. Publishes ms an average of 6 months after acceptance. Byline given. Buys first North American serial rights. Editorial lead time 6 months. Accepts simultaneous submissions. Responds in 3 months to mss. Sample copy for $7. Writer's guidelines online.

Nonfiction Nonfiction Editor. Essays, personal experience. Does not want anything nonliterary. **Buys 4-6 mss/ year.** Send complete ms. Length: 9,000 words maximum. **Pays as funds allow, plus contributor copies.**

Fiction Fiction Editor. Literary short fiction. Experimental, humorous. Does not want anything nonliterary. **Buys 4-6 mss/year.** Send complete ms. Length: 9,000 words maximum. **Pays as funds allow.**

Poetry Poetry Editor. Avant-garde, free verse, traditional. Will not use light verse. **Buys 10-30 poems/year.** Submit maximum 3 poems. **Pays as funds allow.**

Tips ''Open submission period is from October 1-February 1. Manuscripts arriving between February 2 and September 30 will be returned unread.'' The *Bellingham Review* holds 3 annual contests: the 49th Parallel Poetry Award, the Annie Dillard Award in Nonfiction, and the Tobias Wolff Award in Fiction. Submissions December 1-March 15. See the individual listings for these contests under Contests & Awards for full details.

$BLACK WARRIOR REVIEW

P.O. Box 862936, Tuscaloosa AL 35486-0027. (205)348-4518. Website: www.webdelsol.com/bwr. **90% freelance written.** Semiannual magazine of fiction, poetry, essays, art, and reviews. ''We publish contemporary fiction, poetry, reviews, essays, and art for a literary audience. We publish the freshest work we can find.'' Estab. 1974. Circ. 2,000. Pays on publication. Publishes ms an average of 6 months after acceptance. Byline given. Buys first rights. Accepts simultaneous submissions. Responds in 4 months to mss. Sample copy for $8. Writer's guidelines online.

● Stories and poems in recent *Best American Short Stories*, *Best American Poetry* and *Pushcart Prize* anthologies. Responds in 3 months.

Nonfiction Aaron Welborn, editor. Interview/profile, literary/personal essays. **Buys 5 mss/year.** No queries; send complete ms. **Pays up to $100, copies, and a 1-year subscription.**

Fiction Cayenne Sullivan, fiction editor. Publishes novel excerpts if under contract to be published. One story/chapter per envelope, please. Contemporary, short and short-short fiction. Want "work that is conscious of form and well-crafted. We are open to good experimental writing and short-short fiction. No genre fiction please." **Buys 10 mss/year.** Length:7,500 words. **Pays up to $150, copies, and a 1-year subscription.**

Poetry Kimberly Campanello, poetry editor. **Buys 35 poems/year.** Submit maximum 3-6 poems. **Pays up to $75, copies, and a 1-year subscription.**

Tips "Read *BWR* before submitting. Send us only your best work. Address all submissions to the appropriate genre editor."

$ $ BOULEVARD

Opojaz, Inc., 6614 Clayton Rd., PMB 325, Richmond Heights MO 63117. (314)862-2643. Fax: (314)862-2982. Website: www.richardburgin.com. **Contact:** Richard Burgin, editor. **100% freelance written.** Triannual magazine covering fiction, poetry, and essays. "*Boulevard* is a diverse literary magazine presenting original creative work by well-known authors, as well as by writers of exciting promise." Estab. 1985. Circ. 11,000. Pays on publication. Publishes ms an average of 9 months after acceptance. Byline given. Offers no kill fee. Buys first North American serial rights. Accepts queries by mail, phone. Accepts simultaneous submissions. Responds in 2 weeks to queries; 2 months to mss. Sample copy for $8. Writer's guidelines online.

○➤ Break in with "a touching, intelligent, and original story, poem or essay."

Nonfiction Book excerpts, essays, interview/profile, opinion, photo feature. "No pornography, science fiction, children's stories, or westerns." **Buys 10 mss/year.** Send complete ms. Length: 10,000 words maximum. **Pays $20/page, minimum $150.**

Fiction Confessions, experimental, mainstream, novel excerpts. "We do not want erotica, science fiction, romance, western, or children's stories." **Buys 20 mss/year.** Send complete ms. Length: 8,000 words maximum. **$20/page; minimum $150.**

Poetry Avant-garde, free verse, haiku, traditional. "Do not send us light verse." **Buys 80 poems/year.** Submit maximum 5 poems. Length: 200 lines. **$25-250 (sometimes higher).**

Tips "Read the magazine first. The work *Boulevard* publishes is generally recognized as among the finest in the country. We continue to seek more good literary or cultural essays. Send only your best work."

BRAIN, CHILD

The Magazine for Thinking Mothers, March Press, P.O. Box 5566, Charlottesville VA 22905. (434)977-4151. E-mail: editor@brainchildmag.com. Website: www.brainchildmag.com. Co-Editors: Jennifer Niesslein and Stephanie Wilkinson. **90% freelance written.** Quarterly magazine covering the experience of motherhood. "*Brain, Child* reflects modern motherhood—the way it really is. We like to think of *Brain, Child* as a community, for and by mothers who like to think about what raising kids does for (and to) the mind and soul. *Brain, Child* isn't your typical parenting magazine. We couldn't cupcake-decorate our way out of a paper bag. We are more 'literary' than 'how-to,' more *New Yorker* than *Parents*. We shy away from expert advice on childrearing in favor of first-hand reflections by great writers (Jane Smiley, Barbara Ehrenreich, Anne Tyler) on life as a mother. Each quarterly issue is full of essays, features, humor, reviews, fiction, art, cartoons, and our readers' own stories. Our philosophy is pretty simple: Motherhood is worthy of literature. And there are a lot of ways to mother, all of them interesting. We're proud to be publishing articles and essays that are smart, down to earth, sometimes funny, and sometimes poignant." Estab. 2000. Circ. 22,000. Pays on publication. Publishes ms an average of 6 months after acceptance. Byline given. Buys first North American serial, electronic rights. *Brain, Child* anthology rights Editorial lead time 3 months. Submit seasonal material 6 months in advance. Accepts queries by mail, e-mail. Accepts previously published material. Accepts simultaneous submissions. Responds in 1 month to queries; 1-3 months to mss. Sample copy online. Writer's guidelines online.

Nonfiction Essays (including debate), humor, in-depth features. No how-to articles, advice, or tips. **Buys 40-50 mss/year.** Query with published clips for features and debate essays; send complete ms for essays. Length: 800-5,000 words. **Payment varies.** Sometimes pays expenses of writers on assignment.

Photos State availability with submission. Reviews contact sheets, prints, GIF/JPEG files. Model releases required.

Fiction "We publish fiction that has a strong motherhood theme." Mainstream, literary. No genre fiction. **Buys 4 mss/year.** Send complete ms. Length: 800-5,000 words. **Payment varies.**

$ $ ⬚ BRICK

A Literary Journal, Brick, Box 537, Station Q, Toronto ON M4T 2M5, Canada. E-mail: info@brickmag.com. Website: www.brickmag.com. Publisher: Michael Redhill. **Contact:** Vivien Leong, managing editor. **90% free-**

lance written. Semiannual magazine covering literature and the arts. "We publish literary nonfiction of a very high quality on a range of arts and culture subjects." Estab. 1975. Circ. 3,000. Pays on publication. Publishes ms an average of 3 months after acceptance. Byline given. Buys first world, first serial, one-time rights. Editorial lead time 5 months. Accepts queries by mail, e-mail. Responds in 6 weeks to queries; 6 months to mss. Sample copy for $12, plus $3 shipping. Writer's guidelines online.

Nonfiction Essays, historical/nostalgic, interview/profile, opinion, travel. No fiction, poetry, personal real-life experience, or book reviews. **Buys 30-40 mss/year.** Send complete ms. Length: 250-2,500 words. **Pays $75-500 (Canadian).**

Photos State availability with submission. Reviews transparencies, prints, GIF/JPEG files. Buys one-time rights. Offers $25-50/photo.

Tips *"Brick* is interested in polished work by writers who are widely read and in touch with contemporary culture. The magazine is serious, but not fusty. We like to feel the writer's personality in the piece, too."

N CALYX

A Journal of Art & Literature by Women, Calyc, Inc., P.O. Box B, Corvallis OR 97339. (541)753-9384. Fax: (541)753-0515. Biannual publishes prose, poetry, art, essays, interviews and critical and review articles. *"Calyx* exists to publish fine literature and art by women and is committed to publishing the work of all women, including women of color, older women, working class women and other voices that need to be heard. We are committed to discovering and nurturing beginning writers." Estab. 1976. Circ. 6,000. Publishes ms an average of 6-12 months after acceptance. Accepts simultaneous submissions. Responds in 6-12 months to mss. Sample copy for $9.50 plus $2 postage. SASE and by e-mail.

Fiction Length: 5,000 words. **"Combination of payment, free issues and 1 volume subscription.**

Tips Most mss are rejected because "the writers are not familiar with *Calyx*-writers should read *Calyx* and be familar with the publication. We look for good writing, imagination and important/interesting subject matter."

$ THE CHARITON REVIEW

English Dept., Brigham Young University, Provo UT 84602. (660)785-4499. **Contact:** Jim Barnes, editor. **100% freelance written.** Semiannual (fall and spring) magazine covering contemporary fiction, poetry, translation, and book reviews. "We demand only excellence in fiction and fiction translation for a general and college readership." Estab. 1975. Circ. 600. Pays on publication. Publishes ms an average of 6 months after acceptance. Byline given. Buys first North American serial rights. Accepts queries by mail. Responds in 1 week to queries; 1 month to mss. Sample copy for $5 and 7x10 SAE with 4 first-class stamps.

Nonfiction Essays (essay reviews of books). **Buys 2-5 mss/year.** Send complete ms. Length: 1,000-5,000 words. **Pays $15.**

Fiction Fiction editor. Ethnic, experimental, mainstream, novel excerpts, traditional. "We are not interested in slick or sick material." **Buys 6-10 mss/year.** Send complete ms. Length: 1,000-6,000 words. **Pays $5/page (up to $50).**

Poetry Avant-garde, traditional. **Buys 50-55 poems/year.** Submit maximum 5 poems. Length: Open. **Pays $5/page.**

Tips "Read *Chariton.* Know the difference between good literature and bad. Know what magazine might be interested in your work. We are not a trendy magazine. We publish only the best. All sections are open to freelancers. Know your market or you are wasting your time—and mine. Do *not* write for guidelines; the only guideline is excellence."

$ $ THE CHATTAHOOCHEE REVIEW

Georgia Perimeter College, 2101 Womack Rd., Dunwoody GA 30338-4497. (770)551-3019. Website: www.chatta hoochee-review.org. **Contact:** Lawrence Hetrick, editor. Quarterly magazine. "We publish a number of Southern writers, but *Chattahoochee Review* is not by design a regional magazine. All themes, forms, and styles are considered as long as they impact the whole person: heart, mind, intuition, and imagination." Estab. 1980. Circ. 1,350. Pays on publication. Publishes ms an average of 3 months after acceptance. Byline given. Buys first rights. Accepts queries by mail. Responds in 2 weeks to queries; 4 months to mss. Sample copy for $6. Writer's guidelines online.

Nonfiction "We look for distinctive, honest personal essays and creative nonfiction of any kind, including the currently popular memoiristic narrative. We publish interviews with writers of all kinds: literary, academic, journalistic, and popular. We also review selected current offerings in fiction, poetry, and nonfiction, including works on photography and the visual arts, with an emphasis on important southern writers and artisits. We do not often, if ever, publish technical, critical, theoretical, or scholarly work about literature although we are interested in essays written for general readers about writers, their careers, and their work." Essays (interviews with authors, reviews). **Buys 10 mss/year.** Send complete ms. Length: 5,000 words maximum.

Photos State availability with submission. Buys one-time rights. Negotiates payment individually. Identification of subjects required.

Fiction Accepts all subject matter except science fiction and romance. "No juvenile, romance, science fiction." **Buys 12 mss/year.** Send complete ms. Length: 6,000 words maximum. **Pays $20/page, $250 max and 2 contributor's copies.**

Poetry Avant-garde, free verse, haiku, light verse, traditional. **Buys 60 poems/year.** Submit maximum 5 poems. **Pays $30/poem.**

Tips "Become familiar with our journal and the type of work we regularly publish."

$CHELSEA

Chelsea Associates, P.O. Box 773 Cooper Station, New York NY 10276-0773. **Contact:** Alfredo de Palchi, editor. **70% freelance written.** Semiannual magazine. "We stress style, variety, originality. No special biases or requirements. Flexible attitudes, eclectic material. We take an active interest, as always, in cross-cultural exchanges, superior translations, and are leaning toward cosmopolitan, interdisciplinary techniques, but maintain no strictures against traditional modes." Estab. 1958. Circ. 2,200. Pays on publication. Publishes ms an average of 6 months after acceptance. Byline given. Buys first North American serial rights. Accepts queries by mail. Responds in 3-5 months to mss. Sample copy for $6. Writer's guidelines and contest guidelines available for #10 SASE.

• *Chelsea* also sponsors fiction and poetry contests. Poetry Deadline: December 15; Fiction Deadline: June 15. Send SASE for guidelines.

Nonfiction Essays, book reviews (query first with sample). **Buys 6 mss/year.** Send complete ms with SASE. Length: 6,000 words. **Pays $15/page.**

Fiction Mainstream, novel excerpts, literary. **Buys 12 mss/year.** Send complete ms. Length: 5,000-6,000 words. **Pays $15/page.**

Poetry Avant-garde, free verse, traditional. **Buys 60-75 poems/year. Pays $15/page.**

Tips "We only accept written correspondence. We are looking for more super translations, first-rate fiction, and work by writers of color. No need to query; submit complete manuscript. We suggest writers look at a recent issue of *Chelsea*."

$ $CICADA MAGAZINE

Cricket Magazine Group, P.O. Box 300, Peru IL 61354. (815)224-5803 ext. 656. Fax: (815)224-6615. Website: www.cricketmag.com. Editor-in-Chief: Marianne Carus. Executive Editor: DeborahVetter. Associate Editor: Tracy C. Schoenle. Senior Art Director: Ron McCutchan. **Contact:** Submissions Editor. **100% freelance written.** Bimonthly magazine for teenagers and young adults. "*Cicada*, for ages 14 and up, publishes original short stories, poems, and first-person essays written for teens and young adults." Estab. 1998. Circ. 17,000. Pays on publication. Publishes ms an average of 1 year after acceptance. Byline given. Rights vary. Accepts previously published material. Accepts simultaneous submissions. Responds in 3 months to mss. Sample copy for $8.50. Writer's guidelines for SASE and on website.

Nonfiction Looking for first-person experiences that are relevant and interesting to teenagers. Essays, personal experience. Send complete ms. Length: up to 5,000 words. **Pays 25¢/word.**

Reprints Send ms. Payment varies.

Fiction Looking for realistic, contemporary, historical fiction, adventure, humor, fantasy, science fiction. Main protagonist should be age 14 or older. Stories should have a genuine teen sensibility and be aimed at readers in high school or college. Adventure, fantasy, historical, humorous, mainstream, mystery, romance, science fiction, western, sports. Send complete ms. Length: 3,000-15,000 words. **Pays 25¢/word, plus 6 contributor's copies.**

Poetry Looking for serious or humorous; rhymed or free verse. Free verse, light verse, traditional. Length: Up to 25 lines. **Pays up to $3/line.**

Tips "An exact word count should be noted on each manuscript submitted. For poetry, indicate number of lines instead. Word count includes every word, but does not include the title of the manuscript or the author's name."

Ⓝ $THE CINCINNATI REVIEW

P.O. Box 210069, Cincinnati OH 45221-0069. (513)556-3954. E-mail: editors@cincinnatireview.com. Website: www.cincinnatireview.com. Managing Editor: Nicola Mason. **Contact:** James Cummins, poetry editor; Brock Clarke, fiction editor. **100% freelance written.** Semiannual magazine. "A journal devoted to publishing the best new literary fiction and poetry as well as book reviews, essays, and interviews." Estab. 2003. Pays on publication. Publishes ms an average of 6 months after acceptance. Byline given. Buys first North American serial, electronic rights. Accepts queries by mail. Responds in 2 weeks to queries; 1 month to mss. Sample copy for $7. Writer's guidelines online.

Consumer Magazines

Nonfiction Book excerpts, essays, interview/profile, new book fiction and poetry reviews. Query. Length: 1,000-5,000 words. **Pays $25/page.**

Columns/Departments Book Reviews; Literary Fiction and Poetry, 1,500 words. **Buys 20 mss/year.** Query. **Pays $25/page.**

Fiction Brock Clarke, fiction editor. Literary. Does not want genre fiction. **Buys 13 mss/year.** Query. Length: 125-10,000 words. **Pays $25/page.**

Poetry Avant-garde, free verse, traditional. **Buys 120 poems/year.** Submit maximum 10 poems. Query.

$$CITY SLAB

Urban Tales of the Grotesque, City Slab Publications, 1705 Summit Ave., #211, Seattle WA 98122. (206)226-7430. E-mail: dave@cityslab.com. Website: www.cityslab.com. **Contact:** Dave Lindschmidt, editor. **90% freelance written.** Quarterly magazine covering horror and horror/crime mix. *"City Slab* magazine is hard-edged, adult fiction."* Estab. 2002. Pays on publication. Publishes ms an average of 3 months after acceptance. Byline given. Buys first North American serial rights. Accepts queries by mail, e-mail. Responds in 3 weeks to queries; 2 months to mss. Sample copy for $6. Writer's guidelines online.

Nonfiction Essays, interview/profile, photo feature. **Buys 4 mss/year.** Send complete ms. Length: 2,000-3,000 words. **Pays $50-100, plus contributor copies.**

Photos State availability of or send photos with submission. Reviews JPEG files. Buys one-time rights. Offers no additional payment for photos accepted with ms. Model releases required.

Fiction *"City Slab* wants to publish well-thought-out, literary-quality horror."* Erotica, experimental, horror. Does not want to see children/youth in sexually oriented stories. **Buys 24 mss/year.** Send complete ms. Length: 5,000 words maximum. **Pays 1-10¢/word.**

Tips "Read not only the horror greats—Barker, King, Campbell, Lovecraft, etc., but also the classics—Dickens, Hemingway, Oates, Steinbeck to see how a great tale is woven. Recently published fiction by Gerard Hoaurner, Christa Faust, and P.D. Cacek."

N $COFFEE LOUNGE BOOK CLUB

Rembrandt and Co. Publishers International, P.O. Box 13486, St. Petersburg FL 33733. E-mail: ambitionscoffee@hotmail.com. Website: www.rembrandtandcompany.com. **Contact:** Ben Scarlato, publisher. **100% freelance written.** Monthly newsletter covering self-publishing news. "Give us your best work, your most outstanding philosophy on life. The Coffee Lounge wishes to separate certain authors away from others so they can be recognized alone. The Coffee Lounge accepts one author per month, opening the door for just about anything. Of course, not all authors will be accepted, but the opportunity is there. Send stories and poetry as many as you wish to be considered." Estab. 2003. Circ. 100. Pays on publication. Publishes ms an average of 1 month after acceptance. Buys first North American serial rights. Accepts queries by mail, e-mail. Accepts simultaneous submissions. Writer's guidelines free.

Nonfiction Book excerpts, inspirational, interview/profile. **Buys 1 mss/year.** Query with published clips or send complete ms. Length: 200 maximum words. **Pays 1¢/word, plus at least 1 contributor copy.**

Fiction Adventure, confessions, erotica, experimental, historical, horror, humorous, mainstream, mystery, romance, science fiction, serialized novels, suspense. Does not want pornography. **Buys 12 mss/year.** Send complete ms. Length: 200 maximum words.

Poetry Avant-garde, free verse, light verse, traditional. Length: 3 lines.

Tips "Give us your best."

$COLORADO REVIEW

Center for Literary Publishing, Department of English, Colorado State University, Fort Collins CO 80523. (970)491-5449. E-mail: creview@colostate.edu. Website: www.coloradoreview.com. **Contact:** Stephanie G'Schwind, editor. Literary magazine published 3 times/year. Estab. 1972. Circ. 1,300. Pays on publication. Publishes ms an average of within 1 year after acceptance. Byline given. Buys first North American serial rights. Rights revert to author upon publication. Editorial lead time 1 year. Responds in 2 months to mss. Sample copy for $10. Writer's guidelines online.

Nonfiction Personal essays, creative nonfiction. **Buys 6-9 mss/year.** Send complete ms. **Pays $5/page.**

Fiction Short fiction. No genre fiction. Ethnic, experimental, mainstream, contemporary. "No genre fiction." **Buys 15-20 mss/year.** Send complete ms. Length: under 30 ms pages. **Pays $5/page.**

Poetry Considers poetry of any style. Don Revell or Jorie Graham, poetry editors. **Buys 60-100 poems/year.** **Pays $5/page.**

Tips Manuscripts are read from September 1 to April 30. Manuscripts recieved between May 1 and August 30 will be returned unread.

$ $CONFRONTATION

A Literary Journal, Long Island University, Brookville NY 11548. (516)299-2720. Fax: (516)299-2735. E-mail: mtucker@liu.edu. Assistant to Editor: Jonna Semeik. **Contact:** Martin Tucker, editor-in-chief. **75% freelance written.** Semiannual magazine. "We are eclectic in our taste. Excellence of style is our dominant concern." Estab. 1968. Circ. 2,000. Pays on publication. Publishes ms an average of 1 year after acceptance. Byline given. Offers kill fee. Buys first North American serial, first, one-time, all rights. Accepts queries by mail, e-mail, phone. Accepts simultaneous submissions. Responds in 3 weeks to queries; 2 months to mss. Sample copy for $3. Writer's guidelines not available.

• *Confrontation* does not read mss during June, July, or August.

Nonfiction Essays, personal experience. **Buys 15 mss/year.** Send complete ms. Length: 1,500-5,000 words. **Pays $100-300 for assigned articles; $15-300 for unsolicited articles.**

Photos State availability with submission. Buys one-time rights. Offers no additional payment for photos accepted with ms.

Fiction "We judge on quality, so genre is open." Experimental, mainstream, novel excerpts, slice-of-life vignettes, contemporary, prose poem. "No 'proselytizing' literature or genre fiction." **Buys 60-75 mss/year.** Send complete ms. Length: 6,000 words. **Pays $25-250.**

Poetry Avant-garde, free verse, haiku, light verse, traditional. **Buys 60-75 poems/year.** Submit maximum 6 poems. Length: Open. **Pays $10-100.**

Tips "Most open to fiction and poetry. Study our magazine."

$THE CONNECTICUT POETRY REVIEW

The Connecticut Poetry Review Press, P.O. Box 818, Stonington CT 06378. Managing Editor: Harley More. **Contact:** J. Claire White. **60% freelance written.** Annual magazine covering poetry/literature. Estab. 1981. Circ. 500. **Pays on acceptance.** Byline sometimes given. Buys first rights. Editorial lead time 4 months. Submit seasonal material 4 months in advance. Accepts queries by mail. Responds in 1 month to queries; 3 months to mss. Sample copy for $3.50 and #10 SASE. Writer's guidelines for #10 SASE.

Nonfiction Book excerpts, essays. **Buys 18 mss/year.**

Fiction Experimental.

Poetry Avant-garde, free verse, haiku, traditional. No light verse. **Buys 20-30 poems/year.** Submit maximum 4 poems. Length: 3-25 lines. **Pays $5-10.**

$ CONTEMPORARY VERSE 2

The Canadian Journal of Poetry and Critical Writing, Contemporary Verse 2, Inc., 207-100 Arthur St., Winnipeg MB R3B 1H3, Canada. (204)949-1365. Fax: (204)942-5754. E-mail: cv2@mb.sympatico.ca. Website: www.conte mporaryverse2.ca. **Contact:** Clarise Foster, managing editor. **75% freelance written.** Quarterly magazine covering poetry and critical writing about poetry. "*CV2* publishes poetry of demonstrable quality as well as critical writing in the form of interviews, essays, articles, and reviews. With the critical writing we tend to focus on intelligent but accessible to create a discussion of poetry which will interest a broad range of readers, including those who might be skeptical about the value of poetry." Estab. 1975. Circ. 600. Pays on publication. Byline given. Offers 50% kill fee. Not copyrighted. Buys first North American serial, second serial (reprint) rights. Editorial lead time 3-6 months. Submit seasonal material 3-6 months in advance. Accepts queries by mail, e-mail, phone. Responds in 2-3 weeks to queries; 3-8 months to mss. Sample copy for $8. Writer's guidelines online.

Nonfiction Essays, interview/profile, book reviews. No content that is not about poetry. **Buys 10-30 mss/year.** Query. Length: 800-3,000 words. **Pays $40-130 for assigned articles.** Pays in contributor copies only if requested by the author.

Poetry Avant-garde, free verse. No rhyming verse, traditionally inspirational. **Buys 110-120 poems/year.** Submit maximum 6 poems.

$CRAB ORCHARD REVIEW

A Journal of Creative Works, Southern Illinois University at Carbondale, English Department, Faner Hall, Carbondale IL 62901-4503. (618)453-6833. Fax: (618)453-8224. Website: www.siu.edu/~crborchd. "We are a general interest literary journal published twice/year. We strive to be a journal that writers admire and readers enjoy. We publish fiction, poetry, creative nonfiction, fiction translations, interviews and reviews." Estab. 1995. Circ. 2,200. Publishes ms an average of 9-12 months after acceptance. Buys first North American serial rights. Accepts simultaneous submissions. Responds in 3 weeks to queries; 9 months to mss. Sample copy for $8. Writer's guidelines for #10 SASE.

Fiction Jon Tribble, managing editor. Ethnic, excerpted novel. No science fiction, romance, western, horror, gothic or children's. Wants more nove excerpts that also stand alone as pieces. Length: 1,000-6,500 words. **Pays $100 minimum; $20/page maximum, 2 contributor's copies and a year subscription.**

$ CRABGRASS ARIA

1124 Columbia NE, Albuquerque NM 87106. E-mail: art_coop@yahoo.com. Website: www.geocities.com/art_c oop. **Contact:** Charli Valdes, editor. **100% freelance written.** Annual magazine. Estab. 1996. Pays on publication. Buys first North American serial, one-time, electronic, one-time anthology rights. Accepts queries by mail. Accepts simultaneous submissions. Sample copy not available. Writer's guidelines for #10 SASE.

Nonfiction Needs memoir that is original and has an edge to it. Art, travel, environmental with global appeal, profiles and news that elicits personality, local perspectives from around the globe. Strange, fresh ideas and style. Global perspective, international and comparative content. Scholarly articles with zip. Also needs translations. Buys 1-5 translation mss/year. Must have permission of the author. Submit with original and with translator's preface. **Pays $25, plus contributor copies for translations.** Special issues: Themes include Ekphrasis, immigration, Spain, dogs. The magazine is not strictly a theme-oriented magazine. "Please submit your work regardless of upcoming themes." **Buys 2-7 mss/year.** Send complete ms with cover sheet, bio, and publications list. Length: 1,000-10,000 words. **Pays $50 minimum, plus contributor copies.**

Photos Buys one-time rights. Negotiates payment individually. Identification of subjects, model releases required.

Fiction Needs fiction with strong characters, enticing plots, strange and fresh ideas and style. Global perspective, international and comparative content. Code switching, play with language (and languages). No science fiction, horror, fantasy, juvenile, etc. **Buys 2-7 mss/year.** Length: 1,000-10,000 words. **Pays $50, plus contributor copies.**

Poetry No science fiction, horror, fantasy, juvenile, etc. **Buys 6-20 poems/year.**

N $ CREATIVE NONFICTION

Creative Nonfiction Foundation, 5501 Walnut St., Suite 202, Pittsburgh PA 15232. (412)688-0304. Fax: (412)683-9173. E-mail: information@creativenonfiction.org. Website: www.creativenonfiction.org. Managing Editor: Jessica Mesman. **Contact:** Lee Gutkind, editor. **100% freelance written.** Magazine published 3 times/year covering nonfiction—personal essay, memoir, literary journalism. "*Creative Nonfiction* is the first journal to focus exclusively upon the genre of creative nonfiction. It publishes personal essay, memoir, and literary journalism on a broad range of subjects. Interviews with prominent writers and commentary about the genre also appear on its pages." Estab. 1993. Circ. 4,000. Pays on publication. Publishes ms an average of 1 year after acceptance. Byline given. Buys all rights. Editorial lead time 6 months. Accepts simultaneous submissions. Responds in 6 months to mss. Sample copy for $10. Writer's guidelines online.

Nonfiction Essays, interview/profile, personal experience, narrative journalism. No poetry, fiction. **Buys 30 mss/year.** Send complete ms. Length: 5,000 words maximum. **Pays $10/page—more if grant money available for assigned articles.**

Tips "Points to remember when submitting to *Creative Nonfiction*: strong reportage; well-written prose, attentive to language, rich with detail and distinctive voice; an informational quality or 'teaching element;' a compelling, focused, sustained narrative that's well-structured and conveys meaning. Manuscripts will not be accepted via fax."

N $ DAN RIVER ANTHOLOGY

Conservatory of American Letters, P.O. Box 298, Thomaston ME 04861. (207)354-0998. Fax: (207)354-8953. Website: www.americanletters.org. **Contact:** Richard S. Danbury III, series editor. Annual anthology. Deadline every year is March 31, with acceptance/rejection by April 15, proofs out by May 15, and book released December 7. Estab. 1984. Circ. 600. **Pays on acceptance.** Buys first North American serial rights. 50/50 sharing of any subsequent sales. Sample copy for $13.95 paperback, $59.95 cloth, plus $3.25 shipping. Writer's guidelines available for #10 SASE or online.

Fiction "We publish 30-40 pieces of fiction/issue, no theme, no restrictions. There is a reading fee, payable in cash only, of $3 for each 2,500 words or any part. The reading fee goes to the first reader, the company gets none of it." Adventure, ethnic, experimental, fantasy, historical, horror, humorous, mainstream, romance, science fiction, suspense, western, contemporary, prose poem, senior citizen/retirement. "Virtually anything but porn, evangelical, juvenile. Would like to see more first-person adventure." Send complete ms. Length: 800-2,500 words. **Payment "depends on your experience with us, as it is a nonrefundable advance against royalties on all sales that we can attribute to your influence. For first-timers, the advance is about 1¢/word."**

Poetry Poetry is also accepted for publication.

$ ▣ DESCANT

Descant Arts & Letters Foundation, P.O. Box 314, Station P, Toronto ON M5S 2S8, Canada. (416)593-2557. Fax: (416)593-9362. E-mail: descant@web.net. Website: www.descant.on.ca. Editor: Karen Mulhallen. **Contact:** Mary Newberry, managing editor. Quarterly journal. Estab. 1970. Circ. 1,200. Pays on publication. Publishes ms an average of 16 months after acceptance. Editorial lead time 4 months. Accepts queries by mail, e-mail, phone. Sample copy for $8. Writer's guidelines online.

- Pays $100 honorarium, plus 1-year's subscription for accepted submissions of any kind.

Nonfiction Book excerpts, essays, interview/profile, personal experience, historical.

Photos State availability with submission. Reviews contact sheets, prints. Buys one-time rights. Offers no additional payment for photos accepted with ms.

Fiction Karen Mulhallen, editor. Short stories or book excerpts. Maximum length 6,000 words; 3,000 words or less preferred. Ethnic, experimental, historical, humorous. No gothic, religious, beat. Send complete ms. **Pays $100 (Canadian); additional copies $8.**

Poetry Free verse, light verse, traditional. Submit maximum 6 poems.

Tips "Familiarize yourself with our magazine before submitting."

[N] DOUBLETAKE

55 Davis Square, Somerville MA 02144. (617)591-9389. Website: www.doubletakemagazine.org. **Contact:** Fiction Editor. "We strive to present storytelling in its many guises - visual and in words." Pays on publication. Byline given. Buys first North American serial rights. Accepts simultaneous submissions. Responds in 3 months to mss. Sample copy for $12. Writer's guidelines online.

- Send SASE with all submissions.

Fiction R. Jay Magill. "We accept realistic fiction in all of its variety. We look for stories with a strong narrative voice and an urgency in the writing. Realistic fiction in all of its variety; it's very unlikely we'd ever publish science fiction or gothic horror, for example. We would like to see more fiction distinguished by literary excellence and a rare voice." **Buys 12 mss/year.** Send complete ms. Length: No preferred length. **Pays competitively.**

■ The online magazine carries original content not found in the print edition and includes writer's guidelines.

Tips *"Doubletake* looks for writing distinguished by economy, directness, authenticity, and heart."

$ DOWNSTATE STORY

1825 Maple Ridge, Peoria IL 61614. (309)688-1409. E-mail: ehopkins@prairienet.org. Website: www.wiu.edu/users/mfgeh/dss. **Contact:** Elaine Hopkins, editor. Annual magazine covering short fiction with some connection with Illinois or the Midwest. "Short fiction - some connection with Illinois or the Midwest." Estab. 1992. Circ. 500. **Pays on acceptance.** Publishes ms an average of 1 year after acceptance. Buys first rights. Accepts simultaneous submissions. "ASAP" to mss. Sample copy for $8. Writer's guidelines online.

Fiction Adventure, ethnic, experimental, historical, horror, humorous, mainstream, mystery, romance, science fiction, suspense, western. No porn. **Buys 10 mss/year.** Length: 300-2,000 words. **Pays $50.**

Tips Wants more political fiction. Publishes short shorts and literary essays.

$[■] DREAMS & VISIONS

New Frontiers in Christian Fiction, Skysong Press, 35 Peter St. S., Orillia ON L3V 5A8, Canada. (705)329-1770. Fax: (705)329-1770. E-mail: skysong@bconnex.net. Website: www.bconnex.net/~skysong. **Contact:** Steve Stanton, editor. **100% freelance written.** Semiannual magazine. "Innovative literary fiction for adult Christian readers." Estab. 1988. Circ. 200. Pays on publication. Publishes ms an average of 8 months after acceptance. Byline given. Buys first North American serial, one-time, second serial (reprint) rights. Editorial lead time 1 year. Accepts queries by mail, e-mail. Accepts simultaneous submissions. Responds in 3 weeks to queries; 3 months to mss. Sample copy for $4.95. Writer's guidelines online.

Fiction Experimental, fantasy, humorous, mainstream, mystery, novel excerpts, religious, science fiction, slice-of-life vignettes. "We do not publish stories that glorify violence or perversity. All stories should portray a Christian world view or expand upon Biblical themes or ethics in an entertaining or enlightening manner." **Buys 12 mss/year.** Send complete ms. Length: 2,000-6,000 words. **Pays 1¢/word.**

$ DREAMS OF DECADENCE

Vampire Poetry and Fiction, DNA Publications, P.O. Box 2988, Radford VA 24143-2988. (540)763-2925. Fax: (540)763-2924. E-mail: dreamsofdecadence@dnapublications.com. Website: www.dnapublications.com/dreams. **Contact:** Angela Kessler, editor. Quarterly magazine featuring vampire fiction and poetry. Specializes in "vampire fiction and poetry for vampire fans." Estab. 1995. Circ. 7,500. Pays on publication. Publishes ms an average of 6 months after acceptance. Buys first North American serial rights. Accepts simultaneous submissions. Responds in 1 month to queries; 1 month to mss. Sample copy for $6. Writer's guidelines online.

Fiction "I like elegant prose with a Gothic feel. The emphasis is on dark fantasy rather than horror. No vampire feeds, vampire has sex, someone becomes a vampire pieces." Vampires. "I am not interested in seeing the clichés redone." **Buys 30-40 mss/year.** Send complete ms. Length: 1,000-15,000 words. **Pays 1-5¢/word.**

Poetry "Looking for all forms; however, the less horrific and the more explicitly vampiric a poem is, the more likely it is to be accepted." **Pays $3/short poem; $5/long poem; $20/featured poet.**
Tips "We look for atmospheric, well-written stories with original ideas, not rehashes."

ℕ $ELLIPSIS MAGAZINE

Westminster College of Salt Lake City, 1840 S. 1300 E., Salt Lake City UT 84105. (801)832-2321. E-mail: ellipsis@ westminstercollege.edu. Website: www.westminstercollege.edu/ellipsis. **Contact:** *Ellipsis* Editor. Annual magazine. *Ellipsis Magazine* needs good literary poetry, fiction, essays, plays and visual art. Estab. 1967. Circ. 2,500. Pays on publication. Publishes ms an average of 3 months after acceptance. Byline given. Not copyrighted. Buys first North American serial rights. Accepts queries by mail. Accepts simultaneous submissions. Responds in 6 months to mss. Sample copy for $7.50. Writer's guidelines online.
- Reads submissions August 1 to November 1.
Nonfiction Essays. Send ms with SASE and brief bio.
Fiction Martin Murphy (revolving editor; changes every year). Needs good literary fiction and plays. Send complete ms. Length: 6,000 words. **Pays $50 per story and one contributor's copy; additional copies $3.50.**
Poetry All accepted poems are eligible for the *Ellipsis* Award which includes a $100 prize. Past judges have included Jorie Graham, Sandra Cisneros and Stanley Plumly. Submit maximum 3-5 poems. Include SASE and brief bio.

ℕ $EPOCH

Cornell University, 251 Goldwin Smith Hall, Cornell University, Ithaca NY 14853. (607)255-3385. Fax: (607)255-6661. Editor: Michael Koch. **Contact:** Joseph Martin, senior editor. **100% freelance written.** Magazine published 3 times/year. "Well-written literary fiction, poetry, personal essays. Newcomers always welcome. Open to mainstream and avant-garde writing." Estab. 1947. Circ. 1,000. Pays on publication. Publishes ms an average of an average of 6 months after acceptance. Byline given. Offers 100% kill fee. Buys first North American serial rights. Editorial lead time 6 months. Submit seasonal material 8 months in advance. Accepts queries by mail. Responds in 2 weeks to queries; 6 weeks to mss. Sample copy for $5. Writer's guidelines for #10 SASE.
Nonfiction Send complete ms. Essays, interview. No inspirational. **Buys 6-8 mss/year.** Send complete ms. Length: Open. **Pays $5-10/printed page.**
Photos Send photos with submission. Reviews contact sheets, transparencies, any size prints. Buys one-time rights. Negotiates payment individually.
Fiction Ethnic, experimental, mainstream, novel excerpts, literary short stories. "No genre fiction. Would like to see more Southern fiction (Southern US)." **Buys 25-30 mss/year.** Send complete ms. Length: Open. **Pays $5 and up/printed page.**
Poetry Nancy Vieira Couto. Avant-garde, free verse, haiku, light verse, traditional, all types. **Buys 30-75 poems/year.** Submit maximum 7 poems.
Tips "Tell your story, speak your poem, straight from the heart. We are attracted to language and to good writing, but we are most interested in what the good writing leads us to, or where."

$ $☑ EVENT

Douglas College, P.O. Box 2503, New Westminster BC V3L 5B2, Canada. (604)527-5293. Fax: (604)527-5095. E-mail: event@douglas.bc.ca. Website: event.douglas.bc.ca. **Contact:** Carolyn Robertson, assistant editor. **100% freelance written.** Magazine published 3 times/year containing fiction, poetry, creative nonfiction, notes on writing, and reviews. "We are eclectic and always open to content that invites involvement. Generally, we like strong narrative." Estab. 1971. Circ. 1,250. Pays on publication. Publishes ms an average of 8 months after acceptance. Byline given. Buys first North American serial rights. Accepts queries by mail, fax. Accepts simultaneous submissions. Responds in 1 month to queries; 6 months to mss. Sample copy for $5. Writer's guidelines online.
- *Event* does not read mss in July, August, December, and January. No e-mail submissions. All submissions must include SASE (Canadian postage or IRCs only).
Fiction Christine Dewar, fiction editor. "We look for readability, style, and writing that invites involvement." Submit maximum 2 stories. Humorous, contemporary. "No technically poor or unoriginal pieces." **Buys 12-15 mss/year.** Send complete ms. Length: 5,000 words maximum. **Pays $22/page to $500.**
Poetry "We tend to appreciate the narrative and sometimes the confessional modes." Gillian Harding-Russell, poetry editor. Free verse, prose. No light verse. **Buys 30-40 poems/year.** Submit maximum 10 poems. **Pays $25-500.**
Tips "Write well and read some past issues of *Event*."

$FIELD: CONTEMPORARY POETRY & POETICS

Oberlin College Press, 10 N. Professor St., Oberlin OH 44074-1095. (440)775-8408. Fax: (440)775-8124. E-mail: oc.press@oberlin.edu. Website: www.oberlin.edu/ocpress. **Contact:** Linda Slocum, managing editor. **60% free-**

lance written. Biannual magazine of poetry, poetry in translation, and essays on contemporary poetry by poets. No electronic submissions. Estab. 1969. Circ. 1,500. Pays on publication. Byline given. Buys first rights. Editorial lead time 4 months. Accepts queries by mail, e-mail, fax, phone. Responds in 6 weeks to mss. Sample copy for $7. Writer's guidelines online.

Poetry Buys 100 poems/year. Submit maximum 5 with SASE poems. **Pays $15/page.**

Tips "Submit 3-5 of your best poems with a cover letter. No simultaneous submissions and include a SASE. Keep trying! Submissions are read year-round."

$THE FIRST LINE

Blue Cubicle Press, LLC, P.O. Box 250382, Plano TX 75025-0382. E-mail: info@thefirstline.com. Website: www.t hefirstline.com. Co-editors: David LaBounty and Jeff Adams. **Contact:** Robin LaBounty, ms coordinator. **95% freelance written.** Quarterly magazine. *The First Line* is a magazine that explores the different directions writers can take when they start from the same place. All stories must be written with the first line provided by the magazine. Estab. 1999. Circ. 250. Pays on publication. Publishes ms an average of 1 month after acceptance. Byline given. Buys first North American serial, electronic rights. Editorial lead time 2 months. Accepts queries by mail, e-mail. Responds in 1 week to queries; 2 months to mss. Sample copy for $3. Writer's guidelines online.

Nonfiction David LaBounty, editor. Essays, interview/profile, Book Reviews. **Buys 4-8 mss/year.** Query. Length: 300-1,000 words. **Pays $10.**

Fiction Adventure, ethnic, experimental, fantasy, historical, horror, humorous, mainstream, mystery, romance, science fiction, suspense, western. No stories that do not start with the issue's first sentence. **Buys 40-60 mss/ year.** Send complete ms. Length: 300-3,000 words. **Pays $10.**

N $FIVE POINTS

A Journal of Literature and Art, MSC 8R0318 Georgia State University, 33 Gilmer St. SE, Unit 8, Atlanta GA 30303-3083. Fax: (404)651-3167. E-mail: info@langate.gsu.edu. Website: www.webdelsol.com/five_points. Triannual *Five Points* is "committed to publishing work that compels the imagination through the use of fresh and convincing language." Estab. 1996. Circ. 2,000. Publishes ms an average of 6 months after acceptance. Buys first North American serial rights. Sample copy for $7. Editorial calendar online.

Fiction Megan Sexton, associate editor. **Pays $15/page minimum; $250 maximum, free subscription to magazine and 2 contributor's copies; additional copies $4.**

N $FLESH FROM ASHES

Flesh from Ashes Publications, 601 æ N. Main St., Findlay OH 45840. (419)420-9086. E-mail: anakatora@fleshfr omashes.net. Website: www.fleshfromashes.net. **Contact:** Robin Coe, editor. **100% freelance written.** Quarterly magazine using art as a catalyst for social change. "Using the power of art to subvert political and corporate propaganda. Rise from the ashes of your social disillusion and take a creative stand against the political and corporate propaganda that perpetuates spiritual, psychological, and physical death." Estab. 2002. Circ. 1,000. Pays on publication. Publishes ms an average of 3 months after acceptance. Byline given. Buys one-time rights. Editorial lead time 3 months. Submit seasonal material 3 months in advance. Accepts queries by mail, e-mail. Accepts simultaneous submissions. Responds in 6 weeks to queries; 4 months to mss. Sample copy for $4. Writer's guidelines for #10 SASE.

Nonfiction Essays (political), exposé, historical/nostalgic (history of art and political revolution), interview/ profile (of activist artists), opinion (political/social), photo feature (protests, art exhibits/performances). Query. Length: 350-2,000 words. **Pays $5-10.** Sometimes pays expenses of writers on assignment.

Photos Send photos with submission. Reviews GIF/JPEG files. Buys one-time rights. Negotiates payment individually. Captions, identification of subjects, model releases required.

Columns/Departments Movie Reviews; Book Reviews; Music Reviews (all covering political/social issues, including: gay/lesbian issues, human rights, animal rights, environmental justice, corporate accountability), all 200-450 words. **Buys 4-8 mss/year. Pays $5-10.**

Fiction Ethnic, experimental, fantasy, historical, novel excerpts, science fiction. No mss that expound hate or excessive violence. **Buys 4 mss/year.** Query. Length: 500-1,500 words. **Pays $5-10 or contributor copy.**

Poetry Avant-garde, free verse, haiku, light verse, traditional, experimental. **Buys 15-20 poems/year.**

Fillers Anecdotes, facts, gags to be illustrated by cartoonist, newsbreaks, short humor. **Buys 5-15/year. Pays $5-10 or contributor copy.**

Tips "*Flesh from Ashes* focuses on the Marcusean idea of using art as a catalyst for social change. It's important for writers to have a grasp of current political and social issues. However, we are also interested in publishing works that analyze how artists used their work throughout history to influence their environment. We give special attention to art in all mediums that push beyond the current styles and rules of their medium to create new definitions of art."

$ ▣ FRANK

An International Journal of Contemporary Writing & Art, Association Frank, 32 rue Edouard Vaillant, Montreuil, France. (33)(1)48596658. Fax: (33)(1)48596668. E-mail: submissions@readfrank.com. Website: www.readfrank.com or www.frank.ly. **Contact:** David Applefield, editor. **80% freelance written.** Published twice/year magazine covering contemporary writing of all genres. Bilingual. "Writing that takes risks and isn't ethnocentric is looked upon favorably." Estab. 1983. Circ. 4,000. Pays on publication. Publishes ms an average of 1 year after acceptance. Byline given. Buys one-time rights. Editorial lead time 6 months. Responds in 1 month to queries; 2 months to mss. Sample copy for $10. Writer's guidelines online.

Nonfiction Interview/profile, travel. **Buys 2 mss/year.** Query. **Pays $100 for assigned articles.**

Photos State availability with submission. Buys one-time rights. Negotiates payment individually.

Fiction David Applefield. Experimental, novel excerpts, international. "At *Frank*, we publish fiction, poetry, literary and art interviews, and translations. We like work that falls between existing genres and has social or political consciousness." **Buys 8 mss/year.** Send complete ms. Length: 1,000-3,000 words. **Pays $10/printed page.**

Poetry Avant-garde, translations. **Buys 20 poems/year.** Submit maximum 10 poems. **Pays $20.**

Tips "Suggest what you do or know best. Avoid query form letters—we won't read the manuscript. Looking for excellent literary/cultural interviews with leading American writers or cultural figures. Very receptive to new Foreign Dossiers of writing from a particular country."

Ⓝ $ THE GAY & LESBIAN REVIEW

Gay & Lesbian Review, Inc., P.O. Box 180300, Boston MA 02118. (617)421-0082. E-mail: hglr@aol.com. Website: www.glreview.com. **Contact:** Richard Schneider, editor. **100% freelance written.** Bimonthly magazine covers gay & lesbian history, culture, and politics. "In-depth essays on GLBT history, biography, the arts, political issues, written in clear, lively prose targeted to the 'literate nonspecialist.'" Estab. 1994. Circ. 12,000. Pays on publication. Byline given. Buys first rights. Editorial lead time 2 months. Accepts queries by mail, e-mail, phone. Accepts simultaneous submissions. Sample copy for free. Writer's guidelines free.

Nonfiction Essays, historical/nostalgic, humor, interview/profile, opinion, book reviews. Does not want fiction, memoirs, personal reflections. Query. Length: 1,500-5,000 words. **Pays $100.** "Writer can waive payment for five gift subscriptions."

Poetry David Bergman, poetry editor. Avant-garde, free verse, traditional.

Tips "We prefer that a proposal be e-mailed before a completed draft is sent."

$ THE GEORGIA REVIEW

The University of Georgia, 012 Gilbert Hall, University of Georgia, Athens GA 30602-9009. (706)542-3481. Fax: (706)542-0047. E-mail: garev@uga.edu. Website: www.uga.edu/garev. Managing Editor: Annette Hatton. **Contact:** T.R. Hummer, editor. **99% freelance written.** Quarterly journal. "Our readers are educated, inquisitive people who read a lot of work in the areas we feature, so they expect only the best in our pages. All work submitted should show evidence that the writer is at least as well-educated and well-read as our readers. Essays should be authoritative but accessible to a range of readers." Estab. 1947. Circ. 5,000. Pays on publication. Publishes ms an average of 6 months after acceptance. Byline given. Buys first North American serial rights. Accepts queries by mail. Responds in 2 weeks to queries; 3 months to mss. Sample copy for $7. Writer's guidelines online.

● No simultaneous or electronic submissions.

Nonfiction Essays. "For the most part we are not interested in scholarly articles that are narrow in focus and/or overly burdened with footnotes. The ideal essay for *The Georgia Review* is a provocative, thesis-oriented work that can engage both the intelligent general reader and the specialist." **Buys 12-20 mss/year.** Send complete ms. **Pays $40/published page.**

Photos Send photos with submission. Reviews 5×7 prints or larger. Buys one-time rights. Offers no additional payment for photos accepted with ms.

Fiction "We seek original, excellent writing not bound by type. "Ordinarily we do not publish novel excerpts or works translated into English, and we strongly discourage authors from submitting these." **Buys 12-20 mss/year.** Send complete ms. Length: Open. **Pays $40/published page.**

Poetry "We seek original, excellent poetry." **Buys 60-75 poems/year.** Submit maximum 5 poems. **Pays $3/line.**

Tips "Unsolicited manuscripts will not be considered from May 15-August 15 (annually); all such submissions received during that period will be returned unread."

$ THE GETTYSBURG REVIEW

Gettysburg College, Gettysburg PA 17325. (717)337-6770. Fax: (717)337-6775. Website: www.gettysburgreview.com. **Contact:** Peter Stitt, editor. Quarterly magazine. "Our concern is quality. Manuscripts submitted here should be extremely well written." Reading period September-May. Estab. 1988. Circ. 4,000. Pays on publication. Publishes ms an average of within 1 year after acceptance. Byline given. Buys first North American serial rights. Editorial lead time 1 year. Submit seasonal material 9 months in advance. Accepts queries by mail, fax. Accepts simultaneous submissions. Responds in 1 month to queries; 3-6 months to mss. Sample copy for $7. Writer's guidelines online.

Nonfiction Essays. **Buys 20 mss/year.** Send complete ms. Length: 3,000-7,000 words. **Pays $30/page.**

Fiction Mark Drew, assisant editor. High quality, literary. Experimental, historical, humorous, mainstream, novel excerpts, serialized novels, contemporary. "We require that fiction be intelligent, and esthetically written." **Buys 20 mss/year.** Send complete ms. Length: 2,000-7,000 words. **Pays $30/page.**

Poetry Buys 50 poems/year. Submit maximum 3 poems. **Pays $2.50/line.**

$ $ GLIMMER TRAIN STORIES

Glimmer Train Press, Inc., 1211 NW Glisan St., Suite 207, Portland OR 97209. (503)221-0836. Fax: (503)221-0837. E-mail: linda@glimmertrain.com. Website: www.glimmertrain.com. **Contact:** Linda Swanson-Davies, co-editor. **90% freelance written.** Quarterly magazine of literary short fiction. "We are interested in well-written, emotionally-moving short stories published by unknown, as well as known, writers." Estab. 1991. Circ. 16,000. **Pays on acceptance.** Publishes ms an average of 18 months after acceptance. Byline given. Buys first rights. Responds in 3 months to mss. Sample copy for $11 on website. Writer's guidelines online.

Fiction "Open to stories of all themes, all subjects." **Buys 32 mss/year.** Length: up to 12,000. **Pays $500.**

Tips To submit a story, use the form on the website. All stories should be submitted via this electronic format. See *Glimmer Train*'s contest listings in Contest and Awards section.

$ $ ⊡ GRAIN LITERARY MAGAZINE

Saskatchewan Writers Guild, P.O. Box 67, Saskatoon SK S7K 3K1, Canada. (306)244-2828. Fax: (306)244-0255. E-mail: grain@sasktel.net. Website: www.grainmagazine.ca. Buisiness Administrator: Bobbi Clackson-Walker. **Contact:** Kent Bruyneel, editor. **100% freelance written.** Quarterly magazine covering poetry, fiction, creative nonfiction, drama. "*Grain* publishes writing of the highest quality, both traditional and innovative in nature. The *Grain* editors' aim: To publish work that challenges readers; to encourage promising new writers; and to produce a well-designed, visually interesting magazine." Estab. 1973. Circ. 1,600. Pays on publication. Byline given. Buys first, canadian serial rights. Editorial lead time 6 months. Accepts queries by mail. Responds in 1 month to queries; 4 months to mss. Sample copy for $10 or online. Writer's guidelines for #10 SASE or online.

Nonfiction Interested in creative nonfiction.

Photos Submit 12-20 slides and b&w prints, short statement (200 words), and brief résumé. Reviews transparencies, prints. Pays $100 for front cover art, $30/photo.

Fiction Joanne Gerber, fiction editor. Literary fiction of all types. Experimental, mainstream, Contemporary, prose poem. "No romance, confession, science fiction, vignettes, mystery." **Buys 40 mss/year.** Length: "No more than 30 pages." **Pays $40-175.**

Poetry "High quality, imaginative, well-crafted poetry. Submit maximum 10 poems and SASE with postage or IRC's. Avant-garde, free verse, haiku, traditional. No sentimental, end-line rhyme, mundane." **Buys 78 poems/ year. Pays $40-175.**

Tips "Sweat the small stuff. Pay attention to detail, credibility. Make sure you have researched your piece and that the literal and metaphorical support one another."

Ⓝ $ $ $ Ⓞ GRAND STREET

214 Sullivan St., Suite 6C, New York NY 10012. (212)533-2944. Fax: (212)533-2737. Website: www.grandstreet. com. Biannual "We publish new fiction and nonfiction of all types." Estab. 1981. Circ. 7,000. Buys first North American serial rights. Sample copy for $18; varies overseas and Canada.

Fiction Radhika Jones, managing editor. Poetry and essays. Length:9,000 words. **Pays $250-1,000 and 2 contributor's copies.**

⊕ GRANTA

The Magazine of New Writing, Granta Publications, 2-3 Hanover Yard, Noel Rd., London NI 8BE, UK. (44)(0)20 7704 9776. E-mail: editorial@granta.com. Website: www.granta.com. Editor: Ian Jack. **Contact:** Helen Gordon, editorial assistant. **100% freelance written.** Quarterly 256-page paperback book. "*Granta* magazine publishes fiction, reportage, biography and autobiography, history, travel and documentary photography. It does not publish 'writing about writing.' The realistic narrative - the story - is its primary form." Estab. 1979. Circ. 80,000. Pays on publication. Byline given. Offers kill fee, amount determined by arrangement. Buys world English language rights, first serial rights (minimum). "We hold more rights in pieces we commission." Editorial lead time 3 months. Accepts simultaneous submissions. Responds in 3 months to mss. Sample copy for $14.95. Writer's guidelines online.

• Queries not necessary.

Nonfiction No articles or reporting whose relevancy will not last the life span of the magazine. The pieces we publish should last for several years (as the issues themselves do).

Fiction Buys no more than 2 short stories or synopsis and first chapter of a novel. "Please do not send more than 2 stories at a time." Novel excerpts, literary. No genre fiction. Length: No limits on length. **Payment varies.**

Tips "You must be familiar with the magazine and ask yourself honestly if you feel your piece meets our criteria. We receive many submissions every day, many of which are completely unsuitable for *Granta* (however well written)."

Ⓝ $GULF COAST

A Journal of Literature and Fine Art, D, Dept. of English, University of Houston, Houston TX 77204. (713)743-3223. Fax: (713)743-3215. E-mail: gulfcoast@gulfcoast.uh.edu. Website: www.gulfcoastmag.uh.edu. Editor: Mark Doty. Managing Editor: Sasha West. **Contact:** Poetry, Fiction or Nonfiction Editors. **100% freelance written.** Semiannual magazine. "*Gulf Coast*'s mission is to promote and support literary excellence by publishing the best poetry, fiction, literary nonfiction and reviews of both emerging and established writers. *GC* is particularly committed to fostering the careers of young writers." Estab. 1987. Circ. 1,000. Publishes ms an average of 6 months-1 year after acceptance. Buys *small* honorarium for one-time rights rights. Accepts simultaneous submissions. Responds in 6 months to mss. Back issue for $6, 7×10 SAE and 4 first-class stamps. Writer's guidelines for #10 SASE or on website.

Nonfiction James Hall, nonfiction editor. Book excerpts, essays. Send complete ms. **Pays $50-100.**

Fiction Fiction Editors. Literary. **Buys 8-10 mss/year.** Send complete ms. Length: No limit. **Pays $50-100.**

Poetry Buys 60-80 poems/year. Submit maximum 7 poems. **Pays $30-50.**

$HAPPY

240 E. 35th St., Suite 11A, New York NY 10016. E-mail: bayardx@aol.com. **Contact:** Bayard, editor. Quarterly Estab. 1995. Circ. 500. Pays on publication. Publishes ms an average of 6-12 months after acceptance. Byline given. Buys one-time rights. Accepts queries by mail. Accepts simultaneous submissions. Responds in 1 month to queries. Sample copy for $20. Writer's guidelines for #10 SASE.

Fiction "We accept anything that's beautifully written. Genre isn't important. It just has to be incredible writing." Erotica, ethnic, experimental, fantasy, horror, humorous, novel excerpts, science fiction, short stories. No "television rehash or religious nonsense." Want more work that is "strong, angry, empowering, intelligent, God-like, expressive." **Buys 100-130 mss/year.** Send complete ms. Length: 6,000 words maximum. **Pays 1-5¢/word.**

Tips "Don't bore us with the mundane—blast us out of the water with the extreme!"

$HAYDEN'S FERRY REVIEW

Arizona State University, Box 871502, Arizona State University, Tempe AZ 85287-1502. (480)965-1243. E-mail: hfr@asu.edu. Website: www.asu.edu/clas/pipercwcenter/publications/haydensferryreview. **Contact:** Fiction, Poetry, or Art Editor. **85% freelance written.** Semiannual magazine. "*Hayden's Ferry Review* publishes best quality fiction, poetry, and creative nonfiction from new, emerging, and established writers." Estab. 1986. Circ. 1,300. Pays on publication. Publishes ms an average of 6 months after acceptance. Byline given. Buys first North American serial rights. Editorial lead time 3 months. Accepts queries by mail. Accepts simultaneous submissions. Responds in 2 weeks to queries; 3 months to mss. Sample copy for $7.50. Writer's guidelines online.

• No electronic submissions.

Nonfiction Essays, interview/profile, personal experience. **Buys 2 mss/year.** Send complete ms. Length: Open. **Pays $25-100.**

Photos Send photos with submission. Reviews slides. Buys one-time rights. Offers $25/photo.

Fiction Editors change every 1-2 years. Ethnic, experimental, humorous, slice-of-life vignettes, contemporary, prose poem. **Buys 10 mss/year.** Send complete ms. Length: Open. **Pays $25-100.**

Poetry Avant-garde, free verse, haiku, light verse, traditional. **Buys 60 poems/year.** Submit maximum 6 poems. Length: Open. **Pays $25-100.**

$THE HOLLINS CRITIC

P.O. Box 9538, Hollins University, Roanoke VA 24020-1538. E-mail: acockrell@hollins.edu. Website: www.hollins.edu/academics/critic. Editor: R.H.W. Dillard. Managing Editor: Amanda Cockrell. **Contact:** Cathryn Hankla, poetry editor. **100% freelance written.** Magazine published 5 times/year. Estab. 1964. Circ. 400. Pays on publication. Publishes ms an average of 2 years after acceptance. Byline given. Buys first North American serial rights. Accepts queries by mail. Accepts simultaneous submissions. Responds in 2 months to mss. Sample copy for $1.50. Writer's guidelines for #10 SASE.

- No e-mail submissions. Send complete ms.

Poetry "We read poetry only from September 1 to December 15." Avant-garde, free verse, traditional. **Buys 16-20 poems/year.** Submit maximum 5 poems. **Pays $25.**

Tips "We accept unsolicited poetry submissions; all other content is by prearrangement."

⊠ $ THE HUDSON REVIEW

A magazine of literature and the arts, The Hudson Review, Inc., 684 Park Ave., New York NY 10021. (212)650-0020. Fax: (212)774-1911. E-mail: info@hudsonreview.com. Website: www.hudsonreview.com. Managing Editor: Ronald Koury. **Contact:** Paula Deitz, editor. **100% freelance written.** Quarterly magazine publishing fiction, poetry, essays, book reviews; criticism of literature, art, theatre, dance, film and music; and articles on contemporary cultural developments. Estab. 1948. Circ. 5,000. Pays on publication. Publishes ms an average of 6 months after acceptance. Byline given. Only assigned reviews are copyrighted. Editorial lead time 3 months. Accepts queries by mail. Responds in 2 months to queries; 3 months to mss. Sample copy for $9. Writer's guidelines for #10 SASE.

Nonfiction Paula Deitz. Essays, general interest, historical/nostalgic, opinion, personal experience, travel. **Buys 4-6 mss/year.** Send complete ms between January 1 and March 31 only. Length: 3,500 words maximum. **Pays 2¹/₂¢/word.**

Fiction Ronald Koury. Read between September 1 and November 30 only. **Buys 4 mss/year. Pays 2¹/₂¢/word.**

Poetry Read poems only between April 1 and June 30. Shannon Bond, associate editor. **Buys 12-20 poems/ year.** Submit maximum 7 poems. **Pays 50¢/line.**

Tips "We do not specialize in publishing any particular 'type' of writing; our sole criterion for accepting unsolicited work is literary quality. The best way for you to get an idea of the range of work we publish is to read a current issue. We do not consider simultaneous submissions. Unsolicited mss submitted outside of specified reading times will be returned unread. Do not send submissions via e-mail."

$ HUNGER MOUNTAIN

The Vermont College Journal of Arts & Letters, Vermont College/Union Institute & University, 36 College St., Montpelier VT 05602. Fax: (802)828-8649. E-mail: hungermtn@tui.edu. Website: www.hungermtn.org. **Contact:** Caroline Mercurio, managing editor. **30% freelance written.** Semiannual perfect-bound journal covering high quality fiction, poetry, creative nonfiction, interviews, photography, and artwork reproductions. Accepts high quality work from unknown, emerging, or successful writers and artists. No genre fiction, drama, children's writing, or academic articles, please. Estab. 2002. Pays on publication. Publishes ms an average of 1 year after acceptance. Byline given. Buys first North American serial rights. Submit seasonal material 6 months in advance. Accepts queries by mail. Responds in 1 month to queries; 3 months to mss. Sample copy for $10. Writer's guidelines for free, online at website, or by e-mail.

Nonfiction Creative nonfiction only. All book reviews and interviews will be solicited. Book excerpts, essays, opinion, personal experience, photo feature, religious, travel. Special issues: "We will publish special issues, hopefully yearly, but we do not know yet the themes of these issues." No informative or instructive articles, please. Query with published clips. **Pays $5/page (minimum $30).** Sometimes pays expenses of writers on assignment.

Photos Send photos with submission. Reviews contact sheets, transparencies, prints, GIF/JPEG files. Slides preferred. Buys one-time rights. Negotiates payment individually. Query with published clips. **Pays $25-100.**

Poetry Avant-garde, free verse, haiku, traditional, nature, narrative, experimental, etc. No light verse, humor/ quirky/catchy verse, greeting card verse. **Buys 10 poems/year.**

Tips "We want high quality work! Submit in duplicate. Manuscripts must be typed, prose double-spaced. Poets submit at least 3 poems. No multiple genre submissions. We need more b&w photography and short shorts. Fresh viewpoints and human interest are very important, as is originality. We are committed to publishing an outstanding journal of arts & letters. Do not send entire novels, manuscripts, or short story collections. Do not send previously published work."

$ THE ICONOCLAST

1675 Amazon Rd., Mohegan Lake NY 10547-1804. **Contact:** Phil Wagner, editor. **90% freelance written.** Bimonthly literary magazine. "Aimed for a literate general audience with interests in fine (but accessible) fiction and poetry." Estab. 1992. Circ. 600. Pays on publication. Publishes ms an average of 9-12 months after acceptance. Byline given. Buys first North American serial rights. Editorial lead time 1-2 months. Accepts queries by mail. Responds in 2 weeks to queries; 1 month to mss. Sample copy for $2.50. Writer's guidelines for #10 SASE.

Nonfiction Essays, humor, reviews, literary/cultural matters. Does not want "anything that would be found in the magazines on the racks of supermarkets or convenience stores." **Buys 6-10 mss/year.** Query. Length: 250-2,500 words. **Pays 1¢/word.** Pays in contributor copies for previously published articles.

Photos Line drawings preferred. State availability with submission. Reviews 4×6, b&w only prints. Buys one-time rights. Negotiates payment individually.

Columns/Departments Book reviews (fiction/poetry), 250-500 words. **Buys 6 mss/year.** Query. **Pays 1¢/word.**

Fiction Buys more fiction and poetry than anything else. Adventure, ethnic, experimental, fantasy, humorous, mainstream, novel excerpts, science fiction, literary. No character studies, slice-of-life, pieces strong on attitude/weak on plot. **Buys 25 mss/year.** Send complete ms. Length: 250-3,000 words. **Pays 1¢/word.**

Poetry Avant-garde, free verse, haiku, light verse, traditional. No religious, greeting card, beginner rhyming. **Buys 75 poems/year.** Submit maximum 4 poems. Length: 2-50 lines. **Pays $2-5.**

Tips "Professional conduct and sincerity help. Know it's the best you can do on a work before sending it out. Skill is the luck of the prepared. Everything counts. We love what we do, and are serious about it—and expect you to share that attitude. Remember: You're writing for paying subscribers. Ask Yourself: Would I pay money to read what I'm sending? We don't reply to submissions without a SASE, nor do we e-mail replies."

$ INDIANA REVIEW

Indiana University, Ballantine Hall 465, 1020 E. Kirkwood, Bloomington IN 47405-7103. (812)855-3439. Website: www.indiana.edu/~inreview. **Contact:** Esther Lee, editor. **100% freelance written.** Biannual magazine. "*Indiana Review*, a nonprofit organization run by IU graduate students, is a journal of previously unpublished poetry and fiction. Literary interviews and essays also considered. We publish innovative fiction and poetry. We're interested in energy, originality, and careful attention to craft. While we publish many well-known writers, we also welcome new and emerging poets and fiction writers." Estab. 1976. Circ. 2,000. Pays on publication. Publishes ms an average of 3-6 months after acceptance. Byline given. Buys first North American serial rights. Accepts queries by mail. Accepts simultaneous submissions. Responds in 2 weeks to queries; 4 months to mss. Sample copy for $9. Writer's guidelines online.

> ⊶ Break in with 500-1,000 word book reviews of fiction, poetry, nonfiction, and literary criticism published within the last 2 years, "since this is the area in which there's the least amount of competition."

Nonfiction Essays, interview/profile, creative nonfiction, reviews. No "coming of age/slice of life pieces." **Buys 5-7 mss/year.** Send complete ms. Length: 9,000 words maximum. **Pays $5/page ($10/minimum), plus 2 contributor's copies.**

Fiction Danit Brown, fiction editor. "We look for daring stories which integrate theme, language, character, and form. We like polished writing, humor, and fiction which has consequence beyond the world of its narrator." Ethnic, experimental, mainstream, novel excerpts, literary, short fictions, translations. No genre fiction. **Buys 14-18 mss/year.** Send complete ms. Length: 250-10,000 words. **Pays $5/page ($10/minimum), plus 2 contributor's copies.**

Poetry "We look for poems that are skillfull and bold, exhibiting an inventiveness of language with attention to voice and sonics." Experimental, free verse, prose poem, traditional form, lyrical, narrative. Esther Lee, poetry editor. **Buys 80 poems/year.** Submit maximum 6 poems. Length: 5 lines minimum. **Pays $5/page ($10/minimum), plus 2 contributor's copies.**

Tips "We're always looking for non-fiction essays that go beyond merely autobiographical revelation and utilize sophisticated organization and slightly radical narrative strategies. We want essays that are both lyrical and analytical where confession does not mean nostalgia. Read us before you submit. Often reading is slower in summer and holiday months. Only submit work to journals you would proudly subscribe to, then subscribe to a few. Take care to read the latest 2 issues and specifically mention work you identify with and why. Submit work that 'stacks up' with the work we've published." Offers annual poetry, fiction, short-short/prose-poem prizes. See website for details.

$ THE IOWA REVIEW

308 EPB, The University of Iowa, Iowa City IA 52242. (319)335-0462. Fax: (319)335-2535. E-mail: iareview@blue.weeg.uiowa.edu. Website: www.uiowa.edu/~iareview/. **Contact:** David Hamilton, editor. Triannual magazine "Stories, essays, poems for a general readership interested in contemporary literature." Estab. 1970. Circ. 2,500. Pays on publication. Publishes ms an average of 8-12 months after acceptance. Buys first North American serial, nonexclusive anthology, classroom, and online serial rights rights. Responds in 3 months to queries; 3 months to mss. Sample copy for $7 and online. Writer's guidelines online.

• This magazine uses the help of colleagues and graduate assistants. Its reading period for unsolicited work is September 1-December 1. "From January through April, we read entries to our annual Iowa Awards competition. Check our website for further information."

Fiction "We are open to a range of styles and voices and always hope to be surprised by work we then feel we need." **Pays $25 for the first page and $15 for each additional page, plus 2 contributor's copies; additional copies 30% off cover price.**

Tips "We publish essays, reviews, novel excerpts, stories, and poems, and would like for our essays not always to be works of academic criticism. We have no set guidelines as to content or length, but strongly recommend that writers read a sample issue before submitting." **Buys 65-80 unsolicited ms/year.** Submit complete ms with SASE. **Pays $25 for the first page and $15 for each subsequent page of poetry or prose.**

$IRREANTUM

Exploring Mormon Literature, The Association for Mormon Letters, P.O. Box 51364, Provo UT 84605. (801)373-9730. E-mail: irreantum2@cs.com. Website: www.aml-online.org. **Contact:** Christopher Bigelow. Quarterly magazine. "While focused on Mormonism, *Irreantum* is a cultural, humanities-oriented magazine, not a religious magazine. Our guiding principle is that Mormonism is grounded in a sufficiently unusual, cohesive, and extended historical and cultural experience that it has become like a nation, an ethnic culture. We can speak of Mormon literature at least as surely as we can of a Jewish or Southern literature. *Irreantum* publishes stories, one-act dramas, stand-alone novel and drama excerpts, and poetry by, for, or about Mormons (as well as author interviews, essays, and reviews). The magazine's audience includes readers of any or no religious faith who are interested in literary exploration of the Mormon culture, mindset, and worldview through Mormon themes and characters. *Irreantum* is currently the only magazine devoted to Mormon literature." Estab. 1999. Circ. 500. Pays on publication. Publishes ms an average of 3-12 months after acceptance. Buys one-time, electronic rights. Accepts queries by e-mail. Accepts previously published material. Accepts simultaneous submissions. Responds in 2 weeks to queries; 2 months to mss. Sample copy for $6. Writer's guidelines by e-mail.

● Also publishes short shorts, literary essays, literary criticism, and poetry.

Fiction Adventure, ethnic, experimental, fantasy, historical, horror, humorous, mainstream, mystery, religious, romance, science fiction, suspense. **Buys 12 mss/year.** Length: 1,000-5,000 words. **Pays $0-100.**

Tips "*Irreantum* is not interested in didactic or polemnical fiction that primarily attempts to prove or disprove Mormon doctrine, history, or corporate policy. We encourage beginning writers to focus on human elements first, with Mormon elements introduced only as natural and organic to the story. Readers can tell if you are honestly trying to explore human experience or if you are writing with a propagandistic agenda either for or against Mormonism. For conservative, orthodox Mormon writers, beware of sentimentalism, simplistic resolutions, and foregone conclusions."

$THE JOURNAL

The Ohio State University, 164 W. 17th Ave., Columbus OH 43210. (614)292-4076. Fax: (614)292-7816. E-mail: thejournal@osu.edu. Website: www.english.ohio-state.edu/journals/the_journal/. **Contact:** Fiction Editor, Poetry Editor, Nonfiction Editor, Poetry Review Editor. **100% freelance written.** Semiannual magazine. "We're open to all forms; we tend to favor work that gives evidence of a mature and sophisticated sense of the language." Estab. 1972. Circ. 1,500. Pays on publication. Publishes ms an average of 1 year after acceptance. Byline given. Buys first North American serial rights. Accepts queries by mail. Accepts simultaneous submissions. Responds in 2 weeks to queries; 2 months to mss. Sample copy for $7 or online. Writer's guidelines online.

Nonfiction Essays, interview/profile. **Buys 2 mss/year.** Query. Length: 2,000-4,000 words. **Pays $30 maximum.**

Columns/Departments Reviews of contemporary poetry, 1,500 words maximum. **Buys 2 mss/year.** Query. **Pays $30.**

Fiction Novel excerpts, literary short stories. No romance, science fiction or religious/devotional. Length: Open. **Pays $30.**

Poetry Avant-garde, free verse, traditional. **Buys 100 poems/year.** Submit maximum 5 poems. **Pays $30.**

$KALLIOPE

a journal of women's literature & art, Florida Community College at Jacksonville, 11901 Beach Blvd., Jacksonville FL 32246. (904)646-2081. Website: www.fccj.org/kalliope. **Contact:** Mary Sue Koeppel, editor. **100% freelance written.** Biannual magazine. "*Kalliope* publishes poetry, short fiction, reviews, and b&w art, usually by women artists. We look for artistic excellence." Estab. 1978. Circ. 1,600. Pays on publication. Publishes ms an average of 3 months after acceptance. Byline given. Buys first rights. "We accept only unpublished work. Copyright returned to author upon request." Accepts queries by mail. Responds in 1 week to queries; 3 months to mss. Sample copy for $9 (recent issue) or $4 (back copy), or see sample issues on website. Writer's guidelines online.

● *Kalliope's* reading period is September-April.

o→ Break in with a "finely crafted poem or short story or a Q&A with an established, well-published woman poet or literary novelist."

Nonfiction Interview/profile (Q&A), reviews of new works of poetry and fiction. **Buys 6 mss/year.** Send complete ms. Length: 500-2,000 words. **Pays $10 honorarium if funds are available, otherwise 2 copies or subscription.**

Photos "Visual art should be sent in groups of 4-10 works. We require b&w professional quality, glossy prints made from negatives. Please supply photo credits, model releases, date of work, title, medium, and size on the back of each photo submitted. Include artist's résumé where applicable. We welcome an artist's statement of 50-75 words."

Fiction Fiction Editor. Ethnic, experimental, novel excerpts, literary. "Quality short fiction by women writers. No science fiction or fantasy. Would like to see more experimental fiction." **Buys 12 mss/year.** Send complete ms. Length: 100-2,000 words. **Pays $10 honorarium if funds are available, otherwise 2 copies or subscription.**

Poetry Avant-garde, free verse, haiku, traditional. **Buys 75 poems/year.** Submit maximum 3-5 poems. Length: 2-120 lines. **Pays $10 honorarium if funds are available, otherwise 2 copies or subscription.**

Tips "We publish the best of the material submitted to us each issue. (We don't build a huge backlog and then publish from that backlog for years.) Although we look for new writers and usually publish several with each issue alongside already established writers, we love it when established writers send us their work. We've recently published Ruth Stone, Marge Piercy, Maxine Kumin, and 1 of the last poems by Denise Levertov. Send a bio with all submissions."

$THE KENYON REVIEW

Walton House, 104 College Dr., Gambier OH 43022. (740)427-5208. Fax: (740)427-5417. E-mail: kenyonreview @kenyon.edu. Website: www.kenyonreview.org. **Contact:** David H. Lynn, editor. **100% freelance written.** Quarterly magazine covering contemporary literature and criticism. An international journal of literature, culture, and the arts dedicated to an inclusive representation of the best in new writing (fiction, poetry, essays, interviews, criticism) from established and emerging writers. Estab. 1939. Circ. 5,000. Pays on publication. Publishes ms an average of 1 year after acceptance. Byline given. Buys first rights. Editorial lead time 1 year. Submit seasonal material 1 year in advance. Accepts queries by mail. Responds in 3-4 months to queries; 4 months to mss. Sample copy $10 single issue, $13 double issue, includes postage and handling. Please call or e-mail to order. Writer's guidelines online. Length: 3-15 typeset pages preferred. **Pays $10-15/page.**

KIRKUS REVIEWS

VNU Business Media, 770 Broadway, 6th Floor, New York NY 10003. (646)654-5000. Fax: (646)654-4706. E-mail: kirkusrev@kirkusreviews.com. Website: www.kirkusreviews.com. Editor: Anne Larsen. Managing Editor: Chuck Shelton. Semi-monthly magazine. Publication reviews of fiction, nonfiction, juvenile and young adult books for libraries, booksellers, publishers, producers and agents. Sample copy not available.

$THE KIT-CAT REVIEW

244 Halstead Ave., Harrison NY 10528. (914)835-4833. **Contact:** Claudia Fletcher, editor. **100% freelance written.** Quarterly magazine. "*The Kit-Cat Review* is named after the 18th Century Kit-Cat Club, whose members included Addison, Steele, Congreve, Vanbrugh, and Garth. Its purpose is to promote/discover excellence and originality. Some issues are part anthology." The Spring issue includes the winner of the annual Gavin Fletcher Memorial Prize for Poetry of $1,000. The winning poem is published shortly thereafter in a *Kit-Cat Review* ad in the *American Poetry Review*. Estab. 1998. Circ. 500. Pays on publication. Publishes ms an average of 6-12 months after acceptance. Byline given. Buys first rights. Accepts queries by mail, phone. Accepts simultaneous submissions. Responds in 1 week to queries; 2 months to mss. Sample copy for $7 (payable to Claudia Fletcher). Writer's guidelines for SASE.

Nonfiction "Shorter pieces stand a better chance of publication." Book excerpts, essays, general interest, historical/nostalgic, humor, interview/profile, personal experience, travel. **Buys 6 mss/year.** Send complete ms with brief bio and SASE. Length: 5,000 words maximum. **Pays $25-100.**

Fiction Ethnic, experimental, novel excerpts, slice-of-life vignettes. No stories with "O. Henry-type formula endings. Shorter pieces stand a better chance of publication." No science fiction, fantasy, romance, horror, or new age. **Buys 20 mss/year.** Send complete ms. Length: 5,000 words maximum. **Pays $25-200 and 2 contributor's copies; additional copies $5.**

Poetry Free verse, traditional. No excessively obscure poetry. **Buys 100 poems/year. Pays $10-100.**

Tips "Obtaining a sample copy is strongly suggested. Include a short bio, SASE, and word count for fiction and nonfiction submissions."

N $ THE LONDON MAGAZINE

Review of Literature and the Arts, The London Magazine, 32 Addison Grove, London W4 1ER, United Kingdom. (00)44 0208 400 5882. Fax: (00)44 0208 994 1713. E-mail: editorial@thelondonmagazine.net. Website: www.the londonmagazine.net. **Contact:** Sebastian Barker, editor. **100% freelance written.** Bimonthly magazine covering literature and the arts. Estab. 1732. Circ. 5,000. Pays on publication. Publishes ms an average of 4 months after acceptance. Byline given. Kill fee negotiable. Buys first rights. Editorial lead time 3 months. Submit seasonal material 6 months in advance. Accepts queries by mail. Responds in 1 month to queries; 3 months to mss. Sample copy for £5. Writer's guidelines free.

Nonfiction Book excerpts, essays, interview/profile, memoirs. No journalism, reportage, or quasi-marketing. **Buys 16 mss/year.** Send complete ms. Length: 6,000 words maximum. **Pays minimum £20; maximum rate is negotiable.**

Fiction Adventure, confessions, erotica, ethnic, experimental, fantasy, historical, horror, humorous, mainstream, mystery, novel excerpts, religious, romance, science fiction, slice-of-life vignettes, suspense. **Buys 32 mss/year.** Send complete ms. Length: 6,00 words maximum. **Pays minimum £20; maximum rate is negotiable.**

Poetry Avant-garde, free verse, haiku, light verse, traditional. **Buys 60 poems/year.** Submit maximum 6 poems. Length: 1,000 words maximum (negotiable).

N $ LULLABY HEARSE

26 Fifth St., Bangor ME 04401-6022. E-mail: editor@lullabyhearse.com. Website: www.lullabyhearse.com. Editor: Sarah Ruth Jacobs. **95% freelance written.** Quarterly magazine. "*Lullaby Hearse* seeks dark, literary fiction in which the protagonist never gets a free ride. Stories that are event- rather than character-driven or that utilize traditional horror themes will generally get the back door treatment. Stark imagery and powerful characterization are desirable." Estab. 2002. Circ. 200. **Pays on acceptance.** Publishes ms an average of 3 months after acceptance. Buys first rights. Submit seasonal material 5 months in advance. Accepts queries by mail, e-mail. Accepts simultaneous submissions. Responds in 2 weeks to queries; 2 months to mss. Sample copy for $6. Writer's guidelines online.

Nonfiction Book excerpts, interview/profile, reviews of lost cult movie directors and films, reviews of other literary magazines. No essays on the craft of writing. **Buys 20 mss/year.** Send complete ms. Length: 500-2,500 words. **Pays $10-20 for assigned articles; $10-15 for unsolicited articles.**

Photos State availability of or send photos with submission. Reviews contact sheets, 4×6 and up prints, GIF/JPEG files. Offers $10-20/photo. Negotiates payment individually.

Columns/Departments Film Criticism (write-ups of old or obscure movies), 750 words. **Buys 7 mss/year.** Send complete ms. **Pays $10-15.**

Fiction "We look for uniquely structured stories that ultimately cohere in a strong, decisive ending. Black humor is sometimes accepted, but humor alone isn't enough to take a story where it needs to go. Keenness of imagery and overall literary quality are important deciding factors. Crudity crosses the line when it insults the intelligence of the reader." Experimental, horror, science fiction. "Please don't send stories about writers, formulaic horror stories, or crime/mystery narratives that drag themselves down the beaten path. Fantasy and science fiction works are considered, but imagery must always be grounded in reality; miracles will be shot down." **Buys 30 mss/year.** Send complete ms. Length: 1,000-6,000 words. **Pays $10-20.**

Poetry Avant-garde, free verse. No first-person narrated poems that are often lacking in description. Generalized images or statements are undesirable—the shorter the poem, the more overwhelming the imagery should be. **Buys 25 poems/year.** Length: Length: 10 lines minimum.

Tips "Often, subs are rejected because they go overboard on the horror component. Horror is a subtle craft, and its readers have indeed seen almost everything. *Lullaby Hearse* looks for characters and situations that invite the reader to linger after the story is put down. Each story and poem is chosen for its lasting quality, and shorts with predictable punchline endings are the anathema."

$ THE MALAHAT REVIEW

The University of Victoria, P.O. Box 1700, STN CSC, Victoria BC V8W 2Y2, Canada. (250)721-8524. E-mail: malahat@uvic.ca (for queries only). Website: www.malahatreview.com. **Contact:** John Barton, editor. **100% freelance written.** Eager to work with new/unpublished writers. Quarterly magazine covering poetry, fiction, and reviews. "We try to achieve a balance of views and styles in each issue. We strive for a mix of the best writing by both established and new writers." Estab. 1967. Circ. 1,000. **Pays on acceptance.** Publishes ms an average of 6 months after acceptance. Byline given. Offers 100% kill fee. Buys second serial (reprint) rights. first world rights Accepts queries by mail. Responds in 2 weeks to queries; 3 months to mss. Sample copy for $12 (US). Writer's guidelines online.

Nonfiction "Query first about review articles, critical essays, interviews, and visual art, which we generally solicit." Include SASE with Canadian postage or IRCs. **Pays $30/magazine page.**

Fiction Marlene Cookshaw, editor. "General ficton and poetry." **Buys 20 mss/year.** Send complete ms. Length: 20 pages maximum. **Pays $30/magazine page.**

Poetry Avant-garde, free verse, traditional. **Buys 100 poems/year.** Length: 5-10 pages. **Pays $30/magazine page.**

Tips "Please do not send more than 1 manuscript (the one you consider your best) at a time. See *The Malahat Review's* long poem and novella contests in Contest & Awards section."

Ⓝ $ MAN'S STORY 2 MAGAZINE

Man's Story 2 Publishing Co., P.O. Box 1082, Roswell GA 30077. E-mail: glenn@mansstory2.com. Website: www.mansstory2.com. Editor: Glenn Dunn. **50% freelance written.** Quarterly magazine and monthly online zine. "*Man's Story 2 Magazine* strives to recreate the pulp fiction that was published in the magazines of the 1960s. As the title implies, they are stories slanted toward the heterosexual male. Story subjects tend to slant toward the damsel in distress among others." Estab. 2001. Circ. 300. **Pays on acceptance.** Publishes ms an average of 3-6 months after acceptance. Buys one-time, second serial (reprint) rights. Accepts queries by e-mail. Accepts simultaneous submissions. Sample copy online. Writer's guidelines online.

Fiction Adventure, erotica, fantasy, horror, suspense, pulp fiction. **Buys 20-30 mss/year.** Send complete ms. Length: 1,500-5,000 words. **Pays $25-50.**

Tips "Pulp fiction is pretty much a dead art form, and not everyone can write a good pulp fiction story. First read our writer's guidelines. Then, visit our website and/or read one of our magazines, or find an old pulp fiction magazine that was published in the 1960s. If all else fails, e-mail us."

$ $ MANOA

A Pacific Journal of International Writing, English Dept., University of Hawaii, Honolulu HI 96822. (808)956-3070. Fax: (808)956-3083. E-mail: fstewart@hawaii.edu. Website: manoajournal.hawaii.edu. **Contact:** Frank Stewart, editor. Semiannual magazine. "High quality literary fiction, poetry, essays, personal narrative, reviews. Most of each issue devoted to new work from Pacific and Asian nations. Our audience is primarily in the U.S., although expanding in Pacific countries. U.S. writing need not be confined to Pacific settings or subjects." Estab. 1989. Circ. 2,500. Pays on publication. Byline given. Buys first North American serial rights. Non-exclusive, one-time print rights. Editorial lead time 9 months. Accepts simultaneous submissions. Responds in 3 weeks to queries 1 month to poetry mss; 6 months to fiction to mss. Sample copy for $10 (US). Writer's guidelines online.

Nonfiction Book excerpts, essays, interview/profile, creative nonfiction or personal narrative related to literature or nature; book reviews on recent books in arts, humanities and natural sciences, usually related to Asia, the Pacific or Hawaii or published in these places. No Pacific exotica. **Buys 1-2, excluding reviews mss/year.** Send complete ms. Length: 1,000-5,000 words. **Pays $25/printed page.**

Fiction "We're potentially open to anything of literary quality, though usually not genre fiction as such." Mainstream, contemporary, excerpted novel. No Pacific exotica. **Buys 1-2 in the US (excluding translation) mss/year.** Send complete ms. Length: 1,000-7,500 words. **Pays $100-500 normally ($25/printed page).**

Poetry No light verse. **Buys 40-50 poems/year.** Submit maximum 5-6 poems poems. **Pays $25/poem.**

Tips "Although we are a Pacific journal, we are a general interest U.S. literary journal, not limited to Pacific settings or subjects."

$ THE MASSACHUSETTS REVIEW

South College, University of Massachusetts, Amherst MA 01003-9934. (413)545-2689. Fax: (413)577-0740. E-mail: massrev@external.umass.edu. Website: www.massreview.org. **Contact:** Corwin Ericson, managing editor; Paul Jenkins, David Lenson, editors. Quarterly magazine. Estab. 1959. Circ. 1,200. Pays on publication. Publishes ms an average of 18 months after acceptance. Buys first North American serial rights. Accepts queries by mail. Accepts simultaneous submissions. Responds in 3 months to mss. Sample copy for $7. Writer's guidelines online.

• Does not respond to mss without SASE.

Nonfiction Articles on all subjects. No reviews of single books. Send complete ms or query with SASE. Length: 6,500 words maximum. **Pays $50.**

Fiction Short stories. Wants more prose less than 30 pages. **Buys 10 mss/year.** Send complete ms. Length: 25-30 pages maximum. **Pays $50.**

Poetry Submit maximum 6 poems. **Pays 35¢/line to $10 maximum.**

Tips "No manuscripts are considered June-October. No fax or e-mail submissions. No simultaneous submissions."

$ MICHIGAN QUARTERLY REVIEW

3574 Rackham Bldg., 915 E. Washington, University of Michigan, Ann Arbor MI 48109-1070. (734)764-9265. E-mail: mqr@umich.edu. Website: www.umich.edu/~mqr. **Contact:** Laurence Goldstein, editor. **75% freelance written.** Quarterly magazine. "An interdisciplinary journal which publishes mainly essays and reviews, with some high-quality fiction and poetry, for an intellectual, widely read audience." Estab. 1962. Circ. 1,500. Pays on publication. Publishes ms an average of 1 year after acceptance. Byline given. Buys first serial rights. Accepts queries by mail. Responds in 2 months to queries; 2 months to mss. Sample copy for $4. Writer's guidelines online.

• The Laurence Goldstein Award is a $1,000 annual award to the best poem published in the *Michigan Quarterly Review* during the previous year. Prefers to work with published/established writers.

Nonfiction "*MQR* is open to general articles directed at an intellectual audience. Essays ought to have a personal voice and engage a significant subject. Scholarship must be present as a foundation, but we are not interested in specialized essays directed only at professionals in the field. We prefer ruminative essays, written in a fresh style and which reach interesting conclusions. We also like memoirs and interviews with significant historical or cultural resonance." **Buys 35 mss/year.** Query. Length: 2,000-5,000 words. **Pays $100-150.**

Fiction Fiction Editor. No restrictions on subject matter or language. "We are very selective. We like stories which are unusual in tone and structure, and innovative in language. No genre fiction written for a market. Would like to see more fiction about social, political, cultural matters, not just centered on a love relationship or dysfunctional family." **Buys 10 mss/year.** Send complete ms. Length: 1,500-7,000 words. **Pays $10/published page.**

Poetry Buys 10 poems/year. **Pays $10/published page.**

Tips "Read the journal and assess the range of contents and the level of writing. We have no guidelines to offer or set expectations; every manuscript is judged on its unique qualities. On essays—query with a very thorough description of the argument and a copy of the first page. Watch for announcements of special issues which are usually expanded issues and draw upon a lot of freelance writing. Be aware that this is a university quarterly that publishes a limited amount of fiction and poetry that it is directed at an educated audience, one that has done a great deal of reading in all types of literature."

$ MID-AMERICAN REVIEW

Department of English, Bowling Green State University, Bowling Green OH 43403. (419)372-2725. Fax: (419)372-6805. Website: www.bgsu.edu/midamericanreview. **Contact:** Michael Czyzniejewski, editor-in-chief. Willing to work with new/unpublished writers. Biannual magazine of "the highest quality fiction, poetry, and translations of contemporary poetry and fiction." Also publishes critical articles and book reviews of contemporary literature. "We try to put the best possible work in front of the biggest possible audience. We publish serious fiction and poetry, as well as critical studies in contemporary literature, translations and book reviews." Estab. 1981. Pays on publication when funding is available. Publishes ms an average of 6 months after acceptance. Byline given. Buys first North American serial, one-time rights. Accepts queries by mail, phone. Responds in 5 months to mss. Sample copy for $7 (current issue), $5 (back issue); rare back issues $10. Writer's guidelines online.

Oꜛ "Grab our attention with something original—even experimental—but most of all, well-written."

Nonfiction Essays (articles focusing on contemporary authors and topics of current literary interest), short book reviews (500-1,000 words). **Pays $10/page up to $50, pending funding.**

Fiction Michael Czyzniejewski, fiction editor. Character-oriented, literary, experimental, short short. Experimental, Memoir, prose poem, traditional. "No genre fiction. Would like to see more short shorts." **Buys 12 mss/year.** Length: 6,000 words. **Pays $10/page up to $50, pending funding.**

Poetry Karen Craigo, poetry editor. Strong imagery and sense of visio. **Buys 60 poems/year. Pays $10/page up to $50, pending funding.**

Tips "We are seeking translations of contemporary authors from all languages into English; submissions must include the original and proof of permission to translate. We would also like to see more creative nonfiction."

$ miller's pond

H&H Press, RR 2, Box 239, Middlebury Center PA 16935. (570)376-3361. Website: www.millerspondpoetry.com. **Contact:** David Cazden, editor. **100% freelance written.** Annual magazine featuring poetry with poetry book/chapbook reviews and interviews of poets. E-mail submissions must be on the form from the website. Estab. 1998. Circ. 200. Pays on publication. Publishes ms an average of 1 year after acceptance. Byline given. Buys one-time rights. Editorial lead time 1 year. Accepts queries by mail, e-mail. Accepts simultaneous submissions. Responds in 10 months to queries; 10 months to mss. Sample copy for $7, plus $3 p&h. Writer's guidelines online.

Nonfiction Interview/profile (2,000 words), poetry chapbook reviews (500 words). **Buys 1-2 mss/year.** Query or send complete ms. **Pays $5.**

Poetry Free verse. No religious, horror, vulgar, rhymed, preachy, lofty, trite, overly sentimental. **Buys 30-35 poems/year.** Submit maximum 3-5 poems. Length: 40 lines maximum. **Pays $2.**

◼ The online magazine carries original content not found in the print edition and includes writer's guidelines. Contact: Julie Damerell, online editor.

Tips "View our website to see what we like. Study the contemporary masters: Billy Collins, Maxine Kumin, Colette Inez, Vivian Shipley. Always enclose SASE."

N MISSISSIPPI REVIEW

University of Southern Mississippi, Box 5144, Hattiesburg MS 39406-5144. (601)266-4321. Fax: (601)266-5757. Website: www.mississippireview.com. Semiannual "Literary publication for those interested in contemporary literature—writers, editors who read to be in touch with current modes." Estab. 1972. Circ. 1,500. Buys first North American serial rights. Sample copy for $8.

Fiction Rie Fortenberry, managing editor. Experimental, fantasy, humorous, contemporary, avant-garde and "art" fiction. "No juvenile or genre fiction." Length: 30 pages maximum.

$ $ THE MISSOURI REVIEW

1507 Hillcrest Hall, University of Missouri, Columbia MO 65211. (573)882-4474. Fax: (573)884-4671. E-mail: tmr@missourireview.com. Website: www.missourireview.com. Associate Editor: Evelyn Somers. Poetry Editor: Marta Ferguson. **Contact:** Speer Morgan, editor. **90% freelance written.** Triannual magazine. "We publish contemporary fiction, poetry, interviews, personal essays, cartoons, special features—such as 'History as Literature' series and 'Found Text' series—for the literary and the general reader interested in a wide range of subjects." Estab. 1978. Circ. 5,500. Offers signed contract. Byline given. Editorial lead time 6 months. Accepts queries by mail. Responds in 2 weeks to queries; 3 months to mss. Sample copy for $8 or online. Writer's guidelines online.

Nonfiction Evelyn Somers, associate editor. Book excerpts, essays. No literary criticism. **Buys 10 mss/year.** Send complete ms. **Pays $30/printed page, up to $750.**

Fiction Condensed novels, ethnic, humorous, mainstream, novel excerpts, literary. No genre fiction. **Buys 25 mss/year.** Send complete ms. Length: No preferred length. **Pays $30/printed page up to $750.**

Poetry Publishes 3-5 poetry features of 6-12 pages per issue. "Please familiarize yourself with the magazine before submitting poetry." Marta Ferguson, poetry editor. **Buys 50 poems/year. Pays $30/printed page.**

> The online magazine carries original content not found in the print edition and includes writer's guidelines. Contact: Hoa Ngo, online editor.

Tips "Send your best work."

$ MODERN HAIKU

An Independent Journal of Haiku and Haiku Studies, P.O. Box 68, Lincoln IL 62656. Website: www.modernhaiku.org. **Contact:** Lee Gurga, editor. **85% freelance written.** Magazine published 3 times/year. "*Modern Haiku* publishes high quality material only. Haiku and related genres, articles on haiku, haiku book reviews, and translations compose its contents. It has an international circulation and is widely subscribed to by university, school, and public libraries. Estab. 1969. Circ. 625. Pays on acceptance for poetry; on publication for prose. Publishes ms an average of 3 months after acceptance. Byline given. Buys first North American serial rights. Editorial lead time 4 months. Accepts queries by mail. Responds in 1 week to queries; 2 weeks to mss. Sample copy for $8. Writer's guidelines online.

Nonfiction Essays (anything related to haiku). **Buys 40 mss/year.** Send complete ms. **Pays $5/page.**

Columns/Departments Haiku & Senryu; Haibun; Articles (on haiku and related genres); book reviews (books of haiku or related genres), 4 pages maximum. **Buys 15 mss/year.** Send complete ms. **Pays $5/page.**

Poetry Haiku, senryu. Does not want "general poetry, sentimental, and pretty-pretty haiku or overtly pornographic." **Buys 500 poems/year.** Submit maximum 24 poems. **Pays $1.**

Tips "Study the history of haiku, read books about haiku, learn the aesthetics of haiku and methods of composition. Write about your sense perceptions of the suchness of entities, avoid ego-centered interpretations."

$ NEW ENGLAND REVIEW

Middlebury College, Middlebury VT 05753. (802)443-5075. E-mail: nereview@middlebury.edu. Website: www.middlebury.edu/~nereview/. **Contact:** On envelope: Poetry, Fiction, or Nonfiction Editor; on letter: Stephen Donadio, editor. Quarterly magazine. Serious literary only. Reads September 1 to May 31 (postmarked dates). Estab. 1978. Circ. 2,000. Pays on publication. Publishes ms an average of 6 months after acceptance. Byline given. Buys first North American serial, first, second serial (reprint) rights. Accepts simultaneous submissions. Responds in 2 weeks to queries; 3 months to mss. Sample copy for $8. Writer's guidelines online.

● No e-mail submissions.

Nonfiction Serious literary only. Rarely accepts previously published submissions (out of print or previously published abroad only.) **Buys 20-25 mss/year.** Send complete ms. Length: 7,500 words maximum, though exceptions may be made. **Pays $10/page ($20 minimum), and 2 copies.**

Fiction Send 1 story at a time. Serious literary only, novel excerpts. **Buys 25 mss/year.** Send complete ms. Length: Prose length: 10,000 words maximum, double spaced. Novellas: 30,000 words maximum. **Pays $10/page ($20 minimum), and 2 copies.**

Poetry Buys 75-90 poems/year. Submit maximum 6 poems. **Pays $10/page ($20 minimum), and 2 copies.**

Tips "We consider short fiction, including shorts, short-shorts, novellas, and self-contained extracts from novels.

We consider a variety of general and literary, but not narrowly scholarly nonfiction; long and short poems; speculative, interpretive, and personal essays; book reviews; screenplays; graphics; translations; critical reassessments; statements by artists working in various media; interviews; testimonies; and letters from abroad. We are committed to exploration of all forms of contemporary cultural expression in the United States and abroad. With few exceptions, we print only work not published previously elsewhere.''

$NEW LETTERS

University of Missouri-Kansas City, University House, 5101 Rockhill Rd., Kansas City MO 64110-2499. (816)235-1168. Fax: (816)235-2611. E-mail: newletters@umkc.edu. Website: www.newletters.org. Editor: Robert Stewart. **100% freelance written.** Quarterly magazine. ''*New Letters* is intended for the general literate reader. We publish literary fiction, nonfiction, essays, poetry. We also publish art.'' Estab. 1934. Circ. 5,000. Pays on publication. Publishes ms an average of 6 months after acceptance. Byline given. Buys first North American serial rights. Editorial lead time 6 months. Submit seasonal material 6 months in advance. Accepts queries by mail. Responds in 1 month to queries; 3 months to mss. Sample copy for $7 or sample articles on website. Writer's guidelines online.

• Submissions are not read between May 1 and October 1.

Nonfiction Essays. No self-help, how-to, or nonliterary work. **Buys 8-10 mss/year.** Send complete ms. Length: 5,000 words maximum. **Pays $40-100.**

Photos Send photos with submission. Reviews contact sheets, 2x4 transparencies, prints. Buys one-time rights. Pays $10-40/photo.

Fiction Robert Stewart, editor. Ethnic, experimental, humorous, mainstream, Contemporary. No genre fiction. **Buys 15-20 mss/year.** Send complete ms. Length: 5,000 words maximum. **Pays $30-75 for fiction and $15 for single poem.**

Poetry Avant-garde, free verse, haiku, traditional. No light verse. **Buys 40-50 poems/year.** Submit maximum 6 poems. Length: Open. **Pays $10-25.**

Tips ''We aren't interested in essays that are footnoted, essays usually described as scholarly or critical. Our preference is for creative nonfiction or personal essays. We prefer shorter stories and essays to longer ones (an average length is 3,500-4,000 words). We have no rigid preferences as to subject, style, or genre, although commercial efforts tend to put us off. Even so, our only fixed requirement is on *good* writing.''

ℕ $NEW ORLEANS REVIEW

Box 195, Loyola University, New Orleans LA 70118. (504)865-2295. Website: www.loyno.edu/~noreview/. Biannual ''Publishes poetry, fiction, translations, photographs, nonfiction on literature, art and film. Readership: those interested in contemporary literature and culture.'' Estab. 1968. Circ. 1,500. Pays on publication. Buys first North American serial rights. Accepts simultaneous submissions. Responds in 4 months to mss. Sample copy for $7.

Fiction Christopher Chambers, editor. ''Good writing, from conventional to experimental.'' **Pays $25-50 and 2 copies.**

$⊡ THE NEW QUARTERLY

New Directions in Canadian Writing, St. Jerome's University, 200 University Ave. W., Waterloo ON N2L 3G3, Canada. (519)884-8111, ext. 290. E-mail: newquart@watarts.uwaterloo.ca. Website: newquarterly.uwaterloo.ca. Editor: Kim Jernigan. **95% freelance written.** Quarterly book covering Canadian fiction and poetry. ''Emphasis on emerging writers and genres, but we publish more traditional work as well if the language and narrative structure are fresh.'' Estab. 1981. Circ. 1,000. Pays on publication. Publishes ms an average of 4 months after acceptance. Byline given. Buys first Canadian rights. Editorial lead time 6 months. Accepts queries by mail, e-mail. Accepts simultaneous submissions. Responds in 2 weeks to queries; 4 months to mss. Sample copy for $12 (cover price, plus mailing). Writer's guidelines for #10 SASE or online.

• Open to Canadian writers only.

Fiction Kim Jernigan, Rae Crossman, Mark Spielmacher, Rosalynn Worth, fiction editors. *Canadian work only.* ''We are not interested in genre fiction. We are looking for innovative, beautifully crafted, deeply felt literary fiction.'' **Buys 20-25 mss/year.** Send complete ms. Length: 20 pages maximum. **Pays $150/story.**

Poetry *Canadian work only.* Lesley Elliott, Randi Patterson, John Vardon, Erin Noteboom, poetry editors. Avant-garde, free verse, traditional. **Buys 40 poems/year.** Submit maximum 5 poems. Length: 4½ inches typeset.

Tips ''Reading us is the best way to get our measure. We don't have preconceived ideas about what we're looking for other than that it must be Canadian work (Canadian writers, not necessarily Canadian content). We want something that's fresh, something that will repay a second reading, something in which the language soars and the feeling is complexly rendered.''

N $ ⬚ THE NEW WRITER

P.O. Box 60, Cranbrook Kent TN17 2ZR, United Kingdom. 01580 212626. Fax: 01580 212041. E-mail: editor@the newwriter.com. Website: www.thenewwriter.com. Publishes 6 issues per annum Contemporary writing magazine which publishes "the best in fact, fiction and poetry." Estab. 1996. Circ. 1,500. Pays on publication. Publishes ms an average of 1 year after acceptance. Buys one-time rights. Accepts queries by e-mail, fax. Accepts simultaneous submissions. Responds in 2 months to queries; 4 months to mss. Sample copy for SASE and A4 SAE with IRCs only. Writer's guidelines for SASE.

Nonfiction Content should relate to writing. Query. Length: 1,000-2,000 words. **Pays £20-40.**

Fiction No unsolicited manuscripts. Accepts fiction from subscribers only. "We will consider most categories apart from stories written for children. No horror, erotic or cosy fiction." Query with published clips. Length: 2,000-5,000 words. **Pays £10 per story by credit voucher; additional copies for £1.50.**

Poetry Buys 50 poems/year. Submit maximum 3 poems. Length: 40 lines maximum. **Pays £3/poem.**

N $ ⬚ NFG MAGAZINE

Writing with Attitude, NFG Media, Sheppard Centre, P.O. Box 43112, Toronto ON M2N 6N1, Canada. Fax: (416)226-0994. E-mail: mrspeabody@nfg.ca. Website: www.nfg.ca. Editor-in-Chief: Shar O'Brien. Managing Editor: J. Dale Humphries. Senior Editor: Lesleigh Force. **Contact:** Debbie Moorhouse, senior submissions manager. **100% freelance written.** Triannual magazine covering fiction. "We offer fiction without boundaries; content based on merit, not classification. From poetry to short stories, comics to art—if it titillates the mind, twists the subconscious or delivers an unexpected slap, we want to see it. Artists who submit to NFG log in as a member and may check the status of their work as it moves through the editorial process. Work accepted for review is read by a minimum of 5 editors, who leave constructive comments for the author." Estab. October 2001; first issue January 2003. Circ. 5,000. **Pays on acceptance.** Publishes ms an average of 6 months after acceptance. Byline given. Offers 100% kill fee. Buys first, second serial (reprint) rights. Editorial lead time 2 months. Accepts queries by e-mail. Sample copy for $7. Writer's guidelines online.

Nonfiction Kelly A. Harmon, senior articles editor. Book excerpts (unpublished novels), essays, exposé, general interest, historical/nostalgic, humor, inspirational, interview/profile, new product, personal experience, photo feature, technical, travel. **Buys 6 mss/year.** Send complete ms. Length: 7,500 words maximum. **Pays $50 for unsolicited articles.**

Photos Sue Miller, senior art editor. Send photos with submission. Reviews GIF/JPEG files. Buys one-time rights. Offers no additional payment for photos accepted with ms. Identification of subjects, permission for rights required.

Fiction Glen Chapman, senior submissions manager. Adventure, condensed novels, confessions, erotica, ethnic, experimental, fantasy, historical, horror, humorous, mainstream, mystery, novel excerpts, religious, romance, science fiction, serialized novels, slice-of-life vignettes, suspense, western. **Buys 30-40 mss/year.** Send complete ms. Length: 7,500 words maximum. **Pays 3¢/word, minimum $50.**

Poetry Monica S. Kuebler, senior poetry editor. Avant-garde, free verse, haiku, light verse, traditional. **Buys 30-40 poems/year.** Submit maximum 1 poems. **Pays $35/poem.**

Fillers Philip Seiler, senior editor. Anecdotes, facts, gags to be illustrated by cartoonist, newsbreaks, short humor. **Buys 10-20/year.** Length: 1,000 words maximum. **Pays 5¢/word; $15 minimum.**

N $ THE NORTH AMERICAN REVIEW

University of Northern Iowa, 1222 W. 27th St., Cedar Falls IA 50614-0516. (319)273-6455. Fax: (319)273-4326. E-mail: nar@uni.edu. Website: www.webdelsol.com/northamreview/nar/. **Contact:** Grant Tracey, editor. **90% freelance written.** Bimonthly magazine. "The NAR is the oldest literary magazine in America and one of the most respected; though we have no prejudices about the subject matter of material sent to us, our first concern is quality." Estab. 1815. Circ. under 5,000. Pays on publication. Publishes ms an average of 9 months after acceptance. Byline given. Buys first North American serial, first rights. Accepts queries by mail, e-mail, phone. Responds in 4 months to mss. Sample copy for $5. Writer's guidelines online.

● This is the oldest literary magazine in the country and one of the most prestigious. Also one of the most entertaining—and a tough market for the young writer.

○┓ Break in with the "highest quality poetry, fiction, and nonfiction on any topic, but particularly interested in the environment, gender, race, ethnicity, and class."

Nonfiction Ron Sandvik, nonfiction editor. No restrictions; highest quality only. Length: Open. **Pays $5/350 words; $20 minimum, $100 maximum.**

Fiction Grant Tracey, fiction editor. No restrictions; highest quality only. Open (literary). "No flat narrative stories where the inferiority of the character is the paramount concern." Wants to see more "well-crafted literary stories that emphasize family concerns. We'd also like to see more stories engaged with environmental concerns." Length: Open. **$5/350 words; $20 minimum, $100 maximum.**

Poetry No restrictions; highest quality only. Length: Open. **Pays $1/line; $20 minimum, $100 maximum.**

Tips "We like stories that start quickly and have a strong narrative arc. Poems that are passionate about subject, language, and image are welcome, whether they are traditional or experimental, whether in formal or free verse (closed or open form). Nonfiction should combine art and fact with the finest writing. We do not accept simultaneous submissions; these will be returned unread. We read poetry, fiction, and nonfiction year-round."

$ $ NORTH CAROLINA LITERARY REVIEW

A Magazine of North Carolina Literature, Culture, and History, English Dept., East Carolina University, Greenville NC 27858-4353. (252)328-1537. Fax: (252)328-4889. E-mail: bauerm@mail.ecu.edu. Website: www.ecu.edu/nclr. **Contact:** Margaret Bauer, editor. Annual magazine published in fall covering North Carolina writers, literature, culture, history. "Articles should have a North Carolina slant. First consideration is always for quality of work. Although we treat academic and scholarly subjects, we do not wish to see jargon-laden prose; our readers, we hope, are found as often in bookstores and libraries as in academia. We seek to combine the best elements of magazine for serious readers with best of scholarly journal." Estab. 1992. Circ. 750. Pays on publication. Publishes ms an average of 1 year after acceptance. Byline given. Buys first North American serial rights. Rights returned to writer on request. Editorial lead time 6 months. Accepts queries by mail, e-mail. Responds in 1 month to queries; 6 months to mss. Sample copy for $10-15. Writer's guidelines online.

> • Break in with an article related to the special feature topic. Check the website for upcoming topics and deadlines.

Nonfiction North Carolina-related material only. Book excerpts, essays, exposé, general interest, historical/nostalgic, humor, interview/profile, opinion, personal experience, photo feature, travel, reviews, short narratives, surveys of archives. "No jargon-laden academic articles." **Buys 25-35 mss/year.** Query with published clips. Length: 500-5,000 words. **Pays $50-300.**

Photos State availability with submission. Reviews 5×7 or 8×10 prints; snapshot size or photocopy OK. Buys one-time rights. Pays $25-250. Captions and identification of subjects required; releases (when appropriate) required.

Columns/Departments NC Writers (interviews, biographical/bibliographic essays); Reviews (essay reviews of North Carolina-related (fiction, creative nonfiction, poetry). Query with published clips. **Pays $50-300.**

Fiction Must be North Carolina related—either by a North Carolina-connected writer or set in North Carolina. **Buys 3-4 mss/year.** Query. Length: 5,000 words maximum. **Pays $50-300.**

Poetry *North Carolina poets only.* **Buys 8-10 poems/year.** Length: 30-150 lines. **Pays $25-50.**

Fillers Buys 2-10/year. Length: 50-300 words. **Pays $25-50.**

Tips "By far the easiest way to break in is with special issue sections. We are especially interested in reports on conferences, readings, meetings that involve North Carolina writers, and personal essays or short narratives with a strong sense of place. See back issues for other departments. Interviews are probably the other easiest place to break in; no discussions of poetics/theory, etc., except in reader-friendly (accessible) language; interviews should be personal, more like conversations, that explore connections between a writer's life and his/her work."

$ NORTHWEST FLORIDA REVIEW

Gaius Press, P.O. Box 734, Mary Esther FL 32569. E-mail: nwfreview@cs.com. Editor: Mario A. Petaccia. **Contact:** Marie Liberty, fiction. **100% freelance written.** Semiannual magazine. "No special slant or philosophy, just good writing in fiction, poetry, and articles." Estab. 2001. Circ. 1,500. Pays on publication. Byline given. Buys first North American serial rights. Editorial lead time 3 months. Submit seasonal material 9 months in advance. Accepts queries by mail, e-mail. Accepts simultaneous submissions. Responds in 1 month to queries; 3 months to mss. Sample copy for $5. Writer's guidelines for #10 SASE.

> • Not accepting new work until May 2004.

Nonfiction Book excerpts, essays, humor, interview/profile. No religious, technical, travel, or how-to. **Buys 2 mss/year.** Send complete ms. Length: 1,000-3,000 words. **Pays $20.**

Photos Buys one-time rights. Offers no additional payment for photos accepted with ms. Identification of subjects required.

Fiction Experimental, humorous, mainstream, novel excerpts. **Buys 8 mss/year.** Send complete ms. Length: 1,500-5,000 words. **Pays $20.**

Poetry Free verse. No haiku or light verse. **Buys 40-50 poems/year.** Submit maximum 3-5 poems. Length: 10-50 lines. **Pays $5.**

Tips "Read the best magazine or subscribe to *NWFR* to see what we like."

$ NOTRE DAME REVIEW

University of Notre Dame, 840 Flanner Hall, Notre Dame IN 46556. (574)631-6952. Fax: (574)631-4795. E-mail: english.ndreview.1@nd.edu. Website: www.nd.edu/~ndr/review.htm. Executive Editor: Kathleen J. Canavan. Poetry Editor: John Matthias. **Contact:** William O'Rourke, fiction editor. Semiannual magazine. "The *Notre*

Dame Review is an indepenent, noncommercial magazine of contemporary American and international fiction, poetry, criticism, and art. We are especially interested in work that takes on big issues by making the invisible seen, that gives voice to the voiceless. In addition to showcasing celebrated authors like Seamus Heaney and Czelaw Milosz, the *Notre Dame Review* introduces readers to authors they may have never encountered before, but who are doing innovative and important work. In conjunction with the *Notre Dame Review*, the online companion to the printed magazine, the *Notre Dame Re-view* engages readers as a community centered in literary rather than commercial concerns, a community we reach out to through critique and commentary as well as aesthetic experience." Estab. 1995. Circ. 2,000. Pays on publication. Publishes ms an average of 6 months after acceptance. Buys first North American serial rights. Accepts simultaneous submissions. Responds in 4 months to mss. Sample copy for $6. Writer's guidelines online. **Buys 10 mss/year.** Length: 3,000 words. **Pays $5-25.**

Tips "We're looking for high quality work that takes on big issues in a literary way. Please read our back issues before submitting."

$ $▣ ON SPEC MAGAZINE

Copper Pig Writers Society, Box 4727, Edmonton AB T6E 5G6, Canada. E-mail: editor@onspec.ca. Website: www.onspec.ca. **Contact:** Diane L. Walton, editor. **100% freelance written.** Quarterly magazine. "*On Spec Magazine* was launched in 1989 by the nonprofit Copper Pig Writers' Society to provide a voice and a paying market for Canadian writers working in the speculative genre. Aside from the then-biannual *Tesseracts* anthology, there were almost no speculative fiction markets in Canada for Canadian writers. *On Spec* was created to provide this market. *On Spec* is published quarterly by the Copper Pig Writers Society, a collective whose members all writers themselves donate their professional services and their time. Our readers have told us what they want is fiction, fiction and more fiction, and that's what we give them: each 112-page issue of the digest-size magazine typically contains one or two poems and nonfiction pieces, some illustrations, and at least ten short stories, all in the speculative genre." Estab. 1989. **Pays on acceptance.** Byline given. Buys first rights. Accepts queries by mail. Sample copy not available. Writer's guidelines free.

Fiction Fantasy, horror, science fiction. **Buys 40-50 mss/year.** Send complete ms. Length: 1,000-6,000 words. **Pays $50-180 (Canadian).**

Tips "The *On Spec* editors are looking for original, unpublished science fiction—fantasy, horror, ghost stories, fairy stories, magic realism, or any other speculative material. Since our mandate is to provide a market for the Canadian viewpoint, strong preference is given to submissions by Canadians."

$ ONE-STORY

One-Story, LLC, P.O. Box 1326, New York NY 10156. Website: www.one-story.com. Publisher: Maribeth Batcha. Editor: Hannah Tinti. **Contact:** Maribeth Batcha and Hannah Tinti. **100% freelance written.** Literary magazine covering one short story. "*One-Story* is a literary magazine that contains, simply, **one story**. It is a subscription-only magazine. Every 3 weeks subscribers are sent *One Story* in the mail. *One Story* is artfully designed, lightweight, easy to carry, and ready to entertain on buses, in bed, in subways, in cars, in the park, in the bath, in the waiting rooms of doctor's, on the couch, or in line at the supermarket. Subscribers also have access to a website, www.one-story.com, where they can learn more about *One-Story* authors, and hear about *One-Story* readings and events. There is always time to read One Story." Estab. 2002. Circ. 2,500. Pays on publication. Publishes ms an average of 3-6 months after acceptance. Byline given. Buys first North American serial rights. Buys the rights to publish excerpts on website and in promotional materials. Editorial lead time 3-4 months. Accepts simultaneous submissions. Responds in 2-6 months to mss. Sample copy for $5. Writer's guidelines online.

● Accepts submissions via website only.

Fiction Literary short stories. *One-Story* only accepts short stories. Do not send excerpts. Do not send more than 1 story at a time. **Buys 18 mss/year.** Send complete ms. Length: 3,000-8,000 words. **Pays $100.**

Tips "*One-Story* is looking for stories that are strong enough to stand alone. Therefore they must be very good. We want the best you can give. We want our socks knocked off."

Ⓝ OTHER VOICES

University of Illinois at Chicago, 601 S. Morgan St., Chicago IL 60607. (312)413-2209. E-mail: othervoices@listserv.uic.edu. Website: www.othervoicesmagazine.org. **Contact:** Gina Frangello and JoAnne Ruvoli, editors. Semi-annual "Original, fresh, diverse stories and novel excerpts" for literate adults. Estab. 1985. Circ. 1,500. Buys one-time rights. Accepts simultaneous submissions. Responds in 10-12 weeks to mss. Sample copy for $7 (includes postage). Writer's guidelines for #10 SASE.

Fiction Gina Frangello. Humorous, contemporary, excerpted novel and one act-plays. Fiction only. "No taboos, except ineptitude and murkiness. No science fiction, romance, horror, 'chick-lit or futuristic." Length:5,000 words. **Pays in contributor's copies and modest cash gratuity.**

$ $ $ THE PARIS REVIEW

541 E. 72nd St., New York NY 10021. (212)861-0016. Fax: (212)861-4504. Website: www.theparisreview.com. **Contact:** Brigid Hughes, executive editor. Quarterly magazine. "Fiction and poetry of superlative quality, whatever the genre, style or mode. Our contributors include prominent, as well as less well-known and previously unpublished writers. Writers at Work interview series includes important contemporary writers discussing their own work and the craft of writing." Pays on publication. Buys all, first english-language rights. Accepts queries by mail. Accepts simultaneous submissions. Responds in 4 months to mss. Sample copy for $15 (includes postage). Writer's guidelines online.
● Address submissions to proper department.

Fiction Study the publication. Annual Aga Khan Fiction Contest award of $1,000. Query. Length: No length limit. **Pays $500-1,000.**

Poetry Study the publication. Richard Howard, poetry editor.

N $ $ PARNASSUS

Poetry in Review, Poetry in Review Foundation, 205 W. 89th St., #8-F, New York NY 10024. (212)362-3492. Fax: (212)875-0148. E-mail: parnew@aol.com. Website: www.parnassuspoetry.com. Managing Editor: Ben Downing. **Contact:** Herbert Leibowitz, editor. Semiannual magazine covering poetry and criticism. Estab. 1972. Circ. 1,500. Pays on publication. Publishes ms an average of 5 months after acceptance. Byline given. Buys one-time rights. Accepts queries by mail. Responds in 2 months to mss. Sample copy for $15. Writer's guidelines not available.

Nonfiction Essays. **Buys 30 mss/year.** Query with published clips. Length: 1,500-7,500 words. **Pays $50-300.** Sometimes pays writers in contributor copies or other premiums rather than a cash payment upon request.

Poetry Accepts most types of poetry. Avant-garde, free verse, traditional. **Buys 3-4 unsolicited poems/year.**

Tips "Be certain you have read the magazine and are aware of the editor's taste. Blind submissions are a waste of everybody's time. We'd like to see more poems that display intellectual acumen and curiosity about history, science, music, etc. and fewer trivial lyrical poems about the self, or critical prose that's academic and dull. Prose should sing."

$ PEEKS & VALLEYS

Fiction Journal, 702 S. Twyckenham Dr., South Bend IN 46615. E-mail: peeksandvalleys@earthlink.net. Website: www.peeksandvalleys.com. **Contact:** Meagan Church, editor. **100% freelance written.** Quarterly magazine covering short stories. Estab. 1999. **Pays on acceptance.** Publishes ms an average of 8 months after acceptance. Byline given. Buys one-time, second serial (reprint) rights. Editorial lead time 4 months. Submit seasonal material 6 months in advance. Accepts queries by mail, e-mail. Accepts previously published material. Accepts simultaneous submissions. Responds in 2 months to mss. Sample copy for $5.75. Writer's guidelines online.

Fiction Adventure, ethnic, historical, horror, humorous, mainstream, mystery, religious, romance, slice-of-life vignettes, suspense, western. No sci-fi, fantasy, sex, or obscenity. **Buys 30 mss/year.** Send complete ms. Length: 2,600 words. **Pays $5.**

Poetry Light verse, traditional. **Buys 5 poems/year.** Submit maximum 2 poems. Length: 30 lines.

Tips "*Peeks & Valleys* is a fiction journal that seeks quality writing and storytelling of various genres. Readers include people of all ages and backgrounds. We look for writing that leaves an impression and has a purpose—however tangible that may be. Follow the submission guidelines and don't exceed the recommended length. Study the journal to get a clear idea of what is needed. Be sure to check the website for information on the Annual Flash Fiction Contest."

$ ▣ PENINSULAR

Literary Magazine, Cherrybite Publications, Linden Cottage, 45 Burton Rd., Neston Cheshire CH64 4AE, England. 0151 353 0967. E-mail: helicon@globalnet.co.uk. Website: www.cherrybite.co.uk. **Contact:** Shelagh Nugent, editor. Quarterly magazine. "We're looking for brilliant short fiction to make the reader think/laugh/cry. A lively, up-and-coming quality magazine." Estab. 1985. Circ. 400. Pays on publication. Publishes ms an average of 3-6 months after acceptance. Buys one-time rights. Accepts previously published material. Accepts simultaneous submissions. Responds in 1 week to queries; 2 weeks to mss. Sample copy for $5 (cannot accept checks, only dollar bills). Writer's guidelines online.

Fiction Adventure, ethnic, fantasy, historical, horror, humorous, science fiction, gay/lesbian, literary, New Age, psychic/supernatural/occult. No animals telling stories, cliches, pornography, children's fiction, or purple prose. **Buys 40 mss/year.** Length: 1,000-4,000 words. **Pays £5 sterling/1,000 words, or can pay in copies and subscriptions.**

Tips "We look for impeccable presentation and grammar, outstanding prose, original story line and the element of difference that forbids me to put the story down. A good opening paragraph usually grabs me. Read 1 or 2 copies and study the guidelines. A beginning writer should read as much as possible. The trend seems to be for stories written in first person/present tense and for stories without end leaving the reader thinking, 'So what?' Stories not following this trend stand more chance of being published by me!''

$ ⊕ PLANET-THE WELSH INTERNATIONALIST

P.O. Box 44, Aberystwyth Ceredigion SY23 3ZZ, Cymru/Wales UK. 01970-611255. Fax: 01970-611197. E-mail: planet.enquiries@planetmagazine.org.uk. Website: www.planetmagazine.org.uk. **Contact:** John Barnie, fiction editor. Bimonthly journal. "A literary/cultural/political journal centered on Welsh affairs but with a strong interest in minority cultures in Europe and elsewhere." Circ. 1,400. Sample copy for £4. Writer's guidelines online.

Fiction Would like to see more "inventive, imaginative fiction that pays attention to language and experiments with form." No magical realism, horror, science fiction. Length: 1,500-4,000 words. **Pays £40/1,000 words.**

Tips "We do not look for fiction which necessarily has a 'Welsh' connection, which some writers assume from our title. We try to publish a broad range of fiction and our main criterion is quality. Try to read copies of any magazine you submit to. Don't write out of the blue to a magazine which might be completely inappropriate to your work. Recognize that you are likely to have a high rejection rate, as magazines tend to favor writers from their own countries."

$ PLEIADES

Pleiades Press, Department of English & Philosophy, Central Missouri State University, Martin 336, Warrensburg MO 64093. (660)543-4425. Fax: (660)543-8544. E-mail: kdp8106@cmsu2.cmsu.edu. Website: www.cmsu.edu/englphil/pleiades.html. **Contact:** Kevin Prufer, editor. **100% freelance written.** Semiannual journal. "We publish contemporary fiction, poetry, interviews, literary essays, special-interest personal essays, reviews for a general and literary audience." (5½×8½ perfect bound). Estab. 1991. Circ. 3,000. Pays on publication. Publishes ms an average of 9 months after acceptance. Byline given. Buys first North American serial, second serial (reprint) rights. Occasionally requests rights for TV, radio reading, website. Editorial lead time 9 months. Accepts queries by mail. Accepts simultaneous submissions. Responds in 2 months to queries; 2 months to mss. Sample copy for $5 (back issue), $6 (current issue). Writer's guidelines for #10 SASE.

● "We also sponsor the Lena-Miles Wever Todd Poetry Series competition, a contest for the best book manuscript by an American poet. The winner receives $1,000, publication by Pleiades Press, and distribution by Louisiana State University Press. Deadline September 30. Send SASE for guidelines."

Nonfiction Book excerpts, essays, interview/profile, reviews. "Nothing pedantic, slick, or shallow." **Buys 4-6 mss/year.** Send complete ms. Length: 2,000-4,000 words. **Pays $10.**

Fiction Susan Steinberg, fiction editor. Ethnic, experimental, humorous, mainstream, novel excerpts, magic realism. No science fiction, fantasy, confession, erotica. **Buys 16-20 mss/year.** Send complete ms. Length: 2,000-6,000 words. **Pays $10.**

Poetry Avant-garde, free verse, haiku, light verse, traditional. "Nothing didactic, pretentious, or overly sentimental." **Buys 40-50 poems/year.** Submit maximum 6 poems. **Pays $3/poem, and contributor copies.**

Tips "Show care for your material and your readers—submit quality work in a professional format. Include cover letter with brief bio and list of publications. Include SASE."

$ $ PLOUGHSHARES

Emerson College, Department M, 120 Boylston St., Boston MA 02116. Website: www.pshares.org. **Contact:** Don Lee, editor. Triquarterly magazine for "readers of serious contemporary literature. Our mission is to present dynamic, contrasting views on what is valid and important in contemporary literature, and to discover and advance significant literary talent. Each issue is guest-edited by a different writer. We no longer structure issues around preconceived themes." Estab. 1971. Circ. 6,000. Pays on publication. Publishes ms an average of 6 months after acceptance. Offers 50% kill fee for assigned ms not published. kill fee. Buys first North American serial rights. Accepts simultaneous submissions. Responds in 5 months to mss. Sample copy for $9 (back issue). Writer's guidelines online.

● A competitive and highly prestigious market. Rotating and guest editors make cracking the line-up even tougher, since it's difficult to know what is appropriate to send. The reading period is August 1-March 31.

Nonfiction Essays (personal and literary; accepted only occasionally). Length: 6,000 words maximum. **Pays $25/printed page, $50-250.**

Fiction Mainstream. "No genre (science fiction, detective, gothic, adventure, etc.), popular formula or commerical fiction whose purpose is to entertain rather than to illuminate." **Buys 25-35 mss/year.** Length: 300-6,000 words. **Pays $25/printed page, $50-250.**

Poetry Avant-garde, free verse, traditional, blank verse. Length: Open. **Pays $25/printed page, $50-250.**

Tips "We no longer structure issues around preconceived themes. If you believe your work is in keeping with our general standards of literary quality and value, submit at any time during our reading period."

$ POETRY

The Poetry Foundation, 1030 N. Clark St., Chicago IL 60610. (312)787-7070. Fax: (312)787-6650. E-mail: poetry @poetrymagazine.org. Website: www.poetrymagazine.org. Editor: Christian Wiman. Business Manager: Helen Klaviter. Assistant Editors: Danielle Chapman and Fred Sasaki. Reader: Averill Curdy. Circulation Manager: Eugenia Williamson. **Contact:** Editors. **100% freelance written.** Monthly magazine. Estab. 1912. Circ. 12,000. Pays on publication. Publishes ms an average of 9 months after acceptance. Byline given. Buys all rights. Copyright returned to author on request. Accepts queries by mail. Responds in 1 month to queries; 4 months to mss. Sample copy for $5.50 or online at website. Writer's guidelines online.

Nonfiction Reviews (most are solicited). **Buys 14 mss/year.** Query. Length: 1,000-2,000 words. **Pays $150/ page.**

Poetry All styles and subject matter. **Buys 180-250 poems/year.** Submit maximum 4 poems. Length: Open. **Pays $6/line.**

N ⊕ POETRY IRELAND REVIEW

Poetry Ireland, 120 St. Stephen's Green, Dublin. 01-4789974. Fax: 01-4780205. E-mail: poetry@iol.ie. Website: www.poetryireland.ie. Editor: Peter Sirr. Managing Editor: Joseph Woods. Quarterly literary magazine in book form. Estab. 1978. Circ. 5,000. Pays on publication. Not copyrighted. Accepts queries by mail, e-mail, fax, phone. Responds in 1 week to queries; 2 months to mss.

Poetry Avant-garde, free verse, haiku, light verse, traditional. **Buys 200 poems/year.** Submit maximum 6 poems.

$ ⊡ POTTERSFIELD PORTFOLIO

9879 Kempt Head Rd., Ross Ferry NS B1X 1N3, Canada. Website: www.magomania.com. Managing Editor: Douglas Arthur Brown. Biannual magazine. "*Pottersfield Portfolio* is always looking for poetry and fiction that provides fresh insights and delivers the unexpected. The stories and poems that capture our attention will be the ones that most effectively blend an intriguing voice with imaginative language. Our readers expect to be challenged, enlightened and entertained." Estab. 1979. Circ. 2,000. Pays on publication. Publishes ms an average of 6 months after acceptance. Byline given. Buys first North American serial, first canadian serial rights rights. Editorial lead time 6 months. Accepts simultaneous submissions. Responds in 9 months to mss. Sample copy for $9 (US). Writer's guidelines online.

• Non-Canadian submissions by invitation only.

Nonfiction Book excerpts, essays, interview/profile, photo feature. **Buys 6 mss/year.** Query. Length: 500-5,000 words.

Fiction Fiction editor. Experimental, novel excerpts, short fiction. No fantasy, horror, mystery, religious, romance, science fiction, western. **Buys 12-15 mss/year.** Send complete ms. Length: 500-5,000 words. **Pays contributor's copy and $10 Canadian/printed page to a maximum of $50.**

Poetry Poetry editor. Avant-garde, free verse, traditional. **Buys 20-30 poems/year.** Submit maximum 4 poems.

Tips Looking for creative nonfiction, essays.

$ ⊡ THE PRAIRIE JOURNAL

Journal of Canadian Literature, Prairie Journal Trust, P.O. Box 61203, Brentwood P.O., Calgary AB T2L 2K6, Canada. E-mail: prairiejournal@yahoo.com. Website: www.geocities.com/prairiejournal. **Contact:** A. Burke, editor. **100% freelance written.** Semiannual magazine publishing quality poetry, short fiction, drama, literary criticism, reviews, bibliography, interviews, profiles, and artwork. "The audience is literary, university, library, scholarly, and creative readers/writers." Estab. 1983. Circ. 600. Pays on publication. Publishes ms an average of 4-6 months after acceptance. Byline given. Buys first North American serial, electronic, in canada author retains copyright with acknowledgement appreciated rights. Editorial lead time 4-6 months. Accepts queries by mail, e-mail. Responds in 2 weeks to queries; 6 months to mss. Sample copy for $5. Writer's guidelines online.

Nonfiction Essays, humor, interview/profile, literary. No inspirational, news, religious, or travel. **Buys 25-40 mss/year.** Query with published clips. Length: 100-3,000 words. **Pays $100, plus copy.**

Photos State availability with submission. Rights purchased is negotiable. Offers additional payment for photos accepted with ms.

Columns/Departments Reviews (books from small presses publishing poetry, short fiction, essays, and criticism), 200-1,000 words. **Buys 5 mss/year.** Query with published clips. **Pays $10-50.**

Fiction Literary. No genre (romance, horror, western—sagebrush or cowboys), erotic, science fiction, or mystery. **Buys 6 mss/year.** Send complete ms. Length: 100-3,000 words. **Pays $10-75.**

Poetry Avant-garde, free verse, haiku. No heroic couplets or greeting card verse. **Buys 25-35 poems/year.** Submit maximum 6-8 poems. Length: 3-50 lines. **Pays $5-50.**

Tips "We publish many, many new writers and are always open to unsolicited submissions because we are 100% freelance." Do not send U.S. stamps, always use IRCs.

$⊡ PRISM INTERNATIONAL

Department of Creative Writing, Buch E462 Main Mall, University of British Columbia, Vancouver BC V6T 1Z1, Canada. (604)822-2514. Fax: (604)822-3616. E-mail: prism@interchange.ubc.ca. Website: prism.arts.ubc.ca. Executive Editor: Brenda Leifso. **Contact:** Catherine Chen, editor. **100% freelance written.** Eager to work with new/unpublished writers. Quarterly magazine emphasizing contemporary literature, including translations, for university and public libraries, and private subscribers. "An international journal of contemporary writing - fiction, poetry, drama, creative nonfiction and translation." Readership: "public and university libraries, individual subscriptions, bookstores - a world-wide audience concerned with the contemporary in literature." Estab. 1959. Circ. 1,200. Pays on publication. Publishes ms an average of 4 months after acceptance. Buys first North American serial rights. Selected authors are paid an additional $10/page for digital rights. Accepts queries by mail, fax, phone. Responds in 4 months to queries; 4 months to mss. Sample copy for $7 or on website. Writer's guidelines online.

> O⊸ Break in by "sending unusual or experimental work (we get mostly traditional submissions) and playing with forms (e.g., nonfiction, prose poetry, etc.)."

Nonfiction "Creative nonfiction that reads like fiction. Nonfiction pieces should be creative, exploratory, or experimental in tone rather than rhetorical, academic, or journalistic." No reviews, tracts, or scholarly essays. **Pays $20/printed page.**

Fiction Billeh Nickerson, editor. For Drama: one-acts preferred. Also interested in seeing dramatic monologues. **Buys 3-5 mss/year.** Send complete ms. Length: 25 pages maximum. **Pays $20/printed page.** Experimental, novel excerpts, traditional. New writing that is contemporary and literary. Short stories and self-contained novel excerpts. Works of translation are eagerly sought and should be accompanied by a copy of the original. Would like to see more translations. "No gothic, confession, religious, romance, pornography, or sci-fi." Also looking for creative nonfiction that is literary, not journalistic, in scope and tone. **Buys 12-16 mss/year.** Send complete ms. Length: 25 pages maximum. **Pays $20/printed page, and 1-year subscription.**

Poetry Buys 10 poems/issue. Avant-garde, traditional. Submit maximum 6 poems. **Pays $40/printed page, and 1-year subscription.**

Tips "We are looking for new and exciting fiction. Excellence is still our No. 1 criterion. As well as poetry, imaginative nonfiction and fiction, we are especially open to translations of all kinds, very short fiction pieces and drama which work well on the page. Translations must come with a copy of the original language work. We pay an additional $10/printed page to selected authors whose work we place on our online version of *Prism*."

$ QUARTERLY WEST

University of Utah, 255 S. Central Campus Dr., Dept. of English, LNCO 3500, Salt Lake City UT 84112-9109. (801)581-3938. E-mail: dhawk@earthlink.net. Website: www.utah.edu/quarterlywest. **Contact:** David Hawkins, editor-in-chief. Semiannual magazine. "We publish fiction, poetry, and nonfiction in long and short formats, and will consider experimental as well as traditional works." Estab. 1976. Circ. 1,900. Pays on publication. Publishes ms an average of 6 months after acceptance. Buys first North American serial, all rights. Accepts queries by mail. Accepts simultaneous submissions. Responds in 6 months to mss. Sample copy for $7.50 or online. Writer's guidelines online.

Nonfiction Essays, interview/profile, personal experience, travel, book reviews. **Buys 6-8 mss/year.** Send complete ms. Length: 10,000 words maximum. **Pays $20-100.**

Fiction No preferred lengths; interested in longer, fuller short stories and short shorts. Ethnic, experimental, humorous, mainstream, novel excerpts, slice-of-life vignettes, short shorts, translations. No detective, science fiction or romance. **Buys 6-10 mss/year.** Send complete ms. Length: No preferred length; interested in longer, "fuller" short stories, as well as short shorts. **Pays $15-100, and 2 contributor's copies.**

Poetry Avant-garde, free verse, traditional. **Buys 40-50 poems/year.** Submit maximum 5 poems. **Pays $15-100.**

Tips "We publish a special section of short shorts every issue, and we also sponsor a biennial novella contest. We are open to experimental work—potential contributors should read the magazine! Don't send more than 1 story/submission. Biennial novella competition guidelines available upon request with SASE. We prefer work with interesting language and detail—plot or narrative are less important. We don't do Western themes, or religious work."

$ $⊡ QUEEN'S QUARTERLY

A Canadian Review, Queen's University, Kingston ON K7L 3N6, Canada. (613)533-2667. Fax: (613)533-6822. E-mail: qquarter@post.queensu.ca. Website: info.queensu.ca/quarterly. **Contact:** Joan Harcourt, literary editor. **95% freelance written.** Quarterly magazine covering a wide variety of subjects, including science, humanities, arts and letters, politics, and history for the educated reader. "A general interest intellectual review, featuring articles on science, politics, humanities, arts and letters. Book reviews, poetry and fiction." Estab. 1893. Circ.

3,000. Pays on publication. Publishes ms an average of 6-12 months after acceptance. Byline given. Buys first North American serial rights. Responds in 2-3 months to queries. Sample copy online. Writer's guidelines online.

O➤ Submissions can be sent as e-mail attachment or on hard copy with a SASE (Canadian postage).#

Fiction Boris Castel, editor. Historical, mainstream, novel excerpts, short stories, women's. Length: 2,500-3,000 words. **Pays $100-300 for fiction, 2 contributor's copies and 1-year subscription; additional copies $5.**

Poetry **Buys 25 poems/year.** Submit maximum 6 poems.

$ ⊕ QWF (QUALITY WOMEN'S FICTION)

Breaking the Boundaries of Women's Fiction, 18 Warwick Crescent, Harrogate N. Yorks HG2 8JA, United Kingdom. 01788 334302. Fax: 01788 334702. E-mail: jo@qwfmagazine.co.uk. Website: www.qwfmagazine.co.uk. Editor: Jo Good. **Contact:** Sally Zigmond, assistant editor. Bimonthly magazine. *"QWF gets under the skin of the female experience and exposés emotional truth."* Estab. 1994. Circ. 2,000. Pays on publication. Publishes ms an average of 18 months after acceptance. Buys first British serial rights. Accepts queries by mail, e-mail. Accepts previously published material. Responds in 2 weeks to queries; 3 months to mss. Writer's guidelines by e-mail.

Fiction Jo Good, editor. Does not read mss June-August. Erotica, ethnic, experimental, fantasy, horror, humorous, science fiction, feminist, gay, lesbian, literary, New Age, psychic/supernatural/occult, translations. **Buys 72 mss/year.** Length: 1,000-4,500 words. **£10 sterling maximum, or 3 voucher copies to US contributors.**

Tips "Take risks with subject matter. Study at least 1 copy of *QWF*. Ensure story is technically sound."

RARITAN

A Quarterly Review, 31 Mine St., New Brunswick NJ 08903. (732)932-7887. Fax: (732)932-7855. Editor: Jackson Lears. **Contact:** Stephanie Volmer, managing editor. Quarterly magazine covering literature, history, fiction, and general culture. Estab. 1981. Circ. 3,500. Pays on publication. Publishes ms an average of 1 year after acceptance. Byline given. Buys first North American serial rights. Editorial lead time 5 months. Accepts queries by mail. Sample copy not available. Writer's guidelines not available.

● *Raritan* no longer accepts previously published or simultaneous submissions.

Nonfiction Book excerpts, essays. **Buys 50 mss/year.** Send complete ms. Length: 15-30 pages.

$ RIVER STYX

Big River Association, 634 N. Grand Blvd., 12th Floor, St. Louis MO 63103. (314)533-4541. Fax: (314)533-3345. Website: www.riverstyx.org. Senior Editors: Quincy Troupe and Michael Castro. **Contact:** Richard Newman, editor. Triannual magazine. *"River Styx publishes the highest quality fiction, poetry, interviews, essays, and visual art. We are an internationally distributed multicultural literary magazine."* Mss read May-November. Estab. 1975. Pays on publication. Publishes ms an average of 1 year after acceptance. Byline given. Buys first North American serial, one-time rights. Accepts queries by mail. Accepts simultaneous submissions. Responds in 4 months to mss. Sample copy for $7. Writer's guidelines online.

Nonfiction Essays, interview/profile. **Buys 2-5 mss/year.** Send complete ms. **Pays 2 contributor copies, plus 1 year subscription; pays $8/page if funds are available.**

Photos Send photos with submission. Reviews 5×7 or 8×10 b&w and color prints and slides. Buys one-time rights. Pays 2 contributor copies, plus 1-year subscription; $8/page if funds are available.

Fiction Ethnic, experimental, mainstream, novel excerpts, short stories, literary. "No genre fiction, less thinly veiled autobiography." **Buys 6-9 mss/year.** Send complete ms. Length: no more than 23-30 manuscript pages. **Pays 2 contributor copies, plus 1-year subscription; $8/page if funds are available.**

Poetry Avant-garde, free verse, formal. No religious. **Buys 40-50 poems/year.** Submit maximum 3-5 poems. **Pays 2 contributor copies, plus a 1-year subscription; $8/page if funds are available.**

$ ⊡ ROOM OF ONE'S OWN

A Canadian Quarterly of Women's Literature and Criticism, West Coast Feminist Literary Magazine Society, P.O. Box 46160, Station D, Vancouver BC V6J 5G5, Canada. Website: www.roommagazine.com. **Contact:** Growing Room Collective. **100% freelance written.** Quarterly journal of feminist literature. *"Room of One's Own is Canada's oldest feminist literary journal. Since 1975, Room has been a forum in which women can share their unique perspectives on the world, each other and themselves."* Estab. 1975. Circ. 1,000. Pays on publication. Publishes ms an average of 1 year after acceptance. Byline given. Buys first North American serial rights. Editorial lead time 9 months. Responds in 3 months to queries; 6 months to mss. Sample copy for $7 or online. Writer's guidelines online.

Nonfiction Reviews. **Buys 1-2 mss/year.** Send complete ms. Length: 500-1,500 words. **Pays $35 (Canadian), and a 1-year subscription.**

Fiction Feminist literature—short stories, creative nonfiction, essays by, for, and about women. "No humor, science fiction, romance." **Buys 40 mss/year.** Length: 2,000-5,000 words. **Pays $35 (Canadian), and a 1-year subscription.**

Poetry Avant-garde, free verse. "Nothing light, undeveloped." **Buys 40 poems/year.** Submit maximum 6 poems. Length: 3-80 lines. **Pays $35 (Canadian), and a 1-year subscription.**

$ $ THE SAINT ANN'S REVIEW

A Journal of Contemporary Arts and Letters, Saint Ann's School, 129 Pierrepont St., Brooklyn NY 11201. E-mail: sareview@saintanns.k12.ny.us. Website: www.saintannsreview.com. **Contact:** Beth Bosworth, Editor. **100% freelance written.** Semiannual literary magazine. "We seek fully realized work, distinguished by power and craft." Estab. 2000. Circ. 2,000. Pays on publication. Publishes ms an average of 4 months after acceptance. Byline given. Buys first North American serial rights. Submit seasonal material 4 months in advance. Accepts queries by mail. Responds in 1 month to queries; 4 months to mss. Sample copy for $8. Writer's guidelines online.

Nonfiction Book excerpts (occasionally), essays, humor, interview/profile, personal experience, photo feature. **Buys 10 mss/year.** Query with or without published clips or send complete ms. Length: 7,500 words maximum. **Pays $40/published page, $250/maximum.**

Photos Send photos with submission. Reviews transparencies, prints, GIF/JPEG files; black and white art. Buys one-time rights. Offers $50/photo page or art page, $250 maximum.

Columns/Departments Book reviews, 1,500 words. **Buys 10 mss/year.** Send complete ms by mail only. **Pays $40/published page, $250 maximum.**

Fiction Ethnic, experimental, fantasy, historical, humorous, mainstream, slice-of-life vignettes, translations. **Buys 15 mss/year.** Length: 7,500 words maximum. **Pays $40/published page, $250 maximum.**

Poetry Avant-garde, free verse, haiku, light verse, traditional, translations. **Buys 30 poems/year.** Submit maximum 5 poems. **Pays $50/page, $250 maximum.**

$ THE SEWANEE REVIEW

University of the South, 735 University Ave., Sewanee TN 37383-1000. (931)598-1246. E-mail: rjones@sewanee. edu. Website: www.sewanee.edu/sreview/home.html. Editor: George Core. **Contact:** Fiction Editor. Quarterly magazine. "A literary quarterly, publishing original fiction, poetry, essays on literary and related subjects, and book reviews for well-educated readers who appreciate good American and English literature." Estab. 1892. Circ. 3,000. Pays on publication. Buys first North American serial, second serial (reprint) rights. Responds in 6 weeks to mss. Sample copy for $8.50 ($9.50 outside U.S.). Writer's guidelines online.

Fiction Does not read mss June 1-August 31. Literary, contemporary. No erotica, science fiction, fantasy or excessively violent or profane material. **Buys 10-15 mss/year.** Length: 6,000-7,500 words. **Pays $10-12/printed page; 2 contributor copies.**

Tips "Send only 1 story at a time with a serious and sensible cover letter. We think fiction is of greater general interest than any other literary mode."

$ SHENANDOAH

The Washington and Lee University Review, Washington and Lee University, Troubadour Theater, 2nd Floor, Lexington VA 24450-0303. (540)458-8765. Website: shenandoah.wlu.edu. Managing Editor: Lynn Leech. **Contact:** R.T. Smith, editor. Quarterly magazine. Estab. 1950. Circ. 2,000. Pays on publication. Publishes ms an average of 10 months after acceptance. Byline given. Buys first North American serial, one-time rights. Responds in 3 months to mss. Sample copy for $8. Writer's guidelines online.

Nonfiction Book excerpts, essays. **Buys 6 mss/year.** Send complete ms. **Pays $25/page.**

Fiction Mainstream, novel excerpts. No sloppy, hasty, slight fiction. **Buys 15 mss/year.** Send complete ms. **Pays $25/page.**

Poetry No inspirational, confessional poetry. **Buys 70 poems/year.** Submit maximum 6 poems. Length: Open. **Pays $2.50/line.**

$ THE SOUTHERN REVIEW

43 Allen Hall, Louisiana State University, Baton Rouge LA 70803-5001. (225)578-5108. Fax: (225)578-5098. E-mail: bmacon@lsu.edu. Website: www.lsu.edu/thesouthernreview. **Contact:** John Easterly, associate editor. **100% freelance written.** Works with a moderate number of new/unpublished writers each year. Quarterly magazine "with emphasis on contemporary literature in the United States and abroad, and with special interest in Southern culture and history." Reading period: September-May. Estab. 1935. Circ. 3,100. Pays on publication. Publishes ms an average of 6 months after acceptance. Byline given. Buys first North American serial rights. Accepts queries by mail. Responds in 2 months to mss. Sample copy for $8. Writer's guidelines online.

Nonfiction Essays with careful attention to craftsmanship, technique, and seriousness of subject matter. "Willing to publish experimental writing if it has a valid artistic purpose. Avoid extremism and sensationalism.

Essays should exhibit thoughtful and sometimes severe awareness of the necessity of literary standards in our time." Emphasis on contemporary literature, especially southern culture and history. No footnotes. **Buys 25 mss/year.** Length: 4,000-10,000 words. **Pays $12/page.**

Fiction Short stories of lasting literary merit, with emphasis on style and technique; novel excerpts. "We emphasize style and substantial content. No mystery, fantasy or religious mss." Length: 4,000-8,000 words. **Pays $12/page.**

Poetry Length: 1-4 pages. **Pays $20/page.**

N $SPORT LITERATE

Honest Reflections on Life's Leisurely Diversions, 2154 W. Addison, #20, Chicago IL 60618. Website: www.sport literate.com. **Contact:** William Meiners, editor-in-chief. **95% freelance written.** Annual journal covering leisure/sport...life outside the daily grind of making a living. "*Sport Literate* publishes the highest quality creative nonfiction and poetry on themes of leisure and sport. Our writers use a leisure activity to explore a larger theme. This creative allegorical writing serves a broad audience." Estab. 1995. Circ. 1,500. Pays on publication. Publishes ms an average of 6-9 months after acceptance. Byline given. Buys first North American serial rights. Editorial lead time 6 months. Submit seasonal material 4 months in advance. Accepts queries by mail. Responds in 6 weeks to queries; 3 months to mss. Sample copy for $7.75. Writer's guidelines for #10 SASE or on website.

Nonfiction Essays, historical/nostalgic, humor, interview/profile, personal experience, travel, creative nonfiction. No book reviews, straight reporting on sports. **Buys 28 mss/year.** Send complete ms. Length: 250-5,000 words.

Photos Accepts b&w photo essays "that tell a deeper story of folks passing their time." Steve Mend (contact through website).

Poetry Frank Van Zant, poetry editor. Avant-garde, free verse, haiku, light verse, traditional. **Buys 25 poems/ year.** Submit maximum 5 poems. Length: 30 lines maximum. **Pays $20 maximum.**

The online magazine carries original content not found in the print edition and includes writer's guidelines. Contact: Steve Mend, online editor.

Tips "We like to explore all the avenues of the creative nonfiction form—personal essays, literary journalism, travel pieces, historical, humor and interviews—as they relate to our broad definition of sport. We don't publish fiction. Read any publication that you're submitting to. It can be a great time saver."

$STAND MAGAZINE

Department of English, VCU, Richmond VA 23284-2005. (804)828-1331. E-mail: dlatane@vcu.edu. Website: www.people.vcu.edu. Managing Editor: Jon Glover. **Contact:** David Latané, U.S. editor. **75% freelance written.** Quarterly magazine covering short fiction, poetry, criticism, and reviews. "*Stand Magazine* is concerned with what happens when cultures and literatures meet, with translation in its many guises, with the mechanics of language, with the processes by which the policy receives or disables its cultural makers. *Stand* promotes debate of issues that are of radical concern to the intellectual community worldwide." Estab. 1952. Circ. 3,000 worldwide. Pays on publication. Publishes ms an average of 10 months after acceptance. Byline given. first world rights Editorial lead time 2 months. Accepts queries by mail. Responds in 6 weeks to queries; 3 months to mss. Sample copy for $12. Writer's guidelines for #10 SASE with sufficient number of IRCs or online.

Nonfiction "Reviews are commissioned from known freelancers." Reviews of poetry/fiction. **Buys 8 mss/year.** Query. Length: 200-5,000 words. **Pays $30/1,000 words.**

Fiction Adventure, ethnic, experimental, historical, mainstream. "No genre fiction." **Buys 12-14 mss/year.** Send complete ms. Length: 8,000 words maximum. **Payment varies.**

Poetry Avant-garde, free verse, traditional. **Buys 100-120 poems/year.** Submit maximum 6 poems. **Pays $37.50/poem.**

Tips "Poetry/fiction areas are most open to freelancers. *Stand* is published in England and reaches an international audience. North American writers should submit work to the U.S. address. While the topic or nature of submissions does not have to be 'international,' writers may do well to keep in mind the range of *Stand*'s audience."

N $ $ STORIE

all write, Leconte, Via Suor Celestina Donati 13/E, Rome 00167, Italy. Phone/Fax: (+39)06 614 8777. Website: www.storie.it. Assistant Editor: Barbara Pezzopane. Foreign Editor: George Lerner. **Contact:** Gianluca Bassi, editor. Bimonthly magazine. "*Storie* is one of Italy's leading literary magazines. Committed to a truly crossover vision of writing, the bilingual (Italian/English) review publishes high quality fiction and poetry, interspersed with the work of alternative wordsmiths such as filmmakers and musicians. Through writings bordering on narratives and interviews with important contemporary writers, it explores the culture and craft of writing." Estab. 1989. Circ. 20,000. Pays on publication. Publishes ms an average of 2 months after acceptance. Buys first rights (in English and Italian). Accepts queries by mail, e-mail. Responds in 1 month to queries; 6 months to mss. Sample copy for $8. Writer's guidelines online.

Fiction Length: 2,000-6,000 words. **$30-600 and 2 contributor's copies.**

$ SUNDRY: A JOURNAL OF THE ARTS

Sundry Publications, 109 Jepson Ave., St. Clairsville OH 43950. (740)526-0215. E-mail: priesbeck@sundryjournal.com. Website: www.sundryjournal.com. **Contact:** Peter L. Riesbeck, editor-in-chief. **100% freelance written.** Bimonthly magazine. *"Sundry* is a journal of the arts publishing high quality short fiction of nearly any genre. We pride ourselves on our eclectic theme and are eager to work with new, unpublished writers looking to polish their styles. We're especially seeking short fiction from any genre that has a strong narrative quality and that takes the reader somewhere else. Any 'slice-of-life' style stories should be character driven and well-developed. We give special consideration to writers from Ohio, Indiana, West Virginia, Michigan, Pennsylvania, and Kentucky." Estab. 2002. Circ. 500. Pays on publication. Byline given. Buys one-time rights. Editorial lead time 3 months. Submit seasonal material 3 months in advance. Accepts queries by mail, e-mail. Accepts previously published material. Accepts simultaneous submissions. Responds in 2 weeks to queries; 3 months to mss. Sample copy for #10 SASE. Writer's guidelines online.

Nonfiction Essays, general interest, historical/nostalgic, humor. **Buys 10 mss/year.** Submit nonfiction material and queries to Peter Riesbeck via mail or e-mail. Length: Length: 7,500 words maximum. **Pays $10-40.**

Photos Send photos with submission. Reviews GIF/JPEG files. Buys one-time rights. Offers $5-15/photo.

Fiction Ethnic, experimental, historical, humorous, mystery, science fiction, serialized novels, suspense. No erotica, romance, or confessions. **Buys 50 mss/year.** Length: 7,500 words. **Pays $10-50.**

Poetry Send poetry queries and submissions to Gretchen Riesbeck via traditional mail or via e-mail to griesbeck-@sundryjournal.com. Avant-garde, free verse, haiku, light verse, traditional. No sonnets. **Buys 75 poems/ year.** Submit maximum 15 poems. Length: 50 lines maximum.

$ TAMPA REVIEW

University of Tampa Press, 401 W. Kennedy Blvd., Tampa FL 33606. (813)253-6266. Fax: (813)258-7593. Website: tampareview.ut.edu. **Contact:** Richard B. Mathews, editor. Semiannual magazine published in hardback format. An international literary journal publishing art and literature from Florida and Tampa Bay as well as new work and translations from throughout the world. Estab. 1988. Circ. 500. Pays on publication. Publishes ms an average of 10 months after acceptance. Byline given. Buys first North American serial rights. Editorial lead time 18 months. Accepts queries by mail. Responds in 5 months to mss. Sample copy for $7. Writer's guidelines online.

Nonfiction Elizabeth Winston, nonfiction editor. General interest, interview/profile, personal experience, creative nonfiction. No "how-to" articles, fads, journalistic reprise, etc. **Buys 6 mss/year.** Send complete ms. Length: 250-7,500 words. **Pays $10/printed page.**

Photos State availability with submission. Reviews contact sheets, negatives, transparencies, prints, digital files. Buys one-time rights. Offers $10/photo. Captions, identification of subjects required.

Fiction Lisa Birnbaum and Kathleen Ochshorn, fiction editors. Ethnic, experimental, fantasy, historical, mainstream, Literary. "We are far more interested in quality than in genre. Nothing sentimental as opposed to genuinely moving, nor self-conscious style at the expense of human truth." **Buys 6 mss/year.** Send complete ms. Length: 200-5,000 words. **Pays $10/printed page.**

Poetry Don Morrill and Martha Serpas, poetry editors. Avant-garde, free verse, haiku, light verse, traditional, visual/experimental. No greeting card verse, hackneyed, sing-song, rhyme-for-the-sake-of-rhyme. **Buys 45 poems/year.** Submit maximum 10 poems. Length: 2-225 lines.

Tips "Send a clear cover letter stating previous experience or background. Our editorial staff considers submissions between September and December for publication in the following year."

$ THEMA

Box 8747, Metairie LA 70011-8747. (504)887-1263. E-mail: thema@cox.net. Website: members.cox.net/thema. **Contact:** Virginia Howard, editor. **100% freelance written.** Triannual magazine covering a different theme for each issue. Upcoming themes for SASE. *"Thema* is designed to stimulate creative thinking by challenging writers with unusual themes, such as 'safety in numbers' and 'the power of whim.' Appeals to writers, teachers of creative writing, and general reading audience." Estab. 1988. Circ. 350. **Pays on acceptance.** Publishes ms an average of within 6 months after acceptance. Byline given. Buys one-time rights. Accepts queries by mail. Accepts previously published material. Accepts simultaneous submissions. Responds in 1 week to queries; 5 months to mss. Sample copy for $8. Writer's guidelines for #10 SASE.

Reprints Send ms with rights for sale noted and information about when and where the material previously appeared. Pays the same amount paid for original.

Fiction Special Issues Deadlines: Bookstore Cowboy (November 1, 2004); Umbrellas in the Snow (March 1,

2005); The Renaissance Child (July 1, 2005). Adventure, ethnic, experimental, fantasy, historical, humorous, mainstream, mystery, novel excerpts, religious, science fiction, slice-of-life vignettes, suspense, western, contemporary, sports, prose poem. "No erotica." **Buys 30 mss/year.** Length: fewer than 6,000 words preferred. **Pays $10-25.**

Poetry Avant-garde, free verse, haiku, light verse, traditional. "No erotica." **Buys 27 poems/year.** Submit maximum 3 poems. Length: 4-50 lines. **Pays $10.**

Tips "Be familiar with the themes. *Don't submit* unless you have an upcoming theme in mind. Specify the target theme on the first page of your manuscript or in a cover letter. Put your name on *first* page of manuscript only. (All submissions are judged in blind review after the deadline for a specified issue.) Most open to fiction and poetry. Don't be hasty when you consider a theme—mull it over and let it ferment in your mind. We appreciate interpretations that are carefully constructed, clever, subtle, well thought out."

$ $ THE THREEPENNY REVIEW

P.O. Box 9131, Berkeley CA 94709. (510)849-4545. Website: www.threepennyreview.com. **Contact:** Wendy Lesser, editor. **100% freelance written.** Works with small number of new/unpublished writers each year. Quarterly tabloid. "We are a general interest, national literary magazine with coverage of politics, the visual arts, and the performing arts as well." Estab. 1980. Circ. 9,000. **Pays on acceptance.** Publishes an average of 1 year after acceptance. Byline given. Buys first North American serial rights. Responds in 1 month to queries; 2 months to mss. Sample copy for $12 or online. Writer's guidelines online.

• Does not read mss in summer months.

Nonfiction Essays, exposé, historical/nostalgic, personal experience, book, film, theater, dance, music, and art reviews. **Buys 40 mss/year.** Query with or without published clips or send complete ms. Length: 1,500-4,000 words. **Pays $200.**

Fiction No fragmentary, sentimental fiction. **Buys 10 mss/year.** Send complete ms. Length: 800-4,000 words. **Pays $100 per poem or Table Talk piece.**

Poetry Free verse, traditional. No poems "without capital letters or poems without a discernible subject." **Buys 30 poems/year.** Submit maximum 5 poems. **Pays $100.**

Tips "Nonfiction (political articles, memoirs, reviews) is most open to freelancers."

$ TWENTY-FOUR HOURS

3456 N. Hills Dr., #135, Austin TX 78731. (512)342-2327. E-mail: increasethegrease@elvis.com. Website: www. geocities.com/twentyfourhourszine. **Contact:** Josh Medsker, publisher/editor. **80% freelance written.** Quarterly magazine. "*Twenty-Four Hours* is a literary magazine that loves new writers. We want to promote the kind of people who would travel around the country via Greyhound, then come back and publish a zine about it. The only thing we ask is that you put everything you have into your work." Estab. 2001. Circ. 100. Pays on publication. Publishes ms an average of 3 months after acceptance. Byline given. Buys first North American serial, electronic, anthology rights. Editorial lead time 1 month. Accepts queries by mail, e-mail. Responds in 1 month to queries. Sample copy for $3 and an SAE with 3 First-Class stamps. Writer's guidelines online.

Nonfiction Book excerpts, essays, historical/nostalgic, how-to (start a literary zine, start a series of slam poetry events, bind books by hand), interview/profile, personal experience, travel. **Buys 16 mss/year.** Query. **Pays $10, plus 1 contributor copy.** Pays in contributor copies for book reviews, zine reviews, and literary news.

Photos State availability with submission. Reviews GIF/JPEG files. Buys one-time rights and anthology rights. Negotiates payment individually. Captions, identification of subjects required.

Columns/Departments Book Reviews (novels and autobiographies), 500-700 words; Zine Reviews (travel zines and personal zines), 200-300 words; Literary News (local to wherever you are), 100-500 words. **Buys 30 mss/year. Pays in contributor copies.**

Fiction Ethnic, experimental, historical, mainstream, science fiction, slice-of-life vignettes, crime/pulp. **Buys 12 mss/year.** Query with published clips. Length: 3,000 words maximum. **Pays $5, plus 1 contributor copy.**

Poetry Avant-garde, free verse, haiku, slam poetry. **Buys 10 poems/year.** Submit maximum 2 poems. **Pays $5, plus 1 contributor copy.**

Tips "We love literature in all its forms. We cover traditional literary magazine territory such as short fiction and poetry, and also feature interviews with writers and others in the literary world—that's one half. The other half of *Twenty-Four Hours'* mission is to feature zine excerpts, interviews, with zine editors, and to generally promote the zine world to the literary world at large. We highly recommend buying an issue before submitting or querying."

N $ $ VESTAL REVIEW

A flash fiction magazine, 2609 Dartmouth Dr., Vestal NY 13850. Website: www.vestalreview.net. Quarterly "*Vestal Review* is the magazine specializing in flash fiction (stories under 500 words). In our 16 quarterly issues up to date, we had an honor of publishing many good writers, including Aimee Bender, Katharine Weber, and

Mike Resnick. We accept only e-mail submissions.'' Circ. 1,500. Pays on publication. Publishes ms an average of 2-3 months after acceptance. Buys first North American serial, electronic rights. Accepts simultaneous submissions. Responds in 1 week to queries; 2 months to mss. Sample copy for $5. Writer's guidelines online.

Fiction Mark Budman, publisher/editor. Ethnic, horror, mainstream, speculative fiction. Length: 50-500 words. **Pays 3-10¢/word and 1 contributor's copy; additional copies $5.**

N $THE VILLAGE RAMBLER MAGAZINE

The Flying Typewriter, P.O. Box 5070, Chapel Hill NC 27514-5001. (919)545-9789. Fax: (919)545-0921. E-mail: editor@villagerambler.com. Website: www.villagerambler.com. **Contact:** Elizabeth Oliver, editor. **85% freelance written.** Bimonthly magazine. "*The Village Rambler Magazine* is distributed in the Chapel Hill, North Carolina, area and features area and national talent. We are interested in fiction, poetry, and nonfiction." Estab. 2003. Circ. 3,000. Pays on publication. Publishes ms an average of 6-12 months after acceptance. Byline given. Buys all rights, makes work-for-hire assignments. Accepts queries by mail. Accepts previously published material. Responds in 1 month to queries; 3 months to mss. Sample copy for $8. Writer's guidelines for #10 SASE.

Nonfiction Book excerpts, essays, general interest, historical/nostalgic, humor, interview/profile, personal experience, photo feature. **Buys 24 mss/year.** Query. Length: 10,000 words maximum. **Pays $50, plus 2 contributor copies.**

Photos State availability with submission. Reviews 4×6 prints, GIF/JPEG files. Buys all rights. Negotiates payment individually. Captions, identification of subjects, model releases required.

Fiction Ethnic, experimental, historical, humorous, mainstream, novel excerpts, serialized novels, short shorts. No genre fiction (science fiction, horror, romance, or children's). **Buys 6-12 mss/year.** Send complete ms. Length: 10,000 words maximum. **Pays $50, plus 2 contributor copies.**

Poetry "We are open to all types of poetry." **Buys 6-12 poems/year.** Submit maximum 5 poems.

Tips "Send us your strongest work. We are interested in writing that knows its objective and achieves it with talent and technique."

$VIRGINIA QUARTERLY REVIEW

University of Virginia, One West Range, P.O. Box 400223, Charlottesville VA 22904-4223. (434)924-3124. Fax: (434)924-1397. Website: www.virginia.edu/vqr. **Contact:** Ted Genoways, editor. Quarterly magazine. "A national journal of literature and thought. A lay, intellectual audience; people who are not out-and-out scholars but who are interested in ideas and literature." Estab. 1925. Circ. 4,000. Pays on publication. Publishes ms an average of 1 year after acceptance. Byline given. Buys first, "will transfer upon request." rights. Editorial lead time 6 months. Submit seasonal material 6 months in advance. Responds in 2 weeks to queries; 2 months to mss. Sample copy for $5. Writer's guidelines online.

Nonfiction Book excerpts, essays, general interest, historical/nostalgic, humor, inspirational, personal experience, travel. Send complete ms. Length: 2,000-4,000 words. **Pays $100/page maximum.**

Fiction Adventure, ethnic, historical, humorous, mainstream, mystery, novel excerpts, romance, serialized novels. "No pornography." Send complete ms. Length: 3,000-7,000 words. **Pays $100/page maximum.**

Poetry All type. Submit maximum 5 poems. **Pays $5/line.**

$WEST BRANCH

Bucknell Hall, Bucknell University, Lewisburg PA 17837-2029. (570)577-1853. Fax: (570)577-1885. E-mail: westbranch@bucknell.edu. Website: www.bucknell.edu/westbranch. Managing Editor: Andrew Ciotola. **Contact:** Paula Closson Buck, editor. Semiannual literary magazine. "*West Branch* is an aesthetic conversation between the traditional and the innovative in poetry, fiction and nonfiction. It brings writers, new and established, to the rooms where they will be heard, and where they will, no doubt, rearrange the furniture." Pays on publication. Byline given. Buys first North American serial rights. Accepts queries by mail. Sample copy for $3. Writer's guidelines online.

Nonfiction Book excerpts, essays, general interest, historical/nostalgic, opinion, personal experience, travel, literary. **Buys 4-5 mss/year.** Send complete ms. **Pays $20-100 ($10/page).**

Fiction Novel excerpts, short stories. No genre fiction. **Buys 10-12 mss/year.** Send complete ms. **Pays $20-100 ($10/page).**

Poetry Free verse, formal, experimental. **Buys 30-40 poems/year.** Submit maximum 6 poems. **Pays $20-100 ($10/page).**

Tips "Please send only one submission at a time and do not send another work until you have heard about the first. Send no more than 6 poems or 30 pages of prose at once. We accept simultaneous submissions if they are clearly marked as such, and if we are notified immediately upon acceptance elsewhere. Manuscripts must be accompanied by the customary return materials; we cannot respond by e-mail or postcard, except to foreign submissions. All manuscripts should be typed, with the author's name on each page; prose must be double-spaced. We recommend that you acquaint yourself with the magazine before submitting."

$WESTERN HUMANITIES REVIEW

University of Utah, English Department, 255 S. Central Campus Dr., Room 3500, Salt Lake City UT 84112-0494. (801)581-6070. Fax: (801)585-5167. E-mail: whr@mail.hum.utah.edu. Website: www.hum.utah.edu/whr. **Contact:** Paul Ketzle, managing editor. Biannual magazine for educated readers. Estab. 1947. Circ. 1,000. Pays on publication. Publishes ms an average of 1 year after acceptance. Buys all rights. Accepts simultaneous submissions. Sample copy for $10. Writer's guidelines online.

- "We read manuscripts between September 1 and May 1. Manuscripts sent outside of these dates will be returned unread."

Nonfiction Barry Weller, editor-in-chief. Authoritative, readable articles on literature, art, philosophy, current events, history, religion, and anything in the humanities. Interdisciplinary articles encouraged. Departments on films and books. **Buys 4-5 unsolicited mss/year.** Send complete ms. **Pays $5/published page.**

Fiction Karen Brennan and Robin Hemley, fiction editors. Experimental. Does not want genre (romance, sci-fi, etc.). **Buys 8-12 mss/year.** Send complete ms. Length:5,000 words. **Pays $5/published page (when funds available).**

Poetry Richard Howard, poetry editor.

Tips "Because of changes in our editorial staff, we urge familiarity with *recent* issues of the magazine. Inappropriate material will be returned without comment. We do not publish writer's guidelines because we think that the magazine itself conveys an accurate picture of our requirements. Please, *no* e-mail submissions."

N $WRITERS NOTES

Stories, Craft, Experience, Hopewell Publications, LLC, P.O. Box 11, Titusville NJ 08560-0011. E-mail: editor@hopepubs.com. Website: www.writersnotes.com. Managing Editor: Karin Seidel. **Contact:** Christopher Klim, editor. **90% freelance written.** Semiannual magazine covering fiction, nonfiction, poetry, photos, graphic arts, and writing craft. "*Writers Notes* is a community of working writers and curious readers seeking news, information, and entertainment. Good writing is paramount. The editorial staff is open to compelling prose and experience, including photo essays and graphic arts." Estab. 2003. Circ. 1,500. Pays on publication. Publishes ms an average of 18 months after acceptance. Byline given. Buys first, electronic, one-time anthology rights rights. Editorial lead time 6 months. Submit seasonal material 6 months in advance. Accepts queries by mail, e-mail. Accepts simultaneous submissions. Responds in 3 weeks to queries; 3 months to mss. Sample copy online. Writer's guidelines online.

Nonfiction Book excerpts, essays, exposé, general interest, how-to (writing craft), humor, interview/profile, opinion, personal experience, photo feature. Does not want to see "the same tired party line." **Buys 4-5 mss/year.** Query with or without published clips or send complete ms. Length: 250-5,000 words. **Pays $10-50.** Author advertising/promotion offered in magazine.

Photos State availability with submission. Reviews GIF/JPEG files. Buys one-time rights. Negotiates payment individually.

Fiction Adventure, condensed novels, confessions, erotica, experimental, fantasy, horror, humorous, mainstream, mystery, novel excerpts, suspense. Does not want genre-specific formula stories. **Buys 8-10 mss/year.** Send complete ms. Length: 250-5,000 words. **Pays $10-50.**

Poetry All types accepted. Does not want greeting card, saccharin prose. **Buys 2-4 poems/year.** Submit maximum 10 poems.

Tips "There is a form and craft to great stories and articles. You must engage the reader from the first sentence, while informing, entertaining, and lending insight into a facet of writing craft or life in general. A topic or story that jars common thought, without being obtuse or paranoid, expands the mind. If you think we've seen it before, then don't submit it. Finally, we all need more humor. Make sure the work is complete and professional."

N $THE WRITERS POST JOURNAL

Let's Be 'Frank', 1434 Park Blvd., Pittsburgh PA 15216. (412)207-2190. E-mail: submissions@lbfbooks.com. Website: www.lbfbooks.com. Editor: Jacqueline Druga-Marchetti. Managing Editor: Judy Rushe. **Contact:** Michael Evanitz, submissions editor. **90% freelance written.** Monthly magazine. "Based on a literary organization established in 1996. The Writers Post Journal features and focuses on new and emerging literary voices. We also encourage articles on writing." Estab. 2003. Pays on publication. Publishes ms an average of 3 months after acceptance. Buys one-time rights. Editorial lead time 3 months. Submit seasonal material 4 months in advance. Accepts queries by mail, e-mail. Accepts previously published material. Accepts simultaneous submissions. Responds in 2 weeks to queries; 1 month to mss. Sample copy by e-mail. Writer's guidelines online.

Nonfiction Essays, exposé, general interest, how-to, humor, inspirational, opinion, personal experience. Does not want "vulgar material please." **Buys 12-20 mss/year.** Query. Length: 1,700 maximum. **Pays $5-25.** Pays contributor copies for poetic pieces, some short fiction pieces, letters to the editor.

Photos Jacqueline Druga. State availability with submission. Reviews GIF/JPEG files. Buys one-time rights. Offers no additional payment for photos accepted with ms.

Fiction Confessions, ethnic, experimental, horror, humorous, mainstream, religious, romance, science fiction, slice-of-life vignettes, young adult. Does not want porn. **Buys 20-40 mss/year.** Query with or without published clips or send complete ms. Length: 2,000 words maximum. **Pays $5-25.**

Poetry Avant-garde, free verse, light verse. Does not want haiku. **Buys 60 poems/year.** Submit maximum 5 poems. Length: 25 lines maximum.

Tips "Be professional. Be patient. We are not as strict as others if you veer off normal queries. Impress us with freshness. We'd like to see more young writer submissions (12-16)."

$ $ THE YALE REVIEW

Yale University, P.O. Box 208243, New Haven CT 06520-8243. (203)432-0499. Website: www.yale.edu. Associate Editor: Susan Bianconi. **Contact:** J.D. McClatchy, editor. **20% freelance written.** Quarterly magazine. Estab. 1911. Circ. 7,000. Pays prior to publication. Publishes ms an average of 6 months after acceptance. Buys one-time rights. Responds in 2 months to queries; 2 months to mss. Sample copy for $9, plus postage. Writer's guidelines online.

- *The Yale Review* has published work chosen for the Pushcart anthology, *The Best American Poetry*, and the O. Henry Award.

Nonfiction Authoritative discussions of politics, literature and the arts. No previously published submissions. Send complete ms with cover letter and SASE. Length: 3,000-5,000 words. **Pays $400-500.**

Fiction Buys quality fiction. Length: 3,000-5,000 words. **Pays $400-500.**

Poetry **Pays $100-250.**

🆕 $ ZAHIR

Unforgettable Tales, Zahir Publishing, 315 South Coast Hwy. 101, Suite U8, Encinitas CA 92024. E-mail: stempch in@zahirtales.com. Website: www.zahirtales.com. **Contact:** Sheryl Tempchin, editor. **100% freelance written.** Triannual magazine covering speculative fiction. "We publish quality speculative fiction for intelligent adult readers. Our goal is to bridge the gap between literary and genre fiction, and present a publication that is both entertaining and aesthetically pleasing." Estab. 2003. Pays on publication. Publishes ms an average of 2-12 months after acceptance. Byline given. Buys first, second serial (reprint) rights. Accepts queries by e-mail. Accepts previously published material. Responds in 1-2 weeks to queries; 1-3 months to mss. Sample copy for $5 (U.S.), $6.50 elsewhere. Writer's guidelines for #10 SASE, by e-mail, or online.

Fiction Fantasy, science fiction, surrealism, magical realism. No children's stories or stories that deal with excessive violence or anything pornographic. **Buys 18-25 mss/year.** Send complete ms. Length: Length: 6,000 words maximum. **Pays $10, and 2 contributor's copies.**

Tips "We look for great storytelling and fresh ideas. Let your imagination run wild and capture it in concise, evocative prose."

$ $ $ ZOETROPE: ALL STORY

AZX Publications, The Sentinel Bldg., 916 Kearny St., San Francisco CA 94133. (415)788-7500. E-mail: info@all-story.com. Website: www.all-story.com. **Contact:** Francis Ford Coppola, publisher; Tamara Straus, editor. Quarterly magazine specializing in the best of contemporary short fiction. "*Zoetrope: All Story* presents a new generation of classic stories." Estab. 1997. Circ. 20,000. Publishes ms an average of 5 months after acceptance. Byline given. Buys first North American serial rights. Accepts queries by mail. Accepts simultaneous submissions. Responds in 5 months (if SASE included) to mss. Sample copy for $6.95. Writer's guidelines online.

Fiction Literary short stories, one-act plays. **Buys 32-40 mss/year.** Send complete ms. **Pays $1,000.**

- Current and select back issues can be found online. "The website features current news, events, contests, workshops, writer's guidelines, and more. In addition, the site links to Francis Ford Coppola's Virtual Studio, which is host to an online workshop for short story writers."

$ ZYZZYVA

The Last Word: West Coast Writers & Artists, P.O. Box 590069, San Francisco CA 94159-0069. (415)752-4393. Fax: (415)752-4391. E-mail: editor@zyzzyva.org. Website: www.zyzzyva.org. **Contact:** Howard Junker, editor. **100% freelance written.** Works with a small number of new/unpublished writers each year. Magazine published in March, August, and November. "We feature work by writers currently living on the West Coast or in Alaska and Hawaii only. We are essentially a literary magazine, but of wide-ranging interests and a strong commitment to nonfiction." Estab. 1985. Circ. 3,500. **Pays on acceptance.** Publishes ms an average of 3 months after acceptance. Byline given. First North American serial and one-time anthology rights. Accepts queries by mail, e-mail. Responds in 1 week to queries; 1 month to mss. Sample copy for $7 or online. Writer's guidelines online.

Nonfiction Book excerpts, general interest, historical/nostalgic, humor, personal experience. **Buys 50 mss/year.** Query by mail or e-mail. Length: Open. **Pays $50.**

Photos Reviews copies or slides only—scans at 300 dpi, 5½" wide.

Fiction Ethnic, experimental, humorous, mainstream. **Buys 20 mss/year.** Send complete ms. Length: 100-7,500 words. **Pays $50.**

Poetry Buys 20 poems/year. Submit maximum 5 poems. Length: 3-200 lines. **Pays $50.**

Tips "West Coast writers means those currently living in California, Alaska, Washington, Oregon, or Hawaii."

MEN'S

$ $ $ $ CIGAR AFICIONADO

M. Shanken Communications, Inc., 387 Park Ave. S., New York NY 10016. (212)684-4224. Fax: (212)684-5424. Website: www.cigaraficionado.com. Editor: Marvin Shanken. **Contact:** Gordon Mott, executive editor. **75% freelance written.** Bimonthly magazine covering cigars and men's lifestyle. Estab. 1992. Circ. 300,000. **Pays on acceptance.** Publishes ms an average of 9 months after acceptance. Byline given. Offers 25% kill fee. Buys all rights. Editorial lead time 3 months. Submit seasonal material 3 months in advance. Accepts queries by mail, fax. Responds in 2 months to queries. Sample copy and writer's guidelines for SASE.

Nonfiction Buys 80-100 mss/year. Query. Length: 2,000 words. **Payment varies.** Sometimes pays expenses of writers on assignment.

Columns/Departments Length: 1,000 words. **Buys 20 mss/year. Payment varies.**

> ▣ The online magazine carries original content not found in the print edition. Contact: Dave Savona, online editor.

Ⓝ ⊘ DETAILS

Fairchild Publications, Inc., 7 W. 34th St., 4th Floor, New York NY 10001. (212)630-4000. Fax: (212)630-3815. E-mail: detailsletters@fairchildpub.com. Website: www.details.com. Editor: Daniel Peres. Monthly magazine. Lifestyle magazine for today's adult males. Circ. 400,000. Editorial lead time 4 months. Sample copy not available.

- Does not buy freelance materials or use freelance writers.

Ⓝ $ $ $ $ ESQUIRE

Hearst Corp., 1790 Broadway, New York NY 10019. (212)649-4020. Fax: (212)649-4306. E-mail: esquire@hearst .com. Website: www.esquire.com. Editor-in-Chief: David Granger. Senior Editor: A.J. Jacobs. Monthly magazine covering the ever-changing trends in American culture. Monthly magazine for smart, well-off men. General readership is college educated and sophisticated, between ages 30 and 45. Written mostly by contributing editors on contract. Rarely accepts unsolicited manuscripts. Estab. 1933. Circ. 720,000. Publishes ms an average of 2-6 months after acceptance. Retains first worldwide periodical publication rights for 90 days from cover date. Editorial lead time at least 2 months. Accepts simultaneous submissions. Writer's guidelines for SASE.

Nonfiction Focus is the ever-changing trends in American culture. Topics include current events and politics, social criticism, sports, celebrity profiles, the media, art and music, men's fashion. Queries must be sent by letter. **Buys 4 features and 12 shorter mss/year.** Length: Columns average 1,500 words; features average 5,000 words; short front of book pieces average 200-400 words. **Payment varies.**

Photos Uses mostly commissioned photography. Nancy Iacoi, photo editor. Payment depends on size and number of photos.

Fiction Adrienne Miller, literary editor. "Literary excellence is our only criterion." Accepts work chiefly from literary agencies. Novel excerpts, short stories, some poetry, memoirs, and plays. No "pornography, science fiction or 'true romance' stories." Send complete ms. **Pays in cash on acceptance, amount undisclosed.**

Tips "A writer has the best chance of breaking in at *Esquire* by querying with a specific idea that requires special contacts and expertise. Ideas must be timely and national in scope."

Ⓝ ⊘ FHM

For Him Magazine, Emap Metro, LLC, 110 5th Ave., 3rd Floor, New York NY 10011. (212)201-6700. Fax: (212)201-6980. E-mail: fhmedit@emapmetrousa.com. Website: www.fhmus.com. Monthly magazine. Circ. 1,000,000.

- Does not buy freelance material or use freelance writers.

$ GC MAGAZINE

LPI Publishing, P.O. Box 331775, Fort Worth TX 76163. (817)640-1306. Fax: (817)633-9045. E-mail: rosa.gc@sbc global.net. Managing Editor: Rosa Atwood-Flores. **80% freelance written.** Monthly magazine. "*GC Magazine* is a general entertainment magazine for men. We include entertainment celebrity interviews (movies, music, books) along with general interest articles for adult males." Estab. 1994. Circ. 53,000. Pays on publication. Publishes ms an average of 3 months after acceptance. Buys one-time rights. Editorial lead time 3 months.

Submit seasonal material 6 months in advance. Accepts queries by mail, e-mail, fax. Accepts previously published material. Accepts simultaneous submissions. Responds in 1 month to queries. Sample copy for $1.50. Writer's guidelines for #10 SASE.

Nonfiction Book excerpts, essays, exposé, general interest, historical/nostalgic, how-to, humor, interview/profile, opinion, personal experience, technical, travel, dating tips. No religious or "feel good" articles. **Buys 100 mss/year.** Query. Length: 1,000-2,000 words. **Pays 2¢/word.** Sometimes pays expenses of writers on assignment.

Reprints Accepts previously published submissions.

Photos State availability with submission. Reviews 3×5 prints, GIF/JPEG files. Buys one-time rights. Offers no additional payment for photos accepted with ms. Model releases required.

Columns/Departments Actress feature (film actress interviews), 2,500 words; Author feature (book author interviews), 1,500 words; Music feature (singer or band interviews), 1,500 words. **Buys 50 mss/year.** Query. **Pays 2¢/word.**

Tips "Submit material typed and free of errors. Writers should think of magazines like *Maxim* and *Details* when determining article ideas for our magazine. Our primary readership is adult males and we are seeking original and unique articles."

[N] GQ

Conde Nast Publications, Inc., 4 Times Square, New York NY 10036. (212)286-2860. Fax: (212)286-7786. Website: www.gq.com. Editorial Assistant: Sarah Wilson. Managing Editor: Martin Beiser. Senior Correspondent: Alan Richman. Senior Editor: Jason Gary. Senior Editor: John Gillies. Associate Editor: Brian Raftery. Monthly magazine covering subjects ranging from finance, food, entertainment, technology, celebrity profiles, sports and fashion. *Gentleman's Quarterly* is devoted to men's personal style and taste, from what he wears to the way he lives his life. Estab. 1957.

Nonfiction Interview/profile (celebrity).

$ $ $ $ HEARTLAND USA

UST Publishing, 100 W. Putnam Ave., Greenwich CT 06830-5316. (203)622-3456. Fax: (203)863-7296. E-mail: husaedit@att.net. **Contact:** Brad Pearson, editor. **95% freelance written.** Bimonthly magazine for working men. "*HUSA* is a general interest lifestyle magazine for adult males—active outdoorsmen. The editorial mix includes hunting, fishing, sports, automotive, how-to, country music, human interest, and wildlife." Estab. 1991. Circ. 1,200,000. **Pays on acceptance.** Byline given. Offers 20% kill fee. Buys first North American serial, second serial (reprint) rights. Submit seasonal material 1 year in advance. Accepts queries by mail, e-mail, fax. Accepts previously published material. Accepts simultaneous submissions. Responds in 1 month to queries. Sample copy for free. Writer's guidelines for #10 SASE.

Nonfiction Book excerpts, general interest, historical/nostalgic, how-to, humor, inspirational, interview/profile, new product, personal experience, photo feature, technical, travel. "No fiction or dry expository pieces." **Buys 30 mss/year.** Query with or without published clips or send complete ms. Length: 350-1,200 words. **Pays 50¢-$1/word for assigned articles; 25-80¢/word for unsolicited articles.** Sometimes pays expenses of writers on assignment.

Reprints Send photocopy and information about when and where the material previously appeared. Pays 25% of amount paid for an original article.

Photos Send photos with submission. Reviews transparencies. Buys one-time rights. Identification of subjects required.

Tips "Features with the possibility of strong photographic support are open to freelancers, as are our departments. We look for a relaxed, jocular, easy-to-read style, and look favorably on the liberal use of anecdote or interesting quotations. Our average reader sees himself as hardworking, traditional, rugged, confident, uncompromising, and daring."

$ $ $ INDY MEN'S MAGAZINE

The Guy's Guide to the Good Life, Table Moose Media, 8500 Keystone Crossing, Indianapolis IN 46240. (317)255-3850. E-mail: lou@indymensmagazine.com. Website: www.indymensmagazine.com. **Contact:** Lou Harry, editor-in-chief. **50% freelance written.** Monthly magazine. Estab. 2002. Circ. 50,000. Pays on publication. Byline given. Offers 10% kill fee. Buys first North American serial rights. Editorial lead time 3 months. Submit seasonal material 1 year in advance. Accepts queries by e-mail. Accepts simultaneous submissions. Responds in 3 weeks to queries; 2 months to mss. Sample copy for $5. Writer's guidelines by e-mail.

Nonfiction Essays, travel. No generic pieces that could run anywhere. No advocacy pieces. **Buys 50 mss/year.** Query. Length: 100-2,000 words. **Pays $75-500 for assigned articles; $50-400 for unsolicited articles.** Sometimes pays expenses of writers on assignment.

Photos State availability with submission. Reviews contact sheets, transparencies, prints, GIF/JPEG files. Buys one-time rights. Negotiates payment individually. Identification of subjects required.

Columns/Departments Balls (opinionated sports pieces), 1,400 words; Dad Files (introspective parenting essays), 1,400 words; Men At Work (Indianapolis men and their jobs), 100-600 words; Trippin' (experiential travel), 1,500 words. **Buys 30 mss/year.** Query with published clips. **Pays $75-400.**

Fiction "The piece needs to hold our attention from the first paragraph." Adventure, fantasy, historical, horror, humorous, mainstream, mystery, science fiction, suspense. **Buys 12 mss/year.** Send complete ms. Length: 1,000-4,000 words. **Pays $50-250.**

Tips "We don't believe in wasting our reader's time, whether it's in a 50-word item or a 6,000-word Q&A. Our readers are smart, and they appreciate our sense of humor. Write to entertain and engage."

$ $ $ $ THE INTERNATIONAL

The Magazine of Adventure and Pleasure for Men, Tomorrow Enterprises, 2228 E. 20th St., Oakland CA 94606. (510)532-6501. Fax: (510)536-5886. E-mail: tonyattomr@aol.com. **Contact:** Mr. Anthony L. Williams, managing editor. **70% freelance written.** Monthly magazine covering "bush and seaplane flying, seafaring, pleasure touring, etc., with adventure stories from all men who travel on sexual tours to Asia, Latin America, The Caribbean, and the Pacific." Estab. 1997. Circ. 5,000. Pays on publication. Publishes ms an average of 2 months after acceptance. Buys first rights. Editorial lead time 2 months. Submit seasonal material 3 months in advance. Accepts queries by mail, e-mail. Accepts simultaneous submissions. Responds in 2 weeks to queries; 2 months to mss. Writer's guidelines free.

Nonfiction Seafaring storis of all types published with photos. Military and veteran stories also sought as well as ex-pats living abroad. Especially interested in airplane flying stories with photos. Exposé, general interest, historical/nostalgic, humor, interview/profile, opinion, personal experience, photo feature, travel. No pornography, family, or "honeymoon" type travel. **Buys 40-50 mss/year.** Send complete ms. Length: 700 words maximum. **Pays $100-2,000 for assigned articles; $25-1,000 for unsolicited articles.** Sometimes pays expenses of writers on assignment.

Photos Send photos with submission. Reviews negatives, 3×5 prints. Buys one-time or all rights. Offers no additional payment for photos accepted with ms. Identification of subjects required.

Columns/Departments Asia/Pacific Beat; Latin America/Caribbean Beat (nightlife, adventure, air & sea), 450 words; Lifestyles Abroad (expatriate men's doings overseas), 600-1,000 words. **Buys 25 mss/year.** Send complete ms. **Pays $25-1,000.**

Fillers Anecdotes, facts, gags to be illustrated by cartoonist, newsbreaks, short humor. **Buys 25/year.** Length: 200-600 words. **Pays $25-100.**

Tips "If a single male lives in those parts of the world covered, and is either a pleasure tourist, pilot, or seafarer, we are interested in his submissions. He can visit our upcoming website or contact us directly. Stories from female escorts or party girls are also welcomed."

MAXIM

Dennis Publishing, 1040 Avenue of the Americas, 16th Floor, New York NY 10018-3703. (212)302-2626. Fax: (212)302-2635. E-mail: editors@maximmag.com. Website: www.maximonline.com. Editor: Keith Blanchard. Monthly magazine relationships, sex, women, careers and sports. Written for young, professional men interested in fun and informative articles. Circ. 2,500,000. Editorial lead time 5 months. Sample copy for $3.99 at newsstands.

MEN'S JOURNAL

Wenner Media, Inc., 1290 Avenue of the Americas, 2nd Floor, New York NY 10104-0295. (212)484-1616. Fax: (212)484-3434. E-mail: letters@mensjournal.com. Website: www.mensjournal.com. Monthly magazine covering general lifestyle for men, ages 25-49. "*Men's Journal* is for active men with an interest in participatory sports, travel, fitness, and adventure. It provides practical, informative articles on how to spend quality leisure time." Estab. 1992. Circ. 650,000. Accepts queries by mail, fax.

Nonfiction Features and profiles 2,000-7,000 words; shorter features of 400-1,200 words; equipment and fitness stories, 400-1,800 words. Book excerpts, essays, exposé, general interest, historical/nostalgic, how-to, humor, new product, personal experience, photo feature, travel. Query with SASE. **Payment varies.**

$ $ $ $ SMOKE MAGAZINE

Life's Burning Desires, Lockwood Publications, 26 Broadway, Floor 9M, New York NY 10004. (212)391-2060. Fax: (212)827-0945. E-mail: editor@smokemag.com. Website: www.smokemag.com. Editor: Mark Bernardo. Editorial Director: Ted Hoyt. **50% freelance written.** Quarterly magazine covering cigars and men's lifestyle issues. "A large majority of *Smoke's* readers are affluent men, ages 28-50; active, educated and adventurous." Estab. 1995. Circ. 175,000. Pays 2 months after publication. Publishes ms an average of 3 months after acceptance. Byline given. Offers 25% kill fee. Buys first rights. Editorial lead time 2 months. Submit seasonal material 6 months in advance. Accepts queries by mail, e-mail. Accepts simultaneous submissions. Responds in 6 weeks to queries; 3 months to mss. Sample copy for $4.99.

> O— Break in with "good nonfiction that interests guys—beer, cuisine, true-crime, sports, cigars, of course. Be original."

Nonfiction Essays, exposé, general interest, historical/nostalgic, how-to, humor, interview/profile, opinion, personal experience, photo feature, technical, travel, true crime. **Buys 8 mss/year.** Query with published clips. Length: 1,500-3,000 words. **Pays $500-1,200.** Sometimes pays expenses of writers on assignment.

Photos State availability with submission. Reviews 2¼×2¼ transparencies. Negotiates payment individually. Identification of subjects required.

Columns/Departments Smoke Undercover (investigative journalism, personal experience); Smoke Screen (TV/film/entertainment issues); Smoke City (cigar-related travel), all 1,500 words. **Buys 8 mss/year.** Query with published clips. **Pays $500-1,000.**

> ■ The online magazine carries original content not found in the print edition.

Tips "Send a short, clear query with clips. Go with your field of expertise: Cigars, sports, music, true crime, etc."

N STUFF

Dennis Publishing, 1040 Avenue of the Americas, 12th Floor, New York NY 10018. (212)372-3801. Fax: (212)354-4364. E-mail: editors@stuffmagazine.com. Website: www.stuffmagazine.com. Editor: Mike Hammer. Monthly magazine. Targeted towards American men who want sex, sports, gadgets, entertainment and humor. Circ. 1,200,000. Editorial lead time 3 months. Sample copy not available.

$ $ ⊡ UMM (URBAN MALE MAGAZINE)

Canada's Only Lifestyle and Fashion Magazine for Men, UMM Publishing Inc., 70 George St., Suite 200, Ottawa ON K1N 5V9, Canada. (613)723-6216. Fax: (613)723-1702. E-mail: editor@umm.ca. Website: www.umm.ca. **100% freelance written.** Bimonthly magazine covering men's interests. "Our audience is young men, aged 18-24. We focus on Canadian activities, interests, and lifestyle issues. Our magazine is fresh and energetic and we look for original ideas carried out with a spark of intelligence and/or humour (and you'd better spell humour with a 'u')." Estab. 1998. Circ. 90,000. Pays 1 month after publication. Publishes ms an average of 3 months after acceptance. Byline given. Buys first North American serial rights. Editorial lead time 3 months. Submit seasonal material 4 months in advance. Accepts queries by e-mail. Accepts simultaneous submissions. Responds in 6 weeks to queries; 6 weeks to mss.

Nonfiction Book excerpts, exposé, general interest, historical/nostalgic, how-to, humor, interview/profile, new product, personal experience, travel, adventure, cultural, sports, music. **Buys 80 mss/year.** Query with published clips. Length: 1,200-3,500 words. **Pays $100-400.** Sometimes pays expenses of writers on assignment.

Photos State availability with submission. Reviews contact sheets, prints. Buys one-time rights. Negotiates payment individually.

Fillers Anecdotes, facts, short humor. **Buys 35/year.** Length: 100-500 words. **Pays $50-150.**

Tips "Be familiar with our magazine before querying. We deal with all subjects of interest to young men, especially those with Canadian themes. We are very open-minded. Original ideas and catchy writing are key."

MILITARY

$ $ AIR FORCE TIMES

Army Times Publishing Co., 6883 Commercial Dr., Springfield VA 22159. (703)750-8646. Fax: (703)750-8601. Website: www.airforcetimes.com. **Contact:** Lance Bacon, managing editor. Weeklies edited separately for Army, Navy, Marine Corps, and Air Force military personnel and their families. They contain career information such as pay raises, promotions, news of legislation affecting the military, housing, base activities and features of interest to military people. Estab. 1940. **Pays on acceptance.** Byline given. Offers kill fee. Buys first rights. Accepts queries by mail, e-mail, phone. Accepts simultaneous submissions. Responds in 1 month to queries. Sample copy for #10 SASE. Writer's guidelines for #10 SASE.

Nonfiction Features of interest to career military personnel and their families. No advice pieces. **Buys 150-175 mss/year.** Query. Length: 750-2,000 words. **Pays $100-500.**

Columns/Departments Length: 500-900. **Buys 75 mss/year. Pays $75-125.**

> ■ The online magazines carry original content not found in the print editions. Websites: www.armytimes.com; www.navytimes.com; www.airforcetimes.com; www.marinecorpstimes.com. Contact: Neff Hudson, online editor.

Tips Looking for "stories on active duty, reserve and retired military personnel; stories on military matters and localized military issues; stories on successful civilian careers after military service."

$ $ARMY MAGAZINE

2425 Wilson Blvd., Arlington VA 22201-3385. (703)841-4300. Fax: (703)841-3505. E-mail: armymag@ausa.org. Website: www.ausa.org. **Contact:** Mary Blake French, editor-in-chief. **70% freelance written.** Prefers to work with published/established writers. Monthly magazine emphasizing military interests. Estab. 1904. Circ. 90,000. Pays on publication. Publishes ms an average of 5 months after acceptance. Byline given. Buys all rights. Submit seasonal material 3 months in advance. Accepts queries by mail. Sample copy for 9 × 12 SAE with $1 postage or online. Writer's guidelines for 9 × 12 SAE with $1 postage or online.

● *Army Magazine* looks for shorter articles.

Nonfiction "We would like to see more pieces about little-known episodes involving interesting military personalities. We especially want material lending itself to heavy, contributor-supplied photographic treatment. The first thing a contributor should recognize is that our readership is very savvy militarily. 'Gee-whiz' personal reminiscences get short shrift, unless they hold their own in a company in which long military service, heroism and unusual experiences are commonplace. At the same time, *Army* readers like a well-written story with a fresh slant, whether it is about an experience in a foxhole or the fortunes of a corps in battle." Historical/nostalgic (military and original), humor (military feature-length articles and anecdotes), interview/profile, photo feature. No rehashed history. No unsolicited book reviews. **Buys 40 mss/year.** Submit complete ms (hard copy and disk). Length: 1,000-1,500 words. **Pays 12-18¢/word.**

Photos Send photos with submission. Reviews transparencies, prints, slides, high resolution digital photos. Buys all rights. Pays $50-100 for 8 × 10 b&w glossy prints; $50-350 for 8 × 10 color glossy prints or 2¼ × 2¼ transparencies; 35mm and high resolution digital photos. Captions required.

$ $ARMY TIMES

Times News Group, Inc., 6883 Commercial Dr., Springfield VA 22159. (703)750-9000. Fax: (703)750-8622. E-mail: aneill@armytimes.com. Website: www.armytimes.com. **Contact:** Alex Neill, managing editor. Weekly for Army military personnel and their families containing career information such as pay raises, promotions, news of legislation affecting the military, housing, base activities and features of interest to military people. Estab. 1940. Circ. 230,000. **Pays on acceptance.** Byline given. Offers kill fee. Makes work-for-hire assignments. Accepts queries by mail, e-mail. Accepts simultaneous submissions. Responds in 1 month to queries. Sample copy and writer's guidelines for #10 SASE.

○➤ Break in by "proposing specific feature stories that only you can write—things we wouldn't be able to get from 'generic' syndicated or wire material. The story must contain an element of mystery and/or surprise, and be entertaining as well as informative. Above all, your story must have a direct connection to military people's needs and interests."

Nonfiction Features of interest to career military personnel and their families: food, relationships, parenting, education, retirement, shelter, health, and fitness, sports, personal appearance, community, recreation, personal finance, entertainment. No advice please. **Buys 150-175 mss/year.** Query. Length: 750-2,000 words. **Pays $100-500.**

Columns/Departments Length: 500-900 words. **Buys 75 mss/year. Pays $75-125.**

Tips Looking for "stories on active duty, reserve and retired military personnel; stories on military matters and localized military issues; stories on successful civilian careers after military service."

$ $MARINE CORPS TIMES

Army Times Publishing Co., 6883 Commercial Dr., Springfield VA 22159. (703)750-9000. Fax: (703)750-8767. E-mail: rcolenso@marinecorpstimes.com. Website: www.marinecorpstimes.com. **Contact:** Rob Colenso, managing editor, *Marine Corps Times.* Weeklies edited separately for Army, Navy, Marine Corps, and Air Force military personnel and their families. They contain career information such as pay raises, promotions, news of legislation affecting the military, housing, base activities and features of interest to military people. Estab. 1940. Circ. 230,000 (combined). Pays on publication. Byline given. Offers kill fee. Buys first rights. Accepts queries by mail, e-mail, phone. Accepts simultaneous submissions. Responds in 1 month to queries. Sample copy for #10 SASE. Writer's guidelines for #10 SASE.

Nonfiction Features of interest to career military personnel and their families, including stories on current military operations and exercises. No advice pieces. **Buys 150-175 mss/year.** Query. Length: 750-2,000 words. **Pays $100-500.**

Columns/Departments Length: 500-900 words. **Buys 75 mss/year. Pays $75-125.**

▣ The online magazines carry original content not found in the print editions. Websites: www.armytimes.com; www.navytimes.com; www.airforcetimes.com. Contact: Kent Miller, online editor.

Tips Looking for "stories on active duty, reserve and retired military personnel; stories on military matters and localized military issues; stories on successful civilian careers after military service."

$ $ $ $ MILITARY OFFICER

201 N. Washington St., Alexandria VA 22314-2539. (800)234-6622. Fax: (703)838-8179. E-mail: editor@moaa.o rg. Website: www.moaa.org. Editor: Col. Warren S. Lacy, USA-Ret. **Contact:** Managing Editor. **60% freelance written.** Prefers to work with published/established writers. Monthly magazine for officers of the 7 uniformed services and their families. "*Military Officer* covers topics such as current military/political affairs, military history, travel, finance, hobbies, health and fitness, and military family and retirement lifestyles." Estab. 1945. Circ. 389,000. **Pays on acceptance.** Publishes ms an average of 1 year after acceptance. Byline given. Buys first North American serial rights. Accepts queries by mail, e-mail, fax. Responds in 3 months to queries. Sample copy and writer's guidelines for 9×12 SAE with 6 first-class stamps or online.

Nonfiction Current military/political affairs, health and wellness, recent military history, travel, military family life-style. Emphasis now on current military and defense issues. "We rarely accept unsolicited manuscripts." **Buys 48 mss/year.** Query with résumé, sample clips and SASE. Length: 800-2,500 words. **Pays up to $1,800.**

Photos Query with list of stock photo subjects. Original slides and transparencies must be suitable for color separation. Reviews transparencies. Pays $20 for each 8×10 b&w photo (normal halftone) used. Pays $75-250 for inside color; $300 for cover.

■ The online magazine carries original content not found in the print edition and includes writer's guidelines. Contact: Ronda Reid, online editor.

$ $ MILITARY TIMES

Times News Group, Inc. (subsidiary of Gannett Corp.), 6883 Commercial Dr., Springfield VA 22159. Fax: (703)750-8781. E-mail: features@atpco.com. Website: www.militarycity.com. Managing Editor: David Craig. **Contact:** Phillip Thompson, Lifeline editor. **25% freelance written.** Weekly tabloid covering lifestyle topics for active, retired, and reserve military members and their families. "Features need to have real military people in them, and appeal to readers in all the armed services. Our target audience is 90% male, young, fit and adventurous, mostly married and often with young children. They move frequently. Writer queries should approach ideas with those demographics and facts firmly in mind." Circ. 300,000. Pays on publication. Publishes ms an average of 2 months after acceptance. Byline given. Buys first, electronic rights. Editorial lead time 2 months. Submit seasonal material 3 months in advance. Accepts queries by e-mail. Accepts simultaneous submissions. Responds in 6 weeks to queries. Sample copy for $2.50 or online. Writer's guidelines for SAE with 1 first-class stamp or by e-mail.

Nonfiction How-to, interview/profile, new product, technical, travel, sports, recreation, entertainment, health, personal fitness, self-image (fashion, trends), relationships, personal finance, food. "No poems, war memoirs or nostalgia, fiction, travel pieces that are too upscale (luxury cruises) or too focused on military monuments/museums." **Buys 110 mss/year.** Query with published clips. Length: 300-1,500 words. **Pays $100-500.** Sometimes pays expenses of writers on assignment.

Photos State availability with submission. Reviews transparencies. Offers work-for-hire. Offers $75/photo. Captions, identification of subjects required.

Columns/Departments Running (how-to for experienced runners, tips, techniques, problem-solving), 500 words; Personal Fitness (how-to, tips, techniques for working out, improving fitness), 500 words. **Buys 40 mss/year.** Query. **Pays $100-200.**

Tips "Our Lifelines section appears every week with a variety of services, information, and entertainment articles on topics that relate to readers' off-duty lives; or to personal dimensions of their on-duty lives. Topics include food, relationships, parenting, education, retirement, shelter, health and fitness, sports, personal appearances, community, recreation, personal finance, and entertainment. We are looking for articles about military life, its problems and how to handle them, as well as interesting things people are doing, on the job and in their leisure. Keep in mind that our readers come from all of the military services. For instance, a story can focus on an Army family, but may need to include families or sources from other services as well. The editorial 'voice' of the section is familiar and conversational; good-humored without being flippant; sincere without being sentimental; savvy about military life but in a relevant and subtle way, never forgetting that our readers are individuals first, spouses or parents or children second, and service members third."

$ $ NAVAL HISTORY

U.S. Naval Institute, 291 Wood Rd., Annapolis MD 21402-5034. (410)295-1079. Fax: (410)295-1049. E-mail: fschultz@usni.org. Website: www.navalinstitute.org. Associate Editors: Colin Babb and Giles Roblyer. **Contact:** Fred L. Schultz, editor-in-chief. **90% freelance written.** Bimonthly magazine covering naval and maritime history, worldwide. "We are committed, as a publication of the 130-year-old U.S. Naval Institute, to presenting the best and most accurate short works in international naval and maritime history. We do find a place for academicians, but they should be advised that a good story generally wins against a dull topic, no matter how well researched." Estab. 1988. Circ. 40,000. **Pays on acceptance.** Publishes ms an average of 2 years after acceptance. Byline given. Buys all rights. Editorial lead time 6 months. Submit seasonal material 6 months in advance. Accepts queries by mail, e-mail, fax, phone. Responds in 1 month to queries; 2 months to mss. Sample copy for $4.99 and SASE, or on website. Writer's guidelines online.

Nonfiction Book excerpts, essays, historical/nostalgic, humor, inspirational, interview/profile, personal experience, photo feature, technical. **Buys 50 mss/year.** Query. Length: 1,000-3,000 words. **Pays $300-500 for assigned articles; $75-400 for unsolicited articles.**

Photos State availability with submission. Reviews contact sheets, transparencies, 4×6 or larger prints, and digital submissions or CD-ROM. Buys one-time rights. Offers $10 minimum. Captions, identification of subjects, model releases required.

Fillers Anecdotes, newsbreaks (naval-related), short humor. **Buys 40-50/year.** Length: 50-1,000 words. **Pays $10-50.**

Tips "A good way to break in is to write a good, concise, exciting story supported by primary sources and substantial illustrations. Naval history-related news items (ship decommissionings, underwater archaeology, etc.) are also welcome. Because our story bank is substantial, competition is severe. Tying a topic to an anniversary many times is an advantage. We still are in need of Korean and Vietnam War-era material."

$ PARAMETERS

U.S. Army War College Quarterly, U.S. Army War College, 122 Forbes Ave., Carlisle PA 17013-5238. (717)245-4943. E-mail: parameters@carlisle.army.mil. Website: www.carlisle.army.mil/usawc/parameters. **Contact:** Col. Robert H. Taylor, USA Ret., editor. **100% freelance written.** Prefers to work with published/established writers or experts in the field. Readership consists of senior leaders of US defense establishment, both uniformed and civilian, plus members of the media, government, industry and academia. Subjects include national and international security affairs, military strategy, military leadership and management, art and science of warfare, and military history with contemporary relevance. Estab. 1971. Circ. 13,500. Pays on publication. Publishes ms an average of 6 months after acceptance. Byline given. Buys first North American serial rights. Accepts queries by mail, e-mail, phone. Responds in 6 weeks to queries. Sample copy free or online. Writer's guidelines online.

Nonfiction Prefers articles that deal with current security issues, employ critical analysis, and provide solutions or recommendations. Liveliness and verve, consistent with scholarly integrity, appreciated. Theses, studies, and academic course papers should be adapted to article form prior to submission. Documentation in complete endnotes. Send complete ms. Length: 4,500 words average. **Pays $150 average.**

Tips "Make it short; keep it interesting; get criticism and revise accordingly. Write on a contemporary topic. Tackle a subject only if you are an authority. No fax submissions." Encourage e-mail submissions.

$ $ PROCEEDINGS

U.S. Naval Institute, 291 Wood Rd., Annapolis MD 21402-5034. (410)268-6110. Fax: (410)295-7940. E-mail: gkeiser@usni.org. Website: www.usni.org. Editor: Fred H. Rainbow. **Contact:** Gordon Keiser, senior editor. **80% freelance written.** Monthly magazine covering Navy, Marine Corps, Coast Guard issues. Estab. 1873. Circ. 100,000. **Pays on acceptance.** Publishes ms an average of 9 months after acceptance. Byline given. Buys all rights. Editorial lead time 3 months. Responds in 2 months to queries. Sample copy for $3.95. Writer's guidelines online.

Nonfiction Essays, historical/nostalgic, interview/profile, photo feature, technical. **Buys 100-125 mss/year.** Query with or without published clips or send complete ms. Length: 3,000 words. **Pays $60-150/printed page for unsolicited articles.**

Photos State availability of or send photos with submission. Reviews transparencies, prints. Buys one-time rights. Offers $25/photo maximum.

Columns/Departments Comment & Discussion (letters to editor), 750 words; Commentary (opinion), 900 words; Nobody Asked Me, But... (opinion), less than 1,000 words. **Buys 150-200 mss/year.** Query or send complete ms. **Pays $34-150.**

Fillers Anecdotes. **Buys 20/year.** Length: 100 words. **Pays $25.**

$ $ $ $ SOLDIER OF FORTUNE

The Journal of Professional Adventurers, 5735 Arapahoe Ave., Suite A-5, Boulder CO 80303-1340. (303)449-3750. E-mail: editorsof@aol.com. Website: www.sofmag.com. **50% freelance written.** Monthly magazine covering military, paramilitary, police, combat subjects, and action/adventure. "We are an action-oriented magazine; we cover combat hot spots around the world. We also provide timely features on state-of-the-art weapons and equipment; elite military and police units; and historical military operations. Readership is primarily active-duty military, veterans, and law enforcement." Estab. 1975. Circ. 60,000. Byline given. Offers 25% kill fee.

Buys first rights. Responds in 3 weeks to queries; 1 month to mss. Sample copy for $5. Writer's guidelines for #10 SASE.

Nonfiction Exposé, general interest, historical/nostalgic, how-to (on weapons and their skilled use), humor, interview/profile, new product, personal experience, photo feature (No. 1 on our list), technical, travel, combat reports, military unit reports, and solid Vietnam and Operation Iraqi Freedom articles. "No 'How I won the war' pieces; no op-ed pieces unless they are fully and factually backgrounded; no knife articles (staff assignments only). All submitted articles should have good art; art will sell us on an article." **Buys 75 mss/year.** Query with or without published clips or send complete ms. Send mss to articles editor; queries to managing editor. Length: 2,000-3,000 words. **Pays $150-250/page.**

Reprints Send disk copy, photocopy of article and information about when and where the material previously appeared. Pays 25% of amount paid for an original article.

Photos Send photos with submission. Reviews contact sheets, transparencies. Buys one-time rights. Pays $500 for cover photo. Captions, identification of subjects required.

Fillers Bulletin Board editor. Newsbreaks (military/paramilitary related has to be documented). Length: 100-250 words. **Pays $50.**

Tips "Submit a professionally prepared, complete package. All artwork with cutlines, double-spaced typed manuscript with 5.25 or 3.5 IBM-compatible disk, if available, cover letter including synopsis of article, supporting documentation where applicable, etc. Manuscript must be factual; writers have to do their homework and get all their facts straight. One error means rejection. Vietnam features, if carefully researched and art heavy, will always get a careful look. Combat reports, again, with good art, are number one in our book and stand the best chance of being accepted. Military unit reports from around the world are well received as are law-enforcement articles (units, police in action). If you write for us, be complete and factual; pros read *Soldier of Fortune*, and are very quick to let us know if we (and the author) err."

MUSIC

$AMERICAN SONGWRITER MAGAZINE

50 Music Square W., Suite 604, Nashville TN 37203-3227. (615)321-6096. Fax: (615)321-6097. E-mail: info@americansongwriter.com. Website: www.americansongwriter.com. Assistant Editor: Nancy Moran. **Contact:** Vernell Hackett, editor. **30% freelance written.** Bimonthly magazine about songwriters and the craft of songwriting for many types of music, including pop, country, rock, metal, jazz, gospel, and r&b. Estab. 1984. Circ. 5,000. Pays on publication. Publishes ms an average of 2 months after acceptance. Offers 25% kill fee. Buys first North American serial rights. Accepts previously published material. Responds in 2 months to queries. Sample copy for $4. Writer's guidelines for #10 SASE or by e-mail.

Nonfiction General interest, interview/profile, new product, technical, home demo studios, movie and TV scores, performance rights organizations. **Buys 20 mss/year.** Query with published clips. Length: 300-1,200 words. **Pays $25-60.**

Reprints Send tearsheet or photocopy and information about when and where the material previously appeared. Pays same amount as paid for an original article.

Photos Send photos with submission. Reviews 3×5 prints. Buys one-time rights. Offers no additional payment for photos accepeted with ms. Identification of subjects required.

Tips "*American Songwriter* strives to present articles which can be read a year or 2 after they were written and still be pertinent to the songwriter reading them."

N BILLBOARD

VNU Business Media, 770 Broadway, 6th Floor, New York NY 10003-9593. (646)654-5220. Fax: (646)-654-4681. E-mail: info@billboard.com. Website: www.billboard.com. Editor: Keith Girard. Weekly magazine. Contents provide, news, reviews and statistics for all genres of music, including radio play, music video, related internet activity and retail updates. Circ. 34,020. Editorial lead time 2 months. Sample copy not available.

$ $ BLUEGRASS UNLIMITED

Bluegrass Unlimited, Inc., P.O. Box 771, Warrenton VA 20188-0771. (540)349-8181 or (800)BLU-GRAS. Fax: (540)341-0011. E-mail: editor@bluegrassmusic.com. Website: www.bluegrassmusic.com. Editor: Peter V. Kuykendall. **Contact:** Sharon McGraw, managing editor. **20% freelance written.** Prefers to work with published/established writers. Monthly magazine covering bluegrass, acoustic, and old-time country music. Estab. 1966. Circ. 27,000. Pays on publication. Publishes ms an average of 4 months after acceptance. Byline given. Offers negotiated kill fee. Buys first North American serial, one-time, second serial (reprint), all rights. Submit seasonal material 4 months in advance. Accepts queries by mail, e-mail, fax. Responds in 2 weeks to queries; 2 months to mss. Sample copy for free. Writer's guidelines for #10 SASE.

Nonfiction General interest, historical/nostalgic, how-to, interview/profile, personal experience, photo feature, travel. No "fan"-style articles. **Buys 60-70 mss/year.** Query with or without published clips. Length: Open. **Pays 10-13¢/word.**

Reprints Send photocopy with rights for sale noted and information about when and where the material previously appeared. Payment is negotiable.

Photos State availability of or send photos with submission. Reviews 35mm transparencies and 3×5, 5×7 and 8×10 b&w and color prints. Buys all rights. Pays $50-175 for transparencies; $25-60 for b&w prints; $50-250 for color prints. Identification of subjects required.

Fiction Ethnic, humorous. **Buys 3-5 mss/year.** Query. Length: Negotiable. **Pays 10-13¢/word.**

Tips "We would prefer that articles be informational, based on personal experience or an interview with lots of quotes from subject, profile, humor, etc."

$ $CHAMBER MUSIC

Chamber Music America, 305 Seventh Ave., 5th Floor, New York NY 10001-6008. (212)242-2022. Fax: (212)242-7955. Website: www.chamber-music.org. **Contact:** Editor. Bimonthly magazine covering chamber music. Estab. 1977. Circ. 13,000. Pays on publication. Publishes ms an average of 5 months after acceptance. Byline given. Offers kill fee. Buys first rights. Editorial lead time 4 months. Accepts queries by mail, phone.

Nonfiction Book excerpts, essays, humor, opinion, personal experience, issue-oriented stories of relevance to the chamber music fields written by top music journalists and critics, or music practitioners. No artist profiles, no stories about opera or symphonic work. **Buys 35 mss/year.** Query with published clips. Length: 2,500-3,500 words. **Pays $500 minimum.** Sometimes pays expenses of writers on assignment.

Photos State availability with submission. Offers no payment for photos accepted with ms.

$ $ $GUITAR ONE

The Magazine You Can Play, 149 5th St., 9th Floor, New York NY 10010. (212)768-2966. Fax: (212)944-9279. E-mail: editors@guitaronemag.com. Website: www.guitaronemag.com. **Contact:** Troy Nelson, editor-in-chief. **75% freelance written.** Monthly magazine covering guitar news, artists, music, gear. Estab. 1996. Circ. 140,000. Pays on publication. Publishes ms an average of 1 month after acceptance. Byline given. Offers 50% kill fee. Buys one-time rights. Editorial lead time 3 months. Accepts queries by mail, e-mail, fax. Accepts simultaneous submissions. Sample copy online.

Nonfiction Interview/profile (with guitarists). **Buys 15 mss/year.** Query with published clips. Length: 2,000-5,000 words. **Pays $300-1,200 for assigned articles; $150-800 for unsolicited articles.** Sometimes pays expenses of writers on assignment.

Photos State availability with submission. Reviews negatives, transparencies, prints. Buys one-time rights. Negotiates payment individually.

Columns/Departments Opening Axe (newsy items on artists), 450 words; Soundcheck (records review), 200 words; Gear Box (equipment reviews), 800 words.

Tips "Find an interesting feature with a nice angle that pertains to guitar enthusiasts. Submit a well-written draft or samples of work."

N $ $GUITAR PLAYER MAGAZINE

United Entertainment Media, Inc., 2800 Campus Dr., San Mateo CA 94403. (650)513-4300. Fax: (650)513-4616. E-mail: mmolenda@musicplayer.com. Website: www.guitarplayer.com. **Contact:** Michael Molenda, editor-in-chief. **50% freelance written.** Monthly magazine for persons "interested in guitars, guitarists, manufacturers, guitar builders, equipment, careers, etc." Circ. 150,000. **Pays on acceptance.** Publishes ms an average of 3 months after acceptance. Byline given. Buys first serial and all reprint rights Accepts queries by e-mail. Responds in 6 weeks to queries. Writer's guidelines for #10 SASE.

Nonfiction Publishes "wide variety of articles pertaining to guitars and guitarists: interviews, guitar craftsmen profiles, how-to features—anything amateur and professional guitarists would find fascinating and/or helpful. In interviews with 'name' performers, be as technical as possible regarding strings, guitars, techniques, etc. We're not a pop culture magazine, but a magazine for musicians. The essential question: What can the reader take away from a story to become a better player?" **Buys 30-40 mss/year.** Query. Length: Open. **Pays $250-450.** Sometimes pays expenses of writers on assignment.

Photos Reviews 35 mm color transparencies, b&w glossy prints. Buys one-time rights. Payment varies.

$MUSIC FOR THE LOVE OF IT

67 Parkside Dr., Berkeley CA 94705. (510)654-9134. Fax: (510)654-4656. E-mail: tedrust@musicfortheloveofit.com. Website: www.musicfortheloveofit.com. **Contact:** Ted Rust, editor. **20% freelance written.** Bimonthly newsletter covering amateur musicianship. "A lively, intelligent source of ideas and enthusiasm for a musically literate audience of adult amateur musicians." Estab. 1988. Circ. 600. Pays on publication. Publishes ms an

average of 2 months after acceptance. Byline given. Buys one-time rights. Editorial lead time 1 month. Submit seasonal material 1 month in advance. Accepts queries by mail, e-mail, fax, phone. Responds in 1 week to queries; 1 month to mss. Sample copy for $6. Writer's guidelines online.

    O— Break in with "a good article, written from a musician's point of view, with at least 1 photo."

Nonfiction Essays, historical/nostalgic, how-to, personal experience, photo feature. No concert reviews, star interviews, CD reviews. **Buys 6 mss/year.** Query. Length: 500-1,500 words. **Pays $50, or gift subscriptions.**

Photos State availability with submission. Reviews 4×6 prints or larger. Buys one-time rights. Offers no additional payment for photos accepted with ms. Identification of subjects required.

Tips "We're looking for more good how-to articles on musical styles. Love making music. Know something about it."

RELIX MAGAZINE

Music for the Mind, 180 Varick St., 4th Floor, New York NY 10014. (646)230-0100. Website: www.relix.com. **Contact:** Aeve Baldwin, editor-in-chief. **40% freelance written.** Bimonthly magazine focusing on new and independent bands, classic rock, lifestyles, and music alternatives such as roots, improvisational music, psychedelia, and jambands. Estab. 1974. Circ. 100,000. Pays on publication. Publishes ms an average of 4 months after acceptance. Byline given. Buys one-time rights. Accepts queries by mail, e-mail. Accepts previously published material. Responds in 6 months to queries. Sample copy for $5. Writer's guidelines online.

Nonfiction Feature topics include jambands, reggae, Grateful Dead, bluegrass, jazz, country, rock, experimental, electronic, and world music; also deals with environmental, cultural, and lifestyle issues. Historical/nostalgic, humor, interview/profile, new product, photo feature, technical, live reviews, new artists, hippy lifestyles, food, mixed media, books. Query by e-mail with published clips if available or send complete ms. Length: 300-1,500 words. **Pays variable rates.**

Photos "Whenever possible, submit complete artwork with articles."

Columns/Departments Query with published clips or send complete ms. **Pays variable rates.**

Tips "The best part of working with freelance writers is discovering new music we might never have stumbled across."

$ $ $ $ ROLLING STONE

Wenner Media, 1290 Avenue of The Americas, New York NY 10104. (212)484-1616. Fax: (212)484-1664. E-mail: letters@rollingstone.com. Website: www.rollingstone.com. Editor: Jann S. Wenner. Biweekly magazine. Geared towards young adults interested in news of popular music, entertainment and the arts, current news events, politics and American culture. Circ. 1,254,200. Editorial lead time 1 month. Sample copy not available.

SPIN

205 Lexington Ave., 3rd Floor, New York NY 10016. (212)231-7400. Fax: (212)231-7312. E-mail: feedback@spin .com. Website: www.spin.com. Publisher: Jacob Hill. Managing Editor: Jeanann Pannasch. **Contact:** Sia Michel, editor-in-chief. Monthly magazine covering music and popular culture. "*Spin* covers progressive rock as well as investigative reporting on issues from politics, to pop culture. Editorial includes reviews, essays, profiles and interviews on a wide range of music from rock to jazz. It also covers sports, movies, politics, humor, fashion and issues—from AIDS research to the environment. The editorial focuses on the progressive new music scene and young adult culture more from an 'alternative' perspective as opposed to mainstream pop music. The magazine discovers new bands as well as angles for the familiar stars." Estab. 1985. Circ. 540,000.

Nonfiction Features are not assigned to writers who have not established a prior relationship with *Spin*. Cultural, political or social issues. New writers: submit complete ms with SASE. Established writers: query specific editor with published clips.

Columns/Departments Most open to freelancers: Exposure (short articles on popular culture, TV, movies, books), 200-500 words, query Dave Itzhoff, associate editor; Reviews (record reviews), 100 words, queries/mss to Alex Pappademas, associate editor; Noise (music and new artists), query Tracey Pepper, senior editor. Query before submitting.

Tips "The best way to break into the magazine is the Exposure and Reviews sections. We primarily work with seasoned, professional writers who have extensive national magazine experience and very rarely make assignments based on unsolicited queries."

N $ VERMEER MAGAZINE

Rembrandt & Co. Publishers International, P.O. Box 13486, St. Petersburg FL 33733. E-mail: vermeermagazine@ operamail.com. Website: www.rembrandtandcompany.com. Editor: Benjamin Scarlato. Monthly magazine covering media and music subjects. "*Vermeer* is the media and music magazine taking no sides. Music listings are published monthly from classical to heavy metal. Our media room fights for both sides of the negative and the positive in our world of global isolation. Our fiction and poetry rooms are open in all subjects here to flavor this icon of magazines. *Vermeer* is here to stay as the world turns through its negative and positive aspects." Estab. 2003. Circ. 100. Buys first North American serial, one-time rights. Accepts queries by mail, e-mail. Accepts previously published material. Accepts simultaneous submissions. Responds in 2 weeks to queries; 3 months to mss. Sample copy for $2. Writer's guidelines free.

Nonfiction Exposé, general interest, historical/nostalgic, humor, inspirational, new product, media criticism. **Buys 12 mss/year.** Query or send complete ms. Length: 100-200 words. **Pays 1¢/word, plus 1 contributor copy.**

Fiction Adventure, confessions, erotica, ethnic, fantasy, historical, horror, humorous, mainstream, mystery, romance, science fiction, serialized novels, suspense. **Buys 35 mss/year.** Length: 1,000-2,000 words. **Pays 3 contributor copies.**

Poetry Avant-garde, free verse, light verse, traditional. **Buys 24 poems/year.** Submit maximum 5 poems. Length: 5-50 lines.

$ $ $ $ VIBE

215 Lexington Ave., 6th Floor, New York NY 10016. (212)448-7300. Fax: (212)448-7430. E-mail: vibe@vibe.com. Website: www.vibe.com. Managing Editor: Lori Yacovone. **Contact:** Individual editors. Monthly magazine covering urban music and culture. "*Vibe* chronicles and celebrates urban music and the youth culture that inspires and consumes it." Estab. 1993. Circ. 800,000. Pays on publication. Buys first North American serial rights. Editorial lead time 4 months. Responds in 2 months to queries. Sample copy available on newsstands. Writer's guidelines for #10 SASE.

Nonfiction Jamie Katz, deputy editor; Erik Parker, music editor. Cultural, political or social issues. Query with published clips, résumé and SASE. Length: 800-3,000 words. **Pays $1/word.**

Columns/Departments Start (introductory news-based section), 350-740 words, send queries to Noah Callahan-Beaver, senior editor. Revolutions (music reviews), 100-800 words, send queries to Ron Dell Conway, associate music editor. Book reviews, send queries to Serena Kim, features editor. Query with published clips, résumé and SASE. **Pays $1/word.**

Tips "A writer's best chance to be published in *Vibe* is through the Start or Revolutions Sections. Keep in mind that *Vibe* is a national magazine, so ideas should have a national scope. People in Cali should care as much about the story as people in NYC. Also, *Vibe* has a four-month lead time. What we work on today will appear in the magazine four or more months later. Stories must be timely with respect to this fact."

MYSTERY

$ HARDBOILED

Gryphon Publications, P.O. Box 209, Brooklyn NY 11228. Website: www.gryphonbooks.com. **Contact:** Gary Lovisi, editor. **100% freelance written.** Semiannual book covering crime/mystery fiction and nonfiction. "Hard-hitting crime fiction and private-eye stories—the newest and most cutting-edge work and classic reprints." Estab. 1988. Circ. 1,000. Pays on publication. Publishes ms an average of 18 months after acceptance. Byline given. Offers 100% kill fee. Buys first North American serial, one-time rights. Editorial lead time 1 year. Submit seasonal material 9 months in advance. Accepts queries by mail, fax. Accepts previously published material. Accepts simultaneous submissions. Responds in 2 weeks to queries; 1 month to mss. Sample copy for $10 or double issue for $20 (add $1.50 book postage). Writer's guidelines for #10 SASE.

Nonfiction Book excerpts, essays, exposé. **Buys 4-6 mss/year.** Query. Length: 500-3,000 words. **Pays 1 copy.**

Reprints Query first.

Photos State availability with submission.

Columns/Departments Occasional review columns/articles on hardboiled writers. **Buys 2-4 mss/year.** Query.

Fiction Mystery, hardboiled crime, and private-eye stories, all on the cutting edge. No "pastches, violence for the sake of violence." **Buys 40 mss/year.** Query with or without published clips or send complete ms. Length: 500-3,000 words. **Pays $5-50.**

Tips Best bet for breaking in is short hard crime fiction filled with authenticity and brevity.

ALFRED HITCHCOCK'S MYSTERY MAGAZINE

Dell Magazines, 475 Park Ave. S., 11th Floor, New York NY 10016. (212)686-7188. Website: www.themysteryplace.com. Editor: Linda Landrigan. **100% freelance written.** Monthly magazine featuring new mystery short stories. Estab. 1956. Circ. 150,000 readers. Pays on publication. Byline given. Buys first, foreign rights rights. Submit seasonal material 7 months in advance. Responds in 3 months to mss. Sample copy for $5. Writer's guidelines for SASE or on website.

Fiction Linda Landrigan, editor. Original and well-written mystery and crime fiction. "Because this is a mystery magazine, the stories we buy must fall into that genre in some sense or another. We are interested in nearly every kind of mystery, however: stories of detection of the classic kind, police procedurals, private eye tales, suspense, courtroom dramas, stories of espionage, and so on. We ask only that the story be about crime (or the threat or fear of one). We sometimes accept ghost stories or supernatural tales, but those also should involve a crime.'' Mystery. No sensationalism. Send complete ms. Length: Up to 12,000 words. **Payment varies.**

Tips ''No simultaneous submissions, please. Submissions sent to *Alfred Hitchcock's Mystery Magazine* are not considered for or read by *Ellery Queen's Mystery Magazine,* and vice versa.''

$ELLERY QUEEN'S MYSTERY MAGAZINE

Dell Magazines Fiction Group, 475 Park Ave. S., 11th Floor, New York NY 10016. (212)686-7188. Fax: (212)686-7414. E-mail: elleryqueen@dellmagazines.com. Website: www.themysteryplace.com. **Contact:** Janet Hutchings, editor. **100% freelance written.** Magazine published 10 times/year featuring mystery fiction. *"Ellery Queen's Mystery Magazine* welcomes submissions from both new and established writers. We publish every kind of mystery short story: the psychological suspense tale, the deductive puzzle, the private eye case—the gamut of crime and detection from the realistic (including the policeman's lot and stories of police procedure) to the more imaginative (including ''locked rooms'' and ''impossible crimes''). *EQMM* has been in continuous publication since 1941. From the beginning three general criteria have been employed in evaluating submissions: We look for strong writing, an original and exciting plot, and professional craftsmanship. We encourage writers whose work meets these general criteria to read an issue of *EQMM* before making a submission.'' Magazine for lovers of mystery fiction. Estab. 1941. Circ. 180,780. **Pays on acceptance.** Publishes ms an average of 6-12 months after acceptance. Byline given. Buys first North American serial rights. Accepts simultaneous submissions. Responds in 3 months to mss. Sample copy for $5. Writer's guidelines for SASE or online.

Fiction ''We publish every type of mystery: the suspense story, the psychological study, the private-eye story, the deductive puzzle—the gamut of crime and detection from the realistic (including stories of police procedure) to the more imaginative (including 'locked rooms' and 'impossible crimes'). We always need detective stories. Special consideration given to anything timely and original.'' Mystery. No explicit sex or violence, no gore or horror. Seldom publishes parodies or pastiches. **Buys up to 120 mss/year.** Send complete ms. Length: Most stories 2,500-10,000 words. Accepts longer and shorter submissions—including minute mysteries of 250 words, and novellas of up to 20,000 words from established authors. **Pays 5-8¢/word, occasionally higher for established authors.**

Poetry Short mystery verses, limericks. Length: 1 page, double spaced maximum.

Tips ''We have a Department of First Stories to encourage writers whose fiction has never before been in print. We publish an average of 10 first stories every year.''

NATURE, CONSERVATION & ECOLOGY

$ ALTERNATIVES JOURNAL

Canadian Environmental Ideas and Action, Alternatives, Inc., Faculty of Environmental Studies, University of Waterloo, Waterloo ON N2L 3G1, Canada. (519)888-4442. Fax: (519)746-0292. E-mail: editor@alternativesjournal.ca. Website: www.alternativesjournal.ca. **Contact:** Cheryl Lousley, executive editor. **90% freelance written.** Quarterly magazine covering environmental issues with Canadian relevance. Estab. 1971. Circ. 4,800. Pays on publication. Publishes ms an average of 5 months after acceptance. Byline given. Offers 50% kill fee. Buys first rights. Editorial lead time 7 months. Submit seasonal material 5 months in advance. Accepts queries by mail, e-mail, fax. Accepts simultaneous submissions. Sample copy free for Canadian writers only. Writer's guidelines online.

Nonfiction Book excerpts, essays, exposé, humor, interview/profile, opinion. **Buys 50 mss/year.** Query with published clips. Length: 800-3,000 words. **Pays $50-150 (Canadian).** All contributors receive a free subscription in addition to payment. Sometimes pays expenses of writers on assignment.

Photos State availability with submission. Buys one-time rights. Offers $35-75/photo. Identification of subjects required.

$ $ $AMERICAN FORESTS

American Forests, P.O. Box 2000, Washington DC 20013. E-mail: mrobbins@amfor.org. Website: www.americanforests.org. **Contact:** Michelle Robbins, editor. **75% freelance written.** Quarterly magazine ''of trees and forests published by a nonprofit citizens' organization that strives to help people plant and care for trees for ecosystem restoration and healthier communities.'' Estab. 1895. Circ. 25,000. **Pays on acceptance.** Publishes ms an average of 8 months after acceptance. Byline given. Buys one-time rights. Submit seasonal material 5 months in advance. Accepts queries by mail, e-mail. Accepts previously published material. Responds in 2 months to queries. Sample copy for $2. Writer's guidelines online.

☞ Break in with "stories that resonate with city dwellers who love trees, or small, forestland owners (private). This magazine is looking for more urban and suburban-oriented pieces."

Nonfiction All articles should emphasize trees, forests, forestry and related issues. General interest, historical/nostalgic, how-to, humor, inspirational. **Buys 8-12 mss/year.** Query. Length: 1,200-2,000 words. **Pays $250-1,000.**

Reprints Send tearsheet or typed ms with rights for sale noted and information about when and where the material previously appeared. Pays 50% of amount paid for original article.

Photos Originals only. Send photos with submission. Reviews 35mm or larger transparencies, glossy color prints. Buys one-time rights. Offers no additional payment for photos accompanying ms. Captions required.

Tips "We're looking for more good urban forestry stories, and stories that show cooperation among disparate elements to protect/restore an ecosystem. Query should have honesty and information on photo support. We *do not* accept fiction or poetry at this time."

$THE BEAR DELUXE MAGAZINE

Orlo, P.O. Box 10342, Portland OR 97296. (503)242-1047. E-mail: bear@orlo.org. Website: www.orlo.org. **Contact:** Tom Webb, editor. **80% freelance written.** Semiannual magazine. "*The Bear Deluxe Magazine* provides a fresh voice amid often strident and polarized environmental discourse. Street level, solution-oriented, and nondogmatic, *The Bear Deluxe* presents lively creative discussion to a diverse readership." Estab. 1993. Circ. 19,000. Pays on publication. Publishes ms an average of 6 months after acceptance. Byline given. Offers 25% kill fee. Buys first, one-time rights. Editorial lead time 6 months. Submit seasonal material 9 months in advance. Accepts queries by mail, e-mail. Accepts previously published material. Accepts simultaneous submissions. Responds in 3 months to queries; 6 months to mss. Sample copy for $3. Writer's guidelines for #10 SASE or on website.

Nonfiction Book excerpts, essays, exposé, general interest, interview/profile, new product, opinion, personal experience, photo feature, travel, artist profiles. Special issues: Publishes 1 theme/2 years. **Buys 40 mss/year.** Query with published clips. Length: 250-4,500 words. **Pays 5¢/word.** Sometimes pays expenses of writers on assignment.

Photos State availability with submission. Reviews contact sheets, transparencies, 8×10 prints. Buys one-time rights. Offers $30/photo. Identification of subjects, model releases required.

Columns/Departments Reviews (almost anything), 300 words; News Bites (quirk of eco-news), 300 words; Portrait of an Artist (artist profiles), 1,200 words. **Buys 16 mss/year.** Query with published clips. **Pays 5¢/word, subscription, and copies.**

Fiction "Stories must have some environmental context." Adventure, condensed novels, historical, horror, humorous, mystery, novel excerpts, western. "No detective, children's or horror." **Buys 8 mss/year.** Query with or without published clips or send complete ms. Length: 750-4,500 words. **Pays free subscription to the magazine, contributor's copies and 5¢/word; additional copies for postage.**

Poetry Avant-garde, free verse, haiku, light verse, traditional. **Buys 16-20 poems/year.** Submit maximum 5 poems. Length: 50 lines maximum. **Pays $10, subscription, and copies.**

Fillers Facts, newsbreaks, short humor. **Buys 10/year.** Length: 100-750 words. **Pays 5¢/word, subscription, and copies.**

Tips "Offer to be a stringer for future ideas. Get a copy of the magazine and guidelines, and query us with specific nonfiction ideas and clips. We're looking for original, magazine-style stories, not fluff or PR. Fiction, essay, and poetry writers should know we have an open and blind review policy and should keep sending their best work even if rejected once. Be as specific as possible in queries."

$BIRD WATCHER'S DIGEST

Pardson Corp., P.O. Box 110, Marietta OH 45750. (740)373-5285. Fax: (740)373-8443. E-mail: editor@birdwatchersdigest.com. Website: www.birdwatchersdigest.com. **Contact:** William H. Thompson III, editor. **60% freelance written.** Works with a small number of new/unpublished writers each year. Bimonthly magazine covering natural history—birds and bird watching. "*BWD* is a nontechnical magazine interpreting ornithological material for amateur observers, including the knowledgeable birder, the serious novice and the backyard bird watcher; we strive to provide good reading and good ornithology." Estab. 1978. Circ. 90,000. Pays on publication. Publishes ms an average of 2 years after acceptance. Byline given. Buys one-time, second serial (reprint) rights. Submit seasonal material 6 months in advance. Accepts previously published material. Responds in 2 months to queries. Sample copy for $3.99 or online. Writer's guidelines online.

Nonfiction "We are especially interested in fresh, lively accounts of closely observed bird behavior and displays and of bird-watching experiences and expeditions. We often need material on backyard subjects such as bird feeding, housing, gardenening on less common species or on unusual or previously unreported behavior of common species." Book excerpts, how-to (relating to birds, feeding and attracting, etc.), humor, personal experience, travel (limited, we get many). No articles on pet or caged birds; none on raising a baby bird. **Buys 45-60 mss/year.** Send complete ms. Length: 600-3,500 words. **Pays from $100.**

Photos Send photos with submission. Reviews transparencies, prints. Buys one-time rights. Pays $75 minimum for transparencies.

📷 The online magazine carries content not found in the print edition and includes writer's guidelines.

Tips "We are aimed at an audience ranging from the backyard bird watcher to the very knowledgeable birder; we include in each issue material that will appeal at various levels. We always strive for a good geographical spread, with material from every section of the country. We leave very technical matters to others, but we want facts and accuracy, depth and quality, directed at the veteran bird watcher and at the enthusiastic novice. We stress the joys and pleasures of bird watching, its environmental contribution, and its value for the individual and society."

$ $ BIRDER'S WORLD

Enjoying Birds at Home and Beyond, Kalmbach Publishing Co., P.O. Box 1612, Waukesha WI 53187-1612. Fax: (262)798-6468. E-mail: mail@birdersworld.com. Website: www.birdersworld.com. Editor: Charles J. Hagner. Managing Editor: Delilah Smittle. Associate Editor: Matt Schlag-Mendenhall. **Contact:** Rosemary Nowak, editorial assistant. Bimonthly magazine covering wild birds and birdwatching. "*Birder's World* is a magazine designed for people with a broad interest in wild birds and birdwatching. Our readers are curious and generally well-educated with varying degrees of experience in the world of birds. No poetry, fiction, or puzzles please." Estab. 1987. Circ. 70,000. **Pays on acceptance.** Byline given. Offers $100 kill fee. Buys one-time rights. Accepts queries by mail. Writer's guidelines for #10 SASE or by e-mail.

Nonfiction Essays, how-to (attracting birds), interview/profile, personal experience, photo feature (bird photography), travel (birding trips in North America), book reviews, product reviews/comparisons, bird biology, endangered or threatened birds. No poetry, fiction, or puzzles. **Buys 60 mss/year.** Query with published clips or send complete ms. Length: 500-2,400 words. **Pays $200-450.** Sometimes pays expenses of writers on assignment.

Photos State availability with submission. Buys one-time rights. Identification of subjects required.

$ $ $ CALIFORNIA WILD

Natural Science for Thinking Animals, California Academy of Sciences, Golden Gate Park, San Francisco CA 94118. (415)750-7117. Fax: (415)221-4853. E-mail: kkhowell@calacademy.org. Website: www.calacademy.org/calwild. **Contact:** Keith Howell, editor. **75% freelance written.** Quarterly magazine covering natural sciences and the environment. "Our readers' interests range widely from ecology to geology, from endangered species to anthropology, from field identification of plants and birds to armchair understanding of complex scientific issues." Estab. 1948. Circ. 32,000. Pays prior to publication. Publishes ms an average of 3 months after acceptance. Byline given. Offers 50% kill fee; maximum $200. Buys first North American serial, one-time rights. Editorial lead time 3 months. Submit seasonal material 6 months in advance. Accepts queries by mail, fax. Responds in 6 weeks to queries; 6 months to mss. Sample copy for 9×12 SASE or on website. Writer's guidelines online.

Nonfiction Personal experience, photo feature, biological, and earth sciences. Special issues: Mostly California pieces, but also from Pacific Ocean countries. No travel pieces. **Buys 20 mss/year.** Query with published clips. Length: 1,000-3,000 words. **Pays $250-1,000 for assigned articles; $200-800 for unsolicited articles.** Sometimes pays expenses of writers on assignment.

Photos State availability with submission. Reviews transparencies. Buys one-time rights. Offers $75-150/photo. Identification of subjects, model releases required.

Columns/Departments A Closer Look (unusual places); Wild Lives (description of unusual plant or animal); In Pursuit of Science (innovative student, teacher, young scientist), all 1,000-1,500 words; Skywatcher (research in astronomy), 2,000-3,000 words. **Buys 12 mss/year.** Query with published clips. **Pays $200-400.**

Tips "We are looking for unusual and/or timely stories about California environment or biodiversity."

$ $ $ 📷 CANADIAN WILDLIFE

350 Michael Crawford Dr., Kanata ON K2M 2W1, Canada. (613)599-9594. Fax: (613)271-9591. E-mail: wild@cwf-fcf.org. Editor: Kendra Toby. **Contact:** Asha Jhamandas, assistant editor. **90% freelance written.** Magazine published 5 times/year covering wildlife conservation. Includes topics pertaining to wildlife, endangered species, conservation, and natural history. When possible, it is beneficial if articles have a Canadian slant or the topic has global appeal. Estab. 1995. Circ. 15,000. **Pays on acceptance.** Publishes ms an average of 3 months after acceptance. Byline given. Offers 15% kill fee. Buys first North American serial rights. Editorial lead time 3 months. Submit seasonal material 4 months in advance. Accepts queries by mail, e-mail, fax. Responds in 3 weeks to queries; 2 months to mss. Sample copy for $5 (Canadian). Writer's guidelines free.

Nonfiction Book excerpts, interview/profile, photo feature, science/nature. No standard travel stories. **Buys 20**

mss/year. Query with published clips. Length: 800-2,500 words. **Pays $500-1,200 for assigned articles; $300-1,000 for unsolicited articles.**

Photos Send photos with submission. Reviews transparencies. Buys one-time rights. Negotiates payment individually. Captions, identification of subjects, model releases required.

Columns/Departments Vistas (science news), 200-500 words; Book Reviews, 100-150 words. **Buys 15 mss/year.** Query with published clips. **Pays $50-250.**

Tips *"Canadian Wildlife* is a benefit of membership in the Canadian Wildlife Federation. Nearly 15,000 people currently receive the magazine. The majority of these men and women are already well versed in topics concerning the environment and natural science; writers, however, should not make assumptions about the extent of a reader's knowledge of topics."

$ $ $ CONSCIOUS CHOICE

The Journal of Ecology & Natural Living, Dragonfly Chicago, LLC, 920 N. Franklin St., Suite 202, Chicago IL 60610-3179. Fax: (312)751-3973. E-mail: rebecca@consciouschoice.com. Website: www.consciouschoice.com. **Contact:** Rebecca Ephraim, editor. **95% freelance written.** Monthly tabloid covering the environment, natural health and medicine, and personal growth and spirituality. Estab. 1988. Circ. 55,000. Pays on publication. Publishes ms an average of 6 months after acceptance. Byline given. Offers 50% kill fee. Buys first North American serial, electronic rights. Editorial lead time 6 months. Submit seasonal material 6 months in advance. Accepts queries by mail. Accepts simultaneous submissions. Responds in 6 weeks to queries; 1 month to mss. Sample copy online. Writer's guidelines free or by e-mail.

Nonfiction General interest (to cultural creatives), interview/profile (emphasis on narrative, story telling), personal experience, environment. **Buys 24 mss/year.** Query with 2-3 published clips. Length: 1,800 words. **Pays $150-1,000.** Sometimes pays expenses of writers on assignment.

$ $ E THE ENVIRONMENTAL MAGAZINE

Earth Action Network, P.O. Box 5098, Westport CT 06881-5098. (203)854-5559. Fax: (203)866-0602. E-mail: info@emagazine.com. Website: www.emagazine.com. **Contact:** Jim Motavalli, editor. **60% freelance written.** Bimonthly magazine. *"E Magazine* was formed for the purpose of acting as a clearinghouse of information, news, and commentary on environmental issues." Estab. 1990. Circ. 50,000. Pays on publication. Byline given. Buys first North American serial rights. Editorial lead time 3 months. Submit seasonal material 6 months in advance. Accepts queries by mail, e-mail, fax. Accepts simultaneous submissions. Sample copy for $5 or online. Writer's guidelines online.

● The editor reports an interest in seeing more investigative reporting.

Nonfiction On spec or free contributions welcome. Exposé (environmental), how-to, new product, book review, feature (in-depth articles on key natural environmental issues). **Buys 100 mss/year.** Query with published clips. Length: 100-4,000 words. **Pays 30¢/word.**

Photos State availability with submission. Reviews printed samples, e.g., magazine tearsheets, postcards, etc., to be kept on file. Buys one-time rights. Negotiates payment individually. Identification of subjects required.

Columns/Departments In Brief/Currents (environmental news stories/trends), 400-1,000 words; Conversations (Q&As with environmental "movers and shakers"), 2,000 words; Tools for Green Living; Your Health; Eco-Travel; Eco-Home; Eating Right; Green Business; Consumer News (each 700-1,200 words). On spec or free contributions welcome. Query with published clips.

■ Contact: Jim Motavalli, online editor.

Tips "Contact us to obtain writer's guidelines and back issues of our magazine. Tailor your query according to the department/section you feel it would be best suited for. Articles must be lively, well researched, balanced, and relevant to a mainstream, national readership." On spec or free contributions welcome.

$ THE FRUGAL ENVIRONMENTALIST

The Frugal Environmentalist, P.O. Box 45095, Seattle WA 98145-0095. E-mail: info@frugalgreen.com. Website: www.frugalgreen.com. **Contact:** Editor. **10-20% freelance written.** Quarterly magazine covering frugal environmental living. *"The Frugal Environmentalist* is dedicated to showing readers how to make affordable, eco-friendly lifestyle choices. Our audience is concerned about the environment but lacks the money to make expensive lifestyle choices like buying solar panels and taking eco-tourist vacations." Estab. 2003. Pays on publication. Publishes ms an average of 3-6 months after acceptance. Buys first rights; also reserves the right to publish on website and in any anthology of back issues that may be published. Accepts queries by mail. Accepts simultaneous submissions. Responds in 1 month to queries; 2 months to mss. Sample copy for $5. Writer's guidelines for #10 SASE or by e-mail.

Nonfiction How-to (practical advice for affordable ways to make eco-friendly lifestyle choices), personal experience (stories of frugal environmental living). "It's okay to mention environmental problems, but articles should focus mainly on solutions. We are looking for articles that are funny, upbeat and positive, while also providing details about affordable solutions to the challenges of eco-friendly living. We enjoy reading articles of a personal nature, so tell us how you solved a problem in your own life, even if it's for a how-to article." Query or send complete ms. Length: 1,000-2,000 words. **Pays $25-35, plus a 1-year subscription to the magazine.**

Tips "We are actively seeking freelance writers to work with but are not a traditional environmental magazine. If you understand our style and angle, you'll have a much better chance of getting published with us. Writers should think about the practical aspects of environmentalism—i.e., what can ordinary people do in their everyday lives to affect positive change. We are not a political magazine, nor are we focused on 'saving the whales' environmentalism, not unless you can show how a simple, affordable everyday action can help save the whales. For personal experience stories, show us how you've made affordable, eco-friendly lifestyle changes in your own life. While it's good to include the factors that motivated you, focus mostly on what you did, how you did it, and any obstacles you encountered along the way; we want readers to be inspired by your story, and also feel empowered to make changes in their lives based on what you've done. If possible, back up your article with data that illustrates the problem and/or show the readers what good can come of making certain changes. Our overall goal is to empower our readers to make positive changes in their everyday lives, and to prove that you don't have to be rich to be an environmentalist."

$ $ HIGH COUNTRY NEWS

High Country Foundation, P.O. Box 1090, Paonia CO 81428. (970)527-4898. E-mail: greg@hcn.org. Website: www.hcn.org. **Contact:** Greg Hanscom, editor. **80% freelance written.** Weekly tabloid covering Rocky Mountain West, the Great Basin, and Pacific Northwest environment, rural communities, and natural resource issues in 10 western states for environmentalists, politicians, companies, college classes, government agencies, grass roots activists, public land managers, etc. Estab. 1970. Circ. 23,000. Pays on publication. Publishes ms an average of 2 months after acceptance. Byline given. Buys one-time rights. Accepts queries by mail. Responds in 1 month to queries. Sample copy for SAE or online. Writer's guidelines online.

Nonfiction Exposé (government, corporate), interview/profile, personal experience, photo feature (centerspread), reporting (local issues with regional importance). **Buys 100 mss/year.** Query. Length: up to 3,000 words. **Pays 20¢/word minimum.** Sometimes pays expenses of writers on assignment.

Reprints Send tearsheet and information about when and where the material previously appeared. Pays 15¢/word.

Photos Send photos with submission. Reviews b&w prints. Captions, identification of subjects required.

Columns/Departments Roundups (topical stories), 800 words; opinion pieces, 1,000 words.

Tips "We use a lot of freelance material, though very little from outside the Rockies. Familiarity with the newspaper is a must. Start by writing a query letter. We define 'resources' broadly to include people, culture, and aesthetic values, not just coal, oil, and timber."

$ $ $ ⬛ HOOKED ON THE OUTDOORS

2040 30th St., Suite A, Boulder CO 80301. (303)449-5119. E-mail: query@ruhooked.com. Website: www.ruhooked.com. **Contact:** Nancy Coulter-Parker, editor-in-chief. **60% freelance written.** *"Hooked on the Outdoors* magazine is a bimonthly travel and gear guide for outdoorsy folk of all ages, shapes, sizes, religions, and mantras. No matter the background, all have the North American backyard in common. *Hooked* is the outdoor guide for readers who are multi-sport oriented and, just the same, people new to the outdoors, providing affordable, close to home destinations and gear alternative." Estab. 1998. Circ. 150,000. Pays within 30 days of publication. Publishes ms an average of 4 months after acceptance. Byline given. Offers 15% kill fee. Buys first North American serial, electronic rights. Editorial lead time 3 months. Submit seasonal material 1 year in advance. Accepts queries by mail, e-mail. Accepts simultaneous submissions. Responds in 6 weeks to queries. Sample copy for $5 and SAE with $1.75 postage. Writer's guidelines online.

Nonfiction Book excerpts, essays, exposé, general interest, humor, interview/profile, new product, opinion, personal experience, photo feature, travel. **Buys 4 mss/year.** Query with published clips. Length: 350-2,500 words. **Pays 35-50¢/word.** Sometimes pays expenses of writers on assignment.

Photos State availability with submission. Reviews contact sheets. Buys one-time rights. Offers $25-290. Captions, model releases required.

Columns/Departments Buys 30 mss/year. Query with published clips. **Pays 35-50¢/word.**

Tips "Send well thought out, complete queries reflective of research. Writers ought not query on topics already covered."

N $ $ $ MINNESOTA CONSERVATION VOLUNTEER

Minnesota Department of Natural Resources, 500 Lafayette Rd., St. Paul MN 55155-4046. (651)296-0894. Fax: (651)296-0902. E-mail: kathleen.weflen@dnr.state.mn.us. Website: www.dnr.state.mn.us. **Contact:** Kathleen Weflen, editor. **50% freelance written.** Bimonthly magazine covering Minnesota natural resources, wildlife, natural history, outdoor recreation, and land use. *"Minnesota Conservation Volunteer* is a donor-supported magazine advocating conservation and wise use of Minnesota's natural resources. Material must reflect an appreciation of nature and an ethic of care for the environment. We rely on a variety of sources in our reporting. More than 128,000 Minnesota households, businesses, schools, and other groups subscribe to this conservation magazine." Estab. 1940. Circ. 128,000. **Pays on acceptance.** Publishes ms an average of 1 month after acceptance. Byline given. Offers 30% kill fee. Buys first North American serial, rights to post to website, and archive rights. Editorial lead time 8 months. Submit seasonal material 8 months in advance. Accepts queries by mail, e-mail, fax. Accepts previously published material. Accepts simultaneous submissions. Responds in 1 month to queries; 2 months to mss. Sample copy free or on website. Writer's guidelines by e-mail.

Nonfiction Book excerpts, essays, exposé, general interest, historical/nostalgic, humor, interview/profile, opinion, personal experience, photo feature, travel, "Young Naturalist" for children. Does not publish poetry or uncritical advocacy. **Buys 10 mss/year.** Query with published clips. Length: up to 1,500 words. **Pays 50¢/word for full-length feature articles.** Pays expenses of writers on assignment.

Photos State availability with submission. Reviews 35mm or large format transparencies. Buys one-time rights, will negotiate for Web use separately. Offers $100/photo.

Columns/Departments Close Encounters (unusual, exciting, or humorous personal wildlife experience in Minnesota), up to 1,500 words; Sense of Place (first- or third-person essay developing character of a Minnesota place), up to 1,500 words; Viewpoint (well-researched and well-reasoned opinion piece), up to 1,500 words; Minnesota Profile (concise description of emblematic state species or geographic feature), 400 words. **Buys 10 mss/year.** Query with published clips. **Pays 50¢/word.**

Tips "In submitting queries, look beyond topics to *stories:* What is someone doing and why? How does the story end? In submitting a query addressing a particular issue, think of the human impacts and the sources you might consult. Summarize your idea, the story line, and sources in 2 or 3 short paragraphs. While topics must have relevance to Minnesota and give a Minnesota character to the magazine, feel free to round out your research with out-of-state sources."

$ $ $ NATIONAL PARKS

1300 19th St. NW, Suite 300, Washington DC 20036. (202)223-6722. Fax: (202)659-0650. E-mail: npmag@npca. org. Website: www.npca.org/magazine/. Editor-in-chief: Linda Rancourt. **Contact:** Jenell Talley, publications coordinator. **60% freelance written.** Prefers to work with published/established writers. Bimonthly magazine for a largely unscientific but highly educated audience interested in preservation of National Park System units, natural areas, and protection of wildlife habitat. Estab. 1919. Circ. 300,000. **Pays on acceptance.** Publishes ms an average of 2 months after acceptance. Offers 33% kill fee. Responds in 5 months to queries. Sample copy for $3 and 9×12 SASE or online. Writer's guidelines online.

Nonfiction All material must relate to US national parks. Exposé (on threats, wildlife problems in national parks), descriptive articles about new or proposed national parks and wilderness parks; natural history pieces describing park geology, wildlife or plants; new trends in park use; legislative issues. No poetry, philosophical essays, or first-person narratives. No unsolicited mss. Length: 1,500 words. **Pays $1,300 for full-length features; $750 for service articles.**

Photos No color prints or negatives. Send for guidelines. Not responsible for unsolicited photos. Send photos with submission. Reviews color slides. Pays $150-350 inside; $525 for covers. Captions required.

Tips "Articles should have an original slant or news hook and cover a limited subject, rather than attempt to treat a broad subject superficially. Specific examples, descriptive details, and quotes are always preferable to generalized information. The writer must be able to document factual claims, and statements should be clearly substantiated with evidence within the article. *National Parks* does not publish fiction, poetry, personal essays, or 'My trip to...' stories."

N ⊕ NATURE

Nature Publishing Group, The Macmillan Building, 4 Crinan St., London N1 9XW, United Kingdom. (0044)20 7833 4000. Fax: (0044)20 7843 4596. E-mail: nature@nature.com. Website: www.nature.com/nature. Editor: Philip Campbell. Managing Editor: Peter Wrobel. **5% freelance written.** Weekly magazine covering multidisplinary science. "*Nature* is the number one multidisciplinary journal of science, publishing News, Views, Commentary, Reviews, and ground-breaking research." Estab. 1869. Circ. 60,000. Publishes ms an average of 2 months after acceptance. Byline given.

$ $ $ ⊡ NATURE CANADA

Canadian Nature Federation, 1 Nicholas St., Suite 606, Ottawa ON K1N 7B7, Canada. Fax: (613)562-3371. E-mail: naturecanada@cnf.ca. Website: www.cnf.ca. **Contact:** Pamela Feeny, editor. Quarterly magazine covering conservation, natural history and environmental/naturalist community. "Editorial content reflects the goals and priorities of the Canadian Nature Federation as a conservation organization with a focus on our program areas: federally protected areas (national parks, national wildlife areas, etc.), endangered species, and bird conservation through Canada's important bird areas. *Nature Canada* is written for an audience interested in nature conservation. CNF celebrates, preserves, and protects Canadian nature. We promote the awareness and understanding of the connection between humans and nature and how natural systems support life on Earth. We strive to instill a sense of ownership and belief that these natural systems should be protected." Estab. 1971. Circ. 27,000. Pays on publication. Publishes ms an average of 3 months after acceptance. Byline given. Offers $100 kill fee. Buys all CNF rights (including electronic). Author retains resale rights elsewhere. Editorial lead time 4 months. Submit seasonal material 6 months in advance. Responds in 4 months to mss. Sample copy for $5. Writer's guidelines online.

Nonfiction Canadian conservation issues and natural history. **Buys 12 mss/year.** Query with published clips. Length: 2,000 words. **Pays up to 50¢/word (Canadian).**

Photos State availability with submission. Buys one-time rights. Offers $50-200/photo (Canadian). Identification of subjects required.

Columns/Departments Connections (Canadians making a difference for the environment), 650 words; Pathways (protected areas to visit); Terra Firma (grassroots conservation initiatives of our affiliates), 650 words; Species in Danger (news angles about species on Cosewic List). **Buys 16 mss/year.** Query with published clips. **Pays up to 50¢/word (Canadian).**

Tips "Our readers are knowledgeable about nature and the environment so contributors should have a good understanding of the subject. We also deal exclusively with Canadian issues and species, except for those relating directly to our international program. E-mail queries preferred. Do not send unsolicited manuscripts."

$ $ NORTHERN WOODLANDS MAGAZINE

Center for Woodlands Education, Inc., 1776 Center Rd., P.O. Box 471, Corinth VT 05039-0471. (802)439-6292. Fax: (802)439-6296. E-mail: anne@northernwoodlands.org. Website: www.northernwoodlands.org. **Contact:** Anne Margolis. **40-60% freelance written.** Quarterly magazine covering natural history, conservation, and forest management in the Northeast. "*Northern Woodlands* strives to inspire landowners' sense of stewardship by increasing their awareness of the natural history and the principles of conservation and forestry that are directly related to their land. We also hope to increase the public's awareness of the social, economic, and environmental benefits of a working forest." Estab. 1994. Circ. 12,000. **Pays on acceptance.** Publishes ms an average of 6 months after acceptance. Byline given. Buys one-time rights. Editorial lead time 6 months. Submit seasonal material 6 months in advance. Accepts queries by mail, e-mail. Accepts previously published material. Accepts simultaneous submissions. Responds in 2 weeks to queries; 1½ months to mss. Sample copy online. Writer's guidelines online.

Nonfiction Stephen Long, editor. Book excerpts, essays, how-to (related to woodland management), interview/profile. No product reviews, first-person travelogues, cute animal stories, opinion, or advocacy pieces. **Buys 15-20 mss/year.** Query with published clips. Length: 500-3,000 words. **Pays 10¢/word.** Sometimes pays expenses of writers on assignment.

Photos State availability with submission. Reviews transparencies, prints. Buys one-time rights. Offers $25-75/photo. Identification of subjects required.

Columns/Departments Stephen Long, editor. A Place in Mind (essays on places of personal significance), 600-800 words. **Pays $100.** Knots and Bolts (seasonal natural history items or forest-related news items), 300-600 words. **Pays 10¢/word.** Wood Lit (book reviews), 600 words. **Pays $25.** Field Work (profiles of people who work in the woods, the wood-product industry, or conservation field), 1,500 words. **Pays 10¢/word. Buys 30 mss/year.** Query with published clips.

Poetry Jim Schley, poetry editor. Free verse, light verse, traditional. **Buys 4 poems/year.** Submit maximum 5 poems. **Pays $25.**

Tips "We will work with subject-matter experts to make their work suitable for our audience."

$ $ ORION

The Orion Society, 187 Main St., Great Barrington MA 01230. E-mail: orion@orionsociety.org. Website: www.ori ononline.org. Executive Editor: Harlan C. Clifford. **Contact:** Aina Barten, features editor. **30% freelance written.** Quarterly magazine covering the environment. "*Orion* is a quarterly magazine that explores the relationship between people and nature, examines human communities and how they fit into the larger natural community, and strives to renew our spiritual connection to the world. It is a forum of many voices that, collectively, seek to create a philosophy that guides our relationships with nature. *Orion* publishes literary nonfiction, short stories, interviews, poetry, reviews, and visual images related to this exploration. *Orion* is meant as a lively, personal, informative, and provocative dialogue. We look for compelling, reflective writing that connects readers to important issues by heightening awareness of the interconnections between humans and nature. We generally do not select material that is academic or theoretical, nor do we select material that is overly journalistic or overly topical. Literary journalism is welcome." Estab. 1982. Circ. 20,000. Pays on publication. Publishes ms an average of 8 months after acceptance. Byline given. Buys first North American serial rights. Editorial lead time

4 months. Submit seasonal material 6 months in advance. Accepts queries by mail, e-mail. Accepts simultaneous submissions. Responds in 4-8 weeks to queries; 4-6 months to mss. Sample copy online. Writer's guidelines online.

Nonfiction Essays, exposé, historical/nostalgic, humor, personal experience, photo feature, travel. No "What I learned during my walk in the woods"; personal hiking adventure/travel anecdotes; writing that deals with the natural world in only superficial ways. **Buys 8-20 mss/year.** Send complete ms. Length: 600-5,000 words. **Pays 10-20¢/word.** Pays in contributor copies if requested.

Photos State availability with submission. Reviews contact sheets, prints. Buys one-time rights. Negotiates payment individually.

Columns/Departments Features (any subject or slant), 2,500-5,000 words; Arts and the Earth (ways in which the arts are expressing and changing our thinking about nature), 1,200-2,500 words; Profile (stories of individuals working for a healthy world), 1,200-2,500 words; Natural Excursions (encounters with the natural world), 1,200-2,500 words; Deep Green (our spiritual relationship with nature and how it is being re-established), 1,200-2,500 words; Book Reviews (dealing with the context as well as content of environmental texts), 600-800 words; Coda (our endpaper), 600 words. **Buys 5-10 mss/year.** Send complete ms. **Pays 10-20¢/word; $100/book review.**

Fiction Adventure, ethnic, historical, humorous, mainstream, slice-of-life vignettes. No manuscripts that don't carry an environmental message or involve the landscape/nature as a major character. **Buys 0-1 mss/year.** Send complete ms. Length: 1,200-4,000 words. **Pays 10-20¢/word.**

Poetry Avant-garde, free verse, haiku, light verse, traditional. No cliché nature poetry. **Buys 20-30 poems/year.** Submit maximum 8 poems.

Tips "It is absolutely essential that potential submitters read at least one issue of *Orion* before sending work. We are not your typical environmental magazine, and we approach things rather differently than, say, *Sierra* or *Audobon*. We are most impressed by and most likely to work with writers whose submissions show that they know our magazine."

$ SNOWY EGRET

The Fair Press, P.O. Box 29, Terre Haute IN 47808. (812)829-1910. Editor: Philip C. Repp. Managing Editor: Ruth C. Acker. **Contact:** Editors. **95% freelance written.** Semiannual literary magazine featuring nature writing. "We publish works which celebrate the abundance and beauty of nature, and examine the variety of ways in which human beings interact with landscapes and living things. Nature writing from literary, artistic, psychological, philosophical, and historical perspectives." Estab. 1922. Circ. 400. Pays on publication. Publishes ms an average of 6 months after acceptance. Byline given. Buys first North American serial, second serial (reprint), one-time anthology rights, or reprints rights. Editorial lead time 2 months. Accepts queries by mail. Accepts simultaneous submissions. Responds in 1 month to queries; 2 months to mss. Sample copy for 9×12 SASE and $8. Writer's guidelines for #10 SASE.

○┐ Break in with "an essay, story, or short description based on a closely observed first-hand encounter with some aspect of the natural world."

Nonfiction Essays, general interest, interview/profile, personal experience, travel. **Buys 10 mss/year.** Send complete ms. Length: 500-10,000 words. **Pays $2/page.**

Columns/Departments Jane Robertson, Woodnotes editor. Woodnotes (short descriptions of personal encounters with wildlife or natural settings), 200-2,000 words. **Buys 12 mss/year. Pays $2/page.**

Fiction Fiction Editor. Nature-oriented works (in which natural settings, wildlife, or other organisms and/or characters who identify with the natural world are significant components. "No genre fiction, e.g., horror, western romance, etc." **Buys 4 mss/year.** Send complete ms. Length: 500-10,000 words. **Pays $2/page.**

Poetry Avant-garde, free verse, traditional. **Buys 30 poems/year.** Submit maximum 5 poems. **Pays $4/poem or page.**

Tips "The writers we publish invariably have a strong personal identification with the natural world, have examined their subjects thoroughly, and write about them sincerely. They know what they're talking about and show their subjects in detail, using, where appropriate, detailed description and dialogue."

PERSONAL COMPUTERS

Ⓩ BASELINE

Ziff Davis Media, Inc., 28 E. 28th St., New York NY 10016. (212)503-5435. Fax: (212)503-5454. E-mail: baseline @ziffdavis.com. Website: www.baselinemag.com. Editor-in-Chief: Tom Steinert-Threlkeld. Managing Editor: Anna Maria Virzi. **Contact:** Joshua Weinberger, assistant editor. Monthly magazine covering "pricing, planning, and managing the implementation of next generation IT solutions. *Baseline* is edited for senior IT and coroporate management business leaders." Circ. 125,000. Editorial lead time 3 months.

● Managing Editor Maria Virzi says, "Most of the reporting and writing is done by staff writers and editors."

$ $ COMPUTOREDGE

San Diego and Denver's Computer Magazine, The Byte Buyer, Inc., P.O. Box 83086, San Diego CA 92138. (858)573-0315. Fax: (858)573-0205. E-mail: submissions@computoredge.com. Website: www.computoredge.com. Executive Editor: Leah Steward. **Contact:** Patricia Smith, senior editor. **90% freelance written.** "We are the nation's largest regional computer weekly, providing San Diego and Denver with entertaining articles on all aspects of computers. We cater to the novice/beginner/first-time computer buyer. Humor is welcome." Estab. 1983. Circ. 175,000. Pays 1 month after publication. Byline given. Offers $15 kill fee. Buys first North American serial, electronic rights. Submit seasonal material 2 months in advance. Accepts queries by e-mail. Responds in 2 months to queries. Sample copy for SAE with 7 first-class stamps or on website. Writer's guidelines online.

● Accepts electronic submissions only. Put the issue number for which you wish to write in the subject line of your e-mail message. No attachments.

Nonfiction Pays $100 for publication in 1 of the magazines; $150 for publication in 2 of the magazines. General interest (computer), how-to, humor, personal experience. **Buys 150 mss/year.** Send complete ms. Length: 1,000-1,200 words.

Columns/Departments Mac Madness (Macintosh-related), 800-900 words; I Don't Do Windows (alternative operating systems), 800-900 words. **Buys 80 mss/year.** Send complete ms. **Pays $75 for publication in 1 of the magazines; $110 for publication in 2 of the magazines.**

Tips "Be relentless. Convey technical information in an understandable, interesting way. We like light material, but not fluff. Write as if you're speaking with a friend. Avoid the typical 'Love at First Byte' and the 'How My Grandmother Loves Her New Computer' article. We do not accept poetry. Avoid sexual innuendoes/metaphors. Reading a sample issue is advised."

$ $ $ $ MACADDICT

Imagine Media, 150 North Hill Dr., Brisbane CA 94005. (415)468-4684. Fax: (415)468-4686. E-mail: editor@macaddict.com. Website: www.macaddict.com. Managing Editor: Jennifer Morgan. **Contact:** Rik Myslewski, editor-in-chief. **35% freelance written.** Monthly magazine covering Macintosh computers. "*MacAddict* is a magazine for Macintosh computer enthusiasts of all levels. Writers must know, love and own Macintosh computers." Estab. 1996. Circ. 180,000. Pays on publication. Publishes ms an average of 3 months after acceptance. Byline given. Buys all rights. Editorial lead time 3 months. Submit seasonal material 2 months in advance. Accepts queries by mail, e-mail. Responds in 1 month to queries.

Nonfiction How-to, new product, technical. No humor, case studies, personal experience, essays. **Buys 30 mss/year.** Query with or without published clips. Length: 250-7,500 words. **Pays $50-2,500.**

Columns/Departments Reviews (always assigned), 300-750 words; How-to's (detailed, step-by-step), 500-2,500 words; features, 1,000-3,500 words. **Buys 20 mss/year.** Query with or without published clips. **Pays $50-2,500.**

Fillers Narasu Rebbapragada, editor. Get Info. **Buys 20/year.** Length: 50-500 words. **Pays $25-200.**

🔲 The online magazine carries original content not found in the print edition. Contact: Niko Coucouvanis, online editor.

Tips "Send us an idea for a short one to two page how-to and/or send us a letter outlining your publishing experience and areas of Mac expertise so we can assign a review to you (reviews editor is Niko Coucouvanis). Your submission should have great practical hands-on benefit to a reader, be fun to read in the author's natural voice, and include lots of screenshot graphics. We require electronic submissions. Impress our reviews editor with well-written reviews of Mac products and then move up to bigger articles from there."

$ $ $ $ PC MAGAZINE

Ziff-Davis Media, Inc., 28 E. 28th St., New York NY 10016. (212)503-3500. Fax: (212)503-5799. E-mail: pcmag@ziffdavis.com. Website: www.pcmag.com. Editor: Michael Miller. Managing Editor: Paul Ross. Magazine published 22 times/year. Circ. 1,228,658. Editorial lead time 4 months. Sample copy not available.

Ⓝ $ $ $ ⊘ PC UPGRADE

Bedford Communications, 1410 Broadway, 21st Floor, New York NY 10018. E-mail: dcrohn@bedfordmags.com. Website: www.techworthy.com. **Contact:** David Crohn, managing editor. **70% freelance written.** Magazine published 8 times/year covering computer hardware, software and peripherals; industry trends. "Publication is geared toward the computer owner interested in upgrading." Estab. 1991. Pays on publication. Publishes ms an average of 3 months after acceptance. Byline given. Offers 25% kill fee. Buys all rights. Editorial lead time 4 months. Accepts queries by mail, e-mail. Responds in 1 month to queries.

Nonfiction How-to (e.g., how to install a DVD-ROM drive), technical, hands-on reviews. **Buys 80-100 mss/year.** Query with published clips. "Will not accept unsolicited articles or manuscripts." Length: 600-3,500 words. Sometimes pays expenses of writers on assignment.

Tips "Send résumé with feature-length (technology-related, if possible) clips to editorial offices. Unsolicited manuscripts are not accepted or returned."

☑ PC WORLD

PC World Communications, Inc., 501 2nd St., Suite 600, San Francisco CA 94107. (415)243-0500. Fax: (415)442-1891. E-mail: letters@pcworld.com. Website: www.pcworld.com. Editor: Harry McCracken. Managing Editor: Kimberly Brinson. Senior Associate Editor: Grace Aquino. Senior Associate Editor: Sean Captain. Senior Editor: Anush Yegyazarian. **Contact:** Article Proposals. Monthly magazine covering personal computers. "*PC World* was created to give PC-proficient managers advice on which technology products to buy, tips on how to use those products most efficiently, news about the latest technological developments, and alerts regarding current problems with products and manufacturers." Circ. 1,100,000. Editorial lead time 3 months. Accepts queries by mail. Sample copy not available. Writer's guidelines by e-mail.

● "We have very few opportunities for writers who are not already contributing to the magazine."

○━ "One way we discover new talent is by assigning short tips and how-to pieces."

Nonfiction How-to, reviews, news items, features. Query. **Payment varies.**

Tips "Once you're familiar with *PC World*, you can write us a query letter. Your letter should answer the following questions as specifically and consisely as possible. What is the problem, technique, or product you want to discuss? Why will *PC World* readers be interested in it? Which section of the magazine do you think it best fits? What is the specific audience for the piece (e.g., database or LAN users, desktop publishers, and so on)?"

$ $ $ SMART COMPUTING

Sandhills Publishing, 131 W. Grand Dr., Lincoln NE 68521. (800)544-1264. Fax: (402)479-2104. E-mail: editor@smartcomputing.com. Website: www.smartcomputing.com. Managing Editor: Rod Scher. **Contact:** Ron Kobler, editor-in-chief. **45% freelance written.** Monthly magazine. "We focus on plain-English computing articles with an emphasis on tutorials that improve productivity without the purchase of new hardware." Estab. 1990. Circ. 200,000. **Pays on acceptance.** Publishes ms an average of 2 months after acceptance. Byline given. Offers 25% kill fee. Buys all rights. Editorial lead time 4 months. Submit seasonal material 4 months in advance. Accepts queries by mail, e-mail. Accepts simultaneous submissions. Responds in 1 month to queries. Sample copy for $7.99. Writer's guidelines for #10 SASE.

○━ Break in with "any article containing little-known tips for improving software and hardware performance and Web use. We're also seeking clear reporting on key trends changing personal technology."

Nonfiction How-to, new product, technical. No humor, opinion, personal experience. **Buys 250 mss/year.** Query with published clips. Length: 800-3,200 words. **Pays $240-960.** Pays expenses of writers on assignment up to $75.

Photos Send photos with submission. Buys all rights. Offers no additional payment for photos accepeted with ms. Captions required.

■ The online magazine carries original content not found in the print edition. Contact: Rod Scher, online editor.

Tips "Focus on practical, how-to computing articles. Our readers are intensely productivity-driven. Carefully review recent issues. We receive many ideas for stories printed in the last 6 months."

WIRED MAGAZINE

Condé Nast Publications, 520 Third St., 3rd Floor, San Francisco CA 94107-1815. (415)276-5000. Fax: (415)276-5150. E-mail: submit@wiredmag.com. Website: www.wired.com/wired. Publisher: Dean Shutte. Editor-in-chief: Chris Anderson. Managing Editor: Rebecca Smith Hurd. Editor: Blaise Zerega. **Contact:** Chris Baker, editorial assistant. **95% freelance written.** Monthly magazine covering technology and digital culture. "We cover the digital revolution and related advances in computers, communications and lifestyles." Estab. 1993. Circ. 500,000. Pays on publication. Publishes ms an average of 3 months after acceptance. Byline given. Offers 25% kill fee. Buys all rights for items less than 1,000 words, first North American serial rights for pieces over 1,000 words. Editorial lead time 3 months. Responds in 3 weeks to queries. Sample copy for $4.95. Writer's guidelines by e-mail.

Nonfiction Essays, interview/profile, opinion. "No poetry or trade articles." **Buys 85 features, 130 short pieces, 200 reviews, 36 essays, and 50 other mss/year.** Query. Pays expenses of writers on assignment.

Tips "Send query letter with clips to Chris Baker. Read the magazine. We get too many inappropriate queries. We need quality writers who understand our audience, and who understand how to query."

PHOTOGRAPHY

$ $ PC PHOTO
Werner Publishing Corp., 12121 Wilshire Blvd., Suite 1200, Los Angeles CA 90025. Fax: (310)826-5008. E-mail: pceditors@wernerpublishing.com. Website: www.pcphotomag.com. Managing Editor: Chris Robinson. **Contact:** Rob Sheppard, editor. **60% freelance written.** Bimonthly magazine covering digital photography. "Our magazine is designed to help photographers better use digital technologies to improve their photography." Estab. 1997. Circ. 175,000. Pays on publication. Publishes ms an average of 4 months after acceptance. Byline given. Buys one-time rights. Editorial lead time 6 months. Submit seasonal material 6 months in advance. Accepts queries by mail. Responds in 1 month to queries. Sample copy for #10 SASE or online. Writer's guidelines online.

Nonfiction How-to, personal experience, photo feature. **Buys 30 mss/year.** Query. Length: 1,200 words. **Pays $500 for assigned articles; approximately $400 for unsolicited articles.**

Photos Do not send original transparencies or negatives. Send photos with submission. Buys one-time rights. Offers $100-200/photo.

Tips "Since *PCPHOTO* is a photography magazine, we must see photos before any decision can be made on an article, so phone queries are not appropriate. Ultimately, whether we can use a particular piece or not will depend greatly on the photographs and how they fit in with material already in our files. We take a fresh look at the modern photographic world by encouraging photography and the use of new technologies. Editorial is intended to demystify the use of modern equipment by emphasizing practical use of the camera and the computer, highlighting the technique rather than the technical."

$ $ ⊡ PHOTO LIFE
Canada's Photography Magazine, Apex Publications, Inc., One Dundas St. W., Suite 2500, P.O. Box 84, Toronto ON M5G 1Z3, Canada. (800)905-7468. Fax: (800)664-2739. E-mail: editor@photolife.com. Website: www.photo life.com. **Contact:** Anita Dammer, editor-in-chief. **15% freelance written.** Bimonthly magazine. "*Photo Life* is geared to an audience of advanced amateur photographers. *Photo Life* is not a technical magazine per se, but techniques should be explained in enough depth to make them clear." Estab. 1976. Circ. 45,000. Pays on publication. Publishes ms an average of 1 year after acceptance. Byline given. Buys one-time rights. Editorial lead time 4 months. Submit seasonal material 6 months in advance. Accepts queries by mail, e-mail. Accepts simultaneous submissions. Responds in 3 months to queries. Sample copy for $5.50. Writer's guidelines online.

Nonfiction How-to (photo tips, technique), inspirational, photo feature, technical, travel. **Buys 10 mss/year.** Query with published clips or send complete ms. **Pays $100-600 (Canadian).**

Photos Reviews transparencies, prints. Buys one-time rights. Negotiates payment individually. Captions, model releases required.

Tips "We will review any relevant submissions that include a full text or a detailed outline of an article proposal. Accompanying photographs are necessary, as the first decision of acceptance will be based upon images. Most of the space available in the magazine is devoted to our regular contributors. Therefore, we cannot guarantee publication of other articles within any particular period of time. Currently, we are overflowing with travel articles. You are still welcome to submit to this category, but the waiting period may be longer than expected (up to 1½ years). You may, however, use your travel photography to explain photo techniques. A short biography is optional."

$ $ PHOTO TECHNIQUES
Preston Publications, Inc., 6600 W. Touhy Ave., Niles IL 60714. (847)647-2900, ext. 1306. Fax: (847)647-1155. E-mail: jwhite@phototechmag.com. Website: www.phototechmag.com. Publisher: S. Tinsley Preston III. Editor: Joe White. **50% freelance written.** Prefers to work with experienced photographer-writers; happy to work with excellent photographers whose writing skills are lacking. Bimonthly publication covering photochemistry, lighting, optics, processing, and printing, Zone System, digital imaging/scanning/printing, special effects, sensitometry, etc. Aimed at serious amateurs. Article conclusions should be able to be duplicated by readers. Estab. 1979. Circ. 30,000. Pays within 3 weeks of publication. Publishes ms an average of 8 months after acceptance. Byline given. Buys one-time rights. Sample copy for $5. Writer's guidelines by e-mail.

Nonfiction How-to, photo feature, technical (product review), special interest articles within the above listed topics. Query or send complete ms. Length: Open, but most features run approximately 2,500 words or 3-4 magazine pages. **Pays $100-450 for well-researched technical articles.**

Photos Photographers have a much better chance of having their photos published if the photos accompany a written article. Prefers JPEGs scanned at 300 dpi and sent via e-mail or CD-ROM, or prints, slides, and transparencies. Buys one-time rights. Manuscript payment includes payment for photos. Captions, technical information required.

Tips "Study the magazine! Virtually all writers we publish are readers of the magazine. We are now more receptive than ever to articles about photographers, history, aesthetics, and informative backgrounders about specific areas of the photo industry or specific techniques. Successful writers for our magazine are doing what they write about."

POPULAR PHOTOGRAPHY & IMAGING

Hachette Filipacchi Media U.S., Inc., 1633 Broadway, 43rd Floor, New York NY 10019. (212)767-6000. Fax: (212)767-5602. E-mail: popeditor@aol.com. Website: www.popphoto.com. **Contact:** Mason Resnick, managing editor. Monthly magazine edited for amateur to professional photographers. Provides incisive instructional articles, authoritative tests of photographic equipment; covers still and digital imaging; travel, color, nature, and large-format columns, plus up-to-date industry information. Circ. 453,944. Editorial lead time 2 months. Sample copy not available.

POLITICS & WORLD AFFAIRS

[N] THE AMERICAN SPECTATOR

1611 N. Kent St., Suite 901, Arlington VA 22209. (703)807-2011. Fax: (703)807-2013. E-mail: ruddy@spectator.org. Website: www.spectator.org. **Contact:** Katherine Ruddy. Monthly magazine. "For many years, one ideological viewpoint dominated American print and broadcast journalism. Today, that viewpoint still controls the entertainment and news divisions of the television networks, the mass-circulation news magazines, and the daily newspapers. *American Spectator* has attempted to balance the Left's domination of the media by debunking its perceived wisdom and advancing alternative ideas through spirited writing, insightful essays, humor and, most recently, through well-researched investigative articles that have themselves become news." Estab. 1967. Circ. 50,000. Pays on other. Accepts queries by mail.

Nonfiction "Topics include politics, the press, foreign relations, the economy, culture. Stories most suited for publication are timely articles on previously unreported topics with national appeal. Articles should be thoroughly researched with a heavy emphasis on interviewing and reporting, and the facts of the article should be verifiable. We prefer articles in which the facts speak for themselves and shy away from editorial and first person commentary. No unsolicited poetry, fiction, satire, or crossword puzzles. Query with résumé, clips and SASE.

Columns/Departments The Continuing Crisis and Current Wisdom (humor); On the Prowl ("Washington insider news"). Query with résumé, clips and SASE.

$ $ $ $ CALIFORNIA JOURNAL

2101 K St., Sacramento CA 95816. (916)552-7000. Fax: (916)444-2339. E-mail: edit@californiajournal.com. Editor: A.G. Block. **Contact:** Claudia Buck, managing editor. **70% freelance written.** Monthly magazine "with nonpartisan coverage aimed at a literate, well-informed, well-educated readership with strong involvement in California issues, politics, or government." Estab. 1970. Circ. 12,000. Pays on publication. Publishes ms an average of 3 months after acceptance. Byline given. Buys all rights. Accepts queries by mail, fax. Responds in 2 weeks to queries; 2 months to mss.

Nonfiction Political analysis. Interview/profile (of state and local government officials), opinion (on politics and state government in California). No outright advocacy pieces, fiction, poetry, product pieces. **Buys 10 unsolicited mss/year.** Query. Length: 800-2,000 words. **Pays $300-2,000.** Sometimes pays expenses of writers on assignment.

Photos State availability with submission. Reviews contact sheets. Buys all rights. Negotiates payment individually. Identification of subjects required.

Columns/Departments Soapbox (opinion on current affairs), 800 words. **Does not pay.**

Tips "Be well-versed in political and environmental affairs as they relate to California."

$ $ CHURCH & STATE

Americans United for Separation of Church and State, 518 C St. NE, Washington DC 20002. (202)466-3234. Fax: (202)466-3353. E-mail: americansunited@au.org. Website: www.au.org. **Contact:** Joseph Conn, editor. **10% freelance written.** Monthly magazine emphasizing religious liberty and church/state relations matters. Strongly advocates separation of church and state. Readership is well-educated. Estab. 1947. Circ. 40,000. **Pays on acceptance.** Publishes ms an average of 2 months after acceptance. Buys all rights. Accepts queries by mail.

Accepts simultaneous submissions. Responds in 2 months to queries. Sample copy and writer's guidelines for 9×12 SAE with 3 first-class stamps.

Nonfiction Exposé, general interest, historical/nostalgic, interview/profile. **Buys 11 mss/year.** Query. Length: 800-1,600 words. **Pays $150-300 for assigned articles.** Sometimes pays expenses of writers on assignment.

Reprints Send tearsheet, photocopy or typed ms with rights for sale noted and information about when and where the material previously appeared.

Photos Send photos with submission. Buys one-time rights. Pays negotiable fee for b&w prints. Captions required.

Tips "We're looking for feature articles on underreported local church-state controversies. We also consider 'viewpoint' essays that offer a unique or personal take on church-state issues. We are not a religious magazine. You need to see our magazine before you try to write for it."

$ COMMONWEAL

A Review of Public Affairs, Religion, Literature and the Arts, Commonweal Foundation, 475 Riverside Dr., Room 405, New York NY 10115. (212)662-4200. Fax: (212)662-4183. E-mail: editors@commonwealmagazine.org. Website: www.commonwealmagazine.org. Editor: Paul Baumann. **Contact:** Patrick Jordan, managing editor. Biweekly journal of opinion edited by Catholic lay people, dealing with topical issues of the day on public affairs, religion, literature, and the arts. Estab. 1924. Circ. 20,000. Pays on publication. Byline given. Buys all rights. Submit seasonal material 2 months in advance. Responds in 2 months to queries. Sample copy for free. Writer's guidelines online.

Nonfiction Essays, general interest, interview/profile, personal experience, religious. **Buys 30 mss/year.** Query with published clips. Length: 2,000-2,500 words. **Pays $75-100.**

Columns/Departments Upfronts (brief, newsy reportorials, giving facts, information and some interpretation behind the headlines of the day), 750-1,000 words; Last Word (usually of a personal nature, on some aspect of the human condition: spiritual, individual, political, or social), 800 words.

Poetry Rosemary Deen and Daria Donnelly, editors. Free verse, traditional. **Buys 20 poems/year. Pays 75¢/ line.**

Tips "Articles should be written for a general but well-educated audience. While religious articles are always topical, we are less interested in devotional and churchy pieces than in articles which examine the links between 'worldly' concerns and religious beliefs."

🌐 THE ECONOMIST

Economist Group of London, 25 St. James St., London England SW1A 1HG, United Kingdom. (44207)830-7000. Fax: (44207)839-2968. Website: www.economist.com. Weekly magazine. Edited for senior manegement and policy makers in business, government and finance throughout the world. Estab. 1843. Circ. 403,131. Sample copy not available.

$ $ EMPIRE STATE REPORT

The Independent Magazine of Politics, Policy, and the Business of Government, P.O. Box 9001, Mount Vernon NY 10553. (914)699-2020. Fax: (914)699-2025. E-mail: sacunto@cinn.com. Website: www.empirestatereport.c om. **Contact:** Stephen Acunto, Jr., associate publisher/executive editor. Monthly magazine with "timely and independent information on politics, policy, and governance for local and state officials throughout New York State." Estab. 1974. Circ. 16,000. Pays up to 2 months after publication. Byline given. Buys first North American serial rights. Accepts queries by mail, e-mail, fax, phone. Responds in 1 month to queries; 2 months to mss. Sample copy for $4.50 with 9×12 SASE or online. Writer's guidelines online.

    📍 Specifically looking for journalists with a working knowledge of legislative issues in New York State and how they affect businesses, municipalities, and all levels of government.

Nonfiction Essays, exposé, interview/profile, opinion, analysis. **Buys 48 mss/year.** Query with published clips. Length: 500-4,500 words. **Pays $100-700.** Sometimes pays expenses of writers on assignment.

Photos Send photos with submission. Reviews any size prints. Identification of subjects required.

Columns/Departments Empire State Notebook (short news stories about state politics), 300-900 words; Perspective (opinion pieces), 800-850 words. Perspectives does not carry remuneration.

    🖥 The online magazine carries original content not found in the print edition and includes writer's guidelines. Contact: Stephen Acunto Jr.

Tips "We are seeking journalists and nonjournalists from throughout New York State who can bring a new perspective and/or forecast on politics, policy, and the business of government. Query first for columns."

THE LABOR PAPER

Serving Southern Wisconsin, Union-Cooperative Publishing, 3030 39th Ave., Suite 110, Kenosha WI 53144. (262)657-6116. Fax: (262)657-6153. **Contact:** Mark T. Onosko, publisher. **30% freelance written.** Weekly tabloid covering union/labor news. Estab. 1935. Circ. 12,000. Pays on publication. Publishes ms an average of 2 months after acceptance. Byline given. Buys all rights. Editorial lead time 1 month. Submit seasonal material 1 month in advance. Accepts queries by mail, fax. Accepts simultaneous submissions. Sample copy and writer's guidelines free.

Nonfiction Exposé, general interest, historical/nostalgic, humor, inspirational. **Buys 4 mss/year.** Query with published clips. Length: 300-1,000 words. Sometimes pays expenses of writers on assignment.

Photos State availability with submission. Negotiates payment individually. Captions required.

$ PROGRESSIVE POPULIST

Journal from America's Heartland, P.O. Box 150517, Austin TX 78715-0517. (512)447-0455. Fax: (603)649-7871. E-mail: editor@populist.com. Website: www.populist.com. Managing Editor: Art Cullen. **Contact:** Jim Cullen, editor. **90% freelance written.** Biweekly tabloid covering politics and economics. "We cover issues of interest to workers, small businesses, and family farmers and ranchers." Estab. 1995. Circ. 10,000. Pays quarterly. Publishes ms an average of 1 month after acceptance. Byline given. Buys first North American serial, second serial (reprint) rights. Editorial lead time 3 weeks. Submit seasonal material 1 month in advance. Accepts queries by mail, e-mail, fax, phone. Accepts previously published material. Accepts simultaneous submissions. Sample copy and writer's guidelines free.

Nonfiction "We cover politics and economics. We are interested not so much in the dry reporting of campaigns and elections, or the stock markets and GNP, but in how big business is exerting more control over both the government and ordinary people's lives, and what people can do about it." Essays, exposé, general interest, historical/nostalgic, humor, interview/profile, opinion. "We are not much interested in 'sound-off' articles about state or national politics, although we accept letters to the editor. We prefer to see more 'journalistic' pieces, in which the writer does enough footwork to advance a story beyond the easy realm of opinion." **Buys 400 mss/year.** Query. Length: 600-1,000 words. **Pays $15-50.** Pays writers with contributor copies or other premiums if preferred by writer.

Reprints Send photocopy with rights for sale noted and information about when and where the material previously appeared.

Photos State availability with submission. Buys one-time rights. Negotiates payment individually. Identification of subjects required.

Tips "We do prefer submissions by e-mail. I find it's easier to work with e-mail and for the writer it probably increases the chances of getting a response."

$ $ THE PROGRESSIVE

409 E. Main St., Madison WI 53703-2899. (608)257-4626. Fax: (608)257-3373. E-mail: editorial@progressive.org. Website: www.progressive.org. **Contact:** Matthew Rothschild, editor. **75% freelance written.** Monthly Estab. 1909. Pays on publication. Publishes ms an average of 6 weeks after acceptance. Byline given. Accepts queries by mail. Responds in 1 month to queries. Sample copy for 9×12 SAE with 4 first-class stamps or sample articles online. Writer's guidelines online.

Nonfiction Investigative reporting (exposé of corporate malfeasance and governmental wrongdoing); electoral coverage (a current electoral development that has national implications); social movement pieces (important or interesting event or trend in the labor movement, or the GLBT movement, or in the area of racial justice, disability rights, the environment, women's liberation); foreign policy pieces (a development of huge moral importance where the US role may not be paramount); interviews (a long Q&A with a writer, activist, political figure, or musician who is widely known or doing especially worthwhile work); activism (highlights the work of activists and activist groups; increasingly, we are looking for good photographs of a dynamic or creative action, and we accompany the photos with a caption); book reviews (cover two or three current titles on a major issue of concern). Primarily interested in articles that interpret, from a progressive point of view, domestic and world affairs. Occasional lighter features. "*The Progressive* is a *political* publication. General interest is inappropriate. We do not want editorials, satire, historical pieces, philosophical peices or columns." Query. Length: 500-4,000 words. **Pays $250-500.**

Poetry Publishes 1 original poem a month. "We prefer poems that connect up—in one fashion or another, however obliquely—with political concerns. **Pays $150.**

Tips "Sought-after topics include electoral coverage, social movement, foreign policy, activism and book reviews."

$ $ $ $ REASON

Free Minds and Free Markets, Reason Foundation, 3415 S. Sepulveda Blvd., Suite 400, Los Angeles CA 90034. (310)391-2245. Fax: (310)390-8986. E-mail: jsanchez@reason.com. Website: www.reason.com. Editor-in-Chief: Nick Gillespie. **Contact:** Brian Doherty (by mail) or Julian Sanchez (by e-mail). **30% freelance written.** Monthly magazine covering politics, current events, culture, ideas. "*Reason* covers politics, culture and ideas from a dynamic libertarian perspective. It features reported works, opinion pieces, and book reviews." Estab. 1968. Circ. 55,000. **Pays on acceptance.** Byline given. Offers kill fee. Buys first North American serial, first, all rights. Editorial lead time 2 months. Submit seasonal material 3 months in advance. Accepts queries by mail, e-mail. Responds in 6 weeks to queries; 2 months to mss. Sample copy for $4. Writer's guidelines online.

Nonfiction Book excerpts, essays, exposé, general interest, humor, interview/profile, opinion. No products, personal experience, how-to, travel. **Buys 50-60 mss/year.** Query with published clips. Length: 850-5,000 words. **Pays $300-2,000.** Sometimes pays expenses of writers on assignment.

▣ The online magazine carries original content not found in the print edition and includes writer's guidelines. Contact: Nick Gillespie.

Tips "We prefer queries of no more than one or two pages with specifically developed ideas about a given topic rather than more general areas of interest. Enclosing a few published clips also helps."

$ $ TOWARD FREEDOM

A Progressive Perspective on World Events, Toward Freedom, Inc., P.O. Box 468, Burlington VT 05402-0468. (802)657-3733. E-mail: editor@towardfreedom.com. Website: www.towardfreedom.com. **Contact:** Greg Guma, editor. **75% freelance written.** Bimonthly magazine covering politics/culture, focus on Developing World, Europe, and global trends. "*Toward Freedom* is an internationalist journal with a progressive perspective on political, cultural, human rights, and environmental issues around the world. Also covers the United Nations, the post-nationalist movements and U.S. foreign policy." Estab. 1952. Circ. 3,500. Pays on publication. Byline given. Buys first North American serial, one-time rights. Editorial lead time 1 month. Accepts queries by mail, e-mail. Responds in 3 months to queries. Sample copy for $4. Writer's guidelines online.

O─π Break in with "a clear, knowledgeable, and brief query, either by e-mail or U.S. mail, along with the basis of your knowledge about the subject. We're also looking for a new hook for covering subjects we follow, as well as comparisons between the U.S. and other places. We're also eager to break stories that are being 'censored' in mainstream media."

Nonfiction Essays, interview/profile, opinion, personal experience, travel, features, book reviews, foreign, political analysis. **Buys 40-60 mss/year.** Query. Length: 700-2,500 words.

Photos Send photos with submission. Reviews prints. Buys one-time rights. Offers $35 maximum/photo. Identification of subjects required.

Columns/Departments TF Reports (from foreign correspondents); UN; Beyond Nationalism; Art and Book Reviews; 800-1,200 words. **Buys 10-15 mss/year.** Query. **Pays up to 10¢/word.** Last Word (creative commentary), 900 words. **Buys 4 mss/year.** Query. **Pays up to $100.**

▣ The online magazine carries original content not found in the print edition and includes guidelines. Contact: Greg Guma.

Tips "We're looking for articles linking politics and culture; effective first-person storytelling; proposals for global solutions with realistic basis and solid background; provocative viewpoints within the progressive tradition; political humor. We receive too many horror stories about human rights violations, lacking constructive suggestions and solutions; knee-jerk attacks on imperialism."

$ $ WASHINGTON MONTHLY

The Washington Monthly Co., 733 15th St. NW, Suite 520, Washington DC 20005. (202)393-5155. Fax: (202)393-2444. E-mail: editors@washingtonmonthly.com. Website: www.washingtonmonthly.com. Editor-in-Chief: Paul Glastris. **50% freelance written.** Monthly magazine covering politics, policy, media. "We are a neo-liberal publication with a long history and specific views—please read our magazine before submitting." Estab. 1969. Circ. 20,000. Pays on publication. Publishes ms an average of 2 months after acceptance. Byline given. Buys all rights. Editorial lead time 2 months. Submit seasonal material 4 months in advance. Accepts queries by mail, e-mail, fax, phone. Responds in 3 weeks to queries; 2 months to mss. Sample copy for 11×17 SAE with 5 first-class stamps or by e-mail. Writer's guidelines online.

Nonfiction Book excerpts, essays, exposé, general interest, historical/nostalgic, interview/profile, opinion, personal experience, technical, first-person political. "No humor, how-to, or generalized articles." **Buys 20 mss/year.** Query with or without published clips or send complete ms. Length: 1,500-5,000 words. **Pays 10¢/word.**

Photos State availability with submission. Reviews contact sheets, prints. Buys one-time rights. Negotiates payment individually.

Columns/Departments Memo of the Month (memos); On Political Books, Booknotes (both reviews of current political books), 1,500-3,000 words. **Buys 10 mss/year.** Query with published clips or send complete ms. **Pays 10¢/word.**

Tips "Call our editors to talk about ideas. Always pitch articles showing background research. We're particularly looking for first-hand accounts of working in government. We also like original work showing that the government is or is not doing something important. We have writer's guidelines, but do your research first."

WORLD POLICY JOURNAL

World Policy Institute, 66 Fifth Ave., 9th Floor, New York NY 10011. (212)229-5808. Fax: (212)229-5579. E-mail: wrigleyl@newschool.edu. Website: www.worldpolicy.org. **Contact:** Linda Wrigley, managing editor. **10% freelance written.** Quarterly Journal covering international politics, economics, and security isssues, as well as historical and cultural essays, book reviews, profiles, and first-person reporting from regions not covered in the general media. "We hope to bring principle and proportion, as well as a sense of reality and direction to America's discussion of its role in the world." Circ. 8,000. Pays on publication. Publishes ms an average of 3 months after acceptance. Byline given. Buys all rights. Accepts queries by mail. Responds in 3 months to queries. Sample copy for $7.95 and 9×12 SASE with 10 first-class stamps. Writer's guidelines online.

Nonfiction Articles that "define policies that reflect the shared needs and interests of all nations of the world." Query. Length: 2,500-4,500 words. **Pays variable commission rate.**

PSYCHOLOGY & SELF-IMPROVEMENT

ⓝ $PLUS ATTITUDE MAGAZINE

Success Through Positive Action + Positive Attitude, Plus Attitude, 209 W. Millcreek Way, Tooele UT 84074-2929. E-mail: joyehenrie@msn.com. Website: www.plusattitude.com. Editor: Joye L. Henrie. **Contact:** Director of Editorial. **95% freelance written.** Monthly newsletter focused on enhancement in all areas of the lives of our readers. "It is our goal to motivate and inspire our readers to work toward their personal goals of success. Our audience is comprised of individuals who value achievement. Our primary focus isn't necessarily on monetary achievement, so our writers must think in broader terms, beyond the dollar sign. We are open to all styles of writing, as long as the piece speaks to, rather than 'at,' the reader. It has to draw a person in, help him or her visualize the goal, and motivate positive action." Estab. 2003. Pays on publication. Publishes ms an average of 6 months after acceptance. Byline sometimes given. Buys one-time, simultaneous rights. Editorial lead time 4 months. Submit seasonal material 6 months in advance. Accepts queries by mail, e-mail. Accepts previously published material. Accepts simultaneous submissions. Responds in 1 month to queries; 3 months to mss. Sample copy not available. Writer's guidelines for #10 SASE, online or by e-mail.

Nonfiction Book excerpts, essays, general interest, historical/nostalgic, how-to, humor, inspirational, interview/profile, new product, opinion, personal experience, photo feature, technical, travel, anything that encompasses the theme of the publication. Does not want to see religious themes. "While religion is inspirational to many, our publication is not a forum for this. We don't want to see memoirs that disconnect the reader from the picture of success, but we don't discourage memoirs. If in doubt, please query with your idea." **Buys 50 mss/year.** Query with or without published clips or send complete ms. Length: 200-1,200 words. **Pays $10-30.**

Photos State availability with submission. Rights negotiable. Negotiates payment individually. Captions, model releases required.

Columns/Departments Principles of Success (application tools/goal setting), 1,200-1,500 words; Innovators of the Past (historical figures that modeled principles of success), 800-1,000 words; Rags to Riches (present figures that model principles of success), 1,000-1,200 words; Inspirational Retreats (places to visit for relaxation, fun and inspirational), 600-700 words; What Is Plus Attitude? (introduction: ongoing summary), 600-650 words; Dwellings (luxury and/or inspirational homes to own), 600-700 words; PA Forward Thinking Schedule Planner (how to use/benefits), 50-75 words; Fun to Own (the buzz on the latest products), 600-700 words. **Buys 96 mss/year.** Query with or without published clips or send complete ms. **Pays $25-75.**

Fiction "We accept a very limited amount of fiction. The only types of fiction we want to see are pieces that help our readers visualize components of success." Experimental, historical, humorous. **Buys 12 mss/year.** Query with or without published clips or send complete ms. Length: 600-1,000 words. **Pays $10-30.**

Fillers Anecdotes, facts, gags to be illustrated by cartoonist, newsbreaks, short humor. **Buys 24/year.** Length: 25-200 words. **Pays $2-10.**

Tips "We are still a young publication and able to give some level of personal attention to our writers. We still have the leverage to work with writers who have a good piece that needs to be altered some to fit our magazine. If you need further information on the type of content needed, pick up one fo the top selling 'self-help' books, and it should give you some good ideas on the angle we're going for. If you send your query or manuscript in the mail, please include a SASE to receive a response and/or have your material returned."

$ $ $ $PSYCHOLOGY TODAY

Sussex Publishers, Inc., 115 E. 23rd St., 9th Floor, New York NY 10010. (212)260-7210. Fax: (212)260-7445. E-mail: kat@psychologytoday.com. Website: www.psychologytoday.com. **Contact:** Kathleen McGowan, senior editor. Bimonthly magazine. "*Psychology Today* explores every aspect of human behavior, from the cultural trends that shape the way we think and feel to the intricacies of modern neuroscience. We're sort of a hybrid of a science magazine, a health magazine and a self-help magazine. While we're read by many psychologists, therapists and social workers, most of our readers are simply intelligent and curious people interested in the psyche and the self." Estab. 1967. Circ. 331,400. Pays on publication. Publishes ms an average of 3 months after acceptance. Byline given. Buys first North American serial rights. Editorial lead time 5 months. Accepts queries by mail. Responds in 1 month to queries. Sample copy for $3.50. Writer's guidelines for #10 SASE.

Nonfiction "Nearly any subject related to psychology is fair game. We value originality, insight and good reporting; we're not interested in stories or topics that have already been covered *ad nauseum* by other magazines unless you can provide a fresh new twist and much more depth. We're not interested in simple-minded 'pop psychology.'" No fiction, poetry or first-person essays on "How I Conquered Mental Disorder X." **Buys** 20-25 mss/year. Query with published clips. Length: 1,500-4,000 words. **Pays $1,000-2,500.**

Columns/Departments News Editor. News & Trends, 150-300 words. Query with published clips. **Pays $150-300.**

$ ROSICRUCIAN DIGEST

Rosicrucian Order, AMORC, 1342 Naglee Ave., San Jose CA 95191-0001. (408)947-3600. Website: www.rosicrucian.org. **Contact:** Robin M. Thompson, editor-in-chief. Quarterly magazine (international) emphasizing mysticism, science, philosophy, and the arts for educated men and women of all ages seeking alternative answers to life's questions. **Pays on acceptance.** Publishes ms an average of 6 months after acceptance. Byline given. Buys first, second serial (reprint) rights. Accepts queries by mail, phone. Responds in 3 months to queries. Sample copy for free. Writer's guidelines for #10 SASE.

Nonfiction How to deal with life—and all it brings us—in a positive and constructive way. Informational articles—new ideas and developments in science, the arts, philosophy, and thought. Historical sketches, biographies, human interest, psychology, philosophical, and inspirational articles. "We are always looking for good articles on the contributions of ancient civilizations to today's civilizations, the environment, ecology, inspirational (nonreligious) subjects. Know your subject well and be able to capture the reader's interest in the first paragraph. Be willing to work with the editor to make changes in the manuscript." No religious, astrological, or political material, or articles promoting a particular group or system of thought. Most articles are written by members or donated, but we're always open to freelance submissions. No book-length mss. Query. Length: 1,500-2,000 words. **Pays 6¢/word.**

Reprints Prefers typed ms with rights for sale noted and information about when and where the article previously appeared, but tearsheet or photcopy acceptable. Pays 50% of amount paid for an original article.

Tips "We're looking for more pieces on these subjects: our connection with the past—the important contributions of ancient civilizations to today's world and culture and the relevance of this wisdom to now; how to channel teenage energy/angst into positive, creative, constructive results (preferably written by teachers or others who work with young people—written for frustrated parents); and the vital necessity of raising our environmental consciousness if we are going to survive as a species on this planet."

SCIENCE OF MIND MAGAZINE

2600 W. Magnolia Blvd., Burbank CA 91505. (818)526-7757. E-mail: edit@scienceofmind.com. Website: www.scienceofmind.com. Editor: Amanda Pisani. **30% freelance written.** Monthly magazine featuring articles on spirituality, self-help, and inspiration. "Our publication centers on oneness of all life and spiritual empowerment through the application of Science of Mind principles." **Pays on acceptance.** Publishes ms an average of 5 months after acceptance. Byline given. Buys first North American serial rights. Submit seasonal material 6 months in advance. Writer's guidelines online.

Nonfiction Book excerpts, essays, inspirational, interview/profile, personal experience (of Science of Mind), spiritual. **Buys 35-45 mss/year.** Length: 750-2,000 words. **Payment varies. Pays in copies for some features written by readers.**

■ The online version contains material not found in the print edition.

Tips "We are interested in how to use spiritual principles in worldly situations or other experiences of a spiritual nature having to do with Science of Mind principles."

⊠ SHARED VISION

Morphic Media, 873 Beatty St., Suite 203, Vancouver BC V6B 2H6, Canada. (604)733-5062. Fax: (604)731-1050. E-mail: editor@shared-vision.com. Website: www.shared-vision.com. Editor-at-Large: Rex Weyler. **Contact:** Sonya Weir, editor. **75% freelance written.** Monthly magazine covering health and wellness, environment, personal growth, spirituality, social justice, and issues related to food. Estab. 1988. Circ. 40,000 monthly. Byline given. Editorial lead time 3 months. Submit seasonal material 3 months in advance. Accepts queries by mail, e-mail, fax. Accepts previously published material. Sample copy for free. Writer's guidelines by e-mail.

Nonfiction Book excerpts, general interest, inspirational, personal experience, travel, health, environment. Query with published clips.

Columns/Departments Footnotes (first-person inspirational). Query with published clips.

Tips "Reading the magazine is the optimum method. E-mail the editor for writer's guidelines."

REGIONAL

GENERAL

$ $ BLUE RIDGE COUNTRY

Leisure Publishing, 3424 Brambleton Ave., Roanoke VA 24018. (540)989-6138. Fax: (540)989-7603. E-mail: editorial@leisurepublishing.com. Website: www.blueridgecountry.com. **Contact:** Kurt Rheinheimer, editor-in-chief. **75% freelance written.** Bimonthly magazine. "The magazine is designed to celebrate the history, heritage and beauty of the Blue Ridge region. It is aimed at adult, upscale readers who enjoy living or traveling in the mountain regions of Virginia, North Carolina, West Virginia, Maryland, Kentucky, Tennessee, South Carolina, Alabama, and Georgia." Estab. 1988. Circ. 100,000. Pays on publication. Publishes ms an average of 8 months after acceptance. Byline given. Offers $50 kill fee for commissioned pieces only. Buys first, second serial (reprint) rights. Submit seasonal material 6 months in advance. Accepts queries by mail, e-mail, fax. Responds in 2 months to queries; 2 months to mss. Sample copy for 9×12 SAE with 6 first-class stamps or online. Writer's guidelines online.

Nonfiction "Looking for more backroads travel, history and legend/lore pieces." General interest, historical/nostalgic, personal experience, photo feature, travel. **Buys 25-30 mss/year.** Query with or without published clips or send complete ms. Length: 200-1,500 words. **Pays $50-250 for assigned articles; $25-250 for unsolicited articles.**

Photos Send photos with submission. Reviews transparencies. Buys one-time rights. Pays $25-50/photo. Identification of subjects required.

Columns/Departments Country Roads (shorts on people, events, travel, ecology, history, antiques, books); Mountain Inns (reviews of inns); Mountain Delicacies (cookbooks and recipes). **Buys 30-42 mss/year.** Query. **Pays $10-40.**

Tips "Would like to see more pieces dealing with contemporary history (1940s-70s). Freelancers needed for regional departmental shorts and 'macro' issues affecting whole region. Need field reporters from all areas of Blue Ridge region. Also, we need updates on the Blue Ridge Parkway, Appalachian Trail, national forests, ecological issues, preservation movements."

$ CHRONOGRAM

Luminary Publishing, P.O. Box 459, New Paltz NY 12561. Fax: (914)256-0349. E-mail: info@chronogram.com. Website: www.chronogram.com. **Contact:** Brian K. Mahoney, editor. **50% freelance written.** Monthly magazine covering regional arts and culture. "*Chronogram* features accomplished, literary writing on issues of cultural, spiritual, and idea-oriented interest." Estab. 1994. Circ. 20,000. Pays on publication. Publishes ms an average of 3 months after acceptance. Byline given. Buys one-time rights. Editorial lead time 2 months. Submit seasonal material 3 months in advance. Accepts queries by mail, e-mail. Accepts simultaneous submissions. Responds in 2 weeks to queries; 6-8 weeks to mss. Sample copy online. Writer's guidelines online.

Nonfiction Book excerpts, essays, exposé, general interest, historical/nostalgic, humor, interview/profile, opinion, personal experience, photo feature, religious, travel. "No health practitioners writing about their own healing modality." **Buys 24 mss/year.** Query with published clips. Length: 1,000-3,500 words. **Pays $75-150.**

Photos State availability with submission. Reviews contact sheets. Buys one-time rights. Negotiates payment individually. Captions required.

Poetry Phillip Levine, poetry editor. Avant-garde, free verse, haiku, traditional.

Tips "The editor's ears are always open for new voices and all story ideas are invited for pitching. *Chronogram* welcomes all voices and viewpoints as long as they are expressed well. We discriminate solely based on the quality of the writing, nothing else. Clear, thoughtful writing on any subject will be considered for publication in *Chronogram*. We publish a good deal of introspective first-person narratives and find that in the absence of objectivity, subjectivity at least is a quantifiable middle ground between ranting opinion and useless facts."

Ⓝ $ $ GUESTLIFE

Monterey Bay/New Mexico/El Paso/St. Petersburg/Clearwater/Houston/Vancouver, Desert Publications, Inc., 303 N. Indian Canyon Dr., Palm Springs CA 92262. (760)325-2333. Fax: (760)325-7008. E-mail: edit@palmspringslife.com. Website: www.guestlife.com. **Contact:** Olga Reyes, managing editor. **95% freelance written.** Annual prestige hotel room magazine covering history, highlights, and activities of the area named (i.e., *Monterey Bay GuestLife*). "*GuestLife* focuses on its respective area and is placed in hotel rooms in that area for the affluent vacationer." Estab. 1979. Pays on publication. Publishes ms an average of 9 months after acceptance. Byline given. Offers 25% kill fee. Buys electronic, all rights. Editorial lead time 4 months. Submit seasonal material 3 months in advance. Accepts queries by e-mail. Responds in 1 month to queries; 1 month to mss. Sample copy for $10. Writer's guidelines not available.

Nonfiction General interest (regional), historical/nostalgic, photo feature, travel. **Buys 3 mss/year.** Query with published clips. Length: 300-1,500 words. **Pays $100-500.**

Photos State availability with submission. Reviews contact sheets. Buys all rights. Negotiates payment individually. Identification of subjects required.

Fillers Facts. **Buys 3/year.** Length: 50-100 words. **Pays $50-100.**

$ $ NOW AND THEN

The Appalachian Magazine, Center for Appalachian Studies and Services, P.O. Box 70556-ETSU, Johnson City TN 37614. (423)439-5348. Fax: (423)439-6340. E-mail: fischman@mail.etsu.edu. Website: cass.etsu.edu/n&t/. Managing Editor: Nancy Fischman. **80% freelance written.** Triannual magazine covering Appalachian region from Southern New York to Northern Mississippi. *"Now & Then* accepts a variety of writing genres: fiction, poetry, nonfiction, essays, interviews, memoirs, and book reviews. All submissions must relate to Appalachia and to the issue's specific theme. Our readership is educated and interested in the region." Estab. 1984. Circ. 1,000. Pays on publication. Publishes ms an average of 4 months after acceptance. Byline given. Buys all, holds copyright rights. Editorial lead time 6 months. Accepts queries by mail, e-mail, fax. Accepts simultaneous submissions. Responds in 5 months to queries; 5 months to mss. Sample copy for $5. Writer's guidelines online.

Nonfiction Book excerpts, essays, general interest, historical/nostalgic, humor, interview/profile, opinion, personal experience, photo feature, book reviews from and about Appalachia. "We don't consider articles which have nothing to do with Appalachia; articles which blindly accept and employ regional stereotypes (dumb hillbillies, poor and downtrodden hillfolk, and miners)." Query with published clips. Length: 1,000-2,500 words. **Pays $30-250 for assigned articles; $30-100 for unsolicited articles.** Sometimes pays expenses of writers on assignment.

Reprints Send ms with rights for sale noted and information about when and where the material previously appeared. Pays 100% of amount paid for original article (typically $15-60).

Photos State availability with submission. Buys one-time rights. Offers no additional payment for photos accepted with ms. Captions, identification of subjects required.

Fiction "Fiction has to relate to Appalachia and to the issue's theme in some way." Adventure, ethnic, experimental, fantasy, historical, humorous, mainstream, slice-of-life vignettes, excerpted novel, prose poem. "Absolutely has to relate to Appalachian theme. Can be about adjustment to new environment, themes of leaving and returning, for instance. Nothing unrelated to region." **Buys 3-4 mss/year.** Send complete ms. Length: 750-2,500 words. **Pays $30-100.**

Poetry Free verse, haiku, light verse, traditional. "No stereotypical work about the region. I want to be surprised and embraced by the language, the ideas, even the form." **Buys 25-30 poems/year.** Submit maximum 5 poems. **Pays $10.**

Tips "Get a copy of the magazine and read it. Then make sure your submission has a connection to Appalachia (check out http://cass.etsu.edu/cass/apregion.htm) and fits in with an upcoming theme."

ALABAMA

$ $ ALABAMA HERITAGE

University of Alabama, Box 870342, Tuscaloosa AL 35487-0342. (205)348-7467. Fax: (205)348-7473. Website: www.alabamaheritage.com. **Contact:** Donna L. Cox, editor. **75% freelance written.** *"Alabama Heritage* is a nonprofit historical quarterly published by the University of Alabama and the Alabama Department of Archives and History for the intelligent lay reader. We are interested in lively, well-written, and thoroughly researched articles on Alabama/Southern history and culture. Readability and accuracy are essential." Estab. 1986. Pays on publication. Byline given. Buys all rights. Accepts queries by mail. Sample copy for $6, plus $2.50 for shipping. Writer's guidelines for #10 SASE or online.

Nonfiction **Buys 12-16 feature mss/year and 10-14 short pieces**. Historical. "We do not publish fiction, poetry, book reviews, articles on current events or living artists, and personal/family reminiscences." Query. Length: 750-4,000 words. **Pays $50-350.** Sends 10 copies to each author.

Photos Reviews contact sheets. Buys one-time rights. Identification of subjects required.

Tips "Authors need to remember that we regard history as a fascinating subject, not as a dry recounting of dates and facts. Articles that are lively and engaging, in addition to being well researched, will find interested readers among our editors. No term papers, please. All areas are open to freelance writers. Best approach is a written query."

$ $ ALABAMA LIVING

Alabama Rural Electric Assn., P.O. Box 244014, Montgomery AL 36124. (334)215-2732. Fax: (334)215-2733. E-mail: info@areapower.com. Website: www.alabamaliving.com. Editor: Darryl Gates. **Contact:** Editor. **80% freelance written.** Monthly magazine covering topics of interest to rural and suburban Alabamians. "Our magazine is an editorially balanced, informational and educational service to members of rural electric cooperatives. Our mix regularly includes Alabama history, Alabama features, gardening, outdoor, and consumer pieces." Estab. 1948. Circ. 365,000. **Pays on acceptance.** Byline given. Not copyrighted. Editorial lead time 4 months. Submit seasonal material 4 months in advance. Accepts queries by mail, e-mail. Accepts simultaneous submissions. Responds in 1 month to queries. Sample copy for free.

⊶ Break in with a bit of history or nostalgia about Alabama or the Southeast and pieces about "little-known" events in Alabama history or "little-known" sites.

Nonfiction Historical/nostalgic (rural-oriented), inspirational, personal experience (Alabama). Special issues: Gardening (March); Travel (April); Home Improvement (May); Holiday Recipes (December). **Buys 20 mss/ year.** Send complete ms. Length: 500-750 words. **Pays $250 minimum for assigned articles; $75 minimum for unsolicited articles.**

Reprints Send ms with rights for sale noted. Pays $75.

SOUTHERN LIVING

Southern Progress Corp., 2100 Lakeshore Dr., Birmingham AL 35209. (205)445-6000. Fax: (205)445-6700. E-mail: sara_askew_jones@timeinc.com. Website: www.southernliving.com. Editor: John Floyd. Managing Editor: Clay Norden. **Contact:** Sara Askew Jones. Monthly magazine covering the southern lifestyle. Publication addressing the tastes and interest of contemporary southerners. Estab. 1966. Circ. 2,526,799. Buys all rights. Editorial lead time 3 months. Accepts queries by mail. Sample copy for $4.99 at newsstands. Writer's guidelines by e-mail.

Columns/Departments Southern Journal: "Above all, it must be Southern. We need comments on life in this region—written from the standpoint of a person who is intimately familiar with this part of the world. It's personal, almost always involving something that happened to the writer or someone he or she knows very well. We take special note of stories that are contemporary in their point of view." Length: 500-600 words.

ALASKA

$ $ $ ALASKA

Exploring Life on the Last Frontier, 301 Arctic Slope Ave., Suite 300, Anchorage AK 99518. (907)272-6070. E-mail: timwoody@alaskamagazine.com. Website: www.alaskamagazine.com. **Contact:** Tim Woody, managing editor. **70% freelance written.** Eager to work with new/unpublished writers. Magazine published 10 times/ year covering topics "uniquely Alaskan." Estab. 1935. Circ. 180,000. Pays on publication. Publishes ms an average of 6 months after acceptance. Byline given. Buys first, one-time rights. Submit seasonal material 1 year in advance. Accepts queries by mail. Responds in 2 months to queries; 2 months to mss. Sample copy for $3 and 9×12 SAE with 7 first-class stamps. Writer's guidelines online.

⊶ Break in by "doing your homework. Make sure a similar story has not appeared in the magazine within the last 5 years. It must be about Alaska."

Nonfiction Historical/nostalgic, humor, interview/profile, personal experience, photo feature, travel, adventure, outdoor recreation (including hunting, fishing), Alaska destination stories. No fiction or poetry. **Buys 40 mss/ year.** Query. Length: 100-2,500 words. **Pays $100-1,250.**

Photos Send photos with submission. Reviews 35mm or larger transparencies, slides labeled with your name. Captions, identification of subjects required.

Tips "We're looking for top-notch writing—original, well researched, lively. Subjects must be distinctly Alaskan. A story on a mall in Alaska, for example, won't work for us; every state has malls. If you've got a story about a Juneau mall run by someone who is also a bush pilot and part-time trapper, maybe we'd be interested. The point is *Alaska* stories need to be vivid, focused and unique. Alaska is like nowhere else—we need our stories to be the same way."

ARIZONA

$ $ $ $ ARIZONA HIGHWAYS

2039 W. Lewis Ave., Phoenix AZ 85009-9988. (602)712-2024. Fax: (602)254-4505. E-mail: queryeditor@azhighways.com. Website: www.arizonahighways.com. **Contact:** Beth Deveny, senior editor. **100% freelance written.** Magazine that is state-owned, designed to help attract tourists into and through Arizona. Estab. 1925. Circ. 425,000. **Pays on acceptance.** Buys first North American serial rights. Accepts queries by mail, e-mail, fax. Responds in 1 month to queries; 1 month to mss. Sample copy not available. Writer's guidelines online.

⊶ Break in with "a concise query written with flair, backed by impressive clips that reflect the kind of writing that appears in *Arizona Highways*. The easiest way to break into the magazine for writers new to us is to propose short items for the Off-Ramp section, contribute short humor anecdotes for the Humor page, or submit 750-word pieces for the Along the Way column.''

Nonfiction Feature subjects include narratives and exposition dealing with history, anthropology, nature, wildlife, armchair travel, out of the way places, small towns, Old West history, Indian arts and crafts, travel, etc. Travel articles are experience-based. All must be oriented toward Arizona. ''We deal with professionals only, so include a list of current credits.'' **Buys 50 mss/year.** Query with a lead paragraph and brief outline of story. Length: 600-1,800 words. **Pays up to $1/word.** Pays expenses of writers on assignment.

Photos ''We use transparencies of medium format, 4×5, and 35mm when appropriate to the subject matter, or they display exceptional quality or content. If submitting 35mm, we prefer 100 ISO or slower. Each transparency must be accompanied by information attached to each photograph: where, when, what. No photography will be reviewed by the editors unless the photographer's name appears on each and every transparency.'' Peter Ensenberger, director of photography. Buys one-time rights. Pays $125-600.

Columns/Departments Focus on Nature (short feature in first or third person dealing with the unique aspects of a single species of wildlife), 800 words; Along the Way (short essay dealing with life in Arizona, or a personal experience keyed to Arizona), 750 words; Back Road Adventure (personal back-road trips, preferably off the beaten path and outside major metro areas), 1,000 words; Hike of the Month (personal experiences on trails anywhere in Arizona), 500 words; Arizona Humor (amusing short anecdotes about Arizona), 200 words maximum. **Pays $50-1,000, depending on department.**

■ The online magazine carries original content not found in the print edition. Contact: Robert J. Early, editor.

Tips ''Writing must be of professional quality, warm, sincere, in-depth, well peopled, and accurate. Avoid themes that describe first trips to Arizona, the Grand Canyon, the desert, Colorado River running, etc. Emphasis is to be on Arizona adventure and romance as well as flora and fauna, when appropriate, and themes that can be photographed. Double check your manuscript for accuracy. Our typical reader is a 50-something person with the time, the inclination, and the means to travel.''

$ $ DESERT LIVING

342 E. Thomas, Phoenix AZ 85012. (602)667-9798. Fax: (602)508-9454. E-mail: dawson@desertlivingmag.com. Website: www.desertlivingmag.com. **Contact:** Dawson Fearnow, editor. **75% freelance written.** Bimonthly lifestyle and culture magazine ''with an emphasis on modern design, culinary trends, cultural trends, fashion, great thinkers of our time and entertainment.'' Estab. 1997. Circ. 50,000. Pays 1 month after publication. Byline given. Offers 50% kill fee. Buys first, electronic rights. Editorial lead time 3 months. Submit seasonal material 3 months in advance. Accepts queries by mail, e-mail, fax, phone. Responds in 3 weeks to queries; 2 months to mss. Sample copy for e-mail request. Writer's guidelines not available.

Nonfiction General interest, interview/profile, new product, photo feature, travel, architecture. Query with published clips. Length: 300-2,000 words. **Pays $25-400.**

Photos State availability with submission. Reviews contact sheets, negatives, transparencies, prints. Buys one-time or electronic rights. Negotiates payment individually. Identification of subjects, model releases required.

Columns/Departments Design (articles on industrial/product design and firms, 2,000 words. **Buys 100 mss/ year.** Query with published clips.

$ $ TUCSON LIFESTYLE

Conley Publishing Group, Ltd., Suite 12, 7000 E. Tanque Verde Rd., Tucson AZ 85715-5318. (520)721-2929. Fax: (520)721-8665. E-mail: tucsonlife@aol.com. **Contact:** Scott Barker, executive editor. **90% freelance written.** Prefers to work with published/established writers. Monthly magazine covering Tucson-related events and topics. Estab. 1982. Circ. 32,000. **Pays on acceptance.** Publishes ms an average of 6 months after acceptance. Byline given. Buys first North American serial rights. Submit seasonal material 1 year in advance. Accepts queries by mail, e-mail, fax. Responds in 2 months to queries; 3 months to mss. Sample copy for $2.95, plus $3 postage. Writer's guidelines free.

○━ Features are not open to freelancers.

Nonfiction All stories need a Tucson angle. ''Avoid obvious tourist attractions and information that most residents of the Southwest are likely to know. No anecdotes masquerading as articles. Not interested in fish-out-of-water, Easterner-visiting-the-Old-West pieces.'' **Buys 20 mss/year. Pays $50-500.**

Photos Query about electronic formats. Reviews contact sheets, 2¼×2¼ transparencies, 5×7 prints. Buys one-time rights. Pays $25-100/photo. Identification of subjects required.

Columns/Departments Lifestylers (profiles of interesting Tucsonans). Query. **Pays $100-200.**

Tips ''Style is not of paramount importance; good, clean copy with an interesting lead is a must.''

CALIFORNIA

[N] ANGELENO MAGAZINE

Modern Luxury, Inc., 5455 Wilshire Blvd., Suite 1412, Los Angeles CA 90036. (323)930-9400. Fax: (323)930-9402. **Contact:** Amanda Luttrell Garrigus, editor-in-chief. Monthly magazine covering luxury lifestyle. "We cover the good things in life—fashion, fine dining, home design, the arts—from a sophisticated, cosmopolitan, well-to-do perspective." Estab. 1999. Circ. 56,000. Pays 2 months after receipt of invoice. Buys first, all rights. Submit seasonal material 6 months in advance. Responds in 2 months to queries. Sample copy for $7.15 for current issue; $8.20 for back issue.

Nonfiction "All articles must be focused on LA except travel." General interest, how-to (culinary, home design), interview/profile, travel. No fiction; no unsolicited mss. Query with published clips. Length: 500-4,500 words.

Photos State availability with submission. Reviews transparencies, prints, digital (300+ dpi). Buys one-time rights.

$ $ $ $ DIABLO MAGAZINE

The Magazine of the East Bay, Diablo Publications, 2520 Camino Diablo, Walnut Creek CA 94597. Fax: (925)943-1045. E-mail: dmail@diablopubs.com. Website: www.diablomag.com. **50% freelance written.** Monthly magazine covering regional travel, food, homestyle, and profiles in Contra Costa and southern Alameda counties and selected areas of Oakland and Berkeley. Estab. 1979. Circ. 45,000. **Pays on acceptance.** Publishes ms an average of 3 months after acceptance. Byline given. Offers 25% kill fee. Buys first rights. Editorial lead time 3 months. Submit seasonal material 5 months in advance. Accepts queries by mail, e-mail, fax. Sample copy online. Writer's guidelines online.

Nonfiction General interest, interview/profile, new product, photo feature, technical, travel. No restaurant profiles, out of country travel, nonlocal topics. **Buys 60 mss/year.** Query with published clips. Length: 600-3,000 words. **Pays $300-2,000.** Sometimes pays expenses of writers on assignment.

Photos State availability with submission. Buys one-time rights. Negotiates payment individually.

Columns/Departments Tech; Parenting; Homestyle; Food; Books; Health; Profiles; Local Politics, all 1,000 words. Query with published clips.

Tips "We prefer San Francisco Bay area writers who are familiar with the area."

$ $ THE EAST BAY MONTHLY

The Berkeley Monthly, Inc., 1301 59th St., Emeryville CA 94608. (510)658-9811. Fax: (510)658-9902. E-mail: editorial@themonthly.com. **Contact:** Kira Halpern, editor. **95% freelance written.** Monthly tabloid. "We feature distinctive, intelligent articles of interest to *East Bay* readers." Estab. 1970. Circ. 80,000. Pays on publication. Byline given. Buys first, second serial (reprint) rights. Editorial lead time 2+ months. Submit seasonal material 3 months in advance. Accepts queries by mail, e-mail. Accepts simultaneous submissions. Responds in 1 month to queries; 1 month to mss. Sample copy for $1. Writer's guidelines for #10 SASE or by e-mail.

Nonfiction All articles must have a local angle. Topics include essays (first person), exposés, general interest, humor, interview/profile, personal experience, arts, culture, lifestyles. Essays (first-person), exposé, general interest, humor, interview/profile, personal experience, photo feature, arts, culture, lifestyles. No fiction or poetry. Query with published clips. Length: 1,500-3,000 words. **Pays $250-700.**

Reprints Send tearsheet and information about when and where the material previously appeared.

Photos State availability with submission. Negotiates payment individually. Identification of subjects required.

Columns/Departments Shopping Around (local retail news), 2,000 words; First Person, 2,000 words. Query with published clips.

[N] $ $ FOR SENIORS MAGAZINE

Uptown Marketing Publications, 7309 E. Saddlehorn Way, Orange CA 92869. Fax: (714)744-2883. E-mail: articles@upmarketgroup.com. Website: www.upmarketgroup.com. **Contact:** Joan Yankowitz, editor. Quarterly magazine covering Orange County seniors (health, fitness, home, family, legal, finance, travel, leisure). "*For Seniors Magazine* provides Orange County seniors with timely, in-depth editorial on health, fitness, home, family, careers, legal, finance, travel, leisure topics." Estab. 2004. Circ. 170,000. **Pays on acceptance.** Publishes ms an average of 2 months after acceptance. Byline given. Buys first North American serial, electronic rights. Editorial lead time 3 months. Submit seasonal material 3 months in advance. Accepts queries by mail, e-mail, fax. Accepts previously published material. Accepts simultaneous submissions. Responds in 3 months to queries; 3 months to mss. Sample copy online. Writer's guidelines for #10 SASE or online.

Nonfiction Book excerpts, humor, interview/profile, new product, personal experience, photo feature, travel. **Buys 40 mss/year.** Query with or without published clips or send complete ms. Length: 1,000-1,200 words. **Pays 10¢/word.**

Photos Reviews contact sheets. Buys one-time rights. Offers no additional payment for photos accepted with ms. Captions, identification of subjects, model releases required.

Columns/Departments Buys 10 mss/year. Query with or without published clips or send complete ms. **10¢/word.**

Fillers Anecdotes, facts, gags to be illustrated by cartoonist, short humor. **Buys 30/year.** Length: 100-300 words. **Pays 10¢/word.**

Ⓝ $ $ FORTY PLUS MAGAZINE

Uptown Marketing Publications, 7309 E. Saddlehorn Way, Orange CA 92869. Fax: (714)744-2883. E-mail: articles@upmarketgroup.com. Website: www.upmarketgroup.com. **Contact:** Joan Yankowitz, editor. **100% freelance written.** Quarterly magazine covering Orange City baby boomers (health, fitness, careers, home, family, legal, finance, travel, leisure). *"Forty Plus Magazine* provides Orange County California baby boomers with timely, indepth editorial on health, fitness, home, family, careers, legal, finance, travel, leisure topics." Estab. 2004. Circ. 236,000. Pays on publication. Publishes ms an average of 2 months after acceptance. Byline given. Buys first North American serial, second serial (reprint), electronic rights. Editorial lead time 3 months. Submit seasonal material 3 months in advance. Accepts queries by mail, e-mail, fax. Accepts previously published material. Accepts simultaneous submissions. Responds in 3 months to queries; 3 months to mss. Sample copy online. Writer's guidelines for #10 SASE or online.

Nonfiction Book excerpts, humor, interview/profile, new product, personal experience, photo feature, travel. **Buys 40 mss/year.** Query with or without published clips or send complete ms. Length: 1,000-1,200 words. **Pays 10¢/word.**

Photos State availability with submission. Reviews contact sheets. Buys one-time rights. Offers no additional payment for photos accepted with ms. Captions, identification of subjects, model releases required.

Columns/Departments Buys 10 mss/year. Query with or without published clips or send complete ms. **10¢/word.**

Fillers Anecdotes, facts, gags to be illustrated by cartoonist, short humor. **Buys 30/year.** Length: 100-300 words. **Pays 10¢/word.**

$ $ ORANGE COAST MAGAZINE

The Magazine of Orange County, Orange Coast Kommunications, Inc., 3701 Birch St., Suite 100, Newport Beach CA 92660. (949)862-1133. Fax: (949)862-0133. Website: www.orangecoastmagazine.com. **Contact:** Tina Borgatta, editor. **90% freelance written.** Monthly magazine "designed to inform and enlighten the educated, upscale residents of Orange County, California; highly graphic and well researched." Estab. 1974. Circ. 52,000. Pays on publication. Publishes ms an average of 4 months after acceptance. Byline given. Offers 20% kill fee. Buys first North American serial rights. Editorial lead time 5 months. Submit seasonal material 6 months in advance. Accepts queries by mail. Accepts simultaneous submissions. Responds in 2 months to queries; 2 months to mss. Sample copy for #10 SASE and 6 first-class stamps. Writer's guidelines for #10 SASE.

　　○→ Break in with Short Cuts (topical briefs of about 250 words), **pays 30¢/word.**

Nonfiction Absolutely no phone queries. General interest (with Orange County focus), inspirational, interview/profile (prominent Orange County citizens), personal experience, religious, guides to activities and services. Special issues: Health, Beauty, and Fitness (January); Dining (March); International Travel (April); Home Design (June); Family/Education (August); Arts (September); Local Travel (October). "We do not accept stories that do not have specific Orange County angles. We want profiles on local people, stories on issues going on in our community, informational stories using Orange County-based sources. We cannot emphasize the local angle enough." **Buys up to 65 mss/year.** Query with published clips. Length: 1,000-2,000 words. **Pays 30¢/word for assigned articles.**

Photos State availability with submission. Buys one-time rights. Negotiates payment individually. Captions, identification of subjects required.

Columns/Departments Short Cuts (stories for the front of the book that focus on Orange County issues, people, and places), 150-250 words. **Buys up to 25 mss/year.** Query with published clips. **Pays 30¢/word.**

Tips "We're looking for more local personality profiles, analysis of current local issues, local takes on national issues. Most features are assigned to writers we've worked with before. Don't try to sell us 'generic' journalism. *Orange Coast* prefers articles with specific and unusual angles focused on Orange County. A lot of freelance writers ignore our Orange County focus. We get far too many generalized manuscripts."

$ $ PALM SPRINGS LIFE

The California Prestige Magazine, Desert Publications, Inc., 303 N. Indian Canyon, Palm Springs CA 92262. (760)325-2333. Fax: (760)325-7008. E-mail: steve@palmspringslife.com. **Contact:** Steven R. Biller, editor. **80% freelance written.** Monthly magazine covering "affluent resort/southern California/Palm Springs desert resorts. *Palm Springs Life* celebrates the good life." Estab. 1958. Circ. 20,000. Pays on publication. Publishes ms an average of 3 months after acceptance. Byline given. Offers 20% kill fee. Buys all rights. Negotiable Submit seasonal material 6 months in advance. Responds in 4-6 weeks to queries. Sample copy for $3.95. Writer's guidelines not available.

• Increased focus on desert region and business writing opportunities.

Nonfiction Book excerpts, essays, interview/profile, celebrity, fashion, spa, epicurean. Query with published clips. Length: 500-2,500 words. **Pays $100-500.**

Photos State availability with submission. Reviews contact sheets. Buys all rights. Pays $50-200/photo. Captions, identification of subjects, model releases required.

Columns/Departments The Good Life (art, fashion, fine dining, philanthropy, entertainment, luxury living, luxury auto, architecture), 250-750 words. **Buys 12 mss/year.** Query with or without published clips. **Pays $200-350.**

$ PALO ALTO WEEKLY

Embarcadero Publishing Co., 703 High St., P.O. Box 1610, Palo Alto CA 94301. (650)326-8210. Fax: (650)326-3928. Website: www.paloaltoonline.com. **Contact:** Tyler Hanley, editorial assistant. **5% freelance written.** Semiweekly tabloid focusing on local issues and local sources. Estab. 1979. Circ. 48,000. Pays on publication. Publishes ms an average of 1 month after acceptance. Byline given. Offers 50% kill fee. Buys first rights. Submit seasonal material 2 months in advance. Accepts queries by mail. Responds in 2 weeks to queries. Sample copy for 9 × 12 SAE and 2 first-class stamps. Writer's guidelines not available.

• *Palo Alto Weekly* covers sports and has expanded its arts and entertainment coverage. It is still looking for stories in Palo Alto/Stanford area or features on people from the area.

Nonfiction General interest, historical/nostalgic, interview/profile, photo feature. Special issues: Together (weddings—mid-February); Interiors (May, October). Nothing that is not local; no travel. **Buys 25 mss/year.** Query with published clips. Length: 700-1,000 words. **Pays $35-60.** Payment is negotiable.

Photos Send photos with submission. Reviews contact sheets, 5 X 7 prints. Buys one-time rights. Pays $10 minimum/photo. Captions, identification of subjects, model releases required.

Tips "Writers have the best chance if they live within circulation area and know publication and area well. DON'T send generic, broad-based pieces. The most open sections are food, interiors, and sports. Longer 'cover story' submissions may be accepted. Keep it LOCAL."

$ $ SACRAMENTO MAGAZINE

Sacramento Magazines Corp., 706 56th St., Suite 210, Sacramento CA 95819. (916)452-6200. Fax: (916)452-6061. E-mail: krista@sacmag.com. Website: www.sacmag.com. Managing Editor: Darlena Belushin McKay. **Contact:** Krista Minard, editor. **100% freelance written.** Works with a small number of new/unpublished writers each year. Monthly magazine with a strong local angle on local issues, human interest and consumer items for readers in the middle to high income brackets. Estab. 1975. Circ. 29,000. Pays on publication. Publishes ms an average of 3 months after acceptance. Generally buys first North American serial rights and electronic rights, rarely second serial (reprint) rights. Accepts queries by mail. Responds in 2 months to queries; 2 months to mss. Sample copy for $4.50. Writer's guidelines for #10 SASE.

○— Break in with submissions to City Lights.

Nonfiction Local isues vital to Sacramento quality of life. "No e-mail, fax or phone queries will be answered." **Buys 5 unsolicited feature mss/year.** Query. Length: 1,500-3,000 words, depending on author, subject matter and treatment. **Pays $250 and up.** Sometimes pays expenses of writers on assignment.

Photos Send photos with submission. Buys one-time rights. Payment varies depending on photographer, subject matter and treatment. Captions, identification of subjects, location and date required.

Columns/Departments Business, home and garden, first person essays, regional travel, gourmet, profile, sports, city arts (1,000-1,800 words); City Lights (250-300 words). **Pays $50-400.**

$ $ SACRAMENTO NEWS & REVIEW

Chico Community Publishing, 1015 20th St., Sacramento CA 95814. (916)498-1234. Fax: (916)498-7920. E-mail: billf@newsreview.com or jacksong@newsreview.com. Website: www.newsreview.com. **Contact:** Tom Walsh, editor; Bill Forman, news editor; Jackson Griffith, arts and lifestyle editor. **25% freelance written.** Magazine "We are an alternative news and entertainment weekly. We maintain a high literary standard for submissions; unique or alternative slant. Publication aimed at a young, intellectual audience; submissions should have an edge and strong voice." Estab. 1989. Circ. 95,000. Pays on publication. Publishes ms an average of 2 months after acceptance. Byline given. Offers 10% kill fee. Buys first, electronic rights. Editorial lead time 2 months. Submit seasonal material 2 months in advance. Accepts queries by mail, e-mail, fax, phone. Accepts simultaneous submissions. Responds in 1 month to queries; 2 months to mss. Sample copy for 50¢.

Nonfiction Essays, exposé, general interest, humor, interview/profile, personal experience. Does not want to see travel, product stories, business profile. **Buys 20-30 mss/year.** Query with published clips. Length: 750-5,000 words. **Pays $40-500.** Sometimes pays expenses of writers on assignment.

Photos State availability with submission. Reviews 8×10 prints. Buys one-time rights. Negotiates payment individually. Identification of subjects required.

Columns/Departments In the Mix (CD/TV/book reviews), 150-750 words. **Buys 10-15 mss/year.** Query with published clips. **Pays $10-200.**

Ⓝ $ $ SAN DIEGO MAGAZINE

San Diego Magazine Publishing Co., P.O. Box 85409, Suite 250, San Diego CA 92186. (619)230-9292. Fax: (619)230-0490. E-mail: tblair@sandiegomag.com. Website: www.sandiegomag.com. **Contact:** Tom Blair, editor-in-chief. **30% freelance written.** Monthly magazine. "We produce informative and entertaining features and investigative reports about politics; community and neighborhood issues; lifestyle; sports; design; dining; arts; and other facets of life in San Diego." Estab. 1948. Circ. 55,000. Pays on publication. Publishes ms an average of 2 months after acceptance. Byline given. Offers 25% kill fee. Buys first North American serial, second serial (reprint) rights. Editorial lead time 2 months. Submit seasonal material 4 months in advance. Accepts simultaneous submissions. Sample copy not available. Writer's guidelines not available.

Nonfiction Exposé, general interest, historical/nostalgic, how-to, interview/profile, travel, lifestyle. **Buys 12-24 mss/year.** Query with published clips or send complete ms. Length: 1,000-3,000 words. **Pays $250-750.** Sometimes pays expenses of writers on assignment.

Photos State availability with submission. Buys one-time rights. Offers no additional payment for photos accepted with ms.

$ $ $ $ SAN FRANCISCO

Focus on the Bay Area, 243 Vallejo St., San Francisco CA 94111. (415)398-2800. Fax: (415)398-6777. E-mail: letters@sanfran.com. Website: www.sanfran.com. **Contact:** Bruce Kelley, editor-in-chief. **50% freelance written.** Prefers to work with published/established writers. Monthly city/regional magazine. Estab. 1968. Circ. 180,000. Pays on publication. Publishes ms an average of 2 months after acceptance. Byline given. Offers 25% kill fee. Submit seasonal material 5 months in advance. Responds in 2 months to queries; 2 months to mss. Sample copy for $3.95.

Nonfiction All stories should relate in some way to the San Francisco Bay Area (travel excepted). Exposé, interview/profile, travel, arts; politics; public issues; sports; consumer affairs. Query with published clips. Length: 200-4,000 words. **Pays $100-2,000 and some expenses.**

VENTURA COUNTY REPORTER

1567 Spinnaker Dr., Suite 202, Ventura CA 93001. (805)658-2244. Fax: (805)658-7803. E-mail: editor@vcreporter.com. Website: vcreporter.com. **Contact:** Hilary Johnson, editor. **50% freelance written.** Weekly tabloid covering local news (entertainment and environment). Circ. 35,000. Pays on publication. Publishes ms an average of 6 weeks after acceptance. Byline given. Buys first North American serial rights. Accepts queries by mail, e-mail, fax. Responds in 1 month to queries. Sample copy not available. Writer's guidelines not available.

   • Works with a small number of new/unpublished writers each year.

Nonfiction Ventura County slant predominates. Publishes unpaid 500-600 word opinion pieces weekly. General interest (local slant), humor, interview/profile. Length: 2,000-3,000 words. **Payment varies.**

Photos Send photos with submission. Reviews b&w contact sheet.

Columns/Departments Entertainment; Dining News; News; Feature; Culture; Environmental News. Send query with résumé and clips. **Payment varies.**

Tips "We publish views from left, right, and center, with a strong emphasis on stylish, literary writing. Bear in mind that stories must have a local angle for us."

COLORADO

$ $ $ ASPEN MAGAZINE

Ridge Publications, 720 E. Durant Ave., Suite E-8, Aspen CO 81611. (970)920-4040, ext. 25. Fax: (970)920-4044. E-mail: edit@aspenmagazine.com. Website: www.aspenmagazine.com. Editor: Janet C. O'Grady. **Contact:** Dana R. Butler, managing editor. **30% freelance written.** Bimonthly magazine covering Aspen and the Roaring Fork Valley. "All things Aspen, written in a sophisticated, insider-oriented tone." Estab. 1974. Circ. 20,000. Pays within 3 months of publication. Byline sometimes given. Offers 10% kill fee. Buys first North American serial, electronic rights. Editorial lead time 2 months. Accepts queries by mail, e-mail, fax. Accepts simultaneous submissions. Responds in 2 months to queries; 6 months to mss. Sample copy for 9×12 SAE and 10 first-class stamps. Writer's guidelines for #10 SASE.

● Responds only to submissions including a SASE.

Nonfiction Essays, new product, photo feature, historical, environmental and local issues, architecture and design, sports and outdoors, arts. "We do not publish general interest articles without a strong Aspen hook. We do not publish 'theme' (skiing in Aspen) or anniversary (40th year of Aspen Music Festival) articles, fiction, poetry, or prewritten manuscripts." **Buys 30-60 mss/year.** Query with published clips. Length: 50-4,000 words. **Pays $50-1,000.** Sometimes pays expenses of writers on assignment.

Photos State availability with submission. Reviews contact sheets, negatives, transparencies, prints. Identification of subjects, model releases required.

$ $STEAMBOAT MAGAZINE

Sundance at Fish Creek, 405 Anglers Dr., Suite A, P.O. Box 881659, Steamboat Springs CO 80488. (970)871-9413. Fax: (970)871-1922. E-mail: info@steamboatmagazine.com. Website: www.allaboutsteamboat.com. **Contact:** Stacey Kramer, editor. **80% freelance written.** Semiannual magazine "showcasing the history, people, lifestyles, and interests of Northwest Colorado. Our readers are generally well-educated, well-traveled, upscale, active people visiting our region to ski in winter and recreate in summer. They come from all 50 states and many foreign countries. Writing should be fresh, entertaining, and informative." Estab. 1978. Circ. 30,000. Pays 50% on acceptance, 50% on publication. Publishes ms an average of 6 months after acceptance. Byline given. Buys exclusive rights. Submit seasonal material 1 year in advance. Accepts queries by mail, e-mail, fax, phone. Responds in 3 months to queries. Sample copy for $4.95 and SAE with 10 first-class stamps. Writer's guidelines free.

Nonfiction Book excerpts, essays, general interest, historical/nostalgic, humor, interview/profile, photo feature, travel. **Buys 10-15 mss/year.** Query with published clips. Length: 150-1,500 words. **Pays $50-300 for assigned articles.** Sometimes pays expenses of writers on assignment.

Photos "Prefers to review viewing platforms, JPEGs, and dupes. Will request original transparencies when needed." State availability with submission. Buys one-time rights. Pays $50-250/photo. Captions, identification of subjects required.

Tips "Stories must be about Steamboat Springs and the Yampa Valley to be considered. We're looking for new angles on ski/snowboard stories in the winter and activity-related stories, all year round. Please query first with ideas to make sure subjects are fresh and appropriate. We try to make subjects and treatments 'timeless' in nature because our magazine is a 'keeper' with a multi-year shelf life."

N $ $VAIL/BEAVER CREEK MAGAZINE

Rocky Mountain Media, LLC, P.O. Box 1414, Vail CO 81658. (970)949-9170. Fax: (970)949-9176. E-mail: bergerd @vail.net. Website: www.vailweb.com. **Contact:** Don Berger, editor. **80% freelance written.** Semiannual magazine "showcasing the lifestyles and history of the Vail Valley. We are particularly interested in personality profiles, home and design features, the arts, winter and summer recreation and adventure stories, and environmental articles." Estab. 1975. Circ. 30,000. **Pays on acceptance.** Publishes ms an average of 6 months after acceptance. Byline given. Offers 100% kill fee. Buys one-time rights. Editorial lead time 1 year. Submit seasonal material 1 year in advance. Accepts queries by mail, e-mail. Accepts simultaneous submissions. Responds in 1 month to queries; 2 months to mss. Sample copy for $5.95 and SAE with 10 first-class stamps. Writer's guidelines free.

Nonfiction Essays, general interest, historical/nostalgic, humor, interview/profile, personal experience, photo feature. **Buys 20-25 mss/year.** Query with published clips. Length: 500-3,000 words. **Pays 20-30¢/word.** Sometimes pays expenses of writers on assignment.

Reprints Send ms with rights for sale noted and information about when and where the material previously appeared.

Photos State availability with submission. Reviews transparencies. Buys one-time rights. Offers $50-250/photo. Captions, identification of subjects, model releases required.

Tips "Be familiar with the Vail Valley and its 'personality.' Approach a story that will be relevant for several years to come. We produce a magazine that is a 'keeper.'"

CONNECTICUT

$ $ $CONNECTICUT MAGAZINE

Journal Register Co., 35 Nutmeg Dr., Trumbull CT 06611. (203)380-6600. Fax: (203)380-6610. E-mail: dsalm@co nnecticutmag.com. Website: www.connecticutmag.com. Editor: Charles Monagan. **Contact:** Dale Salm, managing editor. **75% freelance written.** Prefers to work with published/established writers who know the state and live/have lived here. Monthly magazine "for an affluent, sophisticated, suburban audience. We want only articles that pertain to living in Connecticut." Estab. 1971. Circ. 93,000. Pays on publication. Publishes ms an average of 4 months after acceptance. Byline given. Offers 20% kill fee. Buys first North American serial rights.

Submit seasonal material 4 months in advance. Accepts queries by mail, e-mail, fax. Responds in 6 weeks to queries. Sample copy not available. Writer's guidelines for #10 SASE.

O→ Freelancers can best break in with "First" (short, trendy pieces with a strong Connecticut angle); find a story that is offbeat and write it in a lively, interesting manner.

Nonfiction Interested in seeing hard-hitting investigative pieces and strong business pieces (not advertorial). Book excerpts, exposé, general interest, interview/profile, topics of service to Connecticut readers. Special issues: Dining/entertainment, northeast/travel, home/garden and Connecticut bride twice/year. Also, business (January) and healthcare once/year. No personal essays. **Buys 50 mss/year.** Query with published clips. Length: 3,000 words maximum. **Pays $600-1,200.** Sometimes pays expenses of writers on assignment.

Photos Send photos with submission. Reviews contact sheets, transparencies. Buys one-time rights. Pays $50 minimum/photo. Identification of subjects, model releases required.

Columns/Departments Business, Health, Politics, Connecticut Calendar, Arts, Dining Out, Gardening, Environment, Education, People, Sports, Media, From the Field (quirky, interesting regional stories with broad appeal). Length: 1,500-2,500 words. **Buys 50 mss/year.** Query with published clips. **Pays $400-700.**

Fillers Short pieces about Connecticut trends, curiosities, interesting short subjects, etc. Length: 150-400 words. **Pays $75-150.**

▣ The online magazine carries original content not found in the print edition. Contact: Charles Monagan, online editor.

Tips "Make certain your idea has not been covered to death by the local press and can withstand a time lag of a few months. Again, we don't want something that has already received a lot of press."

DELAWARE

$ $ DELAWARE TODAY

3301 Lancaster Pike, Suite 5C, Wilmington DE 19805. (302)656-1809. Fax: (302)656-5843. E-mail: editors@delawaretoday.com. Website: www.delawaretoday.com. **50% freelance written.** Monthly magazine geared toward Delaware people, places and issues. "All stories must have Delaware slant. No pitches such as Delawareans will be interested in a national topic." Estab. 1962. Circ. 25,000. Pays on publication. Publishes ms an average of 4 months after acceptance. Byline given. Offers 50% kill fee. all rights for 1 year. Editorial lead time 3 months. Submit seasonal material 6 months in advance. Responds in 2 months to queries. Sample copy for $2.95.

Nonfiction Historical/nostalgic, interview/profile, photo feature, lifestyles, issues. Special issues: Newcomer's Guide to Delaware. **Buys 40 mss/year.** Query with published clips. Length: 100-3,000 words. **Pays $50-750 for assigned articles.** Sometimes pays expenses of writers on assignment.

Photos State availability with submission. Buys one-time rights. Negotiates payment individually. Identification of subjects required.

Columns/Departments Business, Health, History, People, all 1,500 words. **Buys 24 mss/year.** Query with published clips. **Pays $150-250.**

Fillers Anecdotes, newsbreaks, short humor. **Buys 10/year.** Length: 100-200 words. **Pays $50-75.**

Tips "No story ideas that we would know about, i.e., a profile of the governor. Best bets are profiles of quirky/unique Delawareans that we'd never know about or think of."

DISTRICT OF COLUMBIA

$ $ WASHINGTON CITY PAPER

2390 Champlain St. NW, Washington DC 20009. (202)332-2100. Fax: (202)332-8500. E-mail: tscocca@washcp.com. Website: www.washingtoncitypaper.com. **Contact:** Tom Scocca. **50% freelance written.** "Relentlessly local alternative weekly in nation's capital covering city and regional politics, media and arts. No national stories." Estab. 1981. Circ. 93,000. Pays on publication. Publishes ms an average of 6 weeks after acceptance. Byline given. Offers 10% kill fee for assigned stories. Buys first rights. Editorial lead time 7-10 days. Responds in 1 month to queries. Writer's guidelines online.

Nonfiction "Our biggest need for freelancers is in the District Line section of the newspaper: short, well-reported and local stories. These range from carefully-drawn profiles to sharp, hooky approaches to reporting on local institutions. We don't want op-ed articles, fiction, poetry, service journalism or play by play accounts of news conferences or events. We also purchase, but more infrequently, longer 'cover-length' stories that fit the criteria stated above. Full guide to freelance submissions can be found on website." **Buys 100 mss/year.** Query with published clips or send complete ms. Length: District Line: 800-2,500 words; Covers: 4,000-10,000 words. **Pays 10-40¢/word.** Sometimes pays expenses of writers on assignment.

Photos Make appointment to show portfolio to Jandos Rothstein, art director. Pays minimum of $75.

Columns/Departments Music Writing (eclectic). **Buys 100 mss/year.** Query with published clips or send complete ms. **Pays 10-40¢/word.**

Tips "Think local. Great ideas are a plus. We are willing to work with anyone who has a strong idea, regardless of vita."

$ $ $ THE WASHINGTONIAN

1828 L St. NW, #200, Washington DC 20036. (202)296-3600. Fax: (202)862-3526. E-mail: editorial@washingtoni an.com. Website: www.washingtonian.com. **Contact:** Cindy Rich, assistant editor. **20-25% freelance written.** Monthly magazine. "Writers should keep in mind that we are a general interest city-and-regional magazine. Nearly all our articles have a hard Washington connection. And, please, no political satire." Estab. 1965. Circ. 160,000. Pays on publication. Publishes ms an average of 3 months after acceptance. Byline given. Buys first North American serial, limited, nonexclusive electronic rights. Editorial lead time 10 weeks. Accepts queries by mail, fax. Writer's guidelines online.

Nonfiction Book excerpts, exposé, general interest, historical/nostalgic (with specific Washington, D.C. focus), interview/profile, personal experience, photo feature, travel. **Buys 15-30 mss/year.** Query with published clips. **Pays 50¢/word.** Sometimes pays expenses of writers on assignment.

Columns/Departments Bill O'Sullivan. First Person (personal experience that somehow illuminates life in Washington area), 650-700 words. **Buys 9-12 mss/year.** Query. **Pays $325.**

◼ The online magazine carries original content not found in the print edition. Contact: Cheryl Haser, online editor.

Tips "The types of articles we publish include service pieces; profiles of people; investigative articles; rating pieces; institutional profiles; first-person articles; stories that cut across the grain of conventional thinking; articles that tell the reader how Washington got to be the way it is; light or satirical pieces (send the complete manuscript, not the idea, because in this case execution is everything). Subjects of articles include the federal government, local government, dining out, sports, business, education, medicine, fashion, environment, how to make money, how to spend money, real estate, performing arts, visual arts, travel, health, nightlife, home and garden, self-improvement, places to go, things to do, and more. Again, we are interested in almost anything as long as it relates to the Washington area. We don't like puff pieces or what we call 'isn't-it-interesting' pieces. In general, we try to help our readers understand Washington better, to help our readers live better, and to make Washington a better place to live. Also, remember—a magazine article is different from a newspaper story. Newspaper stories start with the most important facts, are written in short paragraphs with a lot of transitions, and usually can be cut from the bottom up. A magazine article usually is divided into sections that are like 400-word chapters of a very short book. The introductory section is very important—it captures the reader's interest and sets the tone for the article. Scenes or anecdotes often are used to draw the reader into the subject matter. The next section then might foreshadow what the article is about without trying to summarize it—you want to make the reader curious. Each succeeding section develops the subject. Any evaluations or conclusions come in the closing section."

FLORIDA

$ $ $ $ BOCA RATON MAGAZINE

JES Publishing, 6413 Congress Ave., Suite 100, Boca Raton FL 33487. (561)997-8683. Fax: (561)997-8909. E-mail: editor@bocamag.com. Website: www.bocamag.com. **Contact:** Marie Speed, editor-in-chief. **70% freelance written.** Bimonthly lifestyle magazine "devoted to the residents of South Florida, featuring fashion, interior design, food, people, places, and issues that shape the affluent South Florida market." Estab. 1981. Circ. 20,000. **Pays on acceptance.** Publishes ms an average of 3 months after acceptance. Byline given. Buys second serial (reprint) rights. Submit seasonal material 7 months in advance. Accepts simultaneous submissions. Responds in 1 month to queries. Sample copy for $4.95 and 10×13 SAE with 10 first-class stamps. Writer's guidelines for #10 SASE.

Nonfiction General interest, historical/nostalgic, humor, interview/profile, photo feature, travel. Special issues: Interior Design (September-October); Real Estate (March-April); Best of Boca (July-August). Query with published clips or send complete ms. Length: 800-2,500 words. **Pays $350-1,500.**

Reprints Send tearsheet. Payment varies.

Photos Send photos with submission.

Columns/Departments Body & Soul (health, fitness and beauty column, general interest); Hitting Home (family and social interactions); History or Arts (relevant to South Florida), all 1,000 words. Query with published clips or send complete ms. **Pays $350-400.**

Tips "We prefer shorter manuscripts, highly localized articles, excellent art/photography."

Consumer Magazines

$ $EMERALD COAST MAGAZINE

Rowland Publishing, Inc., 1932 Miccosukee Rd., Tallahassee FL 32308. E-mail: editorial@rowlandinc.com. Website: www.rowlandinc.com. **Contact:** T. Bart Pfankuch, editor. **50% freelance written.** Bimonthly magazine. Lifestyle publication celebrating life on Florida's Emerald Coast. "All content has an Emerald Coast (Northwest Florida) connection. This includes Panama City, Seaside, Sandestin, Destin, Fort Walton Beach, and Pensacola." Estab. 2000. Circ. 18,000. **Pays on acceptance.** Publishes ms an average of 3 months after acceptance. Byline given. Buys first North American serial rights. Editorial lead time 4 months. Submit seasonal material 6 months in advance. Accepts queries by mail, e-mail. Accepts previously published material. Accepts simultaneous submissions. Responds in 3 months to queries; 3 months to mss. Sample copy for $4. Writer's guidelines by e-mail.

Nonfiction All must have an Emerald Coast slant. Book excerpts, essays, historical/nostalgic, inspirational, interview/profile, new product, personal experience, photo feature. No fiction, poetry, or travel. No general interest—"we are Northwest Florida specific." **Buys 10-15 mss/year.** Query with published clips. Length: 1,800-2,000 words. **Pays $100-250.** Pays in contributor copies as special arrangements through publisher.

Photos Send photos with submission. Reviews prints, GIF/JPEG files. Buys one-time rights. Negotiates payment individually. Captions, identification of subjects, model releases required.

Tips "We're looking for fresh ideas and new slants that are related to Florida's Emerald Coast. Because we work so far in advance, it is difficult to be timely, so be sure to give us ideas that aren't too time specific."

$ $FLORIDA MONTHLY MAGAZINE

Florida Media, Inc., 801 Douglas Ave., Suite 100, Altamonte Springs FL 32714. (407)816-9596. Fax: (407)816-9373. E-mail: exec-editor@floridamagazine.com. Website: www.floridamagazine.com. Publisher: E. Douglas Cifers. Monthly lifestyle magazine covering Florida travel, food and dining, heritage, homes and gardens, and all aspects of Florida lifestyle. Full calendar of events each month. Estab. 1981. Circ. 225,235. Pays on publication. Publishes ms an average of 5 months after acceptance. Byline given. Buys first rights. Editorial lead time 3 months. Submit seasonal material 6 months in advance. Accepts queries by mail, e-mail, fax. Responds in 2 months to queries. Sample copy for $5. Writer's guidelines for #10 SASE.

- Interested in material on areas outside of the larger cities.
- Break in with stories specific to Florida showcasing the people, places, events, and things that are examples of Florida's rich history and culture.

Nonfiction Historical/nostalgic, interview/profile, travel, general Florida interest, out-of-the-way Florida places, dining, attractions, festivals, shopping, resorts, bed & breakfast reviews, retirement, real estate, business, finance, health, recreation, sports. **Buys 50-60 mss/year.** Query with published clips. Length: 500-2,500 words. **Pays $100-400 for assigned articles; $50-250 for unsolicited articles.**

Photos Send photos with submission. Reviews 3×5 color prints and slides. Offers $6/photo. Captions required.

Columns/Departments Golf; Homes & Gardenings; Heritage (all Florida-related); 750 words. **Buys 24 mss/ year.** Query with published clips. **Pays $75-250.**

$FT. MYERS MAGAZINE

And Pat, LLC, 15880 Summerlin Rd., Suite 189, Fort Myers FL 33908. E-mail: ftmyers@optonline.net. Website: www.ftmyersmagazine.com. Director/Designer: Andrew Elias. **Contact:** Pat Simms-Elias, editorial director. **90% freelance written.** Bimonthly magazine covering regional arts and living. Audience: Educated, active, successful and creative residents of Fort Myers and Lee County, Florida, and guests at resorts and hotels in Lee County. Content: Arts, entertainment, media, travel, sports, health, home. Estab. 2001. Circ. 20,000. Pays on publication. Publishes ms an average of 3 months after acceptance. Byline given. Offers 50% kill fee. Buys one-time, second serial (reprint) rights. Editorial lead time 3 months. Submit seasonal material 3 months in advance. Accepts queries by e-mail. Accepts simultaneous submissions. Responds in 3 months to queries; 3 months to mss. Writer's guidelines for #10 SASE or by e-mail.

Nonfiction Essays, general interest, historical/nostalgic, how-to, humor, interview/profile, personal experience, reviews, previews, news, informational. **Buys 60-75 mss/year.** Query with or without published clips or send complete ms. Length: 300-1,500 words. **Pays $40-150.** Will pay in copies or in ad barter at writer's request. Sometimes pays expenses of writers on assignment.

Reprints Accepts previously published submissions.

Photos State availability of or send photos with submission. Reviews 4×5 to 8×10 prints. Buys one-time rights. Negotiates payment individually; generally offers $100/photo or art. Captions, identification of subjects required.

Columns/Departments Media: books, music, video, film, theater, Internet, software (news, previews, reviews, interviews, profiles), 300-1,500 words. Lifestyles: art & design, science & technology, house & garden, health & fitness, sports & recreation, travel & leisure, food & drink (news, interviews, previews, reviews, profiles, advice), 300-1,500 words. **Buys 60 mss/year.** Query with or without published clips or send complete ms. **Pays $40-150.**

$ $ $GULFSHORE LIFE

9051 N. Tamiami Trail, Suite 202, Naples FL 34108. (239)594-9980. Fax: (239)594-9986. E-mail: dlindley@gulfsh orelifemag.com. Website: www.gulfshorelifemag.com. **Contact:** Daniel Lindley, senior editor. **75% freelance written.** Magazine published 10 times/year for "southwest Florida, the workings of its natural systems, its history, personalities, culture and lifestyle." Estab. 1970. Circ. 35,000. Pays on publication. Publishes ms an average of 4 months after acceptance. Byline given. Buys first North American serial rights. Submit seasonal material 8 months in advance. Accepts queries by mail, e-mail, fax. Accepts simultaneous submissions. Sample copy for 9×12 SAE and 10 first-class stamps.

Nonfiction All articles must be related to southwest Florida. Historical/nostalgic, interview/profile, issue/trend. **Buys 100 mss/year.** Query with published clips. Length: 500-3,000 words. **Pays $100-1,000.**

Photos Send photos with submission. Reviews 35mm transparencies, 5×7 prints. Buys one-time rights. Pays $50-100. Identification of subjects, model releases required.

Tips "We buy superbly written stories that illuminate southwest Florida personalities, places and issues. Surprise us!"

Ⓝ $ $JACKSONVILLE

White Publishing Co., 534 Lancaster St., Jacksonville FL 32204. (904)358-8330. Fax: (904)358-8668. E-mail: joe@jacksonvillemag.com. Website: www.jacksonvillemag.com. **Contact:** Joseph White, editor/publisher. **50% freelance written.** Monthly magazine covering life and business in northeast Florida "for upwardly mobile residents of Jacksonville and the Beaches, Orange Park, St. Augustine and Amelia Island, Florida." Estab. 1985. Circ. 25,000. Pays on publication. Byline given. Offers 25-33% kill fee to writers on assignment. Buys first North American serial, second serial (reprint) rights. Editorial lead time 3 months. Submit seasonal material 4 months in advance. Responds in 6 weeks to queries; 1 month to mss. Sample copy for $5 (includes postage).

Nonfiction All articles *must* have relevance to Jacksonville and Florida's First Coast (Duval, Clay, St. John's, Nassau, Baker counties). Book excerpts, exposé, general interest, historical/nostalgic, how-to (service articles), humor, interview/profile, personal experience, photo feature, travel, commentary; local business successes; trends; personalities; community issues; how institutions work. **Buys 50 mss/year.** Query with published clips. Length: 1,200-3,000 words. **Pays $50-500 for feature length pieces.** Sometimes pays expenses of writers on assignment.

Reprints Send photocopy. Payment varies.

Photos State availability with submission. Reviews contact sheets, transparencies. Buys one-time rights. Negotiates payment individually. Captions, model releases required.

Columns/Departments Business (trends, success stories, personalities), 1,000-1,200 words; Health (trends, emphasis on people, hopeful outlooks), 1,000-1,200 words; Money (practical personal financial advice using local people, anecdotes and examples), 1,000-1,200 words; Real Estate/Home (service, trends, home photo features), 1,000-1,200 words; Travel (weekends; daytrips; excursions locally and regionally), 1,000-1,200 words; occasional departments and columns covering local history, sports, family issues, etc. **Buys 40 mss/year. Pays $150-250.**

Tips "We are a writer's magazine and demand writing that tells a story with flair."

$ $TALLAHASSEE MAGAZINE

Rowland Publishing, Inc., 1932 Miccosukee Rd., Tallahassee FL 32308. E-mail: editorial@rowlandinc.com. Website: www.rowlandinc.com. **Contact:** T. Bart Pfankuch, editor. **50% freelance written.** Bimonthly magazine covering life in Florida's Capital Region. "All content has a Tallahassee, Florida connection." Estab. 1978. Circ. 18,000. **Pays on acceptance.** Publishes ms an average of 2 months after acceptance. Byline given. Buys first North American serial rights. Editorial lead time 4 months. Submit seasonal material 6 months in advance. Accepts queries by mail, e-mail. Accepts simultaneous submissions. Responds in 3 months to queries; 3 months to mss. Sample copy for $4. Writer's guidelines by e-mail.

Nonfiction All must have a Tallahassee slant. Book excerpts, essays, historical/nostalgic, inspirational, interview/profile, new product, personal experience, photo feature, travel, sports, business, Calendar items. No fiction, poetry, or travel. No general interest—"we are Tallahassee, Florida specific." **Buys 15 mss/year.** Query with published clips. Length: 1,000-2,000 words. **Pays $100-250.**

Photos Send photos with submission. Reviews prints, GIF/JPEG files. Buys one-time rights. Negotiates payment individually. Captions, identification of subjects, model releases required.

Tips "We're looking for fresh ideas and new slants that are related to Florida's Capital Region. Because we work so far in advance, it is difficult to be timely, so be sure to give us ideas that aren't too time specific."

GEORGIA

$ $ $ $ ATLANTA MAGAZINE

260 Peachtree St., Suite 300, Atlanta GA 30303. (404)527-5500. Fax: (404)527-5585. E-mail: sfreeman@atlantam ag.emmis.com. Website: www.atlantamagazine.com. **Contact:** Scott Freeman, executive editor or Betsy Riley, senior editor. Monthly magazine that explores people, pleasures, useful information, regional happenings, restaurants, shopping, etc., for a general adult audience in Atlanta, including subjects in government, sports, pop culture, urban affairs, arts, and entertainment. ''*Atlanta* magazine articulates the special nature of Atlanta and appeals to an audience that wants to understand and celebrate the uniqueness of the region. The magazine's mission is to engage our community through provacative writing, authoritative reporting, superlative design that illuminates the people, trends, and events that define our city.'' Circ. 69,000. **Pays on acceptance.** Byline given. Offers 25% kill fee. Buys first North American serial rights. Accepts queries by mail, e-mail. Responds in 3 months to queries. Sample copy online.

Nonfiction ''*Atlanta* magazine articulates the special nature of Atlanta and appeals to an audience that wants to understand and celebrate the uniqueness of the city.'' General interest, interview/profile, travel. **Buys 36-40 mss/year.** Query with published clips. Length: 1,500-5,000 words. **Pays $300-2,000.** Pays expenses of writers on assignment.

Columns/Departments Essay, travel. **Length:** 1,000-1,500 words. **Buys 30 mss/year.** Query with published clips. **Pays $500.**

Fiction Rebecca Burns, editor. Novel excerpts. Need short stories for 2 annual reading issues—Winter & Summer. ''We prefer all fiction to be by Georgia writers and/or have a Georgia/Southern theme. Length: 1,500-5,000 words.

Fillers Buys 80/year. Length: 75-175 words. **Pays $50-100.**

Tips ''Writers must know what makes their piece a story rather than just a subject.''

$ $ ATLANTA TRIBUNE: THE MAGAZINE

Black Atlanta's Business & Politics, L&L Communications, 875 Old Roswell Rd, Suite C-100, Roswell GA 30076. (770)587-0501. Fax: (770)642-6501. E-mail: frobinson@atlantatribune.com. Website: www.atlantatribune.com. **Contact:** Fred Robinson, editor. **30% freelance written.** Monthly magazine covering African-American business, careers, technology, wealth-building, politics, and education. ''The *Atlanta Tribune* is written for Atlanta's black executives, professionals and entrepreneurs with a primary focus of business, careers, technology, wealth-building, politics, and education. Our publication serves as an advisor that offers helpful information and direction to the black entrepreneur.'' Estab. 1987. Circ. 30,000. Pays on publication. Byline given. Offers 10% kill fee. Buys electronic, all rights. Editorial lead time 3 months. Submit seasonal material 4 months in advance. Accepts queries by e-mail. Responds in 6 weeks to queries. Sample copy online or mail a request. Writer's guidelines online.

    o→ Break in with ''the ability to write feature stories that give insight into Black Atlanta's business community, technology, businesses, and career and wealth-building opportunities. Also, stories with real social, political or economic impact.''

Nonfiction ''Our special sections include Black History; Real Estate; Scholarship Roundup.'' Book excerpts, how-to (business, careers, technology), interview/profile, new product, opinion, technical. **Buys 100 mss/year.** Query with published clips. Length: 1,400-2,500 words. **Pays $250-600.** Sometimes pays expenses of writers on assignment.

Photos State availability with submission. Reviews $2\frac{1}{4}$ x $2\frac{1}{4}$ transparencies. Buys one-time rights. Negotiates payment individually. Identification of subjects, model releases required.

Columns/Departments Business; Careers; Technology; Wealth-Building; Politics and Education; all 400-600 words. **Buys 100 mss/year.** Query with published clips. **Pays $100-200.**

    ▣ The online version contains material not found in the print edition and includes writer's guidelines. Contact: Monét Cooper, associate managing editor.

Tips ''Send a well-written, convincing query by e-mail that demonstrates that you have thoroughly read previous issues and reviewed our online writer's guidelines.''

$ FLAGPOLE MAGAZINE

Flagpole, P.O. Box 1027, Athens GA 30603. (706)549-9523. Fax: (706)548-8981. E-mail: editor@flagpole.com. Website: www.flagpole.com. **Contact:** Pete McCommons, editor. **75% freelance written.** Local ''alternative'' weekly with a special emphasis on popular (and unpopular) music. ''Will consider stories on national, international musicians, authors, politicians, etc., even if they don't have a local or regional news peg. However, those stories should be original, irreverent enough to justify inclusion. Of course, local/Southern news/feature stories are best. We like reporting, storytelling more than opinion pieces.'' Estab. 1987. Circ. 16,000. Pays on publication. Publishes ms an average of 1 month after acceptance. Byline given. Makes work-for-hire assignments.

Editorial lead time 2 months. Submit seasonal material 2 months in advance. Responds in 2 weeks to queries; 1 month to mss. Sample copy online.

Nonfiction Book excerpts, essays, exposé, interview/profile, new product, personal experience. **Buys 50 mss/year.** Query by e-mail. Length: 600-2,000 words.

Reprints Send tearsheet, photocopy or typed ms with rights for sale noted and information about when and where the material previously appeared.

Photos State availability with submission. Reviews prints. Buys one-time rights. Negotiates payment individually. Captions required.

Columns/Departments Lit. (book reviews), 800 words. **Buys 30 mss/year.** Send complete ms. **Pays 7¢/word.**

Tips "Read our publication online before querying, but don't feel limited by what you see. We can't afford to pay much, so we're open to young/inexperienced writer-journalists looking for clips. Fresh, funny/insightful voices make us happiest, as does reportage over opinion. If you've ever succumbed to the temptation to call a pop record 'ethereal' we probably won't bother with your music journalism. No faxed submissions, please."

$ $ GEORGIA MAGAZINE

Georgia Electric Membership Corp., P.O. Box 1707, Tucker GA 30085. (770)270-6950. E-mail: ann.orowski@geo rgiaemc.com. Website: www.georgiamagazine.org. **Contact:** Ann Orowski, editor. **50% freelance written.** "We are a monthly magazine for and about Georgians, with a friendly, conversational tone and human interest topics." Estab. 1945. Circ. 444,000. Pays on publication. Publishes ms an average of 4 months after acceptance. Byline given. Buys first North American serial, electronic rights. Editorial lead time 2 months. Submit seasonal material 6 months in advance. Accepts simultaneous submissions. Responds in 1 month to subjects of interest to queries. Sample copy for $2. Writer's guidelines for #10 SASE.

Nonfiction General interest (Georgia-focused), historical/nostalgic, how-to (in the home and garden), humor, inspirational, interview/profile, photo feature, travel. **Buys 24 mss/year.** Query with published clips. Length: 800-1,000 words; 500 words for smaller features and departments. **Pays $50-300.**

Photos State availability with submission. Reviews contact sheets, transparencies, prints. Buys one-time rights. Negotiates payment individually. Identification of subjects, model releases required.

$ $ KNOW ATLANTA MAGAZINE

New South Publishing, 1303 Hightower Trail, Suite 101, Atlanta GA 30350. (770)650-1102. Fax: (770)650-2848. E-mail: editor1@knowatlanta.com. Website: www.knowatlanta.com. **Contact:** Geoff Kohl, editor. **80% freelance written.** Quarterly magazine covering the Atlanta area. "Our articles offer information on Atlanta that would be useful to newcomers—homes, schools, hospitals, fun things to do, anything that makes their move more comfortable." Estab. 1986. Circ. 192,000. Pays on publication. Byline given. Offers 100% kill fee. Buys first North American serial rights. Editorial lead time 2 months. Submit seasonal material 2 months in advance. Accepts queries by mail, e-mail, fax. Accepts previously published material. Sample copy for free.

> ○━ "Know the metro Atlanta area, especially hot trends in real estate. Writers who know about international relocation trends and commercial real estate topics are hot."

Nonfiction General interest, how-to (relocate), interview/profile, personal experience, photo feature. No fiction. **Buys 20 mss/year.** Query with clips. Length: 1,000-2,000 words. **Pays $100-500 for assigned articles; $100-300 for unsolicited articles.** Sometimes pays expenses of writers on assignment.

Reprints Accepts previously published submissions.

Photos Send photos with submission, if available. Reviews contact sheets. Buys one-time rights. Negotiates payment individually. Captions, identification of subjects required.

Ⓝ $ $ NORTH GEORGIA JOURNAL

Legacy Communications, Inc., P.O. Box 127, Roswell GA 30077. (770)642-5569. Fax: (770)642-1415. E-mail: info@georgiahistory.ws. Website: www.georgiahistory.ws. **Contact:** Olin Jackson, editor/publisher. **70% freelance written.** Quarterly magazine "for readers interested in travel, history, and lifestyles in Georgia." Estab. 1984. Circ. 18,861. Pays on publication. Publishes ms an average of 5 months after acceptance. Byline given. Offers 25% kill fee. Buys Usually buys all rights. Rights negotiable rights. Editorial lead time 3 months. Submit seasonal material 6 months in advance. Accepts queries by mail, e-mail, fax. Sample copy for 9×12 SAE and 8 first-class stamps, or online. Writer's guidelines for #10 SASE.

Nonfiction Historical/nostalgic, how-to (survival techniques; mountain living; do-it-yourself home construction and repairs, etc.), interview/profile (celebrity), personal experience (anything unique or unusual pertaining to Georgia history), photo feature (any subject of a historic nature which can be photographed in a seasonal context, i.e., old mill with brilliant yellow jonquils in foreground), travel (subjects highlighting travel opportunities in north Georgia). Query with published clips. **Pays $75-350.**

Photos Send photos with submission. Reviews contact sheets, transparencies. Rights negotiable. Negotiates payment individually. Captions, identification of subjects, model releases required.

Fiction Novel excerpts.

Tips "Good photography is crucial to acceptance of all articles. Send written queries then *wait* for a response. *No telephone calls, please.* The most useful material involves a first-person experience of an individual who has explored a historic site or scenic locale and *interviewed* a person or persons who were involved with or have first-hand knowledge of a historic site/event. Interviews and quotations are crucial. Articles should be told in writer's own words."

$$POINTS NORTH MAGAZINE

Serving Atlanta's Stylish Northside, All Points Interactive Media Corp., 568 Peachtree Pkwy., Suite 116, Cumming GA 30041-6820. (770)844-0969. Fax: (770)844-0968. E-mail: managingeditor@ptsnorth.com. Website: www.ptsnorth.com. Managing Editor: Carolyn Williams. **Contact:** Managing Editor. **85% freelance written.** Monthly magazine covering lifestyle (regional). *"Points North* is a first-class lifestyle magazine for affluent residents of suburban communities in north metro Atlanta." Estab. 2000. Circ. 81,000. Pays on publication. Publishes ms an average of 1 month after acceptance. Byline given. Offers negotiable (for assigned articles only) kill fee. Buys electronic, first serial (in the southeast with a 6 month moratorium) rights. Editorial lead time 3 months. Submit seasonal material 6 months in advance. Accepts queries by mail, e-mail, fax. Accepts previously published material. Responds in 6-8 weeks to queries; 6-8 months to mss. Sample copy for $3.

Nonfiction General interest (only topics pertaining to Atlanta area), historical/nostalgic, interview/profile, travel. No political, controversial, advertorial, new age, health and fitness, sports (particularly golf). **Buys 50-60 mss/year.** Query with published clips. Length: 1,200-2,500 words. **Pays $350-500.**

Photos "We do not accept photos until article acceptance. Do not send photos with query." State availability with submission. Reviews slide transparencies, 4×6 prints, GIF/JPEG files. Offers no additional payment for photos accepted with ms. Captions, identification of subjects, model releases required.

Tips "The best way for a freelancer, who is interested in being published, is to get a sense of the types of articles we're looking for by reading the magazine."

HAWAII

N $$HONOLULU MAGAZINE

PacificBasin Communications, 1000 Bishop St., Suite 405, Honolulu HI 96813. (808)537-9500. Fax: (808)537-6455. E-mail: johnh@pacificbasin.net. Website: www.honolulumagazine.com. **Contact:** John Heckathorn, editor. Prefers to work with published/established writers. Monthly magazine covering general interest topics relating to Hawaii residents. Estab. 1888. Circ. 30,000. Pays on publication. Byline given. Makes work-for-hire assignments. Accepts queries by mail, e-mail. Writer's guidelines online.

Nonfiction Historical/nostalgic, interview/profile, sports, politics, lifestyle trends, all Hawaii-related. "We write for Hawaii residents, so travel articles about Hawaii are not appropriate." Query with published clips or send complete ms. Length: Length determined when assignments discussed. **Pays $100-700.** Sometimes pays expenses of writers on assignment.

Photos Jayson Harper, art director. State availability with submission. Pays $50-200. Captions, identification of subjects, model releases required.

Columns/Departments Length determined when assignments discussed. Query with published clips or send complete ms. **Pays $100-300.**

IDAHO

$$SUN VALLEY MAGAZINE

Valley Publishing, LLC, 12 E. Bullion, Suite B, Hailey ID 83333. (208)788-0770. Fax: (208)788-3881. E-mail: info@sunvalleymag.com. Website: www.sunvalleymag.com. **95% freelance written.** Quarterly magazine covering the lifestyle of the Sun Valley area. *Sun Valley Magazine* "presents the lifestyle of the Sun Valley area and the Wood River Valley, including recreation, culture, profiles, history and the arts." Estab. 1973. Circ. 17,000. Pays on publication. Publishes ms an average of 5 months after acceptance. Byline given. Buys first North American serial, electronic rights. Editorial lead time 1 year. Submit seasonal material 14 months in advance. Accepts queries by mail. Accepts previously published material. Accepts simultaneous submissions. Responds in 5 weeks to queries; 2 months to mss. Sample copy for $4.95 and $3 postage. Writer's guidelines for #10 SASE.

Nonfiction "All articles are focused specifically on Sun Valley, the Wood River Valley and immediate surrounding areas." Historical/nostalgic, interview/profile, photo feature, travel. Special issues: Sun Valley home design and architecture, Spring; Sun Valley weddings/wedding planner, summer. Query with published clips. **Pays $40-500.** Sometimes pays expenses of writers on assignment.

Reprints Only occasionally purchases reprints.

Photos State availability with submission. Reviews transparencies. Buys one-time rights and some electronic rights. Offers $60-275/photo. Identification of subjects, model releases required.

Columns/Departments Conservation issues, winter/summer sports, health & wellness, mountain-related activities and subjects, home (interior design), garden. All columns must have a local slant. Query with published clips. **Pays $40-300.**

Tips "Most of our writers are locally based. Also, we rarely take submissions that are not specifically assigned, with the exception of fiction. However, we always appreciate queries."

ILLINOIS

ℕ $ CHICAGO LIFE

1300 W. Belmont Ave., Suite 225, Chicago IL 60657-3260. (773)880-1360. Publisher: Pam Berns. **Contact:** Joan Black, editor. **95% freelance written.** Bimonthly magazine on Chicago life for educated, affluent professionals, 25-60 years old. Estab. 1984. Circ. 50,000. Pays on publication. Byline given. Kill fee varies. Submit seasonal material 8 months in advance. Accepts simultaneous submissions. Responds in 3 months to queries. Sample copy for 9×12 SAE and 7 first-class stamps.

Nonfiction Exposé, travel, environment, health, interior design. **Buys 50 mss/year.** Send complete ms. Length: 400-1,200 words. Sometimes pays expenses of writers on assignment.

Reprints Send photocopy and information about when and where the material previously appeared.

Photos Send photos with submission. Reviews contact sheets, negatives, transparencies, prints. Buys one-time rights. Offers $15-30/photo.

Columns/Departments Law, Book Reviews, Travel, Health, Environment, Home Decorating; **Length:** 500 words. Send complete ms. **Pays $30.**

Fillers Facts. **Pays $15-30.**

Tips "Please send finished work with visuals (photos, if possible). Topics open include environmental concerns, health, interior design, travel."

$ $ $ $ CHICAGO MAGAZINE

500 N. Dearborn, Suite 1200, Chicago IL 60610-4901. E-mail: stritsch@chicagomag.com. Website: www.chicago mag.com. **Contact:** Shane Tritsch, managing editor. **50% freelance written.** Prefers to work with published/established writers. Monthly magazine for an audience which is "95% from Chicago area; 90% college educated; upper income, overriding interests in the arts, politics, dining, good life in the city and suburbs. Most are in 25-50 age bracket, well-read and articulate." Estab. 1968. Circ. 175,000. **Pays on acceptance.** Publishes ms an average of 3 months after acceptance. Buys first rights. Submit seasonal material 4 months in advance. Accepts queries by mail, e-mail. Responds in 1 month to queries. For sample copy, send $3 to Circulation Dept. Writer's guidelines for #10 SASE.

Nonfiction "On themes relating to the quality of life in Chicago: Past, present, and future." Writers should have "a general awareness that the readers will be concerned, influential, longtime Chicagoans. We generally publish material too comprehensive for daily newspapers." Exposé, humor, personal experience, think pieces, profiles, spot news, historical articles. **Buys 100 mss/year.** Query; indicate specifics, knowledge of city and market, and demonstrable access to sources. Length: 200-6,000 words. **Pays $100-3,000 and up.** Pays expenses of writers on assignment.

Photos Usually assigned separately, not acquired from writers. Reviews 35mm transparencies, color and b&w glossy prints.

🖥 The online editor is Deborah Wilk.

Tips "Submit detailed queries, be business-like and avoid clichéd ideas."

ℕ $ $ $ CS

Chicago Social, Modern Luxury, Inc., 200 W. Hubbard, Chicago IL 60610. (312)274-2500. E-mail: gbazer@mode rnluxury.com. Website: www.modernluxury.com. **Contact:** Gina Bazer, editor-in-chief. **70% freelance written.** Monthly Luxury lifestyle magazine. "We cover the good things in life—fashion, fine dining, the arts, etc.—from a sophisticated, cosmopolitan, well-to-do perspective." Circ. 75,000. Pays 2 months after receipt of invoice. Byline given. Offers kill fee. first rights and all rights in this market. Editorial lead time 6 months. Submit seasonal material 3-6 months in advance. Responds in 1 month to queries. Sample copy for $7.15 for current issue; $8.20 for back issue. Writer's guidelines not available.

Nonfiction General interest, how-to (gardening, culinary, home design), interview/profile, photo feature (occasional), travel. No fiction. *No unsolicited mss.* Query with published clips only. Length: 500-4,500 words. **Pays $50-900.** Pays expenses of writers on assignment.

Photos State availability with submission. Reviews transparencies, prints. Buys one-time rights. We pay for film and processing only.

Columns/Departments Few Minutes With (Q&A), 800 words; City Art, Home Design, 2,000 words. Query with published clips only. **Pays $150-400.**

Tips "Send résumé, clips and story ideas. Mention interest and expertise in cover letter. We need writers who are knowledgeable about home design, architecture, art, culinary arts, entertainment, fashion and retail."

N $ ILLINOIS ENTERTAINER

Chicago's Music Monthly, Roberts Publishing Co., 124 W. Polk, #103, Chicago IL 60605. (312)922-9333. Fax: (312)922-9369. E-mail: editors@illinoisentertainer.com. Website: www.illinoisentertainer.com. **Contact:** Althea Legaspi, editor-in-chief. **80% freelance written.** Monthly free magazine covering "popular and alternative music, as well as other entertainment: film, media." Estab. 1974. Circ. 75,000. Pays on publication. Publishes ms an average of 2 months after acceptance. Byline given. Offers 50% kill fee. Buys first North American serial rights. Editorial lead time 2 months. Submit seasonal material 2 months in advance. Accepts queries by mail. Accepts simultaneous submissions. Responds in 2 months to queries. Sample copy for $5.

Nonfiction Exposé, how-to, humor, interview/profile, new product, reviews. No personal, confessional, inspirational articles. **Buys 75 mss/year.** Query with published clips. Length: 600-2,600 words. **Pays $15-160.** Sometimes pays expenses of writers on assignment.

Reprints Send ms with rights for sale noted and information about when and where the material previously appeared. Pays 100% of amount paid for an original article.

Photos Send photos with submission. Reviews contact sheets, transparencies, 5×7 prints. Buys one-time rights. Offers $20-200/photo. Captions, identification of subjects, model releases required.

Columns/Departments Spins (LP reviews), 250-300 words. **Buys 200-300 mss/year.** Query with published clips. **Pays $15.**

The online version contains material not found in the print edition. Contact: Althea Legaspi.

Tips "Send clips, résumé, etc. and be patient. Also, sending queries that show you've seen our magazine and have a feel for it greatly increases your publication chances. Don't send unsolicited material. No e-mail solicitations or queries of any kind."

N $ $ NEWCITY

Chicago's News and Arts Weekly, New City Communications, Inc., 770 N. Halsted, Chicago IL 60622. (312)243-8786. Fax: (312)243-8802. E-mail: brian@newcity.com. Website: www.newcitychicago.com. **Contact:** Brian Hieggelke, editor. **50% freelance written.** Weekly magazine. Estab. 1986. Circ. 70,000. Pays 2-4 months after publication. Publishes ms an average of 1 month after acceptance. Byline given. Offers 20% kill fee in certain cases... first rights and non-exclusive electronic rights. Editorial lead time 2 months. Submit seasonal material 2 months in advance. Accepts queries by e-mail. Responds in 1 month to mss. Sample copy for $3. Writer's guidelines online.

Nonfiction Essays, exposé, general interest, interview/profile, personal experience, travel (related to traveling from Chicago and other issues particularly affecting travelers from this area), service. **Buys 100 mss/year.** Query by e-mail only. Length: 100-4,000 words. **Pays $15-450.** Rarely pays expenses of writers on assignment.

Photos State availability with submission. Reviews contact sheets. Buys one-time rights. Captions, identification of subjects, model releases required.

Columns/Departments Lit (literary supplement), 300-2,000 words; Music, Film, Arts (arts criticism), 150-800 words; Chow (food writing), 300-2,000 words. **Buys 50 mss/year.** Query by e-mail. **Pays $15-300.**

Tips "E-mail a solid, sharply written query that has something to do with what our magazine publishes."

INDIANA

$ $ EVANSVILLE LIVING

Tucker Publishing Group, 100 NW Second St., Suite 220, Evansville IN 47708. (812)426-2115. Fax: (812)426-2134. E-mail: ktucker@evansvilleliving.com. Website: www.evansvilleliving.com. **Contact:** Kristen Tucker, editor/publisher; Shellie Benson, managing editor (sbenson@evansvillelivingmagazine.com). **80-100% freelance written.** Bimonthly magazine covering Evansville, Indiana, and the greater area. *"Evansville Living* is the only full-color, glossy, 100+ page city magazine for the Evansville, Indiana, area. Regular departments include: Home Style, Garden Style, Day Tripping, Sporting Life, and Local Flavor (menus)." Estab. 2000. Circ. 50,000. **Pays on acceptance.** Publishes ms an average of 3 months after acceptance. Byline given. Buys all rights. Editorial lead time 6 months. Submit seasonal material 6 months in advance. Accepts queries by mail, e-mail, fax. Accepts previously published material. Sample copy for $5 or online. Writer's guidelines for free or by e-mail.

Nonfiction Essays, general interest, historical/nostalgic, photo feature, travel. **Buys 60-80 mss/year.** Query with

published clips. Length: 200-2,000 words. **Pays $100-300.** Sometimes pays expenses of writers on assignment.
Reprints Accepts previously published submissions.
Photos State availability with submission. Reviews contact sheets, negatives, transparencies, prints. Buys all rights. Negotiates payment individually. Captions, identification of subjects required.
Columns/Departments Home Style (home); Garden Style (garden); Sporting Life (sports); Local Flavor (menus), all 1,500 words. Query with published clips. **Pays $100-300.**

KANSAS

$ $ KANSAS!

Kansas Department of Commerce, 1000 SW Jackson St., Suite 100, Topeka KS 66612-1354. (785)296-3479. Fax: (785)296-6988. E-mail: ksmagazine@kansascommerce.com. Website: www.kansmag.com. **90% freelance written.** Quarterly magazine emphasizing Kansas travel attractions and events. Estab. 1945. Circ. 52,000. **Pays on acceptance.** Publishes ms an average of 1 year after acceptance. Byline given. Buys one-time rights. Submit seasonal material 8 months in advance. Accepts queries by mail. Responds in 2 months to queries. Sample copy and writer's guidelines available.
Nonfiction "Material must be Kansas-oriented and have good potential for color photographs. The focus is on travel with articles about places and events that can be enjoyed by the general public. In other words, events must be open to the public, places also. Query letter should clearly outline story. We are especially interested in Kansas freelancers who can supply their own quality photos." General interest, photo feature, travel. Query by mail. Length: 750-1,250 words. **Pays $200-350.** Pays mileage only for writers on assignment.
Photos "We are a full-color photo/manuscript publication." Send photos (original transparencies only) with query. Pays $50-75 (generally included in ms rate) for 35mm or larger format transparencies. Captions required.
Tips "History and nostalgia stories do not fit into our format because they can't be illustrated well with color photos. Submit a query letter describing 1 appropriate idea with outline for possible article and suggestions for photos. Do not send unsolicited manuscripts."

KENTUCKY

$ BACK HOME IN KENTUCKY

Back Home in Kentucky, Inc., P.O. Box 710, Clay City KY 40312-0710. (606)663-1011. Fax: (606)663-1808. E-mail: info@backhomeinky.com. **Contact:** Jerlene Rose, editor/publisher. **50% freelance written.** Bimonthly magazine "covering Kentucky heritage, people, places, events. We reach Kentuckians and 'displaced' Kentuckians living outside the state." Estab. 1977. Circ. 8,000. Pays on publication. Publishes ms an average of 6 months after acceptance. Byline given. Buys first North American serial rights. Submit seasonal material 6 months in advance. Responds in 2 months to queries. Sample copy for $3 and 9×12 SAE with $1.23 postage affixed. Writer's guidelines for #10 SASE.
● Interested in profiles of Kentucky gardeners, cooks, craftspeople.
Nonfiction Historical/nostalgic (Kentucky-related eras or profiles), photo feature (Kentucky places and events), travel (unusual/little-known Kentucky places), profiles (Kentucky cooks, gardeners, and craftspersons), memories (Kentucky related). No inspirational or religion. **Buys 20-25 mss/year.** Query with or without published clips or send complete ms. Length: 500-2,000 words. **Pays $50-150 for assigned articles; $25-75 for unsolicited articles.** "In addition to normal payment, writers receive 2 copies of issue containing their article."
Photos Looking for color transparencies for covers (inquire for specific topics). Vertical format. Pays $50-150. Photo credits given. For inside photos, send photos with submission. Reviews transparencies, 4×6 prints. Rights purchased depends on situation. Occasionally offers additional payment for photos accepted with ms. Identification of subjects, model releases required.
Columns/Departments Travel, crafts, gardeners, and cooks (all Kentucky related), 500-750 words. **Buys 10-12 mss/year.** Query with published clips. **Pays $15-40.**
Tips "We work mostly with unpublished or emerging writers who have a feel for Kentucky's people, places, and events. Areas most open are little known places in Kentucky, unusual history, and profiles of interesting Kentuckians, and Kentuckians with unusual hobbies or crafts."

Ⓝ $ $ KENTUCKY LIVING

Kentucky Association of Electric Co-Ops, P.O. Box 32170, Louisville KY 40232. E-mail: e-mail@kentuckyliving.com. Website: www.kentuckyliving.com. **Contact:** Paul Wesslund, editor. Mostly freelance written. Prefers to work with published/established writers. Monthly Feature magazine primarily for Kentucky residents. Estab. 1948. Circ. 470,000. **Pays on acceptance.** Publishes ms an average of 12 months after acceptance. Byline given. first serial rights for Kentucky. Submit seasonal material at least 6 months in advance. Accepts previously published material. Accepts simultaneous submissions. Responds in 1 month to queries. Sample copy for 9 × 12 SAE and 4 first-class stamps.

Nonfiction Kentucky-related profiles (people, places or events), recreation, travel, leisure, lifestyle articles, book excerpts. **Buys 18-24 mss/year.** Query with or without published clips or send complete ms. **Pays $75-125 for "short" features (600-800 words); pays $150-350 for major articles (750-1,500 words).** Sometimes pays expenses of writers on assignment.

Photos State availability of or send photos with submission. Reviews Color slides and prints. Payment for photos included in payment for ms. Identification of subjects required.

Tips "The quality of writing and reporting (factual, objective, thorough) is considered in setting payment price. We prefer general interest pieces filled with quotes and anecdotes. Avoid boosterism. Well-researched, well-written feature articles are preferred. All articles must have a strong Kentucky connection."

$ $ KENTUCKY MONTHLY

Vested Interest Publications, 213 St. Clair St., Frankfort KY 40601. (502)227-0053. Fax: (502)227-5009. E-mail: membry@kentuckymonthly.com or smvest@kentuckymonthly.com. Website: www.kentuckymonthly.com. Publisher: Stephen M. Vest. **Contact:** Michael Embry, editor. **75% freelance written.** Monthly magazine. "We publish stories about Kentucky and by Kentuckians, including those who live elsewhere." Estab. 1998. Circ. 40,000. Pays within 3 months of publication. Publishes ms an average of 3 months after acceptance. Byline given. Buys first North American serial rights. Editorial lead time 3 months. Submit seasonal material 4 months in advance. Accepts queries by mail, e-mail, fax. Accepts simultaneous submissions. Responds in 3 weeks to queries; 1 month to mss. Sample copy online. Writer's guidelines online.

Nonfiction Book excerpts, general interest, historical/nostalgic, how-to, humor, interview/profile, photo feature, religious, travel, all with a Kentucky angle. **Buys 60 mss/year.** Query with or without published clips. Length: 300-2,000 words. **Pays $25-350 for assigned articles; $20-100 for unsolicited articles.**

Photos State availability with submission. Reviews negatives. Buys all rights. Captions required.

Fiction Adventure, historical, mainstream, novel excerpts. **Buys 10 mss/year.** Query with published clips. Length: 1,000-5,000 words. **Pays $50-100.**

Tips "We're looking for more fashion, home, and garden, first-person experience, mystery. Please read the magazine to get the flavor of what we're publishing each month. We accept articles via e-mail, fax, and mail."

$ $ LOUISVILLE MAGAZINE

137 W. Muhammad Ali Blvd., Suite 101, Louisville KY 40202-1438. (502)625-0100. Fax: (502)625-0109. E-mail: loumag@loumag.com. Website: www.louisville.com/loumag. **Contact:** Bruce Allar, editor. **60% freelance written.** Monthly magazine "for and generally about people of the Louisville Metro area. Routinely covers arts, entertainment, business, sports, dining, and fashion. Features range from news analysis/exposé to humorous commentary. We like lean, clean prose, crisp leads." Estab. 1950. Circ. 26,500. Publishes ms an average of 3 months after acceptance. Byline given. Offers 20% kill fee. Buys first North American serial rights. Editorial lead time 6 weeks. Submit seasonal material 6 months in advance. Accepts queries by mail, e-mail, fax. Responds in 3 months to queries. Sample copy online.

Nonfiction Essays, exposé, general interest, historical/nostalgic, interview/profile, photo feature. Special issues: Kentucky Derby (April); Pocket Guide to Louisville (May); Dining & Entertaining Guide (September); Louisville Bride (December). **Buys 75 mss/year.** Query. Length: 500-3,500 words. **Pays $50-600 for assigned articles.**

Photos State availability with submission. Buys one-time rights. Offers $25-50/photo. Identification of subjects required.

Columns/Departments End Insight (essays), 750 words. **Buys 10 mss/year.** Send complete ms. **Pays $100-150.**

LOUISIANA

$ $ SUNDAY ADVOCATE MAGAZINE

P.O. Box 588, Baton Rouge LA 70821-0588. (225)383-1111 ext. 0199. Fax: (225)388-0351. E-mail: glangley@thea dvocate.com. Website: www.theadvocate.com. **Contact:** Tim Belehrad, news/features editor. **5% freelance written.** "Freelance features are put on our website." Estab. 1925. Pays on publication. Publishes ms an average of 3 months after acceptance. Byline given. Buys one-time rights.

   O—☛ Break in with travel articles.

Nonfiction Well-illustrated, short articles; must have local, area, or Louisiana angle, in that order of preference. Buys 24 mss/year. **Pays $100-200.**

Reprints Send tearsheet or typed ms with rights for sale noted and information about when and where the material previously appeared. Pays $100-200.

Photos Photos purchased with ms. Pays $30/published color photo.

Tips "Style and subject matter vary. Local interest is most important. No more than 4 to 5 typed, double-spaced pages."

MAINE

Ⓝ $ MAINE MAGAZINE
The Magazine of Maine's Treasures, County Wide Communications, Inc., P.O. Box 497, 26 Main St., Machias ME 04654. (207)564-7548. Website: www.mainemagazine.com. Publisher/Book Review Editor: Bob Berta. **Contact:** Lester J. Reynolds, managing editor. **30% freelance written.** Monthly Magazine and online covering Maine and its people. Estab. 1977. Circ. 16,000. Pays on acceptance or publication (negotiable). Byline sometimes given. Offers 100% kill fee. Buys electronic, all rights. Editorial lead time 9 months. Submit seasonal material 9 months in advance. Accepts queries by mail. Accepts simultaneous submissions. Responds in 30 days to queries. Sample copy and writer's guidelines for $4 or online at website.

Nonfiction "First person not interesting unless you're related to a rich and famous or unique Mainer." Book excerpts, essays, how-to, humor, inspirational, interview/profile, new product, personal experience, photo feature, religious, travel. Query. Length: 1,000-2,000 words. **Pays $25-50.** Sometimes pays expenses of writers on assignment.

Photos Reviews contact sheets, negatives, transparencies. Buys all rights. Offers $15/photo or negotiates payment individually. Captions, identification of subjects required.

Columns/Departments "We are unsually set here with Maine writers." **Buys 10 or fewer mss/year.** Query. **Pays $10-20.**

Poetry "Many are submitted by readers who love Maine." **Buys 10 or fewer poems/year. Pays $5.**

Tips "We're looking for work that is unique and about Maine—unusual people, places. We always want Stephen King interviews—good luck. We can give you his office address."

MARYLAND

$ $ BALTIMORE MAGAZINE
Inner Harbor E. 1000 Lancaster St., Suite 400, Baltimore MD 21202. (410)752-4200. Fax: (410)625-0280. E-mail: iken@baltimoremag.com. Website: www.baltimoremagazine.net. **Contact:** Ken Iglehart, managing editor. **50-60% freelance written.** Monthly "Pieces must address an educated, active, affluent reader and must have a very strong Baltimore angle." Estab. 1907. Circ. 70,000. Pays within 1 month of publication. Byline given. first rights in all media Submit seasonal material 4 months in advance. Accepts queries by mail, e-mail. Sample copy for $4.45. Writer's guidelines online.

    ⊶ Break in through "Baltimore Inc. and B-Side—these are our shortest, newsiest sections and we depend heavily on tips and reporting from strangers. Please note that we are exclusively local. Submissions without a Baltimore angle may be ignored."

Nonfiction Book excerpts (Baltimore subject or author), essays, exposé, general interest, historical/nostalgic, humor, interview/profile (with a Baltimorean), new product, personal experience, photo feature, travel (local and regional to Maryland *only*). "Nothing that lacks a strong Baltimore focus or angle." Query by mail with published clips or send complete ms. Length: 1,000-3,000 words. **Pays 30-40¢/word.** Sometimes pays expenses of writers on assignment.

Columns/Departments Hot Shot, Health, Education, Sports, Parenting, Politics. Length: 1,000-2,500 words. "The shorter pieces are the best places to break into the magazine." Query with published clips.

    ◻ The online magazine carries original content not found in the print edition. Contact: Mary-Rose Nelson, online editor.

Tips "Writers who live in the Baltimore area can send résumé and published clips to be considered for first assignment. Must show an understanding of writing that is suitable to an educated magazine reader and show ability to write with authority, describe scenes, help reader experience the subject. Too many writers send us newspaper-style articles. We are seeking: 1) *Human interest features*—strong, even dramatic profiles of Baltimoreans of interest to our readers. 2) *First-person accounts* of experience in Baltimore, or experiences of a Baltimore resident. 3) *Consumer*—according to our editorial needs, and with Baltimore sources. Writers should read/familiarize themselves with style of *Baltimore Magazine* before submitting."

CHESAPEAKE LIFE MAGAZINE
Alter Communications, 1040 Park Ave., Suite 200, Baltimore MD 21201. (443)451-6023. Fax: (443)451-6027. E-mail: editor@chesapeakelifemag.com. Website: www.chesapeakelifemag.com. **Contact:** Kessler Burnett, editor. **80% freelance written.** Bimonthly magazine covering restaurant reviews, personalities, home design,

travel, regional calendar of events, feature articles, gardening. *"Chesapeake Life* is a regional magazine covering the Chesapeake areas of Maryland, Virginia, and Southern Delaware.*"* Estab. 1995. Circ. 85,000. Pays on publication. Byline given. Buys first North American serial rights. Editorial lead time 2 months. Accepts queries by mail, e-mail, fax, phone. Writer's guidelines free.

Nonfiction Book excerpts, general interest, historical/nostalgic, interview/profile, photo feature, travel. Query with published clips. Length: Open.

Photos Send photos with submission. Buys one-time rights. Negotiates payment individually.

MASSACHUSETTS

N BOSTON GLOBE MAGAZINE

Boston Globe, P.O. Box 2378, Boston MA 02107-2378. (617)929-2000. Website: www.globe.com/globe/magazi ne. **Contact:** Doug Most, magazine editor. **50% freelance written.** Weekly magazine. Circ. 706,153. Pays on publication. Publishes ms an average of 2 months after acceptance. Buys non exclusive electronic rights Editorial lead time 2 months. Submit seasonal material 3 months in advance. Sample copy for 9×12 SAE and 2 first-class stamps.

Nonfiction Book excerpts (first serial rights only), interview/profile (not Q&A), narratives, trend pieces, profiles. Especially interested in medicine, science, higher education, sports, and the arts. No travelogs or poetry. **Buys up to 100 mss/year.** Query; SASE must be included with ms or queries for return. Length: 1,000-4,000 words. **Payment negotiable.**

Photos Purchased with accompanying ms or on assignment. Reviews contact sheets. Pays standard rates according to size used. Captions required.

BOSTON MAGAZINE

300 Massachusetts Ave., Boston MA 02115. (617)262-9700. Fax: (617)267-1774. E-mail: editor@bostonmagazin e.com. Website: www.bostonmagazine.com. **Contact:** Jon Marcus, editor. **10% freelance written.** Monthly magazine covering the city of Boston. Estab. 1962. Circ. 125,000. Pays on publication. Publishes ms an average of 3 months after acceptance. Byline given. Offers 20% kill fee. Buys first North American serial rights. Editorial lead time 2 months. Submit seasonal material 4 months in advance. Accepts queries by mail, fax. Responds in 2 weeks to queries.

Nonfiction Book excerpts, exposé, general interest, interview/profile, politics; crime; trends; fashion. **Buys 20 mss/year.** Query. *No unsolicited mss.* Length: 1,200-12,000 words. Pays expenses of writers on assignment.

Photos State availability with submission. Buys one-time rights. Negotiates payment individually.

Columns/Departments Dining, Finance, City Life, Personal Style, Politics, Ivory Tower, Media, Wine, Boston Inc., Books, Theater, Music. Query.

Tips "Read *Boston*, and pay attention to the types of stories we use. Suggest which column/department your story might best fit, and keep your focus on the city and its environs. We like a strong narrative style, with a slightly 'edgy' feel—we rarely do 'remember when' stories. Think *city* magazine."

$ $ PROVINCETOWN ARTS

Provincetown Arts, Inc., 650 Commercial St., P.O. Box 35, Provincetown MA 02657. (508)487-3167. Fax: (508)487-3559. E-mail: cbusa@comcast.net. Website: www.provincetownarts.org. **Contact:** Christopher Busa, editor. **90% freelance written.** Annual magazine covering contemporary art and writing. "*Provincetown Arts* focuses broadly on the artists and writers who inhabit or visit the Lower Cape, and seeks to stimulate creative activity and enhance public awareness of the cultural life of the nation's oldest continuous art colony. Drawing upon a 75-year tradition rich in visual art, literature, and theater, *Provincetown Arts* offers a unique blend of interviews, fiction, visual features, reviews, reporting, and poetry." Estab. 1985. Circ. 8,000. Pays on publication. Publishes ms an average of 4 months after acceptance. Offers 50% kill fee. Buys first, one-time, second serial (reprint) rights. Editorial lead time 6 months. Submit seasonal material 6 months in advance. Accepts simultaneous submissions. Responds in 3 weeks to queries; 2 months to mss. Sample copy for $10. Writer's guidelines for #10 SASE.

Nonfiction Book excerpts, essays, humor, interview/profile. **Buys 40 mss/year.** Send complete ms. Length: 1,500-4,000 words. **Pays $150 minimum for assigned articles; $125 minimum for unsolicited articles.**

Photos Send photos with submission. Reviews 8×10 prints. Buys one-time rights. Offers $20-$100/photo. Identification of subjects required.

Fiction Mainstream, novel excerpts. **Buys 7 mss/year.** Send complete ms. Length: 500-5,000 words. **Pays $75-300.**

Poetry Buys 25 poems/year. Submit maximum 3 poems. **Pays $25-150.**

MICHIGAN

$ $ $ ANN ARBOR OBSERVER

Ann Arbor Observer Co., 201 E. Catherine, Ann Arbor MI 48104. Fax: (734)769-3375. E-mail: hilton@aaobserver .com. Website: www.arborweb.com. **Contact:** John Hilton, editor. **50% freelance written.** Monthly magazine. "We depend heavily on freelancers and we're always glad to talk to new ones. We look for the intelligence and judgment to fully explore complex people and situations, and the ability to convey what makes them interesting." Estab. 1976. Circ. 63,000. Pays on publication. Publishes ms an average of 2 months after acceptance. Byline given. Accepts queries by mail, e-mail, fax, phone. Responds in 3 weeks to queries; several months to mss. Sample copy for 12½×15 SAE with $3 postage. Writer's guidelines for #10 SASE.

Nonfiction Historical, investigative features, profiles, brief vignettes. Must pertain to Ann Arbor. **Buys 75 mss/ year.** Length: 100-7,000 words. **Pays up to $1,000.** Sometimes pays expenses of writers on assignment.

Columns/Departments Up Front (short, interesting tidbits), 150 words. **Pays $75.** Inside Ann Arbor (concise stories), 300-500 words. **Pays $150.** Around Town (unusual, compelling ancedotes), 750-1,500 words. **Pays $150-200.**

Tips "If you have an idea for a story, write a 100-200-word description telling us why the story is interesting. We are open most to intelligent, insightful features of up to 5,000 words about interesting aspects of life in Ann Arbor."

ℕ $ $ GRAND RAPIDS MAGAZINE

Gemini Publications, 549 Ottawa Ave. NW, Suite 201, Grand Rapids MI 49503-1444. (616)459-4545. Fax: (616)459-4800. E-mail: cvalade@geminipub.com. Website: www.grmag.com. **Contact:** Carole Valade, editor. "*Grand Rapids* is a general interest life and style magazine designed for those who live in the Grand Rapids metropolitan area or desire to maintain contact with the community." Estab. 1964. Pays on publication. Byline given. Editorial lead time 2 months. Submit seasonal material 2 months in advance. Sample copy for $2 and an SASE with $1.50 postage. Writer's guidelines for #10 SASE.

Nonfiction "*Grand Rapids Magazine* is approximately 60 percent service articles—dining guide, calendar, travel, personal finance, humor and reader service sections—and 40 percent topical and issue-oriented editorial that centers on people, politics, problems and trends in the region. In 2003, the editors added a section called 'Design,' which provides a focus on every aspect of the local design community—from Maya Lin's urban park installation and the new 125-acre sculpture park to architecture and the world's Big Three office furniture manufacturers headquartered here." Query. **Pays $25-500.**

HOUR DETROIT

Hour Media, LLC, 117 W. Third St., Royal Oak MI 48067. (248)691-1800. Fax: (248)691-4531. E-mail: editorial@ hourdetroit.com. Website: www.hourdetroit.com. Managing Editor: George Bulanda. Senior Editor: Rebecca Powers. **Contact:** Ric Bohy, editor. **50% freelance written.** Monthly magazine. "General interest/lifestyle magazine aimed at a middle- to upper-income readership aged 17-70." Estab. 1996. Circ. 45,000. **Pays on acceptance.** Publishes ms an average of 2 months after acceptance. Byline given. Offers 30% kill fee. Buys first North American serial rights. Editorial lead time 6 weeks. Submit seasonal material 1 year in advance. Accepts queries by mail, e-mail, fax. Sample copy for $6.

Nonfiction Book excerpts, exposé, general interest, historical/nostalgic, interview/profile, new product, photo feature, technical. **Buys 150 mss/year.** Query with published clips. Length: 300-2,500 words. Sometimes pays expenses of writers on assignment.

Photos State availability with submission.

ℕ $ $ MICHIGAN HISTORY

Michigan Historical Center, Michigan Dept. of History, Arts & Libraries, 702 W. Kalamazoo, Box 30741, Lansing MI 48909-8241. (800)366-3703. Fax: (517)241-4909. E-mail: editor@michigan.gov. Website: www.michiganhist orymagazine.com. Editor: Roger Rosentreter. **75% freelance written.** Bimonthly magazine covering Michigan history. "We want historical accuracy on Michigan-related content." Estab. 1917. Circ. 30,000. Pays on publication. Publishes ms an average of 16 months after acceptance. Byline given. Buys one-time, electronic rights. Editorial lead time 1 year. Submit seasonal material 1 year in advance. Accepts queries by mail, e-mail, phone. Responds in 3 months to queries; 6 months to mss. Sample copy for free. Writer's guidelines free.

Nonfiction C. Damstra, assistant editor. Book excerpts, general interest, historical/nostalgic, interview/profile, personal experience, photo feature. Nothing already published, fictional. **Buys 20-24 mss/year.** Send complete ms. Length: 1,000-10,000 words. **Pays $100-500.** Sometimes pays expenses of writers on assignment.

Photos C. Schwein, assistant editor. State availability with submission. Reviews contact sheets, negatives, transparencies, prints, GIF/JPEG files. Buys one-time and electronic use rights. Negotiates payment individually. Identification of subjects, model releases required.

Columns/Departments Remember the Time (personal account of historical event, person, experience), 500-2,000 words. **Buys 5 mss/year.** Send complete ms. **Pays $100-400.**

Tips "Send complete manuscripts, including photocopies of photos to use as illustrations. Be historically accurate, interesting, and informative."

$ $ TRAVERSE

Northern Michigan's Magazine, Prism Publications, 148 E. Front St., Traverse City MI 49684. (231)941-8174. Fax: (231)941-8391. E-mail: traverse@traversemagazine.com. Website: www.traversemagazine.com. **20% freelance written.** Monthly magazine covering northern Michigan life. *"Traverse* is a celebration of the life and environment of northern Michigan." Estab. 1981. Circ. 30,000. **Pays on acceptance.** Byline given. Offers 10% kill fee. Buys first North American serial rights. Editorial lead time 1 year. Submit seasonal material 1 year in advance. Accepts queries by mail, e-mail, fax, phone. Accepts simultaneous submissions. Responds in 2 months to queries. Sample copy for $3. Writer's guidelines for #10 SASE.

Nonfiction Book excerpts, essays, general interest, historical/nostalgic, humor, interview/profile, personal experience, photo feature, travel. No fiction or poetry. **Buys 24 mss/year.** Query with published clips or send complete ms. Length: 1,000-3,200 words. **Pays $150-500.** Sometimes pays expenses of writers on assignment.

Photos State availability with submission. Buys one-time rights. Negotiates payment individually.

Columns/Departments Up in Michigan Reflection (essays about northern Michigan); Reflection on Home (essays about northern homes), both 700 words. **Buys 18 mss/year.** Query with published clips or send complete ms. **Pays $100-200.**

Tips "When shaping an article for us, consider first that it must be strongly rooted in our region. The lack of this foundation element is one of the biggest reasons for our rejecting material. If you send us a piece about peaches, even if it does an admirable job of relaying the history of peaches, their medicinal qualities, their nutritional magnificence, and so on, we are likely to reject if it doesn't include local farms as a reference point. We want sidebars and extended captions designed to bring in a reader not enticed by the main subject. We cover the northern portion of the Lower Peninsula and to a lesser degree the Upper Peninsula. General categories of interest include nature and the environment, regional culture, personalities, the arts (visual, performing, literary), crafts, food & dining, homes, history, and outdoor activities (e.g., fishing, golf, skiing, boating, biking, hiking, birding, gardening). We are keenly interested in environmental and land-use issues but seldom use material dealing with such issues as health care, education, social services, criminal justice, and local politics. We use service pieces and a small number of how-to pieces, mostly focused on small projects for the home or yard. Also, we value research. We need articles built with information. Many of the pieces we reject use writing style to fill in for information voids. Style and voice are strongest when used as vehicles for sound research."

MINNESOTA

$ $ LAKE COUNTRY JOURNAL MAGAZINE

Evergreen Press of Brainerd, 201 W. Laurel St., P.O. Box 465, Brainerd MN 56401. (218)828-6424, ext. 14. Fax: (218)825-7816. E-mail: jodi@lakecountryjournal.com. Website: www.lakecountryjournal.com. **Contact:** Jodi Schwen, editor or Beth Hautala, assistant editor. **90% freelance written.** Bimonthly magazine covering central Minnesota's lake country. "We target a specific geographical niche in central Minnesota. The writer must be familiar with our area. We promote positive family values, foster a sense of community, increase appreciation for our natural and cultural environments, and provide ideas for enhancing the quality of our lives." Estab. 1996. Circ. 14,500. Pays on publication. Publishes ms an average of 6 months after acceptance. Byline given. Offers 25% kill fee. Buys first North American serial, second serial (reprint), electronic rights. Submit seasonal material 1 year in advance. Accepts queries by mail, e-mail. Responds in 2 months to queries; 3 months to mss. Sample copy for $6. Writer's guidelines online.

　　O- Break in by "submitting department length first—they are not scheduled as far in advance as features. Always in need of original fillers."

Nonfiction Essays, general interest, how-to, humor, interview/profile, personal experience, photo feature. "No articles that come from writers who are not familiar with our target geographical location." **Buys 30 mss/year.** Query with or without published clips. Length: 1,000-1,500 words. **Pays $100-175.** Sometimes pays expenses of writers on assignment.

Reprints Accepts previously published submissions.

Photos State availability with submission. Reviews transparencies. Buys one-time rights. Negotiates payment individually. Identification of subjects, model releases required.

Columns/Departments Profile-People from Lake Country, 800 words; Essay, 800 words; Health (topics pertinent to central Minnesota living), 500 words; Family Fun, 500 words. **Buys 40 mss/year.** Query with published clips. **Pays $50-75.**

Fiction Adventure, humorous, mainstream, slice-of-life vignettes, literary, also family fiction appropriate to Lake Country and seasonal fiction. **Buys 6 mss/year.** Length:1,500 words. **Pays $100-175.**

Poetry Free verse. ''Never use rhyming verse, avant-garde, experimental, etc.'' **Buys 20 poems/year.** Submit maximum 4 poems. Length: 8-32 lines. **Pays $25.**

Fillers Anecdotes, short humor. **Buys 20/year.** Length: 100-500 words. **Pays $25.**

Tips ''Most of the people who will read your articles live in the north central Minnesota lakes area. All have some significant attachment to the area. We have readers of various ages, backgrounds, and lifestyles. After reading your article, we hope to have a deeper understanding of some aspect of our community, our environment, ourselves, or humanity in general. Tell us something new. Show us something we didn't see before. Help us grasp the significance of your topic. Use analogies, allusions, and other literary techniques to add color to your writing. Add breadth by making the subject relevant to all readers—especially those who aren't already interested in your subject. Add depth by connecting your subject with timeless insights. If you can do this without getting sappy or didactic or wordy or dull, we're looking for you.''

$ $LAKE SUPERIOR MAGAZINE

Lake Superior Port Cities, Inc., P.O. Box 16417, Duluth MN 55816-0417. (218)722-5002. Fax: (218)722-4096. E-mail: edit@lakesuperior.com. Website: www.lakesuperior.com. **Contact:** Konnie LeMay, editor. **60% freelance written.** Works with a small number of new/unpublished writers each year. Please include phone number and address with e-mail queries. Bimonthly magazine covering contemporary and historic people, places and current events around Lake Superior. Estab. 1979. Circ. 20,000. Pays on publication. Publishes ms an average of 10 months after acceptance. Byline given. Buys first North American serial, second serial (reprint) rights. Submit seasonal material 1 year in advance. Accepts queries by mail, e-mail. Responds in 3 months to queries. Sample copy for $3.95 and 5 first-class stamps. Writer's guidelines for #10 SASE.

Nonfiction Book excerpts, general interest, historical/nostalgic, humor, interview/profile (local), personal experience, photo feature (local), travel (local), city profiles, regional business, some investigative. **Buys 45 mss/year.** Query with published clips. Length: 300-2,200 words. **Pays $60-600.** Sometimes pays expenses of writers on assignment.

Photos ''Quality photography is our hallmark.'' Send photos with submission. Reviews contact sheets, 2x2 and larger transparencies, 4×5 prints. Offers $50/image; $150 for covers. Captions, identification of subjects, model releases required.

Columns/Departments Current events and things to do (for Events Calendar section), less than 300 words; Around The Circle (media reviews; short pieces on Lake Superior; Great Lakes environmental issues; themes, letters and short pieces on events and highlights of the Lake Superior Region); I Remember (nostalgic lake-specific pieces), up to 1,100 words; Life Lines (single personality profile with photography), up to 900 words. Other headings include Destinations, Wild Superior, Lake Superior Living, Heritage, Shipwreck, Chronicle, Lake Superior's Own. **Buys 20 mss/year.** Query with published clips. **Pays $60-90.**

Fiction Ethnic, historic, humorous, mainstream, novel excerpts, slice-of-life vignettes, ghost stories. Must be targeted regionally. ''Wants stories that are Lake Superior related.'' **Buys 2-3 mss/year.** Query with published clips. Length: 300-2,500 words. **Pays $1-125.**

The online magazine carries original content not found in the print edition. Contact: Konnie LeMay, online editor.

Tips ''Well-researched queries are attended to. We actively seek queries from writers in Lake Superior communities. We prefer manuscripts to queries. Provide enough information on why the subject is important to the region and our readers, or why and how something is unique. We want details. The writer must have a thorough knowledge of the subject and how it relates to our region. We prefer a fresh, unused approach to the subject which provides the reader with an emotional involvement. Almost all of our articles feature quality photography, color or black and white. It is a prerequisite of all nonfiction. All submissions should include a *short* biography of author/photographer; mug shot sometimes used. Blanket submissions need not apply.''

MINNESOTA MONTHLY

600 U.S. Trust Bldg., 730 S. Second Ave., Minneapolis MN 55402. (612)371-5800. Fax: (612)371-5801. E-mail: editor@minnesotamonthly.com. Website: www.mnmo.com. **Contact:** Jeff Johnson, editor. **50% freelance written.** ''*Minnesota Monthly* is a regional lifestyle publication written for a sophisticated, well-educated audience living in the Twin Cities area and in greater Minnesota.'' Estab. 1967. Circ. 80,000. **Pays on acceptance.** Accepts queries by mail, e-mail. Writer's guidelines online.

''The Journey column/department (2,000 words) is probably the best break-in spot for freelancers. Submit, in its entirety, a diary or journal of a trip, event, or experience that changed your life. Past journeys: being an actress on a cruise ship, a parent's death, making a movie.''

Nonfiction Regional issues, arts, services, places, people, essays, exposé, general interest, historical/nostalgia, interview/profile, new product, photo feature, travel in Minnesota. ''We want exciting, excellent, compelling writing with a strong Minnesota angle.'' Query with résumé, published clips, and SASE. Length: 1,000-4,000 words. **Payment negotiable.**

Columns/Departments Portrait (photo-driven profile), 360 words; Just Asking (sassy interview with a Minnesota character or celebrity), 900 words; Midwest Traveler, 950-2,000 words; Postcards (chatty notes from Midwest towns), 300 words; Journey (diary/journal of a life-changing experience), 2,000 words. Query with résumé, published clips, and SASE. **Payment negotiable.**

Fiction Fiction in the June issue, and a November fiction contest, The Tamarack Awards.

Tips ''Our readers are bright, artsy, and involved in their communities. Writing should reflect that. Stories must all have a strong Minnesota angle. If you can write well, try us! Familiarize yourself with a few recent issues before you query.''

$ $ $ MPLS. ST. PAUL MAGAZINE

MSP Communications, 220 S. 6th St., Suite 500, Minneapolis MN 55402-4507. (612)339-7571. Fax: (612)339-5806. E-mail: banderson@mspcommunications.com. Website: www.mspmag.com. Editor: Brian Anderson. Managing Editor: Jean Marie Hamilton. Monthly magazine. ''*Mpls. St. Paul Magazine* is a city magazine serving upscale readers in the Minneapolis-St. Paul metro area.'' Pays on publication. Buys all rights. Editorial lead time 3 months. Accepts queries by mail, e-mail, fax. Sample copy for $9.25. Writer's guidelines online.

Nonfiction Book excerpts, essays, exposé, general interest, historical/nostalgic, interview/profile, personal experience, photo feature, travel. **Buys 150 mss/year.** Query with published clips. Length: 750-2,500 words. **Pays 50¢/word for assigned articles.**

MISSOURI

N $ $ KANSAS CITY HOMES & GARDENS

Network Communications, Inc., 5301 W. 75th St., Prairie Village KS 66208. (913)648-5757. Fax: (913)648-5783. E-mail: adarr@kc-hg.com. Website: www.kchomesandgardens.com. Publisher: Keith Sauro. Managing Editor: Andrea Darr. Bimonthly magazine. ''Since 1986, Kansas City residents (mainly women) have embraced a local publication that speaks to them. Their home, lifestyle and family are featured with emphasis on high-quality, upscale decorating, building and living.'' Estab. 1986. Circ. 18,000. Pays on publication. Byline given. Buys one-time rights. Editorial lead time 4 months. Submit seasonal material 4 months in advance. Accepts queries by mail, e-mail, fax. Accepts previously published material. Accepts simultaneous submissions. Responds in 1 month to queries; 1 month to mss. Sample copy for $7.50 or online. Writer's guidelines online.

Nonfiction Travel, home and garden. **Buys 8 mss/year.** Query with published clips. Length: 600-1,000 words. **Pays $100-350.** Sometimes pays expenses of writers on assignment.

Reprints Accepts previously published submissions.

Photos State availability of or send photos with submission. Reviews transparencies. Buys one-time rights. Offers no additional payment for photos accepted with ms. Identification of subjects required.

Columns/Departments Time Away (places to take vacations to), 800 words. Query with published clips. **Pays $100-350.**

Tips ''Really read and understand our audience. Who are they and what do they want?''

KANSAS CITY MAGAZINE

118 Southwest Blvd., 3rd Floor, Kansas City MO 64108. (816)421-4111. Fax: (816)221-8350. Website: www.kcmag.com. **Contact:** Leigh Elmore, editor. **75% freelance written.** Monthly magazine. ''Our mission is to celebrate living in Kansas City. We are a consumer lifestyle/general interest magazine focused on Kansas City, its people and places.'' Estab. 1994. Circ. 31,000. **Pays on acceptance.** Publishes ms an average of 3 months after acceptance. Byline given. Offers 10% kill fee. Buys first North American serial rights. Editorial lead time 4 months. Submit seasonal material 6 months in advance. Accepts queries by mail, e-mail, fax. Accepts simultaneous submissions. Sample copy for 8½×11 SAE or online.

Nonfiction Exposé, general interest, interview/profile, photo feature. **Buys 15-20 mss/year.** Query with published clips. Length: 250-3,000 words.

Photos Buys one-time rights. Negotiates payment individually.

Columns/Departments Entertainment (Kansas City only), 1,000 words; Food (Kansas City food and restaurants only), 1,000 words. **Buys 12 mss/year.** Query with published clips.

$ $ MISSOURI LIFE

Missouri Life, Inc., P.O. Box 421, Fayette MO 65248-0421. (660)248-3489. Fax: (660)248-2310. E-mail: info@missourilife.com. Website: www.missourilife.com. Editor-in-Chief: Danita Allen Wood. **Contact:** Martha M. Everett, managing editor. **85% freelance written.** Bimonthly magazine covering the state of Missouri. ''*Missouri Life*'s readers are mostly college-educated people with a wide range of travel and lifestyle interests. Our magazine discovers the people, places, and events—both past and present—that make Missouri a great place to live and/or visit." Estab. 1973. Circ. 20,000. **Pays on acceptance.** Byline given. Buys all, nonexclusive rights. Editorial lead time 3 months. Submit seasonal material 6 months in advance. Accepts queries by mail, e-mail, fax. Responds in 6 weeks to queries. Writer's guidelines online.

Nonfiction General interest, historical/nostalgic, travel, all Missouri related. Length: 300-2,000 words. **Pays $50-600; 20¢/word.**

Photos State availability in query; buys all rights nonexclusive. Offers $50-150/photo. Captions, identification of subjects, model releases required.

Columns/Departments Best of Missouri (people and places, past and present, written in an almanac style), 300 words; Missouri Artist (features a Missouri artist), 500 words; Made in Missouri (products and businesses native to Missouri), 500 words; Missouri Memory (a personal memory of Missouri gone by), 500 words; Missouri Hands (crafts and other items by Missouri craftspeople that don't fall into 'fine art' category), 500 words.

$ RIVER HILLS TRAVELER

Todd Publishing, Route 4, Box 4396, Piedmont MO 63957. (573)223-7143. Fax: (573)223-2117. E-mail: btodd@ri verhillstraveler.com. Website: www.riverhillstraveler.com. **Contact:** Bob Todd, online editor. **50% freelance written.** Monthly tabloid covering "outdoor sports and nature in the southeast quarter of Missouri, the east and central Ozarks. Topics like those in *Field & Stream* and *National Geographic*." Estab. 1973. Circ. 7,500. Pays on publication. Publishes ms an average of 2 months after acceptance. Byline given. Buys one-time rights. Editorial lead time 2 months. Submit seasonal material 1 year in advance. Accepts queries by e-mail. Accepts simultaneous submissions. Responds in 2 months to queries. Sample copy for SAE or online. Writer's guidelines online.

Nonfiction Historical/nostalgic, how-to, humor, opinion, personal experience, photo feature, technical, travel. "No stories about other geographic areas." **Buys 80 mss/year.** Query with writing samples. Length: 1,500 word maximum. **Pays $15-50.** Sometimes pays expenses of writers on assignment.

Reprints Send ms with rights for sale noted and information about when and where the material previously appeared.

Photos Send photos with submission. Buys one-time rights. Negotiates payment individually. Pays $25 for covers.

The online magazine carries original content not found in the print edition and includes writer's guidelines. Contact: Bob Todd, online editor.

Tips "We are a 'poor man's' *Field & Stream* and *National Geographic*—about the eastern Missouri Ozarks. We prefer stories that relate an adventure that causes a reader to relive an adventure of his own or consider embarking on a similar adventure. Think of an adventure in camping or cooking, not just fishing and hunting. How-to is great, but not simple instructions. We encourage good first-person reporting."

$ $ SPRINGFIELD! MAGAZINE

Springfield Communications, Inc., P.O. Box 4749, Springfield MO 65808-4749. (417)882-4917. **Contact:** Robert Glazier, editor. **85% freelance written.** Eager to work with a small number of new/unpublished writers each year. "This is an extremely local and provincial monthly magazine. No *general* interest articles." Estab. 1979. Circ. 10,000. Pays on publication. Publishes ms an average of 3-24 months after acceptance. Byline given. First serial rights. Submit seasonal material 1 year in advance. Responds in 3 months to queries; 6 months to mss. Sample copy for $5.30 and 9½×12½ SAE.

Nonfiction Local interest *only*; no material that could appeal to other magazines elsewhere. Book excerpts (Springfield authors only), exposé (local topics only), historical/nostalgic (top priority, but must be local history), how-to, humor, interview/profile (needs more on females than males), personal experience, photo feature, travel (1 page/month). **Buys 150 mss/year.** Query with published clips by mail only or send complete ms with SASE. Length: 500-3,000 words. **Pays $35-250 for assigned articles.**

Photos Send photos with query or ms. "Needs more photo features of a nostalgic bent." Reviews contact sheets, 4×6 color, 5×7 b&w glossy prints. Buys one-time rights. Pays $5-$35 for b&w, $10-50 for color. Captions, identification of subjects, model releases required.

Columns/Departments Length varies, usually 500-2,500 words. **Buys 150 mss/year.** Query by mail or send complete ms.

Tips "We prefer writers read 8 or 10 copies of our magazine prior to submitting any material for our consideration. The magazine's greatest need is for features which comment on these times in Springfield. We are overstocked with nostalgic pieces right now. We also need profiles about young women and men of distinction."

MONTANA

$ $ MONTANA MAGAZINE

Lee Enterprises, P.O. Box 5630, Helena MT 59604-5630. Fax: (406)443-5480. E-mail: editor@montanamagazine. com. Website: www.montanamagazine.com. **Contact:** Beverly R. Magley, editor. **90% freelance written.** Bimonthly magazine. "Strictly Montana-oriented magazine that features community profiles, contemporary issues, wildlife and natural history, travel pieces." Estab. 1970. Circ. 40,000. Publishes ms an average of 1 year after acceptance. Byline given. Buys one-time rights. Submit seasonal material 1 year in advance. Accepts simultaneous submissions. Responds in 6 months to queries. Sample copy for $5 or online. Writer's guidelines online.

• Accepts queries by e-mail. No phone calls.

Nonfiction Query by September for summer material; March for winter material. Essays, general interest, interview/profile, photo feature, travel. Special issues: Special features on summer and winter destination points. No 'me and Joe' hiking and hunting tales; no blood-and-guts hunting stories; no poetry; no fiction; no sentimental essays. **Buys 30 mss/year.** Query with samples and SASE. Length: 300-3,000 words. **Pays 20¢/word.** Sometimes pays expenses of writers on assignment.

Reprints Send photocopy of article with rights for sale noted and information about when and where the material previously appeared. Pays 50% of amount paid for an original article.

Photos Send photos with submission. Reviews contact sheets, 35mm or larger format transparencies, 5×7 prints. Buys one-time rights. Offers additional payment for photos accepted with ms. Captions, identification of subjects, model releases required.

Columns/Departments Memories (reminisces of early-day Montana life), 800-1,000 words; Outdoor Recreation, 1,500-2,000 words; Community Festivals, 500 words, plus b&w or color photo; Montana-Specific Humor, 800-1,000 words. Query with samples and SASE.

Tips "We avoid commonly known topics so Montanans won't ho-hum through more of what they already know. If it's time to revisit a topic, we look for a unique slant."

NEVADA

$ $ NEVADA MAGAZINE

401 N. Carson St., Carson City NV 89701-4291. (775)687-5416. Fax: (775)687-6159. E-mail: editor@nevadamagazine.com. Website: www.nevadamagazine.com. Editor: David Moore. **Contact:** Joyce Hollister, associate editor. **50% freelance written.** Works with a small number of new/unpublished writers each year. Bimonthly magazine published by the state of Nevada to promote tourism. Estab. 1936. Circ. 80,000. Pays on publication. Publishes ms an average of 8 months after acceptance. Byline given. Buys first North American serial rights. Submit seasonal material 6 months in advance. Accepts queries by mail, e-mail. Responds in 1 month to queries.

○→ Break in with shorter departments, rather than trying to tackle a big feature. Good bets are Dining Out, Recreation, Casinoland, Side Trips, and Roadside Attractions.

Nonfiction "We welcome stories and photos on speculation." Nevada topics only. Historical/nostalgic, humor, interview/profile, personal experience, photo feature, travel, recreational, think pieces. **Buys 40 unsolicited mss/year.** Send complete ms or query. Length: 500-1,800 words. **Pays $50-500.**

Photos Send photo material with accompanying ms. Name, address, and caption should appear on each photo or slide. Also accepts 300 dpi JPEG files. Denise Barr, art director. Buys one-time rights. Pays $20-100 for color transparencies and glossy prints.

Tips "Keep in mind the magazine's purpose is to promote Nevada tourism. Keys to higher payments are quality and editing effort (more than length). Send cover letter; no photocopies. We look for a light, enthusiastic tone of voice without being too cute; articles bolstered by facts and thorough research; and unique angles on Nevada subjects."

NEW HAMPSHIRE

$ $ NEW HAMPSHIRE MAGAZINE

McLean Communications, Inc., 150 Dow St., Manchester NH 03101. (603)624-1442. E-mail: editor@nhmagazine.com. Website: www.nhmagazine.com. **Contact:** Rick Broussard, editor. **50% freelance written.** Monthly magazine devoted to New Hampshire. "We want stories written for, by, and about the people of New Hampshire with emphasis on qualities that set us apart from other states. We feature lifestyle, adventure, and home-related stories with a unique local angle." Estab. 1986. Circ. 24,000. Pays on publication. Byline given. Offers 25% kill fee. Buys all rights. Editorial lead time 3 months. Submit seasonal material 3 months in advance. Accepts queries by mail, e-mail, fax. Accepts simultaneous submissions. Responds in 2 months to queries; 3 months to mss. Writer's guidelines online. Editorial calendar online.

Nonfiction Essays, general interest, historical/nostalgic, photo feature, business. **Buys 30 mss/year.** Query with published clips. Length: 800-2,000 words. **Pays $50-300.** Sometimes pays expenses of writers on assignment.

Photos State availability with submission. Rights purchased vary. Possible additional payment for photos accepted with ms. Captions, identification of subjects, model releases required.

▣ The online magazine carries original content not found in the print edition. Contact: Rick Broussard, online editor.

Tips Network Publications publishes 1 monthly magazine entitled *New Hampshire Magazine* and a "specialty" publication called *Destination New Hampshire*. "In general, our articles deal with the people of New Hampshire—their lifestyles and interests. We also present localized stories about national and international issues, ideas, and trends. We will only use stories that show our readers how these issues have an impact on their daily lives. We cover a wide range of topics, including healthcare, politics, law, real-life dramas, regional history, medical issues, business, careers, environmental issues, the arts, the outdoors, education, food, recreation, etc. Many of our readers are what we call 'The New Traditionalists'—aging Baby Boomers who have embraced solid American values and contemporary New Hampshire lifestyles."

NEW JERSEY

$ $ NEW JERSEY SAVVY LIVING

CTB, LLC, P.O. Box 607, Short Hills NJ 07078-0607. (973)379-7749. Fax: (973)379-4116. E-mail: njsavvyliving@ ctbintl.com. Website: www.njsavvyliving.com. **90% freelance written.** Magazine published 5 times/year covering New Jersey residents with affluent lifestyles. "*Savvy* is a regional magazine for an upscale audience, ages 35-65. We focus on lifestyle topics such as decorating, fashion, people, travel, and gardening." Estab. 1997. Circ. 60,000. Pays on publication. Publishes ms an average of 3 months after acceptance. Byline given. Offers $50 kill fee. variable rights. Editorial lead time 3 months. Accepts queries by mail. Accepts previously published material. Accepts simultaneous submissions. Response time varies to queries. Sample copy for 9 × 12 SAE.

Nonfiction General interest, historical/nostalgic, how-to, humor, inspirational, interview/profile, photo feature, travel, home/decorating. Special issues: Home (April). No investigative, fiction, personal experience, and non-New Jersey topics (excluding travel). **Buys 50 mss/year.** Query with published clips. Length: 900-2,000 words. **Pays $250-500.**

Reprints Accepts previously published submissions (nonconflicting markets only)

Photos State availability with submission. Reviews contact sheets, negatives, transparencies, prints. Buys one-time rights. Offers no additional payment for photos accepted with ms. Captions, identification of subjects, model releases required.

Columns/Departments Wine & Spirits (wine trends); Savvy Shoppers (inside scoop on buying); Intrepid Diner (restaurant review); Home Gourmet (from food to hostess gifts at home), all 900-1,000 words. **Buys 25 mss/ year.** Query with published clips. **Pays $250.**

Fillers Facts, newsbreaks. Length: 125-250 words. **Pays $25-50.**

Tips "Offer ideas of interest to an upscale New Jersey readership. We love articles that utilize local sources and are well focused. Trends are always a good bit, so come up with a hot idea and make us believe you can deliver."

$ $ THE SANDPAPER

Newsmagazine of the Jersey Shore, The SandPaper, Inc., 1816 Long Beach Blvd., Surf City NJ 08008-5461. (609)494-5900. Fax: (609)494-1437. E-mail: letters@thesandpaper.net. **Contact:** Jay Mann, managing editor (jaymann@thesandpaper.net). **10% freelance written.** Weekly tabloid covering subjects of interest to Jersey shore residents and visitors. "*The SandPaper* publishes 2 editions covering many of the Jersey Shore's finest resort communities including Long Beach Island and Ocean City, New Jersey. Each issue includes a mix of news, human interest features, opinion columns, and entertainment/calendar listings." Estab. 1976. Circ. 60,000. Pays on publication. Publishes ms an average of 1 month after acceptance. Byline given. Offers 100% kill fee. Buys first, all rights. Submit seasonal material 3 months in advance. Accepts queries by mail, e-mail, fax, phone. Accepts simultaneous submissions. Responds in 1 month to queries. Sample copy for 9 × 12 SAE with 8 first-class stamps.

○┓ "The opinion page and columns are most open to freelancers." Send SASE for return of ms.

Nonfiction Must pertain to New Jersey shore locale. Essays, general interest, historical/nostalgic, humor, opinion, arts, entertaining news, reviews; also environmental submissons relating to the ocean, wetlands, and pinelands. **Buys 10 mss/year.** Send complete ms. Length: 200-2,000 words. **Pays $25-200.** Sometimes pays expenses of writers on assignment.

Reprints Send photocopy and information about when and where the material previously appeared. Pays 25-50% of amount paid for an original article.

Photos Send photos with submission. Buys one-time or all rights. Offers $8-25/photo.

Columns/Departments Speakeasy (opinion and slice-of-life, often humorous); Commentary (forum for social science perspectives); both 1,000-1,500 words, preferably with local or Jersey Shore angle. **Buys 50 mss/year.** Send complete ms. **Pays $30.**

Tips "Anything of interest to sun worshippers, beach walkers, nature watchers, and water sports lovers is of potential interest to us. There is an increasing coverage of environmental issues. We are steadily increasing the amount of entertainment-related material in our publication. Articles on history of the shore area are always in demand.''

NEW MEXICO

$ $ NEW MEXICO MAGAZINE

Lew Wallace Bldg., 495 Old Santa Fe Trail, Santa Fe NM 87501. (505)827-7447. Website: www.nmmagazine.com. Editor-in-Chief: Emily Drabanski. Associate Publisher: Jon Bowman. Senior Editor: Walter K. Lopez. Associate Editor/Photo Editor: Steve Larese. Book Editor: Carol Kay. **Contact:** Any editor. Monthly magazine emphasizing New Mexico for a college-educated readership with above-average income and interest in the Southwest. Estab. 1923. Circ. 120,000. **Pays on acceptance.** Publishes ms an average of 8 months after acceptance. Buys first North American serial rights. Submit seasonal material 1 year in advance. Accepts queries by mail. Accepts previously published material. Responds in 2 months to queries. Sample copy for $3.95. Writer's guidelines for SASE.

Nonfiction New Mexico subjects of interest to travelers. Historical, cultural, informational articles. ''We are looking for more short, light and bright stories for the 'Poquito Mas' section. Also, we are buying 12 mss per year for our Makin Tracks series.'' Send those submissions to Steve Larese. **Buys 7-10 mss/issue.** General interest, historical/nostalgic, interview/profile, travel. ''No columns, cartoons, poetry or non-New Mexico subjects.'' Query by mail with 3 published writing samples. No phone or fax queries. Length: 250-1,500 words. **Pays $100-600.**

Reprints Rarely publishes reprints but sometimes publishes excerpts from novels and nonfiction books.

Photos Purchased as portfolio or on assignment. ''Photographers interested in photo assignments should send tearsheets to photo editor Steve Larese; slides or transparencies with complete caption information are accepted. Photographers name and telephone number should be affixed to the image mount.'' Buys one-time rights. Captions, model releases required.

Tips ''Your best bet is to write a fun, lively short feature (200-250 words) for our Poquito Mas section that is a superb short manuscript on a little-known person, aspect of history or place to see in New Mexico. Faulty research will ruin a writer's chances for the future. Good style, good grammar. No generalized odes to the state or the Southwest. No sentimentalized, paternalistic views of Indians or Hispanics. No glib, gimmicky 'travel brochure' writing. No first-person vacation stories. We're always looking for well-researched pieces on unusual aspects of New Mexico and lively writing.''

NEW YORK

$ $ ADIRONDACK LIFE

P.O. Box 410, Jay NY 12941-0410. (518)946-2191. Fax: (518)946-7461. E-mail: aledit@adirondacklife.com. Website: www.adirondacklife.com. **Contact:** Mary Thill and Galen Crane, co-editors. **70% freelance written.** Prefers to work with published/established writers. Magazine published 8 issues/year, including special Annual Outdoor Guide, emphasizes the Adirondack region and the North Country of New York State in articles covering outdoor activities, history, and natural history directly related to the Adirondacks. Estab. 1970. Circ. 50,000. Pays 2-3 months after acceptance. Publishes ms an average of 6 months after acceptance. Byline given. Buys first North American serial, web rights. Submit seasonal material 1 year in advance. Accepts queries by mail, e-mail. Sample copy for $3 and 9×12 SAE. Writer's guidelines online. Editorial calendar online.

O─┐ ''For new writers, the best way to break in to the magazine is through departments.''

Nonfiction ''*Adirondack Life* attempts to capture the unique flavor and ethos of the Adirondack mountains and North Country region through feature articles directly pertaining to the qualities of the area.'' Special issues: Outdoors (May); Single-topic Collector's issue (September). **Buys 20-25 unsolicited mss/year.** Query with published clips. Length: 2,500-5,000 words. **Pays 25¢/word.** Sometimes pays expenses of writers on assignment.

Photos All photos must have been taken in the Adirondacks. Each issue contains a photo feature. Purchased with or without ms on assignment. All photos must be individually identified as to the subject or locale and must bear the photographer's name. Send photos with submission. Reviews color transparencies, b&w prints. Pays $150 for full page, b&w, or color; $400 for cover (color only, vertical in format). Credit line given.

Columns/Departments Special Places (unique spots in the Adirondack Park); Watercraft; Barkeater (personal to political essays); Wilderness (environmental issues); Working (careers in the Adirondacks); Home; Yesteryears; Kitchen; Profile; Historic Preservation; Sporting Scene. Length: 1,200-2,400 words. Query with published clips. **Pays 25¢/word.**

Fiction Considers first-serial novel excerpts in its subject matter and region.

Tips "Do not send a personal essay about your meaningful moment in the mountains. We need factual pieces about regional history, sports, culture, and business. We are looking for clear, concise, well-organized manuscripts that are strictly Adirondack in subject. Check back issues to be sure we haven't already covered your topic. Please do not send unsolicited manuscripts via e-mail. Check out our guidelines online."

$BEYOND THE BADGE

47-01 Greenpoint Ave., #114, Sunnyside NY 11104-1709. (347)723-6287. Fax: (360)242-0811. E-mail: badgemag @yahoo.com. **Contact:** Liz Martinez, editor. Quarterly magazine. *Beyond the Badge* is distributed to police officers, peace officers, federal agents, corrections officers, auxiliary police officers, probation and parole officers, civilian employees of law enforcement agencies, etc., in the New York metropolitan area. Estab. 2001. Buys one-time rights. Accepts queries by e-mail. Accepts previously published material. Accepts simultaneous submissions. Sample copy for $5, plus a 9×12 SASE. Writer's guidelines by e-mail.

Nonfiction "We are seeking stories on travel; law enforcement product/news; books with a LE hook; movies and other entertainment that our readers would enjoy knowing about; worthy LE-related Internet sites; the latest developments in forensics and technology; health articles with a LE spin; investigation techniques; innovative international, national, regional, or local (inside and outside of the New York area) approaches to LE or crime prevention issues; other topics of interest to our reader population. General interest. "We see too many pieces that are dry and not enjoyable to read. Even if the topic is serious or scientific, present the material as though you were telling a friend about it." Query. Length: 1,000-1,500 words. **Pays $100.**

Photos Photos are very helpful and much appreciated; however, there is no additional pay for photos. Inclusion of photos does increase chances of publication.

Columns/Departments Book'Em (book reviews/excerpts/author interviews); Internet Guide; Screening Room (movie reviews); Your Finances; Management in Focus; Health Department; Forensics Lab; Technology. Query. **Pays $75.**

Tips "Writers should keep in mind that this is a lifestyle magazine whose readers happen to be cops, not a cop magazine with some lifestyle topics in it."

$ $BUFFALO SPREE MAGAZINE

David Laurence Publications, Inc., 6215 Sheridan Dr., Buffalo NY 14221. (716)634-0820. Fax: (716)810-0075. E-mail: info@buffalospree.com. Website: www.buffalospree.com. **Contact:** Elizabeth Licata, editor. **90% freelance written.** City regional magazine published 8 times/year. Estab. 1967. Circ. 25,000. Pays on publication. Publishes ms an average of 1 month after acceptance. Byline given. Buys first North American serial rights. Accepts queries by mail, e-mail, fax. Responds in 6 months to queries. Sample copy for $3.95 and 9×12 SAE with 9 first-class stamps.

Nonfiction "Most articles are assigned not unsolicited." Interview/profile, travel, issue-oriented features, arts, living, food, regional. Query with résumé and published clips. Length: 1,000-2,000 words. **Pays $125-250.**

Tips "Send a well-written, compelling query or an interesting topic, and *great* clips. We no longer regularly publish fiction or poetry. Prefers material that is Western New York related."

$ $ $CITY LIMITS

New York's Urban Affairs News Magazine, City Limits Community Information Service, 120 Wall St., 20th Floor, New York NY 10005. (212)479-3344. Fax: (212)344-6457. E-mail: citylimits@citylimits.org. Website: www.citylimits.org. **Contact:** Alyssa Katz, editor. **50% freelance written.** Monthly magazine covering urban politics and policy. "*City Limits* is a 27-year-old nonprofit magazine focusing on issues facing New York City and its neighborhoods, particularly low-income communities. The magazine is strongly committed to investigative journalism, in-depth policy analysis and hard-hitting profiles." Estab. 1976. Circ. 4,000. Pays on publication. Publishes ms an average of 3 months after acceptance. Byline given. Offers 50% kill fee. Buys first North American serial, second serial (reprint) rights. Editorial lead time 2 months. Accepts queries by mail, e-mail, fax. Accepts simultaneous submissions. Sample copy for $2.95. Writer's guidelines free.

Nonfiction Book excerpts, exposé, humor, interview/profile, opinion, photo feature. No essays, polemics. **Buys 25 mss/year.** Query with published clips. Length: 400-3,500 words. **Pays $100-1,200 for assigned articles; $100-800 for unsolicited articles.** Pays expenses of writers on assignment.

Photos State availability with submission. Reviews contact sheets, negatives, transparencies. Offers $50-100/ photo.

Columns/Departments Making Change (nonprofit business); Big Idea (policy news); Book Review, all 800 words; Urban Legend (profile); First Hand (Q&A), both 350 words. **Buys 15 mss/year.** Query with published clips. **Pays $100-200.**

Tips "*City Limits*' specialty is covering low-income communities. We want to know how the news of the day is going to affect neighborhoods—at the grassroots. Among the issues we're looking for stories about housing, health care, criminal justice, child welfare, education, economic development, welfare reform, politics and government.''

N $ $ $ HUDSON VALLEY

Today Media, Inc., 22 IBM Rd., Suite 108, Poughkeepsie NY 12601. (845)463-0542. Fax: (845)463-1544. E-mail: rsparling@hvmag.com. Website: www.hudsonvalleymagazine.com. **Contact:** Reed Sparling, editor-in-chief. Monthly magazine for residents of the Hudson Valley. Byline given. Offers 25% kill fee. Buys first North American serial rights. Accepts queries by mail, e-mail. Accepts simultaneous submissions. Responds in 3 months to queries. Sample copy for free. Writer's guidelines for #10 SASE.

Nonfiction Buys 50-80 mss/year. Query with published clips. Length: 200-5,000 words. **Pays $500-800/feature, $50-250/department article, $25-75/short piece.**

N IN NEW YORK

Primedia Broad Reach Magazines, 261 Madison Ave., 9th Floor, New York NY 10016. (212)716-8562. E-mail: trisha.drain@in-newyorkmag.com. Website: www.in-newyorkmag.com. Editor: Trisha McMahon Drain. Monthly magazine. Created exclusively for sophisticated travelers to the New York Metropolitian area and distributed at most hotels, tourist centers and popular sights. Circ. 125,000. Sample copy not available.

$ $ $ $ NEW YORK MAGAZINE

Primedia Magazines, 444 Madison Ave., 14th Floor, New York NY 10022. Website: www.newyorkmetro.com. **Contact:** Sarah Jewler, managing editor. **25% freelance written.** Weekly magazine focusing on current events in the New York metropolitan area. Circ. 433,813. **Pays on acceptance.** Offers 25% kill fee. Buys electronic rights. First World Serial Submit seasonal material 2 months in advance. Responds in 1 month to queries. Sample copy for $3.50 or on website. Writer's guidelines not available.

Nonfiction New York-related journalism that covers lifestyle, politics and business. Query by mail. **Pays $1/ word.** Pays expenses of writers on assignment.

$ $ SYRACUSE NEW TIMES

A. Zimmer, Ltd., 1415 W. Genesee St., Syracuse NY 13204. Fax: (315)422-1721. E-mail: editorial@syracusenewti mes.com. Website: newtimes.rway.com. **Contact:** Molly English, editor. **50% freelance written.** Weekly tabloid covering news, sports, arts, and entertainment. *"Syracuse New Times* is an alternative weekly that can be topical, provocative, irreverent, and intensely local.'' Estab. 1969. Circ. 46,000. Pays on publication. Publishes ms an average of 1 month after acceptance. Byline given. Buys one-time rights. Editorial lead time 3 months. Submit seasonal material 3 months in advance. Accepts simultaneous submissions. Responds in 2 weeks to queries; 1 month to mss. Sample copy for 9×12 SAE and 2 first-class stamps. Writer's guidelines for #10 SASE.

Nonfiction Essays, general interest. **Buys 200 mss/year.** Query by mail with published clips. Length: 250-2,500 words. **Pays $25-200.**

Photos State availability of or send photos with submission. Reviews 8×10 prints, color slides. Buys one-time rights. Offers $10-25/photo or negotiates payment individually. Identification of subjects required.

Tips "Move to Syracuse and query with strong idea.''

TIME OUT NEW YORK

Time Out New York Partners, LP, 475 10th Ave., 12th Floor, New York NY 10018. (646)432-3000. Fax: (646)432-3160. E-mail: letters@timeoutny.com. Website: www.timeoutny.com. Editor-in-Chief: Joe Angio. **Contact:** Samina Virani, editorial assistant. **20% freelance written.** Weekly magazine covering entertainment in New York City. *"Those who want to contribute to *Time Out New York* must be intimate with New York City and its environs.''* Estab. 1995. Circ. 120,000. Pays on publication. Publishes ms an average of 1 month after acceptance. Byline sometimes given. Offers 25% kill fee. Makes work-for-hire assignments. Accepts queries by mail, fax, phone. Responds in 2 months to queries.

    ○→ Pitch ideas to the editor of the section to which you would like to contribute (i.e., film, music, dance, etc.). Be sure to include clips or writing samples with your query letter. No unsolicited mss.

Nonfiction Essays, general interest, how-to, humor, interview/profile, new product, travel (primarily within NYC area), reviews of various entertainment topics. No essays, articles about trends, unpegged articles. Query with published clips. Length: 250-1,500 words.

Columns/Departments Around Town (Billie Cohen); Art (Tim Griffin); Books & Poetry (Maureen Shelly); Technology (Adam Wisnieski); Cabaret (H. Scott Jolley); Check Out (Zoe Wolff); Clubs (Bruce Tantum); Comedy (Joe Grossman); Dance (Gia Kourlas); Eat Out (Salma Abdelnour); Film; Gay & Lesbian (Les Simpson); Kids (Barbara Aria); Music: Classical & Opera (Steve Smith); Music: Rock, Jazz, etc. (Elisabeth Vincentelli); Radio (Ian Landau); Sports (Brett Martin); Television (Michael Freidson); Theater (Jason Zinoman); Video (Michael Freidson).

Tips "We're always looking for quirky, less-known news about what's going on in New York City.''

NORTH CAROLINA

$ $ AAA CAROLINAS GO MAGAZINE

6600 AAA Dr., Charlotte NC 28212. Fax: (704)569-7815. Website: www.aaacarolinas.com. Managing Editor: Sarah B. Davis. **Contact:** Tom Crosby, editor. **20% freelance written.** Member publication for the Carolina affiliate of American Automobile Association covering travel, auto-related issues. "We prefer stories that focus on travel and auto safety in North and South Carolina and surrounding states." Estab. 1922. Circ. 750,000. Pays on publication. Byline given. Buys all rights. Editorial lead time 2 months. Accepts queries by mail. Sample copy and writer's guidelines for #10 SASE.

Nonfiction Travel, auto safety. Length:750 words. **Pays $150.**

Photos Send photos with submission. Reviews slides. Buys all rights. Offers no additional payment for photos accepted with ms. Identification of subjects required.

■ The online magazine carries original content not found in the print edition. Contact: Sarah B. Davis.

Tips "Submit regional stories relating to Carolinas travel."

$ $ CHARLOTTE MAGAZINE

Abarta Media, 127 W. Worthington Ave., Suite 208, Charlotte NC 28203. (704)335-7181. Fax: (704)335-3739. E-mail: editor@charlottemag.com. Website: www.charlottemagazine.com. **Contact:** Richard H. Thurmond, editorial director. **75% freelance written.** Monthly magazine covering Charlotte life. "This magazine tells its readers things they didn't know about Charlotte, in an interesting, entertaining, and sometimes provocative style." Circ. 30,000. Pays within 30 days of acceptance. Publishes ms an average of 3 months after acceptance. Byline given. Offers 25% kill fee. Buys first North American serial rights. Editorial lead time 3 months. Submit seasonal material 6 months in advance. Accepts queries by mail, e-mail. Accepts simultaneous submissions. Responds in 6 months to mss. Sample copy for 8 1/2 × 11 SAE and $2.09.

Nonfiction Book excerpts, exposé, general interest, historical/nostalgic, interview/profile, photo feature, travel. **Buys 90-100 mss/year.** Query with published clips. Length: 200-3,000 words. **Pays 20-40¢/word.** Sometimes pays expenses of writers on assignment.

Photos State availability with submission. Buys one-time rights. Negotiates payment individually. Identification of subjects required.

Columns/Departments Buys 35-50 mss/year. **Pays 20-40¢/word.**

Tips "A story for *Charlotte* magazine could only appear in *Charlotte* magazine. That is, the story and its treatment are particularly germane to this area."

$ $ OUR STATE

Down Home in North Carolina, Mann Media, P.O. Box 4552, Greensboro NC 27404. (336)286-0600. Fax: (336)286-0100. E-mail: editorial@ourstate.com. Website: www.ourstate.com. **95% freelance written.** Monthly magazine covering North Carolina. "*Our State* is dedicated to providing editorial about the history, destinations, out-of-the-way places, and culture of North Carolina." Estab. 1933. Circ. 97,000. Pays on publication. Publishes ms an average of 6-24 months after acceptance. Byline given. Buys first North American serial rights. Editorial lead time 4 months. Submit seasonal material 4 months in advance. Accepts queries by mail, fax. Responds in 6 weeks to queries; 2 months to mss. Sample copy for $6. Writer's guidelines for #10 SASE.

Nonfiction Book excerpts, historical/nostalgic, how-to, humor, personal experience, photo feature, travel. **Buys 60 mss/year.** Send complete ms. Length: 1,200-1,500 words. **Pays $300-500 for assigned articles; $50-125 for unsolicited articles.**

Photos State availability with submission. Reviews 35mm or 4 × 6 transparencies. Buys one-time rights. Negotiates payment individually. Pays $15-350/photo, depending on size; $125-50 for photos assigned to accompany specific story; $500 maximum for cover photos. Identification of subjects required.

Columns/Departments Tar Heel Memories (remembering something specific about North Carolina), 1,200 words; Tar Heel Profile (profile of interesting North Carolinian), 1,500 words; Tar Heel Literature (review of books by North Carolina writers and about North Carolina), 300 words. **Buys 40 mss/year.** Send complete ms. **Pays $50-300.**

Tips "We are developing a style for travel stories that is distinctly *Our State*. That style starts with outstanding photographs, which not only depict an area, but interpret it and thus become an integral part of the presentation. Our stories need not dwell on listings of what can be seen. Concentrate instead on the experience of being there, whether the destination is a hiking trail, a bed and breakfast, a forest, or an urban area. What thoughts and feelings did the experience evoke? We want to know why you went there, what you experienced, and what impressions you came away with. With at least 1 travel story an issue, we run a short sidebar called, 'If You're Going.' It explains how to get to the destination; rates or admission costs if there are any; a schedule of when the attraction is open or list of relevant dates; and an address and phone number for readers to write or call for more information. This sidebar eliminates the need for general-service information in the story."

OHIO

$BEND OF THE RIVER MAGAZINE

P.O. Box 859, Maumee OH 43537. (419)893-0022. **Contact:** R. Lee Raizk, publisher. **90% freelance written.** This magazine reports that it is eager to work with new/unpublished writers. "We buy material that we like whether it is by an experienced writer or not." Monthly magazine for readers interested in northwestern Ohio history and nostalgia. Estab. 1972. Circ. 7,500. Pays on publication. Publishes ms an average of 6 months after acceptance. Byline given. Buys one-time rights. Submit seasonal material 2 months in advance. Responds in 1 month to queries. Sample copy for $1.25. Writer's guidelines not available.

Nonfiction "We deal heavily with Northwestern Ohio history and nostalgia. We are looking for old snapshots of the Toledo area to accompany articles, personal reflection, etc." Historical/nostalgic. Special issues: Deadline for holiday issue is November 1. **Buys 75 unsolicited mss/year.** Query with or without published clips or send complete ms. Length: 1,500 words. **Pays $25 on up.**

Reprints Send tearsheet and information about when and where the material previously appeared. Pays 100% of the amount paid for the original article.

Photos Purchases b&w or color photos with accompanying ms. Pays $5 minimum. Captions required.

Tips "Any Toledo area, well-researched nostalgia, local history will be put on top of the heap. If you send a picture with a manuscript, it gets an A+! We pay a small amount but usually use our writers often and through the years. We're loyal."

$ $ $CINCINNATI MAGAZINE

Emmis Publishing Corp., One Centennial Plaza, 705 Central Ave., Suite 175, Cincinnati OH 45202. (513)421-4300. Fax: (513)562-2746. E-mail: editor@cintimag.emmis.com. **Contact:** Linda Vaccariello, executive editor. Monthly magazine emphasising Cincinnati living. Circ. 30,000. Pays on publication. Byline given. Buys all periodical rights. Sample copy not available. Writer's guidelines not available.

Nonfiction Articles on personalities, business, sports, lifestyle relating to Cincinnati and Northern Kentucky. **Buys 12 mss/year.** Query. Length: 2,500-3,500 words. **Pays $500-1,000.**

Columns/Departments Topics are Cincinnati dining, media, arts and entertainment, people, homes, politics, sports. Length: 1,000-1,500 words. **Buys 10-15 mss/year.** Query. **Pays $300-400.**

Tips "Freelancers may find a market in Home section (10 times/year), special advertising sections on varying topics from golf to cardiac care (query Special Projects Managing Editor Elissa Sonneberg). Always query in writing, with clips. All articles have a local focus. No generics, please. Also: No movie, book, theater reviews, poetry, or fiction."

$ $ $CLEVELAND MAGAZINE

City Magazines, Inc., 1422 Euclid Ave., #730Q, Cleveland OH 44115. (216)771-2833. Fax: (216)781-6318. E-mail: editorial@clevelandmagazine.com. Website: www.clevelandmagazine.com. **Contact:** Steve Gleydura, editorial director. **60% freelance written.** Mostly by assignment. Monthly magazine with a strong Cleveland/Northeast Ohio angle. Estab. 1972. Circ. 50,000. Pays on publication. Publishes ms an average of 3 months after acceptance. Byline given. Buys first, second serial (reprint), electronic rights. Editorial lead time 6 months. Submit seasonal material 8 months in advance. Accepts queries by mail, e-mail, fax. Accepts simultaneous submissions. Responds in 2 months to queries. Sample copy not available.

Nonfiction General interest, historical/nostalgic, humor, interview/profile, travel, home and garden. Query with published clips. Length: 800-4,000 words. **Pays $250-1,200.**

Columns/Departments My Town (Cleveland first-person stories), 1,500 words. Query with published clips. **Pays $300.**

$DARKE COUNTY PROFILE

4952 Bishop Rd., Greenville OH 45331. (937)547-0048. E-mail: profile@woh.rr.com. **Contact:** Diana J. Linder, editor. **15% freelance written.** Monthly magazine covering people and places in the Darke County area. Estab. 1994. Circ. 500. Pays on publication. Publishes ms an average of 3-6 months after acceptance. Byline given. Buys one-time rights. Editorial lead time 3 months. Submit seasonal material 3 months in advance. Accepts previously published material. Responds in 3-6 months to mss. Sample copy for $2. Writer's guidelines by e-mail.

Nonfiction General interest, how-to (crafts), humor, inspirational, personal experience, travel. No foul language, graphic violence, or pornography. **Buys 10-12 mss/year.** Send complete ms. Length: 500-1,500 words. **Pays $15-20.** Pays 1-year subscription for work published for the first time in the *Profile*.

Photos Send photos with submission. Buys one-time rights. Pays $3.50/photo. Captions required.

Fiction Adventure, condensed novels, humorous, mainstream, mystery, romance, suspense, western. No violence, foul language, or sexually explicit material. **Buys 12-14 mss/year.** Send complete ms. Length: 500-1,500 words. **Pays $15-20.**

Fillers Anecdotes, facts, short humor. **Buys 6-12/year.** Length: 250-500 words. **Pays $5-10.**

Tips Write tight and send neatly typed mss with a SASE.

$ $ $ NORTHERN OHIO LIVE

LIVE Publishing Co., 11320 Juniper Rd., Cleveland OH 44106. (216)721-1800. Fax: (216)721-2525. E-mail: ssphar@livepub.com. **Contact:** Sarah R. Sphar, managing editor. **70% freelance written.** Monthly magazine covering Northern Ohio politics, arts, entertainment, education, and dining. "Reader demographic is mid-30s to 50s, though we're working to bring in the late 20s. Our readers are well-educated, many with advanced degrees. They're interested in Northern Ohio's cultural scene and support it." Estab. 1980. Circ. 35,000. Pays on 20th of publication month. Publishes ms an average of 1 month after acceptance. Byline given. Offers 33% kill fee. Buys first North American serial rights. Editorial lead time 3 months. Submit seasonal material 4 months in advance. Responds in 3 weeks to queries; 2 months to mss. Sample copy for $3. Writer's guidelines not available.

Nonfiction All submission/pitches should have a Northern Ohio slant. Essays, exposé, general interest, humor, interview/profile, photo feature, travel. Special issues: Gourmet Guide (restaurants) (May). **Buys 100 mss/ year.** Query with published clips. Length: 1,000-3,500 words. **Pays $100-1,000.** Sometimes pays expenses of writers on assignment.

Reprints Send photocopy and information about when and where the material previously appeared.

Photos State availability with submission. Reviews contact sheets, 4×5 transparencies, 3×5 prints. Buys one-time rights. Negotiates payment individually. Identification of subjects required.

Columns/Departments News & Reviews (arts previews, personality profiles, general interest), 800-1,800 words. **Pays $200-300.** Time & Place (personal essay), 400-450 words. **Pays $100.** Must be local authors. **Buys 60-70 mss/year.** Query with published clips.

Fiction Novel excerpts.

Tips "Don't send submissions not having anything to do with Northern Ohio. Must have some tie to the Northeast Quadrant of Ohio. We are not interested in stories appearing in every other outlet in town. What is the new angle?"

$ $ $ $ OHIO MAGAZINE

Great Lakes Publishing Co., 1422 Euclid Ave., Suite 730, Cleveland OH 44115. (216)771-2833. E-mail: editorial@ ohiomagazine.com. Website: www.ohiomagazine.com. **Contact:** Richard Osborne, editorial director. **50% freelance written.** Monthly magazine emphasizing Ohio-based travel, news and feature material that highlights what's special and unique about the state. Estab. 1978. Circ. 80,000. Pays on publication. Publishes ms an average of 6 months after acceptance. Byline given. Buys first North American serial, one-time, second serial (reprint), all rights. First serial rights Submit seasonal material 6 months in advance. Accepts queries by mail, e-mail, fax. Responds in 3 months to queries; 3 months to mss. Sample copy for $3 and 9×12 SAE or online. Writer's guidelines online.

⚏ Break in by "knowing the magazine—read it thoroughly for several issues. Send good clips—that show your ability to write on topics we cover. We're looking for thoughtful stories on topics that are more contextual and less shallow. I want queries that show the writer has some passion for the subject."

Nonfiction Length: 1,000-3,000 words. **Pays $300-1,200.** Sometimes pays expenses of writers on assignment.

Reprints Send tearsheet or photocopy and information about when and where the material previously appeared. Pays 50% of amount paid for an original article.

Photos Rob McGarr, art director. Rate negotiable.

Columns/Departments Length: 100-1,500 words. **Buys minimum 20 unsolicited mss/year. Pays $50-500.**

Tips "Freelancers should send all queries in writing, not by telephone. Successful queries demonstrate an intimate knowledge of the publication. We are looking to increase our circle of writers who can write about the state in an informative and upbeat style. Strong reporting skills are highly valued."

$ $ OVER THE BACK FENCE

Southern Ohio's Own Magazine, Panther Publishing, LLC, P.O. Box 756, Chillicothe OH 45601. (740)772-2165. Fax: (740)773-7626. E-mail: backfenc@bright.net. Website: www.pantherpublishing.com. Sarah Williamson, managing editor. Quarterly magazine. "We are a regional magazine serving 30 counties in Southern Ohio. *Over The Back Fence* has a wholesome, neighborly style. It appeals to readers from young adults to seniors, showcasing art and travel opportunities in the area." Estab. 1994. Circ. 15,000. Pays on publication. Publishes ms an average of 1 year after acceptance. Byline given. Buys one-time North American serial rights, makes work-for-hire assignments. Editorial lead time 1 year. Submit seasonal material 1 year in advance. Accepts queries by mail. Accepts simultaneous submissions. Responds in 3 months to queries. Sample copy for $4 or on website. Writer's guidelines online.

O— Break in with personality profiles (1,000 words), short features, columns (600 words), and features (1,000 words).

Nonfiction General interest, historical/nostalgic, humor, inspirational, interview/profile, personal experience, photo feature, travel. **Buys 9-12 mss/year.** Query with or without published clips or send complete ms. Length: 750-1,000 words. **Pays 10¢/word minimum, negotiable depending on experience.**

Reprints Send photocopy of article or short story and typed ms with rights for sale noted, and information about when and where the material previously appeared. Payment negotiable.

Photos "If sending photos as part of a text/photo package, please request our photo guidelines and submit color transparencies." Reviews color, 35mm or larger transparencies, prints. Buys one-time rights. $25-100/ photo. Captions, identification of subjects, model releases required.

Columns/Departments The Arts, 750-1,000 words; History (relevant to a designated county), 750-1,000 words; Inspirational (poetry or short story), 600-850 words; Profiles From Our Past, 300-600 words; Sport & Hobby, 750-1,000 words; Our Neighbors (i.e., people helping others), 750-1,000 words. All must be relevant to Southern Ohio. **Buys 24 mss/year.** Query with or without published clips or send complete ms. **Pays 10¢/word minimum, negotiable depending on experience.**

Fiction Humorous. **Buys 4 mss/year.** Query with published clips. Length: 600-800 words. **Pays 10¢/word minimum, negotiable depending on experience.**

Poetry Wholesome, traditional free verse, light verse, and rhyming. **Buys 4 poems/year.** Submit maximum 4 poems. Length: 4-32 lines. **Pays 10¢/word or $25 minimum.**

Tips "Our approach can be equated to a friendly and informative conversation with a neighbor about interesting people, places, and events in Southern Ohio (counties: Adams, Athens, Brown, Clark, Clinton, Coshocton, Fayette, Fairfield, Gallia, Greene, Highland, Hocking, Jackson, Lawrence, Meigs, Morgan, Muskingum, Noble, Perry, Pickaway, Pike, Ross, Scioto, Vinton, Warren, and Washington)."

$ $ THE PLAIN DEALER SUNDAY MAGAZINE

Plain Dealer Publishing Co., Plain Dealer Plaza, 1801 Superior Ave., Cleveland OH 44114. (216)999-4546. Fax: (216)515-2039. E-mail: eburbach@plaind.com. **Contact:** Ellen Stein Burbach, editor. **50% freelance written.** Weekly magazine focusing on Cleveland and Northeastern Ohio. Circ. 500,000. Pays on publication. Publishes ms an average of 2 months after acceptance. Byline given. Buys first, one-time, all web rights. Submit seasonal material 2 months in advance. Accepts queries by mail, e-mail, fax. Responds in 1 month to queries; 2 months to mss. Sample copy for $1.

O— "Start small, with 'North by Northeast' pieces."

Nonfiction Must include focus on northeast Ohio people, places, and issues. Book excerpts, essays, exposé, general interest, historical/nostalgic, humor, inspirational, interview/profile, new product, personal experience, photo feature, travel (only personal essays or local ties). **Buys 50-100 (feature) mss/year.** Query with published clips or send complete ms. Length: 800-4,000 words. **Pays $150-700 for assigned articles.**

Reprints Send ms with rights for sale noted and information about when and where the material previously appeared.

Columns/Departments North by Northeast (short upfront pieces), **pays $25-75;** Essays (personal perspective, memoir OK), **pays $200-250,** 900 words maximum; The Back Burner (food essays with recipe), **pays $200.**

Tips "We're always looking for great stories and superior writers."

OKLAHOMA

$ $ OKLAHOMA TODAY

Colcord Bldg., 15 N. Robinson, Suite 100, Oklahoma City OK 73102-5403. (405)521-2496. Fax: (405)522-4588. E-mail: mccune@oklahomatoday.com. Website: www.oklahomatoday.com. **Contact:** Louisa McCune, editor-in-chief. **80% freelance written.** Works with approximately 25 new/unpublished writers each year. Bimonthly magazine covering people, places, and things Oklahoman. "We are interested in showing off the best Oklahoma has to offer; we're pretty serious about our travel slant but regularly run history, nature, and personality profiles." Estab. 1956. Circ. 45,000. Pays on publication. Publishes ms an average of 6 months after acceptance. Byline given. Buys first worldwide serial rights. Submit seasonal material 1 year in advance. Accepts queries by mail, e-mail. Responds in 4 months to queries. Sample copy for $3.95 and 9×12 SASE or online. Writer's guidelines online.

O— "Start small. Look for possibilities for 'The Range.' Even letters to the editor are good ways to 'get some ink.'"

Nonfiction Book excerpts (on Oklahoma topics), historical/nostalgic (Oklahoma only), interview/profile (Oklahomans only), photo feature (in Oklahoma), travel (in Oklahoma). No phone queries. **Buys 20-40 mss/year.** Query with published clips. Length: 250-3,000 words. **Pays $25-750.**

Photos "We are especially interested in developing contacts with photographers who live in Oklahoma or have shot here. Send samples." Photo guidelines for SASE. Reviews 4×5, 2¼:x2¼, and 35mm color transparencies, high-quality transparencies, slides, and b&w prints. Buys one-time rights to use photos for promotional purposes. Pays $50-750 for color. Captions, identification of subjects required.

Fiction Novel excerpts, occasionally short fiction.

Tips "The best way to become a regular contributor to *Oklahoma Today* is to query us with 1 or more story ideas, each developed to give us an idea of your proposed slant. We're looking for lively, concise, well-researched and reported stories, stories that don't need to be heavily edited and are not newspaper style. We have a 3-person full-time editorial staff, and freelancers who can write and have done their homework get called again and again."

OREGON

$ $OREGON COAST

4969 Highway 101 N. #2, Florence OR 97439-0130. (541)997-8401, ext. 123 or (800)348-8401, ext. 123. E-mail: theresa@ohwy.com. Website: www.ohwy.com. **Contact:** Theresa Baer, managing editor. **65% freelance written.** Bimonthly magazine covering the Oregon Coast. Estab. 1982. Circ. 50,000. Pays after publication. Publishes ms an average of up to 1 year after acceptance. Byline given. Offers 33% (on assigned stories only, not on stories accepted on spec) kill fee. Buys first North American serial rights. Submit seasonal material 6 months in advance. Accepts queries by mail, e-mail. Responds in 3 months to queries. Sample copy for $4.50. Writer's guidelines for #10 SASE.

- This company also publishes *Northwest Travel*.
- ❍ Break in with "great photos with a story that has a great lead and no problems during fact-checking. Like stories that have a slightly different take on 'same-old' subjects and have good anecdotes and quotes. Stories should have satisfying endings."

Nonfiction "A true regional with general interest, historical/nostalgic, humor, interview/profile, personal experience, photo feature, travel, and nature as pertains to Oregon Coast." **Buys 55 mss/year.** Query with published clips. Length: 500-1,500 words. **Pays $75-250, plus 2-5 contributor copies.**

Reprints Send tearsheet or photocopy and information about when and where the material previously appeared. Pays an average of 60% of the amount paid for an original article.

Photos Photo submissions with no ms or stand alone or cover photos. Barb Grano, photo editor. Send photos with submission. Reviews 35mm or larger transparencies. Buys one-time. Captions, identification of subjects, model releases (for cover), photo credits required.

Fillers Newsbreaks (no-fee basis).

Tips "Slant article for readers who do not live at the Oregon Coast. At least 1 historical article is used in each issue. Manuscript/photo packages are preferred over manuscripts with no photos. List photo credits and captions for each historic print or color slide. Check all facts, proper names, and numbers carefully in photo/manuscript packages. Must pertain to Oregon Coast somehow."

PENNSYLVANIA

$ $BERKS COUNTY LIVING

West Lawn Graphic Communications, P.O. Box 642, Shillington PA 19607. (610)775-0640. Fax: (610)775-7412. E-mail: kkramer@berkscountyliving.com. Website: www.berkscountyliving.com. **Contact:** Kristin Kramer, editor. **90% freelance written.** Bimonthly magazine covering topics of interest to people living in Berks County, Pennsylvania. Estab. 2000. Circ. 36,000. Pays on publication. Publishes ms an average of 4 months after acceptance. Byline given. Offers 25% kill fee. Buys first North American serial rights. Editorial lead time 6 months. Submit seasonal material 4 months in advance. Accepts queries by mail, e-mail, fax. Accepts previously published material. Accepts simultaneous submissions. Responds in 1 week to queries; 1 month to mss. Sample copy for 9×12 SAE and 2 first-class stamps. Writer's guidelines for #10 SASE. Editorial calendar online.

Nonfiction Articles must be associated with Berks County, Pennsylvania. Exposé, general interest, historical/nostalgic, how-to, humor, inspirational, interview/profile, new product, photo feature, travel, food, health. **Buys 25 mss/year.** Query. Length: 750-2,000 words. **Pays $150-400.** Sometimes pays expenses of writers on assignment.

Reprints Accepts previously published submissions.

Photos State availability with submission. Reviews 35mm or greater transparencies, any size prints. Buys one-time rights. Negotiates payment individually. Captions, identification of subjects, model releases required.

$ $ CENTRAL PA

WITF, Inc., 1982 Locust Lane, Harrisburg PA 17109. (717)221-2800. Fax: (717)221-2630. E-mail: centralpa@centralpa.org. Website: www.centralpa.org. **Contact:** Steve Kennedy, senior editor. **75% freelance written.** Monthly magazine covering life in Central Pennsylvania. Estab. 1982. Circ. 42,000. Pays on publication. Publishes ms an average of 4 months after acceptance. Offers 20% kill fee. Buys first North American serial rights. Editorial lead time 3 months. Submit seasonal material 6 months in advance. Accepts queries by mail, e-mail, fax. Accepts simultaneous submissions. Responds in 6 weeks to queries. Sample copy for $3.50 and SASE. Writer's guidelines online.

　O→ Break in through Central shorts, essay.

Nonfiction Essays, general interest, historical/nostalgic, how-to, humor, interview/profile, opinion, personal experience, photo feature, travel. Special issues: Dining/Food (January). **Buys 50 mss/year.** Query with published clips or send complete ms. Length: 175-1,500 words. **Pays $50-500.** Sometimes pays expenses of writers on assignment.

Photos State availability with submission. Reviews contact sheets, transparencies, prints. Buys one-time rights. Negotiates payment individually. Identification of subjects required.

Columns/Departments Central Shorts (quirky, newsy, regional), 175 words; Thinking Aloud (essay), 1,100 words; Cameo (interview), 1,000 words. **Buys 90 mss/year.** Query with published clips or send complete ms. **Pays $50-100.**

Tips "Wow us with something you wrote, either a clip or a manuscript on spec. If it's off target but shows you can write well and know the region, we'll ask for more. We're looking for creative nonfiction, with an emphasis on conveying valuable information through near literary-quality narrative. Strong central PA interest an absolute must."

$ $ PENNSYLVANIA

Pennsylvania Magazine Co., P.O. Box 755, Camp Hill PA 17001-0755. (717)697-4660. E-mail: pamag@aol.com. Website: www.pa-mag.com. Publisher: Albert E. Holliday. **Contact:** Matt Holliday, editor. **90% freelance written.** Bimonthly magazine covering people, places, events, and history in Pennsylvania. Estab. 1981. Circ. 33,000. Pays on acceptance except for articles (by authors unknown to us) sent on speculation. Publishes ms an average of 9 months after acceptance. Byline given. 25% kill fee for assigned articles. Buys first North American serial, one-time rights. Submit seasonal material 9 months in advance. Accepts queries by mail, e-mail. Responds in 4-6 weeks to queries. Sample copy for $2.95. Writer's guidelines for #10 SASE.

　O→ Break in with "a text/photo package—learn to take photos or hook up with a photographer who will shoot for our rates."

Nonfiction Features include general interest, historical, photo feature, vacations and travel, people/family success stories—all dealing with or related to Pennsylvania. Will not consider without illustrations; send photocopies of possible illustrations with query or ms. Include SASE. Nothing on Amish topics, hunting, or skiing. **Buys 75-120 mss/year.** Query. Length: 750-2,500 words. **Pays 10-15¢/word.**

Reprints Send photocopy with rights for sale noted and information about when and where the material previously appeared. Pays 5¢/word.

Photos No original slides or transparencies. Photography Essay (highlights annual photo essay contest entries). Reviews 35mm $2\frac{1}{4} \times 2\frac{1}{4}$ color transparencies, 5×7 to 8×10 color prints. Buys one-time rights. Pays $15-25 for inside photos; $100 for covers. Captions required.

Columns/Departments Round Up Panorama (short items about people, unusual events, museums, family and individually owned consumer-related businesses), 250-900 words; Almanac (short historical items), 1,000-2,500 words. All must be illustrated. Include SASE. Query. **Pays 10-15¢/word.**

Tips "Our publication depends upon freelance work—send queries."

$ $ PHILADELPHIA STYLE

Philadelphia's Premier Magazine for Lifestyle & Fashion, Philadelphia Style Magazine, LLC, 141 League St., Philadelphia PA 19147. Fax: (215)468-6530. E-mail: susan@phillystylemag.com. Website: www.phillystylemag.com. Executive Editor: Susan M. Stapleton. **90% freelance written.** Bimonthly magazine covering upscale living in the Philadelphia region. Topics include: fashion (men's and women's), home and design, real estate, dining, beauty, travel, arts and entertainment, and more. "Our magazine is a positive look at the best ways to live in the Philadelphia region. Submitted articles should speak to an upscale, educated audience of professionals that live in the Delaware Valley." Estab. 1999. Circ. 45,000. Pays on publication. Publishes ms an average of 3 months after acceptance. Byline given. Offers 25% kill fee. Buys first rights. Editorial lead time 2-4 months. Submit seasonal material 6 months in advance. Accepts queries by mail, e-mail, fax. Sample copy not available.

　O→ Break in "with ideas for our real estate section (reviews/stories of area neighborhoods, home and design, architecture, and other new ideas you may have)."

Nonfiction General interest, interview/profile, travel, region-specific articles. "We are not looking for articles that do not have a regional spin." **Buys 100+ mss/year.** Query with published clips or send complete ms. Length: 300-2,500 words. **Pays $50-500.**

Columns/Departments Life in the City (fresh, quirky, regional reporting on books, real estate, art, retail, dining, events, and little-known stories/facts about the region), 100-500 words; Vanguard (people on the forefront of Philadelphia's arts, media, fashion, business, and social scene), 500-700 words; In the Neighborhood (reader-friendly reporting on up-and-coming areas of the region including dining, shopping, attractions, and recreation), 2,000-2,500 words. Query with published clips or send complete ms. **Pays $50-500.**

Tips "Mail queries with clips or manuscripts. Articles should speak to a stylish, educated audience."

PHILADELPHIA MAGAZINE

1818 Market St., 36th Floor, Philadelphia PA 19103. (215)564-7700. Website: www.phillymag.com. Monthly magazine. "*Philadelphia* is edited for the area's community leaders and their families. It provides in-depth reports on crucial and controversial issues confronting the region—business trends, political analysis, metropolitan planning, sociological trends—plus critical reviews of the cultural, sports and entertainment scene." Estab. 1908. Circ. 133,083. **Pays on acceptance.** Accepts queries by mail. Sample copy not available. Writer's guidelines not available. Editorial calendar online.

   O→ Break in by sending queries along with clips. "Remember that we are a general interest magazine that focuses exclusively on topics of interest in the Delaware Valley."

Nonfiction "Articles range from law enforcement to fashion, voting trends to travel, transportation to theater, also includes the background studies of the area newsmakers." Query with clips and SASE.

Tips "*Philadelphia Magazine* readers are an affluent, interested and influential group who can afford the best the region has to offer. They're the greater Philadelphia area residents who care about the city and its politics, lifestyles, business and culture."

$ $WESTSYLVANIA

Westsylvania Heritage Corp., P.O. Box 565, 105 Zee Plaza, Hollidaysburg PA 16648-0565. (814)696-9380. Fax: (814)696-9569. E-mail: jschumacher@westsylvania.org. Website: www.westsylvania.com. **Contact:** Jerilynn "Jerry" Schumacher, editor. **90% freelance written.** Quarterly magazine in south-central and southwestern Pennsylvania, plus parts of Ohio, Maryland, West Virginia, Virginia, and Kentucky. "*Westsylvania* magazine celebrates the cultural and natural heritages of south-central and southwestern Pennsylvania. Articles must reflect the writer's keen knowledge of the region. Writers should strive to show what residents are doing to preserve and protect their own legacies. This is not a typical history or travel magazine. Stories should show how the region's history still influences contemporary life." Estab. 1997. Circ. 10,000-14,000. Pays on publication. Publishes ms an average of 4 months after acceptance. Byline given. Offers $50 kill fee. Buys first North American serial, web rights. Editorial lead time 6-12 months. Submit seasonal material 2 months in advance. Accepts queries by mail, e-mail, fax. Accepts simultaneous submissions. Sample copy online. Writer's guidelines online.

   O→ Break in with "a well-written query that spotlights a little-known person, place, or event in the Westsylvania region. We particularly seek stories on what people are doing to preserve their own heritage, such as cleaning up a trout stream, finding new uses for historic buildings, or helping others understand the past through art or music. Some how-to articles accepted. First-person accounts accepted only for assigned columns."

Nonfiction Book excerpts, historical/nostalgic, interview/profile, religious, travel (heritage), business, wildlife, outdoors, photography. *No unsolicited mss.* Buys 30 mss/year. Query with published clips. Length: 750-2,500 words. **Pays $75-300 for assigned articles.**

Photos State photo ideas or availability with submission. Use of high-quality digital images encouraged. Buys one-time rights for magazine and website. Negotiates payments individually. Captions, identification of subjects, model releases required.

Columns/Departments On the Back Porch (introduces readers to a special time or place in Westsylvania), 750 words; Vintage Ventures (stories about businesses 100 or more years old), 750 words; Spirit of Westsylvania (inspirational), 750 words. **Buys 15 mss/year.** Query with published clips. **Pays with free subscription or check up to $125, depending.**

Tips Poorly written queries will receive no response. "Look for stories that are uniquely Westsylvania. We will not accept generic articles that do not have a Westsylvania slant."

WHERE & WHEN

Pennsylvania's Travel Guide, Engle Publishing, 1425 W. Main St., P.O. Box 500, Mount Joy PA 17552. (800)800-1833, ext. 2544. Fax: (717)492-2570. E-mail: wsroyal@engleonline.com. Website: www.whereandwhen.com.

Contact: Wendy Royal, editor. Quarterly magazine covering travel and tourism in Pennsylvania. *"Where & When* presents things to see and do in Pennsylvania." Circ. 100,000.

• This publication is now using mainly staff writers, though this may change in the future.

RHODE ISLAND

$$$ RHODE ISLAND MONTHLY

The Providence Journal Co., 280 Kinsley Ave., Providence RI 02903. Phone/Fax: (401)277-8080. E-mail: paula_b odah@rimonthly.com. Website: www.rimonthly.com. Editor: Paula M. Bodah. **Contact:** Sarah Francis, managing editor. **50% freelance written.** Monthly magazine. *"Rhode Island Monthly* is a general interest consumer magazine with a strict Rhode Island focus." Estab. 1988. Circ. 41,000. **Pays on acceptance.** Publishes ms an average of 3 months after acceptance. Byline given. Offers 25% kill fee. Buys all rights for 90 days from date of publication. Editorial lead time 3 months. Submit seasonal material 6 months in advance. Accepts queries by mail, e-mail, fax. Responds in 6 weeks to queries. Writer's guidelines free.

Nonfiction Exposé, general interest, interview/profile, photo feature. **Buys 40 mss/year.** Query with published clips. Length: 1,800-3,000 words. **Pays $600-1,200.** Sometimes pays expenses of writers on assignment.

SOUTH CAROLINA

CHARLESTON MAGAZINE

P.O. Box 1794, Mt. Pleasant SC 29465-1794. (843)971-9811. Fax: (843)971-0121. E-mail: dshankland@charlesto nmag.com. Website: charlestonmag.com. **Contact:** Darcy Shankland, editor. **80% freelance written.** Bimonthly magazine covering current issues, events, arts and culture, leisure pursuits, travel, and personalities, as they pertain to the city of Charleston and surrounding areas. *"A Lowcountry institution for more than 30 years, Charleston Magazine* captures the essence of Charleston and her surrounding areas—her people, arts and architecture, culture and events, and natural beauty." Estab. 1972. Circ. 25,000. Pays 1 month after publication. Byline given. Buys one-time rights. Submit seasonal material 4 months in advance. Accepts queries by mail, e-mail, fax. Sample copies may be ordered at cover price from office. Writer's guidelines for #10 SASE.

Nonfiction "Must pertain to the Charleston area and its present culture." General interest, humor, interview/profile, opinion, photo feature, travel, food, architecture, sports, current events/issues, art. "Not interested in 'Southern nostalgia' articles or gratuitous history pieces." **Buys 40 mss/year.** Query with published clips and SASE. Length: 150-1,500 words. **Payment negotiated.** Sometimes pays expenses of writers on assignment.

Reprints Send photocopy and information about when and where the material previously appeared. Payment negotiable.

Photos Send photos with submission. Reviews contact sheets, transparencies, slides. Buys one-time rights. Identification of subjects required.

Columns/Departments Channel Markers (general local interest), 50-400 words; Local Seen (profile of local interest), 500 words; In Good Taste (restaurants and culinary trends in the city), 1,000-1,200 words, plus recipes; Chef at Home (profile of local chefs), 1,200 words, plus recipes; On the Road (travel opportunities near Charleston), 1,000-1,200 words; Southern View (personal experience about Charleston life), 750 words; Doing Business (profiles of exceptional local businesses and entrepreneurs), 1,000-1,200 words; Native Talent (local profiles), 1,000-1,200 words; Top of the Shelf (reviews of books with Southern content or by a Southern author), 750 words.

Tips "Charleston, although a city with a 300-year history, is a vibrant, modern community with a tremendous dedication to the arts and no shortage of newsworthy subjects. We're looking for the freshest stories about Charleston—and those don't always come from insiders, but also outsiders who are keenly observant."

$$ HILTON HEAD MONTHLY

Frey Media, Inc., 2 Park Lane, Hilton Head Island SC 29928. Fax: (843)842-5743. E-mail: hhmeditor@hargray.c om. **Contact:** Blanche Tomaszewski, editor. **75% freelance written.** Monthly magazine covering the business, people, and lifestyle of Hilton Head, South Carolina. "Our mission is to provide fresh, upbeat reading about the residents, lifestyle and community affairs of Hilton Head Island, an upscale, intensely pro-active resort community on the East Coast. We are not even remotely 'trendy,' but we like to see how national trends/issues play out on a local level. Especially interested in: home design and maintenance, entrepreneurship, nature, area history, golf/tennis/boating, volunteerism." Circ. 28,000. **Pays on acceptance.** Publishes ms an average of 6 months after acceptance. Byline given. Offers 50% kill fee. Buys first North American serial rights, makes work-for-hire assignments. Editorial lead time 3 months. Submit seasonal material 4 months in advance. Accepts queries by mail, e-mail, fax. Accepts previously published material. Accepts simultaneous submissions. Responds in 1 week to queries; 4 months to mss. Sample copy for $3.

Nonfiction General interest, historical/nostalgic (history only), how-to (home related), humor, interview/profile (Hilton Head residents only), opinion (general humor or Hilton Head Island community affairs), personal experience, travel. No "exposé interviews with people who are not Hilton Head residents; profiles of people, events, or businesses in Beaufort, South Carolina; Savannah, Georgia; Charleston; or other surrounding cities, unless it's within a travel piece." **Buys 225-250 mss/year.** Query with published clips.

Photos State availability with submission. Reviews contact sheets, prints, slides; any size. Buys one-time rights. Negotiates payment individually.

Columns/Departments News; Business; Lifestyles (hobbies, health, sports, etc.); Home; Around Town (local events, charities and personalities); People (profiles, weddings, etc.). Query with synopsis. **Pays 15¢/word.**

Tips "Give us concise, bullet-style descriptions of what the article covers (in the query letter); choose upbeat, pro-active topics; delight us with your fresh (not trendy) description and word choice."

$ SANDLAPPER

The Magazine of South Carolina, The Sandlapper Society, Inc., P.O. Box 1108, Lexington SC 29071-1108. (803)359-9941. Fax: (803)359-0629. E-mail: aida@sandlapper.org. Website: www.sandlapper.org. Editor: Robert P. Wilkins. **Contact:** Aida Rogers, managing editor. **60% freelance written.** Quarterly magazine focusing on the positive aspects of South Carolina. "*Sandlapper* is intended to be read at those times when people want to relax with an attractive, high-quality magazine that entertains and informs them about their state." Estab. 1989. Circ. 18,000 with a readership of 60,000. Pays during the dateline period. Publishes ms an average of 1 year after acceptance. Byline given. Buys first North American serial rights and the right to reprint. Submit seasonal material 6 months in advance. Accepts queries by mail, e-mail, fax. Sample copy online. Writer's guidelines for #10 SASE.

Nonfiction Feature articles and photo essays about South Carolina's interesting people, places, cuisine, things to do. Occasional history articles. Essays, general interest, humor, interview/profile, photo feature. Query with clips and SASE. Length: 500-2,500 words. **Pays $100/published page.** Sometimes pays expenses of writers on assignment.

Photos "*Sandlapper* buys b&w prints, color transparencies, and art. Photographers should submit working cutlines for each photograph. While prints and slides are preferred, we do accept digital images in the following format only: JPEGs at 300 dpi (minimum), at 8æx11-inch size. Please provide digital images on CD or IBM-compatible disk, accompanied by a proof or laser print." Pays $25-75, $100 for cover or centerspread photo.

▣ The online version contains material not found in the print edition. Contact: Dan Harmon.

Tips "We're not interested in articles about topical issues, politics, crime, or commercial ventures. Avoid first-person nostalgia and remembrances of places that no longer exist. We look for top-quality literature. Humor is encouraged. Good taste is a standard. Unique angles are critical for acceptance. Dare to be bold, but not too bold."

SOUTH DAKOTA

$ DAKOTA OUTDOORS

South Dakota,, Hipple Publishing Co., P.O. Box 669 333 W. Dakota Ave., Pierre SD 57501-0669. (605)224-7301. Fax: (605)224-9210. E-mail: office@capjournal.com. Editor: Kevin Hipple. **Contact:** Rachel Engbrecht, managing editor. **85% freelance written.** Monthly magazine on Dakota outdoor life, focusing on hunting and fishing. Estab. 1974. Circ. 7,000. Pays on publication. Publishes ms an average of 1-2 months after acceptance. Byline given. Submit seasonal material 3 months in advance. Accepts queries by mail, e-mail. Accepts simultaneous submissions. Responds in 3 months to queries. Sample copy for 9×12 SAE and 3 first-class stamps. Writer's guidelines by e-mail.

Nonfiction "Topics should center on fishing and hunting experiences and advice. Other topics such as boating, camping, hiking, environmental concerns and general nature will be considered as well." General interest, how-to, humor, interview/profile, personal experience, technical (all on outdoor topics-prefer in the Dakotas). **Buys 120 mss/year.** Send complete ms. Length: 500-2,000 words. **Pays $5-50. Sometimes pays in contributor's copies or other premiums (inquire).**

Reprints Send ms with rights for sale noted and information about when and where the material previously appeared. 50% of amount paid for an original article.

Photos Send photos with submission. Reviews 3×5 or 5×7 prints. Buys one-time rights. Offers no additonal payment for photos accepted with ms or negotiates payment individually. Identification of subjects required.

Columns/Departments Kids Korner (outdoors column addressing kids 12-16 years of age). Length: 50-500 words. **Pays $5-15.**

Fiction Adventure, humorous. Does not want stories about vacations or subjects that don't include hunting and fishing. **Buys 15 mss/year.** Send complete ms. Length: 750-1,500 words.

Fillers Anecdotes, facts, gags to be illustrated by cartoonist, newsbreaks, short humor, line drawings of fish and game. **Buys 10/year.**

Tips "Submit samples of manuscript or previous works for consideration; photos or illustrations with manuscript are helpful."

TENNESSEE

$ $ MEMPHIS

Contemporary Media, 460 Tennessee St., Suite 200, Memphis TN 38103. (901)521-9000. Fax: (901)521-0129. E-mail: memmag@memphismagazine.com. Website: www.memphismagazine.com. **30% freelance written.** Works with a small number of new/unpublished writers. Monthly magazine covering Memphis and the local region. "Our mission is to provide Memphis with a colorful and informative look at the people, places, lifestyles and businesses that make the Bluff City unique." Estab. 1976. Circ. 24,000. Pays on publication. Publishes ms an average of 2 months after acceptance. Byline given. Offers 25% kill fee. Buys first North American serial rights. Editorial lead time 2 months. Submit seasonal material 3 months in advance. Accepts queries by mail, e-mail, fax. Accepts simultaneous submissions. Responds in 2 months to queries. Sample copy for free or online. Writer's guidelines free.

Nonfiction "Virtually all of our material has strong Memphis area connections." Essays, general interest, historical/nostalgic, interview/profile, photo feature, travel, Interiors/exteriors. Special issues: Restaurant Guide and City Guide. **Buys 20 mss/year.** Query with published clips. Length: 500-3,000 words. **Pays 10-30¢/word.** Sometimes pays expenses of writers on assignment.

Photos State availability with submission. Reviews contact sheets, transparencies. Buys one-time rights.

Columns/Departments IntroSpective (personal experiences/relationships), 1,000-1,500 words; CityScape (local events/issues), 1,500-2,000 words; City Beat (peaople, places and things—some quirky), 200-400 words. **Buys 10 mss/year.** Query. **Pays 10-20¢/word.**

Fiction One story published annually as part of contest. Send complete ms. Length: 1,500-3,000 words.

Tips "Send a query letter with specific ideas that apply to our short columns and departments. Good ideas that apply specifically to these sections will often get published."

TEXAS

$ $ $ HOUSTON PRESS

New Times, Inc., 1621 Milam, Suite 100, Houston TX 77002. (713)280-2400. Fax: (713)280-2444. E-mail: melissa .sonzala@houstonpress.com. Website: www.houstonpress.com. Editor: Margaret Downing. Managing Editor: George Flynn. Associate Editor: Cathy Matusow. **Contact:** Melissa Sonzala, editorial administrator. **40% freelance written.** Weekly tabloid covering "news and arts stories of interest to a Houston audience. If the same story could run in Seattle, then it's not for us." Estab. 1989. Pays on publication. Publishes ms an average of 2 weeks after acceptance. Byline given. Buys first North American serial, website rights. Editorial lead time 2 months. Submit seasonal material 3 months in advance. Sample copy for $3.

Nonfiction Exposé, general interest, interview/profile, arts reviews; music. Query with published clips. Length: 300-4,500 words. **Pays $10-1,000.** Sometimes pays expenses of writers on assignment.

Photos State availability with submission. Buys all rights. Negotiates payment individually. Identification of subjects required.

$ $ $ PAPERCITY

Dallas Edition, Urban Publishers, 3303 Lee Parkway, #340, Dallas TX 75219. (214)521-3439. Fax: (214)521-3178. E-mail: trish@papercitymag.com. **Contact:** Trish Donnally, managing editor; Holly Moore, editor-in-chief. **10% freelance written.** Monthly magazine. "*Papercity* covers fashion, food, entertainment, home design and decoratives for urban Dallas, Houston, and San Francisco. Our writing is lively, brash, sexy—it's where to read about the hottest restaurants, great chefs, where to shop, what's cool to buy, where to go and the chicest places to stay—from sexy, small hotels in New York, Los Angeles, London and Morocco, to where to buy the newest trends in Europe. We cover local parties with big photo spreads, and a hip nightlife column." Estab. 1994 (Houston); 1998 (Dallas); 2002 (San Francisco). Circ. 85,000 (Dallas). Pays on publication. Publishes ms an average of 1 month after acceptance. Byline given. Offers 10% kill fee. Buys first North American serial rights. Editorial lead time 2 months. Submit seasonal material 4 months in advance. Accepts queries by mail, e-mail, fax. Accepts simultaneous submissions. Responds in 3 weeks to queries; 1 month to mss. Sample copy for 9 × 12 SAE with $1.50 in first-class stamps. Writer's guidelines for #10 SASE or by e-mail.

Nonfiction General interest, interview/profile, new product, travel, home decor, food. Special issues: Bridal

(February); Travel (April); Restaurants (August). No straight profiles on anyone, especially celebrities. **Buys 10-12 mss/year.** Query with published clips. Length: 150-3,000 words. **Pays 35-50¢/word.**

Photos State availability with submission. Reviews contact sheets, transparencies, prints. Buys one-time rights. Negotiates payment individually.

Tips "Read similar publications such as *W, Tattler, Wallpaper, Martha Stewart Living* for new trends, style of writing, hip new restaurants. We try to be very 'of the moment' so give us something in Dallas, Houston, New York, Los Angeles, London, etc., that we haven't heard yet. Chances are if other hip magazines are writing about it so will we."

$ $ $ TEXAS HIGHWAYS

The Travel Magazine of Texas, Box 141009, Austin TX 78714-1009. (512)486-5858. Fax: (512)486-5879. E-mail: editors@texashighways.com. Website: www.texashighways.com. **Contact:** Jill Lawless, managing editor. **80% freelance written.** Monthly magazine "encourages travel within the state and tells the Texas story to readers around the world." Estab. 1974. Circ. 275,000. **Pays on acceptance.** Publishes ms an average of 1 year after acceptance. Buys first North American serial, electronic rights. Accepts queries by mail. Responds in 2 months to queries. Writer's guidelines online.

Nonfiction "Subjects should focus on things to do or places to see in Texas. Include historical, cultural, and geographical aspects if appropriate. Text should be meticulously researched. Include anecdotes, historical references, quotations and, where relevant, geologic, botanical, and zoological information." Query with description, published clips, additional background materials (charts, maps, etc.) and SASE. Length: 1,200-1,500 words. **Pays 40-50¢/word.**

Tips "We like strong leads that draw in the reader immediately and clear, concise writing. Be specific and avoid superlatives. Avoid overused words. Don't forget the basics—who, what, where, when, why, and how."

TEXAS PARKS & WILDLIFE

3000 South I.H. 35, Suite 120, Austin TX 78704. (512)912-7000. Fax: (512)707-1913. E-mail: michael.berryhill@t pwd.state.tx.us. Website: www.tpwmagazine.com. **Contact:** Michael Berryhill, editorial director. **80% freelance written.** Monthly magazine featuring articles about Texas hunting, fishing, birding, outdoor recreation, game and nongame wildlife, state parks, environmental issues. All articles must be about Texas. Estab. 1942. Circ. 150,000. Pays on publication. Publishes ms an average of 6 months after acceptance. Byline given. Kill fee determined by contract, usually $200-250. Buys first rights. Submit seasonal material 6 months in advance. Accepts queries by mail. Responds in 1 month to queries; 3 months to mss. Sample copy online. Writer's guidelines online.

• *Texas Parks & Wildlife* needs more hunting and fishing material.

Nonfiction General interest (Texas only), how-to (outdoor activities), photo feature, travel (state parks). **Buys 60 mss/year.** Query with published clips. Length: 500-2,500 words.

Photos Send photos to photo editor. Reviews transparencies. Buys one-time rights. Offers $65-350/photo. Captions, identification of subjects required.

Tips "Read outdoor pages of statewide newspapers to keep abreast of news items that can lead to story ideas. Feel free to include more than one story idea in one query letter. All areas are open to freelancers. All articles must have a Texas focus."

VERMONT

$ $ VERMONT LIFE MAGAZINE

6 Baldwin St., Montpelier VT 05602-2109. (802)828-3241. Fax: (802)828-3366. E-mail: tom.slayton@state.vt.us. Website: www.vtlife.com. **Contact:** Thomas K. Slayton, editor-in-chief. **90% freelance written.** Prefers to work with published/established writers. Quarterly magazine. "*Vermont Life* is interested in any article, query, story idea, photograph or photo essay that has to do with Vermont. As the state magazine, we are most favorably impressed with pieces that present positive aspects of life within the state's borders." Estab. 1946. Circ. 80,000. Publishes ms an average of 9 months after acceptance. Byline given. Offers kill fee. Buys first North American serial rights. Submit seasonal material 1 year in advance. Accepts queries by mail, e-mail, fax. Responds in 1 month to queries. Writer's guidelines online.

⚬┐ Break in with "short humorous Vermont anecdotes for our 'Postboy' column."

Nonfiction Wants articles on today's Vermont, those which portray a typical or, if possible, unique aspect of the state or its people. Style should be literate, clear, and concise. Subtle humor favored. No "Vermont clichés," and please do not send first-person accounts of your vacation trip to Vermont. **Buys 60 mss/year.** Query by letter essential. Length: 1,500 words average. **Pays 25¢/word.**

Photos Buys photos with mss; buys seasonal photographs alone. Prefers b&w contact sheets to look at first on assigned material. Color submissions must be 4×5 or 35mm transparencies. Gives assignments but only with experienced photographers. Query in writing. Buys one-time rights. Pays $75-200 inside color; $500 for cover. Captions, identification of subjects, model releases required.

■ The online version contains material not found in the print edition. Contact: Andrew Jackson.

Tips "Writers who read our magazine are given more consideration because they understand that we want authentic articles about Vermont. If a writer has a genuine working knowledge of Vermont, his or her work usually shows it. Vermont is changing and there is much concern here about what this state will be like in years ahead. It is a beautiful, environmentally sound place now and the vast majority of residents want to keep it so. Articles reflecting such concerns in an intelligent, authoritative, non-hysterical way will be given very careful consideration. The growth of tourism makes us interested in intelligent articles about specific places in Vermont, their history and attractions to the traveling public."

VIRGINIA

N $ $ ALBEMARLE

Living in Jefferson's Virginia, Carden Jennings Publishing, 375 Greenbrier Dr., Suite 100, Charlottesville VA 22901. (434)817-2000. Fax: (434)817-2020. E-mail: albemarle@cjp.com. Website: www.cjp.com. **Contact:** Alison Dickie, publisher. **80% freelance written.** Bimonthly magazine. "Lifestyle magazine for central Virginia." Estab. 1987. Circ. 10,000. Pays on publication. Publishes ms an average of 4 months after acceptance. Byline given. Offers 30% kill fee. Buys first North American serial rights. Editorial lead time 6 months. Submit seasonal material 6 months in advance. Accepts queries by mail, e-mail, fax. Accepts simultaneous submissions. Responds in 1 month to queries; 2 months to mss. Sample copy for 10×12 SAE and 5 first-class stamps. Writer's guidelines for #10 SASE.

○— Break in with "a strong idea backed by good clips to prove abilities. Ideas should be targeted to central Virginia and lifestyle, which can be very broad—a renaissance man or woman approach to living."

Nonfiction Essays, historical/nostalgic, interview/profile, photo feature, travel. "No fiction, poetry or anything without a direct tie to central Virginia." **Buys 30-35 mss/year.** Query with published clips. Length: 900-3,500 words. **Pays $75-225 for assigned articles; $75-175 for unsolicited articles.** Sometimes pays expenses of writers on assignment.

Photos State availability with submission. Reviews transparencies. Buys one-time rights. Negotiates payment individually. Captions, identification of subjects, model releases required.

Columns/Departments Etcetera (personal essay), 900-1,200 words; Flavors of Virginia (food), 900-1,100 words; Leisure (travel, sports), 3,000 words. **Buys 20 mss/year.** Query with published clips. **Pays $75-150.**

Tips "Be familiar with the central Virginia area and lifestyle. We prefer a regional slant, which should include a focus on someone or something located in the region, or a focus on someone or something from the region making an impact in other parts of the world. Quality writing is a must. Story ideas that lend themselves to multiple sources will give you a leg up on the competition."

N $ $ THE ROANOKER

Leisure Publishing Co., 3424 Brambleton Ave., P.O. Box 21535, Roanoke VA 24018-9900. (540)989-6138. Fax: (540)989-7603. E-mail: krheinheimer@leisurepublishing.com. Website: www.theroanoker.com. **Contact:** Kurt Rheinheimer, editor. **75% freelance written.** Works with a small number of new/unpublished writers each year. Magazine published 6 times/year. "*The Roanoker* is a general interest city magazine for the people of Roanoke, Virginia and the surrounding area. Our readers are primarily upper-income, well-educated professionals between the ages of 35 and 60. Coverage ranges from hard news and consumer information to restaurant reviews and local history." Estab. 1974. Circ. 12,000. Pays on publication. Publishes ms an average of 4 months after acceptance. Byline given. Buys all rights, makes work-for-hire assignments. Submit seasonal material 4 months in advance. Accepts queries by mail, e-mail, fax. Responds in 2 months to queries. Sample copy for $2 and 9×12 SAE with 5 first-class stamps or online. Editorial calendar online.

Nonfiction "We're looking for more photo feature stories based in western Virginia. We place special emphasis on investigative and exposé articles." Exposé, historical/nostalgic, how-to (live better in western Virginia), interview/profile (of well-known area personalities), photo feature, travel (Virginia and surrounding states), periodic special sections on fashion, real estate, media, banking, investing. **Buys 30 mss/year.** Query with published clips or send complete ms. Length: 1,400 words maximum. **Pays $35-200.**

Reprints Send tearsheet. Pays 50% of amount paid for an original article.

Photos Send photos with submission. Reviews color transparencies. Rights purchased vary. Pays $5-10 for 5×7 or 8×10 b&w prints; $10-50 for color transparencies. Captions, model releases required.

Columns/Departments Skinny (shorts on people, Roanoke-related books, local issues, events, arts and culture).

Tips "We're looking for more pieces on contemporary history (1930s-70s). It helps if freelancer lives in the area. The most frequent mistake made by writers in completing an article for us is not having enough Roanoke-area focus: use of area experts, sources, slants, etc."

WASHINGTON

$ $SEATTLE MAGAZINE

Tiger Oak Publications Inc., 1505 Western Ave., Suite 500, Seattle WA 98101. (206)284-1750. Fax: (206)284-2550. E-mail: rachel@seattlemag.com. Website: www.seattlemagazine.com. **Contact:** Rachel Hart, editor. Monthly magazine "serving the Seattle metropolitan area. Articles should be written with our readers in mind. They are interested in social issues, the arts, politics, homes and gardens, travel and maintaining the region's high quality of life." Estab. 1992. Circ. 45,000. Pays on or about 30 days after publication. Publishes ms an average of 3 months after acceptance. Byline given. Offers 25% kill fee. Buys first rights. Editorial lead time 6 months. Submit seasonal material 6 months in advance. Accepts queries by mail, e-mail, fax. Responds in 2 months to queries. Sample copy for #10 SASE. Writer's guidelines online.

O⊷ Break in by "suggesting short, newsier stories with a strong Seattle focus."

Nonfiction Book excerpts (local), essays, exposé, general interest, humor, interview/profile, photo feature, travel, local/regional interest. No longer accepting queries by mail. Query with published clips. Length: 100-2,000 words. **Pays $50 minimum.** Sometimes pays expenses of writers on assignment.

Photos State availability with submission. Buys one-time rights. Negotiates payment individually.

Columns/Departments Scoop, Urban Safari, Voice, Trips, People, Environment, Hot Button, Fitness, Fashion, Eat and Drink. Query with published clips. **Pays $100-300.**

Tips "The best queries include some idea of a lead and sources of information, plus compelling reasons why the article belongs specifically in *Seattle Magazine*. In addition, queries should demonstrate the writer's familiarity with the magazine. New writers are often assigned front- or back-of-the-book contents, rather than features. However, the editors do not discourage writers from querying for longer articles and are especially interested in receiving trend pieces, in-depth stories with a news hook and cultural criticism with a local angle."

$ $ $SEATTLE WEEKLY

Village Voice, 1008 Western Ave., Suite 300, Seattle WA 98104. (206)623-0500. Fax: (206)467-4377. E-mail: editorial@seattleweekly.com. Website: seattleweekly.com. **Contact:** Knute Berger, editor-in-chief. **20% freelance written.** Weekly tabloid covering arts, politics, food, business and books with local and regional emphasis. Estab. 1976. Circ. 105,000. Pays on publication. Publishes ms an average of 1 month after acceptance. Byline given. Offers variable kill fee. Buys first North American serial rights. Submit seasonal material 2 months in advance. Responds in 1 month to queries. Sample copy for $3.

Nonfiction Book excerpts, exposé, general interest, historical/nostalgic (Northwest), humor, interview/profile, opinion. **Buys 6-8 mss/year.** Query with cover letter, résumé, published clips and SASE. Length: 500-3,000 words. **Pays $50-800.** Sometimes pays expenses of writers on assignment.

Reprints Send tearsheet. Payment varies.

Tips "The *Seattle Weekly* publishes stories on Northwest politics and art, usually written by regional and local writers, for a mostly upscale, urban audience; writing is high-quality magazine style."

WISCONSIN

$ $ $MILWAUKEE MAGAZINE

417 E. Chicago St., Milwaukee WI 53202. (414)273-1101. Fax: (414)273-0016. E-mail: john.fennell@qg.com. Website: www.milwaukeemagazine.com. **Contact:** John Fennell, editor. **40% freelance written.** Monthly magazine. "We publish stories about Milwaukee, of service to Milwaukee-area residents and exploring the area's changing lifestyle, business, arts, politics, and dining." Circ. 40,000. Pays on publication. Publishes ms an average of 2 months after acceptance. Byline given. Offers 20% kill fee. Buys first rights. Submit seasonal material 6 months in advance. Accepts queries by mail, e-mail. Responds in 6 weeks to queries. Sample copy for $4.

Nonfiction Essays, exposé, general interest, historical/nostalgic, interview/profile, photo feature, travel, food and dining, and other services. "No articles without a strong Milwaukee or Wisconsin angle." Length: 2,500-6,000 words for full-length features; 800 words for 2-page "breaker" features (short on copy, long on visuals). **Buys 30-50 mss/year.** Query with published clips. **Pays $400-1,000 for full-length, $150-400 for breaker.** Sometimes pays expenses of writers on assignment.

Columns/Departments Insider (inside information on Milwaukee, exposé, slice-of-life, unconventional angles on current scene), up to 500 words; Mini Reviews for Insider, 125 words. Query with published clips.

Tips "Pitch something for the Insider, or suggest a compelling profile we haven't already done. Submit clips that prove you can do the job. The department most open is Insider. Think short, lively, offbeat, fresh, people-oriented. We are actively seeking freelance writers who can deliver lively, readable copy that helps our readers make the most out of the Milwaukee area. Because we're only human, we'd like writers who can deliver copy on deadline that fits the specifications of our assignment. If you fit this description, we'd love to work with you."

$ $ WISCONSIN TRAILS

P.O. Box 317, Black Earth WI 53515-0317. (608)767-8000. Fax: (608)767-5444. E-mail: lkearney@wistrails.com. Website: www.wistrails.com. **Contact:** Laura Kearney, associate editor. **40% freelance written.** Bimonthly magazine for readers interested in Wisconsin and its contemporary issues, personalities, recreation, history, natural beauty, and arts. Estab. 1960. Circ. 55,000. Pays 1 month from publication. Publishes ms an average of 6 months after acceptance. Byline given. Buys first North American serial, one-time rights. Submit seasonal material 1 year in advance. Accepts queries by mail, e-mail, fax. Responds in 4 months to queries. Sample copy for $4.95. Writer's guidelines for #10 SASE or online.

○── "We're looking for active articles about people, places, events, and outdoor adventures in Wisconsin. We want to publish 1 in-depth article of statewide interest or concern/issue, and several short (600-1,500 words) articles about short trips, recreational opportunities, personalities, restaurants, inns, history, and cultural activities. We're looking for more articles about out-of-the-way Wisconsin places that are exceptional in some way and engaging pieces on Wisconsin's little-known and unique aspects."

Nonfiction "Our articles focus on some aspect of Wisconsin life: an interesting town or event, a person or industry, history or the arts, and especially outdoor recreation. We do not use first-person essays or biographies about people who were born in Wisconsin but made their fortunes elsewhere. No fiction. No articles that are too local for our regional audience, or articles about obvious places to visit in Wisconsin. We need more articles about the new and little-known." **Buys 3 unsolicited mss/year.** Query or send outline. Length: 1,000-3,000 words. **Pays 25¢/word for assigned articles.** Sometimes pays expenses of writers on assignment.

Photos Photographs purchased with or without mss, or on assignment. Color photos usually illustrate an activity, event, region, or striking scenery. Prefer photos with people in scenery. Reviews 35mm or larger transparencies. Pays $45-175 for inside color; $250 for covers. Captions, labels with photographer's name required.

Tips "When querying, submit well-thought-out ideas about stories specific to people, places, events, arts, outdoor adventures, etc., in Wisconsin. Include published clips with queries. Do some research—many queries we receive are pitching ideas for stories we recently have published. Know the tone, content, and audience of the magazine. Refer to our writer's guidelines, or request them, if necessary."

WYOMING

$ WYOMING RURAL ELECTRIC NEWS (WREN)

P.O. Box 549, Gillette WY 82717. (307)682-7527. Fax: (307)682-7528. E-mail: wren@coffey.com. **Contact:** Kris Wendtland, editor. **20% freelance written.** Monthly magazine for audience of small town residents, vacation-home owners, farmers, and ranchers. Estab. 1954. Circ. 35,000. Pays on publication. Publishes ms an average of 1 month after acceptance. Byline given. Buys one-time rights. Submit seasonal material 2 months in advance. Accepts queries by mail, e-mail, fax, phone. Responds in 3 months to queries. Sample copy for $2.50 and 9 × 12 SASE. Writer's guidelines for #10 SASE.

○── "You have just learned something. It is so amazing you just have to find out more. You call around. You search on the Web. You go to the library. Everything you learn about it makes you want to know more. In a matter of days, all your friends are aware that you are into something. You don't stop talking about it. You're totally confident that they find it interesting too. Now, write it down and send it to us. We are excited just wondering what you find so amazing! Come on, tell us! Tell us!"

Nonfiction "We print science, ag, how-to, and human interest but not fiction. Topics of interest in general include: hunting, cooking, gardening, commodities, sugar beets, wheat, oil, coal, hard rock mining, beef cattle, electric technologies such as lawn mowers, car heaters, air cleaners and assorted gadgets, surge protectors, pesticators, etc." Wants science articles with question/answer quiz at end—test your knowledge. Buys electrical appliance articles. Articles welcome that put present and/or future in positive light. No nostalgia. No sad stories. **Buys 4-10 mss/year.** Send complete ms. Length: 500-800 words. **Pays up to $140, plus 4 copies.**

Reprints Send tearsheet or photocopy and information about when and where the material previously appeared.

Photos Color only.

Tips "Always looking for fresh, new writers, original perspectives. Submit entire manuscript. Don't submit a regionally set story from some other part of the country. Photos and illustrations (if appropriate) are always welcomed. We don't care if you misspell words. We don't care if your grammar is poor. We want factual articles that are blunt, to the point, accurate."

CANADIAN/INTERNATIONAL

$ $ ABACO LIFE

Caribe Communications, P.O. Box 37487, Raleigh NC 27627. (919)859-6782. Fax: (919)859-6769. E-mail: jimkerr @mindspring.com. Website: www.abacolife.com. Managing Editor: Cathy Kerr. **Contact:** Jim Kerr, editor/ publisher. **50% freelance written.** Quarterly magazine covering Abaco, an island group in the Northeast Bahamas. *"Abaco Life* editorial focuses entirely on activities, history, wildlife, resorts, people and other subjects pertaining to the Abacos. Readers include locals, vacationers, second-home owners, and other visitors whose interests range from real estate and resorts to scuba, sailing, fishing, and beaches. The tone is upbeat, adventurous, humorous. No fluff writing for an audience already familiar with the area." Estab. 1979. Circ. 10,000. Pays on publication. Publishes ms an average of 2 months after acceptance. Byline given. Offers 40% kill fee. Buys one-time rights. Editorial lead time 2 months. Submit seasonal material 4 months in advance. Accepts queries by mail, e-mail. Accepts simultaneous submissions. Responds in 2 weeks to queries; 2 months to mss. Sample copy for $2. Writer's guidelines free.

Nonfiction General interest, historical/nostalgic, how-to, interview/profile, personal experience, photo feature, travel. "No general first-time impressions. Articles must be specific, show knowledge and research of the subject and area—'Abaco's Sponge Industry'; 'Diving Abaco's Wrecks'; 'The Hurricane of '36.'" **Buys 8-10 mss/year.** Query or send complete ms. Length: 400-2,000 words. **Pays $150-350.**

Photos State availability of or send photos with submission. Reviews transparencies, prints. Buys one-time rights. Offers $25-100/photo. Negotiates payment individually. Captions, identification of subjects, model releases required.

🖳 The online magazine carries original content not found in the print edition. Contact: Jim Kerr, online editor.

Tips "Travel writers must look deeper than a usual destination piece, and the only real way to do that is spend time in Abaco. Beyond good writing, which is a must, we like submissions on Microsoft Word or Works, but that's optional. Color slides are also preferred over prints, and good ones go a long way in selling the story. Read the magazine to learn its style."

$ $ $ $ 🖳 ALBERTAVIEWS

The Magazine About Alberta for Albertans, AlbertaViews, Ltd., Suite 208-320 23rd Ave. SW, Calgary AB T2S 0J2, Canada. (403)243-5334. Fax: (403)243-8599. E-mail: editor@albertaviews.ab.ca. Website: www.albertavie ws.ab.ca. Publisher/Executive Editor: Jackie Flanagan. **Contact:** Michael Hall, assistant editor. **50% freelance written.** Bimonthly magazine covering Alberta culture: politics, economy, social issues, and art. "We are a regional magazine providing thoughtful commentary and background information on issues of concern to Albertans. Most of our writers are Albertans." Estab. 1997. Circ. 30,000. Pays on publication. Publishes ms an average of 3 months after acceptance. Byline given. Offers 50% kill fee. Buys first North American serial, electronic rights. Editorial lead time 4 months. Submit seasonal material 3 months in advance. Accepts queries by e-mail. Responds in 6 weeks to queries; 2 months to mss. Sample copy for free. Writer's guidelines online.

● No phone queries.

Nonfiction Does not want anything not directly related to Alberta. Essays. **Buys 18 mss/year.** Query with published clips. Length: 3,000-5,000 words. **Pays $1,000-1,500 for assigned articles; $350-750 for unsolicited articles.** Sometimes pays expenses of writers on assignment.

Photos State availability with submission. Buys one-time rights, Web rights. Negotiates payment individually.

Fiction Only fiction by Alberta writers. **Buys 6 mss/year.** Send complete ms. Length: 2,500-4,000 words. **Pays $1,000 maximum.**

Ⓝ $ $ 🖳 THE ATLANTIC CO-OPERATOR

Promoting Community Ownership, Atlantic Co-operative Publishers, 123 Halifax St., Moncton, New Brunswick E1C 8N5, Canada. Fax: (506)858-6615. E-mail: editor@theatlanticco-operator.coop. Website: www.theatlanti cco-operator.coop. **Contact:** Mark Higgins, editor. **95% freelance written.** Tabloid published 9 times/year covering co-operatives. "We publish articles of interest to the general public, with a special focus on community ownership and community economic development in Atlantic Canada." Estab. 1933. Pays on publication. Publishes ms an average of 2 months after acceptance. Byline given. Editorial lead time 2 months. Submit seasonal material 2 months in advance. Accepts queries by mail, e-mail, fax. Accepts simultaneous submissions. Responds in 3 weeks to queries. Sample copy not available.

Nonfiction Exposé, general interest, historical/nostalgic, interview/profile. No political stories, economical stories, sports. **Buys 90 mss/year.** Query with published clips. Length: 500-2,000 words. **Pays 22¢/word.** Pays expenses of writers on assignment.

Reprints Accepts previously published submissions.

Photos State availability with submission. Reviews prints, GIF/JPEG files. Buys one-time rights. Offers $25/photo. Identification of subjects required.

Columns/Departments Health and Lifestyle (anything from recipes to travel), 800 words; International Page (co-operatives in developing countries, good ideas from around the world). **Buys 10 mss/year.** Query with published clips. **Pays 15¢/word.**

$ $ $⊠ THE BEAVER

Canada's History Magazine, Canada's National History Society, 478-167 Lombard Ave., Winnipeg MB R3B 0T6, Canada. (204)988-9300. Fax: (204)988-9309. E-mail: beaver@historysociety.ca. Website: www.thebeaver.ca. Associate Editor: Doug Whiteway. **Contact:** Annalee Greenberg, editor. **50% freelance written.** Bimonthly magazine covering Canadian history. Estab. 1920. Circ. 41,000. **Pays on acceptance.** Byline given. Offers $200 kill fee. Buys first North American serial, electronic rights. Editorial lead time 4 months. Submit seasonal material 8 months in advance. Accepts queries by mail. Accepts simultaneous submissions. Responds in 6 weeks to queries; 2 months to mss. Sample copy for 9×12 SAE and 2 first-class stamps. Writer's guidelines online.

⊶ Break in with a "new interpretation based on solid new research; entertaining magazine style."

Nonfiction Photo feature (historical), historical (Canadian focus). Does not want anything unrelated to Canadian history. **Buys 30 mss/year.** Query with published clips. Length: 600-3,500 words. **Pays $400-1,000 for assigned articles; $300-600 for unsolicited articles.** Sometimes pays expenses of writers on assignment.

Photos State availability with submission. Buys one-time rights. Offers no additional payment for photos accepted with ms. Identification of subjects, model releases required.

Columns/Departments Book and other media reviews and Canadian history subjects, 600 words ("These are assigned to freelancers with particular areas of expertise, i.e., women's history, labour history, French regime, etc."). **Buys 15 mss/year. Pays $125.**

Tips *"The Beaver* is directed toward a general audience of educated readers, as well as to historians and scholars. We are in the market for lively, well-written, well-researched, and informative articles about Canadian history that focus on all parts of the country and all areas of human activity. Subject matter covers the whole range of Canadian history, with particular emphasis on social history, politics, exploration, discovery and settlement, aboriginal peoples, business and trade, war, culture and sport. Articles are obtained through direct commission and by submission. Queries should be accompanied by a stamped, self-addressed envelope. *The Beaver* publishes articles of various lengths, including long features (from 1,500-3,500 words) that provide an in-depth look at an event, person or era; short, more narrowly focused features (from 600-1,500 words). Longer articles may be considered if their importance warrants publication. Articles should be written in an expository or interpretive style and present the principal themes of Canadian history in an original, interesting and informative way."

$ BRAZZIL

Brazzil, P.O. Box 50536, Los Angeles CA 90050. (323)255-8062. Fax: (323)257-3487. E-mail: brazzil@brazzil.com. Website: www.brazzil.com. **Contact:** Rodney Mello, editor. **60% freelance written.** Monthly magazine covering Brazilian culture. Estab. 1989. Circ. 12,000. Pays on publication. Publishes ms an average of 2 months after acceptance. Byline given. Offers 10% kill fee. Buys one-time rights. Editorial lead time 2 months. Submit seasonal material 2 months in advance. Accepts queries by mail, e-mail, fax, phone. Accepts simultaneous submissions. Responds in 2 weeks to queries. Sample copy free or online. Writer's guidelines online.

Nonfiction "All subjects have to deal in some way with Brazil and its culture. We assume our readers know very little or nothing about Brazil, so we explain everything." Book excerpts, essays, exposé, general interest, historical/nostalgic, humor, interview/profile, opinion, personal experience, travel. **Buys 15 mss/year.** Query. Length: 800-5,000 words. **Pays $20-50.** Pays writers with contributor copies or other premiums by mutual agreement.

Photos State availability with submission. Reviews prints. Buys one-time rights. Offers no additional payment for photos accepted with ms. Identification of subjects required.

■ The online version of *Brazzil* contains content not included in the print edition. Contact: Rodney Mello, online editor.

Tips "We are interested in anything related to Brazil: politics, economy, music, behavior, profiles. Please document material with interviews and statistical data if applicable. Controversial pieces are welcome."

$ $ $⊠ CANADIAN GEOGRAPHIC

39 McArthur Ave., Ottawa ON K1L 8L7, Canada. (613)745-4629. Fax: (613)744-0947. E-mail: editorial@canadiangeographic.ca. Website: www.canadiangeographic.ca. **Contact:** Rick Boychuk, editor. **90% freelance written.** Works with a small number of new/unpublished writers each year. Bimonthly magazine. *"Canadian Geographic's* colorful portraits of our ever-changing population show readers just how important the relationship between

the people and the land really is." Estab. 1930. Circ. 240,000. **Pays on acceptance.** Publishes ms an average of 3 months after acceptance. Buys first Canadian rights. Accepts queries by mail, e-mail, fax. Responds in 1 month to queries. Sample copy for $5.95 (Canadian) and 9×12 SAE or online.

• *Canadian Geographic* reports a need for more articles on earth sciences. Canadian writers only.

Nonfiction Buys authoritative geographical articles, in the broad geographical sense, written for the average person, not for a scientific audience. Predominantly Canadian subjects by Canadian authors. **Buys 30-45 mss/year.** Query. Length: 1,500-3,000 words. **Pays 80¢/word minimum.** Sometimes pays expenses of writers on assignment.

Photos Pays $75-400 for color photos, depending on published size.

N $ $ THE COTTAGE MAGAZINE

Country Living in Western Canada, OP Publishing, Ltd., 1080 Howe St., Suite 900, Vancouver BC V6Z 2T1, Canada. (604)606-4644. Fax: (604)687-1925. E-mail: editor@cottagemagazine.com. Website: www.cottagemagazine.com. **Contact:** Michael Love, editor. **80% freelance written.** Bimonthly magazine covering do-it-yourself projects, profiles of people and their innovative solutions to building and maintaining their country homes, issues that affect rural individuals and communities, and the R&R aspect of country living. "Our readers want solid, practical information about living in the country—including alternative energy and sustainable living. The also like to have fun in a wide range of recreational pursuits, from canoeing, fishing, and sailing to water skiing, snowmobiling, and entertaining." Estab. 1992. Circ. 10,000. Pays within 1 month of publication. Publishes ms an average of 6 months after acceptance. Byline given. Offers 50% kill fee. Buys first North American serial rights. Accepts queries by e-mail, fax. Accepts simultaneous submissions. Responds in 1 month to queries. Sample copy for $2. Writer's guidelines online.

Nonfiction Buys 18-24 mss/year. Query. Length: Length: Up to 1,500 words. **Pays $200-450 (including visuals).**

Photos Send photos with submission. Reviews with negatives prints, slides. Pays $15-25. Cover submissions also accepted.

Columns/Departments Utilities (solar and/or wind power), 800 words; Weekend Project (a how-to most homeowners can do themselves), 800 words; Government (new regulations, processes, problems), 800 words; Diversions (advisories, ideas, and how-tos about the fun things that people do), 800 words; InRoads (product reviews), 50-600 words; This Land (personal essays or news-based story with a broader context), 800 words; Last Word or Cabin Life (personal essays and experiences), 800 words; Elements (short articles focusing on a single feature of a cottage), 600 words; Alternatives (applied alternative energy), 600 words. Not all columns run every issue. Query. **Pays 20¢/published word.**

Fillers Anecdotes, facts, newsbreaks, seasonal tips. **Buys 12/year.** Length: 50-200 words. **Pays 20¢/word.**

Tips "We serve all of Western Canada, so while it's OK to have a main focus on one region, reference should be made to similarities/differences in other provinces. Even technical articles should have some anecdotal content. Some of our best articles come from readers themselves or from writers who can relay that 'personal' feeling. Cottaging is about whimsy and fun as well as maintenance and chores. Images, images, images: We require sharp, quality photos, and the more, the better."

$ $ OUTDOOR CANADA MAGAZINE

340 Ferrier St., Suite 210, Markham ON L3R 2Z5, Canada. (905)475-8440. Fax: (905)475-9246. E-mail: editorial@outdoorcanada.ca. Website: www.outdoorcanada.ca. **Contact:** Patrick Walsh, editor-in-chief. **90% freelance written.** Works with a small number of new/unpublished writers each year. Magazine published 8 times/year emphasizing hunting, fishing, and related pursuits in Canada *only*. Estab. 1972. Circ. 80,000. Pays on publication. Publishes ms an average of 8 months after acceptance. Byline given. Buys first rights. Submit seasonal material 1 year in advance. Accepts queries by mail, e-mail. Responds in 1 month to queries. Writer's guidelines online.

Nonfiction How-to, fishing, hunting, outdoor issues, outdoor destinations in Canada. **Buys 35-40 mss/year.** Query. Length: 2,500 words. **Pays $500 and up for assigned articles.**

Reprints Send information about when and where the article previously appeared. Payment varies.

Photos Emphasize people in the Canadian outdoors. Pays $100-250 for 35mm transparencies and $400/cover. Captions, model releases required.

Fillers Short news pieces. **Buys 30-40/year.** Length: 100-500 words. **Pays $50 and up.**

The online magazine carries original content not found in the print edition. Contact: Aaron Kylie, online editor.

$ $ $ $ TORONTO LIFE

59 Front St. E., Toronto ON M5E 1B3, Canada. (416)364-3333. Fax: (416)955-4982. E-mail: editorial@torontolife.com. Website: www.torontolife.com. **Contact:** John Macfarlane, editor. **95% freelance written.** Prefers to work

with published/established writers. Monthly magazine emphasizing local issues and social trends, short humor/satire, and service features for upper income, well-educated and, for the most part, young Torontonians. Circ. 91,298. **Pays on acceptance.** Publishes ms an average of 4 months after acceptance. Byline given. Pays 50% kill fee for commissioned articles only. Buys first North American serial rights. Responds in 3 weeks to queries. Sample copy for $4.95 with SAE and IRCs.

Nonfiction Uses most types of articles. **Buys 17 mss/issue.** Query with published clips and SASE. Length: 1,000-6,000 words. **Pays $500-5,000.**

Columns/Departments "We run about 5 columns an issue. They are all freelanced, though most are from regular contributors. They are mostly local in concern and cover politics, business, performing arts, media, design, and food." Length: 2,000 words. Query with published clips and SASE. **Pays $2,000.**

Tips "Submissions should have strong Toronto orientation."

⋈ $⊕ THE UKRANIAN OBSERVER

The Willard Group, 4/6 Desiatynna St., 4th Floor, Kiev 01025, Ukraine. (38044) 230 2080. Fax: (38044) 230 2083. E-mail: scott@twg.com.ua. Website: www.ukraine-observer.com. Editor: Glen Willard. **Contact:** Scott Lewis, managing editor. **75% freelance written.** Monthly magazine covering Ukrainian news, culture, travel, and history. "Our English-language content is entirely Ukraine-centered. A writer unfamiliar with the country, its politics, or its culture is unlikely to be successful with us." Estab. 2000. Circ. 10,000. Pays on publication. Publishes ms an average of 2 months after acceptance. Byline given. Offers 50% kill fee. Buys all rights. Editorial lead time 2 months. Submit seasonal material 4 months in advance. Accepts queries by mail, e-mail. Responds in 2 weeks to queries; 1 month to mss. Sample copy free by post to Ukraine addresses only; $3 USD to foreign addresses. Writer's guidelines by e-mail.

Nonfiction General interest (Ukrainian life, history, culture and travel, and significant Ukrainians abroad), historical/nostalgic (Ukrainian history, particular little-known events with significant impact), interview/profile (prominent Ukrainians or foreign expatriates living in Ukraine), photo feature (current or historical photo essays on Ukrainian life, history, culture, and travel), travel (within Ukraine). Does not want poetry, nostalgic family stories, personal experiences or recollections. **Buys 30-40 mss/year.** Query with or without published clips or send complete ms. Length: 800-1,500 words. **Pays $25-50 for assigned articles; $25 for unsolicited articles.** Sometimes pays expenses of writers on assignment.

Photos Send photos with submission. Reviews negatives, GIF/JPEG files. Buys one-time rights. Pays $10/photo. Captions, identification of subjects, model releases required.

Fiction All fiction should have a Ukrainian setting and/or theme. Adventure, ethnic, historical, humorous, mainstream, slice-of-life vignettes. Does not want erotica. **Buys 12 mss/year.** Query with or without published clips or send complete ms. Length: 3,500-4,500 words. **Pays $25-50.**

Tips "Obtain, read, and follow our writer's guidelines. We follow Western journalism rules. We are not interested in the writer's opinion—our readers want information to be attributed to experts interviewed for the story. An interesting story that has credible sources and lots of good, direct quotes will be a hit with us. Stories covering political or controversial issues should be balanced and fair."

▣ UP HERE

Explore Canada's Far North, Up Here Publishing, Ltd., P.O. Box 1350, Yellowknife NT X1A 2N9, Canada. (867)920-4343. Fax: (867)873-2844. E-mail: liz@uphere.ca. Website: www.uphere.ca. **Contact:** Liz Crompton, editor. **50% freelance written.** Magazine published 8 times/year covering general interest about Canada's Far North. "We publish features, columns, and shorts about people, wildlife, native cultures, travel, and adventure in Yukon, Northwest Territories, and Nunavut. Be informative, but entertaining." Estab. 1984. Circ. 35,000. Pays on publication. Byline given. Offers 50% kill fee. Buys first North American serial rights. Editorial lead time 6 months. Accepts queries by mail, e-mail, fax. Sample copy for $3.50 (Canadian) and 9×12 SASE with $1.45 Canadian postage.

    O→ Break in with "precise queries with well-developed focuses for the proposed story."

Nonfiction Essays, general interest, how-to, humor, interview/profile, personal experience, photo feature, technical, travel, lifestyle/culture, historical. **Buys 25-30 mss/year.** Query. Length: 1,500-3,000 words. **Fees are negotiable.**

Photos "*Please* do not send unsolicited original photos, slides." Send photos with submission. Reviews transparencies, prints. Buys one-time rights. Captions, identification of subjects required.

Columns/Departments Write for updated guidelines, visit website, or e-mail. **Buys 25-30 mss/year.** Query with published clips.

    ▣ The online magazine carries original content not found in the print edition. Contact: Mifi Purvis, online editor.

Tips "We like well-researched, concrete adventure pieces, insights about Northern people and lifestyles, readable natural history. Features are most open to freelancers—travel, adventure, and so on. We don't want a comprehensive 'How I spent my summer vacation' hour-by-hour account. We want stories with angles, articles that look at the North through a different set of glasses. Photos are important; you greatly increase your chances with top-notch images.''

$ $ $⬚ VANCOUVER MAGAZINE

Transcontinental Publications, Inc., Suite 500, 2608 Granville St., Vancouver BC V6H 3V3, Canada. (604)877-7732. Fax: (604)877-4823. E-mail: mmallon@vancouvermagazine.com. Website: www.vancouvermagazine.com. **Contact:** Matthew Mallon, editor. **70% freelance written.** Monthly magazine covering the city of Vancouver. Estab. 1967. Circ. 65,000. **Pays on acceptance.** Byline given. Offers negotiable kill fee. Buys first North American serial rights. Editorial lead time 2 months. Submit seasonal material 6 months in advance. Accepts queries by mail, e-mail, fax, phone. Accepts simultaneous submissions. Responds in 2 weeks to queries; 1 month to mss. Sample copy for $5. Writer's guidelines for #10 SASE or by e-mail.

Nonfiction "We prefer to work with writers from a conceptual stage and have a 6-week lead time. Most stories are under 1,500 words. Please be aware that we don't publish poetry and rarely publish fiction." Book excerpts, essays, historical/nostalgic, humor, interview/profile, new product, personal experience, photo feature, travel. **Buys 200 mss/year.** Query. Length: 200-3,000 words. **Pays 50¢/word.** Sometimes pays expenses of writers on assignment.

Photos State availability with submission. Reviews contact sheets, negatives, transparencies, prints, GIF/JPEG files. Buys negotiable rights. Negotiates payment individually. Captions, identification of subjects, model releases required.

Columns/Departments Sport; Media; Business; City Issues, all 1,500 words. Query. **Pays 50¢/word.**

Tips "Read back issues of the magazine, or visit our website. Almost all of our stories have a strong Vancouver angle. Submit queries by e-mail. Do not send complete stories."

$ $ $ $⬚ WESTWORLD MAGAZINE

Canada Wide Magazines and Communications, 4180 Lougheed Hwy., 4th Floor, Burnaby BC V5C 6A7, Canada. Fax: (604)299-9188. E-mail: arose@canadawide.com. **Contact:** Anne Rose, editor. **80% freelance written.** Quarterly magazine distributed to members of B.C. Automobile Association, with a focus on local (British Columbia), regional, and international travel. Estab. 1983. Circ. 500,000. Pays on acceptance and publication. Byline given. Offers 50% kill fee. Buys first North American serial, second serial (reprint) rights. Editorial lead time at least 6 months. Submit seasonal material 1 year in advance. Accepts simultaneous submissions. Writer's guidelines currently under revision.

● Editorial lineup for following year determined in June; queries held for consideration at that time. No phone calls.

Nonfiction Travel (domestic and international). "No purple prose." Query with published clips and lead paragraph of proposed article. Length: 1,500-2,000 words (features). **Pays 50¢-$1/word.**

Reprints Send photocopy and information about when and where the material previously appeared. Pays approximately 50% of amount paid for an original article.

Photos State availability of photos with submission, do not send photos until requested. Buys one-time rights. Offers writers $35-75/photo. Captions, identification of subjects, model releases required.

Columns/Departments Query with published clips and sample lead paragraph of proposed article. **Pays 50-80¢/word.**

Tips "Please don't send gushy, travelogue articles filled with glowing adjectives about pristine lakes and snow-tipped mountains. We prefer experiential, fact-filled travel stories (emphasis on story) and adventures from professional writers that are a good read, as well as informative and extremely well researched with practical tips and sidebars. Approach an old topic/destination in a fresh/original way."

RELATIONSHIPS

$ $ MARRIAGE PARTNERSHIP

Christianity Today International, 465 Gundersen Dr., Carol Stream IL 60188. Fax: (630)260-0114. E-mail: mp@marriagepartnership.com. Website: www.marriagepartnership.com. Executive Editor: Marshall Shelley. Managing Editor: Ginger E. Kolbaba. **Contact:** Raelynn Eickhoff, editorial coordinator. **50% freelance written.** Quarterly magazine covering Christian marriages. "Our readers are married Christians. Writers must understand our readers." Estab. 1988. Circ. 55,000. **Pays on acceptance.** Publishes ms an average of 9 months after acceptance. Byline given. Offers 50% kill fee. Buys first North American serial rights. Editorial lead time 6 months. Submit seasonal material 1 year in advance. Accepts queries by mail, e-mail, fax. Responds in 10 weeks to queries; 2 months to mss. Sample copy for $5 or online. Writer's guidelines online.

Nonfiction Book excerpts, essays, how-to, humor, inspirational, interview/profile, opinion, personal experience, religious. **Buys 20 mss/year.** Query with or without published clips. Length: 1,200-2,300 words. **Pays 15-30¢/ word for assigned articles; 15¢/word for unsolicited articles.**

Columns/Departments Starting Out (opinion by/for newlyweds), 1,000 words; Soul to Soul (inspirational), 1,500 words; Work It Out (problem-solving), 1,000 words; Back from the Brink (marriage in recovery), 1,800 words. **Buys 10 mss/year.** Query with or without published clips. **Pays 15-30¢/word.**

Tips "Think of topics with a fresh slant. Be ever mindful of our readers. Writers who can communicate with freshness, clarity, and insight will receive serious consideration. We are looking for writers who are willing to candidly speak about their own marriages. We strongly urge writers who are interested in contributing to *Marriage Partnership* to read several issues to become thoroughly acquainted with our tone and slant."

RELIGIOUS

ALIVE NOW

1908 Grand Ave., P.O. Box 340004, Nashville TN 37203-0004. E-mail: alivenow@upperroom.org. Website: www.alivenow.org. **Contact:** Melissa Tidwell. Bimonthly thematic magazine for a general Christian audience interested in reflection and meditation. Circ. 70,000. Writer's guidelines online.

Poetry Avant-garde, free verse. Length: 10-45 lines.

$ $ AMERICA

106 W. 56th St., New York NY 10019. (212)581-4640. Fax: (212)399-3596. E-mail: articles@americamagazine.o rg. Website: www.americamagazine.org. **Contact:** The Rev. Thomas J. Reese, editor. Published weekly for adult, educated, largely Roman Catholic audience. Estab. 1909. **Pays on acceptance.** Byline given. Buys all rights. Responds in 3 weeks to queries. Writer's guidelines online.

Nonfiction "We publish a wide variety of material on religion, politics, economics, ecology, and so forth. We are not a parochial publication, but almost all pieces make some moral or religious point." Articles on theology, spirituality, current political, social issues. "We are not interested in purely informational pieces or personal narratives which are self-contained and have no larger moral interest." Length: 1,500-2,000 words. **Pays $50-300.**

Poetry Only 10-12 poems published a year, thousands turned down. Paul Mariani, poetry editor. **Buys 10-12 poems/year.** Length: 15-30 lines.

$ THE ASSOCIATE REFORMED PRESBYTERIAN

Associate Reformed Presbyterian General Synod, 1 Cleveland St., Suite 110, Greenville SC 29601-3696. (864)232-8297, ext. 237. Fax: (864)271-3729. E-mail: arpmaged@arpsynod.org. Website: www.arpsynod.org. **Contact:** Ben Johnston, editor. **5% freelance written.** Works with a small number of new/unpublished writers each year. Monthly Christian magazine serving a conservative, evangelical, and Reformed denomination. "As the official publication of our denomination, most articles deal with events/news that occurs within the denomination. We also like to feature articles that deal with a Biblical approach to current trends/issues and common problems on a regular basis." Estab. 1976. Circ. 5,200. **Pays on acceptance.** Publishes ms an average of 4 months after acceptance. Byline given. Not copyrighted. Buys first, one-time, second serial (reprint) rights. Submit seasonal material 4 months in advance. Accepts queries by mail, e-mail, fax. Accepts simultaneous submissions. Responds in 1 month to queries. Sample copy for $1.50. Writer's guidelines for #10 SASE or by e-mail.

Nonfiction Book excerpts, essays, inspirational, opinion, personal experience, religious. **Buys 10-15 mss/year.** Query. Length: 400-2,000 words. **Pays $25-75.**

Reprints Send information about when and where the article previously appeared. Pays 100% of amount paid for an original article.

Photos State availability with submission. Buys one-time rights. Offers $25 maximum/photo. Captions, identification of subjects required.

Fiction "Currently overstocked." Religious, children's. "Stories should portray Christian values. No retelling of Bible stories or 'talking animal' stories. Stories for youth should deal with resolving real issues for young people." Length: 300-750 words (children); 1,250 maximum (youth). **Pays $50 maximum.**

Tips "Feature articles are the area of our publication most open to freelancers. Focus on a contemporary problem and offer Bible-based solutions to it. Provide information that would help a Christian struggling in his daily walk. Writers should understand that we are denominational, conservative, evangelical, Reformed, and Presbyterian. A writer who appreciates these nuances would stand a much better chance of being published here than one who does not."

$ $ BGC-WORLD

Baptist General Conference, 2002 S. Arlington Heights Rd., Arlington Heights IL 60005. Fax: (847)228-5376. E-mail: bputman@baptistgeneral.org. Website: www.bgcworld.org. **Contact:** Bob Putman, editor. **35% freelance written.** Nonprofit, religious, evangelical Christian magazine published 10 times/year covering the Baptist General Conference. "*BGC-WORLD* is the official magazine of the Baptist General Conference (BGC). Articles related to the BGC, our churches, or by/about BGC people receive preference." Circ. 38,000. Pays on publication. Byline given. Offers 50% kill fee. Buys first rights. Editorial lead time 6 months. Submit seasonal material 6 months in advance. Accepts queries by e-mail. Responds in 1 month to queries; 2 months to mss. Sample copy for #10 SASE. Writer's guidelines, theme list free.

Nonfiction General interest, photo feature, religious, profile, infographics, sidebars related to theme. No sappy religious pieces, articles not intended for our audience. Ask for a sample instead of sending anything first. **Buys 20-30 mss/year.** Query with published clips. Length: 300-1,200 words. **Pays $60-280.** Sometimes pays expenses of writers on assignment.

Photos State availability with submission. Reviews prints, some high-resolution digital. Buys one-time rights. Offers $15-60/photo. Captions, identification of subjects, model releases required.

Columns/Departments Around the BGC (blurbs of news happening in the BGC), 50-150 words. Send complete ms. **Pays $15-20.**

Tips "Please study the magazine and the denomination. We will send sample copies to interested freelancers and give further information about our publication needs upon request. Freelancers who are interested in working on assignment are welcome to express their interest."

$ $ CATHOLIC DIGEST

185 Willow St., P.O. Box 6001, Mystic CT 06355. (860)536-2611. Fax: (860)536-5600. E-mail: cdsubmissions@bayard-inc.com. Website: www.catholicdigest.org. Editor: Joop Koopman. **Contact:** Articles Editor. **15% freelance written.** Monthly magazine. "Publishes features and advice on topics ranging from health, psychology, humor, adventure, and family, to ethics, spirituality, and Catholics, from modern-day heroes to saints through the ages. Helpful and relevant reading culled from secular and religious periodicals." Estab. 1936. Circ. 350,000. Pays on acceptance for articles. Publishes ms an average of 4 months after acceptance. Byline given. Buys first, one-time, second serial (reprint) rights. Editorial lead time 4 months. Submit seasonal material 5 months in advance. Accepts queries by mail, e-mail, fax. Responds in 2 months to mss. Sample copy free. Writer's guidelines online.

Nonfiction "Most articles we use are reprinted." Book excerpts, essays, general interest, historical/nostalgic, how-to, humor, inspirational, interview/profile, personal experience, religious, travel. **Buys 60 mss/year.** Send complete ms. Length: 750-2,000 words. **Pays $200-400.**

Reprints Send tearsheet or typed ms with rights for sale noted and information about when and where the material previously appeared. Pays $100.

Photos State availability with submission. Reviews contact sheets, transparencies, prints. Negotiates payment individually. Captions, identification of subjects, model releases required.

Columns/Departments Buys 75 mss/year. Send complete ms. **Pays $4-50.**

Fillers Filler Editor. Open Door (statements of true incidents through which people are brought into the Catholic faith, or recover the Catholic faith they had lost), 200-500 words; People Are Like That (original accounts of true incidents that illustrate the instinctive goodness of human nature), 200-500 words; Perfect Assist (original accounts of gracious or tactful remarks or actions), 200-500 words; also publishes jokes, short anecdotes, quizzes, and informational paragraphs. **Buys 200/year.** Length: 1 line minimum, 500 words maximum. **Pays $2/per published line upon publication.**

▣ The online magazine includes writer's guidelines. Contact: Kathleen Stauffer, managing editor.

Tips "Spiritual, self-help, and all wellness is a good bet for us. We would also like to see material with an innovative approach to daily living, articles that show new ways of looking at old ideas, problems. You've got to dig beneath the surface."

$ $ CATHOLIC FORESTER

Catholic Order of Foresters, 355 Shuman Blvd., P.O. Box 3012, Naperville IL 60566-7012. Fax: (630)983-3384. E-mail: cofpr@aol.com. Website: www.catholicforester.com. Editor: Mary Ann File. **Contact:** Patricia Baron, associate editor. **20% freelance written.** Quarterly magazine for members of the Catholic Order of Foresters, a fraternal insurance benefit society. *Catholic Forester* articles cover varied topics to create a balanced issue for the purpose of informing, educating, and entertaining our readers. Circ. 100,000. **Pays on acceptance.** Buys first North American serial rights. Editorial lead time 6 months. Submit seasonal material 6 months in advance. Responds in 3 months to mss. Sample copy for 9 × 12 SAE and 4 first-class stamps. Writer's guidelines online.

Nonfiction Inspirational, religious, travel, health, parenting, financial, money management, humor. **Buys 12-16 mss/year.** Send complete ms by mail, fax, or e-mail. Rejected material will not be returned without accompanying SASE. Length: 500-1,500 words. **Pays 30¢/word.**

Photos State availability with submission. Buys one-time rights. Negotiates payment individually.

Fiction Humorous, religious. **Buys 12-16 mss/year.** Length: 500-1,500 words. **Pays 30¢/word.**

Poetry Light verse, traditional. **Buys 3 poems/year.** Length: 15 lines maximum. **Pays 30¢/word.**

Tips ''Our audience includes a broad age spectrum, ranging from youth to seniors. Nonfiction topics that appeal to our members include health and wellness, money management and budgeting, parenting and family life, interesting travels, insurance, nostalgia, and humor. A good children's story with a positive lesson or message would rate high on our list.''

N $ $ CELEBRATE LIFE

American Life League, P.O. Box 1350, Stafford VA 22555. (540)659-4171. Fax: (540)659-2586. E-mail: clmag@all ,org. Website: www.all.org/. Editor: Nicholas Marmalejo. **Contact:** Melissa Salt, assistant editor. **50% freelance written.** Bimonthly educational magazine covering pro-life education and human interest. ''We are a religious-based publication specializing in pro-life education through human-interest stories and investigative exposés. Our purpose is to inspire, encourage, motivate, and educate pro-life individuals and activists.'' Estab. 1979. Circ. 70,000. Pays on publication. Byline given. Buys first, second serial (reprint) rights, or makes work-for-hire assignments. Submit seasonal material 4 months in advance. Accepts queries by mail, e-mail, fax. Accepts previously published material. Accepts simultaneous submissions. Responds in 6 months to mss. Sample copy for 9×12 SAE SAE and 4 first-class stamps. Writer's guidelines free.

○ Break in with ''interview-based human interest or investigative exposés.''

Nonfiction ''No fiction, book reviews, poetry, allegory, devotionals.'' **Buys 40 mss/year.** Query with published clips or send complete ms. Length: 300-1,500 words.

Photos Buys one-time rights. Identification of subjects required.

Fillers Newsbreaks. **Buys 5/year.** Length: 75-200 words. **Pays $10.**

Online version of magazine: www.all.org/celebrate-life/indexht.

Tips ''We look for inspiring, educational, or motivational human-interest stories. We are religious based and no exceptions pro-life. All articles must have agreement with the principles expressed in Pope John Paul II's encyclical *Evangelium Vitae.* Our common themes include: abortion, post-abortion healing, sidewalk counseling, adoption, and contraception.''

$ $ THE CHRISTIAN CENTURY

104 S. Michigan Ave., Suite 700, Chicago IL 60603-5901. (312)263-7510. Fax: (312)263-7540. E-mail: main@chri stiancentury.org. Website: www.christiancentury.org. **Contact:** David Heim, executive editor. **90% freelance written.** Works with new/unpublished writers. Biweekly magazine for ecumenically-minded, progressive Protestant church people, both clergy and lay. ''Authors must have a critical and analytical perspective on the church and be familiar with contemporary theological discussion.'' Estab. 1884. Circ. 30,000. Pays on publication. Byline given. Buys all rights. Editorial lead time 1 month. Submit seasonal material 4 months in advance. Accepts queries by mail, e-mail. Responds in 1 week to queries; 3 months to mss. Sample copy for $3. Writer's guidelines online.

Nonfiction ''We use articles dealing with social problems, ethical dilemmas, political issues, international affairs, and the arts, as well as with theological and ecclesiastical matters. We focus on issues of church and society, and church and culture.'' Essays, humor, interview/profile, opinion, religious. No inspirational. **Buys 150 mss/ year.** Send complete ms; query appreciated, but not essential. Length: 1,000-3,000 words. **Pays variable amount for assigned articles; $75-150 for unsolicited articles.**

Photos State availability with submission. Reviews any size prints. Buys one-time rights. Offers $25-100/photo.

Fiction Humorous, religious, slice-of-life vignettes. No moralistic, unrealistic fiction. Send complete ms. Length: 1,000-3,000 words. **Pays $75-200.**

Poetry Jill Pelaez Baumgaertner, poetry editor. Avant-garde, free verse, haiku, traditional. No sentimental or didactic poetry. **Buys 50 poems/year.** Length: 20 lines. **Pays $50.**

Tips ''We seek manuscripts that articulate the public meaning of faith, bringing the resources of Christian tradition to bear on such topics as poverty, human rights, economic justice, international relations, national priorities, and popular culture. We are equally interested in articles that probe classical theological themes. We welcome articles that find fresh meaning in old traditions and which adapt or apply religious traditions to new circumstances. Authors should assume that readers are familiar with main themes in Christian history and theology; are not threatened by the historical-critical study of the Bible; and are already engaged in relating faith to social and political issues. Many of our readers are ministers or teachers of religion at the college level.''

$ $ CHRISTIAN HOME & SCHOOL

Christian Schools International, 3350 E. Paris Ave. SE, Grand Rapids MI 49512. (616)957-1070, ext. 239. Fax: (616)957-5022. E-mail: rogers@csionline.org. Executive Editor: Gordon L. Bordewyk. **Contact:** Roger Schmurr, senior editor. **30% freelance written.** Works with a small number of new/unpublished writers each year.

Bimonthly magazine covering family life and Christian education. *"Christian Home & School* is designed for parents in the United States and Canada who send their children to Christian schools and are concerned about the challenges facing Christian families today. These readers expect a mature, Biblical perspective in the articles, not just a Bible verse tacked onto the end." Estab. 1922. Circ. 70,000. Pays on publication. Publishes ms an average of 4 months after acceptance. Byline given. Buys first North American serial rights. Submit seasonal material 4 months in advance. Accepts queries by mail, e-mail. Responds in 1 month to queries. Sample copy and writer's guidelines for 9×12 SAE with 4 first-class stamps. Writer's guidelines only for #10 SASE or online.

- The editor reports an interest in seeing articles on how to experience and express forgiveness in your home, raise polite kids in a rude world, combat procrastination, let kids maintin a relationship with your former spouse, and promote good educational practices in Christian schools.

○→ Break in by picking a contemporary parenting situation/problem and writing to Christian parents.

Nonfiction "We publish features on issues that affect the home and school and profiles on interesting individuals, providing that the profile appeals to our readers and is not a tribute or eulogy of that person." Book excerpts, interview/profile, opinion, personal experience, articles on parenting and school life. **Buys 40 mss/year.** Send complete ms. Length: 1,000-2,000 words. **Pays $175-250.**

Photos "If you have any color photos appropriate for your article, send them along."

Tips "Features are the area most open to freelancers. We are publishing articles that deal with contemporary issues that affect parents. Use an informal easy-to-read style rather than a philosophical, academic tone. Try to incorporate vivid imagery and concrete, practical examples from real life. We look for manuscripts with a mature Christian perspective."

$ $ CHRISTIAN RESEARCH JOURNAL

30162 Tomas, Rancho Santa Margarita CA 92688-2124. (949)858-6100. Fax: (949)858-6111. E-mail: elliot.miller @equip.org. Website: www.equip.org. Managing Editor: Melanie Cogdill. **Contact:** Elliot Miller, editor-in-chief. **75% freelance written.** Quarterly magazine. "The *Journal* is an apologetics magazine probing today's religious movements, promoting doctrinal discernment and critical thinking, and providing reasons for Christian faith and ethics." Pays on publication. Publishes ms an average of 3 months after acceptance. Byline sometimes given. Offers 50% kill fee. Buys first rights. Submit seasonal material 4 months in advance. Accepts queries by mail, e-mail, fax. Accepts simultaneous submissions. Responds in 4 months to queries; 4 months to mss. Sample copy for $6. Writer's guidelines by e-mail at guidelines@equip.org.

Nonfiction Essays, opinion (religious viewpoint), religious, ethics, book reviews, features on cults, witnessing tips. No fiction or general Christian living topics. **Buys 25 mss/year.** Query or send complete ms (if e-mail ms, must mail disk with ms as well). Length: 4,000-6,000 words. **Pays 16¢/word.**

Columns/Departments Features, 4,500 words; Effective Evangelism, 1,700 words; Viewpoint, 875 words; News Watch, 2,500 words. Query or send complete ms to submissions@equip.org.

Tips "We are most open to features on cults, apologetics, Christian discernment, ethics, book reviews, opinion pieces, and witnessing tips. Be familiar with the *Journal* in order to know what we are looking for."

$ $ CHRYSALIS READER

R.R. 1, Box 4510, Dillwyn VA 23936. (434)983-3021. E-mail: chrysalis@hovac.com. Website: www.swedenborg .com. Managing Editor: Susanna van Rensselaer. **Contact:** Patti Cramer, editorial associate. **90% freelance written.** Annual literary magazine on spiritually related topics. "It is very important to send for writer's guidelines and sample copies before submitting. Content of fiction, articles, reviews, poetry, etc., should be directly focused on that issue's theme and directed to the educated, intellectually curious reader." Estab. 1985. Circ. 3,000. Pays at page-proof stage. Publishes ms an average of 9 months after acceptance. Byline given. Buys first rights, makes work-for-hire assignments. Accepts queries by mail, e-mail. Responds in 1 month to queries; 4 months to mss. Sample copy for $10 and 8½×11 SAE. Writer's guidelines online.

- E-mail for themes and guidelines (no mss will be accepted by e-mail).

Nonfiction Relationships (2005), Passages (2006), Discovering Heavenly Realms (2007). Essays, interview/ profile. **Buys 20 mss/year.** Query. Length: no longer than 3,000. **Pays $50-250 for assigned articles; $50-150 for unsolicited articles.**

Photos Send suggestions for illustrations with submission. Buys original artwork for cover and inside copy; b&w illustrations related to theme; **pays $25-150.** Buys one-time rights. Offers no additional payment for photos accepted with ms. Captions, identification of subjects required.

Fiction Robert Tucker, fiction editor. Short fiction more likely to be published. Adventure, experimental, historical, mainstream, mystery, science fiction, fiction (leading to insight), contemporary, spiritual, sports. No religious works. **Buys 10 mss/year.** Query. Length: no longer than 3,000. **Pays $50-150.**

Poetry Rob Lawson, senior editor. Avant-garde and traditional. **Buys 15 poems/year.** Submit maximum 6 poems. **Pays $25, and 5 copies of the issue.**

$ $ CONSCIENCE

The Newsjournal of Catholic Opinion, Catholics for a Free Choice, 1436 U St. NW, Suite 301, Washington DC 20009-3997. (202)986-6093. E-mail: conscience@catholicsforchoice.org. Website: www.catholicsforchoice.org. **Contact:** Editor. **60% freelance written.** Sometimes works with new/unpublished writers. Quarterly newsjournal covering reproductive health and rights including, but not limited to, abortion rights in the church, and church-state issues in US and worldwide. "A feminist, pro-choice perspective is a must, and knowledge of Christianity and specifically Catholicism is helpful." Estab. 1980. Circ. 12,000. Pays on publication. Publishes ms an average of 2 months after acceptance. Byline given. Buys first North American serial rights, makes work-for-hire assignments. Accepts queries by mail, e-mail. Responds in 4 months to queries. Sample copy for 9×12 SAE and 4 first-class stamps. Writer's guidelines for #10 SASE.

Nonfiction Especially needs material that recognizes the complexity of reproductive issues and decisions, and offers original, honest insight. "Writers should be aware that we are a nonprofit organization." Book excerpts, interview/profile, opinion, personal experience (a small amount), issue analysis. **Buys 4-8 mss/year.** Query with published clips or send complete ms. Length: 1,500-3,500 words. **Pays $200 negotiable.**

Reprints Send ms with rights for sale noted and information about when and where the material previously appeared. Pays 20-30% of amount paid for an original article.

Photos Prefers b&w prints. State availability with submission. Identification of subjects required.

Columns/Departments Book Reviews, 600-1,200 words. **Buys 4-8 mss/year. Pays $75.**

Tips "Say something new on the issue of abortion, or sexuality, or the role of religion or the Catholic church, or women's status in the church. Thoughtful, well-researched, and well-argued articles needed. The most frequent mistakes made by writers in submitting an article to us are lack of originality and wordiness."

$ THE COVENANT COMPANION

Covenant Publications of the Evangelical Covenant Church, 5101 N. Francisco Ave., Chicago IL 60625. E-mail: communication@covchurch.org. Website: www.covchurch.org. **Contact:** Donald L. Meyer, editor or Jane K. Swanson-Nystrom, managing editor. **10-15% freelance written.** "As the official monthly periodical of the Evangelical Covenant Church, we seek to inform the denomination we serve and encourage dialogue on issues within the church and in our society." Circ. 16,000. Publishes ms an average of 2 months after acceptance. Byline given. Submit seasonal material 4 months in advance. Accepts queries by mail, e-mail. Accepts simultaneous submissions. Writer's guidelines online.

Nonfiction Inspirational, religious, contemporary issues. **Buys 40 mss/year.** Send complete ms. Unused mss returned only if accompanied by SASE. Length: 500-2,000 words. **Pays $50-100 for assigned articles.**

Reprints Send tearsheet, photocopy or typed ms with rights for sale noted and information about when and where the material previously appeared.

Photos Send photos with submission. Reviews prints. Buys one-time rights. Offers no additional payment for photos accepted with ms. Identification of subjects required.

$ $ $ DECISION

Billy Graham Evangelistic Association, 2 Parkway Plaza, 4828 Parkway Plaza Blvd., Suite 200, Charlotte NC 28217. (704)401-2432. Fax: (704)401-3009. E-mail: submissions@bgea.org. Website: www.decisionmag.org. **Contact:** Bob Paulson, managing editor. **5% freelance written.** Works each year with small number of new/unpublished writers. Magazine published 11 times/year with a mission "to extend the ministry of Billy Graham Evangelistic Association and Samaritan's Purse; to communicate the Good News of Jesus Christ in such a way that readers will be drawn to make a commitment to Christ; and to encourage, strengthen and equip Christians in evangelism and discipleship." Estab. 1960. Circ. 1,000,000. Pays on publication. Publishes ms an average of up to 18 months after acceptance. Byline given. Offers 50% kill fee. Buys first rights. Assigns work-for-hire mss, articles, projects. Editorial lead time 6 months. Submit seasonal material 6 months in advance. Sample copy for 9×12 SAE and 4 first-class stamps. Writer's guidelines online.

- Include telephone number with submission.
- "The best way to break in to our publication is to submit an article that has some connection to the Billy Graham Evangelistic Association or Samaritan's Purse, but also has strong takeaway for the personal lives of the readers."

Nonfiction Personal experience, testimony. **Buys approximately 16 mss/year.** Send complete ms. Length: 400-1,500 words. **Pays $30-260.** Pays expenses of writers on assignment.

Photos State availability with submission. Reviews prints. Buys one-time rights. Captions, identification of subjects, model releases required.

Columns/Departments Finding Jesus (people who have become Christians through Billy Graham Ministries), 500-600 words. **Buys 11 mss/year. Pays $85.**

Poetry Amanda Knoke, assistant editor. Free verse, light verse, traditional. **Buys 6 poems/year.** Submit maximum 7 poems. Length: 4-16 lines. **Pays 60¢/word.**

Tips "Articles should have some connection to the ministry of Billy Graham or Franklin Graham. For example, you may have volunteered in one of these ministries or been touched by them. The article does not need to be entirely about that connection, but it should at least mention the connection. Testimonies and personal experience articles should show how God intervened in your life and how you have been transformed by God. SASE required with submissions."

DEVO'ZINE

Just for Teens, 1908 Grand Ave., P.O. Box 340004, Nashville TN 37203-0004. (615)340-7247. E-mail: devozine@upperroom.org. Website: www.devozine.org. Editor: Sandy Miller. Bimonthly magazine for youth ages 12-18. Offers meditations, scripture, prayers, poems, stories, songs, and feature articles to "aid youth in their prayer life, introduce them to spiritual disciplines, help them shape their concept of God, and encourage them in the life of discipleship." Sample copy not available. Writer's guidelines online.
Nonfiction General interest, inspirational, personal experience, religious, devotional.
Poetry Length: 20 lines.

$ $ DISCIPLESHIP JOURNAL

NavPress, a division of The Navigators, P.O. Box 35004, Colorado Springs CO 80935-0004. (719)531-3514. Fax: (719)598-7128. E-mail: sue.kline@navpress.com. Website: www.discipleshipjournal.com. **Contact:** Sue Kline, editor. **90% freelance written.** Works with a small number of new/unpublished writers each year. Bimonthly magazine. "The mission of *Discipleship Journal* is to help believers develop a deeper relationship with Jesus Christ, and to provide practical help in understanding the scriptures and applying them to daily life and ministry. We prefer those who have not written for us before begin with nontheme articles about almost any aspect of Christian living. We'd like more articles that explain a Bible passage and show how to apply it to everyday life, as well as articles about developing a relationship with Jesus; reaching the world; growing in some aspect of Christian character; or specific issues related to leadership and helping other believers grow." Estab. 1981. Circ. 130,000. **Pays on acceptance.** Publishes ms an average of 6 months after acceptance. Byline given. Buys first North American serial, second serial (reprint), electronic rights. Submit seasonal material 6 months in advance. Accepts queries by mail, e-mail, fax. Responds in 6-8 weeks to queries. Sample copy for $2.56 and 9×12 SAE or online. Writer's guidelines online.
  o— Break in through departments (On the Home Front, Getting into God's Word, DJ Plus) and with non-theme feature articles.
Nonfiction "We'd like to see more articles that encourage involvement in world missions; help readers in personal evangelism, follow-up, and Christian leadership; or show how to develop a real relationship with Jesus." Book excerpts (rarely), how-to (grow in Christian faith and disciplines; help others grow as Christians; serve people in need; understand and apply the Bible), inspirational, interpretation/application of the Bible. No personal testimony; humor; poetry; anything not directly related to Christian life and faith; politically partisan articles. **Buys 80 mss/year.** Query with published clips and SASE only. Length: 500-2,500 words. **Pays 25¢/word for first rights.** Sometimes pays expenses of writers on assignment.
Reprints Send tearsheet and information about when and where the material previously appeared. Pays 5¢/word for reprints.
Tips "Our articles are meaty, not fluffy. Study writer's guidelines and back issues and try to use similar approaches. Don't preach. Polish before submitting. About half of the articles in each issue are related to one theme. We are looking for more practical articles on ministering to others and more articles on growing in Christian character. Be vulnerable. Show the reader that you have wrestled with the subject matter in your own life. Use personal illustrations. We can no longer accept unsolicited manuscripts. Query first."

N $ $ DISCIPLESWORLD

A Journal of News, Opinion, and Mission for the Christian Church, DisciplesWorld, Inc., P.O. Box 11469, Indianapolis IN 46201-0469. E-mail: editor@disciplesworld.com. Website: www.disciplesworld.com. Publisher/Editor: Verity A. Jones. **Contact:** Sherri Wood Emmons, managing editor. **75% freelance written.** Monthly magazine covering faith issues, especially those with a "Disciples slant. We are the journal of the Christian Church (Disciples of Christ) in North America. Our denomination numbers roughly 800,000. Disciples are a mainline Protestant group. Our readers are mostly laity, active in their churches, and interested in issues of faithful living, political and church news, ethics, and contemporary social issues." Estab. 2002. Circ. 14,000. Pays on publication. Publishes ms an average of 6 months after acceptance. Byline given. Buys first North American serial rights. Editorial lead time 3 months. Submit seasonal material 3 months in advance. Accepts queries by mail, e-mail. Accepts simultaneous submissions. Responds in 2 weeks to queries; 2 months to mss. Sample copy for #10 SASE. Writer's guidelines online.
Nonfiction Essays, general interest, inspirational, interview/profile, opinion, personal experience, religious. Does not want preachy or didactic articles. "Our style is conversational rather than academic." **Buys 40 mss/**

year. Query with or without published clips or send complete ms. Length: 400-1,500 words. **Pays $100-300 for assigned articles; $25-300 for unsolicited articles.** Sometimes pays expenses of writers on assignment.

Photos Send photos with submission. Buys one-time rights. Negotiates payment individually. Identification of subjects, model releases required.

Columns/Departments Browsing the Bible (short reflections on the applicability of books of the Bible), 400 words; Speak Out (opinion pieces about issues facing the church), 600 words. **Buys 12-15 mss/year.** Send complete ms. **Pays $100.**

Fiction Ethnic, mainstream, novel excerpts, religious, serialized novels, slice-of-life vignettes. "We're a religious publication, so use common sense! Stories do not have to be overtly 'religious,' but they should be uplifting and positive." **Buys 8-10 mss/year.** Send complete ms. Length: 150-1,500 words. **Pays $25-300.**

Poetry Free verse, light verse, traditional. **Buys 6-10 poems/year.** Submit maximum 3 poems. Length: 30 maximum lines.

Fillers Anecdotes, short humor. **Buys 20/year.** Length: 25-400 words. **Pays $0-100.**

Tips "Send a well-written (and well-proofed!) query explaining what you would like to write about and why you are the person to do it. Write about what you're passionate about. We are especially interested in social justice issues, and we like our writers to take a reasoned and well-argued stand."

$ $ THE DOOR

P.O. Box 1444, Waco TX 76703-1444. (214)827-2625. Fax: (254)752-4915. E-mail: dooreditor@earthlink.net. Website: www.thedoormagazine.com. **Contact:** Robert Darden, senior editor. **90% freelance written.** Works with a large number of new/unpublished writers each year. Bimonthly magazine. "*The Door* is the world's only oldest and largest religious humor and satire magazine." Estab. 1969. Circ. 7,500. Pays on publication. Publishes ms an average of 1 year after acceptance. Buys first rights. Accepts queries by mail. Responds in 3 months to mss. Sample copy for $5.95. Writer's guidelines online.

　O⟶ Read several issues of the magazine first! Get the writer's guidelines.

Nonfiction Looking for humorous/satirical articles on church renewal, Christianity and organized religion. Exposé, humor, interview/profile, religious. No book reviews or poetry. **Buys 45-50 mss/year.** Send complete ms. Length: 1,500 words maximum; 750-1,000 preferred. **Pays $50-250.** Sometimes pays expenses of writers on assignment.

Reprints Send ms with rights for sale noted and information about when and where the material previously appeared.

　▣ The online magazine carries original content not found in the print edition. Contact: Robert Darden.

Tips "We look for someone who is clever, on our wave length, and has some savvy about the evangelical church. We are very picky and highly selective. The writer has a better chance of breaking in with our publication with short articles since we are a bimonthly publication with numerous regular features and the magazine is only 52 pages. The most frequent mistake made by writers is that they do not understand satire. They see we are a humor magazine and consequently come off funny/cute (like *Reader's Digest*) rather than funny/satirical (like *National Lampoon*)."

$ DOVETAIL

A Journal By and For Jewish/Christian Families, Dovetail Institute for Interfaith Family Resources, 775 Simon Greenwell Lane, Boston KY 40107. (502)549-5499. Fax: (502)549-3543. E-mail: di-ifr@bardstown.com. Website: www.dovetailinstitute.org. **Contact:** Debi Tenner, editor, 45 Lilac Lane, Hamden CT 06517. E-mail: debit4rls@aol.com. **75% freelance written.** Bimonthly newsletter for interfaith families. "All articles must pertain to life in an interfaith (primarily Jewish/Christian) family. We are broadening our scope to include other sorts of interfaith mixes. We accept all kinds of opinions related to this topic." Estab. 1992. Circ. 1,500. Pays on publication. Publishes ms an average of 9 months after acceptance. Byline given. Buys first, one-time, second serial (reprint) rights. Editorial lead time 6 months. Submit seasonal material 6 months in advance. Accepts queries by mail, e-mail, fax, phone. Accepts previously published material. Accepts simultaneous submissions. Responds in 3 months to queries. Sample copy for 9×12 SAE and 3 first-class stamps. Writer's guidelines free.

　O⟶ Break in with "a fresh approach to standard interfaith marriage situations."

Nonfiction Book reviews, 500 words. **Pays $15, plus 2 copies.** Book excerpts, interview/profile, opinion, personal experience. No fiction. **Buys 5-8 mss/year.** Send complete ms. Length: 800-1,000 words. **Pays $25, plus 2 copies.**

Photos Send photos with submission. Reviews 5×7 prints. Buys one-time rights. Offers no additional payment for photos accepted with ms. Identification of subjects, model releases required.

Fillers Anecdotes, short humor. **Buys 1-2/year.** Length: 25-100 words. **Pays $10.**

Tips "Write on concrete, specific topics related to Jewish/Christian or other dual-faith intermarriage: no proselytizing, sermonizing, or general religious commentary. Successful freelancers are part of an interfaith family themselves, or have done solid research/interviews with members of interfaith families. We look for honest, reflective personal experience. We're looking for more on alternative or nontraditional families, e.g., interfaith gay/lesbian, single parent raising child in departed partner's faith."

$ $EFCA TODAY

(formerly *Beacon*), Evangelical Free Church of America, 418 Fourth St., NE, Charlottesville VA 22902. Fax: (434)961-2507. E-mail: dianemc@journeygroup.com. Website: www.efca.org/today. **Contact:** Diane McDougall, editor. **1% freelance written.** Quarterly magazine. *"EFCA Today* informs readers of the vision and activities of the Evangelical Free Church of America. Its readers are EFCA leaders—pastors, elders, deacons, Sunday-school teachers, ministry volunteers." Circ. 50,000. **Pays on acceptance.** Publishes ms an average of 3 months after acceptance. Byline given. Offers 50% kill fee. Buys first North American serial, electronic, efca-related church use (if free) rights. Editorial lead time 6 months. Submit seasonal material 6-8 months in advance. Accepts queries by mail, e-mail, fax. Accepts previously published material. Accepts simultaneous submissions. Sample copy for $1 with SAE and 5 first-class stamps. Writer's guidelines free.

Nonfiction How-to, inspirational, religious. No poetry or pieces longer than 1,000 words. **Buys 12-18 mss/year.** Query with published clips. Length: 550-1,000 words. **Pays $126.50-260.** Sometimes pays expenses of writers on assignment.

Photos State availability with submission. Offers no additional payment for photos accepted with ms. Captions, identification of subjects required.

Tips "Be familiar with the Evangelical Free Church of America—its vision and mission—and then look for local church stories that highlight that vision/mission. Keep in mind that *EFCA Today* is geared to church leaders rather than everyone in the pews."

N $ $ENRICHMENT

The General Council of the Assemblies of God, 1445 N. Boonville Ave., Springfield MO 65802. (417)862-2781. Fax: (417)862-0416. E-mail: enrichmentjournal@ag.org. Website: www.enrichmentjournal.ag.org. Executive Editor: Gary Allen. **Contact:** Rick Knoth, managing editor. **15% freelance written.** Quarterly journal covering church leadership and ministry. *"Enrichment* offers enriching and encouraging information to equip and empower spirit-filled leaders." Circ. 33,000. Pays on publication. Publishes ms an average of 1 year after acceptance. Byline given. Buys first rights. Editorial lead time 18 months. Submit seasonal material 18 months in advance. Accepts queries by mail, e-mail, fax, phone. Sample copy for $7. Writer's guidelines free.

Nonfiction Religious. Query with or without published clips or send complete ms. Length: 1,000-3,000 words. **Pays up to 10¢/word.**

$ THE EVANGELICAL BAPTIST

Fellowship of Evangelical Baptist Churches in Canada, 18 Louvigny, Lorraine QC J6Z 1T7, Canada. (450)621-3248. Fax: (450)621-0253. E-mail: eb@fellowship.ca. Website: www.fellowship.ca. **Contact:** Ginette Cotnoir, managing editor. **30% freelance written.** Magazine published 5 times/year covering religious, spiritual, Christian living, denominational, and missionary news. "We exist to enhance the life and ministry of the church leaders of our association of churches—including pastors, elders, deacons, and all the men and women doing the work of the ministry in local churches." Estab. 1953. Circ. 3,000. Pays on publication. Publishes ms an average of 6 months after acceptance. Byline given. Buys one-time, second serial (reprint) rights. Editorial lead time 4 months. Accepts queries by mail, e-mail. Accepts previously published material. Accepts simultaneous submissions. Sample copy for 9×12 SAE with $1.50 in Canadian first-class stamps. Writer's guidelines by e-mail.

> O→ Break in with items for "Church Life (how-to and how-we articles about church ministries) or columns (Joy in the Journey)."

Nonfiction Religious. No poetry, fiction, puzzles. **Buys 12-15 mss/year.** Send complete ms. Length: 500-2,400 words. **Pays $30-150.**

Photos State availability with submission. Reviews prints. Buys one-time rights. Offers no additional payment for photos accepted with ms. Captions required.

Columns/Departments Church Life (practical articles about various church ministries, e.g., worship, Sunday school, missions, seniors, youth, discipleship); Joy in the Journey (devotional article regarding a lesson learned from God in everyday life), all 600-800 words. **Buys 10 mss/year.** Send complete ms. **Pays $25-50.**

$EVANGELICAL MISSIONS QUARTERLY

A Professional Journal Serving the Missions Community, Billy Graham Center/Wheaton College, P.O. Box 794, Wheaton IL 60189. (630)752-7158. Fax: (630)752-7155. E-mail: emqjournal@aol.com. Website: www.billygrahamcenter.org/emis. Editor: A. Scott Moreau. **Contact:** Managing Editor. **67% freelance written.** Quarterly magazine covering evangelical missions. "This is a professional journal for evangelical missionaries, agency executives, and church members who support global missions ministries." Estab. 1964. Circ. 7,000. Pays on publication. Publishes ms an average of 18 months after acceptance. Byline given. Offers negotiable kill fee. Buys electronic, all rights. Editorial lead time 1 year. Accepts queries by mail, e-mail, fax, phone. Accepts previously published material. Responds in 2 weeks to queries. Sample copy free. Writer's guidelines online.

Nonfiction Essays, interview/profile, opinion, personal experience, religious. No sermons, poetry, straight news. **Buys 24 mss/year.** Query. Length: 800-3,000 words. **Pays $50-100.**

Photos Send photos with submission. Buys first rights. Offers no additional payment for photos accepted with ms. Identification of subjects required.

Columns/Departments In the Workshop (practical how to's), 800-2,000 words; Perspectives (opinion), 800 words. **Buys 8 mss/year.** Query. **Pays $50-100.**

$ $ EVANGELIZING TODAY'S CHILD

Child Evangelism Fellowship, Inc., Box 348, Warrenton MO 63383-0348. (636)456-4321. Fax: (636)456-4321. E-mail: etceditor@cefonline.com. Website: www.cefonline.com/etcmag. **Contact:** Elsie Lippy, editor. **50% free-lance written.** Bimonthly magazine. "Our purpose is to equip Christians to win the world's children to Christ and disciple them. Our readership is Sunday school teachers, Christian education leaders, and children's workers in every phase of Christian ministry to children 4-12 years old." Estab. 1942. Circ. 12,000. Pays within 2 months of acceptance. Publishes ms an average of 6 months after acceptance. Byline given. Offers kills fee if assigned. Buys first North American serial, electronic rights. Submit seasonal material 6 months in advance. Accepts queries by mail, e-mail. Responds in 2 months to queries. Sample copy for $2. Writer's guidelines online.

Nonfiction Unsolicited articles welcomed from writers with Christian education training or current experience in working with children. **Buys 35 mss/year.** Query. Length: 900 words. **Pays 10-14¢/word.**

Reprints Send photocopy and information about when and where the material previously appeared. Pays 35% of amount paid for an original article.

$ $ ⬚ FAITH TODAY

Seeking to Inform, Equip, and Inspire Christians Across Canada, Evangelical Fellowship of Canada, MIP Box 3745, Markham ON L3R 0Y4, Canada. (905)479-5885. Fax: (905)479-4742. E-mail: fteditor@efc-canada.com. Website: www.faithtoday.ca. Bimonthly magazine. "*FT* is an interdenominational, evangelical magazine that informs Canadian Christians on issues facing church and society, and on events within the church community. It focuses on the communal life of local congregations and corporate faith interacting with society more than on personal spiritual life. Writers should have a thorough understanding of the Canadian evangelical community." Estab. 1983. Circ. 18,000. Pays on publication. Publishes ms an average of 4 months after acceptance. Byline given. Offers 30-50% kill fee. Buys first rights. Editorial lead time 4 months. Accepts queries by mail, e-mail, fax. Responds in 6 weeks to queries. Sample copy for SASE in Canadian postage. Writer's guidelines online.

    O— Break in by "researching the Canadian field and including in your query a list of the Canadian contacts (Christian or not) that you intend to interview."

Nonfiction Book excerpts (Canadian authors only), essays (Canadian authors only), interview/profile (Canadian subjects only), opinion, religious, news feature. **Buys 75 mss/year.** Query. Length: 400-2,000 words. **Pays $100-500 Canadian, more for cover topic material.** Sometimes pays expenses of writers on assignment.

Reprints Send photocopy. Rarely used. Pays 50% of amount paid for an original article.

Photos State availability with submission. Reviews contact sheets. Buys one-time rights. Identification of subjects required.

Tips "Query should include brief outline and names of the sources you plan to interview in your research. Use Canadian postage on SASE."

$ THE FIVE STONES

Newsletter for Small Churches, The American Baptist Churches—USA, 69 Weymouth St., Providence RI 02906. (401)861-9405. Fax: (401)861-9405. E-mail: pappas@tabcom.org. **Contact:** Anthony G. Pappas, editor. **50% freelance written.** Quarterly magazine covering congregational dynamics in smaller churches. "*The Five Stones* is a resource for leaders in smaller congregations. Target audience: pastors, lay leaders, denominational officers." Estab. 1980. Circ. 500. Pays on publication. Publishes ms an average of 1 year after acceptance. Byline given. Not copyrighted. Buys one-time rights. Editorial lead time 6 months. Submit seasonal material 6 months in advance. Accepts queries by mail, e-mail, fax, phone. Accepts previously published material. Accepts simultaneous submissions. Responds in 6 weeks to queries; 6 months to mss. Sample copy for SASE. Writer's guidelines for SASE or by fax.

Nonfiction "Articles must be specific to small church-related issues." Book excerpts, essays, historical/nostalgic, how-to, humor, inspirational, interview/profile, personal experience, religious. **Buys 8-12 mss/year.** Send complete ms. Length: 500-3,000 words. **Pays $10.**

Reprints Accepts previously published submissions.

Photos State availability with submission. Reviews GIF/JPEG files. Buys one-time rights. Offers no additional payment for photos accepted with ms. Identification of subjects required.

Columns/Departments Small Town; Urban; Stewardship; Evangelism; Mission; Church Life; Reources; Humor (all first-person), all 500-2,500 words. **Buys 20 mss/year.** Send complete ms. **Pays $10.**

Fiction Ethnic, historical, humorous, religious, slice-of-life vignettes. **Buys 4 mss/year.** Send complete ms. Length: 300-3,000 words. **Pays $5 (maximum), and 2 contributor's copies.**

Tips "First-person experiences. Focus on current issues of congregational life. Submit stories of positive events or learnings from negative ones."

$FORWARD IN CHRIST

The Word from the WELS, WELS, 2929 N. Mayfair Rd., Milwaukee WI 53222-4398. (414)256-3210. Fax: (414)256-3862. E-mail: fic@sab.wels.net. Website: www.wels.net. **Contact:** Gary P. Baumler, editor. **5% freelance written.** Monthly magazine covering WELS news, topics, issues. The material usually must be written by or about WELS members. Estab. 1913. Circ. 56,000. Pays on publication. Publishes ms an average of 6 months after acceptance. Byline given. Buys one-time rights. Editorial lead time 3 months. Submit seasonal material 4 months in advance. Accepts queries by mail, e-mail, fax. Responds in 2 months to queries. Sample copy and writer's guidelines free.

Nonfiction Julie Tessmer Weitzke, senior communications assistant. Personal experience, religious. Query. Length: 550-1,200 words. **Pays $75/page, $125/2 pages.** Sometimes pays expenses of writers on assignment.

Photos State availability with submission. Reviews contact sheets. Buys one-time rights, plus 1 month on Web. Negotiates payment individually. Captions, identification of subjects, model releases required.

Tips "Topics should be of interest to the majority of the members of the synod—the people in the pews. Articles should have a Christian viewpoint, but we don't want sermons. We suggest you carefully read at least 5 or 6 issues with close attention to the length, content, and style of the features."

N FOURSQUARE WORLD ADVANCE

International Church of the Foursquare Gospel, 1910 W. Sunset Blvd., Suite 200, Los Angeles CA 90026-0176. E-mail: bshepson@foursquare.org. Website: www.advancemagazine.org. **Contact:** Bill Shepson, editorial director. **90% freelance written.** Quarterly magazine covering devotional/religious material, news, book and product reviews. "The official publication of the International Church of the Foursquare Gospel is distributed without charge to members and friends of the Foursquare Church." Estab. 1917. Circ. 98,000. Pays on publication. Buys all rights. Accepts queries by mail, e-mail. Accepts previously published material. Responds in 2 weeks to queries. Sample copy for free. Writer's guidelines online.

• Does not accept unsolicited mss.

$GOD ALLOWS U-TURNS

True Stories of Hope and Healing. An ongoing book series project, The God Allows U-Turns Project, P.O. Box 717, Faribault MN 55021-0717. Fax: (507)334-6464. E-mail: editor@godallowsuturns.com. Website: www.godallowsuturns.com. **Contact:** Allison Gappa Bottke, editor. **100% freelance written.** Christian inspirational book series. "Each anthology contains approximately 100 uplifting, encouraging, and inspirational true stories written by contributors from all over the world. Multiple volumes are planned." Volumes 1-4 are published by Barbour Publishing, Inc. Estab. 2000. Pays on publication. Byline given. Accepts previously published material. Accepts simultaneous submissions. Writer's guidelines online.

• Accepts stories by mail, e-mail, fax. Prefers submissions via website or e-mail. Responds *only* when a story is selected for publication. For a list of current *God Allows U-Turns* books open to submissions, as well as related opportunities, go to www.godallowsuturns.com. Timelines vary, so send stories any time as they may fit another volume. You may submit the same story to more than 1 volume, but you must send a separate copy to each. When submitting, indicate which volume it is for.

Nonfiction "Open to well-written personal inspirational pieces showing how faith in God can inspire, encourage, and heal. True stories that must touch our emotions." Essays, historical/nostalgic, humor, inspirational, interview/profile, personal experience, religious. **Buys 100+ mss/year. Pays $50, plus 1 copy of anthology.**

Tips "Read a current volume. See the website for a sample story. Keep it real. Ordinary people doing extraordinary things with God's help. These true stories must touch our emotions. Our contributors are a diverse group with no limits on age or denomination."

$ $GROUP MAGAZINE

Group Publishing, Inc., P.O. Box 481, Loveland CO 80539. (970)669-3836. Fax: (970)669-3269. E-mail: kdieterich@youthministry.com. Website: www.groupmag.com. Publisher: Tim Gilmour. **Contact:** Kathy Dietrich. **60% freelance written.** Bimonthly magazine covering youth ministry. "Writers must be actively involved in youth ministry. Articles we accept are practical, not theoretical, and focused for local church youth workers." Estab. 1974. Circ. 57,000. **Pays on acceptance.** Publishes ms an average of 6 months after acceptance. Byline given. Offers $20 kill fee. Buys all rights. Submit seasonal material 7 months in advance. Responds in 2 months to queries. Sample copy for $2 and 9×12 SAE. Writer's guidelines online.

Nonfiction How-to (youth ministry issues). No personal testimony, theological or lecture-style articles. **Buys 50-60 mss/year.** Query. Length: 250-2,200 words. **Pays $40-250.** Sometimes pays expenses of writers on assignment.

Tips "Submit a youth ministry idea to one of our mini-article sections—we look for tried-and-true ideas youth ministers have used with kids."

Ⓝ $ $ GUIDEPOSTS MAGAZINE

16 E. 34th St., New York NY 10016-4397. (212)251-8100. Website: www.guideposts.org. **Contact:** Mary Ann O'Roark, executive editor. **30% freelance written.** Works with a small number of new/unpublished writers each year. Monthly magazine. "*Guideposts* is an inspirational monthly magazine for people of all faiths, in which men and women from all walks of life tell in true, first-person narrative how they overcame obstacles, rose above failures, handled sorrow, gained new spiritual insight, and became more effective people through faith in God." Estab. 1945. Pays on publication. Publishes ms an average of several months after acceptance. Offers 20% kill fee on assigned stories. Buys all rights. Writer's guidelines online.

● "Many of our stories are ghosted articles, so the writer would not get a byline unless it was his/her own story. Because of the high volume of mail the magazine receives, we regret we *cannot* return manuscripts, and will contact writers only if their material can be used."

Nonfiction Articles and features should be true stories written in simple, anecdotal style with an emphasis on human interest. Short mss of approximately 250-750 words (pays $100-250) considered for such features as "Angels Among Us," "His Mysterious Ways," and general 1-page stories. Address short items to Celeste McCauley. For full-length mss, 750-1,500 words, pays $250-500. All mss should be typed, double-spaced, and accompanied by e-mail address, if possible. Annually awards scholarships to high school juniors and seniors in writing contest. **Buys 40-60 unsolicited mss/year.** Length: 250-1,500 words. **Pays $100-500.** Pays expenses of writers on assignment.

Tips "Study the magazine before you try to write for it. Each story must make a single spiritual point that readers can apply to their own daily lives. And it may be easier to just sit down and write them than to have to go through the process of preparing a query. They should be warm, well written, intelligent, and upbeat. We require personal narratives that are true and have some spiritual aspect, but the religious element can be subtle and should *not* be sermonic. A writer succeeds with us if he or she can write a true article using short-story techniques with scenes, drama, tension, and a resolution of the problem presented."

Ⓝ $ HORIZONS

The Magazine of Presbyterian Women, 100 Witherspoon St., Louisville KY 40202-1396. (502)569-5668. Fax: (502)569-8085. Website: www.pcusa.org/horizons/. Bimonthly Magazine owned and operated by Presbyterian women offering "information and inspiration for Presbyterian women by addressing current issues facing the church and the world." Estab. 1988. Circ. 21,000. Pays on publication. Publishes ms an average of 4 months after acceptance. Buys all rights. Accepts queries by e-mail, fax. Accepts simultaneous submissions. Responds in 2 weeks to queries; 3 weeks to mss. Sample copy for $3 and 9X12 SAE. Writer's guidelines for #10 SASE.

Fiction Sharon Dunne, assistant editor. Ethnic, historical, humorous, mainstream, religious, senior citizen/retirement. "No sex/violence or romance." Send complete ms. Length: 800-1,200 words. **Pays $50/page and 2 contributor's copies; additional copies for $2.50.**

$ LIFEGLOW

Christian Record Services, P.O. Box 6097, Lincoln NE 68506. Website: www.christianrecord.org. **Contact:** Gaylena Gibson, editor. **95% freelance written.** Large print Christian publication for sight-impaired over age 25 covering health, handicapped people, uplifting articles. Estab. 1984. Circ. 35,000. **Pays on acceptance.** Publishes ms an average of 3 years after acceptance. Byline given. Buys one-time rights. Accepts previously published material. Accepts simultaneous submissions. Responds in 1 year to mss. Sample copy for 7×10 SAE and 5 first-class stamps. Writer's guidelines for #10 SASE.

○➤ "Write for an interdenominational Christian audience."

Nonfiction Essays, general interest, historical/nostalgic, humor, inspirational, interview/profile, personal experience, travel, adventure, biography, careers, handicapped, health, hobbies, marriage, nature. **Buys 40 mss/year.** Send complete ms. Length: 200-1,400 words. **Pays 4-5¢/word, and complimentary copies.**

Photos Send photos with submission. Buys one-time rights. Negotiates payment individually.

Columns/Departments Baffle U! (puzzle), 150 words, **pays $15-25/puzzle**; Vitality Plus (current health topics), length varies, **pays 4¢/word.** Buys 10 mss/year. Send complete ms.

Fillers Anecdotes, facts, short humor. **Buys very few/year.** Length: 300 words maximum. **Pays 4¢/word.**
Tips "Make sure manuscript has a strong ending that ties everything together and doesn't leave us dangling. Pretend someone else wrote it—would it hold your interest? Draw your readers into the story by being specific rather than abstract or general."

$ $LIGHT AND LIFE MAGAZINE

Free Methodist Church of North America, P.O. Box 535002, Indianapolis IN 46253-5002. (317)244-3660. Fax: (317)248-9055. E-mail: llmauthors@fmcna.org. Website: www.freemethodistchurch.org/magazine. **Contact:** Doug Newton, editor; Cynthia Schnereger, managing editor. Works with a small number of new/unpublished writers each year. Bimonthly magazine for maturing Christians emphasizing a holiness lifestyle, contemporary issues, and a Christ-centered worldview. Includes pull-out discipleship and evangelism tools and encouragement cards, leadership tips and profiles, denominational news. Estab. 1868. Circ. 13,000. Pays on publication. Byline given. Buys first North American serial rights. Sample copy for $4. Writer's guidelines online.
Nonfiction Query. Length: 400-1,200 words. **Pays 15¢/word.**

$ $LIGUORIAN

One Liguori Dr., Liguori MO 63057-9999. (636)464-2500. Fax: (636)464-8449. E-mail: liguorianeditor@liguori.org. Website: www.liguorian.org. Managing Editor: Cheryl Plass. **Contact:** Fr. Allan Weinert, CSSR, editor-in-chief. **25% freelance written.** Prefers to work with published/established writers. Magazine published 10 times/year for Catholics. "Our purpose is to lead our readers to a fuller Christian life by helping them better understand the teachings of the gospel and the church and by illustrating how these teachings apply to life and the problems confronting them as members of families, the church, and society." Estab. 1913. Circ. 220,000. **Pays on acceptance.** Offers 50% kill fee. Buys all rights. Buys all rights but will reassign rights to author after publication upon written request. Submit seasonal material 8 months in advance. Accepts queries by mail, e-mail, fax, phone. Responds in 3 months to mss. Sample copy for 9×12 SAE with 3 first-class stamps or online. Writer's guidelines for #10 SASE and on website.
Nonfiction Pastoral, practical, and personal approach to the problems and challenges of people today. "No travelogue approach or unresearched ventures into controversial areas. Also, no material found in secular publications—fad subjects that already get enough press, pop psychology, negative or put-down articles." **Buys 40-50 unsolicited mss/year.** Length: 400-2,000 words. **Pays 10-12¢/word.** Sometimes pays expenses of writers on assignment.
Photos Photographs on assignment only unless submitted with and specific to article.
Fiction Religious, senior citizen/retirement. Send complete ms. Length: 1,500-2,000 words preferred. **Pays 10-12¢/word and 5 contributor's copies.**

$THE LIVING CHURCH

Living Church Foundation, 816 E. Juneau Ave., P.O. Box 514036, Milwaukee WI 53203. (414)276-5420. Fax: (414)276-7483. E-mail: tlc@livingchurch.org. Managing Editor: John Schuessler. **Contact:** David Kalvelage, editor. **50% freelance written.** Weekly magazine on the Episcopal Church. News or articles of interest to members of the Episcopal Church. Estab. 1878. Circ. 9,500. Does not pay unless article is requested. Publishes ms an average of 3 months after acceptance. Byline given. Buys one-time rights. Editorial lead time 3 weeks. Submit seasonal material 1 month in advance. Accepts queries by mail, e-mail, fax. Responds in 2 weeks to queries; 1 month to mss. Sample copy for free.
Nonfiction Opinion, personal experience, photo feature, religious. **Buys 10 mss/year.** Send complete ms. Length: 1,000 words. **Pays $25-100.** Sometimes pays expenses of writers on assignment.
Photos Send photos with submission. Reviews any size prints. Buys one-time rights. Offers $15-50/photo.
Columns/Departments Benediction (devotional), 250 words; Viewpoint (opinion), under 1,000 words. Send complete ms. **Pays $50 maximum.**
Poetry Light verse, traditional.

$THE LUTHERAN DIGEST

The Lutheran Digest, Inc., P.O. Box 4250, Hopkins MN 55343. (952)933-2820. Fax: (952)933-5708. E-mail: tldi@lutherandigest.com. Website: www.lutherandigest.com. **Contact:** David L. Tank, editor. **95% freelance written.** Quarterly magazine covering Christianity from a Lutheran perspective. "Articles frequently reflect a Lutheran Christian perspective, but are not intended to be sermonettes. Popular stories show how God has intervened in a person's life to help solve a problem." Estab. 1953. Circ. 105,000. **Pays on acceptance.** Publishes ms an average of 6 months after acceptance. Byline given. Buys first, second serial (reprint) rights. Editorial lead time 9 months. Submit seasonal material 9 months in advance. Accepts queries by mail. Accepts previously published material. Accepts simultaneous submissions. Responds in 1 month to queries; 4 months to mss. Sample copy for $3.50. Writer's guidelines online.

O— Break in with "reprints from other publications that will fill less than three pages of *TLD*. Articles of 1 or 2 pages are even better. As a digest, we primarily look for previously published articles to reprint, however, we do publish about twenty to thirty percent original material. Articles from new writers are always welcomed and seriously considered."

Nonfiction General interest, historical/nostalgic, how-to (personal or spiritual growth), humor, inspirational, personal experience, religious, nature, God's unique creatures. Does not want to see "personal tributes to deceased relatives or friends. They are seldom used unless the subject of the article is well known. We also avoid articles about the moment a person finds Christ as his or her personal savior." **Buys 50-60 mss/year.** Send complete ms. Length: 1,500 words. **Pays $35-50.**

Reprints Accepts previously published submissions. "We prefer this as we are a digest and 70-80% of our articles are reprints."

Photos "We seldom print photos from outside sources." State availability with submission. Buys one-time rights.

Tips "An article that tugs on the 'heart strings' just a little and closes leaving the reader with a sense of hope is a writer's best bet to breaking into *The Lutheran Digest*."

$THE LUTHERAN JOURNAL

Apostolic Publishing Co., Inc., P.O. Box 28158, Oakdale MN 55128. (651)702-0086. Fax: (651)702-0074. Publisher: Vance Lichty. **Contact:** Editorial Assistant. Semiannual Magazine published 2 times/year for Lutheran Church members, middle age and older. "A family magazine providing wholesome and inspirational reading material for the enjoyment and enrichment of Lutherans." Estab. 1938. Circ. 200,000. Pays on publication. Byline given. Buys first, all rights. Accepts simultaneous submissions. Responds in 4 months to queries. Sample copy for 9×12 SAE with 60¢ postage.

Nonfiction Historical/nostalgic, how-to, humor, inspirational, interview/profile, personal experience, religious, interesting or unusual church projects, think articles. **Buys 25-30 mss/year.** Send complete ms. Length: 1,500 words maximum; occasionally 2,000 words. **Pays 1-4¢/word.**

Reprints Send tearsheet, photocopy or typed ms with rights for sale noted and information about when and where the material previously appeared. Pays up to 50% of amount paid for an original article.

Photos Send photocopies of b&w and color photos with accompanying ms. Please do not send original photos.

Fiction Religious, romance, senior citizen/retirement. Must be appropriate for distribution in the churches. Send complete ms. Length: 1,000-1,500 words. **Pays $20-50 and one contributor's copy.**

Poetry Buys 2-3 poems/issue, as space allows. **Pays $10-30.**

Tips "We strongly prefer a warm, personal style of writing that speaks directly to the reader. In general, writers should seek to convey information rather than express personal opinion, though the writer's own personality should be reflected in the article's style. Send submissions with SASE so we may respond."

$LUTHERAN PARTNERS

Augsburg Fortress, Publishers, ELCA (DM), 8765 W. Higgins Rd., Chicago IL 60631-4195. (773)380-2884. Fax: (773)380-2829. E-mail: lpartmag@elca.org. Website: www.elca.org/lp. **Contact:** William A. Decker, managing editor. **15-20% freelance written.** Bimonthly magazine covering issues of religious leadership. "We are a leadership magazine for the ordained and rostered lay ministers of the Evangelical Lutheran Church in America (ELCA), fostering an exchange of opinions on matters involving theology, leadership, mission, and service to Jesus Christ. Know your audience: ELCA congregations and the various kinds of leaders who make up this church and their current issues of leadership." Estab. 1979. Circ. 20,000. Pays on publication. Publishes ms an average of 6 months after acceptance. Byline given. Buys first, one-time, second serial (reprint), electronic rights. Editorial lead time 6 months. Submit seasonal material 6 months in advance. Accepts queries by mail, e-mail, fax, phone. Accepts previously published material. Accepts simultaneous submissions. Responds in 1 month to queries; 6 months to mss. Sample copy for $2. Writer's guidelines online.

● The editor reports an interest in seeing articles on various facets of ministry from the perspectives of ELCA Lutheran ethnic authors (Hispanic, African-American, Asian, Native American, Arab-American), as well as material on youth leadership and ministry.

O— Break in through "Jottings" (practical how-to articles involving congregational ministry ideas, 500 words maximum)."

Nonfiction Historical/nostalgic, how-to (leadership in faith communities), humor (religious cartoon), inspirational, opinion (religious leadership issues), religious, book reviews (query book review editor). "No exposés, articles primarily promoting products/services, or anti-religion." **Buys 15-20 mss/year.** Query with published clips or send complete ms. Length: 500-2,000 words. **Pays $25-170.** Pays in copies for book reviews.

Photos State availability with submission. Buys one-time rights. Generally offers no additional payment for photos accepted with ms. Captions, identification of subjects required.

Columns/Departments Review Editor. Partners Review (book reviews), 700 words. Query or submit ms. **Pays in copies.**

Fiction Rarely accepts religious fiction. Query.

Poetry Free verse, haiku, light verse, traditional, hymns. **Buys 6-10 poems/year.** Submit maximum 10 poems. **Pays $50-75.**

Fillers Practical ministry (education, music, youth, social service, administration, worship, etc.) in congregation. **Buys 3-6/year.** Length: 500 words. **Pays $25.**

Tips "Know congregational life, especially from the perspective of leadership, including both ordained pastor and lay staff. Think current and future leadership needs. It would be good to be familiar with ELCA rostered pastors, lay ministers, and congregations."

$ $ THE LUTHERAN

Magazine of the Evangelical Lutheran Church in America, 8765 W. Higgins Rd., Chicago IL 60631-4183. (773)380-2540. Fax: (773)380-2751. E-mail: lutheran@elca.org. Website: www.thelutheran.org. Managing Editor: Sonia Solomonson. **Contact:** David L. Miller, editor. **15% freelance written.** Monthly magazine for "lay people in church. News and activities of the Evangelical Lutheran Church in America, news of the world of religion, ethical reflections on issues in society, personal Christian experience." Estab. 1988. Circ. 600,000. **Pays on acceptance.** Publishes ms an average of 6 months after acceptance. Byline given. Offers 50% kill fee. Buys first rights. Submit seasonal material 4 months in advance. Accepts queries by mail, e-mail. Responds in 6 weeks to queries. Sample copy free. Writer's guidelines online.

O—¬ Break in by checking out the theme list on the website and querying with ideas related to these themes.

Nonfiction Inspirational, interview/profile, personal experience, photo feature, religious. "No articles unrelated to the world of religion." **Buys 40 mss/year.** Query with published clips. Length: 500-1,500 words. **Pays $400-700 for assigned articles; $100-500 for unsolicited articles.** Pays expenses of writers on assignment.

Photos Send photos with submission. Reviews contact sheets, transparencies, prints. Buys one-time rights. Offers $50-175/photo. Captions, identification of subjects required.

Columns/Departments Lite Side (humor—church, religious), In Focus, Living the Faith, Values & Society, In Our Churches, Our Church at Work, 25-100 words. Send complete ms. **Pays $10.**

■ The online magazine carries original content not found in the print edition. Contact: Lorel Fox, online editor.

Tips "Writers have the best chance selling us feature articles."

$ ☑ MENNONITE BRETHREN HERALD

3-169 Riverton Ave., Winnipeg MB R2L 2E5, Canada. (888)669-6575. Fax: (204)654-1865. E-mail: mbherald@m bconf.ca. Website: www.mbherald.com. **Contact:** Susan Brandt, editor. **25% freelance written.** Triweekly family publication "read mainly by people of the Mennonite Brethren faith, reaching a wide cross section of professional and occupational groups, including many homemakers. Readership includes people from both urban and rural communities. It is intended to inform members of events in the church and the world, serve personal and corporate spiritual needs, serve as a vehicle of communication within the church, serve conference agencies and reflect the history and theology of the Mennonite Brethren Church." Estab. 1962. Circ. 16,500. Pays on publication. Publishes ms an average of 6 months after acceptance. Byline given. Not copyrighted. Buys one-time rights. Accepts queries by e-mail, fax. Responds in 6 months to queries. Sample copy for $1 and 9×12 SAE with 2 IRCs. Writer's guidelines online.

● "Articles and manuscripts not accepted for publication will be returned if a SASE (Canadian stamps or IRCs) is provided by the writers."

Nonfiction Articles with a Christian family orientation; youth directed, Christian faith and life, and current issues. Wants articles critiquing the values of a secular society, attempting to relate Christian living to the practical situations of daily living; showing how people have related their faith to their vocations. Send complete ms. Length: 250-1,500 words. **Pays $30-40.** Pays expenses of writers on assignment.

Reprints Send tearsheet, photocopy or typed ms with rights for sale noted and information about when and where the material previously appeared. Pays 70% of amount paid for an original article.

Photos Photos purchased with ms.

Columns/Departments Viewpoint (Christian opinion on current topics), 850 words. Crosscurrent (Christian opinion on music, books, art, TV, movies), 350 words.

Poetry Length: 25 lines maximum.

Tips "We like simple style, contemporary language and fresh ideas. Writers should take care to avoid religious cliches."

$ $ MESSAGE MAGAZINE

Review and Herald Publishing Association, 55 West Oak Ridge Dr., Hagerstown MD 21740. (301)393-4099. Fax: (301)393-4103. E-mail: message@rhpa.org. Website: www.messagemagazine.org. Editor: Ron C. Smith.

Contact: Pat Sparks Harris, executive assistant. **10-20% freelance written.** Bimonthly magazine. *"Message* is the oldest religious journal addressing ethnic issues in the country. Our audience is predominantly black and Seventh-day Adventist; however, *Message* is an outreach magazine geared to the unchurched." Estab. 1898. Circ. 120,000. **Pays on acceptance.** Publishes ms an average of 12 months after acceptance. Byline given. first North American serial rights Editorial lead time 6 months. Submit seasonal material 6 months in advance. Responds in 9 months to queries. Sample copy by e-mail. Writer's guidelines by e-mail.

Nonfiction General interest (to a Christian audience), how-to (overcome depression; overcome defeat; get closer to God; learn from failure, etc.), inspirational, interview/profile (profiles of famous African Americans), personal experience (testimonies), religious. **Buys 10 mss/year.** Send complete ms. Length: 800-1,200 words. **Payment varies.**

Photos State availability with submission. Buys one-time rights. Identification of subjects required.

Columns/Departments Voices in the Wind (community involvement/service/events/health info); Message, Jr. (stories for children with a moral, explain a biblical or moral principle); Recipes (no meat or dairy products— 12-15 recipes and an intro); Healthspan (health issues); all 500 words. Send complete ms. for Message, Jr. and Healthspan. Query editorial assistant with published clips for Voices in the Wind and Recipes. **Pays $50-300.**

Tips "Please look at the magazine before submitting manuscripts. *Message* publishes a variety of writing styles as long as the writing style is easy to read and flows—please avoid highly technical writing styles."

$ 🖂 THE MESSENGER OF THE SACRED HEART

Apostleship of Prayer, 661 Greenwood Ave., Toronto ON M4J 4B3, Canada. (416)466-1195. **Contact:** Rev. F.J. Power, S.J., editor. **20% freelance written.** Monthly magazine for "Canadian and U.S. Catholics interested in developing a life of prayer and spirituality; stresses the great value of our ordinary actions and lives." Estab. 1891. Circ. 11,000. **Pays on acceptance.** Byline given. Buys first North American serial, first rights. Submit seasonal material 5 months in advance. Responds in 1 month to queries. Sample copy for $1 and $7\frac{1}{2} \times 10\frac{1}{2}$ SAE. Writer's guidelines for #10 SASE.

Fiction Rev. F.J. Power, S.J. and Alfred DeManche, editors. Religious, stories about people, adventure, heroism, humor, drama. No poetry. **Buys 12 mss/year.** Send complete ms. Length: 750-1,500 words. **Pays 6¢/word, and 3 contributor's copies.**

Tips "Develop a story that sustains interest to the end. Do not preach, but use plot and characters to convey the message or theme. Aim to move the heart as well as the mind. Before sending, cut out unnecessary or unrelated words or sentences. If you can, add a light touch or a sense of humor to the story. Your ending should have impact, leaving a moral or faith message for the reader."

🅽 $ THE MIRACULOUS MEDAL

The Central Association of the Miraculous Medal, 475 E. Chelten Ave., Philadelphia PA 19144-5785. (215)848-1010. Website: www.cammonline.org. **Contact:** Rev. James Kiernan, editor. **40% freelance written.** Quarterly magazine. Estab. 1915. **Pays on acceptance.** Publishes ms an average of 2 years after acceptance. Buys first North American serial rights. Accepts queries by mail. Responds in 3 months to queries. Sample copy for 6×9 SAE and 2 first-class stamps. Writer's guidelines free.

Fiction Charles Kelly, general manager. Wants good general fiction—not necessarily religious, but if religion is basic to the story, the writer should be sure of his facts. Only restriction is that subject matter and treatment must not conflict with Catholic teaching and practice. Can use seasonal material, Christmas stories. Religious. Should not be pious or sermon-like. Length: 2,000 words maximum. Occasionally uses short-shorts from 1,000-1,500 words. **Pays 3¢/word minimum.**

Poetry Preferably about the Virgin Mary or at least with a religious slant. Length: 20 lines maximum. **Pays $1/ line minimum.**

🅽 $ $ MY DAILY VISITOR

Our Sunday Visitor, Inc., 200 Noll Plaza, Huntington IN 46750. (260)356-8400. E-mail: mdvisitor@osv.com. Website: www.osv.com. **Contact:** Monica Dodds, editor. **99% freelance written.** Bimonthly magazine of Scripture meditations based on the day's Catholic Mass readings. Circ. 33,000. **Pays on acceptance.** Publishes ms an average of 6 months after acceptance. Byline given. Not copyrighted. Buys one-time rights. Accepts queries by mail, e-mail. Responds in 2 months to queries. Sample copy and writer's guidelines for #10 SAE with 3 first-class stamps.

- Sample meditations and guidelines online. Each writer does 1 full month of meditations on assignment basis only.

Nonfiction Inspirational, personal experience, religious. **Buys 12 mss/year.** Query with published clips. Length: 130-140 words times the number of days in month. **Pays $500 for 1 month (28-31) of meditations and 5 free copies.**

Tips "Previous experience in writing Scripture-based Catholic meditations or essays is helpful."

N $ $ ON MISSION

North American Mission Board, SBC, 4200 North Point Pkwy., Alpharetta GA 30022-4176. E-mail: cpipes@namb .net. Website: www.onmission.com. **50% freelance written.** Bimonthly lifestyle magazine that popularizes evangelism and church planting. *"On Mission*'s primary purpose is to help readers and churches become more intentional about personal evangelism. *On Mission* equips Christians for leading people to Christ and encourages churches to reach new people through new congregations." Estab. 1997. Circ. 100,000. **Pays on acceptance.** Publishes ms an average of 6 months after acceptance. Byline given. Buys first, electronic, first north american rights. Editorial lead time 9 months. Submit seasonal material 9 months in advance. Accepts queries by mail, e-mail. Responds in 6 months to queries; 6 months to mss. Sample copy free or online. Writer's guidelines online.

   o-¬ Break in with a 600-word how-to article.

Nonfiction How-to, humor, personal experience (stories of sharing your faith in Christ with a non-Christian). **Buys 30 mss/year.** Query with published clips. Length: 350-1,200 words. **Pays 25¢/word, more for cover stories.** Pays expenses of writers on assignment.

Photos Most are shot on assignment. Buys one-time rights. Captions, identification of subjects required.

Columns/Departments My Mission (personal evangelism), 700 words. **Buys 2 mss/year.** Query. **Pays 25¢/ word.**

Tips "Readers might be intimidated if those featured appear to be 'super Christians' who seem to live on a higher spiritual plane. Try to introduce subjects as three-dimensional, real people. Include anecdotes or examples of their fears and failures, including ways they overcame obstacles. In other words, take the reader inside the heart of the *On Mission* Christian and reveal the inevitable humanness that makes that person not only believable, but also approachable. We want the reader to feel encouraged to become *On Mission* by identifying with people like them who are featured in the magazine."

N $ $ OUR SUNDAY VISITOR

Our Sunday Visitor, Inc., 200 Noll Plaza, Huntington IN 46750. (260)356-8400. Fax: (260)356-8472. E-mail: oursunvis@osv.com. Website: www.osv.com. **Contact:** Editor. **10% freelance written.** (Mostly assigned). Weekly tabloid covering world events and culture from a Catholic perspective. Estab. 1912. Circ. 70,000. **Pays on acceptance.** Publishes ms an average of 1 month after acceptance. Byline given. Buys first rights. Accepts queries by mail, e-mail.

$ PIME WORLD

PIME Missionaries, 17330 Quincy St., Detroit MI 48221-2765. (313)342-4066. Fax: (313)342-6816. E-mail: pimew orld@pimeusa.org. Website: www.pimeusa.org. **Contact:** Christine Bobbitt, publications manager. **10% freelance written.** Bimonthly magazine supplemented with a newsletter, *PIME World's North America.* "Our focus is on educating North American Catholics on the missionary nature of the Church and inviting them to realize their call to be missionaries. The magazine and newsletter also serve the purpose of introducing the missionaries by emphasizing the IR activities throughout the world. Our audience is largely high school educated, conservative in both religion and politics." Estab. 1954. Circ. 12,000. Pays on publication. Publishes ms an average of 5 months after acceptance. Byline given. Buys one-time rights. Editorial lead time 2 months. Submit seasonal material 2 months in advance. Accepts queries by mail, e-mail, fax, phone. Accepts simultaneous submissions. Responds in 2 weeks to queries; 2 months to mss. Sample copy for free. Writer's guidelines for #10 SASE.

Nonfiction Missionary activities of the Catholic church in the world, especially in Bangladesh, Brazil, Myanmar, Cameroon, Guinea Bissau, Hong Kong, India, Ivory Coast, Japan, Papua New Guinea, the Philippines, and Thailand. Query or send complete ms. Length: 200-500 words. **Pays $15 flat rate upon publication; 501-1,000 words pays $25 flat rate upon publication.**

Reprints Accepts previously published submissions.

Photos State availability of or send photos with submission. Buys one-time rights. Pays $10/color photo. Identification of subjects required.

Tips "Articles produced from a faith standpoint dealing with current issues of social justice, evangelization, witness, proclamation, pastoral work in the foreign missions, etc. Interviews of missionaries, both religious and lay, welcome. Good quality color photos greatly appreciated."

$ $ THE PLAIN TRUTH

Christianity Without the Religion, Plain Truth Ministries, 300 W. Green St., Pasadena CA 91129. Fax: (626)304-8172. E-mail: phyllis_duke@ptm.org. Website: www.ptm.org. Editor: Greg Albrecht. **Contact:** Phyllis Duke, assistant editor. **90% freelance written.** Bimonthly magazine. "We seek to reignite the flame of shattered lives by illustrating the joy of a new life in Christ." Estab. 1935. Circ. 70,000. Pays on publication. Publishes ms an average of 8 months after acceptance. Byline given. Offers $50 kill fee. Buys all-language rights for *The Plain Truth* and its affiliated publications. Editorial lead time 6 months. Submit seasonal material 6 months in advance.

Accepts queries by mail, e-mail. Accepts simultaneous submissions. Sample copy for 9×12 SAE and 5 first-class stamps. Writer's guidelines online.

Nonfiction Inspirational, interview/profile, personal experience, religious. **Buys 48-50 mss/year.** Query with published clips and SASE. *No unsolicited mss.* Length: 750-2,500 words. **Pays 25¢/word.**

Reprints Send tearsheet or photocopy of article or typed ms with rights for sale noted and information about when and where the article previously appeared with SASE for response. Pays 15¢/word.

Photos State availability with submission. Reviews transparencies, prints. Buys one-time rights. Negotiates payment individually. Captions required.

▣ The online magazine carries original content not found in the print edition and includes writer's guidelines.

Tips "Material should offer Biblical solutions to real-life problems. Both first-person and third-person illustrations are encouraged. Articles should take a unique twist on a subject. Material must be insightful and practical for the Christain reader. All articles must be well researched and Biblically accurate without becoming overly scholastic. Use convincing arguments to support your Christian platform. Use vivid word pictures, simple and compelling language, and avoid stuffy academic jargon. Captivating anecdotes are vital."

$▣ PRAIRIE MESSENGER

Catholic Journal, Benedictine Monks of St. Peter's Abbey, P.O. Box 190, Muenster SK S0K 2Y0, Canada. (306)682-1772. Fax: (306)682-5285. E-mail: pm.canadian@stpeters.sk.ca. Website: www.stpeters.sk.ca/prairie_messenger. Editor: Rev. Andrew Britz, OSB. **Contact:** Maureen Weber, associate editor. **10% freelance written.** Weekly Catholic journal with strong emphasis on social justice, Third World, and ecumenism. Estab. 1904. Circ. 7,300. Pays on publication. Publishes ms an average of 4 months after acceptance. Byline given. Not copyrighted. Buys first North American serial, first, one-time, second serial (reprint), simultaneous rights. Submit seasonal material 3 months in advance. Accepts queries by mail, e-mail, fax, phone. Responds in 2 months to queries. Sample copy for 9×12 SAE with $1 Canadian postage or IRCs. Writer's guidelines online.

Nonfiction Interview/profile, opinion, religious. "No articles on abortion." **Buys 15 mss/year.** Send complete ms. Length: 250-600 words. **Pays $40-60.** Sometimes pays expenses of writers on assignment.

Photos Send photos with submission. Reviews 3×5 prints. Buys all rights. Offers $20/photo. Captions required.

$▣ PRESBYTERIAN RECORD

50 Wynford Dr., Toronto ON M3C 1J7, Canada. (416)444-1111. Fax: (416)441-2825. E-mail: dharris@presbyterian.ca. Website: www.presbyterian.ca/record. **Contact:** David Harris, editor. **5% freelance written.** Eager to work with new/unpublished writers. Monthly magazine for a church-oriented, family audience. Circ. 45,000. Pays on publication. Publishes ms an average of 4 months after acceptance. Buys first North American serial, one-time, simultaneous rights. Submit seasonal material 3 months in advance. Accepts queries by e-mail. Sample copy for 9×12 SAE with $1 Canadian postage or IRCs.

● Responds in 2 months on accepted ms.

Nonfiction Check a copy of the magazine for style. Inspirational, interview/profile, personal experience, religious. Special issues: Evangelism; Spirituality; Education. No material solely or mainly US in context. No sermons, accounts of ordinations, inductions, baptisms, receptions, church anniversaries, or term papers. **Buys 5-10 unsolicited mss/year.** Query. Length: 700-1,500 words. **Pays $75-150 (Canadian).** Sometimes pays expenses of writers on assignment.

Reprints Send tearsheet, photocopy or typed ms with rights for sale noted and information about when and where the material previously appeared.

Photos When possible, photos should accompany ms; e.g., current events, historical events, and biographies. Pays $50 (Canadian) for glossy photos.

Columns/Departments Items of contemporary and often controversial nature, 700 words; Mission Knocks (new ideas for congregational mission and service), 700 words.

Tips "There is a trend away from maudlin, first-person pieces redolent with tragedy and dripping with simplistic, pietistic conclusions. Writers often leave out those parts which would likely attract readers, such as anecdotes and direct quotes. Using active rather than passive verbs also helps most manuscripts."

$ $ PRESBYTERIANS TODAY

Presbyterian Church (U.S.A.), 100 Witherspoon St., Louisville KY 40202-1396. (502)569-5637. Fax: (502)569-8632. E-mail: today@pcusa.org. Website: www.pcusa.org/today. **Contact:** Eva Stimson, editor. **25% freelance written.** Prefers to work with published/established writers. Denominational magazine published 10 times/year covering religion, denominational activities, and public issues for members of the Presbyterian Church (U.S.A.). "The magazine's purpose is to increase understanding and appreciation of what the church and its members are doing to live out their Christian faith." Estab. 1867. Circ. 58,000. **Pays on acceptance.** Publishes ms an average of 6 months after acceptance. Byline given. Offers 50% kill fee. Buys first North American serial rights. Editorial lead time 3 months. Submit seasonal material 3 months in advance. Accepts queries by mail, e-mail, fax, phone. Responds in 2 weeks to queries; 1 month to mss. Sample copy free. Writer's guidelines online.

◈ Break in with a "short feature for our 'Spotlight' department (300 words)."

Nonfiction "Most articles have some direct relevance to a Presbyterian audience; however, *Presbyterians Today* also seeks well-informed articles written for a general audience that help readers deal with the stresses of daily living from a Christian perspective." How-to (everyday Christian living), inspirational, Presbyterian programs, issues, people. **Buys 20 mss/year.** Send complete ms. Length: 1,000-1,800 words. **Pays $300 maximum for assigned articles; $75-300 for unsolicited articles.**

Photos State availability with submission. Reviews contact sheets, transparencies, color prints, digital images. Buys one-time rights. Negotiates payment individually. Identification of subjects required.

$ $ PRISM MAGAZINE

America's Alternative Evangelical Voice, Evangelicals for Social Action, 10 E. Lancaster Ave., Wynnewood PA 19096. (610)645-9391. Fax: (610)649-8090. E-mail: kristyn@esa-online.org. Website: www.esa-online.org. **Contact:** Kristyn Komarnicki, editor. **50% freelance written.** Bimonthly magazine covering Christianity and social justice. For holistic, Biblical, socially-concerned, progressive Christians. Estab. 1993. Circ. 5,000. Pays on publication. Publishes ms an average of 4-6 months after acceptance. Byline given. Buys first North American serial rights. Editorial lead time 4 months. Submit seasonal material 4 months in advance. Accepts queries by mail, e-mail. Responds in 1 month to queries; 3 months to mss. Sample copy for $3. Writer's guidelines free.

• "We're a nonprofit, some writers are pro bono." Occasionally accepts previously published material.

Nonfiction Book excerpts (to coincide with book release date), essays, interview/profile (ministry). **Buys 10-12 mss/year.** Send complete ms. Length: 500-3,000 words. **Pays $75-300 for assigned articles; $25-200 for unsolicited articles.**

Photos Send photos with submission. Reviews prints, JPEG files. Buys one-time rights. Pays $25/photo published; $150 if photo used on cover.

Tips "We look closely at stories of holistic ministry. It's best to request a sample copy to get to know *PRISM*'s focus/style before submitting—we receive so many submissions that are not appropriate."

$ PURPOSE

616 Walnut Ave., Scottdale PA 15683-1999. (724)887-8500. Fax: (724)887-3111. E-mail: horsch@mph.org. Website: www.mph.org. **Contact:** James E. Horsch, editor. **95% freelance written.** Weekly magazine "for adults, young and old, general audience with varied interests. My readership is interested in seeing how Christianity works in difficult situations. Magazine focuses on Christian discipleship—how to be a faithful Christian in the midst of everday life situations. Uses personal story form to present models and examples to encourage Christians in living a life of faithful discipleship." Estab. 1968. Circ. 10,000. **Pays on acceptance.** Publishes ms an average of 8 months after acceptance. Buys one-time rights. Submit seasonal material 6 months in advance. Accepts queries by e-mail. Accepts previously published material. Accepts simultaneous submissions. Responds in 3 months to queries. Sample copy and writer's guidelines for 6×9 SAE and $2.

Nonfiction Inspirational stories from a Christian perspective. "I want upbeat stories that deal with issues faced by believers in family, business, politics, religion, gender, and any other areas—and show how the Christian faith resolves them. *Purpose* conveys truth through quality fiction or true life stories. Our magazine accents Christian discipleship. Christianity affects all of life, and we expect our material to demonstrate this. I would like story-type articles about individuals, groups, and organizations who are intelligently and effectively working at such problems as hunger, poverty, international understanding, peace, justice, etc., because of their faith. Essays, fiction, and how-to-do-it pieces must include a lot of anecdotal, life exposure examples." **Buys 130 mss/year.**

Reprints Send tearsheet, photocopy or typed ms with rights for sale noted and information about when and where the material previously appeared.

Photos Photos purchased with ms must be sharp enough for reproduction; requires prints in all cases. Captions required.

Fiction "Produce the story with specificity so that it appears to take place somewhere and with real people." Historical, humorous, religious. No militaristic/narrow patriotism or racism. Send complete ms. Length:750 words. **Pays up to 5¢ for stories, and 2 contributor's copies.**

Poetry Free verse, light verse, traditional, blank verse. **Buys 130 poems/year.** Length: 12 lines. **Pays $7.50-20/poem depending on length and quality. Buys one-time rights only.**

Fillers Anecdotal items up to 599 words. **Pays 4¢/word maximum.**

$ QUEEN OF ALL HEARTS

Montfort Missionaries, 26 S. Saxon Ave., Bay Shore NY 11706-8993. (631)665-0726. Fax: (631)665-4349. E-mail: montfort@optonline.net. Website: www.montfortmissionaries.com. **Contact:** Roger Charest, S.M.M., managing editor. **50% freelance written.** Bimonthly magazine covering "Mary, Mother of Jesus, as seen in the sacred scriptures, tradition, history of the church, the early Christian writers, lives of the saints, poetry, art, music, spiritual writers, apparitions, shrines, ecumenism, etc." Magazine of "stories, articles and features on the Mother of God by explaining the Scriptural basis and traditional teaching of the Catholic Church concerning the Mother of Jesus, her influence in fields of history, literature, art, music, poetry, etc." Estab. 1950. Circ. 2,000. **Pays on acceptance.** Publishes ms an average of 6-12 months after acceptance. Byline given. Not copyrighted. Submit seasonal material 6 months in advance. Accepts queries by mail, e-mail, fax, phone. Responds in 2 months to queries. Sample copy for $2.50 with 9X12 SAE.

Nonfiction Essays, inspirational, interview/profile, personal experience, religious (Marialogical and devotional). **Buys 25 mss/year.** Send complete ms. Length: 750-2,500 words. **Pays $40-60.**

Photos Send photos with submission. Reviews transparencies. Buys one-time rights. Pay varies.

Fiction Roger M. Charest, S.M.M., managing editor. Religious. "No mss not about Our Lady, the Mother of God, the Mother of Jesus." **Buys 6 mss/year.** Send complete ms. Length: 1,500-2,500 words. **Pays $40-60.**

Poetry Joseph Tusiani, poetry editor. Free verse. **Buys approximately 10 poems/year.** Submit maximum 2 poems. **Pays in contributor copies.**

$ $ REFORM JUDAISM

Union of American Hebrew Congregations, 633 Third Ave. 7th Floor, New York NY 10017-6778. (212)650-4240. Fax: (212)650-4249. E-mail: rjmagazine@uahc.org. Website: www.uahc.org/rjmag/. **Contact:** Joy Weinberg, managing editor. **30% freelance written.** Quarterly magazine of Reform Jewish issues. "*Reform Judaism* is the official voice of the Union of American Hebrew Congregations, linking the institutions and affiliates of Reform Judaism with every Reform Jew. *RJ* covers developments within the Movement while interpreting events and Jewish tradition from a Reform perspective." Estab. 1972. Circ. 310,000. Pays on publication. Publishes ms an average of 3 months after acceptance. Byline given. Offers kill fee for commissioned articles. Buys first North American serial rights. Submit seasonal material 6 months in advance. Accepts previously published material. Accepts simultaneous submissions. Responds in 2 months to queries; 2 months to mss. Sample copy for $3.50. Writer's guidelines online.

Nonfiction Book excerpts, exposé, general interest, historical/nostalgic, inspirational, interview/profile, opinion, personal experience, photo feature, travel. **Buys 30 mss/year.** Submit complete ms with SASE. Length: Cover stories: 2,500-3,500 words; major feature: 1,800-2,500 words; secondary feature: 1,200-1,500 words; department (e.g., Travel): 1,200 words; letters: 200 words maximum; opinion: 525 words maximum. **Pays 30¢/ word.** Sometimes pays expenses of writers on assignment.

Reprints Send tearsheet, photocopy or typed ms with rights for sale noted and information about when and where the material previously appeared. Usually does not publish reprints.

Photos Send photos with submission. Reviews 8×10/color or slides and b&w prints. Buys one-time rights. Pays $25-75. Identification of subjects required.

Fiction Humorous, religious, ophisticated, cutting-edge, superb writing. **Buys 4 mss/year.** Send complete ms. Length: 600-2,500 words. **Pays 30¢/word.**

🖥 The online magazine carries original content not found in the print edition and includes writer's guidelines.

Tips "We prefer a stamped postcard including the following information/checklist: __Yes, we are interested in publishing; __No, unfortunately the submission doesn't meet our needs; __Maybe, we'd like to hold on to the article for now. Submissions sent this way will receive a faster response."

Ⓝ $ $ THE REPORTER

Women's American ORT, Inc., 250 Park Ave. S., Suite 600, New York NY 10003. (212)505-7700. Fax: (212)674-3057. E-mail: dasher@waort.org. Website: www.waort.org. **Contact:** Dana Asher, editor. **85% freelance written.** Semiannual nonprofit journal published by Jewish women's organization covering Jewish women celebrities, issues of contemporary Jewish culture, Israel, anti-Semitism, women's rights, Jewish travel and the international Jewish community. Estab. 1966. Circ. 50,000. **Pays on acceptance.** Publishes ms an average of 1 year after acceptance. Byline given. Buys first North American serial rights. Submit seasonal material 6 months in advance. Accepts queries by mail, e-mail. Responds in 3 months to queries. Sample copy for 9×12 SAE and 3 first-class stamps. Writer's guidelines for #10 SASE.

⦿ Break in with "a different look at a familiar topic, i.e., 'Jews without God' (Winter 2000). Won't consider handwritten or badly-typed queries. Unpublished writers are welcome. Others, include credits."

Nonfiction Cover feature profiles a dynamic Jewish woman making a difference in Judaism, women's issues, education, entertainment, profiles, business, journalism, arts. Essays, exposé, humor, inspirational, opinion, personal experience, photo feature, religious, travel. Query. Length: 1,800 words maximum. **Pays $200 and up.**

Photos Send photos with submission. Identification of subjects required.

Columns/Departments Education Horizon; Destination (Jewish sites/travel); Inside Out (Advocacy); Women's Business; Art Scene (interviews, books, films); Lasting Impression (uplifting/inspirational).

Fiction Publishes novel excerpts and short stories as part of Lasting Impressions column. Length: 800 words. **Pays $150-300.**

Tips "Send query only by e-mail or postal mail. Show us a fresh look, not a rehash. Particularly interested in stories of interest to younger readers."

$REVIEW FOR RELIGIOUS

3601 Lindell Blvd., Room 428, St. Louis MO 63108-3393. (314)977-7363. Fax: (314)977-7362. E-mail: review@slu.edu. Website: www.reviewforreligious.org. **Contact:** David L. Fleming, S.J., editor. **100% freelance written.** Quarterly magazine for Roman Catholic priests, brothers, and sisters. Estab. 1942. Pays on publication. Publishes ms an average of 9 months after acceptance. Byline given. Buys first North American serial rights. Rarely buys second serial (reprint) rights. Accepts queries by mail, fax. Responds in 2 months to queries. Writer's guidelines online.

Nonfiction Spiritual, liturgical, canonical matters only. Not for general audience. Length: 1,500-5,000 words. **Pays $6/page.**

Tips "The writer must know about religious life in the Catholic Church and be familiar with prayer, vows, community life, and ministry."

$THE SECRET PLACE

Educational Ministries, ABC/USA, P.O. Box 851, Valley Forge PA 19482-0851. (610)768-2240. **Contact:** Kathleen Hayes, senior editor. **100% freelance written.** Quarterly devotional covering Christian daily devotions. Estab. 1938. Circ. 150,000. **Pays on acceptance.** Byline given. Buys first rights. Editorial lead time 1 year. Submit seasonal material 9 months in advance. Sample copy for free. Writer's guidelines for 6×9 SASE.

Nonfiction Inspirational. **Buys about 400 mss/year.** Send complete ms. Length: 100-200 words. **Pays $15 for assigned articles.**

Poetry Avant-garde, free verse, light verse, traditional. **Buys 12-15/year poems/year.** Submit maximum 6 poems. Length: 4-30 lines. **Pays $15.**

$ $SHARING THE VICTORY

Fellowship of Christian Athletes, 8701 Leeds Rd., Kansas City MO 64129. (816)921-0909. Fax: (816)921-8755. E-mail: stv@fca.org. Website: www.fca.org. Editor: Jill Ewert. **50% freelance written.** Prefers to work with published/established writers, but works with a growing number of new/unpublished writers each year. Published 9 times/year. "We seek to encourage and enable athletes and coaches at all levels to take their faith seriously on and off the 'field.'" Estab. 1959. Circ. 80,000. Pays on publication. Publishes ms an average of 4 months after acceptance. Byline given. Buys first rights. Submit seasonal material 6 months in advance. Responds in 3 months to queries; 3 months to mss. Sample copy for $1 and 9×12 SAE with 3 first-class stamps. Writer's guidelines online.

Nonfiction Inspirational, interview/profile (with name athletes and coaches solid in their faith), personal experience, photo feature. **Buys 5-20 mss/year.** Query. Length: 500-1,000 words.

Photos State availability with submission. Reviews contact sheets. Buys one-time rights. Pay based on size of photo.

Tips "Profiles and interviews of particular interest to coed athlete, primarily high school and college age. Our graphics and editorial content appeal to youth. The area most open to freelancers is profiles on or interviews with well-known athletes or coaches (male, female, minorities) who have been or are involved in some capacity with FCA."

$ $SIGNS OF THE TIMES

Pacific Press Publishing Association, P.O. Box 5353, Nampa ID 83653-5353. (208)465-2579. Fax: (208)465-2531. E-mail: mmoore@pacificpress.com. **Contact:** Marvin Moore, editor. **40% freelance written.** Works with a small number of new/unpublished writers each year. Monthly magazine. "We are a monthly Seventh-day Adventist magazine encouraging the general public to practice the principles of the Bible." Estab. 1874. Circ. 200,000. **Pays on acceptance.** Publishes ms an average of 6-18 months after acceptance. Byline given. Offers kill fee. Buys first North American serial, one-time, second serial (reprint) rights. Editorial lead time 1 year. Submit seasonal material 1 year in advance. Responds in 1 month to queries; 2-3 months to mss. Sample copy and writer's guidelines for 9×12 SAE with 3 first-class stamps. Writer's guidelines online.

Nonfiction "We want writers with a desire to share the good news of reconciliation with God. Articles should be people-oriented, well-researched, and should have a sharp focus. Gospel articles deal with salvation and how to experience it. While most of our gospel articles are assigned or picked up from reprints, we do occasionally accept unsolicited manuscripts in this area. Gospel articles should be 1,250 words. Christian lifestyle articles deal with the practical problems of everyday life from a Biblical and Christian perspective. These are typically 1,000-1,200 words. We request that authors include sidebars that give additional information on the topic whenever possible. First-person stories must illuminate a spiritual or moral truth that the individual in the story learned. We especially like stories that hold the reader in suspense or that have an unusual twist at the end. First-person stories are typically 1,000 words long." General interest, how-to, humor, inspirational, interview/profile, personal experience, religious. **Buys 75 mss/year.** Query by mail only with or without published clips or send complete ms. Length: 500-1,500 words. **Pays 10-20¢/word.**

Reprints Send tearsheet, photocopy or typed ms with rights for sale noted and information about when and where the material previously appeared. Pays 50% of amount paid for an original article.

Photos Merwin Stewart, photo editor. Reviews b&w contact sheets, 35mm color transparencies, 5×7 or 8×10 b&w prints. Buys one-time rights. Pays $35-300 for transparencies; $20-50 for prints. Captions, identification of subjects, model releases required.

Fillers "Short fillers can be inspirational/devotional, Christian lifestyle, stories, comments that illuminate a Biblical text—in short, anything that might fit in a general Christian magazine." Length: 500-600 words.

Tips "The audience for *Signs of the Times* includes both Christians and non-Christians of all ages. However, we recommend that our authors write with the non-Christian in mind, since most Christians can easily relate to articles that are written from a non-Christian perspective, whereas many non-Christians will have no interest in an article that is written from a Christian perspective. While *Signs* is published by Seventh-day Adventists, we mention even our own denominational name in the magazine rather infrequently. The purpose is not to hide who we are but to make the magazine as attractive to non-Christian readers as possible. We are especially interested in articles that respond to the questions of everyday life that people are asking and the problems they are facing. Since these questions and problems nearly always have a spiritual component, articles that provide a Biblical and spiritual response are especially welcome. Any time you can provide us with 1 or more sidebars that add information to the topic of your article, you enhance your chance of getting our attention. Two kinds of sidebars seem to be especially popular with readers: those that give information in lists, with each item in the list consisting of only a few words or at the most a sentence, or those that give technical information or long explanations that in the main article might get the reader too bogged down in detail. Whatever their length, sidebars need to be part of the total word count of the article. We like the articles in *Signs of the Times* to have interest-grabbing introductions. One of the best ways to do this is with anecdotes, particularly those that have a bit of suspense or conflict."

$SOCIAL JUSTICE REVIEW

3835 Westminster Place, St. Louis MO 63108-3472. (314)371-1653. Fax: (314)371-0889. E-mail: centbur@juno.com. Website: www.socialjusticereview.org. **Contact:** The Rev. John H. Miller, C.S.C., editor. **25% freelance written.** Works with a small number of new/unpublished writers each year. Bimonthly magazine. Estab. 1908. Publishes ms an average of 1 year after acceptance. Not copyrighted, however special articles within the magazine may be copyrighted, or an occasional special issue has been copyrighted due to author's request. Buys first North American serial rights. Accepts queries by mail. Sample copy for 9×12 SAE and 3 first-class stamps.

Nonfiction Scholarly articles on society's economic, religious, social, intellectual, political problems with the aim of bringing Catholic social thinking to bear upon these problems. Query by mail only with SASE. Length: 2,500-3,000 words. **Pays about 2¢/word.**

Reprints Send ms with rights for sale noted and information about when and where the material previously appeared. Pays about 2¢/word.

Tips "Write moderate essays completely compatible with papal teaching and readable to the average person."

$ $ST. ANTHONY MESSENGER

28 W. Liberty St., Cincinnati OH 45202-6498. (513)241-5615. Fax: (513)241-0399. E-mail: stanthony@americancatholic.org. Website: www.americancatholic.org. **Contact:** Father Pat McCloskey, O.F.M., editor. **55% freelance written.** Monthly general interest magazine for a national readership of Catholic families, most of which have children or grandchildren in grade school, high school, or college. "*St. Anthony Messenger* is a Catholic family magazine which aims to help its readers lead more fully human and Christian lives. We publish articles which report on a changing church and world, opinion pieces written from the perspective of Christian faith and values, personality profiles, and fiction which entertains and informs." Estab. 1893. Circ. 324,000. **Pays on acceptance.** Publishes ms an average of 1 year after acceptance. Byline given. Buys first North American serial, electronic rights. first worldwide serial rights. Submit seasonal material 6 months in advance. Accepts queries by mail, e-mail, fax. Responds in 3 weeks to queries; 2 months to mss. Sample copy for 9×12 SAE with 4 first-class stamps. Writer's guidelines online.

Nonfiction How-to (on psychological and spiritual growth, problems of parenting/better parenting, marriage problems/marriage enrichment), humor, inspirational, interview/profile, opinion (limited use; writer must have special qualifications for topic), personal experience (if pertinent to our purpose), photo feature, informational, social issues. **Buys 35-50 mss/year.** Query with published clips. Length: 1,500-2,500 words. **Pays 16¢/word.** Sometimes pays expenses of writers on assignment.

Fiction Mainstream, religious, senior citizen/retirement. "We do not want mawkishly sentimental or preachy fiction. Stories are most often rejected for poor plotting and characterization; bad dialogue—listen to how people talk; inadequate motivation. Many stories say nothing, are 'happenings' rather than stories." No fetal journals, no rewritten Bible stories. **Buys 12 mss/year.** Send complete ms. Length: 2,000-3,000 words. **Pays 16¢/word maximum and 2 contributor's copies; $1 charge for extras.**

Poetry "Our poetry needs are very limited." Submit maximum 4-5 poems. Length: Up to 20-25 lines; the shorter, the better. **Pays $2/line; $20 minimum.**

Tips "The freelancer should consider why his or her proposed article would be appropriate for us, rather than for *Redbook* or *Saturday Review*. We treat human problems of all kinds, but from a religious perspective. Articles should reflect Catholic theology, spirituality, and employ a Catholic terminology and vocabulary. We need more articles on prayer, scripture, Catholic worship. Get authoritative information (not merely library research); we want interviews with experts. Write in popular style; use lots of examples, stories, and personal quotes. Word length is an important consideration."

$ STANDARD

Nazarene International Headquarters, 6401 The Paseo, Kansas City MO 64131. (816)333-7000. Fax: (816)333-4439. E-mail: cyourdon@nazarene.org or evlead@nazarene.org. Website: www.nazarene.org. **Contact:** Dr. Everett Leadingham, editor, or Charlie L. Roudon, managing editor. **100% freelance written.** Works with a small number of new/unpublished writers each year. Weekly inspirational paper with Christian reading for adults. Inspirational reading for adults. "In *Standard* we want to show Christianity in action, and we prefer to do that through stories that hold the reader's attention." Estab. 1936. Circ. 130,000. **Pays on acceptance.** Publishes ms an average of 14-18 months after acceptance. Byline given. Buys first or reprint rights. Submit seasonal material 6 months in advance. Accepts simultaneous submissions. Writer's guidelines and sample copy for SAE with 2 first-class stamps or by e-mail.

• Accepts submissions by mail, e-mail. No queries needed.

Fiction Prefers fiction-type stories *showing* Christianity in action. Send complete ms. Length: 600-1,800 words. **Pays 3½¢/word for first rights; 2¢/word for reprint rights, and contributor's copies.**

Poetry Free verse, haiku, light verse, traditional. **Buys 50 poems/year.** Submit maximum 5 poems. Length: 30 lines. **Pays 25¢/line.**

Tips "Stories should express Christian principles without being preachy. Setting, plot, and characterization must be realistic."

$ $ TODAY'S CHRISTIAN

Stories of Faith, Hope and God's Love, (formerly *Christian Reader*), Christianity Today, 465 Gundersen Dr., Carol Stream IL 60188. (630)260-6200. Fax: (630)260-0114. E-mail: creditor@christianreader.net. Website: www.christianreader.net. Managing Editor: Edward Gilbreath. **Contact:** Cynthia Thomas, editorial coordinator. **25% freelance written.** Bimonthly magazine for adult evangelical Christian audience. Estab. 1963. Circ. 185,000. Pays on acceptance; on publication for humor pieces. Byline given. Editorial lead time 5 months. Submit seasonal material 8 months in advance. Accepts queries by mail. Accepts simultaneous submissions. Responds in 1 month to queries. Sample copy for 5×8 SAE and 4 first-class stamps. Writer's guidelines online.

Nonfiction Book excerpts, general interest, historical/nostalgic, humor, inspirational, interview/profile, personal experience, photo feature, religious. **Buys 100-125 mss/year.** Query with or without published clips or send complete ms. Length: 250-1,500 words. **Pays $125-600 depending on length.** Pays expenses of writers on assignment.

Reprints Send tearsheet, photocopy or typed ms with rights for sale noted and information about when and where the material previously appeared. Pays 35-50% of amount paid for an original article.

Photos Send photos with submission. Reviews transparencies, prints. Buys one-time rights. Negotiates payment individually. Identification of subjects required.

Columns/Departments Humor Us (adult church humor, kids say and do funny things, and humorous wedding tales), 50-200 words. **Pays $35.**

Fillers Anecdotes, short fillers. **Buys 10-20/year.** Length: 100-250 words. **Pays $35.**

Tips "Most of our articles are reprints or staff written. Freelance competition is keen, so tailor submissions to meet our needs by observing the following: The *Christian Reader* audience is truly a general interest one, including men and women, urban professionals and rural homemakers, adults of every age and marital status, and Christians of every church affiliation. We seek to publish a magazine that people from the variety of ethnic groups in North America will find interesting and relevant."

TRICYCLE

The Buddhist Review, The Buddhist Ray, Inc, 92 Vandam St., New York NY 10013. (212)645-1143. Fax: (212)645-1493. E-mail: editorial@tricycle.com. Website: www.tricycle.com. Editor-in-Chief: James Shaheen. **Contact:** Caitlin Van Dusen, associate editor. **80% freelance written.** Quarterly magazine covering the impact of Buddhism on Western culture. *"Tricycle* readers tend to be well educated and open minded." Estab. 1991. Circ. 60,000. Pays on publication. Byline given. Offers 25% kill fee. Buys one-time rights. Editorial lead time 3 months. Accepts queries by mail, e-mail, fax. Accepts simultaneous submissions. Responds in 3 months to queries; 3 months to mss. Sample copy for $7.50 or online at website. Writer's guidelines online.

Nonfiction Book excerpts, essays, general interest, historical/nostalgic, humor, inspirational, interview/profile, personal experience, photo feature, religious, travel. **Buys 4-6 mss/year.** Length: 1,000-5,000 words.

Photos State availability with submission. Reviews contact sheets. Buys one-time rights. Negotiates payment individually. Captions, identification of subjects required.

Columns/Departments Reviews (film, books, tapes), 600 words; Science and Gen Next, both 700 words. **Buys 6-8 mss/year.** Query.

Poetry *Tricycle* reports that they publish "very little poetry" and do not encourage unsolicited submissions.

Tips *"Tricycle* is a Buddhist magazine, and we can only consider Buddhist-related submissions."

$ $ U.S. CATHOLIC

Claretian Publications, 205 W. Monroe St., Chicago IL 60606. (312)236-7782. Fax: (312)236-8207. E-mail: editors @uscatholic.org. Website: www.uscatholic.org. Editor: Fr. John Molyneux, CMF. Managing Editor: Heidi Schlumpf. Executive Editor: Meinrad Scherer-Emunds. **Contact:** Fran Hurst, editorial assistant. **100% freelance written.** Monthly magazine covering Roman Catholic spirituality. *"U.S. Catholic* is dedicated to the belief that it makes a difference whether you're Catholic. We invite and help our readers explore the wisdom of their faith tradition and apply their faith to the challenges of the 21st century." Estab. 1935. Circ. 40,000. **Pays on acceptance.** Publishes ms an average of 2-3 months after acceptance. Byline given. Buys all rights. Editorial lead time 8 months. Submit seasonal material 6 months in advance. Accepts queries by mail, e-mail, fax, phone. Responds in 1 month to queries; 2 months to mss. Sample copy for large SASE. Guidelines by e-mail or on website.

• Please include SASE with written ms.

Nonfiction Essays, inspirational, opinion, personal experience, religious. **Buys 100 mss/year.** Send complete ms. Length: 2,500-3,500 words. **Pays $250-600.** Sometimes pays expenses of writers on assignment.

Photos State availability with submission.

Columns/Departments Pays $250-600.

Fiction Maureen Abood, literary editor. Ethnic, mainstream, religious, slice-of-life vignettes. **Buys 4-6 mss/ year.** Send complete ms. Length: 2,500-3,000 words. **Pays $300.**

Poetry Maureen Abood, literary editor. Free verse. "No light verse." **Buys 12 poems/year.** Submit maximum 5 poems. Length: 50 lines. **Pays $75.**

▣ THE UNITED CHURCH OBSERVER

478 Huron St., Toronto ON M5R 2R3, Canada. (416)960-8500. Fax: (416)960-8477. E-mail: mduncan@ucobserv er.org. Website: www.ucobserver.org. **Contact:** Muriel Duncan, editor. **20% freelance written.** Prefers to work with published/established writers. Monthly newsmagazine for people associated with The United Church of Canada. Deals primarily with events, trends, and policies having religious significance. Most coverage is Canadian, but reports on international or world concerns will be considered. Pays on publication. Publishes ms an average of 4 months after acceptance. Byline usually given. first serial rights and occasionally all rights. Accepts queries by mail, e-mail, fax.

Nonfiction Occasional opinion features only. Extended coverage of major issues is usually assigned to known writers. Submissions should be written as news, no more than 1,200 words length, accurate, and well-researched. No opinion pieces or poetry. Queries preferred. **Rates depend on subject, author, and work involved.** Pays expenses of writers on assignment as negotiated.

Reprints Send tearsheet or photocopy and information about when and where the material previously appeared. Payment negotiated.

Photos Buys photographs with mss. Color or b&w, electronic mail. Payment varies.

Tips "The writer has a better chance of breaking in at our publication with short articles; this also allows us to try more freelancers. Include samples of previous *news* writing with query. Indicate ability and willingness to do research, and to evaluate that research. The most frequent mistakes made by writers in completing an article for us are organizational problems, lack of polished style, short on research, and a lack of inclusive language."

$THE UPPER ROOM

Daily Devotional Guide, P.O. Box 340004, Nashville TN 37203-0004. (615)340-7252. Fax: (615)340-7267. E-mail: theupperroommagazine@upperroom.org. Website: www.upperroom.org. Editor and Publisher: Stephen D. Bryant. **Contact:** Marilyn Beaty, editorial assistant. **95% freelance written.** Eager to work with new/unpublished writers. Bimonthly magazine "offering a daily inspirational message which includes a Bible reading, text, prayer, 'Thought for the Day,' and suggestion for further prayer. Each day's meditation is written by a different person and is usually a personal witness about discovering meaning and power for Christian living through scripture study which illuminates daily life." Circ. 2.2 million (U.S.); 385,000 outside U.S. Pays on publication. Publishes ms an average of 1 year after acceptance. Byline given. Buys first North American serial, translation rights. Submit seasonal material 14 months in advance. Sample copy and writer's guidelines with a 4×6 SAE and 2 first-class stamps. Guidelines only for #10 SASE or online.

● "Manuscripts are not returned. If writers include a stamped, self-addressed postcard, we will notify them that their writing has reached us. This does not imply acceptance or interest in purchase. Does not respond unless material is accepted for publication."

Nonfiction Inspirational, personal experience, Bible-study insights. Special issues: Lent and Easter; Advent. No poetry, lengthy "spiritual journey" stories. **Buys 365 unsolicited mss/year.** Send complete ms by mail or e-mail. Length:300 words. **Pays $25/meditation.**

Tips "The best way to break in to our magazine is to send a well-written manuscript that looks at the Christian faith in a fresh way. Standard stories and sermon illustrations are immediately rejected. We very much want to find new writers and welcome good material. We are particularly interested in meditations based on Old Testament characters and stories. Good repeat meditations can lead to work on longer assignments for our other publications, which pay more. A writer who can deal concretely with everyday situations, relate them to the Bible and spiritual truths, and write clear, direct prose should be able to write for *The Upper Room*. We want material that provides for interaction on the part of the reader—meditation suggestions, journaling suggestions, space to reflect and link personal experience with the meditation for the day. Meditations that are personal, authentic, exploratory, and full of sensory detail make good devotional writing."

$ $THE WAR CRY

The Salvation Army, 615 Slaters Lane, Alexandria VA 22313. (703)684-5500. Fax: (703)684-5539. E-mail: war_cry@usn.salvationarmy.org. Website: www.thewarcry.com. Managing Editor: Jeff McDonald. **Contact:** Lt. Colonel Marlene Chase, editor-in-chief. **10% freelance written.** Biweekly magazine covering army news and Christian devotional writing. Estab. 1881. Circ. 400,000. **Pays on acceptance.** Publishes ms an average of 2 months-1 year after acceptance. Byline given. Buys first, one-time rights. Editorial lead time 6 weeks. Submit seasonal material 1 year in advance. Accepts previously published material. Accepts simultaneous submissions. Responds in 2 months to mss. Sample copy, theme list, and writer's guidelines free for #10 SASE or online.

● Responds in 4-6 weeks to articles submitted on speculation.

O₋ "A best bet would be a well-written profile of an exemplary Christian or a recounting of a person's experiences that deepened the subject's faith and showed God in action. Most popular profiles are of Salvation Army programs and personnel."

Nonfiction Humor, inspirational, interview/profile, personal experience, religious. No missionary stories, confessions. **Buys 40 mss/year.** Send complete ms. **Pays up to 20¢/word for assigned articles; 15-20¢/word for unsolicited articles.** Sometimes pays expenses of writers on assignment.

Reprints Send ms with rights for sale noted and information about when and where the material previously appeared. Pays 12¢/word.

Photos Buys one-time rights. Offers $35-200/photo. Identification of subjects required.

Fiction Religious. "No fantasy, science fiction or New Age." **Buys 5-10 mss/year.** Send complete ms. Length: 1,200-1,500 words. **Pays up to 10-20¢/word; 12¢ for reprints, and 2 contributor's copies.**

Poetry Free verse. **Buys 10-20/year poems/year.** Submit maximum 5 poems. Length:16 lines. **Pays $20-50.**

Fillers Anecdotes (inspirational). **Buys 10-20/year.** Length: 200-500 words. **Pays 15-20¢/word.**

Tips "We are soliciting more short fiction, inspirational articles and poetry, interviews with Christian athletes, evangelical leaders and celebrities, and theme-focused articles."

$THE WESLEYAN ADVOCATE

The Wesleyan Publishing House, P.O. Box 50434, Indianapolis IN 46250-0434. (317)570-5204. Fax: (317)570-5260. E-mail: communications@wesleyan.org. Executive Editor: Dr. Norman G. Wilson. **Contact:** Jerry Brecheisen, managing editor. Monthly magazine of The Wesleyan Church. Estab. 1842. Circ. 20,000. Pays on publication. Byline given. Buys first rights or simultaneous rights (prefers first rights). Submit seasonal material 6 months in advance. Accepts simultaneous submissions. Responds in 2 weeks to queries. Sample copy for $2. Writer's guidelines for #10 SASE.

Nonfiction Humor, inspirational, religious. No poetry accepted. Send complete ms. Length: 500-700 words. **Pays $25-150.**

Reprints Send photocopy of article and typed ms with rights for sale noted and information about when and where the material previously appeared.

Tips "Write for a guide."

$WOMAN'S TOUCH

Assemblies of God Women's Ministries Department (GPH), 1445 N. Boonville Ave., Springfield MO 65802-1894. (417)862-2781. Fax: (417)862-0503. E-mail: womanstouch@ag.org. Website: www.ag.org/womanstouch. **Contact:** Darla Knoth, managing editor. **50% freelance written.** Willing to work with new/unpublished writers. Bimonthly inspirational magazine for women. "Articles and contents of the magazine should be compatible with Christian teachings as well as human interests. The audience is women of all walks of life." Estab. 1977. Circ. 15,000. Pays on publication. Publishes ms an average of 10 months after acceptance. Byline given. Buys first, second, or one-time and electronic rights. Editorial lead time 10 months. Submit seasonal material 10 months in advance. Accepts queries by mail, e-mail, fax. Responds in 3 months to queries. Sample copy for 9½×11 SAE with 3 first-class stamps or online. Writer's guidelines online.

Nonfiction Book excerpts, general interest, inspirational, personal experience, religious, health. No fiction, poetry. **Buys 30 mss/year.** Send complete ms. Length: 200-600 words. **Pays $10-50 for assigned articles; $10-35 for unsolicited articles.**

Reprints Send photocopy and information about when and where the material previously appeared. Pays 50-75% of amount paid for an original article.

Columns/Departments A Final Touch (inspirational/human interest), 400 words; A Better You (health/wellness), 400 words; A Lighter Touch (true, unpublished anecdotes), 100 words.

     The online magazine carries original content not found in the print edition and includes writer's guidelines. Contact: Darla Knoth, online editor.

Tips "Submit manuscripts on current issues of interest to women. Familiarize yourself with *Woman's Touch* by reading 2 issues before submitting an article."

$WORLD PULSE

Evangelism and Missions Information Service/Wheaton College, P.O. Box 794, Wheaton IL 60189. (630)752-7158. Fax: (630)752-7155. E-mail: pulsenews@aol.com. Website: www.worldpulseonline.com. **Contact:** Managing Editor. **60% freelance written.** Semimonthly newsletter covering mission news and trends in both print and online versions. "We provide current information about evangelical Christian missions and churches around the world. Most articles are news-oriented, although we do publish some features and interviews." Estab. 1965. Circ. 2,700. Pays on publication. Publishes ms an average of 2 months after acceptance. Byline given. Offers negotiable kill fee. Buys first North American serial rights. Editorial lead time 2 months. Accepts queries by e-mail. Sample copy and writer's guidelines free.

Nonfiction Interview/profile, photo feature, religious, technical. No poetry, sermons, or humor. **Buys 50-60 mss/year.** Query with published clips. Length: 300-1,000 words. **Pays $25-100.**

Photos State availability with submission. Reviews prints. Buys one-time rights. Offers $25 for photos/article. Identification of subjects required.

Columns/Departments InterView (Q&A with newsmakers), 300-500 words.

Tips "*Pulse* is not a daily newspaper. Don't write a vanilla news story (with just the 5 Ws and an H). Sprinkle human interest and memorable facts throughout the story. Try to inform and entertain."

RETIREMENT

$$$$AARP THE MAGAZINE

AARP, 601 E St. NW, Washington DC 20049. (202)434-6880. Website: www.aarp.org. **Contact:** Editor. **50% freelance written.** Prefers to work with published/established writers. Bimonthly magazine. "*AARP The Magazine* is devoted to the varied needs and active life interests of AARP members, age 50 and over, covering such topics as financial planning, travel, health, careers, retirement, relationships, and social and cultural change. Its editorial content serves the mission of AARP seeking through education, advocacy and service to enhance the quality of life for all by promoting independence, dignity, and purpose." Circ. 21,500,000. **Pays on acceptance.** Publishes ms an average of 6 months after acceptance. Byline given. Buys exclusive first worldwide publication rights. Submit seasonal material 6 months in advance. Responds in 3 months to queries. Sample copy and writer's guidelines free.

Nonfiction Careers, workplace, practical information in living, financial and legal matters, personal relationships, consumerism. Query first by mail only. *No unsolicited mss.* Length: Up to 2,000 words. **Pays up to $3,000.** Sometimes pays expenses of writers on assignment.

Photos Photos purchased with or without accompanying mss. Pays $250 and up for color; $150 and up for b&w.

Fiction Very occasional short fiction.

Tips "The most frequent mistake made by writers in completing an article for us is poor follow-through with basic research. The outline is often more interesting than the finished piece. We do not accept unsolicited manuscripts."

$ALIVE!

A Magazine for Vibrant Christians Over 50, Vibrant Ministries, (formerly Christian Seniors Fellowship), P.O. Box 46464, Cincinnati OH 45246-0464. (513)825-3681. Editor: J. David Lang. **Contact:** A. June Lang, office editor. **60% freelance written.** Bimonthly magazine for senior adults 50 and older. "We need timely articles about Christian seniors in vital, productive lifestyles, travel or ministries." Estab. 1988. Pays on publication. Byline given. Buys first, second serial (reprint) rights. Submit seasonal material 6 months in advance. Responds in 2 months to mss. Sample copy for 9×12 SAE with 3 first-class stamps. Writer's guidelines for #10 SASE.

• Membership $18/year. Organization membership may be deducted from payment at writer's request.

Nonfiction General interest, humor, inspirational, interview/profile, photo feature, religious, travel. **Buys 25-50 mss/year.** Send complete ms and SASE. Length: 600-1,200 words. **Pays $18-75.**

Reprints Send tearsheet, photocopy or typed ms with rights for sale noted and information about when and where the material previously appeared. Pays 60-75% of amount paid for an original article.

Photos State availability with submission. Buys one-time rights. Offers $10-25. Identification of subjects, model releases required.

Columns/Departments Heart Medicine (humorous personal anecdotes; prefer grandparent/granchild stories or anecdotes re: over-55 persons), 10-100 words. **Buys 50 mss/year.** Send complete ms and SASE. **Pays $2-25.**

Fiction Adventure, humorous, religious, romance, slice-of-life vignettes, motivational, inspirational. **Buys 12 mss/year.** Send complete ms. Length: 600-1,200 words. **Pays $20-60.**

Fillers Anecdotes, facts, gags to be illustrated by cartoonist, short humor. **Buys 15/year.** Length: 50-500 words. **Pays $2-15.**

Tips "Include SASE and information regarding whether manuscript is to be returned or tossed."

$FIFTY SOMETHING MAGAZINE

Linde Graphics Co., 7533-C Tyler Blvd., Mentor OH 44060. (440)953-2200. Fax: (440)953-2202. **Contact:** Linda L. Lindeman-DeCarlo, publisher. **80% freelance written.** Quarterly magazine covering nostalgia. "We are focusing on the 50-and-better reader." Estab. 1990. Circ. 10,000. Pays on publication. Publishes ms an average of 6 months after acceptance. Byline given. Offers 5% kill fee. Buys one-time, second serial (reprint), simultaneous rights. Editorial lead time 6 months. Submit seasonal material 6 months in advance. Accepts previously published material. Accepts simultaneous submissions. Responds in 3 months to queries; 3 months to mss. Sample copy for 9×12 SAE and 4 first-class stamps. Writer's guidelines for #10 SASE.

Nonfiction Book excerpts, essays, exposé, general interest, historical/nostalgic, how-to, humor, inspirational, interview/profile, new product, opinion, personal experience, photo feature, travel. **Buys 20 mss/year.** Length: 500-1,500 words. **Pays $10-100.** Sometimes pays expenses of writers on assignment.

Photos Send photos with submission. Reviews 4×6 prints, GIF/JPEG files. Buys one-time rights. Negotiates payment individually. Captions, identification of subjects, model releases required.

Columns/Departments Health & Fitness (good news/tips), 500 words; Travel (unique trips), 1,000 words; Humor (aging issues), 500 words; Finance (tips), 500 words. **Buys 10 mss/year.** Send complete ms. **Pays $10-100.**

Fiction Adventure, confessions, ethnic, experimental, fantasy, historical, humorous, mainstream, mystery, novel excerpts, romance, slice-of-life vignettes, suspense, western. No erotica or horror. **Buys 10 mss/year.** Send complete ms. Length: 500-1,000 words. **Pays $10-100.**

Poetry Avant-garde, free verse, light verse, traditional. **Buys 10 poems/year.** Submit maximum 5 poems. Length: 10-25 lines.

Fillers Anecdotes, facts, gags to be illustrated by cartoonist, newsbreaks, short humor. **Buys 10/year.** Length: 50-150 words. **Pays $10-100.**

$MATURE YEARS

The United Methodist Publishing House, 201 Eighth Ave. S., Nashville TN 37202-0801. (615)749-6292. Fax: (615)749-6512. E-mail: matureyears@umpublishing.org. **Contact:** Marvin W. Cropsey, editor. **50% freelance written.** Prefers to work with published/established writers. Quarterly magazine "designed to help persons in and nearing the retirement years understand and appropriate the resources of the Christian faith in dealing with specific problems and opportunities related to aging." Estab. 1954. Circ. 55,000. **Pays on acceptance.** Publishes ms an average of 1 year after acceptance. Buys first North American serial rights. Submit seasonal material 14 months in advance. Responds in 2 weeks to queries; 2 months to mss. Sample copy for $5 and 9×12 SAE. Writer's guidelines for #10 SASE or by e-mail.

Nonfiction Especially important are opportunities for older adults to read about service, adventure, fulfillment, and fun. How-to (hobbies), inspirational, religious, travel (special guidelines), older adult health, finance issues. **Buys 75-80 mss/year.** Send complete ms; e-mail submissions preferred. Length: 900-2,000 words. **Pays $45-125.** Sometimes pays expenses of writers on assignment.

Reprints Send tearsheet, photocopy or typed ms with rights for sale noted and information about when and where the material previously appeared. Pays at same rate as for previously unpublished material.

Photos Send photos with submission. Typically buys one-time rights. Negotiates pay individually. Captions, model releases required.

Columns/Departments Health Hints (retirement, health), 900-1,500 words; Going Places (travel, pilgrimage), 1,000-1,500 words; Fragments of Life (personal inspiration), 250-600 words; Modern Revelations (religious/inspirational), 900-1,500 words; Money Matters (personal finance), 1,200-1,800 words; Merry-Go-Round (cartoons, jokes, 4-6 line humorous verse); Puzzle Time (religious puzzles, crosswords). **Buys 4 mss/year.** Send complete ms. **Pays $25-45.**

Fiction Marvin Cropsey, editor. Humorous, religious, slice-of-life vignettes, retirement years nostalgia, intergenerational relationships. "We don't want anything poking fun at old age, saccharine stories or anything not for older adults. Must show older adults (age 55 plus) in a positive manner." **Buys 4 mss/year.** Send complete ms. Length: 1,000-2,000 words. **Pays $60-125.**

Poetry Free verse, haiku, light verse, traditional. **Buys 24 poems/year poems/year.** Submit maximum 6 poems. Length: 3-16 lines. **Pays $5-20.**

ROMANCE & CONFESSION

$TRUE CONFESSIONS

Macfadden Women's Group, 333 Seventh Ave., New York NY 10001. (212)979-4898. Fax: (212)979-4825. E-mail: trueconfessionstales@yahoo.com. **Contact:** Pat Byrdsong, editor. **98% freelance written.** Monthly magazine for high-school-educated, working class women, teens through maturity. "*True Confessions* is a women's magazine featuring true-to-life stories about working class women and their families." Circ. 200,000. Pays 1 month after publication. Publishes ms an average of 4 months after acceptance. Buys all rights. Submit seasonal material 8 months in advance. Accepts queries by e-mail. Responds in 3 months to queries; 15 months to mss. Sample copy for $3.50.

- Eager to work with new/unpublished writers. Prefers writers to query via e-mail before submitting stories.
- O→ "If you have a strong story to tell, tell it simply and convincingly. We always have a need for 4,000-word stories with dramatic impact about dramatic events." Asian-, Latina-, Native- and African-American stories are encouraged.

Nonfiction Timely, exciting, true, emotional first-person stories on the problems that face today's women. The narrators should be sympathetic, and the situations they find themselves in should be intriguing, yet realistic. Many stories may have a strong romantic interest and a high moral tone; however, personal accounts or "confessions," no matter how controversial the topic, are encouraged and accepted. Careful study of current issue is suggested. Send complete ms. No simultaneous submissions. SASE required. Length: 4,000-7,000 words, and mini stories 1,000-1,500 words. **Pays 3¢/word.**

Columns/Departments Family Zoo (pet feature), 50 words or less, **pays $50 for pet photo and story.** All other features are 200-300 words: My Moment With God (a short prayer); Incredible But True (an incredible/mystical/spiritual experience); My Man (a man who has been special in your life); Woman to Woman (a point of view about a contemporary subject matter or a woman overcoming odds). **Pays $65** for all features; **$75** for My Moment With God. Send complete ms and SASE.

Fiction Pat Byrdsong, editorial director. Query. Length: 3,000-7,500 words. **Pays 3¢/word or a flat $100 rate for mini-stories, and 1 contributor's copy.**

Poetry Poetry should rhyme. Length: 4-20 lines. **Pays $10 minimum.**

Tips "Our magazine is almost 100% freelance. We purchase all stories that appear in our magazine. Read 3-4 issues before sending submissions. Do not talk down to our readers. We prefer manuscripts on disk (saved as RTF file) as well as hard copy."

N $TRUE LOVE

Dorchester Media, 333 7th Ave., 11th Floor, New York NY 10001. (212)780-3519. Fax: (212)979-4825. E-mail: away@dorchestermedia.com. Website: www.truestorymail.com. **Contact:** Alison Way, editor-in-chief. Monthly magazine. First person accounts and realistic stories of strong, independent women who have gone through conflict and become better people. Circ. 225,000. Sample copy not available.

- **Buys 15 stories/month.** "We are always on the lookout for new writers. *True Love* is a great place to start a writing career. We are desparate for stories." **Pays 3¢/word.**

$ TRUE ROMANCE

Sterling/MacFadden Partnership, Dorchester Media, 333 Seventh Ave., New York NY 10001. (212)979-4898. E-mail: pvitucci@sterlingmacfadden.com. Website: www.trueromancemag.com. **Contact:** Pat Vitucci, editor. **100% freelance written.** Monthly magazine for women, teens through retired, offering compelling confession stories based on true happenings, with reader identification and strong emotional tone. No third-person material. Estab. 1923. Circ. 225,000. Pays 1 month after publication. Buys all rights. Submit seasonal material 6 months in advance. Accepts queries by mail, e-mail, fax. Responds in 8 months to queries.

Nonfiction Confessions, true love stories, mini-adventures; problems and solutions; dating and marital and child-rearing difficulties. Realistic, yet unique stories dealing with current problems, everyday events; strong emotional appeal; controversial topics of interest to women. **Buys 180 mss/year.** Submit ms. Length: 6,000-9,000 words. **Pays 3¢/word; slightly higher rates for short-shorts.**

Columns/Departments That's My Child (photo and 50 words); Loving Pets (photo and 50 words), **both pay $50;** Cupid's Corner (photo and 500 words about you and spouse), **pays $100;** Passages(2,000-4,000 words about a unique experience), **pays 3¢/word;** Way I Lived It (3,000-5,000 words for literary short stories in first and third person), **pays 3¢/word.**

Poetry Light romantic poetry. Length: 24 lines maximum. **Pays $10-30.**

Tips "A timely, well-written story that is told by a sympathetic narrator who sees the central problem through to a satisfying resolution is *all* important to break into *True Romance*. We are always looking for interesting, emotional, identifiable stories."

$ TRUE STORY

Dorchester Media, 333 7th Ave., 11th Floor, New York NY 10001. (212)780-3500. Fax: (212)979-4825. E-mail: away@dorchestermedia.com. Website: www.truestorymail.com. **Contact:** Alison Way, editor-in-chief. **100% freelance written.** Monthly magazine for young married, blue-collar women, 20-35; high school education; increasingly broad interests; home-oriented, but looking beyond the home for personal fulfillment. Circ. 580,000. Pays 1 month after publication. Buys all rights. Submit seasonal material 1 year in advance. Writer's guidelines online.

- No queries; expect a response in 6 months. "Magazine has been going strong for over 85 years. It has been given a major/minor overhaul and is celebrating its fresh new look."
- ⊙➔ Subject matter can range from light romances to sizzling passion, from all-out tearjerkers to happily-ever-after endings, and everything in between.

Nonfiction "First-person stories covering all aspects of women's interest: love, marriage, family life, careers, social problems, etc. The best direction a new writer can be given is to carefully study several issues of the magazine; then submit a fresh, exciting, well-written true story. We have no taboos. It's the handling and believability that make the difference between a rejection and an acceptance." **Buys about 200 full-length mss/year.** Submit only complete mss and disk for stories. Length: 2,000-12,000 words. **Pays 5¢/word; $100 minimum. Pays a flat rate for columns or departments, as announced in the magazine.**

Tips "*True Story* is unique because all of our stories are written from the hearts of real people, and deal with all of the issues that affect us today—parenthood, relationships, careers, family affairs, and social concerns. All of our stories are written in first person 'as you lived it,' and should be no less than 2,000 words. If you have access to a computer, we require you to send your submission on a disk, along with a clean hard copy of the story. Please keep in mind, all files must be saved as rich text format (RTF)."

RURAL

$ $⊡ THE COUNTRY CONNECTION

Ontario's Magazine of Choice, Pinecone Publishing, P.O. Box 100, Boulter ON K0L 1G0, Canada. (613)332-3651. E-mail: editor@pinecone.on.ca. Website: www.pinecone.on.ca. **Contact:** Joanne Healy, editor. **100% freelance written.** Magazine published 4 times/year covering nature, environment, history and nostalgia, "the arts," and "green travel." "*The Country Connection* is a magazine for true nature lovers and the rural adventurer. Building on our commitment to heritage, cultural, artistic, and environmental themes, we continually add new topics to illuminate the country experience of people living within nature. Our goal is to chronicle rural life in its many aspects, giving 'voice' to the countryside." Estab. 1989. Circ. 4,000. Pays on publication. Publishes ms an average of 4 months after acceptance. Byline given. Buys first rights. Editorial lead time 4 months. Accepts queries by mail, e-mail, phone. Sample copy for $5.69. Writer's guidelines online.

Nonfiction General interest, historical/nostalgic, humor, opinion, personal experience, travel, lifestyle, leisure, art and culture, vegan recipes. No hunting, fishing, animal husbandry, or pet articles. **Buys 60 mss/year.** Send complete ms. Length: 500-2,000 words. **Pays 10¢/word.**

Photos Send photos with submission. Reviews transparencies, prints. Buys one-time rights. Offers $10-50/ photo. Captions required.

Fiction Adventure, fantasy, historical, humorous, slice-of-life vignettes, country living. **Buys 10 mss/year.** Send complete ms. Length: 500-1,500 words. **Pays 10¢/word.**

◻ The online magazine carries original content not found in the print edition. Contact: Joanne Healy.

Tips "Canadian content only. Send manuscript with appropriate support material such as photos, illustrations, maps, etc."

$ COUNTRY FOLK

Salaki Publishing & Design, HC77, Box 580, Pittsburg MO 65724. (417)993-5944. E-mail: salaki@countryfolkmag .com. Website: www.countryfolkmag.com. **Contact:** Susan Salaki, editor. **100% freelance written.** Bimonthly magazine. *"Country Folk* publishes true stories and history of the Ozarks." Estab. 1994. Circ. 10,000. Pays on publication. Publishes ms an average of 3 months after acceptance. Byline given. Buys first rights. Editorial lead time 2 months. Submit seasonal material 3 months in advance. Accepts queries by mail, e-mail, phone. Responds in 1 month to queries; 2 months to mss. Sample copy for $4.75. Writer's guidelines online.

• *Country Folk* has increased from quarterly to bimonthly and doubled its circulation.

Nonfiction Historical/nostalgic (true pieces with family names and real places), how-to, humor, inspirational, personal experience, photo feature, true ghost stories of the Ozarks. **Buys 10 mss/year.** Prefers e-mail submissions. Length: 750-1,000 words. **Pays $5-20.** "Pays writers with contributor copies or other premiums if we must do considerable editing to the work."

Photos Send photos with submission. Buys one-time rights.

Fiction Historical, humorous, mystery, novel excerpts. **Buys 10 mss/year.** Send complete ms. Length: 750-1,000 words. **Pays $5-50.**

Poetry Haiku, light verse, traditional. **Buys 25 poems/year.** Submit maximum 3 poems. **Pays $1-5.**

Fillers Anecdotes, facts, gags to be illustrated by cartoonist, newsbreaks, short humor. **Buys 25/year. Pays $1-5.**

Tips "We want material from people who were born and raised in the Ozarks. We accept submissions in any form, handwritten or typed. Many of the writers and poets whose work we publish are first-time submissions. Most of the work we publish is written by older men and women who have heard stories from their parents and grandparents about how the Ozark region was settled in the 1800s. Almost any writer who writes from the heart about a true experience from his or her youth will get published. Our staff edits for grammar and spelling errors. All the writer has to be concerned about is conveying the story. We also publish recipes, old photos, and humorous anecdotes. Please visit our website to read material we have published in previous issues and/or to print a copy of our writer's guidelines. We look forward to reading your work."

$ $ FARM & RANCH LIVING

Reiman Media Group, 5925 Country Lane, Greendale WI 53129. (414)423-0100. Fax: (414)423-8463. E-mail: editors@farmandranchliving.com. Website: www.farmandranchliving.com. **Contact:** Nick Pabst, editor. **30% freelance written.** Eager to work with new/unpublished writers. Bimonthly magazine aimed at families that farm or ranch full time. *"F&RL is not* a 'how-to' magazine—it focuses on people rather than products and profits." Estab. 1978. Circ. 400,000. Pays on publication. Publishes ms an average of 6 months after acceptance. Byline given. Buys first, one-time rights. Submit seasonal material 6 months in advance. Accepts queries by mail, e-mail, fax. Responds in 6 weeks to queries. Sample copy for $2. Writer's guidelines for #10 SASE.

⊙→ Break in with "photo-illustrated stories about present-day farmers and ranchers."

Nonfiction Humor (rural only), inspirational, interview/profile, personal experience (farm/ranch related), photo feature, nostalgia, prettiest place in the country (photo/text tour of ranch or farm). No how-to articles or stories about "hobby farmers" (doctors or lawyers with weekend farms); no issue-oriented stories (pollution, animal rights, etc.). **Buys 30 mss/year.** Query with or without published clips or send complete ms. Length: 600-1,200 words. **Pays up to $200 for text/photo package. Payment for Prettiest Place negotiable.**

Reprints Send photocopy with rights for sale noted. Payment negotiable.

Photos Scenic. State availability with submission. Buys one-time rights. Pays $75-200 for 35mm color slides.

Fillers Anecdotes, short humor (with farm or ranch slant), jokes. **Buys 10/year.** Length: 50-150 words. **Pays $10-25.**

Tips "Our readers enjoy stories and features that are upbeat and positive. A freelancer must see *F&RL* to fully appreciate how different it is from other farm publications—ordering a sample is strongly advised (not available on newsstands). Photo features (about interesting farm or ranch families) and personality profiles are most open to freelancers.''

$RANGE MAGAZINE

The Cowboy Spirit on American Outback, Purple Coyote, 106 E. Adams, Carson City NV 89706. (775)884-2200. Fax: (775)884-2213. Website: www.rangemagazine.com. Editor: C.J. Hadley. **Contact:** Barbara Wies, associate publisher. **70% freelance written.** Quarterly magazine. ''*RANGE Magazine* covers ranching and farming as available resources.'' Estab. 1991. Pays on publication. Publishes ms an average of 6 months after acceptance. Buys first North American serial rights, makes work-for-hire assignments. Accepts queries by mail. Responds in 6-8 weeks to queries; 3-6 months to mss. Sample copy for free. Writer's guidelines for #10 SASE.

Nonfiction Book excerpts, humor, interview/profile, personal experience, photo feature. No rodeos or anything by a writer not familiar with *RANGE*. Query. Length: 1,000-1,500 words. **Pays $100.** Sometimes pays expenses of writers on assignment.

Photos C.J. Hadley, editor/publisher. State availability with submission. Reviews 35mm transparencies, 4×6 prints. Buys one-time rights. Negotiates payment individually. Captions, identification of subjects, model releases required.

$RURAL HERITAGE

281 Dean Ridge Lane, Gainesboro TN 38562-5039. (931)268-0655. E-mail: editor@ruralheritage.com. Website: www.ruralheritage.com. Publisher: Allan Damerow. **Contact:** Gail Damerow, editor. **98% freelance written.** Willing to work with a small number of new/unpublished writers. Bimonthly magazine devoted to the training and care of draft animals. Estab. 1976. Circ. 6,500. Pays on publication. Publishes ms an average of 6 months after acceptance. Byline given. Buys first English language rights. Submit seasonal material 6 months in advance. Accepts queries by mail, e-mail. Responds in 3 months to queries. Sample copy for $8. Writer's guidelines online.

Nonfiction How-to (farming with draft animals), interview/profile (people using draft animals), photo feature. No articles on *mechanized* farming. **Buys 100 mss/year.** Query or send complete ms. Length: 1,200-1,500 words. **Pays 5¢/word.**

Photos Six covers/year (color transparency or 5×7 horizontal print), animals in harness $100. Photo guidelines for #10 SASE or on website. Send photos with submission. Buys one-time rights. Pays $10. Captions, identification of subjects required.

Poetry Traditional. **Pays $5-25.**

Tips ''Thoroughly understand our subject: working draft animals in harness. We'd like more pieces on plans and instructions for constructing various horse-drawn implements and vehicles. Always welcome are: 1.) Detailed descriptions and photos of horse-drawn implements, 2.) Prices and other details of draft animal and implement auctions and sales.''

$ $RURALITE

P.O. Box 558, Forest Grove OR 97116-0558. (503)357-2105. Fax: (503)357-8615. E-mail: ruralite@ruralite.org. Website: www.ruralite.org. **Contact:** Curtis Condon, editor-in-chief. **80% freelance written.** Works with new, unpublished writers. Monthly magazine aimed at members of consumer-owned electric utilities throughout 10 western states, including Alaska. Publishes 48 regional editions. Estab. 1954. Circ. 325,000. **Pays on acceptance.** Byline given. Buys first, sometimes reprint rights. Accepts queries by mail. Responds in 1 month to queries. Sample copy for 10×13 SAE with 4 first-class stamps; guidelines also online. Writer's guidelines online.

Nonfiction Looking for well-written nonfiction, dealing primarily with human interest topics. Must have strong Northwest perspective and be sensitive to Northwest issues and attitudes. Wide range of topics possible, from energy-related subjects to little-known travel destinations to interesting people living in areas served by consumer-owned electric utilities. Family-related issues, Northwest history (no encyclopedia rewrites), people and events, unusual tidbits that tell the Northwest experience are best chances for a sale. **Buys 50-60 mss/year.** Query first; unsolicited mss submitted without request rarely read by editors. Length: 300-2,000 words. **Pays $50-450.**

Reprints Send ms with rights for sale noted and information about when and where the material previously appeared. Pays 50% of amount paid for an original article.

Photos ''Illustrated stories are the key to a sale. Stories without art rarely make it. Black-and-white prints, color slides, all formats accepted.''

Tips ''Study recent issues. Follow directions when given an assignment. Be able to deliver a complete package (story and photos). We're looking for regular contributors to whom we can assign topics from our story list after they've proven their ability to deliver quality mss.''

SCIENCE

$ $ $ $ AMERICAN ARCHAEOLOGY

The Archaeological Conservancy, 5301 Central Ave. NE, #902, Albuquerque NM 87108-1517. (505)266-9668. Fax: (505)266-0311. E-mail: tacmag@nm.net. Website: www.americanarchaeology.org. Assistant Editor: Tamara Stewart. **Contact:** Michael Bawaya, editor. **60% freelance written.** Quarterly magazine. "We're a popular archaeology magazine. Our readers are very interested in this science. Our features cover important digs, prominent archaeologists, and most any aspect of the science. We only cover North America." Estab. 1997. Circ. 35,000. **Pays on acceptance.** Publishes ms an average of 3 months after acceptance. Byline given. Offers 20% kill fee. Buys one-time, electronic rights. Editorial lead time 3 months. Accepts queries by mail, e-mail, fax. Responds in 3 weeks to queries; 1 month to mss.

Nonfiction Archaeology. No fiction, poetry, humor. **Buys 15 mss/year.** Query with published clips. Length: 1,500-3,000 words. **Pays $700-1,500.** Sometimes pays expenses of writers on assignment.

Photos State availability with submission. Reviews transparencies, prints. Buys one-time rights. Offers $300-1,000/photo shoot. Negotiates payment individually. Identification of subjects required.

Tips "Read the magazine. Features must have a considerable amount of archaeological detail."

$ $ $ $ ARCHAEOLOGY

Archaeological Institute of America, 36-36 33rd St., Long Island NY 11106. (718)472-3050. Fax: (718)472-3051. E-mail: peter@archaeology.org. Website: www.archaeology.org. **Contact:** Peter A. Young, editor-in-chief. **35% freelance written.** Magazine. "*Archaeology* combines worldwide archaeological findings with photography, specially rendered maps, drawings, and charts. Articles cover current excavations, recent discoveries, and special studies of ancient cultures. Regular features: newsbriefs, film and book reviews, current museum exhibits. The only magazine of its kind to bring worldwide archaeology to the attention of the general public." Estab. 1948. Circ. 220,000. Pays on publication. Byline given. Offers 25% kill fee. Buys world rights. Submit seasonal material 6 months in advance. Accepts queries by mail, e-mail, fax. Accepts simultaneous submissions. Sample copy and writer's guidelines free.

Nonfiction Essays, general interest. **Buys 6 mss/year.** Query preferred. Length: 1,000-3,000 words. **Pays $1,500 maximum.** Sometimes pays expenses of writers on assignment.

Photos Send photos with submission. Reviews 4×5 color transparencies, 35mm color slides. Identification of subjects, credits required.

■ The online magazine carries original content not found in the print edition. Contact: Mark Rose, online editor.

Tips "We reach nonspecialist readers interested in art, science, history, and culture. Our reports, regional commentaries, and feature-length articles introduce readers to recent developments in archaeology worldwide."

$ $ ASTRONOMY

Kalmbach Publishing, 21027 Crossroads Circle, P.O. Box 1612, Waukesha WI 53187-1612. (262)796-8776. Fax: (262)798-6468. E-mail: astro@astronomy.com. Editor: David J. Eicher. Managing Editor: Patricia Lantier. **50% of articles submitted and written by science writers; includes commissioned and unsolicited.** Monthly magazine covering the science and hobby of astronomy. "Half of our magazine is for hobbyists (who are active observers of the sky); the other half is directed toward armchair astronomers who are intrigued by the science." Estab. 1973. Circ. 150,000. **Pays on acceptance.** Byline given. Buys first North American serial, one-time, all rights. Responds in 1 month to queries to queries Responds in 3 months (unsolicited mss) to mss. Writer's guidelines for #10 SASE or online.

● "We are governed by what is happening in astronomical research and space exploration. It can be up to a year before we publish a manuscript." Query for electronic submissions.

Nonfiction Book excerpts, new product (announcements), photo feature, technical, space, astronomy. **Buys 75 mss/year.** Query. Length: 500-3,000 words. **Pays $100-1,000.**

Photos Send photos with submission. Pays $25/photo. Captions, identification of subjects, model releases required.

Tips "Submitting to *Astronomy* could be tough. (Take a look at how technical astronomy is.) But if someone is a physics teacher or an amateur astronomer, he or she might want to study the magazine for a year to see the sorts of subjects and approaches we use, and then submit a proposal."

$ $ $ $ SCIENTIFIC AMERICAN

415 Madison Ave., New York NY 10017. (212)754-0550. Fax: (212)755-1976. E-mail: editors@sciam.com. Website: www.sciam.com. **Contact:** Philip Yam, news editor. Monthly magazine covering developments and topics of interest in the world of science. Query before submitting. "*Scientific American* brings its readers directly to the wellspring of exploration and technological innovation. The magazine specializes in first-hand accounts by

the people who actually do the work. Their personal experience provides an authoritative perspective on future growth. Over 100 of our authors have won Nobel Prizes. Complementing those articles are regular departments written by *Scientific American*'s staff of professional journalists, all specialists in their fields. *Scientific American* is the authoritative source of advance information. Authors are the first to report on important breakthroughs, because they're the people who make them. It all goes back to *Scientific American*'s corporate mission: to link those who use knowledge with those who create it." Estab. 1845. Circ. 710,000.

Nonfiction Freelance opportunities mostly in the news scan section; limited opportunity in feature well. **Pays $1/word average.** Pays expenses of writers on assignment.

$ $SKY & TELESCOPE

The Essential Magazine of Astronomy, Sky Publishing Corp., 49 Bay State Rd., Cambridge MA 02138. (617)864-7360. Fax: (617)576-0336. E-mail: editors@skyandtelescope.com. Website: skyandtelescope.coom. Editor: Richard Tresch Fienberg. **Contact:** Bud Sadler, managing editor. **15% freelance written.** Monthly magazine covering astronomy. "*Sky & Telescope* is the magazine of record for astronomy. We cover amateur activities, research news, equipment, book, and software reviews. Our audience is the amateur astronomer who wants to learn more about the night sky." Estab. 1941. Circ. 125,000. Pays on publication. Publishes ms an average of 6 months after acceptance. Byline given. Buys first rights. Editorial lead time 4 months. Submit seasonal material 1 year in advance. Accepts queries by mail, e-mail, fax. Responds in 3 weeks to queries; 1 month to mss. Sample copy for $4.99. Writer's guidelines online.

Nonfiction Essays, historical/nostalgic, how-to, opinion, personal experience, photo feature, technical. No poetry, crosswords, New Age, or alternative cosmologies. **Buys 10 mss/year.** Query. Length: 1,500-2,500 words. **Pays at least 25¢/word.** Sometimes pays expenses of writers on assignment.

Photos Send photos with submission. Reviews contact sheets. Buys one-time rights. Negotiates payment individually. Identification of subjects required.

Columns/Departments Focal Point (opinion), 800 words; Books & Beyond (reviews), 800 words; Amateur Astronomers (profiles), 1,500 words. **Buys 20 mss/year.** Query. **Pays 25¢/word.**

Tips "Good artwork is key. Keep the text lively and provide captions."

$ $WEATHERWISE

The Magazine About the Weather, Heldref Publications, 1319 18th St. NW, Washington DC 20036. (202)296-6267. Fax: (202)296-5149. E-mail: ww@heldref.org. Website: www.weatherwise.org. Associate Editor: Kimbra Cutlip. Assistant Editor: Ellen Fast. **Contact:** Lynn Elsey, managing editor. **75% freelance written.** Bimonthly magazine covering weather and meteorology. "*Weatherwise* is America's only magazine about the weather. Our readers range from professional weathercasters and scientists to basement-bound hobbyists, but all share a common interest in craving information about weather as it relates to the atmospheric sciences, technology, history, culture, society, art, etc." Estab. 1948. Circ. 32,000. Pays on publication. Publishes ms an average of 6 months after acceptance. Byline given. Buys all rights. Editorial lead time 6-9 months. Submit seasonal material 9 months in advance. Accepts queries by mail, e-mail, fax, phone. Responds in 2 months to queries. Sample copy for $4 and 9×12 SAE with 10 first-class stamps. Writer's guidelines online.

O— "First, familiarize yourself with the magazine by taking a close look at the most recent issues. (You can also visit our website, which features the full text of many recent articles.) This will give you an idea of the style of writing we prefer in *Weatherwise*. Then, read through our writer's guidelines (available from our office or on our website) which detail the process for submitting a query letter. As for the subject matter, keep your eyes and ears open for the latest research and/or current trends in meteorology and climatology that may be appropriate for the general readership of *Weatherwise*. And always keep in mind weather's awesome power and beauty—its 'fun, fury, and fascination' that so many of our readers enjoy."

Nonfiction Book excerpts, essays, general interest, historical/nostalgic, how-to, interview/profile, new product, opinion, personal experience, photo feature, technical, travel. Special issues: Photo Contest (September/October deadline June 1). "No blow-by-blow accounts of the biggest storm to ever hit your backyard." **Buys 15-18 mss/year.** Query with published clips. Length: 1,000-2,000 words. **Pays $200-500 for assigned articles; $0-300 for unsolicited articles.**

Photos Reviews contact sheets, negatives, prints, electronic files. Buys one-time rights. Negotiates payment individually. Captions, identification of subjects required.

Columns/Departments Front & Center (news, trends, opinion), 300-400 words; Weather Talk (folklore and humor), 650-1,000 words. **Buys 12-15 mss/year.** Query with published clips. **Pays $0-200.**

Tips "Don't query us wanting to write about broad types like the Greenhouse Effect, the Ozone Hole, El Niño, etc. Although these are valid topics, you can bet you won't be able to cover it all in 2,000 words. With these topics and all others, find the story within the story. And whether you're writing about a historical storm or new technology, be sure to focus on the human element—the struggles, triumphs, and other anecdotes of individuals."

SCIENCE FICTION, FANTASY & HORROR

$ $ ABSOLUTE MAGNITUDE

Science Fiction Adventures, DNA Publications, P.O. Box 2988, Radford VA 24143-2988. E-mail: absolutemagnitude@dnapublications.com. Website: www.dnapublications.com/. Warren Lapine, editor-in-chief. **95% freelance written.** Quarterly magazine featuring science fiction short stories. "We specialize in action/adventure science fiction with an emphasis on hard science fiction short stories." Estab. 1993. Circ. 8,000. **Pays on acceptance.** Publishes ms an average of 1 year after acceptance. Byline given. Buys first, first english language serial rights. Editorial lead time 6 months. Accepts simultaneous submissions. Responds in 1 month to mss. Sample copy for $6. Writer's guidelines online.

- This editor is still looking for tightly plotted stories that are character driven. He is now purchasing more short stories than before. "Do not query—send complete manuscript."

Fiction Warren Lapine. Science fiction. No fantasy, horror, funny science fiction. **Buys 40 mss/year.** Send complete ms. Length: 1,000-20,000 words. **Pays 7-10¢/word.**

Poetry Any form. Best chance with light verse. **Buys 4 poems/issue.** Submit maximum 5 poems. Length: Up to 25,000 words. **Pays $10/poem.**

Tips "We are very interested in working with new writers, but we are not interested in 'drawer-cleaning' exercises. There is no point in sending less than your best effort if you are interested in a career in writing. We do not use fantasy, horror, satire, or funny science fiction. We're looking for character-driven, action/adventure-based technical science fiction. We want tightly plotted stories with memorable characters. Characters should be the driving force behind the action of the story; they should not be thrown in as an afterthought. We need to see both plot development and character growth. Stories which are resolved without action on the protagonist's part do not work for us; characters should not be spectators in situations completely beyond their control or immune to their influence. Some of our favorite writers are Roger Zelazny, Frank Herbert, Robert Silverberg, and Fred Saberhagen."

N $ AMAZING JOURNEYS MAGAZINE

Journey Books Publishing, 3205 Hwy. 431, Spring Hill TN 37174. (615)791-8006. E-mail: journey@journeybookspublishing.com. Website: www.journeybookspublishing.com. Managing Editor: Donnie Clemons. **Contact:** Edward Knight, editor. **80% freelance written.** Quarterly magazine covering science fiction and fantasy. "We are seeking the best in up-and-coming authors who produce great stories that appeal to a wide audience. Each issue will be packed with exciting, fresh material. *Amazing Journeys* will be a fun read, designed to stimulate the senses without offending them. With the introduction of *Amazing Journeys*, we intend to reintroduce the style of writing that made the Golden Age of science fiction "golden." If you are tired of 'shock culture' stories or stories written strictly to appeal to a commercial audience, then *Amazing Journeys* is the right magazine for you." Estab. 2003. **Pays on acceptance.** Publishes ms an average of 6-12 months after acceptance. Byline given. Offers $10 kill fee. Buys first North American serial rights. Editorial lead time 3 months. Accepts queries by mail, e-mail. Responds in 1 week to queries; 2 months to mss. Sample copy for $4.99, plus 1 SAE with 3 First-Class stamps. Writer's guidelines for #10 SASE.

Fiction Fantasy, science fiction. "Absolutely no sexual content will be accepted. Profanity is greatly restricted (none is preferred). **Buys 20 mss/year.** Send complete ms. Length: 2,000-10,000 words. **Pays $10.**

Tips "Send us good, clean stories that are fun to read. Do not try to shock us. Entertain us. We are a conservative market. We are new and very small. We are interested in authors who can help us grow. Also, extra comments on how you, as an author, can broaden our subscription base or sell our magazine is greatly appreciated in your cover letter."

$ $ ANALOG SCIENCE FICTION & FACT

Dell Magazine Fiction Group, 475 Park Ave. S., 11th Floor, New York NY 10016. (212)686-7188. Fax: (212)686-7414. E-mail: analog@dellmagazines.com. Website: www.analogsf.com. **Contact:** Dr. Stanley Schmidt, editor. **100% freelance written.** Eager to work with new/unpublished writers. Monthly magazine for general future-minded audience. Estab. 1930. Circ. 50,000. **Pays on acceptance.** Publishes ms an average of 10 months after acceptance. Byline given. Not copyrighted. Buys first North American serial, nonexclusive foreign serial rights. Sample copy for $5. Writer's guidelines online.

- Break in by telling an "unforgettable story in which an original, thought-provoking, plausible idea plays an indispensible role."

Nonfiction Looking for illustrated technical articles dealing with subjects of not only current but future interest, i.e., topics at the present frontiers of research whose likely future developments have implications of wide interest. **Buys 11 mss/year.** Query by mail only. Length: 5,000 words. **Pays 6¢/word.**

Fiction Stanley Schmidt, editor. "Basically, we publish science fiction stories. That is, stories in which some aspect of future science or technology is so integral to the plot that, if that aspect were removed, the story would collapse. The science can be physical, sociological, or psychological. The technology can be anything from electronic engineering to biogenetic engineering. But the stories must be strong and realistic, with believable people doing believable things—no matter how fantastic the background might be." Science fiction. "No fantasy or stories in which the scientific background is implausible or plays no essential role." **Buys 60-100 unsolicited mss/year.** Length: 2,000-80,000 words. **Pays 4¢/word for novels; 5-6¢/word for novelettes; 6-8¢/word for shorts under 7,500 words; $450-600 for intermediate lengths.**

Tips "In query give clear indication of central ideas and themes and general nature of story line—and what is distinctive or unusual about it. We have no hard-and-fast editorial guidelines, because science fiction is such a broad field that I don't want to inhibit a new writer's thinking by imposing 'Thou Shalt Not's.' Besides, a really good story can make an editor swallow his preconceived taboos. I want the best work I can get, regardless of who wrote it—and I need new writers. So I work closely with new writers who show definite promise, but of course it's impossible to do this with every new writer. No occult or fantasy."

$ARTEMIS MAGAZINE

Science and Fiction for a Space-Faring Age, LRC Publications, Inc., 1380 E. 17th St., Suite 201, Brooklyn NY 11230-6011. E-mail: magazine@lrcpubs.com. Website: www.lrcpublications.com. **Contact:** Ian Randal Strock, editor. **90% freelance written.** Quarterly magazine covering the Artemis Project and manned space flight/colonization in general. "As part of the Artemis Project, we present lunar and space development in a positive light. The magazine is an even mix of science and fiction. We are a proud sponsor of the Artemis Project, which is constructing a commercial, manned moon base. We publish science articles for the intelligent layman, and near-term, near-Earth hard science fiction stories." Estab. 1999. **Pays on acceptance.** Publishes ms an average of 3-12 months after acceptance. Byline given. Buys first world English serial rights. Editorial lead time 3 months. Accepts queries by mail. Responds in 2 months to queries. Sample copy for $5 and a 9×12 SAE with 4 first-class stamps. Writer's guidelines for SASE or on website.

Nonfiction Essays, general interest, how-to (get to, build, or live in a lunar colony), humor, interview/profile, new product, opinion, technical, travel. **Buys 12-16 mss/year.** Query. Length: 5,000 words maximum. **Pays 3-5¢/word.**

Photos State availability of or send photos with submission. Reviews transparencies, prints. Buys one-time rights. Negotiates payment individually. Captions, identification of subjects, model releases required.

Columns/Departments News Notes (news of interest regarding the moon and manned space flight), under 300 words. **Buys 15-20 mss/year.** Send complete ms. **Pays 3-5¢/word.**

Fiction Ian Randal Stock, editor. Science fiction. "We publish near-term, near-Earth, hard science fiction. We don't want to see non-that." Adventure, science fiction. No fantasy, inspirational. **Buys 12-16 mss/year.** Send complete ms. Length: 15,000 words maximum (shorter is better). **Pays 3-5¢/word, and 3 contributor's copies.**

Fillers Newsbreaks, short humor, cartoons. **Buys 4-12/year.** Length: 100 words maximum. **Pays 3-5¢/word.**

Tips "Know your material, and write me the best possible article/story you can. You want us to read your manuscript, so show us the courtesy of reading our magazine. Also, the Artemis Project website (www.asi.org) may be a good source of inspiration."

$ASIMOV'S SCIENCE FICTION

Dell Magazine Fiction Group, 475 Park Ave. S., 11th Floor, New York NY 10016. (212)686-7188. Fax: (212)686-7414. E-mail: asimovs@dellmagazines.com. Website: www.asimovs.com. Executive Editor: Sheila Williams. **Contact:** Gardner Dozois, editor. **98% freelance written.** Works with a small number of new/unpublished writers each year. Magazine published 10 times/year, including 2 double issues. Magazine consists of science fiction and fantasy stories for adults and young adults. Publishes "the best short science fiction available." Estab. 1977. Circ. 50,000. **Pays on acceptance.** Publishes ms an average of 6-12 months after acceptance. Buys first North American serial, nonexclusive foreign serial rights; reprint rights occasionally. Accepts queries by mail. Accepts previously published material. Responds in 2 months to queries; 3 months to mss. Sample copy for $5. Writer's guidelines for #10 SASE or online.

Fiction Science fiction primarily. Some fantasy and humor but no "sword and sorcery." No explicit sex or violence that isn't integral to the story. "It is best to read a great deal of material in the genre to avoid the use of some very old ideas." **Buys 10 mss/issue.** Send complete ms and SASE with *all* submissions. Fantasy, science fiction. No horror or psychic/supernatural. Would like to see more hard science fiction. Length: 750-15,000 words. **Pays 5-8¢/word.**

Poetry Length: 40 lines maximum. **Pays $1/line.**

Tips "In general, we're looking for 'character-oriented' stories, those in which the characters, rather than the science, provide the main focus for the reader's interest. Serious, thoughtful, yet accessible fiction will constitute the majority of our purchases, but there's always room for the humorous as well. Borderline fantasy is fine, but no Sword & Sorcery, please. A good overview would be to consider that all fiction is written to examine or illuminate some aspect of human existence, but that in science fiction the backdrop you work against is the size of the universe. Please do not send us submissions on disk or via e-mail. We've bought some of our best stories from people who have never sold a story before."

$ :: CHALLENGING DESTINY

New Fantasy & Science Fiction, Crystalline Sphere Publishing, RR #6, St. Marys ON N4X 1C8, Canada. (519)885-6012. E-mail: csp@golden.net. Website: challengingdestiny.com. **Contact:** Dave Switzer, editor. **80% freelance written.** Quarterly magazine covering science fiction and fantasy. "We publish all kinds of science fiction and fantasy short stories." Estab. 1997. Circ. 200. Pays on publication. Publishes ms an average of 5 months after acceptance. Byline given. Buys first North American serial rights. Accepts queries by mail. Accepts simultaneous submissions. Responds in 1 week to queries; 1 month to mss. Sample copy for $7.50 (Canadian), $6.50 (US). Writer's guidelines for #10 SASE, 1 IRC, or online.

Fiction David M. Switzer, editor. Fantasy, science fiction. No horror, short short stories. **Buys 24 mss/year.** Send complete ms. Length: 2,000-10,000 words. **Pays 1¢/word (Canadian), plus 2 contributors copies.**

Tips "We're interested in stories where violence is rejected as a means for solving problems. We're also interested in stories with philosophical, political, or religious themes. We're not interested in stories where the good guys kill the bad guys and then live happily ever after. Read an issue to see what kind of stories we publish. Many of the stories we publish are between 4,000 and 8,000 words and have interesting characters, ideas, and plot."

$ FLESH AND BLOOD

Tales of Horror & Dark Fantasy, Flesh & Blood Press, 121 Joseph St., Bayville NJ 08721. E-mail: HorrorJackF@aol .com. Website: www.fleshandbloodpress.com. **Contact:** Jack Fisher, editor-in-chief, or Robert Swartwood, senior editor. **99% freelance written.** Quarterly magazine covering horror/dark fantasy. "We publish fiction with heavy emphasis on the supernatural, fantastic, and/or bizarre." Estab. 1997. Circ. 700. **Pays on acceptance.** Publishes ms an average of 10 months after acceptance. Editorial lead time 1 month. Accepts queries by mail, e-mail. Responds in 2 weeks to queries; 1 month to mss. Sample copy for $6 (check payable to Jack Fisher). Writer's guidelines online.

● The editor reports an interest in seeing powerful vignettes/stories with surrealism-avante-garde(ism) to them and original, unique ghost stories. The magazine recently won Best Magazine of the Year Award in the Jobs in Hell newsletter contest. Also, First Place in *Writer's Digest* zine publishing contest; Bram Stoker Award nominee.

Fiction Horror, slice-of-life vignettes, dark fantasy. "Nothing that isn't dark, strange, odd, and/or offbeat." **Buys 32-36 mss/year.** Length: 100-6,000 words. **4-5¢/word.**

Poetry Avant-garde, free verse, horror/dark fantasy surreal, bizarre. "No rhyming poetry." **Buys 24-36 poems/ year.** Submit maximum 5 poems. **Pays $10-20.**

Tips "We like subtle horror over gore. Don't let the title of the magazine deceive you; we don't want 'flesh' and 'blood'—we want just the opposite: subtle horror, dark fantasy, stories and poems that are strange, unclassifiable, fantastic, bizzare, quirky, weird, but always dark in theme, style, plot, and tone."

$ :: ON SPEC

P.O. Box 4727, Station South, Edmonton AB T6E 5G6, Canada. (780)413-0215. Fax: (780)413-1538. E-mail: editor@earthling.net. Website: www.onspec.ca/. **Contact:** Diane L. Walton. **95% freelance written.** Quarterly magazine covering Canadian science fiction, fantasy and horror. "We publish speculative fiction by new and established writers, with a strong preference for Canadian authored works." Estab. 1989. Circ. 2,000. **Pays on acceptance.** Publishes ms an average of 6-18 months after acceptance. Byline given. Buys first North American serial rights. Editorial lead time 6 months. Accepts queries by mail, phone. Accepts simultaneous submissions. Responds in 2 weeks to queries 2 months after deadline to mss to mss. Sample copy for $7. Writer's guidelines for #10 SASE or on website.

Nonfiction Commissioned only.

Fiction Fantasy, horror, science fiction, magic realism. No media tie-in or shaggy-alien stories. No condensed or excerpted novels, religious/inspirational stories, fairy tales. **Buys 50 mss/year.** Send complete ms. Length: 1,000-6,000 words. **Pays $50-180 for fiction. Short stories (under 1,000 words): $50 plus 1 contributor's copy.**

Poetry "We rarely buy rhyming or religious material." Avant-garde, free verse. **Buys 6 poems/year.** Submit maximum 10 poems. Length: 4-100 lines. **Pays $20.**

Tips "We want to see stories with plausible characters, a well-constructed, consistent, and vividly described setting, a strong plot and believable emotions; characters must show us (not tell us) their emotional responses to each other and to the situation and/or challenge they face. Also: don't send us stories written for television."

We don't like media tie-ins, so don't watch TV for inspiration! Read, instead! Absolutely no e-mailed or faxed submissions. Strong preference given to submissions by Canadians.''

Ⓝ $PENNY BLOOD

New York NY 10012. E-mail: editor@pennyblood.com. Website: www.pennyblood.com. Editor: Nicholas Louras. **70% freelance written.** Semiannual magazine covering horror in entertainment. *"Penny Blood Magazine* is a survey of horror, trash culture, pop culture, and the generally bizarre. We are looking for horror movie retrospectives and articles that explore the stranger aspects of culture.'' Estab. 2004. Circ. 4,000. **Pays on acceptance.** Byline given. Offers 100% kill fee. Buys first North American serial rights. Accepts queries by e-mail. Accepts previously published material. Responds in 2 weeks to queries; 1 month to mss. Sample copy not available. Writer's guidelines online.

Nonfiction Essays, interview/profile. **Buys 20-30 mss/year.** Send complete ms. **Pays $20-125.** Pays in contributor copies for filler material.

Tips ''We accept submissions by e-mail only. We are seeking interviews particularly and our highest pay rates go for these.''

SEX

$FIRST HAND

Experiences For Loving Men, Firsthand, Ltd., 310 Cedar Lane, Teaneck NJ 07666. (201)836-9177. Fax: (201)836-5055. E-mail: firsthand3@aol.com. Publisher: Sal Nolan. **Contact:** Don Dooley, editor. **75% freelance written.** Eager to work with new/unpublished writers. Monthly magazine published 12 times/year covering homosexual erotica. ''Half of the magazine is made up of our readers' own gay sexual experience. Rest is fiction and columns devoted to health, travel, books, etc.'' Estab. 1980. Circ. 70,000. Pays on publication. Publishes ms an average of 9-18 months after acceptance. Byline given. Buys all rights (exceptions made) and second serial (reprint) rights Submit seasonal material 10 months in advance. Responds in 2 months to queries; 4 months to mss. Sample copy for $5.99. Writer's guidelines for #10 SASE.

Reprints Send photocopy. Pays 50% of amount paid for original articles.

Fiction ''We prefer fiction in the first person which is believable—stories based on the writer's actual experience have the best chance. We're not interested in stories which involve underage characters in sexual situations. Other taboos include bestiality, rape—except in prison stories, as rape is an unavoidable reality in prison—and heavy drug use. Writers with questions about what we can and cannot depict should write for our guidelines, which go into this in more detail. We print mostly self-contained stories; we will look at novel excerpts, but only if they stand on their own.'' Erotica. ''Should be written in first person.'' No science fiction or fantasy. Erotica should detail experiences based in reality. Send complete ms. Length: 2,500-3,750 words. **Pays $75.**

Tips ''*First Hand* is a very reader-oriented publication for gay men. Half of each issue is made up of letters from our readers describing their personal experiences, fantasies, and feelings. Our readers are from all walks of life, all races and ethnic backgrounds, all classes, all religious and political affiliations, and so on. They are very diverse, and many live in far-flung rural areas or small towns; for some of them, our magazines are the primary source of contact with gay life, in some cases the only support for their gay identity. Our readers are very loyal and save every issue. We return that loyalty by trying to reflect their interests—for instance, by striving to avoid the exclusively big-city bias so common to national gay publications. So bear in mind the diversity of the audience when you write.''

$$$$HUSTLER

HG Inc., 8484 Wilshire Blvd., Suite 900, Beverly Hills CA 90211. Fax: (323)651-2741. E-mail: dkapelovitz@lfp.com. Website: www.hustler.com. Editor: Bruce David. **Contact:** Dan Kapelovitz, features editor. **60% freelance written.** Magazine published 13 times/year. ''*Hustler* is the no-nonsense men's magazine, one that is willing to speak frankly about society's sacred cows and exposé its hypocrites. The *Hustler* reader expects honest, unflinching looks at hard topics—sexual, social, political, personality profile, true crime.'' Estab. 1974. Circ. 750,000. Pays as boards ship to printer. Publishes ms an average of 3 months after acceptance. Byline given. Offers 20% kill fee. Buys all rights. Editorial lead time 4 months. Submit seasonal material 6 months in advance. Accepts queries by mail, e-mail, fax. Responds in 2 weeks to queries; 1 month to mss. Writer's guidelines for #10 SASE.

● *Hustler* is most interested in well-researched nonfiction reportage focused on sexual practices and subcultures.

Nonfiction Book excerpts, exposé, general interest, how-to, interview/profile, personal experience, trends. **Buys**

30 mss/year. Query. Length: 3,500-4,000 words. **Pays $1,500.** Sometimes pays expenses of writers on assignment.

Columns/Departments Sex play (some aspect of sex that can be encapsulated in a limited space), 2,500 words. **Buys 13 mss/year.** Send complete ms. **Pays $750.**

Fiction "Difficult fiction market. While sex is a required element in *Hustler* fiction, we are not a market for traditional erotica—do not write a 'Hot Letter.' A successful fiction submission will both arouse the reader and take him into a world he may not be able to visit on his own. What an author is able to dream up in front of a computer is rarely as compelling as the product of first-hand experience and keen observation." **Buys 2 mss/year.** Send complete ms. Length: 3,000-3,500 words. **Pays $1,000.**

Fillers Jokes and "Graffilthy," bathroom wall humor. **Pays $50-100.**

Tips "Don't try and mimic the *Hustler* style. If a writer needs to be molded into our voice, we'll do a better job of it than he or she will. Avoid first- and second-person voice. The ideal manuscript is quote-rich, visual and is narratively driven by events and viewpoints that push one another forward."

$ $ $ $ PENTHOUSE

General Media Communications, 11 Penn Plaza, 12th Floor, New York NY 10001. (212)702-6000. Fax: (212)702-6279. Website: www.penthouse.com. Editor: Peter Bloch. Monthly magazine. "*Penthouse* is for the sophisticated male. Its editorial scope ranges from outspoken contemporary comment to photography essays of beautiful women. *Penthouse* features interviews with personalities, sociological studies, humor, travel, food and wines, and fashion and grooming for men." Estab. 1969. Circ. 640,000. Pays 2 months after acceptance. Byline given. Offers 25% kill fee. Buys all rights. Editorial lead time 3 months. Accepts simultaneous submissions. Writer's guidelines for #10 SASE.

Nonfiction Exposé, general interest (to men), interview/profile. **Buys 50 mss/year.** Query with published clips or send complete ms. Length: 4,000-6,000 words. **Pays $3,000.**

Columns/Departments Length: 1,000 words. **Buys 25 mss/year.** Query with published clips or send complete ms. **Pays $500.**

Tips "Because of our long lead time, writers should think at least 6 months ahead. We take chances. Go against the grain; we like writers who look under rocks and see what hides there."

$ $ PENTHOUSE VARIATIONS

General Media Communications, Inc., 11 Penn Plaza, 12th Floor, New York NY 10001. (212)702-6000. E-mail: variations@generalmedia.com. **Contact:** Barbara Pizio, executive editor. **100% freelance written.** Monthly category-oriented, erotica magazine. Estab. 1978. Circ. 200,000. **Pays on acceptance.** Publishes an average of 14 months after acceptance. Buys all rights. Editorial lead time 7 months. Submit seasonal material 10 months in advance. Responds in 1 month to queries; 2 months to mss. Sample copy from (888)312-BACK. Writer's guidelines for #10 SASE or by e-mail.

Nonfiction Book excerpts, interview/profile, personal experience. "No previously published fiction, no humor, no poetry, no children, no one under 21, no relatives, no pets, no coercion." **Buys 50 mss/year.** Query by mail only or send complete ms. Do not submit unsolicited mss via e-mail. Length: 3,000-3,500 words. **Pays $400 maximum.**

Fiction "*Variations* publishes couple-oriented narratives in which a person fully describes his or her favorite sex scenes squarely focused within 1 of the magazine's usual categories, in highly explicit erotic detail, using the best possible language." Erotica. Length: 3,000-3,500 words. **Pays $400 maximum.**

Tips "Read the magazine to familiarize yourself with our voice, style, and categories. Write about what you're familiar with and the most comfortable discussing. We're looking for focused manuscripts which are carefully crafted by excellent writers. We are always glad to work with new writers who choose to go the distance to write successful stories for us."

$ $ $ $ PLAYBOY MAGAZINE

Playboy Enterprises, Inc., 730 5th Ave., New York NY 10019-4105. (212)261-5000. Fax: (212)957-2900. E-mail: editor@playboy.com. Website: www.playboy.com. Publisher: Diane Silberstein. Monthly magazine. "As the world's largest general interest lifestyle magazine for men, *Playboy* spans the spectrum of contemporary men's passions. From hard-hitting investigative journalism to light-hearted humor, the latest in fashion and personal technology to the cutting edge of the popular culture, *Playboy* is and always has been guidebook and dream book for generations of American men...the definitive source of information and ideas for over 10 million readers each month. In addition, *Playboy*'s 'Interview' and '20 Questions' present profiles of politicians, athletes and today's hottest personalities." Estab. 1953. Circ. 3,200,000. Buys first North American serial rights. Editorial lead time 6 months. Accepts queries by mail. Responds in 1 month to queries. Writer's guidelines for #10 SASE or online at website.

• *Playboy* does not consider poetry, plays, story outlines or novel-length mss.

Nonfiction Articles Editor. "*Playboy* regularly publishes nonfiction articles on a wide range of topics—sports, politics, music, topical humor, personality profiles, business and finance, science, technology, and other topics that have a bearing on our readers' lifestyles. You can best determine what we're looking for by becoming familiar with the nonfiction we are currently publishing. We frequently reject ideas and articles simply because they are inappropriate to our publication." General interest, humor, interview/profile. Does not accept unsolicited poetry. Mss should be typed, double-spaced and accompanied by a SASE. Writers who submit mss without a SASE will receive neither the ms nor a printed rejection. Submit brief query that outlines idea, explains why it's right for *Playboy*, and "tells us something about yourself." Length: 4,000-5,000 words.

Fiction Fiction Department. "*Playboy* is considered one of the top fiction markets in the world. We publish serious contemporary stories, mystery, suspense, humor, science fiction and sports stories. It pays to take a close look at the magazine before submitting material; we often reject stories of high quality because they are inappropriate to our publication." Humorous, mainstream, mystery, science fiction, suspense. Does not consider poetry, plays, story outlines or novel-length mss. Writers should remember that the magazine's appeal is chiefly to a well-informed, young male audience. Fairy tales, extremely experimental fiction and out-right pornography all have their place, but it is not in *Playboy*. Handwritten submissions will be returned unread. Writers who submit mss without including a SASE will receive neither the ms nor a printed rejection. "We will not consider stories submitted electronically or by fax." Query. Length: 1,000-6,000 words.

Tips "A bit of advice for writers: Please bear in mind that *Playboy* is not a venue where beginning writers should expect to be published. Nearly all of our writers have long publication histories, working their way up through newspapers and regional publications. Aspiring writers should gain experience and an extensive file of by-lined features before approaching *Playboy*. Please don't call our offices to ask how to submit a story or to explain a story. Don't ask for sample copies, a statement of editorial policy, a reaction to an idea for a story, or a detailed critique. We are unable to provide these, as we receive dozens of submissions daily."

N $ $ $ PLAYGIRL

801 Second Ave., 9th Floor, New York NY 10017. (212)661-7878. Fax: (212)697-6343. E-mail: editorial@playgirlmag.com. Editor-in-Chief: Michele Zipp. **25% freelance written.** Prefers to work with published/established writers. Monthly magazine. "*PLAYGIRL* addresses the needs, interests and desires of women 18 years of age and older. We provide something no other American women's magazine can: An uninhibited approach to exploring sexuality and fantasy that empowers, enlightens, and entertains. We publish features articles of all sorts: interviews with top celebrities; essays and humor pieces on sexually-related topics; first-person accounts of sensual adventures; articles on the latest trends in sex, love, romance, and dating; and how-to stories that give readers sexy news they can use. We also publish erotic fiction and reader fantasies from first-person. The common thread—besides, of course, good, lively writing and scrupulous research—is a fresh, open-minded, inquisitive attitude." Circ. 500,000. Pays within 6 weeks of acceptance. Publishes ms an average of 5 months after acceptance. Byline given. Buys first rights. Submit seasonal material 6 months in advance. Accepts queries by mail. Sample copy not available. Writer's guidelines for #10 SASE.

➤ Break in with pieces for Erotic Encounters. "This section is devoted to female fantasies and pleasures of the flesh. Be creative, wild, and uninhibited in your writings. Write what turns you on, not what you think turns other people on. All submissions considered must be sexually explorative fantasies that empower, enlighten, and entertain. Any fantasies that involve pain, degradation, or extreme negativity will not be published." Send complete ms and mark 'Erotic Encounters' on the envelope.

Nonfiction Average issue: 3 articles; 1 celebrity interview. Essays, exposé (related to women's issues), general interest, interview/profile (Q&A format with major celebrities—pitch first), new product, articles on sexuality, medical breakthroughs, relationships, insightful, lively articles on current issues, investigative pieces particularly geared to *PLAYGIRL*'s focus on sex/dating/relationships. **Buys 6 mss/year.** Query with published clips. Length: 800-1,200 for Erotic Encounters; 1,600-2,500 for articles. **Pays $300-1,000 (varies); $25 for some fantasies, more for celeb interviews.**

Tips "Best bet for first-time writers: Erotic Encounters. No phone calls, please."

$ $ $ SWANK

Swank Publications, 210 Route 4 E., Suite 211, Paramus NJ 07652. (201)843-4004. Fax: (201)843-8636. E-mail: genesismag@aol.com. Website: www.swankmag.com. Editor: Paul Gambino. **Contact:** D.J., associate editor. **75% freelance written.** Works with new/unpublished writers. Monthly magazine on "sex and sensationalism, lurid. High quality adult erotic entertainment." Audience of men ages 18-38, high school and some college education, medium income, skilled blue-collar professionals, union men, some white-collar. Estab. 1954. Circ. 400,000. Pays on publication. Publishes ms an average of 4 months after acceptance. Byline given, pseudonym if wanted. Buys first North American serial rights. Submit seasonal material 6 months in advance. Accepts queries by mail. Accepts previously published material. Responds in 3 weeks to queries; 1 month to mss. Sample copy for $6.95. Writer's guidelines for #10 SASE.

• *Swank* reports a need for more nonfiction, non-sex-related articles.

Nonfiction Exposé (researched), adventure must be accompanied by color photographs. "We buy articles on sex-related topics, which don't need to be accompanied by photos." Interested in unusual lifestyle pieces. How-to, interviews with entertainment, sports and sex industry celebrities. Buys photo pieces on autos, action, adventure. "It is strongly recommended that a sample copy is reviewed before submitting material." **Buys 34 mss/year.** Query with or without published clips. **Pays $350-500.** Sometimes pays expenses of writers on assignment.

Reprints Send tearsheet, photocopy or typed ms with rights for sale noted and information about when and where the material previously appeared. Pays 50% of amount paid for an original article.

Photos "Articles have a much better chance of being purchased if you have accompanying photos." Alex Suarez, art director. Model releases required.

Fiction "All of the fiction used by *Swank* is erotic in some sense—that is, both theme and content are sexual. New angles are always welcome. We will consider stories that are not strictly sexual in theme (humor, adventure, detective stories, etc.). However, these types of stories are much more likely to be considered if they portray some sexual element, or scene, within their context."

Tips "All erotic fiction currently being used by *Swank* must follow certain legal guidelines."

SPORTS

ARCHERY & BOWHUNTING

$ $ BOW & ARROW HUNTING

Y-Visionary Publishing, LP, 265 S. Anita Dr., Suite 120, Orange CA 92868-3310. (714)939-9991. Fax: (714)939-9909. E-mail: editorial@bowandarrowhunting.com. Website: www.bowandarrowhunting.com. **Contact:** Joe Bell, editor. **70% freelance written.** Magazine published 9 times/year covering bowhunting. "Dedicated to serve the serious bowhunting enthusiast. Writers must be willing to share their secrets so our readers can become better bowhunters." Estab. 1962. Circ. 90,000. Pays on publication. Publishes ms an average of 2 months after acceptance. Byline given. Buys all rights. Submit seasonal material 6 months in advance. Accepts queries by mail. Accepts simultaneous submissions. Responds in 1 month to queries; 6 weeks to mss. Sample copy and writer's guidelines free.

Nonfiction How-to, humor, interview/profile, opinion, personal experience, technical. **Buys 60 mss/year.** Send complete ms. Length: 1,700-3,000 words. **Pays $200-450.**

Photos Send photos with submission. Reviews contact sheets, 35mm and 2°x2° transparencies, 5×7 prints. Buys one-time or all rights. Offers no additional payment for photos accepted with ms. Captions required.

Fillers Facts, newsbreaks. **Buys 12/year.** Length: 500 words. **Pays $20-100.**

Tips "Inform readers how they can become better at the sport, but don't forget to keep it fun! Sidebars are recommended with every submission."

$ $ BOWHUNTER

The Number One Bowhunting Magazine, Primedia Consumer Media & Magazine Group, 6405 Flank Dr., Harrisburg PA 17112. (717)657-9555. Fax: (717)657-9552. E-mail: bowhunter_magazine@primediamags.com. Website: www.bowhunter.com. Founder/Editor Emeritus: M.R. James. **Contact:** Jeff Waring, publisher. **50% freelance written.** Bimonthly magazine covering hunting big and small game with bow and arrow. "We are a special-interest publication, produced by bowhunters for bowhunters, covering all aspects of the sport. Material included in each issue is designed to entertain and inform readers, making them better bowhunters." Estab. 1971. Circ. 160,000. **Pays on acceptance.** Publishes ms an average of 3 months to 2 years after acceptance. Byline given. Buys exclusive first, worldwide publication rights. Submit seasonal material 8 months in advance. Accepts queries by mail, e-mail, fax. Responds in 2 weeks to queries; 1 month to mss. Sample copy for $2 and 8 1/2X11 SAE with appropriate postage. Writer's guidelines for #10 SASE or on website.

Nonfiction "We publish a special 'Big Game' issue each Fall (September) but need all material by mid-March. Another annual publication, Whitetail Bowhunter, is staff written or by assignment only. Our latest special issue is the Gear Specia, which highlights the latest in equipment. We don't want articles that graphically deal with an animal's death. And, please, no articles written from the animal's viewpoint." General interest, how-to, interview/profile, opinion, personal experience, photo feature. **Buys 60 plus mss/year.** Query. Length: 250-2,000 words. **Pays $500 maximum for assigned articles; $100-400 for unsolicited articles.** Sometimes pays expenses of writers on assignment.

Photos Send photos with submission. Reviews 35mm and $2\frac{1}{4} \times 2\frac{1}{4}$ transparencies, 5×7 and 8×10 prints. Buys one-time rights. Offers $75-250/photo. Captions required.

Fiction Dwight Schuh, editor. Bowhunting, outdoor adventure. Send complete ms. Length: 500-2,000 words. **Pays $100-350.**

Tips "A writer must know bowhunting and be willing to share that knowledge. Writers should anticipate *all* questions a reader might ask, then answer them in the article itself or in an appropriate sidebar. Articles should be written with the reader foremost in mind; we won't be impressed by writers seeking to prove how good they are—either as writers or bowhunters. We care about the reader and don't need writers with 'I' trouble. Features are a good bet because most of our material comes from freelancers. The best advice is: Be yourself. Tell your story the same as if sharing the experience around a campfire. Don't try to write like you think a writer writes."

Ⓝ $ $ BOWHUNTING WORLD

Ehlert Publishing Group, 6420 Sycamore Lane N., #100, Maple Grove MN 55369. (763)383-4418. Fax: (763)383-4499. E-mail: mstrandlund@ehlertpublishing.com. Website: www.bowhuntingworld.com. **Contact:** Mike Strandlund, editor. **50% freelance written.** Bimonthly magazine with 3 additional issues for bowhunting and archery enthusiasts who participate in the sport year-round. Estab. 1952. Circ. 95,000. **Pays on acceptance.** Publishes ms an average of 5 months after acceptance. Byline given. Buys first, second serial (reprint) rights. Responds in 1 week (e-mail queries) to queries; 6 weeks to mss. Sample copy for $3 and 9×12 SAE with 10 first-class stamps. Writer's guidelines for #10 SASE.

● Accepts queries by mail, but prefers e-mail.

Nonfiction How-to articles with creative slants on knowledgeable selection and use of bowhunting equipment and bowhunting methods. Articles must emphasize knowledgeable use of archery or hunting equipment, and/or specific bowhunting techniques. Contributors must be authorities in the areas of archery and bowhunting. Straight hunting adventure narratives and other types of articles now appear only in special issues. Equipment-oriented aricles must demonstrate wise and insightful selection and use of archery equipment and other gear related to the archery sports. Some product-review, field-test, equipment how-to, and technical pieces will be purchased. We are not interested in articles whose equipment focuses on random mentioning of brands. Technique-oriented aricles most sought are those that briefly cover fundamentals and delve into leading-edge bowhunting or recreational archery methods. **Buys 60 mss/year.** Query with or without published clips or send complete ms. Length: 1,500-2,500 words. **Pays $350-600.**

Photos "We are seeking cover photos that depict specific behavioral traits of the more common big game animals (scraping whitetails, bugling elk, etc.) and well-equipped bowhunters in action. Must include return postage."

Tips "Writers are strongly advised to adhere to guidelines and become familiar with our format, as our needs are very specific. Writers are urged to query by e-mail. We prefer detailed outlines of 6 or so article ideas/query. Assignments are made for the next 18 months."

BASEBALL

$ JUNIOR BASEBALL

America's Youth Baseball Magazine, 2D Publishing, P.O. Box 9099, Canoga Park CA 91309. (818)710-1234. Fax: (818)710-1877. E-mail: dave@juniorbaseball.com. Website: www.juniorbaseball.com. **Contact:** Dave Destler, editor/publisher. **25% freelance written.** Bimonthly magazine covering youth baseball. "Focused on youth baseball players ages 7-17 (including high school) and their parents/coaches. Edited to various reading levels, depending upon age/skill level of feature." Estab. 1996. Circ. 50,000. Pays on publication. Publishes ms an average of 4 months after acceptance. Byline given. Buys all rights. Editorial lead time 3 months. Submit seasonal material 4 months in advance. Accepts simultaneous submissions. Responds in 2 weeks to queries; 1 month to mss. Sample copy for $5 and online.

Nonfiction How-to (skills, tips, features, how to play better baseball, etc.), interview/profile (with major league players; only on assignment), personal experience (from coaches' or parents' perspective). "No trite first-person articles about your kid." No fiction or poetry. **Buys 8-12 mss/year.** Query. Length: 500-1,000 words. **Pays $50-100.**

Photos Photos can be e-mailed in 300 dpi JPEGs. State availability with submission. Reviews 35mm transparencies, 3×5 prints. Offers $10-100/photo; negotiates payment individually. Captions, identification of subjects required.

Columns/Departments When I Was a Kid (a current Major League Baseball player profile); Parents Feature (topics of interest to parents of youth ball players); all 1,000-1,500 words. In the Spotlight (news, events, new products), 50-100 words; Hot Prospect (written for the 14 and older competitive player. High school baseball is included, and the focus is on improving the finer points of the game to make the high school team, earn a college scholarship, or attract scouts, written to an adult level), 500-1,000 words. **Buys 8-12 mss/year. Pays $50-100.**

Tips "Must be well-versed in baseball! Having a child who is very involved in the sport, or have extensive hands-on experience in coaching baseball, at the youth, high school or higher level. We can always use accurate, authoritative skills information and good photos to accompany is a big advantage! This magazine is read by experts."

◙ USA TODAY SPORTS WEEKLY

Gannet Co., Inc., 7950 Jones Branch Dr., McLean VA 22108-0001. (703)854-3400. Fax: (703)854-2034. E-mail: sportsweekly@usatoday.com. Website: www.usatoday.com. Publisher/Executive Editor: Lee Ivory. Weekly magazine providing complete coverage of baseball and football combined into a year-round publication. Circ. 266,526. Editorial lead time 2 months. Sample copy not available.

• All written in-house and on salary.

BICYCLING

Ⓝ $ $ $ ADVENTURE CYCLIST

Adventure Cycling Assn., Box 8308, Missoula MT 59807. (406)721-1776, ext. 222. Fax: (406)721-8754. E-mail: mdeme@adventurecycling.org. Website: www.adventurecycling.org. **Contact:** Mike Deme, editor. **75% freelance written.** Magazine published 9 times/year for Adventure Cycling Association members. Estab. 1975. Circ. 30,000. Pays on publication. Byline given. Buys first rights. Submit seasonal material 3 months in advance. Sample copy and guidelines for 9×12 SAE with 4 first-class stamps.

Nonfiction How-to, humor, interview/profile, photo feature, technical, travel, U.S. or foreign tour accounts; special focus (on tour experience). **Buys 20-25 mss/year.** Query with or without published clips or send complete ms. Length: 800-2,500 words. **Pays $450-1,200.**

Photos Bicycle, scenery, portraits. State availability with submission. Reviews color transparencies. Identification of subjects, model releases required.

Ⓝ $ $ $ BIKE MAGAZINE

Primedia Enthusiast, P.O. Box 1028, Dana Point CA 92629. (949)496-5922. Fax: (949)496-7849. E-mail: bikemag @primedia.com. Website: www.bikemag.com. **Contact:** Ron Ige, editor. **35% freelance written.** Magazine publishes 10 times/year covering mountain biking. Estab. 1993. Circ. 170,000. Pays on publication. Publishes ms an average of 2 months after acceptance. Byline given. Offers 25% kill fee. Buys first North American serial rights. Editorial lead time 4 months. Submit seasonal material 6 months in advance. Responds in 2 months to queries. Sample copy for $8. Writer's guidelines for #10 SASE.

    ○━ *Bike* receives many travel-related queries and is seeking more investigative journalism on matters that affect mountain bikers. Writers have a much better chance of publication if they tackle larger issues that affect mountain bikers, such as trail access or sport controversies (i.e., drugs in cycling). If you do submit a travel article, know that a great location is not a story in itself—there must also be a theme. Examine back issues before submitting a travel story; if *Bike* has covered your location before, they won't again (for at least 4-5 years).

Nonfiction Writers should submit queries in March (April 1 deadline) for consideration for the following year's editions. All queries received by April 1 will be considered and editors will contact writers about stories they are interested in. Queries should include word count. Humor, interview/profile, personal experience, photo feature, travel. **Buys 20 mss/year.** Length: 1,000-2,500 words. **Pays 50¢/word.** Sometimes pays expenses of writers on assignment.

Photos David Reddick, photo editor. Send photos with submission. Reviews color transparencies, b&w prints. Buys one-time rights. Negotiates payment individually. Captions, identification of subjects required.

Columns/Departments Splatter (news), 300 words; Urb (details a great ride within 1 hour of a major metropolitan area), 600-700 words. Query year-round for Splatter and Urb. **Buys 20 mss/year. Pays 50¢/word.**

Tips "Remember that we focus on hard core mountain biking, not beginners. We're looking for ideas that deliver the excitement and passion of the sport in ways that aren't common or predictable. Ideas should be vivid, unbiased, irreverent, probing, fun, humorous, funky, quirky, smart, good. Great feature ideas are always welcome, especially features on cultural matters or issues in the sport. However, you're much more likely to get published in *Bike* if you send us great ideas for short articles. In particular we need stories for our Splatter, a front-of-the-book section devoted to news, funny anecdotes, quotes, and odds and ends. These stories range from 50 to 300 words. We also need personality profiles of 600 words or so for our People Who Ride section. Racers are OK but we're more interested in grassroots people with interesting personalities—it doesn't matter if they're Mother Theresas or scumbags, so long as they make mountain biking a little more interesting. Short descriptions of great rides are very welcome for our Urb column; the length should be from 600-700 words."

$BIKE MIDWEST

Columbus Sports Publications, 1350 W. Fifth Ave., #30, Columbus OH 43212. (614)486-2202. Fax: (614)486-3650. E-mail: nweis@buckeyesports.com. **Contact:** Nicole Weis, editor. **35% freelance written.** Monthly (April-October) tabloid covering bicycling. "We like articles to be in a more casual voice so our readers feel more like a friend than just a customer." Estab. 1986. Circ. 35,000. Pays on publication. Publishes ms an average of 1 month after acceptance. Byline given. Offers 100% or $75 kill fee. Buys all rights. Editorial lead time 1 month. Submit seasonal material 1 month in advance. Accepts queries by mail, e-mail, fax. Accepts simultaneous submissions. Responds in 2 months to queries; 2 months to mss. Sample copy and writer's guidelines free.

Nonfiction Essays, general interest, historical/nostalgic, how-to (bicycle mechanics, i.e., how to change a flat tire, etc.), humor, inspirational, interview/profile, new product, opinion, personal experience, technical, travel. Special issues: April and October issues cover travel and tourism by bicycle. Nothing nonbike related. **Buys 14 mss/year.** Send complete ms. Length: 1,000-2,000 words. **Pays $35-75.**

Reprints Accepts previously published submissions.

Photos Send photos with submission. Reviews negatives, 3½×5 prints. Buys all rights. Offers $25-50/photo. Captions, identification of subjects, model releases required.

Columns/Departments Metal Cowboy (experiences on a bicycle), 1,800 words; Bicycling News (experiences in bicycling), 1,200 words. **Buys 14 mss/year.** Send complete ms. **Pays $35-75.**

Tips "Articles must be informative and/or engaging. Our readers like to be entertained. They also look for lots of information when articles are technical (product reviews, etc.)"

$$CYCLE CALIFORNIA! MAGAZINE

P.O. Box 189, Mountain View CA 94042. (650)961-2663. Fax: (650)968-9030. E-mail: tcorral@cyclecalifornia.com. Website: www.cyclecalifornia.com. **Contact:** Tracy L. Corral, editor/publisher. **75% freelance written.** Magazine published 11 times/year "covering Northern California bicycling events, races, people. Issues (topics) covered include bicycle commuting, bicycle politics, touring, racing, nostalgia, history, anything at all to do with riding a bike." Estab. 1995. Circ. 26,000. Pays on publication. Publishes ms an average of 3 months after acceptance. Byline given. Buys first North American serial rights. Editorial lead time 6 weeks. Submit seasonal material 6 weeks in advance. Accepts queries by mail, e-mail, phone. Accepts simultaneous submissions. Responds in 1 month to queries. Sample copy for 10×13 SAE with 3 first-class stamps. Writer's guidelines for #10 SASE.

Nonfiction Historical/nostalgic, how-to, interview/profile, opinion, personal experience, technical, travel. Special issues: Bicycle Tour & Travel (January/February). No articles about any sport that doesn't relate to bicycling, no product reviews. **Buys 36 mss/year.** Query with or without published clips. Length: 500-1,500 words. **Pays 3-10¢/word.**

Photos Send photos with submission. Reviews 3×5 prints. Buys one-time rights. Negotiates payment individually. Identification of subjects required.

Columns/Departments **Buys 2-3 mss/year.** Query with published clips. **Pays 3-10¢/word.**

Tips "E-mail or call editor with good ideas. While we don't exclude writers from other parts of the country, articles really should reflect a Northern California slant, or be of general interest to bicyclists. We prefer stories written by people who like and use their bikes."

CYCLE WORLD

Hachette Filipacchi Media U.S., Inc., 1499 Monrovia Ave., Newport Beach CA 92663. (949)720-5300. Fax: (949)631-0651. E-mail: cycleworld@hfmus.com. Website: www.cycleworld.com. Editor-in-Chief: David Edwards. Monthly magazine. Geared towards motorcycle owners and buyers, accesory buyers, potential buyers and enthusiasts of the overall sport of motorcycling. Circ. 319,489.

N $$VELONEWS

The Journal of Competitive Cycling, Inside Communications, Inc., 1830 N. 55th St., Boulder CO 80301. (303)440-0601. Fax: (303)444-6788. Website: www.VeloNews.com. **Contact:** Editor. **40% freelance written.** Monthly tabloid covering bicycle racing. Estab. 1972. Circ. 48,000. Pays on publication. Publishes ms an average of 1 month after acceptance. Byline given. Buys one-time worldwide rights. Accepts previously published material. Responds in 3 weeks to queries.

Nonfiction Freelance opportunities include race coverage, reviews (book and videos), health-and-fitness departments. **Buys 80 mss/year.** Query. Length: 300-1,200 words. **Pays $100-400.**

Reprints Send ms with rights for sale noted and information about when and where the material previously appeared.

Photos State availability with submission. Buys one-time rights. Pays $16.50 for b&w prints; $200 for color used on cover. Captions, identification of subjects required.

BOATING

$ $ $ CHESAPEAKE BAY MAGAZINE

Boating at Its Best, Chesapeake Bay Communications, 1819 Bay Ridge Ave., Annapolis MD 21403. (410)263-2662. Fax: (410)267-6924. E-mail: editor@cbmmag.net. Managing Editor: Jane Meneely. **Contact:** Wendy Mitman Clarke, executive editor. **60% freelance written.** Monthly magazine covering boating and the Chesapeake Bay. "Our readers are boaters. Our writers should know boats and boating. Read the magazine before submitting." Estab. 1972. Circ. 46,000. Pays within 2 months after acceptance. Publishes ms an average of 1 year after acceptance. Byline given. Buys first North American serial rights. Editorial lead time 1 year. Submit seasonal material 1 year in advance. Accepts queries by mail, e-mail, fax, phone. Accepts simultaneous submissions. Responds in 2 months to queries; 3 months to mss. Sample copy for $5.19 prepaid.

O→ "Read our Channel 9 column and give us some new ideas. These are short news items, profiles, and updates (200-800 words)."

Nonfiction Destinations, boating adventures, how-to, marina reviews, history, nature, environment, lifestyles, personal and institutional profiles, boat-type profiles, boatbuilding, boat restoration, boating anecdotes, boating news. **Buys 30 mss/year.** Query with published clips. Length: 300-3,000 words. **Pays $100-1,000.** Pays expenses of writers on assignment.

Photos Buys one-time rights. Offers $75-250/photo, $400/day rate for assignment photography. Captions, identification of subjects required.

Tips "Send us unedited writing samples (not clips) that show the writer can write, not just string words together. We look for well-organized, lucid, lively, intelligent writing."

$ $ $ $ CRUISING WORLD

The Sailing Co., 5 John Clarke Rd., Newport RI 02840-0992. (401)845-5100. Fax: (401)845-5180. Website: www.cruisingworld.com. Editor: Herb McCormick. Managing Editor: Elaine Lembo. **Contact:** Tim Murphy, executive editor. **60% freelance written.** Monthly magazine covering sailing, cruising/adventuring, do-it-yourself boat improvements. "*Cruising World* is a publication by and for sailboat owners who spend time in home waters as well as voyaging the world. Its readership is extremely loyal, savvy, and driven by independent thinking." Estab. 1974. Circ. 155,000. **Pays on acceptance for articles;** on publication for photography. Publishes ms an average of 18 months after acceptance. Byline given. Buys 6-month, all-world, first time rights (amendable). Editorial lead time 3 months. Submit seasonal material 1 year in advance. Accepts queries by mail. Responds in 1 month to queries; 4 months to mss. Sample copy for free. Writer's guidelines online.

Nonfiction Book excerpts, essays, exposé, general interest, historical/nostalgic, how-to, humor, interview/profile, new product, opinion, personal experience, photo feature, technical, travel. No travel articles that have nothing to do with cruising aboard sailboats from 20-50 feet in length. **Buys dozens of mss/year.** Send complete ms. **Pays $50-1,500 for assigned articles; $50-1,000 for unsolicited articles.** Sometimes pays expenses of writers on assignment.

Photos Send photos with submission. Reviews negatives, transparencies, color slides preferred. Buys one-time rights. Negotiates payment individually. Also buys stand-alone photos. Captions required.

Columns/Departments Shoreline (sailing news, people, and short features; contact Nim Marsh), 500 words maximum; Hands-on Sailor (refit, voyaging, seamanship, how-to; contact Darrell Nicholson), 1,000-1,500 words. **Buys dozens of mss/year.** Query with or without published clips or send complete ms. **Pays $100-700.**

Tips "*Cruising World's* readers know exactly what they want to read, so our best advice to freelancers is to carefully read the magazine and envision which exact section or department would be the appropriate place for proposed submissions."

GOOD OLD BOAT

The Sailing Magazine for the Rest of Us, Partnership for Excellence, Inc., 7340 Niagara Lane N., Maple Grove MN 55311. (763)420-8923. Fax: (763)420-8921. E-mail: karen@goodoldboat.com. Website: www.goodoldboat.com. **Contact:** Karen Larson, editor. **90% freelance written.** Bimonthly magazine covering sailing. "*Good Old Boat* magazine focuses on maintaining, upgrading, and loving cruising sailboats that are 10 years old and older. Readers see themselves as part of a community of sailors who share similar maintenance and replacement concerns which are not generally addressed in the other sailing publications. Our readers do much of the writing about projects they have done on their boats and the joy they receive from sailing them." Estab. 1998. Circ. 30,000. Pays 2 months in advance of publication. Publishes ms an average of 12-18 months after acceptance. Buys first North American serial rights. Editorial lead time 4 months. Submit seasonal material 12-15 months in advance. Accepts queries by mail, e-mail, fax. Accepts previously published material. Accepts simultaneous submissions. Responds in 1-2 weeks to queries; 2-6 months to mss. Sample copy for free. Writer's guidelines online.

Nonfiction General interest, historical/nostalgic, how-to, interview/profile, personal experience, photo feature, technical. "Articles which are written by nonsailors serve no purpose for us." **Buys 150 mss/year.** Query or send complete ms. **Payment varies, refer to published rates on website.**

Photos State availability of or send photos with submission. "We do not pay additional fees for photos except when they run as covers, center spread photo features, or are specifically requested to support an article."

Tips "Our shorter pieces are the best way to break into our magazine. We publish many Simple Solutions and Quick & Easy pieces. These are how-to tips that have worked for sailors on their boats. In addition, our readers send lists of projects which they've done on their boats and which they could write for publication. We respond to these queries with a thumbs up or down by project. Articles are submitted on speculation, but they have a better chance of being accepted once we have approved of the suggested topic."

$ $HEARTLAND BOATING

The Waterways Journal, Inc., 319 N. Fourth St., Suite 650, St. Louis MO 63102. (314)241-4310. Fax: (314)241-4207. E-mail: info@heartlandboating.com. Website: www.heartlandboating.com. **Contact:** Krista Grueninger, editor. **70% freelance written.** Magazine published 9 times/year covering recreational boating on the inland waterways of mid-America, from the Great Lakes south to the Gulf of Mexico and over to the east. "Our writers must have experience with, and a great interest in, boating, particularly in the area described above. *Heartland Boating*'s content is both informative and humorous—describing boating life as the heartland boater knows it. We are boaters and enjoy the outdoor, water-oriented way of life. The content reflects the challenge, joy, and excitement of our way of life afloat. We are devoted to both power and sailboating enthusiasts throughout middle America; houseboats are included. The focus is on the freshwater inland rivers and lakes of the heartland, primarily the waters of the Tennessee, Cumberland, Ohio, Missouri, Illinois, and Mississippi rivers, the Tennessee-Tombigbee Waterway, The Gulf Intracoastal Waterway, and the lakes along these waterways." Estab. 1989. Circ. 12,000. Pays on publication. Byline given. Buys first North American serial, first, electronic rights. Editorial lead time 3 months. Submit seasonal material 6 months in advance. Accepts queries by mail, e-mail, fax, phone. Accepts previously published material. Responds in 2 months to queries. Sample copy for $5. Writer's guidelines online.

Nonfiction How-to (articles about navigation information and making time spent aboard easier and more comfortable), humor, personal experience (sharing expericenes aboard and on cruises in our coverage area), technical (boat upkeep and maintenance), travel (along the rivers and on the lakes in our coverage area and on-land stops along the way). Special issues: Annual Boat Show/New Products issue in January/February looks at what is coming out on the market for the coming year. **Buys 110 mss/year.** Query with published clips or send complete ms. Length: 850-1,500 words. **Pays $100-300.**

Reprints Send tearsheet, photocopy or typed ms and information about when and where the material previously appeared.

Photos Send photos with submission. Reviews transparencies, prints, digital images. Buys one-time rights. Offers no additional payment for photos accepted with ms.

Columns/Departments Food Afloat (recipes easy to make when aboard), Books Aboard (book reviews), Handy Hints (small boat improvement projects), Waterways History (on-water history tidbits), all 850 words. **Buys 45 mss/year.** Query with published clips or send complete ms. **Pays $75-150.**

Tips "We usually plan an editorial schedule for the coming year in August. Submitting material between May and July will be most helpful for the planning process, although we accept submissions year-round."

$ $HOUSEBOAT MAGAZINE

The Family Magazine for the American Houseboater, Harris Publishing, Inc., 360 B St., Idaho Falls ID 83402. Fax: (208)522-5241. E-mail: hbeditor@houseboatmagazine.com. Website: www.houseboatmagazine.com. **Contact:** Brady L. Kay, managing editor. **40% freelance written.** Monthly magazine for houseboaters, who enjoy reading everything that reflects the unique houseboating lifestyle. If it is not a houseboat-specific article, please do not query. Estab. 1990. Circ. 25,000. Pays on publication. Publishes ms an average of 3 months after acceptance. Byline given. Offers 25% kill fee. Buys first North American serial, electronic rights. Editorial lead time 6 months. Submit seasonal material 6 months in advance. Accepts simultaneous submissions. Responds in 1 month to queries; 2 months to mss. Sample copy for $5. Writer's guidelines online.

● No unsolicited mss. Accepts queries by mail and fax, but e-mail strongly preferred.

Nonfiction How-to, interview/profile, new product, personal experience, travel. **Buys 36 mss/year.** Query. Length: 1,000-1,200 words. **Pays $150-300.**

Photos Often required as part of submission package. Color prints discouraged. Digital prints are unacceptable. Seldom purchases photos without ms, but occasionally buys cover photos. Reviews transparencies, high-resolution electronic images. Buys one-time rights. Offers no additional payment for photos accepted with ms. Captions, model releases required.

Columns/Departments Pays $100-200.

Tips "As a general rule, how-to articles are always in demand. So are stories on unique houseboats or houseboaters. You are less likely to break in with a travel piece that does not revolve around specific people or groups. Personality profile pieces with excellent supporting photography are your best bet.''

N $LAKELAND BOATING

The Magazine for Great Lakes Boaters, O'Meara-Brown Publications, Inc., 727 S. Dearborn, Suite 812, Chicago IL 60605. (312)276-0610. Fax: (312)276-0619. E-mail: lb@omeara-brown.com. Website: www.lakelandboating. com. **50% freelance written.** Magazine covering Great Lakes boating. Estab. 1946. Circ. 38,000. Pays on publication. Byline given. Buys first North American serial rights. Accepts queries by e-mail. Responds in 4 months to queries. Sample copy for $5.50 and 9×12 SAE with 6 first-class stamps. Writer's guidelines free.

Nonfiction Book excerpts, historical/nostalgic, how-to, interview/profile, personal experience, photo feature, technical, travel, must relate to boating in Great Lakes. No inspirational, religious, exposé or poetry. **Buys 20-30 mss/year.** Length: 800-3,00 words. **Pays $100-600.**

Photos State availability with submission. Reviews prefers 35mm transparencies. Buys one-time rights. Captions required.

Columns/Departments Bosun's Locker (technical or how-to pieces on boating), 100-1,000 words. **Buys 40 mss/year.** Query. **Pays $30-100.**

$LIVING ABOARD

Acres, U.S.A., P.O. Box 91299, Austin TX 78709-1299. (512)892-4446. Fax: (512)892-4448. E-mail: editor@living aboard.com. Website: www.livingaboard.com. Managing Editor: Fred Walters. **Contact:** Linda Ridihalgh, editor. **95% freelance written.** Bimonthly magazine covering living on boats/cruising. Estab. 1973. Circ. 7,500. Pays on publication. Publishes ms an average of 3-6 months after acceptance. Byline given. Buys first North American serial, first, one-time, second serial (reprint) rights. Accepts queries by mail, e-mail, fax. Responds in 1-2 weeks to queries; 1-2 months to mss. Sample copy online. Writer's guidelines free.

Nonfiction How-to (buy, furnish, maintain, provision a boat), interview/profile, personal experience, technical (as relates to boats), travel (on the water), Cooking Aboard with Recipes. Send complete ms. **Pays 5¢/word.**

Photos Pays $5/photo; $50/cover photo.

Columns/Departments Cooking Aboard (how to prepare healthy and nutritious meals in the confines of a galley; how to entertain aboard a boat), 1,000-1,500 words; Environmental Notebook (articles pertaining to clean water, fish, waterfowl, water environment), 750-1,000 words. **Buys 6 mss/year.** Send complete ms. **Pays 5¢/word.**

Tips "Articles should have a positive tone and promote the liveaboard lifestyle.''

MOTOR BOATING

Time 4 Media, 18 Marshall St., Suite 114, Norwalk CT 06854-2237. (203)299-5950. Fax: (203)299-5951. E-mail: mailboat@motorboating.com. Website: www.motorboating.com. Editor: Peter Janssen. Managing Editor: John Wooldridge. **Contact:** Jeanne Craig, executive editor. Monthly magazine. Geared toward the owners of power boats 20' to 60'. Monthly magazine devoted to helping its readers make educated decisions about how to buy, equip, maintain, and enjoy their boats. Circ. 155,000. Editorial lead time 6 weeks. Accepts queries by mail. Responds in 6-8 weeks to queries. Sample copy not available.

Nonfiction "We look for articles on adventure travel by boat; investigative stories on issues important to recreational power boaters; and informative service pieces on boat/engine care and maintenance.'' Short tips on boat maintenance and repair. Query with published clips. Length: 1,500-2,000 words.

$NORTHERN BREEZES, SAILING MAGAZINE

Northern Breezes, Inc., 3949 Winnetka Ave. N, Minneapolis MN 55427. E-mail: thom@sailingbreezes.com. Website: www.sailingbreezes.com. Managing Editor: Thom Burns. **70% freelance written.** Magazine published 8 times/year for the Great Lakes and Midwest sailing community. Focusing on regional cruising, racing, and day sailing. Estab. 1989. Circ. 22,300. Pays on publication. Byline given. Buys first North American serial rights. Editorial lead time 1 months. Submit seasonal material 3 months in advance. Accepts queries by mail, e-mail, fax, phone. Accepts previously published material. Responds in 1 month to queries; 2 months to mss. Sample copy for free. Writer's guidelines online.

Nonfiction Book excerpts, how-to (sailing topics), humor, inspirational, interview/profile, new product, personal experience, photo feature, technical, travel. No boating reviews. **Buys 24 mss/year.** Query with published clips. Length: 300-3,500 words.

Reprints Accepts previously published submissions.

Photos Send photos with submission. Reviews negatives, 35mm slides, 3×5 or 4×6 prints. Buys one-time rights. Offers no additional payment for photos accepted with ms. Captions required.

Columns/Departments This Old Boat (sailboat), 500-1,000 words; Surveyor's Notebook, 500-800 words. **Buys 8 mss/year.** Query with published clips. **Pays $50-150.**

Tips "Query with a regional connection already in mind.''

$ $ OFFSHORE

Northeast Boating at Its Best, Offshore Communications, Inc., 500 Victory Rd., Marina Bay, North Quincy MA 02171. (617)221-1400. Fax: (617)847-1871. E-mail: editors@offshoremag.net. Website: www.offshoremag.net. **Contact:** Editorial Department. **80% freelance written.** Monthly magazine covering power and sailboating on the coast from Maine to New Jersey. Estab. 1976. Circ. 35,000. **Pays on acceptance.** Publishes ms an average of 5 months after acceptance. Byline given. Offers 50% kill fee. Buys first North American serial rights. Submit seasonal material 6 months in advance. Accepts queries by mail. Accepts simultaneous submissions. Writer's guidelines for #10 SASE.

Nonfiction Articles on boats, boating, New York, New Jersey, and New England coastal places and people, Northeast coastal history. **Buys 90 mss/year.** Query with or without published clips or send complete ms. Length: 1,200-2,500 words. **Pays $350-500 for features, depending on length.**

Photos Reviews 35mm slides. Buys one-time rights. Pays $150-300. Identification of subjects required.

Tips "Writers must demonstrate a familiarity with boats and with the Northeast coast. Specifically we are looking for articles on boating destinations, boating events (such as races, rendezvous, and boat parades), on-the-water boating adventures, boating culture, maritime museums, maritime history, boating issues (such as safety and the environment), seamanship, fishing, how-to stories, and essays. Note: Since *Offshore* is a regional magazine, all stories must focus on the area from New Jersey to Maine. We are always open to new people, the best of whom may gradually work their way into regular writing assignments. Important to ask for (and follow) our writer's guidelines if you're not familiar with our magazine."

$ $ 🖭 PACIFIC YACHTING

Western Canada's Premier Boating Magazine, OP Publishing, Ltd., 1080 Howe St., Suite 900, Vancouver BC V6Z 2T1, Canada. (604)606-4644. Fax: (604)687-1925. E-mail: editor@pacificyachting.com. Website: www.pacificyachting.com. **90% freelance written.** Monthly magazine covering all aspects of recreational boating on British Columbia's coast. "The bulk of our writers and photographers not only come from the local boating community, many of them were long-time *PY* readers before coming aboard as a contributor. The *PY* reader buys the magazine to read about new destinations or changes to old haunts on the British Columbia coast and to learn the latest about boats and gear." Circ. 19,000. Pays on publication. Publishes ms an average of 6 months after acceptance. Byline given. Buys first North American serial, simultaneous rights. Editorial lead time 4 months. Submit seasonal material 6 months in advance. Accepts queries by mail, e-mail, fax. Sample copy for $5.95, plus postage charged to credit card. Writer's guidelines free.

Nonfiction Historical/nostalgic (British Columbia coast only), how-to, humor, interview/profile, personal experience, technical (boating related), travel, cruising, and destination on the British Columbia coast. "No articles from writers who are obviously not boaters!" Query. Length: 1,500-2,000 words. **Pays $150-500.** Pays expenses of writers on assignment.

Photos Send photos with submission. Reviews transparencies, 4×6 prints, and slides. Buys one-time rights. Offers no additional payment for photos accepted with ms. Offers $25-300 for photos accepted alone. Identification of subjects required.

Columns/Departments Currents (current events, trade and people news, boat gatherings, and festivities), 50-250 words. Reflections; Cruising, both 800-1,000 words. Query. **Pay varies.**

Tips "We strongly encourage queries before submission (written with SAE and IRCs, or by phone or e-mail). Our reader wants you to balance important navigation details with first-person observations, blending the practical with the romantic. Write tight, write short, write with the reader in mind, write to inform, write to entertain. Be specific, accurate, and historic."

$ $ PONTOON & DECK BOAT

Harris Publishing, Inc., 360 B. St., Idaho Falls ID 83402. (208)524-7000. Fax: (208)522-5241. E-mail: brady@pdbmagazine.com. Website: www.pdbmagazine.com. **Contact:** Brady L. Kay, editor. **15% freelance written.** Magazine published 10 times/year. "We are a boating niche publication geared toward the pontoon and deck boating lifestyle and consumer market. Our audience is comprised of people who utilize these boats for varied family activities and fishing. Our magazine is promotional of the PDB industry and its major players. We seek to give the reader a twofold reason to read our publication: to celebrate the lifestyle, and to do it aboard a first-class craft." Estab. 1995. Circ. 84,000. Pays on publication. Byline given. Buys one-time rights. Editorial lead time 2 months. Submit seasonal material 3 months in advance. Accepts simultaneous submissions. Responds in 6 weeks to queries; 3 months to mss. Sample copy and writer's guidelines free.

Nonfiction How-to, personal experience, technical, remodeling, rebuilding. "We are saturated with travel pieces, no general boating, humor, fiction, or poetry." **Buys 15 mss/year.** Query with or without published clips or send complete ms. Length: 600-2,000 words. **Pays $50-300.** Sometimes pays expenses of writers on assignment.

Photos State availability with submission. Reviews transparencies. Rights negotiable. Captions, model releases required.

Columns/Departments No Wake Zone (short, fun quips); Better Boater (how-to). **Buys 6-12 mss/year.** Query with published clips. **Pays $50-150.**

Tips "Be specific to pontoon and deck boats. Any general boating material goes to the slush pile. The more you can tie together the lifestyle, attitudes, and the PDB industry, the more interest we'll take in what you send us."

$ $ $ POWER & MOTORYACHT

Primedia, Inc., 260 Madison Ave., 8th Floor, New York NY 10016. (917)256-2200. Fax: (917)256-2282. E-mail: diane_byrne@primediamags.com. Website: www.powerandmotoryacht.com. Editor: Richard Thiel. Managing Editor: Eileen Mansfield. **Contact:** Diane M. Byrne, executive editor. **25% freelance written.** Monthly magazine covering powerboats 24 feet and larger with special emphasis on the 35-foot-plus market. "Readers have an average of 32 years experience boating, and we give them accurate advice on how to choose, operate, and maintain their boats as well as what electronics and gear will help them pursue their favorite pastime. In addition, since powerboating is truly a lifestyle and not just a hobby for them, *Power & Motoryacht* reports on a host of other topics that affect their enjoyment of the water: chartering, sportfishing, and the environment, among others. Articles must therefore be clear, concise, and authoritative; knowledge of the marine industry is mandatory. Include personal experience and information for marine industry experts where appropriate." Estab. 1985. Circ. 157,000. **Pays on acceptance.** Publishes ms an average of 4-6 months after acceptance. Byline given. Offers 33% kill fee. Buys all rights. Editorial lead time 4-6 months. Submit seasonal material 4-6 months in advance. Accepts queries by mail, e-mail, fax. Accepts simultaneous submissions. Responds in 1 month to queries. Sample copy for 10×12 SASE. Writer's guidelines for #10 SASE.

Nonfiction How-to, interview/profile, personal experience, photo feature, travel. No unsolicited mss or articles about sailboats and/or sailing yachts (including motorsailers). **Buys 20-25 mss/year.** Query with published clips. Length: 800-1,500 words. **Pays $500-1,000 for assigned articles.** Sometimes pays expenses of writers on assignment.

Photos Aimee Colon, art director. State availability with submission. Reviews 8×10 transparencies, GIF/JPEG files (minimum 300 dpi). Buys one-time rights. Offers no additional payment for photos accepted with ms. Captions, identification of subjects required.

Tips "Take a clever or even unique approach to a subject, particularly if the topic is dry/technical. Pitch us on yacht cruises you've taken, particularly if they're in off-the-beaten-path locations."

$ $ ⊠ POWER BOATING CANADA

1020 Brevik Place, Suites 4 & 5, Mississauga ON L4W 4N7, Canada. (905)624-8218. Fax: (905)624-6764. E-mail: editor@powerboating.com. Website: www.powerboating.com. **70% freelance written.** Bimonthly magazine covering recreational power boating. "*Power Boating Canada* offers boating destinations, how-to features, boat tests (usually staff written), lifestyle pieces—with a Canadian slant—and appeal to recreational power boaters across the country." Estab. 1984. Circ. 42,000. Pays on publication. Publishes ms an average of 3 months after acceptance. Byline given. Buys first North American serial rights. Editorial lead time 2 months. Submit seasonal material 3 months in advance. Accepts previously published material. Responds in 1 month to queries; 2 months to mss. Sample copy for free.

Nonfiction "Any articles related to the sport of power boating, especially boat tests." Historical/nostalgic, how-to, interview/profile, personal experience, travel (boating destinations). No general boating articles or personal anecdotes. **Buys 40-50 mss/year.** Query. Length: 1,200-2,500 words. **Pays $150-300 (Canadian).** Sometimes pays expenses of writers on assignment.

Reprints Send photocopy with rights for sale noted and information about when and where the material previously appeared.

Photos Send photos with submission. Reviews contact sheets, negatives, transparencies, prints. Buys one-time rights. Pay varies; no additional payment for photos accepted with ms. Captions, identification of subjects required.

$ $ $ SAIL

98 N. Washington St., 2nd Floor, Boston MA 02114. (617)720-8600. Fax: (617)723-0912. E-mail: sailmail@prime diasi.com. Website: www.sailmagazine.com or www.sailbuyersguide.com. Editor: Peter Nielsen. **Contact:** Amy Ullrich, managing editor. **30% freelance written.** Monthly magazine "written and edited for everyone who sails—aboard a coastal or bluewater cruiser, trailerable, one-design or offshore racer, or daysailer. How-to and technical articles concentrate on techniques of sailing and aspects of design and construction, boat systems, and gear; the feature section emphasizes the fun and rewards of sailing in a practical and instructive way." Estab. 1970. Circ. 180,000. **Pays on acceptance.** Publishes ms an average of 1 year after acceptance. Byline

given. Buys first North American and other rights. Accepts queries by mail, e-mail, fax. Responds in 3 months to queries. Writer's guidelines for SASE or online (download).

Nonfiction How-to, personal experience, technical, distance cruising, destinations. Special issues: "Cruising, chartering, commissioning, fitting-out, special race (e.g., America's Cup), Top 10 Boats." **Buys 50 mss/year.** Query. Length: 1,500-3,000 words. **Pays $200-800.** Sometimes pays expenses of writers on assignment.

Photos Prefers transparencies. Payment varies, up to $700 if photo used on cover. Captions, identification of subjects, credits required.

Columns/Departments Sailing Memories (short essay); Sailing News (cruising, racing, legal, political, environmental); Under Sail (human interest). Query. **Pays $25-400.**

■ The online magazine carries original content not found in the print edition and includes writer's guidelines. Contact: Kimball Livingston, online editor.

Tips "Request an articles' specification sheet. We look for unique ways of viewing sailing. Skim old issues of *Sail* for ideas about the types of articles we publish. Always remember that *Sail* is a sailing magazine. Stay away from gloomy articles detailing all the things that went wrong on your boat. Think constructively and write about how to avoid certain problems. You should focus on a theme or choose some aspect of sailing and discuss a personal attitude or new philosophical approach to the subject. Notice that we have certain issues devoted to special themes—for example, chartering, electronics, commissioning, and the like. Stay away from pieces that chronicle your journey in the day-by-day style of a logbook. These are generally dull and uninteresting. Select specific actions or events (preferably sailing events, not shorebound activities), and build your articles around them. Emphasize the sailing."

N $ $ $ SAILING MAGAZINE

125 E. Main St., Port Washington WI 53074-0249. (262)284-3494. Fax: (262)284-7764. E-mail: editorial@sailing magazine.net. Website: www.sailingonline.com. Publisher: William F. Schanen. Monthly magazine for the experienced sailor. Estab. 1966. Circ. 45,000. Pays on publication. Buys one-time rights. Accepts queries by mail, e-mail. Responds in 2 months to queries. Editorial calendar online.

○→ "Let us get to know your writing with short, newsy, sailing-oriented pieces with good slides for our Splashes section. Query for upcoming theme issues; read the magazine; writing must show the writer loves sailing as much as our readers. We are always looking for fresh stories on new destinations with vibrant writing and top-notch photography. Always looking for short (100-1,500 word) articles or newsy items."

Nonfiction "Experiences of sailing, cruising, and racing or cruising to interesting locations, whether a small lake near you or islands in the Southern Ocean, with first-hand knowledge and tips for our readers. Top-notch photos with maps, charts, cruising information complete the package. No regatta sports unless there is a story involved." Book excerpts, how-to (tech pieces on boats and gear), interview/profile, personal experience, travel (by sail). **Buys 15-20 mss/year.** Length: 750-2,000 words. **Pays $100-800.**

Photos Reviews color transparencies. Pays $50-400. Captions required.

Tips Prefers text in Word on disk for Mac or to e-mail address.

N $ $ SAILING WORLD

World Publications, 5 John Clarke Rd., Box 3400, Newport RI 02840-0992. Fax: (401)848-5180. E-mail: editorial @sailingworld.com. Website: www.sailingworld.com. Editor: John Burnham. **Contact:** David Reed, managing editor. **40% freelance written.** Magazine published 10 times/year covering performance sailing. Estab. 1962. Circ. 60,000. Pays on publication. Publishes ms an average of 4 months after acceptance. Byline given. Buys first North American serial rights. world serial rights Responds in 1 month to queries. Sample copy for $5.

○→ Break in with short articles and fillers such as regatta news reports from your own area.

Nonfiction How-to (for racing and performance-oriented sailors), interview/profile, photo feature, Regatta sports and charter. No travelogs. **Buys 5-10 unsolicited mss/year.** Query. Length: 400-1,500 words. **Pays $600 for up to 2,000 words.** Does not pay expenses of writers on assignment unless pre-approved.

Tips "Send query with outline and include your experience. Prospective contributors should study recent issues of the magazine to determine appropriate subject matter. The emphasis here is on performance sailing: keep in mind that the *Sailing World* readership is relatively educated about the sport. Unless you are dealing with a totally new aspect of sailing, you can and should discuss ideas on an advanced technical level. 'Gee-whiz' impressions from beginning sailors are generally not accepted."

$ $ SEA KAYAKER

Sea Kayaker, Inc., P.O. Box 17029, Seattle WA 98127. (206)789-1326. Fax: (206)781-1141. E-mail: editorial@sea kayakermag.com. Website: www.seakayakermag.com. Editor: Christopher Cunningham. **Contact:** Gretchen Bay, executive editor. **95% freelance written.** "*Sea Kayaker* is a bimonthly publication with a worldwide readership that covers all aspects of kayak touring. It is well known as an important source of continuing education by the most experienced paddlers.'' Estab. 1984. Circ. 30,000. Pays on publication. Publishes ms an average of 6 months after acceptance. Byline given. Offers 10% kill fee. Buys first North American serial rights. Editorial lead time 4 months. Submit seasonal material 4 months in advance. Accepts queries by mail, e-mail, fax, phone. Responds in 2 months to queries. Sample copy for $7.30 (US), samples to other countries extra. Writer's guidelines online.

Nonfiction Essays, historical/nostalgic, how-to (on making equipment), humor, new product, personal experience, technical, travel. Unsolicited gear reviews are not accepted. **Buys 50 mss/year.** Query with or without published clips or send complete ms. Length: 1,500-5,000 words. **Pays 18-20¢/word for assigned articles; 15-17¢/word for unsolicited articles.**

Photos Send photos with submission. Reviews transparencies, prints. Buys one-time rights. Offers $15-400. Captions, identification of subjects required.

Columns/Departments Technique; Equipment; Do-It-Yourself; Food; Safety; Health; Environment; Book Reviews; all 1,000-2,500 words. **Buys 40-45 mss/year.** Query. **Pays 15-20¢/word.**

Tips ''We consider unsolicited manuscripts that include a SASE, but we give greater priority to brief descriptions (several paragraphs) of proposed articles accompanied by at least 2 samples—published or unpublished—of your writing. Enclose a statement as to why you're qualified to write the piece and indicate whether photographs or illustrations are available to accompany the piece.''

SEA MAGAZINE

America's Western Boating Magazine, Duncan McIntosh Co., 17782 Cowan, Suite A, Irvine CA 92614. (949)660-6150. Fax: (949)660-6172. Website: www.goboatingamerica.com. **Contact:** Eston Ellis, managing editor. Monthly magazine covering West Coast power boating. Estab. 1908. Circ. 50,000. Pays on publication. Publishes ms an average of 3 months after acceptance. Byline given. Buys first North American serial rights. Editorial lead time 3 months. Submit seasonal material 6 months in advance. Accepts simultaneous submissions. Responds in 3 months to queries. Writer's guidelines online.

Nonfiction ''News you can use'' is kind of our motto. All articles should aim to help boat owners make the most of their boating experience. How-to, new product, personal experience, technical, travel. **Buys 36 mss/year.** Query with or without published clips or send complete ms. Length: 1,000-1,500 words. **Payment varies.** Sometimes pays expenses of writers on assignment.

Photos State availability with submission. Reviews transparencies. Buys one-time rights. Offers $50-250/photo. Captions, identification of subjects, model releases required.

Ⓝ $WATERFRONT NEWS

Ziegler Publishing Co., Inc., 1515 SW 1st Ave., Ft. Lauderdale FL 33315. (954)524-9450. Fax: (954)524-9464. E-mail: editor@waterfront-news.com. Website: www.waterfront-news.com. **Contact:** Jennifer Heit, editor. **20% freelance written.** Monthly tabloid covering marine and boating topics for the Greater Ft. Lauderdale waterfront community. Estab. 1984. Circ. 39,000. Pays on publication. Publishes ms an average of 2 months after acceptance. Byline given. Buys first, second serial (reprint) rights. , simultaneous rights in certain circumstances Submit seasonal material 3 months in advance. Responds in 1 month to queries. Sample copy for 9×12 SAE and 4 first-class stamps.

O⚊ Travel pieces written for recreational boaters are most needed. Include photos, prints or digital.

Nonfiction Interview/profile (of people important in boating, i.e., racers, boat builders, designers, etc. from south Florida), Regional articles on south Florida's waterfront issues; marine communities. Length: 500-1,000 words. **Pays $100-125 for assigned articles.**

Photos Send photos with submission. Reviews Photos may be submitted digitally, jpeg or tiff files.

Tips ''No fiction. Keep it under 1,000 words. Photos or illustrations help. Send for a sample copy of *Waterfront News* so you can acquaint yourself with our publication and our unique audience. Although we're not necessarily looking for technical articles, it helps if the writer has sailing or powerboating experience. Writers should be familiar with the region and be specific when dealing with local topics.''

Ⓝ $ $WATERWAY GUIDE

326 First St., Suite 400, Annapolis MD 21403. (443)482-9377. E-mail: greich@waterwayguide.com. Website: www.waterwayguide.com. **Contact:** Gary Reich, editor. **90% freelance written.** Triannual magazine covering intracoastal waterway travel for recreational boats. ''Writer must be knowledgeable about navigation and the areas covered by the guide.'' Estab. 1947. Circ. 30,000. Pays on publication. Publishes ms an average of 3 months after acceptance. Byline given. Buys first North American serial, electronic rights, makes work-for-hire assignments. Editorial lead time 4 months. Submit seasonal material 3 months in advance. Accepts queries by mail, phone. Responds in 6 weeks to queries; 2 months to mss. Sample copy for $39.95 with $3 postage.

Nonfiction Essays, historical/nostalgic, how-to, photo feature, technical, travel. **Buys 6 mss/year.** Query with or without published clips or send complete ms. Length: 250-5,000 words. **Pays $50-500.** Pays in contributor copies or other premiums for helpful tips and useful information.

Photos Send photos with submission. Reviews transparencies, 3×5 prints. Buys all rights. Offers $25-50/photo. Captions, identification of subjects required.

Tips "Must have on-the-water experience and be able to provide new and accurate information on geographic areas covered by *Waterway Guide*."

N $ WAVELENGTH MAGAZINE

2735 North Rd., Gabriola Island BC V0R 1X7, Canada. (250)247-8858. E-mail: info@wavelengthmagazine.com. Website: www.wavelengthmagazine.com. **Contact:** Alan Wilson, editor. **75% freelance written.** Bimonthly magazine covering sea kayaking. "We promote safe paddling, guide paddlers to useful products and services and explore coastal environmental issues." Estab. 1991. Circ. 60,000 print and electronic readers. Pays on publication. Publishes ms an average of 4 months after acceptance. Byline given. Offers 10% kill fee. Buys first North American serial, electronic rights. Editorial lead time 4 months. Submit seasonal material 4 months in advance. Accepts queries by mail, e-mail, phone. Responds in 2 months to queries. Sample copy online. Writer's guidelines online.

"Sea kayaking content, even if from a beginner's perspective, is essential. We like a light approach to personal experiences and humor is appreciated. Good detail (with maps and pics) for destinations material. Write to our feature focus."

Nonfiction How-to (paddle, travel), humor, new product, personal experience, technical, travel, trips; advice. **Buys 25 mss/year.** Query. Length: 1,000 words. **Pays $50-75.**

Photos State availability with submission. Reviews 4×6 prints. Buys first and electronic rights. Offers $25-50/photo. Captions, identification of subjects required.

Tips "You must know paddling—although novice paddlers are welcome. A strong environmental or wilderness appreciation component is advisable. We are willing to help refine work with flexible people. E-mail queries preferred. Check out our Editorial Calendar for our upcoming features."

$ $ WOODENBOAT MAGAZINE

The Magazine for Wooden Boat Owners, Builders, and Designers, WoodenBoat Publications, Inc., P.O. Box 78, Brooklin ME 04616. (207)359-4651. Fax: (207)359-8920. Website: www.woodenboat.com. Editor-in-Chief: Jonathan A. Wilson. Senior Editor: Mike O'Brien. Associate Editor: Tom Jackson. **Contact:** Matthew P. Murphy, editor. **50% freelance written.** Bimonthly magazine for wooden boat owners, builders, and designers. "We are devoted exclusively to the design, building, care, preservation, and use of wooden boats, both commercial and pleasure, old and new, sail and power. We work to convey quality, integrity, and involvement in the creation and care of these craft, to entertain, inform, inspire, and to provide our varied readers with access to individuals who are deeply experienced in the world of wooden boats." Estab. 1974. Circ. 106,000. Pays on publication. Publishes ms an average of 1 year after acceptance. Byline given. Offers variable kill fee. Buys first North American serial rights. Accepts previously published material. Accepts simultaneous submissions. Responds in 2 months to queries; 2 months to mss. Sample copy for $4.50. Writer's guidelines for #10 SASE.

Nonfiction Technical (repair, restoration, maintenance, use, design, and building wooden boats). No poetry, fiction. **Buys 50 mss/year.** Query with published clips. Length: 1,500-5,000 words. **Pays $300/1,000 words.** Sometimes pays expenses of writers on assignment.

Reprints Send tearsheet or typed ms with rights for sale noted and information about when and where the material previously appeared.

Photos Send photos with submission. Reviews negatives. Buys one-time rights. Pays $15-75 b&w, $25-350 color. Identification of subjects required.

Columns/Departments Currents pays for information on wooden boat-related events, projects, boatshop activities, etc. Uses same columnists for each issue. Length: 250-1,000 words. Send complete information. **Pays $5-50.**

Tips "We appreciate a detailed, articulate query letter, accompanied by photos, that will give us a clear idea of what the author is proposing. We appreciate samples of previously published work. It is important for a prospective author to become familiar with our magazine. Most work is submitted on speculation. The most common failure is not exploring the subject material in enough depth."

GENERAL INTEREST

$ $ ROCKY MOUNTAIN SPORTS MAGAZINE

Rocky Mountain Sports, Inc., 2525 15th St., #1A, Denver CO 80211. (303)477-9770. Fax: (303)477-9747. E-mail: rheaton@rockymountainsports.com. Website: www.rockymountainsports.com. Publisher: Mary Thorne. **Contact:** Rebecca Heaton, editor. **50% freelance written.** Monthly magazine covering nonteam-related sports in Colorado. *"Rocky* is a magazine for sports-related lifestyles and activities. Our mission is to reflect and inspire the active lifestyle of Rocky Mountain residents." Estab. 1986. Circ. 80,000. Pays on publication. Publishes ms an average of 2 months after acceptance. Byline given. Buys second serial (reprint) rights. Editorial lead time 3 months. Submit seasonal material 5 months in advance. Accepts queries by mail, e-mail, fax. Accepts previously published material. Responds in 3 weeks to queries; 2 months to mss. Sample copy and writer's guidelines for #10 SASE.

 • The editor says she wants to see mountain outdoor sports writing *only*. No ball sports, hunting, or fishing.

 O→ Break in with "Rocky Mountain angle—off-the-beaten-path."

Nonfiction How-to, humor, inspirational, interview/profile, new product, opinion, personal experience, photo feature, travel. Special issues: Skiing & Snowboarding (November); Nordic/Snowshoeing (December); Marathon (January); Running (March); Adventure Travel (April); Triathlon (May); Paddling and Climbing (June); Road Cycling & Camping (July); Mountain Bike & Hiking (August); Women's Sports & Marathon (September); Health Club (October). No articles on football, baseball, basketball, or other sports covered in depth by newspapers. **Buys 24 mss/year.** Query with published clips. Length: 1,500 words maximum. **Pays $150 minimum.**

Reprints Send photocopy and information about when and where the material previously appeared. Pays 20-25% of amount paid for original article.

Photos State availability with submission. Reviews transparencies, prints. Buys one-time rights. Captions, identification of subjects required.

Columns/Departments Starting Lines (short newsy items); Running; Cycling; Climbing; Triathlon; Fitness; Nutrition; Sports Medicine; Off the Beaten Path (sports we don't usually cover). **Buys 20 mss/year.** Query. **Pays $25-300.**

Tips "Have a Colorado angle to the story, a catchy cover letter, good clips, and demonstrate that you've read and understand our magazine and its readers."

$SILENT SPORTS

Waupaca Publishing Co., P.O. Box 152, Waupaca WI 54981-9990. (715)258-5546. Fax: (715)258-8162. E-mail: info@silentsports.net. Website: www.silentsports.net. **75% freelance written.** Monthly magazine covering running, cycling, cross-country skiing, canoeing, kayaking, snowshoeing, in-line skating, camping, backpacking, and hiking aimed at people in Wisconsin, Minnesota, northern Illinois, and portions of Michigan and Iowa. "Not a coffee table magazine. Our readers are participants from rank amateur weekend athletes to highly competitive racers." Estab. 1984. Circ. 10,000. Pays on publication. Publishes ms an average of 3 months after acceptance. Byline given. Offers 20% kill fee. Buys one-time rights. Submit seasonal material 4 months in advance. Accepts queries by mail, e-mail, fax. Accepts previously published material. Responds in 3 months to queries. Sample copy and writer's guidelines for 10×13 SAE with 7 first-class stamps.

 • The editor needs local angles on in-line skating, recreation bicycling, and snowshoeing.

Nonfiction All stories/articles must focus on the Upper Midwest. General interest, how-to, interview/profile, opinion, technical, travel. **Buys 25 mss/year.** Query. Length: 2,500 words maximum. **Pays $15-100.** Sometimes pays expenses of writers on assignment.

Reprints Send ms with rights for sale noted and information about when and where the material previously appeared. Pays 50% of amount paid for an original article.

Photos State availability with submission. Reviews transparencies. Buys one-time rights. Pays $5-15 for b&w story photos; $50-100 for color covers.

Tips "Where-to-go and personality profiles are areas most open to freelancers. Writers should keep in mind that this is a regional, Midwest-based publication. We want only stories/articles with a focus on our region."

$SPORTS ETC

The Northwest's Outdoor Magazine, Sports Etc, 11715 Greenwood Ave. N., Seattle WA 98133. (206)418-0747. Fax: (206)418-0746. E-mail: info@sportsetc.com. Website: www.sportsetc.com. **Contact:** Carolyn Price, editor. **80% freelance written.** Monthly magazine covering outdoor recreation in the Pacific Northwest. "Writers must have a solid knowledge of the sport they are writing about. They must be doers." Estab. 1988. Circ. 40,000. Pays on publication. Publishes ms an average of 3 months after acceptance. Byline given. Buys first rights. Editorial lead time 2 months. Submit seasonal material 4 months in advance. Accepts queries by mail, e-mail, fax. Accepts previously published material. Accepts simultaneous submissions. Sample copy and writer's guidelines for $3.

Nonfiction Interview/profile, new product, travel. Query with published clips. Length: 750-1,500 words. **Pays $10-50.** Sometimes pays expenses of writers on assignment.

Photos Send photos with submission. Reviews negatives, transparencies. Buys all rights. Captions, identification of subjects, model releases required.

Columns/Departments Your Health (health and wellness), 750 words. **Buys 10-12 mss/year.** Query with published clips. **Pays $40-50.**

Tips "*Sports Etc* is written for the serious Pacific Northwest outdoor recreationalist. The magazine's look, style and editorial content actively engage the reader, delivering insightful perspectives on the sports it has come to be known for—alpine skiing, bicycling, adventure racing, triathlon and multi-sport, hiking, in-line skating, kayaking, marathons, mountain climbing, Nordic skiing, running, and snowboarding. *Sports Etc* magazine wants vivid writing, telling images, and original perspectives to produce its smart, entertaining monthly."

SPORTS ILLUSTRATED

Time, Inc., Magazine Co., Sports Illustrated Bldg., 135 W. 50th St., New York NY 10020. (212)522-1212. E-mail: story_queries@simail.com. Associate Publishers: Sheila Buckley and John Rodenburg. **Contact:** Chris Hunt, articles editor; Mark Marvic, senior editor. Weekly magazine. "*Sports Illustrated* reports and interprets the world of sport, recreation, and active leisure. It previews, analyzes, and comments upon major games and events, as well as those noteworthy for character and spirit alone. It features individuals connected to sport and evaluates trends concerning the part sport plays in contemporary life. In addition, the magazine has articles on such subjects as sports gear and swim suits. Special departments deal with sports equipment, books, and statistics." Estab. 1954. Circ. 3,339,000. Accepts queries by mail. Responds in 4-6 weeks to queries.

● Do not send photos or graphics. Please include a SASE for return of materials.

$ $ TWIN CITIES SPORTS

Twin Cities Sports Publishing, Inc., 3009 Holmes Ave. S., Minneapolis MN 55408. (612)825-1034. Fax: (612)825-6452. E-mail: kryan@twincitiessports.com. Website: www.twincitiessports.com. Editor: Jeff Banowetz. **Contact:** Kyle Ryan, managing editor. **75% freelance written.** Monthly magazine covering amateur sports and fitness. "We focus on participatory sports (not team sports) for an active, young audience that likes to exercise." Estab. 1987. Circ. 40,000. Pays on publication. Publishes ms an average of 2 months after acceptance. Byline given. Offers 50% kill fee. Buys first, electronic rights. Editorial lead time 3 months. Submit seasonal material 6 months in advance. Accepts queries by mail, e-mail, fax. Accepts previously published material. Accepts simultaneous submissions. Responds in 3-4 weeks to queries; 1-2 months to mss. Sample copy online. Writer's guidelines by e-mail.

Nonfiction Essays, general interest, historical/nostalgic, how-to (train for a triathlon, set a new 5K P.R., train for an adventure race), humor, inspirational, interview/profile, new product, opinion, personal experience, technical, travel. Special issues: Holiday Gift Guide (December). "We don't publish anything related to team sports (basketball, baseball, football, etc.), golf, tennis. **Buys 24 mss/year.** Query with published clips. Length: 800-3,000 words. **Pays $100-300.** Sometimes pays expenses of writers on assignment.

Photos State availability with submission. Reviews slides transparencies, 3×5 prints, GIF/JPEG files (300 dpi). Buys one-time rights. Negotiates payment individually. Captions, identification of subjects required.

Columns/Departments Running (training, nutrition, profiles), 800 words; Cycling (training, nutrition, profiles), 800 words; Cool Down (first-person essay), 800-1,000 words. **Buys 15 mss/year.** Query with published clips. **Pays $100-250.**

Tips "Read the magazine, know what we cover. E-mail queries or mail with published clips. No phone calls, please."

GOLF

GOLF DIGEST

The Golf Digest Companies, 20 Westport Rd., Box 20, Wilton CT 06897. (203)761-5100. Fax: (203)761-5129. E-mail: editor@golfdigest.com. Website: www.golfdigest.com. Editor: Jerry Tarde. Managing Editor: Roger Schiffman. **Contact:** Craig Bestrom; features editor. Monthly magazine covering the sport of golf. Written for all golf enthusiasts, whether recreational, amateur, or professional player. Estab. 1950. Circ. 1,550,000. Editorial lead time 6 months. Accepts queries by mail. Sample copy for $3.95.

● *Golf Digest* does not accept any unsolicited materials.

Nonfiction Query.

GOLF FOR WOMEN

Advance Magazine Group, 4 Times Square, 7th Floor, New York NY 10036. (212)286-2888. Fax: (212)286-5340. E-mail: editors@golfforwomen.com. Website: www.golfdigest.com/gfw. Managing Editor: Jennifer Sample. **Contact:** Dana White, executive editor. **50% freelance written.** Bimonthly magazine covering golf instruction, travel, lifestyle. "Our magazine is the leading authority on the game for women. We celebrate the traditions and lifestyle of golf, explore issues surrounding the game with incisive features, and we present traditional women's and fashion magazine fare—fashion, beauty, relationship stories—all with a strong golf angle. Travel is also a big component of our coverage. We package everything in a modern, sophisticated way that suits our affluent, educated readers." Circ. 500,000. **Pays on acceptance.** Byline given. Offers variable kill fee (25% standard). Buys all rights, including online. Accepts queries by mail, e-mail, fax.

Nonfiction Book excerpts, essays, general interest, historical/nostalgic, how-to (golf related), humor, inspirational, interview/profile, new product, personal experience, photo feature, travel. **Buys 50 mss/year.** Query. Length: 250-2,500 words. **Payment negotiated.** Sometimes pays expenses of writers on assignment.

Photos State availability with submission. Buys one-time rights and online usage rights. Negotiates payment individually. Model releases required.

Columns/Departments Fitness; Beauty; Get There (travel); Fashion; First Person; Health. **Pays per piece or per word; fees negotiated.**

N $ $ GOLF NEWS MAGAZINE

Premier Golf Magazine Since 1984, Golf News Magazine, P.O. Box 1040, Rancho Mirage CA 92270. (760)321-8800. Fax: (760)328-3013. E-mail: golfnews@aol.com. Website: www.golfnewsmag.com. **Contact:** Dan Poppers, editor/publisher. **70% freelance written.** Monthly magazine covering golf. "Our publication specializes in the creative treatment of the sport of golf, offering a variety of themes and slants as related to golf. If it's good writing and relates to golf, we're interested." Estab. 1984. Circ. 14,000. **Pays on acceptance.** Publishes ms an average of 4 months after acceptance. Byline given. Offers negotiable kill fee. Buys first rights, makes work-for-hire assignments. Editorial lead time 2 months. Submit seasonal material 2 months in advance. Accepts queries by mail, e-mail, fax. Accepts previously published material. Accepts simultaneous submissions. Responds in 1 month to queries; 3 months to mss. Sample copy for $2 and 9×12 SAE with 4 first-class stamps.

Nonfiction "We will consider any topic related to golf that is written well with high standards." Book excerpts, essays, exposé, general interest, historical/nostalgic, how-to, humor, inspirational, interview/profile, opinion, personal experience, photo feature, technical, travel, real estate. **Buys 20 mss/year.** Query with published clips. **Pays $75-350.**

Photos State availability with submission. Buys one-time rights. Negotiates payment individually. Identification of subjects required.

Columns/Departments Submit ideas. **Buys 10 mss/year.** Query with published clips.

■ The online magazine carries content not found in the print edition.

Tips "Solid, creative, good, professional writing. Stay away from cliches and the hackneyed. Only good writers need apply. We are a national award-winning magazine looking for the most creative writers we can find."

$ $ THE GOLFER

551 5th Ave., New York NY 10176. (212)867-7070. Fax: (212)867-8550. E-mail: thegolfer@walrus.com. Editor: H.K. Pickens. **Contact:** Colin Sheehan, senior editor. **40% freelance written.** Bimonthly magazine covering golf. "A sophisticated tone for a lifestyle-oriented magazine." Estab. 1994. Circ. 253,000. Pays on publication. Publishes ms an average of 2 months after acceptance. Byline given. Offers negotiable kill fee. Buys all rights. Editorial lead time 2 months. Submit seasonal material 4 months in advance. Accepts queries by mail, e-mail, fax. Accepts previously published material. Accepts simultaneous submissions. Sample copy for free.

Nonfiction Book excerpts, essays, general interest, historical/nostalgic, how-to, humor, inspirational, interview/profile, new product, opinion, personal experience, photo feature, technical, travel. Send complete ms. Length: 300-2,000 words. **Pays $150-600.**

Reprints Accepts previously published submissions.

Photos Send photos with submission. Reviews any size transparencies. Buys one-time rights.

$ $ $ MINNESOTA GOLFER

6550 York Ave. S., Suite 211, Edina MN 55435. (952)927-4643. Fax: (952)927-9642. E-mail: editor@mngolf.org. Website: www.mngolfer.com. **Contact:** W.P. Ryan, editor. **75% freelance written.** Bimonthly magazine covering golf in Minnesota, the official publication of the Minnesota Golf Association. Estab. 1975. Circ. 70,000. Pays on acceptance or publication. Byline given. Buys first rights. Editorial lead time 3 months. Accepts queries by mail, e-mail, fax.

Nonfiction Book excerpts, historical/nostalgic, humor, inspirational, interview/profile, new product, opinion, personal experience, book reviews. Query with published clips. Length: 400-2,000 words. **Pays $50-750.** Sometimes pays expenses of writers on assignment.

Photos State availability with submission. Reviews contact sheets, transparencies, digital images. Image rights by assignment. Negotiates payment individually. Captions, identification of subjects required.

Columns/Departments Punch shots (golf news and notes); Q Notes (news and information targeted to beginners, junior golfers and women); Great Drives (featuring noteworthy golf holes in Minnesota). Query.

N $ $ $ $ SCORE GOLF MAGAZINE

Canadian Controlled Media Communications, 5397 Eglinton Ave. W, Suite 101, Toronto ON M9C 5K6, Canada. (416)928-2909. Fax: (416)966-1181. E-mail: bobw@scoregolf.com. Website: www.scoregolf.com. Publisher:

(Mr.) Kim Locke. **Contact:** Bob Weeks, vice president of communications. **70% freelance written.** Works with a small number of new/unpublished writers each year. Magazine published 6 times/year covering golf. *"Score Golf Magazine* provides seasonal coverage of the Canadian golf scene, professional, amateur, senior and junior golf for men and women golfers in Canada, the US and Europe through profiles, history, travel, editorial comment and instruction." Estab. 1980. Circ. 150,000 audited. **Pays on acceptance.** Byline given. Offers negotiable kill fee. Buys second serial (reprint), all rights. Submit seasonal material 8 months in advance. Responds in 8 months to queries. Sample copy for $3.50 and 9×12 SAE with IRCs. Writer's guidelines for #10 SASE.

Nonfiction Book excerpts (golf), historical/nostalgic (golf and golf characters), interview/profile (prominent golf professionals), photo feature (golf), travel (golf destinations only). No personal experience, technical, opinion or general interest material. Most articles are by assignment only. **Buys 25-30 mss/year.** Query with published clips. Length: 700-3,500 words. **Pays $200-1,500.**

Photos Send photos with query or ms. Buys all rights. Pays $50-100 for 35mm transparencies (postives) or $30 for 8×10 or 5×7 b&w prints. Captions, identification of subjects, model releases required.

Columns/Departments Profile (historical or current golf personalities or characters); Great Moments ("Great Moments in Canadian Golf"—description of great single moments, usually game triumphs); New Equipment (Canadian availability only); Travel (golf destinations, including "hard" information such as greens fees, hotel accommodations, etc.); Instruction (by special assignment only; usually from teaching golf professionals); The Mental Game (psychology of the game, by special assignment only); History (golf equipment collections and collectors, developments of the game, legendary figures and events), all 700-1,700 words. **Buys 17-20 mss/ year.** Query with published clips or send complete ms. **Pays $140-400.**

Tips "Only writers with an extensive knowledge of golf and familiarity with the Canadian golf scene should query or submit in-depth work to *Score Golf.* Many of our features are written by professional people who play the game for a living or work in the industry. All areas mentioned under Columns/Departments are open to freelancers. Most of our *major* features are done on assignment only."

N T&L GOLF

American Express Publishing Corp., 1120 Avenue of the Americas, 11th Floor, New York NY 10036. E-mail: tlgletters@tlgolf.com. Website: www.tlgolf.com. Editor: John Atwood. Bimonthly magazine. Written for those who see golf not only as a game but as a lifestyle. Circ. 550,000. Sample copy not available.

N $ $ VIRGINIA GOLFER

TPG Sports, Inc., 600 Founders Bridge Blvd., Midlothian VA 23113. (804)378-2300. Fax: (804)378-2369. E-mail: vsgacomm@earthlink.net. Website: www.vsga.org. **Contact:** Andrew Blair, editor. **65% freelance written.** Bimonthly magazine covering golf in Virginia, the official publication of the Virginia Golf Association. Estab. 1983. Circ. 45,000. Pays on publication. Byline given. Buys all rights. Editorial lead time 6 months. Submit seasonal material 3 months in advance. Accepts queries by mail, e-mail. Accepts previously published material. Accepts simultaneous submissions. Sample copy and writer's guidelines free.

Nonfiction Book excerpts, essays, historical/nostalgic, how-to (golf), humor, inspirational, interview/profile, personal experience, photo feature, technical (golf equipment), where to play, golf business. **Buys 30-40 mss/ year.** Query with or without published clips or send complete ms. Length: 500-2,500 words. **Pays $50-200.** Sometimes pays expenses of writers on assignment.

Reprints Accepts previously published submissions.

Photos State availability with submission. Reviews contact sheets. Rights purchased varies. Negotiates payment individually. Captions, identification of subjects required.

Columns/Departments Chip ins & Three Putts (news notes), Rules Corner (golf rules explanations and discussion), Pro Tips, Golf Travel (where to play), Golf Business (what's happening?). Query.

GUNS

$ $ THE ACCURATE RIFLE

Precision Shooting, Inc., 222 McKee St., Manchester CT 06040-4800. (860)645-8776. Fax: (860)643-8215. Website: www.theaccuraterifle.com. **Contact:** Dave Brennan, editor. **30-35% freelance written.** Monthly magazine covering "the specialized field of 'extreme rifle accuracy' excluding rifle competition disciplines." Estab. 2000. Circ. 8,000. Pays on publication. Publishes ms an average of 3 months after acceptance. Byline given. Buys first North American serial rights. Editorial lead time 2 months. Submit seasonal material 3 months in advance. Accepts queries by mail, fax. Responds in 2 weeks to queries; 1 month to mss. Sample copy for free. Writer's guidelines not available.

Nonfiction General interest, historical/nostalgic, how-to, humor, interview/profile, personal experience. "Nothing common to newsstand firearms publications. This has a very sophisticated and knowledgable readership." **Buys 36 mss/year.** Query. Length: 1,800-3,000 words. **Pays $200-500.**

Photos Send photos with submission. Reviews 4×6 prints. Buys one-time rights. Offers no additional payment for photos accepted with ms. Captions required.

Tips "Call the editor first and tell him what topic you propose to write about. Could save time and effort."

$ $ GUN DIGEST

DBI Books, Inc., Division of Krause Publications, 700 E. State St., Iola WI 54990. (888)457-2873. Fax: (715)445-4087. **Contact:** Ken Ramage, editor-in-chief. **50% freelance written.** Prefers to work with published/established writers, but works with a small number of new/unpublished writers each year. Annual journal covering guns and shooting. Estab. 1944. **Pays on acceptance.** Publishes ms an average of 20 months after acceptance. Byline given. Buys all rights. Accepts queries by mail. Responds as time allows to queries.

Nonfiction Buys 25 mss/year. Query. Length: 500-5,000 words. **Pays $100-600 for text/art package.**

Photos Prefers 8×10 b&w prints. Slides, transparencies OK. No digital. State availability with submission. Payment for photos included in payment for ms. Captions required.

Tips Award of $1,000 to author of best article (juried) in each issue.

$ $ MUZZLE BLASTS

National Muzzle Loading Rifle Association, P.O. Box 67, Friendship IN 47021. (812)667-5131. Fax: (812)667-5137. E-mail: mblastdop@seidata.com. Website: www.nmlra.org. Editor: Eric A. Bye. **Contact:** Terri Trowbridge, director of publications. **65% freelance written.** Monthly magazine. "Articles must relate to muzzleloading or the muzzleloading era of American history." Estab. 1939. Circ. 20,000. Pays on publication. Publishes ms an average of 6 months after acceptance. Byline given. Offers $50 kill fee. Buys first North American serial, one-time, second serial (reprint) rights. Editorial lead time 4 months. Submit seasonal material 6 months in advance. Responds in 1 month to mss. Sample copy and writer's guidelines free.

Nonfiction Book excerpts, general interest, historical/nostalgic, how-to, humor, interview/profile, new product, personal experience, photo feature, technical, travel. "No subjects that do not pertain to muzzleloading." **Buys 80 mss/year.** Query. Length: 2,500 words. **Pays $150 minimum for assigned articles; $50 minimum for unsolicited articles.**

Photos Send photos with submission. Reviews 5×7 prints. Buys one-time rights. Negotiates payment individually. Captions, model releases required.

Columns/Departments Buys 96 mss/year. Query. **Pays $50-200.**

Fiction Must pertain to muzzleloading. Adventure, historical, humorous. **Buys 6 mss/year.** Query. Length: 2,500 words. **Pays $50-300.**

Fillers Facts. **Pays $50.**

$ $ PRECISION SHOOTING

Precision Shooting, Inc., 222 McKee St., Manchester CT 06040-4800. (860)645-8776. Fax: (860)643-8215. Website: www.precisionshooting.com. **Contact:** Dave Brennan, editor. **30-35% freelance written.** Monthly magazine covering "the specialized field of 'extreme rifle accuracy' including rifle competition disciplines." Estab. 1956. Circ. 17,500. Pays on publication. Publishes ms an average of 3 months after acceptance. Byline given. Buys first North American serial rights. Editorial lead time 2 months. Submit seasonal material 3 months in advance. Accepts queries by mail, fax. Responds in 2 weeks to queries; 1 month to mss. Sample copy for free. Writer's guidelines not available.

Nonfiction General interest, historical/nostalgic, how-to, humor, interview/profile, personal experience. "Nothing common to newsstand firearms publications. This has a very sophisticated and knowledgeable readership." **Buys 36 mss/year.** Query. Length: 1,800-3,000 words. **Pays $200-500.**

Photos Send photos with submission. Reviews 4×6 prints. Buys one-time rights. Offers no additional payment for photos accepted with ms. Captions required.

Tips "Call the editor first and tell him what topic you propose to write about. Could save time and effort."

$ $ SHOTGUN NEWS

Primedia, Box 1790, Peoria IL 61656. (800)521-2885. Fax: (309)679-5476. E-mail: sgnews@primediasi.com. Website: www.shotgunnews.com. **95% freelance written.** Tabloid published every 10 days covering firearms, accessories, ammunition and militaria. "The nation's oldest and largest gun sales publication. Provides up-to-date market information for gun trade and consumers." Estab. 1946. Circ. 100,000. **Pays on acceptance.** Publishes ms an average of 3 months after acceptance. Byline given. Buys first North American serial rights. Editorial lead time 1 month. Submit seasonal material 3 months in advance. Responds in 1 month to queries. Sample copy for free.

Nonfiction Historical/nostalgic, how-to, technical. No political pieces, fiction or poetry. **Buys 50 mss/year.** Query. Length: 1,000-3,000 words. **Pays $200-500 for assigned articles.** Sometimes pays expenses of writers on assignment.

Photos Send photos with submission. Reviews prints. Buys one-time rights. Offers no additional payment for photos accepted with ms. Captions required.

HIKING & BACKPACKING

$ $ $ $BACKPACKER

Rodale, 33 E. Minor St., Emmaus PA 18098-0099. (610)967-8296. Fax: (610)967-8181. E-mail: pflax@backpacker.com. Website: www.backpacker.com. **Contact:** Peter Flax, features editor. **50% freelance written.** Magazine published 9 times/year covering wilderness travel for backpackers. Estab. 1973. Circ. 295,000. **Pays on acceptance.** Byline given. Buys one-time, all rights. Accepts queries by mail, e-mail, fax. Responds in 6 weeks to queries. Writer's guidelines online.

Nonfiction "What we want are features that let us and the readers 'feel' the place, and experience your wonderment, excitement, disappointment, or other emotions encountered 'out there.' If we feel like we've been there after reading your story, you've succeeded." Essays, exposé, historical/nostalgic, how-to, humor, inspirational, interview/profile, new product, personal experience, technical, travel. No step-by-step accounts of what you did on your summer vacation—stories that chronicle every rest stop and gulp of water. Query with published clips. Length: 750-4,000 words. **Pays $250-5,000.**

Photos State availability with submission. Buys one-time rights. Payment varies.

Columns/Departments Signpost, "News From All Over" (adventure, environment, wildlife, trails, techniques, organizations, special interests—well-written, entertaining, short, newsy item), 50-500 words; Getaways (great hiking destinations, primarily North America), includes weekend, 250-500 words, weeklong, 250-1000, multi-destination guides, 500-1500 words, and dayhikes, 50-200 words, plus travel news and other items; Fitness (in-the-field health column), 750-1,200 words; Food (food-related aspects of wilderness: nutrition, cooking techniques, recipes, products and gear), 500-750 words; Know How (ranging from beginner to expert focus, written by people with solid expertise, details ways to improve performance, how-to-do-it instructions, information on equipment manufacturers, and places readers can go), 300-1,000 words; Senses (capturing a moment in backcountry through sight, sound, smell, and other senses, paired with an outstanding photo), 150-200 words. **Buys 50-75 mss/year.**

🖵 The online magazine carries original content not found in the print edition.

Tips "Our best advice is to read the publication—most freelancers don't know the magazine at all. The best way to break in is with an article for the Weekend Wilderness, Know How, or Signpost Department."

OUTSIDE

Mariah Media, Inc., Outside Plaza, 400 Market St., Santa Fe NM 87501. E-mail: letters@outsidemag.com. Website: www.outsidemag.com. Editor: Hal Espen. **Contact:** Editorial Department. **90% freelance written.** Monthly magazine. "*Outside* is a monthly national magazine for active, educated, upscale adults who love the outdoors and are concerned about its preservation." Estab. 1977. Circ. 550,000. Pays after acceptance. Publishes ms an average of 3 months after acceptance. Byline given. Offers 25% kill fee. Buys first North American serial rights. Submit seasonal material 5 months in advance. Writer's guidelines online. Editorial calendar online.

Nonfiction Book excerpts, essays, general interest, how-to, interview/profile (major figures associated with sports, travel, environment, outdoor), photo feature (outdoor photography), technical (reviews of equipment, how-to), travel (adventure, sports-oriented travel). Do not want to see articles about sports that we don't cover (basketball, tennis, golf, etc.). **Buys 40 mss/year.** Query with published clips. Length: 1,500-4,000 words. Pays expenses of writers on assignment.

Photos "Do not send photos; if we decide to use a story, we may ask to see the writer's photos." Reviews transparencies. Buys one-time rights. Captions, identification of subjects required.

Columns/Departments Dispatches (news, events, short profiles relevant to outdoors), 200-1,000 words; Destinations (places to explore, news, and tips for adventure travelers), 250-400 words; Review (evaluations of products), 200-1,500 words. **Buys 180 mss/year.** Query with published clips.

Tips "Prospective writers should study the magazine before querying. Look at the magazine for our style, subject matter, and standards." The departments are the best areas for freelancers to break in.

HOCKEY

$ $MINNESOTA HOCKEY JOURNAL

Official Publication of Minnesota Hockey, Inc., c/o TPG Sports, Inc., 6160 Summit Dr., Suite 375, Minneapolis MN 55430. (763)595-0808. Fax: (763)595-0016. E-mail: greg@tpgsports.com. Website: www.tpgsports.com. Editor: Greg Anzlec. **50% freelance written.** Journal published 4 times/year. Estab. 2000. Circ. 40,000. Pays on publication. Byline given. Buys all rights. Editorial lead time 6 months. Submit seasonal material 4 months in advance. Accepts previously published material. Accepts simultaneous submissions. Sample copy and writer's guidelines free.

Nonfiction Essays, general interest, historical/nostalgic, how-to (play hockey), humor, inspirational, interview/profile, new product, opinion, personal experience, photo feature, travel, hockey camps, pro hockey, juniors, college, Olympics, youth, etc. **Buys 3-5 mss/year.** Query. Length: 500-1,500 words. **Pays $100-300.**

Reprints Accepts previously published submissions.

Photos State availability with submission. Reviews contact sheets. Rights purchased vary. Negotiates payment individually. Captions, identification of subjects required.

HORSE RACING

$ $THE AMERICAN QUARTER HORSE RACING JOURNAL

American Quarter Horse Association, P.O. Box 32470, Amarillo TX 79120. (806)376-4888. Fax: (806)349-6400. E-mail: richc@aqha.org. Website: www.aqha.com/racing. Executive Editor: Jim Jennings. **Contact:** Richard Chamberlain, editor. **10% freelance written.** Monthly magazine. "The official racing publication of the American Quarter Horse Association. We promote American Quarter Horse racing. Articles include training, breeding, nutrition, sports medicine, health, history, etc." Estab. 1988. Circ. 9,000. **Pays on acceptance.** Publishes ms an average of 3 months after acceptance. Buys first North American serial rights. Submit seasonal material 3 months in advance. Accepts queries by mail, e-mail. Accepts previously published material. Responds in 1 month to queries. Sample copy and writer's guidelines free.

Nonfiction Historical/nostalgic (must be on Quarter Horses or people associated with them), how-to (training), opinion, nutrition, health, breeding. Special issues: Annual Review (March), Yearlings (August), All-American Futurity (September), Stallions (December). Query. Length: 700-1,500 words. **Pays $150-300.**

Reprints Send photocopy and information about when and where the material previously appeared.

Photos Send photos with submission. Additional payment for photos accepted with ms might be offered. Captions, identification of subjects required.

Fiction Novel excerpts.

■ The online magazine carries original content not found in the print edition. Contact: Richard Chamberlain, online editor.

Tips "Query first—must be familiar with Quarter Horse racing and be knowledgeable of the sport. The *Journal* directs its articles to those who own, train, and breed racing Quarter Horses, as well as fans and handicappers. Most open to features covering breeding, raising, training, nutrition, and health care utilizing knowledgeable sources with credentials."

$ $AMERICAN TURF MONTHLY

All Star Sports, Inc., 299 East Shore Rd., Suite 204, Great Neck NY 11023. (516)773-4075. Fax: (516)773-2944. E-mail: editor@americanturf.com. Website: www.americanturf.com. **Contact:** James Corbett, editor-in-chief. **90% freelance written.** Monthly magazine covering Thoroughbred racing, handicapping, and wagering. "Squarely focused on Thoroughbred handicapping and wagering. *ATM* is a magazine for horseplayers, not owners, breeders, or 12-year-old girls enthralled with ponies." Estab. 1946. Circ. 28,000. Pays on publication. Publishes ms an average of 4 months after acceptance. Byline given. Makes work-for-hire assignments. Editorial lead time 2 months. Submit seasonal material 2 months in advance. Accepts queries by mail, e-mail. Responds in 1 month to queries. Sample copy and writer's guidelines free.

Nonfiction Handicapping and wagering features. Special issues: Triple Crown/Kentucky Derby (May); Saratoga/Del Mar (August); Breeder's Cup (November). No historical essays, bilious 'guest editorials,' saccharine poetry, fiction. **Buys 50 mss/year.** Query. Length: 800-2,000 words. **Pays $75-300 for assigned articles; $100-500 for unsolicited articles.**

Photos Send photos with submission. Reviews 3×5 transparencies, prints, 300 dpi TIF images on CD-ROM. Buys one-time rights. Offers $25 interior; $150 for cover. Identification of subjects required.

Fillers Newsbreaks, short humor. **Buys 5/year.** Length: 400 words. **Pays $25.**

■ The online magazine carries original content not found in the print version.

Tips "Send a good query letter specifically targeted at explaining how this contribution will help our readers to cash a bet at the track!"

HUNTING & FISHING

N $ $AMERICAN ANGLER

the Magazine of Fly Fishing & Fly Tying, Abenaki Publishers, Inc., P.O. Box 4100, Bennington VT 05201. E-mail: americananglerl@flyfishingmagazines.com. Website: www.flyfishingmagazines.com. **Contact:** Philip

Monahan, editor. **95% freelance written.** Bimonthly magazine covering fly fishing. *"American Angler* is dedicated to giving fly fishers practical information they can use—wherever they fish, whatever they fish for." Estab. 1976. Circ. 60,000. Pays on publication. Publishes ms an average of 6 months after acceptance. Byline given. Buys first North American serial, one-time rights. Editorial lead time 3 months. Submit seasonal material 5 months in advance. Accepts queries by mail, fax. Accepts previously published material. Accepts simultaneous submissions. Responds in 6 weeks to queries; 2 months to mss. Sample copy for $6. Writer's guidelines for #10 SASE.

Nonfiction How-to (most important), personal experience, photo feature (seldom), technical. No promotional flack fo pay back free trips or freebies, no superficial, broad-brush coverage of subjects. **Buys 45-60 mss/year.** Query with published clips. Length: 800-2,200 words. **Pays $200-400.** Send information about when and where the material previously appeared. Pay negotiable.

Photos "Photographs are important. A fly-tying submission should always include samples of flies to send to our staff photographer, even if photos of the flies are included." Send photos with submission. Reviews contact sheets, transparencies. Buys one-time rights. Offers no additional payment for photos accepted with ms. Captions, identification of subjects required.

Columns/Departments One-page shorts (problem solvers), 350-750 words. Query with published clips. **Pays $100-300.**

Tips "If you are new to this editor, please submit complete queries."

$ $ $ AMERICAN HUNTER

11250 Waples Mill Rd., Fairfax VA 22030-9400. (703)267-1335. Fax: (703)267-3971. E-mail: publications@nrahq .org. Website: www.nra.org. Editor-in-Chief: John Zent. **Contact:** Scott Olmsted, associate editor. Monthly magazine for hunters who are members of the National Rifle Association. *"American Hunter* contains articles dealing with various sport hunting and related activities both at home and abroad. With the encouragment of the sport as a prime game management tool, emphasis is on technique, sportsmanship and safety. In each issue hunting equipment and firearms are evaluated, legislative happenings affecting the sport are reported, lore and legend are retold and the business of the Association is recorded in the Official Journal section." Circ. 1,000,000. **Pays on acceptance.** Byline given. Buys first North American serial, second serial (reprint) rights. Accepts queries by mail, e-mail. Responds in 3 months to queries. Writer's guidelines for #10 SASE.

Nonfiction Factual material on all phases of hunting: Expository how-to, where-to, and general interest pieces; humor: personal narratives; and semi-technical articles on firearms, wildlife management or hunting. Features fall into five categories: Deer, upland birds, waterfowl, big game and varmints/small game. Special issues: Pheasants, whitetail tactics, black bear feed areas, mule deer, duck hunters' transport by land and sea, tech topics to be decided; rut strategies, muzzleloader moose and elk, fall turkeys, staying warm, goose talk, long-range muzzleloading. Not interested in material on fishing, camping, or firearms knowledge. Query. Length: 1,800-2,000 words. **Pays up to $800.**

Reprints Send ms with rights for sale noted and information about when and where the material previously appeared.

Photos No additional payment made for photos used with ms; others offered from $75-600.

Columns/Departments Hunting Guns, Hunting Loads and Public Hunting Grounds. Study back issues for appropriate subject matter and style. Length: 1,200-1,500 words. **Pays $300-450.**

Tips "Although unsolicited manuscripts are welcomed, detailed query letters outlining the proposed topic and approach are appreciated and will save both writers and editors a considerable amount of time. If we like your story idea, you will be contacted by mail or phone and given direction on how we'd like the topic covered. NRA Publications accept all manuscripts and photographs for consideration on a specualtion basis only. Story angles should be narrow, but coverage must have depth. How-to articles are popular with readers and might range from methods for hunting to techniques on making gear used on successful hunts. Where-to articles should contain contacts and information needed to arrange a similar hunt. All submissions are judged on three criteria: Story angle (it should be fresh, interesting, and informative); quality of writing (clear and lively—capable of holding the readers' attention throughout); and quality and quantity of accompanying photos (sharpness, reproduceability, and connection to text are most important.)"

$ $ BASSMASTER MAGAZINE

B.A.S.S. Publications, 5845 Carmichael Pkwy., Montgomery AL 36117. (334)272-9530. Fax: (334)396-8230. E-mail: editorial@bassmaster.com. Website: www.bassmaster.com. **Contact:** James Hall, editor. **80% freelance written.** Magazine published 11 times/year about largemouth, smallmouth, and spotted bass, offering "how-to" articles for dedicated beginning and advanced bass fishermen, including destinations and new product reviews. Estab. 1968. Circ. 600,000. **Pays on acceptance.** Publishes ms an average of less than 1 year after acceptance. Byline given. Buys electronic rights. Editorial lead time 2 months. Submit seasonal material 6 months in advance. Accepts queries by mail, e-mail. Responds in 2 months to queries. Sample copy for $2. Writer's guidelines for #10 SASE.

● Needs destination stories (how to fish a certain area) for the Northwest and Northeast.

Nonfiction Historical/nostalgic, how-to (patterns, lures, etc.), interview/profile (of knowledgeable people in the sport), new product (reels, rods, and bass boats), travel (where to go fish for bass), conservation related to bass fishing. "No first-person, personal experience-type articles." **Buys 100 mss/year.** Query. Length: 500-1,500 words. **Pays $100-600.**

Photos Send photos with submission. Reviews transparencies. Buys all rights. Offers no additional payment for photos accepted with ms, but pays $700 for color cover transparencies. Captions, model releases required.

Columns/Departments Short Cast/News/Views/Notes/Briefs (upfront regular feature covering news-related events such as new state bass records, unusual bass fishing happenings, conservation, new products, and editorial viewpoints). Length: 250-400 words. **Pays $100-300.**

Fillers Anecdotes, newsbreaks. **Buys 4-5/year.** Length: 250-500 words. **Pays $50-100.**

Tips "Editorial direction continues in the short, more direct how-to article. Compact, easy-to-read information is our objective. Shorter articles with good graphics, such as how-to diagrams, step-by-step instruction, etc., will enhance a writer's articles submitted to *Bassmaster Magazine*. The most frequent mistakes made by writers in completing an article for us are poor grammar, poor writing, poor organization, and superficial research. Send in detailed queries outlining specific objectives of article, obtain writer's guidelines. Be as concise as possible."

$ $ ⚑ BC OUTDOORS HUNTING & SHOOTING

OP Publishing, 1080 Howe, Suite 900, Vancouver BC V6Z 2T1, Canada. (604)606-4644. Fax: (604)687-1925. E-mail: bcoutdoors@oppublishing.com. Website: www.oppublishing.com. **Contact:** Tracey Ellis, coordinating editor. **80% freelance written.** Biannual magazine covering hunting, shooting, camping, and backroads. Pays on publication. Publishes ms an average of 3 months after acceptance. Byline given. Offers kill fee. Buys first North American serial rights. Writer's guidelines for 8×10 SAE with 7 Canadian first-class stamps.

Nonfiction "We would like to receive how-to, where-to features dealing with hunting in British Columbia." How-to (new or innovative articles on hunting subjects), personal experience (outdoor adventure), outdoor topics specific to British Columbia. **Buys 50 mss/year.** Query. Length: 1,700-2,000 words. **Pays $300-500.**

Photos State availability with submission. Buys one-time rights. Captions, identification of subjects required.

Tips "Wants in-depth information, professional writing only. Emphasis on environmental issues. Those pieces with a conservation component have a better chance of being published. Subject must be specific to British Columbia. We receive many manuscripts written by people who obviously do not know the magazine or market. The writer has a better chance of breaking in with short, lesser-paying articles and fillers, because we have a stable of regular writers who produce most main features."

⚑ BC OUTDOORS SPORT FISHING AND OUTDOOR ADVENTURE

OP Publishing, 1080 Howe St., Suite 900, Vancouver BC V6Z 2T1, Canada. (604)606-4644. Fax: (604)687-1925. E-mail: bcoutdoors@oppublishing.com. Website: www.bcosportfishing.com. **Contact:** Tracey Ellis, coordinating editor. **80% freelance written.** Magazine published 6 times/year covering fresh and saltwater fishing, camping, and backroads. Pays on publication. Publishes ms an average of 3 months after acceptance. Byline given. Offers kill fee. Buys first North American serial rights. Writer's guidelines for 8×10 SAE with 7 Canadian first-class stamps.

Nonfiction "We would like to receive how-to, where-to features dealing with fishing in British Columbia." How-to (new or innovative articles on fishing subjects), personal experience (outdoor adventure), outdoor topics specific to British Columbia. Query features in early spring. Length: 1,700-2,000 words.

Photos State availability with submission. Buys one-time rights. Captions, identification of subjects required.

Tips "Wants in-depth information, professional writing only. Emphasis on environmental issues. Those pieces with a conservation component have a better chance of being published. Subject must be specific to British Columbia. We receive many manuscripts written by people who obviously do not know the magazine or market. The writer has a better chance of breaking in with short, lesser-paying articles and fillers, because we have a stable of regular writers who produce most main features."

$ $ BUGLE

Rocky Mountain Elk Foundation, P.O. Box 8249, 2291 W. Broadway, Missoula MT 59808. (406)523-4538. Fax: (406)543-7710. E-mail: bugle@rmef.org. Website: www.elkfoundation.org. Editor: Dan Crockett. **Contact:** Paul Queneau, assistant editor. **50% freelance written.** Bimonthly magazine covering elk conservation and elk hunting. *Bugle* is the membership publication of the Rocky Mountain Elk Foundation, a nonprofit wildlife conservation group. "Our readers are predominantly hunters, many of them conservationists who care deeply about protecting wildlife habitat." Estab. 1984. Circ. 132,000. **Pays on acceptance.** Publishes ms an average of 1-36 months after acceptance. Byline given. Offers variable kill fee. Buys one-time rights. Editorial lead time 6 months. Submit seasonal material 6 months in advance. Accepts queries by mail, e-mail, fax. Accepts previously published material. Responds in 1 month to queries; 3 months to mss. Sample copy for $5. Writer's guidelines online.

○━ Preparation: "Read as many issues of *Bugle* as possible to know what the Elk Foundation and magazine are about. Then write a strong query with those things in mind. Send it with clips of other published or unpublished pieces representative of story being proposed."

Nonfiction Book excerpts, essays, general interest (elk related), historical/nostalgic, humor, interview/profile, opinion, personal experience, photo feature. No how-to, where-to. **Buys 20 mss/year.** Query with or without published clips or send complete ms. Length: 1,500-4,500 words. **Pays 20¢/word, and 3 contributor copies; more issues at cost.**

Reprints Send ms with rights for sale noted and information about when and where the material previously appeared. Pays 75% of amount paid for original article.

Columns/Departments Situation Ethics, 1,000-2,000 words; Thoughts & Theories, 1,500-4,000 words; Women in the Outdoors, 1,000-2,500 words. **Buys 13 mss/year.** Query with or without published clips or send complete ms. **Pays 20¢/word.**

Fiction Don Burgess, hunting/human interest editor dburgess@rmef.org. Lee Cromrich, conservation editor lcromrich@rmef.org. Adventure, historical, humorous, novel excerpts, slice-of-life vignettes, western, human interest, natural history, conservation. "We accept fiction and nonfiction stories pertaining in some way to elk, other wildlife, hunting, habitat conservation, and related issues. We would like to see more humor." **Buys 4 mss/year.** Query with or without published clips or send complete ms. Length: 1,500-4,500 words. **Pays 20¢/word.**

Poetry Free verse. **Buys 6 poems/year.** Submit maximum 6 poems.

Tips "Creative queries (250-500 words) that showcase your concept and your style remain the most effective approach. We're hungry for submissions for 3 specific columns: Situation Ethics, Thoughts & Theories, and Women in the Outdoors. Send a SASE for guidelines. We also welcome strong, well-reasoned opinion pieces on topics pertinent to hunting and wildlife conservation, and humorous pieces about elk behavior or encounters with elk (hunting or otherwise). We'd also like to see more humor; more natural history pertaining to elk and elk country; more good, thoughtful writing from women."

$ $ $ FIELD & STREAM

2 Park Ave., Time 4 Media, New York NY 10016-5695. (212)779-5000. Fax: (212)779-5114. E-mail: fsmagazine@aol.com. Website: fieldandstream.com. Editor: Sid Evans. **Contact:** David E. Petzal, deputy editor. **50% free-lance written.** Monthly magazine. "Broad-based service magazine for the hunter and fisherman. Editorial content consists of articles of penetrating depth about national hunting, fishing, and related activities. Also humor and personal essays, nostalgia, fiction, and 'mood pieces' on the hunting or fishing experience and profiles on outdoor people." Estab. 1895. Circ. 1,500,000. **Pays on acceptance.** Byline given. Buys first rights. Accepts queries by mail, e-mail. Responds in 1 month to queries. Sample copy not available. Writer's guidelines for #10 SASE.

Nonfiction Length: 1,500 words for features. Payment varies depending on the quality of work, importance of the article. **Pays $800 and up to $1,000 and more on a sliding scale for major features. Query by mail or e-mail (fsmagazine@aol.com).**

Photos Send photos with submission. Reviews slides (prefers color). Buys first rights. When purchased separately, pays $450 minimum for color.

▣ Online version of magazine carries original content not contained in the print edition. Contact: Elizabeth Burnham.

Tips "Writers are encouraged to submit queries on article ideas. These should be no more than a paragraph or 2, and should include a summary of the idea, including the angle you will hang the story on, and a sense of what makes this piece different from all others on the same or a similar subject. Many queries are turned down because we have no idea what the writer is getting at. Be sure that your letter is absolutely clear. We've found that if you can't sum up the point of the article in a sentence or 2, the article doesn't have a point. Pieces that depend on writing style, such as humor, mood, and nostalgia or essays often can't be queried and may be submitted in manuscript form. The same is true of short tips. All submissions to *Field & Stream* are on an on-spec basis. Before submitting anything, however, we encourage you to *study*, not simply read, the magazine. Many pieces are rejected because they do not fit the tone or style of the magazine, or fail to match the subject of the article with the overall subject matter of *Field & Stream*. Above all, study the magazine before submitting anything."

$ FISHING & HUNTING NEWS

Outdoor Empire Publishing, 424 N. 130th St., Seattle WA 98133. (206)624-3845. Fax: (206)695-8512. E-mail: staff@fishingandhuntingnews.com. Website: www.fhnews.com/. **Contact:** John Marsh, managing editor. **95%**

freelance written. Bimonthly magazine covering fishing and hunting. "We focus on upcoming fishing and hunting opportunities in your area—where to go and what to do once you get there." Estab. 1954. Circ. 96,000. Pays on publication. Publishes ms an average of 1 month after acceptance. Byline given. Buys first North American serial, second serial (reprint), electronic rights. Editorial lead time 1 month. Submit seasonal material 2 months in advance. Accepts queries by mail, e-mail. Sample copy and writer's guidelines free.

Nonfiction How-to (local fishing and hunting), where-to. **Buys 5,000 mss/year.** Query with published clips. Length: 350-2,000 words. **Pays $25-125 and up.** Seldom pays expenses of writers on assignment.

Photos State availability with submission. Buys all rights. Captions required.

Tips "*F&H News* is published in 7 local editions across the western U.S., Great Lakes, and mid-Atlantic states. We look for reports of current fishing and hunting opportunity, plus technique- or strategy-related articles that can be used by anglers and hunters in these areas."

$ $FLORIDA SPORTSMAN

Wickstrom Communications Division of Primedia Special Interest Publications, 2700 S. Kanner Hwy., Stuart FL 34994. (772)219-7400. Fax: (772)219-6900. E-mail: editor@floridasportsman.com. Website: www.floridaspo rtsman.com. **Contact:** Jeff Weakley, editor. **30% freelance written.** Monthly magazine covering fishing, boating, and related sports—Florida and Caribbean only. "*Florida Sportsman* is edited for the boatowner and offshore, coastal, and fresh water fisherman. It provides a how, when, and where approach in its articles, which also includes occasional camping, diving, and hunting stories—plus ecology; in-depth articles and editorials attempting to protect Florida's wilderness, wetlands, and natural beauty." Circ. 115,000. **Pays on acceptance.** Publishes ms an average of 6 months after acceptance. Byline given. Buys nonexclusive additional rights. Submit seasonal material 6 months in advance. Accepts queries by mail. Responds in 2 months to queries; 1 month to mss. Sample copy for free. Writer's guidelines for #10 SASE.

Nonfiction "We use reader service pieces almost entirely—how-to, where-to, etc. One or 2 environmental pieces/issue as well. Writers must be Florida based, or have lengthy experience in Florida outdoors. All articles must have strong Florida emphasis. We do not want to see general how-to-fish-or-boat pieces which might well appear in a national or wide-regional magazine." Essays (environment or nature), how-to (fishing, hunting, boating), humor (outdoors angle), personal experience (in fishing, etc.), technical (boats, tackle, etc., as particularly suitable for Florida specialities). **Buys 40-60 mss/year.** Query. Length: 1,500-2,500 words. **Pays $475.**

Photos Send photos with submission. Reviews 35mm transparencies, 4×5 and larger prints. Buys all rights. Offers no additional payment for photos accepted with ms. Pays up to $750 for cover photos.

Tips "Feature articles are most open to freelancers; however there is little chance of acceptance unless contributor is an accomplished and avid outdoorsman *and* a competent writer-photographer with considerable experience in Florida."

$ $GAME & FISH

2250 Newmarket Pkwy., Suite 110, Marietta GA 30067. (770)953-9222. Fax: (770)933-9510. Website: gameandfi shmag.com. **Contact:** Ken Dunwoody, editorial director. **90% freelance written.** Publishes 30 different monthly outdoor magazines, each one covering the fishing and hunting opportunities in a particular state or region (see individual titles and editors). Estab. 1975. Circ. 550,000. Pays 3 months prior to cover date of issue. Publishes ms an average of 7 months after acceptance. Byline given. Offers negotiable kill fee. Buys first North American serial rights. Submit seasonal material 8 months in advance. Accepts queries by mail, fax. Responds in 3 months to queries. Sample copy for $3.50 and 9×12 SASE. Writer's guidelines for #10 SASE.

Nonfiction Prefers queries over unsolicited mss. Length: 1,500-2,400 words. **Pays $150-300; additional payment made for electronic rights.**

Photos Reviews transparencies, b&w prints. Buys one-time rights. Cover photos $250, inside color $75, and b&w $25. Captions, identification of subjects required.

Fiction Humorous, nostalgia pertaining to hunting and fishing. Length: 1,100-2,500 words. **Pays $150-300; additional payment made for electronic rights.**

Online magazine occasionally carries original content not found in the print edition. Contact: Dave Schaefer.

Tips "Our readers are experienced anglers and hunters, and we try to provide them with useful, specific articles about where, when, and how to enjoy the best hunting and fishing in their state or region. We also cover topics concerning game and fish management. Most articles should be tightly focused and aimed at outdoorsmen in 1 particular state. After familiarizing themselves with our magazine(s), writers should query the appropriate state editor (see individual listings) or send to Ken Dunwoody."

$MICHIGAN OUT-OF-DOORS

P.O. Box 30235, Lansing MI 48909. (517)371-1041. Fax: (517)371-1505. E-mail: dknick@mucc.org. Website: www.mucc.org. **Contact:** Dennis C. Knickerbocker, editor. **75% freelance written.** Monthly magazine emphasizing Michigan outdoor recreation, especially hunting and fishing, conservation, nature, and environmental affairs. Estab. 1947. Circ. 90,000. **Pays on acceptance.** Publishes ms an average of 6 months after acceptance. Byline given. Buys first North American serial rights. Submit seasonal material 6 months in advance. Accepts queries by mail, phone. Responds in 1 month to queries. Sample copy for $3.50. Writer's guidelines for free or on website.

    ○┐ Break in by "writing interestingly about an *unusual* aspect of Michigan natural resources and/or outdoor recreation.

Nonfiction "Stories must have a Michigan slant unless they treat a subject of universal interest to our readers." Exposé, historical/nostalgic, how-to, interview/profile, opinion, personal experience, photo feature. Special issues: Archery Deer and Small Game Hunting (October); Firearm Deer Hunting (November); Cross-country Skiing and Early-ice Lake Fishing (December or January); Camping/Hiking (May); Family Fishing (June). No humor or poetry. **Buys 96 mss/year.** Send complete ms. Length: 1,000-2,000 words. **Pays $90 minimum for feature stories.**

Photos Buys one-time rights. Offers no additional payment for photos accepted with ms; others $20-175. Captions required.

Tips "Top priority is placed on true accounts of personal adventures in the out-of-doors—well-written tales of very unusual incidents encountered while hunting, fishing, camping, hiking, etc."

$ MIDWEST OUTDOORS

MidWest Outdoors, Ltd., 111 Shore Dr., Burr Ridge IL 60527-5885. (630)887-7722. Fax: (630)887-1958. E-mail: glaulunen@midwestoutdoors.com. Website: www.MidWestOutdoors.com. **Contact:** Gene Laulunen, editor. **100% freelance written.** Monthly tabloid emphasizing fishing, hunting, camping, and boating. Estab. 1967. Circ. 45,000. Pays on publication. Publishes ms an average of 3 months after acceptance. Byline given. Buys simultaneous rights. Submit seasonal material 2 months in advance. Accepts previously published material. Accepts simultaneous submissions. Responds in 3 weeks to queries. Sample copy for $1 or online. Writer's guidelines for #10 SASE or online.

    • Submissions may be e-mailed to info@midwestoutdoors.com (Microsoft Word format preferred).

Nonfiction How-to (fishing, hunting, camping in the Midwest), where-to-go (fishing, hunting, camping within 500 miles of Chicago). "We do not want to see any articles on 'my first fishing, hunting, or camping experiences,' 'cleaning my tackle box,' 'tackle tune-up,' 'making fishing fun for kids,' or 'catch and release.'" **Buys 1,800 unsolicited mss/year.** Send complete ms. Length: 1,000-1,500 words. **Pays $15-30.**

Reprints Send tearsheet.

Photos Reviews slides and b&w prints. Buys all rights. Offers no additional payment for photos accompanying ms. Captions required.

Columns/Departments Fishing; Hunting. Send complete ms. **Pays $30.**

Tips "Break in with a great unknown fishing hole or new technique within 500 miles of Chicago. Where, how, when, and why. Know the type of publication you are sending material to."

$ $ NEW JERSEY LAKE SURVEY FISHING MAPS GUIDE

New Jersey Sportsmen's Guides, P.O. Box 100, Somerdale NJ 08083. (856)783-1271. Fax: (856)783-1271. **Contact:** Steve Perrone, editor. **40% freelance written.** Biannual magazine covering freshwater lake fishing. *"New Jersey Lake Survey Fishing Maps Guide* is edited for freshwater fishing for trout, bass, perch, catfish, and other species. It contains 140 pages and approximately 100 full-page maps of the surveyed lakes that illustrate contours, depths, bottom characteristics, shorelines, and vegetation present at each location. The guide includes a 10-page chart which describes over 250 fishing lakes in New Jersey. It also includes more than 125 fishing tips and 'Bass'n Notes.'" Estab. 1989. Circ. 3,500. **Pays on acceptance.** Publishes ms an average of 6 months after acceptance. Byline given. Buys first rights, makes work-for-hire assignments. Editorial lead time 6 months. Accepts queries by mail, fax. Sample copy for $14.50 postage paid.

Nonfiction How-to fishing, freshwater fishing. Length: 500-2,000 words. **Pays $75-250.**

Photos State availability with submission. Reviews transparencies, 4×5 slides, or 4×6 prints. Buys one-time rights. Captions, identification of subjects, model releases required.

Tips "We want queries with published clips of articles describing fishing experiences on New Jersey lakes and ponds."

$ $ NORTH AMERICAN WHITETAIL

The Magazine Devoted to the Serious Trophy Deer Hunter, Game & Fish, 2250 Newmarket Pkwy., Suite 110, Marietta GA 30067. (770)953-9222. Fax: (770)933-9510. Website: northamericanwhitetail.com. **Contact:** Gordon Whittington, editor. **70% freelance written.** Magazine published 8 times/year about hunting trophy-class white-tailed deer in North America, primarily the US. "We provide the serious hunter with highly sophisticated information about trophy-class whitetails and how, when, and where to hunt them. We are not a general hunting magazine or a magazine for the very occasional deer hunter." Estab. 1982. Circ. 130,000. Pays 65 days prior to cover date of issue. Publishes ms an average of 6 months after acceptance. Byline given. Offers negotiable kill fee. Buys first North American serial rights. Submit seasonal material 10 months in advance. Accepts queries by mail, fax, phone. Responds in 3 months to mss. Sample copy for $3.50 and 9×12 SAE with 7 first-class stamps. Writer's guidelines for #10 SASE.

Nonfiction How-to, interview/profile. **Buys 50 mss/year.** Query. Length: 1,000-3,000 words. **Pays $150-400.**

Photos Send photos with submission. Reviews 35mm transparencies, 8×10 prints. Buys one-time rights. Offers no additional payment for photos accepted with ms. Captions, identification of subjects required.

Columns/Departments Trails and Tails (nostalgic, humorous, or other entertaining styles of deer-hunting material, fictional or nonfictional), 1,200 words. **Buys 8 mss/year.** Send complete ms. **Pays $150.**

Tips "Our articles are written by persons who are deer hunters first, writers second. Our hard-core hunting audience can see through material produced by nonhunters or those with only marginal deer-hunting expertise. We have a continual need for expert profiles/interviews. Study the magazine to see what type of hunting expert it takes to qualify for our use, and look at how those articles have been directed by the writers. Good photography of the interviewee and his hunting results must accompany such pieces."

$ $ NORTH CAROLINA GAME & FISH

Game & Fish, Box 741, Marietta GA 30061. (770)953-9222. Fax: (770)933-9510. **Contact:** David Johnson, editor. See *Game & Fish.*

$ $ OKLAHOMA GAME & FISH

Game & Fish, Box 741, Marietta GA 30061. (770)953-9222. Fax: (770)933-9510. **Contact:** Nick Gilmore, editor. See *Game & Fish.*

N $ $ ⊠ ONTARIO OUT OF DOORS

Roger's Media, 1 Mt. Pleasant Rd., Isabella Tower, Toronto ON M4Y 2Y5, Canada. (416)764-1652. Fax: (416)764-1751. E-mail: mail@ontariooutofdoors.com. Website: www.ontariooutofdoors.com. Editor: Burt Myers. **Contact:** John Kerr, managing editor. **90% freelance written.** Magazine published 10 times/year covering the outdoors (hunting, fishing, camping). Estab. 1968. Circ. 93,865. **Pays on acceptance.** Publishes ms an average of 6 months after acceptance. Byline given. Buys first, electronic rights. Editorial lead time 6 months. Submit seasonal material 6 months in advance. Accepts queries by mail, e-mail, fax. Responds in 3 months to queries. Sample copy and writer's guidelines free.

Nonfiction Book excerpts, essays, exposé, how-to (fishing and hunting), humor, inspirational, interview/profile, new product, opinion, personal experience, photo feature, technical, travel (where-to), wildlife management; environmental concerns. "No 'Me and Joe' features or articles written from a women's point of view on how to catch a bass." **Buys 100 mss/year.** Length: 500-2,500 words. **Pays $750 maximum for assigned articles; $700 maximum for unsolicited articles.** Sometimes pays expenses of writers on assignment.

Photos Send photos with submission. Reviews transparencies. Buys one time and electronic rights. Pays $450-750 for covers. Captions required.

Columns/Departments Trips & Tips (travel pieces), 50-150 words; Short News, 50-500 words. **Buys 30-40 mss/year.** Query. **Pays $50-250.**

Fiction Humorous, novel excerpts. **Buys 6 mss/year.** Send complete ms. Length: 1,000 words. **Pays $500 maximum.**

Fillers Facts, newsbreaks. **Buys 40/year.** Length: 25-100 words. **Pays $15-50.**

Tips "With the exception of short news stories, it is suggested that writers query prior to submission."

N $ THE OUTDOORS MAGAZINE

For the Better Hunter, Angler & Trapper, Elk Publishing, Inc., 531 Main St., Colchester VT 05446. (800)499-0447. Fax: (802)879-2015. E-mail: editor@outdoorsmagazine.net. Website: www.outdoorsmagazine.net. **Contact:** James Ehlers, editor. **80% freelance written.** Monthly magazine covering wildlife conservation. "New England hunting, fishing, and trapping magazine with a focus on environmental and conservation issues." Estab. 1996. Circ. 9,500. Pays on publication. Publishes ms an average of 1 year after acceptance. Byline given. Offers 10% kill fee. Buys first North American serial rights. Editorial lead time 1 year. Submit seasonal material 6 months in advance. Accepts queries by mail. Accepts previously published material. Responds in 1 month to queries; 3 month to mss. Sample copy online or by e-mail. Writer's guidelines free.

Nonfiction Book excerpts, essays, exposé, general interest, historical/nostalgic, how-to, interview/profile, new product, opinion, personal experience, technical. **Buys 200 mss/year.** Query with published clips. Length: 750-2,500 words. **Pays $20-150 for assigned articles.**

Photos State availability with submission. Reviews contact sheets. Buys one-time rights. Pays $15-75/photo. Identification of subjects required.

Columns/Departments Buys 100 mss/year. Query with published clips. **Pays $20-60.**

Fillers Anecdotes, facts.

Tips *"Know* the publication, not just read it, so you understand the audience. Patience and thoroughness will go a long way."

$ $PENNSYLVANIA ANGLER & BOATER

Pennsylvania Fish and Boat Commission, P.O. Box 67000, Harrisburg PA 17106-7000. (717)705-7844. E-mail: amichaels@state.pa.us. Website: www.fish.state.pa.us. **Contact:** Art Michaels, editor. **70% freelance written.** Bimonthly magazine covering fishing, boating, and related conservation topics in Pennsylvannia. Circ. 27,000. Pays 2 months after acceptance. Publishes ms an average of 8 months after acceptance. Byline given. Buys varying rights. Submit seasonal material 8 months in advance. Responds in 1 month to queries; 2 months to mss. Sample copy for 9×12 SAE with 9 first-class stamps. Writer's guidelines for #10 SASE.

Nonfiction How-to (and where-to), technical. No saltwater or hunting material. **Buys 75 mss/year.** Query. Length: 500-2,500 words. **Pays $25-300.**

Photos Send photos with submission. Reviews 35mm and larger transparencies. Rights purchased vary. Offers no additional payment for photos accompanying mss. Captions, identification of subjects, model releases required.

N $ $PETERSEN'S HUNTING

Primedia Enthusiast Group, 6420 Wilshire Blvd., Los Angeles CA 90048. (323)782-2563. Fax: (323)782-2477. E-mail: hunting@primedia.com. Website: www.huntingmag.com. **Contact:** Scott Rupp, editor. **10% freelance written.** Magazine published 10 times/year covering sport hunting. "We are a 'how-to' magazine devoted to all facets of sport hunting, with the intent to make our readers more knowledgeable, more successful and safer hunters." Circ. 350,000. Pays on scheduling. Publishes ms an average of 9 months after acceptance. Byline given. Buys all rights. Responds in 1 month to queries. Writer's guidelines on request.

Nonfiction General interest, how-to (on hunting techniques), travel. **Buys 15 mss/year.** Query. Length: 2,400 words. **Pays $350 minimum.**

Photos Send photos with submission. Reviews 35mm transparencies. Buys one-time rights. Captions, identification of subjects, model releases required.

$ $RACK MAGAZINE

Adventures in Trophy Hunting, Buckmasters, Ltd., P.O. Box 244022, Montgomery AL 36124-4022. (800)240-3337. Fax: (334)215-3535. E-mail: mhandley@buckmasters.com. Website: www.rackmag.com. **Contact:** Mike Handley, editor. **10-15% freelance written.** Hunting magazine published monthly (August-January). *"Rack Magazine* caters to deer hunters and chasers of other big game animals who prefer short stories detailing the harvests of exceptional specimens. There are no how-to, destination, or human interest stories; only pieces describing particular hunts." Estab. 1999. Circ. 125,000. Pays on publication. Publishes ms an average of 11 months after acceptance. Byline given. Buys first North American serial, second serial (reprint) rights. Editorial lead time 9 months. Accepts queries by e-mail, phone. Accepts previously published material. Accepts simultaneous submissions. Responds in 1 month to queries. Sample copy for free. Writer's guidelines by e-mail.

Nonfiction Interview/profile, personal experience. *Rack Magazine* does not use how-to, destination, humor, general interest, or hunter profiles. **Buys 35-40 mss/year.** Query. Length: 500-1,500 words. **Pays $250.**

Reprints Accepts previously published submissions.

Photos Send photos with submission. Reviews transparencies. Captions, identification of subjects required.

Tips "We're only interested in stories about record book animals (those scoring high enough to qualify for BTR, B&C, P&Y, SCI, or Longhunter). Whitetails must be scored by a certified BTR/Buckmasters measurer and their antlers must register at least 160-inches on the BTR system. Deer scoring 190 or better on the B&C or P&Y scales would be candidates, but the hunter would have to have his or her buck scored by a BTR measurer."

$ $ROCKY MOUNTAIN GAME & FISH

Game & Fish, Box 741, Marietta GA 30061. Fax: (770)933-9510. **Contact:** Burt Carey, editor. See *Game & Fish.*

N $ $SAFARI MAGAZINE

The Journal of Big Game Hunting, Safari Club International, 4800 W. Gates Pass Rd., Tucson AZ 85745. (520)620-1220. Fax: (520)622-1205. E-mail: tdeuel@safariclub.org. Website: www.safariclub.org. **90% freelance written.** Bimonthly journal covering international big game hunting and wildlife conservation. Circ. 42,000. Pays on publication. Publishes ms an average of 18 months after acceptance. Byline given. Buys first, all rights. Submit seasonal material 1 year in advance. Accepts queries by mail, e-mail. Responds in 2 weeks to queries; 6 weeks to mss. Sample copy for $4. Writer's guidelines for #10 SASE.

⊶ Break in with "engaging, suspenseful, first-person stories of big-game hunts that involve unique circumstances or unusual regions and animals. Conservation stories should include reputable, known sources in the field, plenty of facts, and be supported by scientific data."

Nonfiction Photo feature (wildlife), travel (firearms, hunting techniques, etc.). **Buys 72 mss/year.** Query with or without published clips or send complete ms. Length: 2,000 words. **Pays $300 for professional writers, less if not professional.**

Photos State availability of or send photos with submission. Buys first rights. Payment depends on size in magazine. Pays up to $45 for b&w; $100 color. Captions, identification of subjects, model releases required.

Tips "Study the magazine. Send complete manuscript and photo package. Make it appeal to knowledgeable, world-traveled big game hunters. Features on conservation contributions from big game hunters around the world are open to freelancers. We have enough stories on first-time African safaris. We need North and South American, European, and Asian hunting stories, plus stories dealing with wildlife conservation, especially as it applies to our organization and members."

$ $ SALT WATER SPORTSMAN MAGAZINE

263 Summer St., Boston MA 02210. (617)303-3660. Fax: (617)303-3661. E-mail: editor@saltwatersportsman.com. Website: www.saltwatersportsman.com. **Contact:** Barry Gibson, editor. **85% freelance written.** Monthly magazine. "*Salt Water Sportsman* is edited for serious marine sport fishermen whose lifestyle includes the pursuit of game fish in US waters and around the world. It provides information on fishing trends, techniques, and destinations, both local and international. Each issue reviews offshore and inshore fishing boats, high-tech electronics, innovative tackle, engines, and other new products. Coverage also focuses on sound fisheries management and conservation." Circ. 170,000. **Pays on acceptance.** Publishes ms an average of 5 months after acceptance. Byline given. Offers kill fee. Buys first North American serial rights. Submit seasonal material 8 months in advance. Accepts queries by mail, e-mail, fax. Accepts previously published material. Responds in 1 month to queries. Sample copy for #10 SASE. Writer's guidelines online.

Nonfiction "Readers want solid how-to, where-to information written in an enjoyable, easy-to-read style. Personal anecdotes help the reader identify with the writer." How-to, personal experience, technical, travel (to fishing areas). **Buys 100 mss/year.** Query. Length: 1,200-2,000 words. **Pays $300-750.**

Reprints Send tearsheet. Pays up to 50% of amount paid for original article.

Photos Reviews color slides. Pays $1,500 minimum for 35mm, 2¼×2¼ or 8×10 transparencies for cover. Offers additional payment for photos accepted with ms. Captions required.

Columns/Departments Sportsman's Tips (short, how-to tips and techniques on salt water fishing, emphasis is on building, repairing, or reconditioning specific items or gear). Send complete ms.

Tips "There are a lot of knowledgeable fishermen/budding writers out there who could be valuable to us with a little coaching. Many don't think they can write a story for us, but they'd be surprised. We work with writers. Shorter articles that get to the point which are accompanied by good, sharp photos are hard for us to turn down. Having to delete unnecessary wordage—conversation, clichés, etc.—that writers feel is mandatory is annoying. Often they don't devote enough attention to specific fishing information."

$ $ SHOTGUN SPORTS MAGAZINE

P.O. Box 6810, Auburn CA 95604. (530)889-2220. Fax: (530)889-9106. E-mail: shotgun@shotgunsportsmagazine.com. **Contact:** Linda Martin, production coordinator. **50% freelance written.** Welcomes new writers. Magazine published 11 times/year. "We cover all the shotgun sports and shotgun hunting—sporting clays, trap, skeet, hunting, gunsmithing, shotshell patterning, shotsell reloading, mental training for the shotgun sports, shotgun tests, anything 'shotgun.'" Pays on publication. Publishes ms an average of 1-6 months after acceptance. Buys all rights. Sample copy and writer's guidelines available by contacting Linda Martin, production coordinator.

● Responds within 3 weeks. Subscription: $31 (U.S.); $38 (Canada); $66 (foreign).

Nonfiction Current needs: "Anything with a 'shotgun' subject. Tests, think pieces, roundups, historical, interviews, etc. No articles promoting a specific club or sponsored hunting trip, etc." Submit complete ms with photos by mail with SASE. Can submit by e-mail. Length: 1,000-5,000 words. **Pays $50-200.**

Photos "5×7 or 8×10 b&w or 4-color with appropriate captions. On disk or e-mailed at least 5-inches and 300 dpi (contact Graphics Artist for details)." Reviews transparencies (35 mm or larger), b&w, or 4-color. Send photos with submission.

Tips "Do not fax manuscript. Send good photos. Take a fresh approach. Create a professional, yet friendly article. Send diagrams, maps, and photos of unique details, if needed. For interviews, more interested in 'words of wisdom' than a list of accomplishments. Reloading articles must include source information and backup data. Check your facts and data! If you can't think of a fresh approach, don't bother. If it's not about shotguns or shotgunners, don't send it. Never say, 'You don't need to check my data; I never make mistakes.'"

$ $SPORT FISHING

The Magazine of Saltwater Fishing, 460 N. Orlando Ave., Suite 200, Winter Park FL 32789-7061. (407)571-4576. Fax: (407)571-4577. E-mail: doug.olander@worldpub.net. **Contact:** Doug Olander, editor-in-chief. **50% freelance written.** Magazine covering saltwater sports fishing. Estab. 1986. Circ. 150,000. Pays within 6 weeks of acceptance. Byline given. Offers $100 kill fee. Buys first North American serial, one-time rights. Submit seasonal material 5 months in advance. Accepts queries by mail, e-mail, fax. Responds in 2 weeks to queries. Sample copy for #10 SASE. Writer's guidelines for #10 SASE or by e-mail.

O→ Break in with freelance pieces for the "Tips & Techniques News" and "Fish Tales" departments.

Nonfiction How-to (rigging & techniques tips), technical, conservation, where-to (all on sport fishing). **Buys 32-40 mss/year.** Query. Length: 2,000-3,000 words. **Pays $500 (payment for photos is separate).**

Photos Send photos with submission. Reviews transparencies and returns within 1 week. Buys one-time rights. Pays $75-400 inside; $1,000 cover.

Columns/Departments Fish Tales (humorous sport fishing anecdotes); Rigging (how-to rigging for sport fishing); Technique (how-to technique for sport fishing), 800-1,200 words. **Buys 8-24 mss/year.** Send complete ms. **Pays $250.**

Tips "Don't query unless you are familiar with the magazine; note—*saltwater only*. Find a fresh idea or angle to an old idea. We welcome the chance to work with new/unestablished writers who know their stuff—and how to say it."

$ $TURKEY CALL

Wild Turkey Center, P.O. Box 530, Edgefield SC 29824-0530. (803)637-3106. Fax: (803)637-0034. E-mail: bmccreery@nwtf.net or dhowlett@nwtf.net. Editor: Doug Howlett. **Contact:** Beth McCreery, publishing assistant; Jason Gilbertson, managing editor. **50-60% freelance written.** Eager to work with new/unpublished writers and photographers. Bimonthly educational magazine for members of the National Wild Turkey Federation. Estab. 1973. Circ. 150,000. Pays on acceptance for assigned articles, on publication for unsolicited articles. Publishes ms an average of 6 months after acceptance. Byline given. Buys one-time rights. Accepts queries by mail, e-mail. Accepts previously published material. Responds in 6 weeks to queries. Sample copy for $3 and 9×12 SAE. Writer's guidelines for #10 SASE or online.

• Queries required. Submit complete package if article is assigned. Wants original mss only.

O→ Break in with a knowledgeable, fresh point of view. Articles must be tightly written.

Nonfiction Feature articles dealing with the hunting and management of the American wild turkey. Must be accurate information and must appeal to national readership of turkey hunters and wildlife management experts. May use some fiction that educates or entertains in a special way. Length: Up to 2,500 words. **Pays $100 for short fillers of 600-700 words, $200-500 for features.**

Reprints Send photocopy and information about when and where the material previously appeared. Pays 50% of amount paid for the original article.

Photos "We want quality photos submitted with features." Art illustrations also acceptable. "We are using more and more inside color illustrations." No typical hunter-holding-dead-turkey photos or setups using mounted birds or domestic turkeys. Photos with how-to stories must make the techniques clear (example: how to make a turkey call; how to sculpt or carve a bird in wood). Reviews transparencies. Buys one-time rights. Pays $35 minimum for b&w photos and simple art illustrations; up to $175 for inside color, reproduced any size; $200-400 for covers.

Tips "The writer should simply keep in mind that the audience is 'expert' on wild turkey management, hunting, life history, and restoration/conservation history. He/she must know the subject. We are buying more third person, more fiction, more humor—in an attempt to avoid the 'predictability trap' of a single subject magazine."

$ $WESTERN OUTDOORS

185 Avenida La Pata, San Clemente CA 92673. (949)366-0030. Fax: (949)366-0804. E-mail: lew@wonews.com. **Contact:** Lew Carpenter, editor. **60% freelance written.** Magazine emphasizing fishing, boating for California, Oregon, Washington, Baja California, and Alaska. "We are the West's leading authority on fishing techniques, tackle and destinations, and all reports present the latest and most reliable information." Estab. 1961. Circ. 100,000. **Pays on acceptance.** Publishes ms an average of 6 months after acceptance. Buys first North American serial rights. Submit seasonal material 6 months in advance. Accepts queries by mail, e-mail, fax. Responds in 6 weeks to queries. Sample copy for free. Writer's guidelines for #10 SASE.

Nonfiction Where-to (catch more fish, improve equipment, etc.), how-to informational, photo feature. "We do not accept poetry or fiction." **Buys 36-40 assigned mss/year.** Query. Length: 1,500-2,000 words. **Pays $450-600.**

Photos Reviews 35mm slides. Offers no additional payment for photos accepted with ms; pays $350-500 for covers. Captions required.

Tips "Provide a complete package of photos, map, trip facts and manuscript written according to our news feature format. Excellence of color photo selections make a sale more likely. Include sketches of fishing patterns and techniques to guide our illustrators. Graphics are important. The most frequent mistake made by writers in completing an article for us is that they don't follow our style. Our guidelines are quite clear. One query at a time via mail, e-mail, fax. No phone calls. You can become a regular *Western Outdoors* byliner by submitting professional quality packages of fine writing accompanied by excellent photography. Pros anticipate what is needed, and immediately provide whatever else we request. Furthermore, they meet deadlines!''

N $ $ WESTERN SPORTSMAN

Suite 900, 1080 Howe St., Vancouver BC V6Z 2T1, Canada. E-mail: editor@westernsportsman.com. **Contact:** Tracey Ellis. **90% freelance written.** Bimonthly magazine for fishers, hunters, and others interested in outdoor recreation. ''Note that our coverage area is British Columbia, Alberta, Saskatchewan, Manitoba, Yukon and Northwest Territory. We try to include as much information as possible on all subjects in each edition. Therefore, we often publish fishing articles in our winter issues along with a variety of winter stories.'' Estab. 1968. Circ. 29,000. Pays on publication. Byline given. Rights purchased vary with author and material. Usually buys first North American serial rights. Accepts queries by mail, e-mail, fax. Responds in 1 month to queries. Writer's guidelines for free with SAE.

• Query in early spring.

Nonfiction ''It is necessary that all articles can identify with our coverage area. We are interested in manuscripts from writers who have had an interesting fishing or hunting experience. We also publish other informational pieces as long as they relate to our coverage area. We are most interested in articles which tell about the average guy living on beans, guiding his own boat, stalking his game and generally doing his own thing in our part of Western Canada than a story describing a well-to-do outdoorsmen traveling by motorhome, staying at an expensive lodge with guides doing everything for him except catching the fish or shooting the big game animal. The articles that are submitted to us need to be prepared in a knowledgeable way and include more information than the actual fish catch or animal or bird kill. Discuss the terrain, the people involved on the trip, the water or weather conditions, the costs, the planning that went into the trip, the equipment and other data closely associated with the particular event. We're always looking for new writers.'' **Buys 60 mss/year.** Length: 1,800-2,000 words. **Payment negotiable.**

Photos Photos purchased with ms with no additional payment. Also purchased without ms. Pays $150 for 35mm or larger transparency for front cover.

MARTIAL ARTS

$ $ BLACK BELT

Black Belt Communications, LLC, 24900 Anza Dr., Unit E, Valencia CA 91355. (661)257-4066. Fax: (661)257-3028. E-mail: byoung@sabot.net. Website: www.blackbeltmag.com. **Contact:** Robert Young, executive editor. **80% freelance written.** Works with a small number of new/unpublished writers each year. Monthly magazine emphasizing martial arts for both experienced practitioner and layman. Estab. 1961. Circ. 100,000. Pays on publication. Publishes ms an average of 1 year after acceptance. Buys all rights. Submit seasonal material 6 months in advance. Accepts queries by mail, e-mail, fax. Accepts simultaneous submissions. Responds in 3 weeks to queries. Writer's guidelines online.

Nonfiction Exposé, how-to, interview/profile, new product, personal experience, technical, travel, Informational; Health/fitness; Training. ''We never use personality profiles.'' **Buys 40-50 mss/year.** Query with outline. Length: 1,200 words minimum. **Pays $100-300.**

Photos Very seldom buys photographs without accompanying ms. Total purchase price for ms includes payment for photos. Captions, model releases required.

$ $ JOURNAL OF ASIAN MARTIAL ARTS

Via Media Publishing Co., 821 W. 24th St., Erie PA 16502-2523. (814)455-9517. E-mail: info@goviamedia.com. Website: www.goviamedia.com. **Contact:** Michael A. DeMarco, editor. **90% freelance written.** Quarterly magazine covering ''all historical and cultural aspects related to Asian martial arts, offering a mature, well-rounded view of this uniquely fascinating subject. Although the journal treats the subject with academic accuracy (references at end), writing need not lose the reader!'' Estab. 1991. Pays on publication. Publishes ms an average of 1 year after acceptance. Byline given. Buys first, second serial (reprint) rights. Submit seasonal material 6 months in advance. Responds in 1 month to queries; 2 months to mss. Sample copy for $10. Writer's guidelines for #10 SASE.

Nonfiction ''All articles should be backed with solid, reliable reference material.'' Essays, exposé, historical/nostalgic, how-to (martial art techniques and materials, e.g., weapons), interview/profile, personal experience, photo feature (place or person), religious, technical, travel. ''No articles overburdened with technical/foreign/scholarly vocabulary, or material slanted as indirect advertising or for personal aggrandizement.'' **Buys 30**

mss/year. Query with short background and martial arts experience. Length: 2,000-10,000 words. **Pays $150-500.**

Photos State availability with submission. Reviews contact sheets, negatives, transparencies, prints. Buys one-time and reprint rights. Offers no additional payment for photos accepted with ms. Identification of subjects, model releases required.

Columns/Departments Location (city, area, specific site, Asian or non-Asian, showing value for martial arts, researchers, history); Media Review (film, book, video, museum for aspects of academic and artistic interest).-**Length:** 1,000-2,500 words. **Buys 16 mss/year.** Query. **Pays $50-200.**

Fiction Adventure, historical, humorous, slice-of-life vignettes, translation. No material that does not focus on martial arts culture. **Buys 1 mss/year.** Query. Length: 1,000-10,000 words. **Pays $50-500, or copies.**

Poetry Avant-garde, free verse, haiku, light verse, traditional, translation. "No poetry that does not focus on martial arts culture." **Buys 2 poems/year.** Submit maximum 10 poems. **Pays $10-100, or copies.**

Fillers Anecdotes, facts, gags to be illustrated by cartoonist, newsbreaks, short humor. **Buys 2/year.** Length: 25-500 words. **Pays $1-50, or copies.**

Tips "Always query before sending a manuscript. We are open to varied types of articles; most however require a strong academic grasp of Asian culture. For those not having this background, we suggest trying a museum review, or interview, where authorities can be questioned, quoted, and provide supportive illustrations. We especially desire articles/reports from Asia, with photo illustrations, particularly of a martial art style, so readers can visually understand the unique attributes of that style, its applications, evolution, etc. 'Location' and media reports are special areas that writers may consider, especially if they live in a location of martial art significance."

$KUNG FU TAI CHI

Wisdom for Body and Mind, (formerly *Kungfu Qigong*), Pacific Rim Publishing, 40748 Encyclopedia Circle, Fremont CA 94538. (510)656-5100. Fax: (510)656-8844. E-mail: editor@kungfumagazine.com. Website: www.kungfumagazine.com. **Contact:** Article Submissions. **70% freelance written.** Bimonthly magazine covering Chinese martial arts and culture. "*Kung Fu Tai Chi* covers the full range of Kung Fu culture, including healing, philosophy, meditation, yoga, Fengshui, Buddhism, Taoism, history, and the latest events in art and culture, plus insightful features on the martial arts." Circ. 50,000. Pays on publication. Byline given. Buys first North American serial, electronic rights. Editorial lead time 4 months. Submit seasonal material 4 months in advance. Accepts queries by mail, e-mail, fax, phone. Responds in 2 months to queries; 3 months to mss. Sample copy for $3.99 or online. Writer's guidelines online.

Nonfiction General interest, historical/nostalgic, how-to, interview/profile, personal experience, photo feature, religious, technical, travel, cultural perspectives. No poetry or fiction. **Buys 100 mss/year.** Query. Length: 500-2,500 words. **Pays $35-125.**

Photos Send photos with submission. Reviews 5×7 prints, GIF/JPEG files. Buys one-time rights. Offers no additional payment for photos accepted with ms. Captions, identification of subjects required.

Tips "Check out our website and get an idea of past articles."

$ $T'AI CHI

Leading International Magazine of T'ai Chi Ch'uan, Wayfarer Publications, P.O. Box 39938, Los Angeles CA 90039. (323)665-7773. Fax: (323)665-1627. E-mail: taichi@tai-chi.com. Website: www.tai-chi.com/magazine.htm. **Contact:** Marvin Smalheiser, editor. **90% freelance written.** Bimonthly magazine covering T'ai Chi Ch'uan as a martial art and for health and fitness. "Covers T'ai Chi Ch'uan and other internal martial arts, plus qigong and Chinese health, nutrition, and philosophical disciplines. Readers are practitioners or laymen interested in developing skills and insight for self-defense, health, and self-improvement." Estab. 1977. Circ. 50,000. Pays on publication. Publishes ms an average of 6 months after acceptance. Byline given. Buys first North American serial rights. Editorial lead time 3 months. Submit seasonal material 6 months in advance. Accepts queries by mail, e-mail, fax. Responds in 3 weeks to queries; 3 months to mss. Sample copy for $3.95. Writer's guidelines online.

- **O** Break in by "understanding the problems our readers have to deal with learning and practicing T'ai Chi, and developing an article that deals with 1 or more of those problems.

Nonfiction Book excerpts, essays, how-to (on T'ai Chi Ch'uan, qigong, and related Chinese disciplines), interview/profile, personal experience. "Do not want articles promoting an individual, system, or school." **Buys 100-120 mss/year.** Query with or without published clips or send complete ms. Length: 1,200-4,500 words. **Pays $75-500.** Sometimes pays expenses of writers on assignment.

Photos Send photos with submission. Reviews color transparencies, color or b&w 4×6 or 5×7 prints. Buys one-time and reprint rights. Offers no additional payment for photos accepted with ms, but overall payment takes into consideration the number and quality of photos. Captions, identification of subjects, model releases required.

Tips ''Think and write for practitioners and laymen who want information and insight, and who are trying to work through problems to improve skills and their health. No promotional material.''

MISCELLANEOUS

$ACTION PURSUIT GAMES
CFW Enterprises, Inc., 4201 Vanowen Place, Burbank CA 91505. (818)845-2656. Fax: (818)845-7761. E-mail: editor@actionpursuitgames.com. Website: www.actionpursuitgames.com. **Contact:** Daniel Reeves, editor. **60% freelance written.** Monthly magazine covering paintball. Estab. 1987. Circ. 85,000. Pays on publication. Publishes ms an average of 2 months after acceptance. Byline given. Buys electronic rights. print rights Editorial lead time 3 months. Submit seasonal material 6 months in advance. Accepts queries by e-mail. Sample copy for 9×12 SAE and 5 first-class stamps. Writer's guidelines online.
Nonfiction Essays, exposé, general interest, historical/nostalgic, how-to, humor, interview/profile, new product, opinion, personal experience, technical, travel, all paintball-related. No sexually oriented material. **Buys 100+ mss/year.** Length: 500-1,000 words. **Pays $100.** Sometimes pays expenses of writers on assignment.
Photos Send photos with submission. Reviews transparencies, prints. Buys all rights, web and print. Negotiates payment individually. Captions, identification of subjects, model releases required.
Columns/Departments Guest Commentary, 400 words; TNT (tournament news), 500-800 words; Young Guns, 300 words; Scenario Game Reporting, 300-500 words. **Buys 24 mss/year. Pays $100.**
Fiction Adventure, historical, must be paintball related. **Buys 1-2 mss/year.** Send complete ms. Length: 500 words. **Pays $100.**
Poetry Avant-garde, free verse, haiku, light verse, traditional, must be paintball related. **Buys 1-2 poems/year.** Submit maximum 1 poems. Length: 20 lines.
Fillers Anecdotes, gags to be illustrated by cartoonist. **Buys 2-4/year.** Length: 20-50 words. **Pays $25.**
Tips ''Good graphic support is critical. Read writer's guidelines at website; read website, www.actionpursuitgames.com, and magazine.''

$$AMERICAN CHEERLEADER
Lifestyle Media, Inc., 110 William St., 23rd Floor, New York NY 10038. (646)459-4800. Fax: (646)459-4900. E-mail: snoone@lifestylemedia.com. Website: www.americancheerleader.com. Managing Editor: Marisa Walker. Senior Editor: Jennifer Smith. **Contact:** Sheila Noone, editor-in-chief. **30% freelance written.** Bimonthly magazine covering high school and college cheerleading. ''We try to keep a young, informative voice for all articles— 'for cheerleaders, by cheerleaders.''' Estab. 1995. Circ. 200,000. Pays on publication. Publishes ms an average of 4 months after acceptance. Byline given. Offers 25% kill fee. Buys all rights. Editorial lead time 3 months. Submit seasonal material 4 months in advance. Accepts queries by mail, e-mail. Responds in 3 weeks to queries; 2 months to mss. Sample copy for $2.95. Writer's guidelines free.
Nonfiction How-to (cheering techniques, routines, pep songs, etc.), interview/profile (celebrities and media personalities who cheered). Special issues: Tryouts (April); Camp Basics (June); College (October); Competition (December). No professional cheerleading stories, i.e., no Dallas Cowboy cheerleaders. **Buys 12-16 mss/year.** Query with published clips. Length: 400-1,500 words. **Pays $100-250 for assigned articles; $100 maximum for unsolicited articles.** Sometimes pays expenses of writers on assignment.
Photos State availability with submission. Reviews transparencies, 5×7 prints. Rights purchased varies. Offers $50/photo. Model releases required.
Columns/Departments Gameday Beauty (skin care, celeb how-tos), 600 words; Health & Fitness (teen athletes), 1,000 words; Profiles (winning squads), 1,000 words. **Buys 12 mss/year.** Query with published clips. **Pays $100-250.**
■ The online magazine carries original content not found in the print edition.
Tips ''We invite proposals from freelance writers who are involved in or have been involved in cheerleading— i.e., coaches, sponsors, or cheerleaders. Our writing style is upbeat and 'sporty' to catch and hold the attention of our teenaged readers. Articles should be broken down into lots of sidebars, bulleted lists, Q&As, etc.''

$$$ATV MAGAZINE/ATV SPORT
Ehlert Publishing, 6420 Sycamore Lane, Maple Grove MN 55369. Fax: (763)383-4499. E-mail: ghansen@affinitygroup.com. Website: www.atvnews.com. Managing Editor: Jerrod Kelley. **Contact:** Chaz Rice, editor. **20% freelance written.** Bimonthly magazine covering all-terrain vehicles. ''Devoted to covering all the things ATV owners enjoy, from hunting to racing, farming to trail riding.'' Pays on magazine shipment to printer. Byline given. Buys all rights. Editorial lead time 6 months. Accepts queries by mail, e-mail, fax. Responds in 3 weeks to queries. Sample copy and writer's guidelines for #10 SASE.
Nonfiction How-to, interview/profile, new product, personal experience, photo feature, technical, travel. **Buys**

15-20 mss/year. Query with published clips. Length: 200-2,000 words. **Pays $100-1,000.** Sometimes pays expenses of writers on assignment.

Photos State availability with submission. Rights purchased vary. Negotiates payment individually. Captions, identification of subjects required.

Tips "Writers must have experience with ATVs, and should own one or have regular access to at least one ATV."

$ 🔲 CANADIAN RODEO NEWS

Canadian Rodeo News, Ltd., #223, 2116 27th Ave. NE, Calgary AB T2E 7A6, Canada. (403)250-7292. Fax: (403)250-6926. E-mail: crn@rodeocanada.com. Website: www.rodeocanada.com. **Contact:** Jennifer Jones, editor. **60% freelance written.** Monthly tabloid covering "Canada's professional rodeo (CPRA) personalities and livestock. Read by rodeo participants and fans." Estab. 1964. Circ. 4,000. Pays on publication. Publishes ms an average of 1 month after acceptance. Byline given. Buys first, second serial (reprint) rights. Editorial lead time 1 month. Submit seasonal material 1 month in advance. Accepts queries by mail, e-mail, fax. Accepts simultaneous submissions. Responds in 1 month to queries; 2 months to mss. Sample copy and writer's guidelines free with SASE.

Nonfiction General interest, historical/nostalgic, interview/profile. **Buys 70-80 mss/year.** Query. Length: 500-1,200 words. **Pays $30-60.**

Reprints Send photocopy of article or typed ms with rights for sale noted and information about when and where the material previously appeared. Pays 100% of amount paid for an original article.

Photos Send photos with submission. Reviews 4×6 prints. Buys one-time rights. Offers $15-25/cover photo.

Tips "Best to call first with the story idea to inquire if it is suitable for publication. Readers are very knowledgeable of the sport, so writers need to be as well."

$ $ FENCERS QUARTERLY MAGAZINE

848 S. Kimbrough, Springfield MO 65806. (417)866-4370. E-mail: editor@fencersquarterly.com. Editor-in-Chief: Nick Evangelista. **Contact:** Anita Evangelista, managing editor. **60% freelance written.** Quarterly magazine covering fencing, fencers, history of sword/fencing/dueling, modern techniques and systems, controversies, personalities of fencing, personal experience. "This is a publication for all fencers and those interested in fencing; we favor the grassroots level rather than the highly-promoted elite. Readers will have a grasp of terminology of the sword and refined fencing skills—writers must be familiar with fencing and current changes and controversies. We are happy to air any point of view on any fencing subject, but the material must be well-researched and logically presented." Estab. 1996. Circ. 5,000. Pays prior to or at publication. Publishes ms an average of 6 months after acceptance. Byline given. Offers 25% kill fee. Buys first North American serial, second serial (reprint), electronic rights, makes work-for-hire assignments. Editorial lead time 3 months. Submit seasonal material 6 months in advance. Accepts queries by mail, e-mail. Accepts simultaneous submissions. Sample copy by request. Writer's guidelines by request.

● Responds in 1 week or less for e-mail; 1 month for snail mail if SASE; no reply if no SASE and material not usable.

Nonfiction "All article types acceptable—however, we have seldom used fiction or poetry (though will consider if has special relationship to fencing)." How-to should reflect some aspect of fencing or gear. Personal experience welcome. No articles "that lack logical progression of thought, articles that rant, 'my weapon is better than your weapon' emotionalism, puff pieces, or public relations stuff." **Buys 100 mss/year.** Query with or without published clips or send complete ms. Length: 100-4,000 words. **Pays $100-200 (rarely) for assigned articles; $10-60 for unsolicited articles.**

Photos Send photos by mail or as e-mail attachment. Prefers prints, all sizes. Buys all rights. Negotiates payment individually. Captions, identification of subjects, model releases required.

Columns/Departments Cutting-edge news (sword or fencing related), 100 words; Reviews (books/films), 300 words; Fencing Generations (profile), 200-300 words; Tournament Results (veteran events only, please), 200 words. **Buys 40 mss/year.** Send complete ms. **Pays $10-20.**

Fiction Will consider all as long as strong fencing/sword slant is major element. No erotica. Query with or without published clips or send complete ms. Length: 1,500 words maximum. **Pays $25-100.**

Poetry Will consider all which have distinct fencing/sword element as central. No erotica. Submit maximum 10 poems. Length: Up to 100 lines. **Pays $10.**

Fillers Anecdotes, facts, gags to be illustrated by cartoonist, newsbreaks. **Buys 30/year.** Length: 100 words maximum. **Pays $5.**

Tips "We love new writers! Professionally presented work impresses us. We prefer complete submissions, and e-mail or disk (in rich text format) are our favorites. Ask for our writer's guidelines. Always aim your writing to knowledgeable fencers who are fascinated by this subject, take their fencing seriously, and want to know more about its history, current events, and controversies. Action photos should show proper form—no flailing or tangled-up images, please. We want to know what the 'real' fencer is up to these days, not just what the Olympic contenders are doing. If we don't use your piece, we'll tell you why not.''

$ $ POLO PLAYERS' EDITION

Rizzo Management Corp., 3500 Fairlane Farms Rd., Suite 9, Wellington FL 33414. (561)793-9524. Fax: (561)793-9576. E-mail: info@poloplayersedition.com. Website: www.poloplayersedition.com. **Contact:** Gwen Rizzo, editor. Monthly magazine on polo—the sport and lifestyle. ''Our readers are affluent, well educated, well read, and highly sophisticated.'' Circ. 6,150. **Pays on acceptance.** Publishes ms an average of 2 months after acceptance. Kill fee varies. Buys first North American serial rights, makes work-for-hire assignments. Submit seasonal material 3 months in advance. Accepts queries by mail, e-mail, fax. Accepts simultaneous submissions. Responds in 3 months to queries. Writer's guidelines for #10 SAE with 2 stamps.

Nonfiction Historical/nostalgic, interview/profile, personal experience, photo feature, technical, travel. Special issues: Annual Art Issue/Gift Buying Guide; Winter Preview/Florida Supplement. **Buys 20 mss/year.** Query with published clips or send complete ms. Length: 800-3,000 words. **Pays $150-400 for assigned articles; $100-300 for unsolicited articles.** Sometimes pays expenses of writers on assignment.

Reprints Send tearsheet or typed ms with rights for sale noted and information about when and where the material previously appeared. Pays 50% of amount paid for an original article.

Photos State availability of or send photos with submission. Reviews contact sheets, transparencies, prints. Buys one-time rights. Offers $20-150/photo. Captions required.

Columns/Departments Yesteryears (historical pieces), 500 words; Profiles (clubs and players), 800-1,000 words. **Buys 15 mss/year.** Query with published clips. **Pays $100-300.**

Tips ''Query us on a personality or club profile or historic piece or, if you know the game, state availability to cover a tournament. Keep in mind that ours is a sophisticated, well-educated audience.''

$ RUGBY MAGAZINE

Rugby Press, Ltd., 459 Columbus Ave., #1200, New York NY 10024. (212)787-1160. Fax: (212)787-1161. E-mail: rugbymag@aol.com. Website: www.rugbymag.com. **75% freelance written.** Monthly tabloid. ''*Rugby Magazine* is the journal of record for the sport of rugby in the U.S. Our demographics are among the best in the country.'' Estab. 1975. Circ. 10,000. Pays on publication. Publishes ms an average of 2 months after acceptance. Byline given. Buys all rights. Editorial lead time 1 month. Submit seasonal material 2 months in advance. Accepts queries by mail, e-mail, fax, phone. Accepts simultaneous submissions. Responds in 2 weeks to queries; 1 month to mss. Sample copy for $4. Writer's guidelines free.

Nonfiction Book excerpts, essays, general interest, historical/nostalgic, how-to, humor, interview/profile, new product, opinion, personal experience, photo feature, technical, travel. **Buys 15 mss/year.** Send complete ms. Length: 600-2,000 words. **Pays $50 minimum.** Pays expenses of writers on assignment.

Reprints Send tearsheet or typed ms with rights for sale noted and information about when and where the material previously appeared. Payment varies.

Photos Send photos with submission. Reviews negatives, transparencies, prints. Buys all rights. Offers no additional payment for photos accepted with ms.

Columns/Departments Nutrition (athletic nutrition), 900 words; Referees' Corner, 1,200 words. **Buys 2-3 mss/year.** Query with published clips. **Pays $50 maximum.**

Fiction Condensed novels, humorous, novel excerpts, slice-of-life vignettes. **Buys 1-3 mss/year.** Query with published clips. Length: 1,000-2,500 words. **Pays $100.**

Tips ''Give us a call. Send along your stories or photos; we're happy to take a look. Tournament stories are a good way to get yourself published in *Rugby Magazine*.''

N $ SKYDIVING

1725 N. Lexington Ave., DeLand FL 32724. (386)736-4793. Fax: (386)736-9786. E-mail: editor@skydivingmagazine.com. Website: skydivingmagazine.com. **Contact:** Sue Clifton, editor. **25% freelance written.** Monthly tabloid featuring skydiving for sport parachutists, worldwide dealers and equipment manufacturers. ''*Skydiving* is a news magazine. Its purpose is to deliver timely, useful and interesting information about the equipment, techniques, events, people and places of parachuting. Our scope is national. *Skydiving*'s audience spans the entire spectrum of jumpers, from first-jump students to veterans with thousands of skydives. Some readers are riggers with a keen interest in the technical aspects of parachutes, while others are weekend 'fun' jumpers who want information to help them make travel plans and equipment purchases.'' Circ. 14,200. Pays on publication. Publishes ms an average of 3 months after acceptance. Byline given. Buys one-time rights. Accepts previously published material. Accepts simultaneous submissions. Responds in 1 month to queries. Sample copy for $2. Writer's guidelines online.

Nonfiction Average issue includes 3 feature articles and 3 columns of technical information. ''Send us news and information on how-to, where-to, equipment, techniques, events and outstanding personalities who skydive. We want articles written by people who have a solid knowledge of parachuting." No personal experience or human interest articles. Query. Length: 500-1,000 words. **Pays $25-100.** Sometimes pays expenses of writers on assignment.

Photos State availability with submission. Reviews 5×7 and larger b&w glossy prints. Offers no additional payment for photos accepted with ms. Captions required.

Fillers Newsbreaks. Length: 100-200 words. **Pays $25 minimum.**

Tips "The most frequent mistake made by writers in completing articles for us is that the writer isn't knowledgeable about the sport of parachuting. Articles about events are especially time-sensitive so yours must be submitted quickly. We welcome contributions about equipment. Even short, 'quick look' articles about new products are appropriate for *Skydiving*. If you know of a drop zone or other place that jumpers would like to visit, write an article describing its features and tell them why you liked it and what they can expect to find if they visit it. Avoid first-person articles."

$ $ TENNIS WEEK

Tennis News, Inc., 15 Elm Place, Rye NY 10580. (914)967-4890. Fax: (914)967-8178. **Contact:** Andre Christopher, managing editor. **10% freelance written.** Monthly magazine covering tennis. "For readers who are either tennis fanatics or involved in the business of tennis." Estab. 1974. Circ. 107,253. Pays on publication. Byline given. Buys all rights. Editorial lead time 1 month. Submit seasonal material 1 month in advance. Responds in 1 month to queries. Sample copy for $4.

Nonfiction Buys 15 mss/year. Query with or without published clips. Length: 1,000-2,000 words. **Pays $300.**

N TRANSWORLD SKATEBOARDING

Time 4 Media, 353 Airport Rd., Oceanside CA 92054-1203. (760)722-7777. Fax: (760)722-0653. Website: www.skateboarding.com. Editor-in-Chief: Skin Phillips. Editor: Eric Stricker. Managing Editor: Eric Santianin. Monthly magazine. Written for skateboarding enthusiasts. Circ. 243,000. Editorial lead time 3 months. Sample copy not available.

N $ $ WINDY CITY SPORTS

Windy City Publishing, 1450 W. Randolph St., Chicago IL 60607. (312)421-1551. Fax: (312)421-1454. E-mail: jbanowetz@windycitysportsmag.com. Website: www.windycitysports.com. **Contact:** Jeff Banowetz, editorial director. **50% freelance written.** Monthly tabloid. "Writers should have knowledge of the sport they've been hired to cover. In most cases, these are endurance sports, such as running, cycling, triathlon, or adventure racing. Please read the magazine and visit the website to famliarize yourself with our subject matter and our style. Poorly-tailored queries reflect badly on your journalistic skills. If you query us on a golf story, you will not only suffer the shame of rejection, but your name shall be added to our 'clueless freelancer' list, and we will joke about you at the water cooler." Circ. 110,000. Pays on publication. Publishes ms an average of 1 month after acceptance. Byline given. Buys one-time rights. Editorial lead time 2 months. Accepts queries by e-mail. Sample copy and writer's guidelines online.

Nonfiction Essays, general interest, how-to, humor, interview/profile, opinion, personal experience, photo feature, technical. **Buys up to 35 mss/year.** Query with published clips. Length: 700-1,500 words. **Pays $150-300 for assigned articles; $0-300 for unsolicited articles.** Sometimes pays expenses of writers on assignment.

Photos Send photos with submission. Reviews prints. Buys one-time rights. Negotiates payment individually. Captions, identification of subjects required.

Columns/Departments Cool Down (humorous, personal experience), 800-1,000 words; Nutrition (advice and information on diet), 500-800 words; Health/Wellness (advice and information on general health), 500-800 words. Query with published clips. **Pays $50-150.**

Tips "You should try to make it fun. We like to see anecdotes, great quotes and vivid descriptions. Quote Chicago area people as often as possible. If that's not possible, try to stick to the Midwest or people with Chicago connections."

MOTOR SPORTS

N AUTOMOBILE MAGAZINE

Primedia Broad Reach Magazines, 120 E. Liberty St., 2nd Floor, Ann Arbor MI 48104. (734)994-3500. Fax: (734)994-1153. E-mail: feedback@automobilemag.com. Website: www.automobilemag.com. Editor: Jean Jennings. Managing Editor: Amy Skogstrom. Monthly magazine covering automobiles. Edited for the automotive enthusiast interested in the novelty as well as the tradition of all things automotive. Circ. 644,000. Editorial lead time 6 weeks. Sample copy not available.

N 4-WHEEL & OFF ROAD

Primedia Enthusiast Group, 6420 Wilshire Blvd. 11th Floor, Los Angeles CA 90048-5502. (323)782-2360. Fax: (323)782-2704. E-mail: 4wheeloffroad@primedia.com. Website: www.4wheeloffroad.com. Editor: Rick Pewe. Managing Editor: Craig Johnson. Monthly magazine covering off road driving. Intended for the connoisseur of four wheel drive vehicles and their specific applications. Circ. 379,284. Sample copy not available.

$ THE HOOK MAGAZINE

The Magazine for Antique & Classic Tractor Pullers, Greer Town, Inc., 209 S. Marshall, Box 16, Marshfield MO 65706. (417)468-7000. Fax: (417)859-6075. E-mail: thehook@pcis.net. Website: pcis.net/thehook. Managing Editor: Sherry Linville. **Contact:** Dana Greer Marlin, owner/president. **80% freelance written.** Bimonthly magazine covering tractor pulling. Estab. 1992. Circ. 6,000. Pays on publication. Byline given. Buys one-time, electronic rights. Editorial lead time 6 months. Submit seasonal material 6 months in advance. Accepts queries by mail, e-mail, fax. Accepts previously published material. Accepts simultaneous submissions. Responds in 3 weeks to queries; 2 months to mss. Sample copy for 8½ × 11 SAE with 4 first-class stamps or online. Writer's guidelines for #10 SASE.

> O— "Our magazine is easy to break into. Puller profiles are your best bet. Features on individuals and their tractors, how they got into the sport, what they want from competing."

Nonfiction How-to, interview/profile, new product, personal experience, photo feature, technical, event coverage. **Buys 25 mss/year.** Send complete ms. Length: 500-1,500 words. **Pays $70 for technical articles; $35 for others.**

Photos Send photos with submission. Reviews 3 × 5 prints. Buys one-time and online rights. Negotiates payment individually. Captions, identification of subjects, model releases required.

Fillers Anecdotes, short humor. **Buys 6/year.** Length: 100 words.

Tips "Write 'real'; our readers don't respond well to scholarly tomes. Use your everyday voice in all submissions and your chances will go up radically."

$ $ SAND SPORTS MAGAZINE

Wright Publishing Co., Inc., P.O. Box 2260, Costa Mesa CA 92628. (714)979-2560, ext. 107. Fax: (714)979-3998. Website: www.sandsports.net. **Contact:** Michael Sommer, editor. **20% freelance written.** Bimonthly magazine covering vehicles for off-road and sand dunes. Estab. 1995. Circ. 25,000. Pays on publication. Byline given. Buys first, one-time rights. Editorial lead time 3 months. Submit seasonal material 6 months in advance. Accepts queries by mail. Sample copy and writer's guidelines free.

Nonfiction How-to (technical-mechanical), photo feature, technical. **Buys 20 mss/year.** Query. Length: 1,500 words minimum. **Pays $125-175/page.** Sometimes pays expenses of writers on assignment.

Photos Send photos with submission. Reviews color slides or high res digital images. Buys one-time rights. Negotiates payment individually. Captions, identification of subjects, model releases required.

N $ $ SPEEDWAY ILLUSTRATED

Performance Media, LLC, 107 Elm St., Salisbury MA 01952. (978)465-9099. Fax: (978)465-9033. E-mail: editorial @speedwayillustrated.com. Website: www.speedwayillustrated.com. Executive Editor: Dick Berggren. **Contact:** Rob Sneddon, editor. **80% freelance written.** Monthly magazine covering stock car racing. Estab. 2000. Circ. 130,000. Pays on publication. Byline given. Buys first rights. Editorial lead time 6 weeks. Accepts queries by mail, e-mail, fax. Responds in 2 weeks to queries. Sample copy and writer's guidelines free.

Nonfiction Interview/profile, opinion, personal experience, photo feature, technical. **Buys 30 mss/year.** Query. **Pays variable rate.**

Photos Send photos with submission. Reviews transparencies, digital. Buys all rights. Offers $40-250/photo. Captions, identification of subjects, model releases required.

Tips "We seek short, high-interest value pieces that are accompanied by strong photography, in short—knock our socks off."

OLYMPICS

USA GYMNASTICS

201 S. Capitol Ave., Suite 300, Pan American Plaza, Indianapolis IN 46225. (317)237-5050. Fax: (317)237-5069. E-mail: lpeszek@usa-gymnastics.org. Website: www.usa-gymnastics.org. **Contact:** Luan Peszek, editor. **5% freelance written.** Bimonthly magazine covering gymnastics—national and international competitions. Designed to educate readers on fitness, health, safety, technique, current topics, trends, and personalities related to the gymnastics/fitness field. Readers are gymnasts ages 7-18, parents, and coaches. Estab. 1981. Circ. 95,000. Pays on publication. Publishes ms an average of 4 months after acceptance. Byline given. Buys all rights. Submit

seasonal material 4 months in advance. Accepts queries by e-mail, fax. Accepts simultaneous submissions. Responds in 2 months to queries. Sample copy for $5.

Nonfiction General interest, how-to (related to fitness, health, gymnastics), inspirational, interview/profile, opinion (Open Floor section), photo feature. **Buys 3 mss/year.** Query. Length: 1,500 words maximum. **Payment negotiable.**

Reprints Send photocopy.

Photos Send photos with submission. Buys all rights. Offers no additional payment for photos accepted with ms. Identification of subjects required.

Tips "Any articles of interest to gymnasts (men, women, rhythmic gymnastics, trampoline, and tumbling and sports acrobatics), coaches, judges, and parents. This includes nutrition, toning, health, safety, trends, techniques, timing, etc."

RUNNING

$ $ NEW YORK RUNNER

New York Road Runners, 9 E. 89th St., New York NY 10128. (212)423-2260. Fax: (212)423-0879. E-mail: newyorkrun@nyrrc.org. Website: www.nyrrc.org. **Contact:** Gordon Bakoulis, editor. Bimonthly regional sports magazine covering running, walking, nutrition, and fitness. Estab. 1958. Circ. 45,000. **Pays on acceptance.** Byline given. Offers 33% kill fee. Buys first North American serial rights. Submit seasonal material 4 months in advance. Accepts queries by mail, e-mail, fax. Responds in 2 months to queries. Sample copy for $3. Writer's guidelines for #10 SASE.

• Material should be of interest to members of the New York Road Runners.

Nonfiction Running and marathon articles. Interview/profile (of runners). **Buys 15 mss/year.** Query. Length: 750-1,000 words. **Pays $50-350.**

Columns/Departments Running Briefs (anything noteworthy in the running world, such as new products and volunteer opportunities), 250-500 words. Query.

Tips "Be knowledgeable about the sport of running."

$ $ $ RUNNER'S WORLD

Rodale, 135 N. 6th St., Emmaus PA 18098. (610)967-5171. Fax: (610)967-8883. E-mail: rwedit@rodale.com. Website: www.runnersworld.com. **Contact:** David Willey, editor-in-chief. **5% freelance written.** Monthly magazine on running, mainly long-distance running. "The magazine for and about distance running, training, health and fitness, nutrition, motivation, injury prevention, race coverage, personalities of the sport." Estab. 1966. Circ. 500,000. Pays on publication. Publishes ms an average of 6 months after acceptance. Byline given. Buys all rights. Submit seasonal material 6 months in advance. Accepts queries by mail. Responds in 2 months to queries. Writer's guidelines online.

○→ Break in through columns 'Human Race' and 'Finish Line.' Also 'Warmups,' which mixes international running news with human interest stories. If you can send us a unique human interest story from your region, we will give it serious consideration.

Nonfiction How-to (train, prevent injuries), interview/profile, personal experience. No "my first marathon" stories. No poetry. **Buys 5-7 mss/year.** Query. **Pays $1,500-2,000.** Pays expenses of writers on assignment.

Photos State availability with submission. Buys one-time rights. Identification of subjects required.

Columns/Departments Finish Line (back-of-the-magazine essay, personal experience—humor). **Buys 24 mss/year.** Send complete ms. **Pays $300.**

▣ The online magazine carries original content not found in the print edition. Contact: Matthew Linde.

Tips "We are always looking for 'Adventure Runs' from readers—runs in wild, remote, beautiful, and interesting places. These are rarely race stories but more like backtracking/running adventures. Great color slides are crucial, 2,000 words maximum."

$ $ RUNNING TIMES

The Runner's Best Resource, Fitness Publishing, Inc., 213 Danbury Rd., Wilton CT 06897. (203)761-1113. Fax: (203)761-9933. E-mail: editor@runningtimes.com. Website: www.runningtimes.com. Managing Editor: Marc Chalufour. **Contact:** Jonathan Beverly, editor. **40% freelance written.** Magazine published 10 times/year covering distance running and racing. "*Running Times* is the national magazine for the experienced running participant and fan. Our audience is knowledgeable about the sport and active in running and racing. All editorial relates specifically to running: improving performance, enhancing enjoyment, or exploring events, places, and people in the sport." Estab. 1977. Circ. 75,000. Pays on publication. Publishes ms an average of 3 months after acceptance. Byline given. Buys first North American serial, second serial (reprint), electronic rights. Editorial lead time 4 months. Submit seasonal material 6 months in advance. Accepts queries by mail, e-mail. Responds in 1 month to queries; 2 months to mss. Sample copy for $5. Writer's guidelines online.

Nonfiction Book excerpts, essays, historical/nostalgic, how-to (training), humor, inspirational, interview/profile, new product, opinion, personal experience (with theme, purpose, evidence of additional research and/or special expertise), photo feature, travel, news, reports. No basic, beginner how-to, generic fitness/nutrition, or generic first-person accounts. **Buys 25 mss/year.** Query. Length: 1,500-3,000 words. **Pays $200-500 for assigned articles; $100-300 for unsolicited articles.** Sometimes pays expenses of writers on assignment.

Photos State availability with submission. Buys one-time rights. Negotiates payment individually. Identification of subjects required.

Columns/Departments Training (short topics related to enhancing performance), 1,000 words; Sports-Med (application of medical knowledge to running), 1,000 words; Nutrition (application of nutritional principles to running performance), 1,000 words. **Buys 15 mss/year.** Query. **Pays $50-200.**

Fiction Any genre, with running-related theme or characters. **Buys 1-2 mss/year.** Send complete ms. Length: 1,500-3,000 words. **Pays $100-500.**

Tips "Thoroughly get to know runners and the running culture, both at the participant level and the professional, elite level."

$ $ TRAIL RUNNER

The Magazine of Running Adventure, Big Stone Publishing, 1101 Village Rd. UL-4D, Carbondale CO 81623. (970)704-1442. Fax: (970)963-4965. E-mail: mbenge@bigstonepub.com. Website: www.trailrunnermag.com. **Contact:** Michael Benge, editor. **65% freelance written.** Bimonthly magazine covering all aspects of off-road running. "The only nationally circulated 4-color glossy magazine dedicated to covering trail running." Estab. 1999. Circ. 40,000. Pays on publication. Publishes ms an average of 2 months after acceptance. Byline given. Offers $50 kill fee. Buys first North American serial, electronic rights. Editorial lead time 3 months. Submit seasonal material 5 months in advance. Accepts queries by mail, e-mail. Accepts simultaneous submissions. Responds in 3 weeks to queries; 2 months to mss. Sample copy for $3. Writer's guidelines online.

Nonfiction Essays, exposé, general interest, historical/nostalgic, how-to, humor, inspirational, interview/profile, new product, opinion, personal experience, photo feature, technical, travel, racing. No gear reviews, race results. **Buys 30-40 mss/year.** Query with published clips. Length: 800-2,000 words. **Pays 30-40¢/word.** Sometimes pays expenses of writers on assignment.

Photos Send photos with submission. Reviews 35mm transparencies, prints. Buys one-time rights. Offers $50-250/photo. Identification of subjects, model releases required.

Columns/Departments Monique Cole, senior editor. Training (race training, altitude training, etc.), 800 words; Adventure (off-beat aspects of trail running), 600-800 words; Wanderings (personal essay on any topic related to trail running), 600 words; Urban Escapes (urban trails accessible in and around major US sites), 800 words; Personalities (profile of a trail running personality), 1,000 words. **Buys 5-10 mss/year.** Query with published clips. **Pays 30-40¢/word.**

Fiction Adventure, fantasy, slice-of-life vignettes. **Buys 1-2 mss/year.** Query with published clips. Length: 1,000-1,500 words. **Pays 25-35¢/word.**

Fillers Anecdotes, facts, gags to be illustrated by cartoonist, newsbreaks, short humor. **Buys 50-60/year.** Length: 75-400 words. **Pays 25-35¢/word.**

Tips "Best way to break in is with interesting and unique trail running news, notes, and nonsense from around the world. Also, check the website for more info."

$ $ TRIATHLETE MAGAZINE

The World's Largest Triathlon Magazine, Triathlon Group of North America, 328 Encinitas Blvd., Suite 100, Encinitas CA 92024. (760)634-4100. Fax: (760)634-4110. E-mail: Mhoyer@triathletemag.com. Website: www.triathletemag.com. **Contact:** Meredith Hoyer, managing editor. **50% freelance written.** Monthly magazine. "In general, articles should appeal to seasoned triathletes, as well as eager newcomers to the sport. Our audience includes everyone from competitive athletes to people considering their first event." Estab. 1983. Circ. 50,000. Pays on publication. Byline given. Buys second serial (reprint), all rights. Editorial lead time 3 months. Submit seasonal material 6 months in advance. Accepts queries by mail, e-mail. Accepts simultaneous submissions. Sample copy for $5.

Nonfiction How-to, interview/profile, new product, photo feature, technical. "No first-person pieces about your experience in triathlon or my-first-triathlon stories." **Buys 36 mss/year.** Query with published clips. Length: 1,000-3,000 words. **Pays $200-600.** Sometimes pays expenses of writers on assignment.

Photos State availability with submission. Reviews transparencies. Buys first North American rights. Offers $50-300/photo.

Tips "Writers should know the sport and be familiar with the nuances and history. Training-specific articles that focus on new, but scientifically based, methods are good, as are seasonal training pieces."

SKIING & SNOW SPORTS

Ⓝ $ $ AMERICAN SNOWMOBILER

The Enthusiast Magazine, Recreational Publications, Inc., 2715 Upper Afton Rd., Suite 100, St. Paul MN 55119-4774. (651)738-1953. Fax: (651)738-2302. E-mail: 2editor@amsnow.com. Website: www.amsnow.com. **30% freelance written.** Magazine published 6 times seasonally covering snowmobiling. Estab. 1985. Circ. 90,000. **Pays on acceptance.** Publishes ms an average of 4 months after acceptance. Byline given. Buys all rights. Editorial lead time 4 months. Submit seasonal material 6 months in advance. Accepts queries by mail, e-mail, fax. Responds in 1 month to queries; 2 months to mss. Writer's guidelines for #10 SASE.

> ⚷ Break in with "a packet complete with résumé, published clips and photos (or color copies of available photos) and a complete query with a few paragraphs to get me interested and to give an idea of the angle the writer will be taking. When sending an e-mail, do not attach anything."

Nonfiction Seeking race coverage for online version. General interest, historical/nostalgic, how-to, interview/profile, new product, personal experience, photo feature, travel. **Buys 10 mss/year.** Query with published clips. Length: 1,000-2,000 words. **Pay varies for assigned articles; $100 minimum for unsolicited articles.**

Photos State availability with submission. Buys all rights. Offers no additional payment for photos accepted with ms. Captions, identification of subjects, model releases required.

$ $ $ Ⓩ SKI MAGAZINE

Times Mirror Magazines, 929 Pearl St., Suite 200, Boulder CO 80302. E-mail: editor@skimag.com. Website: www.skimag.com. Editor-in-Chief: Kendall Hamilton. **Contact:** Maureen Drummey, associate editor. **60% freelance written.** Magazine published 8 times/year. "*Ski* is a ski-lifestyle publication written and edited for recreational skiers. Its content is intended to help them ski better (technique), buy better (equipment and skiwear), and introduce them to new experiences, people, and adventures." Estab. 1936. Circ. 430,000. **Pays on acceptance.** Publishes ms an average of 3 months after acceptance. Byline given. Offers 15% kill fee. Buys first North American serial rights. Submit seasonal material 8 months in advance. Accepts queries by mail, e-mail. Sample copy for 9×12 SAE and 5 first-class stamps.

> • Does not accept unsolicited mss, and assumes no responsibility for their return.

Nonfiction Essays, historical/nostalgic, how-to, humor, interview/profile, personal experience. **Buys 5-10 mss/year.** Send complete ms. Length: 1,000-3,500 words. **Pays $500-1,000 for assigned articles; $300-700 for unsolicited articles.** Pays expenses of writers on assignment.

Photos Send photos with submission. Buys one-time rights. Offers $75-300/photo. Captions, identification of subjects, model releases required.

Columns/Departments See magazine.

Fillers Facts, short humor. **Buys 10/year.** Length: 60-75 words. **Pays $50-75.**

Tips "Writers must have an extensive familiarity with the sport and know what concerns, interests, and amuses skiers. Start with short pieces ('hometown hills,' 'dining out,' 'sleeping in'). Columns are most open to freelancers."

$ $ SNOWEST MAGAZINE

Harris Publishing, 360 B St., Idaho Falls ID 83402. (208)524-7000. Fax: (208)522-5241. E-mail: lindstrm@snowest.com. Website: snowest.com. Publisher: Steve Janes. **Contact:** Lane Lindstrom, editor. **10-25% freelance written.** Monthly magazine. "*SnoWest* covers the sport of snowmobiling, products, and personalities in the western states. This includes mountain riding, deep powder, and trail riding, as well as destination pieces, tech tips, and new model reviews." Estab. 1972. Circ. 160,000. Pays on publication. Publishes ms an average of 2 months after acceptance. Byline given. Buys first North American serial rights. Editorial lead time 6 months. Submit seasonal material 3 months in advance. Sample copy and writer's guidelines free.

Nonfiction How-to (fix a snowmobile, make it high performance), new product, technical, travel. **Buys 3-5 mss/year.** Query with published clips. Length: 500-1,500 words. **Pays $150-300.**

Photos Send photos with submission. Buys one-time rights. Negotiates payment individually. Captions, identification of subjects required.

WATER SPORTS

Ⓝ $ DIVER

Seagraphic Publications, Ltd., Box 1312, Station A, Delta BC V4M 3Y8, Canada. (604)948-9337. Fax: (604)948-9985. E-mail: divermag@axion.net. Website: www.divermag.com. Publisher: Peter Vassilopoulos. **Contact:** Martina Campbell, editor. Magazine published 8 times/year emphasizing scuba diving, ocean science, and technology for a well-educated, outdoor-oriented readership. Circ. 7,000. Accepts queries by mail, e-mail.

Nonfiction "Well-written and illustrated Canadian and North American regional dive destination articles. Most travel articles are committed up to a year in advance, and there is limited scope for new material." Reading period for unsolicited articles July through August. Length: 500-1,000 words. **Pays $2.50/column inch.**

Photos Reviews 5×7 prints, JPEG/TIFF files (300 dpi), slides, maps, drawings. Captions, identification of subjects required.

$ $ PADDLER MAGAZINE

World's No. 1 Canoeing, Kayaking and Rafting Magazine, Paddlesport Publishing, P.O. Box 775450, Steamboat Springs CO 80477-5450. (970)879-1450. E-mail: rico@paddlermagazine.com. Website: www.paddlermagazine. com. **70% freelance written.** Bimonthly magazine covering paddle sports. "*Paddler* magazine is written by and for those knowledgeable about river running, flatwater canoeing and sea kayaking. Our core audience is the intermediate to advanced paddler, yet we strive to cover the entire range from beginners to experts. Our editorial coverage is divided between whitewater rafting, whitewater kayaking, canoeing and sea kayaking. We strive for balance between the Eastern and Western U.S. paddling scenes and regularly cover international expeditions. We also try to integrate the Canadian paddling community into each publication." Estab. 1991. Circ. 80,000. Pays on publication. Publishes ms an average of 6 months after acceptance. Byline given. Buys first North American serial, one-time electronic rights rights. Editorial lead time 3 months. Submit seasonal material 6 months in advance. Accepts queries by mail, e-mail. Responds in 6 months to queries. Sample copy for $3 with 8½×11 SASE. Writer's guidelines online.

o→ Break in through "The Hotline section at the front of the magazine."

Nonfiction Book excerpts, essays, general interest, historical/nostalgic, how-to, humor, inspirational, interview/profile, new product, opinion, personal experience, photo feature, technical, travel (must be paddlesport related). **Buys 75 mss/year.** Query. Length: 100-3,000 words. **Pays 10-25¢/word (more for established writers) for assigned articles; 10-20¢/word for unsolicited articles.** Sometimes pays expenses of writers on assignment.

Photos Submissions should include photos or other art. State availability with submission. Reviews contact sheets, negatives, transparencies. Buys one-time rights. Offers $25-200/photo.

Columns/Departments Hotline (timely news and exciting developments relating to the paddling community. Stories should be lively and newsworthy), 150-750 words; Paddle People (unique people involved in the sport and industry leaders), 600-800 words; Destinations (informs paddlers of unique places to paddle—we often follow regional themes and cover all paddling disciplines); submissions should include map and photo, 800 words. Marketplace (gear reviews, gadgets and new products, and is about equipment paddlers use, from boats and paddles to collapsible chairs, bivy sacks and other accessories), 250-800 words. Paddle Tales (short, humorous anecdotes), 75-300 words. Skills (a "How-to" forum for experts to share tricks of the trade, from playboating techniques to cooking in the backcountry), 250-1,000 words. Query. **Pays 20-25¢/word.**

Tips "We prefer queries, but will look at manuscripts on speculation. No phone queries please. Be familiar with the magazine and offer us unique, exciting ideas. Most positive responses to queries are on spec, but we will occasionally make assignments."

$ $ SPORT DIVER

World Publications, 460 N. Orlando Ave., Suite 200, Winter Park FL 32789-2988. (407)628-4802. E-mail: editor@sportdiver.com. Website: www.sportdiver.com. Editor: Ty Sawyer. **75% freelance written.** Magazine published 10 times/year covering scuba diving. "We portray the adventure and fun of diving—the reasons we all started diving in the first place." Estab. 1993. Circ. 250,000. Pays on publication. Byline given. Offers 25% kill fee. Buys first North American serial rights. Editorial lead time 3 months. Submit seasonal material 4 months in advance. Accepts queries by e-mail. Responds in 2 weeks to queries; 3 months to mss. Writer's guidelines online.

Nonfiction Personal experience, travel, diving. No nondiving related articles. **Buys 150 mss/year.** Query with SASE. Length: 500-2,000 words. **Pays $300-500.**

Photos State availability with submission. Reviews transparencies. Buys one-time rights. Offers $50-200/photo; $1,000 for covers. Captions required.

Columns/Departments Divebriefs (shorts), 150-450 words. Query. **Pays $50-250.**

Tips "Know diving, and even more importantly, know how to write. It's getting much more difficult to break into the market due to a recent series of takeovers."

Ⓝ $ $ SWIMMING TECHNIQUE

Sports Publications, Inc., P.O. Box 20337, Sedona AZ 86341. (520)284-4005. Fax: (520)284-2477. E-mail: swimworld@aol.com. Website: www.swiminfo.com. Senior Editor: Mr. Bob Ingram. **Contact:** Dr. Phillip Whitten, editor. **75% freelance written.** Quarterly magazine for professional swim coaches, covering swimming techniques and training. "Covers all aspects of swimming technique and training." Estab. 1963. Circ. 9,000. Pays on publication. Publishes ms an average of 4 months after acceptance. Byline given. Buys first, all rights. Editorial lead time 4

months. Submit seasonal material 4 months in advance. Accepts queries by mail, e-mail, fax, phone. Accepts previously published material. Responds in 1 month to queries. Sample copy for $5. Writer's guidelines free.
Nonfiction Book excerpts, essays, how-to (swim & technique), interview/profile, opinion, personal experience, technical. **Buys 16-20 mss/year.** Query with published clips. Length: 500-4,000 words. **Pays 12-15¢/word.** Sometimes pays expenses of writers on assignment.
Photos Send photos with submission. Buys all rights. Negotiates payment individually. Captions, identification of subjects required.

Ⓝ $ $SWIMMING WORLD

Sports Publications, Inc., P.O. Box 20337, Sedona AZ 86341. (520)284-4005. Fax: (520)284-2477. E-mail: swimworld@aol.com. Website: www.swiminfo.com. Senior Editor: Bob Ingram. **Contact:** Dr. Phillip Whitten, editor-in-chief. **50% freelance written.** Monthly magazine. *"Swimming World* is recognized as the authoritative source in the sport of swimming. It publishes articles about all aspects of competitive swimming.'' Estab. 1959. Circ. 39,700. Pays on publication. Byline given. Kill fee negotiated. Buys all rights. Editorial lead time 2 months. Submit seasonal material 3 months in advance. Accepts queries by mail, e-mail, fax, phone. Accepts simultaneous submissions. Responds in 1 month to queries. Sample copy for $5 and SAE with 4 first-class stamps. Writer's guidelines free.
Nonfiction Book excerpts, essays, exposé, general interest, historical/nostalgic, how-to, humor, inspirational, interview/profile, new product, opinion, personal experience, photo feature, technical, travel. **Buys 30 mss/year.** Query. Length: 300-3,000 words. **Pays $75-400.** Sometimes pays expenses of writers on assignment.
Photos State availability with submission. Reviews prints. Buys negotiable rights. Negotiates payment individually. Captions, identification of subjects, model releases required.
Columns/Departments Buys 18 mss/year. Query with published clips. **Pays $75-200.**

$THE WATER SKIER

USA Water Ski, 1251 Holy Cow Rd., Polk City FL 33868-8200. (863)324-4341. Fax: (863)325-8259. E-mail: satkinson@usawaterski.org. Website: www.usawaterski.org. Scott Atkinson, editor. **10-20% freelance written.** Magazine published 9 times/year. *"The Water Skier* is the membership magazine of USA Water Ski, the national governing body for organized water skiing in the United States. The magazine has a controlled circulation and is available only to USA Water Ski's membership, which is made up of 20,000 active competitive water skiers and 10,000 members who are supporting the sport. These supporting members may participate in the sport but they don't compete. The editorial content of the magazine features distinctive and informative writing about the sport of water skiing only.'' Estab. 1951. Circ. 30,000. Byline given. Offers 30% kill fee. Editorial lead time 4 months. Submit seasonal material 6 months in advance. Responds in 2 weeks to queries. Sample copy for $3.50. Writer's guidelines for #10 SASE.
○┐ Most open to material for feature articles (query editor with your idea).
Nonfiction Historical/nostalgic (has to pertain to water skiing), interview/profile (call for assignment), new product (boating and water ski equipment), travel (water ski vacation destinations). **Buys 10-15 mss/year.** Query. Length: 1,500-3,000 words. **Pays $100-150.**
Reprints Send photocopy. Payment negotiable.
Photos State availability with submission. Reviews contact sheets. Buys all rights. Negotiates payment individually. Captions, identification of subjects required.
Columns/Departments The Water Skier News (small news items about people and events in the sport), 400-500 words. Other topics include safety, training (3-event, barefoot, disabled, show ski, ski race, kneeboard, and wakeboard); champions on their way; new products. Query. **Pays $50-100.**
▣ The online magazine carries original content not found in the print edition. Contact: Scott Atkinson, online editor.
Tips "Contact the editor through a query letter (please, no phone calls) with an idea. Avoid instruction, these articles are written by professionals. Concentrate on articles about the people of the sport. We are always looking for interesting stories about people in the sport. Also, short news features which will make a reader say to himself, 'Hey, I didn't know that.' Keep in mind that the publication is highly specialized about the sport of water skiing.''

TEEN & YOUNG ADULT

BOP

(formerly *Teen Beat*), Laufer Media, 6430 Sunset Blvd., Hollywood CA 90028. (323)462-4267. Fax: (323)462-4341. Editor: Leesa Coble. Monthly magazine. Top teen entertainment magazine covers today's hottest stars. Features, news, gossip, quizzes. Circ. 200,000. Sample copy not available.

$ $ BREAKAWAY MAGAZINE

Focus on the Family, 8605 Explorer Dr., Colorado Springs CO 80920. (719)531-3400. Website: www.breakaway mag.com. Associate Editor: Jeremy V. Jones. **Contact:** Michael Ross, editor. **25% freelance written.** Monthly magazine covering extreme sports, Christian music artists, and new technology relevant to teen boys. "This fast-paced, 4-color publication is designed to creatively teach, entertain, inspire, and challenge the emerging teenager. It also seeks to strengthen a boy's self-esteem, provide role models, guide a healthy awakening to girls, make the Bible relevant, and deepen their love for family, friends, church, and Jesus Christ." Estab. 1990. Circ. 96,000. **Pays on acceptance.** Publishes ms an average of 5-12 months after acceptance. Byline given. Offers $25 kill fee. Buys first North American serial, first, one-time, electronic rights. Editorial lead time 3 months. Submit seasonal material 6 months in advance. Accepts queries by mail. Responds in 2-3 months to queries; 2-3 months to mss. Sample copy for $1.50 and 9×12 SASE with 3 first-class stamps. Writer's guidelines for #10 SASE.

Nonfiction Inspirational, interview/profile, personal experience. **Buys up to 6 mss/year.** Send complete ms. Length: 700-2,000 words. **Pays 12-15¢/word.**

Columns/Departments Truth Encounter (spiritual/Biblical application devotional for teen guys), 600 words. **Buys 2-3 mss/year.** Send complete ms. **Pays 12-15¢/word.**

Fiction Adventure, humorous, religious, suspense. "Avoid Christian jargon, clichés, preaching, and other dialogue that isn't realistic or that interrupts the flow of the story." **Buys 3-4 mss/year.** Send complete ms. Length: 600-2,000 words. **Pays 12-15¢/word.**

Tips "Some of our readers get spiritual nurture at home and at church; many don't. To reach both groups, the articles must be written in ways that are compelling, bright, out of the ordinary. Nearly every adult in a boy's life is an authority figure. We would like you, through the magazine, to be seen as a friend! We also want *Breakaway* to be a magazine any pre-Christian teen could pick up and understand without first learning 'Christianese.' Stories should spiritually challenge, yet be spiritually inviting."

$ COLLEGEBOUND TEEN MAGAZINE

(formerly *College Bound*), The College Bound Network, 1200 South Ave., Suite 202, Staten Island NY 10314. (718)761-4800. Fax: (718)761-3300. E-mail: editorial@collegebound.net. Website: www.collegeboundteen.c om. Editor-in-Chief: Gina LaGuardia. **Contact:** Dawn Papandrea, managing editor. **70% freelance written.** Monthly magazine. "*CollegeBound Teen Magazine* is designed to provide high school students with an inside look at all aspects of college life academics and socials. College students from around the country (and those young at heart!) are welcome to serve as correspondents to provide our teen readership with real-life accounts and cutting-edge, expert advice on the college admissions process and beyond." Estab. 1987. Circ. 100,000 (regional issues). Pays 6 weeks upon publication. Publishes ms an average of 3-4 months after acceptance. Byline given. Buys first North American serial, first, electronic rights. Editorial lead time 4 months. Submit seasonal material 4 months in advance. Accepts queries by mail, e-mail. Accepts previously published material. Responds in 6 weeks to queries; 2 months to mss. Sample copy for 9×12 SAE and $2.27 postage. Writer's guidelines online.

Nonfiction How-to (apply for college, prepare for the interview, etc.), personal experience (college experiences). No fillers, poetry, or fiction. **Buys 250+ mss/year.** Query with published clips. Length: 650-1,500 words. **Pays $50-100, plus 2 or 3 issues of magazine.**

Photos Gina LaGuardia, editor-in-chief. State availability with submission. Buys one-time rights. Offers no additional payment for photos accepted with ms. Captions, identification of subjects required.

Columns/Departments "Most departments are written in-house." **Buys 25 mss/year.** Query with published clips. **Pays $40-70.**

Tips "We're looking for well-researched, well-reported articles packed with real-life student anecdotes and expert insight on everything from dealing with dorm life, choosing the right college, and joining a fraternity or sorority, to college dating, cool campus happenings, scholarship scoring strategies, and other college issues."

$ $ $ $ COSMOGIRL!

A Cool New Magazine for Teens, The Hearst Corp., 224 W. 57th St., 3rd Floor, New York NY 10019. (212)649-3851. E-mail: inbox@cosmogirl.com. Website: www.cosmogirl.com. Editor: Susan Schulz. Monthly magazine covering fashion, beauty, photos and profiles of young celebs, advice, health and fitness, dating, relationships and finance. "CosmoGIRL! has the voice of a cool older sister. The magazine is conversational, funny, down-to-earth, and honest. We never talk down to our readers, who are 12- to 22-year-old young women." Estab. 1999. Circ. 1,350,000. Byline given. Offers 25% kill fee. Buys all rights. Editorial lead time 3-4 months. Accepts queries by mail. Responds in 2 months to queries. Writer's guidelines by e-mail.

Nonfiction Look at the masthead of a current issue for the appropriate editor. Looking for features with a news bent that pertains to teenagers' lives; quizzes; relationship stories; dynamic first-person stories. Interview/

profile, opinion, personal experience. **Pays $1/word.** Pays expenses of writers on assignment.

Photos Put name, phone # and address on back of all photos. Send photos with submission.

$FLORIDA LEADER

(for high school students), Oxendine Publishing, Inc., P.O. Box 14081, Gainesville FL 32604-2081. (352)373-6907. Fax: (352)373-8120. E-mail: stephanie@studentleader.com. Website: www.floridaleader.com. **Contact:** Stephanie Reck, editor. Triannual magazine covering high school and pre-college youth. Estab. 1983. Circ. 50,000. Pays on publication. Publishes ms an average of 3 months after acceptance. Buys all rights. Submit seasonal material 4 months in advance. Accepts queries by mail, e-mail, fax. Accepts simultaneous submissions. Responds in 2 months to queries. Sample copy for $3.50 and 8×11 SAE, with 3 first-class stamps. Writer's guidelines online.

Nonfiction Practical tips for going to college, student life, and leadership development. "No lengthy individual profiles or articles without primary and secondary sources of attribution." How-to, new product. Length: 250-1,000 words. **Payment varies. Pays students or first-time writers with contributor's copies.**

Photos Send photos with submission. Reviews contact sheets, negatives, transparencies. Buys all rights. Offers $50/photo maximum. Captions, identification of subjects, model releases required.

Columns/Departments College Life, The Lead Role, In Every Issue (quizzes, tips), Florida Forum (features Florida high school students), 250-1,000 words. **Buys 2 mss/year.** Query. **Pays $35-75.**

Fillers Facts, newsbreaks, tips, book reviews. Length: 100-300 words. **Pays no payment.**

Tips "Read other high school and college publications for current issues, interests. Send manuscripts or outlines for review. All sections open to freelance work. Always looking for lighter, humorous articles as well as features on Florida colleges and universities, careers, jobs. Multi-sourced (5-10) articles are best."

$ $GUIDEPOSTS FOR TEENS

Guideposts, 1050 Broadway, Suite 6, Chesterton IN 46304. (219)929-4429. Fax: (219)926-3839. E-mail: gp4t@guideposts.org. Website: www.gp4teens.com. Editor-in-Chief: Mary Lou Carney. **Contact:** Betsy Kohn, managing editor. **90% freelance written.** Bimonthly magazine serving as an inspiration for teens. "*Guideposts for Teens* is a general interest magazine for teenage girls (ages 11-17). We are an inspirational publication that offers true, first-person stories about real teens. Our watchwords are 'wholesome,' 'current,' 'fun,' and 'inspiring.' We also publish shorter pieces on fashion, beauty, celebrity, boys, embarrassing moments, and advice columns." Estab. 1998. Circ. 250,000. **Pays on acceptance.** Byline sometimes given. Offers 25% kill fee. Buys all rights. Editorial lead time 6 months. Submit seasonal material 6 months in advance. Accepts queries by mail, e-mail. Accepts simultaneous submissions. Responds in 6 weeks to queries; 6 weeks to mss. Sample copy for $4.50. Writer's guidelines online.

Nonfiction Nothing written from an adult point of view. How-to, humor, inspirational, interview/profile, personal experience, religious. **Buys 80 mss/year.** Query. Length: 200-1,500 words. **Pays $300-500 for assigned articles; $100-300 for unsolicited articles.** Pays expenses of writers on assignment.

Photos State availability with submission. Buys one-time rights. Negotiates payment individually. Identification of subjects required.

Columns/Departments Quiz (teen-relevant topics, teen language), 1,000 words; Positive Thinker (first-person stories of teens who've overcome something remarkable and kept a positive outlook), 300-500 words; My Own Thing (profiles of teen girls who followed their passion to do something extraordinary that helps others), 300-500 words; My Bad Day (first-person "strange but true"/miracle stories), 250 words; Winner's Circle (profiles of teen girls excelling at sports on national/world level), 500 words. **Buys 40 mss/year.** Query with published clips. **Pays $175-400.**

The online magazine carries original content not found in the print edition. Contact: Chris Lyon, managing editor.

Tips "We are eagerly looking for a number of things: teen how-to pieces, quizzes, DIYs, fashion/beauty. Most of all, though, we are about TRUE STORIES in the *Guideposts* tradition. Teens in dangerous, inspiring, miraculous situations. These first-person (ghostwritten) true narratives are the backbone of *GP4T*—and what sets us apart from other publications."

$GUMBO MAGAZINE

The National Magazine Written by Teens for Teens, Strive Media Institute, 1818 N. Dr. Martin Luther King Dr., Milwaukee WI 53212. (414)374-3511. Fax: (414)374-3512. E-mail: info@mygumbo.com. Website: www.mygumbo.com. Editor: Corbin Robinson. **Contact:** Amy Muehlbauer, managing editor. **25% freelance written.** Bimonthly magazine covering teen issues (arts, entertainment, social issues, etc.). "All articles must be written by teens (13-19 year-olds) and for teens. Tone is modern, hip, and urban. No adults may write for magazine." Estab. 1998. Circ. 25,000. Pays on publication. Publishes ms an average of 6 months after acceptance. Byline given. Buys one-time rights. Editorial lead time 6 months. Submit seasonal material 6 months in advance.

Accepts queries by mail, e-mail, fax. Accepts previously published material. Accepts simultaneous submissions. Responds in 2 weeks to queries; 2 months to mss. Sample copy for free. Writer's guidelines free.

Nonfiction General interest, humor, inspirational, interview/profile, opinion, personal experience, photo feature, technical, book & CD reviews. Does not want unsolicited articles or fiction other than poetry. All news stories require approval from Managing Editor prior to submission. **Buys 50-70 mss/year.** Query. Length: 500-1,000 words. **Pays $25.** Sometimes pays expenses of writers on assignment.

Photos State availability of or send photos with submission. Reviews prints, GIF/JPEG files. Buys one-time rights. Offers no additional payment for photos accepted with ms. Captions, identification of subjects required.

Poetry Any poetry is acceptable provided author is 13-19 years of age. Avant-garde, free verse, haiku, light verse, traditional. Submit maximum 3 poems. Length: 5-50 lines.

Tips "Writers need to apply online or mail in an application from an issue of the magazine."

$ INSIGHT

A Spiritual Lift for Teens, The Review and Herald Publishing Association, 55 W. Oak Ridge Dr., Hagerstown MD 21740. E-mail: insight@rhpa.org. Website: www.insightmagazine.org. **Contact:** Dwain Neilson Esmond, editor. **80% freelance written.** Weekly magazine covering spiritual life of teenagers. "*Insight* publishes true dramatic stories, interviews, and community and mission service features that relate directly to the lives of Christian teenagers, particularly those with a Seventh-day Adventist background." Estab. 1970. Circ. 20,000. Pays on publication. Publishes ms an average of 4 months after acceptance. Byline given. Buys first, second serial (reprint) rights. Editorial lead time 6 months. Submit seasonal material 6 months in advance. Accepts queries by mail, e-mail, fax. Responds in 1 month to mss. Sample copy for $2 and #10 SASE. Writer's guidelines online.

- "'Big Deal' appears in *Insight* often, covering a topic of importance to teens. Each feature contains: An opening story involving real teens (can be written in first-person), "Scripture Picture" (a sidebar that discusses what the Bible says about the topic) and another sidebar (optional) that adds more perspective and help.

Nonfiction How-to (teen relationships and experiences), humor, interview/profile, personal experience, photo feature, religious. **Buys 120 mss/year.** Send complete ms. Length: 500-2,000 words. **Pays $25-150 for assigned articles; $25-125 for unsolicited articles.**

Reprints Send ms with rights for sale noted and information about when and where the material previously appeared. Pays $50.

Photos State availability with submission. Reviews contact sheets, negatives, transparencies, prints. Buys one-time rights. Negotiates payment individually. Model releases required.

Columns/Departments Big Deal (topic of importance to teens) 1,200-1,700 words; Interviews (Christian culture figures, especially musicians), 2,000 words; It Happened to Me (first-person teen experiences containing spiritual insights), 1,000 words; On the Edge (dramatic true stories about Christians), 2,000 words; So I Said…(true short stories in the first person of common, everyday events and experiences that taught the writer something), 300-500 words. Send complete ms. **Pays $25-125.**

Tips "Skim 2 months of *Insight*. Write about your teen experiences. Use informed, contemporary style and vocabulary. Become a Christian if you haven't already."

Ⓝ $ $ KEYNOTER MAGAZINE

Key Club International, 3636 Woodview Trace, Indianapolis IN 46268-3196. E-mail: keynoter@kiwanis.org. Website: www.keyclub.org. **Contact:** Executive Editor. **65% freelance written.** Monthly magazine for youth (December/January combined issue), distributed to members of Key Club International, a high school service organization for young men and women. Estab. 1946. Circ. 171,000. **Pays on acceptance.** Publishes ms an average of 5 months after acceptance. Byline given. Buys first North American serial rights. Submit seasonal material 7 months in advance. Accepts queries by mail, e-mail. Accepts simultaneous submissions. Responds in 2 months to queries. Sample copy for 65¢ and 8½ × 11 SAE. Writer's guidelines online.

Nonfiction "We would like to receive self-help and school-related nonfiction on leadership, community service, and teen issues." Book excerpts (included in articles), general interest (for intelligent teen audience), historical/nostalgic (generally not accepted), how-to (advice on how teens can enhance the quality of lives or communities), humor (accepted if adds to story), interview/profile (rarely purchased), new product (affecting teens), photo feature (if subject is right), technical (understandable and interesting to teen audience), travel (must apply to club travel schedule), academic, self-help, subjects that entertain and inform teens on topics that relate directly to their lives. "*Please, no first-person confessions, fiction, or articles that are written down to our teen readers. No filler, or book, movie, or music reviews.*" **Buys 10-15 mss/year.** Query with SASE. Length: 1,200-1,500 words. Sometimes pays expenses of writers on assignment.

Reprints Send tearsheet or photocopy and information about when and where the material previously appeared.

Photos State availability with submission. Reviews negatives, color contact sheets. Buys one-time rights. Payment for photos included in payment for ms. Identification of subjects required.

Tips "We want to see articles written with attention to style and detail that will enrich the world of teens. Articles must be thoroughly researched and must draw on interviews with nationally and internationally respected sources. Our readers are 13-18, mature, and dedicated to community service. We are very committed to working with good writers, and if we see something we like in a well-written query, we'll try to work it through to publication."

$ $LISTEN MAGAZINE

Celebrating Positive Choices, The Health Connection, 55 W. Oak Ridge Dr., Hagerstown MD 21740. (301)393-4010. E-mail: editor@listenmagazine.org. Website: www.listenmagazine.org. **Contact:** Anita Jacobs, editor. **50% freelance written.** Monthly magazine specializing in tobacco, drug, and alcohol prevention, presenting positive alternatives to various tobacco, drug, and alcohol dependencies. "*Listen* is used in many high school classes and by professionals: medical personnel, counselors, law enforcement officers, educators, youth workers, etc. *Listen* publishes true-to-lifestories about giving teens choices about real-life situations and moral issues in a secular way." Circ. 40,000. Publishes ms an average of 6 months after acceptance. Byline given. Pays on acceptance for first rights for use in *Listen*, reprints, and associated material. Accepts queries by mail, e-mail, fax. Accepts previously published material. Accepts simultaneous submissions. Responds in 2 months to queries. Sample copy for $2 and 9×12 SASE. Writer's guidelines for SASE, by e-mail, fax or on website.

   O─¬ Break in with "a fresh approach with a surprise ending."

Nonfiction Seeks articles that deal with causes of drug use such as poor self-concept, family relations, social skills, peer pressure. Especially interested in youth-slanted articles or personality interviews encouraging nonalcoholic and nondrug ways of life and showing positive alternatives. Also interested in good activity articles of interest to teens; an activity that teens would want to do instead of taking abusive substances because they're bored. Teenage point of view is essential. Also seeks narratives which portray teens dealing with youth conflicts, especially those related to the use of or temptation to use harmful substances. Growth of the main character should be shown. "Submit an article with an ending that catches you by surprise. We don't want typical alcoholic story/skid-row bum, or AA stories. We are also being inundated with drunk-driving accident stories. Unless yours is unique, consider another topic." **Buys 30-50 unsolicited mss/year.** Query. Length: 1,000-1,200 words. **Pays 5-10¢/word.** Sometimes pays expenses of writers on assignment.

Reprints Send photocopy of article or typed ms with rights for sale noted and information about when and where the material previously appeared. Pays their regular rates.

Photos Color photos preferred, but b&w acceptable. Purchased with accompanying ms. Captions required.

Fiction Anti-drug, alcohol, tobacco, positive role models. Query with published clips or send complete ms. Length: 1,000-1,200. **Pays $50-150, and 3 contributor's copies; additional copies $2.**

Fillers Word square/general puzzles are also considered. **Pays $15.**

Tips "True stories are good, especially if they have a unique angle. Other authoritative articles need a fresh approach. In query, briefly summarize article idea and logic of why you feel it's good. Make sure you've read the magazine to understand our approach."

$ $LIVE

A Weekly Journal of Practical Christian Living, Gospel Publishing House, 1445 N. Boonville Ave., Springfield MO 65802-1894. (417)862-2781. Fax: (417)862-6059. E-mail: rl-live@gph.org. Website: www.radiantlife.org. **Contact:** Paul W. Smith, senior editor, adult resources. **100% freelance written.** Weekly magazine for weekly distribution covering practical Christian living. "*LIVE* is a take-home paper distributed weekly in young adult and adult Sunday school classes. We seek to encourage Christians in living for God through fiction and true stories which apply Biblical principles to everyday problems." Estab. 1928. Circ. 70,000. **Pays on acceptance.** Publishes ms an average of 18 months after acceptance. Byline given. Buys first, second serial (reprint) rights. Editorial lead time 12 months. Submit seasonal material 18 months in advance. Accepts queries by mail, e-mail, fax. Accepts simultaneous submissions. Responds in 2 weeks to queries; 6 weeks to mss. Sample copy for #10 SASE. Writer's guidelines for #10 SASE.

   O─¬ Break in with "true stories that demonstrate how the principles in the Bible work in everyday circumstances as well as crises."

Nonfiction Inspirational, religious. No preachy articles or stories that refer to religious myths (e.g., Santa Claus, Easter Bunny, etc.). **Buys 50-100 mss/year.** Send complete ms. Length: 400-1,500 words. **Pays 7-10¢/word.**

Reprints Send tearsheet, photocopy or typed ms with rights for sale noted and information about when and where the material previously appeared. Pays 7¢/word.

Photos Send photos with submission. Reviews 35mm transparencies and 3×4 prints or larger. Buys one-time rights. Offers $35-60/photo. Identification of subjects required.

Fiction Paul W. Smith, editor. Religious, inspirational, prose poem. No preachy fiction, fiction about Bible characters, or stories that refer to religious myths (e.g., Santa Claus, Easter Bunny, etc.). No science or Bible fiction. No controversial stories about such subjects as feminism, war or capital punishment. **Buys 20-50 mss/ year.** Send complete ms. Length: 800-1,600 words. **Pays 7-10¢/word.**

Poetry Free verse, haiku, light verse, traditional. **Buys 15-24 poems/year.** Submit maximum 3 poems. Length: 12-25 lines. **Pays $35-60.**

Fillers Anecdotes, short humor. **Buys 12-36/year.** Length: 300-600 words. **Pays 7-10¢/word.**

Tips "Don't moralize or be preachy. Provide human interest articles with Biblical life application. Stories should consist of action, not just thought-life; interaction, not just insight. Heroes and heroines should rise above failures, take risks for God, prove that scriptural principles meet their needs. Conflict and suspense should increase to a climax! Avoid pious conclusions. Characters should be interesting, believable, and realistic. Avoid stereotypes. Characters should be active, not just pawns to move the plot along. They should confront conflict and change in believable ways. Describe the character's looks and reveal his personality through his actions to such an extent that the reader feels he has met that person. Readers should care about the character enough to finish the story. Feature racial, ethnic, and regional characters in rural and urban settings."

$ $ THE NEW ERA

50 E. North Temple, Salt Lake City UT 84150. (801)240-2951. Fax: (801)240-2270. E-mail: cur-editorial-newera@ ldschurch.org. **Contact:** Richard Romney, managing editor. **20% freelance written.** Monthly magazine for young people (ages 12-18) of the Church of Jesus Christ of Latter-day Saints (Mormon), their church leaders and teachers. Estab. 1971. Circ. 230,000. **Pays on acceptance.** Publishes ms an average of 1 year after acceptance. Byline given. Buys all rights. Submit seasonal material 1 year in advance. Accepts queries by mail, e-mail, fax. Responds in 2 months to queries. Sample copy for $1.50 and 9×12 SAE with 2 first-class stamps. Writer's guidelines for SASE.

Nonfiction Material that shows how the Church of Jesus Christ of Latter-day Saints is relevant in the lives of young people today. Must capture the excitement of being a young Latter-day Saint. Special interest in the experiences of young Mormons in other countries. No general library research or formula pieces without the *New Era* slant and feel. How-to, humor, inspirational, interview/profile, personal experience, informational. Query. Length: 150-1,200 words. **Pays 3-12¢/word.** Pays expenses of writers on assignment.

Photos Uses b&w photos and transparencies with manuscripts. Individual photos used for *Photo of the Month.* Payment depends on use, $10-125 per photo.

Columns/Departments Of All Things (news of young Mormons around the world); How I Know; Scripture Lifeline. **Pays 3-12¢/word.**

Poetry Must relate to editorial viewpoint. Free verse, light verse, traditional, blank verse, all other forms. **Pays 25¢/line minimum.**

Tips "The writer must be able to write from a Mormon point of view. We're especially looking for stories about successful family relationships and personal growth. We anticipate using more staff-produced material. This means freelance quality will have to improve. Try breaking in with a department piece for 'How I Know' or 'Scripture Lifeline.' Well-written, personal experiences are always in demand."

N $ $ $ $ SEVENTEEN

1440 Broadway, 13th Floor, New York NY 10018. (917)934-6500. Fax: (917)934-6574. Website: www.seventeen. com. Features Assistant: Melanie Abrahams. Features Editor: Sarah Nanus. **20% freelance written.** Monthly magazine. "*Seventeen* is a young woman's first fashion and beauty magazine. Tailored for young women in their teens and early twenties, *Seventeen* covers fashion, beauty, health, fitness, food, college, entertainment, fiction, plus crucial personal and global issues." Estab. 1944. Circ. 2,400,000. **Pays on acceptance.** Publishes ms an average of 6 months after acceptance. Byline given. Offers 25% kill fee. Buys one-time rights. Accepts queries by mail. Responds in 3 months to queries. Sample copy not available. Writer's guidelines available online.

O— Break in with the Who Knew section, which contains shorter items, or *Quiz.*

Nonfiction Articles and features of general interest to young women who are concerned with intimate relationships and how to realize their potential in the world; strong emphasis on topicality and service. Send brief outline and query, including typical lead paragraph, summing up basic idea of article, with clips of previously published works. Articles are commissioned after outlines are submitted and approved. Length: 1,200-2,500 words. **Pays $1/word, occasionally more for assigned articles.** Pays expenses of writers on assignment.

Photos Photos usually by assignment only. Elizabeth Kildahl, photo editor.

Fiction Thoughtful, well-written stories on subjects of interest to girls between the ages of 12 and 21. Avoid formula stories—"She's blonde and pretty; I'm not"—no heavy moralizing or condescension of any sort. We also have an annual fiction contest. No science fiction, action/adventure or pornography. Query with published clips or send complete ms. Length: 750-3,000 words. **Pays $500-2,000.**

⬛ The online magazine carries original content not found in the print edition. Contact: Fiona Gibb, editorial director.

Tips "Writers have to ask themselves whether or not they feel they can find the right tone for a *Seventeen* article—a tone which is empathetic, yet never patronizing; lively, yet not superficial. Not all writers feel comfortable with, understand, or like teenagers. If you don't like them, *Seventeen* is the wrong market for you. An excellent way to break in to the magazine is by contributing ideas for quizzes or the 'My Story' (personal essay) column."

$ $ SPIRIT

Lectionary-based Weekly for Catholic Teens, Good Ground Press, 1884 Randolph Ave., St. Paul MN 55105-1700. (651)690-7010. Fax: (651)690-7039. E-mail: jmcsj9@aol.com. Managing Editor: Therese Sherlock, CSJ. **Contact:** Joan Mitchell, CSJ, editor. **50% freelance written.** Weekly newsletter for religious education of Catholic high schoolers. "We want realistic fiction and nonfiction that raises current ethical and religious questions and that deals with conflicts that teens face in multi-racial contexts. The fact we are a religious publication does *not* mean we want pious, moralistic fiction." Estab. 1981. Circ. 26,000. Pays on publication. Publishes ms an average of 6 months after acceptance. Byline given. Buys all rights. Editorial lead time 6 months. Submit seasonal material 6 months in advance. Accepts queries by mail, e-mail, fax. Accepts simultaneous submissions. Responds in 1 month to queries. Sample copy and writer's guidelines free.

Nonfiction "No Christian confessional, born-again pieces." Interview/profile, personal experience, religious, Roman Catholic leaders, human interest features, social justice leaders, projects, humanitarians. **Buys 4 mss/year.** Query with published clips or send complete ms. Length: 1,000-1,200 words. **Pays $200-225 for assigned articles; $150 for unsolicited articles.**

Photos State availability with submission. Reviews 8×10 prints. Buys one-time rights. Offers $85-125/photo. Identification of subjects required.

Fiction "We want realistic pieces for and about teens—nonpedantic, nonpious. We need good Christmas stories that show spirit of the season, and stories about teen relationship conflicts (boy/girl, parent/teen)." Conflict vignettes. **Buys 10 mss/year.** Query with published clips or send complete ms. Length: 1,000-1,200 words. **Pays $150-200.**

Tips "Writers must be able to write from and for teen point of view rather than adult or moralistic point of view. In nonfiction, interviewed teens must speak for themselves. Query to receive call for stories, spec sheet, sample issues."

Ⓝ $ $ ⊘ TEEN MAGAZINE

Hearst Magazines, 3000 Ocean Park Blvd., Suite 3048, Santa Monica CA 90405. (310)664-2950. Fax: (310)664-2959. Website: www.teenmag.com. **Contact:** Jane Fort, editor-in-chief (fashion, beauty, TeenPROM); Damon Romine, deputy editor (entertainment, movies, TV, music, books, covers); Heather Hewitt, managing editor (manufacturing, advertising, new products, what's hot). Quarterly magazine. "We are a pure Jr. high school female audience. *TEEN* teens are upbeat and want to be informed." Estab. 1957. **Pays on acceptance.** Byline given. Buys all rights.

● No unsolicited materials accepted.

Nonfiction How-to, interview/profile, travel, arts/crafts, fashion, games/puzzles, careers, cooking, health, multicultural, problem-solving, social issues. Does not want to see adult-oriented, adult point of view." **Pays $50-500.**

Fiction Does not want to see "that which does not apply to our market—i.e., science fiction, history, religious, adult-oriented." **Pays $100-400.**

Ⓝ $ $ $ $ TEEN PEOPLE

Times, Inc., 1271 Avenue of The Americas, New York NY 10020. (212)522-1264. Fax: (212)467-4633. E-mail: teenpeople@aol.com. Website: www.teenpeople.com. Editor: Amy Barnett. Monthly magazine that mixes entertainment with real world issues. Circ. 1,470,000. Sample copy not available.

Ⓝ TEEN VOGUE

Condé Nast Publications, 4 Times Square, 9th Floor, New York NY 10036. (212)286-8085. Fax: (212)286-7543. Website: www.teenvogue.com. Editor: Amy Astley. Magazine published 10 times/year. Written for sophisticated teenage girls age 12 to 17 years old. Circ. 450,000. Editorial lead time 2 months. Sample copy not available.

TIGER BEAT

Laufer Media, 6430 Sunset Blvd., Suite 700, Hollywood CA 90028. (323)462-4267. Fax: (323)462-4341. Editor: Leesa Coble. Monthly magazine. Leading teen entertainment magazine written for girls. Features news, gossip and features on today's hottest stars. Circ. 200,000. Editorial lead time 2 months. Sample copy not available.

$ $◻ WHAT MAGAZINE

What! Publishers Inc., 108-93 Lombard Ave., Winnipeg MB R3B 3B1, Canada. (204)985-8160. Fax: (204)957-5638. E-mail: what@whatmagazine.ca. **Contact:** Barbara Chabai, editor/publisher. **40% freelance written.** Magazine published 5 times during the school year covering teen issues and pop culture. *"What Magazine* is distributed to high school students across Canada. We produce a mag that is empowering, interactive and entertaining. We respect the reader—today's teens are smart and creative (and critical)." Estab. 1987. Circ. 250,000. Pays 1 month after publication. Publishes ms an average of 3 months after acceptance. Byline given. Offers negotiable kill fee. Buys first North American serial rights. Editorial lead time 5 months. Submit seasonal material 5 months in advance. Accepts queries by mail, e-mail, fax. Responds in 2 months to queries; 1 month to mss. Sample copy for 9×12 SAE with Canadian postage. Writer's guidelines for #10 SAE with Canadian postage.

Nonfiction General interest, interview/profile, issue-oriented features. No cliché teen material. **Buys 6-10 mss/year.** Query with published clips. Length: 700-1,900 words. **Pays $175-400 (Canadian).** Sometimes pays expenses of writers on assignment.

Photos Send photos with submission. Reviews transparencies, 4×6 prints. Negotiates payment individually. Identification of subjects required.

Tips "We have an immediate need for savvy freelancers to contribute features, short articles, interviews, and reviews that speak to our intelligent teen audience. Looking for fresh talent and new ideas in the areas of entertainment, pop culture, teen issues, international events as they relate to readers, celebs and 'real people' profiles, lifestyle articles, extreme sports and any other stories of relevance to today's Canadian teen."

$WINNER

Saying No To Drugs and Yes To Life, The Health Connection, 55 W. Oak Ridge Dr., Hagerstown MD 21740. (301)393-3294. Fax: (301)393-3294. E-mail: winner@healthconnection.org. Website: www.winnermagazine.org. **Contact:** Anita Jacobs, editor. **30% freelance written.** Monthly magazine covering positive lifestyle choices for students in grades 4-6. *"Winner* is a teaching tool to help students learn the dangers in abusive substances, such as tobacco, alcohol, and other drugs, as well as at-risk behaviors. It also focuses on everyday problems such as dealing with divorce, sibling rivalry, coping with grief, and healthy diet, to mention just a few." Estab. 1956. Circ. 12,000. **Pays on acceptance.** Publishes ms an average of 6-9 months after acceptance. Byline sometimes given. Offers 50% kill fee. Buys first North American serial, first rights. Editorial lead time 5 months. Submit seasonal material 6-8 months in advance. Accepts queries by mail, e-mail, fax, phone. Accepts simultaneous submissions. Responds in 4-6 weeks to queries; 2-3 months to mss. Sample copy for $2 and 9×12 SAE with 2 first-class stamps. Writer's guidelines for SASE, by e-mail, fax or on website.

Nonfiction General interest, humor, drug/alcohol/tobacco activities, personalities, family relationships, friends. No occult, mysteries. "I prefer true-to-life stories." Query or send complete ms. Length: 600-650 words. **Pays $50-80.** Sometimes pays expenses of writers on assignment.

Photos Doug Bendall, designer. State availability of or send photos with submission. Reviews GIF/JPEG files. Buys one-time rights. Negotiates payment individually. Model releases required.

Columns/Departments Personality (kids making a difference in their community), 600-650 words; Fun & Games (dangers of tobacco, alcohol, and other drugs), 400 words. **Buys 9 mss/year.** Query. **Pays $50-80.**

Fiction True-to-life stories dealing with problems preteens face. No suspense or mystery. **Buys 18 mss/year.** Send complete ms. Length: 600-650 words. **Pays $50-80.**

YM

Gruner & Jahr, 15 E. 26th St., New York NY 10010. E-mail: jbanin@ym.com; mglassman@ym.com. Website: www.ym.com. Editor-in-Chief: Linda Fears. Executive Editor: Tamara Glenny. **Contact:** Jana Banin or Melissa Glassman. **75% freelance written.** Magazine published 11 times/year covering teenage girls/dating. "We are a national magazine for young women ages 13-24. They're bright, enthusiastic, and inquisitive. Our goal is to guide them—in effect, to be a 'best friend' and help them through the many exciting, yet often challenging, experiences of young adulthood." Estab. 1940s. Circ. 2,200,000. **Pays on acceptance.** Byline given. Offers 25% kill fee. Buys all rights. Editorial lead time 4 months. Submit seasonal material 5 months in advance. Accepts simultaneous submissions. Responds in 1 month to queries. Writer's guidelines free.

Nonfiction How-to, interview/profile, personal experience, first-person stories. Special issues: "YM publishes 1 special prom issue a year." Query with published clips. Length: 2,000 words maximum. Pays expenses of writers on assignment.

Tips "Our relationship articles are loaded with advice from psychologists and real teenagers. Areas most open to freelancers are: 2,000-word stories covering a personal triumph over adversity—incorporating a topical social/political problem; 2,000-word relationship stories; 1,200-word relationship articles; and 800-word quizzes. All articles should be lively and informative, but not academic in tone, and any 'expert' opinions (psychologists, authors, and teachers) should be included as a supplement to the feelings and experiences of young women. Do not call our offices."

$ YOUNG & ALIVE

Christian Record Services, P.O. Box 6097, Lincoln NE 68506. Website: www.christianrecord.org. **Contact:** Gaylena Gibson, editor. **95% freelance written.** Large-print Christian material for sight-impaired people age 12-25 (also in braille), covering health, handicapped people, uplifting articles. "Write for an interdenominational Christian audience—we also like to portray handicapped individuals living normal lives or their positive impact on those around them." Submit seasonal material anytime. Estab. 1976. Circ. 25,000 large print; 3,000 braille. **Pays on acceptance.** Publishes ms an average of 3 years after acceptance. Byline given. Buys one-time rights. Accepts simultaneous submissions. Responds in 1 year to mss. Sample copy for 7×10 SAE with 5 first-class stamps. Writer's guidelines for #10 SASE or included with sample copy.

Nonfiction Essays, general interest, historical/nostalgic, humor, inspirational, personal experience, travel, adventure (true), biography, camping, careers, handicapped, health, hobbies, holidays, nature, sports. **Buys 40 mss/year.** Send complete ms. Length: 200-1,400 words. **Pays 4-5¢/word, and complimentary copies.**

Photos Send photos with submission. Reviews 3×5 to 10×12 prints. Buys one-time rights. Negotiates payment individually. Model releases required.

Fillers Anecdotes, facts, short humor. Length: 300 words maximum. **Pays 4¢/word.**

Tips "Make sure article has a strong ending that ties everything together. Pretend someone else wrote it—would it hold your interest? Draw your readers into the story by being specific rather than abstract or general."

$ $ YOUNG SALVATIONIST

The Salvation Army, P.O. Box 269, Alexandria VA 22313-0269. (703)684-5500. Fax: (703)684-5539. E-mail: ys@usn.salvationarmy.org. Website: www.thewarcry.com. **Contact:** Lt. Col. Marlene Chase, editor. **80% freelance written.** Monthly magazine for high school teens. "Only material with Christian perspective with practical real-life application will be considered." Circ. 48,000. **Pays on acceptance.** Publishes ms an average of 6 months after acceptance. Byline given. Buys first North American serial, first, one-time, second serial (reprint) rights. Submit seasonal material 6 months in advance. Responds in 2 months to mss. Sample copy for 9×12 SAE with 3 first-class stamps or on website. Writer's guidelines and theme list for #10 SASE or on website.

● Works with a small number of new/unpublished writers each year. Accepts complete mss by mail and e-mail.

○ᴜ "Our greatest need is for nonfiction pieces based in real life rather than theory or theology. Practical living articles are especially needed. We receive many fiction submissions but few good nonfiction."

Nonfiction "Articles should deal with issues of relevance to teens (high school students) today; avoid 'preachiness' or moralizing." How-to, humor, inspirational, interview/profile, personal experience, photo feature, religious. **Buys 60 mss/year.** Send complete ms. Length: 1,000-1,500 words. **Pays 15¢/word for first rights.**

Reprints Send tearsheet, photocopy or typed ms with rights for sale noted and information about when and where the material previously appeared. Pays 10¢/word for reprints.

Fiction Only a small amount is used. Adventure, fantasy, humorous, religious, romance, science fiction, (all from a Christian perspective). **Buys few mss/year.** Length: 500-1,200 words. **Pays 15¢/word.**

Tips "Study magazine, familiarize yourself with the unique 'Salvationist' perspective of *Young Salvationist*; learn a little about the Salvation Army; media, sports, sex, and dating are strongest appeal."

TRAVEL, CAMPING & TRAILER

$ AAA GOING PLACES

Magazine for Today's Traveler, AAA Auto Club South, 1515 N. Westshore Blvd., Tampa FL 33607. (813)289-5923. Fax: (813)288-7935. Editor-In-Chief: Sandy Klim. **50% freelance written.** Bimonthly magazine on auto tips, cruise travel, tours. Estab. 1982. Circ. 2,500,000. Pays on publication. Publishes ms an average of 6 months after acceptance. Byline given. Buys one-time rights. Submit seasonal material 9 months in advance. Accepts simultaneous submissions. Responds in 2 months to queries; 2 months to mss. Sample copy not available. Writer's guidelines for SAE.

Nonfiction Travel stories feature domestic and international destinations with practical information and where to stay, dine, and shop, as well as personal anecdotes and historical background; they generally relate to tours currently offered by AAA Travel Agency. Historical/nostalgic, how-to, humor, interview/profile, personal experience, photo feature, travel. Special issues: Cruise Guide (September/October) and Europe Issue (January/February). **Buys 15 mss/year.** Send complete ms. Length: 500-1,500 words. **Pays $50/printed page.**

Photos State availability with submission. Reviews 2×2 transparencies. Offers no additional payment for photos accepted with ms. Captions required.

Columns/Departments AAAway We Go (local attractions in Florida, Georgia, or Tennessee).

Tips "We prefer lively, upbeat stories that appeal to a well-traveled, sophisticated audience, bearing in mind that AAA is a conservative company."

N $ $ AAA MIDWEST TRAVELER

AAA Auto Club of Missouri, 12901 N. 40 Dr., St. Louis MO 63141. (314)523-7350 ext. 6301. Fax: (314)523-6982. E-mail: dreinhardt@aaamissouri.com. Website: www.aaatravelermags.com. Editor: Michael J. Right. **Contact:** Deborah Reinhardt, managing editor. **80% freelance written.** Bimonthly magazine covering travel and automotive safety. "We provide members with useful information on travel, auto safety and related topics." Estab. 1901. Circ. 440,000. **Pays on acceptance.** Byline given. Offers $50 kill fee. Not copyrighted. Buys first North American serial, second serial (reprint), electronic rights. Editorial lead time 1 year. Submit seasonal material 6 months in advance. Accepts queries by mail, e-mail, fax. Accepts simultaneous submissions. Responds in 1 month to queries; 1 month to mss. Sample copy for 10×13 SAE and 4 first-class stamps. Writer's guidelines for #10 SASE.

Nonfiction Travel. No humor, fiction, poetry or cartoons. **Buys 20-30 mss/year.** Query; query with published clips the first time. Length: 800-1,200 words. **Pays $250-350.**

Photos State availability with submission. Reviews transparencies, prints. Buys one-time and electronic rights. Offers no additional payment for photos accepted with ms. Captions required.

Tips "Send queries between December and February, as we plan our calendar for the following year. Request a copy. Serious writers ask for media kit to help them target their piece. Travel destinations and tips are most open to freelancers; all departments and auto-related news handled by staff. We see too many 'Here's a recount of our family vacation' manuscripts. Go easy on first-person accounts."

$ $ ARUBA NIGHTS

Nights Publications, Inc., 1831 Rene Levesque Blvd. W., Montreal QC H3H 1R4, Canada. (514)931-1987. Fax: (514)931-6273. E-mail: editor@nightspublications.com. Website: www.nightspublications.com. **Contact:** Sonya Plowman, editor. **90% freelance written.** Annual magazine covering the Aruban vacation lifestyle experience with an upscale, upbeat touch. Estab. 1988. Circ. 225,000. **Pays on acceptance.** Publishes ms an average of 9 months after acceptance. Byline given for feature articles. Buys North American and Caribbean serial rights. Editorial lead time 1 month. Accepts queries by mail, e-mail, fax. Responds in 2 weeks to queries; 1 month to mss. Writer's guidelines by e-mail.

O— *Aruba Nights* is looking for more articles on nightlife experiences.

Nonfiction General interest, historical/nostalgic, how-to (relative to Aruba vacationers), humor, inspirational, interview/profile, opinion, personal experience, photo feature, travel, ecotourism, Aruban culture, art, activities, entertainment, topics relative to vacationers in Aruba. "No negative pieces." **Buys 5-10 mss/year.** Send complete ms, include SAE with Canadian postage or IRC. Length: 250-750 words. **Pays $100-250.**

Photos State availability with submission. Reviews transparencies. Buys one-time rights. Pays $50/photo. Captions, identification of subjects, model releases required.

Tips "Be descriptive and entertaining and make sure stories are factually correct. Stories should immerse the reader in a sensory adventure. Focus on specific, individual aspects of the Aruban lifestyle and vacation experience (e.g., art, music, culture, a colorful local character, a personal experience, etc.), rather than generalized overviews. Provide an angle that will be entertaining to vacationers who are already there. E-mail submissions preferred."

$ $ ASU TRAVEL GUIDE

ASU Travel Guide, Inc., 1525 Francisco Blvd. E., San Rafael CA 94901. (415)459-0300. Fax: (415)459-0494. E-mail: christopher_gil@asutravelguide.com. Website: www.asutravelguide.com. **Contact:** Christopher Gil, managing editor. **80% freelance written.** Quarterly guidebook covering international travel features and travel discounts for well-traveled airline employees. Estab. 1970. Circ. 40,000. **Pays on acceptance.** Publishes ms an average of 4 months after acceptance. Byline given. Buys first North American serial, first, second serial (reprint) rights. Submit seasonal material 6 months in advance. Accepts previously published material. Accepts simultaneous submissions. Responds in 1 year to queries; 1 year to mss. Sample copy for 6×9 SAE and 5 first-class stamps. Writer's guidelines for #10 SASE.

Nonfiction International travel articles "similar to those run in consumer magazines. Not interested in amateur efforts from inexperienced travelers or personal experience articles that don't give useful information to other travelers." Destination pieces only; no "Tips on Luggage" articles. Unsolicited mss or queries without SASE will not be acknowledged. No telephone queries. Travel (international). **Buys 16 mss/year.** Length: 1,800 words. **Pays $200.**

Reprints Send tearsheet and information about when and where the material previously appeared. Pays 100% of amount paid for an original article.

Photos "Interested in clear, high-contrast photos." Reviews 5×7 and 8×10 b&w or color prints, JPEGs (300 dpi). Payment for photos is included in article price; photos from tourist offices are acceptable.

Tips "Query with samples of travel writing and a list of places you've recently visited. We appreciate clean and simple style. Keep verbs in the active tense and involve the reader in what you write. Avoid 'cute' writing, coined words, and stale clichés. The most frequent mistakes made by writers in completing an article for us are: 1) Lazy writing—using words to describe a place that could describe any destination such as 'there is so much to do in (fill in destination) that whole guidebooks have been written about it'; 2) Including fare and tour package information—our readers make arrangements through their own airline."

$⬚ BONAIRE NIGHTS

Nights Publications, Inc., 1831 René Levesque Blvd. W., Montreal QC H3H 1R4, Canada. (514)931-1987. Fax: (514)931-6273. E-mail: editor@nightspublications.com. **Contact:** Sonya N. Plowman, editor. **90% freelance written.** Annual magazine covering Bonaire vacation experience. Estab. 1993. Circ. 65,000. Byline given for features. Buys North American and Caribbean serial rights. Editorial lead time 1 month. Accepts queries by mail, e-mail, fax. Responds in 2 weeks to queries; 1 month to mss. Writer's guidelines by e-mail.

Nonfiction General interest, historical/nostalgic, how-to, humor, interview/profile, opinion, personal experience, photo feature, travel, lifestyle, local culture, art, architecture, activities, scuba diving, snorkeling, ecotourism. **Buys 6-9 mss/year.** E-mail submissions preferred. Mailed mss must include an e-mail address for correspondence. Length: 250-750 words. **Pays $100.**

Photos State availability with submission. Pays $50/published photo. Captions, identification of subjects, model releases required.

Tips "Focus on the Bonaire lifestyle, what sets it apart from other islands. We want personal experience on specific attractions and culture, not generalized overviews. Be positive and provide an angle that will appeal to vacationers who are already there. Our style is upbeat, friendly, fluid, and descriptive."

⬚ CAMPING CANADA'S RV LIFESTYLE MAGAZINE

1020 Brevik Place, Unit 5, Mississauga ON L4W 4N7, Canada. (905)624-8218. Fax: (905)624-6764. E-mail: editor@rvlifemag.com. Website: www.rvlifemag.com. **50% freelance written.** Magazine published 7 times/year (monthly January-June and November). "*Camping Canada's RV Lifestyle Magazine* is geared to readers who enjoy travel/camping. Upbeat pieces only. Readers vary from owners of towable trailers or motorhomes to young families and entry-level campers (no tenting)." Estab. 1971. Circ. 51,000. Pays on publication. Byline given. Buys first North American serial rights. Editorial lead time 2 months. Responds in 1 month to queries; 2 months to mss. Sample copy for free. Writer's guidelines not available.

Nonfiction How-to, personal experience, technical, travel. No inexperienced, unresearched, or too general pieces. **Buys 20-30 mss/year.** Query. Length: 1,200-2,000 words. **Payment varies.**

Photos Send photos with submission. Buys one-time rights. Offers no additional payment for photos accepted with ms.

Tips "Pieces should be slanted toward RV living. All articles must have an RV slant. Canadian content regulations require 95% Canadian writers."

$ CAMPING TODAY

Official Publication of the Family Campers & RVers, 126 Hermitage Rd., Butler PA 16001-8509. (724)283-7401. **Contact:** DeWayne Johnston, June Johnston, editors. **30% freelance written.** Monthly official membership publication of the FCRV. *Camping Today* is "the largest nonprofit family camping and RV organization in the United States and Canada. Members are heavily oriented toward RV travel, both weekend and extended vacations. Concentration is on member activities in chapters. Group is also interested in conservation and wildlife. The majority of members are retired." Estab. 1983. Circ. 10,000. Pays on publication. Publishes ms an average of 6 months after acceptance. Byline given. Buys one-time rights. Submit seasonal material 3 months in advance. Accepts simultaneous submissions. Responds in 2 months to queries; 2 months to mss. Sample copy and guidelines for 4 first-class stamps. Writer's guidelines for #10 SASE.

Nonfiction Humor (camping or travel related), interview/profile (interesting campers), new product, technical (RVs related), travel (interesting places to visit by RV, camping). **Buys 10-15 mss/year.** Query by mail only or send complete ms with photos. Length: 750-2,000 words. **Pays $50-150.**

Reprints Send ms with rights for sale noted and information about when and where the material previously appeared. Pays 35-50% of amount paid for original article.

Photos "Need b&w or sharp color prints inside (we can make prints from slides) and vertical transparencies for cover." Send photos with submission. Captions required.

Tips "Freelance material on RV travel, RV maintenance/safety, and items of general camping interest throughout the United States and Canada will receive special attention. Good photos increase your chances."

$ $ $COAST TO COAST MAGAZINE

Affinity Group, Inc., 2575 Vista Del Mar Dr., Ventura CA 93001. (805)667-4100. Fax: (805)667-4217. E-mail: vlaw@affinitygroup.com. Website: www.coastresorts.com. **Contact:** Valerie Law, editorial director. **80% free-lance written.** Magazine published 8 times/year for members of Coast to Coast Resorts. *"Coast to Coast* focuses on travel, recreation, and good times, with most stories targeted to recreational vehicle owners." Estab. 1983. Circ. 150,000. **Pays on acceptance.** Publishes ms an average of 4 months after acceptance. Byline given. Offers 33% kill fee. Buys first North American serial rights. Editorial lead time 5 months. Submit seasonal material 5 months in advance. Accepts queries by mail, e-mail, fax. Accepts previously published material. Accepts simultaneous submissions. Responds in 6-8 weeks to queries; 1-2 months to mss. Sample copy for $4 and 9 × 12 SASE. Writer's guidelines for #10 SASE.

Nonfiction Book excerpts, essays, general interest, how-to, interview/profile, new product, personal experience, photo feature, technical, travel. No poetry, cartoons. **Buys 70 mss/year.** Query with published clips or send complete ms. Length: 800-2,500 words. **Pays $75-1,000.**

Reprints Send photocopy and information about when and where the material previously appeared. Pays approximately 50% of amount paid for original article.

Columns/Departments Pays $150-400.

Tips "Send clips or other writing samples with queries, or story ideas will not be considered."

$ $⬚ CURACAO NIGHTS

Nights Publications, Inc., 1831 Rene Levesque Blvd. W., Montreal QC H3H 1R4, Canada. (514)931-1987. Fax: (514)931-6273. E-mail: editor@nightspublications.com. **Contact:** Sonya N. Plowman, editor. **90% freelance written.** Annual magazine covering the Curacao vacation experience. "We are seeking upbeat, entertaining lifestyle articles; colorful profiles of locals; lively features on culture, activities, nightlife, ecotourism, special events, gambling, how-to features, humor. Our audience is North American vacationers." Estab. 1989. Circ. 155,000. Byline given. Buys North American and Caribbean serial rights. Editorial lead time 1 month. Accepts queries by mail, e-mail, fax. Responds in 2 weeks to queries; 1 month to mss. Writer's guidelines by e-mail.

Nonfiction General interest, historical/nostalgic, how-to (help a vacationer get the most from their vacation), humor, interview/profile, opinion, personal experience, photo feature, travel, ecotourism, lifestyle, local culture, art, activities, nightlife, topics relative to vacationers in Curacao. "No negative pieces, generic copy, or stale rewrites." **Buys 5-10 mss/year.** Query with published clips, include SASE and either Canadian postage or IRC, though e-mail submissions are preferred. Length: 250-750 words. **Pays $100-300.**

Photos State availability with submission. Reviews transparencies. Buys one-time rights. Pays $50/photo. Captions, identification of subjects, model releases required.

Tips "Demonstrate your voice in your query letter. Focus on individual aspects of the island lifestyle and vacation experience (e.g., art, music, culture, a colorful local character, a personal experience, etc.), rather than a generalized overview. Provide an angle that will be entertaining to vacationers who are already on the island. Our style is upbeat, friendly, and fluid."

Ⓝ $ $DURANGO MAGAZINE

For People Who Love Durango, Schultz & Associates, Inc., P.O. Box 3408, Durango CO 81302. (970)385-4030. Fax: (970)385-4436. E-mail: drgomag@animas.net. Website: www.durangomagazine.com. **Contact:** Julianne W. Schultz, editor/publisher. **75% freelance written.** Semiannual magazine covering travel and tourism, city and regional. "Readers want to know what to see and do in the Durango area. Locals need more in-depth information than visitors, but subjects of interest to both are covered. People profiles, area attractions, history, arts & culture, outdoor pursuits, entertainment are subjects covered." Estab. 1986. Circ. 325,000. Pays on publication. Publishes ms an average of 3 months after acceptance. Byline given. Offers 50% kill fee. Buys first North American serial rights. Editorial lead time 4 months. Submit seasonal material 5 months in advance. Accepts queries by mail, e-mail. Accepts previously published material. Accepts simultaneous submissions. Responds in 6 weeks to queries. Sample copy for $3.95, plus mailing. Writer's guidelines free.

Nonfiction Book excerpts, historical/nostalgic, humor, interview/profile, personal experience, photo feature, travel. Does not want to see anything not assigned. Query with or without published clips. **Pays 30-50¢/word.** Sometimes pays expenses of writers on assignment.

Photos State availability of or send photos with submission. Buys one-time rights. Negotiates payment individually. Identification of subjects required.

$ $ $ $ENDLESS VACATION MAGAZINE

Endless Vacation, 9998 N. Michigan Rd., Carmel IN 46032-9640. (317)805-8120. Fax: (317)805-9507. Website: www.evmediakit.com.; www.rci.com. **Contact:** Julie Woodard, senior editor. Prefers to work with published/ established writers. Bimonthly magazine. *"Endless Vacation* is the vacation-idea magazine edited for people who love to travel. Each issue offers articles for America's dedicated and frequent leisure travelers—time-share owners. Articles and features explore the world through a variety of vacation opportunities and options for travelers who average 4 weeks of leisure travel each year." Estab. 1974. Circ. 1,541,107. **Pays on acceptance.** Publishes ms an average of 6 months after acceptance. Byline given. Buys first North American serial rights. Accepts queries by mail, e-mail, fax. Accepts simultaneous submissions. Responds in 2 months to queries. Sample copy for $5 and 9×12 SAE with 5 first-class stamps. Writer's guidelines for #10 SASE.

Nonfiction Most articles are from established writers already published in *Endless Vacation. Accepts very few unsolicited pieces.* **Buys 30 feature mss/year.** Query with published clips (no phone calls). Length: 500-1,500 words. **Pays $500-1,500 for feature articles.** Sometimes pays expenses of writers on assignment.

Photos Reviews transparencies, 35mm slides. Buys one-time rights. Pays $300-1,300/photo. Identification of subjects required.

Columns/Departments Weekender (on domestic weekend vacation travel); Healthy Traveler; Cruise Currents; Family Vacationing; Destinations, up to 1,200 words. Also Taste (on food-related travel topics) and news items for Ready, Set, Go column on travel news, products, and the useful and unique in travel, 100-200 words. **Pays $100-900.**

Tips "Study the magazine and the writer's guidelines before you query us. Also check out www.evmediakit.com, which includes a reader profile and the magazine's current editorial calendar. The best way to break in to writing for *Endless Vacation* is through departments (Weekender, for example) and smaller pieces (Ready, Set, Go and Taste). Queries should be well developed."

[N] $ESCAPEES MAGAZINE

Sharing the RV Lifestyle, Escapees Inc., 100 Rainbow Dr., Livingston TX 77351-9300. (936)327-8873. Fax: (936)327-4388. E-mail: editor@escapees.com. Website: www.escapees.com. Editor: Janice Lasko. **Contact:** Ann Rollo or Tammy Johnson, editorial assistants. **90% freelance written.** Bimonthly magazine published for members of Escapees RV Club. "Articles must be RV related. *Escapees Magazine* readers are seeking RVing knowledge beyond what is found in conventional RV magazines." Estab. 1978. Circ. 35,000. Pays on publication. Publishes ms an average of 6 months after acceptance. Byline given. Buys first North American serial, first, one-time, second serial or electronic rights. Editorial lead time 6 months. Submit seasonal material 6 months in advance. Accepts previously published material. Writer's guidelines online.

Nonfiction All articles must be RV related. General interest, historical/nostalgic, how-to, humor, inspirational, interview/profile, new product, personal experience, photo feature, technical, travel, mechanical; finances; working; volunteering; boondocking. Travelogues, consumer advocacy issues, poetry and recipes are not generally published. **Buys 100-125 mss/year.** Send complete ms. Length: 1,400 words maximum. **Pays $150 maximum.**

Reprints Accepts previously published submissions.

Photos Send photos with submission. Reviews contact sheets, transparencies, prints. Buys one-time rights. Negotiates payment individually. Captions required.

Fiction All fiction must be RV related. Adventure, historical, humorous, mainstream, mystery, slice-of-life vignettes, western. **Buys 2-6 mss/year.** Send complete ms. Length: 1,400 words maximum. **Pays $150 maximum.**

Tips "Please do not send queries. Send complete manuscripts."

$ $FAMILY MOTOR COACHING

Official Publication of the Family Motor Coach Association, 8291 Clough Pike, Cincinnati OH 45244-2796. (513)474-3622. Fax: (513)388-5286. E-mail: magazine@fmca.com. Website: www.fmca.com. Director of Communications: Pamela Wisby Kay. **Contact:** Robbin Gould, editor. **80% freelance written.** "We prefer that writers be experienced RVers." Monthly magazine emphasizing travel by motorhome, motorhome mechanics, maintenance, and other technical information. "*Family Motor Coaching* magazine is edited for the members and prospective members of the Family Motor Coach Association who own or are about to purchase self-contained, motorized recreational vehicles known as motorhomes. Featured are articles on travel and recreation, association news and activities, plus articles on new products and motorhome maintenance and repair. Approximately 1/3 of editorial content is devoted to travel and entertainment, 1/3 to association news, and 1/3 to new products, industry news, and motorhome maintenance." Estab. 1963. Circ. 140,000. **Pays on acceptance.** Publishes ms an average of 8 months after acceptance. Byline given. Buys first North American serial rights. Submit seasonal material 4 months in advance. Accepts queries by mail, e-mail, fax. Responds in 3 months to queries. Sample copy for $3.99; $5 if paying by credit card. Writer's guidelines for #10 SASE.

Nonfiction How-to (do-it-yourself motorhome projects and modifications), humor, interview/profile, new product, technical, motorhome travel (various areas of North America accessible by motorhome), bus conversions, nostalgia. **Buys 90-100 mss/year.** Query with published clips. Length: 1,000-2,000 words. **Pays $100-500, depending on article category.**

Photos State availability with submission. Prefers North American serial rights but will consider one-time rights on photos only. Offers no additional payment for b&w contact sheets, 35mm 2¼ X 2¼ color transparencies, or high-resolution electronic images (300 dpi and at least 4 X 5 in size). Captions, model releases, photo credits required.

Tips "The greatest number of contributions we receive are travel; therefore, that area is the most competitive. However, it also represents the easiest way to break in to our publication. Articles should be written for those traveling by self-contained motorhome. The destinations must be accessible to motorhome travelers and any peculiar road conditions should be mentioned."

$ $ $ FRONTIER MAGAZINE

Adventure Media, 3983 S. McCarran Blvd., No. 434, Reno NV 89502. (775)856-3532. Fax: (775)829-2457. E-mail: laurah@adventuremedia.com. Website: www.frontiermag.com. **Contact:** Laura Hengstler, editor. **60% freelance written.** Monthly magazine covering travel, with special emphasis on the Rocky Mountain states. "*Frontier Magazine* is a sophisticated yet fun-to-read magazine that celebrates the Rocky Mountain lifestyle. It celebrates those attitudes, traditions, and issues that define the modern west." Estab. 1998. Circ. 250,000. Pays on publication. Publishes ms an average of 4 months after acceptance. Byline given. Offers 25% kill fee. Buys first North American serial rights. Editorial lead time 4 months. Submit seasonal material 4 months in advance. Accepts queries by mail, e-mail. Responds in 2 months to queries; 2 months to mss. Sample copy for $2 (shipping and handling). Writer's guidelines online. Editorial calendar online.

Nonfiction Essays, general interest, historical/nostalgic, humor (essays), interview/profile, photo feature, travel. Special issues: Golf guide (October); Ski guide (November). "We do not accept fiction, religious, or how-to articles." **Buys 15 mss/year.** Query with published clips. Length: 350-1,500 words. **Pays 25-50¢/word.**

Photos State availability with submission. Reviews duplicate slides only. Buys one-time rights. Negotiates payment individually. Identification of subjects required.

Columns/Departments Local Color (tourist-oriented events around the route system), 50-500 words; Creature Comforts (hotel/restaurant reviews), 700 words; Local Flavor (restaurants, chefs, or specialty cuisine along the Frontier Airline route system). **Buys 30 mss/year.** Query with published clips. **Pays $50-150.**

Tips "Know the airline's route system—we accept stories only from/about these areas. Submit clips with all queries."

🅽 $ GO MAGAZINE

AAA Carolinas, 6600 AAA Dr., Charlotte NC 28212. (704)569-7733. Fax: (704)569-7815. E-mail: trcrosby@aaaqa .com. Website: www.aaacarolinas.com. **Contact:** Sarah Davis, assistant editor. Bimonthly magazine covering travel, automotive, safety (traffic), and insurance. "Consumer-oriented membership publication providing information on things such as car buying, vacations, travel safety problems, etc." Estab. 1928. Circ. 750,000. Pays on publication. Makes work-for-hire assignments. Editorial lead time 2 months. Accepts queries by mail, fax. Responds in 6 weeks to queries; 3 months to mss. Sample copy for 1 SAE and 4 first-class stamps. Writer's guidelines for #10 SASE.

Nonfiction How-to (fix auto, travel safety, etc.), travel, automotive insurance, traffic safety. **Buys 12-14 mss/ year.** Query with published clips. Length: 600-900 words. **Pays $150/published story.**

Photos Send photos with submission. Buys one-time rights. Offers no additional payment for photos accepted with ms.

🅽 $ $ HIGHWAYS

The Official Publication of the Good Sam Club, Affinity Group, Inc., 2575 Vista Del Mar Dr., Ventura CA 93001. (805)667-4100. Fax: (805)667-4454. E-mail: goodsam@goodsamclub.com. Website: www.goodsamclub.com/ highways. **Contact:** Dee Reed, managing editor. **30% freelance written.** Monthly magazine covering recreational vehicle lifestyle. "All of our readers own some type of RV—a motorhome, trailer, pop-up, tent—so our stories need to include places that you can go with large vehicles, and campgrounds in and around the area where they can spend the night." Estab. 1966. Circ. 975,000. **Pays on acceptance.** Publishes ms an average of 6 months after acceptance. Byline given. Offers 50% kill fee. Buys first North American serial, electronic rights. Accepts queries by e-mail. Responds in 2 weeks to queries. Sample copy and writer's guidelines free or online.

Nonfiction How-to (repair/replace something on an RV), humor, technical, travel (all RV related). **Buys 15-20 mss/year.** Query. Length: 800-1,100 words.

Photos Send photos with submission. Reviews contact sheets, negatives, transparencies, prints. Buys one-time rights. No additional payment for photos accepted with ms. Captions, identification of subjects, model releases required.

Columns/Departments On the Road (issue related); RV Insight (for people new to the RV lifestyle); Action Line (consumer help); Tech Topics (tech Q&A); Hot Stove (cooking in an RV); Product Previews (new products). No plans on adding new columns/departments.

Tips "Know something about RVing. People who drive motorhomes or pull trailers have unique needs that have to be incorporated into our stories. We're looking for well-written, first-person stories that convey the fun of this lifestyle and way to travel.''

$ $ 🌐 INTERNATIONAL LIVING

Agora Ireland, Ltd., 5 Catherine St., Waterford Ireland. 353-51-304-557. Fax: 353-51-304-561. E-mail: lchestnutt @internationalliving.com. Website: www.internationalliving.com. Managing Editor: Laura Sheridan. **Contact:** Lynn Chestnutt, editorial assistant. **50% freelance written.** Monthly newsletter covering retirement, travel, investment, and real estate overseas. "We do not want descriptions of how beautiful places are. We want specifics, recommendations, contacts, prices, names, addresses, phone numbers, etc. We want offbeat locations and off-the-beaten-track spots." Estab. 1981. Circ. 500,000. Pays on publication. Publishes ms an average of 3 months after acceptance. Byline given. Offers 25-50% kill fee. Buys all rights. Editorial lead time 2 months. Submit seasonal material 3 months in advance. Accepts queries by mail, e-mail, fax. Accepts simultaneous submissions. Responds in 2 months to mss. Sample copy for #10 SASE. Writer's guidelines online.

○▸ Break in by writing about something real. If you find it a chore to write the piece you're sending us, then chances are, we don't want it.

Nonfiction How-to (get a job, buy real estate, get cheap airfares overseas, start a business, etc.), interview/ profile (entrepreneur abroad), new product (travel), personal experience, travel, shopping, cruises. Special issues: "We produce special issues each year focusing on Asia, Eastern Europe, and Latin America." No descriptive, run-of-the-mill travel articles. **Buys 100 mss/year.** Send complete ms. Length: 500-2,000 words. **Pays $200-500 for assigned articles; $100-400 for unsolicited articles.**

Photos State availability with submission. Reviews contact sheets, negatives, transparencies, prints. Buys all rights. Offers $50/photo. Identification of subjects required.

Fillers Facts. **Buys 20/year.** Length: 50-250 words. **Pays $25-50.**

▪ The online magazine carries original content not found in the print version. Contact: Len Galvin, online editor (lgalvin@internationalliving.com).

Tips "Make recommendations in your articles. We want first-hand accounts. Tell us how to do things: how to catch a cab, order a meal, buy a souvenir, buy property, start a business, etc. *International Living*'s philosophy is that the world is full of opportunities to do whatever you want, whenever you want. We will show you how."

$ THE INTERNATIONAL RAILWAY TRAVELER

Hardy Publishing Co., Inc., P.O. Box 3747, San Diego CA 92163. (619)260-1332. Fax: (619)296-4220. E-mail: irteditor@aol.com. Website: www.irtsociety.com. **Contact:** Gena Holle, editor. **100% freelance written.** Monthly newsletter covering rail travel. Estab. 1983. Circ. 3,500. Pays within 1 month of the publication date. Byline given. Offers 25% kill fee. Buys first North American serial, electronic rights. Editorial lead time 4 months. Submit seasonal material 6 months in advance. Responds in 1 month to queries; 2 months to mss. Sample copy for $6. Writer's guidelines for #10 SASE or via e-mail.

Nonfiction General interest, how-to, interview/profile, new product, opinion, personal experience, travel, book reviews. **Buys 48-60 mss/year.** Query with published clips or send complete ms. Length: 800-1,200 words. **Pays 3¢/word.**

Photos Include SASE for return of photos. Send photos with submission. Reviews contact sheets, negatives, transparencies, 8×10 (preferred) and 5×7 prints, digital photos preferred (300 dpi at least). Buys first North American serial rights, Electronic rights. Offers $10 b&w; $20 cover photo. Costs of converting slides and negatives to prints are deducted from payment. Captions, identification of subjects required.

Tips "We want factual articles concerning world rail travel which would not appear in the mass-market travel magazines. *IRT* readers and editors love stories and photos on off-beat train trips as well as more conventional train trips covered in unconventional ways. With *IRT*, the focus is on the train travel experience, not a blow-by-blow description of the view from the train window. Be sure to include details (prices, passes, schedule info, etc.) for readers who might want to take the trip. E-mail queries, submissions encouraged. Digital photo submissions (at least 300 dpi) are encouraged. Please stay within word-count guidelines.''

$ $ $ $ ISLANDS

Islands Media Corp., 6267 Carpinteria Ave., Suite 200, Santa Barbara CA 93140. (805)745-7100. Fax: (805)745-7102. E-mail: editorial@islands.com. Website: www.islands.com. **Contact:** Lisa Gosselin, editor. **95% freelance written.** Magazine published 8 times/year covering "accessible and once-in-a-lifetime islands from many different perspectives: travel, culture, lifestyle. We ask our authors to give us the essence of the island and do it with literary flair." Estab. 1981. Circ. 220,000. **Pays on acceptance.** Publishes ms an average of 8 months after acceptance. Byline given. Offers 25% kill fee. Buys all rights. Accepts queries by mail, e-mail, fax. Responds in 2 months to queries; 6 weeks to mss. Sample copy for $6. Writer's guidelines for #10 SASE or online.

Nonfiction Book excerpts, essays, general interest, interview/profile, personal experience, photo feature, travel, island-related material. **Buys 25 feature mss/year.** Query with published clips or send complete ms. Length: 2,000-4,000 words. **Pays $750-3,500.** Sometimes pays expenses of writers on assignment.

Photos "Fine color photography is a special attraction of *Islands*, and we look for superb composition, technical quality, and editorial applicability." Label slides with name and address, include very detailed captions, and submit in protective plastic sleeves. Reviews 35mm transparencies. Buys one-time rights. Pays $75-300 for 35mm transparencies. Identification of subjects required.

Columns/Departments Horizons section and ArtBeat (all island related), 200-600 words; Crossroads (columns and experiences that highlight island life), 500-1,500 words; IslandWise (travel experiences, classic island hotels, classic island eatery, great enrichment experience), 700-1,000 words; Insiders (10 things to do in well-visited islands), 800 words. **Buys 50 mss/year.** Query with published clips. **Pays $25-1,000.**

Tips "A freelancer can best break in to our publication with front- or back-of-the-book stories. Stay away from general topics."

N $PATHFINDERS

Travel Information for People of Color, 6325 Germantown Ave., Philadelphia PA 19144. (215)438-2140. Fax: (215)438-2144. E-mail: editors@pathfinderstravel.com. Website: www.pathfinderstravel.com. **Contact:** Joseph P. Blake, managing editor. **75% freelance written.** Quarterly magazine covering travel for people of color, primarily African-Americans. "We look for lively, original, well-written stories that provide a good sense of place, with useful information and fresh ideas about travel and the travel industry. Our main audience is African-Americans, though we do look for articles relating to other persons of color: Native Americans, Hispanics and Asians." Estab. 1997. Circ. 100,000. **Pays on acceptance.** Byline given. Buys first North American serial, electronic rights. Accepts queries by mail, e-mail. Responds in 1 month to queries; 2 months to mss. Sample copy at bookstores (Barnes & Noble, Borders, Waldenbooks). Writer's guidelines online.

> O→ Break in through *Looking Back*, 600-word essay on travel from personal experience that provides a historical perspective and U.S. travel with cultural perspective. Also Chef's Table column, featuring information on African American chefs.

Nonfiction Interested in seeing more Native American stories, places that our readers can visit and rodeos (be sure to tie-in African-American cowboys). Essays, historical/nostalgic, how-to, personal experience, photo feature, travel (all vacation travel oriented). "No more pitches on Jamaica. We get these all the time." **Buys 16-20 mss/year.** Send complete ms. Length: 1,200-1,400 words for cover stories; 1,000-1,200 words for features. **Pays $125-150.**

Photos State availability with submission.

Columns/Departments Chef's Table, Post Cards from Home; Looking Back; City of the Month, 500-600 words. Send complete ms. **Pays $100.**

Tips "We prefer seeing finished articles rather than queries. All articles are submitted on spec. Articles should be saved in either WordPerfect of Microsoft Word, double-spaced and saved as a text-only file. Include a hard copy. E-mail articles are accepted only by request of the editor. No historical articles."

N $ $PILOT GETAWAYS MAGAZINE

Airventure Publishing LLC, P.O. Box 550, Glendale CA 91209-0550. (818)241-1890. Fax: (818)241-1895. E-mail: editor@pilotgetaways.com. Website: www.pilotgetaways.com. **Contact:** John Kounis, editor. **90% freelance written.** Quarterly magazine covering aviation travel for private pilots. "*Pilot Getaways* is a travel magazine for private pilots. Our articles cover destinations that are easily accessible by private aircraft, including details such as airport transportation, convenient hotels, and attractions. Other regular features include Fly-in dining, Flying Tips, and Bush Flying." Estab. 1998. Circ. 20,000. Pays on publication. Byline given. Buys first North American serial, electronic rights. Editorial lead time 4 months. Submit seasonal material 9 months in advance. Accepts queries by mail, e-mail, fax, phone. Accepts simultaneous submissions. Responds in 2 weeks to queries; 2 months to mss. Sample copy and writer's guidelines free.

Nonfiction Travel (specifically travel guide articles). "We rarely publish articles about events that have already occurred, such as travel logs about trips the authors have taken or air show reports." **Buys 30 mss/year.** Query. Length: 1,000-3,500 words. **Pays $100-500.**

Reprints Accepts previously published submissions.

Photos State availability with submission. Reviews contact sheets, negatives, 35mm transparencies, prints, GIF/JPEG files. Buys one-time rights. Negotiates payment individually. Captions, identification of subjects required.

Columns/Departments Weekend Getaways (short fly-in getaways), 2,000 words; Fly-in Dining (reviews of airport restaurants), 1,200 words; Flying Tips (tips and pointers on flying technique), 1,000 words; Bush Flying (getaways to unpaved destinations), 1,500 words. **Buys 20 mss/year.** Query. **Pays $100-500.**

Tips "*Pilot Getaways* follows a specific format, which is factual and informative. We rarely publish travel logs that chronicle a particular journey. Rather, we prefer travel guides with phone numbers, addresses, prices, etc., so that our readers can plan their own trips. The exact format is described in our writer's guidelines.''

$ $ $ PORTHOLE CRUISE MAGAZINE

Panoff Publishing, 4517 NW 31st Ave., Ft. Lauderdale FL 33309-3403. (954)377-7777. Fax: (954)377-7000. E-mail: rgrizzle@ppigroup.com. Website: www.porthole.com. **Contact:** Ralph Grizzle, editor. **70% freelance written.** Bimonthly magazine covering the cruise industry. *"Porthole Cruise Magazine* entices its readers into taking a cruise vacation by delivering information that is timely, accurate, colorful, and entertaining.'' Estab. 1992. Circ. 35,000. Pays on publication. Publishes ms an average of 6 months after acceptance. Byline given. Offers 20% kill fee. Buys electronic, first international serial rights. Editorial lead time 8 months. Submit seasonal material 5 months in advance. Accepts queries by mail, e-mail, fax. Accepts simultaneous submissions. Sample copy for 8×11 SAE and $3 postage.

Nonfiction General interest (cruise related), historical/nostalgic, how-to (pick a cruise, not get seasick, travel tips), humor, interview/profile (crew on board or industry executives), new product, personal experience, photo feature, travel (off-the-beaten-path, adventure, ports, destinations, cruises), onboard fashion, spa articles, duty-free shopping, port shopping, ship reviews. No articles on destinations that can't be reached by ship. **Buys 30 mss/year.** Query with published clips or send complete ms. Length: 1,000-1,200 words. **Pays $400-650 for assigned articles.**

Reprints Send photocopy of article or typed ms with rights for sale noted and information about when and where the material previously appeared. Negotiates payment.

Photos Linda Douthat, creative director. State availability with submission. Reviews transparencies, prints. Buys one-time rights. Negotiates payment individually. Captions, identification of subjects, model releases required.

$ $ THE SOUTHERN TRAVELER

AAA Auto Club of Missouri, 12901 N. Forty Dr., St. Louis MO 63141. (314)523-7350. Fax: (314)523-6982. Website: www.aaatravelermags.com. Editor: Michael J. Right. **Contact:** Deborah Reinhardt, managing editor. **80% freelance written.** Bimonthly magazine. Estab. 1997. Circ. 170,000. **Pays on acceptance.** Byline given. Not copyrighted. Buys first North American serial, second serial (reprint) rights. Accepts simultaneous submissions. Responds in 1 month to queries; 1 month to mss. Sample copy for 12½ X 9½ SAE and 3 first-class stamps. Writer's guidelines online. Editorial calendar online.

　O⟶ Query, with best chance for good reception January-March for inclusion in following year's editorial calendar.

Nonfiction "We feature articles on regional and world travel, area history, auto safety, highway and transportation news." **Buys 30 mss/year.** Query. Length: 2,000 words maximum. **Pays $300 maximum.**

Reprints Send ms with rights for sale noted and information about when and where the material previously appeared. Pays $125-200.

Photos State availability with submission. Reviews transparencies. One-time photo reprint rights. Offers no additional payment for photos accepted with ms. Captions required.

Tips "Editorial schedule is set 6-9 months in advance (available online). Some stories available throughout the year, but most are assigned early. Travel destinations and tips are most open to freelancers; auto-related topics handled by staff. Make story bright and quick to read. We see too many 'Here's what I did on my vacation' manuscripts. Go easy on first-person accounts.''

N $ $ $ $ SPA

Healthy Living, Travel & Renewal, Islands Media, 6267 Carpinteria Ave., Suite 200, Santa Barbara CA 93140. (805)745-7100. Fax: (805)745-7105. E-mail: info@spamagazine.com. Website: www.spamagazine.com. Bimonthly magazine covering health spas: treatments, travel, cuisine, fitness, beauty. "Approachable and accessible, yet authoritative and full of advice, *Spa* is the place to turn for information and tips on nutrition, spa cuisine/recipes, beauty, health, skin care, travel (to spas), fitness, wellness, and renewal. Sometimes humorous and light, sometimes thoughtful and introspective, *Spa* is always helpful, insightful and personal.'' Byline given. Offers 25% kill fee. Buys first North American serial, all rights. Editorial lead time 3 months. Accepts queries by mail. Sample copy for $6.

Nonfiction Essays, how-to (beauty), humor, personal experience, travel. Does not want "a general article on a spa you have visited.'' **Buys 30 mss/year.** Query with published clips. Length: 1,500-3,000 words. **Pays $1,125-2,500.** Sometimes pays expenses of writers on assignment.

Columns/Departments Being Well (news and trends on health and healing, wellness and workouts); Spa Talk (new spas, spa programs, treatments); Lotions & Potions (beauty, fragrance); Living Wardrobe (personal style, fashion); Living Well (home, garden, books, music, internet). **Buys 60 mss/year.** Query with published clips. **Pays $100-1,500.**

$ $ ⊠ ST. MAARTEN NIGHTS

Nights Publications, Inc., 1831 Rene Levesque Blvd. W., Montreal QC H3H 1R4, Canada. (514)931-1987. Fax: (514)931-6273. E-mail: editor@nightspublications.com. Website: www.nightspublications.com. **Contact:** Sonya N. Plowman, editor. **90% freelance written.** Annual magazine covering the St. Maarten/St. Martin vacation experience seeking "upbeat, entertaining, lifestyle articles. Our audience is the North American vacationer." Estab. 1981. Circ. 225,000. **Pays on acceptance.** Publishes ms an average of 9 months after acceptance. Byline given. Buys North American and Caribbean serial rights. Editorial lead time 1 month. Accepts queries by mail, e-mail, fax. Responds in 2 weeks to queries; 1 month to mss. Writer's guidelines by e-mail.

● E-mail queries preferred. All submissions must include an e-mail address for correspondence.

O⇥ "Let the reader experience the story; utilize the senses; be descriptive."

Nonfiction Lifestyle with a lively, upscale touch. Include SASE with Canadian postage or IRC. General interest, historical/nostalgic, how-to (gamble), humor, interview/profile, opinion, personal experience, photo feature, travel, colorful profiles of islanders, sailing, ecological, ecotourism, local culture, art, activities, entertainment, nightlife, special events, topics relative to vacationers in St. Maarten/St. Martin. **Buys 8-10 mss/year.** Query with published clips. Length: 250-750 words. **Pays $100-300.**

Photos State availability with submission. Reviews transparencies. Buys one-time rights. Pays $50/photo. Captions, identification of subjects, model releases required.

Tips "Our style is upbeat, friendly, fluid, and descriptive. Our magazines cater to tourists who are already at the destination, so ensure your story is of interest to this particular audience. We welcome stories that offer fresh angles to familiar tourist-related topics."

$ $ ▦ TIMES OF THE ISLANDS

The International Magazine of the Turks & Caicos Islands, Times Publications, Ltd., P.O. Box 234, Southwind Plaza, Providenciales Turks & Caicos Islands, British West Indies. (649)946-4788. Fax: (649)946-4788. E-mail: timespub@tciway.tc. Website: www.timespub.tc. **Contact:** Kathy Borsuk, editor. **60% freelance written.** Quarterly magazine covering the Turks & Caicos Islands. "*Times of the Islands* is used by the public and private sector to inform visitors and potential investors/developers about the Islands. It goes beyond a superficial overview of tourist attractions with in-depth articles about natural history, island heritage, local personalities, new development, offshore finance, sporting activities, visitors' experiences, and Caribbean fiction." Estab. 1988. Circ. 6,000-9,000. Pays on publication. Publishes ms an average of 6 months after acceptance. Byline given. Buys second serial (reprint) rights. Publication rights for 6 months with respect to other publications distributed in Caribbean. Editorial lead time 4 months. Submit seasonal material at least 4 months in advance. Accepts queries by mail, fax. Accepts simultaneous submissions. Responds in 6 weeks to queries; 2 months to mss. Sample copy for $6. Writer's guidelines online.

Nonfiction Book excerpts, essays, general interest (Caribbean art, culture, cooking, crafts), historical/nostalgic, humor, interview/profile (locals), personal experience (trips to the Islands), photo feature, technical (island businesses), travel, book reviews, nature, ecology, business (offshore finance), watersports. **Buys 20 mss/year.** Query. Length: 500-3,000 words. **Pays $200-600.**

Reprints Send photocopy and information about when and where the material previously appeared. Payment varies.

Photos Send photos with submission. Reviews slides, prints, digital photos. Pays $15-100/photo. Identification of subjects required.

Columns/Departments On Holiday (unique experiences of visitors to Turks & Caicos), 500-1,500 words. **Buys 4 mss/year.** Query. **Pays $200.**

Fiction Adventure, ethnic, historical, humorous, mystery, novel excerpts. **Buys 2-3 mss/year.** Query. Length: 1,000-3,000 words. **Pays $250-400.**

Tips "Make sure that the query/article specifically relates to the Turks and Caicos Islands. The theme can be general (ecotourism, for instance), but the manuscript should contain specific and current references to the Islands. We're a high-quality magazine, with a small budget and staff, and are very open-minded to ideas (and manuscripts). Writers who have visited the Islands at least once would probably have a better perspective from which to write."

N $ $ TRAILER LIFE

America's No. 1 RV Magazine, Affinity Group, Inc., 2575 Vista Del Mar Dr., Ventura CA 93001. Fax: (805)667-4484. E-mail: info@trailerlife.com. Website: www.trailerlife.com. **40% freelance written.** Monthly magazine. "*Trailer Life* magazine is written specifically for active people whose overall lifestyle is based on travel and recreation in their RV. Every issue includes product tests, travel articles, and other features—ranging from lifestyle to vehicle maintenance." Estab. 1941. Circ. 285,000. **Pays on acceptance.** Publishes ms an average of 6 months after acceptance. Byline given. Offers 30% kill fee for assigned articles that are not acceptable. Buys first North American serial, electronic rights. Editorial lead time 4 months. Submit seasonal material 6 months in advance. Accepts queries by mail. Responds in 2 months to queries; 2 months to mss. Sample copy for free. Writer's guidelines for #10 SASE.

> O→ Break in with a "small piece for the Campground Spotlight or Etc. section; a short article on an interesting RV trip."

Nonfiction Historical/nostalgic, how-to (technical), humor, new product, opinion, personal experience, travel. No vehicle tests, product evaluations or road tests; tech material is strictly assigned. No diaries or trip logs, no non-RV trips; nothing without an RV-hook. **Buys 75 mss/year.** Query with or without published clips. Length: 250-2,500 words. **Pays $125-700.** Sometimes pays expenses of writers on assignment.

Photos Send photos with submission. Reviews transparencies, b&w contact sheets. Buys one-time and occasionally electronic rights. Offers no additional payment for photos accepted with ms, does pay for supplemental photos. Identification of subjects, model releases required.

Columns/Departments Campground Spotlight (report with 1 photo of campground recommended for RVers), 250 words; Bulletin Board (news, trends of interest to RVers), 100 words; Etcetera (useful tips and information affecting RVers), 240 words. **Buys 70 mss/year.** Query or send complete ms. **Pays $75-250.**

Tips "Prerequisite: Must have RV focus. Photos must be magazine quality. These are the two biggest reasons why manuscripts are rejected. Our readers are travel enthusiasts who own all types of RVs (travel trailers, truck campers, van conversions, motorhomes, tent trailers, fifth-wheels) in which they explore North America and beyond, embrace the great outdoors in national, state and private parks. They're very active and very adventurous."

$TRANSITIONS ABROAD

P.O. Box 745, Bennington VT 05201. Phone/Fax: (802)442-4827. E-mail: editor@transitionsabroad.com. Website: www.transitionsabroad.com. **Contact:** Sherry Schwartz, editor. **80-90% freelance written.** Bimonthly magazine resource for low-budget international travel, often with an educational or work component. Focus is on the alternatives to mass tourism. Estab. 1977. Circ. 12,000. Pays on publication. Byline given. Buys first, second serial (reprint) rights. Accepts queries by e-mail. Responds in 1 month to queries; 1 month to mss. Sample copy for $6.45. Writer's guidelines online.

> O→ Break in by sending "a concisely written fact-filled article—or even a letter to Info Exchange—of no more than 1,000 words with up-to-date practical information, based on your own experience, on how readers can combine travel and learning or travel and work."

Nonfiction Lead articles (up to 1,500 words) provide first-hand practical information on independent travel to featured country or region (see topics schedule). Also, how to find educational and specialty travel opportunities, practical information (evaluation of courses, special interest and study tours, economy travel), travel (new learning and cultural travel ideas). Foreign travel only. Few destination ("tourist") pieces or first-person narratives. *Transitions Abroad* is a resource magazine for independent, educated, and adventurous travelers, not for armchair travelers or those addicted to packaged tours or cruises. Emphasis on information—which must be usable by readers—and on interaction with people in host country. **Buys 20 unsolicited mss/year.** Prefer e-mail queries that indicate familiarity with the magazine. Query with credentials and SASE. Include author's bio and e-mail with submissions. Length: 500-1,500 words. **Pays $2/column inch.**

Photos Photos increase likelihood of acceptance. Send photos with submission. Buys one-time rights. Pays $10-45 for color prints or color slides (prints preferred), $150 for covers. Captions, identification of subjects required.

Columns/Departments Worldwide Travel Bargains (destinations, activities, and accomodations for budget travelers—featured in every issue); Tour and Program Notes (new courses or travel programs); Travel Resources (new information and ideas for independent travel); Working Traveler (how to find jobs and what to expect); Activity Vacations (travel opportunities that involve action and learning, usually by direct involvement in host culture); Responsible Travel (information on community-organized tours). Length: 1,000 words maximum. **Buys 60 mss/year.** Send complete ms. **Pays $20-50.**

Fillers Info Exchange (information, preferably first hand—having to do with travel, particularly offbeat educational travel and work or study abroad). **Buys 10/year.** Length: 750 words maximum. **Pays complimentary 1-year subscription.**

> ▣ The online magazine carries original content not found in the print edition and includes writer's guidelines.

Tips "We like nuts and bolts stuff, practical information, especially on how to work, live, and cut costs abroad. Our readers want usable information on planning a travel itinerary. Be specific: names, addresses, current costs. We are very interested in educational and long-stay travel and study abroad for adults and senior citizens. *Overseas Travel Planner* published each year in July provides best information sources on work, study, and independent travel abroad. Each bimonthly issue contains a worldwide directory of educational and specialty travel programs."

Consumer Magazines

$ $ $ $ TRAVEL + LEISURE

American Express Publishing Corp., 1120 Ave. of the Americas, New York NY 10036. (212)382-5600. E-mail: tlquery@aexp.com. Website: www.travelandleisure.com. Editor-in-Chief: Nancy Novogrod. Managing Editor: Michael S. Cain. **Contact:** Editor. **80% freelance written.** *"Travel + Leisure* is a monthly magazine edited for affluent travelers. It explores the latest resorts, hotels, fashions, foods, and drinks, as well as political, cultural, and economic issues affecting travelers." Circ. 925,000. **Pays on acceptance.** Byline given. Offers 25% kill fee. Buys first world rights, as well as rights to republish in international editions and online. Accepts queries by mail, e-mail. Responds in 6 weeks to queries; 6 weeks to mss. Sample copy for $5.50 from (800)888-8728. Writer's guidelines online.

> O— There is no single editorial contact for *Travel + Leisure.* It is best to find the name of the editor of each section, as appropriate for your submission.

Nonfiction Travel. **Buys 40-50 feature (3,000-5,000 words) and 200 short (125-500 words) mss/year.** Query (e-mail preferred). **Pays $4,000-6,000/feature; $100-500/short piece.** Pays expenses of writers on assignment.
Photos Discourages submission of unsolicited transparencies. Buys one-time rights. Payment varies. Captions required.
Columns/Departments Length: 2,500-3,500 words. **Buys 125-150 mss/year. Pays $2,000-3,500.**
Tips "Queries should not be generic, but should specify what is new or previously uncovered in a destination or travel-related subject area."

$ TRAVEL NATURALLY

Nude Recreation, Internaturally, Inc. Publishing Co., P.O. Box 317, Newfoundland NJ 07435-0317. (973)697-3552. Fax: (973)697-8313. Website: www.internaturally.com. **Contact:** Bernard Loibl, editor. **90% freelance written.** Quarterly magazine covering wholesome family nude recreation and travel locations. *"Travel Naturally* nude recreation looks at why millions of people believe that removing clothes in public is a good idea, and at places specifically created for that purpose—with good humor, but also in earnest. *Travel Naturally* nude recreation takes you to places where your personal freedom is the only agenda, and to places where textile-free living is a serious commitment." Estab. 1981. Circ. 35,000. Pays on publication. Byline given. Buys first, one-time rights. Editorial lead time 4 months. Submit seasonal material 4 months in advance. Accepts queries by mail, e-mail, fax. Accepts simultaneous submissions. Sample copy for $9. Writer's guidelines free.
Nonfiction Frequent contributors and regular columnists, who develop a following through *Travel Naturally*, are paid from the Frequent Contributors Budget. Payments increase on the basis of frequency of participation. General interest, interview/profile, personal experience, photo feature, travel. **Buys 12 mss/year.** Send complete ms. Length: 2 pages. **Pays $70/published page, including photos.**
Reprints Accepts previously published submissions.
Photos Send photos with submission. Reviews contact sheets, negatives, transparencies, prints. Buys one-time rights. Payment for photos included in payment forms.
Fillers Sherry Stafford, associate editor. Anecdotes, facts, gags to be illustrated by cartoonist, newsbreaks, short humor.
Tips *"Travel Naturally* nude recreation invokes the philosophies of naturism and nudism, but also activities and beliefs in the mainstream that express themselves, barely: spiritual awareness, New Age customs, pagan and religious rites, alternative and fringe lifestyle beliefs, artistic expressions, and many individual nude interests. Our higher purpose is simply to help restore our sense of self. Although the term 'nude recreation' may, for some, conjure up visions of sexual frivolities inappropriate for youngsters—because that can also be technically true—these topics are outside the scope of *Travel Naturally* magazine. Here the emphasis is on the many varieties of human beings, of all ages and backgrounds, recreating in their most natural state, at extraordinary places, their reasons for doing so, and the benefits they derive. We incorporate a travel department to advise and book vacations in locations reviewed in travel articles."

$ WESTERN RV NEWS & RECREATION

(formerly *Western RV News*), P.O. Box 847, Redmond OR 97756. (541)548-2255. Fax: (541)548-2288. E-mail: editor@westernrvnews.com. Website: www.westernrvnews.com. **Contact:** Terie Snyder, editor. **50% freelance written.** Monthly magazine for owners of recreational vehicles and those interested in the RV lifestyle. Estab. 1966. Pays on publication. Publishes ms an average of 6 months after acceptance. Byline given. Buys first, second serial (reprint) rights. Accepts queries by mail, e-mail, fax. Accepts simultaneous submissions. Responds in 2 months to queries; 2 months to mss. Sample copy for 9 × 12 SAE and 5 first-class stamps. Writer's guidelines for #10 SASE.
Nonfiction How-to (RV oriented, purchasing considerations, maintenance), humor (RV experiences), new product (with ancillary interest to RV lifestyle), personal experience (varying or unique RV lifestyles), technical (RV systems or hardware), travel. "No articles without an RV slant." **Buys 100 mss/year.** Submit complete ms on paper, disk, or by e-mail. Length: 250-1,400 words. **Pays 8¢/word for first rights.**

Reprints Photocopy of article or typed ms with rights for sale noted and information about when and where the material previously appeared. Pays 5¢/word.

Photos Color slides and prints are accepted with article at a rate of $5/photo used. Digital photos are also accepted through e-mail or on disk (CD, Zip, etc.), but must be at a minimum resolution of 300 dpi at published size (generally, 5×7 inches is adequate). Captions, identification of subjects, model releases required.

Fillers Encourage anecdotes, RV-related tips, and short humor. Length: 50-250 words. **Pays $5-25.**

Tips "Highlight the RV lifestyle! Western travel articles should include information about the availability of RV sites, dump stations, RV parking, and accessibility. Thorough research and a pleasant, informative writing style are paramount. Technical, how-to, and new product writing is also of great interest. Photos enhance the possibility of article acceptance."

$ $ WOODALL'S REGIONALS

2575 Vista Del Mar Dr., Ventura CA 93001. E-mail: editor@woodallpub.com. Website: www.woodalls.com. **Contact:** Tim Conway, assistant editor. Monthly magazine for RV and camping enthusiasts. Woodall's Regionals include *Camper Ways*, *Midwest RV Traveler*, *Northeast Outdoors*, *Florida RV Traveler*, *Southern RV*, *Texas RV*, and *Southwest RV Traveler*. Byline given. Buys first rights. Accepts queries by mail, e-mail. Responds in 1-2 months to queries. Sample copy for free. Writer's guidelines free.

Nonfiction "We need interesting and tightly focused feature stories on RV travel and lifestyle, campground spotlights and technical articles that speak to both novices and experienced RVers." **Buys 500 mss/year.** Query with published clips. Length: 500-1,700 words. **Pays $180-250/feature; $75-100/department article and short piece.**

WOMEN'S

Ⓝ Ⓩ ALLURE

Conde Nast Publications, 4 Times Square, 10th Floor, New York NY 10036. (212)286-7441. Fax: (212)286-2690. E-mail: alluremag@aol.com. Website: www.allure.com. Editor: Linda Wells. Senior Editor: Catherine Scroop and Jillian MacKenzie. Articles Editor: Sarah Van Boven. Monthly magazine covering fashion, beauty, fitness, etc. Geared towards the professional modern woman. Circ. 957,276. Sample copy not available.

- Does not buy freelance material or use freelance writers.

$ $ $ BRIDAL GUIDE

R.F.P., LLC, 3 E. 54th St., 15th Floor, New York NY 10022. (212)838-7733. Fax: (212)308-7165. Website: www.bridalguide.com. Editor-in-Chief: Diane Forden. **Contact:** Cybele Eidenschenk, executive editor; Sherri Eisenberg, travel editor for travel features. **20% freelance written.** Bimonthly magazine covering relationships, sexuality, fitness, wedding planning, psychology, finance, travel. Only works with experienced/published writers. **Pays on acceptance.** Accepts queries by mail. Responds in 3 months to queries; 3 months to mss. Sample copy for $5 and SAE with 4 first-class stamps. Writer's guidelines available.

Nonfiction "Please do not send queries concerning beauty, fashion, or home design stories since we produce them in-house. We do not accept personal wedding essays, fiction, or poetry. Address travel queries to travel editor." All correspondence accompanied by an SASE will be answered. **Buys 100 mss/year.** Query with published clips from national consumer magazines. Length: 1,000-2,000 words. **Pays 50¢/word.**

Photos Photography and illustration submissions should be sent to the art department. Robin Zachary, art director; Amber Katz, associate art director.

Columns/Departments The only columns written by freelancers cover wedding-planning issues.

Tips "We are looking for service-oriented, well-researched pieces that are journalistically written. Writers we work with use at least 3 top expert sources, such as physicians, book authors, and business people in the appropriate field. Our tone is conversational, yet authoritative. Features are also generally filled with real-life anecdotes. We also do features that are completely real-person based—such as roundtables of bridesmaids discussing their experiences, or grooms-to-be talking about their feelings about getting married. In queries, we are looking for a well-thought-out idea, the specific angle of focus the writer intends to take, and the sources he or she intends to use. Queries should be brief and snappy—and titles should be supplied to give the editor an even better idea of the direction the writer is going in."

$ $ $ $ CONDÉ NAST BRIDE'S

Condé Nast, 4 Times Square, 6th Floor, New York NY 10036. Fax: (212)286-8331. Website: www.brides.com. Editor-in-Chief: Millie Bratten. **Contact:** Sally Kilbridge, managing editor. **75% freelance written.** Bimonthly magazine covering all things related to the bride—engagement, the wedding, and marriage. All articles are written for the engaged woman planning her wedding. Estab. 1934. Circ. 500,000. **Pays on acceptance.** Publishes ms an average of 6 months after acceptance. Byline given. Offers 15% kill fee. Buys all rights. Editorial lead time 6 months. Submit seasonal material 1 year in advance. Accepts queries by mail. Responds in 3 months to queries. Sample copy not available. Writer's guidelines for #10 SASE.

Nonfiction Topic (1) Personal essays on wedding planning, aspects of weddings or marriage. Length: 700 words. Written by brides, grooms, attendants, family members, friends in the first person. The writer's unique experience qualifies them to tell this story. (2) Articles on specific relationship and lifestyle issues. Length: 800 words. Select a specialized topic in the areas of relationships, religion, in-laws, second marriage, finances, sex. Written either by experts (attorneys, doctors, financial planners, marriage counselors, etc) or freelancers who interview and quote experts and real couples. (3) In-depth explorations of relationship and lifestyle issues. Length: 1,000 words. Well-researched articles on finances, sex, wedding, and marriage trends. Should include statistics, quotes from experts and real couples, a resolution of the issues raised by each couple. Book excerpts, essays, how-to, personal experience. No humor. **Buys 36 mss/year.** Query with published clips. Length: 700-1,000 words. **Pays $1/word for assigned articles.** Pays expenses of writers on assignment.

Photos State availability with submission. Negotiates payment individually.

Columns/Departments Length: 750 words. Query with published clips. **Pays $1/word.**

Tips "We look for relationship pieces that will help a newlywed couple enjoy the engagement and adjust to marriage. Wedding planning articles are usually written by experts or depend on a lot of interviews with experts. Writers should have a good idea of what we would and would not do: Read the 3 or 4 most recent issues. What separates us from the competition is quality-writing, photographs, amount of information. All articles are assigned with some consumer slant, with the exception of personal essays."

⊘ COSMOPOLITAN

The Hearst Corp., 224 W. 57th St., New York NY 10019. (212)649-2000. **Contact:** Michele Promaulayko, executive editor. **25% freelance written.** Monthly magazine for 18- to 35-year-old single, married, divorced women. "*Cosmopolitan* is edited for young women for whom beauty, fashion, fitness, career, relationships, and personal growth are top priorities. Nutrition, home/lifestyle and celebrities are other interests reflected in the editorial lineup." Estab. 1886. Circ. 2,300,100. **Pays on acceptance.** Byline given. Offers 10-15% kill fee. Buys all magazine rights and occasionally negotiates first North American rights. Submit seasonal material 6 months in advance. Sample copy for $2.95.

  ● "We do not accept unsolicited manuscripts and rarely accept queries."

Nonfiction Book excerpts, how-to, humor, opinion, personal experience, anything of interest to young women.

Tips "Combine information with entertainment value, humor and relatability." Needs "information- and emotion- and fun-packed relationship and sex service stories; first-person stories that display triumph over tragedy."

ℕ $$$$ELLE

Hachette Filipacchi Media U.S., Inc., 1633 Broadway, 44th Floor, New York NY 10019. (212)767-5800. Fax: (212)489-4211. Website: www.elle.com. Editor: Robbie Myers. Beauty & Fitness Director: Emily Dougherty. Senior Beauty Editor: Megan Deem. Assistant Editor: Eva Chen. Special Projects Fashion Editor: Kym Canter. Fashion Assistant: Francesca Mills. Monthly magazine. Edited for the modern, sophisticated, affluent, well-traveled woman in her twenties to early thirties. Circ. 1,100,000. Editorial lead time 3 months. Sample copy not available.

$$$$FAMILY CIRCLE MAGAZINE

Gruner & Jahr, 375 Lexington Ave., New York NY 10017-5514. (212)499-2000. Fax: (212)499-1987. E-mail: nclark@familycircle.com. Website: www.familycircle.com. Editor-in-Chief: Susan Ungaro. **Contact:** Nancy Clark, deputy editor. **80% freelance written.** Magazine published every 3 weeks. "We are a national women's service magazine which covers many stages of a woman's life, along with her everyday concerns about social, family, and health issues." Estab. 1932. Circ. 5,000,000. Byline given. Offers 20% kill fee. Buys one-time, all rights. Editorial lead time 4 months. Submit seasonal material 4 months in advance. Responds in 2 months to queries; 2 months to mss. Sample copy not available. Writer's guidelines online.

  ○→ Break in with "Women Who Make A Difference." Send queries to Nancy Clark, deputy editor.

Nonfiction "We look for well-written, well-reported stories told through interesting anecdotes and insightful writing. We want well-researched service journalism on all subjects." Essays, humor, opinion, personal experience, women's interest subjects such as family and personal relationships, children, physical and mental health, nutrition and self-improvement. No fiction or poetry. **Buys 200 mss/year.** Query with SASE. Length: 1,000-2,500 words. **Pays $1/word.** Pays expenses of writers on assignment.

Columns/Departments Women Who Make a Difference (profiles of volunteers who have made a significant impact on their community), 1,500 words; Profiles in Courage/Love (dramatic narratives about women and families overcoming adversity), 2,000 words; Full Circle (opinion/point of view on current issue/topic of general interest to our readers), 750 words; Humor, 750 words. **Buys 200 mss/year.** Query with published clips and SASE. **Pays $1/word.**

Tips "Query letters should be concise and to the point. Also, writers should keep close tabs on *Family Circle* and other women's magazines to avoid submitting recently run subject matter."

Ⓝ Ⓞ FIRST FOR WOMEN

Bauer Publishing Co., 270 Sylvan Ave., Englewood Cliffs NJ 07632-2523. (201)569-6699. Fax: (201)569-6264. E-mail: firstfw@aol.com. Website: www.firstforwomen.com. Magazine published 17 times/year. Circ. 1,300,000.
  • Does not buy freelance material or use freelance writers.

$ $ $ $ Ⓓ FLARE MAGAZINE

One Mt. Pleasant Rd., 8th Floor, Toronto ON M4Y 2Y5, Canada. (416)764-1829. Fax: (416)764-2866. E-mail: editors@flare.com. Website: www.flare.com. **Contact:** Kim Izzo, features editor. Monthly magazine for women ages 17-34. Byline given. Offers 50% kill fee. Buys first North American serial, electronic rights. Accepts queries by e-mail. Response time varies to queries. Sample copy for #10 SASE. Writer's guidelines online.

Nonfiction Looking for "women's fashion, beauty, health, sociological trends and celebrities." **Buys 24 mss/year.** Query. Length: 200-1,200 words. **Pays $1/word.** Pays expenses of writers on assignment.

Ⓝ $ $ $ $ GLAMOUR

Conde Nast Publications, Inc., 4 Times Square, 16th floor, New York NY 10036. (212)286-2860. Fax: (212)286-7731. Website: www.glamour.com. Senior Beauty Editor: Laurel Naversen. Monthly magazine covering subjects ranging from fashion, beauty and health, personal relationships, career, travel, food and entertainment. *Glamour* is edited for the contemporary woman, and informs her of the trends and recommends how she can adapt them to her needs, and motivates her to take action. Estab. 1939.

Nonfiction Personal experience (relationships), travel.

Ⓝ $ $ $ $ GOOD HOUSEKEEPING

Hearst Corp., 250 W. 55th St., New York NY 10019. (212)649-2200. Fax: (212)649-2340. Website: www.goodhousekeeping.com. Editor-in-Chief: Ellen Levine. **Contact:** Judith Coyne, executive editor . Monthly magazine. "*Good Housekeeping* is edited for the 'New Traditionalist.' Articles which focus on food, fitness, beauty, and child care draw upon the resources of the Good Housekeeping Institute. Editorial includes human interest stories, articles that focus on social issues, money management, health news, travel, and 'The Better Way,' an 8-page hard-fact guide to better living." Circ. 5,000,000. **Pays on acceptance.** Byline given. Offers 25% kill fee. Buys first North American serial rights. Submit seasonal material 6 months in advance. Responds in 2-3 months to queries; 2-3 months to mss. For sample copy, call (800)925-0485. Writer's guidelines for #10 SASE.

Nonfiction Consumer, social issues, dramatic narrative, nutrition, work, relationships, psychology, trends. **Buys 4-6 mss/issue mss/year.** Query. Length: 1,500-2,500 words. Pays expenses of writers on assignment.

Photos Photos purchased on assignment mostly. Melissa Paterno, art director. Libby Fudo, photo editor. State availability with submission. Pays $100-350 for b&w; $200-400 for color photos. Model releases required.

Columns/Departments The Better Way, editor: Mary Kate Hogan (consumer advice, how-to, shopping strategies, money savers, health), 300-500 words. Profiles (inspirational, activist or heroic women), 400-600 words. Query with published clips. **Pays $1/word for items 300-600 words.**

Fiction Laura Mathews, fiction editor. No longer accepts unagented fiction submissions. Because of heavy volume of fiction submissions, *Good Housekeeping* is not accepting unsolicited submissions at this time. Agented submissions only. Length: 1,500 words (short-shorts); novel according to merit of material; average 5,000 word short stories. **Pays $1,000 minimum.**

Tips "Always send a SASE and clips. We prefer to see a query first. Do not send material on subjects already covered in-house by the Good Housekeeping Institute—these include food, beauty, needlework and crafts."

Ⓝ $ $ $ $ HARPER'S BAZAAR

The Hearst Corp., 1700 Broadway, 37th Floor, New York, NY 10019. (212)903-5000. Editor-in-Chief: Glenda Bailey. Senior Beauty Editor: Melissa Foss. Associate Beauty Editor: Victoria Kirby. **Contact:** Features Department. "*Harper's Bazaar* is a monthly specialist magazine for women who love fashion and beauty. It is edited for sophisticated women with exceptional taste. *Bazaar* offers ideas in fashion and beauty, and reports on issues and interests relevant to the lives of modern women." Estab. 1867. Circ. 711,000. Pays on publication. Byline given. Offers 25% kill fee. Worldwide rights. Responds in 2 months to queries. Sample copy not available. Writer's guidelines not available.

Nonfiction Buys 36 mss/year. Query with published clips. Length: 2,000-3,000 words. **Payment negotiable.**

Columns/Departments Length: 500-700 words. **Payment negotiable.**

N̲ I DO FOR BRIDES

Pinnacle Publishing Co., 4798 Long Island Dr. NW, Atlanta GA 30342. (404)255-1234. Fax: (404)255-2575. E-mail: editor@idoforbrides.com. Website: www.idoforbrides.com. **Contact:** Linda Sherbert, editor-in-chief. **30% freelance written.** Quarterly magazine covering the bridal industry. The magazine includes tips for wedding preparation, bridal attire, honeymoon and wedding destinations. Publishes 5 regional versions: Alabama; Georgia; Ohio; Tennessee; and Washington DC, Maryland, and Virginia. Estab. 1996. Circ. 160,000. Pays on other. Publishes ms an average of 8 months after acceptance. Byline given. Buys all rights. Editorial lead time 8 months. Submit seasonal material 8 months in advance. Accepts queries by mail, e-mail. Accepts simultaneous submissions.

Nonfiction Book excerpts, essays, general interest, historical/nostalgic, how-to (bridal-related), humor, inspirational, interview/profile, new product, opinion, personal experience, photo feature, religious, travel. **Buys 8 mss/year.** Query. Length: 300-1,000 words. **Pays variable rate.**

N̲ INSTYLE

Time, Inc., 1271 Avenue of the Americas, 18th Floor, New York NY 10020. (212)522-1212. Fax: (212)522-0867. E-mail: letters@instylemag.com. Website: www.instyle.com. Editor: Norman Pearlstine. Managing Editor: Charla Lawhon. Monthly magazine. Written to be the most trusted style adviser and lifestyle resource for women. Circ. 1,670,000. Editorial lead time 4 months. Sample copy not available.

N̲ JANE

Fairchild Publications, Inc., 7 W. 34th St., 3rd Floor, New York NY 10001. (212)630-3900. Fax: (212)630-3925. E-mail: jane@fairchildpub.com. Website: www.janemag.com. Editor: Jane Pratt. Beauty/Health Director: Erin Flaherty. Deputy Editor: Stephanie Trong. Assistant Beauty Editor: Jill Schuck. Monthly magazine for confident, media-savvy 18-34 year old women. Written in an honest, first person tone by women (and some men) who are living the lifestyle they are covering. Circ. 678,000. Sample copy not available.

- Only accepting submissions for fiction and column called "It happened to me." Most writing is done in-house.

N̲ $ $ $ $ ⊘ LADIES' HOME JOURNAL

Meredith Corp., 125 Park Ave., 20th Floor, New York NY 10017-5516. (212)557-6600. Fax: (212)455-1313. Website: www.lhj.com. Publisher: Lynn Lehmkuhl. Deputy Articles Editor: Nancy Bilyeau. Assistant to the Editor-in-Chief: Lisa Dicus. **Contact:** Diane Salvatore, editor-in-chief. **50% freelance written.** Monthly magazine focusing on issues of concern to women 30-45. They cover a broader range of news and political issues than many women's magazines. *"Ladies' Home Journal* is for active, empowered women who are evolving in new directions. It addresses informational needs with highly focused features and articles on a variety of topics including beauty and fashion, food and nutrition, health and medicine, home decorating and design, parenting and self-help, personalities and current events." Circ. 13,371,000. **Pays on acceptance.** Publishes ms an average of 4-12 months after acceptance. Offers 25% kill fee. Buys first North American serial rights. Rights bought vary with submission. Accepts queries by mail. Accepts simultaneous submissions. Responds in 3 months to queries. Sample copy not available. Writer's guidelines online.

Nonfiction Submissions on the following subjects should be directed to the editor listed for each: investigative reports, news-related features, psychology/relationships/sex (Roberta Caploe, executive editor); celebrities/entertainment (Laura Barostein). Query with published clips. Length: 2,000-3,000 words. **Pays $2,000-4,000.** Pays expenses of writers on assignment.

Photos LHJ arranges for its own photography almost all the time. State availability with submission. Rights bought vary with submission. Offers variable payment for photos accepted with ms. Captions, identification of subjects, model releases required.

Columns/Departments Query the following editor or box for column ideas. First Person (Roberta Caploe, executive editor). Query. **Pays $750-2,000.**

Fiction Editor. Only short stories and novels submitted by an agent or publisher will be considered. No poetry of any kind. **Buys 12 mss/year.** Send complete ms. Length: 2,000-2,500.

  ■ The online magazine carries original content not found in the print edition.

N̲ ⊘ LIFETIME MAGAZINE

Hearst Corp., 1790 Broadway, 11th Floor, New York NY 10019. (212)649-2800. Fax: (212)649-3845. Website: www.lifetimetv.com/magazine. Monthly magazine. Circ. 500,000.

- Does not buy freelance material or use freelance writers.

$ $⊡ THE LINK & VISITOR

Baptist Women of Ontario and Quebec, 1-315 Lonsdale Rd., Toronto ON M4V 1X3, Canada. (416)544-8550. E-mail: linkvis@baptistwomen.com. **Contact:** Editor. **50% freelance written.** Magazine published 6 times/ year "designed to help Baptist women grow their world, faith, relationships, creativity, and mission vision-evangelical, egalitarian, Canadian." Estab. 1878. Circ. 4,000. Pays on publication. Publishes ms an average of 6 months after acceptance. Byline given. Buys one-time, second serial (reprint), simultaneous rights, makes work-for-hire assignments. Editorial lead time 2 months. Submit seasonal material 4 months in advance. Accepts simultaneous submissions. Sample copy for 9×12 SAE with 2 first-class Canadian stamps. Writer's guidelines free.

Nonfiction "Articles must be Biblically literate. No easy answers, American mindset or U.S. focus, retelling of Bible stories, sermons." Inspirational, interview/profile, religious. **Buys 30-35 mss/year.** Send complete ms. Length: 750-2,000 words. **Pays 5-10¢/word (Canadian).** Sometimes pays expenses of writers on assignment.

Photos State availability with submission. Reviews prints. Buys one-time rights. Offers no additional payment for photos accepted with ms. Captions required.

Tips "We cannot use unsolicited manuscripts from non-Canadian writers. When submitting by e-mail, please send stories as messages, not as attachments."

$LONG ISLAND WOMAN

Maraj, Inc., P.O. Box 176, Malverne NY 11565. E-mail: editor@liwomanonline.com. Website: www.liwomanonline.com. **Contact:** A. Nadboy, managing editor. **40% freelance written.** Monthly magazine covering issues of importance to women—health, family, finance, arts, entertainment, fitness, travel, home. Estab. 2001. Circ. 40,000. Pays within 1 month of publication. Publishes ms an average of 3 months after acceptance. Byline given. Offers 33% kill fee. Buys one-time rights for print and online use. Editorial lead time 3 months. Submit seasonal material 3 months in advance. Accepts queries by mail, e-mail. Accepts previously published material. Accepts simultaneous submissions. Responds in 8 weeks to queries; 3 months to mss. Sample copy for $5. Writer's guidelines online. Editorial calendar online.

• Responds if interested in using reprints that were submitted.

Nonfiction Book excerpts, general interest, how-to, humor, interview/profile, new product, travel, reviews. **Buys 25-30 mss/year.** Query with published clips or send complete ms. Length: 500-1,800 words. **Pays $50-150 for assigned articles; $35-120 for unsolicited articles.**

Reprints Accepts previously published submissions.

Photos State availability of or send photos with submission. Reviews 5×7 prints. Captions, identification of subjects, model releases required.

Columns/Departments Humor; Health Issues; Family Issues; Financial and Business Issues; Book Reviews and Books; Arts and Entertainment; Travel and Leisure; Home and Garden; Fitness.

N ⊘ LUCKY

Conde Nast Publications, Inc., 4 Times Square, 8th Floor, New York NY 10036. (212)286-2860. Fax: (212)286-8083. E-mail: talktous@luckymag.com. Website: luckymag.com. Editor-in-Chief: Kim France. Fashion Assistants: Fiona Lennon, Ariela Suster, Heather Sumerville, Melissa Lamkin. Market Editors: Madeline Muney-Passarelli, Liz Kiernan. Fashion Director: Hope Greenberu. Senior Market Editor: Anne Kwon-Keane. Accessories Director: Ashley Kennedy. Senior Fashion Editors: Jennifer Smith, Lauren Rockwell. Fashion News Editor: Joyce Chang. Executive Editor: Gigi Guerra. Beauty Director: Jean Godfrey-June. Senior Beauty Editor: Lori Bergamotto. Associate Beauty Editor: Liz Flahne. Creative Director: Andrea Linett. West Coast Editor: Marlien Rentmeester. Associate Fashion Editor: Beth Siriani. Monthly magazine. Written as a lifestyle and shopping resource for young women. Circ. 779,521. Editorial lead time 3 months. Sample copy not available.

• All writers are on staff.

N $ $ $ $ MARIE CLAIRE

The Hearst Publishing Corp., 1790 Broadway, 3rd Floor, New York NY 10019. (212)649-5000. Fax: (212)649-5050. E-mail: marieclaire@hearst.com. Website: www.marieclaire.com. Editor: Lesley Jane Seymour. Monthly magazine. Written for today's younger working woman with a smart service-oriented view. Estab. 1937. Circ. 952,223. Editorial lead time 6 months. Sample copy not available.

$ $ $ $ MS. MAGAZINE

433 S. Beverly Dr., Beverly Hills CA 90212. (310)556-2515. Fax: (310)556-2514. E-mail: info@msmagazine.com. Website: www.msmagazine.com. Editor-in-Chief: Elaine Lafferty. **Contact:** Manuscripts Editor. **30% freelance written.** Quarterly magazine on women's issues and news. Estab. 1972. Circ. 150,000. Byline given. Offers 30% kill fee. Buys first North American serial rights. Responds in 2 months to queries; 2 months to mss. Sample copy for $9. Writer's guidelines online.

• No unsolicited fiction or poetry.

Nonfiction International and national (U.S.) news, the arts, books, popular culture, feminist theory and scholarship, ecofeminism, women's health, spirituality, political and economic affairs, photo essays. **Buys 4-5 feature**

(3,500 words) and 4-5 short (500 words) mss/year. Query with published clips. Length: 300-3,500 words. **Pays $1/word, 50¢/word for news stories.** Pays expenses of writers on assignment.

Reprints Send tearsheet or typed ms with rights for sale noted and information about when and where the material previously appeared. Pays 50% of amount paid for original article.

Photos State availability with submission. Buys one-time rights. Identification of subjects, model releases required.

Columns/Departments Length: 3,000 words maximum. **Buys 4-5 mss/year. Pays $1/word.**

Tips Needs "international and national women's news, investigative reporting, personal narratives, humor, world-class fiction and poetry, and prize-winning journalists and feminist thinkers."

N Ø O, THE OPRAH MAGAZINE

Hearst Corp., 1700 Broadway, 38th Floor, New York NY 10019-5905. (212)903-5187. Fax: (212)977-1947. Website: www.oprah.com. Monthly magazine. Circ. 2,200,000.

• Does not buy freelance material or use freelance writers.

$ $ GRACE ORMONDE WEDDING STYLE

Elegant Publishing, Inc., P.O. Box 89, Barrington RI 02806. (401)245-9726. Fax: (401)245-5371. E-mail: yanni@weddingstylemagazine.com. Website: www.weddingstylemagazine.com. Editor: Grace Ormonde. **Contact:** Yannis Tzoumas, editorial director/publisher. Annual magazine covering wedding and special event planning resource. "*Grace Ormonde Wedding Style* is a wedding and special event planning magazine with editorial covering home and home decorating, women's health issues, cooking, beauty, and travel." Estab. 1997. Circ. 400,000. Pays on publication. Publishes ms an average of 4 months after acceptance. Accepts queries by mail, e-mail, fax. Sample copy not available. Writer's guidelines not available.

Nonfiction General interest, how-to, interview/profile, personal experience, travel. **Buys 35 mss/year.** Query. Length: 300-3,500 words. **Pays $100-300.** Sometimes pays expenses of writers on assignment.

Photos State availability with submission. Reviews transparencies. Negotiates payment individually.

Columns/Departments Wedding related (flowers, beauty, etc.), 450 words, buys 25 mss/year; Women's Health, 3,000 words, buys 1 ms/year; Home Decorating/Cooking, 400 words, buys 5 mss/year; Travel, 350 words, buys 3 mss/year. Query. **Pays $100-300.**

$ $ $ Ø REDBOOK MAGAZINE

Hearst Corp., 224 W. 57th St., 6th Floor, New York NY 10019. (212)649-2000. Fax: (212)581-8114. E-mail: redbook@hearst.com. Website: www.redbookmag.com. Editor-in-chief: Ellen Kunes. Market/Sittings Editor: Samantha Schoengold. Assistant Articles Editor: Amanda May. Features Director: Andrea Bauman. Deputy Editor: Lisa Lombardi. Monthly magazine. "*Redbook* addresses young married women between the ages of 28 and 44. Most of our readers are married with children 10 and under; over 60 percent work outside the home. The articles entertain, educate and inspire our readers to confront challenging issues. Each article must be timely and relevant to *Redbook* readers' lives." Estab. 1903. Circ. 2,300,000. **Pays on acceptance.** Publishes ms an average of 6 months after acceptance. Rights purchased vary with author and material. Responds in 3 months to queries; 3 months to mss. Sample copy not available. Writer's guidelines online.

O→ "Please review at least the past six issues of *Redbook* to better understand subject matter and treatment."

Nonfiction Articles Department. Subjects of interest: Social issues, parenting, sex, marriage, news profiles, true crime, dramatic narratives, health. Query with published clips and SASE. Length: Articles: 2,500-3,000 words; short articles, 1,000-1,500 words.

Tips "Most *Redbook* articles require solid research, well-developed anecdotes from on-the-record sources, and fresh, insightful quotes from established experts in a field that pass our 'reality check' test. Articles must apply to women in our demographics."

N $ $ $ $ SELF

Condé Nast, 4 Times Square, New York NY 10036. (212)286-2860. Fax: (212)286-8110. E-mail: comments@self.com. Website: www.self.com. Editor-in-Chief: Lucy Danziger. **Contact:** Dana Points, executive editor. Monthly magazine for women ages 20-45. "Self-confidence, self-assurance, and a healthy, happy lifestyle are pivotal to *Self* readers. This healthy lifestyle magazine delivers by addressing real-life issues from the inside out, with unparalleled energy and authority. From beauty, fitness, health and nutrition to personal style, finance, and happiness, the path to total well-being begins with *Self*." Circ. 1,300,000. **Pays on acceptance.** Byline given on features and most short items. Buys one-time rights. Accepts simultaneous submissions. Responds in 1 month to queries. Sample copy not available. Writer's guidelines for #10 SASE.

• *SELF* magazine does not accept unsolicited mss.

O→ Break in with "an original, news-driven story idea conveyed with lively and compelling writing and storytelling."

Nonfiction Considers proposals for major pieces on health, nutrition, psychology, fitness, family relationships and sociological issues. **Buys 40 mss/year.** Query with published clips. Length: 1,500-5,000 words. **Pays $1-2/word.**

Columns/Departments Uses short, news-driven items on health, fitness, nutrition, money, jobs, love/sex, psychology and happiness, travel. Length: 300-1,000 words. **Buys 50 mss/year.** Query with published clips. **Pays $1-2/word.**

▣ The online version contains material not found in the print edition. Contact: Catherine Winters.

Ⓝ $ $▱ TODAY'S BRIDE

Family Communications, 65 The East Mall, Toronto ON M8Z SW3, Canada. (416)537-2604. Fax: (416)538-1794. E-mail: info@canadianbride.com. Website: www.todaysbride.ca.; www.canadianbride.com. Editor: Bettie Bradley. **Contact:** Tracy Cooper, assistant editor. **20% freelance written.** Semiannual magazine. "Magazine provides information to engaged couples on all aspects of wedding planning, including tips, fashion advice, etc. There are also beauty, home, groom, and honeymoon travel sections." Estab. 1979. Circ. 102,000. **Pays on acceptance.** Byline given. Buys all rights. Editorial lead time 6 months. Accepts queries by mail, e-mail, fax. Accepts simultaneous submissions. Responds in 2 weeks-1 month to queries. Sample copy not available. Writer's guidelines not available.

Nonfiction Humor, opinion, personal experience. No travel pieces. Query with or without published clips or send complete ms. Length: 800-1,400 words. **Pays $250-300.**

Photos Send photos with submission. Reviews transparencies, prints. Rights purchased negotiated on individual basis. Negotiates payment individually. Identification of subjects required.

Tips "Send us tight writing about topics relevant to all brides and grooms. Stories for grooms, especially those written by/about grooms, are also encouraged."

$ $▱ TODAY'S CHRISTIAN WOMAN

465 Gundersen Dr., Carol Stream IL 60188-2498. (630)260-6200. Fax: (630)260-0114. E-mail: tcwedit@christianitytoday.com. Website: www.todayschristianwoman.net. Editor: Jane Johnson Struck. Managing Editor: Camerin Courtney. **Contact:** Holly Robaina, assistant editor. **50% freelance written.** Bimonthly magazine for Christian women of all ages, single and married, homemakers, and career women. "*Today's Christian Woman* seeks to help women deal with the contemporary issues and hot topics that impact their lives, as well as provide depth, balance, and a Biblical perspective to the relationships they grapple with daily in the following arenas: family, friendship, faith, marriage, single life, self, work, and health." Estab. 1978. Circ. 260,000. **Pays on acceptance.** Publishes ms an average of 6-12 months after acceptance. Byline given. Buys first rights. Submit seasonal material 9 months in advance. Accepts queries by mail, e-mail, fax. Responds in 2 months to queries; 2 months to mss. Sample copy for $5. Writer's guidelines for #10 SASE or online.

Nonfiction How-to, narrative, inspirational. *Practical* spiritual living articles, 1,500-1,800 words. Humor (light, first-person pieces that include some spiritual distinctive), 1,000-1,500 words. Issues (third-person, anecdotal articles that report on scope of trends or hot topics, and provide perspective and practical take away on issues, plus sidebars), 1,800 words. How-to, inspirational. Query. No unsolicited mss. "The query should include article summary, purpose, and reader value, author's qualifications, suggested length, date to send, and SASE for reply." **Pays 20-25¢/word.**

Columns/Departments Faith @ Work (recent true story of how you shared your faith with someone on the job), 100-200 words; **pays $25.** Readers' Picks (a short review of your current favorite CD or book, and why), 200 words; **pays $25.** My Story (first-person, true-life dramatic story of how you solved a problem or overcame a difficult situation), 1,500-1,800 words; **pays $300.** Small Talk (true humorous or inspirational anecdotes about children), 50-100 words; **pays $25.** Does not return or acknowledge submissions to these departments.

Tips "Articles should be practical and contain a distinct evangelical Christian perspective. While *TCW* adheres strictly to this underlying perspective in all its editorial content, articles should refrain from using language that assumes a reader's familiarity with Christian or church-oriented terminology. Bible quotes and references should be used selectively. All Bible quotes should be taken from the New International Version if possible. All articles should be highly anecdotal, personal in tone, and universal in appeal."

Ⓝ $ $ $ $VOGUE

Condé Nast, 4 Times Square, 12th Floor, New York NY 10036-6518. (212)286-2860. Website: www.vogue.com. **Contact:** Laurie Jones, managing editor. Monthly magazine. "*Vogue* mirrors the changing roles and concerns of women, covering not only evolutions in fashion, beauty and style, but the important issues and ideas of the arts, health care, politics and world affairs." Estab. 1892. Circ. 1,174,677. **Pays on acceptance.** Byline sometimes given. Offers 25% kill fee. Responds in 3 months to queries. Sample copy not available. Writer's guidelines for #10 SASE.

Nonfiction "Needs fresh voices on unexpected topics." **Buys 5 unsolicited mss/year.** Query with published clips. Length: 2,500 words maximum. **Pays $1-2/word.**

Tips "Sophisticated, surprising and compelling writing a must." Please note: *Vogue* accepts *very* few unsolicited manuscripts. Most stories are generated in-house and are written by staff.

W

Fairchild Publications, Inc., 7 W. 34th St., 3rd Floor, New York NY 10001. (212)630-4000. Fax: (212)630-3566. Website: www.fairchildpub.com. Editor: Julie Belcove. Monthly magazine. Written for today's contemporary woman whose fashion sensibility and sense of style define her own look, in her own way. Circ. 471,265. Editorial lead time 6 weeks. Sample copy not available.

N $ $ WEDDINGBELLS

(Canada), WEDDINGBELLS, Inc., 34 King St. E., Suite 1200, Toronto ON M5C 2X8, Canada. E-mail: editorial@weddingbells.com. Website: www.weddingbells.com. **Contact:** Crys Stewart. **10% freelance written.** Semiannual magazine covering bridal, wedding, setting up home. Estab. 1985. Circ. 107,000 (Canada), 325,000 (USA). Pays on completion of assignment. Publishes ms an average of 6 months after acceptance. Offers 25% kill fee. Buys first North American serial, second serial (reprint), electronic rights. Accepts queries by mail, fax. Responds in 2 months to queries; 2 months to mss. Sample copy not available. Writer's guidelines not available.

Nonfiction Book excerpts, bridal service pieces. **Buys 22 mss/year.** Query with published clips. **Pays variable rates for assigned articles.** Sometimes pays expenses of writers on assignment.

WEDDINGBELLS, (U.S.)

WEDDINGBELLS, Inc., 34 King St. E., Suite 1200, Toronto ON M5C 2X8, Canada. (416)363-1574. Fax: (416)363-6004. E-mail: editorialdept@weddingbells.com. Website: www.weddingbells.com. Editor: Crys Stewart. **Contact:** Michael Killingsworth, managing editor. **10% freelance written.** Semiannual magazine covering bridal, wedding, setting up home. Estab. 2000. Circ. 350,000. Pays on completion of assignment. Publishes ms an average of 6 months after acceptance. Byline sometimes given. Offers 25% kill fee. Buys first North American serial, second serial (reprint), electronic rights. Accepts queries by mail, fax. Responds in 2 months to queries.

• Does not accept unsolicited materials.

Nonfiction Book excerpts, bridal service pieces. **Buys 22 mss/year.** Query with published clips. **Pays variable rates for assigned articles.**

N $ $ WOMAN'S DAY

54-58 Park St., Sydney NSW 2000, Australia. 9282 8000. Fax: 9267 4360. Weekly "Magazine for women of all ages (and the men in their lives enjoy it too)." Buys Purchases the first Australian and New Zealand rights rights. Accepts queries by e-mail, fax.

Fiction Julie Redlich, fiction editor. **Payment is usually $350 (Australian) for under 1,000 words; $450 for longer stories, up to 2,500 words.**

N $ $ $ WOMAN'S OWN

Harris Publications, Inc., 1115 Broadway, New York NY 10010. (212)807-7100. Fax: (212)627-4678. E-mail: editor@womansown.com. Website: womansown.com. **50% freelance written.** Magazine published 8 times/year. "Woman's Own is a self-improvement/lifestyle magazine for women 25-45. It is a service publication which offers advice, inspiration and tips on relationships, self esteem, beauty, health and jobs." Estab. 1993. Circ. 200,000. Pays on publication. Publishes ms an average of 2 months after acceptance. Byline given. Offers 25% kill fee. Buys first North American serial, one-time, second serial (reprint) rights. Editorial lead time 4 months. Submit seasonal material 5 months in advance. Accepts simultaneous submissions. Responds in 3 weeks to queries; 1 month to mss. Sample copy for $4. Writer's guidelines for #10 SASE.

Nonfiction Book excerpts, inspirational, interview/profile, personal experience, travel. No fiction, poetry, recipes or humor. **Buys 30 mss/year.** Query with published clips or send complete ms. Length: 900-2,000 words. **Pays $350-900 for assigned articles; $250 for unsolicited articles.** Pays expenses of writers on assignment.

Photos State availability with submission. Reviews transparencies, Prints. Buys one-time rights. Negotiates payment individually. Captions, model releases required.

Columns/Departments Women Doing It Their Way (real women entrepreneurs or women who overcome obstacles to find success), 100-250 words; Money Matters (saving money, ideas, best ideas), 900-1,200 words. **Buys 10 mss/year.** Query with published clips or send complete ms. **Pays $200-400.**

Tips "Be very specific, very narrowly focused about what you want to write about. Keep queries concise. Do not try to oversell an idea. If it's good, it'll sell itself."

Ⓝ $ $ $ WOMAN'S WORLD

Bauer Publishing Co., 270 Sylvan Ave., Englewood Cliffs NJ 07632. (201)569-6699. Fax: (201)569-3584. Editor-in-Chief: Stephanie Saible. **Contact:** Kathleen Fitzpatrick, senior editor; Johnene Granger, fiction editor. **95% freelance written.** Weekly magazine covering "human interest and service pieces of interest to family-oriented women across the nation. *Woman's World* is a women's service magazine. It offers a blend of fashion, food, parenting, beauty, and relationship features coupled with the true-life human interest stories." "We publish short romances and mini-mysteries for all woman, ages 18-68." Estab. 1980. Circ. 1,625,779. **Pays on acceptance.** Publishes ms an average of 4 months after acceptance. for First North American Serial rights for 6 months. Submit seasonal material 4 months in advance. Accepts queries by mail. Responds in 2 months to mss. Sample copy not available. Writer's guidelines for #10 SASE.

Nonfiction Dramatic personal women's stories and articles on self-improvement, medicine, and health topics. Please specify "Real-Life Story" on envelope. Features include Emergency (real-life drama); My Story; Medical Miracle; Triumph; Courage; My Guardian Angel; Happy Ending (queries to Kathy Fitzpatrick). Also service stories on parenting, marriage, and work (queries to Irene Daria). **Pays $500/1,000 words.**

Fiction Johnene Granger, fiction editor. Short story, romance, and mainstream of 1,100 words and mini-mysteries of 1,000 words. "Each of our stories has a light romantic theme and can be written from either a masculine or feminine point of view. Women characters may be single, married, or divorced. Plots must be fast moving with vivid dialogue and action. The problems and dilemmas inherent in them should be contemporary and realistic, handled with warmth and feeling. The stories must have a positive resolution." Specify "Fiction" on envelope. Always enclose SASE. Responds in 4 months. No phone or fax queries. Pays $1,000 for romances on acceptance for North American serial rights for 6 months. "The 1,000 word mini-mysteries may feature either a 'whodunnit' or 'howdunnit' theme. The mystery may revolve around anything from a theft to murder. However, we are not interested in sordid or grotesque crimes. Emphasis should be on intricacies of plot rather than gratuitous violence. The story must include a resolution that clearly states the villain is getting his or her come-uppance." Submit complete mss. Specify "Mini-Mystery" on envelope. Enclose SASE. No phone queries. Mystery, romance. Not interested in science fiction, fantasy, historical romance, or foreign locales. No explicit sex, graphic language, or seamy settings. Send complete ms. Length: Romances—1,100 words; mysteries—1,000 words. **Pays $1,000/romances; $500/mysteries.**

Tips "The whole story should be sent when submitting fiction. Stories slanted for a particular holiday should be sent at least 6 months in advance."

WOMEN ALIVE

Encouraging Excellence in Holy Living, Women Alive, Inc., P.O. Box 480052, Kansas City MO 64145. Phone/Fax: (913)402-1369. E-mail: ahinthorn@kc.rr.com. Website: www.womenalivemagazine.org. Managing Editor: Jeanette Littleton. **Contact:** Aletha Hinthorn, editor. **50% freelance written.** Bimonthly magazine covering Christian living. "*Women Alive* encourages and equips women to live holy lives through teaching them to live out Scripture." Estab. 1984. Circ. 4,000. Pays on publication. Publishes ms an average of 6 months after acceptance. Byline given. Buys first North American serial, first, one-time, second serial (reprint), simultaneous rights. Editorial lead time 4 months. Submit seasonal material 4 months in advance. Accepts queries by mail, e-mail. Accepts simultaneous submissions. Responds in 6 weeks to mss. Sample copy for 9 × 12 SAE and 3 first-class stamps. Writer's guidelines for 9 × 12 SAE with 3 first-class stamps.

Nonfiction Inspirational, opinion, personal experience, religious. **Buys 30 mss/year.** Send complete ms. Length: 500-1,500 words.

Photos State availability with submission. Offers no additional payment for photos accepted with ms.

Trade Journals

Many writers who pick up *Writer's Market* for the first time do so with the hope of selling an article to one of the popular, high-profile consumer magazines found on newsstands and in bookstores. Many of those writers are surprised to find an entire world of magazine publishing exists outside the realm of commercial magazines and that they may have never known about—trade journals. Writers who *have* discovered trade journals have found a market that offers the chance to publish regularly in subject areas they find interesting, editors who are typically more accessible than their commercial counterparts, and pay rates that rival those of the big-name magazines. **(Note: All of the magazines listed in the Trade Journals section are paying markets. However, some of the magazines are not identified by payment rates ($-$$$) because the magazines preferred not to disclose specific payment information.)**

Trade journal is the general term for any publication focusing on a particular occupation or industry. Other terms used to describe the different types of trade publications are business, technical, and professional journals. They are read by truck drivers, bricklayers, farmers, fishermen, heart surgeons, and just about everyone else working in a trade or profession. Trade periodicals are sharply angled to the specifics of the professions on which they report. They offer business-related news, features, and service articles that will foster their readers' professional development.

Trade magazine editors tell us their readers are a knowledgeable and highly interested audience. Writers for trade magazines have to either possess knowledge about the field in question or be able to report it accurately from interviews with those who do. Writers who have or can develop a good grasp of a specialized body of knowledge will find trade magazine editors who are eager to hear from them.

An ideal way to begin your foray into trade journals is to write for those that report on your present profession. Whether you've been teaching dance, farming, or working as a paralegal, begin by familiarizing yourself with the magazines that serve your occupation. After you've read enough issues to have a feel for the kinds of pieces the magazines run, approach the editors with your own article ideas. If you don't have experience in a profession but can demonstrate an ability to understand (and write about) the intricacies and issues of a particular trade that interests you, editors will still be willing to hear from you.

Information on trade publications listed in the previous edition of *Writer's Market*, but not included in this edition, can be found in the General Index.

ADVERTISING, MARKETING & PR

$ $ BIG IDEA

Detroit's Connection to the Communication Arts, Big Idea, 2145 Crooks Rd., Suite 208, Troy MI 48084. (248)458-5500. Fax: (248)458-7099. E-mail: info@bigideaweb.com. Website: www.bigideaweb.com. **Contact:** Conny Coon, managing editor (send e-mail queries to ccoon@bigideaweb.com). **75% freelance written.** Monthly magazine covering creative and communication arts in Southeastern Michigan. "We are a trade magazine specifically for creative professionals in the advertising, marketing and communication arts industry in Southeastern Michigan. Detroit is the third largest advertising market in the U.S. We are the resource for anyone in the agency, film and video, printing, post production, interactive, art and design, illustration, or photography." Estab. 1994. Circ. 10,000. **Pays on acceptance.** Publishes ms an average of 2 months after acceptance. Byline sometimes given. Offers 100% kill fee. Editorial lead time 2 months. Accepts queries by mail, e-mail, fax. Accepts previously published material. Responds in 6 weeks to queries. and 4 first-class stamps.

Nonfiction Conny Coon, VP Editorial. **Buys 10-12 mss/year.** Query with published clips. Length: 1,500-2,500 words. **Pays $100-350 for assigned articles.** Sometimes pays expenses of writers on assignment.

Photos State availability with submission. Reviews GIF/JPEG files. Offers no additional payment for photos accepted with ms. Captions, identification of subjects, model releases required.

$ $ $ BRAND PACKAGING

Stagnito Communications, 155 Pfingsten Rd., Suite 205, Deerfield IL 60015. (847)205-5660, ext. 4113. Fax: (847)205-5680. E-mail: bswientek@stagnito.com. Website: www.brandpackaging.com. Senior Editor: Jim George. **Contact:** Bob Swientek, editor. **15% freelance written.** Magazine published 10 times/year covering how packaging can be a marketing tool. "We publish strategies and tactics to make products stand out on the shelf. Our market is brand managers who are marketers but need to know something about packaging." Estab. 1997. Circ. 33,000. **Pays on acceptance.** Publishes ms an average of 2 months after acceptance. Byline given. Makes work-for-hire assignments. Editorial lead time 3 months. Submit seasonal material 3 months in advance. Accepts queries by mail, fax. Sample copy for free.

Nonfiction How-to, interview/profile, new product. **Buys 10 mss/year.** Send complete ms. Length: 600-2,400 words. **Pays 40-50¢/word.**

Photos State availability with submission. Reviews contact sheets, 35mm transparencies, 4×5 prints. Buys one-time rights. Negotiates payment individually. Identification of subjects required.

Columns/Departments Emerging Technology (new packaging technology), 600 words. **Buys 10 mss/year.** Query. **Pays $150-300.**

Tips "Be knowledgeable on marketing techniques and be able to grasp packaging techniques. Be sure you focus on packaging as a marketing tool. Use concrete examples. We are not seeking case histories at this time."

$ DECA DIMENSIONS

1908 Association Dr., Reston VA 20191. (703)860-5000. Fax: (703)860-4013. E-mail: deca_dimensions@deca.org. Website: www.deca.org. **Contact:** Cindy Sweeney, editor. **30% freelance written.** Quarterly magazine covering marketing, professional development, business, career training during school year (no issues published May-August). "*DECA Dimensions* is the membership magazine for DECA—The Association of Marketing Students—primarily ages 15-19 in all 50 states, the U.S. territories, Germany, and Canada. The magazine is delivered through the classroom. Students are interested in developing professional, leadership, and career skills." Estab. 1947. Circ. 160,000. Pays on publication. Byline given. Buys first, second serial (reprint) rights. Editorial lead time 3 months. Submit seasonal material 4 months in advance. Accepts queries by mail, e-mail, fax, phone. Accepts simultaneous submissions. Sample copy for free.

Nonfiction "Interested in seeing trends/forecast information of interest to audience (How do you forecast? Why? What are the trends for the next 5 years in fashion or retail?)." Essays, general interest, how-to (get jobs, start business, plan for college, etc.), interview/profile (business leads), personal experience (working), leadership development. **Buys 10 mss/year.** Send complete ms. Length: 800-1,000 words. **Pays $125 for assigned articles; $100 for unsolicited articles.**

Reprints Send ms and information about when and where the material previously appeared. Pays 85% of amount paid for an original article.

Columns/Departments Professional Development; Leadership, 350-500 words. **Buys 6 mss/year.** Send complete ms. **Pays $75-100.**

N $ FORMAT MAGAZINE

Minnesota Advertising & Communications Monthly, Decker Publications, 315 5th Ave. NW, St. Paul MN 55112. (651)628-2468. Fax: (651)633-1862. E-mail: format@deckerpublications.com. Website: www.formatmagazine.com. **Contact:** Gabe Castaneda, editor. **90% freelance written.** Monthly magazine covering the marketing communication industry in Minnesota. Estab. 1954. Circ. 6,000. Pays on publication. Byline given. Buys one-time rights. Editorial lead time 1 months. Accepts queries by mail. Accepts simultaneous submissions. Sample copy for #10 SASE. Writer's guidelines for #10 SASE or online.

Nonfiction General interest, historical/nostalgic, humor, interview/profile, photo feature. **Buys 2 mss/year.** Send complete ms. Length: 300-800 words. **Pays $25-50.**

Photos Send photos with submission. Buys one-time rights. Negotiates payment individually. Identification of subjects required.

Columns/Departments Advertising (ad humor), 400 words. **Buys 12 mss/year.** Send complete ms. **Pays $25-50.**

Fillers Anecdotes, facts, gags to be illustrated by cartoonist, newsbreaks, short humor. **Buys 12/year.** Length: 100-300 words. **Pays $10-25.**

MEDIA INC.

Pacific Northwest Media, Marketing and Creative Services News, P.O. Box 24365, Seattle WA 98124-0365. (206)382-9220. Fax: (206)382-9437. E-mail: media@media-inc.com. Website: www.media-inc.com. Publisher: James Baker. **Contact:** Hilary Smith, editor. **30% freelance written.** Bimonthly magazine covering Northwest US media, advertising, marketing, and creative-service industries. Audience is Northwest ad agencies, marketing professionals, media, and creative-service professionals. Estab. 1987. Circ. 10,000. Byline given. Responds in 1 month to queries. Sample copy for 9×12 SAE and 6 first-class stamps.

Tips "It is best if writers live in the Pacific Northwest and can report on local news and events in Media Inc.'s areas of business coverage."

$ $ $ PROMO MAGAZINE

Insights and Ideas for Building Brands, Primedia, 11 Riverbend Dr., Stamford CT 06907. (203)358-4226. Fax: (203)358-9900. E-mail: kjoyce@primediabusiness.com. Website: www.promomagazine.com. **Contact:** Kathleen Joyce, editor. **5% freelance written.** Monthly magazine covering promotion marketing. "*Promo* serves marketers, and stories must be informative, well written, and familiar with the subject matter." Estab. 1987. Circ. 25,000. Pays on publication. Publishes ms an average of 2 months after acceptance. Byline given. Offers 25% kill fee. Buys first North American serial rights. Editorial lead time 3 months. Submit seasonal material 3 months in advance. Responds in 1 month to queries. Sample copy for $5.

Nonfiction Exposé, general interest, how-to (marketing programs), interview/profile, new product (promotion). "No general marketing stories not heavily involved in promotions." Generally does not accept unsolicited mss, query first. **Buys 6-10 mss/year.** Query with published clips. Length: Variable. **Pays $1,000 maximum for assigned articles; $500 maximum for unsolicited articles.** Sometimes pays expenses of writers on assignment.

Photos State availability with submission. Reviews contact sheets, negatives. Negotiates payment individually. Captions, identification of subjects, model releases required.

Tips "Understand that our stories aim to teach marketing professionals about successful promotion strategies. Case studies or new promos have the best chance."

$ $ SIGN BUILDER ILLUSTRATED

America's How-To Sign Magazine, Simmons-Boardman Publishing Corp., 345 Hudson St., 12th Floor, New York NY 10014. (252)355-5806. Fax: (252)355-5690. E-mail: jwooten@sbpub.com. Website: www.signshop.com. Associate Editor: Chris Ytuarte. **Contact:** Jeff Wooten, editor. **40% freelance written.** Monthly magazine covering sign and graphic industry. "*Sign Builder Illustrated* targets sign professionals where they work: on the shop floor. Our topics cover the broadest spectrum of the sign industry, from design to fabrication, installation, maintenance and repair. Our readers own a similarly wide range of shops, including commercial, vinyl, sign erection and maintenance, electrical and neon, architectural, and awnings." Estab. 1987. Circ. 14,500. **Pays on acceptance.** Publishes ms an average of 3 months after acceptance. Byline given. Offers 10% kill fee. Buys all rights. Editorial lead time 3 months. Submit seasonal material 4 months in advance. Accepts queries by mail, e-mail, fax, phone. Accepts simultaneous submissions. Responds in 1 month to queries. Sample copy for free. Writer's guidelines free.

Nonfiction Historical/nostalgic, how-to, humor, interview/profile, photo feature, technical. **Buys 50-60 mss/year.** Query. Length: 1,000-1,500 words. **Pays $250-550 for assigned articles.**

Photos Send photos with submission. Reviews 3×5 prints. Buys all rights. Negotiates payment individually. Captions, identification of subjects required.

Tips "Be very knowledgeable about a portion of the sign industry you are covering. We want our readers to come away from each article with at least one good idea, one new technique, or one more 'trick of the trade.' At the same time, we don't want a purely textbook listing of 'do this, do that.' Our readers enjoy *Sign Builder Illustrated* because the publication speaks to them in a clear and lively fashion, from one sign professional to another. We want to engage the reader who has been in the business for some time. While there might be a place for basic instruction in new techniques, our average paid subscriber has been in business over twenty years, employs over seven people, and averages of $800,000 in annual sales. These people aren't neophytes content with retread articles they can find anywhere. It's important for our writers to use anecdotes and examples drawn from the daily sign business."

N $ $ SIGNCRAFT

The Magazine for Today's Sign Maker, SignCraft Publishing Co., Inc., P.O. Box 60031, Fort Myers FL 33906. (239)939-4644. Fax: (239)939-0607. E-mail: signcraft@signcraft.com. Website: www.signcraft.com. **Contact:** Tom McIltrot, editor. **10% freelance written.** Bimonthly magazine covering the sign industry. "Like any trade magazine, we need material of direct benefit to our readers. We can't afford space for material of marginal interest." Estab. 1980. Circ. 14,000. Pays on publication. Publishes ms an average of 6 months after acceptance. Byline given. Offers negotiable kill fee. Buys first North American serial, all rights. Accepts queries by mail, e-mail, fax. Responds in 1 month to queries. Sample copy and writer's guidelines for $3.

Nonfiction "All articles should be directly related to quality commercial signs. If you are familiar with the sign trade, we'd like to hear from you." Interview/profile. **Buys 10 mss/year.** Query with or without published clips. Length: 500-2,000 words.

$ $ SIGNS OF THE TIMES

The Industry Journal Since 1906, ST Publications, Dept. WM, 407 Gilbert Ave., Cincinnati OH 45202-2285. (513)421-2050. Fax: (513)421-5144. E-mail: swormstedt@stmediagroup.com. Website: www.signweb.com. **Contact:** Wade Swormstedt, editor/publisher. **15-30% freelance written.** Monthly magazine covering the sign and outdoor advertising industries. Estab. 1906. Circ. 17,000. Pays on publication. Publishes ms an average of 3 months after acceptance. Byline given. Buys variable rights. Accepts queries by mail, e-mail, fax, phone. Responds in 3 months to queries. Sample copy and writer's guidelines for 9 × 12 SAE with 10 first-class stamps.

Nonfiction Historical/nostalgic (regarding the sign industry), how-to (carved signs, goldleaf, etc.), interview/profile (focusing on either a signshop or a specific project), photo feature (query first), technical (sign engineering, etc.). Nothing "nonspecific on signs, an example being a photo essay on 'signs I've seen.' We are a trade journal with specific audience interests." **Buys 15-20 mss/year.** Query with published clips. **Pays $150-500.**

Reprints Send tearsheet or typed ms with rights for sale noted and information about when and where the material previously appeared. Payment is negotiated.

Photos "Sign industry-related photos only. We sometimes accept photos with funny twists or misspellings." Send photos with submission.

Fillers Open to queries; request rates.

■ The online version contains material not found in the print edition.

Tips "Be thoroughly familiar with the sign industry, especially in the CAS-related area. Have an insider's knowledge plus an insider's contacts."

ART, DESIGN & COLLECTIBLES

$ $ AIRBRUSH ACTION MAGAZINE

Action, Inc., 3209 Atlantic Ave., Allenwood NJ 08720. (732)223-7878. Fax: (732)223-2855. E-mail: editor@airbrushaction.com. Website: www.airbrushaction.com. **80% freelance written.** Bimonthly magazine covering the spectrum of airbrush applications: Illustration, T-shirt airbrushing, fine art, automotive and sign painting, hobby/craft applications, wall murals, fingernails, temporary tattoos, artist profiles, reviews and more. Estab. 1985. Circ. 35,000. Pays 1 month after publication. Publishes ms an average of 6 months after acceptance. Byline given. Buys all rights. Editorial lead time 6 months. Submit seasonal material 6 months in advance. Accepts queries by mail, e-mail, fax, phone. Accepts simultaneous submissions.

Nonfiction Current primary focus on automotive, motorcycle, and helmet kustom kulture arts. How-to, humor, inspirational, interview/profile, new product, personal experience, technical. Nothing unrelated to airbrush. Query with published clips. **Pays 15¢/word.** Sometimes pays expenses of writers on assignment.

Photos Send photos with submission. Buys all rights. Negotiates payment individually. Captions, identification of subjects, model releases required.

Columns/Departments Query with published clips.

■ The online version contains material not found in the print edition.

Tips "Send bio and writing samples. Send well-written technical information pertaining to airbrush art. We publish a lot of artist profiles—they all sound the same. Looking for new pizzazz!"

$ $ ANTIQUEWEEK

DMG World Media (USA), P.O. Box 90, Knightstown IN 46148-0090. (800)876-5133. Fax: (800)695-8153. E-mail: connie@antiqueweek.com. Website: www.antiqueweek.com. Managing Editor: Connie Swaim. **80% freelance**

written. Weekly tabloid covering antiques and collectibles with 2 editions: Eastern and Central, plus monthly *AntiqueWest.* "AntiqueWeek has a wide range of readership from dealers and auctioneers to collectors, both advanced and novice. Our readers demand accurate information presented in an entertaining style." Estab. 1968. Circ. 50,000. Pays on publication. Byline given. Offers 10% kill fee or $25. Buys first, second serial (reprint) rights. Submit seasonal material 1 month in advance. Accepts queries by mail, e-mail, fax. Sample copy for free. Writer's guidelines for #10 SASE.

Nonfiction Historical/nostalgic, how-to, interview/profile, opinion, personal experience, antique show and auction reports, feature articles on particular types of antiques and collectibles. **Buys 400-500 mss/year.** Query. Length: 1,000-2,000 words. **Pays $50-250.**

Reprints Send tearsheet or typed ms with rights for sale noted and information about when and where the material previously appeared.

Photos Send photos with submission. Identification of subjects required.

Tips "Writers should know their topics thoroughly. Feature articles must be well researched and clearly written. An interview and profile article with a knowledgeable collector might be the break for a first-time contributor. We seek a balanced mix of information on traditional antiques and 20th century collectibles."

$ THE APPRAISERS STANDARD

New England Appraisers Association, 5 Gill Terrace, Ludlow VT 05149-1003. (802)228-7444. Fax: (802)228-7444. E-mail: llt44@ludl.tds.net. Website: www.newenglandappraisers.net. **Contact:** Linda L. Tucker, publisher/editor. **50% freelance written.** Works with a small number of new/unpublished writers each year. Quarterly publication covering the appraisals of antiques, art, collectibles, jewelry, coins, stamps, and real estate. "The writer should be knowledgeable on the subject, and the article should be written with appraisers in mind, with prices quoted for objects, good pictures, and descriptions of articles being written about." Estab. 1980. Circ. 1,300. Pays on publication. Publishes ms an average of 1 year after acceptance. Short bio and byline given. Buys first and simultaneous rights. Submit seasonal material 2 months in advance. Accepts queries by mail, e-mail. Accepts simultaneous submissions. Responds in 1 month to queries; 2 months to mss. Sample copy for 9×12 SAE with 78¢ postage. Writer's guidelines for #10 SASE.

Nonfiction "All geared toward professional appraisers." Interview/profile, personal experience, technical, travel. Query with or without published clips or send complete ms. Length: 700 words. **Pays $50.**

Reprints Send ms with rights for sale noted and information about when and where the material previously appeared.

Photos Send photos with submission. Reviews negatives, prints. Buys one-time rights. Offers no additional payment for photos accepted with ms. Identification of subjects required.

Tips "Interviewing members of the association for articles, reviewing, shows, and large auctions are all ways for writers who are not in the field to write articles for us. Articles should be geared to provide information which will help the appraisers with ascertaining value, detecting forgeries or reproductions, or simply providing advice on appraising the articles.

ARCHITECTURAL RECORD

McGraw-Hill, 2 Penn Plaza, 9th Floor, New York NY 10121. (212)904-2594. Fax: (212)904-4256. E-mail: rivy@m cgraw-hill.com. Website: www.architecturalrecord.com. Editor: Robert Ivy, FAIA. Managing Editor: Ingrid Whitehead. **50% freelance written.** Monthly magazine covering architecture and design. "Our readers are architects, designers, and related professionals." Estab. 1891. Circ. 110,000. Pays on publication. Publishes ms an average of 2 months after acceptance. Byline given. Offers 25% kill fee. Buys all rights. Editorial lead time 2 months. Submit seasonal material 2 months in advance. Accepts queries by mail. Responds in 2 weeks to queries; 2 months to mss. Sample copy and writer's guidelines online.

$ $ ART MATERIALS RETAILER

Fahy-Williams Publishing, 171 Reed St., P.O. Box 1080, Geneva NY 14456-8080. (315)789-0458. Fax: (315)789-4263. E-mail: tmanzer@fwpi.com. Website: www.artmaterialsretailer.com. **Contact:** Tina Manzer, editor. **10% freelance written.** Quarterly magazine. Estab. 1998. Pays on publication. Byline given. Buys one-time rights. Editorial lead time 2 months. Submit seasonal material 3 months in advance. Accepts simultaneous submissions. Responds in 3 weeks to queries; 3 months to mss. Sample copy for free. Writer's guidelines free.

Nonfiction Book excerpts, how-to, interview/profile, personal experience. **Buys 2 mss/year.** Send complete ms. Length: 1,500-3,000 words. **Pays $50-250.** Sometimes pays expenses of writers on assignment.

Photos State availability with submission. Reviews transparencies. Buys one-time rights. Offers no additional payment for photos accepted with ms. Identification of subjects required.

Fillers Anecdotes, facts, newsbreaks. **Buys 5/year.** Length: 500-1,500 words. **Pays $50-125.**

Tips "We like to review manuscripts rather than queries. Artwork (photos, drawings, etc.) is a real plus. We enjoy (our readers enjoy) practical, nuts and bolts, news-you-can-use articles."

$ARTS MANAGEMENT

110 Riverside Dr., Suite 4E, New York NY 10024. (212)579-2039. **Contact:** A.H. Reiss, editor. **1% freelance written.** Magazine published 5 times/year for cultural institutions. Estab. 1962. Circ. 6,000. Pays on publication. Byline given. Buys all rights. Accepts queries by mail. Responds in 2 months to queries. Writer's guidelines for #10 SASE.

- *Arts Management* is almost completely staff-written and uses very little outside material.

Nonfiction Short articles, 400-900 words, tightly written, expository, explaining how arts administrators solved problems in publicity, fund raising, and general administration; actual case histories emphasizing the how-to. Also short articles on the economics and sociology of the arts and important trends in the nonprofit cultural field. Must be fact filled, well organized, and without rhetoric. No photographs or pictures. **Pays 2-4¢/word.**

$ $ $HOW

Design Ideas at Work, F + W Publications, Inc., 4700 E. Galbraith Rd., Cincinnati OH 45236. (513)531-2222. Fax: (513)531-2902. E-mail: editorial@howdesign.com. Website: www.howdesign.com. **Contact:** Bryn Mooth, editor. **75% freelance written.** Bimonthly magazine covering graphic design profession. "*HOW: Design Ideas at Work* strives to serve the business, technological and creative needs of graphic-design professionals. The magazine provides a practical mix of essential business information, up-to-date technological tips, the creative whys and hows behind noteworthy projects, and profiles of professionals who are impacting design. The ultimate goal of *HOW* is to help designers, whether they work for a design firm or for an inhouse design department, run successful, creative, profitable studios." Estab. 1985. Circ. 40,000. **Pays on acceptance.** Byline given. Buys first North American serial rights. Responds in 6 weeks to queries. Sample copy for cover price plus $1.50 (cover price varies per issue). Writer's guidelines and editorial calendar online.

Nonfiction Features cover noteworthy design projects, interviews with leading creative professionals, profiles of established and up-and-coming firms, business and creativity topics for graphic designers. Special issues: Self-Promotion Annual (September/October); Business Annual (November/December); International Annual of Design (March/April); Creativity/Paper/Stock Photography (May/June); Digital Design Annual (July/August). No how-to articles for beginning artists or fine-art-oriented articles. **Buys 40 mss/year.** Query with published clips and samples of subject's work, artwork or design. Length: 1,500-2,000 words. **Pays $700-900.** Sometimes pays expenses of writers on assignment.

Photos State availability with submission. Reviews Information updated and verified. Buys one-time rights. Captions required.

Columns/Departments Design Disciplines (focuses on lucrative fields for designers/illustrators); Workspace (takes an inside look at the design of creatives' studios), 1,200-1,500 words. **Buys 35 mss/year.** Query with published clips. **Pays $250-400.**

Tips "We look for writers who can recognize graphic designers on the cutting-edge of their industry, both creatively and business-wise. Writers must have an eye for detail, and be able to relay *HOW*'s editorial style in an interesting, concise manner—without omitting any details. Showing you've done your homework on a subject—and that you can go beyond asking 'those same old questions'—will give you a big advantage."

$ $INTERIOR BUSINESS MAGAZINE

The Lawn & Landscape Media Group, 4012 Bridge Ave., Cleveland OH 44113. (800)456-0707. Fax: (216)961-0364. E-mail: acybulski@interiorbusinessonline.com. Website: www.interiorbusinessonline.com. Publisher: Bob West. **Contact:** Ali Cybulski, editor. **5-10% freelance written.** Magazine covering interior landscaping. "*Interior Business* addresses the concerns of the professional interior landscape contractor. It's devoted to the business management needs of interior landscape professionals." Estab. 2000. Circ. 6,000. Pays on publication. Publishes ms an average of 3 months after acceptance. Editorial lead time 3 months. Submit seasonal material 5 months in advance. Responds in 1 week to queries.

Nonfiction Interior landscaping. "No articles oriented to the consumer or homeowner." **Buys 2 mss/year.** Length: 1,000-2,500 words. **Pays $250-500.**

Tips "Know the audience. It's the professional business person, not the consumer."

[N] $ $ $PRINT

America's Graphic Design Magazine, F + W Publications, 116 E. 27th St., 6th Floor, New York NY 10016. (212)447-1430. Fax: (212)447-5231. E-mail: info@printmag.com. Website: www.printmag.com. **75% freelance written.** Bimonthly magazine covering graphic design and visual culture. "*PRINT*'s articles, written by design specialists and cultural critics, focus on the social, political, and historical context of graphic design, and on the places where consumer culture and popular culture meet. We aim to produce a general interest magazine for professionals, with engagingly written text and lavish illustrations. By covering a broad spectrum of topics, both international and local, we try to demonstrate the significance of design in the world at large." Estab. 1940. Circ. 45,000. **Pays on acceptance.** Publishes ms an average of 3 months after acceptance. Byline given.

Offers 50% kill fee. Buys first North American serial rights. Editorial lead time 3 months. Submit seasonal material 3 months in advance. Accepts queries by e-mail. Responds in 2 weeks to queries; 1 month to mss. Sample copy not available.

Nonfiction Essays, interview/profile, opinion. **Buys 35-40 mss/year.** Query with published clips. Length: 1,000-2,500 words. **Pays $1,250.** Sometimes pays expenses of writers on assignment.

Columns/Departments Query with published clips. **Pays $800.**

Tips "Be well-versed in issues related to the field of graphic design; don't submit ideas that are too general or geared to nonprofessionals."

$TEXAS ARCHITECT

Texas Society of Architects, 816 Congress Ave., Suite 970, Austin TX 78701. (512)478-7386. Fax: (512)478-0528. E-mail: editor@texasarchitect.org. Website: www.texasarchitect.org. **Contact:** Stephen Sharpe, editor. **30% freelance written.** Mostly written by unpaid members of the professional society. Bimonthly journal covering architecture and architects of Texas. "*Texas Architect* is a highly visually-oriented look at Texas architecture, design, and urban planning. Articles cover varied subtopics within architecture. Readers are mostly architects and related building professionals." Estab. 1951. Circ. 12,000. Pays on publication. Publishes ms an average of 3 months after acceptance. Byline given. Buys one-time, all rights, makes work-for-hire assignments. Submit seasonal material 4 months in advance. Accepts queries by mail, e-mail. Responds in 6 weeks to queries. Writer's guidelines online.

Nonfiction Interview/profile, photo feature, technical, book reviews. Query with published clips. Length: 100-2,000 words. **Pays $50-100 for assigned articles.**

Photos Send photos with submission. Reviews contact sheets, 35mm or 4×5 transparencies, 4×5 prints. Buys one-time rights. Offers no additional payment for photos accepted with ms. Identification of subjects required.

Columns/Departments News (timely reports on architectural issues, projects, and people), 100-500 words. **Buys 10 mss/year.** Query with published clips. **Pays $50-100.**

AUTO & TRUCK

$ $AUTOINC.

Automotive Service Association, P.O. Box 929, Bedford TX 76095. (800)272-7467. Fax: (817)685-0225. E-mail: editor@asashop.org. Website: www.autoinc.org. Assistant Editor: Levy Joffrion. **Contact:** Angie Wilson, VP/Communications. **10% freelance written.** Monthly magazine covering independent automotive repair. "The mission of *AutoInc.*, ASA's official publication, is to be the informational authority for ASA and industry members nationwide. Its purpose is to enhance the professionalism of these members through management, technical and legislative articles, researched and written with the highest regard for accuracy, quality, and integrity." Estab. 1952. Circ. 15,000. Pays on publication. Publishes ms an average of 3 months after acceptance. Byline given. Buys all rights. Editorial lead time 2 months. Accepts queries by mail, e-mail, fax. Accepts simultaneous submissions. Responds in 6 weeks to queries; 2 months to mss. Sample copy for $5 or online. Writer's guidelines online.

Nonfiction How-to (automotive repair), technical. No coverage of staff moves or financial reports. **Buys 6 mss/year.** Query with published clips. Length: 1,200 words. **Pays $250.** Sometimes pays phone expenses of writers on assignment.

Photos State availability of or send photos with submission. Reviews 2×3 transparencies, 3×5 prints. Buys one-time and electronic rights. Negotiates payment individually. Captions, identification of subjects, model releases required.

Tips "Learn about the automotive repair industry, specifically the independent shop segment. Understand the high-tech requirements needed to succeed today."

$ $BUSINESS FLEET

Managing 10-50 Company Vehicles, Bobit Publishing, 21061 S. Western Ave., Torrance CA 90501-1711. (310)533-2592. Fax: (310)533-2503. E-mail: steve.elliott@bobit.com. Website: www.businessfleet.com. **Contact:** Steve Elliott, executive editor. **10% freelance written.** Bimonthly magazine covering businesses which operate 10-50 company vehicles. "While it's a trade publication aimed at a business audience, *Business Fleet* has a lively, conversational style. The best way to get a feel for our 'slant' is to read the magazine." Estab. 2000. Circ. 100,000. Pays on publication. Publishes ms an average of 3 months after acceptance. Byline given. Offers 25% kill fee. Buys first, second serial (reprint), electronic rights. Editorial lead time 2 months. Submit seasonal material 2 months in advance. Accepts queries by mail, e-mail, fax. Responds in 3 weeks to queries; 2 months to mss. Sample copy and writer's guidelines free.

Nonfiction How-to, interview/profile, new product, personal experience, photo feature, technical. **Buys 16**

mss/year. Query with published clips. Length: 500-2,000 words. **Pays $100-400.** Pays with contributor copies or other premiums by prior arrangement. Sometimes pays expenses of writers on assignment.
Photos State availability with submission. Reviews 3×5 prints. Buys one-time, reprint, and electronic rights. Negotiates payment individually. Captions required.

🔲 The online magazine carries original content not included in the print edition. Contact: Steve Elliott, online editor.

Tips "Our mission is to educate our target audience on more economical and efficient ways of operating company vehicles, and to inform the audience of the latest vehicles, products, and services available to small commercial companies. Be knowledgeable about automotive and fleet-oriented subjects."

$ $FLEET EXECUTIVE

The Magazine of Vehicle Management, The National Association of Fleet Administrators, Inc., 100 Wood Ave. S., Suite 310, Iselin NJ 08830-2716. (732)494-8100. Fax: (732)494-6789. E-mail: publications@nafa.org. Website: www.nafa.org. **Contact:** Carolann McLaughlin, managing editor. **50% freelance written.** Magazine published 8 times/year covering automotive fleet management. "*NAFA Fleet Executive* focuses on car, van, and light-duty truck management in U.S. and Canadian corporations, government agencies, and utilities. Editorial emphasis is on general automotive issues; improving jobs skills, productivity, and professionalism; legislation and regulation; alternative fuels; safety; interviews with prominent industry personalities; technology; Association news; public service fleet management; and light-duty truck fleet management." Estab. 1957. Circ. 4,000. Pays on publication. Publishes ms an average of 4 months after acceptance. Buys all rights. Editorial lead time 2 months. Accepts queries by mail, e-mail, fax. Accepts simultaneous submissions. Responds in 1 month to queries. Sample copy online. Writer's guidelines free.
Nonfiction "NAFA hosts its Fleet Management Institute, an educational conference and trade show, which is held in a different city in the U.S. and Canada each year. *Fleet Executive* would consider articles on regional attractions, particularly those that might be of interest to those in the automotive industry, for use in a conference preview issue of the magazine. The preview issue is published one month prior to the conference. Information about the conference, its host city, and conference dates in a given year may be found on NAFA's website, www.nafa.org, or by calling the association at (732)494-8100." Interview/profile, technical. **Buys 24 mss/year.** Query with published clips. Length: 500-3,000 words. **Pays $500 maximum.**
Photos State availability with submission. Reviews electronic images.
Tips "The sample articles online at www.nafa.org/fleetexecutive should help writers get a feel of the journalistic style we require."

$ $GLASS DIGEST

Ashlee Publishing, 18 E. 41st St., New York NY 10017. (212)376-7722. Fax: (212)376-7723. E-mail: publisher@ashlee.com. Website: www.ashlee.com. **15-20% freelance written.** Monthly magazine covering flat glass, architectural metal, glazing, auto glass. Estab. 1921. Pays on publication. Publishes ms an average of 2 months after acceptance. Byline given. Buys first, all rights, makes work-for-hire assignments. Editorial lead time 3 months. Accepts queries by mail, e-mail, fax. Accepts simultaneous submissions.
Nonfiction Photo feature, technical, architectural designs & trends. "No reports on stained glass hobbyists or art glass." **Buys 16-20 mss/year.** Query. Length: 1,000-2,000 words. **Pays $100-400.** Sometimes pays expenses of writers on assignment.
Photos State availability with submission. Negotiates payment individually. Identification of subjects required.
Tips "Architecturally interesting projects with good photography make excellent features for *Glass Digest*."

NORTHWEST MOTOR

Journal for the Automotive Industry, Northwest Automotive Publishing Co., P.O. Box 46937, Seattle WA 98146-0937. (206)935-3336. Fax: (206)937-9732. E-mail: jerry@nwmotor.com. Website: www.nwmotor.com. **Contact:** J.B. Smith, editor. **5% freelance written.** Monthly magazine covering the automotive industry. Estab. 1909. Circ. 12,500. Pays on publication. Byline given. Offers 10% kill fee. Buys all rights. Editorial lead time 1 month. Submit seasonal material 2 months in advance. Accepts queries by mail, e-mail. Accepts simultaneous submissions. Sample copy for $2. Writer's guidelines for #10 SASE.

○┓ Break in by sending a listing of available articles.

Nonfiction Interested in seeing automotive environmental articles. Book excerpts, general interest, how-to, new product, photo feature, technical. **Buys 6 mss/year.** Query. Length: 250-1,200 words. **Payment varies.** Sometimes pays expenses of writers on assignment.
Photos Send photos with submission. Reviews 3×5 prints. Buys all rights. Negotiates payment individually.
Columns/Departments Buys 4-6 mss/year. Query. **Payment varies.**
Fillers Anecdotes, facts. **Buys 4-9/year.** Length: 15-100 words. **Pays variable amount.**

OLD CARS WEEKLY

News & Marketplace, Krause Publications, 700 E. State St., Iola WI 54990-0001. (715)445-4612. Fax: (715)445-4087. Website: www.collect.com. **50% freelance written.** Weekly tabloid covering old cars. Estab. 1971. Circ. 65,000. Pays in the month after publication date. Publishes ms an average of 6 months after acceptance. Byline given. For sample copy call circulation department. Writer's guidelines for #10 SASE.

Nonfiction How-to, technical, auction prices realized lists. No "Grandpa's Car," "My First Car" or "My Car" themes. **Buys 1,600 mss/year.** Send complete ms. Length: 400-1,600 words. **Payment varies.**

Photos Send photos with submission. Pays $5/photo. Offers no additional payment for photos accepted with ms. Captions, identification of subjects required.

Tips "Ninety percent of our material is done by a small group of regular contributors. Many new writers break in here, but we are usually overstocked with material and never seek nostalgic or historical pieces from new authors. Our big need is for well-written items that fit odd pieces in a tabloid page layout. Budding authors should try some short, catchy items that help us fill odd-ball 'news holes' with interesting writing. Authors with good skills can work up to longer stories. A weekly keeps us too busy to answer mail and phone calls. The best queries are 'checklists' where we can quickly mark a 'yes' or 'no' to article ideas."

$ $ $ OVERDRIVE

The Voice of the American Trucker, Randall Publishing Co./Overdrive, Inc., 3200 Rice Mine Rd., Tuscaloosa AL 35406. (205)349-2990. Fax: (205)750-8070. E-mail: mheine@randallpub.com. Website: www.etrucker.net. Editor: Linda Longton. **Contact:** Max Heine, editorial director. **5% freelance written.** Monthly magazine for independent truckers. Estab. 1961. Circ. 100,000. Pays on publication. Publishes ms an average of 2 months after acceptance. Byline given. Offers 10% kill fee. Buys all North American rights, including electronic rights. Responds in 2 months to queries. Sample copy for 9×12 SASE.

Nonfiction All must be related to independent trucker interest. Essays, exposé, how-to (truck maintenance and operation), interview/profile (successful independent truckers), personal experience, photo feature, technical. Query with or without published clips or send complete ms. Length: 500-2,000 words. **Pays $200-1,000 for assigned articles.**

Photos Send photos with submission. Reviews transparencies, prints, slides. Buys all rights. Offers $25-150/photo.

Tips "Talk to independent truckers. Develop a good knowledge of their concerns as small-business owners, truck drivers, and individuals. We prefer articles that quote experts, people in the industry, and truckers, to first-person expositions on a subject. Get straight facts. Look for good material on truck safety, on effects of government regulations, and on rates and business relationships between independent truckers, brokers, carriers, and shippers."

N $ PML

The Market Letter for Porsche Automobiles, PML Consulting, P.O. Box 567, Socorro NM 87801. Fax: (505)838-1222. E-mail: phil@pmletter.com. Website: www.pmletter.com. **Contact:** Phil Van Buskirk, owner. **100% freelance written.** Monthly magazine covering technical tips, personality profiles and race coverage of Porsche automobiles. Estab. 1981. Circ. 1,500. Pays on publication. Publishes ms an average of 2 months after acceptance. Byline given. Buys one-time rights. Editorial lead time 2 months. Submit seasonal material 2 months in advance. Accepts queries by mail, e-mail, fax, phone. Accepts previously published material. Accepts simultaneous submissions. Responds in 2 weeks to queries; 1 month to mss. Sample copy for $5. Writer's guidelines for #10 SASE.

Nonfiction General interest, historical/nostalgic, how-to, humor, interview/profile, new product, personal experience, photo feature, technical, travel, race results. **Buys 30-40 mss/year.** Query with published clips. Length: 500-2,000 words. **Pays $30-50 and up, depending on length and topic.** Sometimes pays expenses of writers on assignment.

Photos Send photos with submission. Reviews 8×10 b&w prints. Buys one-time rights. Negotiates payment individually. Captions, identification of subjects, model releases required.

Fillers Anecdotes, facts, gags to be illustrated by cartoonist, newsbreaks, short humor. **Pays negotiable amount.**

Tips "Check any auto-related magazine for types, styles of articles. We are looking for people doing anything unusual or interesting in the Porsche world. Submit well-prepared, thoroughly-edited articles with photos."

$ ROAD KING MAGAZINE

For the Professional Driver, Parthenon Publishing, 28 White Bridge Rd., Suite 209, Nashville TN 37205. (615)627-2250. Fax: (615)690-3401. E-mail: submissions@roadking.com. Website: www.roadking.com. **80% freelance written.** Bimonthly magazine. "*Road King* is published bimonthly for long-haul truckers. It celebrates the lifestyle and work and profiles interesting and/or successful drivers. It also reports on subjects of interest to our audience, including outdoors, vehicles, music and trade issues." Estab. 1963. Circ. 229,900. **Pays on**

acceptance. Publishes ms an average of 4 months after acceptance. Byline given. Offers negotiable kill fee. Buys first North American serial, electronic rights. Editorial lead time 3 months. Submit seasonal material 4 months in advance. Accepts queries by mail, e-mail. Responds in 2 months to queries. Sample copy for 9 × 12 SAE and 5 first-class stamps. Writer's guidelines online.

Nonfiction How-to (trucking-related), humor, interview/profile, new product, personal experience, photo feature, technical, travel. Special issues: Road Gear (the latest tools, techniques and industry developments to help truckers run a smarter, more efficient trucking business); Haul of Fame (salutes drivers whose work or type of rig makes them unique); At Home on the Road ("creature comfort" products, services and information for the road life, including what's new, useful, interesting or fun for cyber-trucking drivers); Fleet Focus (asks fleet management about what their companies offer, and drivers about why they like it there); Weekend Wheels (from Harleys to Hondas, most drivers have a passion for their "other" set of wheels. This section looks at this aspect of drivers' lives). "No fiction, poetry." **Buys 20 mss/year.** Query with published clips. Length: 850-2,000 words. **Payment negotiable.** Sometimes pays expenses of writers on assignment.

Photos State availability with submission. Reviews contact sheets. Buys negotiable rights. Negotiates payment individually. Identification of subjects, model releases required.

Columns/Departments Lead Driver (profile of outstanding trucker), 250-500 words; Roadrunner (new products, services suited to the business of trucking or to truckers' lifestyles), 100-250 words. **Buys 6-10 mss/year.** Query. **Payment negotiable.**

Fillers Anecdotes, facts, gags to be illustrated by cartoonist, short humor. Length: 100-250 words. **Pays $50.**

  ◼ The online magazine of *Road King* carries original content not found in the print edition.

$ $RV TRADE DIGEST

Your Source for Management, Marketing and Production Information, Cygnus Business Media, Inc., 1233 Janeville Ave., Fort Atkinson WI 53538. (920)568-8349. Fax: (920)563-1702. E-mail: editor@rvtradedigest.com. Website: www.rvtradedigest.com. **Contact:** Greg Gerber, editor-in-chief. **15% freelance written.** Monthly magazine. "RV Trade Digest seeks to help RV dealers become more profitable and efficient. We don't want fluff and theory. We want tested and proven ideas other dealers can apply to their own businesses. We believe sharing best practices helps everyone in the industry stay strong." Estab. 1980. Circ. 16,000. Pays 30 days after publication. Publishes ms an average of 3 months after acceptance. Byline given. Buys first North American serial rights. Editorial lead time 3 months. Submit seasonal material 4 months in advance. Accepts queries by mail, e-mail. Accepts simultaneous submissions. Responds in 2 months to queries. Sample copy for free. Writer's guidelines free.

Nonfiction How-to (install, service parts, accessories), interview/profile (of industry leaders or successful RV dealers), new product (with emphasis on how to best sell and market the product), technical, business subjects, mobile electronics. Does not want articles about RV travel experience. **Buys 8-12 mss/year.** Length: 1,000-2,000 words. **Pays $300-500.** Pays expenses of writers on assignment.

Photos Send photos with submission. Reviews transparencies, prints. Buys one-time rights. Negotiates payment individually. Model releases required.

Columns/Departments Dealer Pro-File, Profit Central, Modern Manager, Shop Talk, Industry Insider.

Tips "Send complete manuscript. Propose an idea that will have broad appeal to the RV industry in that it will be interesting and useful to RV dealers, manufacturers, and suppliers. Queries must include background/experience and published clips."

Ⓝ $ $SPORT TRUCK & SUV ACCESSORY BUSINESS

Covering the Light Truck-Van-SUV Aftermarket, Cygnus Business Media, 1233 Janesville Ave., Ft. Atkinson WI 53538. (920)563-6388. Fax: (920)563-1702. E-mail: pat.walker@cygnuspub.com. Website: www.sportstruck.com. **Contact:** Pat Walker, editor. **25% freelance written.** "Sport Truck & SUV Accessory Business is a bimonthly trade magazine designed to provide light truck accessory dealers and installers with advice on improving their retail business practices, plus timely information about industry trends and events. Each issue's editorial package includes a dealer profile, plus features aimed at meeting the distinct needs of store owners, managers and counter sales people. The magazine also provides aftermarket, OEM and trade association news, three separate new product sections, plus an analysis of light truck sales." Estab. 1996. Circ. 15,000. Pays 30 days after publication. Publishes ms an average of 3 months after acceptance. Byline given. Buys first North American serial rights. Editorial lead time 3 months. Submit seasonal material 4 months in advance. Accepts simultaneous submissions. Responds in 1 month to queries. Sample copy, writer's guidelines free.

  ○→ Break in with "a feature on a top truck or SUV retailer in your area."

Nonfiction General interest, interview/profile, new product, technical, Considers cartoons. No travel, installation how-to's. **Buys 20-30 mss/year.** Query. Length: 1,000-2,000 words. **Pays $300-500.**

Photos Send photos with submission. Reviews transparencies, prints. Buys one-time rights. Negotiates payment individually. Model releases required.

Tips "Send query with or without completed manuscripts. Background/experience and published clips are required."

$ $⊞ TODAY'S TRUCKING

New Communications Group, 451 Attwell Dr., Toronto ON M9W 5C4, Canada. (416)614-2200. Fax: (416)614-8861. E-mail: editors@todaystrucking.com. Website: www.todaystrucking.com. Editor: Stephen Petit. **Contact:** Rolf Lockwood. **15% freelance written.** Monthly magazine covering the trucking industry in Canada. "We reach nearly 30,000 fleet owners, managers, owner-operators, shop supervisors, equipment dealers, and parts distributors across Canada. Our magazine has a strong service slant, combining useful how-to journalism with analysis of news, business issues, and heavy-duty equipment trends. Before you sit down to write, please take time to become familiar with *Today's Trucking*. Read a few recent issues." Estab. 1987. Circ. 30,000. **Pays on acceptance.** Byline given. Buys first North American serial, second serial (reprint) rights. Editorial lead time 2 months. Submit seasonal material 3 months in advance. Accepts queries by mail, e-mail, fax. Sample copy and writer's guidelines free.

Nonfiction How-to, interview/profile, technical. **Buys 20 mss/year.** Query with published clips. Length: 500-2,000 words. **Pays 40¢/word.** Sometimes pays expenses of writers on assignment.

Photos State availability with submission.

Columns/Departments Pays 40¢/word.

$ $⊞ WESTERN CANADA HIGHWAY NEWS

Craig Kelman & Associates, 3C-2020 Portage Ave., Winnipeg MB R3J 0K4, Canada. (204)985-9785. Fax: (204)985-9795. E-mail: terry@kelman.mb.ca. **Contact:** Terry Ross, managing editor. **30% freelance written.** Quarterly magazine covering trucking. "The official magazine of the Alberta, Saskatchewan, and Manitoba trucking associations." Estab. 1995. Circ. 4,500. Pays on publication. Publishes ms an average of 2 months after acceptance. Byline given. Buys one-time rights. Editorial lead time 3 months. Submit seasonal material 3 months in advance. Accepts simultaneous submissions. Responds in 1 month to queries; 1 month to mss. Sample copy for 10×13 SAE with 1 IRC. Writer's guidelines for #10 SASE.

Nonfiction Essays, general interest, how-to (run a trucking business), interview/profile, new product, opinion, personal experience, photo feature, technical, profiles in excellence (bios of trucking or associate firms enjoying success). **Buys 8-10 mss/year.** Query. Length: 500-3,000 words. **Pays 18-25¢/word.** Sometimes pays expenses of writers on assignment.

Photos State availability with submission. Reviews 4×6 prints. Buys one-time rights. Identification of subjects required.

Columns/Departments Safety (new safety innovation/products), 500 words; Trade Talk (new products), 300 words. Query. **Pays 18-25¢/word.**

Tips "Our publication is fairly time-sensitive re: issues affecting the trucking industry in Western Canada. Current 'hot' topics are international trucking, security, driver fatigue, health and safety, emissions control, and national/international highway systems."

AVIATION & SPACE

$ $AIRCRAFT MAINTENANCE TECHNOLOGY

Cygnus Business Media, 1233 Janesville Ave., Fort Atkinson WI 53538. (920)563-6388. Fax: (920)563-1702. E-mail: editor@amtonline.com. Website: www.amtonline.com. Editor: Joe Escobar. **10% freelance written.** Magazine published 10 times/year covering aircraft maintenance. "*Aircraft Maintenance Technology* provides aircraft maintenance professionals worldwide with a curriculum of technical, professional, and managerial development information that enables them to more efficiently and effectively perform their jobs. Estab. 1989. Circ. 41,500 worldwide. Pays on publication. Publishes ms an average of 2 months after acceptance. Byline given. Buys all rights, makes work-for-hire assignments. Editorial lead time 3 months. Submit seasonal material 6 months in advance. Accepts queries by mail, e-mail, fax. Accepts simultaneous submissions. Responds in 2 weeks to queries; 1 month to mss. Sample copy for free. Writer's guidelines for #10 SASE or by e-mail.

Nonfiction How-to, technical, safety; human factors. Special issues: Aviation career issue (August). No travel/pilot-oriented pieces. **Buys 10-12 mss/year.** Query with published clips. Length: 600-1,500 words, technical articles 2,000 words. **Pays $200.**

Photos State availability with submission. Buys one-time rights. Offers no additional payment for photos accepted with ms. Captions, identification of subjects, model releases required.

Columns/Departments Professionalism, 1,000-1,500 words; Safety Matters, 600-1,000 words; Human Factors, 600-1,000 words. **Buys 10-12 mss/year.** Query with published clips. **Pays $200.**

Tips "This is a technical magazine, which is approved by the FAA and Transport Canada for recurrency training for technicians. Freelancers should have a strong background in aviation, particularly maintenance, to be considered for technical articles. Columns/Departments: Freelancers still should have a strong knowledge of aviation to slant professionalism, safety, and human factors pieces to that audience.''

$ $ AIRPORT OPERATIONS

Flight Safety Foundation, Suite 300, 601 Madison St., Alexandria VA 22314-1756. (703)739-6700. Fax: (703)739-6708. E-mail: rozelle@flightsafety.org. Website: www.flightsafety.org. **Contact:** Roger Rozelle, director of publications. **25% freelance written.** Bimonthly newsletter covering safety aspects of airport operations. *"Airport Operations* directs attention to ground operations that involve aircraft and other equipment, airport personnel and services, air traffic control (ATC), and passengers." Estab. 1974. Circ. 2,000. Pays on publication. Publishes ms an average of 3 months after acceptance. Byline given. Buys all rights. Editorial lead time 3 months. Accepts queries by mail, e-mail, fax. Accepts previously published material. Responds in 3 weeks to queries. Sample copy online. Writer's guidelines online.

Nonfiction Technical. No argumentation, crusading, inspiration, anecdotes, or humor. **Buys 6 mss/year.** Query. Length: 2,500-8,750 words. **Pays $200/printed page, plus 6 copies of publication.**

Photos Send photos with submission. Reviews contact sheets, negatives, 35mm or larger transparencies, 5×7 minimum prints, GIF/JPEG files. Buys all rights. Offers $25/photo. Captions, identification of subjects, model releases required.

Tips "Study the guidelines carefully. Be concerned above all with accuracy, fairness, and objectivity, but if you have information that you believe meets those standards, do not hesitate to query even if you aren't sure of format or style. If you have the content we need, our editorial staff will work with you to put the material into shape."

$ $ AVIATION INTERNATIONAL NEWS

The Newsmagazine of Corporate, Business, and Regional Aviation, The Convention News Co., 214 Franklin Ave., Midland Park NJ 07432. (201)444-5075. Fax: (201)444-4647. E-mail: rpadfield@ainonline.com. Website: www.ainonline.com. Editor *AIN* Monthly Edition: Nigel Moll. **Contact:** R. Randall Padfield, editor-in-chief. **30-40% freelance written.** Monthly magazine (with onsite issues published at 3 conventions and 2 international air shows each year) covering business and commercial aviation with news features, special reports, aircraft evaluations, and surveys on business aviation worldwide, written for business pilots and industry professionals. "While the heartbeat of *AIN* is driven by the news it carries, the human touch is not neglected. We pride ourselves on our people stories about the industry's 'movers and shakers' and others in aviation who make a difference." Estab. 1972. Circ. 40,000. **Pays on acceptance and upon receipt of writer's invoice.** Publishes ms an average of 2 months after acceptance. Byline given. Offers variable kill fee. Buys first North American serial and second serial (reprint) rights and makes work-for-hire assignments. Editorial lead time 2 months. Submit seasonal material 3 months in advance. Accepts queries by mail, e-mail, fax. Responds in 6 weeks to queries; 2 months to mss. Sample copy for $10. Writer's guidelines for 9×12 SAE with 3 first-class stamps.

- Do not send mss by e-mail unless requested.
- Break in with "local news stories relating to business, commercial and regional airline aviation—think turbine-powered aircraft (no stories about national airlines, military aircraft, recreational aviation or history."

Nonfiction "We hire freelancers to work on our staff at 3 aviation conventions and 2 international airshows each year. Must have strong reporting and writing skills and knowledge of aviation." How-to (aviation), interview/profile, new product, opinion, personal experience, photo feature, technical. No puff pieces. "Our readers expect serious, real news. We don't pull any punches. *AIN* is not a 'good news' publication: It tells the story, both good and bad." **Buys 150-200 mss/year.** Query with published clips. Length: 200-3,000 words. **Pays 30¢/word to first timers, higher rates to proven AIN freelancers.** Pays expenses of writers on assignment.

Photos Send photos with submission. Reviews contact sheets, transparencies, prints, TIFF files (300 dpi). Buys one-time rights. Negotiates payment individually. Captions required.

- "*AIN Alerts,* our online mini-newsletter, is posted on our website twice a week and carries original content not found in our print publications. It includes 10-12 news items of about 100 words each." Contact: Gordon Gilbert, ggilbert@ainonline.com.

Tips "Our core freelancers are professional pilots with good writing skills, or good journalists and reporters with an interest in aviation (some with pilot licenses) or technical experts in the aviation industry. The ideal *AIN* writer has an intense interest in and strong knowledge of aviation, a talent for writing news stories, and journalistic cussedness. Hit me with a strong news story relating to business aviation that takes me by surprise—something from your local area or area of expertise. Make it readable, fact-filled, and in the inverted-pyramid style. Double-check facts and names. Interview the right people. Send me good, clear photos and illustrations. Send me well-written, logically ordered copy. Do this for me consistently and we may take you along on our staff to one of the conventions in the U.S. or an airshow in Paris, Singapore, London, or Dubai."

$ $AVIATION MAINTENANCE

PBI Media LLC, 1201 Seven Locks Rd., Suite 300, Potomac MD 20854. (301)354-1831. Fax: (301)340-8741. E-mail: am@pbimedia.com. Website: www.aviationmx.com. Managing Editor: Joy Finnegan. **Contact:** Matt Thurber, editor. **60% freelance written.** Monthly magazine covering aircraft maintenance from small to large aircraft. *Aviation Maintenance* delivers news and information about the aircraft maintenance business for mechanics and management at maintenance shops, airlines, and corporate flight departments. Estab. 1982. Circ. 25,000. **Pays on acceptance.** Publishes ms an average of 2 months after acceptance. Byline given. Kill fee varies. Buys all rights. Editorial lead time 3 months. Submit seasonal material 3 months in advance. Accepts queries by mail, e-mail, fax, phone. Responds in 1 week to queries; 1 month to mss. Sample copy online. Writer's guidelines free.

Nonfiction Exposé, interview/profile, technical. No fiction, technical how-to, or poetry. **Buys 50 mss/year.** Query with or without published clips. Length: 200-500 words. **Pays 35¢/word.** Pays expenses of writers on assignment.

Photos State availability with submission. Buys all rights. Negotiates payment individually. Captions, identification of subjects required.

Columns/Departments Intelligence (news), 200-500 words; Postflight (profile of aircraft mechanic), 800 words, plus photo. **Buys 12 mss/year.** Query with or without published clips. **Pays $200-250.**

Tips "Writer must be intimately familiar with or involved in aviation, either as a pilot or preferably a mechanic or a professional aviation writer. Best place to break in is in the Intelligence News section or with a Postflight profile of an interesting mechanic."

$AVIATION MECHANICS BULLETIN

Flight Safety Foundation, Suite 300, 601 Madison St., Alexandria VA 22314-1756. (703)739-6700. Fax: (703)739-6708. E-mail: rozelle@flightsafety.org. Website: www.flightsafety.org. **Contact:** Roger Rozelle, director of publications. **25% freelance written.** Bimonthly newsletter covering safety aspects of aviation maintenance (airline and corporate). Estab. 1953. Circ. 2,000. Pays on publication. Publishes ms an average of 3 months after acceptance. Byline given. Buys all rights. Editorial lead time 3 months. Accepts queries by mail, e-mail, fax. Accepts previously published material. Responds in 3 weeks to queries. Sample copy online. Writer's guidelines online.

Nonfiction Technical. No argumentation, crusading, inspiration, anecdotes, or humor. **Buys 6 mss/year.** Query. Length: 2,000-5,500 words. **Pays $100/printed pocket-sized page, plus 6 copies of publication.**

Photos Send photos with submission. Reviews contact sheets, negatives, 35mm or larger transparencies, 5×7 minimum prints, GIF/JPEG files. Buys all rights. Offers $25/photo. Captions, identification of subjects, model releases required.

Tips "Study guidelines carefully. Be concerned above all with accuracy, but if you have information that you believe meets those standards, do not hesitate to query even if you aren't sure of format or style. If you have the content we need, our editorial staff will work with you to put the material into shape."

$ $CABIN CREW SAFETY

Flight Safety Foundation, Suite 300, 601 Madison St., Alexandria VA 22314-1756. (703)739-6700. Fax: (703)739-6708. E-mail: rozelle@flightsafety.org. Website: www.flightsafety.org. **Contact:** Roger Rozelle, director of publications. **25% freelance written.** Bimonthly newsletter covering safety aspects of aircraft cabins (airline and corporate aviation) for cabin crews and passengers. Estab. 1956. Circ. 2,000. Pays on publication. Publishes ms an average of 3 months after acceptance. Byline given. Buys all rights. Editorial lead time 3 months. Accepts queries by mail, e-mail, fax. Accepts previously published material. Responds in 3 weeks to queries. Sample copy online. Writer's guidelines online.

Nonfiction Technical. No argumentation, crusading, inspiration, anecdotes, or humor. **Buys 6 mss/year.** Query. Length: 2,500-8,750 words. **Pays $200/printed page, plus 6 copies of publication.**

Photos Send photos with submission. Reviews contact sheets, negatives, 35mm or larger transparencies, 5×7 minimum prints, GIF/JPEG files. Buys all rights. Offers $25/photo. Captions, identification of subjects, model releases required.

Tips "Study guidelines carefully. Be concerned above all with accuracy, fairness, and objectivity, but if you have information that you believe meets those standards, do not hesitate to query even if you aren't sure of format or style. If you have the content we need, our editorial staff will work with you to put the material into shape."

$ $FLIGHT SAFETY DIGEST

Flight Safety Foundation, Suite 300, 601 Madison St., Alexandria VA 22314-1756. (703)739-6700. Fax: (703)739-6708. E-mail: rozelle@flightsafety.org. Website: www.flightsafety.org. **Contact:** Roger Rozelle, director of publications. **25% freelance written.** Monthly magazine covering significant issues in airline and corporate aviation

safety. *"Flight Safety Digest* offers the page space to explore subjects in greater detail than in other Foundation periodicals." Estab. 1982. Circ. 2,000. Pays on publication. Publishes ms an average of 3 months after acceptance. Byline given. Buys all rights. Editorial lead time 3 months. Accepts queries by mail, e-mail, fax. Accepts previously published material. Responds in 3 weeks to queries. Sample copy online. Writer's guidelines online.
Nonfiction Technical. No argumentation, crusading, inspiration, anecdotes, or humor. **Buys 6 mss/year.** Query. Length: 4,000-15,000 words. **Pays $200/printed page, plus 6 copies of publication.**
Photos Send photos with submission. Reviews contact sheets, negatives, 35mm or larger transparencies, 5×7 minimum prints, GIF/JPEG files. Buys all rights. Offers $25/photo. Captions, identification of subjects, model releases required.
Tips "Study guidelines carefully. Be concerned above all with accuracy, fairness, and objectivity, but if you have information that you believe meets those standards, do not hesitate to query even if you aren't sure of format or style. If you have the content we need, our editorial staff will work with you to put the material into shape."

$ $ GROUND SUPPORT MAGAZINE

Cygnus Business Media, 1233 Janesville Ave., Fort Atkinson WI 53538. (920)563-1622. Fax: (920)563-1699. E-mail: karen.reinhardt@cygnuspub.com. Website: www.groundsupportmagazine.com. **Contact:** Karen Reinhardt, editor. **20% freelance written.** Magazine published 10 times/year. "Our readers are those aviation professionals who are involved in ground support—the equipment manufacturers, the suppliers, the ramp operators, ground handlers, airport and airline managers. We cover issues of interest to this community—deicing, ramp safety, equipment technology, pollution, etc." Estab. 1993. Circ. 15,000. Pays on publication. Publishes ms an average of 2 months after acceptance. Buys all rights. Editorial lead time 2 months. Accepts queries by mail, e-mail, fax. Responds in 3 weeks to queries; 3 months to mss. Sample copy for 9×11 SAE and 5 first-class stamps.
Nonfiction How-to (use or maintain certain equipment), interview/profile, new product, opinion, photo feature, technical aspects of ground support and issues, industry events, meetings, new rules and regulations. **Buys 12-20 mss/year.** Send complete ms. Length: 500-2,000 words. **Pays $100-300.**
Photos Send photos with submission. Reviews 35mm prints, electronic preferred, slides. Buys all rights. Offers additional payment for photos accepted with ms. Identification of subjects required.
Tips "Write about subjects that relate to ground services. Write in clear and simple terms—personal experience is always welcome. If you have an aviation background or ground support experience, let us know."

$ $ HELICOPTER SAFETY

Flight Safety Foundation, Suite 300, 601 Madison St., Alexandria VA 22314-1756. (703)739-6700. Fax: (703)739-6708. E-mail: rozelle@flightsafety.org. Website: www.flightsafety.org. **Contact:** Roger Rozelle, director of publications. **50% freelance written.** Bimonthly newsletter covering safety aspects of helicopter operations. *"Helicopter Safety* highlights the broad spectrum of real-world helicopter operations. Topics have ranged from design principles and primary training to helicopter utilization in offshore applications and in emergency medical service (EMS)." Estab. 1956. Circ. 2,000. Pays on publication. Publishes ms an average of 3 months after acceptance. Byline given. Buys all rights. Editorial lead time 3 months. Accepts queries by mail, e-mail, fax. Accepts previously published material. Responds in 3 weeks to queries. Sample copy online. Writer's guidelines online.
Nonfiction Technical. No argumentation, crusading, inspiration, anecdotes, or humor. **Buys 6 mss/year.** Query. Length: 2,500-8,750 words. **Pays $200/printed page, plus 6 copies of publication.**
Photos Send photos with submission. Reviews contact sheets, negatives, 35mm or larger transparencies, 5×7 minimum prints. Buys all rights. Offers $25/photo. Captions, identification of subjects, model releases required.
Tips "Study guidelines carefully. Be concerned above all with accuracy, fairness, and objectivity, but if you have information that you believe meets those standards, do not hesitate to query even if you aren't sure of format or style. If you have the content we need, our editorial staff will work with you to put the material into shape."

$ $ HUMAN FACTORS & AVIATION MEDICINE

Flight Safety Foundation, Suite 300, 601 Madison St., Alexandria VA 22314-1756. (703)739-6700. Fax: (703)739-6708. E-mail: rozelle@flightsafety.org. Website: www.flightsafety.org. **Contact:** Roger Rozelle, director of publications. **50% freelance written.** Bimonthly newsletter covering medical aspects of aviation, primarily for airline and corporate aviation pilots. *"Human Factors & Aviation Medicine* allows specialists, researchers, and physicians to present information critical to the training, performance, and health of aviation professionals." Estab. 1953. Circ. 2,000. Pays on publication. Publishes ms an average of 3 months after acceptance. Byline given. Buys all rights. Editorial lead time 3 months. Accepts queries by mail, e-mail, fax. Accepts previously published material. Responds in 3 weeks to queries. Sample copy online. Writer's guidelines online.

Nonfiction Technical. No argumentation, crusading, inspiration, anecdotes, or humor. **Buys 6 mss/year.** Query. Length: 2,500-8,750 words. **Pays $200/printed page, plus 6 copies of publication.**

Photos Send photos with submission. Reviews contact sheets, negatives, 35mm or larger transparencies, 5×7 minimum prints, GIF/JPEG files. Buys all rights. Offers $25/photo. Captions, identification of subjects, model releases required.

Tips "Study guidelines carefully. Be concerned above all with accuracy, fairness, and objectivity, but if you have information that you believe meets those standards, do not hesitate to query even if you aren't sure of format or style. If you have the content we need, our editorial staff will work with you to put the material into shape."

$ $ $ PROFESSIONAL PILOT

Queensmith Communications, 30 S. Quaker Lane, Suite 300, Alexandria VA 22314. (703)370-0606. Fax: (703)370-7082. E-mail: editorial@propilotmag.com. Website: www.propilotmag.com. **Contact:** Paul Richfield, executive editor. **75% freelance written.** Monthly magazine covering regional airline, corporate and various other types of professional aviation. "The typical reader has a sophisticated grasp of piloting/aviation knowledge and is interested in articles that help him/her do the job better or more efficiently." Estab. 1967. Circ. 44,000. Pays on publication. Publishes ms an average of 2-3 months after acceptance. Byline given. Kill fee negotiable. Buys all rights. Accepts queries by mail, e-mail, fax, phone.

○┐ "Affiliation with an active flight department, weather activity of Air Traffic Control (ATC) is helpful. Our readers want tool tech stuff from qualified writers with credentials."

Nonfiction "Typical subjects include new aircraft design, new product reviews (especially avionics), pilot techniques, profiles of regional airlines, fixed base operations, profiles of corporate flight departments and technological advances." All issues have a theme such as regional airline operations, maintenance, avionics, helicopters, etc. **Buys 40 mss/year.** Query. Length: 750-2,500 words. **Pays $200-1,000, depending on length. A fee for the article will be established at the time of assignment.** Sometimes pays expenses of writers on assignment.

Photos Send photos with submission. Prefers transparencies or slides. Buys all rights. Additional payment for photos negotiable. Captions, identification of subjects required.

Tips Query first. "Freelancer should be a professional pilot or have background in aviation. Authors should indicate relevant aviation experience and pilot credentials (certificates, ratings and hours). We place a greater emphasis on corporate operations and pilot concerns."

BEAUTY & SALON

AMERICAN SALON

Advanstar, 1 Park Ave., 2nd Floor, New York NY 10016. (212)951-6640. Fax: (212)951-6624. E-mail: rmcclain@advanstar.com. Website: www.advanstar.com. **Contact:** Robbin McClain, editor. **5% freelance written.** Monthly magazine covering "business stories of interest to salon owners and stylists, distributors and manufacturers of professional beauty products." Estab. 1878. Circ. 132,000. **Pays on acceptance.** Publishes ms an average of 3 months after acceptance. Byline given. Buys first North American serial, first rights. Editorial lead time 3 months. Accepts queries by mail. Sample copy for free. Writer's guidelines free.

○┐ Break in with "extensive experience (in writing and the beauty industry); topic of article must be relevant. Very hard to get into our mag."

$ $ BEAUTY STORE BUSINESS

Creative Age Communications, 7628 Densmore Ave., Van Nuys CA 91406-2042. (818)782-7328, ext. 353. Fax: (818)782-7450. E-mail: klissak@creativeage.com. **Contact:** Keith Lissak, executive editor. **50% freelance written.** Magazine published 11 times/year covering beauty store business management and news. "The primary readers of the publication are owners, managers, and buyers at open-to-the-public beauty stores, including general-market and multicultural market-oriented ones with or without salon services. Our secondary readers are those at beauty stores only open to salon industry professionals. We also go to beauty distributors." Estab. 1994. Circ. 15,000. **Pays on acceptance.** Publishes ms an average of 3 months after acceptance. Byline given. Offers negotiable kill fee. Buys all rights. Editorial lead time 3 months. Submit seasonal material 4 months in advance. Accepts queries by mail, e-mail, fax. Responds in 1 week to queries 2 weeks, if interested, to mss. Sample copy for free.

Nonfiction "If your business-management article will help a specialty retailer, it should be of assistance to our readers. We're also always looking for writers who are fluent in Korean." How-to (business management, merchandising, e-commerce, retailing), interview/profile (industry leaders). **Buys 20-30 mss/year.** Query.

Length: 1,800-2,200 words. **Pays $250-525 for assigned articles.** Sometimes pays expenses of writers on assignment.

Photos Do not send computer art electronically. State availability with submission. Reviews transparencies, computer art (artists work on Macs, request 300 dpi, on CD or Zip Disk, saved as JPEG, TIFF, or EPS). Buys all rights. Negotiates payment individually. Captions, identification of subjects required.

$ $🖳 COSMETICS

Canada's Business Magazine for the Cosmetics, Fragrance, Toiletry, and Personal Care Industry, Rogers, 1 Mt. Pleasant Rd., 7th Floor, Toronto ON M4Y 2Y5, Canada. (416)764-1680. Fax: (416)764-1704. E-mail: ron.wood@ cosmetics.rogers.com. Website: www.cosmeticsmag.com. **Contact:** Ronald A. Wood, editor. **10% freelance written.** Bimonthly magazine. "Our main reader segment is the retail trade—department stores, drugstores, salons, estheticians—owners and cosmeticians/beauty advisors; plus manufacturers, distributors, agents, and suppliers to the industry." Estab. 1972. Circ. 13,000. **Pays on acceptance.** Publishes ms an average of 3 months after acceptance. Byline given. Offers 50% kill fee. Buys all rights. Editorial lead time 4 months. Submit seasonal material 4 months in advance. Accepts queries by mail. Responds in 1 month to queries. Sample copy for $6 (Canadian) and 8% GST.

Nonfiction General interest, interview/profile, photo feature. **Buys 1 mss/year.** Query. Length: 250-1,200 words. **Pays 25¢/word.** Sometimes pays expenses of writers on assignment.

Photos Send photos with submission. Reviews 2½ up to 8×10 transparencies, 4×6 up to 8×10 prints, 35mm slides, e-mail pictures in 300 dpi JPEG format. Buys all rights. Offers no additional payment for photos accepted with ms. Captions, identification of subjects, model releases required.

Columns/Departments "All articles assigned on a regular basis from correspondents and columnists that we know personally from the industry."

⬛ The online magazine carries original content not found in the print edition. Contact: Jim Hicks, publisher/online editor.

Tips "Must have broad knowledge of the Canadian cosmetics, fragrance, and toiletries industry and retail business. 99.9% of freelance articles are assigned by the editor to writers involved with the Canadian cosmetics business."

$ $ DAYSPA

For the Salon of the Future, Creative Age Publications, 7628 Densmore Ave., Van Nuys CA 91406. (818)782-7328. Fax: (818)782-7450. E-mail: dayspa@creativeage.com. Website: www.dayspamagazine.com. Managing Editor: Linda Jacobson-Kossoff. **Contact:** Linda Lewis, executive editor. **50% freelance written.** Monthly magazine covering the business of day spas, skin care salons, wellness centers. "*Dayspa* includes only well-targeted business articles directed at the owners and managers of high-end, multi-service salons, day spas, resort spas, and destination spas." Estab. 1996. Circ. 31,000. **Pays on acceptance.** Publishes ms an average of 4 months after acceptance. Byline given. Buys first, one-time rights. Editorial lead time 4 months. Submit seasonal material 4 months in advance. Accepts queries by mail, e-mail, fax, phone. Responds in 2 months to queries. Sample copy for $5.

Nonfiction Buys 40 mss/year. Query. Length: 1,200-3,000 words. **Pays $150-500.**

Photos Send photos with submission. Buys one-time rights. Negotiates payment individually. Identification of subjects, model releases required.

Columns/Departments Legal Pad (legal issues affecting salons/spas); Money Matters (financial issues), both 1,200-1,500 words. **Buys 20 mss/year.** Query. **Pays $150-300.**

$ DERMATOLOGY INSIGHTS

A Patient's Guide to Healthy Skin, Hair, and Nails, American Academy of Dermatology, 930 E. Woodfield Rd., Schaumburg IL 60173. (847)330-0230. E-mail: dmonti@aad.org. Website: www.aad.org. Managing Editor: Lara Lowery. **Contact:** Dean Monti, editor. **30% freelance written.** Semiannual magazine covering dermatology. *Dermatology Insights* contains "educational and informative articles for consumers about dermatological subjects." Estab. 2000. **Pays on acceptance.** Publishes ms an average of 4 months after acceptance. Byline given. Buys all rights, makes work-for-hire assignments. Editorial lead time 4 months. Submit seasonal material 4 months in advance. Accepts queries by mail, e-mail. Responds in 3 weeks to queries; 1 month to mss. Sample copy for free. Writer's guidelines not available.

Nonfiction General interest, how-to, interview/profile, new product, personal experience, photo feature, technical. **Buys 10-15 mss/year.** Query. Length: 750 words maximum. **Pays flat rate of $40/hour.** Sometimes pays expenses of writers on assignment.

Photos State availability with submission. Buys all rights. Negotiates payment individually. Identification of subjects required.

Columns/Departments Patient Perspective (patient's first-hand account). **Buys 2-3 mss/year.** Query. **Pays flat rate of $40/hour.**

MASSAGE & BODYWORK

Associated Bodywork & Massage Professionals, 1271 Sugarbush Dr., Evergreen CO 80439-9766. (303)674-8478 or (800)458-2267. Fax: (303)674-0859. E-mail: editor@abmp.com. Website: www.massageandbodywork.com. **Contact:** Leslie A. Young, Ph.D., editor-in-chief. **85% freelance written.** Bimonthly magazine covering therapeutic massage/bodywork. "A trade publication for the massage therapist, bodyworker, and skin care professionals. An all-inclusive publication encompassing everything from traditional Swedish massage to energy work to other complementary therapies (i.e., homeopathy, herbs, aromatherapy, etc.)." **Pays on acceptance.** Publishes ms an average of 6 months after acceptance. Buys first North American serial, one-time, electronic rights. Editorial lead time 6 months. Submit seasonal material 6 months in advance. Accepts queries by mail, e-mail, fax, phone. Responds in 1 month to queries; 5 months to mss. Writer's guidelines online.

Nonfiction Essays, exposé, how-to (technique/modality), interview/profile, opinion, personal experience, technical, travel. No fiction. **Buys 60-75 mss/year.** Query with published clips. Length: 1,000-3,000 words.

Reprints Accepts previously published submissions.

Photos State availability with submission. Reviews contact sheets. Buys one-time rights. Negotiates payment individually. Captions, identification of subjects, model releases required.

Columns/Departments Buys 20 mss/year.

Tips "Know your topic. Offer suggestions for art to accompany your submission. *Massage & Bodywork* looks for interesting, tightly focused stories concerning a particular modality or technique of massage, bodywork, somatic and skin care therapies. The editorial staff welcomes the opportunity to review manuscripts which may be relevant to the field of massage, bodywork, and skin care practices, in addition to more general pieces pertaining to complementary and alternative medicine. This would include the widely varying modalities of massage and bodywork (from Swedish massage to Polarity therapy), specific technical or ancillary therapies, including such topics as biomagnetics, aromatherapy, and facial rejuvenation. Reference lists relating to technical articles should include the author, title, publisher, and publication date of works cited. Word count: 1,500-4,000 words; longer articles negotiable."

$ $ MASSAGE MAGAZINE

Exploring Today's Touch Therapies, 200 7th Ave., #240, Santa Cruz CA 95062. (831)477-1176. E-mail: edit@massagemag.com. Website: www.massagemag.com. **Contact:** Karen Menehan, editor. **60% freelance written.** Bimonthly magazine covering massage and other touch therapies. Estab. 1985. Circ. 50,000. **Pays on acceptance.** Publishes ms an average of 1 year after acceptance. Byline given. Buys first North American serial rights. Accepts queries by mail, e-mail. Responds in 2 months to queries; 3 months to mss. Sample copy and writer's guidelines free. Writer's guidelines online.

Nonfiction Book excerpts, essays, general interest, how-to, inspirational, interview/profile, personal experience, photo feature, technical, experiential. Length: 600-2,000 words. **Pays $75-300 for assigned articles.**

Reprints Send tearsheet of article and typed ms with rights for sale noted and information about when and where the material previously appeared. Pays 50-75% of amount paid for an original article.

Photos Send photos with submission via e-mail. Buys one-time rights. Offers $25-100/photo. Identification of subjects, identification of photographer required.

Columns/Departments Profiles; Table Talk (news briefs); Practice Building (business); Technique; Body/Mind. Length: 800-1,200 words. **$75-300 for assigned articles.**

Fillers Facts, newsbreaks. Length: 100-800 words. **Pays $125 maximum.**

Tips "Our readers seek practical information on how to help their clients, improve their techniques, and/or make their businesses more successful, as well as feature articles that place massage therapy in a positive or inspiring light. Since most of our readers are professional therapists, we do not publish articles on topics like 'How Massage Can Help You Relax.' Please study a few back issues so you know what types of topics and tone we're looking for."

$ $ NAILPRO

The Magazine for Nail Professionals, Creative Age Publications, 7628 Densmore Ave., Van Nuys CA 91406. (818)782-7328. Fax: (818)782-7450. E-mail: jmills@creativeage.com. Website: www.nailpro.com. **Contact:** Jodi Mills, executive editor. **75% freelance written.** Monthly magazine written for manicurists and nail technicians working in full-service salons or nails-only salons. It covers technical and business aspects of working in and operating a nail-care service, as well as the nail-care industry in general. Estab. 1989. Circ. 65,000. **Pays on acceptance.** Publishes ms an average of 6 months after acceptance. Byline given. Buys first North American serial rights. Editorial lead time 3 months. Submit seasonal material 3 months in advance. Accepts queries by

mail, e-mail, fax. Accepts simultaneous submissions. Responds in 6 weeks to queries. Sample copy for $2 and
8½×11 SASE.

Nonfiction Book excerpts, how-to, humor, inspirational, interview/profile, personal experience, photo feature,
technical. No general interest articles or business articles not geared to the nail-care industry. **Buys 50 mss/
year.** Query. Length: 1,000-3,000 words. **Pays $150-450.**

Reprints Send ms with rights for sale noted and information about when and where the material previously
appeared. Pays 25-50% of amount paid for an original article.

Photos Send photos with submission. Reviews transparencies, prints. Buys one-time rights. Negotiates payment
individually. Identification of subjects, model releases required.

Columns/Departments Building Business (articles on marketing nail services/products), 1,200-2,000 words;
Shop Talk (aspects of operating a nail salon), 1,200-2,000 words. **Buys 50 mss/year.** Query. **Pays $200-300.**

■ The online magazine carries original content not found in the print edition. Contact: Jodi Mills.

$ $◪ NAILS

Bobit Publishing, 21061 S. Western Ave., Torrance CA 90501-1711. (310)533-2400. Fax: (310)533-2504. E-mail:
nailsmag@nailsmag.com. Website: www.nailsmag.com. **Contact:** Cyndy Drummey, editor. **10% freelance
written.** Monthly magazine. "*NAILS* seeks to educate its readers on new techniques and products, nail anatomy
and health, customer relations, working safely with chemicals, salon sanitation, and the business aspects of
running a salon." Estab. 1983. Circ. 55,000. **Pays on acceptance.** Byline given. Buys all rights. Submit seasonal
material 4 months in advance. Accepts queries by mail, e-mail, fax. Responds in 3 months to queries. Sample
copy for #10 SASE. Writer's guidelines for #10 SASE.

Nonfiction Historical/nostalgic, how-to, inspirational, interview/profile, personal experience, photo feature,
technical. "No articles on one particular product, company profiles or articles slanted toward a particular
company or manufacturer." **Buys 20 mss/year.** Query with published clips. Length: 1,200-3,000 words. **Pays
$200-500.** Sometimes pays expenses of writers on assignment.

Photos State availability with submission. Reviews contact sheets, transparencies, prints (any standard size
acceptable). Buys all rights. Offers $50-200/photo. Captions, identification of subjects, model releases required.

■ The online version contains material not found in the print edition. Contact: Hannah Lee.

Tips "Send clips and query; *do not send unsolicited manscripts.* We would like to see ideas for articles on a
unique salon or a business article that focuses on a specific aspect or problem encountered when working in
a salon. The Modern Nail Salon section, which profiles nail salons and full-service salons, is most open to
freelancers. Focus on an innovative business idea or unique point of view. Articles from experts on specific
business issues—insurance, handling difficult employees, cultivating clients—are encouraged."

$ $SKIN INC. MAGAZINE

The Complete Business Guide for Face & Body Care, Allured Publishing Corp., 362 S. Schmale Rd., Carol Stream
IL 60188. (630)653-2155. Fax: (630)653-2192. E-mail: taschetta-millane@allured.com. Website: www.skininc.c
om. Publisher: Marian Raney. **Contact:** Melinda Taschetta-Millane, associate publisher/editor. **30% freelance
written.** Magazine published 12 times/year. "Manuscripts considered for publication that contain original and
new information in the general fields of skin care and makeup, dermatological and esthetician-assisted surgical
techniques. The subject may cover the science of skin, the business of skin care and makeup, and plastic
surgeons on healthy (i.e., nondiseased) skin. Subjects may also deal with raw materials, formulations, and
regulations concerning claims for products and equipment." Estab. 1988. Circ. 16,000. Pays on publication.
Publishes ms an average of 6 months after acceptance. Byline given. Buys all rights. Editorial lead time 6
months. Submit seasonal material 1 year in advance. Accepts queries by mail, e-mail, fax, phone. Responds in
2 weeks to queries; 1 month to mss. Sample copy for free. Writer's guidelines free.

Nonfiction General interest, how-to, interview/profile, personal experience, technical. **Buys 6 mss/year.** Query
with published clips. Length: 2,000 words. **Pays $100-300 for assigned articles; $50-200 for unsolicited articles.**

Photos State availability with submission. Reviews 3×5 prints. Buys one-time rights. Offers no additional
payment for photos accepted with ms. Captions, identification of subjects, model releases required.

Columns/Departments Finance (tips and solutions for managing money), 2,000-2,500 words; Personnel (managing personnel), 2,000-2,500 words; Marketing (marketing tips for salon owners), 2,000-2,500 words; Retail
(retailing products and services in the salon environment), 2,000-2,500 words. Query with published clips.
Pays $50-200.

Fillers Facts, newsbreaks. **Buys 6/year.** Length: 250-500 words. **Pays $50-100.**

Tips "Have an understanding of the skin care industry."

BEVERAGES & BOTTLING

$ $ ⌧ BAR & BEVERAGE BUSINESS MAGAZINE

Mercury Publications, Ltd., 1839 Inkster Blvd., Winnipeg MB R2X 1R3, Canada. (204)954-2085. Fax: (204)954-2057. E-mail: mp@mercury.mb.ca. Website: www.mercury.mb.ca/. Editor: Kelly Gray. **Contact:** Kristi Balon, editorial production manager. **33% freelance written.** Bimonthly magazine providing information on the latest trends, happenings, buying-selling of beverages and product merchandising. Estab. 1998. Circ. 16,077. Pays 30-45 days from receipt of invoice. Byline given. Offers 33% kill fee. Buys all rights. Submit seasonal material 3 months in advance. Accepts simultaneous submissions. Sample copy and writer's guidelines free or by e-mail.

  • Does not accept queries. Assigns stories to Canadian writers.

Nonfiction How-to (making a good drink, training staff, etc.), interview/profile. Industry reports, profiles on companies. Query with published clips. Length: 500-9,000 words. **Pays 25-35¢/word.** Sometimes pays expenses of writers on assignment.

Photos State availability with submission. Reviews negatives, transparencies, 3×5 prints, JPEG, EPS or TIFF files. Buys all rights. Negotiates payment individually. Captions required.

Columns/Departments Out There (bar & bev news in various parts of the country), 100-500 words. Query. **Pays $0-100.**

$ BEER, WINE & SPIRITS BEVERAGE RETAILER

The Marketing & Merchandising Magazine for Off-Premise Innovators, Oxford Publishing Co., 307 W. Jackson Ave., Oxford MS 38655-2154. (662)236-5510. Fax: (662)236-5541. E-mail: brenda@oxpub.com. Website: www. beverage-retailer.com. **Contact:** Brenda Owen, editor. **2-5% freelance written.** Magazine published 6 times a year covering alcohol beverage retail industry (off-premise). "Our readership of off-premise beverage alcohol retailers (owners and operators of package liquor stores, wine cellars, beer barns, etc.) appreciates our magazine's total focus on helping them increase their revenue and profits. We particulary emphasize stories on retailers' own ideas and efforts to market their products and their stores' images." Estab. 1997. Circ. 20,000. **Pays on acceptance.** Publishes ms an average of 7 months after acceptance. Byline given. Buys first North American serial rights. Editorial lead time 6 months. Submit seasonal material 6 months in advance. Accepts queries by mail. Responds in 2 weeks to queries; 1 month to mss. Sample copy for $5 or online at website.

  ○⌐ Break in with a "successful retailer" profile or product feature that shows your grasp on moneymaking tips, marketing, and merchandising ideas.

Nonfiction General interest, how-to, interview/profile, industry commentary. "No book reviews; no product stories narrowly focused on one manufacturer's product; no general stories on beverage categories (scotch, tequila, etc.) unless trend-oriented." **Buys 4-6 mss/year.** Query with published clips or send complete ms. Length: 350-800 words. **Pays $100 for assigned articles.** Pays phone expenses only of writers on assignment.

Photos State availability of or send photos with submission. Reviews contact sheets, transparencies (all sizes), prints (all sizes). Buys all rights. Offers no additional payment for photos accepted with ms on most features. Negotiates payment individually on cover stories and major features. Captions, identification of subjects, model releases required.

Columns/Departments Successful Retailers (What business practice, unique facility feature, or other quality makes this business so successful?), 350-400 words; Marketing & Merchandising (brief stories of innovative efforts by retailers—displays, tastings and other events, celebrity appearances, special sales, etc.) 50-350 words. Query with published clips or send complete ms. **Pays $25-100.**

Tips "Rely solely on off-premise beverage alcohol retailers (and, in some cases, leading industry experts) as your sources. Make certain every line of your story focuses on telling the reader how to improve his business' revenue and profits. Keep your story short, and include colorful, intelligent, and concise retailer quotes. Include a few relevant and irresistible statistics. We particularly appreciate trend or analysis stories when we get them early enough to publish them in a timely fashion."

$ $ THE BEVERAGE JOURNAL

Michigan Edition, MI Licensed Beverage Association, 920 N. Fairview Ave., Lansing MI 48912. (517)374-9611. Fax: (517)374-1165. E-mail: editor@mlba.org. Website: www.mlba.org. **Contact:** Peter Broderick, editor. **40-50% freelance written.** Monthly magazine covering hospitality industry. "A monthly trade magazine devoted to the beer, wine, and spirits industry in Michigan. It is dedicated to serving those who make their living serving the public and the state through the orderly and responsible sale of beverages." Estab. 1983. Circ. 4,200. Pays on publication. Buys one-time, second serial (reprint) rights, makes work-for-hire assignments. Editorial lead time 3 months. Submit seasonal material 3 months in advance. Accepts queries by mail, e-mail. Responds in 2 weeks to queries; 1 month to mss. Sample copy for $5 or online.

Nonfiction Essays, general interest, historical/nostalgic, how-to (make a drink, human resources, tips, etc.), humor, interview/profile, new product, opinion, personal experience, photo feature, technical. **Buys 24 mss/ year.** Send complete ms. Length:1,000 words. **Pays $20-200.**

Reprints Accepts previously published submissions.

Columns/Departments Interviews (legislators, others), 750-1,000 words; personal experience (waitstaff, customer, bartenders), 500 words. "Open to essay content ideas." **Buys 12 mss/year.** Send complete ms. **Pays $25-100.**

Tips "We are particularly interested in nonfiction concerning responsible consumption/serving of alcohol. We are looking for product reviews, company profiles, personal experiences, and news articles that would benefit our audience. Our audience is a busy group of business owners and hospitality professionals striving to obtain pertinent information that is not too wordy."

$ $ PATTERSON'S CALIFORNIA BEVERAGE JOURNAL

Interactive Color, Inc., 4910 San Fernando Rd., Glendale CA 91204. (818)291-1125. Fax: (818)547-4607. E-mail: mmay@interactivecolor.com. Website: www.beveragelink.com. **Contact:** Meridith May, associate publisher/ senior editor. **25% freelance written.** Monthly magazine covering the alcohol, beverage, and wine industries. *"Patterson's* reports on the latest news in product information, merchandising, company appointments, developments in the wine industry, and consumer trends. Our readers can be informed, up-to-date and confident in their purchasing decisions." Estab. 1962. Circ. 25,000. Byline given. Offers negotiable kill fee. Editorial lead time 1 month. Submit seasonal material 1 month in advance. Accepts queries by mail, e-mail, fax. Sample copy for free. Writer's guidelines free.

Nonfiction Interview/profile, new product, market reports. "No consumer-oriented articles or negative slants on industry as a whole." **Buys 200 mss/year.** Query with published clips. Length: 500-750 words. **Pays $60-200.**

Photos State availability with submission. Reviews transparencies. Buys all rights. Offers no additional payment for photos accepted with ms. Captions, identification of subjects required.

Columns/Departments Query with published clips.

$ $ $ VINEYARD & WINERY MANAGEMENT

P.O. Box 2358, Windsor CA 95492-2358. (707)836-6820. Fax: (707)836-6825. E-mail: gparnell@vwm-online.com. Website: www.vwm-online.com. **Contact:** Graham Parnell, managing editor. **70% freelance written.** Bimonthly magazine of professional importance to grape growers, winemakers, and winery sales and business people. Estab. 1975. Circ. 6,500. Pays on publication. Byline given. Buys first North American serial, simultaneous rights. Accepts queries by e-mail. Responds in 3 weeks to queries; 1 month to mss. Sample copy for free. Writer's guidelines for #10 SASE.

Nonfiction Subjects are technical in nature and explore the various methods people in these career paths use to succeed and the equipment and techniques they use successfully. Business articles and management topics are also featured. The audience is national with western dominance. How-to, interview/profile, new product, technical. **Buys 30 mss/year.** Query. Length: 1,800-5,000 words. **Pays $30-1,000.** Sometimes pays expenses of writers on assignment.

Photos State availability with submission. Reviews contact sheets, negatives, transparencies, digital photos. Black & white often purchased for $20 each to accompany story material; 35mm and/or 4×5 transparencies for $50 and up; 6/year of vineyard and/or winery scene related to story. Captions, identification of subjects required.

Tips "We're looking for long-term relationships with authors who know the business and write well. Electronic submissions required; query for formats."

$ $ WINES & VINES MAGAZINE

The Authoritative Voice of the Grape and Wine Industry Since 1919, The Hiaring Co., 1800 Lincoln Ave., San Rafael CA 94901. (415)453-9700. Fax: (415)453-2517. E-mail: edit@winesandvines.com. Website: www.winesandvines.com. **50% freelance written.** Monthly magazine covering the international winegrape and winemaking industry. "Since 1919 *Wines & Vines Magazine* has been the authoritative voice of the wine and grape industry—from prohibition to phylloxera, we have covered it all. Our paid circulation reaches all 50 states and foreign countries. Because we are intended for the trade—including growers, winemakers, winery owners, wholesalers, restauranteurs, and serious amateurs—we accept more technical, informative articles. We do not accept wine reviews, wine country tours, or anything of a wine consumer nature." Estab. 1919. Circ. 4,000. **Pays on acceptance.** Publishes ms an average of 3 months after acceptance. Byline given. Buys first, electronic rights. Editorial lead time 2 months. Submit seasonal material 4 months in advance. Accepts queries by e-mail. Responds in 2-3 weeks to queries. Sample copy for $5. Writer's guidelines free.

Nonfiction Interview/profile, new product, technical. No wine reviews, wine country travelogues, 'lifestyle' pieces, or anything aimed at wine consumers. "Our readers are professionals in the field." **Buys 60 mss/year.**

Query with published clips. Length: 800-1,800 words. **Pays 15-25¢/word for assigned articles.**

Photos State availability of or send photos with submission. Reviews transparencies, prints, GIF/JPEG files (JPEG, 300 dpi minimum). Buys one-time rights. Offers $10/published original photos. Captions, identification of subjects required.

BOOK & BOOKSTORE

$THE BLOOMSBURY REVIEW

A Book Magazine, Dept. WM, Owaissa Communications Co., Inc., P.O. Box 8928, Denver CO 80201. (303)455-3123. Fax: (303)455-7039. E-mail: bloomsb@aol.com. **Contact:** Marilyn Auer, editor. **75% freelance written.** Bimonthly tabloid covering books and book-related matters. "We publish book reviews, interviews with writers and poets, literary essays, and original poetry. Our audience consists of educated, literate, nonspecialized readers." Estab. 1980. Circ. 50,000. Pays on publication. Publishes ms an average of 4-6 months after acceptance. Byline given. Buys first, one-time rights. Accepts queries by mail. Responds in 4 months to queries. Sample copy for $5 and 9×12 SASE. Writer's guidelines for #10 SASE.

Nonfiction "Summer issue features reviews, etc., about the American West. We do not publish fiction." Essays, interview/profile, book reviews. **Buys 60 mss/year.** Query with published clips or send complete ms. Length: 800-1,500 words. **Pays $10-20. Sometimes pays writers with contributor copies or other premiums "if writer agrees."**

Reprints Considered but not encouraged. Send photocopy of article and information about when and where the article previously appeared.

Photos State availability with submission. Reviews prints. Buys one-time rights. Offers no additional payment for photos accepted with ms.

Columns/Departments Book reviews and essays, 500-1,500 words. **Buys 6 mss/year.** Query with published clips or send complete ms. **Pays $10-20.**

Poetry Ray Gonzalez, poetry editor. Avant-garde, free verse, haiku, traditional. **Buys 20 poems/year.** Submit maximum 5 poems. **Pays $5-10.**

Tips "We appreciate receiving published clips and/or completed manuscripts. Please—no rough drafts. Book reviews should be of new books (within 6 months of publication)."

$ $ FOREWORD MAGAZINE

ForeWord Magazine, Inc., 129½ E. Front St., Traverse City MI 49684. (231)933-3699. Fax: (231)933-3899. E-mail: alex@forewordmagazine.com. Website: www.forewordmagazine.com. **Contact:** Alex Moore, managing editor. **95% freelance written.** Bimonthly magazine covering independent and university presses for booksellers and librarians with articles, news, book reviews. Estab. 1998. Circ. 8,000. Pays 2 months after publication. Publishes ms an average of 2-3 months after acceptance. Byline given. Buys all rights. Editorial lead time 3-4 months. Submit seasonal material 5 months in advance. Accepts queries by mail, e-mail. Responds in 1 month to queries; 1 month to mss. Sample copy for $10 and 8½×11 SASE with $1.50 postage.

Nonfiction Reviews, 85% nonfiction and 15% fiction/poetry. Query with published clips. Length: 400-1,500 words. **Pays $25-200 for assigned articles.**

Tips "Be knowledgeable about the needs of booksellers and librarians—remember we are an industry trade journal, not a how-to or consumer publication. We review books prior to publication, so book reviews are always assigned—but send us a note telling subjects you wish to review in as well as a résumé."

THE HORN BOOK MAGAZINE

The Horn Book, Inc., 56 Roland St., Suite 200, Boston MA 02129. (617)628-0225. Fax: (617)628-0882. E-mail: magazine@hbook.com. Website: www.hbook.com. **Contact:** Roger Sutton, editor-in-chief. **75% freelance written.** Prefers to work with published/established writers. Bimonthly magazine covering children's literature for librarians, booksellers, professors, teachers and students of children's literature. Estab. 1924. Circ. 16,000. Pays on publication. Publishes ms an average of 4 months after acceptance. Byline given. Submit seasonal material 6 months in advance. Accepts queries by mail, e-mail, fax. Accepts simultaneous submissions. Responds in 2 months to queries. Sample copy and writer's guidelines online.

Nonfiction Interested in seeing strong, authoritative pieces about children's books and contemporary culture. Writers should be familiar with the magazine and its contents. Interview/profile (children's book authors and illustrators), topics of interest to the children's bookworld. **Buys 20 mss/year.** Query or send complete ms. Length: 1,000-2,800 words. **Pays honorarium upon publication.**

Tips "Writers have a better chance of breaking into our publication with a query letter on a specific article they want to write."

BRICK, GLASS & CERAMICS

$ $ GLASS MAGAZINE

For the Architectural Glass Industry, National Glass Association, 8200 Greensboro Dr., Suite 302, McLean VA 22102. (866)342-5642. Fax: (703)442-0630. E-mail: charles@glass.org. Website: www.glass.org. **Contact:** Charles Cumpston, editor. **10% freelance written.** Prefers to work with published/established writers. Monthly magazine covering the architectural glass industry. Circ. 23,291. **Pays on acceptance.** Publishes ms an average of 6 months after acceptance. Byline given. Kill fee varies. Buys first rights. Accepts queries by mail, e-mail, fax. Responds in 2 months to mss. Sample copy for $5 and 9×12 SAE with 10 first-class stamps.

Nonfiction Interview/profile (of various glass businesses; profiles of industry people or glass business owners), new product, technical (about glazing processes). **Buys 5 mss/year.** Query with published clips. Length: 1,000 words minimum. **Pays $150-300 for assigned articles.**

Photos State availability with submission.

Tips *Glass Magazine* is doing more inhouse writing; freelance cut by half. "Do not send in general glass use stories. Research the industry first, then query."

$ STAINED GLASS

Stained Glass Association of America, 10009 E. 62nd St., Raytown MO 64133. (800)438-9581. Fax: (816)737-2801. E-mail: sgaa@stainedglass.org. Website: www.stainedglass.org. **Contact:** Richard Gross, editor. **70% freelance written.** Quarterly magazine. "Since 1906, *Stained Glass* has been the official voice of the Stained Glass Association of America. As the oldest, most respected stained glass publication in North America, *Stained Glass* preserves the techniques of the past as well as illustrates the trends of the future. This vital information, of significant value to the professional stained glass studio, is also of interest to those for whom stained glass is an avocation or hobby." Estab. 1906. Circ. 8,000. Pays on publication. Publishes ms an average of 1 year after acceptance. Byline given. Buys one-time rights. Editorial lead time 6 months. Submit seasonal material 8 months in advance. Accepts queries by mail, e-mail, fax. Responds in 3 months to queries. Sample copy and writer's guideline free.

O─ Break in with "excellent photography and in-depth stained glass architectural knowledge."

Nonfiction Strong need for technical and how to create architectural type stained glass. Glass etching, use of etched glass in stained glass compositions, framing. How-to, humor, interview/profile, new product, opinion, photo feature, technical. **Buys 9 mss/year.** Query or send complete ms but must include photos or slides—very heavy on photos. **Pays $125/illustrated article; $75/nonillustrated.**

Reprints Accepts previously published submissions from nonstained glass publications only. Send tearsheet of article. Payment negotiable.

Photos Send photos with submission. Reviews 4×5 transparencies, send slides with submission. Buys one-time rights. Pays $75 for non-illustrated. Pays $125, plus 3 copies for line art or photography. Identification of subjects required.

Columns/Departments Teknixs (technical, how-to, stained and glass art), word length varies by subject. "Columns must be illustrated." **Buys 4 mss/year.** Query or send complete ms, but must be illustrated.

Tips "We need more technical articles. Writers should be extremely well versed in the glass arts. Photographs are extremely important and must be of very high quality. Submissions without photographs or illustrations are seldom considered unless something special and writer states that photos are available. However, prefer to see with submission."

$ $ US GLASS, METAL & GLAZING

Key Communications, Inc., P.O. Box 569, Garrisonville VA 22463. (540)720-5584. Fax: (540)720-5687. E-mail: echilcoat@glass.com. Website: www.usglassmag.com. **Contact:** Ellen Giard Chilcoat, editor. **25% freelance written.** Monthly magazine for companies involved in the flat glass trades. Estab. 1966. Circ. 27,000. Pays on publication. Publishes ms an average of 3 months after acceptance. Byline given. Buys all rights. Editorial lead time 3 months. Submit seasonal material 2 months in advance. Accepts queries by mail, e-mail, fax. Accepts simultaneous submissions. Responds in 1 month to queries; 2 months to mss. Sample copy and writer's guidelines on website.

Nonfiction **Buys 12 mss/year.** Query with published clips. **Pays $300-600 for assigned articles.** Sometimes pays expenses of writers on assignment.

Photos State availability with submission. Reviews contact sheets. Buys first North American rights. Offers no additional payment for photos accepted with ms. Captions, identification of subjects required.

◼ The online magazine carries original content not found in the print edition. Contact: Holly Carter.

BUILDING INTERIORS

$$PWC

Painting & Wallcovering Contractor, Finan Publishing Co., Inc., 107 W. Pacific Ave., St. Louis MO 63119-2323. (314)961-6644. Fax: (314)961-4809. E-mail: jbeckner@finan.com. Website: www.paintstore.com. **Contact:** Jeffery Beckner, editor. **90% freelance written.** Bimonthly magazine. *"PWC provides news you can use: Information helpful to the painting and wallcovering contractor in the here and now."* Estab. 1928. Circ. 30,000. Pays 1 month after acceptance. Publishes ms an average of 1 month after acceptance. Byline given. Offers variable kill fee. Buys first North American serial rights. Editorial lead time 2 months. Submit seasonal material 2 months in advance. Accepts simultaneous submissions. Responds in 2 weeks to queries. Sample copy for free.

Nonfiction Essays, exposé, how-to (painting and wallcovering), interview/profile, new product, opinion, personal experience. **Buys 40 mss/year.** Query with published clips. Length: 1,500-2,500 words. **Pays $300 minimum.** Pays expenses of writers on assignment.

Reprints Send photocopy and information about when and where the material previously appeared. Negotiates payment.

Photos State availability of or send photos with submission. Reviews contact sheets, negatives, transparencies, digital prints. Buys all rights. Offers no additional payment for photos accepted with ms. Identification of subjects required.

Columns/Departments Anything of interest to the small businessman, 1,250 words. **Buys 2 mss/year.** Query with published clips. **Pays $50-100.**

Tips "We almost always buy on an assignment basis. The way to break in is to send good clips, and I'll try and give you work."

$$QUALIFIED REMODELER

The Business Management Tool for Professional Remodelers, Cygnus Business Media, 1233 Janesville Ave., Fort Atkinson WI 53538. E-mail: jonathan.sweet@cygnusb2b.com. Website: www.qualifiedremodeler.com. Editor: Patrick O'Toole. **Contact:** Jonathan Sweet, managing editor. **5% freelance written.** Monthly magazine covering residential remodeling. Estab. 1975. Circ. 83,500. **Pays on acceptance.** Publishes ms an average of 1 month after acceptance. Byline given. Buys all rights. Editorial lead time 3 months. Submit seasonal material 2 months in advance. Accepts queries by mail, e-mail, fax, phone. Sample copy online.

Nonfiction How-to (business management), new product, photo feature, best practices articles, innovative design. **Buys 12 mss/year.** Query with published clips. Length: 1,200-2,500 words. **Pays $300-600 for assigned articles; $200-400 for unsolicited articles.** Sometimes pays expenses of writers on assignment.

Photos Send photos with submission. Reviews negatives, transparencies. Buys one-time rights. Negotiates payment individually.

Columns/Departments Query with published clips. **Pays $200-400.**

◼ The online version contains material not found in the print edition.

Tips "We focus on business management issues faced by remodeling contractors. For example, sales, marketing, liability, taxes, and just about any matter addressing small business operation."

$$$REMODELING

Hanley-Wood, LLC, One Thomas Circle NW, Suite 600, Washington DC 20005. (202)452-0800. Fax: (202)785-1974. E-mail: chartman@hanley-wood.com. Website: www.remodelingmagazine.com. Editor-in-Chief: Sal Alfano. **Contact:** Christine Hartman, managing editor. **10% freelance written.** Monthly magazine covering residential and light commercial remodeling. "We cover the best new ideas in remodeling design, business, construction and products." Estab. 1985. Circ. 80,000. Pays on publication. Publishes ms an average of 3 months after acceptance. Byline given. Offers 5¢/word kill fee. Buys first North American serial rights. Accepts queries by mail, e-mail, fax. Responds in 1 month to queries. Sample copy for free.

Nonfiction Interview/profile, new product, technical, small business trends. **Buys 6 mss/year.** Query with published clips. Length: 250-1,000 words. **Pays 50¢/word.** Sometimes pays expenses of writers on assignment.

Photos State availability with submission. Reviews 4×5 transparencies, slides, 8×10 prints. Buys one-time rights. Offers $25-125/photo. Captions, identification of subjects, model releases required.

◼ The online magazine carries original content not included in the print edition. Contact: John Butterfield, online editor.

Tips "We specialize in service journalism for remodeling contractors. Knowledge of the industry is essential."

$ $ WALLS & CEILINGS

2401 W. Big Beaver Rd., Suite 700, Troy MI 48084. (248)244-6244. Fax: (248)362-5103. E-mail: morettin@bnpm edia.com. Website: www.wconline.com. **Contact:** Nick Moretti, editor. **20% freelance written.** Monthly magazine for contractors involved in lathing and plastering, drywall, acoustics, fireproofing, curtain walls, and movable partitions, together with manufacturers, dealers, and architects. Estab. 1938. Circ. 30,000. Pays on publication. Publishes ms an average of 6 months after acceptance. Byline given. Buys all rights. Submit seasonal material 4 months in advance. Accepts queries by mail, e-mail, phone. Accepts simultaneous submissions. Responds in 6 months to queries. Sample copy for 9 × 12 SAE with $2 postage. Writer's guidelines for #10 SASE.

O→ Break in with technical expertise in drywall, plaster, stucco.

Nonfiction How-to (drywall and plaster construction and business management), technical. **Buys 20 mss/year.** Query or send complete ms. Length: 1,000-1,500 words. **Pays $50-500.** Sometimes pays expenses of writers on assignment.

Reprints Send tearsheet or photocopy with rights for sale noted and information about when and where the material previously appeared. Pays 50% of the amount paid for an original article.

Photos Send photos with submission. Reviews contact sheets, negatives, transparencies, prints. Buys one-time rights. Captions, identification of subjects required.

■ The online magazine carries original content not included in the print edition.

BUSINESS MANAGEMENT

$ $ $ $ ACROSS THE BOARD

The Conference Board Magazine, The Conference Board, 845 Third Ave., New York NY 10022-6679. (212)759-0900. Fax: (212)836-3828. E-mail: atb@conference-board.org. Website: www.acrosstheboardmagazine.com. **Contact:** Al Vogl, editor. **60% freelance written.** Bimonthly magazine covering business—focuses on higher management. "*Across the Board* is a nonprofit magazine of ideas and opinions for leaders in business, government, and other organizations. The editors present business perspectives on timely issues, including management practices, foreign policy, social issues, and science and technology. *Across the Board* is neither an academic business journal not a 'popular' manual. That means we aren't interested in highly technical articles about business strategy. It also means we don't publish oversimple 'how-to' articles. We are an idea magazine, but the ideas should have practical overtones. We let *Forbes, Fortune* and *Business Week* do most of the straight reporting, while we do some of the critical thinking; that is, we let writers explore the implications of the news in depth. *Across the Board* tries to provide different angles on important topics, and to bring to its readers' attention issues that they might otherwise not devote much thought to." Circ. 30,000. Pays on publication. Publishes ms an average of 4 months after acceptance. Byline given. Offers 20% kill fee. Buys first rights. Editorial lead time 6 months. Submit seasonal material 6 months in advance. Accepts queries by mail, e-mail, fax. Accepts simultaneous submissions. Responds in 3 weeks to queries. Sample copy for free. Writer's guidelines online.

Nonfiction Book excerpts, essays, humor, opinion, personal experience. No new product information. **Buys 30 mss/year.** Query with published clips or send complete ms. Length: 500-4,000 words. **Pays $50-2,500.** Sometimes pays expenses of writers on assignment.

Photos State availability with submission. Reviews contact sheets. Buys one-time or all rights. Negotiates payment individually. Captions, identification of subjects required.

Tips "We emphasize the human side of organizational life at all levels. We're as concerned with helping managers who are 'lonely at the top' as with motivating workers and enhancing job satisfaction."

Ⓝ $ $ AMERICAN DRYCLEANER/COIN-OP/AMERICAN LAUNDRY NEWS

Crain Communications Inc., 500 N. Dearborn, Suite 1000, Chicago IL 60610. (312)337-7700. Fax: (312)337-8654. E-mail: drycleaner@crain.com. Website: www.crain.com. **Contact:** Ian Murphy, editor. **20% freelance written.** Monthly tabloid covering drycleaning, coin laundry, coin car cleaning, institutional laundry. Estab. 1934. Circ. 25,000. Pays on publication. Publishes ms an average of 1 month after acceptance. Byline given. Offers 10% kill fee. Buys first, second serial (reprint), all rights. Editorial lead time 2 months. Submit seasonal material 2 months in advance. Accepts queries by mail, e-mail, fax, phone. Accepts simultaneous submissions. Responds in 1 month to queries; 4 months to mss. Sample copy for 6 × 9 SAE and 2 first-class stamps.

Nonfiction How-to (general biz, industry-specific), interview/profile, new product, personal experience, technical. No inspirational, consumer-geared. **Buys 12-15 mss/year.** Query. Length: 600-2,000 words. **Pays $50-500 for assigned articles; $25-250 for unsolicited articles.** Sometimes pays expenses of writers on assignment.

Photos State availability with submission. Reviews contact sheets, negatives, 4 × 5 or slide transparencies, 3 × 5-5 × 7 prints. Buys one-time rights. Negotiates payment individually. Identification of subjects required.

Columns/Departments General Business, 1,200 words. **Buys 72 mss/year.** Send complete ms. **Pays $50-150.**

Tips "Each magazine is geared toward small-business owners in these specific industries. Writers will find professional experience in the industry is a plus; general small-business articles are often used, but tailored to each magazine's audience."

$ $ $ BEDTIMES

The Business Journal for the Sleep Products Industry, International Sleep Products Association, 501 Wythe St., Alexandria VA 22314-1917. (703)683-8371. E-mail: jpalm@sleepproducts.org. Website: www.sleepproducts.org. **Contact:** Julie Palm, editor-in-chief. **20-40% freelance written.** Monthly magazine covering the mattress manufacturing industry. "Our news and features are straight forward—we are not a lobbying vehicle for our association. No special slant or philosophy." Estab. 1917. Circ. 4,000. **Pays on acceptance.** Publishes ms an average of 4 months after acceptance. Byline sometimes given. Buys first North American serial rights. Editorial lead time 2 months. Accepts queries by e-mail, fax. Accepts simultaneous submissions. Responds in 1 month to queries. Sample copy for $4. Writer's guidelines free for #10 SASE or by e-mail.

> Break in with "Headlines"—short news stories. We also use freelancers for our monthly columns on "New Products," "Newsmakers," and "Snoozebriefs." Query first.

Nonfiction Interview/profile, photo feature. "No pieces that do not relate to business in general or mattress industry in particular." **Buys 15-25 mss/year.** Query with published clips. Length: 500-3,500 words. **Pays 25-50¢/word for short features; $1,000 for cover story.**

Photos State availability with submission. Buys one-time rights. Negotiates payment individually. Identification of subjects required.

Columns/Departments Millennium Milestones (companies marking anniversaries from 25-150 years), 1,000 words. **Buys 10-12 mss/year.** Query with 3 published clips. **Pays $350 or more, depending on length and degree of difficulty in getting the story.**

Tips "Cover stories are a major outlet for freelance submissions. Once a story is written and accepted, the author is encouraged to submit suggestions to the graphic designer of the magazine regarding ideas for the cover illustration as well as possible photos/graphs/charts, etc. to be used with the story itself. Topics have included annual industry forecast; physical expansion of industry facilities; e-commerce; flammability and home furnishings; the risks and rewards of marketing overseas; the evolving family business; the shifting workplace environment; and what do consumers really want?"

Ⓝ $ $ $ $ BLACK MBA MAGAZINE

Official Publication of NBMBAA, P&L Publishing Ltd., 9730 S. Western Ave., Suite 320, Evergreen Park IL 60805. (708)422-1506. Fax: (708)422-1507. E-mail: pam@blackmbamagazine.com. Website: www.blackmbamagazine.com. Editor: Diane Hayes. Associate Editor: Robert Miller. **80% freelance written.** Quarterly magazine covering business career strategy, economic development, and financial management. Estab. 1997. Circ. 40,000. Pays on publication. Publishes ms an average of 1 month after acceptance. Byline given. Offers 10-20% or $500 kill fee. Buys all rights. Editorial lead time 2-3 months. Submit seasonal material 3-4 months in advance. Accepts queries by mail, e-mail, fax. Sample copy not available.

Photos State availability of or send photos with submission. Reviews ZIP disk. Buys one-time rights. Offers no additional payment for photos accepted with ms. Identification of subjects required.

Columns/Departments Management Strategies (leadership development), 1,200-1,700 words; Features (business management, entreprenuerial finance); Finance; Technology. Send complete ms. **Pays $800-1,900.**

☒ CA MAGAZINE

Canadian Institute of Chartered Accountants, 277 Wellington St. W, Toronto ON M5V 3H2, Canada. (416)204-3261. Fax: (416)204-3409. E-mail: christian.bellavance@cica.ca. Website: www.camagazine.com. **Contact:** Christian Bellavance, editor-in-chief. **30% freelance written.** Magazine published 10 times/year covering accounting. "CA Magazine is the leading accounting publication in Canada and the preferred information source for chartered accountants and financial executives. It provides a forum for discussion and debate on professional, financial, and other business issues." Estab. 1911. Circ. 74,834. **Pays on acceptance.** Publishes ms an average of 3 months after acceptance. Byline given. Offers 30% kill fee. Buys all rights. Editorial lead time 4 months. Accepts queries by e-mail. Responds in 1 month to queries. Sample copy and writer's guidelines online.

Nonfiction Book excerpts, financial/accounting business. **Buys 30 mss/year.** Query. Length: 2,500-3,500 words. **Pays honorarium for chartered accountants; freelance rate varies.**

$ $ CBA MARKETPLACE

CBA Service Corp., P.O. Box 62000, Colorado Springs CO 80962. E-mail: publications@cbaonline.org. Website: www.cbaonline.org. **Contact:** Cindy Parolini, publications manager. **20% freelance written.** Monthly magazine covering the Christian retail industry. "Writers must have knowledge of and direct experience in the Christian retail industry. Subject matter must specifically pertain to the Christian retail audience." Estab. 1968. **Pays on**

acceptance. Publishes ms an average of 3 months after acceptance. Byline given. Buys all rights. Editorial lead time 3 months. Submit seasonal material 6 months in advance. Accepts queries by mail, e-mail. Responds in 2 months to queries. Sample copy for $9.50 or online.

Nonfiction Christian retail. **Buys 24 mss/year.** Query. Length: 750-1,500 words. **Pays 20-30¢/word.**

Fillers Cartoons. **Buys 12/year. Pays $150.**

Tips "Only experts on Christian retail industry, completely familiar with retail audience and their needs and considerations, should submit a query. Do not submit articles unless requested."

$ $ CONTRACT MANAGEMENT

National Contract Management Association, 8260 Greensboro Dr., Suite 200, McLean VA 22102. (571)382-0082. Fax: (703)448-0939. E-mail: miedema@ncmahq.org. Website: www.ncmahq.org. **Contact:** Amy Miedema, director of communications. **10% freelance written.** Monthly magazine covering contract and business management. "Most of the articles published in *Contract Management (CM)* are written by members, although one does not have to be an NCMA member to be published in the magazine. Articles should concern some aspect of the contract management profession, whether at the level of a beginner or that of the advanced practitioner." Estab. 1960. Circ. 23,000. Pays on publication. Publishes ms an average of 3 months after acceptance. Byline given. Buys one-time rights. Editorial lead time 10 weeks. Submit seasonal material 3 months in advance. Accepts queries by mail, e-mail, fax, phone. Accepts previously published material. Accepts simultaneous submissions. Responds in 2 weeks to queries; 1 month to mss. Sample copy and writer's guidelines free.

Nonfiction Essays, general interest, how-to, humor, inspirational, new product, opinion, technical. No company or CEO profiles—please read a copy of publication before submitting. **Buys 6-10 mss/year.** Query with published clips. Length: 2,500-3,000 words. **Pays $300, association members paid in 3 copies.**

Reprints Accepts previously published submissions.

Photos State availability with submission. Buys one-time rights. Offers no additional payment for photos accepted with ms. Captions, identification of subjects required.

Columns/Departments Professional Development (self-improvement in business), 1,000-1,500 words; Back to Basics (basic how-tos and discussions), 1,500-2,000 words. **Buys 2 mss/year.** Query with published clips. **Pays $300.**

Tips "Query and read at least 1 issue. Visit website to better understand our audience."

$ $ CONTRACTING PROFITS

Trade Press Publishing, 2100 W. Florist Ave., Milwaukee WI 53209. (414)228-7701. E-mail: stacie.whitacre@tradepress.com. Website: www.cleanlink.com/cp. **Contact:** Stacie H. Whitacre, editor. **40% freelance written.** Magazine published 10 times/year covering "building service contracting, business management advice." "We are the pocket MBA for this industry—focusing not only on cleaning-specific topics, but also discussing how to run businesses better and increase profits through a variety of management articles." Estab. 1995. Circ. 32,000. Pays within 30 days of acceptance. Byline given. Buys all rights. Editorial lead time 2 months. Submit seasonal material 3 months in advance. Accepts queries by mail, e-mail. Sample copy online. Writer's guidelines free.

Nonfiction Exposé, how-to, interview/profile, technical. "No product-related reviews or testimonials." **Buys 30 mss/year.** Query with published clips. Length: 1,000-1,500 words. **Pays $100-500.** Sometimes pays expenses of writers on assignment.

Columns/Departments Query with published clips.

Tips "Read back issues on our website and be able to understand some of those topics prior to calling."

CONVENTION SOUTH

Covey Communications Corp., P.O. Box 2267, Gulf Shores AL 36547-2267. (251)968-5300. Fax: (251)968-4532. E-mail: info@conventionsouth.com. Website: www.conventionsouth.com. Editor: J. Talty O'Connor. **Contact:** Kristen McIntosh, executive editor. **50% freelance written.** Monthly business journal for meeting planners who plan events in the South. Topics relate to the meetings industry—how-to articles, industry news, destination spotlights. Estab. 1983. Circ. 16,000. Pays on publication. Publishes ms an average of 2 months after acceptance. Byline given. Buys first, second serial (reprint) rights. Editorial lead time 3 months. Submit seasonal material 4 months in advance. Accepts queries by mail, e-mail, fax. Accepts simultaneous submissions. Responds in 2 months to queries. Sample copy for free. Writer's guidelines for #10 SASE.

Nonfiction How-to (relative to meeting planning/travel), interview/profile, photo feature, technical, travel. **Buys 50 mss/year.** Query. Length: 750-1,250 words. **Payment negotiable.** Pays in contributor copies or other premiums if arranged in advance. Sometimes pays expenses of writers on assignment.

Reprints Send photocopy and information about when and where the material previously appeared. Payment negotiable.

Photos Send photos with submission. Reviews 5×7 prints. Buys one-time rights. Offers no additional payment for photos accepted with ms. Captions, identification of subjects required.

Columns/Departments How-to (related to meetings), 700 words. **Buys 12 mss/year.** Query with published clips. **Payment negotiable.**

Tips "Know who our audience is and make sure articles are appropriate for them."

$ $ EXECUTIVE UPDATE

Greater Washington Society of Association Executives, Reagan Building & International Trade Center, 1300 Pennsylvania Ave. NW, Washington DC 20004. (202)326-9545. Fax: (202)326-0999. E-mail: sbriscoe@gwsae.o rg. Website: www.executiveupdate.com. **Contact:** Scott Briscoe, editor. **60% freelance written.** Monthly magazine "exploring a broad range of association management issues and for introducing and discussing management and leadership philosophies. It is written for individuals at all levels of association management, with emphasis on senior staff and CEOs." Estab. 1979. Circ. 14,000. **Pays on acceptance.** Publishes ms an average of 6 months after acceptance. Byline given. Offers 20% kill fee. Buys first rights. Editorial lead time 3 months. Submit seasonal material 6 months in advance. Accepts queries by mail, e-mail, fax, phone. Accepts simultaneous submissions. Responds in 1 month to queries; 2 months to mss. Sample copy and writer's guidelines free. Writer's guidelines online.

Nonfiction How-to, humor, interview/profile, opinion, personal experience, travel, management and workplace issues. **Buys 24-36 mss/year.** Query with published clips. Length: 1,750-2,250 words. **Pays $500-700.** Pays expenses of writers on assignment.

Columns/Departments Intelligence (new ways to tackle day-to-day issues), 500-700 words; Off the Cuff (guest column for association executives). Query. **Pays $100-200.**

$ $ EXPANSION MANAGEMENT MAGAZINE

Growth Strategies for Companies On the Move, Penton Media, Inc., 1300 E. 9th St., Cleveland OH 44114. (216)931-9578. Fax: (216)931-9866. Editor: Bill King. **Contact:** Ken Krizner, managing editor. **50% freelance written.** Monthly magazine covering economic development. Estab. 1986. Circ. 45,000. **Pays on acceptance.** Publishes ms an average of 1 month after acceptance. Byline given. Buys all rights, makes work-for-hire assignments. Editorial lead time 2 months. Sample copy for $7. Writer's guidelines free.

Nonfiction "*Expansion Management* presents articles and industry reports examining relocation trends, strategic planning, work force hiring, economic development agencies, and relocation consultants and state, province, and county reviews and profiles to help readers select future expansions and relocation sites." **Buys 120 mss/ year.** Query with published clips. Length: 800-1,200 words. **Pays $200-400 for assigned articles.** Sometimes pays expenses of writers on assignment.

Photos Send photos with submission. Buys one-time rights. Offers no additional payment for photos accepted with ms. Captions required.

Tips "Send clips first, then call me."

$ $ $ EXPO

Atwood Publishing, LLC, 11600 College Blvd., Overland Park KS 66210. (913)469-1185. Fax: (913)469-0806. E-mail: dvasos@expoweb.com. Website: www.expoweb.com. **Contact:** Danica O'Donnell Vasos, editor-in-chief. **80% freelance written.** Magazine covering expositions. "*EXPO* is the information and education resource for the exposition industry. It is the only magazine dedicated exclusively to the people with direct responsibility for planning, promoting and operating trade and consumer shows. Our readers are show managers and their staff, association executives, independent show producers and industry suppliers. Every issue of *EXPO* contains in-depth, how-to features and departments that focus on the practical aspects of exposition management, including administration, promotion and operations." Pays on publication. Byline given. Offers 50% kill fee. Buys first North American serial rights. Editorial lead time 3 months. Accepts queries by mail, e-mail, fax. Responds in 3 weeks to queries. Sample copy for free. Writer's guidelines online.

Nonfiction How-to, interview/profile. Query with published clips. Length: 600-2,400 words. **Pays 50¢/word.** Pays expenses of writers on assignment.

Photos State availability with submission.

Columns/Departments Profile (personality profile), 650 words; Exhibitor Matters (exhibitor issues) and EXPO-Tech (technology), both 600-1,300 words. **Buys 10 mss/year.** Query with published clips.

Tips "*EXPO* now offers shorter features and departments, while continuing to offer in-depth reporting. Editorial is more concise, using synopsis, bullets and tidbits whenever possible. Every article needs sidebars, call-outs, graphs, charts, etc., to create entry points for readers. Headlines and leads are more provocative. And writers should elevate the level of shop talk, demonstrating that *EXPO* is the leader in the industry. We plan our editorial calendar about one year in advance, but we are always open to new ideas. Please query before submitting a story to *EXPO*—tell us about your idea and what our readers would learn. Include your qualifications to write about the subject and the sources you plan to contact.''

$ $ $FAMILY BUSINESS

The Guide for Family Companies, Family Business Publishing Co., 1845 Walnut St., Philadelphia PA 19103. Fax: (215)405-6078. E-mail: bspector@familybusinessmagazine.com. Website: www.familybusinessmagazine.com. **Contact:** Barbara Spector, executive editor. **50% freelance written.** Quarterly magazine covering family-owned companies. ''Written expressly for family company owners and advisors. Focuses on issues—business and human dynamic—special to family enterprises. Offers practical guidance and tried-and-true solutions for business stakeholders.'' Estab. 1989. Circ. 6,000. **Pays on acceptance.** Publishes ms an average of 3-6 months after acceptance. Byline given. Offers 30% kill fee. Buys first, electronic rights. Editorial lead time 4 months. Submit seasonal material 6 months in advance. Accepts queries by e-mail. Writer's guidelines online.
Nonfiction Book excerpts, how-to (family business related only), interview/profile, personal experience. No ''articles that aren't specifically related to multi-generational family companies (no general business advice). No success stories—there must be an underlying family or business lesson.'' **Buys 12 mss/year.** Query with published clips. Length: 2,000-2,500 words. **Pays $50-1,000.**
Photos State availability with submission. Buys one-time rights. Offers $50-500 maximum/shoot. Captions, identification of subjects, model releases required.

$HOMEBUSINESS JOURNAL

Steffen Publishing Co., 9584 Main St., Holland Patent NY 13354. Fax: (315)865-4000. E-mail: joanne@homebusinessjournal.net. Website: www.homebusinessjournal.net. **Contact:** Joanne Steffen, managing editor. **90% freelance written.** Bimonthly magazine covering home businesses. ''*HomeBusiness Journal* publishes material pertinent to home-based entrepreneurs.'' Circ. 25,000. Pays on publication. Publishes ms an average of 3-4 months after acceptance. Byline given. Buys first North American serial, second serial (reprint) rights. Editorial lead time 4-6 months. Submit seasonal material 4 months in advance. Accepts queries by mail, e-mail, fax. Accepts previously published material. Accepts simultaneous submissions. Responds in 1-2 months to queries. Sample copy for 9×12 SAE and 5 first-class stamps. Writer's guidelines online.
Nonfiction ''All above article types as they apply to home business issues.'' Book excerpts, general interest, how-to, humor, interview/profile, tax, marketing, finance. No highly technical, ''small,'' or ''mid-size'' business articles, advertorials. **Buys 50 mss/year.** Query. Length: 700-1,100 words. **Pays $75.**
Photos State availability with submission. Reviews 3×5 prints, GIF/JPEG files. Buys one-time rights. Offers no additional payment for photos accepted with ms. Identification of subjects, model releases required.
Columns/Departments Neighborhood CEO (profiling home-based entrepreneurs), 700 words. **Buys 24 mss/year.** Query. **Pays $75.**
Tips ''Visit our website to view articles previously published, have a good understanding of the issues home-based entrepreneurs face, and work on creative angles for queries.''

$ $IN TENTS

The Magazine for the Tent Rental and Fabric Structure Industries, Industrial Fabrics Association International, 1801 County Rd. B W., Roseville MN 55113-4061. (651)225-6970. Fax: (651)225-6966. E-mail: bktaylor@ifai.com. Website: www.ifai.com. **Contact:** Betsy Taylor, editor. **50% freelance written.** Quarterly magazine covering tent-rental and fabric structure industries. Estab. 1994. Circ. 12,000. **Pays on acceptance.** Publishes ms an average of 2 months after acceptance. Byline given. Buys all rights. Editorial lead time 3 months. Accepts queries by mail, e-mail, fax. Sample copy and writer's guidelines free.
> **⚬⚞** Break in with familiarity of tent rental, special events, tent manufacturing, and fabric structure industries. Or lively, intelligent writing on technical subjects.

Nonfiction How-to, interview/profile, new product, photo feature, technical. **Buys 10-12 mss/year.** Query. Length: 800-2,000 words. **Pays $100-500.** Sometimes pays expenses of writers on assignment.
Photos State availability with submission. Reviews contact sheets, negatives, transparencies, prints, digital images. Buys one-time rights. Negotiates payment individually. Captions, identification of subjects, model releases required.
Tips ''We look for lively, intelligent writing that makes technical subjects come alive.''

$ $MAINEBIZ

Maine's Business News Source, Mainebiz Publications, Inc., 30 Milk St., 3rd Floor, Portland ME 04101. (207)761-8379. Fax: (207)761-0732. E-mail: mcavallaro@mainebiz.biz. Website: www.mainebiz.biz. Editor: Scott Sutherland. **Contact:** Michaela Cavallaro, managing editor. **50% freelance written.** Biweekly tabloid covering business in Maine. ''*Mainebiz* is read by business decision makers across the state. They look to the publication for business news and analysis.'' Estab. 1994. Circ. 13,000. Pays on publication. Publishes ms an average of 1 month after acceptance. Byline given. Offers 10% kill fee. Buys all rights. Editorial lead time 1 month. Submit seasonal material 2 months in advance. Accepts queries by mail, e-mail. Responds in 3 weeks to queries. Sample copy online. Writer's guidelines online.

Nonfiction "All pieces are reported and must comply with accepted journalistic standards. We only publish stories about business in Maine. Period." Essays, exposé, interview/profile, business trends. Special issues: See website for editorial calendar. **Buys 50+ mss/year.** Query with published clips. Length: 500-2,500 words. **Pays $50-250.** Pays expenses of writers on assignment.

Photos State availability with submission. Reviews GIF/JPEG files. Buys one-time rights. Negotiates payment individually. Identification of subjects required.

Tips "Stories should be well-thought-out with specific relevance to Maine. Arts and culture-related queries are welcome, as long as there is a business angle. We appreciate unusual angles on business stories, and regularly work with new freelancers. Please, no queries unless you have read the paper."

⊘ NORTHEAST EXPORT

A Magazine for New England Companies Engaged in International Trade, Commerce Publishing Company, Inc., P.O. Box 254, Northborough MA 01532. (508)351-2925. Fax: (508)351-6905. E-mail: editor@northeast-export.com. Website: www.northeast-export.com. **Contact:** Carlos Cunha, editor. **30% freelance written.** Bimonthly business-to-business magazine. "*Northeast Export* is the only publication directly targeted at New England's international trade community. All stories relate to issues affecting New England companies and feature only New England-based profiles and examples. Estab. 1997. Circ. 13,500. **Pays on acceptance.** Byline given. Offers 10% kill fee. Buys all rights. Editorial lead time 2 months. Accepts queries by mail, e-mail, fax. Sample copy for free.

Nonfiction How-to, interview/profile, travel, industry trends/analysis. **Buys 10-12 mss/year.** Query with published clips and SASE. *No unsolicited mss.* Length: 800-2,000 words. **Payment varies.**

Photos State availability of or send photos with submission. Reviews 2¼ transparencies, 5×7 prints. Buys one-time rights. Negotiates payment individually. Captions, identification of subjects, model releases required.

Tips "We're looking for writers with availability; the ability to write clearly about tough, sometimes very technical subjects; the fortitude to slog through industry jargon to get the story straight; a knowledge of international trade issues and/or New England transportation infrastructure. We're interested in freelancers with business writing and magazine experience, especially those with contacts in the New England manufacturing, finance, and transportation communities."

$ $ PORTABLE RESTROOM OPERATOR

Rangoon Moon, Inc., P.O. Box 904, Dahlonega GA 30533. (706)864-6838. Fax: (706)864-9851. E-mail: sesails@yahoo.com. Website: www.1promag.com. Managing Editor: M.A. Watson. **Contact:** Kevin Gralton, editor. **50% freelance written.** Magazine published 9 times/year covering portable sanitation. Estab. 1998. **Pays on acceptance.** Publishes ms an average of 2 months after acceptance. Byline given. Editorial lead time 1 month. Submit seasonal material 2 months in advance. Accepts queries by mail, e-mail, fax.

Nonfiction Quality articles that will be of interest to our readers. Studies on governmental changes, OSHA regulations, and sanitation articles that deal with portable restrooms are of strong interest. Exposé (government relations, OSHA, EPS associated, trends, public attitudes, etc.), general interest (state portable restroom associations, conventions, etc.), historical/nostalgic, humor, inspirational, new product, personal experience, technical. Query or send complete ms. Length: Length is not important. **Pays 15¢/word.**

Photos No negatives. "We need good contrast." Send photos with submission. Buys one-time rights. Pays $15 for b&w and color prints that are used. Captions, model releases required.

Tips "Material must pertain to portable sanitation industry."

PROFESSIONAL COLLECTOR

Pohly & Partners, 27 Melcher St., 2nd Floor, Boston MA 02210-1516. (617)451-1700. Fax: (617)338-7767. E-mail: procollector@pohlypartners.com. Website: www.pohlypartners.com. **Contact:** Karen English, editor. **50% freelance written.** Magazine published 3 times/year for Western Union's Financial Services, Inc.'s Quick Collect Service, covering debt collection business/lifestyle issues. "We gear our articles directly to the debt collectors and their managers. Each issue offers features covering the trends and players, the latest technology, and other issues affecting the collections industry. It's all designed to help collectors be more productive and improve their performance." Estab. 1993. Circ. 161,000. Pays on publication. Byline given. Buys first North American serial rights. Editorial lead time 9 months. Submit seasonal material 9 months in advance. Accepts queries by mail, e-mail, fax. Sample copy for free. Writer's guidelines online.

Nonfiction General interest, how-to (tips on good collecting), humor, interview/profile, new product, book reviews. **Buys 10-15 mss/year.** Query with published clips. Length: 400-1,000 words. **Payment negotiable for assigned articles.** Sometimes pays expenses of writers on assignment.

Photos State availability with submission. Reviews contact sheets, 3×5 prints. Buys one-time rights. Negotiates payment individually. Captions, identification of subjects, model releases required.

Columns/Departments Industry Roundup (issues within industry), 500-1,000 words; Tips, 750-1,000 words; Q&A (questions & answers for collectors), 1,500 words. **Buys 15-20 mss/year.** Query with published clips. **Payment negotiable.**

Tips "Writers should be aware that *Professional Collector* is a promotional publication, and that its content must support the overall marketing goals of Western Union. It helps to have extensive insider knowledge about the debt collection industry."

$ $ PROGRESSIVE RENTALS

The Voice of the Rental-Purchase Industry, Association of Progressive Rental Organizations, 1504 Robin Hood Trail, Austin TX 78703. (800)204-2776. Fax: (512)794-0097. Website: www.aprovision.org. **Contact:** Julie Stephen Sherrier, editor. **50% freelance written.** Bimonthly magazine covering the rent-to-own industry. "*Progressive Rentals* is the only publication representing the rent-to-own industry and members of APRO. The magazine covers timely news and features affecting the industry, association activities, and member profiles. Awarded best 4-color magazine by the American Society of Association Executives in 1999." Estab. 1980. Circ. 5,500. **Pays on acceptance.** Publishes ms an average of 2 months after acceptance. Byline given. Offers 25% kill fee. Buys first North American serial rights. Editorial lead time 2 months. Submit seasonal material 4 months in advance. Accepts queries by mail, e-mail, fax, phone. Accepts simultaneous submissions. Responds in 1 month to queries; 2 months to mss. Sample copy for free.

Nonfiction Exposé, general interest, how-to, inspirational, interview/profile, technical, industry features. **Buys 12 mss/year.** Query with published clips. Length: 1,200-2,500 words. **Pays $150-700.** Sometimes pays expenses of writers on assignment.

RENTAL MANAGEMENT

American Rental Association, 1900 19th St., Moline IL 61265. (309)764-2475. Fax: (309)764-1533. E-mail: brian.alm@ararental.org. Website: www.rentalmanagementmag.com. **Contact:** Brian R. Alm, editor. **30% freelance written.** Monthly magazine for the equipment rental industry worldwide (*not* property, real estate, appliances, furniture, or cars), emphasizing management topics in particular but also marketing, merchandising, technology, etc. Estab. 1970. Circ. 20,000. **Pays on acceptance.** Publishes ms an average of 3 months after acceptance. Byline given. Buys first North American serial rights. Editorial lead time 2 months. Submit seasonal material 3 months in advance. Accepts queries by mail, e-mail, fax.

Nonfiction Business management and marketing. **Buys 25-30 mss/year.** Query with published clips. Does not respond to unsolicited work unless being considered for publication. Length: 600-1,500 words. **Payment negotiable.** Sometimes pays expenses of writers on assignment.

Reprints Send tearsheet or typed ms with rights for sale noted and information about when and where the material previously appeared.

Photos State availability with submission. Reviews contact sheets; negatives; 35mm or $2\frac{1}{4}$; transparencies; any size prints; 300 dpi EPS, TIF, JPG, on e-mail or CD. Buys one-time rights. Negotiates payment individually. Identification of subjects required.

Columns/Departments "We are adequately served by existing columnists and have a long waiting list of others to use pending need." **Buys 20 mss/year.** Query with published clips. **Payment negotiable.**

Tips "Show me you can write maturely, cogently, and fluently on management matters of direct and compelling interest to the small-business owner or manager in a larger operation; no sloppiness, no unexamined thoughts, no stiffness or affectation—genuine, direct, and worthwhile English. Knowledge of the equipment rental industry is a distinct plus."

N $ $ RETAIL INFO SYSTEMS NEWS

Where Retail Management Shops for Technology, Edgell Communications, 4 Middlebury Blvd., Suite 1, Randolph NJ 07869-1111. (973)252-0100. Fax: (973)252-9020. E-mail: jskorupa@edgellmail.com. Website: www.risnews.com. **Contact:** Joe Skorupa, editor. **65% freelance written.** Monthly magazine. "Readers are functional managers/executives in all types of retail and consumer goods firms. They are making major improvements in company operations and in alliances with customers/suppliers." Estab. 1988. Circ. 20,000. Pays on publication. Publishes ms an average of 2 months after acceptance. Byline sometimes given. Buys first North American serial, second serial (reprint), electronic, all rights. Editorial lead time 3 months. Submit seasonal material 3 months in advance. Accepts queries by mail. Sample copy online.

Nonfiction Essays, exposé, how-to, humor, interview/profile, technical. **Buys 80 mss/year.** Query with published clips. Length: 700-1,900 words. **Pays $600-1,200 for assigned articles.** Sometimes pays in contributor copies as negotiated. Sometimes pays expenses of writers on assignment.

Photos State availability of or send photos with submission. Buys one-time rights plus reprint, if applicable. Negotiates payment individually. Identification of subjects required.

Columns/Departments News/trends (analysis of current events), 150-300 words. **Buys 4 mss/year.** Query with published clips. **Pays $100-300.**

Tips "Case histories about companies achieving substantial results using advanced management practices and/or advanced technology are best."

$ $ SECURITY DEALER

Cygnus Publishing, 445 Broad Hollow Rd., Melville NY 11747. (631)845-2700. Fax: (631)845-2736. E-mail: susan.brady@secdealer.com. Managing Editor: Erin Plonski. **Contact:** Susan A. Brady, editor-in-chief. **25% freelance written.** Monthly magazine for electronic alarm dealers, burglary and fire installers, with technical, business, sales and marketing information. Circ. 25,000. Pays 3 weeks after publication. Publishes ms an average of 4 months after acceptance. Byline sometimes given. Buys first North American serial rights. Accepts simultaneous submissions.

Nonfiction How-to, interview/profile, technical. No consumer pieces. Query by mail only. Length: 1,000-3,000 words. **Pays $300 for assigned articles; $100-200 for unsolicited articles.** Sometimes pays expenses of writers on assignment.

Photos State availability with submission. Reviews contact sheets, transparencies. Offers $25 additional payment for photos accepted with ms. Captions, identification of subjects required.

Columns/Departments Closed Circuit TV, Access Control (both on application, installation, new products), 500-1,000 words. **Buys 25 mss/year.** Query by mail only. **Pays $100-150.**

Tips "The areas of our publication most open to freelancers are technical innovations, trends in the alarm industry, and crime patterns as related to the business as well as business finance and management pieces."

$ $ SMART BUSINESS

Cleveland Edition, Smart Business Network, Inc., 14725 Detroit Ave., #200, Cleveland OH 44107. (216)228-6397. Fax: (216)529-8924. E-mail: dsklein@sbnonline.com. Website: www.sbnonline.com. **Contact:** Dustin S. Klein, executive editor. **5% freelance written.** Monthly business magazine with an audience made up of business owners and top decision makers. "Smart Business is smart ideas for growing companies. Best practices, winning strategies. The pain—and joy—of running a business. Every issue delves into the minds of the most innovative executives in each of our regions to report on how market leaders got to the top and what strategies they use to stay there." Estab. 1989. Pays on publication. Publishes ms an average of 2 months after acceptance. Byline given. Offers 50% kill fee. Buys first North American serial, second serial (reprint), electronic rights. Editorial lead time 3 months. Submit seasonal material 3 months in advance. Accepts queries by mail, e-mail. Responds in 2 weeks to queries; 1 month to mss. Sample copy online. Writer's guidelines by e-mail.

• Publishes local editions in Cleveland, Akron/Canton, Columbus, Pittsburgh, Atlanta, Chicago, and Indianapolis.

Nonfiction How-to, interview/profile. No breaking news or straight personality profiles. **Buys 2-5 mss/year.** Query with published clips. Length: 300-1,500 words. **Pays $200-500.** Sometimes pays expenses of writers on assignment.

Reprints Accepts previously published submissions.

Photos State availability with submission. Reviews negatives, prints. Buys one-time, reprint, or Web rights. Offers no additional payment for photos accepted with ms. Identification of subjects required.

Columns/Departments Another View (business management related), 400-500 words. **Buys 6-8 mss/year.** Query.

The online magazine carries original content not found in the print edition. Contact: Dustin S. Klein, executive editor.

Tips "The best way to submit to Smart Business is to read us—either online or in print. Remember, our audience is made up of top level business executives and owners."

$ $ SMART BUSINESS

Pittsburgh Edition, (formerly SBM), SBN, Inc., 11632 Frankstown Rd., #313, Pittsburgh PA 15235. (412)371-0451. Fax: (412)371-0452. E-mail: rmarano@sbnonline.com. Website: www.sbnonline.com. **Contact:** Ray Marano, editor. **5% freelance written.** Monthly magazine. "We provide information and insight designed to help companies grow. Our focus is on local companies with 50 or more employees and their successful business strategies, with the ultimate goal of educating entrepreneurs. Our target audience is business owners and other top executives." Estab. 1994. Circ. 16,000. Pays on publication. Publishes ms an average of 2 months after acceptance. Byline given. Buys all rights, makes work-for-hire assignments. Editorial lead time 2 months. Submit seasonal material 4 months in advance. Accepts queries by mail, e-mail, fax. Responds in 1 month to queries. Sample copy for $3. Writer's guidelines free.

O→ "Right now we have very little need for freelance work."

Nonfiction How-to, interview/profile, opinion, annual energy and telecommunication supplements, among others. "No basic profiles about 'interesting' companies or stories about companies with no ties to Pittsburgh." Query with published clips. Length: 250-1,000 words. **Pays $150-300 for assigned articles.**

Reprints Accepts reprints (mainly columns from business professionals).

Photos State availability with submission. Reviews negatives, transparencies, digital. Buys one-time or all rights. Negotiates payment individually. Identification of subjects required.

Tips "Have articles localized to the Pittsburgh and surrounding areas. We look for articles that will help our readers, educate them on a business strategy that another company may be using that can help our readers' companies grow."

$ $STAMATS MEETINGS MEDIA

550 Montgomery St., #750, San Francisco CA 94111. Fax: (415)788-0301. E-mail: tyler.davidson@meetingsmedia.com. Website: www.meetingsmedia.com. Destinations Editor: Lori Tenny. **Contact:** Tyler Davidson, editor (columnists, cover stories). **75% freelance written.** Monthly tabloid covering meeting, event, and conference planning. Estab. 1986. Circ. *Meetings East* and *Meetings South* 22,000; *Meetings West* 26,000. Pays 1 month after publication. Publishes ms an average of 1 month after acceptance. Byline given. Buys first North American serial, electronic rights. Editorial lead time 3 months. Submit seasonal material 3 months in advance. Accepts queries by mail, e-mail, fax. Responds in 3 weeks to queries. Sample copy for 9×13 SAE and 5 first-class stamps. Editorial calendar online.

O→ Queries and pitches are accepted on columns and cover stories only. All other assignments (Features and Site Inspections) are based exclusively on editorial calendar. Interested writers should send a résumé and 2-3 relevant clips, which must show familiarity with meetings/conventions topics, by e-mail.

Nonfiction How-to, travel (as it pertains to meetings and conventions). "No first-person fluff. We are a business magazine." **Buys 150 mss/year.** Query with published clips. Length: 1,200-2,000 words. **Pays $500 flat rate/package.**

Photos State availability with submission. Buys one-time rights. Offers no additional payment for photos accepted with ms. Identification of subjects required.

Tips "We're always looking for freelance writers who are local to our destination stories. For Site Inspections, get in touch in late September or early October, when we usually have the following year's editorial calendar available."

$THE STATE JOURNAL

West V Media Management, LLC, 13 Kanawha Blvd. W., Suite 100, Charleston WV 25302. (304)344-1630. Fax: (304)343-6138. E-mail: dpage@statejournal.com. Website: www.statejournal.com. **Contact:** Dan Page, editor. **30% freelance written.** "We are a weekly journal dedicated to providing stories of interest to the business community in West Virginia." Estab. 1984. Circ. 10,000. Pays on publication. Publishes ms an average of 3 weeks after acceptance. Byline given. Buys first rights. Submit seasonal material 4 months in advance. Accepts queries by mail, e-mail, fax. Sample copy for #10 SASE. Writer's guidelines for #10 SASE.

Nonfiction General interest, interview/profile, new product, (All business related). **Buys 400 mss/year.** Query. Length: 250-1,500 words. **Pays $50.** Sometimes pays expenses of writers on assignment.

Photos State availability with submission. Reviews contact sheets. Buys one-time rights. Offers $15/photo. Captions required.

Tips "Localize your work—mention West Virginia specifically in the article; or talk to business people in West Virginia."

$ $SUSTAINABLE INDUSTRIES JOURNAL NW

Sustainable Industries Media, LLC, 3941 SE Hawthorne Blvd., Portland OR 97214. Fax: (503)226-7917. E-mail: brian@sijournal.com. Website: www.sijournal.com. Associate Editor: April Streeter. **Contact:** Brian J. Back, editor. **20% freelance written.** Monthly magazine covering environmental innovation in business (Northwest focus). "We seek high quality, balanced reporting aimed at business readers. More compelling writing than is typical in standard trade journals." Estab. 2003. Circ. 2,500. Pays on publication. Publishes ms an average of 1-3 months after acceptance. Byline sometimes given. Not copyrighted. Buys all rights. Editorial lead time 1-2 months. Accepts queries by mail, e-mail, fax. Accepts simultaneous submissions.

Nonfiction General interest, how-to, interview/profile, new product, opinion, news briefs. Special issues: Issue themes rotate on the following topics: Agriculture & Natural Resources; Green Building; Energy; Government; Manufacturing & Technology; Retail & Service; Transportation & Tourism—though all topics are covered in each issue. No prosaic essays or extra-long pieces. Query with published clips. Length: 500-1,500 words. **Pays $0-500.**

Photos State availability with submission. Reviews prints, GIF/JPEG files. Buys all rights. Offers no additional payment for photos accepted with ms.

Columns/Departments Business trade columns on specific industries, 500-1,000 words. Guest columns accepted, but not compensated. Query.

N $ $ ⊕ VENECONOMY/VENECONOMÍA

VenEconomía, Edificio Gran Sabana, Piso 1, Avendia Abraham Lincoln No. 174, Blvd. de Sabana Grande, Caracas, Venezuela. (+58)212-761-8121. Fax: (+58)212-762-8160. E-mail: editor@veneconía.com. Website: www.veneconomía.com or www.veneconomy.com. Managing Editor: Robert Bottome. **Contact:** Francisco Toro, political editor. **70% freelance written.** Monthly business magazine covering business, political and social issues in Venezuela. "*VenEconomy*'s subscribers are mostly businesspeople, both Venezuelans and foreigners doing business in Venezuela. Some academics and diplomats also read our magazine. The magazine is published monthly both in English and Spanish—freelancers may query us in either language. Our slant is decidedly pro-business, but not dogmatically conservative. Development, human rights, political and environmental issues are covered from a business-friendly angle." Estab. 1983. Pays on publication. Publishes ms an average of 1 month after acceptance. Byline given. Offers 50% kill fee. Makes work-for-hire assignments. Editorial lead time 1-2 months. Submit seasonal material 1 month in advance. Accepts queries by e-mail. Accepts simultaneous submissions. Responds in 2 weeks to queries; 4 months to mss. Sample copy by e-mail.

Nonfiction Essays, exposé, interview/profile, new product, opinion. No first-person stories or travel articles. **Buys 50 mss/year.** Query. Length: 1,100-3,200 words. **Pays 10-15¢/word for assigned articles.** Sometimes pays expenses of writers on assignment.

Tips "A Venezuela tie-in is absolutely indispensable. While most of our readers are businesspeople, *VenEconomy* does not limit itself strictly to business-magazine fare. Our aim is to give our readers a sophisticated understanding of the main issues affecting the country as a whole. Stories about successful Venezuelan companies, or foreign companies doing business successfully with Venezuela are particularly welcome. Stories about the oil-sector, especially as it relates to Venezuela, are useful. Other promising topics for freelancers outside Venezuela include international trade and trade negotiations, U.S.-Venezuela bilateral diplomatic relations, international investors' perceptions of business prospects in Venezuela, and international organizations' assessments of environmental, human rights, or democracy and development issues in Venezuela, etc. Both straight reportage and somewhat more opinionated pieces are acceptable, articles that straddle the borderline between reportage and opinion are best. Before querying, ask yourself: Would this be of interest to me if I was doing business in or with Venezuela?"

$ $ $ WORLD TRADE

"For the Executive with Global Vision," 23421 S. Pointe Dr., Suite 280, Laguna Hills CA 92653. (949)830-1340. Fax: (949)830-1328. E-mail: laras@worldtrademag.com. Website: www.worldtrademag.com. Editorial Director: Neil Shister. **Contact:** Lara Sowinski, associate editor. **50% freelance written.** Monthly magazine covering international business. Estab. 1988. Circ. 75,000. Pays on publication. Publishes ms an average of 1 month after acceptance. Byline given. Buys all rights. Editorial lead time 3 months. Accepts queries by mail, fax.

Nonfiction "See our editorial calendar online at wwww.worldtrademag.com." Interview/profile, technical, market reports, finance, logistics. **Buys 40-50 mss/year.** Query with published clips. Length: 450-1,500 words. **Pays 50¢/word.**

Photos State availability with submission. Reviews transparencies, prints. Buys all rights. Negotiates payment individually. Identification of subjects required.

Columns/Departments International Business Services, 800 words; Shipping, Supply Chain Management, Logistics, 800 words; Software & Technology, 800 words; Economic Development (US, International), 800 words. **Buys 40-50 mss/year. Pays 50¢/word.**

Tips "We seek writers with expertise in their subject areas, as well as solid researching and writing skills. We want analysts more than reporters. We don't accept unsolicited manuscripts, and we don't want phone calls—Please read *World Trade* before sending a query."

CHURCH ADMINISTRATION & MINISTRY

THE AFRICAN AMERICAN PULPIT

P.O. Box 15347, Pittsburgh PA 15237. Phone/Fax: (412)364-1688. E-mail: info@theafricanamericanpulpit.com. Website: www.theafricanamericanpulpit.com. Editors: Martha Simmons, Frank A. Thomas. **Contact:** Victoria McGoey, project manager. **100% freelance written.** Quarterly magazine covering African-American preaching.

"*The African American Pulpit* is a quarterly journal that serves as a repository for the very best of African-American preaching and provides practical and creative resources for persons in ministry." Estab. 1997. Circ. 2,000. Pays on publication. Publishes ms an average of 6 months after acceptance. Byline always given. Editorial lead time 9 months. Submit seasonal material 1 year in advance. Accepts queries by mail, e-mail, fax, phone. Accepts simultaneous submissions. Writer's guidelines online.

Nonfiction Sermons/articles relating to African-American preaching and the African-American Church. Book excerpts, essays, how-to (craft a sermon), inspirational, interview/profile, opinion, religious. **Buys 60 mss/year.** Send complete ms. Length: 1,500-3,000 words.

$THE CHRISTIAN COMMUNICATOR

9731 N. Fox Glen Dr., #6F, Niles IL 60714-4222. (847)296-3964. Fax: (847)296-0754. E-mail: lin@wordprocommunications.com. **Contact:** Lin Johnson, managing editor. **90% freelance written.** Monthly magazine covering Christian writing and speaking. Circ. 4,000. Pays on publication. Publishes ms an average of 6-12 months after acceptance. Byline given. Buys first, second serial (reprint) rights. Editorial lead time 3 months. Submit seasonal material 9 months in advance. Accepts queries by e-mail. Responds in 4-6 weeks to queries; 4-6 weeks to mss. Sample copy free with SAE and 5 first-class stamps. Writer's guidelines free with SASE or by e-mail.

Nonfiction Essays, how-to, inspirational, interview/profile, opinion, book reviews. **Buys 90 mss/year.** Query or send complete ms only by e-mail. Length: 300-1,000 words. **Pays $10.**

Columns/Departments Speaking, 650-1,000 words. **Buys 11 mss/year.** Query. **Pays $10.**

Poetry Free verse, light verse, traditional. **Buys 11 poems/year.** Submit maximum 3 poems. Contact: Gretchen Sousa, poetry editor (gretloriat@earthlink.net) Length: 4-20 lines. **Pays $5.**

Fillers Anecdotes, short humor. **Buys 10-30/year.** Length: 50-300 words. **Pays cassette tape.**

Tips "We primarily use 'how to' articles and personality features on experienced writers and editors. However, we're willing to look at any other pieces geared to the writing life."

Ⓝ $CHURCH EDUCATOR

Educational Ministries, Inc., 165 Plaza Dr., Prescott AZ 86303. (928)771-8601. Fax: (928)771-8621. E-mail: edmin2@aol.com. **Contact:** Linda Davidson, editor. **95% freelance written.** Monthly magazine covering resources for Christian educators. "*Church Educator* has programming ideas for the Christian educator in the mainline Protestant church. We are *not* on the conservative, fundamental side theologically, so slant articles to the liberal side. Programs should offer lots of questions and not give pat answers." Estab. 1978. Circ. 4,500. Pays 60 days after publication. Publishes ms an average of 2 months after acceptance. Byline given. Buys first rights. Editorial lead time 3 months. Submit seasonal material 7 months in advance. Accepts queries by mail, e-mail, fax, phone. Accepts simultaneous submissions. Responds in 2 weeks to queries; 4 months to mss. Sample copy for 9×12 SAE and 4 first-class stamps. Writer's guidelines free.

Nonfiction How-to, religious. Special issues: How to recruit volunteers; Nurturing faith development of children. No testimonials. **Buys 200 mss/year.** Send complete ms. Length: 500-2,000 words. **Pays 3¢/word.**

Fiction Religious. "No 'How God Saved My Life' or 'How God Answers Prayers.'" **Buys 10 mss/year.** Send complete ms. Length: 500-1,500 words. **Pays 3¢/word.**

Tips "We are always looking for material on the seasons of the church year: Advent, Lent, Pentecost, Epiphany. Write up a program for one of those seasons directed toward children, youth, adults or intergenerational."

Ⓝ $CREATOR MAGAZINE

Bimonthly Magazine of Balanced Music Ministries, P.O. Box 480, Healdsburg CA 95448. (707)837-9071. E-mail: creator@creatormagazine.com. Website: www.creatormagazine.com. **Contact:** Rod Ellis, editor. **35% freelance written.** Bimonthly magazine. "Most readers are church music directors and worship leaders. Content focuses on the spectrum of worship styles from praise and worship to traditional to liturgical. All denominations subscribe. Articles on worship, choir rehearsal, handbells, children's/youth choirs, technique, relationships, etc." Estab. 1978. Circ. 6,000. Pays on publication. Publishes ms an average of 3 months after acceptance. Byline given. Buys first, one-time, second serial (reprint) rights. Occasionally buys no rights. Editorial lead time 3 months. Submit seasonal material 4 months in advance. Accepts queries by mail. Accepts simultaneous submissions. Sample copy for 9×12 SAE and 5 first-class stamps. Writer's guidelines free.

Nonfiction Essays, how-to (be a better church musician, choir director, rehearsal technician, etc.), humor (short personal perspectives), inspirational, interview/profile (call first), new product (call first), opinion, personal experience, photo feature, religious, technical (choral technique). Special issues: July/August is directed toward adult choir members, rather than directors. **Buys 20 mss/year.** Query or send complete ms. Length: 1,000-10,000 words. **Pays $30-75 for assigned articles; $30-60 for unsolicited articles.** Pays expenses of writers on assignment.

Photos State availability of or send photos with submission. Reviews negatives, 8×10 prints. Buys one-time rights. Offers no additional payment for photos accepted with ms. Captions required.

Columns/Departments Hints & Humor (music ministry short ideas, anecdotes [cute] ministry experience), 75-250 words; Inspiration (motivational ministry stories), 200-500 words; Children/Youth (articles about specific choirs), 1,000-5,000 words. **Buys 15 mss/year.** Query or send complete ms. **Pays $20-60.**

■ The online magazine carries original content not found in the print edition.

Tips "Request guidelines and stick to them. If theme is relevant and guidelines are followed, we'll probably publish."

$CROSS & QUILL

The Christian Writers Newsletter, Christian Writers Fellowship International, 1624 Jefferson Davis Rd., Clinton SC 29325-6401. (864)697-6035. E-mail: cwfi@cwfi-online.org. Website: www.cwfi-online.org. **Contact:** Sandy Brooks, editor/publisher. **75% freelance written.** Bimonthly journal featuring information and encouragement for writers. "We serve Christian writers and others in Christian publishing. We like informational and how-to articles." Estab. 1976. Circ. 1,000. Pays on publication. Publishes ms an average of 6-12 months after acceptance. Byline given. Buys first, second serial (reprint) rights. Editorial lead time 6 months. Submit seasonal material 6 months in advance. Accepts queries by mail, e-mail. Responds in 1 month to queries; 2 months to mss. Sample copy for $2 with 9×11 SAE and 2 first-class stamps. Writer's guidelines online or for SAE.

● "Paste article submissions into an e-mail form. We do not download submissions as attached files due to the risk of viruses. Double-space between paragraphs. Please use plain text. Do not use boldface or bullets. Submit articles to cqarticles@aol.com."

O→ Break in by writing "good informational, substantive how-to articles. Right now we're particularly looking for articles on juvenile writing and owning and operating writers groups—successes and learning experiences; also organizing and operating writers workshops and conferences."

Nonfiction How-to, humor, inspirational, interview/profile, new product, technical, devotional. **Buys 25 mss/year.** Send complete ms. Length: 300-800 words. **Pays $10-25.** Sometimes pays in contributor copies or subscriptions for fillers, poetry.

Photos State availability with submission.

Poetry Free verse, haiku, light verse, traditional. **Buys 6 poems/year.** Submit maximum 3 poems. Length: 12 lines. **Pays $5.**

Tips "Study guidelines and follow them. Acceptances of philosophical, personal reflection, or personal experiences is rare."

$ $GROUP MAGAZINE

Group Publishing, Inc., 1515 Cascade Ave., Loveland CO 80538. (970)669-3836. Fax: (970)292-4360. E-mail: greditor@grouppublishing.com. Website: www.groupmag.com. Editor: Rick Lawrence. **Contact:** Kathy Dieterich, assistant editor. **50% freelance written.** Bimonthly magazine for Christian youth workers. "*Group* is the interdenominational magazine for leaders of Christian youth groups. *Group*'s purpose is to supply ideas, practical help, inspiration, and training for youth leaders." Estab. 1974. Circ. 55,000. **Pays on acceptance.** Byline sometimes given. Buys all rights. Editorial lead time 4 months. Submit seasonal material 5 months in advance. Accepts queries by mail, e-mail, fax. Responds in 6 weeks to queries; 2 months to mss. Sample copy for $2, plus 10×12 SAE and 3 first-class stamps. Writer's guidelines online.

Nonfiction Inspirational, personal experience, religious. No fiction. **Buys 100 mss/year.** Query. Length: 175-2,000 words. **Pays $125-350.** Sometimes pays expenses of writers on assignment.

Columns/Departments Try This One (short ideas for group use), 300 words; Hands-On-Help (tips for youth leaders), 175 words; Strange But True (profiles remarkable youth ministry experience), 500 words. **Pays $40.**

ℕ $ $THE JOURNAL OF ADVENTIST EDUCATION

General Conference of SDA, 12501 Old Columbia Pike, Silver Spring MD 20904-6600. (301)680-5075. Fax: (301)622-9627. E-mail: 74617.1231@compuserve.com. Website: education.gc.adventist.org/jae. **Contact:** Beverly J. Robinson-Rumble, editor. Bimonthly (except skips issue in summer) professional journal covering teachers and administrators in Seventh Day Adventist school systems. Estab. 1939. Circ. 7,500. Pays on publication. Publishes ms an average of 1 year after acceptance. Byline given. Buys first rights. Editorial lead time 1 year. Accepts queries by mail, e-mail, fax, phone. Responds in 6 weeks to queries; 4 months to mss. Sample copy for 10×12 SAE and 5 first-class stamps. Writer's guidelines free.

Nonfiction Theme issues have assigned authors. Book excerpts, essays, how-to (education-related), personal experience, photo feature, religious, education. "No brief first-person stories about Sunday Schools." Query. Length: 1,000-1,500 words. **Pays $25-300.**

Reprints Send tearsheet or photocopy and information about when and where the material previously appeared.

Photos State availability of or send photos with submission. Reviews Prints. Buys one-time rights. Negotiates payment individually. Captions required.

Tips "Articles may deal with educational theory or practice, although the *Journal* seeks to emphasize the practical. Articles dealing with the creative and effective use of methods to enhance teaching skills or learning in the classroom are especially welcome. Whether theoretical or practical, such essays should demonstrate the skillful integration of Seventh-day Adventist faith/values and learning."

$KIDS' MINISTRY IDEAS

Review and Herald Publishing Association, 55 W. Oak Ridge Dr., Hagerstown MD 21740. (301)393-4115. Fax: (301)393-4055. E-mail: kidsmin@rhpa.org. Editor: Tamara Michalenko Terry. **Contact:** Editor. **95% freelance written.** "A quarterly resource for those leading children to Jesus, *Kids' Ministry Ideas* provides affirmation, pertinent and informative articles, program ideas, resource suggestions, and answers to questions from a Seventh-day Adventist Christian perspective." Estab. 1991. Circ. 3,000. **Pays on acceptance.** Publishes ms an average of 3 months after acceptance. Byline given. Buys first North American serial, electronic rights. Editorial lead time 3 months. Submit seasonal material 3 months in advance. Accepts queries by mail, e-mail, fax. Responds in 3 weeks to queries; 3 months to mss. Sample copy and writer's guidelines free.

Nonfiction Inspirational, new product (related to children's ministry), articles fitting the mission of *Kids' Ministry Ideas*. **Buys 40-60 mss/year.** Send complete ms. Length: 300-1,000 words. **Pays $30-100 for assigned articles; $30-70 for unsolicited articles.**

Photos State availability with submission. Buys one-time rights. Captions required.

Columns/Departments Buys 20-30 mss/year. Query. **Pays $30-100.**

Tips "Request writers' guidelines and a sample issue."

$ $LEADERSHIP

A Practical Journal for Church Leaders, Christianity Today International, 465 Gundersen Dr., Carol Stream IL 60188. (630)260-6200. Fax: (630)260-0114. E-mail: ljeditor@leadershipjournal.net. Website: www.leadershipjournal.net. Editor: Marshall Shelley. Managing Editor: Eric Reed. **Contact:** Dawn Zemke, editorial coordinator. **75% freelance written.** Works with a small number of new/unpublished writers each year. Quarterly magazine. Writers must have a "knowledge of and sympathy for the unique expectations placed on pastors and local church leaders. Each article must support points by illustrating from real life experiences in local churches." Estab. 1980. Circ. 65,000. **Pays on acceptance.** Publishes ms an average of 6 months after acceptance. Byline given. Offers 33% kill fee. Buys first, electronic rights. Editorial lead time 6 months. Submit seasonal material 6 months in advance. Accepts queries by mail, e-mail, fax. Responds in 3 weeks to queries; 2 months to mss. Sample copy for $5 or online. Writer's guidelines online.

Nonfiction How-to, humor, interview/profile, personal experience, sermon illustrations. "No articles from writers who have never read our journal." **Buys 60 mss/year.** Query. Length: 300-3,000 words. **Pays $35-400.** Sometimes pays expenses of writers on assignment.

Columns/Departments Eric Reed, managing editor. Growing Edge (book/software reviews), 500 words. **Buys 8 mss/year.** Query.

Tips "Every article in *Leadership* must provide practical help for problems that church leaders face. *Leadership* articles are not essays expounding a topic or editorials arguing a position or homilies explaining Biblical principles. They are how-to articles, based on first-person accounts of real-life experiences in ministry. They allow our readers to see 'over the shoulder' of a colleague in ministry who then reflects on those experiences and identifies the lessons learned. As you know, a magazine's slant is a specific personality that readers expect (and it's what they've sent us their subscription money to provide). Our style is that of friendly conversation rather than directive discourse—what I learned about local church ministry rather than what you need to do."

N $MOMENTUM

Official Journal of the National Catholic Educational Association, National Catholic Educational Association, 1077 30th St. NW, Suite 100, Washington DC 20007-3852. (202)337-6232. Fax: (202)333-6706. E-mail: momentum@ncea.org. Website: www.ncea.org. **Contact:** Brian E. Gray, editor. **65% freelance written.** Quarterly educational journal covering educational issues in Catholic schools, parishes, and private schools. "*Momentum* is a membership journal of the National Catholic Educational Association. The audience is educators and administrators in Catholic and private schools K-12, and parish programs." Estab. 1970. Circ. 28,000. Pays on publication. Publishes ms an average of 3 months after acceptance. Byline given. Buys first rights. Accepts queries by e-mail. Sample copy for $5 SASE and 8 first-class stamps. Writer's guidelines online.

Nonfiction Educational trends, issues, research. No articles unrelated to educational and catechesis issues. **Buys 40-60 mss/year.** Query and send complete ms. Length: 1,500 words. **Pays $75 maximum.**

Photos State availability with submission. Reviews Prints. Offers no additional payment for photos accepted with ms. Captions, identification of subjects required.

Columns/Departments From the Field (practical application in classroom), 700 words; Justice and Peace Education (examples); DRE Direction (parish catechesis), all 900 words. **Buys 10 mss/year.** Query and send complete ms. **Pays $50.**

$ PASTORAL LIFE

Society of St. Paul, P.O. Box 595, Canfield OH 44406-0595. (330)533-5503. E-mail: plmagazine@hotmail.com. Website: www.albahouse.org. **Contact:** Rev. Matthew Roehrig, editor. **66% freelance written.** Works with new/unpublished writers. "Monthly magazine designed to focus on the current problems, needs, issues, and all important activities related to all phases of Catholic pastoral work and life." Estab. 1953. Circ. 2,000. Pays on publication. Publishes ms an average of 4 months after acceptance. Byline given. Buys first rights. Accepts queries by mail, e-mail, phone. Responds in 1 month to queries. Sample copy and writer's guidelines for 6×9 SAE and 4 first-class stamps.

Nonfiction "*Pastoral Life* is a professional review, principally designed to focus attention on current problems, needs, issues, and important activities related to all phases of pastoral work and life." **Buys 30 unsolicited mss/year.** Query with outline before submitting ms. Length: 1,000-3,500 words. **Pays 4¢/word minimum.**

Tips "Articles should have application for priests and Christian leadership to help them in their ministries and lives."

$ $ THE PRIEST

Our Sunday Visitor, Inc., 200 Noll Plaza, Huntington IN 46750-4304. (260)356-8400. Fax: (260)356-8472. E-mail: tpriest@osv.com. Website: www.osv.com. Editor: Msgr. Owen F. Campion. **Contact:** Murray Hubley, associate editor. **40% freelance written.** Monthly magazine. "We run articles that will aid priests in their day-to-day ministry. Includes items on spirituality, counseling, administration, theology, personalities, the saints, etc." **Pays on acceptance.** Byline given. Buys first North American serial rights. Editorial lead time 3 months. Submit seasonal material 4 months in advance. Accepts queries by mail, e-mail, fax, phone. Responds in 5 weeks to queries; 3 months to mss. Sample copy and writer's guidelines free.

Nonfiction Essays, historical/nostalgic, humor, inspirational, interview/profile, opinion, personal experience, photo feature, religious. **Buys 96 mss/year.** Send complete ms. Length: 1,500-5,000 words. **Pays $200 minimum for assigned articles; $50 minimum for unsolicited articles.**

Photos Send photos with submission. Reviews transparencies, prints. Buys one-time rights. Negotiates payment individually. Captions, identification of subjects required.

Tips "Please do not stray from the magisterium of the Catholic Church."

Ⓝ $ $ REV.

P.O. Box 481, Loveland CO 80539-0481. (970)669-3836. Fax: (970)679-4392. E-mail: therev@onlinerev.com. Website: www.revmagazine.com. Editor: Paul Allen. **25% freelance written.** Bimonthly magazine for pastors. "We offer practical solutions to revolutionize and revitalize ministry." Estab. 1997. Circ. 45,000. **Pays on acceptance.** Publishes ms an average of 6 months after acceptance. Byline given. Makes work-for-hire assignments. Editorial lead time 6 months. Submit seasonal material 8 months in advance. Accepts queries by mail, e-mail. Responds in 2 months to queries. Writer's guidelines online.

○⇥ Break in with short, practical department pieces.

Nonfiction Ministry, leadership, and personal articles with practical application. "No devotions, articles for church members, theological pieces." **Buys 18-24 mss/year.** Query or send complete ms. Length: 1,800-2,000 words. **Pays $300-400.**

Columns/Departments Work (preaching, worship, discipleship, outreach, church business & administration, leadership); Life (personal growth, pastor's family); Culture (trends, facts), all 250-300 words. **Buys 25 mss/year.** Send complete ms. **Pays $35-50.**

Fillers Cartoons. **Buys 3/year. Pays $50.**

Tips "We're most open to submissions for our departments. Remember that we focus on practical articles with an edgy tone."

$ TEACHERS INTERACTION

Concordia Publishing House, 3558 S. Jefferson Ave., St. Louis MO 63118-3968. (314)268-1083. Fax: (314)268-1329. E-mail: tom.nummela@cph.org. Editorial Associate: Jean Muser. **Contact:** Tom Nummela, editor. **20% freelance written.** Quarterly magazine of practical, inspirational, theological articles for volunteer Sunday school teachers. Material must be true to the doctrines of the Lutheran Church—Missouri Synod. Estab. 1960. Circ. 12,000. Pays on publication. Publishes ms an average of 1 year after acceptance. Byline given. Buys all rights. Submit seasonal material 1 year in advance. Accepts queries by mail, e-mail, fax. Responds in 3 months to mss. Sample copy for $4.99. Writer's guidelines for #10 SASE.

Nonfiction How-to (practical help/ideas used successfully in own classroom), inspirational, personal experience (of a Sunday School classroom nature—growth). No theological articles. **Buys 6 mss/year.** Send complete ms. Length: 1,200 words. **Pays up to $110.**

Fillers "*Teachers Interaction* buys short Interchange items—activities and ideas planned and used successfully in a church school classroom." **Buys 48/year.** Length: 200 words maximum. **Pays $20.**

Tips "Practical or 'it happened to me' experiences articles would have the best chance. Also short items—ideas used in classrooms; seasonal and in conjunction with our Sunday school material, Our Life in Christ. Our format emphasizes volunteer Sunday school teachers."

$ $ TODAY'S CATHOLIC TEACHER

The Voice of Catholic Education, Peter Li Education Group, 2621 Dryden Rd., Suite 300, Dayton OH 45439. (937)293-1415. Fax: (937)293-1310. E-mail: mnoschang@peterli.com. Website: www.catholicteacher.com. **Contact:** Mary C. Noschang, editor. **60% freelance written.** Magazine published 6 times/year during school year covering Catholic education for grades K-12. "We look for topics of interest and practical help to teachers in Catholic elementary schools in all curriculum areas including religion technology, discipline, motivation." Estab. 1972. Circ. 50,000. Pays on publication. Publishes ms an average of 2 months after acceptance. Byline given. first and all rights and makes work-for-hire assignments Editorial lead time 3 months. Submit seasonal material 6 months in advance. Accepts queries by mail, e-mail, fax. Accepts simultaneous submissions. Responds in 1 month to queries; 3 months to mss. Sample copy for $3 or on website. Writer's guidelines online.
Nonfiction Interested in articles detailing ways to incorporate Catholic values into academic subjects other than religion class. Essays, how-to, humor, interview/profile, personal experience. "No articles pertaining to public education." **Buys 15 mss/year.** Query or send complete ms. Length: 1,500-3,000 words. **Pays $150-300.** Sometimes pays expenses of writers on assignment.
Photos State availability with submission. Reviews transparencies, prints. Buys one-time rights. Offers $20-50/photo. Captions, identification of subjects, model releases required.
Tips "Although our readership is primarily classroom teachers, *Today's Catholic Teacher* is read also by principals, supervisors, superintendents, boards of education, pastors, and parents. *Today's Catholic Teacher* aims to be for Catholic educators a source of information not available elsewhere. The focus of articles should span the interests of teachers from early childhood through junior high. Articles may be directed to just 1 age group yet have wider implications. Preference is given to material directed to teachers in grades four through eight. The desired magazine style is direct, concise, informative, and accurate. Writing should be enjoyable to read, informal rather than scholarly, lively, and free of educational jargon."

N $ TODAY'S CHRISTIAN PREACHER

Right Ideas, Inc., P.O. Box 100, Morgantown PA 19543. (610)856-6830. Fax: (610)856-6831. E-mail: publications @rightideas.us. Editor: Jerry Thacker. **Contact:** Elaine Williams, assistant editor. **10% freelance written.** Quarterly magazine offering articles for pastors. "*Today's Christian Preacher* is designed to meet the personal needs of the man of God." Estab. 1992. Circ. 25,000. Pays on publication. Publishes ms an average of 1 year after acceptance. Buys simultaneous rights. Editorial lead time 1 year. Submit seasonal material 1 year in advance. Accepts queries by mail, e-mail, fax. Accepts simultaneous submissions. Responds in 1 month to queries; 3 months to mss. Sample copy for 9 × 12 SAE and 4 first-class stamps. Writer's guidelines for #10 SASE.
   O→ Break in with "concise, practical information for the pastor in his personal life, not sermons or church issues."
Nonfiction Inspirational, religious, articles to help the man of God in his personal life. **Buys 2 mss/year.** Send complete ms. Length: 800-1,000 words. **Pays $150 for assigned articles.**
Photos Offers no additional payment for photos accepted with ms.

$ WORLD PULSE

Evangelism and Missions Information Service/Wheaton College, P.O. Box 794, Wheaton IL 60189. (630)752-7158. Fax: (630)752-7155. E-mail: pulsenews@aol.com. Website: www.worldpulseonline.com. **Contact:** Editor. **60% freelance written.** Semimonthly print and online newsletter covering mission news and trends. "We provide current information about evangelical Christian missions and churches around the world. Most articles are news-oriented, although we do publish some features and interviews." Estab. 1965. Circ. 3,000. Pays on publication. Publishes ms an average of 2 months after acceptance. Byline given. Buys first rights. Editorial lead time 2 months. Sample copy and writer's guidelines free.
   ● Prefers queries by e-mail.
   O→ Break in with "coverage of the subjects requested, bringing to the task both the topic's essential components, but with a dash of style, as well."
Nonfiction Interview/profile, photo feature, religious, technical. Does not want anything that does not cover the world of evangelical missions. **Buys 50-60 mss/year.** Query with published clips. Length: 300-1,000 words. **Pays $25-100.**
Photos Send photos with submission. Reviews contact sheets. Pays $25 for use of all photos accompanying an article.
Tips "Have a knowledge of and appreciation for the evangelical missions community, as well as for cross-cultural issues. Writing must be economical, with a judicious use of quotes and examples."

$ $ $WORSHIP LEADER MAGAZINE

26311 Junipero Serra, #130, San Juan Capistrano CA 92675. (949)240-9339. Fax: (949)240-0038. E-mail: editor@ wlmag.com. Website: www.worshipleader.com. **80% freelance written.** Bimonthly magazine covering all aspects of Christian worship. *"Worship Leader Magazine* exists to challenge, serve, equip, and train those involved in leading the 21st century Church in worship. The intended readership is the worship team (all those who plan and lead) of the local church." Estab. 1992. Circ. 50,000. Pays on publication. Byline given. Offers 50% kill fee. Buys first North American serial, all rights. Editorial lead time 3 months. Submit seasonal material 6 months in advance. Responds in 6 weeks to queries; 3 months to mss. Sample copy for $5. Writer's guidelines online.

Nonfiction General interest, how-to (related to purpose/audience), inspirational, interview/profile, opinion. **Buys 15-30 mss/year.** Query with published clips. Length: 1,200-2,000 words. **Pays $200-800 for assigned articles; $200-500 for unsolicited articles.** Sometimes pays expenses of writers on assignment.

Photos State availability with submission. Buys one-time rights. Negotiate payment individually. Identification of subjects required.

Tips "Our goal has been and is to provide the tools and information pastors, worship leaders, and ministers of music, youth, and the arts need to facilitate and enhance worship in their churches. In achieving this goal, we strive to maintain high journalistic standards, Biblical soundness, and theological neutrality. Our intent is to present the philosophical, scholarly insight on worship, as well as the day-to-day, 'putting it all together' side of worship, while celebrating our unity and diversity."

$ $YOUR CHURCH

Helping You With the Business of Ministry, Christianity Today, Inc., 465 Gundersen Dr., Carol Stream IL 60188. (630)260-6200. Fax: (630)260-0114. E-mail: yceditor@yourchurch.net. Website: www.yourchurch.net. Managing Editor: Mike Schreiter. **90% freelance written.** Bimonthly magazine covering church administration and products. "Articles pertain to the business aspects of ministry pastors are called upon to perform: administration, purchasing, management, technology, building, etc." Estab. 1955. Circ. 85,000 (controlled). **Pays on acceptance.** Publishes ms an average of 3-4 months after acceptance. Byline given. Buys first, electronic rights. Editorial lead time 6 weeks. Submit seasonal material 5 months in advance. Accepts queries by mail, e-mail, fax. Accepts previously published material. Responds in 1 month to queries; 3 months to mss. Sample copy for 9×12 SAE and 4 first-class stamps. Writer's guidelines free.

Nonfiction How-to, new product, technical. **Buys 50-60 mss/year.** Send complete ms. Length: 1,000-4,000 words. **Pays 15-20¢/word.** Sometimes pays expenses of writers on assignment.

Tips "The editorial is generally geared toward brief and helpful articles dealing with some form of church business. Concise, bulleted points from experts in the field are typical for our articles."

$YOUTH AND CHRISTIAN EDUCATION LEADERSHIP

Pathway Press, 1080 Montgomery Ave., P.O. Box 2250, Cleveland TN 37320-2250. (423)478-7597. Fax: (423)478-7616. E-mail: wanda_griffith@pathwaypress.org. Website: www.pathwaypress.org. **Contact:** Wanda Griffith, editor. **25% freelance written.** Quarterly magazine covering Christian education. *"Youth and Christian Education Leadership* is written for teachers, youth pastors, children's pastors, and other local Christian education workers." Estab. 1976. Circ. 12,000. Pays on publication. Publishes ms an average of 6 months after acceptance. Buys first or one-time rights. Editorial lead time 3 months. Submit seasonal material 6 months in advance. Accepts queries by mail, e-mail. Accepts simultaneous submissions. Responds in 3 months to mss. Sample copy for $1 and 9×12 SASE. Writer's guidelines online or by e-mail.

Nonfiction How-to, humor (in-class experience), inspirational, interview/profile, motivational, seasonal short skits. **Buys 16 mss/year.** Send complete ms; include SSN. Send SASE for return of ms. Length: 400-1,200 words. $25-50.

Reprints Send typed, double-spaced ms with rights for sale noted and information about when and where the material previously appeared. Pays 80% of amount paid for an original article.

Photos State availability with submission. Reviews contact sheets, transparencies. Buys one-time rights. Negotiates payment individually.

Columns/Departments Sunday School Leadership; Reaching Out (creative evangelism); The Pastor and Christian Education; Preschool; Elementary; Teen; Adult; Drawing Closer; Kids Church; all 500-1,000 words. Send complete ms with SASE. **Pays $25-50.**

Tips "Become familiar with the publication's content and submit appropriate material. We are continually looking for 'fresh ideas' that have proven to be successful."

CLOTHING

APPAREL

1500 Hampton St., Suite 150, Columbia SC 29201. (203)312-0600. Fax: (203)312-0341. E-mail: kdesmarteau@ap parelmag.com. Website: www.apparelmag.com. Editor-in-Chief: Kathleen DesMarteau. **25% freelance written.**

Monthly magazine for CEO's and top management in apparel and soft goods businesses including manufacturers and retailers. Circ. 19,000. Pays on receipt of article. Byline given. Buys all rights. Responds in 2 weeks to queries. Sample copy for free. Writer's guidelines free.

Columns/Departments R&D; Winning Strategies; International Watch; Best Practices; Retail Strategies; Production Solutions.

Tips ''Articles should be written in a style appealing to busy top managers and should in some way foster thought or new ideas, or present solutions/alternatives to common industry problems/concerns. CEOs are most interested in quick read pieces that are also informative and substantive. Articles should not be based on opinions but should be developed through interviews with industry manufacturers, retailers, or other experts, etc. Sidebars may be included to expand upon certain aspects within the article. If available, illustrations, graphs/charts, or photographs should accompany the article.''

$ $ EMB-EMBROIDERY/MONOGRAM BUSINESS

VNU Business Publications, 1115 Northmeadows Pkwy., Roswell GA 30076. (800)241-9034. Fax: (770)569-5105. E-mail: mallison@embmag.com. Website: www.embmag.com. **Contact:** Melanie Allison, senior editor. **30% freelance written.** Monthly magazine covering computerized embroidery and digitizing design. ''Readable, practical business and/or technical articles that show our readers how to succeed in their profession.'' Estab. 1994. Circ. 26,000. **Pays on acceptance.** Publishes ms an average of 3 months after acceptance. Byline given. Buys all rights. Editorial lead time 3 months. Submit seasonal material 6 months in advance. Accepts queries by mail, e-mail. Accepts simultaneous submissions. Sample copy for $10. Writer's guidelines not available.

Nonfiction How-to (embroidery, sales, marketing, design, general business info), interview/profile, new product, photo feature, technical (computerized embroidery). **Buys 4-6 mss/year.** Query. Length: 800-2,000 words. **Pays $200 and up for assigned articles.**

Photos Send photos with submission. Reviews transparencies, prints. Negotiates payment individually.

Tips ''Show us you have specified knowledge, experience, or contacts in the embroidery industry or a related field.''

$ $ $ MADE TO MEASURE

Halper Publishing Co., 830 Moseley Rd., Highland Park IL 60035. Fax: (847)780-2902. E-mail: mtm@halper.com. Website: www.madetomeasuremag.com. **Contact:** Rick Levine, editor/publisher. **50% freelance written.** Semiannual magazine covering uniforms and career apparel. ''A semi-annual magazine/buyers' reference containing leading sources of supply, equipment, and services of every description related to the Uniform, Career Apparel, and allied trades, throughout the entire US.'' Estab. 1930. Circ. 25,000. **Pays on acceptance.** Publishes ms an average of 2 months after acceptance. Byline given. Buys first North American serial rights. Editorial lead time 4 months. Submit seasonal material 4 months in advance. Accepts queries by mail, e-mail. Accepts simultaneous submissions. Responds in 3 weeks to queries. Sample copy online.

Nonfiction ''Please only consider sending queries related to stories to companies that wear or make uniforms, career apparel, or identifying apparel.'' Historical/nostalgic, interview/profile, new product, personal experience, photo feature, technical. **Buys 6-8 mss/year.** Query with published clips. Length: 1,000-3,000 words. **Pays $400-1,200.** Sometimes pays expenses of writers on assignment.

Photos State availability with submission. Reviews contact sheets, any prints. Buys one-time rights. Negotiates payment individually.

Tips ''We look for features about large and small companies who wear uniforms (restaurants, hotels, industrial, medical, public safety, etc.).''

$ $ TEXTILE WORLD

Billian Publishing Co., 2100 Powers Ferry Rd., Suite 300, Atlanta GA 30339. (770)955-5656. Fax: (770)952-0669. E-mail: editor@textileindustries.com. Website: www.textileindustries.com. **Contact:** James Borneman, editor-in-chief. **5% freelance written.** Monthly magazine covering ''the business of textile, apparel, and fiber industries with considerable technical focus on products and processes. No puff pieces pushing a particular product.'' Estab. 1868. Pays on publication. Byline given. Buys first North American serial rights.

Nonfiction Technical, business. **Buys 10 mss/year.** Query. Length: 500 words minimum. **Pays $200/published page.**

Photos Send photos with submission. Reviews prints. Buys one-time rights. Offers no additional payment for photos accepted with ms. Captions required.

CONFECTIONERY & SNACK FOODS

$ $ PACIFIC BAKERS NEWS

3155 Lynde St., Oakland CA 94601. (510)532-5513. E-mail: bakersnews@aol.com. **Contact:** C.W. Soward, publisher. **30% freelance written.** Eager to work with new/unpublished writers. Monthly newsletter for commercial bakeries in the western states. Estab. 1961. Pays on publication. No byline given; uses only 1-paragraph news items.

Nonfiction Uses bakery business reports and news about bakers. Buys only brief "boiled-down news items about bakers and bakeries operating only in Alaska, Hawaii, Pacific Coast and Rocky Mountain states. We welcome clippings. We need monthly news reports and clippings about the baking industry and the donut business." No pictures, jokes, poetry, or cartoons. Length: 10-200 words. **Pays 10¢/word for news, and 6¢/word for clips.**

CONSTRUCTION & CONTRACTING

$ $ ADVANCED MATERIALS & COMPOSITES NEWS AND COMPOSITES eNEWS

International Business & Technology Intelligence on High Performance M&P, Composites Worldwide, Inc., 991C Lomas Santa Fe Dr., MC469, Solana Beach CA 92075-2141. (858)755-1372. Fax: (858)755-5271. E-mail: info@compositesnews.com. Website: www.compositesnews.com. Managing Editor: Susan Loud. **Contact:** Steve Loud, editor. **1% freelance written.** Bimonthly newsletter covering advanced materials and fiber-reinforced polymer composites, plus a weekly electronic version called *Composite eNews*, reaching over 15,000 subscribers and many more pass-along readers. *Advanced Materials & Composites News* "covers markets, applications, materials, processes, and organizations for all sectors of the global hi-tech materials world. Audience is management, academics, researchers, government, suppliers, and fabricators. Focus on news about growth opportunities." "We target, contact, and use the freelancers with the most industry knowledge, usually people we know personally from the FRP composites industry." Estab. 1978. Circ. 15,000 +. Pays on publication. Publishes ms an average of 1 month after acceptance. Byline sometimes given. Buys all rights. Editorial lead time 1 week. Submit seasonal material 1 month in advance. Accepts queries by e-mail. Responds in 1 week to queries; 1 month to mss. Sample copy for #10 SASE. Editorial calendar online.

> ⊶ "We target, contact, and use the freelancers with the most industry knowledge, usually people who know personally from the FRP composites industry."

Nonfiction New product, technical, industry information. **Buys 4-6 mss/year.** Query. Length: 300 words. **Pays $200.**

Photos State availability with submission. Reviews 4×5 transparencies, prints, 35mm slides, JPEGs (much preferred). Buys all rights. Offers no additional payment for photos accepted with ms. Captions, identification of subjects, model releases required.

$ $ AUTOMATED BUILDER

CMN Associates, Inc., 1445 Donlon St., Suite 16, Ventura CA 93003. (805)642-9735. Fax: (805)642-8820. E-mail: info@automatedbuilder.com. Website: www.automatedbuilder.com. Editor-in-Chief: Don Carlson. **Contact:** Bob Mendel. **10% freelance written.** Monthly magazine specializing in management for industrialized (manufactured) housing and volume home builders. "Our material is technical in content and concerned with new technologies or improved methods for in-plant building and components related to building. Online content is uploaded from the monthly print material." Estab. 1964. Circ. 25,000. **Pays on acceptance.** Publishes ms an average of 3 months after acceptance. Byline given. Buys first North American serial rights. Editorial lead time 2 months. Submit seasonal material 2 months in advance. Accepts queries by mail, e-mail, fax. Responds in 2 weeks to queries. Sample copy for free.

Nonfiction Case history articles on successful home building companies which may be 1) production (big volume) home builders; 2) mobile home manufacturers; 3) modular home manufacturers; 4) prefabricated (panelized) home manufacturers; 5) house component manufacturers; or 6) special unit (in-plant commercial building) manufacturers. Also uses interviews, photo features, and technical articles. "No architect or plan 'dreams.' Housing projects must be built or under construction." **Buys 6-8 mss/year.** Query. Phone queries OK. Length: 250-500 words. **Pays $300.**

Photos Wants 4×5, 5×7, or 8×10 glossies. State availability with submission. Reviews 35mm or larger (35mm preferred) transparencies. Offers no additional payment for photos accepted with ms. Captions, identification of subjects required.

Tips "Stories often are too long, too loose; we prefer 500-750 words. We prefer a phone query on feature articles. If accepted on query, article usually will not be rejected later."

$ $ BUILDERNEWS MAGAZINE

(formerly *NW Builder Magazine*), Pacific NW Sales & Marketing, Inc., 500 W. 8th St., Suite 270, Vancouver WA 98660. (360)906-0793. Fax: (360)906-0794. E-mail: editor@buildernewsmag.com. Website: www.builderne wsmag.com. "Articles must address pressing topics for builders in our region with a special emphasis on the business aspects of construction." Estab. 1996. Circ. 35,000. Pays on acceptance of revised ms. Publishes ms an average of 1 month after acceptance. Byline given. Buys first North American serial, electronic rights. Editorial lead time 2 months. Submit seasonal material 3 months in advance. Accepts queries by mail, e-mail, fax. Responds in 1 week to queries; 1 month to mss. Sample copy for free or online. Writer's guidelines free.

Nonfiction How-to, interview/profile, new product, technical. No personal bios unless they teach a valuable lesson to those in the building industry. **Buys 400 mss/year.** Query. Length: 500-2,500 words. **Pays $200-500.** Sometimes pays expenses of writers on assignment.

Photos State availability with submission. Buys first North American serial and electronic rights. Offers no additional payment for photos accepted with ms. Captions, identification of subjects, model releases required.

Columns/Departments Engineering; Construction; Architecture & Design; Tools & Materials; Heavy Equipment; Business & Economics; Legal Matters; E-build; Building Green, all 750-2,500 words. Query.

Tips "Writers should have an understanding of the residential building industry and its terminology and be prepared to provide a résumé, writing samples, and story synopsis."

$ $ CONCRETE CONSTRUCTION

Hanley-Wood, LLC., 426 S. Westgate St., Addison IL 60101. (630)543-0870. Fax: (630)543-5399. E-mail: preband @hanley-wood.com. Website: www.worldofconcrete.com. Editor: William Palmer. **Contact:** Pat Reband, managing editor. **20% freelance written.** Monthly magazine for concrete contractors, engineers, architects, specifiers and others who design and build residential, commercial, industrial, and public works, cast-in-place concrete structures. It also covers job stories and new equipment in the industry. Estab. 1956. Circ. 80,000. **Pays on acceptance.** Publishes ms an average of 4 months after acceptance. Byline given. Editorial lead time 4 months. Submit seasonal material 4 months in advance. Accepts queries by mail, e-mail, fax. Responds in 2 weeks to queries; 1 month to mss. Sample copy for free. Writer's guidelines free.

Nonfiction How-to, new product, personal experience, photo feature, technical, job stories. **Buys 7-10 mss/ year.** Query with published clips. Length: 2,000 words maximum. **Pays $250 or more for assigned articles; $200 minimum for unsolicited articles.** Pays expenses of writers on assignment.

Photos Send photos with submission. Reviews contact sheets, negatives, transparencies, prints. Buys one-time rights. Offers no additional payment for photos accepted with ms. Captions required.

Tips "Have a good understanding of the concrete construction industry. How-to stories accepted only from industry experts. Job stories must cover procedures, materials, and equipment used as well as the project's scope."

$ $ $ THE CONCRETE PRODUCER

Hanley-Wood, LLC, 426 S. Westgate St., Addison IL 60101. (630)543-0870. Fax: (630)543-3112. Website: www. worldofconcrete.com. **Contact:** Rick Yelton, editor. **30% freelance written.** Monthly magazine covering concrete production. "Our audience consists of producers who have succeeded in making concrete the preferred building material through management, operating, quality control, use of the latest technology, or use of superior materials." Estab. 1982. Circ. 18,000. **Pays on acceptance.** Publishes ms an average of 2 months after acceptance. Byline given. Editorial lead time 4 months. Accepts queries by mail, e-mail, fax, phone. Responds in 1 week to queries; 2 months to mss. Sample copy for $4. Writer's guidelines free.

Nonfiction How-to (promote concrete), new product, technical. **Buys 10 mss/year.** Send complete ms. Length: 500-2,000 words. **Pays $200-1,000.** Sometimes pays expenses of writers on assignment.

Photos Scan photos at 300 dpi. State availability with submission. Reviews transparencies, prints. Offers no additional payment for photos accepted with ms. Captions, identification of subjects required.

$ HARD HAT NEWS

Lee Publications, Inc., 6113 State Highway 5, Palatine Bridge NY 13428. (518)673-3237. Fax: (518)673-2381. E-mail: rdecamp@leepub.com. Website: www.hardhat.com. **Contact:** Ralph DeCamp, editor. **80% freelance written.** Biweekly tabloid covering heavy construction, equipment, road, and bridge work. "Our readers are contractors and heavy construction workers involved in excavation, highways, bridges, utility construction, and underground construction." Estab. 1980. Circ. 58,000. Byline given. Editorial lead time 2 weeks. Submit seasonal material 2 weeks in advance. Accepts queries by mail, e-mail, fax, phone. Sample copy and writer's guidelines free.

○┰ "We especially need writers with some knowledge of heavy construction, although anyone with good composition and interviewing skills is welcome. Focus on major construction in progress in your area."

Nonfiction Also 'Job Stories,' (a brief overall description of the project, the names and addresses of the companies and contractors involved, and a description of the equipment used, including manufacturers' names and model numbers. Quotes from the people in charge, as well as photos, are important, as are the names of the dealers providing the equipment). Interview/profile, new product, opinion, photo feature, technical. Send complete ms. Length: 50-800 words. **Pays $2.50/inch.** Sometimes pays expenses of writers on assignment.

Photos Send photos with submission. Reviews prints, slides. Offers $15/photo. Captions, identification of subjects required.

Columns/Departments New Products; Association News; Parts and Repairs; Attachments; Trucks and Trailers; People on the Move.

Tips "Every issue has a focus—see our editorial calender. Special consideration is given to a story that coincides with the focus. A color photo is necessary for the front page. Vertical shots work best. We need more writers in metro NY area. Also, we are expanding our distribution into the Mid-Atlantic states and need writers in Virginia, Tennessee, North Carolina, and South Carolina."

$ $ HEAVY EQUIPMENT NEWS

Cygnus Business Media, 33 Inverness Center Pkwy., Suite 200, Birmingham AL 35242. Fax: (205)380-1384. E-mail: clare.martin@cygnusb2b.com. Website: www.heavyequipmentnews.com. **Contact:** Clare Martin, assistant editor. **30-40% freelance written.** Monthly magazine covering construction equipment and construction industry. "*Heavy Equipment News* is an editorial-driven publication for the construction contractor, focusing on job sites, asphalt-road building, concrete, business management, equipment selection, and material handling." Estab. 1995. Circ. 60,000. **Pays on acceptance.** Publishes ms an average of 3 months after acceptance. Byline given. Offers 10% kill fee. Buys first North American serial, second serial (reprint), electronic rights. Editorial lead time 6 months. Submit seasonal material 6 months in advance. Accepts queries by mail, e-mail, fax. Responds in 2 weeks to queries; 1 month to mss. Sample copy for #10 SASE. Writer's guidelines free.

Nonfiction How-to, interview/profile, new product, personal experience, technical. **Buys 12 mss/year.** Query with published clips. Length: 1,200-1,500 words. **Pays $500.**

Photos Reviews transparencies, prints. Buys all rights. Offers no additional payment for photos accepted with ms. Captions, identification of subjects required.

Columns/Departments Asphalt Road; Concrete Batch; Point of View; Truck Stop. Query with published clips. **Pays $300.**

$ $ MC MAGAZINE

The Voice of the Manufactured Concrete Products Industry, National Precast Concrete Association, 10333 N. Meridian St., Suite 272, Indianapolis IN 46290. (317)571-9500. Fax: (317)571-0041. E-mail: rhyink@precast.org. Website: www.precast.org. **Contact:** Ron Hyink, managing editor. **75% freelance written.** Bimonthly magazine covering manufactured concrete products. "*MC Magazine* is a publication for owners and managers of factory-produced concrete products used in construction. We publish business articles, technical articles, company profiles, safety articles, and project profiles, with the intent of educating our readers in order to increase the quality and use of precast concrete." Estab. 1995. Circ. 8,500. **Pays on acceptance.** Publishes ms an average of 6 months after acceptance. Byline given. Buys first North American serial, second serial (reprint), all rights. Editorial lead time 3 months. Accepts queries by mail, e-mail, fax. Accepts simultaneous submissions. Responds in 1 month to queries; 2 months to mss. Sample copy online. Writer's guidelines online.

Nonfiction How-to (business), interview/profile, technical (concrete manufacturing). "No humor, essays, fiction, or fillers." **Buys 8-14 mss/year.** Query or send complete ms. Length: 1,500-2,500 words. **Pays $250-750.** Sometimes pays expenses of writers on assignment.

Photos State availability with submission. Buys all rights. Offers no additional payment for photos accepted with ms. Captions required.

Tips "Understand the audience and the purpose of the magazine. Understanding audience interests and needs is important and expressing a willingness to tailor a subject to get the right slant is critical. Our primary freelance needs are about general business or technology topics. Of course, if you are an engineer or a writer specializing in industry, construction, or manufacturing technology, other possibilities may exist. Writing style should be concise, yet lively and entertaining. Avoid clichés. We require a third-person perspective, encourage a positive tone and active voice. For stylistic matters, follow the *AP Style Book*."

MICHIGAN CONTRACTOR & BUILDER

1917 Savannah Lane, Ypsilanti MI 48198-3674. (734)482-0272. Fax: (734)482-0291. E-mail: akalousdian@reedbusiness.com. **Contact:** Aram Kalousdian. **25% freelance written.** Weekly magazine covering the commercial construction industry in Michigan (no home building). "*Michigan Contractor & Builder's* audience is contractors, equipment suppliers, engineers, and architects. The magazine reports on construction projects in Michigan. It does not cover homebuilding. Stories should focus on news or innovative techniques or materials in construction." Estab. 1907. Circ. 3,700. Pays 1 month after publication. Byline given. Buys all rights. Accepts queries by mail, e-mail, fax, phone. Sample copy for free.

Nonfiction Michigan construction projects. **Buys 52 mss/year.** Query with published clips. Length: 1,500 words with 5-7 photos. **Payment is negotiable.**

Photos Send photos with submission. Reviews original prints. Buys all rights. Offers no additional payment for photos accepted with ms. Captions required.

$ $ PENNSYLVANIA BUILDER

Pennsylvania Builders Association, 600 N. 12th St., Lemoyne PA 17043. (717)730-4380. Fax: (717)730-4396. E-mail: pba@pahomes.org. Website: www.pahomes.org. **10% freelance written.** "Quarterly trade publication for builders, remodelers, subcontractors, and other affiliates of the home building industry in Pennsylvania." Estab. 1988. Circ. 12,200. Pays on publication. Publishes ms an average of 1 year after acceptance. Byline given. Buys one-time rights. Editorial lead time 3 months. Submit seasonal material 9 months in advance. Accepts queries by mail, e-mail. Accepts simultaneous submissions. Responds in 2 weeks to queries; 3 months to mss. Sample copy for free. Writer's guidelines by e-mail. Editorial calendar online.

Nonfiction General interest, how-to, new product, technical. No personnel or company profiles. **Buys 1-2 mss/year.** Send complete ms. Length: 800-1,200 words. **Pays $250.** Sometimes pays expenses of writers on assignment.

Reprints Accepts previously published submissions.

Photos Send photos with submission. Reviews negatives, transparencies, prints. Buys one-time rights. Negotiates payment individually. Captions, identification of subjects required.

$ $ PERMANENT BUILDINGS & FOUNDATIONS (PBF)

R.W. Nielsen Co., 350 E. Center St., Suite 201, Provo UT 84606-3262. (801)373-0013. E-mail: rnielsen@permane ntbuildings.com. Website: www.permanentbuildings.com. **Contact:** Roger W. Nielsen, editor. **50% freelance written.** Magazine published 8 times/year. "*PBF* readers are contractors who build residential and light commercial concrete buildings. Editorial focus is on new technologies to build solid, energy efficient structures, insulated concrete walls, waterproofing, underpinning, roofing and the business of contracting and construction." Estab. 1989. Circ. 30,000. Pays on publication. Byline given. Buys first North American serial rights. Editorial lead time 1 month. Submit seasonal material 2 months in advance. Accepts queries by mail, e-mail. Responds immediately to queries; 1 month to mss. Sample copy for 9×12 SASE or online. Writer's guidelines free or online.

Nonfiction How-to (construction methods, management techniques), humor, interview/profile, new product, technical, book reviews, tool reviews. Special issues: Water Proofing and Repair (February); Buyer's Guide (October); Insulated Concrete Forming Report (November); Concrete Homes (January); Commercial Market (July). **Buys 5-10 mss/year.** Query. Length: 500-1,500 words. **Pays 20-40¢/word for assigned articles; $50-500 for unsolicited articles.**

Photos State availability with submission. Reviews contact sheets. Buys North American rights. Offers no additional payment for photos accepted with ms. Captions, identification of subjects required.

Columns/Departments Marketing Tips, 250-500 words; Q&A (solutions to contractor problems), 200-500 words. Query.

$ $ REEVES JOURNAL

Business News Publishing Co., 23241 South Pointe Dr., Suite 280, Laguna Hills CA 92653. (949)830-0881. Fax: (949)859-7845. E-mail: john@reevesjournal.com. Website: www.reevesjournal.com. **Contact:** John Fultz, editor. **25% freelance written.** Monthly magazine covering building subcontractors—plumbers, HVAC contractors. Estab. 1920. Circ. 13,800. Pays on publication. Byline given. Buys first North American serial, electronic rights. Editorial lead time 3 months. Accepts queries by mail, e-mail, fax. Responds in 1 month to queries; 2 months to mss. Sample copy for free. Writer's guidelines for #10 SASE.

● "Knowledge of building construction, water science, engineering is extremely helpful. Even better—former plumbing, HVAC experience, and a great command of the English language."

Nonfiction "Only articles applicable to plumbing/HVAC subcontracting trade in the western US." How-to, interview/profile, new product, technical. Query with published clips. Length: 1,500-2,000 words. **Pays $100-350.** Pays phone expenses.

Photos State availability with submission. Buys all rights. Negotiates payment individually. Captions, identification of subjects required.

■ The online magazine carries original content not found in the print edition. Contact: John Fultz.

Tips "Know the market—we're not just another builder publication. Our target audience is the plumbing, HVAC contractor—new construction, mechanical, and service and repair. We cover the western U.S. (plus Texas)."

$ $ UNDERGROUND CONSTRUCTION

Oildom Publishing Co. of Texas, Inc., P.O. Box 941669, Houston TX 77094-8669. (281)558-6930. Fax: (281)558-7029. E-mail: rcarpenter@oildompublishing.com. Website: www.oildompublishing.com. **Contact:** Robert Carpenter, editor. **35% freelance written.** Monthly magazine covering underground oil and gas pipeline, water and sewer pipeline, cable construction for contractors and owning companies. Circ. 34,500. Publishes ms an average of 6 months after acceptance. Buys first North American serial rights. Accepts queries by mail, e-mail, fax, phone. Responds in 1 month to mss.

Nonfiction How-to, job stories. Query with published clips. Length: 1,000-2,000 words. **Pays $3-500.** Sometimes pays expenses of writers on assignment.

Photos Send photos with submission. Reviews color prints and slides. Buys one-time rights. Captions required.

Tips "We supply guidelines outlining information we need." The most frequent mistake made by writers in completing articles is unfamiliarity with the field.

DRUGS, HEALTHCARE & MEDICAL PRODUCTS

$ $ $ VALIDATION TIMES

Washington Information Source Co., 6506 Old Stage Rd., Suite 100, Rockville MD 20852-4326. (703)779-8777. Fax: (703)779-2508. E-mail: editors@fdainfo.com. Website: www.fdainfo.com. **Contact:** Dawn Gould, managing editor. Monthly newsletter covering regulation of pharmaceutical and medical devices. "We write to executives who have to keep up on changing FDA policies and regulations, and on what their competitors are doing at the agency." Estab. 1992. Pays on publication. Publishes ms an average of 1 month after acceptance. Byline given. Makes work-for-hire assignments. Editorial lead time 1 month. Submit seasonal material 1 month in advance. Accepts queries by mail. Responds in 1 month to queries. Sample copy and writer's guidelines free.

Nonfiction How-to, technical, regulatory. No lay interest pieces. **Buys 50-100 mss/year.** Query. Length: 600-1,500 words. **Pays $100/half day; $200 full day "to cover meetings and same rate for writing."** Sometimes pays expenses of writers on assignment.

Tips "If you're covering a conference for non-competing publications, call me with a drug or device regulatory angle."

EDUCATION & COUNSELING

$ ARTS & ACTIVITIES

Publishers' Development Corp., Dept. WM, 12345 World Trade Dr., San Diego CA 92128. (858)605-0242. Fax: (858)605-0247. Website: www.artsandactivities.com. **Contact:** Maryellen Bridge, editor-in-chief. **95% freelance written.** Eager to work with new/unpublished writers. Monthly (except July and August) magazine covering art education at levels from preschool through college for educators and therapists engaged in arts and crafts education and training. Estab. 1932. Circ. 20,000. Pays on publication. Publishes ms an average of 1 year after acceptance. Byline given. Buys first North American serial rights. Submit seasonal material 6 months in advance. Accepts queries by mail. Responds in 3 months to queries. Sample copy for 9 × 12 SAE and 8 first-class stamps. Writer's guidelines online.

- Editors here are seeking more materials for upper elementary and secondary levels on printmaking, ceramics, 3-dimensional design, weaving, fiber arts (stitchery, tie-dye, batik, etc.), crafts, painting, and multicultural art.

Nonfiction Historical/nostalgic (arts, activities, history), how-to (classroom art experiences, artists' techniques), interview/profile (of artists), opinion (on arts activities curriculum, ideas of how to do things better, philosophy of art education), personal experience (this ties in with the how-to, we like it to be personal, no recipe style), articles of exceptional art programs. **Buys 80-100 mss/year.** Length: 200-2,000 words. **Pays $35-150.**

Tips "Frequently in unsolicited manuscripts, writers obviously have not studied the magazine to see what style of articles we publish. Send for a sample copy to familiarize yourself with our style and needs. The best way to find out if his/her writing style suits our needs is for the author to submit a manuscript on speculation. We prefer an anecdotal style of writing, so that readers will feel as though they are there in the art room as the lesson/project is taking place. Also, good quality photographs of student artwork are important. We are a visual art magazine!"

$ 🖰 THE ATA MAGAZINE

The Alberta Teachers' Association, 11010 142nd St., Edmonton AB T5N 2R1, Canada. (780)447-9400. Fax: (780)455-6481. E-mail: postmaster@teachers.ab.ca. Website: www.teachers.ab.ca. Editor: Tim Johnston. **Contact:** Raymond Gariepy, associate editor. Quarterly magazine covering education. Estab. 1920. Circ. 39,500. Pays on publication. Publishes ms an average of 4 months after acceptance. Byline given. Buys one-time rights.

Editorial lead time 2 months. Submit seasonal material 2 months in advance. Accepts queries by mail, e-mail, fax, phone. Accepts simultaneous submissions. Responds in 2 months to queries. Sample copy free. Writer's guidelines online.

Nonfiction Education-related topics. Query with published clips. Length: 500-1,250 words. **Pays $75 (Canadian).**

Photos Send photos with submission. Reviews 4×6 prints. Negotiates rights. Negotiates payment individually. Captions required.

$CLASS ACT

Class Act, Inc., 3 Riverdale Court, Henderson KY 42419. E-mail: classact@lightpower.net. Website: classactpress .com. **Contact:** Susan Thurman, editor. **50% freelance written.** Newsletter published 9 times/year covering English/language arts education. "Our writers must know English as a classroom subject and should be familiar with writing for teens. If you can't make your manuscript interesting to teenagers, we're not interested." Estab. 1993. Circ. 300. **Pays on acceptance.** Publishes ms an average of 6 months after acceptance. Byline given. Offers 100% kill fee. Buys all rights. Editorial lead time 2 months. Submit seasonal material 3 months in advance. Accepts simultaneous submissions. Responds in 1 month to queries. Sample copy for $3 and SASE. Writer's guidelines online.

- Accepts queries by mail and e-mail, but no attachments.
- Break in with "an original, ready-for-classroom-use article that provides tips for writing (but geared to a teenage audience)."

Nonfiction How-to (games, puzzles, assignments relating to English education). "No Masters theses; no esoteric articles; no poetry; no educational theory or jargon." **Buys 12 mss/year.** Send complete ms. Length: 100-2,000 words. **Pays $10-40.**

Columns/Departments Writing Assignments (innovative, thought-provoking for teens), 500-1,500 words; Puzzles, Games (English education oriented), 200 words; Teacher Tips (bulletin boards, time-saving devices), 100 words. "E-mailed mss (not attachments) are encouraged. Articles on disk (MS Word) also are encouraged." Send complete ms. **Pays $10-40.**

Fillers Teacher tips. **Pays $10.**

Tips "Please know the kind of language used by junior/senior high students. Don't speak above them. Also, it helps to know what these students don't know, in order to explain or emphasize the concepts. Clip art is sometimes used but is not paid extra for. We like material that's slightly humorous while still being educational. We are especially open to innovative writing assignments, educational puzzles and games, and instructions on basics. Again, be familiar with this age group. Remember we are geared for English teachers."

$ $ $EARLYCHILDHOOD NEWS

Excelligence Learning Corp., 2 Lower Ragsdale, Suite 125, Monterey CA 93940. (831)333-2000. Fax: (831)333-5510. E-mail: mshaw@excelligencemail.com. Website: www.earlychildhoodnews.com. **Contact:** Megan Shaw, editor. **80% freelance written.** Bimonthly magazine covering early childhood education. Targets teachers and parents of young children, infants to age 8. Estab. 1988. Circ. 55,000. Pays on publication. Publishes ms an average of 2-3 months after acceptance. Byline given. Buys all rights. Editorial lead time 2-4 months. Submit seasonal material 4 months in advance. Accepts queries by mail, e-mail, fax. Responds in 4-6 weeks to queries; 2-4 months to mss. Sample copy for free. Writer's guidelines free.

Nonfiction Essays, general interest, inspirational, interview/profile, research-based. Special issues: Math and Assessment and Observation (January/February); Learning through Play (March/April); Science and Art (May/June); Back to School (August/September); Literacy and Safety (October); Infants and Toddlers and Music (November/December). No personal stories. **Buys 40-50 mss/year.** Query. Length: 500-3,000 words. **Pays $100 minimum; $800-1,000 maximum for assigned articles; $100-300 for unsolicited articles.**

Poetry "Poems should have a teacher-directed audience." Light verse, traditional. No "poetry not related to children, teachers, or early childhood." **Buys 6 poems/year.** Length: 10-60 lines. **Pays $100-250.**

Tips "Knowing about the publication and the types of articles we publish is greatly appreciated. Query letters are preferred over complete manuscripts."

$ $HISPANIC OUTLOOK IN HIGHER EDUCATION

210 Route 4 E., Suite 310, Paramus NJ 07652. (201)587-8800, ext 100. Fax: (201)587-9105. E-mail: sloutlook@aol .com. Website: www.hispanicoutlook.com. Editor: Adalyn Hixson. **Contact:** Sue Lopez-Isa, managing editor. **50% freelance written.** Biweekly magazine. "We're looking for higher education story articles, with a focus on Hispanics and the advancements made by and for Hispanics in higher education." Circ. 28,000. Pays on publication. Publishes ms an average of 2 months after acceptance. Byline given. Editorial lead time 2 months. Submit seasonal material 3 months in advance. Accepts queries by mail, e-mail, fax. Accepts simultaneous submissions. Sample copy for free.

O—¬ Break with "issues articles such as new laws in higher education."

Nonfiction Historical/nostalgic, interview/profile (of academic or scholar), opinion (on higher education), personal experience, all regarding higher education only. **Buys 20-25 mss/year.** Query with published clips. Length: 1,800-2,200 words. **Pays $500 minimum for assigned articles.** Pays expenses of writers on assignment.

Photos Send photos with submission. Reviews color or b&w prints, digital images must be 300 dpi (call for e-mail photo address). Offers no additional payment for photos accepted with ms.

Tips "Articles explore the Hispanic experience in higher education. Special theme issues address sports, law, health, corporations, heritage, women, and a wide range of similar issues; however, articles need not fall under those umbrellas."

$ $PTO TODAY

The Magazine for Parent Group Leaders, PTO Today, Inc., 200 Stonewall Blvd., Suite 6A, Wrentham MA 02093. (800)644-3561. Fax: (508)384-6108. E-mail: editor@ptotoday.com. Website: www.ptotoday.com. **Contact:** Craig Bystrynski, editor. **65% freelance written.** Magazine published 6 times during the school year covering the work of school parent-teacher groups. "We celebrate the work of school parent volunteers and provide resources to help them do that work more effectively." Estab. 1999. Circ. 80,000. Pays on publication. Publishes ms an average of 2 months after acceptance. Byline given. Offers 30% kill fee. Buys first North American serial, electronic, all rights. Editorial lead time 4 months. Submit seasonal material 4 months in advance. Accepts queries by e-mail. Sample copy online. Writer's guidelines by e-mail.

Nonfiction Exposé, general interest, how-to (anything related to PTO/PTA), interview/profile, new product, personal experience. **Buys 40 mss/year.** Query. Length: 600-2,000 words. **Pays 20-40¢/word for assigned articles; $50-500 for unsolicited articles.** Sometimes pays expenses of writers on assignment.

Photos State availability with submission. Buys one-time rights. Negotiates payment individually. Identification of subjects required.

Tips "It's difficult for us to find talented writers with strong experience with parent groups. This experience is a big plus. Also, it helps to review our writer's guidelines before querying."

⑬ $RELIGION TEACHER'S JOURNAL

The First and Best Magazine for Catechists, Bayard, Inc., P.O. Box 180, 185 Willow St., Mystic CT 06355. (800)321-0411, ext. 163. Fax: (860)536-5674. E-mail: aberger@twentythirdpublications.com. Website: www.religionteachersjournal.com. **Contact:** Alison J. Berger, editor. **40% freelance written.** Magazine published 7 times during the school year, with combined November/December and April/May issues, covering topics for catechists and religion teachers teaching religion to teens and children. *Religion Teacher's Journal* enriches and empowers catechists and religion teachers in their important ministry of faith formation by providing up-to-date religious knowledge, information, practice, and methods in catechesis." Estab. 1966. Circ. 34,000. **Pays on acceptance.** Publishes ms an average of 3-12 months after acceptance. Byline given. Buys first North American serial rights. Editorial lead time 5 months. Submit seasonal material 6 months in advance. Accepts queries by mail, e-mail, fax. Accepts simultaneous submissions. Responds in 2-3 weeks to queries; 1 month to mss. Sample copy for 9×12 SAE and 3 first-class stamps. Writer's guidelines free.

Nonfiction How-to (short activities that can be used in religion lessons), personal experience (in teaching religion—a practical approach), religious. Special issues: Sacraments/Christmas Season (January); Lent/Reconciliation (February); Prayer/Easter/Baptism (March); Catechist Formation/Summer (April/May); Back to School/Teaching Techniques—as applied to religion sessions (September); Scripture/Saints (October); Advent/Christmas/Thanksgiving (November/December). No fiction. Query or send complete ms. Length: 600-1,300 words. **Pays $50-125 for unsolicited articles.**

$SCHOOL ARTS MAGAZINE

50 Portland St., Worcester MA 01608-9959. Fax: (610)683-8229. Website: www.davis-art.com. **Contact:** Eldon Katter, editor. **85% freelance written.** Monthly magazine (September-May), serving arts and craft education profession, K-12, higher education, and museum education programs written by and for art teachers. Estab. 1901. Pays on publication. Publishes ms an average of 3 months after acceptance. Buys all rights. Accepts queries by mail, phone. Responds in 3 months to queries. Sample copy for free. Writer's guidelines online.

O—¬ Break in with "professional quality photography to illustrate art lessons."

Nonfiction Articles on art and craft activities in schools. Should include description and photos of activity in progress, as well as examples of finished artwork. Query or send complete ms and SASE. Length: 600-1,400 words. **Pays $30-150.**

▪ The online version contains material not found in the print edition.

Tips "We prefer articles on actual art projects or techniques done by students in actual classroom situations. Philosophical and theoretical aspects of art and art education are usually handled by our contributing editors.

Our articles are reviewed and accepted on merit and each is tailored to meet our needs. Keep in mind that art teachers want practical tips, above all—more hands-on information than academic theory. Write your article with the accompanying photographs in hand.'' The most frequent mistakes made by writers are ''bad visual material (photographs, drawings) submitted with articles, a lack of complete descriptions of art processes, and no rationale behind programs or activities. Familiarity with the field of art education is essential. Review recent issues of *School Arts*.''

[N] SCHOLASTIC DYNAMATH

Scholastic, Inc., 557 Broadway, New York NY 10012-3902. (212)343-6100. Fax: (212)343-6945. E-mail: dynamath@scholastic.com. Website: www.scholastic.com. Editor: Matthew Friedman. Magazine published 8 times/year. Intended to show 3rd through 6th graders that math can be fun and relevent to their lives. Circ. 200,000. Sample copy not available.

[N] SCHOLASTIC MATH MAGAZINE

Scholastic, Inc., 557 Broadway, New York NY 10012-3902. (212)343-6100. Fax: (212)343-4459. E-mail: mathmag@scholastic.com. Website: www.scholastic.com. Editor: Jack Silbert. Monthly magazine. Aimed at encouraging the interest of 6th, 7th, 8th and 9th graders in mathmatics. Circ. 200,000. Sample copy available.

$ $ $ TEACHER MAGAZINE

Editorial Projects in Education, 6935 Arlington Rd., Suite 100, Bethesda MD 20814. (310)280-3100. Fax: (301)280-3150. E-mail: info@teachermagazine.org. Website: www.teachermagazine.org. Managing Editor: Samantha Stainburn. **Contact:** Rich Shea, executive editor. **40% freelance written.** Magazine published 8 times/year covering the teaching profession. ''One of the major thrusts of the current school reform movement is to make teaching a true profession. *Teacher Magazine* plays a central role in that effort. It is a national communications network that provides teachers with the information they need to be better practitioners and effective leaders.'' Estab. 1989. Circ. 120,000. Pays on publication. Publishes ms an average of 1 month after acceptance. Byline given. Offers 25% kill fee. Buys first North American serial, electronic rights. Editorial lead time 3 months. Submit seasonal material 4 months in advance. Accepts queries by mail, e-mail, fax. Responds in 2 months to queries. Sample copy online. Writer's guidelines free.

Nonfiction Book excerpts, essays, interview/profile, personal experience, photo feature, investigative. No ''how-to'' articles. **Buys 56 mss/year.** Query with published clips. Length: 1,000-5,000 words. **Pays 50¢/word.** Sometimes pays expenses of writers on assignment.

Photos State availability with submission. Reviews contact sheets, transparencies, prints. Buys one-time rights. Negotiates payment individually. Identification of subjects, model releases required.

Columns/Departments Current events, forum. Query with published clips. **Pays 50¢/word.**

Tips ''Sending us a well-researched query letter accompanied by clips that demonstrate you can tell a good story is the best way to break into *Teacher Magazine*. Describe the characters in your proposed article. What scenes do you hope to include in the piece?''

$ TEACHERS OF VISION

Christian Educators Association, P.O. Box 41300, Pasadena CA 91114. (626)798-1124. Fax: (626)798-2346. E-mail: judy@ceai.org. Website: www.ceai.org. Editor: Forrest L. Turpen. **Contact:** Judy Turpen, contributing editor. **50% freelance written.** Magazine published 6 times/year for Christian teachers in public education. ''*Teachers of Vision*'s articles inspire, inform, and equip teachers and administrators in the educational arena. Readers look for teacher tips, integrating faith & work, and general interest education articles. Topics include union issues, religious expression and activity in public schools, and legal rights of Christian educators. Our audience is primarily public school educators. Other readers include teachers in private schools, university professors, school administrators, parents and school board members.'' Estab. 1953. Circ. 10,000. Pays on publication. Publishes ms an average of 6 months after acceptance. Byline given. Buys first North American serial, second serial (reprint) rights. Editorial lead time 6 months. Submit seasonal material 6 months in advance. Accepts queries by mail, e-mail, fax. Accepts simultaneous submissions. Responds in 1 month to queries; 3-4 months to mss. Sample copy for 9×12 SAE and 4 first-class stamps. Writer's guidelines online.

Nonfiction How-to, humor, inspirational, interview/profile, opinion, personal experience, religious. ''Nothing preachy.'' **Buys 15-20 mss/year.** Query or send complete ms if 2,000 words or less. Length: 600-2,500 words. **Pays $30-40.**

Reprints Accepts previously published submissions.

Photos State availability with submission. Buys one-time and reprint rights. Offers no additional payment for photos accepted with ms.

Columns/Departments Query. **Pays $10-30.**

Fillers Send with SASE—must relate to public education.

Tips "We are looking for material on living out one's faith in appropriate, legal ways in the public school setting."

$ $TEACHING THEATRE

Educational Theatre Association, 2343 Auburn Ave., Cincinnati OH 45219-2819. (513)421-3900. Fax: (513)421-7077. E-mail: jpalmarini@edta.org. Website: www.edta.org. **Contact:** James Palmarini, editor. **65% freelance written.** Quarterly magazine covering education theater K-12, primary emphasis on middle and secondary level education. *"Teaching Theatre* emphasizes the teaching, theory, philosophy issues that are of concern to teachers at the elementary, secondary, and—as they relate to teaching K-12 theater— college levels. We publish work that explains specific approaches to teaching (directing, acting, curriculum development and management, etc.); advocates curriculum reform; or offers theories of theater education." Estab. 1989. Circ. 3,500. **Pays on acceptance.** Publishes ms an average of 3 months after acceptance. Byline given. Buys one-time, electronic rights. Editorial lead time 2 months. Accepts previously published material. Accepts simultaneous submissions. Responds in 1 month to queries; 3 months to mss. Sample copy for $2. Writer's guidelines online.

Nonfiction *"Teaching Theatre*'s audience is well educated, and most have considerable experience in their field; *generalist* articles are discouraged; readers already *possess* basic skills." Book excerpts, essays, how-to, interview/profile, opinion, technical theater. **Buys 20 mss/year.** Query. **Pays $100-300.**

Photos State availability with submission. Reviews contact sheets, 5×7 and 8×10 transparencies, prints. Offers no additional payment for photos accepted with ms.

Tips Wants articles that address the needs of the busy but experienced high school theater educators. "Fundamental pieces, on the value of theater education are *not* of value to us—our readers already know that."

$ $ $ $TEACHING TOLERANCE

The Southern Poverty Law Center, 400 Washington Ave., Montgomery AL 36104. (334)956-8200. Fax: (334)956-8488. Website: www.teachingtolerance.org. **65% freelance written.** Semiannual magazine. *"Teaching Tolerance* is dedicated to helping K-12 teachers promote tolerance and understanding between widely diverse groups of students. Includes articles, teaching ideas, and reviews of other resources available to educators." Estab. 1991. Circ. 600,000. **Pays on acceptance.** Byline given. Buys all rights. Editorial lead time 6 months. Submit seasonal material 6 months in advance. Accepts queries by mail, fax. Sample copy and writer's guidelines free or online. Writer's guidelines online.

Nonfiction Essays, how-to (classroom techniques), personal experience (classroom), photo feature. "No jargon, rhetoric or academic analysis. No theoretical discussions on the pros/cons of multicultural education." **Buys 6-8 mss/year.** Query with published clips. Length: 1,000-3,000 words. **Pays $500-3,000 for assigned articles.** Pays expenses of writers on assignment.

Photos State availability with submission. Reviews contact sheets, transparencies. Buys one-time rights. Captions, identification of subjects required.

Columns/Departments Essays (personal reflection, how-to, school program), 400-800 words; Idea Exchange (special projects, successful anti-bias activities), 250-500 words; Student Writings (short essays dealing with diversity, tolerance & justice), 300-500 words. **Buys 8-12 mss/year.** Query with published clips. **Pays $50-1,000.**

The online magazine carries original content not found in the print edition and includes writer's guidelines. Contact: Tim Walker, online editor.

Tips "We want lively, simple, concise writing. The writing style should be descriptive and reflective, showing the strength of programs dealing successfully with diversity by employing clear descriptions of real scenes and interactions, and by using quotes from teachers and students. We ask that prospective writers study previous issues of the magazine and writer's guidelines before sending a query with ideas. Most open to articles that have a strong classroom focus. We are interested in approaches to teaching tolerance and promoting understanding that really work—approaches we might not have heard of. We want to inform our readers; we also want to inspire and encourage them. We know what's happening nationally; we want to know what's happening in your neighborhood classroom."

$TECH DIRECTIONS

Prakken Publications, Inc., P.O. Box 8623, Ann Arbor MI 48107-8623. (734)975-2800. Fax: (734)975-2787. E-mail: susanne@techdirections.com. Website: www.techdirections.com. **Contact:** Susanne Peckham, managing editor. **100% freelance written.** Eager to work with new/unpublished writers. Monthly (except June and July) magazine covering issues, trends, and activities of interest to science, technical, and technology educators at the elementary through post-secondary school levels. Estab. 1934. Circ. 40,000. Pays on publication. Publishes ms an average of 1 year after acceptance. Byline given. Buys all rights. Responds in 1 month to queries. Sample copy for $5. Writer's guidelines online.

Nonfiction Uses articles pertinent to the various teaching areas in science and technology education (woodwork, electronics, drafting, physics, graphic arts, computer training, etc.). Prefers authors who have direct connection with the field of science and/or technical education. "The outlook should be on innovation in educational programs, processes, or projects that directly apply to the technical education area." Main focus: technical career and education. General interest, how-to, personal experience, technical, think pieces. **Buys 50 unsolicited mss/ year.** Length: 2,000-3,000 words. **Pays $50-150.**

Photos Send photos with submission. Reviews color prints. Payment for photos included in payment for ms. Will accept electronic art as well.

Columns/Departments Direct from Washington (education news from Washington DC); Technology Today (new products under development); Technologies Past (profiles the inventors of last century); Mastering Computers, Technology Concepts (project orientation).

Tips "We are most interested in articles written by technology and science educators about their class projects and their ideas about the field. We need more and more technology-related articles, especially written for the community college level."

ELECTRONICS & COMMUNICATION

$ $THE ACUTA JOURNAL OF TELECOMMUNICATIONS IN HIGHER EDUCATION

ACUTA, 152 W. Zandale Dr., Suite 200, Lexington KY 40503-2486. (859)278-3338. Fax: (859)278-3268. E-mail: pscott@acuta.org. Website: www.acuta.org. **Contact:** Patricia Scott, communications manager. **20% freelance written.** Quarterly professional association journal covering telecommunications in higher education. "Our audience includes, primarily, middle to upper management in the telecommunications department on college/ university campuses. They are highly skilled, technology-oriented professionals who provide data, voice, and video communications services for residential and academic purposes." Estab. 1997. Circ. 2,200. Pays on publication. Publishes ms an average of 6 months after acceptance. Byline given. Buys first rights. Editorial lead time 6 months. Accepts queries by mail, e-mail, fax, phone. Responds in 1 month to queries; 2 months to mss. Sample copy for 9×12 SAE and 6 first-class stamps. Writer's guidelines free.

> O→ Break in with a campus study or case profile. "Contact me with your idea for a story. Convince me that you can handle the level of technical depth required."

Nonfiction "Each issue has a focus. Available with writer's guidelines. We are only interested in articles described in article types." How-to (telecom), technical (telecom), case study, college/university application of technology. **Buys 6-8 mss/year.** Query. Length: 1,200-4,000 words. **Pays 8-10¢/word.** Sometimes pays expenses of writers on assignment.

Photos State availability with submission. Reviews prints. Offers no additional payment for photos accepted with ms. Captions, model releases required.

Tips "Our audience expects every article to be relevant to telecommunications on the college/university campus, whether it is related to technology, facilities, or management. Writers must read back issues to understand this focus and the level of technicality we expect."

AMERICA'S NETWORK

Advanstar Communications, 201 E. Sandpointe Ave., Suite 600, Santa Ana CA 92707. (714)513-8459. Fax: (714)513-8845. E-mail: belliott@advanstar.com. Website: www.americasnetwork.com. Managing Editor: Al Senia. **Contact:** Bonnie Elliott. Magazine published 22 times/year. Edited for telecommunications executives and professionals who are responsible for the design, construction, sales, purchase, operationsand maintenance of telephone/telecom systems. Circ. 62,780. Editorial lead time 3 months.

$ $DIGITAL OUTPUT

The Business Guide for Electronic Publishers, The Doyle Group, 5150 Palm Valley Rd., Suite 103, Ponte Vedra Beach FL 32082. (904)285-6020. Fax: (904)285-9944. E-mail: mmcenaney@digitaloutput.net. Website: www.digitaloutput.net. **Contact:** Mike McEnaney, editor. **50% freelance written.** Monthly magazine covering electronic prepress, desktop publishing, and digital imaging, with articles ranging from digital capture and design to electronic prepress and digital printing. "*Digital Output* is a national business publication for electronic publishers and digital imagers, providing monthly articles which examine the latest technologies and digital methods and discuss how to profit from them. Our readers include service bureaus, prepress and reprographic houses, designers, commercial printers, wide-format printers, ad agencies, corporate communications and others." Estab. 1994. Circ. 30,000. Pays on publication. Publishes ms an average of 2 months after acceptance. Byline given. Offers 10-20% kill fee. Buys one-time rights including electronic rights for archival posting. Editorial lead time 3 months. Submit seasonal material 3 months in advance. Accepts queries by mail, e-mail. Responds in 3 weeks to queries; 1 month to mss. Sample copy for $4.50 or online.

Nonfiction How-to, interview/profile, technical, case studies. **Buys 36 mss/year.** Query with published clips or hyperlinks to posted clips. Length: 1,500-4,000 words. **Pays $250-600.**

Photos State availability with submission.

Tips "Our readers are graphic arts professionals. Freelance writers we use are deeply immersed in the technology of commercial printing, desktop publishing, digital imaging, color management, PDF workflow, inkjet printing, and similar topics."

$ $ ELECTRONIC SERVICING & TECHNOLOGY

The Professional Magazine for Electronics and Computer Servicing, P.O. Box 12487, Overland Park KS 66282-2487. (913)492-4857. Fax: (913)492-4857. E-mail: cpersedit@aol.com. **Contact:** Conrad Persson, editor. **80% freelance written.** Monthly magazine for service technicians, field service personnel, and avid servicing enthusiasts, who service audio, video, and computer equipment. Estab. 1950. Circ. 15,000. Pays on publication. Publishes ms an average of 4 months after acceptance. Byline given. Buys one-time rights. Editorial lead time 2 months. Accepts queries by mail, e-mail, fax, phone. Accepts simultaneous submissions. Responds in 1 month to queries; 2 months to mss. Sample copy for free. Writer's guidelines free.

> ○┮ Break in by knowing how to service consumer electronics products and being able to explain it in writing in good English.

Nonfiction Book excerpts, how-to (service consumer electronics), new product, technical. **Buys 40 mss/year.** Query or send complete ms. **Pays $50/page.**

Reprints Send ms with rights for sale noted and information about when and where the material previously appeared.

Photos Send photos with submission. Buys one-time rights. Offers no additional payment for photos accepted with ms.

Columns/Departments Business Corner (business tips); Computer Corner (computer servicing tips); Video Corner (understanding/servicing TV and video), all 1,000-2,000 words. **Buys 30 mss/year.** Query, or send complete ms. **Pays $100-300.**

Tips "Writers should have a strong background in electronics, especially consumer electronics servicing. Understand the information needs of consumer electronics service technicians, and be able to write articles that address specific areas of those needs."

$ $ $ SOUND & VIDEO CONTRACTOR

Primedia Business, 6400 Hollis St., Suite 12, Emeryville CA 94608. (510)985-3203. Fax: (510)653-5142. E-mail: mjohnson@primediabusiness.com. **Contact:** Mark Johnson, editor. **60% freelance written.** Monthly magazine covering "professional audio, video, security, acoustical design, sales, and marketing." Estab. 1983. Circ. 24,000. **Pays on acceptance.** Publishes ms an average of 3 months after acceptance. Byline given. Buys one-time, all rights. Editorial lead time 3 months. Accepts queries by mail, e-mail, fax, phone. Accepts simultaneous submissions. Responds ASAP to queries and to mss. Sample copy and writer's guidelines free.

Nonfiction Historical/nostalgic, how-to, photo feature, technical, professional audio/video applications, installations, product reviews. No opinion pieces, advertorial, interview/profile, exposé/gossip. **Buys 60 mss/year.** Query. Length: 1,000-2,500 words. **Pays $200-1,200 for assigned articles; $200-650 for unsolicited articles.**

Reprints Accepts previously published submissions.

Photos Send photos with submission. Reviews transparencies, prints. Offers no additional payment for photos accepted with ms. Identification of subjects required.

Columns/Departments Security Technology Review (technical install information); Sales & Marketing (techniques for installation industry); Video Happenings (Pro video/projection/storage technical info), all 1,500 words. **Buys 30 mss/year.** Query. **Pays $200-350.**

Tips "We want materials and subject matter that would be of interest to audio/video/security/low-voltage product installers/contractors/designers professionals. If the piece allows our readers to save time, money and/or increases their revenues, then we have reached our goals. Highly technical is desirable."

$ $ SQL SERVER MAGAZINE

Penton Media, 221 E. 29th St., Loveland CO 80538. (970)663-4700. E-mail: articles@sqlmag.com. Website: www.sqlmag.com. Editor: Kathy Blomstrom. **Contact:** Suzanne Cone, assistant managing editor. **35% freelance written.** Monthly magazine covering Microsoft SQL Server. "*SQL Server Magazine* is the only magazine completely devoted to helping developers and DBAs master new and emerging SQL Server technologies and issues. It provides practical advice and lots of code examples for SQL Server developers and administrators, and includes how-to articles, tips, tricks, and programming techniques offered by SQL Server experts." Estab. 1999. Circ. 20,000. Pays on publication. Publishes ms an average of 6 months after acceptance. Byline given. Offers $100 kill fee. Buys all rights. Editorial lead time 4+ months. Accepts queries by mail, e-mail. Responds in 6 weeks to queries; 2-3 months to mss. Sample copy online. Writer's guidelines online.

Nonfiction How-to, technical, SQL Server administration and programming. Nothing promoting third-party products or companies. **Buys 25-35 mss/year.** Query with or without published clips, or send complete ms. Length: 1,800-3,000 words. **Pays $200 for feature articles; $500 for Focus articles.** Pays in contributor copies if the writer requests the substitution.

Columns/Departments R2R Editor. Reader to Reader (helpful SQL Server hints and tips from readers), 200-400 words. Send all column/department submissions to r2r@sqlmag.com. **Buys 6-12 mss/year.** Send complete ms. **Pays $50.**

Tips "Read back issues and make sure that your proposed article doesn't overlap previous coverage. When proposing articles, state specifically how your article would contain new information compared to previously published information, and what benefit your information would be to *SQL Server Magazine*'s readership."

ENERGY & UTILITIES

$ $ ALTERNATIVE ENERGY RETAILER

Zackin Publications, Inc., P.O. Box 2180, Waterbury CT 06722-2180. (800)325-6745. Fax: (203)755-3480. E-mail: griffin@aer-online.com. Website: www.aer-online.com/aer/. **Contact:** Michael Griffin, editor. **5% freelance written.** Prefers to work with published/established writers. Monthly magazine on selling home hearth products—chiefly solid fuel and gas-burning appliances. "We seek detailed how-to tips for retailers to improve business. Most freelance material purchased is about retailers and how they succeed." Estab. 1980. Circ. 10,000. Pays on publication. Publishes ms an average of 2 months after acceptance. Buys first North American serial rights. Submit seasonal material 4 months in advance. Accepts queries by mail, e-mail, fax, phone. Responds in 2 weeks to queries. Sample copy for 9 × 12 SAE and 4 first-class stamps. Writer's guidelines online.

● Submit articles that focus on hearth market trends and successful sales techniques.

Nonfiction How-to (improve retails profits and business know-how), interview/profile (of successful retailers in this field). No "general business articles not adapted to this industry." **Buys 10 mss/year.** Query. Length: 1,000 words. **Pays $200.**

Photos State availability with submission. Reviews color transparencies. Buys one-time rights. Pays $25-125 maximum for 5 × 7 b&w prints. Identification of subjects required.

Tips "A freelancer can best break into our publication with features about readers (retailers). Stick to details about what has made this person a success."

$ $ ELECTRICAL APPARATUS

The Magazine of Electromechanical & Electronic Application & Maintenance, Barks Publications, Inc., 400 N. Michigan Ave., Chicago IL 60611-4198. (312)321-9440. Fax: (312)321-1288. Senior Editor: Kevin N. Jones. **Contact:** Elsie Dickson, editorial director. Monthly magazine for persons working in electrical and electronic maintenance, chiefly in industrial plants, who install and service electrical motors, transformers, generators, controls, and related equipment. Estab. 1967. Circ. 17,000. Pays on publication. Publishes ms an average of 2 months after acceptance. Byline given. Buys all rights unless other arrangements made. Accepts queries by mail, fax. Responds in 1 week to queries; 1 month to mss. Sample copy for $4.

Nonfiction Technical. Length: 1,500-2,500 words. **Pays $250-500 for assigned articles.**

Tips "All feature articles are assigned to staff and contributing editors and correspondents. Professionals interested in appointments as contributing editors and correspondents should submit résumé and article outlines, including illustration suggestions. Writers should be competent with a camera, which should be described in résumé. Technical expertise is absolutely necessary, preferably an E.E. degree, or practical experience. We are also book publishers and some of the material in *EA* is now in book form, bringing the authors royalties. Also publishes an annual directory, subtitled *ElectroMechanical Bench Reference*."

$ NATIONAL PETROLEUM NEWS

833 W. Jackson, 7th Floor, Chicago IL 60607. (312)846-4600. Fax: (312)977-1042. E-mail: dwight@mail.aip.c om. Website: www.npn-net.com. **Contact:** Darren Wight, editor. **15% freelance written.** Prefers to work with published/established writers. Monthly magazine for decision-makers in the petroleum marketing and convenience store industry. Estab. 1909. Circ. 38,000. Pays on acceptance if done on assignment. Publishes ms an average of 2 months after acceptance. variable rights, depending upon author and material; usually buys all rights Accepts queries by mail, e-mail, fax. Sample copy not available.

● This magazine is particularly interested in articles on national industry-related material.

Nonfiction Material related directly to developments and issues in the petroleum marketing and convenience store industry and "how-to" and "what-with" case studies. "No unsolicited copy, especially with limited attribution regarding information in story." **Buys 9-10 mss/year.** Length: 2,500 words maximum. **Pays $50-150/printed page.** Sometimes pays expenses of writers on assignment.

Trade Journals

Reprints Send typed ms on disk with rights for sale noted and information about when and where the article previously appeared.

Photos Pays $150/printed page. Payment for color and b&w photos.

$ $ PUBLIC POWER

Dept. WM, 2301 M St. NW, Washington DC 20037-1484. (202)467-2948. Fax: (202)467-2910. E-mail: jlabella@appanet.org. Website: www.appanet.org. **Contact:** Jeanne LaBella, editor. **60% freelance written.** Prefers to work with published/established writers. Bimonthly trade journal. Estab. 1942. **Pays on acceptance.** Publishes ms an average of 3 months after acceptance. Byline given. Accepts queries by mail, e-mail, fax. Responds in 6 months to queries. Sample copy and writer's guidelines free.

Nonfiction Features on municipal and other local publicly owned electric utilities. **Pays $600 and up.**

Photos Reviews electronic photos (minimum 300 dpi at reproduction size), transparencies, slides, and prints.

Tips "We look for writers who are familiar with energy policy issues."

$ $ $ TEXAS CO-OP POWER

Texas Electric Cooperatives, Inc., 2550 S. IH-35, Austin TX 78704. (512)454-0311. Website: www.texascoopower.com. Editor: Kaye Northcott. Managing Editor: Carol Moczygemba. **50% freelance written.** Monthly magazine covering rural and suburban Texas life, people, and places. "*Texas Co-op Power* provides 950,000 households and businesses educational and technical information about electric cooperatives in a high-quality and entertaining format to promote the general welfare of cooperatives, their member-owners, and the areas in which they serve." Estab. 1948. Circ. 950,000. **Pays on acceptance.** Publishes ms an average of 6 months after acceptance. Byline given. Buys first, electronic rights. Editorial lead time 3 months. Submit seasonal material 6 months in advance. Accepts queries by mail, e-mail, fax. Accepts simultaneous submissions. Responds in 1 month to queries; 2 months to mss. Sample copy online. Writer's guidelines for #10 SASE.

Nonfiction General interest, historical/nostalgic, interview/profile, photo feature, travel. **Buys 30 mss/year.** Query with published clips. Length: 1,000-2,000 words. **Pays $400-1,000.** Sometimes pays expenses of writers on assignment.

Photos State availability with submission. Reviews transparencies, prints. Buys one-time rights. Negotiates payment individually. Identification of subjects, model releases required.

Tips "We're looking for Texas-related, rural-based articles, often first-person, always lively and interesting."

N $ $ UTILITY AND TELECOM FLEETS

Practical Communications, Inc., 2615 Three Oaks Rd., Suite 1B, Cary IL 60013. (847)639-2200. Fax: (847)639-9542. E-mail: cbirkland@truklink.com. Website: www.utilityfleets.com. **Contact:** Carol Birkland, editor. **20% freelance written.** published 8 times/year magazine for fleet managers and maintenance supervisors for electric gas and water utilities, telephone, interconnect and cable TV companies, public works departments and related contractors. "Case history/application features are also welcome." Estab. 1987. Circ. 18,000. Pays on publication. Publishes ms an average of 1 month after acceptance. Byline given. Buys all rights. Submit seasonal material 2 months in advance. Accepts queries by e-mail. Responds in 2 months to mss. Sample copy and writer's guidelines free.

Nonfiction How-to (ways for performing fleet maintenance/improving management skills/vehicle tutorials), technical, case history/application features. No advertorials in which specific product or company is promoted. **Buys 4-5 mss/year.** Query with published clips. Length: 1,000-2,800 words. **Pays 30¢/word if experienced in auto writing; 20¢/word if not.**

Photos Prefers high resolution, electronic images. Send photos with submission. Reviews contact sheets, negatives, 3×5 transparencies, prints. Buys one-time rights. Offers no additional payment for photos accepted with ms. Captions required.

Tips "Working with a utility or telephone company and gathering information about a construction, safety or fleet project is the best approach for a freelancer."

ENGINEERING & TECHNOLOGY

$ $ $ CABLING NETWORKING SYSTEMS

(formerly *Cabling Systems*), Southam, Inc., 1450 Don Mills Rd., Don Mills ON M3B 2X7, Canada. (416)442-2124. Fax: (416)442-2214. E-mail: pbarker@cnsmagazine.com. Website: www.cablingsystems.com. **Contact:** Paul Barker. **50% freelance written.** Magazine published 8 times/year covering structured cabling/telecommunications industry. "*Cabling Systems* is written for engineers, designers, contractors, and end users who design, specify, purchase, install, test and maintain structured cabling and telecommunications products and systems."

Estab. 1998. Circ. 11,000. Pays on publication. Publishes ms an average of 1 month after acceptance. Byline given. Buys all rights. Editorial lead time 3 months. Submit seasonal material 1 month in advance. Accepts queries by mail, e-mail, phone. Accepts simultaneous submissions. Sample copy online. Writer's guidelines free.

Nonfiction Technical (case studies, features). "No reprints or previously written articles. All articles are assigned by editor based on query or need of publication." **Buys 12 mss/year.** Query with published clips. Length: 1,500-2,500 words. **Pays 40-50¢/word.** Sometimes pays expenses of writers on assignment.

Photos State availability with submission. Reviews contact sheets, prints. Negotiates payment individually. Captions, identification of subjects required.

Columns/Departments Focus on Engineering/Design, Focus on Installation, Focus on Maintenance/Testing, all 1,500 words. **Buys 7 mss/year.** Query with published clips. **Pays 40-50¢/word.**

Tips "Visit our website to see back issues, and visit links on our website for background."

$ $ $ CANADIAN CONSULTING ENGINEER

Business Information Group, 1450 Don Mills Rd., Toronto ON M3B 2X7, Canada. (416)442-2266. Fax: (416)442-2214. E-mail: bparsons@ccemag.com. Website: www.canadianconsultingengineer.com. **Contact:** Bronwen Parsons, editor. **20% freelance written.** Bimonthly magazine covering consulting engineering in private practice. Estab. 1958. Circ. 8,900. Pays on publication. Publishes ms an average of 4 months after acceptance. Byline given depending on length of story. Offers 50% kill fee. Buys first North American serial rights. Editorial lead time 6 months. Responds in 3 months to mss. Sample copy for free.

• Canadian content only.

Nonfiction Historical/nostalgic, new product, technical, engineering/construction projects, environmental/construction issues. **Buys 8-10 mss/year.** Length: 300-1,500 words. **Pays $200-1,000 (Canadian).** Sometimes pays expenses of writers on assignment.

Photos State availability with submission. Buys one-time rights. Negotiates payment individually.

Columns/Departments Export (selling consulting engineering services abroad); Management (managing consulting engineering businesses); On-Line (trends in CAD systems); Employment. Length: 800 words. **Buys 4 mss/year.** Query with published clips,. **Pays $250-400.**

$ $ $ CAREER RECRUITMENT MEDIA

211 W. Wacker Dr., #900, Chicago IL 60606. (312)525-3100. E-mail: valerie.anderson@careermedia.com. Website: www.careermedia.com. **50% freelance written.** "Recruitment publications for college engineering/computer science/allied health students. Our readers are smart, savvy and hip. The writing must be, too." **Pays on acceptance.** Publishes ms an average of 2 months after acceptance. Byline given. Offers $50 kill fee. Buys all rights. Editorial lead time 2 months. Submit seasonal material 6 months in advance. Accepts queries by mail, e-mail. Accepts simultaneous submissions. Responds in 2 weeks to queries; 3 months to mss. Sample copy and writer's guidelines free.

Nonfiction Book excerpts, exposé, interview/profile, personal experience. Special issues: Minorities; Women. **Buys 40 mss/year.** Send complete ms. Length: 1,500-3,000 words. **Pays $200-800 for assigned articles; $50-300 for unsolicited articles.** Sometimes pays expenses of writers on assignment.

Photos Send photos with submission. Reviews 3×5 prints. Buys one-time rights. Offers no additional payment for photos accepted with ms. Identification of subjects required.

Columns/Departments Industry Focus (analysis of hiring market within particular industry), 1,500 words. **Buys 6 mss/year.** Query. **Pays $200-300.**

Tips "Know the hiring market for entry-level professionals and be able to communicate to college students at their level."

N $ $ COMPOSITES FABRICATION MAGAZINE

The Official Publication of the American Composites Manufacturers Association, American Composites Manufacturers Association, 1010 N. Glebe Rd., Suite 450, Arlington VA 22201. (703)525-0511. Fax: (703)525-0743. E-mail: arusnak@acmanet.org. Website: www.cfmagazine.org. **Contact:** Andrew Rusnak, editor. Monthly magazine covering any industry that uses reinforced composites: marine, aerospace, infrastructure, automotive, transportation, corrosion, architecture, tub and shower, sports, and recreation. "Primarily, we publish educational pieces, the how-to of the shop environment. We also publish marketing, business trends, and economic forecasts relevant to the composites industry." Estab. 1979. Circ. 12,000. **Pays on acceptance.** Publishes ms an average of 2-3 months after acceptance. Byline given. Buys all rights. Editorial lead time 2 months. Accepts queries by e-mail. Accepts previously published material. Accepts simultaneous submissions. Responds in 1 week to queries; 1 month to mss. Sample copy for free. Writer's guidelines by e-mail.

Nonfiction How-to (composites manufacturing), new product, technical, marketing, related business trends and forecasts. Special issues: "Each January we publish a World Market Report where we cover all niche markets and all geographic areas relevant to the composites industry. Freelance material will be considered strongly for this issue." "No need to query company or personal profiles unless there is an extremely unique or novel angle." **Buys 5-10 mss/year.** Query. Length: 1,500-4,000 words. **Pays 20-40¢/word (negotiable).** Sometimes pays expenses of writers on assignment.

Columns/Departments "We publish columns on HR, relevant government legislation, industry lessons learned, regulatory affairs, and technology. Average word length for columns is 500 words. We would entertain any new column idea that hits hard on industry matters." Query. **Pays $300-350.**

Tips "The best way to break into the magazine is to empathize with the entrepreneurial and technical background of readership, and come up with an exclusive, original, creative story idea. We pride ourselves on not looking or acting like any other trade publication (composites industry or otherwise). Our editor is very open to suggestions, but they must be unique. Don't waste his time with canned articles dressed up to look exclusive. This is the best way to get on the 'immediate rejection list.'"

DESIGN NEWS

Reed Business Information, 275 Washington St., Newton MA 02458-1646. (617)558-4660. Fax: (617)558-4402. E-mail: dnonline@reedbusiness.com. Website: www.designnews.com. Editor: Karen Auguston Field. Magazine published 18 times/year dedicated to reporting on the latest technology that OEM design engineers can use in their jobs. Circ. 170,000. Editorial lead time 4-6 months. Sample copy not available.

ECN ELECTRONIC COMPONENT NEWS

Reed Business Information, 301 Gibraltar Dr., P.O. Box 650, Morris Plains NJ 07950-0650. (973)292-5100. Fax: (973)292-0783. E-mail: akalnoskas@reedbusiness.com. Website: www.ecnmag.com. Editor: Aimee Kalnoskas. Managing Editor: Jean Miller. Monthly magazine. Provides design engineers and engineering management in electronics OEM with a monthly update on new products and literature. Circ. 131,052. Editorial lead time 2 months. Sample copy not available.

N $ $ FLOW CONTROL

The Magazine of Fluid Handling Technology, Witter Publishing Corp., 20 Commerce St., Flemington NJ 08822. (908)788-0343 ext. 124. Fax: (908)788-3782. E-mail: mmigliore@witterpublishing.com. Website: www.flowcontrolnetwork.com. Managing Editor: Annu Mangat. **Contact:** Matt Migliore, editor. **90% freelance written.** Monthly magazine covering fluid handling systems. "*Flow Control* is the technology resource for the fluid handling industry's critical disciplines of control, containment and measurement. *Flow Control* provides solutions for system design, operational and maintenance challenges in all process and OEM applications." Estab. 1995. Circ. 40,000. Pays on publication. Publishes ms an average of 1 month after acceptance. Byline given. Buys all rights. Accepts queries by mail, e-mail, fax, phone. Writer's guidelines online.

Nonfiction How-to (design or maintenance), technical. No glorified product releases. **Buys 18 mss/year.** Query with published clips or send complete ms. Length: 1,000-2,500 words. **Pays $250-350.** Sometimes pays writers with contributor copies or other premiums.

Photos Offers no additional payment for photos accepted with ms. Captions, identification of subjects required.

Columns/Departments Query with published clips or send complete ms. **Pays $250.**

Tips "Anyone involved in flow control technology and/or applications may submit a manuscript for publication. Articles should be informative and analytical, containing sufficient technical data to support statements and material presented. Articles should not promote any individual product, service, or company. Case history features, describing the use of flow control technologies in specific applications, are welcomed."

LASER FOCUS WORLD MAGAZINE

PennWell, 98 Spit Brook Rd., Nashua NH 03062-2801. (603)891-0123. Fax: (603)891-0574. E-mail: carols@pennwell.com. Website: www.laserfocusworld.com. Publisher: Christine Shaw. Group Editorial Director: Stephen G. Anderson. **Contact:** Carol Settino, managing editor. **1% freelance written.** Monthly magazine for physicists, scientists, and engineers involved in the research and development, design, manufacturing, and applications of lasers, laser systems, and all other segments of optoelectronic technologies. Estab. 1968. Circ. 66,000. Publishes ms an average of 6 months after acceptance. Byline given unless anonymity requested. Buys all rights. Accepts queries by mail, e-mail, fax, phone. Responds in 1 month to queries. Sample copy and writer's guidelines free. Writer's guidelines online.

Nonfiction Lasers, laser systems, fiberoptics, optics, detectors, sensors, imaging, and other optoelectronic materials, components, instrumentation, and systems. "Each article should serve our reader's need by either stimulating ideas, increasing technical competence, or improving design capabilities in the following areas: natural light and radiation sources, artificial light and radiation sources, light modulators, optical materials and components, image detectors, energy detectors, information displays, image processing, information storage and processing, subsystem and system testing, support equipment, and other related areas. No flighty prose, material not written for our readership, or irrelevant material. Query first with a clear statement and outline of why the article would be important to our readers.

Photos Drawings: Rough drawings acceptable, are finished by staff technical illustrator. Send photos with submission. Reviews 4×5 color transparencies, 8×10 b&w glossies.

Tips "The writer has a better chance of breaking in at our publication with short articles because shorter articles are easier to schedule, but must address more carefully our requirements for technical coverage. Most of our submitted materials come from technical experts in the areas we cover. The most frequent mistake made by writers in completing articles for us is that the articles are too commercial, i.e., emphasize a given product or technology from one company. Also articles are not the right technical depth, too thin, or too scientific."

$ $LIGHTING DESIGN & APPLICATION

Illuminating Engineering Society of North America, 120 Wall St., 17th Floor, New York NY 10005-4001. (212)248-5000. Fax: (212)248-5017. E-mail: cbeardsley@iesna.org. Website: www.iesna.org. **Contact:** Paul Tarricone, editor. **20% freelance written.** Monthly magazine. "LD&A is geared to professionals in lighting design and the lighting field in architecture, retail, entertainment, etc. From designers to educators to sales reps, LD&A has a very unique, dedicated, and well-educated audience." Estab. 1971. Circ. 10,000. **Pays on acceptance.** Publishes ms an average of 4 months after acceptance. Byline given. Buys first rights. Editorial lead time 4 months. Submit seasonal material 6 months in advance. Accepts queries by mail, e-mail, fax, phone. Accepts simultaneous submissions. Responds in 2 weeks to queries. Sample copy for free.

Nonfiction "Every year we have entertainment, outdoor, retail and arts, and exhibits issues. Historical/nostalgic, how-to, opinion, personal experience, photo feature, technical. "No articles blatantly promoting a product, company, or individual." **Buys 6-10 mss/year.** Query. Length: 1,500-2,200 words. **Pays $300-400 for assigned articles.**

Photos Send photos with submission. Reviews 4×5 transparencies. Offers no additional payment for photos accepted with ms. Captions required.

Columns/Departments Essay by Invitation (industry trends), 1,200 words. Query. **Does not pay for columns.**

Tips "Most of our features detail the ins and outs of a specific lighting project. From Ricky Martin at the Grammys to the Getty Museum, LD&A gives its readers an in-depth look at how the designer(s) reached their goals."

$ $ $MINNESOTA TECHNOLOGY

Inside Technology and Manufacturing Business, Minnesota Technology, Inc., 111 Third Ave. S., Minneapolis MN 55401. (612)373-2900. Fax: (612)339-5214. E-mail: editor@mntech.org. Website: mntechnologymag.com. **Contact:** Chris Mikko, editor. **75% freelance written.** Magazine published 5 times/year. "Minnesota Technology is read 5 times a year by owners and top management of Minnesota's technology and manufacturing companies. The magazine covers technology trends and issues, global trade, management techniques, and finance. We profile new and growing companies, new products, and the innovators and entrepreneurs of Minnesota's technology sector." Estab. 1991. Circ. 20,000. **Pays on acceptance.** Publishes ms an average of 3 months after acceptance. Byline given. Offers 25% kill fee. Buys first North American serial rights. Editorial lead time 2 months. Submit seasonal material 1 year in advance. Accepts queries by mail, e-mail, fax. Responds in 1 month to queries. Sample copy for 9×12 SAE and 5 first-class stamps. Writer's guidelines online.

Nonfiction General interest, how-to, interview/profile. **Buys 45 mss/year.** Query with published clips. Length: 500-2,000 words. **Pays $150-1,000.**

Columns/Departments Feature Well (Q&A format, provocative ideas from busines and industry leaders), 2,000 words; Up Front (mini profiles, anecdotal news items), 250-500 words. **Buys 30 mss/year.** Query with published clips. **Pays $150-300.**

▣ The online magazine includes writer's guidelines. Contact: Linda Ball, online editor.

Tips "Query with ideas for short profiles of fascinating Minnesota technology people and business written to interest even the most nontechnical person."

Ⓝ $ $MINORITY ENGINEER

An Equal Opportunity Career Publication for Professional and Graduating Minority Engineers, Equal Opportunity Publications, Inc., 445 Broad Hollow Rd., Suite 425, Melville NY 11747. (631)421-9421. Fax: (516)421-0359. E-mail: info@eop.com. Website: www.eop.com. **Contact:** James Schneider, editor. **60% freelance written.** Prefers to work with published/established writers. Triannual magazine covering career guidance for minority engineering students and minority professional engineers. Estab. 1969. Circ. 15,000. Pays on publication. Publishes ms an average of 6 months after acceptance. Byline given. Buys first rights. Accepts queries by mail, e-mail, fax, phone. Accepts simultaneous submissions. Sample copy and writer's guidelines for 9×12 SAE with 5 first-class stamps.

Nonfiction "We're interested in articles dealing with career guidance and job opportunities for minority engineers." Book excerpts, general interest (on specific minority engineering concerns), how-to (land a job, keep a job, etc.), interview/profile (minority engineer role models), opinion (problems of ethnic minorities), personal experience (student and career experiences), technical (on career fields offering opportunities for minority engineers), articles on job search techniques, role models. No general information. Query. Length: 1,000-2,000 words. **Pays 10¢/word, $15/photo used.** Sometimes pays expenses of writers on assignment.

Reprints Send ms with rights for sale noted and information about when and where the material previously appeared. Pays 100% of amount paid for an original article.

Photos State availability with submission. Reviews transparencies, Prints. Buys all rights. Pays $15. Captions required.

Tips "Articles should focus on career guidance, role model and industry prospects for minority engineers. Prefer articles related to careers, not politically or socially sensitive."

N $ $ WOMAN ENGINEER

An Equal Opportunity Career Publication for Graduating Women and Experienced Professionals, Equal Opportunity Publications, Inc., 445 Broad Hollow Rd., Suite 425, Melville NY 11747. (631)421-9421. Fax: (631)421-0359. E-mail: jschneider@eop.com. Website: www.eop.com. **Contact:** James Schneider, editorial director. **60% freelance written.** Works with a small number of new/unpublished writers each year. Triannual magazine covering career guidance for women engineering students and professional women engineers. Estab. 1968. Circ. 16,000. Pays on publication. Publishes ms an average of 1 year after acceptance. Byline given. Buys first North American serial rights. Accepts queries by e-mail. Responds in 3 months to queries. Sample copy and writer's guidelines free.

Nonfiction "Interested in articles dealing with career guidance and job opportunities for women engineers. Looking for manuscripts showing how to land an engineering position and advance professionally. We want features on job-search techniques, engineering disciplines offering career opportunities to women; companies with career advancement opportunities for women; problems facing women engineers and how to cope with such problems; and role-model profiles of successful women engineers, especially in major U.S. corporations." Query. Length: 1,000-2,500 words. **Pays 10¢/word.**

Photos Reviews color slides but will accept b&w. Buys all rights. Pays $15. Captions, identification of subjects required.

Tips "We are looking for 800-1,000 word first-person 'As I See It, personal perspectives.'"

ENTERTAINMENT & THE ARTS

$ $ $ AMERICAN CINEMATOGRAPHER

The International Journal of Film & Digital Production Techniques, American Society of Cinematographers, 1782 N. Orange Dr., Hollywood CA 90028. (323)969-4333. Fax: (323)876-4973. E-mail: stephen@theasc.com. Website: cinematographer.com. Senior Editor: Rachael Bosley. **Contact:** Stephen Pizzello, editor. **90% freelance written.** Monthly magazine covering cinematography (motion picture, TV, music video, commercial). "*American Cinematographer* is a trade publication devoted to the art and craft of cinematography. Our readers are predominantly film-industry professionals." Estab. 1919. Circ. 45,000. Pays on publication. Publishes ms an average of 2-3 months after acceptance. Byline given. Offers 50% kill fee. Buys all rights. Editorial lead time 2 months. Submit seasonal material 3 months in advance. Accepts queries by mail, e-mail, phone. Responds in 2 weeks to queries; 2 months to mss. Sample copy and writer's guidelines free.

Nonfiction Interview/profile, new product, technical. No reviews, opinion pieces. **Buys 20-25 mss/year.** Query with published clips. Length: 1,500-4,000 words. **Pays $600-1,200.** Pays in contributor copies if the writer is promoting his/her own product or company. Sometimes pays expenses of writers on assignment.

Tips "Familiarity with the technical side of film production and the ability to present that information in an articulate fashion to our audience are crucial."

$ $ BOXOFFICE MAGAZINE

RLD Publishing Co., 155 S. El Molino Ave., Suite 100, Pasadena CA 91101. (626)396-0250. Fax: (626)396-0248. E-mail: editorial@boxoffice.com. Website: www.boxoffice.com. Editor-in-chief: Kim Williamson. **Contact:** Christine James, managing editor. **15% freelance written.** Monthly magazine about the motion picture industry for members of the film industry: theater owners, film producers, directors, financiers, and allied industries. Estab. 1920. Circ. 8,000. Pays on publication. Publishes ms an average of 3 months after acceptance. Byline given. Buys all rights, including electronic publishing. Submit seasonal material 5 months in advance. Accepts queries by mail, e-mail, fax. Sample copy for $5.

O— *"Boxoffice Magazine* is particularly interested in freelance writers who can write business articles on the exhibition industry or technical writers who are familiar with projection/sound equipment and new technologies such as digital cinema."

Nonfiction "We are a general news magazine about the motion picture and theater industry and are looking for stories about trends, developments, problems, or opportunities facing the industry. Almost any story will be considered, including corporate profiles, but we don't want gossip or celebrity coverage." Book excerpts, essays, interview/profile, new product, personal experience, photo feature, technical, investigative "all regarding movie theater business." Query with published clips. Length: 800-2,500 words. **Pays 10¢/word.**

Photos State availability with submission. Reviews prints, slides. Pays $10 maximum. Captions required.

◼ The online version of this magazine carries original content. Contact: Kim Williamson.

Tips "Request a sample copy, indicating you read about *Boxoffice* in *Writer's Market*. Write a clear, comprehensive outline of the proposed story, and enclose a résumé and clip samples."

$ $ CAMPUS ACTIVITIES

Cameo Publishing Group, P.O. Box 509, Prosperity SC 29127. (800)728-2950. Fax: (803)321-2049. E-mail: cameo publishing@mac.com. Website: www.campusactivitiesmagazine.com or www.cameopublishing.com. Editor: Ian Kirby. Managing Editor: Laura Moore. **Contact:** WC Kirby, publisher. **75% freelance written.** Magazine published 8 times/year covering entertainment on college campuses. *Campus Activities* goes to entertainment buyers on every campus in the U.S. Features stories on artists (national and regional), speakers, and the programs at individual schools. Estab. 1991. Circ. 9,872. Pays on publication. Publishes ms an average of 2 months after acceptance. Byline given. Offers 15% kill fee if accepted and not run. Buys first, second serial (reprint), electronic rights. Editorial lead time 2 months. Submit seasonal material 2 months in advance. Accepts queries by mail, e-mail, fax. Accepts simultaneous submissions. Responds in 1 month to queries; 2 months to mss. Sample copy for $3.50. Writer's guidelines free.

Nonfiction Interview/profile, photo feature. Accepts no unsolicited articles. **Buys 40 mss/year.** Query. Length: 1,400-3,000 words. **Pays 13¢/word.** Sometimes pays expenses of writers on assignment.

Photos State availability with submission. Reviews contact sheets, negatives, 3×5 transparencies, 8×10 prints, electronic media at 300 dpi or higher. Buys one-time rights. Negotiates payment individually. Identification of subjects required.

Tips "Writers who have ideas, proposals, and special project requests should contact the publisher prior to any commitment to work on such a story. The publisher welcomes innovative and creative ideas for stories and works with writers on such proposals which have significant impact on our readers."

$ $ DANCE TEACHER

The Practical Magazine of Dance, Lifestyle Media, Inc., 250 W. 57th St., Suite 420, New York NY 10107. (212)265-8890, ext. 20. Fax: (212)265-8908. E-mail: csims@lifestyleventures.com. Website: www.dance-teache r.com. **Contact:** Caitlin Sims, editor. **80% freelance written.** Monthly magazine. "Our readers are professional dance educators, business persons, and related professionals in all forms of dance." Estab. 1979. Circ. 8,000. Pays on publication. Publishes ms an average of 3 months after acceptance. Byline given. Negotiates rights and permission to reprint on request. Submit seasonal material 6 months in advance. Accepts queries by mail, e-mail, fax, phone. Responds in 3 months to mss. Sample copy for 9×12 SAE and 6 first-class stamps. Writer's guidelines online.

Nonfiction How-to (teach, business), interview/profile, new product, personal experience, photo feature. Special issues: Summer Programs (January); Music & More (July); Costumes and Production Preview (November); College/Training Schools (December). No PR or puff pieces. All articles must be well researched. **Buys 50 mss/ year.** Query. Length: 700-2,000 words. **Pays $100-250.**

Photos Send photos with submission. Reviews contact sheets, negatives, transparencies, prints. Limited photo budget.

◼ The online magazine carries original content. Contact: Caitlin Sims.

Tips "Read several issues—particularly seasonal. Stay within writer's guidelines."

$ $ DRAMATICS MAGAZINE

Educational Theatre Association, 2343 Auburn Ave., Cincinnati OH 45219-2815. (513)421-3900. Fax: (513)421-7077. E-mail: dcorathers@edta.org. Website: www.edta.org. **Contact:** Donald Corathers, editor-in-chief. **70% freelance written.** Monthly magazine for theater arts students, teachers, and others interested in theater arts education. "*Dramatics* is designed to provide serious, committed young theater students and their teachers with the skills and knowledge they need to make better theater; to be a resource that will help high school juniors and seniors make an informed decision about whether to pursue a career in theater, and about how to do so; and to prepare high school students to be knowledgeable, appreciative audience members for the rest of their lives." Estab. 1929. Circ. 37,000. **Pays on acceptance.** Publishes ms an average of 3 months after acceptance. Byline given. Buys first North American serial rights. Submit seasonal material 3 months in advance. Accepts queries by mail, e-mail, fax. Accepts previously published material. Accepts simultaneous submissions. Responds in 3 months to queries; longer than 3 months on unsolicited mss. Sample copy for 9×12 SAE with 5 first-class stamps. Writer's guidelines online.

> ⊶ "The best way to break in is to know our audience—drama students, teachers, and others interested in theater—and to write for them."

Nonfiction How-to (technical theater, directing, acting, etc.), humor, inspirational, interview/profile, photo feature, technical. **Buys 30 mss/year.** Send complete ms. Length: 750-3,000 words. **Pays $50-400.** Sometimes pays expenses of writers on assignment.

Reprints Send tearsheet, photocopy, or typed ms with rights for sale noted and information about when and where the material previously appeared. Pays up to 75% of amount paid for original.

Photos Query. Purchased with accompanying ms. Reviews transparencies. Total price for ms usually includes payment for photos.

Fiction Drama (one-act and full-length plays). Prefers unpublished scripts that have been produced at least once. "No plays for children, Christmas plays, or plays written with no attention paid to the conventions of theater." **Buys 5-9 mss/year.** Send complete ms. **Pays $100-400.**

Tips "Writers who have some practical experience in theater, especially in technical areas, have a leg-up here, but we'll work with anybody who has a good idea. Some freelancers have become regular contributors. Others ignore style suggestions included in our writer's guidelines."

$ $ $ EMMY MAGAZINE

Academy of Television Arts & Sciences, 5220 Lankershim Blvd., North Hollywood CA 91601-3109. (818)754-2800. Fax: (818)761-8524. E-mail: emmymag@emmys.org. Website: www.emmys.tv. **Contact:** Gail Polevoi, editor. **90% freelance written.** Prefers to work with published/established writers. Bimonthly magazine on television for TV professionals. Circ. 14,000. Pays on publication or within 6 months. Publishes ms an average of 4 months after acceptance. Byline given. Offers 25% kill fee. Buys first North American serial rights. Accepts queries by mail, e-mail. Responds in 1 month to queries. Sample copy for 9×12 SAE and 6 first-class stamps. Writer's guidelines online.

Nonfiction Articles on contemporary issues, trends, and VIPs (especially those behind the scenes) in broadcast and cable TV; programming and new technology. "Looking for profiles of fascinating people who work 'below the line' in television. Also, always looking for new writers who understand technology and new media and can write about it in an engaging manner. We require TV industry expertise and clear, lively writing." Query with published clips. Length: 1,500-2,000 words. **Pays $1,000-1,200.**

Columns/Departments Most written by regular contributors, but newcomers can break in with filler items in In the Mix or short profiles in Labors of Love. Length: 250-500 words, depending on department. Query with published clips. **Pays $250-500.**

Tips "Please review recent issues before querying us. Query with published, television-related clips. No fanzine, academic, or nostalgic approaches, please. Demonstrate experience in covering the business of television and your ability to write in a lively and compelling manner about programming trends and new technology. Identify fascinating people behind the scenes, not just in the executive suites but in all ranks of the industry."

$ $ RELEASE PRINT

The Magazine of Film Arts Foundation, Film Arts Foundation, 145 9th St., Suite 101, San Francisco CA 94103. (415)552-8760. Fax: (415)552-0882. E-mail: writersguidelines@filmarts.org. Website: www.filmarts.org. Managing Editor: Shari Kizirian. **Contact:** Editor. **80% freelance written.** Monthly magazine covering U.S. independent filmmaking. "We have a knowledgeable readership of film and videomakers. They are interested in the financing, production, exhibition, and distribution of independent films and videos. They are interested in practical and technical issues and, to a lesser extent, aesthetic ones." Estab. 1977. Circ. 5,000. Pays on publication. Publishes ms an average of 3 months after acceptance. Byline given. Buys all rights for commissioned works. For works submitted on spec, buys first rights and requests acknowledgement of Release Print in any subsequent publication. Editorial lead time 4 months. Accepts queries by mail. Responds in 3 weeks to queries; 2 months to mss. Sample copy for $5 (payable to Film Arts Foundation) and 9×12 SASE with $1.52 postage. Writer's guidelines by e-mail.

> ⊶ Break in with a proposal for an article or interview of an American experimental, documentary or very low budget feature film/video maker with ties to the San Francisco Bay area (or an upcoming screening in this area). Submit at least 4 months prior to publication date.

Nonfiction Interview/profile, technical, book recommendations, case studies. No film criticism or reviews. **Buys 30-35 mss/year.** Query. Length: 500-2,000 words. Sometimes pays expenses of writers on assignment.

Photos Send photos with submission. Reviews prints. Buys one-time rights. Offers no additional payment for photos accepted with ms. Identification of subjects required.

Columns/Departments Book Reviews (independent film & video), 800-1,000 words. **Buys 4 mss/year.** Query. **Pays 10¢/word.**

$SCREEN MAGAZINE

Screen Enterprises, Inc., 222 W. Ontario St., Suite 500, Chicago IL 60610. (312)640-0800. Fax: (312)640-1928. E-mail: editorial@screenmag.com. Website: www.screenmag.com. **Contact:** Julie Mynatt, editor. **5% freelance written.** Biweekly Chicago-based trade magazine covering advertising and film production in the Midwest and national markets. "*Screen* is written for Midwest producers (and other creatives involved) of commercials, AV, features, independent corporate and multimedia." Estab. 1979. Circ. 15,000. Pays on publication. Publishes ms an average of a few weeks after acceptance. Byline given. Makes work-for-hire assignments. Accepts queries by e-mail. Responds in 3 weeks to queries. Sample copy online.

Nonfiction Interview/profile, new product, technical. "No general AV; nothing specific to other markets; no no-brainers or opinion." **Buys 26 mss/year.** Query with published clips. Length: 750-1,500 words. **Pays $50.**

Photos Send photos with submission. Reviews prints. Offers no additional payment for photos accepted with ms. Captions required.

Tips "Our readers want to know facts and figures. They want to know the news about a company or an individual. We provide exclusive news of this market, in as much depth as space allows without being boring, with lots of specific information and details. We write knowledgably about the market we serve. We recognize the film/video-making process is a difficult one because it 1) is often technical, 2) has implications not immediately discerned."

$SOUTHERN THEATRE

Southeastern Theatre Conference, 3309 Northampton Dr., Greensboro NC 27408. (336)294-3292. Fax: (336)292-6041. E-mail: deanna@setc.org. Website: www.setc.org. **Contact:** Deanna Thompson, editor. **100% freelance written.** Quarterly magazine covering theatre. "*Southern Theatre* is the magazine covering all aspects of theater in the Southeast, from innovative theater companies to important trends to people making a difference in the region. All stories must be written in a popular magazine style but with subject matter appropriate for theater professionals (not the general public). The audience includes members of the Southeastern Theatre Conference, founded in 1949 and the nation's largest regional theater organization. These members include individuals involved in professional, community, college/university, children's and secondary school theater. The magazine also is purchased by more than 100 libraries." Estab. 1962. Circ. 3,600. **Pays on acceptance.** Publishes ms an average of 3 months after acceptance. Byline given. Buys first North American serial, first, one-time, second serial (reprint), electronic rights. Editorial lead time 3 months. Submit seasonal material 6 months in advance. Accepts queries by mail, e-mail. Responds in 6 weeks to queries; 3 months to mss. Sample copy for $6. Writer's guidelines online.

Nonfiction Looking for stories on design/technology, playwriting, acting, directing, all with a Southeastern connection. General interest (innovative theaters and theater programs; trend stories), interview/profile (people making a difference in Southeastern theater). Special issues: Playwriting (fall issue, all stories submitted by January 1). No scholarly articles. **Buys 15-20 mss/year.** Query with or without published clips or send complete ms. Length: 1,000-3,000 words. **Pays $50 for feature stories.** Pays in contributor copies for book reviews, sidebars, and other short stories.

Photos State availability of or send photos with submission. Reviews transparencies, prints. Offers no additional payment for photos accepted with ms. Captions, identification of subjects, model releases required.

Columns/Departments Outside the Box (innovative solutions to problems faced by designers and technicians), 800-1,000 words; Words, Words, Words (reviews of books on theater), 400-550 words. **Buys 2-4 mss/year.** Query or send complete ms. **No payment for columns.**

Tips "Look for a theater or theater person in your area that is doing something different or innovative that would be of interest to others in the profession, then write about that theater or person in a compelling way. We also are looking for well-written trend stories (talk to theaters in your area about trends that are affecting them), and we especially like stories that help our readers do their jobs more effectively. Send an e-mail detailing a well-developed story idea, and ask if we're interested."

FARM

AGRICULTURAL EQUIPMENT

$ $IMPLEMENT & TRACTOR

Agri USA, 2302 W. First St., Cedar Falls IA 50613. (319)277-3599. Fax: (319)277-3783. E-mail: mshepherd@cfu.net. Website: www.agra-usa.com. **Contact:** Mary Shepherd, editor. **10% freelance written.** Bimonthly magazine covering farm equipment, light construction, commercial turf, and lawn and garden equipment. *"Implement & Tractor* offers technical and business news for agricultural equipment dealers, manufacturers, consultants and others involved as suppliers to the industry. Writers must know U.S. and global machinery and the industry trends." Estab. 1895. Circ. 7,000. Pays on publication. Publishes ms an average of 3-4 months after acceptance. Byline given. Buys all rights. Editorial lead time 2 months. Accepts queries by mail, e-mail, fax. Responds in 2 months to queries. Sample copy for $6.

Nonfiction Interview/profile (dealer or manufacturer), review machinery with photos. No general farm machinery articles or farmer profiles articles. Query with published clips. Length: 600-1,200 words. **Pays $100-250.**

Photos State availability with submission. Reviews contact sheets. Buys one-time rights. Offers no additional payment for photos accepted with ms. Captions, identification of subjects required.

Tips "Know the equipment industry, have an engineer's outlook for analyzing machinery and a writer's skills to communicate that information. Technical background is helpful, as is mechanical aptitude."

CROPS & SOIL MANAGEMENT

$ $ AMERICAN FRUIT GROWER

Meister Media Worldwide, 37733 Euclid Ave., Willoughby OH 44094. (440)942-2000. Fax: (440)942-0662. E-mail: afg_edit@meistermedia.com. Website: www.fruitgrower.com. **Contact:** Brian Sparks, managing editor. **3% freelance written.** Annual magazine covering commercial fruit growing. "How-to" articles are best. Estab. 1880. Circ. 44,000. Pays on publication. Publishes ms an average of 4 months after acceptance. Byline given. Buys first rights. Editorial lead time 2 months. Submit seasonal material 4 months in advance. Accepts queries by mail, e-mail, fax, phone. Responds in 2 weeks to queries; 2 months to mss. Sample copy for free. Writer's guidelines free.

Nonfiction How-to (better grow fruit crops). **Buys 6-10 mss/year.** Query with published clips or send complete ms. Length: 800-1,200 words. **Pays $200-250.** Sometimes pays expenses of writers on assignment.

Photos Send photos with submission. Reviews prints, slides. Buys one-time rights. Negotiates payment individually.

$ $ COTTON GROWER MAGAZINE

Meister Media Worldwide, 65 Germantown Court, #202, Cordova TN 38018. (901)756-8822. Fax: (901)756-8879. E-mail: wlspencer@meistermedia.com. Editor: Bill Spencer. **Contact:** Frank Giles, senior editor. **5% freelance written.** Monthly magazine covering cotton production, cotton markets and related subjects. Readers are mostly cotton producers who seek information on production practices, equipment and products related to cotton. Estab. 1901. Circ. 43,000. **Pays on acceptance.** Publishes ms an average of 2 months after acceptance. Byline given. Buys first rights. Editorial lead time 2 months. Submit seasonal material 2 months in advance. Accepts queries by mail, e-mail, fax, phone. Accepts simultaneous submissions. Sample copy for free. Writer's guidelines not available.

Nonfiction Interview/profile, new product, photo feature, technical. No fiction or humorous pieces. **Buys 5-10 mss/year.** Query with published clips. Length: 500-800 words. **Pays $200-400.** Sometimes pays expenses of writers on assignment.

Photos State availability with submission. Reviews transparencies. Buys all rights. Offers no additional payment for photos accepted with ms. Captions, identification of subjects required.

$ THE FRUIT GROWERS NEWS

Great American Publishing, P.O. Box 128, Sparta MI 49345. (616)887-9008. Fax: (616)887-2666. E-mail: editor@fruitgrowersnews.com. Website: www.fruitgrowersnews.com. Publisher: Matt McCallum. **Contact:** Kimberly Warren, associate editor. **25% freelance written.** Monthly tabloid covering agriculture. "Our objective is to provide commercial fruit growers of all sizes with information to help them succeed." Estab. 1970. Circ. 28,000. Pays on publication. Publishes ms an average of 2 months after acceptance. Makes work-for-hire assignments. Editorial lead time 1 month. Submit seasonal material 1 month in advance. Accepts queries by mail, e-mail, fax. Accepts simultaneous submissions. Responds in 2 weeks to queries; 1 month to mss. Sample copy for free.

Nonfiction Essays, general interest, how-to, interview/profile, new product, opinion, technical. No advertorials, other "puff pieces." **Buys 72 mss/year.** Query with published clips. Length: 800-1,200 words. **Pays $100-125.** Sometimes pays expenses of writers on assignment.

Photos Send photos with submission. Reviews prints. Buys one-time rights. Offers $15/photo. Captions required.

$ GRAIN JOURNAL

Country Publications, Inc., 3065 Pershing Ct., Decatur IL 62526. (217)877-8660. Fax: (217)877-6647. E-mail: ed@grainnet.com. Website: www.grainnet.com. **Contact:** Ed Zdrojewski, editor. **5% freelance written.** Bimonthly magazine covering grain handling and merchandising. *"Grain Journal* serves the North American grain industry, from the smallest country grain elevators and feed mills to major export terminals." Estab. 1972. Circ. 12,000. Pays on publication. Publishes ms an average of 2 months after acceptance. Byline sometimes given. Buys first rights. Editorial lead time 2 months. Submit seasonal material 2 months in advance. Accepts simultaneous submissions. Sample copy for free.

Nonfiction How-to, interview/profile, new product, technical. Query. Length: 750 words maximum. **Pays $100.**

Photos Send photos with submission. Reviews contact sheets, negatives, transparencies, 3×5 prints. Buys one-time rights. Offers $50-100/photo. Captions, identification of subjects required.

Tips "Call with your idea. We'll let you know if it is suitable for our publication."

$ ONION WORLD

Columbia Publishing, P.O. Box 9036, Yakima WA 98909-0036. (509)248-2452, ext. 152. Fax: (509)248-4056. E-mail: brent@freshcut.com. Website: www.onionworld.net. **Contact:** Brent Clement, managing editor or Carrie Kennington, editor. **25% freelance written.** Monthly magazine covering the world of onion production and marketing for onion growers and shippers. Estab. 1985. Circ. 5,500. Pays on publication. Publishes ms an average of 1 month after acceptance. Byline given. Not copyrighted. Buys first North American serial rights. Submit seasonal material 1 month in advance. Accepts queries by mail, e-mail, fax, phone. Accepts simultaneous submissions. Responds in 1 month to queries. Sample copy for 9×12 SAE and 5 first-class stamps.

- Columbia Publishing also produces *Fresh Cut, The Tomato Magazine, Potato Country, RVgolfer,* and *Carrot Country.*

Nonfiction General interest, historical/nostalgic, interview/profile. **Buys 30 mss/year.** Query. Length: 1,200-1,250 words. **Pays $5/column inch for assigned articles.**

Reprints Send photocopy and information about when and where the material previously appeared. Pays 50% of amount paid for an original article.

Photos Send photos with submission. Buys all rights. Offers no additional payment for photos accepted with ms, unless it's a cover shot. Captions, identification of subjects required.

Tips "Writers should be familiar with growing and marketing onions. We use a lot of feature stories on growers, shippers, and others in the onion trade—what they are doing, their problems, solutions, marketing plans, etc."

$ $ RICE JOURNAL

SpecCom International, Inc., 5808 Faringdon Place, Raleigh NC 27609-3930. (919)872-5040. Fax: (919)876-6531. E-mail: editor@ricejournal.com. Website: www.ricejournal.com. Editor: Mary Ann Rood. **5% freelance written.** Monthly (January-June) magazine covering rice farming. "Articles must discuss rice production practices. Readers are rice farmers. The most accessible article is an on-farm interview with 1 or more farmers who use the featured agronomic practice. Must include photo of the farmer involved in a farming activity." Estab. 1897. Circ. 10,000. Pays on publication. Byline given. Buys first rights. Editorial lead time 2 months. Accepts queries by mail, e-mail, fax. Responds in 2 weeks to queries; 2 months to mss. Sample copy online. Writer's guidelines for #10 SASE.

Nonfiction How-to, personal experience, photo feature, technical, farmer production tips. Special issues: Land Preparation (January); Water Management (February); Weed Control (March); Rice Diseases and Management (April); Insect Control, Tracked Vehicles (May); Harvest, Curing (June). No recipes, cooking. **Buys 2 mss/year.** Query. Length: 600-2,000 words. **Pays $50-400.**

Photos State availability with submission. Buys one-time rights. Offers no additional payment for photos accepted with ms. Captions, identification of subjects required.

$ THE VEGETABLE GROWERS NEWS

Great American Publishing, P.O. Box 128, Sparta MI 49345. (616)887-9008. Fax: (616)887-2666. E-mail: editor@ vegetablegrowersnews.com. Website: www.vegetablegrowersnews.com. Publisher: Matt McCallum. **Contact:** Kimberly Warren, associate editor. **25% freelance written.** Monthly tabloid covering agriculture. "Our objective is to provide commercial vegetable growers of all sizes with information to help them succeed." Estab. 1970. Circ. 28,000. Pays on publication. Publishes ms an average of 2 months after acceptance. Makes work-for-hire assignments. Editorial lead time 1 month. Submit seasonal material 1 month in advance. Accepts queries by mail, e-mail, fax. Accepts simultaneous submissions. Responds in 2 weeks to queries; 1 month to mss. Sample copy for free.

Nonfiction Essays, general interest, how-to, interview/profile, new product, opinion, technical. No advertorials, other "puff pieces." **Buys 72 mss/year.** Query with published clips. Length: 800-1,200 words. **Pays $100-125.** Sometimes pays expenses of writers on assignment.

Photos Send photos with submission. Reviews prints. Buys one-time rights. Offers $15/photo. Captions required.

DAIRY FARMING

N $ DAIRY GOAT JOURNAL

Central Countryside Publications, Ltd., W. 11654 State Hwy. 64, Withee WI 54498. (715)785-7979. Fax: (715)785-7414. E-mail: csymag@tds.net. Website: www.dairygoatjournal.com. **Contact:** Jennifer Schultz, editor. **45% freelance written.** Monthly journal. "We are looking for clear and accurate articles about dairy goat owners, their herds, cheesemaking, and other ways of marketing products. Some readers own two goats; others own 1,500 and are large commercial operations." Estab. 1917. Circ. 8,000, including copies to more than 70 foreign countries. Pays on publication. Byline given.

Nonfiction Information on personalities and on public issues affecting dairy goats and their owners. How-to articles with plenty of practical information. Health and husbandry articles should be written with appropriate experience or academic credentials. **Buys 100 mss/year.** Query with published clips. Length: 750-2,500 words. **Pays $50-150.** Pays expenses of writers on assignment.

Photos Color or b&w. Vertical cover. Goats and/or people. Pays $100 maximum for covers; $20-70 for inside use or for b&w. Identification of subjects required.

$ $ HOARD'S DAIRYMAN

W.D. Hoard and Sons, Co., 28 Milwaukee Ave. W., Fort Atkinson WI 53538-0801. (920)563-5551. Fax: (920)563-7298. E-mail: hoards@hoards.com. Website: www.hoards.com. Editor: W.D. Knox. **Contact:** Steven A. Larson, managing editor. Tabloid published 20 times/year covering dairy industry. "We publish semi-technical information published for dairy-farm families and their advisors." Estab. 1885. Circ. 100,000. **Pays on acceptance.** Publishes ms an average of 4 months after acceptance. Byline given. Buys first rights. Editorial lead time 2 months. Submit seasonal material 3 months in advance. Accepts queries by mail, e-mail, fax. Responds in 2 weeks to queries; 1 month to mss. Sample copy for 12x15 SAE and $3. Writer's guidelines for #10 SASE.

Nonfiction How-to, technical. **Buys 60 mss/year.** Query. Length: 800-1,500 words. **Pays $150-350.**

Photos Send photos with submission. Reviews 2 X 2 transparencies. Offers no additional payment for photos accepted with ms.

$ ☒ WESTERN DAIRY FARMER

Bowes Publishers, Ltd., 4504—61 Ave., Leduc AB T9E 3Z1, Canada. (780)980-7488. Fax: (780)986-6397. E-mail: editor-wdf-caf@webcoleduc.com. Website: www.westerndairyfarmer.com. **Contact:** Diana Macleod, editor. **70% freelance written.** Bimonthly magazine covering the dairy industry. "*Western Dairy Farmer* is a trade publication dealing with issues surrounding the dairy industry. The magazine features innovative articles on animal health, industry changes, new methods of dairying, and personal experiences. Sometimes highlights successful farmers." Estab. 1991. Circ. 6,300. Pays on publication. Publishes ms an average of 4 months after acceptance. Byline given. Buys all rights. Editorial lead time 2 months. Submit seasonal material 2 months in advance. Accepts queries by mail, e-mail, fax. Responds in 2 weeks to queries; 2 months to mss. Sample copy for 9×12 SAE.

Nonfiction "All topics/submissions must be related to the dairy industry." General interest, how-to, interview/profile, new product, personal experience (only exceptional stories), technical. "Not interested in anything vague, trite, or not dairy related." **Buys 50 mss/year.** Query or send complete ms. Length: 900-1,200 words. **Pays $75-150.**

Photos State availability with submission. Reviews GIF/JPEG files. Buys all rights. Offers no additional payment for photos accepted with ms. Captions, identification of subjects, model releases required.

Tips "Know the industry inside and out. Provide contact names and phone numbers (both for writers and subjects) with submissions. Remember, this is a specialized trade publication, and our readers are well-acquainted with the issues and appreciate new up-to-date information."

$ $ WESTERN DAIRYBUSINESS

Heritage Complex, Suite 218, 4500 S. Laspina, Tulare CA 93274. (559)687-3160. Fax: (559)687-3166. E-mail: rgoble@dairybusiness.com. Website: www.dairybusiness.com. **Contact:** Ron Goble, editor. **10% freelance written.** Prefers to work with published/established writers. Monthly magazine dealing with large-herd commercial dairy industry. Rarely publishes information about non-Western producers or dairy groups and events. Estab. 1922. Circ. 17,000. Pays on publication. Publishes ms an average of 3 months after acceptance. Byline given. Buys first North American serial rights. Submit seasonal material 3 months in advance. Accepts queries by mail, e-mail. Responds in 1 month to queries. Sample copy for 9×12 SAE and 4 first-class stamps.

Nonfiction Special emphasis on: environmental stewardship, herd management systems, business management, facilities/equipment, forage/cropping. Interview/profile, new product, opinion, industry analysis. "No religion, nostalgia, politics, or 'mom and pop' dairies." Query, or send complete ms. Length: 300-1,500 words. **Pays $25-400 for assigned articles.**

Reprints Seldom accepts previously published submissions. Send information about when and where the article previously appeared. Pays 50% of amount paid for an original article.

Photos Photos are a critical part of story packages. Send photos with submission. Reviews contact sheets, 35mm or 2¼×2¼ transparencies. Buys one-time rights. Pays $25 for b&w; $50-100 for color. Captions, identification of subjects required.

Tips "Know the market and the industry, be well-versed in large-herd dairy management and business."

LIVESTOCK

$ $ ANGUS BEEF BULLETIN

Angus Productions, Inc., 3201 Frederick Ave., St. Joseph MO 64506. (816)383-5200. Fax: (816)233-6575. E-mail: shermel@angus.org. Website: www.angusebeefbulletin.com. **Contact:** Shauna Hermel, editor. **45% freelance written.** Tabloid published 4 times/year covering commercial cattle industry. "The *Bulletin* is mailed free to commercial cattlemen who have purchased an Angus bull and had the registration transferred to them and to others who sign a request card." Estab. 1985. Circ. 67,000. Pays on publication. Publishes ms an average of 3 months after acceptance. Byline given. Buys first, electronic rights. Editorial lead time 3 months. Submit seasonal material 3 months in advance. Accepts queries by mail, e-mail. Accepts simultaneous submissions. Responds in 3 weeks to queries; 3 months to mss. Sample copy for $5. Writer's guidelines for #10 SASE.

Nonfiction How-to (cattle production), interview/profile, technical (cattle production). **Buys 10 mss/year.** Query with published clips. Length: 800-2,500 words. **Pays $50-600.** Pays expenses of writers on assignment.

Photos Send photos with submission. Reviews 5×7 transparencies, 5×7 glossy prints. Buys all rights. Offers $25/photo. Identification of subjects required.

Tips "Read the publication and have a firm grasp of the commercial cattle industry and how the Angus breed fits in that industry."

$ $ $ ANGUS JOURNAL

Angus Productions Inc., 3201 Frederick Ave., St. Joseph MO 64506-2997. (816)383-5200. Fax: (816)233-6575. E-mail: shermel@angusjournal.com. Website: www.angusjournal.com. **Contact:** Shauna Hermel, editor. **40% freelance written.** Monthly magazine covering Angus cattle. "The *Angus Journal* is the official magazine of the American Angus Association. Its primary function as such is to report to the membership association activities and information pertinent to raising Angus cattle." Estab. 1919. Circ. 17,000. Pays on publication. Publishes ms an average of 3 months after acceptance. Byline given. Buys first, electronic rights. Editorial lead time 2 months. Submit seasonal material 3 months in advance. Accepts queries by mail, e-mail, fax. Accepts simultaneous submissions. Responds in 3 weeks to queries; 2 months to mss. Sample copy for $5. Writer's guidelines for #10 SASE.

Nonfiction How-to (cattle production), interview/profile, technical (related to cattle). **Buys 20-30 mss/year.** Query with published clips. Length: 800-3,500 words. **Pays $50-1,000.** Pays expenses of writers on assignment.

Photos Send photos with submission. Reviews 5×7 glossy prints. Buys all rights. Offers $25-400/photo. Identification of subjects required.

The online magazine carries original content not included in the print edition. Contact: Shauna Hermel, online editor.

Tips "Read the magazine and have a firm grasp of the cattle industry."

$ $ THE BRAHMAN JOURNAL

17269 FM 1887, Hempstead TX 77445. (979)826-4347. Fax: (979)826-8352. **Contact:** Vicki Lambert, editor. **10% freelance written.** Monthly magazine covering Brahman cattle. Estab. 1971. Circ. 4,000. Pays on publication. Publishes ms an average of 2 months after acceptance. Byline given. Not copyrighted. Buys first North American serial, one-time, second serial (reprint) rights, makes work-for-hire assignments. Submit seasonal material 3 months in advance. Sample copy for 9×12 SAE and 5 first-class stamps.

Nonfiction General interest, historical/nostalgic, interview/profile. Special issues: Pre-Houston, International Sale Catalog (February); Houston Livestock Show Issue (March); Performance, Houston Results (April); Herd Bull Issue (May); Youth Issue (June); All-American Issue (July); International Issue (August); All-American Results (September); Pre-National Show (October); Calendar Issue (November); Directory Issue (December). **Buys 3-4 mss/year.** Query with published clips. Length: 1,200-3,000 words. **Pays $100-250 for assigned articles.**

Reprints Send ms with rights for sale noted. Pays 50% of amount paid for an original article.

Photos Photos needed for article purchase. Send photos with submission. Reviews 4×5 prints. Buys one-time rights. Offers no additional payment for photos accepted with ms. Captions required.

$ $ THE CATTLEMAN

Texas and Southwestern Cattle Raisers Association, 1301 W. 7th St., Ft. Worth TX 76102-2660. (817)332-7064. Fax: (817)332-5446. E-mail: anita@texascattleraisers.org. Website: www.thecattlemanmagazine.com. Editor: Lionel Chambers; Managing Editor: Ellen Humphries. **Contact:** Anita Braddock, director. **25% freelance written.** Monthly magazine covering the Texas/Oklahoma beef cattle industry. "We specialize in in-depth, management-type articles related to range and pasture, beef cattle production, animal health, nutrition, and marketing. We want 'how-to' articles." Estab. 1914. Circ. 15,400. **Pays on acceptance.** Publishes ms an average of 2 months after acceptance. Byline given. Buys exclusive and one-time rights, plus rights to post on website in month of publication. Editorial lead time 2 months. Submit seasonal material 6 months in advance. Accepts queries by mail, e-mail, fax. Sample copy for free. Writer's guidelines online.

　　○┓ Break in with "clips from other cattle magazines and demonstrated knowledge of our audiences."

Nonfiction How-to, interview/profile, new product, personal experience, technical, ag research. Special issues: Editorial calendar theme issues include: Horses (January); Range and Pasture (February); Livestock Marketing (July); Hereford and Wildlife (August); Feedlots (September); Bull Buyers (October); Ranch Safety (December). Does not want to see anything not specifically related to beef production in the Southwest. **Buys 20 mss/year.** Query with published clips. Length: 1,500-2,000 words. **Pays $200-350 for assigned articles; $100-350 for unsolicited articles.** Sometimes pays expenses of writers on assignment.

Photos Reviews transparencies, prints, digital files. Buys one-time rights. Offers no additional payment for photos accepted with ms. Identification of subjects required.

Tips "In our most recent readership survey, subscribers said they were most interested in the following topics in this order: range/pasture, property rights, animal health, water, new innovations, and marketing. *The Cattleman* prefers to work on an assignment basis. However, prospective contributors are urged to write the managing editor of the magazine to inquire of interest on a proposed subject. Occasionally, the editor will return a manuscript to a potential contributor for cutting, polishing, checking, rewriting, or condensing. Be able to demonstrate background/knowledge in this field. Include tearsheets from similar magazines."

$ $ FEED LOT MAGAZINE

Feed Lot Magazine, Inc., P.O. Box 850, Dighton KS 67839. (620)397-2838. Fax: (620)397-2839. E-mail: feedlot @st-tel.net. Website: www.feedlotmagazine.com. **Contact:** Robert A. Strong, editor (rstrong@st-tel.net). **40% freelance written.** Bimonthly magazine. "The editorial information content fits a dual role: large feedlots and their related cow/calf, operations, and large 500pl cow/calf, 100pl stocker operations. The information covers all phases of production from breeding, genetics, animal health, nutrition, equipment design, research through finishing fat cattle. *Feed Lot* publishes a mix of new information and timely articles which directly affect the cattle industry." Estab. 1993. Circ. 12,000. Pays on publication. Publishes ms an average of 2 months after acceptance. Byline given. Offers 50% kill fee. Buys all rights. Editorial lead time 2 months. Submit seasonal material 6 months in advance. Accepts queries by mail, e-mail, fax. Responds in 1 month to queries. Sample copy and writer's guidelines for $1.50.

Nonfiction Interview/profile, new product (cattle-related), photo feature. Send complete ms. Length: 100-400 words. **Pays 20¢/word.**

Reprints Send tearsheet or typed ms with rights for sale noted and information about when and where the material previously appeared. Pays 50% of amount paid for an original article.

Photos State availability of or send photos with submission. Reviews contact sheets. Buys all rights. Negotiates payment individually. Captions, model releases required.

Tips "Know what you are writing about—have a good knowledge of the subject."

N $ SHEEP! MAGAZINE

Countryside Publications, Ltd., W. 11564 State Hwy. 64, Withee WI 54498. (715)785-7979. Fax: (715)785-7414. E-mail: csymag@tds.net. Website: www.sheepmagazine.com. **Contact:** Nathan Griffin, editor/publisher. **35% freelance written.** Prefers to work with published/established writers. Bimonthly magazine. "We're looking for clear, concise, useful information for sheep raisers who have a few sheep to a 1,000 ewe flock." Estab. 1980. Circ. 4,000. Pays on publication. Byline given. Offers $30 kill fee. Buys all rights or makes work-for-hire assignments. Submit seasonal material 3 months in advance.

Nonfiction Information (on personalities and/or political, legal, or environmental issues affecting the sheep industry). Health and husbandry articles should be written by someone with extensive experience or appropriate credentials (i.e., a veterinarian or animal scientist); features (on small businesses that promote wool products and stories about local and regional sheep producers' groups and their activities); first-person narratives. Book excerpts, how-to (on innovative lamb and wool marketing and promotion techniques, efficient record-keeping systems, or specific aspects of health and husbandry), interview/profile (on experienced sheep producers who detail the economics and management of their operation), new product (of value to sheep producers; should be written by someone who has used them), technical (on genetics health and nutrition). **Buys 80 mss/year.** Query with published clips, or send complete ms. Length: 750-2,500 words. **Pays $45-150.**

Photos Color—vertical compositions of sheep and/or people—for cover. Use only b&w inside magazine. Black & white, 35mm photos or other visuals improve chances of a sale. Buys all rights. Identification of subjects required.

Tips "Send us your best ideas and photos! We love good writing!"

MANAGEMENT

$ AG JOURNAL

Arkansas Valley Publishing, P.O. Box 500, La Junta CO 81050-0500. (800)748-1997. Fax: (719)384-2867. E-mail: ag-edit@centurytel.net. Website: www.agjournalonline.com. **Contact:** Pat R. Ptolemy, editor. **20% freelance written.** Weekly journal covering agriculture. "The Ag Journal covers people, issues and events relevant to ag producers in our seven state region (Colorado, Kansas, Oklahoma, Texas, Wyoming, Nebraska, New Mexico)." Estab. 1949. Circ. 11,000. Pays on publication. Publishes ms an average of 2 weeks after acceptance. Byline given. Buys first, one-time rights, makes work-for-hire assignments. Editorial lead time 1 month. Submit seasonal material 1 month in advance. Accepts queries by e-mail. Accepts previously published material. Responds in 2 weeks to queries. Sample copy and writer's guidelines free.

Nonfiction How-to, interview/profile, new product, opinion, photo feature, technical. Query by e-mail only. **Pays 4¢/word.** Sometimes pays expenses of writers on assignment.

Photos State availability with submission. Buys one-time rights. Offers $8/photo. Captions, identification of subjects required.

Tips "Query by e-mail."

$ $ NEW HOLLAND NEWS

P.O. Box 1895, New Holland PA 17557-0903. Website: www.newholland.com/na. **Contact:** Gary Martin, editor. **60% freelance written.** Works with a small number of new/unpublished writers each year. Magazine published 8 times/year covering agriculture; designed to entertain and inform farm families. Estab. 1960. **Pays on acceptance.** Publishes ms an average of 10 months after acceptance. Byline given. Offers negotiable kill fee. Buys first North American serial rights. Submit seasonal material 6 months in advance. Accepts queries by mail. Responds in 2 months to queries. Sample copy and writer's guidelines for 9×12 SAE with 2 first-class stamps.

○➤ Break in with an "agricultural 'economic' success story with all the management details."

Nonfiction "We need strong photo support for articles of 1,200-1,700 words on farm management and farm human interest." Inspirational, photo feature. **Buys 40 mss/year.** Query. **Pays $700-900.** Pays expenses of writers on assignment.

Photos Send photos with submission. Reviews color transparencies. Buys one-time rights. Pays $50-300, $500 for cover shot. Captions, identification of subjects, model releases required.

Tips "The writer must have an emotional understanding of agriculture and the farm family and must demonstrate in the article an understanding of the unique economics that affect farming in North America. We want to know about the exceptional farm managers, those leading the way in agriculture. Use anecdotes freely."

SMALL FARM TODAY

The How-to Magazine of Alternative and Traditional Crops, Livestock, and Direct Marketing, Missouri Farm Publishing, Inc., Ridge Top Ranch 3903 W. Ridge Trail Rd., Clark MO 65243-9525. (573)687-3525. Fax: (573)687-3148. E-mail: smallfarm@socket.net. Website: www.smallfarmtoday.com. Editor: Ron Macher. **Contact:** Paul Berg, managing editor. Bimonthly magazine "for small farmers and small-acreage landowners interested in diversification, direct marketing, alternative crops, horses, draft animals, small livestock, exotic and minor breeds, home-based businesses, gardening, vegetable and small fruit crops." Estab. 1984 as *Missouri Farm Magazine.* Circ. 12,000. Pays 60 days after publication. Publishes ms an average of 6 months after acceptance. Byline given. Buys first serial and nonexclusive reprint rights (right to reprint article in an anthology) Submit seasonal material 4 months in advance. Accepts queries by mail, e-mail, fax. Responds in 3 months to queries. Sample copy for $3. Writer's guidelines online.

○➤ Break in with a detailed "how-to" story with budget information on a specific crop or animal.

Nonfiction Practical and how-to (small farming, gardening, alternative crops/livestock). Special issues: Poultry (January); Wool & Fiber (March); Aquaculture (July); Equipment (November). Query letters recommended. Length: 1,200-2,600 words.

Reprints Send tearsheet, photocopy, or typed ms with rights for sale noted and information about when and where the material previously appeared. Pays 57% of amount paid for an original article.

Photos Send photos with submission. Buys one-time and nonexclusive reprint rights (for anthologies). Offers $6 for inside photos and $10 for cover photos. Pays $4 for negatives or slides. Captions required.

Tips "No poetry or humor. Your topic must apply to the small farm or acreage. It helps to provide more practical and helpful information without the fluff. We need 'how-to' articles (how-to grow, raise, market, build, etc.), as well as articles about small farmers who are experiencing success through diversification, specialty/alternative crops and livestock, and direct marketing."

MISCELLANEOUS

$ BEE CULTURE

P.O. Box 706, Medina OH 44256-0706. Fax: (330)725-5624. E-mail: kim@beeculture.com. Website: www.beeculture.com. **Contact:** (Mr.) Kim Flottum, editor. **50% freelance written.** Monthly magazine for beekeepers and those interested in the natural science of honey bees, with environmentally-oriented articles relating to honey bees or pollination. Estab. 1873. Pays on both publication and acceptance. Publishes ms an average of 4 months after acceptance. Buys first North American serial rights. Accepts queries by mail, e-mail, fax, phone. Responds in 1 month to mss. Sample copy for 9×12 SAE and 5 first-class stamps. Writer's guidelines online.

○→ Break in with marketing strategies, interviews of successful beekeepers or beekeeping science, making management of bees easier or less expensive.

Nonfiction Interested in articles giving new ideas on managing bees. Also looking for articles on honey bee/environment connections or relationships. Also uses success stories about commercial beekeepers. Interview/profile, personal experience, photo feature. No "how I began beekeeping" articles. No highly advanced, technical, and scientific abstracts, or impractical advice. Length: 2,000 words average. **Pays $60-100/published page and up.**

Reprints Send photocopy and information about when and where the material previously appeared. Pays 50% of amount paid for an original article, on negotiation.

Photos "B&W or color prints, 5×7 standard, but 3×5 are OK. 35mm slides, mid-format transparencies are excellent. Electronic images accepted and encouraged." Pays $7-10 each, $50 for cover photos.

Tips "Do an interview story on commercial beekeepers who are cooperative enough to furnish accurate, factual information on their operations. Frequent mistakes made by writers in completing articles are that they are too general in nature and lack management knowledge."

REGIONAL

$ ◨ CENTRAL ALBERTA FARMER

Bowes Publishers, Ltd., 4504—61 Ave., Leduc AB T9E 3Z1, Canada. (780)986-2271. Fax: (780)986-6397. E-mail: editor-wdf-caf@webcoleduc.com. Website: www.albertafarmer.com. **Contact:** Diana MacLeod, editor. **10% freelance written.** Monthly tabloid covering farming issues specific to or affecting farmers in central Alberta, Canada. "*Central Alberta Farmer* is an industry magazine-type product that deals with issues in farming. It also highlights value-added efforts in agriculture and features stories on rural lifestyles." Estab. 1993. Circ. 36,000. Pays on publication. Publishes ms an average of 3 months after acceptance. Byline given. Buys all rights. Editorial lead time 3 months. Submit seasonal material 4 months in advance. Accepts queries by mail, e-mail, fax. Accepts simultaneous submissions. Responds in 2 weeks to queries; 2 months to mss. Sample copy for 9×12 SAE.

Nonfiction "All articles must be related to an aspect of farming in the area *Central Alberta Farmer* covers. Freelance articles must be exceptional. Not many are accepted." General interest, how-to, interview/profile, new product, personal experience, technical. "Not interested in anything trite or trivial." **Buys 5 mss/year.** Query or send complete ms. Length: 1,000-1,500 words. **Pays $20-30.**

Photos State availability with submission. Reviews GIF/JPEG files. Buys all rights. Offers no additional payment for photos accepted with ms. Captions, identification of subjects, model releases required.

Tips "Know the industry well. Provide names and phone numbers with submissions (both yours and the people in the article). This is a difficult publication to break into because most copy is generated in-house. So, your submission must be far above average."

$ $ FLORIDA GROWER

The Voice of Florida Agriculture for More Than 90 Years, Meister Media Worldwide, 1555 Howell Branch Rd., Suite C-204, Winter Park FL 32789. (407)539-6552. E-mail: flg_edit@meisternet.com. Website: www.floridagrower.net. **Contact:** Roy Padrick, managing editor. **10% freelance written.** Monthly magazine "edited for the Florida farmer with commercial production interest primarily in citrus, vegetables, and other ag endeavors. Our goal is to provide articles which update and inform on such areas as production, ag financing, farm labor relations, technology, safety, education, and regulation." Estab. 1907. Circ. 12,200. Pays on publication. Byline given. Buys all rights. Editorial lead time 2 months. Submit seasonal material 3 months in advance. Accepts queries by mail, e-mail, fax, phone. Responds in 1 month to queries. Sample copy for 9 × 12 SAE and 5 first-class stamps. Writer's guidelines free.

Nonfiction Interview/profile, photo feature, technical. Query with published clips. Length: 700-1,000 words. **Pays $150-250.**

Photos Send photos with submission.

$ FLORIDAGRICULTURE

Florida Farm Bureau Federation, P.O. Box 147030, Gainesville FL 32614. (352)374-1521. Fax: (352)374-1530. E-mail: ealbanesi@sfbcic.com. Website: www.fb.com/flfb. **Contact:** Ed Albanesi, editor. **Less than 5% freelance written.** Monthly tabloid covering Florida agriculture. Promotes agriculture to its 125,000 members families. Estab. 1943. Circ. 125,000. **Pays on acceptance.** Publishes ms an average of 3 months after acceptance. Byline sometimes given. Buys all rights. Editorial lead time 3 months. Submit seasonal material 3 months in advance. Accepts queries by mail, e-mail. Responds in 1 week to queries; 1 month to mss. Sample copy for $3.

Nonfiction Sportsmen articles with a Florida connection. **Buys fewer than 2 mss/year.** Query. Length: 500-1,500 words. **Pays $50-100 for assigned articles.**

Photos State availability with submission. Buys up to 3 uses. Negotiates payment individually. Captions, identification of subjects required.

$ THE LAND

Minnesota's Favorite Ag Publication, Free Press Co., P.O. Box 3169, Mankato MN 56002-3169. (507)345-4523. E-mail: kschulz@the-land.com. Website: www.the-land.com. **Contact:** Kevin Schulz, editor. **40% freelance written.** Weekly tabloid covering farming in Minnesota. "Although we're not tightly focused on any one type of farming, our articles must be of interest to farmers. In other words, will your article topic have an impact on people who live and work in rural areas?" Prefers to work with Minnesota writers. Estab. 1976. Circ. 33,000. **Pays on acceptance.** Publishes ms an average of 2 months after acceptance. Byline given. Buys first North American serial rights. Editorial lead time 2 months. Submit seasonal material 2 months in advance. Accepts queries by mail, e-mail. Responds in 3 weeks to queries; 2 months to mss. Sample copy for free. Writer's guidelines for #10 SASE.

Nonfiction General interest (ag), how-to (crop, livestock production, marketing). "Nothing that doesn't pertain to Minnesota agricultural or rural life." **Buys 80 mss/year.** Query. Length: 500-750 words. **Pays $30-60 for assigned articles.**

Photos Send photos with submission. Reviews contact sheets. Buys one-time rights. Negotiates payment individually.

Columns/Departments Query. **Pays $10-50.**

Tips "Be enthused about rural Minnesota life and agriculture and be willing to work with our editors. We try to stress relevance. When sending me a query, convince me the story belongs in a Minnesota farm publication."

$ $ MAINE ORGANIC FARMER & GARDENER

Maine Organic Farmers & Gardeners Association, 662 Slab City Rd., Lincolnville ME 04849. (207)763-3043. E-mail: jenglish@midcoast.com. Website: www.mofga.org. **Contact:** Jean English, editor. **40% freelance written.** Prefers to work with published/established local writers. Quarterly magazine. "*MOF&G* promotes and encourages sustainable agriculture and environmentally sound living. Our primary focus is organic farming, gardening, and forestry, but we also deal with local, national, and international agriculture, food, and environmental issues." Estab. 1976. Circ. 10,000. Pays on publication. Publishes ms an average of 8 months after acceptance. Byline and bio offered. Buys first North American serial, first, one-time, second serial (reprint) rights. Submit seasonal material 1 year in advance. Accepts queries by mail, e-mail. Accepts simultaneous submissions. Responds in 2 months to queries. Sample copy for $2 and SAE with 7 first-class stamps from MOFGA, P.O. Box 170, Unity ME 04988. Writer's guidelines free.

Nonfiction Book reviews; how-to based on personal experience, research reports, interviews. Profiles of farmers, gardeners, plants. Information on renewable energy, recycling, nutrition, health, nontoxic pest control, organic farm management and marketing. "We use profiles of New England organic farmers and gardeners and news reports (500-1,000 words) dealing with U.S./international sustainable ag research and development, rural development, recycling projects, environmental and agricultural problems and solutions, organic farms with broad impact, cooperatives and community projects." **Buys 30 mss/year.** Query with published clips or send complete ms. Length: 250-3,000 words. **Pays $25-300.**

Reprints Send ms with rights for sale noted and information about when and where the material previously appeared. Pays 50% of amount paid for an original article.

Photos State availability of b&w photos with query; send 3 × 5 b&w photos with ms. State availability with submission. Buys one-time rights. Captions, identification of subjects, model releases required.

Tips "We are a nonprofit organization. Our publication's primary mission is to inform and educate, but we also want readers to enjoy the articles."

FINANCE

$ $ $☑ ADVISOR'S EDGE

Canada's Magazine for the Financial Professional, Rogers Media, Inc., 156 Front St. W., 4th Floor, Toronto ON M5J 2L6, Canada. (416)764-3802. Fax: (416)642-4949. E-mail: dgage@rmpublishing.com. Website: www.advis orsedge.ca. **Contact:** Deanne Gage, managing editor. Monthly magazine covering the financial industry (financial advisors and investment advisors). "*Advisor's Edge* focuses on sales and marketing opportunities for the financial advisor (how they can build their business and improve relationships with clients." Estab. 1998. Circ. 36,000. Pays on publication. Publishes ms an average of 3 months after acceptance. Byline given. Offers 25% kill fee. Buys one-time, electronic rights. Editorial lead time 3 months. Accepts queries by e-mail. Sample copy online.
Nonfiction "We are looking for articles that help advisors do their jobs better." How-to, interview/profile. No articles that aren't relevant to how a financial advisor does his/her job. **Buys 12 mss/year.** Query with published clips. Length: 1,500-2,000 words. **Pays $900 (Canadian).** Pays in contributor copies only if an industry contributor (i.e., an advisor).

$ $ $ $ BANKING STRATEGIES

Bank Administration Institute (BAI), Chicago IL. E-mail: kcline@bai.org. Website: www.bai.org/bankingstrateg ies. **Contact:** Kenneth Cline, senior editor. **70% freelance written.** Magazine covering banking and financial services. "Magazine covers banking from a strategic and managerial perspective for its senior financial executive audience. Each issue includes in-depth trend articles and interviews with influential executives." Offers variable kill fee. Buys all rights. Accepts queries by e-mail. Responds almost immediately to queries.
Nonfiction How-to (articles that help institutions be more effective and competitive in the marketplace), interview/profile (executive interviews). "No topic queries, we assign stories to freelancers. I'm looking for qualifications as opposed to topic queries. I need experienced writers/reporters." **Buys 30 mss/year.** E-queries preferred.
Pays $1.25/word for assigned articles.
Tips "Demonstrate ability and financial services expertise. I'm looking for freelancers who can write according to our standards, which are quite high."

$ $ $ COLLECTIONS & CREDIT RISK

The Authority for Commercial and Consumer Professionals, Thomson Media, 300 S. Wacker Dr., Suite 1800, Chicago IL 60606. (312)913-1334. Fax: (312)913-1369. E-mail: catherine.ladwig@thomsonmedia.com. Website: www.creditcollectionsworld.com. **Contact:** Catherine (Kit) Ladwig, editor. **33% freelance written.** Monthly journal covering debt collections and credit risk management. "*Collections & Credit Risk* reports and analyzes events and trends affecting consumer and commercial credit practices and debt collections. The entire credit cycle is covered from setting credit policy and making loan decisions to debt recovery, collections, bankruptcy, and debt sales." Estab. 1996. Circ. 30,000. **Pays on acceptance.** Publishes ms an average of 3 months after acceptance. Byline given. Kill fee determined case by case. Buys all rights. Editorial lead time 3 months. Accepts queries by mail, e-mail, fax. Sample copy free or online.
  ⚷ Break in with "a query with clips of business trend stories using 8-10 sources and demonstrating strong analysis."
Nonfiction Interview/profile, technical, business news and analysis. "No unsolicited submissions accepted—freelancers work on assignment only." **Buys 30-40 mss/year.** Query with published clips. Length: 1,000-2,500 words. **Pays $800-1,000.** Sometimes pays expenses of writers on assignment.
  ▣ The online version contains material not found in the print version.
Tips "This is a business news and analysis magazine focused on events and trends affecting the credit-risk management and collections professions. Our editorial approach is modeled after *Business Week, Forbes, Fortune, Wall Street Journal.* No fluff accepted."

ℕ $ $ COMMUNITY BANKER

900 19th St. NW, Suite 400, Washington DC 20006. (202)857-3100. Fax: (202)857-5581. E-mail: mharwood@acb ankers.org. Website: www.americascommunitybankers.com/magazine. **Contact:** Melanie Harwood, editor. **25% freelance written.** Monthly magazine. "*America's Community Banker* is written for senior managers and executives of community financial institutions. The magazine covers all aspects of financial institution management, with an emphasis on strategic business issues and trends. Recent features have included bank technology, trends in home mortgage finance and alternative bank funding." Circ. 14,000. **Pays on acceptance.**

Publishes ms an average of 2 months after acceptance. Byline given. Buys first North American serial rights. Editorial lead time 3 months. Submit seasonal material 6 months in advance. Responds in 1 month to queries. Sample copy and writer's guidelines free.

Nonfiction "Articles must be well-researched and backed up by a variety of sources, preferably senior managers of financial institutions or experts associated with the banking industry." How-to (articles on various aspects of a financial institution's operations). **Buys 6 mss/year.** Query with published clips. Length: 1,000-2,700 words. **Pays 50¢/word.**

Photos Send photos with submission. Reviews contact sheets, negatives, prints. Buys one-time rights. Identification of subjects required.

Columns/Departments Nationwide News (news items on banking and finance), 100-500 words; Technology Report (news on techology for community bankers); and Surveys and Trends (information on the banking business and business in general). **Buys 25 mss/year.** Query with published clips.

Tips "The best way to develop a relationship with *America's Community Banker* is through our two departments, Nationwide News and Technology Report. If writers can prove themselves reliable there first, major feature assignments may follow."

$ $ CREDIT UNION MANAGEMENT

Credit Union Executives Society, 5510 Research Park Dr., Madison WI 53711. (608)271-2664. Fax: (608)271-2303. E-mail: editors@cues.org. Website: www.cumanagement.org. **Contact:** Mary Arnold or Theresa Sweeney, editors. **44% freelance written.** Monthly magazine covering credit union, banking trends management, HR, marketing issues. "Our philosophy mirrors the credit union industry of cooperative financial services." Estab. 1978. Circ. 7,413. **Pays on acceptance.** Publishes ms an average of 2 months after acceptance. Editorial lead time 3 months. Submit seasonal material 4 months in advance. Accepts queries by mail, e-mail, fax, phone. Accepts simultaneous submissions. Responds in 2 weeks to queries; 1 month to mss. Sample copy and writer's guidelines free.

Nonfiction Book excerpts, how-to (be a good mentor/leader, recruit, etc.), interview/profile, technical. **Buys 74 mss/year.** Query with published clips. Length: 700-2,400 words. **Pays $250-350.** Pays phone expenses only of writers on assignment.

Columns/Departments Management Network (book/Web reviews, briefs), 300 words; Trends (marketing trends), 700 words; Point of Law, 700 words; Plugged In (new technology/operations trends), 700 words. Query with published clips. **Pays $250-350.**

Tips "The best way is to e-mail an editor; include résumé. Follow up with mailing cover letter and clips. Knowledge of financial services is very helpful."

$ $ EQUITIES MAGAZINE, LLC

P.O. Box 130H, Scarsdale NY 10583. (914)723-6702. Fax: (914)723-0176. E-mail: equitymag@aol.com. Website: www.equitiesmagazine.com. **50% freelance written.** "We are a seven-issues-a-year financial magazine covering the fastest-growing public companies in the world. We study the management of companies and act as critics reviewing their performances. We aspire to be 'The Shareholder's Friend.' We want to be a bridge between quality public companies and sophisticated investors." Estab. 1951. Circ. 18,000. Pays on publication. Publishes ms an average of 2 months after acceptance. Byline given. Buys all rights. Accepts queries by mail. Sample copy for 9×12 SAE and 5 first-class stamps.

Nonfiction "We must know the writer first as we are careful about whom we publish. A letter of introduction with résumé and clips is the best way to introduce yourself. Financial writing requires specialized knowledge and a feel for people as well, which can be a tough combination to find." Carries guest columns by famous money managers who are not writing for cash payments, but to showcase their ideas and approach. Exposé, new product, technical. **Buys 30 mss/year.** Query with published clips. Length: 300-1,500 words. **Pays $250-750 for assigned articles, more for very difficult or invetigative pieces.** Pays expenses of writers on assignment.

Photos Send color photos with submission. Reviews contact sheets, negatives, transparencies, prints. Offers no additional payment for photos accepted with ms. Identification of subjects required.

Columns/Departments Pays $25-75 for assigned items only.

Tips "Give us an idea for a story on a specific publically-owned company, whose stock is traded on NASDAQ, the NYSE, or American Stock Exchange. Anyone who enjoys analyzing a business and telling the story of the people who started it, or run it today, is a potential *Equities* contributor. But to protect our readers and ourselves, we are careful about who writes for us. We do not want writers who are trading the stocks of the companies they profile. Business writing is an exciting area and our stories reflect that. If a writer relies on numbers and percentages to tell his story, rather than the individuals involved, the result will be numbingly dull."

$ $ $ THE FEDERAL CREDIT UNION

National Association of Federal Credit Unions, 3138 N. 10th St., Arlington VA 22201. (703)522-4770. Fax: (703)524-1082. E-mail: tfcu@nafcu.org. Website: www.nafcu.org. Executive Editor: Jay Morris. **Contact:** Robin Johnston, publisher/managing editor. **30% freelance written.** "Looking for writers with financial, banking, or credit union experience, but will work with inexperienced (unpublished) writers based on writing skill. Published bimonthly, *The Federal Credit Union* is the official publication of the National Association of Federal Credit Unions. The magazine is dedicated to providing credit union management, staff, and volunteers with in-depth information (HR, technology, security, board management, etc.) they can use to fulfill their duties and better serve their members. The editorial focus includes coverage of management issues, operations, technology as well as volunteer-related issues." Estab. 1967. Circ. 8,000. Pays on publication. Publishes ms an average of 3 months after acceptance. Byline given. Buys first North American serial rights, rights to publish and archive online. Submit seasonal material 5 months in advance. Accepts queries by mail, e-mail, fax. Accepts simultaneous submissions. Responds in 2 months to queries. Sample copy for 10×13 SAE and 5 first-class stamps. Writer's guidelines for #10 SASE.

○→ Break in with "pithy, informative, thought-provoking items for our 'Management Insight' section (for free or a small fee of $50-200)."

Nonfiction Humor, inspirational, interview/profile. Query with published clips and SASE. Length: 1,200-2,000 words. **Pays $400-1,000.**

Photos Send photos with submission. Reviews 35mm transparencies, 5×7 prints, high-resolution photos. Buys all rights. Offers no additional payment for photos accepted with ms. Pays $50-500. Identification of subjects, model releases required.

◼ The online magazine carries original content not found in the print edition, as well as some print copy. Contact: Robin Johnston.

Tips "We would like more articles on how credit unions are using technology to serve their members and more articles on leading-edge technologies they can use in their operations. If you can write on current trends in technology, human resources, or strategic planning, you stand a better chance of being published than if you wrote on other topics."

FINANCIAL PLANNING

Thomson Media, State St. Plaza, 26th Floor, New York NY 10001. (212)803-8696. Fax: (212)843-9608. E-mail: jennifer.liptow@thomsonmedia.com. Website: www.financial-planning.com. **Contact:** Jennifer Liptow. **30-40% freelance written.** Monthly magazine covering investment strategies, estate planning, practice management and other issues facing professional financial planners and money managers. Estab. 1971. Circ. 100,000. Pays on publication. Publishes ms an average of 3 months after acceptance. Byline given. Offers 15% kill fee. Buys all rights. Editorial lead time 3 months. Submit seasonal material 4 months in advance. Accepts queries by mail, e-mail. Responds in 3 weeks to queries; 1 month to mss. Sample copy for $10. Writer's guidelines free.

Nonfiction Book excerpts, how-to, interview/profile, new product, opinion, technical. No product endorsements. **Buys 25-30 mss/year.** Query (e-mail preferred). Length: 1,800-2,500 words. **Payment varies.** Sometimes pays expenses of writers on assignment.

Photos State availability with submission. Reviews contact sheets, any size prints. Offers no additional payment for photos accepted with ms. Identification of subjects required.

◼ The online magazine carries original content not included in the print edition. Contact: John Whelan, online editor.

Tips "Avoid articles that are too general—ours is a professional readership who require thoughtful, in-depth analysis of financial issues. A submission that includes charts, graphs, and statistical data is much more likely to pique our interest than overviews of investing."

ILLINOIS BANKER

Illinois Bankers Association, 133 S. Fourth St., Suite 300, Springfield IL 62701. (217)789-9340. Fax: (217)789-5410. **Contact:** Debbie Jemison, editor. "Our audience is approximately 3,000 bankers and vendors related to the banking industry. The purpose of the publication is to educate and inform readers on major public policy issues affecting banking today, as well as provide new ideas that can be applied to day-to-day operations and management. Writers may not sell or promote a product or service." Estab. 1891. Circ. 2,500. Publishes ms an average of 3 months after acceptance. Byline given. Buys first North American serial rights. Editorial lead time 2 months. Accepts simultaneous submissions. Responds in 3 months to queries. Sample copy and writer's guidelines free.

Nonfiction "It is *IBA* policy that writers do not sell or promote a particular product, service, or organization within the content of an article written for publication." Essays, historical/nostalgic, interview/profile, new product, opinion, personal experience. Query. Length: 1,000-1,500 words.

Photos State availability with submission. Reviews contact sheets, negatives, transparencies, prints. Captions, identification of subjects required.

Tips "Articles published in *Illinois Banker* address current issues of key importance to the banking industry in Illinois. Our intention is to keep readers informed of the latest industry news, developments, and trends, as well as provide necessary technical information. We publish articles on any topic that affects the banking industry, provided the content is in agreement with Association policy and position. Because we are a trade association, most articles need to be reviewed by an advisory committee before publication; therefore, the earlier they are submitted the better. Some recent topics include: agriculture, bank architecture, commercial and consumer credit, marketing, operations/cost control, security, and technology. In addition, articles are also considered on the topics of economic development and business/banking trends in Illinois and the Midwest region."

INVESTMENT NEWS

Crain Communications, 711 Third Ave., New York NY 10017-4014. (212)210-0100. Fax: (212)210-0444. E-mail: jpavia@crain.com. Website: www.investmentnews.com. Editor: Jim Pavia. **10% freelance written.** Weekly magazine, newsletter, tabloid covering financial planning and investing. "It covers the business of personal finance to keep its audience of planners, brokers and other tax investment professionals informed of the latest news about their industry." Estab. 1997. Circ. 60,000. Pays on publication. Publishes ms an average of 1 month after acceptance. Byline given. Negotiate kill fee. Buys all rights, makes work-for-hire assignments. Editorial lead time 2 weeks. Submit seasonal material 1 month in advance. Sample copy for free. Writer's guidelines free.

Tips "Come to us with a specific pitch-preferably based on a news tip. We prefer to be contacted by fax or e-mail."

MORTGAGE BANKING

The Magazine of Real Estate Finance, Mortgage Bankers Association of America, 1919 Pennsylvania Ave., NW, Washington DC 20006. (202)557-2853. Fax: (202)721-0245. E-mail: janet_hewitt@mbaa.org. Website: www.mbaa.org. Deputy Editor: Lesley Hall. **Contact:** Janet Hewitt, editor-in-chief. Monthly magazine covering real estate finance. "Timely examinations of major news and trends in the business of mortgage lending for both commercial and residential real estate." Estab. 1939. Circ. 8,000. **Pays on acceptance.** Publishes ms an average of 2 months after acceptance. Byline given. Negotiates kill fee. Buys one-time rights, makes work-for-hire assignments. Editorial lead time 2 months. Submit seasonal material 3 months in advance. Accepts queries by mail, e-mail, fax. Accepts simultaneous submissions. Responds in 1 month to queries; 4 months to mss. Sample copy and writer's guidelines free.

Nonfiction Book excerpts, essays, interview/profile, opinion. Special issues: Commercial Real Estate Special Supplemental Issue (January); Internet Guide Supplemental Issue (September). **Buys 30 mss/year.** Query. Length: 3,000-4,000 words. **Writers' fees negotiable.** Sometimes pays expenses of writers on assignment.

Photos State availability with submission. Reviews prints. Buys one-time rights. Negotiates payment individually. Identification of subjects, model releases required.

Columns/Departments Book reviews (current, relevant material), 300 words; executive essay (industry executive's personal views on relevant topic), 750-1,000 words. **Buys 2 mss/year.** Query. **Pay negotiated.**

Tips "Trends in technology, current and upcoming legislation that will affect the mortgage industry are good focus."

$ $ $ $ ON WALL STREET

Thomson Media, 40 W. 57th St., New York NY 10019. (212)803-8782. Fax: (212)631-9731. E-mail: evan.cooper @thomsonmedia.com. Website: www.onwallstreet.com. **Contact:** Evan Cooper, editor-in-chief. **50% freelance written.** Monthly magazine for stockbrokers. "We help 95,000 stockbrockers build their business." Estab. 1991. Circ. 95,000. Pays on publication. Publishes ms an average of 1 month after acceptance. Byline given. Offers 50% kill fee. Buys first North American serial rights. Editorial lead time 2 months. Submit seasonal material 2 months in advance. Accepts queries by mail, e-mail. Accepts simultaneous submissions. Responds in 1 week to queries; 1 month to mss. Sample copy for free. Writer's guidelines free.

Nonfiction How-to, interview/profile. "No investment-related articles about hot stocks, nor funds or hot alternative investments." **Buys 30 mss/year.** Query. Length: 1,000-3,000 words. **Pays $1/word.**

Photos State availability with submission. Reviews contact sheets. Buys one-time rights. Negotiates payment individually. Identification of subjects required.

Tips "Writers should know what stockbrokers need to expand their business—industry-specific knowledge of cold-calling, selling investment ideas."

$ $ SERVICING MANAGEMENT

The Magazine for Loan Servicing Professionals, Zackin Publications, P.O. Box 2180, Waterbury CT 06722-2180. (800)325-6745 ext. 241. Fax: (203)755-3480. E-mail: bates@sm-online.com. Website: www.sm-online.com. **Contact:** Michael Bates, editor. **15% freelance written.** Monthly magazine covering residential mortgage servicing. Estab. 1989. Circ. 20,000. **Pays on acceptance.** Publishes ms an average of 2 months after acceptance. Byline given. Buys all rights. Accepts queries by mail, e-mail, fax. Responds in 2 weeks to queries. Sample copy and writer's guidelines free. Writer's guidelines online.

> O→ Break in by "submitting a query for Servicing Reports, a monthly department featuring news and information about mortgage servicing and the industry. It should be informative, topical and include comments by industry professionals."

Nonfiction How-to, interview/profile, new product, technical. **Buys 10 mss/year.** Query. Length: 1,500-2,500 words. Will pay industry experts with contributor copies or other premiums rather than a cash payment.

Photos State availability with submission. Reviews contact sheets. Buys all rights. Offers no additional payment for photos accepted with ms. Identification of subjects required.

Columns/Departments Buys 5 mss/year. Query. **Pays $200.**

TRADERS MAGAZINE

Thomson Media Group, 1 State St. Plaza, 17th Floor, New York NY 10001. (212)803-8366. Fax: (212)295-1725. E-mail: john.byrne@thomsonmedia.com. Website: www.tradersmagazine.com. **Contact:** John Aidan Byrne, editor. **35% freelance written.** Monthly magazine plus 2 specials covering equity trading and technology. "Provides comprehensive coverage of how institutional trading is performed on NASDAQ and the New York Stock Exchange." Pays on publication. Publishes ms an average of 2 months after acceptance. Byline given. Buys all rights. Editorial lead time 2 months. Submit seasonal material 3 months in advance. Accepts queries by mail, e-mail, phone. Sample copy free to writers on assignment.

> O→ Needs more "buy-side" stories (on mutual fund, pension fund traders, etc.), "sell-side" stories on hot-button topics.

Nonfiction Book excerpts, exposé, general interest, historical/nostalgic, how-to, humor, interview/profile, new product, opinion, personal experience, religious, technical. Special issues: Correspondent clearing (every market) and market making survey of broker dealers. No stories that are related to fixed income and other non-equity topics. **Buys 12-20 mss/year.** Query with published clips or send complete ms. Length: 750-2,800 words.

Columns/Departments Special Features (market regulation and human interest), 1600 words; Trading & Technology, 1,600 words; Washington Watch (market regulation), 750 words. Query with published clips.

Fiction Ethnic, historical, humorous, mystery, science fiction, slice-of-life vignettes. No erotica. **Buys 1 mss/year.** Query with or without published clips or send complete ms. Length: 2,100-2,800 words.

> ◼ The online magazine carries original content not found in the print edition. "We welcome controversy in both mediums."

Tips "Boil it all down and don't bore the hell out of readers. Advice from a distinguished scribe which we pass along. Learn to explain equity market making and institutional trading in a simple, direct manner. Don't waffle. Have a trader explain the business to you if necessary. The *Traders Magazine* is highly regarded among Wall Street insiders, trading honchos, and Washington pundits alike."

FISHING

$ $ PACIFIC FISHING

Northwest Publishing Center, 1710 S. Norman St., Seattle WA 98144. (206)709-1840. E-mail: brad@pacificfishing.com. Website: www.pfmag.com. **Contact:** Brad Warren, editor. **75% freelance written.** Works with some new/unpublished writers. Monthly magazine for commercial fishermen and others in the commercial fishing industry throughout Alaska, the west coast, and the Pacific. "*Pacific Fishing* views the fisherman as a small businessman and covers all aspects of the industry, including harvesting, processing, and marketing." Estab. 1979. Circ. 8,000. Pays on publication. Publishes ms an average of 2 months after acceptance. Byline given. Buys first North American serial and unlimited re-use rights. Accepts queries by mail, e-mail, fax, phone. Variable response time to queries. Sample copy and writer's guidelines for 9×12 SAE with 10 first-class stamps.

> O→ Study the magazine before querying.

Nonfiction "Articles must be concerned specifically with commercial fishing. We view fishermen as small business operators and professionals who are innovative and success-oriented. To appeal to this reader, *Pacific Fishing* offers 4 basic features: Technical, how-to articles that give fishermen hands-on tips that will make their operation more efficient and profitable; practical, well-researched business articles discussing the dollars and cents of fishing, processing and marketing; profiles of a fisherman, processor, or company with emphasis on practical business and technical areas; and in-depth analysis of political, social, fisheries management, and

Trade Journals

resource issues that have a direct bearing on commercial fishermen.'' **Buys 20 mss/year.** Query noting whether photos are available, and enclose samples of previous work and SASE. Length: varies, one-paragraph news items to 3,000-word features. **Pays 20¢/word for most assignments.** Sometimes pays expenses of writers on assignment.

Photos ''We need good, high-quality photography, especially color, of commercial fishing. We prefer 35mm color slides or JPEG files of at least 300 dpi.'' Our rates are $200 for cover; $50-100 for inside color; $25-75 for b&w; $10 for table of contents.

Tips ''Read the magazine before sending a query. Make your pitch fit the magazine. If you haven't read it, don't waste your time and ours.''

FLORISTS, NURSERIES & LANDSCAPERS

$ $ DIGGER

Oregon Association of Nurseries, 29751 SW Town Center Loop W., Wilsonville OR 97070. (503)682-5089. Fax: (503)682-5727. E-mail: csivesind@oan.org. Website: www.oan.org. **Contact:** Cam Sivesind, manager of publications and communications. **50% freelance written.** Monthly magazine covering nursery and greenhouse industry. ''Our readers are mainly nursery and greenhouse operators and owners who propagate nursery stock/crops, so we write with them in mind.'' Circ. 5,500. Pays on receipt of copy. Publishes ms an average of 2 months after acceptance. Byline given. Offers 100% kill fee. Buys first North American serial rights. Editorial lead time 6 weeks. Submit seasonal material 2 months in advance. Accepts queries by mail, e-mail, fax, phone. Sample copy and writer's guidelines free.

Nonfiction General interest, how-to (propagation techniques, other crop-growing tips), interview/profile, personal experience, technical. Special issues: Farwest Edition (August)—this is a triple-size issue that runs in tandem with our annual trade show (12,500 circulation for this issue). ''No articles not related or pertinent to nursery and greenhouse industry.'' **Buys 20-30 mss/year.** Query. Length: 800-2,000 words. **Pays $125-400 for assigned articles; $100-300 for unsolicited articles.** Sometimes pays expenses of writers on assignment.

Photos State availability with submission. Reviews negatives, 5×7 prints, slides. Buys one-time rights. Offers $25-150/photo. Captions, identification of subjects required.

Tips ''Our best freelancers are familiar with or have experience in the horticultural industry. Some 'green' knowledge is a definite advantage.''

$ GROWERTALKS

Ball Publishing, 335 N. River St., P.O. Box 9, Batavia IL 60510. (630)208-9080. Fax: (630)208-9350. E-mail: beytes@growertalks.com. Website: www.growertalks.com. **Contact:** Chris Beytes, editor. **50% freelance written.** Monthly magazine. ''*GrowerTalks* serves the commercial greenhouse grower. Editorial emphasis is on floricultural crops: bedding plants, potted floral crops, foliage and fresh cut flowers. Our readers are growers, managers, and owners. We're looking for writers who've had experience in the greenhouse industry.'' Estab. 1937. Circ. 9,500. Pays on publication. Publishes ms an average of 3 months after acceptance. Byline given. Buys first North American serial rights. Editorial lead time 4 months. Submit seasonal material 3 months in advance. Accepts queries by mail, e-mail, fax. Responds in 1 month to queries. Sample copy and writer's guidelines free.

Nonfiction How-to (time- or money-saving projects for professional flower/plant growers), interview/profile (ornamental horticulture growers), personal experience (of a grower), technical (about growing process in greenhouse setting). ''No articles that promote only 1 product.'' **Buys 36 mss/year.** Query. Length: 1,200-1,600 words. **Pays $125 minimum for assigned articles; $75 minimum for unsolicited articles.**

Photos State availability with submission. Reviews 2½×2½ slides and 3×5 prints. Buys one-time rights. Negotiates payment individually. Captions, identification of subjects, model releases required.

The online magazine carries original content not included in the print edition. Contact: Chris Beytes, online editor.

Tips ''Discuss magazine with ornamental horticulture growers to find out what topics that have or haven't appeared in the magazine interest them.''

$ $ THE GROWING EDGE

New Moon Publishing, Inc., P.O. Box 1027, Corvallis OR 97339. (541)757-8477. Fax: (541)757-0028. Website: www.growingedge.com. **Contact:** Tom Weller, editor. **85% freelance written.** Bimonthly magazine covering indoor and outdoor high-tech gardening techniques and tips. Estab. 1980. Circ. 20,000. Pays on publication. Publishes ms an average of 3 months after acceptance. Byline given. first serial and reprint rights Submit seasonal material 6 months in advance. Accepts queries by mail, e-mail. Responds in 3 months to queries. Sample copy for $3. Writer's guidelines online.

O⇥ Break in with "a detailed, knowledgeable e-mail story pitch."

Nonfiction How-to, interview/profile, personal experience (must be technical), book reviews, general horticulture and agriculture. Query. Length: 500-3,500 words. **Pays 20¢/word (10¢ for first rights, 5¢ for nonexclusive reprint and nonexclusive electronic rights).**

Reprints Send tearsheet, photocopy or typed ms with rights for sale noted and information about when and where the material previously appeared. Payment negotiable.

Photos Buys first and reprint rights. Pays $25-175. Pays on publication. Credit line given.

Tips Looking for more hydroponics articles and information that will give the reader/gardener/farmer the "growing edge" in high-tech gardening and farming on topics such as high intensity grow lights, water conservation, drip irrigation, advanced organic fertilizers, new seed varieties, and greenhouse cultivation.

$ $ ORNAMENTAL OUTLOOK

Your Connection To The South's Horticulture Industry, Meister Media Worldwide, 1555 Howell Branch Rd., Suite C204, Winter Park FL 32789. (407)539-6552. Fax: (407)539-6544. E-mail: oo.edit@meistermedia.com. Website: www.ornamentaloutlook.com. **Contact:** Tacy Callies, editor. **20% freelance written.** Monthly magazine. "*Ornamental Outlook* is written for commercial growers of ornamental plants in the Southeast U.S. Our goal is to provide interesting and informative articles on such topics as production, legislation, safety, technology, pest control, water management, and new varieties, as they apply to Southeast growers." Estab. 1991. Circ. 11,000. Pays 30 days after publication. Publishes ms an average of 4 months after acceptance. Byline given. Buys all rights. Editorial lead time 2 months. Submit seasonal material 3 months in advance. Accepts queries by mail, e-mail, fax, phone. Responds in 3 months to queries. Sample copy for 9×12 SAE and 5 first-class stamps. Writer's guidelines free.

Nonfiction Interview/profile, photo feature, technical. "No first-person articles. No word-for-word meeting transcripts or all-quote articles." Query with published clips. Length: 600-1,000 words. **Pays $150-300/article including photos.**

Photos Send photos with submission. Reviews contact sheets, transparencies, prints. Buys one-time rights. Captions, identification of subjects required.

Tips "I am most impressed by written queries that address specific subjects of interest to our audience, which is the Southeast grower of commercial horticulture. Our biggest demand is for features, about 700 words, that follow subjects listed on our editorial calendar (which is sent with guidelines). Please do not send articles of national or consumer interest."

$ $ TREE CARE INDUSTRY MAGAZINE

Tree Care Industry Association, 3 Perimeter Rd. Unit 1, Manchester NH 03103-3341. (800)733-2622 or (603)314-5380. Fax: (603)314-5386. E-mail: garvin@treecareindustry.org. Website: www.treecareindustry.org. Mark Garvin, editor. **50% freelance written.** Monthly magazine covering tree care and landscape maintenance. Estab. 1990. Circ. 28,500. Pays within 30 days of publication. Publishes ms an average of 3 months after acceptance. Byline given. Buys first North American serial, electronic rights. Editorial lead time 10 weeks. Submit seasonal material 3 months in advance. Accepts queries by mail, e-mail, fax, phone. Responds in 2 weeks to queries; 2 months to mss. Sample copy for 9×12 SAE and 6 first-class stamps. Writer's guidelines free.

Nonfiction Book excerpts, historical/nostalgic, interview/profile, new product, technical. **Buys 40 mss/year.** Query with published clips. Length: 900-3,500 words. **Pays negotiable rate.**

Photos Send photos with submission. Reviews prints. Buys one-time and web rights. Negotiate payment individually. Captions, identification of subjects required.

Columns/Departments Management Exchange (business management-related); 1,200-1,800 words; Industry Innovations (inventions), 1,200 words; From The Field (OP/ED from practitioners), 600 words. **Buys 40 mss/year.** Send complete ms. **Pays $100 and up.**

Tips "Preference is given to writers with background and knowledge of the tree care industry; our focus is relatively narrow."

GOVERNMENT & PUBLIC SERVICE

$ CHIEF OF POLICE MAGAZINE

National Association of Chiefs of Police, 3801 Biscayne Blvd., Miami FL 33137. Fax: (721)264-0333. E-mail: policeinfo@aphf.org. Website: www.aphf.org. **Contact:** Jim Gordon, executive editor. Bimonthly journal for law enforcement commanders (command ranks). Circ. 13,500. **Pays on acceptance.** Publishes ms an average of 6 months after acceptance. Byline given. Buys first rights. Submit seasonal material 6 months in advance. Accepts queries by mail, e-mail, fax. Accepts simultaneous submissions. Responds in 2 weeks to queries. Sample copy for $3 and 9×12 SAE with 5 first-class stamps. Writer's guidelines online.

○⇁ Break in with "a story concerning command officers or police family survivors."

Nonfiction "We want stories about interesting police cases and stories on any law enforcement subject or program that is positive in nature." General interest, historical/nostalgic, how-to, humor, inspirational, interview/profile, new product, personal experience, photo feature, religious, technical. "No exposé types or anti-police." **Buys 50 mss/year.** Send complete ms. Length: 600-2,500 words. **Pays $25-75 for assigned articles; $25-100 for unsolicited articles.** Sometimes pays expenses of writers on assignment.

Photos Send photos with submission. Reviews 5×6 prints. Buys one-time rights. Pays $5-10 for b&w; $10-25 for color. Captions required.

Columns/Departments New Police (police equipment shown and tests), 200-600 words. **Buys 6 mss/year.** Send complete ms. **Pays $5-25.**

Fillers Anecdotes, short humor, law-oriented cartoons. **Buys 100/year.** Length: 100-1,600 words. **Pays $5-25.**

Tips "Writers need only contact law enforcement officers right in their own areas and we would be delighted. We want to recognize good commanding officers from sergeant and above who are involved with the community. Pictures of the subject or the department are essential and can be snapshots. We are looking for interviews with police chiefs and sheriffs on command level with photos."

$ $COUNTY

Texas Association of Counties, P.O. Box 2131, Austin TX 78768. (512)478-8753. Fax: (512)477-1324. E-mail: jiml@county.org. Website: www.county.org. **Contact:** Jim Lewis, editor. **15% freelance written.** Bimonthly magazine covering county and state government in Texas. "We provide elected and appointed county officials with insights and information that help them do their jobs and enhances communications among the independent office-holders in the courthouse." Estab. 1988. Circ. 5,500. **Pays on acceptance.** Publishes ms an average of 2 months after acceptance. Byline given. Makes work-for-hire assignments. Editorial lead time 2 months. Submit seasonal material 4 months in advance. Accepts queries by mail, e-mail, phone. Responds in 2 weeks to queries; 1 month to mss. Sample copy and writer's guidelines for 8×10 SAE with 3 first-class stamps.

Nonfiction Historical/nostalgic, photo feature, government innovations. **Buys 5 mss/year.** Query with published clips. Length: 1,000-3,000 words. **Pays $500-700.** Sometimes pays expenses of writers on assignment.

Photos State availability with submission. Buys all rights. Negotiates payment individually. Captions, identification of subjects, model releases required.

Columns/Departments Safety; Human Resources; Risk Management (all directed toward education of Texas county officials), maximum length 1,000 words. **Buys 2 mss/year.** Query with published clips. **Pays $500.**

Tips "Identify innovative practices or developing trends that affect Texas county officials, and have the basic journalism skills to write a multi-sourced, informative feature."

$ $FIRE CHIEF

Primedia Business, 330 N. Wabash, Suite 2300, Chicago IL 60611. (312)595-1080. Fax: (312)595-0295. E-mail: jwilmoth@primediabusiness.com. Website: www.firechief.com. **Contact:** Janet Wilmoth, editor. **60% freelance written.** Monthly magazine. "*Fire Chief* is the management magazine of the fire service, addressing the administrative, personnel, training, prevention/education, professional development and operational issues faced by chiefs and other fire officers, whether in paid, volunteer, or combination departments. We're potentially interested in any article that can help them do their jobs better, whether that's as incident commanders, financial managers, supervisors, leaders, trainers, planners, or ambassadors to municipal officials or the public." Estab. 1956. Circ. 53,000. Pays on publication. Publishes ms an average of 6 months after acceptance. Byline given. Kill fee negotiable. Buys first, one-time, second serial (reprint), all rights. Editorial lead time 2 months. Submit seasonal material 4 months in advance. Accepts queries by mail, e-mail, fax. Responds in 1 month to queries; 2 months to mss. Sample copy and writer's guidelines free or online.

Nonfiction "If your department has made some changes in its structure, budget, mission, or organizational culture (or really did reinvent itself in a serious way), an account of that process, including the mistakes made and lessons learned, could be a winner. Similarly, if you've observed certain things that fire departments typically could do a lot better and you think you have the solution, let us know." How-to, technical. **Buys 50-60 mss/year.** Query with published clips. Length: 1,500-8,000 words. **Pays $50-400.** Sometimes pays expenses of writers on assignment.

Photos State availability with submission. Reviews transparencies, prints. Buys one-time or reprint rights. Captions, identification of subjects required.

Columns/Departments Training Perspectives; EMS Viewpoints; Sound Off; Volunteer Voice, all 1,000-1,800 words.

Tips "Writers who are unfamiliar with the fire service are very unlikely to place anything with us. Many pieces that we reject are either too unfocused or too abstract. We want articles that help keep fire chiefs well informed and effective at their jobs."

$ $ FIREHOUSE MAGAZINE

Cygnus Business Media, 445 Broad Hollow Rd., Suite 21, Melville NY 11747. (631)845-2700. Fax: (631)845-7109. E-mail: editors@firehouse.com. Website: www.firehouse.com. Editor-in-Chief: Harvey Eisner. **Contact:** Elizabeth Friszell, associate editor. **85% freelance written.** Works with a small number of new/unpublished writers each year. Monthly magazine. *"Firehouse* covers major fires nationwide, controversial issues and trends in the fire service, the latest firefighting equipment and methods of firefighting, historical fires, firefighting history and memorabilia. Fire-related books, fire safety education, hazardous-materials incidents, and the emergency medical services are also covered." Estab. 1976. Circ. 127,000. Pays on publication. Byline given. Accepts queries by mail, e-mail, fax. Sample copy for 9×12 SAE and 8 first-class stamps. Writer's guidelines online.

Nonfiction Book excerpts (of recent books on fire, EMS, and hazardous materials), historical/nostalgic (great fires in history, fire collectibles, the fire service of yesteryear), how-to (fight certain kinds of fires, buy and maintain equipment, run a fire department), technical (on almost any phase of firefighting, techniques, equipment, training, administration), trends in the fire service. No profiles of people or departments that are not unusual or innovative, reports of nonmajor fires, articles not slanted toward firefighters' interests. No poetry. **Buys 100 mss/year.** Query with or without published clips. Length: 500-3,000 words. **Pays $50-400 for assigned articles.**

Photos Send photos with submission. Pays $25-200 for transparencies and color prints. Cannot accept negatives. Captions, identification of subjects required.

Columns/Departments Training (effective methods); Book Reviews; Fire Safety (how departments teach fire safety to the public); Communicating (PR, dispatching); Arson (efforts to combat it). Length: 750-1,000. **Buys 50 mss/year.** Query or send complete ms. **Pays $100-300.**

Tips "Have excellent fire service credentials and be able to offer our readers new information. Read the magazine to get a full understanding of the subject matter, the writing style, and the readers before sending a query or manuscript. Send photos with manuscript or indicate sources for photos. Be sure to focus articles on firefighters."

$ FOREIGN SERVICE JOURNAL

2101 E. St. NW, Washington DC 20037-2990. (202)338-4045. Fax: (202)338-8244. E-mail: journal@afsa.org. Website: www.afsa.org. **Contact:** Shawn Dorman. **75% freelance written.** Monthly magazine for Foreign Service personnel and others interested in foreign affairs and related subjects. Estab. 1924. Pays on publication. Publishes ms an average of 3 months after acceptance. Byline given. Buys first North American serial rights. Accepts queries by mail, e-mail, fax. Responds in 1 month to queries. Sample copy for $3.50 and 10×12 SAE with 6 first-class stamps. Writer's guidelines for #10 SASE.

○┅ Break in through "Postcard from Abroad—short items (600 words) on life abroad."

Nonfiction Uses articles on "diplomacy, professional concerns of the State Department and Foreign Service, diplomatic history and articles on Foreign Service experiences. Much of our material is contributed by those working in the profession. Informed outside contributions are welcomed, however." Essays, exposé, humor, opinion, personal experience. **Buys 15-20 unsolicited mss/year.** Query. Length: 1,000-3,000 words. **Offers $60 honorarium.**

Tips "We're more likely to want your article if it has something to do with diplomacy or U.S. foreign policy."

$ $ THE JOURNAL OF SAFE MANAGEMENT OF DISRUPTIVE AND ASSAULTIVE BEHAVIOR

Crisis Prevention Institute, Inc., 3315-K N. 124th St., Brookfield WI 53005. Fax: (262)783-5906. E-mail: info@crisisprevention.com. Website: www.crisisprevention.com. **20% freelance written.** Semiannual journal covering safe management of disruptive and assaultive behavior. "Our audience is human service and business professionals concerned about workplace violence issues. *CPI* is the world leader in violence prevention training." Estab. 1980. Circ. 12,000. Pays on publication. Publishes ms an average of 6 months after acceptance. Byline given. Offers 50% kill fee. Buys one-time, second serial (reprint) rights. Editorial lead time 6 months. Submit seasonal material 3 months in advance. Responds in 1 month to queries. Sample copy and writer's guidelines free.

Nonfiction "Each issue is specifically devoted to one topic. Inquire about topics by e-mail." Interview/profile, new product, opinion, personal experience, research. Inquire for editorial calendar. **Buys 5-10 mss/year.** Query. Length: 1,500-3,000 words. **Pays $50-300 for assigned articles; $50-100 for unsolicited articles.**

Tips "For more information on CPI, please refer to our website."

$ $ LAW AND ORDER

Hendon Co., 130 N. Waukegan Rd., Deerfield IL 60015. (847)444-3300. Fax: (847)444-3333. E-mail: esanow@hendonpub.com. Website: www.lawandordermag.com. **Contact:** Ed Sanow, editor-in-chief. **90% freelance written.** Prefers to work with published/established writers. Monthly magazine covering the administration and operation of law enforcement agencies, directed to police chiefs, sheriffs, and supervisors. Estab. 1953. Circ.

42,000. Pays on publication. Publishes ms an average of 6 months after acceptance. Byline given. Buys first North American serial rights. Submit seasonal material 3 months in advance. Accepts queries by mail, e-mail, fax, phone. Responds in 1 month to queries. Sample copy for 9×12 SAE. Writer's guidelines online.

Nonfiction General police interest. How-to (do specific police assignments), new product (how applied in police operation), technical (specific police operation). Special issues: Weapons (January); Buyers Guide (February); S.W.A.T. (March); Community Relations (April); Science & Technology (May); Training (June); Mobile Patrol (July); Communications (August); Uniforms (September); IACP (October); Investigative (November); Computing & the Internet (December). No articles dealing with courts (legal field) or convicted prisoners. No nostalgic, financial, travel, or recreational material. **Buys 150 mss/year.** Query; no simultaneous queries. Length: 2,000-3,000 words. **Pays 10-25¢/word.**

Photos Send photos with submission. Reviews transparencies, prints. Buys all rights. Pays $25-40/photo. Identification of subjects required.

Tips *"L&O* is a respected magazine that provides up-to-date information that police chiefs can use. Writers must know their subject as it applies to this field. Case histories are well received. We are upgrading editorial quality—stories must show some understanding of the law enforcement field. A frequent mistake is not getting photographs to accompany article."

$ $ LAW ENFORCEMENT TECHNOLOGY

Cygnus Business Media, P.O. Box 803, 1233 Janesville Ave., Fort Atkinson WI 53538-0803. (920)563-1726. Fax: (920)563-1702. E-mail: ronnie.garrett@cygnuspub.com. Editor: Ronnie Garrett. **50% freelance written.** Monthly magazine covering police management and technology. Estab. 1974. Circ. 35,000. Pays on publication. Publishes ms an average of 6 months after acceptance. Byline given. Offers 25% kill fee. Buys first North American serial rights. Editorial lead time 6 months. Submit seasonal material 6 months in advance. Responds in 1 month to queries; 2 months to mss. Writer's guidelines for #10 SASE.

Nonfiction Book excerpts, how-to, interview/profile, photo feature, police management and training. **Buys 15 mss/year.** Query. Length: 800-1,800 words. **Pays $75-400 for assigned articles.**

Reprints Send ms with rights for sale noted and information about when and where the material previously appeared. Payment negotiable.

Photos Send photos with submission. Reviews contact sheets, negatives, 5×7 or 8×10 prints. Buys one-time rights. Offers no additional payment for photos accepted with ms. Captions required.

Tips "Writer should have background in police work or currently work for a police agency. Most of our articles are technical or supervisory in nature. Please query first after looking at a sample copy."

$ $ NATIONAL FIRE & RESCUE

SpecComm International, Inc., 5808 Faringdon Place, Suite 200, Raleigh NC 27609. (919)872-5040. Fax: (919)876-6531. E-mail: ppowell@nfrmag.com. Website: www.nfrmag.com. **Contact:** Phill Powell, editor. **80% freelance written.** *"National Fire & Rescue* is a bimonthly magazine devoted to informing the nation's fire and rescue services, with special emphasis on fire departments serving communities of less than 100,000. It is the *Popular Science* for fire and rescue with easy-to-understand information on science, technology, and training." Estab. 1980. Circ. 30,000. Pays on publication. Publishes ms an average of 5 months after acceptance. Byline given. Offers 50% kill fee. Buys first North American serial rights. Editorial lead time 2 months. Submit seasonal material 3 months in advance. Accepts simultaneous submissions. Responds in 1 month to queries. Call for writer's guidelines.

Nonfiction Book excerpts, how-to, humor, inspirational, interview/profile, new product, personal experience, photo feature. No pieces marketing specific products or services. **Buys 40 mss/year.** Query with published clips. Length: 600-2,000 words. **Pays $100-350 for assigned articles; $100-200 for unsolicited articles.** Pays expenses of writers on assignment.

Photos State availability with submission. Buys one-time rights. Offers $50-200/photo. Identification of subjects required.

Columns/Departments Leadership (management); Training; Special Operations, all 800 words. **Buys 16 mss/year.** Send complete ms. **Pays $100-200.**

Tips "Discuss your story ideas with the editor."

$ $ $ $ NFPA JOURNAL

National Fire Protection Association, P.O. Box 9101, Quincy MA 02269-9101. (617)984-7567. Fax: (617)984-7090. E-mail: nfpajournal@nfpa.org. Website: www.nfpajournal.org. Publisher: Kathie Robinson. **Contact:** John Nicholson, managing editor. Bimonthly magazine covering fire safety, fire science, fire engineering. "The *NFPA Journal,* the official journal of the NFPA, reaches all of the association's various fire safety professionals. Covering major topics in fire protection and suppression, fire protection advances, and public education."

Estab. 1969. Circ. 74,000. **Pays on acceptance.** Byline given. Buys all rights. Accepts queries by e-mail, fax. Writer's guidelines online.

Nonfiction Technical. No fiction, product pieces, or human interest. Query. Length: 2,000-2,500 words. **Negotiates payment individually.**

Tips "Query or call. Be familiar with our publication and audience. We happily send out sample issues and guidelines. We appreciate and value quality writers who can provide well-written material on technical subjects related to fire and life safety."

$ $ 9-1-1 MAGAZINE

Official Publications, Inc., 18201 Weston Place, Tustin CA 92780-2251. (714)544-7776. Fax: (714)838-9233. E-mail: publisher@9-1-1magazine.com. Website: www.9-1-1magazine.com. **Contact:** Randall Larson, editor (editor@9-1-1magazine.com). **85% freelance written.** Bimonthly magazine for knowledgeable emergency communications professionals and those associated with this respectful profession. "Serving law enforcement, fire and emergency medical services, *9-1-1 Magazine* provides valuable information to readers in all aspects of the public safety communications and response community. Each issue contains a blending of product-related, technical, operational, and people-oriented stories, covering the skills, training, and equipment which these professionals have in common." Estab. 1989. Circ. 20,000. Pays on publication. Publishes ms an average of 4-6 months after acceptance. Byline given. Offers 20% kill fee. Buys one-time, second serial (reprint) rights. Accepts queries by mail, e-mail, fax. Responds in 1 month to queries; 2 months to mss. Sample copy for 9×12 SAE and 5 first-class stamps. Writer's guidelines online.

Nonfiction New product, photo feature, technical, incident report. **Buys 20-30 mss/year.** Query by e-mail. We prefer queries, but will look at manuscripts on speculation. Most positive responses to queries are considered on spec, but occasionally we will make assignments. Length: 1,000-2,500 words. **Pays 10¢/word.**

Photos Send photos with submission. Reviews color transparencies, prints, hi-res digital (300 dpi). Buys one-time rights. Offers $50-100/interior, $300/cover. Captions, identification of subjects required.

■ The online version of this magazine contains material not found in the print version.

Tips "We are looking for writers knowledgable in this field. As a trade magazine, stories should be geared for professionals in the emergency services and dispatch field, not the lay public. We use poetry or fiction. Our primary considerations in selecting material are: quality, appropriateness of material, brevity, knowledge of our readership, accuracy, accompanying photography, originality, wit and humor, a clear direction and vision, and proper use of language."

$ $ $ PLANNING

American Planning Association, 122 S. Michigan Ave., Suite 1600, Chicago IL 60603. (312)431-9100. Fax: (312)431-9985. E-mail: slewis@planning.org. Website: www.planning.org. **Contact:** Sylvia Lewis, editor. **30% freelance written.** Monthly magazine emphasizing urban planning for adult, college-educated readers who are regional and urban planners in city, state or federal agencies or in private business or university faculty or students. Estab. 1972. Circ. 35,000. Pays on publication. Publishes ms an average of 2 months after acceptance. Byline given. Buys all rights. Accepts queries by mail, e-mail, fax. Responds in 5 weeks to queries. Sample copy and writer's guidelines for 9×12 SAE with 5 first-class stamps. Writer's guidelines online.

Nonfiction "It's best to query with a fairly detailed, 1-page letter or e-mail. We'll consider any article that's well-written and relevant to our audience. Articles have a better chance if they are timely and related to planning, and if they appeal to a national audience. All articles should be written in magazine feature style." Exposé (on government or business, but topics related to planning, housing, land use, zoning), general interest (trend stories on cities, land use, government), how-to (successful government or citizen efforts in planning, innovations, concepts that have been applied), technical (detailed articles on the nitty-gritty of planning, transportation, computer mapping, but no footnotes or mathematical models). Special issues: Transportation Issue (May 2005); Technology Issue (July 2005). Also needs news stories up to 500 words. **Buys 44 features and 33 news story mss/year.** Length: 500-3,000 words. **Pays $150-1,500.**

Photos "We prefer that authors supply their own photos, but we sometimes take our own or arrange for them in other ways." State availability with submission. Buys one-time rights. Pays $100 minimum for photos used on inside pages and $300 for cover photos. Captions required.

$ $ POLICE AND SECURITY NEWS

DAYS Communications, Inc., 1208 Juniper St., Quakertown PA 18951-1520. (215)538-1240. Fax: (215)538-1208. E-mail: jdevery@policeandsecuritynews.com. **Contact:** James Devery, editor. **40% freelance written.** Bimonthly tabloid on public law enforcement and private security. "Our publication is designed to provide educational and entertaining information directed toward management level. Technical information written for the expert in a manner that the nonexpert can understand." Estab. 1984. Circ. 22,000. Pays on publication. Publishes ms an average of 2 months after acceptance. Byline given. Buys first North American serial rights.

Accepts queries by mail, e-mail, fax, phone. Accepts simultaneous submissions. Sample copy and writer's guidelines for 9×12 SAE with $2.18 postage.

Nonfiction Al Menear, articles editor. Exposé, historical/nostalgic, how-to, humor, interview/profile, opinion, personal experience, photo feature, technical. **Buys 12 mss/year.** Query. Length: 200-4,000 words. **Pays 10¢/word. Sometimes pays in trade-out of services.**

Reprints Send tearsheet, photocopy, or typed ms with rights for sale noted and information about when and where the material previously appeared.

Photos State availability with submission. Reviews 3×5 prints. Buys one-time rights. Offers $10-50/photo.

Fillers Facts, newsbreaks, short humor. **Buys 6/year.** Length: 200-2,000 words. **Pays 10¢/word.**

Ⓝ $ POLICE TIMES

American Federation of Police & Concerned Citizens, Inc., 6350 Horizon Dr., Titusville FL 32780. (321)264-0911. Fax: (321)264-0033. E-mail: policeinfo@aphf.org. Website: www.aphf.org/pt.html. **Contact:** Jim Gordon, executive editor. **80% freelance written.** Eager to work with new/unpublished writers. Quarterly magazine covering "law enforcement (general topics) for men and women engaged in law enforcement and private security, and citizens who are law and order concerned." Circ. 55,000. **Pays on acceptance.** Publishes ms an average of 6 months after acceptance. Byline given. Buys second serial (reprint) rights. Submit seasonal material 4 months in advance. Accepts queries by mail, fax. Accepts simultaneous submissions. Sample copy for $2.50 and 9×12 SAE with 3 first-class stamps. Writer's guidelines for #10 SASE.

Nonfiction Book excerpts, essays (on police science), exposé (police corruption), general interest, historical/nostalgic, how-to, humor, interview/profile, new product, personal experience (with police), photo feature, technical (all police related). Special issues: "We produce a special edition on police killed in the line of duty. It is mailed May 15 so copy must arrive six months in advance. Photos required." No anti-police materials. **Buys 50 mss/year.** Send complete ms. Length: 200-4,000 words. **Pays $25-100. Payment includes right to publish on organization's website.**

Photos Send photos with submission. Reviews 5×6 prints. Buys all rights. Offers $5-25/photo. Identification of subjects required.

Columns/Departments Legal Cases (lawsuits involving police actions); New Products (new items related to police services); Awards (police heroism acts). Length: 200-1,000. **Buys variable number of mss/year.** Send complete ms. **Pays $25-75.**

Fillers Fillers are usually humorous stories about police officer and citizen situations. Special stories on police cases, public corruptions, etc., are most open to freelancers. Anecdotes, facts, newsbreaks. **Buys 100/year.** Length: 50-100 words. **Pays $5-10.**

TRANSACTION/SOCIETY

35 Berrue Circle, Piscataway NJ 08854. (732)445-2280. Fax: (732)445-3138. E-mail: ihorowitz@transactionpub.com. Website: www.transactionpub.com. **Contact:** Irving Louis Horowitz, editor. **10% freelance written.** Prefers to work with published/established writers. Bimonthly magazine for social scientists (policymakers with training in sociology, political issues, and economics). Estab. 1962. Circ. 15,000. Pays on publication. Publishes ms an average of 6 months after acceptance. Byline given. Buys all rights. Responds in 3 months to queries. Sample copy and writer's guidelines for 9×12 SAE with 5 first-class stamps.

Nonfiction Andrew McIntosh, managing editor. "Articles of wide interest in areas of specific interest to the social science community. Must have an awareness of problems and issues in education, population, and urbanization that are not widely reported. Articles on overpopulation, terrorism, international organizations." Book excerpts, essays, interview/profile, photo feature. No general think pieces. Query. **Pays for assigned articles only.**

Photos Douglas Harper, photo editor. Pays $200 for photographic essays done on assignment or upon publication.

Tips "Submit an article on a thoroughly unique subject, written with good literary quality. Present new ideas and research findings in a readable and useful manner. A frequent mistake is writing to satisfy a journal, rather than the intrinsic requirements of the story itself. Avoid posturing and editorializing."

GROCERIES & FOOD PRODUCTS

AUTOMATIC MERCHANDISER MAGAZINE

Cygnus Business Media, P.O. Box 803, Fort Atkinson WI 53538. (800)547-7377. Fax: (920)568-2305. E-mail: stacey.meacham@amonline.com. Website: www.amonline.com. Editor: Elliot Maras. **Contact:** Stacey Meacham, managing editor. **30% freelance written.** Monthly magazine covering vending and office coffee. Estab.

1940. Circ. 16,000. **Pays on acceptance.** Byline given. Buys first rights. Editorial lead time 1 months. Accepts queries by mail, e-mail, fax. Accepts simultaneous submissions. Sample copy online.

$ $ $ DISTRIBUTION CHANNELS

AWMA's Magazine for Candy, Tobacco, Grocery, and General Merchandise Marketers, American Wholesale Marketers Association, 2750 Prosperity Ave., Suite 530, Fairfax VA 22031. (703)208-3358. Fax: (703)573-5738. E-mail: tracic@awmanet.org. Website: www.awmanet.org. **Contact:** Traci Carneal, editor-in-chief. **50% free-lance written.** Magazine published 10 times/year. "We cover trends in candy, tobacco, groceries, beverages, snacks, and other product categories found in convenience stores, grocery stores, and drugstores, plus distribution topics. Contributors should have prior experience writing about the food, retail, and/or distribution industries. Editorial includes a mix of columns, departments, and features (2-6 pages). We also cover AWMA programs." Estab. 1948. Circ. 11,000. **Pays on acceptance.** Publishes ms an average of 2 months after acceptance. Byline given. Editorial lead time 4 months. Accepts queries by mail, e-mail, fax. Writer's guidelines online.

Nonfiction How-to, technical, industry trends; also profiles of distribution firms. No comics, jokes, poems, or other fillers. **Buys 50 mss/year.** Query with published clips. Length: 1,200-3,600 words. **Pays 50¢/word.** Sometimes pays industry members who author articles. Pays expenses of writers on assignment.

Photos Authors must provide artwork (with captions) with articles.

Tips "We're looking for reliable, accurate freelancers with whom we can establish a long-term working relationship. We need writers who understand this industry. We accept very few articles on speculation. Most are assigned. To consider a new writer for an assignment, we must first receive his or her résumé, at least 2 writing samples, and references."

$ $ $ $ FOOD PRODUCT DESIGN MAGAZINE

Weeks Publishing, 3400 Dundee Rd., Suite 100, Northbrook IL 60062. (847)559-0385. Fax: (847)559-0389. E-mail: weeksfpd@aol.com. **Contact:** Lynn Kuntz, editor. **50% freelance written.** Monthly magazine covering food processing industry. "The magazine written for food technologists by food technologists. No foodservice/restaurant, consumer, or recipe development." Estab. 1991. Circ. 30,000. **Pays on acceptance.** Publishes ms an average of 2 months after acceptance. Byline given. Buys one-time, all rights, makes work-for-hire assignments. Editorial lead time 4 months. Sample copy for 9 × 12 SAE and 5 first-class stamps.

Nonfiction Technical. **Buys 30 mss/year.** Length: 1,500-7,000 words. **Pays $100-1,500.** Sometimes pays expenses of writers on assignment.

Reprints Accepts previously published submissions depending on where it was published.

Photos State availability with submission. Reviews transparencies, Prints. Buys rights depending on photo. Offers no additional payment for photos accepted with ms. Captions required.

Columns/Departments Pays $100-500.

Tips "If you haven't worked in the food industry in Research & Development, or QA/QC, don't bother to call us. If you can't communicate technical information in a way that is clear, easy-to-understand and well organized, don't bother to call us. While perfect grammar is not expected, good grammar and organization is."

$ $ FOODSERVICE DIRECTOR

VNU Business Media, 770 Broadway, New York NY 10003. (646)654-7403. Fax: (646)654-7410. E-mail: jpond@fsdmag.com. Website: www.fsdmag.com. Editor-In-Chief: James Pond. Feature Editor: Karen Weisberg. News Editor: Jennifer Alexis. **20% freelance written.** Monthly tabloid covering noncommercial foodservice operations for operators of kitchens and dining halls in schools, colleges, hospitals/health care, office and plant cafeterias, military, airline/transportation, correctional institutions. Estab. 1988. Circ. 45,000. Pays on publication. Byline sometimes given. Buys all rights for print and online usage. Submit seasonal material 3 months in advance. Accepts simultaneous submissions. Sample copy for free.

Nonfiction How-to, interview/profile. **Buys 60-70 mss/year.** Query with published clips. Length: 700-900 words. **Pays $250-500.**

Photos Send photos with submission. Reviews transparencies. Buys all rights. Offers no additional payment for photos accepted with ms. Identification of subjects required.

Columns/Departments Equipment (case studies of kitchen/serving equipment in use), 700-900 words; Food (specific category studies per publication calendar), 750-900 words. Query.

$ $ FRESH CUT MAGAZINE

The Magazine for Value-added Produce, Columbia Publishing, 417 N. 20th Ave., Yakima WA 98902. (509)248-2452. Fax: (509)248-4056. E-mail: rick@freshcut.com. **Contact:** Rick Stedman, editor. **40% freelance written.** Monthly magazine covering minimally processed fresh fruits and vegetables, packaged salads, etc. "We want informative articles about processing produce. We also want stories about how these products are sold at retail, in restaurants, etc." Estab. 1993. Circ. 18,464. Pays on publication. Publishes ms an average of 2 months after acceptance. Byline given. Buys all rights. Editorial lead time 2 months. Submit seasonal material 3 months in advance. Accepts queries by mail, e-mail, fax, phone. Responds in 1 month to queries; 2 months to mss. Sample copy for 9×12 SAE. Writer's guidelines for #10 SASE.

Nonfiction Historical/nostalgic, new product, opinion, technical. Special issues: Retail (May); Foodservice (February, July); Packaging Technology (December). **Buys 2-4 mss/year.** Query with published clips. **Pays $5/ column inch for assigned articles; $75-125 for unsolicited articles.**

Reprints Send tearsheet with rights for sale noted and information about when and where the material previously appeared. Pays 50% of amount paid for an original article.

Photos Send photos with submission. Reviews transparencies. Buys one-time rights. Offers no additional payment for photos accepted with ms. Identification of subjects required.

Columns/Departments Packaging; Food Safety; Processing/Engineering. **Buys 20 mss/year.** Query. **Pays $125- 200.**

Fillers Facts. Length: 300 words maximum. **Pays $25-50.**

$ $ HEALTH PRODUCTS BUSINESS

CYGNUS Business Media, Inc., 445 Broad Hollow Rd., Suite 21, Melville NY 11747. (631)845-2700. Fax: (631)845-2723. Website: www.healthproductsbusiness.com. **Contact:** Michael Schiavetta, editor. **70% freelance written.** Monthly magazine covering natural health products. ''The business magazine for natural products retailers.'' Estab. 1954. Circ. 18,000. Pays on publication. Publishes ms an average of 3 months after acceptance. Byline given. Buys first North American serial rights. Editorial lead time 4 months. Submit seasonal material 3 months in advance. Accepts queries by mail, fax. Sample copy for $3.

Nonfiction Query first. **Pays $200-450 for articles on natural health retailing.**

Photos State availability with submission.

   The online version of this publication contains material not found in the print edition. Contact: Michael Schiavetta, editor.

Tips ''We are always looking for well-written features with a lot of detailed information, but new writers should always query first to receive information. We prefer writers with industry experience/interest. AP Style, a plus.''

$ $ PRODUCE MERCHANDISING

Vance Publishing Corp., 10901 W. 84th Terrace, Lenexa KS 66214. (913)438-8700. Fax: (913)438-0691. E-mail: eashby@producemerchandising.com. Website: www.producemerchandising.com. **Contact:** Elizabeth Ashby, editor. **33% freelance written.** Monthly magazine. ''The magazine's editorial purpose is to provide information about promotions, merchandising, and operations in the form of ideas and examples. *Produce Merchandising* is the only monthly journal on the market that is dedicated solely to produce merchandising information for retailers.'' Circ. 12,000. **Pays on acceptance.** Publishes ms an average of 3 months after acceptance. Byline given. Buys all rights. Editorial lead time 3 months. Accepts queries by mail. Responds in 2 weeks to queries. Sample copy for free.

Nonfiction How-to, interview/profile, new product, photo feature, technical (contact the editor for a specific assignment). **Buys 48 mss/year.** Query with published clips. Length: 1,000-1,500 words. **Pays $200-600.** Pays expenses of writers on assignment.

Photos State availability of or send photos with submission. Reviews color slides and 3×5 or larger prints. Buys all rights. Offers no additional payment for photos accepted with ms. Captions, identification of subjects, model releases required.

Columns/Departments Contact editor for a specific assignment. **Buys 30 mss/year.** Query with published clips. **Pays $200-450.**

Tips ''Send in clips and contact the editor with specific story ideas. Story topics are typically outlined up to a year in advance.''

$ $ THE PRODUCE NEWS

482 Hudson Terrace, Englewood Cliffs NJ 07632. (201)503-9100. Fax: (201)503-9104. E-mail: groh@theproduce news.com. Website: www.theproducenews.com. Publisher: Gordon M. Hochberg. **Contact:** John Groh, editor. **10% freelance written.** Works with a small number of new/unpublished writers each year. Weekly magazine for commercial growers and shippers, receivers and distributors of fresh fruits and vegetables, including chain store produce buyers and merchandisers. Estab. 1897. Pays on publication. Publishes ms an average of 2 weeks after acceptance. Accepts queries by mail, e-mail, fax. Responds in 1 month to queries. Sample copy for 10×13 SAE and 4 first-class stamps., Writer's guidelines for 10×13 SAE with 4 first-class Stamps.

Nonfiction News stories (about the produce industry). Buys profiles, spot news, coverage of successful business operations and articles on merchandising techniques. Query. **Pays $1/column inch minimum.** Sometimes pays expenses of writers on assignment.

Photos Black and white glossies or color prints. Pays $8-10/photo.

Tips "Stories should be trade-oriented, not consumer-oriented. As our circulation grows in the next year, we are interested in stories and news articles from all fresh-fruit-growing areas of the country."

$ $⧉ WESTERN GROCER MAGAZINE

Mercury Publications Ltd., 1839 Inkster Blvd., Winnipeg MB R2X 1R3, Canada. (204)954-2085. Fax: (204)954-2057. E-mail: mp@mercury.mb.ca. Website: www.mercury.mb.ca/. Editor: Frank Yeo. **Contact:** Kristi Balon, editorial production manager. **75% freelance written.** Bimonthly magazine covering the grocery industry. Reports profiles on independent food stores, supermarkets, manufacturers and food processors, brokers, distributors, and wholesalers. Estab. 1916. Circ. 15,500. Pays 30-45 days from receipt of invoice. Byline given. Offers 33% kill fee. Buys all rights. Submit seasonal material 3 months in advance. Sample copy and writer's guidelines free or by e-mail.

  • Assigns stories to Canadian writers based on editorial needs of publication.

Nonfiction How-to, interview/profile. Industry reports and profiles on companies. Query with published clips. Length: 500-9,000 words. **Pays 25-35¢/word.** Sometimes pays expenses of writers on assignment.

Photos State availability with submission. Reviews negatives, transparencies, 3×5 prints, JPEG, EPS, or TIF files. Buys all rights. Negotiates payment individually. Captions required.

Tips "Send an e-mailed, faxed, or mailed query outlining your experience, interests, and pay expectations. A requirement also is clippings."

HOME FURNISHINGS & HOUSEHOLD GOODS

FINE FURNISHINGS INTERNATIONAL

FFI, Grace McNamara, Inc., 4215 White Bear Parkway, Suite 100, St. Paul MN 55110. Fax: (651)653-4308. E-mail: ffiedit@gwmcnamara.com. Website: www.ffimagazine.com. **Contact:** Kate Lundquist, managing editor. Quarterly magazine covering the high-end furniture industry. Estab. 1997. Circ. 25,000. Pays on publication. Buys all rights. Editorial lead time 3-5 months. Accepts queries by mail, e-mail. Sample copy for $5.

Nonfiction Interior designer profiles, high-end residential furnishings, international trade events, and interior-design associations are all featured in our trade publication.

Tips "Writers must have a knowledge of interior design and furnishings that allows them to speak with authority to our to-the-trade audience of interior designers and architects."

$ $ $ HOME FURNISHINGS RETAILER

National Home Furnishings Association (NHFA), 3910 Tinsley Dr., High Point NC 27265. (336)801-6156. Fax: (336)801-6102. E-mail: tkemerly@nhfa.org. **Contact:** Trisha Kemerly, editor. **75% freelance written.** Monthly magazine published by NHFA covering the home furnishings industry. "We hope that home furnishings retailers view our magazine as a profitability tool. We want each issue to help them make money or save money." Estab. 1927. Circ. 15,000. **Pays on acceptance.** Publishes ms an average of 6 weeks after acceptance. Byline given. Buys first North American serial rights. Editorial lead time 3 months. Accepts queries by mail, e-mail. Responds in 1 month to queries. Sample copy available with proper postage. Writer's guidelines for #10 SASE.

  ⊶ Break in by "e-mailing queries that pertain to our market—furniture retailers. We publish articles that give our readers tangible ways to improve their business."

Nonfiction Query with published clips. Length: 3,000-5,000 words (features). **Pays $350-500 for assigned articles.**

Photos State availability with submission. Reviews transparencies. Buys one-time rights. Negotiates payment individually. Identification of subjects required.

Columns/Departments Columns cover business and product trends that shape the home furnishings industry. Advertising and Marketing; Finance; Technology; Training; Creative Leadership; Law; Style and Operations. Length: 1,200-1,500 words. Query with published clips.

Tips "Our readership includes owners of small 'ma and pa' furniture stores, executives of medium-sized chains (2-10 stores), and executives of big chains. Articles should be relevant to retailers and provide them with tangible information, ideas, and products to better their business."

HOME LIGHTING & ACCESSORIES

1011 Clifton Ave., Clifton NJ 07013. (973)779-1600. Fax: (973)779-3242. E-mail: linda@homelighting.com. Website: www.homelighting.com. **Contact:** Linda Longo, editor. **25% freelance written.** Prefers to work with published/established writers. Monthly magazine for lighting showrooms/department stores. Estab. 1923. Circ. 10,000. Pays on publication. Publishes ms an average of 6 months after acceptance. Buys first rights. Submit seasonal material 6 months in advance. Accepts queries by mail, e-mail. Responds in 2 months to queries. Sample copy for 9×12 SAE and 4 first-class stamps.

Nonfiction Interview/profile (with lighting retailers), personal experience (as a businessperson involved with lighting), technical (concerning lighting or lighting design), profile (of a successful lighting retailer/lamp buyer). Special issues: Outdoor (March); Tribute To Tiffanies (August). **Buys less than 10 mss/year.** Query.

Reprints Send tearsheet and information about when and where the material previously appeared.

Photos State availability with submission. Offers no additional payment for 5×7 or 8×10 b&w glossy prints. Captions required.

Tips "Have a unique perspective on retailing lamps and lighting fixtures. We often use freelancers located in a part of the country where we'd like to profile a specific business or person. Anyone who has published an article dealing with any aspect of home furnishings will have high priority."

WINDOW FASHIONS

Grace McNamara, Inc., 4215 White Bear Pkwy., Suite 100, St. Paul MN 55110. Fax: (651)653-4308. E-mail: wfedit@gracemcnamarainc.com. Website: www.window-fashions.com. **Contact:** Linda Henry, senior editor. **30% freelance written.** Monthly magazine "dedicated to the advancement of the window fashions industry, *Window Fashions* Design & Education magazine provides comprehensive information on design and business principles, window fashion aesthetics, and product applications. The magazine serves the window-treatment and wall-coverings industry, including designers, retailers, dealers, specialty stores, workrooms, manufacturers, fabricators, and others associated with the field of interior design. Writers should be thoroughly knowledgable on the subject, and submittals need to be comprehensive." Estab. 1981. Circ. 30,000. Pays on publication. Publishes ms an average of 3 months after acceptance. Byline given. Buys all rights. Editorial lead time 3 months. Submit seasonal material 4 months in advance. Accepts queries by mail, e-mail. Accepts simultaneous submissions. Sample copy for $5.

Nonfiction How-to (window fashion installation), interview/profile (of designers), personal experience. "No broad topics not specific to the window fashions industry." **Buys 24 mss/year.** Query or send complete ms. Length: 800-1,000 words.

Tips "The most helpful experience is if a writer has knowledge of interior design or, specifically, window treatments. We already have a pool of generalists, although we welcome clips from writers who would like to be considered for assignments. Our style is professional business writing—no flowery prose. Articles tend to be to the point, as our readers are busy professionals who read for information, not for leisure. Most of all we need creative ideas and approaches to topics in the field of window treatments and interior design. A writer needs to be knowledgeable in the field because our readers would know if information were inaccurate."

HOSPITALS, NURSING & NURSING HOMES

AMERICAN JOURNAL OF NURSING

333 7th Ave., 20th Floor, New York NY 10001. (800)933-6525. Fax: (212)886-1206. E-mail: ajn@lww.com. Website: www.ajn.edmgr.com. **Contact:** Diana Mason, editor-in-chief. Monthly magazine covering nursing and health care. Estab. 1900. Circ. 342,000. Pays on publication. Publishes ms an average of 6 months after acceptance. Byline given. Accepts queries by mail. Responds in 2 weeks to queries; 10 weeks to mss. Sample copy for free. Writer's guidelines online.

Nonfiction Practical, hands-on clinical evidence-based articles of interest to nurses in all settings; professional issues; personal experience. Now accepting commentaries, poetry, short stories, and personal essays. Opinion, personal experience.

Photos Now accepting paintings, drawings, photos of sculpture, and other artwork. Reviews b&w and color transparencies, prints. Identification of subjects, model releases required.

Tips "Send an outline with query letter."

$ $ $ HOSPITALS & HEALTH NETWORKS

Health Forum, 1 N. Franklin, 29th Floor, Chicago IL 60606. (312)422-2100. E-mail: bsantamour@healthforum.com. Website: www.hhnmag.com. **Contact:** Bill Santamour, managing editor. **25% freelance written.** Monthly magazine covering hospitals. "We are a business publication for hospital and health system executives. We use only writers who are thoroughly familiar with the hospital field. Submit résumé and up to five samples of health care-related articles. We assign all articles and do not consider manuscripts." Estab. 1926. Circ. 85,000. **Pays on acceptance.** Publishes ms an average of 3 months after acceptance. Byline given. Offers variable kill fee. Buys all rights. Editorial lead time 2-3 months. Accepts queries by e-mail. Responds in 2-4 months to queries.

Nonfiction Interview/profile, technical. Query with published clips. Length: 350-2,000 words. **Pays $300-1,500 for assigned articles.**

Tips "If you demonstrate via published clips that you are thoroughly familiar with the business issues facing health-care executives, and that you are a polished reporter and writer, we will consider assigning you an article for our InBox section to start out. These are generally 350 words on a specific development of interest to hospitals and health system executives. Persistence does not pay with us. Once you've sent your résumé and clips, we will review them. If we have no assignment at that time, we will keep promising freelance candidates on file for future assignments."

$ $ $❒ LONG TERM CARE

The Ontario Long Term Care Association, 345 Renfrew Dr., Suite 102-202, Markham ON L3R 9S9, Canada. (905)470-8995. Fax: (905)470-9595. E-mail: hlrpublishing@bellnet.ca. Website: www.oltca.com. Co-Editor: Tracey Ann Schofield. **Contact:** Heather Lang, editor. Quarterly magazine covering "practical articles of interest to staff working in a long term care setting (nursing home, retirement home); professional issues; information must be applicable to a Canadian setting; focus should be on staff and for resident well-being." Estab. 1990. Circ. 6,000. Pays on publication. Publishes ms an average of 4 months after acceptance. Byline given. Buys one-time rights. Editorial lead time 3 months. Submit seasonal material 5 months in advance. Responds in 3 months to queries. Sample copy for free. Writer's guidelines online.

Nonfiction General interest, how-to (practical, of use to long term care practitioners), inspirational, interview/profile. No product-oriented articles. Query with published clips. Length: 800-1,500 words. **Pays up to $500 (Canadian).**

Photos Send photos with submission. Reviews contact sheets, 5×5 prints. Buys one-time rights. Offers no additional payment for photos accepted with ms. Captions, model releases required.

Columns/Departments Resident Health (nursing, rehabilitation, food services); Resident Life (activities, volunteers, spiritual and pastoral care); Environment (housekeeping, laundry, maintenance, safety, landscape and architecture, staff health and well being), all 800 words. Query with published clips. **Pays up to $1,000 (Canadian).**

Tips "Articles must be positive, upbeat, and contain helpful information that staff and managers working in the long term care field can use. Focus should be on staff and resident well being. Articles that highlight new ways of doing things are particularly useful. Please call the editor to discuss ideas. Must be applicable to Canadian settings."

NURSEWEEK

NurseWeek Publishing, 1156-C Aster Ave., Sunnyvale CA 94086. (800)859-2091. Fax: (408)249-3756. E-mail: richardh@nurseweek.com. Website: www.nurseweek.com. **Contact:** Richard Hellmann, executive news editor. Magazine. *NurseWeek* is an independent biweekly news magazine supported by advertising revenue, sales of continuing education, and trade shows. Its editorial mission is to provide nurses with the latest news, resources, and opportunities to help them succeed in their lives and careers. Five regional editions: California, Mountain West, South Central, Midwest, and Great Lakes. Assigns articles. **Pays on acceptance.**

▣ NurseWeek.com is updated daily with news content and posts new job listings on a daily basis.

$ $ $ NURSING SPECTRUM

Florida Edition, Nursing Spectrum, 1001 W. Cypress Creek Rd., Suite 330, Ft. Lauderdale FL 33309. (954)776-1455. Fax: (954)776-1456. E-mail: pclass@nursingspectrum.com. Website: www.nursingspectrum.com. **Contact:** Phyllis Class, RN, editorial director. **80% freelance written.** Biweekly magazine covering registered nursing. "We support and recognize registered nurses. All articles must have at least 1 RN in byline. We prefer articles that feature nurses in our region, but articles of interest to all nurses are welcome, too. We look for substantive, yet readable articles. Our bottom line—timely, relevant, and compelling articles that support nurses and help them excel in their clinical and professional careers." Estab. 1991. Circ. 90,000. Pays on publication. Byline given. Buys all rights. Editorial lead time 3 months. Submit seasonal material 4 months in advance. Accepts queries by mail, e-mail, fax, phone. Responds in 1 month to queries; 4 months to mss. Sample copy and writer's guidelines free. Writer's guidelines online.

○▬ "Having an original idea is paramount and the first step in writing an article. We are looking for success stories, nurses to be proud of, and progress that is helping patients. If you and your colleagues have dealt with and learned from a thorny issue, tell us how. What is new in your field? Consider your audience: all RNs, well educated, and of various specialties. Will they relate, be inspired, learn something? The best articles are both interesting and informative."

Nonfiction General interest, how-to (career management), humor, interview/profile, personal experience, photo feature. Special issues: Critical Care; Nursing Management. "No articles that do not have at least 1 RN on the byline." **Buys 125 plus mss/year.** Length: 700-1,200 words. **Pays $50-800 for assigned articles.** Sometimes pays expenses of writers on assignment.

Photos Buys one-time rights. Negotiates payment individually. Captions, identification of subjects, model releases required.

Columns/Departments Perspectives in Leadership (nurse managers); Advanced Practice (advanced practice nurses); Humor Infusion (cartoon, amusing anecdotes); Career Fitness (career tips, types of careers). **Buys 75 mss/year.** Query with published clips. **Pays $50-120.**

Tips "Write in 'magazine' style—as if talking to another RN. Use to-the-point, active language. Narrow your focus. Topics such as 'The Future of Nursing' or 'Dealing With Change' are too broad and nonspecific. Use informative but catchy titles and subheads (we can help with this). If quoting others be sure quotes are meaningful and add substance to the piece. To add vitality, you may use statistics and up-to-date references. Try to paint a complete picture, using pros and cons. Be both positive and realistic."

$ $ $NURSING SPECTRUM

Greater Philadelphia/Tri-State edition, Nursing Spectrum, 2002 Renaissance Blvd., Suite 250, King of Prussia PA 19406. (610)292-8000. Fax: (610)292-0179. E-mail: dnovak@nursingspectrum.com. Website: www.nursings pectrum.com. **Contact:** Donna Novak, editorial director. **80% freelance written.** Biweekly magazine covering registered nursing. "We support and recognize registered nurses. All articles must have at least one RN in byline. We prefer articles that feature nurses in our region, but articles of interest to all nurses are welcome, too. We look for substantive, yet readable articles. Our bottom line—timely, relevant, and compelling articles that support nurses and help them excel in their clinical and professional careers." Estab. 1992. Circ. 74,000. Byline given. Writer's guidelines online.

• See *Nursing Spectrum, Florida Edition* for article needs.

$ $ $NURSING SPECTRUM

New England edition, Nursing Spectrum, 1050 Waltham St., Suite 330, Waltham MA 02421. (781)863-2300. Fax: (781)863-6277. E-mail: jborgatti@nursingspectrum.com. Website: www.nursingspectrum.com. **Contact:** Joan Borgatti, RN, editor. **80% freelance written.** Biweekly magazine covering registered nursing. "We support and recognize registered nurses. All articles must have at least one RN in byline. We prefer articles that feature nurses in our region, but articles of interest to all nurses are welcome, too. We look for substantive, yet readable articles. Our bottom line—timely, relevant, and compelling articles that support nurses and help them excel in their clinical and professional careers." Estab. 1997. Circ. 80,000. Byline given. Accepts queries by mail, e-mail, fax, phone. Writer's guidelines online.

• See *Nursing Spectrum, Florida Edition* for article needs.

The online version carries original content not found in the print edition. Contact: Cynthia Saver, RN, editor.

$ $ $NURSING SPECTRUM

Washington, DC/Baltimore edition, Nursing Spectrum, 803 W. Broad St., Suite 500, Falls Church VA 22046. (703)237-6515. Fax: (703)237-6299. E-mail: pmeredith@nursingspectrum.com. Website: www.nursingspectru m.com. **Contact:** Pam Meredith, RN, editor. **80% freelance written.** Biweekly journal covering registered nursing. "We support and recognize registered nurses. All articles must have at least one RN in byline. We prefer articles that feature nurses in our region, but articles of interest to all nurses are welcome, too. We look for substantive, yet readable articles. Our bottom line—timely, relevant, and compelling articles that support nurses and help them excel in their clinical and professional careers." Estab. 1990. Circ. 1 million. Writer's guidelines online.

• See *Nursing Spectrum, Florida Edition* for article needs.

$ $NURSING2004

Lippincott Williams & Wilkins, 323 Norristown Rd., Suite 200, Ambler PA 19002. (215)646-8700. Fax: (215)367-2155. E-mail: nursing@lww.com. Website: www.nursing2004.com. Editor-in-Chief: Cheryl L. Mee, RN, BC, MSN. Managing Editor: Jane Benner. **Contact:** Pat Wolf, editorial dept. **100% freelance written.** Monthly magazine "Written by nurses for nurses; we look for practical advice for the direct caregiver that reflects the author's experience." "Any form acceptable, but focus must be nursing." Estab. 1971. Circ. over 300,000. Pays on publication. Publishes ms an average of 18 months after acceptance. Byline given. Offers 50% kill fee. Buys all rights. Submit seasonal material 8 months in advance. Responds in 2 weeks to queries; 3 months to mss. Sample copy for $5. Writer's guidelines online.

Nonfiction Book excerpts, exposé, how-to (specifically as applies to nursing field), inspirational, opinion, personal experience, photo feature. No articles from patients' point of view, poetry, etc. **Buys 100 mss/year.** Query. Length: 100 words minimum. **Pays $50-400 for assigned articles.**

Reprints Send photocopy and information about when and where the material previously appeared. Pays 50% of amount paid for an original articles.

Photos State availability with submission. Buys all rights. Offers no additional payment for photos accepted with ms. Model releases required.

Tips "Basically, *Nursing2004* is a how-to journal, full of hands-on, practical articles. We look for the voice of experience from authors and for articles that help our readers deal with problems they face. We're always interested in taking a look at manuscripts that fall into the following categories: clinical articles, drug articles, charting/documentation, emotional problems, legal problems, ethical dilemmas, difficult or challenging cases."

HOTELS, MOTELS, CLUBS, RESORTS & RESTAURANTS

$ $ BARTENDER MAGAZINE

Foley Publishing, P.O. Box 158, Liberty Corner NJ 07938. (908)766-6006. Fax: (908)766-6607. E-mail: barmag@aol.com. Website: www.bartender.com. Editor: Jaclyn M. Wilson. **Contact:** Jackie Foley, publisher. **100% freelance written.** Prefers to work with published/established writers; eager to work with new/unpublished writers. Quarterly magazine emphasizing liquor and bartending for bartenders, tavern owners, and owners of restaurants with full-service liquor licenses. Circ. 148,225. Pays on publication. Publishes ms an average of 3 months after acceptance. Byline given. Buys first North American serial, first, one-time, second serial (reprint), simultaneous, all rights. Submit seasonal material 3 months in advance. Accepts simultaneous submissions. Responds in 2 months to mss. Sample copy for 9 × 12 SAE and 4 first-class stamps.

Nonfiction General interest, historical/nostalgic, how-to, humor, interview/profile (with famous bartenders or ex-bartenders), new product, opinion, personal experience, photo feature, travel, nostalgia, unique bars, new techniques, new drinking trends, bar sports, bar magic tricks. Special issues: Annual Calendar and Daily Cocktail Recipe Guide. Send complete ms and SASE. Length: 100-1,000 words.

Reprints Send tearsheet and information about when and where the material previously appeared. Pays 25% of amount paid for an original article.

Photos Send photos with submission. Pays $7.50-50 for 8 × 10 b&w glossy prints; $10-75 for 8 × 10 color glossy prints. Captions, model releases required.

Columns/Departments Bar of the Month; Bartender of the Month; Drink of the Month; Creative Cocktails; Bar Sports; Quiz; Bar Art; Wine Cellar; Tips from the Top (from prominent figures in the liquor industry); One For the Road (travel); Collectors (bar or liquor-related items); Photo Essays. **Length:** 200-1,000 words. Query by mail only with SASE. **Pays $50-200.**

Fillers Anecdotes, newsbreaks, short humor, clippings, jokes, gags. Length: 25-100 words. **Pays $5-25.**

Tips "To break in, absolutely make sure that your work will be of interest to all bartenders across the country. Your style of writing should reflect the audience you are addressing. The most frequent mistake made by writers in completing an article for us is using the wrong subject."

$ $ CHEF

The Food Magazine for Professionals, Talcott Communications Corp., 20 W. Kinzie, 12th Floor, Chicago IL 60610. (312)849-2220. Fax: (312)849-2174. E-mail: chef@talcott.com. Website: www.chefmagazine.com. **Contact:** Editor. **40% freelance written.** Monthly magazine covering chefs in all food-service segments. "*Chef* is the one magazine that communicates food production to a commercial, professional audience in a meaningful way." Circ. 42,000. **Pays on acceptance.** Byline given. Offers 10% kill fee. Buys first North American serial, second serial (reprint) rights. Editorial lead time 2 months. Submit seasonal material 4 months in advance. Accepts queries by mail, e-mail, fax. Writer's guidelines free.

Nonfiction Book excerpts, essays, exposé, general interest, historical/nostalgic, how-to (create a dish or perform a technique), inspirational, interview/profile, new product, opinion, personal experience, photo feature, technical. **Buys 30-50 mss/year.** Query. Length: 750-1,500 words. **Pays $250-500.** Sometimes pays expenses of writers on assignment.

Reprints Accepts previously published submissions.

Photos State availability with submission. Reviews transparencies. Buys one-time rights. Negotiates payment individually. Captions, identification of subjects required.

Columns/Departments Flavor (traditional and innovative applications of a particular flavor) 1,000-1,200 words; Dish (professional chef profiles), 1,000-1,200 words; Savor (themed recipes), 1,000-1,500 words. **Buys 12-18 mss/year.** Query. **Pays $250-500.**

Tips "Know food and apply it to the business of chefs. Always query first, after you've read our magazine. Tell us how your idea can be used by our readers to enhance their businesses in some way."

$ $ CHRISTIAN CAMP & CONFERENCE JOURNAL

Christian Camping International U.S.A., P.O. Box 62189, Colorado Springs CO 80962-2189. (719)260-9400. Fax: (719)260-6398. E-mail: editor@cciusa.org. Website: www.christiancamping.org. **Contact:** Justin Boles, managing editor or Alison Hayhoe, editor. **75% freelance written.** Prefers to work with published/established writers. Bimonthly magazine emphasizing the broad scope of organized camping with emphasis on Christian camps and conference centers. "All who work in youth camps and adult conferences read our magazine for inspiration and to get practical help in ways to serve in their operations." Estab. 1963. Circ. 8,500. Pays on publication. Publishes ms an average of 4 months after acceptance. Byline given. Buys negotiable rights. Submit seasonal material 6 months in advance. Accepts queries by mail, e-mail. Responds in 1 month to queries. Sample copy for $4.95 plus 9×12 SASE. Writer's guidelines online.

Nonfiction General interest (trends in organized camping in general, Christian camping in particular), how-to (anything involved with organized camping, including motivating staff, programming, record keeping, and camper follow-up), inspirational, interview/profile (with movers and shakers in Christian camping; submit a list of basic questions first). **Buys 15-20 mss/year.** Query required. Length: 500-3,000 words. **Pays 16¢/word.**

Reprints Send photocopy and information about when and where the material previously appeared. Pays 50% of amount paid for an original article.

Photos Price negotiable for 35mm color transparencies.

Tips "The most frequent mistake made by writers is that they send articles unrelated to our readers. Ask for our publication guidelines first. Profiles/interviews are the best bet for freelancers."

CLUB MANAGEMENT

The Resource for Successful Club Operations, Finan Publishing Company, 107 W. Pacific Ave., St. Louis MO 63119-2323. (314)961-6644. Fax: (314)961-4809. E-mail: tfinan@finan.com. Website: www.club-mgmt.com. **Contact:** Tom Finan, editor. Bimonthly magazine covering club management, private club market, hospitality industry. Estab. 1925. Circ. 16,702. Pays on publication. Publishes ms an average of 2 months after acceptance. Buys first North American serial, electronic rights. Accepts queries by mail, e-mail, fax.

Nonfiction General interest, historical/nostalgic, how-to, interview/profile, personal experience, photo feature, technical, travel. **Buys 100 mss/year.** Query with published clips. Length: 2,000-2,500 words.

Photos State availability with submission.

Columns/Departments Sports (private club sports: golf, tennis, yachting, fitness, etc.).

Tips "We don't accept blind submissions. Please submit a résumé and clips of writer's work. Send copies, not originals."

$ $ EL RESTAURANTE MEXICANO

P.O. Box 2249, Oak Park IL 60303-2249. (708)445-9454. Fax: (708)445-9477. E-mail: kfurore@restmex.com. **Contact:** Kathleen Furore, editor. Bimonthly magazine covering Mexican restaurants. "*El Restaurante Mexicano* offers features and business-related articles that are geared specifically to owners and operators of Mexican, Tex-Mex, Southwestern, and Latin cuisine restaurants." Estab. 1997. Circ. 27,000. Pays on publication. Publishes ms an average of 3 months after acceptance. Byline given. Buys first North American serial rights. Responds in 2 months to queries. Sample copy for free.

Nonfiction Looking for stories about unique Mexican restaurants and about business issues that affect Mexican restaurant owners. "No specific knowledge of food or restaurants is needed; the key qualification is to be a good reporter who knows how to slant a story toward the Mexican restaurant operator." **Buys 2-4 mss/year.** Query with published clips. Length: 800-1,500 words. **Pays $225.** Pays expenses of writers on assignment.

Tips "Query with a story idea, and tell how it pertains to Mexican restaurants."

$ $ FLORIDA HOTEL & MOTEL JOURNAL

The Official Publication of the Florida Hotel & Motel Association, Accommodations, Inc., P.O. Box 1529, Tallahassee FL 32302-1529. (850)224-2888. Fax: (850)668-2884. E-mail: journal@fhma.net. Website: www.flahotel.com. **Contact:** Lytha Page Belrose, editor. **10% freelance written.** Prefers to work with published/established writers. Bimonthly magazine acting as a reference tool for managers and owners of Florida's hotels, motels, and resorts. Estab. 1978. Circ. 8,500. Pays on publication. Publishes ms an average of 1-2 months after acceptance. Byline given. Buys first rights. Editorial lead time 1-9 months. Submit seasonal material 4-5 months in advance. Accepts queries by mail. Accepts previously published material. Responds in 2-4 months to queries. Sample copy and writer's guidelines free. Writer's guidelines online.

● Preference is given to articles that include references to member properties and general managers affiliated with the Florida Hotel and Motel Association. Since the Association acquires new members weekly, queries may be made prior to the scheduling of interviews. This does not preclude the use of materials or ideas based on non-member properties, but member property sources are preferable.

Nonfiction How-to (pertaining to hotel management), interview/profile, new product, personal experience, technical. No travel tips or articles aimed at the traveling public, and no promotion of individual property, destination, product, or service. Query with published clips. Length: 500-1,500 words. **Pays 10¢/published word.** Pays in contributor copies if the article is reprinted with persmission, or the author is a paid representative of a company which is publicized in some manner through the article. Sometimes pays expenses of writers on assignment.

Photos State availability with submission. Buys all rights. Offers no additional payment for photos accepted with ms. Captions, identification of subjects, model releases required.

Columns/Departments Management Monograph, 500-1,000 words (expert information for hotel and motel management); Florida Scene, 500 words (Florida-specific, time-sensitive information for hotel managers or owners); National Scene, 500-1,000 words (USA-specific, time-sensitive information for hotel managers or owners); Fillers and Features, 500-700 words (information specific to editorial focus for the issue). Query. **Pays in contributor copies.**

Fillers Anecdotes, facts, short humor. Length: 50-1,000 words. **Pays in contributor copies.**

Tips "We use press releases provided to this office that fit the profile of our magazine's departments, targeting items of interest to the general managers of Florida's lodging operations. Feature articles are written based on an editorial calendar. We also publish an annual buyer's guide that provides a directory of all FH&MA member companies and allied member companies."

$ $ $ $ HOSPITALITY TECHNOLOGY

Edgell Communications, 4 Middlebury Blvd., Randolph NJ 07869. (973)252-0100. Fax: (973)252-9020. E-mail: rpaul@edgellmail.com. Website: www.htmagazine.com. **Contact:** Reid Paul, managing editor. **70% freelance written.** Magazine published 9 times/year. "We cover the technology used in foodservice and lodging. Our readers are the operators, who have significant IT responsibilities." Estab. 1996. Circ. 16,000. **Pays on acceptance.** Publishes ms an average of 1 month after acceptance. Byline given. Buys all rights, makes work-for-hire assignments. Editorial lead time 2 months. Accepts queries by mail, e-mail, fax, phone. Responds in 2 weeks to queries.

Nonfiction How-to, interview/profile, new product, technical. Special issues: "We publish two studies each year, the Restaurant Industry Technology Study and the Lodging Industry Technology Study." No unsolicited mss. **Buys 40 mss/year.** Query with published clips. Length: 800-1,200 words. **Pays $1/word.** Sometimes pays expenses of writers on assignment.

Ⓝ $ $ ⌨ HOTELIER

Kostuch Publications, Ltd., 23 Lesmill Rd., Suite 101, Don Mills ON M3B 3P6, Canada. (416)447-0888. Fax: (416)447-5333. E-mail: rcaira@foodservice.ca. Website: www.foodserviceworld.com. Associate Editor: Iris Benaroia. **Contact:** Rosanna Caira, editor. **40% freelance written.** Bimonthly magazine covering the Canadian hotel industry. Estab. 1989. Circ. 9,000. Pays on publication. Byline given. Buys first North American serial rights. Editorial lead time 3 months. Submit seasonal material 2 months in advance. Accepts queries by mail, fax. Sample copy and writer's guidelines free.

Nonfiction How-to, new product. No case studies. **Buys 30-50 mss/year.** Query with or without published clips. Length: 700-1,500 words. **Pays 35¢/word (Canadian) for assigned articles.** Sometimes pays expenses of writers on assignment.

Photos Send photos with submission. Offers $30-75/photo.

$ $ $ PIZZA TODAY

The Monthly Professional Guide to Pizza Profits, Macfadden Protech, LLC, 908 S. 8th St., Suite 200, Louisville KY 40203. (502)736-9500. Fax: (502)736-9502. E-mail: jwhite@pizzatoday.com. Website: www.pizzatoday.com. **Contact:** Jeremy White, editor-in-chief. **30% freelance written.** Works only with published/established writers. Monthly magazine for the pizza industry, covering trends, features of successful pizza operators, business and management advice, etc. Estab. 1983. Circ. 40,000. **Pays on acceptance.** Publishes ms an average of 2 months after acceptance. Byline given. Offers 10-30% kill fee. Buys all rights. Submit seasonal material 3 months in advance. Accepts queries by mail, e-mail, fax. Responds in 2 months to queries; 3 weeks to mss. Sample copy for 10×13 SAE and 6 first-class stamps. Writer's guidelines for #10 SASE.

Nonfiction Interview/profile, entrepreneurial slants, pizza production and delivery, employee training, hiring, marketing, and business management. No fillers, humor or poetry. **Buys 50 mss/year.** Length: 1,000 words. **Pays 50¢/word, occasionally more.** Sometimes pays expenses of writers on assignment.

Photos Reviews contact sheets, negatives, transparencies, color slides, 5×7 prints. Captions required.

Tips "We currently need articles that cover ways pizzeria operators can increase profits through the bar area."

Ⓝ $ $ ⌨ WESTERN HOTELIER MAGAZINE

Mercury Publications, Ltd., 1839 Inkster Blvd., Winnipeg MB R2X 1R3, Canada. (204)954-2085. Fax: (204)954-2057. E-mail: mp@mercury.mb.ca. Website: www.mercury.mb.ca/. Editor: Kelly Gray. **Contact:** Kristi Balon, editorial production manager. **45% freelance written.** Quarterly magazine covering the hotel industry. "*Western Hotelier* is dedicated to the accommodation industry in Western Canada and U.S. western border states. WH offers the West's best mix of news and feature reports geared to hotel management. Feature reports are written on a sector basis and are created to help generate enhanced profitability and better understanding."

Circ. 4,342. Pays 30-45 days from receipt of invoice. Byline given. Offers 33% kill fee. Buys all rights. Submit seasonal material 3 months in advance. Accepts queries by mail, e-mail, fax. Accepts simultaneous submissions. Responds in 2 weeks to queries. Sample copy and writer's guidelines free or by e-mail.
Nonfiction How-to (train staff), interview/profile. Industry reports and profiles on companies. Query with published clips. Length: 500-9,000 words. **Pays 25-35¢/word.** Sometimes pays expenses of writers on assignment.
Photos State availability with submission. Reviews negatives, transparencies, 3×5 prints, JPEG, EPS or TIF files. Buys all rights. Negotiates payment individually. Captions required.
Columns/Departments Across the West (hotel news from various parts of Western Canada), 100-500 words. Query. **Pays $0-100.**
Fillers Facts. Length: 100 words.
Tips "Send an e-mailed, faxed or mailed query outlining your experience, interests and pay expectations. A requirement also is clippings."

Ⓝ $ $🖳 WESTERN RESTAURANT NEWS
Mercury Publications, Ltd., 1839 Inkster Blvd., Winnipeg MB R2X 1R3, Canada. (204)954-2085. Fax: (204)954-2057. E-mail: mp@mercury.mb.ca. Website: www.mercury.mb.ca/. Editor: Kelly Gray. **Contact:** Kristi Balon, editorial production manager. **33% freelance written.** Bimonthly magazine covering the restaurant trade. Reports profiles and industry reports on associations, regional business developments, etc. "*Western Restaurant News Magazine* is the authoritative voice of the foodservice industry in Western Canada. Offering a total package to readers, *WRN* delivers concise news articles, new product news, and coverage of the leading trade events in the West, across the country, and around the world." Estab. 1994. Circ. 14,532. Pays 30-45 days from receipt of invoice. Byline given. Offers 33% kill fee. Buys all rights. Submit seasonal material 3 months in advance. Accepts queries by mail, e-mail, fax. Accepts simultaneous submissions. Sample copy and writer's guidelines free or by e-mail.
Nonfiction How-to, interview/profile. Industry reports and profiles on companies. Query with published clips. Length: 500-9,000 words. **Pays 25-35¢/word.** Sometimes pays expenses of writers on assignment.
Photos State availability with submission. Reviews negatives; transparencies; 3×5 prints; JPEG, EPS, or TIFF files. Buys all rights. Negotiates payment individually. Captions required.
Columns/Departments Across the West (restaurant news from Western Canada), 100-500 words. Query. **Payment varies.**
Fillers Facts. Length: 100 words.
Tips "Send an e-mailed, faxed, or mailed query outlining your experience, interests, and pay expectations. A requirement also is clippings."

INDUSTRIAL OPERATIONS

Ⓝ $ $🖳 CANADIAN PLASTICS
The Business Information Group, 1450 Don Mills Rd, Don Mills ON M3B 2X7, Canada. (416)442-2290. Fax: (416)442-2213. E-mail: mlegault@canplastics.com. Associate Editor: Cindy Macdonald. **Contact:** Michael LeGault, editor. **20% freelance written.** Monthly magazine covering plastics. "*Canadian Plastics Magazine* reports on and interprets development in plastics markets and technologies for plastics processors and end-users based in Canada." Estab. 1942. Circ. 11,000. Pays on publication. Publishes ms an average of 3 months after acceptance. Byline sometimes given. Offers 25% kill fee. Editorial lead time 2 months. Submit seasonal material 4 months in advance. Responds in 2 weeks to queries; 1 month to mss. Sample copy for free.
Nonfiction Technical, industry news (Canada only). **Buys 6 mss/year.** Query with published clips. Length: 400-1,600 words. **Pays $120-500.** Sometimes pays expenses of writers on assignment.
Photos State availability with submission.
Tips "Give the editor a call."

Ⓝ $ $ CAST POLYMER CONNECTION
International Cast Polymer Alliance of the American Composites Manufacturers Association, 1010 N. Glebe Rd., Suite 450, Arlington VA 22201-5761. (703)525-0511. Fax: (703)525-0743. E-mail: jsikorski@acmanet.org. Website: www.icpa-hq.org. Editor: Andy Rusnak. Managing Editor: Jessica Howard. **Contact:** Jennifer Sikorski, assistant editor. Bimonthly magazine covering cultured marble and solid surface industries. "Articles should focus on small business owners and manufacturers." Circ. 2,000. Pays on publication. Publishes ms an average of 3 months after acceptance. Byline given. Buys all rights. Accepts queries by mail, e-mail.
Nonfiction "We are interested in how-to articles on technical processes, industry-related manufacturing techniques, and small-business operations." Historical/nostalgic, how-to, interview/profile, photo feature, techni-

cal. **Buys 3-5 mss/year.** Query. Length: 2,000-5,000 words. **Pays $200-350.** Occasionally arrange adspace to swap for editorial. Sometimes pays expenses of writers on assignment.

$ $ COMMERCE & INDUSTRY

Mercury Publications, Ltd., 1839 Inkster Blvd., Winnipeg MB R2X 1R3, Canada. (204)954-2085. Fax: (204)954-2057. E-mail: mp@mercury.mb.ca. Website: www.mercury.mb.ca/. Publisher/Editor: Frank Yeo. **Contact:** Kristi Balon, editorial production manager. **75% freelance written.** Bimonthly magazine covering the business and industrial sectors. Industry reports and company profiles provide readers with an in-depth insight into key areas of interest in their profession. Estab. 1947. Circ. 18,876. Pays 30-45 days from receipt of invoice. Byline given. Offers 33% kill fee. Buys all rights. Submit seasonal material 3 months in advance. Accepts queries by mail, e-mail, fax. Accepts simultaneous submissions. Responds in 2 weeks to queries. Sample copy and writer's guidelines free or by e-mail.

Nonfiction How-to, interview/profile. Industry reports and profiles on companies. Query with published clips. Length: 500-9,000 words. **Pays 25-35¢/word.** Sometimes pays expenses of writers on assignment.

Photos State availability with submission. Reviews negatives; transparencies; 3×5 prints; JPEG, EPS or TIF files. Buys all rights. Negotiates payment individually. Captions required.

Tips "Send an e-mailed, faxed, or mailed query outlining your experience, interests, and pay expectations. A requirement also is clippings."

INDUSTRIAL FABRIC PRODUCTS REVIEW

Industrial Fabrics Association International, 1801 County Rd. B W., Roseville MN 55113-4061. (651)222-2508. Fax: (651)225-6966. E-mail: gdnordstrom@ifai.com. Website: www.ifai.com. **Contact:** Galynn Nordstrom, editorial director. **50% freelance written.** Monthly magazine covering industrial textiles and products made from them for company owners, salespeople, and researchers in a variety of industrial textile areas. Estab. 1915. Circ. 11,000. Pays on publication. Publishes ms an average of 2 months after acceptance. Byline given. Buys all rights. Accepts queries by mail, e-mail, phone. Responds in 1 month to queries. Editorial calendar online.

> ⛐ Break in by "researching the industry/magazine audience and editorial calendar. We rarely buy material not directed specifically at our markets."

Nonfiction Technical, marketing, and other topics related to any aspect of industrial fabric industry from fiber to finished fabric product. Special issues: New Products, New Fabrics, and Equipment. No historical or apparel-oriented articles. **Buys 50-60 mss/year.** Query with phone number. Length: 1,200-3,000 words.

Tips "We encourage freelancers to learn our industry and make regular, solicited contributions to the magazine. We do not buy photography."

$ $ MODERN MATERIALS HANDLING

Reed Business Information, 275 Washington St., Newton MA 02458. (617)558-4374. Fax: (617)558-4327. E-mail: gforger@reedbusiness.com. Website: www.reedbusiness.com. **Contact:** Gary Forger, chief editor. **40% freelance written.** Magazine published 11 times/year covering warehousing, distribution centers, inventory. "*Warehousing Management* is an 11 times-a-year glossy national magazine read by managers of warehouses and distribution centers. We focus on lively, well-written articles telling our readers how they can achieve maximum facility productivity and efficiency. Heavy management components. We cover technology, too." Estab. 1945. Circ. 42,000. Pays on acceptance (allow 4-6 weeks for invoice processing). Publishes ms an average of 1 month after acceptance. Byline given. Editorial lead time 3 months. Accepts queries by mail, e-mail, fax. Sample copy for free. Writer's guidelines free.

> • "*Warehousing Management* is now a subaddition of *Modern Materials Handling*, a magazine that has been around for 58 years."

Nonfiction Articles must be on-point, how-to pieces for managers. How-to, new product, technical. Special issues: State-of-the-Industry Report, Peak Performer, Salary and Wage survey, Warehouse of the Year. Doesn't want to see anything that doesn't deal with our topic—warehousing. No general-interest profiles or interviews. **Buys 25 mss/year.** Query with published clips. **Pays $300-650.**

Photos State availability with submission. Reviews negatives, transparencies, prints. Buys all rights. Offers no additional payment for photos accepted with ms. Captions, identification of subjects required.

> ▣ The online magazine carries original content not found in the print edition and includes writer's guidelines.

Tips "Learn a little about warehousing, distributors and write well. We typically don't accept specific article queries, but welcome introductory letters from journalists to whom we can assign articles. But authors are welcome to request an editorial calendar and develop article queries from it."

$ $ $ PEM PLANT ENGINEERING & MAINTENANCE

CLB Media, Inc., 209-3228 S. Service Rd., Burlington ON L7N 3H8, Canada. (905)634-2100. Fax: (905)634-2238. E-mail: rrobertson@clbmedia.ca. Website: www.pem-mag.com. **Contact:** Rob Robertson, editor. **30%**

freelance written. Bimonthly magazine looking for "informative articles on issues that affect plant floor operations and maintenance." Circ. 18,500. Pays on publication. Publishes ms an average of 3 months after acceptance. Byline given. Buys one-time rights. Editorial lead time 4 months. Submit seasonal material 4 months in advance. Accepts simultaneous submissions. Responds in 3 weeks to queries; 1 month to mss. Sample copy and writer's guidelines free. Writer's guidelines online.

Nonfiction How-to (how-to keep production downtime to a minimum, how-to better operate an industrial operation), new product, technical. **Buys 6 mss/year.** Query with published clips. Length: 750-4,000 words. **Pays $500-1,400 (Canadian).** Sometimes pays expenses of writers on assignment.

Photos State availability with submission. Reviews transparencies, prints. Buys one-time rights. Negotiates payment individually. Captions required.

Tips "Information can be found at our website. Call us for sample issues, ideas, etc."

$ $ QUALITY DIGEST

40 Declaration Dr., Suite 100, Chico CA 95973. (530)893-4095. Fax: (530)893-0395. E-mail: rg@qualitydigest.com. Website: www.qualitydigest.com. **Contact:** Robert Green, managing editor. **75% freelance written.** Monthly magazine covering quality improvement. Estab. 1981. Circ. 75,000. **Pays on acceptance.** Byline given. Buys all rights. Submit seasonal material 4 months in advance. Accepts queries by mail, e-mail, fax. Accepts simultaneous submissions. Responds in 3 months to mss. Sample copy and writer's guidelines free.

Nonfiction Book excerpts, how-to (implement quality programs and solve problems for benefits, etc.), interview/profile, opinion, personal experience, technical. **Buys 2-5 mss/year.** Query with or without published clips or send complete ms. Length: 800-3,000 words. **Pays $200-600 for assigned articles. Pays in contributor copies for unsolicited mss.** Sometimes pays expenses of writers on assignment.

Reprints Send tearsheet and information about when and where the material previously appeared.

Photos Send photos with submission. Reviews any size prints. Buys one-time rights. Offers no additional payment for photos accepted with ms. Captions, identification of subjects, model releases required.

🔳 The online magazine carries original content not found in the print edition and includes writer's guidelines. Contact: Dirk Dusharme.

Tips "Please be specific in your articles. Explain what the problem was, how it was solved and what the benefits are. Tell the reader how the technique described will benefit him or her. We feature shorter, tighter, more focused articles than in the past. This means we have more articles in each issue. We're striving to present our readers with concise, how-to, easy-to-read information that makes their job easier."

$ $ WEIGHING & MEASUREMENT

WAM Publishing Co., P.O. Box 2247, Hendersonville TN 37077. (615)824-6920. Fax: (615)824-7092. E-mail: wampub@wammag.com. Website: www.wammag.com. **Contact:** David M. Mathieu, editor. Bimonthly magazine for users of industrial scales. Estab. 1914. Circ. 13,900. **Pays on acceptance.** Byline given. Offers 20% kill fee. Buys all rights. Accepts queries by mail, e-mail, fax, phone. Responds in 2 weeks to queries. Sample copy for $2.

Nonfiction Interview/profile (with presidents of companies), personal experience (guest editorials on government involvement in business, etc.), technical, Profile (about users of weighing and measurement equipment); Product reviews. **Buys 15 mss/year.** Query on technical articles; submit complete ms for general interest material. Length: 1,000-2,500 words. **Pays $175-300.**

Ⓝ $ $ WESTERN PACKING NEWS

3155 Lynde St., Oakland CA 94601. (510)532-5513. E-mail: westpacknews@aol.com. **Contact:** C.W. Soward, editor. Monthly newsletter covering canning, freezing, drying—food processing industries. Estab. 1938. Circ. 1,200. Pays on publication. Publishes ms an average of 1 month after acceptance. Not copyrighted. Editorial lead time 1 month. Submit seasonal material 1 month in advance. Accepts queries by mail, e-mail. Accepts previously published material. Responds in 1 month to queries. Sample copy for free. Writer's guidelines free.

Nonfiction New product. Query. **Pays 6-10¢/word.**

INFORMATION SYSTEMS

Ⓝ $ $ $ $ BOARDWATCH MAGAZINE

Light Reading, 23 Leonard St., New York NY 10013. (212)925-0020. E-mail: editors@boardwatch.com. Website: www.boardwatch.com. **Contact:** Joanne "Jo" Maitland, senior editor. **70% freelance written.** Monthly magazine covering Internet/information technology/networking. Estab. 1987. Circ. 29,000. **Pays on acceptance.** Publishes ms an average of 2 months after acceptance. Byline given. Offers $300 kill fee. Buys first North American serial, second serial (reprint), electronic rights. First worldwide rights Editorial lead time 2 months.

Submit seasonal material 2 months in advance. Accepts queries by e-mail. Accepts simultaneous submissions. Sample copy online. Writer's guidelines free.

Nonfiction Exposé, interview/profile, new product, opinion, personal experience, technical. "No general interest internet—this is a trade publication for technical readers." **Buys 12 mss/year.** Query. Length: 800-3,000 words. **Pays $800-3,000.**

Photos State availability with submission. Buys one-time rights. Negotiates payment individually. Identification of subjects required.

Columns/Departments "Columns on all issues of internet access providers and telecommunications are welcome." **Buys 180 mss/year.** Query. **Pays $100-500.**

Tips "Submissions by e-mail are best; technical knowledge and experience in providing access or telecommunications very helpful."

N $ $ $ CARD TECHNOLOGY

The Magazine of Smart Cards, Networks, and ID Solutions, Thomson Media, 300 S. Wacker Dr., Suite 1800, Chicago IL 60606. (312)913-1334. Fax: (312)913-1340. E-mail: don.davis@thomsonmedia.com. Website: www.cardtechnology.com. **Publisher:** Andy Rowe. **Contact:** Don Davis, editor/associate publisher. **20% freelance written.** Monthly magazine covering smart cards, biometrics, and related technologies. "*Card Technology* covers all uses of smart cards worldwide, as well as other advanced plastic card technologies. Aimed at senior management, not technical staff. Our readership is global, as is our focus." Estab. 1996. Circ. 22,000. **Pays on acceptance.** Byline given. Offers negotiable kill fee. Buys all rights. Editorial lead time 1 month. Submit seasonal material 2 months in advance. Accepts queries by e-mail. Responds in 1 week to queries; 1 month to mss. Sample copy for free.

Nonfiction Interview/profile, opinion. **Buys 15 mss/year.** Query with published clips. Length: 2,000-4,000 words. **Pays $500-1,500.** Sometimes pays expenses of writers on assignment.

Photos State availability with submission. Reviews contact sheets, negatives, transparencies, prints. Rights negotiable. Negotiates payment individually. Identification of subjects required.

■ The online magazine carries original content not found in the print edition. Contact: Don Davis.

Tips "We are especially interested in finding freelancers outside of North America who have experience writing about technology issues for business publications."

$ $ COMPUTER GRAPHICS WORLD

PennWell, 98 Spit Brook Rd., Nashua NH 03062-2801. (603)891-0123. Fax: (603)891-0539. E-mail: phill@pennwell.com. Website: www.cgw.com. **Contact:** Phil LoPiccolo, editor. **25% freelance written.** Monthly magazine. "*Computer Graphics World* specializes in covering computer-aided 3D modeling, animation, and visualization, and their uses in entertainment applications." Estab. 1978. Circ. 50,000. **Pays on acceptance.** Publishes ms an average of 3 months after acceptance. Byline given. Offers 20% kill fee. Buys all rights. Editorial lead time 4 months. Submit seasonal material 3 months in advance. Sample copy for free.

Nonfiction New product, opinion, technical, user application stories, professional-user, techonology innovations. "We do not want to run articles that are geared to computer programmers. Our focus as a magazine is on users involved in specific applications." **Buys 10-20 mss/year.** Query with published clips. Length: 1,200-2,000 words. **Pays $500 minimum.**

Columns/Departments Technology stories (describes innovation and its implication for computer graphics users), 750-1,000 words; Reviews (offers hands-on review of important new products), 750 words. Query with published clips. **Pays $300-500.**

Tips "Freelance writers will be most successful if they have some familiarity with computers and know how to write from a user's perspective. They do not need to be computer experts, but they do have to understand how to explain the impact of the technology and the applications in which a user is involved. Our feature section, and our application story section are open to freelancers. The trick to winning acceptance for your story is to have a well-developed idea that highlights a fascinating new trend or development in computer graphics technology or profiles a unique use of the technology by a single user or a specific class of users."

$ $ $ DESKTOP ENGINEERING

Complete Computing Resource for Engineers, Helmers Publishing, P.O. Box 874, Peterborough NH 03458. (603)924-9631. Fax: (603)924-4004. E-mail: de-editors@helmers.com. Website: www.deskeng.com. **Contact:** Jonathan Gourlay, features editor. **90% freelance written.** Monthly magazine covering microcomputer hardware/software for hands-on design and mechanical engineers and engineering management. Estab. 1995. Circ. 62,000. Pays on publication. Publishes ms an average of 4 months after acceptance. Byline given. Buys all rights. Editorial lead time 3 months. Accepts queries by mail, e-mail, fax, phone. Responds in 6 weeks to queries; 6 months to mss. Sample copy free; editorial calendar online. Writer's guidelines online.

Nonfiction How-to, new product, technical, reviews. "No fluff." **Buys 120 mss/year.** Query. Length: 750-1,500 words. **Pays 60¢/word for assigned articles; negotiable for unsolicited articles.** Sometimes pays expenses of writers on assignment.

Photos Send photos with submission. Negotiates payment individually. Captions required.

Columns/Departments Product Briefs (new products), 50-100 words; Reviews (software, hardware), 500-1,500 words. **Buys 30 mss/year.** Query. **Payment varies.**

    ◼ The online magazine carries original content not found in the print edition. Contact: Jonathan Gourlay.

Tips "Call the editors or e-mail them for submission tips."

ℕ E-DOC

The Magazine of Information and Image Management, Association for Information and Image Management, 1100 Wayne Ave., Silver Spring MD 20910. (301)587-8202. Fax: (301)587-2711. E-mail: bduhon@aiim.org. Website: www.aiim.org. **30% freelance written.** Prefers to work with writers with business/high tech experience. Bimonthly magazine on document and information management. "Specifically we feature coverage of the business issues surrounding implementation and use of document and information management technologies." Estab. 1943. Circ. 30,000. Pays on submission. Publishes ms an average of 3 months after acceptance. Byline given. Offers $50 kill fee. Buys first North American serial, second serial (reprint) rights. Accepts queries by mail, e-mail, fax, phone. Accepts simultaneous submissions. Sample copy online. Writer's guidelines online.

Nonfiction Interview/profile, photo feature, technical. **Buys 10-20 mss/year.** Query. Length: 1,500 words. Sometimes pays expenses of writers on assignment.

Photos State availability with submission. Reviews negatives, 4×5 transparencies. Buys all rights. Offers no additional payment for photos accepted with ms. Captions, identification of subjects required.

Columns/Departments Trends (developments across industry segments); Technology (innovations of specific technology); Management (costs, strategies of managing informaiton); Point/Counterpoint. Length: 500-1,500 words. Query.

Fillers Facts. Length: 150-500 words.

Tips "We would encourage freelancers who have access to our editorial calendar to contact us regarding article ideas, inquiries, etc. Our feature section is the area where the need for quality freelance coverage of our industry is most desirable. The most likely candidate for acceptance is someone who has a proven background in business writing, and/or someone with demonstrated knowledge of high-tech industries as they relate to information management."

$ $ $ GAME DEVELOPER

CMP Media LLC, 600 Harrison St., San Francisco CA 94107. (415)947-6000. Fax: (415)947-6090. E-mail: editors @gdmag.com. Website: www.gdmag.com. **Contact:** Jamil Moledina, managing editor. **90% freelance written.** Monthly magazine covering computer game development. Estab. 1994. Circ. 35,000. Pays on publication. Publishes ms an average of 3-6 months after acceptance. Byline given. Buys first North American serial, first, electronic, all rights. Editorial lead time 3 months. Submit seasonal material 4 months in advance. Accepts queries by e-mail. Sample copy for free. Writer's guidelines online.

Nonfiction How-to, personal experience, technical. **Buys 50 mss/year.** Query. Length: 3,000-5,000 words. **Pays $150/page.**

Photos State availability with submission.

    ◼ The online magazine carries original content not found in the print edition and includes writer's guidelines. Contact: Alex Dunne, executive producer.

Tips "We're looking for writers who are professional game developers with published game titles. We do not target the hobbyist or amateur market."

ℕ $ $ $ $ GOVERNMENT COMPUTER NEWS

Post Newsweek Tech Media, 10 G St., NE, Suite 500, Washington DC 20002. (202)772-2500. Fax: (202)772-2516. E-mail: ttemin@gcn.com. Website: www.gcn.com. **Contact:** Thomas Temin, editorial director. Biweekly for government information technology managers. **Pays on acceptance.** Byline given. Offers variable kill fee. Buys all rights. Responds in 1 month to queries. Sample copy for free. Writer's guidelines for #10 SASE.

Nonfiction **Buys 30 mss/year.** Query. Length: 600-750 words. **Pays $800-2,000.** Pays expenses of writers on assignment.

Columns/Departments Length: 400-600 words. No freelance columns accepted. **Buys 75 mss/year.** Query. **Pays $250-400.**

Fillers Buys 10/year. Length: 300-500 words. **Pays $250-450.**

Tips Needs "technical case histories of applications of computers to governmental missions and trends in information technology."

Ⓝ $ $ $ $ INFORMATION WEEK

600 Community Dr., Manhasset NY 11030. (516)562-5000. Fax: (516)562-5036. E-mail: bevans@cmp.com. Website: www.informationweek.com. Editor-in-Chief: Bob Evans. Senior Editor-At-Large: John Foley. **20% freelance written.** Weekly magazine for information systems managers. Estab. 1985. Circ. 440,000. **Pays on acceptance.** Publishes ms an average of 1 month after acceptance. Byline given. Offers 25% kill fee. Buys first rights. Non-exclusive serial rights Accepts simultaneous submissions. Responds in 1 month to mss. Sample copy for free. Writer's guidelines for #10 SASE.

Nonfiction Book excerpts, how-to, interview/profile, new product, technical, News analysis, company profiles. **Buys 30 mss/year.** Query with published clips. Length: 1,500-4,000 words. **Pays $1.10/word minimum.** Pays expenses of writers on assignment.

Reprints Considers prviously published submissions.

Tips Needs "feature articles on technology trends—all with a business angle. We look at implementations by users, new products, management issues, intranets, the Internet, web, networks, PCs, objects, workstations, sewers, etc. Our competitors are tabloids—we're better written, more selective, and more analytical."

Ⓝ $ $ $ INTELLIGENT ENTERPRISE

Enterprise Solutions for Business Intelligence, CMP Media Inc., 2800 Campus Dr., San Mateo CA 94403. (650)513-4300. Fax: (650)513-4613. E-mail: dstodder@cmp.com. Website: www.intelligententerprise.com. **Contact:** David Stodder, editor-in-chief. **98% freelance written.** 18 times/year magazine covering e-business and business intelligence. "Intelligent Enterprise is a new magazine covering the strategies, trends and products for managing enterprise information solutions in a cohesive, coherent infrastructure—what we call the information supply chain. Most of our readers work within or are consultants serving the needs of corporate information systems organizations. Our readers are educated, technically astute, and experienced; they use their knowledge to guide them through a dynamic, market-driven industry. They are expoloring business intelligence, data warehousing, knowledge management, multitier client/server, the Internet/intranet, and object technology." Estab. 1998. Circ. 100,000. Pays on publication. Publishes ms an average of 3 months after acceptance. Byline given. Buys all rights. Submit seasonal material 4 months in advance. Accepts queries by mail, e-mail, phone. Sample copy online. Writer's guidelines online.

Nonfiction Technical. **Buys 60 mss/year.** Query. Length: 350-3,000 words. **Pays $0-1,000.** Sometimes pays expenses of writers on assignment.

◼ The online version of *Intelligent Enterprise* contains material not found in the print edition.

Tips "To write for *Intelligent Enterprise*, you must have a minimum of three years field experience. You must also have a working knowledge of theories and techniques beyond your own personal experience (unless you've done absolutely everything there is to do). Be familiar with the magazine in terms of style, content, and editorial focus. *Intelligent Enterprise* readers make the best *Intelligent Enterprise* writers and have enthusiasm for the job."

$ $ $ iSERIES NEWS

Penton Technology Media, 221 E. 29th St., Loveland CO 80538. (970)203-2824. Fax: (970)667-2321. E-mail: mratchford@pentontech.com. Website: www.iseriesnetwork.com. **Contact:** Mary Ann Ratchford. **40% freelance written.** Magazine published 14 times/year. "Programming, networking, IS management, technology for users of IBM AS/400 platform." Estab. 1982. Circ. 30,000 (international). Pays on publication. Publishes ms an average of 3 months after acceptance. Byline given. Offers 50% kill fee. Buys first, second serial (reprint), all rights. Editorial lead time 4 months. Submit seasonal material 4 months in advance. Accepts queries by mail, e-mail, fax, phone. Responds in 3 weeks to queries; 5 weeks to mss. Writer's guidelines online.

Nonfiction Book excerpts, opinion, technical. **Buys 70 mss/year.** Query. Length: 1,500-2,500 words. **Pays 17-50¢/word for assigned articles.** Pays in contributor copies upon request of the author. Sometimes pays expenses of writers on assignment.

Reprints Send photocopy. Payment negotiable.

Photos State availability with submission. Offers no additional payment for photos accepted with ms.

Columns/Departments Dialog Box (computer industry opinion), 1,500 words; Load'n'go (complete utility). **Buys 24 mss/year.** Query. **Pays $250-1,000.**

◼ The online magazine carries original content not found in the print edition and includes writer's guidelines. Contact: Lori Piotrowski.

Tips "Be familiar with IBM AS/400 computer platform."

$ JOURNAL OF INFORMATION ETHICS

McFarland & Co., Inc., Publishers, 720 Fourth Ave. S., St. Cloud State University, St. Cloud MN 56301. (320)255-4822. Fax: (320)255-4778. E-mail: hauptman@stcloudstate.edu. **Contact:** Robert Hauptman, LRTS, editor. **90% freelance written.** Semiannual scholarly journal. "Addresses ethical issues in all of the information sciences with a deliberately interdisciplinary approach. Topics range from electronic mail monitoring to library acquisition of controversial material. The *Journal*'s aim is to present thoughtful considerations of ethical dilemmas that arise in a rapidly evolving system of information exchange and dissemination.'' Estab. 1992. Pays on publication. Publishes ms an average of 2 years after acceptance. Byline given. Buys all rights. Submit seasonal material 8 months in advance. Accepts queries by mail, e-mail, fax, phone. Sample copy for $21. Writer's guidelines free.

Nonfiction Essays, opinion, book reviews. **Buys 10 mss/year.** Send complete ms. Length: 500-3,500 words. **Pays $25-50 depending on length.**

Tips ''Familiarize yourself with the many areas subsumed under the rubric of information ethics, e.g., privacy, scholarly communication, errors, peer review, confidentiality, e-mail, etc. Present a well-rounded discussion of any fresh, current, or evolving ethical topic within the information sciences or involving real-world information collection/exchange.''

SYS ADMIN

CMP Media, LLC, 1601 W. 23rd St., Suite 200, Lawrence KS 66046. (785)838-7555. Fax: (785)841-2047. E-mail: rendsley@cmp.com. Website: www.sysadminmag.com. Editor-in-Chief: Amber Ankerholz. **Contact:** Rikki Endsley, associate managing editor. **90% freelance written.** Monthly magazine. ''*Sys Admin* is written for UNIX systems administrators. Articles are practical and technical. Our authors are practicing UNIX systems administrators.'' Estab. 1992. Circ. 60,000. Pays on publication. Publishes ms an average of 6 months after acceptance. Byline given. Buys all rights. Editorial lead time 4 months. Accepts queries by mail, e-mail, fax, phone. Accepts simultaneous submissions. Responds in 1 month to queries. Sample copy for free. Writer's guidelines online.

Nonfiction Technical. **Buys 40-60 mss/year.** Query. Length: 3,000 words. **Payment varies.**

WINDOWS DEVELOPER MAGAZINE

CMP Media LLC, 600 Harrison St., San Francisco CA 94107. (650)513-4307. E-mail: wdeditor@cmp.com. Website: www.wd-mag.com. Editor: John Dorsey. **90% freelance written.** Monthly magazine. ''*WD* is written for advanced Windows programmers. Articles are practical, advanced, code-intensive, and not product-specific. We expect our authors to be working Windows programmers.'' Estab. 1990. Circ. 58,000. **Pays on acceptance.** Publishes ms an average of 6 months after acceptance. Byline given. Offers $150 kill fee. Buys all rights. Editorial lead time 3 months. Accepts simultaneous submissions. Responds in 2 weeks to queries. Sample copy for free. Writer's guidelines online.

Nonfiction Technical. **Buys 70-80 mss/year.** Query. Length: Varies. **Payment varies.**

INSURANCE

$ $ $ $ ADVISOR TODAY

2901 Telestar Court, Falls Church VA 22042. (703)770-8204. E-mail: amseka@advisortoday.com. Website: www.advisortoday.com. **Contact:** Ayo Mseka, editor-in-chief. **25% freelance written.** Monthly magazine covering life insurance and financial planning. ''Writers must demonstrate an understanding at what insurance agents and financial advisors do to earn business and serve their clients.'' Estab. 1906. Circ. 110,000. Pays on acceptance or publication (by mutual agreement with editor). Publishes ms an average of 3 months after acceptance. Makes work-for-hire assignments. Editorial lead time 3 months. Submit seasonal material 6 months in advance. Accepts queries by mail, e-mail, fax, phone. Sample copy for free. Writer's guidelines online.

O— Break in with queries for ''pieces about sales techniques and product disclosure issues.''

Nonfiction Insurance. **Buys 8 mss/year.** Query. Length: 1,500-6,000 words. **Pays $800-2,000.**

Tips Prior to January 2000, *Advisor Today* was published under the title *LAN* (Life Association News).

$ $ GEICO DIRECT

K.L. Publications, 2001 Killebrew Dr., Suite 105, Bloomington MN 55425-1879. (952)854-0155. Fax: (952)854-9440. E-mail: klpub@aol.com. **Contact:** Jan Brenny, editor. **60% freelance written.** Semiannual magazine published for the Government Employees Insurance Company (GEICO) policyholders. Estab. 1988. Circ. 5,000,000. **Pays on acceptance.** Byline given. Buys first North American serial rights. Accepts queries by mail. Responds in 3 months to queries. Writer's guidelines for #10 SASE.

O— Break in by ''submitting an idea (or editorial approach) for auto/home safety or themed regional travel— 1 theme with several destinations around the country—that is unique, along with proof of research and writing ability.''

Nonfiction Americana, home and auto safety, car care, financial, lifestyle. How-to (auto/home related only), technical (auto), travel. Query with published clips. Length: 1,000-2,200 words. **Pays $300-650.**

Photos Reviews 35mm transparencies, websites. Payment varies.

Columns/Departments Moneywise; Your Car. Length: 500-600 words. Query with published clips. **Pays $175-350.**

Tips "We prefer work from published/established writers, especially those with specialized knowledge of the insurance industry, safety issues, and automotive topics."

JEWELRY

$ $ AJM: THE AUTHORITY ON JEWELRY MANUFACTURING

Manufacturing Jewelers and Suppliers of America, 45 Royal Little Dr., Providence RI 02904. (401)274-3840. Fax: (401)274-0265. E-mail: tinaw@ajm-magazine.com. Website: www.ajm-magazine.com. **Contact:** Tina Wojtkielo, editor. **75% freelance written.** Monthly magazine. "AJM is a monthly magazine providing technical, marketing and business information for finished jewelry manufacturers and supporting industries." Estab. 1956. **Pays on acceptance.** Publishes ms an average of 6 months after acceptance. Byline given. all rights for limited period of 18 months Editorial lead time 1 year. Submit seasonal material 6 months in advance. Accepts queries by mail, e-mail, fax. Responds in 2 months to mss. Sample copy and writer's guidelines free.

Nonfiction All articles should focus on jewelry manufacturing techniques, especially how-to and technical articles. How-to, new product, technical. "No generic articles for a wide variety of industries, articles for hobbyists, or articles written for a consumer audience. Our focus is professional jewelry manufacturers and designers, and articles for AJM should be carefully targeted for this audience." **Buys 40 mss/year.** Query. Length: 2,500-3,000 words. **Pays $300-500 for assigned articles.** Sometimes pays expenses of writers on assignment.

Reprints Occasionally accepts previously published submissions. Query.

Photos State availability with submission. Buys one-time rights. Negotiates payment individually. Captions required.

Tips "Because our editorial content is highly focused and specific, we assign most article topics rather than relying on outside queries. We are, as a result, always seeking new writers comfortable with business and technical topics who will work with us long term and whom we can develop into 'experts' in jewelry manufacturing. We invite writers to send an introductory letter and clips highlighting business and technical writing skills if they would like to be considered for a specific assignment."

$ THE DIAMOND REGISTRY BULLETIN

580 Fifth Ave., #806, New York NY 10036. (212)575-0444. Fax: (212)575-0722. E-mail: diamond58@aol.com. Website: www.diamondregistry.com. **Contact:** Joseph Schlussel, editor-in-chief. **50% freelance written.** Monthly newsletter. Estab. 1969. Pays on publication. Buys all rights. Submit seasonal material 1 month in advance. Accepts queries by mail, e-mail. Accepts simultaneous submissions. Responds in about 3 weeks to mss. Sample copy for $5.

Nonfiction How-to (ways to increase sales in diamonds, improve security, etc.), interview/profile (of interest to diamond dealers or jewelers), prevention advice (on crimes against jewelers). Send complete ms. Length: 50-500 words. **Pays $75-150.**

Tips "We seek ideas to increase sales of diamonds."

$ $ THE ENGRAVERS JOURNAL

P.O. Box 318, Brighton MI 48116. (810)229-5725. Fax: (810)229-8320. E-mail: sdavis@engraversjournal.com. Website: www.engraversjournal.com. Publisher: Michael J. Davis. **Contact:** Sonja Davis, general manager. **60% freelance written.** Monthly magazine covering the recognition and identification industry (engraving, marking devices, awards, jewelry, and signage.). "We provide practical information for the education and advancement of our readers, mainly retail business owners." Estab. 1975. **Pays on acceptance.** Publishes ms an average of 1 year after acceptance. Byline given. Buys one-time rights, makes work-for-hire assignments. Accepts queries by mail, e-mail, fax. Responds in 2 weeks to mss. Sample copy for free. Writer's guidelines free.

    To break in, submit well-written, fairly in-depth general business articles. Topics and article style should focus on the small retail business owner, and should be helpful and informative.

Nonfiction General interest (industry related), how-to (small business subjects, increase sales, develop new markets, use new sales techniques, etc.), technical. No general overviews of the industry. Length: 1,000-5,000 words. **Pays $200 and up.**

Reprints Send tearsheet, photocopy or typed ms with rights for sale noted and information about when and where the material previously appeared. Pays 50-100% of amout paid for original article.

Photos Send photos with submission. Pays variable rate. Captions, identification of subjects, model releases required.

Tips "Articles should always be down to earth, practical, and thoroughly cover the subject with authority. We do not want the 'textbook' writing approach, vagueness, or theory—our readers look to us for sound practical information. We use an educational slant, publishing both trade-oriented articles and general business topics of interest to a small retail-oriented readership."

$ $ LUSTRE

The Jeweler's Magazine on Design & Style, Cygnus Publishing Co., 19 W. 44th St., Suite 1405, New York NY 10036. (212)921-1091. Fax: (212)921-5539. E-mail: steve.feldman@cygnuspub.com. Website: www.lustremag.com. **Contact:** Steve Feldman, publisher. Bimonthly Trade magazine covering fine jewelry and related accessories. "*LUSTRE* is dedicated to helping the retail jeweler stock, merchandise, sell and profit from upscale, high-quality brand name and designer jewelry. Many stories are how-to. We also offer sophisticated graphics to showcase new products." Estab. 1997. Circ. 12,200. Pays on publication. Publishes ms an average of 4 months after acceptance. Byline given. Offers 50% kill fee. Buys all rights. Editorial lead time 4 months. Submit seasonal material 4 months in advance. Accepts queries by mail. Responds in 4 weeks to queries. Sample copy for free.

Nonfiction How-to, new product. **Buys 18 mss/year.** Query with published clips. Length: 1,000-2,500 words. **Pays $500.** Sometimes pays expenses of writers on assignment.

Photos State availability with submission. Buys one-time rights, plus usage for 1 year after publication date (but not exclusive usage). Offers no additional payment for photos accepted with ms. Captions, identification of subjects required.

Columns/Departments Celebrity Link (tie in designer jewelry with celebrity), 500 words; Details (news about designer jewelry), 500 words; International Eye, 500 words. **Buys 8 mss/year.** Query. **Pays $500.**

Tips "Step 1: Request an issue; call (212) 921-1091; ask for assistant. Step 2: Write a letter to Lorraine with clips. Step 3: Lorraine will call back. Background in jewelry is helpful."

MODERN JEWELER

Cygnus Business Media, 19 W. 44th St., Suite 1405, New York NY 10036-5902. (212)921-1091. Fax: (212)921-5539. Website: www.modernjeweler.com. Publisher: Tim Murphy. **20% freelance written.** Monthly magazine covering fine jewelry and watches. Estab. 1901. Circ. 33,000. **Pays on acceptance.** Publishes ms an average of 2 months after acceptance. Byline given. Buys all rights. Editorial lead time 2 months. Submit seasonal material 2 months in advance. Accepts queries by mail, fax. Responds in 3 weeks to queries; 3 months to mss. Sample copy for SAE.

Nonfiction Technical.

Photos State availability with submission. Reviews transparencies, prints.

Tips "Requires knowledge of retail business, experience in dealing with retail and manufacturing executives and analytical writing style. We don't frequently use writers who have no ties to or experience with the jewelry manufacturing industry."

JOURNALISM & WRITING

$ $ $ $ AMERICAN JOURNALISM REVIEW

1117 Journalism Bldg., University of Maryland, College Park MD 20742. (301)405-8803. Fax: (301)405-8323. E-mail: editor@ajr.org. Website: www.ajr.org. Editor: Rem Rieder. **Contact:** Lori Robertson, managing editor. **80% freelance written.** Bimonthly magazine covering print, broadcast, and online journalism. "Mostly journalists subscribe. We cover ethical issues, trends in the industry, coverage that falls short." Circ. 25,000. Pays within 1 month after publication. Publishes ms an average of 2 months after acceptance. Byline given. Offers 25% kill fee. Buys first North American serial, electronic rights. Editorial lead time 1 month. Accepts queries by mail, e-mail, fax. Responds in 1 month to queries. Sample copy for $4.95 pre-paid or online. Writer's guidelines online.

Nonfiction Exposé, personal experience, ethical issues. **Buys many mss/year.** Query with published clips or send complete ms. Length: 2,000-4,000 words. **Pays $1,500-2,000.** Pays expenses of writers on assignment.

Fillers Jill Rosen, assistant managing editor. Anecdotes, facts, short humor, short pieces. Length: 150-1,000 words. **Pays $100-250.**

Tips "Write a short story for the front-of-the-book section. We prefer queries to completed articles. Include in a page what you'd like to write about, who you'll interview, why it's important, and why you should write it."

$ BOOK DEALERS WORLD

North American Bookdealers Exchange, P.O. Box 606, Cottage Grove OR 97424. (561)258-2625. Fax: (561)258-2625. Website: www.bookmarketingprofits.com. **Contact:** Al Galasso, editorial director. **50% freelance written.** Quarterly magazine covering writing, self-publishing, and marketing books by mail. Circ. 20,000. Pays on publication. Publishes ms an average of 3 months after acceptance. Byline given. Buys first North American serial, second serial (reprint) rights. Accepts simultaneous submissions. Responds in 1 month to queries. Sample copy for $3.

Nonfiction Book excerpts (writing, mail order, direct mail, publishing), how-to (home business by mail, advertising), interview/profile (of successful self-publishers), positive articles on self-publishing, new writing angles, marketing. **Buys 10 mss/year.** Send complete ms. Length: 1,000-1,500 words. **Pays $25-50.**

Reprints Send ms with rights for sale noted and information about when and where the material previously appeared. Pays 80% of amount paid for an original article.

Columns/Departments Publisher Profile (on successful self-publishers and their marketing strategy). Length: 250-1,000 words. **Buys 20 mss/year.** Send complete ms. **Pays $5-20.**

Fillers Fillers concerning writing, publishing, or books. **Buys 6/year.** Length: 100-250 words. **Pays $3-10.**

Tips "Query first. Get a sample copy of the magazine."

$BYLINE

P.O. Box 5240, Edmond OK 73083-5240. (405)348-5591. E-mail: mpreston@bylinemag.com. Website: www.bylinemag.com. **Contact:** Marcia Preston, editor/publisher. **80% freelance written.** Eager to work with new/unpublished writers or experienced ones. Magazine published 11 times/year for writers and poets. Estab. 1981. **Pays on acceptance.** Publishes ms an average of 3 months after acceptance. Byline given. Buys first North American serial rights. Editorial lead time 3-4 months. Submit seasonal material 6 months in advance. Accepts queries by mail, e-mail. Accepts simultaneous submissions. Responds in 2 months or less to queries. Sample copy for $4 postpaid. Writer's guidelines online.

- Please *do not send* complete mss by e-mail.

- "First Sale is probably the easiest way to break in. Do not submit full manuscript by e-mail."

Nonfiction "We're always searching for appropriate, well-written features on topics we haven't covered for a couple of years." Needs articles of 1,500-1,800 words connected with writing and selling. No profiles of writers. **Buys approximately 75 mss/year.** Prefers queries; will read complete mss. Send SASE. Length: 1,500-1,800 words. **Pays $75.**

Columns/Departments End Piece (humorous, philosophical, or motivational personal essay related to writing), 700 words, **pays $35;** First Sale (account of a writer's first sale), 250-300 words, **pays $20;** Only When I Laugh (writing-related humor), 50-400 words; **pays $15-25;** Great American Bookstores (unique, independent bookstores), 500-600 words. Send complete ms. **Pays $30-40.**

Fiction Mainstream, genre, literary. No science fiction, erotica, or extreme violence. **Buys 11 mss/year.** Send complete ms. Length: 2,000-4,000 words. **Pays $100.**

Poetry "All poetry should connect in some way with the theme of writing or the creative process." Sandra Soli, poetry editor. Free verse, haiku, light verse, traditional. **Buys 100 poems/year.** Submit maximum 3 poems. Length: Under 30 lines. **Pays $10, plus free issue.**

Tips "We're open to freelance submissions in all categories. We're always looking for clear, concise feature articles on topics that will help writers write better, market smarter, and be more successful. Strangely, we get many more short stories than we do features, but we buy more features. If you can write a friendly, clear, and helpful feature on some aspect of writing better or selling more work, we'd love to hear from you."

$■ CANADIAN WRITER'S JOURNAL

P.O. Box 1178, New Liskeard ON P0J 1P0, Canada. (705)647-5424. Fax: (705)647-8366. E-mail: cwj@cwj.ca. Website: www.cwj.ca. **Contact:** Deborah Ranchuk, editor. **75% freelance written.** Bimonthly magazine for writers. Accepts well-written articles by all writers. Estab. 1984. Circ. 350. Pays on publication. Publishes ms an average of 9 months after acceptance. Byline given. Buys one-time rights. Accepts queries by mail, e-mail, fax, phone. Responds in 2 months to queries. Sample copy for $8, including postage. Writer's guidelines online.

Nonfiction Looking for articles on how to break into niche markets. How-to (articles for writers). **Buys 200 mss/year.** Query optional. **Pays $7.50/published magazine page (approx. 450 words).**

Reprints Send ms with rights for sale noted and information about when and where the material previously appeared.

Fiction Requirements being met by annual contest. Send SASE for rules, or see guidelines on website. "Does not want gratuitous violence, sex subject matter."

Poetry Short poems or extracts used as part of articles on the writing of poetry.

Tips "We prefer short, tightly written, informative how-to articles. U.S. writers note that U.S. postage cannot be used to mail from Canada. Obtain Canadian stamps, use IRCs, or send small amounts in cash."

$ $ $E CONTENT MAGAZINE

Digital Content Strategies & Resources, Online, Inc., 213 Danbury Rd., Wilton CT 06897. (203)761-1466. Fax: (203)761-1444. E-mail: michelle.manafy@infotoday.com. Website: www.econtentmag.com. **Contact:** Michelle

Manafy, editor. **90% freelance written.** Monthly magazine covering digital content trends, strategies, etc. *"E Content* is a business publication. Readers need to stay on top of industry trends and developments." Estab. 1979. Circ. 12,000. Pays within 1 month of publication. Byline given. Offers 20-50% kill fee. Buys all rights. Editorial lead time 4 months. Accepts queries by e-mail. Responds in 3 weeks to queries; 1 month to mss. Sample copy and writer's guidelines online. Writer's guidelines online.

Nonfiction Exposé, how-to, interview/profile, new product, opinion, technical, news features, strategic and solution-oriented features. No academic or straight Q&A. **Buys 48 mss/year.** Query with published clips. Length: 1,000-2,000 words. **Pays 40-50¢/word.** Sometimes pays expenses of writers on assignment.

Photos State availability with submission. Buys one-time rights. Negotiates payment individually. Captions required.

Columns/Departments Profiles (short profile of unique company, person or product), 1,200 words; New Features (breaking news of content-related topics), 500 words maximum. **Buys 40 mss/year.** Query with published clips. **Pays 30-40¢/word.**

Tips "Take a look at the website. Most of the time, an e-mail query with specific article ideas works well. A general outline of talking points is good, too. State prior experience."

$ 💟 FELLOWSCRIPT

InScribe Christian Writers' Fellowship, 333 Hunter's Run, Edmonton AB T6R 2N9, Canada. (780)988-5622. Fax: (780)430-0139. E-mail: submissions@inscribe.org. Website: www.inscribe.org. **Contact:** Elsie Montgomery, editor. **100% freelance written.** Quarterly Writers' newsletter featuring Christian writing. "Our readers are Christians with a commitment to writing. Among our readership are best-selling authors and unpublished beginning writers. Submissions to us should include practical information, something the reader can put into practice immediately." Estab. 1983. Circ. 250. Pays on publication. Publishes ms an average of 2-6 months after acceptance. Byline given. Buys one-time, second serial (reprint) rights. Editorial lead time 3 months. Submit seasonal material 4 months in advance. Accepts queries by mail, e-mail, fax, phone. Accepts simultaneous submissions. Responds in 1 month to queries; 2-6 months to mss. Sample copy for $3.50, 9×12 SAE, and 2 first-class stamps or IRCs. Writer's guidelines online.

> ○━ "The best bet to break in at *FellowScript* is to write something very specific that will be useful to writers. We receive far too many 'general' submissions which try to cover too much territory in 1 article. Choose your topic and keep a narrow focus."

Nonfiction All must pertain to writing and the writing life. Essays, exposé, how-to (for writers), inspirational, interview/profile, new product, personal experience, photo feature, religious. "Does not want poetry, fiction or think piece, commentary articles." **Buys 30-45 mss/year.** Send complete ms. Length: 400-1,200 words. **Pays 2¹/₂¢/word (first rights); 1¹/₂¢/word reprints (Canadian).**

Photos State availability with submission.

Columns/Departments Book reviews, 150-300 words; Market Updates, 50-300 words. **Buys 1-3 mss/year.** Send complete ms. **Pays 1 copy.**

Fillers Facts, newsbreaks. **Buys 5-10/year.** Length: 25-300 words. **Pays 1 copy.**

Tips "Send your complete manuscript by post or e-mail (pasted into the message, no attachments). E-mail is preferred. Tell us a bit about yourself. Write in a casual, first-person, anecdotal style. Be sure your article is full of practical material, something that can be applied. Most of our accepted freelance submissions fall into the 'how-to' category, and involve tasks, crafts, or procedures common to writers. Please do not swamp us with inspirational articles (e.g., 'How I sold My First Story'), as we receive too many of these already."

$ 🌐 FREELANCE MARKET NEWS

An Essential Guide for Freelance Writers, The Writers Bureau Ltd., Sevendale House, 7 Dale St., Manchester M1 1JB, England. (+44)161 228 2362. Fax: (+44)161 228 3533. E-mail: fmn@writersbureau.com. Website: www.writersbureau.com. **Contact:** Angela Cox, editor. **15% freelance written.** Monthly newsletter covering freelance writing. Estab. 1968. **Pays on acceptance.** Publishes ms an average of 3 months after acceptance. Byline given. Buys all rights. Editorial lead time 3 months. Submit seasonal material 3 months in advance. Accepts queries by mail, e-mail, fax. Accepts previously published material. Accepts simultaneous submissions. Sample copy for #10 SASE. Writer's guidelines for #10 SASE.

Nonfiction How-to (sell your writing/improve your writing). **Buys 12 mss/year.** Length: "Articles should be around 700 words." **Pays £50/1,000 words.**

Columns/Departments New Markets (magazines which have recently been published); Fillers & Letters, Overseas Markets (obviously only English-language publications); Market Notes (established publications accepting articles, fiction, reviews, or poetry). All should be between 40 and 200 words. **Pays £35/1,000 words.**

$ $ FREELANCE WRITER'S REPORT

CNW Publishing, Inc., Main St., P.O. Box A, North Stratford NH 03590-0167. (603)922-8338. Fax: (603)922-8339. E-mail: fwrwm@writers-editors.com. Website: www.writers-editors.com. **Contact:** Dana K. Cassell, editor. **25% freelance written.** Monthly newsletter. *"FWR* covers the marketing and business/office management aspects of running a freelance writing business. Articles must be of value to the established freelancer; nothing basic." Estab. 1982. Pays on publication. Publishes ms an average of 6 months after acceptance. Byline given. Buys one-time rights. Editorial lead time 2 months. Submit seasonal material 2 months in advance. Accepts queries by mail, e-mail. Accepts simultaneous submissions. Responds in 1 week to queries; 1 month to mss. Sample copy for 6×9 SAE with 2 first-class stamps (for back copy); $4 for current copy. Writer's guidelines online.

O— Most needed are filler tips of up to 325 words.

Nonfiction Book excerpts, how-to (market, increase income or profits). No articles about the basics of freelancing. **Buys 50 mss/year.** Send complete ms. Length: Up to 900 words. **Pays 10¢/word.**

Reprints Accepts previously published submissions.

■ The online magazine carries original content not found in the print edition and includes writer's guidelines.

Tips "Write in a terse, newsletter style."

$ MAINE IN PRINT

Maine Writers & Publishers Alliance, 1326 Washington St., Bath ME 04530. (207)386-1400. Fax: (207)386-1401. E-mail: info@mainewriters.org. Website: www.mainewriters.org. Bimonthly newsletter for writers, editors, teachers, librarians, etc., focusing on Maine literature and the craft of writing. Estab. 1975. Circ. 3,000. Pays on publication. Publishes ms an average of 2 months after acceptance. Byline given. Buys one-time rights. Editorial lead time 2 months. Accepts queries by mail. Accepts simultaneous submissions. Sample copy and writer's guidelines free.

Nonfiction Essays, how-to (writing), interview/profile, technical. No creative writing, fiction, or poetry. **Buys 20 mss/year.** Query with published clips. Length: 400-1,500 words. **Pays $25-50 for assigned articles.**

Reprints Send tearsheet and information about when and where the material previously appeared. Pays $25.

Photos State availability with submission. Offers no additional payment for photos accepted with ms.

Columns/Departments Front-page articles (writing related), 500-1,500 words. **Buys 20 mss/year.** Query. **Pays $25 minimum.**

Tips "Become a member of Maine Writers & Publishers Alliance. Become familiar with Maine literary scene."

$ $ $ ☒ MASTHEAD

The Magazine About Magazines, North Island Publishing, 1606 Sedlescomb Dr., Unit 8, Mississauga ON L4X 1M6, Canada. (905)625-7070. Fax: (905)625-4856. Website: www.mastheadonline.com. **40% freelance written.** Journal published 10 times/year covering the Canadian magazine industry. "With its lively mix of in-depth features, news stories, service pieces, surveys, tallies, and spirited commentary, this independent journal provides detailed coverage and analysis of the events, issues, personalities, and technologies shaping Canada's magazine industry." Estab. 1987. Circ. 4,200. Pays on publication. Publishes ms an average of 2 months after acceptance. Byline given. Offers 50% kill fee. Buys first North American serial rights. Editorial lead time 1 month. Accepts queries by mail. Accepts simultaneous submissions. Responds in 2 weeks to queries; 1 month to mss. Sample copy for free. Writer's guidelines free or by e-mail.

Nonfiction "We generally pay $600-850 for a cover story running 2,000-2,500 words, depending on the amount of research, etc., required. For the most part, *Masthead* generates feature ideas in-house and then assigns the stories to regular contributors. When space permits, we sometimes run shorter features or service pieces (1,000-1,500 words) for a flat rate of $350." Book excerpts, essays, exposé, historical/nostalgic, how-to, humor, interview/profile, new product, opinion, personal experience, technical. No articles that have nothing to do with Canadian magazines. Length: 100-3,000 words. **Pays $30-850 (Canadian).** Sometimes pays expenses of writers on assignment.

Photos State availability with submission. Negotiates payment individually. Identification of subjects required.

Columns/Departments Back of the Book, the guest column, pays freelancers a flat rate of $350 and runs approximately 950 words. Back of the Book columns examine and/or comment on issues or developments relating to any department: editorial, art, production, circulation, publishing, advertising, etc. **Buys 10 mss/year.** Query with published clips. **Pays $350 (Canadian).**

Fiction Novel excerpts. No excerpts that have nothing to do with Canadian magazines. Query with published clips.

■ The online magazine carries original content.

Tips "Have a solid understanding of the Canadian magazine industry. A good way to introduce yourself is to propose small articles on new magazines."

$ $ ⊞ MSLEXIA

For Women Who Write, Mslexia Publications Ltd., P.O. Box 656, Newcastle upon Tyne NE99 1PZ, United Kingdom. (0044) 191 261 6656. E-mail: postbag@mslexia.demon.co.uk. Website: www.mslexia.co.uk. Editor:

Debbie Taylor. **Contact:** Melanie Ashby, deputy editor. **60% freelance written.** Quarterly magazine offering advice and publishing opportunities for women writers, plus poetry and prose submissions on a different theme each issue. *"Mslexia* tells you all you need to know about exploring your creativity and getting into print. No other magazine provides *Mslexia*'s unique mix of advice and inspiration; news, reviews, interviews; competitions, events, grants; all served up with a challenging selection of new poetry and prose. *Mslexia* is read by authors and absolute beginners. A quarterly master class in the business and psychology of writing, it's the essential magazine for women who write." Estab. 1998. Circ. 12,000. Pays on publication. Publishes ms an average of 1 month after acceptance. Byline given. Offers 50% kill fee. Buys one-time rights. Editorial lead time 3 months. Submit seasonal material 3 months in advance. Accepts queries by mail, e-mail, phone. Accepts simultaneous submissions. Responds in 3 months to mss. Sample copy online. Writer's guidelines online or by e-mail.

• This publication does not accept e-mail submissions except from overseas writers.

Nonfiction How-to, interview/profile, opinion, personal experience. No general items about women or academic features. "We are only interested in features (for tertiary-educated readership) about women's writing and literature." **Buys 40 mss/year.** Query with published clips. Length: 500-2,000 words. **Pays $70-400 for assigned articles; $70-300 for unsolicited articles.** Pays in contributor copies for poetry and prose submitted for the New Writing section of the magazine. Sometimes pays expenses of writers on assignment.

Columns/Departments "We are open to suggestions, but would only commission 1 new column/year, probably from a UK-based writer." **Buys 12 mss/year.** Query with published clips.

Fiction Sheila Mulhern, editorial assistant. "See guidelines on our website. Submissions not on one of our current themes will be returned (if submitted with a SASE) or destroyed." **Buys 30 mss/year.** Send complete ms. Length: 50-3,000 words.

Poetry Sheila Mulhern, editorial assistant. Avant-garde, free verse, haiku, traditional. **Buys 40 poems/year.** Submit maximum 4 poems.

Tips "Read the magazine; subscribe if you can afford it. *Mslexia* has a particular style and relationship with its readers which is hard to assess at a quick glance. The majority of our readers live in the UK, so feature pitches should be aware of this. We never commission work without seeing a written sample first. We rarely accept unsolicited manuscripts, but prefer a short letter suggesting a feature, plus a brief bio and writing sample."

$NEW WRITER'S MAGAZINE

Sarasota Bay Publishing, P.O. Box 5976, Sarasota FL 34277-5976. (941)953-7903. E-mail: newriters@aol.com. Website: www.newriters.com. **Contact:** George S. Haborak, editor. **95% freelance written.** Bimonthly magazine. *"New Writer's Magazine* believes that *all* writers are *new* writers in that each of us can learn from one another. So, we reach pro and nonpro alike." Estab. 1986. Circ. 5,000. Pays on publication. Byline given. Buys first rights. Accepts queries by mail. Responds in 1 month to queries; 1 month to mss. Sample copy for $3. Writer's guidelines for #10 SASE.

Nonfiction General interest, how-to (for new writers), humor, interview/profile, opinion, personal experience (with pro writer). **Buys 50 mss/year.** Send complete ms. Length: 700-1,000 words. **Pays $10-50.**

Photos Send photos with submission. Reviews 5×7 prints. Offers no additional payment for photos accepted with ms. Captions required.

Fiction Experimental, historical, humorous, mainstream, slice-of-life vignettes. "Again we do *not* want anything that does not have a tie-in with the writing life or writers in general." **Buys 2-6 mss/year.** Send complete ms. Length: 700-800 words. **Pays $20-40.**

Poetry Free verse, light verse, traditional. Does not want anything *not* for writers. **Buys 10-20 poems/year.** Submit maximum 3 poems. Length: 8-20 lines. **Pays $5 minimum.**

Fillers For cartoons, writing lifestyle slant. Buys 20-30/year. Pays $10 maximum. Anecdotes, facts, newsbreaks, short humor. **Buys 5-15/year.** Length: 20-100 words. **Pays $5 maximum.**

Tips "Any article with photos has a good chance, especially an up close and personal interview with an established professional writer offering advice, etc. Short profile pieces on new authors also receive attention."

$OHIO WRITER

Poets' & Writers' League of Greater Cleveland, P.O. Box 91801, Cleveland OH 44101. (216)421-0403. Fax: (216)791-1727. E-mail: pwlgc@yahoo.com. Website: www.pwlgc.com. **75% freelance written.** Bimonthly magazine covering writing and Ohio writers. Estab. 1987. Pays on publication. Publishes ms an average of 4 months after acceptance. Byline given. Buys one-time, second serial (reprint) rights. Editorial lead time 4 months. Submit seasonal material 4 months in advance. Accepts queries by mail, e-mail, fax, phone. Responds in 6 weeks to mss. Sample copy for $2.50. Writer's guidelines for #10 SASE.

Nonfiction "All articles must related to the writing life or Ohio writers, or Ohio publishing scene." Essays, how-to, humor, inspirational, interview/profile, opinion, personal experience. **Buys 24 mss/year.** Send complete ms and SASE. Length: 2,000-2,500 words. **Pays $25 minimum, up to $50 for lead article, other payment under arrangement with writer.**

Reprints Send ms with rights for sale noted and information about when and where the material previously appeared. Pays 50% of amount paid for an original article.

Columns/Departments Subjectively Yours (opinions, controversial stance on writing life), 1,500 words; Reviews (Ohio writers, publishers, or publishing), 400-600 words; Focus on (Ohio publishing scene, how to write/ publish certain kind of writing, e.g., travel), 1,500 words. **Buys 6 mss/year.** Send complete ms. **Pays $25-50; $5/book review.**

Tips "We look for articles about writers and writing, with a special emphasis on activities in our state. However, we publish articles by writers throughout the country that offer something helpful about the writing life. Profiles and interviews of writers who live in Ohio are always needed. *Ohio Writer* is read by both beginning and experienced writers and hopes to create a sense of community among writers of different genres, abilities, and backgrounds. We want to hear a personal voice, one that engages the reader. We're looking for intelligent, literate prose that isn't stuffy."

$ $POETS & WRITERS MAGAZINE

72 Spring St., New York NY 10012. E-mail: editor@pw.org. Website: www.pw.org. **Contact:** The Editors. **100% freelance written.** Bimonthly Professional trade journal for poets and fiction writers and creative nonfiction writers. Estab. 1973. Circ. 70,000. Pays on acceptance of finished draft. Publishes ms an average of 4 months after acceptance. Byline given. Offers 20% kill fee. Buys first North American serial rights. Submit seasonal material 4 months in advance. Accepts queries by mail. Responds in 6 weeks to mss. Sample copy for $4.95 to Sample Copy Dept. Writer's guidelines for #10 SASE.

• No poetry or fiction.

Nonfiction How-to (craft of poetry or fiction writing), interview/profile (with poets or fiction writers). "We do not accept submissions by fax or e-mail." **Buys 35 mss/year.** Query with published clips or send complete ms. Length: 500-2,500 depending on topic words.

Photos State availability with submission. Reviews b&w prints. Offers no additional payment for photos accepted with ms.

Columns/Departments Literary and Publishing News, 500-1,000 words; Profiles of Emerging and Established Poets and Fiction Writers, 2,000-3,000 words; Regional Reports (literary activity in US), 1,000-2,00 words. Query with published clips or send complete ms. **Pays $150-300.**

$THE WIN INFORMER

The Professional Association for Christian Writers, Writers Information Network, P.O. Box 11337, Bainbridge Island WA 98110. (206)842-9103. Fax: (206)842-0536. E-mail: writersinfonetwork@juno.com. Website: www.c hristianwritersinfo.net. **Contact:** Elaine Wright Colvin, editor. **33¹/₃% freelance written.** Bimonthly magazine for this professional association for Christian writers covering the CBA and religious publishing industry. Estab. 1983. Circ. 1,000. **Pays on acceptance.** Publishes ms an average of 1-4 months after acceptance. Byline given. Buys first North American serial rights. Editorial lead time 2 months. Submit seasonal material 2 months in advance. Accepts queries by e-mail. Responds in 1 month to mss. Sample copy for $10, 9 × 12 SAE with 4 first-class stamps. Writer's guidelines online.

O→ Break in by "getting involved in the Christian publishing (CBA) industry; interview CBA published authors, CBA editors, or CBA bookstore managers."

Nonfiction For advanced/professional writers only. How-to (writing), humor, inspirational, interview/profile, new product, opinion, personal experience, religious, technical. No beginners basics material used. Send complete ms. Submit material in the body of e-mail only. Length: 100-1,000 words. **Pays $5-50, sometimes pays other than cash.** Sometimes pays expenses of writers on assignment.

Columns/Departments Industry News; Book Publisher News; Editor/Agent Hot News; News of the Magazines; Awards & Bestsellers; Conference Tips; Conference Schedule; New Book Alert; Bulletin Board; Winmember Websites. Send complete ms in body of e-mail or as an e-mail attachment.

Tips "The *Win Informer* is sometimes referred to as ChristianWritersInfo.net."

$WRITER'S APPRENTICE

For Aspiring, Beginning, and Intermediate Writers, Prairie River Publishing, 607 N. Cleveland St., Merrill WI 54452. (715)536-3167. Fax: (715)536-3167. E-mail: tina@writersapprentice.com. Website: www.writersapprent ice.com. **Contact:** Tina L. Miller, editor-in-chief. **90% freelance written.** Monthly trade magazine (beginning in 2005), 3 issues in 2004. "*Writer's Apprentice* magazine offers real, practical advice for writers—whether writing for pleasure or publication. Specifics, resources, information, encouragement, and answers to the questions they have." Estab. 2002. Circ. 10,000. Pays on publication. Byline given. Not copyrighted. Buys first rights. Editorial lead time 6-9 months. Submit seasonal material 6-9 months in advance. Accepts queries by mail, e-mail, fax. Responds in 3-4 weeks to queries; 6 months to mss. Sample copy for 9×12 SAE and 4 first-class stamps. Writer's guidelines online.

Nonfiction Essays, general interest, how-to, humor, inspirational, interview/profile, personal experience, technical. No fiction, poetry, or stories/articles that do not have a practical, take-away value. Query or send complete ms. Length: 300-900 words. **Pays $15-50.**

Photos State availability with submission. Reviews GIF/JPEG files. Buys one-time rights. Negotiates payment individually. Identification of subjects, model releases required.

Columns/Departments The Writing Life (back page essays), 300-600 words. Send complete ms. **Pays $10-25.**

Tips ''Pretend your best friend wants to become a writer. Think of all the questions he/she will have. What can you teach him/her that you already know? How can you share the benefit of your experience? What advice would you give? How would you help him/her get started? Become this imaginary new writer's mentor. Write it down in a concise article on a specific topic, and we're very likely to buy it. But remember: It's got to be real, practical, focused, informative, do-able, and contain resources or a how-to. No 'fluff' stories or stories that are too generic.''

$ $WRITER'S DIGEST

F + W Publications, 4700 E. Galbraith Rd., Cincinnati OH 45236. (513)531-2690, ext. 1483. E-mail: wdsubmissions@fwpubs.com. Website: www.writersdigest.com. **Contact:** Submissions Editor. **70% freelance written.** Monthly magazine about writing and publishing. ''Our readers write fiction, nonfiction, plays, and scripts. They're interested in improving writing skills and the ability to sell their work and find new outlets for their talents.'' Estab. 1920. Circ. 150,000. **Pays on acceptance.** Publishes ms an average of 9-12 months after acceptance. Byline given. Offers 25% kill fee. Buys first world serial rights for one-time editorial use, possible electronic posting, and magazine promotional use. Pays 25% reprint fee and 10% for electronic use in fee-charging mediums. Sample copy for $5.25/copy to Lyn Menke, at the address above. ''A helpful index of each year's contents is published in the December issue. You also may purchase copies online.'' Writer's guidelines online.

- *Writer's Digest* strongly prefers e-queries and responds in 2 months to e-queries and mail queries w/SASE. The magazine does not accept or read e-queries with attachments.
- ''Break in through Markets Spotlight or with a 1,000-word profile of a niche writing market.''

Nonfiction ''What we need is the how-to article: How to write compelling leads and conclusions, how to improve your character descriptions, how to become more efficient and productive. We like plenty of examples, anecdotes, and details in our articles. On how-to technique articles, we prefer to work with writers with a proven track record of success. For example, don't pitch us an article on creating effective dialogue if you've never had a work of fiction published. Don't query about setting up a book tour if you've never done one. We like our articles to speak directly to the reader through the use of the first-person voice. We are seldom interested in author interviews, and 'evergreen' topics are not accepted unless they are timely and address industry trends. Must have fax to receive galleys. Don't send articles today that would have fit in *WD* 5 years ago. No articles titled 'So You Want to Be a Writer,' and no first-person pieces without something readers can learn from in the sharing of the story. Avoid the 'and then I wrote' article that is a promotional vehicle for you without tips on how others can put your experience to work.'' **Buys 75 mss/year.** ''We only accept electronic final manuscripts.'' Length: 800-1,200 words. **Pays 30-50¢/word.**

Tips ''Keep an eye on Inkwell—an expanded upfront section of the magazine. It's the best place for new writers to try and break in, so read it thoroughly to get a feel for the types of articles we include. Please note that all product reviews and book reviews are handled in house. We welcome short reader tips, but we do not pay for these. This is one section of the magazine where you can benefit from sending the complete written piece as opposed to a query. We accept Inkwell submissions via e-mail or mail. Note that our standing columns and departments are not open to freelance submissions. Further, we buy at most 2 interviews/profiles/year; nearly all that we publish are staff-written. Candidates for First Impressions interviews (all of which are conducted in-house; candidates must be first-time authors) should send galleys and information about themselves at least 5 months before their book's publication date to Christine Mersch at the address above.''

$ $THE WRITER

Kalmbach Publishing Co., 21027 Crossroads Circle, P.O. Box 1612, Waukesha WI 53187-1612. E-mail: editor@writermag.com. Website: www.writermag.com. **Contact:** Elfrieda Abbe, editor. **90% freelance written.** Prefers to buy work of published/established writers. Estab. 1887. **Pays on acceptance.** Buys first North American serial rights. Accepts queries by mail, e-mail. Sample copy for $4.95. Writer's guidelines online.

- No phone queries.

Nonfiction Practical articles for writers on how to write for publication, and how and where to market manuscripts in various fields. Considers all submissions promptly. No assignments. Length: 800-3,000 words.

Reprints Send tearsheet or photocopy and information about when and where the material previously appeared.

Tips ''We are looking for articles with plenty of practical, specific advice, tips, and techniques that aspiring and beginning writers can apply to their own work. New types of publications and our continually updated market listings in all fields will determine changes of focus and fact.''

$WRITERS' JOURNAL

The Complete Writer's Magazine, Val-Tech Media, P.O. Box 394, Perham MN 56573-0394. (218)346-7921. Fax: (218)346-7924. E-mail: writersjournal@lakesplus.com. Website: www.writersjournal.com. Managing Editor: John Ogroske. **Contact:** Leon Ogroske, editor. **90% freelance written.** Bimonthly trade magazine covering writing. *''Writers' Journal* is read by thousands of aspiring writers whose love of writing has taken them to the next step: Writing for money. We are an instructional manual giving writers the tools and information necessary to get their work published. We also print works by authors who have won our writing contests.'' Estab. 1980. Circ. 26,000. Pays on publication. Publishes ms an average of 10 months after acceptance. Byline given. Buys one-time rights. Editorial lead time 8 months. Submit seasonal material 8 months in advance. Accepts queries by mail, e-mail. Accepts simultaneous submissions. Responds in 6 weeks to queries; 6 months to mss. Sample copy for $5.

Nonfiction Looking for articles on fiction writing (plot development, story composition, character development, etc.) and writing ''how-to.'' Book excerpts, essays, exposé, general interest (to writers), humor, inspirational, interview/profile, new product, opinion, personal experience, photo feature, technical. No erotica. **Buys 45 mss/year.** Send complete ms. Length: 800-2,500 words. **Pays with a 1-year subscription, money depending on article and budget, and in contributor copies or other premiums if author agrees**.

Photos State availability with submission. Reviews contact sheets, prints. Buys one-time rights. Negotiates payment individually. Model releases required.

Columns/Departments For Beginners Only (helpful advice to beginners), 800-2,500 words. **Buys 30 mss/year.** Send complete ms. **Pays $20, money depending on article, and a 1-year subscription.**

Fiction ''We only publish winners of our fiction contests—16 contests/year.'' Length: 2,000 words.

Poetry Esther Leiper-Jefferson, poetry editor. Also publishes winners of the three poetry contests. No erotica. **Buys 25 poems/year.** Submit maximum 4 poems. Length: 25 lines. **Pays $5.**

Fillers Anecdotes, facts, short humor, cartoons. **Buys 20/year.** Length: 200 words. **Pays up to $10.**

Tips ''Appearance must be professional with no grammatical or spelling errors, submitted on white paper, double spaced with easy-to-read font. We want articles that will help writers improve technique in writing, style, editing, publishing, and story construction. We are interested in how writers use new and fresh angles to break into the writing markets.''

$WRITING THAT WORKS

The Business Communications Report, Communications Concepts, Inc., 7481 Huntsman Blvd., #720, Springfield VA 22153-1648. (703)643-2200. Fax: (703)643-2329. E-mail: jd@writingthatworks.com. Website: www.apexaw ards.com. **Contact:** John De Lellis, editor/publisher. Monthly newsletter on business writing and communications. ''Our readers are company writers, editors, communicators, and executives. They need specific, practical advice on how to write well as part of their job.'' Estab. 1983. Pays within 45 days of acceptance. Publishes ms an average of 3 months after acceptance. Byline sometimes given. Buys all rights. Editorial lead time 3 months. Accepts queries by mail, e-mail. Responds in 1 month to queries. Sample copy and writer's guidelines online. Writer's guidelines online.

Nonfiction Practical, short, how-to articles and quick tips on business writing techniques geared to company writers, editors, publication staff and communicators. ''We're always looking for shorts—how-to tips on business writing.'' How-to. **Buys 120 mss/year.** Accepts electronic final mss. Length: 100-500 words. **Pays $35-150.**

Columns/Departments Writing Techniques (how-to business writing advice); Style Matters (grammar, usage, and editing); Online Publishing (writing, editing, and publishing for the Web); Managing Publications; PR & Marketing (writing).

Fillers Short tips on writing or editing. Mini-reviews of communications websites for business writers, editors, and communicators. Length: 100-150 words. **Pays $35.**

Tips ''We do not use material on how to get published or how to conduct a freelancing business. Format your copy to follow *Writing That Works* style. Include postal and e-mail addresses, phone numbers, website URLs, and prices for products/services mentioned in articles.''

N $ $ $ $WRITTEN BY

The Magazine of the Writers Guild of America, West, 7000 W. Third St., Los Angeles CA 90048. (323)782-4522. Fax: (323)782-4800. E-mail: writtenby@wga.org. Website: www.wga.org. **40% freelance written.** Magazine published 9 times/year. *''Written By* is the premier magazine written by and for America's screen and TV writers. We focus on the craft of screenwriting and cover all aspects of the entertainment industry from the perspective of the writer. We are read by all screenwriters and most entertainment executives.'' Estab. 1987.

Circ. 12,000. **Pays on acceptance.** Publishes ms an average of 2 months after acceptance. Byline given. Offers 10% kill fee. Buys first North American serial, electronic rights. Editorial lead time 4 months. Submit seasonal material 4 months in advance. Accepts queries by mail, e-mail, fax, phone. Writer's guidelines for #10 SASE.

○→ Break in with "an exclusive profile or Q&A with a major TV or screenwriter."

Nonfiction Book excerpts, essays, historical/nostalgic, humor, interview/profile, opinion, personal experience, photo feature, technical (software). No "how to break into Hollywood," "how to write scripts"-type beginner pieces. **Buys 20 mss/year.** Query with published clips. Length: 500-3,500 words. **Pays $500-3,500 for assigned articles.** Sometimes pays expenses of writers on assignment.

Photos State availability with submission. Reviews transparencies. Buys one-time rights. Offers no additional payment for photos accepted with ms. Captions, identification of subjects, model releases required.

Columns/Departments Pays $1,000 maximum.

▣ The online version of this publication contains material not found in the print edition.

Tips "We are looking for more theoretical essays on screenwriting past and/or present. Also the writer must always keep in mind that our audience is made up primarily of working writers who are inside the business, therefore all articles need to have an 'insider' feel and not be written for those who are still trying to break in to Hollywood. We prefer a hard copy of submission or e-mail."

LAW

$ $ $ $ ABA JOURNAL

The Lawyer's Magazine, American Bar Association, 750 N. Lake Shore Dr., Chicago IL 60611. (312)988-6018. Fax: (312)988-6014. E-mail: releases@abanet.org. Website: www.abajournal.com. Editor: Danial J. Kim. **Contact:** Debra Weiss, managing editor. **10% freelance written.** Monthly magazine covering law. "The *ABA Journal* is an independent, thoughtful, and inquiring observer of the law and the legal profession. The magazine is edited for members of the American Bar Association." Circ. 389,000. **Pays on acceptance.** Byline given. Makes work-for-hire assignments. Accepts queries by mail, e-mail. Sample copy and writer's guidelines free. Writer's guidelines online.

Nonfiction Legal features. "We don't want anything that does not have a legal theme. No poetry or fiction." **Buys 5 mss/year.** Query with published clips. Length: 700-3,500 words. **Pays $400-2,000 for assigned articles.**

Columns/Departments The National Pulse/Ideas from the Front (reports on legal news and trends), 650 words; eReport (reports on legal news and trends), 500-1,500 words. The *ABA Journal eReport* is our weekly online newsletter sent out to members. **Buys 25 mss/year.** Query with published clips. **Pays $300, regardless of story length.**

$ $ $ BENCH & BAR OF MINNESOTA

Minnesota State Bar Association, 600 Nicollet Ave., Suite 380, Minneapolis MN 55402-1641. (612)333-1183. Fax: (612)333-4927. Website: www.mnbar.org. **Contact:** Judson Haverkamp, editor. **5% freelance written.** Magazine published 11 times/year. "Audience is mostly Minnesota lawyers. *Bench & Bar* seeks reportage, analysis, and commentary on trends and issues in the law and the legal profession, especially in Minnesota. Preference to items of practical/human interest to professionals in law." Estab. 1931. Circ. 16,000. **Pays on acceptance.** Publishes ms an average of 3 months after acceptance. Byline given. Buys first North American serial rights, makes work-for-hire assignments. Responds in 1 month to queries. Writer's guidelines for free online or by mail.

Nonfiction How-to (how to handle particular types of legal, ethical problems in office management, representation, etc.), humor, interview/profile, technical (/legal). "We do not want one-sided opinion pieces or advertorial." **Buys 2-3 mss/year.** Query with or without published clips or send complete ms. Length: 1,500-3,000 words. **Pays $300-800.** Sometimes pays expenses of writers on assignment.

Photos State availability with submission. Reviews 5×7 prints. Buys one-time rights. Pays $25-100 upon publication. Identification of subjects, model releases required.

$ $ $ $ CALIFORNIA LAWYER

Daily Journal Corporation, 1145 Market St., 8th Floor, San Francisco CA 94103. (415)296-2415. Fax: (415)296-0288. E-mail: peter_allen@dailyjournal.com. Website: www.dailyjournal.com. Managing Editor: Tema Goodwin. **Contact:** Peter Allen, editor. **30% freelance written.** Monthly magazine of law-related articles and general-interest subjects of appeal to lawyers and judges. "Our primary mission is to cover the news of the world as it affects the law and lawyers, helping our readers better comprehend the issues of the day and to cover changes and trends in the legal profession. Our readers are all 140,000 California lawyers, plus judges, legislators and corporate executives. Although we focus on California and the West, we have subscribers in every state. *California Lawyer* is a general interest magazine for people interested in law. Our writers are journalists." Estab.

1981. Circ. 140,000. **Pays on acceptance.** Publishes ms an average of 3 months after acceptance. Byline given. Offers 25% kill fee. Buys first North American serial, electronic rights. Editorial lead time 3 months. Accepts queries by mail, e-mail, fax. Sample copy and writer's guidelines for #10 SASE.

    ⚷ Break in by "showing us clips—we usually start people out on short news stories."

Nonfiction Essays, general interest, interview/profile, News and feature articles on law-related topics. "We are interested in concise, well-written and well-researched articles on issues of current concern, as well as well-told feature narratives with a legal focus. We would like to see a description or outline of your proposed idea, including a list of possible sources." **Buys 12 mss/year.** Query with or without published clips, or send complete ms. Length: 500-5,000 words. **Pays $50-2,000.** Pays expenses of writers on assignment.

Photos Jake Flaherty, art director. State availability with submission. Reviews Prints. Identification of subjects, model releases required.

Columns/Departments California Esq. (current legal trends). 300 words. **Buys 6 mss/year.** Query with or without published clips. **Pays $50-250.**

$ $ $ $ CORPORATE LEGAL TIMES

656 W. Randolph St., #500-E, Chicago IL 60661-2114. (312)654-3500. E-mail: rvosper@cltmag.com. Website: www.corporatelegaltimes.com. **Contact:** Robert Vosper, managing editor. **50% freelance written.** Monthly tabloid. "*Corporate Legal Times* is a monthly national magazine that gives general counsel and inhouse attorneys information on legal and business issues to help them better manage corporate law departments. It routinely addresses changes and trends in law departments, litigation management, legal technology, corporate governance and inhouse careers. Law areas covered monthly include: Intellectual property, international, technology, project finance, e-commerce and litigation. All articles need to be geared toward the inhouse attorney's perspective." Estab. 1991. Circ. 45,000. Pays on publication. Publishes ms an average of 3 months after acceptance. Byline given. Buys all rights. Editorial lead time 3 months. Submit seasonal material 3 months in advance. Accepts queries by mail, e-mail. Responds in 3 weeks to queries. Sample copy for $17. Writer's guidelines online.

Nonfiction Interview/profile, news about legal aspects of business issues and events. **Buys 12-25 mss/year.** Query with published clips. Length: 500-3,000 words. **Pays $500-2,000.**

Photos Freelancers should state availability of photos with submission. State availability with submission. Reviews color transparencies, b&w prints. Buys all rights. Offers $25-150/photo. Identification of subjects required.

Tips "Our publication targets general counsel and inhouse lawyers. All articles need to speak to them—not to the general attorney population. Query with clips and a list of potential in-house sources."

$ $ $ JOURNAL OF COURT REPORTING

National Court Reporters Association, 8224 Old Courthouse Rd., Vienna VA 22182. (703)556-6272. Fax: (703)556-6291. E-mail: jschmidt@ncrahq.org. **Contact:** Jacqueline Schmidt, editor. **20% freelance written.** Monthly (bimonthly July/August and November/December) magazine. "The *Journal of Court Reporting* has two complementary purposes: to communicate the activities, goals and mission of its publisher, the National Court Reporters Association; and, simultaneously, to seek out and publish diverse information and views on matters significantly related to the information/court reporting and captioning profession." Estab. 1905. Circ. 34,000. **Pays on acceptance.** Publishes ms an average of 3 months after acceptance. Byline given. Buys one-time rights, makes work-for-hire assignments. Editorial lead time 3 months. Accepts simultaneous submissions. Sample copy for $6. Writer's guidelines free.

Nonfiction Essays, historical/nostalgic, how-to, interview/profile, new product, technical. **Buys 10 mss/year.** Query. Length: 1,200 words. **Pays $55-1,000.** Sometimes pays expenses of writers on assignment.

Photos State availability with submission. Buys one-time rights. Offers no additional payment for photos accepted with ms. Captions, identification of subjects, model releases required.

LAW OFFICE COMPUTING

James Publishing, 3505 Cadillac Ave., Suite H, Costa Mesa CA 92626. (714)755-5468. Fax: (714)751-5508. E-mail: editorloc@jamespublishing.com. Website: www.lawofficecomputing.com. **Contact:** Amanda Clifford, editor and publisher. **90% freelance written.** Bimonthly magazine covering legal technology industry. "*Law Office Computing* is a magazine written for attorneys and other legal professionals. It covers the legal technology field and features software reviews, profiles of prominent figures in the industry, and 'how-to' type articles." Estab. 1991. Circ. 7,000. Pays on publication. Publishes ms an average of 2 months after acceptance. Byline given. Buys first North American serial rights. Editorial lead time 4 months. Submit seasonal material 4 months in advance. Accepts queries by mail, e-mail, fax. Sample copy for free. Writer's guidelines online.

Nonfiction How-to, interview/profile, new product, technical. Special issues: Looking for Macintosh and Linux articles. **Buys 30 mss/year.** Query. Length: 2,000-3,500 words. **Pays on a case-by-case basis.** Sometimes pays expenses of writers on assignment.

Photos State availability with submission.

Columns/Departments Tech profile (profile firm using technology), 1,200 words; My Solution, 1,500 words; Software reviews: Short reviews (a single product), 400-800 words; Software Shootouts (2 or 3 products going head-to-head), 1,000-1,500 words; Round-Ups/Buyer's Guides (8-15 products), 300-500 words/product. Each type of software review article has its own specific guidelines. Request the appropriate guidelines from editor. **Buys 6 mss/year.** Query. **Pays on a case-by-case basis.**

Tips "If you are a practicing attorney, legal MIS, or computer consultant, try the first-person My Solution column or a short review. If you are a professional freelance writer, technology profiles or a news story regarding legal technology are best, since most of our other copy is written by legal technology professionals."

LEGAL ASSISTANT TODAY

James Publishing, Inc., P.O. Box 25202, Santa Ana CA 92799. (714)755-5468. Fax: (714)751-5508. E-mail: aclifford@jamespublishing.com. Website: www.legalassistanttoday.com. **Contact:** Amanda Clifford, editor/publisher. Bimonthly magazine "geared toward all legal assistants/paralegals throughout the United States and Canada, regardless of specialty (litigation, corporate, bankruptcy, environmental law, etc.). How-to articles to help paralegals perform their jobs more effectively are most in demand, as is career and salary information, and timely news and trends pieces." Estab. 1983. Circ. 10,000. Pays on publication. Byline given. Buys first North American serial, electronic rights. non-exclusive electronic/Internet right and non-exclusive rights to use the article, author's name, image, and biographical data in advertising and promotion. Editorial lead time 10 weeks. Submit seasonal material 3 months in advance. Accepts queries by mail, e-mail, fax. Accepts simultaneous submissions. Responds in 2 months to mss. Sample copy and writer's guidelines free. Writer's guidelines online.

Nonfiction Interview/profile (unique and interesting paralegals in unique and particular work-related situations), news (brief, hard news topics regarding paralegals), features (present information to help paralegals advance their careers).

Photos Send photos with submission.

Tips "Fax a detailed outline of a 3,000 to 4,500-word feature about something useful to working legal assistants. Writers must understand our audience. There is some opportunity for investigative journalism as well as the usual features, profiles, and news. How-to articles are especially desired. If you are a great writer who can interview effectively, and really dig into the topic to grab readers' attention, we need you."

$ $ THE NATIONAL JURIST

Crittenden Magazines, P.O. Box 939039, San Diego CA 92193. (858)503-7562. Fax: (858)503-7588. E-mail: keith@crittendenmagazines.com. **Contact:** Keith Carter, managing editor. **5% freelance written.** Bimonthly magazine covering law literature. Estab. 1991. Circ. 100,000. Pays on publication. Buys all rights. Accepts queries by mail, e-mail, fax, phone.

Nonfiction General interest, how-to, humor, interview/profile. **Buys 4 mss/year.** Query. Length: 750-3,000 words. **Pays $100-500 for assigned articles.**

Photos State availability with submission. Reviews contact sheets. Negotiates payment individually.

Columns/Departments Pays $100-500.

$ $ THE PENNSYLVANIA LAWYER

Pennsylvania Bar Association, P.O. Box 186, 100 South St., Harrisburg PA 17108-0186. E-mail: editor@pabar.org. Executive Editor: Marcy Carey Mallory. Editor: Geoff Yuda. **Contact:** Donald C. Sarvey, editorial director. **25% freelance written.** Prefers to work with published/established writers. Bimonthly magazine published as a service to the legal profession and the members of the Pennsylvania Bar Association. Estab. 1979. Circ. 30,000. **Pays on acceptance.** Publishes ms an average of 6 months after acceptance. Byline given. Buys first, one-time rights. Submit seasonal material 6 months in advance. Accepts queries by mail, e-mail. Responds in 2 months to queries; 2 months to mss. Sample copy for $2. Writer's guidelines for #10 SASE or by e-mail.

Nonfiction All features must relate in some way to Pennsylvania lawyers or the practice of law in Pennsylvania. How-to, interview/profile, law-practice management, technology. **Buys 8-10 mss/year.** Query. Length: 1,200-2,000 words. **Pays $50 for book reviews; $75-400 for assigned articles; $150 for unsolicited articles.** Sometimes pays expenses of writers on assignment.

Photos State availability with submission. Reviews contact sheets. Buys one-time rights. Negotiates payment individually. Identification of subjects required.

$ $ $ STUDENT LAWYER

The Magazine of the Law Student Division, American Bar Association, 750 N. Lake Shore Dr., Chicago IL 60611. (312)988-6048. Fax: (312)988-6081. E-mail: abastulawyer@abanet.org. Website: www.abanet.org/lsd. **Contact:**

Ira Pilchen, editor. **85% freelance written.** Works with a small number of new writers each year. Monthly magazine. *"Student Lawyer* is a legal-affairs features magazine that competes for a share of law students' limited spare time, so the articles we publish must be informative, lively, well-researched good reads." Estab. 1972. Circ. 35,000. **Pays on acceptance.** Publishes ms an average of 3 months after acceptance. Byline given. Buys first rights. Editorial lead time 5 months. Submit seasonal material 6 months in advance. Accepts queries by mail, e-mail, phone. Writer's guidelines online.

Nonfiction Essays (on legal affairs), interview/profile (prominent person in law-related fields), opinion (on matters of current legal interest). No fiction, please. Query with published clips. Length: 2,000-2,500 words. **Pays $500-1,200 for features.** Sometimes pays expenses of writers on assignment.

Columns/Departments Profile (profiles out-of-the-ordinary lawyers), 1,200 words; Coping (dealing with law school), 1,200 words; Online (Internet and the law), 1,200 words; Leagal-ease (language and legal writing), 1,200 words; Jobs (marketing to legal employers), 1,200 words; Opinion (opinion on legal issue), 800 words. Query with published clips. **Pays $200-500.**

Tips *"Student Lawyer* actively seeks good, new reporters and writers eager to prove themselves. Legal training definitely not essential; writing talent is. The writer should not think we are a law review; we are a features magazine with the law (in the broadest sense) as the common denominator. Find issues of national scope and interest to write about; be aware of subjects the magazine—and other media—have already covered and propose something new. Write clearly and well. Expect to work with editor to polish manuscripts to perfection. We do not make assignments to writers whose work we are not familiar. If you're interested in writing for us, send a detailed, thought-out query with 3 previously published clips. We are always willing to look at material on spec. Sorry, we don't return manuscripts."

LUMBER

$ $ PALLET ENTERPRISE

Industrial Reporting Inc., 10244 Timber Ridge Dr., Ashland VA 23005. (804)550-0323. Fax: (804)550-2181. E-mail: editor@ireporting.com. Website: www.palletenterprise.com. Assistant Publisher: Chaille Brindley. **Contact:** Tim Cox, editor. **40% freelance written.** Monthly magazine covering lumber and pallet operations. Articles should offer technical, solution-oriented information. Anti-forest articles are not accepted. Articles should focus on machinery and unique ways to improve profitability/make money. Estab. 1981. Circ. 14,500. Pays on publication. Buys first, one-time, electronic rights, makes work-for-hire assignments. May buy all rights. Rights purchased depends on the writer and the article. Editorial lead time 2 months. Submit seasonal material 2 months in advance. Accepts queries by mail, e-mail, fax, phone. Accepts previously published material. Accepts simultaneous submissions. Sample copy online. Writer's guidelines free.

Nonfiction "We only want articles of interest to pallet manufacturers, pallet recyclers, and lumber companies/sawmills." Interview/profile, new product, opinion, technical, industry news; environmental; forests operation/plant features. No lifestyle, humor, general news, etc. **Buys 20 mss/year.** Query with published clips. Length: 1,000-3,000 words. **Pays $200-400 for assigned articles; $100-400 for unsolicited articles.** Call editor to discuss circumstances under which writers are paid in contributor copies. Sometimes pays expenses of writers on assignment.

Photos State availability with submission. Reviews 3×5 prints. Buys one time rights and Web rights. Negotiates payment individually. Captions, identification of subjects required.

Columns/Departments Green Watch (environmental news/opinion affecting U.S. forests), 1,500 words. **Buys 12 mss/year.** Query with published clips. **Pays $200-400.**

Tips "Provide unique environmental or industry-oriented articles. Many of our freelance articles are company features of sawmills, pallet manufacturers, pallet recyclers, and wood waste processors."

$ $ SOUTHERN LUMBERMAN

Hatton-Brown Publishers, P.O. Box 681629, Franklin TN 37068-1629. (615)791-1961. Fax: (615)591-1035. E-mail: southernlumberman@forestind.com. Website: www.southernlumberman.com. **Contact:** Nanci P. Gregg, editor. **20% freelance written.** Works with a small number of new/unpublished writers each year. Monthly journal for the sawmill industry. Estab. 1881. Circ. 15,000. Pays on publication. Publishes ms an average of 3 months after acceptance. Byline given. Buys first North American serial rights. Submit seasonal material 6 months in advance. Responds in 1 month to queries; 2 months to mss. Sample copy for $3 and 9×12 SAE with 5 first-class stamps. Writer's guidelines for #10 SASE.

Nonfiction How-to (sawmill better), technical, equipment analysis, sawmill features. **Buys 10-15 mss/year.** Query with or without published clips or send complete ms. Length: 500-2,000 words. **Pays $150-350 for assigned articles; $100-250 for unsolicited articles.** Sometimes pays expenses of writers on assignment.

Reprints Send tearsheet or photocopy of article and information about when and where the article previously appeared. Pays 25-50% of amount paid for an original article.

Photos Always looking for news feature types of photos featuring forest products, industry materials or people. Send photos with submission. Reviews transparencies, 4×5 color prints. Pays $10-25/photo. Captions, identification of subjects required.

Tips "Like most, we appreciate a clearly-worded query listing merits of suggested story—what it will tell our readers they need/want to know. We want quotes, we want opinions to make others discuss the article. Best hint? Find an interesting sawmill operation owner and start asking questions—I bet a story idea develops. We need color photos too. Find a sawmill operator and ask questions—what's he doing bigger, better, different. We're interested in new facilities, better marketing, improved production."

$ $ TIMBERLINE

Timber Industry Newsline/Trading Post, Industrial Reporting, Inc., 10244 Timber Ridge Dr., Ashland VA 23005. (804)550-0323. Fax: (804)550-2181. E-mail: editor@ireporting.com. Website: www.timberlinemag.com. Assistant Publisher: Chaille Brindley. **Contact:** Tim Cox, editor. **50% freelance written.** Monthly tabloid covering the forest products industry. Articles should offer technical, solution-oriented information. Anti-forest products, industry articles are not accepted. Articles should focus on machinery and unique ways to improve profitability and make money. Estab. 1994. Circ. 30,000. Pays on publication. Byline given. Buys first, one-time, electronic rights, makes work-for-hire assignments. May purchase all rights. Rights purchased depends on the writer and the article. Editorial lead time 2 months. Submit seasonal material 2 months in advance. Accepts queries by mail, e-mail, fax, phone. Accepts previously published material. Accepts simultaneous submissions. Sample copy online. Writer's guidelines free.

Nonfiction "We only want articles of interest to loggers, sawmills, wood treatment facilities, etc. Readers tend to be pro-industry/conservative, and opinion pieces must be written to appeal to them." Historical/nostalgic, interview/profile, new product, opinion, technical, Industry News; Environmental Operation/Plant Features. No lifestyles, humor, general news, etc. **Buys 25 mss/year.** Query with published clips. Length: 1,000-3,000 words. **Pays $200-400 for assigned articles; $100-400 for unsolicited articles.** Call editor to discuss circumstances under which writers are paid in contributor copies. Sometimes pays expenses of writers on assignment.

Photos State availability with submission. Reviews 3×5 prints. Buys one time rights and Web rights. Negotiates payment individually. Captions, identification of subjects required.

Columns/Departments From the Hill (legislative news impacting the forest products industry), 1,800 words; Green Watch (environmental news/opinion affecting U.S. forests), 1,500 words. **Buys 12 mss/year.** Query with published clips. **Pays $200-400.**

Tips "Provide unique environmental or industry-oriented articles. Many of our freelance articles are company features of logging operations or sawmills."

$ $ TIMBERWEST

Timber/West Publications, LLC, P.O. Box 610, Edmonds WA 98020-0160. Fax: (425)771-3623. E-mail: timberwest@forestnet.com. Website: www.forestnet.com. **Contact:** Diane Mettler, managing editor. **75% freelance written.** Monthly magazine covering logging and lumber segment of the forestry industry in the Northwest. "We publish primarily profiles on loggers and their operations, with an emphasis on the machinery, in Washington, Oregon, Idaho, Montana, Northern California, and Alaska. Some timber issues are highly controversial and although we will report on the issues, this is a pro-logging publication. We don't publish articles with a negative slant on the timber industry." Estab. 1975. Circ. 10,000. **Pays on acceptance.** Byline given. Not copyrighted. Buys first North American serial, second serial (reprint) rights. Editorial lead time 3 months. Accepts queries by mail, fax. Responds in 3 weeks to queries. Sample copy for $2. Writer's guidelines for #10 SASE.

Nonfiction Historical/nostalgic, interview/profile, new product. No articles that put the timber industry in a bad light—such as environmental articles against logging. **Buys 50 mss/year.** Query with published clips. Length: 1,100-1,500 words. **Pays $350.** Pays expenses of writers on assignment.

Photos Send photos with submission. Reviews contact sheets, transparencies, prints, GIF/JPEG files. Buys all rights. Offers no additional payment for photos accepted with ms. Captions, identification of subjects required.

Fillers Facts, newsbreaks. **Buys 10/year.** Length: 400-800 words. **Pays $100-250.**

Tips "We are always interested in profiles of loggers and their operations in Alaska, Oregon, Washington, Montana, and Northern California. Also articles pertaining to current industry topics, such as fire abatement, sustainable forests, or new technology. Read an issue to get a clear idea of the type of material *TimberWest* publishes. The audience is primarily loggers and topics that focus on an 'evolving' timber industry versus a 'dying' industry will find a place in the magazine. When querying, a clear overview of the article will enhance acceptance."

MACHINERY & METAL

$ $ $ CUTTING TOOL ENGINEERING

CTE Publications, Inc., 400 Skokie Blvd., Suite 395, Northbrook IL 60062-7903.. (847)498-9100. Fax: (847)559-4444. Website: www.ctemag.com. Managing Editor: Allan Richter. **Contact:** Don Nelson, publisher. **40% freelance written.** Monthly magazine covering industrial metal cutting tools and metal cutting operations. *"Cutting Tool Engineering* serves owners, managers and engineers who work in manufacturing, specifically manufacturing that involves cutting or grinding metal or other materials. Writing should be geared toward improving manufacturing processes."* Circ. 35,000. Pays 1 week before publication. Publishes ms an average of 2 months after acceptance. Byline given. Offers 50% kill fee. Buys all rights. Editorial lead time 2 months. Accepts queries by mail, fax. Responds in 2 months to mss. Sample copy and writer's guidelines free.

Nonfiction How-to, opinion, personal experience, technical. "No fiction, articles that don't relate to manufacturing." **Buys 30 mss/year.** Length: 1,500-3,000 words. **Pays $450-1,000.** Pays expenses of writers on assignment.

Photos State availability with submission. Reviews transparencies, prints. Buys all rights. Negotiates payment individually. Captions required.

Tips "For queries, write two clear paragraphs about how the proposed article will play out. Include sources that would be in the article."

$ $ $ THE FABRICATOR

The Croydon Group, Ltd., 833 Featherstone Rd., Rockford IL 61107. (815)399-8700. Fax: (815)484-7700. E-mail: dand@thefabricator.com. Website: www.thefabricator.com. **Contact:** Dan Davis, executive editor. **15% freelance written.** Monthly magazine covering metal forming and fabricating. Our purpose is to disseminate information about modern metal forming and fabricating techniques, machinery, tooling and management concepts for the metal fabricator. Estab. 1971. Circ. 55,000. Pays on publication. Byline given. Buys all rights. Editorial lead time 6 months. Accepts queries by mail, e-mail. Responds in 2 weeks to queries; 1 month to mss. Sample copy and writer's guidelines free. Writer's guidelines online.

Nonfiction How-to, technical, company profile. Special issues: Forecast issue (January). No unsolicited case studies. Query with published clips. Length: 800-1,200 words. **Pays 40-80¢/word.** Sometimes pays expenses of writers on assignment.

Photos Request guidelines for digital images. State availability with submission. Reviews transparencies, prints. Rights purchased depends on photographer requirements. Negotiates payment individually. Captions, identification of subjects required.

⬛ The online magazine carries original content not found in the print edition. Contact: Laurie Harshbarger.

MACHINE DESIGN

Penton Media, Penton Media Bldg., 1300 E. 9th St., Cleveland OH 49114-1503. (216)931-9412. Fax: (216)621-8469. E-mail: mdeditor@penton.com. Website: www.machinedesign.com. Editor: Ronald Khol. **Contact:** Kenneth Korane, managing editor. Semimonthly magazine covering machine design. Covers the design engineering of manufactured products, across the entire spectrum of the idustry for people who perform design engineering functions. Circ. 185,163. Editorial lead time 3 weeks. Accepts queries by mail, e-mail. Sample copy not available.

Nonfiction How-to, new product, technical. Query with or without published clips or send complete ms.

Columns/Departments Query with or without published clips or send complete ms.

$ MATERIAL HANDLING WHOLESALER

Specialty Publications International, Inc., P.O. Box 725, Dubuque IA 52004-0725. (877)638-6190 or (563)557-4495. Fax: (563)557-4499. E-mail: editorial@mhwmag.com. Website: www.mhwmag.com. **Contact:** Cathy Murphy, editor. **100% freelance written.** Monthly magazine covering material handling industry. *MHW* is published monthly for new and used equipment dealers, equipment manufacturers, manufacturer reps, parts suppliers, and service facilities serving the material handling industry. Estab. 1979. Circ. 12,000. Pays on publication. Publishes ms an average of 2 months after acceptance. Byline given. Buys first rights. Editorial lead time 1 month. Submit seasonal material 2 months in advance. Accepts queries by mail, e-mail, fax. Accepts simultaneous submissions. Sample copy for $31 annually-3rd class. Writer's guidelines free.

Nonfiction General interest, how-to, inspirational, new product, opinion, personal experience, photo feature, technical, material handling news.

Photos Send photos with submission. Reviews 3×5 prints. Buys all rights. Offers no additional payment for photos accepted with ms.

Columns/Departments Aftermarket (aftermarket parts and service); Battery Tech (batteries for lifts-MH equipment); Marketing Matters (sales trends in MH industry); Internet at Work (internet trends), all 1,200 words. **Buys 3 mss/year.** Query. **Pays $0-50.**

▣ The online version of this publication contains material not found in the print edition. Contact: Cathy Murphy, online editor.

MODERN MACHINE SHOP

Gardner Publications, Inc., 6915 Valley Ave., Cincinnati OH 45244-3029. (513)527-8800. Fax: (513)527-8801. E-mail: malbert@mmsonline.com. Website: www.mmsonline.com. **Contact:** Mark Albert, editor-in-chief. **5% freelance written.** Monthly magazine. Estab. 1928. Pays 1 month following acceptance. Publishes ms an average of 6 months after acceptance. Byline given. Accepts queries by mail, e-mail, fax, phone. Responds in 1 month to mss. Call for sample copy. Writer's guidelines online.

○┐ Advances in metalworking technology are occurring rapidly. Articles that show how this new technology, as embodied in specific products, is being implemented in shops and plants are sought after. Writers are strongly encouraged to call to discuss an idea.

Nonfiction Uses only articles dealing with all phases of metalworking, manufacturing, and machine shop work, with photos. "Ours is an industrial publication, and contributing authors should have a working knowledge of the metalworking industry. We regularly use contributions from machine shop owners, engineers, other technical experts, and suppliers to the metalworking industry. Almost all of these contributors pursue these projects to promote their own commercial interests." **Buys 5 or fewer unsolicited mss/year.** Query. Length: 1,000-3,500 words. **Pays current market rate.**

▣ The online magazine carries original content not found in the print edition. Contact: A.J. Sweatt (ajsweatt@mmsonline.com).

Tips "Although our focus remains on the basics of metalworking/machining processes, we are giving added coverage to lean manufacturing, business strategies, and marketing as critical factors in competitiveness."

MSI

Reed Business Information, 2000 Clearwater Dr., Oak Brook IL 60523-8809. (630)288-8756. Fax: (630)288-8105. E-mail: kparker@reedbusiness.com. Website: www.msimag.com. **Contact:** Kevin Parker, editorial director. Monthly magazine. "*Manufacturing Systems* is about the use of information technology to improve productivity in discrete manufacturing and process industries." Estab. 1984. Circ. 105,000. Pays on publication. Publishes ms an average of 3 months after acceptance. Byline sometimes given. Buys all rights. Editorial lead time 3 months. Submit seasonal material 4 months in advance. Accepts queries by e-mail. Sample copy for free. Writer's guidelines online.

Nonfiction Technical. **Buys 30 mss/year.** Query.

Photos No additional payment for photos. Captions required.

$ $ ORNAMENTAL AND MISCELLANEOUS METAL FABRICATOR

National Ornamental And Miscellaneous Metals Association, 532 Forest Pkwy., Suite A, Forest Park GA 30297. Fax: (404)366-1852. E-mail: todd@nomma.org. **Contact:** Todd Daniel, editor. **20% freelance written.** Bimonthly magazine "to inform, educate, and inspire members of the ornamental and miscellaneous metalworking industry." Estab. 1959. Circ. 8,000. Pays when article is received. Byline given. Buys one-time rights. Editorial lead time 2 months. Accepts queries by mail, e-mail, fax. Responds in 1 month to queries. Sample copy for 9×12 SAE and 6 first-class stamps. Writer's guidelines for $1.

Nonfiction Book excerpts, essays, exposé, general interest, historical/nostalgic, how-to, humor, inspirational, interview/profile, new product, opinion, personal experience, photo feature, technical. **Buys 8-12 mss/year.** Query. Length: 1,200-2,000 words. **Pays $350-375.** Pays expenses of writers on assignment.

Reprints Send tearsheet, photocopy, or typed ms with rights for sale noted and information about when and where the material previously appeared. Pays 100% of amount paid for an original article.

Photos State availability with submission. Reviews contact sheets, negatives, transparencies, prints. May offer additonal payment for photos accepted with ms. Model releases required.

Tips "Make article relevant to our industry. Don't write in passive voice."

$ $ $ PRACTICAL WELDING TODAY

The Croydon Group, Ltd., 833 Featherstone Rd., Rockford IL 61107-6302. (815)227-8282. Fax: (815)484-7715. E-mail: stephaniev@thefabricator.com. Website: www.thefabricator.com. **Contact:** Stephanie Vaughan, associate editor. **15% freelance written.** Bimonthly magazine covering welding. "We generally publish how-to, educational articles that teach people about a process or how to do something better." Estab. 1997. Circ. 40,000. Pays on publication. Byline given. Buys all rights. Editorial lead time 6 months. Accepts queries by mail, e-mail. Responds in 2 weeks to queries; 2 months to mss. Sample copy and writer's guidelines free. Writer's guidelines online.

Nonfiction How-to, technical, company profiles. Special issues: Forecast issue on trends in welding (January/February). No promotional, one-sided, persuasive articles, unsolicited case studies. **Buys 5 mss/year.** Query with published clips. Length: 800-1,200 words. **Pays 40-80¢/word.** Sometimes pays expenses of writers on assignment.

Photos State availability with submission. Reviews contact sheets. Rights purchased depends on photographer requirements. Negotiates payment individually. Captions, identification of subjects required.

Tips "Follow our author guidelines and editorial policies to write a how-to piece from which our readers can benefit."

$ $ SPRINGS

The International Magazine of Spring Manufacturers, Spring Manufacturers Institute, 2001 Midwest Rd., Suite 106, Oak Brook IL 60523-1335. (630)495-8588. Fax: (630)495-8595. Website: www.smihq.org. **Contact:** Rita Schauer, editor. **10% freelance written.** Quarterly magazine covering precision mechanical spring manufacture. Articles should be aimed at spring manufacturers. Estab. 1962. Circ. 10,800. Pays on publication. Publishes ms an average of 3-6 months after acceptance. Byline given. Buys first rights. Editorial lead time 4 months. Accepts simultaneous submissions. Sample copy free. Writer's guidelines online.

Nonfiction General interest, how-to, interview/profile, opinion, personal experience, technical. **Buys 4-6 mss/ year.** Length: 2,000-10,000 words. **Pays $100-600 for assigned articles; $50-300 for unsolicited articles.**

Photos State availability with submission. Reviews transparencies, prints. Buys one-time rights. Offers no additional payment for photos accepted with ms. Captions required.

Fillers Facts, newsbreaks. **Buys 4/year.** Length: 200-1,000 words. **Pays $25-50.**

Tips "Call the editor. Contact springmakers and spring industry suppliers and ask about what interests them. Include interviews/quotes from people in the spring industry in the article. The editor can supply contacts."

$ $ $ STAMPING JOURNAL

Fabricators & Manufacturers Association (FMA), 833 Featherstone Rd., Rockford IL 61107. (815)399-8700. Fax: (815)381-1370. E-mail: katm@thefabricator.com. Website: www.thefabricator.com. **Contact:** Kathleen McLaughlin, associate editor. **15% freelance written.** Bimonthly magazine covering metal stamping. "We look for how-to, educational articles—nonpromotional." Estab. 1989. Circ. 35,000. Pays on publication. Byline given. Buys all rights. Editorial lead time 6 months. Accepts queries by mail, e-mail, fax, phone. Responds in 2 weeks to queries; 2 months to mss. Sample copy and writer's guidelines free.

Nonfiction How-to, technical, company profile. Special issues: Forecast issue (January). No unsolicited case studies. **Buys 5 mss/year.** Query with published clips. Length: 1,000 words. **Pays 40-80¢/word.** Sometimes pays expenses of writers on assignment.

Photos State availability with submission. Reviews contact sheets. Rights purchased depends on photographer requirements. Negotiates payment individually. Captions, identification of subjects required.

■ The online magazine contains material not found in the print edition. Contact: Vicki Bell, online editor.

Tips "Articles should be impartial and should not describe the benefits of certain products available from certain companies. They should not be biased toward the author's or against a competitor's products or technologies. The publisher may refuse any article that does not conform to this guideline."

$ $ $ TPJ—THE TUBE & PIPE JOURNAL

Fabricators & Manufacturers Association (FMA), 833 Featherstone Rd., Rockford IL 61107. (815)399-8700. Fax: (815)381-1370. E-mail: ericl@thefabricator.com. Website: www.thefabricator.com. Executive Editor: Dan Davis. **Contact:** Eric Lundin, associate editor. **15% freelance written.** Magazine published 8 times/year covering metal tube and pipe. Educational perspective—emphasis is on "how-to" articles to accomplish a particular task or how to improve on a process. New trends and technologies are also important topics. Estab. 1990. Circ. 30,000. Pays on publication. Byline given. Buys all rights. Editorial lead time 6 months. Accepts queries by mail, e-mail. Responds in 2 weeks to queries; 2 months to mss. Sample copy and writer's guidelines free. Writer's guidelines online.

Nonfiction Any new or improved tube production or fabrication process—includes manufacturing, bending, and forming tube (metal tube only). How-to, technical. Special issues: Forecast issue (January). No unsolicited case studies. **Buys 5 mss/year.** Query with published clips. Length: 800-1,200 words. **Pays 40-80¢/word.** Sometimes pays expenses of writers on assignment.

Photos State availability with submission. Reviews contact sheets. Rights purchased depends on photographer requirements. Negotiates payment individually. Captions, identification of subjects required.

Tips "Submit a detailed proposal, including an article outline, to the editor."

$ $ WIRE ROPE NEWS & SLING TECHNOLOGY

VS Enterprises, P.O. Box 871, Clark NJ 07066. (908)486-3221. Fax: (732)396-4215. E-mail: vsent@aol.com. Website: www.wireropenews.com. **100% freelance written.** Bimonthly magazine "published for manufacturers and distributors of wire rope, chain, cordage, related hardware, and sling fabricators. Content includes technical articles, news and reports describing the manufacturing and use of wire rope and related products in marine, construction, mining, aircraft and offshore drilling operations." Estab. 1979. Circ. 4,300. **Pays on acceptance.** Publishes ms an average of 6 months after acceptance. Byline sometimes given. Buys all rights. Editorial lead time 2 months. Submit seasonal material 2 months in advance. Accepts queries by mail, fax. Accepts simultaneous submissions.

Nonfiction General interest, historical/nostalgic, interview/profile, photo feature, technical. **Buys 30 mss/year.** Send complete ms. Length: 2,500-5,000 words. **Pays $300-500.**

Photos Send photos with submission. Reviews contact sheets, 5×7 prints, digital. Buys all rights. Offers no additional payment for photos accepted with ms. Identification of subjects required.

Tips "We are accepting more submissions and queries by e-mail."

MAINTENANCE & SAFETY

CANADIAN OCCUPATIONAL SAFETY

CLB Media, Inc., 3228 S. Service Rd., Suite 209, Burlington ON L7N 3H8, Canada. (905)634-2100 ext. 35. Fax: (905)634-2238. E-mail: mmorra@clbmedia.ca. Website: www.cos-mag.com. **Contact:** Michelle Morra, editor. **40% freelance written.** Bimonthly magazine. "We want informative articles dealing with issues that relate to occupational health and safety in Canada." Estab. 1989. Circ. 14,000. Pays on publication. Publishes ms an average of 3 months after acceptance. Byline given. Buys one-time rights. Editorial lead time 4 months. Submit seasonal material 4 months in advance. Accepts queries by mail, e-mail, fax, phone. Responds in 3 weeks to queries; 1 month to mss. Sample copy and writer's guidelines free.

Nonfiction How-to, interview/profile. **Buys 30 mss/year.** Query with published clips. Length: 500-2,000 words. **Payment varies.** Sometimes pays expenses of writers on assignment.

Photos State availability with submission. Reviews transparencies. Buys one-time rights. Negotiates payment individually. Captions required.

Tips "Present us with an idea for an article that will interest workplace health and safety professionals, with cross-Canada appeal."

$ $EXECUTIVE HOUSEKEEPING TODAY

The International Executive Housekeepers Association, 1001 Eastwind Dr., Suite 301, Westerville OH 43081. (614)895-7166. Fax: (614)895-1248. E-mail: avance@ieha.org. Website: www.ieha.org. **Contact:** Andi Vance, editor. **50% freelance written.** Monthly magazine for "nearly 5,000 decision makers responsible for housekeeping management (cleaning, grounds maintenance, laundry, linen, pest control, waste management, regulatory compliance, training) for a variety of institutions: hospitality, healthcare, education, retail, government." Estab. 1930. Circ. 5,500. **Pays on acceptance.** Publishes ms an average of 6 months after acceptance. Byline given. Buys first North American serial rights. Editorial lead time 2 months. Submit seasonal material 3 months in advance. Accepts queries by mail, e-mail, fax, phone.

Nonfiction General interest, interview/profile, new product (related to magazine's scope), personal experience (in housekeeping profession), technical. **Buys 30 mss/year.** Query with published clips. Length: 500-1,500 words. **Pays $150-250.**

Photos State availability with submission. Buys one-time rights. Offers no additional payment for photos accepted with ms. Identification of subjects required.

Columns/Departments Federal Report (OSHA/EPA requirements), 1,000 words; Industry News; Management Perspectives (industry specific), 500-1,500 words. Query with published clips. **Pays $150-250.**

Tips "Have a background in the industry or personal experience with any aspect of it."

$ $PEST CONTROL MAGAZINE

7500 Old Oak Blvd., Cleveland OH 44130. (440)243-8100. Fax: (440)891-2683. Website: www.pestcontrolmag.com. **Contact:** Susan Porter, associate publisher/executive editor. Monthly magazine for professional pest management professionals and sanitarians. Estab. 1933. Circ. 20,000. Pays on publication. Licenses rights. Submit seasonal material 3 months in advance. Accepts queries by mail, e-mail, phone. Responds in 1 month to mss. Sample copy not available. Writer's guidelines online.

○→ Break in with "information directly relating to the field—citing sources that are either industry experts (university or otherwise) or direct quotes from pest/management professionals."

Nonfiction Prefers contributors with pest control industry background. All articles must have trade or business orientation. How-to, humor, inspirational, interview/profile, new product, personal experience (stories about pest management operations and their problems), case histories, new technological breakthroughs. No general information type of articles desired. **Buys 3 mss/year.** Query. Length: 1,000-1,400 words. **Pays $150-400 minimum.**

Photos Certain digital photos accepted; please query on specs. State availability with submission. Pays $50-

500 for 8×10 color or transparencies for front cover graphics. No additional payment for photos used with ms. **Columns/Departments** Regular columns use material oriented to this profession. Length: 550 words.

🔳 The online magazine carries original material not found in the print edition. Contact: Heather Gooch.

MANAGEMENT & SUPERVISION

$ $🔲 CONTACT MANAGEMENT

Canada's Professional Customer Contact Solutions Forum, August Communications, 225-530 Century St., Winnipeg MB R3H 0Y4, Canada. (888)573-1136. Fax: (866)957-0217. E-mail: t.rehberg@august.ca. Website: www.contactmanagement.ca. **Contact:** Trina Rehberg, editor. **90% freelance written.** Quarterly magazine covering Canadian contact centres. "*Contact Management* is the only magazine specifically targeted at Canadian contact centres. Direct mailed to managers, executives, and suppliers, the magazine explores topics important to the successful execution and planning of the day-to-day activities in a modern Canadian contact centre." Estab. 2000. Circ. 5,200. Pays 1 month after publication. Publishes ms an average of 2 months after acceptance. Byline given. Buys all rights. Editorial lead time 3 months. Submit seasonal material 3 months in advance. Accepts queries by mail, e-mail, fax. Responds in 1 week to queries. Sample copy for free.

Nonfiction Exposé, how-to, interview/profile, new product, technical. **Buys 12 mss/year.** Query with published clips. Length: 700-2,250 words. **Pays 15-40¢/word for assigned articles.**

Photos State availability with submission. Reviews GIF/JPEG files. Buys all rights. Negotiates payment individually. Identification of subjects required.

Columns/Departments Buys 6 mss/year. Query with published clips. **Pays 15-40¢/word.**

HR MAGAZINE

On Human Resource Management, Society for Human Resource Management, 1800 Duke St., Alexandria VA 22314-3499. (703)548-3440. Fax: (703)535-6488. E-mail: hrmag@shrm.org. Website: www.shrm.org. **70% freelance written.** Monthly magazine covering human resource management professions with special focus on business news that affects the workplace including compensation, benefits, recruiting, training and development, management trends, court decisions, legislative actions, and government regulations. Accepts queries and mss via website; responds in 45 days. Estab. 1948. Circ. 165,000. **Pays on acceptance.** Publishes ms an average of 2 months after acceptance. Byline given. Buys all rights. Editorial lead time 4 months. Sample copy for free. Writer's guidelines online.

● Must submit queries via website.

○━ Break in by having "relevant writing experience and a sharp, narrowly-focused article idea on something new or not well-covered elsewhere."

Nonfiction Technical, expert advice and analysis, news features. **Buys 50 mss/year.** Query. Length: 1,800-2,500 words. Pays expenses of writers on assignment.

Photos State availability with submission. Buys one-time rights. Identification of subjects, model releases required.

Tips "Readers are members of the Society for Human Resource Management (SHRM), mostly HR managers with private employers."

$ $ $ HUMAN RESOURCE EXECUTIVE

LRP Publications Magazine Group, 747 Dresher Rd., P.O. Box 980, Dept. 500, Harsham PA 19044. (215)784-0910. Fax: (215)784-0275. E-mail: dshadovitz@lrp.com. Website: www.hrexecutive.com. **Contact:** David Shadovitz, editor. **30% freelance written.** "Monthly magazine serving the information needs of chief human resource professionals/executives in companies, government agencies, and nonprofit institutions with 500 or more employees." Estab. 1987. Circ. 75,000. **Pays on acceptance.** Publishes ms an average of 2 months after acceptance. Byline given. Pays 50% kill fee on assigned stories. Buys all rights. Accepts queries by mail, e-mail, fax. Responds in 1 month to mss. Writer's guidelines online.

Nonfiction Book excerpts, interview/profile. **Buys 16 mss/year.** Query with published clips. Length: 1,800 words. **Pays $200-1,000.** Sometimes pays expenses of writers on assignment.

Photos State availability with submission. Reviews contact sheets. Buys first and repeat rights. Offers no additional payment for photos accepted with ms. Identification of subjects required.

$ $ INCENTIVE

VNU Business Publications, 770 Broadway, New York NY 10003. (646)654-7636. Fax: (646)654-7650. E-mail: edit@incentivemag.com. Website: www.incentivemag.com. **Contact:** Danine Alati, editor-in-chief. Monthly magazine covering sales promotion and employee motivation: managing and marketing through motivation. Estab. 1905. Circ. 41,000. **Pays on acceptance.** Publishes ms an average of 3 months after acceptance. Byline given. Buys all rights. Accepts queries by mail, e-mail, fax. Responds in 1 month to queries; 2 months to mss. Sample copy for 9×12 SAE.

Nonfiction General interest (motivation, demographics), how-to (types of sales promotion, buying product categories, using destinations), interview/profile (sales promotion executives), travel (incentive-oriented), Corporate case studies. **Buys 48 mss/year.** Query with published clips. Length: 1,000-2,000 words. **Pays $250-700 for assigned articles; does not pay for unsolicited articles.** Pays expenses of writers on assignment.

Reprints Send tearsheet and information about when and where the material previously appeared. Pays 50% of the amount paid for an original article.

Photos Send photos with submission. Reviews contact sheets, transparencies. Offers some additional payment for photos accepted with ms. Identification of subjects required.

Tips "Read the publication, then query."

$ $SKATEPARK

Harris Publishing, 360 B St., Idaho Falls ID 83402. (208)524-7000. Fax: (208)522-5241. E-mail: brady@skatepark mag.com. Website: www.skateparkmag.com. Executive Editor: Steve Smede. **Contact:** Brady L. Kay, editor. **25% freelance written.** Magazine published 8 times/year covering skatepark market. *"SkatePark* targets a park and recreation management readership. Articles should focus on the skatepark market as a whole, not the sport of skateboarding itself." Estab. 2001. Circ. 20,000. Pays on publication. Publishes ms an average of 6 months after acceptance. Byline given. Offers $50 kill fee. Buys first North American serial, electronic rights. Editorial lead time 2 months. Submit seasonal material 1 year in advance. Accepts queries by mail, e-mail. Accepts simultaneous submissions. Responds in 2 weeks to queries; 2 months to mss. Sample copy for $5. Writer's guidelines for #10 SASE.

Nonfiction How-to, interview/profile, new product, opinion, photo feature, technical, travel. *"SkatePark* does not publish articles about skaters, X-Games, pros, etc. Writers should find interesting and informative article ideas that focus on skateparks and related issues." **Buys 4-6 mss/year.** Query with or without published clips. Length: 800-1,500 words. **Pays $50-300 for assigned articles.** Sometimes pays expenses of writers on assignment.

Photos State availability of or send photos with submission. Reviews 35mm transparencies, GIF/JPEG files. Buys one-time rights. Offers no additional payment for photos accepted with ms. Captions, identification of subjects, model releases required.

Columns/Departments How'd They Do That? (explores a specific challenge and how subject was able to overcome it), 800-1,200 words. **Buys 2 mss/year.** Query. **Pays $100-300.**

Tips "We are looking for articles that managers can use as a resource when considering skatepark construction, management, or safety. We are not a traditional skateboarding magazine. We are a trade journal that offers up-to-date industry news and features that promote the skatepark industry."

$ $TODAY'S PLAYGROUND

The National Magazine for Today's Playground Design & Standards, Harris Publishing, 360 B St., Idaho Falls ID 83402. (208)524-7000. Fax: (208)522-5241. E-mail: brady@todaysplayground.com. Website: www.todayspla yground.com. Executive Editor: Steve Smede. **Contact:** Brady L. Kay, editor. **25% freelance written.** Magazine published 10 times/year covering playgrounds and the play equipment market. *"Today's Playground* targets a park and recreation management readership. Articles should focus on the playground market as a whole, including aquatic play and surfacing." Estab. 2000. Circ. 35,000. Pays on publication. Publishes ms an average of 6 months after acceptance. Byline given. Buys first North American serial, electronic rights. Editorial lead time 2 months. Submit seasonal material 1 year in advance. Accepts queries by mail, e-mail. Accepts simultaneous submissions. Responds in 2 weeks to queries; 2 months to mss. Sample copy for $5. Writer's guidelines for #10 SASE.

Nonfiction How-to, interview/profile, new product, opinion, personal experience, photo feature, technical, travel. *"Today's Playground* does not publish any articles that do not directly relate to the playground industry." **Buys 4-6 mss/year.** Query with or without published clips. Length: 800-1,500 words. **Pays $50-300 for assigned articles.** Sometimes pays expenses of writers on assignment.

Photos State availability of or send photos with submission. Reviews 35mm transparencies, GIF/JPEG files. Buys one-time rights. Offers no additional payment for photos accepted with ms. Captions, identification of subjects, model releases required.

Columns/Departments Playground Profile (an article that profiles a unique play area and focuses on community involvement, unique design, or human interest), 800-1,200 words. **Buys 2 mss/year.** Query. **Pays $100-300.**

Tips "We are looking for articles that managers can use as a resource when considering playground construction, management, safety, etc. Writers should find unique angles to playground-related features. We are a trade journal that offers up-to-date industry news and features that promote the playground industry."

MARINE & MARITIME INDUSTRIES

$ $ MARINE BUSINESS JOURNAL

The Voice of the Marine Industries Nationwide, 330 N. Andrews Ave., Ft. Lauderdale FL 33301. (954)522-5515. Fax: (954)522-2260. E-mail: sboating@southernboating.com. Website: www.marinebusinessjournal.com. **Contact:** Bill Lindsey, executive editor. **25% freelance written.** Bimonthly magazine that covers the recreational boating industry. "*The Marine Business Journal* is aimed at boating dealers, distributors and manufacturers, naval architects, yacht brokers, marina owners and builders, marine electronics dealers, distributors and manufacturers, and anyone involved in the U.S. marine industry. Articles cover news, new product technology, and public affairs affecting the industry." Estab. 1986. Circ. 26,000. Pays on publication. Publishes ms an average of 1 month after acceptance. Byline given. Buys first North American serial, one-time, second serial (reprint) rights. Accepts queries by mail, e-mail. Responds in 2 weeks to queries. Sample copy for $2.50, 9×12 SAE with 7 first-class stamps. Writer's guidelines for #10 SASE.

Nonfiction Buys 20 mss/year. Query with published clips. Length: 500-2,000 words. **Pays $100-200.** Sometimes pays expenses of writers on assignment.

Photos State availability with submission. Reviews 35mm or larger transparencies, 5×7 prints. Buys one-time rights. Offers $25-50/photo. Captions, identification of subjects, model releases required.

Tips "Query with clips. It's a highly specialized field, written for professionals by professionals, almost all on assignment or by staff."

$ $ PROFESSIONAL MARINER

Journal of the Maritime Industry, Navigator Publishing, P.O. Box 569, Portland ME 04112. (207)822-4350. Fax: (207)772-2879. E-mail: editors@professionalmariner.com. Website: www.professionalmariner.com. **Contact:** John Gormley, editor. **75% freelance written.** Bimonthly magazine covering professional seamanship and maritime industry news. Estab. 1993. Circ. 29,000. Pays on publication. Byline given. Buys all rights. Editorial lead time 3 months. Accepts queries by mail, e-mail, fax, phone. Accepts simultaneous submissions.

Nonfiction For professional mariners on vessels and ashore. Seeks submissions on industry news, regulations, towing, piloting, technology, engineering, business, maritime casualties, and feature stories about the maritime industry. Does accept "sea stories" and personal professional experiences as correspondence pieces. **Buys 15 mss/year.** Query. Length: Varies; short clips to long profiles/features. **Pays 20¢/word.** Sometimes pays expenses of writers on assignment.

Photos Send photos with submission. Reviews prints, slides. Buys one-time rights. Negotiates payment individually. Captions, identification of subjects required.

Tips "Remember that our audience is professional mariners and other marine professionals. Stories must be written at a level that will benefit this group."

MEDICAL

$ $ SOUTHERN CALIFORNIA PHYSICIAN

LACMA Services, Inc., 523 W. 6th St., 10th Floor, Los Angeles CA 90014-1210. (213)630-1147. Fax: (213)630-1152. E-mail: editor@socalphys.com. Website: www.socalphys.com. **Contact:** Barbara Feiner, editor-in-chief. **50% freelance written.** Monthly magazine covering the practice of medicine in Southern California. "*Southern California Physician* covers political, legislative, economic, and social/public health issues relevant to practicing medicine in today's challenging healthcare environment." Estab. 2001. Circ. 20,000. **Pays on acceptance.** Publishes ms an average of 6 months after acceptance. Byline given. Offers 50% kill fee. Buys first North American serial, electronic rights. Editorial lead time 6 months. Submit seasonal material 6 months in advance. Accepts queries by mail, e-mail. Accepts simultaneous submissions. Responds in 4-6 weeks to queries; 2 months to mss. Sample copy for $3.50.

Nonfiction Book excerpts, essays, how-to, interview/profile, opinion, personal experience. No fiction, poetry, new products, or press releases masquerading as stories. **Buys 50 mss/year.** Query with published clips. Length: 1,000-2,500 words. **Pays $100-500.** Sometimes pays expenses of writers on assignment.

Photos State availability with submission. Buys one-time rights. Offers $25-100/photo. Captions, identification of subjects, model releases required.

Columns/Departments Politics As Unusual (California legislation), 1,500 words; Careers & Recruitment (job-related issues), 1,000 words; Hot Topics (time-sensitive news), 1,500 words; Medtropolis (profiles of physicians), 1,500 words. **Buys 25 mss/year.** Query with published clips. **Pays $100-300.**

Tips "I generally prefer to work on assignment, as my needs tend to be quite specific. The best way to connect with us is to let us know you're interested in receiving an assignment, describe your areas of expertise/interest, and send clips of your strongest work."

Trade Journals

Ⓝ $ $ $ AMA ALLIANCE TODAY

American Medical Association Alliance, Inc., 515 N. State St., 9th Floor, Chicago IL 60610. (312)464-4470. Fax: (312)464-5020. E-mail: amaa@ama-assn.org. Website: www.ama-assn.org/go/alliance. **Contact:** Megan Pellegrini, editor. **25% freelance written.** Magazine published 3 times/year for physicians' spouses. Works with both established and new writers. Estab. 1965. Circ. 35,000. **Pays on acceptance.** Publishes ms an average of 6 months after acceptance. Buys first rights. Accepts queries by mail, e-mail, fax. Accepts simultaneous submissions. Sample copy for 9 × 12 SAE and 2 first-class stamps.

O─ Break in with a "solid understanding of issues affecting physicians and their families with a special emphasis on the perspective of the physician's spouse or child."

Nonfiction All articles must be related to the experiences of physicians' spouses. Current health issues; financial topics, physicians' family circumstances, business management and volunteer leadership how-to's. Query with clear outline of article—what points will be made, what conclusions drawn, what sources will be used. Length: 1,000 words. **Pays $300-800.**

Photos Uses all color visuals. State availability with submission.

Tips "Emphasize trends in healthcare as they affect the spouses and children of physicians."

$ $ CONTINUING CARE

Stevens Publishing, 5151 Beltline Rd., Dallas TX 75254. (972)687-6786. Fax: (972)687-6770. E-mail: sbienkowski @stevenspublishing.com. Website: www.ccareonline.com. **Contact:** Sandra Bienkowski, editor. **10% freelance written.** Monthly journal covering care management. "*Continuing Care* provides practical information for managed care professionals in case management and discharge planning of high-risk, high-cost patient cases in home health care, rehabilitation, and long-term care settings. *Continuing Care* encourages practical articles on case management, focusing on quality outcome of patient care at a cost-effective price to the health care payer. The magazine also informs readers on professional and business news, insurance and reimbursement issues, and legal and legislative news." Estab. 1971. Circ. 22,000. Pays on publication. Byline given. Offers no kill fee. Buys all rights. Editorial lead time 4 months. Submit seasonal material 4 months in advance. Accepts queries by mail, e-mail, fax, phone. Accepts simultaneous submissions. Sample copy for free. Writer's guidelines free.

Nonfiction Essays, exposé, general interest, new product, opinion, technical. **Buys 4 mss/year.** Query with published clips. Length: 1,500-2,000 words. **Pays $0-500.** Sometimes pays in contributor copies.

Photos Send photos with submission. Offers $0-500/photo. Captions, identification of subjects required.

Columns/Departments Managed Care, 2,000 words. **Buys 3 mss/year.** Query with published clips. **Pays $0-50.**

Ⓝ $ $ FIRE-RESCUE MAGAZINE

Jems Communications, 525 B St., Suite 1900, San Diego CA 92101. E-mail: frm.editor@jems.com. Website: www.jems.com. **Contact:** Michelle Garrido, deputy editor. **75% freelance written.** Monthly magazine covering technical aspects of being a firefighter/rescuer. Estab. 1988. Circ. 50,000. y. Buys first North American serial, one-time rights. Submit seasonal material 6 months in advance. Accepts queries by mail, e-mail. Responds in 3 weeks to queries; 2 months to mss. Sample copy and writer's guidelines for 9 × 12 SAE with 5 first-class stamps or online. Writer's guidelines online.

Nonfiction How-to, new product, photo feature, technical, Incident review/report. Special issues: Fire suppression, incident command, vehicle extrication, rescue training, mass-casualty incidents, water rescue/major issues facing the fire service. **Buys 15-20 mss/year.** Query with published clips or send complete ms. Length: 1,000-3,000 words. **Pays $125-250.** Sometimes pays expenses of writers on assignment.

Photos Send photos with submission. Reviews contact sheets, negatives, 2 × 2 and 35mm transparencies, 5 × 7 prints. Buys one-time rights. Offers $20-200.

▣ The online magazine carries original content not found in the print edition.

Tips "Read our magazine, spend some time with a fire department. We focus on all aspects of fire and rescue. Emphasis on techniques and new technology, with color photos as support."

$ $ $ HEALTHPLAN

AAHP-HIAA, 601 Pennsylvania Ave., Suite 500, Washington DC 20004. (202)778-3200. Fax: (202)331-7487. E-mail: gfauntleroy@aahp.org. Website: www.aahp.org. Editor: Larry A. Key. **Contact:** Glenda Fauntleroy, managing editor. **75% freelance written.** Bimonthly magazine. "*Healthplan* is geared toward administrators in America's health insurance companies. Articles should inform and generate interest and discussion about topics on anything from patient care to regulatory issues." Estab. 1990. Circ. 12,000. Pays within 30 days of acceptance of article in final form. Publishes ms an average of 2 months after acceptance. Byline given. Offers 30% kill fee. Buys all rights. Editorial lead time 2 months. Submit seasonal material 4 months in advance. Accepts queries by mail, e-mail, fax. Accepts simultaneous submissions. Sample copy for free.

Nonfiction Book excerpts, how-to (how industry professionals can better operate their health plans), opinion. "We do not accept stories that promote products." Query with published clips or send complete ms. Length: 1,800-2,500 words. **Pays 65¢/word minimum for assigned articles.** Pays phone expenses of writers on assignment. Buys all rights.

Tips "Look for health plan success stories in your community; we like to include case studies on a variety of topics—including patient care, provider relations, regulatory issues—so that our readers can learn from their colleagues. Our readers are members of our trade association and look for advice and news. Topics relating to the quality of health plans are the ones more frequently assigned to writers, whether a feature or department. We also welcome story ideas. Just send us a letter with the details."

$ $ JEMS

The Journal of Emergency Medical Services, Jems Communications, 525 B St., Suite 1900, San Diego CA 92101. (800)266-5367, ext. 6847. E-mail: a.j.heightman@elsevier.com. Website: www.jems.com. **Contact:** A.J. Heightman, editor. **95% freelance written.** Monthly magazine directed to personnel who serve the pre-hospital emergency medicine industry: Paramedics, EMTs, emergency physicians and nurses, administrators, EMS consultants, etc. Estab. 1980. Circ. 45,000. Pays on publication. Publishes ms an average of 6 months after acceptance. Byline given. all North American serial rights Submit seasonal material 6 months in advance. Accepts queries by mail, e-mail, fax. Responds in 2-3 months to queries. Sample copy and writer's guidelines free. Writer's guidelines online.

Nonfiction Essays, exposé, general interest, how-to, humor, interview/profile, new product, opinion, personal experience, photo feature, technical, continuing education. **Buys 50 mss/year.** Query. **Pays $200-400.**

Photos State availability with submission. Reviews 4×6 prints. Buys one-time rights. Offers $25 minimum per photo. Identification of subjects, model releases required.

Columns/Departments Length: 850 words maximum. "Columns and departments are staff-written with the exception of commentary on EMS issues and practices." Query with or without published clips. **Pays $50-250.**

Tips "Please submit a 1-page query letter before you send a manuscript. Your query should answer these questions: 1) What specifically are you going to tell *JEMS* readers? 2) Why do *JEMS* readers need to know this? 3) How will you make your case (i.e., literature review, original research, interviews, personal experience, observation)? Your query should explain your qualifications, as well as include previous writing samples."

$ $ $ MANAGED CARE

780 Township Line Rd., Yardley PA 19067-4200. (267)685-2784. Fax: (267)685-2966. E-mail: editors@managedc aremag.com. Website: www.managedcaremag.com. **Contact:** John Marcille, editor. **50% freelance written.** Monthly magazine. "We emphasize practical, usable information that helps HMO medical directors, pharmacy directors, and primary care physicians cope with the options, challenges, and hazards in the rapidly changing health care industry. Our regular readers understand that 'health care reform' isn't a piece of legislation; it's an evolutionary process that's already well under way. But we hope to help our readers also keep the faith that led them to medicine in the first place." Estab. 1992. Circ. 60,000. **Pays on acceptance.** Publishes an average of 6 weeks after acceptance. Byline given. Offers 20% kill fee. Buys all rights. Editorial lead time 3 months. Submit seasonal material 4 months in advance. Accepts queries by mail, e-mail, fax. Responds in 3 weeks to queries; 2 months to mss. Sample copy for free. Writer's guidelines on request.

Nonfiction "I strongly recommend submissions via e-mail. You'll get a faster response." Book excerpts, general interest (trends in health-care delivery and financing, quality of care, and employee concerns), how-to (deal with requisites of managed care, such as contracts with health plans, affiliation arrangements, accreditation, computer needs, etc.), original research and review articles that examine the relationship between health care delivery and financing. Also considered occasionally are personal experience, opinion, interview/profile, and humor pieces, but these must have a strong managed care angle and draw upon the insights of (if they are not written by) a knowledgeable MD or managed care professional. **Buys 40 mss/year.** Query with published clips. Length: 1,000-3,000 words. **Pays 60¢/word.** Pays expenses of writers on assignment.

Photos State availability with submission. Reviews contact sheets, negatives, transparencies, prints. Buys first-time rights. Negotiates payment individually.

Tips "Know our audience (health plan executives) and their needs. Study our website to see what we cover."

$ $ $ $ MEDICAL ECONOMICS

5 Paragon Dr., Montvale NJ 07645-1742. (201)358-7367. Fax: (201)722-2688. E-mail: helen.mckenna@medec.c om. Website: www.memag.com. **Contact:** Helen A. McKenna, outside copy editor. Semimonthly magazine (24 times/year). "*Medical Economics* is a national business magazine read by M.D.s and D.O.s in office-based practice. Our purpose is to be informative and useful to practicing physicians in the professional and financial management of their practices. We look for contributions from writers who know—or will make the effort to learn—the nonclinical concerns of today's physician. These writers must be able to address those concerns in

feature articles that are clearly written and that convey authoritative information and advice. Our articles focus very narrowly on a subject and explore it in depth.'' Circ. 170,000. **Pays on acceptance.** Offers 25% kill fee. Buys first world publication rights. Accepts queries by mail, e-mail, fax. Sample copy online. Writer's guidelines online.

Nonfiction Articles about private physicians in innovative, pioneering, and/or controversial situations affecting medical care delivery, patient relations, or malpractice prevention/litigation; personal finance topics. ''We do not want overviews or pieces that only skim the surface of a general topic. We address physician readers in a conversational, yet no-nonsense tone, quoting recognized experts on office management, personal finance, patient relations, and medical-legal issues.'' Query with published clips. Length: 1,000-1,800 words. **Pays $1,200-2,000 for assigned articles.** Pays expenses of writers on assignment.

Photos Will negotiate an additional fee for photos accepted for publication.

Tips ''We look for articles about physicians who run high-quality, innovative practices suited to the age of managed care. We also look for how-to service articles—on practice-management and personal-finance topics— which must contain anecdotal examples to support the advice. Read the magazine carefully, noting its style and content. Then send detailed proposals or outlines on subjects that would interest our mainly primary-care physician readers.''

MEDICAL IMAGING

6701 Center Dr. W., Suite 450, Los Angeles CA 90045. (310)642-4400. Fax: (310)641-0790. E-mail: alucas@medp ubs.com. Website: www.medicalimagingmag.com. **Contact:** Andi Lucas, editor. **70% freelance written.** Monthly magazine covering diagnostic imaging equipment. Estab. 1986. Circ. 26,000. Pays on publication. Publishes ms an average of 2 months after acceptance. Byline given. Buys all rights. Editorial lead time 2 months. Sample copy for $10 prepaid.

Nonfiction Interview/profile, technical. ''No general interest/human interest stories about healthcare. Articles *must* deal with our industry, diagnostic imaging.'' **Buys 6 mss/year.** Query with published clips. Length: 1,500-2,500 words.

Photos State availability with submission. Reviews negatives. Buys all rights. Offers no additional payment for photos accepted with ms. Identification of subjects, model releases required.

Tips ''Send a letter with an interesting story idea that is applicable to our industry, diagnostic imaging. Then follow up with a phone call. Areas most open to freelancers are features and technology profiles. You don't have to be an engineer or doctor, but you have to know how to talk and listen to them.''

$ $ $ $ MODERN PHYSICIAN

Essential Business News for the Executive Physician, Crain Communications, 360 N. Michigan Ave., 7th Floor, Chicago IL 60601. (312)649-5439. Fax: (312)649-5393. E-mail: dburda@crain.com. Website: www.modernphysi cian.com. **Contact:** David Burda, editor. **10% freelance written.** Monthly magazine covering business and management news for doctors. ''*Modern Physician* offers timely topical news features with lots of business information—revenues, earnings, financial data.'' Estab. 1997. Circ. 32, 552. **Pays on acceptance.** Publishes ms an average of 2 months after acceptance. Byline given. Buys all rights. Editorial lead time 2 months. Accepts queries by mail, e-mail. Responds in 6 weeks to queries. Sample copy for free. Writer's guidelines sent after query.

O━ Break in with a regional story involving business or physicians.

Nonfiction Length: 750-1,000 words. **Pays 75¢-$1/word.**

🖵 The online magazine carries original content not found in the print edition.

Tips ''Read the publication, know our audience, come up with a good story idea that we haven't thought of yet.''

$ $ THE NEW PHYSICIAN

1902 Association Dr., Reston VA 20191. **Contact:** Rebecca Sernett, editor. **30% freelance written.** Magazine published 9 times/year for medical students, interns, residents, and educators. Circ. 38,000. **Pays on acceptance.** Publishes ms an average of 5 months after acceptance. Accepts simultaneous submissions. Responds in 3 months to mss. Sample copy for 10×13 SAE and 5 first-class stamps. Writer's guidelines for #10 SASE.

Nonfiction Articles on social, political, economic issues in medical education/health care. **Buys 3 mss/year.** Query or send complete ms. Length: 800-3,000 words. **Pays 25-40¢/word.** Sometimes pays expenses of writers on assignment.

Reprints Send photocopy and information about when and where the material previously appeared. Payment varies.

Tips ''Although we are published by the American Medical Student Association, we are not a 'house organ.' We are a professional magazine for readers with a progressive view on health care issues and a particular interest in improving medical education and the health care system. Our readers demand sophistication on the issues we cover. Freelancers should be willing to look deeply into the issues in question and not be satisfied with a cursory review of those issues.''

$ $PHYSICIAN

Focus on the Family, 8605 Explorer Dr., Colorado Springs CO 80920. (719)531-3400. Fax: (719)531-3499. E-mail: physician@macmail.fotf.org. Website: www.family.org. Editorial Director: Charles Johnson. **Contact:** Scott Denicola, editor. **20% freelance written.** Bimonthly magazine. ''The goal of our magazine is to encourage physicians in their faith, family, and medical practice. Writers should understand the medical lifestyle.'' Estab. 1989. Circ. 89,000. **Pays on acceptance.** Publishes ms an average of 6 months after acceptance. Byline given. Buys first North American serial, electronic rights. Editorial lead time 1 year. Accepts queries by mail, e-mail, fax. Responds in 2 months to queries. Sample copy for SASE.

Nonfiction General interest, interview/profile, personal experience, religious, technical. ''No patient's opinions of their doctor.'' **Buys 20-30 mss/year.** Query. Length: 900-2,400 words. **Pays $100-500 for assigned articles.** Sometimes pays expenses of writers on assignment. Accepts previously published submissions.

Photos State availability with submission. Reviews transparencies. Buys one-time rights. Negotiates payment individually.

Tips ''Most writers are M.D.'s.''

N $ $ $ $THE PHYSICIAN AND SPORTSMEDICINE

McGraw-Hill, 4530 W. 77th St., Minneapolis MN 55435. (952)835-3222. Fax: (952)835-3460. E-mail: jim-wappes @mcgraw-hill.com. Website: www.physsportsmed.com. **Contact:** Jim Wappes, executive editor. **5% freelance written.** Monthly magazine covering medical aspects of sports and exercise. Prefers to work with published/ established writers. ''We publish articles that are of practical, clinical interest to our physician audience.'' Estab. 1973. Circ. 115,000. **Pays on acceptance.** Publishes ms an average of 4 months after acceptance. Byline given. Buys all rights. Responds in 2 months to queries. Sample copy for $10. Writer's guidelines for #10 SASE or on website.

● This publication is relying more heavily on the clinical component of the journal, meaning review articles written by physicians who have expertise in a specific specialty.

Nonfiction New developments and issues in sports medicine. Query. Length: 250-2,500 words. **Pays $150-1,800.**

Photos Mary Schill, photo editor. State availability with submission.

N $ $ $PHYSICIANS' TRAVEL & MEETING GUIDE

Quadrant HealthCom, Inc., 26 Main St., Chatham NJ 07928-2402. (973)701-2716. E-mail: bea.riemschneider@c meplanner.com. Website: www.cmeplanner.com. **Contact:** Bea Riemschneider, editorial director. **60% freelance written.** Monthly magazine covering travel for physicians and their families. *Physicians' Travel & Meeting Guide* supplies continuing medical education events listings and extensive travel coverage of international and national destinations. Circ. 142,541. **Pays on acceptance.** Byline given. Buys first North American serial rights. Submit seasonal material 4-6 months in advance. Accepts queries by mail, e-mail. Responds in 3 months to queries.

Nonfiction Photo feature, travel. **Buys 25-35 mss/year.** Query with published clips. Length: 450-3,000 words. **Pays $150-1,000 for assigned articles.**

Photos State availability of or send photos with submission. Reviews 35mm; 4×5 transparencies. Buys one-time rights. Captions, identification of subjects required.

$ $PODIATRY MANAGEMENT

Kane Communications, Inc., P.O. Box 750129, Forest Hills NY 11375. (718)897-9700. Fax: (718)896-5747. E-mail: bblock@prodigy.net. Website: www.podiatrym.com. Publisher: Scott C. Borowsky. **Contact:** Barry Block, editor. Magazine published 9 times/year for practicing podiatrists. ''Aims to help the doctor of podiatric medicine to build a bigger, more successful practice, to conserve and invest his money, to keep him posted on the economic, legal, and sociological changes that affect him.'' Estab. 1982. Circ. 14,500. Pays on publication. Byline given. Buys first North American serial, second serial (reprint) rights. Submit seasonal material 4 months in advance. Accepts queries by e-mail. Accepts simultaneous submissions. Responds in 2 weeks to queries. Sample copy for $3 and 9×12 SAE. Writer's guidelines for #10 SASE.

Nonfiction Book excerpts, general interest (taxes, investments, estate, estate planning, recreation, hobbies), how-to (establish and collect fees, practice management, organize office routines, supervise office assistants, handle patient relations), interview/profile (about interesting or well-known podiatrists), personal experience. Special issues: ''These subjects are the mainstay of the magazine, but offbeat articles and humor are always welcome.'' **Buys 25 mss/year.** Length: 1,200-3,000 words. **Pays $250-600.**

Reprints Send photocopy. Pays 33% of amount paid for an original article.

Photos State availability with submission. Buys one-time rights. Pays $15 for b&w contact sheet.

Tips "We have been persuading writers to use e-mail for the past few years because of the speed, ease of editing, and general efficiency of the process. The tragic events of 9/11/01 along with the anthrax issue now make the policy mandatory—and the trees will also appreciate it!"

$ $⬛ STITCHES

The Journal of Medical Humour, Stitches Publishing, Inc., 240 Edward St., Aurora ON L4G 3S9, Canada. (905)713-4336. Fax: (905)727-0017. E-mail: simon@stitchesmagazine.com. **Contact:** Simon Hally, editor. **90% freelance written.** Monthly magazine covering humor for physicians. "*Stitches* is read primarily by physicians in Canada. Stories with a medical slant are particularly welcome, but we also run a lot of nonmedical material. It must be funny and, of course, brevity is the soul of wit." Estab. 1990. Circ. 39,000. Pays on publication. Publishes ms an average of 2 months after acceptance. Byline given. Buys first North American serial, electronic rights. Editorial lead time 1 month. Submit seasonal material 4 months in advance. Responds in 6 weeks to queries; 2 months to mss. Sample copy and writer's guidelines free.

Nonfiction Humor, personal experience. **Buys 30 mss/year.** Send complete ms. Length: 200-2,000 words. **Pays 40¢/word (Canadian).**

Fiction Humorous. **Buys 40 mss/year.** Send complete ms. Length: 200-2,000 words. **Pays 25¢/word (US) to US contributors.**

Poetry Humorous. **Buys 5 poems/year.** Submit maximum 5 poems. Length: 2-30 lines. **Pays 35¢/word (US) to US contributors.**

Tips "Due to the nature of humorous writing, we have to see a completed manuscript, rather than a query, to determine if it is suitable for us. Along with a short cover letter, that's all we require."

$ $⬛ STRATEGIC HEALTH CARE MARKETING

Health Care Communications, 11 Heritage Lane, P.O. Box 594, Rye NY 10580. (914)967-6741. Fax: (914)967-3054. E-mail: healthcomm@aol.com. Website: www.strategichealthcare.com. **Contact:** Michele von Dambrowski, editor. **90% freelance written.** Monthly newsletter covering health care marketing and management in a wide range of settings, including hospitals, medical group practices, home health services, and managed care organizations. Emphasis is on strategies and techniques employed within the health care field and relevant applications from other service industries. Works with published/established writers only. Estab. 1984. Pays on publication. Publishes ms an average of 2 months after acceptance. Byline given. Offers 25% kill fee. Buys first North American serial rights. Accepts queries by mail, e-mail. Responds in 1 month to queries. Sample copy for 9×12 SAE and 3 first-class stamps. Guidelines sent with sample copy only.

- *Strategic Health Care Marketing* is specifically seeking writers with expertise/contacts in managed care, patient satisfaction, and e-health.

Nonfiction "Preferred format for feature articles is the case history approach to solving marketing problems. Crisp, almost telegraphic style." How-to, interview/profile, new product, technical. **Buys 50 mss/year.** *No unsolicited mss.* Length: 700-3,000 words. **Pays $100-500.** Sometimes pays expenses of writers on assignment with prior authorization.

Photos Photos, unless necessary for subject explanation, are rarely used. State availability with submission. Reviews contact sheets. Buys one-time rights. Offers $10-30/photo. Captions, model releases required.

▣ The online magazine carries original content not found in the print edition. Contact: Mark Gothberg.

Tips "Writers with prior experience on business beat for newspaper or newsletter will do well. We require a sophisticated, in-depth knowledge of health care and business. This is not a consumer publication—the writer with knowledge of both health care and marketing will excel. Absolutely no unsolicited manuscripts; any received will be returned or discarded unread."

$ $ $ $ UNIQUE OPPORTUNITIES

The Physician's Resource, U O, Inc., 214 S. 8th St., Suite 502, Louisville KY 40202. Fax: (502)587-0848. E-mail: bett@uoworks.com. Website: www.uoworks.com. Editor: Mollie Vento Hudson. **Contact:** Bett Coffman, associate editor. **55% freelance written.** Bimonthly magazine covering physician relocation and career development. "Published for physicians interested in a new career opportunity. It offers physicians useful information and first-hand experiences to guide them in making informed decisions concerning their first or next career opportunity. It provides features and regular columns about specific aspects of the search process." Estab. 1991. Circ. 80,000 physicians. Pays 30 days after acceptance. Publishes ms an average of 2 months after acceptance. Byline given. Offers 15% kill fee. Buys first North American serial, electronic rights. Editorial lead time 3 months. Submit seasonal material 6 months in advance. Responds in 2 months to queries. Sample copy for 9×12 SAE and 6 first-class stamps. Writer's guidelines online.

Nonfiction Features: Practice options and information of interest to physicians in career transition. **Buys 14**

mss/year. Query with published clips. Length: 1,500-3,500 words. **Pays $750-2,000.** Sometimes pays expenses of writers on assignment.

Photos State availability with submission. Buys electronic rights. Negotiates payment individually. Identification of subjects, model releases required.

Columns/Departments Remarks (opinion from physicians and industry experts on physician career issues), 900-1,500 words. **No payment.**

■ The online magazine carries original content not found in the print edition.

Tips "Submit queries via letter or e-mail with ideas for articles that directly pertain to physician career issues, such as specific or unusual practice opportunities, relocation or practice establishment subjects, etc. Feature articles are most open to freelancers. Physician sources are most important, with tips and advice from both the physicians and business experts. Physicians like to know what other physicians think and do and appreciate suggestions from other business people."

MUSIC

$ CLASSICAL SINGER MAGAZINE

Classical Publications, Inc., P.O. Box 95490, South Jordan UT 84095-0490. (801)254-1025. Fax: (801)254-3139. E-mail: editor@classicalsinger.com. Website: www.classicalsinger.com. **Contact:** Ms. CJ Williamson, editor. Monthly magazine covering classical singers. Estab. 1988. Circ. 6,000. Pays on publication. Publishes ms an average of 3 months after acceptance. Byline given. Buys second serial (reprint), all rights. Editorial lead time 3 months. Submit seasonal material 3 months in advance. Accepts queries by e-mail. Accepts previously published material. Responds in 1 month to queries. Potential writers will be given password to website version of magazine and writer's guidelines online.

   ○┱ E-mail, mail, or fax writing sample. If accepted, editor will give assignment. Most future correspondence is done via e-mail. All mss must be submitted electronically in Word 98 or higher.

Nonfiction Editorial calendar available on request. "The best way to find materials for articles is to look on the General Interest forum on our website and see what singers are interested in." Book excerpts, exposé (carefully done), how-to, humor, interview/profile, new product, personal experience, photo feature, religious, technical, travel, crossword puzzles on opera theme. No reviews. Query with published clips. Length: 500-3,000 words. **Pays 5¢/word ($50 minimum). Writers also receive 10 copies of the magazine.** Pays telephone expenses of writers with assignments when Xerox copy of bill submitted.

Photos Send photos with submission. Buys all rights. Captions required.

■ The online magazine carries original content not found in the print edition. Contact editor by e-mail.

Tips "*Classical Singer Magazine* has a full-color, glossy cover, glossy b&w pages inside. It ranges in size from 40 pages during the summer to 92 pages in September. The mission statement is: 'Information for a classical singer's career, support for a classical singer's life, and enlightenment for a classical singer's art.'"

CLAVIER MAGAZINE

The Instrumentalist Publishing Co., 200 Northfield Rd., Northfield IL 60093. (847)446-5000. Fax: (847)446-6263. **Contact:** Judy Nelson, editor. **1% freelance written.** Magazine published 10 times/year featuring practical information on teaching subjects that are of value to studio piano teachers and interviews with major artists. Estab. 1937. Circ. 14,000. Pays on publication. Publishes ms an average of 18 months after acceptance. Byline given. Buys all rights. Submit seasonal material 6 months in advance. Accepts queries by mail, fax, phone. Responds in 6 weeks to queries. Sample copy and writer's guidelines free.

Nonfiction "Articles should be of interest and direct practical value to concert pianists, harpsichordists, and organists who are teachers of piano, organ, harpsichord, and electronic keyboards. Topics may include pedagogy, technique, performance, ensemble playing, and accompanying." Historical/nostalgic, how-to, interview/profile, photo feature. Length: 10-12 double-spaced pages. **Pays small honorarium.**

Reprints Occasionally we will reprint a chapter in a book.

Photos Digital artwork should be sent in TIF, EPS, JPEG files for PhotoShop at 300 dpi. Send photos with submission. Reviews negatives, 2¼×2¼ transparencies, 3×5 prints. Buys all rights. Offers no additional payment for photos accepted with ms. Identification of subjects required.

N $ ⊘ INTERNATIONAL BLUEGRASS

International Bluegrass Music Association, 2 Music Circle S., Suite 100, Nashville TN 37203. (615)256-3222. Fax: (615)256-0450. E-mail: info@ibma.org. Website: www.ibma.org; www.discoverbluegrass.com. **Contact:** Nancy Cardwell. **10% freelance written.** Bimonthly newsletter. "We are the business publication for the bluegrass music industry. IBMA believes that our music has growth potential. We are interested in hard news and features concerning how to reach that potential and how to conduct business more effectively." Estab.

1985. Circ. 4,500. Pays on publication. Publishes ms an average of 2 months after acceptance. Byline given. Not copyrighted. Buys one-time rights. Submit seasonal material 4 months in advance. Accepts queries by mail, e-mail, phone. Accepts simultaneous submissions. Responds in 1 month to queries. Sample copy for 6×9 SAE and 2 first-class stamps.

Nonfiction Unsolicited mss are not accepted, but unsolicited news about the industry is accepted. Book excerpts, essays, how-to (conduct business effectively within bluegrass music), new product, opinion. No interview/profiles/feature stories of performers (rare exceptions) or fans. **Buys 6 mss/year.** Query with or without published clips. Length: 1,000-1,200 words. **Pays up to $150/article for assigned articles.**

Reprints Send photocopy of article and information about when and where the article previously appeared. Does not pay for reprints.

Photos Send photos with submission. Buys one-time rights. Offers no additional payment for photos accepted with ms. Captions, identification of subjects, photographer's name required.

Columns/Departments Staff written.

Tips "We're interested in a slant strongly toward the business end of bluegrass music. We're especially looking for material dealing with audience development and how to book bluegrass bands outside of the existing market."

$ $ $ MIX MAGAZINE

Primedia Business Magazines, 6400 Hollis St., Suite 12, Emeryville CA 94608. Fax: (510)653-5142. Website: www.mixonline.com. Editorial Director: George Petersen. **Contact:** Blair Jackson. **50% freelance written.** Monthly magazine covering pro audio. "*Mix* is a trade publication geared toward professionals in the music/sound production recording and post-production industries. We include stories about music production, sound for picture, live sound, etc. We prefer in-depth technical pieces that are applications-oriented." Estab. 1977. Circ. 50,000. Pays on publication. Publishes ms an average of 3 months after acceptance. Byline given. Offers 50% kill fee. Buys all rights. Editorial lead time 10 weeks. Submit seasonal material 3 months in advance. Responds in 2 weeks to queries; 1 month to mss. Sample copy for $6. Writer's guidelines free.

Nonfiction How-to, interview/profile, new product, technical, Project/Studio Spotlights. Special issues: Sound for picture supplement (April, September), Design issue. **Buys 60 mss/year.** Query. Length: 500-2,000 words. **Pays $300-800 for assigned articles; $300-400 for unsolicited articles.**

Photos State availability with submission. Reviews 4×5 transparencies, prints. Buys one-time rights. Negotiates payment individually. Captions, identification of subjects required.

Tips "Send Blair Jackson a letter outlining the article, including a description of the topic, information sources, what qualifies writers for the story, and mention of available graphics. A writing sample is also helpful."

MUSIC CONNECTION

The West Coast Music Trade Magazine, Music Connection, Inc., 4215 Coldwater Canyon Blvd., Studio City CA 91604. (818)755-0101. Fax: (818)755-0102. E-mail: markn@musicconnection.com. Website: www.musicconnection.com. **Contact:** Mark Nardone, senior editor. **40% freelance written.** "Biweekly magazine geared toward working musicians and/or other industry professionals, including producers/engineers/studio staff, managers, agents, publicists, music publishers, record company staff, concert promoters/bookers, etc." Estab. 1977. Circ. 75,000. Pays after publication. Publishes ms an average of 2 months after acceptance. Byline given. Kill fee varies. Buys all rights. Editorial lead time 2 months. Submit seasonal material 2 months in advance. Sample copy for $5.

Nonfiction How-to (music industry related), interview/profile, new product, technical. Query with published clips. Length: 1,000-5,000 words. **Payment varies.** Sometimes pays expenses of writers on assignment.

Photos State availability with submission. Reviews transparencies, prints. Buys one-time rights. Negotiates payment individually. Identification of subjects required.

Tips "Articles must be informative music/music industry-related pieces, geared toward a trade-reading audience comprised mainly of musicians. No fluff."

$ $ $ OPERA NEWS

Metropolitan Opera Guild, Inc., 70 Lincoln Center Plaza, New York NY 10023-6593. (212)769-7080. Fax: (212)769-8500. Website: www.operanews.com. Editor: F. Paul Driscoll. **Contact:** Kitty March, editor. **75% freelance written.** Monthly magazine for people interested in opera; the opera professional as well as the opera audience. Estab. 1936. Circ. 105,000. Pays on publication. Publishes ms an average of 4 months after acceptance. Byline given. Buys first serial rights only. Editorial lead time 4 months. Sample copy for $5. Writer's guidelines not available.

O— Break in by "showing incisive knowledge of opera and the opera scene. We look for knowledgeable and informed writers who are capable of discussing opera in detailed musical terms—but in an engaging way."

Nonfiction Most articles are commissioned in advance. Monthly issues feature articles on various aspects of opera worldwide. Emphasis is on high quality writing and an intellectual interest to the opera-oriented public. Historical/nostalgic, interview/profile, informational, think pieces, opera, CD, and DVD reviews. Query. Length: 1,500-2,800 words. **Pays $450-1,200.** Sometimes pays expenses of writers on assignment.

Photos State availability with submission. Buys one-time rights.

Columns/Departments Buys 24 mss/year.

N $ $VENUES TODAY

The News Behind the Headlines, 18350 Mount Langley, #200, Fountain Valley CA 92647. Fax: (714)378-5400. E-mail: natasha@venuestoday.com. Website: www.venuestoday.com. Editor: Linda Deckard. **Contact:** Natasha Emmons, managing editor. **70% freelance written.** Weekly magazine covering live entertainment industry and the buildings that host shows and sports. "We need writers who can cover an exciting industry from the business side, not the conusmer side. The readers are venue managers, concert promoters, those in the concert and sports business, not the audience for concerts and sports. So we need business journalists who can cover the latest news and trends in the market." Estab. 2002. Pays on publication. Publishes ms an average of 1 month after acceptance. Byline given. Buys all rights. Editorial lead time 2 months. Submit seasonal material 2 months in advance. Accepts queries by mail, e-mail, fax. Accepts simultaneous submissions. Responds in 1 week to queries. Sample copy online. Writer's guidelines free.

Nonfiction Interview/profile, photo feature, technical, travel. Does not want customer slant, marketing pieces. Query with published clips. Length: 500-1,500 words. **Pays $60-250.** Pays expenses of writers on assignment.

Photos State availability with submission. Reviews GIF/JPEG files. Buys one-time rights. Negotiates payment individually. Captions, identification of subjects required.

Columns/Departments Venue News (new buildings, trend features, etc.); Bookings (show tours, business side); Marketing (of shows, sports, convention centers); Concessions (food, drink, merchandise). Length: 500-1,200 words. **Buys 250 mss/year.** Query with published clips. **Pays $60-250.**

Fillers Gags to be illustrated by cartoonist. **Buys 6/year. Pays $100.**

OFFICE ENVIRONMENT & EQUIPMENT

$ $OFFICE DEALER

Updating the Office Products Industry, OfficeVision, Inc., 252 N. Main St., Suite 200, Mt. Airy NC 27030. (336)783-0000. Fax: (336)783-0045. E-mail: scullen@os-od.com. Website: www.os-od.com. **Contact:** Scott Cullen, managing editor. **80% freelance written.** Bimonthly magazine covering the office product industry. "*Office Dealer* serves independent resellers of office supplies, furniture, and equipment." Estab. 1987. Circ. 15,300. Pays on publication. Byline given. Buys all rights. Editorial lead time 3 months. Submit seasonal material 5 months in advance. Accepts queries by mail, e-mail, fax. Accepts simultaneous submissions. Responds in 1 month to queries. Sample copy and writer's guidelines free.

Nonfiction Interview/profile, new product, technical. **Buys 10 mss/year.** Length: 700-1,500 words. **Pays $300-500.**

Tips "See editorial calendar posted online. Feature articles are written by our staff or by freelance writers. We may accept corporate 'byline' articles. Queries should be a single page or less and include an SASE for response. Samples of a writer's past work and clips concerning the proposed story are helpful."

$ $OFFICE SOLUTIONS

The Magazine for Office Professionals, OfficeVision Inc., 252 N. Main St., Suite 200, Mt. Airy NC 27030. (336)783-0000. Fax: (336)783-0045. E-mail: scullen@os-od.com. Website: www.os-od.com. **Contact:** Scott Cullen, managing editor. **80% freelance written.** Bimonthly magazine covering the office personnel and environment. "*Office Solutions* subscribers are responsible for the management of their personnel and office environments." Estab. 1984. Circ. 81,250. Pays on publication. Byline given. Buys all rights. Editorial lead time 3 months. Submit seasonal material 4 months in advance. Accepts queries by mail, e-mail, fax. Accepts simultaneous submissions. Responds in 1 month to queries. Sample copy and writer's guidelines free.

Nonfiction "Our audience is responsible for general management of an office environment and personnel, so articles should be broad in scope and not too technical in nature." Interview/profile, new product, technical, human resources. **Buys 18 mss/year.** Query. Length: 1,500-2,200 words. **Pays $200-450.**

Tips "See editorial calendar posted online. Feature articles are written by our staff or by freelance writers. Queries should be a single page or less and include an SASE for response. Samples of a writer's past work and clips concerning the proposed story are helpful."

PAPER

$ $ THE PAPER STOCK REPORT

News and Trends of the Paper Recycling Markets, McEntee Media Corp., 9815 Hazelwood Ave., Cleveland OH 44149. (440)238-6603. Fax: (440)238-6712. E-mail: psr@recycle.cc. Website: www.recycle.cc. **Contact:** Ken McEntee, editor. Biweekly newsletter covering market trends, news in the paper recycling industry. "Audience is interested in new innovative markets, applications for recovered scrap paper, as well as new laws and regulations impacting recycling." Estab. 1990. Circ. 2,000. Pays on publication. Publishes ms an average of 1 month after acceptance. Byline given. Buys first, all rights. Editorial lead time 2 months. Submit seasonal material 2 months in advance. Accepts queries by mail, e-mail, fax, phone. Accepts simultaneous submissions. Responds in 1 month to queries. Sample copy for #10 SAE with 55¢ postage.

Nonfiction Book excerpts, essays, exposé, general interest, historical/nostalgic, interview/profile, new product, opinion, photo feature, technical, all related to paper recycling. **Buys 0-13 mss/year.** Send complete ms. Length: 250-1,000 words. **Pays $50-250 for assigned articles; $25-250 for unsolicited articles.** Pays expenses of writers on assignment.

Photos State availability with submission. Reviews contact sheets. Negotiates payment individually. Identification of subjects required.

■ The online magazine carries original content not found in the print edition. Contact: Ken McEntee, online editor.

Tips "Article must be valuable to readers in terms of presenting new market opportunities or cost-saving measures."

Ⓝ $ $Ⓜ PULP & PAPER CANADA

1 Holiday St., #705, East Tower, Pointe-Claire QC H9R 5N3, Canada. (514)630-5955. Fax: (514)630-5980. E-mail: anyao@pulpandpapercanada.com. Publisher: Jim Bussiere. **Contact:** Anya Orzechowska, managing editor. **5% freelance written.** Monthly magazine. Prefers to work with published/established writers. Estab. 1903. Circ. 10,361. Pays on publication. Byline given. Negotiates kill fee. Buys first North American serial rights. Accepts queries by mail, e-mail. Responds in 1 month to queries. Sample copy for free.

Oⁿ Break in with an article about a Canadian paper mill case study, e.g., problem/solution type or maintenance-related articles.

Nonfiction Articles with photographs (b&w glossy) or other good quality illustrations will get priority review. How-to (related to processes and procedures in the industry), interview/profile (of Canadian leaders in pulp and paper industry), technical (relevant to modern pulp and/or paper industry). No fillers, short industry news items, or product news items. **Buys 5 mss/year.** Query with published clips or send complete ms. Length: 1,200 words maximum (with photos). **Pays $160 (Canadian)/published page including photos, graphics, charts, etc.**

Tips "Any return postage must be in either Canadian stamps or International Reply Coupons only."

$ $ RECYCLED PAPER NEWS

Independent Coverage of Environmental Issues in the Paper Industry, McEntee Media Corp., 9815 Hazelwood Ave., Cleveland OH 44149. (440)238-6603. Fax: (440)238-6712. E-mail: rpn@recycle.cc. Website: www.recycle. cc. **Contact:** Ken McEntee, president. **10% freelance written.** Monthly newsletter. "We are interested in any news impacting the paper recycling industry, as well as other environmental issues in the paper industry, i.e., water/air pollution, chlorine-free paper, forest conservation, etc., with special emphasis on new laws and regulations." Estab. 1990. Pays on publication. Publishes ms an average of 2 months after acceptance. Buys first, all rights. Editorial lead time 1 month. Submit seasonal material 1 month in advance. Accepts queries by mail, e-mail, fax, phone. Accepts simultaneous submissions. Responds in 2 months to queries. Sample copy for 9×12 SAE and 55¢ postage. Writer's guidelines for #10 SASE.

Nonfiction Book excerpts, essays, how-to, interview/profile, new product, opinion, personal experience, photo feature, technical, new business, legislation, regulation, business expansion. **Buys 0-5 mss/year.** Query with published clips. **Pays $10-500.** Pays writers with contributor copies or other premiums by prior agreement.

Reprints Accepts previously published submissions.

Columns/Departments Query with published clips. **Pays $10-500.**

Tips "We appreciate leads on local news regarding recycling or composting, i.e., new facilities or businesses, new laws and regulations, unique programs, situations that impact supply and demand for recyclables, etc. International developments are also of interest."

PETS

$ $ PET AGE

H.H. Backer Associates, Inc., 200 S. Michigan Ave., Suite 840, Chicago IL 60604-2383-2404. (312)663-4040. Fax: (312)663-5676. E-mail: petage@hhbacker.com. Editor-In-Chief/Associate Publisher: Karen Long MacLeod. **Contact:** Cathy Foster, senior editor. **90% freelance written.** Monthly magazine for pet/pet supplies retailers, covering the complete pet industry. Prefers to work with published/established writers. Will consider new writers. Estab. 1971. Circ. 23,022. **Pays on acceptance.** Publishes ms an average of 3 months after acceptance. Byline given. Buys first North American serial, one-time rights. Sample copy and writer's guidelines available.

Nonfiction How-to articles on marketing/merchandising companion animals and supplies; how-to articles on retail store management; industry trends and issues; animal health care and husbandry. No profiles of industry members and/or retail establishments or consumer-oriented pet articles. **Buys 80 mss/year.** Query with published clips. Length: 1,500-2,200 words. **Pays 15¢/word for assigned articles.** Pays documented telephone expenses.

Photos Reviews transparencies, slides, and 5×7 glossy prints. Buys one-time rights. Captions, identification of subjects required.

Tips "This is a business publication for busy people, and must be very informative in easy-to-read, concise style. Articles about animal care or business practices should have the pet-retail angle or cover issues specific to this industry."

$ $ PET COMMERCE

August Communications, 225-530 Century St., Winnipeg MB R3H 0Y4, Canada. (888)573-1136. Fax: (866)957-0217. E-mail: s.vivian@august.ca. Website: www.petcommerce.ca. Editorial Director: Adam Peeler. **Contact:** Shelley Vivian, editor. **60% freelance written.** Bimonthly magazine covering pet retail and supply industry. Estab. 1997. Circ. 8,416. Pays 1 month after publication. Byline given. Offers 50% kill fee. Buys all rights. Editorial lead time 3 months. Submit seasonal material 3 months in advance. Accepts queries by mail, e-mail, fax. Responds in 1 week to queries. Sample copy online.

Nonfiction General interest, how-to, interview/profile, new product. Special issues: Annual Pond issue (February/March); Pre-PIJAC Convention issue (June/July); PIJAC Trade Show issue (August/September); Post PIJAC Convention issue (October/November). No consumer-related articles. **Buys 35-40 mss/year.** Query with published clips. Length: 1,500-3,000 words. **Pays 15-30¢/word for assigned articles.**

Photos Send photos with submission. Reviews GIF/JPEG files. Buys all rights. Negotiates payment individually. Captions, identification of subjects, model releases required.

Columns/Departments Clinic Corner (profile of vet), 2,000 words; Company Profile (profile of pet company), 2,000 words. **Buys 12 mss/year.** Query with published clips. **Pays 15-30¢/word.**

$ $ PET PRODUCT NEWS

Fancy Publications, P.O. Box 6050, Mission Viejo CA 92690. (949)855-8822. Fax: (949)855-3045. **Contact:** Carol Boker, editor. **70% freelance written.** Monthly magazine. "*Pet Product News* covers business/legal and economic issues of importance to pet product retailers, suppliers, and distributors, as well as product information and animal care issues. We're looking for straightforward articles on the proper care of dogs, cats, birds, fish, and exotics (reptiles, hamsters, etc.) as information the retailers can pass on to new pet owners." Estab. 1947. Circ. 26,000. Pays on publication. Byline given. Offers $50 kill fee. Buys first North American serial rights. Editorial lead time 3 months. Submit seasonal material 4 months in advance. Accepts queries by mail, fax. Responds in 2 weeks to queries. Sample copy for $5.50. Writer's guidelines for #10 SASE.

Nonfiction General interest, interview/profile, new product, photo feature, technical. "No cute animal stories or those directed at the pet owner." **Buys 150 mss/year.** Query. Length: 500-1,500 words. **Pays $175-350.**

Columns/Departments The Pet Dealer News™ (timely news stories about business issues affecting pet retailers), 800-1,000 words; Industry News (news articles representing coverage of pet product suppliers, manufacturers, distributors, and associations), 800-1,000 words; Pet Health News™ (pet health and articles relevant to pet retailers), 800-1,000 words; Dog & Cat (products and care of), 1,000-1,500 words; Fish & Bird (products and care of), 1,000-1,500 words; Small Mammals (products and care of), 1,000-1,500 words; Pond/Water Garden (products and care of), 1,000-1,500 words. **Buys 120 mss/year.** Query. **Pays $150-300.**

Tips "Be more than just an animal lover. You have to know about health, nutrition, and care. Product and business articles are told in both an informative and entertaining style. Talk to pet store owners and see what they need to know to be better business people in general, who have to deal with everything from balancing the books and free trade agreements to animal rights activists. All sections are open, but you have to be knowledgeable on the topic, be it taxes, management, profit building, products, nutrition, animal care, or marketing."

PLUMBING, HEATING, AIR CONDITIONING & REFRIGERATION

$ $ ☑ HEATING PLUMBING AIR CONDITIONING

One Mount Pleasant Rd., Toronto ON M4Y 2Y5, Canada. (416)764-1549. **Contact:** Kerry Turner, editor. **20% freelance written.** Monthly magazine. For a prompt reply, "enclose a sheet on which is typed a statement either approving or rejecting the suggested article which can either be checked off, or a quick answer written in and signed and returned." Estab. 1923. Circ. 16,500. Pays on publication. Publishes ms an average of 3 months after acceptance. Accepts queries by mail, e-mail, phone. Responds in 2 months to queries.

○→ Break in with technical, "how-to," Canadian-specific applications/stories.

Nonfiction News, business management articles that inform, educate, motivate, and help readers to be more efficient and profitable. Readers design, manufacture, install, sell, service maintain, or supply all mechanical components and systems in residential, commercial, institutional, and industrial installations across Canada. How-to, technical. Length: 1,000-1,500 words. **Pays 25¢/word.** Sometimes pays expenses of writers on assignment.

Reprints Send tearsheet or photocopy with rights for sale noted and information about when and where the material previously appeared.

Photos Prefers 4×5 or 5×7 glossies, high resolution JPEGS. Photos purchased with ms.

Tips "Topics must relate directly to the day-to-day activities of *HPAC* readers in Canada. Must be detailed, with specific examples, quotes from specific people or authorities—show depth. We specifically want material from other parts of Canada besides southern Ontario. U.S. material must relate to Canadian readers' concerns. We primarily want articles that show *HPAC* readers how they can increase their sales and business step-by-step based on specific examples of what others have done."

$ $ HVACR NEWS

Trade News International, 4444 Riverside Dr., #202, Burbank CA 91505-4048. Fax: (818)848-1306. E-mail: news@hvacrnews.com. Website: www.hvacrnews.com. **Contact:** Gary McCarty. Monthly tabloid covering heating, ventilation, air conditioning, and refrigeration. "We are a national trade publication writing about news and trends for those in the trade." Estab. 1981. Circ. 50,000. Pays on publication. Byline sometimes given. Buys first North American serial rights. Editorial lead time 2 months. Submit seasonal material 2 months in advance. Accepts queries by mail, e-mail. Responds in 1 month to queries. Sample copy online. Writer's guidelines by e-mail.

Nonfiction General interest, how-to, interview/profile, photo feature, technical. **Buys 25 mss/year.** Query with published clips. Length: 250-1,000 words. **Pays 25¢/word.** Sometimes pays expenses of writers on assignment.

Photos Send photos with submission. Buys one-time rights. Offers $10 minimum. Negotiates payment individually. Identification of subjects required.

Columns/Departments Technical only. **Buys 24 mss/year. Pays 20¢/word.**

Tips "Writers must be knowledgeable about the HVACR industry."

$ $ SNIPS MAGAZINE

Business News Publishing Co., 2401 W. Big Beaver Rd., Suite 700, Troy MI 48084. (248)244-6416. Fax: (248)362-0317. E-mail: mcconnellm@bnpmedia.com. Website: www.snipsmag.com. **Contact:** Michael McConnell, managing editor. **2% freelance written.** Monthly magazine for sheet metal, warm air heating, ventilating, air conditioning, and roofing contractors. Estab. 1932. Publishes ms an average of 3 months after acceptance. Buys all rights. Accepts queries by mail, e-mail, fax, phone. Call for writer's guidelines.

○→ Break in with a "profile of a local contractor in our industries."

Nonfiction Material should deal with information about contractors who do sheet metal, warm air heating, airconditioning, ventilation, and metal roofing work; also about successful advertising and/or marketing campaigns conducted by these contractors and the results. Length: Under 1,000 words unless on special assignment. **Pays $200-300.**

Photos Negotiable.

PRINTING

$ $ IN-PLANT GRAPHICS

North American Publishing Co., 401 N. Broad St., Philadelphia PA 19108. (215)238-5321. Fax: (215)238-5457. E-mail: bobneubauer@napco.com. Website: www.ipgonline.com. **Contact:** Bob Neubauer, editor. **10% freelance written.** "*In-Plant Graphics* features articles designed to help in-house printing departments increase productivity, save money, and stay competitive. *IPG* features advances in graphic arts technology and shows in-plants how to put this technology to use. Our audience consists of print shop managers working for (nonprint related) corporations (i.e., hospitals, insurance companies, publishers, nonprofits), universities, and government departments. They often oversee graphic design, prepress, printing, bindery, and mailing departments." Estab. 1951. Circ. 23,000. Pays on publication. Publishes ms an average of 5 months after acceptance. Byline given. Buys all rights. Editorial lead time 2 months. Submit seasonal material 3 months in advance. Accepts queries by mail, e-mail, fax. Writer's guidelines online.

Nonfiction "Stories include profiles of successful in-house printing operations (not commercial or quick printers); updates on graphic arts technology (new features, uses); reviews of major graphic arts and printing conferences (seminar and new equipment reviews)." New product (graphic arts), technical (graphic arts/printing/prepress). No articles on desktop publishing software or design software. No Internet publishing articles. **Buys 5 mss/year.** Query with published clips. Length: 800-1,500 words. **Pays $300-450.** Pays writers with contributor copies or other premiums for consultants who agree to write just for exposure.

Photos State availability with submission. Reviews transparencies, prints. Buys one-time rights. Negotiates payment individually. Captions, identification of subjects required.

■ The online magazine carries original content not found in the print edition. Contact: Bob Neubauer.

Tips "To get published in *IPG*, writers must contact the editor with an idea in the form of a query letter that includes published writing samples. Writers who have covered the graphic arts in the past may be assigned stories for an agreed-upon fee. We don't want stories that tout only 1 vendor's products and serve as glorified commercials. All profiles must be well balanced, covering a variety of issues. If you can tell us about an in-house printing operation that is doing innovative things, we will be interested."

$ $ SCREEN PRINTING

407 Gilbert Ave., Cincinnati OH 45202-2285. (513)421-2050. Fax: (513)421-5144. E-mail: screen@stmediagroup. com. Website: www.screenweb.com. **Contact:** Tom Frecska, editor. **30% freelance written.** Monthly magazine for the screen printing industry, including screen printers (commercial, industrial, and captive shops), suppliers and manufacturers, ad agencies and allied professions. Works with a small number of new/unpublished writers each year. Estab. 1953. Circ. 17,500. Pays on publication. Publishes ms an average of 3 months after acceptance. Byline given. Buys all rights. Accepts queries by mail, e-mail, fax. Response time varies to queries. Sample copy available. Writer's guidelines for #10 SASE.

Nonfiction "Because the screen printing industry is a specialized but diverse trade, we do not publish general interest articles with no pertinence to our readers. Subject matter is open, but should fall into 1 of 4 categories—technology, management, profile, or news. Features in all categories must identify the relevance of the subject matter to our readership. Technology articles must be informative, thorough, and objective—no promotional or 'advertorial' pieces accepted. Management articles may cover broader business or industry specific issues, but they must address the screen printer's unique needs. Profiles may cover serigraphers, outstanding shops, unique jobs and projects, or industry personalities; they should be in-depth features, not PR puff pieces, that clearly show the human interest or business relevance of the subject. News pieces should be timely (reprints from nonindustry publications will be considered) and must cover an event or topic of industry concern." Unsolicited mss not returned. **Buys 10-15 mss/year.** Query. **Pays $400 minimum for major features.**

Photos Cover photos negotiable; b&w or color. Published material becomes the property of the magazine.

■ The online magazine carries information from the print edition, as well as original content not found in the print edition. Contact: John Tymoski.

Tips "Be an expert in the screen-printing industry with supreme or special knowledge of a particular screen-printing process, or have special knowledge of a field or issue of particular interest to screen-printers. If the author has a working knowledge of screen printing, assignments are more readily available. General management articles are rarely used."

PROFESSIONAL PHOTOGRAPHY

$ $ NEWS PHOTOGRAPHER

National Press Photographers Association, Inc., 3200 Croasdaile Dr., #306, Durham NC 27705. (919)383-7246. Fax: (919)383-7261. E-mail: info@nppa.org. Website: www.nppa.org. **Contact:** Editor. Published 12 times/year. "*News Photographer* magazine is dedicated to the advancement of still and television news photography. The magazine presents articles, interviews, profiles, history, new products, electronic imaging, and news related to the practice of photojournalism." Estab. 1946. Circ. 11,000. **Pays on acceptance.** Publishes ms an average of 4 months after acceptance. Byline given. Offers 100% kill fee. Buys one-time, and archival electronic rights rights. Editorial lead time 2 months. Submit seasonal material 2 months in advance. Accepts queries by mail, e-mail, fax, phone. Accepts previously published material. Accepts simultaneous submissions. Responds in 1 month to queries. Sample copy for 9×12 SAE and 3 first-class stamps. Writer's guidelines free.

Nonfiction Historical/nostalgic, how-to, interview/profile, new product, opinion, personal experience, photo feature, technical. **Buys 10 mss/year.** Query. Length: 1,500 words. **Pays $300.** Pays expenses of writers on assignment.

Photos State availability with submission. Reviews high resolution, digital images only. Buys one-time rights. Negotiates payment individually. Captions, identification of subjects required.

Columns/Departments Query.

$ $ THE PHOTO REVIEW

140 E. Richardson Ave., Suite 301, Langhorne PA 19047. (215)891-0214. Fax: (215)891-9358. E-mail: info@phot oreview.org. Website: www.photoreview.org. **Contact:** Stephen Perloff, editor-in-chief. **50% freelance written.** Quarterly magazine covering art photography and criticism. *"The Photo Review* publishes critical reviews of photography exhibitions and books, critical essays, and interviews. We do not publish how-to or technical articles." Estab. 1976. Circ. 2,000. Pays on publication. Publishes ms an average of 9-12 months after acceptance. Byline given. Buys first rights. Editorial lead time 3 months. Submit seasonal material 6 months in advance. Accepts queries by mail. Accepts simultaneous submissions. Responds in 2 months to queries; 3 months to mss. Sample copy for $7. Writer's guidelines for #10 SASE.

Nonfiction Interview/profile, photography essay, critical review. No how-to articles. **Buys 20 mss/year.** Send complete ms. Length: 2-20 typed pages. **Pays $10-250.**

Reprints Send tearsheet, photocopy, or typed ms with rights for sale noted and information about when and where the material previously appeared. Payment varies.

Photos Send photos with submission. Reviews contact sheets, transparencies, prints. Buys all rights. Offers no additional payment for photos accepted with ms. Captions required.

N $ $ PHOTOGRAPHIC PROCESSING

Cygnus Business Media, 445 Broad Hollow Rd., Suite 21, Melville NY 11747. (631)845-2700. Fax: (631)845-7109. E-mail: bill.schiffner@cygnusb2b.com. Website: www.labsonline.com. Publisher: Arthur Hotz. **Contact:** Bill Schiffner, editor-in-chief. **30% freelance written.** Monthly magazine covering photographic (commercial/minilab) and electronic processing markets. Estab. 1965. Circ. 19,000. Pays on publication. Publishes ms an average of 4 months after acceptance. Byline given. Offers $75 kill fee. Editorial lead time 3 months. Submit seasonal material 3 months in advance. Accepts simultaneous submissions. Sample copy and writer's guidelines free.

Nonfiction How-to, interview/profile, new product, photo processing/digital imaging features. **Buys 20-30 mss/year.** Query with published clips. Length: 1,500-2,200 words. **Pays $275-350 for assigned articles; $250-275 for unsolicited articles.**

Photos Looking for digitally manipulated covers. Send photos with submission. Reviews 4×5 transparencies, 4×6 prints. Buys one-time rights. Offers no additional payment for photos accepted with ms. Captions required.

Columns/Departments Surviving in 2000 (business articles offering tips to labs on how to make their businesses run better), 1,500-1,800 words; Business Side (getting more productivity out of your lab). **Buys 10 mss/year.** Query with published clips. **Pays $150-250.**

SHUTTERBUG/EDIGITALPHOTO.COM

Primedia, 1419 Chaffee Dr., Suite 1, Titusville FL 32780. Fax: (321)225-3149. E-mail: editorial@shutterbug.net. Website: www.shutterbug.net. Managing Editor: Bonnie Paulk. **Contact:** George Schaub, editor. **90% freelance written.** Monthly covering photography and digial imaging. "Written for the avid amateur, part-time, and full-time professional photographers. Covers equipment techniques, profiles, technology and news in both silver-halide and digital imaging." Estab. 1972. Circ. 90,000. Pays on publication. Publishes ms an average of 90 days after acceptance. Byline given. Buys first North American serial, second serial (reprint), electronic rights. Editorial lead time 3 months. Submit seasonal material 6 months in advance. Accepts queries by mail. Responds in 1 month to queries; 1 month to mss. Sample copy not available.

Nonfiction How-to, interview/profile, new product, photo feature, technical, travel. **Buys 100 mss/year.** Query with or without published clips. Length: 1,000-2,000 words. **Payment rate depends on published length.** Sometimes pays expenses of writers on assignment.

Photos Send photos with submission. Reviews contact sheets, transparencies, CD-ROMs. Buys one-time rights. Offers no additional payment for photos accepted with ms. Captions, model releases required.

REAL ESTATE

$ $ AREA DEVELOPMENT MAGAZINE

Sites and Facility Planning, Halcyon Business Publications, Inc., 400 Post Ave., Westbury NY 11590. (516)338-0900, ext. 211. Fax: (516)338-0100. E-mail: gerri@areadevelopment.com. Website: www.areadevelopment.c

om. **Contact:** Geraldine Gambale, editor. **80% freelance written.** Prefers to work with published/established writers. Monthly magazine covering corporate facility planning and site selection for industrial chief executives worldwide. Estab. 1965. Circ. 45,000. Pays on publication. Publishes ms an average of 2 months after acceptance. Byline given. Buys all rights. Accepts queries by mail, e-mail, fax. Responds in 3 months to queries. Sample copy for free. Writer's guidelines for #10 SASE.

Nonfiction Related areas of site selection and facility planning such as taxes, labor, government, energy, architecture, and finance. Historical/nostalgic (if it deals with corporate facility planning), how-to (experiences in site selection and all other aspects of corporate facility planning), interview/profile (corporate executives and industrial developers). **Buys 75 mss/year.** Query. Length: 1,500-2,000 words. **Pays 30¢/word.** Sometimes pays expenses of writers on assignment.

Photos State availability with submission. Reviews transparencies. Negotiates payment individually. Captions, identification of subjects required.

> The online version of this publication contains material not found in the print edition. Contact: Geraldine Gambale, online editor.

$ $ CANADIAN PROPERTY MANAGEMENT

Mediaedge Communications Inc., 5255 Yonge St., Suite 1000, Toronto ON M2N 6P4, Canada. (416)512-8186. Fax: (416)512-8344. E-mail: barbc@mediaedge.ca. Website: www.mediaedge.ca. **Contact:** Barb Carss, editor. **10% freelance written.** Magazine published 8 times/year covering Canadian commercial, industrial, institutional (medical and educational), residential properties. "*Canadian Property Management* magazine is a trade journal supplying building owners and property managers with Canadian industry news, case law reviews, technical updates for building operations and events listings. Feature building and professional profile articles are regular features." Estab. 1985. Circ. 14,500. Pays on publication. Publishes ms an average of 3 months after acceptance. Byline given. Buys all rights. Editorial lead time 2 months. Submit seasonal material 2 months in advance. Accepts queries by mail, e-mail, fax, phone. Accepts simultaneous submissions. Responds in 3 weeks to queries; 2 months to mss. Sample copy for $5, subject to availability. Writer's guidelines free.

Nonfiction Interview/profile, technical. "No promotional articles (e.g., marketing a product or service geared to this industry)!" Query with published clips. Length: 700-1,200 words. **Pays 35¢/word.**

Photos State availability with submission. Reviews transparencies, 3×5 prints, digital (at least 300 dpi). Offers no additional payment for photos accepted with ms. Captions, identification of subjects, model releases required.

Tips "We do not accept promotional articles serving companies or their products. Freelance articles that are strong, information-based pieces that serve the interests and needs of property managers and building owners stand a better chance of being published. Proposals and inquiries with article ideas are appreciated the most. A good understanding of the real estate industry (management structure) is also helpful for the writer."

$ $ $ $ COMMERCIAL INVESTMENT REAL ESTATE

CCIM, 430 N. Michigan Ave., Suite 800, Chicago IL 60611-4092. (312)321-4460. Fax: (312)321-4530. E-mail: magazine@ccim.com. Website: www.ciremagazine.com. **Contact:** Jennifer Norbut, editor. **10% freelance written.** Bimonthly magazine. "*CIRE* offers practical articles on current trends and business development ideas for commercial investment real estate practitioners." Estab. 1982. Circ. 17,000. **Pays on acceptance.** Publishes ms an average of 4 months after acceptance. Byline given. Buys all rights. Editorial lead time 4 months. Submit seasonal material 4 months in advance. Accepts queries by mail, e-mail, fax. Responds in 2 weeks to queries; 1 month to mss. Sample copy online. Writer's guidelines online.

> Break in by sending résumé and feature-length clips, "including commercial real estate-related clips if available. We keep writers' materials on file for assigning articles."

Nonfiction How-to, technical, business strategies. **Buys 6-8 mss/year.** Query with published clips. Length: 2,000-3,500 words. **Pays $1,000-1,600.**

Photos May ask writers to have sources. Send images to editors.

Tips "Always query first with a detailed outline and published clips. Authors should have a background in writing on business or real estate subjects."

$ $ THE COOPERATOR

The Co-op and Condo Monthly, Yale Robbins, Inc., 31 E. 28th St., 12th Floor, New York NY 10016. (212)683-5700. Fax: (212)696-1268. E-mail: debbie@cooperator.com. Website: www.cooperator.com. **Contact:** Debra A. Estock, managing editor. **70% freelance written.** Monthly tabloid covering real estate in the New York City metro area. "*The Cooperator* covers condominium and cooperative issues in New York and beyond. It is read by condo unit owners and co-op shareholders, real estate professionals, board members and managing agents, and other service professionals." Estab. 1980. Circ. 40,000. Pays on publication. Publishes ms an average of 3 months after acceptance. Byline given. Buys all rights, makes work-for-hire assignments. Submit seasonal material 3 months in advance. Accepts queries by mail, e-mail, fax. Responds in 1 month to queries. Sample copy and writer's guidelines free.

Nonfiction All articles related to co-op and condo ownership. Interview/profile, new product, personal experience. No submissions without queries. Query with published clips. Length: 1,500-2,000 words. **Pays $300.** Sometimes pays expenses of writers on assignment.

Photos State availability with submission. Reviews contact sheets, negatives, transparencies, prints, digital. Rights purchased vary. Negotiates payment individually. Captions, identification of subjects required.

Columns/Departments Profiles of co-op/condo-related businesses with something unique; Building Finance (investment and financing issues); Buying and Selling (market issues, etc.); Management/Board Relations and Interacting With Professionals (issues dealing with board members and the professionals that help run the building); Interior Design (architectural and interior/exterior design, lobby renovation, etc.); Building Maintenance (issues related to maintaining interior/exterior, facades, lobbies, elevators, etc.); Legal Issues Related to Co-Ops/Condos; Real Estate Trends, all 1,500 words. **Buys 50 mss/year.** Query with published clips. **Pays $300.**

Tips "You must have experience in business, legal, or financial. Must have published clips to send in with résumé and query."

$ $ FLORIDA REALTOR MAGAZINE

Florida Association of Realtors, 7025 Augusta National Dr., Orlando FL 32822-5017. (407)438-1400. Fax: (407)438-1411. E-mail: flrealtor@far.org. Website: floridarealtormagazine.com. Assistant Editor: Leslie Stone. **Contact:** Tracey Lawton, editor-in-chief. **30% freelance written.** Journal published 11 times/year covering Florida real estate. "As the official publication of the Florida Association of Realtors, we provide helpful articles for our 100,000 members. We try to stay up on the trends and issues that affect business in Florida's real estate market." Estab. 1925. Circ. 100,000. Pays on publication. Publishes ms an average of 2 months after acceptance. Byline given. Editorial lead time 2 months. Accepts queries by mail, e-mail, fax. Accepts simultaneous submissions. Sample copy online.

Nonfiction Book excerpts, how-to, inspirational, interview/profile, new product, all with real estate angle—Florida-specific is good. "No fiction, poetry." **Buys varying number of mss/year.** Query with published clips. Length: 800-1,500 words. **Pays $300-700.** Sometimes pays expenses of writers on assignment.

Photos State availability with submission. Buys one-time rights. Negotiates payment individually. Captions, identification of subjects, model releases required.

Columns/Departments Written in-house. Publishes: Promotional Strategies, 900 words; Technology & You, 1,000 words; Realtor Advantage, 1,000 words. **Buys varying number of mss/year. Payment varies.**

Fillers Short humor. **Buys varying number/year.**

Tips "Build a solid reputation for specializing in real estate-specific writing in state/national publications. Query with specific article ideas."

JOURNAL OF PROPERTY MANAGEMENT

Institute of Real Estate Management, 430 N. Michigan Ave., 7th Floor, Chicago IL 60611. (312)329-6058. Fax: (312)410-7958. E-mail: adruckman@irem.org. Website: www.irem.org. **Contact:** Amanda Druckman, managing editor. **30% freelance written.** Bimonthly magazine covering real estate management. "The *Journal* has a feature/information slant designed to educate readers in the application of new techniques and to keep them abreast of current industry trends." Circ. 20,000. **Pays on acceptance.** Publishes ms an average of 3 months after acceptance. Byline given. Buys all rights. Accepts queries by mail, e-mail, fax. Responds in 6 weeks to queries; 1 month to mss. Sample copy for free. Writer's guidelines online.

Nonfiction Demographic shifts in business employment and buying patterns, marketing. How-to, interview/profile, technical (building systems/computers). "No non-real estate subjects, personality or company humor." **Buys 8-12 mss/year.** Query with published clips. Length: 750-1,500 words. Sometimes pays expenses of writers on assignment.

Reprints Send tearsheet, photocopy or typed ms. Pays 35% of amount paid for an original article.

Photos State availability with submission. Reviews contact sheets. Buys one-time rights. May offer additional payment for photos accepted with ms. Identification of subjects, model releases required.

Columns/Departments Insurance; Tax Issues; Technology; Maintentance; Personal Development; Legal Issues. Length: 500 words. **Buys 6-8 mss/year.** Query.

NATIONAL RELOCATION & REAL ESTATE

RIS Media, 50 Water St., Norwalk CT 06854. (203)855-1234. Fax: (203)852-7208. E-mail: maria@rismedia.com. Website: rismedia.com. **Contact:** Maria Patterson, executive editor. **10-30% freelance written.** Monthly magazine covering residential real estate and corporate relocation. "Our readers are professionals within the relocation and real estate industries; therefore, we require our writers to have sufficient knowledge of the workings of these industries in order to ensure depth and accuracy in reporting." Estab. 1980. Circ. 45,000. **Pays on acceptance.** Byline usually given. Offers kill fee. Buys all rights. Editorial lead time 2 months. Accepts queries by mail, e-mail. Responds in 2 weeks to queries. Sample copy for free.

Nonfiction Exposé, how-to (use the Internet to sell real estate, etc.), interview/profile, new product, opinion, technical. Query with published clips. Length: 250-1,200 words. Pays unsolicited article writers with contributor copies upon use. Sometimes pays expenses of writers on assignment.

Photos Prefers digital media via e-mail. Send photos with submission. Reviews transparencies. Offers no additional payment for photos accepted with ms. Captions required.

Columns/Departments Query with published clips.

◼ The online news carries original content not found in the print edition. Website features daily news service, written submissions and other information on publication. Contact: Ed Silverstein.

Tips "All queries must be done in writing. Phone queries are unacceptable. Any clips or materials sent should indicate knowledge of the real estate and relocation industries. In general, we are open to all knowledgeable contributors."

$ $ OFFICE BUILDINGS MAGAZINE

Yale Robbins, Inc., 31 E. 28th St., New York NY 10016. (212)683-5700. Fax: (212)545-0764. E-mail: info@yrinc.com. Website: www.yrinc.com.; www.mrofficespace.com. **Contact:** Debbie Estock, executive editor. **15% freelance written.** "Annual magazine covering market statistics, trends, and thinking of area professionals on the current and future state of the real estate market." Estab. 1987. Circ. 10,500. Pays 1 month after publication. Byline sometimes given. Offers kill fee. Buys all rights. Editorial lead time 2 months. Accepts queries by mail, e-mail, fax. Sample copy and writer's guidelines free.

Nonfiction Survey of specific markets. **Buys 15-20 mss/year.** Query with published clips. Length: 1,500-2,000 words. **Pays $600-700.** Sometimes pays expenses of writers on assignment.

$ $ PROPERTIES MAGAZINE

Properties Magazine, Inc., P.O. Box 112127, Cleveland OH 44111. (216)251-0035. Fax: (216)251-0064. E-mail: kkrych@propertiesmag.com. Editor: Kenneth C. Krych. **25% freelance written.** Monthly magazine covering real estate, residential, commerical construction. *"Properties Magazine* is published for executives in the real estate, building, banking, design, architectural, property management, tax, and law community—busy people who need the facts presented in an interesting and informative format." Estab. 1946. Circ. over 10,000. Pays on publication. Publishes ms an average of 2 months after acceptance. Byline given. Buys first rights. Editorial lead time 2 months. Submit seasonal material 2 months in advance. Accepts queries by mail, fax. Responds in 3 weeks to queries. Sample copy for $3.95.

Nonfiction General interest, how-to, humor, new product. Special issues: Environmental issues (September); Security/Fire Protection (October); Tax Issues (November); Computers In Real Estate (December). **Buys 30 mss/year.** Send complete ms. Length: 500-2,000 words. **Pays 50¢/column line.** Sometimes pays expenses of writers on assignment.

Photos Send photos with submission. Reviews prints. Buys one-time rights. Offers no additional payment for photos accepted with ms. Negotiates payment individually. Captions required.

Columns/Departments Buys 25 mss/year. Query or send complete ms. **Pays 50¢/column line.**

$ $ ◩ REM

The Real Estate Magazine, House Publications, 115 Thorncliff Park Dr., Toronto ON M4C 3E4, Canada. (416)425-3504. Fax: (416)406-0882. E-mail: jim@remonline.com. Website: www.remonline.com. **Contact:** Jim Adair, editor. **35% freelance written.** Monthly trade journal covering real estate. *"REM* provides Canadian real estate agents and brokers with news and opinion they can't get anywhere else. It is an independent publication and not affiliated with any real estate board, association, or company." Estab. 1989. Circ. 50,000. **Pays on acceptance.** Publishes ms an average of 2 months after acceptance. Offers 25% kill fee. Buys first Canadian serial rights. Editorial lead time 3 months. Submit seasonal material 3 months in advance. Accepts queries by mail, e-mail, fax. Accepts previously published material. Accepts simultaneous submissions. Sample copy for free.

Nonfiction Book excerpts, exposé, inspirational, interview/profile, new product, personal experience. No articles geared to consumers about market conditions or how to choose a realtor. Must have Canadian content. **Buys 60 mss/year.** Query. Length: 500-1,500 words. **Pays $200-400.**

Photos Send photos with submission. Reviews transparencies, prints, GIF/JPEG files. Buys one-time rights. Offers $25/photo. Captions, identification of subjects required.

Tips "Stories must be of interest or practical use for Canadian realtors. Check out our website to see the types of stories we require."

RESOURCES & WASTE REDUCTION

$ $ COMPOSTING NEWS

The Latest News in Composting and Scrap Wood Management, McEntee Media Corp., 9815 Hazelwood Ave., Cleveland OH 44149. (440)238-6603. Fax: (440)238-6712. E-mail: cn@recycle.cc. **Contact:** Ken McEntee, editor. **5% freelance written.** Monthly newsletter. "We are interested in any news impacting the composting industry including new laws, regulations, new facilities/programs, end-uses, research, etc." Estab. 1992. Circ. 1,000. Pays on publication. Publishes ms an average of 1 month after acceptance. Buys first, all rights. Editorial lead time 1 month. Submit seasonal material 1 month in advance. Accepts queries by mail, e-mail, fax, phone. Accepts previously published material. Accepts simultaneous submissions. Responds in 2 months to queries. Sample copy for 9×12 SAE and 55¢ postage. Writer's guidelines for #10 SASE.

Nonfiction Book excerpts, essays, general interest, how-to, interview/profile, new product, opinion, personal experience, photo feature, technical, new business, legislation, regulation, business expansion. **Buys 0-5 mss/year.** Query with published clips. Length: 100-5,000 words. **Pays $10-500.** Pays writers with contributor copies or other premiums by prior agreement.

Columns/Departments Query with published clips. **Pays $10-500.**

■ The online magazine carries original content not found in the print edition. Contact: Ken McEntee.

Tips "We appreciate leads on local news regarding composting, i.e., new facilities or business, new laws and regulations, unique programs, situations that impact supply and demand for composting. International developments are also of interest."

$ $ $ EROSION CONTROL

The Journal for Erosion and Sediment Control Professionals, Forester Communications, Inc., 2946 De La Vina St., Santa Barbara CA 93105. (805)682-1300. Fax: (805)682-0200. E-mail: eceditor@forester.net. Website: www.erosioncontrol.com. **Contact:** Janice Kaspersen, editor. **60% freelance written.** Magazine published 7 times/year covering all aspects of erosion prevention and sediment control. "*Erosion Control* is a practical, hands-on, 'how-to' professional journal. Our readers are civil engineers, landscape architects, builders, developers, public works officials, road and highway construction officials and engineers, soils specialists, farmers, landscape contractors, and others involved with any activity that disturbs significant areas of surface vegetation." Estab. 1994. Circ. 20,000. Pays 30 days after acceptance. Publishes ms an average of 3 months after acceptance. Byline given. Buys all rights. Editorial lead time 4 months. Submit seasonal material 4 months in advance. Accepts queries by mail, e-mail, fax, phone. Responds in 3 weeks to queries. Sample copy and writer's guidelines free.

Nonfiction Photo feature, technical. **Buys 15 mss/year.** Query with published clips. Length: 3,000-4,000 words. **Pays $700-850.** Sometimes pays expenses of writers on assignment.

Photos Send photos with submission. Reviews transparencies, prints. Buys all rights. Offers no additional payment for photos accepted with ms. Captions, identification of subjects, model releases required.

Tips "Writers should have a good grasp of technology involved, good writing and communication skills. Most of our freelanced articles include extensive interviews with engineers, contractors, developers, or project owners, and we often provide contact names for articles we assign."

$ $ MSW MANAGEMENT

The Journal for Municipal Solid Waste Professionals, Forester Communications, Inc., P.O. Box 3100, Santa Barbara CA 93130. (805)682-1300. Fax: (805)682-0200. E-mail: editor@forester.net. Website: www.mswmanag ement.net. **Contact:** John Trotti, editor. **70% freelance written.** Bimonthly magazine. "*MSW Management* is written for public sector solid waste professionals—the people working for the local counties, cities, towns, boroughs, and provinces. They run the landfills, recycling programs, composting, incineration. They are responsible for all aspects of garbage collection and disposal; buying and maintaining the associated equipment; and designing, engineering, and building the waste processing facilities, transfer stations, and landfills." Estab. 1991. Circ. 25,000. Pays on publication. Byline given. Buys all rights. Editorial lead time 4 months. Submit seasonal material 4 months in advance. Accepts queries by mail, e-mail, fax, phone. Accepts simultaneous submissions. Responds in 6 weeks to queries; 2 months to mss. Sample copy and writer's guidelines free. Writer's guidelines online.

Nonfiction Photo feature, technical. "No rudimentary, basic articles written for the average person on the street. Our readers are experienced professionals with years of practical, in-the-field experience. Any material submitted that we judge as too fundamental will be rejected." **Buys 15 mss/year.** Query. Length: 3,000-4,000 words. **Pays $350-750.** Sometimes pays expenses of writers on assignment.

Photos Send photos with submission. Reviews transparencies, prints. Buys all rights. Offers no additional payment for photos accepted with ms. Captions, identification of subjects, model releases required.

■ The online version of *MSW Management* includes material not found in the print edition. Contact: John Trotti.

Tips "We're a small company, easy to reach. We're open to any and all ideas as to possible editorial topics. We endeavor to provide the reader with usable material, and present it in full color with graphic embellishment whenever possible. Dry, highly technical material is edited to make it more palatable and concise. Most of our feature articles come from freelancers. Interviews and quotes should be from public sector solid waste managers and engineers—not PR people, not manufacturers. Strive to write material that is 'over the heads' of our readers. If anything, attempt to make them 'reach.' Anything submitted that is too basic, elementary, fundamental, rudimentary, etc., cannot be accepted for publication."

$ $ $STORMWATER

The Journal for Surface Water Quality Professionals, Forester Communications, Inc., 2946 De La Vina St., Santa Barbara CA 93105. (805)682-1300. Fax: (805)682-0200. E-mail: sweditor@forester.net. Website: www.stormh2 o.com. **Contact:** Janice Kaspersen, editor. **10% freelance written.** "*Stormwater* is a practical business journal for professionals involved with surface water quality issues, protection, projects, and programs. Our readers are municipal employees, regulators, engineers, and consultants concerned with stormwater management." Estab. 2000. Circ. 20,000. Publishes ms an average of 3 months after acceptance. Byline given. Editorial lead time 4 months. Submit seasonal material 4 months in advance. Accepts queries by mail, e-mail. Responds in 3 weeks to queries. Writer's guidelines free.

Nonfiction Technical. **Buys 8-10 mss/year.** Query with published clips. Length: 3,000-4,000 words. **Pays $700-850.** Sometimes pays expenses of writers on assignment.

Photos Send photos with submission. Buys all rights. Offers no additional payment for photos accepted with ms. Captions, identification of subjects, model releases required.

Tips "Writers should have a good grasp of the technology and regulations involved in stormwater management and good interviewing skills. Our freelanced articles include extensive interviews with engineers, stormwater managers, and project owners, and we often provide contact names for articles we assign. See past editorial content online."

WASTE AGE MAGAZINE

The Business Magazine For Waste Industry Professionals, Intertec Publishing, 6151 Powers Ferry Rd. NW, Atlanta GA 30339-2941. (770)618-0310. Fax: (770)618-0349. E-mail: ptom@primediabusiness.com. Editorial Director: Bill Wolpin. **Contact:** Patti Tom, editor. **50% freelance written.** Monthly magazine. "*Waste Age* reaches individuals and firms engaged in the removal, collection, processing, transportation, and disposal of solid/hazardous liquid wastes. This includes: private refuse contractors; landfill operators; municipal, county, and other government officials; recyclers and handlers of secondary materials; major generators of waste, such as plants and chain stores; engineers, architects, and consultants; manufactures and distributors of equipment; universities, libraries, and associations; and legal, insurance, and financial firms allied to the field. Readers include: owners, presidents, vice-presidents, directors, superintendents, engineers, managers, supervisors, consultants, purchasing agents, and commissioners." Estab. 1958. Circ. 40,000. Pays on publication. Publishes ms an average of 4 months after acceptance. Byline given. Editorial lead time 2 months. Responds in 1 week to queries; 1 month to mss. Sample copy for free. Writer's guidelines free.

Nonfiction How-to (practical information on improving solid waste management, i.e., how to rehabilitate a transfer station, how to improve recyclable collection, how to manage a landfill, etc.), interview/profile (of prominent persons in the solid waste industry.). "No feel-good 'green' articles about recycling. Remember our readers are not the citizens but the governments and private contractors. No 'why you should recycle' articles." **Buys over 50 mss/year.** Query. Length: 500-2,000 words. Pays expenses of writers on assignment.

Photos Send photos with submission. Reviews contact sheets, negatives, transparencies, prints, digital. Negotiates payment individually. Identification of subjects required.

Tips "Read the magazine and understand our audience. Write useful articles with sidebars that the readers can apply to their jobs. Use the Associated Press style book. Freelancers can send in queries or manuscripts, or can fax or e-mail a letter of interest (including qualifications/résumé) in possible assignments. Writers must be deadline-oriented."

$ $WATER WELL JOURNAL

National Ground Water Association, 601 Dempsey Rd., Westerville OH 43081. Fax: (614)898-7786. E-mail: jross@ngwa.org. Website: www.ngwa.org. **Contact:** Jill Ross, director of publications. **15% freelance written.** Monthly magazine covering the ground water industry; well drilling. "Each month the *Water Well Journal* covers the topics of drilling, rigs and heavy equipment, pumping systems, water quality, business management, water supply, on-site waste water treatment, and diversification opportunities, including geoexchange installations, environmental remediation, irrigation, dewatering, and foundation installation. It also offers updates on regulatory issues that impact the ground water industry." Estab. 1948. Circ. 26,500. Pays on publication. Publishes ms an average of 3 months after acceptance. Byline given. Buys all rights. Editorial lead time 2 months. Submit seasonal material 3 months in advance. Accepts queries by mail, e-mail, fax, phone. Responds in 2 weeks to queries; 1 month to mss. Sample copy for 9×12 SAE and 2 first-class stamps. Writer's guidelines free.

Nonfiction Essays (sometimes), historical/nostalgic (sometimes), how-to (recent examples include how to chlorinate a well; how to buy a used rig; how to do bill collections), interview/profile, new product, personal experience, photo feature, technical, business management. No company profiles; extended product releases. **Buys up to 20 mss/year.** Query with published clips. Length: 1,000-4,000 words. **Pays $100-600.**

Photos State availability with submission. Offers $50-250/photo. Captions, identification of subjects required.

Tips "Some previous experience or knowledge in groundwater/drilling/construction industry helpful. Published clips a must."

SELLING & MERCHANDISING

$ $ BALLOONS AND PARTIES MAGAZINE

Partilife Publications, 65 Sussex St., Hackensack NJ 07601. (201)441-4224. Fax: (201)342-8118. E-mail: mark@balloonsandparties.com. Website: www.balloonsandparties.com. **Contact:** Mark Zettler, publisher. **10% freelance written.** International trade journal for professional party decorators and for gift delivery businesses published 5 times/year. Estab. 1986. Circ. 7,000. Pays on publication. Publishes ms an average of 3 months after acceptance. Byline given. Buys all rights. Submit seasonal material 6 months in advance. Accepts queries by mail, e-mail, fax, phone. Responds in 6 weeks to queries. Sample copy for 9×12 SAE.

Nonfiction Essays, how-to, interview/profile, new product, personal experience, photo feature, technical, craft. **Buys 12 mss/year.** Query with or without published clips or send complete ms. Length: 500-1,500 words. **Pays $100-300 for assigned articles; $50-200 for unsolicited articles.** Sometimes pays expenses of writers on assignment.

Reprints Send ms with rights for sale noted and information about when and where the material previously appeared Length: up to 2,500 words. Pays 10¢/word.

Photos Send photos with submission. Reviews 2×2 transparencies, 3×5 prints. Buys all rights. Captions, identification of subjects, model releases required.

Columns/Departments Problem Solver (small business issues); Recipes That Cook (centerpiece ideas with detailed how-to), 400-1,000 words. Send complete ms with photos.

Tips "Show unusual, lavish, and outstanding examples of balloon sculpture, design and decorating, and other craft projects. Offer specific how-to information. Be positive and motivational in style."

$ $ COLLEGE STORE

National Association of College Stores, 500 E. Lorain, Oberlin OH 44074. (216)775-7777. Fax: (216)775-4769. E-mail: thecollegestore@nacs.org. Website: www.nacs.org. **Contact:** Keith Galestock, editor. **10% freelance written.** Bimonthly magazine. "*College Store* is the journal of record for the National Association of College Stores and serves its members by publishing information and expert opinion on all phases of college store retailing." Estab. 1928. Circ. 10,000. **Pays on acceptance.** Byline given. Buys all rights. Editorial lead time 3 months. Submit seasonal material 6 months in advance. Accepts queries by mail, e-mail. Responds in 1 month to queries. Writer's guidelines online.

Nonfiction "Articles must have clearly defined connection to college stores and collegiate retailing." How-to, interview/profile, personal experience, technical (unique attributes of collete stores/personnel). **Buys 1-3 unsolicited mss/year.** Query with published clips. Length: 1,500-3,000 words. **Pays $400 minimum for assigned articles; $200 minimum for unsolicited articles.**

Reprints Send tearsheet or photocopy with rights for sale noted. Pay negotiable.

Tips "It's best if writers work (or have worked) in a college store. Articles on very specific retailing successes are most open to freelancers—they should include information on how well an approach worked and the reasons for it, whether they're specific to a campus or region, etc."

$ $ $ CONSUMER GOODS TECHNOLOGY

Edgell Communications, 4 Middlebury Blvd., Randolph NJ 07867. (973)252-0100. Fax: (973)252-9020. E-mail: tclark@edgellmail.com. Website: www.consumergoods.com. **Contact:** Tim Clark, managing editor. **40% freelance written.** Monthly tabloid benchmarking business technology performance. Estab. 1987. Circ. 25,000. Pays on publication. Publishes ms an average of 2 months after acceptance. Byline given. Buys first North American serial, second serial (reprint), electronic, all rights. Editorial lead time 3 months. Accepts queries by e-mail. Sample copy online. Writer's guidelines by e-mail.

Nonfiction "We create several supplements annually, often using freelance." Essays, exposé, interview/profile.

Buys 60 mss/year. Query with published clips. Length: 700-1,900 words. **Pays $600-1,200.** Sometimes pays expenses of writers on assignment.

Photos Buys all rights. Negotiates payment individually. Identification of subjects, model releases required.

Columns/Departments Columns 400-750 words—featured columnists. **Buys 4 mss/year.** Query with published clips. **Pays 75¢-$1/word.**

Tips "All stories in *Consumer Goods Technology* are told through the voice of the consumer goods executive. We only quote VP-level or C-level CG executives. No vendor quotes. We're always on the lookout for freelance talent. We look in particular for writers with an in-depth understanding of the business issues faced by consumer goods firms and the technologies that are used by the industry to address those issues successfully. 'Bits and bytes' tech writing is not sought; our focus is on benchmarketing the business technology performance of CG firms, CG executives, CG vendors, and CG vendor products. Our target reader is tech-savvy, CG C-level decision maker. We write to, and about, our target reader."

$ $ CONVENIENCE STORE DECISIONS

Donohue-Meehan Publishing, Two Greenwood Square, #410, Bensalem PA 19020. (215)245-4555. Fax: (215)245-4060. E-mail: bdonahue@penton.com. Website: www.c-storedecisions.com. Editor-in-Chief: Jay Gordon. **Contact:** Bill Donahue, managing editor. **15-20% freelance written.** Monthly magazine covering convenience retail/petroleum marketing. "*CSD* is received by top-level executives in the convenience retail and petroleum marketing industry. Writers should have knowledge of the industry and the subjects it encompasses." Estab. 1990. Circ. 42,000. Pays on publication. Byline given. Buys all rights, makes work-for-hire assignments. Editorial lead time 2-4 months. Submit seasonal material 3 months in advance. Accepts queries by mail, e-mail, fax. Accepts simultaneous submissions. Responds in 3 weeks to queries. Sample copy and writer's guidelines free.

    O→ Break in with a "demonstrated knowledge of finance and business, with special emphasis on retail. Keen powers of observation and attention to detail are also prized."

Nonfiction Interview/profile (retailers), photo feature, technical. No self-serving, vendor-based stories. **Buys 12-15 mss/year.** Query with published clips. Length: 400-2,000 words. **Pays $200-600 for assigned articles.** Sometimes pays expenses of writers on assignment.

Photos State availability with submission. Buys all rights. Negotiates payment individually. Identification of subjects required.

Tips Offer experience. "We get queries from freelancers daily. We are looking for writers with industry experience. We need real-life, retailer-based work. Bring us a story."

$ $ COUNTRY SAMPLER'S COUNTRY BUSINESS

Emmis Communications, 707 Kautz Rd., St. Charles IL 60174. (630)377-8000, ext. 866. Fax: (630)377-8194. E-mail: cbiz@sampler.emmis.com. Website: www.country-business.com. **Contact:** Susan Wagner, editor. **40% freelance written.** Magazine published 7 times/year covering gift and home decor retail. "*Country Business* articles are written for independent retailers of gifts and home accents. Articles should include solid business advice on the various aspects of running a retail business." Estab. 1983. Circ. 35,000. Pays 1 month after acceptance of final ms. Publishes ms an average of 6-8 months after acceptance. Byline given. Offers $50 kill fee. Buys all rights, makes work-for-hire assignments. Editorial lead time 4-6 months. Submit seasonal material 6 months in advance. Accepts queries by mail, e-mail. Accepts simultaneous submissions. Sample copy for free. Writer's guidelines by e-mail.

Nonfiction How-to, interview/profile, technical, finance, legal, marketing, small business. No fiction, poetry, fillers, photos, artwork, profiles of businesses, unless queried and first assigned. **Buys 20-30 mss/year.** Query with published clips or send complete ms. Length: 1,000-2,500 words. **Pays $275-500 for assigned articles; $200-350 for unsolicited articles.** Sometimes pays expenses of writers on assignment.

Columns/Departments Display & Design (store design and product display), 1,500 words; Retailer Profile (profile of retailer—assigned only), 1,800 words; Vendor Profile (profile of manufacturer—assigned only), 1,200 words; Technology (Internet, computer-related articles as applies to small retailers), 1,500 words; Marketing (marketing ideas and advice as applies to small retailers), 1,500 words; Finance (financial tips and advice as applies to small retailers), 1,500 words; Legal (legal tips and advice as applies to small retailers), 1,500 words; Employees (tips and advice on hiring, firing, and working with employees as applies to small retailers), 1,500 words. **Buys 15 mss/year.** Query with published clips or send complete ms. **Pays $250-350.**

Ⓝ $ EVENTS MEDIA NETWORK, INC.

P.O. Box 1132, Medford NJ 08055. (609)953-9544. Fax: (609)953-2010. **Contact:** Jonathon Tuttle, assistant to the editor. **20% freelance written.** Bimonthly magazine covering special events across North America, including festivals, fairs, auto shows, home shows, trade shows, etc., and attractions including museums, amusement parks, and zoos. Covers 15 categories of shows/events. Byline given. Buys first rights. Submit seasonal material 3 months in advance. Accepts queries by mail. Sample copy and writer's guidelines free.

Nonfiction How-to, interview/profile, new product, event review. Special issues: Annual special event directory, covering over 38,000 events. No submissions unrelated to selling at events. Query. Length: 400-750 words. **Pays $2.50/column inch.**

Reprints Send photocopy of article and information about when and where the article previously appeared.

Photos Send photos with submission. Reviews contact sheets. Buys one-time rights. Offers $20/photo. Captions required.

Columns/Departments Five columns monthly (dealing with background of event, special events, and attractions, or unique facets of industry in North America). Length: 250-500 words. Query with published clips. **Pays $3/column inch.**

$ $ GIFTWARE NEWS

Talcott Corp., 20 W. Kinzie, 12th Floor, Chicago IL 60610. (312)849-2220. Fax: (312)849-2174. **Contact:** John Saxtan, editor-in-chief. **20% freelance written.** Monthly magazine covering gifts, collectibles, and tabletops for giftware retailers. Estab. 1976. Circ. 35,000. Pays on publication. Publishes ms an average of 2 months after acceptance. Byline given. Buys all rights. Submit seasonal material 6 months in advance. Responds in 2 months to mss. Sample copy for $5.

Nonfiction How-to (sell, display), new product. **Buys 50 mss/year.** Query with published clips or send complete ms. Length: 1,500-2,000 words. **Pays $400-500 for assigned articles; $200-300 for unsolicited articles.**

Photos Send photos with submission. Reviews 4×5 transparencies, 5×7 prints, electronic images. Offers no additional payment for photos accepted with ms. Identification of subjects required.

Columns/Departments Stationery, giftbaskets, collectibles, holiday, merchandise, tabletop, wedding market and display—all for the gift retailer. Length: 1,500-2,500 words. **Buys 10 mss/year.** Send complete ms. **Pays $100-250.**

Tips "We are not looking so much for general journalists but rather experts in particular fields who can also write."

$ $ NEW AGE RETAILER

Continuity Publishing, 1300 N. State St., #105, Bellingham WA 98225. (800)463-9243. Fax: (360)676-0932. E-mail: ray@newageretailer.com. Website: www.newageretailer.com. **Contact:** Ray Hemachandra, editor-in-chief. **60% freelance written.** Bimonthly magazine for retailers of spiritual and New Age books, music, and giftware. "The goal of the articles in *New Age Retailer* is usefulness—we strive to give store owners and managers practical, in-depth information they can begin using immediately. We have 3 categories of articles: retail business methods that give solid information about the various aspects of running an independent store; inventory articles that discuss a particular New Age subject or trend; and education articles that help storeowners and managers gain knowledge and stay current in New Age subjects." Estab. 1987. Circ. 10,000. Pays on publication. Publishes ms an average of 4 months after acceptance. Byline given. Offers 10% kill fee. Buys first North American serial, second serial (reprint), simultaneous, electronic rights. Editorial lead time 4 months. Submit seasonal material 4 months in advance. Accepts queries by mail, e-mail, fax, phone. Accepts simultaneous submissions. Responds in 1 month to queries; 2 months to mss. Sample copy for $5. Writer's guidelines online.

Nonfiction Book excerpts, how-to, interview/profile, new product, opinion, personal experience, technical, business principles, spiritual. No self-promotion for writer's company or product. Writer must understand independent retailing or New Age subjects. **Buys approximately 25 mss/year.** Query with published clips. Length: 2,500-3,500 words. **Pays $150-350 for assigned articles; $100-300 for unsolicited articles.**

Photos State availability of or send photos with submission. Reviews 2x3 minimum size prints, digital images at 300 dpi. Buys one-time rights. Negotiates payment individually. Captions required.

Tips "Describe your expertise in independent retailing or the New Age market and independent retailing. Have an idea for an article ready to pitch. Promise only what you can deliver."

$ $ NICHE

The Magazine For Craft Gallery Retailers, The Rosen Group, 3000 Chestnut Ave., Suite 304, Baltimore MD 21211. (410)889-3093. Fax: (410)243-7089. E-mail: hoped@rosengrp.com. **Contact:** Hope Daniels, editor-in-chief. **80% freelance written.** Quarterly trade magazine for the progressive craft gallery retailer. Each issue includes retail gallery profiles, store design trends, management techniques, financial information, and merchandising strategies for small business owners, as well as articles about craft artists and craft mediums. Estab. 1988. Circ. 25,000. Pays on publication. Publishes ms an average of 9 months after acceptance. Byline given. Buys first North American serial rights. Editorial lead time 9 months. Submit seasonal material 1 year in advance. Accepts queries by mail, e-mail, fax. Responds in 2 months to queries; 2 months to mss. Sample copy for $3.

Nonfiction *Niche* is looking for in-depth articles on store security, innovative merchandising/display, design trends, or marketing and promotion. Stories of interest to independent retailers, such as gallery owners, may be submitted. Interview/profile, photo feature, articles targeted to independent retailers and small business owners. **Buys 20-28 mss/year.** Query with published clips. **Pays $300-700.** Sometimes pays expenses of writers on assignment.

Photos Send photos with submission. Reviews 4×5 transparencies, slides, e-images. Negotiates payment individually. Captions required.

Columns/Departments Retail Details (short items at the front of the book, general retail information); Artist Profiles (biographies of American Craft Artists); Retail Resources (including book/video/seminar reviews and educational opportunities pertaining to retailers). Query with published clips. **Pays $25-100.**

$O&A MARKETING NEWS

KAL Publications, Inc., 559 S. Harbor Blvd., Suite A, Anaheim CA 92805. (714)563-9300. Fax: (714)563-9310. E-mail: kathy@kalpub.com. Website: www.kalpub.com. **Contact:** Kathy Laderman, editor-in-chief. **3% freelance written.** Bimonthly tabloid. *"O&A Marketing News* is editorially directed to people engaged in the distribution, merchandising, installation, and servicing of gasoline, oil, TBA, quick lube, carwash, convenience store, alternative fuel, and automotive aftermarket products in the 13 Western states." Estab. 1966. Circ. 7,500. Pays on publication. Publishes ms an average of 2 months after acceptance. Byline sometimes given. Buys first, electronic rights. Editorial lead time 1 month. Submit seasonal material 1 month in advance. Accepts queries by mail, e-mail, fax. Accepts simultaneous submissions. Responds in 2 months to queries; 2 months to mss. Sample copy for 9×13 SAE and 10 first-class stamps. Writer's guidelines not available.

Nonfiction Interview/profile, photo feature, industry news. Nothing that doesn't pertain to the petroleum marketing industry in the 13 Western states. **Buys 35 mss/year.** Send complete ms. Length: 100-500 words. **Pays $1.25/column inch.**

Photos State availability of or send photos with submission. Reviews contact sheets, 4×6 prints. electronic rights. Offers $5/photo. Captions, identification of subjects required.

Columns/Departments Oregon News (petroleum marketing news in state of Oregon). **Buys 7 mss/year.** Send complete ms. **Pays $1.25/column inch.**

Fillers Gags to be illustrated by cartoonist, short humor. **Buys 7/year.** Length: 1-200 words. **Pays column inch.**

Tips "Seeking Western industry news pertaining to the petroleum marketing industry. It can be something simple—like a new gas station or quick lube opening. News from 'outlying' states such as Montana, Idaho, Wyoming, New Mexico, and Hawaii is always needed—but any timely, topical news-oriented stories will be considered."

N $ $ $ $OPERATIONS & FULFILLMENT

Primedia, Inc., 11 Riverbend Dr. S., P.O. Box 4949, Stamford CT 06907-2524. (203)358-4106. E-mail: barnn@primediabusiness.com. Website: www.opsandfulfillment.com. **Contact:** Barbara Arnn, managing editor. **25% freelance written.** Monthly magazine covering catalog/direct mail operations. *"Operations & Fulfillment (O&F)* is a monthly publication that offers practical solutions for catalog online, and direct response operations management. The magazine covers such critical areas as material handling, bar coding, facility planning, transportation, call centers, warehouse management, information systems, online fulfillment and human resources." Estab. 1993. Circ. 17,600. Pays on publication. Publishes ms an average of 2 months after acceptance. Buys first North American serial rights. Editorial lead time 2 months. Accepts queries by mail, e-mail, phone. Responds in 1 week to queries. Sample copy and writer's guidelines free.

Nonfiction Book excerpts, how-to, interview/profile, new product, technical. **Buys 4-6 mss/year.** Query with published clips. Length: 2,500-3,000 words. **Pays $1,000-1,800.**

Photos "In addition to the main article, you must include at least one sidebar of about 400 words that contains a detailed example or case study of how a direct-to-customer catalog company implements or benefits from the process you're writing about; a check list or set of practical guidelines (e.g., "Twelve Ways to Ship Smarter") that describe how to implement what you suggest in the article; supporting materials such as flow charts, graphs, diagrams, illustrations and photographs (these must be clearly labeled and footnoted); and an author biography of no more than 75 words." Send photos with submission. Captions, identification of subjects required.

Tips "Writers need some knowledge of the direct-to-customer industry. They should be able to deal clearly with highly technical material; provide attention to detail and painstaking research."

PARTY & PAPER RETAILER

107 Mill Plain Rd., Suite 204, Danbury CT 06811-6100. (203)730-4090. Fax: (203)730-4094. E-mail: editor@partypaper.com. Website: www.partypaper.com. **Contact:** Nicholas Messina, Jr., managing editor. **90% freelance written.** Monthly magazine covering "every aspect of how to do business better for owners of party and fine

stationery shops. Tips and how-tos on display, marketing, success stories, merchandising, operating costs, e-commerce, retail technology, etc." Estab. 1986. Circ. 20,000. Pays on publication. Offers 15% kill fee. Buys first North American serial rights. Editorial lead time 6 months. Submit seasonal material 6 months in advance. Accepts queries by mail, e-mail, fax. Responds in 2 months to queries. Sample copy for $6.

○→ Especially interested in news items on party retail industry for our Press Pages. Also, new column on Internet retailing ("Cyberlink") which covers all www-related topics.

Nonfiction Book excerpts, how-to (retailing related), new product. No articles written in first person. **Buys 100 mss/year.** Query with published clips. Length: 800-1,800 words. Pays phone expenses only of writers on assignment.

Reprints Send tearsheet or photocopy of article and information about when and where the article previously appeared.

Photos State availability with submission. Reviews transparencies. Buys one-time rights. Negotiates payment individually. Captions, identification of subjects required.

Columns/Departments Shop Talk (successful party/stationery store profile), 1,800 words; Storekeeping (selling, employees, market, running store), 800 words; Cash Flow (anything finance related), 800 words. **Buys 30 mss/year.** Query with published clips. **Payment varies.**

$ $ SPECIALTY COFFEE RETAILER

The Coffee Business Monthly, Adams Business Media, 833 W. Jackson, 7th Floor, Chicago IL 60607. (773)881-9273. Fax: (773)881-9274. E-mail: jbanks@aip.com. Website: www.specialty-coffee.com. **Contact:** Jennifer Banks, editor-in-chief. **60% freelance written.** Monthly magazine covering coffee—retail and roasting, tea. "*Specialty Coffee Retailer* is the business monthly for the specialty coffee industry. The magazine provides practical business information for the profitable operation of a coffeehouse, cart/kiosk/drive-through, or tea house. Featured topics include business management and finance, marketing and promotion, site selection, store design, equipment selection and maintenance, drink preparation, tea trends, new products and more." Estab. 1994. Circ. 7,500. Pays on publication. Publishes ms an average of 2 months after acceptance. Byline given. Buys first North American serial, electronic rights. Editorial lead time 2 months. Submit seasonal material 5 months in advance. Accepts queries by mail, e-mail, fax. Accepts simultaneous submissions. Sample copy by e-mail.

Nonfiction How-to (select a roaster, blend coffees, purchse tea, market chai). No opinion, essays, book reviews, humor, personal experience. **Buys 36 mss/year.** Query with published clips. Length: 1,800-2,500 words. **Pays $300-425.** Sometimes pays expenses of writers on assignment.

Photos Send photos with submission. Reviews transparencies, 3×5 prints. Offers no additional payment for photos accepted with ms.

Tips "Be willing to contact industry experts for inclusion in stories."

$ $ TRAVEL GOODS SHOWCASE

The source for luggage, business cases, and accessories, Travel Goods Association, 5 Vaughn Dr., Suite 105, Princeton NJ 08540. (609)720-1200. Fax: (609)720-0620. E-mail: john@travel-goods.org. Website: www.travel-goods.org. Editor: Michele M. Pittenger. **Contact:** John Misiano, senior editor. **5-10% freelance written.** Magazine published 5 times/year. covering travel goods, accessories, trends, and new products. "*Travel Goods Showcase* contains articles for retailers, dealers, manufacturers, and suppliers, about luggage, business cases, personal leather goods, handbags, and accessories. Special articles report on trends in fashion, promotions, selling and marketing techniques, industry statistics, and other educational and promotional improvements and advancements." Estab. 1975. Circ. 11,500. **Pays on acceptance.** Publishes ms an average of 2 months after acceptance. Byline given. Offers $50 kill fee. Editorial lead time 3 months. Submit seasonal material 2 months in advance. Accepts queries by mail, e-mail. Responds in 2 weeks to queries; 1 month to mss. Sample copy and writer's guidelines free.

Nonfiction Interview/profile, new product, technical, travel, retailer profiles with photos. "No manufacturer profiles." **Buys 3 mss/year.** Query with published clips. Length: 1,200-1,600 words. **Pays $200-500.**

Ⓝ $ $ $ VERTICAL SYSTEMS RESELLER

The news source for channel management, Edgell Communications, Inc., 4 Middlebury Blvd., Suite 1, Randolph NJ 07869-1111. (973)252-0100. Fax: (973)252-9020. E-mail: dbreeman@edgellmail.com. Website: www.vertical systemsreseller.com. Publisher/Editor: Michael Kachmar. **Contact:** Daniel Breeman, managing editor. **60% freelance written.** Monthly journal covering channel strategies that build business. Estab. 1992. Circ. 30,000. **Pays on acceptance.** Publishes ms an average of 2 months after acceptance. Byline given. Editorial lead time 3 months. Accepts queries by mail, e-mail, fax. Accepts simultaneous submissions. Responds in 2 weeks to queries; 2 months to mss. Sample copy online.

Nonfiction Interview/profile, opinion, technical, technology/channel issues. **Buys 36 mss/year.** Query with published clips. Length: 1,000-1,700 words. **Pays $200-800 for assigned articles.** Sometimes pays expenses of writers on assignment.

Photos Send photos with submission. Offers no additional payment for photos accepted with ms. Identification of subjects, model releases required.

SPORT TRADE

$ $ AQUATICS INTERNATIONAL

Hanley-Wood, LLC, 4160 Wilshire Blvd., Los Angeles CA 90010. Fax: (323)801-4986. E-mail: gthill@hanleywood.com. Website: www.aquaticsintl.com. **Contact:** Gary Thill, editor. Magazine published 10 times/year covering public swimming pools and waterparks. Estab. 1989. Circ. 30,000. Pays on publication. Publishes ms an average of 3 months after acceptance. Byline given. international rights in perpetuity and makes work-for-hire assignments. Editorial lead time 3 months. Responds in 1 month to queries. Sample copy for $10.50.

Nonfiction How-to, interview/profile, technical. **Buys 6 mss/year.** Query with published clips. Length: 1,500-2,500 words. **Pays $525 for assigned articles.**

Columns/Departments Pays $250.

Tips "Send query letter with samples."

N $ $ ARROWTRADE MAGAZINE

A Magazine for Retailers, Distributors & Manufacturers of Bowhunting Equipment, Arrow Trade Publishing Corp., 3479 409th Ave. NW, Braham MN 55006. (320)396-3473. Fax: (320)396-3206. E-mail: atrade@ecenet.com. **Contact:** Tim Dehn, editor and publisher. **35% freelance written.** Bimonthly magazine covering the archery industry. "Our readers are interested in articles that help them operate their business better. They are primarily owners or managers of sporting goods stores and archery pro shops." Estab. 1996. Circ. 10,000. **Pays on acceptance.** Publishes ms an average of 2 months after acceptance. Byline given. Buys first North American serial rights. Editorial lead time 2 months. Accepts queries by mail, e-mail, fax. Responds in 2 weeks to queries; 2 weeks to mss. Sample copy for 9×12 SAE and 10 first-class stamps. Writer's guidelines not available.

> *ArrowTrade Magazine* needs queries from veterans interested in writing for our industry audience. Our readers are primarily retailers of bowhunting equipment. "Find an unusual business combination, like someone selling archery plus cowboy boots, motorcycles, taxidermy—and submit it, 1,100-1,400 words for 'Archery Plus.'"

Nonfiction Interview/profile, new product. "Generic business articles won't work for our highly specialized audience." **Buys 21 mss/year.** Query with published clips. Length: 1,800-3,800 words. **Pays $350-550.**

Photos Send photos with submission. Reviews contact sheets, negatives, 35mm transparencies, 4×6 prints, digital photos on CD or ZIP disk. Offers no additional payment for photos accepted with ms. Captions required.

Columns/Departments Dealer Workbench (repair and tuning bows), 1,600 words; Bow Report (tests and evaluations of current models), 2,400 words; Archery Plus (short profiles of retailers who combine archery with other product lines.). **Buys 12 mss/year.** Query with published clips. **Pays $250-375.**

Tips "Our readers are hungry for articles that help them decide what to stock and how to do a better job selling or servicing it. Articles needed typically fall into one of these categories: business profiles on outstanding retailers, manufacturers or distributors; equipment articles that cover categories of gear, citing trends in the market and detailing why products have been designed a certain way and what type of use they're best suited for; basic business articles that help dealers do a better job of promoting their business, managing their inventory, training their staff, etc. Good interviewing skills are a must, as especially in the equipment articles we like to see a minimum of 6 sources."

N $ $ BOATING INDUSTRY INTERNATIONAL

The Management Magazine for the Recreational Marine Industry, National Trade Publications, 414 S. Manlius St., Fayetteville NY 13066. (315)637-5726. Fax: (315)637-6229. E-mail: lwalz@affinitygroup.com. Website: www.boating-industry.com. **Contact:** Liz Walz, executive editor. **10-20% freelance written.** Bimonthly magazine covering recreational marine industry management. "We write for those in the industry—not the consumer. Our subject is the business of boating. All of our articles must be analytical and predictive, telling our readers where the industry is going, rather than where it's been." Estab. 1929. Circ. 23,000. **Pays on acceptance.** Publishes ms an average of 2 months after acceptance. Byline given. Offers 50% kill fee. Buys first, electronic rights. Editorial lead time 2 months. Submit seasonal material 2 months in advance. Accepts queries by mail, e-mail, fax. Responds in 1 month to queries. Sample copy online. Writer's guidelines free.

> "We actively solicit items for our electronic news service. See the News Flash section of our website. This is an excellent way to break in, especially for writers based outside the U.S."

Nonfiction Technical, business. **Buys 30 mss/year.** Query with published clips. Length: 250-2,500 words. **Pays $25-250.** Sometimes pays expenses of writers on assignment.

Photos State availability with submission. Reviews 2×2 transparencies, 4×6 prints. Buys one-time rights. Negotiates payment individually. Captions, identification of subjects required.

$ $CROSSFIRE

Paintball Digest, 570 Mantus Rd., P.O. Box 690, Sewell NJ 08080. (888)834-6026. E-mail: editor@paintball2xtremes.com. Website: www.crossfiremag.com. **Contact:** John Amodea, executive editor. **100% freelance written.** Monthly magazine covering paintball sport. *"Crossfire* will cover all aspects of the paintball industry from tactics to safety."* Pays on publication. Byline given. Makes work-for-hire assignments. Editorial lead time 1 year. Submit seasonal material 2 months in advance. Accepts queries by mail, e-mail, fax. Accepts simultaneous submissions. Responds in 2 weeks to queries. Sample copy for free.

Nonfiction How-to, humor, interview/profile, new product, personal experience, photo feature, technical, travel, Tournament coverage, industry news. **Buys 1-3 mss/year.** Send complete ms. Length: 700-1,900 words. **Pays 7-22¢/word.**

Photos Send photos with submission. Reviews negatives. Buys all rights. Negotiates payment individually. Captions, identification of subjects, model releases required.

Fillers Facts, gags to be illustrated by cartoonist, newsbreaks. **Buys 24/year.** Length: 25-100 words. **Pays 7-22¢/word.**

Tips "Paintball or extreme sport participation is a plus."

$ $FITNESS MANAGEMENT

Issues and Solutions in Fitness Services, Leisure Publications, Inc., 4160 Wilshire Blvd., Los Angeles CA 90010. (323)964-4800. Fax: (323)964-4835. E-mail: edit@fitnessmanagement.com. Website: www.fitnessmanagement.com. Publisher: Chris Ballard. **Contact:** Ronale Tucker Rhodes, editor. **50% freelance written.** Monthly magazine. "Readers are owners, managers, and program directors of physical fitness facilities. *FM* helps them run their enterprises safely, efficiently, and profitably. Ethical and professional positions in health, nutrition, sports medicine, management, etc., are consistent with those of established national bodies." Estab. 1985. Circ. 26,000. Pays on publication. Publishes ms an average of 5 months after acceptance. Byline given. Offers 50% kill fee. Buys all rights (all articles published in *FM* are also published and archived on its website). Submit seasonal material 6 months in advance. Accepts queries by mail, e-mail, fax. Responds in 3 months to queries. Sample copy for $5. Writer's guidelines for #10 SASE.

Nonfiction How-to (manage fitness center and program), new product (no pay), photo feature (facilities/programs), technical, News of fitness research and major happenings in fitness industry. No exercise instructions or general ideas without examples of fitness businesses that have used them successfully. **Buys 50 mss/year.** Query. Length: 750-2,000 words. **Pays $60-300 for assigned articles.** Pays expenses of writers on assignment.

Photos Send photos with submission. Reviews contact sheets, 2×2 and 4×5 transparencies, prefers glossy prints, 5×7 to 8×10. Captions, model releases required.

The online magazine carries original content not found in the print edition. Includes sample articles.

Tips "We seek writers who are expert in a business or science field related to the fitness-service industry or who are experienced in the industry. Be current with the state of the art/science in business and fitness and communicate it in human terms (avoid intimidating academic language; tell the story of how this was learned and/or cite examples or quotes of people who have applied the knowledge successfully)."

$ $GOLF COURSE MANAGEMENT

Golf Course Superintendents Association of America, 1421 Research Park Dr., Lawrence KS 66049. (785)841-2240. Fax: (785)932-3665. E-mail: shollister@gcsaa.org. Website: www.gcsaa.org. **Contact:** Scott Hollister, editor. **85% freelance written.** Monthly magazine covering the golf course superintendent. "*GCM* helps the golf course superintendent become more efficient in all aspects of their job." Estab. 1924. Circ. 40,000. **Pays on acceptance.** Publishes ms an average of 6 months after acceptance. Byline given. Buys first North American serial rights, Web rights, and makes work-for-hire assignments. Editorial lead time 6 months. Submit seasonal material 6 months in advance. Accepts simultaneous submissions. Responds in 3 weeks to queries; 1 month to mss. Sample copy and writer's guidelines free.

Nonfiction How-to, interview/profile. No articles about playing golf. **Buys 40 mss/year.** Query. Length: 1,500-2,500 words. **Pays $300-450 for assigned articles.** Sometimes pays expenses of writers on assignment.

Photos Send photos with submission. Buys all rights. Offers no additional payment for photos accepted with ms. Identification of subjects required.

Tips "Writers should have prior knowledge of the golf course superintendent profession."

IDEA FITNESS JOURNAL

(formerly *Idea Health & Fitness Source*), IDEA Health & Fitness Association, Inc., 10455 Pacific Center Court, San Diego CA 92121. (858)535-8979. Fax: (858)535-8234. E-mail: websters@ideafit.com. Website: www.ideafit. com. **Contact:** Sandy Todd Webster, editor-in-chief. **70% freelance written.** Magazine published 10 times/ year "for fitness professionals—personal trainers, group fitness instructors, and studio and health club owners— covering topics such as exercise science, nutrition, injury prevention, entrepreneurship in fitness, fitness-oriented research, and program design." Estab. 1984. Circ. 20,000. **Pays on acceptance.** Publishes ms an average of 4 months after acceptance. Byline given. Buys all rights. Accepts queries by mail, e-mail, fax. Accepts simultaneous submissions. Responds in 2 months to queries. Sample copy for $5. Writer's guidelines online.

Nonfiction How-to, technical. No general information on fitness; our readers are pros who need detailed information. **Buys 15 mss/year.** Query. Length: 1,000-3,000 words. **Payment varies.**

Photos State availability with submission. Buys all rights. Offers no additional payment for photos with ms. Model releases required.

Columns/Departments Research (detailed, specific info; must be written by expert), 750-1,500 words; Industry News (short reports on research, programs, and conferences), 150-300 words; Fitness Handout (exercise and nutrition info for participants), 750 words. **Buys 80 mss/year.** Query. **Payment varies.**

Tips "We don't accept fitness information for the consumer audience on topics such as why exercise is good for you. Writers who have specific knowledge of, or experience working in, the fitness industry have an edge."

$ $ NSGA RETAIL FOCUS

National Sporting Goods Association, 1601 Feehanville Dr., Suite 300, Mt. Prospect IL 60056-6035. (847)296-6742. Fax: (847)391-9827. E-mail: info@nsga.org. Website: www.nsga.org. **Contact:** Larry N. Weindruch, editor/publisher. **20% freelance written.** Works with a small number of new/unpublished writers each year. Bimonthly magazine. "*NSGA Retail Focus* serves as a bimonthly trade journal for sporting goods retailers who are members of the association." Estab. 1948. Circ. 2,000. Pays on publication. Publishes ms an average of 1 month after acceptance. Byline given. Offers kill fee. Buys first, second serial (reprint), electronic rights. Submit seasonal material 6 months in advance. Accepts queries by e-mail. Sample copy for 9×12 SAE and 5 first-class stamps.

Nonfiction Interview/profile, photo feature. "No articles written without sporting goods retail businesspeople in mind as the audience. In other words, no generic articles sent to several industries." **Buys 12 mss/year.** Query with published clips. **Pays $150-300.** Sometimes pays expenses of writers on assignment.

Photos State availability with submission. Reviews high-resolution, digital images. Buys one-time rights. Payment negotiable.

Columns/Departments Personnel Management (succinct tips on hiring, motivating, firing, etc.); Sales Management (in-depth tips to improve sales force performance); Retail Management (detailed explanation of merchandising/inventory control); Store Design; Visual Merchandising; all 1,500 words. **Buys 12 mss/year.** Query. **Pays $150-300.**

$ $ PADDLE DEALER

The Trade Magazine for Paddlesports, Paddlesport Publishing, Inc., P.O. Box 775450, Steamboat Springs CO 80477. (970)879-1450. Fax: (970)870-1404. E-mail: matt@paddlermagazine.com. Website: www.paddlermagazine.com. Editor: Eugene Buchanan. **Contact:** Matt Hansen, managing editor. **70% freelance written.** Quarterly magazine covering the canoeing, kayaking and rafting industry. Estab. 1993. Circ. 7,500. Pays on publication. Publishes ms an average of 6 months after acceptance. Byline given. first North American serial and one-time electronic rights. Editorial lead time 2 months. Submit seasonal material 6 months in advance. Accepts queries by mail, e-mail, fax. Accepts simultaneous submissions. Responds in 3 months to queries. Sample copy for 8½×11 SAE and $1.78. Writer's guidelines for #10 SASE.

Nonfiction New product, technical, business advice. **Buys 8 mss/year.** Query or send complete ms. Length: 2,300 words. **Pays 15-20¢/word.** Sometimes pays expenses of writers on assignment.

Photos State availability with submission. Reviews transparencies, 5×7 prints. Buys one-time rights.

Columns/Departments Profiles, how-to, great ideas, computer corner. **Buys 12 mss/year.** Query or send complete ms. **Pays 10-20¢/word.**

$ $ POOL & SPA NEWS

Hanley-Wood, LLC, 4160 Wilshire Blvd., Los Angeles CA 90010. (323)801-4972. Fax: (323)801-4986. E-mail: etaylor@hanleywood.com. Website: poolspanews.com. **Contact:** Erika Taylor, editor. **15% freelance written.** Semimonthly magazine covering the swimming pool and spa industry for builders, retail stores, and service firms. Estab. 1960. Circ. 16,300. Pays on publication. Publishes ms an average of 2 months after acceptance. Buys all rights. Accepts queries by mail, e-mail. Responds in 1 month to queries. Sample copy for $5 and 9×12 SAE and 11 first-class stamps.

Trade Journals

Nonfiction Interview/profile, technical. Send résumé with published clips. Length: 500-2,000 words. **Pays $150-500.** Pays expenses of writers on assignment.

Reprints Send ms with rights for sale noted and information about when and where the material previously appeared. Payment varies.

Photos Payment varies.

Columns/Departments Payment varies.

■ The online magazine carries original content not found in the print edition. Contact: Margi Millunzi, online editor.

$ $REFEREE

Referee Enterprises, Inc., P.O. Box 161, Franksville WI 53126. Fax: (262)632-5460. E-mail: jarehart@referee.com. Website: www.referee.com. Editor: Bill Topp. **Contact:** Jim Arehart, associate editor. **75% freelance written.** Monthly magazine covering sports officiating. "Referee is a magazine for and read by sports officials of all kinds with a focus on baseball, basketball, football, softball, and soccer officiating." Estab. 1976. Circ. 40,000. **Pays on acceptance.** Publishes ms an average of 6 months after acceptance. Byline given. Kill fee negotiable. Buys all rights. Editorial lead time 6 months. Accepts queries by mail, e-mail, fax. Responds in 2 weeks to queries; 1 month to mss. Sample copy for #10 SASE. Writer's guidelines online.

Nonfiction Book excerpts, essays, historical/nostalgic, how-to (sports officiating related), humor, interview/profile, opinion, photo feature, technical (as it relates to sports officiating). "We don't want to see articles with themes not relating to sport officiating. General sports articles, although of interest to us, will not be published." **Buys 40 mss/year.** Query with published clips. Length: 500-2,500 words. **Pays $100-400.** Sometimes pays expenses of writers on assignment.

Photos State availability with submission. Reviews contact sheets, negatives, transparencies, prints. Purchase of rights negotiable. Offers $35-40 per photo. Identification of subjects required.

Tips "Query first and be persistent. We may not like your idea but that doesn't mean we won't like your next one. Professionalism pays off."

$ $SKI AREA MANAGEMENT

Beardsley Publications, P.O. Box 644, Woodbury CT 06798. (203)263-0888. Fax: (203)266-0452. E-mail: samedit@saminfo.com. Website: www.saminfo.com. **Contact:** Rick Kahl, editor. **85% freelance written.** Bimonthly magazine covering everything involving the management and development of ski resorts. "We are the publication of record for the North American ski industry. We report on new ideas, developments, marketing, and regulations with regard to ski and snowboard resorts. Everyone from the CEO to the lift operator of winter resorts reads our magazine to stay informed about the people and procedures that make ski areas successful." Estab. 1962. Circ. 4,500. Pays on publication. Byline given. Offers kill fee. Buys all rights. Editorial lead time 2 months. Submit seasonal material 3 months in advance. Accepts queries by mail, e-mail. Responds in 2 weeks to queries. Sample copy for 9×12 SAE with $3 postage or online. Writer's guidelines for #10 SASE.

Nonfiction Historical/nostalgic, how-to, interview/profile, new product, opinion, personal experience, technical. "We don't want anything that does not specifically pertain to resort operations, management, or financing." **Buys 25-40 mss/year.** Query. Length: 500-2,500 words. **Pays $50-400.**

Reprints Accepts previously published submissions.

Photos Send photos with submission. Reviews transparencies, prints. Buys one-time rights or all rights. Offers no additional payment for photos accepted with ms. Identification of subjects required.

■ The online magazine carries original content not found in the print edition. Contact: Olivia Rowan.

Tips "Know what you are writing about. We are read by people dedicated to skiing and snowboarding and to making the resort experience the best possible for their customers. It is a trade publication read by professionals."

$ $THOROUGHBRED TIMES

Thoroughbred Times Co., Inc., 2008 Mercer Rd., P.O. Box 8237, Lexington KY 40533. (859)260-9800. **Contact:** Mark Simon, editor. **10% freelance written.** Weekly tabloid "written for professionals who breed and/or race thoroughbreds at tracks in the U.S. Articles must help owners and breeders understand racing to help them realize a profit." Estab. 1985. Circ. 23,000. Pays on publication. Publishes ms an average of 1 month after acceptance. Byline given. Offers 50% kill fee. Buys first publication rights. Submit seasonal material 2 months in advance. Responds in 2 weeks to mss. Sample copy not available.

Nonfiction General interest, historical/nostalgic, interview/profile, technical. **Buys 52 mss/year.** Query. Length: 500-2,500 words. **Pays 10-20¢/word.** Sometimes pays expenses of writers on assignment.

Photos State availability with submission. Reviews prints. Buys one-time rights. Offers $25/photo. Identification of subjects required.

Columns/Departments Vet Topics; Business of Horses; Pedigree Profiles; Bloodstock Topics; Tax Matters; Viewpoints; Guest Commentary.

Tips "We are looking for farm stories and profiles of owners, breeders, jockeys, and trainers."

STONE, QUARRY & MINING

$ $▣ CANADIAN MINING JOURNAL

Business Information Group, 1450 Don Mills Rd., Toronto ON M3B 2X7, Canada. (416)510-6742. Fax: (416)442-2175. E-mail: jwerniuk@canadianminingjournal.com. **Contact:** Jane Werniuk, editor. **5% freelance written.** Magazine covering mining and mineral exploration by Canadian companies. *"Canadian Mining Journal* provides articles and information of practical use to those who work in the technical, administrative, and supervisory aspects of exploration, mining, and processing in the Canadian mineral exploration and mining industry." Estab. 1879. Circ. 10,000. Pays on publication. Publishes ms an average of 3 months after acceptance. Byline given. Buys one-time, electronic rights, makes work-for-hire assignments. Submit seasonal material 3 months in advance. Accepts queries by mail, e-mail, fax, phone. Responds in 1 week to queries; 1 month to mss.

Nonfiction Opinion, technical, operation descriptions. **Buys 6 mss/year.** Query with published clips. Length: 500-1,400 words. **Pays $100-600.** Pays expenses of writers on assignment.

Photos State availability with submission. Reviews 4×6 prints or high-resolution files. Buys one-time rights. Negotiates payment individually. Captions, identification of subjects, credits required.

Columns/Departments Guest editorial (opinion on controversial subject related to mining industry), 600 words. **Buys 3 mss/year.** Query with published clips. **Pays $150.**

Tips "I need articles about mine sites that it would be expensive/difficult for me to reach. I also need to know that the writer is competent to understand and describe the technology in an interesting way."

$ COAL PEOPLE MAGAZINE

Al Skinner, Inc., Dept. WM, 629 Virginia St. W, P.O. Box 6247, Charleston WV 25362. (304)342-4129. Fax: (304)343-3124. Editor/Publisher: Al Skinner. **Contact:** Christina Karawan, president. **50% freelance written.** Monthly magazine. "Most stories are about people or historical—either narrative or biographical on all levels of coal people, past and present—from coal execs down to grass roots miners. Most stories are upbeat—showing warmth of family or success from underground up!" Estab. 1976. Circ. 11,000. Pays on publication. Publishes ms an average of 3 months after acceptance. Byline given. Buys first, second serial (reprint) rights, makes work-for-hire assignments. Submit seasonal material 2 months in advance. Responds in 3 months to mss. Sample copy for 9×12 SAE and 10 first-class stamps.

Nonfiction Book excerpts (and film if related to coal), historical/nostalgic (coal towns, people, lifestyles), humor (including anecdotes and cartoons), interview/profile (for coal personalities), personal experience (as relates to coal mining), photo feature (on old coal towns, people, past and present). Special issues: Calendar issue for more than 300 annual coal shows, association meetings, etc. (January); Surface Mining/Reclamation Award (July); Christmas in Coal Country (December). No poetry, fiction, or environmental attacks on the coal industry. **Buys 32 mss/year.** Query with published clips. Length: 5,000 words. **Pays $90 for assigned articles.**

Reprints Send tearsheet and information about when and where the material previously appeared. Pays 50% of amount paid for an original article.

Photos Send photos with submission. Reviews contact sheets, transparencies, 5×7 prints. Buys one-time reprint rights. Captions, identification of subjects required.

Columns/Departments Editorials—anything to do with current coal issues (nonpaid); Mine'ing Our Business (bull pen column—gossip—humorous anecdotes); Coal Show Coverage (freelance photojournalist coverage of any coal function across the US). Length: 300-500 words. **Buys 10 mss/year.** Query. **Pays $50.**

Fillers Anecdotes. Length: 300 words. **Pays $35.**

Tips "We are looking for good feature articles on coal people, towns, companies—past and present, color slides (for possible cover use), and b&w photos to complement stories. Could also use a few news writers to take photos and do journalistic coverage on coal events across the country. Slant stories more toward people and less on historical. More faces and names than old town, company store photos. Include more quotes from people who lived these moments!" The following geographical areas are covered: Eastern Canada; Mexico; Europe; China; Russia; Poland; Australia; Alabama; Tennessee; Virginia; Washington; Oregon; North and South Dakota; Arizona; Colorado; Alaska; and Wyoming.

$ $ COLORED STONE

Lapidary Journal/Primedia, Inc., 60 Chestnut Ave., Suite 201, Devon PA 19333-1312. (610)964-6300. Fax: (610)293-0977. E-mail: cs_editorial@primediamags.com. Website: www.colored-stone.com. **Contact:** Morgan Beard, editor-in-chief. **50% freelance written.** Bimonthly magazine covering the colored gemstone industry. *"Colored Stone* covers all aspects of the colored gemstone (i.e., no diamonds) trade. Our readers are manufacturing jewelers and jewelry designers, gemstone dealers, miners, retail jewelers, and gemologists." Estab. 1987. Circ. 11,000. **Pays on acceptance.** Publishes ms an average of 2 months after acceptance. Byline given. Buys one-time, all rights. Editorial lead time 2 months. Submit seasonal material 4 months in advance. Accepts queries by mail, e-mail, fax. Accepts simultaneous submissions. Responds in 1 month to queries; 2 months to mss. Sample copy and writer's guidelines free. Writer's guidelines online.

Nonfiction Exposé, interview/profile, new product, technical. "No articles intended for the general public." **Buys 35-45 mss/year.** Query with published clips. Length: 400-2,200 words. **Pays $200-600.**

Photos State availability with submission. Reviews any size transparencies, 4×6 prints and up. Buys one-time rights. Offers $15-50/photo. Captions, identification of subjects, model releases required.

Tips "A background in the industry is helpful but not necessary. Please, no recycled marketing/new technology/ etc. pieces."

$ CONTEMPORARY STONE & TILE DESIGN

Business News Publishing Co., 210 Route 4 E., Suite 311, Paramus NJ 07652. (201)291-9001. Fax: (201)291-9002. E-mail: cstd@stoneworld.com. Website: www.stoneworld.com. Publisher: Alex Bachrach. **Contact:** Michael Reis, editor, or Jennifer Adams, editor. Quarterly magazine covering the full range of stone and tile design and architecture—from classic and historic spaces to current projects. Estab. 1995. Circ. 14,000. Pays on publication. Publishes ms an average of 3 months after acceptance. Byline given. Buys first rights. Submit seasonal material 6 months in advance. Responds in 3 weeks to queries. Sample copy for $10.

Nonfiction Overall features on a certain aspect of stone design/tile work, or specific articles on individual architectural projects. Interview/profile (prominent architect/designer or firm), photo feature, technical, architectural design. **Buys 8 mss/year.** Query with published clips. Length: 1,500-3,000 words. **Pays $6/column inch.** Pays expenses of writers on assignment.

Photos State availability with submission. Reviews transparencies, prints. Buys one-time rights. Pays $10/ photo accepted with ms. Captions, identification of subjects required.

Columns/Departments Upcoming Events (for the architecture and design community); Stone Classics (featuring historic architecture); question and answer session with a prominent architect or designer. Length: 1,500-2,000 words. **Pays $6/inch.**

Tips "The visual aspect of the magazine is key, so architectural photography is a must for any story. Cover the entire project, but focus on the stonework or tile work and how it relates to the rest of the space. Architects are very helpful in describing their work and often provide excellent quotes. As a relatively new magazine, we are looking for freelance submissions and are open to new feature topics. This is a narrow subject, however, so it's a good idea to speak with an editor before submitting anything."

$ $ PIT & QUARRY

Advanstar Communications, 7500 Old Oak Blvd., Cleveland OH 44130. (440)891-2607. Fax: (440)891-2675. E-mail: mkuhar@advanstar.com. Website: www.pitandquarry.com. Managing Editor: Darren Constantino. **Contact:** Mark S. Kuhar, editor. **10-20% freelance written.** Monthly magazine covering nonmetallic minerals, mining, and crushed stone. Audience has "knowledge of construction-related markets, mining, minerals processing, etc." Estab. 1916. Circ. 25,000. **Pays on acceptance.** Publishes ms an average of 6 months after acceptance. Byline given. Buys first North American serial rights. Editorial lead time 6 months. Accepts queries by mail, e-mail, fax, phone. Accepts simultaneous submissions. Responds in 1 month to queries; 4 months to mss. Sample copy for 9×12 SAE and 4 first-class stamps.

Nonfiction How-to, interview/profile, new product, technical. No humor or inspirational articles. **Buys 12-15 mss/year.** Query. Length: 1,000-1,500 words. **Pays $250-700 for assigned articles; $250-500 for unsolicited articles.** Pays writers with contributor copies or other premiums for simple news items, etc. Sometimes pays expenses of writers on assignment.

Photos State availability with submission. Buys one-time rights. Offers no additional payment for photos accepted with ms. Identification of subjects, model releases required.

Columns/Departments Brand New; Techwatch; E-business; Software corner; Equipment Showcase. Length: 250-750 words. **Buys 5-6 mss/year.** Query. **Pays $250-300.**

■ The online magazine sometimes carries original content not found in the print edition.

Tips "Be familiar with quarry operations (crushed stone or sand and gravel), as opposed to coal or metallic minerals mining. Know construction markets. We always need equipment-focused features on specific quarry operations."

$ STONE WORLD

Business News Publishing Co., 210 Route 4 E., Suite 311, Paramus NJ 07652. (201)291-9001. Fax: (201)291-9002. E-mail: info@stoneworld.com. Website: www.stoneworld.com. **Contact:** Michael Reis, editor, or Jennifer Adams, managing editor. Monthly magazine on natural building stone for producers and users of granite, marble, limestone, slate, sandstone, onyx and other natural stone products. Estab. 1984. Circ. 21,000. Pays on publication. Publishes ms an average of 4 months after acceptance. Byline given. Buys first North American serial, second serial (reprint) rights. Submit seasonal material 6 months in advance. Responds in 2 months to queries. Sample copy for $10.

Nonfiction How-to (fabricate and/or install natural building stone), interview/profile, photo feature, technical, architectural design, artistic stone uses, statistics, factory profile, equipment profile, trade show review. **Buys 10 mss/year.** Query with or without published clips or send complete ms. Length: 600-3,000 words. **Pays $6/ column inch.** Pays expenses of writers on assignment.

Reprints Send photocopy with rights for sale noted and information about when and where the material previously appeared. Pays 50% of amount paid for an original article.

Photos State availability with submission. Reviews transparencies, prints, slides, digital images. Buys one-time rights. Pays $10/photo accepted with ms. Captions, identification of subjects required.

Columns/Departments News (pertaining to stone or design community); New Literature (brochures, catalogs, books, videos, etc., about stone); New Products (stone products); New Equipment (equipment and machinery for working with stone); Calendar (dates and locations of events in stone and design communities). Query or send complete ms. Length 300-600 words. **Pays $6/inch.**

Tips "Articles about architectural stone design accompanied by professional color photographs and quotes from designing firms are often published, especially when one unique aspect of the stone selection or installation is highlighted. We are also interested in articles about new techniques of quarrying and/or fabricating natural building stone."

TOY, NOVELTY & HOBBY

$ $ MODEL RETAILER

Resources for Successful Hobby Retailing, Kalmbach Publishing Co., 21027 Crossroads Circle, Waukesha WI 53187-1612. (262)796-8776. Fax: (262)796-1383. E-mail: staff@modelretailer.com. Website: www.modelretaile r.com. **Contact:** Mark Savage, editor. **5% freelance written.** Monthly magazine. "*Model Retailer* covers the business of hobbies, from financial and shop management issues to industry trends and the latest product releases. Our goal is to provide hobby shop entrepreneurs with the tools and information they need to be successful retailers." Estab. 1987. Circ. 6,000 (controlled circulation). **Pays on acceptance.** Publishes ms an average of 3 months after acceptance. Byline given. Buys first rights. Editorial lead time 3 months. Submit seasonal material 6 months in advance. Accepts queries by mail, e-mail, fax. Sample copy and writer's guidelines free. Writer's guidelines online.

Nonfiction How-to (business), new product. "No articles that do not have a strong hobby or small retail component." **Buys 2-3 mss/year.** Query with published clips. Length: 750-2,000 words. **Pays $250-500 for assigned articles; $100-250 for unsolicited articles.** Sometimes pays expenses of writers on assignment.

Photos State availability with submission. Reviews 4×6 prints. Buys one-time rights. Negotiates payment individually. Captions, identification of subjects required.

Columns/Departments Shop Management; Sales Marketing; Technology Advice; Industry Trends, all 500-750 words. **Buys 2-3 mss/year.** Query with published clips. **Pays $100-200.**

PEN WORLD INTERNATIONAL

World Publications, Inc., 3946 Glade Valley Dr., Kingwood TX 77339-2059. (281)359-4363. Fax: (281)359-5748. E-mail: editor@penworld.com. Website: www.penworld.com. Editor: Marie Picon. Magazine published 7 times/year. Published for the collectors and connoiseurs of contemporary and vintage writing instruments. Circ. 105,994. Sample copy not available.

TRANSPORTATION

BUS CONVERSIONS

The First and Foremost Bus Converters Magazine, MAK Publishing, 7246 Garden Grove Blvd., Westminster CA 92683. (714)799-0062. Fax: (714)799-0042. E-mail: editor@busconversions.com. Website: www.busconversion s.com. **Contact:** Tiffany Christian, editor. **95% freelance written.** Monthly magazine covering the bus conversion industry. Estab. 1992. Circ. 10,000. Pays on publication. Buys first North American serial rights. Accepts queries by mail, e-mail.

Nonfiction Each month, *Bus Conversions* publishes a minimum of 2 coach reviews, usually anecdotal stories told by those who have completed their own bus conversion. Publishes some travel/destination stories (all of which are related to bus/RV travel). Looking for articles on engine swaps, exterior painting, and furniture. How-to (articles on the electrical, plumbing, mechanical, decorative, and structural aspects of bus conversions; buses that are converted into RVs).

Trade Journals

Photos Include color photos (glossy) with submission. Photos not returned unless an SASE is included.
Columns/Departments Industry Update; Products of Interest; Ask the Experts; One For the Road; Road Fix.
Tips "Most of our writers are our readers. Knowledge of bus conversions and the associated lifestyle is a prerequisite."

$ $ CLEAR DAY LIMOUSINE DIGEST

Digest Publications, 29 Fostertown Rd., Medford NJ 08055. (609)953-4900. Fax: (609)953-4905. E-mail: info@limodigest.com. Website: www.limodigest.com. **Contact:** Susan Keehn, editor. **33% freelance written.** Monthly magazine covering ground transportation. "*Limousine Digest* is 'the voice of the luxury ground transportation industry.' We cover all aspects of ground transportation from vehicles to operators, safety issues, and political involvement." Estab. 1990. Circ. 14,000. Pays on publication. Publishes ms an average of 2 months after acceptance. Byline given. Makes work-for-hire assignments. Editorial lead time 1 year. Submit seasonal material 2 months in advance. Accepts queries by mail, e-mail, fax, phone. Accepts simultaneous submissions. Sample copy for free.
Nonfiction Historical/nostalgic, how-to (start a company, market your product), humor, inspirational, interview/profile, new product, personal experience, photo feature, technical, travel, industry news, business. **Buys 7-9 mss/year.** Send complete ms. Length: 700-1,900 words. **Pays 15-25¢/word. Will pay authors in advertising trade-outs.**
Reprints Accepts previously published submissions.
Photos Must include photos to be considered. Send photos with submission. Reviews negatives. Buys all rights. Negotiates payment individually. Captions, identification of subjects, model releases required.
Columns/Departments New Model Showcase (new limousines, sedans, buses), 1,000 words; Player Profile (industry members profiled), 700 words; Hall of Fame (unique vehicles featured), 500-700 words; Association News (association issues), 400 words. **Buys 5 mss/year.** Query. **Pays 15-25¢/word.**

$ $ METRO MAGAZINE

Bobit Publishing Co., 3520 Challenger St., Torrance CA 90503. E-mail: info@metro-magazine.com. Website: www.metro-magazine.com. Editor: Steve Hirano. **Contact:** Joseph Campbell, managing editor. **10% freelance written.** Magazine published 10 times/year covering transit bus, passenger rail, and motorcoach operations. "*Metro Magazine* delivers business, government policy, and technology developments that are *industry specific* to public transportation." Estab. 1904. Circ. 20,500. **Pays on acceptance.** Publishes ms an average of 2 months after acceptance. Byline given. Offers 10% kill fee. Buys all rights. Editorial lead time 3 months. Submit seasonal material 3 months in advance. Accepts queries by e-mail. Responds in 2 weeks to queries; 1 month to mss. Sample copy for $8. Writer's guidelines by e-mail.
Nonfiction How-to, interview/profile (of industry figures), new product (related to transit—bus and rail—private bus), technical. **Buys 6-10 mss/year.** Query. Length: 400-1,500 words. **Pays $80-400.**
Photos State availability with submission. Buys all rights. Negotiates payment individually. Captions, identification of subjects, model releases required.
Columns/Departments Query. **Pays 20¢/word.**
■ The online magazine carries original content not found in the print edition. Contact: Joseph Campbell.

$ $ SCHOOL BUS FLEET

Bobit Publishing Co., 21061 S. Western Ave., Torrance CA 90501. (310)533-2400. Fax: (310)533-2502. E-mail: sbf@bobit.com. Website: www.schoolbusfleet.com. **Contact:** Steve Hirano, editor. **10% freelance written.** Magazine covering school transportation of K-12 population. "Most of our readers are school bus operators, public and private." Estab. 1965. Circ. 24,000. **Pays on acceptance.** Publishes ms an average of 3 months after acceptance. Byline given. Offers 25% kill fee or $50. Buys first North American serial rights. Editorial lead time 3 months. Submit seasonal material 3 months in advance. Accepts queries by mail, e-mail, fax. Responds in 1 month to queries. Sample copy for free. Writer's guidelines free.
Nonfiction Interview/profile, new product, technical. **Buys 6 mss/year.** Query with published clips. Length: 600-1,800 words. **Pays 20-25¢/word.** Sometimes pays expenses of writers on assignment.
Photos State availability with submission. Reviews transparencies, 4×6 prints. Buys one-time rights. Negotiates payment individually. Captions, identification of subjects required.
Columns/Departments Shop Talk (maintenance information for school bus mechanics), 650 words. **Buys 2 mss/year.** Query with published clips. **Pays $100-150.**
Tips "Freelancers should submit ideas about innovations in school bus safety and operations."

TRAVEL

$ $ $ CRUISE INDUSTRY NEWS

Cruise Industry News, 441 Lexington Ave., Suite 1209, New York NY 10017. (212)986-1025. Fax: (212)986-1033. E-mail: oivind@cruiseindustrynews.com. Website: www.cruiseindustrynews.com. **Contact:** Oivind Mathisen, editor. **20% freelance written.** Quarterly magazine covering cruise shipping. "We write about the *business* of cruise shipping for the industry. That is, cruise lines, shipyards, financial analysts, etc." Estab. 1991. Circ. 10,000. Pays on acceptance or on publication. Publishes ms an average of 4 months after acceptance. Byline given. Offers 25% kill fee. Buys first rights. Editorial lead time 3 months. Accepts queries by mail. Reponse time varies to queries. Sample copy for $15. Writer's guidelines for #10 SASE.

Nonfiction Interview/profile, new product, photo feature, travel, Business. No travel stories. **Buys more than 20 mss/year.** Query with published clips. Length: 500-1,500 words. **Pays $500-1,000 for assigned articles.** Sometimes pays expenses of writers on assignment.

Photos State availability with submission. Buys one-time rights. Pays $25-50/photo.

$ $ LEISURE GROUP TRAVEL

Premier Tourism Marketing, 4901 Forest Ave., Downers Grove IL 60515. (630)964-1431. Fax: (630)852-0414. E-mail: info@premiertourismmarketing.com. Website: www.premiertourismmarketing.com. **Contact:** John Kloster, editor-in-chief. **35% freelance written.** Bimonthly magazine covering group travel. We cover destinations and editorial relevant to the group travel market. Estab. 1994. Circ. 15,012. Pays on publication. Byline given. Buys first rights, including online publication rights. Editorial lead time 6 months. Submit seasonal material 6 months in advance. Accepts queries by mail, e-mail. Sample copy online.

Nonfiction Travel. **Buys 75 mss/year.** Query with published clips. Length: 1,200-3,000 words. **Pays $0-1,000.**

Tips "Experience in writing for 50+ travel marketplace a bonus."

Ⓝ $ $ $ RV BUSINESS

TL Enterprises, Inc., 2575 Vista del Mar Dr., Ventura CA 93001. (805)667-4100. Fax: (805)667-4484. E-mail: rvb@tl.com. Website: www.rvbusiness.com. **Contact:** John Sullaway, editor. **50% freelance written.** Monthly magazine. "*RV Business* caters to a specific audience of people who manufacture, sell, market, insure, finance, service and supply, components for recreational vehicles." Estab. 1972. Circ. 21,000. **Pays on acceptance.** Publishes ms an average of 2 months after acceptance. Byline given. Offers kill fee. Buys first North American serial rights. Editorial lead time 3 months. Accepts queries by mail, e-mail. Sample copy for free.

Nonfiction New product, photo feature, industry news and features. "No general articles without specific application to our market." **Buys 300 mss/year.** Query with published clips. Length: 125-2,200 words. **Pays $35-1,500.** Sometimes pays expenses of writers on assignment.

Columns/Departments Top of the News (RV industry news), 75-400 words; Business Profiles, 400-500 words; Features (indepth industry features), 800-2,000 words. **Buys 300 mss/year.** Query. **Pays $35-1,500.**

Tips "Query. Send 1 or several ideas and a few lines letting us know how you plan to treat it/them. We are always looking for good authors knowledgeable in the RV industry or related industries. We need more articles that are brief, factual, hard hitting, and business oriented. Review other publications in the field, including enthusiast magazines."

$ $ SPECIALTY TRAVEL INDEX

Alpine Hansen, 305 San Anselmo Ave., Suite 309, San Anselmo CA 94960. (415)455-1643. Fax: (415)455-1648. E-mail: info@specialtytravel.com. Website: www.specialtytravel.com. **90% freelance written.** Semiannual magazine covering adventure and special interest travel. Estab. 1980. Circ. 45,000. Pays on receipt and acceptance of all materials. Byline given. Buys one-time rights. Editorial lead time 3 month. Submit seasonal material 3 months in advance. Accepts queries by mail, e-mail. Writer's guidelines on request.

Nonfiction How-to, personal experience, photo feature, travel. **Buys 15 mss/year.** Query. Length: 1,250 words. **Pays $200 minimum.**

Reprints Send tearsheet. Pays 100% of amount paid for an original article.

Photos State availability with submission. Reviews 35mm transparencies, 5×7 prints. Negotiates payment individually. Captions, identification of subjects required.

Tips "Write about group travel and be both creative and factual. The articles should relate to both the travel agent booking the tour and the client who is traveling."

$ STAR SERVICE

NORTHSTAR Travel Media, 200 Brookstown Ave., Suite 301, Winston-Salem NC 27101. (336)714-3328. Fax: (336)714-3168. E-mail: csheaffer@ntmllc.com. Website: www.starserviceonline.com. **Contact:** Cindy Sheaffer, editor-in-chief. "Eager to work with new/unpublished writers as well as those working from a home base abroad, planning trips that would allow time for hotel reporting, or living in major ports for cruise ships." Worldwide guide to accommodations and cruise ships, sold to travel professionals on subscription basis. Estab. 1960. Pays 1 month after acceptance. Buys all rights. Writer's guidelines and list of available assignments for #10 SASE.

● E-mail queries preferred.

○┐ Break in by "being willing to inspect hotels in remote parts of the world."

Nonfiction Objective, critical evauations of hotels and cruise ships suitable for international travelers, based on personal inspections. Freelance correspondents ordinarily are assigned to update an entire state or country. "Assignment involves on-site inspections of all hotels and cruise ships we review; revising and updating published reports; and reviewing new properties. Qualities needed are thoroughness, precision, perserverance, and keen judgment. Solid research skills and powers of observation are crucial. Travel writing experience is highly desirable. Reviews must be colorful, clear, and documented with hotel's brochure, rate sheet, etc. We accept no advertising or payment for listings, so reviews should dispense praise and criticism where deserved." Now accepting queries for destination assignments with deadlines through October 2004. Query should include details on writer's experience in travel and writing, clips, specific forthcoming travel plans, and how much time would be available for hotel or ship inspections. Sponsored trips are acceptable. **Buys 4,500 mss/year. Pays $30/report used.**

Tips "We may require sample hotel or cruise reports on facilities near freelancer's hometown before giving the first assignment. No byline because of sensitive nature of reviews."

$ $ TRAVEL TIPS

Premier Tourism Marketing, 4901 Forest Ave., Downers Grove IL 60515. (630)964-1431. Fax: (630)852-0414. E-mail: info@premiertourismmarketing.com. Website: www.premiertourismmarketing.com. **Contact:** John Kloster, editor-in-chief. **75% freelance written.** Bimonthly magazine covering group travel. "We cover destinations and editorial relevant to the group travel market." Estab. 1994. Circ. 12,500. Pays on publication. Byline given. Buys first, electronic rights. Editorial lead time 6 months. Submit seasonal material 6 months in advance. Accepts queries by mail, e-mail. Sample copy online.

Nonfiction Travel. **Buys 36-50 mss/year.** Query with published clips. Length: 1,200-3,000 words. **Pays $0-500.**

Tips "Experience in writing for 50+ travel marketplace a bonus."

$ $ VACATION INDUSTRY REVIEW

Interval International, 6262 Sunset Dr., Miami FL 33143. **Contact:** Matthew McDaniel, editor-in-chief. **30% freelance written.** Quarterly magazine covering leisure lodgings (timeshare resorts, fractionals, and other types of vacation-ownership properties). "The international readership of *VIR* consists of people who develop, finance, market, sell, and manage timeshare resorts and mixed-use projects, such as hotels, resorts, and second-home communities with a vacation-ownership component worldwide; and suppliers of products and services to the vacation-ownership industry." Prefers to work with published/established writers. Estab. 1982. Circ. 30,000. Pays on publication. Publishes ms an average of 6 months after acceptance. Byline given. Makes work-for-hire assignments. Accepts queries by mail. Sample copy for 9×12 SAE and 3 first-class stamps or online. Writer's guidelines for #10 SASE.

  O— Break in by writing a letter to tell us about yourself and enclosing 2 or 3 (nonreturnable) samples of published work that show you can meet our specialized needs.

Nonfiction How-to, interview/profile, technical. No consumer travel, hotel, or nonvacation real-estate material. **Buys 6-8 mss/year.** Query with published clips. Length: 800-1,500 words. **Pays 30¢/word.**

Photos Only send photos on assignment. Reviews 35mm transparencies, 5×7 or larger prints, electronic images. Generally offers no additional payment for photos accepted with ms. Captions, identification of subjects required.

Tips "We do not want consumer-oriented destination travel articles. We want articles about the business aspects of the vacation-ownership industry: entrepreneurship, project financing, design and construction, sales and marketing, operations, management—anything that will help our readers plan, build, sell, and run a quality timeshare or vacation-ownership property that satisfies the owners/guests and earns a profit for the developer and marketer. We're also interested in owner associations at vacation-ownership resorts (not residential condos). Requires electronic submissions. Query for details."

VETERINARY

$ $ VETERINARY ECONOMICS

Business Solutions for Practicing Veterinarians, Advanstar Veterinary Healthcare Communications, 8033 Flint, Lenexa KS 66214. (913)492-4300. Fax: (913)492-4157. E-mail: ve@advanstar.com. Website: www.vetmedpub.com. Managing Editor: Jessica Harper. **Contact:** Marnette Falley, editor. **20% freelance written.** Monthly magazine covering veterinary practice management. "We address the business concerns and management needs of practicing veterinarians." Estab. 1960. Circ. 54,000. Pays on publication. Publishes ms an average of 6 months after acceptance. Byline given. Buys all rights. Editorial lead time 3 months. Submit seasonal material 3 months in advance. Accepts queries by mail, e-mail, fax. Accepts simultaneous submissions. Responds in 3 months to queries. Sample copy and writer's guidelines free. Writer's guidelines online.

Nonfiction How-to, interview/profile, personal experience. **Buys 24 mss/year.** Query with or without published clips or send complete ms. Length: 1,000-2,000 words. **Pays $50-400.**

Photos Send photos with submission. Reviews transparencies, prints. Buys one-time rights. Offers no additional payment for photos accepted with ms. Captions, identification of subjects required.

Columns/Departments Practice Tips (easy, unique business tips), 200-300 words. Send complete ms. **Pays $35.**

Tips "Among the topics we cover: Veterinary hospital design, client relations, contractual and legal matters, investments, day-to-day management, marketing, personal finances, practice finances, personnel, collections, and taxes. We also cover news and issues within the veterinary profession; for example, articles might cover the effectiveness of Yellow Pages advertising, the growing number of women veterinarians, restrictive-covenant cases, and so on. Freelance writers are encouraged to submit proposals or outlines for articles on these topics. Most articles involve interviews with a nationwide sampling of veterinarians; we will provide the names and phone numbers if necessary. We accept only a small number of unsolicited manuscripts each year; however, we do assign many articles to freelance writers. All material submitted by first-time contributors is read on speculation, and the review process usually takes 12 to 16 weeks. Our style is concise yet conversational, and all manuscripts go through a fairly rigorous editing process. We encourage writers to provide specific examples to illustrate points made throughout their articles."

Contests & Awards

The contests and awards listed in this section are arranged by subject. Nonfiction writers can turn immediately to nonfiction awards listed alphabetically by the name of the contest or award. The same is true for fiction writers, poets, playwrights and screenwriters, journalists, children's writers, and translators. You'll also find general book awards, fellowships offered by arts councils and foundations, and multiple category contests.

New contests and awards are announced in various writer's publications nearly every day. However, many lose their funding or fold—and sponsoring magazines go out of business just as often. We have contacted the organizations whose contests and awards are listed here with the understanding that they are valid through 2005-2006. **Contact names**, **entry fees**, and **deadlines** have been highlighted and set in bold type for your convenience.

To make sure you have all the information you need about a particular contest, always send a SASE to the contact person in the listing before entering a contest. The listings in this section are brief, and many contests have lengthy, specific rules and requirements that we could not include in our limited space. Often a specific entry form must accompany your submission.

When you receive a set of guidelines, you will see that some contests are not for some writers. The writer's age, previous publication, geographic location, and length of the work are common matters of eligibility. Read the requirements carefully to ensure you don't enter a contest for which you are not qualified. You should also be aware that every year, more and more contests, especially those sponsored by "little" literary magazines, are charging entry fees.

Winning a contest or award can launch a successful writing career. Take a professional approach by doing a little extra research. Find out who the previous winner of the award was by investing in a sample copy of the magazine in which the prize-winning article, poem, or short story appeared. Attend the staged reading of an award-winning play. Your extra effort will be to your advantage in competing with writers who simply submit blindly.

Information on contests and awards listed in the previous edition of *Writer's Market*, but not included in this edition, can be found in the General Index.

GENERAL

THE ANISFIELD-WOLF BOOK AWARDS

The Cleveland Foundation, 6100 Rockside Woods Blvd., Suite 350, Cleveland OH 44131. Website: www.anisfi eld-wolf.org. **Contact:** Laura Scharf. "The Anisfield-Wolf Book Award annually honors books which contribute to our understanding of racism or our appreciation of the diversity of human culture published during the year of the award." Judged by a 5-member panel chaired by Dr. Henry Louis Gates of Harvard University and including Joyce Carol Oates, Rita Dove, Steven Pinker, and Simon Schama. Any work addressing issues of racial bias or human diversity may qualify. **Deadline: January 31.** Guidelines for SASE. Prize: $10,000.

▣ ANTIDOTE ESSAY CONTEST

Conversely, 3053 Filmore St., #121, San Francisco CA 94123. E-mail: contest@conversely.com. Website: www.c onversely.com. **Contact:** Alejandro Gutierrez. "Annual contest held to foster interest in our 'Antidote' essay section. Personal opinion essays are welcome, as are social observations, intimate critiques, and satires. Topic choice is open as long as it falls within the theme of romantic (male-female) relationships." Writers can obtain guidelines and submission procedures online at www.conversely.com/Masth/conte.shtml. **Deadline: June 30. Charges $5 entry fee.** Prize: 1st Prize: $250; 2nd Prize: $125; winning essay may also be published. Judged by *Conversely* editors. Acquires Acquires 90-day exclsuive electronic rights and one-time print anthology rights (nonexclusive) for winning entries. Open to US residents only.

ARTSLINK PROJECTS AWARD

CEC Artslink, 12 W. 31st St., New York NY 10001. (212)643-1985, ext. 22. Fax: (212)643-1996. E-mail: artslink@ cecip.org. Website: www.cecip.org. **Contact:** Jennifer Gullace, program manager. Offered annually to enable artists of all media to work in Central Europe, Russia, and Eurasia with colleagues there on collaborative projects. Check website for deadline and other information. Prize: Up to $10,000.

▣ BBC WILDLIFE MAGAZINE NATURE WRITING AWARD

BBC Wildlife Magazine, Broadcasting House, Whiteladies Rd., Bristol BS8 2LR, United Kingdom. +44 (0)117 973 8402. Fax: +44 (0)117 946 7075. E-mail: nina.epton@bbc.co.uk. **Contact:** Nina Epton. Offered annually for unpublished work. "We are looking for new and established writers who are able to capture their observations of and feelings about nature on paper. The main conditions are that the essay should not be pure fiction, a poem, or written from an animal's point of view. It should not exceed 800 words. There are 4 categories: adult amateur, adult professional/semi-professional, young essay writer (age 13-17), young essay writer (age 12 or under). Entrants must buy the relevant copy of *BBC Wildlife Magazine* containing the entry form and rules. This is usually our May issue, but it's best to check with the office first." Prize-winners in this competition grant, free of charge, the right for all or part of their essay to be published, broadcast, transmitted, and read in all media (now known or hereafter created), or on stage, in connection with this competition. This includes the right for the essays to be published in *BBC Wildlife* (or any resulting anthology) and syndicated, if the organizers so wish. **Deadline: Varies from year to year (usually the end of June). Best to contact the office and ask for details.** Guidelines for SASE. Prize: Varies slightly from year to year. Normally a top prize of £1,000 for the overall winner. If the winner is a professional or semi-professional writer, there will also be a £200 prize for the best essay by an amateur. Runners-up (to a maximum of 6) will each win £150. The winning essays will be published in *BBC Wildlife Magazine*. Open to any writer.

▣ THE BOARDMAN TASKER AWARD FOR MOUNTAIN LITERATURE

The Boardman Tasker Charitable Trust, Pound House, Llangennith, Swansea Wales, United Kingdom. (00 44) 1792-386-215. Fax: (00 44) 1792-386-215. E-mail: margaretbody@lineone.net. Website: www.boardmantasker. com. **Contact:** Margaret Body. Offered annually to reward a work of nonfiction or fiction, in English or in translation, which has made an outstanding contribution to mountain literature. Books must be published in the UK between November 1 of previous year and October 31 of year of the prize. Writers may obtain information, but entry is by publishers only. "No restriction of nationality, but work must be published or distributed in the UK." **Deadline: August 1.** Guidelines for SASE. Prize: £2,000.

THE RALPH WALDO EMERSON AWARD

The Phi Beta Kappa Society, 1606 New Hampshire Ave. NW, Washington DC 20009. (202)265-3808. Fax: (202)986-1601. E-mail: sbeasley@pbk.org. Website: www.pbk.org/scholarships/books. **Contact:** Ms. Sandra Beasley. Estab. 1960. "The Ralph Waldo Emerson Award is offered annually for scholarly studies that contribute significantly to interpretations of the intellectual and cultural condition of humanity. This award may recognize work in the fields of history, philosophy, and religion; these fields are conceived in sufficiently broad terms to permit the inclusion of appropriate work in related fields such as anthropology and the social sciences. Biographies of public figures may be eligible if their critical emphasis is primarily on the intellectual and cultural condition of humanity." Work must have appeared in print May 1, 2003-April 30, 2004. Entries must be submitted by the publisher. Entries must be preceded by a letter certifying that the book(s) conforms to all the conditions of eligibility and stating the publication date of each entry. If accepted, 8 copies of each entry are required for the Emerson Award. Ineligible entries will be returned by Phi Beta Kappa. Books will not be entered officially in the competition until all copies and the letter of certification have been received. **Deadline: April 30.** Prize: $2,500. Judged by a rotating panel of distinguished scholars and experts in the field. Open only to original works in English, and authors of US residency and publication.

THE MARIAN ENGEL AWARD

The Writers' Trust of Canada, 40 Wellington St. E., Suite 300, Toronto ON M5E 1C7, Canada. (416)504-8222. Fax: (416)504-9090. E-mail: info@writerstrust.com. Website: www.writerstrust.com. The Engel Award is presented annually at the Great Literary Awards Event, held in Tornoto each Spring, to a female Canadian writer for a body of work in hope of continued contribution to the richness of Canadian literature. Prize: $15,000. Open to Canadian residents only.

THE TIMOTHY FINDLEY AWARD

The Writers' Trust of Canada, 40 Wellington St. E., Suite 300, Toronto ON M5E 1C7, Canada. (416)504-8222. Fax: (416)504-9090. E-mail: info@writerstrust.com. Website: www.writerstrust.com. **Contact:** James Davies. The Findley Award is presented annually at The Great Literary Awards Event held in Toronto each spring, to a male Canadian writer for a body of work in hope of continued contribution to the richness of Canadian literature. Prize: $15,000. Open to Canadian residents only.

FOREWORD MAGAZINE BOOK OF THE YEAR AWARDS

ForeWord Magazine, 129½ E. Front St., Traverse City MI 49684. (231)933-3699. Fax: (231)933-3899. Website: www.forewordmagazine.com. Awards offered annually. Eligibility: Books must have a 2004 copyright. **Deadline: January 15.** Prize: $1,500 cash prize will be awarded to a Best Fiction and Best Nonfiction choice as determined by the editors of *ForeWord Magazine*. Judged by a jury of librarians, booksellers, and reviewers who are selected to judge the categories for entry and select winners and finalists based on editorial excellence and professional production as well as the originality of the narrative and the value the book adds to its genre. Open to any writer.

FRIENDS OF THE DALLAS PUBLIC LIBRARY AWARD

The Texas Institute of Letters, Texas Institute of Letters, 3700 Mockingbird, Dallas TX 75205. (214)528-2655. E-mail: franvick@aol.com. Website: www.stedwards.edu/newc/marks/til/owards.htm. **Contact:** Fran Vick, secretary. Offered annually for submissions published January 1-December 31 of previous year to recognize the writer of the book making the most important contribution to knowledge. Writer must have been born in Texas, have lived in the state at least 2 consecutive years at some time, or the subject matter of the book should be associated with the state. **Deadline: January 3.** Guidelines for SASE. Prize: $1,000.

FRONTIERS IN WRITING

Panhandle Professional Writers, P.O. Box 176, Clarendon TX 79226. E-mail: fiw2004@yahoo.com. Website: users.arn.net/~ppw. Offered annually for unpublished work to encourage new writers and to bring them to the attention of the publishing industry. **Deadline: March 1.** Guidelines for SASE. **Charges variable fee.** Prize: Varies, see guidelines.

THE JANE GESKE AWARD

Prairie Schooner, 201 Andrews Hall, P.O. Box 880334, Lincoln NE 68588-0334. (402)472-0911. Fax: (402)472-9771. E-mail: kgrey2@unl.edu. Website: www.unl.edu/schooner/psmain.htm. **Contact:** Hilda Raz. Offered annually for work published in *Prairie Schooner* in the previous year. Prize: $250. Open to any writer.

INDEPENDENT PUBLISHER BOOK AWARDS

Jenkins Group/Independent Publisher Online, 400 W. Front St., #4A, Traverse City MI 49684. (231)933-4954, ext. 1011. Fax: (231)933-0448. E-mail: jimb@bookpublishing.com. Website: www.independentpublisher.com. **Contact:** Jim Barnes. "The Independent Publisher Book Awards were conceived as a broad-based, unaffiliated awards program open to all members of the independent publishing industry. The staff at *Independent Publisher* magazine saw the need to bring increased recognition to the thousands of exemplary independent, university, and self-published titles produced each year. The IPPY Awards reward those who exhibit the courage, innovation, and creativity to bring about change in the world of publishing. Independent spirit and expertise comes from publishers of all areas and budgets, and we judge books with that in mind. For 20 years our mission at

Independent Publisher has been to recognize and encourage the work of publishers who exhibit the courage and creativity necessary to take chances, break new ground, and bring about changes, not only to the world of publishing, but to our society, our environment, and our collective spirit. Entries will be accepted in 55 categories." **Deadline: April 15.** Guidelines for SASE. **Charges $60 until November 15; $65 until January 15; $70 until April 15.** Prize: $500, and a trophy to 1 book in each of the following categories: Most Original Concept; Best Corporate Branding Book; Best Book Arts Craftsmanship; Most Inspirational to Youth; Best Health Book; Most Likely to Save the Planet; Most Unique Design; Story Teller of the Year; Most Life-Changing; Business Breakthrough of the Year. Judged by a panel of experts representing the fields of design, writing, bookselling, library, and reviewing. Open to any published writer.

JACK KAVANAGH MEMORIAL YOUTH BASEBALL RESEARCH AWARD

Society for American Baseball Research (SABR), 239 E. Chilton Dr., Tempe AZ 85283. E-mail: fdelhichpt@aol.com. Website: www.sabr.org. **Contact:** Rodney Johnson, contest/award director. Offered annually for unpublished work. Purpose is to stimulate interest in baseball research by youth under age of 21. Deadline is typically 1 month prior to our National Convention, usually held in late June or early July. Guidelines for SASE. Prize: Award is $200 cash prize, publication in *SABR Journal* and/or website, 3-year SABR membership, plaque honoring award. Up to 3 finalists also receive 1-year SABR membership. Judged by the Youth/Education Awards Committee. Acquires nonexclusive rights to SABR to publish the entrants' submissions in printed and/or electronic form. Writers must be under 21 as of June 1 of the year the award is given. Writers must submit a copy of birth certificate or drivers license with their submission as proof of age.

Ⓝ CORETTA SCOTT KING AWARDS

American Library Association, 50 E. Huron St., Chicago IL 60611. (800)545-2433, ext. 4294. E-mail: olos@ala.org. Website: www.ala.org/srrt/csking. Offered annually to an African-American author and illustrator to promote understanding and appreciation of culture and contributions of all people. Guidelines for SASE. Prize: $1,000, and set of encyclopedias from World Book & Encyclopedia Britannica.

Ⓝ KORET JEWISH BOOK AWARDS

Koret Foundation, 33 New Montgomery St., Suite 1090, San Francisco CA 94105-4526. (415)882-7740. Fax: (415)882-7775. E-mail: koretinstitute@koretfoundation.org. Website: www.koretfoundation.org. **Contact:** Steven J. Zipperstein, Ph.D., director, Koret Institute. Annual awards established "to help readers identify the best Jewish books now available in the English language." Books must be published in English; translations are eligible. Edited volumes and anthologies are not eligible. Books must be submitted by publishers on behalf of authors. There are 4 categories: Biography, Autobiography, and Literary Studies; Fiction; History; Philosophy and Thought. **Deadline: Visit website for details, since deadlines change annually.** Guidelines for SASE. Prize: $10,000 to the winner in each category.

DOROTHEA LANGE—PAUL TAYLOR PRIZE

Center for Documentary Studies at Duke University, 1317 W. Pettigrew St., Durham NC 27705. (919)660-3663. Fax: (919)681-7600. E-mail: alexad@duke.edu. Website: cds.aas.duke.edu/l-t/. **Contact:** Alexa Dilworth. Offered annually to "promote the collaboration between a writer and a photographer in the formative or fieldwork stages of a documentary project. Collaborative submissions on any subject are welcome." Guidelines for SASE or on website. **Deadline: January 31. Submissions accepted during January only.** Prize: $10,000.

FENIA AND YAAKOV LEVIANT MEMORIAL PRIZE

Modern Language Association of America, 26 Broadway, 3rd Floor, New York NY 10004-1789. (646)576-5141. Fax: (646)458-0030. E-mail: awards@mla.org. Website: www.mla.org. **Contact:** Annie Reiser, coordinator of book prizes and special projects. This prize is to honor, in alternating years, an outstanding English translation of a Yiddish literary work or an outstanding scholarly work in any language in the field of Yiddish. Offered every two years. In 2004, it will be awarded to a scholarly work published between 1999 and 2003. In 2006 it will be awarded to a translation published between 2002 and 2005. Open to MLA members and nonmembers. Authors or publishers may submit titles. Guidelines for SASE or by e-mail. **Deadline: May 1, 2004.** Prize: $500, and a certificate, to be presented at the Modern Language Association's annual convention in December.

Ⓝ DEANN LUBELL PROFESSIONAL WRITER'S COMPETITION

National League of American Pen Women — Palm Springs Branch, P.O. Box 1166, 45300 Portola Ave., Palm Desert CA 92261-9998. (760) 568-0550. E-mail: wynlady@yahoo.com. **Contact:** Kristin Johnson. Awards prizes for published articles, published poetry, published short stories, and Web articles. Professional writers only. Offered every 2 years (odd years) to previously published work published within the last 5 years. **Deadline: Next contest not offered until 2005.** Guidelines for SASE. Open to any writer.

THE GLENNA LUSCHEI PRAIRIE SCHOONER AWARD

Prairie Schooner, 201 Andrews Hall, P.O. Box 880334, Lincoln NE 68588-0334. (402)472-0911. Fax: (402)472-9771. E-mail: kgrey2@unl.edu. Website: www.unl.edu/schooner/psmain.htm. **Contact:** Hilda Raz. Offered annually for work published in *Prairie Schooner* in the previous year. Prize: $1,000. Open to any writer.

◩ THE GRANT MACEWAN YOUNG WRITER'S SCHOLARSHIP

Alberta Community Development, 9th Floor Standard Life Centre, 10405 Jasper Ave., Edmonton AB T5J 4R7, Canada. Website: www.cd.gov.ab.ca. This annual award was created by the government of Alberta to honor the life and contributions of the late Dr. Grant MacEwan. Open to young Alberta writers (16-25) who create a literary work reflecting Alberta and/or Dr. MacEwan's interests. **Deadline: December 31.** Guidelines for SASE. Prize: 4 scholarships of $2,500 each. Judged by a panel of Alberta authors and educators.

MISSISSIPPI REVIEW PRIZE

Mississippi Review, U.S.M. Box 5144, Hattiesburg MS 39406. (601)266-4321. Fax: (601)266-5757. E-mail: rief@netdoor.com. Website: www.mississippireview.com. **Contact:** Rie Fortenberry, contest director. Offered annually for unpublished fiction and poetry. Guidelines available online or with SASE. **Deadline: October 1. Charges $15 fee.** Prize: $1,000 each for fiction and poetry winners.

◩ THE W.O. MITCHELL LITERARY PRIZE

The Writers' Trust of Canada, 40 Wellington St. E., Suite 300, Toronto ON M5E 1C7, Canada. (416)504-8222. Fax: (416)504-9090. E-mail: info@writerstrust.com. Website: www.writerstrust.com. **Contact:** James Davies. Offered annually for a writer who has produced an outstanding body of work and has acted during his/her career as a "caring mentor" for other writers. They must also have published a work of fiction or had a new stage play produced during the 3-year period for each competition. Every third year the W.O. Mitchell Literary Prize will be awarded to a writer who works in French. Prize: $15,000. Open to Canadian residents only.

MLA PRIZE IN UNITED STATES LATINA & LATINO AND CHICANA & CHICANO LITERARY AND CULTURAL STUDIES

(formerly MLA Prize in Chicana & Chicano and Latina & Latino Literary and Cultural Studies), Modern Language Association of America, 26 Broadway, 3rd Floor, New York NY 10004-1789. (646)576-5141. Fax: (646)458-0030. E-mail: awards@mla.org. Website: www.mla.org. **Contact:** Coordinator of Book Prizes. Award for an outstanding scholarly study in any language of United States Latina & Latino and Chicana & Chicano literature or culture. *Open to current MLA members only.* Authors or publishers may submit titles. **Deadline: May 1.** Guidelines for SASE. Prize: $1,000, and a certificate to be presented at the Modern Language Association's annual convention in December.

NATIONAL OUTDOOR BOOK AWARDS

Box 8128, Idaho State University, Pocatello ID 83209. (208)282-3912. E-mail: wattron@isu.edu. Website: www.isu.edu/outdoor/books. **Contact:** Ron Watters. Eight categories: History/biography, outdoor literature, instructional texts, outdoor adventure guides, nature guides, childrens' books, design/artistic merit, and nature and the environment. Additionally, a special award, the Outdoor Classic Award, is given annually to books which, over a period of time, have proven to be exceptionally valuable works in the outdoor field. Application forms and eligibilty requirements are available online. **Deadline: September 1. Charges $65 fee.** Prize: Winning books are promoted nationally and are entitled to display the National Outdoor Book Award (NOBA) medallion.

OHIOANA WALTER RUMSEY MARVIN GRANT

Ohioana Library Association, 274 E. First Ave., Suite 300, Columbus OH 43201. (614)466-3831. Fax: (614)728-6974. E-mail: ohioana@sloma.state.oh.us. Website: www.oplin.lib.oh.us/products/ohioana/marvin.doc. **Contact:** Linda Hengst. Offered annually to encourage young writers; open to writers under age 30 who have not published a book. Entrants must have been born in Ohio or have lived in Ohio for at least 5 years. Enter 6 pieces of prose totaling 10-60 pages. **Deadline: January 31.** Prize: $1,000.

PEN CENTER USA LITERARY AWARDS

PEN Center USA, 672 S. Lafayette Park Place, Suite 42, Los Angeles CA 90057. (213)365-8500. Fax: (213)365-9616. E-mail: awards@penusa.org. Website: www.penusa.org. **Contact:** Literary Awards Coordinator. Offered for work published or produced in the previous calendar year. Open to writers living west of the Mississippi River. Award categories: drama, screenplay, teleplay, journalism. Guidelines for SASE or download from website. **Deadline: 4 copies must be received by January 31.** Prize: $1,000.

THE PRAIRIE SCHOONER READERS' CHOICE AWARDS

Prairie Schooner, 201 Andrews Hall, P.O. Box 880334, Lincoln NE 68588-0334. (402)472-0911. Fax: (402)472-9771. E-mail: kgrey2@unl.edu. Website: www.unl.edu/schooner/psmain.htm. **Contact:** Hilda Raz. Annual awards (usually 4-6) for work published in *Prairie Schooner* in the previous year. Prize: $250. Open to any writer.

PULITZER PRIZES

The Pulitzer Prize Board, 709 Journalism, 2950 Broadway, Mail Code 3865, Columbia University, New York NY 10027. (212)854-3841. Website: www.pulitzer.org. **Contact:** Sig Gissler, administrator. Estab. 1917. Journalism in US newspapers (published daily or weekly), and in letters, drama, and music by Americans. **Deadline: February 1 (journalism); March 1 (music and drama); July 1 and November 1 (letters). Charges $50.** Prize: $10,000.

DAVID RAFFELOCK AWARD FOR PUBLISHING EXCELLENCE

National Writers Association, 3140 S. Peoria, #295, Aurora CO 80014. (303)841-0246. Fax: (303)841-2607. E-mail: sandywrter@aol.com. Website: www.nationalwriters.com. **Contact:** Sandy Whelchel. Contest is offered annually for books published the previous year. The purpose of this contest is to assist published authors in marketing their works and to reward outstanding published works. **Deadline: May 1.** Guidelines for SASE. **Charges $100 fee.** Prize: Publicity tour, including airfare, valued at $5,000.

ROCKY MOUNTAIN ARTISTS' BOOK COMPETITION

Hemingway Western Studies Center, Boise State University, 1910 University Dr., Boise ID 83725. (208)426-1999. Fax: (208)426-4373. E-mail: ttrusky@boisestate.edu. Website: www.boisestate.edu/hemingway/. **Contact:** Tom Trusky. Offered annually "to publish multiple edition artists' books of special interest to Rocky Mountain readers. Topics must be public issues (race, gender, environment, etc.). Authors may hail from Topeka or Ulan Bator, but their books must initially have regional appeal." Acquires first rights. Open to any writer. **Deadline: September 1-December 1.** Guidelines for SASE. Prize: $500, publication, standard royalties.

WILLIAM SANDERS SCARBOROUGH PRIZE

Modern Language Association of America, 26 Broadway, 3rd Floor, New York NY 10004-1789. (646)576-5141. Fax: (646)458-0030. E-mail: awards@mla.org. Website: www.mla.org. **Contact:** Annie Reiser, coordinator of book prizes and special projects. Offered annually for work published in the previous year. "Given in honor of a distinguished man of letters and the first African-American member of the Modern Language Association, this prize will be awarded to an outstanding scholarly study of black American literature or culture." Open to MLA members and nonmembers. Authors or publishers may enter titles. Guidelines for SASE or by e-mail. **Deadline: May 1.** Prize: $1,000, and a certificate, to be presented at the Modern Language Association's annual convention in December.

JOANNA CATHERINE SCOTT NOVEL EXCERPT PRIZE

National League of American Pen Women, Nob Hill, San Francisco Bay Area Branch, 1544 Sweetwood Dr., Colma CA 94015. E-mail: pennobhill@aol.com. Website: www.soulmakingcontest.us. **Contact:** Eileen Malone. Send first chapter or the first 20 pages, whichever comes first. Include a 1-page synopsis. Annually. **Deadline: November 30.** Guidelines for SASE. **Charges $5/entry (make checks payable to NLAPW, Nob Hill Branch).** Prize: 1st Place: $100; 2nd Place: $50; 3rd Place: $25. Open to any writer.

BYRON CALDWELL SMITH AWARD

Hall Center for the Humanities, 1540 Sunflower Rd., Lawrence KS 66045-7618. (785)864-4798. Website: www.hallcenter.ku.edu. **Contact:** Janet Crow, executive director. Offered in odd years to an individual who lives or is employed in Kansas, and who has authored an outstanding book published in the previous 2 calendar years. Translations are eligible. **Deadline: March 3.** Guidelines for SASE. Prize: $2,000.

N WHITING WRITERS' AWARDS

Mrs. Giles Whiting Foundation, 1133 Avenue of the Americas, 22nd Floor, New York NY 10036. Website: whitingfoundation.org. **Contact:** Barbara Bristol, director, writers' program. "The Foundation gives annually $35,000 each to up to 10 writers of poetry, fiction, nonfiction, and plays. The awards place special emphasis on exceptionally promising emerging talent." Direct applications and informal nominations are not accepted by the Foundation.

WORLD FANTASY AWARDS ASSOCIATION

P.O. Box 43, Mukilteo WA 98275-0043. Website: www.worldfantasy.org. **Contact:** Peter Dennis Pautz, president. Estab. 1975. Offered annually for previously published work recommended by previous convention attendees in several categories, including life achievement, novel, novella, short story, anthology, collection, artist, special award-pro, and special award nonpro. Works are recommended by attendees of current and previous 2 years' conventions, and a panel of judges. **Deadline: July 1.**

NONFICTION

AMWA MEDICAL BOOK AWARDS COMPETITION

American Medical Writers Association, 40 W. Gude Dr., Suite 101, Rockville MD 20850-1192. (301)294-5303. Fax: (301)294-9006. E-mail: norine@amwa.org. Website: www.amwa.org. **Contact:** Book Awards Committee. Offered annually to honor the best medical book published in the previous year in each of three categories: Books for Physicians, Books for Allied Health Professionals, and Trade Books. **Deadline: March 1. Charges $20 fee.**

ANTHEM ESSAY CONTEST

The Ayn Rand Institute, P.O. Box 57044, Irvine CA 92619-7044. (949)222-6550. Fax: (949)222-6558. E-mail: essay@aynrand.org. Website: www.aynrand.org/contests. **Contact:** Marilee Dahl. Estab. 1992. Offered annually to encourage analytical thinking and excellence in writing, and to exposé students to the philosophic ideas of Ayn Rand. "For information contact your English teacher or guidance counselor or visit our website." **Deadline: March 18.** Prize: 1st Place: $2,000; 2nd Place (10): $500; 3rd Place (20): $200; Finalist (45): $50; Semifinalist (175): $30. 9th and 10th graders.

ATLAS SHRUGGED ESSAY CONTEST

Dept. W, The Ayn Rand Institute, 2121 Alton Pkwy., Suite 250, Irvine CA 92606. (949)222-6550. Fax: (949)222-6558. E-mail: essay@aynrand.org. Website: www.aynrand.org/contests. **Contact:** Marilee Dahl. Offered annually to encourage analytical thinking and excellence in writing, and to exposé students to the philosophic ideas of Ayn Rand. Essays are judged both on style and content. Essay length: 1,000-1,200 words. Guidelines on website. Open to students enrolled full-time in an undergraduate or graduate program. **Deadline: September 16.** Prize: 1st Place: $5,000; 2nd Place (3 awards): $1,000; 3rd Place (5 awards): $400; Finalists (20 awards): $100; Semifinalists (20 awards): $50.

BANCROFT PRIZE

Columbia University-Office of the University Librarian, 517 Butter Library, Mail Code 1101, 535 W. 114th St., New York NY 10027. Website: www.columbia.edu/cu/lweb/eguides/amerihist/bancroft.html. **Contact:** Bancroft Prize Committee. Offered annually for work published previously. Winning submissions will be chosen in either or both of the following categories: American history (including biography) and diplomacy. **Deadline: December 1.** Guidelines for SASE. Prize: $4,000 for the winning entry in each category. Open to all writers except previous recipients of the Bancroft Prize.

RAY ALLEN BILLINGTON PRIZE

Organization of American Historians, 112 N. Bryan Ave., Bloomington IN 47408-4199. (812)855-7311. Fax: (812)855-0696. E-mail: awards@oah.org. Website: www.oah.org. **Contact:** Award and Prize Committee Coordinator. Offered in even years for the best book in American frontier history, defined broadly so as to include the pioneer periods of all geographical areas and comparison between American frontiers and others. Guidelines available on website. **Deadline: October 1.** Prize: $1,000, a certificate, and a medal.

BIOGRAPHERS' CLUB PRIZE

Biographers' Club, The Secretary, 17 Sutherland St., London, England SW1V 4JU. (020)7828 1274. Fax: (020)7828 7608. E-mail: lownie@globalnet.co.uk. Website: www.booktrust.org.uk. **Contact:** Andrew Lownie. The annual prize is sponsored by the Daily Mail, and all previous winners have gone on to secure publishing contracts—some for 6-figure sums. Entries should consist of a 15-20 page synopsis and 10 pages of a sample chapter for a biography. **Deadline: August 1.** Prize: £1,000. Judged by 3 distinguished biographers. Judges have included Michael Holroyd, Victoria Glendinning, Selina Hastings, Frances Spalding, Lyndall Gordon, Anne de Courcy, Nigel Hamilton, Anthony Sampson, and Mary Lovell. Judges for 2004 are Anne Chisholm, David Ellis, and Anna Swan. Open to any biographer who has not previously been commissioned or written a book.

BIRKS FAMILY FOUNDATION AWARD FOR BIOGRAPHY

Canadian Authors Association, Box 419, 320 S. Shores Rd., Campbellford ON K0L 1L0, Canada. (705)653-0323. Fax: (705)653-0593. E-mail: admin@canauthors.org. Website: www.canauthors.org. **Contact:** Alec McEachern. Offered annually for a biography about a Canadian. Entry form required. Obtain entry form from contact name or download from website. **Deadline: December 15.** Guidelines for SASE. **Charges $35 (Canadian) entry fee.** Prize: $2,500, and a silver medal.

BOWLING WRITING COMPETITION

American Bowling Congress Publications, 5301 S. 76th St., Greendale WI 53129-1127. Fax: (414)321-8356. E-mail: abcpr@bowling.com. Website: www.bowl.com. **Contact:** Bill Vint, editor. Estab. 1935. Offered for feature, editorial, and news all relating to the sport of bowling. **Deadline: December 15.** Prize: 1st Place in each division: $300. In addition, News and Editorial: $225; $200; $175; $150; $75; and $50; Feature: $225; $200; $175; $150; $125; $100; $75; $50; and $50; with 5 honorable mention certificates awarded in each category.

⊞ BRITISH COUNCIL PRIZE

North American Conference on British Studies Dept., Austin TX 78712-1163. (512)475-7204. Fax: (512)475-7222. E-mail: harling@pop.uky.edu. **Contact:** Philip Harling, executive secretary. Offered annually for best book by a North American scholar published in previous year in any field of British Studies after 1800. Open to American or Canadian citizens or permanent residents. **Deadline: April 1.** Guidelines for SASE. Prize: $1,000.

THE BROSS PRIZE

The Bross Foundation, Lake Forest College, 555 N. Sheridan, Lake Forest IL 60045. (847)735-5175. Fax: (847)735-6192. E-mail: rmiller@lfc.edu. **Contact:** Professor Ron Miller. Offered every 10 years for unpublished work "to award the best book or treatise on the relation between any discipline or topic of investigation and the Christian religion." Next contest in 2010. Manuscripts awarded prizes become property of the college. Open to any writer. **Deadline: September 1 of contest year.** Guidelines for SASE. Prize: Award varies depending on interest earned.

⊠ JOHN BULLEN PRIZE

Canadian Historical Association, 395 Wellington St., Ottawa ON K1A 0N3, Canada. (613)233-7885. Fax: (613)567-3110. E-mail: cha-shc@archives.ca. Website: www.cha-shc.ca. Offered annually for an outstanding historical dissertation for a doctoral degree at a Canadian university. Open only to Canadian citizens or landed immigrants. **Deadline: November 30.** Guidelines for SASE. Prize: $500.

⊠ CANADIAN AUTHORS ASSOCIATION LELA COMMON AWARD FOR CANADIAN HISTORY

Box 419, 320 S. Shores Rd., Campbellford ON K0L 1L0, Canada. (705)653-0323. Fax: (705)653-0593. E-mail: canauth@redden.on.ca. Website: www.canauthors.org. **Contact:** Alec McEachern. Offered annually for a work of historical nonfiction on a Canadian topic by a Canadian author. Entry form required. Obtain entry form from contact name or download from website. **Deadline: December 15.** Guidelines for SASE. **Charges $25 (Canadian) entry fee.** Prize: $2,500, and a silver medal.

⊠ CANADIAN LIBRARY ASSOCIATION STUDENT ARTICLE CONTEST

Canadian Library Association, 328 Frank St., Ottawa ON K2P 0X8, Canada. (613)232-9625, ext. 318. Fax: (613)563-9895. Website: www.cla.ca. **Contact:** Brenda Shields. Offered annually to "unpublished articles discussing, analyzing, or evaluating timely issues in librarianship or information science." Open to all students registered in or recently graduated from a Canadian library school, a library techniques program, or faculty of education library program. Submissions may be in English or French. **Deadline: April 1.** Guidelines for SASE. Prize: 1st Place: $150, publication, and trip to CLA's annual conference; 1st runner-up: $150, and $75 in CLA publications; 3rd runner-up: $100, and $75 in CLA publications.

THE DOROTHY CHURCHILL CAPPON CREATIVE NONFICTION AWARD

New Letters, 5101 Rockhill Rd., Kansas City MO 64110. (816)235-1168. Fax: (816)235-2611. E-mail: newletters@umkc.edu. Website: www.newsletters.org. **Contact:** Aleatha Ezra. Contest is offered annually for unpublished work to discover and reward emerging writers and to give experienced writers a place to try new genres. Acquires first North American serial rights. Open to any writer. Guidelines for SASE or online. **Deadline: Third week of May. Charges $15 fee (includes a 1-year subscription to *New Letters*).** Prize: 1st Place: $1,000, and publication in a volume of *New Letters*; 1st runner-up will receive a copy of a recent book of poetry or fiction courtesy of our affiliate BkMk Press. All entries will receive consideration for publication in future editions of *New Letters*.

MORTON N. COHEN AWARD

Modern Language Association of America, 26 Broadway, 3rd Floor, New York NY 10004-1789. (646)576-5141. Fax: (646)458-0030. E-mail: awards@mla.org. Website: www.mla.org. **Contact:** Coordinator of Book Prizes. Estab. 1989. Awarded in odd-numbered years for a distinguished edition of letters. At least 1 volume of the edition must have been published during the previous 2 years. Editors need not be members of the MLA. **Deadline: May 1.** Guidelines for SASE. Prize: $1,000, and a certificate.

ⓝ CARR P. COLLINS AWARD

The Texas Institute of Letters, 3700 Mockingbird, Dallas TX 75205. (214)528-2655. E-mail: franvick@aol.com. Website: www.stedwards.edu/newc/marks/til/awards.htm. **Contact:** Fran Vick. Offered annually for work published January 1-December 31 of the previous year to recognize the best nonfiction book by a writer who was born in Texas or who has lived in the state for at least 2 consecutive years at one point or a writer whose work has some notable connection with Texas. **Deadline: January 3.** Guidelines for SASE. Prize: $5,000.

ⓝ COMPETITION FOR WRITERS OF B.C. (BRITISH COLUMBIA) HISTORY

B.C. Historical Federation, P.O. Box 130, Whonnock BC V2W 1V9, Canada. (604)462-8942. **Contact:** Helmi Braches, coordinator. Offered annually to nonfiction books published during contest year "to promote the history of British Columbia." Book must contain any facet of B.C. history. Submit 2 copies to the contest and they become the property of B.C. Historical Federation. Open to any writer. **Deadline: December 31.** Prize: 1st Place: $300 and The Lieutenant Governor's Medal for Historical Writing; 2nd Place: $200; 3rd Place: $100.

⊕ THE THOMAS COOK TRAVEL BOOK AWARD

Jarden Press, Ltd., Unit 27 Wyndham St., Hull HU3 1HD, United Kingdom. 01482 610707. E-mail: joantba2003@ hotmail.com. Website: www.thetravelbookaward.com. **Contact:** Joan Lee. Annual award to reward and encourage the art of travel writing and to inspire in the reader the wish to travel. Books should have been published for the first time during January 1 and December 31; should be available in the English language (but may be translations); should be a minimum of 150 pages; and must be travel narratives (i.e., not guidebooks). **Deadline: April 16.** Guidelines for SASE. Prize: £10,000. Judged by a panel of 7 or 8 judges from travel literature/media/ publishing (changes annually). Open to any writer.

AVERY O. CRAVEN AWARD

Organization of American Historians, 112 N. Bryan Ave., Bloomington IN 47408-4199. (812)855-9852. Fax: (812)855-0696. E-mail: awards@oah.org. Website: www.oah.org. **Contact:** Award and Prize Committee Coordinator. Offered annually for the most original book on the coming of the Civil War, the Civil War years, or the Era of Reconstruction, with the exception of works of purely military history. Guidelines on website. **Deadline: October 1.** Prize: $500, and a certificate.

A CUP OF COMFORT

Adams Media Corp./F+W Publications Co., 57 Littlefield St., Avon MA 02322. Fax: (541)427-6790. E-mail: cupofcomfort@adamsmedia.com. Website: www.cupofcomfort.com. "A Cup of Comfort is the best-selling book series featuring from-the-heart, slice-of-life true stories about the relationships and experiences that deeply affect our lives. This paid and bylined publishing opportunity is open to aspiring and experienced writers as well as to people from all walks of life." Stories must be true, written in English, uplifting, positive, and/or inspiring, and appropriate for a mainstream audience. This prize includes publication in an anthology: Four anthologies are published each year, 2 in Spring and 2 in Fall; and some years an additional "niche" volume (i.e., cookbook, collection of prayers, etc.) are also compiled. Contest is offered 4 or 5 times/year. Deadline for Spring publications is usually August or September of previous year; for Fall publications January of same year. Finalists are selected throughout the submission period, so early entry is encouraged. Guidelines for SASE or by e-mail. Open to aspiring and published writers. Allow 6-9 months for response. Prize: Grand Prize: $500; $100 for each other story published in each book (50-60 stories/anthology). Acquires limited rights for a specified period of time; applies only to those stories selected for publication.

MERLE CURTI AWARD

Organization of American Historians, 112 N. Bryan Ave., Bloomington IN 47408-4199. (812)855-9852. Fax: (812)855-0696. E-mail: awards@oah.org. Website: www.oah.org. **Contact:** Award and Prize Committee Coordinator. Offered annually for books in the fields of American social, intellectual, and/or cultural history. Guidelines available on website. **Deadline: October 1.** Guidelines for SASE. Prize: $1,000, a certificate, and a medal.

ANNIE DILLARD AWARD IN CREATIVE NONFICTION

Bellingham Review, Mail Stop 9053, Western Washington University, Bellingham WA 98225. (360)650-4863. E-mail: bhreview@cc.wwu.edu. Website: www.wwu.edu/~bhreview. **Contact:** Brenda Miller. Offered annually for unpublished essays on any subject and in any style. Guidelines for SASE or on website. **Deadline: December 1-March 15. Charges $15/1st entry, $10/additional entry.** Prize: 1st Place: $1,000, plus publication and copies. All finalists considered for publication. All entrants receive subscription.

GORDON W. DILLON/RICHARD C. PETERSON MEMORIAL ESSAY PRIZE

American Orchid Society, Inc., 16700 AOS Lane, Delray Beach FL 33446-4351. (561)404-2043. Fax: (561)404-2045. E-mail: jmengel@aos.org. Website: www.aos.org. **Contact:** Jane Mengel. Estab. 1985. "An annual contest open to all writers. The theme is announced each May in *Orchids* magazine. All themes deal with an aspect of orchids, such as repotting, growing, hybridizing, etc. Unpublished submissions only." Themes in past years have included Orchid Culture, Orchids in Nature, and Orchids in Use. Buys one-time rights. **Deadline: November 30.** Prize: Cash award, and certificate. Winning entry usually published in the May issue of *Orchids* magazine.

ⓃⓈ THE DONNER PRIZE

The Award for Best Book on Canadian Public Policy, The Donner Canadian Foundation, 394A King St. E., Toronto ON M5A 1K9, Canada. (416)368-8253 or (416)368-3763. Fax: (416)363-1448. E-mail: meisnerpublicity @sympatico.ca. Website: www.donnerbookprize.com. **Contact:** Meisner Publicity, prize manager; Sherry Naylor or Susan Meisner. Offered annually for nonfiction published January 1-December 31 that highlights the importance of public policy and to reward excellent work in this field. Entries must be published in either English or French. Open to Canadian citizens. **Deadline: November 30.** Guidelines for SASE. Prize: Winner: $30,000; 5 shortlist authors: $5,000 each.

THE FREDERICK DOUGLASS BOOK PRIZE

Gilder Lehrman Center for the Study of Slavery, Resistance & Abolition of Yale University, P.O. Box 208206, New Haven CT 06520-8206. (203)432-3339. Fax: (203)432-6943. E-mail: gilder.lehrman.center@yale.edu. Website: www.yale.edu/glc. **Contact:** Robert P. Forbes, associate director. Write or fax, Attention: Douglass Prize. Offered annually for books published the previous year. "The annual prize of $25,000 is awarded for the most outstanding book published on the subject of slavery, resistance, and/or abolition. Works related to the American Civil War are eligble only if their primary focus is slavery, resistance, or abolition." **Deadline: March 29.** Guidelines for SASE. Prize: $25,000, and a bronze medallion.

Ⓢ THE DRAINIE-TAYLOR BIOGRAPHY PRIZE

The Writers' Trust of Canada, 40 Wellington St. E., Suite 300, Toronto ON M5E 1C7, Canada. (416)504-8222. Fax: (416)504-9090. E-mail: info@writerstrust.com. Website: www.writerstrust.com. **Contact:** James Davies. Awarded annually to a Canadian author for a significant work of biography, autobiography, or personal memoir. Award presented at the Great Literary Awards event held in Toronto each spring. Prize: $10,000.

Ⓝ EVERETT E. EDWARDS MEMORIAL AWARD

Agricultural History, P.O. Box 5075, Minard Hall, NDSU, Fargo ND 58105-5075. (701)231-5831. Fax: (701)231-5832. E-mail: ndsu.agricultural.history@ndsu.nodak.edu. Website: agriculturalhistory.ndsu.nodak.edu. **Contact:** Claire Strom. Offered annually for best graduate paper written during the calendar year on any aspect of agricultural and rural studies, broadly interpreted, submitted by a graduate student. Open to submission by any graduate student. **Deadline: December 31.** Prize: $200 and publication of the paper in the scholarly journal, *Agricultural History*.

EVANS BIOGRAPHY & HANDCART AWARDS

(formerly David W. and Beatrice C. Evans Biography & Handcart Awards), Mountain West Center for Regional Studies, Utah State University, 0735 Old Main Hill, Logan UT 84322-0735. (435)797-3630. Fax: (435)797-3899. E-mail: mwc@cc.usu.edu. Website: www.usu.edu/~pioneers/mwc.html. Estab. 1983. Offered to encourage the writing of biography about people who have played a role in Mormon Country. (Not the religion, the country: Intermountain West with parts of Southwestern Canada and Northwestern Mexico.) Publishers or authors may nominate books. Criteria for consideration: Work must be a biography or autobiography on "Mormon Country"; must be submitted for consideration for publication year's award; new editions or reprints are not eligible; mss are not accepted. Submit 5 copies. **Deadline: December 1.** Guidelines for SASE. Prize: $10,000 and $1,000.

Ⓢ EVENT CREATIVE NONFICTION CONTEST

Event, P.O. Box 2503, New Westminster BC V3L 5B2, Canada. (604)527-5293. Fax: (604)527-5095. E-mail: event@douglas.bc.ca. Website: event.douglas.bc.ca. **Contact:** Ian Cockfield, managing editor. Offered annually for unpublished creative nonfiction. Guidelines for SASE (Canadian postage/IRCs only). Acquires first North American serial rights for the 3 winning entries. Open to any writer, except Douglas College employees. **Deadline: April 15. Charges $25 entry fee, which includes 1-year subscription; US residents, pay in US funds.** Prize: 3 winners will each receive $500, plus payment for publication.

◼ WALLACE K. FERGUSON PRIZE

Canadian Historical Association, 395 Wellington St., Ottawa ON K1A 0N3, Canada. (613)233-7885. Fax: (613)567-3110. E-mail: cha-shc@archives.ca. Website: www.cha-shc.ca. Offered to a Canadian who has published the outstanding scholarly book in a field of history other than Canadian history. **Deadline: December 2.** Guidelines for SASE. Prize: $1,000. Open to Canadian citizens and landed immigrants only.

◼ GILBERT C. FITE DISSERTATION AWARD

Agricultural History, P.O. Box 5075, Minard Hall, NDSU, Fargo ND 58105-5075. (701)231-5831. Fax: (701)231-5832. E-mail: ndsu.agricultural.history@ndsu.nodak.edu. Website: agriculturalhistory.ndsu.nodak.edu. **Contact:** Claire Strom. Award is presented to the author of the best dissertation on agricultural history, broadly construed, completed during the calendar year. **Deadline: December 31.** Guidelines for SASE. Prize: $300 honorararium.

ROSALIE FLEMING MEMORIAL ESSAY AND CREATIVE NONFICTION PRIZE

National League of American Pen Women, Nob Hill, San Francisco Branch, 1544 Sweetwood Dr., Colma CA 94015. E-mail: pennobhill@aol.com. Website: www.soulmakingcontest.us. **Contact:** Eileen Malone. All prose works must be typed, page numbered, stapled, and double-spaced. Each essay/entry, up to 3,000 words. Annually. **Deadline: November 30.** Guidelines for SASE. **Charges $5/entry (make checks payable to NLAPW, Nob Hill Branch).** Prize: 1st Place: $100; 2nd Place: $50; 3rd Place: $25. Open to any writer.

THE FOUNTAINHEAD ESSAY CONTEST

The Ayn Rand Institute, Dept. W, P.O. Box 57044, Irvine CA 92619-7044. E-mail: essay@aynrand.org. Website: www.aynrand.org/contests/. Estab. 1985. Offered annually to encourage analytical thinking and excellence in writing, and to exposé students to the philosophic ideas of Ayn Rand. "For information contact your English teacher or guidance counselor, or visit our website." Length: 800-1,600 words. **Deadline: April 15.** Prize: 1st Place: $10,000; 2nd Place (5): $2,000; 3rd Place (10): $1,000; Finalist (35): $100; Semifinalist (200): $50. 11th and 12th graders.

GEORGE FREEDLEY MEMORIAL AWARD

Theatre Library Association, Benjamin Rosenthal Library, Queens College, C.U.N.Y., 65-30 Kissena Blvd., Flushing NY 11367. (718)997-3672. Fax: (718)997-3753. E-mail: rlw$lib@qc1.qc.edu. Website: tla.library.unt.edu. **Contact:** Richard Wall, book awards committee chair. Estab. 1968. Offered for a book published in the US within the previous calendar year on a subject related to live theatrical performance (including cabaret, circus, pantomime, puppetry, vaudeville, etc.). Eligible books may include biography, history, theory, criticism, reference, or related fields. **Deadline: February 15 of year following eligibility.** Prize: $500, and certificate to the winner; $200, and certificate for honorable mention.

THE CHRISTIAN GAUSS AWARD

The Phi Beta Kappa Society, 1606 New Hampshire Ave. NW, Washington DC 20009. (202)265-3808. Fax: (202)986-1601. E-mail: sbeasley@pbk.org. Website: www.pbk.org/scholarships/books. **Contact:** Sandra Beasley. The Christian Gauss Award is offered annually for books published between May 1 and April 30 in the field of literary scholarship or criticism. "The prize was established in 1950 to honor the late Christian Gauss, the distinguished Princeton University scholar, teacher, and dean, who also served as President of the Phi Beta Kappa Society. To be eligible, a literary biography must have a predominantly critical emphasis." Entries must be submitted by the publisher. Entries must be preceded by a letter certifying that the book(s) conform to all conditions of eligibility and stating the publication date of each entry. If accepted, 8 copies of each entry are required for the Gauss Award. Ineligible entries will be returned by Phi Beta Kappa. Books will not be entered officially in the competition until all copies and the letter of certification have been received. **Deadline: April 30.** Prize: $2,500. Judged by a rotating panel of distinguished scholars and experts in the field. Open only to original works in English and authors of US residency and publication.

◼ ◼ LIONEL GELBER PRIZE

Munk Center for International Studies, University of Toronto, 1 Devonshire Place, Toronto ON M5S 3K7, Canada. (416)946-8901. Fax: (416)946-8915. E-mail: gelberprize.munk@utoronto.ca. Website: www.utoronto.ca/mcis/gelber. **Contact:** Prize Manager. Offered annually for the year's most outstanding work of nonfiction in the field of international relations. Books must be published in English or English translation September 1-August 31 of the current year, and submitted by the publisher. Publishers should submit 6 copies of each title (up to 3 titles can be submitted). **Deadline: October 31.** Prize: $15,000 (Canadian funds).

⬛ GOVERNOR GENERAL'S LITERARY AWARD FOR LITERARY NONFICTION

Canada Council for the Arts, 350 Albert St., P.O. Box 1047, Ottawa ON K1P 5V8, Canada. (613)566-4414, ext. 5576. Fax: (613)566-4410. E-mail: joanne.larocque-poirier@canadacouncil.ca. Website: www.canadacouncil .ca/prizes/ggla. **Contact:** Joanne Larocque-Poirier. Offered for work published September 1-September 30. Given annually to the best English language and the best French language work of literary nonfiction by a Canadian. Publishers submit titles for consideration. **Deadline: March 15 or August 7, depending on the book's publication date.** Prize: Each laureate receives $15,000, and nonwinning finalists receive $1,000.

JAMES T. GRADY—JAMES H. STACK AWARD FOR INTERPRETING CHEMISTRY FOR THE PUBLIC

American Chemical Society, 1155 16th St. NW, Washington DC 20036-4800. (202)872-4408. Fax: (202)776-8211. E-mail: awards@acs.org. Website: www.acs.org/awards/grady-stack.html. **Contact:** Alicia Harris. Offered annually for previously published work to recognize, encourage, and stimulate outstanding reporting directly to the public, which materially increases the public's knowledge and understanding of chemistry, chemical engineering, and related fields. Guidelines online at website. Rules of eligibility: A nominee must have made noteworthy presentations through a medium of public communication to increase the American public's understanding of chemistry and chemical progress. This information shall have been disseminated through the press, radio, television, films, the lecture platform, books, or pamphlets for the lay public. **Deadline: February 1.** Prize: $3,000, medallion with a presentation box, and certificate, plus travel expenses to the meeting at which the award will be presented.

JOHN GUYON NONFICTION PRIZE

Crab Orchard Review, English Department, Southern Illinois University Carbondale, Carbondale IL 62901-4503. E-mail: jtribble@siu.edu. Website: www.siu.edu/ ~ crborchd. **Contact:** Jon C. Tribble, managing editor. Offered annually for unpublished work. This competition seeks to reward excellence in the writing of creative nonfiction. This is not a prize for academic essays. *Crab Orchard Review* acquires first North American serial rights to submitted works. **Deadline: February 1-March 15.** Guidelines for SASE. **Charges $15/essay (limit of 3 essays of up to 6,500 words each).** Prize: $1,500, and publication. U.S. citizens only.

ALBERT J. HARRIS AWARD

International Reading Association, Division of Research and Policy, 800 Barksdale Rd., Newark DE 19714-8139. (302)731-1600, ext. 423. Fax: (302)731-1057. E-mail: research@reading.org. Website: www.reading.org. **Contact:** Marcella Moore. Offered annually to recognize outstanding published works on the topics of reading disabilities and the prevention, assessment, or instruction of learners experiencing difficulty learning to read. Open to any writer. Copies of the applications and guidelines can be downloaded in PDF format from the International Reading Association's website. **Deadline: September 15.** Prize: Monetary award and recognition at the International Reading Association's annual convention.

ELLIS W. HAWLEY PRIZE

Organization of American Historians, 112 N. Bryan Ave., Bloomington IN 47408-4199. (812)855-7311. Fax: (812)855-0696. E-mail: awards@oah.org. Website: www.oah.org. **Contact:** Award and Prize Committee Coordinator. Offered annually for the best book-length historical study of the political economy, politics, or institutions of the US, in its domestic or international affairs, from the Civil War to the present. Books must be written in English. Guidelines available on website. **Deadline: October 1.** Prize: $500, and a certificate.

HENDRICKS MANUSCRIPT AWARD

New Netherland Project, New York State Library, Cultural Exchange Center, 8th Floor, Madison Ave., Empire State Plaza Station, Albany NY 12220-0536. (518)474-6067. Fax: (518)473-0472. E-mail: cgehring@mail.nysed.g ov. Website: www.nnp.org. **Contact:** Charles Gehring. Offered annually for the best published or unpublished ms focusing on any aspect of the Dutch colonial experience in North America. **Deadline: February 15.** Guidelines for SASE. Prize: $2,000.

L. KEMPER AND LEILA WILLIAMS PRIZE

The Historic New Orleans Collection and Louisiana Historical Association, 533 Royal St., New Orleans LA 70130-2179. Fax: (504)598-7108. E-mail: johnl@hnoc.org. Website: www.hnoc.org. **Contact:** Chair, Williams Prize Committee. Director: John H. Lawrence. Offered annually for the best published work on Louisiana history, published during the previous calendar year. **Deadline: January 15.** Prize: $1,500, and a plaque.

THE KIRIYAMA PRIZE

(formerly The Kiriyama Pacific Rim Book Prize), Kiriyama Pacific Rim Institute, 650 Delancey St., Suite 101, San Francisco CA 94107. (415)777-1628. Fax: (415)777-1646. E-mail: admin@kiriyamaprize.org. Website: www

.kiriyamaprize.org. **Contact:** Jeannine Cuevas, prize manager. Offered for work published from January 1 through December 31 of the current prize year to promote books that will contribute to greater mutual understanding and increased cooperation throughout the Pacific Rim and South Asia. Guidelines and entry form on request, or may be downloaded from the prize website. Books must be submitted for entry by the publisher. Proper entry forms must be submitted. Contact the administrators of the prize for complete rules and entry forms. **Deadline: late Fall each year; specific date TBA.** Prize: $30,000 to be divided equally between the author of 1 fiction and of 1 nonfiction book.

KATHERINE SINGER KOVACS PRIZE

Modern Language Association of America, 26 Broadway, 3rd Floor, New York NY 10004-1789. (646)576-5141. Fax: (646)458-0030. E-mail: awards@mla.org. Website: www.mla.org. **Contact:** Coordinator of Book Prizes. Estab. 1990. Offered annually for a book published during the previous year in English in the field of Latin American and Spanish literatures and cultures. Books should be broadly interpretive works that enhance understanding of the interrelations among literature, the other arts, and society. Author need not be a member of the MLA. **Deadline: May 1.** Guidelines for SASE. Prize: $1,000, and a certificate.

⊕ KRASZNA-KRAUSZ PHOTOGRAPHY & MOVING IMAGE BOOK AWARDS

Kraszna-Krausz Foundation, 122 Fawnbrake Ave., London, England SE24-0BZ. (+44)20-7738-6701. E-mail: awards@k-k.org.uk. Website: www.k-k.org.uk. **Contact:** Andrea Livingstone. These annual awards recognize outstanding achievements in the publishing and writing of books (published between June and May) on the art, history, practice, and technology of photography and the moving image (film, TV, etc.). All submissions must be made by the publisher of the title. **Deadline: July 1.** Guidelines for SASE. Prize: Main Awards (2): £5,000 UK Sterling; Finalist Awards: up to £1,000 UK Sterling. Judged by an international panel of 3 judges which changes annually. Open to any writer.

LERNER-SCOTT PRIZE

Organization of American Historians, 112 N. Bryan Ave., Bloomington IN 47408-4199. (812)855-9852. Fax: (812)855-0696. E-mail: awards@oah.org. Website: www.oah.org. **Contact:** Award and Prize Committee Coordinator. Offered annually for the best doctoral dissertation in US women's history. Guidelines available at website. **Deadline: October 1 for a dissertation completed in the previous academic year (July 1-June 30).** Prize: $1,000, and a certificate.

LINCOLN PRIZE AT GETTYSBURG COLLEGE

Gettysburg College and Lincoln & Soldiers Institute, 233 N. Washington St., Gettysburg PA 17325. (717)337-6590. Fax: (717)337-6596. E-mail: lincolnprize@gettysburg.edu. Website: www.gettysburg.edu/lincoln_prize. Offered annually for the finest scholarly work in English on the era of the American Civil War. The award will usually go to a book published in the previous year; however articles, essays, and works of fiction may be submitted. Guidelines for SASE or on website. **Deadline: November 1.** Prize: $50,000.

Ⓝ WALTER D. LOVE PRIZE

North American Conference on British Studies, History Department, University of Texas, Austin TX 78712. (512)475-7204. Fax: (512)475-7222. E-mail: harling@pop.uky.edu. **Contact:** Philip Harling, executive secretary. Offered annually for best article in any field of British Studies. Open to American or Canadian writers. **Deadline: April 1.** Guidelines for SASE. Prize: $150.

JAMES RUSSELL LOWELL PRIZE

Modern Language Association of America, 26 Broadway, 3rd Floor, New York NY 10004-1789. (646)576-5141. Fax: (646)458-0030. E-mail: awards@mla.org. Website: www.mla.org. **Contact:** Coordinator of Book Prizes. Offered annually for literary or linguistic study, or critical edition or biography published in previous year. *Open to MLA members only.* **Deadline: March 1.** Guidelines for SASE. Prize: $1,000, and a certificate.

◼ SIR JOHN A. MACDONALD PRIZE

Canadian Historical Association, 395 Wellington St., Ottawa ON K1A 0N3, Canada. (613)233-7885. Fax: (613)567-3110. E-mail: cha-shc@archives.ca. Website: www.cha-shc.ca. Offered annually to award a previously published nonfiction work of Canadian history "judged to have made the most significant contribution to an understanding of the Canadian past." Open to Canadian citizens only. **Deadline: December 2.** Guidelines for SASE. Prize: $1,000.

◼ GRANT MACEWAN AUTHOR'S AWARD

Alberta Community Development, 9th Floor Standard Life Centre, 10405 Jasper Ave., Edmonton AB T5J 4R7, Canada. Website: www.cd.gov.ab.ca. This annual award was created by the government to honor the life and contributions of the late Dr. Grant MacEwan. Books submitted must reflect Alberta and/or Dr. MacEwan's interests and must have been published between January 1 and December 31. **Deadline: December 31.** Guidelines for SASE. Prize: $25,000. Judged by a jury of prominent Alberta authors. Residents of Alberta only.

HOWARD R. MARRARO PRIZE

Modern Language Association of America, 26 Broadway, 3rd Floor, New York NY 10004-1789. (646)576-5141. Fax: (646)458-0030. E-mail: awards@mla.org. Website: www.mla.org. **Contact:** Coordinator of Book Prizes. Offered in even-numbered years for a scholarly book or essay on any phase of Italian literature or comparative literature involving Italian, published in previous year. Authors must be members of the MLA. **Deadline: May 1, 2004.** Guidelines for SASE. Prize: $1,000, and a certificate.

MID-LIST PRESS FIRST SERIES AWARD FOR CREATIVE NONFICTION

Mid-List Press, 4324 12th Ave. S., Minneapolis MN 55407-3218. Fax: (612)823-8387. E-mail: guide@midlist.org. Website: www.midlist.org. **Contact:** Lane Stiles, publisher. Open to any writer who has never published a book of creative nonfiction. Submit either a collection of essays or a single book-length work; minimum length 50,000 words. Accepts simultaneous submissions. Guidelines and entry form for SASE or on website. **Deadline: July 1. Charges $30 (US dollars) fee.** Prize: Awards include publication and an advance against royalties.

KENNETH W. MILDENBERGER PRIZE

Modern Language Association of America, 26 Broadway, 3rd Floor, New York NY 10004-1789. (646)576-5141. Fax: (646)458-0030. E-mail: awards@mla.org. Website: www.mla.org. **Contact:** Coordinator of Book Prizes. Offered annually for a publication from the previous year in the field of teaching foreign languages and literatures. Author need not be a member. **Deadline: May 1.** Guidelines for SASE. Prize: $1,000, a certificate, and a year's membership in the MLA.

MLA PRIZE FOR A DISTINGUISHED BIBLIOGRAPHY

Modern Language Association of America, 26 Broadway, 3rd Floor, New York NY 10004-1789. (646)576-5141. Fax: (646)458-0030. E-mail: awards@mla.org. Website: www.mla.org. **Contact:** Coordinator of Book Prizes. Offered in even-numbered years for enumerative and descriptive bibliographies published in monographic, book, or electronic format in the 2 years prior to the competition. Open to any writer or publisher. **Deadline: May 1, 2004.** Guidelines for SASE. Prize: $1,000, and a certificate.

MLA PRIZE FOR A DISTINGUISHED SCHOLARLY EDITION

Modern Language Association of America, 26 Broadway, 3rd Floor, New York NY 10004-1789. (646)576-5141. Fax: (646)458-0030. E-mail: awards@mla.org. Website: www.mla.org. **Contact:** Coordinator of Book Prizes. Offered in odd-numbered years. To qualify for the award, an edition should be based on an examination of all available relevant textual sources; the source texts and the edited text's deviations from them should be fully described; the edition should employ editorial principles appropriate to the materials edited, and those principles should be clearly articulated in the volume; the text should be accompanied by appropriate textual and other historical contextual information; the edition should exhibit the highest standards of accuracy in the presentation of its text and apparatus; and the text and apparatus should be presented as accessibly and elegantly as possible. Editor need not be a member of the MLA. **Deadline: May 1.** Guidelines for SASE. Prize: $1,000, and a certificate.

MLA PRIZE FOR A FIRST BOOK

Modern Language Association of America, 26 Broadway, 3rd Floor, New York NY 10004-1789. (646)576-5141. Fax: (646)458-0030. E-mail: awards@mla.org. Website: www.mla.org. **Contact:** Coordinator of Book Prizes. Offered annually for the first book-length scholarly publication by a current member of the association. To qualify, a book must be a literary or linguistic study, a critical edition of an important work, or a critical biography. Studies dealing with literary theory, media, cultural history, and interdisciplinary topics are eligible; books that are primarily translations will not be considered. **Deadline: April 1.** Guidelines for SASE. Prize: $1,000, and a certificate.

MLA PRIZE FOR INDEPENDENT SCHOLARS

Modern Language Association of America, 26 Broadway, 3rd Floor, New York NY 10004-1789. (646)576-5141. Fax: (646)458-0030. E-mail: awards@mla.org. Website: www.mla.org. **Contact:** Coordinator of Book Prizes. Offered annually for a book in the field of English, or another modern language, or literature published in the previous year. Authors who are enrolled in a program leading to an academic degree or who hold tenured or tenure-track positions in higher education are not eligible. Authors need not be members of MLA. Guidelines and application form for SASE. **Deadline: May 1.** Prize: $1,000, a certificate, and a year's membership in the MLA.

GEORGE JEAN NATHAN AWARD FOR DRAMATIC CRITICISM

Cornell University, Department of English, Goldwin Smith Hall, Ithaca NY 14853. (607)255-6801. Fax: (607)255-6661. E-mail: english_chair@cornell.edu. Website: www.arts.cornell.edu/english/nathan/index.html. **Contact:** Chair, Department of English. Offered annually to the American "who has written the best piece of drama criticism during the theatrical year (July 1-June 30), whether it is an article, an essay, treatise, or book." Only published work may be submitted; author must be an American citizen. Guidelines for SASE. Prize: $10,000, and a trophy.

■ NATIONAL BUSINESS BOOK AWARD

PricewaterhouseCoopers and BMO Financial Group, 77 King St. W., Toronto ON M5K 1G8, Canada. (416)941-8344. Fax: (416)941-8345. E-mail: mafreedman@freedmanandassociates.com. Website: www.pwc.com. **Contact:** Faye Mattachione. Offered annually for books published January 1-December 31 to recognize excellence in business writing in Canada. Publishers nominate books. **Deadline: December 31.** Prize: $10,000.

NATIONAL WRITERS ASSOCIATION NONFICTION CONTEST

The National Writers Association, 3140 S. Peoria, #295, Aurora CO 80014. (303)841-0246. Fax: (303)841-2607. E-mail: sandywrter@aol.com. Website: www.nationalwriters.com. **Contact:** Sandy Whelchel, director. Annual contest "to encourage writers in this creative form and to recognize those who excel in nonfiction writing." **Deadline: December 31.** Guidelines for SASE. **Charges $18 fee.** Prize: 1st Place: $200; 2nd Place: $100; 3rd Place: $50.

■ THE NATURAL WORLD BOOK PRIZE

The Wildlife Trusts & Booktrust, Book House, 45 E. Hill, Wandsworth, London SW18 2QZ, United Kingdom. Fax: (00 44) 8516 2978. E-mail: tarryn@booktrust.org.uk. Website: www.booktrust.org.uk. **Contact:** Amanda Spivack. "This annual award rewards the book that most imaginatively promotes the understanding and conservation of our natural environment and its wildlife in an accessible and enjoyable fashion. The books must be accessible to the general, nonspecific reader and be published between June 1 and May 31. Entries must be full length, unified, and substantial new works by an author of any nationality, but the book must be published in the UK by a UK publisher." Prize: £5,000 to the author(s) or editor(s) of the winning book. The judges reserve the right to award a discretionary prize of £1,000 to a runner up.

■ C.B. OLDMAN PRIZE

International Association of Music Libraries United Kingdom and Ireland Branch, c/o Queen Mother Library, Meston Walk, Aberdeen AB24 3VE, United Kingdom. (01224) 272590. Fax: (01224) 487048. Website: www.music.ox.ac.uk/IAML/. **Contact:** Graham Muncy. Contest for the best book of music bibliography, librarianship, or reference by an author domiciled in the United Kingdom or Ireland. Annually, Must Be Previously Published. **Deadline: December 31.** Prize: £200. Judged by a committee of 3 whose members spend 3 years (staggered so that there is only one newcomer annually).

OUTSTANDING DISSERTATION OF THE YEAR AWARD

International Reading Association, 800 Barksdale Rd., P.O. Box 8139, Newark DE 19714-8139. (302)731-1600, ext. 423. Fax: (302)731-1057. E-mail: research@reading.org. Website: www.reading.org. **Contact:** Marcella Moore. Offered annually to recognize dissertations in the field of reading and literacy. *Applicants must be members of the International Reading Association.* Copies of the applications and guidelines can be downloaded in PDF format from the International Reading Association's website. **Deadline: October 1.** Prize: $1,000.

FRANK LAWRENCE AND HARRIET CHAPPELL OWSLEY AWARD

Southern Historical Association, Dept. of History University of Georgia, Athens GA 30602-1602. (706)542-8848. Fax: (706)542-2455. Website: www.uga.edu/~sha. **Contact:** Secretary-Treasurer. Estab. 1934. Managing Editor: John B. Boles. Offered in odd-numbered years for recognition of a distinguished book in Southern history published in even-numbered years. Publishers usually submit the books. **Deadline: March 1.**

■ THE PEARSON WRITERS' TRUST NONFICTION PRIZE

The Writers' Trust of Canada, 40 Wellington St. E., Suite 300, Toronto ON M5E 1C7, Canada. (416)504-8222. Fax: (416)504-9090. E-mail: info@writerstrust.com. **Contact:** James Davies. Offered annually for a work of nonfiction published in the previous year. Award presented at the Great Literary Awards event held in Toronto each spring. Applications for SASE. **Deadline: Late July or mid-November, depending on publication date.** Prize: $15,000 (Canadian), and up to 4 runners-up prizes of $2,000 (Canadian).

LOUIS PELZER MEMORIAL AWARD

Organization of American Historians, *Journal of American History*, 1215 E. Atwater Ave., Bloomington IN 47401. (812)855-9852. Fax: (812)855-0696. E-mail: awards@oah.org. Website: www.oah.org. **Contact:** Joanne Meyerowitz, committee chair. Offered annually for the best essay in American history by a graduate student. The essay may be about any period or topic in the history of the US, and the author must be enrolled in a graduate program at any level, in any field. Length: 7,000 words (including endnotes) maximum. Guidelines available on website. **Deadline: December 1.** Prize: $500, a medal, a certificate, and publication of the essay in the *Journal of American History*.

PEN AWARD FOR THE ART OF THE ESSAY

(formerly PEN/Spielvogel-Diamonstein Award), PEN American Center, 568 Broadway, New York NY 10012. (212)334-1660. Fax: (212)334-2181. E-mail: awards@pen.org. **Contact:** Stephen Motika. Offered for the best previously unpublished collection of essays on any subject by an American writer. "The $5,000 prize is awarded to preserve the dignity and esteem that the essay form imparts to literature." The essays included in books submitted may have been previously published in magazines, journals, or anthologies, but must not have collectively appeared before in book form. Books will be judged on literary character and distinction of the writing. Publishers, agents, or the authors must submit 4 copies of each eligible title. **Deadline: December 15.** Prize: $5,000. Authors must be American citizens or permanent residents.

PEN/MARTHA ALBRAND AWARD FOR FIRST NONFICTION

PEN American Center, 568 Broadway, New York NY 10012. (212)334-1660. Fax: (212)334-2181. E-mail: awards @pen.org. **Contact:** Stephen Motika, coordinator. Offered annually for a first published book of general nonfiction distinguished by qualities of literary and stylistic excellence. Eligible books must have been published in the calendar year under consideration. Authors must be American citizens or permanent residents. Although there are no restrictions on the subject matter of titles submitted, nonliterary books will not be considered. Books should be of adult nonfiction for the general or academic reader. Publishers, agents, and authors themselves must submit 3 copies of each eligible title. **Deadline: December 15.** Prize: $1,000.

PEN/MARTHA ALBRAND AWARD FOR THE ART OF THE MEMOIR

PEN American Center, 568 Broadway, New York NY 10012. (212)334-1660. Fax: (212)334-2181. E-mail: awards @pen.org. **Contact:** Stephen Motika. Offered annually to an American author for his/her memoir published in the current calendar year, distinguished by qualities of literary and stylistic excellence. Send 3 copies of each eligible book. Open to American writers. **Deadline: December 15.** Prize: $1,000.

PEN/JERARD FUND

PEN American Center, 568 Broadway, New York NY 10012. (212)334-1660. Fax: (212)334-2181. E-mail: awards @pen.org. **Contact:** Stephen Motika. Estab. 1986. Biennial grant offered in odd-numbered years for an American woman writer of nonfiction for a book-length work-in-progress. **Deadline: January 3, 2005.** Prize: $5,500 grant.

THE PHI BETA KAPPA AWARD IN SCIENCE

The Phi Beta Kappa Society, 1606 New Hampshire Ave. NW, Washington DC 20009. (202)265-3808. Fax: (202)986-1601. E-mail: sbeasley@pbk.org. Website: www.pbk.org/scholarships/books. **Contact:** Sandra Beasley. Estab. 1959. "The Phi Beta Kappa Award in Science is offered annually for outstanding contributions by scientists to the literature of science. The intent of the award is to encourage literate and scholarly interpretations of the physical and biological sciences and mathematics; monographs and compendiums are not eligible. To be eligible, biographies of scientists must have a substantial critical emphasis on their scientific research." Entries must have been published May 1-April 30. Entries must be submitted by the publisher. Entries must be preceded by a letter certifying that the book(s) conforms to all the conditions of eligibility and stating the publication date of each entry. If accepted, 6 copies of each entry are required for the Science Award. Ineligible entries will be returned by Phi Beta Kappa. Books will not be entered officially in the competition until all copies and the letter of certification have been received. **Deadline: April 30.** Prize: $2,500. Open only to original works in English and authors of US residency and publication.

N PRESERVATION FOUNDATION CONTESTS

The Preservation Foundation, Inc., 3102 W. End Ave., Suite 200, Nashville TN 37203. E-mail: preserve@storyho use.org. Website: www.storyhouse.org. **Contact:** Richard Loller. Contest offered annually for unpublished nonfiction. "Our annual contests are to encourage those with a story to tell to share it with others before it is lost or forgotten. General nonfiction category (1,500-5,000 words)—any appropriate nonfiction topic. Travel nonfiction category (1,500-5,000 words)—must be true story of trip by author or someone known personally by author." Contest is for previously unpublished writers. **First entry is free, $5/additional entry per contest.**

Deadline: September 30. Prize: 1st prize: $100 in each category. Certificates for runners-up and finalists. Open to any writer.

JAMES A. RAWLEY PRIZE

Organization of American Historians, 112 N. Bryan Ave., Bloomington IN 47408-4199. (812)855-7311. Fax: (812)855-0696. E-mail: awards@oah.org. Website: www.oah.org. **Contact:** Award and Prize Committee Coordinator. Offered annually for a book dealing with the history of race relations in the US. Books must have been published in the current calendar year. Before submitting a nomination, a listing of current committee members and details about individual prizes must be obtained from the OAH website. **Deadline: October 1; books to be published after October 1 of the calendar year may be submitted as page proofs.** Prize: $1,000, and a certificate.

PHILLIP D. REED MEMORIAL AWARD FOR OUTSTANDING WRITING ON THE SOUTHERN ENVIRONMENT

Southern Environmental Law Center, 201 W. Main St., Charlottesville VA 22902. (434)977-4090. Fax: (434)977-1483. E-mail: selcva@selcva.org. Website: www.SouthernEnvironment.org. **Contact:** Cathryn McCue, award director. Offered annually for nonfiction pieces that pertain to the natural resources in at least 1 of the following: Alabama, Georgia, North Carolina, South Carolina, Tennessee, Virginia. Two categories for works published in previous calendar year: books and journalism. Minimum length: 3,000 words. Prize: $1,000 each. Category for unpublished advocacy piece. Length 2,000-5,000 words. Prize: $250.

⌧ EVELYN RICHARDSON NONFICTION AWARD

Writers' Federation of Nova Scotia, 1113 Marginal Rd., Halifax NS B3H 4P7, Canada. (902)423-8116. Fax: (902)422-0881. E-mail: talk@writers.ns.ca. Website: www.writers.ns.ca. **Contact:** Jane Buss, executive director. "Nova Scotia's highest award for a book of nonfiction written by a Nova Scotian, the Evelyn Richardson Nonfiction Award is presented annually by the Writers' Federation of Nova Scotia. The Award is named for Nova Scotia writer Evelyn Richardson, whose book *We Keep a Light* won the Governor General's Literary Award for nonfiction in 1945." There is **no entry fee** or form. Full-length books of nonfiction written by Nova Scotians, and published as a whole for the first time in the previous calendar year, are eligible. Publishers: Send 4 copies and a letter attesting to the author's status as a Nova Scotian, and the author's current mailing address and telephone number. **Deadline: First Friday in December.** Prize: $1,000.

⌧ ROGERS COMMUNICATION LITERARY NONFICTION CONTEST

(formerly Prism International Prize for Literary Nonfiction), PRISM International, Creative Writing Program, UBC, Buch E462—1866 Main Mall, Vancouver BC V6T 1Z1, Canada. (604)822-2514. Fax: (604)822-3616. E-mail: prism@interchange.ubc.ca. Website: prism.arts.ubc.ca. **Contact:** Mark Mallet, executive editor. Offered annually for published and unpublished writers to promote and reward excellence in literary nonfiction writing. *PRISM* buys first North American serial rights upon publication. "We also buy limited Web rights for pieces selected for website." Open to anyone except students and faculty of the Creative Writing Program at UBC or people who have taken a creative writing course at UBC in the 2 years prior to contest deadline. All entrants receive a 1-year subscription to *PRISM*. **Deadline: September 30.** Guidelines for SASE. **Charges $25, plus $7 for each additional entry (outside Canada use US funds).** Prize: $500 for the winning entry, plus $20/page for the publication of the winner in *PRISM*'s winter issue.

⌘ THE ROYAL SOCIETY OF LITERATURE AWARD UNDER THE W.H. HEINEMANN BEQUEST

Royal Society of Literature, Somerset House Strand, London, England WC2R 1LA. (44)2078454676. Fax: (44)2078454679. E-mail: info@rslit.org. Website: www.rslit.org. Offered annually for previously published work appearing in print between January and December 2004. "W.H. Heinemann's Bequest was 'the encouragement of genuine contributions to literature.' Most often awarded to works of nonfiction, though novels, if of sufficient distinction, will not be overlooked." **Deadline: December 15.** Guidelines for SASE. Prize: £5,000. Judged by 3 Fellows of the Royal Society of Literature. Open to any writer.

THE CORNELIUS RYAN AWARD

The Overseas Press Club of America, 40 W. 45th St., New York NY 10036. (212)626-9220. Fax: (212)626-9210. Website: www.opcofamerica.org. **Contact:** Sonya Fry, executive director. Offered annually for excellence in a nonfiction book on international affairs. Generally publishers nominate the work, but writers may also submit in their own name. The work must be published and on the subject of foreign affairs. **Deadline: End of January. Charges $125 fee.** Prize: $1,000, and certificate.

▨ THEODORE SALOUTOS AWARD

Agricultural History, P.O. Box 5075, Minard Hall, NDSU, Fargo ND 58105-5075. (701)231-5831. Fax: (701)231-5832. E-mail: ndsu.agricultural.history@ndsu.nodak.edu. Website: agriculturalhistory.ndsu.nodak.edu. **Contact:** Claire Strom. Offered annually for best book on US agricultural history broadly interpreted. Open nominations. **Deadline: December 31.** Prize: $500.

▨ SASKATCHEWAN NONFICTION AWARD

Saskatchewan Book Awards, Inc., Box 1921, Regina SK S4P 3E1, Canada. (306)569-1585. Fax: (306)569-4187. E-mail: director@bookawards.sk.ca. Website: www.bookawards.sk.ca. **Contact:** Joyce Wells, executive director. Offered annually for work published September 15-September 14. This award is presented to a Saskatchewan author for the best book of nonfiction, judged on the quality of writing. **Deadline: First deadline: July 31; Final deadline: September 14.** Guidelines for SASE. **Charges $20 (Canadian).** Prize: $2,000.

▨ SASKATCHEWAN SCHOLARLY WRITING AWARD

Saskatchewan Book Awards, Inc., Box 1921, Regina SK S4P 3E1, Canada. (306)569-1585. Fax: (306)569-4187. E-mail: director@bookawards.sk.ca. Website: www.bookawards.sk.ca. **Contact:** Joyce Wells, executive director. Offered annually for work published September 15 to September 14 annually. This award is presented to a Saskatchewan author for the best contribution to scholarship. The work must recognize or draw on specific theoretical work within a community of scholars, and participate in the creation and transmission of knowledge. **Deadline: First deadline: July 31; Final deadline: September 14.** Guidelines for SASE. **Charges $20 (Canadian).** Prize: $2,000.

THE BARBARA SAVAGE 'MILES FROM NOWHERE' MEMORIAL AWARD

The Mountaineers Books, 1001 SW Klickitat Way, Suite 201, Seattle WA 98134. (206)223-6303. Fax: (206)223-6306. E-mail: mbooks@mountaineersbooks.org. Website: www.mountaineersbooks.org. **Contact:** Mary Metz. Offered in even-numbered years for previously unpublished book-length nonfiction personal adventure narrative. Narrative must be based on an outdoor adventure involving hiking, mountain climbing, bicycling, paddle sports, skiing, snowshoeing, nature, conservation, ecology, or adventure travel not dependent upon motorized transport. Subjects *not* acceptable include hunting, fishing, or motorized or competitive sports. **Deadline: March 1, 2004.** Guidelines for SASE. Prize: $3,000 cash award, a $12,000 guaranteed advance against royalties, and publication by The Mountaineers.

ALDO AND JEANNE SCAGLIONE PRIZE FOR COMPARATIVE LITERARY STUDIES

Modern Language Association of America, 26 Broadway, 3rd Floor, New York NY 10004-1789. (646)576-5141. Fax: (646)458-0030. E-mail: awards@mla.org. Website: www.mla.org. **Contact:** Coordinator of Book Prizes. Offered annually for outstanding scholarly work published in the preceding year in the field of comparative literary studies involving at least 2 literatures. *Author must be a member of the MLA.* Works of scholarship, literary history, literary criticism, and literary theory are eligible; books that are primarily translations are not eligible. **Deadline: May 1.** Guidelines for SASE. Prize: $2,000, and a certificate.

ALDO AND JEANNE SCAGLIONE PRIZE FOR FRENCH AND FRANCOPHONE STUDIES

Modern Language Association of America, 26 Broadway, 3rd Floor, New York NY 10004-1789. (646)576-5141. Fax: (646)458-0030. E-mail: awards@mla.org. Website: www.mla.org. **Contact:** Coordinator of Book Prizes. Offered annually for work published in the preceding year that is an outstanding scholarly work in the field of French or francophone linguistic or literary studies. *Author must be a member of the MLA.* Works of scholarship, literary history, literary criticism, and literary theory are eligible; books that are primarily translations are not eligible. **Deadline: May 1.** Guidelines for SASE. Prize: $2,000, and a certificate.

ALDO AND JEANNE SCAGLIONE PRIZE FOR ITALIAN STUDIES

Modern Language Association of America, 26 Broadway, 3rd Floor, New York NY 10004-1789. (646)576-5141. Fax: (646)458-0030. E-mail: awards@mla.org. Website: www.mla.org. **Contact:** Coordinator of Book Prizes. Offered in odd-numbered years for a scholarly book on any phase of Italian literature or culture, or comparative literature involving Italian, including works on literary or cultural theory, science, history, art, music, society, politics, cinema, and linguistics, preferably but not necessarily relating other disciplines to literature. Books must have been published in year prior to competition. *Authors must be members of the MLA.* **Deadline: May 1.** Guidelines for SASE. Prize: $2,000, and a certificate.

ALDO AND JEANNE SCAGLIONE PRIZE FOR STUDIES IN GERMANIC LANGUAGES & LITERATURE

Modern Language Association of America, 26 Broadway, 3rd Floor, New York NY 10004-1789. (646)576-5141. Fax: (646)458-0030. E-mail: awards@mla.org. Website: www.mla.org. **Contact:** Coordinator of Book Prizes.

Offered in even-numbered years for outstanding scholarly work appearing in print in the previous 2 years and written by a member of the MLA on the linguistics or literatures of the Germanic languages. Works of literary history, literary criticism, and literary theory are eligible; books that are primarily translations are not eligible. **Deadline: May 1.** Guidelines for SASE. Prize: $2,000, and a certificate.

ALDO AND JEANNE SCAGLIONE PRIZE FOR STUDIES IN SLAVIC LANGUAGES AND LITERATURES

Modern Language Association of America, 26 Broadway, 3rd Floor, New York NY 10004-1789. (646)576-5141. Fax: (646)458-0030. E-mail: awards@mla.org. Website: www.mla.org. **Contact:** Coordinator of Book Prizes. Offered each odd-numbered year for books published in the previous 2 years. Membership in the MLA is not required. Works of literary history, literary criticism, philology, and literary theory are eligible; books that are primarily translations are not eligible. **Deadline: May 1.** Guidelines for SASE. Prize: $2,000, and a certificate.

SCIENCE WRITING AWARDS IN PHYSICS AND ASTRONOMY

American Institute of Physics, 1 Physics Ellipse, College Park MD 20740-3843. (301)209-3096. Fax: (301)209-0846. E-mail: fgonzale@aip.org. Website: www.aip.org/aip/writing. **Contact:** Flory Gonzalez. Offered for published articles, booklets, or books "that improve the general public's appreciation and understanding of physics and astronomy." Four categories: articles or books intended for children, preschool-15 years old; broadcast media for radio or television programming; journalism, written by a professional journalist; and finally, books or articles by a scientist. Guidelines by phone, e-mail, or website. **Deadline: March 1.** Prize: $3,000, engraved Windsor chair, and certificate awarded in each category.

MINA P. SHAUGHNESSY PRIZE

Modern Language Association of America, 26 Broadway, 3rd Floor, New York NY 10004-1789. (646)576-5141. Fax: (646)458-0030. E-mail: awards@mla.org. Website: www.mla.org. **Contact:** Coordinator of Book Prizes. Offered annually for a scholarly book in the fields of language, culture, literacy or literature with strong application to the teaching of English published during preceding year. Authors need not be members of the MLA. **Deadline: May 1.** Guidelines for SASE. Prize: $1,000, a certificate, and a year's membership in the MLA.

SOUTHERN CALIFORNIA GENEALOGICAL SOCIETY'S WRITERS CONTEST

Southern California Genealogical Society, 417 Irving Dr., Burbank CA 91504-2408. (818)843-7247. Fax: (818)843-7262. E-mail: scgs@earthlink.net. Website: www.scgsgenealogy.com. **Contact:** Writing Contest. **Category 1:** Research-oriented family, local, or ancestral history (3,000 words maximum). **Category 2:** Miscellaneous (must relate to family or local history), can include how-to articles, memoirs, accounts of ancestral events or dramas, reflections, personality sketches, humor, etc. (1,000-2,000 words). **Category 3:** Miscellaneous (must relate to family or local history), can include how-to articles, memoirs, accounts of ancestral events or dramas, reflections, personality sketches, humor, etc. (1,000 words or less). **Deadline: December 31 (must be received November 1-December 31).** Guidelines for SASE. Prize: **Categories 1 & 2:** 1st Prize: $250; 2nd Prize: $125; 3rd Prize: $75. **Category 3:** 1st Prize: $125; 2nd Prize: $75; 3rd Prize: $50. All Honorable Mentions receive a 1-year subscription to *The Searcher.* Judged by newspaper editors from Book Review sections. Open to any writer.

SWACKHAMER PEACE ESSAY CONTEST

Nuclear Age Peace Foundation, PMB 121, 1187 Coastal Village Rd., Suite 1, Santa Barbara CA 93108-2794. (805)965-3443. Fax: (805)568-0466. E-mail: youth@napf.org. Website: www.wagingpeace.org. **Contact:** David Krieger. Offered annually for unpublished work. "The Swackhamer Peace Essay Contest seeks suggestions for constructive approaches from high school students to the problems of war and peace. The topic of the 2004 contest is: If you were invited to give a nationally televised speech to the American people, including the President and the Congress, what would you say to convince them that the United States should take a leadership role in the global elimination of nuclear weapons?" All essays become the property of the Nuclear Age Peace Foundation. The prize-winning essays will be published by the Foundation and will be sent to the Secretary General of the United Nations for transmittal to the UN General Assembly, to the President of the United States, and to other key world and national leaders. The winning essays will also be made widely available for use by newspapers, magazines, and broadcasting networks. Other essays, including honorable mentions, may be published by the Foundation and used on its website or in publications. **Deadline: June 1 (postmarked).** Guidelines for SASE. Prize: 1st Place: $1,500; 2nd Place: $1,000; 3rd Place: $500. Honorable Mentions may also be awarded. Judged by a committee of judges selected by the Nuclear Age Peace Foundation. Open to all high school students throughout the world.

THE THEATRE LIBRARY ASSOCIATION AWARD

Theatre Library Association, Benjamin Rosenthal Library, Queens College, C.U.N.Y., 65-30 Kissena Blvd., Flushing NY 11367. (718)997-3672. Fax: (718)997-3753. E-mail: rlw$lib@qc1.qc.edu. Website: tla.library.unt.edu.

Contact: Richard Wall, book awards committee chair. Estab. 1973. Offered for a book published in the US within the previous calendar year on a subject related to recorded or broadcast performance (including motion pictures, television, and radio). Eligible books may include biography, history, theory, criticism, reference, or related fields. **Deadline: February 15 of year following eligibility.** Prize: $500, and certificate to the winner; $200 and certificate for honorable mention.

FREDERICK JACKSON TURNER AWARD

Organization of American Historians, 112 N. Bryan Ave., Bloomington IN 47408-4199. (812)855-7311. Fax: (812)855-0696. E-mail: awards@oah.org. Website: www.oah.org. **Contact:** Award and Prize Committee Coordinator. Offered annually for an author's first book on some significant phase of American history and also to the press that submits and publishes it. The entry must comply with the following rules: 1) The work must be the first book-length study of history published by the author; 2) If the author has a Ph.D., he/she must have received it no earlier than 7 years prior to submission of the ms for publication; 3) The work must be published in the calendar year before the award is given; 4) The work must deal with some significant phase of American history. Before submitting a nomination, a listing of current committee members and details about individual prizes must be obtained from the OAH website. **Deadline: October 1.** Prize: $1,000, certificate, and medal.

TURNING WHEEL YOUNG WRITER'S AWARD

Turning Wheel: The Journal of Socially Engaged Buddhism, P.O. Box 3470, Berkeley CA 94703. (510)655-6169, ext. 303. Fax: (510)655-1369. E-mail: sue@bpf.org. Website: www.bpf.org. **Contact:** Susan Moon, editor. Contest for "essays from a socially engaged Buddhist perspective by emerging writers (30 and under) on an aspect of the issue's theme." Contest is ongoing—award is given twice per year. Open to writers 30 and under who have not previously published in *Turning Wheel*. **Deadline: September 1 and March 1; details and coming themes posted on website.** Guidelines for SASE. Prize: $500, and publication in *Turning Wheel*. Judged by *Turning Wheel* Editor Susan Moon, and the *Turning Wheel* Editorial Committee. Acquires first publication rights.

THE ELIE WIESEL PRIZE IN ETHICS ESSAY CONTEST

The Elie Wiesel Foundation for Humanity, 529 Fifth Ave., Suite 1802, New York NY 10017. (212)490-7777. Fax: (212)490-6006. E-mail: info@eliewieselfoundation.org. Website: www.eliewieselfoundation.org. "Since 1989, The Elie Wiesel Foundation has sponsored the Prize in Ethics Essay Contest. This annual competition is intended to challenge undergraduate juniors and seniors in colleges and universities throughout the United States to analyze ethical questions and concerns facing them in today's complex society. All students are encouraged to write thought-provoking, personal essays." **Deadline: Early December.** Guidelines for SASE. Prize: 1st Prize: $5,000; 2nd Prize: $2,500; 3rd Prize: $1,500; Honorable Mentions (2): $500. Judged by a distinguished panel of readers who evaluate all contest entries, and a jury, including Elie Wiesel, chooses the winners.

WRITERS' JOURNAL ANNUAL TRAVEL WRITING CONTEST

Val-Tech Media, P.O. Box 394, Perham MN 56573. (218)346-7921. Fax: (218)346-7924. E-mail: writersjournal@lakesplus.com. Website: www.writersjournal.com. **Contact:** Leon Ogroske. Offered annually for unpublished work. Buys one-time rights. Open to any writer. 2,000 word maximum. No e-mail submissions accepted. Guidelines for SASE and online. **Deadline: November 30. Charges $5 fee.** Prize: 1st Place: $50; 2nd Place: $25; 3rd Place: $15, plus honorable mentions. Prize-winning stories and selected honorable mentions will be published in *Writer's Journal* magazine.

⚏ THE WRITERS' TRUST OF CANADA'S SHAUGHNESSY COHEN AWARD FOR POLITICAL WRITING

The Writers' Trust of Canada, 40 Wellington St. E., Suite 300, Toronto ON M5E 1C7, Canada. (416)504-8222. Fax: (416)504-9090. E-mail: info@writerstrust.com. Website: www.writerstrust.com. **Contact:** James Davies. Awarded annually for "a nonfiction book of outstanding literary merit that enlarges our understanding of contemporary Canadian political and social issues." Presented at the Great Literary Awards event each spring in Toronto. Prize: $10,000.

LAMAR YORK PRIZE FOR NONFICTION CONTEST

The Chattahoochee Review, 2101 Womack Rd., Dunwoody GA 30338-4497. (770)551-3019. Website: www.chattahoochee-review.org. **Contact:** Lawrence Hetrick, contest director. Offered annually for unpublished creative nonfiction and nonscholarly essays. *The Chattahoochee Review* buys first rights only for winning essay/ms for the purpose of publication in the summer issue. **Deadline: January 31.** Guidelines for SASE. **Charges $10 fee/entry.** Prize: $1,000, plus publication for 1 or more winners. Judged by the editorial staff of *The Chattahoochee Review*. Open to any writer.

FICTION

AIM MAGAZINE SHORT STORY CONTEST

P.O. Box 1174, Maywood IL 60153-8174. (708)344-4414. E-mail: apiladoone@aol.com. Website: www.aimmaga zine.org. **Contact:** Myron Apilado, editor. Estab. 1974. $100 prize offered to contest winner for best unpublished short story (4,000 words maximum) "promoting brotherhood among people and cultures." **Deadline: August 15.** Open to any writer.

N THE ALLEGHENY REVIEW LITERARY AWARDS

The Allegheny Review, Allegheny College, Box 32, Meadville PA 16335. E-mail: review@allegheny.edu. Website: review.allegheny.edu. **Contact:** Senior Editor. Offered annually for unpublished work. Accepts inquiries by e-mail and phone. Guidelines for SASE. **Charges $5.** Prize: $250 and guaranteed publication. Judged by the editorial staff, and semi-finalists are then reveiwed by a published author (Penelope Pelicone in 2001) who picks the winners. Open to currently enrolled, undergraduate students.

SHERWOOD ANDERSON SHORT FICTION AWARD

Mid-American Review, Dept. of English, Box W, Bowling Green State University, Bowling Green OH 43403. (419)372-2725. E-mail: mikeczy@bgnet.bgsu.edu. Website: www.bgsu.edu/midamericanreview. **Contact:** Michael Czyzniejewski, fiction editor. Offered annually for unpublished mss. Contest is open to all writers not associated with judge or *Mid-American Review*. **Deadline: October 1.** Guidelines for SASE. **Charges $10.** Prize: $500, plus publication in the spring issue of *Mid-American Review*. Judged by editors and a well-known writer, e.g. Peter Ho Davies or Melanie Rae Thon. Open to any writer.

N ANNUAL GIVAL PRESS SHORT STORY CONTEST

Gival Press, LLC, P.O. Box 3812, Arlington VA 22203. (703)351-0079. Fax: (703)351-0079. E-mail: givalpress@ya hoo.com. Website: www.givalpress.com. **Contact:** Robert L. Giron. Offered annually for a previously unpublished original, not a translation, short story in English of at least 5,000-15,000 words of literary quality. Guidelines by mail with SASE, by e-mail, or online. **Deadline: August 8. Charges $20 (USD) reading fee.** Prize: $1,000, plus publication on website. Open to any writer.

N ANNUAL HIDDEN TALENTS SHORT STORY CONTEST

Tall Tales Press Book Publishing, Inc., 20 Tuscany Valley Park NW, Calgary AB T3L 2B6, Canada. (403)874-4293. E-mail: talltalespress@shaw.ca. Website: www.talltalespress.com. **Contact:** Steve Van Bakel. Annual contest to "promote new writers and give them the opportunity to have their work published. There are 2 categories: the adult section and the junior writer for all those under the age of 18." **Deadline: May 31.** Guidelines for SASE. **Charges $10 (Canadian) for adult submissions; $5 (Canadian) for junior writer submissions.** Prize: Adult—1st Place: $500; 2nd Place: $250; 3rd Place: $100; 4th Place: $75; Honorable Mentions: $25. Junior Writers—1st Place: $200; 2nd Place: $100; 3rd Place: $50; 4th Place: $25; Honorable Mentions: $10. "We acquire first-time publishing rights to all stories entered. After that, all rights remain with the author." Judged by 4 published authors and the publisher of Tall Tales Press Book Publishing, Inc. Open to any writer.

ANTHOLOGY ANNUAL CONTEST

P.O. Box 4411, Mesa AZ 85211-4411. Website: www.anthology.org. Annual competition for short stories. All prize-winning stories are published in January/February of following year. Open to any writer, any genre. Erotica and graphic horror are not encouraged. **Deadline: August 31.** Guidelines for SASE. **Charges $5/short story.** Prize: $150. Judged by a panel of local writers and *Anthology* staff. Acquires one-time rights.

ANTIETAM REVIEW LITERARY AWARD

Antietam Review, 41 S. Potomac St., Hagerstown MD 21740. (301)791-3132. Fax: (240)420-1754. **Contact:** Mary Jo Vincent, business manager. "We consider all fiction manuscripts sent to *Antietam Review* Literary Contest as entries for inclusion in each issue. We look for well-crafted, serious literary prose fiction under 5,000 words. Contributors may submit up to three poems. Editors seek well-crafted pieces of no more than 30 lines." Offered annually for unpublished work. Reading period: June 1-September 1. Guidelines for SASE. **Charges $15/story; $15/3 poems.** Prize: $100. Writers from Maryland, Pennsylvania, Virginia, Washington DC and Delaware.

THE ISAAC ASIMOV AWARD

International Association for the Fantastic in the Arts and *Asimov*'s magazine, School of Mass Communications, University of South Florida, 4202 E. Fowler, Tampa FL 33620. (813)974-6792. Fax: (813)974-2592. E-mail: rwilber@chuma.cas.usf.edu. **Contact:** Rick Wilber, administrator. "The annual award honors the legacy of one of science fiction's most distinguished authors through an award aimed at unpublished, undergraduate writers."

Deadline: December 15. Guidelines for SASE. **Charges $10 for up to 3 submissions.** Prize: $500, and consideration for publication in *Asimov*'s. Winner receives expense-paid trip to Ft. Lauderdale, Florida, to attend conference on the Fantastic in mid-March where award is given. Judged by *Asimov*'s editors. Open to full-time, college undergraduates only.

AUTHORMANIA.COM WRITING CONTEST

AuthorMania.com, Route 4, Box 201-A, Buna TX 77612. E-mail: TeddyBearTeam@aol.com. Website: www.authormania.com. **Contact:** Cindy Thomas, contest director. Annual contest for unpublished short stories on any topic (no adult or hate), but no more than 5,000 words. ''Enter as many times as you wish, but each entry must be mailed separately, and each must include an entry fee. No handwritten submissions.'' **Deadline: February 14. Charges $20 entry fee.** Prize: $1,000, and publication on AuthorMania.com. Open to any writer.

BARD FICTION PRIZE

Bard College, P.O. Box 5000, Annandale-on-Hudson NY 12504-5000. (845)758-7087. E-mail: bfp@bard.edu. Estab. 2001. Annually. Guidelines for SASE. Prize: $30,000 cash award, and appointment as writer-in-residence at Bard College for 1 semester. Open to younger American writers.

BONOMO MEMORIAL LITERATURE PRIZE

Italian Americana, URI/CCE, 80 Washington St., Providence RI 02903. (401)277-5306. Fax: (401)277-5100. E-mail: bonomoal@etal.uri.edu. Website: www.uri.edu/prov/italian/italian.html. **Contact:** Carol Bonomo Albright, editor. Offered annually for the best fiction, essay, or memoir that is published annually by an Italian-American. Send submission of 20 pages maximum, double-spaced in duplicate to be considered for publication/prize. Acquires first North American serial rights. Prize: $250.

▣ THE MAN BOOKER PRIZE

Colman Getty PR, Middlesex House, 34-42 Cleveland St., London W1T 4JE, United Kingdom. (020) 7631 2666. Fax: (020) 7631 2699. E-mail: sue@colmangettypr.co.uk. Website: www.themanbookerprize.com. **Contact:** Colman Getty PR. ''The Booker Prize for Fiction was set up in 1968 as a result of discussions between Booker plc and the Publishers Association about the need for a signifiant literary award in Britain, along the lines of the Prix Goncourt and similar awards in France. In 2002 the sponsorship of the Prize was awarded to The Man Group, and the prize is now known as The Man Booker Prize.'' Books are only accepted through UK publishers. However, publication outside the UK does not disqualify a book once it is published in the UK. Open to any full-length novel (published October 1-September 30) written by a citizen of the Commonwealth or the Republic of Ireland. No novellas, collections of short stories, translations, or self-published books. **Deadline: July.** Prize: The winner receives £50,000, and the short-listed authors receive £2,500. Judged by judges appointed by the Booker Prize Management Committee. Citizens of the Commonwealth or Republic of Ireland.

BOSTON REVIEW SHORT STORY CONTEST

Boston Review, E53-407 MIT, Cambridge MA 02139. Website: bostonreview.mit.edu. Stories should not exceed 4,000 words and must be previously unpublished. **Deadline: October 1. Charges $20 fee (check or money order payable to *Boston Review*).** Prize: $1,000, and publication in a later issue of *Boston Review*.

BOULEVARD SHORT FICTION CONTEST FOR EMERGING WRITERS

Boulevard Magazine, 6614 Clayton Rd., PMB #325, Richmond Heights MO 63117. Website: www.richardburgin.com. **Contact:** Richard Burgin, senior editor. Offered annually for unpublished short fiction to award a writer who has not yet published a book of fiction, poetry, or creative nonfiction with a nationally distributed press. ''We hold first North American rights on anything not previously published.'' Open to any writer with no previous publication by a nationally known press. Guidelines for SASE or on website. **Deadline: December 15. Charges $15 fee/story; includes 1-year subscription to *Boulevard*.** Prize: $1,500, and publication in 1 of the next year's issues.

▣ BRAZOS BOOKSTORE SHORT STORY AWARD

3700 Mockingbird Lane, Dallas TX 75205. (214)528-2655. E-mail: franvick@aol.com. **Contact:** Fran Vick. Offered annually for work published January 1-December 31 of previous year to recognize the best short story. The story submitted must have appeared in print for the first time to be eligible. Writers must have been born in Texas, must have lived in Texas for at least 2 consecutive years, or the subject matter of the work must be associated with Texas. **Deadline: January 3.** Guidelines for SASE. Prize: $750.

SANDRA BROWN AWARD FOR OUTSTANDING SHORT FICTION

descant, Texas Christian University's literary journal, TCU Box 297270, Fort Worth TX 76129. (817)257-6537. Fax: (817)257-6239. E-mail: descant@tcu.edu. **Contact:** Dave Kuhne, editor. Offered annually for unpublished short stories. Winning entries published in *descant*. Publication retains copyright but will transfer it to the author upon request. **Deadline: September-April.** Guidelines for SASE. Prize: $250. Open to any writer.

THE CAINE PRIZE FOR AFRICAN WRITING
2 Drayson Mews, London, England W8 4LY, United Kingdom. (020) 7376 0440. Fax: (020) 7938 3728. E-mail: caineprize@jftaylor.com. Website: www.caineprize.com. **Contact:** Nick Elam. Annual award for a short story (3,000-15,000 words) by an African writer. "An 'African writer' is normally taken to mean someone who was born in Africa; who is a national of an African country; or whose parents are African, and whose work has reflected African sensibilities." Entries must have appeared for the first time in the 5 years prior to the closing date for submissions, which is January 31 each year. Publishers should submit 12 copies of the published original with a brief cover note (no pro forma application). **Deadline: January 31.** Guidelines for SASE. Prize: $15,000 (£10,000). Judged by a panel of judges appointed each year.

CANADIAN AUTHORS ASSOCIATION JUBILEE AWARD FOR SHORT STORIES
P.O. Box 419, 320 S. Shores Rd., Campbellford ON K0L 1L0, Canada. (705)653-0323. Fax: (705)653-0593. E-mail: admin@canauthors.org. Website: www.canauthors.org. **Contact:** Alec McEachern. Offered annually for a collection of short stories by a Canadian author. Entry form required. Obtain entry form from contact name or download from website. **Deadline: December 15.** Guidelines for SASE. **Charges $35 fee (Canadian).** Prize: $2,500, and a silver medal.

CANADIAN AUTHORS ASSOCIATION MOSAID TECHNOLOGIES INC. AWARD FOR FICTION
Box 419, 320 South Shores Rd., Campbellford ON K0L 1L0, Canada. (705)653-0323. Fax: (705)653-0593. E-mail: admin@canauthors.org. Website: www.canauthors.org. **Contact:** Alec McEachern. Offered annually for a full-length novel by a Canadian citizen. Entry form required. Obtain entry form from contact name or download from website. **Deadline: December 15.** Guidelines for SASE. **Charges $35 fee (Canadian).** Prize: $2,500, and a silver medal.

CAPE FEAR CRIME FESTIVAL SHORT STORY CONTEST
Atticus, Inc., 5828 Greenville Loop Rd., Wilmington NC 28409. (910)264-2101. Fax: (910)256-4770. E-mail: booklady@ec.rr.com. Website: www.galleone.com/cfcf.htm. **Contact:** Nicole Smith, contest director. "The CFCF Short Story Contest was created in concert with the annual Cape Fear Crime Festival, a mystery writer and reader's conference held in North Carolina. The purpose of the annual Story Contest is to provide a forum in which to discover, publish, and promote new writers, and to introduce readers to promising authors through the publication of the contest's annual chapbook. Contest organizers are also interested in bridging the imagined gap between genre and nongenre fiction." No specific categories, as long as the story has a strong mystery or crime theme. **Deadline: June 1.** Guidelines for SASE. **Charges $8/entry—unlimited entries.** Prize: 1st Place: $100; 2nd Place: $75; 3rd Place: $50. All winning stories will be published in the Story Contest chapbook, which is distributed to hundreds of Festival attendees. Winning authors will also receive free registration to the Cape Fear Crime Festival, and a free Saturday night dinner featuring a celebrated mystery author. Each winning story is subject to editorial review and will be copyedited for grammatical errors, spelling mistakes, and libelous language. All editorial changes will be shared with the winning authors before the chapbook goes to press. Judged by a panel of local bookstore employees, editors, and librarians, to determine the semifinalists. Semifinalist stories are then passed on to a celebrity judge who determines which stories win 1st, 2nd, and 3rd Place. 2004 celebrity judge is author Margaret Maron. Acquires Prize winning stories may be included in a Cape Fear Crime Anthology to be published at a later date. Open to any writer.

THE ALEXANDER PATTERSON CAPPON FICTION AWARD
New Letters, 5101 Rockhill Rd., Kansas City MO 64110. (816)235-1168. Fax: (816)235-2611. E-mail: newletters@umkc.edu. Website: www.newletters.org. **Contact:** Aleatha Ezra. Offered annually for unpublished work to discover and reward new and upcoming writers. Buys first North American serial rights. Open to any writer. **Deadline: Third week in May.** Guidelines for SASE. **Charges $15 (includes a 1-year subscription to *New Letters*).** Prize: 1st Place: $1,000, and publication in a volume of *New Letters*; 2 runners-up will receive a complimentary copy of a recent book of poetry or fiction from our affiliate BkMk Press. All entries will be given consideration for publication in future issues of *New Letters*.

CAPTIVATING BEGINNINGS SHORT STORY CONTEST
(formerly Captivating Beginnings Contest), *Lynx Eye*, 542 Mitchell Dr., Los Osos CA 93402. (805)528-8146. Fax: (805)528-7876. E-mail: pamccully@aol.com. **Contact:** Pam McCully, co-editor. Annual award for unpublished stories "with engrossing beginnings, stories that will enthrall and absorb readers." **Deadline: January 31.**

Guidelines for SASE. **Charges $5/story.** Prize: $100, plus publication; $10 each for 4 honorable mentions, plus publication. Judged by *Lynx Eye* editors. Open to any writer.

G.S. SHARAT CHANDRA PRIZE FOR SHORT FICTION

BkMk Press, University of Missouri-Kansas City, 5101 Rockhill Rd., Kansas City MO 64110. (816)235-2558. Fax: (816)235-2611. E-mail: bkmk@umkc.edu. Website: www.umkc.edu/bkmk. **Contact:** Ben Furnish. Offered annually for the best book-length ms collection (unpublished) of short fiction in English by a living author. Translations are not eligible. Initial judging is done by a network of published writers. Final judging is done by a writer of national reputation. Guidelines for SASE, by e-mail, or on website. **Deadline: December 1 (postmarked). Charges $25 fee.** Prize: $1,000, plus book publication by BkMk Press.

CHILDREN'S WRITERS FICTION CONTEST

Stepping Stones, P.O. Box 8863, Springfield MO 65801-8863. (417)863-7369. E-mail: verwil@alumni.pace.edu. **Contact:** V.R. Williams, director. Offered annually for unpublished fiction. **Deadline: July 31.** Guidelines for SASE. **Charges $10.** Prize: $260, and/or publication in *Hodge Podge*. Judged by Goodin, Williams, Goodwin and/or associates. "Entries are judged for clarity, grammar, punctuation, imagery, content, and suitability for children." Open to any writer.

🌐 THE ARTHUR C. CLARKE AWARD

Sir Arthur C. Clarke, 60 Bournemouth Rd., Folkestone, Kent CT19 5AZ, United Kingdom. E-mail: arthurcclarkeaward@yahoo.co.uk. Website: www.clarkeaward.com. **Contact:** Paul Kincaid. Annual award presented to the best science fiction novel, published between January 1 and December 31 of the year in question, receiving its first British publication during the calendar year. **Deadline: 2nd week in December.** Prize: £2,003 (rising by £1 each year), and an engraved bookend. Judged by representatives of the British Science Fiction Association, the Science Fiction Foundation, and the Science Museum. Open to any writer.

🌐 COMMONWEALTH WRITERS PRIZE

The Commonwealth Foundation, c/o Booktrust, Book House, 45 E. Hill, Wandsworth London SW18 2QZ, United Kingdom. Fax: (00 44) 20 8516 2978. E-mail: tarryn@booktrust.org.uk. Website: www.commonwealthwriters.com. **Contact:** Tarryn McKay. The purpose of the annual award is "to encourage and reward the upsurge of new Commonwealth fiction and ensure that works of merit reach a wider audience outside their country of origin. The Commonwealth Foundation established the Commonwealth Writers Prize in 1987. For the purpose of the Prize, the Commonwealth is split into 4 regions—Africa, Caribbean and Canada, Eurasia, and Southeast Asia and South Pacific. Each region has 2 regional winners, 1 for the Best Book and 1 for the Best First Book. To be eligible for the Best Book Award, the author must have at least 1 work of fiction previously published between January 1 and December 1. To be eligible for the Best First Book Award, the book must be the author's first work of fiction (including a collection of short stories) to be published." This prize is publisher entry only, except in the case of some African and Asian countries where self-published works may be accepted at the administrator's discretion. Please contact Booktrust on this matter. All entries must be from Commonwealth citizens. All work must be written in English, translations are not eligible. **Deadline: November 15.** Prize: £10,000 to the overall best book; £3,000 to the overall best first book; £1,000 to 8 regional winners, 2 from each of the 4 regions. Judged by 4 panels of judges, 1 for each region. Each region has a chairperson and 2 judges. Once the regional winners are announced, the chairpersons read all 8 books and meet to decide which of the winners will receive the overall awards. This judging is headed by an eminent critic/author.

DAVID DORNSTEIN MEMORIAL CREATIVE WRITING CONTEST FOR YOUNG ADULT WRITERS

The Coalition for the Advancement of Jewish Education, 261 W. 35th St., Floor 12A, New York NY 10001. (212)268-4210. Fax: (212)268-4214. E-mail: cajeny@caje.org. Website: www.caje.org. **Contact:** Operations Manager. Contest offered annually for an unpublished short story based on a Jewish theme or topic. Writer must prove age of 18-35 years old. Submit only 1 story each year. Guidelines on website or available on request from CAJE office. **Deadline: December 31.** Prize: 1st Place: $700; 2nd Place: $200; 3rd Place: $100, and publication in the *Jewish Education News*.

JACK DYER FICTION PRIZE

Crab Orchard Review, Dept. of English, Southern Illinois University Carbondale, Carbondale IL 62901-4503. E-mail: jtribble@siu.edu. Website: www.siu.edu/~crborchd. **Contact:** Jon C. Tribble, managing editor. Offered annually for unpublished short fiction. *Crab Orchard Review* acquires first North American serial rights to all submitted work. Open to any writer. **Deadline: February 1-March 15.** Guidelines for SASE. **Charges $15/entry (can enter up to 3 stories, each story submitted requires a separate fee and can be up to 6,000 words),** which includes a 1-year subscription to *Crab Orchard Review*. Prize: $1,500, and publication. Open to US citizens only.

FANTASTICAL VISIONS SHORT STORY CONTEST

Fantasist Enterprises, P.O. Box 9381, Wilmington DE 19809. E-mail: contest@fantasistent.com. Website: www.fantasistent.com. **Contact:** William H. Horner III. Offered annually for writers of quality, unpublished, short fantasy fiction. **Deadline: October 15.** Guidelines for SASE. **Charges no entry fee for 1 entry; however there is a $5 fee for 2 entries, and each additional entry is $3.** Prize: 1st Prize: $150; 2nd Prize: $100; 3rd Prize: $50, plus all 3 receive pro rata share of 25% of the net price of the book. All honorable mention winners will receive 1/2-2¢/word, as an advance on pro rata share of 25% of the net price of the book. Winning stories will be published in an annual anthology of fiction. Judged by William H. Horner III, editor-in-chief; Courtenay Dudek, assistant editor; and a handful of volunteer readers. Acquires first anthology rights to winning and honorable mention stories. Copyright remains in name of authors. Open to any writer.

THE WILLIAM FAULKNER-WILLIAM WISDOM CREATIVE WRITING COMPETITION

(formerly The William Faulkner Creative Writing Competition), The Pirate's Alley Faulkner Society, 624 Pirate's Alley, New Orleans LA 70116-3254. (504)586-1609. E-mail: faulkhouse@aol.com. Website: www.wordsandmusic.org. **Contact:** Rosemary James, director. Offered annually for unpublished mss to encourage publisher interest in a promising writer's novels, novellas, novels-in-progress, short stories, personal essays, poems, or short stories by high school students. The Society retains the right to publish excerpts of longer fiction; short stories, essays, poems in toto. Open to all authors working in English. Additional information on the competition and the festival is on the website. **Deadline: April 30. Charges entry fee: Novel—$35; novella—$30; novel-in-progress—$30; short story, personal essay, and individual poem—$25; high school short story—$10 (paid by school).** Prize: Novel: $7,500; novella: $2,500; novel-in-progress: $2,000; short story: $1,500; personal essay: $1,000; individual poem: $750; high school: $750 for student and $250 for sponsoring teacher. The Society also awards gold medals in William Faulkner's likeness; airfare and hotel expenses for winners to attend Words & Music: A Literary Feast in New Orleans, encompassing a major national writers' conference, and the Faulkner Society's gala annual meeting and Salute to All Great Writers: Past, Present, and Yet To Come, at which winners are presented by their judges. Note: For foreign residents the Society pays airfare only from selected US points of entry.

🌐 FISH ANNUAL SHORT STORY PRIZE

Fish Publishing, Durrus, Bantry, Co. Cork, Ireland. +353(0)27 61246. E-mail: info@fishpublishing.com. Website: www.fishpublishing.com. **Contact:** Prize Coordinator. Offered annually for unpublished fiction mss. **Deadline: November 30. Charges $15 for 1st story; $10 for each additional story.** Prize: 1st Prize: $1,500; 2nd Prize: 1 week at Anam Cara Writers' Retreat in the west of Ireland. The top 15 stories will be published in Fish's anthology, which is launched at the West Cork Writers Festival in June, and will be read by literary agents, including Shirley Stewart, Merric Davidson, and Andrew Russell. Judged by a panel of international judges which changes every year. Open to any writer.

Ⓝ F. SCOTT FITZGERALD SHORT STORY CONTEST

F. Scott Fitzgerald Literary Conference, Inc., 111 Maryland Ave., Rockville MD 20850. (301)309-9461. Fax: (301)294-8073. **Contact:** Michelle Beadle. Offered annually for unpublished short stories. **Deadline: July 9.** Guidelines for SASE. **Charges $25 fee; no entry fee for students.** Prize: Adults: 1st Place: $1,000; 2nd-4th Place: $200 each. Students: 1st Place: $250; 2nd-4th Place: $100 each.

Ⓝ H.E. FRANCIS SHORT STORY AWARD

The Ruth Hindman Foundation and the University of Alabama in Huntsville English Department, Dept. of English, University of Alabama in Huntsville, Huntsville AL 35899. Website: www.uah.edu/colleges/liberal/english/whatnewcontest.html. **Contact:** Patricia Sammon, editor. Offered annually for unpublished work not to exceed 5,000 words. Acquires first time publication rights. **Deadline: December 31.** Guidelines for SASE. **Charges $15 reading fee (make check payable to the Ruth Hindman Foundation).** Prize: $1,000. Judged by a panel of nationally recognized, award-winning authors, directors of creative writing programs, and editors of literary journals.

THE JOHN GARDNER FICTION BOOK AWARD

Creative Writing Program, Binghamton University-State University of New York, P.O. Box 6000, Binghamton NY 13902-6000. (607)777-6134. Fax: (607)777-2408. E-mail: mgillan@binghamton.edu. Website: www.binghamton.edu/english. **Contact:** Maria Mazziotti Gillan, director, creative writing program. Offered annually for work that appeared in print between January 1 and December 31 of year preceding award. **Deadline: April 1.**

Guidelines for SASE. Prize: $1,000. Judged by a professional writer not on the Binghamton University faculty. Open to any writer.

THE JOHN GARDNER MEMORIAL PRIZE FOR FICTION

Harpur Palate at Binghamton University, Dept. of English, Binghamton University, P.O. Box 6000, Binghamton NY 13902-6000. (607)355-4761. Website: harpurpalate.binghamton.edu. **Contact:** Editor. Contest offered annually for previously published fiction in any genre, up to 8,000 words. **Deadline: January 1-March 1.** Guidelines for SASE. **Charges $10/story.** Prize: $500, and publication in summer issue of *Harpur Palate*. Name and contact information should appear in the cover letter only. Acquires first North American serial rights. Open to any writer.

■ DANUTA GLEED LITERARY AWARD FOR FIRST BOOK OF SHORT FICTION

The Writers' Union of Canada, 40 Wellington St. E., 3rd Floor, Toronto ON M5E 1C7, Canada. (416)703-8982, ext. 223. Fax: (416)504-7656. E-mail: projects@writersunion.ca. Website: www.writersunion.ca. **Contact:** Deborah Windsor. Offered annually to Canadian writers for the best first collection of published short stories in the English language. Must have been published in the previous calendar year. Submit 4 copies. **Deadline: January 31.** Guidelines for SASE. Prize: 1st Place: $5,000; $500 to each of 2 runners-up.

GLIMMER TRAIN VERY SHORT FICTION AWARD

Glimmer Train Press, Inc., 1211 NW Glisan St., #207, Portland OR 97209. (503)221-0836. Fax: (503)221-0837. E-mail: eds@glimmertrain.com. Website: glimmertrain.com. **Contact:** Linda Swanson-Davies. Offered twice yearly to encourage the art of the very short story. Word count: 2,000 maximum. Open April 1-July 31 (Summer contest) or November 1-January 31 (Winter contest). Follow online submission process on website. Results will be e-mailed to all entrants on November 1 (for Summer contest) and May 1 (for Winter contest). **Charges $10 fee/story.** Prize: 1st Place: $1,200, publication in *Glimmer Train Stories* (circulation 13,000), and 20 copies of that issue. Runners-up: $500/$300, respectively, and consideration for publication.

GLIMMER TRAIN'S FALL SHORT-STORY AWARD FOR NEW WRITERS

Glimmer Train Press, Inc., 1211 NW Glisan St., Suite 207, Portland OR 97209. (503)221-0836. Fax: (503)221-0837. E-mail: eds@glimmertrain.com. Website: www.glimmertrain.com. **Contact:** Linda Swanson-Davies. Offered for any writer whose fiction hasn't appeared in a nationally-distributed publication with a circulation over 5,000. Word limit: 12,000 words. **Open August 1-September 30.** Follow online submission procedure on website. Notification on January 2.'' **Charges $12 fee/story.** Prize: Winner receives $1,200, publication in *Glimmer Train Stories*, and 20 copies of that issue. First/second runners-up receive $500/$300, respectively.

GLIMMER TRAIN'S SPRING SHORT-STORY AWARD FOR NEW WRITERS

Glimmer Train Press, Inc., 1211 NW Glisan St., Suite 207, Portland OR 97209. (503)221-0836. Fax: (503)221-0837. E-mail: eds@glimmertrain.com. Website: www.glimmertrain.com. **Contact:** Linda Swanson-Davies. Offered for any writer whose fiction hasn't appeared in a nationally-distributed publication with a circulation over 5,000. Word limit: 12,000 words. Contest open February 1-March 31. Follow online submission procedure at www.glimmertrain.com. Notification on July 1.'' **Charges $12 fee/story.** Prize: Winner receives $1,200, publication in *Glimmer Train Stories* and 20 copies of that issue. First/second runners-up receive $500/$300, respectively.

GLIMMER TRAIN'S SUMMER FICTION OPEN

Glimmer Train Press, Inc., 1211 NW Glisan St., Suite 207, Portland OR 97209. (503)221-0836. Fax: (503)221-0837. E-mail: eds@glimmertrain.com. Website: www.glimmertrain.com. **Contact:** Linda Swanson-Davies. Offered annually for unpublished stories as ''a platform for all themes, all lengths (up to 25,000 words), all writers.'' Open to any writer. Follow online submission procedure on website. **Deadline: June 30. Charges $15 fee/story.** Prize: 1st Place: $2,000, publication in *Glimmer Train Stories*, and 20 copies of that issue; 2nd Place: $1,000, and possible publication in *Glimmer Train Stories*; 3rd Place: $600, and possible publication in *Glimmer Train Stories*.

GLIMMER TRAIN'S WINTER FICTION OPEN

Glimmer Train, Inc., 1211 NW Glisan St., Suite 207, Portland OR 97209. (503)221-0836. Fax: (503)221-0837. E-mail: eds@glimmertrain.com. Website: www.glimmertrain.com. **Contact:** Linda Swanson-Davies. Offered annually for unpublished work as ''a platform for all themes, all lengths (up to 25,000 words), and all writers.'' Follow online submission procedure on website. **Deadline: January 11. Charges $15/story.** Prize: 1st Place: $2,000, publication in *Glimmer Train Stories*, and 20 copies of that issue; 2nd Place: $1,000, possible publication in *Glimmer Train Stories*; 3rd Place: $600, possible publication in *Glimmer Train Stories*. Open to any writer.

⊕ THE PHILLIP GOOD MEMORIAL PRIZE

QWF Magazine, P.O. Box 1768, Rugby CV21 4ZA, United Kingdom. 01788 334302. E-mail: jo@qwfmagazine.co. uk. Website: www.qwfmagazine.co.uk. **Contact:** The Competition Secretary. Estab. 1998. Annual international short story competition open to all writers over 18. **Deadline: August 21.** Guidelines for SASE. **Charges £5 for each story up to 5,000 words (checks payable to J.M. Good).** Prize: 1st Prize: £300; 2nd Prize: £150; 3rd Prize: £75. Judged by Lynne Barrett-Lee. Acquires Copyright remains with the author, but permissions will be requested to include the winning entries in the anthology or *QWF Magazine*.

⊠ GOVERNOR GENERAL'S LITERARY AWARD FOR FICTION

Canada Council for the Arts, 350 Albert St., P.O. Box 1047, Ottawa ON K1P 5V8, Canada. (613)566-4414, ext. 5576. Fax: (613)566-4410. E-mail: joanne.larocque-poirier@canadacouncil.ca. Website: www.canadacouncil .ca/prizes/ggla. **Contact:** Joanne Larocque-Poirier. Offered annually for the best English-language and the best French-language work of fiction by a Canadian published September 1, 2003-September 30, 2004. Publishers submit titles for consideration. **Deadline: March 15 or August 7, depending on the book's publication date.** Prize: Each laureate receives $15,000, and nonwinning finalists receive $1,000.

DRUE HEINZ LITERATURE PRIZE

University of Pittsburgh Press, 3400 Forbes Ave., 5th Floor, Eureka Bldg., Pittsburgh PA 15260. (412)383-2492. Fax: (412)383-2466. E-mail: susief@pitt.edu. Website: www.pitt.edu/ ~ press. **Contact:** Sue Borello, assistant to the director. Estab. 1981. Offered annually to writers who have published a book-length collection of fiction or a minimum of 3 short stories or novellas in commercial magazines or literary journals of national distribution. Does not return mss. **Deadline: Submit in May and June only.** Guidelines for SASE. Prize: $15,000.

LORIAN HEMINGWAY SHORT STORY COMPETITION

Hemingway Days Festival, P.O. Box 993, Key West FL 33041-0993. (305)294-0320. E-mail: info@shortstorycomp etition.com. Website: www.shortstorycompetition.com. Estab. 1981. Mail for guideline requests only. Guidelines for SASE or by e-mail. Offered annually for unpublished short stories up to 3,000 words. **Deadline: May 15. Charges $10/story postmarked by May 1, $15/story postmarked by May 15; no stories accepted after May 15.** Prize: 1st Place: $1,000; 2nd and 3rd Place: $500; runners-up awards; honorable mentions will also be awarded.

ℕ TOM HOWARD/JOHN H. REID SHORT STORY CONTEST

John H. Reid, c/o Winning Writers, 351 Pleasant St., PMB 222, Northampton MA 01060-3961. E-mail: johnreid@ mail.qango.com. Website: www.geocities.com/rastar330/prose.htm. **Contact:** John Howard Reid. Prefers electronic inquiries. Maximum of 8,000 words. 1st-3rd Prize must give John H. Reid a free license to publish the winning works in an anthology. Other winners are at liberty to decline the offer of publication. Annually. **Deadline: March 31.** Guidelines for SASE. **Charges $10 USD/story/essay/prose work.** Prize: 1st Prize: $1,000; 2nd Prize: $400; 3rd Prize: $200. Highly commended entries share a prize pool of $280. Judged by John Howard Reid. Open to any writer.

L. RON HUBBARD'S WRITERS OF THE FUTURE CONTEST

P.O. Box 1630, Los Angeles CA 90078. (323)466-3310. E-mail: contests@authorservicesinc.com. Website: www. writersofthefuture.com. **Contact:** Contest Administrator. Offered for unpublished work "to find, reward, and publicize new speculative fiction writers so they may more easily attain professional writing careers." Open to new and amateur writers who have not professionally published a novel or short novel, more than 1 novelette, or more than 3 short stories. Eligible entries are short stories or novelettes (under 17,000 words) of science fiction or fantasy. Guidelines for SASE, online, or via e-mail. **Deadline: December 31, March 31, June 30, September 30. No entry fee; entrants retain all rights to their stories; judging by professional writers only.** Prize: Awards quarterly 1st Place: $1,000; 2nd Place: $750; and 3rd Place: $500. Annual Grand Prize: $4,000.

INDIANA REVIEW FICTION CONTEST

Indiana Review, BH 465/Indiana University, Bloomington IN 47405-7103. (812)855-3439. Fax: (812)855-4253. E-mail: inreview@indiana.edu. Website: www.indiana.edu/ ~ inreview. **Contact:** Danit Brown. Maximum story length is 15,000 words (no minimum). Offered annually for unpublished work. **Deadline: Early October.** Guidelines for SASE. **Charges $15 fee (includes a year's subscription).** Prize: $1,000. Judged by guest judges. Aimee Bender judged the 2003 contest. Open to any writer.

JERRY JAZZ MUSICIAN NEW SHORT FICTION AWARD

Jerry Jazz Musician, 2207 NE Broadway, Portland OR 97232. (503)287-5570. Fax: (801)749-9896. E-mail: jm@jer ryjazzmusician.com. Website: www.jerryjazz.com. **Contact:** Joe Maita. Contest is offered 3 times/year. "We value creative writing and wish to encourage writers of short fiction to pursue their dream of being published. *Jerry Jazz Musician*, an online magazine, would like to provide another step in the career of an aspiring writer. Three times a year, *Jerry Jazz Musician* awards a writer who submits, in our opinion, the best original, previously unpublished work of approximately 3,000-5,000 words. The winner will be announced via a special mailing of our *Jerry Jazz* newsletter. Publishers, artists, musicians, and interested readers are among those who subscribe to the newsletter. Additionally, the work will be published on the home page of *Jerry Jazz Musician* and featured there for at least 4 weeks. The *Jerry Jazz Musician* reader tends to have interests in music, history, literature, art, film, and theater, particularly that of the counter-culture of mid-20th century America. Writing should appeal to a reader with these characteristics.'' Guidelines available online. **Deadline: September 15, 2004; January 31, 2005; and May 15, 2005.** Prize: $200. Judged by the editors of *Jerry Jazz Musician*. Open to any writer.

JESSE H. JONES AWARD

3700 Mockingbird Lane, Dallas TX 75205. (214)528-2655. E-mail: franvick@aol.com. **Contact:** Fran Vick. Offered annually for work published January 1-December 31 of year before award is given to recognize the writer of the best book of fiction entered in the competition. Writers must have been born in Texas, or have lived in the state for at least 2 consecutive years at some time, or the subject matter of the work should be associated with the state. **Deadline: January 3.** Guidelines for SASE. Prize: $6,000.

JAMES JONES FIRST NOVEL FELLOWSHIP

Wilkes University, English Department, Kirby Hall, Wilkes-Barre PA 18766. (570)408-4530. Fax: (570)408-7829. E-mail: english@wilkes.edu. Website: www.wilkes.edu/humanities/jones.asp. **Contact:** Jacqueline Mosher, coordinator. Offered annually for unpublished novels, novellas, and closely-linked short stories (all works in progress). ''The award is intended to honor the spirit of unblinking honesty, determination, and insight into modern culture exemplified by the late James Jones.'' The competition is open to all American writers who have not previously published novels. **Deadline: March 1. Charges $20 fee.** Prize: $6,000; $250 honorarium (runner-up).

JUST DESSERTS SHORT-SHORT FICTION CONTEST

Passages North, Dept. of English, Northern Michigan University, 1401 Presque Isle Ave., Marquette MI 49855. (906)227-1203. Fax: (906)227-1096. E-mail: passages@nmu.edu. Website: myweb.nmu.edu/~passages. **Contact:** Katie Hanson. Offered every even year to publish new voices in literary fiction. Guidelines available for SASE or download from website. **Deadline: Submit September 15-January 15. Charges $8 reading fee/story.** Prize: $1,000, and publication for the winner; 2 honorable mentions also published; all entrants receive a copy of *Passages North*.

SERENA MCDONALD KENNEDY AWARD

(formerly Snake Nation Press Annual Award for Short Fiction), Snake Nation Press, 110 W. Force St., Valdosta GA 31601. (229)244-0752. E-mail: jeana@snakenationpress.org. Website: www.snakenationpress.org. **Contact:** Jean Arambula. Contest for a collection of unpublished short stories by a new or underpublished writer. Entries accepted year round. **Deadline: September 1.** Guidelines for SASE. **Charges $20 reading fee.** Prize: $1,000, and publication. Judged by an independent judge. Open to any writer.

E.M. KOEPPEL SHORT FICTION AWARD

Writecorner Press, Koeppel Contest, P.O. Box 16369, Jacksonville FL 32245. Website: writecorner.com. **Contact:** Mary Sue Koeppel and Robert B. Gentry. Estab. 2004. Any number of unpublished stories may be entered by any writer. Only the first title page may appear on submission. Guidelines for SASE or online. **Deadline: October 1-April 30. Charges $15/story or $25 for 2 stories.** Prize: 1st Place: $1,100; Editor's Choices: $100 each. Open to any writer.

THE LAWRENCE FOUNDATION AWARD

Prairie Schooner, 201 Andrews Hall, P.O. Box 880334, Lincoln NE 68588-0334. (402)472-0911. Fax: (402)472-9771. E-mail: kgrey2@unl.edu. Website: www.unl.edu/schooner/psmain.htm. **Contact:** Hilda Raz. Offered annually for the best short story published in *Prairie Schooner* in the previous year. Prize: $1,000.

LITERAL LATTÉ FICTION AWARD

Literal Latté, 61 4th Ave., Suite 240, New York NY 10003. (212)260-5532. E-mail: litlatte@aol.com. Website: www.literal-latte.com. Offered annually for unpublished fiction. Guidelines for SASE or on website. Open to any writer. **Deadline: January 15. Charges $10/story fee or $15/story including 1-year subscription.** Prize: 1st Prize: $1,000 and publication in *Literal Latté*; 2nd Prize: $300; 3rd Prize: $200.

LONG FICTION CONTEST

International, White Eagle Coffee Store Press, P.O. Box 383, Fox River Grove IL 60021. (847)639-9200. E-mail: wecspress@aol.com. Website: members.aol.com/wecspress. **Contact:** Frank E. Smith, publisher. Offered annually since 1993 for unpublished work to recognize and promote long short stories of 8,000-14,000 words (about 30-50 pages). Sample of previous winner: $5.95, including postage. Open to any writer, no restrictions on materials. **Deadline: December 15.** Guidelines for SASE. **Charges $15 fee, $5 for second story in same envelope.** Prize: (A.E. Coppard Prize) $500, and publication, plus 25 copies of chapbook.

⚅ ⚄ THE MALAHAT REVIEW NOVELLA PRIZE

The Malahat Review, University of Victoria, P.O. Box 1700 STN CSC, Victoria BC V8W 2Y2, Canada. (250)721-8524. E-mail: malahat@uvic.ca. Website: malahatreview.ca. **Contact:** Editor. "In alternate years, we hold the Long Poem and Novella contests." Offered to promote unpublished novellas. Obtains first world rights. After publication rights revert to the author. Open to any writer. **Deadline: March 1.** Guidelines for SASE. **Charges $35 fee (includes a 1-year subscription to *Malahat*).** Prize: $500, plus payment for publication ($30/page) and an additional year's subscription.

MALICE DOMESTIC GRANTS FOR UNPUBLISHED WRITERS

Malice Domestic, P.O. Box 31137, Bethesda MD 20284-1137. Website: www.malicedomestic.org. **Contact:** Grants chair. Offered annually for unpublished work in the mystery field. Malice awards 2 grants to unpublished writers in the Malice Domestic genre at its annual convention in May. The competition is designed to help the next generation of Malice authors get their first work published and to foster quality Malice literature. Malice Domestic literature is loosely described as mystery stories of the Agatha Christie type—i.e., "traditional mysteries," which usually feature an amateur detective, characters who know each other, and no excessive gore, gratuitous violence, or explicit sex. Writers who have been published previously in the mystery field, including publication of a mystery novel, short story, or nonfiction work, are ineligible to apply. Members of the Malice Domestic Board of Directors and their families are ineligible to apply. Malice encourages applications from minority candidates. Guidelines on website. **Deadline: December 15.** Prize: $1,000. Writers who have been published previously in the mystery field, including the publication of a mystery novel, short story or nonfiction work, are ineligible to apply.

MARY MCCARTHY PRIZE IN SHORT FICTION

Sarabande Books, P.O. Box 4456, Louisville KY 40204. (502)458-4028. Fax: (502)458-4065. E-mail: info@sarabndebooks.org. Website: www.SarabandeBooks.org. **Contact:** Kirby Gann, managing editor. Offered annually to publish an outstanding collection of stories, novellas, or short novel (less than 300 pages). All finalists considered for publication. **Deadline: January 1-February 15.** Guidelines for SASE. **Charges $20 fee.** Prize: $2,000, and publication (standard royalty contract).

MID-LIST PRESS FIRST SERIES AWARD FOR SHORT FICTION

Mid-List Press, 4324 12th Ave. S., Minneapolis MN 55407-3218. Fax: (612)823-8387. E-mail: guide@midlist.org. Website: www.midlist.org. **Contact:** Lane Stiles, publisher. Open to any writer who has never published a book-length collection of short fiction (short stories, novellas); minimum 50,000 words. Accepts simultaneous submissions. Guidelines and entry form for SASE or on website. **Deadline: July 1. Charges $30 (US dollars) fee.** Prize: Awards include publication and an advance against royalties.

MID-LIST PRESS FIRST SERIES AWARD FOR THE NOVEL

Mid-List Press, 4324-12th Ave. S., Minneapolis MN 55407-3218. (612)822-3733. Fax: (612)823-8387. E-mail: guide@midlist.org. Website: www.midlist.org. **Contact:** Lane Stiles, publisher. Offered annually for unpublished novels to locate and publish quality mss by first-time writers, particularly those mid-list titles that major publishers may be rejecting. Guidelines for SASE or on website. Open to any writer who has never published a novel. **Deadline: February 1. Charges $30 (US dollars) fee.** Prize: Advance against royalties, plus publication.

MILKWEED NATIONAL FICTION PRIZE

Milkweed Editions, 1011 Washington Ave. S., Suite 300, Minneapolis MN 55415. (612)332-3192. Fax: (612)215-2550. Website: www.milkweed.org. **Contact:** Elisabeth Fitz, first reader. Estab. 1986. Annual award for unpublished works. "Milkweed is looking for a novel, novella, or a collection of short stories. Manuscripts should be of high literary quality and must be double-spaced and between 150-400 pages in length. Due to new postal regulations, writers who need their work returned must include a check for $5 rather than a SAS book mailer. Manuscripts not accompanied by a check for postage will be recycled." Winner will be chosen from the mss Milkweed accepts for publication each year. All mss submitted to Milkweed will automatically be considered for the prize. Submission directly to the contest is no longer necessary. "Must be written in English. Writers should have previously published a book of fiction or 3 short stories (or novellas) in magazines/journals with national distribution." Catalog available on request for $1.50. Guidelines for SASE or online. **Deadline: Open.** Prize: Publication by Milkweed Editions, and a cash advance of $5,000 against royalties agreed upon in the contractual arrangement negotiated at the time of acceptance.

C. WRIGHT MILLS AWARD

The Society for the Study of Social Problems, 901 McClung Tower, University of Tennessee, Knoxville TN 37996-0490. (865)689-1531. Fax: (865)689-1534. E-mail: mkoontz3@utk.edu. Website: www.sssp1.org. **Contact:** Michele Smith Koontz, administrative officer. Offered annually for a book published the previous year that most effectively critically addresses an issue of contemporary public importance; brings to the topic a fresh, imaginative perspective; advances social scientific understanding of the topic; displays a theoretically informed view and empirical orientation; evinces quality in style of writing; and explicitly or implicitly contains implications for courses of action. **Deadline: January 15.** Prize: $500 stipend.

N ⊕ KATHLEEN MITCHELL AWARD

Cauz Group Pty., Ltd., P.O. Box 777, Randwick NSW 2031, Australia. 61-2-93321559. Fax: 61-2-93321298. E-mail: psalter@cauzgroup.com.au. **Contact:** Petrea Salter. Offered in even years for novels published in the previous 2 years. Author must have been under age 30 when the novel was published. Entrants must be Australian or British born or naturalized Australian citizens, and have resided in Australia for the last year. The award is for a novel of the highest literary merit. **Deadline: March 31.** Guidelines for SASE. Prize: $7,500 (Australian).

NATIONAL WRITERS ASSOCIATION NOVEL WRITING CONTEST

The National Writers Association, 3140 S. Peoria, #295, Aurora CO 80014. (303)841-0246. Fax: (303)841-2607. **Contact:** Sandy Whelchel, director. Annual contest "to help develop creative skills, to recognize and reward outstanding ability, and to increase the opportunity for the marketing and subsequent publication of novel manuscripts." **Deadline: April 1. Charges $35 fee.** Prize: 1st Place: $500; 2nd Place: $300; 3rd Place: $200.

NATIONAL WRITERS ASSOCIATION SHORT STORY CONTEST

The National Writers Association, 3140 S. Peoria, #295, Aurora CO 80014. (303)841-0246. Fax: (303)841-2607. **Contact:** Sandy Whelchel, director. Annual contest "to encourage writers in this creative form, and to recognize those who excel in fiction writing." **Deadline: July 1.** Guidelines for SASE. **Charges $15 fee.** Prize: 1st Place: $200; 2nd Place: $100; 3rd Place: $50.

NEW YORK STORIES FICTION PRIZE

New York Stories, English Department, E-103, LaGuardia Community College/CUNY, 31-10 Thomson Ave., Long Island City NY 11101. E-mail: nystories@lagcc.cuny.edu. Website: www.newyorkstories.org. **Contact:** Daniel Lynch, contest director. Offered annually for unpublished work to showcase new, quality short fiction. Stories must not exceed 6,500 words. Open to any writer. **Deadline: September 15.** Guidelines for SASE. **Charges $15 fee (payable to New York Stories).** Prize: 1st Place: $500 and publication; 2nd Place: $250, and consideration for publication.

FRANK O'CONNOR AWARD FOR SHORT FICTION

descant, Texas Christian University's literary journal, TCU Box 297270, Fort Worth TX 76129. (817)257-6537. Fax: (817)257-6239. E-mail: descant@tcu.edu. **Contact:** Dave Kuhne, editor. Offered annually for unpublished short stories. Publication retains copyright but will transfer it to the author upon request. **Deadline: September-April.** Guidelines for SASE. Prize: $500.

THE FLANNERY O'CONNOR AWARD FOR SHORT FICTION

The University of Georgia Press, 330 Research Dr., Athens GA 30602-4901. (706)369-6130. Fax: (706)369-6131. Website: www.ugapress.org. Estab. 1981. Does not return mss. Manuscripts must be 200-275 pages long. Authors do not have to be previously published. **Deadline: Submission Period: April 1-May 31.** Guidelines for SASE. **Charges $20 fee.** Prize: $1,000, and publication under standard book contract.

THE OHIO STATE UNIVERSITY PRIZE IN SHORT FICTION

The Ohio State University Press and the MFA Program in Creative Writing at The Ohio State University, 1070 Carmack Rd., Columbus OH 43210-1002. (614)292-1462. Fax: (614)292-2065. E-mail: ohiostatepress@osu.edu. Website: ohiostatepress.org. Offered annually to published and unpublished writers. Submissions may include short stories, novellas, or a combination of both. Manuscripts must be 150-300 typed pages; novellas must not exceed 125 pages. No employee or student of The Ohio State University is eligible. **Deadline: postmarked during month of November. Charges $20 fee.** Prize: $1,500, publication under a standard book contract.

▣ ONCEWRITTEN.COM FICTION CONTEST

Oncewritten.com, P.O. Box 3046, Hollywood CA 90078-3046. E-mail: contests@oncewritten.com. Website: www.oncewritten.com. The purpose of this biannual contest is to find high quality short fiction to feature on the website and in *Off the Press*, our biweekly newsletter, which is distributed specifically to people interested in reading about new authors." **Deadline: September 30; March 31.** Guidelines for SASE. **Charges $15.** Prize: Grand Prize: $1,000; 1st Prize: $100; both include publication on website and in newsletter. Judged by editor and 1 industry professional. The first fiction contest will be judged by Rob Roberge, a published author and teacher of creative writing at UCLA extension. Open to any writer.

▣ ONCEWRITTEN.COM IN THE MIDNIGHT HOUR HALLOWEEN CONTEST

Oncewritten.com, P.O. Box 3046, Hollywood CA 90078-3046. E-mail: monica@oncewritten.com. Website: www.oncewritten.com. **Contact:** Monica Poling. "The purpose of this contest is to find high quality, previously unpublished Halloween fiction to feature on the website and in *Off the Press*, our biweekly newsletter, which is distributed specifically to people interested in reading about new authors." **Deadline: September 1.** Guidelines for SASE. **Charges $10.** Prize: Grand Prize: $500; 1st Prize: $100; both include publication on website and in newsletter. Judged by editor and 1 industry professional. This year the contest will be judged by Ian Rabin, a professional screenwriter. Open to any writer.

▣ THE OPUS FANTASY WRITING CONTEST

Fantasy Arts Enterprises, 397 S. Revere St., Aurora CO 80012-2369. (303)523-0527. Fax: (360)283-6047. E-mail: opusfest@carpovita.com. Website: www.faefests.com. **Contact:** Sage Bergquist. Offered annually for unpublished work. **Deadline: April 15.** Guidelines for SASE. **Charges $3/submission.** Prize: Grand Prize: 1 year's advisement with a professional writer from the Opus Fantasy Arts Festival guest list; 2nd Prize: $75; 3rd Prize: $50. All prize winners also receive print publication in *Opus Imagico*, and 2 copies of the publication. Judged by veteran editor Sage Bergquist and guest editors. The 2004 guest editor was Wynette Hoffman from Alien Perspective Publications. Final judging is done by the professional writer who is to conduct the internship. In 2004, it was Robert Asprin; in 2003, Michael Stackpole. Acquires first serial rights. Open to any writer.

⊕ ORANGE PRIZE FOR FICTION

Orange PCS, c/o Booktrust, Book House, 45 E. Hill, Wandsworth, London SW18 2QZ, United Kingdom. Fax: (00 44) 20 8516 2978. E-mail: tarryn@booktrust.org.uk. Website: www.orangeprize.com. **Contact:** Ms. Becky Shaw. This annual award is for a full-length novel written by a woman which fulfills the criteria of excellence in writing, relevance to people's everyday and imaginative lives, accessibility, and originality. The award is open to any full-length novel written in English between April 1, 2004, and March 31, 2005, by a woman of any nationality. Translations are not eligible, neither are novellas or collections of short stories. Books from all genres are encouraged, but all books must be unified and substantial works written by a single author. All entries must be published in the UK between the publication dates, but may have been previously published outside the UK. Publisher entry only. **Deadline: November 26.** Prize: £30,000 and a statuette known as a "Bessie." Judged by a panel of women.

▣ OTTAWA PUBLIC LIBRARY ANNUAL SHORT STORY CONTEST

Ottawa Public Library, Community Partnerships and Programming, 101 Centrepointe Dr., Ottawa ON K2G 5K7, Canada. (613)580-2424, ext. 41468. E-mail: esme.bailey@library.ottawa.on.ca. Website: www.library.ottawa.on.ca. **Contact:** Esme Bailey. Offered annually for unpublished short stories (written in French or English) to encourage writing in the community. Open to residents of Ottawa, Ontario, age 18 or older. Guidelines online at www.library.ottawa.on.ca/english/story, or call (613)580-2424. **Deadline: March 2. Charges $5/story.** Prize: 1st Prize: $500; 2nd Prize: $250; 3rd Prize: $100.

▣ THE PARABLE AWARD

420 N. Meridian St., #5798, Newberg OR 97132. E-mail: write_the_word@yahoo.com. Website: parableaward.tripod.com. **Contact:** Christine Hahn-Steichen, editor. "The annual Parable Award was created to promote excellence in the field of Christian fiction writing. It is open to works that draw the reader into a closer relationship with, and a better understanding of, the Triune God. It can belong to any genre of fiction, and can be written for children, youth, or adults. Please visit our website for details and submission guidelines." The contest is open to anyone "who believes that Jesus Christ is their Leader and Savior from evil, and who belongs to a recognized Christian denomination (this includes all major branches of evangelical Protestantism, Catholicism, and Orthodoxy)." **Deadline: December 1. Charges $1.** Prize: $25.

PATERSON FICTION PRIZE

One College Blvd., Paterson NJ 07505-1179. (973)684-6555. Fax: (973)684-5843. E-mail: mgillan@pccc.cc.nj.us. Website: www.pccc.cc.nj.us/poetry. **Contact:** Maria Mazziotti Gillan, director. Offered annually for a novel or collection of short fiction published the previous calendar year. **Deadline: April 1.** Guidelines for SASE. Prize: $1,000.

WILLIAM PEDEN PRIZE IN FICTION

The Missouri Review, 1507 Hillcrest Hall, Columbia MO 65211. (573)882-4474. Fax: (573)884-4671. Website: www.missourireview.com. **Contact:** Hoa Ngo, managing editor. Offered annually "for the best story published in the past volume year of the magazine. All stories published in *The Missouri Review* are automatically considered." Prize: $1,000, and reading/reception.

PEN/FAULKNER AWARDS FOR FICTION

PEN/Faulkner Foundation, 201 E. Capitol St., Washington DC 20003. (202)675-0345. Fax: (202)608-1719. E-mail: delaney@folger.edu. Website: www.penfaulkner.org. **Contact:** Janice F. Delaney, executive director. Offered annually for best book-length work of fiction by an American citizen published in a calendar year. **Deadline: October 31.** Prize: $15,000 (one winner); $5,000 (4 nominees).

PHOEBE WINTER FICTION CONTEST

Phoebe, George Mason University, 4400 University Dr., Fairfax VA 22030-4444. (703)993-2915. E-mail: phoebe@gmu.edu. Website: www.gmu.edu/pubs/phoebe. **Contact:** Lisa Ampleman. Offered annually for unpublished work. **Deadline: December 1.** Guidelines for SASE. **Charges $12.** Prize: $1,000, and publication in Fall issue. All entrants receive a free issue. Judged by outside judge—recognized fiction writer hired by *Phoebe*—who changes each year. Acquires first serial rights, if work is accepted for publication. Open to any writer.

POCKETS FICTION-WRITING CONTEST

The Upper Room, 1908 Grand Ave., P.O. Box 340004, Nashville TN 37203-0004. (615)340-7333. E-mail: pockets @upperroom.org. Website: www.pockets.org. **Contact:** Lynn W. Gilliam. Offered annually for unpublished work to discover new writers. **Deadline: March 1-August 15.** Guidelines for SASE. Prize: $1,000, and publication in *Pockets*.

THE KATHERINE ANNE PORTER PRIZE FOR FICTION

Nimrod International Journal, 600 S. College Ave., Tulsa OK 74104. (918)631-3080. Fax: (918)631-3033. E-mail: nimrod@utulsa.edu. Website: www.utulsa.edu/nimrod. **Contact:** Francine Ringold. This annual award was established to discover new, unpublished writers of vigor and talent. **Deadline: April 30.** Guidelines for SASE. **Charges $20 (includes a 1-year subscription to *Nimrod*).** Prize: 1st Place: $2,000, and publication; 2nd Place: $1,000, and publication. Judged by the *Nimrod* editors (finalists), and a recognized author selects the winners. Acquires *Nimrod* retains the right to publish any submission. Open to US residents only.

◪ PRISM INTERNATIONAL ANNUAL SHORT FICTION CONTEST

Prism International, Creative Writing Program, UBC, Buch E462, 1866 Main Mall, Vancouver BC V6T 1Z1, Canada. (604)822-2514. Fax: (604)822-3616. E-mail: prism@interchange.ubc.ca. Website: prism.arts.ubc.ca. **Contact:** Fiction Contest Manager. Offered annually for unpublished work to award the best in contemporary fiction. Works of translation are eligible. Guidelines for SASE, by e-mail, or on website. Acquires first North American serial rights upon publication, and limited Web rights for pieces selected for website. Open to any writer except students and faculty in the Creative Writing Department at UBC, or people who have taken a creative writing course at UBC with the 2 years prior to the contest deadline. **Deadline: January 31. Charges $25/story, $7 each additional story (outside Canada pay US currency); includes subscription.** Prize: 1st Place: $2,000; Runners-up (5): $200 each; winner and runners-up published.

◪ THOMAS H. RADDALL ATLANTIC FICTION PRIZE

Writers' Federation of Nova Scotia, 1113 Marginal Rd., Halifax NS B3H 4P7, Canada. (902)423-8116. Fax: (902)422-0881. E-mail: talk@writers.ns.ca. Website: www.writers.ns.ca. **Contact:** Jane Buss, executive director. "This award was established by the Writers' Federation of Nova Scotia and the Writers' Development Trust in 1990 to honor the achievement of Thomas H. Raddall, and to recognize the best Atlantic Canadian adult fiction. Thomas Head Raddall is probably best-known for *His Majesty's Yankees* (1942), *The Governor's Lady* (1960), *The Nymph and the Lamp* (1950), and *Halifax, Warden of the North* (1948)." There is no entry fee or form. Full-length books of fiction written by Atlantic Canadians, and published as a whole for the first time in the previous calendar year, are eligible. Entrants must be native or resident Atlantic Canadians who have either been born in Newfoundland, Prince Edward Island, Nova Scotia, or New Brunswick, and spent a substantial portion of their lives living there, or who have lived in 1 or a combination of these provinces for at least 24 consecutive months prior to entry deadline date. Publishers: Send 4 copies and a letter attesting to the author's status as an Atlantic Canadian, and the author's current mailing address and telephone number. **Deadline: First Friday in December.** Prize: $10,000.

RAMBUNCTIOUS REVIEW FICTION CONTEST
Rambunctious Review, 1221 W. Pratt Blvd., Chicago IL 60626. Annual themed contest for unpublished stories. Acquires one-time publication rights. Open to any writer. **Deadline: December 31.** Guidelines for SASE. **Charges $3/story.** Prize: 1st Prize: $100; 2nd Prize: $75; 3rd Prize: $50; all winning stories will be published in future issues of *Rambunctious Review*. Acquires one-time publication rights.

N ⊕ REAL WRITERS SHORT STORY AWARDS
Real Writers Support & Appraisal Service, P.O. Box 170, Chesterfield S42 6UL, United Kingdom. E-mail: info@real-writers.com. Website: www.real-writers.com. **Contact:** Lynne Patrick, coordinator. Annual contest for unpublished short stories to provide an outlet for writers of short fiction and to open up opportunities for development. "We have a good working relationship with a major publisher." **Deadline: November 30.** Guidelines for SASE. **Charges £5 sterling (payable by credit card, so converted to dollars of current exchange rate).** Prize: £2500 sterling and section prizes. Judged by an experienced team of readers who select a shortlist from which prize winners are chosen by a smaller team which includes literary agents and editors, and is led by a senior editor from a major publishing house. "We buy first British serial rights for publication in an anthology." Applies only to prize winners. Open to any writer.

N HAROLD U. RIBALOW PRIZE
Hadassah WZOA, 50 W. 58th St., New York NY 10019. (212)451-6289 or (212)451-6293. Fax: (212)451-6257. E-mail: hadamag@aol.com or atigay@aol.com. **Contact:** Dorothy Silfen, coordinator. Editor: Alan Tigay. Offered annually for English-language books of fiction (novel or short stories) on a Jewish theme published the previous year. Books should be submitted by the publisher. Administered annually by *Hadassah Magazine*. **Deadline: March 31.** Prize: $2,000. "The official announcement of the winner will be made in early fall."

RIVER CITY WRITING AWARDS IN FICTION
The University of Memphis/Hohenberg Foundation, Dept. of English, Memphis TN 38152. (901)678-4591. E-mail: rivercity@memphis.edu. Website: www.people.memphis.edu/~rivercity. Offered annually for unpublished short stories of 7,500 words maximum. Guidelines for SASE or on website. **Deadline: March 15. Charges $12/story, which is put toward a 1-year subscription for** *River City*. Prize: 1st Place: $1,500; 2nd Place: $350; 3rd Place: $150.

⊠ THE ROGERS WRITERS' TRUST FICTION PRIZE
The Writers' Trust of Canada, 40 Wellington St. E, Suite 300, Toronto ON M5E 1C7, Canada. (416)504-8222. Fax: (416)504-9090. E-mail: info@writerstrust.com. Website: www.writerstrust.com. **Contact:** James Davies. Awarded annually for a distinguished work of fiction, either a novel or short story collection, published within the previous year. Presented at the Great Literary Awards event held in Toronto each spring. Prize: $10,000. Open to Canadian residents only.

N ⊕ ROONEY PRIZE FOR IRISH LITERATURE
Strathin, Templecarrig, Delgany, Co. Wicklow, Republic of Ireland. (01) 287 4769. Fax: (01) 287 2595. E-mail: rooneyprize@ireland.com. **Contact:** Thelma Cloake. Estab. 1976. Annual award for a published, Irish writer under the age of 40. Prize: 8,000 Euros. Judged by Michael Allen, Ingrid Craigie, Seamus Hosey, Niall MacMonagle, Paul Mercier, Deirdre Purcell, and Jim Sherwin (chairman).

⊠ SASKATCHEWAN FICTION AWARD
Saskatchewan Book Awards, Inc., Box 1921, Regina SK S4P 3E1, Canada. (306)569-1585. Fax: (306)569-4187. E-mail: director@bookawards.sk.ca. Website: www.bookawards.sk.ca. **Contact:** Joyce Wells, executive director. Offered annually for work published September 15, 2002 to September 14, 2003 annually. This award is presented to a Saskatchewan author for the best book of fiction (novel or short fiction), judged on the quality of writing. **Deadline: First deadline: July 31; Final deadline: September 14.** Guidelines for SASE. **Charges $20 (Canadian).** Prize: $2,000.

MICHAEL SHAARA AWARD FOR EXCELLENCE IN CIVIL WAR FICTION
US Civil War Center, LSU, Raphael Semmes Dr., Baton Rouge LA 70803. (225)578-3151. Fax: (225)578-4876. E-mail: lwood@lsu.edu. Website: www.cwc.lsu.edu. **Contact:** Leah Jewett, director. Offered annually for fiction

published for the first time in January 1-December 31 of the year of the award "to encourage examination of the Civil War from unique perspectives or by taking an unusual approach." All Civil War novels are eligible. To nominate a novel, send 5 copies of the novel to the address above with a cover letter. Nominations should be made by publishers, but authors and critics can nominate as well. **Deadline: December 31.** Guidelines for SASE. Prize: $2,500, which includes travel stipend.

MARY WOLLSTONECRAFT SHELLEY PRIZE FOR IMAGINATIVE FICTION
(formerly Ursula K. Leguin Prize for Imaginative Fiction), *Rosebud*, P.O. Box 459, Cambridge WI 53523. E-mail: jrodclark@smallbytes.net. Website: www.rsbd.net. **Contact:** J. Roderick Clark, editor. Biennial (odd years) contest for unpublished stories. Next contest closes October 1, 2005. Entries are welcome any time. Acquires first rights. Open to any writer. **Deadline: September 30. Charges $10/story fee.** Prize: $1,000, plus publication in *Rosebud*.

ELIZABETH SIMPSON SMITH AWARD
Charlotte Writers Club, P.O. Box 220954, Charlotte NC 28222-0954. E-mail: elizabethsimpsonsmithaward@charlottewritersclub.org. Website: www.charlottewritersclub.org. Offered annually for unpublished short stories by North Carolina and South Carolina residents. Guidelines for SASE or online. **Deadline: May 31. Charges $15 fee.** Prize: $500.

SHEILA K. SMITH SHORT STORY PRIZE
National League of American Pen Women, Nob Hill, San Francisco Bay Area, 1544 Sweetwood Dr., Colma CA 94015-2029. E-mail: pennobhill@aol.com. Website: www.soulmakingcontest.us. **Contact:** Eileen Malone. One story/entry, up to 5,000 words. All prose works must be typed, page numbered, stapled, and double-spaced. Annually. **Deadline: November 30.** Guidelines for SASE. **Charges $5/entry (make checks payable to NLAPW, Nob Hill Branch).** Prize: 1st Place: $100; 2nd Place: $50; 3rd Place: $25. Open to any writer.

KAY SNOW WRITING AWARDS
Willamette Writers, 9045 SW Barbur Blvd., Suite 5A, Portland OR 97219. (503)452-1592. Fax: (503)452-0372. E-mail: wilwrite@teleport.com. Website: www.willamettewriters.com. **Contact:** Marlene Moore. Contest offered annually to "offer encouragement and recognition to writers with unpublished submissions." Acquires right to publish excerpts from winning pieces 1 time in their newsletter. **Deadline: May 15.** Guidelines for SASE. **Charges $15 fee; no fee for student writers.** Prize: 1st Place: $300; 2nd Place: $150; 3rd Place: $50; excerpts published in Willamette Writers newsletter, and winners acknowledged at banquet during writing conference. Student writers win $50 in categories for grades 1-5, 6-8, and 9-12. $500 Liam Callen Memorial Award goes to best overall entry.

THE SOUTHERN REVIEW/LOUISIANA STATE UNIVERSITY SHORT FICTION AWARD
Louisiana State University, 43 Allen Hall, Baton Rouge LA 70803. (225)578-5108. Fax: (225)578-5098. E-mail: bmacon@lsu.edu or jeaster@lsu.edu. Offered for first collections of short stories by Americans published in the US during the previous year. Publisher or author may enter by mailing 2 copies of the collection. **Deadline: January 31.**

SPOKANE PRIZE FOR SHORT FICTION
Eastern Washington University Press, 705 W. First Ave., Spokane WA 99201. (800)508-9095. Fax: (509)623-4283. E-mail: ewupress@ewu.edu. Website: ewupress.ewu.edu. **Contact:** Scott Poole. "Annual award to publish the finest work the literary world has to offer." **Deadline: May 15.** Guidelines for SASE. **Charges $25.** Prize: $1,500, and publication. Judged by EWU Press staff. Open to any writer.

THE STORYCOVE FLASH FICTION CONTEST
Word Smitten, LLP, P.O. Box 5067, St. Petersburg FL 33737. E-mail: story@wordsmitten.com. Website: www.wordsmitten.com. Offered annually for unpublished, original fiction with memorable characters and interesting consequences with 500 or fewer words. Submit story embedded in an e-mail (no attachments) with your name at the top of the e-mail. Guidelines for SASE, by e-mail, and on website. **Deadline: May 1. Charges $10/entry.** Prize: $150, and publication in Native Shore Fiction/Word Smitten Summer edition. Judged by recognized authors. In last year's major fiction competition, Peter Meinke, winner of the Flannery O'Connor Award, was our judge. Acquires One-time rights for publication, then all rights revert to author. Open to any writer.

🔲 THE SUNDAY STAR SHORT STORY CONTEST
The Toronto Star, 1 Yonge St., 5th Floor, Toronto ON M5A 4L1, Canada. Website: www.thestar.com. Annual contest for unpublished work offered "to encourage good, quality short story writing." Must be a Canadian

citizen if living outside Canada, or a resident of Canada and at least 16 years or older. Guidelines on website or on "StarPhone (416)350-3000, ext. 2747." **Deadline: December 31. Charges $5.** Prize: 1st Place: $5,000, plus tuition fee for the Humber School of Writers Creative Correspondence Program; 2nd Place: $2,000; 3rd Place: $1,000; 7 runners-up receive $200 each. Judged by Ryerson Writing Centre (initial judging). Final judging by panel of writers and editors from *The Star*.

THE PETER TAYLOR PRIZE FOR THE NOVEL

Knoxville Writers' Guild and University of Tennessee Press, P.O. Box 2565, Knoxville TN 37901-2565. Website: www.knoxvillewritersguild.org. **Contact:** Brian Griffin. Offered annually for unpublished work to discover and publish novels of high literary quality. Guidelines for SASE or on website. Open to US residents writing in English. Members of the Knoxville Writers' Guild do the initial screening. A widely published novelist chooses the winner from a pool of finalists. 2004 judge: Barry Hannah; 2003 judge: John Casey. **Deadline: February 1-April 30. Charges $20 fee.** Prize: $1,000, publication by University of Tennessee Press (a standard royalty contract).

〖N〗 THOROUGHBRED TIMES FICTION CONTEST

P.O. Box 8237, Lexington KY 40533. (859)260-9800. Fax: (859)260-9812. E-mail: copy@thoroughbredtimes.com. Website: www.thoroughbredtimes.com. **Contact:** Amy Owens. Offered every 2 years for unpublished work to recognize outstanding fiction written about the Thoroughbred racing industry. Maximum length: 5,000 words. *Thoroughbred Times* receives first North American serial rights and reserves the right to publish any and all entries in the magazine. **Deadline: December 31.** Prize: 1st Place: $800, and publication in *Thoroughbred Times*; 2nd Place: $400, and publication; 3rd Place: $250, and publication.

THREE OAKS PRIZE FOR FICTION

Story Line Press, P.O. Box 1240, Ashland OR 97520-0055. (541)512-8792. Fax: (541)512-8793. E-mail: mail@storylinepress.com. Website: www.storylinepress.com. Offered annually to find and publish the best work of fiction. Open to any writer. **Deadline: April 30.** Guidelines for SASE. **Charges $25.** Prize: $1,500 advance, and book publication.

〖N〗 STEVEN TURNER AWARD FOR BEST FIRST WORK OF FICTION

3700 Mockingbird Lane, Dallas TX 75205. (214)528-2655. E-mail: franvick@aol.com. **Contact:** Fran Vick. Offered annually for work published January 1-December 31 for the best first book of fiction. Writers must have been born in Texas, or have lived in the state for at least 2 consecutive years at some time, or the subject matter of the work should be associated with the state. **Deadline: January 3.** Guidelines for SASE. Prize: $1,000.

〖N〗 〖▣〗 WCDR SHORT FICTION CONTEST

The Writers' Circle of Durham Region, P.O. Box 323, Ajax ON L1S 3C5, Canada. Fax: (905)985-6454. E-mail: secretary@wcdr.org. Website: www.wcdr.org. **Contact:** Aprille Janes. Annual contest for unpublished short fiction. **Deadline: February 15. Charges $20 (Canadian).** Prize: 1st Prize: $500; 2nd Prize: $300; 3rd Prize: $200. Judged by novelist Joan Barfoor, novelist Greg Ward, and editor of *Storyteller Magazine*, Terry Tyo, in 2004. Open to Canadian residents only.

WHIM'S PLACE CHANGING OF THE SEASONS FLASH FICTION WRITING CONTEST

WhimsPlace.com, P.O. Box 14931, Lenexa KS 66285. E-mail: contest@whimsplace.com. Website: www.whimsplace.com/contest/contest.asp. **Contact:** Betsy Gallup. Offered quarterly for flash fiction. "We love flash fiction! That's why we're having a contest. We also feel that contests are a great way to boost an ego, enhance a résumé, and to just have some plain old fashion fun with your writing. We expect good writing, however. It must be tightly written, organized, and proofread at least 100 times." Submissions are accepted only through Whim's Place online submission form. Entries over 500 words will automatically be disqualified. **Deadline: March 30; June 30; September 30; December 30. Charges $5.** Prize: 1st Place: $150; 2nd Place: $100; 3rd Place: $50; Honorable Mentions (8): $25. Judged by Whim's Place staff members, and an appointed guest judge each season. The special judge will be a published author or an editor. Open to any writer.

TOBIAS WOLFF AWARD IN FICTION

Bellingham Review, Mail Stop 9053, Western Washington University, Bellingham WA 98225. (360)650-4863. E-mail: bhreview@cc.wwu.edu. Website: www.wwu.edu/~bhreview/. **Contact:** Brenda Miller. Offered annually for unpublished work. Guidelines for SASE or online. **Deadline: December 1-March 15. Charges $15 entry fee for 1st entry, and $10 for each additional entry.** Prize: $1,000, plus publication and subscription. All finalists considered for publication. All entrants receive subscription.

WORD SMITTEN'S TENTEN FICTION COMPETITION

Word Smitten, LLP, P.O. Box 5067, St. Petersburg FL 33737-5067. E-mail: story@wordsmitten.com. Website: www.wordsmitten.com. Contest offered annually for unpublished short stories that require exactly 1,010 words. "The word count does not include the story title, but we recommend you keep it short. Excise those adverbs! Cut those adjectives. Make us laugh or make us weep. Above all, pay rigorous attention to the word count. It's why we call it the TenTen. It's a challenge to be precise, be witty, be short!" For more details visit website. Guidelines by e-mail or on website. **Deadline: July 1. Charges $15/entry.** Prize: $1,010, and publication in *Native Shore Fiction/Word Smitten* Summer edition. Judged by recognized authors. "In last year's major competition, Peter Meinke, winner of The Flannery O'Connor Award was our judge." Acquires Buys one-time rights for publication, and then all rights revert to author. Open to any writer.

WORLD'S BEST SHORT SHORT STORY FICTION CONTEST

English Department, Writing Program, Florida State University, Tallahassee FL 32306. (850)644-2773. E-mail: southeastreview@english.fsu.edu. Website: www.english.fsu.edu/southeastreview. **Contact:** James Kimbrell, editor, *The Southeast Review.* Estab. 1986. Annual award for unpublished short short stories (no more than 500 words). **Deadline: February 15. Charges $10 fee/story.** Prize: $500, an all-expense-paid-trip to read at FSU, and a box of Florida oranges.

Ⓝ ⊞ WRITERS' FORUM INTERNATIONAL STORY COMPETITION

Writers' FORUM, P.O. Box 3229, Bournemouth BH1 1ZS. E-mail: editorial@writers-forum.com. Website: www.writers-forum.com. Annual contest for unpublished stories (crime, mystery, romance, sport, humor, fantasy, erotica, science fiction) between 1,500 and 3,000 words. *Writers' FORUM* also awards a prize in each issue. **Deadline: The 5th day of June, August, September, October, November, and December.** Guidelines for SASE. **Charges £10 reading fee (£6 reading fee for subscribers).** Prize: Annually awards £1,000 for best short story with £250 (2) to runners-up. Awards £150-250 each issue. Open to any writer.

WRITERS' JOURNAL ANNUAL FICTION CONTEST

Val-Tech Media, P.O. Box 394, Perham MN 56573. (218)346-7921. Fax: (218)346-7924. E-mail: writersjournal@lakesplus.com. Website: www.writersjournal.com. **Contact:** Leon Ogroske. Offered annually for previously unpublished fiction. Open to any writer. Guidelines for SASE and online. **Deadline: January 30. Charges $5 reading fee.** Prize: 1st Place: $50; 2nd Place: $25; 3rd Place: $15, plus honorable mentions. Prize-winning stories and selected honorable mentions published in *Writers' Journal.*

WRITERS' JOURNAL ANNUAL HORROR/GHOST CONTEST

Val-Tech Media, P.O. Box 394, Perham MN 56573. (218)346-7921. Fax: (218)346-7924. E-mail: writersjournal@lakesplus.com. Website: www.writersjournal.com. **Contact:** Leon Ogroske. Offered annually for previously unpublished works. Open to any writer. Guidelines for SASE and online. **Deadline: March 30. Charges $5 fee.** Prize: 1st Place: $50; 2nd Place: $25; 3rd Place: $15, plus honorable mentions. Prize-winning stories and selected honorable mentions published in *Writers' Journal.*

WRITERS' JOURNAL ANNUAL ROMANCE CONTEST

Val-Tech Media, P.O. Box 394, Perham MN 56573. (218)346-7921. Fax: (218)346-7924. E-mail: writersjournal@lakesplus.com. Website: www.writersjournal.com. **Contact:** Leon Ogroske. Offered annually for previously unpublished works. Open to any writer. Guidelines for SASE and online. **Deadline: July 30. Charges $5 fee.** Prize: 1st Place: $50; 2nd Place: $25; 3rd Place: $15, plus honorable mentions. Prize-winning stories and selected honorable mentions published in *Writers' Journal.*

WRITERS' JOURNAL ANNUAL SHORT STORY CONTEST

Val-Tech Media, P.O. Box 394, Perham MN 56573. (218)346-7921. Fax: (218)346-7924. E-mail: writersjournal@lakesplus.com. Website: www.writersjournal.com. **Contact:** Leon Ogroske. Offered annually for previously unpublished short stories. Open to any writer. Guidelines for SASE and online. **Deadline: May 30. Charges $7 reading fee.** Prize: 1st Place: $300; 2nd Place: $100; 3rd Place: $50, plus honorable mentions. Prize-winning stories and selected honorable mentions published in *Writers' Journal.*

WRITER'S REPERTORY SHORT FICTION LITERARY AWARD

Center for Teaching and Learning, University of Illinois at Springfield, One University Plaza, MS BRK 489, Springfield IL 62703. (217)206-7459. E-mail: writersrepertory@hotmail.com. Website: www.uis.edu/ctl. **Contact:** Maureen Skubee. "We are seeking unpublished short fiction (15 pages maximum). Writer's Repertory is a student-run organization seeking exposure for both the organization and the Center for Teaching and Learning. The contest grew out of a graduate assistant's yearlong project." Entries are limited to the first 200 entries, after 200, entries will be returned unread. **Deadline: January 31.** Guidelines for SASE. **Charges $5 entry fee.** Prize: 1st Place: $300, and publication in *The Alchemist Review* (the student-run literary journal produced by the English Department at the University of Illinois at Springfield), and 2 copies of the journal; 2nd Place: $100, and 1 copy of *The Alchemist Review*; 3rd Place: 1 copy of *The Alchemist Review*. Judged by graduate students in the English Department with a primary focus on creative writing. Open to any writer.

ZOETROPE SHORT STORY CONTEST

Zoetrope: All-Story, 916 Kearny St., San Francisco CA 94133. (415)788-7500. Fax: (415)989-7910. Website: www.all-story.com. **Contact:** Francis Ford Coppola, publisher. Annual contest for unpublished short stories. Guidelines for SASE or on website. Open to any writer. Please mark envelope clearly "short fiction contest." **Deadline: October 1. Charges $15 fee.** Prize: 1st Place: $1,000, 2nd Place: $500, 3rd Place: $250, plus 10 honorable mentions.

POETRY

🌐 ACADEMI CARDIFF INTERNATIONAL POETRY COMPETITION

Academi, P.O. Box 438, Cardiff, Wales CF10 5 YA, United Kingdom. E-mail: competitions@academi.org. Website: www.academi.org. **Contact:** Peter Finch, contest/award director. "This annual competition is open to everyone—the only criteria being that poems submitted must be of 50 lines or less, written in English, and previously unpublished. All entries must be accompanied by payment and an entry form, which may be downloaded from the Academi website." **Deadline: January 30.** Guidelines for SASE. **Charges £5/poem.** Prize: 1st Prize: £5,000; 2nd Prize: £700; 3rd Prize: £300; 4th-8th Prize: £200. All cash awards include publication in the *New Welsh Review*, Wales' leading literary journal, and on the Academi website. Judged by Robert Minhinnick and Ruth Padel.

AKRON POETRY PRIZE

University of Akron Press, 374B Bierce Library, Akron OH 44325-1703. (330)972-5342. Fax: (330)972-6896. E-mail: uapress@uakron.edu. Website: www.uakron.edu/uapress/poetry.html. **Contact:** Elton Glaser, poetry editor. Annual book contest for unpublished poetry. "The Akron Poetry Prize brings to the public writers with original and compelling voices. Books must exhibit three essential qualities: mastery of language, maturity of feeling, and complexity of thought." Guidelines available online or for SASE. The final selection will be made by a nationally prominent poet. The University of Akron Press has the right to publish the winning ms, inherent with winning the Poetry Prize. Open to all poets writing in English. **Deadline: May 15-June 30. Charges $25 fee.** Prize: Winning poet receives $1,000, and publication of book.

ANHINGA PRIZE FOR POETRY

Anhinga Press, P.O. Box 10595, Tallahassee FL 32302. (850)442-1408. Fax: (850)442-6363. E-mail: info@anhinga.org. Website: www.anhinga.org. **Contact:** Rick Campbell. Offered annually for a book-length collection of poetry by an author who has not published more than 1 book of poetry. Guidelines for SASE or on website. Open to any writer writing in English. **Deadline: February 15-May 1. Charges $20 fee.** Prize: $2,000, and publication.

ANNUAL GIVAL PRESS OSCAR WILDE AWARD

Gival Press, LLC, P.O. Box 3812, Arlington VA 22203. (703)351-0079. Fax: (703)351-0079. E-mail: givalpress@yahoo.com. Website: www.givalpress.com. **Contact:** Robert L. Giron. Award given to the best previously unpublished original poem written in English of any length, in any style, typed, double-spaced on 1 side only, which best relates alternative lifestyles, often referred to as gay/lesbian/bisexual/transgendered life, by a poet who is 18 or older. Entrants are asked to submit their poems in the following manner: (1) without any kind of identification, with the exception of titles, and (2) with a separate cover page with the following information: name, address (street, city, and state with zip code), telephone number, e-mail address (if available) and a list of poems by title. Checks drawn on American banks should be made out to Gival Press, LLC, and mailed to: Gival Press, LLC, P.O. Box 3812, Arlington VA, 22203. **Deadline: June 27 (postmarked). Charges $5 reading fee (USD).** Prize: $100 (USD), and the poem, along with information about the poet, will be published on the website of Gival Press. Open to any writer.

ANNUAL GIVAL PRESS POETRY CONTEST

Gival Press, LLC, P.O. Box 3812, Arlington VA 22203. (703)351-0079. Fax: (703)351-0079. E-mail: givalpress@yahoo.com. Website: www.givalpress.com. **Contact:** Robert L. Giron. Offered annually for a previously unpublished poetry collection of at least 45 pages, which may include previously published poems. The competition seeks to award well-written, original poetry in English on any topic, in any style. Guidelines for SASE, by e-mail, or on website. Entrants are asked to submit their poems in the following manner: (1) without any kind of identification, with the exception of the titles, and (2) with a separate cover page with the following information: name, address (street, city, state, and zip code), telephone number, e-mail address (if available), and a list of the poems by title. Checks drawn on American banks should be made out to Gival Press, LLC, and mailed to: Gival Press, LLC, P.O. Box 3812, Arlington VA 22203. **Deadline: December 15 (postmarked). Charges $20 reading fee (USD).** Prize: $1,000, plus publication, standard contract, and 20 author's copies. Open to any writer.

THE ANNUAL PRAIRIE SCHOONER STROUSSE AWARD

Prairie Schooner, 201 Andrews Hall, P.O. Box 880334, Lincoln NE 68588-0334. (402)472-0911. Fax: (402)472-9771. E-mail: kgrey2@unl.edu. Website: www.unl.edu/schooner/psmain.htm. **Contact:** Hilda Raz. Offered annually for the best poem or group of poems published in *Prairie Schooner* in the previous year. Prize: $500.

APR/HONICKMAN FIRST BOOK PRIZE

The American Poetry Review, 117 S. 17th St., Suite 910, Philadelphia PA 19103-5009. (215)496-0439. Fax: (215)569-0808. Website: www.aprweb.org. Offered annually for a poet's first unpublished book-length ms. Judging is by a different distinguished poet each year. Past judges include Gerald Stern, Louise Glück, Robert Creeley, Adrienne Rich, Derek Walcott, and Jorie Graham. Open to US citizens. **Deadline: October 31.** Guidelines for SASE. **Charges $25 fee.** Prize: Publication by *APR* (distrubution by Copper Canyon Press through Consortium), $3,000 cash prize, plus $1,000 to support a book tour.

ATLANTIC POETRY PRIZE

Writers' Federation of Nova Scotia, 1113 Marginal Rd., Halifax NS B3H 4P7, Canada. (902)423-8116. Fax: (902)422-0881. E-mail: talk@writers.ns.ca. Website: www.writers.ns.ca. **Contact:** Jane Buss, executive director. Full-length books of adult poetry written by Atlantic Canadians, and published as a whole for the first time in the previous calendar year, are eligible. Entrants must be native or resident Atlantic Canadians who have either been born in Newfoundland, Prince Edward Island, Nova Scotia, or New Brunswick, and spent a susbstantial portion of their lives living there, or who have lived in one or a combination of these provinces for at least 24 consecutive months prior to entry deadline date. Publishers: Send 4 copies and a letter attesting to the author's status as an Atlantic Canadian and the author's current mailing address and telephone number. **Deadline: First Friday in December.** Prize: $1,000.

THE BACKWATERS PRIZE

The Backwaters Press, 3502 N. 52nd St., Omaha NE 68104-3506. (402)451-4052. E-mail: gkosm62735@aol.com. Website: www.thebackwaterspress.homestead.com. **Contact:** Greg Kosmicki. Offered annually to find the best collection of poems, or single long poem, no collaborations, to publish and help further the poet's career. Collections must be unpublished, however parts of the ms may have been published as a chapbook, or individual poems may have been previously published in magazines. **Deadline: June 4. Charges $25 fee.** Prize: $1,000, and publication of the winning ms in an edition of at least 500 copies in perfect bound format.

THE BASKERVILLE PUBLISHERS POETRY AWARD

descant, Texas Christian University's literary journal, TCU, Box 297270, Fort Worth TX 76129. (817)257-6537. Fax: (817)257-6239. E-mail: descant@tcu.edu. **Contact:** Dave Kuhne, editor. Annual award for an outstanding poem published in an issue of *descant*. **Deadline: September-April.** Guidelines for SASE. Prize: $250. Acquires Publication retains copyright, but will transfer it to the author upon request. Open to any writer.

BBC WILDLIFE MAGAZINE POET OF THE YEAR AWARD

BBC Wildlife Magazine, Broadcasting House, Whiteladies Rd., Bristol BS8 2LR, United Kingdom. +44 (0)117 973 8402. Fax: +44 (0)117 946 7075. E-mail: nina.epton@bbc.co.uk. **Contact:** Nina Epton. Offered annually for unpublished poetry. "The poem (no longer than 50 lines) must be on the subject of the natural world and/or our relationship with it. There are no restrictions on the form the poem takes—it can be a song of praise, an ode, or a lament, in rhyme, free or blank verse. There are 5 categories: adult, age 15-17, age 12-14, age 8-11, age 7 and under. Entrants must buy the relevant copy of *BBC Wildlife Magazine* containing the entry form and rules. This is usually our April issue, but it's best to check with the office first. By entering the competition, entrants grant, free of charge, the right for all or part of their poem to be published, broadcast, transmitted, and read in all media (now known or hereafter created), or on stage, including the right for the poems to be published in *BBC Wildlife Magazine* and any resulting anthology, if the organizers wish." **Deadline: Varies from year to year. Best to contact the office, and ask for details.** Guidelines for SASE. Prize: £500 to the overall winner; £100 for the runners-up; £50 for young poets. Open to any writer.

ℕ BEST ROMANTIC POETRY

Generation X National Journal, 411 West Front, Wayland IA 52654. (319)601-9128. E-mail: lstoops01@sprintpcs .com. **Contact:** Kathy Stoops. Estab. 2004. ''We are looking for beautiful, descriptive poetry. Sensual, erotic, lovely. Looking for beauty in fluidity, language, and the beginning of a love affair between 2 people. How would you woo your potential lover? We're not looking for trashy work. Anything that resembles the media's portrait of falling in love. Are one-night affairs really romantic? Not really.'' **Deadline: March 1. Charges $15/ first poem, $5/additional poems (limit 5).** Prize: 1st Place: $100; 2nd Place: $50; 3rd Place: $25; 4th Place: $15. All entrants receive 1-year subscription. Open to any writer.

THE BINGHAMTON UNIVERSITY MILT KESSLER POETRY BOOK AWARD

Binghamton University Creative Writing Program, Dept. of English, General Literature & Rhetoric, P.O. Box 6000, Binghamton NY 13902-6000. (607)777-2713. E-mail: cwpro@binghamton.edu. Website: english.bingham ton.edu/cwpro/bookawards/bookawards.htm. **Contact:** Maria Mazziotti Gillan, creative writing program director. Estab. 2001. Offered annually for previously published work. Open to any writer over 40. Book must be published, be 48 pages or more with a press run of 500 copies or more. ''Please explain any special criteria (such as residency) or nominating process that must be met before a writer's entry will be considered.'' Each book submitted must be accompanied by an application form. Publisher may submit more than 1 book for prize consideration. Send 3 copies of each book. Guidelines available online or for SASE. Must have appeared in print between January 1 and December 31 of year preceding award. **Deadline: March 1.** Prize: $1,000. Judged by professional poet not on Binghamton University faculty. Any writer over the age of 40.

BLUESTEM POETRY AWARD

Dept. of English, Emporia State University 1200, Emporia KS 66801. (620)341-5216. Fax: (620)341-5547. E-mail: bluestem@emporia.edu. Website: www.emporia.edu/bluestem. **Contact:** Philip Heldrich, director. Offered annually ''to recognize outstanding poetry.'' Full-length, single-author collections, at least 48 pages long. **Deadline: March 1. Charges $20 fee.** Prize: $1,000, and a published book.

ℕ THE FREDERICK BOCK PRIZE

Poetry, 1030 N. Clark St., Suite 420, Chicago IL 60610. (312)787-7070. E-mail: poetry@poetrymagazine.org. Website: www.poetrymagazine.org. Offered annually for poems published in *Poetry* during the preceding year (October through September). *Poetry* buys all rights to the poems published in the magazine. Copyrights are returned to the authors on request. Any writer may submit poems to *Poetry*. Guidelines for SASE. Prize: $300.

THE BORDIGHERA ITALIAN-AMERICAN POETRY PRIZE

Sonia Raiziss-Giop Foundation, 57 Montague St. #8G, Brooklyn NY 11201-3356. E-mail: daniela@garden.net. Website: www.ItalianAmericanWriters.com. **Contact:** Daniela Gioseffi. Offered annually ''to find the best unpublished manuscripts of poetry in English, by an American of Italian descent, to be translated into quality Italian and published bilingually.'' **Deadline: May 31.** Guidelines for SASE. Prize: $2,000, and bilingual book publication to be divided between poet and translator.

BOSTON REVIEW POETRY CONTEST

Boston Review, E-53-407 MIT, Cambridge MA 02139. Website: bostonreview.net. Submit up to 5 unpublished poems, no more than 10 pages total. **Deadline: June 1. Charges $15 fee (check or money order payable to *Boston Review*).** Prize: $1,000, and publication in the October/November issue of *Boston Review*.

☒ bp NICHOL CHAPBOOK AWARD

Phoenix Community Works Foundation, 316 Dupont St., Toronto ON M5R 1V9, Canada. (416)964-7919. Fax: (416)964-6941. E-mail: info@pcwf.ca. Website: www.pcwf.ca. **Contact:** Philip McKenna, award director. Offered annually to a chapbook (10-48 pages) of poetry in English, published in Canada in the previous year. Must submit 3 nonreturnable copies. **Deadline: March 30.** Prize: $1,000 (Canadian). Open to any writer. Author or publisher may make submissions. Send 3 copies (nonreturnable), plus a short cv of the author.

ℕ BARBARA BRADLEY AWARD

New England Poetry Club, 16 Cornell St., Arlington MA 02474. E-mail: contests@nepoetryclub.org. Website: www.nepoetryclub.org/contests.htm. **Contact:** Elizabeth Crowell. Offered annually for a lyric poem under 21 lines, written by a woman. **Deadline: May 1-June 30.** Guidelines for SASE. **Charges $10 entry fee for nonmembers (up to 3 poems), but only 1 poem/contest.** Prize: $200.

BRITTINGHAM PRIZE IN POETRY/FELIX POLLAK PRIZE IN POETRY

University of Wisconsin Press, Dept. of English, 600 N. Park St., University of Wisconsin, Madison WI 53706. Website: www.wisc.edu/wisconsinpress/poetryguide.html. **Contact:** Ronald Wallace, contest director. Estab.

1985. Offered for unpublished book-length mss of original poetry. Submissions must be *received* by the press *during* the month of September, accompanied by a SASE for contest results. Does *not* return mss. One entry fee covers both prizes. Guidelines for SASE or online. **Charges $25 fee (payable to University of Wisconsin Press).** Prize: $1,000, and publication of the 2 winning mss.

THE DOROTHY BRUNSMAN POETRY PRIZE

Bear Star Press, 185 Hollow Oak Dr., Cohasset CA 95973. (530)891-0360. E-mail: bspencer@bearstarpress.com. Website: www.bearstarpress.com. **Contact:** Beth Spencer. Offered annually to support the publication of 1 volume of poetry. Guidelines on website. Open to poets living in the Western States (those in Mountain or Pacific Time Zones, plus Alaska and Hawaii). **Deadline: November 30. Charges $16 fee.** Prize: $1,000, and publication.

⚡ CAA JACK CHALMERS POETRY AWARD

Box 419, 320 S. Shores Rd., Campbellford ON K0L 1L0, Canada. (705)653-0323. Fax: (705)653-0593. E-mail: admin@canauthors.org. Website: www.canauthors.org. **Contact:** Alec McEachern. Offered annually for a volume of poetry by a Canadian citizen. Entry form required. Obtain form from contact name or download from website. **Deadline: December 15.** Guidelines for SASE. **Charges $35 fee (Canadian).** Prize: $2,500, and a silver medal.

GERALD CABLE BOOK AWARD

Silverfish Review Press, P.O. Box 3541, Eugene OR 97403. (541)344-5060. E-mail: sfrpress@earthlink.net. **Contact:** Rodger Moody, series editor. Purpose is to publish a poetry book by a deserving author who has yet to publish a full-length book collection. Open to any writer. Guidelines for SASE or by e-mail. **Deadline: October 15. Charges $20 reading fee.** Prize: $1,000, 10% of the press run, and publication by the Press for a book-length ms of original poetry.

CAMPBELL CORNER POETRY CONTEST

Graduate Studies/Sarah Lawrence College, One Meadway, Bronxville NY 10708. (914)395-2371. Fax: (914)395-2664. **Contact:** Dean of Graduate Studies. **Deadline: March 15.** Guidelines for SASE. **Charges $25.** Prize: $2,500. The work will also be published on Campbell Corner's Language Exchange. Judged by Phillis Levin, Beth Ann Fennelly, and David Baker. Open to any writer.

HAYDEN CARRUTH AWARD

Copper Canyon Press, P.O. Box 271, Port Townsend WA 98368. (360)385-4925. Fax: (360)385-4985. E-mail: poetry@coppercanyonpress.org. Website: www.coppercanyonpress.org. **Contact:** Office Manager. Offered annually for unpublished work. Contest is for new and emerging poets who have published no more than 2 full-length books of poetry. Chapbooks of 32 pages or less are not considered to be full length, and books published in other genres do not count toward the 2-book limit. **Deadline: November 1-30 (reading period).** Guidelines for SASE. **Charges $25 fee.** Prize: $1,000 advance, and book publication by Copper Canyon Press.

THE CENTER FOR BOOK ARTS POETRY CHAPBOOK COMPETITION

The Center for Book Arts, 28 W. 27th St., 3rd Floor, New York NY 10001. (212)481-0295. Fax: (212)481-9853. E-mail: info@centerforbookarts.org. Website: www.centerforbookarts.org. **Contact:** Rory Golden. Offered annually for unpublished collections of poetry. Individual poems may have been previously published. Collection must not exceed 500 lines or 24 pages. **Deadline: December 1 (postmarked).** Guidelines for SASE. **Charges $15 fee.** Prize: $500 award, $500 honorarium for a reading, publication, and 10 copies of chapbook. Judged by Sharon Dolin and C.K. Williams (2004 judges). Open to any writer.

JOHN CIARDI POETRY AWARD FOR LIFETIME ACHIEVEMENT

Italian Americana, URI/CCE, 80 Washington St., Providence RI 02903-1803. Fax: (401)277-5100. E-mail: bonom oal@etal.uri.edu. Website: www.uri.edu/prov/italian/italian.html. **Contact:** Carol Bonomo Albright, editor. Offered annually for lifetime achievement to a mature Italian American poet who has published in all aspects of poetry: creative, critical, etc. Applicants should have at least 2 books published. Open to Italian-Americans only. Guidelines for SASE. Prize: $1,000.

JOHN CIARDI PRIZE FOR POETRY

BkMk Press, University of Missouri-Kansas City, 5101 Rockhill Rd., Kansas City MO 64110. (816)235-2558. Fax: (816)235-2611. E-mail: bkmk@umkc.edu. Website: www.umkc.edu/bkmk. **Contact:** Ben Furnish. Offered annually for the best book-length collection (unpublished) of poetry in English by a living author. Translations are not eligible. Initial judging is done by a network of published writers. Final judging is done by a writer of national reputation. Guidelines for SASE, by e-mail, or on website. **Deadline: December 1 (postmarked). Charges $25 fee.** Prize: $1,000, plus book publication by BkMk Press.

⊠ CLEVELAND STATE UNIVERSITY POETRY CENTER PRIZES

Cleveland State University Poetry Center, 2121 Euclid Ave., Cleveland OH 44115-2214. (216)687-3986. Fax: (216)687-6943. E-mail: poetrycenter@csuohio.edu. Website: www.csuohio.edu/poetrycenter. **Contact:** Rita Grabowski, Poetry Center coordinator. Estab. 1962. Offered annually to identify, reward, and publish the best unpublished book-length poetry ms submitted (40 pages of poetry, minimum) in 2 categories: First Book and Open Competition (for poets who have published a collection at least 48 pages long, with a press run of 500). "Submission implies willingness to sign standard contract for publication if manuscript wins." Does not return mss. Guidelines for SASE or online. **Deadline: Submissions accepted November-January only (postmarked February 1). Charges $20 fee.** Prize: $1,000, and publication.

THE COLORADO PRIZE FOR POETRY

Colorado Review/Center for Literary Publishing, Dept. of English, Colorado State University, Ft. Collins CO 80523. (970)491-5449. E-mail: creview@colostate.edu. Website: www.coloradoreview.com. **Contact:** Stephanie G'Schwind, managing editor. Offered annually to an unpublished collection of poetry. Guidelines for SASE or online. **Deadline: January 15. Charges $25 fee.** Prize: $1,500, and publication of book.

BETSY COLQUITT AWARD FOR POETRY

descant, Texas Christian University's literary journal, TCU Box 297270, Fort Worth TX 76129. (817)257-6537. Fax: (817)257-6239. E-mail: descant@tcu.edu. **Contact:** Dave Kuhne, editor. Offered annually for unpublished poems or series of poems. Publication retains copyright but will transfer it to the author upon request. **Deadline: September-April.** Guidelines for SASE. Prize: $500.

CONTEMPORARY POETRY SERIES

University of Georgia Press, 330 Research Dr., Suite B100, Athens GA 30602-4901. (706)369-6135. Fax: (706)369-6131. Website: www.ugapress.org. Offered 2 times/year. Two awards: 1 for poets who have not had a full-length book of poems published **(deadline in September)**, and 1 for poets with at least 1 full-length publication **(deadline in January)**. Guidelines for SASE. **Charges $20 fee.**

CRAB ORCHARD AWARD SERIES IN POETRY

Crab Orchard Review and Southern Illinois University Press, Dept. of English, Carbondale IL 62901-4503. Website: www.siu.edu/~crborchd. **Contact:** Jon C. Tribble, series editor. Offered annually for collections of unpublished poetry. Visit website for current deadlines. Guidelines for SASE. **Charges $25 fee.** Prize: 1st Place: $3,500, and publication; 2nd Place: $1,500, and publication. Open to US citizens and permanent residents.

ALICE FAY DI CASTAGNOLA AWARD

Poetry Society of America, 15 Gramercy Park S., New York NY 10003. (212)254-9628. Fax: (212)673-2352. Website: www.poetrysociety.org. **Contact:** Brett Lauer, programs associate. Offered annually for a manuscript-in-progress of poetry or verse-drama. Guidelines for SASE or on website. Award open only to PSA members. **Deadline: October 1-December 21.** Prize: $1,000. Members only.

DISCOVERY/*THE NATION*

The Joan Leiman Jacobson Poetry Prizes, The Unterberg Poetry Center of the 92nd Street YM-YWHA, 1395 Lexington Ave., New York NY 10128. (212)415-5759. Website: www.92y.org. Open to poets who have not published a book of poems (chapbooks, self-published books included). Must have guidelines; send SASE, call, or see website. **Deadline: January. Charges $8 fee.**

⊠ MILTON DORFMAN POETRY PRIZE

Rome Art & Community Center, 308 W. Bloomfield St., Rome NY 13440. (315)336-1040. Fax: (315)336-1090. Website: www.borg.com/~racc. Estab. 1990. "The purpose of the Milton Dorfman Poetry Prize is to offer poets an outlet for their craft. All submissions must be previously unpublished." **Deadline: January 1-April 30.** Guidelines for SASE. **Charges $8 fee/poem.** Prize: 1st Place: $500; 2nd Place: $250; 3rd Place: $150. Judged by a professional, published poet. Awards ceremony and poetry reading in June.

T.S. ELIOT PRIZE FOR POETRY

Truman State University Press, 100 E. Normal St., Kirksville MO 63501-4221. (660)785-7336. Fax: (660)785-4480. E-mail: tsup@truman.edu. Website: tsup.truman.edu. **Contact:** Nancy Rediger. Annual competition for unpublished poetry collection. Guidelines for SASE, on website, or by e-mail. **Deadline: October 31 (post-marked). Charges $25 fee.** Prize: $2,000, and publication.

ROBERT G. ENGLISH/POETRY IN PRINT

P.O. Box 30981, Albuquerque NM 87190-0981. (505)888-3937. Fax: (505)888-3937. Website: www.poets.com/RobertEnglish.html. **Contact:** Robert G. English, owner. Offered annually "to help a poetry writer accomplish their own personal endeavors. Hopefully the prize amount of the Poetry in Print award will grow to a higher significance. The contest is open to any writer of any age. Hopefully to prepare writers other than just journalists with a stronger desire to always tell the truth." No limit to number of entries; 60-line limit/poem. "Please enclose SASE." **Deadline: August 1. Charges $10/poem.** Prize: $1,000.

JANICE FARRELL POETRY PRIZE

National League of American Pen Women, Nob Hill, San Francisco Branch, 1544 Sweetwood Dr., Colma CA 94015-2029. E-mail: pennobhill@aol.com. Website: www.soulmakingcontest.us. **Contact:** Eileen Malone. Poetry may be double- or single-spaced. One-page poems only, and only 1 poem/page. All poems must be titled. Three poems/entry. Annually. **Deadline: November 30.** Guidelines for SASE. **Charges $5/entry (make checks payable to NLAPW, Nob Hill Branch).** Prize: 1st Place: $100; 2nd Place: $50; 3rd Place: $25. Judged by a local San Francisco successfully published poet. Open to any writer.

FIELD POETRY PRIZE

Oberlin College Press/FIELD, 10 N. Professor St., Oberlin OH 44074-1095. (440)775-8408. Fax: (440)775-8124. E-mail: oc.press@oberlin.edu. Website: www.oberlin.edu/ocpress. **Contact:** Linda Slocum, managing editor. Offered annually for unpublished work. "The FIELD Poetry Prize contest seeks to encourage the finest in contemporary poetry writing." Open to any writer. **Deadline: Submit in May only.** Guidelines for SASE. **Charges $22 fee, which includes a 1-year subscription to _FIELD_.** Prize: $1,000, and book published in Oberlin College Press's FIELD Poetry Series.

FIVE POINTS JAMES DICKEY PRIZE FOR POETRY

Five Points, MSC 8R0318, Georgia State University, 33 Gilmer St. SE, Unit 8, Atlanta GA 30303-3083. (404)651-0071. Fax: (404)651-3167. E-mail: msexton@gsu.edu. Website: www.webdelsol.com/Five_Points. **Contact:** Megan Sexton. Offered annually for unpublished poetry. Send 3 unpublished poems, no longer than 50 lines each, name and addresses on each poem, SASE for receipt and notification of winner. Winner announced in Spring issue. **Deadline: November 30.** Guidelines for SASE. **Charges $15 fee (includes 1-year subscription).** Prize: $1,000, plus publication.

FOLEY POETRY CONTEST

America Press, 106 W. 56th St., New York NY 10019. (212)581-4640. Fax: (212)399-3596. Website: www.americamagazine.org. **Contact:** Paul Mariani, poetry editor. Estab. 1909. Offered annually for unpublished works between January and April. **Deadline: January 1-April 16.** Guidelines for SASE. Prize: $1,000, usually awarded in June. Open to any writer.

THE 49th PARALLEL POETRY AWARD

Bellingham Review, Mail Stop 9053, Western Washington University, Bellingham WA 98225. (360)650-4863. E-mail: bhreview@cc.wwu.edu. Website: www.wwu.edu/~bhreview/. **Contact:** Brenda Miller. Estab. 1977. Offered annually for unpublished poetry. Guidelines available on website or for SASE. **Deadline: December 1-March 15. Charges $15 for first entry (up to 3 poems), $10 each additional entry (including each additional poem).** Prize: 1st Place: $1,000, and publication. All finalists considered for publication, all entrants receive subscription.

FOUR WAY BOOKS POETRY PRIZES

Four Way Books, P.O. Box 535, Village Station, New York NY 10014. (212)334-5430. Fax: (212)334-5435. E-mail: four_way_editors@yahoo.com. Website: www.fourwaybooks.com. **Contact:** C. Lowen, contest coordinator. Four Way Books runs different prizes annually. For guidelines send a SASE or download from website. **Deadline: March 31.** Prize: Cash honorarium, and book publication.

ROBERT FROST POETRY AWARD

The Robert Frost Foundation, Heritage Place, 439 S. Union, Lawrence MA 01843. (978)725-8828. Fax: (978)725-8828. E-mail: frostfoundation@comcast.com. Website: www.frostfoundation.org. **Contact:** Poetry Contest. Offered annually for unpublished work "to recognize poets writing today in the tradition of Frost and other American greats. Poems should be written in the spirit of Frost, as interpreted by the poet's knowledge of

Frost's poetry, life, persona, etc.'' More than 1 poem may be entered. Open to any writer. **Deadline: September 1.** Guidelines for SASE. **Charges $10 fee/poem.** Prize: $1,000.

ALLEN GINSBERG POETRY AWARDS

The Poetry Center at Passaic County Community College, One College Blvd., Paterson NJ 07505-1179. (973)684-6555. Fax: (973)684-5843. E-mail: mgillan@pccc.cc.nj.us. Website: www.pccc.cc.nj.us/poetry. **Contact:** Maria Mazziotti Gillan, executive director. Offered annually for unpublished poetry ''to honor Allen Ginsberg's contribution to American literature.'' The college retains first publication rights. Open to any writer. **Deadline: April 1.** Guidelines for SASE. **Charges $13, which covers the cost of a subscription to** *The Paterson Literary Review*. Prize: $1,000.

◼ GOVERNOR GENERAL'S LITERARY AWARD FOR POETRY

Canada Council for the Arts, 350 Albert St., P.O. Box 1047, Ottawa ON K1P 5V8, Canada. (613)566-4414, ext. 5576. Fax: (613)566-4410. E-mail: joanne.larocque-poirier@canadacouncil.ca. Website: www.canadacouncil .ca/prizes/ggla. **Contact:** Joanne Larocque-Poirier. Offered for the best English-language and the best French-language work of poetry by a Canadian published September 1-September 30. Publishers submit titles for consideration. **Deadline: March 15 or August 7, depending on the book's publication date.** Prize: Each laureate receives $15,000, and nonwinning finalists receive $1,000.

GREEN ROSE PRIZE IN POETRY

New Issues Poetry & Prose, Dept. of English, Western Michigan University, 1903 W. Michigan Ave., Kalamazoo MI 49008-5331. (269)387-8185. Fax: (269)387-2562. E-mail: herbert.scott@wmich.edu. Website: www.wmich. edu/newissues. **Contact:** Herbert Scott, editor. Offered annually for unpublished poetry. The university will publish a book of poems by a poet writing in English who has published 1 or more full-length books of poetry. Guidelines for SASE or on website. *New Issues Poetry & Prose* obtains rights for first publication. Book is copyrighted in author's name. **Deadline: September 30. Charges $20 fee.** Prize: $2,000, and publication of book. Author also receives 10% of the printed edition.

◼ THE GRIFFIN POETRY PRIZE

The Griffin Trust for Excellence in Poetry, 6610 Edwards Blvd., Mississauga ON L5T 2V6, Canada. (905)565-5993. E-mail: info@griffinpoetryprize.com. Website: www.griffinpoetryprize.com. **Contact:** Ruth Smith. Offered annually for work published between January 1 and December 31. **Deadline: December 31.** Prize: 2 $40,000 (Canadian) prizes. One prize will go to a living Canadian poet or translator, the other to a living poet or translator from any country, which may include Canada. Judged by a panel of qualified English-speaking judges of stature. Judges are chosen by the Trustees of The Griffin Trust For Excellence in Poetry. Open to any writer.

◼ GROLIER POETRY PRIZE

Grolier Poetry Book Shop, Inc., and Ellen LaForge Memorial Poetry Foundation, Inc., 6 Plympton St., Cambridge MA 02138. (617)253-4452. E-mail: jjhildeb@mit.edu. **Contact:** John Hildebidle. Estab. 1973. When e-mailing, please put ''Grolier Poetry Prize'' in subject line. The Prize is intended to encourage and introduce developing poets, is open to all poets who have not published a previous volume (chapbook, small press, trade, or vanity) of poetry. Submissions (in duplicate) should include no more than 5 poems (none simultaneously submitted or previously published), running 10 double-spaced pages or 5 single-spaced pages. Separate cover sheet should include poet's address and telephone number, e-mail address, titles of poems, and brief biography. Enclose a self-addressed, stamped postcard for notification of receipt. The author's name and other identifying information should not appear on the same pages as the poems. Entries must be submitted in duplicate. Mss will not be returned. Annually. **Deadline: May 1. Charges $7 fee.**

GREG GRUMMER POETRY AWARD

Phoebe, George Mason University, 4400 University Dr., Fairfax VA 22030-4444. (703)993-2915. E-mail: phoebe@ gmu.edu. Website: www.gmu.edu/pups/phoebe. **Contact:** Lisa Ampleman. Offered annually for unpublished work. **Deadline: December 1.** Guidelines for SASE. **Charges $12 fee.** Prize: $1,000, and publication in Fall issue. All entrants receive free Fall issue. Judged by outside judge—a recognized poet hired by *Phoebe* each year. Acquires first serial rights, if work is to be published. Open to any writer.

VIOLET REED HAAS POETRY CONTEST

Snake Nation Press, 110 W. Force St., Valdosta GA 31601. (229)244-0752. E-mail: jeana@snakenationpress.org. Website: www.snakenationpress.org. **Contact:** Jean Arambula. Offered annually for poetry mss of 50-75 pages. **Deadline: June 15. Charges $10 reading fee.** Prize: $500, and publication. Judged by an independent judge.

KATHRYN HANDLEY PROSE-POEM PRIZE

National League of American Pen Women, Nob Hill, San Francisco Branch, 1544 Sweetwood Dr., Colma CA 94015-2029. E-mail: pennobhill@aol.com. Website: www.soulmakingcontest.us. **Contact:** Eileen Malone. Poetry may be double- or single-spaced. One-page poems only, and only 1 poem/page. Three poems/entry. Annually. **Deadline: November 30.** Guidelines for SASE. **Charges $5/entry (make checks payable to NLAPW, Nob Hill Branch).** Prize: 1st Place: $100; 2nd Place: $50; 3rd Place: $25. Open to any writer.

ℕ THE BEATRICE HAWLEY AWARD

Alice James Poetry Cooperative, 238 Main St., Farmington ME 04938. Phone/Fax: (207)778-7071. E-mail: ajb@umf.main.edu. Website: www.alicejamesbooks.org. **Contact:** April Ossmann, director. Offered annually for unpublished poetry. Open to U.S. residents only. **Deadline: December 1.** Guidelines for SASE. **Charges $20.** Prize: $2,000, and publication.

ℕ CECIL HEMLEY MEMORIAL AWARD

Poetry Society of America, 15 Gramercy Park S., New York NY 10003. (212)254-9628. Fax: (212)673-2352. E-mail: brett@poetrysociety.org. Website: www.poetrysociety.org. **Contact:** Brett Lauer, programs associate. Offered for unpublished lyric poems on a philosophical theme. *Open to PSA members only.* **Deadline: December 22.** Guidelines for SASE. Prize: $500.

ℕ THE BESS HOKIN PRIZE

Poetry, 1030 N. Clark St., Suite 420, Chicago IL 60610. (312)787-7070. E-mail: poetry@poetrymagazine.org. Website: www.poetrymagazine.org. Offered annually for poems published in *Poetry* during the preceding year (October-September). *Poetry* buys all rights to the poems published in the magazine. Copyrights are returned to the authors on request. Any writer may submit poems to *Poetry*. Guidelines for SASE. Prize: $500.

ℕ FIRMAN HOUGHTON AWARD

New England Poetry Club, 16 Cornell St., Arlington MA 02474. E-mail: contests@nepoetryclug.org. Website: www.nepoetryclub.org/contests.htm. **Contact:** Elizabeth Crowell. Offered annually for a lyric poem worthy of the former NEPC president. **Deadline: June 30.** Guidelines for SASE. **Charges nonmembers $10 for 3 poems, but only 1 poem/contest.** Prize: $250.

ℕ LYNDA HULL POETRY AWARD

Denver Quarterly, Dept. of English, University of Denver, Denver CO 80208. (303)871-2892. Fax: (303)871-2853. **Contact:** Bin Ramke, editor. Estab. 1965. Annual award for best poem published in a volume year. All poems published in *Denver Quarterly* are automatically entered. Do not submit between May 15 and September 15. Guidelines for SASE. Prize: $500. Open to any writer.

INDIANA REVIEW POETRY PRIZE

(formerly Indiana Review Poetry Contest), *Indiana Review*, BH 465, Indiana University, Bloomington IN 47405-7103. (812)855-3439. Fax: (812)855-4253. E-mail: inreview@indiana.edu. Website: www.indiana.edu/~inreview. **Contact:** Esther Lee. Offered annually for unpublished work. Judged by guest judges; Cornelius Eady judged the 2004 contest. Open to any writer. Send no more than 4 poems, 15-page maximum combined (no minimum). **Deadline: Late March.** Guidelines for SASE. **Charges $15 fee (includes a year's subscription).** Prize: $1,000.

IOWA POETRY PRIZES

University of Iowa Press, 100 Kuhl House, Iowa City IA 52242. (319)335-2000. Fax: (319)335-2055. E-mail: uipress@uiowa.edu. Website: www.uiowapress.org. Offered annually to encourage poets and their work. Submit mss by April 30; put name on title page only. Open to writers of English (US citizens or not). Manuscripts will not be returned. Previous winners are not eligible. **Deadline: April. Charges $20 fee.**

IRA LEE BENNETT HOPKINS PROMISING POET AWARD

International Reading Association, P.O. Box 8139, Newark DE 19714-8139. (302)731-1600. Fax: (302)731-1057. E-mail: exec@reading.org. Website: www.reading.org. Offered every 3 years to a promising new poet of children's poetry (for children and young adults up to grade 12) who has published no more than 2 books of children's poetry. **Deadline: December 1.** Guidelines for SASE. Prize: $500.

RANDALL JARRELL/HARPERPRINTS POETRY CHAPBOOK COMPETITION

North Carolina Writers' Network, 3501 Highway 54 W., Studio C, Chapel Hill NC 27516. E-mail: mail@ncwriters.org. Website: www.ncwriters.org. **Contact:** Lisa Robinson Bailey. Offered annually for unpublished work "to honor Randall Jarrell and his life at UNC-Greensboro by recognizing the best poetry submitted." Competition is open to North Carolina residents who have not published a full-length collection of poems. **Deadline: January 31. Charges $10 (NCWN members), $15 (nonmembers) entry fee.** Prize: $200, chapbook publication, and a reading and reception.

ROBINSON JEFFERS TOR HOUSE PRIZE FOR POETRY
Robinson Jeffers Tor House Foundation, P.O. Box 2713, Carmel CA 93921. (831)624-1813. Fax: (831)624-3696. E-mail: thf@torhouse.org. Website: www.torhouse.org. **Contact:** Elliot Ruchowitz-Roberts. "The Annual Prize for Poetry is a living memorial to American poet Robinson Jeffers (1887-1962). It honors well-crafted, unpublished poetry in all styles, ranging from experimental work to traditional forms including short narrative poems." **Deadline: March 15.** Guidelines for SASE. **Charges $10 for first 3 poems; $15 for up to 6 poems; $2.50 for each additional poem.** Prize: $1,000; $200 for Honorable Mention. Judged by a distinguished panel of published poets and editors (preliminary judging). Final judging by a poet nationally known. Past judges have been Mary Oliver, Donald Hall, Dana Gioia, Sherod Santos, Jane Hirshfield, Pattiann Rogers, Billy Collins, and John Haines. Open to any writer.

THE JUNIPER PRIZE
University of Massachusetts, Amherst MA 01003. (413)545-2217. Fax: (413)545-1226. E-mail: info@umpress.umass.edu. Website: www.umass.edu/umpress/juniper.html. **Contact:** Alice I. Maldonado, assistant editor/Web manager. Estab. 1964. Awarded annually for an original ms of poems. In alternating years, the program is open to poets either with or without previously published books. **Deadline: September 30. Charges $25 fee.** Prize: The University of Massachusetts Press publishes the winning ms, and a $1,000 prize is awarded in lieu of royalties on the first print run.

KALLIOPE'S ANNUAL SUE SANIEL ELKIND POETRY CONTEST
Kalliope, 11901 Beach Blvd., Jacksonville FL 32246. (904)646-2081. Website: www.fccj.org/kalliope. **Contact:** Mary Sue Koeppel, editor. Offered annually for unpublished work. "Poetry may be in any style and on any subject. Maximum poem length is 50 lines. Only unpublished poems are eligible." No limit on number of poems entered by any 1 poet. The winning poem is published as are the finalists' poems. Copyright then returns to the authors. Guidelines for SASE and on website. **Deadline: November 1. Charges $4/poem, or $10 for 3 poems.** Prize: $1,000, publication of poem in *Kalliope*.

BARBARA MANDIGO KELLY PEACE POETRY AWARDS
Nuclear Age Peace Foundation, PMB 121, 1187 Coast Village Rd., Suite 1, Santa Barbara CA 93108-2794. (805)965-3443. Fax: (805)568-0466. E-mail: development@napf.org. Website: www.wagingpeace.org. **Contact:** Carah Ong. "The Barbara Mandigo Kelly Peace Poetry Contest was created to encourage poets to explore and illuminate positive visions of peace and the human spirit. The contest honors the late Barbara Kelly, a Santa Barbara poet and longtime supporter of peace issues. Awards are given in three categories: adult (over 18 years), youth between 12 and 18 years, and youth under 12." Contest is offered annually. All submitted articles should be unpublished. **Deadline: July 1 (postmarked).** Guidelines for SASE. **Charges $15 for up to 3 poems; no fee for youth entries.** Prize: Adult: $1,000; Youth (13-18): $200; Youth (12 and under): $200. Honorable Mentions may also be awarded. Judged by a committee of poets selected by the Nuclear Age Peace Foundation. The Foundation reserves the right to publish and distribute the award-winning poems, including honorable mentions. Open to any writer.

ⓃTHE KENYON REVIEW PRIZE IN POETRY FOR A FIRST BOOK
Zoo Press, P.O. Box 22990, Lincoln NE 68542. E-mail: editors@zoopress.org. Website: www.zoopress.org. **Contact:** David Baker, poetry editor. "Zoo Press aims to publish the best emerging writers writing in the English language, and will endeavor to do it at the rate of at least 10 manuscripts of admirable quality a year, providing we can find them. We're confident that we can through contests such as The Kenyon Review Prize in Poetry for a First Book." Contestants should send only 1 copy of each ms. Manuscripts must be between 48 and 100 pages, typed single-spaced, with no more than 1 poem/page. The ms must be paginated and contain a table of contents. A title page must be submitted with each ms and should include the author's name, address, telephone number, e-mail (if avaialable), and the ms title. **Deadline: April 15 (postmarked).** Guidelines for SASE. **Charges $25.** Prize: $3,500 as an advance against royalties, and an invitation to read from the winning ms at Kenyon College if such a reading is held. Judged by David Baker (final judge). Open to any writer.

THE MILTON KESSLER MEMORIAL PRIZE FOR POETRY
Harpur Palate at Binghamton University, Dept. of English, Binghamton University, P.O. Box 6000, Binghamton NY 13902-6000. (607)355-4761. Website: harpurpalate.binghamton.edu. **Contact:** Editor. Contest offered annually for previously unpublished poems in any style, form, or genre of no more than 10 pages per submission.

Deadline: August 1-October 1. Guidelines for SASE. **Charges $10/5 poems.** Prize: $500, and publication in Winter issue of *Harpur Palate*. Name and contact information should appear in the cover letter only. Acquires first North American serial rights. Open to any writer.

(HELEN AND LAURA KROUT MEMORIAL) OHIOANA POETRY AWARD
Ohioana Library Association, 274 E. First Ave., Columbus OH 45201. (614)466-3831. Fax: (614)728-6974. E-mail: ohioana@sloma.state.oh.us. Website: www.oplin.lib.oh.us/OHIOANA/. **Contact:** Linda R. Hengst. Offered annually "to an individual whose body of published work has made, and continues to make, a significant contribution to poetry, and through whose work, interest in poetry has been developed." Recipient must have been born in Ohio or lived in Ohio at least 5 years. **Deadline: December 31.** Guidelines for SASE. Prize: $1,000.

GERALD LAMPERT MEMORIAL AWARD
The League of Canadian Poets, 920 Yonge St., Suite 608, Toronto ON M4W 3C7, Canada. (416)504-1657. Fax: (416)504-0096. E-mail: promotion@poets.ca. Website: www.poets.ca. Offered annually for a first book of poetry by a Canadian poet published in the preceding year. Guidelines for SASE and on website. **Deadline: November 1. Charges $15 fee.** Prize: $1,000. Open to Canadian citizens and landed immigrants only.

THE JAMES LAUGHLIN AWARD
The Academy of American Poets, 588 Broadway, Suite 604, New York NY 10012-3210. (212)274-0343. Fax: (212)274-9427. E-mail: murphy@poets.org. Website: www.poets.org. **Contact:** Awards Coordinator. Offered annually for a ms of original poetry, in English, by a poet who has already published 1 book of poems in a standard edition (40 pages or more in length and 500 or more copies). Only mss that have come under contract with a US publisher between May 1 of the preceding year and April 30 of the year of the deadline are eligible. **Deadline: May 15.** Guidelines for SASE. Prize: $5,000, and the Academy will purchase at least 10,000 hardcover copies for distribution.

THE LEDGE ANNUAL POETRY CHAPBOOK CONTEST
The Ledge Magazine, 40 Maple Ave., Bellport NY 11713. **Contact:** Timothy Monaghan. Offered annually to publish an outstanding collection of poems. Open to any writer. **Deadline: October 31.** Guidelines for SASE. **Charges $15 fee.** Prize: $1,000, publication of chapbook, and 50 copies; all entrants receive a copy of winning chapbook.

THE LEDGE POETRY AWARDS
The Ledge Magazine, 40 Maple Ave., Bellport NY 11713. **Contact:** Timothy Monaghan. Offered annually for unpublished poems of exceptional quality and significance. All poems considered for publication in the magazine. Open to any writer. **Deadline: April 30.** Guidelines for SASE. **Charges $10 for 3 poems; $3/additional poem ($15 subscription gains free entry for the first 3 poems).** Prize: 1st Place: $1,000, and publication in *The Ledge Magazine*; 2nd Place: $250, and publication in *The Ledge Magazine*; 3rd Place: $100, and publication in *The Ledge Magazine*.

LENA-MILES WEVER TODD POETRY SERIES
Pleiades Press & Winthrop University, Dept. of English, Central Missouri State University, Warrensburg MO 64093. (660)543-8106. Fax: (660)543-8544. E-mail: kdp8106@cmsu2.cmsu.edu. Website: www.cmsu.edu/engl phil/pleiades.html. **Contact:** Kevin Prufer. Offered annually for an unpublished book of poetry by an American or Canadian poet. Guidelines for SASE or by e-mail. The winning book is copyrighted by the author and Pleiades Press. **Deadline: Generally September 30; e-mail for firm deadline. Charges $15, which includes a copy of the winning book.** Prize: $1,000, and publication of winning book in paperback edition. Distribution through Louisiana State University Press. Open to any writer living in the US or Canada.

THE LEVINSON PRIZE
Poetry, 1030 N. Clark St., Suite 420, Chicago IL 60610. (312)787-7070. E-mail: poetry@poetrymagazine.org. Website: www.poetrymagazine.org. Offered annually for poems published in *Poetry* during the preceding year (October-September). *Poetry* buys all rights to the poems published in the magazine. Copyrights are returned to the authors on request. Any writer may submit poems to *Poetry*. Guidelines for SASE. Prize: $500.

THE LARRY LEVIS PRIZE FOR POETRY
Prairie Schooner, 201 Andrews Hall, P.O. Box 880334, Lincoln NE 68588-0334. (402)472-0911. Fax: (402)472-9771. E-mail: kgrey2@unl.edu. Website: www.unl.edu/schooner/psmain.htm. **Contact:** Hilda Raz. Offered annually for poetry published in *Prairie Schooner* in the previous year. Prize: $1,000.

⧄ THE RUTH LILLY POETRY PRIZE

The Modern Poetry Association, 1030 N. Clark St., Suite 420, Chicago IL 60610. E-mail: poetry@poetrymagazine. org. Website: www.poetrymagazine.org. Estab. 1986. Offered annually to a poet whose accomplishments in the field of poetry warrant extraordinary recognition. No applicants or nominations are accepted. **Deadline: Varies.** Prize: $100,000.

⧄ LITERAL LATTÉ POETRY AWARD

Literal Latté, 61 4th Ave., Suite 240, New York NY 10003. (212)260-5532. E-mail: LitLatte@aol.com. Website: www.literal-latte.com. Offered annually for unpublished poetry. **Deadline: July 19.** Guidelines for SASE. **Charges $10 reading free/set of up to 4 poems, or $15/set of 8 poems (includes 1-year subscription).** Prize: 1st-$1,000; 2nd-$300; 3rd-$200; winners published in *Literal Latté*. Open to any writer.

FRANCES LOCKE MEMORIAL POETRY AWARD

The Bitter Oleander Press, 4983 Tall Oaks Dr., Fayetteville NY 13066-9776. (315)637-3047. Fax: (315)637-5056. E-mail: info@bitteroleander.com. Website: www.bitteroleander.com. **Contact:** Paul B. Roth. Offered annually for unpublished, imaginative poetry. Open to any writer. **Deadline: June 15.** Guidelines for SASE. **Charges $10 for 5 poems, $2 for each additional poem.** Prize: $1,000, and 5 copies of issue.

LOUISIANA LITERATURE PRIZE FOR POETRY

Louisiana Literature, SLU—Box 792, Southeastern Louisiana University, Hammond LA 70402. (504)549-5022. Fax: (504)549-5021. E-mail: lalit@selu.edu. Website: www.selu.edu/orgs/lalit/. **Contact:** Jack Bedell, contest director. Estab. 1984. Offered annually for unpublished poetry. All entries considered for publication. **Deadline: April 1.** Guidelines for SASE. **Charges $12 fee.** Prize: $400.

LOUISE LOUIS/EMILY F. BOURNE STUDENT POETRY AWARD

Poetry Society of America, 15 Gramercy Park S., New York NY 10003. (212)254-9628. Fax: (212)673-2352. Website: www.poetrysociety.org. **Contact:** Brett Lauer, programs associate. Offered annually for unpublished work to promote excellence in student poetry. Open to American high school or preparatory school students (grades 9-12). Guidelines for SASE and on website. Judged by prominent American poets. **Deadline: October 1-December 21. Charges $5 for a student submitting a single entry; $20 for a high school submitting unlimited number of its students' poems.** Prize: $250.

⧄ PAT LOWTHER MEMORIAL AWARD

920 Yonge St., Suite 608, Toronto ON M4W 3C7, Canada. (416)504-1657. Fax: (416)504-0096. E-mail: promotion @poets.ca. Website: www.poets.ca. Estab. 1966. Offered annually to promote new Canadian poetry/poets and also to recognize exceptional work in each category. Submissions to be published in the preceding year. Enquiries from publishers welcome. Open to Canadians living at home and abroad. The candidate must be a Canadian citizen or landed imigrant, though the publisher need not be Canadian. Call, write, fax, or e-mail for rules. **Deadline: November 1. Charges $15 fee/title.** Prize: $1,000.

⧄ LYRIC POETRY AWARD

Poetry Society of America, 15 Gramercy Park S., New York NY 10003. (212)254-9628. Fax: (212)673-2352. E-mail: brett@poetrysociety.org. Website: www.poetrysociety.org. **Contact:** Brett Lauer, programs associate. Offered annually for unpublished work to promote excellence in lyric poetry. Line limit 50. *Open to PSA members only.* **Deadline: December 22.** Guidelines for SASE. Prize: $500.

THE MACGUFFIN NATIONAL POET HUNT

The MacGuffin, 18600 Haggerty, Livonia MI 48152. E-mail: macguffin@schoolcraft.cc.mi.us. Website: www.ma cguffin.org. **Contact:** Managing Editor. "The purpose of the National Poet Hunt contest is to judge each piece blindly in its own right. It is not judged against another poet, only on the merits of the piece of itself. By sponsoring this contest, we've been able to publish new poets and give confidence to those who've entered by assuring those writers that the pieces would be judged on their own merits and that that work would be read by a renowned published poet." Offered annually for unpublished work. **Deadline: End of May.** Guidelines for SASE. **Charges $15 for a 5-poem entry.** Prize: First Prize: $500; 2nd Prize: $250; 3rd Prize: $100, and up to 3 Honorable Mentions. All winning poems published in the fall issue of *The MacGuffin*. Judged by a well-known poet. Past judges include Molly Peacock, Gary Gildner, and Richard Tillinghast. Acquires First rights (if piece is published). Once published, all rights revert to the author. Open to any writer.

⧄ THE MALAHAT REVIEW LONG POEM PRIZE

The Malahat Review, Box 1700 STNCSC, Victoria BC V8W 2Y2, Canada. E-mail: malahat@uvic.ca (queries only). Website: malahatreview.ca. **Contact:** Editor. Offered every 2 years to unpublished long poems. Preliminary reading by editorial board; final judging by the editor and 2 recognized poets. Obtains first world rights. After publication rights revert to the author. Open to any writer. **Deadline: March 1.** Guidelines for SASE. **Charges $35 fee (includes a 1-year subscription to the *Malahat*, published quarterly).** Prize: 2 prizes of $400, plus payment for publication ($30/page), and an additional year's subscription.

MORTON MARR POETRY PRIZE

Southwest Review, P.O. Box 750374, Dallas TX 75275-0374. (214)768-1037. Fax: (214)768-1408. E-mail: swr@m ail.smu.edu. Website: www.southwestreview.org. **Contact:** Willard Spiegelman. Annual award given to a poem by a writer who has not yet published a first book. Contestants may submit no more than 6 poems in a ''traditional'' form (i.e., sonnet, sestina, villanelle, rhymed stanzas, blank verse, etc.). A cover letter with name, address, and other relevant information may accompany the poems which must be printed without any identifying information. Guidelines for SASE or online. **Deadline: November 30. Charges $5/poem.** Prize: $1,000, and publication in *The Southwest Review*. Open to any writer who has not yet published a first book.

THE LENORE MARSHALL POETRY PRIZE

The Nation and The Academy of American Poets, 588 Broadway, Suite 604, New York NY 10012-3210. (212)274-0343. Fax: (212)274-9427. E-mail: rmurphy@poets.org. Website: www.poets.org. **Contact:** Ryan Murphy, awards coordinator. Offered annually for book of poems published in US during previous year and nominated by the publisher. Self-published books are not eligible. **Deadline: April 1-June 15 (postmarked).** Prize: $25,000.

ℕ LUCILLE MEDWICK MEMORIAL AWARD

Poetry Society of America, 15 Gramercy Park S., New York NY 10003. (212)254-9628. Fax: (212)673-2352. E-mail: brett@poetrysociety.org. Website: www.poetrysociety.org. **Contact:** Brett Lauer, programs associate. Original poem in any form on a humanitarian theme. Guidelines subject to change. *Open to PSA members only*. **Deadline: December 22.** Guidelines for SASE. Prize: $500.

MID-LIST PRESS FIRST SERIES AWARD FOR POETRY

Mid-List Press, 4324 12th Ave. S., Minneapolis MN 55407-3218. Fax: (612)823-8387. E-mail: guide@midlist.org. Website: www.midlist.org. **Contact:** Lane Stiles, publisher. Estab. 1990. Offered annually for unpublished book of poetry to encourage new poets. Guidelines for SASE or on website. Contest is open to any writer who has never published a book of poetry. ''We do not consider a chapbook to be a book of poetry.'' **Deadline: February 1. Charges $30 (US dollars) fee.** Prize: Publication, and an advance against royalties.

MISSISSIPPI VALLEY NON-PROFIT POETRY CONTEST

Midwest Writing Center, P.O. Box 3188, Rock Island IL 61204-3188. (563)359-1057. **Contact:** Max Molleston, chairman. Estab. 1972. Offered annually for unpublished poetry: adult general, student division, Mississippi Valley, senior citizen, religious, rhyming, jazz, humorous, haiku, history, and ethnic. Up to 5 poems may be submitted. **Deadline: April 1. Charges $8 fee, $5 for students.** Prize: Cash prizes total $1,200.

MORSE POETRY PRIZE

Northeastern University English Department, 406 Holmes Hall, Boston MA 02115. (617)437-2512. E-mail: g.rotel la@neu.edu. Website: www.casdn.neu.edu/~english. **Contact:** Guy Rotella. Offered annually for previously published poetry book-length mss of first or second books. **Deadline: September 15. Charges $15 fee.** Prize: $1,000, and publication by Northeastern University Press.

KATHRYN A. MORTON PRIZE IN POETRY

Sarabande Books, P.O. Box 4456, Louisville KY 40204. (502)458-4028. Fax: (502)458-4065. E-mail: sarabanden @aol.com. Website: www.SarabandeBooks.org. **Contact:** Kirby Gann, managing editor. Offered annually to publish an outstanding collection of poetry. All finalists considered for publication. **Deadline: January 1-February 15.** Guidelines for SASE. **Charges $20 fee.** Prize: $2,000 and publication with standard royalty contract.

SHEILA MOTTON AWARD

New England Poetry Club, 16 Cornell St., Apt. 2, Arlington MA 02476-7710. **Contact:** Elizabeth Crowell. For a poetry book published in the last 2 years. Send 2 copies of the book and **$10 entry fee**. Prize: $500.

ERIKA MUMFORD PRIZE

16 Cornell St., Apt. 2, Arlington MA 02476-7710. **Contact:** Elizabeth Crowell. Offered annually for a poem in any form about foreign culture or travel. **Deadline: June 30.** Guidelines for SASE. **Charges $10 for up to 3 entries in NEPC contests.** Prize: $250.

NATIONAL WRITERS ASSOCIATION POETRY CONTEST
The National Writers Association, 3140 S. Peoria, #295, Aurora CO 80014. (303)841-0246. Fax: (303)841-2607. **Contact:** Sandy Whelchel, director. Annual contest "to encourage the writing of poetry, an important form of individual expression but with a limited commercial market." Guidelines for SASE. **Charges $10 fee.** Prize: 1st Place: $100; 2nd Place: $50; 3rd Place: $25.

HOWARD NEMEROV SONNET AWARD
The Formalist: A Journal of Metrical Poetry, 320 Hunter Dr., Evansville IN 47711. **Contact:** Mona Baer. Offered annually for an unpublished sonnet to encourage poetic craftsmanship and to honor the memory of the late Howard Nemerov, third US Poet Laureate. Final judge for year 2003: Dana Gioia. Acquires first North American serial rights for those sonnets chosen for publication. Upon publication all rights revert to the author. Open to the international community of writers. **Deadline: June 15.** Guidelines for SASE. **Charges $3 entry fee/sonnet.** Prize: $1,000, and publication in *The Formalist*; 11 other finalists also published.

THE PABLO NERUDA PRIZE FOR POETRY
Nimrod International Journal, 600 S. College Ave., Tulsa OK 74104. (918)631-3080. Fax: (918)631-3033. E-mail: nimrod@utulsa.edu. Website: www.utulsa.edu/nimrod. **Contact:** Francine Ringold. Annual award to discover new writers of vigor and talent. **Deadline: April 30.** Guidelines for SASE. **Charges $20 (includes a 1-year subscription to** *Nimrod*). Prize: 1st Place: $2,000, and publication; 2nd Place: $1,000, and publication. Judged by the *Nimrod* editors (finalists), and a recognized author selects the winners. Acquires *Nimrod* retains the right to publish any submission. Open to US residents only.

NEW ISSUES FIRST BOOK OF POETRY PRIZE
New Issues Poetry & Prose, Dept. of English, Western Michigan University, 1903 W. Michigan Ave., Kalamazoo MI 49008-5331. (269)387-8185. Fax: (269)387-2562. E-mail: herbert.scott@wmich.edu. Website: www.wmich.edu/newissues. **Contact:** Herbert Scott, editor. Offered annually for publication of a first book of poems by a poet writing in English who has not previously published a full-length collection of poems in an edition of 500 or more copies. *New Issues Poetry & Prose* obtains rights for first publication. Book is copyrighted in author's name. Guidelines for SASE or on website. **Deadline: November 30. Charges $15.** Prize: $2,000, and publication of book. Author also receives 10% of the printed edition.

THE NEW LETTERS POETRY AWARD
New Letters, 5101 Rockhill Rd., Kansas City MO 64110. (816)235-1168. Fax: (816)235-2611. E-mail: newletters@umkc.edu. Website: www.newletters.org. **Contact:** Aleatha Ezra. Offered annually for unpublished work to discover and reward new and upcoming writers. Buys first North American serial rights. Open to any writer. **Deadline: Third week of May. Charges $15 fee (includes a year's subscription to** *New Letters*). Prize: 1st Place: $1,000, and publication in *New Letters*; Runners-Up receive a complimentary copy of a recent book of poetry or fiction from our affiliate BkMk Press. All entries will be given consideration for publication in future issues of *New Letters*. Guidelines and samples available online.

NEW RIVER POETS QUARTERLY POETRY AWARDS
New River Poets, a chapter of Florida State Poets Association, Inc., 5545 Meadowbrook St., Zephyrhills FL 33541-2715. **Contact:** June Owens, awards coordinator. Offered quarterly (February, May, August, and November) for previously published and unpublished work to acknowledge and reward outstanding poetic efforts. Previous winners have been Maureen Tolman Flannery, John McBride, and Gwendolyn Carr. **Deadline: February 15, May 15, August 15, and November 15.** Guidelines for SASE. **Charges $5 fee for 1-4 poems, $1 each additional poem (no limit).** Prize: Awarded each quarter. 1st Prize: $65; 2nd Prize: $45; 3rd Prize: $35. Judged by the 1st-Place winning authors in each quarterly competition who judge the unscreened entries in a subsequent competition. Open to any writer.

⊠ THE JOHN FREDERICK NIMS MEMORIAL PRIZE
Poetry, 1030 N. Clark St., Suite 420, Chicago IL 60610. (312)787-7070. E-mail: poetry@poetrymagazine.org. Website: www.poetrymagazine.org. Offered annually for poems published in *Poetry* during the preceding year (October-September). Judged by the editors of *Poetry*. *Poetry* buys all rights to the poems published in the magazine. Copyrights are returned to the authors on request. Any writer may submit poems to *Poetry*. Guidelines for SASE. Prize: $500.

⊠ NO LOVE LOST III
Hidden Brook Press, 412-701 King St. W., Toronto ON M5V 2W7, Canada. (416)504-3966. Fax: (801)751-1837. E-mail: writers@hiddenbrookpress.com. Website: www.hiddenbrookpress.com/an-nll.htm. No Love Lost III is

an annual international poetry anthology contest. "Love, hate, lust, desire, passion, jealousy, and ambivalence. Including brotherly, sisterly, parental love, love of country, city." Send 3 unpublished poems with SASE. Electronic and hard copy submissions required. Annually, Must Be Unpublished. **Deadline: November 30. Charges $15 for 3 poems (includes purchase of book).** Prize: 1st Prize: $100; 2nd Prize: $75; 3rd Prize: $50; 4th Prize: $40; 5th Prize: $30; 6th Prize: $25; 7th Prize: $20; 8th Prize: $15; 9th-10th Prize: $10, plus up to 12 Honorable Mentions. Up to 300 poems published. Open to any writer.

THE OHIO STATE UNIVERSITY PRESS/*THE JOURNAL* AWARD IN POETRY

The Ohio State University Press and *The Journal*, 1070 Carmack, Columbus OH 43210. (614)292-6930. Fax: (614)292-2065. E-mail: ohiostatepress@osu.edu. Website: www.ohiostatepress.org. **Contact:** David Citino, poetry editor. Offered annually for unpublished work, minimum of 48 pages of original poetry. **Deadline: Entries accepted September 1-30. Charges $25 fee.** Prize: $2,000, and publication.

🆕 ONCEWRITTEN.COM POETRY CONTEST

Oncewritten.com, P.O. Box 3046, Hollywood CA 90078-3046. E-mail: contests@oncewritten.com. Website: www.oncewritten.com. The purpose of this biannual contest is "to find high quality, previously unpublished poetry to feature on the website and in *Off the Press*, our biweekly newsletter, which is distributed specifically for people interested in reading about new authors." **Deadline: January 31; July 31.** Guidelines for SASE. **Charges $10.** Prize: Grand Prize: $500; 1st Prize: $100; both include publication on website and in newsletter. Judged by editor and 1 industry professional. The first contest will be judged by Sarah Provost, a published author and long-time teacher of creative writing. Open to any writer.

🔲 THE OPEN WINDOW IV

Hidden Brook Press, 412-701 King St. W., Toronto ON M5V 2W7, Canada. (416)504-3966. Fax: (801)751-1837. E-mail: writers@hiddenbrookpress.com. Website: www.hiddenbrookpress.com/an-ow.htm. An annual poetry anthology contest. "A wide open window theme including family, nature, death, rhyming, city, country, war and peace, social...long, short haiku, or any other genre." Send sets of 3 poems with short bio (35-40 words) and a SASE. Electronic and hard copy submissions required. **Deadline: July 15. Charges $15 for 3 poems.** Prize: 1st Prize: $100; 2nd Prize: $75; 3rd Prize: $50; 4th Prize: $40; 5th Prize: $30; 6th Prize: $25; 7th Prize: $20; 8th Prize: $15; 9th-10th Prize: $10, plus up to 12 honorable mentions. All winners, honorable mentions, and runners up receive 1 copy of the book for each published poem. Open to any writer.

GUY OWEN AWARD

Southern Poetry Review, Dept. of Languages, Literature, and Philosophy, Armstrong Atlantic State University, Savannah GA 31419-1997. (912)927-5289. Fax: (912)927-5399. E-mail: parhamro@mail.armstrong.edu. Website: www.spr.armstrong.edu. **Contact:** Robert Parham. This annual contest was established to "honor the founder of *Southern Poetry Review* and to sustain its ongoing publication." **Deadline: See website.** Guidelines for SASE. **Charges $15 entry fee (includes 1-year subscription to *Southern Poetry Review*).** Prize: $1,000, and publication of winning poem in *Southern Poetry Review*. Judged by a different established poet each year. Open to any writer.

🆕 THE PARIS REVIEW PRIZE IN POETRY

Zoo Press, P.O. Box 22990, Lincoln NE 68542. E-mail: editors@zoopress.org. Website: www.zoopress.org. **Contact:** Richard Howard. "Zoo Press aims to publish the best emerging writers writing in the English language, and will endeavor to do it at the rate of at least 10 manuscripts of admirable quality a year, providing we can find them. We're confident we can through contests such as The Paris Review Prize in Poetry." **Deadline: October 31 (postmarked).** Guidelines for SASE. **Charges $25.** Prize: $5,000 as an advance against royalties, and an invitation to read at the annual Paris Review Awards Reading in New York City, if such a gala is held. Judged by Richard Howard (final judge). Open to any writer.

THE PATERSON POETRY PRIZE

The Poetry Center at Passaic County Community College, One College Blvd., Paterson NJ 07505-6555. (973)684-6555. Fax: (973)684-5843. E-mail: mgillan@pccc.cc.nj.us. Website: www.pccc.edu/poetry. **Contact:** Maria Mazziotti Gillan, director. Offered annually for a book of poetry published in the previous year. **Deadline: February 1.** Guidelines for SASE. Prize: $1,000.

PEARL POETRY PRIZE

Pearl Editions, 3030 E. Second St., Long Beach CA 90803. (562)434-4523. Fax: (562)434-4523. E-mail: pearlmag @aol.com. Website: www.pearlmag.com. **Contact:** Marilyn Johnson, editor/publisher. Offered annually "to provide poets with further opportunity to publish their poetry in book-form and find a larger audience for their work." Manuscripts must be original works written in English. Guidelines for SASE or on website. **Deadline: July 15. Charges $20.** Prize: $1,000, and publication by Pearl Editions. Open to all writers. Manuscripts must be original work (no translations) and in English.

PEN/JOYCE OSTERWEIL AWARD FOR POETRY

PEN American Center, 568 Broadway, Suite 401, New York NY 10012. (212)334-1660, ext. 110. E-mail: awards@pen.org. Website: www.pen.org. **Contact:** Peter Meyer, literary awards manager. *Candidates may only be nominated by members of PEN.* This award "recognizes the high literary character of the published work to date of a new and emerging American poet of any age, and the promise of further literary achievement." Nominated may not have published more than 1 book of poetry. Offered every 2 years (odd years). **Deadline: January 3.** Prize: $5,000. Judged by a panel of 3 judges selected by the PEN Awards Committee.

PEN/VOELCKER AWARD FOR POETRY

PEN American Center, 568 Broadway, Suite 401, New York NY 10012. (212)334-1600, ext. 110. E-mail: awards@pen.org. Website: www.pen.org. **Contact:** Peter Meyer, literary awards manager. *Candidates can be nominated for Award only by members of PEN.* Award given to an American poet "whose distinguished and growing body of work to date represents a notable and accomplished presence in American literature." Offered every 2 years (even years). **Deadline: January 1 (nominations).** Prize: $5,000 stipend. Judged by a panel of 3-5 poets or other writers.

PHILBRICK POETRY AWARD

Providence Athenaeum, 251 Benefit St., Providence RI 02903. (401)421-6970. Fax: (401)421-2860. E-mail: smarkley@providenceathenaeum.org. Website: www.providenceathenaeum.org. **Contact:** Sandy Markley. Offered annually for New England poets who have not yet published a book. Previous publication of individual poems in journals or anthologies is allowed. Judged by nationally-known poets. John Ashbery is the 2004 judge. Guidelines for SASE or on website. **Deadline: June 15-October 15. Charges $8 fee (includes copy of previously published chapbook).** Prize: $500, publication of winning ms as a chapbook, and a public reading at Providence Athenaeum with the final judge/award presenter.

POET'S CORNER AWARD

Broken Jaw Press and BS Poetry Society, Box 596 Stn. A, Fredericton NB E3B 5A6, Canada. (506)454-5127. Fax: (506)454-5127. E-mail: jblades@nbnet.nb.ca. Website: www.brokenjaw.com. Offered annually to recognize the best book-length ms by a Canadian poet. Guidelines for SASE or on website at www.brokenjaw.com/poetscorner.htm. **Deadline: December 31. Charges $20 fee (which includes copy of winning book upon publication).** Prize: $500, plus trade publication of poetry ms.

THE POETRY BUSINESS BOOK & PAMPHLET COMPETITION

The Poetry Business, The Studio, Byram Arcade, Westgate, Huddersfield HD1 1ND, United Kingdom. (00 44) 1484 434840. Fax: (00 44) 1484 426566. E-mail: edit@poetrybusiness.co.uk. Website: www.poetrybusiness.co.uk. "The purpose of this annual contest is to find and publish new or less-well-known poets. Entrants should submit a short manuscript. The winners will have a chapbook published; these winners can then submit an extended manuscript. The overall winner will have a full-length book published under our own imprint (Smith/Doorstop Books)." No poetry by or for children. Work must be in English. **Deadline: October 31.** Guidelines for SASE. **Charges £18.** Prize: Book publication, plus share of a cash prize. Judged by the directors of The Poetry Business, who are experienced editors, plus a well-known poet. Open to any writer.

THE POETRY CENTER BOOK AWARD

The Poetry Center, San Francisco State University, 1600 Holloway Ave., San Francisco CA 94132-9901. (415)338-2227. Fax: (415)338-0966. E-mail: poetry@sfsu.edu. Website: www.sfsu.edu/~poetry. Estab. 1980. Offered annually for books of poetry and chapbooks, published in year of the prize. "Prize given for an extraordinary book of American poetry." Please include a cover letter noting author name, book title(s), name of person issuing check, and check number. Will not consider anthologies or translations. **Deadline: December 31. Charges $10 reading fee/entry.** Prize: $500, and an invitation to read in the Poetry Center Reading Series.

POETRY IN PRINT POETRY CONTEST

Poetry in Print, P.O. Box 30981, Albuquerque NM 87190-0981. (505)888-3937. Fax: (505)888-3937. **Contact:** Robert G. English. No limit to the number of entries; 60 lines of poetry accepted. **Deadline: August 1. Charges $10.** Prize: $1,000. Open to any writer.

⁑ POETRY IN THE ARTS AWARD

5801 Highland Pass, Austin TX 78731. (512)453-7920. E-mail: jlj@poetryinarts.org. Website: www.poetryinarts.org. **Contact:** J.L. Johnson. Monthly contests and awards, and an annual grand prize for the best poem; several free contests that are bonus incentives of the organization's open submission policy, and free youth contests and a scholarship. "Literary publishers typically offer contests as a revenue raiser to at least offset their award outlays and publishing expenses. The difference is that we pay out annually in the range of $6,000 in awards to our fee-paid contests, free contests, youth contests and scholarships, and publish numerous nonwinners." Author retains copyright. Submission constitutes grant of license to publish. Award winners grant exclusive right to publish for a period of 13 months, which includes publication online and in an anthology, and the right for republication in a future collection. Accepts electronic submissions. **Deadline: Monthly deadlines. Charges $10.** Prize: Annual Prize: $1,000. Monthly Awards—1st Place: $100; 2nd Place: $50; 3rd Place: $25; Honorable Mention (3): $10; also publication in anthology. Judged by award-winning poets from across the literary spectrum. Open to any writer.

⁑ ⊕ THE POETRY LIFE PRIZE

Poetry Life magazine, No. 1, Blue Ball Corner, Walter Lane, Winchester Hampshire SO23 0ER. Website: freespace.virgin.net/poetry.life/. **Contact:** Adrian Bishop, editor. Annual award for unpublished poetry in any style (up to 80 lines/poem). Poems are regarded as copies and will not be returned. **Deadline: March 31. Charges £4/poem (make checks payable to *Poetry Life*).** Prize: 1st Prize: £250, plus publication of a collection of the winner's poems in *Poetry Life* magazine and on the *Poetry Life* website; 2nd-5th Prize: £100.

⁑ POETRY SOCIETY OF VIRGINIA CONTESTS

Poetry Society of Virginia, P.O. Box 650962, Richmond VA 23235. E-mail: contest@poetrysocietyofvirginia.org. Website: www.poetrysocietyofvirginia.org. **Contact:** Guy Terrell, adult categories; Shann Palmer, student categories. Annual contest for unpublished poetry in several categories. Some categories are open to any writer, others are open only to members or students. Guidelines for SASE or on website. **Deadline: January 19. Charges $3/poem for nonmembers, free for members, free for student categories.** Prize: $25-100 in each category.

POETS OUT LOUD PRIZE

Poets Out Loud, Fordham University at Lincoln Center, 113 W. 60th St., Room 924, New York NY 10023. (212)636-6792. Fax: (212)636-7153. E-mail: pol@fordham.edu. Website: www.poetsoutloud.com. Annual competition for an unpublished, full-length poetry ms (50-80 pages). Winning volume is published each fall by Fordham University Press in paper and cloth editions. **Deadline: October 31.** Guidelines for SASE. **Charges $25 entry fee.** Prize: $1,000, book publication, and a gala reading with prize judge. Judged by a group of judges of national reputation. Open to any writer.

RAINMAKER AWARDS IN POETRY

ZONE 3, Austin Peay State University, P.O. Box 4565, Clarksville TN 37044. (931)221-7031. Fax: (931)221-7393. E-mail: zone3@apsu01.apsu.edu. **Contact:** Susan Wallace, managing editor. Offered annually for unpublished poetry. Previous judges include Carolyn Forché, Marge Piercy, Howard Nemerov, and William Stafford. Open to any poet. Guidelines for SASE. **Charges $8 fee (includes 1-year subscription).** Prize: 1st Place: $500; 2nd Place: $300; 3rd Place: $100.

RAMBUNCTIOUS REVIEW POETRY CONTEST

Rambunctious Review, 1221 W. Pratt Blvd., Chicago IL 60626. Annual themed contest for unpublished poems. Acquires one-time publication rights. Open to any writer. **Deadline: December 31.** Guidelines for SASE. **Charges $2/poem.** Prize: 1st Prize: $100; 2nd Prize: $75; 3rd Prize: $50; all winning entries will be published in future issues of *Rambunctious Review*.

LEVIS READING PRIZE

Virginia Commonwealth University, Dept. of English, P.O. Box 842005, Richmond VA 23284-2005. (804)828-1329. Fax: (804)828-8684. E-mail: eng_grad@vcu.edu. Website: www.has.vcu.edu/eng/resources/levis_prize.htm. **Contact:** Jeff Lodge. Offered annually for books of poetry published in the previous year to encourage poets early in their careers. The entry must be the writer's first or second published book of poetry. Previously published books in other genres, or previously published chapbooks, do not count as books for this purpose. **Deadline: January 15.** Guidelines for SASE. Prize: $1,000 honorarium, and an expense-paid trip to Richmond to present a public reading.

RED ROCK POETRY AWARD

Red Rock Review, Community College of Southern Nevada, English Department J2A, 3200 E. Cheyenne Ave., North Las Vegas NV 89030. (702)651-4094. Fax: (702)651-4639. E-mail: richard_logsdon@ccsn.nevada.edu. Website: www.ccsn.nevada.edu/english/redrockreview/contest.htm. **Contact:** Richard Logsdon. Offered annually for unpublished poetry. Open to any writer. **Deadline: October 31.** Guidelines for SASE. **Charges $6 for 3 poems.** Prize: $500.

RIVER CITY WRITING AWARDS IN POETRY

The University of Memphis/Hohenberg Foundation, Dept. of English, Memphis TN 38152. (901)678-4591. E-mail: rivercity@memphis.edu. Website: www.people.memphis.edu/~rivercity. Offered annually for unpublished poems of 2 pages maximum. Guidelines for SASE or on website. **Deadline: March 15. Charges $5 fee/poem.** Prize: 1st Place: $1,000; 2nd and 3rd Place: Publication, and 1-year subscription. Open to any writer.

RIVER STYX INTERNATIONAL POETRY CONTEST

River Styx Magazine, 634 N. Grand Blvd., 12th Floor, St. Louis MO 63103. (314)533-4541. Fax: (314)533-3345. Website: www.riverstyx.org. **Contact:** Richard Newman, editor; Melissa Gurley Banks, managing editor. Offered annually for unpublished poetry. Poets may send up to 3 poems, not more than 14 pages. Open to any writer. 2004 judge: Maura Stanton. Past judges include Miller Williams, Billy Collins, Marylin Hacker, Mark Doty, Molly Peacock, and Philip Levine. **Deadline: May 31.** Guidelines for SASE. **Charges $20 reading fee (which includes a 1-year subscription).** Prize: $1,000, and publication in August issue.

NICHOLAS ROERICH POETRY PRIZE

Story Line Press, Three Oaks Farm, P.O. Box 1240, Ashland OR 97520-0055. (541)512-8792. Fax: (541)512-8793. E-mail: mail@storylinepress.com. Website: www.storylinepress.com. **Contact:** Roerich Prize Coordinator. Estab. 1988. Offered annually for full-length book of poetry. Any writer who has not previously published a full-length collection of poetry (48 pages or more) in English is eligible to apply. Guidelines for SASE or on website. **Deadline: May 1-October 31. Charges $20 fee.** Prize: $1,000, publication, and reading at the Nicholas Roerich Museum in New York.

THE RUNES AWARD

RUNES, A Review of Poetry/Arctos Press, P.O. Box 401, Sausalito CA 94966. Fax: (415)331-3092. E-mail: runesrev@aol.com. Website: http://members.aol.com/runes. **Contact:** CB Follett or Susan Terris. Offered annually for unpublished poems. Prefer poems less than 100 lines. Theme for Runes 2005 is Signals, 2006 is Hearth. Guidelines for SASE or online. **Deadline: May 31 postmark (regular and contest submissions accepted in April and May only). Charges $15 for 3 poems (includes a 1-year subscription to *RUNES, A Review of Poetry*)**; additional poems $3 each. Prize: $1,000, plus publication in *RUNES, A Review of Poetry*. Judged by Lucille Clifton (2005 competition). There is no charge for Regular Submissions, same themes, with equal chance at publication. Acquires one-time publication rights. Open to any writer.

BENJAMIN SALTMAN POETRY AWARD

Red Hen Press, P.O. Box 3537, Granada Hills CA 91394. (818)831-0649. Fax: (818)831-6659. E-mail: editors@redhen.org. Website: www.redhen.org. **Contact:** Kate Gale. Offered annually for unpublished work "to publish a winning book of poetry." Open to any writer. **Deadline: October 31.** Guidelines for SASE. **Charges $20 fee.** Prize: $1,000, and publication.

✂ SASKATCHEWAN POETRY AWARD

Saskatchewan Book Awards, Inc., Box 1921, Regina SK S4P 3E1, Canada. (306)569-1585. Fax: (306)569-4187. E-mail: director@bookawards.sk.ca. Website: www.bookawards.sk.ca. **Contact:** Joyce Wells, executive director. Offered annually for work published September 15-September 14 annually. This award is presented to a Saskatchewan author for the best book of poetry, judged on the quality of writing. **Deadline: First deadline: July 31; Final deadline: September 14.** Guidelines for SASE. **Charges $20 (Canadian).** Prize: $2,000.

THE HELEN SCHAIBLE INTERNATIONAL SHAKESPEAREAN/PETRARCHAN SONNET CONTEST

Poets' Club of Chicago, 1212 S. Michigan Ave., #2702, Chicago IL 60605. **Contact:** Tom Roby, chair. Offered annually for original and unpublished Shakespearean or Petrarchan sonnets. One entry/author. Submit 2 copies, typed and double-spaced; 1 with name and address, 1 without. All rules printed here. Send SASE for winners list. **Deadline: September 1.** Prize: 1st Place: $50; 2nd Place: $35; 3rd Place: $15; 3 Honorable Mentions.

✂ SEEDS 7

(formerly Seeds 6), Hidden Brook Press, 412-701 King St. W., Toronto ON M5V 2W7, Canada. (416)504-3966. Fax: (801)751-1837. E-mail: writers@hiddenbrookpress.com. Website: www.hiddenbrookpress.com/contest1.

htm. "The *SEEDS* International Poetry Chapbook Anthology Contest is interested in all types and styles of poetry. See the *SEEDS* website for examples of the type of poetry we have published in the past." Annually. **Deadline: October 1. Charges $12 for 3 poems.** Prize: 1st Prize: $100; 2nd Prize: $75; 3rd Prize: $50; 4th Prize: $40; 5th Prize: $30; 6th Prize: $25; 7th Prize: $20; 8th Prize: $15; 9th-10th Prize: $10, plus 15-25 Honorable Mentions. Winning poems published in the *SEEDS International Poetry Chapbook Anthology*. All winning and honorable mention submissions receive 1 copy of the book for each published poem. Open to any writer.

SLAPERING HOL PRESS CHAPBOOK COMPETITION

The Hudson Valley Writers' Center, 300 Riverside Dr., Sleepy Hollow NY 10591. (914)332-5953. Fax: (914)332-4825. E-mail: info@writerscenter.org. Website: www.writerscenter.org. **Contact:** Stephanie Strickland or Margo Stever, co-editors. The annual competition is open to poets who have not published a book or chapbook, though individual poems may have already appeared. Limit: 16-20 pages. The press was created in 1990 to provide publishing opportunities for emerging poets. **Deadline: May 15.** Guidelines for SASE. **Charges $10 fee.** Prize: $1,000, publication of chapbook, 10 copies of chapbook, and a reading at The Hudson Valley Writers' Center.

SLIPSTREAM ANNUAL POETRY CHAPBOOK COMPETITION

Slipstream, Box 2071, Niagara Falls NY 14301. (716)282-2616 (after 5 P.M. EST). E-mail: editors@slipstreampres s.org. Website: www.slipstreampress.org. **Contact:** Dan Sicoli, co-editor. Offered annually to help promote a poet whose work is often overlooked or ignored. Open to any writer. **Deadline: December 1.** Guidelines for SASE. **Charges $15.** Prize: $1,000, and 50 copies of published chapbook.

THE SOW'S EAR POETRY PRIZE

The Sow's Ear Poetry Review, 355 Mount Lebanon Rd., Donalds SC 29638-9115. (864)379-8061. E-mail: errol@kit enet.net. **Contact:** Errol Hess, managing editor. Estab. 1988. Offered for previously unpublished poetry. Guidelines for SASE or by e-mail. All submissions considered for publication. **Deadline: Submit September-October. Charges $3 fee/poem.** Prize: $1,000, publication, plus option of publication for 20-25 finalists.

SPOKANE PRIZE FOR POETRY

Eastern Washington University Press, 705 W. First Ave., Spokane WA 99201. (800)508-9095. Fax: (509)623-4283. E-mail: ewupress@ewu.edu. Website: www.ewupress.ewu.edu. **Contact:** Scott Poole. "Annual award to publish the finest work the literary world has to offer." **Deadline: May 1.** Guidelines for SASE. **Charges $25.** Prize: $1,500, and publication. Judged by anonymous judges. Open to any writer.

SPOON RIVER POETRY REVIEW EDITORS' PRIZE

Spoon River Poetry Review, Campus Box 4241, English Department, Illinois State University, Normal IL 61790-4241. (309)438-7906. Website: www.litline.org/spoon. **Contact:** Lucia Cordell Getsi, editor. Offered annually for unpublished poetry "to identify and reward excellence." Guidelines on website. Open to all writers. **Deadline: April 15. Charges $16 (entitles entrant to a year's subscription valued at $15).** Prize: 1st Place: $1,000; Runners-Up (2) prizes: $100 each; publication of 1st Place, runners-up, and selected honorable mentions.

SPS STUDIOS POETRY CARD CONTEST

SPS Studios, Inc., publishers of Blue Mountain Arts, P.O. Box 1007, Boulder CO 80306. (303)449-0536. Fax: (303)447-0939. E-mail: editorial@spsstudios.com. Website: www.sps.com. "We're looking for original poetry, which can be rhyming or nonrhyming, although we find nonrhyming poetry reads better. Poems may also be considered for possible publication on greeting cards or in book anthologies, but that is separate from the contest." Contest is offered biannually. Guidelines online. **Deadline: December 31 and June 30.** Prize: 1st Prize: $300; 2nd Prize: $150; 3rd Prize: $50. Judged by SPS Studios editorial staff. Open to any writer.

THE EDWARD STANLEY AWARD

Prairie Schooner, 201 Andrews Hall, P.O. Box 880334, Lincoln NE 68588-0334. (402)472-0911. Fax: (402)472-9771. E-mail: kgrey2@unl.edu. Website: www.unl.edu/schooner/psmain.htm. **Contact:** Hilda Raz. Offered annually for poetry published in *Prairie Schooner* in the previous year. Prize: $1,000.

THE AGNES LYNCH STARRETT POETRY PRIZE

University of Pittsburgh Press, 3400 Forbes Ave., Pittsburgh PA 15260. Website: www.pitt.edu/~press. **Contact:** Sue Borello. Estab. 1980. Series Editor: Ed Ochester. Offered annually for first book of poetry for poets who have not had a full-length book published. Mandatory guidelines for SASE. **Deadline: March and April only. Charges $20 fee.** Prize: $5,000.

THE ELIZABETH MATCHETT STOVER MEMORIAL AWARD

Southwest Review, P.O. Box 750374, Dallas TX 75275-0374. (214)768-1037. Fax: (214)768-1408. E-mail: swr@m ail.smu.edu. Website: www.southwestreview.org. **Contact:** Elizabeth Mills and Willard Spiegelman. Offered annually for unpublished poems or group of poems. Please note that mss are submitted for publication, not for the prizes themselves. Guidelines for SASE and on website. Prize: $250. Judged by Elizabeth Mills, senior editor, and Willard Spiegelman, editor-in-chief. Open to any writer.

▦ STROKESTOWN INTERNATIONAL POETRY COMPETITION

Strokestown International Poetry Festival, Bawn St., Strokestown, County Roscommon, Ireland. (+353) 71 9633759. E-mail: slaw@eircom.net. Website: www.strokestownpoetryprize.com. **Contact:** M.J.C. Harpur. This annual competition was established "to promote excellence in poetry, and participation in the reading and writing of it." **Deadline: February 19.** Guidelines for SASE. **Charges Charges $5 (4 Euros, £3).** Prize: 1st Prize: 4,000 euros (approximately $3,900) for a poem in English of up to 70 lines; 2nd Prize: 1,000 euros; 3rd Prize: 500 euros. All 10 shortlisted poets are invited to read at the Strokestown International Poetry Festival for a fee and travel expenses. Acquires first publication rights. Open to any writer.

⃝N ⃝ THE DAN SULLIVAN MEMORIAL POETRY CONTEST

The Writers' Circle of Durham Region, P.O. Box 323, Ajax ON L1S 3C5, Canada. (905)259-6520. E-mail: info@wc dr.org. Website: www.wcdr.org. **Contact:** Nancy Del Col, contest/award director. Estab. 1995. Annual contest for unpublished poetry. **Deadline: February 15. Charges $10/submission for adults; $5/entry for children, youth. Payment must be payable in Canadian funds to The Writers' Circle of Dunham Region.** Prize: **Children:** 1st Prize: $75; 2nd Prize: $50; 3rd Prize: $25; **Youth:** 1st Prize: $150; 2nd Prize: $100; 3rd Prize: $75; **Adult:** 1st Prize: $300; 2nd Prize: $200; 3rd Prize: $100. Judged by First round judging is done by Durham local judges. Second round judging is done by published Canadian poets. Open to Canadian residents only.

HOLLIS SUMMERS POETRY PRIZE

Ohio University Press, Scott Quadrangle, Athens OH 45701. (740)593-1155. Fax: (740)593-4536. Website: www. ohio.edu/oupress. **Contact:** David Sanders. Offered annually for unpublished poetry books. Books will be eligible if individual poems or sections have been published previously. Open to any writer. **Deadline: October 31.** Guidelines for SASE. **Charges $15.** Prize: $500, and publication of the ms in book form.

MAY SWENSON POETRY AWARD

Utah State University Press, 7800 Old Main Hill, Logan UT 84322-7800. (435)797-1362. Fax: (435)797-0313. E-mail: michael.spooner@usu.edu. Website: www.usu.edu/usupress. **Contact:** Michael Spooner. Offered annually in honor of May Swenson, one of America's major poets. Contest for unpublished mss in English, 50-100 pages; not only a "first book" competition. Entries are screened by 6 professional writers and teachers. The finalists are judged by a nationally known poet. Former judges include: Alicia Ostriker, Mark Doty, John Hollander, and Mary Oliver. Open to any writer. **Deadline: September 30.** Guidelines for SASE. **Charges $25 fee.** Prize: $1,000, publication of ms, and royalties.

TRANSCONTINENTAL POETRY AWARD

Pavement Saw Press, P.O. Box 6291, Columbus OH 43206. (614)445-0534. E-mail: info@pavementsaw.org. Website: pavementsaw.org. **Contact:** David Baratier, editor. Offered annually for a first book of poetry. Judged by Editor David Baratier and a guest judge (2003 judge Judith Vollmer). Guidelines on website. **Deadline: August 15. Charges $15 fee.** Prize: $1,500, 30 copies for judge's choice, standard royalty contract for editor's choice. Open to any writer.

KATE TUFTS DISCOVERY AWARD

Claremont Graduate University, 160 E. 10th St., Harper B7, Claremont CA 91711-6165. (909)621-8974. Fax: (909)607-8438. Website: www.cgu.edu/tufts. **Contact:** Betty Terrell, awards coordinator. Estab. 1993. Offered annually for a first book by a poet of genuine promise. Entries must be a published book completed September 15, 2003-September 15, 2004. Open to US residents only. Guidelines for SASE or on website. **Deadline: September 15.** Prize: $10,000.

KINGSLEY TUFTS POETRY AWARD

Claremont Graduate University, 160 E. 10th St., Harper B7, Claremont CA 91711-6165. (909)621-8974. Fax: (909)607-8438. Website: www.cgu.edu/tufts. **Contact:** Betty Terrell, awards coordinator. Estab. 1992. Offered annually "for a work by a poet, one who is past the very beginning but who has not yet reached the acknowledged pinnacle of his or her career." Guidelines for SASE or on website. **Deadline: September 15.** Prize: $100,000.

DANIEL VAROUJAN AWARD

New England Poetry Club, 16 Cornell St., #2, Arlington MA 02476-7710. **Contact:** Elizabeth Crowell. Offered annually for "an unpublished poem worthy of Daniel Varoujan, a poet killed by the Turks at the onset of the first genocide of this century which decimated three-fourths of the Armenian population." Send poems in duplicate. Open to any writer. **Deadline: June 30.** Guidelines for SASE. **Charges $10 for 3 entries in NEPC contests paying $3,000 in prizes.** Prize: $1,000.

CHAD WALSH POETRY PRIZE

Beloit Poetry Journal, P.O. Box 151, Farmington ME 04938. (207)778-0020. Website: www.bpj.org. **Contact:** Lee Sharkey and John Rosenwald, editors. Offered annually to honor the memory of poet Chad Walsh, a founder of the *Beloit Poetry Journal*. The editors select a strong poem or group of poems from the poems published in the journal that year. Prize: $3,000.

WAR POETRY CONTEST

Winning Writers, 39 Avenue A, Dept. 111, New York NY 10009. (866)946-9748. Fax: (212)280-0539. E-mail: warcontest@winningwriters.com. Website: www.winningwriters.com/annualcontest.htm. **Contact:** Adam Cohen. "This annual contest seeks outstanding, unpublished poetry on the theme of war. 1-3 poems should be submitted, up to a maximum total of 500 lines. English language. No translations, please." **Deadline: March 1-May 31.** Guidelines for SASE. **Charges $10.** Prize: 1st Prize: $1,000, and publication on WinningWriters.com; 2nd Prize: $500, and publication on WinningWriters.com; 3rd Prize: $250, and publication on WinningWriters.com; Honorable Mentions (10): $50. Judged by award-winning poet Jendi Reiter. Acquires nonexclusive right to publish submissions on WinningWriters.com. Open to any writer.

THE WASHINGTON PRIZE

The Word Works, Inc., P.O. Box 42164, Washington DC 20015. E-mail: editor@wordworksdc.com. Website: www.wordworksdc.com. **Contact:** Miles David Moore. Offered annually "for the best full-length poetry manuscript (48-64 pp.) submitted to The Word Works each year. The Washington Prize contest is the only forum in which we consider unsolicited manuscripts." Submissions accepted in the month of February. Acquires first publication rights. Open to any American writer. **Deadline: March 1 (postmarked).** Guidelines for SASE. **Charges $20 fee.** Prize: $1,500, and book publication; all entrants receive a copy of the winning book.

WERGLE FLOMP POETRY CONTEST

Winning Writers, 39 Avenue A, Dept. 111, New York NY 10009. (866)946-9748. Fax: (212)280-0539. E-mail: flompcontest@winningwriters.com. Website: www.winningwriters.com/contestflomp.htm. **Contact:** Adam Cohen. "This annual contest seeks the best parody poem that has been sent to a 'vanity poetry contest' as a joke. Vanity contests are characterized by low standards. Their main purpose is to entice poets to buy expensive products like anthologies, chapbooks, CDs, plaques, and silver bowls. Vanity contests will often praise remarkably bad poems in their effort to sell as much stuff to as many people as possible. The Wergle Flomp Prize will be awarded for the best bad poem. One poem of any length should be submitted, along with the name of the vanity contest that was spoofed. The poem should be in English. Inspired gibberish is also accepted. Online submission at WinningWriters.com is preferred." **Deadline: April 1.** Guidelines for SASE. Prize: $817.70, and publication on WinningWriters.com; 2nd Prize: $132, and publication on WinningWriters.com; 3rd prize: $57.95, and publication on WinningWriters.com. Honorable Mentions will also be published on WinningWriters.com. Judged by award-winning poet Jendi Reiter. Acquires nonexclusive right to publish submissions on WinningWriters.com and in e-mail newsletter. Open to any writer.

WHITE PINE PRESS POETRY PRIZE

White Pine Press, P.O. Box 236, Buffalo NY 14201. E-mail: wpine@whitepine.org. Website: www.whitepine.org. **Contact:** Elaine LaMattina, managing editor. Offered annually for previously published or unpublished poets. Manuscript: Up to 80 pages of original work; translations are not eligible. Poems may have appeared in magazines or limited-edition chapbooks. Open to any US citizen. **Deadline: November 30 (postmarked). Charges $20 fee.** Prize: $1,000, and publication. Judged by a poet of national reputation. All entries are screened by the editorial staff of White Pine Press.

Ⓝ THE WALT WHITMAN AWARD

The Academy of American Poets, 588 Broadway, Suite 604, New York NY 10012-3210. (212)274-0343. Fax: (212)274-9427. E-mail: rmurphy@poets.org. Website: www.poets.org. **Contact:** Awards Director. Offered annually to publish and support a poet's first book. Submissions must be in English by a single poet. Translations are not eligible. Contestants must be living citizens of the US and have neither published nor committed to publish a volume of poetry 40 pages or more in length in an edition of 500 or more copies. **Deadline: September**

15-November 15. Guidelines for SASE. **Charges $25 fee.** Prize: $5,000, a residency for 1 month at the Vermont Studio Center, and publication by Louisiana State University Press.

WICK POETRY CHAPBOOK SERIES 'OPEN' COMPETITION

Wick Poetry Program, Dept. of English, Kent State University, P.O. Box 5190, Kent OH 44242-0001. (330)672-2067. Fax: (330)672-2567. E-mail: wickpoet@kent.edu. Website: dept.kent.edu/wick. Offered annually for a chapbook of poems by a poet currently living in Ohio. **Deadline: October 31.** Guidelines for SASE. **Charges $5 fee.** Prize: Publication of the chapbook by the Kent State University Press.

WICK POETRY CHAPBOOK SERIES 'STUDENT' COMPETITION

Wick Poetry Program, Dept. of English, Kent State University, P.O. Box 5190, Kent OH 44242-0001. (330)672-2067. Fax: (330)672-2567. E-mail: wickpoet@kent.edu. Website: dept.kent.edu/wick. Offered annually for publication of a chapbook of poems by a poet currently enrolled in an Ohio college or university. **Deadline: October 31.** Guidelines for SASE. Prize: Publication of the chapbook by the Kent State University Press.

STAN AND TOM WICK POETRY PRIZE

Wick Poetry Program, Dept. of English, Kent State University, P.O. Box 5190, Kent OH 44242-0001. (330)672-2067. Fax: (330)672-2567. E-mail: wickpoet@kent.edu. Website: dept.kent.edu/wick. Open to anyone writing in English who has not previously published a full-length book of poems (a volume of 48 pages or more published in an edition of 500 or more copies). **Deadline: May 1.** Guidelines for SASE. **Charges $20 fee.** Prize: $2,000, and publication by the Kent State University Press.

THE RICHARD WILBUR AWARD

The University of Evansville Press, University of Evansville, Evansville IN 47722. **Contact:** The Editors. Offered in even-numbered years for an unpublished poetry collection. Guidelines for SASE and online at http://english.evansville.edu/english/WilburAwardGuidelines.htm. **Deadline: December 1, 2004. Charges $25 fee.** Prize: $1,000, and publication by the University of Evansville Press.

WILLIAM CARLOS WILLIAMS AWARD

Poetry Society of America, 15 Gramercy Park S., New York NY 10003. (212)254-9628. Fax: (212)673-2352. Website: www.poetrysociety.org. **Contact:** Brett Lauer, programs associate. Offered annually for a book of poetry published by a small press, nonprofit, or university press. Winning books are distributed to PSA members upon request and while supplies last. Books must be submitted directly by publishers. Entry forms are required. **Deadline: October 1-December 21. Charges $20 fee.** Prize: $500-1,000.

N ROBERT H. WINNER MEMORIAL AWARD

Poetry Society of America, 15 Gramercy Park S., New York NY 10003. (212)254-9628. Fax: (212)673-2352. E-mail: brett@poetrysociety.org. Website: www.poetrysociety.org. **Contact:** Brett Lauer, programs associate. Recognizing and rewarding the work of someone in midlife. Open to poets over 40, still unpublished or with 1 book. For guidelines send SASE or on website. **Deadline: December 22. Charges $15 fee for nonmembers; free to PSA members.** Prize: $2,500.

N THE J. HOWARD AND BARBARA M.J. WOOD PRIZE

Poetry, 1030 N. Clark St., Suite 420, Chicago IL 60610. (312)787-7070. E-mail: poetry@poetrymagazine.org. Website: www.poetrymagazine.org. Offered annually for poems published in *Poetry* during the preceding year (October-September). *Poetry* buys all rights to the poems published in the magazine. Copyrights are returned to the authors on request. Any writer may submit poems to *Poetry*. Guidelines for SASE. Prize: $5,000.

JAMES WRIGHT POETRY AWARD

Mid-American Review, Dept. of English, Bowling Green State University, Bowling Green OH 43403. (419)372-2725. Fax: (419)372-6805. Website: www.bgsu.edu/midamericanreview. **Contact:** Michelle Boisseau, poetry editor. Offered annually for unpublished poetry. Open to all writers not associated with *Mid-American Review* or judge. **Deadline: October 1.** Guidelines for SASE. **Charges $10.** Prize: $500, publication in Spring issue of *Mid-American Review*. Judged by editors and a well known writer, e.g., Kathy Fagan, Bob Hicok.

N THE WRITER MAGAZINE/EMILY DICKINSON AWARD

Poetry Society of America, 15 Gramercy Park S., New York NY 10003. (212)254-9628. Fax: (212)673-2352. E-mail: brett@poetrysociety.org. Website: www.poetrysociety.org. **Contact:** Brett Lauer, programs associate. Offered annually for a poem inspired by Emily Dickinson, though not necessarily in her style. For guidelines send SASE; also online. Guidelines subject to change. *Open to PSA members only*. **Deadline: December 22.** Prize: $250.

WRITERS' JOURNAL POETRY CONTEST

Val-Tech Media, P.O. Box 394, Perham MN 56573. (218)346-7921. Fax: (218)346-7924. E-mail: writersjournal@l akesplus.com. Website: www.writersjournal.com. **Contact:** Esther M. Leiper. Offered for previously unpublished poetry. Guidelines for SASE or online. **Deadline: April 30, August 30, December 30. Charges $3/each poem entered.** Prize: 1st Place: $50; 2nd Place: $25; 3rd Place: $15; 1st, 2nd, 3rd Place, and selected honorable mention winners will be published in *Writers' Journal* magazine.

PLAYWRITING & SCRIPTWRITING

⚑ ALBERTA PLAYWRITING COMPETITION

Alberta Playwrights' Network, 2633 Hochwald Ave. SW, Calgary AB T3E 7K2, Canada. (403)269-8564; (800)268-8564. Fax: (403)265-6773. E-mail: apn@nucleus.com. Website: www.nucleus.com/ ~ apn. Offered annually for unproduced plays with full-length and Discovery categories. Discovery is open only to previously unproduced playwrights. Open only to residents of Alberta. **Deadline: January 15. Charges $40 fee (Canadian).** Prize: Full length: $3,500 (Canadian); Discovery: $1,500 (Canadian); written critique, workshop of winning play, reading of winning plays at a Showcase Conference.

ANNUAL INTERNATIONAL ONE-PAGE PLAY COMPETITION

Lamia Ink!, P.O. Box 202, Prince Street Station, New York NY 10012. **Contact:** Cortland Jessup, founder/artistic director. Offered annually for previously published or unpublished 1-page plays. Acquires "the rights to publish in our magazine and to be read or performed at the prize awarding festival." Playwright retains copyright. **Deadline: March 15.** Guidelines for SASE. **Charges $2/play or $5/3 plays.** Prize: $200, staged reading, and publication of 12 finalists.

⚑ AUSTIN HEART OF FILM FESTIVAL FEATURE LENGTH SCREENPLAY COMPETITION

1604 Nueces, Austin TX 78701. (512)478-4795. Fax: (512)478-6205. E-mail: austinfilm@aol.com. Website: www.austinfilmfestival.com. Offered annually for unpublished screenplays. The Austin Film Festival is looking for quality screenplays which will be read by industry professionals. Two competitions: Adult/Family Category and Comedy Category. Guidelines for SASE or call (800)310-3378. The writer must hold the rights when submitted; it must be original work. The screenplay must be between 90 and 120 pages. It must be in standard screenplay format (industry standard). **Deadline: May 15. Charges $40 entry fee.** Prize: $5,000 in each category.

BAKER'S PLAYS HIGH SCHOOL PLAYWRITING CONTEST

Baker's Plays, P.O. Box 699222, Quincy MA 02269-9222. (617)745-0805. Fax: (617)745-9891. Website: www.ba kersplays.com. **Contact:** Deirdre Shaw, managing editor. Offered annually for unpublished work by high school-age students. Plays can be about any subject, so long as the play can be reasonably produced on the high school stage. Plays may be of any length. Submissions must be accompanied by the signature of the sponsoring high school drama or English teacher, and it is recommended that the play receive a production or a public reading prior to the submission. Multiple submissions and co-authored scripts are welcome. Teachers may not submit a student's work. The ms must be firmly bound, typed, and come with SASE that includes enough postage to cover the return of the ms. Plays that do not come with a SASE will not be returned. Do not send originals; copies only. **Deadline: January 31.** Guidelines for SASE. Prize: 1st Place: $500, and publication by Baker's Plays; 2nd Place: $250; 3rd Place: $100.

BAY AREA PLAYWRIGHTS FESTIVAL

Produced by The Playwrights Foundation, 131 10th St., 3rd Floor, San Francisco CA 94103. (415)626-0453, ext. 106. E-mail: literary@playwrightsfoundation.org. Website: www.playwrightsfoundation.org. **Contact:** Amy Mueller, artistic director; Christine Young, literary manager. Offered annually for unpublished plays by established and emerging theater writers nationally to support and encourage development of a new work. Unproduced full-length play only. Open to all writers. Guidelines for SASE and on website. **Deadline: January 16 (postmarked).** Prize: Small stipend and in-depth development process with dramaturg and director, and a professionally staged reading in San Francisco.

BIG BREAK INTERNATIONAL SCREENWRITING COMPETITION

Final Draft, Inc., 26707 W. Aguora Rd., Suite 205, Calabasas CA 91302. (800)231-4055. Fax: (818)995-4422. E-mail: bigbreak@finaldraft.com. Website: www.finaldraft.com/bigbreak. **Deadline: March 15.** Guidelines for

SASE. **Charges $50.** Prize: 1st Prize: $10,000; 2nd Prize: $3,000; 3rd Prize: $1,000. Judged by industry professionals. Open to any writer.

ⓝ BUNTVILLE CREW'S AWARD BLUE

Buntville Crew, 118 N. Railroad Ave., Buckley IL 60918-0445. E-mail: buntville@yahoo.fr. **Contact:** Steven Packard, artistic director. Presented annually for the best unpublished/unproduced play script, under 15 pages, written by a student enrolled in any Illinois high school in the 2004-2005 school year. Submit 1 copy of the script in standard play format, a brief biography, and a SASE (scripts will not be returned). Include name, address, telephone number, age, and name of school. **Deadline: May 31.** Guidelines for SASE. Prize: Cash prize, and possible productions in Buckley and/or New York City. Judged by panel selected by the theater.

ⓝ BUNTVILLE CREW'S DAS GOLDKIEL

Buntville Crew, 118 N. Railroad Ave., Buckley IL 60918-0445. E-mail: buntvill@yahoo.fr. **Contact:** Steven Packard, artistic director. Annual award for best unpublished/unproduced full-length play script. Plays may be in English, French, German, or Spanish (no translations, no adaptations). Submit 1 copy of the script in standard play format, a résumé, and a SASE (scripts will not be returned). Include name, address, and telephone number. **Deadline: May 31.** Guidelines for SASE. **Charges $8.** Prize: $250; possible production in Buckley and/or New York City. Judged by panel selected by the theater. Open to any writer.

ⓝ BUNTVILLE CREW'S PRIX HORS PAIR

Buntville Crew, 118 N. Railroad Ave., Buckley IL 60918-0445. E-mail: buntville@yahoo.fr. **Contact:** Steven Packard, artistic director. Annual award for unpublished/unproduced play script under 15 pages. Plays may be in English, French, German, or Spanish (no translations, no adaptations). Submit 1 copy of the script in standard play format, a résumé, and a SASE (scripts will not be returned). Include name, address, and telephone number. **Deadline: May 31.** Guidelines for SASE. **Charges $8.** Prize: $200; possible production in Buckley and/or New York City. Judged by panel selected by the theater. Open to any writer.

ⓒ CAA CAROL BOLT AWARD FOR DRAMA

Canadian Authors Association with the support of the Playwrights Union of Canada and Playwrights Canada Press, 320 S. Shores Rd., P.O. Box 419, Campbellford ON K0L 1L0, Canada. (705)653-0323. Fax: (705)653-0593. E-mail: admin@canauthors.org. Website: www.canauthors.org. **Contact:** Alec McEachern. Annual contest for the best English-language play for adults by an author who is Canadian or landed immigrant. Submissions should be previously published or performed in the year prior to the giving of the award. For instance, in 2004 for this year's award to be given in July 2005. Open to Canadian citizens or landed immigrants. **Deadline: December 15, except for plays published or performed in December, in which case the deadline is January 15.** Guidelines for SASE. **Charges $35 (Canadian funds) fee.** Prize: $1,000, and a silver medal. Judged by a trustee for the award (appointed by the CAA). The trustee appoints up to 3 judges. The identities of the trustee and judges are confidential. Short lists are not made public. Decisions of the trustee and judges are final, and they may choose not to award a prize.

CALIFORNIA YOUNG PLAYWRIGHTS CONTEST

Playwrights Project, 450 B St., Suite 1020, San Diego CA 92101-8093. (619)239-8222. Fax: (619)239-8225. E-mail: write@playwrightsproject.com. Website: www.playwrightsproject.com. **Contact:** Cecelia Kouma, managing director. Offered annually for previously unpublished plays by young writers to stimulate young people to create dramatic works, and to nurture promising writers. Scripts must be a minimum of 10 standard typewritten pages; send 2 copies. Scripts will *not* be returned. All entrants receive detailed evaluation letter. Writers must be California residents under age 19 as of the deadline date. **Deadline: June 1.** Guidelines for SASE. Prize: Professional production of 3-5 winning plays at the Old Globe in San Diego, plus royalty.

COE COLLEGE PLAYWRITING FESTIVAL

Coe College, 1220 First Ave. NE, Cedar Rapids IA 52402-5092. (319)399-8624. Fax: (319)399-8557. E-mail: swolvert@coe.edu. Website: www.public.coe.edu/departments/theatre/. **Contact:** Susan Wolverton. Estab. 1993. Offered biennially for unpublished work to provide a venue for new works for the stage. "There is usually a theme for the festival. We are interested in full-length productions, not one acts or musicals. There are no specific criteria although a current résumé and synopsis is requested." Open to any writer. **Deadline: November 1. Notification: January 15.** Guidelines for SASE. Prize: $325, plus 1-week residency as guest artist with airfare, room and board provided.

THE CUNNINGHAM COMMISSION FOR YOUTH THEATRE

The Theatre School, DePaul University, 2135 N. Kenmore, Chicago IL 60614. (773)325-7938. Fax: (773)325-7920. E-mail: lgoetsch@depaul.edu. Website: theatreschool.depaul.edu/programs/prize.htm. **Contact:** Lara

Goetsch. Chicago-area playwrights only. Commission will result in a play for younger audiences that "affirms the centrality of religion, broadly defined, and the human quest for meaning, truth, and community." **Deadline: December 1.** Guidelines for SASE. Prize: $5,000 ($2,000 when commission is contracted, $1,000 if script moves to workshop, $2,000 as royalty if script is produced by The Theatre School).

N DAYTON PLAYHOUSE FUTUREFEST

The Dayton Playhouse, 1301 E. Siebenthaler Ave., Dayton OH 45414-5357. (937)333-7469. Fax: (937)333-2827. Website: www.daytonplayhouse.com. **Contact:** Dave Seyer, executive director. "Three plays selected for full productions, 3 for readings at July FutureFest weekend; the 6 authors will be given travel and lodging to attend the festival." Professionally adjudicated. Guidelines for SASE or online. **Deadline: October 30.** Prize: $1,000; and $100 to the other 5 playwrights.

DRURY UNIVERSITY ONE-ACT PLAY CONTEST

Drury University, 900 N. Benton Ave., Springfield MO 65802-3344. E-mail: msokol@drury.edu. **Contact:** Mick Sokol. Offered in even-numbered years for unpublished and professionally unproduced plays. One play/playwright. Guidelines for SASE or by e-mail. **Deadline: December 1.**

DUBUQUE FINE ARTS PLAYERS ANNUAL ONE-ACT PLAY CONTEST

Dubuque Fine Arts Players, 1686 Lawndale, Dubuque IA 52001. E-mail: gary.arms@clarke.edu. **Contact:** Gary Arms. "We select 3 one-act plays each year. We award cash prizes of up to $600 for a winning entry. We produce the winning plays in August." Offered annually for unpublished work. Guidelines and application form for SASE. **Deadline: January 31. Charges $10.** Prize: 1st Prize: $600; 2nd Prize: $300; 3rd Prize: $200. Judged by 3 groups who read all the plays; each play is read at least twice. Plays that score high enough, enter the second round. The top 10 plays are read by a panel consisting of 3 directors and 2 other final judges. Open to any writer.

EMERGING PLAYWRIGHT'S AWARD

Urban Stages, 17 E. 47th St., New York NY 10017-1920. (212)421-1380. Fax: (212)421-1387. E-mail: tlreilly@urbanstages.org. Website: www.urbanstages.org. **Contact:** T.L. Reilly, producing director. Estab. 1986. Submissions required to be unproduced in New York City. Send script, letter of introduction, production history, author's name, résumé, and SASE. Submissions accepted year-round. Plays selected in August and January for award consideration. One submission/person. **Deadline: Ongoing. Charges $5.** Prize: $1,000 (in lieu of royalties), and a staged production of winning play in New York City. Open to US residents only.

ESSENTIAL THEATRE PLAYWRITING AWARD

The Essential Theatre, P.O. Box 8172, Atlanta GA 30306. (404)212-0815. E-mail: pmhardy@aol.com. **Contact:** Peter Hardy. Offered annually for unproduced, full-length plays by Georgia writers. No limitations as to style or subject matter. **Deadline: April 15.** Prize: $400, and full production.

SHUBERT FENDRICH MEMORIAL PLAYWRITING CONTEST

Pioneer Drama Service, Inc., P.O. Box 4267, Englewood CO 80155. (303)779-4035. Fax: (303)779-4315. E-mail: playwrights@pioneerdrama.com. Website: www.pioneerdrama.com. **Contact:** Lori Conary, assistant editor. Offered annually for unpublished, but previously produced, submissions to encourage the development of quality theatrical material for educational and community theater. Rights acquired only if published. Authors already published by Pioneer Drama are not eligible. **Deadline: March 1 (postmarked).** Guidelines for SASE. Prize: $1,000 royalty advance, publication.

FIREHOUSE THEATRE PROJECT NEW PLAY COMPETITION

The Firehouse Theatre Project, 1609 W. Broad St., Richmond VA 23220. (804)355-2001. E-mail: harry@firehousetheatre.org. Website: www.firehousetheatre.org. **Contact:** Literary Manager FTP. "This annual award is intended to encourage American playwrights to continue to produce new scripts for the theater; thereby maintaining a fertile base for American voices in the dramatic literature of current times and the years to come. The scripts must be full-length theatrical scripts in English on any topic. All scripts must be submitted by an agent or accompanied by a professional letter of recommendation from a director, literary manager, or dramaturg. Translations, adaptations, musicals, one-acts, film and television screenplays are ineligible and will not be considered." Open to US residents only. Submissions must be unpublished. Visit website for complete submission guidelines. **Deadline: June 1.** Prize: 1st Prize: $1,000 with a production or a fully produced staged reading at the 2005 FTP Festival of New American Plays (January 2005); 2nd Prize: $500 with a staged reading at the 2005 FTP Festival; 3rd Prize: $250 with a possible staged reading at the 2005 FTP Festival. Judged by a committee selected by the executive board of the Firehouse Theatre Project. Acquires the right to produce the winning scripts for the 2005 FTP Festival of New American Plays. Following the Festival production dates, all rights are relinquished to the author.

FULL-LENGTH PLAY COMPETITION

West Coast Ensemble, P.O. Box 38728, Los Angeles CA 90038. (323)876-9337. Fax: (323)876-8916. Website: www.wcensemble.org. **Contact:** Les Hanson, artistic director. Offered annually "to nurture, support, and encourage" unpublished playwrights. Permission to present the play is granted if work is selected as finalist. **Deadline: December 31.** Guidelines for SASE. Prize: $500, and presentation of play.

[N] JOHN GASSNER MEMORIAL PLAYWRITING COMPETITION

New England Theatre Conference, PMB 502, 198 Tremont St., Boston MA 02116. E-mail: mail@netconline.org. Website: www.netconline.org. Offered annually to unpublished full-length plays and scripts. Open to New England residents and NETC members. Playwrights living outside New England may participate by joining NETC. **Deadline: April 15.** Guidelines for SASE. **Charges $10 fee.** Prize: 1st Place: $1,000; 2nd Place: $500.

[N] GOVERNOR GENERAL'S LITERARY AWARD FOR DRAMA

Canada Council for the Arts, 350 Albert St., P.O. Box 1047, Ottawa ON K1P 5V8, Canada. (613)566-4414, ext. 5576. Fax: (613)566-4410. E-mail: joanne.larocque-poirier@canadacouncil.ca. Website: www.canadacouncil .ca/prizes/ggla. **Contact:** Joanne Larocque-Poirier. Offered for the best English-language and the best French-language work of drama by a Canadian published September 1, 2004-September 30, 2005. Publishers submit titles for consideration. **Deadline: March 15 or August 7, 2005, depending on the book's publication date.** Prize: Each laureate receives $15,000, and nonwinning finalists receive $1,000.

[N] AURAND HARRIS MEMORIAL PLAYWRITING AWARD

The New England Theatre Conference, Inc., PMB 502, 198 Tremont St., Boston MA 02116-4750. (617)851-8535. E-mail: mail@netconline.org. Website: www.netconline.org. Offered annually for an unpublished full-length play for young audiences. Guidelines for SASE. "No phone calls, please." Open to New England residents and/ or members of the New England Theatre Conference. **Deadline: May 1.** Guidelines for SASE. **Charges $20 fee.** Prize: 1st Place: $1,000; 2nd Place: $500. Open to any writer.

HENRICO THEATRE COMPANY ONE-ACT PLAYWRITING COMPETITION

Henrico Recreation & Parks, P.O. Box 27032, Richmond VA 23273. (804)501-5138. Fax: (804)501-5284. E-mail: per22@co.henrico.va.us. Website: www.co.henrico.va.us/rec. **Contact:** Amy A. Perdue. Offered annually for previously unpublished or unproduced plays or musicals to produce new dramatic works in one-act form. "Scripts with small casts and simpler sets given preference. Controversial themes and excessive language should be avoided." **Deadline: July 1.** Guidelines for SASE. Prize: $300; Runner-Up: $200. Winning entries may be produced; videotape sent to author.

HOLLYWOOD SCREENPLAY AWARDS

433 N. Camden Dr., #600, Beverly Hills CA 90210. (310)288-1882. Fax: (310)475-0193. E-mail: hollyinfo@holly woodnetwork.com. Website: www.hollywoodawards.com. **Contact:** Carlos de Abreu. Annual contest "to discover new screenplay writers." Judged by reputable industry professionals (producers, development executives, story analysts). Open to any writer. **Deadline: November 30.** Guidelines for SASE. **Charges $55 fee.** Prize: Cash prizes, plus professional development guidance, and access to agents, producers, and studios.

JEWEL BOX THEATRE PLAYWRIGHTING COMPETITION

Jewel Box Theatre, 3700 N. Walker, Oklahoma City OK 73118-7099. (405)521-1786. **Contact:** Charles Tweed, production director. Estab. 1982. Offered annually for full-length plays. Send SASE in October for guidelines. **Deadline: January 15.** Prize: $500.

[N] THE KAUFMAN & HART PRIZE FOR NEW AMERICAN COMEDY

Arkansas Repertory Theatre, P.O. Box 110, Little Rock AR 72203-0110. (501)378-0445. Website: www.therep.o rg. **Contact:** Brad Mooy, literary manager. Offered every 2 years for unpublished, unproduced, full-length comedies (no musicals or children's plays). Scripts may be submitted with the recommendation of an agent or theater professional only. Must be at least 65 pages, with minimal set requirements and a cast limit of 12. One entry/playwright. Open to US citizens only. **Deadline: February 1. Notification April.** Prize: $10,000, a staged reading, and transportation.

MARC A. KLEIN PLAYWRITING AWARD FOR STUDENTS

Dept. of Theater and Dance, Case Western Reserve University, 10900 Euclid Ave., Cleveland OH 44106-7077. (216)368-4868. Fax: (216)368-5184. E-mail: ksg@case.edu. Website: www.cwru.edu/artsci/thtr. **Contact:** Ron

Wilson, reading committee chair. Estab. 1975. Offered annually for an unpublished, professionally unproduced full-length play, by a student at an American college or university. **Deadline: December 1.** Prize: $1,000, which includes $500 to cover residency expenses; production.

KUMU KAHUA/UHM THEATRE DEPARTMENT PLAYWRITING CONTEST

Kumu Kahua Theatre, Inc./University of Hawaii at Manoa, Dept. of Theatre and Dance, 46 Merchant St., Honolulu HI 96813. (808)536-4222. Fax: (808)536-4226. E-mail: kkt@pixi.com. Website: www.kumukahua.c om. **Contact:** Harry Wong III, artistic director. Offered annually for unpublished work to honor full-length and short plays. Guidelines available every September. First 2 categories open to residents and nonresidents. For Hawaii Prize, plays must be set in Hawaii or deal with some aspect of the Hawaiian experience. For Pacific Rim prize, plays must deal with the Pacific Islands, Pacific Rim, or Pacific/Asian-American experience—short plays only considered in 3rd category. **Deadline: January 2.** Prize: $500 (Hawaii Prize); $400 (Pacific Rim); $200 (Resident).

L.A. DESIGNERS' THEATRE-COMMISSIONS

L.A. Designers' Theatre, P.O. Box 1883, Studio City CA 91614-0883. (323)650-9600 or (323)654-2700 T.D.D. Fax: (323)654-3210. E-mail: ladesigners@juno.com. **Contact:** Richard Niederberg, artistic director. Quarterly contest "to promote new work and push it onto the conveyor belt to filmed or videotaped entertainment." All submissions must be registered with copyright office and be unpublished. Material will not be returned. "Do not submit anything that will not fit in a #10 envelope. No rules, guidelines, fees, or entry forms. Just present an idea that can be commissioned into a full work." Proposals for uncompleted works are encouraged. Unpopular political, religious, social, or other themes are encouraged; 'street' language and nudity are acceptable. Open to any writer. **Deadline: March 15, June 15, September 15, December 15.** Prize: Production or publication of the work in the Los Angeles market. "We only want 'first refusal.'"

LOVE CREEK ANNUAL SHORT PLAY FESTIVAL

Love Creek Productions, c/o Granville, 162 Nesbit St., Weehawken NJ 07086-6817. E-mail: creekread@aol.com. **Contact:** Cynthia Granville-Callahan, festival manager. Estab. 1985. *E-mail address is for information only.* Annual festival for unpublished plays, unproduced in New York in the previous year, under 40 minutes, at least 2 characters, larger casts preferred. "We established the Festival as a playwriting competition in which scripts are judged on their merits in performance." All entries must specify "festival" on envelope and must include letter giving permission to produce script, if chosen, and stating whether equity showcase is acceptable. "We are giving strong preference to scripts featuring females in major roles in casts which are predominantly female." **Deadline: Ongoing.** Guidelines for SASE. Prize: Cash prize awarded to overall winner.

LOVE CREEK MINI FESTIVALS

Love Creek Productions, c/o Granville, 162 Nesbit St., Weehawken NJ 07086-6817. E-mail: creekread@aol.com. **Contact:** Cynthia Granville-Callahan, festival literary manager. *E-mail address is for information only.* "The Mini Festivals are an outgrowth of our annual Short Play Festival in which we produce scripts concerning a particular issue or theme which our artistic staff selects according to current needs, interests, and concerns of our members, audiences, and playwrights submitting to our Short Play Festival throughout the year." Considers scripts unpublished, unproduced in New York City in the past year, under 40 minutes, at least 2 characters, larger casts preferred. Submissions must list name of festival on envelope and must include letter giving permission to produce script, if chosen, and stating whether equity showcase is acceptable. Finalists receive a mini-showcase production in New York City. Write for upcoming themes. "We are giving strong preference to scripts featuring females in major roles in casts which are predominantly female." **Deadline: Ongoing.** Guidelines for SASE. Prize: Winner of overall festival series receives a cash prize.

MAXIM MAZUMDAR NEW PLAY COMPETITION

Alleyway Theatre, One Curtain Up Alley, Buffalo NY 14202-1911. (716)852-2600. Fax: (716)852-2266. E-mail: email@alleyway.com. Website: alleyway.com. **Contact:** Literary Manager. Estab. 1990. Annual competition. Full Length: Not less than 90 minutes, no more than 10 performers. One-Act: Less than 20 minutes, no more than 6 performers. Children's plays. Musicals must be accompanied by audio tape. Finalists announced October 1. "Playwrights may submit work directly. There is no entry form. Annual playwright's **fee $5;** may submit 1 in each category, but pay only 1 fee. Please specify if submission is to be included in competition. Alleyway Theatre must receive first production credit in subsequent printings and productions." **Deadline: July 1.** Prize: Full length: $400, production, and royalties; One-act: $100, production, plus royalties.

Ⓝ MCKNIGHT ADVANCEMENT GRANT

The Playwrights' Center, 2301 Franklin Ave. E., Minneapolis MN 55406-1099. (612)332-7481, ext. 10. Fax: (612)332-6037. E-mail: info@pwcenter.org. Website: www.pwcenter.org. **Contact:** Kristen Gandrow, director of new play development. Offered annually for either published or unpublished playwrights to recognize those whose work demonstrates exceptional artistic merit and potential and whose primary residence is in the state of Minnesota. The grants are intended to significantly advance recipients' art and careers, and can be used to support a wide variety of expenses. Applications available December 1. Guidelines for SASE. Additional funds of up to $1,500 are available for workshops and readings. The Playwrights' Center evaluates each application and forwards finalists to a panel of 3 judges from the national theater community. Applicant must have been a citizen or permanent resident of the US and a legal resident of the state of Minnesota since July 1, 2004. (Residency must be maintained during fellowship year.) Applicant must have had a minimum of 1 work fully produced by a professional theater at the time of application. **Deadline: February 4.** Prize: $25,000 which can be used to support a wide variety of expenses, including writing time, artistic costs of residency at a theater or arts organization, travel and study, production, or presentation.

N MCLAREN MEMORIAL COMEDY PLAY WRITING COMPETITION

Midland Community Theatre, 2000 W. Wadley, Midland TX 79705. (432)682-2544. Fax: (432)682-6136. Website: www.mctmidland.org. **Contact:** Alathea Blischke, McLaren co-chair. Estab. 1990. Offered annually in 2 divisions: one-act and full-length. All entries must be comedies for adults, teens, or children; musical comedies accepted. Work must have never been professionally produced or published. See website for competition guidelines and required entry form. **Charges $10 fee/script.** Prize: $400 for winning full-length play; $200 for winning one-act play; staged readings for finalists in each category.

MOVING ARTS PREMIERE ONE-ACT COMPETITION

Moving Arts, 514 S. Spring St., Los Angeles CA 90013-2304. (213)622-8906. Fax: (213)622-8946. E-mail: treynichols@movingarts.org. Website: www.movingarts.org. **Contact:** Trey Nichols, literary director. Offered annually for unproduced one-act plays in the Los Angeles area and "is designed to foster the continued development of one-act plays." All playwrights are eligible except Moving Arts resident artists. Guidelines for SASE or by e-mail. **Deadline: February 28 (postmarked). Charges $10 fee/script.** Prize: 1st Place: $200, plus a full production with a 4-8 week run; 2nd and 3rd Place: Program mention and possible production.

N MOXIE FILMS/NEW CENTURY (PLAYWRITING)

New Century Writer, 107 Suffolk St., Studio #517, New York NY 10002. (212)982-5008. Fax: (212)353-9070. E-mail: drew@moxie-films.com. Website: www.moxie-films.com. Offered annually to discover and encourage emerging writers of stage plays and musicals. All genres. Winners announced on website in December. Guidelines/entry form on website. Open to all playwrights, both nonproduced and those with a limited production history. Call if in doubt about your eligibility. **Deadline: August 31. Charges $35-40 entry fee.** Prize: 1st Place: $2,000; 2nd Place: $500; 3rd Place: $250; 4th-10th Place: $100.

N MOXIE FILMS/NEW CENTURY (SCREENWRITING)

107 Suffolk St., Studio #517, New York NY 10002. (212)982-5008. Fax: (212)353-9070. E-mail: drew@moxie-films.com. Website: www.moxie-films.com. Offered annually to discover and encourage emerging writers of screenplays, stage plays, TV scripts, TV movie scripts, and musicals. All genres. Winners announced on website in December. Guidelines/entry form available on website. Open to all writers, both nonproduced and those with limited production history. Call if in doubt about your eligibility. **Deadline: August 31. Charges $35-40 entry fee.** Prize: 1st Place: $3,000; 2nd Place: $1,000; 3rd Place: $500; 4th-10th Place: $200.

MUSICAL STAIRS

West Coast Ensemble, P.O. Box 38728, Los Angeles CA 90038. (323)876-9337. Fax: (323)876-8916. **Contact:** Les Hanson. Offered annually for unpublished writers "to nurture, support, and encourage musical creators." Permission to present the musical is granted if work is selected as finalist. **Deadline: June 30.** Prize: $500, and presentation of musical.

NANTUCKET SHORT PLAY COMPETITION AND FESTIVAL

Nantucket Theatrical Productions, Box 2177, Nantucket MA 02584. (508)228-5002. **Contact:** Jim Patrick, artistic director. Offered annually for unpublished plays to "seek the highest quality of playwriting distilled into a short-play format." Selected plays receive staged readings. Plays must be less than 40 pages. **Deadline: January 1. Charges $10 fee.** Prize: $200, plus staged readings.

NATIONAL AUDIO DRAMA SCRIPT COMPETITION

National Audio Theatre Festivals, 115 Dikeman St., Hempstead NY 11150. (516)483-8321. Fax: (516)538-7583. Website: www.natf.org. **Contact:** Sue Zizza. Offered annually for unpublished radio scripts. "NATF is particularly interested in stories that deserve to be told because they enlighten, intrigue, or simply make us laugh out loud. Contemporary scripts with strong female roles, multi-cultural casting, and diverse viewpoints will be favorably received." Preferred length is 25 minutes. Guidelines on website. Open to any writer. NATF will have the right to produce the scripts for the NATF Live Performance Workshop; however, NATF makes no commitment to produce any script. The authors will retain all other rights to their work. **Deadline: November 15. Charges $25 fee (US currency only).** Prize: $800 split between 2-4 authors, and free workshop production participation.

NATIONAL CANADIAN ONE-ACT PLAYWRITING COMPETITION

Ottawa Little Theatre, 400 King Edward Ave., Ottawa ON K1N 7M7, Canada. (613)233-8948. Fax: (613)233-8027. E-mail: olt@on-aibn.com. Website: www.o-l-t.com. **Contact:** Elizabeth Holden, office manager. Estab. 1913. Purpose is "to encourage literary and dramatic talent in Canada." Guidelines for #10 SASE with Canadian postage or #10 SAE with 1 IRC. **Deadline: August 31.** Prize: 1st Place: $1,000; 2nd Place: $700; 3rd Place: $500.

NATIONAL CHILDREN'S THEATRE FESTIVAL

Actors' Playhouse at the Miracle Theatre, 280 Miracle Mile, Coral Gables FL 33134. (305)444-9293. Fax: (305)444-4181. Website: www.actorsplayhouse.org. **Contact:** Earl Maulding. Offered annually for unpublished musicals for young audiences. Target age is between 3-12. Script length should be 45-60 minutes. Maximum of 8 actors to play any number of roles. Settings which lend themselves to simplified scenery. Bilingual (English/Spanish) scripts are welcomed. Call or visit website for guidelines. Open to any writer. **Deadline: June 1. Charges $10 fee.** Prize: 1st Place: $500, and full production.

NATIONAL LATINO PLAYWRITING AWARD

(formerly National Latino Playwrights Award), Arizona Theatre Co. in affiliation with Centro Cultural Mexicano, 40 E. 14th St., Tucson AZ 85701. (520)884-8210, ext. 5510. Fax: (520)628-9129. E-mail: eromero@arizonatheatre.org. Website: www.arizonatheatre.org. **Contact:** Elaine Romero, playwright-in-residence. Offered annually for unproduced (professionally), unpublished plays over 50 pages in length. "The plays may be in English, bilingual, or in Spanish (with English translation). The award recognizes exceptional full-length plays by Latino playwrights on any subject." Open to Latino playwrights currently residing in the US, its territories, and/or Mexico. **Deadline: December 30.** Guidelines for SASE. Prize: $1,000.

NATIONAL ONE-ACT PLAYWRITING COMPETITION

Little Theatre of Alexandria, 600 Wolfe St., Alexandria VA 22314. Website: www.thelittletheatre.com/oneact. Estab. 1978. Offered annually to encourage original writing for theater. Submissions must be original, unpublished, unproduced, one-act stage plays. "We usually produce top 2 or 3 winners." Guidelines for SASE or on website. **Deadline: Submit scripts for contest from January 1-May 31. Charges $20/play; 2-play limit.** Prize: 1st Place: $350; 2nd Place: $250; 3rd Place: $150.

NATIONAL TEN-MINUTE PLAY CONTEST

Actors Theatre of Louisville, 316 W. Main St., Louisville KY 40202-4218. (502)584-1265. E-mail: tpalmer@actorstheatre.org. Website: www.actorstheatre.org. **Contact:** Tanya Palmer, literary manager. Offered annually for previously (professionally) unproduced 10-minute plays (10 pages or less). "Entries must *not* have had an Equity or Equity-waiver production." One submission/playwright. Scripts are not returned. Please write or call for submission guidelines. Open to US residents. **Deadline: December 1 (postmarked).** Prize: $1,000.

NEW AMERICAN COMEDY WORKSHOP

Ukiah Players Theatre, 1041 Low Gap Rd., Ukiah CA 95482. (707)462-1210. Fax: (707)462-1790. E-mail: players@pacific.net. Website: ukiahplayerstheatre.org. **Contact:** Kate Magruder, executive director. Offered every 2 years to playwrights seeking to develop their unproduced, full-length comedies into funnier, stronger scripts. Two scripts will be chosen for staged readings; 1 of these may be chosen for full production. Guidelines for SASE or online. **Deadline: November 30 of odd-numbered years.** Prize: Playwrights chosen for readings will receive a $25 royalty/performance. The playwright chosen for full production will receive a $50 royalty/performance, travel (up to $500) to Ukiah for development workshop/rehearsal, lodging, and per diem.

NEW WORKS FOR THE STAGE

COE College Theatre Arts Department, 1220 First Ave. NE, Cedar Rapids IA 52402. (319)399-8624. Fax: (319)399-8557. E-mail: swolvert@coe.edu. Website: www.public.coe.edu/departments/theatre. **Contact:** Susan Wolverton. Offered every 2 years (odd years) "to encourage new work, to provide an interdisciplinary forum for the discussion of issues found in new work, to offer playwright contact with theater professionals who can provide response to new work." Full-length, original unpublished and unproduced scripts only. No musicals, adaptations, translations, or collaborations. Submit 1-page synopsis, résumé, and SASE if the script is to be returned. **Deadline: November 1, 2004.** Prize: $325, plus travel, room and board for residency at the college.

'THE NEXT STAGE' NEW PLAY READING FESTIVAL
The Cleveland Play House, 8500 Euclid Ave., Cleveland OH 44106-0189. Fax: (216)795-7005. E-mail: sgordon@c levelandplayhouse.com. Website: www.clevelandplayhouse.com. **Contact:** Seth Gordon, director of new play development. Offered annually for unpublished/unproduced submissions. "'The Next Stage' is our annual new play reading series. Up to 6 writers are brought to our theater for 1 week of rehearsal/development. The plays are then given public staged readings, and at least 1 is chosen for a full production in the upcoming season." **Deadline: Ongoing.** Guidelines for SASE. Prize: Staged reading of play, fee, travel, and housing, consideration for full production. Writers sign a 3-month option for production of script.

DON AND GEE NICHOLL FELLOWSHIPS IN SCREENWRITING
Academy of Motion Picture Arts & Sciences, 1313 N. Vine St., Los Angeles CA 90028. (310)247-3059. E-mail: nicholl@oscars.org. Website: www.oscars.org/nicholl. **Contact:** Greg Beal, program coordinator. Estab. 1985. Offered annually for unproduced screenplays to identify talented new screenwriters. Applications available mid-January-April 30. Recipients announced late October. Open to writers who have not earned more than $5,000 writing for films or TV. **Deadline: May 1. Charges $30 fee.** Prize: $30,000 in fellowships (up to 5/year).

OGLEBAY INSTITUTE TOWNGATE THEATRE PLAYWRITING CONTEST
Oglebay Institute, Stifel Fine Arts Center, 1330 National Rd., Wheeling WV 26003. (304)242-7700. Fax: (304)242-7747. Website: www.oionline.com. **Contact:** Kate H. Crosbie, director of performing arts. Estab. 1976. Offered annually for unpublished works. "All full-length nonmusical plays that have never been professionally produced or published are eligible." Open to any writer. **Deadline: January 1; winner announced May 31.** Guidelines for SASE. Prize: Run of play and cash award.

ONE ACT MARATHON
Attic Theatre & Film Center, 5429 W. Washington Blvd., Los Angeles CA 90016. (323)525-0600. E-mail: attictheat re1@aol.com. Website: www.attictheatre.org. **Contact:** Literary Manager. Offered annually for unpublished and unproduced work. Guidelines for SASE or online. **Deadline: October 30. Charges $15.** Prize: 1st Place: $250; 2nd Place: $100; 1st-3rd Place scripts will be produced. Acquires 6-month window for 1st-6th Place entries for exclusive option.

MILDRED & ALBERT PANOWSKI PLAYWRITING AWARD
Forest Roberts Theatre, Northern Michigan University, Marquette MI 49855-5364. (906)227-2559. Fax: (906)227-2567. Website: www.nmu.edu/theatre. **Contact:** Megan Marcellini, award coordinator. Estab. 1977. Offered annually for unpublished, unproduced, full-length plays. Guidelines and application for SASE. **Deadline: August 15-November 15 (due at office on the 15th).** Prize: $2,000, a fully-mounted production, and transportation to Marquette to serve as Artist-in-Residence the week of the show.

PERISHABLE THEATRE'S WOMEN'S PLAYWRITING FESTIVAL
P.O. Box 23132, Providence RI 02903. (401)331-2695. Fax: (401)331-7811. E-mail: info@perishable.org. Website: www.perishable.org. **Contact:** Rebecca Wolf, festival coordinator. Offered annually for unproduced, one-act plays (up to 30 minutes in length when fully produced) to encourage women playwrights. Judged by reading committee, the festival director, and the artistic director of the theater. Open to women playwrights exclusively. **Deadline: October 15 (postmarked).** Guidelines for SASE. **Charges $5 fee/playwright (limit 2 plays/playwright).** Prize: $500, and travel to Providence.

PETERSON EMERGING PLAYWRIGHT COMPETITION
Catawba College Theatre Arts Department, 2300 W. Innes St., Salisbury NC 28144. (704)637-4440. Fax: (704)637-4207. E-mail: lfkesler@catawba.edu. Website: www.catawba.edu. **Contact:** Linda Kesler, theatre arts department staff. Offered annually for full-length unpublished work "to assist emerging playwrights in the development of new scripts, hopefully leading to professional production. Competition is open to all subject matter except children's plays. Playwrights may submit more than 1 entry." Open to any writer. Guidelines for SASE or by e-mail. **Deadline: December 1.** Prize: Production of the winning play at Catawba College; $2,000 cash award; transportation to and from Catawba College for workshop and performance; lodging and food while in residence; professional response to the performance of the play.

ROBERT J. PICKERING AWARD FOR PLAYWRIGHTING EXCELLENCE

Coldwater Community Theater, c/o 89 Division, Coldwater MI 49036. (517)279-7963. Fax: (517)279-8095. **Contact:** J. Richard Colbeck, committee chairperson. Estab. 1982. Previously unproduced monetarily. "To encourage playwrights to submit their work, to present a previously unproduced play in full production." Submit script with SASE. "We reserve the right to produce winning script." **Deadline: December 31.** Guidelines for SASE. Prize: 1st Place: $300; 2nd Place: $100; 3rd Place: $50.

PILGRIM PROJECT GRANTS

156 Fifth, #400, New York NY 10010. (212)627-2288. Fax: (212)627-2184. E-mail: davida@firstthings.com. **Contact:** Davida Goldman. Grants for a reading, workshop production, or full production of plays that deal with questions of moral significance. **Deadline: Ongoing.** Guidelines for SASE. Prize: Grants of $1,000-7,000.

PLAYHOUSE ON THE SQUARE NEW PLAY COMPETITION

Playhouse on the Square, 51 S. Cooper, Memphis TN 38104. **Contact:** Jackie Nichols. Submissions required to be unproduced. **Deadline: April 1.** Guidelines for SASE. Prize: $500, and production.

PLAYWRIGHT DISCOVERY AWARD

VSA Arts, 1300 Connecticut Ave. NW, Suite 700, Washington DC 20036. (202)628-2800. Fax: (202)737-0725. E-mail: info@vsarts.org. Website: www.vsarts.org. **Contact:** Director, Performing Arts. Invites students with and without disabilities (grades 6-12) to submit a one-act play that explores the experience of living with a disability. Two plays will be selected for production at the John F. Kennedy Center for the Performing Arts. **Deadline: April 15.** Guidelines for SASE. Prize: Monetary award, and a trip to Washington DC to view the production or staged reading.

ℕ PLAYWRIGHTS/SCREENWRITERS FELLOWSHIPS

NC Arts Council, Dept. of Cultural Resources, Raleigh NC 27699-4632. (919)715-1519. Fax: (919)733-4834. E-mail: debbie.mcgill@ncmail.net. Website: www.ncarts.org. **Contact:** Deborah McGill, literature director. Offered every even year for an unpublished play to support the development and creation of new work. **Deadline: November 1, 2004.** Guidelines for SASE. Prize: $8,000. Judged by a panel of film and theater professionals (playwrights, screenwriters, directors, producers, etc.). Artists must be current North Carolina residents who have lived in the state for at least 1 year as of the application deadline. Grant recipients must maintain their North Carolina status during the grant year and may not pursue academic or professional degrees during that period.

PRIME TIME TELEVISION COMPETITION

Austin Film Festival, 1604 Nueces, Austin TX 78701. (512)478-4795. Fax: (512)478-6205. E-mail: austinfilm@aol.com. Website: www.austinfilmfestival.com. Offered annually for unpublished work to discover talented television writers, and introduce their work to production companies. Categories: drama and sitcom. Contest open to writers who do not earn a living writing for television or film. **Deadline: June 15.** Guidelines for SASE. **Charges $30.** Prize: $1,000 in each category.

PRINCESS GRACE AWARDS PLAYWRIGHT FELLOWSHIP

Princess Grace Foundation—USA, 150 E. 58th St., 25th Floor, New York NY 10155. (212)317-1470. Fax: (212)317-1473. E-mail: pgfusa@pgfusa.com. Website: www.pgfusa.com. **Contact:** Christine Giancatarino, grants coordinator. Offered annually for unpublished, unproduced submissions to support playwright-through-residency program with New Dramatists, Inc., located in New York City. Entrants must be U.S. citizens or have permanent U.S. status. Guidelines for SASE or on website. **Deadline: March 31.** Prize: $7,500, plus residency with New Dramatists, Inc., in New York City, and representation/publication by Samuel French, Inc.

ℕ REGENT UNIVERSITY'S 13TH ANNUAL ONE-ACT PLAY COMPETITION

Regent University, 1000 Regent University Dr., Virginia Beach VA 23464. (757)226-4223. E-mail: theatre@regent.edu. Website: www.regent.edu/theatre. Annual contest to encourage new, unpublished playwrights in their endeavors. **Deadline: September 1.** Prize: 1st Prize: $250, and play produced during the one-act play festival in March; 2nd and 3rd Prize: Honorable Mention and play produced during festival. Judged by Regent University MFA in Script and Screenwriting faculty. Open to any writer.

THE SCREENWRITER'S PROJECT

Indiefest: Film Festival & Market, P.O. Box 148849, Chicago IL 60614-8849. (773)665-7600. E-mail: info@indiefestchicago.com. Website: www.indiefestchicago.com. Offered annually to give both experienced and first-time writers the opportunity to begin a career as a screenwriter. **Deadline: March 1; May 1; June 1.** Guidelines for SASE. **Charges $20-100.** Prize: Various cash awards and prizes.

SCRIPTAPALOOZA SCREENWRITING COMPETITION

supported by Writers Guild of America and sponsored by Write Brothers, Inc., 7775 Sunset Blvd., PMB #200, Hollywood CA 90046. (323)654-5809. E-mail: info@scriptapalooza.com. Website: www.scriptapalooza.com. Annual contest open to unpublished scripts from any genre. Open to any writer, 18 or older. Submit 1 copy of a 90-130-page screenplay. Body pages must be numbered, and scripts must be in industry-standard format. All entered scripts are being read and judged by over 50 production companies. **Deadline: Early Deadline: January 5; Deadline: March 4; Late Deadline: April 15.** Guidelines for SASE. **Charges Early Deadline Fee: $40; Fee: $45; Late Deadline Fee: $50.** Prize: 1st Place: $10,000, and software package from Write Brothers, Inc; 2nd and 3rd Place, plus 10 Runners-Up: Software package from Write Brothers, Inc. The top 13 scripts will be considered by over 50 production companies.

◨ REVA SHINER FULL-LENGTH PLAY CONTEST

Bloomington Playwrights Project, 312 S. Washington St., Bloomington IN 47401. (812)334-1188. E-mail: bppwrite@newplays.org. Website: www.newplays.org. **Contact:** CATrueblood, contest award/director. Annual award for unpublished/unproduced plays. The Bloomington Playwrights Project is a script-developing organization. Winning playwrights are expected to become part of the development process, working with the director in person or via long-distance. **Deadline: January 15.** Guidelines for SASE. **Charges $5 reading fee.** Prize: $500, and possible production. Judged by the literary committee of the BPP. Open to any writer.

SIENA COLLEGE INTERNATIONAL PLAYWRIGHTS COMPETITION

Siena College Theatre Program, 515 Loudon Rd., Loudonville NY 12211-1462. (518)783-2381. Fax: (518)783-2381. E-mail: maciag@siena.edu. Website: www.siena.edu/theatre. **Contact:** Gary Maciag, director. Offered every 2 years for unpublished plays "to allow students to explore production collaboration with the playwright. In addition, it provides the playwright an important development opportunity. Plays should be previously unproduced, unpublished, full-length, nonmusicals, and free of copyright and royalty restrictions. Plays should require unit set, or minimal changes, and be suitable for a college-age cast of 3-10. There is a required 4-6 week residency." Guidelines for SASE. Guidelines are available after November 1 in odd-numbered years. Winning playwright must agree that the Siena production will be the world premiere of the play. **Deadline: February 1-June 30 in even-numbered years.** Prize: $2,000 honorarium; up to $2,000 to cover expenses for required residency; full production of winning script.

DOROTHY SILVER PLAYWRITING COMPETITION

The Eugene S. & Blanche R. Halle Theatre of the Jewish Community Center of Cleveland, 3505 Mayfield Rd., Cleveland Heights OH 44118. (216)382-4000, ext. 274. Fax: (216)382-5401. E-mail: halletheatre@clevejcc.org. Website: www.clevejcc.org. **Contact:** Kris Barnes, box office manager. Estab. 1948. All entries must be original works, not previously produced, suitable for a full-length presentation; directly concerned with the Jewish experience. **Deadline: May 1.** Prize: Cash award, plus staged reading.

◨ SOUTH CUMBERLAND PLAYWRIGHTS CONTEST

The South Cumberland Cultural Society (SCCS), P.O. Box 333, Monteagle TN 37356. Annual award for unproduced dramatic, comedic, or musical plays that focus on the history, culture, and personalities of the South Cumberland region. Entries may be full-length plays or a series of shorter pieces. Entries should constitute a full evening in the theater and run at least 70 minutes. They may include interactive, dinner murder mysteries, or nonsectarian holiday specials. SCCS shall have the option of first production of any prize-winning play within 2 years of the announcement of the award. SCCS shall have the right to retain all entries for its archives. Open to any writer resident in Tennessee. **Deadline: October 1.** Prize: 1st Place: $500; 2nd Place: $300; 3rd Place: $200. Judged by a panel of theater professionals independent of the SCCS.

SOUTHERN PLAYWRIGHTS COMPETITION

Jacksonville State University, 700 Pelham Rd. N., Jacksonville AL 36265-1602. (256)782-5414. Fax: (256)782-5441. E-mail: swhitton@jsucc.jsu.edu. Website: www.jsu.edu/depart/english/southpla.htm. **Contact:** Steven J. Whitton. Estab. 1988. Offered annually to identify and encourage the best of Southern playwriting. Playwrights must be a native or resident of Alabama, Arkansas, Florida, Georgia, Kentucky, Louisiana, Missouri, North Carolina, South Carolina, Tennessee, Texas, Virginia, or West Virginia. **Deadline: February 15.** Guidelines for SASE. Prize: $1,000, and production of the play.

SOUTHWEST THEATRE ASSOCIATION NATIONAL NEW PLAY CONTEST

Southwest Theatre Association, c/o David H. Fennema, Dept. of Music and Theatre Arts, Cameron University, Lawton OK 73505-6377. E-mail: davidf@cameron.edu. Website: www.southwest-theater.com. **Contact:** David H. Fennema, chair. Annual contest for unpublished, unproduced work to promote the writing and production of new one-act or full-length plays. No musicals, translations, adaptations of previously produced or published work, or children's plays. Guidelines for SASE or by e-mail. Open to writers who reside in the US. One entry/writer. **Deadline: March 15. Charges $10 (make check payable to SWTA).** Prize: $300 honorarium, a reading at the annual SWTA conference, complimentary registration at conference, 1-year membership in SWTA, award plaque, and possibility of excerpt publication in the professional journal of SWTA.

STANLEY DRAMA AWARD

Dept. of Theatre Wagner College, One Campus Rd., Staten Island NY 10301. (718)390-3157. Fax: (718)390-3323. **Contact:** Dr. Felicia J. Ruff, director. Offered for original full-length stage plays, musicals, or one-act play sequences that have not been professionally produced or received trade book publication. **Deadline: October 1.** Guidelines for SASE. **Charges $20 submission fee.** Prize: $2,000.

🛐 TCG/METLIFE FOUNDATION EXTENDED COLLABORATION GRANTS

Theatre Communications Group, Inc., 520 8th Ave., 24th Floor, New York NY 10018-4156. (212)609-5900. Fax: (212)609-5901. E-mail: grants@tcg.org. Website: www.tcg.org. **Contact:** Sheela Kangal, senior artistic programs associate. Program is "designed to allow writers to work collaboratively with other artists for a period beyond the sponsoring theater's normal preproduction and rehearsal schedule. Grants of $5,500 will be awarded 2 times in 2004. Only artistic leaders of TCG member theaters can apply on behalf of the writer. Applications will be automatically mailed to TCG member theaters."

🎭 THEATRE BC'S ANNUAL CANADIAN NATIONAL PLAYWRITING COMPETITION

Theatre BC, P.O. Box 2031, Nanaimo BC V9R 6X6, Canada. (250)714-0203. Fax: (250)714-0213. E-mail: pwc@theatrebc.org. Website: www.theatrebc.org. **Contact:** Robb Mowbray, executive director. Offered annually to unpublished plays "to promote the development and production of previously unproduced new plays (no musicals) at all levels of theater. Categories: Full Length (2 acts or longer); One Act (less than 60 minutes); and an open Special Merit (juror's discretion). Guidelines for SASE or on website. Winners are also invited to New Play Festival: Up to 18 hours with a professional dramaturg, registrant actors, and a public reading in Kamloops (every Spring). Production and publishing rights remain with the playwright. Open to Canadian residents. All submissions are made under pseudonyms. E-mail inquiries welcome. **Deadline: Fourth Monday in July. Charges $35/entry, and optional $25 for written critique.** Prize: Full Length: $1,000; One Act: $750; Special Merit: $500.

THEATRE CONSPIRACY ANNUAL NEW PLAY CONTEST

Theatre Conspiracy, 10091 McGregor Blvd., Ft. Myers FL 33919. (239)936-3239. Fax: (239)936-0510. E-mail: info@theatreconspiracy.org. **Contact:** Bill Taylor, award director. Offered annually for unproduced full-length plays with 8 or less characters and simple production demands. Open to any writer. Send SASE for reply. **Deadline: November 30. Charges $5 fee.** Prize: $700, and full production.

🎭 THEATRE IN THE RAW ONE-ACT PLAY WRITING CONTEST

Theatre In the Raw, 3521 Marshall St., Vancouver BC V5N 4S2, Canada. (604)708-5448. E-mail: theatreintheraw@hotmail.com. **Contact:** Artistic Director. Biennial contest for an original one-act play, presented in proper stage-play format, that is unpublished and unproduced. The play (with no more than 6 characters) cannot be longer than 25 double-spaced, typed pages equal to 30 minutes. **Deadline: September 30. Charges $25 entry fee, $40 for 2 plays (payable to Theatre In the Raw).** Prize: 1st Prize: $150, at least 1 dramatic reading or staging of the play at a Theatre In the Raw Cafe/Venue, or as part of a mini-tour program for the One-Act Play Series Nights; 2nd Prize: $50; 3rd Prize: $40.

THEATREFEST REGIONAL PLAYWRITING FESTIVAL

(formerly TheatreFest Regional Playwriting Contest), TheatreFest, Montclair State University, Upper Montclair NJ 07043. (973)655-7071. Fax: (973)655-5335. E-mail: blakec@mail.montclair.edu. Website: www.montclair.edu/theatrefest. **Contact:** John Wooten, artistic director. Offered annually for unpublished work to encourage and nurture the work of American dramatists. Open to any writer in the tri-state area (New Jersey, New York, Connecticut). Guidelines are available September-January, send a SASE for guidelines. **Deadline: January 31.** Prize: 1st Place: $1,500, and equity production; Runners-up (2): $500 and possible workshop.

⚡ THEATREPEI NEW VOICES PLAYWRITING COMPETITION

P.O. Box 1573, Charlottetown PE C1A 7N3, Canada. (902)894-3558. Fax: (902)368-7180. E-mail: theatre@isn.n et. **Contact:** Dawn Binkley, general manager. Offered annually. Open to individuals who have been residents of Prince Edward Island for 6 months preceding the deadline for entries. **Deadline: February 14.** Guidelines for SASE. **Charges $5 fee.** Prize: Monetary.

TRUSTUS PLAYWRIGHTS' FESTIVAL

Trustus Theatre, Box 11721, Columbia SC 29211-1721. (803)254-9732. Fax: (803)771-9153. E-mail: trustus@trus tus.org. Website: www.trustus.org. **Contact:** Jon Tuttle, literary manager. Offered annually for professionally unproduced full-length plays; cast limit of 8; prefer challenging, innovative dramas and comedies; no musicals, plays for young audiences, or "hillbilly" southern shows. Guidelines and application for SASE. **Deadline: Applications received between December 1, 2004, and February 28, 2005, only.** Prize: Public staged-reading and $250, followed after a 1-year development period by full production, $500, plus travel/accommodations to attend opening.

⚡ UBC'S CREATIVE WRITING RESIDENCY PRIZE IN STAGEPLAY

PRISM International and the Dept. of Theatre, Film, and Creative Writing at the University of British Columbia, c/o *PRISM International*, Creative Writing Program, UBC, Buch. E462-1866 Main Mall, Vancouver BC V6T 1Z1, Canada. (604)822-0231. E-mail: resprize@mail.arts.ubc.ca. Website: www.creativewriting.ubc.ca/resprize. UBC's Creative Writing Residency Prize in Stageplay is the result of a cooperative venture between the literary magazine *PRISM International* and the Dept. of Theatre, Film, and Creative Writing at the University of British Columbia. The prize will be awarded tri-annually. Plays should be original, previously unproduced, with 2 or more acts, and have a running time of at least 75, and no more than 120, minutes. Scripts should be in stageplay format and in English. The winner will be announced October 1. For complete rules and entry guidelines, visit the official website. **Deadline: April 30.** Prize: $10,000 (Canadian), plus expenses for a 1-month residency at the University, during which time, the winning playwright will be available for consultation with students. The winning play will be published as part of *PRISM*'s regular volume year. The theater program at UBC has an option to produce the winning play as part of their regular season at the Freddie Wood Theatre, The Chan Centre for the Performing Arts, or in co-production with a local theater company. open to professional and emerging playwrights from Canada and around the world.

UNICORN THEATRE NEW PLAY DEVELOPMENT

Unicorn Theatre, 3828 Main St., Kansas City MO 64111. (816)531-7529, ext. 18. Fax: (816)531-0421. Website: www.unicorntheatre.org. **Contact:** Herman Wilson, literary assistant. Offered annually to encourage and assist the development of an unpublished and unproduced play. Acquires 2% subsidiary rights of future productions for a 5-year period. **Deadline: Ongoing.** Guidelines for SASE. Prize: $1,000 royalty, and production.

VERMONT PLAYWRIGHT'S AWARD

The Valley Players, P.O. Box 441, Waitsfield VT 05673. (802)496-3751. E-mail: valleyplayers@madriver.com. Website: www.valleyplayers.com. **Contact:** Jennifer Howard, chair. Offered annually for unpublished, nonmusical, full-length plays suitable for production by a community theater group to encourage development of playwrights in Vermont, New Hampshire, and Maine. **Deadline: February 1.** Prize: $1,000.

⚡⚡ THE HERMAN VOADEN NATIONAL PLAYWRITING COMPETITION

Drama Department, Queen's University, Kingston ON K7L 3N6, Canada. (613)533-2104. E-mail: hannaca@post. queensu.ca. Website: www.queensu.ca/drama. **Contact:** Carol Anne Hanna. Offered every 2 years for unpublished plays to discover and develop new Canadian plays. See website for deadlines, guidelines. Open to Canadian citizens or landed immigrants. **Charges $30 entry fee.** Prize: $3,000, $2,000, and 8 honorable mentions. 1st- and 2nd-prize winners are offered a 1-week workshop and public reading by professional director and cast. The 2 authors will be playwrights-in-residence for the rehearsal and reading period.

VSA ARTS PLAYWRIGHT DISCOVERY AWARD

VSA Arts, 1300 Connecticut Ave. NW, Suite 700, Washington DC 20036. (202)628-2800. Fax: (202)737-0725. Website: www.vsarts.org. **Contact:** Performing Arts Coordinator. The VSA Arts Playwright Discovery Award challenges students grades 6-12 of all abilities to express their views about disability by writing a one-act play. Two plays will be produced at The Kennedy Center in Washington, D.C. The Playwright Discovery Teacher Award honors teachers who bring disability awareness to the classroom through the art of playwriting. Recipient receives funds for playwriting resources, a scholarship, a trip to Washington, D.C., and national recognition. **Deadline: April 16.**

WEST COAST ENSEMBLE FULL-PLAY COMPETITION

West Coast Ensemble, P.O. Box 38728, Los Angeles CA 90038. (323)876-9337. Fax: (323)876-8916. **Contact:** Les Hanson, artistic director. Estab. 1982. Offered annually for unpublished plays in Southern California. No musicals or children's plays for full-play competition. No restrictions on subject matter. **Deadline: December 31.**

JACKIE WHITE MEMORIAL NATIONAL CHILDREN'S PLAYWRITING CONTEST

Columbia Entertainment Co., 309 Parkade, Columbia MO 65202. (573)874-5628. **Contact:** Betsy Phillips, director. Offered annually for unpublished plays. "Searching for good scripts, either adaptations or plays with original story lines, suitable for audiences of all ages." Script must include at least 7 well-developed roles. **Deadline: June 1.** Guidelines for SASE. **Charges $10 fee.** Prize: $500. Company reserves the right to grant prize money without production. All entrants receive written evaluation.

WRITE A PLAY! NYC

Young Playwrights, Inc., 306 W. 38th St., Suite 300, New York NY 10018. (212)594-5440. Fax: (212)594-5441. E-mail: writeaplay@aol.com. Website: youngplaywrights.org. **Contact:** Literary Department. Offered annually for plays by NYC elementary, middle, and high school students only. **Deadline: April 1.** Prize: Varies.

YEAR END SERIES (YES) NEW PLAY FESTIVAL

Dept. of Theatre, Nunn Dr., Northern Kentucky University, Highland Heights KY 41099-1007. (859)572-6362. Fax: (859)572-6057. E-mail: forman@nku.edu. **Contact:** Sandra Forman, project director. Receives submissions from May 1-October 31 in even-numbered years for the Festivals which occur in April of odd-numbered years. Open to all writers. **Deadline: October 31.** Guidelines for SASE. Prize: $500, and an expense-paid visit to Northern Kentucky University to see the play produced.

ANNA ZORNIO MEMORIAL CHILDREN'S THEATRE PLAYWRITING COMPETITION

University of New Hampshire, Dept. of Theatre and Dance, PCAC, 30 College Rd., Durham NH 03824-3538. (603)862-2919. Fax: (603)862-0298. E-mail: mike.wood@unh.edu. Website: www.unh.edu/theatre-dance. **Contact:** Michael Wood. Offered every 4 years for unpublished well-written plays or musicals appropriate for young audiences with a maximum length of 60 minutes. Guidelines and entry forms for SASE. May submit more than 1 play, but not more than 3. Open to all playwrights in US and Canada. All ages are invited to participate. **Deadline: September 1.** Prize: $1,000, and play produced and underwritten as part of the season by the UNH Department of Theatre and Dance. Winner will be notified in November 2004.

JOURNALISM

AAAS SCIENCE JOURNALISM AWARDS

American Association for the Advancement of Science, Office of News and Information, 1200 New York Ave. NW, Washington DC 20005. (202)326-6440. E-mail: media@aaas.org. Website: www.aaas.org. Offered annually for previously published work July 1-June 30 to reward excellence in reporting on science and its applications in daily newspapers with circulation over 100,000; newspapers with circulation under 100,000; general circulation magazines; radio; television and online." Sponsored by the Whitaker Foundation. **Deadline: August 1.** Prize: $2,500, plaque, trip to AAAS Annual Meeting.

THE AMERICAN LEGION FOURTH ESTATE AWARD

The American Legion, 700 N. Pennsylvania, Indianapolis IN 46206. (317)630-1253. Fax: (317)630-1368. E-mail: pr@legion.org. Website: www.legion.org. Offered annually for journalistic works published the previous calendar year. "Subject matter must deal with a topic or issue of national interest or concern. Entry must include cover letter explaining entry, and any documention or evidence of the entry's impact on the community, state, or nation. No printed entry form." Guidelines for SASE or on website. Judged by a volunteer panel of 4 practicing print or broadcast journalists and/or educators. Judges submit their recommendation to the National Public Relations Commission for final approval. **Deadline: January 31.** Prize: $2,000 stipend to defray expenses of recipient accepting the award at The American Legion National Convention in August.

AMY WRITING AWARDS

The Amy Foundation, P.O. Box 16091, Lansing MI 48901. (517)323-6233. Fax: (517)323-7293. E-mail: amyfoundtn@aol.com. Website: www.amyfound.org. **Contact:** James Russell, president. Estab. 1985. Offered annually for nonfiction articles containing scripture published in the previous calendar year in the secular media. **Dead-**

line: **January 31.** Prize: 1st Prize: $10,000; 2nd Prize: $5,000; 3rd Prize: $4,000; 4th Prize: $3,000; 5th Prize: $2,000; and 10 prizes of $1,000.

JOHN AUBUCHON FREEDOM OF THE PRESS AWARD

(formerly Freedom of the Press Award), National Press Club, General Manager's Office, National Press Club, National Press Bldg., Washington DC 20045. (202)662-7532. Fax: (202)662-7512. E-mail: jbooze@npcpress.org. Website: npc.press.org. **Contact:** Joann Booze. Offered annually "to recognize members of the news media who have, through the publishing or broadcasting of news, promoted or helped to protect the freedom of the press" during the previous calendar year. Categories: A US journalist or team for work published or broadcast in the US; a foreign journalist or team for work published or broadcast in their home country. Guidelines on website. Open to professional journalists. **Deadline: April 1.** Prize: $1,000 in each category.

☘ AVENTIS PASTEUR MEDAL FOR EXCELLENCE IN HEALTH RESEARCH JOURNALISM

Canadians for Health Research, P.O. Box 126, Westmount QC H3Z 2T1, Canada. (514)398-7478. Fax: (514)398-8361. E-mail: info@chrcrm.org. Website: www.chrcrm.org. **Contact:** Linda Bazinet. Offered annually for work published the previous calendar year in Canadian newspapers or magazines. Applicants must have demonstrated an interest and effort in reporting health research issues within Canada. Guidelines available from CHR or on website. **Deadline: February.** Prize: $2,500, and a medal. The winner's name also appears on a permanent plaque at the Canadian Medical Hall of Fame in London, Ontario.

ERIK BARNOUW AWARD

Organization of American Historians, 112 N. Bryan Ave., Bloomington IN 47408-4199. (812)855-7311. Fax: (812)855-0696. E-mail: awards@oah.org. Website: www.oah.org. **Contact:** Award & Prize Committee Coordinator. One or 2 awards are given annually in recognition of outstanding reporting or programming on network or cable television, or in documentary film, concerned with American history, the study of American history, and/or the promotion of history. Entries must have been released the year of the contest. Guidelines available on website. **Deadline: December 1.** Prize: $1,000, and a certificate.

THE WHITMAN BASSOW AWARD

Overseas Press Club of America, 40 W. 45th St., New York NY 10036. (212)626-9220. Fax: (212)626-9210. Website: www.opcofamerica.org. **Contact:** Sonya Fry, executive director. Offered annually for best reporting in any medium on international environmental issues. Work must be published by US-based publications or broadcast. **Deadline: End of January. Charges $125 fee.** Prize: $1,000, and certificate.

MIKE BERGER AWARD

Columbia University Graduate School of Journalism, 2950 Broadway, MC 3800, New York NY 10027-7004. (212)854-5974. Fax: (212)854-3800. E-mail: jf680@columbia.edu. Website: www.jrn.columbia.edu. **Contact:** Jane M. Folpe, program coordinator. Offered annually honoring "human-interest reporting about daily life in New York City in the tradition of the late Meyer 'Mike' Berger. All newspaper reporters whose beat is New York City, whether they report for dailies, weeklies, or monthlies, are eligible." **Deadline: March 15.** Prize: Cash prize.

NICHOLAS BLAKE FOREIGN FREE-LANCE REPORTING GRANT

Family of Nicholas Blake, Nicholas Blake Grant Program, 1500A Lafayette Rd., Box 320, Portsmouth NH 03801. Estab. 2001. Contest offered annually for material published between January 1, 2004-December 31, 2004. The purpose of the grant program is to support current freelance print journalists who specialize in foreign reporting on national (or significant regional) political or armed conflicts within foreign countries. The grant program was created in honor of Nicholas C. Blake, an American freelance journalist who was murdered by security forces in 1985 while pursuing a story on the Guatemalan civil war. The grant program seeks to recognize that freelance foreign reporting is an important but under-emphasized branch of print journalism and to reward high-quality, innovative foreign reporting by these journalists. The program is intended to recognize the difficult conditions under which many freelance foreign print reporters work, and to foster their important role in foreign reporting by providing them needed financial support. An additional goal is to assist in the career development of these individuals, whether it is freelance reporting or as foreign correspondents with news organizations. Complete grant submission guidelines can be obtained by sending an e-mail request to nblakegrant@aol.com. **Deadline: September 1-December 31, 2004.** Prize: $5,000 grant. Open to freelance print journalists reporting from foreign countries.

HEYWOOD BROUN AWARD

The Newspaper Guild-CWA, 501 Third St. NW, Washington DC 20001-2797. (202)434-7173. Fax: (202)434-1472. E-mail: azipser@cwa-union.org. Website: www.newsguild.org. **Contact:** Andy Zipser. Offered annually for works published the previous year. "This annual competition is intended to encourage and recognize individual journalistic achievement by members of the working media, particularly if it helps right a wrong or correct an injustice. First consideration will be given to entries on behalf of individuals or teams of no more than 2." Guidelines for SASE or online. **Deadline: Last Friday in January.** Prize: $5,000, and plaque.

HARRY CHAPIN MEDIA AWARDS
World Hunger Year, 505 Eighth Ave., Suite 2100, New York NY 10018-6582. (212)629-8850, ext. 122. Fax: (212)465-9274. E-mail: media@worldhungeryear.org. Website: www.worldhungeryear.org. **Contact:** Lisa Ann Batitto. Estab. 1982. Open to works published the previous calendar year. Critical issues of domestic and world hunger, poverty and development (newspaper, periodical, TV, radio, photojournalism, books). **Deadline: Early February. Charges $25 for 1 entry, $40 for 2 entries, or $50 for 3-5 entries.** Prize: Several prizes from $1,000-2,500.

CONGRESSIONAL FELLOWSHIP PROGRAM
American Political Science Association, 1527 New Hampshire Ave. NW, Washington DC 20036-1206. (202)483-2512. Fax: (202)483-2657. E-mail: apsa@apsanet.org. Website: www.apsanet.org/about/cfp. **Contact:** Program Coordinator. Offered annually for professional journalists who have 2-10 years of full-time professional experience in newspaper, magazine, radio, or television reporting at time of application to learn more about the legislative process through direct participation. Visit our website for deadlines. Open to journalists and scholars. Prize: $38,000, and travel allowance for 3 weeks' orientation and legislation aide assignments December-August.

THE JANE CUNNINGHAM CROLY PRINT JOURNALISM AWARD FOR EXCELLENCE IN COVERING ISSUES OF CONCERN TO WOMEN
The General Federation of Women's Clubs, 1734 N St. NW, Washington DC 20036. (202)347-3168. Fax: (202)835-0246. E-mail: gfwc@gfwc.org. Website: www.gfwc.org. An annual award "to honor the print journalist whose writing demonstrates a concern for the rights and the advancement of women in our society and/or an awareness of women's sensitivity, strength, and courage, and/or an attempt to counteract existing sexism." Open to women and men who write for newspapers, magazines, Internet publications, or news services in the United States—either on staff or in a freelance capacity. Three articles must be submitted by each person. Articles must have been published between January 1 and December 31, 2003. **Deadline: March 3.** Guidelines for SASE. **Charges $50 (the fee is reduced by $10 for subsequent entries from other writers at the same news organization).** Prize: $1,000 presented at GFWC's annual International Convention. GFWC pays airfare and expenses. The winner is asked to deliver an address on some aspect of the media and issues of concern to women. Judged by 2 prominent journalists, and 1 leader of a major woman's organization.

ROBIN GOLDSTEIN AWARD FOR WASHINGTON REGIONAL REPORTING
National Press Club, Administered by the National Press Foundation, General Manager's Office, National Press Club, National Press Bldg., Washington DC 20045. (202)662-8744. E-mail: jbooze@npcpress.org. Website: npc.press.org. **Contact:** Joann Booze. Offered annually for a Washington newspaper correspondent "who best exemplifies the standards set by the late Robin Goldstein, who established the Washington bureaus of the Asbury Park (NJ) Press and the Orange County (CA) Register. Working alone in each bureau, Goldstein proved that one dedicated reporter can do it all for the hometown readers—news, features, enterprise, analysis and columns. This contest honors reporters who demonstrate excellence and versatility in covering Washington from a local angle." Guidelines on website. **Deadline: April 1.** Prize: $1,000.

EDWIN M. HOOD AWARD FOR DIPLOMATIC CORRESPONDENCE
National Press Club, General Manager's Office, National Press Club, National Press Bldg., Washington DC 20045. (202)662-8744. E-mail: jbooze@npcpress.org. Website: npc.press.org. **Contact:** Joann Booze. Offered annually to recognize excellence in reporting on diplomatic and foreign policy issues. Categories: newspaper and broadcast. Guidelines on website. **Deadline: April 1.** Prize: $500 in each category.

ICIJ AWARD FOR OUTSTANDING INTERNATIONAL INVESTIGATIVE REPORTING
International Consortium of Investigative Journalists, A Project of the Center for Public Integrity, 910 17th St. NW, 7th Floor, Washington DC 20006. (202)466-1300. Fax: (202)466-1101. E-mail: info@icij.org. Website: www.icij.org. **Contact:** Laura Peterson or Andre Verloy. Offered annually for works produced in print, broadcast, and online media between June 1, 2004, and June 1, 2005, are eligible. Work must be on a transnational, investigative topic. Guidelines for SASE or on website. **Deadline: July 15.** Prize: 1st Place: $20,000; up to 5 finalist awards of $1,000 each.

INVESTIGATIVE JOURNALISM GRANT

Fund For Investigative Journalism, P.O. Box 60184, Washington DC 20039-0184. (202)362-0260. Fax: (301)576-0804. E-mail: johnchyde@yahoo.com. Website: www.fij.org. **Contact:** John Hyde. Offered 3 times/year for original investigative newspaper and magazine stories, radio and TV documentaries, books and media criticism. Guidelines on website or by e-mail. The Fund also offers an annual $25,000 FIJ Book Prize in November for the best book chosen by the board during the year. **Deadline: February 1, June 1, and October 1.** Prize: Grants of $500-10,000.

THE IOWA AWARD/THE TIM McGINNIS AWARD

The Iowa Review, 308 EPB, University of Iowa, Iowa City IA 52242. (319)335-0462. E-mail: iowa-review@uiowa.edu. Website: www.uiowa.edu/~iareview. **Contact:** David Hamilton. "Offered annually for work already published in our magazine, usually within the previous year. The Iowa Award is a judge's choice of the best work of the year. The McGinnis Award is the editors' choice of a work from whatever we publish during the year before that usually expresses an off-beat and (we hope) sophisticated sense of humor. The Iowa Awards result from an annual contest, the submissions for which arrive in January. We send finalists in fiction, poetry, and nonfiction to outside judges to name the winners and publish each winner and several runners-up in our December issue. Please see our online guidelines for current information." Prize: $1,000 for each Iowa Award; $500 for McGinnis Award.

ANSON JONES, M.D. AWARD

Texas Medical Association, 401 W. 15th St., Austin TX 78701-1680. (512)370-1381. Fax: (512)370-1629. E-mail: brent.annear@texmed.org. Website: www.texmed.org. **Contact:** Brent Annear, media relations manager. Offered annually "to the media of Texas for excellence in communicating health information to the public." Open only to Texas media or writers published in Texas. Guidelines posted online. **Deadline: January 15.** Prize: $1,000 for winners of each of the categories.

ROBERT L. KOZIK AWARD FOR ENVIRONMENTAL REPORTING

National Press Club, General Manager's Office, National Press Bldg., Washington DC 20045. (202)662-8744. E-mail: jbooze@npcpress.org. Website: npc.press.org. **Contact:** Joann Booze. Offered annually to recognize excellence in environmental reporting at the local, national, or international level that impacted or prompted action to remedy an environmental situation. Categories: print and broadcast. Guidelines on website. **Deadline: April 1.** Prize: $500, and Kozik medal in each category.

N C HERB LAMPERT STUDENT WRITING AWARD

Canadian Science Writers' Association, P.O. Box 1543, Kingston ON K7L 5C7, Canada. (800)796-8595. E-mail: awards@sciencewriters.ca. Website: www.interlog.com/~cswa. Offered annually to any student science writer who has an article published in a student or other newspaper or magazine or aired on a radio or TV station in Canada. Open to any Canadian residents or citizens. **Deadline: February 15.** Guidelines for SASE. Prize: $1,000 for print and broadcast winners.

LIVINGSTON AWARDS FOR YOUNG JOURNALISTS

Mollie Parnis Livingston Foundation, Wallace House, 620 Oxford, Ann Arbor MI 48104. (734)998-7575. Fax: (734)998-7979. E-mail: livingstonawards@umich.edu. Website: www.livawards.org. **Contact:** Charles Eisendrath. Offered annually for journalism published January 1-December 31 the previous year to recognize and further develop the abilities of young journalists. Includes print, online, and broadcast. Guidelines on website. Judges include Mike Wallace, Ellen Goodman, and Tom Brokaw. Open to journalists who are 34 years or younger as of December 31 of previous year and whose work appears in US-controlled print or broadcast media. **Deadline: February 1.** Prize: (3)$10,000: 1 each for local reporting, national reporting, and international reporting.

FELIX MORLEY JOURNALISM COMPETITION

Institute for Humane Studies, 3301 N. Fairfax Dr., Suite 440, Arlington VA 22201. (800)697-8799. Fax: (703)993-4890. Website: www.theihs.org/morley. Offered annually for nonfiction published July 1, 2002-November 29, 2003, to reward young journalists who effectively address individual rights and free markets in their work. Writers must be either full-time students or be 25 years old as of the December 1 deadline. Prize: 1st Place: $2,500; 2nd Place: $1,000; 3rd Place: $750; and $250 to several runners-up. Writers must be either full-time students or 25 years of age or younger as of the deadline.

N FRANK LUTHER MOTT—KAPPA TAU ALPHA RESEARCH AWARD IN JOURNALISM

University of Missouri School of Journalism, 3 Neff Hall, Columbia MO 65211. (573)882-7685. E-mail: umcjourkta@missouri.edu. Website: www.missouri.edu/~ktahq. **Contact:** Dr. Keith Sanders, executive director, Kappa

Tau Alpha. Offered annually for best researched book in mass communication. Submit 6 copies; no forms required. **Deadline: December 9.** Prize: $1,000.

NATIONAL MAGAZINE AWARDS

National Magazine Awards Foundation, 109 Vanderhoof Ave., Suite 207, Toronto ON M4G 2H7, Canada. (416)422-1358. Fax: (416)422-3762. E-mail: nmaf@bellnet.ca. Website: www.magazine-awards.com. **Contact:** Pat Kendall. Offered annually for work by Canadian citizens or landed immigrants published in a Canadian magazine during the previous calendar year. Awards presented for writers, art directors, illustrators and photographers in written and visual categories. **Deadline: early January. Charges $60 per entry.** Prize: Gold, Silver, Honourable Mention. Open to Canadian residents only.

NATIONAL PRESS CLUB CONSUMER JOURNALISM AWARD

National Press Club, National Press Bldg., Washington DC 20045. (202)662-8744. E-mail: jbooze@npcpress.org. Website: npc.press.org. **Contact:** Joann Booze. Offered annually to recognize excellence in reporting on consumer topics in the following categories: newspapers, periodicals, television, and radio. Entries must have been published/broadcast in the previous calendar year. Include a letter detailing how the piece or series resulted in action by consumers, the government, the community or an individual. Guidelines on website. **Deadline: April 1.** Prize: $500 for each category.

NATIONAL PRESS CLUB JOSEPH D. RYLE AWARD FOR EXCELLENCE IN WRITING ON THE PROBLEMS OF GERIATRICS

National Press Club, General Manager's Office, National Press Bldg., Washington DC 20045. (202)662-8744. Fax: (202)662-7512. Website: npc.press.org. **Contact:** Joann Booze. Offered annually for work published in the previous year. This award emphasizes excellence and objectivity in coverage of the problems faced by the elderly. Guidelines on website. Open to professional print journalists. **Deadline: April 1.** Prize: $2,000.

NATIONAL PRESS CLUB ONLINE JOURNALISM AWARD

National Press Club, General Manager's Office, National Press Bldg., Washington DC 20045. (202)662-8744. E-mail: jbooze@npcpress.org. Website: npc.press.org. **Contact:** Joanne Booze. Offered annually to recognize the most significant contributions to journalism by the online media in 2 categories: Best Journalism Site (this award honors the best journalistic use of the online medium); and Distinguished Online Contribution (this award goes to the best individual contribution to public service using online technology). Guidelines on website. **Deadline: April 1.** Prize: $1,000 in each category.

NATIONAL PRESS CLUB SANDY HUME MEMORIAL AWARD FOR EXCELLENCE IN POLITICAL JOURNALISM

National Press Club, General Manager's Office, National Press Bldg., Washington DC 20045. (202)662-8744. Fax: (202)662-7512. E-mail: jbooze@npcpress.org. Website: npc.press.org. **Contact:** Joann Booze. Offered annually for work published in the previous calendar year. "This award honors excellence and objectivity in political coverage by reporters 34 years old or younger. Named in memory of Sandy Hume, the reporter for *The Hill* who broke the story of the aborted 1997 coup against House Speaker Newt Gingrich, this prize can be awarded for a single story of great distinction or for continuing coverage of 1 political topic." Guidelines on website. Open to professional journalists 34 or younger. **Deadline: April 1.** Prize: $1,000.

NATIONAL PRESS CLUB WASHINGTON CORRESPONDENCE AWARD

National Press Club, National Press Bldg., Washington DC 20045. (202)662-8744. E-mail: jbooze@npcpress.org. Website: npc.press.org. **Contact:** Joann Booze. Offered annually to honor the work of reporters who cover Washington for the benefit of the hometown audience. "This award is for a single report or series on one topic, not for national reporting, nor for a body of work. Entrants must demonstrate a clear knowledge of how Washington works and what it means to the folks back home." Guidelines on webiste. **Deadline: April 1.** Prize: $1,000.

NEWSLETTER JOURNALISM AWARD

National Press Club, National Press Bldg., Washington DC 20045. (202)662-8744. E-mail: jbooze@npcpress.org. Website: npc.press.org. **Contact:** Joann Booze. Offered annually to acknowledge excellence in newsletter journalism in 2 categories: Best analytical or interpretive reporting piece or best exclusive story. Entries must be published by an independent newsletter and serve the audience and mission of the newsletter. Guidelines on website. **Deadline: April 1.** Prize: $2,000 for each category.

THE MADELINE DANE ROSS AWARD

Overseas Press Club of America, 40 W. 45th St., New York NY 10036. (212)626-9220. Fax: (212)626-9210. E-mail: sonya@opcofamerica.org. Website: www.opcofamerica.org. **Contact:** Sonya Fry, executive director. Offered annually for best international reporting in the paint medium showing a concern for the human condition. Work must be published by US-based publications or broadcast. Printable application available on website. **Deadline: Late January; date changes each year. Charges $125 fee.** Prize: $1,000, and certificate.

ARTHUR ROWSE AWARD FOR PRESS CRITICISM

General Manager's Office, National Press Club, National Press Bldg., Washington DC 20045. (202)662-8744. E-mail: jbooze@npcpress.org. Website: npc.press.org. **Contact:** Joann Booze. Offered annually for work published or broadcast the previous calendar year. "This award, sponsored by former *US News & World Report* reporter Arthur Rowse, honors excellence in examining the role and work of the news media. Categories: Single Entry (3 categories) and Body of Work (2 categories). Single Entry: newspapers, magazines, newsletters, and online; TV and radio; books. Body of Work: newspapers, magazines, newsletters, and online; TV and radio. Guidelines on website. Open to professional journalists (with the exception of those entering as book authors). **Deadline: April 1.** Prize: $1,000 in each category.

N ⬚ SCIENCE IN SOCIETY JOURNALISM AWARDS

Canadian Science Writers' Association, P.O. Box 1543, Kingston ON K7L 5C7, Canada. (800)796-8595. E-mail: awards@sciencewriters.ca. Website: www.interlog.com/~cswa. Offered annually for work published/aired January 1-December 31 of previous year to recognize outstanding contributions to science journalism in all media. Three newspaper, 3 magazine, 2 TV, 2 radio, 1 special publication, student sciences writing award (Herb Lampert Student Writing Award). Each Material becomes property of CSWA. Does not return mss. Open to Canadian citizens or residents of Canada. **Deadline: January 31.** Guidelines for SASE. **Charges $10 entry fee.** Prize: $1,000, and a plaque.

WRITING FOR CHILDREN & YOUNG ADULTS

⬚ THE GEOFFREY BILSON AWARD FOR HISTORICAL FICTION FOR YOUNG PEOPLE

The Canadian Children's Book Centre, 40 Orchard View Blvd., Suite 101, Toronto ON M4R 1B9, Canada. (416)975-0010. Fax: (416)975-8970. E-mail: brenda@bookcentre.ca. Website: www.bookcentre.ca. **Contact:** (Ms.) Brenda Halliday, librarian. Created in Geoffrey Bilson's memory in 1988. Offered annually for a previously published "outstanding work of historical fiction for young people by a Canadian author." Open to Canadian citizens and residents of Canada for at least 2 years. **Deadline: January 15.** Prize: $1,000. Judged by a jury selected by the Canadian Children's Book Centre.

⬚ BOOKSTART BABY BOOK AWARD

(formerly Sainsbury's Baby Book Award), c/o Booktrust, Book House, 45 E. Hill, Wandsworth, London SW18 2QZ, United Kingdom. Fax: (00 44) 20 8516 2978. E-mail: tarryn@booktrust.org.uk. Website: www.booktrusted.com. **Contact:** Kate Mervyn Jones. The Bookstart Baby Book Award was established in 1999 and is awarded annually. The award is given to the best book, published between September 1, 2003 and August 31, 2004, in the opinion of the judges for a baby under 1 year of age. Authors and illustrators must be of British nationality, or other nationals who have been residents in the British Isles for at least 10 years. Books can be any format. **Deadline: June.** Prize: £2,000, and a crystal award. In addition, the publisher receives a crystal award naming them as "The Bookstart Baby Book Award Publisher of the Year."

BOSTON GLOBE-HORN BOOK AWARDS

The Boston Globe, Horn Book, Inc., 56 Roland St., Suite 200, Boston MA 02129. (617)628-0225. Website: www.hbook.com. **Contact:** Marika Hoe. Offered annually for excellence in literature for children and young adults (published June 1, 2003-May 31, 2004). Categories: picture book, fiction and poetry, nonfiction. Judges may also name several honor books in each category. Books must be published in the United States. Guidelines for SASE or online. **Deadline: May 3.** Prize: Winners receive $500, and engraved silver bowl; honor book recipients receive an engraved silver plate. Judged by a panel of 3 judges selected each year.

MARGUERITE DE ANGELI PRIZE

Delacorte Press Books for Young Readers, Random House, Inc., 1745 Broadway, New York NY 10019. (212)782-9000. Fax: (212)782-9452. Website: www.randomhouse.com/kids. Estab. 1992. Offered annually for an unpublished fiction ms suitable for readers 8-12 years of age, set in North America, either contemporary or historical.

Guidelines on website. **Deadline: April 1-June 30.** Prize: $1,500 in cash, publication, and $7,500 advance against royalties; world rights acquired.

DELACORTE PRESS CONTEST FOR A FIRST YOUNG ADULT NOVEL

Random House, Inc., 1745 Broadway, 9th Floor, New York NY 10019. Website: www.randomhouse.com/kids/games/delacorte.html. Offered annually "to encourage the writing of contemporary young adult fiction." Open to US and Canadian writers who have not previously published a young adult novel. Guidelines on website. **Deadline: October 1-December 31 (postmarked).** Prize: $1,500 cash, publication, and $7,500 advance against royalties. Judged by the editors of Delacorte Press Books for Young Readers.

⚫ THE NORMA FLECK AWARD FOR A CANADIAN CHILDREN'S NONFICTION BOOK

The Canadian Children's Book Centre, 40 Orchard View Blvd., Suite 101, Toronto ON M4R 1B9, Canada. (416)975-0010. Fax: (416)975-8970. E-mail: info@bookcentre.ca. Website: www.bookcentre.ca. **Contact:** Shannon Howe, program coordinator. The Norma Fleck Award was established by the Fleck Family Foundation in May 1999 to honor the life of Norma Marie Fleck, and to recognize exceptional Canadian nonfiction books for young people. Publishers are welcome to nominate books using the online form found at www.bookcentre.ca. Offered annually for books published between May 1, 2004, and April 30, 2005. Open to Canadian citizens or landed immigrants. **Deadline: March 31.** Schedule decided upon annually. Prize: $10,000 goes to the author (unless 40% or more of the text area is composed of original illustrations, in which case the award will be divided equally between the author and the artist). $5,000 in matching funding will be made available for promotional purposes to all of the shortlisted titles. Judged by a minimum of 3 jury members and the total number, if more, will be an uneven number. The jury will always include at least 3 of the following: a teacher, a librarian, a bookseller, and a reviewer. There should be at least 1 new jury member each year. A juror will have a deep understanding of, and some involvement with, Canadian children's books. The Canadian Children's Book Centre will select the jury members.

⚫ FRIENDS OF THE AUSTIN PUBLIC LIBRARY AWARD FOR BEST CHILDREN'S OR YOUNG ADULTS' BOOK

(formerly Book Publishers of Texas Award for Children's or Young People's Book), 3700 Mockingbird Lane, Dallas TX 75205. (214)528-2655. E-mail: franvick@aol.com. **Contact:** Fran Vick. Offered annually for work published January 1-December 31 of previous year to recognize the best book for children or young people. Writer must have been born in Texas or have lived in the state for at least 2 consecutive years at one time, or the subject matter is associated with the state. **Deadline: January 3.** Guidelines for SASE. Prize: $500.

⚫ GOVERNOR GENERAL'S LITERARY AWARD FOR CHILDREN'S LITERATURE

Canada Council for the Arts, 350 Albert St., P.O. Box 1047, Ottawa ON K1P 5V8, Canada. (613)566-4414, ext. 5576. Fax: (613)566-4410. E-mail: joanne.larocque-poirier@canadacouncil.ca. Website: www.canadacouncil.ca/prizes/ggla. **Contact:** Joanne Larocque-Poirier. Offered for the best English-language and the best French-language works of children's literature by a Canadian in 2 categories: text and illustration. Books must have been published between September 1, 2004, and September 30, 2005. Publishers submit titles for consideration. **Deadline: April 15 or August 7, 2005, depending on the book's publication date.** Prize: Each laureate receives $15,000, and nonwinning finalists receive $1,000.

GUIDEPOSTS YOUNG WRITERS CONTEST

Guideposts, 16 E. 34th St., New York NY 10016. (212)251-8100. E-mail: ywcontest@guideposts.org. Website: gp4teens.com. Offered annually for unpublished high school juniors and seniors. Stories "needn't be about a highly dramatic situation, but it should record an experience that affected you and deeply changed you. Remember, *Guideposts* stories are true, not fiction, and they show how faith in God has made a specific difference in a person's life. We accept submissions after announcement is placed in the October issue each year. If the manuscript is placed, we require all rights to the story in that version." Open only to high school juniors or seniors. **Deadline: November 24.** Prize: 1st Place: $10,000; 2nd Place: $8,000; 3rd Place: $6,000; 4th Place: $4,000; 5th Place: $3,000; 6th-10th Place: $1,000; 11th-20th Place: $250 gift certificate for college supplies.

HIGHLIGHTS FOR CHILDREN FICTION CONTEST

Highlights for Children, 803 Church St., Honesdale PA 18431-1824. (570)253-1080. Website: www.highlights.com. **Contact:** Marileta Robinson, senior editor. Offered for stories for children ages 2-12; category varies each year. Stories should be previously unpublished and limited to 800 words for older readers, 500 words for younger readers. No crime or violence, please. Specify that ms is a contest entry. **Deadline: January 1-February 28 (postmarked).** Guidelines for SASE. Prize: $1,000 to 3 winners, and publication of stories in *Highlights*. All other submissions will be considered for purchase by *Highlights for Children*.

INTERNATIONAL READING ASSOCIATION CHILDREN'S BOOK AWARDS

International Reading Association, P.O. Box 8139, Newark DE 19714-8139. (302)731-1600, ext. 293. Fax: (302)731-1057. Website: www.reading.org. **Contact:** Beth Cady. Offered annually for an author's first or second published book in fiction and nonfiction in 3 categories: primary (preschool-age 8), intermediate (ages 9-13), and young adult (ages 14-17). Recognizes newly published authors who show unusual promise in the children's book field. Guidelines and deadlines for SASE. Prize: $500, and a medal for each category.

CORETTA SCOTT KING BOOK AWARD

Coretta Scott King Task Force, American Library Association, 50 E. Huron St., Chicago IL 60611. (800)545-2433. E-mail: feedback@ala.org. Website: www.ala.org. Offered annually for children's books by African-American authors and/or illustrators published the previous year. Three categories: preschool-grade 4; grades 5-8; grades 9-12. **Deadline: December 1.** Guidelines for SASE. Prize: Honorarium, framed citation, and a set of *Encyclopedia Britannica* or *World Book Encyclopedias.*

ANNE SPENCER LINDBERGH PRIZE IN CHILDREN'S LITERATURE

The Charles A. & Anne Morrow Lindbergh Foundation, 2150 Third Ave. N., Suite 310, Anoka MN 55303. (763)576-1596. Fax: (763)576-1664. E-mail: info indberghfoundation.org. Website: www.lindberghfoundation.org. **Contact:** Executive Director. Offered every 2 years in even years for a children's fantasy novel published in the English language in that or the preceding year. Entries must include 4 copies of the book and an **application fee of $25** (payable to the Lindbergh Foundation) for each title submitted. Open to any writer. **Deadline: November 1.**

✣ THE VICKY METCALF AWARD FOR CHILDREN'S LITERATURE

The Writers' Trust of Canada, 40 Wellington St. E., Suite 300, Toronto ON M5E 1C7, Canada. (416)504-8222. Fax: (416)504-9090. E-mail: info@writerstrust.com. Website: www.writerstrust.com. **Contact:** James Davies. The Metcalf Award is presented annually at The Great Literary Awards Event held in Toronto each spring, to a Canadian writer for a body of work in children's literature. Prize: $15,000. Open to Canadian residents only.

MILKWEED PRIZE FOR CHILDREN'S LITERATURE

Milkweed Editions, 1011 Washington Ave. S., Suite 300, Minneapolis MN 55415. (612)332-3192. Fax: (612)215-2550. Website: www.milkweed.org. **Contact:** Elisabeth Fitz, first reader. Estab. 1993. Annual prize for unpublished works. "Milkweed is looking for a novel intended for readers aged 8-13. Manuscripts should be of high literary quality and must be double-spaced, 90-200 pages in length. The Milkweed Prize for Children's Literature will be awarded to the best manuscript for children ages 8-13 that Milkweed accepts for publication during each calendar year by a writer not previously published by Milkweed Editions." All mss submitted to Milkweed will automatically be considered for the prize. Submission directly to the contest is not necessary. Must review guidelines, available at website or for SASE. Catalog for $1.50 postage. Prize: $5,000 advance on royalties agreed upon at the time of acceptance.

🌐 NESTLÉ SMARTIES BOOK PRIZE

Nestlé Smarties, % Booktrust, Book House, 45 E. Hill, Wandsworth, London SW18 2QZ, United Kingdom. Fax: (00 44) 20 8516 2978. E-mail: tarryn@booktrust.org.uk. Website: www.booktrusted.com. **Contact:** Kate Mervyn Jones. "The Nestlé Smarties Book Prize was established in 1985 to encourage high standards and stimulate interest in children's books. The prize is split into 3 age categories: 5 and under, 6-8, and 9-11. Within the last couple of years, a new category, the Kids' Club Network Special Award has been introduced. The books are judged by our adult panel, who shortlist 3 outstanding books in each category, and the final decision of who gets Gold, Silver, Bronze, and the KCN Special Award is left to our young judges. The young judges are chosen from classes of school children who complete a task for their age category, the best 50 from each category go on to judge the 3 books in their age category. The KCN children judge the 6-8 books. From the 200 classes who judge the books, 1 class from each category is invited to present the award at the ceremony in London. The children are chosen from projects they submit with their votes." Open to works of fiction or poetry for children written in English by a citizen of the UK, or an author resident in the UK. All work must be submitted by a UK publisher. **Deadline: July.** Prize: Gold Award winners in each age category: £2,500; Silver Award winners in each age category: £1,500; Bronze Award winners in each age category: £500; certificate for the KCN Special Award winner.

(ALICE WOOD MEMORIAL) OHIOANA AWARD FOR CHILDREN'S LITERATURE

Ohioana Library Association, 274 E. First Ave., Suite 300, Columbus OH 43201. (614)466-3831. Fax: (614)728-6974. E-mail: ohioana@sloma.state.oh.us. Website: www.oplin.lib.oh.us/OHIOANA/. **Contact:** Linda R. Hengst. Offered to an author whose body of work has made, and continues to make, a significant contribution to literature for children or young adults and through their work as a writer, teacher, administrator, or through community service, interest in children's literature has been encouraged and children have become involved with reading. Nomination forms for SASE. Recipient must have been born in Ohio or lived in Ohio at least 5 years. **Deadline: December 31.** Prize: $1,000.

PATERSON PRIZE FOR BOOKS FOR YOUNG PEOPLE

The Poetry Center at Passaic County Community College, One College Blvd., Paterson NJ 07505-1179. (973)684-6555. Fax: (973)684-5843. E-mail: mgillan@pccc.cc.nj.us. Website: www.pccc.cc.nj.us/poetry. **Contact:** Maria Mazziotti Gillan, director. Offered annually for books published the previous calendar year. Three categories: pre-kindergarten-grade 3; grades 4-6; and grades 7-12. Open to any writer. **Deadline: April 1.** Guidelines for SASE. Prize: $500 in each category.

PEN/PHYLLIS NAYLOR WORKING WRITER FELLOWSHIP

PEN American Center, 568 Broadway, New York NY 10012. (212)334-1660. Fax: (212)334-2181. E-mail: awards @pen.org. **Contact:** Stephen Motika. Offered annually to a "writer of children's or young-adult fiction in financial need, who has published at least 2 books, and no more than 5, in the past 10 years, which may have been well reviewed and warmly received by literary critics, but which have not generated sufficient income to support the author." Writers must be nominated by an editor or fellow writer. **Deadline: January 15.** Prize: $5,000.

PRIX ALVINE-BELISLE

Association pour L'avancement des sciences et des techniques de la documentation, ASTED, Inc., 3414 av. Parc #202, Montreal QC H2X 2H5, Canada. (514)281-5012. Fax: (514)281-8219. E-mail: info@asted.org. Website: www.asted.org. **Contact:** Louis Cabral, executive director. Offered annually for work published the previous year before the award to promote authors of French youth literature in Canada. **Deadline: April 1.** Prize: $1,000.

SASKATCHEWAN CHILDREN'S LITERATURE AWARD

Saskatchewan Book Awards, Inc., Box 1921, Regina SK S4P 3E1, Canada. (306)569-1585. Fax: (306)569-4187. E-mail: director@bookawards.sk.ca. Website: www.bookawards.sk.ca. **Contact:** Joyce Wells, executive director. Offered annually for work published September 15, 2002-September 14, 2003. This award is presented to a Saskatchewan author for the best book of children's or young adult's literature, judged on the quality of writing. **Deadline: First Deadline: July 31; Final Deadline: September 14.** Guidelines for SASE. **Charges $20 (Canadian).** Prize: $2,000.

SYDNEY TAYLOR BOOK AWARD

Association of Jewish Libraries, 15 E. 26th St., 10th Floor, New York NY 10010. (212)725-5359. E-mail: heidi@cb iboca.org. Website: www.jewishlibraries.org. **Contact:** Heidi Estrin, chair. Offered annually for work published in the year of the award. "Given to distinguished contributions to Jewish literature for children. One award for older readers, one for younger." Publishers submit books. **Deadline: December 31.** Guidelines for SASE. Prize: Certificate, cash award, and gold seal for cover of winning book.

TEDDY AWARD FOR BEST CHILDREN'S BOOK

Writers' League of Texas, 1501 W. Fifth St., Suite E-2, Austin TX 78703. (512)499-8914. Fax: (512)499-0441. E-mail: wlt@writersleague.org. Website: www.writersleague.org. **Contact:** Stephanie Sheppard, director. Offered annually for work published June 1-May 31. Honors an outstanding book for children published by a member of the Writers' League of Texas. Writer's League of Texas dues may accompany entry fee. **Deadline: May 31.** Guidelines for SASE. **Charges $20 fee.** Prize: $1,000, and trophy.

TORONTO MUNICIPAL CHAPTER IODE BOOK AWARD

Toronto Municipal Chapter IODE, 40 St. Clair Ave. E., Suite 205, Toronto ON M4T 1M9, Canada. (416)925-5078. Fax: (416)925-5127. **Contact:** Theo Heras (Lillian Smith Library, 239 College St., Toronto). Offered annually for childrens' books published by a Canadian publisher. Author and illustrator must be Canadian citizens residing in or around Toronto. **Deadline: Late November.** Prize: $1,000.

PAUL A. WITTY SHORT STORY AWARD

Executive Office, International Reading Association, P.O. Box 8139, Newark DE 19714-8139. (302)731-1600, ext. 293. Fax: (302)731-1057. E-mail: exec@reading.org. Website: www.reading.org. Offered to reward author of an original short story published in a children's periodical during 2004 which serves as a literary standard that encourages young readers to read periodicals. Write for guidelines or download from website. **Deadline: December 1.** Prize: $1,000.

WORK-IN-PROGRESS GRANT

Society of Children's Book Writers and Illustrators (SCBWI) and Judy Blume, 8271 Beverly Blvd., Los Angeles CA 90048. (323)782-1010. E-mail: scbwi@scbwi.org. Website: www.scbwi.org. Two grants—1 designated specifically for a contemporary novel for young people—to assist SCBWI members in the completion of a specific project. Open to SCBWI members only. **Deadline: March 1.** Guidelines for SASE.

WRITING FOR CHILDREN COMPETITION

(formerly The Writer's Union of Canada Writing for Children Competition), The Writers' Union of Canada, 40 Wellington St. E., 3rd Floor, Toronto ON M5E 1C7. (416)703-8982, ext. 223. Fax: (416)504-7656. E-mail: projects@writersunion.ca. Website: www.writersunion.ca. **Contact:** Projects Coordinator. Offered annually "to discover developing Canadian writers of unpublished children's/young adult fiction or nonfiction." Open to Canadian citizens or landed immigrants who have not been published in book format, and who do not currently have a contract with a publisher. **Deadline: April 24. Charges $15 entry fee.** Prize: $1,500; the winner and 11 finalists' pieces will be submitted to 3 Canadian publishers of children's books.

TRANSLATION

AMERICAN TRANSLATORS ASSOCIATION STUDENT TRANSLATION PRIZE

American Translators Association, 225 Reinekers Lane, Suite 590, Alexandria VA 22314. (703)683-6100. Fax: (703)683-6122. E-mail: ata@atanet.org. Website: www.atanet.org. Support is granted for a promising project to an unpublished student enrolled in a translation program at a US college or university. Must be sponsored by a faculty member. **Deadline: April 15.** Prize: $500, and up to $500 toward expenses for attending the ATA Annual Conference.

ASF TRANSLATION PRIZE

The American-Scandinavian Foundation, 58 Park Ave., New York NY 10016-3007. (212)879-9779. Fax: (212)686-2115. E-mail: ahenkin@amscan.org. Website: www.amscan.org. **Contact:** Andrey Henkin. Offered annually to a translation of Scandinavian literature into English of a Nordic author born within the last 200 years. "The Prize is for an outstanding English translation of poetry, fiction, drama, or literary prose originally written in Danish, Finnish, Icelandic, Norwegian, or Swedish that has not been previously published in the English language." **Deadline: June 1.** Guidelines for SASE. Prize: $2,000, publication of an excerpt in an issue of *Scandinavian Review*, and a commemorative bronze medallion. Runner-up receives the Leif and Inger Sjöberg Prize: $1,000, publication of an excerpt in an issue of *Scandinavian Review*, and a commemorative bronze medallion.

SOEURETTE DIEHL FRASER TRANSLATION AWARD

3700 Mockingbird Lane, Dallas TX 75205. (214)528-2655. E-mail: franvick@aol.com. **Contact:** Fran Vick. Offered every 2 years (books published 2002-2003 are eligible) to recognize the best translation of a literary book into English. Translator must have been born in Texas or have lived in the state for at least two consecutive years at some time. **Deadline: January 3.** Guidelines for SASE. Prize: $1,000.

GERMAN PRIZE FOR LITERARY TRANSLATION

American Translators Association, 225 Reinekers Lane, Suite 590, Alexandria VA 22314. (703)683-6100, ext. 3006. Fax: (703)683-6122. E-mail: ata@atanet.org. Website: www.atanet.org. **Contact:** Walter W. Bacack. Offered in odd-numbered years for a previously published book translated from German to English. In even-numbered years, the Lewis Galentiere Prize is awarded for translations other than German to English. **Deadline: May 15.** Prize: $1,000, a certificate of recognition, and up to $500 toward expenses for attending the ATA Annual Conference.

JOHN GLASSCO TRANSLATION PRIZE

Literary Translators' Association of Canada, c/o 272 Heneker, Sherbrooke QC J1J 3G4, Canada. (819)820-1244. E-mail: patricia.godbout@courrier.usherb.ca. Website: www.attlc-ltac.org/glasscoe.htm. Estab. 1981. Offered annually for a translator's first book-length literary translation into French or English, published in Canada during the previous calendar year. The translator must be a Canadian citizen or landed immigrant. Eligible genres include fiction, creative nonfiction, poetry, and children's books. **Deadline: June 30.** Prize: $1,000.

GOVERNOR GENERAL'S LITERARY AWARD FOR TRANSLATION

Canada Council for the Arts, 350 Albert St., P.O. Box 1047, Ottawa ON K1P 5V8, Canada. (613)566-4414, ext. 5576. Fax: (613)566-4410. E-mail: joanne.larocque-poirier@canadacouncil.ca. Website: www.canadacouncil

.ca/prizes/ggla. **Contact:** Joanne Larocque-Poirier. Offered for the best English-language and the best French-language work of translation by a Canadian published September 1, 2004-September 30, 2005. Publishers submit titles for consideration. **Deadline: March 15 or August 7, 2005, depending on the book's publication date.** Prize: Each laureate receives $15,000, and nonwinning finalists receive $1,000.

JAPAN-U.S. FRIENDSHIP COMMISSION PRIZE FOR THE TRANSLATION OF JAPANESE LITERATURE

Donald Keene Center of Japanese Culture at Columbia University, 507 Kent Hall, MC 3920, Columbia University, New York NY 10027. (212)854-5036. Fax: (212)854-4019. E-mail: donald-keene-center@columbia.edu. Website: www.columbia.edu/cu/ealac/dkc. "The Donald Keene Center of Japanese Culture at Columbia University annually awards $5,000 in Japan-U.S. Friendship Commission Prizes for the Translation of Japanese Literature. A prize is given for the best translation of a modern work of literature or for the best classical literary translation, or the prize is divided between a classical and modern work. Translators of any nationality are welcome to apply. To qualify, works must be book-length translations of Japanese literary works: novels, collections of short stories, literary essays, memoirs, drama or poetry. Submissions will be judged on the literary merit of the translation and the accuracy with which it reflects the spirit of the Japanese original. Eligible works include unpublished manuscripts, works in press, or books published during the 2 years prior to the prize year." **Deadline: February 1.** Guidelines for SASE. Judged by a panel of distinguished writers, editors, translators, and scholars.

THE HAROLD MORTON LANDON TRANSLATION AWARD

The Academy of American Poets, 584 Broadway, Suite 604, New York NY 10012-3210. (212)274-0343. Fax: (212)274-9427. E-mail: rmurphy@poets.org. Website: www.poets.org. **Contact:** Ryan Murphy, awards coordinator. Offered annually to recognize a published translation of poetry from any language into English. Open to living US citizens. Anthologies by a number of translators are ineligible. **Deadline: December 31.** Guidelines for SASE. Prize: $1,000.

▦ THE MARSH AWARD FOR CHILDREN'S LITERATURE IN TRANSLATION

The Marsh Christian Trust/Administered by NCRCL, University of Surrey Roehampton, Digby Stuart College, Roehampton Lane, London, England SW15 5PH. 020 8392 3014. Fax: 020 3892 3819. **Contact:** Dr. Gillian Lathey. Offered every 2 years to raise awareness in the UK of the quality of children's books written in other languages and of the work of their translators. Entries must be submitted by British publishing companies and published between June 30, 2002 and June 30, 2004. No translations first published in the USA or Australia are eligible for this award. **Deadline: June 30, 2004.** Guidelines for SASE. Prize: £1,000. Judged by critics and translators of children's books.

PEN AWARD FOR POETRY IN TRANSLATION

PEN American Center, 568 Broadway, New York NY 10012. (212)334-1660, ext. 110. E-mail: awards@pen.org. Website: www.pen.org. **Contact:** Peter Meyer, literary awards manager. This award "recognizes book-length translations of poetry from any language into English, published during the current calendar year. All books must have been published in the U.S. Translators may be of any nationality. U.S. residency/citizenship not required." Annually, Must Be Previously Published. **Deadline: December 16.** Prize: $3,000. Judged by a single translator of poetry appointed by the PEN Translation Committee.

PEN/BOOK-OF-THE-MONTH CLUB TRANSLATION PRIZE

PEN American Center, 568 Broadway, New York NY 10012. (212)334-1660. Fax: (212)334-2181. E-mail: awards @pen.org. **Contact:** Stephen Motika. Offered for a literary book-length translation into English published in the calendar year. No technical, scientific, or reference books. Publishers, agents, or translators may submit 3 copies of each eligible title. **Deadline: December 15.** Prize: $3,000.

THE RAIZISS/DE PALCHI TRANSLATION FELLOWSHIP

The Academy of American Poets, 588 Broadway, Suite 604, New York NY 10012-3210. (212)274-0343. Fax: (212)274-9427. E-mail: rmurphy@poets.org. Website: www.poets.org. **Contact:** Awards Director. Offered in even-numbered years to recognize outstanding unpublished translations of modern Italian poetry into English. Applicants must verify permission to translate the poems or that the poems are in the public domain. Open to any US citizen. **Deadline: September 1-November 1.** Guidelines for SASE. Prize: $20,000, and a 6-week residency at the American Academy in Rome.

LOIS ROTH AWARD FOR A TRANSLATION OF A LITERARY WORK

Modern Language Association, 26 Broadway, 3rd Floor, New York NY 10004-1789. (646)576-5141. Fax: (646)458-0030. E-mail: awards@mla.org. Website: www.mla.org. **Contact:** Coordinator of Book Prizes. Offered every 2 years (odd years) for an outstanding translation into English of a book-length literary work published the previous year. Translators need not be members of the MLA. **Deadline: May 1.** Guidelines for SASE. Prize: $1,000, and a certificate.

ALDO AND JEANNE SCAGLIONE PRIZE FOR A TRANSLATION OF A LITERARY WORK

Modern Language Association, 26 Broadway, 3rd Floor, New York NY 10004-1789. (646)576-5141. Fax: (646)458-0030. E-mail: awards@mla.org. Website: www.mla.org. **Contact:** Coordinator of Book Prizes. Offered in even-numbered years for the translation of a book-length literary work appearing in print during the previous year. Translators need not be members of the MLA. **Deadline: April 1.** Guidelines for SASE. Prize: $2,000, and a certificate.

ALDO AND JEANNE SCAGLIONE PRIZE FOR A TRANSLATION OF A SCHOLARLY STUDY OF LITERATURE

Modern Language Association of America, 26 Broadway, 3rd Floor, New York NY 10004-1789. (646)576-5141. Fax: (646)458-0030. E-mail: awards@mla.org. Website: www.mla.org. **Contact:** Coordinator of Book Prizes. Offered in odd-numbered years "for an outstanding translation into English of a book-length work of literary history, literary criticism, philology, or literary theory published during the previous biennium." Translators need not be members of the MLA. **Deadline: May 1.** Guidelines for SASE. Prize: $2,000, and a certificate.

MULTIPLE WRITING AREAS

Ⓝ ABILENE WRITERS GUILD ANNUAL CONTEST

Abilene Writers Guild, P.O. Box 2562, Abilene TX 79604-2562. E-mail: AWG@abilenewritersguild.org. Website: abilenewritersguild.org. **Contact:** Jan Carrington, contest award/director. Offered annually for unpublished work in the following categories: Rhymed Poetry (up to 50 lines); Unrhymed Poetry (up to 50 lines); Children's Stories for Ages 3-10 (1,000 words maximum); Articles of General Interest (1,500 words maximum); Compositions of Inspiration (1,500 words maximum); Memoir/Composition of Nostalgia (1,500 words maximum); Fiction for Adults (1,500 words maximum); Adventure/Science Fiction/Mystery/Fantasy/Horror Novels (no more than 10 pages of 1st chapter and a 1-page synopsis of book); Mainstream/Romance/Western/Other Novel (no more than 10 pages of 1st chapter and a 1-page synopsis of book). All rights remain with the writer. **Deadline: July 1-August 2.** Guidelines for SASE. **Charges $5-10 depending on type of entry.** Prize: Each Category: 1st Place: $100; 2nd Place: $65; 3rd Place: $35. Judged by professional writers and editors, different ones each year and for each category, not announced until after entries are received. Open to any writer.

AMERICAN LITERARY REVIEW CONTEST

American Literary Review, P.O. Box 311307, University of North Texas, Denton TX 76203-1307. (940)565-2755. E-mail: americanliteraryreview@yahoo.com. Website: www.engl.unt.edu/alr. **Contact:** Managing Editor. Offered annually for unpublished work. This contest alternates annually between poetry and fiction. Open to any writer. Guidelines for SASE or online. **Deadline: Varies each year. Charges $10 entry fee.** Prize: $1,000, and publication.

AMERICAN MARKETS NEWSLETTER COMPETITION

American Markets Newsletter, 1974 46th Ave., San Francisco CA 94116. E-mail: sheila.oconnor@juno.com. **Contact:** Sheila O'Connor. "Accepts fiction and nonfiction up to 2,000 words. Entries are eligible for cash prizes and all entries are eligible for worldwide syndication whether they win or not. Here's how it works. Send us your double-spaced manuscripts with your story/article title, byline, word count, and address on the first page above your article/story's first paragraph (no need for separate cover page). There is no limit to the number of entries you may send." Annually. **Deadline: December 31.** Guidelines for SASE. **Charges $10 for 1 entry; $15 for 2 entries; $20 for 3 entries; and $25 for 4 or 5 entries.** Prize: 1st Place: $300; 2nd Place: $100; 3rd Place: $50. Judged by a panel of independent judges. Open to any writer.

ARIZONA AUTHORS' ASSOCIATION ANNUAL NATIONAL LITERARY CONTEST AND BOOK AWARDS

Arizona Authors' Association, P.O. Box 87857, Phoenix AZ 85080-7857. (602)769-2066. Fax: (623)780-0468. E-mail: info@azauthors.com. Website: www.azauthors.com. **Contact:** Toby Heathcote, contest coordinator. Offered annually for previously unpublished poetry, short stories, essays, and articles. New awards for published books in fiction, anthology, nonfiction, and children's. Winners announced at an award banquet in Phoenix in November, and short pieces and excerpts published in *Arizona Literary Magazine*. **Deadline: July 1. Charges $10 fee for poetry; $15 for short stories and essays, and $30 for published books.** Prize: $100, publication of unpublished novel, radio interview for published book winners.

ARTS & LETTERS PRIZES

Arts & Letters Journal of Contemporary Culture, Campus Box 89, GC&SU, Milledgeville GA 31061. (478)445-1289. E-mail: al@gcsu.edu. Website: al.gcsu.edu. **Contact:** The Editors. Offered annually for unpublished work. **Deadline: April 1 (postmarked). Charges $15/entry (payable to GC&SU), which includes a 1-year subscription to the journal.** Prize: $1,000 for winners in fiction, poetry, and drama (one-act play). Fiction and poetry winners will attend a weekend program in October, and the drama winner will attend a Spring festival that includes a production of the prize-winning play. Judged by editors (initial screening); 2003 final judges: Kelly Cherry (fiction), Molly Peacock (poetry), Tina Howe (drama). Open to any writer.

☒ ASTED/GRAND PRIX DE LITTERATURE JEUNESSE DU QUEBEC-ALVINE-BELISLE

Association pour l'avancement des sciences et des techniques de la documentation, 3414 Avenue du Parc, Bureau 202, Montreal QC H2X 2H5, Canada. (514)281-5012. Fax: (514)281-8219. E-mail: info@asted.org. Website: www.asted.org. **Contact:** Marie-Hélène Parent, president. "Prize granted for the best work in youth literature edited in French in the Quebec Province. Authors and editors can participate in the contest." Offered annually for books published during the preceding year. **Deadline: June 1.** Prize: $1,000.

☒ ATLANTIC WRITING COMPETITION FOR UNPUBLISHED MANUSCRIPTS

Writers' Federation of Nova Scotia, 1113 Marginal Rd., Halifax NS B3H 4P7. (902)423-8116. Fax: (902)422-0881. E-mail: talk@writers.ns.ca. Website: www.writers.ns.ca. **Contact:** Monika Sormova, executive assistant. "Established in 1975 under the auspices of the Nova Scotia Branch of the Canadian Authors' Association, the Atlantic Writing Competition has been sponsored by the Writers' Federation of Nova Scotia since 1976. We encourage all writers in Atlantic Canada to explore and celebrate their talents by sending in their new, untried work. Manuscripts are read by a team of 2 or 3 judges. WFNS chooses judges carefully, trying to balance skills, points of view, and taste. Judges are professionals who work as writers, editors, booksellers, librarians, or teachers. Because our aim is to help Atlantic Canadian writers grow, judges return written comments when the competition is concluded. Anyone resident in the Atlantic Provinces for at least 6 months prior to the contest deadline is eligible to enter. Only 1 entry/category is allowed. Writers whose work has been professionally published in book form, or frequently in periodical or media production, may not enter in the genre in which they have been published or produced. Entries must be the original, unpublished work of the writer, and must not have been accepted for publication or submitted elsewhere. The same work may not be submitted again. Entry forms will be available on the WFNS website in April, or contact the office for a copy of the form. For more information on the Atlantic Writing Competition, visit our website at www.writers.ns.ca/competitions." **Deadline: First Friday in August. Charges $15 fee ($10 for WFNS members); $25 for novel ($20 for WFNS members).** Prize: **Novel**, 1st Place: $200; 2nd Place: $150; 3rd Place: $100. **Writing for Children**, 1st Place: $150; 2nd Place: $75; 3rd Place: $50. **Poetry**, 1st Place: $100; 2nd Place: $75; 3rd Place: $50. **Short Story**, 1st Place: $100; 2nd Place: $75; 3rd Place: $50. **Essay/Magazine Article**, 1st Place: $150; 2nd Place: $75; 3rd Place: $50.

AWP AWARD SERIES

Association of Writers & Writing Programs, Carty House, Mail Stop 1E3, George Mason University, Fairfax VA 22030. (703)993-4301. Fax: (703)993-4302. E-mail: awp@gmu.edu. Website: awpwriter.org. **Contact:** Supriya Bhatnagar. Offered annually to foster new literary talent. Categories: poetry (Donald Hall Poetry Prize), short fiction, novel, and creative nonfiction. Guidelines for SASE and on website. Open to any writer. **Deadline: Must be postmarked January 1-February 28. Charges $20 for nonmembers, $10 for members.** Prize: Cash honorarium ($4,000 for Donald Hall Prize for Poetry, and $2,000 each for novel, short fiction, and creative nonfiction), and publication by a participating press.

☒ AWP INTRO JOURNALS PROJECT

The Associated Writing Programs, Dept. of English, Bluffton College, 280 W. College Ave., Suite 1, Bluffton OH 45817. E-mail: awp@gmu.edu. Website: www.awpwriter.org. **Contact:** Jeff Gundy. "This is a prize for students in AWP member-university creative writing programs only. Authors are nominated by the head of the Creative Writing Department. Each school may nominate no more than 1 work of nonfiction, 1 work of short fiction, and 3 poems." **Deadline: December 1.** Guidelines for SASE. Prize: $50, plus publication in participating journal. Judged by AWP. Open to students in AWP member-university creative writing programs only.

EMILY CLARK BALCH AWARD

Virginia Quarterly Review, 1 West Range, P.O. Box 400223, Charlottesville VA 22904-4233. (434)924-3124. Fax: (434)924-1397. Website: www.virginia.edu/vqr. **Contact:** Ted Genoways, editor. Annual award for the best short story/poetry accepted and published by the *Virginia Quarterly Review* during a calendar year. No deadline. Prize: $500.

BERTELSMANN FOUNDATION'S WORLD OF EXPRESSION SCHOLARSHIP PROGRAM

Bertelsmann, 1745 Broadway, New York NY 10019. E-mail: worldofexpression@randomhouse.com. Website: www.worldofexpression.org. Offered annually for unpublished work to NYC public high school seniors. Three categories: poetry, fiction/drama, and personal essay. **Deadline: February 1.** Guidelines for SASE. Prize: 72 awards given in literary (3) and nonliterary (2) categories. Awards range from $500-10,000. Applicants must be seniors (under age 21) at a New York high school. No college essays or class assignments will be accepted.

THE BOSTON AUTHORS CLUB BOOK AWARDS

The Boston Authors Club, 121 Follen Rd., Lexington MA 02421. **Contact:** Andrew McAleer, president. Julia Ward Howe Prize offered annually for books published the previous year. Two awards are given, 1 for trade books of fiction, nonfiction, or poetry, and the second for children's books. Authors must live or have lived within 100 miles of Boston. **Deadline: January 2.** Prize: Certificate and honorarioum of $500 in each category.

THE BRIAR CLIFF POETRY & FICTION COMPETITION

The Briar Cliff Review, Briar Cliff University, 3303 Rebecca St., Sioux City IA 51104-0100. (712)279-5321. Fax: (712)279-5410. E-mail: currans@briarcliff.edu. Website: www.briarcliff.edu/bcreview. **Contact:** Tricia Currans-Sheehan, editor. Offered annually for unpublished poetry and fiction. **Deadline: Submissions between August 1 and November 1. No mss returned.** Guidelines for SASE. **Charges $15.** Prize: $500, and publication in Spring issue. Judged by editors. "We guarantee a considerate reading." Open to any writer.

ARCH & BRUCE BROWN FOUNDATION

The Arch & Bruce Brown Foundation, PMB 503, 31855 Date Palm Dr., Suite 3, Cathedral City CA 92234. E-mail: archwrite@aol.com. Website: www.aabbfoundation.org. **Contact:** Arch Brown, president. Annual contest for unpublished, "gay-positive works based on history." Type of contest changes each year: short fiction (2004); playwriting (2005); full-length fiction (2006). **Deadline: November 30.** Guidelines for SASE. Prize: $1,000 (not limited to a single winner). Open to any writer.

CECIL A. BROWNLOW PUBLICATION AWARD

IHS Aviation Information, administered by Flight Safety Foundation, Suite 300, 601 Madison St., Alexandria VA 22314. (703)739-6700. Fax: (703)739-6708. E-mail: rozelle@flightsafety.org. Website: www.flightsafety.org. **Contact:** Roger Rozelle, director of publications. Offered annually for work published July 1-June 30. Nominees should represent standards of excellence in reporting/writing accurately and objectively about commercial aviation safety or business/corporate aviation safety through outstanding articles, books, or other communication media. Nominations may be made on behalf of individuals, print or electronic media, or organizations. The contributions of individuals during a lifetime are eligible, as are long-term achievements of publications. **Deadline: August 1.** Guidelines for SASE. Prize: $1,000, travel to the FSF International Air Safety Seminar (IASS), held annually in a different international location (where the award will be presented), and a wood-framed, hand-lettered citation. Judged by a panel of aviation safety specialist editors. Open to any writer.

☑ BURNABY WRITERS' SOCIETY CONTEST

Burnaby Writers' Society, 6584 Deer Lake Ave., Burnaby BC V5G 3T7, Canada. E-mail: lonewolf@portal.ca. Website: www.bws.bc.ca. **Contact:** Eileen Kernaghan. Offered annually for unpublished work. Open to all residents of British Columbia. Categories vary from year-to-year. Send SASE for current rules. Purpose is to encourage talented writers in all genres. **Deadline: May 31.** Guidelines for SASE. **Charges $5 fee.** Prize: 1st Place: $200; 2nd Place: $100; 3rd Place: $50; and public reading.

BYLINE MAGAZINE AWARDS

P.O. Box 5240, Edmond OK 73083-5240. (405)348-5591. E-mail: mpreston@bylinemag.com. Website: www.bylinemag.com. **Contact:** Marcia Preston, award director. Contest includes several monthly contests, open to anyone, in various categories that include fiction, nonfiction, poetry, and children's literature; an annual poetry chapbook award which is open to any poet; and an annual *ByLine* Short Fiction and Poetry Award open only to our subscribers. For chapbook award and subscriber awards, publication constitutes part of the prize, and winners grant first North American rights to *ByLine*. **Deadline: Varies. Charges $3-5 for monthly contests and $15 for chapbook contest.** Prize: **Monthly contests:** Cash and listing in magazine; **Chapbook Award:** Publication of chapbook, 50 copies and $200; *ByLine* **Short Fiction and Poetry Award:** $250 in each category, plus publication in the magazine.

☑ CANADIAN AUTHORS ASSOCIATION AWARDS PROGRAM

P.O. Box 419, Campbellford ON K0L 1L0, Canada. (705)653-0323. Fax: (705)653-0593. E-mail: admin@canauthors.org. Website: www.canauthors.org. **Contact:** Alec McEachern. Offered annually for short stories, fiction, poetry, history, and biography. Entrants must be Canadians by birth, naturalized Canadians, or landed immigrants. Entry form required for all awards. Obtain entry form from contact name or download from website. **Deadline: December 15.** Guidelines for SASE. **Charges $35 (Canadian) fee/title entered.** Prize: $2,500, and a silver medal.

CELTIC VOICE WRITING CONTEST

Bardsong Press, P.O. Box 775396, Steamboat Springs CO 80477-5396. (970)870-1401. Fax: (970)879-2657. E-mail: bard@bardsongpress.com. Website: www.bardsongpress.com. Offered annually for unpublished work to encourage and celebrate Celtic heritage and culture through poetry, short stories, essays, and creative nonfiction. Guidelines for SASE or on website. **Deadline: September 30. Charges $10 fee.** Prize: Cash award for category winners. Publication in *Bardsong* for winners and honorable mentions.

CHAUTAUQUA LITERARY JOURNAL ANNUAL CONTESTS

Chautauqua Literary Journal, a publication of the Writers' Center at Chautauqua, Inc., P.O. Box 2039, York Beach ME 03910. E-mail: cljeditor@aol.com (for contest entries only). **Contact:** Richard Foerster, editor. Offered annually for unpublished work to award literary excellence in the categories of poetry and prose (short stories and/or creative nonfiction). Guidelines for SASE or by e-mail. **Deadline: September 30 (postmarked). Charges $15/entry.** Prize: $1,500 in each of the 2 categories or poetry and prose, plus publication in *Chautauqua Literary Journal*. Judged by the editor and editorial advisory staff of the *Chautauqua Literary Journal*. Acquires first North American serial rights and one-time nonexclusive reprint rights. Open to any writer.

CHICAGO LITERARY AWARD

Left Field Press/*Another Chicago Magazine*, 3709 N. Kenmore, Chicago IL 60613-2905. E-mail: editors@anotherchicagomag.com. Website: www.anotherchicagomag.com. **Contact:** Editors. Offered annually for unpublished works to recognize excellence in poetry and fiction. Guidelines for SASE and on website. Buys first North American serial rights. Open to any writer. **Deadline: December 15. Charges $12 fee.** Prize: $1,000, and publication.

CHICANO/LATINO LITERARY CONTEST

Dept. of Spanish and Portuguese, University of California-Irvine, Irvine CA 92697. (949)824-5443. Fax: (949)824-2803. E-mail: cllp@uci.edu. Website: www.hnet.uci.edu/spanishandportuguese/contest.html. **Contact:** Adriana Gallardo. Estab. 1974. Offered annually "to promote the dissemination of unpublished Chicano/Latino literature in Spanish or English, and to encourage its development. The call for entries will be genre specific, rotating through four categories: novel (2003), short story (2004), poetry (2005), drama (2006)." The contest is open to all citizens or permanent residents of the US. **Deadline: June 1.** Guidelines for SASE. Prize: 1st Place: $1,000, and publication, transportation to receive the award; 2nd Place: $500; 3rd Place: $250.

N ⊠ THE CITY OF VANCOUVER BOOK AWARD

Office of Cultural Affairs, 453 W. 12th Ave., Vancouver BC V5Y 1V4, Canada. (604)873-7487. Fax: (604)871-6048. E-mail: oca@city.vancouver.bc.ca. Website: www.city.vancouver.bc.ca/oca. Offered annually for books published the previous year which exhibit excellence in 1 or more of 4 categories: content, illustration, design, and format. The book must contribute significantly to the appreciation and understanding of the city of Vancouver and heighten awareness of 1 or more of the following: Vancouver's history, the city's unique character, or achievements of the city's residents. The book may be fiction, nonfiction, poetry, or drama written for adults or children, and may deal with any aspects of the city: history, geography, current affairs, or the arts. Guidelines on website. Prize: $2,000.

CLEVERKITTY CATERWAULING CONTEST

Cleverkitty.com, 6764 Sugar Hill Dr., Nashville TN 37211. (615)941-6765. E-mail: caterwauling@cleverkitty.com. Website: www.cleverkitty.com. **Contact:** Kim Cady, contest director. "Our website celebrates all things feline. Our annual contest is for writers of all kinds of short literature, fiction or nonfiction (stories concerning real-life experiences are accepted) relating to "The Cat." There are no separate categories at this time. The pieces will be judged for impact and overall excellence." **Deadline: August 31.** Prize: 1st Place: $100; 2nd Place: $50; 3rd Place: $20. In addition, all winners will receive a membership in the "Best Friends Animal Society" (one of the premier animal welfare organizations in the USA). Open to all writers.

CNW/FFWA ANNUAL FLORIDA STATE WRITING COMPETITION

Florida Freelance Writers Association, P.O. Box A, North Stratford NH 03590-0167. E-mail: contest@writers-editors.com. Website: www.writers-editors.com. **Contact:** Dana K. Cassell, executive director. Annual award "to recognize publishable talent." Divisions & Categories: Nonfiction (previously published article/essay/column/nonfiction book chapter; unpublished or self-published article/essay/column/nonfiction book chapter); Fiction (unpublished or self-published short story or novel chapter); Children's Literature (unpublished or self-published short story/nonfiction article/book chapter/poem); Poetry (unpublished or self-published free verse/traditional). **Deadline: March 15.** Guidelines for SASE. **Charges $5 (active or new CNW/FFWA members) or $10 (nonmembers) for each fiction/nonfiction entry under 3,000 words; $10 (members) or $20 (nonmembers) for each entry of 3,000 words or longer; and $3 (members) or $5 (nonmembers) for each poem.** Prize: 1st Place: $100, plus certificate; 2nd Place: $75, plus certificate; 3rd Place: $50, plus certificate. Honorable Mention certificates will be awarded in each category as warranted. Judged by editors, librarians, and writers. Open to any writer.

◨ COMPACT FICTION/SHORT POEM COMPETITION

Pottersfield Portfolio, 9879 Kempt Head Rd., Ross Ferry NS B1X 1N3, Canada. Website: www.magomania.com. **Contact:** Editor. Offered annually for unpublished work: Stories of 1,500 words or less and poems of 20 lines or less. Maximum of 2 stories or 3 poems per author. Buys first Canadian serial rights; copyright remains with author. Guidelines for SASE or on website. **Deadline: May 1. Charges $20 for the first entry, $5 for each subsequent entry in the same category.** Prize: $250 for the best story and the best poem, publication, and a 1-year subscription to *Pottersfield Portfolio*.

VIOLET CROWN BOOK AWARDS

Writers' League of Texas, 1501 W. Fifth St., Suite E-2, Austin TX 78703. (512)499-8914. Fax: (512)499-0441. E-mail: wlt@writersleague.org. Website: www.writersleague.org. **Contact:** Helen Ginger, director. Offered annually for work published June 1-May 31. Honors 3 outstanding books published in fiction, nonfiction, and literary categories by Writers' League of Texas members. Membership dues may accompany entry fee. **Deadline: May 31.** Guidelines for SASE. **Charges $20 fee.** Prize: $1,000 prizes (3), and trophies.

THE CRUCIBLE POETRY AND FICTION COMPETITION

Crucible, Barton College, College Station, Wilson NC 27893. (252)399-6456. E-mail: tgrimes@barton.edu. **Contact:** Terrence L. Grimes, editor. Offered annually for unpublished mss. **Deadline: Late April.** Guidelines for SASE. Prize: $150 (1st Prize); $100 (2nd Prize) and publication in *Crucible*. Judged by in-house editorial board. Open to any writer.

◨ CWW ANNUAL AWARDS COMPETITION

Council for Wisconsin Writers, 4465 N. Oakland Ave., Milwaukee WI 53211. E-mail: mbowen@foleylaw.com. Website: www.wisconsinwriters.org/index.htm. Offered annually for work published by Wisconsin writers the previous calendar year. Thirteen awards: Major/life achievement; short fiction; scholarly book; short nonfiction; nonfiction book; juvenile fiction book; children's picture book; poetry book; fiction book; outdoor writing; juevnile nonfiction book; drama (produced); outstanding service to Wisconsin writers. Open to Wiscconsin residents. **Deadline: January 31.** Guidelines for SASE. **Charges $25 fee for nonmembers, $10 for members.** Prize: $100-1,500, and certificate.

DANA AWARDS IN PORTFOLIO, THE NOVEL, SHORT FICTION AND POETRY

(formerly Dana Awards in the Novel, Short Fiction and Poetry), 7207 Townsend Forest Court, Browns Summit NC 27214-9634. (336)656-7009. E-mail: danaawards@pipeline.com. Website: www.danaawards.com. **Contact:** Mary Elizabeth Parker, chair. Four awards offered annually for unpublished work written in English. Purpose is monetary award for work that has not been previously published or received monetary award, but will accept work published simply for friends and family. Works previously published online are not eligible. No work accepted by or for persons under 16 for any of the 4 awards. Awards: **Portfolio:** For any group of 3 mss (novel, short fiction, or poetry, any combination of 3 mss). Also for this award, novel mss must be first 50 pages only, poetry mss must be 5 poems only. **Novel:** For the first 50 pages of a novel completed or in progress. **Short fiction:** Short fiction (no memoirs) up to 10,000 words. **Poetry:** For best group of 5 poems based on excellence of all 5 (no light verse, no single poem over 100 lines). **Deadline: October 31 (postmarked). Charges varied fee/portfolio award—must see full guidelines for fee schedule; $20 fee/novel entry, $15 fee/short fiction or poetry entry.** Prize: $3,000 for portfolio award; $1,000 each for other categories.

◨ DOG WRITERS ASSOCIATION OF AMERICA ANNUAL WRITING CONTEST

Dog Writers Association of America, 825 College Blvd., Suite 102, PMB 524, Oceanside CA 92057. (760)630-3828. E-mail: lizpalika@cox.net. Website: www.dwaa.org. **Contact:** Liz Palika, contest chair. Offered annually for submissions published between September 1-August 31 in the following categories: newspaper articles; books; pqems; mystery; club newsletters; videos; and children's books. Only published work is eligible. Books must be first published within the competition period, and the actual date of publication must appear on the entry form; revisions and updates are not eligible. **Deadline: August 31.** Guidelines for SASE. **Charges $10 for members; $15 for nonmembers.** Prize: Cash awards, and plaques.

EATON LITERARY AGENCY'S ANNUAL AWARDS PROGRAM

Eaton Literary Agency, P.O. Box 49795, Sarasota FL 34230. (941)366-6589. Fax: (941)365-4679. E-mail: eatonlit @aol.com. **Contact:** Richard Lawrence, vice president. Offered annually for unpublished mss. Annually, Must Be Unpublished. **Deadline: March 31 (mss under 10,000 words); August 31 (mss over 10,000 words).** Guidelines for SASE. Prize: $2,500 (over 10,000 words); $500 (under 10,000 words). Judged by an independent agency in conjunction with some members of Eaton's staff. Open to any writer.

N EMERGING LESBIAN WRITERS FUND AWARD

ASTRAEA Lesbian Action Foundation, 116 E. 16th St., 7th Floor, New York NY 10003. (212)529-8021. Fax: (212)982-3321. E-mail: info@astraea.org. Website: www.astraea.org. **Contact:** Christine Lipat, senior program officer. Offered annually to encourage and support the work of new lesbian writers of fiction and poetry. Guidelines for SASE or on website. Entrants must be a lesbian writer of either fiction or poetry, a US resident, work includes some lesbian content, at least 1 piece of writing (in any genre) has been published in a newspaper, magazine, journal, anthology, or professional website, and not more than 1 book. (Published work may be in any discipline; self-published books are not included in the 1 book maximum.) **Deadline: March 8 (postmarked). Charges $5 fee.** Prize: $10,000 grants.

THE VIRGINIA FAULKNER AWARD FOR EXCELLENCE IN WRITING

Prairie Schooner, 201 Andrews Hall, P.O. Box 880334, Lincoln NE 68588-0334. (402)472-0911. Fax: (402)472-9771. E-mail: kgrey2@unl.edu. Website: www.unl.edu/schooner/psmain.htm. **Contact:** Hilda Raz. Offered annually for work published in *Prairie Schooner* in the previous year. Prize: $1,000.

FINELINE COMPETITION FOR PROSE POEMS, SHORT SHORTS, AND ANYTHING IN BETWEEN

Mid-American Review, Dept. of English, Box W, Bowling Green State University, Bowling Green OH 43403. (419)372-2725. Website: www.bgsu.edu/midamericanreview. **Contact:** Michael Czyzniejewski, editor-in-chief. Offered annually for previously unpublished submissions. Contest open to all writers not associated with current judge or *Mid-American Review*. **Deadline: October 1.** Guidelines for SASE. **Charges $10/group of 3 pieces or $5 each. All $10-and-over participants receive prize issue.** Prize: $500, plus publication in spring issue of *Mid-American Review*; 10 finalists receive notation plus possible publication. Judged by well-known writer, e.g., Michael Martone, Alberto Rios, Stephen Dunn. Open to any writer.

THE FLORIDA REVIEW EDITOR'S AWARD

Dept. of English, University of Central Florida, Orlando FL 32816. (407)823-2038. E-mail: flreview@mail.ucf.e du. Website: www.flreview.com. Annual awards for the best unpublished fiction, poetry, and memoir. **Deadline: April 2.** Guidelines for SASE. **Charges $15.** Prize: $1,000 (in each genre) and publication in *The Florida Review*. Judged by the editors in each genre. Acquires first rights. Open to any writer.

N ☼ FREEFALL SHORT FICTION AND POETRY CONTEST

The Alexandra Writers' Centre Society, 922 9th Ave. SE, Calgary AB T2G 0S4, Canada. (403)264-4730. E-mail: awcs@telusplanet.net. Website: www.alexandrawriters.org. Offered annually for unpublished work in the categories of poetry (5 poems/entry) and fiction (3,000 words or less). The purpose of the award in both categories is to recognize writers and offer publication credits in a literary magazine format. **Deadline: October 1.** Guidelines for SASE. **Charges $10 entry fee.** Prize: 1st Prize: $200 (Canadian); 2nd Prize: $100 (Canadian). Both prizes include publication in the Spring edition of *FreeFall Magazine*. Winners will also be invited to read at the launch of that issue if such a launch takes place. Honorable mentions in each category will be published and may be asked to read. Travel expenses not included. Judged by current *FreeFall* editors (who are also published authors in Canada). Acquires first Canadian serial rights (ownership reverts to author after one-time publication). Open to any writer.

N FUGUE CONTEST IN PROSE AND POETRY

Fugue, Literary Journal of University of Idaho, English Department, 200 Brink Hall, Moscow ID 83844-1102. Website: www.class.uidaho.edu/english/fugue. **Contact:** Senior Editor. Annual award for fiction, every 2 years for nonfiction and poetry, to recognize the most compelling work being produced. **Deadline: Annually April 1 (fiction); April 1, 2006 (poetry); April 1, 2005, and April 1, 2007 (nonfiction).** Guidelines for SASE. **Charges $15/submission.** Prize: **Fiction:** $1,000 for winning story, and publication for top 3 winners. **Poetry:** $1,000 for winning poem(s), and publication for top 3 winners. **Nonfiction:** $1,000 for winning essay, and publication for top 3 winners. Judged by established authors. In 2004, Ehud Havazelet judged fiction, and Ellen Bryant

Voigt judged poetry. Other past judges have included Scott Russell Sanders, Rick Moody, and Mark Doty. Acquires first North American serial rights and electronic rights. Open to any writer.

ⓝ GULF COAST POETRY & SHORT FICTION PRIZE
Gulf Coast, English Department, University of Houston, Houston TX 77204-3013. (713)743-3223. Website: www. gulfcoast.uh.edu. Offered annually for poetry and short stories. Open to any writer. **Deadline: March 31.** Guidelines for SASE. **Charges $15 fee, which includes subscription.** Prize: $1,000, and publication in *Gulf Coast* for best poem and short story.

INDIANA REVIEW ½ K (SHORT-SHORT/PROSE-POEM) PRIZE
(formerly Indiana Review ½ K (Short-Short/Prose-Poem) Contest), *Indiana Review*, BH 465, Indiana University, Bloomington IN 47405-7103. (812)855-3439. Fax: (812)855-4253. E-mail: inreview@indiana.edu. Website: www.indiana.edu/~inreview. **Contact:** Esther Lee. Maximum story/poem length is 500 words. Offered annually for unpublished work. **Deadline: Early June.** Guidelines for SASE. **Charges $15 fee for no more than 3 pieces (includes a year's subscription).** Prize: $1,000. Judged by guest judges. Juliana Baggott was 2004 judge. Open to any writer.

IOWA AWARD IN POETRY, FICTION, & ESSAY
The Iowa Review, 308 EPB, The University of Iowa, Iowa City IA 52242. (319)335-0462. Fax: (319)335-2535. E-mail: iowa-review@uiowa.edu. Website: www.uiowa.edu/~iareview. **Deadline: February 1. Charges $15 entry fee.** Prize: $1,000, and publication.

ROBERT F. KENNEDY BOOK AWARDS
1367 Connecticut Ave., NW, Suite 200, Washington DC 20036. (202)463-7575. Fax: (202)463-6606. E-mail: info@rfkmemorial.org. Website: www.rfkmemorial.org. **Contact:** Book Award Director. Offered annually for work published the previous year "which most faithfully and forcefully reflects Robert Kennedy's purposes—his concern for the poor and the powerless, his struggle for honest and even-handed justice, his conviction that a decent society must assure all young people a fair chance, and his faith that a free democracy can act to remedy disparities of power and opportunity." **Deadline: January 31. Charges $25 fee.** Prize: $2,500, and a bust of Robert F. Kennedy.

ⓝ LABYRINTH SOCIETY WRITING CONTEST
The Labyrinth Society, P.O. Box 736, Trumansburg NY 14886-0736. Website: www.labyrinthsociety.org. **Contact:** David Gallagher. Estab. 2004. The Labyrinth Society is looking for short stories, essays, and poems that reflect the many experiences available through the labyrinth. "We want to see your best writing. Stories will be judged on creativity, content, general appeal, and the extent to which the labyrinth is highlighted." Entry forms are available online or by sending a request and SASE to The Labyrinth Society. Must Be Unpublished. **Deadline: June 15 (postmarked). Charges $10 (send checks only).** Prize: Grand Prize: Free registration for The Labyrinth Society's Annual Gathering/Conference ($500 + value), or $150 if unable to attend; First Prize: $75; Second Prize: $50; Third Prize: $25. Open to any writer.

LARRY LEVIS EDITORS' PRIZE IN POETRY/THE MISSOURI REVIEW EDITOR'S PRIZE IN FICTION & ESSAY
The Missouri Review, 1507 Hillcrest Hall, Columbia MO 65211. (573)882-4474. Fax: (573)884-4671. Website: www.missourireview.com. **Contact:** Hoa Ngo. Offered annually for unpublished work in 3 categories: fiction, essay, and poetry. Guidelines for SASE after June. **Deadline: October 15. Charges $15 fee (includes a 1-year subscription).** Prize: $2,000 in each genre, plus publication; 3 finalists in each category receive a minimum of $100.

THE HUGH J. LUKE AWARD
Prairie Schooner, 201 Andrews Hall, P.O. Box 880334, Lincoln NE 68588-0334. (402)472-0911. Fax: (402)472-9771. E-mail: kgrey2@unl.edu. Website: www.unl.edu/schooner/psmain.htm. **Contact:** Hilda Raz. Offered annually for work published in *Prairie Schooner* in the previous year. Prize: $250.

ⓝ JOHN T. LUPTON AWARDS
Books for Life Foundation, 450 S. Galena St., Aspen CO 81611. (970)544-3398. E-mail: help@booksforlifefoundation.com. Website: www.booksforlifefoundation.com. Offered annually to encourage writers to complete professionally written query letters and book proposals for submission to literary agents and publishers to maximize their opportunity to become published authors through traditional means. The contest is open to authors who have not been traditionally published (self-published authors are eligible). Writers should submit a profession-

ally written query letter and book proposal for a book not previously published. Book categories include fiction (any genre); nonfiction (biography, autobiography, memoir, inspirational, religious, how-to, etc.). See website for complete submission guidelines. **Deadline: May 5 (postmarked). Charges $25 (fee waived for those attending the Book Expo America Writers Conference co-sponsored by *Writer's Digest*).** Prize: $25,000. $10,000 is awarded to the winner in each category (nonfiction and fiction), plus $2,500 to each winner to cover expenses and entertainment at Book Expo America. Judged by staff members and literary consultants for the Books for Life Foundation. Open to any writer.

⚡ THE LUSH TRIUMPHANT

subTerrain Magazine, P.O. Box 3008, MPO, Vancouver BC V6B 3 × 5, Canada. E-mail: subter@portal.ca. Website: www.subterrain.ca. Annual contest for fiction, poetry, and creative nonfiction. All entries must be previously unpublished and not currently under consideration in any other contest or competition. Entries will not be returned. Results of the competition will be announced in the Summer 2003 issue of *subTerrain*. All entrants receive a complimentary 1-year subscription to *subTerrain*. **Deadline: May 15. Charges $20/entry (entrants may submit as many entries in as many categories as they like).** Prize: The winning entries in each category will receive $500 and will be published in the Fall issue of *subTerrain*. The 1st runner-up in each category will be published in a future issue of *subTerrain*. Open to any writer.

⚡ BRENDA MACDONALD RICHES FIRST BOOK AWARD

Saskatchewan Book Awards, Inc., 120-2505 11th Ave., Regina SK S4P 0K6, Canada. (306)569-1585. Fax: (306)569-4187. E-mail: director@bookawards.sk.ca. Website: www.bookawards.sk.ca. **Contact:** Joyce Wells, executive director. Offered annually for work published September 15 of year past to September 14 of current year. This award is presented to a Saskatchewan author for the best first book, judged on the quality of writing. Books from the following categories will be considered: children's; drama; fiction (short fiction by a single author, novellas, novels); nonfiction (all categories of nonfiction writing except cookbooks, directories, how-to books, or bibliographies of minimal critical content); poetry. **Deadline: First deadline: July 31; Final deadline: September 14.** Guidelines for SASE. **Charges $20 (Canadian).** Prize: $2,000.

🌐 THE MAIL ON SUNDAY/JOHN LLEWELLYN RHYS PRIZE

(formerly John Llewellyn Rhys Prize), *The Mail on Sunday*, c/o Book House, 45 E. Hill, Wandsworth, London SW18 2QZ, United Kingdom. Fax: (00 44) 20 8516 2978. E-mail: tarryn@booktrust.org.uk. Website: www.booktrust.org.uk. **Contact:** Kate Mervyn Jones. "The Prize was founded in 1942 by Jane Oliver, the widow of John Llewellyn Rhys, a young writer killed in action in World War II. This is one of Britain's oldest and most prestigious literary awards, with an unequalled reputation of singling out the fine young writers—from poets to novelists, biographers and travel writers—early in their careers." Entries can be any work of literature written by a British Commonwealth writer aged 35 or under at the time of publication. Books must be written in English, published between January 1 and December 31 and translations are not eligible. **Deadline: August.** Prize: £5,000 to the winner and £500 to shortlisted authors.

⚡ MANITOBA WRITING AND PUBLISHING AWARDS

c/o Manitoba Writers' Guild, 206-100 Arthur St., Winnipeg MB R3B 1H3, Canada. (204)942-6134 or toll-free (888)637-5802. Fax: (204)942-5754. E-mail: mbwriter@mts.net. Website: www.mbwriter.mb.ca. **Contact:** Robyn Maharaj or Jamis Paulson. Offered annually: The McNally Robinson Book of Year Award (adult); The McNally Robinson Book for Young People Awards (8 and under and 9 and older); The John Hirsch Award for Most Promising Manitoba Writer; The Mary Scorer Award for Best Book by a Manitoba Publisher; The Carol Shields Winnipeg Book Award; The Eileen McTavish Sykes Award for Best First Book; The Margaret Laurence Award for Fiction; The Alexander Kennedy Isbister Award for Non-Fiction; The Manuela Dias Book Design of the Year Award; The Best Illustrated Book of the Year Award; and the biennial Le Prix Littéraire Rue-Deschambault. Guidelines and submission forms available on website at www.mbwriter.mb.ca/mwapa.html. Open to Manitoba writers only. **Deadline: December 1 (books published December 1-31 will be accepted until mid-January).** Prize: Several prizes up to $5,000 (Canadian).

MASTERS LITERARY AWARDS

Titan Press, P.O. Box 17897, Encino CA 91416-7897. **Contact:** Contest Coordinator. Offered annually and quarterly for work published within 2 years (preferred) and unpublished work (accepted). Fiction, 15-page maximum; poetry, 5 pages or 150-lines maximum; and nonfiction, 10 pages maximum. "A selection of winning entries may appear in our national literary publication." Winners may also appear on the Internet. Titan Press retains one-time publishing rights to selected winners. **Deadline: Ongoing (nominations made March 15, June 15, September 15, December 15).** Guidelines for SASE. **Charges $15.** Prize: $1,000, and possible publication in the *Titan Press Internet* journal.

THE MCGINNIS-RITCHIE MEMORIAL AWARD

Southwest Review, P.O. Box 750374, Dallas TX 75275-0374. (214)768-1037. Fax: (214)768-1408. E-mail: swr@mail.smu.edu. Website: www.southwestreview.org. **Contact:** Elizabeth Mills & Willard Spiegelman. The McGinnis-Ritchie Memorial Award is given annually to the best works of fiction and nonfiction that appeared in the magazine in the previous year. Manuscripts are submitted for publication, not for the prizes themselves. Guidelines for SASE or on website. Prize: 2 cash prizes of $500 each. Judged by Elizabeth Mills, senior editor, and Willard Spiegelman, editor-in-chief. Open to any writer.

MID-LIST PRESS FIRST SERIES AWARDS

Mid-List Press, 4324 12th Ave. S., Minneapolis MN 55407-3218. (612)822-3733. Fax: (612)823-8387. E-mail: guide@midlist.org. Website: www.midlist.org. **Contact:** Lane Stiles. Offered annually for authors who have yet to publish books in any of 4 categories: creative nonfiction, short fiction, poetry, and novels. Guidelines for SASE or online at website. **Deadline: Varies. Charges $30 fee (US dollars).** Prize: An advance against royalties and publication. Open to any writer who has not published a book-length work in the category for which he or she is submitting.

MOUNTAINS & PLAINS BOOKSELLERS ASSOCIATION REGIONAL BOOK AWARD

Mountains & Plains Booksellers Association, 19 Old Town Square, Suite 238, Fort Collins CO 80525. (970)484-5856. Fax: (970)407-1479. E-mail: lisa@mountainsplains.org. Website: www.mountainsplains.org. **Contact:** Lisa D. Knudsen. The purpose of these annual awards is to honor outstanding books published between November and October, which are set in our region. The Mountains & Plains region includes Colorado, Wyoming, New Mexico, Utah, Idaho, Texas, Montana, Kansas, Arizona, Nebraska, Oklahoma, North Dakota, and South Dakota. **Deadline: October 1.** Guidelines for SASE. **Charges $50.** Prize: Each award includes a framed copy of the poster. Press releases are sent out nationally and regionally, MPBA's 250 bookstores receive free posters, and the winning titles are featured on the back of the MPBA regional catalog, *Reading the West*. The prizes are awarded at a banquet in Denver in March. Judged by 3 panels of judges, 1 each for adult fiction, adult nonfiction and the arts, and children's. Each panel consists of 3 persons selected by the Awards Committee. The panelists represent a cross-section of the book community in our region, including, at various times, members of the media, librarians, and booksellers. Open to any writer.

NEW ENGLAND WRITERS FREE VERSE AND FICTION CONTESTS

New England Writers, P.O. Box 5, Windsor VT 05089-0005. (802)674-2315. E-mail: newvtpoet@aol.com. Website: www.newenglandwriters.org. **Contact:** Dr. Frank and Susan Anthony. Poetry line limit: 30 lines. Fiction word limit: 1,000 words. Guidelines for SASE or online. **Deadline: Postmarked June 15. Charges $5 for 3 poems or 1 fiction (multiple entries welcome).** Prize: The winning poems and fiction are published in *The Anthology of New England Writers*. The free verse contest has Robert Penn Warren Awards of $300, $200, and $100, with 10 Honorable Mentions of $20. The short fiction contest has 1 Marjory Bartlett Sanger Award of $300, with 5 Honorable Mentions of $30. Judged by published, working university professors of the genre. Open to any writer, not just New England.

NEW LETTERS LITERARY AWARDS

New Letters, University House, 5101 Rockhill Rd., Kansas City MO 64110-2499. (816)235-1168. Fax: (816)235-2611. E-mail: newletters@umkc.edu. Website: www.newletters.org. **Contact:** Aleatha Ezra. Award has 3 categories (fiction, poetry, and creative nonfiction) with 1 winner in each. Offered annually for previously unpublished work. Guidelines for SASE or online. **Deadline: May 19.** Deadline is always the closest Friday to May 15. **Charges $15 fee (includes a year's subscription to *New Letters* magazine).** Prize: 1st Place: $1,000, plus publication; First Runners-Up: A copy of a recent book of poetry or fiction courtesy of our affiliate BkMk Press. Preliminary judges are regional writers of prominence and experience. All judging is done anonymously. Winners picked by a final judge of national repute. Previous judges include Maxine Kumin, Albert Goldbarth, Charles Simic, Janet Burroway. Acquires first North American serial rights. Open to any writer.

NEW WRITERS AWARDS

Great Lakes Colleges Association New Writers Awards, The Philadelphia Center, North American Building, 121 S. Broad St., 7th Floor, Philadelphia PA 19107. (215)735-7300. Fax: (215)735-7373. E-mail: clark@philactr.edu. **Contact:** Dr. Mark A. Clark, faculty of writing, literature, and education, award director. Offered annually to the best first book of poetry and the best first book of fiction among those submitted by publishers. An honorarium of at least $300 will be guaranteed the author by each of the colleges visited. Open to any first book of poetry or fiction submitted by a publisher. **Deadline: February 28.** Guidelines for SASE. Prize: Winning authors tour the GLCA colleges, where they will participate in whatever activities they and the college deem appropriate.

⬛ NLAPW VIRGINIA LIEBELER BIENNIAL GRANTS FOR MATURE WOMEN

National League of American Pen Women, Inc., 1300 17th St. NW, Washington DC 20036-1973. (202)785-1997. Offered in even years for career enhancement in the creative arts. Three categories: art, letters, and music. Open to women 35 and over who are US citizens. No phone calls. **Deadline: December 1, 2005.** Guidelines for SASE. **Charges $8.** Prize: $1,000 grant in each category.

⬛ THE NOMA AWARD FOR PUBLISHING IN AFRICA

Kodansha Ltd., Japan, P.O. Box 128, Witney, Oxon OX8 5XU, United Kingdom. (+44) (0)1993-775235. Fax: (+44) (0)1993-709265. E-mail: maryljay@aol.com. Website: www.nomaward.org. **Contact:** Mary Jay, secretary to the Noma Award Managing Committee. "The Noma Award is open to African writers and scholars whose work is published in Africa, rather than outside. The spirit within which the annual Award is given is to encourage and reward genuinely autonomous African publishers, and African writers. The Award is given for an outstanding new book in any of these 3 categories: scholarly or academic; books for children; and literature and creative writing (including fiction, drama, poetry, and essays on African literature)." Entries must be submitted by publishers in Africa, who are limited to 3 entries (in any combination of the eligible categories). The Award is open to any author who is indigenous to Africa (a national, irrespective of place of domicile). Guidelines at website or from Secretariat. **Deadline: February 28.** Prize: $10,000 (U.S.). Judged by an impartial committee chaired by Mr. Walter Bgoya, comprising African scholars and book experts, and representatives of the international book community, is entrusted with the selection of the annual prize. This Managing Committee is the Jury. The Jury is assisted by independent opinion and assessment from a large and distinguished pool of subject specialists from throughout the world, including many in Africa.

⬛ OHIOANA BOOK AWARDS

Ohioana Library Association, 274 E. 1st Ave., Suite 300, Columbus OH 43201-3673. (614)466-3831. Fax: (614)728-6974. E-mail: ohioana@sloma.state.oh.us. Website: www.oplin.lib.oh.us/OHIOANA. **Contact:** Linda Hengst, director. Offered annually to bring national attention to Ohio authors and their books (published in the last 2 years). Categories: Fiction, nonfiction, juvenile, poetry, and books about Ohio or an Ohioan. Books about Ohio or an Ohioan need not be written by an Ohioan. For other book categories, writers must have been born in Ohio or lived in Ohio for at least 5 years. **Deadline: December 31.** Guidelines for SASE.

OREGON BOOK AWARDS

Literary Arts, 219 NW 12th Ave., #201, Portland OR 97209. (503)227-2583. E-mail: la@literary-arts.org. Website: www.literary-arts.org. **Contact:** Kristy Athens, award coordinator. The annual Oregon Book Awards celebrate Oregon authors in the areas of poetry, fiction, nonfiction, drama, and young readers' literature published between April 1 and March 31. **Deadline: May 28.** Guidelines for SASE. Prize: Finalists are invited on a statewide reading tour and are promoted in bookstores and libraries across the state. Winners receive a cash prize. Judged by out-of-state judges who are selected for their expertise in a genre. Past judges include Dorothy Allison, Chris Offutt, and Maxine Kumin. Oregon residents only.

⬛ PAINTED BRIDE QUARTERLY'S POETRY & FICTION CONTEST

Painted Bride Quarterly, Rutgers University, Armitage Hall, Camden NJ 08102. Website: pbq.rutgers.edu. **Contact:** Kathy Volk Miller. Offered annually to celebrate new and emerging writers, as well as reward excellence in writing. **Deadline: Reading period between June 1 and September 30 (deadline is September 30). Charges Poetry: $5 (maximum 3 poems/submission); Fiction $10 (maximum 5,000 words).** Prize: $1,000, plus publication in a celected copy of *Painted Bride Quarterly*. One award/year for poetry, and 1 award/year for fiction. Judged by Carole Simmons Oles (poetry) and Victor Lavalle (fiction), 2003 contest. Open to any writer.

PEACE WRITING INTERNATIONAL WRITING AWARDS

Peace and Justice Studies Association, 2582 Jimmie, Fayetteville AR 72703-3420. (479)442-4600. E-mail: jbennet @uark.edu. Website: www.omnicenter.org. **Contact:** Dick Bennett. Offered annually for unpublished books. "PeaceWriting encourages writing about war and international nonviolent peacemaking and peacemakers. PeaceWriting seeks book manuscripts about the causes, consequences, and solutions to violence and war, and about the ideas and practices of nonviolent peacemaking and the lives of nonviolent peacemakers." Three categories: Nonfiction Prose (history, political science, memoirs); Imaginative Literature (novels, plays, collections of short stories, collections of poetry, collections of short plays); and Works for Young People. Open to any writer. Enclose SASE for ms return. **Deadline: December 1.** Guidelines for SASE. Prize: $500 for best nonfiction; $500 for best imaginative work; and $500 for best work for young people.

PEN CENTER USA ANNUAL LITERARY AWARDS

(formerly PEN Center USA West Annual Literary Awards), PEN Center USA, 672 S. Lafayette Park Place, Suite 42, Los Angeles CA 90057. (213)365-8500. Fax: (213)365-9616. E-mail: awards@penusa.org. Website:

www.penusa.org. **Contact:** Literary Awards Coordinator. Offered annually for fiction, nonfiction, poetry, children's literature, or translation published January 1-December 31 of the current year. Open to authors west of the Mississippi River. Guidelines for SASE or online. **Deadline: December 17. Charges $35 fee.** Prize: $1,000.

ⓝ PNWA LITERARY CONTEST

Pacific Northwest Writers Association, P.O. Box 2016, Edmonds WA 98020-9516. (425)673-2665. Fax: (425)771-9588. E-mail: staff@pnwa.org. Website: www.pnwa.org. **Contact:** Dana Murphy-Love. Annual contest for unpublished mss that awards prize money in 10 categories. Categories include: Stella Cameron Romance Genre; Screenwriting; Poetry; Adult Genre Novel; Jean Auel Adult Mainstream Novel; Adult Short Story; Juvenile/Young Adult Novel; Juvenile Short Story or Picture Book; Nonfiction Book/Memoir; Adult Article/Essay/Short Memoir. Each entry receives 2 critiques. **Deadline: February.** Guidelines for SASE. **Charges $35/entry (members); $45/entry (nonmembers).** Prize: 1st Place: $600; 2nd Place: $300; 3rd Place: $150. 1st, 2nd, and 3rd Places awarded in 10 categories. Judged by industry experts. Open to any writer.

⚟ POSTCARD STORY COMPETITION

The Writers' Union of Canada, 40 Wellington St. E., 3rd Floor, Toronto ON M5E 1C7, Canada. (416)703-8982, ext. 223. Fax: (416)504-7656. E-mail: projects@writersunion.ca. Website: www.writersunion.ca. **Contact:** Project Coordinator. Offered annually for original and unpublished fiction, nonfiction, prose, verse, dialogue, etc. with a maximum 250 words in length. Open to Canadian citizens or landed immigrants only. **Deadline: February 14.** Guidelines for SASE. **Charges $5 entry fee.** Prize: $500.

THE PRESIDIO LA BAHIA AWARD

Sons of the Republic of Texas, 1717 Eighth St., Bay City TX 77414-5033. (979)245-6644. Fax: (979)244-3819. E-mail: srttexas@srttexas.org. Website: www.srttexas.org. **Contact:** Scott Dunbar, chairman. Offered annually "to promote suitable preservation of relics, appropriate dissemination of data, and research into our Texas heritage, with particular attention to the Spanish Colonial period." **Deadline: September 30.** Guidelines for SASE. Prize: $2,000 total; 1st Place: Minimum of $1,200, 2nd and 3rd prizes at the discretion of the judges. Judged by members of the Sons of the Republic of Texas on the Presidio La Bahia Award Committee. Open to any writer.

⚟ QWF LITERARY AWARDS

Quebec Writers' Federation, 1200 Atwater Ave., Montreal QC H3Z 1X4, Canada. (514)933-0878. E-mail: admin@qwf.org. Website: www.qwf.org. Offered annually for a book published October 1-September 30 to honor excellence in English-language writing in Quebec. Categories: fiction, nonfiction, poetry and first book, and translation. Author must have resided in Quebec for 3 of the past 5 years. **Deadline: May 31 for books, and August 15 for books and finished proofs.** Guidelines for SASE. **Charges $10/title.** Prize: $2,000 in each category; $1,000 for first book.

⚟ REGINA BOOK AWARD

Saskatchewan Book Awards, Inc., 120-2505 11th Ave., Regina SK S4P 0K6, Canada. (306)569-1585. Fax: (306)569-4187. E-mail: director@bookawards.sk.ca. Website: www.bookawards.sk.ca. **Contact:** Joyce Wells, executive director. Offered annually for work published September 15 of year past to September 14 of current year. In recognition of the vitality of the literary community in Regina, this award is presented to a Regina author for the best book, judged on the quality of writing. Books from the following categories will be considered: children's; drama; fiction (short fiction by a single author, novellas, novels); nonfiction (all categories of nonfiction writing except cookbooks, directories, how-to books, or bibliographies of minimal critical content); poetry. **Deadline: First deadline: July 31; Final deadline: September 14.** Guidelines for SASE. **Charges $20 (Canadian).** Prize: $2,000.

ⓝ MARY ROBERTS RINEHART FUND

English Department, MSN 3E4, George Mason University, Fairfax VA 22030-4444. (703)993-1180. E-mail: writing@gmu.edu. Website: www.gmu.edu/departments/writing/rinehart.htm. Offered annually for unpublished authors "who, in order to finish projected work, need financial assistance otherwise unavailable." Grants by nomination to unpublished creative writers for fiction, poetry, and nonfiction with a strong narrative quality. Submissions must include nominating letter from person in appropriate field. Send e-mail for guidelines. **Deadline: November 30.** Prize: 3 grants worth $2,000 each.

SUMMERFIELD G. ROBERTS AWARD

Sons of the Republic of Texas, 1717 Eighth St., Bay City TX 77414-5033. (979)245-6644. Fax: (979)244-3819. E-mail: srttexas@srttexas.org. Website: www.srttexas.org. **Contact:** Leonard G. Cloud, chairman. Offered annually for submissions published during the previous calendar year "to encourage literary effort and research about historical events and personalities during the days of the Republic of Texas, 1836-1846, and to stimulate interest in the period." **Deadline: January 15.** Guidelines for SASE. Prize: $2,500. Judged by the last 3 winners of the contest. Open to any writer.

▣ SASKATCHEWAN BOOK OF THE YEAR AWARD

Saskatchewan Book Awards, Inc., Box 1921, Regina SK S4P 3E1, Canada. (306)569-1585. Fax: (306)569-4187. E-mail: director@bookawards.sk.ca. Website: www.bookawards.sk.ca. **Contact:** Joyce Wells, executive director. Offered annually for work published September 15-September 14 annually. This award is presented to a Saskatchewan author for the best book, judged on the quality of writing. Books from the following categories will be considered: children's; drama; fiction (short fiction by a single author, novellas, novels); nonfiction (all categories of nonfiction writing except cookbooks, directories, how-to books, or bibliographies of minimal critical content); poetry. Visit website for more details. **Deadline: First deadline: July 31; Final deadline: September 14.** Guidelines for SASE. **Charges $20 (Canadian).** Prize: $2,000.

▣ SASKATOON BOOK AWARD

Saskatchewan Book Awards, Inc., Box 1921, Regina SK S4P 3E1, Canada. (306)569-1585. Fax: (306)569-4187. E-mail: director@bookawards.sk.ca. Website: www.bookawards.sk.ca. **Contact:** Joyce Wells, executive director. Offered annually for work published September 15, 2002-September 14, 2002. In recognition of the vitality of the literary community in Saskatoon, this award is presented to a Saskatoon author for the best book, judged on the quality of writing. Books from the following categories will be considered: children's; drama; fiction (short fiction by a single author, novellas, novels); nonfiction (all categories of nonfiction writing except cookbooks, directories, how-to books, or bibliographies of minimal critical content); poetry. **Deadline: First deadline: July 31; Final deadline: September 14.** Guidelines for SASE. **Charges $20 (Canadian).** Prize: $2,000.

▣ MARGARET & JOHN SAVAGE FIRST BOOK AWARD

(formerly Cunard First Book Award), Writers' Federation of Nova Scotia, 1113 Marginal Rd., Halifax NS B3H 4P7. (902)423-8116. Fax: (902)422-0881. E-mail: talk@writers.ns.ca. Website: www.writers.ns.ca. **Contact:** Jane Buss, executive director. This award was established by the Atlantic Book Week Steering Committee to honor the first published book by an Atlantic-Canadian author. Full-length books of fiction, nonfiction, or poetry written by Atlantic Canadians, and published as a whole for the first time in the previous calendar year, are eligible. Entrants must be native or resident Atlantic Canadians who have either been born in Newfoundland, Prince Edward Island, Nova Scotia, or New Brunswick, and spent a susbstantial portion of their lives living there, or who have lived in 1 or a combination of these provinces for at least 24 consecutive months prior to entry deadline date. Entries submitted to the Atlantic Poetry Prize, Evelyn Richardson Nonfiction Award, Thomas Head Raddall Atlantic Fiction Award, Dartmouth Book Award, and/or Ann Connor Brimer Award are automatically entered in the competition. Publishers: Send 4 copies and a letter attesting to the author's status as an Atlantic Canadian and the author's current mailing address and telephone number. **Deadline: First Friday in December.** Prize: $500.

THE MONA SCHREIBER PRIZE FOR HUMOROUS FICTION & NONFICTION

11362 Homedale St., Los Angeles CA 90049. (310)471-3280. E-mail: brashcyber@pcmagic.net. Website: www.brashcyber.com. **Contact:** Brad Schreiber. **Deadline: December 1. Charges $5 fee (payable to Mona Schreiber Prize).** Prize: 1st Place: $500; 2nd Place: $250; 3rd Place: $100. Judged by Brad Schreiber, author, journalist, consultant, instructor at UCLA Extension Writers' Program, "Writing Humorous Fiction and Nonfiction." Open to any writer.

SHOCK YOUR MAMA HUMOR COMPETITION

Abbott Productions, P.O. Box 188, Reno OH 45773-0188. E-mail: info@shockyourmama.com. Website: www.shockyourmama.com. **Contact:** Mary Ann Abbott, editor. Quarterly contest for published and unpublished humor writers. Fiction, nonfiction, and poetry, 1,500 words maximum. Guidelines for SASE or online. **Deadline: June 1, September 1, December 1, March 1. Charges $5 entry fee.** Prize: $25 prize to each winner. 1 winner each quarter from all categories combined. All winners published on website. Judged by editor and staff. Open to any writer.

▣ SHORT GRAIN WRITING CONTEST

Grain Magazine, Box 67, Saskatoon SK S7K 3K1, Canada. (306)244-2828. Fax: (306)244-0255. E-mail: grainmag @sasktel.net. Website: www.grainmagazine.ca. **Contact:** Bobbi Clackson-Walker. Offered annually for unpublished dramatic monologues, postcard stories (narrative fiction) and prose (lyric) poetry, and nonfiction creative prose. Maximum length for short entries, 500 words; Long Grain of Truth (nonfiction), 5,000 words or less.

Entry guidelines online. All entrants receive a 1-year subscription to *Grain Magazine*. *Grain* purchases first Canadian serial rights only; copyright remains with the author. Open to any writer. No fax or e-mail submissions. **Deadline: January 31. Charges $25 fee for 2 entries, plus $5 for additional entries; US and international entries $25, plus $5 postage in US funds (non-Canadian).** Prize: $6,000; three prizes of $500 in each category.

SHORT PROSE COMPETITION FOR DEVELOPING WRITERS
The Writers' Union of Canada, 40 Wellington St. E., 3rd Floor, Toronto ON M5E 1C7, Canada. (416)703-8982, ext. 223. Fax: (416)504-7656. E-mail: projects@writersunion.ca. Website: www.writersunion.ca. **Contact:** Project Coordinator. Offered annually "to discover developing Canadian writers of unpublished prose fiction and nonfiction." Length: 2,500 words maximum. Open to Canadian citizens or landed immigrants who have not been published in book format, and who do not currently have a contract with a publisher. **Deadline: November 3.** Guidelines for SASE. **Charges $25 entry fee.** Prize: $2,500, and possible publication in a literary journal.

THE BERNICE SLOTE AWARD
Prairie Schooner, 201 Andrews Hall, PO Box 880334, Lincoln NE 68588-0334. (402)472-0911. Fax: (402)472-9771. E-mail: kgrey2@unl.edu. Website: www.unl.edu/schooner/psmain.htm. **Contact:** Hilda Raz. Offered annually for the best work by a beginning writer published in *Prairie Schooner* in the previous year. Prize: $500.

SOUTHWEST REVIEW AWARDS
Southern Methodist University, P.O. Box 750374, Dallas TX 75275-0374. (214)768-1037. Fax: (214)768-1408. E-mail: swr@mail.smu.edu. Website: www.southwestreview.org. **Contact:** Elizabeth Mills. "The $500 John H. McGinnis Memorial Award is given each year for fiction and nonfiction that has been published in the *Southwest Review* in the previous year. Stories or articles are not submitted directly for the award, but simply for publication in the magazine. The Elizabeth Matchett Stover Award, an annual prize of $250, is awarded to the author of the best poem or group of poems published in the *Southwest Review* during the preceding year. Stories or articles are not submitted directly for the award, but simply for publication in the magazine. Morton Marr Poetry Prize gives an annual award of $1,000 to a poem by a writer who has not yet published a first book. Contest entry fee is $5/poem. Entry deadline is November 30."

WALLACE STEGNER FELLOWSHIPS
Creative Writing Program, Stanford University, Dept. of English, Stanford CA 94305-2087. (650)723-2637. Fax: (650)723-3679. E-mail: vfhess@stanford.edu. Website: www.stanford.edu/dept/english/cw/. **Contact:** Virginia Hess, program administrator. Offered annually for a 2-year residency at Stanford for emerging writers to attend the Stegner workshop to practice and perfect their craft under the guidance of the creative writing faculty. Guidelines available online. **Deadline: December 1 (postmark). Charges $50 fee.** Prize: Living stipend (currently $22,000/year) and required workshop tuition of $6,500/year.

TENNESSEE WRITERS ALLIANCE LITERARY COMPETITION
Tennessee Writers Alliance, P.O. Box 120396, Nashville TN 37212. Website: www.tn-writers.org. **Contact:** Jane Hicks, competition director. Offered annually for unpublished short fiction and poetry. Membership open to all, regardless of residence, for $25/year; $15/year for students. "For more information and guidelines visit our website or send a SASE." **Deadline: July 1. Charges $10 fee for members, $15 fee for nonmembers.** Prize: 1st Place: $500; 2nd Place: $250; 3rd Place: $100.

TORONTO BOOK AWARDS
City of Toronto c/o Toronto Protocol, 100 Queen St. W., 10th Floor, West Tower, City Hall, Toronto ON M5H 2N2, Canada. (416)392-8191. Fax: (416)392-1247. E-mail: bkurmey@toronto.ca. Website: www.toronto.ca/book_awards. **Contact:** Bev Kurmey, protocol officer. Offered annually for previously published fiction, nonfiction, or juvenile books that are "evocative of Toronto." Previously published entries must have appeared in print between January 1 and December 31 the year prior to the contest year. **Deadline: February 27.** Guidelines for SASE. Prize: Awards total $15,000. $1,000 to shortlist finalists (usually 4-6) with remainder to the winner. Judged by independent judging committee of 5 people chosen through an application and selection process.

WESTERN HERITAGE AWARDS
National Cowboy & Western Heritage Museum, 1700 NE 63rd St., Oklahoma City OK 73111. (405)478-6404. Fax: (405)478-4714. E-mail: editor@nationalcowboymuseum.org. Website: www.nationalcowboymuseum.org. **Contact:** M.J. VanDeventer, publications director. Offered annually for excellence in representation of great stories of the American West published November 30-December 1. Competition includes 7 literary categories:

nonfiction, western novel, juvenile book, art book, short story, poetry book, and magazine article. **Charges $35 entry fee.**

⚡ WESTERN MAGAZINE AWARDS

Western Magazine Awards Foundation, #901-207 W. Hastings St., Vancouver BC V6B 1H7, Canada. (604)669-3717. Fax: (604)669-3701. E-mail: wma@direct.ca. Website: www.westernmagazineawards.com. Offered annually for magazine work published January 1-December 31 of previous calendar year. Entry categories include business, culture, science, technology and medicine, entertainment, fiction, political issues, and much more. Guidelines for SASE or on website. Applicant must be Canadian citizen, landed immigrant, or full-time resident. The work must have been published in a magazine whose main editorial office is in Western Canada, the Northwest Territories, and Yukon. **Deadline: February 27. Charges $27 for work in magazines with circulation under 20,000; $35 for work in magazines with circulation over 20,000.** Prize: $500.

WESTMORELAND POETRY & SHORT STORY CONTEST

Westmoreland Arts & Heritage Festival, RR 2, Box 355A, Latrobe PA 15650-9415. (724)834-7474. Fax: (724)850-7474. E-mail: info@artsandheritage.com. **Contact:** Donnie A. Gutherie. Offered annually for unpublished work. Writers are encouraged to submit short stories from all genres. The purpose of the contest is to provide writers varied competition in 2 categories: short story and poetry. Entries must be 4,000 words or less. No erotica or pornography. **Deadline: March.** Guidelines for SASE. **Charges $10 fee/story, $10 fee/2 poems.** Prize: Up to $200 in prizes.

WILLA LITERARY AWARD

Women Writing the West, 6131 Island Rd., Etna CA 96027. (530)468-5331. Fax: (530)467-4131. E-mail: gfiorini @sisqtel.net. Website: www.womenwritingthewest.org. **Contact:** Gail Jenner, contest director. "The WILLA Literary Award honors the best in literature featuring women's stories set in the West published each year. Women Writing the West (WWW), a nonprofit association of writers and other professionals writing and promoting the Women's West, underwrites and presents the nationally recognized award annually (for work published between January 1 and December 31). The award is named in honor of Pulitzer Prize winner Willa Cather, one of the country's foremost novelists. The award is given in 7 categories: historical fiction, contemporary fiction, original softcover, nonfiction, memoir/essay nonfiction, poetry, and children's/young adult fiction/nonfiction." **Deadline: February 1.** Guidelines for SASE. **Charges $50 entry fee.** Prize: Each winner receives $100, and a trophy award. Each finalist receives a plaque. Award announcement is in early August, and awards are presented to the winners and finalists at the annual WWW Fall Conference. Judged by professional librarians, not affiliated with WWW. Open to any writer.

WIND CONTESTS

Wind, P.O. Box 24548, Lexington KY 40524. (859)277-6849. Website: www.wind.wind.org. **Contact:** Chris Green, editor. Offered annually for unpublished poems, chapbooks, and short stories. Consult website or send SASE for guidelines. **Deadline: March 1 for poems; July 30 for short stories; October 31 for chapbooks.** Guidelines for SASE. **Charges $3/poem, $10/short story, and $15/chapbook.** Prize: $500, and publication in *Wind* for winning poem and short story; $100 plus 25 copies of winning chapbook; chapbook is published as summer issue of *Wind*. All entries receive copy of chapbook. All finalists receive a 1-year subscription to the magazine. Enclose SASE for results. Authors are responsible for copyright clearance on previously published poems. Open to all writers.

Ⓝ ⚡ WINNERS' CIRCLE INTERNATIONAL WRITING CONTEST

Canadian Authors Association, 599-B Yonge St., Suite 514, Toronto ON M4Y 1Z4, Canada. Website: www.tacob. org/winnerscircle.htm. Offered annually to encourage new short stories which help authors to get published. First publishing rights required but copyright owned by writer. SAE plus 90 cents postage for "How to Write a Short Story" booklet. Registration and rules only, send SASE. Do not send entry by e-mail or fax. **Deadline: January 31. Charges $25 fee, payable to Canadian Authors Association.** Prize: 1st Prize: $500; 2nd Prize: $200; 3rd Prize: $100, and 20 Honorable Mentions.

L.L. WINSHIP/PEN NEW ENGLAND AWARD

PEN New England, Emerson College, 120 Boylston St., Boston MA 02116. E-mail: awards@pen-ne.org. Website: www.pen-ne.org. Offered annually for work published in the previous calendar year. This annual prize is offered for the best book by a New England author or with a New England topic or setting. Open to fiction, nonfiction, and poetry. **Deadline: December 15.** Guidelines for SASE.

WOMEN IN THE ARTS ANNUAL FICTION CONTEST

Women in the Arts, P.O. Box 2907, Decatur IL 62524. (217)872-0811. **Contact:** Vice President. Annual competition for essays, fiction, fiction for children, plays, rhymed poetry, and unrhymed poetry. **Deadline: November 1.** Guidelines for SASE. **Charges $2/submission.** Prize: 1st Prize: $50; 2nd Prize: $35; 3rd Prize: $15. Judged by professional writers. Open to any writer.

JOHN WOOD COMMUNITY COLLEGE ADULT CREATIVE WRITING CONTEST

1301 S. 48th St., Quincy IL 62305. Website: www.jwcc.edu. **Contact:** Sherry L. Sparks, contest coordinator. Categories include serious poetry, light poetry, nonfiction, fiction. "No identification should appear on manuscripts, but send a separate 3×5 card for each entry with name, address, phone number, e-mail address, word count, title of work, and category in which each work should be entered." Only for previously unpublished work: serious or light poetry (2 page/poem maximum), fiction (2,000 words maximum), nonfiction (2,000 words maximum). Guidelines for SASE or online. Period of Contest: January 1-April 1. Contest in conjunction with Mid Mississippi Review Writer's Conference. **Charges $5/poem; $7/fiction or nonfiction.** Prize: Cash prizes dictated by the number of entries received.

◻ THE WORD GUILD CANADIAN WRITING AWARDS

The Word Guild, Box 487, Markham ON L3P 3R1. E-mail: info@thewordguild.com. Website: www.thewordguild.com. This contest is offered "to encourage writers who are Christian by giving recognition to excellence." Open to Canadian citizens only. The Castle Quay Award is open to Canadian citizens only and someone who has never had a book published. The Youth! Write Award is open to Canadian citizens only ages 15-25. **Categories for work published in 2002:** Nonfiction Books (life stories, personal growth, relationships, culture, leadership and philosophy, and special—books of poetry, anthology, etc.); Novels (literary/mainstream); Children & Young Adult Books (novels and nonfiction); Self-Published Books; Articles (news, feature, column/editorial/opinion, personal experience, devotional/inspirational, humor); Letter to the Editor; Short Story (fiction); Children & Young Adult (articles and short stories); Poetry (rhymed or free verse; maximum of 40 lines). **Categories for unpublished work:** Castle Quay Books Unpublished Mss 1st-Time Author Award (must send entire mss—see guidelines on website); Youth! Write Award (specific details on website). Annually. **Deadline: January 10 for published work; April 1 for unpublished work.** Guidelines for SASE. **Charges $40 (Canadian)/$30 (US) for books; $20 (Canadian)/$15 (US) for short items.** Prize: Book Awards: $200; Short Items: $100; Castle Quay Books Award: Ms published; Youth! Write Award: Registration at the God Uses Ink conference, plus runners-up awards. Judged by writers, editors, etc.

◻ ◻ WRITERS GUILD OF ALBERTA AWARDS

Writers Guild of Alberta, Percy Page Centre, 11759 Groat Rd., Edmonton AB T5M 3K6, Canada. (708)422-8174. Fax: (702)422-2663. E-mail: mail@writersguild.ab.ca. Website: www.writersguild.ab.ca. **Contact:** Executive Director. Offers the following awards: Wilfred Eggleston Award for Nonfiction; Georges Bugnet Award for Fiction (novel); Howard O'Hagan Award for Short Fiction; Stephan G. Stephansson Award for Poetry; R. Ross Annett Award for Children's Literature; Gwen Pharis Ringwood Award for Drama; and Isabel Miller Young Writers Award (poetry or fiction); John Whyte Essay Competition. Eligible books will have been published anywhere in the world between January 1 and December 31. The authors must have been residents of Alberta for at least 12 of the 18 months prior to December 31. Unpublished mss, except in the drama category, are not eligible. Anthologies are not eligible. Full-length radio plays which have been published in anthologies are eligible. Works may be submitted by authors, publishers, or any interested parties. **Deadline: December 31.** Guidelines for SASE. Prize: Winning authors will receive $1,000; the Isabel Miller Young Writers Award offers prizes of $300, $200, and $100.

◻ WRITERS NOTES BOOK AWARDS

Writers Notes Magazine, P.O. Box 11, Titusville NJ 08560. Fax: (609)818-1913. E-mail: info@hopepubs.com. Website: www.writersnotes.com. **Contact:** Christopher Klim, senior editor. Annual contest for previously published writing. Recognizes excellence in independent publishing in many unique categories: Art (titles capture the experience, execution, or demonstration of the arts); General Fiction (nongenre-specific fiction); Commercial Fiction (genre-specific fiction); Children (titles for young children); Young Adult (titles aimed at the juvenile and teen markets); Culture (titles demonstrating the human or world experience); Business (titles with application to today's business environment and emerging trends); Reference (titles from traditional and emerging reference areas); Home (titles with practical applications to home or home-related issues); Health/Self-Help (titles promoting the evaluation of mind and/or body); Legacy (titles over 2 years of age that hold particular relevance to any subject matter or form). **Deadline: January 15.** Guidelines for SASE. **Charges $40.** Prize: $100, and national coverage in *Writers Notes Magazine*. Judged by authors, editors, agents, publishers, book producers, artists, experienced category readers, and health and business professionals. Open to any writer.

N WRITERS NOTES WRITING AWARDS

Writers Notes Magazine, P.O. Box 11, Titusville NJ 08560. Fax: (609)818-1913. E-mail: info@hopepubs.com. Website: www.writersnotes.com. **Contact:** Christopher Klim, senior editor. Annual contests for unpublished fiction and nonfiction (5,000 words or less). Purchases first publication and one-time anthology rights for winning entries. **Deadline: July 31.** Guidelines for SASE. **Charges $15.** Prize: For both categories—Winner: $150; 1st Runners-up: $50; Honorable Mention: Publication contract. All winners will be published in Fall issue or offered a writing contract for future issue. Judged by authors, editors, journalists, agents, and experienced category readers. Open to any writer.

ARTS COUNCILS & FOUNDATIONS

N ☙ ADVANCED ARTIST AWARD

Government of Yukon, Box 2703 (L-3), Whitehouse YT Y1A 2C6, Canada. (867)667-5264. Fax: (867)393-6456. E-mail: laurel.parry@gov.yk.ca. **Contact:** Laurel Parry, manager arts section. "Grants to senior artists toward projects that contribute to their artistic development. Open to all disciplines. Open only to Yukon artists." **Deadline: April 1 and October 1.** Guidelines for SASE. Prize: Level A artists: Up to $5,000; Level B artists: Up to $2,500. Judged by peer assessment: made up of senior Yukon artists representing the various disciplines seen in applicants for that round.

ALABAMA STATE COUNCIL ON THE ARTS FELLOWSHIP-LITERATURE

Alabama State Council on the Arts, 201 Monroe St., Montgomery AL 36130. (334)242-4076, ext. 224. Fax: (334)240-3269. E-mail: randy@arts.state.al.us. Website: www.arts.state.al.us. **Contact:** Randy Shoults. Literature fellowship offered every year, for previously published or unpublished work to set aside time to create and to improve skills. Two-year Alabama residency required. Guidelines available. **Deadline: March 1.** Prize: $10,000 or $5,000.

N ALASKA STATE COUNCIL ON THE ARTS CAREER OPPORTUNITY GRANT AWARD

Alaska State Council on the Arts, 411 W. 4th Ave., Suite 1E, Anchorage AK 99501-2343. (907)269-6610. Fax: (907)269-6601. E-mail: aksca_info@eed.state.ak.us. Website: www.eed.state.ak.us/aksca. **Contact:** Charlotte Fox, executive director. Grants help artists take advantage of impending, concrete opportunities that will significantly advance their work or careers. **Deadline: Applications must be received by the first of the month preceding the proposed activity.** Prize: Up to $1,000. Alaskan residents only.

AMERICAN PRINTING HISTORY ASSOCIATION FELLOWSHIP IN PRINTING HISTORY

American Printing History Association, P.O. Box 4519, Grand Central Station, New York NY 10163. E-mail: marksl@udel.edu. Website: www.printinghistory.org. **Contact:** Mark Samuels Lasner, VP for programs. Annual award for research in any area of the history of printing in all its forms, including all the arts and technologies relevant to printing, the book arts, and letter forms. Applications are especially welcome from those working in the area of American printing history, but the subject of research has no geographical or chronological limitations, and may be national or regional in scope, biographical, analytical, technical, or bibliographic in nature. Printing history-related study with a recognized printer or book artist may also be supported. The fellowship can be used to pay for travel, living, and other expenses. Applicants are asked to submit an application form, a curriculum vitae, and a 1-page proposal. Two confidential letters of recommendation specific to this fellowship should be sent separately by the recommenders. **Deadline: December 1.** Guidelines for SASE. Prize: Up to $2,000. Judged by a committee. Open to any writer.

N ARROWHEAD REGIONAL ARTS COUNCIL INDIVIDUAL ARTIST CAREER DEVELOPMENT GRANT

Arrowhead Regional Arts Council, 1301 Rice Lake Rd., Suite 111, Duluth MN 55811. (218)722-0952 or (800)569-8134. Fax: (218)722-4459. E-mail: aracouncil@aol.com. Website: www.aracouncil.org. **Contact:** Robert DeArmond, executive director. For writers residing in the 7 counties of Northeastern Minnesota. **Deadline: April 29; July 30; November 24.** Guidelines for SASE. Prize: Up to $1,000. Judged by ARAC Board. Applicants must live in the 7-county region of Northeastern Minnesota.

ART COOPERATIVE FICTION FELLOWSHIP

Cottonwood Art Co-operative, 1124 Columbia NE, Albuquerque NM 87106. E-mail: art_coop@yahoo.com. Website: www.geocities.com/art_coop. **Contact:** Editor-in-Chief. Offered annually. For most recent information, please visit website or write for guidelines with SASE. Submit with cover sheet, bio, and publications list. Open to any writer. **Deadline: December 1 (postmark). Charges $15 for 3-50 page portfolio. For additional**

flat fee of $15 and SASE, feedback provided on fiction. Prize: Cash award to be determined, not less than $250, and publication to support serious, aspiring authors. Open to any writer.

ART COOPERATIVE POETRY FELLOWSHIP

Cottonwood Art Co-operative, 1124 Columbia NE, Albuquerque NM 87106. E-mail: art_coop@yahoo.com. Website: www.geocities.com/art_coop. **Contact:** Editor-in-Chief. Contest offered annually. For most recent information, please visit website or write for guidelines with SASE. Submit with cover sheet, bio, and publications list. Open to any writer. **Deadline: December 1. Charges $15 for up to 3 poems, $2 each thereafter. For additional flat $15 fee and SASE, feedback provided on poems.** Prize: Cash award to be determined, not less than $250, and publication to support serious, aspiring poets. Open to any writer.

ART COOPERATIVE TRAVELING FELLOWSHIP

Cottonwood Art Co-operative, 1124 Columbia NE, Albuquerque NM 87106. E-mail: art_coop@yahoo.com. Website: www.geocities.com/art_coop. **Contact:** Editor-in-Chief. For most recent information, please visit website or write for guidelines with SASE. Submit cover letter explaining project and location, anticipated budget, bio, and publications list. Submit 3-50 page portfolio of fiction or creative nonfiction, 10-20 pages of poetry, or slides of visual artwork with SASE. **Deadline: December 1. Charges $20 fee. For an additional flat $15 fee and SASE, feedback is provided.** Prize: Cash award to be determined, and publication to support serious, aspiring poets, essayists, fiction writers, and visual artists in completing a project that requires travel. Open to any writer/artist.

ARTIST TRUST/WASHINGTON STATE ARTS COMMISSION FELLOWSHIP AWARDS

Artist Trust, 1835 12th Ave., Seattle WA 98122-2437. (206)467-8734. E-mail: info@artisttrust.org. Website: www.artisttrust.org. **Contact:** Fionn Meade, director of grant programs. "The fellowship is a merit-based award of $6,000 to practicing professional Washington State artists of exceptional talent and demonstrated ability." Applicants must be individual artists; Washington State residents; not matriculated students; and generative artists. Offered every 2 years in odd years. Guidelines and application online or for SASE. **Deadline: June.** Prize: $6,000. Judged by a selection panel of artists and/or arts professionals in the field chosen by the Artist Trust staff.

🆕 BARRINGTON AREA ARTS COUNCIL/WHETSTONE PRIZES

Box 1266, Barrington IL 60010-1266. (847)382-5626. Fax: (847)382-3685. E-mail: baacwhetstone@hotmail.com. **Contact:** Lani Ori, Charles White, Dale Griffith, Anna Husain. Must Be Unpublished. **Deadline: Open until publication.** Guidelines for SASE. Prize: The Whetstone Prize, usually $250 to a single author for best fiction, nonfiction, or poetry selected for publication in *Whetstone* (an annual literary journal); The John Patrick McGrath Memorial Award, $250 to a single author, for fiction or poetry. Judged by co-editors of *Whetstone*. Open to any writer.

BUSH ARTIST FELLOWS PROGRAM

The Bush Foundation, E-900 First National Bank Bldg., 332 Minnesota St., St. Paul MN 55101. (651)227-0891. Fax: (651)297-6485. Website: www.bushfoundation.org. **Contact:** Kathi Polley, program assistant. Estab. 1976. Award for Minnesota, North Dakota, South Dakota, and western Wisconsin residents 25 years or older (students are not eligible) "to buy 12-18 months of time for the applicant to further his/her own work." All application categories rotate on a 2-year cycle. Publishing, performance, and/or option requirements for eligibility. Applications available August 2004. **Deadline: October.** Prize: Up to 15 fellowships/year, $44,000 each.

CHESTERFIELD WRITERS FILM PROJECT FELLOWSHIP

The Chesterfield Writers Film Project, 1158 26th St., PMB 544, Santa Monica CA 90403. (213)683-3977. E-mail: info@chesterfield-co.com. Website: www.chesterfield-co.com. **Contact:** Edward Rugoff. This annual contest is offered "to nurture the talent of aspiring screenwriters." **Deadline: May 15.** Guidelines for SASE. **Charges $39.50.** Prize: "We award up to 5 $20,000 fellowships. In addition, each fellow participates in a 10-month screenwriting workshop under the guidance of a professional screenwriter and a Paramount Studio executive." Judged by Chesterfield staff. Open to any writer.

🆕 CHLA RESEARCH FELLOWSHIPS & SCHOLARSHIPS

Children's Literature Association, P.O. Box 138, Battle Creek MI 49016-0138. (269)965-8180. Fax: (269)965-8180. E-mail: kkiessling@childlitassn.org. Website: www.childlitassn.org. **Contact:** ChLA Scholarship Chair. Offered annually. "The fellowships are available for proposals dealing with criticism or original scholarship with the expectation that the undertaking will lead to publication and make a significant contribution to the field of children's literature in the area of scholarship or criticism." Funds are not intended for work leading to the completion of a professional degree. Guidelines for SASE or online. **Deadline: February 1.** Prize: $250-1,000.

CONNECTICUT COMMISSION ON THE ARTS ARTIST FELLOWSHIPS

One Financial Plaza, Hartford CT 06103-2601. (860)566-4770. Fax: (860)566-6462. E-mail: artsinfo@ctarts.org. Website: www.ctarts.org/artfellow.htm. **Contact:** Linda Dente, program manager. **Deadline: September 15.** Prize: $5,000, and $2,500. Judged by peer professionals (writers, editors). Connecticut residents only.

DELAWARE DIVISION OF THE ARTS

820 N. French St., Wilmington DE 19801. (302)577-8284. Fax: (302)577-6561. E-mail: kristin.pleasanton@state. de.us. Website: www.artsdel.org. **Contact:** Kristin Pleasanton, coordinator. Award offered annually "to help further careers of Delaware's emerging and established professional artists." Annually. **Deadline: August 1.** Guidelines for SASE. Prize: $10,000 for masters, $5,000 for established professionals; $2,000 for emerging professionals. Judged by out-of-state professionals in each division. Delaware residents only.

N DOBIE/PAISANO FELLOWSHIPS

Jo Frank Dobie House, 702 E. Dean Keeton St., Austin TX 78705. Fax: (512)471-9997. E-mail: nslate@mail.utexa s.edu. Website: www.utexas.edu/ogs/paisano. **Contact:** Paula Michelle Marks. The Dobie-Paisano Fellowships provide an opportunity for creative writers to live for an extended period of time at a place of literary association. At the time of the application, 1 of the following requirements must be met: 1.) be a native Texan, or 2.) have lived in Texas at some time for at least 3 years, or 3.) have published writing that has a Texas subject. Criteria for making the awards include quality of work, character of proposed project, and suitability of the applicant for life at Paisano. Applicants must submit examples of their work in triplicate. Guidelines for SASE or online. Annually. **Deadline: January 30. Charges $10 fee.** Prize: 2 fellowships of $2,000/month for 6 months, and 6 months in residence at the late J. Frank Dobie's ranch near Austin, Texas, the first beginning September 1 and the second March 1. The fellowships are known as the Ralph A. Johnston Memorial Fellowship and the Jesse H. Jones Writing Fellowship. Winners are announced in early May. Three copies of the application must be submitted with the rest of the entry and mailed in 1 package. Entries must be submitted on the form.

DOCTORAL DISSERTATION FELLOWSHIPS IN JEWISH STUDIES

National Foundation for Jewish Culture, 330 7th Ave., 21st Floor, New York NY 10001. (212)629-0500. Fax: (212)629-0508. E-mail: grants@jewishculture.org. Website: www.jewishculture.org/grants. **Contact:** Kristin L. Runk. Offered annually to students. Deadline varies, usually early January. Open to students who have completed their course work and need funding for research in order to write their dissertation thesis or a Ph.D. in a Jewish field of study. Guidelines for SASE. Prize: $8,000-10,000 grant.

N FELLOWSHIPS FOR CREATIVE WRITERS

National Endowment for the Arts Literature Program, Nancy Hanks Center, 1100 Pennsylvania Ave. NW, Washington DC 20506-0001. (202)682-5034. Website: www.arts.gov. "Fellowships in prose (fiction and creative nonfiction) and poetry are available to creative writers of exceptional talent. Fellowships enable recipients to set aside time for writing, research, travel, and general career advancement." Guidelines on website. **Deadline: Poetry: March 1.** Prize: $20,000 grants.

HAWAI'I AWARD FOR LITERATURE

State Foundation on Culture and the Arts, 250 S. Hotel St., 2nd Floor, Honolulu HI 96813. (808)586-0769. Fax: (808)586-0308. E-mail: sfca@sfca.state.hi.us. Website: www.state.hi.us/sfca. **Contact:** Hawai'i Literary Arts Council (Box 11213, Honolulu HI 96828-0213. (808)956-7357. Fax: (808)956-6345. E-mail: lwasa@hawaii.edu). "The annual award honors the lifetime achievement of a writer whose work is important to Hawai'i and/or Hawai'i's people." Nominations are a public process; inquiries should be directed to the Hawai'i Literary Arts Council at address listed. "Cumulative work is considered. Self nominations are allowed, but not usual. Fiction, poetry, drama, certain types of nonfiction, screenwriting and song lyrics are considered. The award is not intended to recognize conventional academic writing and reportage, nor is it intended to recognize more commercial types of writing, e.g., advertising copy, tourist guides, and how-to manuals." **Deadline: November.** Prize: Governor's reception and cash award.

THE HODDER FELLOWSHIP

The Council of the Humanities, Joseph Henry House, Princeton University, Princeton NJ 08544. (609)258-4717. Fax: (609)258-2783. E-mail: humcounc@princeton.edu. Website: www.princeton.edu/~humcounc/. The Hodder Fellowships is awarded to exceptional humanists at the early stages of their careers, typically after they have published one book and are working on a second. Preference is given to individuals outside academia.

Hodder Fellows spend an academic year in residence in Princeton, pursuing independent projects. Candidates are invited to submit a résumé, a sample of previous work (10-page maximum, not returnable), a project proposal of 2-3 pages, and SASE for acknowledgement. Letters of recommendation are not required. **Deadline: November 1 (postmarked).** Prize: $55,000 stipend.

ILLINOIS ART COUNCIL ARTISTS FELLOWSHIP PROGRAM IN POETRY & PROSE

Illinois Art Council, 100 W. Randolph, Suite 10-500, Chicago IL 60601. (312)814-6740. Fax: (312)814-1471. E-mail: info@arts.state.il.us. Website: www.state.il.us/agency/iac. **Contact:** Director of Literature. Offered biannually for Illinois writers of exceptional talent to enable them to pursue their artistic goals. Applicant must have been a resident of Illinois for at least 1 year prior to the deadline. Guidlines for SASE. **Deadline: September 1, 2005 (prose).** Prize: Nonmatching award of $7,000; finalist award of $700.

CHRISTOPHER ISHERWOOD FELLOWSHIPS

Christopher Isherwood Foundation, Box 650, Montrose AL 36559. E-mail: james@isherwoodfoundation.org. Website: www.isherwoodfoundation.org. **Contact:** James P. White, executive director. Awards are given annually to selected novelists who have published a novel. **Deadline: October 1.** Prize: Fellowship consists of $3,000. Judged by advisory board.

KANSAS ARTS COMMISSION INDIVIDUAL ARTIST FELLOWSHIPS/MINI-FELLOWSHIPS

Kansas Arts Commission, 700 SW Jackson St., Suite 1004, Topeka KS 66603-3761. (785)296-3335. Fax: (785)296-4989. E-mail: kac@arts.state.ks.us. Website: arts.state.ks.us. **Contact:** Karen Brady. Offered annually for Kansas artists, both published and unpublished. Fellowships are offered in 10 artistic disciplines, rotating 5 disciplines every other year, and are awarded based on artistic merit. The fellowship disciplines are: music composition; choreography; film/video; interdisciplinary/performance art; playwriting; fiction; poetry; 2-dimensional visual art; 3-dimensional visual art; and crafts. Mini-fellowships (up to 12) are awarded annually to emerging artists in the same 10 disciplines. Guidelines on website. **Deadline: Varies.** Prize: Fellowship: $5,000. Mini-fellowship: $500. Open to Kansas residents only.

◩ KORET JEWISH STUDIES PUBLICATIONS PROGRAM

Koret Foundation, 33 New Montgomery St., Suite 1090, San Francisco CA 94105-4526. (415)882-7740. Fax: (415)882-7775. E-mail: info@koretfoundation.org. Website: www.koretfoundation.org. **Contact:** Call Koret Foundation and ask for JSPP Program Officer. "In 1998, the Koret Foundation launched the Jewish Studies Publications Program (JSPP) to provide publication subsidies to first-time authors of original scholarly monographs in the field of Jewish studies. The program was designed to help previously unpublished scholars bring their work to light. As of February 2004, these grants have assisted in the publication of 55 books. Koret is the only Jewish foundation that has such a program, and the response of publishers and authors has been very positive. The subsidy grants are payable only to nonprofit institutions, organizations, and publishers. The grant funds are to support costs that an interested publisher may not otherwise be able to meet." Equal consideration will be given to applicants whose mss have not yet been accepted by a publisher. **Deadline: Posted on Koret Foundation's website in November.** Guidelines for SASE. Prize: Grants ranging from $3,000-4,000.

◩ KORET YOUNG WRITER ON JEWISH THEMES AWARD

Koret Foundation, 33 New Montgomery St., Suite 1090, San Francisco CA 94105-4526. (415)882-7740. Fax: (415)882-7775. E-mail: koretinstitute@koretfoundation.org. Website: www.koretfoundation.org. **Contact:** Steven J. Zipperstein, Ph.D., director, Koret Institute. Annual award for "1 writer whose work contains Jewish themes. The residency allows time for writing, teaching 1 course at Stanford, and giving several workshops in collaboration with Jewish community organizations in the San Francisco Bay Area." Applicants must be 35 years of age or younger and have published no more than 1 book at the time of application. Scholarly work will not be considered. This award is for fiction, nonfiction, or poetry. **Deadline: December 1.** Prize: $25,000, plus 3-months residency at Stanford University. Judged by a distinguished panel of judges who remain anonymous.

LITERARY GIFT OF FREEDOM

(formerly Gift of Freedom), A Room of Her Own Foundation, P.O. Box 778, Placitas NM 87043. E-mail: info@aroomofherownfoundation.org. Website: www.aroomofherownfoundation.org. **Contact:** Darlene Chandler Bassett. Award offered every other year to provide very practical help both materially and in professional guidance and moral support, to women who need assistance in making their creative contribution to the world. Guidelines available on website. **Deadline: February 1. Charges $25.** Prize: Up to $50,000 over two years, also a mentor for advice and dialogue, and access to the Advisory Council for professional and business consultation. Judged by members of AROHO's Board of Directors, Advisory Council, and volunteers from a wide variety of backgrounds. Any female resident citizen of the US.

MASSACHUSETTS CULTURAL COUNCIL ARTISTS GRANTS PROGRAM

Massachusetts Cultural Council, 10 St. James Ave., Boston MA 02116-3803. (617)727-3668. Fax: (617)727-0044. E-mail: mcc@art.state.ma.us. Website: www.massculturalcouncil.org. Awards in poetry, fiction, and playwriting/new theater works (among other discipline categories) are $5,000 each in recognition of exceptional original work. Criteria: Artistic excellence and creative ability, based on work submitted for review. Judged by independent peer panels composed of artists and art professionals. Legal residents of Massachusetts for the last 2 years and at time of award (18 years or older). This excludes students in directly related degree programs, grant recipients within the last 3 years.

MONEY FOR WOMEN

Barbara Deming Memorial Fund, Inc., P.O. Box 630125, The Bronx NY 10463. **Contact:** Susan Pliner. "Small grants to individual feminists in fiction, nonfiction, and poetry, whose work addresses women's concerns and/or speaks for peace and justice from a feminist perspective." Guidelines and required entry forms for SASE. "The Fund does not give educational assistance, monies for personal study or loans, monies for dissertation, research projects, or self-publication, grants for group projects, business ventures, or emergency funds for hardships." Open to citizens of the US or Canada. The fund also offers 2 awards, the Gertrude Stein Award for outstanding works by a lesbian and the Fannie Lou Hamer Award for work which combats racism and celebrates women of color. No special application necessary for these 2 awards. Recipients will be chosen from all the proposals. **Deadline: December 31 (fiction) and June 30 (nonfiction and poetry).** Prize: Grants up to $1,500.

JENNY McKEAN/MOORE VISITING WRITER

English Department, George Washington University, Washington DC 20052. (202)994-6180. Fax: (202)994-7915. E-mail: dmca@gwu.edu. Website: www.gwu.edu/~english. **Contact:** David McAleavey. Offered annually to provide 1-year visiting writers to teach 1 George Washington course and 1 free community workshop each semester. Guidelines for SASE or on website. This contest seeks someone specializing in a different genre each year; in 2004-2005, a fiction writer. **Deadline: November 15.** Prize: Annual stipend approximately $50,000, plus reduced-rent townhouse (not guaranteed).

WILLIAM MORRIS SOCIETY IN THE US FELLOWSHIP

William Morris Society in the US, P.O. Box 53263, Washington DC 20009. E-mail: us@morrissociety.org. Website: www.morrissociety.org. **Contact:** Mark Samuels Lasner. Offered annually "to promote study of the life and work of William Morris (1834-96), British poet, designer, and socialist. Award may be for research or a creative project." Curriculum vitae, 1-page proposal, and 2 letters of recommendation required for application. Applicants must be US citizens or permanent residents. **Deadline: December 1.** Prize: Up to $1,000, multiple, partial awards possible.

⁅N⁆ LARRY NEAL WRITERS' COMPETITION

DC Commission on the Arts and Humanities, 410 Eighth St., NW 5th Floor, Washington DC 20004. (202)724-1475. Fax: (202)727-4135. E-mail: lionellt@hotmail.com. Website: www.capaccess.org/dccah. **Contact:** Lionell C. Thomas, grants and legislative officer. Offered annually for unpublished poetry, fiction, essay, and dramatic writing. Call or visit website for current deadlines. Open to Washington DC residents only. Prize: Cash awards.

NEBRASKA ARTS COUNCIL INDIVIDUAL ARTISTS FELLOWSHIPS

Nebraska Arts Council, 3838 Davenport St., Omaha NE 68131-2329. (402)595-2122. Fax: (402)595-2334. E-mail: ltubach@nebraskaartscouncil.org. Website: www.nebraskaartscouncil.org. **Contact:** Lisa Tubach. Estab. 1991. Offered every 3 years (literature alternates with other disciplines) to recognize exemplary achievements by originating artists in their fields of endeavor and support the contributions made by Nebraska artists to the quality of life in this state. "Generally, distinguished achievement awards are $5,000 and merit awards are $1,000-2,000. Funds available are announced in September prior to the deadline." Must be a resident of Nebraska for at least 2 years prior to submission date; 18 years of age; not enrolled in an undergraduate, graduate, or certificate-granting program in English, creative writing, literature, or related field. **Deadline: November 15, 2005.** Prize: $5,000, and merit awards are $1,000-2,000.

⁅N⁆ NEW HAMPSHIRE INDIVIDUAL ARTISTS' FELLOWSHIPS

New Hampshire State Council on the Arts, 2½ Beacon St., Concord NH 03301. (603)271-2789. Fax: (603)271-3584. Website: www.nh.gov/nharts. **Contact:** Julie Mento. Estab. 1981. Offered to publicly recognized, professional New Hampshire artists for their artistic excellence and professional commitment, as judged by their peers. Fiction writers and poets, playwrights and screenwriters, as well as performing and visual disciplines. **Deadline: First Friday in May.**

NEW JERSEY STATE COUNCIL ON THE ARTS FELLOWSHIP PROGRAM

New Jersey State Council on the Arts, 225 W. State St., P.O. Box 306, Trenton NJ 08625. (609)292-6130. Fax: (609)989-1440. E-mail: njsca@njartscouncil.org. Website: www.njartscouncil.org. **Contact:** Don Ehman, program associate. Offered every other year. Writers may apply in either poetry, playwriting, or prose. Fellowship awards are intended to provide support for the artist during the year to enable him or her to continue producing new work. Send for guidelines and application, or visit website. Must be New Jersey residents; may *not* be undergraduate or graduate matriculating students. **Deadline: July 15.** Prize: $7,000-12,000.

N NEW YORK FOUNDATION FOR THE ARTS ARTISTS' FELLOWSHIPS

New York Foundation for the Arts, 155 Avenue of the Americas, 14th Floor, New York NY 10013-1507. (212)366-6900, ext. 217. E-mail: nyfaafp@nyfa.org. Website: www.nyfa.org. "Artists' Fellowships are cash grants of $7,000 awarded in 16 disciplines on a biannual rotation made to individual originating artists living and working in the State of New York. Awards are based upon the recommendations of peer panels and are not project support. The Fellowships may be used by each recipient as she/he sees fit. Deadlines in October. Results announced in April. The New York Foundation for the Arts supports artists at all stages of their careers and from diverse backgrounds." All applicants must be 18 years of age, and a New York resident for 2 years prior to the time of application. **Deadline: October 1.** Prize: Grants of $7,000.

N NORTH CAROLINA ARTS COUNCIL REGIONAL ARTIST PROJECT GRANTS

North Carolina Arts Council, Dept. of Cultural Resources, Raleigh NC 27699-4634. (919)715-1519. Fax: (919)733-4834. E-mail: debbie.mcgill@ncmail.net. Website: www.ncarts.org. **Contact:** Debbie McGill, literature director. Annually. **Deadline: Varies; generally late summer/early fall.** Prize: $500-3,000 general range awarded to writers to pursue projects that further their artistic development. Open to any writer living in North Carolina.

N NORTH CAROLINA WRITERS' FELLOWSHIPS

North Carolina Arts Council, Dept. of Cultural Resources, Raleigh NC 27699-4632. (919)715-1519. Fax: (919)733-4834. E-mail: debbie.mcgill@ncmail.net. Website: www.ncarts.org. **Contact:** Deborah McGill, literature director. Offered every even year to support writers in the development and creation of their work. **Deadline: November 1.** Guidelines for SASE. Prize: $8,000. Judged by a panel of literary professionals (writers, editors). Writers must be current residents of North Carolina for at least 1 year and may not pursue academic or professional degrees while receiving grant.

OREGON LITERARY FELLOWSHIPS

Literary Arts, Inc., 219 NW 12th Ave., #201, Portland OR 97209. (503)227-2583. E-mail: la@literary-arts.org. Website: www.literary-arts.org. **Contact:** Kristy Athens, award coordinator. The annual Oregon Literary Fellowships support Oregon writers with a monetary award. Guidelines for SASE or online. **Deadline: June 25.** Prize: $500-3,000. Fellows are also offered residencies at Caldera, a writers' retreat in Central Oregon. Judged by out-of-state judges who are selected for their expertise in a genre. Oregon residents only.

ALICIA PATTERSON JOURNALISM FELLOWSHIP

Alicia Patterson Foundation, 1730 Pennsylvania Ave. NW, Suite 850, Washington DC 20006. (202)393-5995. Fax: (301)951-8512. E-mail: info@aliciapatterson.org. Website: www.aliciapatterson.org. **Contact:** Margaret Engel. Offered annually for previously published submissions to give 8-10 full-time print journalists or photojournalists a year of in-depth research and reporting. Applicants must have 5 years of professional print journalism experience and be US citizens. Fellows write 4 magazine-length pieces for the *Alicia Patterson Reporter*, a quarterly magazine, during their fellowship year. Fellows must take a year's leave from their jobs, but may do other freelance articles during the year. Write, call, fax, or check website for applications. **Deadline: October 1.** Prize: $35,000 stipend for calendar year.

THE CHARLES PICK FELLOWSHIP

School of English and American Studies, University of East Anglia, Norwich NR4 7TJ, United Kingdom. Website: www.vea.ac.uk/eas/fellowships/pick.shtml. "The Charles Pick Fellowship is dedicated to the memory of the distinguished publisher and literary agent, Charles Pick. Applicants must be writers of fictional or nonfictional prose (no more than 2,500 words) in English who have not yet published a book." All applicants must provide reference from an editor, agent, or accredited teacher of creative writing. **Deadline: January 31.** Guidelines for SASE. Prize: £10,000. Judged by a distinguished panel of writers. Open to any writer.

THE PULLIAM JOURNALISM FELLOWSHIPS

The Indianapolis Star, a Gannett Co. publication, P.O. Box 145, Indianapolis IN 46206-0145. (317)444-6001 or (800)669-7827. Fax: (317)444-6750. E-mail: russell.pulliam@indystar.com. Website: www.indystar.com/pjf. **Contact:** Russell B. Pulliam. Offered annually as an intensive 10-week summer "training school" for college students with firm commitments to, and solid training in, newspaper journalism. "Call or e-mail us in September, and we'll send an application packet." **Deadline: March 1.** Prize: $6,600 for 10-week session, June-August.

🅽 REQUEST FOR PROPOSAL

Rhode Island State Council on the Arts, 83 Park St. Suite 6, Providence RI 02903-1037. (401)222-3880. Fax: (401)222-3018. E-mail: info@arts.ri.gov. Website: www.arts.ri.gov. **Contact:** Randall Rosenbaum, executive director. "Request for Proposal grants enable an artist to create new work and/or complete works-in-progress by providing direct financial assistance. By encouraging significant development in the work of an individual artist, these grants recognize the central contribution artists make to the creative environment of Rhode Island." Guidelines online. Open to Rhode Island residents age 18 or older; students not eligible. **Deadline: October 1 and April 1.** Prize: Nonmatching grants of $1,500-4,000.

RHODE ISLAND STATE COUNCIL ON THE ARTS FELLOWSHIPS (LITERATURE)

Rhode Island State Council on the Arts, 83 Park St., 6th Floor, Providence RI 02903. (401)222-3880. Fax: (401)222-3018. E-mail: info@arts.ri.gov. Website: www.arts.ri.gov. **Contact:** Fellowship Coordinator. Offered every year for previously published or unpublished works in the categories of poetry, fiction, and playwriting/screenwriting. Open to Rhode Island residents only. Guidelines available on website. **Deadline: April 1.** Prize: $5,000 fellowship; $1,000 runner-up.

🔳 THE SASKATCHEWAN ARTS BOARD INDIVIDUAL ASSISTANCE GRANT PROGRAM

The Saskatchewan Arts Board, 2135 Broad St., Regina SK S4P 3V7, Canada. (306)787-4056. Fax: (306)787-4199. E-mail: grants@artsboard.sk.ca. Website: www.artsboard.ck.ca. **Contact:** Dianne Warren, literary arts consultant. "The Individual Assistance Grant Program assists the Saskatchewan Arts Board in fulfilling its mandate by providing grants to Saskatchewan artists and individuals active in the arts in the province. These grants support the creation of new work in any art form or development and performance of work; study in a formal or informal setting; research in the arts; or travel to attend events or participate in eligible activities." Applicants must be residents of Saskatchewan and at minimum must have achieved a level of emerging professional in their field. **Deadline: October 1 and March 15.** Prize: **Awards**: $20,000 (maximum) to artists or individuals working in the arts who have achieved a senior level of accomplishment, and who have made a sustained and progressive nationally or internationally recognized contribution to their discipline or to the arts in general. $12,000 (maximum) to artists or individuals working in the arts who have been practicing professionally in their discipline or in the arts for a sustained period of time, and are able to demonstrate a regionally or nationally recognized contribution to their discipline or to the arts in general. $4,000 (maximum) to artists or individuals working in the arts striving to achieve a professional level in their discipline and who can demonstrate their commitment to the achievement of a professional level in their discipline through training, mentorships, or peer recognition and are producing a growing repertoire of work. Judged by a panel of adjudicators consisting of a jury of professionals in each artistic discipline.

THE SOCIETY FOR THE SCIENTIFIC STUDY OF SEXUALITY STUDENT RESEARCH GRANT

The Society for the Scientific Study of Sexuality, P.O. Box 416, Allentown PA 18105-0416. (610)530-2483. Fax: (610)530-2485. E-mail: thesociety@inetmail.att.net. Website: www.sexscience.org. **Contact:** Ilsa Lottes. Offered twice a year for unpublished works. "The student research grant award is granted twice yearly to help support graduate student research on a variety of sexually related topics." Guidelines and entry forms for SASE. Open to students pursuing graduate study. **Deadline: February 1 and September 1.** Prize: $1,000.

VERMONT ARTS COUNCIL

136 State St., Drawer 33, Montpelier VT 05633-6001. (802)828-3291. Fax: (802)828-3363. E-mail: mbailey@vermontartscouncil.org. Website: www.vermontartscouncil.org. **Contact:** Michele Bailey. Offered quarterly for previously published or unpublished works. Opportunity Grants are for specific projects of writers (poetry, playwriters, fiction, nonfiction) as well as not-for-profit presses. Also available are Artist Development funds to provide technical assistance for Vermont writers. Write or call for entry information. Open to Vermont residents only. Prize: $250-5,000.

WISCONSIN ARTS BOARD ARTIST FELLOWSHIP AWARDS

Wisconsin Arts Board, 101 E. Wilson St. 1st Floor, Madison WI 53702. (608)266-0190. Fax: (608)267-0380. E-mail: artsboard@arts.state.wi.us. Website: www.arts.state.wi.us. **Contact:** Mark Fraire, grant programs and services specialist. Offered every 2 years (even years), rewarding outstanding, professionally active Wisconsin artists by supporting their continued development, enabling them to create new work, complete work in progress, or pursue activities which contribute to their artistic growth. If the deadline falls on a weekend, the deadline is extended to the following Monday. Application is found on the Wisconsin Arts Board website at www.arts.state.wi.us on August 2, 2004. The Arts Board requires permission to use the work sample, or a portion thereof, for publicity or educational purposes. Contest open to professionally active artists who have resided in Wisconsin 1 year prior to application. Artists who are full-time students pursuing a degree in the fine arts at the time of application are not eligible. **Deadline: September 13, 2006.** Prize: $8,000 fellowship awarded to 7 Wisconsin writers.

🖥 DAVID T.K. WONG FELLOWSHIP

School of English and American Studies, University of East Anglia, Norwich NR4 7TJ, United Kingdom. Website: www.vea.ac.uk/eas/fellowships/wong/wong.shtml. Offered annually for mss of no more than 5,000 words (in English). The purpose of the award is to promote "excellence in the writing of literature." The Fellowship is awarded to a writer planning to produce a work of prose fiction in English which deals seriously with some aspect of life in the Far East. **Deadline: October 31.** Guidelines for SASE. **Charges £5.** Prize: £25,000. Judged by a distinguished international panel. Open to any writer.

🅽 WRITERS' RESIDENCIES—HEADLANDS CENTER FOR THE ARTS

NC Arts Council, Dept. of Cultural Resources, Raleigh NC 27699-4634. (919)715-1519. Fax: (919)733-4834. E-mail: debbie.mcgill@ncmail.net. Website: www.ncarts.org. **Contact:** Deborah McGill, literature director. Annually. **Deadline: June 4.** Guidelines for SASE. Prize: Room, board, round-trip travel, and a $500 monthly stipend for 2-month residency. Judged by a panel assembled by Headlands. In addition, a member of Headlands staff comes to North Carolina to interview a short list of finalists, in order to narrow that list down to 1 grant recipient. Applicants must be residents of North Carolina and have lived in the state at least 1 year prior to the application deadline. NCAC grant recipients must maintain their North Carolina residency status during the grant year and may not pursue academic or professional degrees during that period.

Glossary

Advance. A sum of money a publisher pays a writer prior to the publication of a book. It is usually paid in installments, such as one-half on signing the contract; one-half on delivery of a complete and satisfactory manuscript.

Agent. A liaison between a writer and editor or publisher. An agent shops a manuscript around, receiving a commission when the manuscript is accepted. Agents usually take a 10-15% fee from the advance and royalties.

Assignment. Editor asks a writer to produce a specific article for an agreed-upon fee.

Auction. Publishers sometimes bid for the acquisition of a book manuscript that has excellent sales prospects. The bids are for the amount of the author's advance, advertising and promotional expenses, royalty percentage, etc. Auctions are conducted by agents.

Avant-garde. Writing that is innovative in form, style, or subject, often considered difficult and challenging.

Backlist. A publisher's list of its books that were not published during the current season, but that are still in print.

Bimonthly. Every two months.

Bio. A sentence or brief paragraph about the writer.

Biweekly. Every two weeks.

Boilerplate. A standardized contract.

Byline. Name of the author appearing with the published piece.

Category fiction. A term used to include all various labels attached to types of fiction.

Chapbook. A small booklet, usually paperback, of poetry, ballads, or tales.

Circulation. The number of subscribers to a magazine.

Clips. Samples, usually from newspapers or magazines, of your *published* work.

Coffee-table book. An oversize book, heavily illustrated.

Commercial novels. Novels designed to appeal to a broad audience. These are often broken down into categories such as western, mystery, and romance. See also *genre*.

Contributor's copies. Copies of the issues of magazines sent to the author in which the author's work appears.

Copyediting. Editing a manuscript for grammar, punctuation, and printing style, not subject content.

Copyright. A means to protect an author's work.

Cover letter. A brief letter, accompanying a complete manuscript, especially useful if responding to an editor's request for a manuscript.

Creative nonfiction. Nonfictional writing that uses an innovative approach to the subject and creative language.

CV. Curriculum vita. A brief listing of qualifications and career accomplishments.

Electronic submission. A submission made by modem or on computer disk.

Erotica. Fiction or art that is sexually oriented.

Fair use. A provision of the copyright law that says short passages from copyrighted material may be used without infringing on the owner's rights.

Feature. An article giving the reader information of human interest rather than news.

Filler. A short item used by an editor to "fill" out a newspaper column or magazine page. It could be a joke, an anecdote, etc.

Frontlist. A publisher's list of its books that are new to the current season.

Galleys. The first typeset version of a manuscript that has not yet been divided into pages.

Genre. Refers either to a general classification of writing, such as the novel or the poem, or to the categories within those classifications, such as the problem novel or the sonnet.

Ghostwriter. A writer who puts into literary form an article, speech, story, or book based on another person's ideas or knowledge.

Graphic novel. An adaptation of a novel in graphic form, long comic strip, or heavily illustrated story, of 40 pages or more, produced in paperback form.

Honorarium. Token payment—small amount of money, or a byline and copies of the publication.

How-to. Books and magazine articles offering a combination of information and advice in describing how something can be accomplished.

Imprint. Name applied to a publisher's specific line or lines of books.

Kill fee. Fee for a complete article that was assigned but which was subsequently cancelled.

Lead time. The time between the acquisition of a manuscript by an editor and its actual publication.

Literary fiction. The general category of serious, nonformulaic, intelligent fiction.

Mainstream fiction. Fiction that transcends popular novel categories such as mystery, romance, and science fiction.

Mass market. Nonspecialized books of wide appeal directed toward a large audience.

Memoir. A narrative recounting a writer's (or fictional narrator's) personal or family history.

Midlist. Those titles on a publisher's list that are not expected to be big sellers, but are expected to have limited sales.

Model release. A paper signed by the subject of a photograph giving the photographer permission to use the photograph.

Multiple submissions. Sending more than one idea at the same time.

Narrative nonfiction. A narrative presentation of actual events.

Net royalty. A royalty payment based on the amount of money a book publisher receives on the sale of a book after booksellers' discounts, special sales discounts, and returns.

Novella. A short novel, or a long short story; approximately 7,000 to 15,000.

On spec. An editor expresses an interest in a proposed article idea and agrees to consider the finished piece for publication "on speculation." The editor is under no obligation to buy the finished manuscript.

Payment on acceptance. The editor sends you a check for your article, story, or poem as soon as he decides to publish it.

Payment on publication. The editor doesn't send you a check for your material until it is published.

Pen name. The use of a name other than your legal name on articles, stories, or books when you wish to remain anonymous. Also called a pseudonym.

Photo feature. Feature in which the emphasis is on the photographs rather than on accompanying written material.

Proofreading. Close reading and correction of a manuscript's typographical errors.

Proposal. A summary of a proposed book submitted to a publisher, particularly used for nonfiction manuscripts. A proposal often contains an individualized cover letter, one-page overview of the book, marketing information, competitive books, author information, chapter-by-chapter outline, and two to three sample chapters.

Query. A letter that sells an idea to an editor. Usually a query is brief (no more than one page) and uses attention-getting prose.

Remainders. Copies of a book that are slow to sell and can be purchased from the publisher at a reduced price.

Reporting time. The time it takes for an editor to report to the author on his/her query or manuscript.

Royalties, standard hardcover book. 10% of the retail price on the first 5,000 copies sold; 12½% on the next 5,000; 15% thereafter.

Royalties, standard mass paperback book. 4 to 8% of the retail price on the first 150,000 copies sold.

Royalties, standard trade paperback book. No less than 6% of list price on the first 20,000 copies; 7½% thereafter.

Self-publishing. In this arrangement, the author keeps all income derived from the book, but he pays for its manufacturing, production, and marketing.

Semimonthly. Twice per month.

Semiweekly. Twice per week.

Serial. Published periodically, such as a newspaper or magazine.

Serial fiction. Fiction published in a magazine in installments, often broken off at a suspenseful spot.

Short-short. A complete short story of 1,500 words maximum, and around 250 words minimum.

Sidebar. A feature presented as a companion to a straight news report (or main magazine article) giving sidelights on human-interest aspects or sometimes elucidating just one aspect of the story.

Simultaneous submissions. Sending the same article, story, or poem to several publishers at the same time. Some publishers refuse to consider such submissions.

Slant. The approach or style of a story or article that will appeal to readers of a specific magazine.

Slice-of-life vignette. A short fiction piece intended to realistically depict an interesting moment of everyday living.

Slush pile. The stack of unsolicited or misdirected manuscripts received by an editor or book publisher.

Subsidy publisher. A book publisher who charges the author for the cost to typeset and print his book, the jacket, etc., as opposed to a royalty publisher who pays the author.

Synopsis. A brief summary of a story, novel, or play. As part of a book proposal, it is a comprehensive summary condensed in a page or page and a half, single-spaced.

Tabloid. Newspaper format publication on about half the size of the regular newspaper page.

Tearsheet. Page from a magazine or newspaper containing your printed story, article, poem, or ad.

TOC. Table of Contents.

Unsolicited manuscript. A story, article, poem, or book that an editor did not specifically ask to see.

YA. Young adult books.

Book Publishers Subject Index

This index will help you find publishers that consider books on specific subjects. Remember that a publisher may be listed here only under a general subject category such as Art and Architecture, while the company publishes *only* art history or how-to books. Be sure to consult each company's individual listing, its book catalog, and several of its books before you send your query or proposal.

FICTION

Adventure

Feminist

Gay/Lesbian

Gothic

Literary

Mainstream/Contemporary

Occult

Picture Books

Americana

NONFICTION

Agriculture/ Horticulture

Biography

Subject Index

Business/Economics

Child Guidance/ Parenting

Children's/Juvenile

Coffee Table Book

Computers/Electronic

Contemporary Culture

Cookbook

Cooking/Foods/Nutrition

Subject Index

Gift Book

Government/Politics

History

Hobby

Subject Index

How-To

Humor

Illustrated Book

Language/Literature

3 GREAT OPPORTUNITIES to WRITE and WIN!

Writer's Digest Annual Writing Competition

More than $30,000 in prizes! Win a meeting with professional editors and agents in New York City or participation in the Maui Writers Conference. Enter in one or more of 10 categories.

Writer's Digest Short Short Story Competition

Show us your shorts! Enter your bold, brilliant but brief fiction (1,500 words or less). First Place winner receives $3,000, 2nd place $1,500, 3rd place $500 and 4th through 10th places $100 each — plus a listing in *Writer's Digest*. Top prize winners will also be considered for publication!

Writer's Digest International Self-Published Book Awards

This is the only competition exclusively for self-published books! The Grand Prize winner receives $2,500. Nine First Place winners receive $500 each. Other prizes include promotion of your work in *Writer's Digest* and *Publishers Weekly* and marketing advice from self-publishing gurus!

**For more information, visit us online at
www.writersdigest.com/contests,
email writing-competition@fwpubs.com,
or call 1-513-531-2690 ext. 1328**

Writer's Digest Competitions, 4700 East Galbraith Road, Cincinnati, Ohio 45236

Writer'sDigest
WRITE BETTER
GET PUBLISHED

Literary Criticism

Subject Index

Money/Finance

Multicultural

Nature/Environment

New Age

Psychology

Religion

Science

Self-Help

Sex

Textbook

World Affairs

General Index

This index lists every market appearing in the book; use it to find specific companies you wish to approach. Markets that appeared in the 2004 edition of *Writer's Market*, but are not included in this edition are identified by a code explaining why the market was omitted: (**ED**)—Editorial Decision, (**GLA**)—Included in *Guide to Literary Agents*, (**NS**)—Not Accepting Submissions, (**NR**)—No or Late Response to Listing Request, (**OB**)—Out of Business, (**RR**)—Removed by Market's Request, (**UC**)—Unable to Contact, (**RP**)—Business Restructured or Purchased, (**NP**)—No Longer Pays or Pays in Copies Only, (**SR**)—Subsidy/Royalty Publisher, (**UF**)—Uncertain Future, (**Web**)—a listing that appears on our website at www.WritersMarket.com.

DISCOVER
A World of WRITING
SUCCESS

Are you ready to be praised, published, and paid for your writing? It's time to invest in your future with *Writer's Digest*! Beginners and experienced writers alike have been relying on *Writer's Digest*, the world's leading magazine for writers, for more than 80 years — and it keeps getting better! Each issue is brimming with:

- Inspiration from writers who have been in your shoes
- Detailed info on the latest contests, conferences, markets, and opportunities in every genre
- Tools of the trade, including reviews of the latest writing software and hardware
- Writing prompts and exercises to overcome writer's block and rekindle your creative spark
- Expert tips, techniques, and advice to help you get published
- And so much more!

That's a lot to look forward to every month. Let *Writer's Digest* put you on the road to writing success!

NO RISK!
Send No Money Now!

☐ **Yes!** Please rush me my 2 FREE issues of *Writer's Digest* — the world's leading magazine for writers. If I like what I read, I'll get a full year's subscription (12 issues, including the 2 free issues) for only $19.96. That's 67% off the newsstand rate! If I'm not completely happy, I'll write "cancel" on your invoice, return it and owe nothing. The 2 FREE issues are mine to keep, no matter what!

Name _____

Address _____

City _____

State_____ZIP _____

Subscribers in Canada will be charged an additional US$10 (includes GST/HST) and invoiced. Outside the U.S. and Canada, add US$10 and remit payment in U.S. funds with this order. Annual newsstand rate: $59.88. Please allow 4-6 weeks for first-issue delivery.

Writer's Digest

www.writersdigest.com

J4FWMK

Get **2 FREE** TRIAL ISSUES of *Writer's Digest*

Packed with creative inspiration, advice, and tips to guide you on the road to success, *Writer's Digest* offers everything you need to take your writing to the next level! You'll discover how to:

- Create dynamic characters and page-turning plots
- Submit query letters that publishers won't be able to refuse
- Find the right agent or editor
- Make it out of the slush-pile and into the hands of publishers
- Write award-winning contest entries
- And more!

See for yourself by ordering your 2 FREE trial issues today!

RUSH!
2 Free Issues!

BUSINESS REPLY MAIL
FIRST-CLASS MAIL   PERMIT NO. 340   FLAGLER BEACH FL

POSTAGE WILL BE PAID BY ADDRESSEE

Writer's Digest

PO BOX 421365
PALM COAST FL 32142-7104

General Index